PHILIP'S

WORLD ATLAS

Philip's are grateful to the following for acting as specialist geography consultants on 'The World in Focus' front section:

Professor D. Brunsden, Kings College, University of London, UK
Dr C. Clarke, Oxford University, UK
Dr I. S. Evans, Durham University, UK
Professor P. Haggett, University of Bristol, UK
Professor K. McLachlan, University of London, UK
Professor M. Monmonier, Syracuse University, New York, USA
Professor M-L. Hsu, University of Minnesota, Minnesota, USA
Professor M. J. Tooley, University of St Andrews, UK
Dr T. Unwin, Royal Holloway, University of London, UK

THE WORLD IN FOCUS
Cartography by Philip's

Picture Acknowledgements:
Robin Scagell/Galaxy Picture Library page 3
Thinkstock/iStockphoto page 7 (bottom left & bottom right), /Digital Vision page 7 (centre)

WORLD CITIES
Cartography by Philip's

Page 10, Dublin: The town plan of Dublin is based on Ordnance Survey Ireland by permission of the Government Permit Number 8798. © Ordnance Survey Ireland and Government of Ireland.

Page 11, Edinburgh, and page 15, London: This product includes mapping data licensed from Ordnance Survey® with the permission of the Controller of Her Majesty's Stationery Office. © Crown copyright 2012. All rights reserved. Licence number 100011710.

All satellite images in this section courtesy of Fugro NPA Ltd, Edenbridge, Kent, UK (www.fugro-npa.com).

Published in Great Britain in 2012 by Philip's,
a division of Octopus Publishing Group Limited
(www.octopusbooks.co.uk)
Endeavour House, 189 Shaftesbury Avenue, London WC2H 8JY
An Hachette UK Company (www.hachette.co.uk)

Copyright © 2012 Philip's

Cartography by Philip's

HARDBACK EDITION: ISBN 978-1-84907-236-6
PAPERBACK EDITION: ISBN 978-1-84907-237-3

A CIP catalogue record for this book is available from the British Library.

Printed in Singapore

Details of other Philip's titles and services can be found on our website at:
www.philips-maps.co.uk

PHILIP'S

WORLD ATLAS

IN ASSOCIATION WITH
THE ROYAL GEOGRAPHICAL SOCIETY
WITH THE INSTITUTE OF BRITISH GEOGRAPHERS

Contents

World Statistics

Countries	vi
Physical Dimensions	vii
User Guide	viii

The World in Focus

Planet Earth	2–3
Restless Earth	4–5
Landforms	6–7
Oceans	8–9
Climate	10–11
Water and Vegetation	12–13
Environment	14–15
Population	16–17
The Human Family	18–19
Wealth	20–21
Quality of Life	22–23
Energy	24–25
Production	26–27
Trade	28–29
Travel and Tourism	30–31

World Cities

Amsterdam	2
Athens	2
Atlanta	3
Baghdad	3
Bangkok	3
Barcelona	4
Beijing	4
Berlin	5
Boston	6
Brussels	6
Budapest	7
Buenos Aires	7
Cairo	7
Cape Town	8
Copenhagen	8
Chicago	9
Dubai	9
Delhi	10
Dublin	10
Edinburgh	11
Guangzhou (Canton)	11
Helsinki	11
Hong Kong	12
Istanbul	12
Jakarta	12
Jerusalem	13
Johannesburg	13
Karachi	13
Kolkata (Calcutta)	14
Lagos	14
Las Vegas	14
Lima	14
London	15
Lisbon	16
Los Angeles	16
Madrid	17
Manila	17
Melbourne	18
Mexico City	18
Milan	18
Miami	19
Moscow	19
Montréal	20
Mumbai (Bombay)	20
Munich	21
New Orleans	21
New York	22
Orlando	23
Osaka	23
Oslo	23
Paris	24
Prague	25
Rio de Janeiro	25
Rome	26
San Francisco	26
St Petersburg	27
Santiago	27
São Paulo	27
Seoul	27
Shanghai	28
Singapore	28
Stockholm	29
Sydney	29
Tokyo	30
Tehran	31
Toronto	31
Venice	32
Vienna	32
Warsaw	33
Washington	33
Index to City Maps	34–39
World Cities Satellite Images	40–48

World Maps

Map Symbols	1
The World: Political 1:95 000 000	2–3
Arctic Ocean 1:35 000 000	4
Antarctica 1:35 000 000	5

Europe

Europe: Physical 1:20 000 000	6
Europe: Political 1:20 000 000	7
Scandinavia 1:6 000 000 Iceland 1:6 000 000 Færoe Islands 1:6 000 000	8–9
Ireland 1:2 000 000	10
Scotland 1:2 000 000	11
England and Wales 1:2 000 000	12–13
British Isles 1:5 000 000	14

Netherlands, Belgium and Luxembourg 1:2 500 000	15
Central Europe 1:5 000 000	16–17
Eastern Europe and Turkey 1:10 000 000	18–19
France 1:5 000 000	20
Spain and Portugal 1:5 000 000	21
Italy and the Balkan States 1:5 000 000	22–23

Asia

Asia: Physical 1:47 000 000		24
Asia: Political 1:47 000 000		25
Russia and Northern Asia 1:20 000 000		26–27
Japan 1:5 000 000		28–29

China and the Far East 1:15 000 000 Hong Kong, Macau and Shenzhen 1:1 000 000	30–31

Northern China and Korea 1:6 000 000	32–33

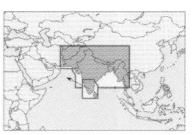

Southern China 1:6 000 000	34–35
Indonesia and the Philippines 1:12 500 000 Java and Madura 1:7 500 000 Bali 1:2 000 000	36–37
Mainland South-east Asia 1:6 000 000 Ko Phuket 1:1 000 000 Ko Samui 1:1 000 000 Pinang 1:1 000 000 Singapore 1:1 000 000	38–39
South Asia 1:10 000 000	40–41

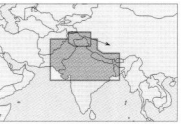

Northern India, Pakistan and Nepal 1:6 000 000 Jammu and Kashmir 1:6 000 000	42–43

Southern India and Sri Lanka
1:6 000 000
Andaman and Nicobar Islands
1:6 000 000

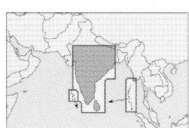

44–45

The Middle East
1:7 000 000

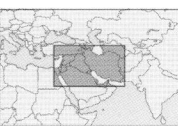

46–47

The Near East 1:2 500 000

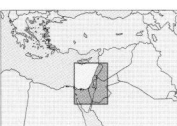

48

**Arabia and the Horn
of Africa** 1:15 000 000

49

Africa

Africa: Physical
1:42 000 000   50

Africa: Political
1:42 000 000   51

Northern Africa
1:15 000 000
Azores 1:15 000 000
Cape Verde Islands 1:10 000 000

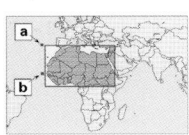

52–53

Central and Southern Africa
1:15 000 000
Comoros 1:8 000 000
Seychelles 1:2 500 000
Réunion 1:2 500 000
Mauritius 1:2 500 000
Madagascar 1:15 000 000

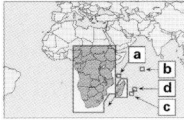

54–55

Southern Africa
1:8 000 000

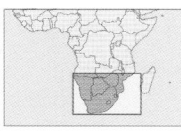

56–57

Australia and Oceania

**Australia and Oceania:
Physical and Political**
1:50 000 000   58

New Zealand 1:6 000 000
Fiji 1:6 000 000
Samoan Islands 1:6 000 000
Tonga 1:6 000 000
Tahiti and Moorea 1:1 000 000

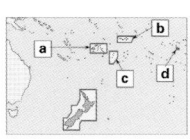

59

Western Australia
1:8 000 000

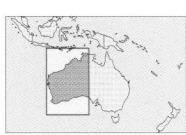

60–61

Eastern Australia
1:8 000 000
Torres Strait 1:8 000 000
Whitsunday Islands 1:2 500 000
Tasmania 1:8 000 000

62–63

Pacific Ocean
1:54 000 000   64–65

North America

North America: Physical
1:35 000 000   66

North America: Political
1:35 000 000   67

Canada 1:15 000 000

68–69

Western Canada 1:7 000 000

70–71

Eastern Canada 1:7 000 000

72–73

United States 1:15 000 000
Hawai'i 1:15 000 000
Alaska 1:15 000 000

74–75

United States – West
1:6 700 000

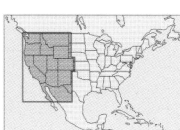

76–77

**Central and Southern
California and Western
Washington**
1:2 500 000

78–79

**United States – Midwest and
North-east**
1:6 700 000

80–81

North-eastern United States
1:2 500 000

82–83

United States – South
1:6 700 000

84–85

Mexico 1:8 000 000

86–87

**Central America and the
West Indies** 1:8 000 000
Jamaica 1:3 000 000
Guadeloupe 1:2 000 000
Martinique 1:2 000 000
Puerto Rico 1:3 000 000
Virgin Islands 1:2 000 000
St Lucia 1:1 000 000
Barbados 1:1 000 000

88–89

South America

South America: Physical
1:35 000 000   90

South America: Political
1:35 000 000   91

South America – North
1:16 000 000
Trinidad and Tobago 1:2 500 000

92–93

Central South America
1:8 000 000

94–95

South America – South
1:16 000 000

96

Index to World Maps

97–176

World Statistics: Countries

This alphabetical list includes the principal countries and territories of the world. If a territory is not completely independent, the country it is associated with is named. The area figures give the total area of land, inland water and ice. The population figures are 2011 estimates where available. The annual income is the Gross Domestic Product per capita in US dollars. The figures are the latest available, usually 2011 estimates.

Country/Territory	Area km² Thousands	Area miles² Thousands	Population Thousands	Capital	Annual Income US $
Afghanistan	652	252	29,835	Kabul	1,000
Albania	28.7	11.1	2,995	Tirana	7,800
Algeria	2,382	920	34,995	Algiers	7,200
American Samoa (US)	0.20	0.08	67	Pago Pago	8,000
Andorra	0.47	0.18	85	Andorra La Vella	37,200
Angola	1,247	481	13,339	Luanda	5,900
Anguilla (UK)	0.10	0.04	15	The Valley	12,200
Antigua & Barbuda	0.44	0.17	88	St John's	22,100
Argentina	2,780	1,074	41,770	Buenos Aires	17,400
Armenia	29.8	11.5	2,968	Yerevan	5,400
Aruba (Netherlands)	0.19	0.07	106	Oranjestad	21,800
Australia	7,741	2,989	21,767	Canberra	40,800
Austria	83.9	32.4	8,217	Vienna	41,700
Azerbaijan	86.6	33.4	8,372	Baku	10,200
Azores (Portugal)	2.2	0.86	236	Ponta Delgada	15,000
Bahamas	13.9	5.4	313	Nassau	30,900
Bahrain	0.69	0.27	1,215	Manama	27,300
Bangladesh	144	55.6	158,571	Dhaka	1,700
Barbados	0.43	0.17	287	Bridgetown	23,600
Belarus	208	80.2	9,578	Minsk	14,900
Belgium	30.5	11.8	10,431	Brussels	37,600
Belize	23.0	8.9	321	Belmopan	8,300
Benin	113	43.5	9,325	Porto-Novo	1,500
Bermuda (UK)	0.05	0.02	70	Hamilton	69,900
Bhutan	47.0	18.1	708	Thimphu	6,000
Bolivia	1,099	424	10,119	La Paz/Sucre	4,800
Bosnia-Herzegovina	51.2	19.8	4,622	Sarajevo	8,200
Botswana	582	225	2,065	Gaborone	16,300
Brazil	8,514	3,287	203,430	Brasília	11,600
Brunei	5.8	2.2	395	Bandar Seri Begawan	49,400
Bulgaria	111	42.8	7,149	Sofia	13,500
Burkina Faso	274	106	16,751	Ouagadougou	1,500
Burma (Myanmar)	677	261	53,414	Rangoon/Naypyidaw	1,300
Burundi	27.8	10.7	10,216	Bujumbura	400
Cambodia	181	69.9	14,702	Phnom Penh	2,300
Cameroon	475	184	19,711	Yaoundé	2,300
Canada	9,971	3,850	34,031	Ottawa	40,300
Canary Is. (Spain)	7.2	2.8	2,117	Las Palmas/Santa Cruz	19,900
Cape Verde Is.	4.0	1.6	516	Praia	4,000
Cayman Is. (UK)	0.26	0.10	51	George Town	43,800
Central African Republic	623	241	4,950	Bangui	800
Chad	1,284	496	10,759	Ndjaména	1,900
Chile	757	292	16,889	Santiago	16,100
China	9,597	3,705	1,336,718	Beijing	8,400
Colombia	1,139	440	44,726	Bogotá	10,100
Comoros	2.2	0.86	795	Moroni	1,200
Congo	342	132	4,244	Brazzaville	4,600
Congo (Dem. Rep. of the)	2,345	905	71,713	Kinshasa	300
Cook Is. (NZ)	0.24	0.09	11	Avarua	9,100
Costa Rica	51.1	19.7	4,577	San José	11,500
Croatia	56.5	21.8	4,484	Zagreb	18,300
Cuba	111	42.8	11,087	Havana	9,900
Curaçao (Netherlands)	0.44	0.17	142	Willemstad	15,000
Cyprus	9.3	3.6	1,120	Nicosia	29,100
Czech Republic	78.9	30.5	10,190	Prague	25,900
Denmark	43.1	16.6	5,530	Copenhagen	40,200
Djibouti	23.2	9.0	757	Djibouti	2,600
Dominica	0.75	0.29	73	Roseau	13,600
Dominican Republic	48.5	18.7	9,957	Santo Domingo	9,300
East Timor	14.9	5.7	1,178	Dili	3,100
Ecuador	284	109	15,007	Quito	8,300
Egypt	1,001	387	82,080	Cairo	6,500
El Salvador	21.0	8.1	6,072	San Salvador	7,600
Equatorial Guinea	28.1	10.8	668	Malabo	19,300
Eritrea	118	45.4	5,939	Asmara	700
Estonia	45.1	17.4	1,283	Tallinn	20,200
Ethiopia	1,104	426	90,874	Addis Ababa	1,100
Falkland Is. (UK)	12.2	4.7	3	Stanley	35,400
Faroe Is. (Denmark)	1.4	0.54	49	Tórshavn	30,500
Fiji	18.3	7.1	883	Suva	4,600
Finland	338	131	5,259	Helsinki	38,300
France	552	213	65,312	Paris	35,000
French Guiana (France)	90.0	34.7	229	Cayenne	8,300
French Polynesia (France)	4.0	1.5	295	Papeete	18,000
Gabon	268	103	1,577	Libreville	16,000
Gambia, The	11.3	4.4	1,798	Banjul	2,100
Gaza Strip (OPT)*	0.36	0.14	1,657	–	2,900
Georgia	69.7	26.9	4,586	Tbilisi	5,400
Germany	357	138	81,472	Berlin	37,900
Ghana	239	92.1	24,791	Accra	3,100
Gibraltar (UK)	0.006	0.002	29	Gibraltar Town	43,000
Greece	132	50.9	10,760	Athens	27,600
Greenland (Denmark)	2,176	840	58	Nuuk	37,400
Grenada	0.34	0.13	108	St George's	13,300
Guadeloupe (France)	1.7	0.66	452	Basse-Terre	7,900
Guam (US)	0.55	0.21	183	Agana	15,000
Guatemala	109	42.0	13,824	Guatemala City	5,000
Guinea	246	94.9	10,601	Conakry	1,100
Guinea-Bissau	36.1	13.9	1,597	Bissau	1,100
Guyana	215	83.0	775	Georgetown	7,500
Haiti	27.8	10.7	9,720	Port-au-Prince	1,200
Honduras	112	43.3	8,144	Tegucigalpa	4,300
Hungary	93.0	35.9	9,976	Budapest	19,600
Iceland	103	39.8	311	Reykjavik	38,000
India	3,287	1,269	1,189,173	New Delhi	3,700
Indonesia	1,905	735	245,613	Jakarta	4,700
Iran	1,648	636	77,891	Tehran	12,200
Iraq	438	169	30,400	Baghdad	3,900
Ireland	70.3	27.1	4,671	Dublin	39,500
Israel	20.6	8.0	7,473	Jerusalem	31,000
Italy	301	116	61,017	Rome	30,100
Ivory Coast (Côte d'Ivoire)	322	125	21,504	Yamoussoukro	1,600
Jamaica	11.0	4.2	2,868	Kingston	9,000
Japan	378	146	126,476	Tokyo	34,300
Jordan	89.3	34.5	6,508	Amman	5,900
Kazakhstan	2,725	1,052	15,522	Astana	13,000
Kenya	580	224	41,071	Nairobi	1,700
Kiribati	0.73	0.28	101	Tarawa	6,200
Korea, North	121	46.5	24,457	Pyŏngyang	1,800
Korea, South	99.3	38.3	48,755	Seoul	31,700
Kosovo	10.9	4.2	1,826	Pristina	6,500
Kuwait	17.8	6.9	2,596	Kuwait City	40,700
Kyrgyzstan	200	77.2	5,587	Bishkek	2,400
Laos	237	91.4	6,477	Vientiane	2,700

Country/Territory	Area km² Thousands	Area miles² Thousands	Population Thousands	Capital	Annual Income US $
Latvia	64.6	24.9	2,205	Riga	15,400
Lebanon	10.4	4.0	4,143	Beirut	15,600
Lesotho	30.4	11.7	1,925	Maseru	1,400
Liberia	111	43.0	3,787	Monrovia	400
Libya	1,760	679	6,598	Tripoli	14,100
Liechtenstein	0.16	0.06	35	Vaduz	141,100
Lithuania	65.2	25.2	3,536	Vilnius	18,700
Luxembourg	2.6	1.0	503	Luxembourg	84,700
Macedonia (FYROM)	25.7	9.9	2,077	Skopje	10,400
Madagascar	587	227	21,926	Antananarivo	900
Madeira (Portugal)	0.78	0.30	267	Funchal	22,700
Malawi	118	45.7	15,879	Lilongwe	900
Malaysia	330	127	28,729	Kuala Lumpur/Putrajaya	15,600
Maldives	0.30	0.12	395	Malé	8,400
Mali	1,240	479	14,160	Bamako	1,300
Malta	0.32	0.12	408	Valletta	25,700
Marshall Is.	0.18	0.07	67	Majuro	2,500
Martinique (France)	1.1	0.43	397	Fort-de-France	14,400
Mauritania	1,026	396	3,282	Nouakchott	2,200
Mauritius	2.0	0.79	1,304	Port Louis	15,000
Mayotte (France)	0.37	0.14	231	Mamoudzou	4,900
Mexico	1,958	756	113,714	Mexico City	15,100
Micronesia, Fed. States of	0.70	0.27	107	Palikir	2,200
Moldova	33.9	13.1	4,314	Kishinev	3,400
Monaco	0.001	0.0004	31	Monaco	63,400
Mongolia	1,567	605	3,133	Ulan Bator	4,500
Montenegro	14.0	5.4	662	Podgorica	11,200
Montserrat (UK)	0.10	0.39	5	Brades	3,400
Morocco	447	172	31,968	Rabat	5,100
Mozambique	802	309	22,949	Maputo	1,100
Namibia	824	318	2,148	Windhoek	7,300
Nauru	0.02	0.008	9	Yaren	5,000
Nepal	147	56.8	29,392	Katmandu	1,300
Netherlands	41.5	16.0	16,847	Amsterdam/The Hague	42,300
Netherlands Antilles (Neths)	0.8	0.31	229	Willemstad	1,600
New Caledonia (France)	18.6	7.2	256	Nouméa	15,000
New Zealand	271	104	4,290	Wellington	27,900
Nicaragua	130	50.2	5,666	Managua	3,200
Niger	1,267	489	16,469	Niamey	800
Nigeria	924	357	155,216	Abuja	2,600
Northern Mariana Is. (US)	0.46	0.18	46	Saipan	12,500
Norway	324	125	4,692	Oslo	53,300
Oman	310	119	3,028	Muscat	26,200
Pakistan	796	307	187,343	Islamabad	2,800
Palau	0.46	0.18	21	Melekeok	8,100
Panama	75.5	29.2	3,460	Panamá	13,600
Papua New Guinea	463	179	6,188	Port Moresby	2,500
Paraguay	407	157	6,459	Asunción	5,500
Peru	1,285	496	29,249	Lima	10,000
Philippines	300	116	101,834	Manila	4,100
Poland	323	125	38,442	Warsaw	20,100
Portugal	88.8	34.3	10,760	Lisbon	23,200
Puerto Rico (US)	8.9	3.4	3,989	San Juan	16,300
Qatar	11.0	4.2	848	Doha	102,700
Réunion (France)	2.5	0.97	839	St-Denis	6,200
Romania	238	92.0	21,905	Bucharest	12,300
Russia	17,075	6,593	138,740	Moscow	16,700
Rwanda	26.3	10.2	11,370	Kigali	1,300
St Kitts & Nevis	0.26	0.10	50	Basseterre	16,400
St Lucia	0.54	0.21	162	Castries	12,900
St Vincent & Grenadines	0.39	0.15	104	Kingstown	11,700
Samoa	2.8	1.1	193	Apia	6,000
San Marino	0.06	0.02	32	San Marino	36,200
São Tomé & Príncipe	0.96	0.37	180	São Tomé	2,000
Saudi Arabia	2,150	830	26,132	Riyadh	24,000
Senegal	197	76.0	12,644	Dakar	1,900
Serbia	77.5	29.9	7,311	Belgrade	10,700
Seychelles	0.46	0.18	89	Victoria	24,700
Sierra Leone	71.7	27.7	5,364	Freetown	800
Singapore	0.68	0.26	4,741	Singapore City	59,900
Slovak Republic	49.0	18.9	5,477	Bratislava	23,400
Slovenia	20.3	7.8	2,003	Ljubljana	29,100
Solomon Is.	28.9	11.2	572	Honiara	3,300
Somalia	638	246	9,926	Mogadishu	600
South Africa	1,221	471	49,004	Cape Town/Pretoria	11,000
Spain	498	192	46,755	Madrid	30,600
Sri Lanka	65.6	25.3	21,284	Colombo	5,600
Sudan	1,886	728	35,680	Khartoum	3,000
Sudan, South	620	239	8,260	Juba	1,500
Suriname	163	63.0	492	Paramaribo	9,500
Swaziland	17.4	6.7	1,370	Mbabane	5,200
Sweden	450	174	9,089	Stockholm	40,600
Switzerland	41.3	15.9	7,640	Bern	43,400
Syria	185	71.5	22,518	Damascus	5,100
Taiwan	36.0	13.9	23,072	Taipei	37,900
Tajikistan	143	55.3	7,627	Dushanbe	2,000
Tanzania	945	365	42,747	Dodoma	1,500
Thailand	513	198	66,720	Bangkok	9,700
Togo	56.8	21.9	6,772	Lomé	900
Tonga	0.65	0.25	106	Nuku'alofa	7,500
Trinidad & Tobago	5.1	2.0	1,228	Port of Spain	20,300
Tunisia	164	63.2	10,629	Tunis	9,500
Turkey	775	299	78,786	Ankara	14,600
Turkmenistan	488	188	4,998	Ashkhabad	7,500
Turks & Caicos Is. (UK)	0.43	0.17	45	Cockburn Town	11,500
Tuvalu	0.03	0.01	11	Fongafale	3,400
Uganda	241	93.1	34,612	Kampala	1,300
Ukraine	604	233	45,135	Kiev	7,200
United Arab Emirates	83.6	32.3	5,149	Abu Dhabi	48,500
United Kingdom	242	93.4	62,698	London	35,900
United States of America	9,629	3,718	313,232	Washington, DC	48,100
Uruguay	175	67.6	3,309	Montevideo	15,400
Uzbekistan	447	173	28,129	Tashkent	3,300
Vanuatu	12.2	4.7	225	Port-Vila	4,900
Venezuela	912	352	27,636	Caracas	12,400
Vietnam	332	128	90,549	Hanoi	3,300
Virgin Is. (UK)	0.15	0.06	25	Road Town	38,500
Virgin Is. (US)	0.35	0.13	110	Charlotte Amalie	14,500
Wallis & Futuna Is. (France)	0.20	0.08	15	Mata-Utu	3,800
West Bank (OPT)*	5.9	2.3	2,569	–	2,900
Western Sahara	266	103	507	El Aaiún	2,500
Yemen	528	204	24,133	Sana'	2,500
Zambia	753	291	13,881	Lusaka	1,600
Zimbabwe	391	151	12,084	Harare	500

*OPT = Occupied Palestinian Territory

World Statistics: Physical Dimensions

Each topic list is divided into continents and within a continent the items are listed in order of size. The bottom part of many of the lists is selective in order to give examples from as many different countries as possible. The order of the continents is the same as in the atlas, beginning with Europe and ending with South America. The figures are rounded as appropriate.

World, Continents, Oceans

	km^2	$miles^2$	%
The World	509,450,000	196,672,000	–
Land	149,450,000	57,688,000	29.3
Water	360,000,000	138,984,000	70.7
Asia	44,500,000	17,177,000	29.8
Africa	30,302,000	11,697,000	20.3
North America	24,241,000	9,357,000	16.2
South America	17,793,000	6,868,000	11.9
Antarctica	14,100,000	5,443,000	9.4
Europe	9,957,000	3,843,000	6.7
Australia & Oceania	8,557,000	3,303,000	5.7
Pacific Ocean	155,557,000	60,061,000	46.4
Atlantic Ocean	76,762,000	29,638,000	22.9
Indian Ocean	68,556,000	26,470,000	20.4
Southern Ocean	20,327,000	7,848,000	6.1
Arctic Ocean	14,056,000	5,427,000	4.2

Ocean Depths

Atlantic Ocean	m	ft
Puerto Rico (Milwaukee) Deep	8,605	28,232
Cayman Trench	7,680	25,197
Gulf of Mexico	5,203	17,070
Mediterranean Sea	5,121	16,801
Black Sea	2,211	7,254
North Sea	660	2,165

Indian Ocean	m	ft
Java Trench	7,450	24,442
Red Sea	2,635	8,454

Pacific Ocean	m	ft
Mariana Trench	11,022	36,161
Tonga Trench	10,882	35,702
Japan Trench	10,554	34,626
Kuril Trench	10,542	34,587

Arctic Ocean	m	ft
Molloy Deep	5,608	18,399

Southern Ocean	m	ft
South Sandwich Trench	7,235	23,737

Mountains

Europe		m	ft
Elbrus	*Russia*	5,642	18,510
Dykh-Tau	*Russia*	5,205	17,076
Shkhara	*Russia/Georgia*	5,201	17,064
Koshtan-Tau	*Russia*	5,152	16,903
Kazbek	*Russia/Georgia*	5,047	16,558
Pushkin	*Russia/Georgia*	5,033	16,512
Katyn-Tau	*Russia/Georgia*	4,979	16,335
Shota Rustaveli	*Russia/Georgia*	4,860	15,945
Mont Blanc	*France/Italy*	4,808	15,774
Monte Rosa	*Italy/Switzerland*	4,634	15,203
Dom	*Switzerland*	4,545	14,911
Liskamm	*Switzerland*	4,527	14,852
Weisshorn	*Switzerland*	4,505	14,780
Taschorn	*Switzerland*	4,490	14,730
Matterhorn/Cervino	*Italy/Switzerland*	4,478	14,691
Grossglockner	*Austria*	3,797	12,457
Mulhacén	*Spain*	3,478	11,411
Zugspitze	*Germany*	2,962	9,718
Olympus	*Greece*	2,917	9,570
Galdhøpiggen	*Norway*	2,469	8,100
Ben Nevis	*UK*	1,344	4,409

Asia		m	ft
Everest	*China/Nepal*	8,850	29,035
K2 (Godwin Austen)	*China/Kashmir*	8,611	28,251
Kanchenjunga	*India/Nepal*	8,598	28,208
Lhotse	*China/Nepal*	8,516	27,939
Makalu	*China/Nepal*	8,481	27,824
Cho Oyu	*China/Nepal*	8,201	26,906
Dhaulagiri	*Nepal*	8,167	26,795
Manaslu	*Nepal*	8,156	26,758
Nanga Parbat	*Kashmir*	8,126	26,660
Annapurna	*Nepal*	8,078	26,502
Gasherbrum	*China/Kashmir*	8,068	26,469
Broad Peak	*China/Kashmir*	8,051	26,414
Xixabangma	*China*	8,012	26,286
Kangbachen	*Nepal*	7,858	25,781
Trivor	*Pakistan*	7,720	25,328
Pik Imeni Ismail Samani	*Tajikistan*	7,495	24,590
Demavend	*Iran*	5,604	18,386
Ararat	*Turkey*	5,165	16,945
Gunong Kinabalu	*Malaysia (Borneo)*	4,101	13,455
Fuji-San	*Japan*	3,776	12,388

Africa		m	ft
Kilimanjaro	*Tanzania*	5,895	19,340
Mt Kenya	*Kenya*	5,199	17,057
Ruwenzori (Margherita)	*Ug./Congo (D.R.)*	5,109	16,762
Meru	*Tanzania*	4,565	14,977
Ras Dashen	*Ethiopia*	4,553	14,937
Karisimbi	*Rwanda/Congo (D.R.)*	4,507	14,787
Mt Elgon	*Kenya/Uganda*	4,321	14,176
Batu	*Ethiopia*	4,307	14,130
Toubkal	*Morocco*	4,165	13,665
Mt Cameroun	*Cameroon*	4,070	13,353

Oceania		m	ft
Puncak Jaya	*Indonesia*	4,884	16,024
Puncak Trikora	*Indonesia*	4,730	15,518
Puncak Mandala	*Indonesia*	4,702	15,427
Mt Wilhelm	*Papua New Guinea*	4,508	14,790
Mauna Kea	*USA (Hawai'i)*	4,205	13,796
Mauna Loa	*USA (Hawai'i)*	4,169	13,678
Aoraki Mt Cook	*New Zealand*	3,753	12,313
Mt Kosciuszko	*Australia*	2,228	7,310

North America		m	ft
Mt McKinley (Denali)	*USA (Alaska)*	6,194	20,321
Mt Logan	*Canada*	5,959	19,551
Pico de Orizaba	*Mexico*	5,610	18,405
Mt St Elias	*USA/Canada*	5,489	18,008
Popocatépetl	*Mexico*	5,452	17,887
Mt Foraker	*USA (Alaska)*	5,304	17,401
Iztaccihuatl	*Mexico*	5,286	17,342
Mt Lucania	*Canada*	5,226	17,146
Mt Steele	*Canada*	5,073	16,644
Mt Bona	*USA (Alaska)*	5,005	16,420
Mt Whitney	*USA*	4,418	14,495
Tajumulco	*Guatemala*	4,220	13,845
Chirripó Grande	*Costa Rica*	3,837	12,589
Pico Duarte	*Dominican Rep.*	3,175	10,417

South America		m	ft
Aconcagua	*Argentina*	6,962	22,841
Bonete	*Argentina*	6,872	22,546
Ojos del Salado	*Argentina/Chile*	6,863	22,516
Pissis	*Argentina*	6,779	22,241
Mercedario	*Argentina/Chile*	6,770	22,211
Huascarán	*Peru*	6,768	22,204
Llullaillaco	*Argentina/Chile*	6,723	22,057
Nevado de Cachi	*Argentina*	6,720	22,047
Yerupaja	*Peru*	6,632	21,758
Sajama	*Bolivia*	6,520	21,391
Chimborazo	*Ecuador*	6,267	20,561
Pico Cristóbal Colón	*Colombia*	5,800	19,029
Pico Bolivar	*Venezuela*	5,007	16,427

Antarctica		m	ft
Vinson Massif		4,897	16,066
Mt Kirkpatrick		4,528	14,855

Rivers

Europe		km	miles
Volga	*Caspian Sea*	3,700	2,300
Danube	*Black Sea*	2,850	1,770
Ural	*Caspian Sea*	2,535	1,575
Dnieper	*Black Sea*	2,285	1,420
Kama	*Volga*	2,030	1,260
Don	*Black Sea*	1,990	1,240
Petchora	*Arctic Ocean*	1,790	1,110
Oka	*Volga*	1,480	920
Dniester	*Black Sea*	1,400	870
Vyatka	*Kama*	1,370	850
Rhine	*North Sea*	1,320	820
N. Dvina	*Arctic Ocean*	1,290	800
Elbe	*North Sea*	1,145	710

Asia		km	miles
Yangtse	*Pacific Ocean*	6,380	3,960
Yenisey–Angara	*Arctic Ocean*	5,550	3,445
Huang He	*Pacific Ocean*	5,464	3,395
Ob–Irtysh	*Arctic Ocean*	5,410	3,360
Mekong	*Pacific Ocean*	4,500	2,795
Amur	*Pacific Ocean*	4,442	2,760
Lena	*Arctic Ocean*	4,402	2,735
Irtysh	*Ob*	4,250	2,640
Yenisey	*Arctic Ocean*	4,090	2,540
Ob	*Arctic Ocean*	3,680	2,285
Indus	*Indian Ocean*	3,100	1,925
Brahmaputra	*Indian Ocean*	2,900	1,800
Syrdarya	*Aralkum Desert*	2,860	1,775
Salween	*Indian Ocean*	2,800	1,740
Euphrates	*Indian Ocean*	2,700	1,675
Amudarya	*Aralkum Desert*	2,540	1,575

Africa		km	miles
Nile	*Mediterranean*	6,695	4,160
Congo	*Atlantic Ocean*	4,670	2,900
Niger	*Atlantic Ocean*	4,180	2,595
Zambezi	*Indian Ocean*	3,540	2,200
Oubangi/Uele	*Congo (D.R.)*	2,250	1,400
Kasai	*Congo (D.R.)*	1,950	1,210
Shaballe	*Indian Ocean*	1,930	1,200
Orange	*Atlantic Ocean*	1,860	1,155
Cubango	*Okavango Delta*	1,800	1,120
Limpopo	*Indian Ocean*	1,770	1,100
Senegal	*Atlantic Ocean*	1,640	1,020

Australia		km	miles
Murray–Darling	*Southern Ocean*	3,750	2,330
Darling	*Murray*	3,070	1,905
Murray	*Southern Ocean*	2,575	1,600
Murrumbidgee	*Murray*	1,690	1,050

North America		km	miles
Mississippi–Missouri	*Gulf of Mexico*	5,971	3,710
Mackenzie	*Arctic Ocean*	4,240	2,630
Missouri	*Mississippi*	4,088	2,540
Mississippi	*Gulf of Mexico*	3,782	2,350
Yukon	*Pacific Ocean*	3,185	1,980
Rio Grande	*Gulf of Mexico*	3,030	1,880
Arkansas	*Mississippi*	2,340	1,450
Colorado	*Pacific Ocean*	2,330	1,445
Red	*Mississippi*	2,040	1,270
Columbia	*Pacific Ocean*	1,950	1,210
Saskatchewan	*Lake Winnipeg*	1,940	1,205

South America		km	miles
Amazon	*Atlantic Ocean*	6,450	4,010
Paraná–Plate	*Atlantic Ocean*	4,500	2,800
Purus	*Amazon*	3,350	2,080
Madeira	*Amazon*	3,200	1,990
São Francisco	*Atlantic Ocean*	2,900	1,800
Paraná	*Plate*	2,800	1,740
Tocantins	*Atlantic Ocean*	2,750	1,710
Orinoco	*Atlantic Ocean*	2,740	1,700
Paraguay	*Paraná*	2,550	1,580
Pilcomayo	*Paraná*	2,500	1,550
Araguaia	*Tocantins*	2,250	1,400

Lakes

Europe		km^2	$miles^2$
Lake Ladoga	*Russia*	17,700	6,800
Lake Onega	*Russia*	9,700	3,700
Saimaa system	*Finland*	8,000	3,100
Vänern	*Sweden*	5,500	2,100

Asia		km^2	$miles^2$
Caspian Sea	*Asia*	371,000	143,000
Lake Baikal	*Russia*	30,500	11,780
Tonlé Sap	*Cambodia*	20,000	7,700
Lake Balqash	*Kazakhstan*	18,500	7,100
Aral Sea	*Kazakhstan/Uzbekistan*	17,160	6,625

Africa		km^2	$miles^2$
Lake Victoria	*East Africa*	68,000	26,300
Lake Tanganyika	*Central Africa*	33,000	13,000
Lake Malawi/Nyasa	*East Africa*	29,600	11,430
Lake Chad	*Central Africa*	25,000	9,700
Lake Bangweulu	*Zambia*	9,840	3,800
Lake Turkana	*Ethiopia/Kenya*	8,500	3,290

Australia		km^2	$miles^2$
Lake Eyre	*Australia*	8,900	3,400
Lake Torrens	*Australia*	5,800	2,200
Lake Gairdner	*Australia*	4,800	1,900

North America		km^2	$miles^2$
Lake Superior	*Canada/USA*	82,350	31,800
Lake Huron	*Canada/USA*	59,600	23,010
Lake Michigan	*USA*	58,000	22,400
Great Bear Lake	*Canada*	31,800	12,280
Great Slave Lake	*Canada*	28,500	11,000
Lake Erie	*Canada/USA*	25,700	9,900
Lake Winnipeg	*Canada*	24,400	9,400
Lake Ontario	*Canada/USA*	19,500	7,500
Lake Nicaragua	*Nicaragua*	8,200	3,200

South America		km^2	$miles^2$
Lake Titicaca	*Bolivia/Peru*	8,300	3,200
Lake Poopo	*Bolivia*	2,800	1,100

Islands

Europe		km^2	$miles^2$
Great Britain	*UK*	229,880	88,700
Iceland	*Atlantic Ocean*	103,000	39,800
Ireland	*Ireland/UK*	84,400	32,600
Novaya Zemlya (N.)	*Russia*	48,200	18,600
Sicily	*Italy*	25,500	9,800
Corsica	*France*	8,700	3,400

Asia		km^2	$miles^2$
Borneo	*South-east Asia*	744,360	287,400
Sumatra	*Indonesia*	473,600	182,860
Honshu	*Japan*	230,500	88,980
Celebes	*Indonesia*	189,000	73,000
Java	*Indonesia*	126,700	48,900
Luzon	*Philippines*	104,700	40,400
Hokkaido	*Japan*	78,400	30,300

Africa		km^2	$miles^2$
Madagascar	*Indian Ocean*	587,040	226,660
Socotra	*Indian Ocean*	3,600	1,400
Réunion	*Indian Ocean*	2,500	965

Oceania		km^2	$miles^2$
New Guinea	*Indonesia/Papua NG*	821,030	317,000
New Zealand (S.)	*Pacific Ocean*	150,500	58,100
New Zealand (N.)	*Pacific Ocean*	114,700	44,300
Tasmania	*Australia*	67,800	26,200
Hawai'i	*Pacific Ocean*	10,450	4,000

North America		km^2	$miles^2$
Greenland	*Atlantic Ocean*	2,175,600	839,800
Baffin Is.	*Canada*	508,000	196,100
Victoria Is.	*Canada*	212,200	81,900
Ellesmere Is.	*Canada*	212,000	81,800
Cuba	*Caribbean Sea*	110,860	42,800
Hispaniola	*Dominican Rep./Haiti*	76,200	29,400
Jamaica	*Caribbean Sea*	11,400	4,400
Puerto Rico	*Atlantic Ocean*	8,900	3,400

South America		km^2	$miles^2$
Tierra del Fuego	*Argentina/Chile*	47,000	18,100
Falkland Is. (E.)	*Atlantic Ocean*	6,800	2,600

User Guide

The reference maps which form the main body of this atlas have been prepared in accordance with the highest standards of international cartography to provide an accurate and detailed representation of the Earth. The scales and projections used have been carefully chosen to give balanced coverage of the world, while emphasizing the most densely populated and economically significant regions. A hallmark of Philip's mapping is the use of hill shading and relief colouring to create a graphic impression of landforms: this makes the maps exceptionally easy to read. However, knowledge of the key features employed in the construction and presentation of the maps will enable the reader to derive the fullest benefit from the atlas.

Map sequence

The atlas covers the Earth continent by continent: first Europe; then its land neighbour Asia (mapped north before south, in a clockwise sequence), then Africa, Australia and Oceania, North America and South America. This is the classic arrangement adopted by most cartographers since the 16th century. For each continent, there are maps at a variety of scales. First, physical relief and political maps of the whole continent; then a series of larger-scale maps of the regions within the continent, each followed, where required, by still larger-scale maps of the most important or densely populated areas. The governing principle is that by turning the pages of the atlas, the reader moves steadily from north to south through each continent, with each map overlapping its neighbours.

Map presentation

With very few exceptions (for example, for the Arctic and Antarctica), the maps are drawn with north at the top, regardless of whether they are presented upright or sideways on the page. In the borders will be found the map title; a locator diagram showing the area covered; continuation arrows showing the page numbers for maps of adjacent areas; the scale; the projection used; the degrees of latitude and longitude; and the letters and figures used in the index for locating place names and geographical features. Physical relief maps also have a height reference panel identifying the colours used for each layer of contouring.

Map symbols

Each map contains a vast amount of detail which can only be conveyed clearly and accurately by the use of symbols. Points and circles of varying sizes locate and identify the relative importance of towns and cities; different styles of type are employed for administrative, geographical and regional place names. A variety of pictorial symbols denote features such as glaciers and marshes, as well as man-made structures including roads, railways, airports and canals.

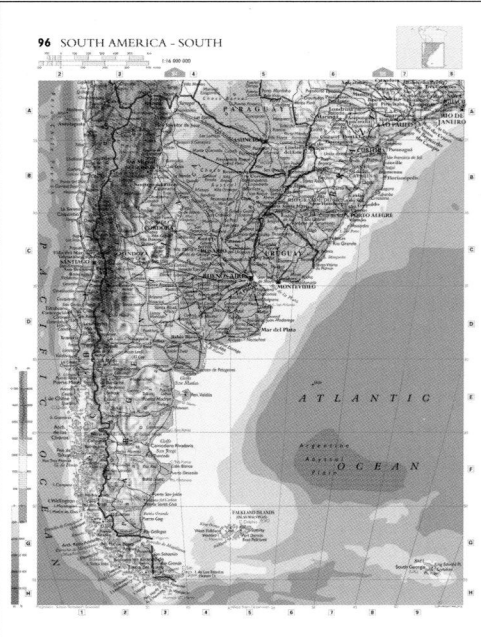

International borders are shown by red lines. Where neighbouring countries are in dispute, for example in the Middle East, the maps show the *de facto* boundary between nations, regardless of the legal or historical situation. The symbols are explained on the first page of the World Maps section of the atlas.

Map scales

The scale of each map is given in the numerical form known as the 'representative fraction'. The first figure is always one, signifying one unit of distance on the map; the second figure, usually in millions, is the number by which the map unit must be multiplied to give the equivalent distance on the Earth's surface. Calculations can easily be made in centimetres and kilometres, by dividing the Earth units figure by 100 000 (i.e. deleting the last five 0s). Thus 1:1 000 000 means 1 cm = 10 km. The calculation for inches and miles is more laborious, but 1 000 000 divided by 63 360 (the number of inches in a mile) shows that the ratio 1:1 000 000 means approximately 1 inch = 16 miles. The table below provides distance equivalents for scales down to 1:50 000 000.

LARGE SCALE		
1:1 000 000	1 cm = 10 km	1 inch = 16 miles
1:2 500 000	1 cm = 25 km	1 inch = 39.5 miles
1:5 000 000	1 cm = 50 km	1 inch = 79 miles
1:6 000 000	1 cm = 60 km	1 inch = 95 miles
1:8 000 000	1 cm = 80 km	1 inch = 126 miles
1:10 000 000	1 cm = 100 km	1 inch = 158 miles
1:15 000 000	1 cm = 150 km	1 inch = 237 miles
1:20 000 000	1 cm = 200 km	1 inch = 316 miles
1:50 000 000	1 cm = 500 km	1 inch = 790 miles
SMALL SCALE		

Measuring distances

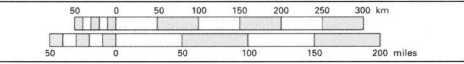

Although each map is accompanied by a scale bar, distances cannot always be measured with confidence because of the distortions involved in portraying the curved surface of the Earth on a flat page. As a general rule, the larger the map scale (i.e. the lower the number of Earth units in the representative fraction), the more accurate and reliable will be the distance measured. On small-scale maps such as those of the world and of entire continents, measurement may only be accurate along the 'standard parallels', or central axes, and should not be attempted without considering the map projection.

Latitude and longitude

Accurate positioning of individual points on the Earth's surface is made possible by reference to the geometrical system of latitude and longitude. Latitude *parallels* are drawn west–east around the Earth and numbered by degrees north and south of the Equator, which is designated 0° of latitude. Longitude *meridians* are drawn north–south and numbered by degrees east and west of the *prime meridian*, 0° of longitude, which passes through Greenwich in England. By referring to these co-ordinates and their subdivisions of minutes ($^1/_{60}$th of a degree) and seconds ($^1/_{60}$th of a minute), any place on Earth can be located to within a few hundred metres. Latitude and longitude are indicated by blue lines on the maps; they are straight or curved according to the projection employed. Reference to these lines is the easiest way of determining the relative positions of places on different maps, and for plotting compass directions.

Name forms

For ease of reference, both English and local name forms appear in the atlas. Oceans, seas and countries are shown in English throughout the atlas; country names may be abbreviated to their commonly accepted form (for example, Germany, not The Federal Republic of Germany). Conventional English forms are also used for place names on the smaller-scale maps of the continents. However, local name forms are used on all large-scale and regional maps, with the English form given in brackets only for important cities – the large-scale map of Russia and Central Asia thus shows Moskva (Moscow). For countries which do not use a Roman script, place names have been transcribed according to the systems adopted by the British and US Geographic Names Authorities. For China, the Pin Yin system has been used, with some more widely known forms appearing in brackets, as with Beijing (Peking). Both English and local names appear in the index, the English form being cross-referenced to the local form.

THE
WORLD
IN FOCUS

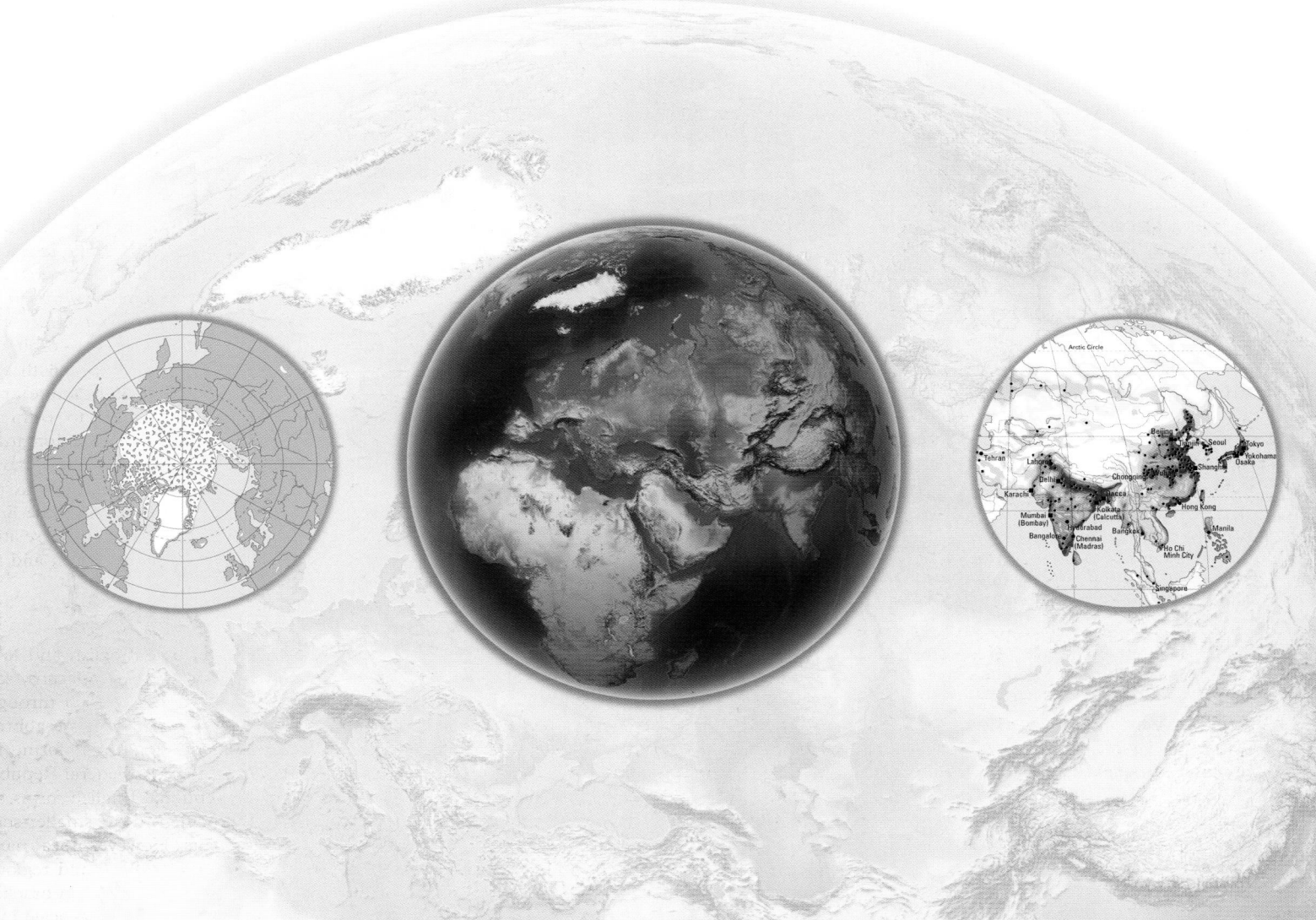

PLANET EARTH	2	WATER AND VEGETATION	12	QUALITY OF LIFE	22
RESTLESS EARTH	4	ENVIRONMENT	14	ENERGY	24
LANDFORMS	6	POPULATION	16	PRODUCTION	26
OCEANS	8	THE HUMAN FAMILY	18	TRADE	28
CLIMATE	10	WEALTH	20	TRAVEL AND TOURISM	30

Planet Earth

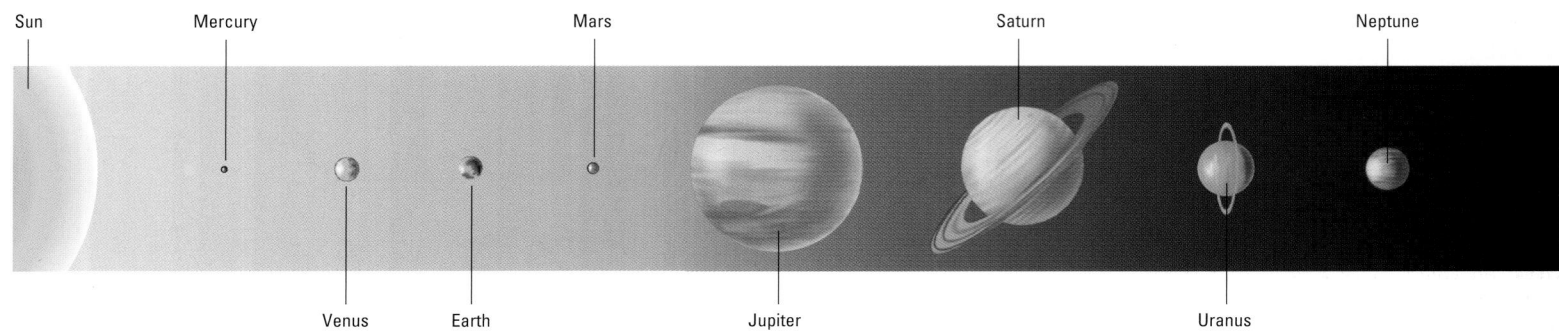

Sun · Mercury · Venus · Earth · Mars · Jupiter · Saturn · Uranus · Neptune

THE SOLAR SYSTEM

A minute part of one of the billions of galaxies (collections of stars) that populate the Universe, the Solar System lies about 26,000 light-years from the centre of our own Galaxy, the 'Milky Way'. Thought to be about 5 billion years old, it consists of a central Sun with eight planets and their moons revolving around it, attracted by its gravitational pull. The planets orbit the Sun in the same direction – anti-clockwise when viewed from above the Sun's north pole – and almost in the same plane. Their orbital distances, however, vary enormously.

The Sun's diameter is 109 times that of the Earth, and the temperature at its core – caused by continuous thermonuclear fusions of hydrogen into helium – is estimated to be 15 million degrees Celsius. It is the Solar System's only source of light and heat.

PROFILE OF THE PLANETS

	Mean distance from Sun (million km)	Mass (Earth = 1)	Period of orbit (Earth days/years)	Period of rotation (Earth days)	Equatorial diameter (km)	Number of known satellites*
Mercury	57.9	0.06	87.97 days	58.65	4,879	0
Venus	108.2	0.82	224.7 days	243.02	12,104	0
Earth	149.6	1.00	365.3 days	1.00	12,756	1
Mars	227.9	0.11	687.0 days	1.029	6,792	2
Jupiter	778	317.8	11.86 years	0.411	142,984	67
Saturn	1,427	95.2	29.45 years	0.428	120,536	62
Uranus	2,871	14.5	84.02 years	0.720	51,118	27
Neptune	4,498	17.2	164.8 years	0.673	49,528	13

* Number of known satellites at mid-2012

All planetary orbits are elliptical in form, but only Mercury follows a path that deviates noticeably from a circular one. In 2006, Pluto was demoted from its former status as a planet and is now regarded as a member of the Kuiper Belt of icy bodies at the fringes of the Solar System.

THE SEASONS

Seasons occur because the Earth's axis is tilted at an angle of approximately 23½°. When the northern hemisphere is tilted to a maximum extent towards the Sun, on 21 June, the Sun is overhead at the Tropic of Cancer (latitude 23½° North). This is midsummer, or the summer solstice, in the northern hemisphere.

On 22 or 23 September, the Sun is overhead at the Equator, and day and night are of equal length throughout the world. This is the autumnal equinox in the northern hemisphere. On 21 or 22 December, the Sun is overhead at the Tropic of Capricorn (23½° South), the winter solstice in the northern hemisphere. The overhead Sun then tracks north until, on 21 March, it is overhead at the Equator. This is the spring (vernal) equinox in the northern hemisphere.

In the southern hemisphere, the seasons are the reverse of those in the north.

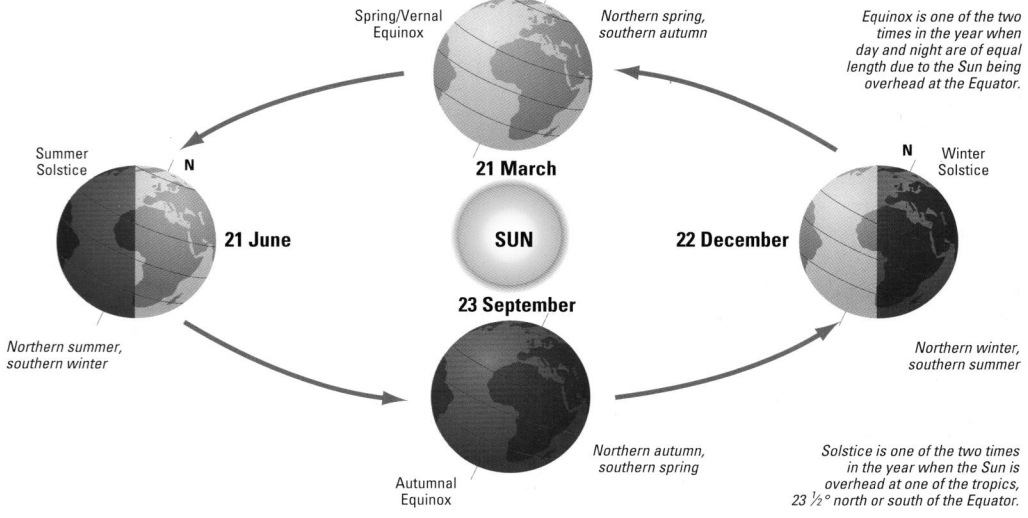

DAY AND NIGHT

The Sun appears to rise in the east, reach its highest point at noon, and then set in the west, to be followed by night. In reality, it is not the Sun that is moving but the Earth rotating from west to east. The moment when the Sun's upper limb first appears above the horizon is termed sunrise; the moment when the Sun's upper limb disappears below the horizon is sunset.

At the summer solstice in the northern hemisphere (21 June), the Arctic has total daylight and the Antarctic total darkness. The opposite occurs at the winter solstice (21 or 22 December). At the Equator, the length of day and night are almost equal all year.

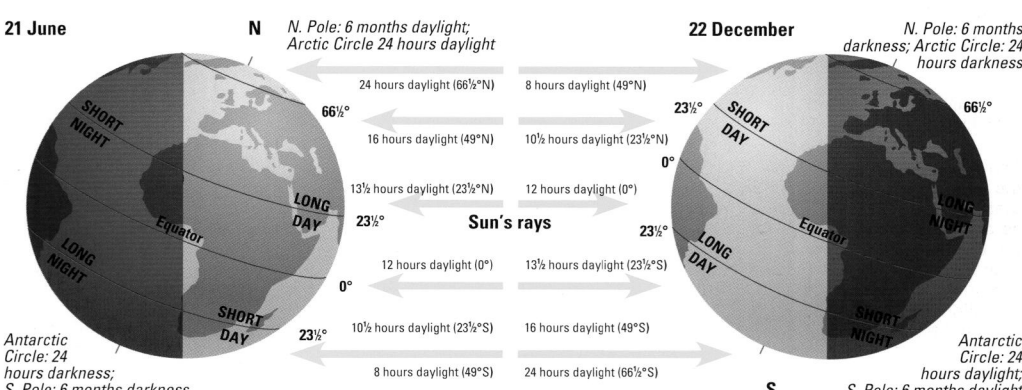

TIME

Year: The time taken by the Earth to revolve around the Sun, or 365.24 days.

Leap Year: A calendar year of 366 days, 29 February being the additional day. It offsets the difference between the calendar and the solar year.

Month: The 12 calendar months of the year are approximately equal in length to a lunar month.

Week: An artificial period of 7 days, not based on astronomical time.

Day: The time taken by the Earth to complete one rotation on its axis.

Hour: 24 hours make one day. The day is divided into hours a.m. (ante meridiem or before noon) and p.m. (post meridiem or after noon), although most timetables now use the 24-hour system, from midnight to midnight.

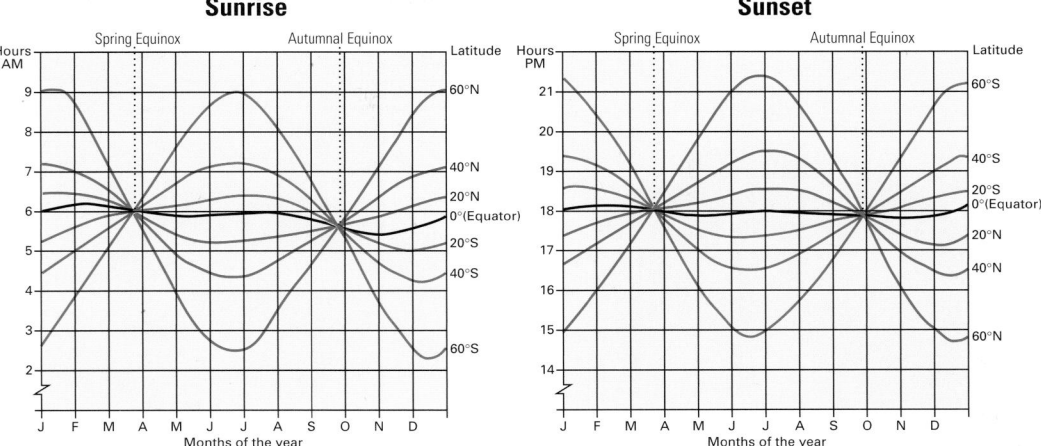

THE MOON

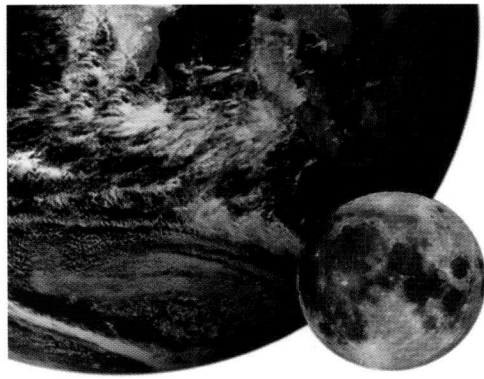

The Moon rotates more slowly than the Earth, taking just over 27 days to make one complete rotation on its axis. This corresponds to the Moon's orbital period around the Earth, and therefore the Moon always presents the same hemisphere towards us; some 41% of the Moon's far side is never visible from the Earth. The interval between one New Moon and the next is 29½ days – this is called a lunation, or lunar month. The Moon shines only by reflected sunlight, and emits no light of its own. During each lunation the Moon displays a complete cycle of phases, caused by the changing angle of illumination from the Sun.

PHASES OF THE MOON

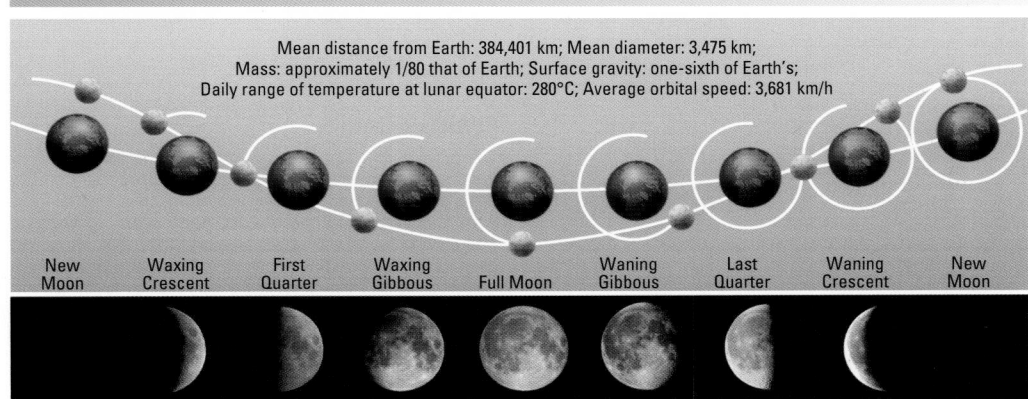

Mean distance from Earth: 384,401 km; Mean diameter: 3,475 km; Mass: approximately 1/80 that of Earth; Surface gravity: one-sixth of Earth's; Daily range of temperature at lunar equator: 280°C; Average orbital speed: 3,681 km/h

ECLIPSES

When the Moon passes between the Sun and the Earth, the Sun becomes partially eclipsed (1). A partial eclipse becomes a total eclipse if the Moon proceeds to cover the Sun completely (2) and the dark central part of the lunar shadow touches the Earth. The broad geographical zone covered by the Moon's outer shadow (P) has only a very small central area (often less than 100 km wide) that experiences totality. Totality can never last for more than 7½ minutes at maximum, but is usually much briefer than this. Lunar eclipses take place when the Moon moves through the shadow of the Earth, and can be partial or total. Any single location on Earth can experience a maximum of four solar and three lunar eclipses in any single year, while a total solar eclipse occurs an average of once every 360 years for any given location.

TIDES

The daily rise and fall of the ocean's tides are the result of the gravitational pull of the Moon and that of the Sun, though the effect of the latter is not as strong as that of the Moon. This effect is greatest on the hemisphere facing the Moon and causes a tidal 'bulge'.

Spring tides occur when the Sun, Earth and Moon are aligned; high tides are at their highest, and low tides fall to their lowest. When the Moon and Sun are furthest out of line (near the Moon's First and Last Quarters), neap tides occur, producing the smallest range between high and low tides.

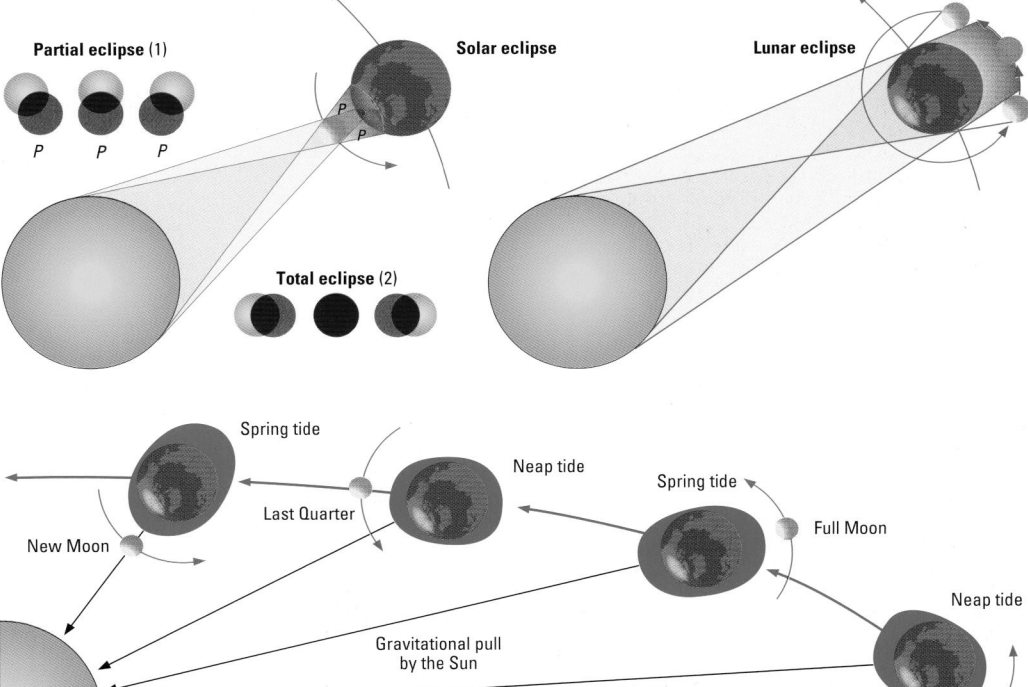

Restless Earth

THE EARTH'S STRUCTURE

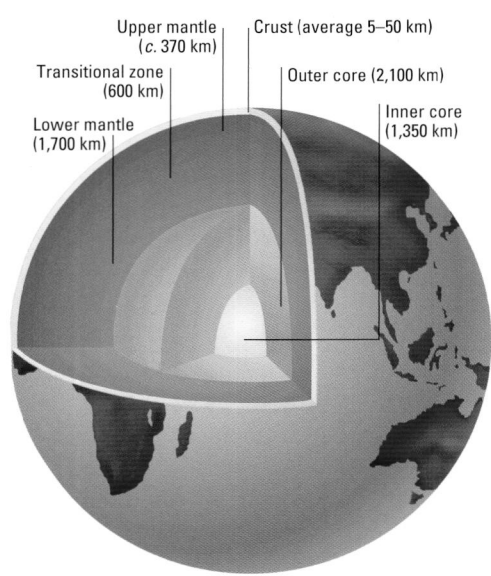

Upper mantle (c. 370 km)
Crust (average 5–50 km)
Transitional zone (600 km)
Outer core (2,100 km)
Lower mantle (1,700 km)
Inner core (1,350 km)

CONTINENTAL DRIFT

About 200 million years ago the original Pangaea landmass began to split into two continental groups, which further separated over time to produce the present-day configuration.

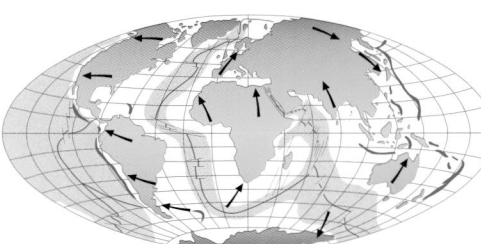

180 million years ago

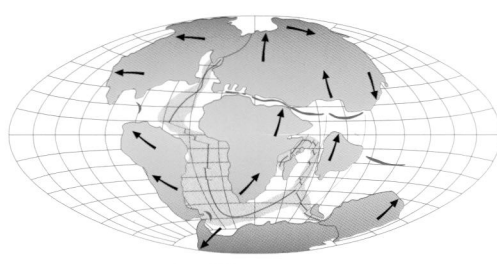

135 million years ago

Trench
Rift
New ocean floor
Zones of slippage

Present day

NOTABLE EARTHQUAKES SINCE 1900

Year	Location	Richter Scale	Deaths
1906	San Francisco, USA	8.3	3,000
1906	Valparaiso, Chile	8.6	22,000
1908	Messina, Italy	7.5	83,000
1915	Avezzano, Italy	7.5	30,000
1920	Gansu (Kansu), China	8.6	180,000
1923	Yokohama, Japan	8.3	143,000
1927	Nan Shan, China	8.3	200,000
1932	Gansu (Kansu), China	7.6	70,000
1933	Sanriku, Japan	8.9	2,990
1934	Bihar, India/Nepal	8.4	10,700
1935	Quetta, India (now Pakistan)	7.5	60,000
1939	Chillan, Chile	8.3	28,000
1939	Erzincan, Turkey	7.9	30,000
1960	S. W. Chile	9.5	2,200
1960	Agadir, Morocco	5.8	12,000
1962	Khorasan, Iran	7.1	12,230
1964	Anchorage, USA	9.2	125
1970	N. Peru	7.8	70,000
1972	Managua, Nicaragua	6.2	5,000
1976	Guatemala	7.5	22,500
1976	Tangshan, China	8.2	255,000
1978	Tabas, Iran	7.7	25,000
1980	El Asnam, Algeria	7.3	20,000
1985	Mexico City, Mexico	8.1	4,200
1988	N.W. Armenia	6.8	55,000
1990	N. Iran	7.7	36,000
1993	Maharashtra, India	6.4	30,000
1994	Los Angeles, USA	6.6	51
1995	Kobe, Japan	7.2	5,000
1998	Rostaq, Afghanistan	7.0	5,000
1999	Izmit, Turkey	7.4	15,000
1999	Taipei, Taiwan	7.6	1,700
2001	Gujarat, India	7.7	14,000
2003	Bam, Iran	6.6	30,000
2004	Sumatra, Indonesia	9.0	250,000
2005	N. Pakistan	7.6	74,000
2006	Java, Indonesia	6.4	6,200
2007	S. Peru	8.0	600
2008	Sichuan, China	7.9	70,000
2010	Haiti	7.0	230,000
2011	Christchurch, New Zealand	6.3	182
2011	N. Japan	9.0	28,000

EARTHQUAKES

Earthquake magnitude is usually rated according to either the Richter or the Modified Mercalli scale, both devised by seismologists in the 1930s. The Richter scale measures absolute earthquake power with mathematical precision: each step upwards represents a tenfold increase in shockwave amplitude. Theoretically, there is no upper limit, but most of the largest earthquakes measured have been rated at between 8.8 and 8.9. The 12–point Mercalli scale, based on observed effects, is often more meaningful, ranging from I (earthquakes noticed only by seismographs) to XII (total destruction); intermediate points include V (people awakened at night; unstable objects overturned), VII (collapse of ordinary buildings; chimneys and monuments fall), and IX (conspicuous cracks in ground; serious damage to reservoirs).

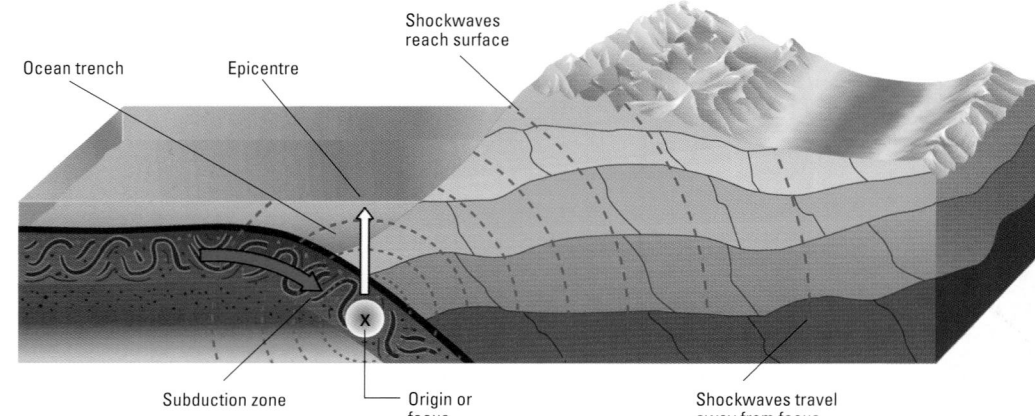

Shockwaves reach surface
Ocean trench
Epicentre
Subduction zone
Origin or focus
Shockwaves travel away from focus

DISTRIBUTION OF EARTHQUAKES

Mobile land areas
Submarine zones of mobile land areas
Stable land platforms
Submarine extensions of stable land platforms

● 1995 Principal earthquakes and dates (since 1900)

Earthquakes are a series of rapid vibrations originating from the slipping or faulting of parts of the Earth's crust when stresses within build up to breaking point. They usually happen at depths varying from 8 km to 30 km. Severe earthquakes cause extensive damage when they take place in populated areas, destroying structures and severing communications. Most initial loss of life occurs due to secondary causes such as falling masonry, fires and flooding.

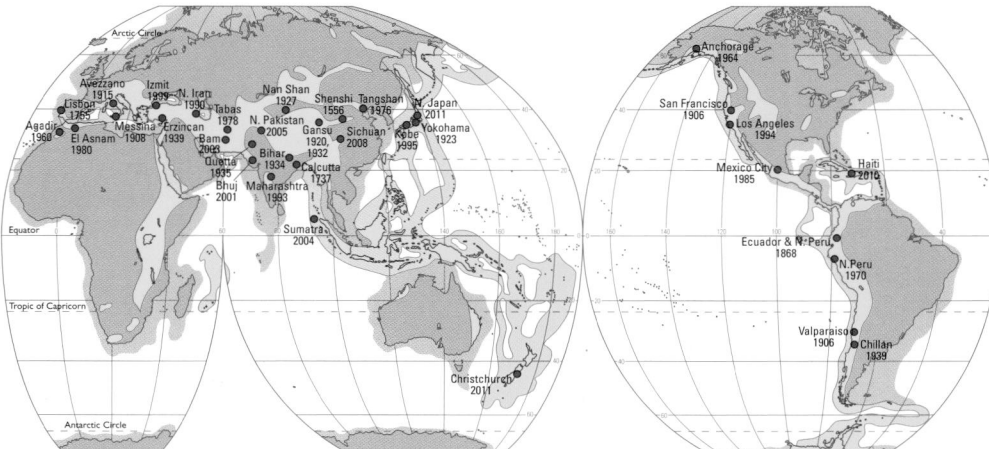

Projection: Interrupted Mollweide

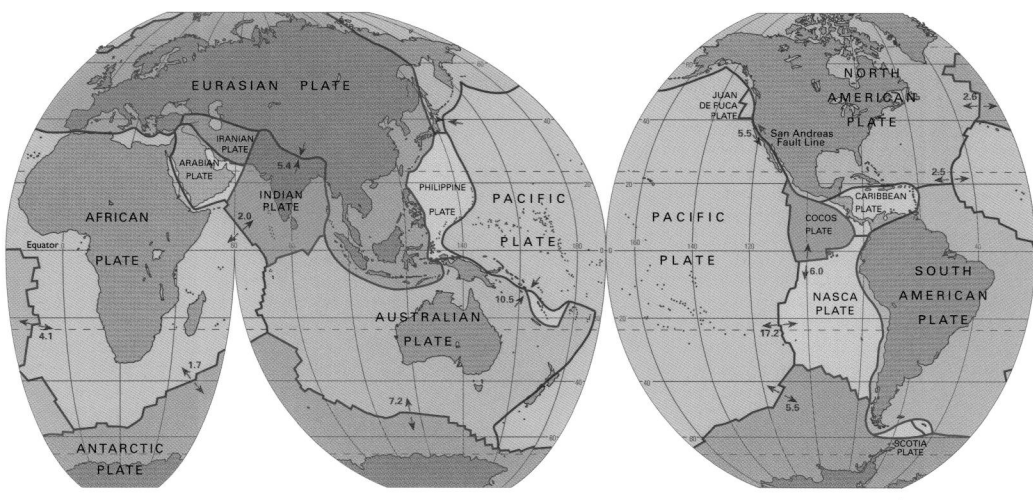

The drifting of the continents is a feature that is unique to planet Earth. The complementary, almost jigsaw-puzzle fit of the coastlines on each side of the Atlantic Ocean inspired Alfred Wegener's theory of continental drift in 1915. The theory suggested that the ancient supercontinent, which Wegener named Pangaea, incorporated all of the Earth's landmasses and gradually split up to form today's continents.

The original debate about continental drift was a prelude to a more radical idea: plate tectonics. The basic theory is that the Earth's crust is made up of a series of rigid plates which float on a soft layer of the mantle and are moved about by continental convection currents within the Earth's interior. These plates diverge and converge along margins marked by seismic activity. Plates diverge from mid-ocean ridges where molten lava pushes upwards and forces the plates apart at rates of up to 40 mm [1.6 in] a year.

The three diagrams, left, give some examples of plate boundaries from around the world. Diagram (a) shows sea-floor spreading at the Mid-Atlantic Ridge as the American and African plates slowly diverge. The same thing is happening in (b) where sea-floor spreading at the Mid-Indian Ocean Ridge is forcing the Indian plate to collide into the Eurasian plate. In (c) oceanic crust (sima) is being subducted beneath lighter continental crust (sial).

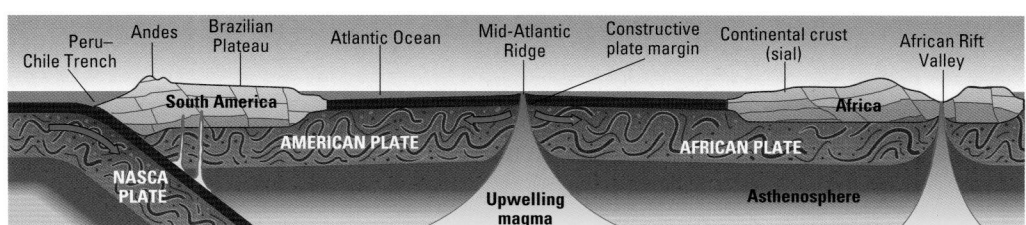

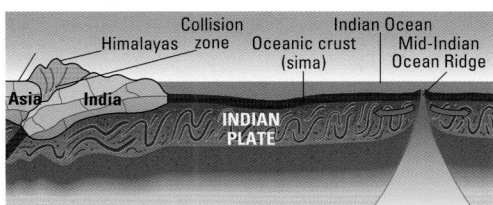

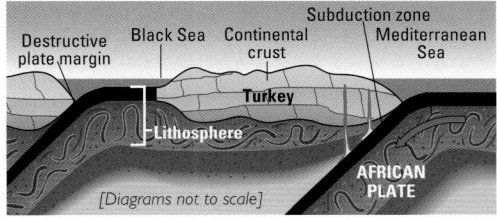

VOLCANOES

Volcanoes occur when hot liquefied rock beneath the Earth's crust is pushed up by pressure to the surface as molten lava. Some volcanoes erupt in an explosive way, throwing out rocks and ash, whilst others are effusive and lava flows out of the vent. There are volcanoes which are both, such as Mount Fuji. An accumulation of lava and cinders creates cones of variable size and shape. As a result of many eruptions over centuries, Mount Etna in Sicily has a circumference of more than 120 km [75 miles].

Climatologists believe that volcanic ash, if ejected high into the atmosphere, can influence temperature and weather for several years afterwards. The 1991 eruption of Mount Pinatubo in the Philippines ejected more than 20 million tonnes of dust and ash 32 km [20 miles] into the atmosphere and is believed to have accelerated ozone depletion over a large part of the globe.

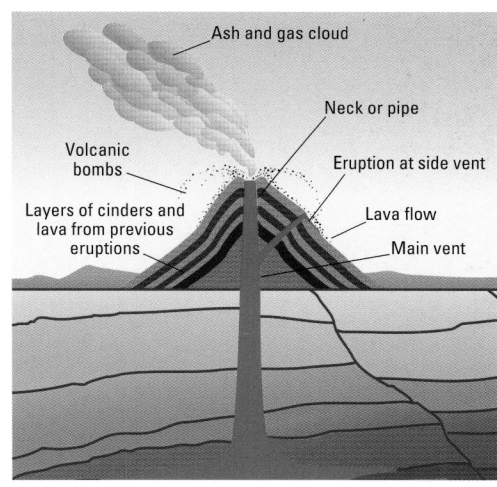

DISTRIBUTION OF VOLCANOES

Volcanoes today may be the subject of considerable scientific study but they remain both dramatic and unpredictable: in 1991 Mount Pinatubo, 100 km [62 miles] north of the Philippines capital Manila, suddenly burst into life after lying dormant for more than six centuries. Most of the world's active volcanoes occur in a belt around the Pacific Ocean, on the edge of the Pacific plate, called the 'ring of fire'. Indonesia has the greatest concentration with 90 volcanoes, 12 of which are active. The most famous, Krakatoa, erupted in 1883 with such force that the resulting tidal wave killed 36,000 people, and tremors were felt as far away as Australia.

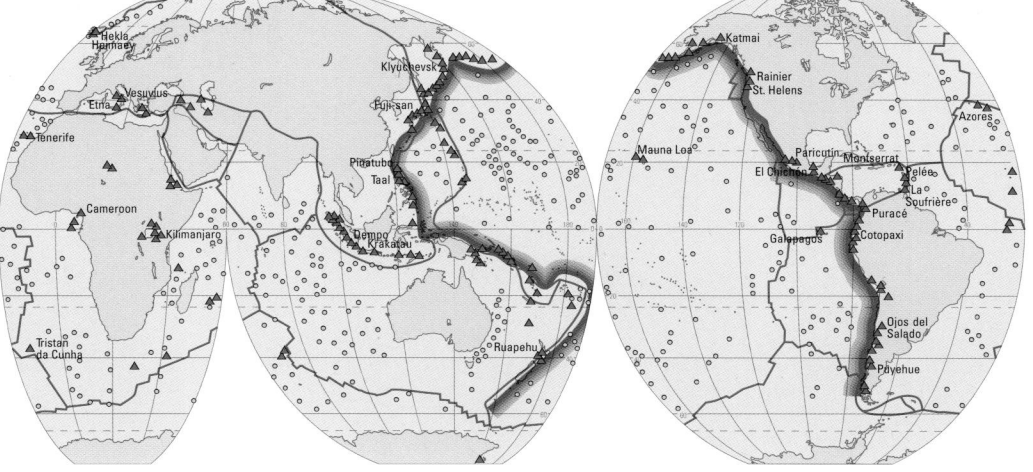

■■■ 'Ring of Fire'

○ Submarine volcanoes

▲ Land volcanoes active since 1700

—— Boundaries of tectonic plates

Landforms

THE ROCK CYCLE

James Hutton first proposed the rock cycle in the late 1700s after he observed the slow but steady effects of erosion.

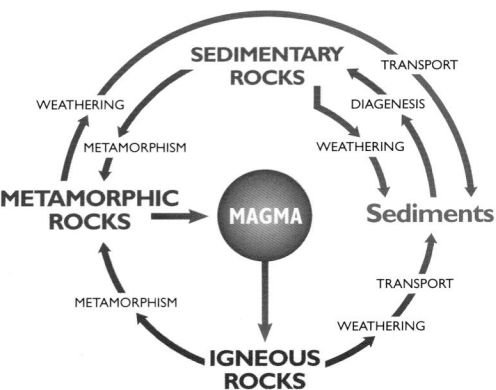

Above and below the surface of the oceans, the features of the Earth's crust are constantly changing. The phenomenal forces generated by convection currents in the molten core of our planet carry the vast segments or 'plates' of the crust across the globe in an endless cycle of creation and destruction. A continent may travel little more than 25 mm [1 in] per year, yet in the vast span of geological time this process throws up giant mountain ranges and creates new land.

Destruction of the landscape, however, begins as soon as it is formed. Wind, water, ice and sea, the main agents of erosion, mount a constant assault that even the most resistant rocks cannot withstand. Mountain peaks may dwindle by as little as a few millimetres each year, but if they are not uplifted by further movements of the crust they will eventually be reduced to rubble and transported away.

Water is the most powerful agent of erosion – it has been estimated that 100 billion tonnes of sediment are washed into the oceans every year.

Three Asian rivers account for 20% of this total: the Huang He, in China, and the Brahmaputra and the Ganges in Bangladesh.

Rivers and glaciers, like the sea itself, generate much of their effect through abrasion – pounding the land with the debris they carry with them. But as well as destroying they also create new landforms, many of them spectacular: vast deltas like those of the Mississippi and the Nile, or the deep fjords cut by glaciers in British Columbia, Norway and New Zealand.

Geologists once considered that landscapes evolved from 'young', newly uplifted mountainous areas, through a 'mature' hilly stage, to an 'old age' stage when the land was reduced to an almost flat plain, or peneplain. This theory, called the 'cycle of erosion', fell into disuse when it became evident that so many factors, including the effects of plate tectonics and climatic change, constantly interrupt the cycle, which takes no account of the highly complex interactions that shape the surface of our planet.

MOUNTAIN BUILDING

Mountains are formed when pressures on the Earth's crust caused by continental drift become so intense that the surface buckles or cracks. This happens where oceanic crust is subducted by continental crust or, more dramatically, where two tectonic plates collide: the Rockies, Andes, Alps, Urals and Himalayas resulted from such impacts. These are all known as fold mountains because they were formed by the compression of the rocks, forcing the surface to bend and fold like a crumpled rug. The Himalayas were formed from the folded former sediments of the Tethys Sea, which was trapped in the collision zone between the Indian and Eurasian plates.

The other main mountain-building process occurs when the crust fractures to create faults, allowing rock to be forced upwards in large blocks; or when the pressure of magma within the crust forces the surface to bulge into a dome, or erupts to form a volcano. Large mountain ranges may reveal a combination of these features; the Alps, for example, have been compressed so violently that the folds are fragmented by numerous faults and intrusions of molten igneous rock.

Over millions of years, even the greatest mountain ranges can be reduced by the agents of erosion (most notably rivers) to a low rugged landscape known as a peneplain.

Types of faults: Faults occur where the crust is being stretched or compressed so violently that the rock strata break in a horizontal or vertical movement. They are classified by the direction in which the blocks of rock have moved. A normal fault results when a vertical movement causes the surface to break apart; compression causes a reverse fault. Horizontal movement causes shearing, known as a strike-slip fault. When the rock breaks in two places, the central block may be pushed up in a horst fault, or sink (creating a rift valley) in a graben fault.

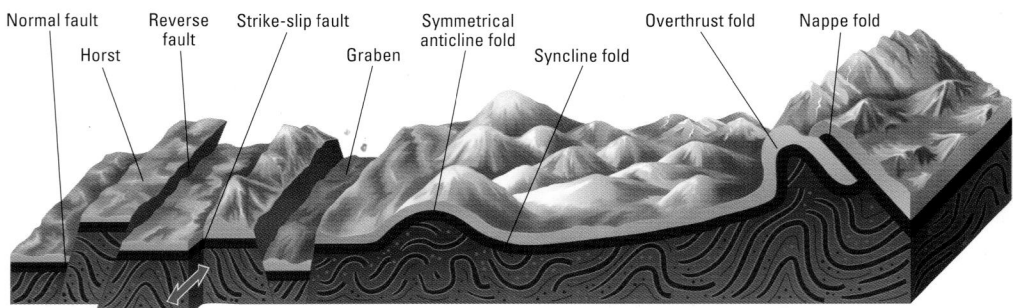

Types of fold: Folds occur when rock strata are squeezed and compressed. They are common, therefore, at destructive plate margins and where plates have collided, forcing the rocks to buckle into mountain ranges. Geographers give different names to the degrees of fold that result from continuing pressure on the rock. A simple fold may be symmetric, with even slopes on either side, but as the pressure builds up, one slope becomes steeper and the fold becomes asymmetric. Later, the ridge or 'anticline' at the top of the fold may slide over the lower ground or 'syncline' to form a recumbent fold. Eventually, the rock strata may break under the pressure to form an overthrust and finally a nappe fold.

CONTINENTAL GLACIATION

Ice sheets were at their greatest extent about 200,000 years ago. The maximum advance of the last Ice Age was about 18,000 years ago, when ice covered virtually all of Canada and reached as far south as the Bristol Channel in Britain.

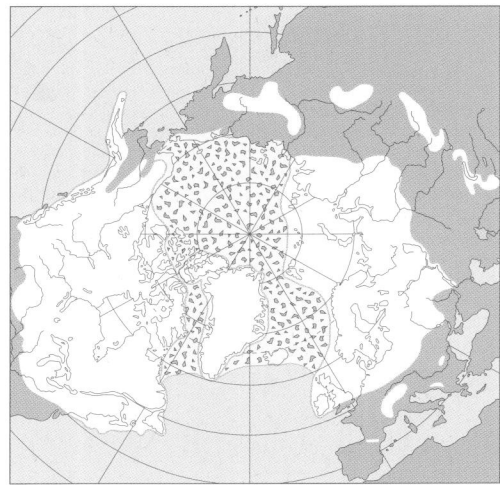

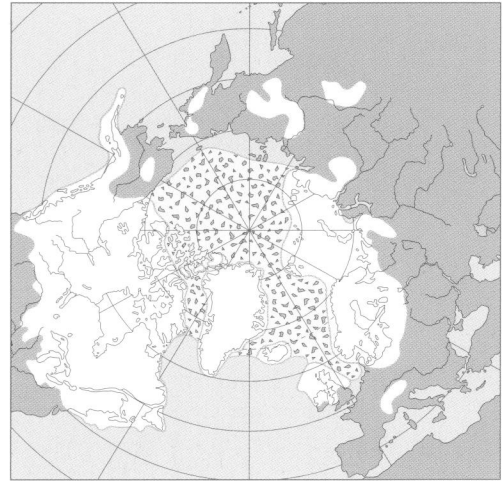

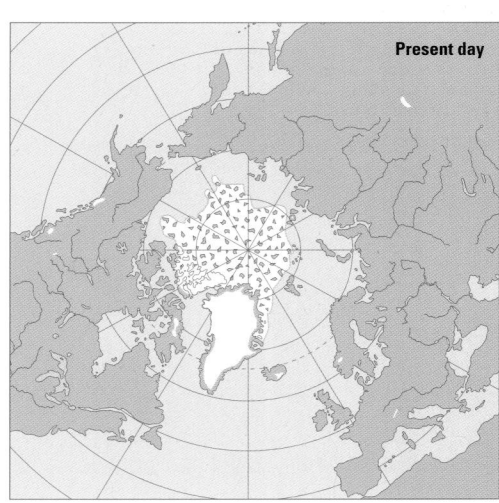

Present day

NATURAL LANDFORMS

A stylized diagram to show some of the major natural landforms found in the mid-latitudes.

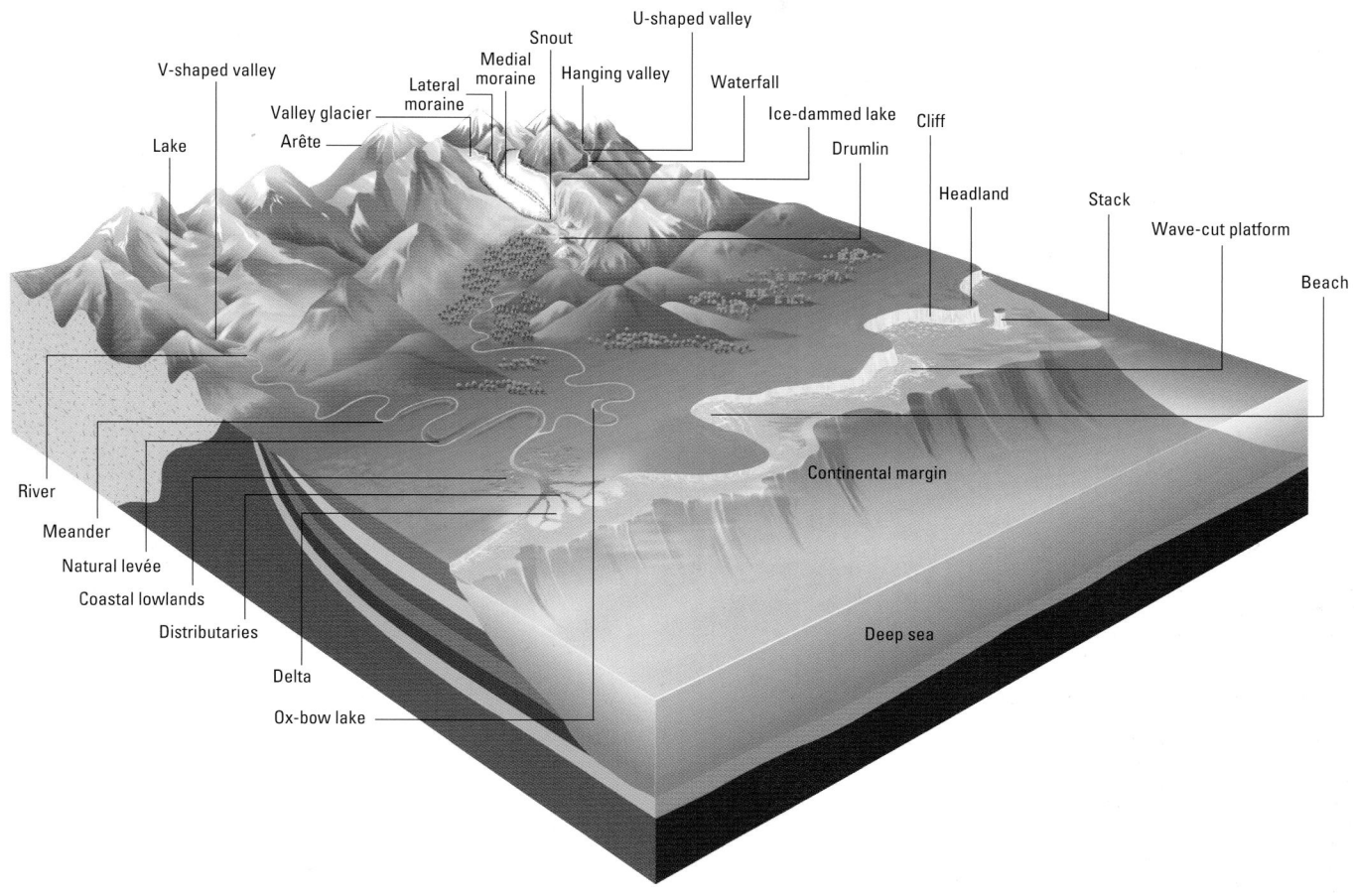

DESERT LANDSCAPES

The popular image that deserts are all huge expanses of sand is wrong. Despite harsh conditions, deserts contain some of the most varied and interesting landscapes in the world. They are also one of the most extensive environments – the hot and cold deserts together cover almost 40% of the Earth's surface.

The three types of hot desert are known by their Arabic names: sand desert, called *erg*, covers only about one-fifth of the world's desert; the rest is divided between *hammada* (areas of bare rock) and *reg* (broad plains covered by loose gravel or pebbles).

In areas of *erg*, such as the Namib Desert, the shape of the dunes reflects the character of local winds. Where winds are constant in direction, crescent-shaped *barchan* dunes form. In areas of bare rock, wind-blown sand is a major agent of erosion. The erosion is mainly confined to within 2 m [6.5 ft] of the surface, producing characteristic mushroom-shaped rocks.

Erg

Hammada

Reg

SURFACE PROCESSES

Catastrophic changes to natural landforms are periodically caused by such phenomena as avalanches, landslides and volcanic eruptions, but most of the processes that shape the Earth's surface operate extremely slowly in human terms. One estimate, based on a study in the United States, suggested that 1 m [3 ft] of land was removed from the entire surface of the country, on average, every 29,500 years. However, the time-scale varies from 1,300 years to 154,200 years depending on the terrain and climate.

In hot, dry climates, mechanical weathering, a result of rapid temperature changes, causes the outer layers of rock to peel away, while in cold mountainous regions, boulders are prised apart when water freezes in cracks in rocks. Chemical weathering, at its greatest in warm, humid regions, is responsible for hollowing out limestone caves and decomposing granites.

The erosion of soil and rock is greatest on sloping land and the steeper the slope, the greater the tendency for mass wasting – the movement of soil and rock downhill under the influence of gravity. The mechanisms of mass wasting (ranging from very slow to very rapid) vary with the type of material, but the presence of water as a lubricant is usually an important factor.

Running water is the world's leading agent of erosion and transportation. The energy of a river depends on several factors, including its velocity and volume, and its erosive power is at its peak when it is in full flood. Sea waves also exert tremendous erosive power during storms when they hurl pebbles against the shore, undercutting cliffs and hollowing out caves.

Glacier ice forms in mountain hollows and spills out to form valley glaciers, which transport rocks shattered by frost action. As glaciers move, rocks embedded into the ice erode steep-sided, U-shaped valleys. Evidence of glaciation in mountain regions includes cirques, knife-edged ridges, or arêtes, and pyramidal peaks.

Oceans

THE GREAT OCEANS

Relative sizes of the world's oceans

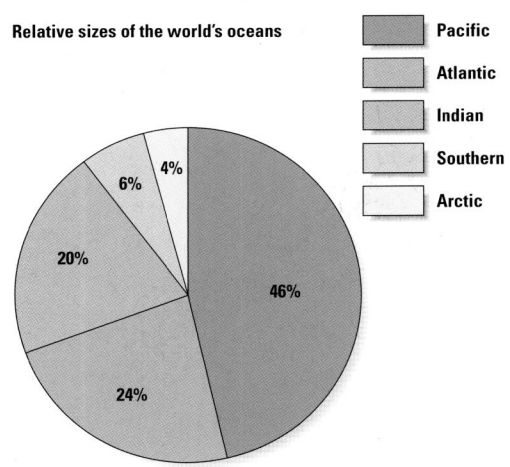

Pacific
Atlantic
Indian
Southern
Arctic

From ancient times to about the 15th century, the legendary 'Seven Seas' comprised the Red Sea, Mediterranean Sea, Persian Gulf, Black Sea, Adriatic Sea, Caspian Sea and Indian Sea.

The Earth is a watery planet: more than 70% of its surface – over 360,000,000 sq km [140,000,000 sq miles] – is covered by the oceans and seas. The mighty Pacific alone accounts for nearly 36% of the total, and more than 46% of the sea area. Gravity holds in around 1,400 million cubic km [320 million cubic miles] of water, of which over 97% is saline.

The vast underwater world starts in the shallows of the seaside and plunges to depths of more than 11,000 m [36,000 ft]. The continental shelf, part of the landmass, drops gently to around 200 m [650 ft]; here the seabed falls away suddenly at an angle of 3° to 6° – the continental slope. The third stage, called the continental rise, is more gradual with gradients varying from 1 in 100 to 1 in 700. At an average depth of 5,000 m [16,500 ft] there begins the aptly-named abyssal plain – massive submarine depths where sunlight fails to penetrate and few creatures can survive.

From these plains rise volcanoes which, taken from base to top, rival and even surpass the tallest continental mountains in height. Mauna Kea, on Hawai'i, reaches a total of 10,203 m [33,400 ft], some 1,355 m [4,500 ft] higher than Mount Everest, though scarcely 40% is visible above sea level.

In addition, there are underwater mountain chains up to 1,000 km [600 miles] across, whose peaks sometimes appear above sea level as islands, such as Iceland and Tristan da Cunha.

OCEAN DEPTHS

Average and maximum depths of the world's great oceans, in metres

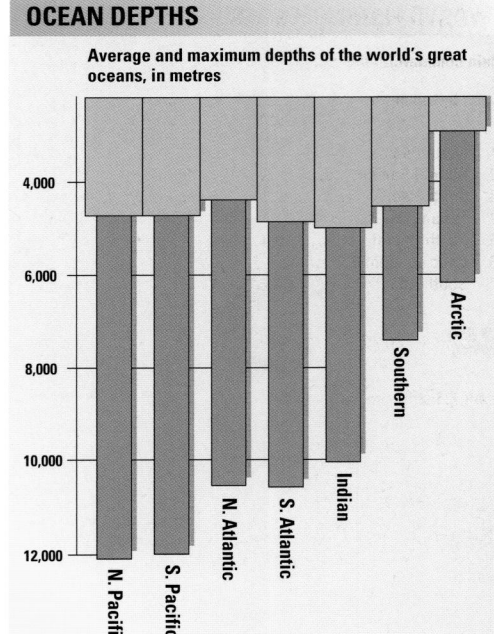

OCEAN CURRENTS

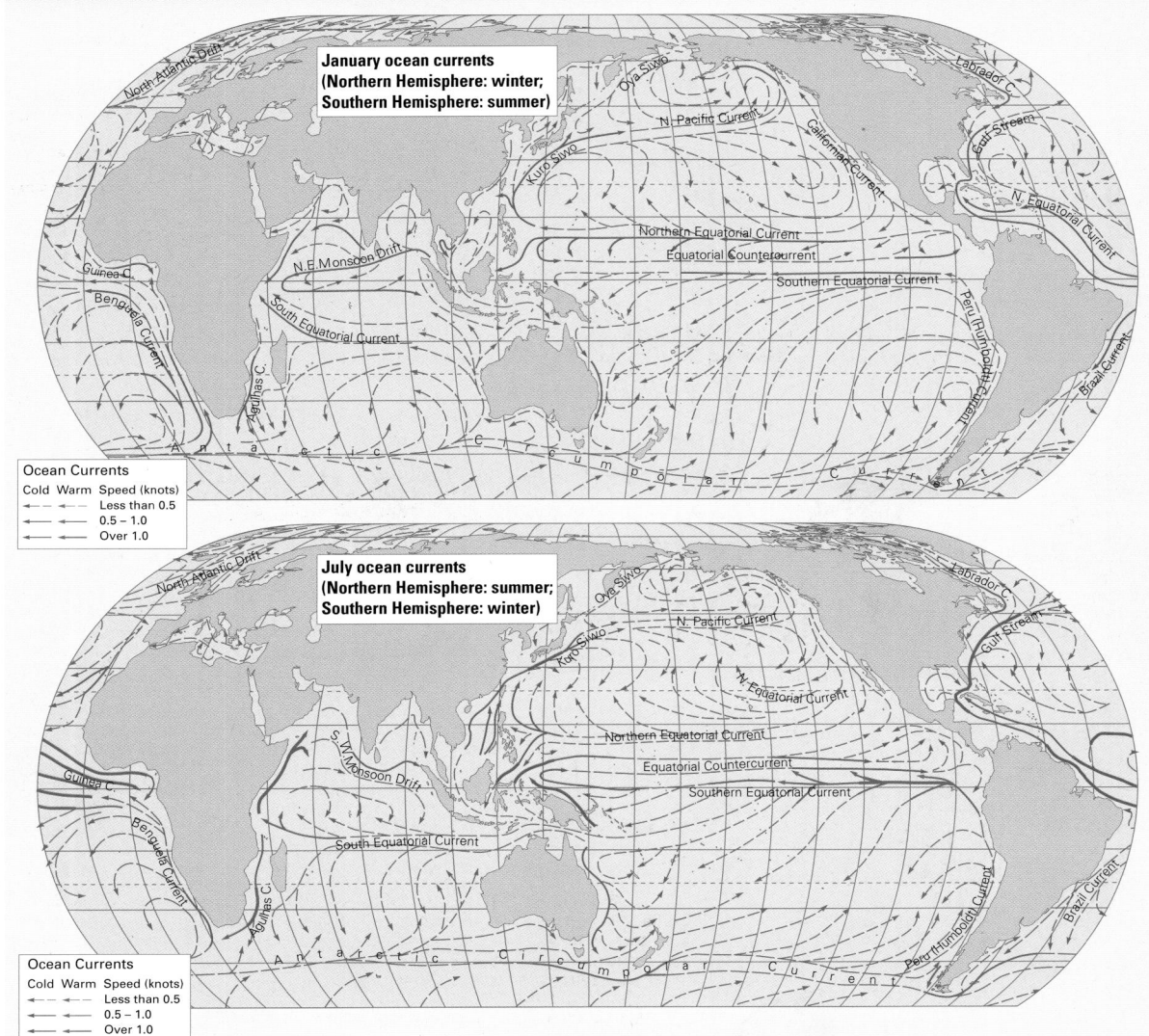

January ocean currents (Northern Hemisphere: winter; Southern Hemisphere: summer)

July ocean currents (Northern Hemisphere: summer; Southern Hemisphere: winter)

Ocean Currents
Cold Warm Speed (knots)
Less than 0.5
0.5 – 1.0
Over 1.0

Moving immense quantities of energy as well as billions of tonnes of water every hour, the ocean currents are a vital part of the great heat engine that drives the Earth's climate. They themselves are produced by a twofold mechanism. At the surface, winds push huge masses of water before them; in the deep ocean, below an abrupt temperature gradient that separates the churning surface waters from the still depths, density variations cause slow vertical movements.

The pattern of circulation of the great surface currents is determined by the displacement known as the Coriolis effect. As the Earth turns beneath a moving object – whether it is a tennis ball or a vast mass of water – it appears to be deflected to one side. The deflection is most obvious near the Equator, where the Earth's surface is spinning eastwards at 1,700 km/h [1,050 mph]; currents moving polewards are curved clockwise in the northern hemisphere and anti-clockwise in the southern.

The result is a system of spinning circles known as 'gyres'. The Coriolis effect piles up water on the left of each gyre, creating a narrow, fast-moving stream that is matched by a slower, broader returning current on the right. North and south of the Equator, the fastest currents are located in the west and in the east respectively. In each case, warm water moves from the Equator and cold water returns to it. Cold currents often bring an upwelling of nutrients with them, supporting the world's most economically important fisheries.

Depending on the prevailing winds, some currents on or near the Equator may reverse their direction in the course of the year – a seasonal variation on which Asian monsoon rains depend, and whose occasional failure can bring disaster to millions of people.

WORLD FISHING AREAS

Main commercial fishing areas (numbered FAO regions)

Catch by top marine fishing areas, million tonnes (2009)

% world catch by area

1.	North Pacific	23.6%
2.	Central Pacific	11.6%
3.	South Pacific	12.3%
4.	Indian	11.2%
5.	North Atlantic	11.0%
6.	Central Atlantic	3.5%
7.	South Atlantic	2.5%

Principal fishing areas

Leading fishing nations

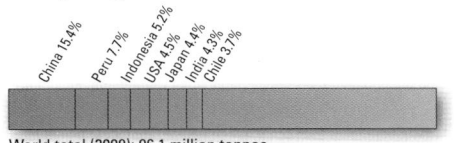

China 15.4% • Peru 7.7% • Indonesia 5.2% • USA 4.5% • Japan 4.4% • India 4.3% • Chile 3.7%

World total (2009): 96.1 million tonnes
(Marine catch 90% : Inland catch 10%)

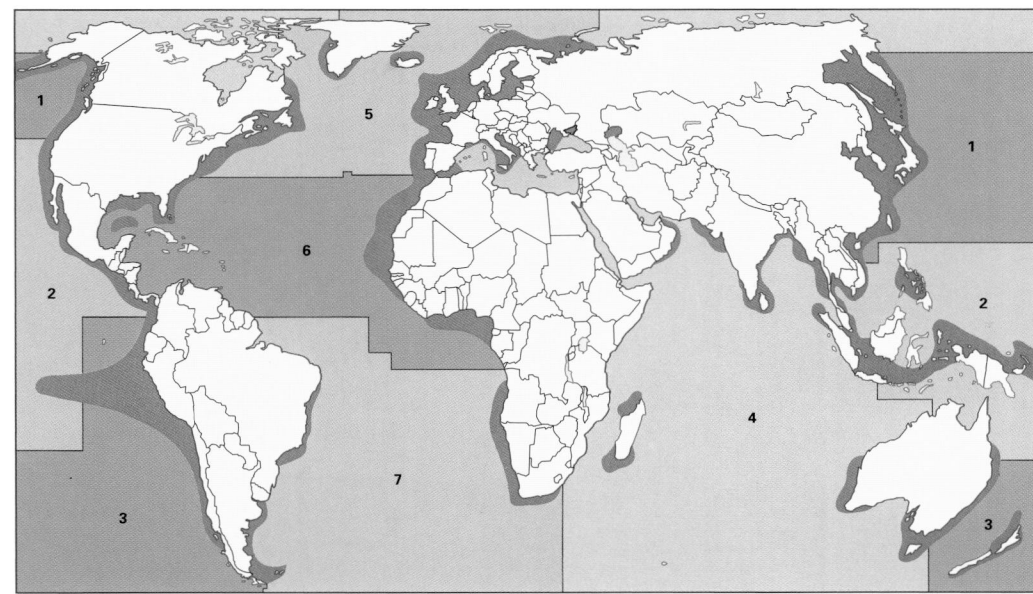

MARINE POLLUTION

Sources of marine oil pollution

Tanker operations
Municipal wastes
Tanker accidents
Bilge and fuel oils
Natural seeps
Industrial waste
Urban runoff
Coastal oil refining
Offshore oil rigs
River runoffs
Other

(Pie chart values: 22%, 22%, 12.5%, 9%, 7.5%, 6%, 3.5%, 3%, 1.5%, 1%, 12%)

OIL SPILLS

Major oil spills from tankers and combined carriers

Year	Vessel	Location	Spill (barrels)*	Cause
1979	Atlantic Empress	West Indies	1,890,000	collision
1983	Castillo De Bellver	South Africa	1,760,000	fire
1978	Amoco Cadiz	France	1,628,000	grounding
1991	Haven	Italy	1,029,000	explosion
1988	Odyssey	Canada	1,000,000	fire
1967	Torrey Canyon	UK	909,000	grounding
1972	Sea Star	Gulf of Oman	902,250	collision
1977	Hawaiian Patriot	Hawaiian Is.	742,500	fire
1979	Independenta	Turkey	696,350	collision
1993	Braer	UK	625,000	grounding
1996	Sea Empress	UK	515,000	grounding
2002	Prestige	Spain	463,250	storm

Other sources of major oil spills

1983	Nowruz oilfield	Persian Gulf	4,250,000†	war
1979	Ixtoc 1 oilwell	Gulf of Mexico	4,200,000	blow-out
2010	Deepwater Horizon	Gulf of Mexico	3.6 – 4,610,000	blow-out

* 1 barrel = 0.136 tonnes/159 lit./35 Imperial gal./42 US gal. † estimated

RIVER POLLUTION

Sources of river pollution, USA

Agriculture
Mining
Forestry
Urban runoff
Hydro-engineering
Construction
Land disposal
Other

(Pie chart values: 64%, 9%, 9%, 6%, 5%, 4%, 2%, 1%)

EL NIÑO

El Niño, 'The Little Boy' in Spanish, was originally the name given by local fishermen to the warm current that can appear off the Pacific coast of South America. In a normal year, south-easterly trade winds drive surface waters westwards off the coast of South America, drawing cold, nutrient-rich water up from below. In an El Niño year, warm water from the west Pacific suppresses upwelling in the east, depriving the region of nutrients and driving the fish away. The water is warmed by as much as 7°C, disturbing the tropical atmosphere circulation. During an intense El Niño, the south-east trade winds change direction and become equatorial westerlies, resulting in climatic extremes in many regions of the world, such as drought in parts of Australia and India, and heavy rainfall in south-eastern USA.

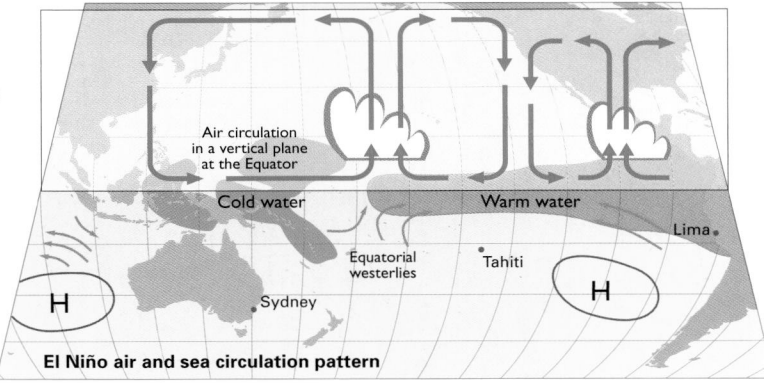

El Niño air and sea circulation pattern

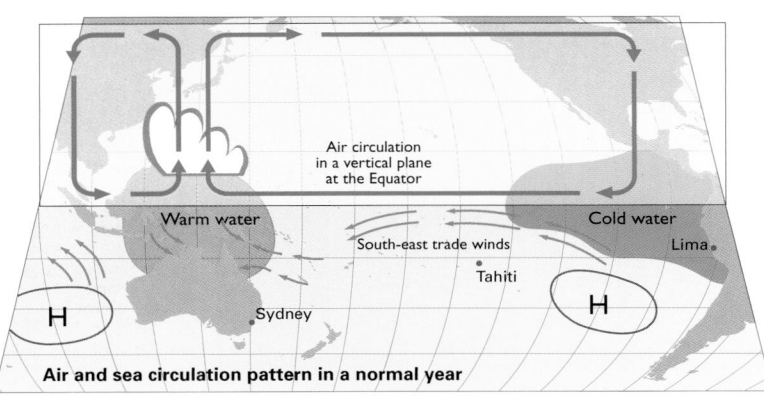

Air and sea circulation pattern in a normal year

El Niño events occur about every 4 to 7 years and typically last for around 12 to 18 months. El Niño usually results in reduced rainfall across northern and eastern Australia.This can lead to widespread and severe drought, as well as increased temperatures and bushfire risk. However, each El Niño event is unique in terms of its strength as well as its impact. It is measured by the Southern Oscillation Index (SOI) and the changes in ocean temperatures.

La Niña, or 'The Little Girl', is associated with cooler waters in the central and eastern Pacific. A La Niña year can result in cooler land temperatures across the tropics and subtropics, and more storms in the North Atlantic.

Climate

CLIMATE REGIONS

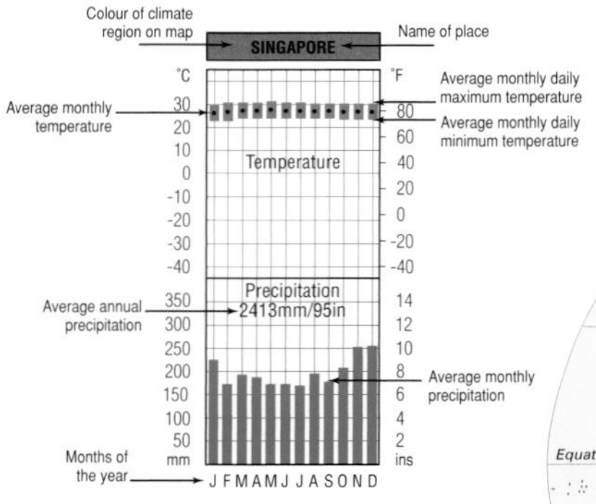

Colour of climate region on map
SINGAPORE
Name of place
°C
°F
Average monthly temperature
Average monthly daily maximum temperature
Average monthly daily minimum temperature
Temperature
Precipitation
2413mm/95in
Average annual precipitation
Average monthly precipitation
Months of the year
mm
ins
J F M A M J J A S O N D

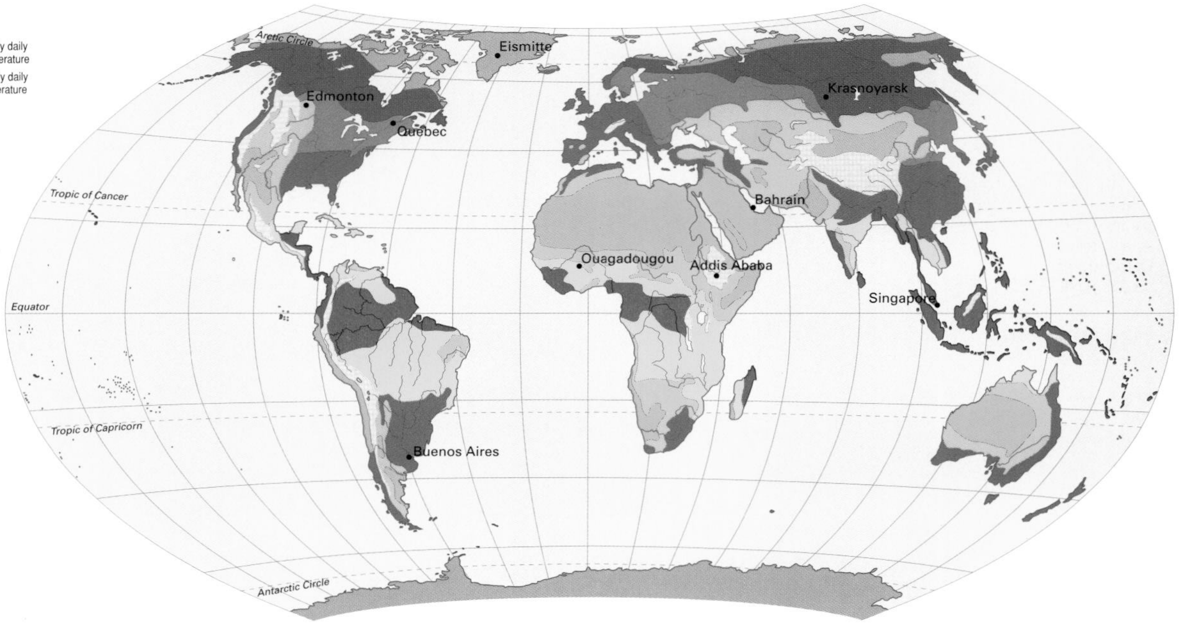

Arctic Circle
Eismitte
Edmonton
Québec
Krasnoyarsk
Tropic of Cancer
Bahrain
Ouagadougou
Addis Ababa
Singapore
Equator
Tropic of Capricorn
Buenos Aires
Antarctic Circle

- Tropical climate (hot with rain all year)
- Desert climate (hot and very dry)
- Savanna climate (hot with dry season)
- Steppe climate (warm and dry)
- Mild climate (warm and wet)
- Continental climate (wet with cold winter)
- Subarctic climate (very cold winter)
- Polar climate (very cold and dry)
- Mountainous climate (altitude affects climate)

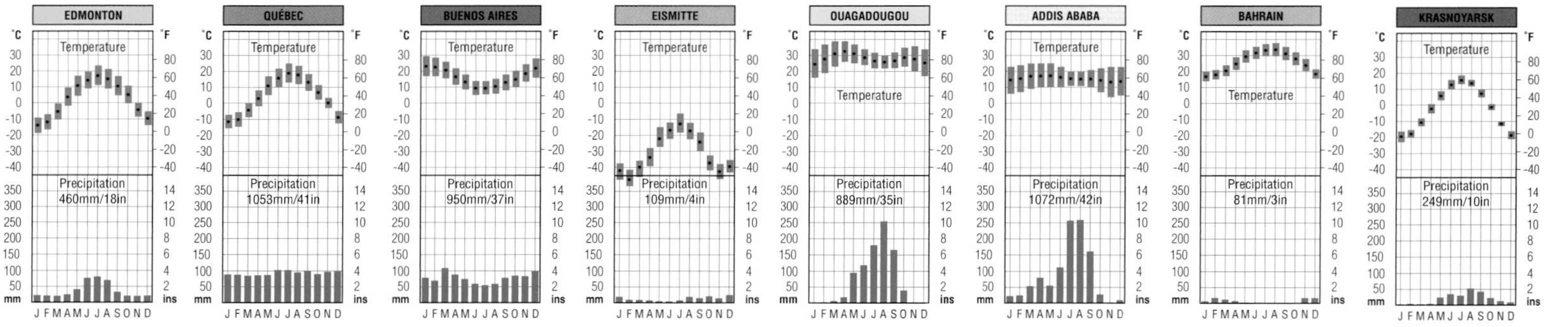

EDMONTON
Precipitation 460mm/18in
QUÉBEC
Precipitation 1053mm/41in
BUENOS AIRES
Precipitation 950mm/37in
EISMITTE
Precipitation 109mm/4in
OUAGADOUGOU
Precipitation 889mm/35in
ADDIS ABABA
Precipitation 1072mm/42in
BAHRAIN
Precipitation 81mm/3in
KRASNOYARSK
Precipitation 249mm/10in
Temperature
°C
°F
mm
ins
J F M A M J J A S O N D

THE MONSOON

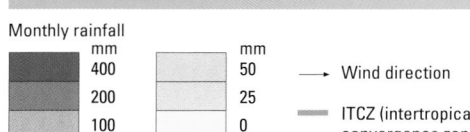

Monthly rainfall

mm		mm	
400		50	
200		25	
100		0	

→ Wind direction

ITCZ (intertropical convergence zone)

In early March, which normally marks the end of the subcontinent's cool season and the start of the hot season, winds blow outwards from the mainland. But as the overhead sun and the ITCZ move northwards, the land is intensely heated, and a low-pressure system develops. The south-east trade winds, which are drawn across the Equator, change direction and are sucked into the interior, bringing heavy rain. By November, the overhead sun and the ITCZ have again moved southwards and the wind directions are again reversed. Cool winds blow from the Asian interior to the sea, losing any moisture on the Himalayas before descending to the coast.

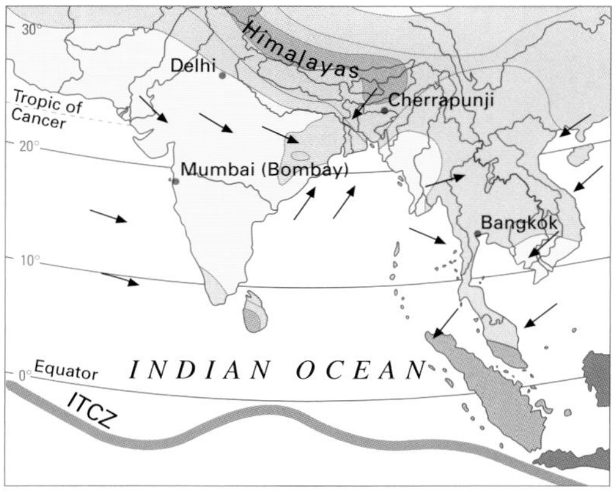

30°
Delhi
Himalayas
Tropic of Cancer
Cherrapunji
20°
Mumbai (Bombay)
Bangkok
10°
0° Equator
INDIAN OCEAN
ITCZ

March – Start of the hot, dry season, the ITCZ is over the southern Indian Ocean.

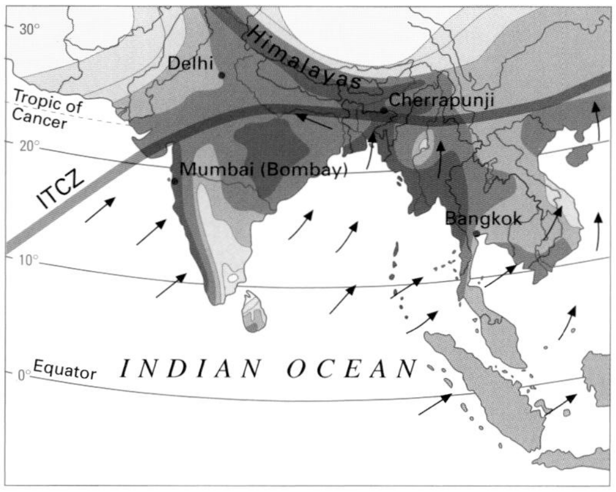

30°
Delhi
Himalayas
Tropic of Cancer
Cherrapunji
20°
ITCZ
Mumbai (Bombay)
Bangkok
10°
0° Equator
INDIAN OCEAN

July – The rainy season, the ITCZ has migrated northwards; winds blow onshore.

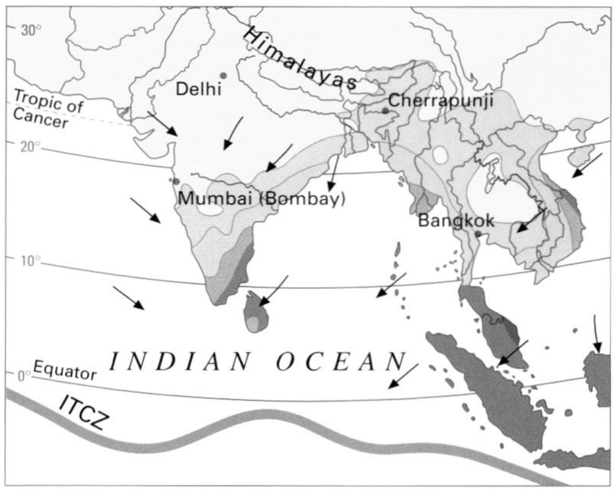

30°
Himalayas
Delhi
Cherrapunji
Tropic of Cancer
20°
Mumbai (Bombay)
Bangkok
10°
0° Equator
INDIAN OCEAN
ITCZ

November – The ITCZ has returned south, the offshore winds are cool and dry.

CLIMATE

Climate is weather in the long term: the seasonal pattern of hot and cold, wet and dry, averaged over time (usually 30 years). At the simplest level, it is caused by the uneven heating of the Earth. Surplus heat at the Equator passes towards the poles, levelling out the energy differential. Its passage is marked by a ceaseless churning of the atmosphere and the oceans, further agitated by the Earth's diurnal spin and the motion it imparts to moving air and water. The heat's means of transport – by winds and ocean currents, by the continual evaporation and recondensation of water molecules – is the weather itself. There are four basic types of climate, each of which can be further subdivided: tropical, desert (dry), temperate and polar.

COMPOSITION OF DRY AIR

Nitrogen	78.09%	Sulphur dioxide	trace
Oxygen	20.95%	Nitrogen oxide	trace
Argon	0.93%	Methane	trace
Water vapour	0.2–4.0%	Dust	trace
Carbon dioxide	0.03%	Helium	trace
Ozone	0.00006%	Neon	trace

CLIMATE RECORDS

Temperature
Highest recorded shade temperature: Al Aziziyah, Libya, 57.7°C [135.9°F], 13 September 1922.

Highest mean annual temperature: Dallol, Ethiopia, 34.4°C [94°F], 1960–66.

Longest heatwave: Marble Bar, W. Australia, 162 days over 38°C [100°F], 23 October 1923 to 7 April 1924.

Lowest recorded temperature (outside poles): Verkhoyansk, Siberia, –68°C [–93.6°F], 7 February 1982.

Lowest mean annual temperature: Polus Nedostupnosti, Pole of Cold, Antarctica, –57.8°C [–72°F].

Precipitation
Driest place: Quillagua, Chile, mean annual rainfall 0.5 mm [0.02 in], 1964–2001.

Wettest place (average): Mt Wai-ale-ale, Hawai'i, USA, mean annual rainfall 11,680 mm [459.8 in].

Wettest place (12 months): Cherrapunji, Meghalaya, N. E. India, 26,461 mm [1,042 in], August 1860 to July 1861. Cherrapunji also holds the record for the most rainfall in one month: 2,930 mm [115 in], July 1861.

Wettest place (24 hours): Fac Fac, Réunion, Indian Ocean, 1,825 mm [71.9 in], 15–16 March 1952.

Heaviest hailstones: Gopalganj, Bangladesh, up to 1.02 kg [2.25 lb], 14 April 1986 (killed 92 people).

Heaviest snowfall (continuous): Bessans, Savoie, France, 1,730 mm [68 in] in 19 hours, 5–6 April 1969.

Heaviest snowfall (season/year): Mt Baker, Washington, USA, 28,956 mm [1,140 in], June 1998 to June 1999.

Pressure and winds
Highest barometric pressure: Agata, Siberia (at 262 m [862 ft] altitude), 1,083.8 mb, 31 December 1968.

Lowest barometric pressure: Typhoon Tip, Guam, Pacific Ocean, 870 mb, 12 October 1979.

Highest recorded wind speed: Bridge Creek, Oklahoma, USA, 512 km/h [318 mph], 3 May 1999. Measured by Doppler radar monitoring a tornado.

Windiest place: Port Martin, Antarctica, where winds of more than 64 km/h [40 mph] occur for not less than 100 days a year.

Conversions
°C = (°F − 32) × 5/9; °F = (°C × 9/5) + 32; 0°C = 32°F
1 in = 25.4 mm; 1 mm = 0.0394 in; 100 mm = 3.94 in

TEMPERATURE

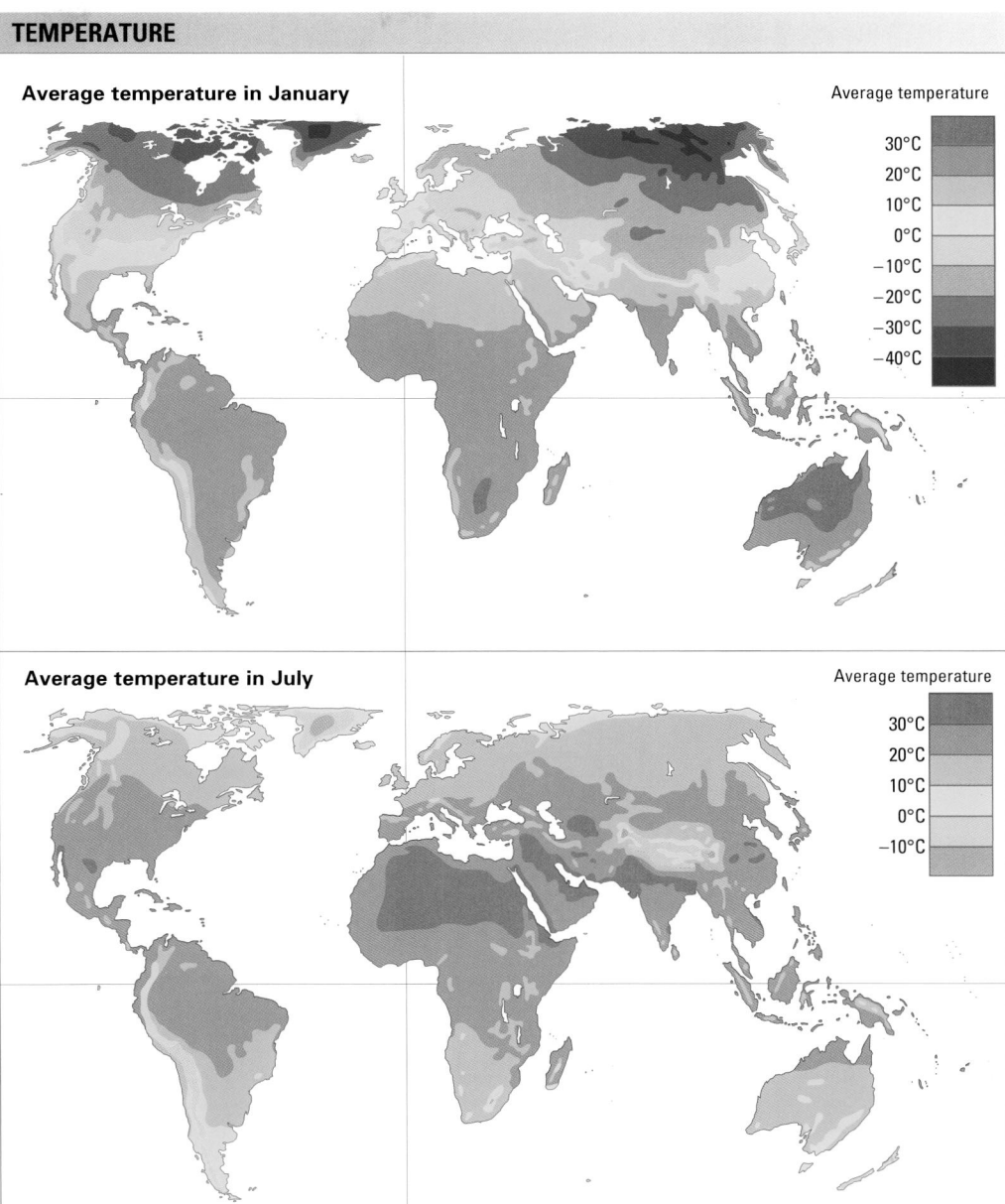

Average temperature in January

Average temperature
- 30°C
- 20°C
- 10°C
- 0°C
- −10°C
- −20°C
- −30°C
- −40°C

Average temperature in July

Average temperature
- 30°C
- 20°C
- 10°C
- 0°C
- −10°C

PRECIPITATION (RAINFALL AND SNOW)

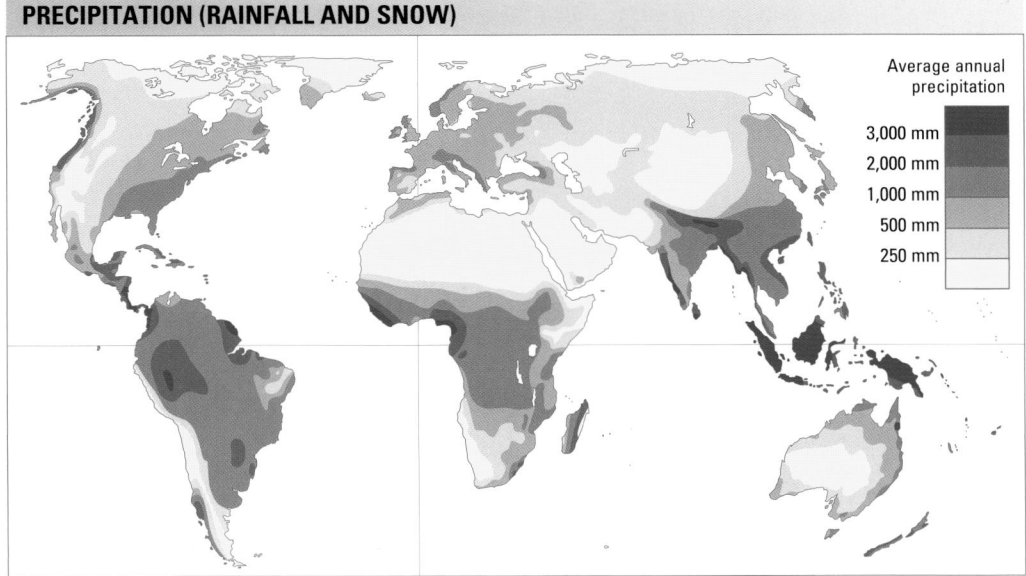

Average annual precipitation
- 3,000 mm
- 2,000 mm
- 1,000 mm
- 500 mm
- 250 mm

Water and Vegetation

THE HYDROLOGICAL CYCLE

The world's water balance is regulated by the constant recycling of water between the oceans, atmosphere and land. The movement of water between these three reservoirs is known as the hydrological cycle. The oceans play a vital role in the hydrological cycle: 74% of the total precipitation falls over the oceans and 84% of the total evaporation comes from the oceans.

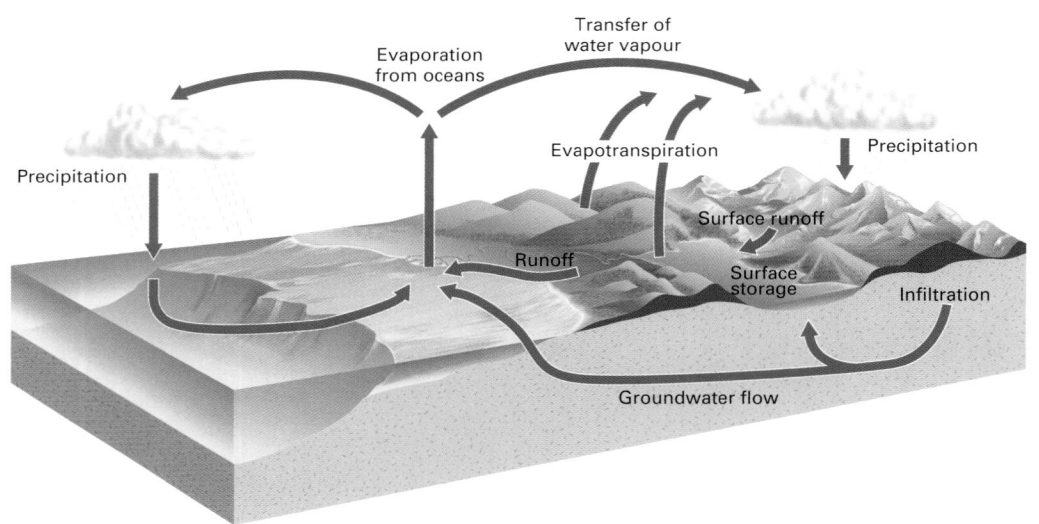

WATER DISTRIBUTION

The distribution of planetary water, by percentage. Oceans and ice caps together account for more than 99% of the total; the breakdown of the remainder is estimated.

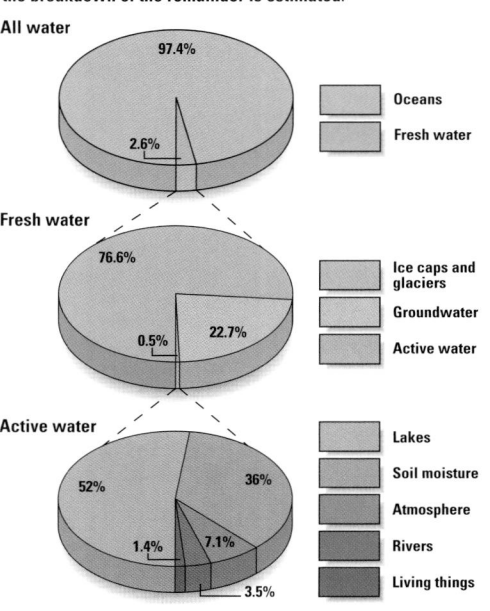

All water
- 97.4% — Oceans
- 2.6% — Fresh water

Fresh water
- 76.6% — Ice caps and glaciers
- 22.7% — Groundwater
- 0.5% — Active water

Active water
- 52% — Lakes
- 36% — Soil moisture
- 7.1% — Atmosphere
- 3.5% — Rivers
- 1.4% — Living things

WATER UTILIZATION

The percentage breakdown of water usage by sector, selected countries (2009)

Legend: Domestic | Industrial | Agriculture

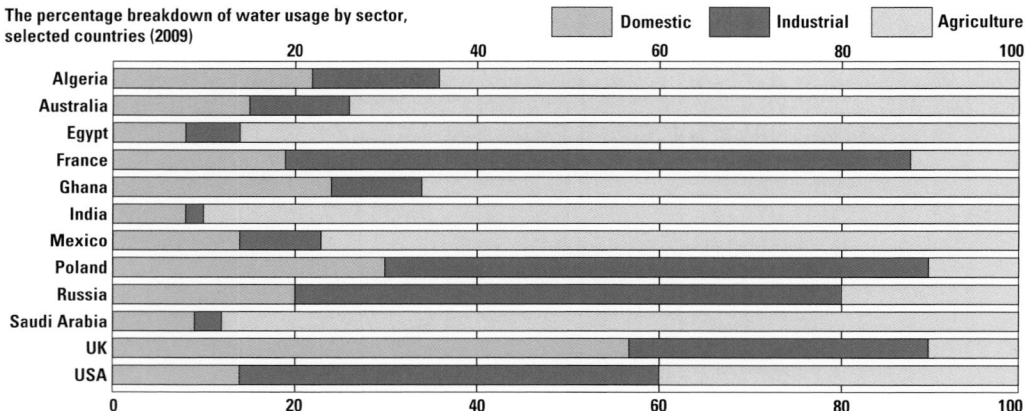

Countries listed: Algeria, Australia, Egypt, France, Ghana, India, Mexico, Poland, Russia, Saudi Arabia, UK, USA

WATER USAGE

Almost all the world's water is 3,000 million years old, and all of it cycles endlessly through the hydrosphere, though at different rates. Water vapour circulates over days or even hours, deep ocean water circulates over millennia, and ice-cap water remains solid for millions of years.

Fresh water is essential to all terrestrial life. Humans cannot survive more than a few days without it, and even the hardiest desert plants and animals could not exist without some water. Agriculture requires huge quantities of fresh water: without large-scale irrigation most of the world's people would starve. In the USA, agriculture uses 40% and industry 46% of all water withdrawals.

According to the latest figures, the average North American uses 1.5 million litres of water per year. This is more than six times the average African, who uses just 186,000 litres of water each year. Europeans and Australians use 694,000 litres per year.

WATER SUPPLY

Percentage of total population with access to safe drinking water (2008)

- Over 90% with safe water
- 80 – 90% with safe water
- 70 – 80% with safe water
- Less than 70% with safe water
- No data available

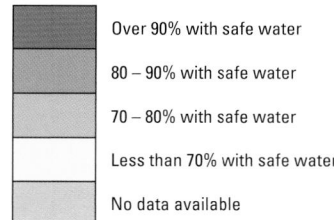

Least well-provided countries

Country	%	Country	%
Niger	48%	Madagascar	41%
Fiji	47%	Papua New Guinea	41%
Mozambique	47%	Ethiopia	38%
Congo (Dem. Rep.)	46%	Somalia	30%
Equatorial Guinea	43%	Western Sahara	26%

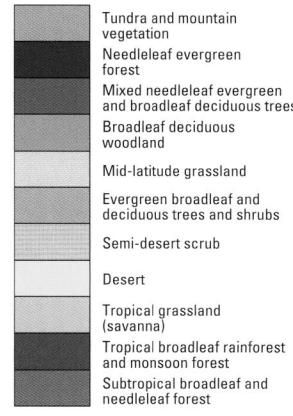

NATURAL VEGETATION

Regional variation in vegetation

- Tundra and mountain vegetation
- Needleleaf evergreen forest
- Mixed needleleaf evergreen and broadleaf deciduous trees
- Broadleaf deciduous woodland
- Mid-latitude grassland
- Evergreen broadleaf and deciduous trees and shrubs
- Semi-desert scrub
- Desert
- Tropical grassland (savanna)
- Tropical broadleaf rainforest and monsoon forest
- Subtropical broadleaf and needleleaf forest

The map shows the natural 'climax vegetation' of regions, as dictated by climate and topography. In most cases, however, agricultural activity has drastically altered the vegetation pattern. Western Europe, for example, lost most of its broadleaf forest many centuries ago, while irrigation has turned some natural semi-desert into productive land.

LAND USE BY CONTINENT (2010)

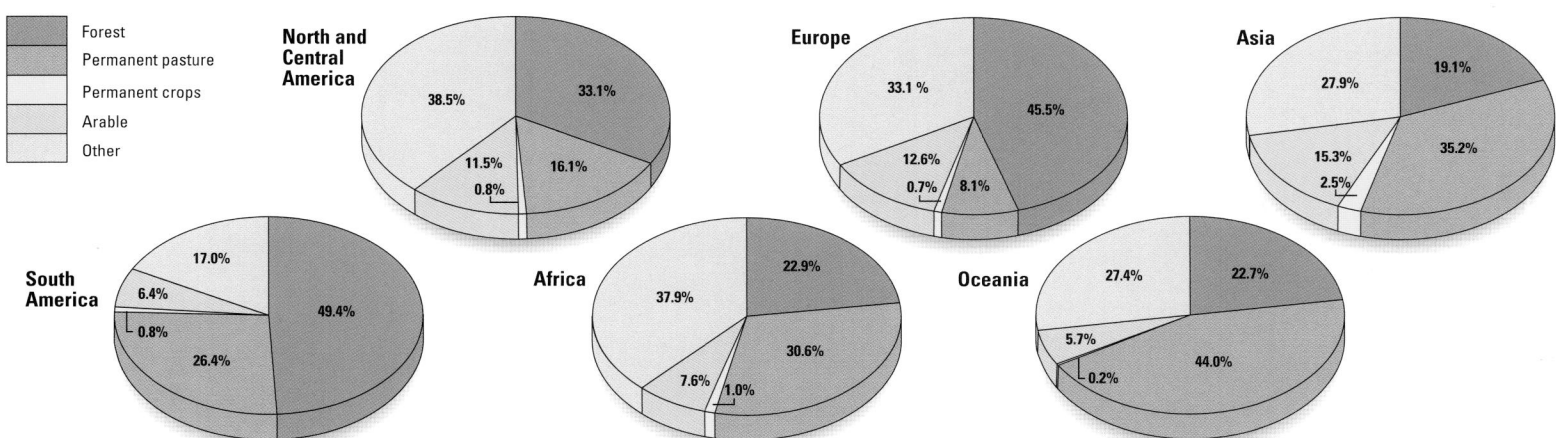

Legend:
- Forest
- Permanent pasture
- Permanent crops
- Arable
- Other

North and Central America: 33.1%, 16.1%, 0.8%, 11.5%, 38.5%

Europe: 45.5%, 8.1%, 0.7%, 12.6%, 33.1%

Asia: 19.1%, 35.2%, 2.5%, 15.3%, 27.9%

South America: 49.4%, 26.4%, 0.8%, 6.4%, 17.0%

Africa: 22.9%, 30.6%, 1.0%, 7.6%, 37.9%

Oceania: 22.7%, 44.0%, 0.2%, 5.7%, 27.4%

FORESTRY: PRODUCTION

Forest and woodland (million hectares)	Annual production (2010; million cubic metres)	
	Fuelwood	Industrial roundwood*
World 4,038.7	*1,868.0*	*1,616.3*
Europe 1,004.2	149.5	504.2
S. America 867.9	197.9	196.2
Africa 677.9	616.7	74.2
N. & C. America 705.4	128.4	520.2
Asia 590.8	765.0	268.0
Oceania 192.5	10.5	53.5

Paper and Board

Top producers (2010)**		Top exporters (2010)**	
China	96.5	Germany	13,254
USA	75.7	Finland	11,851
Japan	27.3	USA	11,707
Germany	23.2	Canada	10,910
Canada	12.7	Sweden	10,579
Finland	11.7		
World	399.8		

* roundwood is timber as it is felled
** in million tonnes

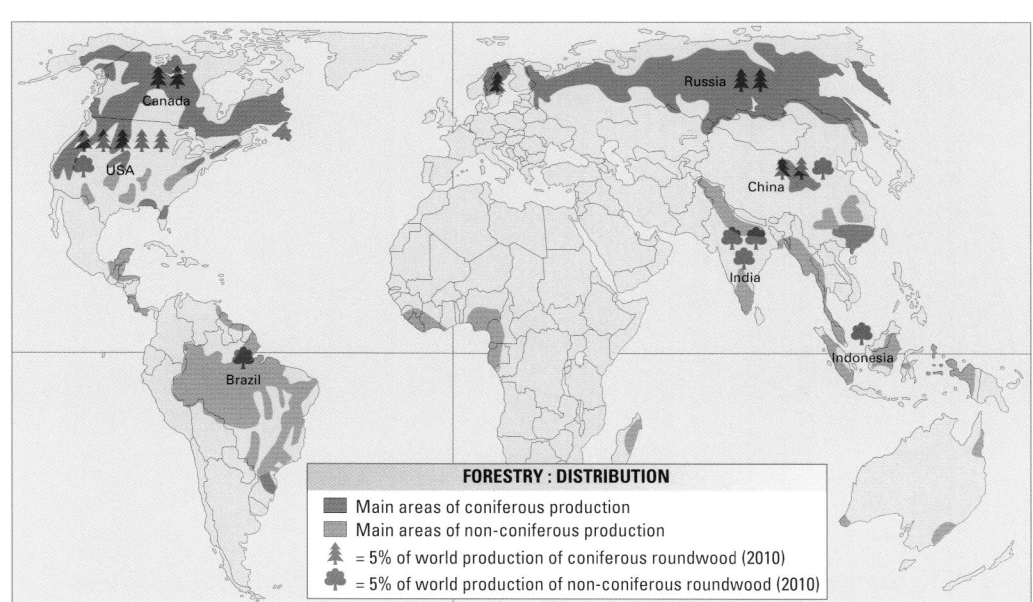

FORESTRY : DISTRIBUTION
- Main areas of coniferous production
- Main areas of non-coniferous production
- 🌲 = 5% of world production of coniferous roundwood (2010)
- 🌳 = 5% of world production of non-coniferous roundwood (2010)

Environment

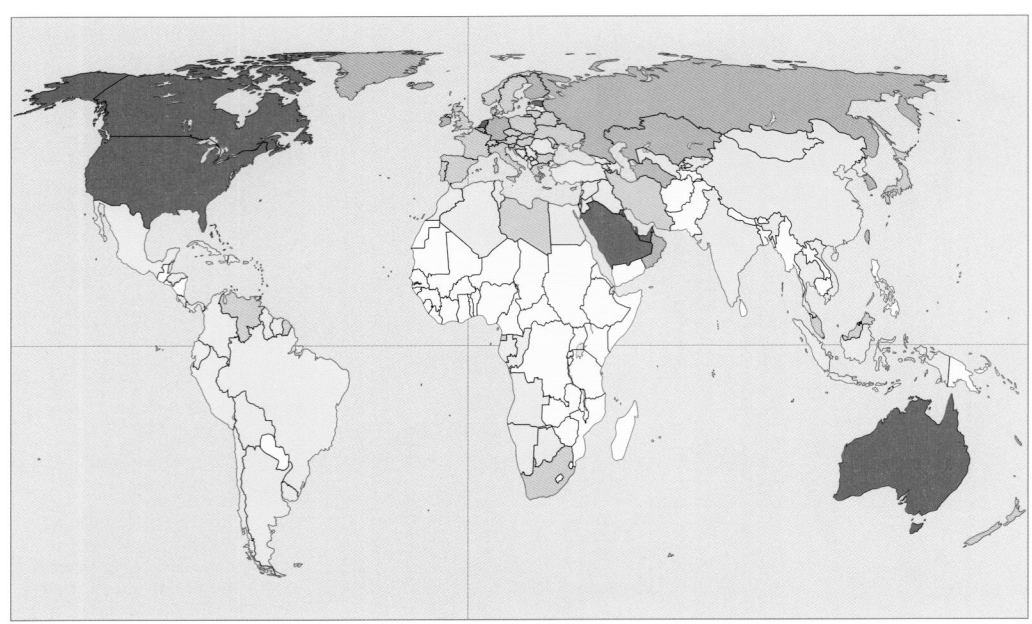

CARBON DIOXIDE EMISSIONS

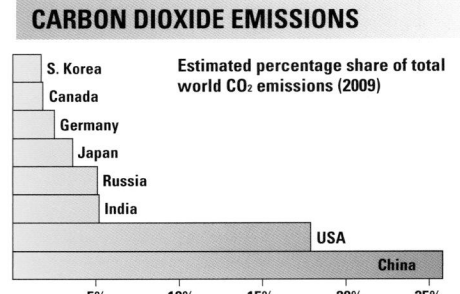

Estimated percentage share of total world CO_2 emissions (2009)

S. Korea
Canada
Germany
Japan
Russia
India
USA
China

5%   10%   15%   20%   25%

PREDICTED CHANGE IN PRECIPITATION

The difference between actual annual average precipitation, 1960–1990, and the predicted annual average precipitation, 2070–2100. It should be noted that these predicted annual mean changes mask quite significant seasonal detail.

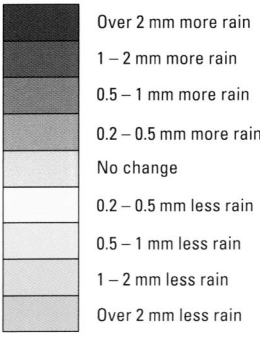

	Over 2 mm more rain
	1 – 2 mm more rain
	0.5 – 1 mm more rain
	0.2 – 0.5 mm more rain
	No change
	0.2 – 0.5 mm less rain
	0.5 – 1 mm less rain
	1 – 2 mm less rain
	Over 2 mm less rain

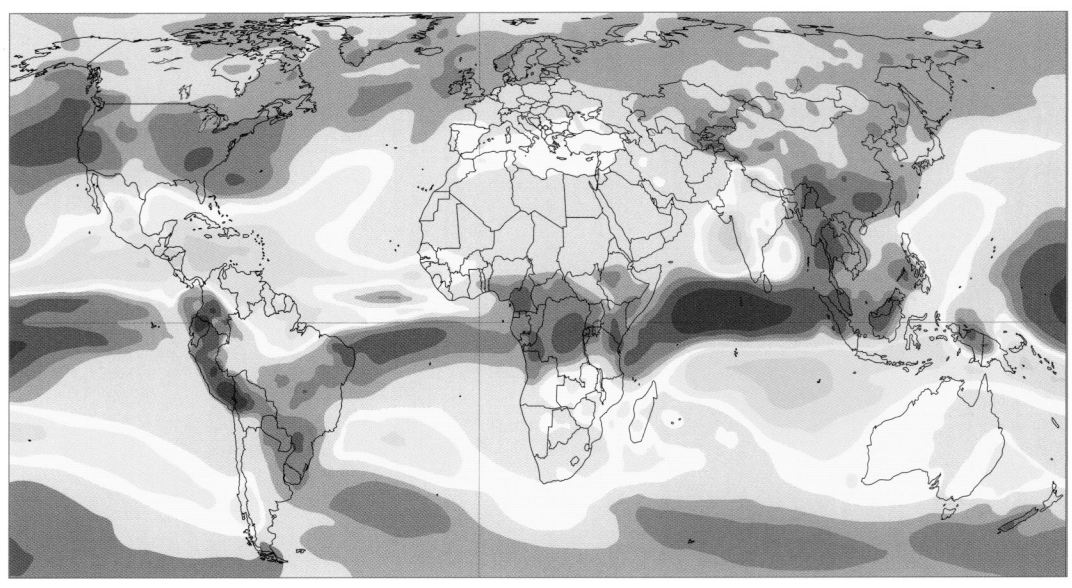

PREDICTED CHANGE IN TEMPERATURE

The difference between actual annual average surface air temperature, 1960–1990, and the predicted annual average surface air temperature, 2070–2100. This map shows the predicted increase, assuming a 'medium growth' of global economy and assuming that no measures are taken to combat the emission of greenhouse gases.

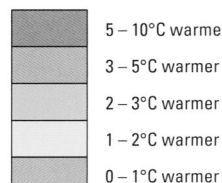

	5 – 10°C warmer
	3 – 5°C warmer
	2 – 3°C warmer
	1 – 2°C warmer
	0 – 1°C warmer

Source: The Hadley Centre of Climate Prediction and Research, The Met. Office

GLOBAL WARMING PROJECTIONS

Projected Change in Global Warming

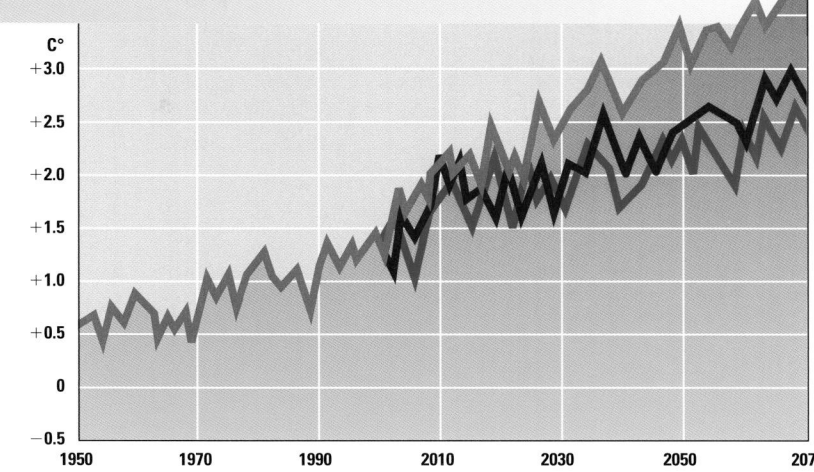

∿ Rise in average temperatures assuming present trends in CO_2 emissions continue

∿ Assuming some cuts are made in emissions

∿ Assuming drastic cuts are made in emissions

Climate models are used to provide the best scientifically-based estimates of the future global climate. A typical method is to run the models for some decades ahead and then to compare the predicted average with a past 30-year period. A range of climate models are used, run with different scenarios that express the breadth of possibilities of, for example, industrial development and the degree of atmospheric pollution 'clean-up' by industrial nations.

The diagram on the right shows global observed and predicted surface mean temperature change from 1950 to 2070 with three prediction scenarios. The first (red) assumes rapid economic growth and continued population increases. The second (blue) assumes some attempts are made to cut greenhouse gas emissions, while the green line involves the greater use of cleaner technologies, with global population peaking mid-century then declining.

GREENHOUSE EFFECT

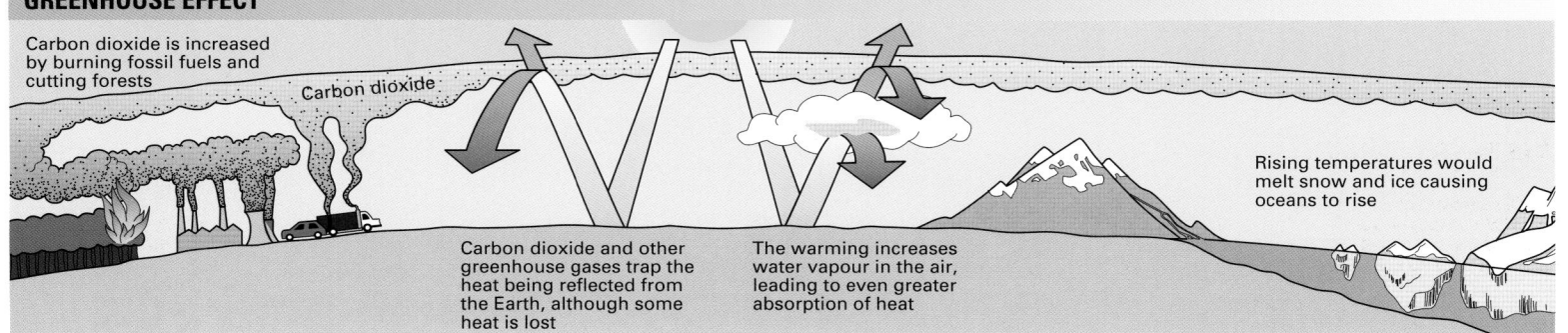

Carbon dioxide is increased by burning fossil fuels and cutting forests

Carbon dioxide

Carbon dioxide and other greenhouse gases trap the heat being reflected from the Earth, although some heat is lost

The warming increases water vapour in the air, leading to even greater absorption of heat

Rising temperatures would melt snow and ice causing oceans to rise

DESERTIFICATION AND DEFORESTATION

- Existing deserts
- Areas with a high risk of desertification
- Areas with a moderate risk of desertification
- Former areas of rainforest
- Existing rainforest

FOREST CLEARANCE

Thousands of hectares of forest cleared annually, tropical countries surveyed 1980–85, 1990–95, 2000–2005 and 2005–10. Loss as a percentage of remaining stocks is shown in figures on each column. Gain is indicated as a minus figure.

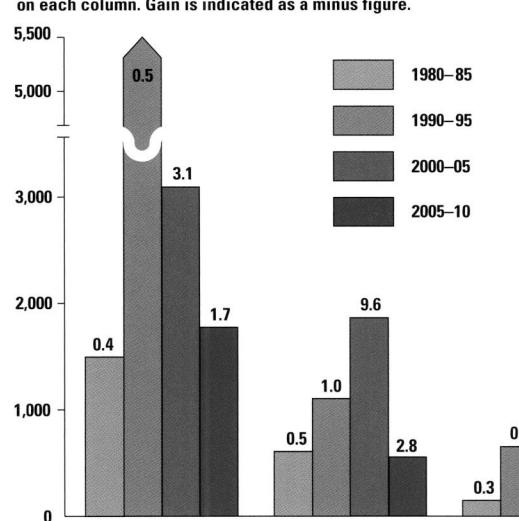

- 1980–85
- 1990–95
- 2000–05
- 2005–10

Brazil: 0.4, 0.5, 3.1, 1.7
Indonesia: 0.5, 1.0, 9.6, 2.8
India: 0.3, 0.0, 0.7, −0.9
Burma: 0.3, 1.4, 4.7, 3.7
Thailand: 2.4, 2.6, 2.0, −0.3
Vietnam: 0.7, 1.4, −12.2, −4.4
Philippines: 1.0, 3.5, 4.2, −3.0
Costa Rica: 4.0, 3.0, −0.6, −3.7

DEFORESTATION

The Earth's remaining forests are under attack from three directions: expanding agriculture, logging, and growing consumption of fuelwood, often in combination. Sometimes deforestation is the direct result of government policy, as in the efforts made to resettle the urban poor in some parts of Brazil; just as often, it comes about despite state attempts at conservation.

Loggers, licensed or unlicensed, blaze a trail into virgin forest, often destroying twice as many trees as they harvest. Landless farmers follow, burning away most of what remains to plant their crops, completing the destruction. However, some countries such as Vietnam, Philippines and Costa Rica have successfully implemented reafforestation programmes.

Population

DEMOGRAPHIC PROFILES

Developed nations such as the UK have populations evenly spread across the age groups and, usually, a growing proportion of elderly people. The great majority of the people in developing nations, however, are in the younger age groups, about to enter their most fertile years. In time, these population profiles should resemble the world profile (even Nigeria has made recent progress by reducing its birth rate), but the transition will come about only after a few more generations of rapid population growth.

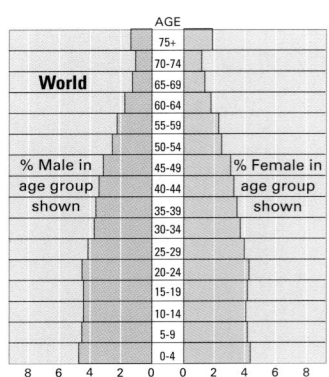

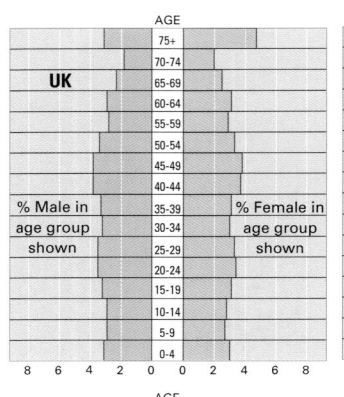

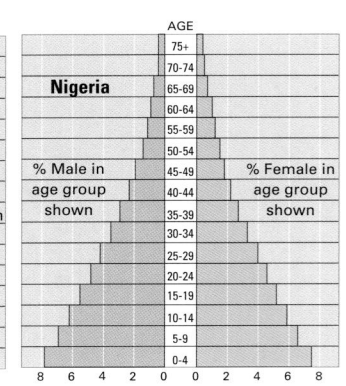

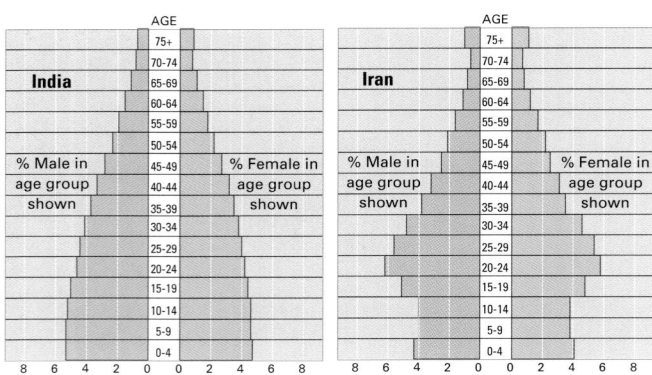

MOST POPULOUS NATIONS

Totals in millions (2011 estimates)

1. China	1,337	9. Russia	139	17. Turkey	79
2. India	1,189	10. Japan	126	18. Iran	78
3. USA	313	11. Mexico	113	19. Congo (Dem. Rep.)	72
4. Indonesia	246	12. Philippines	101	20. Thailand	67
5. Brazil	203	13. Vietnam	91	21. France	65
6. Pakistan	187	14. Ethiopia	91	22. UK	63
7. Bangladesh	159	15. Egypt	82	23. Italy	61
8. Nigeria	155	16. Germany	81	24. Burma (Myanmar)	53

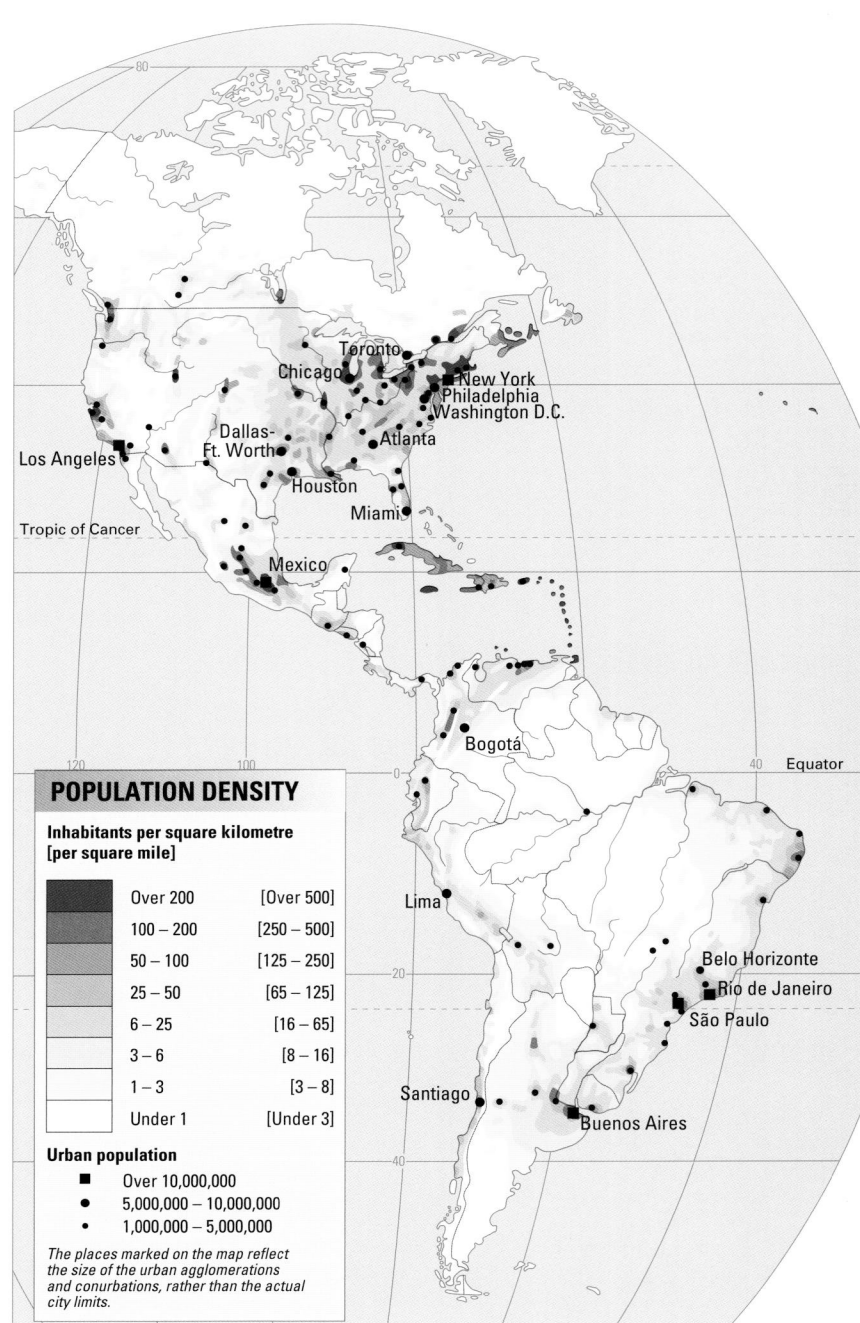

POPULATION DENSITY

Inhabitants per square kilometre [per square mile]

Over 200	[Over 500]
100 – 200	[250 – 500]
50 – 100	[125 – 250]
25 – 50	[65 – 125]
6 – 25	[16 – 65]
3 – 6	[8 – 16]
1 – 3	[3 – 8]
Under 1	[Under 3]

Urban population

■ Over 10,000,000

● 5,000,000 – 10,000,000

• 1,000,000 – 5,000,000

The places marked on the map reflect the size of the urban agglomerations and conurbations, rather than the actual city limits.

Projection: *Interrupted Mollweide's Homolographic*

CONTINENTAL COMPARISONS

North and Central America · Europe · Africa · South America · Asia · Australasia

Each square in the diagram above represents 1% of the total world population.

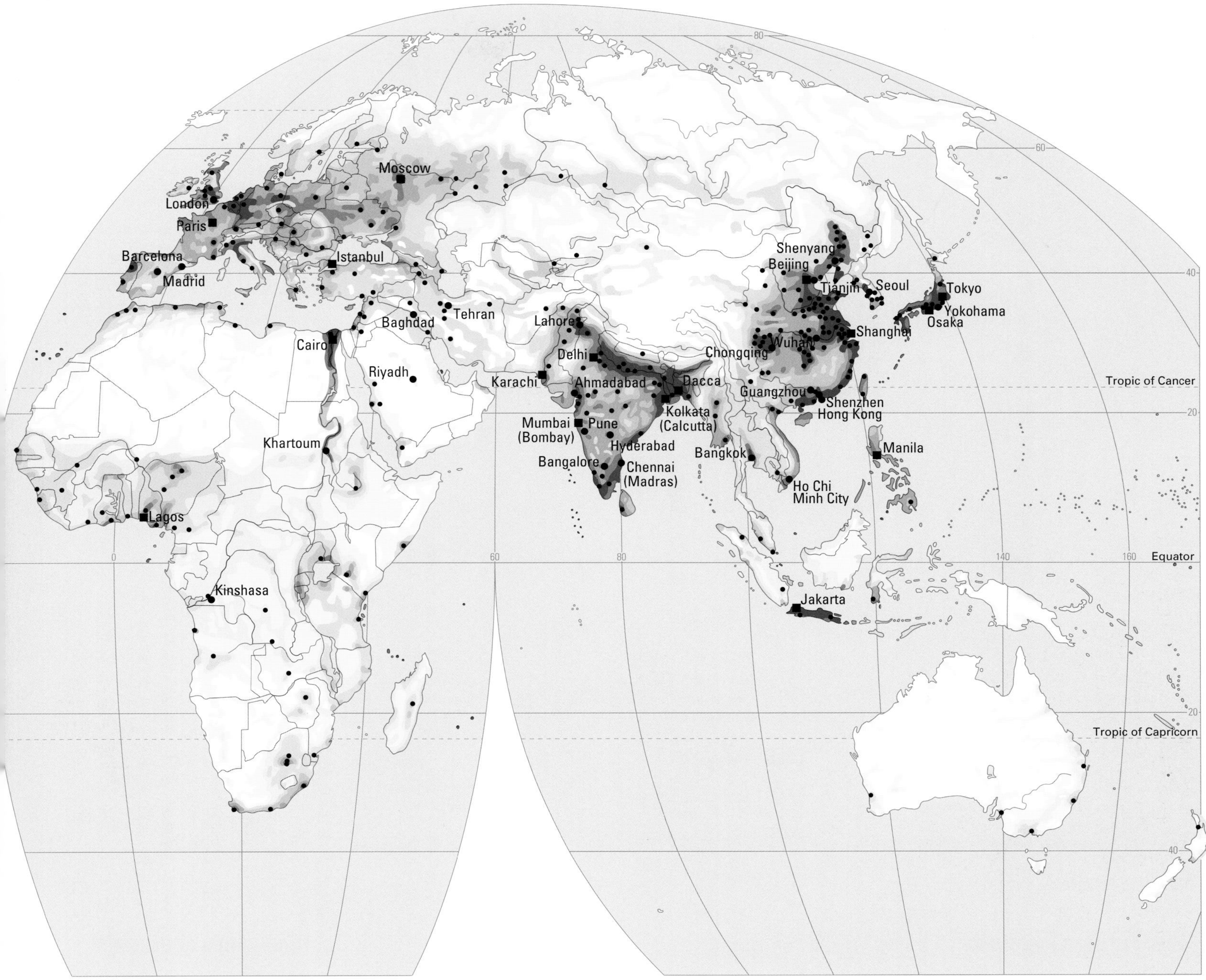

Moscow

London
Paris

Barcelona
Madrid

Istanbul

Baghdad
Tehran

Cairo

Riyadh

Khartoum

Lagos

Kinshasa

Lahore
Delhi
Karachi
Ahmadabad
Mumbai (Bombay)
Pune
Bangalore
Hyderabad
Chennai (Madras)
Kolkata (Calcutta)
Dacca

Shenyang
Beijing
Tianjin
Seoul
Tokyo
Yokohama
Osaka
Shanghai
Wuhan
Chongqing
Guangzhou
Shenzhen
Hong Kong
Bangkok
Ho Chi Minh City

Manila

Jakarta

Tropic of Cancer

Equator

Tropic of Capricorn

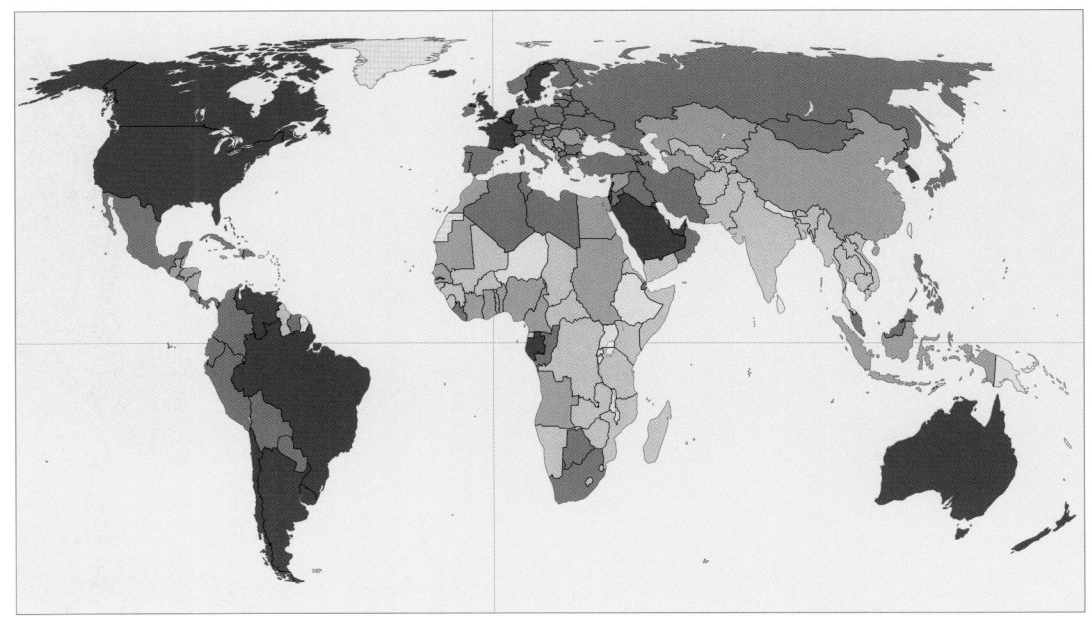

URBAN POPULATION

Percentage of total population living in towns and cities (2010)

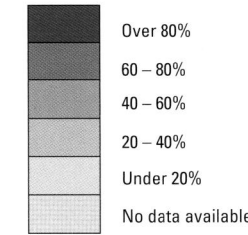

- Over 80%
- 60 – 80%
- 40 – 60%
- 20 – 40%
- Under 20%
- No data available

Most urbanized

Singapore	100%
Kuwait	98%
Belgium	97%
Qatar	96%
Malta	95%

Least urbanized

Burundi	11%
Papua New Guinea	13%
Uganda	13%
Trinidad & Tobago	14%
Sri Lanka	15%

The Human Family

PREDOMINANT LANGUAGES

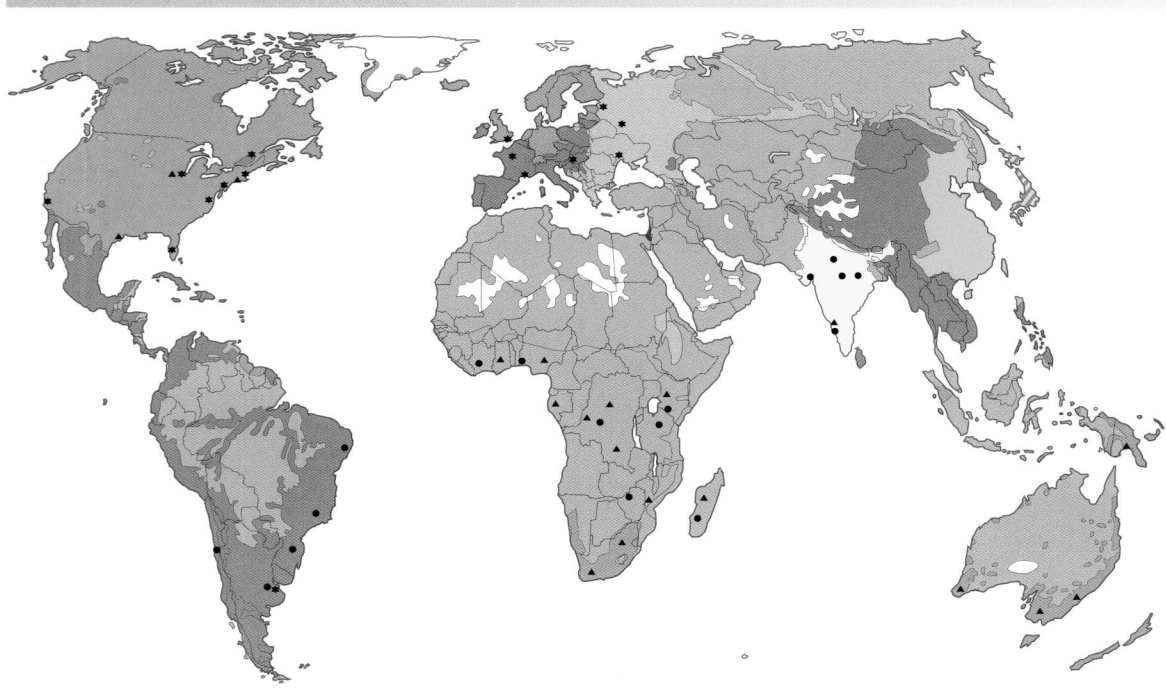

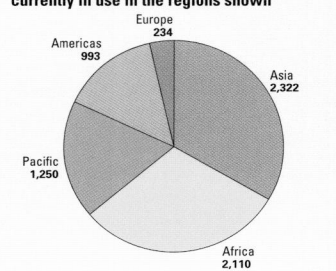

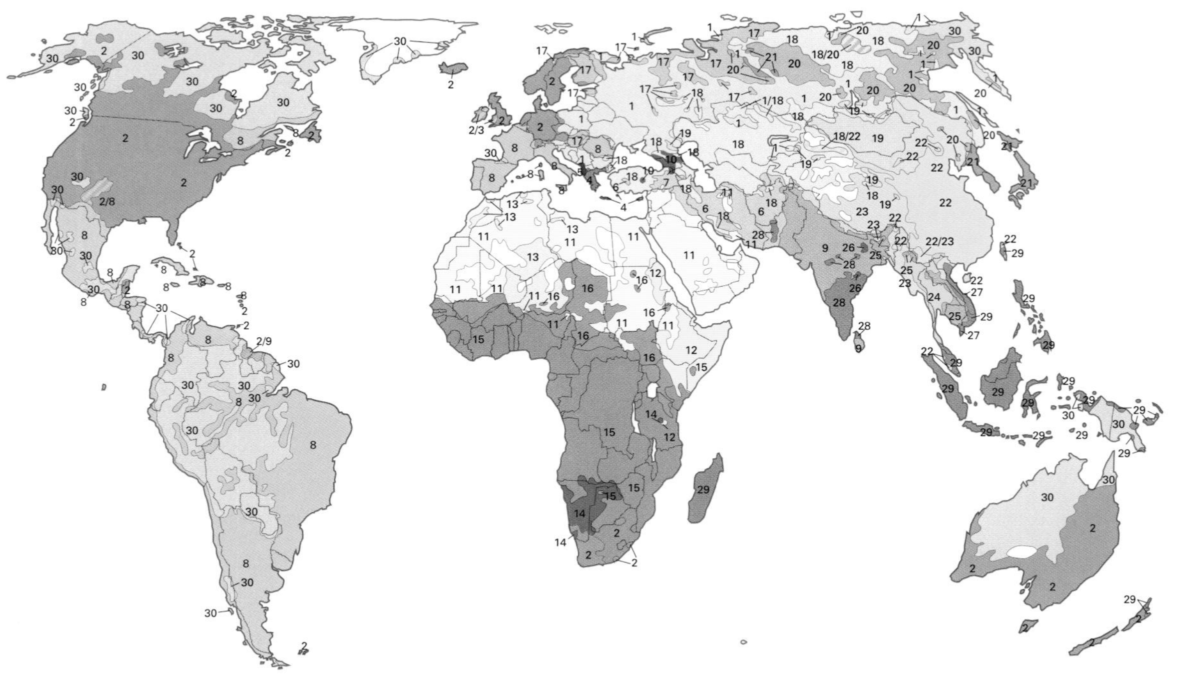

INDO-EUROPEAN FAMILY
- 1 Balto-Slavic group (incl. Russian, Ukrainian)
- 2 Germanic group (incl. English, German)
- 3 Celtic group
- 4 Greek
- 5 Albanian
- 6 Iranian group
- 7 Armenian
- 8 Romance group (incl. Spanish, Portuguese, French, Italian)
- 9 Indo-Aryan group (incl. Hindi, Bengali, Urdu, Punjabi, Marathi)

- 10 CAUCASIAN FAMILY

AFRO-ASIATIC FAMILY
- 11 Semitic group (incl. Arabic)
- 12 Kushitic group
- 13 Berber group

- 14 KHOISAN FAMILY
- 15 NIGER-CONGO FAMILY
- 16 NILO-SAHARAN FAMILY
- 17 URALIC FAMILY

ALTAIC FAMILY
- 18 Turkic group (incl. Turkish)
- 19 Mongolian group
- 20 Tungus-Manchu group
- 21 Japanese and Korean

SINO-TIBETAN FAMILY
- 22 Sinitic (Chinese) languages (incl. Mandarin, Wu, Yue)
- 23 Tibetic-Burmic languages

- 24 TAI FAMILY

AUSTRO-ASIATIC FAMILY
- 25 Mon-Khmer group
- 26 Munda group
- 27 Vietnamese

- 28 DRAVIDIAN FAMILY (incl. Telugu, Tamil)
- 29 AUSTRONESIAN FAMILY (incl. Malay-Indonesian, Javanese)
- 30 OTHER LANGUAGES

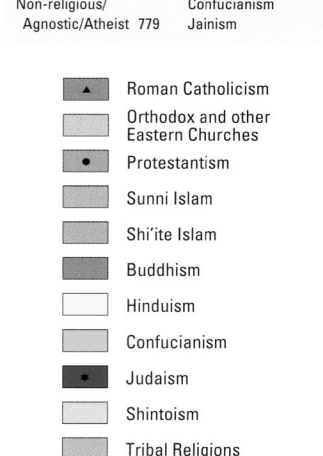

LANGUAGES OF THE WORLD

Language can be classified by ancestry and structure. For example, the Romance and Germanic groups are both derived from an Indo-European language believed to have been spoken 5,000 years ago.

First-language speakers, in millions (2009)
Mandarin Chinese 845, Spanish 329, English 328, Arabic 221, Hindi 182, Bengali 181, Portuguese 178, Russian 144, Japanese 122, German 90, Javanese 85, Wu Chinese 77, Telugu 70, Vietnamese 69, Marathi 68, French 68, Korean 66, Tamil 66, Punjabi 63, Italian 62.

Distribution of Living Languages

The figures refer to the number of languages currently in use in the regions shown

Europe 234
Americas 993
Asia 2,322
Pacific 1,250
Africa 2,110

PREDOMINANT RELIGIONS

RELIGIOUS ADHERENTS

Religious adherents in millions (2009)

Christianity	2,264	Buddhism	484
Roman Catholic	*1,143*	Chinese folk	455
Protestant	*413*	Ethnic religions	259
Orthodox	*273*	New religions	64
Anglican	*85*	Sikhism	24
Islam	1,523	Spiritism	14
Sunni	*1,279*	Judaism	15
Shi'ite	*213*	Taoism	9
Hinduism	935	Baha'i	7
Non-religious/		Confucianism	6
Agnostic/Atheist	779	Jainism	6

- Roman Catholicism
- Orthodox and other Eastern Churches
- Protestantism
- Sunni Islam
- Shi'ite Islam
- Buddhism
- Hinduism
- Confucianism
- Judaism
- Shintoism
- Tribal Religions

UNITED NATIONS

Created in 1945 to promote peace and co-operation, and based in New York, the United Nations is the world's largest international organization, with 193 members and an annual budget of US $5.2 billion (2012). Each member of the General Assembly has one vote, while the five permanent members of the 15-nation Security Council – China, France, Russia, the UK and the USA – each hold a veto. The Secretariat is the UN's principal administrative arm. The 54 members of the Economic and Social Council are responsible for economic, social, cultural, educational, health and related matters. The UN has 16 specialized agencies – based in Canada, France, Switzerland and Italy, as well as the USA – which help members in fields such as education (UNESCO), agriculture (FAO), medicine (WHO) and finance (IFC). By the end of 1994, all the original 11 trust territories of the Trusteeship Council had become independent.

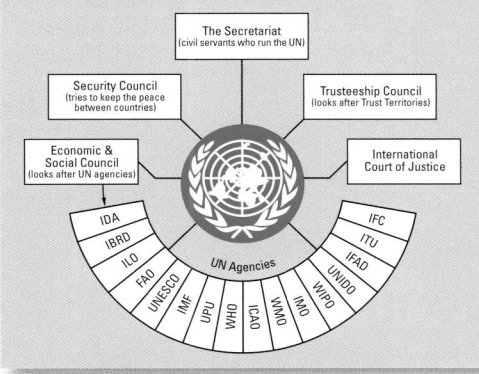

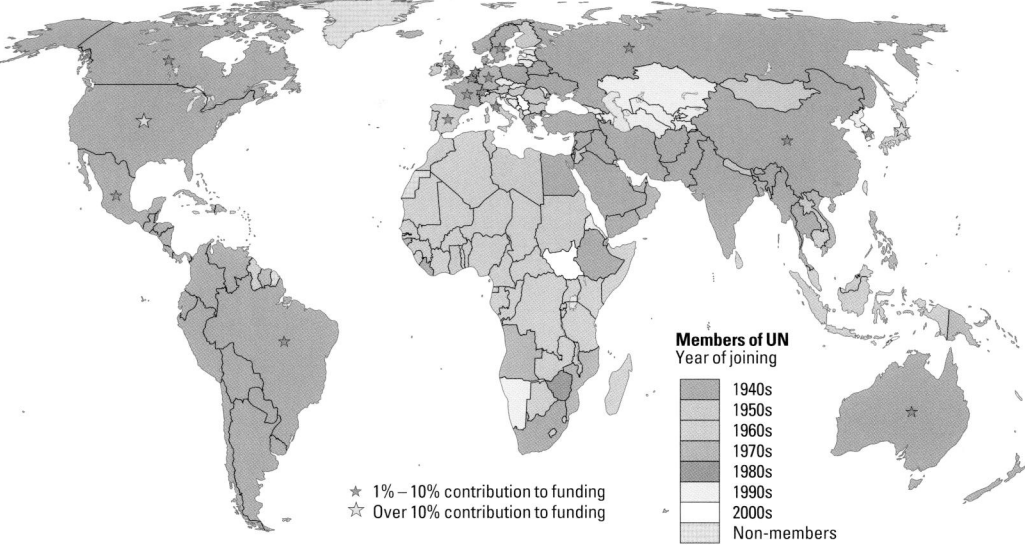

Members of UN
Year of joining

- 1940s
- 1950s
- 1960s
- 1970s
- 1980s
- 1990s
- 2000s
- Non-members

★ 1% – 10% contribution to funding
☆ Over 10% contribution to funding

MEMBERSHIP OF THE UN From the original 51, membership of the UN has now grown to 193. Recent additions include East Timor, Switzerland, Montenegro and South Sudan. There are only two independent states which are not members of the UN – Taiwan and the Vatican City. All the successor states of the former USSR had joined by the end of 1992. The official languages of the UN are Chinese, English, French, Russian, Spanish and Arabic.

FUNDING The UN budget for 2012 was US $5.2 billion. Contributions are assessed by the members' ability to pay, with the maximum 22% of the total (USA's share), and the minimum 0.001%. The 27-member EU pays 40% of the budget.

PEACEKEEPING The UN has been involved in 67 peacekeeping operations worldwide since 1948.

INTERNATIONAL ORGANIZATIONS

ACP African-Caribbean-Pacific (formed in 1963). Members have economic ties with the EU.
APEC Asia-Pacific Economic Co-operation (formed in 1989). It aims to enhance economic growth and prosperity for the region and to strengthen the Asia-Pacific community. APEC is the only intergovernmental grouping in the world operating on the basis of non-binding commitments, open dialogue, and equal respect for the views of all participants. There are 21 member economies.
ARAB LEAGUE (formed in 1945). The League's aim is to promote economic, social, political and military co-operation. There are 22 member nations.
ASEAN Association of South-east Asian Nations (formed in 1967). Cambodia joined in 1999.
AU The African Union replaced the Organization of African Unity (formed in 1963) in 2002. Its 53 members represent over 94% of Africa's population. Arabic, English, French and Portuguese are recognized as working languages.
COLOMBO PLAN (formed in 1951). Its 25 members aim to promote economic and social development in Asia and the Pacific.
COMMONWEALTH The Commonwealth of Nations evolved from the British Empire. Pakistan was suspended in 1999, but reinstated in 2004. Zimbabwe was suspended in 2002 and, in response to its continued suspension, Zimbabwe left the Commonwealth in 2003. Fiji was suspended in 2006 following a military coup. Rwanda joined the Commonwealth in 2009, as the 54th member state, becoming only the second country which was not formerly a British colony to be admitted to the group.
EU European Union (evolved from the European Community in 1993). Cyprus, the Czech Republic, Estonia, Hungary, Latvia, Lithuania, Malta, Poland, the Slovak Republic and Slovenia joined the EU in May 2004; Bulgaria and Romania joined in 2007. The other 15 members of the EU are Austria, Belgium, Denmark, Finland, France, Germany, Greece, Ireland, Italy, Luxembourg, Netherlands, Portugal, Spain, Sweden and the UK. Together, the 27 members aim to integrate economies, co-ordinate social developments and bring about political union.
LAIA Latin American Integration Association (1980). Its aim is to promote freer regional trade.
NATO North Atlantic Treaty Organization (formed in 1949). It continues despite the winding-up of the Warsaw Pact in 1991. Bulgaria, Estonia, Latvia, Lithuania, Romania, the Slovak Republic and Slovenia became members in 2004, Albania and Croatia in 2009.

OAS Organization of American States (formed in 1948). It aims to promote social and economic co-operation between countries in developed North America and developing Latin America.
OECD Organization for Economic Co-operation and Development (formed in 1961). It comprises 30 major free-market economies. Poland, Hungary and South Korea joined in 1996, and the Slovak Republic in 2000. The 'G8' is its 'inner group' of leading industrial nations, comprising Canada, France, Germany, Italy, Japan, Russia, the UK and the USA.
OPEC Organization of Petroleum Exporting Countries (formed in 1960). It controls about three-quarters of the world's oil supply. Gabon formally withdrew from OPEC in August 1996.

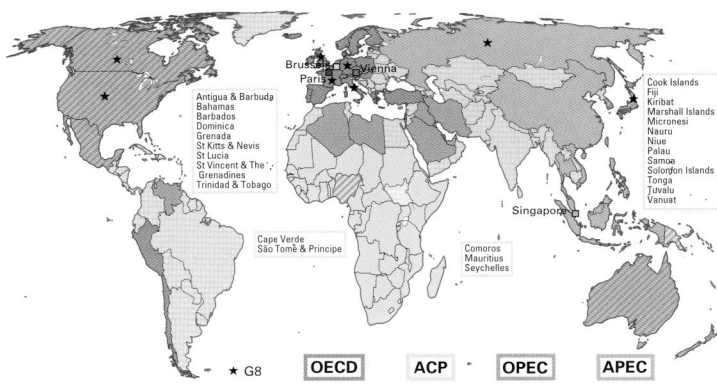

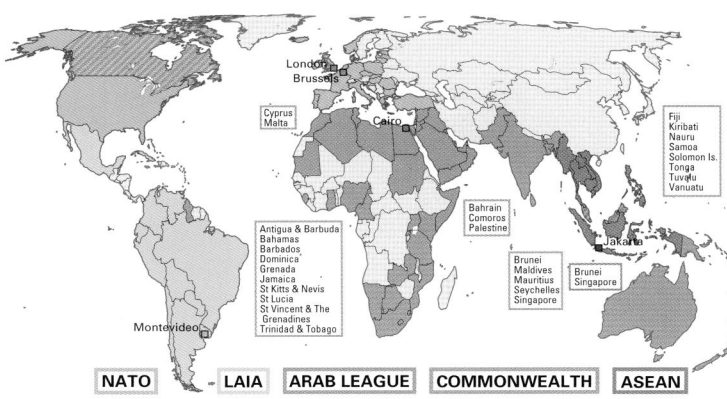

Wealth

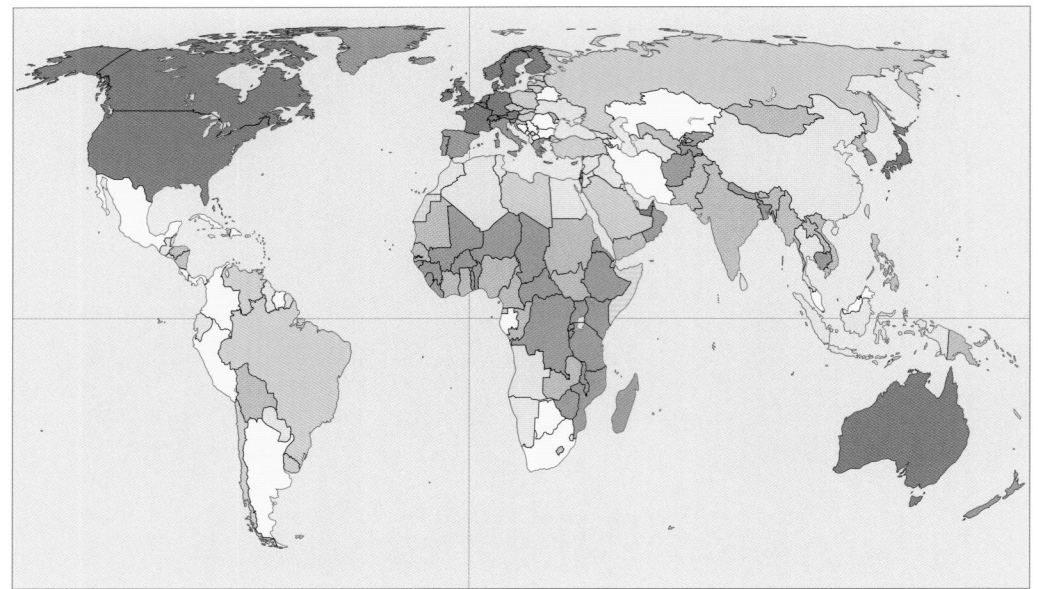

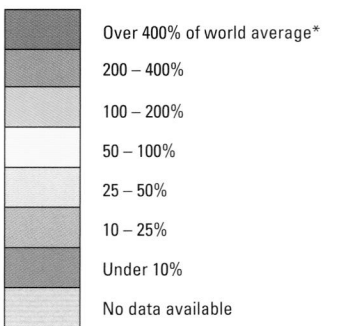
WEALTH CREATION

The Gross National Income (GNI) of the world's largest economies, US $ million (2010)

1.	USA	14,645,600	21. Belgium	499,500
2.	China	5,720,800	22. Poland	474,900
3.	Japan	5,334,400	23. Sweden	470,000
4.	Germany	3,522,000	24. Saudi Arabia	439,000
5.	France	2,749,800	25. Norway	411,800
6.	UK	2,387,100	26. Austria	394,600
7.	Italy	2,125,800	27. Argentina	348,400
8.	Brazil	1,830,400	28. Venezuela	334,100
9.	India	1,553,900	29. Iran	330,600
10.	Canada	1,475,900	30. Denmark	327,400
11.	Spain	1,462,900	31. Greece	305,000
12.	Russia	1,403,800	32. South Africa	304,600
13.	Taiwan	1,016,400	33. Thailand	286,600
14.	Mexico	1,008,000	34. Finland	256,000
15.	South Korea	972,300	35. Colombia	255,300
16.	Australia	957,500	36. Portugal	232,900
17.	Netherlands	814,800	37. Hong Kong (China)	231,700
18.	Turkey	719,900	38. Malaysia	220,400
19.	Indonesia	599,200	39. Israel	207,200
20.	Switzerland	559,700	40. North Korea	205,000

THE WEALTH GAP

The world's richest and poorest countries, by Gross National Income (GNI) per capita in US $ (2010)

Richest countries		Poorest countries	
1. Monaco	183,150	1. Burundi	170
2. Liechtenstein	137,070	2. Congo (Dem. Rep.)	180
3. Norway	84,290	3. Liberia	200
4. Luxembourg	77,160	4. Malawi	330
5. Switzerland	71,530	5. Eritrea	340
6. Denmark	59,050	6. Sierra Leone	340
7. San Marino	50,670	7. Niger	370
8. Sweden	50,110	8. Ethiopia	390
9. Netherlands	49,050	9. Guinea	400
10. Finland	47,720	10. Afghanistan	410
11. USA	47,390	11. Madagascar	430
12. Austria	47,060	12. Mozambique	440
13. Belgium	45,910	13. Nepal	440
14. Australia	43,590	14. Togo	440
15. Canada	43,270	15. Gambia, The	450
16. Germany	43,110	16. Zimbabwe	460
17. France	42,390	17. Central African Rep.	470
18. United Arab Emirates	41,930	18. Uganda	500
19. Japan	41,850	19. Rwanda	520
20. Andorra	41,130	20. Tanzania	530

CONTINENTAL SHARES

Shares of population and of wealth (GNI) by continent (2010)

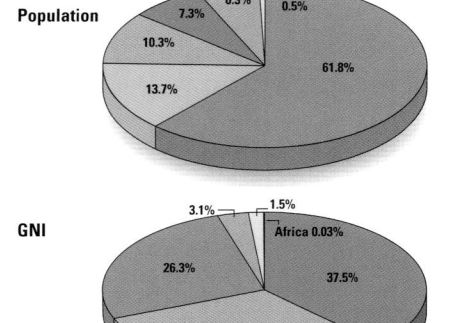

Population

GNI

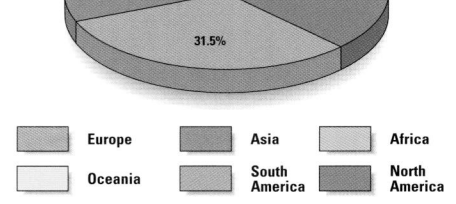

Europe Asia Africa

Oceania South America North America

Highest average inflation		Lowest average inflation	
Belarus	41%	Bahrain	0.3%
Venezuela	29%	Switzerland	0.4%
Ethiopia	29%	Japan	0.4%

INTERNATIONAL AID

Official Development Assistance (ODA) provided and received, per capita (2010)

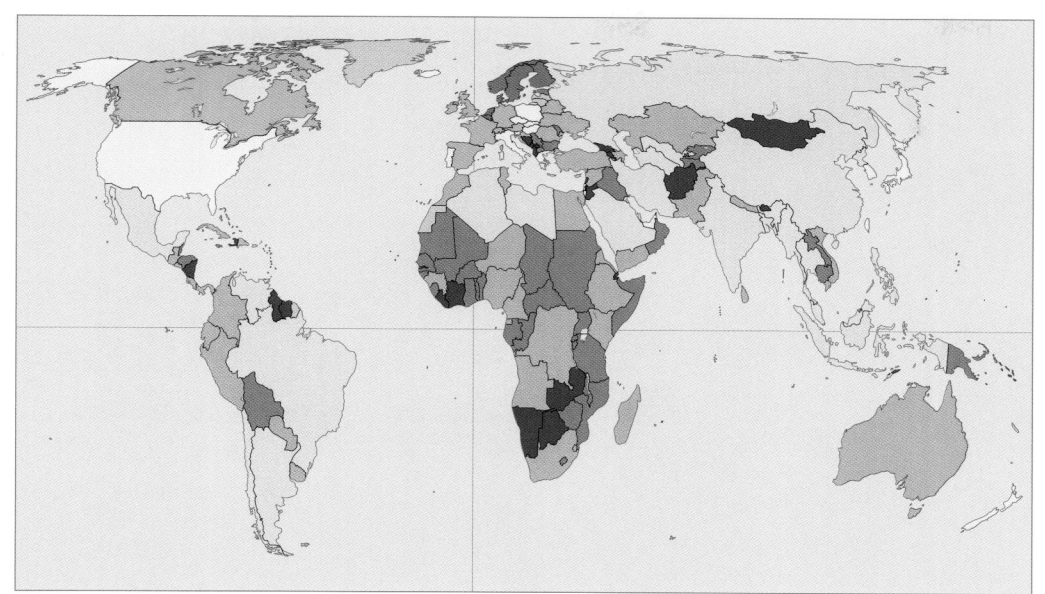

Over $250 per person
$100 – $250 per person
$50 – $100 per person
} Providers

Under $10 per person
$10 – $50 per person
$50 – $100 per person
Over $100 per person
} Receivers

No data available

DEBT AND AID

International debtors and the aid they receive

Although aid grants make a vital contribution to many of the world's poorer countries, they are usually dwarfed by the burden of debt that the developing economies are expected to repay. It is estimated that the total debt burden of developing countries is US$4,000 billion.

Debt, US$ per capita (2009)

Aid, US$ per capita (2009)

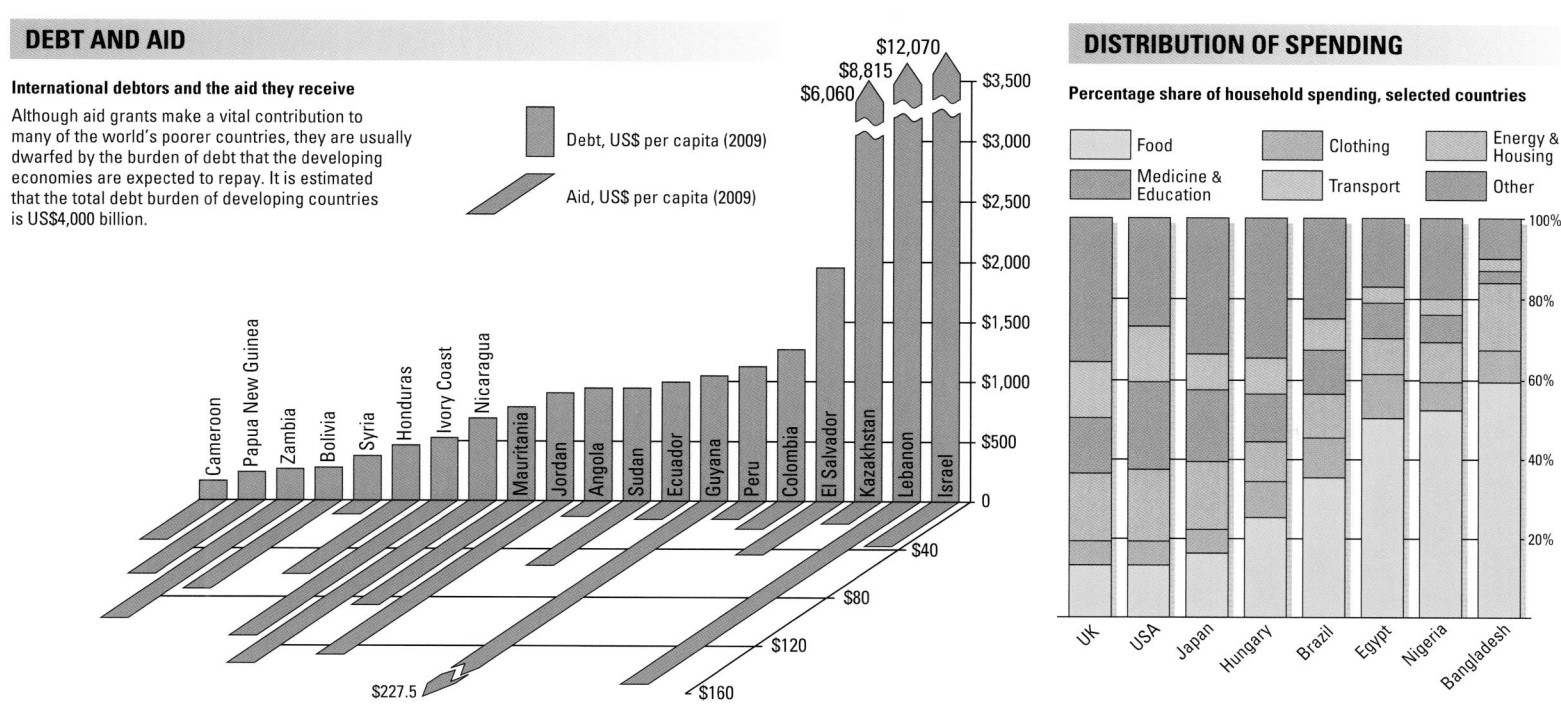

DISTRIBUTION OF SPENDING

Percentage share of household spending, selected countries

Food
Clothing
Energy & Housing
Medicine & Education
Transport
Other

UK, USA, Japan, Hungary, Brazil, Egypt, Nigeria, Bangladesh

WEALTH INDICATORS

Number of passenger vehicles, Internet users and mobile phones for each 1,000 people, selected countries (2010)

Passenger vehicles
Internet users
Mobile phones

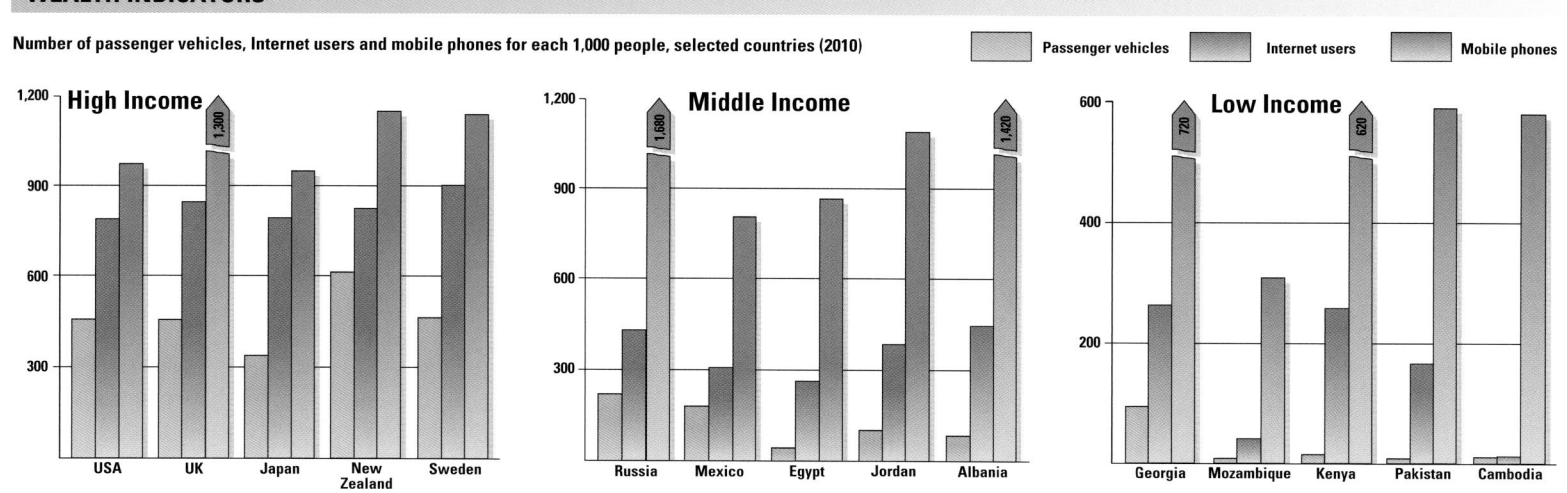

High Income — USA, UK, Japan, New Zealand, Sweden

Middle Income — Russia, Mexico, Egypt, Jordan, Albania

Low Income — Georgia, Mozambique, Kenya, Pakistan, Cambodia

Quality of Life

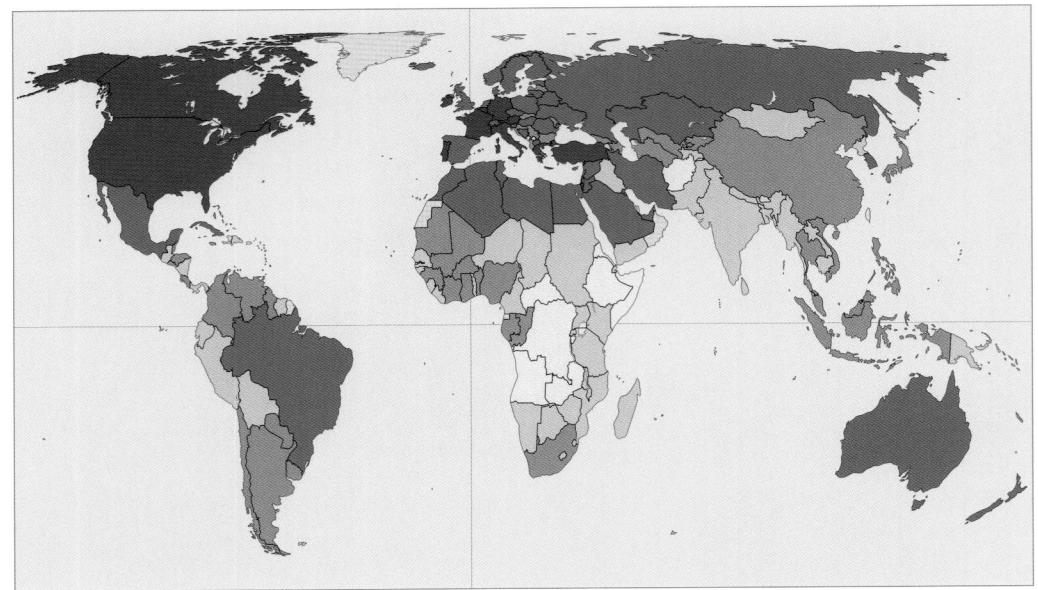

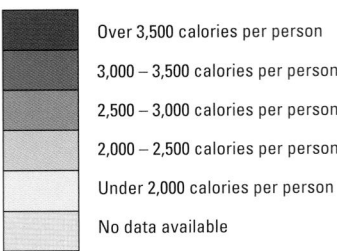
HOSPITAL CAPACITY

Hospital beds available for each 1,000 people (2009)

Highest capacity		Lowest capacity	
Japan	13.8	Cambodia	0.1
North Korea	12.3	Ethiopia	0.2
South Korea	12.2	Madagascar	0.3
Belarus	11.2	Niger	0.3
Russia	9.7	Guinea	0.3
Ukraine	8.7	Senegal	0.3
Germany	8.2	Uganda	0.4
Azerbaijan	7.7	Bangladesh	0.4
Austria	7.7	Mauritania	0.4
Barbados	7.6	Afghanistan	0.4
Kazakhstan	7.6	Ivory Coast	0.4
Czech Republic	7.2	Somalia	0.4
France	7.1	Sierra Leone	0.4
Hungary	7.0	Chad	0.4
Lithuania	6.8	Philippines	0.5

Although the ratio of people to hospital beds gives a good approximation of a country's health provision, it is not an absolute indicator. Raw numbers may mask inefficiency and other weaknesses: the high availability of beds in Belarus, for example, has not prevented infant mortality rates over three times as high as in the United Kingdom and the United States.

LIFE EXPECTANCY

Years of life expectancy at birth, selected countries (2012)

The chart shows combined data for both sexes. On average, women live longer than men worldwide, even in developing countries with high maternal mortality rates. Overall, life expectancy is steadily rising, though the difference between rich and poor nations remains dramatic.

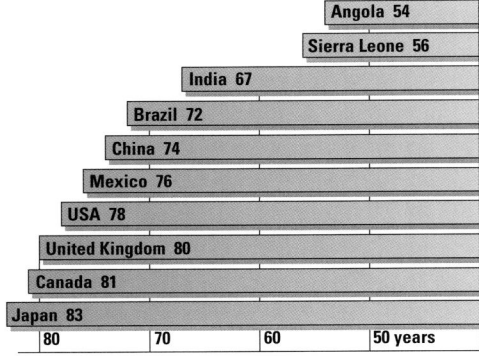

Angola 54
Sierra Leone 56
India 67
Brazil 72
China 74
Mexico 76
USA 78
United Kingdom 80
Canada 81
Japan 83

80   70   60   50 years

CAUSES OF DEATH

Causes of death for selected countries by percentage

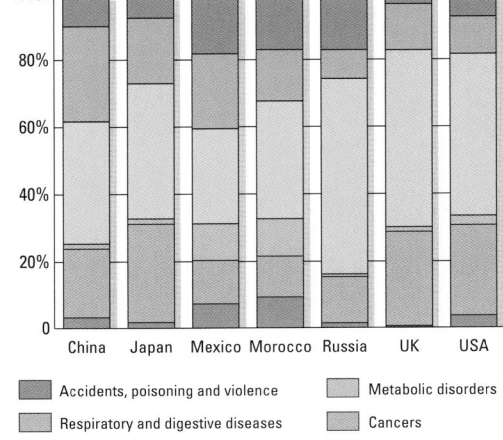

China   Japan   Mexico   Morocco   Russia   UK   USA

- Accidents, poisoning and violence
- Respiratory and digestive diseases
- Nervous and circulatory diseases
- Metabolic disorders
- Cancers
- Infectious and parasitic diseases

INFANT MORTALITY

Number of babies who died under the age of one, per 1,000 live births (2011)

Over 100 deaths per 1,000 births

50 – 100 deaths per 1,000 births

20 – 50 deaths per 1,000 births

10 – 20 deaths per 1,000 births

Under 10 deaths per 1,000 births

No data available

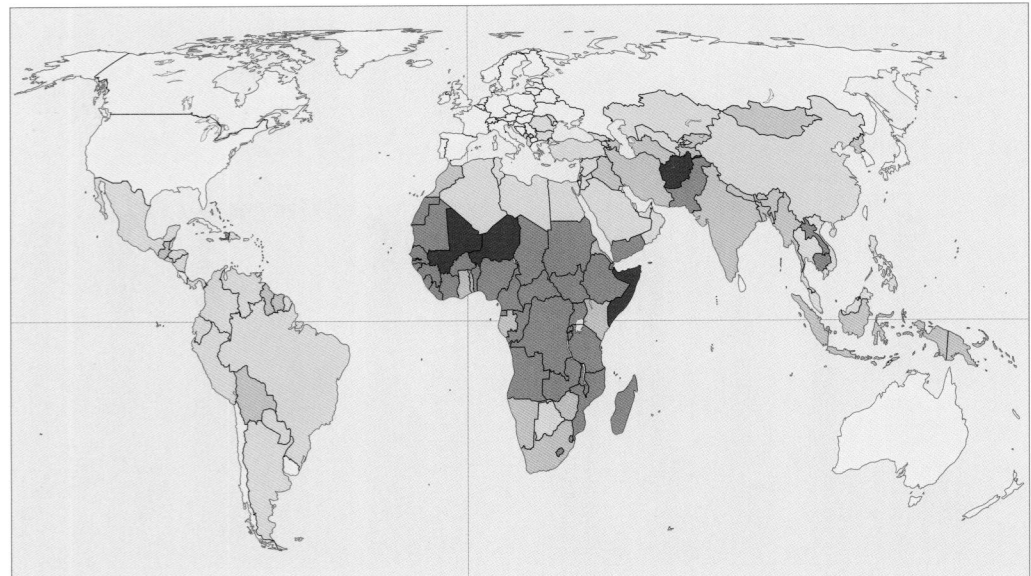

Highest infant mortality		Lowest infant mortality	
Afghanistan	122 deaths	Japan	2 deaths
Niger	110 deaths	Singapore	3 deaths
Mali	109 deaths	Sweden	3 deaths

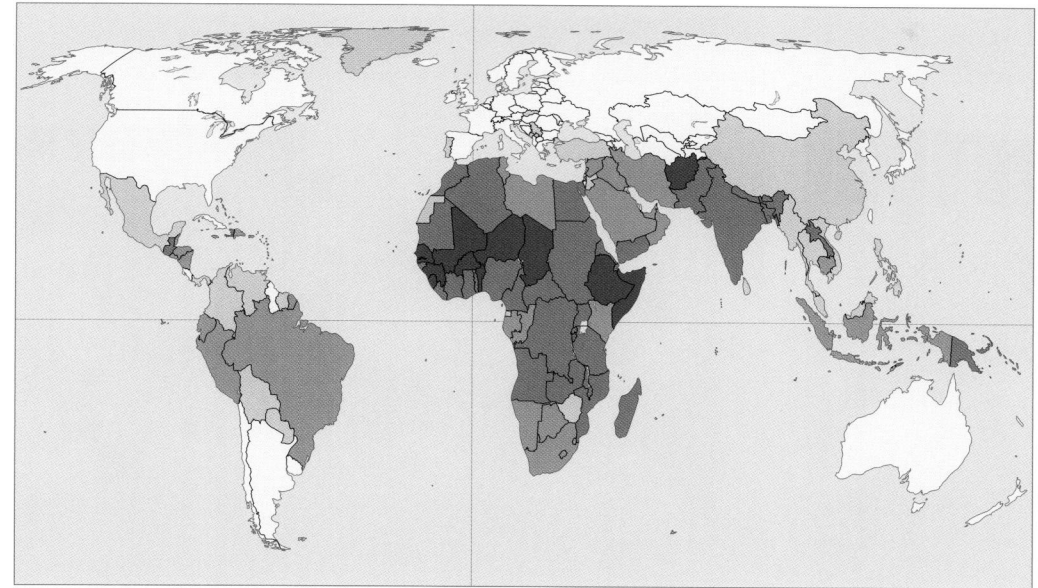

Percentage of the total adult population unable to read or write (2010)

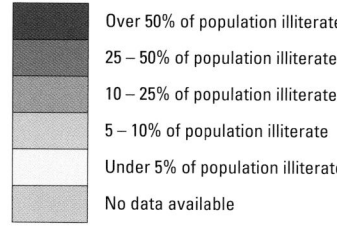

Over 50% of population illiterate

25 – 50% of population illiterate

10 – 25% of population illiterate

5 – 10% of population illiterate

Under 5% of population illiterate

No data available

Countries with the highest and lowest illiteracy rates as percentage of population

Highest		Lowest	
Mali	74%	Australia	0%
Burkina Faso	71%	Denmark	0%
Niger	71%	Finland	0%
Ethiopia	70%	Liechtenstein	0%
Chad	66%	Luxembourg	0%

FERTILITY AND EDUCATION

Fertility rates compared with female education, selected countries (2010)

Percentage of females aged 12–17 in secondary education

Fertility rate: average number of children borne per woman

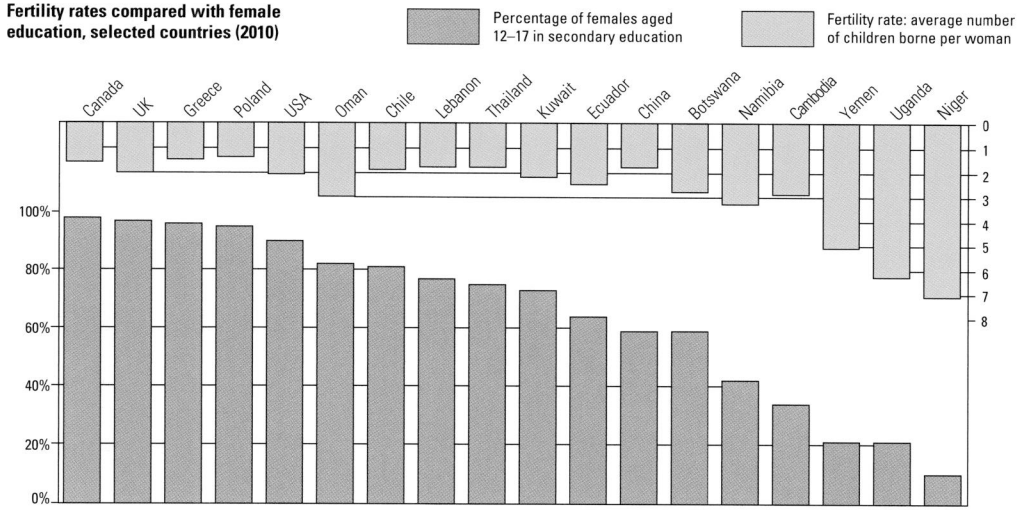

LIVING STANDARDS

At first sight, most international contrasts in living standards are swamped by differences in wealth. The rich not only have more money, they have more of everything, including years of life. Those with only a little money are obliged to spend most of it on food and clothing, the basic maintenance costs of their existence; air travel and tourism are unlikely to feature on their expenditure lists. However, poverty and wealth are both relative: slum dwellers living on social security payments in an affluent industrial country have far more resources at their disposal than an average African peasant, but feel their own poverty nonetheless. A middle-class Indian lawyer cannot command the earnings of a counterpart living in New York, London or Rome; nevertheless, he rightly sees himself as prosperous.

The rich not only live longer, on average, than the poor, they also die from different causes. Infectious and parasitic diseases, all but eliminated in the developed world, remain a scourge in the developing nations. On the other hand, more than two-thirds of the populations of OECD nations eventually succumb to cancer or circulatory disease.

HUMAN DEVELOPMENT INDEX

The Human Development Index (HDI), calculated by the UN Development Programme (UNDP), gives a value to countries using indicators of life expectancy, education and standards of living (2011). Higher values show more developed countries.

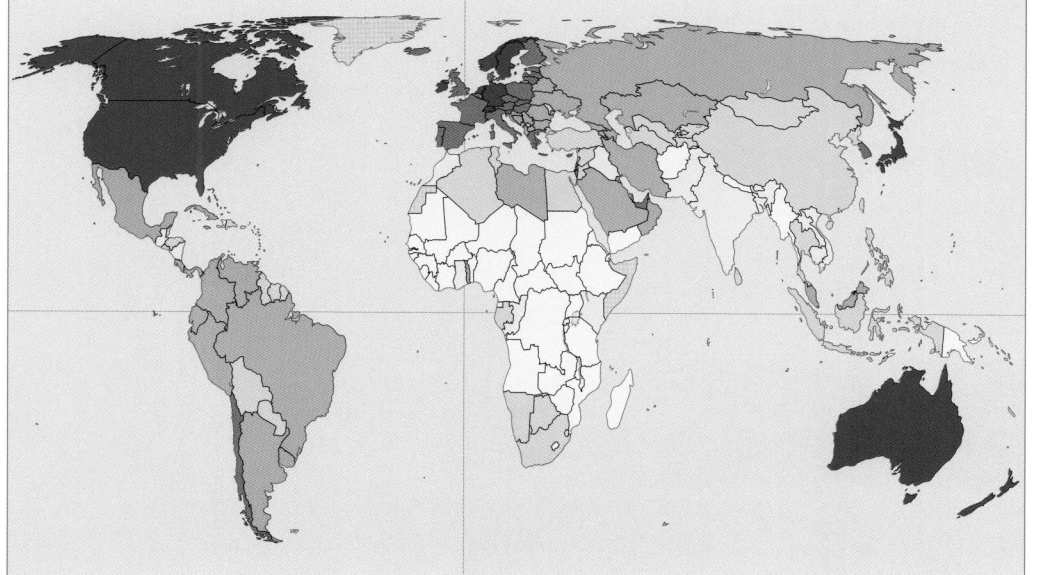

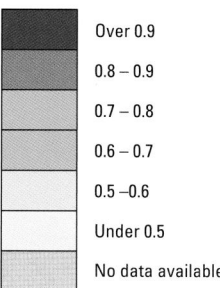

Over 0.9

0.8 – 0.9

0.7 – 0.8

0.6 – 0.7

0.5 – 0.6

Under 0.5

No data available

Highest values		Lowest values	
Norway	0.943	Congo (Dem. Rep.)	0.286
Australia	0.929	Niger	0.295
Netherlands	0.910	Burundi	0.316
USA	0.910	Mozambique	0.322
Canada	0.908	Chad	0.328

Energy

ENERGY PRODUCTION

Each square represents 1% of world primary energy production, by region (2009)

North America   Western Europe   Eastern Europe & Russia

Middle East

Africa

Asia

South America

Oceania

ENERGY CONSUMPTION

Each square represents 1% of world primary energy production, by region (2009)

North America   Western Europe   Eastern Europe & Russia

Middle East

Africa

Asia

South America

Oceania

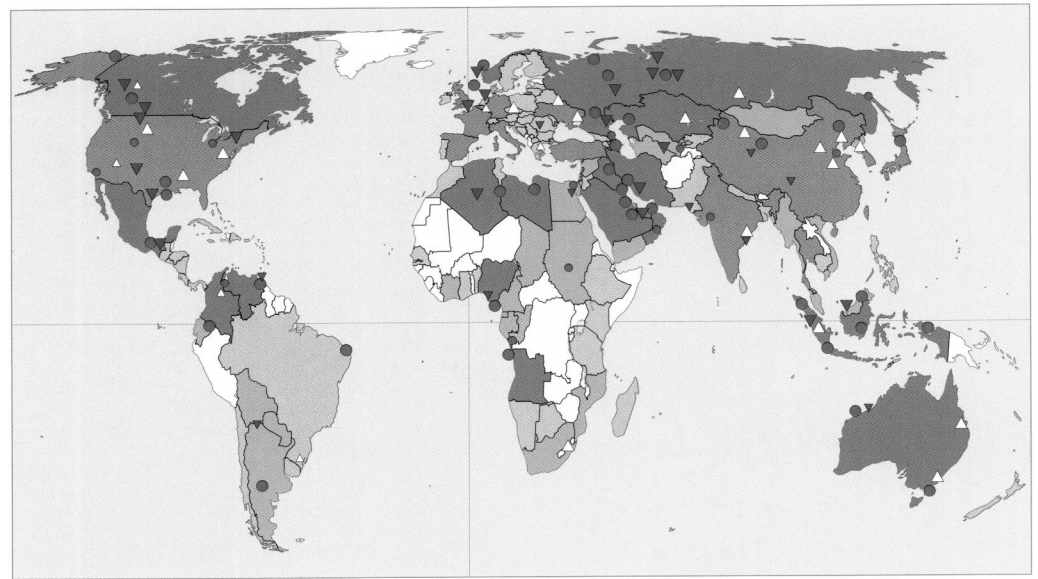

ENERGY BALANCE

Difference between energy production and consumption in millions of tonnes of oil equivalent (MtOe) (2009)

Energy surplus

	Over 35 MtOe surplus
	1 – 35 MtOe surplus
	Between 1 deficit – 1 surplus (approx. balance)
	1 – 35 MtOe deficit
	Over 35 MtOe deficit
	No data available

Energy deficit

- Principal oilfields   • Secondary oilfields
- ▼ Principal gasfields   ▾ Secondary gasfields
- △ Principal coalfields   △ Secondary coalfields

WORLD ENERGY CONSUMPTION

Energy consumed by world regions, measured in million tonnes of oil equivalent (2010)
Total world consumption was 11,843 MtOe. Only energy from oil, natural gas, coal, nuclear and hydroelectric sources are included. Excluded are biomass fuels such as wood, peat and animal waste, and wind, solar and geothermal energy which, though important locally in some countries, are not always reliably documented statistically.

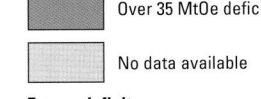 Oil   Gas   Coal   Nuclear   Hydro

World energy consumption, by source (2010)

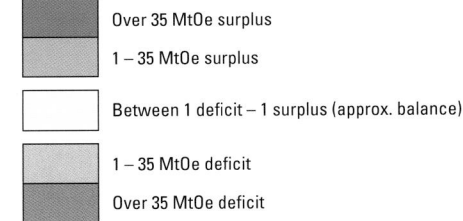

6.6%
5.3%
34.0%
30.0%
24.1%

Africa

South and Central America

Middle East

North America

Europe and Eurasia

Asia Pacific

| 500 | 1,000 | 1,500 | 2,000 | 2,500 | 3,000 | 3,500 | 4,000 | 4,500 | 5,000 |

million tonnes of oil equivalent

Source: BP Statistical Review of World Energy 2011

ENERGY

Energy is used to keep us warm or cool, fuel our industries and our transport systems, and even feed us; high-intensity agriculture, with its use of fertilizers, pesticides and machinery, is heavily energy-dependent. Although we live in a high-energy society, there are vast discrepancies between rich and poor; for example, a North American consumes six times as much energy as a Chinese person. But even developing nations have more power at their disposal than was imaginable a century ago.

The distribution of energy supplies, most importantly fossil fuels (coal, oil and natural gas), is very uneven. In addition, the diagrams and map opposite show that the largest producers of energy are not necessarily the largest consumers. The movement of energy supplies around the world is therefore an important component of international trade.

As the finite reserves of fossil fuels are depleted, renewable energy sources, such as solar, hydro-thermal, wind, tidal and biomass, will become increasingly important around the world.

NUCLEAR POWER

Major producers by percentage of world total and by percentage of domestic electricity generation (2010)

Country	% of world total production	Country	% of nuclear as proportion of domestic electricity
1. USA	30.7%	1. France	74.7%
2. France	15.5%	2. Slovakia	53.1%
3. Japan	10.6%	3. Belgium	49.2%
4. Russia	6.2%	4. Ukraine	47.4%
5. South Korea	5.3%	5. Hungary	42.1%
6. Germany	5.1%	6. Sweden	37.7%
7. Canada	3.2%	7. Switzerland	37.3%
8. Ukraine	3.2%	8. Bulgaria	33.1%
9. China	2.7%	9. Czech Republic	32.6%
10. UK	2.2%	10. South Korea	29.7%

Although the 1980s were a bad time for the nuclear power industry (fears of long-term environmental damage were heavily reinforced by the 1986 disaster at Chernobyl), the industry picked up in the early 1990s. Despite this, growth has recently been curtailed whilst countries review their energy mix, in light of the March 2011 Japanese earthquake and tsunami which seriously damaged the Fukushima nuclear power station.

HYDROELECTRICITY

Major producers by percentage of world total and by percentage of domestic electricity generation (2010)

Country	% of world total production	Country	% of hydroelectric as proportion of domestic electricity
1. China	21.0%	1. Norway	94.8%
2. Brazil	11.6%	2. Brazil	81.7%
3. Canada	10.7%	3. Colombia	70.7%
4. USA	7.6%	4. Venezuela	65.8%
5. Russia	4.9%	5. Canada	58.1%
6. Norway	3.4%	6. New Zealand	56.4%
7. India	3.2%	7. Peru	56.0%
8. Japan	2.5%	8. Switzerland	50.6%
9. Venezuela	2.2%	9. Austria	48.9%
10. Sweden	2.0%	10. Ecuador	44.3%

Countries heavily reliant on hydroelectricity are usually small and non-industrial: a high proportion of hydroelectric power more often reflects a modest energy budget than vast hydroelectric resources. The USA, for instance, produces only 6% of its power requirements from hydroelectricity; yet that 6% amounts to almost half the hydropower generated by most of Africa.

ELECTRICITY PRODUCTION

Percentage of electricity generated by source (2010)

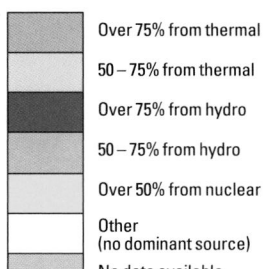

- Over 75% from thermal
- 50 – 75% from thermal
- Over 75% from hydro
- 50 – 75% from hydro
- Over 50% from nuclear
- Other (no dominant source)
- No data available
- ● Selected geothermal plants
- ◆ Selected hydroelectric plants

Conversion Rates

1 barrel = 0.136 tonnes or 159 litres or 35 Imperial gallons or 42 US gallons

1 tonne = 7.33 barrels or 1,185 litres or 256 Imperial gallons or 261 US gallons

1 tonne oil = 1.5 tonnes hard coal or 3.0 tonnes lignite or 12,000 kWh

1 Imperial gallon = 1.201 US gallons or 4.546 litres or 277.4 cubic inches

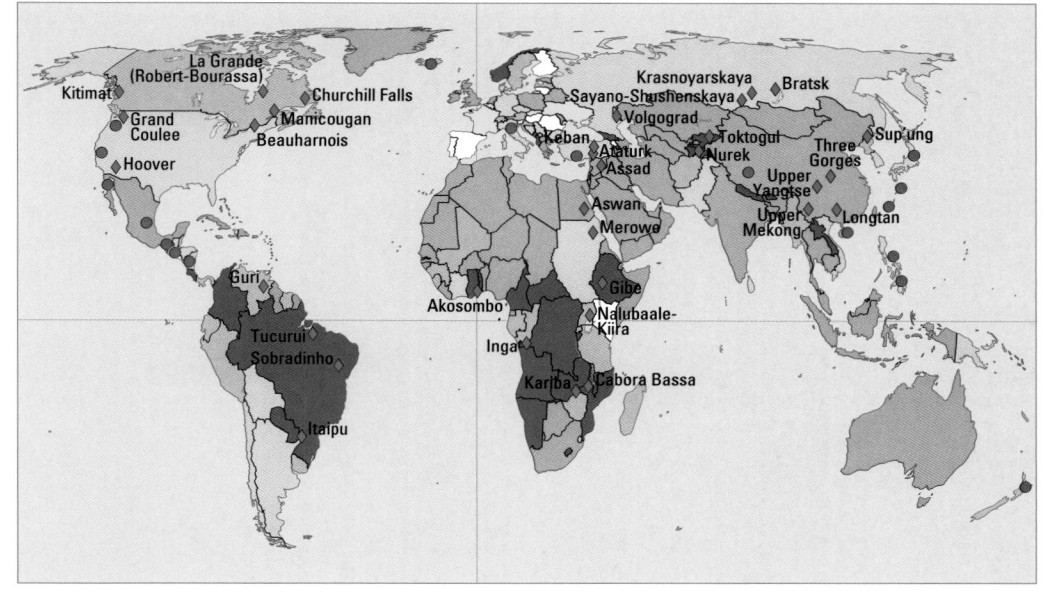

Measurements
For historical reasons, oil is traded in 'barrels'. The weight and volume equivalents (shown right) are all based on average-density 'Arabian light' crude oil.

The energy equivalents given for a tonne of oil are also somewhat imprecise: oil and coal of different qualities will have varying energy contents, a fact usually reflected in their price on world markets.

ENERGY RESERVES

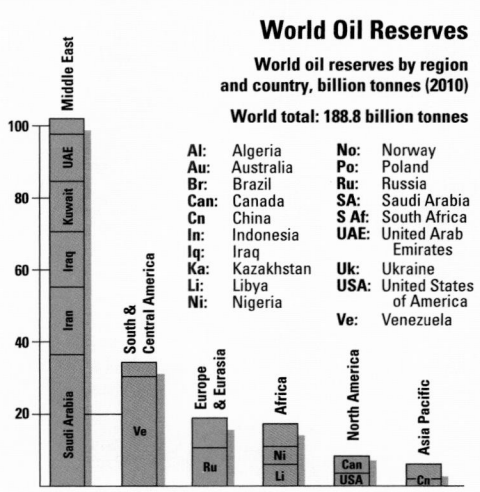

World Oil Reserves

World oil reserves by region and country, billion tonnes (2010)

World total: 188.8 billion tonnes

Al: Algeria	No: Norway
Au: Australia	Po: Poland
Br: Brazil	Ru: Russia
Can: Canada	SA: Saudi Arabia
Cn: China	S Af: South Africa
In: Indonesia	UAE: United Arab Emirates
Iq: Iraq	Uk: Ukraine
Ka: Kazakhstan	USA: United States of America
Li: Libya	Ve: Venezuela
Ni: Nigeria	

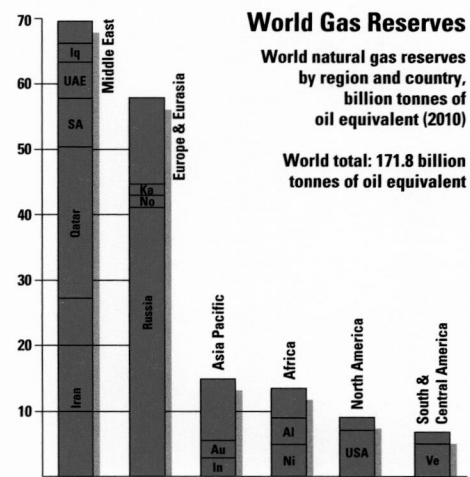

World Gas Reserves

World natural gas reserves by region and country, billion tonnes of oil equivalent (2010)

World total: 171.8 billion tonnes of oil equivalent

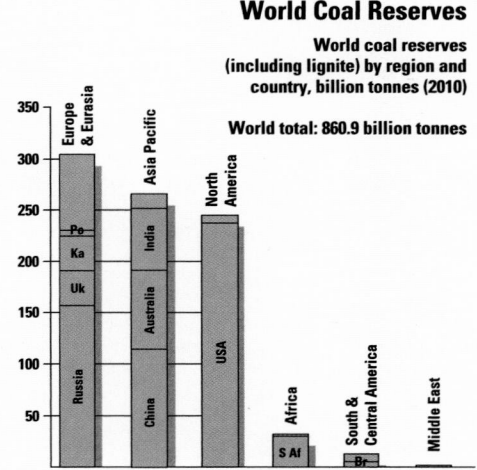

World Coal Reserves

World coal reserves (including lignite) by region and country, billion tonnes (2010)

World total: 860.9 billion tonnes

Production

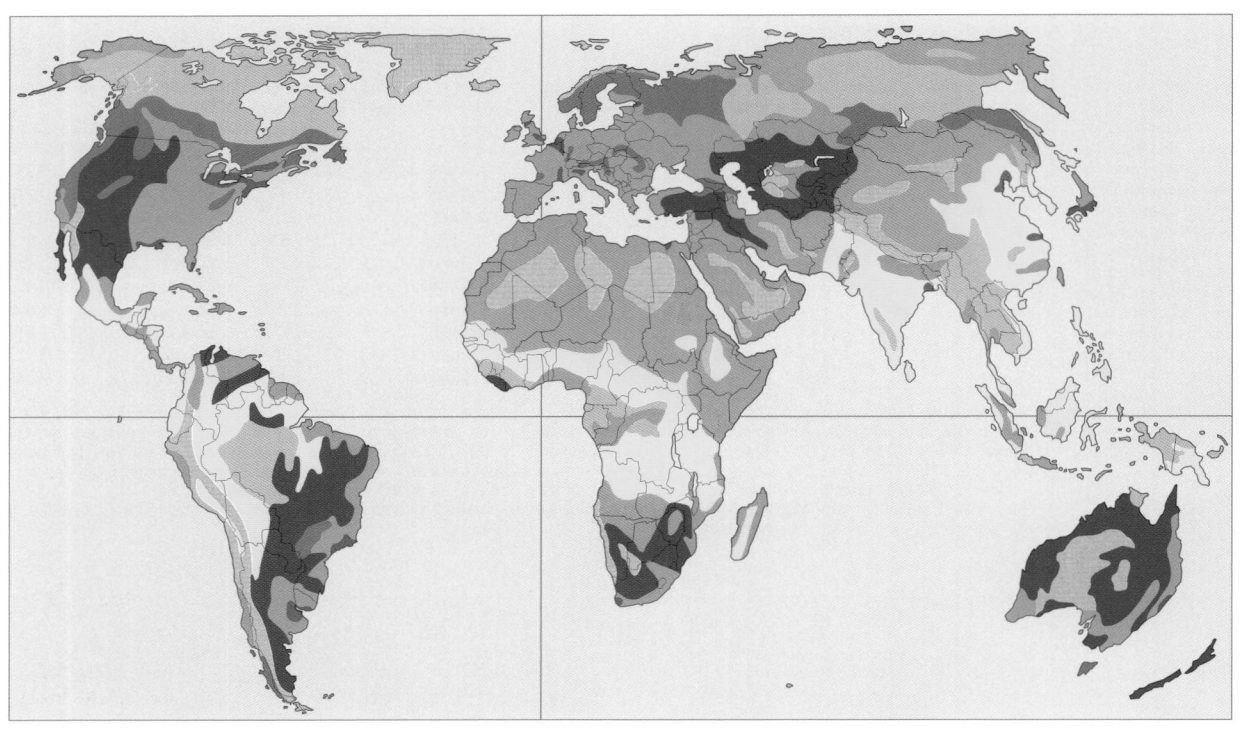

AGRICULTURE

Predominant type of farming or land use

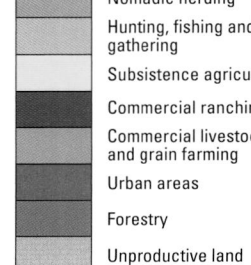

- Nomadic herding
- Hunting, fishing and gathering
- Subsistence agriculture
- Commercial ranching
- Commercial livestock and grain farming
- Urban areas
- Forestry
- Unproductive land

The development of agriculture has transformed human existence more than any other. The whole business of farming is constantly developing: due mainly to the new varieties of rice and wheat, world grain production has more than doubled since 1965. New machinery and modern agricultural techniques enable farmers to produce food for the world's developed economies, but the poorer third world relies very much on subsistence agriculture.

STAPLE CROPS

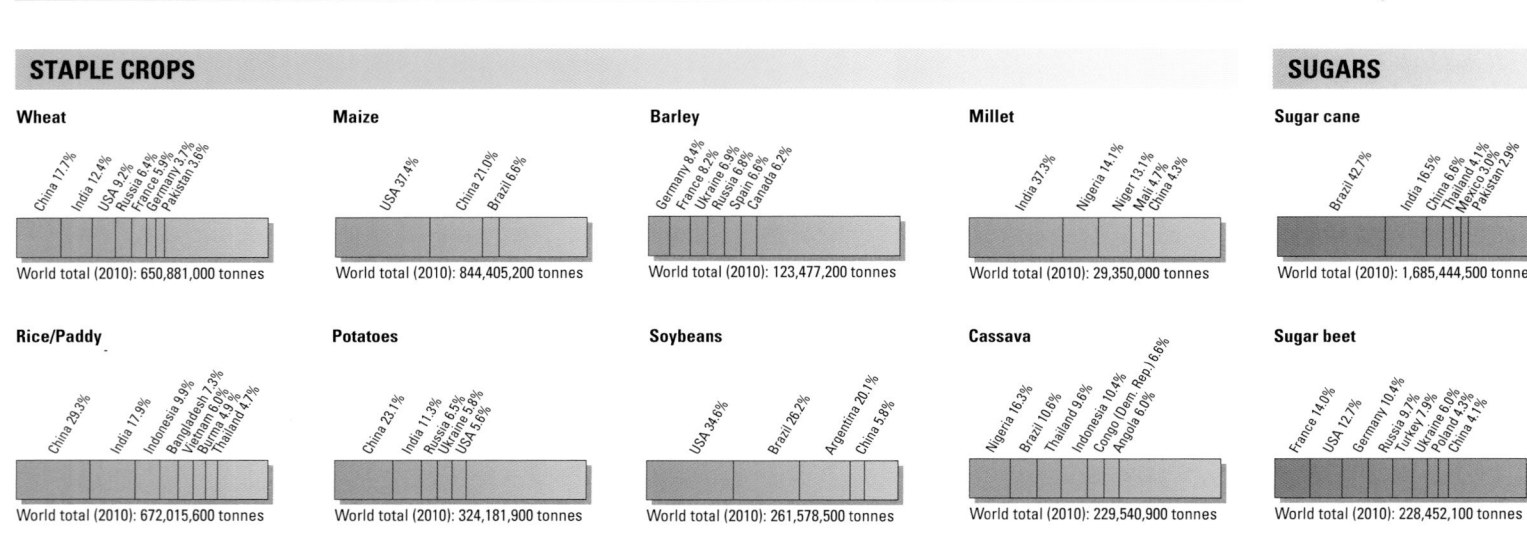

Wheat

China 17.7%, India 12.4%, USA 9.2%, Russia 6.4%, France 5.5%, Germany 3.7%, Pakistan 3.6%

World total (2010): 650,881,000 tonnes

Maize

USA 37.4%, China 21.0%, Brazil 6.6%

World total (2010): 844,405,200 tonnes

Barley

Germany 8.4%, France 8.2%, Ukraine 6.9%, Russia 6.6%, Spain 6.6%, Canada 6.2%

World total (2010): 123,477,200 tonnes

Millet

India 37.3%, Nigeria 14.1%, Niger 13.1%, Mali 4.7%, China 4.3%

World total (2010): 29,350,000 tonnes

Rice/Paddy

China 29.3%, India 17.9%, Indonesia 9.9%, Bangladesh 7.3%, Vietnam 6.0%, Burma 4.9%, Thailand 4.7%

World total (2010): 672,015,600 tonnes

Potatoes

China 23.1%, India 11.3%, Russia 6.5%, Ukraine 5.8%, USA 5.6%

World total (2010): 324,181,900 tonnes

Soybeans

USA 34.6%, Brazil 26.2%, Argentina 20.1%, China 5.8%

World total (2010): 261,578,500 tonnes

Cassava

Nigeria 16.3%, Brazil 10.5%, Thailand 9.6%, Indonesia 10.4%, Congo (Dem. Rep.) 6.6%, Angola 6.0%

World total (2010): 229,540,900 tonnes

SUGARS

Sugar cane

Brazil 42.7%, India 16.5%, China 6.6%, Thailand 4.1%, Mexico 3.0%, Pakistan 2.9%

World total (2010): 1,685,444,500 tonnes

Sugar beet

France 14.0%, USA 12.7%, Germany 10.4%, Russia 9.7%, Ukraine 6.0%, Poland 4.3%, China 4.1%

World total (2010): 228,452,100 tonnes

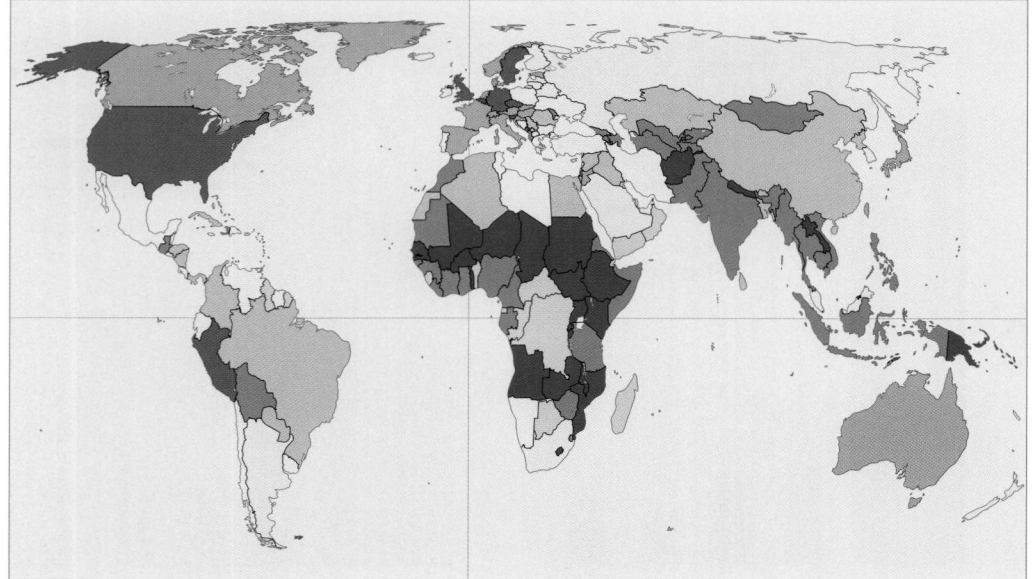

EMPLOYMENT

The number of workers employed in manufacturing for every 100 workers engaged in agriculture (2010)

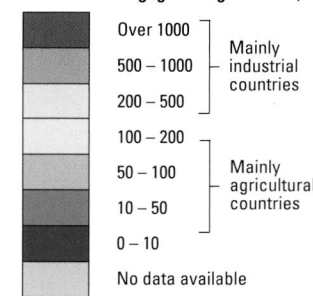

- Over 1000 ⎫
- 500 – 1000 ⎬ Mainly industrial countries
- 200 – 500 ⎭
- 100 – 200
- 50 – 100 ⎫
- 10 – 50 ⎬ Mainly agricultural countries
- 0 – 10 ⎭
- No data available

Countries with the highest number of workers employed in manufacturing per 100 workers engaged in agriculture (2010)

1. Singapore 30,200
2. San Marino 18,150
3. Bahrain 7,900
4. Micronesia, Fed. States .. 3,820
5. Peru 3,400
6. USA 2,900
7. Sweden 2,560
8. Liechtenstein 2,540
9. Malta 1,910
10. Slovenia 1,590

MINERAL PRODUCTION

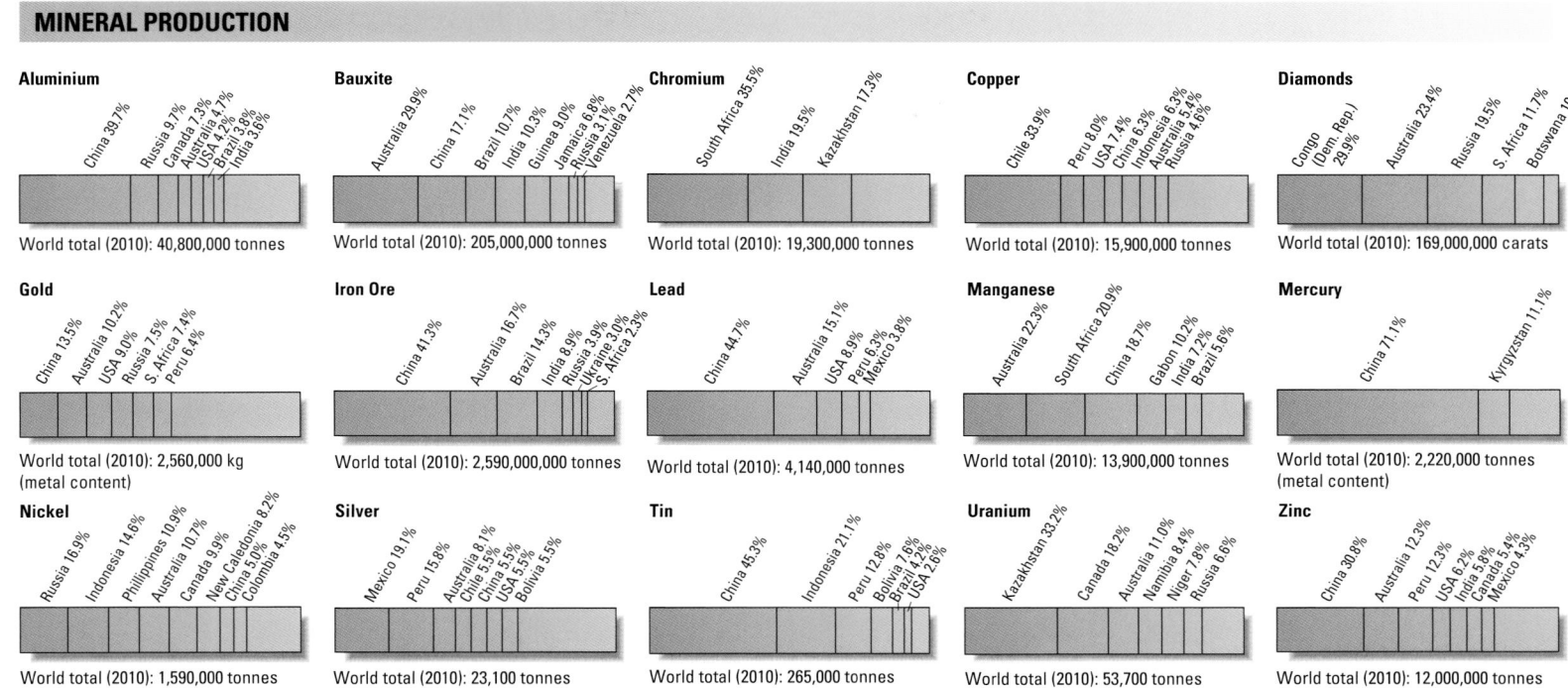

Aluminium
China 38.7% · Russia 9.7% · Canada 7.3% · Australia 4.7% · USA 4.2% · Brazil 3.8% · India 3.6%
World total (2010): 40,800,000 tonnes

Bauxite
Australia 29.9% · China 17.1% · Brazil 10.7% · India 10.3% · Guinea 9.0% · Jamaica 6.8% · Russia 3.1% · Venezuela 2.7%
World total (2010): 205,000,000 tonnes

Chromium
South Africa 35.5% · India 19.5% · Kazakhstan 17.3%
World total (2010): 19,300,000 tonnes

Copper
Chile 33.9% · Peru 8.0% · USA 7.4% · China 6.3% · Indonesia 5.4% · Australia 5.4% · Russia 4.6%
World total (2010): 15,900,000 tonnes

Diamonds
Congo (Dem. Rep.) 23.9% · Australia 23.4% · Russia 19.5% · S. Africa 11.7% · Botswana 10.4%
World total (2010): 169,000,000 carats

Gold
China 13.5% · Australia 10.2% · USA 9.0% · Russia 7.5% · S. Africa 7.4% · Peru 6.4%
World total (2010): 2,560,000 kg (metal content)

Iron Ore
China 41.3% · Australia 16.7% · Brazil 14.3% · India 8.9% · Russia 3.9% · Ukraine 3.0% · S. Africa 2.3%
World total (2010): 2,590,000,000 tonnes

Lead
China 44.7% · Australia 15.1% · USA 8.9% · Peru 6.3% · Mexico 3.8%
World total (2010): 4,140,000 tonnes

Manganese
Australia 22.3% · South Africa 20.9% · China 18.7% · Gabon 10.2% · India 7.2% · Brazil 5.6%
World total (2010): 13,900,000 tonnes

Mercury
China 71.1% · Kyrgyzstan 11.1%
World total (2010): 2,220,000 tonnes (metal content)

Nickel
Russia 16.9% · Indonesia 14.6% · Phillippines 10.9% · Australia 10.7% · Canada 9.9% · New Caledonia 8.2% · China 5.0% · Colombia 4.5%
World total (2010): 1,590,000 tonnes

Silver
Mexico 19.1% · Peru 15.8% · Australia 8.1% · Chile 5.5% · China 5.5% · USA 5.5% · Bolivia 5.5%
World total (2010): 23,100 tonnes (metal content)

Tin
China 45.3% · Indonesia 21.1% · Peru 12.8% · Bolivia 7.6% · Brazil 4.2% · USA 2.6%
World total (2010): 265,000 tonnes

Uranium
Kazakhstan 33.2% · Canada 18.2% · Australia 11.0% · Namibia 8.4% · Niger 7.8% · Russia 6.6%
World total (2010): 53,700 tonnes

Zinc
China 30.8% · Australia 12.3% · Peru 12.3% · USA 6.2% · India 5.8% · Canada 5.4% · Mexico 4.3%
World total (2010): 12,000,000 tonnes

MINERAL DISTRIBUTION

The map shows the richest sources of the most important minerals

Precious metals
◇ Diamonds
○ Gold
◉ Silver

Iron and ferro-alloys
⬙ Chromium
◈ Cobalt
◇ Iron ore
◇ Manganese
◈ Molybdenum
◇ Nickel ore
◈ Tungsten

Non-ferrous metals
◈ Bauxite
(◈ Aluminium)
◇ Copper
◇ Lead
◈ Mercury
◇ Zinc

Fertilizers
▲ Phosphates
▲ Potash

The map does not show undersea deposits, most of which are currently inaccessible.

INDUSTRIAL PRODUCTION

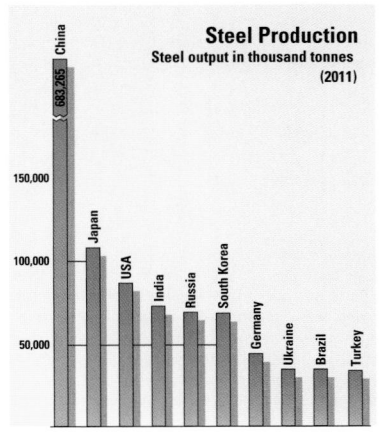

Steel Production
Steel output in thousand tonnes (2011)
China 683,265 · Japan · USA · India · Russia · South Korea · Germany · Ukraine · Brazil · Turkey

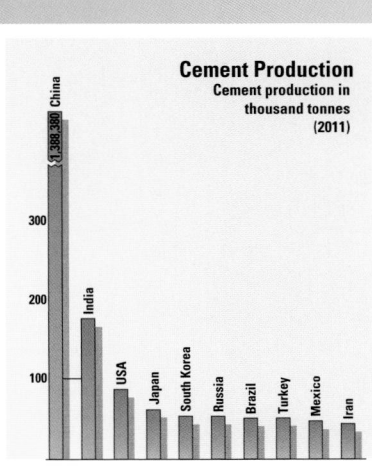

Cement Production
Cement production in thousand tonnes (2011)
China 1,380,390 · India · USA · Japan · South Korea · Russia · Brazil · Turkey · Mexico · Iran

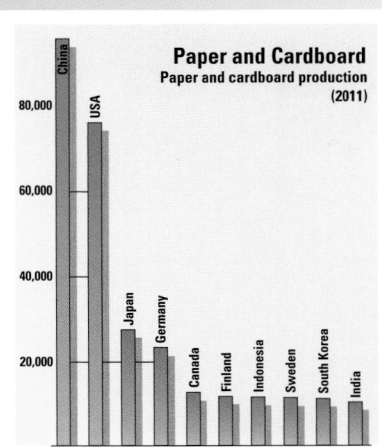

Paper and Cardboard
Paper and cardboard production (2011)
China · USA · Japan · Germany · Canada · Finland · Indonesia · Sweden · South Korea · India

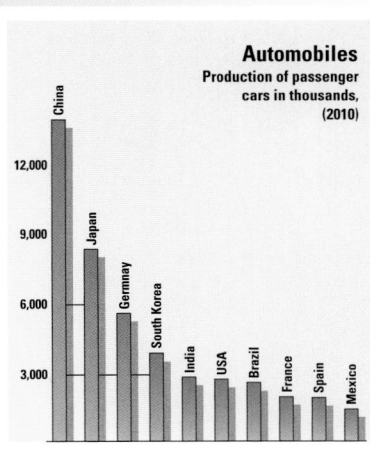

Automobiles
Production of passenger cars in thousands, (2010)
China · Japan · Germany · South Korea · India · USA · Brazil · France · Spain · Mexico

Trade

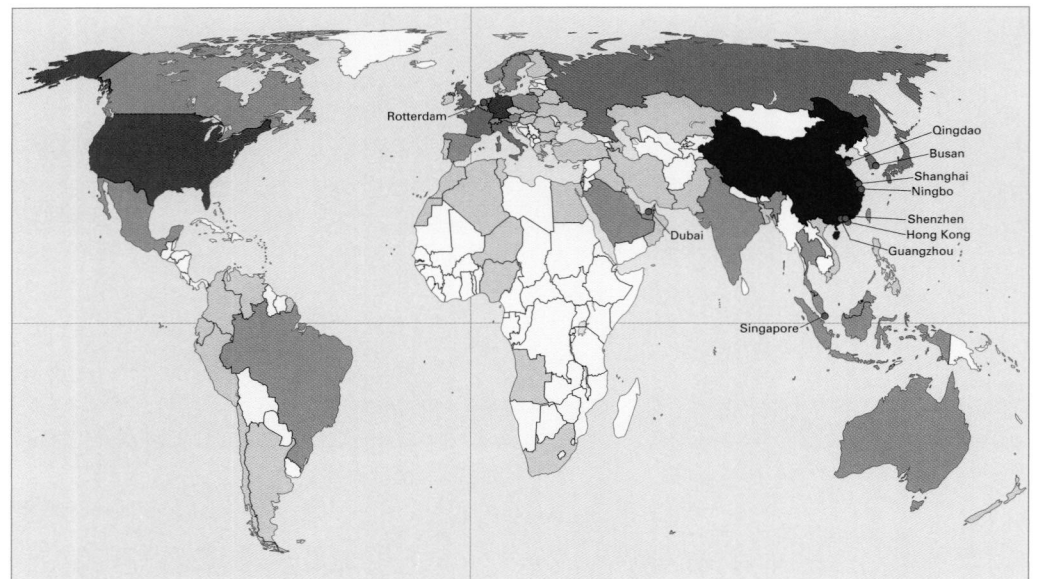

SHARE OF WORLD TRADE

Percentage share of total world exports by value (2011)

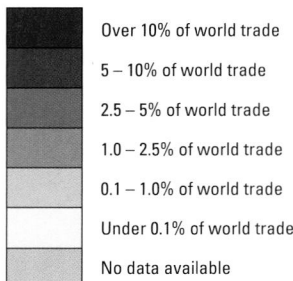

- Over 10% of world trade
- 5 – 10% of world trade
- 2.5 – 5% of world trade
- 1.0 – 2.5% of world trade
- 0.1 – 1.0% of world trade
- Under 0.1% of world trade
- No data available

- ● Top ten container ports

Countries with the largest share of world trade

1. China	10.5%	6. Netherlands	3.2%
2. Germany	8.5%	7. South Korea	3.1%
3. USA	8.3%	8. Italy	2.8%
4. Japan	4.4%	9. UK	2.7%
5. France	3.2%	10. Russia	2.7%

THE MAIN TRADING NATIONS

The imports and exports of the top ten trading nations as a percentage of world trade (2010). Each country's trade in manufactured goods is shown in dark blue

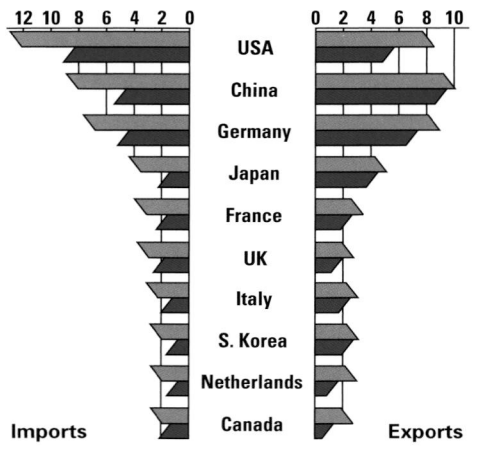

MAJOR EXPORTS

Leading manufactured items and their exporters

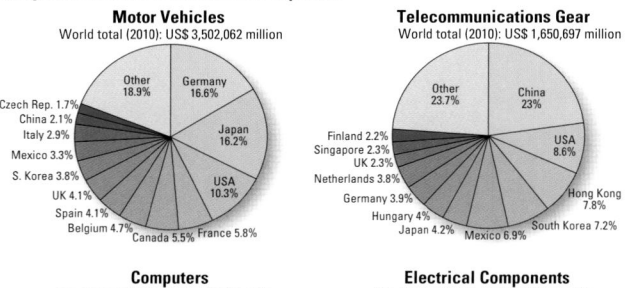

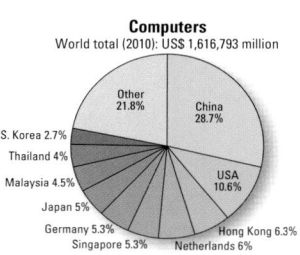

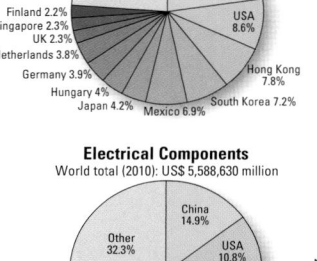

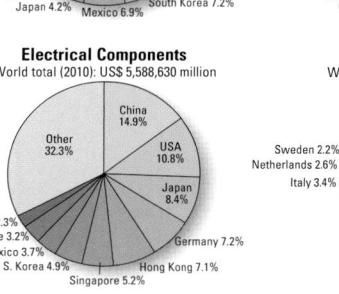

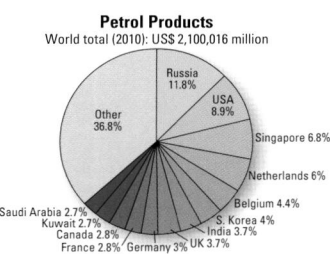

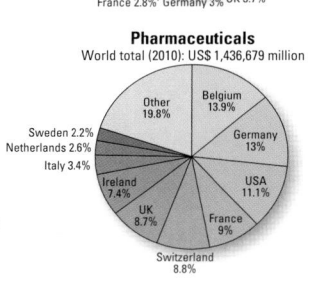

BALANCE OF TRADE

Value of exports in proportion to the value of imports (2011)

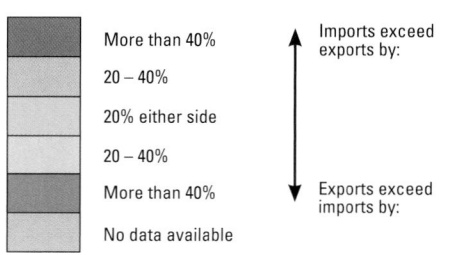

- More than 40%
- 20 – 40%
- 20% either side
- 20 – 40%
- More than 40%
- No data available

Imports exceed exports by:

Exports exceed imports by:

The total world trade balance should amount to zero, since exports must equal imports on a global scale. In practice, at least $100 billion in exports go unrecorded, leaving the world with an apparent deficit and many countries in a better position than public accounting reveals. However, a favourable trade balance is not necessarily a sign of prosperity: many poorer countries must maintain a high surplus in order to service debts, and do so by restricting imports below the levels needed to sustain successful economies.

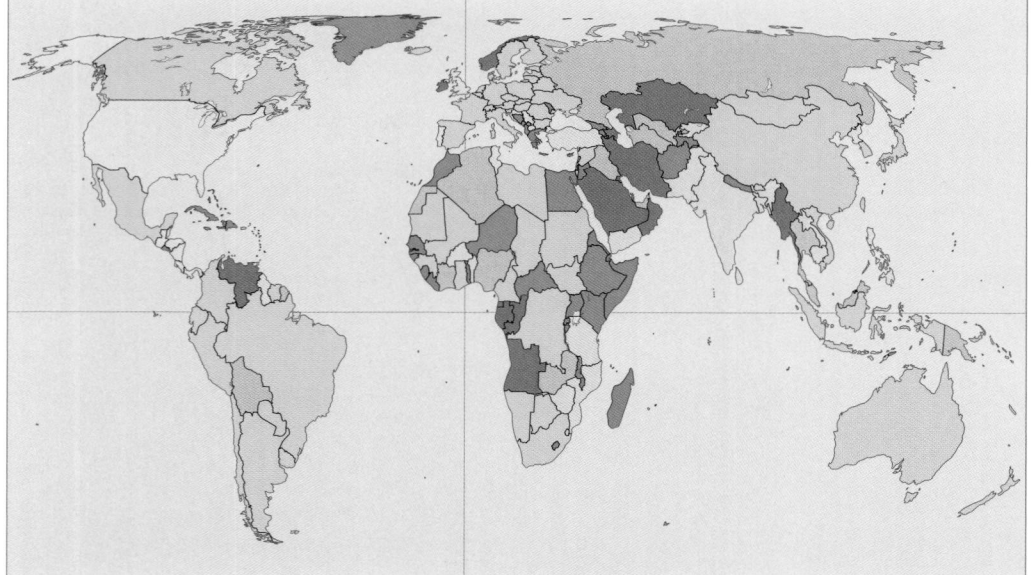

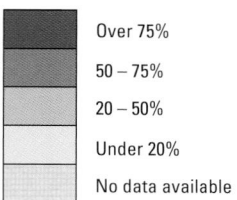

TRADE IN PRIMARY EXPORTS

Primary exports as a percentage of total export value (2009)

- Over 75%
- 50 – 75%
- 20 – 50%
- Under 20%
- No data available

Primary exports are raw materials or partly processed products that form the basis for manufacturing. They are the necessary requirements of industries and include agricultural products, minerals, fuels and timber, as well as many semi-manufactured goods such as cotton, which has been spun but not woven, wood pulp or flour. Many developed countries have few natural resources and rely on imports for the majority of their primary products. The countries of South-east Asia export hardwoods to the rest of the world, while some South American countries are heavily dependent on coffee exports.

MERCHANT FLEETS

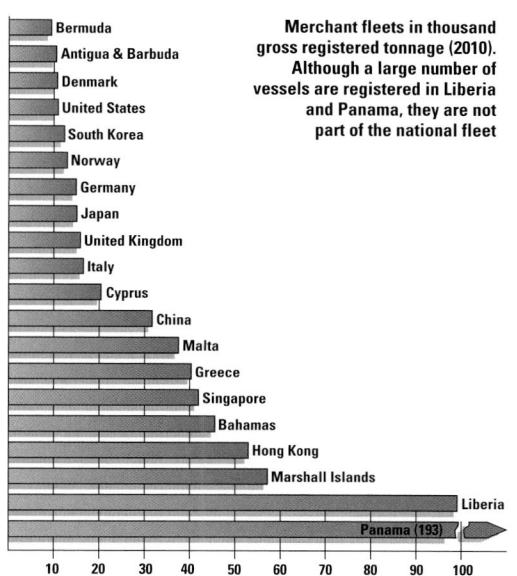

Merchant fleets in thousand gross registered tonnage (2010). Although a large number of vessels are registered in Liberia and Panama, they are not part of the national fleet

Bermuda
Antigua & Barbuda
Denmark
United States
South Korea
Norway
Germany
Japan
United Kingdom
Italy
Cyprus
China
Malta
Greece
Singapore
Bahamas
Hong Kong
Marshall Islands
Liberia
Panama (193)

10 20 30 40 50 60 70 80 90 100

TOP TEN PORTS

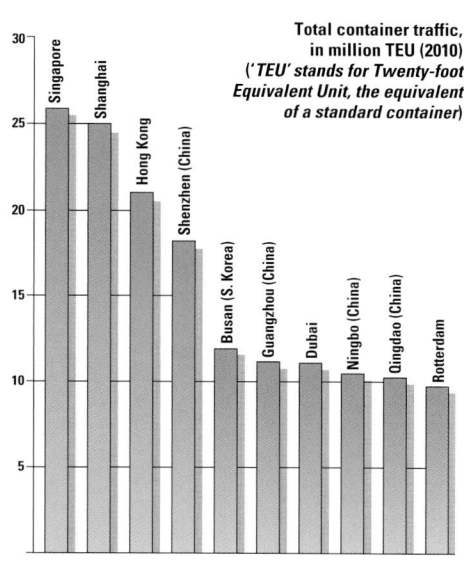

Total container traffic, in million TEU (2010) ('TEU' stands for Twenty-foot Equivalent Unit, the equivalent of a standard container)

Singapore
Shanghai
Hong Kong
Shenzhen (China)
Busan (S. Korea)
Guangzhou (China)
Dubai
Ningbo (China)
Qingdao (China)
Rotterdam

TYPES OF VESSELS

World fleet by type of vessel (2010)

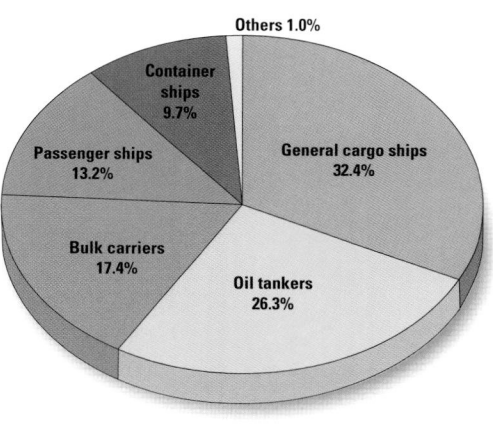

- Others 1.0%
- Container ships 9.7%
- Passenger ships 13.2%
- Bulk carriers 17.4%
- Oil tankers 26.3%
- General cargo ships 32.4%

EXPORTS PER CAPITA

Value of exports in US $, divided by total population (2011)

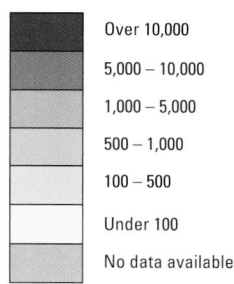

- Over 10,000
- 5,000 – 10,000
- 1,000 – 5,000
- 500 – 1,000
- 100 – 500
- Under 100
- No data available

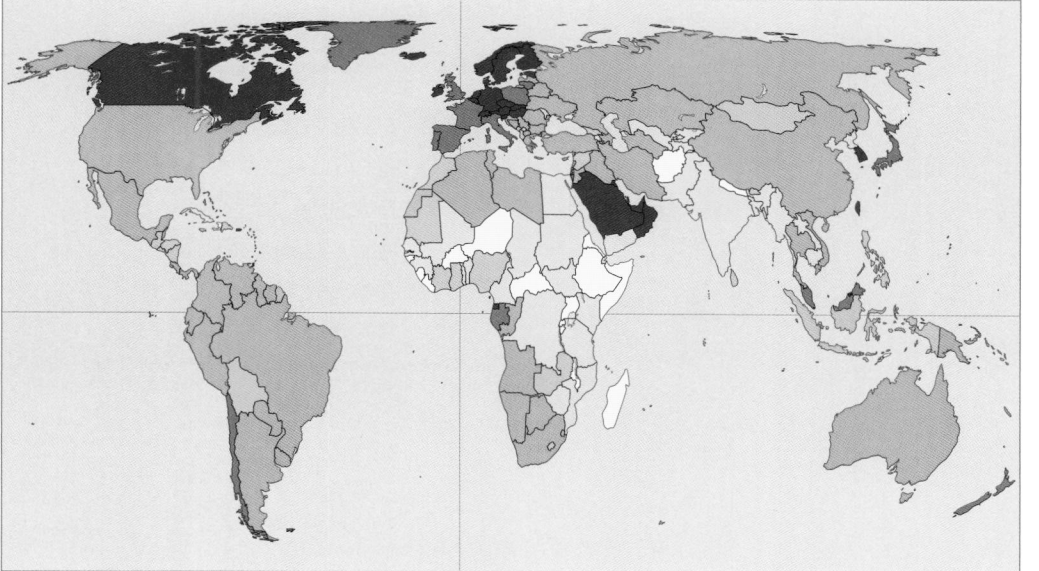

Countries with highest exports per capita

Qatar	$122,993
Singapore	$91,146
Liechtenstein	$80,316
San Marino	$77,223
Norway	$55,373
UAE	$51,528

Travel and Tourism

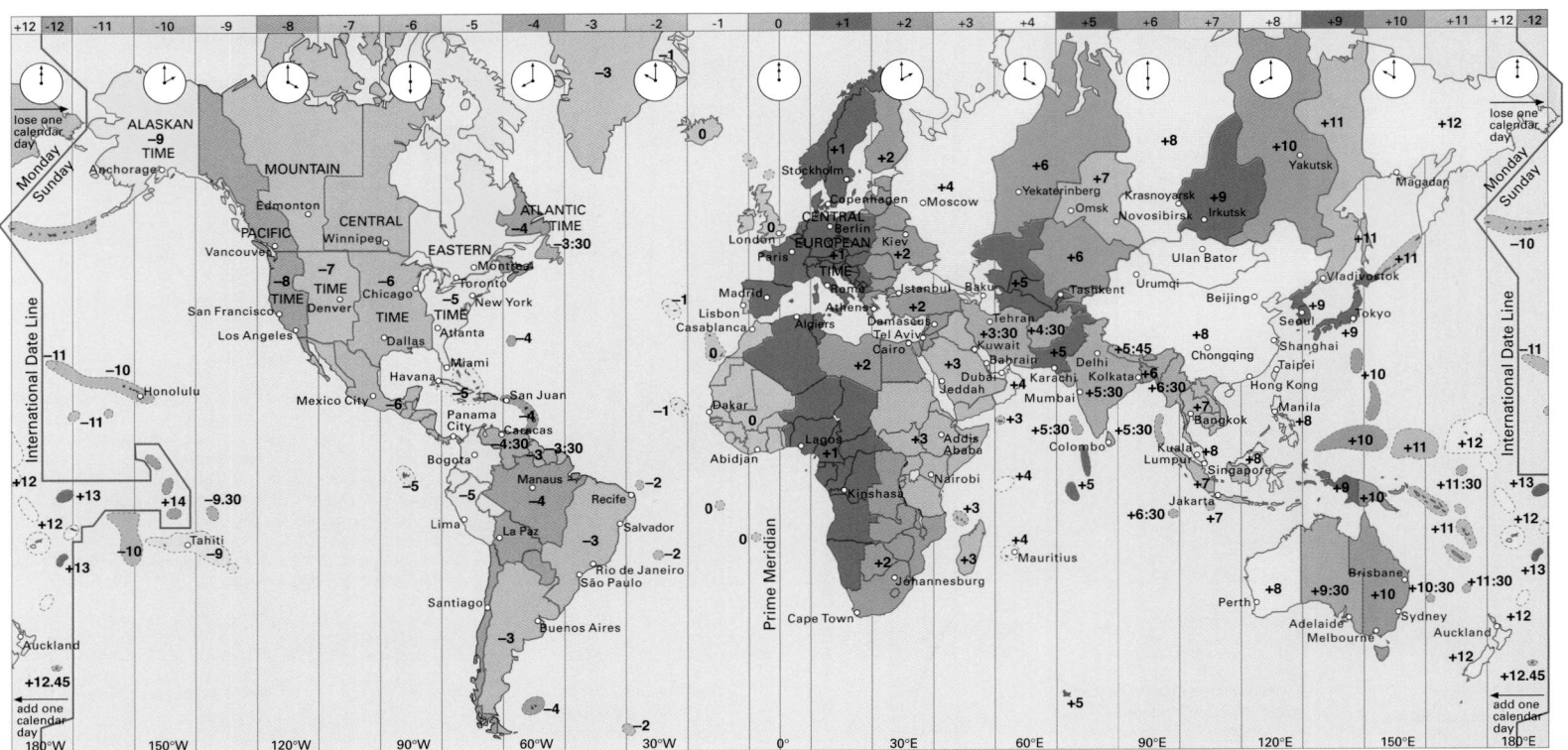

Projection: *Mercator*

TIME ZONES

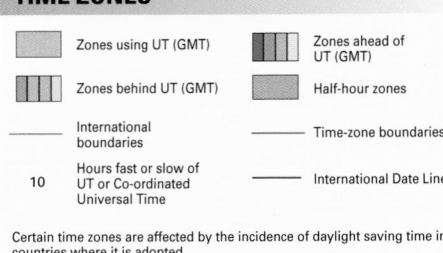

Zones using UT (GMT)	Zones ahead of UT (GMT)
Zones behind UT (GMT)	Half-hour zones

International boundaries	Time-zone boundaries
10 Hours fast or slow of UT or Co-ordinated Universal Time	International Date Line

Certain time zones are affected by the incidence of daylight saving time in countries where it is adopted.

Actual solar time, when it is noon at Greenwich, is shown along the top of the map.

The world is divided into 24 time zones, each centred on meridians at 15° intervals, which is the longitudinal distance the sun travels every hour. The meridian running through Greenwich, London, passes through the middle of the first zone.

RAIL AND ROAD: THE LEADING NATIONS

	Total rail network ('000 km), 2010		Passenger km per head per year, 2010		Total road network ('000 km), 2009		Vehicle km per head per year, 2009		Number of vehicles per km of roads, 2009
1.	USA 228.5	Switzerland 2,258	USA 6,486.2	Peru 38,553	Kuwait 271
2.	Russia 85.3	Japan 1,910	China 3,799.4	USA 34,560	Hong Kong 241
3.	China 65.5	Slovakia 1,420	India 3,428.0	Tunisia 25,225	Macau 238
4.	India 63.3	Denmark 1,322	Brazil 1,841.5	Pakistan 25,199	UAE 220
5.	Canada 58.3	France 1,320	Canada 1,419.3	Ecuador............23,570	Singapore 218
6.	Germany 33.7	Austria 1,227	Japan 1,201.3	Chile................22,671	Taiwan 170
7.	France 33.6	Ukraine............1,097	France 1,030.2	South Korea 21,763	South Korea 157
8.	UK 31.5	Russia 1,075	Russia............. 953.0	Singapore 21,563	ABC Islands 154
9.	Brazil 29.8	Belgium 972	Australia 815.5	Morocco 18,455	Israel 128
10.	Mexico 26.7	Germany 961	Sweden 697.8	Croatia............17,723	Malta 123
11.	Argentina 25.0	Netherlands 922	Spain 680.3	Finland 17,639	Thailand 121
12.	South Africa 22.1	UK 887	Germany 644.8	Canada.............17,498	Bahrain 114
13.	Ukraine 21.7	Kazakhstan 879	Italy 490.0	Denmark 16,903	Jordan 112
14.	Japan 20.0	Belarus 779	Turkey 427.2	Thailand 16,823	Puerto Rico 110
15.	Poland 19.7	Italy 735	Indonesia 404.3	Isreal 16,721	Dom. Rep. 105

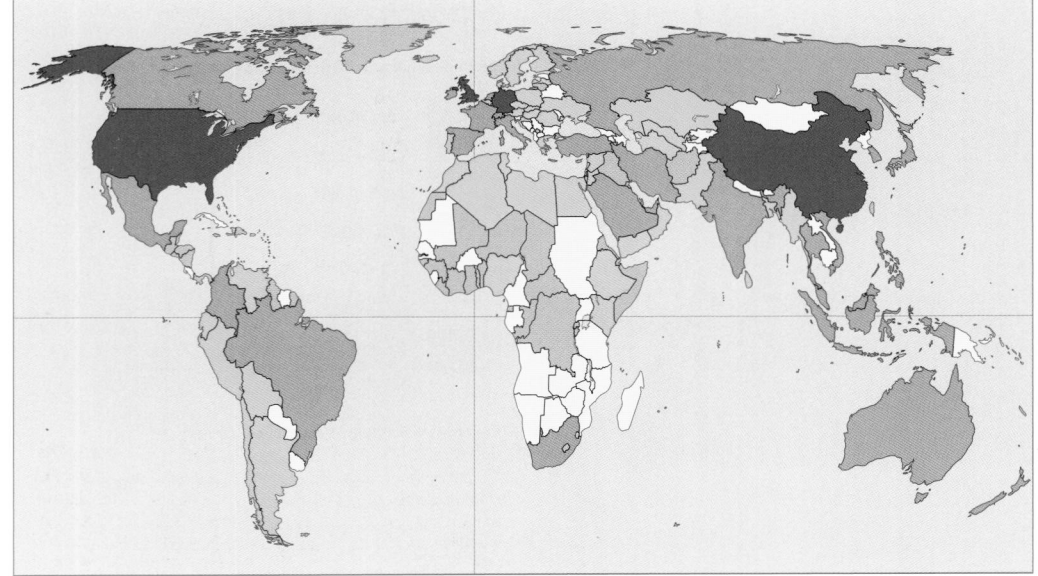

AIR TRAVEL

Number of air passengers carried (2009)

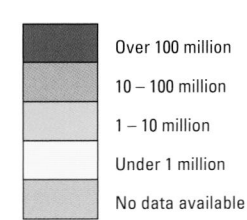

	Over 100 million
	10 – 100 million
	1 – 10 million
	Under 1 million
	No data available

World's busiest airports (2011) – total passengers
1. Atlanta Hartsfield Internat'l.
2. Beijing Capital International
3. London Heathrow
4. Chicago O'Hare International
5. Tokyo Haneda
6. Los Angeles International
7. Paris Charles de Gaulle
8. Dallas Fort Worth Internat'l.
9. Frankfurt International
10. Hong Kong International

World's busiest airports (2011) – international passengers
1. London Heathrow
2. Paris Charles de Gaulle
3. Hong Kong International
4. Dubai International
5. Amsterdam
6. Frankfurt International
7. Singapore Changi
8. Bangkok Suvarnabhumi
9. Incheon International
10. Madrid Barajas

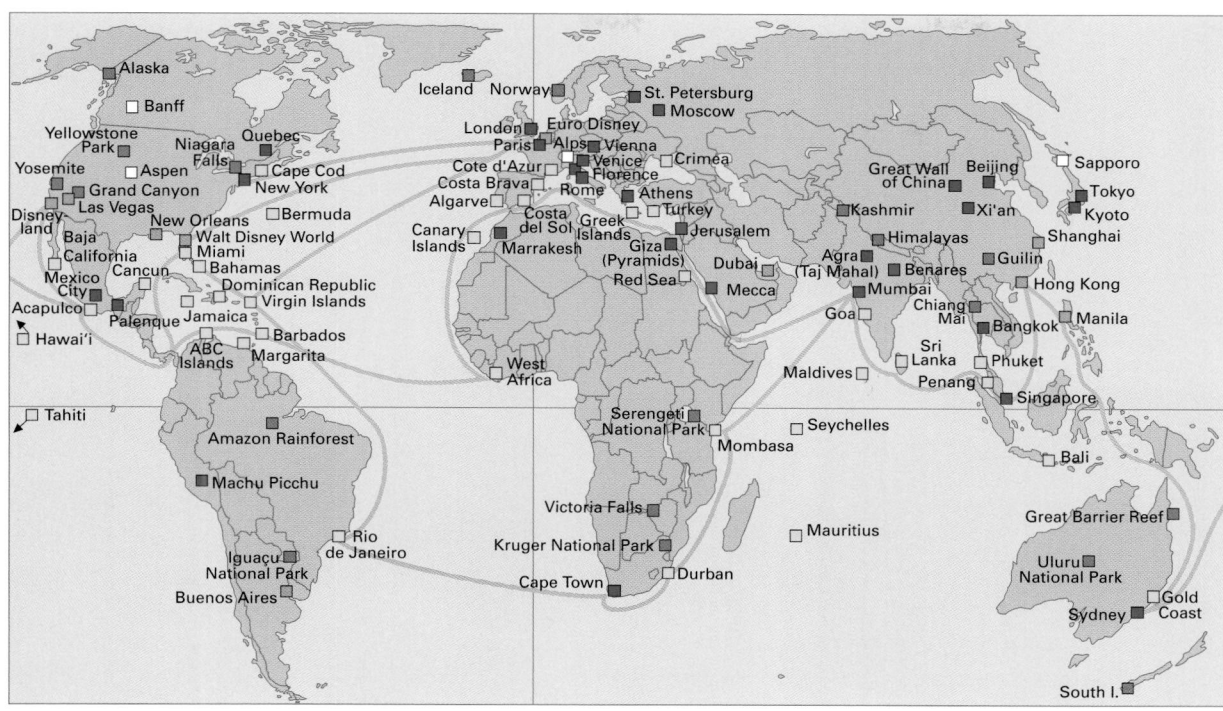

TOURIST CENTRES

- ■ Cultural and historical centres
- □ Coastal resorts
- □ Ski resorts
- ■ Centres of entertainment
- ■ Places of pilgrimage
- ■ Places of great natural beauty
- ⸺ Popular holiday cruise routes

VISITORS TO THE USA

Overseas arrivals to the USA, in thousands (2011)

1.	Canada	21,028
2.	Mexico	13,414
3.	UK	3,835
4.	Japan	3,249
5.	Germany	1,823
6.	Brazil	1,508
7.	France	1,504
8.	South Korea	1,145
9.	China	1,089
10.	Australia	1,037

TOURIST SPENDING

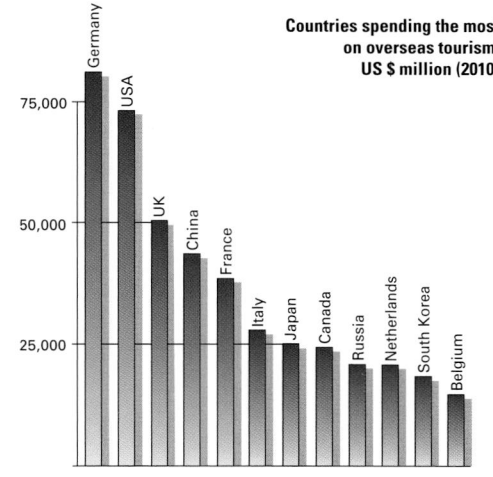

Countries spending the most on overseas tourism, US $ million (2010)

THE MAIN DESTINATIONS

		Arrivals from abroad millions (2010)	% of world total (2010)
1.	France	76.8	9.0%
2.	USA	59.7	6.4%
3.	China	55.7	5.9%
4.	Spain	52.7	5.6%
5.	Italy	43.6	4.6%
6.	UK	28.1	3.0%
7.	Turkey	27.0	2.9%
8.	Germany	26.9	2.6%
9.	Malaysia	24.6	2.6%
10.	Mexico	22.4	2.4%

The 940 million international arrivals in 2010 represented an additional 62 million over the 2009 level – making a new record year for the industry. Growth was common to all regions, but was particularly strong in Asia and the Pacific, and in the Middle East.

TOURIST EARNINGS

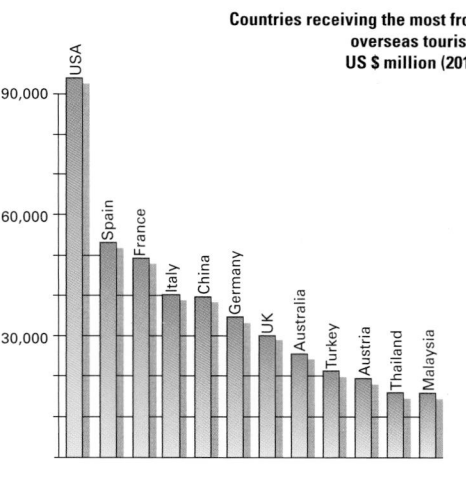

Countries receiving the most from overseas tourism, US $ million (2010)

IMPORTANCE OF TOURISM

Tourism receipts as a percentage of Gross National Income (2010)

- Over 10%
- 5 – 10%
- 2.5 – 5%
- 1 – 2.5%
- Under 1%
- No data available

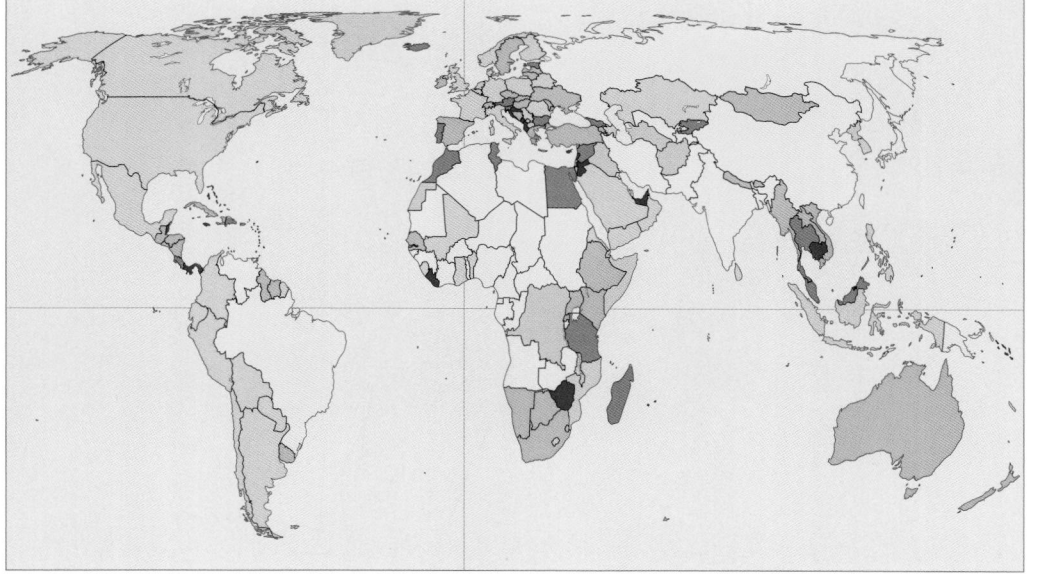

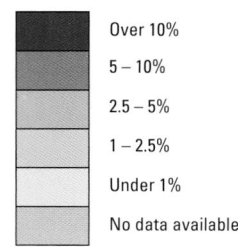

Countries with the highest tourism receipts as % of GNI (2010)

1.	Bermuda (UK)	90.8	6.	Virgin Is. (UK)	32.6
2.	Palau	53.9	7.	Barbados	30.4
3.	Maldives	39.3	8.	St Lucia	28.8
4.	Cayman Is. (UK)	38.8	9.	Liechtenstein	27.2
5.	Seychelles	35.7	10.	Antigua & Barbuda	25.8

HONG KONG, CHINA

© RapidEye AG/Fugro NPA

WORLD CITIES

AMSTERDAM	2	HELSINKI	11	MONTRÉAL	20	TOKYO	30
ATHENS	2	HONG KONG	12	MUMBAI	20	TEHRAN	31
ATLANTA	3	ISTANBUL	12	MUNICH	21	TORONTO	31
BAGHDAD	3	JAKARTA	12	NEW ORLEANS	21	VENICE	32
BANGKOK	3	JERUSALEM	13	NEW YORK	22	VIENNA	32
BARCELONA	4	JOHANNESBURG	13	ORLANDO	23	WARSAW	33
BEIJING	4	KARACHI	13	OSAKA	23	WASHINGTON	33
BERLIN	5	KOLKATA	14	OSLO	23		
BOSTON	6	LAGOS	14	PARIS	24	INDEX	34–39
BRUSSELS	6	LAS VEGAS	14	PRAGUE	25		
BUDAPEST	7	LIMA	14	RIO DE JANEIRO	25	WORLD CITIES	
BUENOS AIRES	7	LONDON	15	ROME	26	SATELLITE IMAGES	
CAIRO	7	LISBON	16	SAN FRANCISCO	26	BEIJING	40
CAPE TOWN	8	LOS ANGELES	16	ST PETERSBURG	27	CAPE TOWN	41
COPENHAGEN	8	MADRID	17	SANTIAGO	27	LAS VEGAS	42
CHICAGO	9	MANILA	17	SÃO PAULO	27	LONDON	43
DUBAI	9	MELBOURNE	18	SEOUL	27	MEXICO CITY	44
DELHI	10	MEXICO CITY	18	SHANGHAI	28	MUMBAI	45
DUBLIN	10	MILAN	18	SINGAPORE	28	NEW YORK	46
EDINBURGH	11	MIAMI	19	STOCKHOLM	29	RIO DE JANEIRO	47
GUANGZHOU	11	MOSCOW	19	SYDNEY	29	SYDNEY	48

CITY MAPS

Motorway, freeway, expressway – with Interstate route number		Primary road – with US route number	41	Principal station	*Estación del Norte*
Motorway, freeway, expressway – with European road number	E51	Secondary road – with State route number	19	Height above sea level (m)	705
		Other road with road number	96	Principal airport with location identifier	YYZ
				Other airport	
Road junction		Ferry		Central area coverage	
Under construction				Urban area	
		Railroad			
Tunnel		Point of interest	Zoo	Woodlands and parks	

CENTRAL AREA MAPS

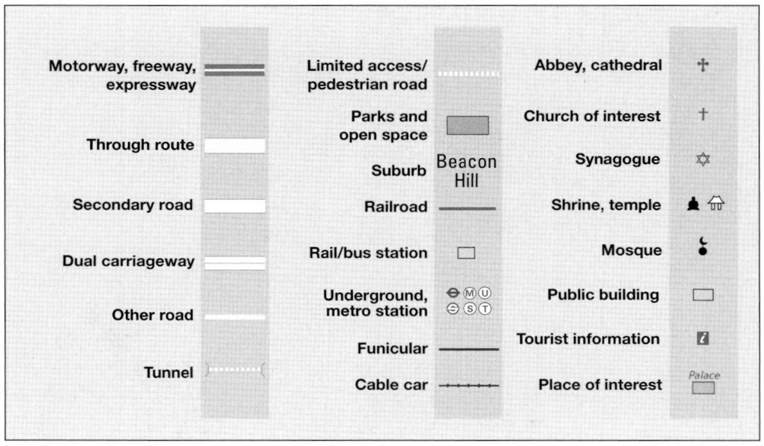

Motorway, freeway, expressway		Limited access/ pedestrian road		Abbey, cathedral	
Through route		Parks and open space		Church of interest	
		Suburb	Beacon Hill	Synagogue	
Secondary road		Railroad		Shrine, temple	
Dual carriageway		Rail/bus station		Mosque	
Other road		Underground, metro station		Public building	
		Funicular		Tourist information	
Tunnel		Cable car		Place of interest	*Palace*

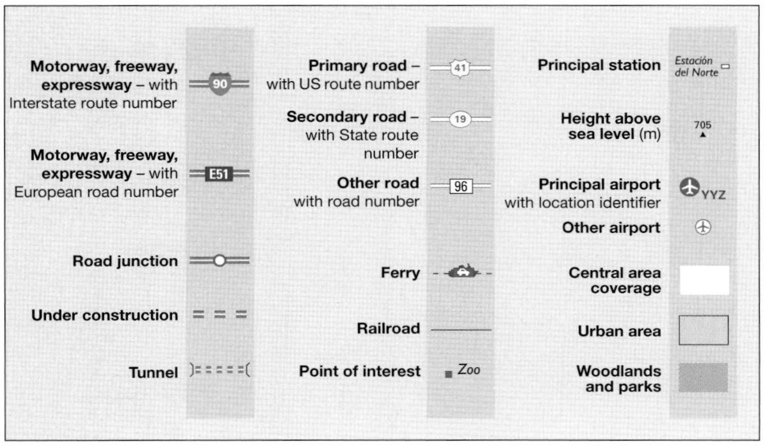

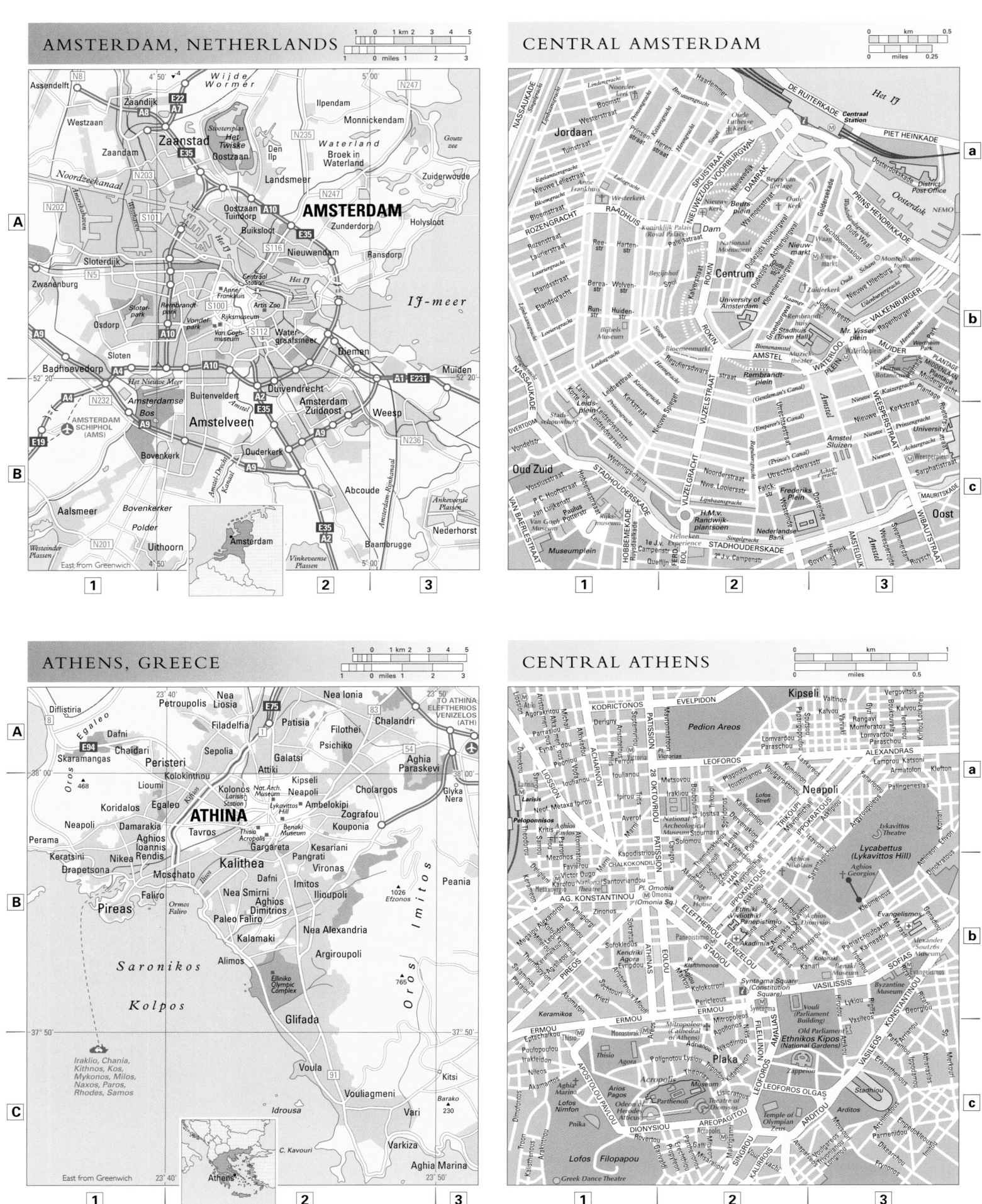

AMSTERDAM, NETHERLANDS

CENTRAL AMSTERDAM

ATHENS, GREECE

CENTRAL ATHENS

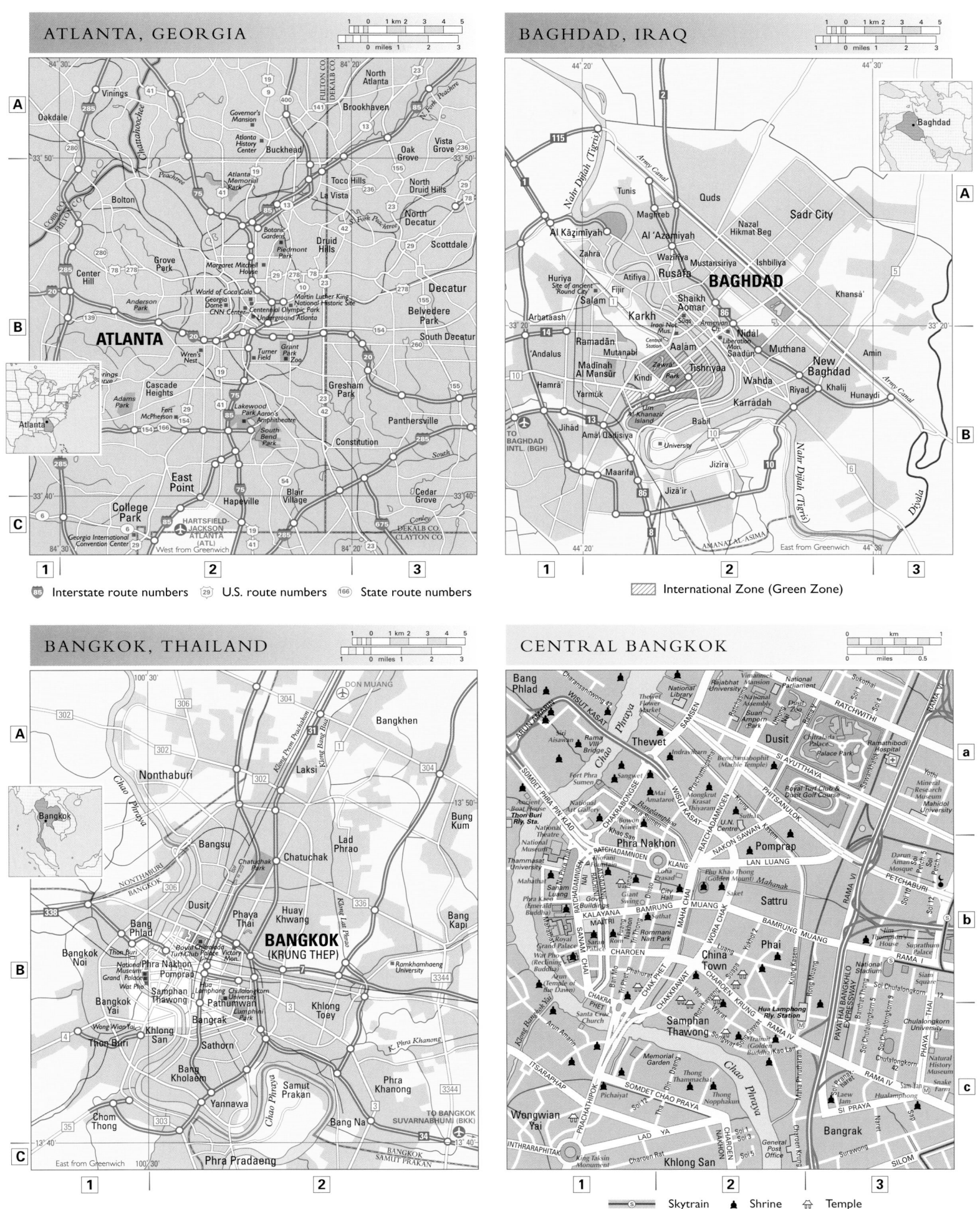

ATLANTA, GEORGIA

Interstate route numbers · U.S. route numbers · State route numbers

BAGHDAD, IRAQ

International Zone (Green Zone)

BANGKOK, THAILAND

CENTRAL BANGKOK

Skytrain · Shrine · Temple

BARCELONA, SPAIN

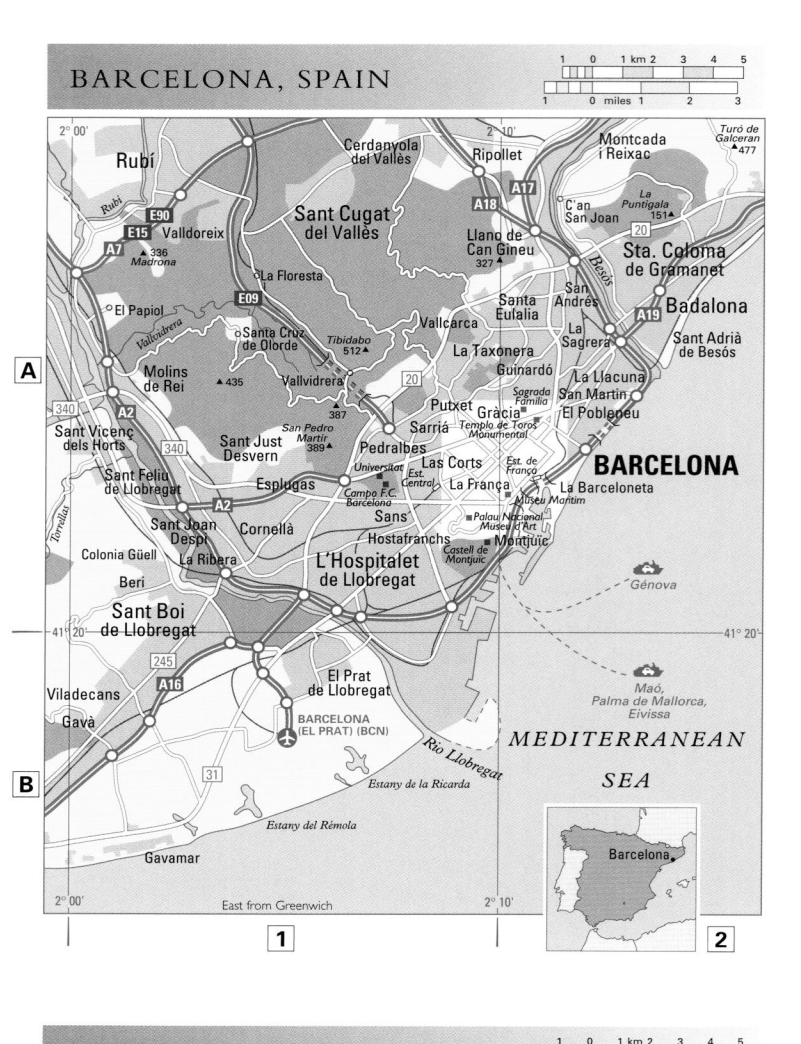

CENTRAL BARCELONA

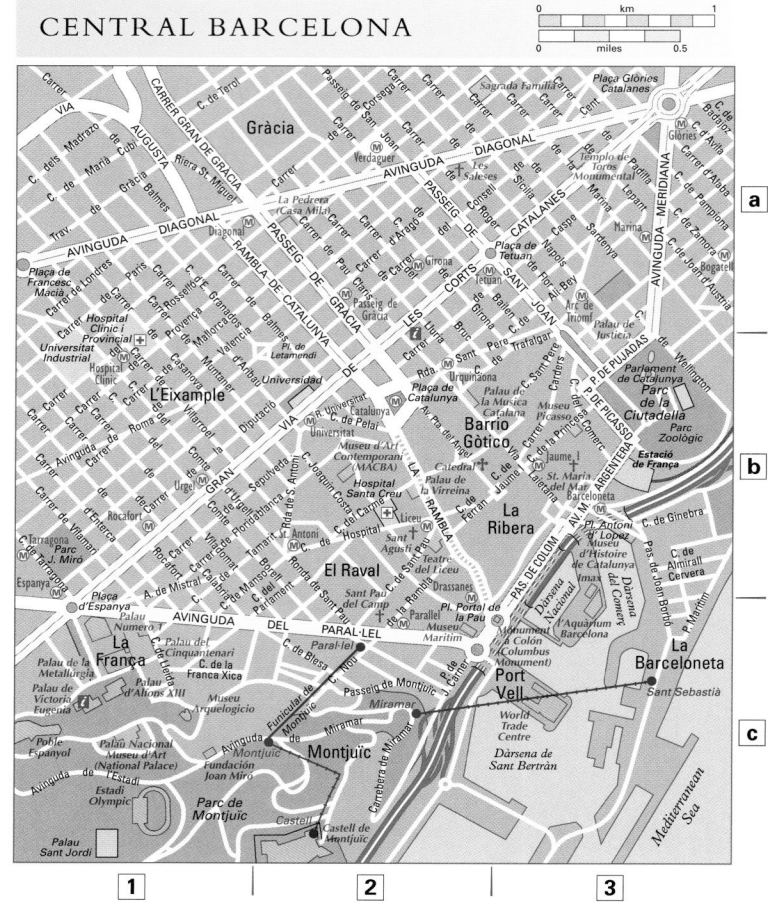

BEIJING, CHINA

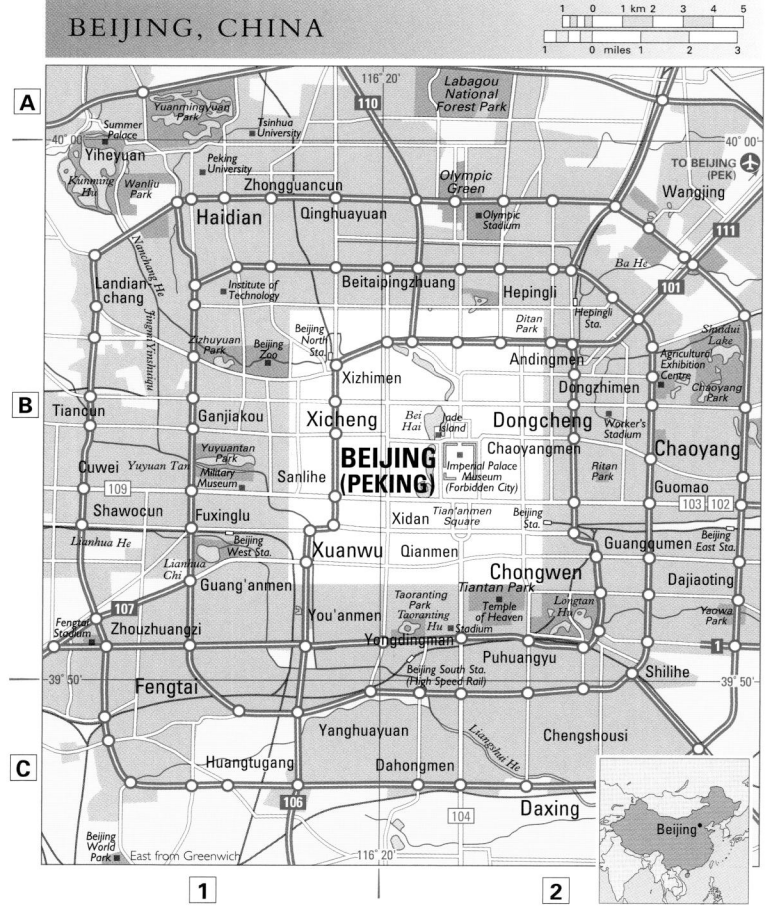

CENTRAL BEIJING

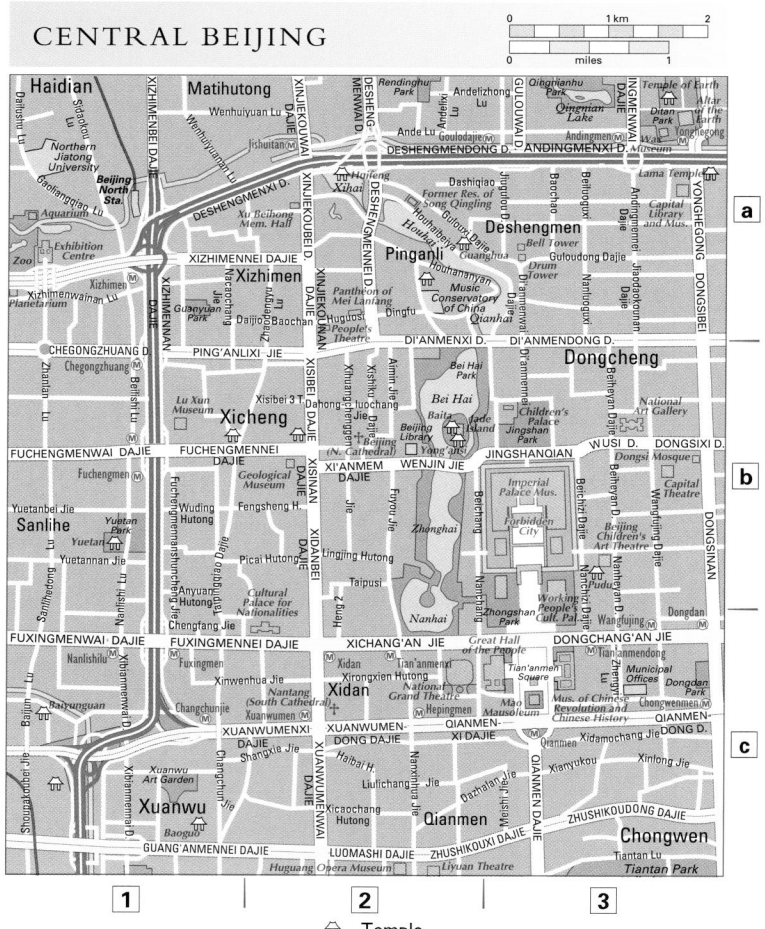

⛩ Temple

BERLIN, GERMANY

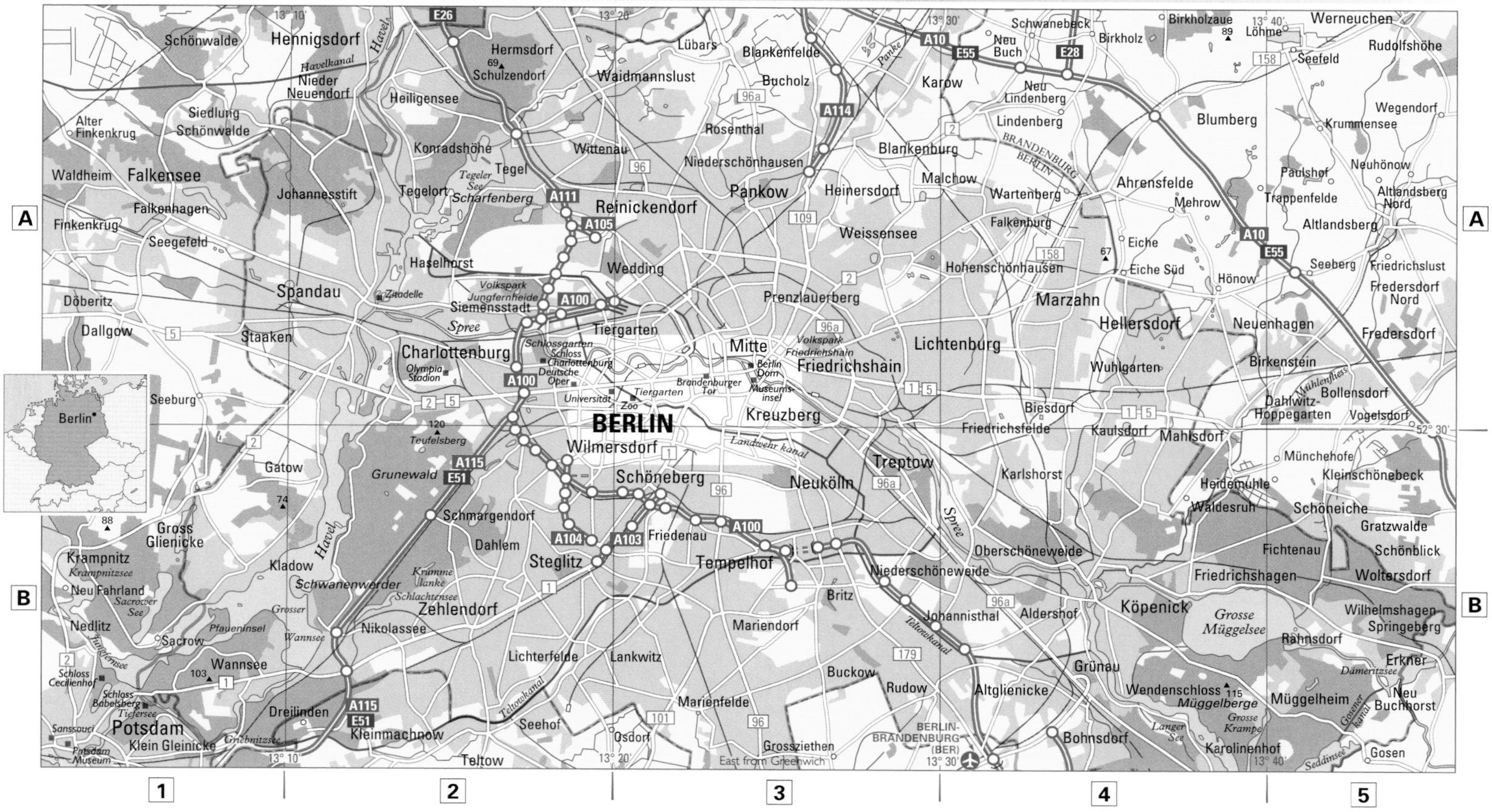

1 0 1 km 2 3 4 5
1 0 miles 1 2 3

Schönwalde Hennigsdorf E26 Hermsdorf Schwanebeck Birkholzaue Werneuchen
Siedlung Schulzendorf Lübars Blankenfelde Buch Neu Buch Birkholz Löhme Rudolfshöhe
Alter Finkenkrug Nieder Neuendorf Heiligensee Waidmannslust Bucholz Karow A10 E55 E28 Seefeld
Waldheim Falkensee Johannesstift Tegelort Tegel Wittenau Niederschönhausen Rosenthal A114 Neu Lindenberg Blumberg Krummensee
Finkenkrug Falkenhagen Scharfenberg A111 Reinickendorf Pankow Heinersdorf Malchow Wartenberg Ahrensfelde Mehrow Trappenfelde Neuhönow
Döberitz Seegefeld Haselhorst A105 Wedding Weissensee Hohenschönhausen Eiche Eiche Süd Hönow A10 E55 Seeberg Friedrichslust Wegendorf
Spandau Volkspark Jungfernheide A100 Tiergarten Prenzlauerberg Marzahn Hellersdorf Neuenhagen Fredersdorf Nord
Dallgow Staaken Siemensstadt Charlottenburg Mitte Berlin Dom Lichtenburg Wuhlgarten Birkenstein Fredersdorf
Olympia Stadion Schloss Charlottenburg Berlin Friedrichshain Biesdorf Dahlwitz Hoppegarten Vogelsdorf
Teufelsberg **BERLIN** Kreuzberg Friedrichsfelde Kaulsdorf Mahlsdorf
Gatow Grunewald Wilmersdorf Schöneberg Neukölln Karlshorst Heidemühle Kleinschönebeck
A115 E51 Schmargendorf Treptow Oberschöneweide Schöneiche Gratzwalde
Krampnitz Gross Glienicke Dahlem A104 Friedenau Tempelhof Niederschöneweide Waldesruh Fichtenau Schönblick
Neu Fahrland Kladow Steglitz A103 A100 Britz Johannisthal Aldershof Köpenick Grosse Müggelsee Rahnsdorf Wilhelmshagen Springeberg
Nedlitz Sacrow Zehlendorf Lichterfelde Lankwitz Mariendorf Grünau Müggelberge Müggelheim Erkner Neu Buchhorst
Schloss Cecilienhof Wannsee Nikolassee Buckow Rudow Altglienicke Bohnsdorf Müggelsee Gosen
Potsdam Dreilinden A115 E51 Kleinmachnow Seehof Osdorf Grossziethen BERLIN-BRANDENBURG (BER) Karolinenhof
Sanssouci Klein Gleinicke Teltow East from Greenwich

CENTRAL BERLIN

0 km 1
0 miles 0.5

Scheunenviertel Rosa-Luxemburg-Pl.
Charlottenburg Tiergarten Hauptbahnhof Lehrter bahnhof Hackescher Mkt. Alexanderplatz Kongresshalle
Zoologischer Garten Bellevue Schlosspark Tiergarten Unter den Linden Museumsinsel Mitte Jannowitzbrücke
Savignypl. Kurfürstendamm Potsdamer Platz Checkpoint Charlie Jewish Museum Sporthalle
Wilmersdorf Kurfürstendamm Schöneberger Ufer Anhalter Bf. Kreuzberg
Deutsches Technikmuseum Berlin Tempelhofer Ufer Yorckstrasse Viktoriapark

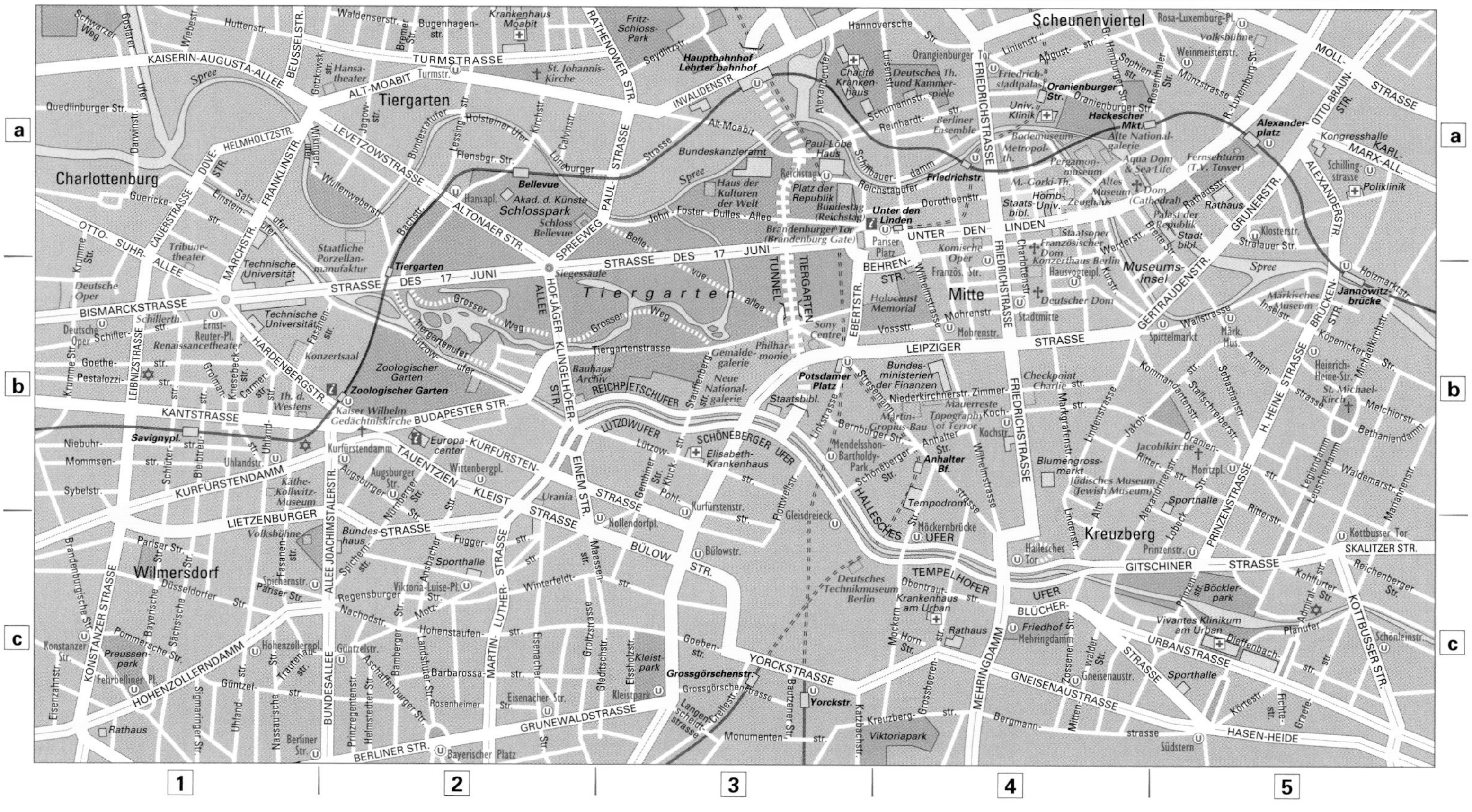

COPYRIGHT PHILIP'S

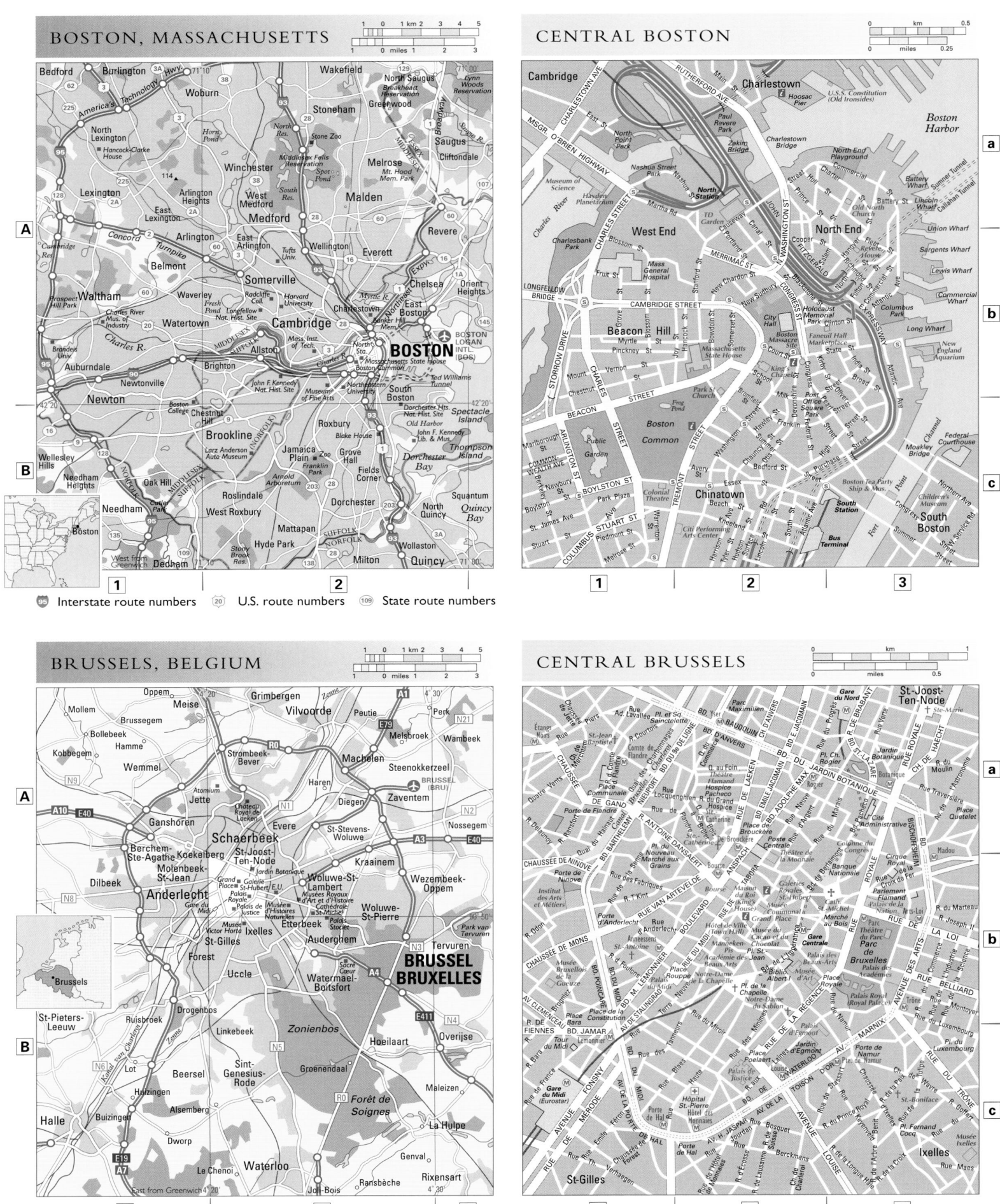

BOSTON, MASSACHUSETTS

CENTRAL BOSTON

95 Interstate route numbers   20 U.S. route numbers   109 State route numbers

BRUSSELS, BELGIUM

CENTRAL BRUSSELS

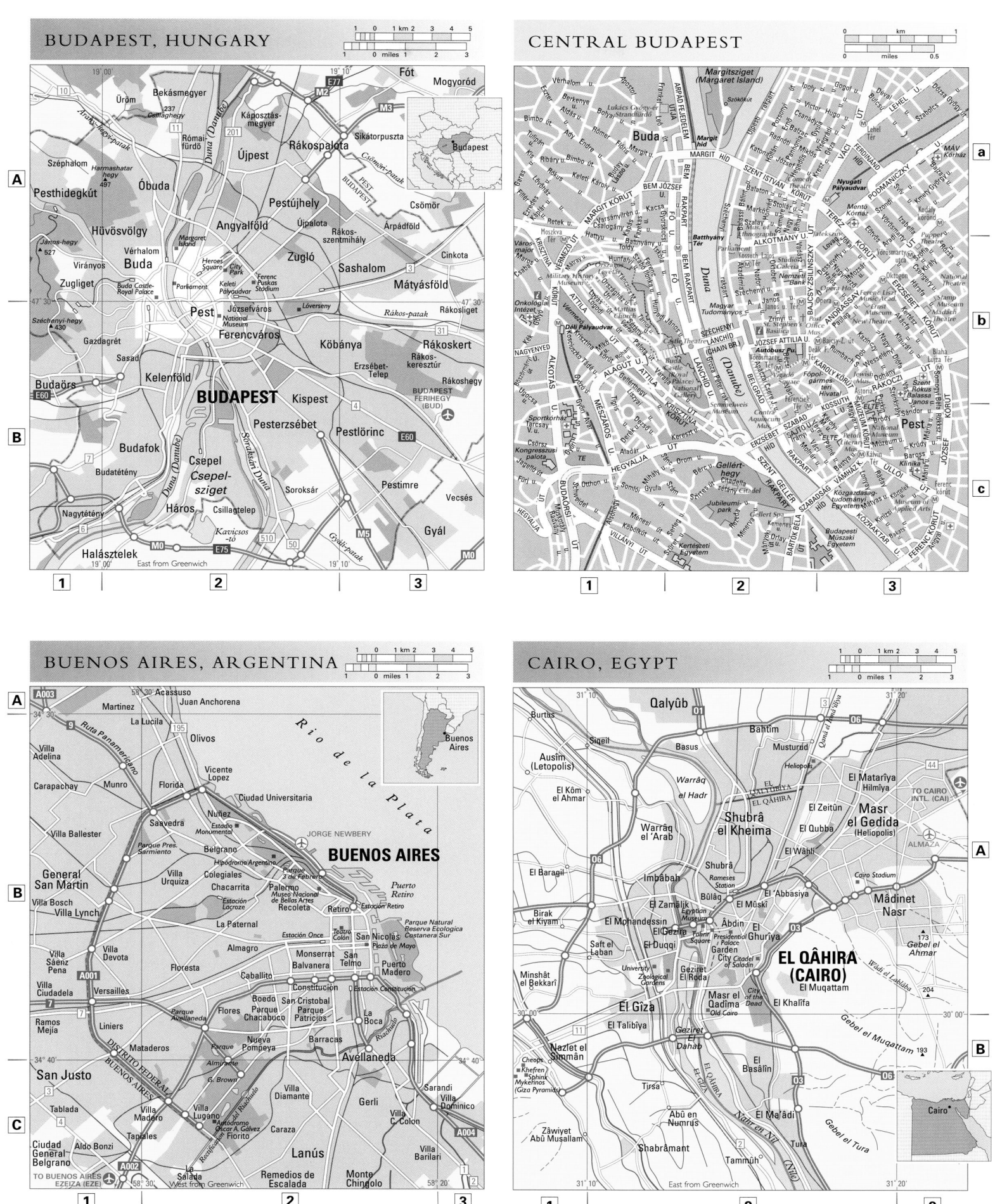

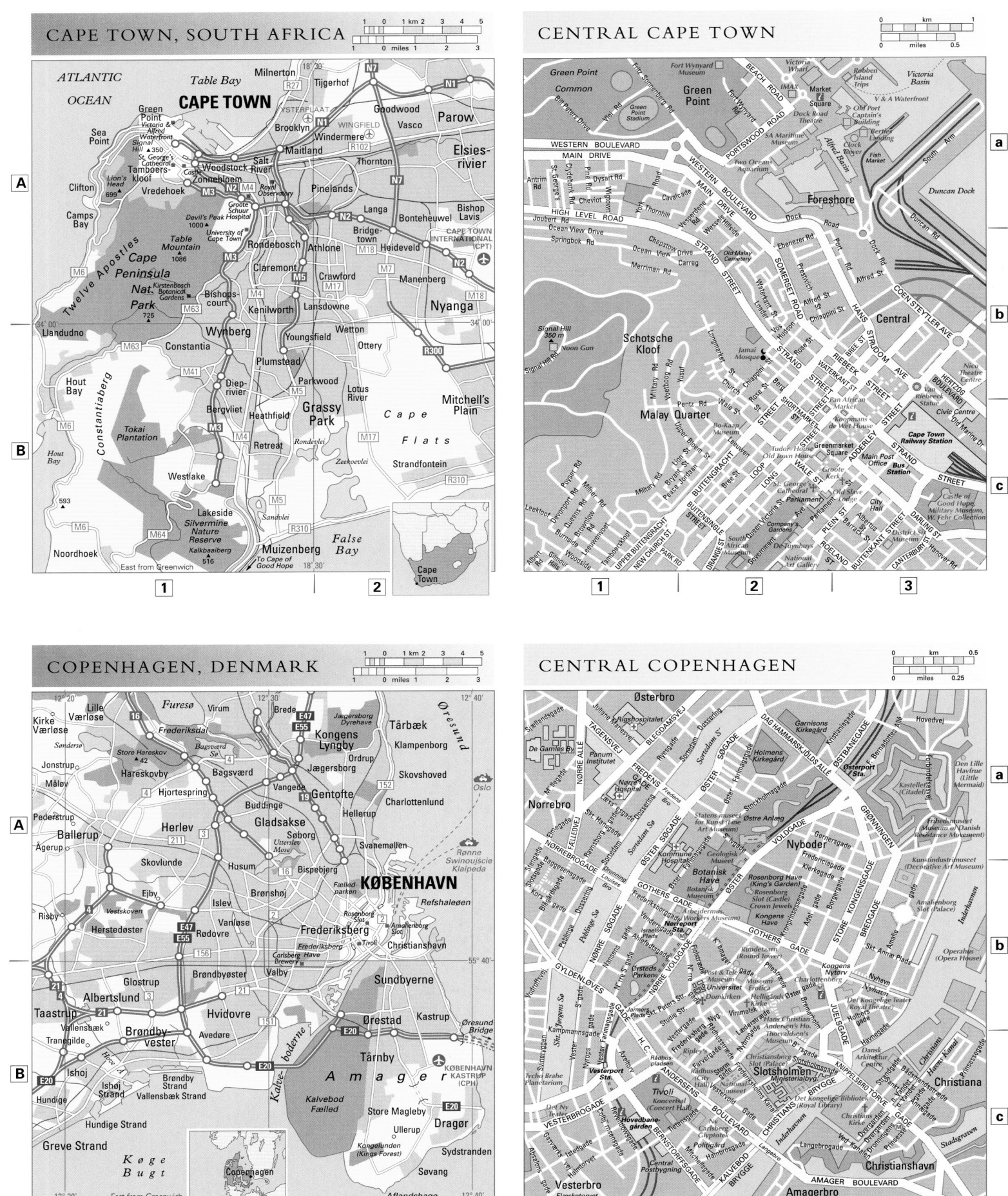

CAPE TOWN, SOUTH AFRICA

ATLANTIC OCEAN

Table Bay

Milnerton

CAPE TOWN

Green Point
Victoria & Alfred Waterfront
Signal Hill ▲350
Sea Point
Clifton
Lion's Head 699
Camps Bay
St. George's Cathedral
Tamboers-kloof
Woodstock
Zonnebloem
Vredehoek
Groote Schuur
Devil's Peak Hospital
Royal Observatory

Tijgerhof
R27
Goodwood
Brooklyn
Vasco
Parow
Maitland
Windermere
Thornton
R102
Elsies-rivier
Salt River
Pinelands
Langa
Bishop Lavis
Bonteheuwel
Bridge-town
Heideveld

N7
N1
WINGFIELD
N1
N4
M3

Cape Peninsula Nat. Park
Twelve Apostles
Table Mountain 1086
University of Cape Town
Kirstenbosch Botanical Gardens 725
1000 ▲
Bishops-court
Rondebosch
Claremont
Kenilworth
Athlone
Crawford
Manenberg
Nyanga

M6
M3
M4
M5
M17
M7
M18
N2

Llandudno
Constantiaberg
Hout Bay
Hout Bay 593
Noordhoek

Wynberg
Constantia
Diep-rivier
Plumstead
Bergvliet
Heathfield
Retreat
Westlake
Lakeside
Silvermine Nature Reserve
Kalkbaaiberg 516

M63
M41
M5
M3
M4
M5
M6
M64

Youngsfield
Wetton
Ottery
Parkwood
Lotus River
Grassy Park
Ronderlei
Zeekoevlei
Sandvlei
Muizenberg

Wynberg
Mitchell's Plain
Cape Flats
Strandfontein

R300
M17
R310
R310

Table Mountain

To Cape of Good Hope
East from Greenwich

False Bay

Cape Town

CENTRAL CAPE TOWN

Green Point Common
Green Point
Fort Wynyard Museum
BEACH ROAD
IMAX
Market Square
Victoria Wharf
Robben Island Trips
Victoria Basin
V & A Waterfront
Old Port Captain's Building
Bertie Landing
Clock Tower
Fish Market

Green Point Stadium
WESTERN BOULEVARD
MAIN DRIVE
PORTSWOOD ROAD
WESTERN BOULEVARD
Two Oceans Aquarium
SA Maritime Museum
Alfred Basin
Dock Road
South Arm
Duncan Dock

Antrim Rd
St George's Rd
Chesham Rd
Dysart Rd
Cheviot Rd
Wigtown Rd
HIGH LEVEL ROAD
Joubert Rd
Ocean View Drive
Springbok Rd
MAIN DRIVE
Thornhill
Vesperdene
London Rd
STRAND STREET
SOMERSET ROAD
Chepstow Rd
Ocean View Drive
Old Malay Cemetery
Carreg
Merriman Rd
Prestwich
Waterkant
Alfred St
Chiappini St
Alfred St
Dock Road
Ebenezer Rd
HANS STRIJDOM AVE
COEN STEYTLER AVE

Foreshore

Signal Hill 350 m
Noon Gun
Signal Hill Rd
Military Rd
Yusuf
Voetboog Rd
Church St
Bloem St
Schotsche Kloof
Jamai Mosque
STRAND
BREE STREET
LOOP STREET
LONG STREET
SHORTMARKET STREET
WATERKANT ST
RIEBEEK ST
BURG ST
Pan African Market
Koopmans de Wet House

Central
HERTZOG BOULEVARD
Nico Theatre Centre
Van Riebeeck Statue
Civic Centre
Old Marine Dr
Cape Town Railway Station
Bus Station

Malay Quarter
Bo-Kaap Museum
Upper Bloem St
Pentz Rd
Wale St
Rose St
Buitengracht
Greenmarket Square
Old Town House
Tudor House

Leeuloop
Poysen Rd
Queens Rd
Devonport Rd
Brownlow Rd
Military Rd
Bryant St
Pepys St
Jordaan
Bree St
Peach St
St George's Cathedral
Parliament
Old Slave Lodge
Main Post Office
STRAND
ADDERLEY
City Hall
DARLING STREET

Albert Rd
Gilmour Rd
Woodside Rd
UPPER BUITENGRACHT
BUITENSINGLE STREET
NEW CHURCH ST
ORANGE ST
Burnside Rd
Tamboerskloof Rd
PARK RD
South African Museum
Company's Gardens
Government
De Tuynhuys
National Art Gallery
South Queen Victoria
Parliament
PLEIN ST
Castle Barracks
ROELAND
Albertus St
BUITENKANT STREET
District Six Museum
CANTERBURY ST
Hanover Rd
Castle of Good Hope, Military Museum, W. Fehr Collection

COPENHAGEN, DENMARK

Kirke Værløse
Lille Værløse
Furesø
Virum
Brede
Jægersborg Dyrehave
Tårbæk
Øresund
E47
E55

Frederiksdal
Kongens Lyngby
Klampenborg
Store Hareskov 42
Hareskovby
Bagsværd Sø
Bagsværd
Ordrup
Skovshoved
Jonstrup
Måløv
Sønderse
Hjortespring
Vangede
Jægersborg
Gentofte
Hellerup
Charlottenlund

Pederstrup
Ballerup
Ågerup
Herlev
Gladsakse
Søborg
Utterslev Mose
Svanemøllen
211
3

Risby
Skovlunde
Ejby
Husum
Brønshøj
Islev
Vanløse
Frederiksberg
Rosenborg Slot
Amalienborg Slot
Refshaleøen

Herstedøster
Vestskoven
Rødovre
Fælled-parken
KØBENHAVN
E47
E55
156

Glostrup
Albertslund
Brøndbyøster
Frederiksberg
Frederiksberg Have
Carlsberg Brewery
Valby
Christianshavn
21
21
3

Taastrup
Vallensbæk
Brøndby vester
Avedøre
Hvidovre
Sundbyerne
151

Tranegilde
Brøndby Strand
Vallensbæk Strand
Ørestad
Kastrup
Øresund Bridge
E20
E20

Ishøj
Ishøj Strand
Kalveboderne
Tårnby
KØBENHAVN KASTRUP (CPH)
E20

Hundige
Greve Strand
Kalvebod Fælled
Store Magleby
Dragør
Ullerup
Sydstranden
Søvang

Køge Bugt
Kongelunden (Kings Forest)
Aflandshage
East from Greenwich

Copenhagen

Oslo
Rønne
Swinoujscie
Klaipeda
Amager

CENTRAL COPENHAGEN

Østerbro
Rigshospitalet
Garnisons Kirkegård
Hovedvej
De Gamles By
Panum Institutet
Holmens Kirkegård
Østerport Sta.
Den Lille Havfrue (Little Mermaid)

Nørrebro
Nørre Hospital
Statens museum for Kunst (Fine Art Museum)
Østre Anlæg
Kastellet (Citadel)
Frihedsmuseet (Museum of Danish Resistance Movement)

Kommune Hospital
Geologisk Museet
Nyboder
Kunstindustrimuseet (Decorative Art Museum)
Botanisk Have
Botanisk Museum
Rosenborg Have (King's Garden)
Rosenborg Slot (Castle) Crown Jewels
Kongens Have
Amalienborg Slot (Palace)

Nørreport Sta.
Arbejdermus (Workers' Museum)
GOTHERS GADE
Skt. Annæ Plads
Operahus (Opera House)

Ørsteds Parken
Rundetaarn (Round Tower)
Universitet
Domkirken
Helligånd Kirke
Charlottenborg
Nyhavn
Det Kongelige Teater (Royal Theatre)
Holbergs g

Hans Christian Andersen's Ho.
Thorvaldsens Museum
Dansk Arkitektur Centre

Tycho Brahe Planetarium
Ripley's
Rådhus pladsen
Nationalmuseum
Slotsholmen
Ministerialbyg
Christiansborg Slot (Palace)
Det Kgl. Bibliotek (Royal Library)
Christiania

Det Ny Teater
Tivoli
Koncertsal (Concert Hall)
Vesterport Sta.
Ny Carlsberg Glyptotek
Hovedbane-gården
Central Postbygning
Slotsholmsgade
Christians Kirke
VESTERBROGADE
CHRISTIANS BOULEVARD
Christianshavn

Vesterbro
Amagerbro
AMAGER BOULEVARD
Flæsketorvet

CENTRAL CHICAGO

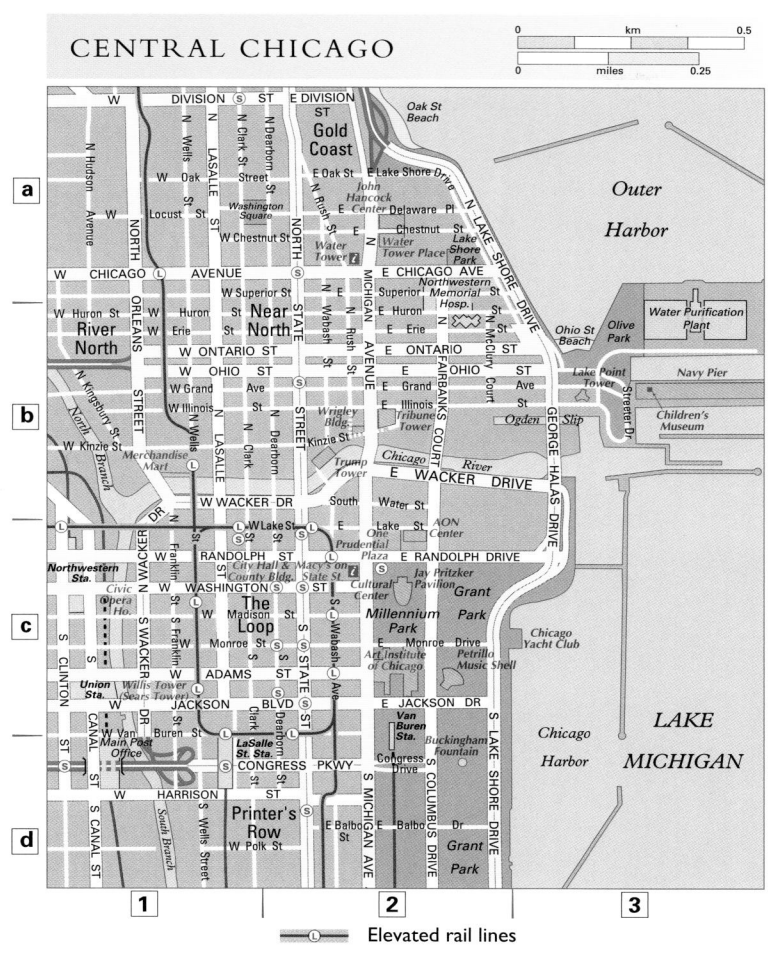

Elevated rail lines

CHICAGO, ILLINOIS

DUBAI, U.A.E.

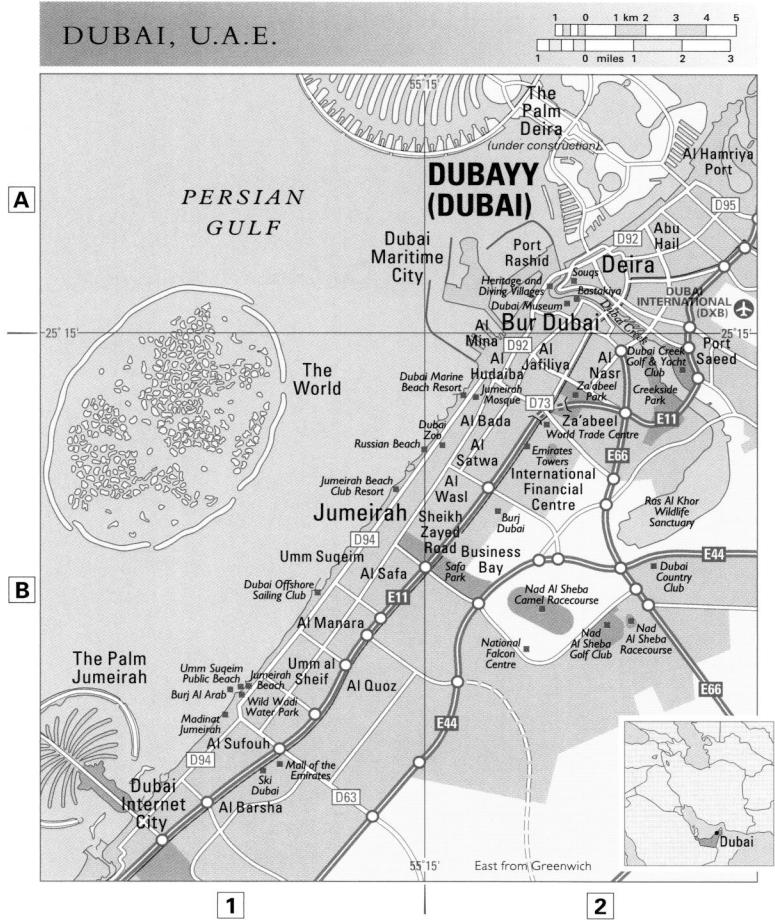

East from Greenwich

Interstate route numbers   U.S. route numbers   State route numbers

COPYRIGHT PHILIP'S

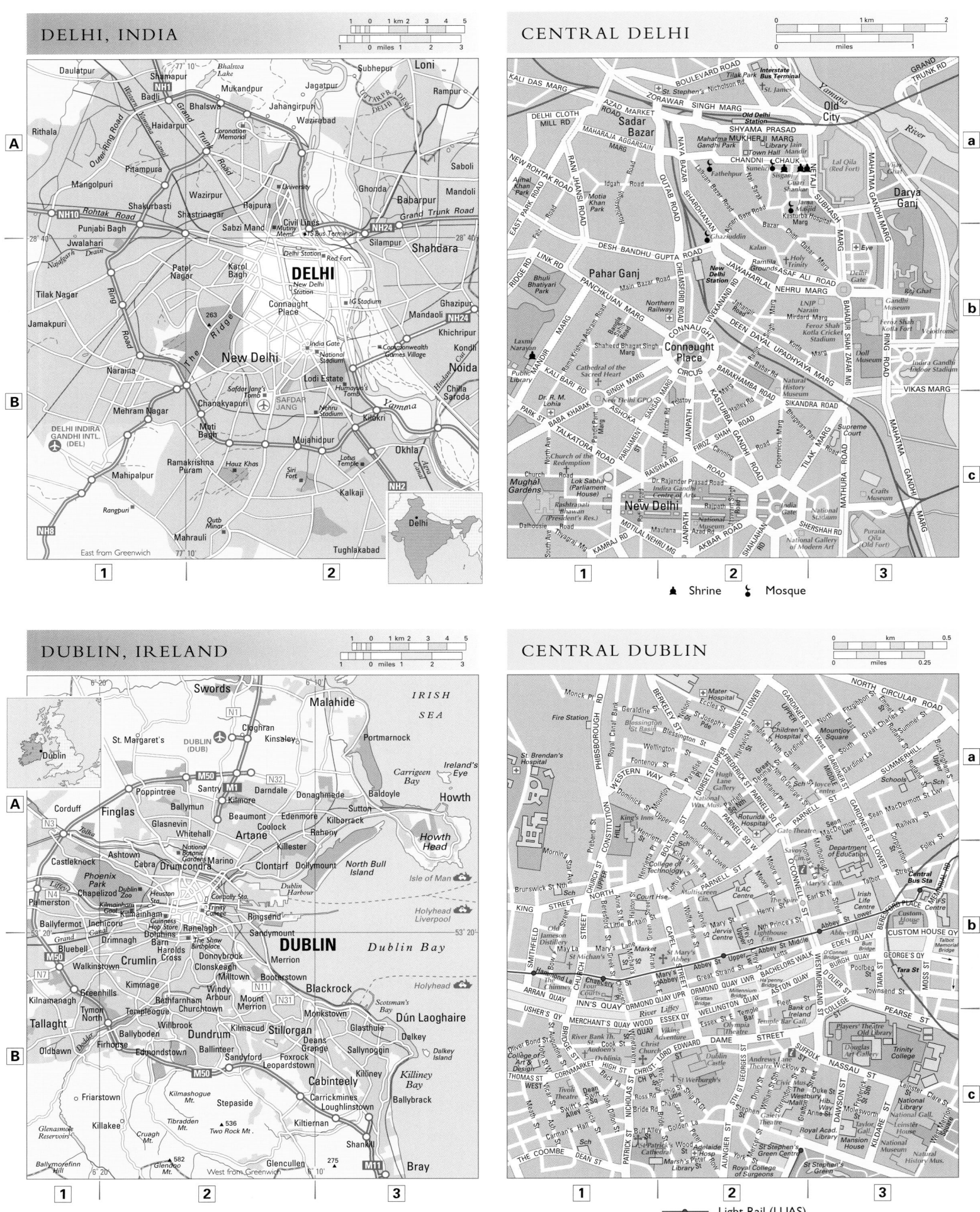

DELHI, INDIA

CENTRAL DELHI

🔔 Shrine   ⚲ Mosque

DUBLIN, IRELAND

CENTRAL DUBLIN

— Light Rail (LUAS)

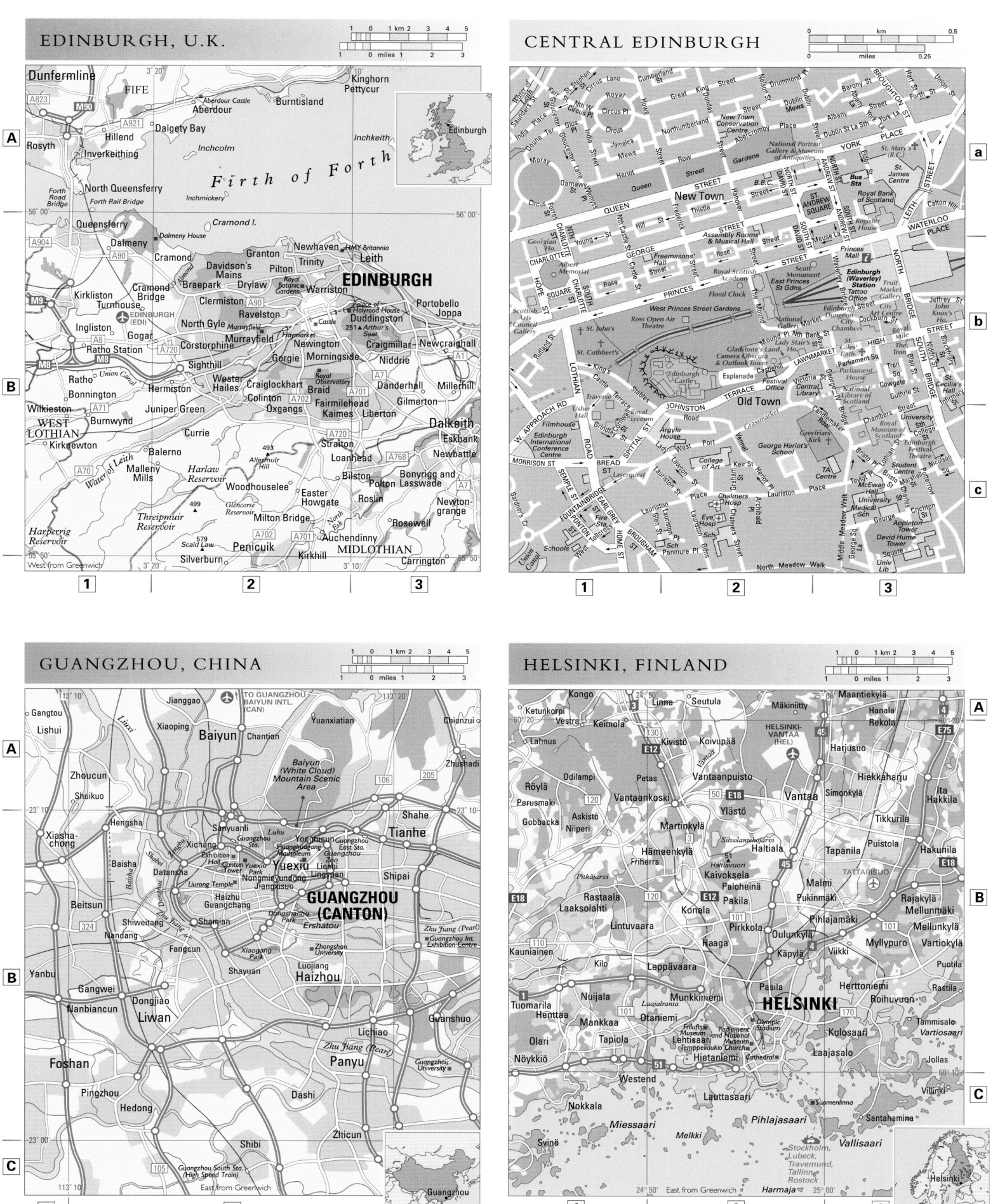

EDINBURGH, U.K.

CENTRAL EDINBURGH

GUANGZHOU, CHINA

HELSINKI, FINLAND

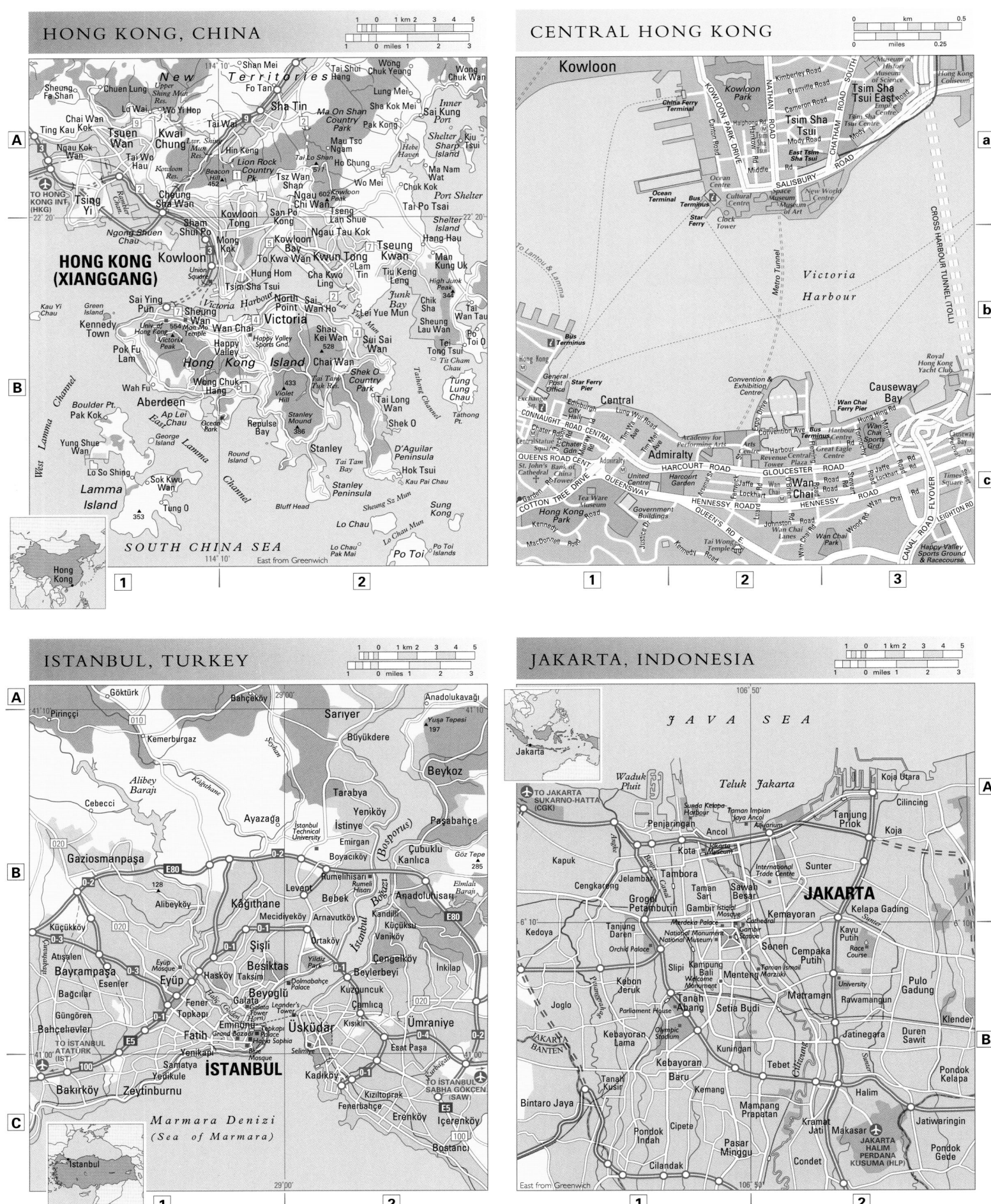

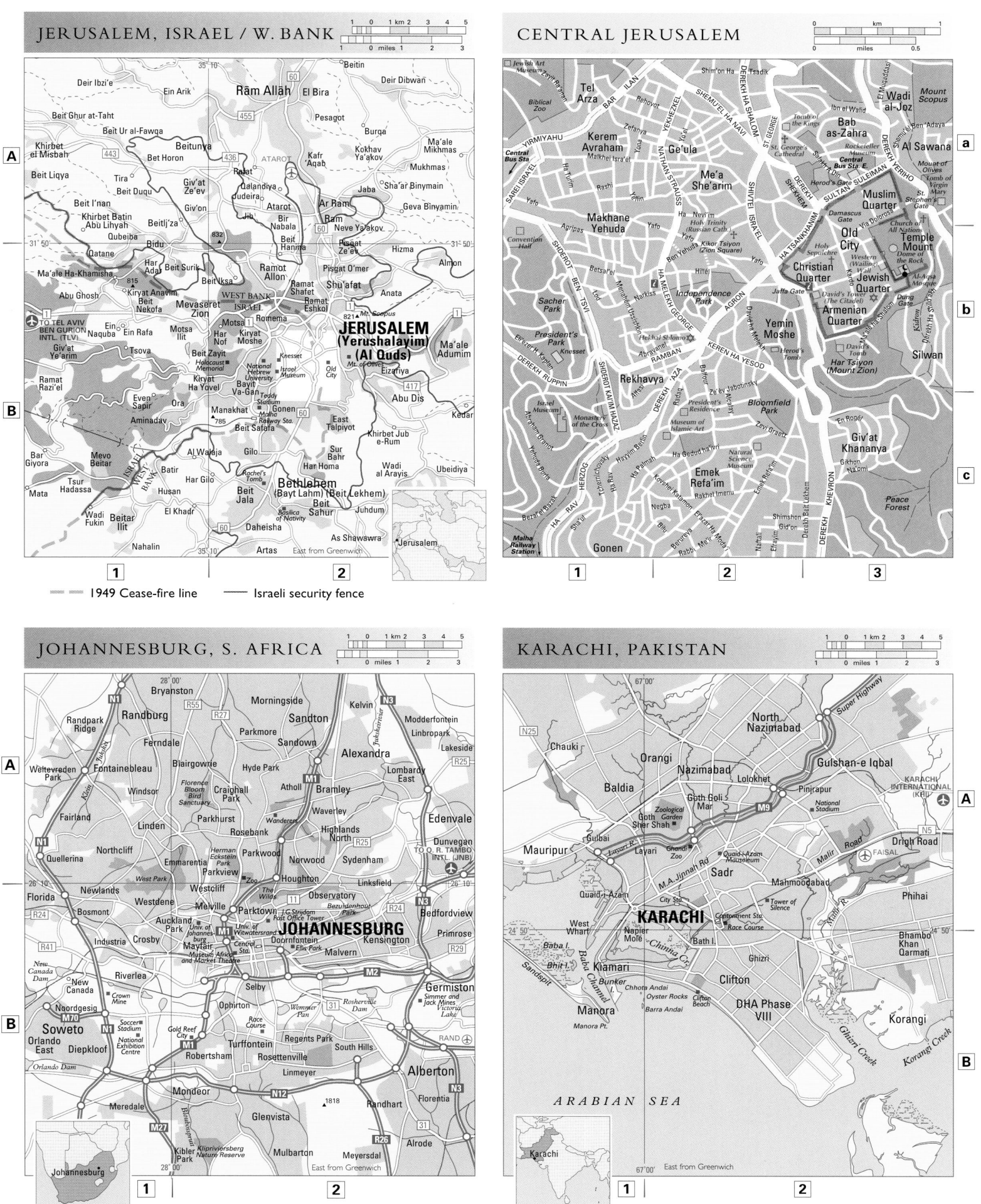

JERUSALEM, ISRAEL / W. BANK

1949 Cease-fire line — Israeli security fence

CENTRAL JERUSALEM

JOHANNESBURG, S. AFRICA

KARACHI, PAKISTAN

ARABIAN SEA

COPYRIGHT PHILIP'S

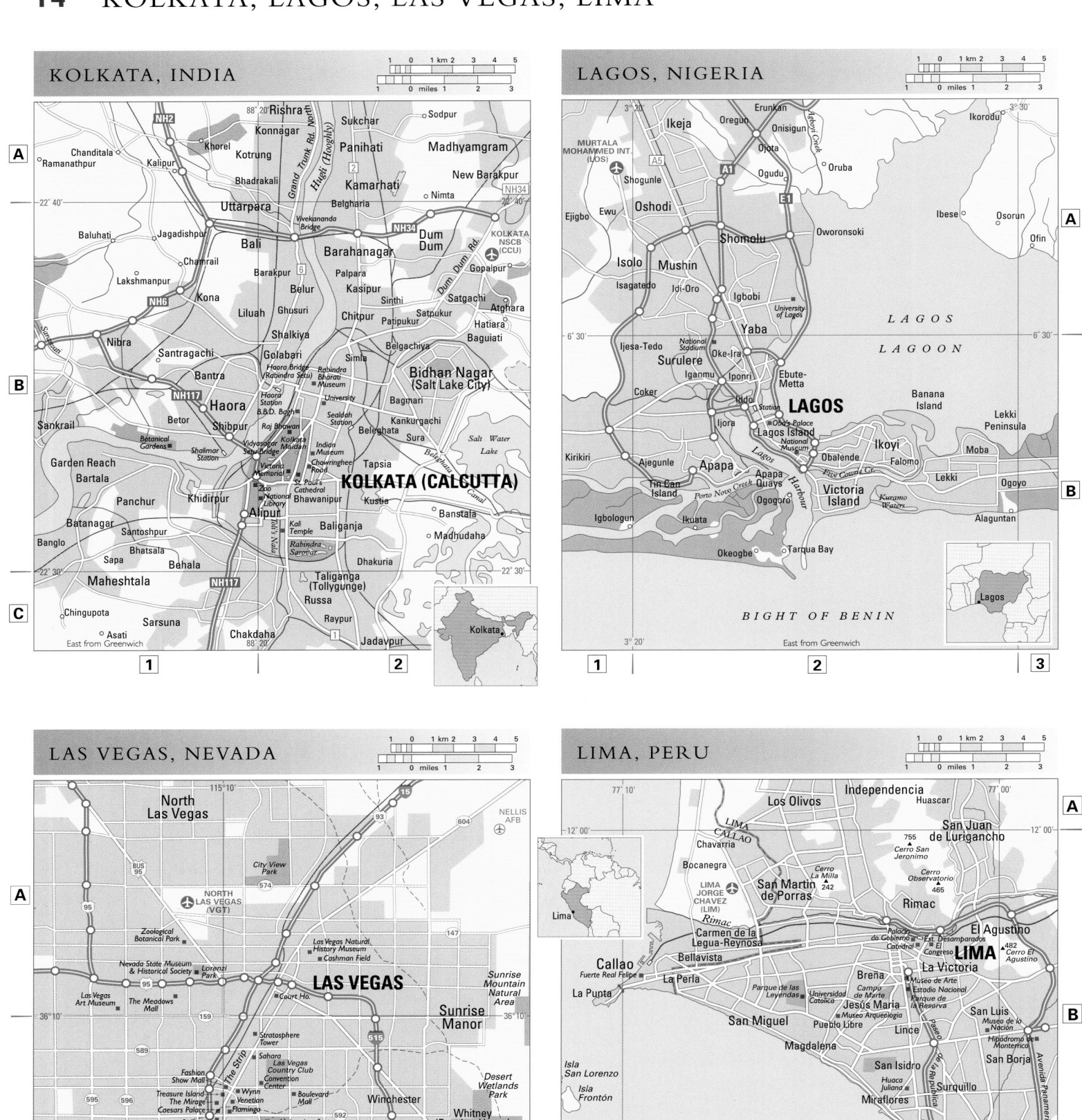

KOLKATA, INDIA

| | 1 | 0 | 1 km 2 | 3 | 4 | 5 |
| 1 | 0 miles 1 | | 2 | | 3 | |

Rishra
Sodpur
88° 20'
Konnagar
Sukchar
Chanditala
Khorel
Panihati
Madhyamgram
Ramanathpur
Kotrung
Kalipur
Bhadrakali
New Barakpur
22° 40'
Uttarpara
Kamarhati
Nimta
NH34
Belgharia
Baluhati
Jagadishpur
Dum
Vivekananda
NH34
Dum
KOLKATA
Bali
Bridge
Barahanagar
NSCB
Chamrail
Barakpur
Palpara
(CCU)
Lakshmanpur
Belur
Kasipur
Gopalpur
Kona
Liluah
Ghusuri
Chitpur
Sinthi
Satgachi
Shalkiya
Patipukur
Satpukur
Atghara
Nibra
Simla
Hatiara
Santragachi
Golabari
Belgachiya
Baguiati
Bantra
Haora Bridge
Rabindra
Haora
(Rabindra Setu)
Bharati
University
Bidhan Nagar
NH117
Haora
Museum
Bagmari
(Salt Lake City)
Station
Sealdah
Sankrail
Betor
Shibpur
B.B.D. Bagh
Kankurgachi
Vidyasagar
Raj Bhawan
Station
Sura
Botanical
Setu Bridge
Kolkata
Indian
Beleghata
Gardens
Shalimar
Maidan
Museum
Garden Reach
Station
Chowringhee
Tapsia
Salt Water
Bartala
Victoria
Road
Lake
Memorial
St. Paul's
KOLKATA (CALCUTTA)
Cathedral
Panchur
Khidirpur
Zoo
Bhawanipur
Kustia
Batanagar
Santoshpur
National
Aliput
Library
Banstala
Banglo
Bhatsala
Kali
Baliganja
Madhudaha
Sapa
Behala
Temple
Dhakuria
22° 30'
Maheshtala
NH117
Rabindra
Taliganga
Sarovar
(Tollygunge)
Chingupota
Russa
Sarsuna
Raypur
Asati
Chakdaha
88° 20'
Jadavpur

LAGOS, NIGERIA

| | 1 | 0 | 1 km 2 | 3 | 4 | 5 |
| 1 | 0 miles 1 | | 2 | | 3 | |

Erunkan
Ikorodu
3° 30'
Ikeja
Oregun
Onisigun
MURTALA
Ojota
Oruba
MOHAMMED INT.
Shogunle
(LOS)
Ibese
Osorun
A1
Ogudu
Ejigbo
Ewu
Oshodi
Ofin
Shomolu
Oworonsoki
Isolo
Mushin
Idi-Oro
University
LAGOS
Isagatedo
Igbobi
of Lagos
LAGOON
Ijesa-Tedo
Yaba
National
Oke-Ira
Surulere
Stadium
Iganmu
Iponri
Ebute-
Banana
Metta
Island
Coker
Iddo
Station
LAGOS
Lekki
Peninsula
Ijora
Lagos Island
Kirikiri
Ajegunle
Oba's Palace
Moba
National
Ikoyi
Tin Can
Apapa
Museum
Obalende
Falomo
Island
Apapa Quays
Lekki
Ogogoro
Victoria
Kuramo
Ogoyo
Igbologun
Ikuata
Porto Novo Creek
Island
Waters
Alaguntan
Okeogbe
Tarqua Bay
3° 20'
BIGHT OF BENIN

LAS VEGAS, NEVADA

| | 1 | 0 | 1 km 2 | 3 | 4 | 5 |
| 1 | 0 miles 1 | | 2 | | 3 | |

North
115° 10'
Las Vegas
15
93
NELLIS
AFB
604
City View
Park
BUS
95
574
NORTH
LAS VEGAS
95
(VGT)
147
Zoological
Botanical Park
Las Vegas Natural
History Museum
Nevada State Museum
Lorenzi
Cashman Field
& Historical Society
Park
95
LAS VEGAS
Sunrise
Las Vegas
Court Ho.
Mountain
Art Museum
The Meadows
159
Natural
Mall
Area
36° 10'
Sunrise
Stratosphere
Manor
Tower
515
589
Sahara
Fashion
Las Vegas
Desert
Show Mall
Country Club
Wetlands
Convention
Park
Center
592
Treasure Island
Wynn
Boulevard
The Mirage
Venetian
Mall
Caesars Palace
Flamingo
Winchester
Bellagio
Paris
593
Monte Carlo
MGM
University of
Whitney
New York
Grand
Nevada L.V.
(East Las Vegas)
New York
Thomas & Mack
595
596
Luxor
Center
Tropicana
Liberace
Spring Valley
Museum
Paradise
Mandalay
LAS VEGAS
Bay
McCARRAN
Sam Boyd
INTL. (LAS)
582
Stadium
Town Square
Galleria
Mall
Civic Center
at Sunset
Sunset
Park
93
Las Vegas
95
Outlet Center
Henderson
160
595
15
Enterprise
215
115° 10'
West from Greenwich

15 Interstate route numbers   95 U.S. route numbers   147 State route numbers

LIMA, PERU

| | 1 | 0 | 1 km 2 | 3 | 4 | 5 |
| 1 | 0 miles 1 | | 2 | | 3 | |

Independencia
77° 00'
77° 10'
Los Olivos
Huascar
LIMA
12° 00'
CALLAO
San Juan
Chavarria
de Lurigancho
755
Bocanegra
Cerro San
Cerro
Jeronimo
LIMA
La Milla
Cerro
JORGE
San Martin
242
Observatorio
CHAVEZ
de Porras
465
(LIM)
Rimac
Rimac
Palacio
El Agustino
de Gobierno
482
Carmen de la
Est.
Cerro El
Legua-Reynosa
Catedral
El
Agustino
Callao
Bellavista
Congreso
LIMA
Fuerte Real Felipe
Breña
La Victoria
La Perla
Museo de Arte
Campo
San Luis
La Punta
Parque de las
de Marte
Estadio Nacional
Leyendas
Universidad
Jesús María
Parque de
Museo de la
Católica
Parque de la Reserva
Nación
San Miguel
Museo Arqueologia
Lince
San Borja
Pueblo Libre
Magdalena
San Isidro
Surquillo
Huaca
Isla
Juliana
San Lorenzo
Miraflores
Santiago de
Isla
Surco
Frontón
Vista Alegre
PACIFIC OCEAN
Berranco
12° 10'
LAS PALMAS
Cerro Morro Solar
La Campiña
273
Chorrillos
Punta La Chira
La Encantada
77° 10'
West from Greenwich
77° 00'

COPYRIGHT PHILIP'S

LONDON, U.K.

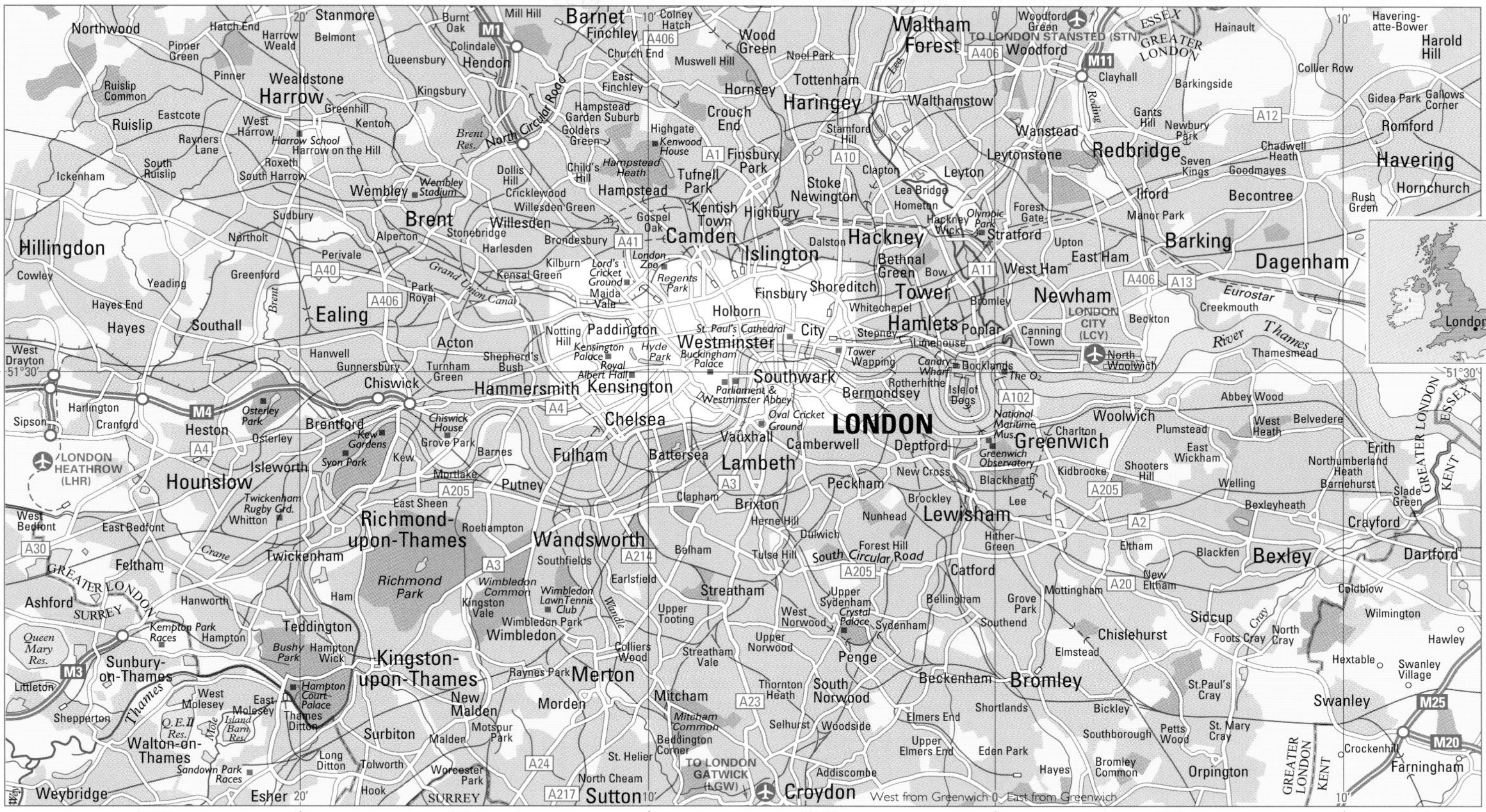

1	2	3	4	5

CENTRAL LONDON

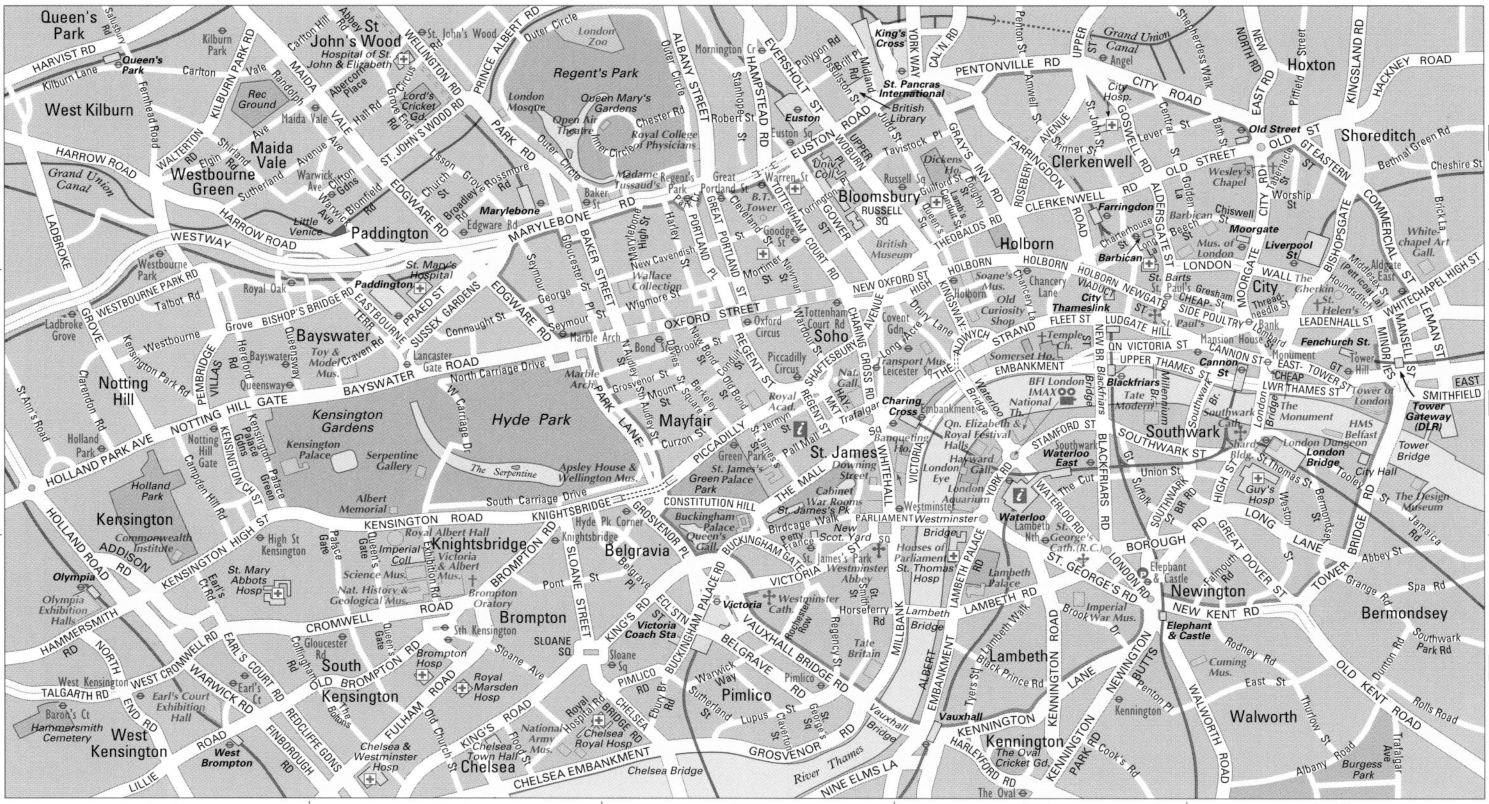

1	2	3	4	5

Congestion Charging Zone

LISBON, PORTUGAL

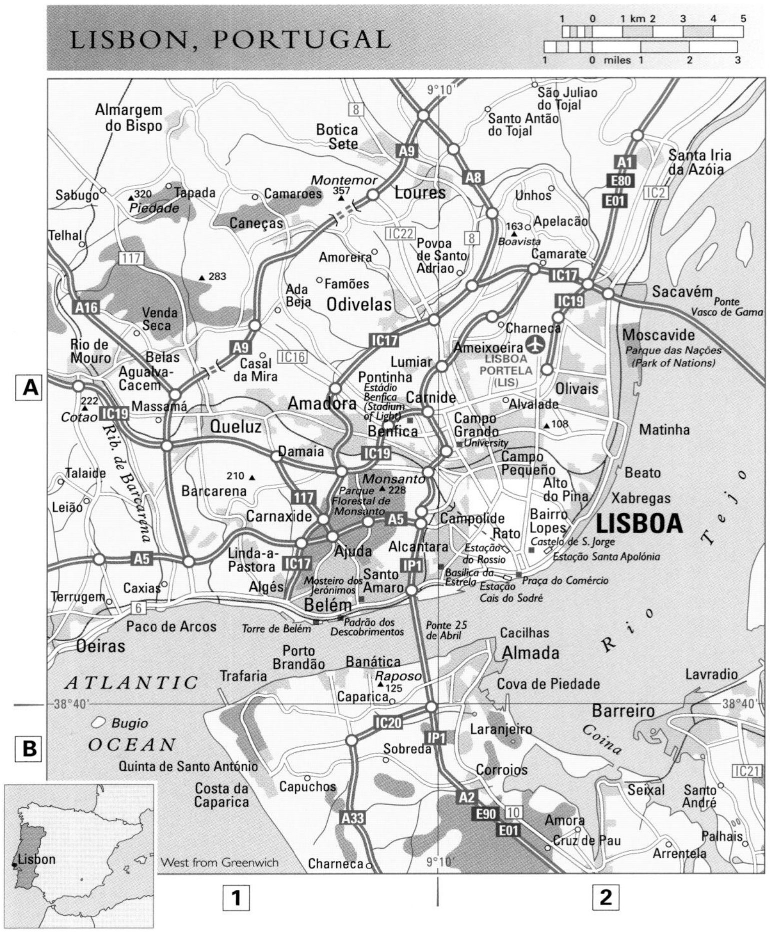

1 0 1 km 2 3 4 5
1 0 miles 1 2 3

Almargem do Bispo, Botica Sete, São Julião do Tojal, Santo Antão do Tojal, Santa Iria da Azóia, Sabugo, 320, Tapada, Piedade, Camarões, Montemor 357, Loures, Unhas, Apelação, Telhal, Caneças, Póvoa de Santo Adrião, Camarate, 163, Boavista, Amoreira, Ada Beja, Famões, Odivelas, Sacavém, Ponte Vasco da Gama, Rio de Mouro, 222, Cotao, Casal da Mira, Lumiar, Pontinha, Catnide, Alvalade, Olivais, Moscavide, Parque das Nações (Park of Nations), Venda Seca, Aguava-Cacem, Massamá, Amadora, Benfica, Estádio Benfica (Stadium) of Ulpio, Campo Grande University, LISBOA PORTELA (LIS), Queluz, Damaia, 210, Parque Florestal de Monsanto, 228, Campo Pequeno, Alto do Pina, Beato, Xabregas, Matinha, Talaide, Bárcarena, Carnaxide, Campolide, Rato, Bairro Lopes, Castelo de S. Jorge, LISBOA, Leião, Linda-a-Pastora, Ajuda, Alcântara, Estação do Rossio, Estação Santa Apolónia, Caxias, Algés, Santo Amaro, Mosteiro dos Jerónimos, Basílica da Estrela, Estação Cais do Sodré, Praça do Comércio, Terrugem, Belém, Torre de Belém, Padrão dos Descobrimentos, Ponte 25 de Abril, Cacilhas, Rio Tejo, Oeiras, Paço de Arcos, Porto Brandão, Banática, 125, Almada, Lavradio, Trafaria, Raposo, Caparica, Cova da Piedade, 38°40', Bugio, Barreiro, Coina, OCEAN, Quinta de Santo António, Sobreda, Laranjeiro, Costa da Caparica, Capuchos, Corroios, 38°40', Amora, Seixal, Santo André, Cruz de Pau, Arrentela, Palhais, Charneca, 9°10', West from Greenwich, 9°10'

ATLANTIC OCEAN

Lisbon (locator map)

1 · 2

CENTRAL LISBON

0 km ... 0 miles 0.5

Palácio da Justiça, Penitenciária, M. S. Sebastião, Praça Duque de Saldanha, Pinheiro Chagas, Instituto Superior Técnico, Hosp. Infantil, Maternidade, Av. Duque de Ávila, Parque Eduardo VII, Pavilhão dos Desportos, Estefânia, Av. Alm. Barroso, RUA PASCOAL DE MELO, Praça do Chile, Amoreiros, Praça Marquês de Pombal, Penha França, Rato, Hospital M. Bombarda, Anjos, Bairro Lopes, Hospital de Santa Marta, Graça, Academia das Ciências, Jardim Botânico, Instituto de Medicina Legal, Palácio de Assembleia Nacional, Bairro Alto, Museu do Arqueológico, Estação do Rossio, Praça Rossio, Castelo de São Jorge (St. George's Castle), Estação Santa Apolónia, Elevador de Santa Justa, Theatro Nac. de São Carlos, Biblioteca Nacional, Sé Catedral, Alfama, Military Museum, Baixa, AV. VINTE E QUATRO DE JULHO, RUA DO ARSENAL, R. DA ALFÂNDEGA, INFANTE DOM HENRIQUE, AV. RIBEIRA DAS NAUS, Dom José I, Estação Fluvial, Rio Tejo (Tagus), Estação Cais do Sodré

1 · 2 · 3

a · b · c

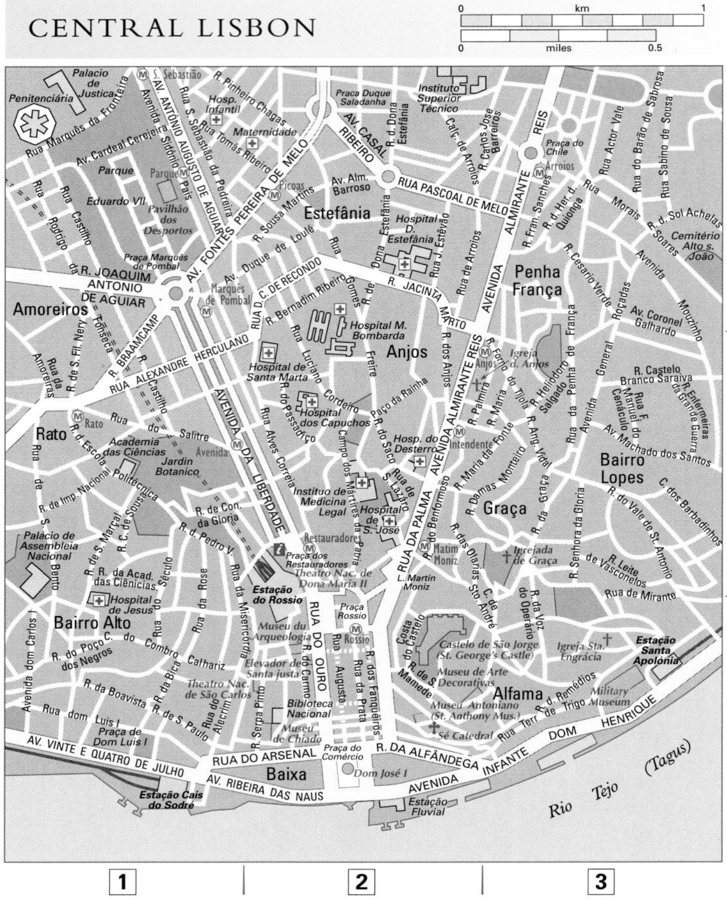

LOS ANGELES, CALIFORNIA

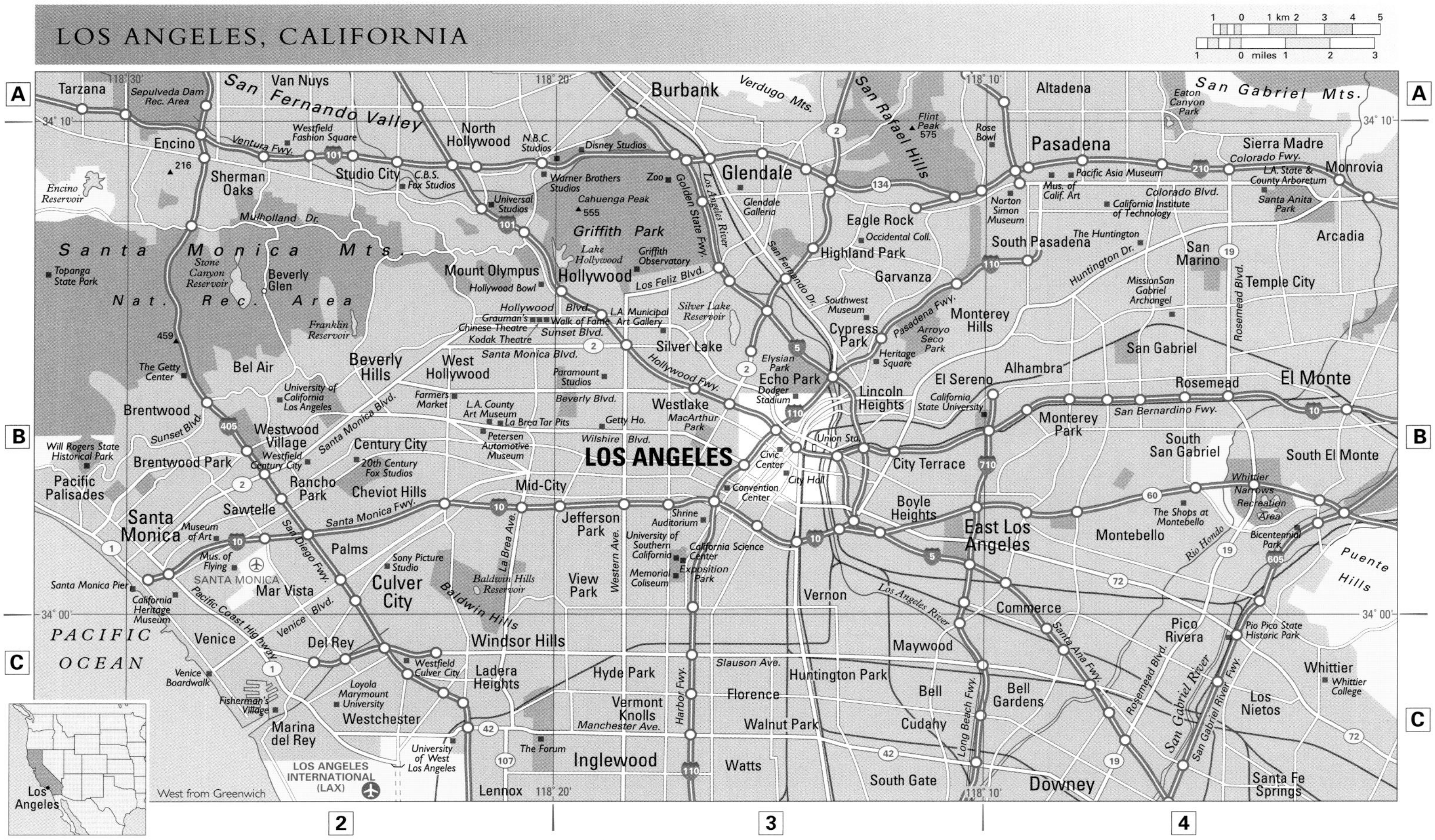

1 0 1 km 2 3 4 5
1 0 miles 1 2 3

118°30', Tarzana, Van Nuys, San Fernando Valley, Burbank, Verdugo Mts., 118°20', Altadena, San Gabriel Mts., Eaton Canyon Park, 34°10', Encino, 216, Westfield Fashion Square, North Hollywood, N.B.C. Studios, Disney Studios, Flint Peak 575, Rose Bowl, Pasadena, Sierra Madre, Colorado Fwy., Monrovia, Encino Reservoir, Sherman Oaks, Studio City, C.B.S. Fox Studios, Warner Brothers Studios, Zoo, Glendale, Glendale Galleria, Eagle Rock, Pacific Asia Museum, L.A. State & County Arboretum, Santa Anita Park, Mulholland Dr., Universal Studios, Cahuenga Peak 555, Griffith Park, Griffith Observatory, Norton Simon Museum, Mus. of Calif. Art, California Institute of Technology, Arcadia, Santa Monica Mts., Lake Hollywood, Highland Park, Occidental Coll., South Pasadena, The Huntington, San Marino, Topanga State Park, Stone Canyon Reservoir, Beverly Glen, Mount Olympus, Hollywood Bowl, Hollywood, Los Feliz Blvd., Garvanza, Southwest Museum, MissionSan Gabriel Archangel, Temple City, Nat. Rec. Area, Franklin Reservoir, 459, Grauman's Chinese Theatre, Kodak Theatre, Walk of Fame, L.A. Municipal Art Gallery, Sunset Blvd., Silver Lake Reservoir, Cypress Park, Pasadena Fwy., Arroyo Seco Park, Monterey Hills, San Gabriel, Rosemead Blvd., The Getty Center, Bel Air, Beverly Hills, West Hollywood, Santa Monica Blvd., Silver Lake, Hollywood Fwy., Echo Park, Elysian Park, Lincoln Heights, Alhambra, Brentwood, University of California Los Angeles, Westwood Village, Century City, Farmers Market, L.A. County Art Museum, La Brea Tar Pits, Getty Ho., Westlake, MacArthur Park, California State University, Monterey Park, San Bernardino Fwy., Will Rogers State Historical Park, Pacific Palisades, Brentwood Park, Westfield Century City, 20th Century Fox Studios, Rancho Park, Cheviot Hills, Petersen Automotive Museum, Wilshire Blvd., Civic Center, City Hall, City Terrace, South San Gabriel, South El Monte, LOS ANGELES, Union Sta., Convention Center, Boyle Heights, East Los Angeles, Montebello, The Shops at Montebello, Whittier Narrows Recreation Area, Santa Monica, Museum of Art, Mus. of Flying, SANTA MONICA, Palms, Sony Picture Studio, Mid-City, Jefferson Park, University of Southern California, Shrine Auditorium, Los Angeles River, Vernon, 34°00', Mar Vista, Baldwin Hills Reservoir, View Park, Memorial Coliseum, California Science Center, Exposition Park, Commerce, Rio Hondo, Bicentennial Park, Puente Hills, Pico Rivera, Pio Pico State Historic Park, Santa Monica Pier, California Heritage Museum, Culver City, Baldwin Hills, Windsor Hills, Venice, Venice Boardwalk, Del Rey, Westfield Culver City, Ladera Heights, Hyde Park, Vermont Knolls, Maywood, Bell, Bell Gardens, Whittier, PACIFIC OCEAN, Fisherman's Village, Marina del Rey, Loyola Marymount University, Westchester, University of West Los Angeles, The Forum, Inglewood, Manchester Ave., Walnut Park, Cudahy, Los Nietos, Whittier College, LOS ANGELES INTERNATIONAL (LAX), Lennox, 118°20', Watts, South Gate, Downey, 118°10', Santa Fe Springs, West from Greenwich

A · B · C

Los Angeles (locator map)

2 · 3 · 4

🛡 Interstate route numbers   ◯ State route numbers

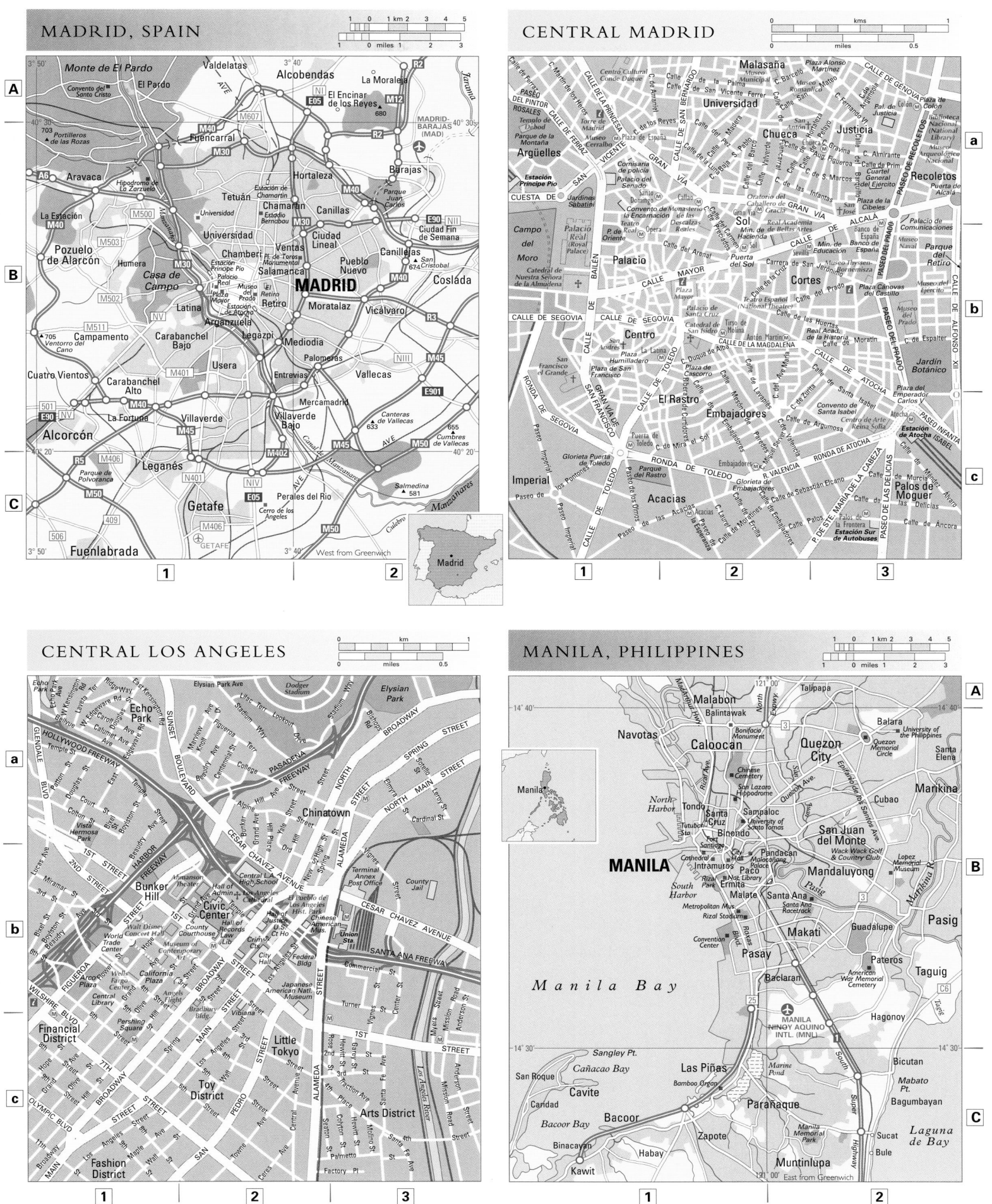

MADRID, SPAIN

Monte de El Pardo
Convento del Santo Cristo
El Pardo
Valdelatas
Alcobendas
La Moraleja
El Encinar de los Reyes
Portilleros de las Rozas
Fuencarral
Barajas
MADRID-BARAJAS (MAD)
Aravaca
Hortaleza
Tetuán
Estación de Chamartín
Canillas
La Estación
Universidad
Chamartín
Estadio Bernabéu
Ciudad Lineal
Ciudad Fin de Semana
Pozuelo de Alarcón
Humera
Chamberí
Ventas
Pueblo Nuevo
Coslada
Casa de Campo
Salamanca
MADRID
Latina
Retiro
Moratalaz
Vicálvaro
Campamento
Arganzuela
Legazpi
Mediodía
Carabanchel Bajo
Usera
Palomeras
Vallecas
Cuatro Vientos
Carabanchel Alto
Entrevías
Mercamadrid
La Fortuna
Villaverde
Villaverde Bajo
Canteras de Vallecas
Cumbres de Vallecas
Alcorcón
Salmedina
Leganés
Parque de Polvoranca
Perales del Rio
Getafe
Cerro de los Ángeles
Fuenlabrada
West from Greenwich
Madrid

CENTRAL MADRID

Malasaña
Universidad
Chueca
Justicia
Argüelles
Recoletos
Estación Príncipe Pío
Gran Vía
Sol
Palacio
Palacio Real (Royal Palace)
Campo del Moro
Cortes
Centro
El Rastro
Embajadores
Jardín Botánico
Imperial
Acacias
Palos de Moguer
Estación de Atocha
Estación Sur de Autobuses

CENTRAL LOS ANGELES

Echo Park
Dodger Stadium
Elysian Park
Chinatown
Bunker Hill
Civic Center
Little Tokyo
Financial District
Toy District
Arts District
Fashion District

MANILA, PHILIPPINES

Malabon
Talipapa
Navotas
Balintawak
Balara
University of the Philippines
Caloocan
Bonifacio Monument
Quezon City
Quezon Memorial Circle
Santa Elena
Chinese Cemetery
Marikina
North Harbor
Tondo
Sampaloc
Cubao
Santa Cruz
San Juan del Monte
Binondo
Pandacan
Wack Wack Golf & Country Club
Lopez Memorial Museum
MANILA
Intramuros
Malacañang Palace
Paco
Mandaluyong
Ermita
Pasig
South Harbor
Malate
Santa Ana
Guadalupe
Pasig
Metropolitan Mus.
Rizal Stadium
Makati
Pateros
Taguig
Convention Center
Pasay
Baclaran
American War Memorial Cemetery
Manila Bay
MANILA NINOY AQUINO INTL. (MNL)
Hagonoy
Sangley Pt.
Las Piñas
Bicutan
San Roque
Cañacao Bay
Cavite
Caridad
Bacoor
Parañaque
Mabato Pt.
Bagumbayan
Bacoor Bay
Bacoor
Zapote
Manila Memorial Park
Binacayan
Habay
Muntinlupa
Sucat
Bule
Laguna de Bay
Kawit
East from Greenwich

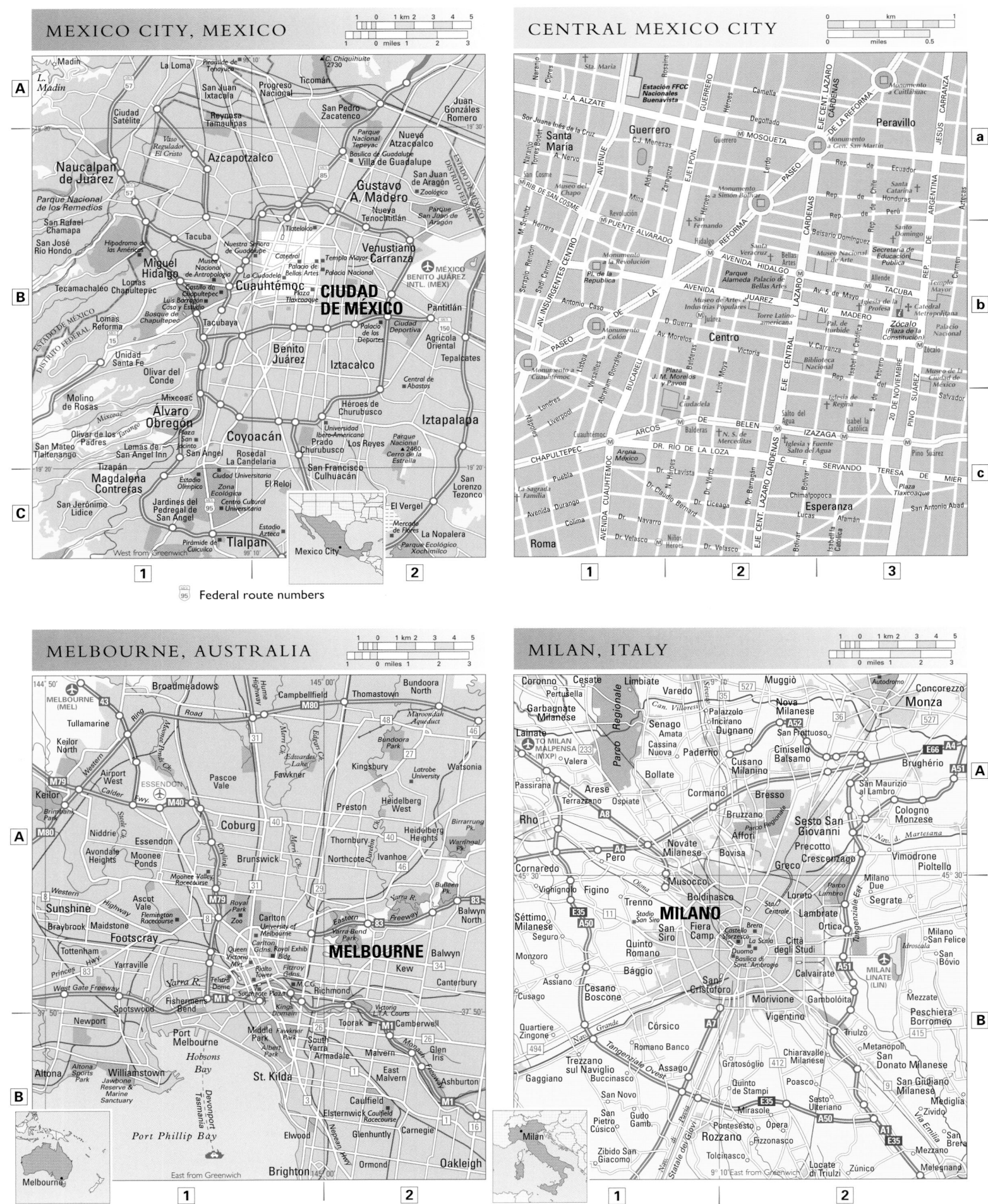

MEXICO CITY, MEXICO

CENTRAL MEXICO CITY

⬡ Federal route numbers

MELBOURNE, AUSTRALIA

MILAN, ITALY

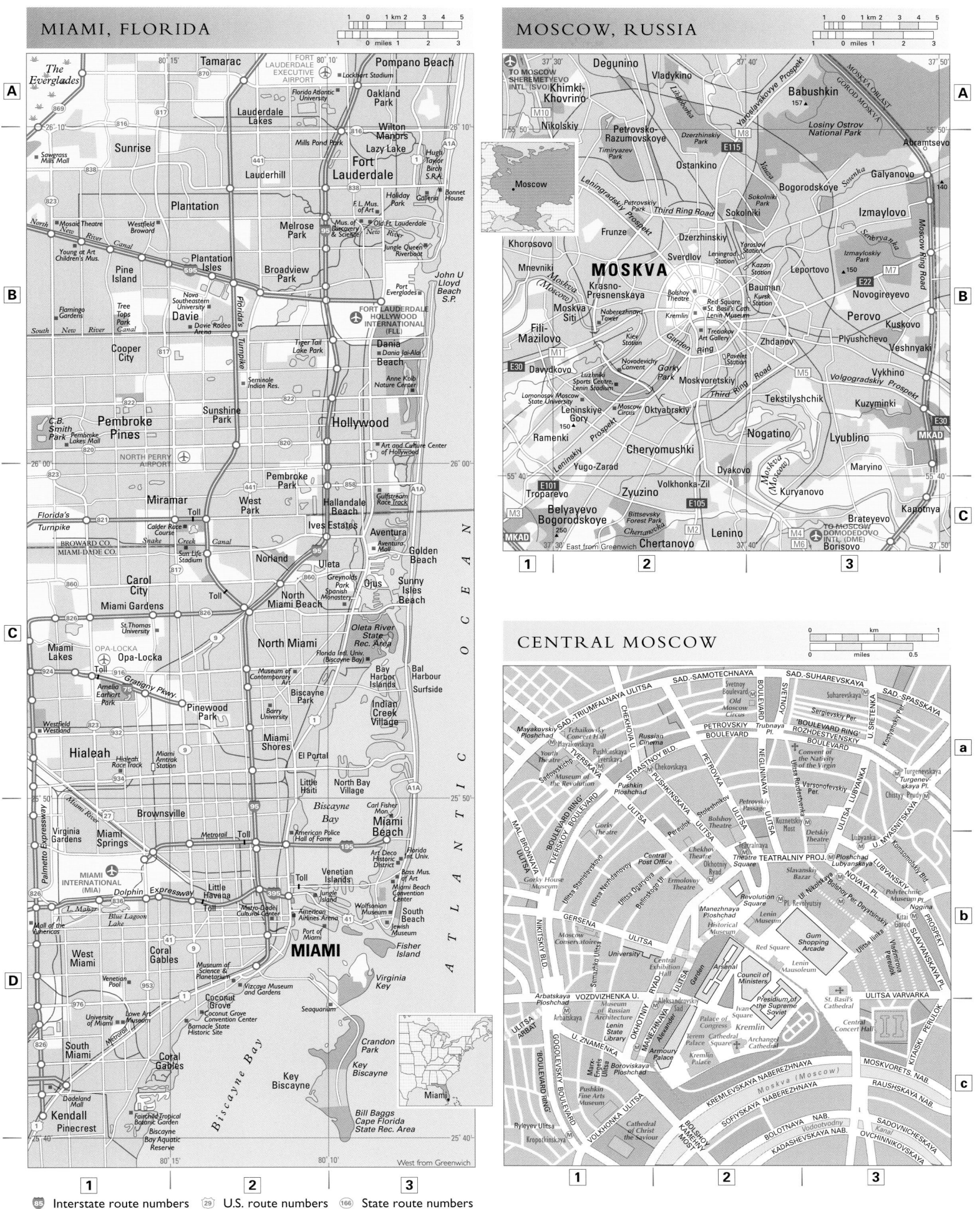

MIAMI, FLORIDA

The Everglades
Tamarac
Pompano Beach
FORT LAUDERDALE EXECUTIVE AIRPORT
Lockhart Stadium
Oakland Park
Sawgrass Mills Mall
Sunrise
Florida Atlantic University
Lauderdale Lakes
Wilton Manors
Lazy Lake
Mills Pond Park
Fort Lauderdale
Hugh Taylor Birch S.R.A.
Lauderhill
Bonnet House
Plantation
Melrose Park
F. L. Mus. of Art
Old Ft. Lauderdale
Mus. of Discovery & Science
Jungle Queen Riverboat
North New River Canal
Mosaic Theatre
Westfield Broward
Young at Art Children's Mus.
Pine Island
Plantation Isles
Broadview Park
Port Everglades
John U Lloyd Beach S.P.
Nova Southeastern University
Flamingo Gardens
Tree Tops Park
Davie
Davie Rodeo Arena
Tiger Tail Lake Park
Dania
Dania Jai-Alai
Dania Beach
South New River Canal
Cooper City
Seminole Indian Res.
Anne Kolb Nature Center
C.B. Smith Park
Pembroke Pines
Pembroke Lakes Mall
Sunshine Park
Hollywood
Art and Culture Center of Hollywood
NORTH PERRY AIRPORT
Pembroke Park
Hallandale Beach
Miramar
Toll
West Park
Gulfstream Race Track
Florida's Turnpike
Calder Race Course
BROWARD CO. MIAMI-DADE CO.
Ives Estates
Aventura
Aventura Mall
Golden Beach
Snake Creek Canal
Norland
Uleta
Greynolds Park Spanish Monastery
Ojus
Sunny Isles Beach
Carol City
Toll
North Miami Beach
Oleta River State Rec. Area
Miami Gardens
St. Thomas University
Bal Harbour
Museum of Contemporary Art
Surfside
Miami Lakes
OPA-LOCKA
Opa-Locka
Toll
North Miami
Bay Harbor Islands
Amelia Earhart Park
Biscayne Park
Indian Creek Village
Gratigny Pkwy.
Florida Intl. Univ. (Biscayne Bay)
Westfield Westland
Pinewood Park
Barry University
Miami Shores
Hialeah
Hialeah Race Track
Miami Amtrak Station
El Portal
Little Haiti
North Bay Village
Brownsville
Biscayne Bay
Carl Fisher Mon.
Miami Beach
Virginia Gardens
Miami Springs
Metrorail
Toll
American Police Hall of Fame
Art Deco Historic District
Florida Intl. Univ.
Bass Mus. of Art
Miami Beach Convention Center
MIAMI INTERNATIONAL (MIA)
Dolphin
Expressway
Little Havana
Toll
Jungle Island
Wolfsonian Museum
South Beach
Jewish Museum
L. Mahar
Blue Lagoon Lake
American Airlines Arena
Port of Miami
Metro-Dade Cultural Center
MIAMI
Fisher Island
Mall of the Americas
West Miami
Venetian Pool
Coral Gables
Museum of Science and Planetarium
Virginia Key
University of Miami
Lowe Art Museum
Vizcaya Museum and Gardens
Coconut Grove
Coconut Grove Convention Center
Barnacle State Historic Site
Seaquarium
South Miami
Coral Gables
Fairchild Tropical Botanic Garden
Crandon Park
Dadeland Mall
Kendall
Pinecrest
Biscayne Bay Aquatic Reserve
Key Biscayne
Key Biscayne
Bill Baggs Cape Florida State Rec. Area
West from Greenwich

Miami

MOSCOW, RUSSIA

TO MOSCOW SHEREMETYEVO INTL. (SVO)
Degunino
Vladykino
Khimki-Khovrino
Nikolskiy
GOROD MOSKVA
Babushkin
Petrovsko-Razumovskoye
Timiryazev Park
Losiny Ostrov National Park
Abramtsevo
Dzerzhinskiy Park
Khorosovo
Ostankino
Galyanovo
Frunze
Sokolniki Park
Bogorodskoye
Sokolniki
Izmaylovo
Mnevniki
Leningradskiy Prospekt
Petrovskiy Park
Yaroslovl Station
Izmaylovskiy Park
MOSKVA
Sverdlov
Kazan Station
Serebryanka
Krasno-Presnenskaya
Moskva (Moskva)
Bolshoy Theatre
Red Square, St. Basil's Cath.
Kursk Station
Leporto vo
Novogireyevo
Moskva Siti
Naberezhnaya Tower
Kremlin
Lenin Museum
Kiev Station
Tretiakov Art Gallery
Perovo
Kuskovo
Fili-Mazilovo
Garden
Zhdanov
Plyushchevo
Veshnyaki
Davdkovo
Novodevichy Convent
Gorky Park
Pavelet Station
Vykhino
E30
Lomonosov Moscow State University
Moskvoretskiy
Volgogradskiy Prospekt
Leninskiye Gory
Luzhniki Sports Centre, Lenin Stadium
Moscow Circus
Oktyabrskiy
Third Ring Road
Tekstilyshchik
Kuzminki
Ramenki
Leninskiy Prospekt
Nogatino
Lyublino
Cheryomushki
Yugo-Zarad
Troparevo
Zyuzino
Volkhonka-Zil
Dyakovo
Maryino
Belyayevo Bogorodskoye
Bittsevsky Forest Park
Chertanovka
Lenino
Kapotnya
MKAD
Chertanovo
Brateyevo
TO MOSCOW DOMODEDOVO INTL. (DME)
Borisovo
East from Greenwich

CENTRAL MOSCOW

SAD.-SAMOTECHNAYA
SAD.-SUHAREVSKAYA
SAD.-SPASSKAYA
Svetnoy Boulevard, Old Moscow Circus
SAD.-TRIUMFALNAYA ULITSA
CHEKHOVA UL.
SVETNOY BOULEVARD
Suharevskaya
Mayakovskiy Ploshchad
Tchaikovsky Concert Hall
Russian Cinema
PETROVSKIY BOULEVARD
Sergievskiy Per.
U. SRETENKA
Mayakovskaya
Trubnaya Pl.
ROZHDESTVENSKIY BOULEVARD
Youth Theatre
TVERSKAYA
Sadovnichiy
Pushkinskaya, Tverskaya
STRASTNOY BLD.
Chekovskaya
Convent of the Nativity of the Virgin
Museum of the Revolution
Pushkin Ploshchad
PUSHKINSKAYA ULITSA
PETROVKA
Varsonofevskiy Per.
U. LUBYANKA
Turgenevskaya
Turgenev-skaya Pl.
MAL. BRONNAYA ULITSA
BOULEVARD RING
TVERSKOY BOULEVARD
Stoleshnik
Petrovskiy Passage
Kuznetskiy Most
Detskiy Theatre
Chistyy Prudy
Gorky Theatre
Bolshoy Theatre
ULITSA
Lubyanka
Ploshchad Lubyanskaya
U. MYASNITSKAYA
Ulitsa Stanislavsky
Ulitsa Ogareva
Belinskogo U.
Ermolovoy Theatre
Chekhov Theatre
Teatralnaya
Slavyanskiy Bazar
NOVAYA PL.
Polytechnic Museum
Nogina
GERSENA
NIKITSKIY BLD.
Central Post Office
Okhotny Ryad
TEATRALNIY PROJ.
Revolution Square
Bolshoy Per. Dryatinskiy
PROSPEKT
Moscow Conservatoire
Teatralnaya Square
Pl. Revolyutsiy
Lenin Museum
Kitai Gorod
University
Semashko Ulitsa
Historical Museum
Manezhnaya Ploshchad
Gum Shopping Arcade
SLAVYANSKAYA PL.
Central Exhibition Hall
MANEZHNAYA
Red Square
Lenin Mausoleum
Kitaiskiy Perulok
Arbatskaya Ploshchad
VOZDVIZHENKA U.
OKHOTNIY RYAD
Garden
Arsenal
ULITSA VARVARKA
Museum of Russian Architecture
Aleksandrovsky Sad
Council of Ministers
St. Basil's Cathedral
ULITSA ARBAT
U. ZNAMENKA
Lenin State Library
Alexander Garden
Ivan the Great
Presidium of the Supreme Soviet
MOSKVORETS. NAB.
Terem Palace
Palace of Congress
Kremlin Square
Kremlin
Archangel Cathedral
Central Concert Hall
RAUSHSKAYA NAB.
GOGOLEVSKIY BOULEVARD
Armoury Palace
Kremlin Palace
Marx Engels Ulitsa
Borovitskaya Ploshchad
SOFIYSKAYA NAB.
Pushkin Fine Arts Museum
VOLKHONKA ULITSA
Moskva (Moscow)
KREMLEVSKAYA NABEREZHNAYA
BOLOTNAYA NAB.
SADOVNICHESKAYA
BOULEVARD RING
Ryleyev Ulitsa
Cathedral of Christ the Saviour
BOLSHOY KAMENNY MOST
BOLOTNAYA NAB.
Vodootvodny Kanal
OVCHINNIKOVSKAYA
Kropotkinskaya
KADASHEVSKAYA NAB.

85 Interstate route numbers   29 U.S. route numbers   166 State route numbers

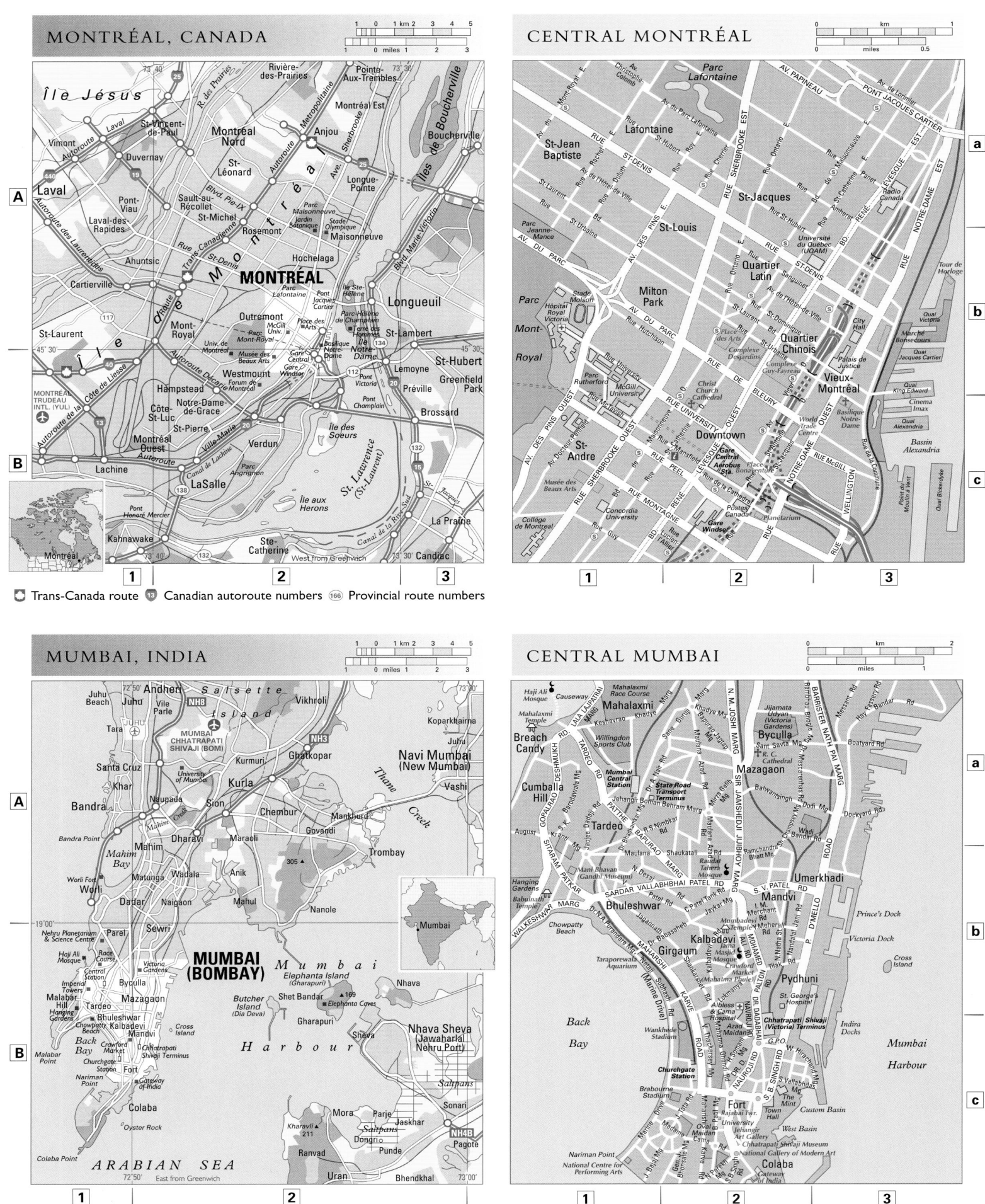

MONTRÉAL, CANADA

CENTRAL MONTRÉAL

Trans-Canada route   Canadian autoroute numbers   Provincial route numbers

MUMBAI, INDIA

CENTRAL MUMBAI

MUNICH, GERMANY

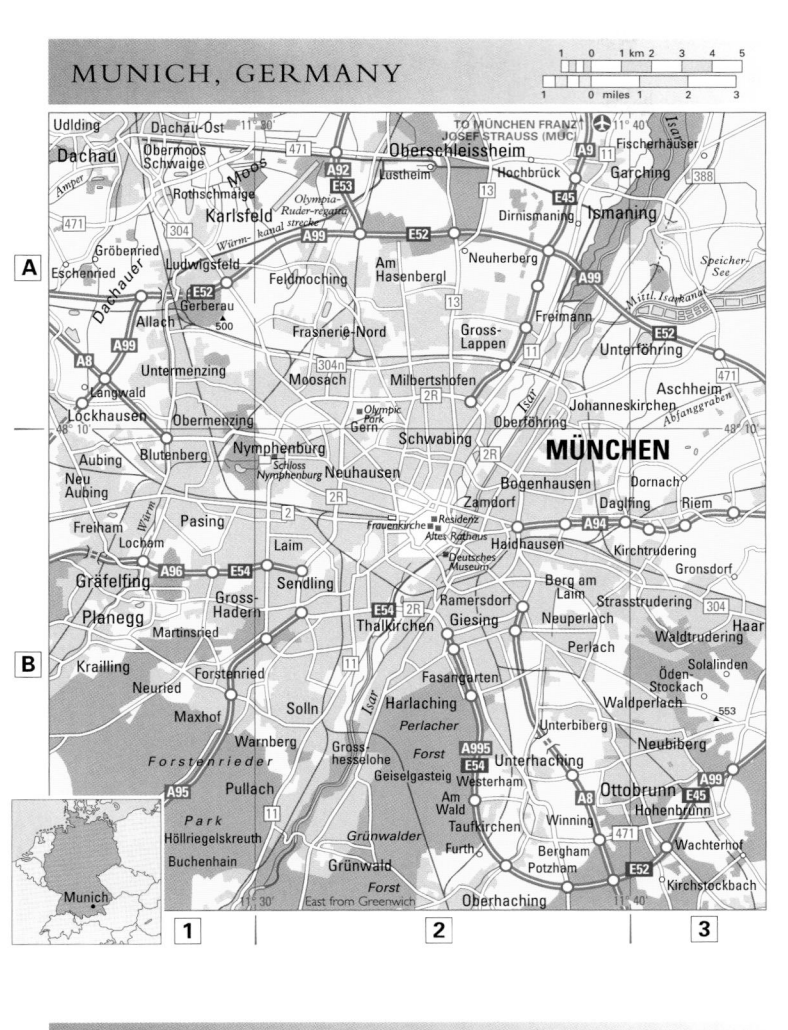

CENTRAL MUNICH

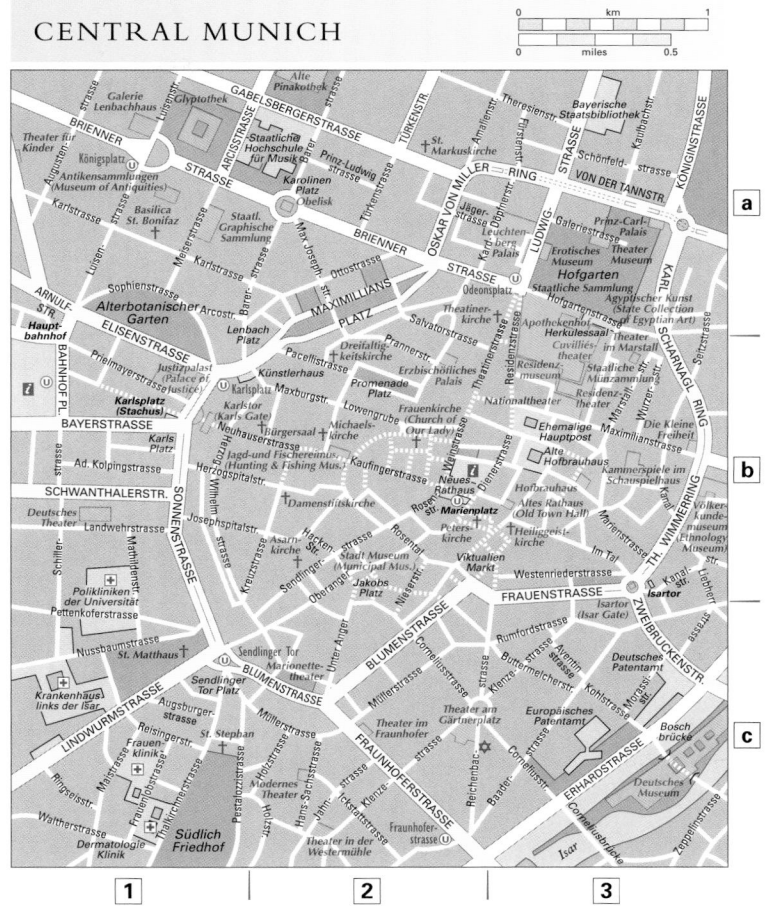

NEW ORLEANS, LOUISIANA

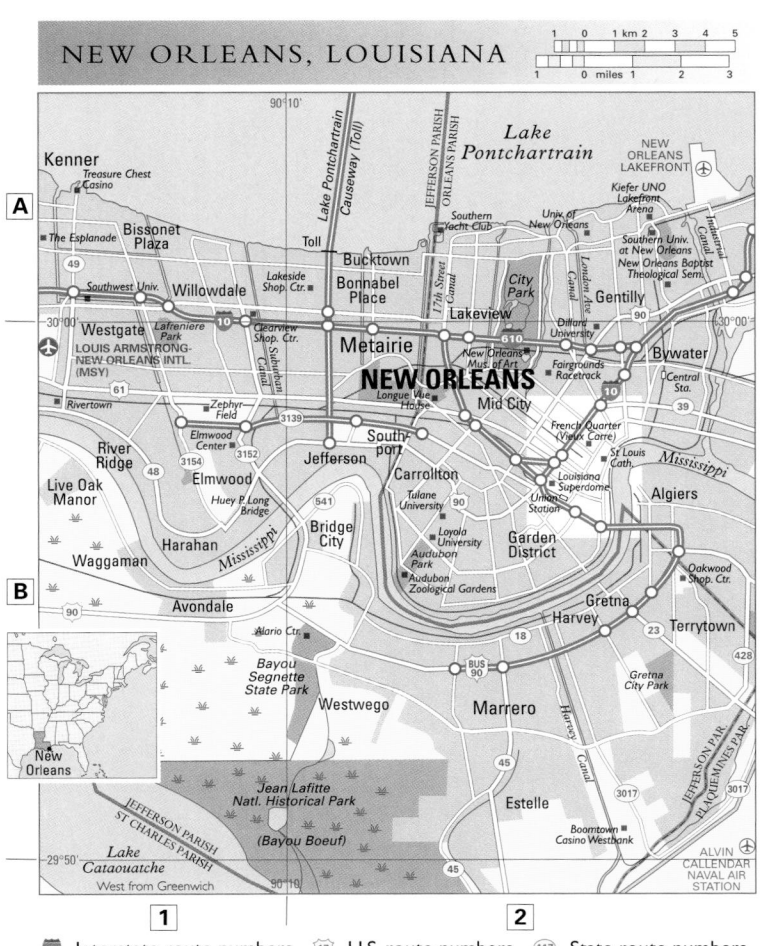

CENTRAL NEW ORLEANS

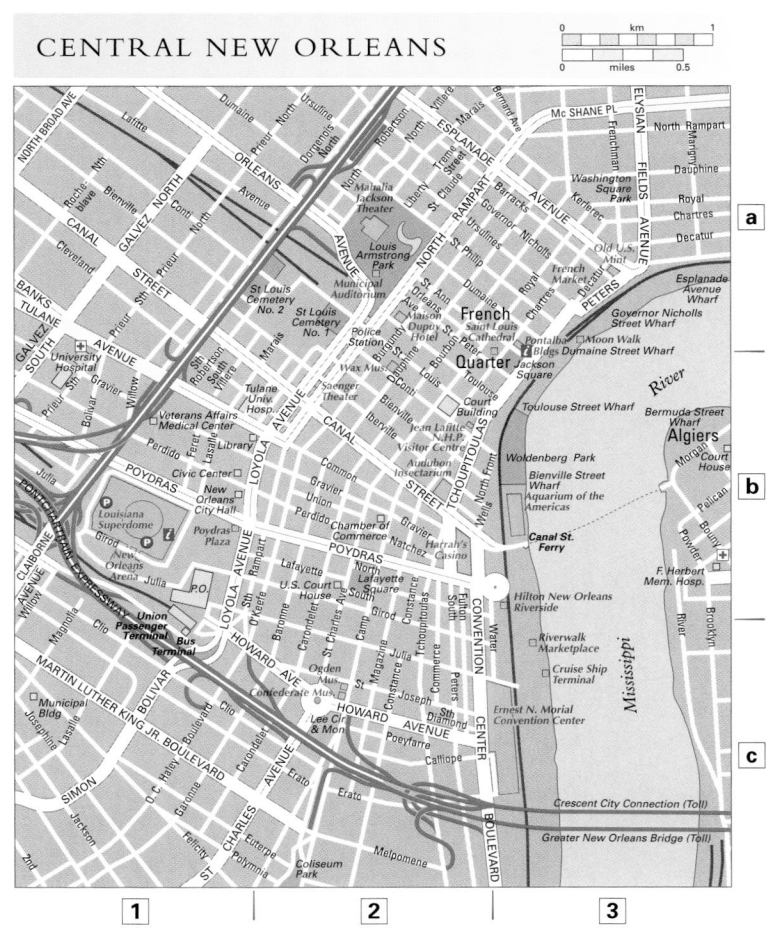

Interstate route numbers   U.S. route numbers   State route numbers

COPYRIGHT PHILIP'S

NEW YORK, NEW YORK

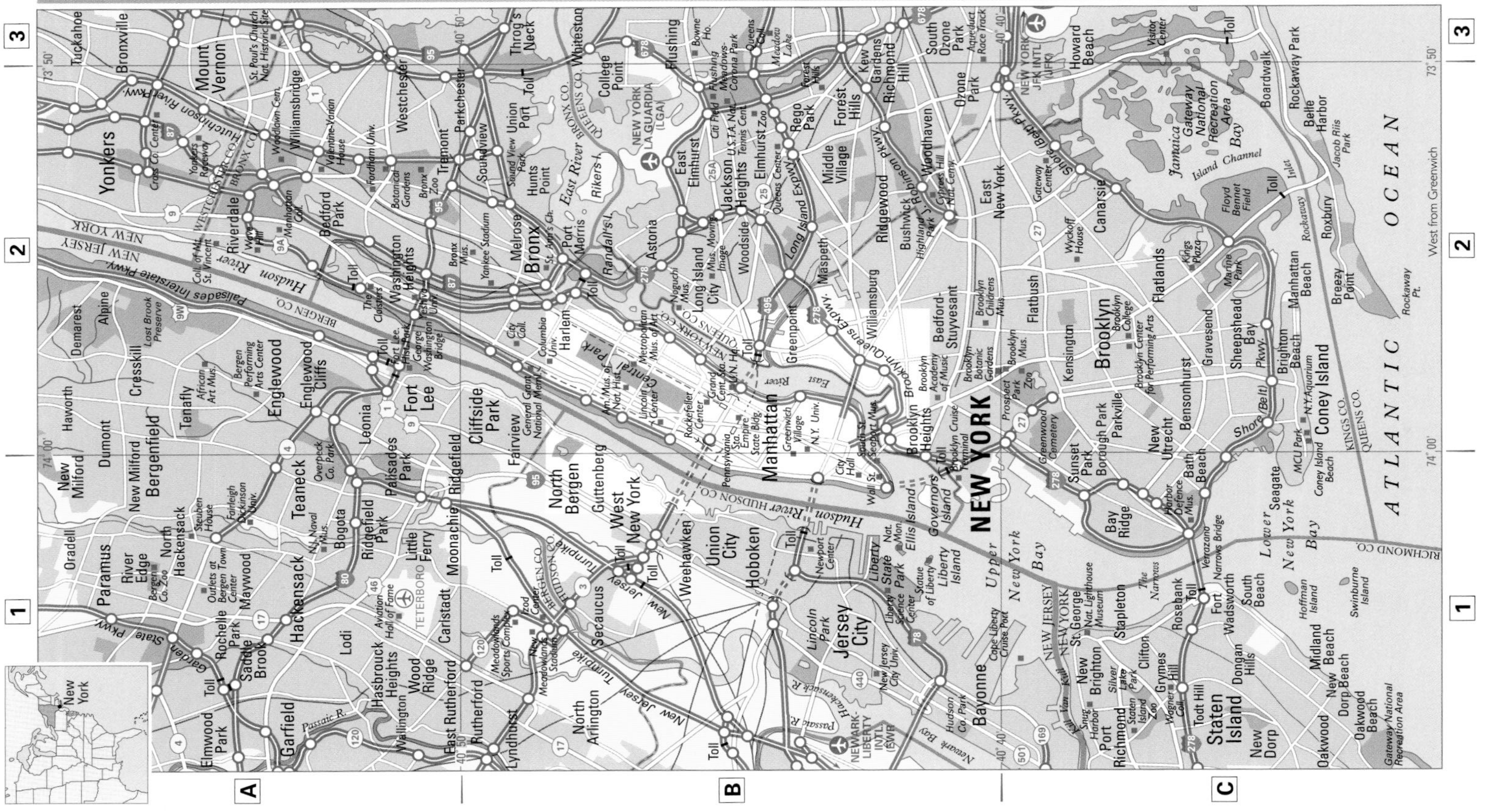

km miles

ATLANTIC OCEAN

NEW JERSEY

Yonkers · Mount Vernon · Bronxville · Tuckahoe · Westchester · Pelham · Williamsbridge · Throg's Neck · Whitestone · Flushing · College Point · South Ozone Park · Howard Beach · Rockaway Park · Bay Harbor

Bronx · Washington Heights · Tremont · Melrose · Hunts Point · Astoria · Long Island City · Woodside · Middle Village · Ridgewood · Maspeth · Bushwick · East New York · Canarsie · Flatlands

Englewood · Fort Lee · Cliffside Park · Fairview · North Bergen · West New York · Weehawken · Union City · Hoboken · Harlem · Manhattan · Central Park · Brooklyn Heights · NEW YORK · Greenpoint · Williamsburg · Bedford-Stuyvesant · Flatbush · Brooklyn · Gravesend · Sheepshead Bay · Brighton Beach · Coney Island

Paramus · Hackensack · Teaneck · Ridgefield Park · Secaucus · Jersey City · Bayonne · Staten Island · New Brighton · Bay Ridge · Sunset Park · Bensonhurst · New Utrecht

NEWARK INTL. (EWR) · LIBERTY · NEW JERSEY · New Dorp · Oakwood

New York (inset)

A   B   C

CENTRAL NEW YORK

km miles

Harlem · Upper West Side · Central Park · Upper East Side · Midtown · Manhattan · Queens · Long Island City · Greenpoint · Williamsburg · Brooklyn

Hudson River · West New York · Guttenberg · Weehawken · Union City · Hoboken

East River · Roosevelt Island · Queensboro Bridge · United Nations Headquarters · Grand Central Sta. · Times Square · Port Authority Bus Terminal · Penn Sta. · Chelsea · Greenwich Village · East Village · Stuyvesant Town · Lower East Side

Little Italy · China Town · Soho · Tribeca · West Village · Lower Manhattan · Brooklyn Heights · Fort Greene · Brooklyn

Battery Park · Ellis & Liberty Ferry · Staten Island Ferry · Governors Island · Brooklyn-Battery Tunnel · Williamsburg Bridge · Manhattan Bridge · Brooklyn Bridge

a   b   c   d   e   f

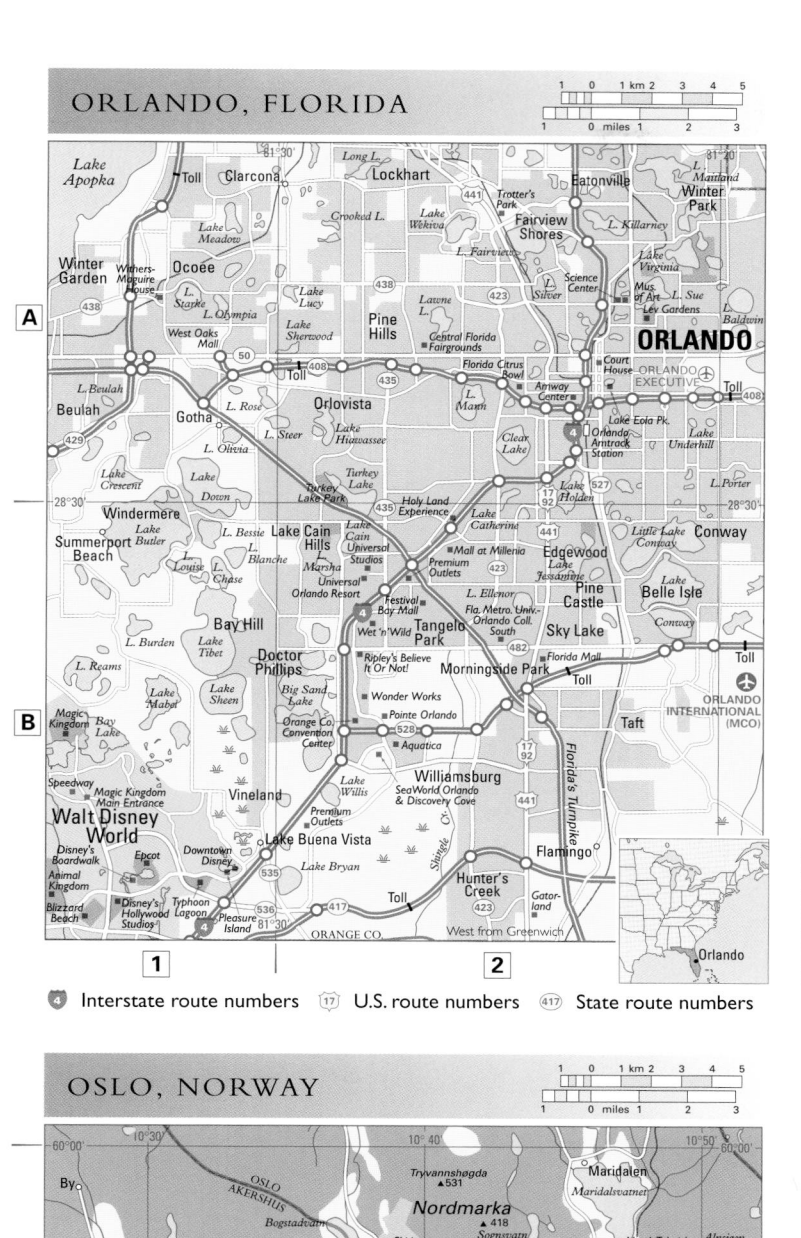

ORLANDO, FLORIDA

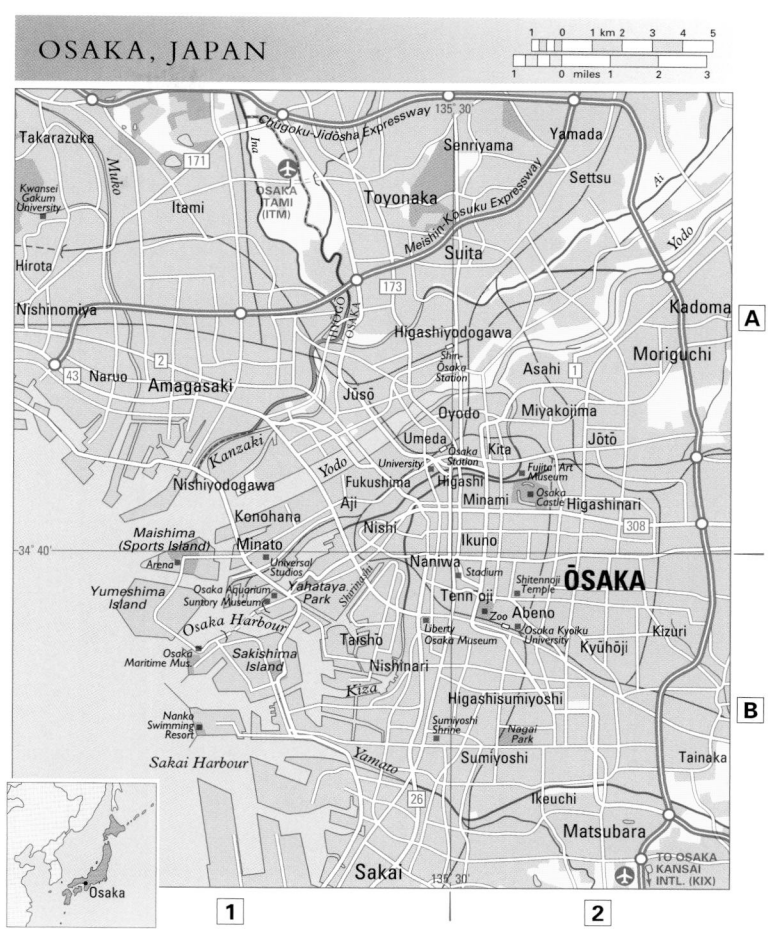

OSAKA, JAPAN

Interstate route numbers   U.S. route numbers   State route numbers

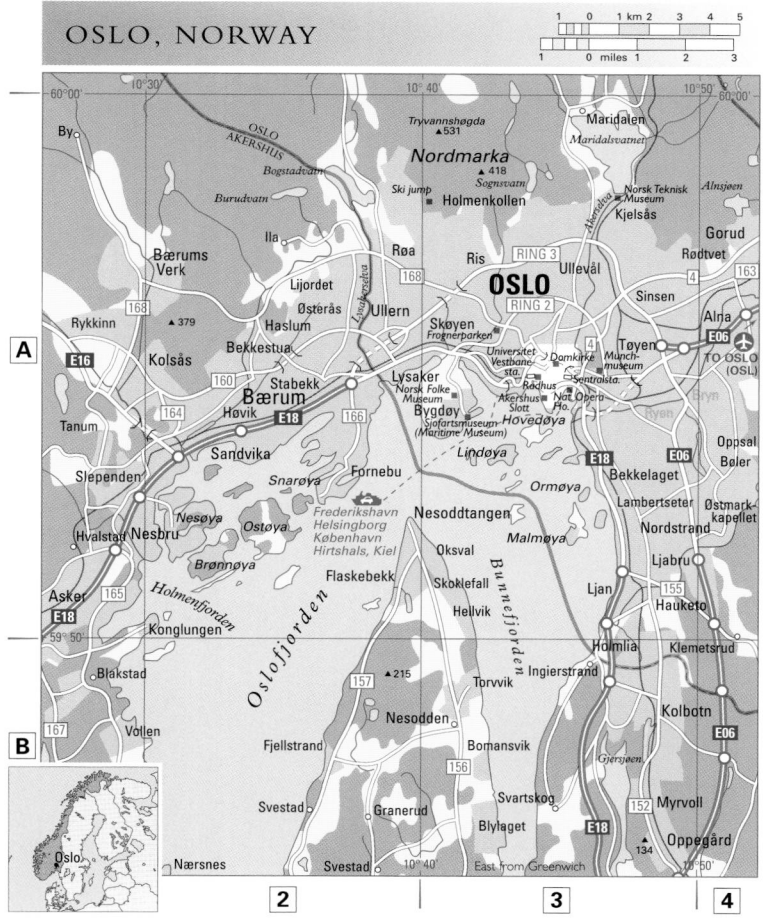

OSLO, NORWAY

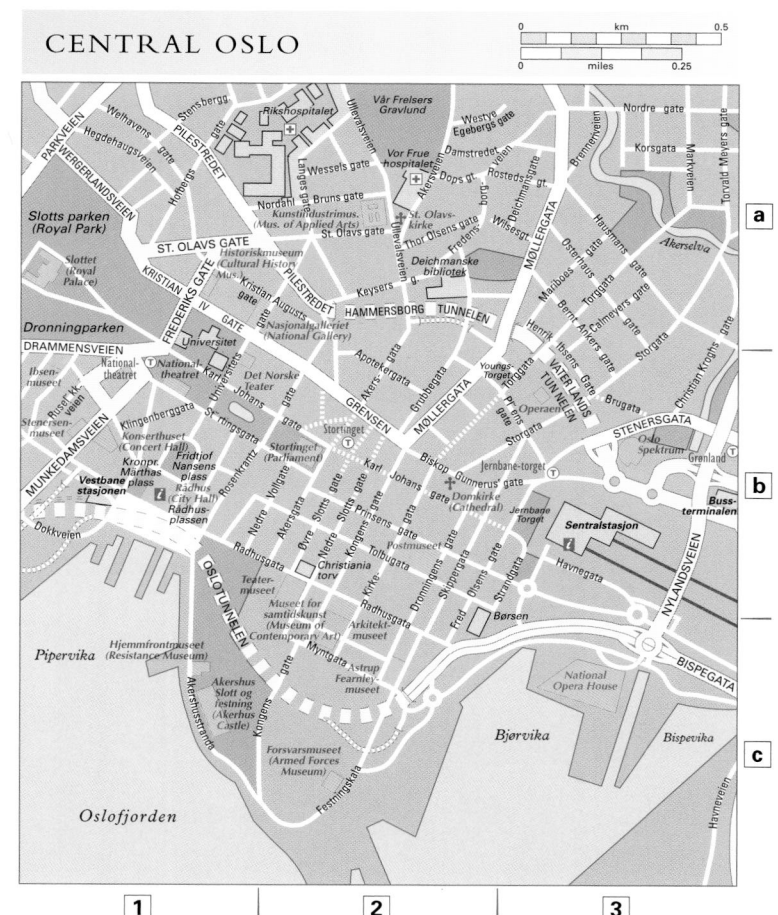

CENTRAL OSLO

COPYRIGHT PHILIP'S

PARIS, FRANCE

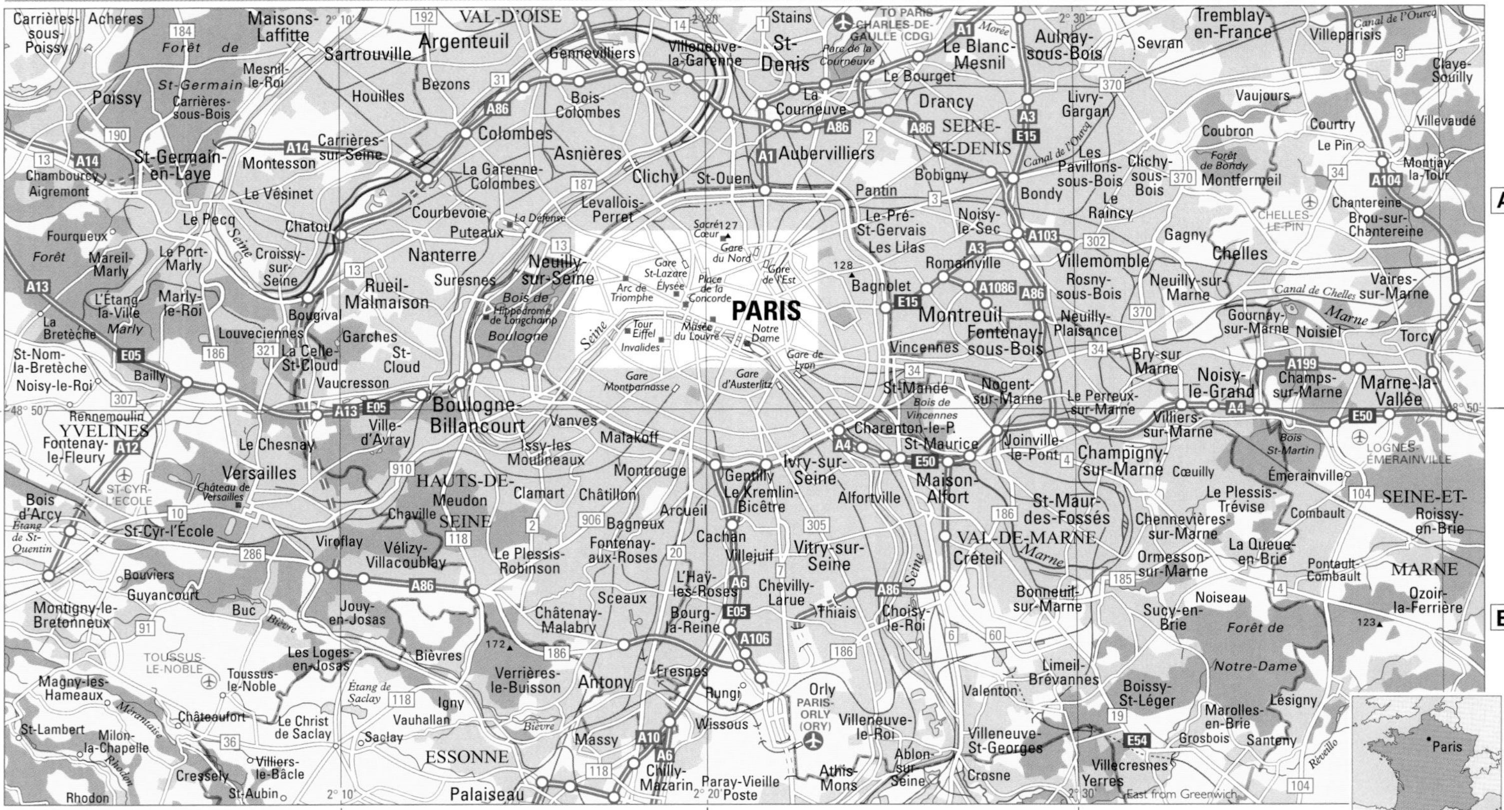

1 0 1 km 2 3 4 5
1 0 miles 1 2 3

Carrières-sous-Poissy · Achères · Maisons-Laffitte · Forêt de · VAL-D'OISE · Argenteuil · Gennevilliers · Villeneuve-la-Garenne · Stains · St-Denis · TO PARIS CHARLES-DE-GAULLE (CDG) · Le Blanc-Mesnil · Aulnay-sous-Bois · Sevran · Tremblay-en-France · Villeparisis · Canal de l'Ourcq · Claye-Souilly · Villevaudé

Poissy · St-Germain-le-Roi · Mesnil-le-Roi · Sartrouville · Houilles · Bezons · Bois-Colombes · Colombes · Asnières · La Courneuve · Le Bourget · Drancy · Livry-Gargan · Coubron · Courtry · Le Pin · Montjay-la-Tour

St-Germain-en-Laye · Montesson · Carrières-sur-Seine · La Garenne-Colombes · Clichy · St-Ouen · Aubervilliers · SEINE-ST-DENIS · Bobigny · Les Pavillons-sous-Bois · Montfermeil · Chantereine · Brou-sur-Chantereine

A

Le Pecq · Le Vésinet · Chatou · Courbevoie · Puteaux · La Défense · Levallois-Perret · Pantin · Le Pré-St-Gervais · Les Lilas · Noisy-le-Sec · Romainville · Villemomble · Rosny-sous-Bois · Neuilly-sur-Marne · Gagny · Chelles · Vaires-sur-Marne

Fourqueux · Mareil-Marly · Le Port-Marly · Croissy-sur-Seine · Nanterre · Neuilly-sur-Seine · Gare St-Lazare · Arc de Triomphe · Place de la Concorde · Gare du Nord · Gare de l'Est · Bagnolet · **PARIS** · Montreuil · Fontenay-sous-Bois · Noisiel · Torcy

L'Étang-la-Ville · Marly-le-Roi · Louveciennes · Rueil-Malmaison · Bougival · Garches · St-Cloud · Bois de Boulogne · Musée du Louvre · Notre Dame · Vincennes · Nogent-sur-Marne · Le Perreux-sur-Marne · Noisy-le-Grand · Champs-sur-Marne · Marne-la-Vallée

St-Nom-la-Bretèche · Noisy-le-Roi · La Celle-St-Cloud · Vaucresson · Tour Eiffel · Musée Invalides · Gare Montparnasse · Gare d'Austerlitz · Gare de Lyon · St-Mandé · Bois de Vincennes · Champigny-sur-Marne · Émerainville

YVELINES · Fontenay-le-Fleury · Versailles · Ville-d'Avray · Boulogne-Billancourt · Vanves · Malakoff · Charenton-le-P. · St-Maurice · Joinville-le-Pont · Bry-sur-Marne · Villiers-sur-Marne · SEINE-ET-MARNE

B

Bois d'Arcy · Château de Versailles · St-Cyr-l'École · HAUTS-DE-SEINE · Meudon · Clamart · Châtillon · Montrouge · Issy-les-Moulineaux · Gentilly · Le Kremlin-Bicêtre · Ivry-sur-Seine · Alfortville · Maisons-Alfort · St-Maur-des-Fossés · Chennevières-sur-Marne · Le Plessis-Trévise · Combault · MARNE · Ozoir-la-Ferrière

Viroflay · Vélizy-Villacoublay · Le Plessis-Robinson · Bagneux · Fontenay-aux-Roses · Cachan · Arcueil · Villejuif · Vitry-sur-Seine · Créteil · Ormesson-sur-Marne · La Queue-en-Brie · Roissy-en-Brie

Bouviers · Guyancourt · Buc · Sceaux · Châtenay-Malabry · L'Haÿ-les-Roses · Chevilly-Larue · Thiais · Choisy-le-Roi · Bonneuil-sur-Marne · Sucy-en-Brie · Noiseau · Forêt de Notre-Dame

Montigny-le-Bretonneux · TOUSSUS-LE-NOBLE · Bièvres · Verrières-le-Buisson · Antony · Fresnes · Rungis · Orly PARIS-ORLY (ORY) · Villeneuve-le-Roi · Valenton · Limeil-Brévannes · Boissy-St-Léger · Lésigny · Santeny

Magny-les-Hameaux · Milon-la-Chapelle · Le Christ de Saclay · Saclay · Vauhallan · Igny · Massy · Wissous · Athis-Mons · Ablon-sur-Seine · Crosne · Marolles-en-Brie · Grosbois · Villecresnes · Yerres

St-Lambert · Châteaufort · Les Loges-en-Josas · Jouy-en-Josas · ESSONNE · Chilly-Mazarin · Paray-Vieille-Poste · East from Greenwich

Cressely · St-Aubin · Palaiseau · Rhodon

1 2 3 4

CENTRAL PARIS

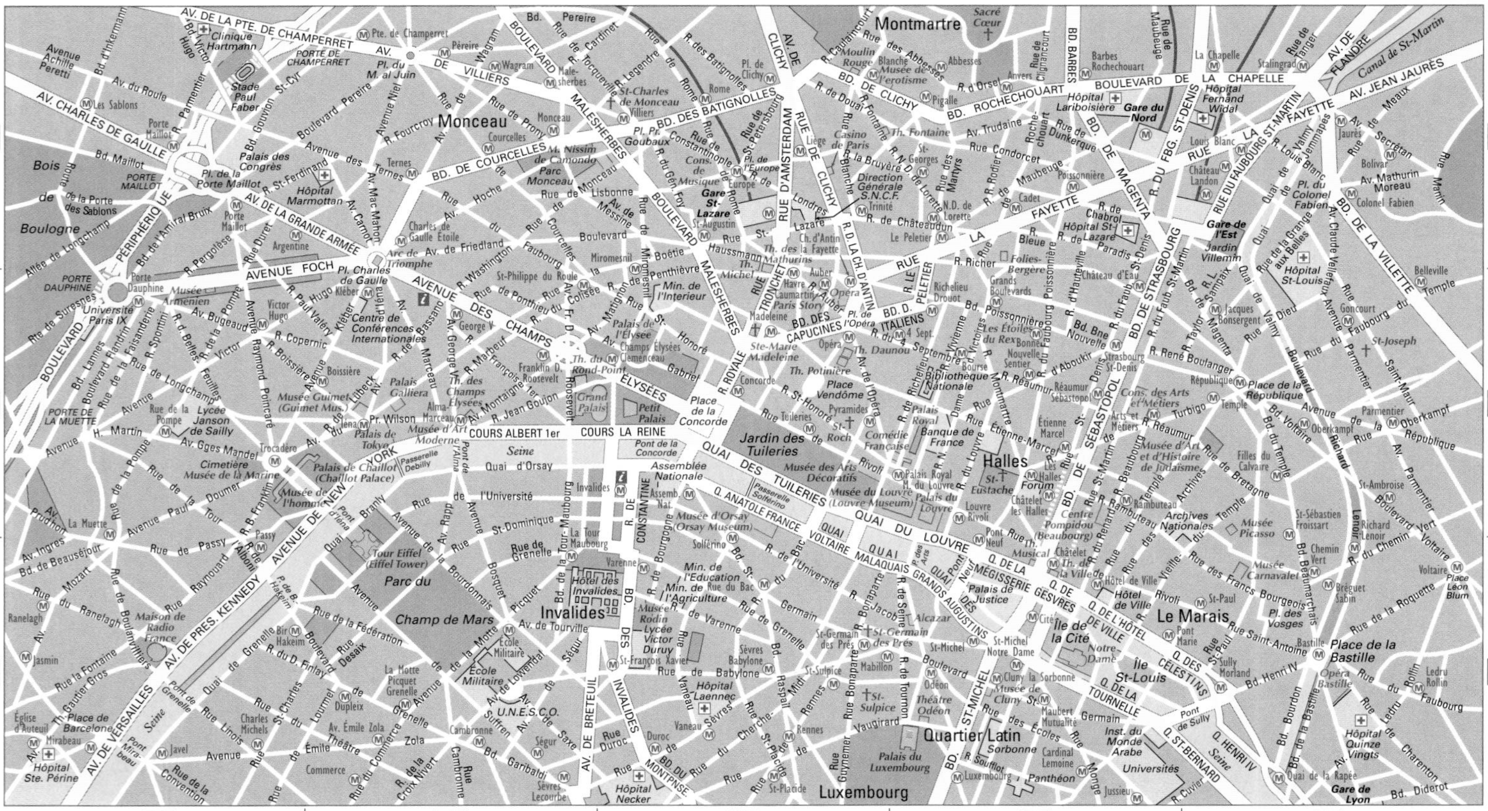

0 km 1
0 miles 0.5

Montmartre · Sacré Cœur · Av. de Clichy · Bd. de la Chapelle · Gare du Nord · Av. de Flandre · Canal de St-Martin

a

Monceau · Parc Monceau · Gare St-Lazare · Gare de l'Est · Jardin Villemin

Bois de Boulogne · PORTE MAILLOT · Avenue Foch · Arc de Triomphe · Hôpital St-Louis · Belleville

b

PORTE DAUPHINE · AVENUE DES CHAMPS ÉLYSÉES · Place de la Concorde · Jardin des Tuileries · Halles · Centre Pompidou · Place de la République

Musée Guimet · Palais de Tokyo · Grand Palais · Petit Palais · Musée du Louvre · Musée d'Orsay

Tour Eiffel Tower · Parc du Champ de Mars · Invalides · Assemblée Nationale · Île de la Cité · Le Marais · Place de la Bastille

c

U.N.E.S.C.O. · Hôpital Laennec · St-Sulpice · Quartier Latin · Palais du Luxembourg · Panthéon · Gare de Lyon · Luxembourg

1 2 3 4 5

PRAGUE, CZECH REPUBLIC

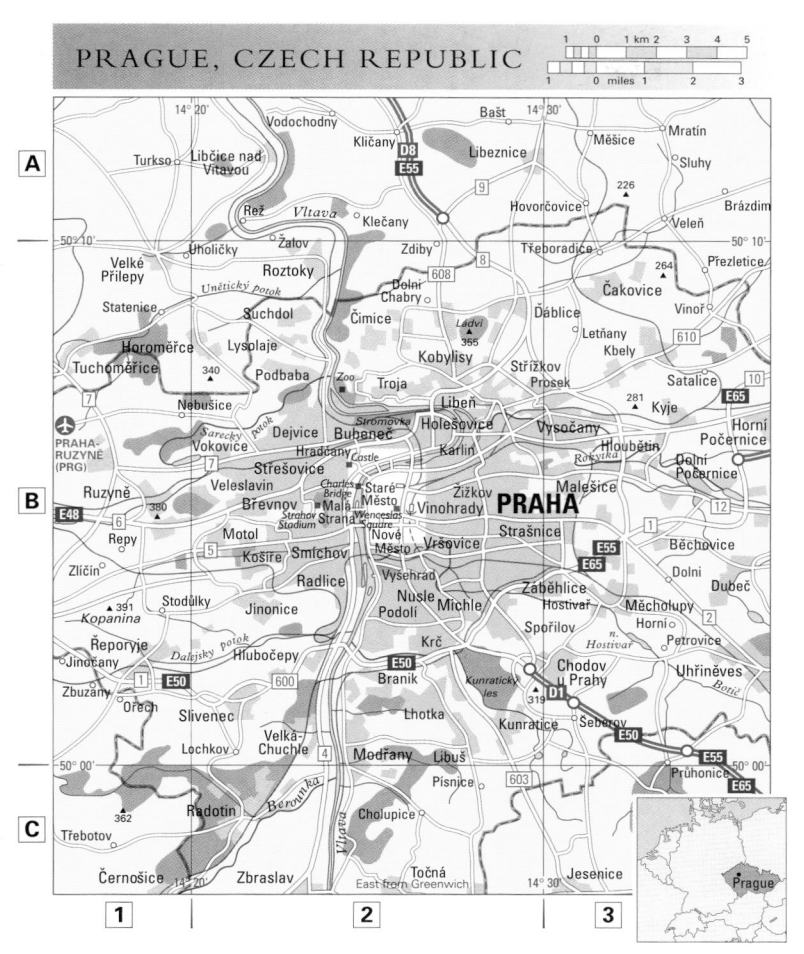

CENTRAL PRAGUE

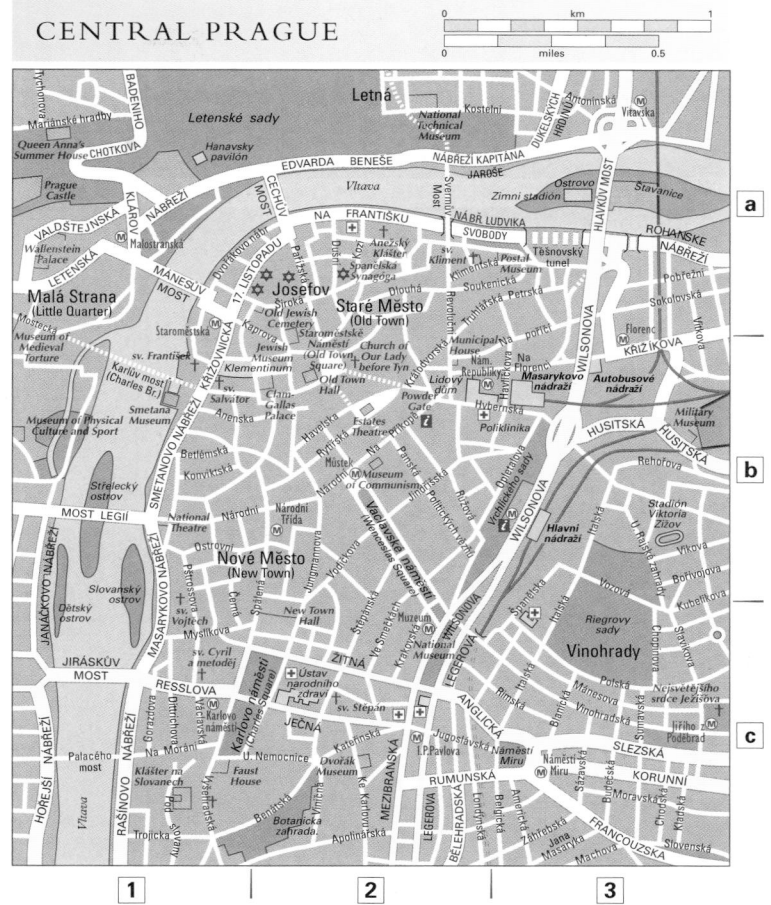

RIO DE JANEIRO, BRAZIL

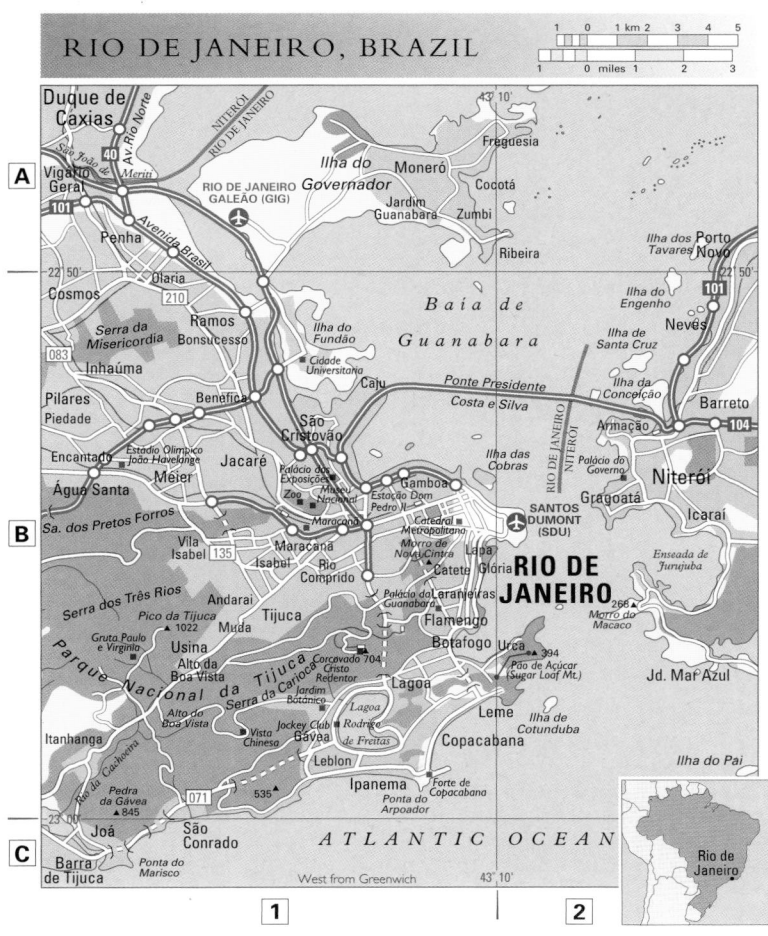

CENTRAL RIO DE JANEIRO

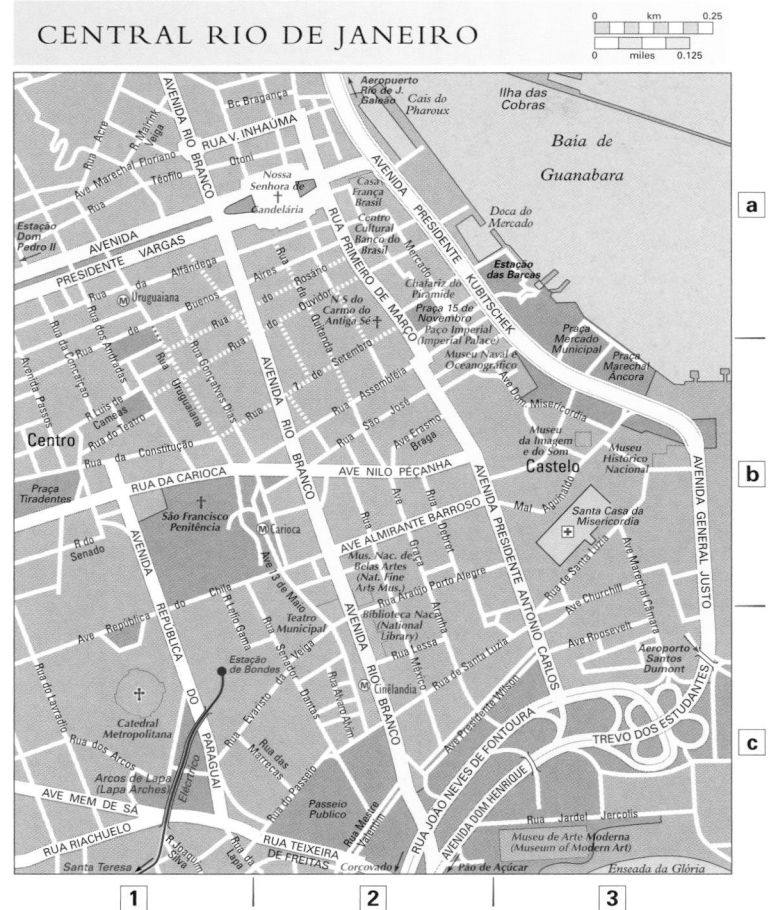

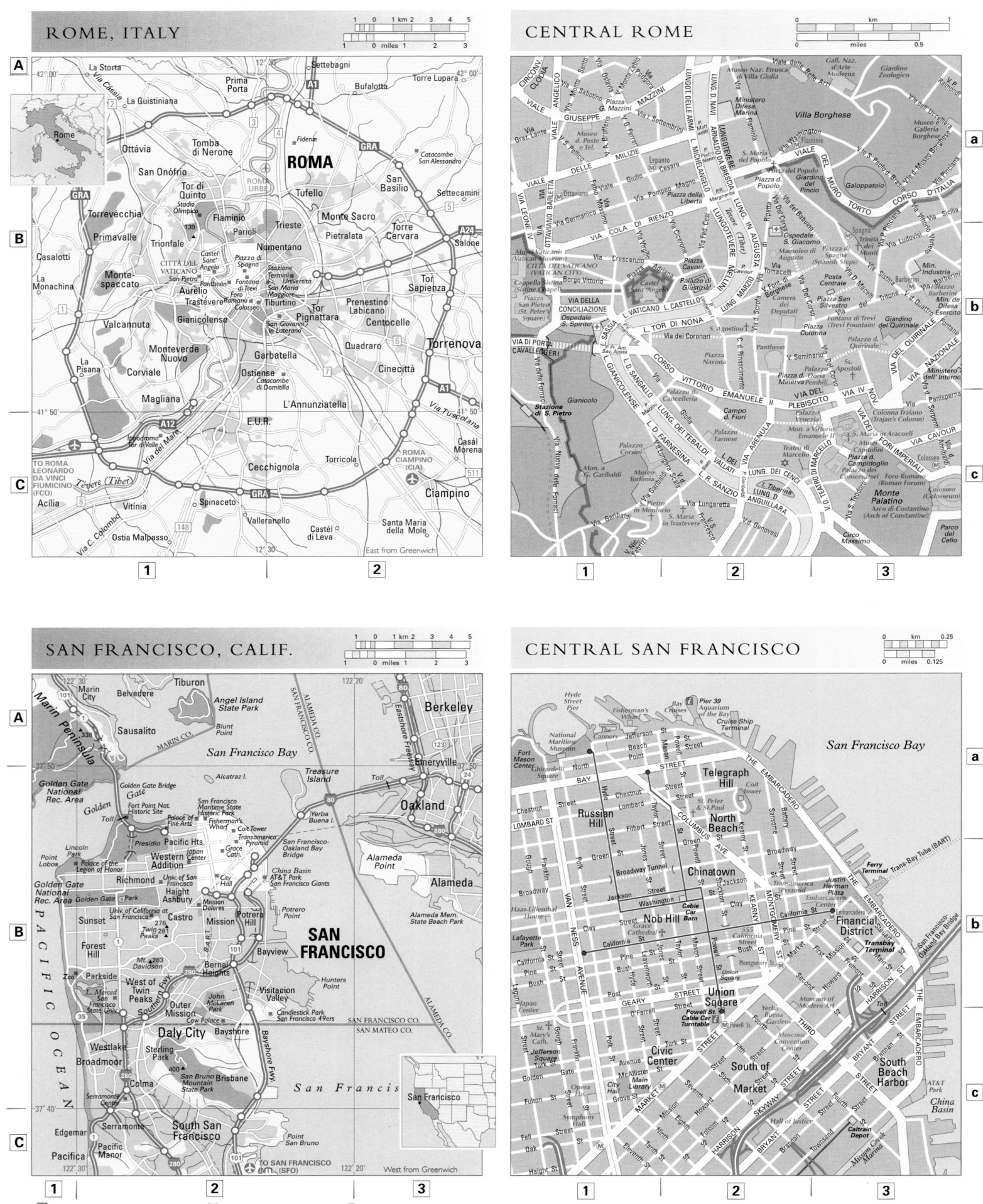

ROME, ITALY

CENTRAL ROME

SAN FRANCISCO, CALIF.

CENTRAL SAN FRANCISCO

Interstate route numbers   U.S. route numbers   State route numbers

Cable Car route

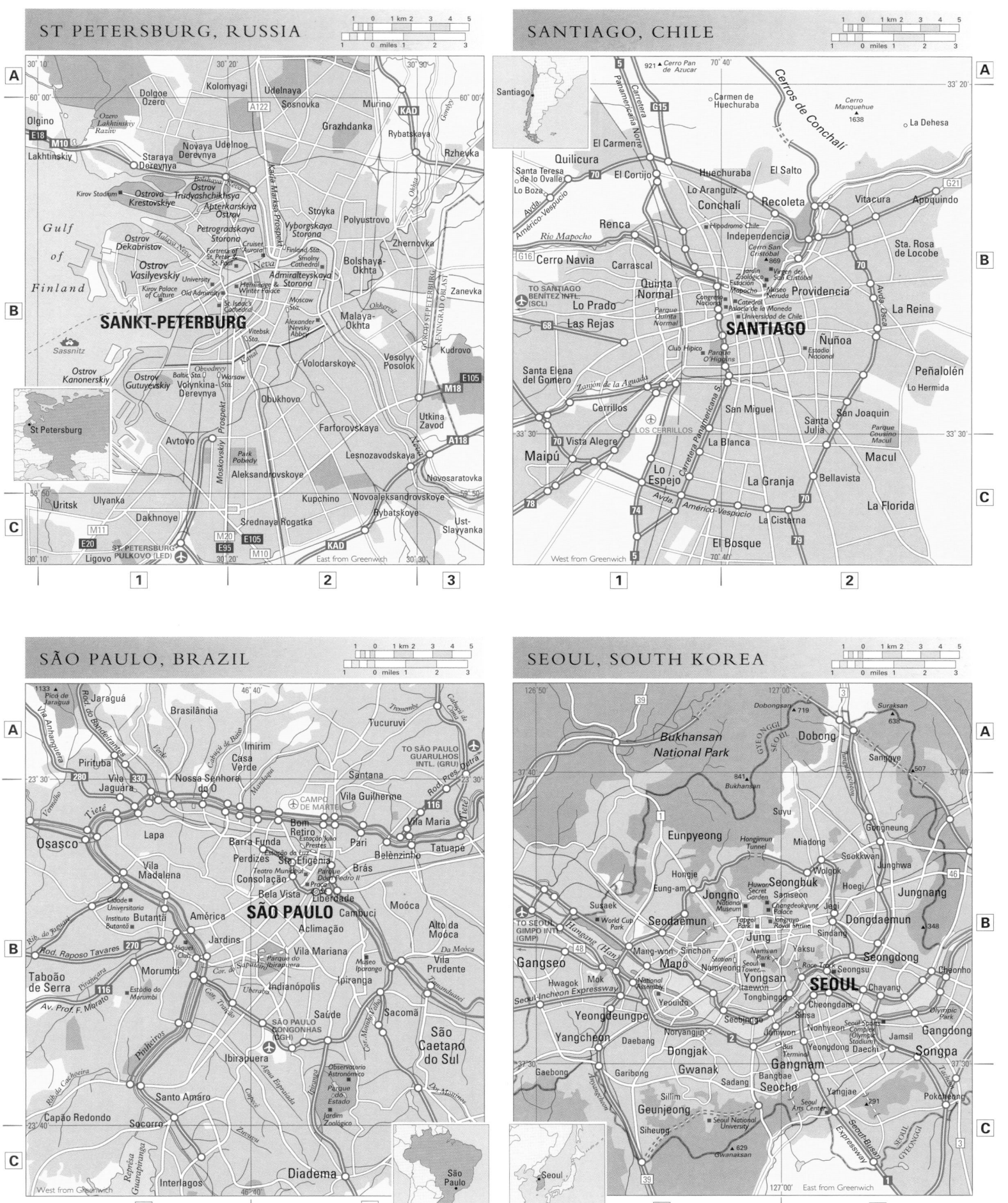

ST PETERSBURG, RUSSIA

Gulf of Finland

Sankt-Peterburg

SANTIAGO, CHILE

Santiago

SANTIAGO

SÃO PAULO, BRAZIL

SÃO PAULO

SEOUL, SOUTH KOREA

Bukhansan National Park

SEOUL

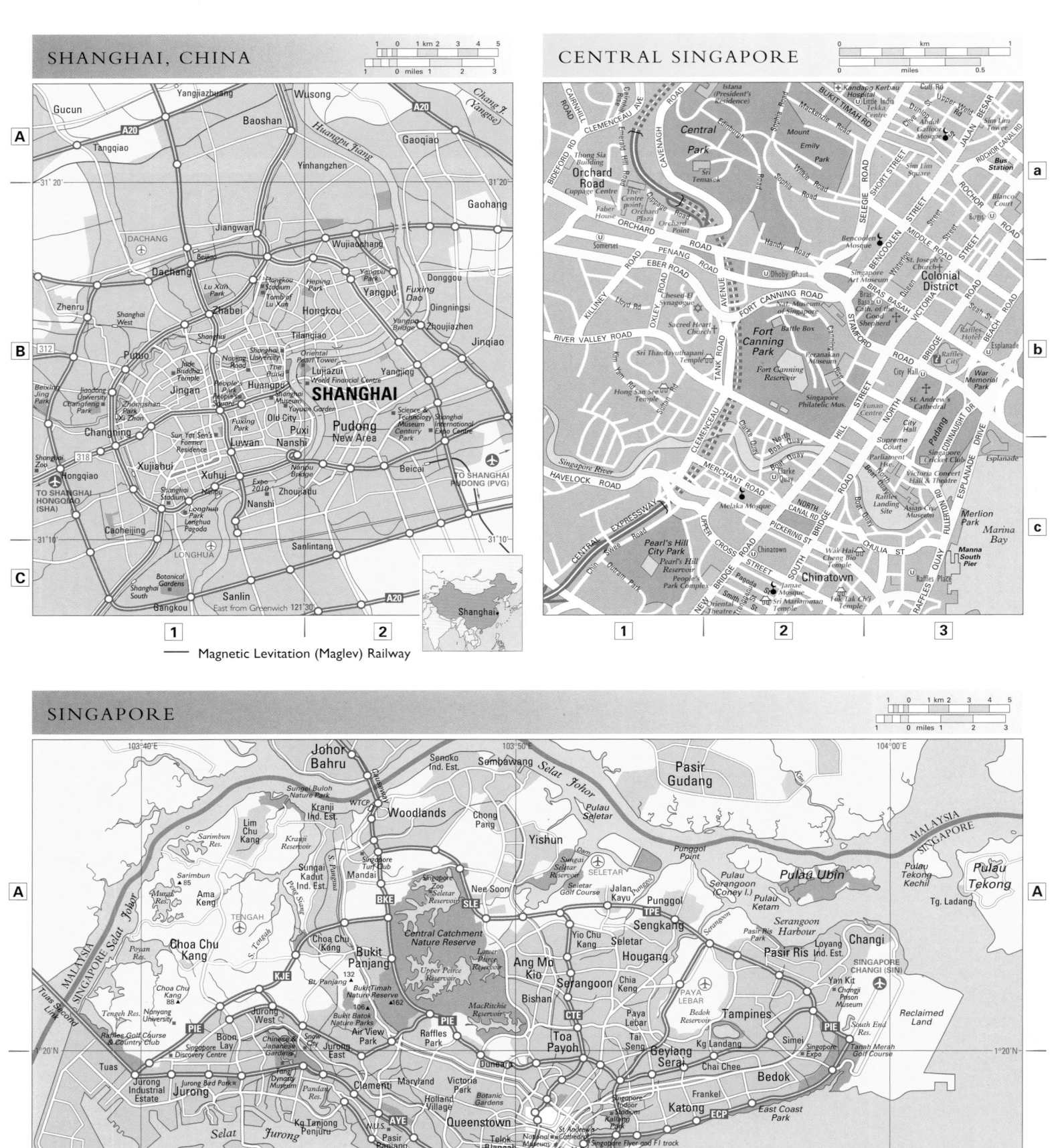

SHANGHAI, CHINA

CENTRAL SINGAPORE

Magnetic Levitation (Maglev) Railway

SINGAPORE

STOCKHOLM, SWEDEN

CENTRAL STOCKHOLM

SYDNEY, AUSTRALIA

CENTRAL SYDNEY

—Ⓜ— Monorail

COPYRIGHT PHILIP'S

TOKYO, JAPAN

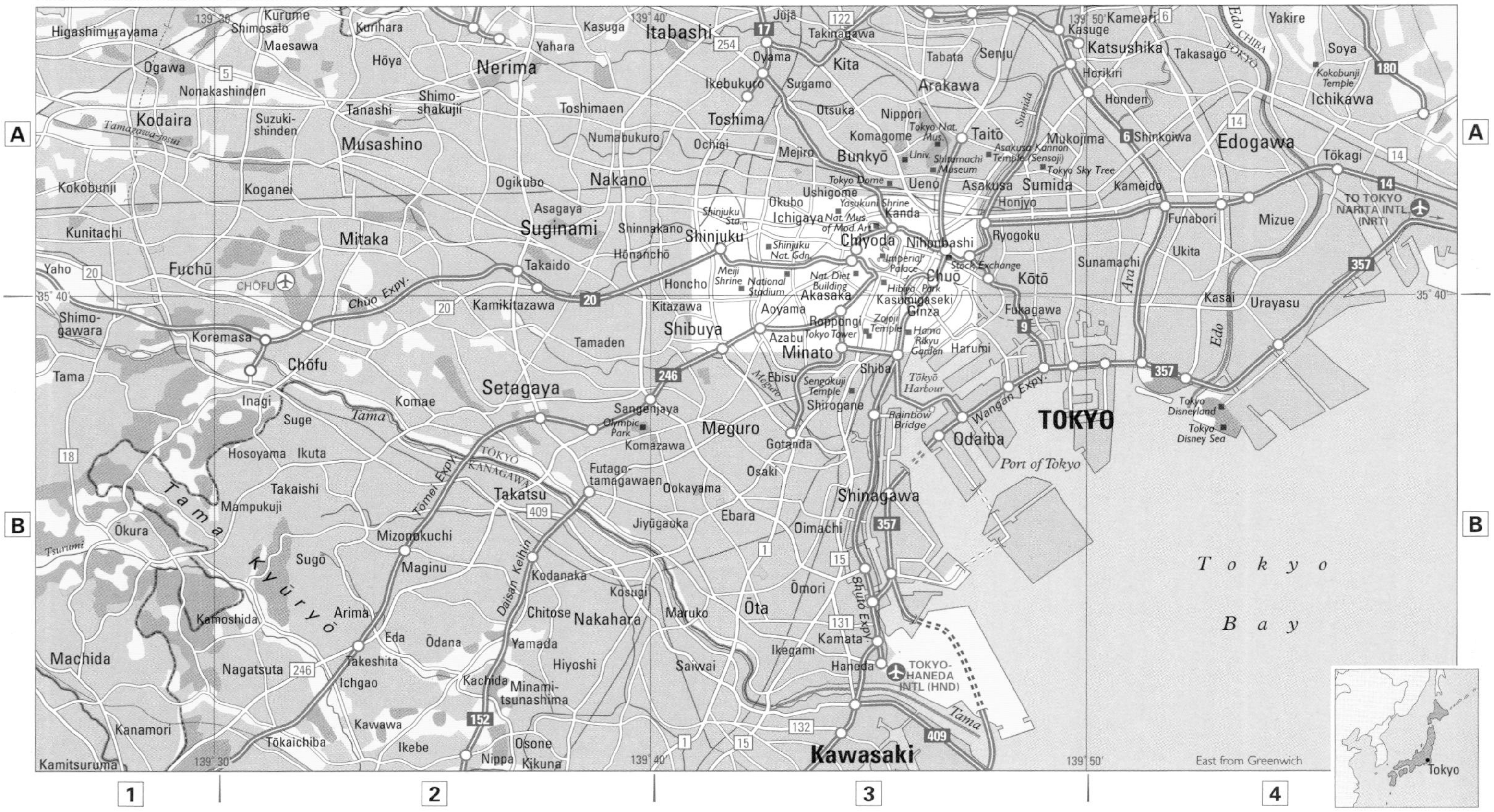

CENTRAL TOKYO

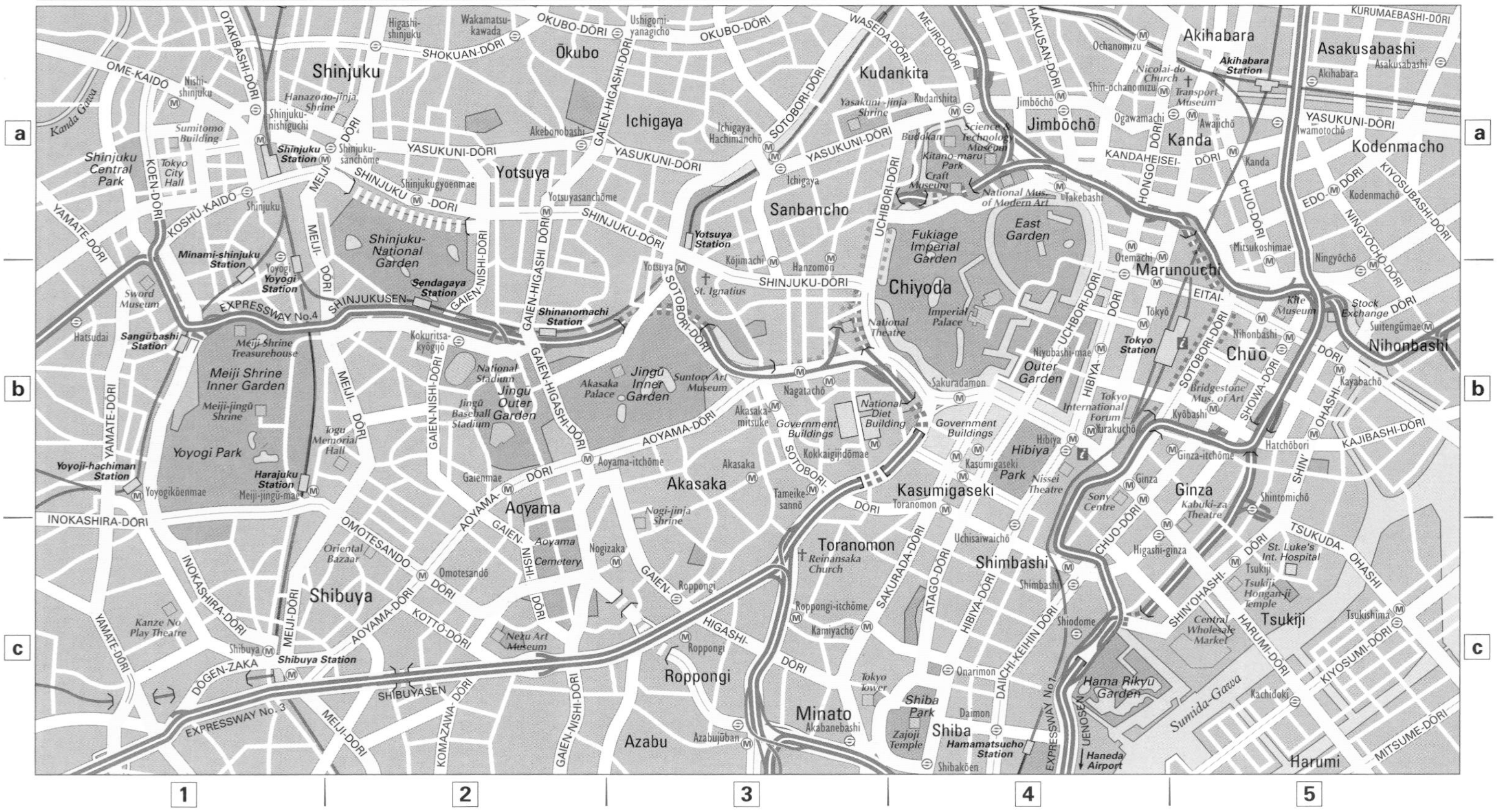

Ⓢ Toei Subway   Ⓜ Tokyo Metro

TEHRAN, IRAN

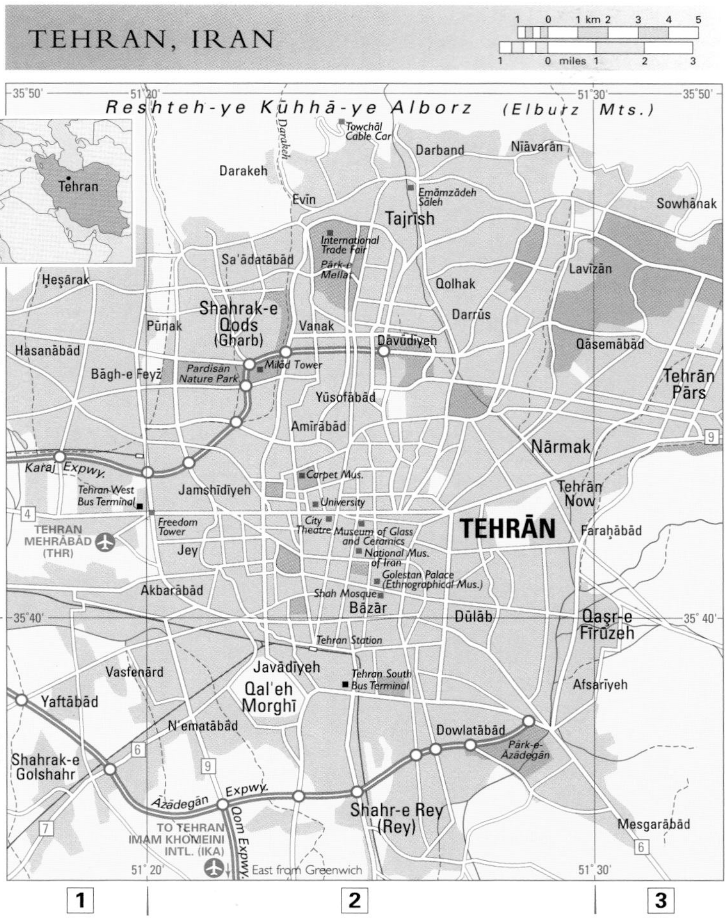

Scale: 1 0 1 km 2 3 4 5 / 1 0 miles 1 2 3

Reshteh-ye Kūhhā-ye Alborz (Elburz Mts.)

Tehran (inset)

Darakeh
Darband
Niāvarān
Towchāl Cable Car
Emāmzādeh Sāleh
Sowhānak
Evīn
Tajrīsh
Darrūs
Lavīzān
Sa'ādatābād
Qolhak
Vanak
Qāsemābād
Davūdiyeh
Tehrān Pārs
Shahrak-e Qods (Gharb)
Pūnak
Yūsofābād
Pardisan Nature Park
Mīlād Tower
Nārmak
Amīrābād
Tehrān Now
Karaj Expwy.
Jamshīdīyeh
Carpet Mus.
University
Tehrān West Bus Terminal
Freedom Tower
City Theatre
Museum of Glass and Ceramics
National Mus. of Iran
Farahābād
TEHRĀN MEHRĀBĀD (THR)
Jey
Shah Mosque
Golestan Palace (Ethnographical Mus.)
Akbarābād
Bāzār
Dūlāb
Qasr-e Fīrūzeh
Hasanābād
Hešārak
Bāgh-e Feyz
Tehrān Station
Vasfenārd
Javādiyeh
Qal'eh Morghī
Tehrān South Bus Terminal
Afsarīyeh
Yaftābād
N'ematābād
Dowlatābād
Pārk-e Azādegān
Shahrak-e Golshahr
Āzādegān Expwy.
Shahr-e Rey (Rey)
Mesgarābād
TO TEHRAN IMAM KHOMEINI INTL. (IKA)
Qom Expwy.
East from Greenwich

CENTRAL TORONTO

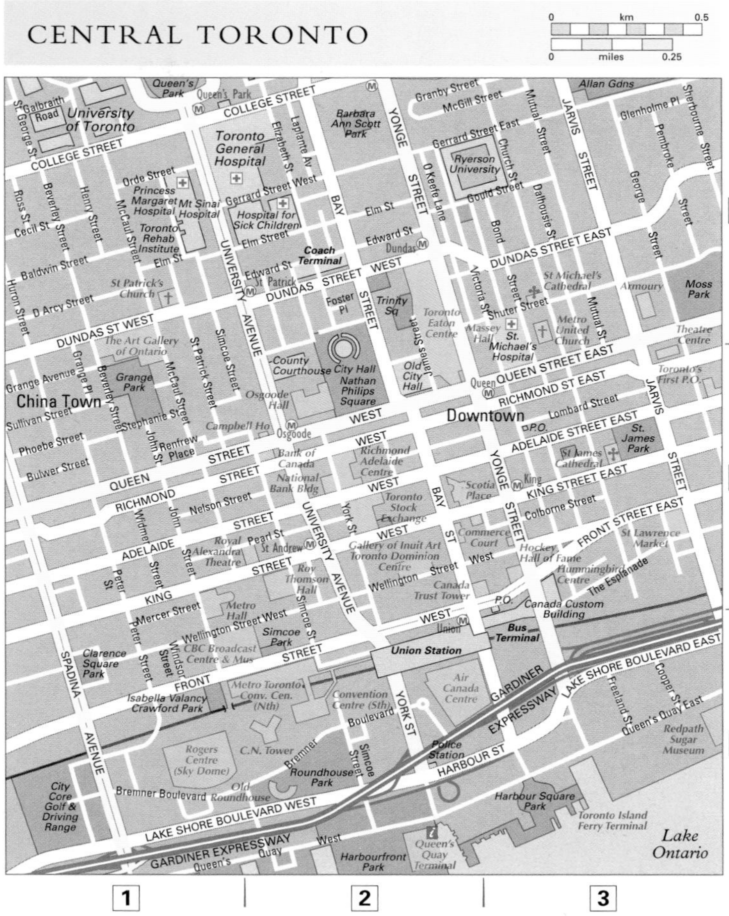

Scale: 0 km 0.5 / 0 miles 0.25

University of Toronto
Queen's Park
College Street
Toronto General Hospital
Galbraith Road
Ryerson University
Gerrard Street East
Barbara Ann Scott Park
Granby Street
McGill Street
Allan Gdns
Glenholme Pl
Orde Street
Princess Margaret Hospital
Mt Sinai Hospital
Hospital for Sick Children
Cecil St
Elm St
Coach Terminal
Dundas Street East
St Michael's Cathedral
Moss Park
Baldwin Street
Toronto Rehab Institute
D'Arcy Street
St Patrick's Church
Foster Pl
Trinity Sq
Toronto Eaton Centre
Metro United Church
Theatre Centre
The Art Gallery of Ontario
County Courthouse
City Hall
Nathan Phillips Square
Massey Hall
St Michael's Hospital
China Town
Grange Park
Osgoode Hall
Old City Hall
Queen Street East
Toronto's First P.O.
Phoebe Street
Campbell Ho
Queen Street West
Downtown
Adelaide Street East
St James Cathedral
St James Park
Bulwer Street
Bank of Canada
Richmond Adelaide Centre
Richmond St East
Scotia Plaza
Colborne Street
King Street East
Nelson Street
Toronto Stock Exchange
Royal Alexandra Theatre
Gallery of Inuit Art
Toronto Dominion Centre
Commerce Court
St Lawrence Market
Adelaide Street West
St Andrew
Royal Pearl St
Canada Trust Tower
Roy Thomson Hall
Hockey Hall of Fame
Hummingbird Centre
The Esplanade
Clarence Square Park
CBC Broadcast Centre & Mus.
Metro Hall
Wellington Street West
Union Station
Bus Terminal
P.O.
Canada Custom Building
Front Street East
Isabella Valancy Crawford Park
Metro Toronto Conv. Cen. (Nth)
Convention Centre (Sth)
Police Station
Lake Shore Boulevard East
Rogers Centre (Sky Dome)
C.N. Tower
Roundhouse Park
Air Canada Centre
Redpath Sugar Museum
City Core Golf & Driving Range
Bremner Boulevard West
Gardiner Expressway
Harbour St
Harbour Square Park
Lake Shore Boulevard West
Gardiner Expressway
Queen's Quay
Harbourfront Park
Harbourfront Terminal
Queen's Quay Terminal
Toronto Island Ferry Terminal
Lake Ontario

TORONTO, CANADA

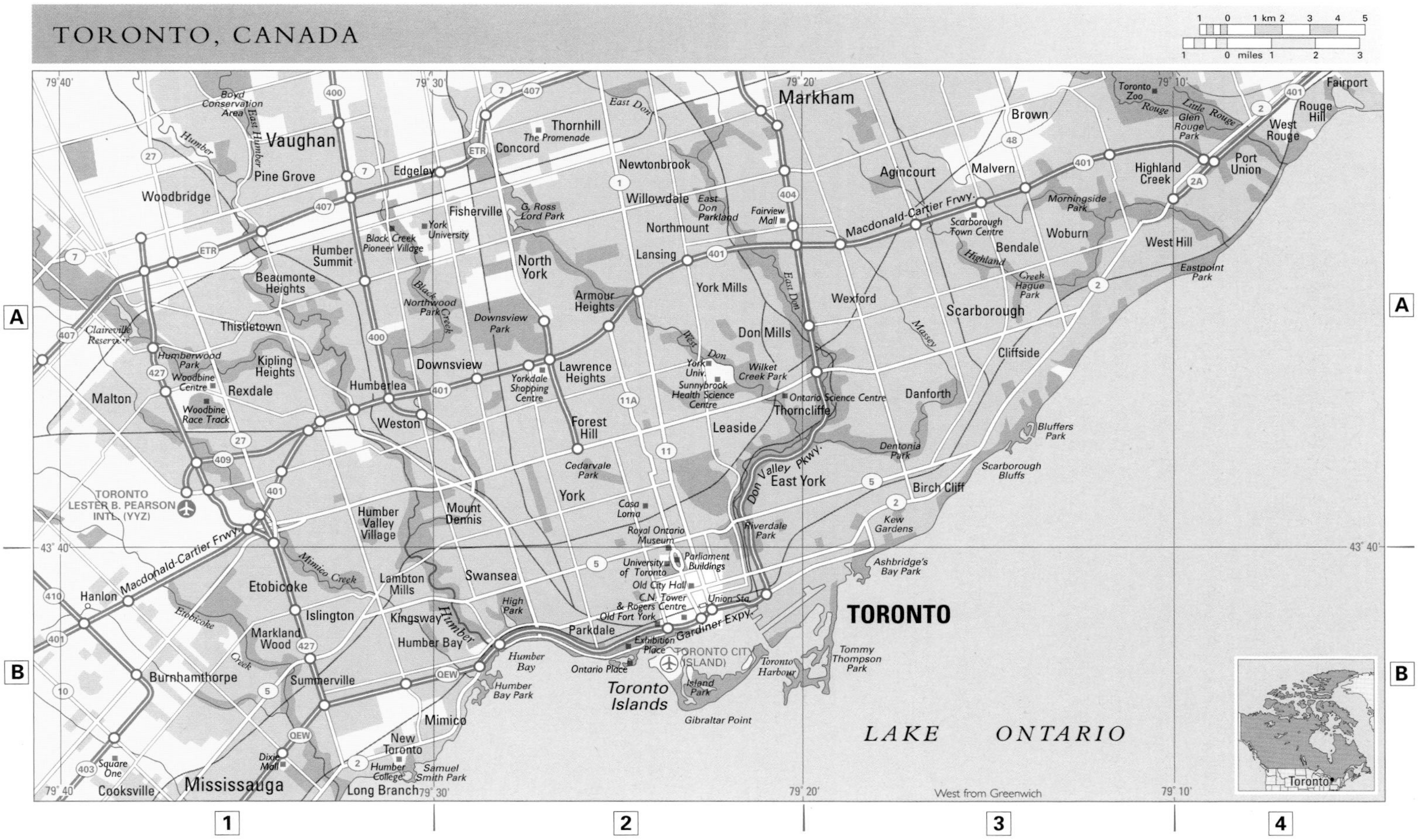

Scale: 1 0 1 km 2 3 4 5 / 1 0 miles 1 2 3

Boyd Conservation Area
Markham
Fairport
Toronto Zoo
Rouge Hill
Vaughan
Thornhill
Concord
East Don
Brown
West Rouge
Port Union
Pine Grove
Edgeley
The Promenade
Newtonbrook
Agincourt
Malvern
Highland Creek
Woodbridge
Fisherville
Willowdale
Fairview Mall
Scarborough Town Centre
Morningside Park
Humber Summit
York University
Black Creek Pioneer Village
Northmount
East Don Parkland
Macdonald-Cartier Frwy
Bendale
Woburn
West Hill
Beaumonte Heights
Northwood Park
North York
Lansing
York Mills
Wexford
Eastpoint Park
Thistletown
Downsview Park
Armour Heights
Don Mills
Scarborough
Humberwood Park
Woodbine Centre
Kipling Heights
Downsview
Lawrence Heights
Yorkdale Shopping Centre
York Univ. Sunnybrook Health Science Centre
Wilket Creek Park
Ontario Science Centre
Cliffside
Bluffers Park
Rexdale
Humberlea
Weston
Forest Hill
Thorncliffe
Danforth
Malton
Woodbine Race Track
Cedarvale Park
Leaside
Dentonia Park
Scarborough Bluffs
TORONTO LESTER B. PEARSON INTL. (YYZ)
York
Casa Loma
Royal Ontario Museum
East York
Birch Cliff
Kew Gardens
Hanlon
Humber Valley Village
Mount Dennis
University of Toronto
Parliament Buildings
Ashbridge's Bay Park
Etobicoke
Lambton Mills
Swansea
Old City Hall
C.N. Tower & Rogers Centre
Old Fort York
Union Sta.
Islington
High Park
Parkdale
Exhibition Place
Gardiner Expy.
TORONTO
Kingsway
Humber Bay
TORONTO CITY (ISLAND)
Toronto Harbour
Tommy Thompson Park
Markland Wood
Summerville
Humber Bay Park
Ontario Place
Island Park
Burnhamthorpe
Mimico
New Toronto
Toronto Islands
Gibraltar Point
Dixie Mall
Square One
Humber College
Samuel Smith Park
Cooksville
Mississauga
Long Branch
West from Greenwich
LAKE ONTARIO
Toronto (inset)

427 Provincial route numbers

COPYRIGHT PHILIP'S

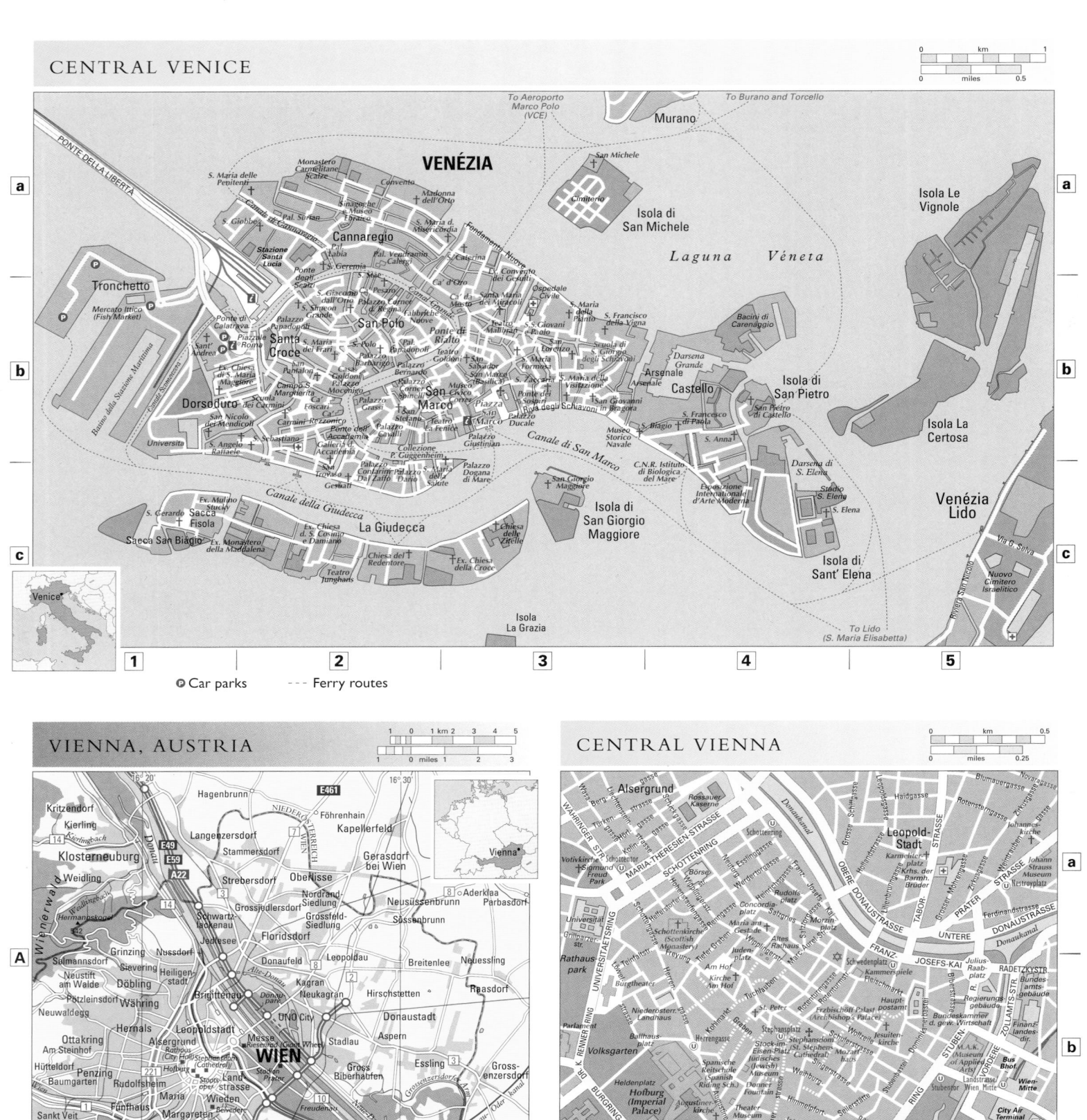

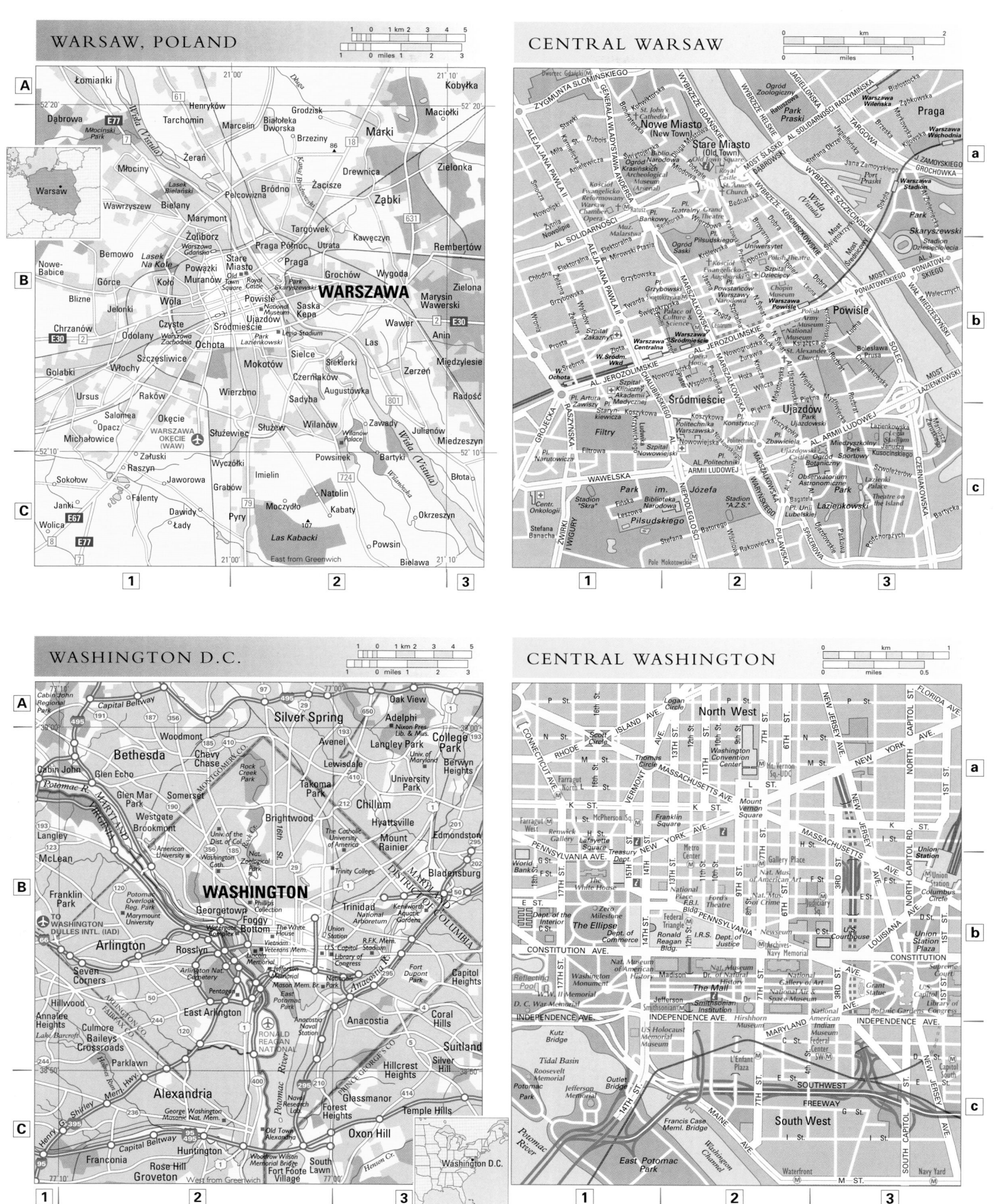

WARSAW, POLAND

CENTRAL WARSAW

WASHINGTON D.C.

CENTRAL WASHINGTON

85 Interstate route numbers   29 U.S. route numbers   166 State route numbers

INDEX TO CITY MAPS

The index contains the names of all the principal places and features shown on the City Maps. Each name is followed by an additional entry in italics giving the name of the City Map within which it is located.

The number in bold type which follows each name refers to the number of the City Map page where that feature or place will be found.

The letter and figure which are immediately after the page number give the grid square on the map within which the feature or place is situated.

The letter represents the latitude and the figure the longitude. The full geographic reference is provided in the border of the City Maps.

The location given is the centre of the city, suburb or feature and is not necessarily the name. Rivers, canals and roads are indexed to their name. Rivers carry the symbol → after their name.

An explanation of the alphabetical order rules and a list of the abbreviations used are to be found at the beginning of the World Map Index.

A

Aalām *Baghdad* **3** B2
Aalsmeer *Amsterdam* **2** B1
Abbey Wood *London* **15** B4
Abcoude *Amsterdam* **2** B2
Ābdīn *Cairo* **7** A2
Abeno *Osaka* **23** B2
Aberdeen *Hong Kong* **12** B1
Aberdour *Edinburgh* **11** A2
Aberdour Castle *Edinburgh* **11** A2
Abfanggraben → *Munich* **21** A3
Ablon-sur-Seine *Paris* **24** B3
Abramtsevo *Moscow* **19** B3
Abu Dis *Jerusalem* **13** B2
Abū en Numrus *Cairo* **7** B2
Abu Ghosh *Jerusalem* **13** B1
Abu Hail *Dubai* **9** A2
Acassuso *Buenos Aires* **7** A2
Achères *Paris* **24** A1
Acilia *Rome* **26** C1
Aclimação *São Paulo* **27** B2
Acropolis *Athens* **2** B2
Acton *London* **15** A2
Açúcar, Pão de *Rio de Janeiro* **25** B2
Ada Beja *Lisbon* **16** A1
Adams Park *Atlanta* **3** B2
Addiscombe *London* **15** B3
Adelphi *Washington* **33** A3
Aderklaa *Vienna* **32** A3
Adler Planetarium *Chicago* **9** B3
Admiralteyskaya Storona *St. Petersburg* **27** B2
Affori *Milan* **18** A2
Aflandshage *Copenhagen* **8** B3
Afsarīyeh *Tehran* **31** B2
Agboyi Cr. → *Lagos* **14** A2
Agerup *Copenhagen* **8** A1
Agesta *Stockholm* **29** B2
Aghia Marina *Athens* **2** C3
Aghia Paraskevi *Athens* **2** A2
Aghios Dimitrios *Athens* **2** B2
Aghios Ioannis Rendis *Athens* **2** B2
Agincourt *Toronto* **31** A3
Agra Canal *Delhi* **10** B2
Agricola Oriental *Mexico City* **18** B2
Água Espraiada → *São Paulo* **27** B2
Agualva-Cacem *Lisbon* **16** A1
Ahrensfelde *Berlin* **5** A4
Ahuntsic *Montreal* **20** A1
Ai → *Osaka* **23** A2
Aigremont *Paris* **24** A1
Air View Park *Singapore* **28** A2
Airport West *Melbourne* **18** A1
Ajegunle *Lagos* **14** B2
Aji *Osaka* **23** B1
Ajuda *Lisbon* **16** A1
Akalla *Stockholm* **29** A1
Akasaka *Tokyo* **30** A3
Akbarābād *Tehran* **31** A2
Akershus Slott *Oslo* **23** A3
Al 'Azamīyah *Baghdad* **3** A2
Al Bada *Dubai* **9** B2
Al Barsha *Dubai* **9** B1
Al Hamriya Port *Dubai* **9** A2
Al Hudaiba *Dubai* **9** B2
Al Jafiliya *Dubai* **9** B2
Al Manara *Dubai* **9** B1
Al Mina *Dubai* **9** B2
Al Nasr *Dubai* **9** B2
Al Quds = Jerusalem *Jerusalem* **13** B2
Al Quoz *Dubai* **9** B1
Al Safa *Dubai* **9** B1
Al Satwa *Dubai* **9** B2
Al Sufouh *Dubai* **9** B1
Al Walaja *Jerusalem* **13** B1
Al Wasl *Dubai* **9** B2
Alaguntan *Lagos* **14** B2
Alameda *San Francisco* **26** B3
Alameda Memorial State Beach Park *San Francisco* **26** B3
Albern *Vienna* **32** B2
Albert Park *Melbourne* **18** B1
Alberton *Johannesburg* **13** B2
Albertslund *Copenhagen* **8** B2
Alcantara *Lisbon* **16** A1
Alcatraz I. *San Francisco* **26** B2
Alcobendas *Madrid* **17** A2
Alcorcón *Madrid* **17** B1
Aldershof *Berlin* **5** B4
Aldo Bonzi *Buenos Aires* **7** C1
Aleksandrovskoye *St. Petersburg* **27** B2
Alexander Nevsky Abbey *St. Petersburg* **27** B2
Alexandra *Johannesburg* **13** A2
Alexandra *Singapore* **28** B2
Alexandria *Washington* **33** C2
Alfortville *Paris* **24** B3
Algés *Lisbon* **16** A1
Algiers *New Orleans* **21** B2
Alhambra *Los Angeles* **16** B4
Alibey → *Istanbul* **12** B1
Alibey Barajı *Istanbul* **12** B1
Alibeyköy *Istanbul* **12** B1
Alimos *Athens* **2** B2
Alipur *Kolkata* **14** B1
Allach *Munich* **21** A1
Allambie Heights *Sydney* **29** A2
Allermuir Hill *Edinburgh* **11** B2
Allston *Boston* **6** A2
Almada *Lisbon* **16** A2
Almagro *Buenos Aires* **7** B2
Almargem do Bispo *Lisbon* **16** A1
Almirante G. Brown, Parque *Buenos Aires* **7** C2
Almon *Jerusalem* **13** B2
Almond → *Edinburgh* **11** B2
Alna *Oslo* **23** A4
Alnsjøen *Oslo* **23** A4
Alperton *London* **15** A2
Alpine *New York* **22** A2
Alrode *Johannesburg* **13** B2
Alsemberg *Brussels* **6** B2
Alsergrund *Vienna* **32** A2
Alsip *Chicago* **9** C2
Älsten *Stockholm* **29** B1
Älta *Stockholm* **29** B3
Altadena *Los Angeles* **16** A4
Alte-Donau → *Vienna* **32** A2
Alter Finkenkrug *Berlin* **5** A1
Altes Rathaus *Munich* **21** B2
Altglienicke *Berlin* **5** B4
Altlandsberg *Berlin* **5** A5
Altlandsberg Nord *Berlin* **5** A5
Altmannsdorf *Vienna* **32** B1
Alto da Boa Vista *Rio de Janeiro* **25** B1
Alto da Moóca *São Paulo* **27** B2
Alto do Pina *Lisbon* **16** A2
Altona *Melbourne* **18** B1
Alvalade *Lisbon* **16** A2
Alvik *Stockholm* **29** B1
Alvin Callendar Naval Air Station *New Orleans* **21** B2
Älvsjo *Stockholm* **29** B2
Älvvik *Stockholm* **29** A3
Am Hasenbergl *Munich* **21** A2
Am Steinhof *Vienna* **32** A1
Am Wald *Munich* **21** B2
Ama Keng *Singapore* **28** A2
Amadora *Lisbon* **16** A1
Amagasaki *Osaka* **23** A1
Amager *Copenhagen* **8** B3
Amāl Qādisiya *Baghdad* **3** B2
Amalienborg Slot *Copenhagen* **8** A3
Amata *Milan* **18** A1
Ambelokipi *Athens* **2** B2
Ameixoeira *Lisbon* **16** A2
Amelia Earhart Park *Miami* **19** C1
América *São Paulo* **27** B1
American Univ. *Washington* **33** B2
Amin *Baghdad* **3** B2
Aminadav *Jerusalem* **13** B1
Amirābād *Tehran* **31** A2
Amora *Lisbon* **16** B2
Amoreira *Lisbon* **16** A1
Amper → *Munich* **21** A1
Amstel-Drecht-Kanaal *Amsterdam* **2** B2
Amstelveen *Amsterdam* **2** B2
Amsterdam *Amsterdam* **2** A2
Amsterdam ✕ (AMS) *Amsterdam* **2** B1
Amsterdam-Rijnkanaal *Amsterdam* **2** B3
Amsterdam Zuidoost *Amsterdam* **2** B2
Amsterdamse Bos *Amsterdam* **2** B1
Anacostia *Washington* **33** B3
Anacostia → *Washington* **33** B3
Anadoluhisarı *Istanbul* **12** B2
Anadolukavağı *Istanbul* **12** A2
Anata *Jerusalem* **13** B2
Ancol *Jakarta* **12** A1
'Andalus *Baghdad* **3** B1
Andarai *Rio de Janeiro* **25** B1
Anderlecht *Brussels* **6** A1
Anderson Park *Atlanta* **3** B2
Andingmen *Beijing* **4** B2
Ang Mo Kio *Singapore* **28** A3
Ängby *Stockholm* **29** A1
Angel I. *San Francisco* **26** A2
Angel Island State Park ⌂ *San Francisco* **26** A2
Angke, Kali → *Jakarta* **12** A1
Angyalföld *Budapest* **7** A2
Anik *Mumbai* **20** A2
Anin *Warsaw* **33** B2
Anjou *Montreal* **20** A2
Annalee Heights *Washington* **33** B1
Anne Frankhuis *Amsterdam* **2** A2
Antony *Paris* **24** B2
Aoyama *Tokyo* **30** B3
Ap Lei Chau *Hong Kong* **12** B1
Apapa *Lagos* **14** B2
Apapa Quays *Lagos* **14** B2
Apelação *Lisbon* **16** A2
Apopka, L. *Orlando* **23** A1
Apoquindo *Santiago* **27** B2
Apterkarskiy Ostrov *St. Petersburg* **27** B2
Ar Kazimiyah *Baghdad* **3** B1
Ar Ram *Jerusalem* **13** A2
Ara → *Tokyo* **30** A4
Arakawa *Tokyo* **30** A3
Arany-hegyi-patak → *Budapest* **7** A2
Aravaca *Madrid* **17** B1
Arbataash *Baghdad* **3** A1
Arc de Triomphe *Paris* **24** A2
Arcadia *Los Angeles* **16** B4
Arcueil *Paris* **24** B2
Arese *Milan* **18** A1
Arganzuela *Madrid* **17** B1
Argenteuil *Paris* **24** A2
Argiroupoli *Athens* **2** B2
Arima *Tokyo* **30** B2
Arlanda, Stockholm ✕ (ARN) *Stockholm* **29** A1
Arlington *Boston* **6** A1
Arlington *Washington* **33** B2
Arlington Heights *Boston* **6** A1
Arlington Nat. Cemetery *Washington* **33** B2
Armação *Rio de Janeiro* **25** B2
Armadale *Melbourne* **18** B2
Armour Heights *Toronto* **31** A2
Arncliffe *Sydney* **29** B1
Arnold Arboretum *Boston* **6** B2
Árpádföld *Budapest* **7** A3
Arrentela *Lisbon* **16** B2
Arroyo Seco Park *Los Angeles* **16** B3
Årsta *Stockholm* **29** B2
Artane *Dublin* **10** A2
Artas *Jerusalem* **13** B2
Arthur's Seat *Edinburgh* **11** B3
Arts, Place des *Montreal* **20** A2
As Shawawra *Jerusalem* **13** B2
Asagaya *Tokyo* **30** A2
Asahi *Osaka* **23** A2
Asakusa *Tokyo* **30** A3
Asati *Kolkata* **14** C1
Aschheim *Munich* **21** A3
Ascot Vale *Melbourne* **18** A1
Ashbridge's Bay Park *Toronto* **31** B3
Ashburn *Chicago* **9** C2
Ashburton *Melbourne* **18** B2
Ashfield *Sydney* **29** B1
Ashford *London* **15** B1
Ashtown *Dublin* **10** A2
Askisto *Helsinki* **11** B1
Askrikefjärden *Stockholm* **29** A3
Asnières *Paris* **24** A2
Aspern *Vienna* **32** A2
Assago *Milan* **18** B1
Assendelft *Amsterdam* **2** A1
Assiano *Milan* **18** B1
Astoria *New York* **22** B2
Astrolabe Park *Sydney* **29** B2
Atarot *Jerusalem* **13** A2
Atarot ✕ (JRS) *Jerusalem* **13** A2
Atghara *Kolkata* **14** B2
Athens = Athina *Athens* **2** B2
Athina *Athens* **2** B2
Athina ✕ (ATH) *Athens* **2** A3
Athinai = Athina *Athens* **2** B2
Athis-Mons *Paris* **24** B3
Athlone *Cape Town* **8** A2
Atholl *Johannesburg* **13** A2
Atifiya *Baghdad* **3** A2
Atişalen *Istanbul* **12** B1
Atlanta *Atlanta* **3** B2
Atlanta Hartsfield-Jackson Int. ✕ (ATL) *Atlanta* **3** C2
Atlanta History Center *Atlanta* **3** B2
Atlanta Zoo *Atlanta* **3** B2
Atomium *Brussels* **6** A2
Attiki *Athens* **2** B2
Atzgersdorf *Vienna* **32** B1
Aubervilliers *Paris* **24** A3
Aubing *Munich* **21** B1
Auburndale *Boston* **6** A1
Auchendinny *Edinburgh* **11** B2
Auckland Park *Johannesburg* **13** B2
Auderghem *Brussels* **6** B2
Audubon Park *New Orleans* **21** B2
Augustówka *Warsaw* **33** B2
Aulnay-sous-Bois *Paris* **24** A3
Aurelio *Rome* **26** B1
Ausīm *Cairo* **7** A1
Austerlitz, Gare d' *Paris* **24** A3
Austin *Chicago* **9** B2
Avedøre *Copenhagen* **8** B2
Avellaneda *Buenos Aires* **7** C2
Avenel *Washington* **33** B3
Aventura *Miami* **19** C3
Avondale *Chicago* **9** B2
Avondale *New Orleans* **21** B1
Avondale Heights *Melbourne* **18** A1
Avtovo *St. Petersburg* **27** B1
Ayazağa *Istanbul* **12** B1
Ayer Chawan, Pulau *Singapore* **28** B2
Ayer Merbau, Pulau *Singapore* **28** B2
Azabu *Tokyo* **30** B3
Azcapotzalco *Mexico City* **18** B1
Azteca, Estadio *Mexico City* **18** C2
Azucar, Cerro Pan de *Santiago* **27** A1

B

Baambrugge *Amsterdam* **2** B2
Baba Channel *Karachi* **13** B1
Baba I. *Karachi* **13** B1
Babarpur *Delhi* **10** A2
Babushkin *Moscow* **19** A3
Back B. *Mumbai* **20** B1
Baclaran *Manila* **17** B2
Bacoor *Manila* **17** C1
Bacoor B. *Manila* **17** C1
Badalona *Barcelona* **4** A2
Badhoevedorp *Amsterdam* **2** A1
Badli *Delhi* **10** A1
Bærum *Oslo* **23** A2
Bağcılar *Istanbul* **12** B1
Baggio *Milan* **18** B1
Bāgh-e-Feyz *Tehran* **31** A1
Baghdād *Baghdad* **3** A2
Baghdād al Muthana ✕ (BGW) *Baghdad* **3** B2
Baghdad Int. ✕ (SDA) *Baghdad* **3** B1
Bagmari *Kolkata* **14** B2
Bagneux *Paris* **24** B2
Bagnolet *Paris* **24** A3
Bagsværd *Copenhagen* **8** A2
Bagsværd Sø *Copenhagen* **8** A2
Baguiati *Kolkata* **14** B2
Bagumbayan *Manila* **17** C2
Baha'i Temple *Chicago* **9** A2
Bahçeköy *Istanbul* **12** A1
Bahçelievler *Istanbul* **12** B1
Bahtīm *Cairo* **7** A2
Baile Átha Cliath = Dublin *Dublin* **10** A2
Baileys Crossroads *Washington* **33** B2
Bailly *Paris* **24** A1
Bairro Lopes *Lisbon* **16** A2
Baisha *Guangzhou* **11** B2
Baiyun *Guangzhou* **11** A2
Baiyun Mountain Scenic Area *Guangzhou* **11** A2
Bakırköy *Istanbul* **12** C1
Bal Harbor *Miami* **19** C3
Balara *Manila* **17** B2
Baldia *Karachi* **13** A1
Baldoyle *Dublin* **10** A3
Baldwin, L. *Orlando* **23** A3
Baldwin Hills *Los Angeles* **16** B2
Baldwin Hills Res. *Los Angeles* **16** B2
Balgowlah *Sydney* **29** A2
Balgowlah Heights *Sydney* **29** A2
Balham *London* **15** B3
Bali *Kolkata* **14** A1
Baliganja *Kolkata* **14** B2
Balingsnäs *Stockholm* **29** B2
Balingsta *Stockholm* **29** B2
Balintawak *Manila* **17** B1
Ballerup *Copenhagen* **8** A2
Ballinteer *Dublin* **10** B2
Ballyboden *Dublin* **10** B2
Ballybrack *Dublin* **10** B3
Ballyfermot *Dublin* **10** A1
Ballymorefinn Hill *Dublin* **10** B1
Ballymun *Dublin* **10** A2
Balmain *Sydney* **29** B2
Baluhati *Kolkata* **14** B1
Balvanera *Buenos Aires* **7** B2
Balwyn *Melbourne* **18** A2
Balwyn North *Melbourne* **18** A2
Banana Island *Lagos* **14** B2
Banática *Lisbon* **16** A1
Bandra *Mumbai* **20** A1
Bandra Pt. *Mumbai* **20** A1
Bang Kapi *Bangkok* **3** B2
Bang Na *Bangkok* **3** B2
Bangbae *Seoul* **27** C1
Bangkhen *Bangkok* **3** A2
Bangkok *Bangkok* **3** B2
Bangkok Don Muang Int. ✕ (BKK) *Bangkok* **3** A2
Bangkok Noi *Bangkok* **3** B1
Bangkok Yai *Bangkok* **3** B1
Banglo *Kolkata* **14** B1
Bangrak *Bangkok* **3** B2
Bangsu *Bangkok* **3** B2
Banks, C. *Sydney* **29** C2
Banksmeadow *Sydney* **29** B2
Banstala *Kolkata* **14** B2
Bantra *Kolkata* **14** B1
Baoshan *Shanghai* **28** A1
Bar Giyora *Jerusalem* **13** B1
Barahanagar *Kolkata* **14** B2
Barajas *Madrid* **17** B2
Barajas, Madrid ✕ (MAD) *Madrid* **17** B2
Barakpur *Kolkata* **14** A2
Barcarena *Lisbon* **16** A1
Barcarena, Rib. de → *Lisbon* **16** A1
Barcelona *Barcelona* **4** A2
Barcelona ✕ (BCN) *Barcelona* **4** B1
Barcroft, L. *Washington* **33** B2
Barking *London* **15** A4
Barkingside *London* **15** A4
Barnes *London* **15** B2
Barnet *London* **15** A2
Barra Andai *Karachi* **13** B2
Barra Funda *São Paulo* **27** B2
Barracas *Buenos Aires* **7** B2
Barrackpur = Barakpur *Kolkata* **14** A2
Barranco *Lima* **14** B2
Barreiro *Lisbon* **16** B2
Barreto *Rio de Janeiro* **25** B2
Bartala *Kolkata* **14** B1
Barton Park *Sydney* **29** B1
Bartyki *Warsaw* **33** C2
Basus *Cairo* **7** A2
Batanagar *Kolkata* **14** B1
Bath Beach *New York* **22** C1
Bath I. *Karachi* **13** B2
Batir *Jerusalem* **13** B1
Batok, Bukit *Singapore* **28** A2
Battersea *London* **15** B3
Bauman *Moscow* **19** B3
Baumgarten *Vienna* **32** A1
Bay, L. *Orlando* **23** A2
Bay Harbor Islands *Miami* **19** C3
Bay Hill *Orlando* **23** B1
Bay Ridge *New York* **22** C1
Bayit Va-Gan *Jerusalem* **13** B2
Bayonne *New York* **22** B1
Bayou Boeuf *New Orleans* **21** B1
Bayou Segnette State Park ⌂ *New Orleans* **21** B2
Bayrampaşa *Istanbul* **12** B1
Bayshore *San Francisco* **26** B2
Bayt Lahm *Jerusalem* **13** B2
Bayview *San Francisco* **26** B2
Bāzār *Tehran* **31** A2
Beacon Hill *Hong Kong* **12** A2
Beato *Lisbon* **16** A2
Beaumont *Dublin* **10** A2
Beaumonte Heights *Toronto* **31** A1
Bebek *Istanbul* **12** B2
Běchovice *Prague* **25** B3
Beckenham *London* **15** B3
Beckton *London* **15** A4
Becontree *London* **15** A4
Beddington Corner *London* **15** B3
Bedford *Boston* **6** A1
Bedford Park *Chicago* **9** C2
Bedford Park *New York* **22** A2
Bedford Stuyvesant *New York* **22** B2
Bedford View *Johannesburg* **13** B2
Bedok *Singapore* **28** B3
Bedok, Res. *Singapore* **28** A3
Beersel *Brussels* **6** B1
Behala *Kolkata* **14** B1
Bei Hai *Beijing* **4** B2
Beicai *Shanghai* **28** B2
Beijing *Beijing* **4** B1
Beit Duqu *Jerusalem* **13** A1
Beit Ghur at-Tahti *Jerusalem* **13** A1
Beit Ghur el-Fawqa *Jerusalem* **13** A1
Beit Hanina *Jerusalem* **13** B2
Beit Ij'za *Jerusalem* **13** A1
Beit Iksa *Jerusalem* **13** B2
Beit I'nan *Jerusalem* **13** A1
Beit Jala *Jerusalem* **13** B2
Beit Lekhem = Bayt Lahm *Jerusalem* **13** B2
Beit Liqya *Jerusalem* **13** A1
Beit Nekofa *Jerusalem* **13** B1
Beit Sahur *Jerusalem* **13** B2
Beit Sofafa *Jerusalem* **13** B2
Beit Surik *Jerusalem* **13** B1
Beit Ur al-Fawqa *Jerusalem* **13** A1
Beit Zayit *Jerusalem* **13** B1
Beitaipingzhuang *Beijing* **4** B1
Beitar Illit *Jerusalem* **13** B1
Beitin *Jerusalem* **13** A2
Beitsun *Guangzhou* **11** B2
Beitunya *Jerusalem* **13** A2
Beixing Jing Park *Shanghai* **28** B1
Békásmegyer *Budapest* **7** A2
Bekkelaget *Oslo* **23** A3
Bekkestua *Oslo* **23** A2
Bel Air *Los Angeles* **16** B2
Bela Vista *São Paulo* **27** B2
Bélanger *Montreal* **20** A1
Belas *Lisbon* **16** A1
Beleghata *Kolkata* **14** B2
Belém *Lisbon* **16** A1
Belém, Torre de *Lisbon* **16** A1
Belenzinho *São Paulo* **27** B2
Belgachiya *Kolkata* **14** B2
Belgharia *Kolkata* **14** B2
Belgrano *Buenos Aires* **7** B2
Bell *Los Angeles* **16** C3
Bell Gardens *Los Angeles* **16** C4
Bellavista *Lima* **14** B2
Bellavista *Santiago* **27** C2
Belle Harbor *New York* **22** C2
Bellingham *London* **15** B3
Belmont *Boston* **6** A1
Belmont *London* **15** A2
Belmont Cragin *Chicago* **9** B2
Belmont Harbor *Chicago* **9** B3
Belmore *Sydney* **29** B1
Belur *Kolkata* **14** B2
Belvedere *London* **15** B4
Belvedere *San Francisco* **26** A2
Belvedere Park *Atlanta* **3** B3
Belyayevo Bogorodskoye *Moscow* **19** C2
Bemowo *Warsaw* **33** B1
Benaki Museum *Athens* **2** B2
Bendale *Toronto* **31** A3
Benefica *Rio de Janeiro* **25** B1
Benfica *Lisbon* **16** A1
Benitez Int. ✕ (SCL) *Santiago* **27** B1
Benito Juárez, Int. ✕ (MEX) *Mexico City* **18** B2
Bensonhurst *New York* **22** C2
Berchem-Ste-Agathe *Brussels* **6** A1
Berg am Laim *Munich* **21** B2
Bergenfield *New York* **22** A2
Bergham *Munich* **21** B2
Bergvliet *Cape Town* **8** B1
Beri *Barcelona* **4** A1
Berkeley *San Francisco* **26** A3
Berlin *Berlin* **5** A3
Berlin Brandenburg ✕ (BER) *Berlin* **5** B4
Berlin Dom *Berlin* **5** A3
Bermondsey *London* **15** B3
Bernabeu, Estadio *Madrid* **17** B1
Bernal Heights *San Francisco* **26** B2
Berwyn *Chicago* **9** B2
Berwyn Heights *Washington* **33** B3
Besiktas *Istanbul* **12** B2
Besós → *Barcelona* **4** A2
Bessie, L. *Orlando* **23** B1
Bet Horon *Jerusalem* **13** A1
Bethesda *Washington* **33** B2
Bethlehem = Bayt Lahm *Jerusalem* **13** B2
Bethnal Green *London* **15** A3
Betor *Kolkata* **14** B1
Beulah *Orlando* **23** A1
Beulah, L. *Orlando* **23** A1
Beverley Hills *Sydney* **29** B1
Beverley Park *Sydney* **29** B1
Beverly *Chicago* **9** C3
Beverly Arts Center *Chicago* **9** C2
Beverly Glen *Los Angeles* **16** B2
Beverly Hills *Los Angeles* **16** B2
Beverly Hills-Morgan Park Historic District *Chicago* **9** C2
Bexley *Sydney* **29** B1
Bexley □ *London* **15** B4
Bexleyheath *London* **15** B4
Beykoz *Istanbul* **12** B2
Beylerbeyi *Istanbul* **12** B2
Beyoğlu *Istanbul* **12** B1
Bezons *Paris* **24** A2
Bezuidenhout Park *Johannesburg* **13** B2
Bhadrakali *Kolkata* **14** A2
Bhalswa *Delhi* **10** A2
Bhambo Khan Qarmati *Karachi* **13** B2
Bhatsala *Kolkata* **14** B1
Bhawanipur *Kolkata* **14** B2
Bhendkhal *Mumbai* **20** B2
Bhit I. *Jerusalem* **13** B1
Bhuleshwar *Mumbai* **20** B1
Białołeka Dworska *Warsaw* **33** B2
Bicentennial Park *Los Angeles* **16** B4
Bicentennial Park *Sydney* **29** B1
Bickley *London* **15** B4
Bicutan *Manila* **17** C2
Bidhan Nagar *Kolkata* **14** B2
Bidu *Jerusalem* **13** B1
Bielany *Warsaw* **33** B1
Bielawa *Warsaw* **33** C2
Biesdorf *Berlin* **5** A4
Bièvre → *Paris* **24** B1
Bièvres *Paris* **24** B2
Big Sand L. *Orlando* **23** B2
Bill Baggs Cape Florida State Recr. Area ⌂ *Miami* **19** D3
Bilston *Edinburgh* **11** B2
Binacayan *Manila* **17** C1
Binondo *Manila* **17** B1
Bintaro Jaya *Jakarta* **12** B1
Bir Nabala *Jerusalem* **13** A2
Birak el Kiyam *Cairo* **7** A1
Birch Cliff *Toronto* **31** A3
Birkenstein *Berlin* **5** A5
Birkholz *Berlin* **5** A4
Birkholzaue *Berlin* **5** A4
Birrarrung Park *Melbourne* **18** A2
Biscayne Bay Aquatic Reserve *Miami* **19** E2
Biscayne Park *Miami* **19** C2
Bishop Lavis *Cape Town* **8** A2
Bishopscourt *Cape Town* **8** A1
Bispebjerg *Copenhagen* **8** A3
Bissonet Plaza *New Orleans* **21** A1
Bittsevsky Forest Park *Moscow* **19** C2
Björknas *Stockholm* **29** B3
Black Cr. → *Toronto* **31** A2
Black Creek Pioneer Village *Toronto* **31** A1
Blackfen *London* **15** B4
Blackheath *London* **15** B4
Blackrock *Dublin* **10** B2
Bladensburg *Washington* **33** B3
Blair Village *Atlanta* **3** C2
Blairgowrie *Johannesburg* **13** A2
Blake House *Boston* **6** B2
Blakehurst *Sydney* **29** B1
Blakstad *Oslo* **23** B1
Blanche, L. *Orlando* **23** B1
Blankenburg *Berlin* **5** A3
Blankenfelde *Berlin* **5** A3
Blizne *Warsaw* **33** B1
Blota *Warsaw* **33** C3
Blue Island *Chicago* **9** D2
Blue Lagoon L. *Miami* **19** D1
Blue Mosque = Sultanahme Camil *Istanbul* **12** B1
Bluebell *Dublin* **10** B1
Bluff Hd. *Hong Kong* **12** B2
Bluffers Park *Toronto* **31** A3
Blumberg *Berlin* **5** A4
Blunt Pt. *San Francisco* **26** A2
Blutenberg *Munich* **21** B1
Blylaget *Oslo* **23** B3
Boa Vista, Alto do *Rio de Janeiro* **25** B1
Boardwalk *New York* **22** C3
Boavista *Lisbon* **16** A2
Bobigny *Paris* **24** A3
Bocanegra *Lima* **14** A2
Boedo *Buenos Aires* **7** B2
Bogenhausen *Munich* **21** B2
Bogorodskoye *Moscow* **19** B3
Bogota *New York* **22** A1
Bogstadvatnet *Oslo* **23** A2
Bohnsdorf *Berlin* **5** B4
Bois-Colombes *Paris* **24** A2
Bois-d'Arcy *Paris* **24** B1
Boissy-St-Léger *Paris* **24** B4
Boldinasco *Milan* **18** B1
Bøler *Oslo* **23** A4
Bollate *Milan* **18** A1
Bollebeek *Brussels* **6** A1
Bollensdorf *Berlin* **5** A5
Bollmora *Stockholm* **29** B3
Bolshaya Okhta *St. Petersburg* **27** B2
Bolton *Atlanta* **3** B2
Bom Retiro *São Paulo* **27** B2
Bombay = Mumbai *Mumbai* **20** B2
Bondi *Sydney* **29** B2
Bondy *Paris* **24** A3
Bondy, Forêt de *Paris* **24** A4
Bonifacio Monument *Manila* **17** B1
Bonnabel Place *New Orleans* **21** A2
Bonneuil-sur-Marne *Paris* **24** B4
Bonnington *Edinburgh* **11** B1
Bonnyrigg and Lasswade *Edinburgh* **11** B3
Bonsucesso *Rio de Janeiro* **25** B1
Bonteheuwel *Cape Town* **8** A2
Boo *Stockholm* **29** A3
Booterstown *Dublin* **10** B2
Borisovo *Moscow* **19** C3
Borle *Mumbai* **20** A2
Boronia Park *Sydney* **29** A1
Bosmont *Johannesburg* **13** B1
Bosön *Stockholm* **29** A3
Bosporus = İstanbul Boğazı *Istanbul* **12** B2
Bostancı *Istanbul* **12** C2
Boston *Boston* **6** A2
Boston Common *Boston* **6** A2
Boston Logan Int. ✕ (BOS) *Boston* **6** A2
Botafogo *Rio de Janeiro* **25** B1
Botany *Sydney* **29** B2
Botany B. *Sydney* **29** B2
Botany Bay △ *Sydney* **29** B2
Botič → *Prague* **25** B3
Botica Sete *Lisbon* **16** A1
Boucherville *Montreal* **20** A3
Boucherville, Îs. de *Montreal* **20** A3
Bougival *Paris* **24** A1
Boulder Pt. *Hong Kong* **12** B1
Boulogne, Bois de *Paris* **24** A2
Boulogne-Billancourt *Paris* **24** A2
Bourg-la-Reine *Paris* **24** B2
Bouviers *Paris* **24** B1
Bovenkerk *Amsterdam* **2** B2
Bovenkerker Polder *Amsterdam* **2** B2
Bovisa *Milan* **18** A2
Bow *London* **15** A3
Boyacıköy *Istanbul* **12** B2
Boyd Conservation Area *Toronto* **31** A1
Boyle Heights *Los Angeles* **16** B3
Braepark *Edinburgh* **11** B1
Braid *Edinburgh* **11** B2
Bramley *Johannesburg* **13** A2
Brandeis Univ. *Boston* **6** A1
Brandenburger Tor *Berlin* **5** A3
Brani, Pulau *Singapore* **28** B3
Branik *Prague* **25** B2
Brännkyrka *Stockholm* **29** B2
Brás *São Paulo* **27** B2
Brasilândia *São Paulo* **27** A1
Brateyevo *Moscow* **19** C3
Braybrook *Melbourne* **18** A1
Brázdim *Prague* **25** A3
Breakheart Reservation *Boston* **6** A2
Brede *Copenhagen* **8** A3
Breezy Point *New York* **22** C2
Breitenlee *Vienna* **32** A3
Breña *Lima* **14** B2
Brent □ *London* **15** A2
Brent Res. *London* **15** A2
Brentford *London* **15** B2
Brentwood *Los Angeles* **16** B2
Brentwood Park *Los Angeles* **16** B2
Brera *Milan* **18** B2
Bresso *Milan* **18** A2
Brevik *Stockholm* **29** B3
Břevnov *Prague* **25** B2
Brickyard, The *Chicago* **9** B2
Bridge City *New Orleans* **21** B2
Bridgeport *Chicago* **9** B3
Bridgetown *Cape Town* **8** A2
Bridgeview *Chicago* **9** C2
Brighton *Boston* **6** A2
Brighton *Melbourne* **18** B1
Brighton Beach *New York* **22** C2
Brighton-Le-Sands *Sydney* **29** B1
Brighton Park *Chicago* **9** C2
Brightwood *Washington* **33** B2
Brigittenau *Vienna* **32** A2
Brimbank Park *Melbourne* **18** A1
Brisbane Pt. *San Francisco* **26** B2
Britz *Berlin* **5** B3
Brixton *London* **15** B3
Broadmeadows *Melbourne* **18** A1
Broadmoor *San Francisco* **26** B2
Broadview *Chicago* **9** B1
Broadview Park *Miami* **19** B2
Brockley *London* **15** B3
Bródno *Warsaw* **33** B2
Bródnowski, Kanal *Warsaw* **33** B2
Broek *Amsterdam* **2** A2
Bromley □ *London* **15** B4
Bromley Common *London* **15** B4
Bromma *Stockholm* **29** A1
Bromma ✕ (BMA) *Stockholm* **29** A1
Brøndby Strand *Copenhagen* **8** B2
Brøndbyøster *Copenhagen* **8** B2
Brøndbyvester *Copenhagen* **8** B2
Brondesbury *London* **15** A2
Brønnøya *Oslo* **23** A2
Brønshøj *Copenhagen* **8** A2
Bronxville *New York* **22** A2
Brookfield Zoo *Chicago* **9** B1
Brookhaven *Atlanta* **3** A2
Brookline *Boston* **6** B2
Brooklyn *Cape Town* **8** A1
Brooklyn *New York* **22** B2
Brooklyn Heights *New York* **22** B2
Brookmont *Washington* **33** B2
Brossard *Montreal* **20** B3
Brou-sur-Chantereine *Paris* **24** A4
Brown *Toronto* **31** A3
Brownsville *Miami* **19** D1
Brughério *Milan* **18** A2
Brunswick *Melbourne* **18** A1
Brussegem *Brussels* **6** A1
Brussel *Brussels* **6** A2
Brussel ✕ (BRU) *Brussels* **6** A2
Brussels = Brussel *Brussels* **6** A2
Bruxelles = Brussel *Brussels* **6** A2
Bruzzano *Milan* **18** A2
Bry-sur-Marne *Paris* **24** A4
Bryan, L. *Orlando* **23** B2
Bryanston *Johannesburg* **13** A1
Bryn *Oslo* **23** A1
Brzeziny *Warsaw* **33** B2
Bubeneč *Prague* **25** B2
Buc *Paris* **24** B1
Buchenhain *Munich* **21** B1
Buchholz *Berlin* **5** A3
Buckhead *Atlanta* **3** A2
Buckingham Palace *London* **15** A3
Buckow *Berlin* **5** B3
Bucktown *New Orleans* **21** A2
Buda *Budapest* **7** A2
Buda Castle = Budavaripalota *Budapest* **7** A2
Budafok *Budapest* **7** B2
Budaörs *Budapest* **7** B1
Budapest *Budapest* **7** B2
Budapest ✕ (BUD) *Budapest* **7** B3
Budatétény *Budapest* **7** B2
Budavaripalota *Budapest* **7** A2
Buddinge *Copenhagen* **8** A3
Buenos Aires *Buenos Aires* **7** B2
Buenos Aires Ezeiza ✕ (EZE) *Buenos Aires* **7** C1
Bufalotta *Rome* **26** B2
Bugio *Lisbon* **16** B1
Buiksloot *Amsterdam* **2** A2
Buitenveldert *Amsterdam* **2** B2
Buizingen *Brussels* **6** B1
Bukhansan *Seoul* **27** B1
Bukit Panjang *Singapore* **28** A2
Bukit Panjang Nature Reserve *Singapore* **28** A2
Bukit Timah Nature Reserve *Singapore* **28** A2
Bukum, Pulau *Singapore* **28** B2
Būlāq *Cairo* **7** A2
Bule *Manila* **17** C2
Bullen Park *Melbourne* **18** A2
Bund, The *Shanghai* **28** B1
Bundoora North *Melbourne* **18** A2
Bundoora Park *Melbourne* **18** A2
Bunker Hill Memorial *Boston* **6** A2
Bunker I. *Karachi* **13** B1
Bunkyō *Tokyo* **30** A3
Bunnefjorden *Oslo* **23** A3
Buona Vista Park *Singapore* **28** B2
Bur Dubai *Dubai* **9** A2
Burbank *Chicago* **9** C2
Burbank *Los Angeles* **16** A3
Burden, L. *Orlando* **23** B1
Burj Al Arab *Dubai* **9** B1
Burj Dubai *Dubai* **9** B2
Burlington *Boston* **6** A1
Burnham Park *Chicago* **9** C3
Burnham Park Harbor *Chicago* **9** B3
Burnhamthorpe *Toronto* **31** B1
Burnt Oak *London* **15** A2
Burntisland *Edinburgh* **11** A2
Burnwynd *Edinburgh* **11** B1
Burqa *Jerusalem* **13** A2
Burtus *Cairo* **7** A1
Burudvatn *Oslo* **23** A2
Burwood *Sydney* **29** B1
Bushwick *New York* **22** B2
Bushy Park *London* **15** B1
Business Bay *Dubai* **9** B2
Butantã *São Paulo* **27** B1
Butcher I. *Mumbai* **20** B2
Butler, L. *Orlando* **23** B1
Büyükdere *Istanbul* **12** B2
Byculla *Mumbai* **20** B2
Bygdøy *Oslo* **23** A3
Bywater *New Orleans* **21** B2

C

C.B.S. Fox Studios *Los Angeles* **16** B2
C.N. Tower *Toronto* **31** B2
Caballito *Buenos Aires* **7** B2
Cabin John *Washington* **33** B1
Cabin John Regional Park ⌂ *Washington* **33** A1
Cabinteely *Dublin* **10** B3
Cabra *Dublin* **10** A2
Cabuçú de Baixo → *São Paulo* **27** A1
Cabuçú de Cima → *São Paulo* **27** A2
Cachan *Paris* **24** B2
Cachoeira, Rib. da → *São Paulo* **27** B1
Cacilhas *Lisbon* **16** A2
Cahuenga Park *Los Angeles* **16** B3
Cain, L. *Orlando* **23** B2
Cairo = El Qâhira *Cairo* **7** A2
Cairo Int. ✕ (CAI) *Cairo* **7** A3
Caju *Rio de Janeiro* **25** B1
Čakovice *Prague* **25** B3
Calcutta = Kolkata *Kolkata* **14** B2
California Inst. of Tech. *Los Angeles* **16** B4
California Los Angeles, Univ. of *Los Angeles* **16** B2
California State Univ. *Los Angeles* **16** B3
Callao *Lima* **14** B2
Caloocan *Manila* **17** B1
Calumet, L. *Chicago* **9** C3

Calumet City Chicago 9 D3
Calumet Park Chicago 9 C3
Calumet Sag Channel ➜ Chicago 9 C2
Calvairate Milan 18 B2
Camarate Lisbon 16 A2
Camaroes Lisbon 16 A1
Camberwell London 15 B3
Camberwell Melbourne 18 B2
Cambridge Boston 6 A2
Cambuci São Paulo 27 B2
Camden □ London 15 A3
Çamlıca Istanbul 12 B2
Camp Springs Washington 33 C3
Campamento Madrid 17 B1
Campbellfield Melbourne 18 A1
Camperdown Sydney 29 B2
Campo, Casa de Madrid 17 B1
Campo F.C. Barcelona Barcelona 4 A1
Campo Grando Lisbon 16 A2
Campo Pequeño Lisbon 16 A2
Campolide Lisbon 16 A2
Camps Bay Cape Town 8 A1
C'an San Joan Barcelona 4 A2
Cañacao B. Manila 17 C1
Canarsie New York 22 C2
Canary Wharf London 15 A3
Candiac Montreal 20 B3
Caneças Lisbon 16 A1
Canillas Madrid 17 B2
Canillejas Madrid 17 B2
Canning Town London 15 A4
Canteras de Vallecas Madrid 17 B2
Canterbury Melbourne 18 A2
Canterbury Sydney 29 B1
Canton = Guangzhou Guangzhou 11 B2
Canton Tower Guangzhou 11 B2
Caoheijing Shanghai 28 B1
Capão Redondo São Paulo 27 B1
Caparica Lisbon 16 A2
Caparica, Costa da Lisbon 16 B1
Cape Flats Cape Town 8 B2
Cape Town Cape Town 8 A1
Cape Town Int. ✈ (CPT) Cape Town 8 A2
Capitol Heights Washington 33 B3
Captain Cook Bridge Sydney 29 C1
Captain Cook Landing Place Park Sydney 29 C2
Capuchos Lisbon 16 B1
Carabanchel Alto Madrid 17 B1
Carabanchel Bajo Madrid 17 B1
Carapachay Buenos Aires 7 B1
Caraza Buenos Aires 7 C2
Caridad Manila 17 C1
Carioca, Sa. da Rio de Janeiro 25 B1
Carlstadt New York 22 A1
Carlton Melbourne 18 A1
Carlton Gardens Melbourne 18 A1
Carmen de Huechuraba Santiago 27 B1
Carmen de la Legua -Reynosa Lima 14 B2
Carnaxide Lisbon 16 A1
Carnegie Melbourne 18 B2
Carnide Lisbon 16 A1
Carol City Miami 19 C1
Carollton New Orleans 21 B2
Carrascal Santiago 27 B1
Carrickmines Dublin 10 B3
Carrières-sous-Bois Paris 24 A1
Carrières-sous-Poissy Paris 24 A1
Carrières-sur-Seine Paris 24 A2
Carrigeen B. Dublin 10 A3
Cartierville Montreal 20 A1
Casa Loma Toronto 31 A2
Casa Verde São Paulo 27 A1
Casal da Mira Lisbon 16 A1
Casál Morena Rome 26 C2
Casalotti Rome 26 B1
Cascade Heights Atlanta 3 B2
Castèl di Leva Rome 26 C2
Castèl Sant'Angelo Rome 26 B1
Castleknock Dublin 10 A1
Castleton Corners New York 22 C1
Catahouatche, L. New Orleans 21 B1
Catete Rio de Janeiro 25 B1
Catford London 15 B3
Catherine, L. Orlando 23 B2
Caulfield Melbourne 18 B2
Cavite Manila 17 C1
Caxias Lisbon 16 A1
Cebecci Istanbul 12 B1
Cecchignola Rome 26 C2
Cecilienhof, Schloss Berlin 5 B1
Cedar Grove Atlanta 3 C3
Cedarvale Park Toronto 31 A2
Cempaka Putih Jakarta 12 B2
Çengelköy Istanbul 12 B2
Cengkareng Jakarta 12 A1
Centennial Olympic Park Atlanta 3 B2
Centennial Park Sydney 29 B2
Center Hill Atlanta 3 B2
Centocelle Rome 26 B2
Central, Gare Montreal 20 B2
Central Park New York 22 B2
Century City Los Angeles 16 B2
Cerdanyola del Vallès Barcelona 4 A1
Cerillos Santiago 27 B1
Cerro de la Estrella △ Mexico City 18 B2
Cerro de los Angeles Madrid 17 C1
Cerro Navia Santiago 27 B1
Cesano Boscone Milan 18 B1
Cesate Milan 18 A1
Cha Kwo Ling Hong Kong 12 B2
Chacarrita Buenos Aires 7 B2
Chadwell Heath London 15 A4
Chai Chee Singapore 28 B3
Chai Wan Hong Kong 12 B2
Chai Wan Kok Hong Kong 12 A1
Chaidari Athens 2 A1
Chakdaha Kolkata 14 C1
Chalandri Athens 2 A2
Chamartin Madrid 17 B1
Chamberi Madrid 17 B1
Chambourcy Paris 24 A1
Champigny-sur-Marne Paris 24 B4
Champlain, Pont Montreal 20 B2
Champs-sur-Marne Paris 24 A4
Chamrail Kolkata 14 B1
Chanakyapuri Delhi 10 B2
Chanditala Kolkata 14 A1
Changfeng Park Shanghai 28 B1
Changhai = Shanghai Shanghai 28 B2
Changi Singapore 28 A3
Changi, Singapore ✈ (SIN) Singapore 28 A3
Changning Shanghai 28 B1
Chanteceine Paris 24 A4
Chantian Guangzhou 11 A2
Chaoyang Beijing 4 B2
Chaoyangmen Beijing 4 B2
Chapelizod Dublin 10 A1
Chapultepec, Bosque de Mexico City 18 B1
Chapultepec, Castillo de Mexico City 18 B1
Charenton-le-Pont Paris 24 B3
Charleroi, Kanal de ➜ Brussels 6 B1
Charles Bridge = Karlův most Prague 25 B2
Charles Gates Dawes House Chicago 9 A2
Charlestown Boston 6 A2
Charlottenburg Berlin 5 A2
Charlottenburg, Schloss Berlin 5 A2
Charlottenlund Copenhagen 8 A3
Charlton London 15 B4
Charneca Lisbon 16 A2
Charneca Lisbon 16 B1
Chase, L. Orlando 23 B1
Châteaufort Paris 24 B1
Châtenay-Malabry Paris 24 B2
Chatham Chicago 9 C3
Châtillon Paris 24 B2
Chatou Paris 24 A1
Chatpur Kolkata 14 B2
Chatswood Sydney 29 A2
Chatuchak Bangkok 3 B2
Chatuchak Park Bangkok 3 B2
Chauki Karachi 13 A1
Chavarria Lima 14 B2
Chaville Paris 24 B2
Chayang Seoul 27 B2
Chelles Paris 24 A4
Chelles, Canal de Paris 24 A4
Chells-le-Pin ✈ Paris 24 A4
Chelsea Boston 6 A2
Chelsea London 15 B2
Chembur Mumbai 20 A2
Chengshousi Beijing 4 C2
Chennevières-sur-Marne Paris 24 B4
Cheongdam Seoul 27 B2
Cheonho Seoul 27 B2
Cheops Cairo 7 B1
Chertanovka ➜ Moscow 19 C2
Chertanovo Moscow 19 C2
Cheryomushki Moscow 19 B2
Chestnut Hill Boston 6 B1
Cheung Sha Wan Hong Kong 12 A1
Cheverly Washington 33 B3
Chevilly-Larue Paris 24 B3
Cheviot Hills Los Angeles 16 B2
Chevy Chase Washington 33 B2
Chhatrapati Shivaji, Mumbai ✈ (BOM) Mumbai 20 A2
Chhatrapati Shivaji Terminus Mumbai 20 B2
Chia Keng Singapore 28 A3
Chiaravalle Milanese Milan 18 B2
Chicago Chicago 9 B3
Chicago, Univ. of Chicago 9 C3
Chicago Harbor Chicago 9 B3
Chicago Lawn Chicago 9 C2
Chicago Ridge Chicago 9 C2
Chicago River, North Branch ➜ Chicago 9 B2
Chicago Sanitary and Ship Canal Chicago 9 C2
Chicago State Univ. Chicago 9 C3
Chienzui Guangzhou 11 A3
Chik Sha Hong Kong 12 B2
Child's Hill London 15 A2
Chile, Univ. de Santiago 27 B2
Chilla Saroda Delhi 10 B2
Chillum Washington 33 B3
Chilly-Mazarin Paris 24 B2
Chingupota Kolkata 14 C1
Chinna Cr. ➜ Karachi 13 B2
Chiquihuite, Cerro Mexico City 18 A2
Chislehurst London 15 B4
Chiswick London 15 B2
Chiswick House London 15 B2
Chitose Tokyo 30 B2
Chitralada Palace Bangkok 3 B2
Chiyoda Tokyo 30 A3
Choa Chu Kang Singapore 28 A2
Chodov u Prahy Prague 25 B3
Chōfu Tokyo 30 B2
Choisy-le-Roi Paris 24 B3
Cholargos Athens 2 B2
Cholupice Prague 25 C2
Chom Thong Bangkok 3 B1
Chong Pang Singapore 28 A2
Chongwen Beijing 4 B2
Chorrillos Lima 14 C2
Chowpatty Beach Mumbai 20 B1
Christianshavn Copenhagen 8 A3
Chrzanów Warsaw 33 B1
Chuen Lung Hong Kong 12 A1
Chuk Kok Hong Kong 12 A2
Chulalongkorn Univ. Bangkok 3 B2
Chuō Tokyo 30 A3
Church End London 15 A2
Church of our Lady = Frauenkirche Munich 21 B2
Churchtown Dublin 10 B2
Ciampino Rome 26 C2
Ciampino ✈ (CIA) Rome 26 C2
Cicero Chicago 9 B2
Cilandak Jakarta 12 B1
Cilincing Jakarta 12 A2
Ciliwung ➜ Jakarta 12 B2
Čimice Prague 25 B2
Cinecittà Rome 26 B2
Cinisello Bàlsamo Milan 18 A2
Cinkota Budapest 7 A3
Cipete Jakarta 12 B1
Città degli Studi Milan 18 B2
Città del Vaticano = Vatican City ■ Rome 26 B1
City, The London 15 A3
City Hall = Rådhus Oslo 23 A3
City Hall = Stadshuset Stockholm 29 B2
City of the Dead Cairo 7 A2
City Park New Orleans 21 A2
City Terrace Los Angeles 16 B3
Ciudad de México Mexico City 18 B2
Ciudad Deportiva Mexico City 18 B2
Ciudad Fin de Semana Madrid 17 B2
Ciudad General Belgrano Buenos Aires 7 C1
Ciudad Lineál Madrid 17 B2
Ciudad Satélite Mexico City 18 A1
Ciudad Universitaria Buenos Aires 7 B2
Ciudad Universitaria Mexico City 18 C1
Clairville Res. Toronto 31 A1
Clamart Paris 24 B2
Clapham London 15 B3
Clapton London 15 A3
Claremont Cape Town 8 A1
Clayhall London 15 A4
Clear, L. Orlando 23 A2
Clermiston Edinburgh 11 B2
Clichy Paris 24 A2
Clichy-sous-Bois Paris 24 A4
Cliffside Toronto 31 A3
Cliffside Park New York 22 B2
Clifton Cape Town 8 A1
Clifton Karachi 13 B2
Clifton New York 22 C1
Clifton Beach Karachi 13 B2
Cliftondale Boston 6 A2
Cloghran Dublin 10 A2
Clonskeagh Dublin 10 B2
Clontarf Dublin 10 A2
Clontarf Sydney 29 A2
Clovelly Sydney 29 B2
CNN Center Atlanta 3 B2
Cobras, I. das Rio de Janeiro 25 B2
Coburg Melbourne 18 A1
Coconut Grove Miami 19 D2
Cocotá Rio de Janeiro 25 A1
Cœuilly Paris 24 B4
Coina Lisbon 16 B2
Coker Lagos 14 B2
Colaba Mumbai 20 B1
Colaba Pt. Mumbai 20 B1
Colegiales Buenos Aires 7 B2
Colindale London 15 A2
Colinton Edinburgh 11 B2
College Park Atlanta 3 C2
College Park Washington 33 B3
College Point New York 22 B2
Collégien Paris 24 A4
Collier Row London 15 A4
Colliers Wood London 15 B2
Colma San Francisco 26 B2
Colney Hatch London 15 A3
Cologno Monzese Milan 18 A2
Colombes Paris 24 A2
Colonia Güell Barcelona 4 A1
Colosseo Rome 26 B1
Colosseum = Colosseo Rome 26 B1
Combault Paris 24 B4
Comércio, Praça do Lisbon 16 A2
Commerce Los Angeles 16 B4
Conceição, I. da Rio de Janeiro 25 B2
Conchali Santiago 27 B2
Concord Sydney 29 B1
Concord Toronto 31 A2
Concorde, Place de la Paris 24 A2
Concorezzo Milan 18 A2
Condet Jakarta 12 A2
Coney I. = Serangoon, Pulau Singapore 28 A3
Coney Island New York 22 C2
Congonhas São Paulo ✈ (CGH) São Paulo 27 B2
Conley ➜ Atlanta 3 C3
Connaught Place Delhi 10 B2
Consolação São Paulo 27 B2
Constantia Cape Town 8 B1
Constitución Buenos Aires 7 B2
Constitution Atlanta 3 B2
Conway Orlando 23 B2
Conway, L. Orlando 23 B2
Coogee Sydney 29 B2
Cooksville Toronto 31 B1
Coolock Dublin 10 A2
Cooper City Miami 19 B1
Copacabana Rio de Janeiro 25 B1
Copenhagen = København Copenhagen 8 A2
Coral Gables Miami 19 D1
Coral Hills Washington 33 B3
Corcovado, Cristo Redentor Rio de Janeiro 25 B1
Corduff Dublin 10 A1
Cormano Milan 18 A2
Cornaredo Milan 18 A1
Corsico Milan 18 B1
Corstorphine Edinburgh 11 B2
Corviale Rome 26 B1
Coslada Madrid 17 B2
Cossigny Paris 24 B4
Cotao Lisbon 16 A1
Côte-St-Luc Montreal 20 B2
Cotunduba, I. de Rio de Janeiro 25 B2
Coubron Paris 24 A4
Courbevoie Paris 24 A2
Courtry Paris 24 A4
Cowley London 15 A1
Coyoacán Mexico City 18 B2
Craighall Park Johannesburg 13 A2
Craiglockhart Edinburgh 11 B2
Craigmillar Edinburgh 11 B3
Cramond Edinburgh 11 B2
Cramond Bridge Edinburgh 11 B1
Cramond I. Edinburgh 11 B2
Crandon Park Miami 19 D3
Cranford London 15 B1
Crawford Cape Town 8 A2
Crayford London 15 B5
Creekmouth London 15 A4
Crescent, L. Orlando 23 A1
Crescenzago Milan 18 A2
Cressely Paris 24 B1
Cresskill New York 22 A2
Crestwood Chicago 9 D2
Créteil Paris 24 B3
Cricklewood London 15 A2
Cristo Redentor, Corcovado Rio de Janeiro 25 B1
Crockenhill London 15 B4
Croissy-Beaubourg Paris 24 B4
Croissy-sur-Seine Paris 24 A1
Crosby Johannesburg 13 B1
Crosne Paris 24 B3
Cross I. Mumbai 20 B2
Crouch End London 15 A3
Crown Mine Johannesburg 13 B1
Crows Nest Sydney 29 A2
Croydon London 15 B3
Croydon Park Sydney 29 B1
Cruagh Mt. Dublin 10 B2
Crumlin Dublin 10 B2
Cruz de Pau Lisbon 16 B2
Crystal Palace London 15 B3
Csepel Budapest 7 B2
Csepelsziget Budapest 7 B2
Csillaghegy Budapest 7 A2
Csillagtelep Budapest 7 B2
Csömör Budapest 7 A3
Csömöri-patak ➜ Budapest 7 A3
Cuatro Vientos Madrid 17 B1
Cuauhtémoc Mexico City 18 B2
Cubao Manila 17 B2
Çubuklu Istanbul 12 B2
Cudahy Los Angeles 16 C3
Cuicuilco, Pirámide de Mexico City 18 C1
Culmore Washington 33 B2
Culver City Los Angeles 16 B2
Cupecé ➜ São Paulo 27 B1
Currie Edinburgh 11 B2
Cusago Milan 18 B1
Cusano Milanino Milan 18 A2
Cutler Park Boston 6 B1
Çuvuşabaşi ➜ Istanbul 12 B1
Cuwei Beijing 4 B1
Cypress Hills New York 22 B2
Cypress Park Los Angeles 16 B3
Czerniaków Warsaw 33 B2
Czyste Warsaw 33 B1

D

D.H.A. Phase VIII Karachi 13 B2
Da Moóca ➜ São Paulo 27 B2
Ďáblice Prague 25 B2
Dąbrowa Warsaw 33 B1
Dachang Shanghai 28 B1
Dachang ✈ Shanghai 28 B1
Dachau Munich 21 A1
Dachau-Ost Munich 21 A1
Dachauer Moos Munich 21 A1
Dadar Mumbai 20 A1
Daebang Seoul 27 B1
Daechi Seoul 27 B2
Dafni Athens 2 B2
Dagenham London 15 A4
Daglfing Munich 21 B2
Dahab, Gezîret el Cairo 7 B2
Daheisha Jerusalem 13 B2
Dahlem Berlin 5 B2
Dahlwitz-Hoppegarten Berlin 5 A5
Dahongmen Beijing 4 C2
Daiba = Odaiba Tokyo 30 B3
Dajiaoting Beijing 4 B2
Dakhnoye St. Petersburg 27 C1
Dalejsky potok ➜ Prague 25 B2
Dalgety Bay Edinburgh 11 A1
Dalkeith Edinburgh 11 B3
Dalkey Dublin 10 B3
Dalkey I. Dublin 10 B3
Dallgow Berlin 5 A1
Dalmeny Edinburgh 11 B1
Dalston London 15 A3
Daly City San Francisco 26 B2
Damaia Lisbon 16 A1
Damarakia Athens 2 B1
Dämeritzsee Berlin 5 B5
Dan Ryan Woods Chicago 9 C2
Danderhall Edinburgh 11 B3
Danderyd Stockholm 29 A2
Danforth Toronto 31 A3
Dania Beach Miami 19 B3
Darakeh Tehran 31 A2
Darband Tehran 31 A2
Darling Point Sydney 29 B2
Darndale Dublin 10 A2
Darrūs Tehran 31 A2
Dartford London 15 B5
Dashi Guangzhou 11 B2
Datansha Guangzhou 11 B2
Datun Beijing 4 B2
Daulatpur Delhi 10 A1
Davidson, Mt. San Francisco 26 B2
Davidson's Mains Edinburgh 11 B2
Davie Miami 19 B2
Dāvūdiyeh Tehran 31 A2
Davydkovo Moscow 19 B1
Dawidy Warsaw 33 C1
Daxing Beijing 4 C2
Decatur Atlanta 3 B3
Dedham Boston 6 B1
Degunino Moscow 19 A2
Deir Dibwan Jerusalem 13 A2
Deir Ibzi'e Jerusalem 13 A1
Deira Dubai 9 A2
Dejvice Prague 25 B2
Dekabristov, Ostrov St. Petersburg 27 B1
Del Rey Los Angeles 16 C2
Delhi Delhi 10 B2
Delhi Indira Gandhi Int. ✈ (DEL) Delhi 10 B1
Demarest New York 22 A2
Den Ilp Amsterdam 2 A2
Denistone Heights Sydney 29 A1
Dentonia Park Toronto 31 A3
DePaul Univ. Chicago 9 B3
Deptford London 15 B3
Desert Wetlands Park Las Vegas 14 B2
Deutsche Oper Berlin 5 A2
Deutsches Museum Munich 21 B2
Devil's Peak Cape Town 8 A1
Dhakuria Kolkata 14 B2
Dharavi Mumbai 20 A2
Dia Deva = Butcher I. Mumbai 20 B2
Diadema São Paulo 27 C2
Diegen Brussels 6 A2
Diemen Amsterdam 2 A2
Diepkloof Johannesburg 13 B1
Dieprivier Cape Town 8 B1
Dilbeek Brussels 6 A1
Dilli = Delhi Delhi 10 B2
Dirnismaning Munich 21 A2
Disney-M.G.M. Studios Orlando 23 B1
Disney Studios Los Angeles 16 B3
Dixmoor Chicago 9 D2
Djakarta = Jakarta Jakarta 12 A2
Djursholm Stockholm 29 A2
Döberitz Berlin 5 A1
Döbling Vienna 32 A2
Dobong Seoul 27 B2
Dobongsan Seoul 27 A2
Docklands London 15 A3
Doctor Phillips Orlando 23 B2
Dodder ➜ Dublin 10 B1
Dodger Stadium Los Angeles 16 B3
Dogs, Isle of London 15 B3
Dolgoe Ozero St. Petersburg 27 A1
Dollis Hill London 15 A2
Dollymount Dublin 10 A2
Dolni Prague 25 B3
Dolni Chabry Prague 25 B2
Dolni Počernice Prague 25 B3
Dolphins Barn Dublin 10 B2
Dolton Chicago 9 D3
Dom Pedro II, Parque São Paulo 27 B2
Don Mills Toronto 31 A2
Don Muang Int. ✈ (BKK) Bangkok 3 A2
Donaghmede Dublin 10 A3
Donau-Oder Kanal Vienna 32 A3
Donaufeld Vienna 32 A2
Donaupark Vienna 32 A2
Donaustadt Vienna 32 A2
Dongan Hills New York 22 C1
Dongcheng Beijing 4 B2
Dongdaemung Seoul 27 B2
Donggou Shanghai 28 B2
Dongjak Seoul 27 B1
Dongjiao Guangzhou 11 B2
Dongri Mumbai 20 B2
Dongshanhu Park Guangzhou 11 B2
Dongzhimen Beijing 4 B2
Donnybrook Dublin 10 B2
Doornfontein Johannesburg 13 B2
Dorchester Boston 6 B2
Dorchester B. Boston 6 B2
Dorchester Heights Nat. Historical Site ⌂ Boston 6 B2
Dornach Munich 21 B3
Dorval Int., Montréal ✈ (YUL) Montreal 20 B1
Dos Moninos ➜ São Paulo 27 B2
Douglas Park Chicago 9 B2
Dover Heights Sydney 29 B2
Dowlatābād Tehran 31 B2
Down, L. Orlando 23 A1
Downey Los Angeles 16 C4
Downsview Toronto 31 A2
Downsview Park Toronto 31 A2
Dragor Copenhagen 8 B3
Drancy Paris 24 A3
Drapetsona Athens 2 B1
Dreilinden Berlin 5 B2
Drewnica Warsaw 33 B2
Drigh Road Karachi 13 A2
Drimnagh Dublin 10 B2
Drogenbos Brussels 6 B1
Drottningholm Stockholm 29 B1
Druid Hills Atlanta 3 B3
Drumcondra Dublin 10 A2
Drummoyne Sydney 29 B1
Drylaw Edinburgh 11 B2
Dubai = Dubayy Dubai 9 A2
Dubai Creek Dubai 9 A2
Dubai Int. ✈ (DXB) Dubai 9 A2
Dubai Int. Financial Centre Dubai 9 B2
Dubai Internet City Dubai 9 B1
Dubai Maritime City Dubai 9 A2
Dubayy Dubai 9 A2
Dubeč Prague 25 B3
Dublin Dublin 10 A2
Dublin ✈ (DUB) Dublin 10 A2
Dublin B. Dublin 10 B3
Dublin Harbour Dublin 10 A2
Duddingston Edinburgh 11 B3
Dugnano Milan 18 A2
Duivendrecht Amsterdam 2 B2
Dūlāb Tehran 31 B2
Dulwich London 15 B3
Dum Dum Kolkata 14 B2
Dumont New York 22 A2
Dún Laoghaire Dublin 10 B3
Dundrum Dublin 10 B2
Dunearn Singapore 28 B2
Dunleary = Dún Laoghaire Dublin 10 B3
Dunning Chicago 9 B2
Dunvegan Johannesburg 13 A2
Duomo Milan 18 B2
Duque de Caxias Rio de Janeiro 25 A1
Duren Sawit Jakarta 12 B2
Dusit Bangkok 3 B2
Dworp Brussels 6 B1
Dyakovo Moscow 19 B2
Dyker Beach Park New York 22 C1
Dzerzhinskiy Moscow 19 B2
Dzerzhinskiy Park Moscow 19 B2

E

E.U.R. = Esposizione Universale di Roma Rome 26 C1
Eagle Rock Los Angeles 16 B3
Ealing □ London 15 A2
Earlsfield London 15 B2
Earlwood Sydney 29 B1
East Arlington Boston 6 A2
East Arlington Washington 33 B2
East Bedfont London 15 B1
East Boston Boston 6 A2
East Don ➜ Toronto 31 A2
East Don Parkland Toronto 31 A2
East Elmhurst New York 22 B2
East Finchley London 15 A2
East Flatbush New York 22 C2
East Ham London 15 A4
East Humber ➜ Toronto 31 A1
East Lamma Channel Hong Kong 12 B1
East Las Vegas = Whitney Las Vegas 14 B2
East Lexington Boston 6 A1
East Los Angeles Los Angeles 16 B3
East Molesey London 15 B1
East New York New York 22 B2
East Pines Washington 33 B3
East Point Atlanta 3 B2
East Potomac Park Washington 33 B2
East River ➜ New York 22 B2
East Rutherford New York 22 A1
East Sheen London 15 B2
East Talpiyot Jerusalem 13 B2
East Wickham London 15 B4
East York Toronto 31 A2
Eastcote London 15 A1
Easter Howgate Edinburgh 11 B2
Eastpoint Park Toronto 31 A4
Estelle New Orleans 21 B2
Eastwood Sydney 29 A1
Eaton Canyon Park Los Angeles 16 A4
Ebara Tokyo 30 B3
Ebisu Tokyo 30 B3
Ebute-Metta Lagos 14 B2
Eda Tokyo 30 B2
Edendale Johannesburg 13 A2
Edenmore Dublin 10 A2
Edgars Cr. ➜ Melbourne 18 A1
Edgeley Toronto 31 A1
Edgemar San Francisco 26 C2
Edgewater New York 22 B2
Edgewood Orlando 23 B2
Edinburgh Edinburgh 11 B2
Edinburgh ✈ (EDI) Edinburgh 11 B1
Edinburgh Castle Edinburgh 11 B2
Edison Park Chicago 9 A2
Edmondston Washington 33 B3
Edmondstown Dublin 10 B2
Edo ➜ Tokyo 30 B4
Edogawa Tokyo 30 A4
Edsberg Stockholm 29 A1
Edwards L. Melbourne 18 A1
Efzonos Athens 2 B2
Egaleo Athens 2 B2
Egaleo, Oros Athens 2 B1
Eiche Berlin 5 A4
Eiche Süd Berlin 5 A4
Eiffel, Tour Paris 24 A2
Ein Arik Jerusalem 13 A1
Ein Naquba Jerusalem 13 B1
Ein Rafa Jerusalem 13 B1
Eizariya Jerusalem 13 B2
Ejby Copenhagen 8 A2
Ejigbo Lagos 14 A1
Ekeberg Oslo 23 A3
Eknäs Stockholm 29 B3
El 'Abbasiya Cairo 7 A2
El Agustino Lima 14 B2
El Agustino, Cerro Lima 14 B3
El Baragil Cairo 7 A1
El Basâtîn Cairo 7 B2
El Bira Jerusalem 13 A2
El Bosque Santiago 27 C2
El Carmen Santiago 27 B1
El Cortijo Santiago 27 B1
El Cristo, Vaso Regulador Mexico City 18 B1
El Duqqi Cairo 7 A2
El Encinar de los Reyes Madrid 17 A2
El Gezira Cairo 7 A2
El Ghuriya Cairo 7 A2
El Gîza Cairo 7 A2
El Khadr Jerusalem 13 B1
El Khalîfa Cairo 7 A2
El Kôm el Ahmar Cairo 7 A2
El Ma'âdi Cairo 7 B2
El Matariya Cairo 7 A2
El Mohandessin Cairo 7 A2
El Monte Los Angeles 16 B4
El Muqattam Cairo 7 A2
El Mûskî Cairo 7 A2
El Pardo Madrid 17 A1
El Pobleneu Barcelona 4 A2
El Portal Miami 19 C2
El Prat Barcelona ✈ (BCN) Barcelona 4 B1
El Prat de Llobregat Barcelona 4 B1
El Qâhira Cairo 7 A2
El Qubba Cairo 7 A2
El Reloj Mexico City 18 C2
El Retiro Madrid 17 B1
El Salto Santiago 27 B2
El Sereno Los Angeles 16 B3
El Talibîya Cairo 7 B2
El Vergel Mexico City 18 C2
El Wâhli Cairo 7 A2
El Zamâlik Cairo 7 A2
El Zeitûn Cairo 7 A2
Elefthérios Venizelos ✈ (ATH) Athens 2 A3
Elephanta Caves Mumbai 20 B2
Elephanta I. Mumbai 20 B2
Ellboda Stockholm 29 A3
Ellenor, L. Orlando 23 B2
Elliniko Olympic Complex Athens 2 B2
Ellis I. New York 22 B1
Elmers End London 15 B3
Elmhurst New York 22 B2
Elmstead London 15 B4
Elmwood New Orleans 21 B1
Elmwood Park Chicago 9 B2
Elmwood Park New York 22 A1
Elsiesrivier Cape Town 8 A2
Elsternwick Melbourne 18 B2
Eltham London 15 B4
Elwood Melbourne 18 B1
Élysée Paris 24 A2
Elysian Park Los Angeles 16 B3
Emāmzādeh Sāleh Tehran 31 A2
Emerainville Paris 24 B4
Emeryville San Francisco 26 A3
Eminönü Istanbul 12 B1
Emirates, Mall of the Dubai 9 B1
Emirgan Istanbul 12 B2
Emmarentia Johannesburg 13 A2
Empire State Building New York 22 B2
Encantado Rio de Janeiro 25 B1
Encino Los Angeles 16 B2
Encino Res. Los Angeles 16 B1
Enebyberg Stockholm 29 A1
Enfield Sydney 29 B1
Engenho, I. do Rio de Janeiro 25 B2
Englewood Chicago 9 C3
Englewood New York 22 A2
Englewood Cliffs New York 22 A2
Enmore Sydney 29 B2
Enskede Stockholm 29 B2
Enterprise Las Vegas 14 B1
Entrevias Madrid 17 B1
Epcot Orlando 23 B1
Epping Sydney 29 A1
Erenköy Istanbul 12 C2
Erith London 15 B5
Erlaa Vienna 32 B1
Ermington Sydney 29 A1
Ermita Manila 17 B1
Ershatou Guangzhou 11 B2
Erskineville Sydney 29 B2
Erunkan Lagos 14 A2
Erzsébet-Telep Budapest 7 B3
Eschenried Munich 21 A1
Esenler Istanbul 12 B1
Esher London 15 B1
Eskbank Edinburgh 11 B3
Esplanade Shanghai 28 c3
Esplugas Barcelona 4 A1
Esposizione Universale di Roma Rome 26 C1
Essendon Melbourne 18 A1
Essendon ✈ (MEB) Melbourne 18 A1
Essingen Stockholm 29 B1
Essling Vienna 32 A3
Est, Gare de l' Paris 24 A3
Estado, Parque do São Paulo 27 B2
Estelle New Orleans 21 B2
Estrela, Basilica da Lisbon 16 A2
Etobicoke Toronto 31 B1
Etobicoke Cr. ➜ Toronto 31 B1
Etterbeek Brussels 6 B2
Eung-am Seoul 27 B1
Eunpyeong Seoul 27 B1
Evanston Chicago 9 A2
Even Sapir Jerusalem 13 B1
Evere Brussels 6 A2
Everett Boston 6 A2
Evergreen Park Chicago 9 C2
Evīn Tehran 31 A2
Ewu Lagos 14 A1
Exhibition Place Toronto 31 B2
Expo 2010 Shanghai 28 B1
Exposições, Palácio das Rio de Janeiro 25 B1
Eyüp Istanbul 12 B1
Ezeiza ✈ (EZE) Buenos Aires 7 C1

F

Faber, Mt. Singapore 28 B2
Fælledparken Copenhagen 8 A3
Fägelön Stockholm 29 B1
Fagersjö Stockholm 29 B2
Fairland Johannesburg 13 A1
Fairmilehead Edinburgh 11 B2
Fairport Toronto 31 A4
Fairview New York 22 B2
Fairview, L. Orlando 23 A2
Falenty Warsaw 33 C1
Faliro Athens 2 B1
Faliro, Ormos Athens 2 B1
Falkenburg Berlin 5 A4
Falkenhagen Berlin 5 A1
Falkensee Berlin 5 A1
Falomo Lagos 14 B2
False Bay Cape Town 8 B2
Famões Lisbon 16 A1
Fangcun Guangzhou 11 B2
Farahābād Tehran 31 A2
Farforovskaya St. Petersburg 27 B2
Farningham London 15 B5
Farsta Stockholm 29 B2
Fasanerie-Nord Munich 21 A2
Fasangarten Munich 21 B2
Fatih Istanbul 12 B1
Favoriten Vienna 32 B2
Fawkner Melbourne 18 A1
Fawkner Park Melbourne 18 B1
Feldkirchen Munich 21 B3
Feldmoching Munich 21 A2
Feltham London 15 B1
Fener Istanbul 12 B1
Fenerbahçe Istanbul 12 C2
Fengtai Beijing 4 C1
Fengtai Stadium Beijing 4 B1
Ferencváros Budapest 7 B2
Ferihegy, Budapest ✈ (BUD) Budapest 7 B3
Ferndale Johannesburg 13 A2
Fichtenau Berlin 5 B5
Field Museum of Natural History Chicago 9 B3
Fields Corner Boston 6 B2
Fiera Camp Milan 18 B1
Figino Milan 18 B1
Fijir Baghdad 3 A2
Filadelfia Athens 2 A2
Fili-Mazilovo Moscow 19 B1
Filothei Athens 2 A2
Finchley London 15 A2
Fine Arts, Museum of Boston 6 A2
Finglas Dublin 10 A2
Finsbury London 15 A3
Finsbury Park London 15 A3
Fiorito Buenos Aires 7 C2
Firhouse Dublin 10 B2
Fischerhäuser Munich 21 A3
Fisher I. Miami 19 D3
Fishermans Bend Melbourne 18 A1
Fisherman's Village Los Angeles 16 C2
Fisherville Toronto 31 A2
Fisksätra Stockholm 29 B3
Fitzroy Gardens Melbourne 18 A1
Five Cowrie Cr. ➜ Lagos 14 B2
Five Dock Sydney 29 B1
Fjellstrand Oslo 23 B2
Flamengo Rio de Janeiro 25 B1
Flamingo Orlando 23 B2
Flaminio Rome 26 B1
Flaskebekk Oslo 23 A2
Flatbush New York 22 C2
Flatlands New York 22 C2
Flaten Stockholm 29 B2
Flemington Racecourse Melbourne 18 A1
Flint Pk. Los Angeles 16 B3
Florence Los Angeles 16 C3
Florence Bloom Bird Sanctuary ⌂ Johannesburg 13 A2
Florentia Johannesburg 13 B2
Flores Buenos Aires 7 B2
Flores, Merconcado de Mexico City 18 C2
Floresta Buenos Aires 7 B2
Florida Buenos Aires 7 B2
Florida Johannesburg 13 B1
Floridsdorf Vienna 32 A2
Flushing New York 22 B3
Flushing Meadows Corona Park New York 22 B2
Flysta Stockholm 29 A1
Fo Tan Hong Kong 12 A2
Foggy Bottom Washington 33 B2
Föhrenhain Vienna 32 A2
Fontainebleau Johannesburg 13 A1
Fontenay-aux-Roses Paris 24 B2
Fontenay-le-Fleury Paris 24 B1
Fontenay-sous-Bois Paris 24 A3
Foots Cray London 15 B4
Footscray Melbourne 18 A1
Forbidden City = Imperial Palace Museum Beijing 4 B2
Forest Brussels 6 B1
Forest Gate London 15 A4
Forest Heights Washington 33 C2
Forest Hill London 15 B3
Forest Hill Toronto 31 A2
Forest Hills New York 22 B2
Forest Park Chicago 9 B2
Forest Park New York 22 B2
Forest View Chicago 9 C2
Fornebu Oslo 23 A2
Foro Romano Rome 26 B1
Forstenried Munich 21 B1
Forstenrieder Park Munich 21 B1
Fort Mumbai 20 B1
Fort Dupont Park Washington 33 B3
Fort Foote Village Washington 33 C2
Fort Lauderdale Miami 19 B3
Fort Lauderdale Executive ✈ (FXE) Miami 19 A2
Fort Lauderdale-Hollywood Int. ✈ (FLL) Miami 19 B3
Fort Lee New York 22 A2
Forth, Firth of Edinburgh 11 A3
Forth Rail Bridge Edinburgh 11 A1
Forth Road Bridge Edinburgh 11 A1
Foshan Guangzhou 11 B1
Föt Budapest 7 A3
Fourqueux Paris 24 A1
Fox Studios Sydney 29 B2
Foxrock Dublin 10 B2
Franconia Washington 33 C2
Frank Lloyd Wright Home Chicago 9 B2
Frankel Singapore 28 B3
Franklin Park Boston 6 B2
Franklin Park Washington 33 B2
Franklin Res. Los Angeles 16 B2
Franz Josef Strauss ✈ (MUC) Munich 21 A3
Frauenkirche Munich 21 B2
Frederiksberg Copenhagen 8 A3
Frederiksdal Copenhagen 8 A2
Fredersdorf Berlin 5 A5
Freguesia Rio de Janeiro 25 A1
Freidrichshain, Volkspark Berlin 5 A3
Freiham Munich 21 B1
Freimann Munich 21 A2
French Quarter New Orleans 21 B2
Fresh Pond Boston 6 A1
Fresnes Paris 24 B2
Freudenau Vienna 32 A2
Friarstown Dublin 10 B1
Friedenau Berlin 5 B3
Friedrichsfelde Berlin 5 A4
Friedrichshagen Berlin 5 B4
Friedrichshain Berlin 5 A3
Friedrichslust Berlin 5 A5
Friherrs Helsinki 11 B1
Frilufts Museum Helsinki 11 B2
Frontón, I. Lima 14 B1
Frunze Moscow 19 B2
Fuchū Tokyo 30 A1
Fuencarral Madrid 17 B1
Fuenlabrada Madrid 17 C1
Fukagawa Tokyo 30 B3
Fukushima Osaka 23 A1
Fulham London 15 B2
Funabori Tokyo 30 A4
Fundão, I. do Rio de Janeiro 25 B1
Fünfhaus Vienna 32 A2
Furesø Copenhagen 8 A2
Fürth Munich 21 B2
Futago-tamagawaen Tokyo 30 B2
Fuxing Dao Shanghai 28 B2
Fuxing Park Shanghai 28 B1
Fuxinglu Beijing 4 B1

G

G. Ross Lord Park Toronto 31 A2
Gaebong Seoul 27 C1
Gage Park Chicago 9 C2
Gagny Paris 24 A4
Galata Istanbul 12 B1
Galata Tower Istanbul 12 B1
Galatsi Athens 2 A2
Galeão, Int. de ✈ (GIG) Rio de Janeiro 25 A1
Galyanovo Moscow 19 B3
Gambir Jakarta 12 A1
Gamboa Rio de Janeiro 25 B1
Gambolòita Milan 18 B2
Gamlebyen Oslo 23 A3
Gangdong Seoul 27 B2
Gangnam Seoul 27 B1
Gangseo Seoul 27 B1
Gangtou Guangzhou 11 A1
Gangwei Guangzhou 11 B2
Ganjiakou Beijing 4 B1
Ganshoren Brussels 6 A1
Gants Hill London 15 A4
Gaohang Shanghai 28 B2
Gaoqiao Shanghai 28 A2
Garbagnate Milanese Milan 18 A1
Garbatella Rome 26 B2
Garches Paris 24 A2
Garching Munich 21 A3
Garden City Cairo 7 A2
Garden District New Orleans 21 B2
Garden Reach Kolkata 14 B1
Garder Oslo 23 B2
Garfield New York 22 A1
Garfield Park Chicago 9 B2
Gargareta Athens 2 B2
Garibong Seoul 27 C1
Garvanza Los Angeles 16 B3
Gåshaga Stockholm 29 A3
Gateway ⌂ New York 22 C2
Gateway of India Mumbai 20 B2
Gatow Berlin 5 B1
Gavà Barcelona 4 B1
Gavamar Barcelona 4 B1
Gávea Rio de Janeiro 25 B1
Gávea, Pedra da Rio de Janeiro 25 B1
Gazdagrét Budapest 7 B1
Gaziosmanpaşa Istanbul 12 B1
Gebel el Ahmar Cairo 7 A3
Gebel el Muqattam Cairo 7 A2
Gebel el Tura Cairo 7 B2
Geiselgasteig Munich 21 B2
General San Martín Buenos Aires 7 B1
Gennevilliers Paris 24 A2
Gentilly New Orleans 21 B2
Gentilly Paris 24 B3
Gentofte Copenhagen 8 A3
Genval Brussels 6 B2
George I. Hong Kong 12 B1
Georges River Bridge Sydney 29 C1
Georgetown Washington 33 B2
Georgia Dome Atlanta 3 B2
Gerasdorf bei Wien Vienna 32 A2
Gerberau Munich 21 A1
Gerli Buenos Aires 7 C2
Germiston Johannesburg 13 B2
Gern Munich 21 B2
Getafe Madrid 17 C1
Getty Center, The Los Angeles 16 B2
Geunjeong Seoul 27 C1
Geva Binyamin Jerusalem 13 A2
Geylang Serai Singapore 28 B3
Gharapuri = Elephanta I. Mumbai 20 B2
Gharapuri Mumbai 20 B2
Gharb = Shahrak-e Qods Tehran 31 A2
Ghatkopar Mumbai 20 A2
Ghazipur Delhi 10 B2
Ghizri Karachi 13 B2
Ghizri Cr. ➜ Karachi 13 B2
Ghonda Delhi 10 A2
Ghusuri Kolkata 14 B2
Gianicolense Rome 26 B1
Giant Wheel = Riesenrad Vienna 32 A2
Gibraltar Pt. Toronto 31 B2
Gidea Park London 15 A5
Giesing Munich 21 B2
Gilmerton Edinburgh 11 B3
Gilo Jerusalem 13 B2
Gimmersta Stockholm 29 B3
Ginza Tokyo 30 B3
Giv'at Ram Jerusalem 13 B2
Giv'at Ye'arim Jerusalem 13 B1
Giv'at Ze'ev Jerusalem 13 A2
Giv'on Jerusalem 13 A1
Giza = El Gîza Cairo 7 A2
Giza Pyramids Cairo 7 B1
Gjersjøen Oslo 23 B3
Gladesville Sydney 29 B1
Gladsakse Copenhagen 8 A2
Glasnevin Dublin 10 A2
Glassmanor Washington 33 C3
Glasthule Dublin 10 B3
Glen Iris Melbourne 18 B2
Glen Mar Park Washington 33 B2
Glen Rouge Park Toronto 31 A4
Glenasmole Reservoirs Dublin 10 B1
Glencoe Chicago 9 A2
Glencorse Res. Edinburgh 11 B2
Glencullen Dublin 10 B2
Glendale Los Angeles 16 B3
Glendoo Mt. Dublin 10 B2
Glenhuntly Melbourne 18 B2
Glenview Chicago 9 A2
Glenview Countryside Chicago 9 A2
Glenvista Johannesburg 13 B2
Glifada Athens 2 B2
Glostrup Copenhagen 8 B2
Gogar Edinburgh 11 B2
Göktürk Istanbul 12 A1
Golabari Kolkata 14 B2
Golabki Warsaw 33 B1
Gold Coast Chicago 9 B3
Golden Beach Miami 19 C3
Golden Gate San Francisco 26 B2
Golden Gate ⌂ San Francisco 26 A2
Golden Gate Bridge San Francisco 26 B2

Golden Gate Park San Francisco 26 B2
Golden Horn = Haliç Istanbul 12 B1
Golders Green London 15 A2
Golestan Palace Tehran 31 A2
Golf Chicago 9 A2
Gonen Jerusalem 13 B2
Gongneung Seoul 27 B2
Goodmayes London 15 A4
Goodwood Cape Town 8 A2
Gopalpur Kolkata 14 B2
Górce Warsaw 33 B1
Gore Hill Sydney 29 A2
Gorelyy → St. Petersburg 27 A3
Gorgie Edinburgh 11 B2
Gorky Park Moscow 19 B2
Gosen Berlin 5 B5
Gosener kanal Berlin 5 B5
Gospel Oak London 15 A3
Gotanda Tokyo 30 B3
Goth Goli Mar Karachi 13 A2
Goth Sher Shah Karachi 13 A1
Gotha Orlando 23 A1
Gournay-sur-Marne Paris 24 A4
Governador, I. do Rio de Janeiro 25 A1
Governors I. New York 22 B1
Grabów Warsaw 33 C1
Gràcia Barcelona 4 A2
Gräfelfing Munich 21 B1
Gragoatá Rio de Janeiro 25 B2
Grand Bazaar = Kapali Carsi Istanbul 12 B1
Grand Central Station New York 22 B2
Grand Palace Bangkok 3 B1
Grand Place Brussels 6 A2
Grande Place Brussels 6 A2
Grankulla = Kauniainen Helsinki 11 B1
Grant Park Chicago 9 B3
Granton Edinburgh 11 B2
Grassy Park Cape Town 8 B2
Gratosóglio Milan 18 B2
Gratzwalde Berlin 5 B5
Gravesend New York 22 C2
Grazhdanka St. Petersburg 27 B2
Great Western Forum Los Angeles 16 C2
Greco Milan 18 A2
Green I. Hong Kong 12 B1
Green Point Cape Town 8 A1
Green Point Stadium Cape Town 8 A1
Greenfield Park Montreal 20 B3
Greenford London 15 A1
Greenhill London 15 A2
Greenhills Dublin 10 B1
Greenwich □ London 15 B3
Greenwich Observatory London 15 B3
Greenwich Village New York 22 B2
Greenwood Boston 6 A2
Grefsen Oslo 23 A3
Gresham Park Atlanta 3 B2
Gretna New Orleans 21 B2
Gretna City Park New Orleans 21 B2
Greve Strand Copenhagen 8 B1
Greynolds Park Miami 19 C3
Griebnitzsee Berlin 5 B1
Griffith Park Los Angeles 16 B3
Grimbergen Brussels 6 A2
Grinzing Vienna 32 A2
Gröbenried Munich 21 A1
Grochów Warsaw 33 B2
Grodzisk Warsaw 33 B2
Groenendaal Brussels 6 B2
Grogol Petamburin Jakarta 12 A1
Gronsdorf Munich 21 B3
Grorud Oslo 23 A4
Gross-Glienicke Berlin 5 B1
Gross-Hadern Munich 21 B1
Gross-Lappen Munich 21 A2
Grosse Krampe Berlin 5 B5
Grosse Müggelsee Berlin 5 B4
Grosse Point Lighthouse Chicago 9 A2
Grossenzersdorf Vienna 32 A3
Grossenzersdorfer Arm → Vienna 32 A3
Grosser Biberhaufen Vienna 32 A2
Grosser Wannsee Berlin 5 B2
Grossfeld-Siedlung Vienna 32 A2
Grosshesselohe Munich 21 B2
Grossjedlersdorf Vienna 32 A2
Grossziethen Berlin 5 B3
Ground Zero = National September 11 Memorial and Museum New York 22 B1
Grove Hall Boston 6 B2
Grove Park Atlanta 3 B2
Grove Park London 15 B4
Grove Park London 15 B2
Groveton Washington 33 C2
Grünau Berlin 5 B4
Grunewald Berlin 5 B2
Grünwald Munich 21 B2
Grünwalder Forst Munich 21 B2
Grymes Hill New York 22 C1
Guadalupe Manila 17 B2
Guadalupe, Basilica de Mexico City 18 B2
Guanabara, B. de Rio de Janeiro 25 B1
Guanabara, Jardim Rio de Janeiro 25 A1
Guanabara, Palácio da Rio de Janeiro 25 B1
Guang'anmen Beijing 4 B1
Guangqumen Beijing 4 B2
Guangzhou Guangzhou 11 B2
Guanshuo Guangzhou 11 B3
Gucun Shanghai 28 A1
Gudō Stockholm 29 B3
Güell, Parque de Barcelona 4 A2
Guinardó Barcelona 4 A2
Gulbai Karachi 13 A1
Gulshan-e Iqbal Jerusalem 13 A2
Güngören Istanbul 12 B1
Gunnersbury London 15 B2
Guomao Beijing 4 B2
Gustavo A. Madero Mexico City 18 B2
Guttenberg New York 22 B1
Gutuyevskiy, Ostrov St. Petersburg 27 B1
Guyancourt Paris 24 B1
Gwanak Seoul 27 C1
Gwanaksan Seoul 27 C1
Gyál Budapest 7 B3
Gyáli-patak → Budapest 7 B2

H

Haaga Helsinki 11 B2
Haar Munich 21 B3
Habay Manila 17 C1
Hackbridge London 15 B3
Hackensack New York 22 A1
Hackensack → New York 22 B1
Hackney □ London 15 A3
Hackney Wick London 15 A3
Hadr, Warrāq el Cairo 7 A2
Haga Stockholm 29 A2
Hagenbrunn Vienna 32 A2
Hägersten Stockholm 29 B1
Häggvik Stockholm 29 A1
Hagonoy Manila 17 B2
Hague Park Toronto 31 A3
Haidari = Chaidari Athens 2 A1
Haidarpur Delhi 10 A1
Haidhausen Munich 21 B2
Haidian Beijing 4 B1
Haight-Ashbury San Francisco 26 B2
Hainault London 15 A4
Haizhou Guangzhou 11 B2
Haizhu Guangchang Guangzhou 11 B2
Hakunila Helsinki 11 B3
Halandri = Chalandri Athens 2 A2
Halásztelek Budapest 7 B1
Haliç Istanbul 12 B1
Halim Perdana Kusuma Int. ✕ (HLP) Jakarta 12 B2
Hallandale Beach Miami 19 C3
Halle Brussels 6 B1
Haltiala Helsinki 11 B2
Haltiavuori Helsinki 11 B2
Ham London 15 B2
Hämeenkylä Helsinki 11 B1
Hammarby Stockholm 29 B2
Hamme Brussels 6 A1
Hammersmith London 15 B2
Hampstead London 15 A2
Hampstead Montreal 20 B2
Hampstead Garden Suburb London 15 A2
Hampstead Heath London 15 A2
Hampton London 15 B1
Hampton Court Palace London 15 B1
Hampton Wick London 15 B2
Hamrā' Baghdad 3 B1
Hanala Helsinki 11 A3
Haneda Tokyo 30 B3
Haneda, Tōkyō ✕ (HND) Tokyo 30 B3
Hang Hau Hong Kong 12 B2
Hanging Gardens Mumbai 20 B1
Hanlon Toronto 31 B1
Hanwell London 15 A1
Hanworth London 15 B1
Haora Kolkata 14 B1
Hapeville Atlanta 3 C2
Happy Valley Hong Kong 12 B2
Har Adar Jerusalem 13 B1
Har Gilo Jerusalem 13 B2
Har Homa Jerusalem 13 B2
Har Nof Jerusalem 13 B2
Harahan New Orleans 21 B1
Harbour Front Centre Singapore 28 B2
Haren Brussels 6 A2
Hareskovby Copenhagen 8 A2
Haringey □ London 15 A3
Harjusuo Helsinki 11 B3
Harlaching Munich 21 B2
Harlaw Res. Edinburgh 11 B2
Harlem New York 22 B2
Harlesden London 15 A2
Harlington London 15 B1
Harmaja Helsinki 11 C2
Harmashatar hegy Budapest 7 A2
Harolds Cross Dublin 10 B2
Háros Budapest 7 B2
Harperrig Res. Edinburgh 11 B1
Harrow □ London 15 A1
Harrow on the Hill London 15 A1
Harrow School London 15 A1
Harrow Weald London 15 A1
Hartsfield-Jackson Atlanta Int. ✕ (ATL) Atlanta 3 C2
Harumi Tokyo 30 B3
Harvard Univ. Boston 6 A2
Harvey Chicago 9 D3
Harvey New Orleans 21 B2
Harwood Heights Chicago 9 B2
Ḩasanābād Tehran 31 A1
Hasbrouck Heights New York 22 A1
Haselhorst Berlin 5 A2
Hasköy Istanbul 12 B1
Hasle Oslo 23 B2
Haslum Oslo 23 A2
Hässelby Stockholm 29 A1
Hästhagen Stockholm 29 B2
Hatch End London 15 A1
Hatiara Kolkata 14 B2
Hauketo Oslo 23 A3
Hauz Khas Delhi 10 B2
Havel → Berlin 5 A2
Havelkanal Berlin 5 A2
Havering □ London 15 A5
Havering-atte-Bower London 15 A5
Haworth New York 22 A2
Hawthorne Racecourse Chicago 9 C2
Hayes London 15 B4
Hayes London 15 A1
Hayes End London 15 A1
Hayford Chicago 9 C2
Heathfield Cape Town 8 B1
Heathrow, London ✕ (LHR) London 15 B1
Hebe Haven Hong Kong 12 A2
Hedong Guangzhou 11 B2
Heidelberg Heights Melbourne 18 A2
Heidelberg West Melbourne 18 A2
Heidemühle Berlin 5 B5
Heideveld Cape Town 8 A2
Heiligensee Berlin 5 A2
Heiligenstadt Vienna 32 A2
Heinersdorf Berlin 5 A3
Hélène de Champlain, Parc ⌂ Montreal 20 A2
Helenelund Stockholm 29 A1
Heliopolis = Masr el Gedida Cairo 7 A2
Hellersdorf Berlin 5 A4
Hellerup Copenhagen 8 A3
Helsingfors = Helsinki Helsinki 11 B2
Helsinki Helsinki 11 B2
Helsinki-Vantaa ✕ (HEL) Helsinki 11 B2
Hen and Chicken B. Sydney 29 B1
Henderson Las Vegas 14 B2
Hendon London 15 A2
Hengsha Guangzhou 11 B2
Hennigsdorf Berlin 5 A2
Henryków Warsaw 33 B1
Henson Cr. → Washington 33 C3
Henttaa Helsinki 11 B1
Heping Park Shanghai 28 B2
Hepingli Beijing 4 B2
Herlev Copenhagen 8 A2
Herman Eckstein Park Johannesburg 13 A2
Hermannskogel Vienna 32 A1
Hermiston Edinburgh 11 B2
Hermitage and Winter Palace St. Petersburg 27 B2
Hermsdorf Berlin 5 A2
Hernals Vienna 32 A2
Herne Hill London 15 B3
Héroes de Churubusco Mexico City 18 B2
Herons, Î. aux Montreal 20 B2
Herstedøster Copenhagen 8 A1
Herttoniemi Helsinki 11 B3
Ḩeşārak Tehran 31 A1
Heston London 15 B1
Hetzendorf Vienna 32 B1
Hextable London 15 B5
Hialeah Miami 19 C1
Hialeah Race Track Miami 19 C1
Hiawassa, L. Orlando 23 A2
Hickory Hills Chicago 9 C2
Hiekkaharju Helsinki 11 B3
Hietaniemi Helsinki 11 B2
Hietzing Vienna 32 A1
Higashi Osaka 23 A2
Higashimurayama Tokyo 30 A1
Higashinari Osaka 23 A2
Higashisumiyoshi Osaka 23 B2
Higashiyodogawa Osaka 23 A1
High Park Toronto 31 B2
Highbury London 15 A3
Highgate London 15 A3
Highland Cr. → Toronto 31 A3
Highland Creek Toronto 31 A3
Highland Park Los Angeles 16 B3
Highlands North Johannesburg 13 A2
Hillcrest Heights Washington 33 C3
Hillend Edinburgh 11 A1
Hillingdon □ London 15 A1
Hillwood Washington 33 B2
Hilmīya Cairo 7 A2
Hin Keng Hong Kong 12 A2
Hirota Osaka 23 A1
Hirschstetten Vienna 32 A2
Hither Green London 15 B3
Hiyoshi Tokyo 30 B2
Hizma Jerusalem 13 B2
Hjortekær Copenhagen 8 A3
Hjortespring Copenhagen 8 A2
Hlubočepy Prague 25 B2
Ho Chung Hong Kong 12 A2
Hoboken New York 22 B1
Hobsons B. Melbourne 18 B1
Hochbrück Munich 21 A2
Hochelaga Montreal 20 A2
Hoegi Seoul 27 B2
Hoeilaart Brussels 6 B2
Hofburg Vienna 32 A2
Hoffman I. New York 22 C1
Hohenbrunn Munich 21 B3
Hohenschönhausen Berlin 5 A4
Holargos = Cholargos Athens 2 B2
Holborn London 15 A3
Holden, L. Orlando 23 B2
Holešovice Prague 25 B2
Holiday Park Miami 19 B3
Holland Village Singapore 28 B2
Höllriegelskreuth Munich 21 B1
Hollywood Los Angeles 16 B3
Hollywood Miami 19 B3
Hollywood Bowl Los Angeles 16 B2
Holmenkollen Oslo 23 A3
Holmgård Stockholm 29 B1
Holmlia Oslo 23 B3
Holocaust Memorial Jerusalem 13 B2
Holyrood House, Palace of Edinburgh 11 B3
Holysloot Amsterdam 2 A3
Homerton London 15 A3
Hometown Chicago 9 C2
Hōnanchō Tokyo 30 A2
Honcho Tokyo 30 A3
Honden Tokyo 30 A4
Hondo, Rio → Los Angeles 16 B4
Hong Kong Hong Kong 12 B1
Hong Kong, Univ. of Hong Kong 12 B1
Hong Kong I. Hong Kong 12 B2
Hongje Seoul 27 B1
Hongjimun Tunnel Seoul 27 B1
Hongkou Shanghai 28 B1
Hongqiao Shanghai 28 B1
Honjyo Tokyo 30 A3
Honoré Mercier, Pont Montreal 20 B1
Honow Berlin 5 A4
Hook London 15 B2
Horikiri Tokyo 30 A4
Horn Pond Boston 6 A1
Hornchurch London 15 A5
Horni Prague 25 B3
Horní Počernice Prague 25 B3
Hornsey London 15 A3
Horoměřice Prague 25 B1
Hortaleza Madrid 17 B2
Hosoyama Tokyo 30 B2
Hostafranchs Barcelona 4 A1
Hostivař Prague 25 B3
Houbětin Prague 25 B3
Hougang Singapore 28 A3
Houghton Johannesburg 13 B2
Houilles Paris 24 A2
Hounslow □ London 15 B1
Hout Bay Cape Town 8 B1
Hove Å → Copenhagen 8 B2
Hovedøya Oslo 23 A3
Høvik Oslo 23 A2
Hovorčovice Prague 25 A3
Howard Beach New York 22 C2
Howrah = Haora Kolkata 14 B1
Howth Dublin 10 A3
Howth Hd. Dublin 10 A3
Hōya Tokyo 30 A2
Hradčany Prague 25 B2
Huanghuagang Mausoleum Guangzhou 11 B2
Huangpu Shanghai 28 B2
Huangpu Jiang → Shanghai 28 B1
Huangtugang Beijing 4 C1
Huascar Lima 14 A2
Huay Khwang Bangkok 3 B2
Huddinge Stockholm 29 B2
Huechuraba Santiago 27 B1
Hugh Taylor Birch State Recr. Area ⌂ Miami 19 B3
Huizingen Brussels 6 B1
Humayun's Tomb Delhi 10 B2
Humber → Toronto 31 A1
Humber B. Toronto 31 B2
Humber Bay Toronto 31 B2
Humber Bay Park Toronto 31 B2
Humber College Toronto 31 B1
Humber Summit Toronto 31 A1
Humber Valley Village Toronto 31 A1
Humberlea Toronto 31 A1
Humberwood Park Toronto 31 A1
Humboldt Park Chicago 9 B2
Humera Madrid 17 B1
Hunaydī Baghdad 3 B2
Hundige Copenhagen 8 B1
Hundige Strand Copenhagen 8 B2
Hung Hom Hong Kong 12 B2
Hunters Hill Sydney 29 B1
Hunters Pt. San Francisco 26 B2
Huntington Washington 33 C2
Huntington Park Los Angeles 16 C3
Ḩurīya Baghdad 3 A1
Hurstville Sydney 29 B1
Husan Jerusalem 13 B1
Husby Stockholm 29 A1
Husum Copenhagen 8 A2
Hütteldorf Vienna 32 A1
Hüvösvölgy Budapest 7 A2
Huwon Secret Garden Seoul 27 B1
Hvalstad Oslo 23 A1
Hvalstrand Oslo 23 A2
Hvidovre Copenhagen 8 B2
Hwagok Seoul 27 B1
Hyattsville Washington 33 B3
Hyde Park Boston 6 B2
Hyde Park Chicago 9 C3
Hyde Park Johannesburg 13 A2
Hyde Park London 15 A2
Hyde Park Los Angeles 16 C3

I

Ibese Lagos 14 A2
Ibirapuera São Paulo 27 B1
Ibirapuera, Parque do São Paulo 27 B2
Icaraí Rio de Janeiro 25 B2
İçerenköy Istanbul 12 C2
Ichgao Tokyo 30 B2
Ichigaya Tokyo 30 A3
Ichikawa Tokyo 30 A4
Ickenham London 15 A1
Iddo Lagos 14 B2
Idi-Oro Lagos 14 A2
Iganmu Lagos 14 B2
Igbobi Lagos 14 A2
Igbologun Lagos 14 B1
Igny Paris 24 B2
IJ, Het → Amsterdam 2 A2
IJ-meer Amsterdam 2 A3
Ijesa-Tedo Lagos 14 B1
Ijora Lagos 14 B2
Ikebe Tokyo 30 B2
Ikebukuro Tokyo 30 A3
Ikegami Tokyo 30 B3
Ikeja Lagos 14 A2
Ikeuchi Osaka 23 B2
Ikorodu Lagos 14 A2
Ikoyi Lagos 14 B2
Ikuata Lagos 14 B2
Ikuno Osaka 23 A2
Ikuta Tokyo 30 B2
Ila Oslo 23 A3
Ilford London 15 A4
Ilioupoli Athens 2 B2
Illinois at Chicago, Univ. of Chicago 9 B3
Illinois Institute of Technology Chicago 9 B3
Ilpendam Amsterdam 2 A2
Ilsos → Athens 2 B2
Imbābah Cairo 7 A2
Imbiah Lookout Singapore 28 B2
Imielin Warsaw 33 C2
Imirim São Paulo 27 A2
Imitos Athens 2 B2
Imitos, Oros Athens 2 B2
Imperial Palace Museum Beijing 4 B2
Inagi Tokyo 30 B2
Inchcolm Edinburgh 11 A2
Inchicore Dublin 10 A1
Inchkeith Edinburgh 11 A3
Inchmickery Edinburgh 11 A2
Incirano Milan 18 A1
Independencia Lima 14 A2
Independencia Santiago 27 B2
India Gate Delhi 10 B2
Indian Creek Village Miami 19 C3
Indianópolis São Paulo 27 B2
Indira Gandhi Int. ✕ (DEL) Delhi 10 B1
Industria Johannesburg 13 B1
Industrial Canal New Orleans 21 A2
Ingierstrand Oslo 23 B3
Inglewood Los Angeles 16 C3
Ingliston Edinburgh 11 B1
Inhaúma Rio de Janeiro 25 B1
Inner Port Shelter Hong Kong 12 A2
Interlagos São Paulo 27 C1
Intramuros Manila 17 B1
Invalides Paris 24 A2
Inverkeithing Edinburgh 11 A1
Inzersdorf Vienna 32 B2
Ipanema Rio de Janeiro 25 B1
Ipiranga São Paulo 27 B2
Ipiranga → São Paulo 27 B2
Iponri Lagos 14 B2
Ireland's Eye Dublin 10 A3
Irving Park Chicago 9 B2
Isabel Rio de Janeiro 25 B1
Isagatedo Lagos 14 A1
Isar → Munich 21 B2
Ishbīlīya Baghdad 3 A2
Ishøj Strand Copenhagen 8 B2
Island Park Toronto 31 B2
Islev Copenhagen 8 A2
Isleworth London 15 B2
Islington Toronto 31 B1
Islington □ London 15 A3
Ismā'ilīya, Qanâ el Cairo 7 A2
Ismaning Munich 21 A3
Ismayloskiy Park Moscow 19 B3
Isolo Lagos 14 A2
Issy-les-Moulineaux Paris 24 B2
İstanbul Istanbul 12 C1
İstanbul Boğazı Istanbul 12 B2
İstinye Istanbul 12 B2
Itä Hakkila Helsinki 11 B3
Itaewon Seoul 27 B1
Itami Osaka 23 A1
Itanhanga Rio de Janeiro 25 B1
Ivanhoe Melbourne 18 A2
Ives Estates Miami 19 C2
Ivry-sur-Seine Paris 24 B3
Ixelles Brussels 6 B2
Izmaylovo Moscow 19 B3
Iztacalco Mexico City 18 B2
Iztapalapa Mexico City 18 B2

J

Jaba Jerusalem 13 A2
Jabotabek = Jakarta Jakarta 12 A2
Jacaré Rio de Janeiro 25 B1
Jackson Heights New York 22 B2
Jackson Park Chicago 9 C3
Jacques-Cartier Montreal 20 A3
Jacques-Cartier, Pont Montreal 20 A2
Jadavpur Kolkata 14 C2
Jade Buddha Temple Shanghai 28 B1
Jægersborg Copenhagen 8 A3
Jægersborg Dyrehave Copenhagen 8 A3
Jagadishpur Kolkata 14 B1
Jagatpur Delhi 10 A2
Jaguaré, Rib. do → São Paulo 27 B1
Jahangirpur Delhi 10 A2
Jakarta Jakarta 12 A2
Jakarta, Teluk Jakarta 12 A1
Jakarta Halim Perdana Kusuma Int. ✕ (HLP) Jakarta 12 B2
Jalan Kayu Singapore 28 A3
Jamaica B. New York 22 C3
Jamaica Plain Boston 6 B2
Jamakpuri Delhi 10 B1
Jamshīdīyeh Tehran 31 A2
Jamsil Seoul 27 B2
Jamwon Seoul 27 B2
Janki Warsaw 33 C1
Jaraguá São Paulo 27 A1
Jaraguá, Pico de São Paulo 27 A1
Jardim Paulista São Paulo 27 B1
Järvatältet Stockholm 29 A1
Jaskhar Mumbai 20 B2
Jatinegara Jakarta 12 B2
Javādīyeh Tehran 31 B2
Jawaharlal Nehru Port = Nhava Sheva Mumbai 20 B2
Jaworowa Warsaw 33 C1
Jean Lafitte Nat. Historical Park ⌂ New Orleans 21 B1
Jedlesee Vienna 32 A2
Jefferson New Orleans 21 B2
Jefferson Memorial Washington 33 B2
Jefferson Park Chicago 9 B2
Jefferson Park Los Angeles 16 B3
Jegi Seoul 27 B2
Jelambar Jakarta 12 A1
Jelonki Warsaw 33 B1
Jerónimos, Mosteiro dos Lisbon 16 A1
Jersey City New York 22 B1
Jerusalem Jerusalem 13 B2
Jessamine, L. Orlando 23 B2
Jésus, Î. Montreal 20 A1
Jesús María Lima 14 B2
Jette Brussels 6 A1
Jey Tehran 31 B2
Jianggao Guangzhou 11 A2
Jiangwan Shanghai 28 B1
Jib Jerusalem 13 A2
Jihād Baghdad 3 B1
Jingan Shanghai 28 B1
Jinočany Prague 25 B1
Jinonice Prague 25 B2
Jinqiao Shanghai 28 B2
Jiulong = Kowloon Hong Kong 12 B1
Jiyūgaoka Tokyo 30 B3
Jīzā'ir Baghdad 3 B2
Jīzīra Baghdad 3 B2
Joglo Jakarta 12 B1
Johannesburg Johannesburg 13 B2
Johannesburg, Univ. of Johannesburg 13 B2
Johanneskirchen Munich 21 A2
Johannestift Berlin 5 A2
Johannisthal Berlin 5 B4
John F. Kennedy Nat. Historic Site ⌂ Boston 6 A2
John McLaren Park San Francisco 26 B2
John U. Lloyd Beach ⌂ Miami 19 B3
Joinville-le-Pont Paris 24 B3
Joli-Bois Brussels 6 B2
Jollas Helsinki 11 B3
Jongmyo Royal Shrine Seoul 27 B1
Jongno Seoul 27 B1
Jonstrup Copenhagen 8 A2
Joppa Edinburgh 11 B3
Jorge Chavez, Int. ✕ (LIM) Lima 14 B2
Jorge Newbery ✕ (AEP) Buenos Aires 7 B2
Józefa Piłsudskiego Park Warsaw 33 B1
Jōtō Osaka 23 A2
Jouy-en-Josas Paris 24 B2
Juan Anchorena Buenos Aires 7 A2
Juan González Romero Mexico City 18 A2
Juárez Int. ✕ (MEX) Mexico City 18 B2
Judeira Jerusalem 13 A2
Juhdum Jerusalem 13 B2
Juhu Mumbai 20 A2
Jūjā Tokyo 30 A3
Jukskeirivier → Johannesburg 13 A2
Julianów Warsaw 33 B2
Jumeirah Dubai 9 B1
Jung Seoul 27 B1
Jungfernheide, Volkspark Berlin 5 A2
Jungfernsee Berlin 5 B1
Junghwa Seoul 27 B2
Jungnang Seoul 27 B2
Jungnangcheon → Seoul 27 B1
Juniper Green Edinburgh 11 B2
Junk B. Hong Kong 12 B2
Jurong Singapore 28 B2
Jurong, Selat Singapore 28 B2
Jurong Industrial Estate Singapore 28 B1
Jurujuba, Enseada de Rio de Janeiro 25 B2
Jūsō Osaka 23 A1
Justice Chicago 9 C2
Jwalahari Delhi 10 B1

K

Kaapstad = Cape Town Cape Town 8 A1
Kabaty Warsaw 33 C2
Kadıköy Istanbul 12 C2
Kadoma Osaka 23 A2
Kafr 'Aqab Jerusalem 13 A2
Kāğıthane Istanbul 12 B1
Kāğıthane → Istanbul 12 B1
Kagran Vienna 32 A2
Kahnawake Montreal 20 B1
Kaimes Edinburgh 11 B2
Kaiserebersdorf Vienna 32 B2
Kaivoksela Helsinki 11 B2
Kalamaki Athens 2 B2
Kalbadevi Mumbai 20 B2
Kalipur Kolkata 14 A1
Kalithea Athens 2 B2
Kalkaji Delhi 10 B2
Kalookan = Caloocan Manila 17 B1
Kalvebod Fælled Copenhagen 8 B3
Kalveboderne Copenhagen 8 B3
Kamarhati Kolkata 14 A2
Kamata Tokyo 30 B3
Kameari Tokyo 30 A4
Kameido Tokyo 30 A4
Kami-Itabashi Tokyo 30 A3
Kamikitazawa Tokyo 30 B2
Kamitsuruma Tokyo 30 B1
Kamoshida Tokyo 30 B2
Kampong Landang Singapore 28 A3
Kampong Tanjong Penjuru Singapore 28 B2
Kampung Bali Jakarta 12 B1
Kanamori Tokyo 30 B1
Kanda Tokyo 30 A3
Kandilli Istanbul 12 B2
Kankurgachi Kolkata 14 B2
Kanlıca Istanbul 12 B2
Kanonerskiy, Ostrov St. Petersburg 27 B1
Kansai Int. ✕ (KIX) Osaka 23 B2
Kanzaki → Osaka 23 A1
Kapali Carsi Istanbul 12 B1
Kapellerfeld Vienna 32 A2
Káposztásmegyer Budapest 7 A2
Kapotnya Moscow 19 C3
Käppala Stockholm 29 A3
Kapuk Jakarta 12 A1
Käpylä Helsinki 11 B2
Karachi Karachi 13 A2
Karachi Int. ✕ (KHI) Karachi 13 A2
Karkh Baghdad 3 A2
Karlin Prague 25 B2
Karlsfeld Munich 21 A1
Karlshorst Berlin 5 B4
Karlův most Prague 25 B2
Karol Bagh Delhi 10 B2
Karolinenhof Berlin 5 B4
Karow Berlin 5 A3
Karrādah Baghdad 3 B2
Kärsön Stockholm 29 B1
Kasai Tokyo 30 B4
Kasipur Kolkata 14 B2
Kastrup Copenhagen 8 B3
Kastrup, København ✕ (CPH) Copenhagen 8 B3
Kasuga Tokyo 30 A2
Kasuge Tokyo 30 A3
Kasumigaseki Tokyo 30 B3
Katong Singapore 28 B3
Katsushika Tokyo 30 A4
Kau Pai Chau Hong Kong 12 B2
Kau Yi Chau Hong Kong 12 B1
Kaulsdorf Berlin 5 B4
Kauniainen Helsinki 11 B1
Kawasaki Tokyo 30 B3
Kawawa Tokyo 30 B2
Kawęczyn Warsaw 33 B2
Kayu Putih Jakarta 12 B2
Kbely Prague 25 B3
Kebayoran Baru Jakarta 12 B1
Kebayoran Lama Jakarta 12 B1
Kebon Jeruk Jakarta 12 B1
Kedar Jerusalem 13 B2
Kedoya Jakarta 12 B1
Keilor Melbourne 18 A1
Keilor North Melbourne 18 A1
Keimola Helsinki 11 A1
Kelapa Gading Jakarta 12 A2
Kelenföld Budapest 7 B2
Kelvin Johannesburg 13 A2
Kemang Jakarta 12 B1
Kemayoran Jakarta 12 B2
Kemerburgaz Istanbul 12 B1
Kempton Park Races London 15 B1
Kendall Miami 19 D1
Kenilworth Cape Town 8 A1
Kenilworth Chicago 9 A2
Kennedy Town Hong Kong 12 B1
Kenner New Orleans 21 A1
Kensal Green London 15 A2
Kensington Johannesburg 13 B2
Kensington London 15 A2
Kensington New York 22 C2
Kensington Sydney 29 B2
Kensington Palace London 15 A2
Kentish Town London 15 A3
Kenton London 15 A2
Kenwood House London 15 A3
Kepa Warsaw 33 B2
Keppel Harbour Singapore 28 B2
Kesariani Athens 2 B2
Kew London 15 B2
Kew Melbourne 18 A2
Kew Gardens London 15 B2
Kew Gardens Toronto 31 B3
Key Biscayne Miami 19 D3
Khalīj Baghdad 3 B2
Khansā' Baghdad 3 A2
Kharavli Mumbai 20 B2
Khefren Cairo 7 B1
Khichripur Delhi 10 B2
Khidirpur Kolkata 14 B1
Khimki-Khovrino Moscow 19 A2
Khirbet Batin Abu Lihyah Jerusalem 13 A1
Khirbet el-Misbah Jerusalem 13 A1
Khirbet Jub e-Rum Jerusalem 13 B2
Khlong San Bangkok 3 B2
Khlong Toey Bangkok 3 B2
Khorel Kolkata 14 A1
Khorosovo Moscow 19 B1
Kiamari Karachi 13 B1
Kierling Vienna 32 A1
Kierlingbach → Vienna 32 A1
Kifisos → Athens 2 B2
Kikuna Tokyo 30 B2
Kilbarrack Dublin 10 A3
Kilburn London 15 A2
Kilkakee Dublin 10 B2
Killester Dublin 10 A2
Killiney Dublin 10 B3
Killiney B. Dublin 10 B3
Kilmacud Dublin 10 B2
Kilmainham Dublin 10 A2
Kilmainham Gaol Dublin 10 A2
Kilmashogue Mt. Dublin 10 B2
Kilmore Dublin 10 A2
Kilnamanagh Dublin 10 B1
Kilo Helsinki 11 B1
Kilokri Delhi 10 B2
Kilternan Dublin 10 B2
Kimmage Dublin 10 B2
Kindi Baghdad 3 B2
Kinghorn Edinburgh 11 A2
Kings Domain Melbourne 18 A1
Kings Forest = Kongelunden Copenhagen 8 B3
Kingsbury London 15 A2
Kingsbury Melbourne 18 A2
Kingsford Sydney 29 B2
Kingsford Smith, Sydney ✕ (SYD) Sydney 29 B2
Kingston-upon-Thames □ London 15 B2
Kingston Vale London 15 B2
Kingsway Toronto 31 B1
Kinsaley Dublin 10 A2
Kipling Heights Toronto 31 A1
Kipseli Athens 2 B2
Kirchstockbach Munich 21 B3
Kirchtrudering Munich 21 B3
Kirikiri Lagos 14 B1
Kirke Værløse Copenhagen 8 A1
Kirkhill Edinburgh 11 B2
Kirkliston Edinburgh 11 B1
Kirknewton Edinburgh 11 B1
Kirov Palace of Culture St. Petersburg 27 B1
Kiryat Anavim Jerusalem 13 B1
Kiryat Ha Yovel Jerusalem 13 B1
Kısıklı Istanbul 12 B2
Kispest Budapest 7 B2
Kista Stockholm 29 A1
Kita Osaka 23 A2
Kita Tokyo 30 A3
Kitazawa Tokyo 30 B3
Kiu Tsiu Hong Kong 12 A2
Kivistö Helsinki 11 B2
Kiza → Osaka 23 B1
Kızıltoprak Istanbul 12 C2
Kizuri Osaka 23 B2
Kjelsås Oslo 23 A3
Kladow Berlin 5 B1
Klampenborg Copenhagen 8 A3
Klečany Prague 25 A2
Kledering Vienna 32 B2
Klein Jukskei → Johannesburg 13 A1
Kleinmachnow Berlin 5 B2
Kleinschönebeck Berlin 5 B5
Klemetsrud Oslo 23 A4
Klender Jakarta 12 A2
Klíčany Prague 25 A2
Klipriviersberg Nature Reserve Johannesburg 13 B2
Klosterneuburg Vienna 32 A1
Kōbānya Budapest 7 B2
Kobbegem Brussels 6 A1
København Copenhagen 8 A2
København ✕ (CPH) Copenhagen 8 B3
Kobylisy Prague 25 B2
Kobyłka Warsaw 33 A3
Kodaira Tokyo 30 A1
Kodanaka Tokyo 30 B2
Koekelberg Brussels 6 A1
Koganei Tokyo 30 A2
Kogarah Sydney 29 B1
Koivupää Helsinki 11 B2
Koja Jakarta 12 A2
Koja Utara Jakarta 12 A2
Kokhav Ya'akov Jerusalem 13 A2
Kokobunji Tokyo 30 A1
Kokobunji-Temple Tokyo 30 A4
Kolarängen Stockholm 29 B3
Kolbotn Oslo 23 B3
Kolkata Kolkata 14 B2
Kolkata Maidan Kolkata 14 B1
Kolkata Netaji Subhash Chandra Bose Int. ✕ (CCU) Kolkata 14 B2
Koło Warsaw 33 B1
Kolokinthou Athens 2 B2
Kolomyagi St. Petersburg 27 A1
Kolonos Athens 2 B2
Kolsås Oslo 23 A2
Komae Tokyo 30 B2
Komagome Tokyo 30 A3
Komazawa Tokyo 30 B3
Kona Kolkata 14 B1
Konala Helsinki 11 B2
Kondli Delhi 10 B2
Kongelunden Copenhagen 8 B3
Kongens Lyngby Copenhagen 8 A3
Kongo Helsinki 11 A1
Konnagar Kolkata 14 A2
Konohana Osaka 23 A1
Konradshöhe Berlin 5 A2
Kopanina Prague 25 B1
Koparkhairna Mumbai 20 A2
Köpenick Berlin 5 B4
Korangi Karachi 13 B2
Koremasa Tokyo 30 B1
Koridalos Athens 2 B1
Kosino Moscow 19 B4
Kosugi Tokyo 30 B2
Kota Jakarta 12 A1
Kōtō Tokyo 30 A3
Kotrung Kolkata 14 A2
Kouponia Athens 2 B2
Kowloon Hong Kong 12 B1
Kowloon Peak Hong Kong 12 A2
Kowloon Res. Hong Kong 12 A1
Kowloon Tong Hong Kong 12 A2
Kraainem Brussels 6 A2
Krailling Munich 21 B1
Krampnitz Berlin 5 B1
Krampnitzsee Berlin 5 B1
Kranji Industrial Estate Singapore 28 A2
Kranji Res. Singapore 28 A2
Krasno-Presnenskaya Moscow 19 B2
Krč Prague 25 B2
Kremlin Moscow 19 B2
Krestovskiye, Ostrov St. Petersburg 27 B1
Kreuzberg Berlin 5 A3
Kritzendorf Vienna 32 A1
Krumme Lanke Berlin 5 B2
Krummensee Berlin 5 A5
Krung Thep = Bangkok Bangkok 3 B2
Krusboda Stockholm 29 B3
Kuangchou = Guangzhou Guangzhou 11 B2
Küçükköy Istanbul 12 B1
Küçüksu Istanbul 12 B2
Kudrovo St. Petersburg 27 B3
Kulosaari Helsinki 11 B3
Kumla Stockholm 29 B3
Kungens kurva Stockholm 29 B1
Kungliga Slottet Stockholm 29 B2
Kungshatt Stockholm 29 B1
Kungsholmen Stockholm 29 A2
Kuningan Jakarta 12 B1
Kunitachi Tokyo 30 A1
Kunming Hu Beijing 4 B1
Kunratice Prague 25 B2
Kupchino St. Petersburg 27 B2
Kuramo Waters Lagos 14 B2
Kurbağalı → Istanbul 12 C2
Kurihara Tokyo 30 A2
Kurla Mumbai 20 A2
Kurmuri Mumbai 20 A2
Kurume Tokyo 30 A2
Kuryanovo Moscow 19 C3
Kuskovo Moscow 19 B3
Kustia Kolkata 14 B2
Kuzguncuk Istanbul 12 B2
Kuzyminki Moscow 19 B3
Kwai Chung Hong Kong 12 A1
Kwangchow = Guangzhou Guangzhou 11 B2
Kwun Tong Hong Kong 12 B2
Kyje Prague 25 B3
Kyūhōji Osaka 23 B2

L

L.A. County Art Museum Los Angeles 16 B2
La Barceloneta Barcelona 4 A2
La Blanca Santiago 27 C2
La Boca Buenos Aires 7 B2
La Bretèche Paris 24 A1
La Campiña Lima 14 C2
La Celle-St-Cloud Paris 24 A1
La Cisterna Santiago 27 C2
La Courneuve Paris 24 A3
La Dehesa Santiago 27 B2
La Encantada Lima 14 C2
La Estación Madrid 17 B1
La Floresta Barcelona 4 A1
La Florida Santiago 27 C2
La Fortuna Madrid 17 B1
La França Barcelona 4 A1
La Garenne-Colombes Paris 24 A2
La Giustiniana Rome 26 B1
La Granja Santiago 27 C2
La Guardia, New York ✕ (LGA) New York 22 B2
La Hulpe Brussels 6 B2
La Llacuna Barcelona 4 A2
La Loma Mexico City 18 A1
La Lucila Buenos Aires 7 B2
La Maladrerie Paris 24 A1
La Milla, Cerro Lima 14 B2
La Monachina Rome 26 B1
La Moraleja Madrid 17 A2
La Nopalera Mexico City 18 C2
La Paternal Buenos Aires 7 B2
La Perla Lima 14 B2
La Perouse Sydney 29 B2
La Pisana Rome 26 B1
La Prairie Montreal 20 B3
La Punta Lima 14 B1
La Puntigala Barcelona 4 A2
La Queue-en-Brie Paris 24 B4
La Reina Santiago 27 B2
La Ribera Barcelona 4 A1
La Sagrera Barcelona 4 A2
La Salada Buenos Aires 7 C2
La Scala Milan 18 B2
La Storta Rome 26 A1
La Taxonera Barcelona 4 A2
La Victoria Lima 14 B2
La Vista Atlanta 3 B2
Laajalahti Helsinki 11 B1
Laajasalo Helsinki 11 B3
Laaksolahti Helsinki 11 B1
Labagou Nat. Forest Park Beijing 4 A2
Lablāba, W. el → Cairo 7 A2
Lachine Montreal 20 B1
Lachine, Canal de Montreal 20 B2
Lad Phrao Bangkok 3 B2
Ladera Heights Los Angeles 16 C2
Ládví Prague 25 B2
Łady Warsaw 33 C1
Lafontaine, Parc Montreal 20 A2
Lagoa Rio de Janeiro 25 B1
Lagos Lagos 14 B2
Lagos Harbour Lagos 14 B2
Lagos-Ikeja ✕ (LOS) Lagos 14 A1
Lagos Island Lagos 14 B2
Lagos Lagoon Lagos 14 B2
Laguna de B. Manila 17 C2
Laim Munich 21 B2
Lainate Milan 18 A1
Lainz Vienna 32 B1
Lake Buena Vista Orlando 23 B1
Lake Cain Hills Orlando 23 B2
Lakemba Sydney 29 B1
Lakeside Cape Town 8 B1
Lakeside Johannesburg 13 A2
Lakeview Chicago 9 B3
Lakeview New Orleans 21 A2
Lakewood Park Atlanta 3 B2
Lakhtinskiy St. Petersburg 27 B1
Lakhtinskiy Razliv, Oz. St. Petersburg 27 B1
Lakshmanpur Kolkata 14 B1
Laksi Bangkok 3 A2
Lal Qila Delhi 10 B2
Lam Tin Hong Kong 12 B2
Lambert Oslo 23 A3
Lambeth □ London 15 B3
Lambrate Milan 18 B2
Lambro, Parco Milan 18 B2
Lambton Mills Toronto 31 B1
Lamma I. Hong Kong 12 B1
Landianchang Beijing 4 B1
Landsmeer Amsterdam 2 A2
Landstrasse Vienna 32 A2
Landwehr kanal Berlin 5 B3
Lane Cove Sydney 29 A1
Lane Cove Nat. Park △ Sydney 29 A1
Langa Cape Town 8 A2
Langenzersdorf Vienna 32 A2
Langer See Berlin 5 B4
Langley Washington 33 B1
Langley Park Washington 33 B3
Langwald Munich 21 A1
Lankwitz Berlin 5 B3
L'Annunziatella Rome 26 C2
Lansdowne Cape Town 8 A2
Lansing Toronto 31 A2
Lanus Buenos Aires 7 C2
Lapa Rio de Janeiro 25 B1
Laranjeiras Rio de Janeiro 25 B1
Las Arenas Barcelona 4 A1
Las Corts Barcelona 4 A1
Las Kabacki Warsaw 33 C2
Las Pinas Manila 17 C1
Las Rejas Santiago 27 B1
Las Vegas Las Vegas 14 A2
Las Vegas McCarran Int. ✕ (LAS) Las Vegas 14 B2
LaSalle Montreal 20 B2
LaSalle Street Station Chicago 9 B3
Lasek Bielański Warsaw 33 B1
Lasek Na Kole Warsaw 33 B1
Latina Madrid 17 B1
Lauderdale Lakes Miami 19 B1
Lauderhill Miami 19 B2
Lauttasaari Helsinki 11 C2
Laval-des-Rapides Montreal 20 A1
Lavīzān Tehran 31 A2
Lavradio Lisbon 16 A2
Lawndale Chicago 9 B2
Lawne L. Orlando 23 A2
Lawrence Heights Toronto 31 A2
Layari Karachi 13 A1
Layari → Karachi 13 A1
Lazienkowski Park Warsaw 33 B2
Lazy Lake Miami 19 B3
Le Blanc-Mesnil Paris 24 A3
Le Bourget Paris 24 A3
Le Chenoi Brussels 6 B2
Le Chesnay Paris 24 B1
Le Christ de Saclay Paris 24 B2
Le Kremlin-Bicêtre Paris 24 B3
Le Mesnil-le-Roi Paris 24 A1
Le Pecq Paris 24 A1
Le Perreux Paris 24 A3
Le Pin Paris 24 A4

Le Plessis-Robinson *Paris* 24 B2
Le Plessis-Trévise *Paris* 24 B4
Le Port-Marly *Paris* 24 A1
Le Pré-St-Gervais *Paris* 24 A3
Le Raincy *Paris* 24 A4
Le Vésinet *Paris* 24 A1
Lea Bridge *London* 15 A3
Leaside *Toronto* 31 A2
Leblon *Rio de Janeiro* 25 B1
Lee *London* 15 B4
Leganés *Madrid* 17 C1
Legazpi *Madrid* 17 B1
Lehtisaari *Helsinki* 11 B2
Lei Yue Mun *Hong Kong* 12 B2
Leião *Lisbon* 16 A1
Leichhardt *Sydney* 29 B1
Leith *Edinburgh* 11 B3
Lekki *Lagos* 14 B2
Lekki Peninsula *Lagos* 14 B2
Leme *Rio de Janeiro* 25 B1
Lemoyne *Montreal* 20 B3
Lenin *Moscow* 19 B2
Lenino *Moscow* 19 C2
Leninskiye Gory *Moscow* 19 B2
Lennox *Los Angeles* 16 C2
Leonia *New York* 22 A2
Leopardstown *Dublin* 10 B2
Leopoldau *Vienna* 32 A2
Leopoldsdorf *Vienna* 32 B2
Leopoldstadt *Vienna* 32 A2
Leportovo *Moscow* 19 B3
Leppävaara *Helsinki* 11 B1
Les Lilas *Paris* 24 A3
Les Loges-en-Josas *Paris* 24 B1
Les Pavillons-sous-Bois *Paris* 24 A4
Lésigny *Paris* 24 B4
Lesnozavodskaya *St. Petersburg* 27 B2
Lester B. Pearson Int., Toronto ✈ (YYZ) *Toronto* 31 A1
L'Étang-la-Ville *Paris* 24 A1
Letňany *Prague* 25 B3
Letopolis = Ausîm *Cairo* 7 A1
Levallois-Perret *Paris* 24 A2
Levent *Istanbul* 12 B2
Lewisdale *Washington* 33 B3
Lewisham ☐ *London* 15 B3
Lexington *Boston* 6 A1
Leyton *London* 15 A3
Leytonstone *London* 15 A4
L'Haÿ-les-Roses *Paris* 24 B3
L'Hospitalet de Llobregat *Barcelona* 4 A1
Lhotka *Prague* 25 B2
Liangshui He → *Beijing* 4 C2
Lianhua Chi *Beijing* 4 B1
Lianhua He → *Beijing* 4 B1
Libčice nad Vitavou *Prague* 25 A2
Libeň *Prague* 25 B2
Liberdade *São Paulo* 27 B2
Liberton *Edinburgh* 11 B3
Liberty I. *New York* 22 B1
Liberty Ōsaka Museum *Osaka* 23 B1
Liberty State Park ⌂ *New York* 22 B1
Libeznice *Prague* 25 A2
Libuš *Prague* 25 B2
Lichiao *Guangzhou* 11 B2
Lichtenburg *Berlin* 5 A4
Lichterfelde *Berlin* 5 B2
Lidingö *Stockholm* 29 A2
Lieshi Lingyuan *Guangzhou* 11 B2
Liesing *Vienna* 32 B1
Liesing → *Vienna* 32 B2
Ligovo *St. Petersburg* 27 C1
Lijordet *Oslo* 23 A2
Likhoborka → *Moscow* 19 A2
Lilla Värtan *Stockholm* 29 A3
Lille Værløse *Copenhagen* 8 A2
Liluah *Kolkata* 14 B1
Lim Chu Kang *Singapore* 28 A2
Lima *Lima* 14 B2
Lima Jorge Chavez, Int. ✈ (LIM) *Lima* 14 B2
Limbiate *Milan* 18 A1
Limehouse *London* 15 A3
Limeil-Brévannes *Paris* 24 B3
Linate, Milano ✈ (LIN) *Milan* 18 B2
Linbropark *Johannesburg* 13 A2
Lincoln Center for Performing Arts *New York* 22 B2
Lincoln Heights *Los Angeles* 16 B3
Lincoln Memorial *Washington* 33 B2
Lincoln Park *Chicago* 9 B3
Lincoln Park *New York* 22 B1
Lincoln Park *San Francisco* 26 B1
Lincoln Park Zoo *Chicago* 9 B3
Lincolnwood *Chicago* 9 A2
Linda-a-Pastora *Lisbon* 16 A1
Linden *Johannesburg* 13 A2
Lindenberg *Berlin* 5 A4
Lindøya *Oslo* 23 A3
Liniers *Buenos Aires* 7 B1
Linkebeek *Brussels* 6 B2
Linksfield *Johannesburg* 13 A2
Linmeyer *Johannesburg* 13 B2
Linna *Helsinki* 11 A2
Lintuvaara *Helsinki* 11 B1
Lion Rock Country Park ⌂ *Hong Kong* 12 A2
Lion's Head *Cape Town* 8 A1
Lioumi *Athens* 2 B2
Lisboa *Lisbon* 16 A2
Lisboa ✈ (LIS) *Lisbon* 16 A2
Lisbon = Lisboa *Lisbon* 16 A2
Lishui *Guangzhou* 11 B1
Little B. *Sydney* 29 B2
Little Calumet → *Chicago* 9 D3
Little Ferry *New York* 22 A1
Little Haiti *Miami* 19 C2
Little Havana *Miami* 19 D1
Little Italia *Shanghai* 28 a2
Little Lake Conway *Orlando* 23 B2
Little Rouge → *Toronto* 31 A4
Liuhang *Shanghai* 28 A1
Liurong Temple *Guangzhou* 11 B2
Live Oak Manor *New Orleans* 21 B1
Livry-Gargan *Paris* 24 A4
Liwan *Guangzhou* 11 B2
Ljan *Oslo* 23 A3
Llano de Can Gineu *Barcelona* 4 A2
Lo Aranguiz *Santiago* 27 B2
Lo Boza *Santiago* 27 B1
Lo Chau *Hong Kong* 12 B2
Lo Chau Pak Mai *Hong Kong* 12 B2
Lo Espejo *Santiago* 27 C1
Lo Hermida *Santiago* 27 B2
Lo Prado *Santiago* 27 B1
Lo So Shing *Hong Kong* 12 B1
Lo Wai *Hong Kong* 12 A1
Loanhead *Edinburgh* 11 B3
Lobau *Vienna* 32 A3
Lobos, Pt. *San Francisco* 26 B1
Locham *Munich* 21 B1
Lochkov *Prague* 25 B2
Lockhausen *Munich* 21 A1
Lodi *New York* 22 A1
Lodi Estate *Delhi* 10 B2
Logan Int., Boston ✈ (BOS) *Boston* 6 A2
Logan Square *Chicago* 9 B2
Lognes-Émerainville ✈ (XLG) *Paris* 24 B4
Löhme *Berlin* 5 A5
Lolokhet *Karachi* 13 A2
Lomas Chapultepec *Mexico City* 18 B1
Lomas de San Angel Inn *Mexico City* 18 B1
Lombardy East *Johannesburg* 13 A2
Lomianki *Warsaw* 33 A1
Lomus Reforma *Mexico City* 18 B1
London *London* 15 B3
London Avenue Canal *New Orleans* 21 A2
London City ✈ (LCY) *London* 15 A4
London Heathrow ✈ (LHR) *London* 15 B1
London Zoo *London* 15 A3
Long B. *Sydney* 29 B2
Long Branch *Toronto* 31 B1
Long Ditton *London* 15 B2
Long Island City *New York* 22 B2
Longchamp, Hippodrome de *Paris* 24 A2
Longhua Pagoda *Shanghai* 28 B1
Longhua Park *Shanghai* 28 B1
Longtan Hu → *Beijing* 4 B2
Longue-Pointe *Montreal* 20 A2
Longueuil *Montreal* 20 A3
Loni *Delhi* 10 A2
Lord's Cricket Ground *London* 15 A2
Loreto *Milan* 18 B2
Los Angeles *Los Angeles* 16 B3
Los Angeles Int. ✈ (LAX) *Los Angeles* 16 C2
Los Cerrillos ✈ (ULC) *Santiago* 27 B1
Los Nietos *Los Angeles* 16 C4
Los Olivos *Lima* 14 A2
Los Remedios ⌂ *Mexico City* 18 B1
Los Reyes *Mexico City* 18 B2
Losiny Ostrov ⌂ *Moscow* 19 A3
Lot *Brussels* 6 B1
Lotus River *Cape Town* 8 B2
Lotus Temple *Delhi* 10 B2
Loughlinstown *Dublin* 10 B3
Louis Armstrong New Orleans Int. ✈ (MSY) *New Orleans* 21 B1
Louise, L. *Orlando* 23 B1
Louisiana Superdome *New Orleans* 21 B2
Loures *Lisbon* 16 A1
Louveciennes *Paris* 24 A1
Louvre, Musée du *Paris* 24 A3
Lower B. *New York* 22 C1
Lower New York B. = Lower B. *New York* 22 C1
Lower Peirce Res. *Singapore* 28 A2
Lower Shing Mun Res. *Hong Kong* 12 A1
Loyola Univ. *Chicago* 9 B3
Lu Xun, Tomb of *Shanghai* 28 B1
Lu Xun Park *Shanghai* 28 B1
Lübars *Berlin* 5 A3
Lucy, L. *Orlando* 23 A2
Ludwigsfeld *Munich* 21 A1
Luhu *Guangzhou* 11 B2
Lumiar *Lisbon* 16 A2
Lundtofte *Copenhagen* 8 A3
Lung Mei *Hong Kong* 12 A2
Luojiang *Guangzhou* 11 B2
Lustheim *Munich* 21 A2
Luwan *Shanghai* 28 B1
Luzhniki Sports Centre *Moscow* 19 B2
Lyndhurst *New York* 22 B1
Lynn Woods Res. *Boston* 6 A2
Lyon, Gare de *Paris* 24 A3
Lyons *Chicago* 9 C2
Lysaker *Oslo* 23 A2
Lysakerelva → *Oslo* 23 A2
Lysolaje *Prague* 25 B2
Lyublino *Moscow* 19 B3

M

Ma Nam Wat *Hong Kong* 12 A2
Ma On Shan Country Park ⌂ *Hong Kong* 12 A2
Ma'ale Adumim *Jerusalem* 13 B2
Ma'ale Ha Khamisha *Jerusalem* 13 B1
Ma'ale Mikhmas *Jerusalem* 13 A2
Maantiekylä *Helsinki* 11 A3
Maarifa *Baghdad* 3 B2
Mabato Pt. *Manila* 17 C2
Mabel, L. *Orlando* 23 B1
Macaco, Morro do *Rio de Janeiro* 25 B2
McCarran Int., Las Vegas ✈ (LAS) *Las Vegas* 14 B2
McCook *Chicago* 9 C2
McGill Univ. *Montreal* 20 A2
Machelen *Brussels* 6 A2
Machida *Tokyo* 30 B1
Maciołki *Warsaw* 33 B2
McKinley Park *Chicago* 9 C2
McLean *Washington* 33 B1
Macopocho → *Santiago* 27 B1
MacRitchie Res. *Singapore* 28 A2
Macul *Santiago* 27 C2
Madhudaha *Kolkata* 14 B2
Madhyamgram *Kolkata* 14 A2
Madin *Mexico City* 18 A1
Madín, L. *Mexico City* 18 A1
Madīnah Al Mansūr *Baghdad* 3 B2
Mâdinet Nasr *Cairo* 7 A2
Madrid *Madrid* 17 B1
Madrid Barajas ✈ (MAD) *Madrid* 17 B2
Madrona *Barcelona* 4 A1
Maesawa *Tokyo* 30 A2
Magdalena *Lima* 14 B2
Magdalena Contreras *Mexico City* 18 C1
Magelungen *Stockholm* 29 B2
Maghreb *Baghdad* 3 A2
Maginu *Tokyo* 30 B2
Magliana *Rome* 26 B1
Magny-les-Hameaux *Paris* 24 B1
Mahar, L. *Miami* 19 D1
Maheshtala *Kolkata* 14 C1
Mahim *Mumbai* 20 A2
Mahim B. *Mumbai* 20 A1
Mahipalpur *Delhi* 10 B1
Mahlsdorf *Berlin* 5 A4
Mahmoodabad *Karachi* 13 A2
Mahrauli *Delhi* 10 B2
Mahul *Mumbai* 20 A2
Maida Vale *London* 15 A2
Maidstone *Melbourne* 18 A1
Maipú *Santiago* 27 C1
Maisonneuve, Parc *Montreal* 20 A2
Maisons-Alfort *Paris* 24 B3
Maisons-Laffitte *Paris* 24 A1
Maissoneuve *Montreal* 20 A2
Maitland *Cape Town* 8 A1
Makasar *Jakarta* 12 A2
Makati *Manila* 17 B2
Mäkiniitty *Helsinki* 11 A2
Malá Strana *Prague* 25 B2
Malabar *Sydney* 29 B2
Malabar Hill *Mumbai* 20 B1
Malabar Pt. *Mumbai* 20 B1
Malabon *Manila* 17 B1
Malacañang Palace *Manila* 17 B1
Malahide *Dublin* 10 A3
Malakoff *Paris* 24 B2
Mälarhöjaen *Stockholm* 29 B1
Malate *Manila* 17 B1
Malaya Neva *St. Petersburg* 27 B1
Malaya Okhta *St. Petersburg* 27 B2
Malchow *Berlin* 5 A3
Malden *Boston* 6 A2
Malden *London* 15 B2
Maleizen *Brussels* 6 B3
Malešice *Prague* 25 B3
Malir → *Karachi* 13 B2
Malleny Mills *Edinburgh* 11 B2
Malmi *Helsinki* 11 B2
Malmøya *Oslo* 23 A3
Målov *Copenhagen* 8 A1
Malpense, Milano ✈ (MXP) = Milano Malpense ✈ (MXP) *Milan* 18 A1
Malton *Toronto* 31 A1
Malvern *Johannesburg* 13 B2
Malvern *Melbourne* 18 B2
Malvern *Toronto* 31 A3
Mampang Prapatan *Jakarta* 12 B1
Mampukuji *Tokyo* 30 B2
Man Budrukh *Mumbai* 20 A2
Man Khurd *Mumbai* 20 A2
Manakhat *Jerusalem* 13 B2
Mandai *Singapore* 28 A2
Mandaluyong *Manila* 17 B2
Mandaoli *Delhi* 10 B2
Mandaqui → *São Paulo* 27 A2
Mandoli *Delhi* 10 A2
Mandvi *Mumbai* 20 B2
Manenberg *Cape Town* 8 A2
Mang Kung Uk *Hong Kong* 12 B2
Mang-won *Seoul* 27 B1
Mangolpuri *Delhi* 10 A1
Manguinhos ✈ *Rio de Janeiro* 25 B1
Manhattan *New York* 22 B2
Manhattan Beach *New York* 22 C2
Manila *Manila* 17 B1
Manila Ninoy Aquino Int. ✈ (MNL) *Manila* 17 B2
Mankkaa *Helsinki* 11 B1
Manly *Sydney* 29 A2
Mann, L. *Orlando* 23 A2
Mann's Chinese Theatre *Los Angeles* 16 B2
Mannswörth *Vienna* 32 B3
Manor Park *London* 15 A4
Manora *Karachi* 13 B1
Manora Pt. *Karachi* 13 B1
Manquehue, Cerro *Santiago* 27 B2
Manzanares, Canal de *Madrid* 17 C2
Mapo *Seoul* 27 B1
Mar Vista *Los Angeles* 16 B2
Maracanã *Rio de Janeiro* 25 B1
Maraoli *Mumbai* 20 A2
Marcelin *Warsaw* 33 B1
Mareil-Marly *Paris* 24 A1
Margaret I. = Margitsziget *Budapest* 7 a2
Margareten *Vienna* 32 A2
Margitsziget *Budapest* 7 a2
Maria *Vienna* 32 A2
Maridalen *Oslo* 23 A3
Maridalsvatnet *Oslo* 23 A3
Mariendorf *Berlin* 5 B3
Marienfelde *Berlin* 5 B3
Marikina *Manila* 17 B2
Marikina → *Manila* 17 B2
Marin City *San Francisco* 26 A1
Marin Pen. *San Francisco* 26 A1
Marina Bay Sands *Singapore* 28 B3
Marina del Rey *Los Angeles* 16 C2
Marino *Dublin* 10 A2
Marisco, Ponta do *Rio de Janeiro* 25 C1
Markham *Chicago* 9 D2
Markham *Toronto* 31 A2
Marki *Warsaw* 33 B2
Markland Wood *Toronto* 31 B1
Marly, Forêt de *Paris* 24 A1
Marly-le-Roi *Paris* 24 A1
Marne-la-Vallée *Paris* 24 A4
Marolles-en-Brie *Paris* 24 B4
Maroubra *Sydney* 29 B2
Marquette Park *Chicago* 9 C2
Marrero *New Orleans* 21 B2
Marrickville *Sydney* 29 B1
Marsfield *Sydney* 29 A1
Marsha, L. *Orlando* 23 B2
Marte, Campo de *São Paulo* 27 B2
Martesana, Naviglio della *Milan* 18 A2
Martin Luther King Nat. Historic Site ⌂ *Atlanta* 3 B2
Martinez *Buenos Aires* 7 A1
Martinkylä *Helsinki* 11 B2
Martinsried *Munich* 21 B1
Maruko *Tokyo* 30 B3
Maryino *Moscow* 19 B3
Maryland *Singapore* 28 B2
Marymont *Warsaw* 33 B1
Marysin Wawerski *Warsaw* 33 B2
Marzahn *Berlin* 5 A4
Mascot *Sydney* 29 B2
Masmo *Stockholm* 29 B1
Maspeth *New York* 22 B2
Masr el Gedida *Cairo* 7 A2
Masr el Qadima *Cairo* 7 A2
Massachusetts Inst. of Tech. *Boston* 6 A2
Massamá *Lisbon* 16 A1
Massey → *Toronto* 31 A3
Massy *Paris* 24 B2
Mata *Jerusalem* 13 B1
Matinha *Lisbon* 16 A2
Matramam *Jakarta* 12 B2
Matsubara *Ōsaka* 23 B2
Mattapan *Boston* 6 B2
Mátyásföld *Budapest* 7 A3
Mau Tso Ngam *Hong Kong* 12 A2
Mauer *Vienna* 32 B1
Mauripur *Karachi* 13 A1
Maxhof *Munich* 21 B1
Mayfair *Johannesburg* 13 B2
Maywood *Chicago* 9 B1
Maywood *Los Angeles* 16 C3
Maywood *New York* 22 A1
Maywood Park Race Track *Chicago* 9 B1
Mazagaon *Mumbai* 20 B2
Meadowbank Park *Sydney* 29 A1
Měcholupy *Prague* 25 B3
Měčice *Prague* 25 A3
Mecidiyeköy *Istanbul* 12 B2
Medford *Boston* 6 A2
Mediodia *Madrid* 17 B2
Meguro *Tokyo* 30 B3
Meguro → *Tokyo* 30 B3
Mehrābād ✈ (THR) *Tehran* 31 A1
Mehram Nagar *Delhi* 10 B1
Mehrow *Berlin* 5 A4
Meidling *Vienna* 32 A2
Méier *Rio de Janeiro* 25 B1
Meiji Shrine *Tokyo* 30 A3
Meise *Brussels* 6 A1
Mejiro *Tokyo* 30 A3
Melbourne *Melbourne* 18 A1
Melbourne ✈ (MEL) *Melbourne* 18 A1
Melkki *Helsinki* 11 C2
Mellunkylä *Helsinki* 11 B3
Mellunmäki *Helsinki* 11 B3
Melrose *Boston* 6 A2
Melrose *New York* 22 B2
Melrose Park *Miami* 19 B3
Melsbroek *Brussels* 6 A2
Melville *Johannesburg* 13 B2
Menteng *Jakarta* 12 B1
Mérantaise → *Paris* 24 B1
Mercamadrid *Madrid* 17 B2
Merced, L. *San Francisco* 26 B2
Meredale *Johannesburg* 13 B1
Merlimau, Pulau *Singapore* 28 B2
Merri Cr. → *Melbourne* 18 A1
Merrion *Dublin* 10 B2
Merrionette Park *Chicago* 9 C2
Merton ☐ *London* 15 B2
Mesgarābād *Tehran* 31 B3
Messe *Vienna* 32 A2
Metairie *New Orleans* 21 A2
Metanópoli *Milan* 18 B2
Metro Toronto Zoo *Toronto* 31 A3
Metropolitan Museum of Art *New York* 22 B2
Meudon *Paris* 24 B2
Mevaseret Zion *Jerusalem* 13 B1
Mevo Beitar *Jerusalem* 13 B1
México, Ciudad de *Mexico City* 18 B2
Mexico City Int. ✈ (MEX) *Mexico City* 18 B2
Meyersdal *Johannesburg* 13 B2
Mezzate *Milan* 18 B2
Miadong *Seoul* 27 B2
Miami *Miami* 19 D2
Miami → *Miami* 19 D1
Miami Beach *Miami* 19 D3
Miami Gardens *Miami* 19 C1
Miami Int. ✈ (MIA) *Miami* 19 D1
Miami Lakes *Miami* 19 C1
Miami Shores *Miami* 19 C2
Miami Springs *Miami* 19 D1
Miasto *Warsaw* 33 B2
Michałowice *Warsaw* 33 B1
Michle *Prague* 25 B2
Mid-City *Los Angeles* 16 B2
Mid City *New Orleans* 21 B2
Middle Harbour *Sydney* 29 A2
Middle Hd. *Sydney* 29 A2
Middle Park *Melbourne* 18 B1
Middle Village *New York* 22 B2
Middlesex Fells Reservation *Boston* 6 A2
Midland Beach *New York* 22 C1
Midlothian *Chicago* 9 D2
Midwood *New York* 22 C2
Miedzeszyn *Warsaw* 33 B3
Międzylesie *Warsaw* 33 B3
Miessaari *Helsinki* 11 C1
Miguel Hidalgo *Mexico City* 18 B1
Milan = Milano *Milan* 18 B1
Milanese, Parco Regionale ⌂ *Milan* 18 A1
Milano *Milan* 18 B1
Milano Due *Milan* 18 B2
Milano Linate ✈ (LIN) *Milan* 18 B2
Milano Malpense ✈ (MXP) *Milan* 18 A1
Milano San Felice *Milan* 18 B2
Milbertshofen *Munich* 21 A2
Mill Hill *London* 15 A2
Millennium Dome *London* 15 A4
Miller Meadow *Chicago* 9 B2
Millerhill *Edinburgh* 11 B3
Milltown *Dublin* 10 B2
Milnerton *Cape Town* 8 A1
Milon-la-Chapelle *Paris* 24 B1
Milton *Boston* 6 B2
Milton Bridge *Edinburgh* 11 B2
Mimico *Toronto* 31 B2
Mimico Creek → *Toronto* 31 B1
Minami *Osaka* 23 A2
Minamitsunashima *Tokyo* 30 B2
Minato *Osaka* 23 B1
Minato *Tokyo* 30 B3
Minshât el Bekkari *Cairo* 7 A1
Miraflores *Lima* 14 B2
Miramar *Miami* 19 C1
Misericordia, Sa. da *Rio de Janeiro* 25 B1
Mission *San Francisco* 26 B2
Mississauga *Toronto* 31 B1
Mitaka *Tokyo* 30 A2
Mitcham *London* 15 B2
Mitcham Common *London* 15 B3
Mitchell Museum of the American Indian *Chicago* 9 A2
Mitchell's Plain *Cape Town* 8 B2
Mitte *Berlin* 5 A3
Mittel Isarkanal → *Munich* 21 A3
Mixcoac *Mexico City* 18 B1
Miyakojima *Osaka* 23 A2
Mizonokuchi *Tokyo* 30 B2
Mizue *Tokyo* 30 A4
Młocinski, Park *Warsaw* 33 B1
Młociny *Warsaw* 33 B1
Mnevniki *Moscow* 19 B1
Moba *Lagos* 14 B2
Moczydło *Warsaw* 33 C2
Modderfontein *Johannesburg* 13 A2
Modřany *Prague* 25 B2
Mogyoród *Budapest* 7 A3
Moinho Velho, Cor. → *São Paulo* 27 B2
Mok Dong *Seoul* 27 B1
Mokotów *Warsaw* 33 B2
Molenbeek-St-Jean *Brussels* 6 A1
Molino de Rosas *Mexico City* 18 B1
Mollem *Brussels* 6 A1
Mollins de Rey *Barcelona* 4 A1
Mondeor *Johannesburg* 13 B2
Moneda, Palacio de la *Santiago* 27 B2
Monerō *Rio de Janeiro* 25 A1
Mong Kok *Hong Kong* 12 B2
Monkstown *Dublin* 10 B3
Monnickendam *Amsterdam* 2 A3
Monrovia *Los Angeles* 16 B4
Monsanto *Lisbon* 16 A1
Monsanto, Parque Florestal de *Lisbon* 16 A1
Mont-Royal *Montreal* 20 A2
Mont-Royal, Parc *Montreal* 20 A2
Montcada i Reixac *Barcelona* 4 A2
Monte Chingolo *Buenos Aires* 7 C2
Montebello *Los Angeles* 16 B4
Montemor *Lisbon* 16 A1
Monterey Hills *Los Angeles* 16 B3
Monterey Park *Los Angeles* 16 B4
Montespaccato *Rome* 26 B1
Montesson *Paris* 24 A1
Monteverde Nuovo *Rome* 26 B1
Montfermeil *Paris* 24 A4
Montigny-le-Bretonneux *Paris* 24 B1
Montjay-la-Tour *Paris* 24 A4
Montjuïc *Barcelona* 4 A2
Montparnasse, Gare *Paris* 24 A2
Montréal *Montreal* 20 A2
Montréal, Î. de *Montreal* 20 A2
Montréal, Univ. de *Montreal* 20 B2
Montréal Est *Montreal* 20 A2
Montréal Nord *Montreal* 20 A2
Montréal Ouest *Montreal* 20 B1
Montréal Trudeau Int. ✈ (YUL) *Montreal* 20 B1
Montreuil *Paris* 24 A3
Montrouge *Paris* 24 B2
Montserrat *Buenos Aires* 7 B2
Monza *Milan* 18 A2
Monzoro *Milan* 18 B1
Moóca *São Paulo* 27 B2
Moonachie *New York* 22 B1
Moonee Ponds *Melbourne* 18 A1
Moonee Valley Racecourse *Melbourne* 18 A1
Moosach *Munich* 21 A2
Mora *Mumbai* 20 B2
Moratalaz *Madrid* 17 B2
Mörby *Stockholm* 29 A2
Morden *London* 15 B2
Morée → *Paris* 24 A3
Morgan Park *Chicago* 9 C3
Moriguchi *Osaka* 23 A2
Morivione *Milan* 18 B2
Morningside *Edinburgh* 11 B2
Morningside *Johannesburg* 13 A2
Morningside Park *Orlando* 23 B2
Morningside Park *Toronto* 31 A3
Morro Solar, Cerro *Lima* 14 C2
Mortlake *London* 15 B2
Mortlake *Sydney* 29 B1
Morton Grove *Chicago* 9 A2
Morumbi *São Paulo* 27 B1
Moscavide *Lisbon* 16 A2
Moschato *Athens* 2 B2
Moscow = Moskva *Moscow* 19 B2
Moskva *Moscow* 19 B2
Moskvoretskiy *Moscow* 19 B2
Mosman *Sydney* 29 B2
Moti Bagh *Delhi* 10 B2
Motol *Prague* 25 B2
Motsa *Jerusalem* 13 B2
Motsa Illit *Jerusalem* 13 B1
Motspur Park *London* 15 B2
Mottingham *London* 15 B4
Mount Dennis *Toronto* 31 A2
Mount Greenwood *Chicago* 9 C2
Mount Hood Memorial Park ⌂ *Boston* 6 A2
Mount Merrion *Dublin* 10 B2
Mount Olympus *Los Angeles* 16 B2
Mount Rainier *Washington* 33 B3
Mount Vernon *New York* 22 A3
Müggelberge *Berlin* 5 B4
Müggelheim *Berlin* 5 B5
Muggiò *Milan* 18 A2
Mühleiten *Vienna* 32 A3
Mühlenfliess → *Berlin* 5 A5
Muiden *Amsterdam* 2 A3
Muizenberg *Cape Town* 8 B1
Mujahidpur *Delhi* 10 B2
Mukandpur *Delhi* 10 A2
Mukhmas *Jerusalem* 13 A2
Muko → *Osaka* 23 A1
Mukojima *Tokyo* 30 A3
Mulbarton *Johannesburg* 13 B2
Mullach Íde = Malahide *Dublin* 10 A3
Mumbai *Mumbai* 20 B2
Mumbai Chhatrapati Shivaji Int. ✈ (BOM) *Mumbai* 20 A2
Mumbai Harbour *Mumbai* 20 B2
Munch-museum *Oslo* 23 A3
Münchehofe *Berlin* 5 B5
München *Munich* 21 B2
München Franz Josef Strauss Int. ✈ (MUC) *Munich* 21 A2
Munich = München *Munich* 21 B2
Munkkiniemi *Helsinki* 11 B2
Munro *Buenos Aires* 7 B1
Muntinlupa *Manila* 17 C2
Murai Res. *Singapore* 28 A2
Muranów *Warsaw* 33 B1
Murino *St. Petersburg* 27 B2
Murrayfield *Edinburgh* 11 B2
Murtala Mohammed Int. ✈ (LOS) *Lagos* 14 A1
Musashino *Tokyo* 30 A2
Museumsinsel *Berlin* 5 A3
Mushin *Lagos* 14 A2
Musocco *Milan* 18 B1
Mustansiriya *Baghdad* 3 A2
Musturud *Cairo* 7 A2
Muswell Hill *London* 15 A3
Mutanabi *Baghdad* 3 B2
Muthana *Baghdad* 3 B2
Myllypuro *Helsinki* 11 B3
Mystic → *Boston* 6 A2

N

N.S.C.B. Int. ✈ (CCU) *Kolkata* 14 B2
Naberezhnaya Tower *Moscow* 19 B2
Nacka *Stockholm* 29 B3
Nærsnes *Oslo* 23 B1
Nagatsuta *Tokyo* 30 B2
Nagytétény *Budapest* 7 B1
Nahalin *Jerusalem* 13 B1
Najafgarh Drain → *Delhi* 10 B1
Nakahara *Tokyo* 30 B2
Nakano *Tokyo* 30 A2
Namsan Park *Seoul* 27 B1
Namyeong *Seoul* 27 B1
Nanbiancun *Guangzhou* 11 B1
Nanchang He → *Beijing* 4 B1
Nandang *Guangzhou* 11 B2
Nangal Dewat *Delhi* 10 B1
Naniwa *Osaka* 23 B1
Nanole *Mumbai* 20 A2
Nanpu Bridge *Shanghai* 28 B2
Nanshi *Shanghai* 28 B1
Nanterre *Paris* 24 A2
Napier Mole *Karachi* 13 B1
Naraina *Delhi* 10 B1
Nariman Pt. *Mumbai* 20 B1
Närmak *Tehran* 31 A2
Naruo *Osaka* 23 A1
Näsby *Stockholm* 29 A2
Näsbypark *Stockholm* 29 A2
National Arboretum *Washington* 33 B2
National Maritime Museum *London* 15 B3
National September 11 Memorial and Museum *New York* 22 B1
National University (N.U.S.) *Singapore* 28 B2
National Zoological Park *Washington* 33 B2
Nationals Park *Washington* 33 B2
Nativity, Basilica of *Jerusalem* 13 B2
Natolin *Warsaw* 33 C2
Naucalpan de Juárez *Mexico City* 18 B1
Naupada *Mumbai* 20 A2
Navi Mumbai *Mumbai* 20 A2
Naviglio di Pavia *Milan* 18 B1
Naviglio Grande *Milan* 18 B1
Navotas *Manila* 17 B1
Navy Pier *Chicago* 9 B3
Nazal Hikmat Beg *Baghdad* 3 A2
Nazimabad *Karachi* 13 A2
Nazlet el Simmân *Cairo* 7 B1
Nea Alexandria *Athens* 2 B2
Nea Ionia *Athens* 2 A2
Nea Liosia *Athens* 2 A2
Nea Smirni *Athens* 2 B2
Neapoli *Athens* 2 B2
Near North *Chicago* 9 B3
Nebušice *Prague* 25 B1
Nederhorst *Amsterdam* 2 B3
Nedlitz *Berlin* 5 B1
Nee Soon *Singapore* 28 A2
Needham *Boston* 6 B1
Needham Heights *Boston* 6 B1
Nellis Air Force Base ✈ (LSV) *Las Vegas* 14 A2
N'ematābād *Tehran* 31 B2
Nerima *Tokyo* 30 A3
Nesodden *Oslo* 23 B3
Nesoddtangen *Oslo* 23 A3
Nesøya *Oslo* 23 A2
Netaji Subhash Chandra Bose Int. ✈ (CCU) *Kolkata* 14 B2
Neu Aubing *Munich* 21 B1
Neu Buch *Berlin* 5 A4
Neu Buchhorst *Berlin* 5 B5
Neu Fahrland *Berlin* 5 B1
Neu Lindenberg *Berlin* 5 A4
Neubiberg *Munich* 21 B3
Neuenhagen *Berlin* 5 A4
Neuessling *Vienna* 32 A3
Neuhausen *Munich* 21 B2
Neuherberg *Munich* 21 A2
Neuhönow *Berlin* 5 A5
Neuilly-Plaisance *Paris* 24 A4
Neuilly-sur-Marne *Paris* 24 A4
Neuilly-sur-Seine *Paris* 24 A2
Neukagran *Vienna* 32 A2
Neukettenhof *Vienna* 32 B2
Neukölln *Berlin* 5 B3
Neuperlach *Munich* 21 B2
Neuried *Munich* 21 B1
Neustift am Walde *Vienna* 32 A1
Neusüssenbrunn *Vienna* 32 A2
Neuwaldegg *Vienna* 32 A1
Neve Ya'akov *Jerusalem* 13 A2
Neves *Rio de Janeiro* 25 B2
New Baghdād *Baghdad* 3 B2
New Barakpur *Kolkata* 14 A2
New Brighton *New York* 22 C1
New Canada *Johannesburg* 13 B1
New Canada Dam *Johannesburg* 13 B1
New Cross *London* 15 B3
New Delhi *Delhi* 10 B2
New Dorp *New York* 22 C1
New Dorp Beach *New York* 22 C1
New Malden *London* 15 B2
New Milford *New York* 22 A1
New Mumbai = Navi Mumbai *Mumbai* 20 A2
New Orleans *New Orleans* 21 B2
New Orleans Int. ✈ (MSY) *New Orleans* 21 B1
New River → *Miami* 19 B3
New Territories *Hong Kong* 12 A1
New Toronto *Toronto* 31 B1
New Utrecht *New York* 22 C2
New York *New York* 22 B2
New York La Guardia ✈ (LGA) *New York* 22 B2
Newark B. *New York* 22 B1
Newbattle *Edinburgh* 11 B3
Newbury Park *London* 15 A4
Newcraighall *Edinburgh* 11 B3
Newham ☐ *London* 15 A4
Newhaven *Edinburgh* 11 B2
Newington *Edinburgh* 11 B2
Newlands *Johannesburg* 13 B1
Newport *Melbourne* 18 B1
Newton *Boston* 6 B1
Newtonbrook *Toronto* 31 A2
Newtongrange *Edinburgh* 11 B3
Newtonville *Boston* 6 A1
Newtown *Sydney* 29 B2
Ngau Chi Wan *Hong Kong* 12 A2
Ngau Tau Kok *Hong Kong* 12 B2
Ngong Shuen Chau *Hong Kong* 12 B1
Ngua Kok Wan *Hong Kong* 12 A1
Nhava Sheva *Mumbai* 20 B2
Niāvarān *Tehran* 31 A2
Nibra *Kolkata* 14 B1
Nidāl *Baghdad* 3 B2
Niddrie *Edinburgh* 11 B3
Niddrie *Melbourne* 18 A1
Nieder Neuendorf *Berlin* 5 A2
Niederschöneweide *Berlin* 5 B3
Niederschönhausen *Berlin* 5 A3
Niemeyer *Rio de Janeiro* 25 B1
Nieuwendam *Amsterdam* 2 A2
Nihonbashi *Tokyo* 30 A3
Niipperi *Helsinki* 11 B1
Nikea *Athens* 2 B1
Nikolassee *Berlin* 5 B2
Nikolskiy *Moscow* 19 B1
Niles *Chicago* 9 A2
Nimta *Kolkata* 14 A2
Ninoy Aquino Int. ✈ (MNL) *Manila* 17 B2
Nippa *Tokyo* 30 B2
Nippori *Tokyo* 30 A3
Nishi *Osaka* 23 A1
Nishinari *Osaka* 23 B1
Nishinomiya *Osaka* 23 A1
Nishiyodogawa *Osaka* 23 A1
Niterói *Rio de Janeiro* 25 B2
Nockeby *Stockholm* 29 B1
Noel Park *London* 15 A3
Nogatino *Moscow* 19 B3
Nogent-sur-Marne *Paris* 24 A3
Noida *Delhi* 10 B2
Noiseau *Paris* 24 B4
Noisiel *Paris* 24 A4
Noisy-le-Grand *Paris* 24 A4
Noisy-le-Roi *Paris* 24 A1
Noisy-le-Sec *Paris* 24 A3
Nokkala *Helsinki* 11 C1
Nomentano *Rome* 26 B2
Nonakashinden *Tokyo* 30 A2
Nongminyundong Jiangxisuo *Guangzhou* 11 B2
Nonhyeon *Seoul* 27 B2
Nonthaburi *Bangkok* 3 A1
Noordgesig *Johannesburg* 13 B1
Noordzeekanaal *Amsterdam* 2 A1
Nord, Gare du *Paris* 24 A3
Nordmarka *Oslo* 23 A3
Nordrand-Siedlung *Vienna* 32 A2
Nordstrand *Oslo* 23 A3
Norland *Miami* 19 C2
Norridge *Chicago* 9 B2
Norrmalm *Stockholm* 29 A2
North Arlington *New York* 22 B1
North Atlanta *Atlanta* 3 A3
North Bay Village *Miami* 19 C3
North Bergen *New York* 22 B1
North Bull I. *Dublin* 10 A3
North Cheam *London* 15 B2
North Cray *London* 15 B4
North Decatur *Atlanta* 3 B3
North Druid Hills *Atlanta* 3 B3
North Esk → *Edinburgh* 11 B2
North Gyle *Edinburgh* 11 B2
North Hackensack *New York* 22 A1
North Harbor *Manila* 17 B1
North Hd. *Sydney* 29 A2
North Hollywood *Los Angeles* 16 B2
North Las Vegas *Las Vegas* 14 A1
North Las Vegas ✈ (VGT) *Las Vegas* 14 A1
North Lexington *Boston* 6 A1
North Miami *Miami* 19 C2
North Miami Beach *Miami* 19 C2
North Nazimabad *Karachi* 13 A2
North Perry ✈ (HWO) *Miami* 19 B2
North Pt. *Hong Kong* 12 B2
North Queensferry *Edinburgh* 11 A1
North Quincy *Boston* 6 B2
North Res. *Boston* 6 A2
North Riverside *Chicago* 9 B2
North Saugus *Boston* 6 A2
North Shore Channel → *Chicago* 9 B2
North Station *Boston* 6 A2
North Sydney *Sydney* 29 B2
North Woolwich *London* 15 A4
North York *Toronto* 31 A2
Northbridge *Sydney* 29 A2
Northbridge Park *Sydney* 29 A2
Northbrook *Chicago* 9 A2
Northcliff *Johannesburg* 13 A1
Northcote *Melbourne* 18 A2
Northeastern Univ. *Boston* 6 A2
Northfield *Chicago* 9 A2
Northmount *Toronto* 31 A2
Northolt *London* 15 A1
Northumberland Heath *London* 15 B5
Northwestern Station *Chicago* 9 B3
Northwestern Univ. *Chicago* 9 A2
Northwood *London* 15 A1
Northwood Park *Toronto* 31 A1
Norwood *Johannesburg* 13 A2
Norwood Park *Chicago* 9 B2
Noryangjin *Seoul* 27 B1
Nossa Senhora do Ó *São Paulo* 27 B1
Nossegem *Brussels* 6 A3
Notre-Dame *Paris* 24 A3
Notre-Dame, Basilique *Montreal* 20 B2
Notre-Dame, Bois *Paris* 24 B4
Notre-Dame-de-Grace *Montreal* 20 B2
Notting Hill *London* 15 A2
Nova Milanese *Milan* 18 A2
Novate Milanese *Milan* 18 A1
Novaya Derevnya *St. Petersburg* 27 A1
Nové Město *Prague* 25 B2
Novoaleksandrovskoye *St. Petersburg* 27 B2
Novodevichy Convent *Moscow* 19 B2
Novogireyevo *Moscow* 19 B3
Novosaratovka *St. Petersburg* 27 B3
Nowe-Babice *Warsaw* 33 B1
Nöykkiö *Helsinki* 11 B1
Nueva Atzacoalco *Mexico City* 18 B2
Nueva Pompeya *Buenos Aires* 7 C2
Nueva Tenochtitlán *Mexico City* 18 B2
Nuijala *Helsinki* 11 B1
Numabukuro *Tokyo* 30 A2
Nuñez *Buenos Aires* 7 B2
Nunhead *London* 15 B3
Ñuñoa *Santiago* 27 B2
Nusle *Prague* 25 B2
Nussdorf *Vienna* 32 A2
Nyanga *Cape Town* 8 A2
Nymphenburg *Munich* 21 B2
Nymphenburg, Schloss *Munich* 21 B2

O

O.R. Tambo Int. ✈ (JNB) *Johannesburg* 13 A2
Oak Forest *Chicago* 9 D2
Oak Grove *Atlanta* 3 A3
Oak Hill *Boston* 6 B1
Oak Lawn *Chicago* 9 C2
Oak Park *Chicago* 9 B2
Oak View *Washington* 33 A3
Oakdale *Atlanta* 3 A2
Oakland *San Francisco* 26 B3
Oakland Park *Miami* 19 A3
Oaklawn *Washington* 33 C3
Oakleigh *Melbourne* 18 B2
Oakwood Beach *New York* 22 C1
Oatley *Sydney* 29 B1
Obalende *Lagos* 14 B2
Oba's Palace *Lagos* 14 B2
Oberföhring *Munich* 21 B2
Oberhaching *Munich* 21 B2
Oberlaa *Vienna* 32 B2
Oberlisse *Vienna* 32 A2
Obermenzing *Munich* 21 A1
Obermoos Schwaige *Munich* 21 A1
Oberschleissheim *Munich* 21 A2
Oberschöneweide *Berlin* 5 B4
Observatory *Johannesburg* 13 B2
Óbuda *Budapest* 7 A2
Obukhovo *St. Petersburg* 27 B2
Obvodnyy Kanal *St. Petersburg* 27 B1
Ocean Park *Hong Kong* 12 B2
Ochota *Warsaw* 33 B1
Ocoee *Orlando* 23 A1
Odaiba *Tokyo* 30 B3
Ōdana *Tokyo* 30 B2
Öden-Stockach *Munich* 21 B3
Odilampi *Helsinki* 11 B1
Odivelas *Lisbon* 16 A1
Odolany *Warsaw* 33 B1
Oeiras *Lisbon* 16 A1
Ofin *Lagos* 14 A3
Ogawa *Tokyo* 30 A1
Ogden Park *Chicago* 9 C2
Ogikubo *Tokyo* 30 A2
Ogogoro *Lagos* 14 B2
Ogoyo *Lagos* 14 B2
Ogudu *Lagos* 14 A2
O'Higgins, Parque *Santiago* 27 B2
Ōimachi *Tokyo* 30 B3
Ojota *Lagos* 14 A2
Ojus *Miami* 19 C3
Oke-Ira *Lagos* 14 B2
Okęcie *Warsaw* 33 B1
Okęcie, Warszawa ✈ (WAW) *Warsaw* 33 B1
Okeogbe *Lagos* 14 B2
Okhla *Delhi* 10 B2
Okhta → *St. Petersburg* 27 B2
Okkervil → *St. Petersburg* 27 B2
Okrzeszyn *Warsaw* 33 C2
Oksval *Oslo* 23 A3
Oktyabrskiy *Moscow* 19 B2
Ōkubo *Tokyo* 30 A3
Ōkura *Tokyo* 30 B1
Olari *Helsinki* 11 B1
Olaria *Rio de Janeiro* 25 B1
Old Admiralty *St. Petersburg* 27 B1
Old City *Jerusalem* 13 B2
Old City *Shanghai* 28 B1
Old Fort York *Toronto* 31 B2
Old Harbor *Boston* 6 B2
Old Town = Stare Miasto *Warsaw* 33 B2
Old Town *Chicago* 9 B3
Old Town Hall = Altes Rathaus *Munich* 21 B2
Oldbawn *Dublin* 10 B1
Oleta River State Rec. Area *Miami* 19 C3
Olgino *St. Petersburg* 27 B1
Olimpico, Estadio *Mexico City* 18 C1
Olivais *Lisbon* 16 A2
Olivar de los Padres *Mexico City* 18 B1
Olivar del Conde *Mexico City* 18 B1
Olives, Mt. of *Jerusalem* 13 B2
Olivia, L. *Orlando* 23 A1
Olivos *Buenos Aires* 7 B2
Olona → *Milan* 18 B1
Olympia, L. *Orlando* 23 B1
Olympic Green *Beijing* 4 B2
Olympic Park *London* 15 A3
Olympic Stadium = Turner Field *Atlanta* 3 B2
Olympic Stadium *Beijing* 4 B2
Olympic Stadium *Helsinki* 11 B2
Olympique, Stade *Montreal* 20 A2
Ōmori *Tokyo* 30 B3
One World Trade Center *New York* 22 e1
Onisigun *Lagos* 14 A2
Ontario Science Centre *Toronto* 31 A2
Ōokayama *Tokyo* 30 B3
Oostzaan Tuindorp *Amsterdam* 2 A2
Opa-Locka *Miami* 19 C1
Opa-Locka ✈ (OPF) *Miami* 19 C1
Opacz *Warsaw* 33 B1
Ophirton *Johannesburg* 13 B2
Oppegård *Oslo* 23 B3
Oppem *Brussels* 6 A1
Oppsal *Oslo* 23 A4
Ora *Jerusalem* 13 B1
Oradell *New York* 22 A1
Oradell Res. *New York* 22 A1
Orangi *Karachi* 13 A2
Ordrup *Copenhagen* 8 A3
Óřech *Prague* 25 B2
Oregun *Lagos* 14 A2
Orestad *Copenhagen* 8 B3
Orient Heights *Boston* 6 A3
Oriental Pearl Tower *Shanghai* 28 B2
Orland Park *Chicago* 9 D2
Orlando *Orlando* 23 A2
Orlando Dam *Johannesburg* 13 B1
Orlando East *Johannesburg* 13 B1
Orlando Executive ✈ (ORL) *Orlando* 23 A2
Orlando Int. ✈ (MCO) *Orlando* 23 B3
Orlovista *Orlando* 23 A2
Orly *Paris* 24 B3
Orly, Paris ✈ (ORY) *Paris* 24 B3
Ormesson-sur-Marne *Paris* 24 B4
Ormond *Melbourne* 18 B2
Ormøya *Oslo* 23 A3
Orpington *London* 15 B4
Ortaköy *Istanbul* 12 B2
Ortica *Milan* 18 B2
Oruba *Lagos* 14 A2
Ōsaka *Osaka* 23 B2
Ōsaka Castle *Osaka* 23 A2
Ōsaka Harbour *Osaka* 23 B1
Ōsaka Itami Int. ✈ (ITM) *Osaka* 23 A1
Ōsaka Kansai Int. ✈ (KIX) *Osaka* 23 B2
Ōsaki *Tokyo* 30 B3
Osasco *São Paulo* 27 B1
Osdorf *Berlin* 5 B3
Osdorp *Amsterdam* 2 A1
Oshodi *Lagos* 14 A2
Oslo *Oslo* 23 A3
Oslo ✈ (OSL) *Oslo* 23 A4
Ōsone *Tokyo* 30 B2
Osorun *Lagos* 14 A2
Ospiate *Milan* 18 A1
Ostankino *Moscow* 19 B2
Osterley *London* 15 B1
Osterley Park *London* 15 B1
Östermalm *Stockholm* 29 A2
Österskär *Stockholm* 29 A3
Óstia Malpasso *Rome* 26 C1
Ostiense *Rome* 26 B1
Østmarkkapellet *Oslo* 23 A4
Østøya *Oslo* 23 A2
Ōta *Tokyo* 30 B3
Otaniemi *Helsinki* 11 B1
Ōtsuka *Tokyo* 30 A3
Ottakring *Vienna* 32 A1
Ottávia *Rome* 25 B1
Ottery *Cape Town* 8 B2

Ottobrunn Munich 21 B3
Ouderkerk Amsterdam 2 B2
Oulunkylä Helsinki 11 B2
Ourcq, Canal de l' Paris 24 A3
Outer Mission San Francisco 26 B2
Outremont Montreal 20 A2
Overijse Brussels 6 B3
Oworonsoki Lagos 14 A2
Oxgangs Edinburgh 11 B2
Oxon Hill Washington 33 C3
Oyodo Osaka 23 A1
Oyster Rock Mumbai 20 B1
Oyster Rocks Karachi 13 B2
Ozoir-la-Ferrière Paris 24 B4
Ozone Park New York 22 B2

P

Pacific Heights
San Francisco 26 B2
Pacific Manor San Francisco 26 C2
Pacific Palisades Los Angeles 16 B1
Pacifica San Francisco 26 C2
Paco Manila 17 B1
Paco de Arcos Lisbon 16 A1
Paddington London 15 A2
Paddington Sydney 29 B2
Paderno Milan 18 A1
Pagewood Sydney 29 B2
Pagote Mumbai 20 B2
Pai, I. do Rio de Janeiro 25 B2
Pak Kok Hong Kong 12 B1
Pak Kong Hong Kong 12 A2
Pakila Helsinki 11 B2
Palacio Real Madrid 17 B1
Palaiseau Paris 24 B2
Palazzolo Milan 18 A1
Paleo Faliro Athens 2 B2
Palermo Buenos Aires 7 B2
Palhais Lisbon 16 B2
Palisades Park New York 22 A1
Palm Deira, The Dubai 9 A2
Palm Jumeirah, The Dubai 9 B1
Palmerston Dublin 10 A1
Palms Los Angeles 16 B2
Paloheinä Helsinki 11 B2
Palomeras Madrid 17 B2
Palos Heights Chicago 9 D2
Palos Hills Chicago 9 C2
Palos Park Chicago 9 C1
Palpara Kolkata 14 B2
Panchur Kolkata 14 B1
Pandacan Manila 17 B2
Pandan, Selat Singapore 28 B2
Pandan Res. Singapore 28 B2
Pangrati Athens 2 B2
Pangsua, Sungei ➜
Singapore 28 A2
Panihati Kolkata 14 A2
Panjang, Bukit Singapore 28 A2
Panke ➜ Berlin 5 A3
Pankow Berlin 5 A3
Pantheon Rome 26 B1
Panthersville Atlanta 3 B3
Pantin Paris 24 A3
Pantitlán Mexico City 18 B2
Panyu Guangzhou 11 B2
Papiol Barcelona 4 A1
Paradise Las Vegas 14 B2
Paramount Studios
Los Angeles 16 B3
Paramus New York 22 A1
Paranaque Manila 17 B1
Paray-Vieille-Poste Paris 24 B3
Pardisān Nature Park
Tehran 31 A2
Parel Mumbai 20 B1
Pari São Paulo 27 B2
Parioli Rome 26 B1
Paris Paris 24 A3
Paris Orly ✈ (ORY) Paris 24 B3
Parje Mumbai 20 B2
Pārk-e Āzādegān Tehran 31 B2
Pārk-e Mellat Tehran 31 A2
Park Ridge Chicago 9 A1
Park Royal London 15 A2
Parkchester New York 22 B2
Parkdale Toronto 31 B2
Parkhurst Johannesburg 13 A2
Parklawn Washington 33 B2
Parkmore Johannesburg 13 A2
Parkside San Francisco 26 B2
Parktown Johannesburg 13 B2
Parkview Johannesburg 13 A2
Parkville New York 22 C2
Parkwood Cape Town 8 B1
Parkwood Johannesburg 13 A2
Parow Cape Town 8 A2
Parque Chacabuco
Buenos Aires 7 B2
Parque Patricios Buenos Aires 7 B2
Parramatta ➜ Sydney 29 A1
Paşabahçe Istanbul 12 B2
Pasadena Los Angeles 16 B4
Pasar Minggu Jakarta 12 B1
Pasay Manila 17 B1
Pascoe Vale Melbourne 18 A1
Pasig Manila 17 B2
Pasig ➜ Manila 17 B2
Pasila Helsinki 11 B2
Pasing Munich 21 B1
Pasir Panjang Singapore 28 B2
Pasir Ris Singapore 28 A3
Passaic New York 22 A1
Passaic ➜ New York 22 B1
Passirana Milan 18 A1
Patel Nagar Delhi 10 B1
Pateros Manila 17 B2
Pathumwan Bangkok 3 B2
Patipukur Kolkata 14 B2
Patisia Athens 2 A2
Paulo E. Virginia, Gruta
Rio de Janeiro 25 B1
Paulshof Berlin 5 A5
Paya Lebar Singapore 28 A3
Peakhurst Sydney 29 B1
Peania Athens 2 B3
Pearson Int. Toronto ✈
(YYZ) Toronto 31 A1
Peckham London 15 B3
Pederstrup Copenhagen 8 A2
Pedralbes Barcelona 4 A1
Pedregal de San Angel,
Jardines del Mexico City 18 C1
Peip'ing = Beijing Beijing 4 B1
Peking = Beijing Beijing 4 B1
Pelcowizna Warsaw 33 B2
Pembroke Park Miami 19 C2
Pembroke Pines Miami 19 B1
Peñalolén Santiago 27 B2
Peng Siang ➜ Singapore 28 A2
Penge London 15 B3
Penha Rio de Janeiro 25 A1
Penicuik Edinburgh 11 B2
Penjaringan Jakarta 12 A1
Pentagon Washington 33 B2
Penzing Vienna 32 A1
People's Park Shanghai 28 B1
People's Square Shanghai 28 B1
Perales del Río Madrid 17 C2
Perchtoldsdorf Vienna 32 B1
Perdizes São Paulo 27 B2
Peristeri Athens 2 A2
Perivale London 15 A2
Perk Brussels 6 A2
Perlach Munich 21 B2
Perlacher Forst Munich 21 B2
Pero Milan 18 A1
Peropok, Bukit Singapore 28 B2
Perovo Moscow 19 B3
Pertusella Milan 18 A1
Pesagot Jerusalem 13 A2
Pesanggrahag, Kali ➜
Jakarta 12 B1
Peschiera Borromeo Milan 18 B2
Pesek, Pulau Singapore 28 B2
Pest Budapest 7 B2
Pesterzsébet Budapest 7 B2
Pesthidegkút Budapest 7 A1
Pestimre Budapest 7 B3
Pestlőrinc Budapest 7 B3
Pestújhely Budapest 7 A2
Petas Helsinki 11 B2
Petrogradskaya Storona
St. Petersburg 27 B2
Petroupoli Athens 2 A2
Petrovice Prague 25 B3
Petrovskiy Park Moscow 19 B2
Petrovsko-Razumovskoye
Moscow 19 B2
Pettycur Edinburgh 11 A2
Peutie Brussels 6 A2
Pfaueninsel Berlin 5 B1
Phaya Thai Bangkok 3 B2
Phihai Karachi 13 A2
Phillip B. Sydney 29 B2
Phoenix Chicago 9 D3
Phoenix Park Dublin 10 A2
Phra Khanong Bangkok 3 B2
Phra Nakhon Bangkok 3 B2
Phra Pradaeng Bangkok 3 C2
Phranakhon Bangkok 3 B1
Pico Rivera Los Angeles 16 C4
Piedade Lisbon 16 A1
Piedade Rio de Janeiro 25 B1
Piedade, Cova da Lisbon 16 A2
Piedmont Park Atlanta 3 B2
Pierre Elliott Trudeau ✈
(YUL) Montreal 20 B1
Pietralata Rome 26 B2
Pihlajamäki Helsinki 11 B2
Pihlajasaari Helsinki 11 C2
Pilares Rio de Janeiro 25 B1
Pilton Edinburgh 11 B2
Pine Castle Orlando 23 B2
Pine Grove Toronto 31 A1
Pine Hills Orlando 23 A2
Pine Island Miami 19 B1
Pinecrest Miami 19 D1
Pinewood Park Miami 19 C2
Pingzhou Guangzhou 11 B2
Pinheiros ➜ São Paulo 27 B1
Pinjrapur Karachi 13 A2
Pinner London 15 A1
Pinner Green London 15 A1
Pioltello Milan 18 A2
Piræus = Pireas Athens 2 B1
Piraiévs = Pireas Athens 2 B1
Pirajuçara ➜ São Paulo 27 B1
Pireas Athens 2 B1
Pirinççi Istanbul 12 B1
Pirituba São Paulo 27 A1
Pirkkola Helsinki 11 B2
Pisgat O'mer Jerusalem 13 B2
Pisgat Ze'ev Jerusalem 13 B2
Pisnice Prague 25 C2
Pitampura Delhi 10 A1
Pitkäjärvi Helsinki 11 B1
Planegg Munich 21 B1
Plantation Miami 19 B2
Plantation Isles Miami 19 B2
Plaza Mayor Madrid 17 B1
Pleasure Island Orlando 23 B1
Plumstead Cape Town 8 B1
Plumstead London 15 B4
Plyushchevo Moscow 19 B3
Po Toi Hong Kong 12 B2
Po Toi O Hong Kong 12 B2
Poasco Milan 18 B2
Podbaba Prague 25 B2
Podolí Prague 25 B2
Pointe-Aux-Trembles
Montreal 20 A2
Poissy Paris 24 A1
Pok Fu Lam Hong Kong 12 B1
Pokcheong Seoul 27 C2
Polton Edinburgh 11 B3
Polvoranca, Parque de
Madrid 17 C1
Polyustrovo St. Petersburg 27 B2
Pompano Beach Miami 19 A3
Pomprap Bangkok 3 B2
Pondok Gede Jakarta 12 B2
Pondok Indah Jakarta 12 B1
Pont-Viau Montreal 20 A1
Pontault-Combault Paris 24 B4
Pontinha Lisbon 16 A1
Poplar London 15 A3
Poppintree Dublin 10 A2
Port Botany Sydney 29 B2
Port Mearnóg =
Portmarnock Dublin 10 A3
Port Melbourne Melbourne 18 B1
Port Rashid Dubai 9 A2
Port Richmond New York 22 C1
Port Saeed Dubai 9 B2
Port Shelter Hong Kong 12 A2
Port Union Toronto 31 A4
Portage Park Chicago 9 B2
Portela, Lisboa ✈ (LIS)
Lisbon 16 A2
Porter, L. Orlando 23 A3
Portmarnock Dublin 10 A3
Porto Brandão Lisbon 16 A1
Pôrto Novo Rio de Janeiro 25 A2
Porto Novo Cr. ➜ Lagos 14 B2
Portobello Edinburgh 11 B3
Portrero San Francisco 26 B3
Posen Chicago 9 D2
Potomac Overlook Reg.
Park ⌂ Washington 33 B2
Potrero Pt. San Francisco 26 B2
Potsdam Berlin 5 B1
Potzham Munich 21 B2
Pötzleinsdorf Vienna 32 A1
Póvoa de Santo Adriao
Lisbon 16 A2
Powązki Warsaw 33 B1
Powiśle Warsaw 33 B2
Powsin Warsaw 33 C2
Powsinek Warsaw 33 C2
Poyan Res. Singapore 28 A2
Pozuelo de Alarcón Madrid 17 B1
Prado, Museo del Madrid 17 B1
Prado Churubusco
Mexico City 18 B2
Praga Warsaw 33 B2
Prague = Praha Prague 25 B2
Praha Prague 25 B2
Praha ✈ (PRG) Prague 25 B1
Praires, R. des ➜ Montreal 20 A2
Prater Vienna 32 A2
Precotto Milan 18 A2
Prenestino Labicano Rome 26 B2
Prenzlauerberg Berlin 5 A3
Preston Melbourne 18 A1
Pretos Forros, Sa. dos
Rio de Janeiro 25 B1
Préville Montreal 20 B3
Přezletice Prague 25 B3
Prima Porta Rome 26 B1
Primavalle Rome 26 B1
Primrose Johannesburg 13 B2
Progreso Nacional
Mexico City 18 A2
Prosek Prague 25 B3
Prospect Hill Park Boston 6 A1
Providencia Santiago 27 B2
Průhonice Prague 25 C3
Psichiko Athens 2 A2
Pudong New Area Shanghai 28 B2
Pueblo Libre Lima 14 B2
Pueblo Nuevo = El
Pobleneu Barcelona 4 A2
Pueblo Nuevo Madrid 17 B2
Puerto Madero Buenos Aires 7 B2
Puhuangyu Beijing 4 B2
Puistola Helsinki 11 B3
Pukinmäki Helsinki 11 B2
Pulkovo Int. ✈ (LED)
St. Petersburg 27 C1
Pullach Munich 21 B1
Pullman Historic District
Chicago 9 C3
Pulo Gadung Jakarta 12 B2
Pūnak Tehran 31 A2
Punchbowl Sydney 29 B1
Punde Mumbai 20 B2
Punggol Singapore 28 A3
Punggol, Sungei ➜
Singapore 28 A3
Punggol Pt. Singapore 28 A3
Punjabi Bagh Delhi 10 A1
Puotila Helsinki 11 B3
Puteaux Paris 24 A2
Putney London 15 B2
Putuo Shanghai 28 B1
Putxet Barcelona 4 A1
Puxi Shanghai 28 B1
Pyramids Cairo 7 B1
Pyry Warsaw 33 C1

Q

Qalandiya Jerusalem 13 A2
Qal'eh Morghī Tehran 31 B2
Qāsemābād Tehran 31 A3
Qasr-e Fīrūzeh Tehran 31 B3
Qatane Jerusalem 13 B1
Qianmen Beijing 4 B2
Qinghuayuan Beijing 4 B1
Qingningsi Shanghai 28 B2
Qolhak Tehran 31 A2
Quadraro Rome 26 B2
Quaid-i-Azam Karachi 13 A1
Quartiere Zingone Milan 18 B1
Qubeiba Jerusalem 13 A1
Quds Baghdad 3 A2
Queen Mary Res. London 15 B1
Queen Victoria Market
Melbourne 18 A1
Queensbury London 15 A2
Queenscliffe Sydney 29 A2
Queensferry Edinburgh 11 B1
Queenstown Singapore 28 B2
Quellerina Johannesburg 13 A1
Queluz Lisbon 16 A1
Quezon City Manila 17 B2
Quilicura Santiago 27 B1
Quincy Boston 6 B2
Quincy B. Boston 6 B3
Quinta Normal Santiago 27 B1
Quinto de Stampi Milan 18 B2
Quinto Romano Milan 18 B1
Quirinale Rome 26 B1
Qutb Minar Delhi 10 B2

R

R.F.K. Memorial Stadium
Washington 33 B3
Raasdorf Vienna 32 A3
Radcliffe College Boston 6 A2
Rådhus Oslo 23 A3
Radlice Prague 25 B2
Radość Warsaw 33 B3
Radotín Prague 25 C2
Rafat Jerusalem 13 A2
Raffles Park Singapore 28 B2
Raheny Dublin 10 A3
Rahnsdorf Berlin 5 B5
Rajakylä Helsinki 11 B3
Rajpura Delhi 10 A2
Rákos-patak ➜ Budapest 7 B3
Rákoshegy Budapest 7 B3
Rákoskeresztúr Budapest 7 B3
Rákoskert Budapest 7 B3
Rákosliget Budapest 7 B3
Rákospalota Budapest 7 A2
Rákosszentmihály Budapest 7 A2
Raków Warsaw 33 B1
Ram Jerusalem 13 A2
Rām Allāh Jerusalem 13 A2
Ramadān Baghdad 3 B2
Ramakrishna Puram Delhi 10 B1
Rāmallāh = Rām Allāh
Jerusalem 13 A2
Ramanathpur Kolkata 14 A1
Ramat Allon Jerusalem 13 B2
Ramat Eshkol Jerusalem 13 B2
Ramat Razi'el Jerusalem 13 B1
Ramat Shafet Jerusalem 13 B2
Rambler Channel
Hong Kong 12 A1
Ramenki Moscow 19 B1
Ramersdorf Munich 21 B2
Rameses Station Cairo 7 A2
Ramos Rio de Janeiro 25 B1
Ramos Mejía Buenos Aires 7 B1
Ramot Jerusalem 13 B2
Rampur Delhi 10 A2
Ramsgate Sydney 29 B1
Rancho Park Los Angeles 16 B2
Rand ✈ (QRA) Johannesburg 13 B2
Randalls I. New York 22 B2
Randburg Johannesburg 13 A1
Randhart Johannesburg 13 B2
Randpark Ridge
Johannesburg 13 A1
Randwick Sydney 29 B2
Ranelagh Dublin 10 A2
Rangpuri Delhi 10 B1
Rannersdorf Vienna 32 B2
Ransbèche Brussels 6 B2
Ransdorp Amsterdam 2 A2
Ranvad Mumbai 20 B2
Raposo Lisbon 16 A1
Rastaala Helsinki 11 B1
Rastila Helsinki 11 B3
Raszyn Warsaw 33 C1
Rathfarnham Dublin 10 B2
Ratho Edinburgh 11 B1
Ratho Station Edinburgh 11 B1
Rato Lisbon 16 A2
Ravelston Edinburgh 11 B2
Rawamangun Jakarta 12 B2
Rayners Lane London 15 A1
Raynes Park London 15 B2
Raypur Kolkata 14 C2
Real Felipe, Fuerte Lima 14 B2
Reams, L. Orlando 23 B1
Reclining Buddha = Wat
Pho Bangkok 3 B1
Recoleta Buenos Aires 7 B2
Recoleta Santiago 27 B2
Red Fort = Lal Qila Delhi 10 B2
Red Square Moscow 19 B2
Redbridge ⌂ London 15 A4
Redfern Sydney 29 B2
Refshaleøen Copenhagen 8 A3
Regents Park Johannesburg 13 B2
Regent's Park London 15 A3
Rego Park New York 22 B2
Reinickendorf Berlin 5 A3
Rekola Helsinki 11 B3
Rembertów Warsaw 33 B2
Rembrandtpark Amsterdam 2 A2
Remedios de Escalada
Buenos Aires 7 C2
Rémola, Estany del Barcelona 4 B1
Renca Santiago 27 B1
Rennemoulin Paris 24 A1
Řeporyje Prague 25 B1
Repulse Bay Hong Kong 12 B2
Repy Prague 25 B1
Residenz Munich 21 B2
Retiro Buenos Aires 7 B2
Retiro Madrid 17 B1
Retiro, Puerto Buenos Aires 7 B2
Retreat Cape Town 8 B1
Reutov Moscow 19 B4
Réveillon ➜ Paris 24 B4
Revere Boston 6 A2
Rexdale Toronto 31 A1
Reynosa Tamaulipas
Mexico City 18 A1
Rho Milan 18 A1
Rhodes Sydney 29 A1
Rhodon Paris 24 B1
Rhodon ➜ Paris 24 B1
Rialto Towers Melbourne 18 A1
Ribeira Rio de Janeiro 25 A1
Ricarda, Estany de la
Barcelona 4 B1
Richmond Melbourne 18 A2
Richmond San Francisco 26 B2
Richmond Hill New York 22 B2
Richmond Park London 15 B2
Richmond-upon-
Thames ⌂ London 15 B2
Ridge, The Delhi 10 B2
Ridgefield New York 22 B1
Ridgefield Park New York 22 A1
Ridgewood New York 22 B2
Riem Munich 21 B3
Riesenrad Vienna 32 A2
Rijksmuseum Amsterdam 2 A2
Rikers I. New York 22 B2
Rimac Lima 14 B2
Ringsend Dublin 10 A2
Rinkeby Stockholm 29 A1
Rio Comprido Rio de Janeiro 25 B1
Rio de Janeiro Rio de Janeiro 25 B1
Rio de Janeiro Galeão ✈
(GIG) Rio de Janeiro 25 A1
Rio de Mouro Lisbon 16 A1
Ripollet Barcelona 4 A1
Ris Oslo 23 A3
Risby Copenhagen 8 A1
Rishra Kolkata 14 A2
Rithala Delhi 10 A1
Rive Sud, Canal de la
Montreal 20 B2
River Edge New York 22 A1
River Forest Chicago 9 B2
River Grove Chicago 9 B1
River Ridge New Orleans 21 B1
Riverdale Chicago 9 D3
Riverdale New York 22 A2
Riverdale Washington 33 B3
Riverdale Park Toronto 31 A2
Riverlea Johannesburg 13 B1
Riverside Chicago 9 C2
Riverwood Sydney 29 B1
Rivière-des-Praires
Montreal 20 A2
Rixensart Brussels 6 B3
Riyad Baghdad 3 B2
Rizal Park Manila 17 B1
Rizal Stadium Manila 17 B1
Roa Oslo 23 A2
Robbins Chicago 9 D2
Robertsham Johannesburg 13 B2
Rochelle Park New York 22 A1
Rock Cr. ➜ Washington 33 B2
Rock Creek Park
Washington 33 B2
Rockaway Beach New York 22 C3
Rockaway Pt. New York 22 C2
Rockdale Sydney 29 B1
Rockefeller Center
New York 22 B2
Roda, Gezîret el Cairo 7 A2
Roda I. = Roda, Gezîret el
Cairo 7 A2
Rodaon Vienna 32 B1
Rødovre Copenhagen 8 A2
Rodrigo de Freitas, L.
Rio de Janeiro 25 B1
Roehampton London 15 B2
Rogers Park Chicago 9 A3
Roihuvuori Helsinki 11 B3
Roissy-en-Brie Paris 24 B4
Rokytka ➜ Prague 25 B3
Roma Rome 26 B1
Roma Urbe ✈ Rome 26 B2
Római-Fürdő Budapest 7 A2
Romainville Paris 24 A3
Roman Forum = Foro
Romano Rome 26 B1
Romano Banco Milan 18 B1
Rome = Roma Rome 26 B1
Romema Jerusalem 13 B2
Romford London 15 A5
Ronald Reagan Nat.
Washington ✈ (DCA)
Washington 33 B2
Rondebosch Cape Town 8 A1
Roppongi Tokyo 30 B3
Rose, L. Orlando 23 A1
Rose Bowl Los Angeles 16 B4
Rose Hill Washington 33 C2
Rosebank Johannesburg 13 A2
Rosebank New York 22 C1
Rosebery Sydney 29 B2
Rosedal La Candelaria
Mexico City 18 B2
Roseland Chicago 9 C3
Rosemead Los Angeles 16 B4
Rosemont Chicago 9 B1
Rosemont Montreal 20 A2
Rosenborg Slot Copenhagen 8 A3
Rosenthal Berlin 5 A3
Rosettenville Johannesburg 13 B2
Rosewell Edinburgh 11 B3
Rosherville Dam
Johannesburg 13 B2
Rösjön Stockholm 29 A2
Roslags-Näsby Stockholm 29 A2
Roslin Edinburgh 11 B3
Roslindale Boston 6 B2
Rosny-sous-Bois Paris 24 A4
Rosslyn Washington 33 B2
Rosyth Edinburgh 11 A1
Rotherhithe London 15 B3
Rothneusiedl Vienna 32 B2
Rothschmaige Munich 21 A1
Rouge Hill Toronto 31 A4
Round I. Hong Kong 12 B2
Roxbury Boston 6 B2
Roxeth London 15 A1
Royal Botanic Gardens
Edinburgh 11 B2
Royal Exhibition Building
Melbourne 18 A1
Royal Observatory
Edinburgh 11 B2
Royal Palace = Kungliga
Slottet Stockholm 29 B2
Royal Palace = Palacio
Real Madrid 17 B1
Royal Park Melbourne 18 A1
Röylä Helsinki 11 B1
Rozas, Portilleros de las
Madrid 17 B1
Roztoky Prague 25 B2
Rozzano Milan 18 B1
Rubí ➜ Barcelona 4 A1
Rudolfsheim Vienna 32 A2
Rudolfshöhe Berlin 5 A5
Rudow Berlin 5 B3
Rueil-Malmaison Paris 24 A2
Ruisbroek Brussels 6 B1
Ruislip London 15 A1
Rumelihisarı Istanbul 12 B2
Rungis Paris 24 B3
Rusāfa Baghdad 3 A2
Rush Green London 15 A5
Russa Kolkata 14 C2
Rutherford New York 22 B1
Ruzyně Prague 25 B1
Ruzyne, Praha ✈ (PRG)
Prague 25 B1
Rybatskaya St. Petersburg 27 B2
Rydboholm Stockholm 29 A3
Ryde Sydney 29 A1
Ryogoku Tokyo 30 A3
Rzhevka St. Petersburg 27 B3

S

Sa'ādatābād Tehran 31 A2
Saadūn Baghdad 3 B2
Saavedra Buenos Aires 7 B2
Saboli Delhi 10 A2
Sabugo Lisbon 16 A1
Sabzi Mand Delhi 10 A2
Sacavém Lisbon 16 A2
Saclay Paris 24 B2
Saclay, Étang de Paris 24 B1
Sacomã São Paulo 27 B2
Sacré Cœur Paris 24 A3
Sacrow Berlin 5 B1
Sacrower See Berlin 5 B1
Sadang Seoul 27 C1
Saddle ➜ New York 22 A1
Saddle Brook New York 22 A1
Sadr Karachi 13 A2
Sadr City Baghdad 3 A2
Sadyba Warsaw 33 B2
Safdar Jang's Tomb Delhi 10 B2
Saft el Laban Cairo 7 A2
Sagene Oslo 23 A3
Sagrada Familia, Templo
de Barcelona 4 A2
Sahar, Mumbai ✈ (BOM)
Mumbai 20 A2
Sai Kung Hong Kong 12 A2
Sai Wan Ho Hong Kong 12 B2
Sai Ying Pun Hong Kong 12 B1
St-Aubin Paris 24 B1
St-Cloud Paris 24 A2
St-Cyr-l'École Paris 24 B1
St-Cyr-l'École ✈ Paris 24 B1
St-Denis Paris 24 A3
St-Germain, Forêt de Paris 24 A1
St-Germain-en-Laye Paris 24 A1
St-Gilles Brussels 6 B2
St. Helier London 15 B2
St-Hubert Montreal 20 B3
St-Hubert, Galeries
Royales Brussels 6 A2
St. Isaac's Cathedral
St. Petersburg 27 B1
St-Jacques ➜ Montreal 20 B3
St-Josse-Ten-Noode Brussels 6 A2
St. Kilda Melbourne 18 B1
St-Lambert Montreal 20 A3
St-Lambert Paris 24 B1
St-Laurent Montreal 20 A1
St-Léonard Montreal 20 A2
St-Mandé Paris 24 A3
St. Margaret's Dublin 10 A2
St-Martin, Bois Paris 24 B4
St. Mary Cray London 15 B4
St-Maur-des-Fossés Paris 24 B3
St-Maurice Paris 24 B3
St-Michel Montreal 20 A2
St-Ouen Paris 24 A3
St. Paul's Cray London 15 B4
St. Peters Sydney 29 B2
St. Peter's Square = San
Pietro, Piazza Rome 26 B1
St. Petersburg = Sankt-
Peterburg St. Petersburg 27 B1
St. Petersburg Pulkovo
Int. ✈ (LED) St. Petersburg 27 C1
St-Pierre Montreal 20 B2
St-Pieters Leew Brussels 6 B1
St-Quentin, Étang de Paris 24 B1
St. Stephen's Cathedral =
Stephansdom Vienna 32 A2
St-Stevens-Woluwe Brussels 6 A2
St-Vincent-de-Paul
Montreal 20 A2
St. Xavier Univ. Chicago 9 C2
Ste-Catherine Montreal 20 B2
Ste-Hélène, Î. Montreal 20 A2
Saiwai Tokyo 30 B3
Sakai Osaka 23 B1
Sakai Harbour Osaka 23 B1
Sakra, Pulau Singapore 28 B2
Salam Baghdad 3 A2
Salamanca Madrid 17 B1
Sallynoggin Dublin 10 B3
Salmannsdorf Vienna 32 A1
Salmedina Madrid 17 C2
Salomea Warsaw 33 B1
Salsette I. Mumbai 20 A2
Salt Lake City = Bidhan
Nagar Kolkata 14 B2
Salt River Cape Town 8 A1
Salt Water L. Kolkata 14 B2
Saltsjö-Duvnäs Stockholm 29 B3
Samatya Istanbul 12 C1
Sampaloc Manila 17 B1
Samphan Thawong Bangkok 3 B2
Samseon Seoul 27 B2
Samuel Smith Park Toronto 31 B1
Samut Prakan Bangkok 3 B2
San Andrés Barcelona 4 A2
San Angel Mexico City 18 B1
San Basilio Rome 26 B2
San Borja Lima 14 B3
San Bóvio Milan 18 B2
San Bruno, Pt. San Francisco 26 C2
San Bruno Mountain
State Park ⌂
San Francisco 26 B2
San Cristóbal Buenos Aires 7 B2
San Cristobal Madrid 17 B2
San Cristóbal, Cerro
Santiago 27 B2
San Cristóbal, Virgen del
Santiago 27 B2
San Cristoforo Milan 18 B1
San Donato Milanese Milan 18 B2
San Francisco San Francisco 26 B2
San Francisco B.
San Francisco 26 B3
San Francisco Culhuacán
Mexico City 18 C2
San Fruttuoso Milan 18 A2
San Gabriel Los Angeles 16 B4
San Gabriel ➜ Los Angeles 16 C4
San Giuliano Milanese
Milan 18 B2
San Isidro Lima 14 B2
San Jerónimo Lídice
Mexico City 18 C1
San Joaquín Santiago 27 B2
San José Rio Hondo
Mexico City 18 B1
San Juan ➜ Manila 17 B2
San Juan de Aragón
Mexico City 18 B2
San Juan de Aragón,
Parque Mexico City 18 B2
San Juan de Lurigancho
Lima 14 A2
San Juan del Monte Manila 17 B2
San Juan Ixtacala
Mexico City 18 A1
San Just Desvern Barcelona 4 A1
San Justo Buenos Aires 7 C1
San Lorenzo Tezonco
Mexico City 18 C2
San Luis Lima 14 B2
San Marino Los Angeles 16 B4
San Martín Barcelona 4 A2
San Martín de Porras Lima 14 B2
San Mateo Tlaltenango
Mexico City 18 B1
San Miguel Lima 14 B2
San Miguel Santiago 27 B2
San Nicolás Buenos Aires 7 B2
San Onófrio Rome 26 B1
San Pedro Mártir Barcelona 4 A1
San Pedro Zacatenco
Mexico City 18 A2
San Pietro, Piazza Rome 26 B1
San Po Kong Hong Kong 12 A2
San Rafael Chamapa
Mexico City 18 B1
San Rafael Hills Los Angeles 16 A3
San Roque Manila 17 B2
San Siro Milan 18 B1
San Souci Sydney 29 B1
San Telmo Buenos Aires 7 B2
San Vicenç dels Horts
Barcelona 4 A1
Sandown Johannesburg 13 A2
Sandown Park Races
London 15 B1
Sandton Johannesburg 13 A2
Sandvika Oslo 23 A2
Sandyford Dublin 10 B2
Sandymount Dublin 10 B2
Sangenjaya Tokyo 30 B2
Sanggye Seoul 27 B2
Sangley Pt. Manila 17 C1
Sankrail Kolkata 14 B1
Sankt-Peterburg
St. Petersburg 27 B1
Sankt Veit Vienna 32 A1
Sanlihe Beijing 4 B1
Sanlin Shanghai 28 C1
Sanlintang Shanghai 28 C1
Sans Barcelona 4 A1
Sanssouci Berlin 5 B1
Sant Ambrogio, Basilica di
Milan 18 B2
Sant Boi de Llobregat
Barcelona 4 A1
Sant Cugat Barcelona 4 A1
Sant Feliu de Llobregat
Barcelona 4 A1
Sant Joan Despi Barcelona 4 A1
Santa Ana Manila 17 B2
Santa Anita Park
Los Angeles 16 B4
Santa Coloma de
Gramenet Barcelona 4 A2
Santa Cruz Manila 17 B1
Santa Cruz Mumbai 20 A1
Santa Cruz, I. de
Rio de Janeiro 25 B2
Santa Cruz de Olorde
Barcelona 4 A1
Santa Efigênia São Paulo 27 B2
Santa Elena Manila 17 B2
Santa Elena del Gomero
Santiago 27 B2
Santa Eulàlia Barcelona 4 A2
Santa Fe Springs Los Angeles 16 C4
Santa Iria da Azóia Lisbon 16 A2
Santa Julia Santiago 27 C2
Santa Monica Los Angeles 16 B2
Santa Monica Mts.
Los Angeles 16 B2
Santa Rosa de Locobe
Santiago 27 B2
Santa Teresa de la Ovalle
Santiago 27 B1
Santahamina Helsinki 11 C3
Santana São Paulo 27 A2
Santeny Paris 24 B4
Santiago Santiago 27 B2
Santiago Benitez ✈ (SCL)
Santiago 27 B1
Santiago de Surco Lima 14 B2
Santo Amaro Lisbon 16 A1
Santo Amaro São Paulo 27 B2
Santo André Lisbon 16 B2
Santo Antão do Tojal Lisbon 16 A2
Santo Antônio, Qta. de
Lisbon 16 B1
Santo Tomas, Univ. of
Manila 17 B1
Santos Dumont ✈ (SDU)
Rio de Janeiro 25 B2
Santoshpur Kolkata 14 B1
Santragachi Kolkata 14 B1
Santry Dublin 10 A2
Sanyuanli Guangzhou 11 B2
São Caetano do Sul
São Paulo 27 B2
São Conrado Rio de Janeiro 25 B1
São Cristóvão Rio de Janeiro 25 B1
São Jorge, Castelo de Lisbon 16 A2
São Julião do Tojal Lisbon 16 A2
São Paulo São Paulo 27 B2
São Paulo Congonhas ✈
(CGH) São Paulo 27 B2
Sapa Kolkata 14 B1
Sapateiro, Cor. do ➜
São Paulo 27 B1
Sarandí Buenos Aires 7 C2
Saraswati ➜ Kolkata 14 A1
Sarecky potok ➜ Prague 25 B2
Sarimbun Singapore 28 A2
Sarimbun Res. Singapore 28 A2
Sarıyer Istanbul 12 A2
Sarriá Barcelona 4 A1
Sarsuna Kolkata 14 C1
Sartrouville Paris 24 A2
Sasad Budapest 7 B2
Sashalom Budapest 7 A3
Saska Warsaw 33 B2
Satalice Prague 25 B3
Satgachi Kolkata 14 B2
Satpukur Kolkata 14 B2
Sätra Stockholm 29 B1
Saúde São Paulo 27 B2
Saugus Boston 6 A2
Saugus ➜ Boston 6 A2
Sault-au-Récollet Montreal 20 A2
Sausalito San Francisco 26 A2
Sawah Besar Jakarta 12 A1
Sawtelle Los Angeles 16 B2
Scald Law Edinburgh 11 B2
Scarborough Toronto 31 A3
Scarborough Bluffs Toronto 31 A3
Sceaux Paris 24 B2
Schaerbeek Brussels 6 A2
Scharfenberg Berlin 5 A2
Schiller Woods Chicago 9 B1
Schiphol, Amsterdam ✈
(AMS) Amsterdam 2 B1
Schlachtensee Berlin 5 B2
Schlossgarten Berlin 5 A2
Schmargendorf Berlin 5 B2
Schönblick Berlin 5 B5
Schönbrunn Vienna 32 A1
Schöneberg Berlin 5 B3
Schönefeld Berlin 5 B4
Schöneiche Berlin 5 B5
Schönwalde Berlin 5 A1
Schulzendorf Berlin 5 A2
Schwabing Munich 21 B2
Schwanebeck Berlin 5 A4
Schwanenwerder Berlin 5 B2
Schwarzlackenau Vienna 32 A2
Schwechat Vienna 32 B2
Schwechat, Wien ✈ (VIE)
Vienna 32 B3
Science and Industry,
Museum of Chicago 9 C3
Scopus, Mt. Jerusalem 13 B2
Scottdale Atlanta 3 B3
Scutari = Üsküdar Istanbul 12 B2
Sea Point Cape Town 8 A1
Seacliff San Francisco 26 B2
Seaforth Sydney 29 A2
Seagate New York 22 C1
SeaWorld Orlando 23 B2
Šeberov Prague 25 B3
Secaucus New York 22 B1
Seddinsee Berlin 5 B5
Seeberg Berlin 5 A5
Seeburg Berlin 5 A1
Seefeld Berlin 5 A5
Seegefeld Berlin 5 A1
Seehof Berlin 5 B2
Segeltorp Stockholm 29 B1
Segrate Milan 18 B2
Seguro Milan 18 B1
Seixal Lisbon 16 B2
Selby Johannesburg 13 B2
Seletar Singapore 28 A3
Seletar, Pulau Singapore 28 A3
Seletar Hills Singapore 28 A3
Seletar Res. Singapore 28 A2
Selhurst London 15 B3
Sembawang Singapore 28 A2
Senago Milan 18 A1
Sendling Munich 21 B2
Senju Tokyo 30 A3
Senkang Singapore 28 A3
Senriyama Osaka 23 A2
Sentosa Singapore 28 B2
Seobinggo Seoul 27 B1
Seocho Seoul 27 C1
Seodaemun Seoul 27 B1
Seokkwan Seoul 27 B2
Seongbuk Seoul 27 B2
Seongdong Seoul 27 B2
Seongsu Seoul 27 B2
Seoul Seoul 27 B2
Seoul Nat. Univ. Seoul 27 C1
Seoul Tower Seoul 27 B1
Sepolia Athens 2 A2
Sepulveda Dam Rec.
Area ⌂ Los Angeles 16 A2
Serangoon Singapore 28 A3
Serangoon, Pulau Singapore 28 A3
Serangoon, Sungei ➜
Singapore 28 A3
Serangoon Harbour
Singapore 28 A3
Seraya, Pulau Singapore 28 B2
Serebryanka ➜ Moscow 19 B3
Serramonte San Francisco 26 C2
Sesto San Giovanni Milan 18 A2
Sesto Ulteriano Milan 18 B2
Setagaya Tokyo 30 B2
Seter Oslo 23 A3
Setia Budi Jakarta 12 B1
Settebagni Rome 26 A2
Settecamini Rome 26 B2
Séttimo Milanese Milan 18 B1
Settsu Osaka 23 A2
Seutula Helsinki 11 A2
Seven Corners Washington 33 B2
Seven Kings London 15 A4
Seventeenth Street Canal
New Orleans 21 A2
Sévesco ➜ Milan 18 A1
Sevran Paris 24 A4
Sewri Mumbai 20 B2
Sforzesco, Castello Milan 18 B2
Sha Kok Mei Hong Kong 12 A2
Sha Tin Hong Kong 12 A2
Sha'ar Binyamin Jerusalem 13 A2
Shabramant Cairo 7 B2
Shah Mosque Tehran 31 A2
Shahdara Delhi 10 A2
Shahe Guangzhou 11 B2
Shahr-e Rey Tehran 31 B2
Shahrak-e Golshahr Tehran 31 B1
Shahrak-e Qods Tehran 31 A2
Shaikh Aomar Baghdad 3 A2
Shakurbasti Delhi 10 A1
Shalkiya Kolkata 14 B2
Sham Shui Po Hong Kong 12 B1
Shamapur Delhi 10 A1
Shamian Guangzhou 11 B2
Sham Mei Hong Kong 12 A2
Shanghai Shanghai 28 B2
Shanghai Hongqiao Int. ✈
(SHA) Shanghai 28 B1
Shanghai Pudong Int. ✈
(PVG) Shanghai 28 B2
Shankill Dublin 10 B3
Sharp I. Hong Kong 12 A2
Shastrinagar Delhi 10 A2
Shau Kei Wan Hong Kong 12 B2
Shawocun Beijing 4 B1
Shayuan Guangzhou 11 B2
Sheen, L. Orlando 23 B1
Sheepshead Bay New York 22 C2
Sheikh Zayed Road Dubai 9 B2
Shek O Hong Kong 12 B2
Shelter I. Hong Kong 12 B2
Shepherds Bush London 15 A2
Shepperton London 15 B1
Sheremetyevo ✈ (SVO)
Moscow 19 A1
Sherman Oaks Los Angeles 16 B2
Sherman Park Chicago 9 C2
Sherwood, L. Orlando 23 A2
Shet Bandar Mumbai 20 B2
Sheung Fa Shan Hong Kong 12 A1
Sheung Lau Wan
Hong Kong 12 B2
Sheung Wan Hong Kong 12 B1
Sheva Mumbai 20 B2
Sheva Nhava Mumbai 20 B2
Shiba Tokyo 30 B3
Shibpur Kolkata 14 B1
Shibuya Tokyo 30 B3
Shilihe Beijing 4 B2
Shimogawara Tokyo 30 B1
Shimosalo Tokyo 30 A2
Shimoshakujii Tokyo 30 A2
Shinagawa Tokyo 30 B3
Shing Mun Res. Hong Kong 12 A1
Shinjuku Tokyo 30 A3
Shinjuku Nat. Garden
Tokyo 30 A3
Shinkoiwa Tokyo 30 A4
Shinnakano Tokyo 30 A3
Shipai Guangzhou 11 B3
Shirinashi ➜ Osaka 23 B1
Shirogane Tokyo 30 B3
Shitennoji Temple Osaka 23 B2
Shiweitang Guangzhou 11 B2
Shogunle Lagos 14 A2
Shomolu Lagos 14 A2
Shooters Hill London 15 B4
Shoreditch London 15 A3
Shortlands London 15 B4
Shu'afat Jerusalem 13 B2
Shubrâ Cairo 7 A2
Shubrâ el Kheima Cairo 7 A2
Shuikou Guangzhou 11 A2
Sidcup London 15 B4
Siebenhirten Vienna 32 B1
Siedlung Berlin 5 A1
Siekierki Warsaw 33 B2
Sielce Warsaw 33 B2
Siemensstadt Berlin 5 A2
Sierra Madre Los Angeles 16 B4
Sievering Vienna 32 A2
Sighthill Edinburgh 11 B2
Signal Hill Cape Town 8 A1
Siheung Seoul 27 C1
Sikátorpuszta Budapest 7 A3
Silampur Delhi 10 B2
Sillim Seoul 27 C1
Silver, L. Orlando 23 A2
Silver Hill Washington 33 B3
Silver Lake Los Angeles 16 B3
Silver Spring Washington 33 A2
Silvermine Nature
Reserve Cape Town 8 B1
Silvolantekojärvi Helsinki 11 B2
Simei Singapore 28 A3
Simla Kolkata 14 B2
Simmering Vienna 32 A2
Simmering Heide Vienna 32 A2
Simonkylä Helsinki 11 B3
Sinchon Seoul 27 B1
Sindang Seoul 27 B2
Singapore ■ Singapore 28 B3
Singapore Changi ✈ (SIN)
Singapore 28 A3
Sinki, Selat Singapore 28 B2
Sinsa Seoul 27 B2
Sint-Genesius-Rode Brussels 6 B2
Sion Mumbai 20 A2
Sipson London 15 B1
Siqeil Cairo 7 A1
Şişli Istanbul 12 B1
Skansen Stockholm 29 B2
Skärholmen Stockholm 29 B1
Skarpäng Stockholm 29 A2
Skarpnäck Stockholm 29 B2
Skaryszewski, Park
Warsaw 33 B2
Skogskyrkogården
Stockholm 29 B2
Skokie Chicago 9 A2
Skokie ➜ Chicago 9 A2
Skokie Heritage Museum
Chicago 9 A2
Skoklefall Oslo 23 A3
Sköndal Stockholm 29 B2
Skovlunde Copenhagen 8 A2
Skovshoved Copenhagen 8 A3
Skuru Stockholm 29 B3
Sky Lake Orlando 23 B2
Slade Green London 15 B5
Slependen Oslo 23 A2
Slipi Jakarta 12 B1
Slivenec Prague 25 B2
Sloten Amsterdam 2 A1
Sloterdijk Amsterdam 2 A1
Sloterpark Amsterdam 2 A1
Sluhy Prague 25 A3
Służew Warsaw 33 B2
Służewiec Warsaw 33 B2
Smíchov Prague 25 B2
Smith Forest Preserve
Chicago 9 B2
Smolny St. Petersburg 27 B2
Smolny Cathedral
St. Petersburg 27 B2
Snake Creek Canal Miami 19 C2
Snarøya Oslo 23 A2
Snättringe Stockholm 29 B1
Søborg Copenhagen 8 A2
Sobreda Lisbon 16 B1
Söderby Stockholm 29 A3
Södermalm Stockholm 29 B2
Sodpur Kolkata 14 A2
Soeurs, Î. des Montreal 20 B2
Sognsvatn Oslo 23 A3
Soignes, Forêt de Brussels 6 B2
Sok Kwu Wan Hong Kong 12 B1
Sokolniki Moscow 19 B3
Sokolniki Park Moscow 19 B3
Sokołów Warsaw 33 C1
Solalinden Munich 21 B3
Sollentuna Stockholm 29 A1
Solln Munich 21 B2
Solna Stockholm 29 A1
Somerset Washington 33 B2
Somerville Boston 6 A2

Sonari *Mumbai* **20** B2
Sonderso *Copenhagen* **8** A2
Songpa *Seoul* **27** B2
Sony Pictures Studio
  Los Angeles **16** B2
Sord = Swords *Dublin* **10** A2
Soroksár *Budapest* **7** B2
Soroksári Duna → = *Budapest* **7** B2
Sosenka *Moscow* **19** B2
Sosnovka *St. Petersburg* **27** B2
Sŏul = Seoul *Seoul* **27** B2
Soundview *New York* **22** B2
South Beach *Miami* **19** D3
South Beach *New York* **22** C1
South Bend Park *Atlanta* **3** B3
South Boston *Boston* **6** A2
South Decatur *Atlanta* **3** B3
South Deering *Chicago* **9** C3
South El Monte *Los Angeles* **16** B4
South Gate *Los Angeles* **16** C3
South Harbor *Manila* **17** B1
South Harrow *London* **15** A1
South Hd. *Sydney* **29** B2
South Hills *Johannesburg* **13** B2
South Holland *Chicago* **9** C3
South Lawn *Washington* **33** C2
South Miami *Miami* **19** D1
South Norwood *London* **15** B3
South of Market
  San Francisco **26** B2
South Ozone Park
  New York **22** B3
South Pasadena *Los Angeles* **16** B4
South Res. *Boston* **6** A2
South Ruislip *London* **15** A1
South San Francisco
  San Francisco **26** C2
South San Gabriel
  Los Angeles **16** B4
South Shore *Chicago* **9** C3
Southall *London* **15** A1
Southborough *London* **15** B4
Southend *London* **15** B3
Southern California, Univ.
  of *Los Angeles* **16** B3
Southfields *London* **15** B2
Southport *New Orleans* **21** B2
Southwark □ *London* **15** B3
Southwest Museum
  Los Angeles **16** B3
Sovang *Copenhagen* **8** B3
Soweto *Johannesburg* **13** B1
Sowhānak *Tehran* **31** A3
Soya *Tokyo* **30** A4
Spandau *Berlin* **5** A2
Spånga *Stockholm* **29** A1
Spectacle I. *Boston* **6** A2
Speicher-See *Munich* **21** A3
Speising *Vienna* **32** B1
Sphinx *Cairo* **7** B1
Spinaceto *Rome* **26** C1
Spit Junction *Sydney* **29** A2
Spořilov *Prague* **25** B3
Spot Pond *Boston* **6** A2
Spotswood *Melbourne* **18** B1
Spring Valley *Las Vegas* **14** B1
Springeberg *Berlin* **5** B5
Springfield *Washington* **33** C1
Squantum *Boston* **6** B2
Srednaya Rogatka
  St. Petersburg **27** C2
Środmieście *Warsaw* **33** B2
Staaken *Berlin* **5** A1
Stabekk *Oslo* **23** A2
Stadlau *Vienna* **32** A2
Stadshuset *Stockholm* **29** B2
Stains *Paris* **24** A3
Stamford Hill *London* **15** A3
Stammersdorf *Vienna* **32** A2
Stanley Pen. *Hong Kong* **12** B2
Stanmore *London* **15** A1
Stapleton *New York* **22** C1
Staraya Derevnya
  St. Petersburg **27** B1
Staré Město *Prague* **25** B2
Stare Miasto *Warsaw* **33** B2
Starke, L. *Orlando* **23** A1
Staten Island Zoo *New York* **22** C1
Staten Islands Ferry
  Terminal *New York* **22** C1
Statenice *Prague* **25** B1
Stedelijk Museum
  Amsterdam **2** A2
Steele Creek *Melbourne* **18** A1
Steenokkerzeel *Brussels* **6** A3
Steer, L. *Orlando* **23** A1
Steglitz *Berlin* **5** B2
Stepaside *Dublin* **10** B2
Stephansdom *Vienna* **32** B2
Stepney *London* **15** A3
Sterling Park *San Francisco* **26** B2
Sticklinge udde *Stockholm* **29** A2
Stickney *Chicago* **9** C2
Stillorgan *Dublin* **10** B2
Stockholm *Stockholm* **29** B2
Stockholm Arlanda ✈
  (ARN) *Stockholm* **29** A1
Stocksund *Stockholm* **29** A2
Stoclet, Palais *Brussels* **6** B2
Stodůlky *Prague* **25** B1
Stoke Newington *London* **15** A3
Stone Canyon Res.
  Los Angeles **16** B2
Stone Zoo *Boston* **6** A2
Stonebridge *London* **15** A2
Stoneham *Boston* **6** A2
Stony Brook Res. *Boston* **6** B2
Stony Creek → *Chicago* **9** C2
Stora Värtan *Stockholm* **29** A2
Store Hareskov *Copenhagen* **8** A2
Store Magleby *Copenhagen* **8** B3
Storholmen *Stockholm* **29** A2
Stoyka *St. Petersburg* **27** B2
Straiton *Edinburgh* **11** B3
Strandfontein *Cape Town* **8** B2
Strašnice *Prague* **25** B3
Strasstrudering *Munich* **21** B3
Stratford *London* **15** A4
Strathfield *Sydney* **29** B1
Streatham *London* **15** B3
Streatham Vale *London* **15** B3
Strebersdorf *Vienna* **32** A1
Strip, The *Las Vegas* **14** B2
Střížkov *Prague* **25** B2
Strombeek-Bever *Brussels* **6** A2
Stromovka *Prague* **25** B2
Studio City *Los Angeles* **16** B2
Stureby *Stockholm* **29** B2
Stuvsta *Stockholm* **29** B2
Subhepur *Delhi* **10** A2
Suburban Canal
  New Orleans **21** B1
Sucat *Manila* **17** C2
Suchdol *Prague* **25** B1
Sucy-en-Brie *Paris* **24** B4
Sue, L. *Orlando* **23** A2
Sugamo *Tokyo* **30** A3
Sugar Loaf Mt. = Açúcar,
  Pão de *Rio de Janeiro* **25** B2
Suge *Tokyo* **30** B2

Suginami *Tokyo* **30** A2
Sugō *Tokyo* **30** B2
Sui Sai Wan *Hong Kong* **12** B1
Suita *Osaka* **23** A1
Suitland *Washington* **33** B3
Sukchar *Kolkata* **14** A1
Sultanahme Camil *Istanbul* **12** B1
Sumida *Tokyo* **30** A3
Sumida → *Tokyo* **30** A3
Sumiyoshi *Osaka* **23** B2
Sumiyoshi Shrine *Osaka* **23** B1
Summerville *Toronto* **31** B1
Summit *Chicago* **9** C2
Sunamachi *Tokyo* **30** A4
Sunbury-on-Thames
  London **15** B1
Sundbyberg *Stockholm* **29** A1
Sundbyerne *Copenhagen* **8** B3
Sung Kong *Hong Kong* **12** B2
Sungei Kadut Industrial
  Estate *Singapore* **28** A2
Sungei Selatar Res.
  Singapore **28** A3
Sunny Isles Beach *Miami* **19** C3
Sunrise *Miami* **19** B1
Sunrise Manor *Las Vegas* **14** A2
Sunrise Mountain Natural
  Area *Las Vegas* **14** A2
Sunset Park *Las Vegas* **14** B2
Sunset Park *New York* **22** C2
Sunshine Park *Miami* **19** B2
Sunter *Jakarta* **12** A1
Sunter, Kali → *Jakarta* **12** B2
Suomenlinna *Helsinki* **11** C2
Sur Bahr *Jerusalem* **13** B2
Sura *Kolkata* **14** B2
Suraksan *Seoul* **27** A2
Surbiton *London* **15** B2
Suresnes *Paris* **24** A2
Surfside *Miami* **19** C3
Surquillo *Lima* **14** B2
Surrey Hills *Sydney* **29** B2
Surulere *Lagos* **14** B2
Susaek *Seoul* **27** B1
Süssenbrunn *Vienna* **32** A2
Sutton *London* **15** B2
Sutton *Dublin* **10** A3
Sutton *London* **15** B2
Suyu *Seoul* **27** B2
Suzukishinden *Tokyo* **30** A2
Svanemøllen *Copenhagen* **8** A3
Sveaborg = Suomenlinna
  Helsinki **11** C2
Sverdlov *Moscow* **19** B2
Svestad *Oslo* **23** B2
Svinö *Helsinki* **11** C1
Swanley *London* **15** B4
Swansea *Toronto* **31** B2
Swinburne I. *New York* **22** C1
Swords *Dublin* **10** A2
Sydenham *Johannesburg* **13** A2
Sydney *Sydney* **29** B2
Sydney, Univ. of *Sydney* **29** B2
Sydney Harbour △ *Sydney* **29** B2
Sydney Harbour Bridge
  Sydney **29** B2
Sydney Kingsford Smith ✈
  (SYD) *Sydney* **29** B2
Sydstranden *Copenhagen* **8** B3
Sylvania *Sydney* **29** C1
Syon Park *London* **15** B2
Szczęśliwice *Warsaw* **33** B1
Széchenyi-hegy *Budapest* **7** B2
Széphalom *Budapest* **7** A1

T

Taastrup *Copenhagen* **8** B1
Tabata *Tokyo* **30** A3
Tablada *Buenos Aires* **7** C1
Table B. *Cape Town* **8** A1
Table Mountain △
  Cape Town **8** A1
Table Mt. *Cape Town* **8** A1
Taboão da Serra *São Paulo* **27** B1
Täby *Stockholm* **29** A2
Tacuba *Mexico City* **18** B1
Tacubaya *Mexico City* **18** B1
Tafelbaai = Table B.
  Cape Town **8** A1
Taft *Orlando* **23** B2
Tagig → *Manila* **17** B2
Taguig *Manila* **17** B2
Tahrir Square *Cairo* **7** A2
Tai Lo Shan *Hong Kong* **12** A2
Tai Po Tsai *Hong Kong* **12** A2
Tai Seng *Singapore* **28** A3
Tai Shui Hang *Hong Kong* **12** A2
Tai Tam B. *Hong Kong* **12** B2
Tai Tam Tuk Res.
  Hong Kong **12** B2
Tai Wai *Hong Kong* **12** A1
Tai Wan Tau *Hong Kong* **12** B2
Tai Wo Hau *Hong Kong* **12** A1
Tainaka *Osaka* **23** B2
Taishō *Osaka* **23** B1
Tajrīsh *Tehran* **31** A2
Takaido *Tokyo* **30** A2
Takaishi *Tokyo* **30** B2
Takarazuka *Osaka* **23** A1
Takasago *Tokyo* **30** A4
Takatsu *Tokyo* **30** B2
Takeshita *Tokyo* **30** B2
Takinegawa *Tokyo* **30** A3
Takoma Park *Washington* **33** B2
Taksim *Istanbul* **12** B1
Talaide *Lisbon* **16** A1
Taliganga *Kolkata* **14** B2
Taligapa *Manila* **17** A2
Tallaght *Dublin* **10** B1
Tallkrogen *Stockholm* **29** B2
Tama *Tokyo* **30** B1
Tama → *Tokyo* **30** B2
Tama Kyūryō *Tokyo* **30** B2
Tamaden *Tokyo* **30** B2
Tamagawa-josui → *Tokyo* **30** A1
Taman Sari *Jakarta* **12** A1
Tamanduateí → *São Paulo* **27** B2
Tamarac *Miami* **19** B1
Tamboerskloof *Cape Town* **8** A1
Tambora *Jakarta* **12** A1
Tammisalo *Helsinki* **11** B3
Tammū *Cairo* **7** B1
Tampines *Singapore* **28** A3
Tanah Bukit *Singapore* **28** A3
Tanah Kusir *Jakarta* **12** B1
Tangelo Park *Orlando* **23** B2
Tanjung Duren *Jakarta* **12** A1
Tanjung Priok *Jakarta* **12** A2
Tanum *Oslo* **23** A1
Tapada *Lisbon* **16** A1
Tapanila *Helsinki* **11** B3
Tapiola *Helsinki* **11** B1
Tapsia *Kolkata* **14** B2
Tara *Mumbai* **20** A1
Tarabya *Istanbul* **12** A2
Tårbæk *Copenhagen* **8** A3
Tarchomin *Warsaw* **33** B1
Tardeo *Mumbai* **20** A1
Targówek *Warsaw* **33** B2
Tárnby *Copenhagen* **8** B3

Tarqua Bay *Lagos* **14** B2
Tathong Channel
  Hong Kong **12** B2
Tathong Pt. *Hong Kong* **12** B2
Tatuapé *São Paulo* **27** B2
Taufkirchen *Munich* **21** B2
Tavares, I. dos *Rio de Janeiro* **25** A2
Tavros *Athens* **2** B2
Teaneck *New York* **22** A1
Tebet *Jakarta* **12** B2
Tecamachalco *Mexico City* **18** B1
Ted Williams Tunnel *Boston* **6** A2
Teddington *London* **15** B1
Tegel *Berlin* **5** A2
Tegeler See *Berlin* **5** A2
Tegelort *Berlin* **5** A2
Teheran = Tehrān *Tehran* **31** A2
Tehrān *Tehran* **31** A2
Tehrān Mehrābād ✈
  (THR) *Tehran* **31** A2
Tehrān Pārs *Tehran* **31** A3
Tei Tong Tsui *Hong Kong* **12** B2
Tejo, Rio → *Lisbon* **16** A2
Tekstilshchik *Moscow* **19** B3
Telhal *Lisbon* **16** A1
Teltow *Berlin* **5** B2
Teltow kanal *Berlin* **5** B3
Temple City *Los Angeles* **16** B4
Temple Hills *Washington* **33** C3
Temple of Heaven *Beijing* **4** B2
Templeogue *Dublin* **10** B2
Temppeliaukio Church
  Helsinki **11** B2
Tenafly *New York* **22** A2
Tenayuca, Piramide de
  Mexico City **18** A1
Tengah → *Singapore* **28** A2
Tennōji *Osaka* **23** B2
Tepalcates *Mexico City* **18** B2
Tepeyac △ *Mexico City* **18** B2
Terrazzano *Milan* **18** A1
Terre des Hommes *Montreal* **20** A2
Terruguem *Lisbon* **16** A1
Terrytown *New Orleans* **21** B2
Tervuren *Brussels* **6** B3
Tervuren, Park van *Brussels* **6** B3
Tetuán *Madrid* **17** B1
Teufelsberg *Berlin* **5** B2
Thalkirchen *Munich* **21** B2
Thames Ditton *London* **15** B1
Thamesmead *London* **15** A4
Thana Cr. → *Mumbai* **20** A2
Thiais *Paris* **24** B3
Thisio *Athens* **2** B2
Thistletown *Toronto* **31** A1
Thomastown *Melbourne* **18** A2
Thompson I. *Boston* **6** B3
Thon Buri *Bangkok* **3** B1
Thornbury *Melbourne* **18** A2
Thorncliffe *Toronto* **31** B2
Thornhill *Toronto* **31** A2
Thornton *Cape Town* **8** A2
Thornton Heath *London* **15** B3
Threipmuir Res. *Edinburgh* **11** B2
Throg's Neck *New York* **22** B3
Tiancun *Beijing* **4** B1
Tianhe *Guangzhou* **11** B3
Tibet, L. *Orlando* **23** B1
Tibidabo *Barcelona* **4** A1
Tibradden Mt. *Dublin* **10** B2
Tiburon *San Francisco* **26** A2
Tiburtino *Rome* **26** B2
Ticomán *Mexico City* **18** A2
Tiefersee *Berlin* **5** B1
Tiergarten *Berlin* **5** A3
Tijgerhof *Cape Town* **8** A2
Tijuca *Rio de Janeiro* **25** B1
Tijuca, Pico da *Rio de Janeiro* **25** B1
Tikkurila *Helsinki* **11** B3
Tilak Nagar *Delhi* **10** B1
Tilangiao *Shanghai* **28** B1
Timah, Bukit *Singapore* **28** A2
Timiryazev Park *Moscow* **19** A2
Tin Can I. *Lagos* **14** B2
Ting Kau *Hong Kong* **12** A1
Tira *Jerusalem* **13** A1
Tirsa *Cairo* **7** B2
Tishriyaa *Baghdad* **3** B2
Tiu Keng Leng *Hong Kong* **12** B2
Tizapán *Mexico City* **18** C1
Tlalnepantla → *Mexico City* **18** A1
Tlalpan *Mexico City* **18** C1
To Kwai Wan *Hong Kong* **12** B2
Toa Payoh *Singapore* **28** A3
Točná *Prague* **25** C2
Toco Hills *Atlanta* **3** A3
Todt Hill *New York* **22** C1
Tōkagi *Tokyo* **30** A4
Tokai Plantation *Cape Town* **8** B1
Tōkaichiba *Tokyo* **30** B2
Tōkyō B. *Tokyo* **30** A3
Tōkyō = Tōkyō-Wan
  Tokyo **30** B4
Tōkyō Disneyland *Tokyo* **30** B4
Tōkyō Haneda ✈ (HND)
  Tokyo **30** B3
Tōkyō Harbour *Tokyo* **30** A3
Tōkyō Sky Tree *Tokyo* **30** A3
Tōkyō-Wan *Tokyo* **30** B4
Tolka → *Dublin* **10** A1
Tollygunge = Taliganga
  Kolkata **14** B2
Tolworth *London* **15** B2
Tomba di Nerone *Rome* **26** B1
Tommy Thompson Park
  Toronto **31** B2
Tondo *Manila* **17** B1
Tongbiogo *Seoul* **27** B2
Tongqiao *Shanghai* **28** A1
Toorak *Melbourne* **18** B2
Topanga State Park △
  Los Angeles **16** B1
Topkapi *Istanbul* **12** B1
Topkapi Palace *Istanbul* **12** B1
Tor di Quinto *Rome* **26** B1
Tor Pignattara *Rome* **26** B2
Tor Sapienza *Rome* **26** B2
Torcy *Paris* **24** A4
Toronto *Toronto* **31** B2
Toronto, Univ. of *Toronto* **31** B2
Toronto City Centre ✈
  (YTZ) *Toronto* **31** B2
Toronto Harbour *Toronto* **31** B2
Toronto Lester B. Pearson
  Int. ✈ (YYZ) *Toronto* **31** A1
Torre Lupara *Rome* **26** B1
Torre Nova *Rome* **26** B2
Torrevecchia *Rome* **26** B1
Toshima *Tokyo* **30** A3
Toshimaen *Tokyo* **30** A2
Tottenham *London* **15** A3
Tottenham *Melbourne* **18** A1
Toussus-le-Noble *Paris* **24** B1
Toussus-le-Noble ✈ (TNF)
  Paris **24** B1
Towchāl Cable Car *Tehran* **31** A2
Tower Hamlets □ *London* **15** A3

Tower of London *London* **15** A3
Towra Pt. *Sydney* **29** C2
Tøyen *Oslo* **23** A3
Toyonaka *Osaka* **23** A1
Traição, Cor. → *São Paulo* **27** B2
Tranegilde *Copenhagen* **8** B3
Trångsund *Stockholm* **29** B2
Trappenfelde *Berlin* **5** A4
Trastévere *Rome* **26** B1
Treasure I. *San Francisco* **26** B2
Trebradice *Prague* **25** B3
Trebotov *Prague* **25** C1
Tree Tops Park *Miami* **19** B1
Tremblay-en-France *Paris* **24** A4
Tremembe → *São Paulo* **27** A2
Tremont *New York* **22** B2
Trenno *Milan* **18** B1
Treptow *Berlin* **5** B3
Três Rios, Sa. dos
  Rio de Janeiro **25** B1
Trevi, Fontana de *Rome* **26** B1
Trezzano sul Naviglio *Milan* **18** B1
Trieste *Rome* **26** B2
Trinidad *Washington* **33** B3
Trinity *Edinburgh* **11** B2
Trinity College *Dublin* **10** A2
Trionfale *Rome* **26** B1
Triulzo *Milan* **18** B2
Troja *Prague* **25** B2
Trollbäcken *Stockholm* **29** B3
Trombay *Mumbai* **20** A2
Troparevo *Moscow* **19** C1
Trudeau, Montréal ✈
  (YUL) *Montreal* **20** A1
Trudyashchikhsya,
  Ostrov *St. Petersburg* **27** B1
Tryvasshøgda *Oslo* **23** A3
Tseng Lan Shue *Hong Kong* **12** A2
Tsenge *Copenhagen* **8** A3
Tseung Kwan *Hong Kong* **12** B2
Tsim Sha Tsui *Hong Kong* **12** B2
Tsing Yi *Hong Kong* **12** A1
Tsova *Jerusalem* **13** B1
Tsuen Wan *Hong Kong* **12** A1
Tsur Hadassa *Jerusalem* **13** B1
Tsurumi → *Tokyo* **30** B2
Tsz Wan Shan *Hong Kong* **12** A2
Tuas *Singapore* **28** B1
Tuchoměřice *Prague* **25** B1
Tuckahoe *New York* **22** A2
Tucuruvi *São Paulo* **27** A2
Tufello *Rome* **26** B2
Tufnell Park *London* **15** A3
Tufts Univ. *Boston* **6** A2
Tughlakabad *Delhi* **10** B2
Tukwila *Melbourne* **18** A1
Tulse Hill *London* **15** B3
Tung Lung Chau *Hong Kong* **12** B2
Tung O *Hong Kong* **12** B1
Tunis *Bangkok* **3** B1
Tuomarila *Helsinki* **11** B1
Tureberg *Stockholm* **29** A1
Turffontein *Johannesburg* **13** B2
Turkey L. *Orlando* **23** A2
Turkey Lake Park *Orlando* **23** A2
Turner Field *Atlanta* **3** B2
Turnham Green *London* **15** B2
Turnhouse *Edinburgh* **11** B1
Tuscolana, Via *Rome* **26** B2
Twelve Apostles *Cape Town* **8** A1
Twentieth Century Fox
  Studios *Los Angeles* **16** B2
Twickenham *London* **15** B1
Twickenham Rugby
  Ground *London* **15** B1
Twin Peaks *San Francisco* **26** B2
Two Rock Mt. *Dublin* **10** B2
Tymon North *Dublin* **10** B1

U

U.S. Capitol *Washington* **33** B2
U.S. Cellular Field *Chicago* **9** C3
Ubeidiya *Jerusalem* **13** B2
Uberaba → *São Paulo* **27** B2
Ubin, Pulau *Singapore* **28** A3
Uccle *Brussels* **6** B2
Udelnaya *St. Petersburg* **27** A2
Udelnoe *St. Petersburg* **27** B1
Uddling *Munich* **21** A1
Ueno *Tokyo* **30** A3
Üholíčky *Prague* **25** B1
Uhříněves *Prague* **25** B3
Uithoorn *Amsterdam* **2** B1
Ujazdów *Warsaw* **33** B2
Ujpalota *Budapest* **7** A2
Ujpest *Budapest* **7** A2
Ukita *Tokyo* **30** A4
Uleta *Miami* **19** C3
Ullerup *Copenhagen* **8** B3
Ulleval *Oslo* **23** A3
Ulriksdal *Stockholm* **29** A1
Ulyanka *St. Petersburg* **27** C1
Um Al Khanazir I. *Baghdad* **3** B2
Umeda *Osaka* **23** A1
Umm al Sheif *Dubai* **9** B1
Umm Suqeim *Dubai* **9** B1
Ümraniye *Istanbul* **12** B2
Underground Atlanta
  Atlanta **3** B2
Underhill, L. *Orlando* **23** B2
Unětický potok → *Prague* **25** B2
Unhos *Lisbon* **16** A2
Unidad Santa Fe
  Mexico City **18** B1
Union City *New York* **22** B1
Union Port *New York* **22** B2
Union Square *Hong Kong* **12** B1
Union Station *Toronto* **31** B2
United Center *Chicago* **9** B2
United Nations
  Headquarters *New York* **22** B2
Universal Studios
  Los Angeles **16** B2
Universal Studios *Orlando* **23** B2
Universidad *Madrid* **17** B1
University Park *Washington* **33** B3
Unterbiberg *Munich* **21** B2
Unterföhring *Munich* **21** A3
Unterhaching *Munich* **21** B2
Unterlaa *Vienna* **32** B2
Untermenzing *Munich* **21** A1
Upper B. *New York* **22** C1
Upper End *New York* **22** C1
Upper Town End *London* **15** B1
Upper New York B. =
  Upper B. *New York* **22** C1
Upper Norwood *London* **15** B3
Upper Peirce Res. *Singapore* **28** A2
Upper Sydenham *London* **15** B3
Upper Tooting *London* **15** B3
Upton *London* **15** A4
Uptown *Chicago* **9** B3
Uran *Mumbai* **20** B2
Urawa *Tokyo* **30** A3
Urbe ✈ *Rome* **26** B2
Urca *Rio de Janeiro* **25** B2
Uritsk *St. Petersburg* **27** C1
Üröm *Budapest* **7** A2
Ursus *Warsaw* **33** B1
Ursvik *Stockholm* **29** A1
Usera *Madrid* **17** B1

Ushigome *Tokyo* **30** A3
Usina *Rio de Janeiro* **25** B1
Üsküdar *Istanbul* **12** B2
Ust-Slavyanka
  St. Petersburg **27** C3
Uteke *Stockholm* **29** A3
Utrata *Warsaw* **33** C1
Uttarpara *Kolkata* **14** B1
Utterslev Mose *Copenhagen* **8** A2

V

Vaclavské náměstí *Prague* **25** B2
Vadaul *Mumbai* **20** A2
Vaires-sur-Marne *Paris* **24** A4
Valby *Copenhagen* **8** B2
Valcannuta *Rome* **26** B1
Valdelatas *Madrid* **17** A1
Valenton *Paris* **24** B3
Valera *Milan* **18** A1
Vallcarca *Barcelona* **4** A1
Valldoreix *Barcelona* **4** A1
Vallecas *Madrid* **17** B2
Vallecas, Cumbres de
  Madrid **17** B2
Vallensbæk *Copenhagen* **8** B2
Vallensbæk Strand
  Copenhagen **8** B2
Vallentunasjön *Stockholm* **29** A2
Valleranello *Rome* **26** C1
Vallisaari *Helsinki* **11** C3
Vallvidrera *Barcelona* **4** A1
Valvidrera → *Barcelona* **4** A1
Van Gogh Museum
  Amsterdam **2** A2
Vanak *Tehran* **31** A2
Vanda = Vantaa *Helsinki* **11** B2
Vangede *Copenhagen* **8** A3
Vaniköy *Istanbul* **12** B2
Vanløse *Copenhagen* **8** A2
Vantaa *Helsinki* **11** B2
Vantaankoski *Helsinki* **11** B2
Vantaanpuisto *Helsinki* **11** B2
Vanves *Paris* **24** B2
Varedo *Milan* **18** A1
Varkiza *Athens* **2** C2
Vartiokylä *Helsinki* **11** B3
Vartiosaari *Helsinki* **11** B3
Vasamuseet *Stockholm* **29** B2
Vasco *Cape Town* **8** A2
Vasfenārd *Tehran* **31** B2
Vashi *Mumbai* **20** B2
Vasilyevskiy, Ostrov
  St. Petersburg **27** B1
Vatican City ■ *Rome* **26** B1
Vaucluse *Sydney* **29** B2
Vaucluse House *Sydney* **29** B2
Vaucresson *Paris* **24** A1
Vaughan *Toronto* **31** A1
Vauhallan *Paris* **24** B2
Vaujours *Paris* **24** A4
Vauxhall *London* **15** B3
Veleslavin *Prague* **25** B1
Vélizy-Villacoublay *Paris* **24** B2
Velka-Chuchle *Prague* **25** B2
Velké Přílepy *Prague* **25** B1
Venda Seca *Lisbon* **16** A1
Venetian Islands *Miami* **19** D3
Venice *Los Angeles* **16** C2
Ventas *Madrid* **17** B1
Ventorno del Cano *Madrid* **17** B1
Venustiano Carranza
  Mexico City **18** B2
Verde → *São Paulo* **27** A1
Verdugo Mts. *Los Angeles* **16** A2
Verdun *Montreal* **20** B2
Vérhalom *Budapest* **7** A2
Vermelho → *São Paulo* **27** B2
Vermont Knolls *Los Angeles* **16** C3
Vernon *Los Angeles* **16** B3
Verrières-le-Buisson *Paris* **24** B2
Versailles *Buenos Aires* **7** B1
Versailles *Paris* **24** B2
Veshnyaki *Moscow* **19** B3
Vesolyy Posolok
  St. Petersburg **27** B2
Vestra *Helsinki* **11** B1
Vestskoven *Copenhagen* **8** A2
Vicálvaro *Madrid* **17** B2
Vicente Lopez *Buenos Aires* **7** B2
Victoria *Hong Kong* **12** B1
Victoria, Pont *Montreal* **20** B2
Victoria and Alfred
  Waterfront *Cape Town* **8** A1
Victoria Gardens *Mumbai* **20** B2
Victoria Harbour *Hong Kong* **12** B1
Victoria Island *Lagos* **14** B2
Victoria L. *Johannesburg* **13** B2
Victoria Lawn Tennis
  Courts *Melbourne* **18** B2
Victoria Park *Singapore* **28** B2
Victoria Peak *Hong Kong* **12** B1
Victoria Terminus =
  Chhatrapati Shivaji
  Terminus *Mumbai* **20** B2
Vienna = Wien *Vienna* **32** A2
Vietnam Veterans
  Memorial *Washington* **33** B2
Vietnam War Museum
  Chicago **9** B3
Vieux Carré = French
  Quarter *New Orleans* **21** B2
View Park *Los Angeles* **16** B3
Vigário Geral *Rio de Janeiro* **25** A1
Vigentino *Milan* **18** B2
Viggbyholm *Stockholm* **29** A2
Vignolo *Milan* **18** B1
Viikki *Helsinki* **11** B3
Vikhroli *Mumbai* **20** A2
Vila Guilherme *São Paulo* **27** B2
Vila Isabel *Rio de Janeiro* **25** B1
Vila Jaguára *São Paulo* **27** B1
Vila Madalena *São Paulo* **27** B2
Vila Maria *São Paulo* **27** B2
Vila Mariana *São Paulo* **27** B2
Vila Prudente *São Paulo* **27** B2
Viladecans *Barcelona* **4** B1
Vile Parle *Mumbai* **20** A2
Villa Adelina *Buenos Aires* **7** B1
Villa Ballester *Buenos Aires* **7** B1
Villa Barilari *Buenos Aires* **7** C2
Villa Bosch *Buenos Aires* **7** B1
Villa C. Colon *Buenos Aires* **7** C2
Villa Ciudadela *Buenos Aires* **7** B1
Villa de Guadalupe
  Mexico City **18** B2
Villa Devoto *Buenos Aires* **7** B1
Villa Diamante *Buenos Aires* **7** C2
Villa Dominico *Buenos Aires* **7** C2
Villa Lugano *Buenos Aires* **7** C2
Villa Lynch *Buenos Aires* **7** B1
Villa Madero *Buenos Aires* **7** C1
Villa Saenz Pena
  Buenos Aires **7** B1
Villa Urquiza *Buenos Aires* **7** B1
Villaverde *Madrid* **17** B1
Villaverde Bajo *Madrid* **17** B1
Ville-d'Avray *Paris* **24** B2

Villecresnes *Paris* **24** B4
Villejuif *Paris* **24** B3
Villemomble *Paris* **24** A4
Villeneuve-la-Garenne
  Paris **24** A2
Villeneuve-le-Roi *Paris* **24** B3
Villeneuve-St-Georges *Paris* **24** B3
Villeparisis *Paris* **24** A4
Villevaudé *Paris* **24** A4
Villiers-le-Bâcle *Paris* **24** B1
Villiers-sur-Marne *Paris* **24** B4
Villinki *Helsinki* **11** C3
Villoresi, Canale *Milan* **18** A1
Vilvoorde *Brussels* **6** A2
Vimodrone *Milan* **18** A2
Vimont *Montreal* **20** A1
Vincennes *Paris* **24** A3
Vincennes, Bois de *Paris* **24** A3
Vineland *Orlando* **23** B1
Vinings *Atlanta* **3** A2
Vinohrady *Prague* **25** B2
Vinoř *Prague* **25** B3
Violet Hill *Hong Kong* **12** B2
Virányos *Budapest* **7** A1
Virginia, L. *Orlando* **23** A2
Virginia Gardens *Miami* **19** D1
Virginia Key *Miami* **19** D3
Viroflay *Paris* **24** B2
Vironas *Athens* **2** B2
Virum *Copenhagen* **8** A3
Visitacion Valley
  San Francisco **26** B2
Vista Alegre *Lima* **14** B3
Vista Alegre *Santiago* **27** C1
Vista Grove *Atlanta* **3** A3
Vitacura *Santiago* **27** B2
Vitinia *Rome* **26** C1
Vitry-sur-Seine *Paris* **24** B3
Vladykino *Moscow* **19** A2
Vokovice *Prague* **25** B1
Volgelsdorf *Berlin* **5** B5
Volkhonka-Zil *Moscow* **19** C2
Vollen *Oslo* **23** B2
Volodarskoye *St. Petersburg* **27** B2
Volynkina-Derevnya
  St. Petersburg **27** B1
Vondelpark *Amsterdam* **2** A2
Vösendorf *Vienna* **32** B2
Voula *Athens* **2** C2
Vouliagmeni *Athens* **2** C2
Vredehoek *Cape Town* **8** A1
Vršovice *Prague* **25** B2
Vyborgskaya Storona
  St. Petersburg **27** B1
Vykhino *Moscow* **19** B3
Vyšehrad *Prague* **25** B2

W

Wachterhof *Munich* **21** B2
Wadala *Mumbai* **20** A2
Wadi al-Arayis *Jerusalem* **13** B2
Wadi Fukin *Jerusalem* **13** B1
Waduk Pluit *Jakarta* **12** A1
Waggaman *New Orleans* **21** B1
Wah Fu *Hong Kong* **12** B1
Wahda *Baghdad* **3** B2
Währing *Vienna* **32** A2
Waidmannslust *Berlin* **5** A3
Wakefield *Boston* **6** A2
Waldesruh *Berlin* **5** B5
Waldperlach *Munich* **21** B3
Waldtrudering *Munich* **21** B3
Walkinstown *Dublin* **10** B1
Wall Street *New York* **22** B1
Walt Disney World *Orlando* **23** B1
Waltham *Boston* **6** A1
Waltham Forest □ *London* **15** A3
Walthamstow *London* **15** A3
Walton-on-Thames *London* **15** B1
Wambeek *Brussels* **6** A3
Wan Chai *Hong Kong* **12** B1
Wandle → *London* **15** B2
Wandsworth □ *London* **15** B2
Wangjing *Beijing* **4** B2
Wannsee *Berlin* **5** B1
Wansdorf *Berlin* **5** A1
Wanstead *London* **15** A4
Wapping *London* **15** A3
Wards I. *New York* **22** B2
Warnberg *Munich* **21** B2
Warner Brothers Studios
  Los Angeles **16** B2
Warrāq el 'Arab *Cairo* **7** A2
Warringal Park *Melbourne* **18** A2
Warriston *Edinburgh* **11** B2
Warsaw = Warszawa
  Warsaw **33** B1
Warszawa *Warsaw* **33** B1
Warszawa ✈ (WAW)
  Warsaw **33** B1
Wartenberg *Berlin* **5** A4
Washington *Washington* **33** B1
Washington Heights
  New York **22** B2
Washington Park *Chicago* **9** C3
Washington Ronald
  Reagan Nat. ✈ (DCA)
  Washington **33** B2
Wat Pho *Bangkok* **3** B1
Water of Leith → *Edinburgh* **11** B1
Watergraafsmeer *Amsterdam* **2** A2
Waterland *Amsterdam* **2** A2
Waterloo *Brussels* **6** B2
Watermeal-Boitsfort *Brussels* **6** B2
Watertown *Boston* **6** A1
Watsonia *Melbourne* **18** A2
Watts *Los Angeles* **16** C3
Waverley *Boston* **6** A1
Waverley *Johannesburg* **13** A2
Waverley *Sydney* **33** B1
Wawrzyszew *Warsaw* **33** B1
Wazirabad *Delhi* **10** A2
Waziriya *Baghdad* **3** A2
Wazirpur *Delhi* **10** A1
Wealdstone *London* **15** A1
Wedding *Berlin* **5** A3
Weehawken *New York* **22** B1
Weesp *Amsterdam* **2** B3
Weidling *Vienna* **32** A1
Weidlingbach *Vienna* **32** A1
Weissensee *Berlin* **5** A3
Welamunson *Berlin* **5** A1
Wellesley Hills *Boston* **6** B1
Welling *London* **15** B4
Wellington *Boston* **6** A2
Weltevreden Park
  Johannesburg **13** B1
Wembley *London* **15** A2
Wemmel *Brussels* **6** A1
Wènmer Pan *Johannesburg* **13** B2
Wenceslas Square =
  Vaclavské náměstí
  Prague **25** B2
Wendenschloss *Berlin* **5** B4
Wennington *London* **15** A5
Werneuchen-Bahn *Berlin* **5** A5
Shanghai *Shanghai* **28** B1
West Don → *Toronto* **31** A2
West Drayton *London* **15** B1
West Ham *London* **15** A4
West Harrow *London* **15** A1

Worli *Mumbai* **20** B1
Worth *Chicago* **9** C2
Wren's Nest *Atlanta* **3** B2
Wrigley Field *Chicago* **9** B3
Wuhlgarten *Berlin* **5** A5
Wujiaochang *Shanghai* **28** B1
Würm → *Munich* **21** B1
Wusong *Shanghai* **28** A2
Wyczółki *Warsaw* **33** C1
Wygoda *Warsaw* **33** B2
Wynberg *Cape Town* **8** B1

X

Xabregas *Lisbon* **16** A2
Xiaogang Park *Guangzhou* **11** B2
Xiaoping *Guangzhou* **11** A2
Xiashachong *Guangzhou* **11** B3
Xichang *Guangzhou* **11** B3
Xicheng *Beijing* **4** B2
Xidan *Beijing* **4** B2
Xizhimen *Beijing* **4** B1
Xochimilco, Parque
  Ecológico *Mexico City* **18** C2
Xuanwu *Beijing* **4** B2
Xuhui *Shanghai* **28** B1
Xujiahui *Shanghai* **28** B1

Y

Yaba *Lagos* **14** A2
Yaftābād *Tehran* **31** B1
Yahara *Tokyo* **30** A2
Yaho *Tokyo* **30** A1
Yakire *Tokyo* **30** A4
Yaksu *Seoul* **27** B2
Yamada *Osaka* **23** A2
Yamada *Tokyo* **30** B2
Yamato → *Osaka* **23** B1
Yan Kit *Singapore* **28** A3
Yanbu *Guangzhou* **11** B2
Yangcheon *Seoul* **27** B1
Yangjiazhuang *Shanghai* **28** A2
Yangjae *Seoul* **27** B2
Yangma *Shanghai* **28** B2
Yangpu Park *Shanghai* **28** B2
Yannawa *Bangkok* **3** B2
Yarmūk *Baghdad* **3** B2
Yarra Bend Park *Melbourne* **18** A2
Yarraville *Melbourne* **18** B1
Yauza → *Moscow* **19** B4
Yeading *London* **15** A1
Yedikule *Istanbul* **12** C1
Yenikapı *Istanbul* **12** B1
Yeniköy *Istanbul* **12** B2
Yeongdeungpo *Seoul* **27** B1
Yeongdong *Seoul* **27** B2
Yeouido *Seoul* **27** B1
Yerba Buena I.
  San Francisco **26** B2
Yerres *Paris* **24** B4
Yerushalayim =
  Jerusalem *Jerusalem* **13** B2
Yildiz Park *Istanbul* **12** B2
Yinhangzhen *Shanghai* **28** A2
Yishun *Singapore* **28** A2
Ylästö *Helsinki* **11** B2
Yodo → *Osaka* **23** A2
Yongdingman *Beijing* **4** B2
Yongfucun *Guangzhou* **11** B2
Yongsan *Seoul* **27** B1
Yonkers *New York* **22** A2
York *Toronto* **31** A1
York Mills *Toronto* **31** A2
York Univ. *Toronto* **31** A1
You'anmen *Beijing* **4** B2
Youngsfield *Cape Town* **8** B1
Yuanmingyuan Park *Beijing* **4** B1
Yuanxiatian *Guangzhou* **11** A2
Yuexiu *Guangzhou* **11** B2
Yuexiu Park *Guangzhou* **11** B2
Yugo-Zarad *Moscow* **19** B2
Yung Shue Wan *Hong Kong* **12** B1
Yūsofābād *Tehran* **31** A2

Z

Za'abeel *Dubai* **9** B2
Zaandam *Amsterdam* **2** A1
Zaandijk *Amsterdam* **2** A1
Zaanstad *Amsterdam* **2** A1
Zábéhlice *Prague* **25** B3
Zabki *Warsaw* **33** B2
Zacisze *Warsaw* **33** B2
Zahrā *Baghdad* **3** A1
Zalov *Prague* **25** B2
Zaluski *Warsaw* **33** C1
Zamdorf *Munich* **21** B2
Zanevka *St. Petersburg* **27** B2
Zapote *Manila* **17** C1
Zaventem *Brussels* **6** A2
Zawady *Warsaw* **33** B2
Zāwiyet Abū Musallam
  Cairo **7** B1
Zawrā' Park *Baghdad* **3** B2
Zbraslav *Prague* **25** C2
Zbuzany *Prague* **25** B1
Zdiby *Prague* **25** B2
Zeekoevlei *Cape Town* **8** B2
Zehlendorf *Berlin* **5** B2
Zenne → *Brussels* **6** A2
Zephyr Field *New Orleans* **21** B1
Zeraň *Warsaw* **33** B2
Zeytinburnu *Istanbul* **12** C1
Zhabei *Shanghai* **28** B1
Zhdanov *Moscow* **19** B3
Zhenru *Shanghai* **28** B1
Zhernovka *St. Petersburg* **27** B2
Zhicun *Guangzhou* **11** B2
Zhongguancun *Beijing* **4** B1
Zhongshan Park *Shanghai* **28** B1
Zhoucun *Guangzhou* **11** A2
Zhoujiadu *Shanghai* **28** B2
Zhoujiazhen *Shanghai* **28** A2
Zhouzhuangzi *Beijing* **4** B1
Zhulebino *Moscow* **19** B3
Zhushadi *Guangzhou* **11** A3
Zielona *Warsaw* **33** B2
Zielonka *Warsaw* **33** B2
Zizhuyuan Park *Beijing* **4** B1
Žižkov *Prague* **25** B2
Zlíčin *Prague* **25** B1
Zografou *Athens* **2** B2
Zoliborz *Warsaw* **33** B1
Zonnebloem *Cape Town* **8** A1
Züglget *Budapest* **7** A2
Zugló *Budapest* **7** A2
Zuiderwoude *Amsterdam* **2** A2
Zur880 *Rio de Janeiro* **25** A2
Zuverva → *São Paulo* **27** C1
Zwanenburg *Amsterdam* **2** A1
Zwölfaxing *Vienna* **32** B2

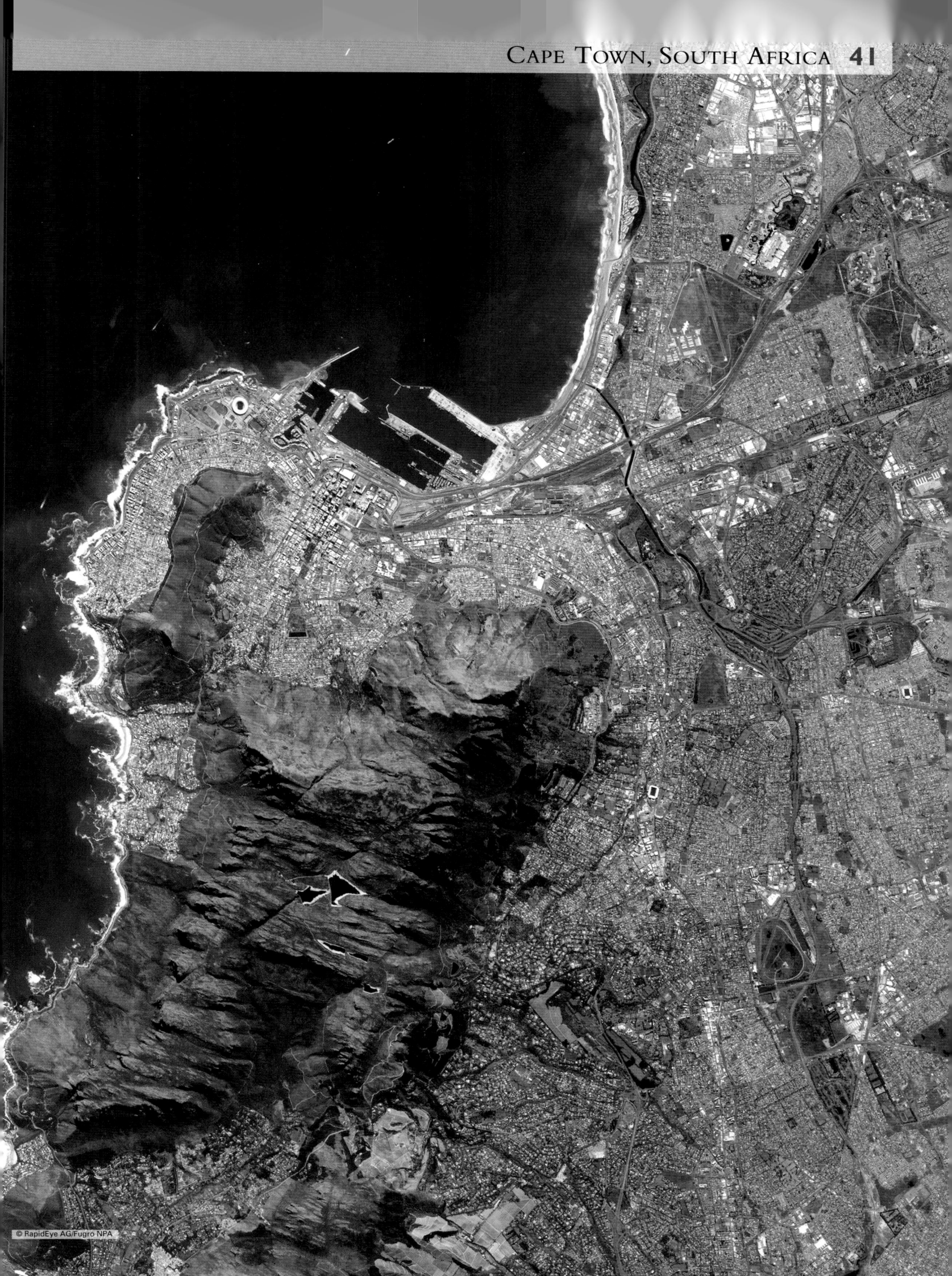

© Fugro NPA/USGS Landsat

© RapidEye AG/Fugro NPA

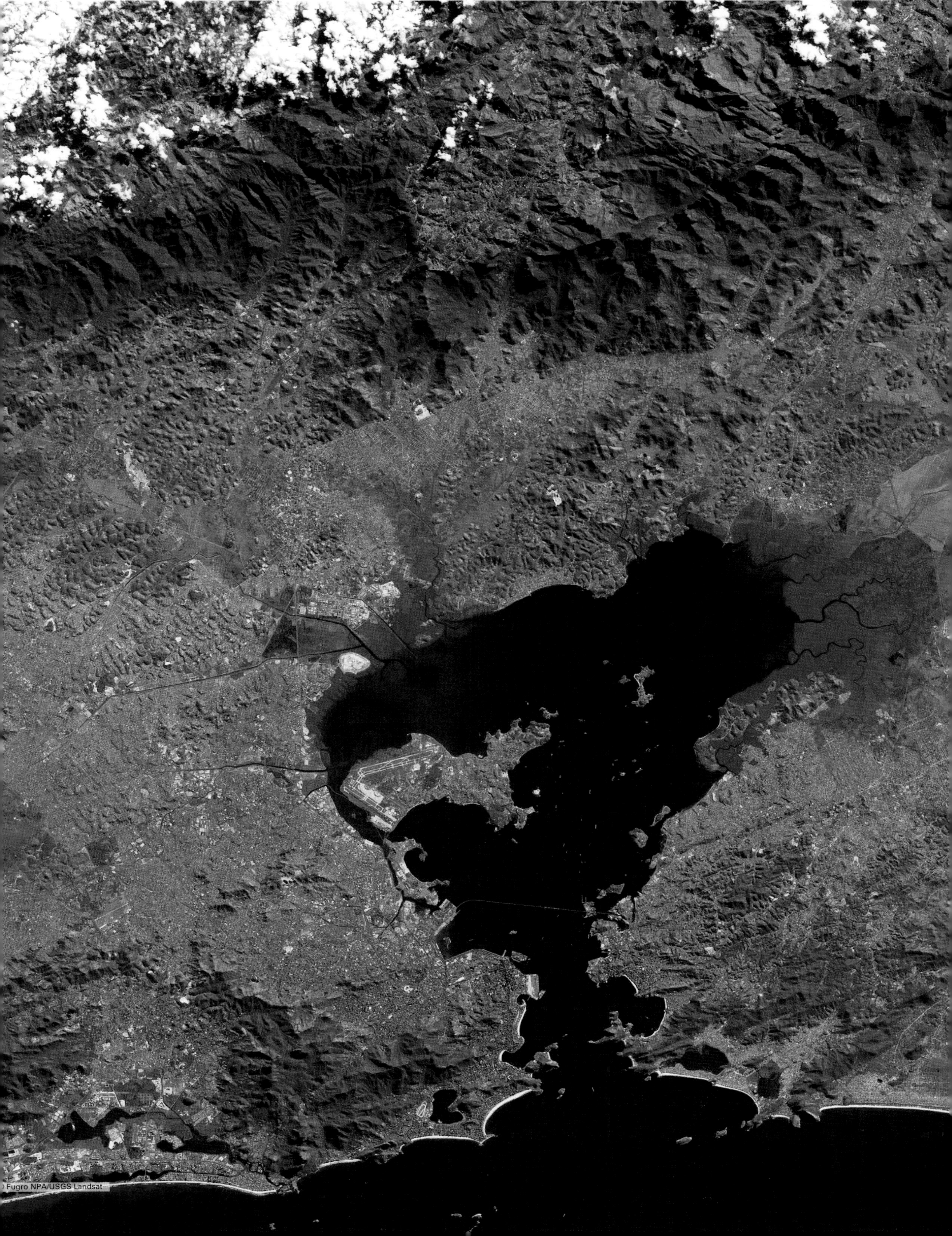

© Fugro NPA/USGS Landsat

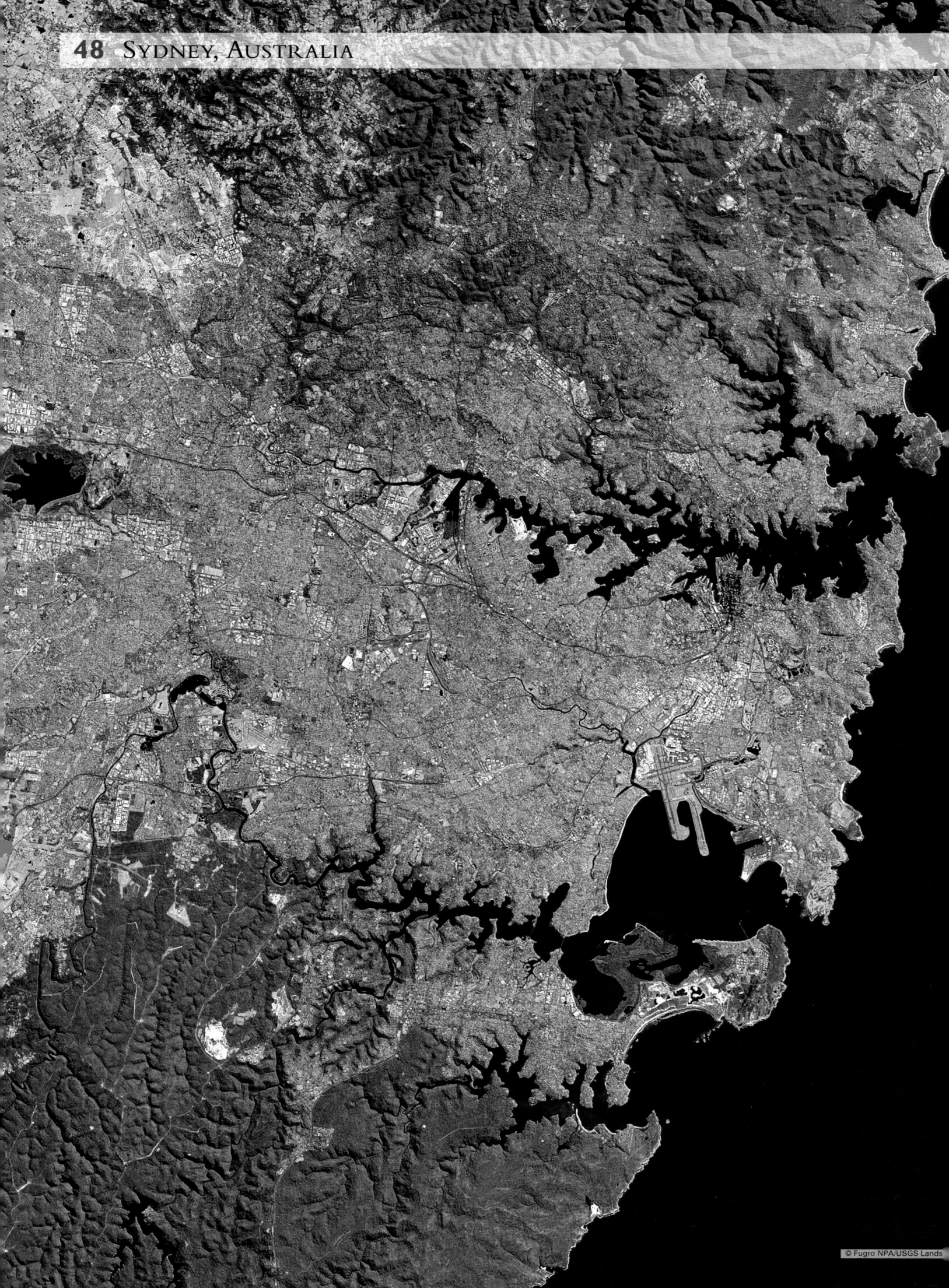

WORLD MAPS

SETTLEMENTS

■ **PARIS**   ◉ **Rotterdam**   ◉ **Livorno**   ◉ **Brugge**   ◎ Exeter   ○ Torremolinos   ○ Oberammergau   ○ Thira

Settlement symbols and type styles vary according to the scale of each map and indicate the importance
of towns on the map rather than specific population figures

● Vaduz   Capital cities have red infills   ∴   Ruins or archaeological sites

⬠   Urban agglomerations   ⌣   Wells in desert

ADMINISTRATION

―――― International boundaries   ·········· Internal boundaries   **PERU**   Country names

――――· International boundaries   ⬡ National parks   KENT   Administrative
(undefined or disputed)   area names

International boundaries show the *de facto* situation where there are rival claims to territory

COMMUNICATIONS

―――― Motorways, freeways   ―――― Principal railways   LHR ⊕   Principal airports
and expressways

―――― Principal roads   – – – – Railways   ⊕   Other airports
under construction

――― Other roads   ――― Other railways   ········· Principal canals

+---+ Road tunnels   +---+ Railway tunnels   ⤨   Passes

PHYSICAL FEATURES

⌒ Perennial streams   ⬭ Intermittent lakes   ▲ 8850 Elevations in metres

– – – Intermittent streams   ⸙ Swamps and marshes   ▼ 8500 Sea depths in metres

⬭ Perennial lakes   ⬭ Permanent ice   *1134* Height of lake surface
and glaciers   above sea level in metres

⠂⠄ Sand deserts

ELEVATION AND DEPTH TINTS

Height of land above sea level   Land below sea level   Depth of sea

in metres	6000	4000	3000	2000	1500	1000	400	200	0						in feet
in feet	18 000	12 000	9000	6000	4500	3000	1200	600		6000	12 000	15 000	18 000	24 000	
									0	200	2000	4000	5000	6000	8000	in metres

Some of the maps have different contours to highlight and clarify the principal relief features

Equatorial Scale 1:95 000 000

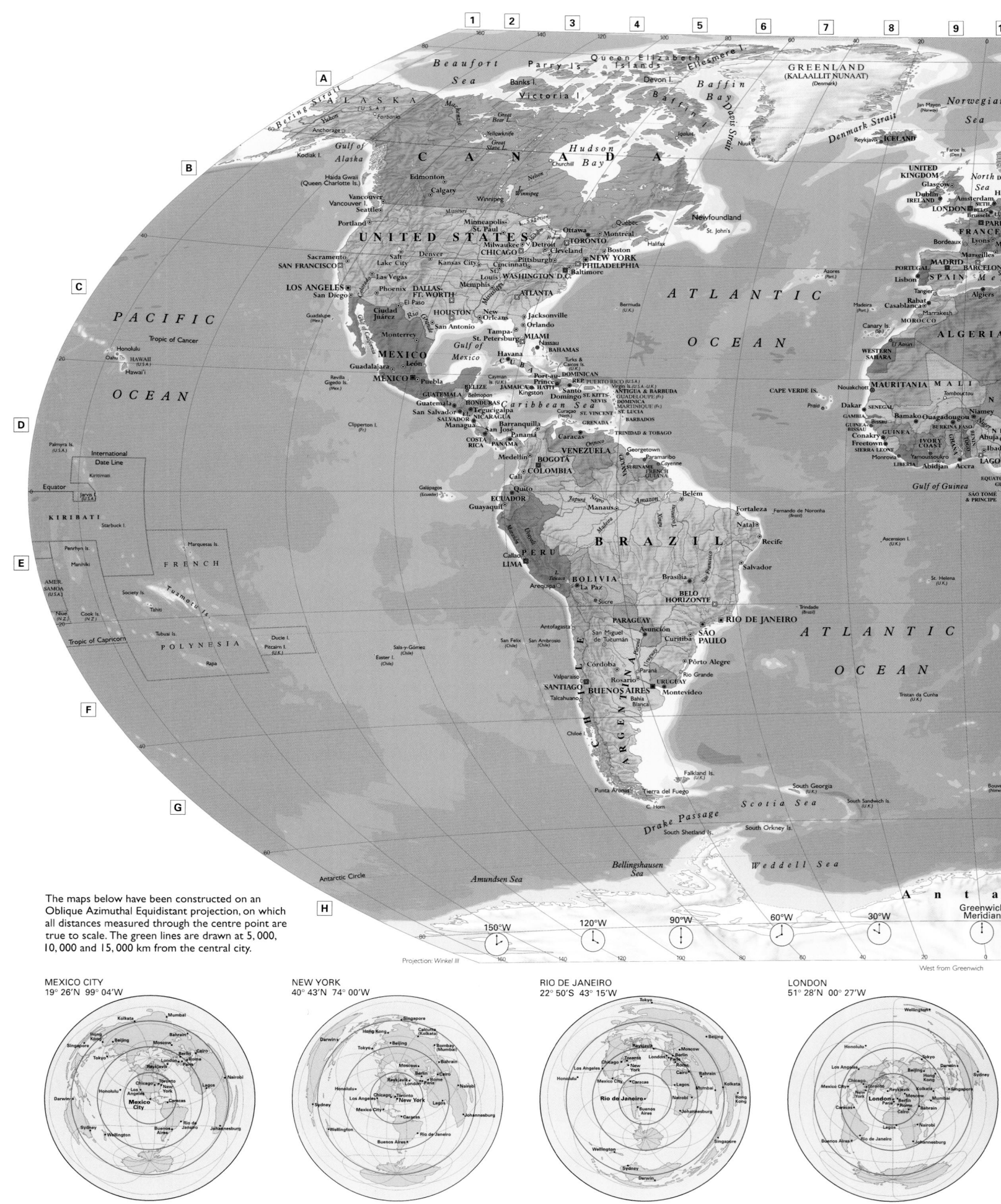

The maps below have been constructed on an Oblique Azimuthal Equidistant projection, on which all distances measured through the centre point are true to scale. The green lines are drawn at 5,000, 10,000 and 15,000 km from the central city.

Projection: Winkel III

West from Greenwich

MEXICO CITY
19° 26'N 99° 04'W

NEW YORK
40° 43'N 74° 00'W

RIO DE JANEIRO
22° 50'S 43° 15'W

LONDON
51° 28'N 00° 27'W

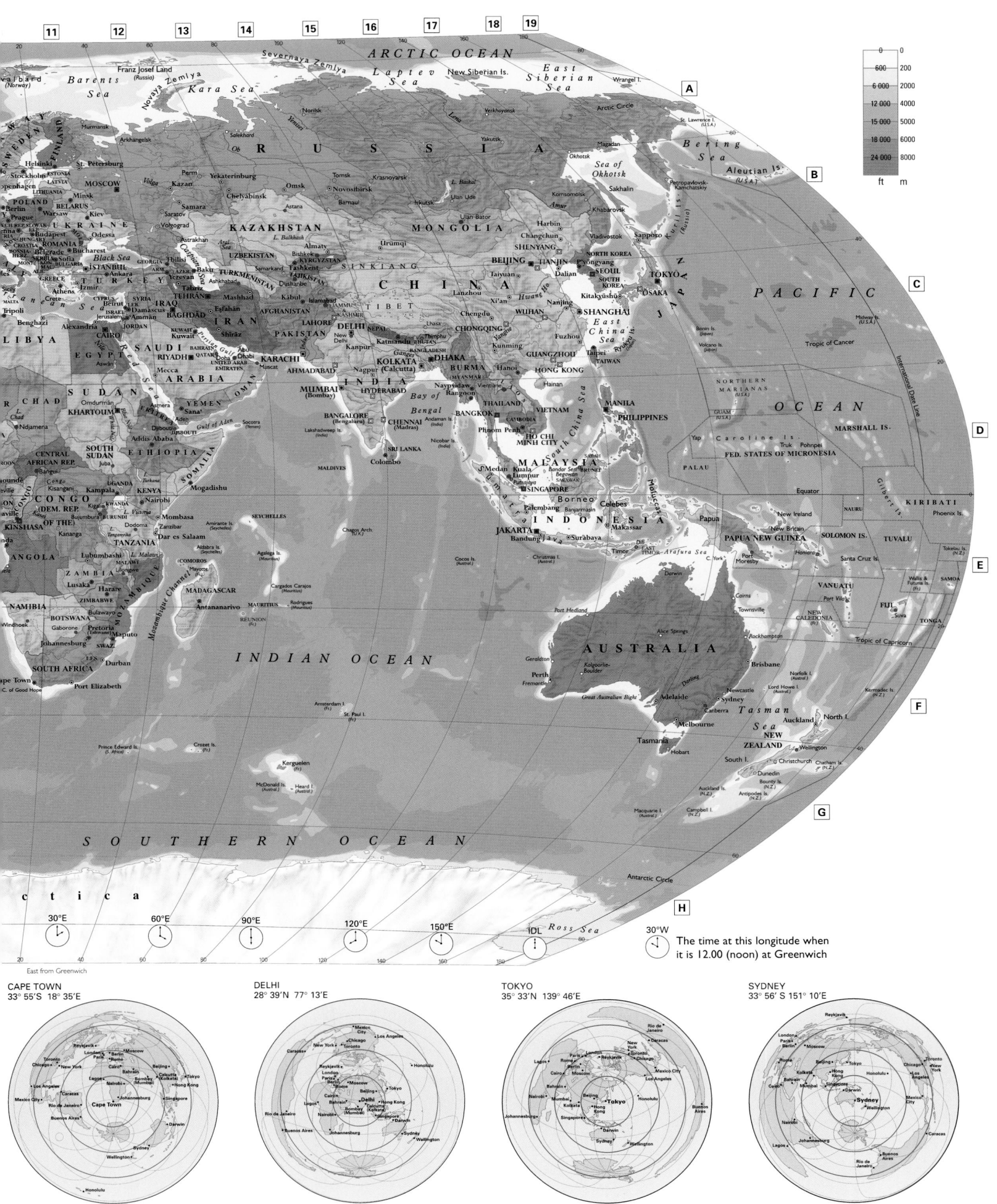

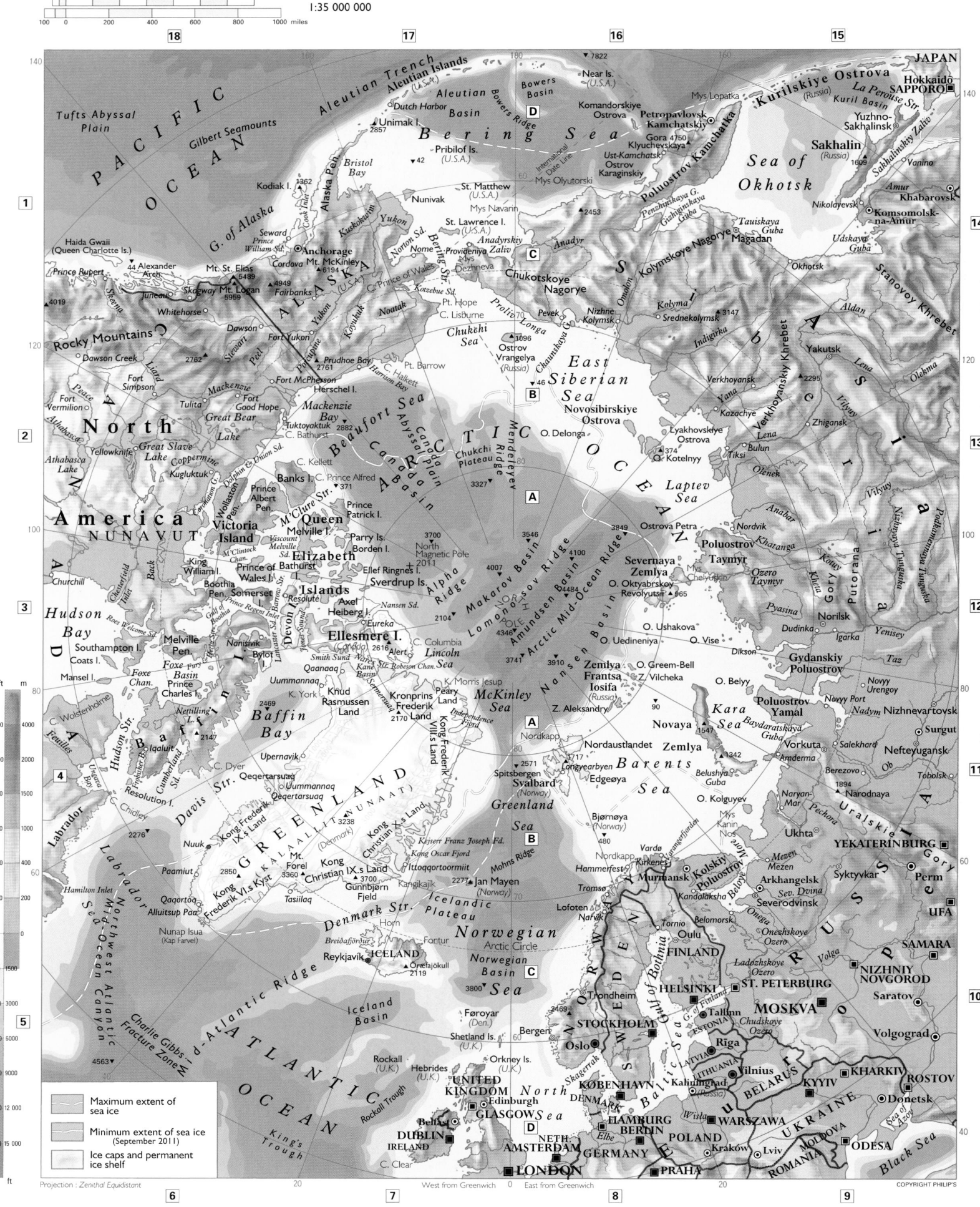

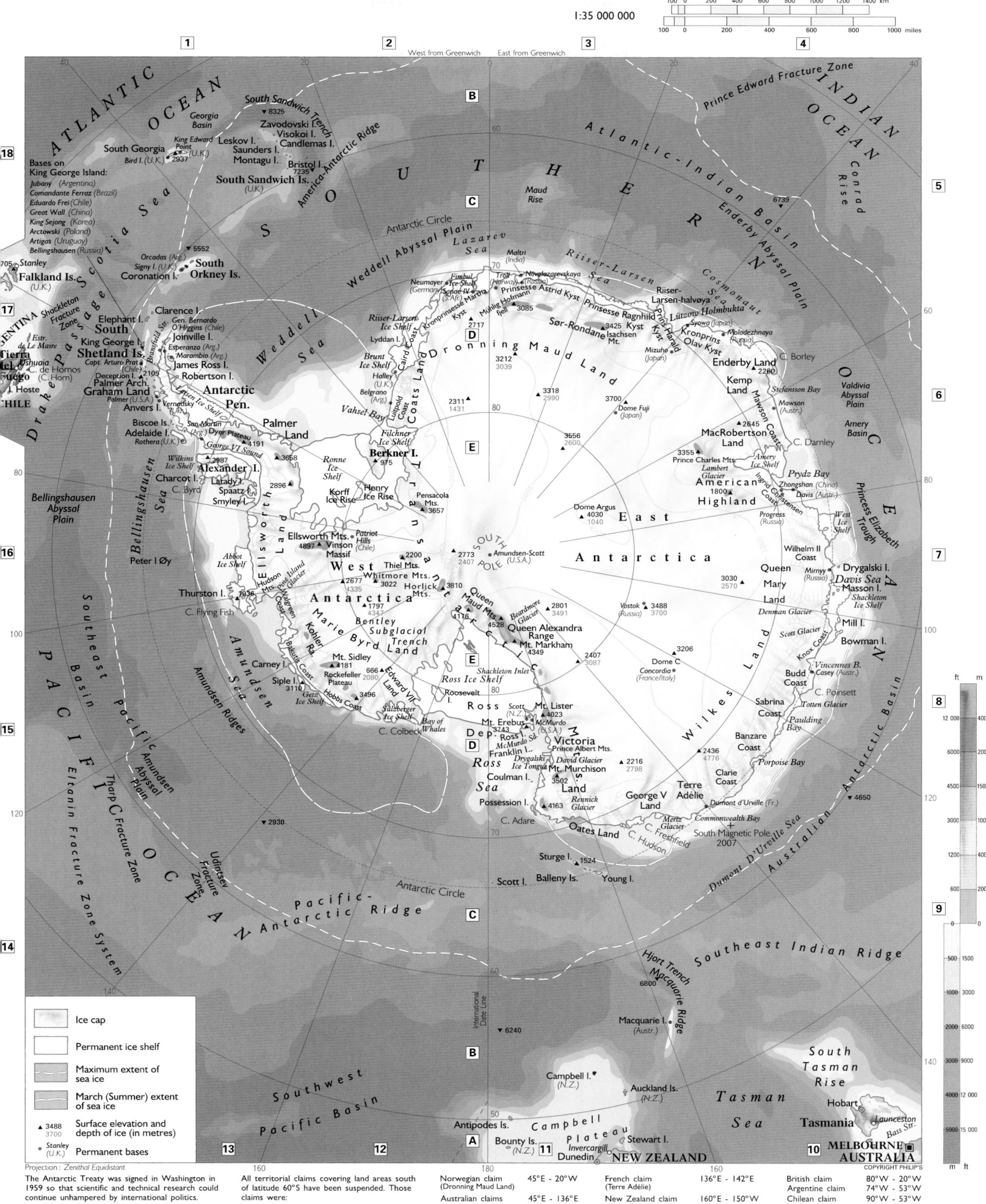

1:35 000 000

| 100 | 0 | 200 | 400 | 600 | 800 | 1000 | 1200 | 1400 km |
| 100 | 0 | 200 | 400 | 600 | 800 | 1000 miles |

Legend:

- Ice cap
- Permanent ice shelf
- Maximum extent of sea ice
- March (Summer) extent of sea ice
- ▲ 3488 / 3700 Surface elevation and depth of ice (in metres)
- • *Stanley* / (U.K.) Permanent bases

Projection: Zenithal Equidistant

COPYRIGHT PHILIP'S

The Antarctic Treaty was signed in Washington in 1959 so that scientific and technical research could continue unhampered by international politics.

All territorial claims covering land areas south of latitude 60°S have been suspended. Those claims were:

Norwegian claim (Dronning Maud Land)	45°E – 20°W	French claim (Terre Adélie)	136°E – 142°E	British claim	80°W – 20°W
Australian claims	45°E – 136°E 142°E – 160°E	New Zealand claim (Ross Dependency)	160°E – 150°W	Argentine claim Chilean claim	74°W – 53°W 90°W – 53°W

Bases on King George Island:
Jubany (Argentina)
Comandante Ferraz (Brazil)
Eduardo Frei (Chile)
Great Wall (China)
King Sejong (Korea)
Arctowski (Poland)
Artigas (Uruguay)
Bellingshausen (Russia)

1:20 000 000

Projection Bonne

COPYRIGHT PHILIP'S

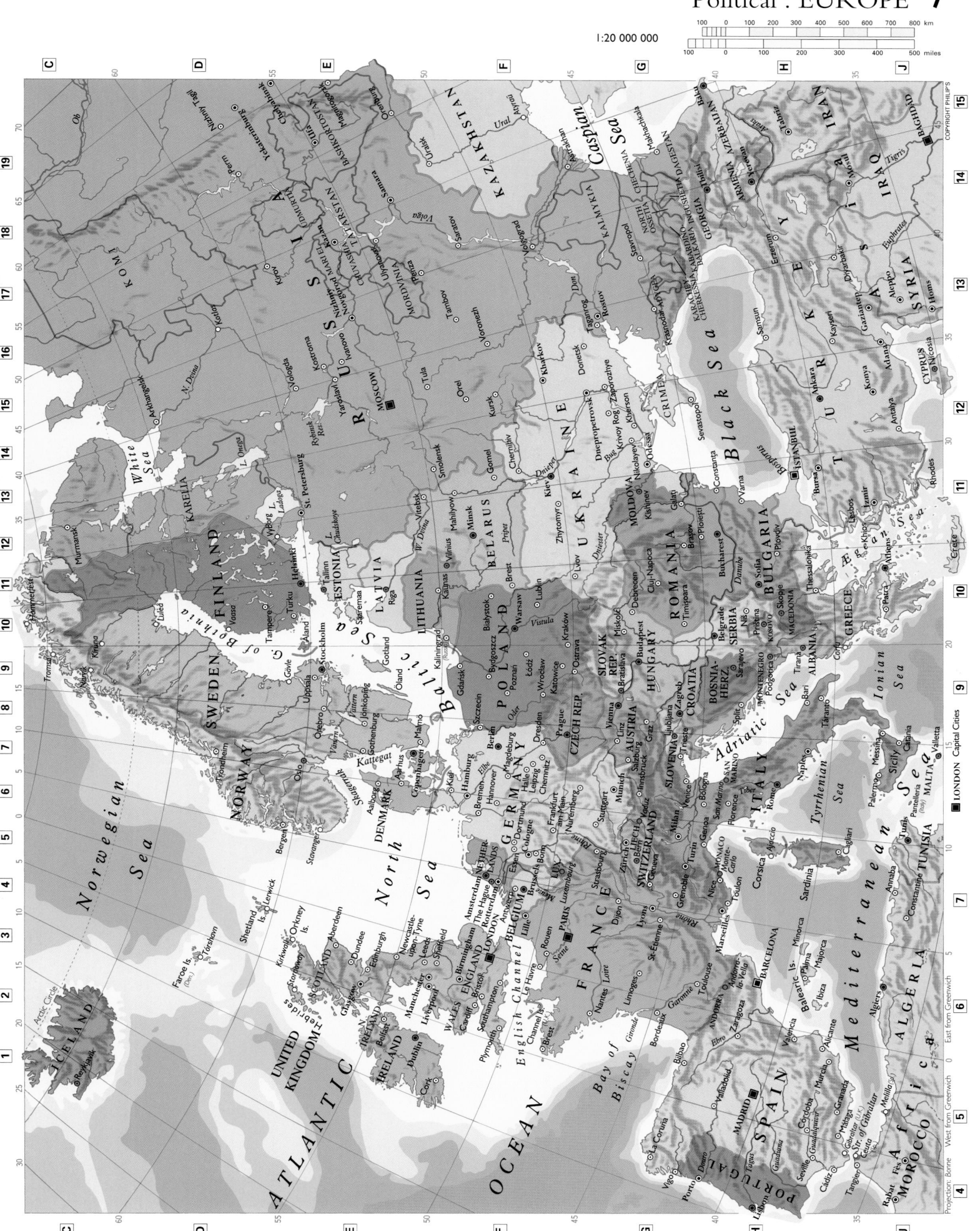

BARENTS SEA

RUSSIA

KARELIA

FINLAND

Lapp land

SWEDEN

NORWAY

ATLANTIC OCEAN

ICELAND
on same scale

FAEROE ISLANDS
on same scale

Føroyar
(Faeroe Is.)
(Den.)

1:6 000 000

50   0   25   50   75   100 125 150 175 km

50   0   25   50   75   100 125 miles

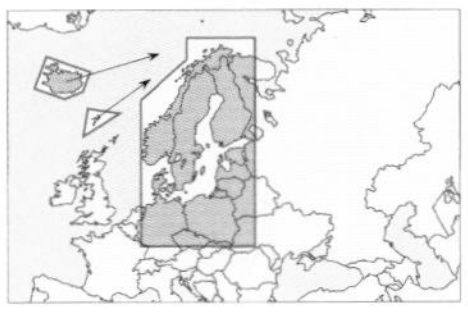

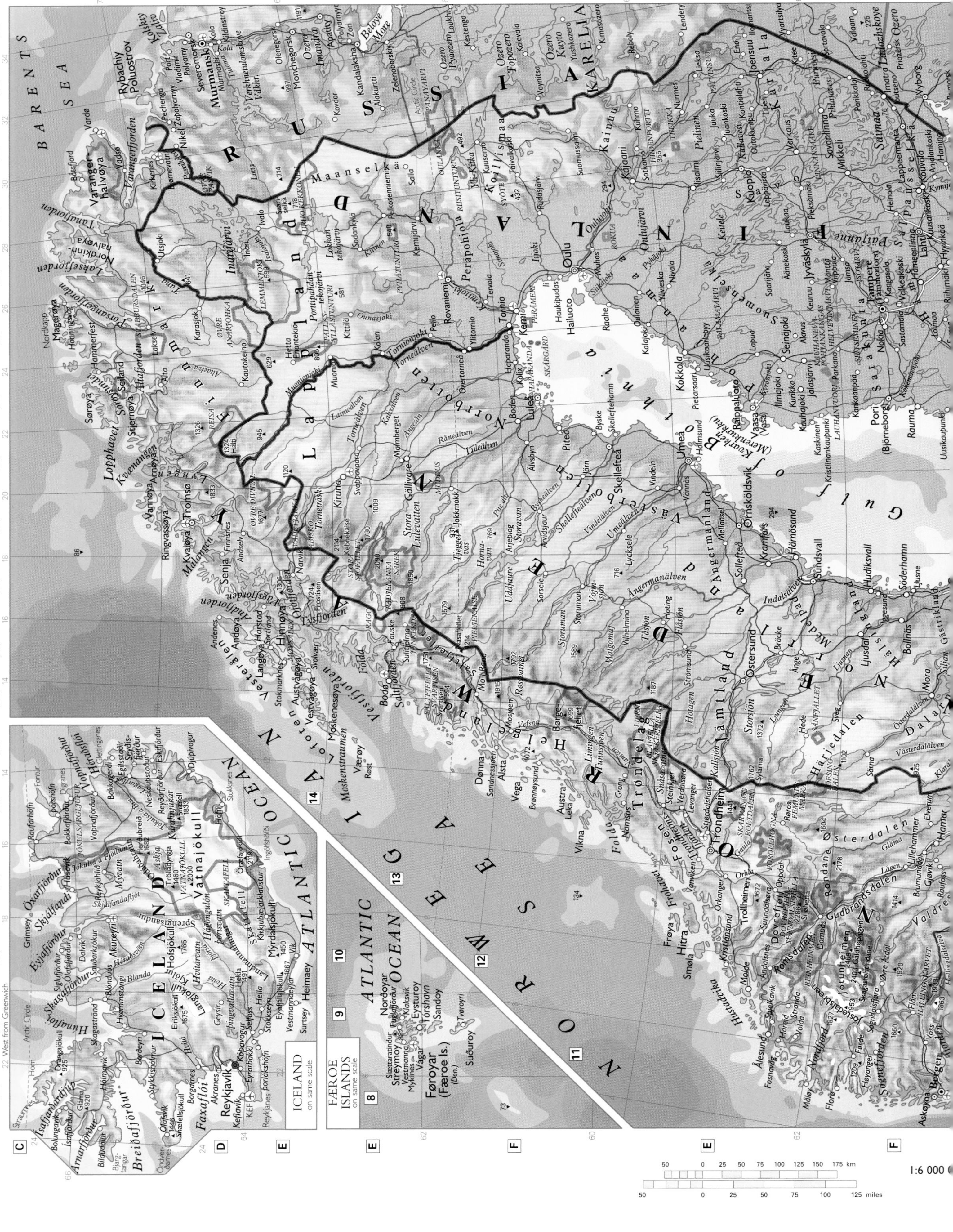

Projection: Conical with two standard parallels

East from Greenwich

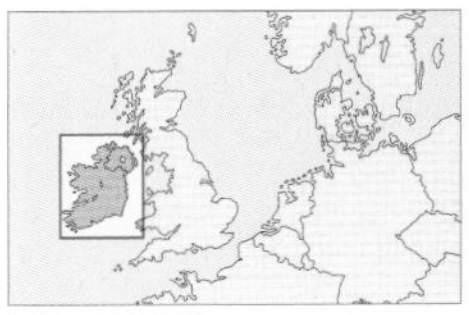

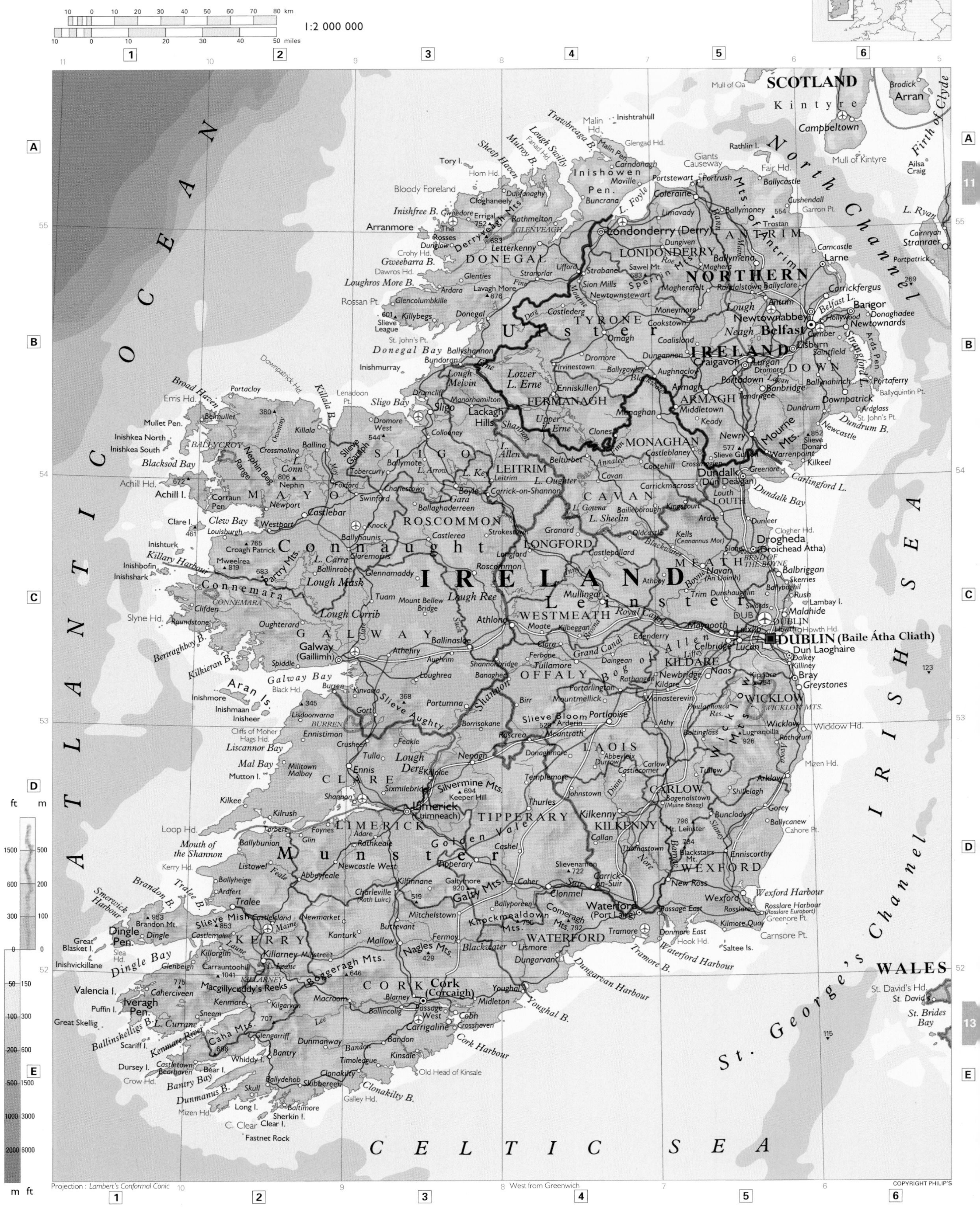

1:2 000 000

10 0 10 20 30 40 50 60 70 80 km
10 0 10 20 30 40 50 miles

SCOTLAND

ATLANTIC OCEAN

NORTHERN IRELAND

IRELAND

Ulster
Connaught
Leinster
Munster

DONEGAL
LONDONDERRY
TYRONE
FERMANAGH
ANTRIM
DOWN
ARMAGH
MONAGHAN
CAVAN
LEITRIM
SLIGO
MAYO
ROSCOMMON
LONGFORD
WESTMEATH
MEATH
LOUTH
GALWAY
OFFALY
KILDARE
DUBLIN
WICKLOW
LAOIS
CLARE
LIMERICK
TIPPERARY
KILKENNY
CARLOW
WEXFORD
KERRY
CORK
WATERFORD

DUBLIN (Baile Átha Cliath)
Belfast
Londonderry (Derry)
Cork (Corcaigh)
Limerick (Luimneach)
Galway (Gaillimh)
Waterford (Port Láirge)

NORTH Channel
IRISH SEA
St. George's Channel
CELTIC SEA

WALES

Dublin (Baile Átha Cliath)

Projection : Lambert's Conformal Conic
West from Greenwich

COPYRIGHT PHILIP'S

ft m
1500 500
600 200
300 100
0
50 150
100 300
200 600
500 1500
1000 3000
2000 6000
m ft

1:2 000 000

Key to Scottish unitary
authorities on map
1 CITY OF ABERDEEN
2 DUNDEE CITY
3 WEST DUNBARTONSHIRE
4 EAST DUNBARTONSHIRE
5 CITY OF GLASGOW
6 INVERCLYDE
7 RENFREWSHIRE
8 EAST RENFREWSHIRE
9 NORTH LANARKSHIRE
10 FALKIRK
11 CLACKMANNANSHIRE
12 WEST LOTHIAN
13 CITY OF EDINBURGH
14 MIDLOTHIAN

ORKNEY IS.
on same scale

ORKNEY

SHETLAND IS.
on same scale

SHETLAND

Projection : Lambert's Conformal Conic

West from Greenwich

COPYRIGHT PHILIP'S

1:2 000 000

80 km
50 miles

Key to English unitary authorities on map

25 HARTLEPOOL
26 DARLINGTON
27 STOCKTON-ON-TEES
28 MIDDLESBROUGH
29 REDCAR AND CLEVELAND
30 BLACKPOOL
31 BLACKBURN WITH DARWEN
32 HALTON
33 WARRINGTON
34 KINGSTON UPON HULL
35 NORTH EAST LINCOLNSHIRE
36 STOKE-ON-TRENT
37 TELFORD AND WREKIN
38 DERBY CITY
39 CITY OF NOTTINGHAM
40 LEICESTER CITY
41 RUTLAND
42 PETERBOROUGH
43 MILTON KEYNES
44 LUTON
45 NORTH SOMERSET
46 CITY OF BRISTOL
47 BATH AND NORTH EAST SOMERSET
48 SWINDON
49 READING
50 WOKINGHAM
51 WINDSOR AND MAIDENHEAD
52 SLOUGH
53 BRACKNELL FOREST
54 THURROCK
55 SOUTHEND-ON-SEA
56 MEDWAY
57 PLYMOUTH
58 TORBAY
59 POOLE
60 BOURNEMOUTH
61 SOUTHAMPTON
62 PORTSMOUTH
63 BRIGHTON AND HOVE
64 BEDFORD
65 CENTRAL BEDFORDSHIRE

Key to Welsh unitary authorities on map

15 SWANSEA
16 NEATH PORT TALBOT
17 BRIDGEND
18 RHONDDA CYNON TAFF
19 MERTHYR TYDFIL
20 CAERPHILLY
21 BLAENAU GWENT
22 TORFAEN
23 CARDIFF
24 NEWPORT

NORTH

SEA

IRISH SEA

North Channel

NORTHERN
IRELAND

SCOTLAND

ENGLAND

WALES

Newcastle-upon-Tyne
Sunderland
Middlesbrough
Hartlepool
Carlisle
Kingston upon Hull
Leeds
MANCHESTER
Sheffield
LIVERPOOL
Nottingham
Derby
Stoke-on-Trent
Chester
Lincoln
Glasgow
Edinburgh
Belfast

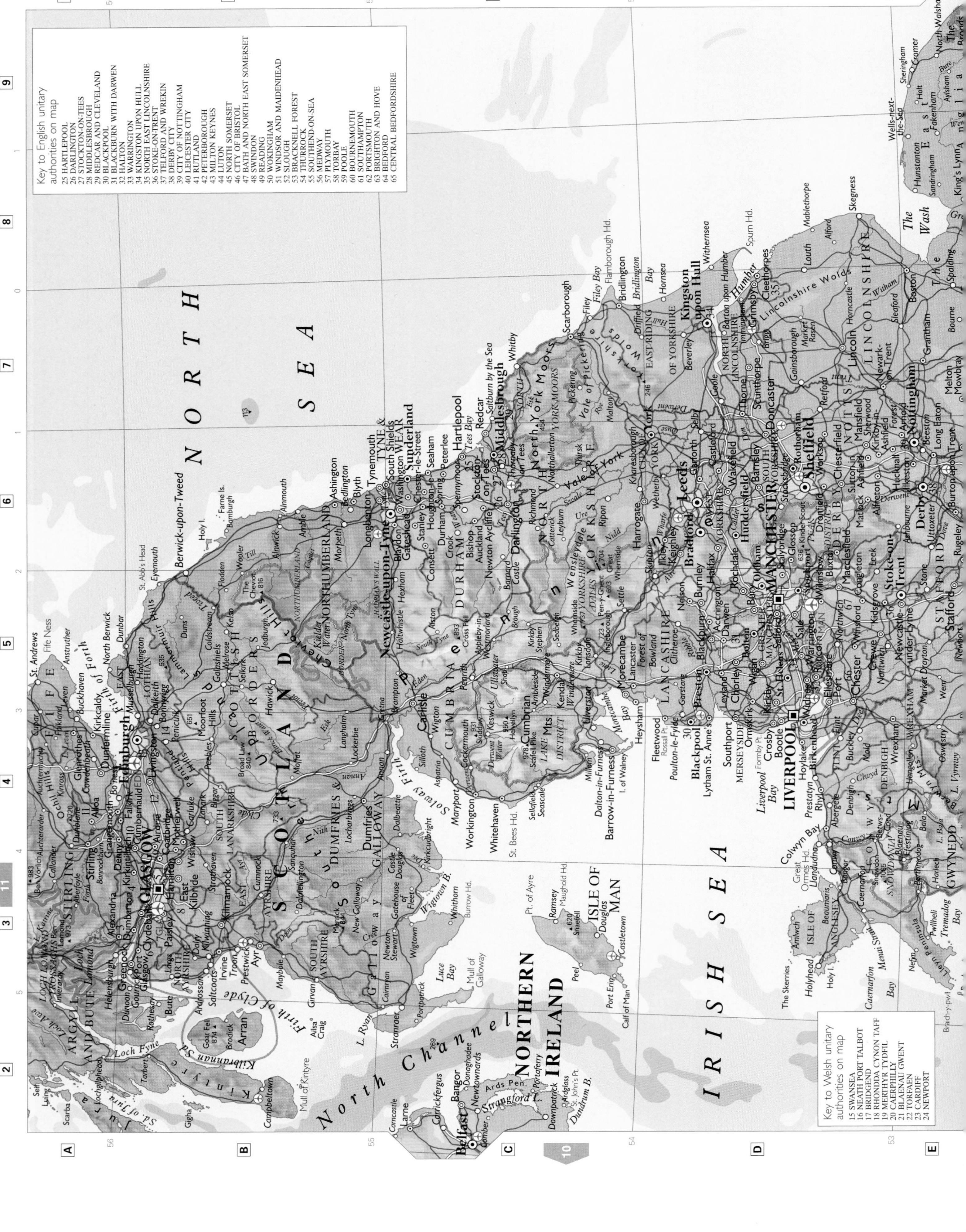

ISLES OF SCILLY
on same scale

Projection : Lambert's Conformal Conic

1:5 000 000

Projection: Conical with two standard parallels

East from Greenwich
COPYRIGHT PHILIP'S

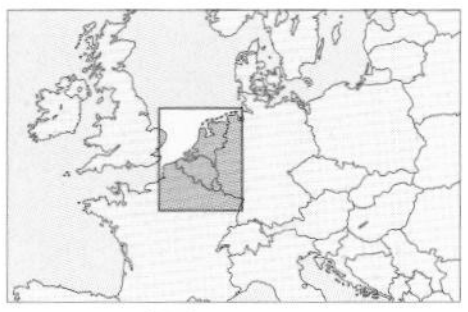

1:2 500 000

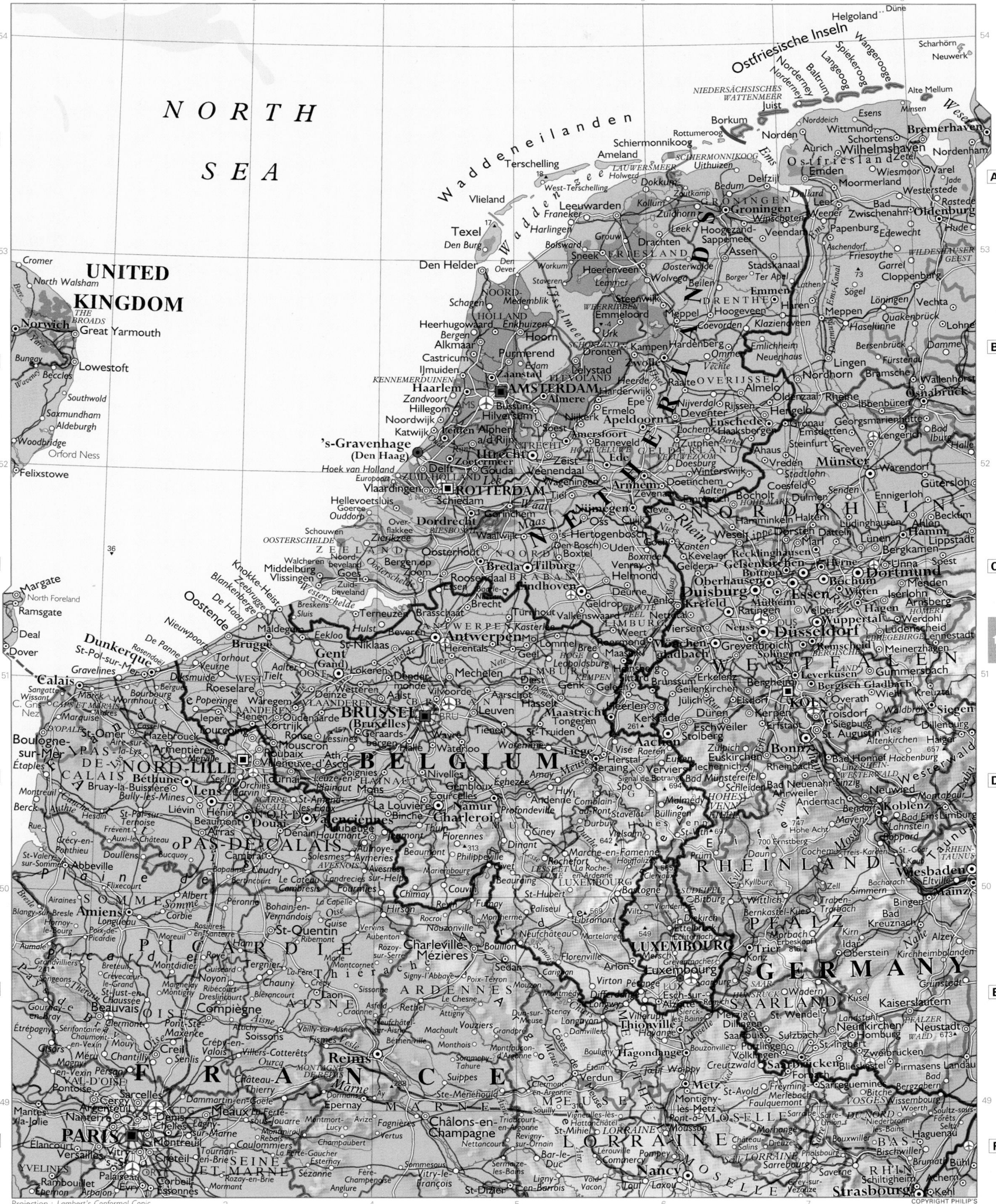

10 0 10 20 30 40 50 60 70 80 90 km
10 0 10 20 30 40 50 60 miles

Major features and labels

NORTH SEA

UNITED KINGDOM

NETHERLANDS

BELGIUM

GERMANY

FRANCE

LUXEMBOURG

Waddeneilanden

Ostfriesische Inseln

Major towns: Amsterdam, 's-Gravenhage (Den Haag), Rotterdam, Utrecht, Haarlem, Groningen, Leeuwarden, Arnhem, Nijmegen, Eindhoven, Breda, Tilburg, Maastricht, Antwerpen, Brussel (Bruxelles), Gent (Gand), Brugge, Liège, Namur, Charleroi, Mons, Luxembourg, Köln, Bonn, Düsseldorf, Dortmund, Essen, Münster, Bremerhaven, Oldenburg, Wiesbaden, Mainz, Koblenz, Saarbrücken, Lille, Amiens, Reims, Paris, Strasbourg, Metz, Nancy, Calais, Dunkerque, Boulogne-sur-Mer

Regions: HOLLAND, FRIESLAND, DRENTHE, OVERIJSSEL, GELDERLAND, ZEELAND, NOORD-BRABANT, LIMBURG, FLEVOLAND, NORDRHEIN-WESTFALEN, RHEINLAND, PFALZ, SAARLAND, PAS-DE-CALAIS, PICARDIE, AISNE, ARDENNES, LORRAINE, MARNE, MEUSE, MOSELLE

Projection : Lambert's Conformal Conic

COPYRIGHT PHILIP'S

ft m
1500 500
600 200

High-speed rail routes

Underlined towns give their name to the administrative area in which they stand.

1:5 000 000

50 0 25 50 75 100 125 150 175 km
50 0 25 50 75 100 125 miles

NORTH SEA

BALTIC SEA

DENMARK

UNITED KINGDOM

NETHERLANDS

BELGIUM

GERMANY

LUXEMBOURG

FRANCE

SWITZERLAND

AUSTRIA

ITALY

SLOVENIA

CZECH

ADRIATIC SEA

HAMBURG · BERLIN · BREMEN · Hannover · Magdeburg · Leipzig · Dresden · Köln (Cologne) · Bonn · Frankfurt · Stuttgart · Nürnberg · MÜNCHEN (Munich) · AMSTERDAM · ROTTERDAM · BRUSSELS (Bruxelles) · PARIS · LYON · MARSEILLE · MONACO · TORINO (Turin) · MILANO · ZÜRICH · Bern · Genève · PRAHA (Prague) · Szczecin · BERLIN · Ljubljana · ZAGREB

Projection: Conical with two standard parallels

ft m
12000 4000
9000 3000
6000 2000
4500 1500
3000 1000
1500 500
600 200
150 50
0

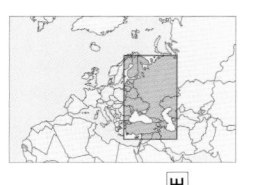

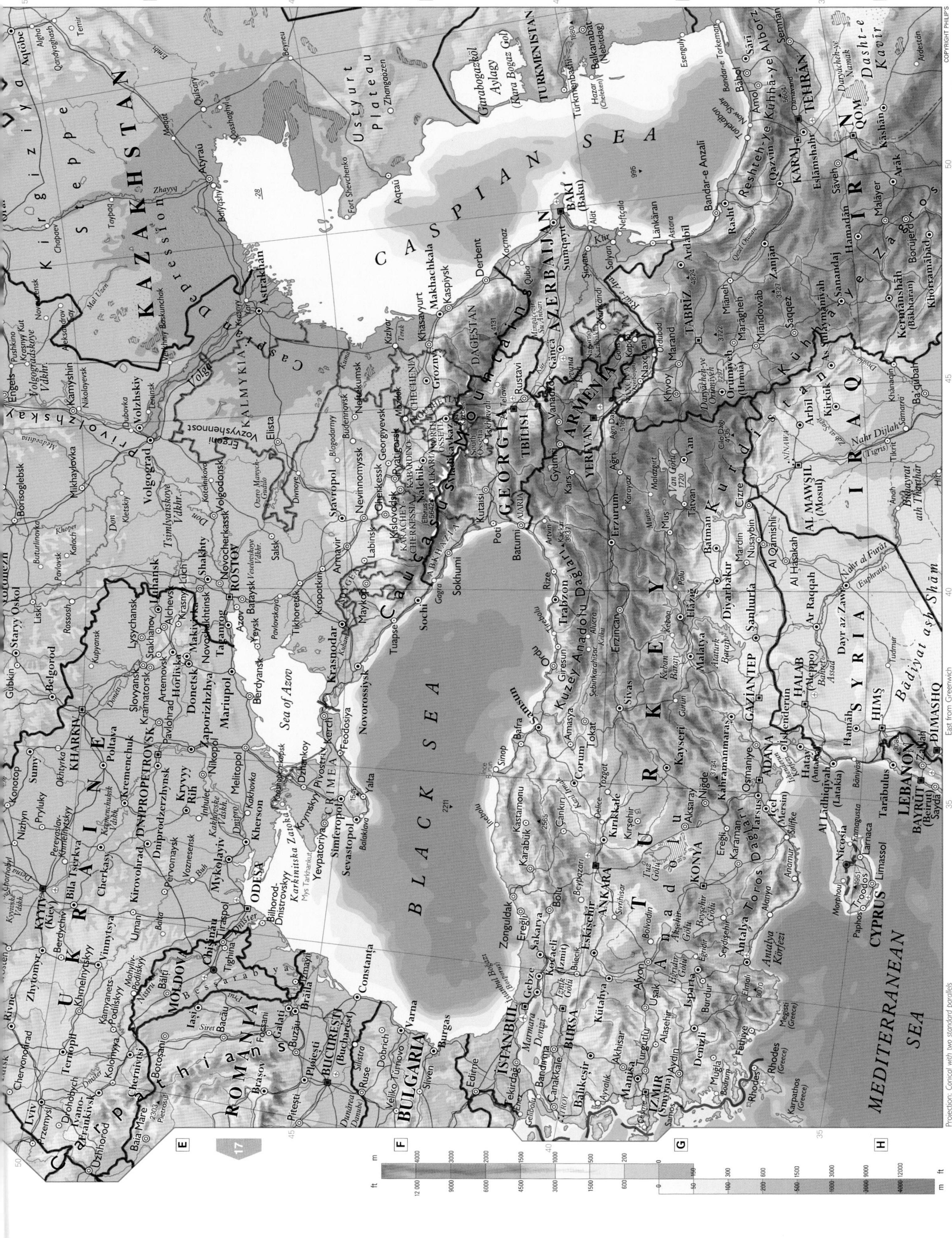

E 45 F 40 G 35 H

CASPIAN SEA

BLACK SEA

MEDITERRANEAN SEA

Sea of Azov

KAZAKHSTAN

Kirgiziya Steppe

Ustyurt Plateau

Caspian Depression

TURKMENISTAN

UKRAINE

ROMANIA

BULGARIA

MOLDOVA

TURKEY

GEORGIA

ARMENIA

AZERBAIJAN

SYRIA

IRAQ

IRAN

LEBANON

CYPRUS

KALMYKIA

CHECHENIA

DAGESTAN

Caucasus Mountains

Kuzey Anadolu Dağları

Toros Dağları

İÇ Anadolu

Orta Toros Dağları

Dasht-e Kavir

Bādiyat ash Shām

BAKİ (Baku)

TBİLİSİ

YEREVAN

TEHRĀN

QOM

KARAJ

TABRĪZ

ANKARA

İSTANBUL

İZMİR (Smyrna)

BURSA

KONYA

ADANA

GAZİANTEP

HALAB (Aleppo)

HIMŞ

DIMASHQ

BAYRŪT (Beirut)

Nicosia

AL MAWŞIL (Mosul)

ROSTOV

KHARKIV

DNİPROPETROVSK

Volgograd

Krasnodar

Astrakhan

ODESA

BUCUREŞTI (Bucharest)

KYIV (Kiev)

CHIŞİNĂU

Projection: Conical with two standard parallels

East from Greenwich

COPYRIGHT PHILIP'S

m 6000 4000 3000 2000 1500 1000 500 200 0

ft 12 000 9000 6000 4500 3000 1500 600 300 0 150 600 1500 3000 9000 12000 ft

m 150 300 600 1000 2000 3000 4000 m

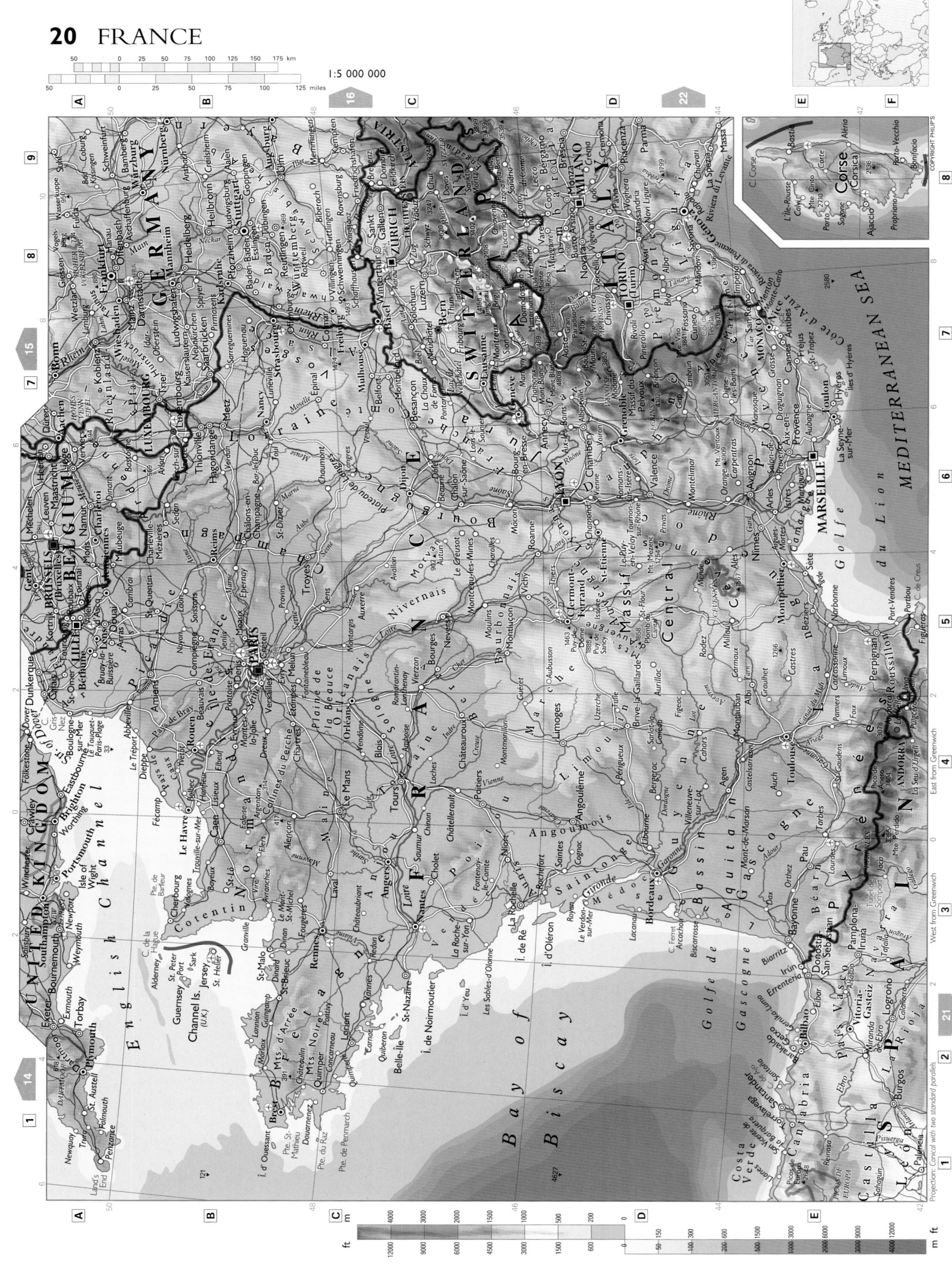

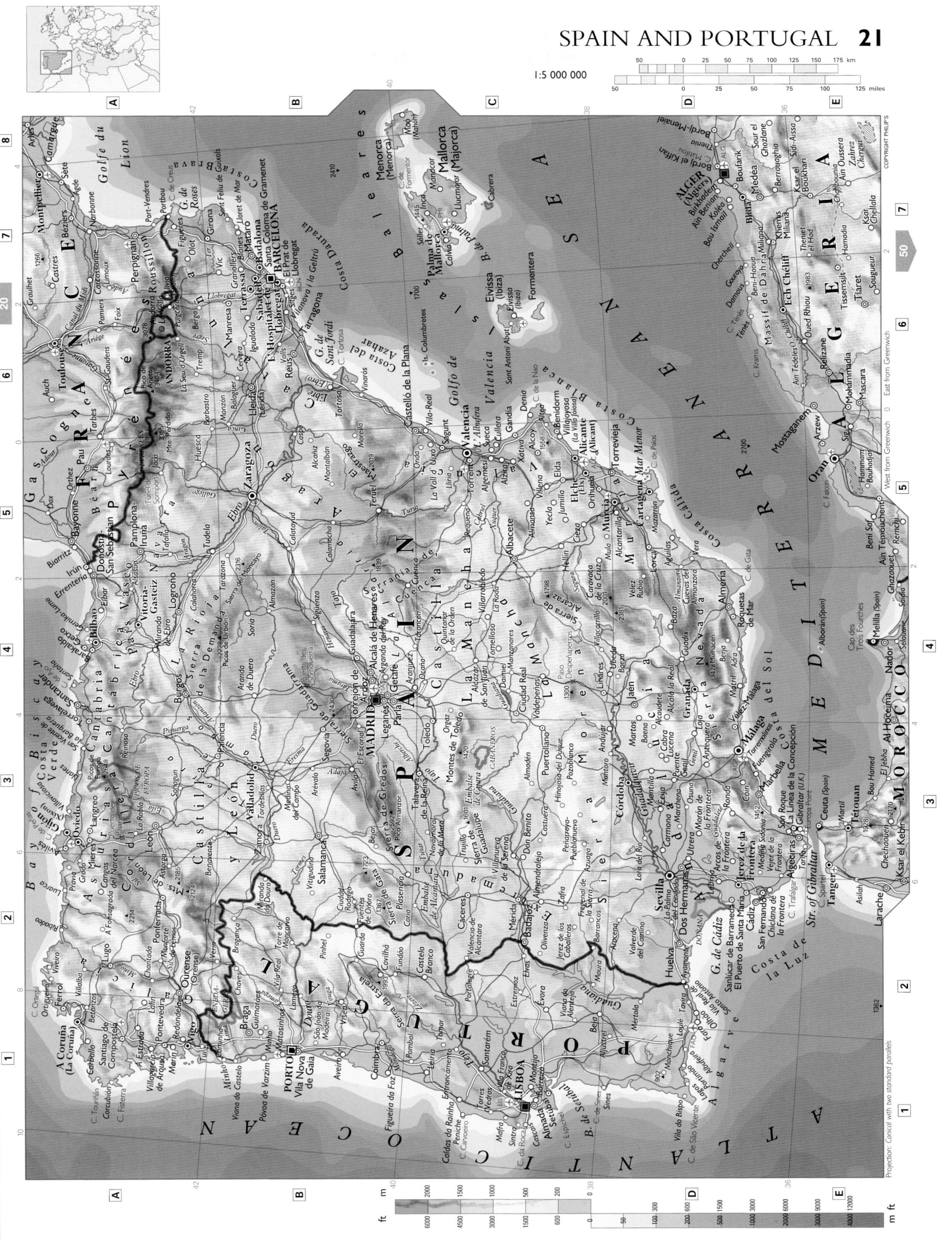

1:5 000 000

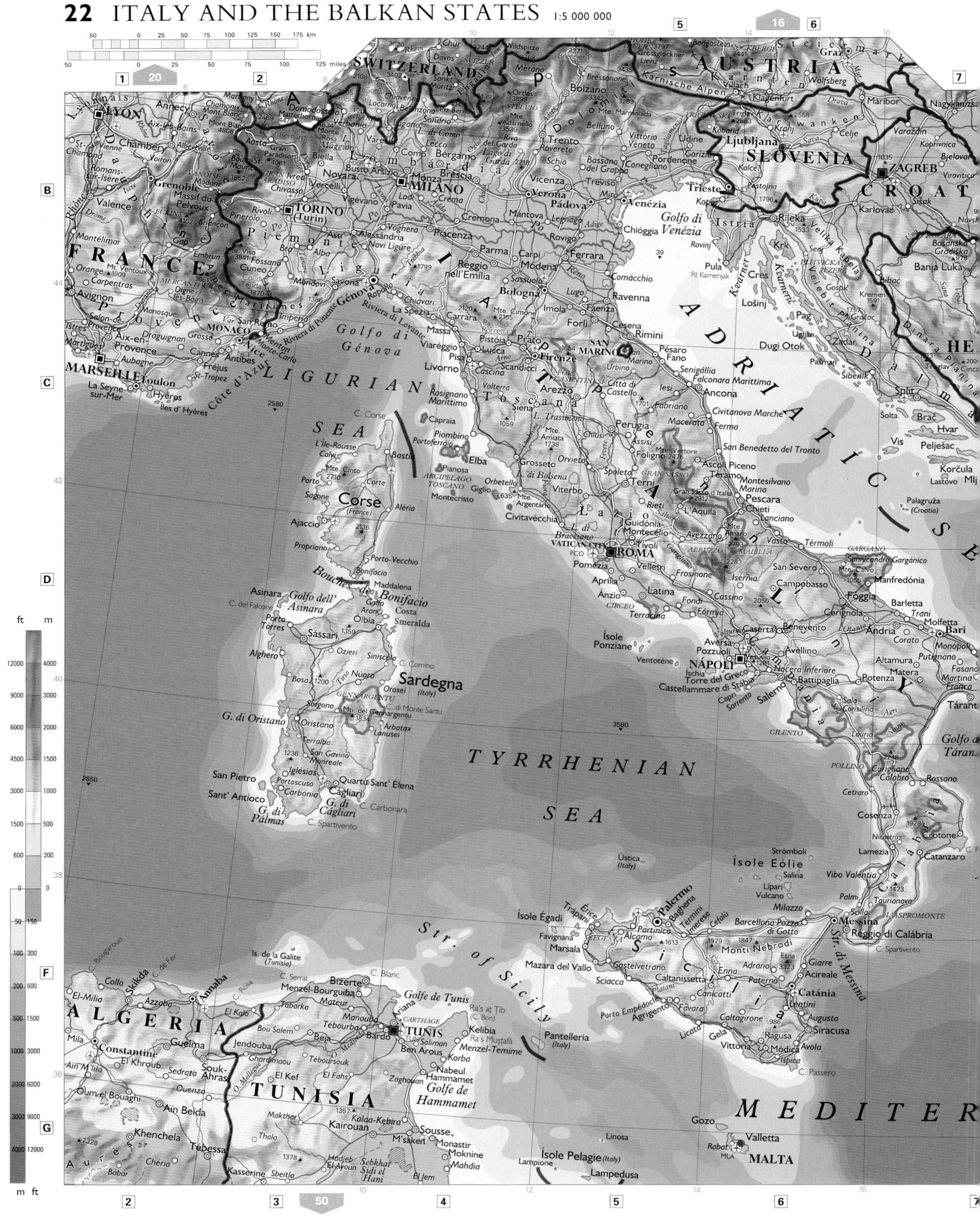

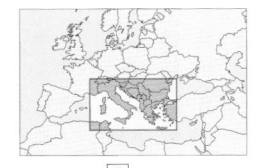

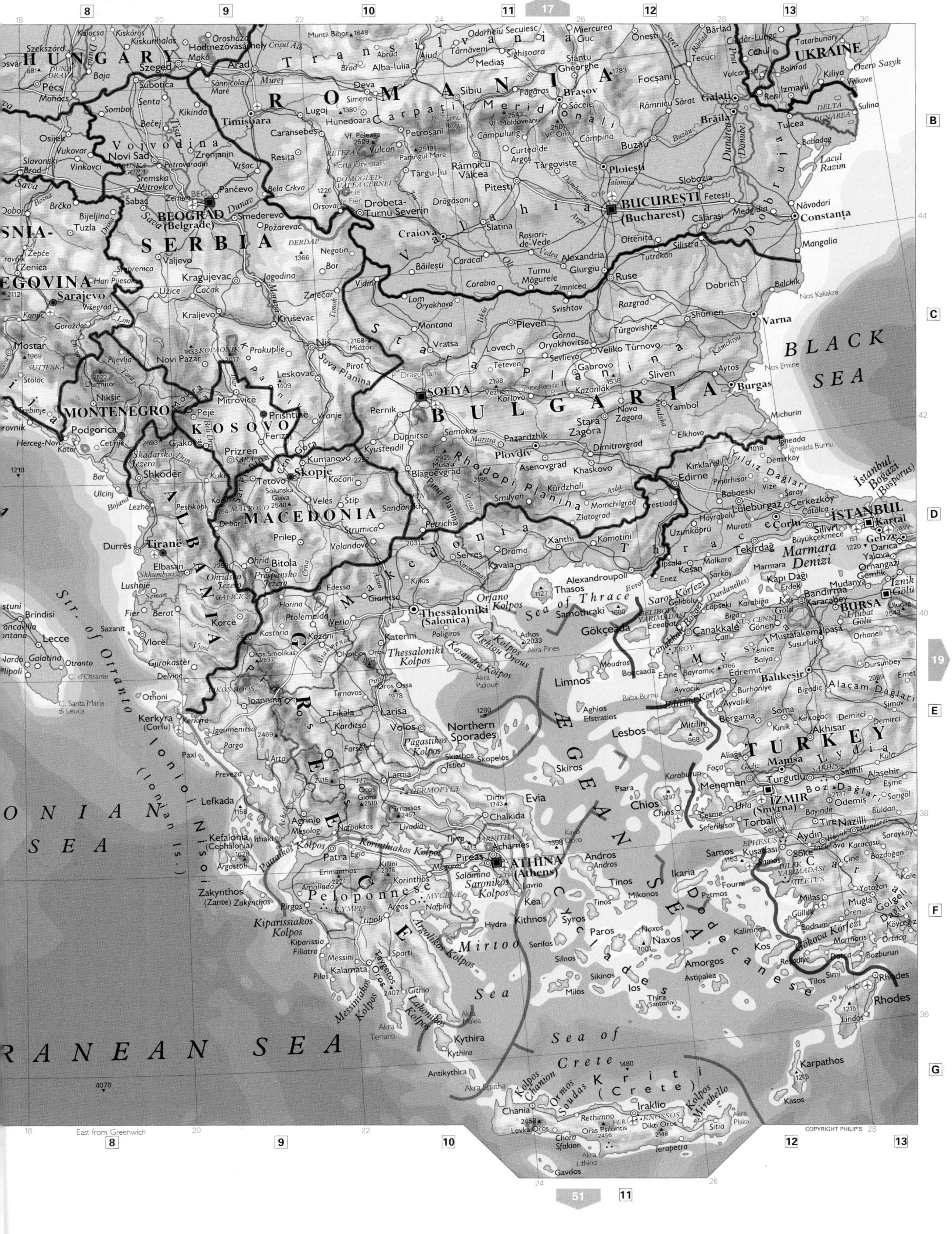
HUNGARY
ROMANIA
UKRAINE
SERBIA
BULGARIA
MONTENEGRO
KOSOVO
ALBANIA
MACEDONIA
GREECE
TURKEY
BLACK SEA
IONIAN SEA
MEDITERRANEAN SEA
Aegean Sea
Sea of Crete
Sea of Thrace
Mirtoo Sea
Marmara Denizi
Transilvania
Carpații Meridionali
Walachia
Dobruja
Stara Planina
Rhodopi Planina
Pindos Oros
Makedonia
Thraki
Peloponnese
Cyclades
Dodecanese
Kriti (Crete)
BEOGRAD (Belgrade)
BUCUREȘTI (Bucharest)
SOFIYA
ATHINA (Athens)
İSTANBUL
Sarajevo
Skopje
Tiranë
Podgorica
Prishtinë
Thessaloniki (Salonica)
İZMIR (Smyrna)
BURSA
Constanța
Varna
Burgas
Plovdiv
Edirne
Patra
Iraklio
Rhodes
Limnos
Lesbos
Chios
Samos
Evia
Naxos
Kythira
Karpathos
Gökçeada
Kerkyra (Corfu)
Kefalonia (Cephalonia)
Zakynthos (Zante)
Str. of Otranto
Brindisi
Lecce
East from Greenwich
COPYRIGHT PHILIP'S

1:47 000 000

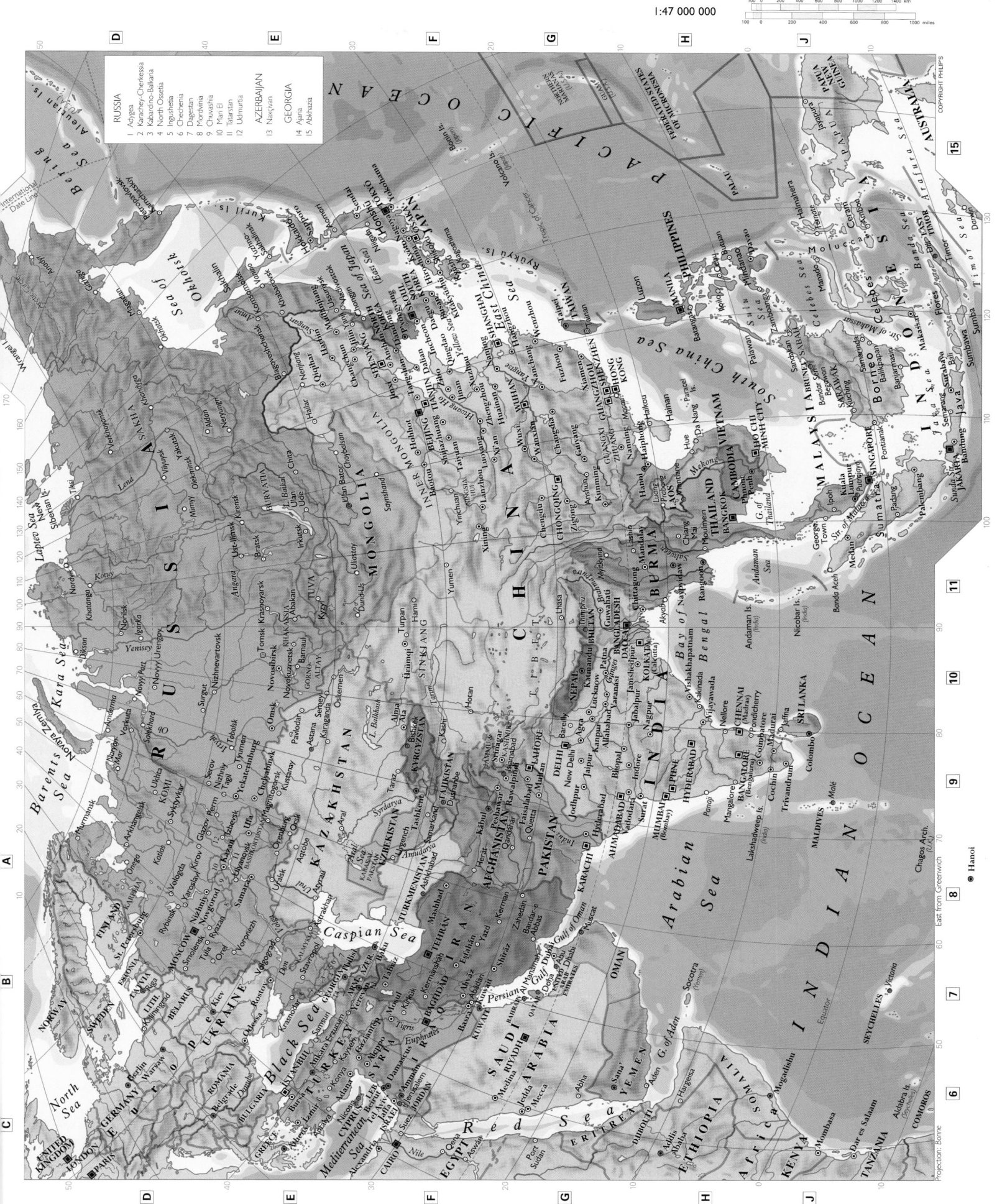

1:47 000 000

COPYRIGHT PHILIPS

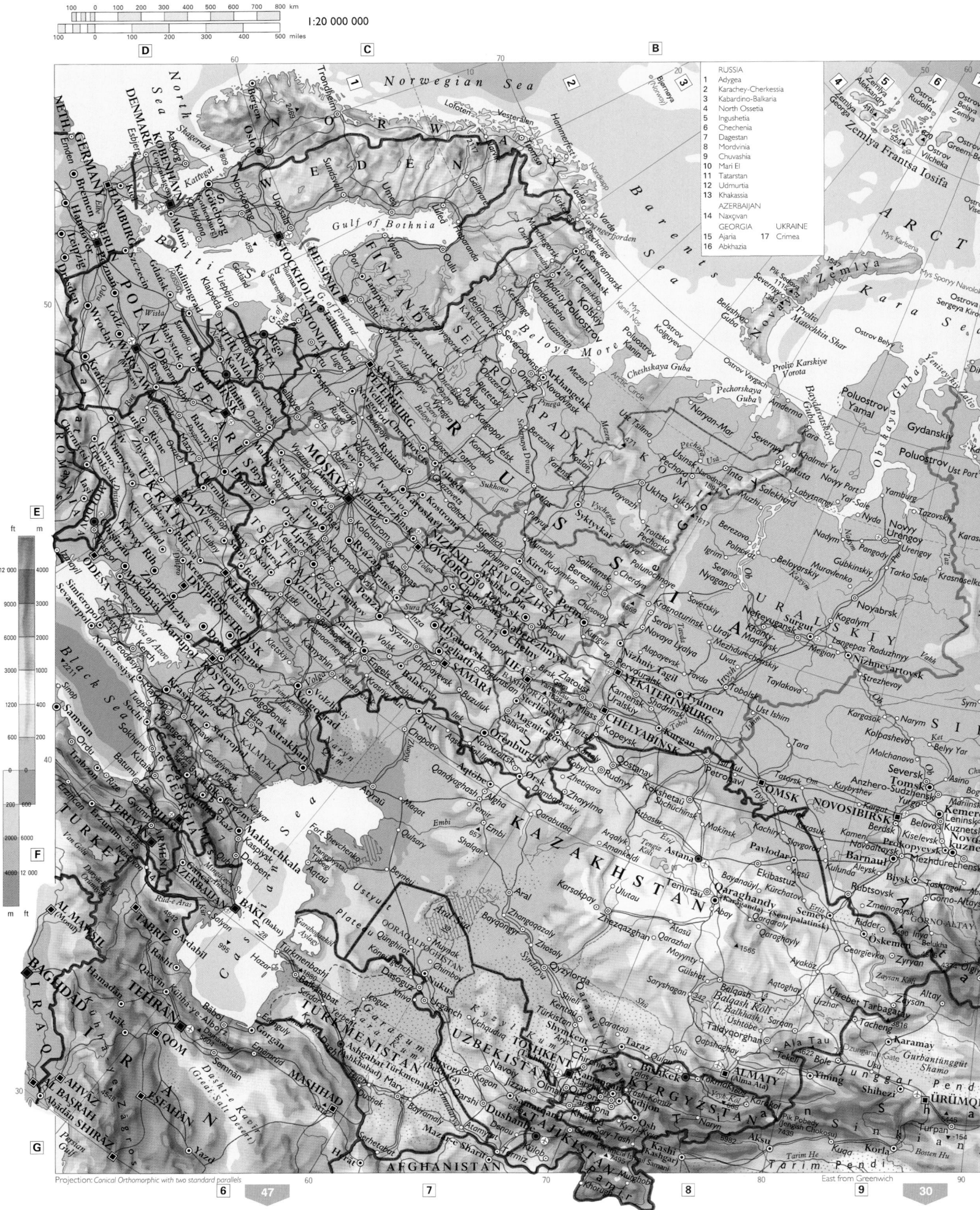

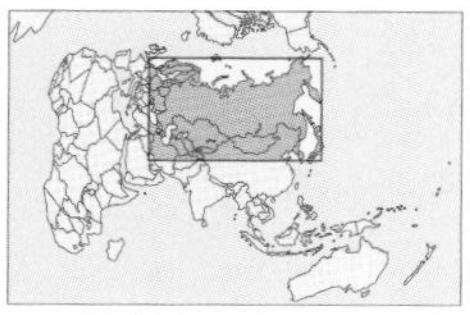

A 4 B 70 C

8 9 10 11 12 13 14 15 16 17 18 19

Mys Dezhneva
(East C.)

60

ARCTIC OCEAN

Laptev Sea

East Siberian Sea

Chukchi Sea

Bering Strait

Bering Sea

Severnaya Zemlya

Ostrov Shmidta
Mys Arkticheskiy
Ostrov Komsomolets
Ostrov Ushakova
Ostrov Pioner
Ostrov Oktyabrskoy Revolyutsii
Ostrov Bolshevik
Ostrova Sergeya Kirova

Ostrova Novosibirskiye
Ostrov Kotelnyy
Lyakhovskiye Ostrova
Ostrov Bolshoy Lyakhovskiy
Novaya Sibir
Ostrov Vrangelya

Proliv Vilkitskogo
Mys Chelyuskin

Poluostrov Taymyr
Gory Byrranga
Oz. Taymyr
Nordvik

D

Koryakskoye Nagorye

Sredinnyy Khrebet
Poluostrov Kamchatka
Petropavlovsk-Kamchatskiy

Kolymskoye Nagorye

Khrebet Cherskogo

Verkhoyansk
Verkhoyanskiy Khrebet

DALNEVOSTOCHNYY

Sea of Okhotsk

Sakhalin
Aleksandrovsk-Sakhalinskiy
Yuzhno-Sakhalinsk

Arctic Circle

Yakutsk
Lena

R U S S I A

Magadan
Okhotsk

Kurilskiye Ostrova

50

Stanovoy Khrebet

Yablonovyy Khrebet

Bratsk
Irkutsk
Ozero Baikal
Ulan Ude
Chita

Amur

Komsomolsk-na-Amure

Khabarovsk
Sikhote Alin

Hokkaido
SAPPORO
Hakodate

E

Krasnoyarsk

BURYATIYA

Ulaanbaatar

Hentiyn Nuruu

D o n g b e i
(Manchuria)

QIQIHAR
DAQING Yichan
HARBIN
JIXI
JIAMUSI

Vladivostok
Yanji

Sea of Japan
(East Sea)

Honshu

40

M O N G O L I A
(Aerhtai Shan)

Hangayn Nuruu

G o b i

C H I N A

CHANGCHUN
JILIN
FUSHUN
SHENYANG
ANSHAN
NORTH KOREA
PYONGYANG
NAMP'O

Hamhung
Wonsan

SEOUL
SOUTH KOREA
INCHEON
DAEJEON
DAEGU
BUSAN
GWANGJU

JAPAN
KYOTO
KOBE
OSAKA

BAOTOU
HOHHOT
BEIJING
TANGSHAN
DALIAN

ZHANGJIAKOU
CHIFENG
JINXI
Dandong
Yingkou

COPYRIGHT PHILIP'S

10 30 11 12 31 13 14
100 110 120 130

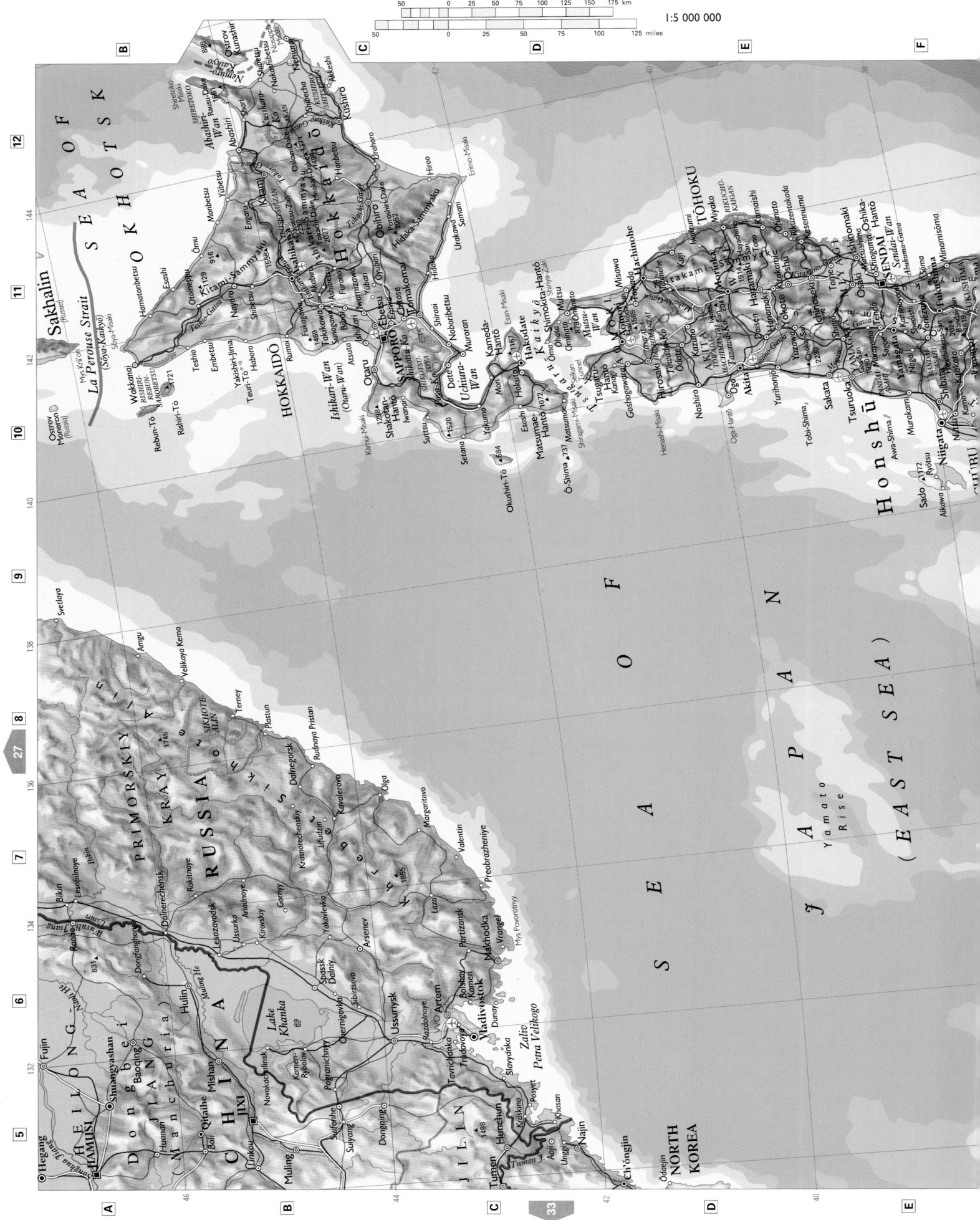

50 0 25 50 75 100 125 150 175 km

50 0 25 50 75 100 125 miles

1:5 000 000

B **C** **D** **E** **F**

SEA OF OKHOTSK

Sakhalin

La Pérouse Strait (Sōya-Kaikyō)

Ostrov Moneron (Russia)

Mys Krilʹon

HOKKAIDŌ

Wakkanai

SAPPORO

HOKKAIDO

Hakodate

Tsugaru-Hantō

Ishikari-Wan (Otaru-Wan)

Uchiura-Wan

Okushiri-Tō

Ō-Shima

Svetlaya

Angu

Velikaya Kema

Terney

Plastun

Rudnaya Pristanʹ

SIKHOTE-ALIN

PRIMORSKIY KRAY

RUSSIA

Dalnegorsk

Kavalerovo

Olga

Margaritovo

Valentin

Preobrazheniye

CHINA

Manchuria

Heilongjiang

Dongbei

HAMUSI

Hegang

Fujin

Shuangyashan

Huanan

Boli

Qitaihe

Mishan

JILIN

Lake Khanka

Ussuriysk

VLADIVOSTOK

Nakhodka

Zaliv Petra Velikogo

NORTH KOREA

Chʻŏngjin

Najin

Tumen

Hunchun

TOHOKU

Hachinohe

AKITA

Akita

Morioka

Niigata

Sado

SENDAI

Sendai-Wan

Honshū

CHŪBU

SEA OF JAPAN (EAST SEA)

Yamato Rise

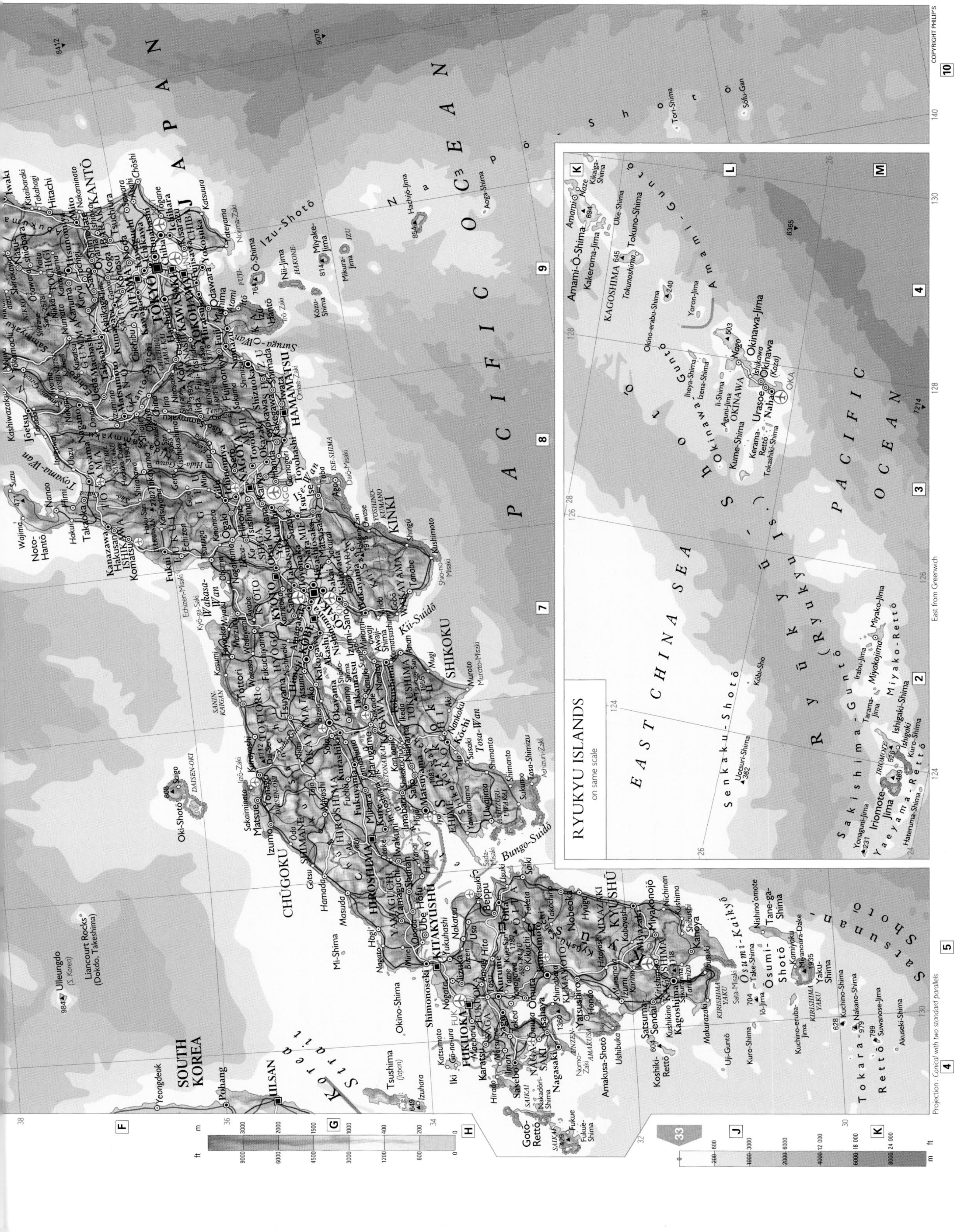

J A P A N

PACIFIC OCEAN

EAST CHINA SEA

SOUTH KOREA

KANTŌ

TOKYO
KAWASAKI
YOKOHAMA
CHIBA
NAGOYA
HAMAMATSU
KYOTO
KOBE
OSAKA
HIROSHIMA
KITAKYUSHU
FUKUOKA
NAGASAKI
KAGOSHIMA

CHŪGOKU
SHIKOKU
KYUSHU
KINKI
KIso

ULSAN
Pohang
Yeongdeok
Ulleungdo (S. Korea)
Liancourt Rocks (Dokdo, Takeshima)

Tsushima (Japan)

Kōrai Strait / Korea Strait

Izu-Shotō
Hachijō-Jima
Miyake-Jima

RYUKYU ISLANDS
on same scale

Amami-Ō-Shima
KAGOSHIMA
Okinawa-Jima
OKINAWA
Naha
Okino-erabu-Shima
Tokuno-Shima
Kakeroma-Jima

Sakishima-Guntō
Yaeyama-Shima
Miyako-Rettō
Iriomote
Ishigaki-Shima
Yonaguni-Jima

Senkaku-Shotō

Ryūkyū Islands
Amami-Guntō
Okinawa-Guntō

Satsunan-Shotō
Tokara-Rettō
Ōsumi-Shotō
Tane-ga-Shima
Yaku-Shima

Goto-Rettō
Fukue-Shima

Bungo-Suidō
Kii-Suidō
Tosa-Wan
Ise-Wan
Wakasa-Wan
Tōyama-Wan
Suruga-Wan

Noto-Hantō

East from Greenwich

Projection: Conical with two standard parallels

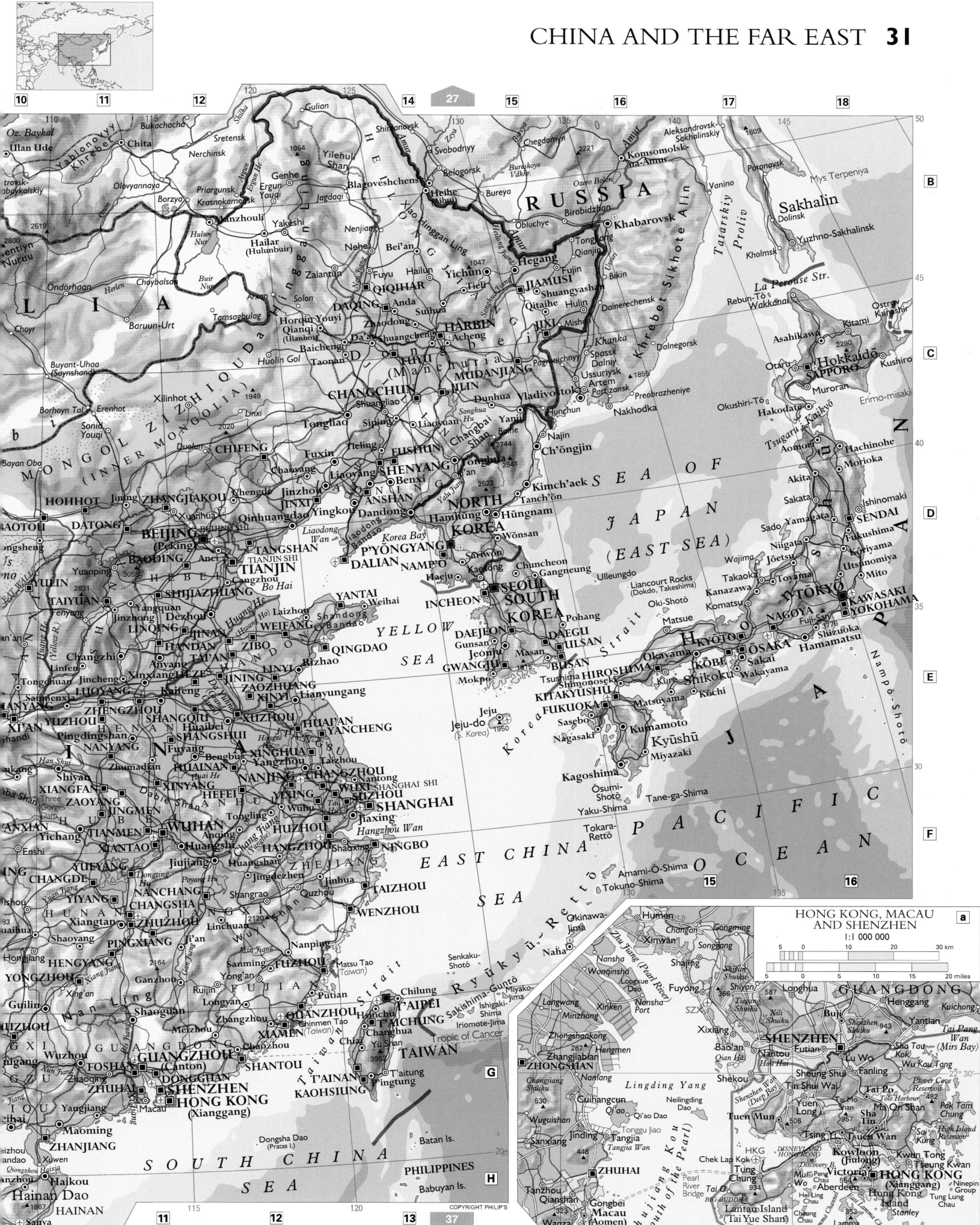

HONG KONG, MACAU
AND SHENZHEN
1:1 000 000

COPYRIGHT PHILIP'S

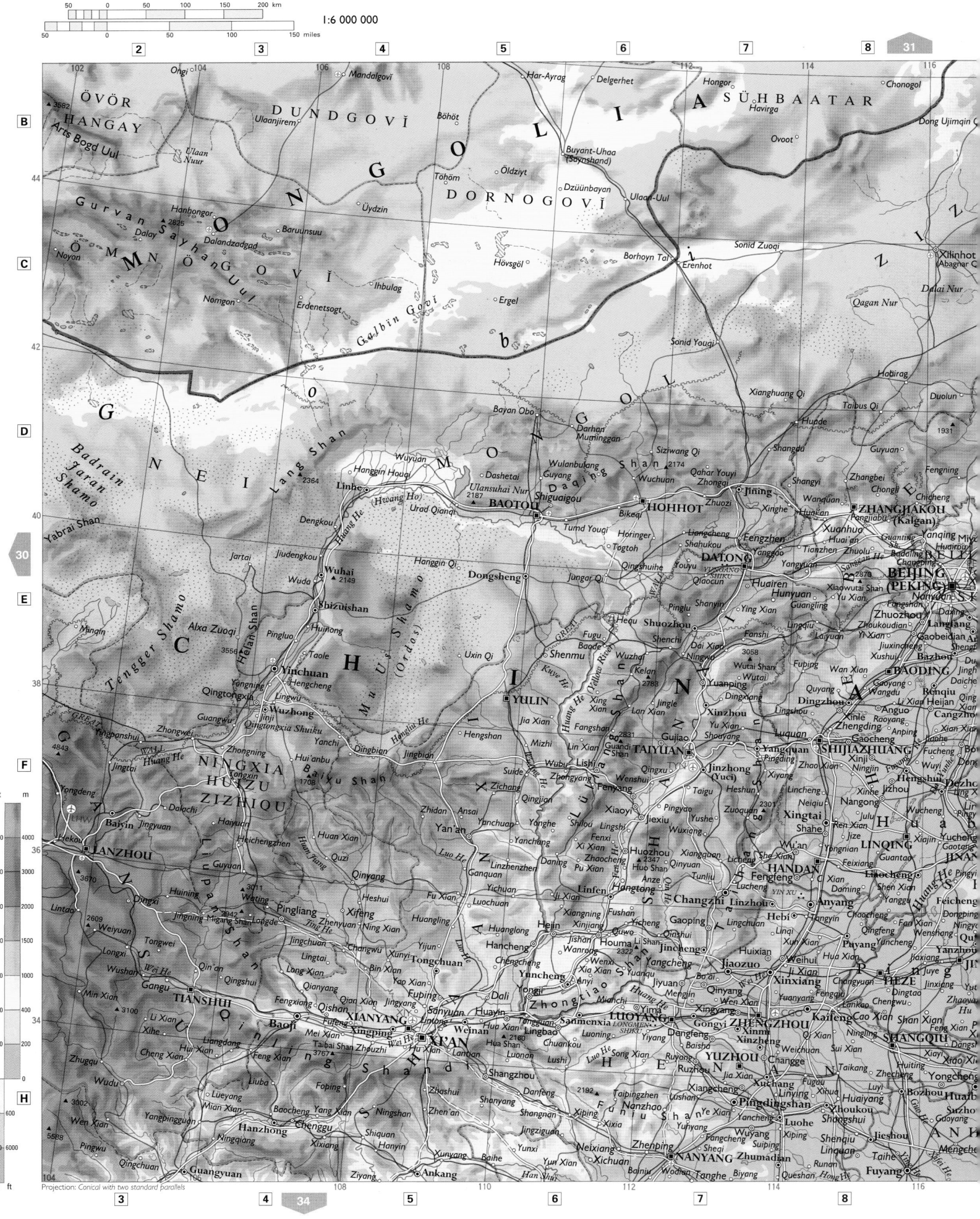

Projection: Conical with two standard parallels

Horqin Youyi Qianqi (Ulanhot)
Zhenlai
Maoxing Zhaoyuan
HARBIN
Bin Xian
HXI
Novokachalinsk
Lake Khanka
Huolin Gol
Hulin He
Baicheng
Da'an
Songhua Jiang
Shuangcheng Acheng
Shangzhi
Linkou
Muling
RUSSIA
Xi Ujimqin Qi
Tuquan
Taonan
Songhua
Changchunling
Yimianpo
Yushu
Hailin
Maqiaohe
Suifenhe
Golenki
1949
Jarud Qi
Ar Horqin Qi
Tongyu
Qagan Nur Qian
Gorlos
FUYU
Beitaolaizhao
Wuchang
Shenjingzi
Kaoshan
Shonhetun
Shulan
Mingyuegou
Dongning
Ussuriyska
MUDANJIANG
Xiaobenzi
Pogranichnyy
Nong'an
Dehui
Gangyang
Wulajie
Ning'an
Muling
Suiyang

YELLOW SEA
(Huang Hai)

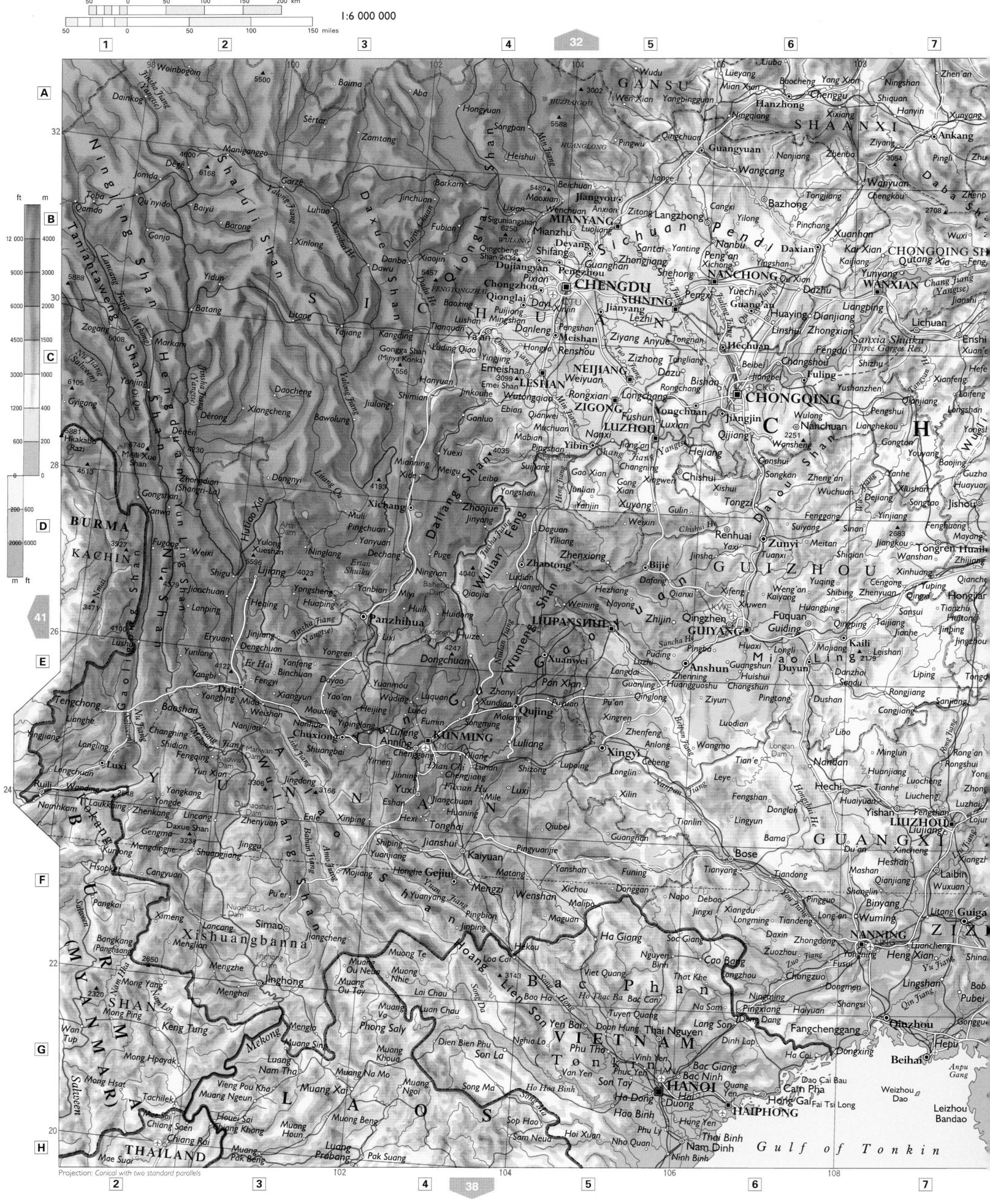

33
A
B
C
D
E
F
G
H
8
9
10
11
12
13
14
HENAN
ANHUI
JIANGSU
ZHEJIANG
JIANGXI
HUNAN
FUJIAN
GUANGDONG
TAIWAN
NANYANG
XINYANG
XIANGFAN
ZAOYANG
HEFEI
HUAINAN
NANJING
CHANGZHOU
WUXI
SUZHOU
SHANGHAI
SHANGHAI SHI
HANGZHOU
XIAOSHAN
NINGBO
HUZHOU
JINGMEN
TIANMEN
XIANTAO
WUHAN
YUEYANG
CHANGDE
YIYANG
CHANGSHA
ZHUZHOU
PINGXIANG
NANCHANG
HENGYANG
YONGZHOU
WENZHOU
TAIZHOU
FUZHOU
QUANZHOU
XIAMEN (Amoy)
T'AIPEI
T'AICHUNG
T'AINAN
KAOHSIUNG
GUANGZHOU (CANTON)
HUIZHOU
DONGGUAN
SHENZHEN
FOSHAN
JIANGMEN
ZHONGSHAN
ZHUHAI
HONG KONG (XIANGGANG)
SHANTOU
ZHANJIANG (Xiashan)
Macau
Shaoguan
Meizhou
Chaozhou
Jieyang
Wuzhou
Guilin
Dongting Hu
Poyang Hu
Tai Hu
Chang Jiang (Yangtse)
Tropic of Cancer
Taiwan Strait
Luzon Strait
SOUTH CHINA SEA
Dongsha Dao (Pratas I.)
East from Greenwich
112
114
116
118
120
122
32
30
28
26
24
22
20
COPYRIGHT PHILIP'S

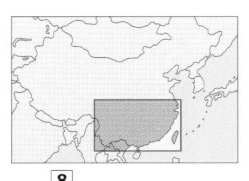

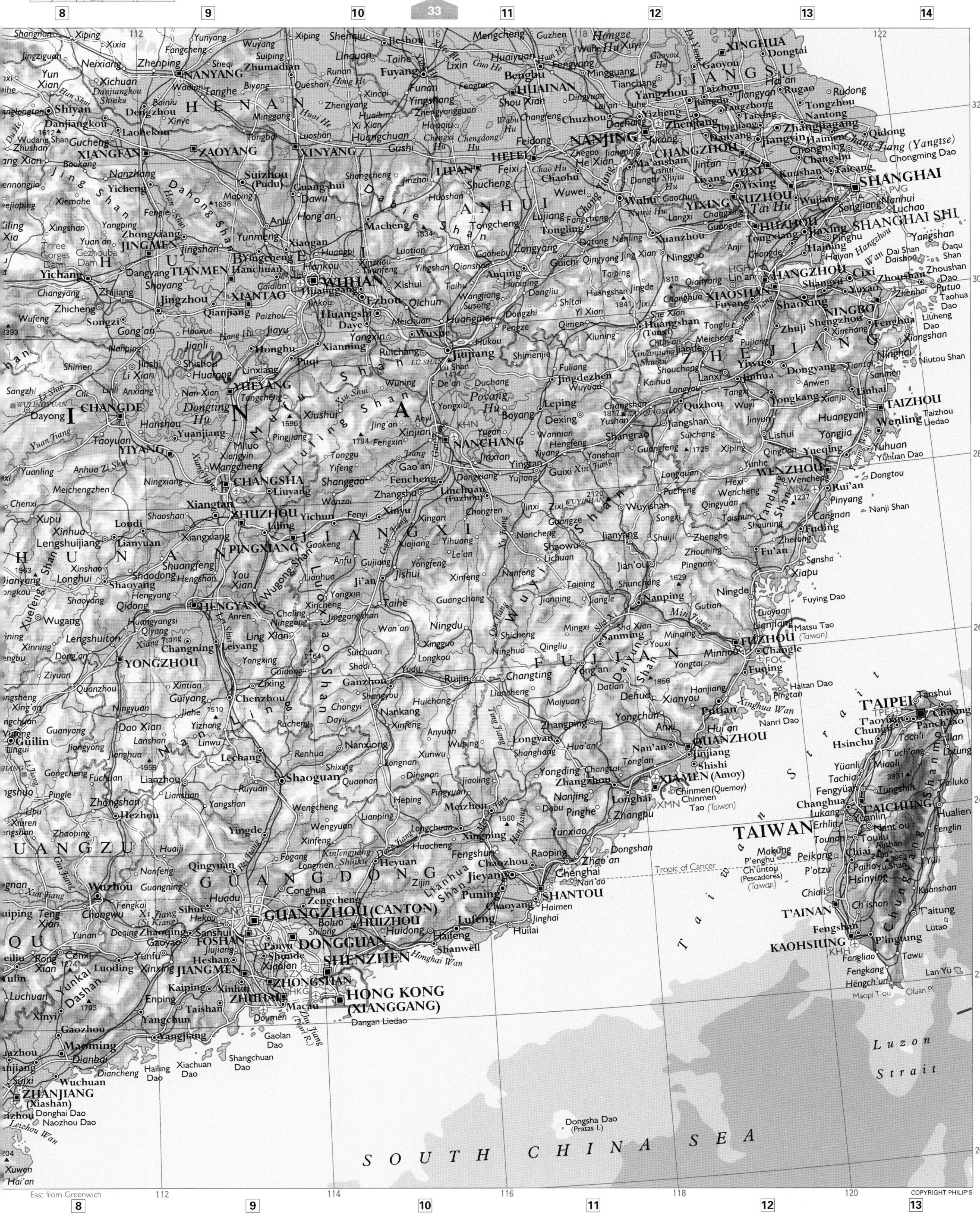

1:12 500 000

Projection: Mercator

East from Greenwich

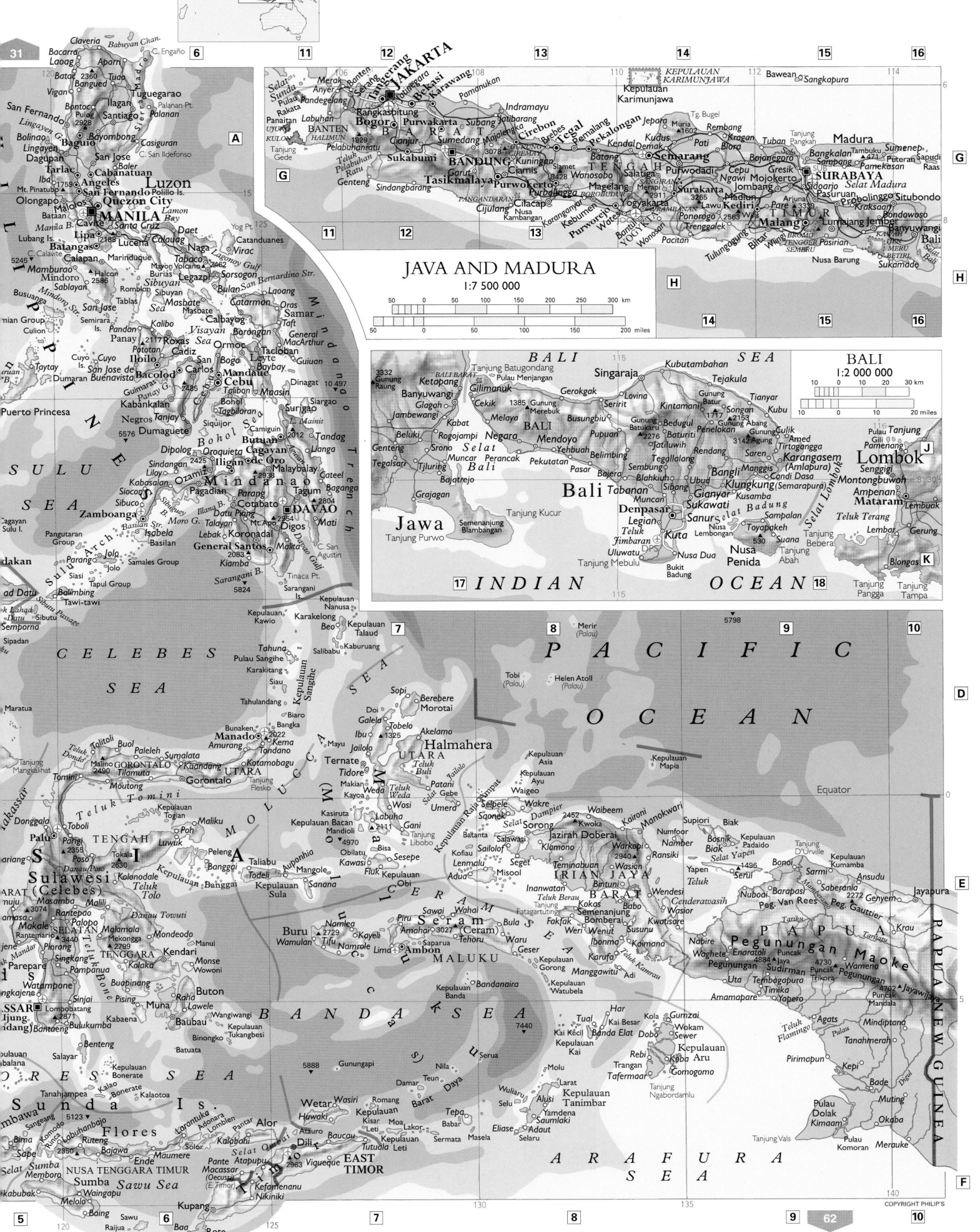

JAVA AND MADURA
1:7 500 000

BALI
1:2 000 000

1:6 000 000

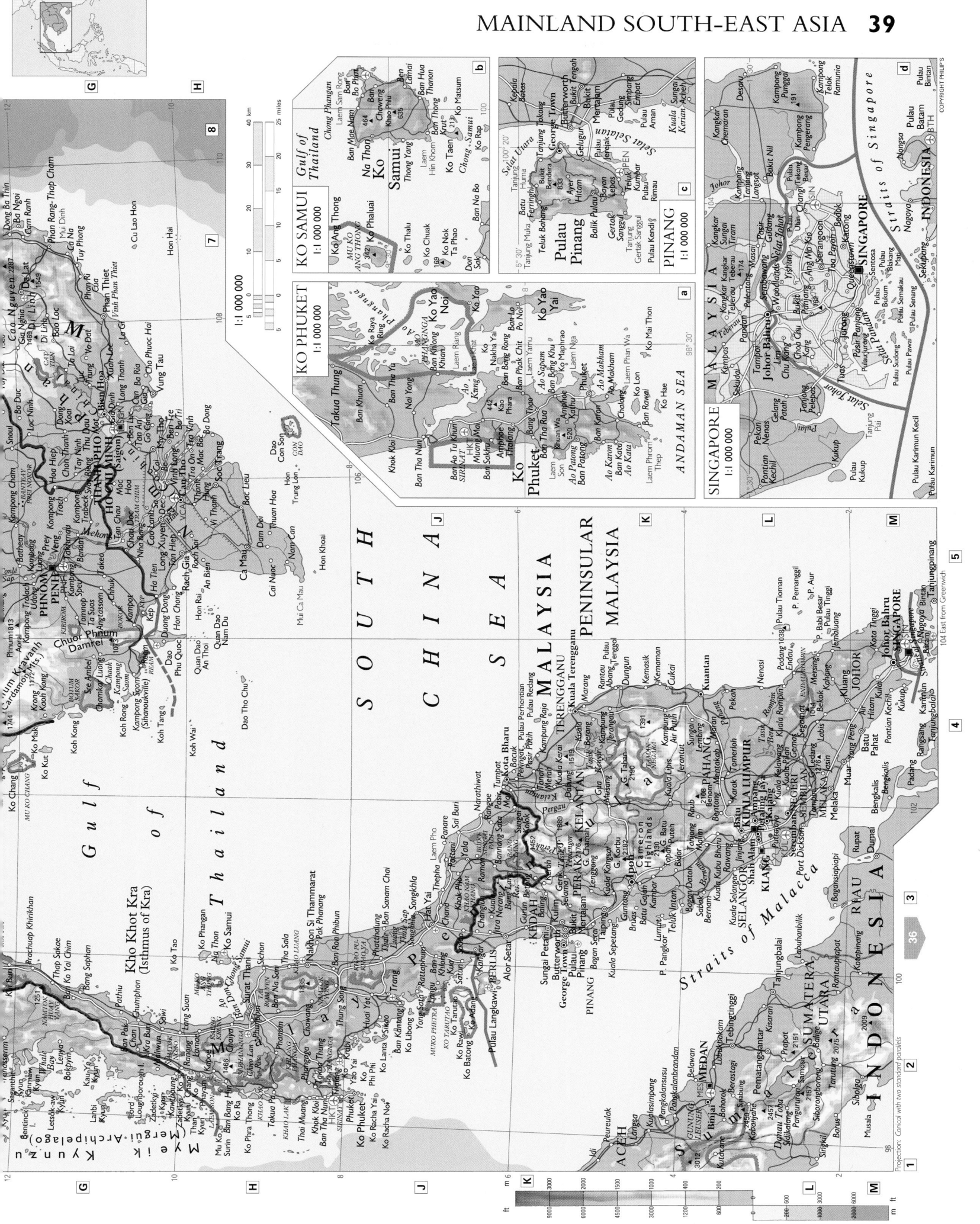

KO SAMUI
1:1 000 000

PINANG
1:1 000 000

KO PHUKET
1:1 000 000

SINGAPORE
1:1 000 000

Pulau Pinang

Gulf of Thailand

Ko Samui

MU KO ANG THONG

ANDAMAN SEA

Ko Phuket

SOUTH CHINA SEA

PENINSULAR MALAYSIA

MALAYSIA

Straits of Singapore

INDONESIA

Gulf of Thailand

Kho Khot Kra (Isthmus of Kra)

Kyunzu (Mergui Archipelago)

Straits of Malacca

SUMATERA UTARA

INDONESIA

Projection: Conical with two standard parallels

1:10 000 000

continuation southwards
on same scale

Projection: _Conical with two standard parallels_

12
13
14
30
15
16
17
18
19
20
21
22
B
C
D
E
F
G
H
J
K
L
M
38
39
JIANG UYGUR ZIZHIQU
(SINKIANG)
Muz Tag
7723
Pulu
Hoh Xil Shan
Kunlun Shankou
QINGHAI
Gyaring Hu
4237
Ngoring Hu
Bayan Har Shan
6094
Huang He
Dogai Coring
Tanggula (Dangla) Shan
CHINA
XIZANG ZIZHIQU
(TIBET)
Yushu
Dainkog
5180
Tanggula Shankou
Amdo
Nangqên
Dêgê
Garzê
Baqên
Dêngqên
Qamdo
Siling Co
4495
Nagqu
Ombu
Tangra Yumco
Gyaring Co
Xainza
Nam Co
4627
Lhari
Nu Jiang
Lhorong
Xinlong
SICHUAN
Yidun
Litang
Yajiang
Zhaxizê
Markam
Nyainqentanglha Shan
7088
Lhünzub
Gongbo'gyamda
Namcha Barwa
7756
Riga
Goqên
Lancang Jiang (Mekong)
Jinsha Jiang
Kangrinboqe Feng (Kailash)
6714
Mapam Yumco
Coqên
Dongco
Lhasa
Maquan He (Tsangpo)
Xigazê
Gyangzê
Yarlung Zangbo Jiang
Nang Xian
Jido
Zayü
6740
Zhongdian
7059
Zhongba
Saga
Lhazê
Simikot
Mugu
Jumla
Mustang
NEPAL
Dhaulagiri
8167
Annapurna
8078
Muktinath
Xixabangma Feng
8012
Pokhara
Nyalam
Mt. Everest
8850
Kanchenjunga
8598
KATHMANDU
Bhaktapur
SIKKIM
Thimphu
Gangtok
Punakha
BHUTAN
Tongsa Dzong
Taga Dzong
Gamba
Dinggyê
K'ula Kangri
7553
Cona
Lhünzê
7090
Kangto
ARUNACHAL PRADESH
Dibrugarh
Tinsukia
Sibsagar
North Lakhimpur
Jorhat
Hukawng Valley
KACHIN
Putao
Weixi
5596
Lijiang
Jianchuan
Dali
Yunlong
YUNNAN
Baoshan
Tengchong
Myitkyina
Bhamo
Lashio
Nepalganj
Lakhimpur
Bahraich
Gonda
Basti
LUCKNOW
Faizabad
Gorakhpur
Rae Bareli
Sultanpur
Azamgarh
Jaunpur
VARANASI
Mirzapur
Sasaram
Aurangabad
Gaya
Siwan
Chhapra
BIHAR
Motihari
Muzaffarpur
Darbhanga
Birganj
Raxaul
Bettiah
PATNA
Ara
Munger
Bhagalpur
Katihar
Purnia
Kishanganj
Shiliguri
Darjiling
Jalpaiguri
Rangpur
Dinajpur
Bogra
Rajshahi
Pabna
Tangail
Mymensingh
Sylhet
Shillong
MEGHALAYA
Cherrapunji
GUWAHATI
Tezpur
Nagaon
Dimapur
Kohima
NAGALAND
Imphal
MANIPUR
Silchar
Aizawl
MIZORAM
Agartala
TRIPURA
Comilla
DHAKA
BANGLADESH
Narayanganj
Chandpur
Khulna
Jessore
Barisal
Patuakhali
Noakhali
CHITTAGONG
Cox's Bazar
Brahmaputra
Giridih
DHANBAD
Hazaribag
JHARKHAND
ASANSOL
Durgapur
RANCHI
JAMSHEDPUR
Barddhaman
Haora
KOLKATA
(CALCUTTA)
Kharagpur
Haldia
Raurkela
Sambalpur
Bilaspur
Korba
CHHATTISGARH
Raipur
BHILAINAGAR-DURG
Dhamtari
Baleshwar
Bhadrak
Cuttack
Bhubaneshwar
Puri
ODISHA
Chilka L.
Brahmapur
Jagdalpur
Vizianagaram
VISHAKHAPATNAM
Kakinada
VIJAYAWADA
Machilipatnam
Mouths of the Ganges
The Sundarbans
BAY OF BENGAL
INDIAN OCEAN
Sittwe (Akyab)
Ramree I.
Cheduba I.
Sandoway
Arakan Coast
Chin Hills
BURMA (MYANMAR)
MANDALAY
Monywa
Sagaing
Myingyan
Pakokku
Meiktila
Magwe
NAYPYIDAW
Pyinmana
Taunggyi
SHAN
KAYAH
Prome
Henzada
Bassein
Pegu
RANGOON
IRRAWADDY
G. of Martaban
Moulmein
MON
Mouths of the Irrawaddy
Preparis North Channel
Preparis South Channel
Coco Kyunzu
Moscos Is.
Tavoy
THAILAND
Chiang Mai
Lampang
Tak
Tropic of Cancer
East from Greenwich
COPYRIGHT PHILIP'S

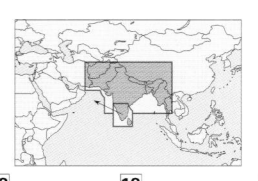

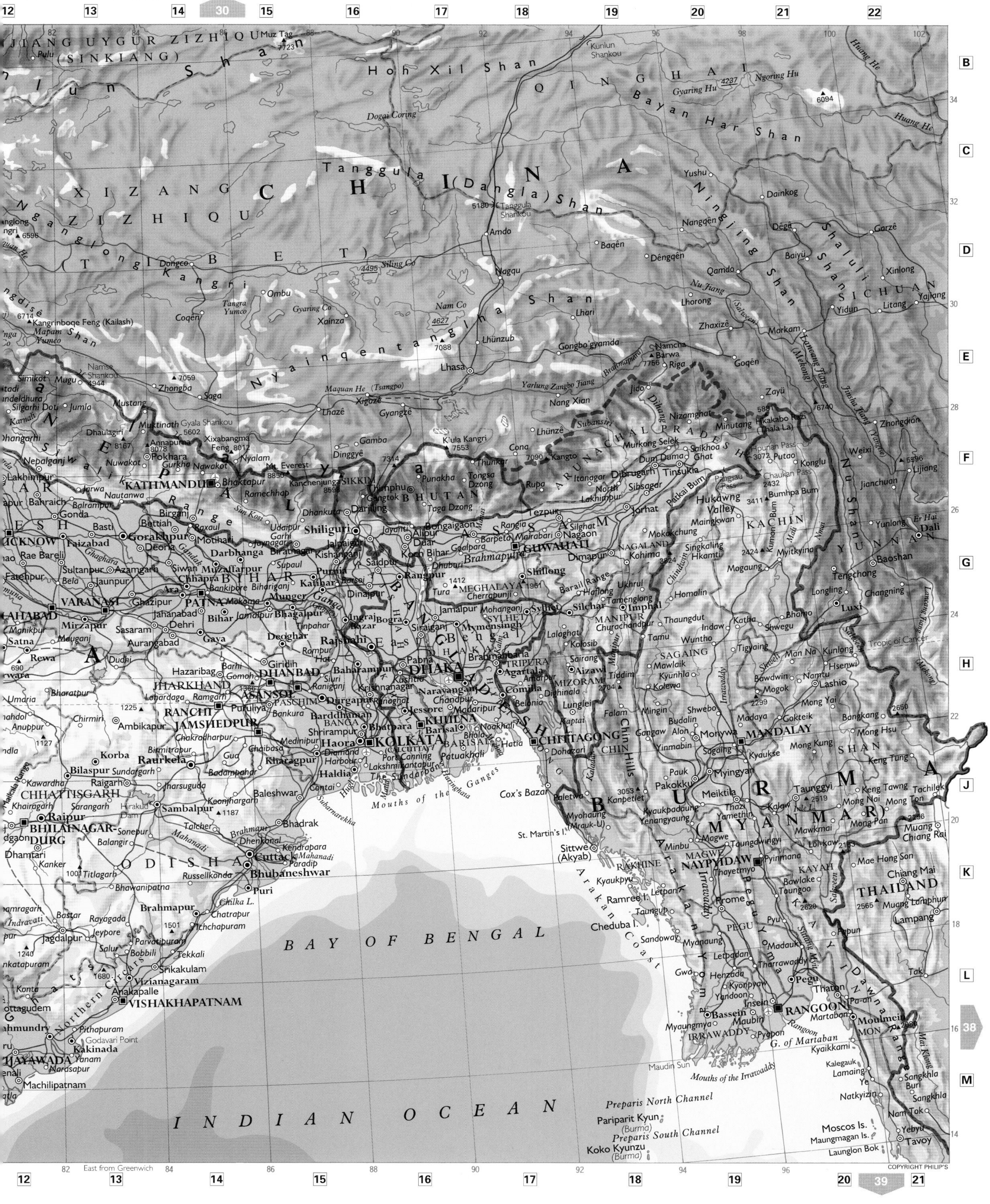

1:6 000 000

JAMMU AND KASHMIR
on same scale
AFGHANISTAN
CHINA
KHYBER PAKHTUNKHWA (N.W. FRONTIER)
Gilgit-Baltistan (Northern Areas)
JAMMU & KASHMIR
ISLAMABAD
RAWALPINDI
SRINAGAR
PUNJAB
HIMACHAL PRADESH
Aksai Chin
Karakoram Pass
Siachen Glacier
K2
Nanga Parbat
Ladakh Range
Zaskar Mountains
Kunlun Shan
Nganglong Kangri
Gangdisê Shan
CHINA
XIZANG ZIZHIQU (TIBET)
NEPAL
KATHMANDU
Mt. Everest (Chomolungma or Sagarmatha)
Annapurna
Dhaulagiri
SIKKIM
BHUTAN
Thimphu
UTTARAKHAND
UTTAR PRADESH
LUCKNOW
KANPUR
ALLAHABAD
VARANASI
BIHAR
PATNA
JHARKHAND
RANCHI
DHANBAD
JAMSHEDPUR
CHHATTISGARH
MADHYA PRADESH
JABALPUR
PASCHIM BANGA
KOLKATA
ODISHA
BANGLADESH
DHAKA
KHULNA
ASSAM
Mouths of the Ganges
The Sandheads
Garo Hills
East from Greenwich
COPYRIGHT PHILIP'S

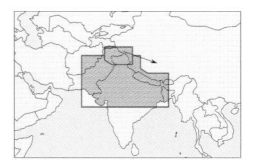

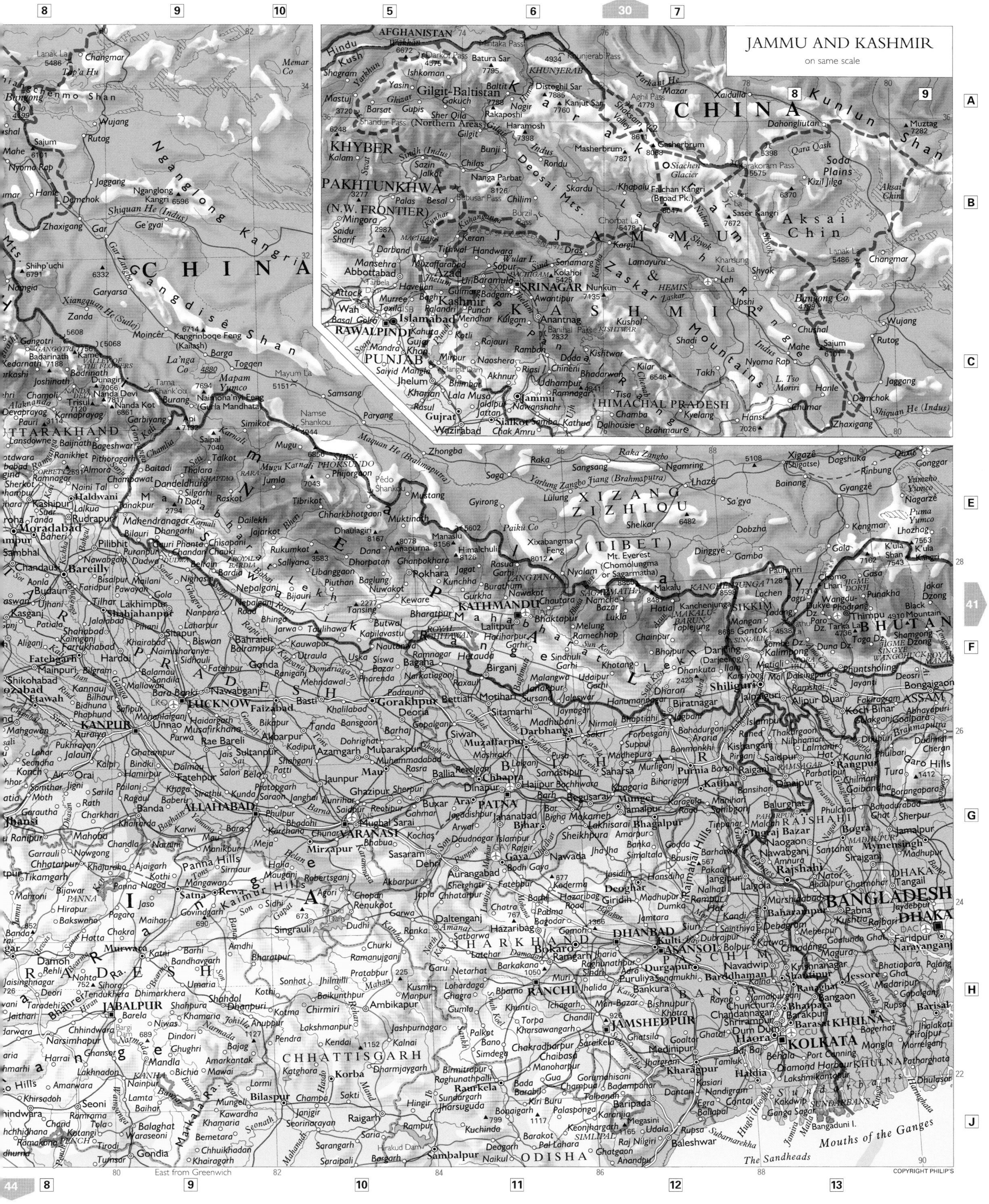

1:6 000 000

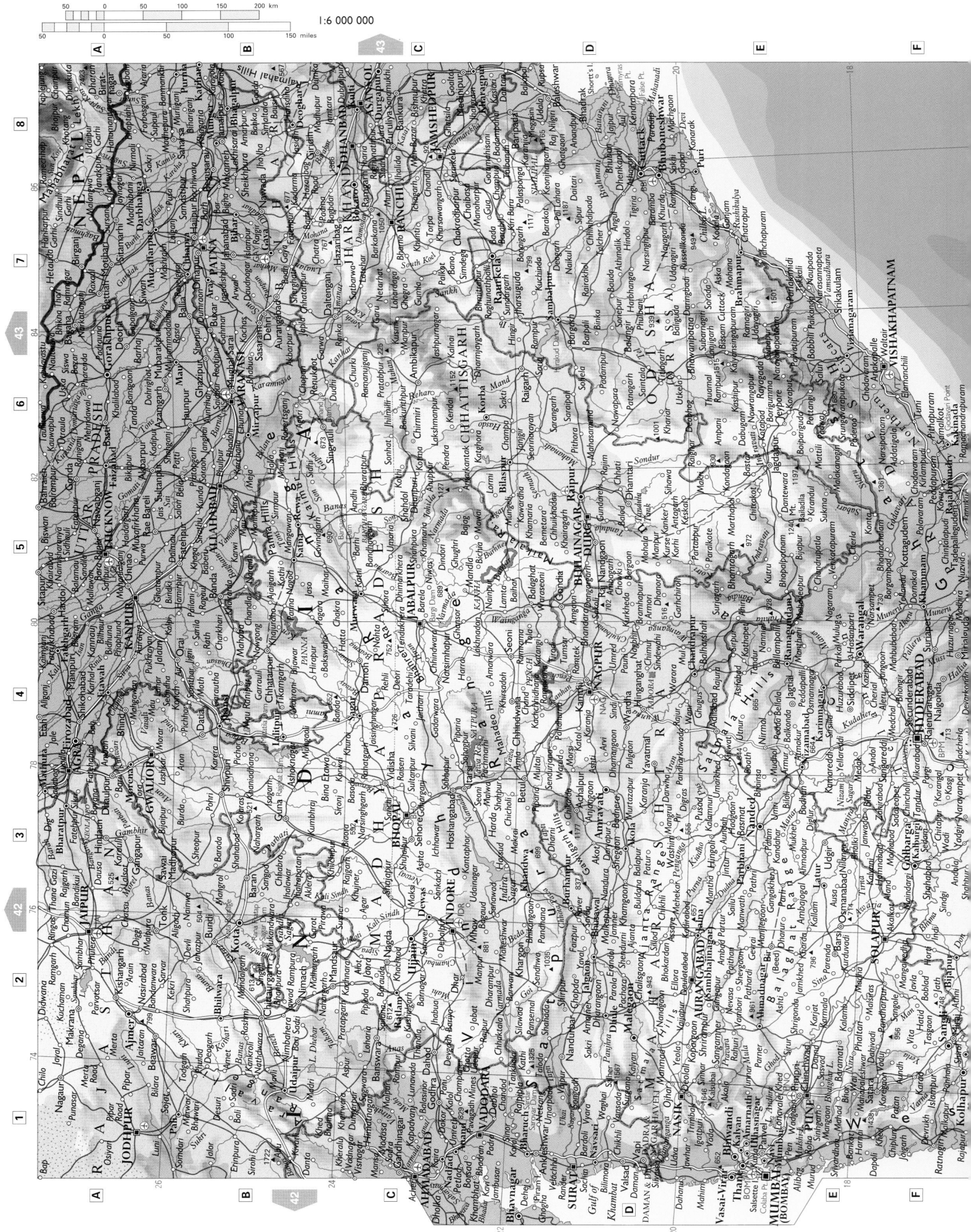

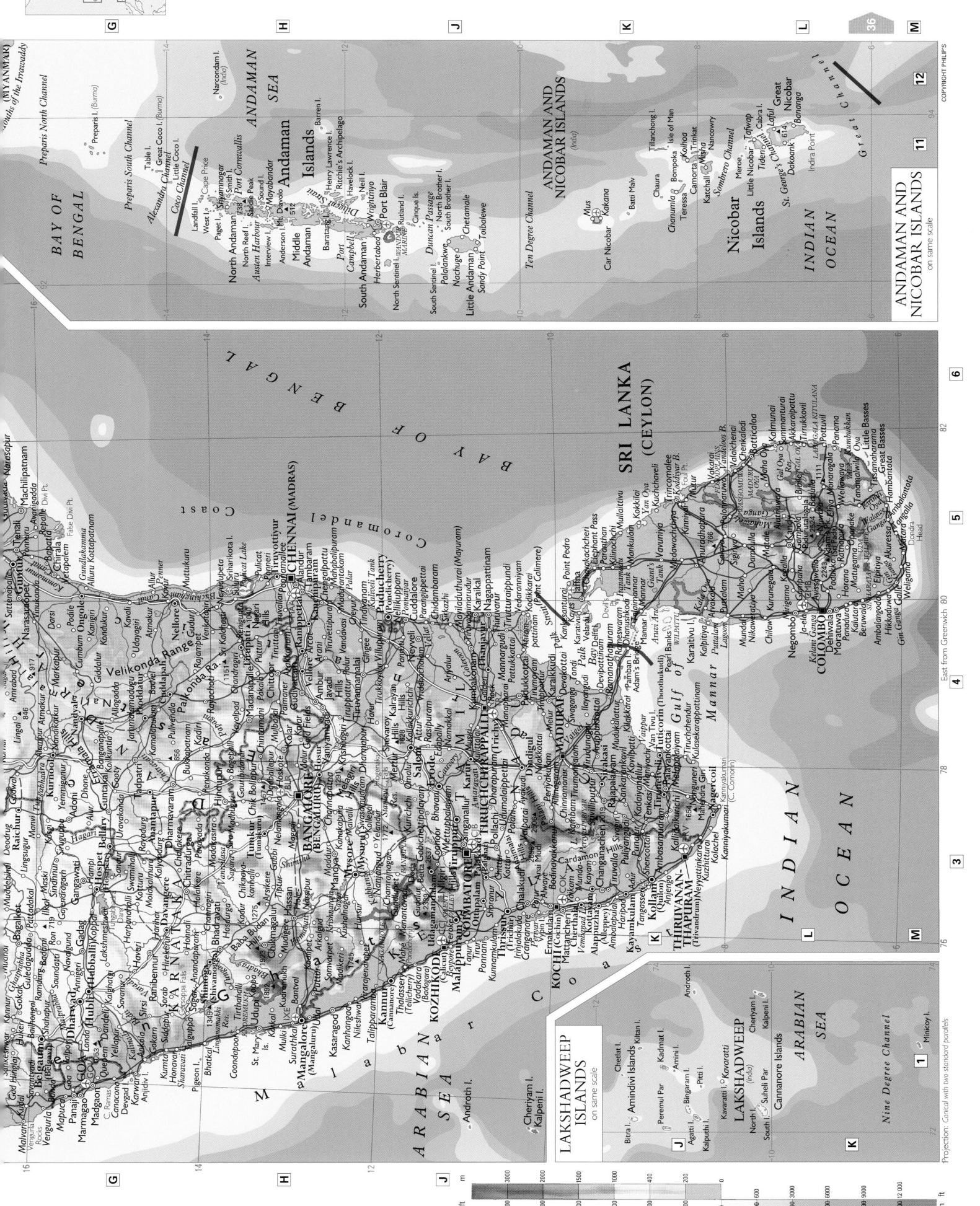

LAKSHADWEEP
ISLANDS
on same scale

ANDAMAN AND
NICOBAR ISLANDS
on same scale

Projection: Conical with two standard parallels

1:7 000 000

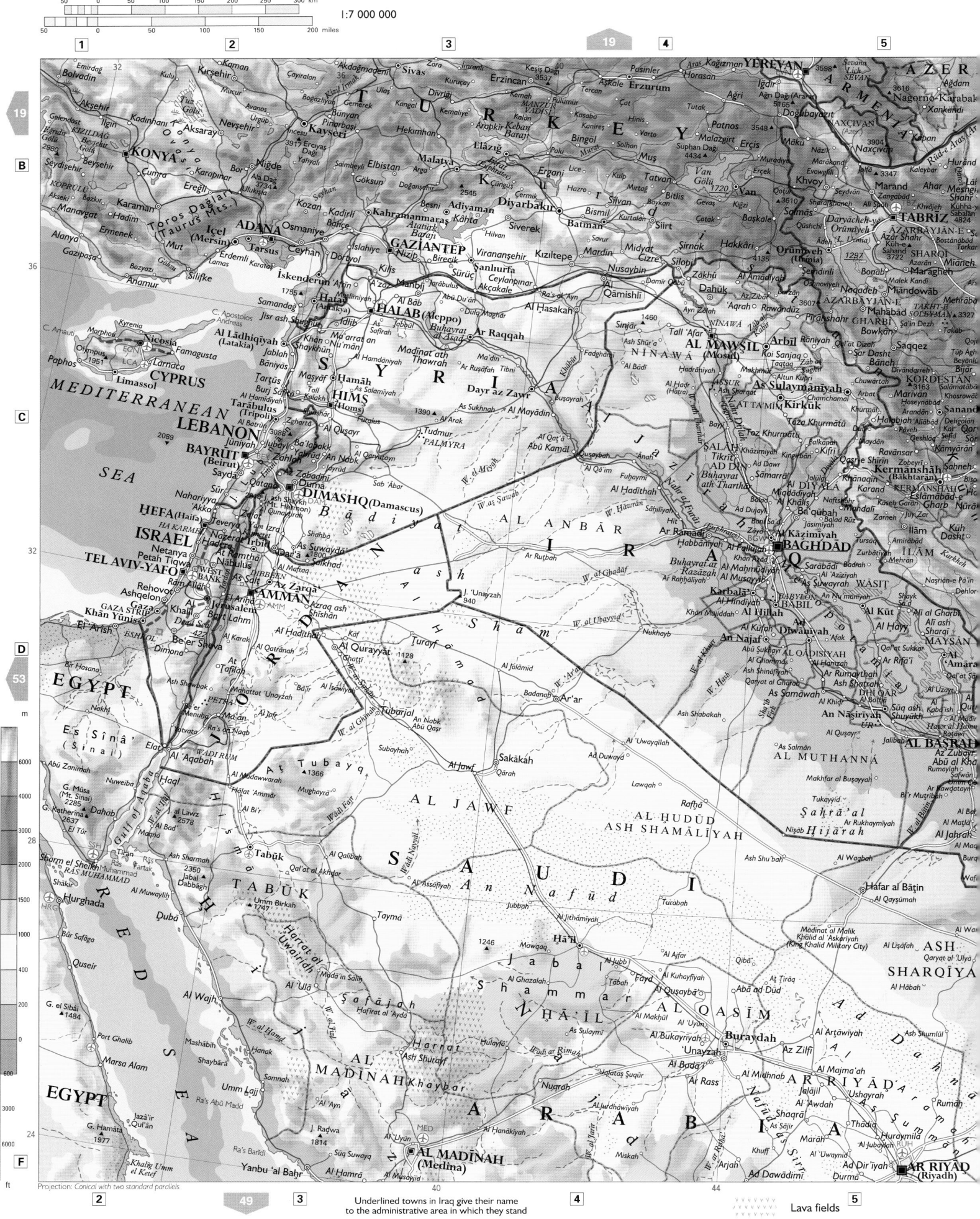

Underlined towns in Iraq give their name
to the administrative area in which they stand

Lava fields

6
7
8
26
9
10
TURKMENISTAN
Garagum
(Kara Kum)
Türkmenbashi
Ashgabat
Mary
Türkmenabat (Chardzhou)
BAKI (Baku)
CASPIAN SEA
Kopet Dagh
GOLESTĀN
KHORĀSĀN-E SHEMĀLĪ
MASHHAD
Gorgān
Sārī
Rasht
GĪLĀN
MĀZANDARĀN
Reshteh-ye Kūhhā-ye Alborz (Elburz Mts.)
Damāvand 5604
TEHRĀN
KARAJ
QAZVĪN
QOM
SEMNĀN
Dasht-e Kavīr (Great Salt Desert)
KHORĀSĀN-E RAZAVĪ
Herāt
AFGHANISTAN
FARĀH
40
HAMADĀN
MARKAZĪ
Arāk
Kāshān
I R A N
ESFAHĀN
Yazd
YAZD
Dasht-e Lūt
KHORĀSĀN-E JANŪBĪ
Zābol
Dasht-e Mārgow
NĪMRŪZ
Zāhedān
PAKISTAN
Kermān
KERMĀN
Shīrāz
FĀRS
BŪSHEHR
AHVĀZ
KHŪZESTĀN
Ābādān
KUWAIT
AL KUWAYT (Kuwait)
SĪSTĀN VA BALŪCHESTĀN
HORMOZGĀN
Bandar-e Abbās
Str. of Hormuz
PERSIAN GULF
BAHRAIN
Al Manāmah
QATAR
Ad Dawhah (Doha)
Ad Dammām
DUBAYY (Dubai)
Abū Zāby (Abu Dhabi)
UNITED ARAB EMIRATES
OMAN
Gulf of Oman
Makran
Chāh Bahār
B
C
D
E
F
49
East from Greenwich
COPYRIGHT PHILIP'S

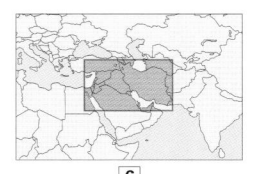

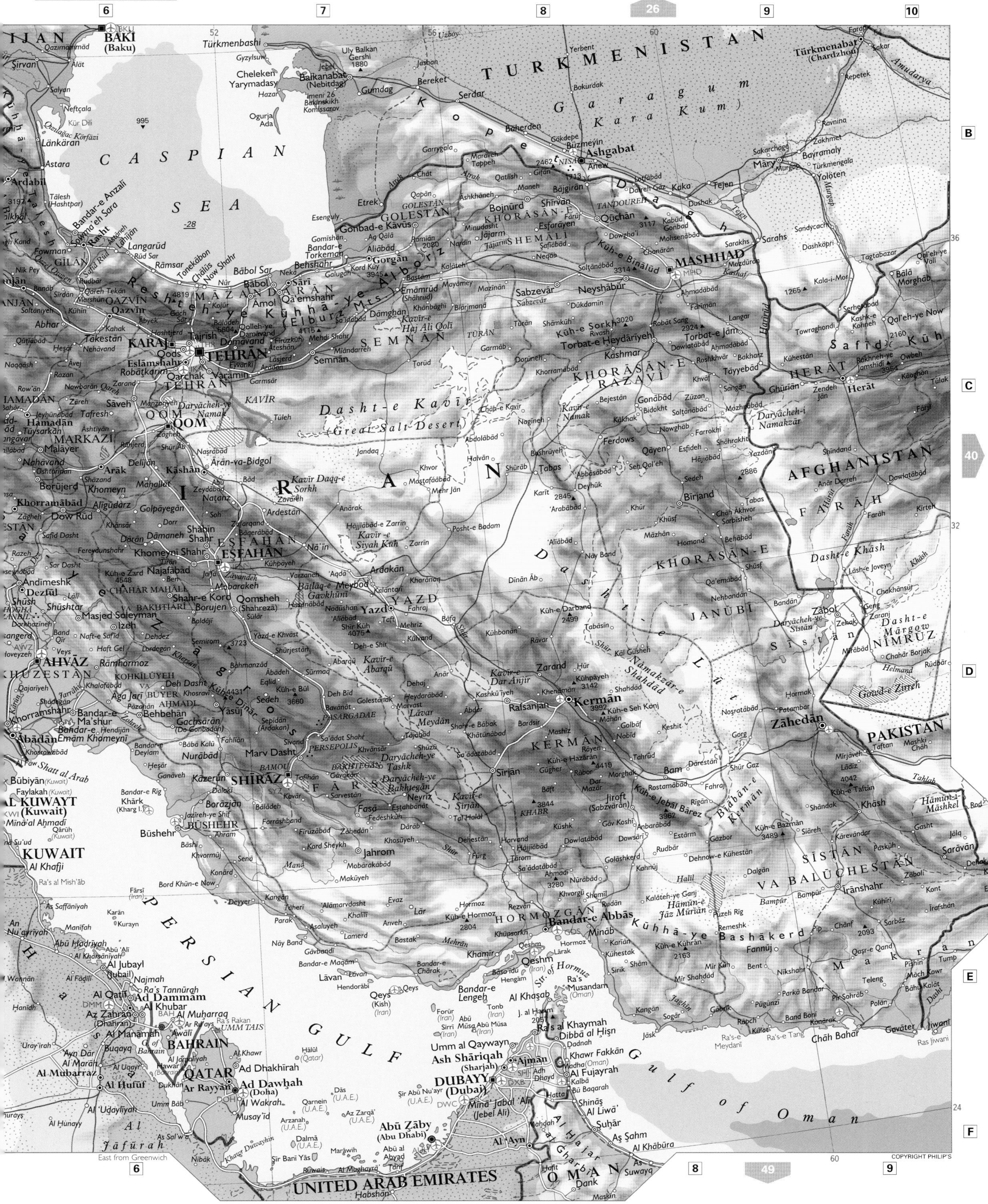

1:2 500 000

10 0 10 20 30 40 50 60 70 80 100 km
10 0 10 20 30 40 50 60 miles

46

CYPRUS
Paphos
PFO
Episkopi
Kivides
Zyyi
Limassol
Akrotiri Bay
Episkopi Bay
C. Gata

Hims
(Homs)
Al Hamidiyah
Kalakh
Shinshār
Furqlus
Halbā
ASH SHAMĀL
Al Hirmil
Al Quşayr
HIMŞ
Tarābulus
(Tripoli)
Zgharta
Qurnat as Sawdā'
Al Batrūn
3088
Al Burayj
2464
Al Qaryatayn

M E D I T E R R A N E A N
2775
Jubayl
Qartabā
Al Labwah
An Nabk
Bi'r Ghadir
Ibrāhīm
2616
Ba'labakk
Yabrūd

S E A
2089
Jūniyah
2628
J. Sannin
BAYRŪT
(Beirut)
BEY
Ash Shuwayfāt
'Alayh
Zahlah
Jayrūd
LEBANON
Ad Dāmūr
JABAL LUBNĀN
Hawsh Mūssā
Az Zabadānī
1942
J. al Bārūk
Dumayr
Khān Abū Shāmat
SYRIA

DIMASHQ
Saydā (Sidon)
Jazzīn
ash Shaykh
(Mt. Hermon)
Dūmā
DIMASHQ (Damascus)
2814
Darayyā
Qatanā
Jaramānah
DAM.
An Nabaṭīyah
at Tahta
Marj 'Uyūn
Al 'Aiyūn
Al Hājānah
AL JANŪB
Al Kiswah
Sūr (Tyre)
Qiryat Shemona
1197
Qunayṭirah
As Sanamayn
Burāq
Ma'alot-Tarshiha
Hagalil
Zefat
Ar Rafid
DAR'Ā
Nahariyya
1208
(Galilee)
Yam Kinneret
Shaykh Miskin
Izra'
Shahbā'
SUWAYDĀ
'Akko (Acre)
Qiryat Karmi'el
Sea of Galilee
Fiq
Saham al Jawlan
As Suwaydā
Mifraz Hefa
Yam HAZAFON
Teverya (Tiberias)
210
Salah
Hefa (Haifa)
Qiryat Ata
Nazerat (Nazareth)
Darā
1900
Har HaKarmel 546
HA KARMEL
'Afula
Taibe
Yarmūk
IRBID
As Suwaydā
Umm el Fahm
TEL MEGIDDO
Bet She'an
AJLŪN
JABAL AD DURŪZ
Malah
CAESAREA
Shomron
Jenin
'Ajlūn
ad Dará
Salkhad
ISRAEL
Hadera
Hama-Karkur
Tūbas
SAMARIA
1247
Jarash
Al Mafraq
Umm al Qittayn
Netanya
Tulkarm
JARASH
HAMERKAZ
Nabulus
Al Ramtha
Buşrā ash Shām
Herzliyya
Ra'anana
Kefar Sava
SHILO
AL BALQA'
AL MAFRAQ
Benē Beraq
Petah Tiqwa
N. az Zarqā
As Salt
Az Zarqā
TEL AVIV-YAFO
Ramat Gan
289
Tila' al Ali
Ar Ruşayfah
Bat Yam
Holon
Lod
WEST BANK
Wadi as Sir
AMMĀN
Rishon le Ziyyon
Ramla
Rām Allāh
El Arīhā (Jericho)
Al Quwaysimah
Yavne
Rehovot
Na'ūr
Azraq ash Shishan
Qiryat Malakhi
Jerusalem
(Yerushalayim)
(Al Quds)
Ma'daba
AZ ZARQĀ
Ashqelon
Bet Shemesh
Bayt Lahm (Bethlehem)
MA'DĀBA
Qiryat Gat
TEL LAKHISH
'AMMĀN
Beit Lāhīya
Jabālya
N. Shiqma
Al Khalīl (Hebron)
Dead Sea
UMM AR RASAS
GAZA STRIP
Gaza
Sederot
422
Deir al Balah
Nuşeirāt
Rahat
Az Zāhirīyah
'En Gedi
Dhibān
Khān Yūnis
ESHKOL
Arad
Al Hodithah
Rafah
Be'er Sheva (Beersheba)
MASADA
Al Qaţrānah
Bûr Sa'îd (Port Said)
Bûr Fu'ad
Râs Burûn
Bor Mashash
'En Boqeq
333
BŪR SA'ĪD
Khalig el Tîna
Sabkhet el Bardawîl
El Daheir
Dimona
Sedom
1305
Al Karak
Romani
Bîr el Abd
El 'Arîsh
HADAROM
W. al Hasā
AL KARAK
W. Bā'ir
El Qantara
Bîr el Garârât
Bîr Lahfân
Al Mazar
JORDAN
Wâhid
Bîr Qatia
Bîr el Duweidar
Qezi'ot
333
Bîr Madkûr
Bîr el Jafir
Abu Aweigila
Muweilih
Sedé Boqer
Birein
At Ţafilah
Bā'ir
SHAMÂL SÎNÎ
892
El Quseima
121
AT ŢAFĪLAH
Dana
Ismâ'ilîya
Talâta
Bîr el Mâlhi
Mizpe Ramon
1072
Shawbak
ISMÂ'ILÎYA
Khamsa
Bîr Hasana
N. Paran
Nijil
El Buheirat
el Murrat
el Kubra
G. Yi 'Allaq
1094
Bîr Beida
El 'Agrûd
PETRA
Mahattat 'Unayzah
1736
Gineifa
Bîr el Thamâda
W. el Bruk
W. Chraiya
Ruim Tal'at
al Jamâlah
Wâdi Mûsa
Ma'ān
E G Y P T
Mamarr Mitlâ
Bîr Gebeil Hisn
El 'Agrûd
El Thamad
Ma'ān
MA'ĀN
El Suweis (Suez)
Bûr Taufîq
948
G. el Kabrît
El Kuntilla
Yotvata
Bi'r al Mârî
Adabiya
Uyûn Mûsa
Nakhl
W. Ruda
Ra's an Naqb
S A U D I
Ain Sudr
W. el Giddi
'En Avrona
1435
Khalig
el Suweis
Gebel el Tih
Rum
1754
WADI RUM
Batn al Ghûl
Ghubbet el Bûs
1272
El Wabeira
Râs Sudr
Elat
1592
Al 'Aqabah
AL 'AQABAH
At Tubayq
A R A B I A
Bîr el Biarât
Râs el Matarma
W. Abu Ga'da
Bîr Tâba
Gulf of Aqaba
Al Mudawwarah
EL SUWEIS
Bîr Wuseit
1165
Haql

Projection: Polyconic
East from Greenwich
COPYRIGHT PHILIP'S

1974 Cease Fire Lines

1:15 000 000

100   0   100   200   300   400   500   600 km
100   0   100   200   300   400 miles

| 1 | 2 | 3 | 46 | 4 | 5 | 47 | 6 | 7 |

LEBANON
BAYRŪT (Beirut)
SYRIA
DIMASHQ (Damascus)
Ba'qūbah
Arāk
Kāshān
Khvor
Tabas
AFGHANISTAN
ISRAEL
HAIFA
'AMMĀN
Ar Ramādī
BAGHDĀD
Khomeynī Shahr
Birjand
Farāh

A
TEL AVIV-YAFO
Ashqelon
Jabal ad Durūz 1800
Ar Rutbah
Karbalā'
Al Kūt
Dezfūl
EŞFAHĀN
Shahr-e Kord
Yazd
4548
4075

A
Bûr Sa'îd (Port Said)
Jerusalem
GAZA STRIP
Ismā'iliya
El Suweis (Suez)
Al Hillah
An Najaf
Al 'Amārah
AHVĀZ
Khorramābād
Anār
Rafsanjān
Daryācheh-ye Sīstān
Zābol

Moān
Al Qurayyat
Ar'ar
An Nāşirīyah
Khorramshahr
AL BAŞRAH (Basra)
Ābādān
Yāsūj 4431
Marv Dasht
SHĪRĀZ
Kermān
Zāhedān

Elat
Al 'Aqabah
Sakākah
AL KUWAYT
KUWAIT
Kāzerūn
PERSEPOLIS 1100
4419
Bam
4042

B
Hurghada 2187
Sharm el Sheikh
Dubā
Al Muwaylih
An Nafūd
Ḥā'il
Hafar al Bātin
Būshehr
Deyyer
Jahrom
Neyrīz
Sīrjān
Bandār-e Abbās
Īrānshahr

2578
Tabūk
1747
Al Jubayl
Al Qatīf
BAHRAIN
Khārk
Khamīr
Qeshm
2163
Gābrīk
Jāsk

C
Qena
Quseir
Al Wajh
Buraydah
Ad Dammām
Az Zahrān (Dhahran)
QATAR
Al Manāmah
Ra's al-Khaymah
Ra's Musandam
Str. of Hormuz (Oman)
Ash Shāriqah (Sharjah)
'Ajmān
Gulf of Oman

THEBES
KARNAK
El Uqsur (Luxor)
Isna
Marsa Alam
Umm Lajj
Unayzah
Al Mubarraz
Al Hufūf
Ad Dawhah (Doha)
DUBAYY (Dubai)
Al Fujayrah
Suḥār

C
Idfū
Kôm Ombo
Aswân
1814
AR RIYĀD (Riyadh)
SAUDI
Shaqrā
Abū Zaby (Abu Dhabi)
UNITED ARAB EMIRATES
Al 'Ayn
As Sib
Matrah
Masqat (Muscat)

1977
Ras Bânâs
Bîr Shalatein
AL MADĪNAH (Medina)
'Afif
Tropic of Cancer
As Sulaymānīyah
Harad
Ibrī
Izki
Şūr
3019

EGYPT
Buheiret en Naser (L. Nasser)
Halaib Triangle
Yanbu al Bahr
Rābigh
ARABIA
As Sulayyil
Al 'Ubaylah
Nizwā

ABU SIMBEL
Wadi Halfa
Halaib
2216
JIDDAH (Jedda)
MAKKAH (Mecca)
Al Hawiyah
Aţ Ţā'if 2565
Layla
Al 'Ubaylah
Rub' al Khāli
(Empty Quarter)
OMAN
Maşīrah
Khalūf

Kosha
Es Sahrâ en Nûbîya
Muhammad Qol
2259
Ras Abu Shagara
Al Līth
Turabah
Qal'at Bīshah
As Sulayyil
Khalīj Maşīrah

D
Delgo
3rd Cataract
Dongola
Abu Hamed
Bûr Sûdân
Suakin
Al Qunfudhah
3013
Abhā
Najrān
Ash Sharawrah
Zufār
Salālah
Haymā'
Ra's al Madrakah
J. al Hallānīyat

D
Merowe Dam
Kareima
SUDAN
Berber
Atbara
Ed Dâmer
1596
Sinkat
Haiya
Karora
2780
Khamīs Mushayt
Jīzān
Mirbāt

6th Cataract
Wad Hamid
Shendî
Adarama
Nakfa
Dahlak Kebir
Farasān
Hajjah
Khamir
Shibām
Hadramawt
Al Ghaydah
Ra's Fartak

E
Omdurmân
EL KHARTÛM (Khartoum)
Kassalâ
Akordat
Mitsiwa
Zula
Al Luhayyah
Kamarān
3760
ŞAN'Ā'
YEMEN
2469
Ash Shihr
Sayhūt
Al Mukallā

El Manaqil
Khashm el Girba
Asmera
ERITREA
Adigrat
Aksum
Adwa
Tekeze Dam
Ras Dashen 4533
3018
Al Hudaydah
Dhamār
Ibb
Ta'izz
J. Manar 3200
Nişāb
2185
'Abd al Kūrī (Yemen)
Socotra
Hadiboh
1503

Ed Dueim
Wâd Medanî
Gedaref
Gonder
Mekele
-125
Danakil Desert
Al Mukhā
Madīnat ash Sha'b
Shuqrā
Ahwar
Bereeda
Ras Asir

F
Kôstî
Gezira
Sennar
Singa
4190
Alamata
2028
Aseb
Bab el Mandeb
Adan (Aden)
Gulf of Aden
Boosaaso
El Gal
Xaafuun
Ras Xaafuun

Umm Ruwaba
Jibalan
Nubah
Ed Damazin
Roseires Res.
L. Tana
1830
Debre Tabor
DJIBOUTI
Djibouti
L. Assal
Tadjoura
Saylac
Berbera
Karin
Shimbiris 2416
Ceerigaabo
Qardho (Gardo)
Bender Beyla

Bahir Dar
Abay (Blue Nile)
Bure
Debre Markos
L. Abbé
Somaliland
Hargeisa
Burco (Burao)
Garoowe
Eyl

G
Malakal
Sobat
Nekemte
Ethiopian Highlands
4012
Dire Dawa
Jijiga
Harer
Las Anod (Laascaanood)
SOMALIA
Galmudug Puntland
Eyl

SOUTH SUDAN
Pibor Post
Bôr
Dembidolo
Metu
Gore
Gambela
3302
ADDIS ABEBA
Debre Zeyit
Nazret
Awash
3381
ETHIOPIA
Ogaden
Kebri Dehar
Gaalkacyo (Galcaio)
Qardho

INDIAN

Tali Post
Gimbi
Jima
3686
Awasa
Shashemene
Asela
Ginir
Goba 4307
Imi
Gode
Shebele
Ferfer
Hobyo

F
Juba
Mongalla
Kapoeta
Elemi Triangle
Lokitaung 1794
2141
Arba Minch
L. Shamo
Dila
Kibre Mengist
Negele
Genale
Dolo
Sina Dhago
Ceeldheere

OCEAN

G
Yei
Kajo Kaji
Torit
3187
2749
L. Turkana
Mega
Moyale
El Wak
Luuq (Lugh)
Baydhabo (Baidoa)
Jawhar (Giohar)

UGANDA
Arua
Gulu
Lira
Moroto
3084
375
South Horr
Marsabit
Wajir
Buurhakaba (Bur Acaba)
Wanleweyne (Uanle Uen)
MUQDISHO (Mogadishu)

Pakwach
Murchison Falls
Soroti
Mt. Elgon 4321
2752
Lodwar
Dif
Buuraxaba
Marka (Merca)

L. Albert
L. Kyoga
Mbale
KENYA
Kitale
Jamaame (Giamama)
Jilib (Gelib)

Projection: Sanson-Flamsteed's Sinusoidal
Equator
Kismaayo (Chisimaio)

| 1 | 54 | 2 | 3 | East from Greenwich | 4 | 5 | 6 |

COPYRIGHT PHILIP'S

Lava fields

ft   m
12 000   4000
9000   3000
6000   2000
4500   1500
3000   1000
1200   400
600   200
0   0
200   600
1000   3000
2000   6000
4000   12 000
m   ft

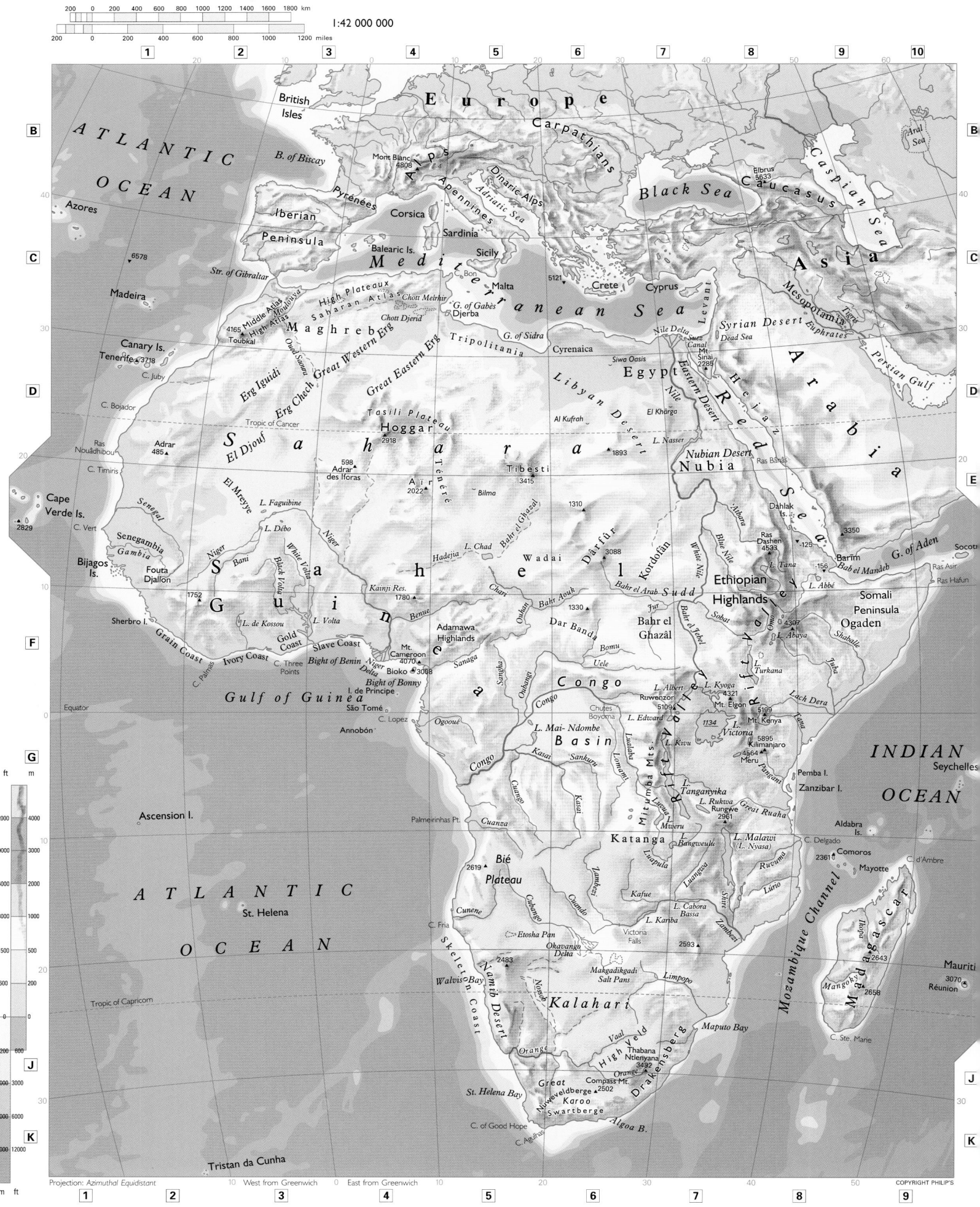

1:42 000 000

Projection: Azimuthal Equidistant

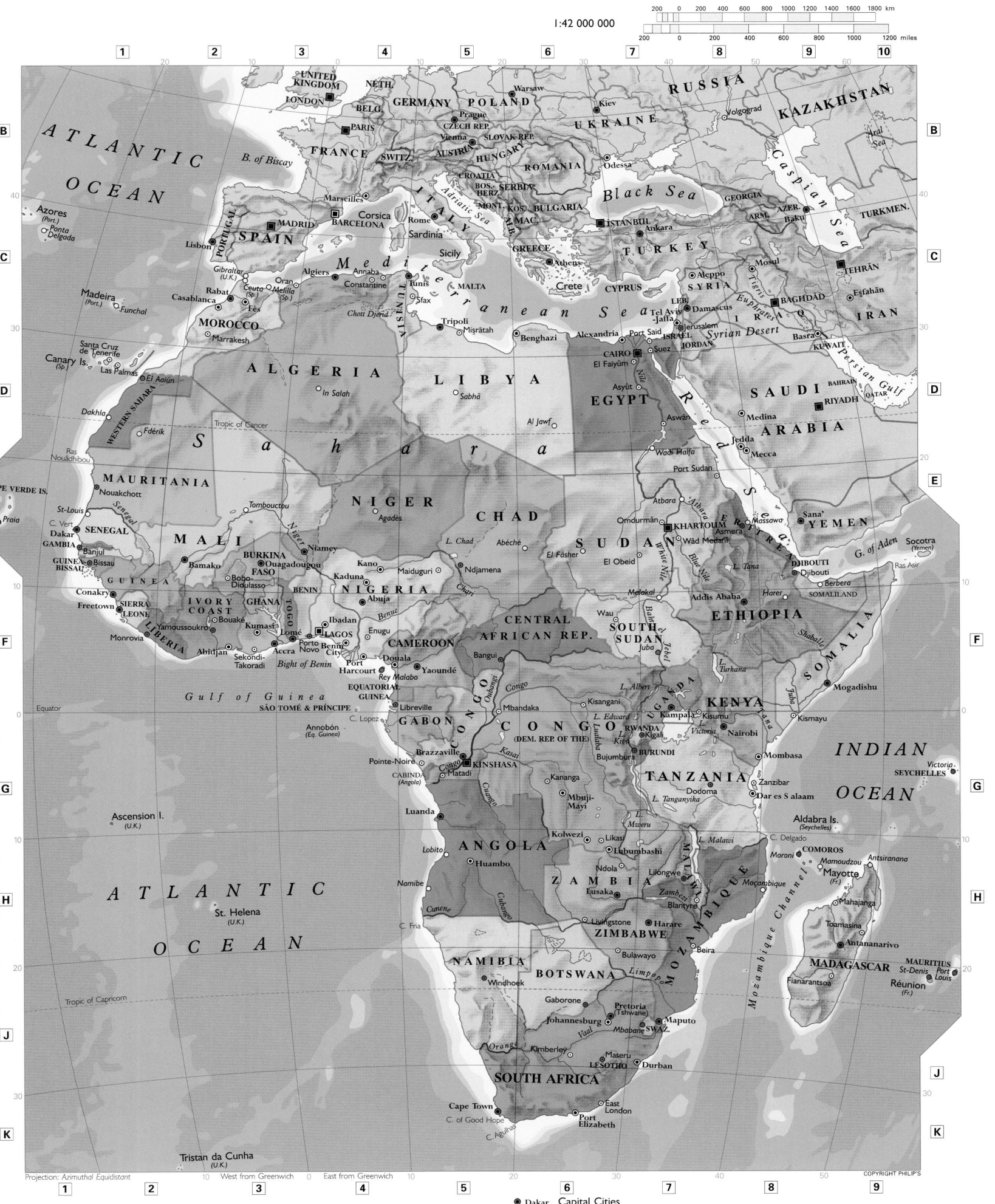

1:42 000 000

● Dakar Capital Cities

Projection: Azimuthal Equidistant

COPYRIGHT PHILIP'S

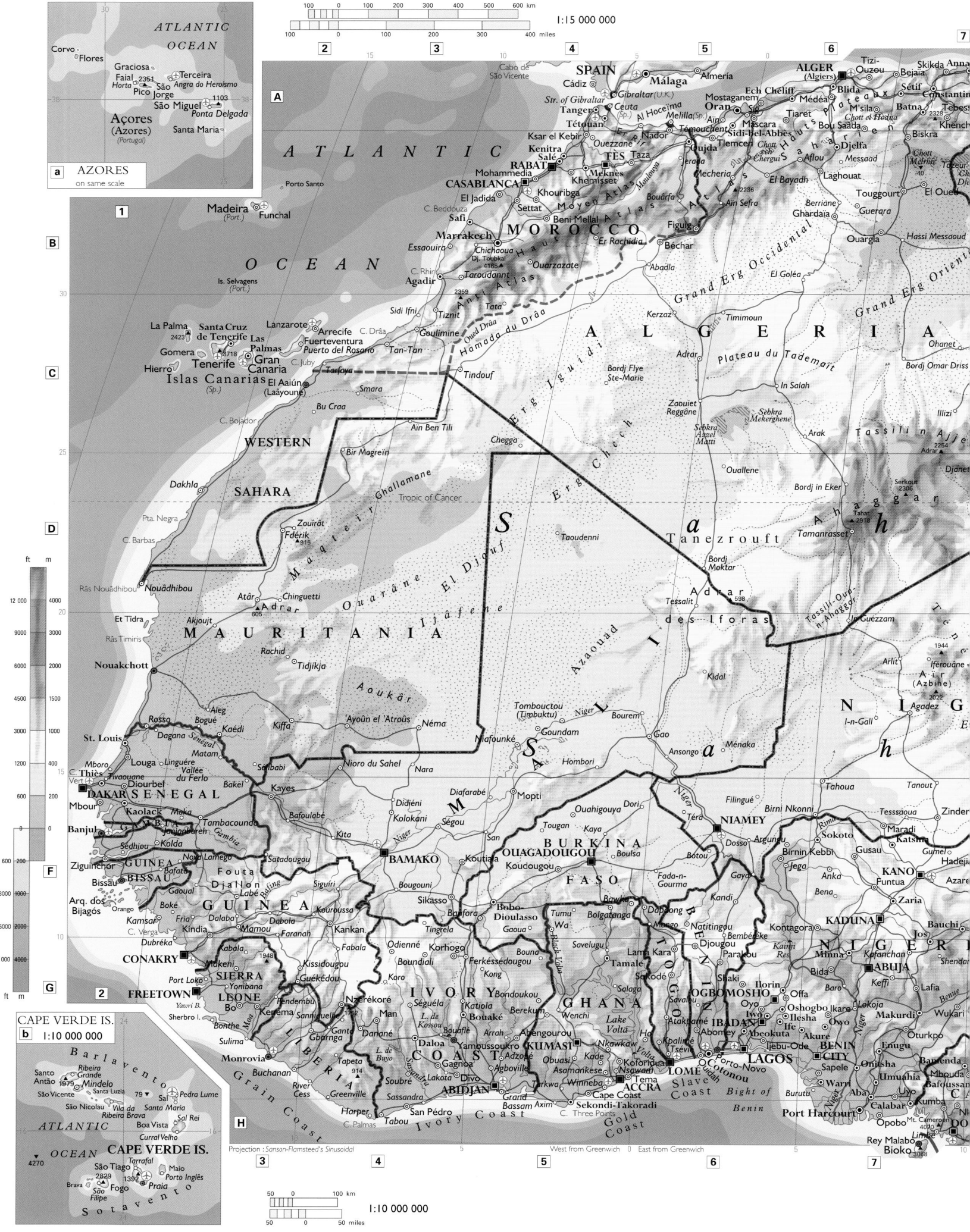

1:15 000 000

ATLANTIC OCEAN

AZORES
on same scale

a

Corvo
Flores
Graciosa
Faial 2351
Horta
Pico
São Jorge
Terceira
Angra do Heroismo

Açores
(Azores)
(Portugal)

São Miguel 1103
Ponta Delgada
Santa Maria

CAPE VERDE IS.
b 1:10 000 000

Barlavento

Santo
Antão 1979
Mindelo
Santa Luzia
São Vicente
São Nicolau
Santo
Ribeira Brava
Sal
Pedra Lume
Santa Maria
Sal Rei
Boa Vista
Curral Velho

ATLANTIC

OCEAN

CAPE VERDE IS.

4270

São Tiago
Tarrafal
Maio
Porto Inglês
Praia
Brava 2829 1392
São Filipe
Fogo

Sotavento

1:10 000 000

Projection : Sanson-Flamsteed's Sinusoidal

Lava fields

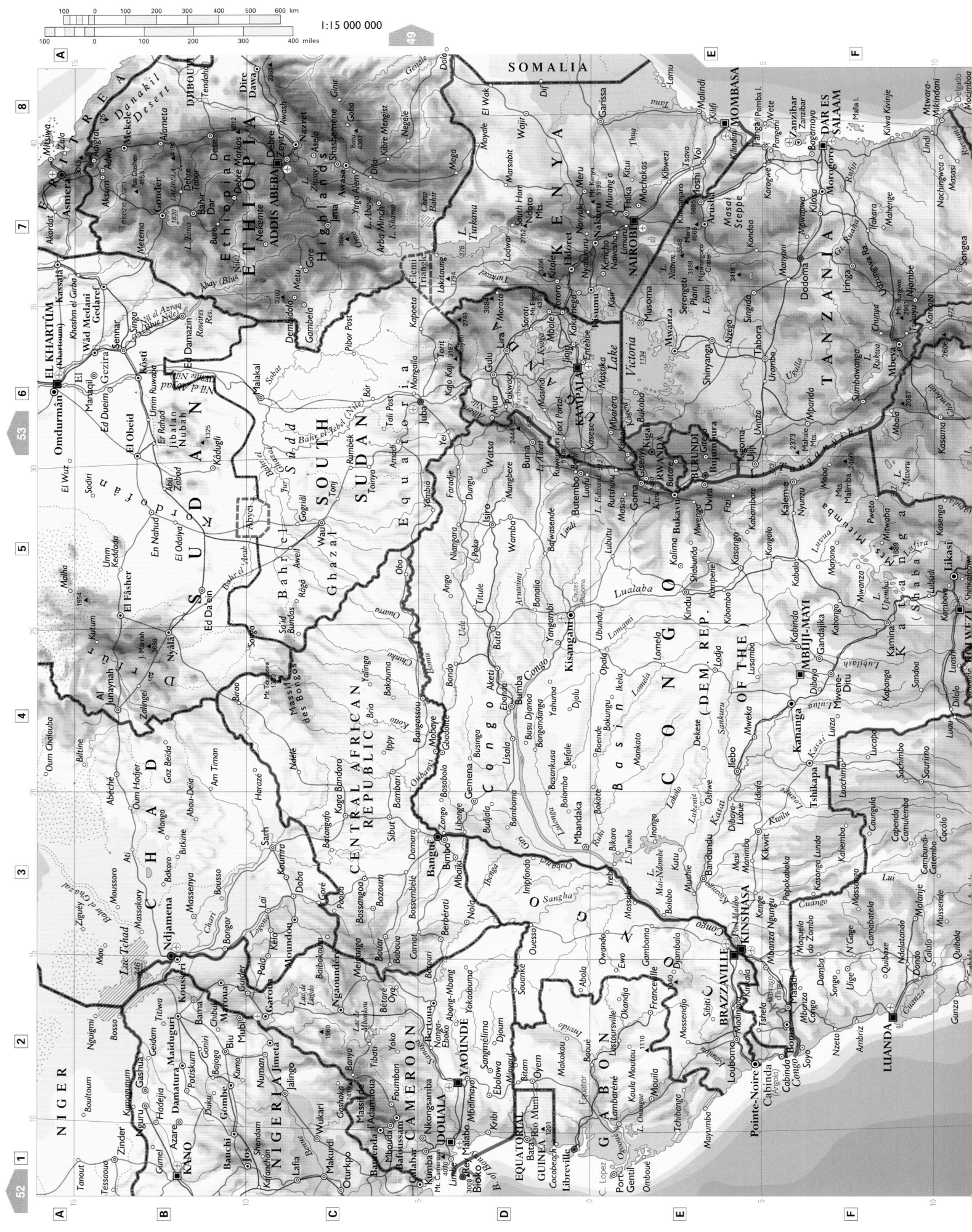

1:15 000 000

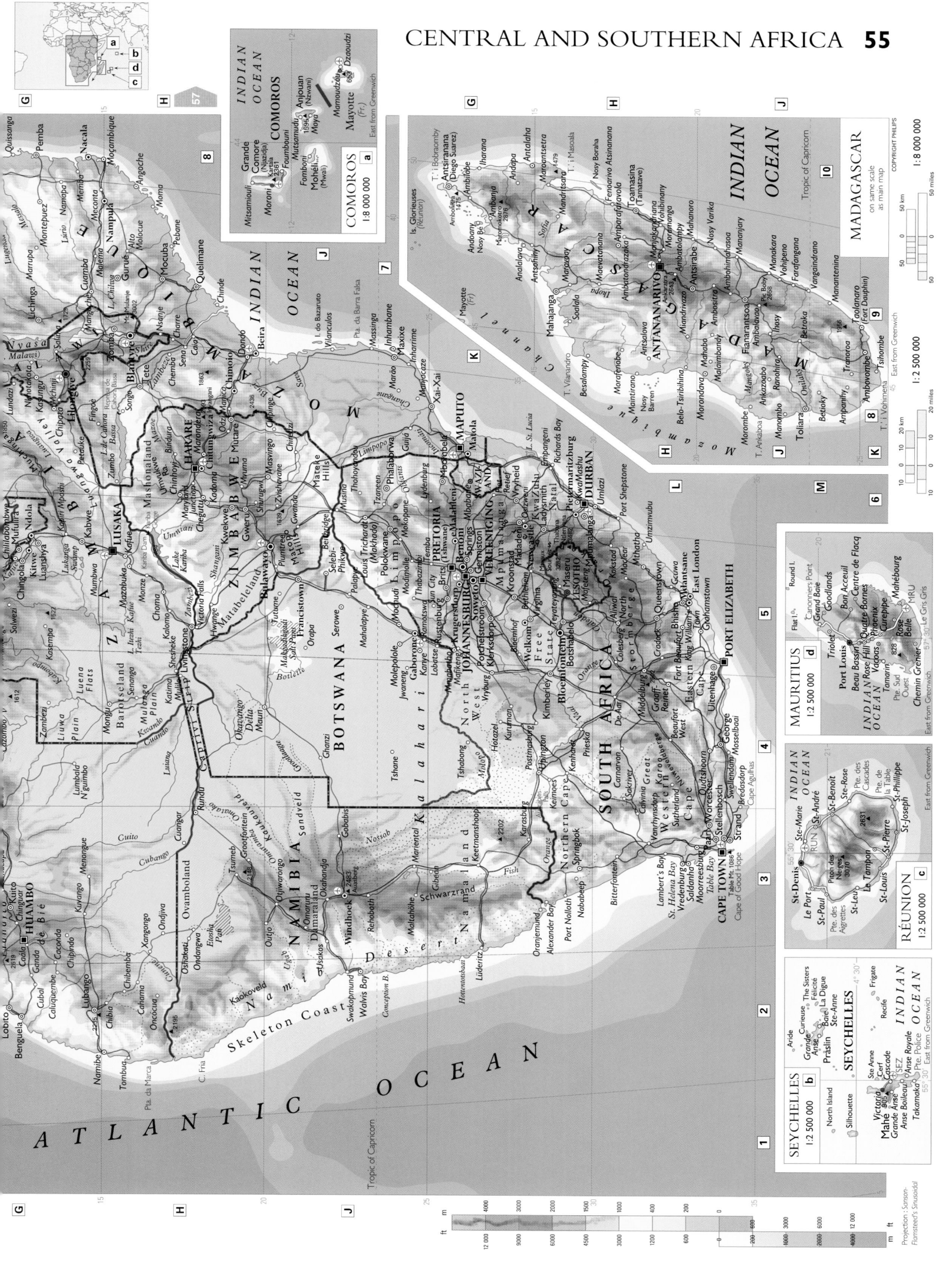

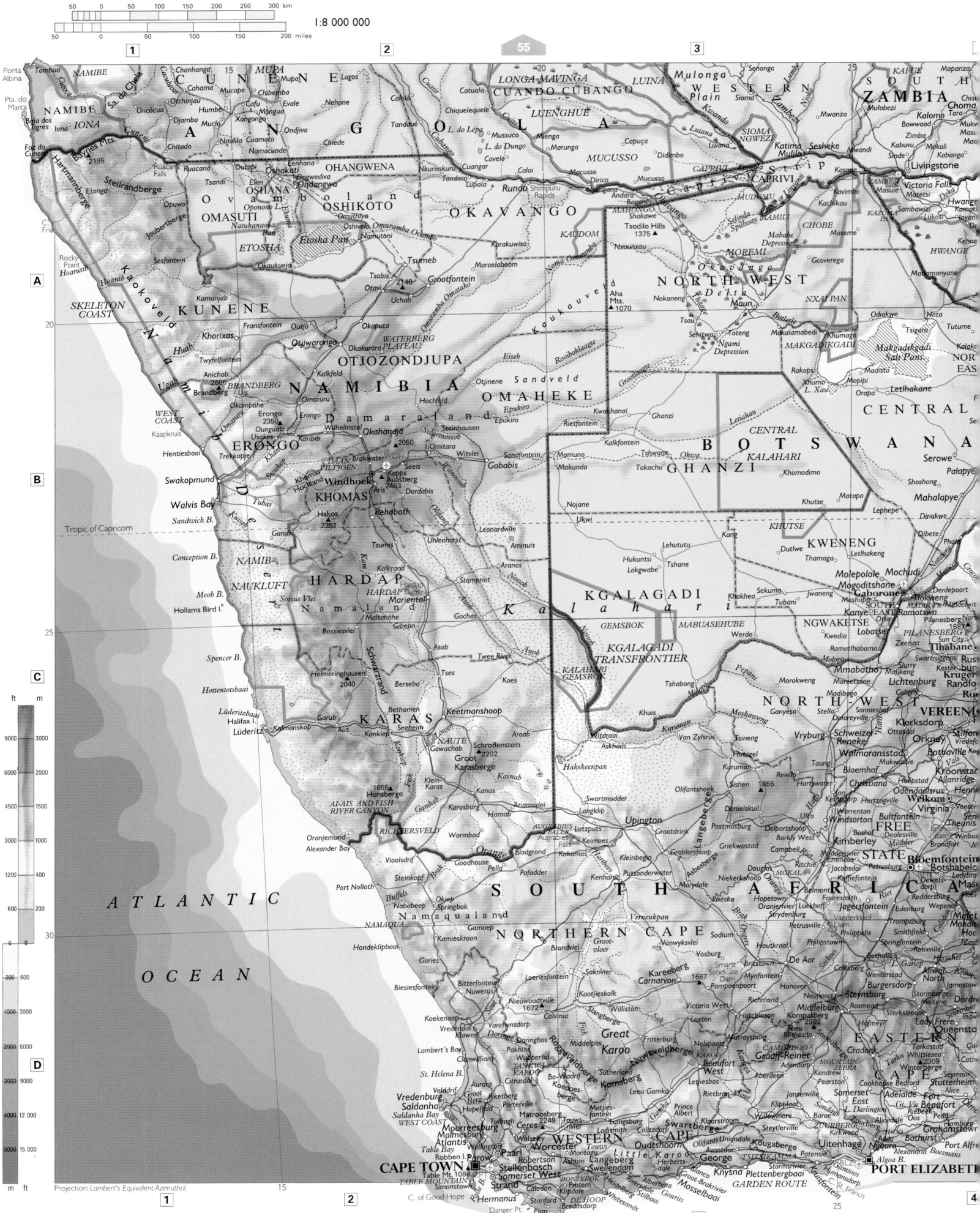

Projection: Lambert's Equivalent Azimuthal

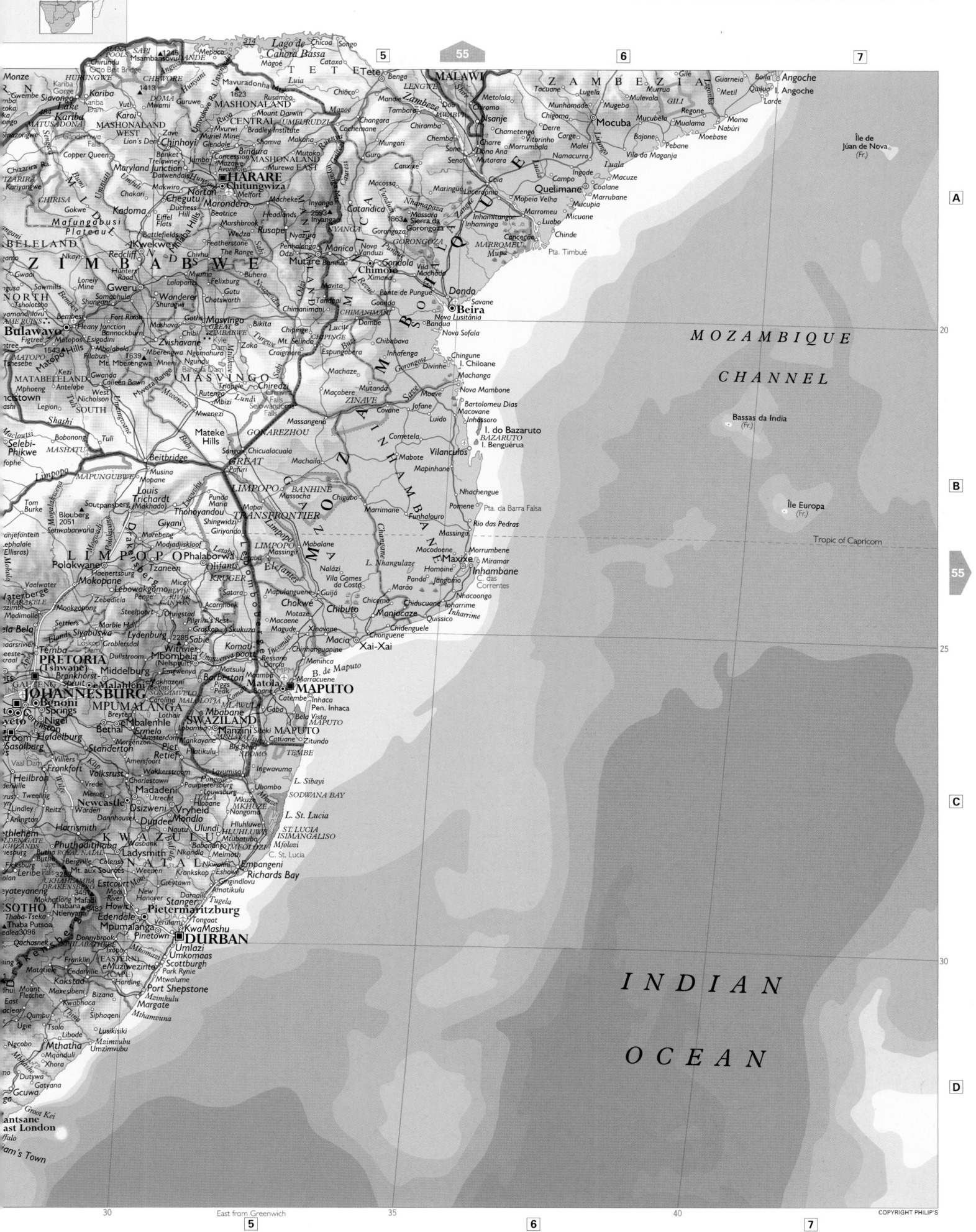

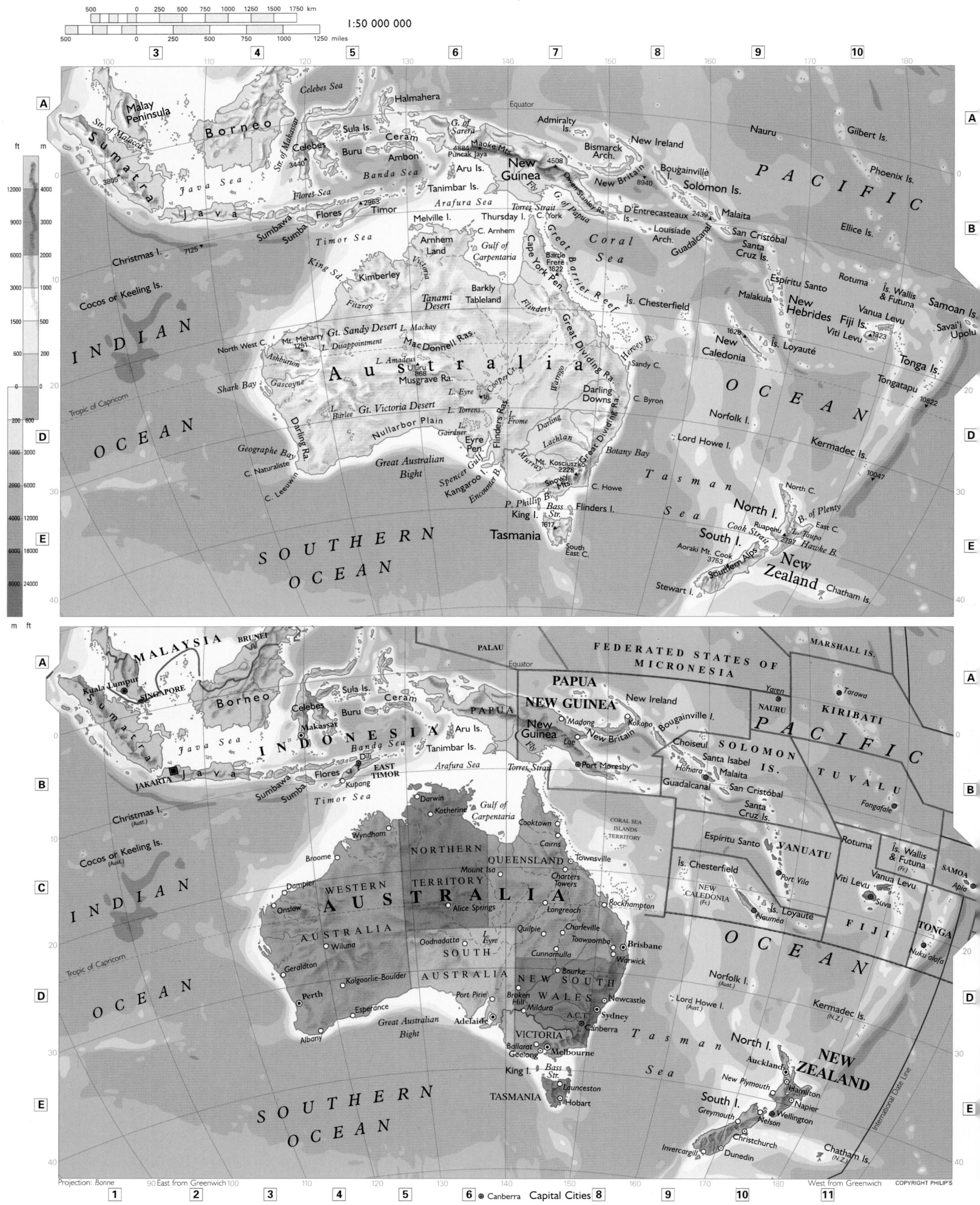

500   0   250   500   750   1000   1250   1500   1750 km

1:50 000 000

500   0   250   500   750   1000   1250 miles

Physical map (top):

Malay Peninsula, Borneo, Celebes Sea, Halmahera, Equator, Admiralty Is., Nauru, Gilbert Is., PACIFIC

Str. of Malacca, Sumatra, Celebes, Sula Is., Ceram, G. of Sarera, Maoke Mts., New Ireland, Bismarck Arch., Bougainville, Phoenix Is.

3440, Buru, Ambon, Aru Is., 4884, Puncak Jaya, New Guinea, 4508, New Britain, 8940, Solomon Is., Malaita

3805, Java Sea, Java, Banda Sea, Tanimbar Is., Fly, Owen Stanley Ra., D'Entrecasteaux, 2439, Espíritu Santo, Rotuma, Îs. Wallis & Futuna, Samoan Is.

Flores Sea, Sumbawa, Sumba, Flores, Timor, Arafura Sea, Torres Strait, C. York, G. of Papua, Louisiade Arch., Guadalcanal, San Cristóbal, Santa Cruz Is., Ellice Is.

Christmas I., 7125, Timor Sea, Melville I., Thursday I., C. Arnhem, Barle Frere 1622, Coral Sea, Îs. Chesterfield, Malakula, New Hebrides, Fiji Is., Savai'i, Upolu

Cocos or Keeling Is., Arnhem Land, Victoria, Gulf of Carpentaria, Cape York Pen., Great Barrier Reef, 1628, Viti Levu, 1323

INDIAN, King Sd., Kimberley, Tanami Desert, Barkly Tableland, Flinders, Great Dividing Ra., New Caledonia, Îs. Loyauté, Tonga Is.

OCEAN, Fitzroy, Gt. Sandy Desert, L. Mackay, MacDonnell Ras., Warrego, Hervey B., Sandy C., OCEAN, Tongatapu, 10822

North West C., Mt. Meharry 1251, L. Disappointment, Australia, L. Amadeus, Uluru 868, Musgrave Ra., Cooper Cr., Darling Downs, C. Byron, Norfolk I., Lord Howe I., Kermadec Is.

Tropic of Capricorn, Ashburton, Shark Bay, Gascoyne, L. Eyre, L. Torrens, L. Frome, Darling, Lachlan, Tasman Sea, 10047

Geographe Bay, Darling Ra., L. Barlee, Gt. Victoria Desert, Gairdner, Eyre Pen., Flinders Ras., Murray, Mt. Kosciuszko 2228, Snowy Mts., Botany Bay, North I., B. of Plenty, East C.

C. Naturaliste, C. Leeuwin, Nullarbor Plain, Spencer Gulf, Kangaroo I., Encounter B., Great Australian Bight, C. Howe, Ruapehu 2797, L. Taupo, Hawke B.

Aoraki Mt. Cook 3753, Southern Alps, New Zealand, Chatham Is.

SOUTHERN, P. Philip B., King I., Bass Str., Flinders I., Tasman Sea, South I., Cook Strait

OCEAN, South East C., Tasmania, 1617, Stewart I.

Political map (bottom):

MALAYSIA, BRUNEI, PALAU, FEDERATED STATES OF MICRONESIA, MARSHALL IS., Equator

Kuala Lumpur, SINGAPORE, Borneo, Sula Is., Ceram, PAPUA, PAPUA NEW GUINEA, New Ireland, Yaren, Tarawa, NAURU, KIRIBATI, PACIFIC

Sumatra, Makassar, Celebes, Buru, Aru Is., New Guinea, Madang, Kokopo, Bougainville I., Choiseul, SOLOMON IS.

JAKARTA, Java, Java Sea, INDONESIA, Banda Sea, Dili, Tanimbar Is., Fly, Lae, New Britain, Santa Isabel, TUVALU

Christmas I. (Aust.), Sumbawa, Flores, Kupang, EAST TIMOR, Arafura Sea, Torres Strait, Port Moresby, Honiara, Malaita, San Cristóbal, Fongafale

Cocos or Keeling Is. (Aust.), Sumba, Timor Sea, Darwin, Katherine, Gulf of Carpentaria, Cooktown, CORAL SEA ISLANDS TERRITORY, Santa Cruz Is., Espíritu Santo, VANUATU, Rotuma, Îs. Wallis & Futuna (Fr.), SAMOA

INDIAN, Wyndham, NORTHERN, Cairns, Mount Isa, QUEENSLAND, Townsville, Port Vila, Apia

Broome, TERRITORY, Charters Towers, NEW CALEDONIA (Fr.), Îs. Chesterfield, Viti Levu, Vanua Levu

OCEAN, Dampier, WESTERN, Longreach, Îs. Loyauté, Suva, FIJI

Onslow, AUSTRALIA, Alice Springs, Rockhampton, Nouméa, OCEAN, TONGA

Tropic of Capricorn, Wiluna, Oodnadatta, L. Eyre, Quilpie, Charleville, Toowoomba, Brisbane, Norfolk I. (Aust.), Nuku'alofa

Geraldton, Kalgoorlie-Boulder, SOUTH, AUSTRALIA, Cunnamulla, Warwick, Bourke, NEW SOUTH WALES, Lord Howe I. (Aust.), Kermadec Is. (N.Z.)

Perth, Esperance, Port Pirie, Broken Hill, Mildura, Newcastle, A.C.T., Sydney, Canberra, North I., Tasman Sea, NEW ZEALAND

Albany, Great Australian Bight, Adelaide, VICTORIA, Ballarat, Geelong, Melbourne, King I., Bass Str., Auckland, New Plymouth, Hamilton, Napier

SOUTHERN, TASMANIA, Launceston, Hobart, South I., Greymouth, Nelson, Wellington

OCEAN, Invercargill, Dunedin, Christchurch, Chatham Is. (N.Z.)

Projection: Bonne   90 East from Greenwich 100   West from Greenwich   COPYRIGHT PHILIP'S

Canberra Capital Cities

1:6 000 000

50　0　50　100　150　200 km
50　0　50　100　150 miles

4　64　5　6　7

FIJI a
on same scale

Great Sea Reef　Kia　Udu Pt.　Ringgold Is.
Yaqaga　Labasa　Natewa Bay　Rabi　PACIFIC OCEAN
Vanua Levu　Buca
Yasawa Group　Yasawa　Yadua　Buo　Savusavu　Somosomo　Qamea
Nacula　Nabouwalu　Bay　Taveuni　Naitaba　Vanua Balavu
Naviti　Bligh Water　Rakiraki　Namenalala　Nasau　Vacata　Kanacea
Viwa　Vomo　Tavua　Makogai　Vatu　Mago　Northern Lau Group
Waya　Mananuca Group　Lautoka　Tomanivi　Lawaki　Levuka　Wakaya　Vanua Vara　Cicia
Malolo　Naqvi　KOROYAWITU　Ovalau　Batiki　Sawaleke　Nairai　Tuvuca
Sigatoka　Korolevu　Keiyasi　Yunidevu　Gau　Nayau　Lakeba Passage　Lakeba
Vatulele　Yanuca　Beqa　Suva　FIJI　Vanua Vatu　Tubou　Oneata　Moce
Ono　Moala　Nayau　Namuka-i-Lau　Yagasa Cluster
Kadavu　Tavuki　Vunisea　Totoya　Matuku　Fulaga　Ogea Group　Ogea Levu　Ogea Driki
KADAVU PASSAGE　KORO SEA　Lau Group
East from Greenwich　West from Greenwich

SAMOA
Asau　Safune　Pu'apu'a　PACIFIC OCEAN
Savai'i　Falelima　Salelologa　Apia　Falefa
Taga　Mulifanua　Manono　Amaile
OLE PUPU PUE　Satupa itea　Faleolo　Safata Bay　'Upolu
AMERICAN SAMOA (U.S.A.)
Ofu　Olosega　Ta'u
Tutuila　Leone　Pago Pago　Manu'a Is.
Vaitogi
SAMOAN ISLANDS b
on same scale
International Date Line
West from Greenwich

TONGA c
on same scale
PACIFIC OCEAN
Fonualei　Toku
Vava'u　Neiafu
Vava'u Group
Home Reef　Late
Disney Reef
Ofolanga　Ha'ano
Tofua　Kao　Foa　Lifuka　Ha'apai Group
Kotu Group　Uiha
Fonuafo'ou　Nomuka　Oto Tolu Group
Hunga Ha'apai　Nomuka Group　Mango　Tonumea
TONGA
Nuku'alofa　Tongatapu
Tongatapu Group　Eua
West from Greenwich

TASMAN SEA

North Island

C. Reinga　C. Maria van Diemen　North C.
Houhora Heads　Rangaunu B.　Doubtless B.
Ahipara B.　Kaitaia　Mangonui　Whangaroa Harb.
Tauroa Pt.　Awanui　Okaihau　B. of Islands
Hokianga Harbour　Rawene　Waitangi　C. Brett
Waipoua Forest　Kaikohe　Opua
Dargaville　Hikurangi
Whangarei
Whangarei Harb.
Waipu　Bream Hd.
Bream B.　Little Barrier I.
Kaipara Harbour　Warkworth　C. Rodney　Great Barrier I.
Helensville　C. Colville　Cuvier I.
Hauraki Gulf　Coromandel
Takapuna　AUCKLAND　Whitianga
Manukau　Papakura　Thames　Whangamata
Waiuku　Pukekohe　Mayor I.
Waikato　Mercer　Paeroa　Waihi　Tauranga Harb.
Huntly　Te Aroha　Tauranga　Whakatane
Hamilton　Morrinsville　Mount Maunganui　Bay of Plenty
Raglan　Te Awamutu　Cambridge　Te Puke　Whakaari (White I.)
Kawhia　Tauranga　C. Runaway
Kawhia Harbour　Putaruru　Rotorua　Raukumara Ra.　East C.
Otorohanga　L. Rotorua　Taneatua　Hikurangi 1763
Te Kuiti　Waitomo Caves　Mokau　Wairakei　Murupara　UREWERA　Waipiro
Mokau Bight　Taumarunui　Taupo　Rangitaiki　L. Waikaremoana　Tolaga Bay
New Plymouth　Inglewood　Turangi　Kaimanawa Mts.　Tarawera　Ormond　Gisborne
Mt. Taranaki or Mt. Egmont 2518　Stratford　Raetihi　Nuhaka　Poverty Bay
Opunake　Kapuni　Eltham　Ruapehu 2797　TONGARIRO　Wairoa　Hawke Bay
Hawera　Waverley　Taihape　Ruahine Ra.　Napier　C. Kidnappers
Patea　Mangaweka　Hunterville　Hastings
Wanganui　Marton　Halcombe　Feilding　Waipawa　Waipukurau
Bulls　Palmerston North　Woodville　Danevirke
Foxton　Shannon　Pahiatua　C. Turnagain
Levin　Otaki　Masterton
Paraparaumu　Kapiti I.　Carterton　Greytown
Upper Hutt　Martinborough　Wairarapa
Petone　Lower Hutt　Wellington
Cook Strait

South Island

C. Farewell　Collingwood　Golden B.　D'Urville I.
KAHURANGI　Takaka　ABEL TASMAN
Tasman Mts.　Tasman B.　Motueka　Pelorus Sd.
Karamea　Nelson　Havelock　Picton
Karamea Bight　Richmond　Wakefield　Blenheim
Seddonville　Tadmor　NELSON LAKES　Seddon
Granity　Matiri Ra.　Murchison　L. Rotoiti　Ward
Westport　Lyell　Inangahua　L. Rotoroa　Mt. Travers 2337　Tapuae-o-Uenuku 2885
PAPAROA　Reefton　Spenser Mts.　Kaikoura
Punakaiki　Lewis Pass　Hanmer Springs
Blackball　Greymouth　Waiau　Clarence
Runanga　Stillwater　L. Brunner　ARTHUR'S PASS　Culverden
Hokitika　Jacksons　Waikari　Amberley　Pegasus Bay
Ross　Otira　Springfield　Oxford　Waipara
Whitecliffs　Rangiora　Kaiapoi
Westland Bight　Riccarton　New Brighton
WESTLAND　Mt. Cook 3753　Staveley　Christchurch
Aoraki　Methven　Lincoln　Banks Pen.
Mount Cook　Fairlie　Rakaia　Lyttelton
Southern Alps (Tiritiri o te Moana)　Tekapo　Ashburton　Akaroa
Jackson B.　Ohau　L. Ellesmere　Lake River
MOUNT ASPIRING　Pukaki　Canterbury Plains　Rakaia
Mt. Aspiring 3033　Temuka　Timaru　Canterbury Bight
Milford Sd.　Earnslaw 2819　Wanaka　St. Andrews
Sutherland Falls　L. Wanaka　Waimate
Bligh Sound　Milford　Arrowtown　Kurow　Waitaki
George Sound　Queenstown　Cromwell　Oamaru
Secretary I.　Anau　Kingston　Roxburgh　Maheno　Hampden
Doubtful Sd.　L. Manapouri　Garvie Mts.　Alexandra　Dunback
FIORDLAND　Manapouri　Mataura　Waikouaiti　Port Chalmers
Resolution I.　Mossburn　Edievale　Otago Harbour
Dusky Sd.　Lumsden　Balclutha　C. Saunders
Chalky Inlet　Clifden　Tuatapere　Nightcaps　Milton　Dunedin
Preservation Inlet　Orepuki　Hedgehope　Kaitangata
Solander I.　Riverton　Winton　Gore　Clinton　Nugget Pt.
Invercargill　Mataura　Wyndham　Tahakopa
Te Waewae B.　Bluff　Foveaux Str.
Halfmoon Bay　Ruapuke I.
Stewart I. (Rakiura)　RAKIURA
South West C.　Port Pegasus

PACIFIC OCEAN

64

TAHITI & MOOREA d
1:1 000 000

Pte. Aroa
Papetoai　B. de Matavai　Pte. Vénus
Paopao　Arue　Mahina
Mt. Tohiea 1207　Papeete　Papenoo
Moorea (France)　Pirae　Tiarei
Haapiti　Faaa　Afareaitu　Hitiaa
Pte. Nuupere　Mt. Aorai 2060　Mt. Orohena 2241　Faaone
Punaauia　Mt. Teufaira 1799　Lac Vaihiria　Taravao
Paea　Afaahiti
Maraa　Papara　Isthme de Taravao
Atimaono　Mataiea　Afaahiti　Pte. Tatutua
Vairao　Mt. Rooniu 1332　Tautira
Teahupoo　Presqu'île de Taiarapu
West from Greenwich

Projection: Conical with two standard parallels
East from Greenwich
COPYRIGHT PHILIP'S

1　2　3　4

10　0　10 km
10　0　10 miles
1:1 000 000

ft　m
9000　3000
6000　2000
3000　1200
400
600　200
0　0
200　600
2000　6000
4000　12 000
6000　18 000
m　ft

1:8 000 000

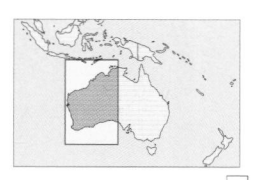

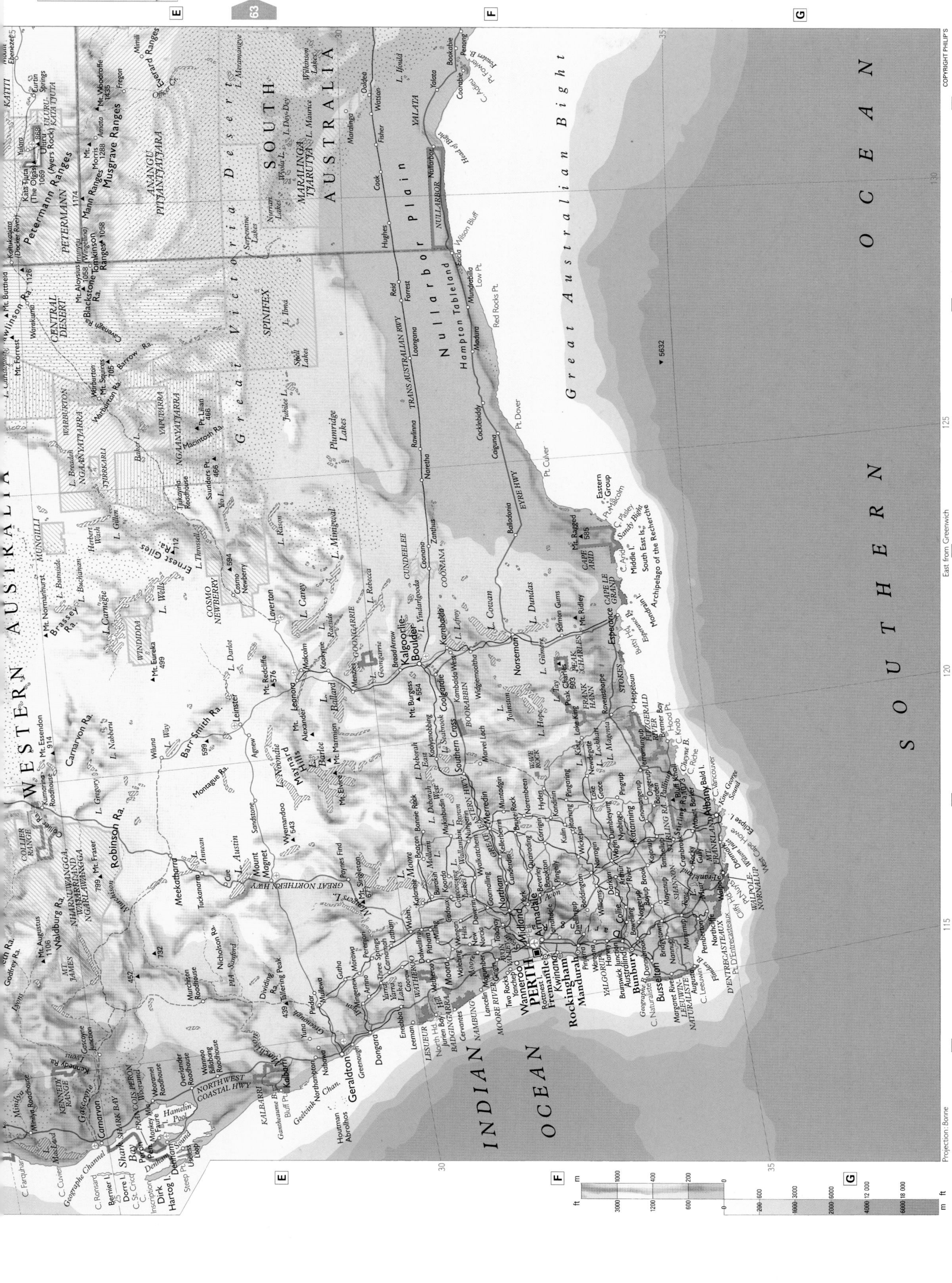
WESTERN AUSTRALIA
SOUTH AUSTRALIA
INDIAN OCEAN
SOUTHERN OCEAN
Great Australian Bight
Great Victoria Desert
Nullarbor Plain
Hampton Tableland
PERTH
Fremantle
Rockingham
Mandurah
Bunbury
Busselton
Albany
Esperance
Kalgoorlie-Boulder
Coolgardie
Norseman
Geraldton
Carnarvon
Leonora
Laverton
Southern Cross
Merredin
Northam
Eucla
Great Eastern Hwy
Eyre Hwy
Trans Australian Rwy
Musgrave Ranges
Petermann Ranges
Everard Ranges
Robinson Ra.
Aboriginal lands
Projection: Bonne
East from Greenwich
COPYRIGHT PHILIP'S

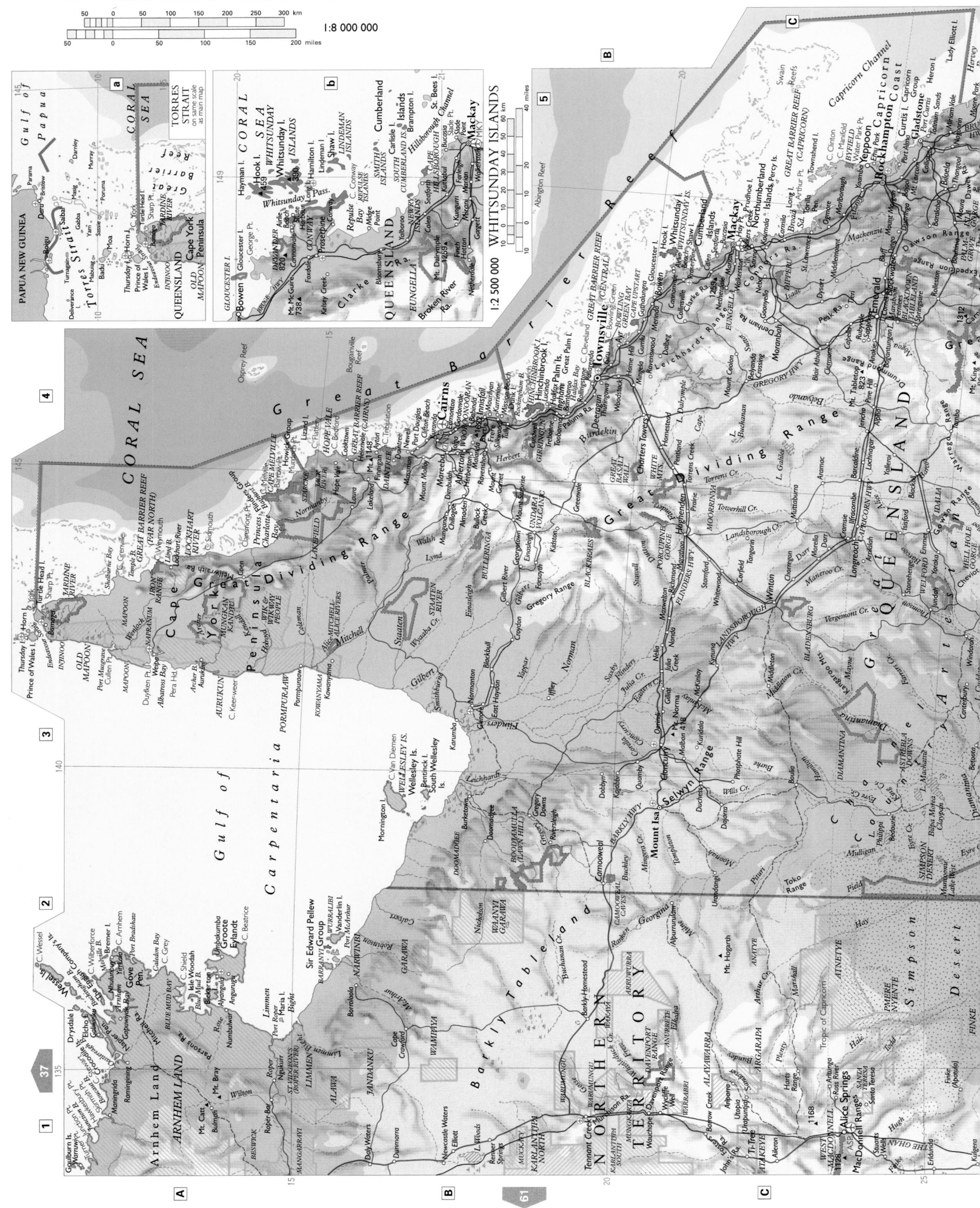

1:8 000 000

PAPUA NEW GUINEA

a

TORRES STRAIT
on same scale
as main map

WHITSUNDAY ISLANDS

b

1:2 500 000

RUSSIA

Yekaterinburg
Tomsk
Novosibirsk
Irkutsk
Chita
Oz. Baykal
Okhotsk
Sea of Okhotsk
Poluostrov Kamchatka
Komandorskiye Ostrova (Russia)
Aleutian Basin
Near Is. (U.S.A.)
Andreanof
Bering Sea

KAZAKHSTAN
Astana (Aqmola)
Semey
Aral Sea
Balqash Köl
Almaty
Ürümqi
MONGOLIA
Ulaanbaatar
Changchun
Harbin
Blagoveshchensk
Khabarovsk
Vladivostok
Sapporo
Hakodate
Sakhalin
Kurilskiye Ostrova (Russia)
Kuril-Kamchatka Trench
Petropavlovsk-Kamchatskiy
La Pérouse Str.
Northwest
Emperor Trough
Aleutian Trench
Aleutia
7822
Chinook Trou

TOSHKENT
KYRGYZSTAN
TAJIKISTAN
AFGHANISTAN
Kābul
Srinagar
PAKISTAN
Lahore
Delhi
Kanpur

CHINA
Altai
Kunlun Shan
XIZANG
Lanzhou
Xi'an
Beijing
Tianjin
Taiyuan
Shenyang
NORTH KOREA
SOUTH KOREA
Dalian
Seoul
Qingdao
Nagoya
Kyōto
Osaka
JAPAN
Shikoku
Kyūshū
Sendai
Tōkyō
Yokohama
Sea of Japan
Shatsky Rise
Pacific
Pacific Chain
10,542
Hoo
Midway Is. (U.S.A.)
Ho

Lhasa
Himalaya
Mt. Everest 8850
Kathmandu
NEPAL
Brahmaputra
Ganga
BANGLADESH
Kolkata (Calcutta)
Dhaka
INDIA
Hyderabad
Chennai (Madras)

Chongqing
Wuhan
Nanjing
Changsha
Kunming
Guangzhou
Hangzhou
Shanghai
East China Sea
Yellow Sea
Fuzhou
Taipei
TAIWAN
Macau
Hong Kong
Hainan
Hanoi
10,554
Japan Trench
Kitakyushu
Fuji-San 3776

Ryūkyū-retto (Japan)
Okinawa
Iwo-Jima (Japan)
Ogasawara Gunto (Japan)
Kazan-Retto (Japan)
Minami-Tori-Shima (Japan)
Lisianski I. (U.S.A.)
Wake I. (U.S.A.)
International Date Line
Mid-Pacific Mount

Philippine Sea
C. Engano
Paracel Is.
Luzon
Manila
Mindoro
Samar
PHILIPPINES
Palawan
Mindanao
Davao
10,497
Mindanao Trench

West Mariana Basin
NORTHERN MARIANAS (U.S.A.)
Tinian
Saipan
East Mariana Basin
Mariana Trench
Challenger Deep 11,022
GUAM (U.S.A.)
Yap
Caroline Is.
Chuuk
MARSHALL IS.
Bikini Atoll
Enewetak Atoll
Ralik Chain
Kwajalein
Majuro
Jaluit I.
Pohnpei
Palikir
Butaritari
Howland I. (U.S.)
Baker I. (U.S.)
Tarawa
Gilbert Is.
Banaba
Phoenix Is.
Abariringa
Enderbury

BURMA
Mandalay
LAOS
THAILAND
Bangkok
CAMBODIA
Phnom Penh
VIETNAM
Thanh Pho Ho Chi Minh
G. of Thailand
South China Sea
Bay of Bengal
Rangoon
Andaman Is. (India)
Nicobar Is. (India)
SRI LANKA
Colombo
Sumatera
Sunda East Ridge

MALAYSIA
Kuala Lumpur
Singapore
BRUNEI
SABAH
SARAWAK
Celebes Sea
Sulu Sea
Melekeok
PALAU
West Caroline Basin
Eauripik Rise
FED. STATES OF MICRONESIA
East Caroline Basin
Micronesia
NAURU
Yaren
Melanesian Basin
Solomon Rise
Melanesia
KIRIBATI

Borneo
Sulawesi
Halmahera
Buru
Seram
Maluku
INDONESIA
Makassar
Jakarta
Surabaya
Jawa
Java Sea
Flores Sea
Bali
Flores
Sumbawa
Sumba
Banda Sea
4181
7440
PAPUA
Puncak Jaya 4884
New Guinea
Admiralty Is.
Bismarck Arch.
New Ireland
New Britain
PAPUA NEW GUINEA
Kokopo
Lae
Port Moresby
Bougainville
8940
SOLOMON IS.
Honiara
Guadalcanal
Santa Cruz I. 9165
Fongafale
TUVALU

EAST TIMOR
Dili
Timor
Arafura Sea
Torres Strait
C. York
Louisiade Arch.
Rotuma
Wallis & Futuna (Fr.)
SAMOA
Apia

INDIAN OCEAN
Cocos Is. (Austral.)
Christmas I. (Austral.)
North Australian Basin
C. Arnhem
Darwin
Gulf of Carpentaria
Cairns
Townsville
Coral Sea Basin
Coral Sea
Espiritu Santo
VANUATU
Port Vila
Îs. Chesterfield
West Fiji Basin
Vanua Levu
Viti Levu
Suva
FIJI
Nuku'alofa
TONGA
7570
South Fiji Basin
Tonga Trench

Wharton Basin
Broken Ridge
Exmouth Plateau
North West C.
Broome
Mount Isa
AUSTRALIA
Alice Springs
L. Eyre
Rockhampton
Brisbane
Great Dividing Ra.
Darling
Middleton Basin
Lord Howe I. (Austral.)
NEW CALEDONIA (Fr.)
Nouméa
Norfolk I. (Austral.)
Norfolk Ridge
New Caledonia Trough
Lord Howe Rise
10,822
Kermadec Is. (N.Z.)
Kermadec Trench 10,047

Geraldton
Perth Basin
Perth
Naturaliste Plateau
Albany
Great Australian Bight
Adelaide
Murray
Canberra
Sydney
Mt Kosciuszko 2228
Melbourne
South Australian Basin
Tasman Sea
Auckland
NEW ZEALAND
Wellington
Christchurch
Chatham Rise
Chatham Is. (N.Z.)

Nouvelle Amsterdam (Fr.)
I. St. Paul (Fr.)
Mid Indian Ridge
Tasmania
Hobart
Bass Str.
East Tasman Plateau
Tasman Sea
Aoraki Mt. Cook 3753
Dunedin
Bounty Trough
Invercargill
Bounty Is. (N.Z.)

Îs. Crozet (Fr.)
Kerguelen (Fr.)
Heard I. (Austral.)
SOUTHERN OCEAN
South Tasman Rise
Auckland Is. (N.Z.)
Antipodes Is. (N.Z.)
Campbell I. (N.Z.)
Campbell Plateau
Macquarie I. (Austral.)

ft m
12 000 4000
9000 3000
6000 2000
3000 1000
1500 500
600 200
0 0
200 600
1000 3000
2000 6000
4000 12 000
6000 18 000
8000 24 000
m ft

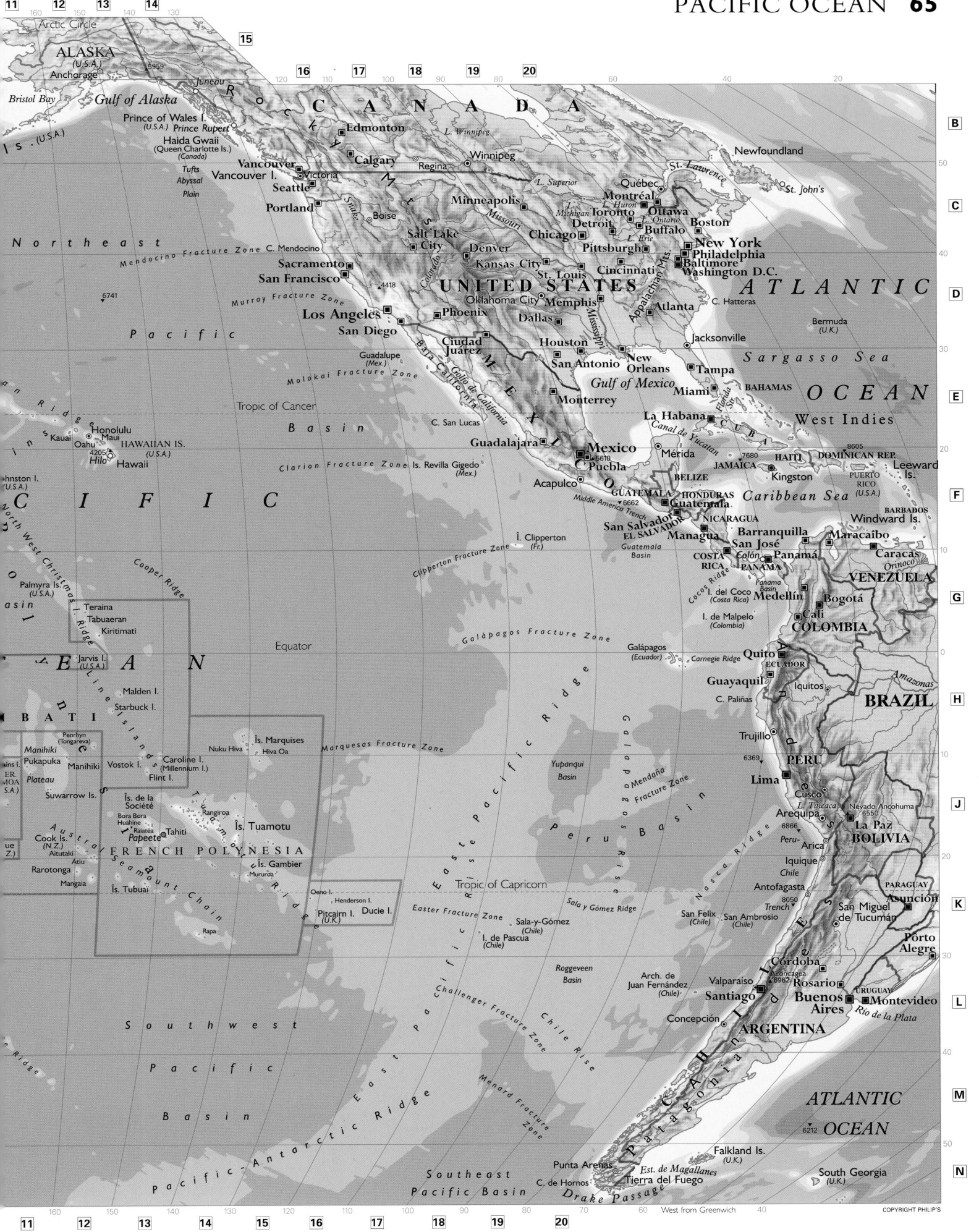

Arctic Circle

ALASKA
(U.S.A.)
Anchorage

Bristol Bay
Gulf of Alaska
5959

Is. (U.S.A.)

Prince of Wales I.
(U.S.A.) Prince Rupert
Haida Gwaii
(Queen Charlotte Is.)
(Canada)
Tufts
Abyssal
Plain

Juneau

ROCKY

CANADA

Edmonton

Calgary

L. Winnipeg

Newfoundland

Vancouver
Vancouver I.
Seattle
Victoria
Portland
Boise
Regina
Winnipeg

St. Lawrence
Québec
St. John's
Montréal

Northeast
Mendocino Fracture Zone C. Mendocino

Pacific

6741

Minneapolis

Salt Lake
City
Sacramento
San Francisco
4418

Denver
Kansas City

L. Superior
Toronto
L. Michigan
Chicago
L. Huron
Detroit L. Ontario Ottawa Boston
Buffalo
Pittsburgh
L. Erie

Cincinnati

New York
Philadelphia
Baltimore
Washington D.C.

ATLANTIC

UNITED STATES
St. Louis
Memphis

Los Angeles
San Diego

Phoenix
Oklahoma City
Dallas

Atlanta

C. Hatteras

Bermuda
(U.K.)

Murray Fracture Zone

Guadalupe
(Mex.)

Ciudad
Juárez

M

Houston
San Antonio

New
Orleans
Jacksonville

Tampa

Sargasso Sea

OCEAN

Tropic of Cancer

Molokai Fracture Zone

Basin

C. San Lucas

Monterrey

Gulf of Mexico
Miami

Florida Str.
BAHAMAS

La Habana
CUBA
West Indies

Honolulu
Maui
HAWAIIAN IS.
(U.S.A.)

Kauai
Oahu
4205
Hilo
Hawaii

Clarion Fracture Zone Is. Revilla Gigedo
(Mex.)

Guadalajara
Mexico
5610
Puebla
Acapulco

Mérida

7680
Canal de Yucatán

8605
HAITI
DOMINICAN REP.
JAMAICA
Kingston
PUERTO
RICO
(U.S.A.)
Leeward
Is.

Johnston I.
(U.S.A.)

CIFIC

Middle America Trench 6662

GUATEMALA
Guatemala
HONDURAS

BELIZE

Caribbean Sea

BARBADOS
Windward Is.

Palmyra Is.
(U.S.A.)

Î. Clipperton
(Fr.)

Clipperton Fracture Zone

Guatemala
Basin

San Salvador
EL SALVADOR
Managua
NICARAGUA

Barranquilla
San José

Maracaíbo

Teraina
Tabuaeran
Kiritimati

COSTA
RICA

Colón
Panamá
PANAMA

Caracas
Orinoco
VENEZUELA

Cooper Ridge

Panama
Basin

Medellín

I. del Coco
(Costa Rica)

I. de Malpelo
(Colombia)

Bogotá
Cali
COLOMBIA

Jarvis I.
(U.S.A.)

Equator

Galápagos Fracture Zone

Galápagos
(Ecuador)

Carnegie Ridge

Quito
ECUADOR

Malden I.
Starbuck I.

BATI

Guayaquil

Iquitos

Amazonas

BRAZIL

Penrhyn
(Tongareva)
Manihiki
Pukapuka
Manihiki
Plateau
Suwarrow Is.

Vostok I.
Caroline I.
(Millennium I.)
Flint I.

Nuku Hiva
Hiva Oa

Îs. Marquises

Marquesas Fracture Zone

Yupanqui
Basin

Trujillo

6369
Lima

PERU

Cusco

Îs. de la
Société
Bora Bora
Huahine
Raiatea
Papeete Tahiti

Rangiroa

Îs. Tuamotu

Mendaña
Fracture Zone

Peru Basin

Cook Is.
(N.Z.)
Aitutaki
Atiu
Rarotonga
Mangaia

FRENCH POLYNESIA

Îs. Gambier
Mururoa

L. Titicaca
6550

Nevado Ancohuma

Arequipa
6866
Peru-Chile
Arica

La Paz
BOLIVIA

Îs. Tubuai

Tropic of Capricorn

Iquique
Chile

Oeno I.
Henderson I.
Pitcairn I. Ducie I.
(U.K.)

Easter Fracture Zone

Sala y Gómez Ridge
Sala-y-Gómez
(Chile)
I. de Pascua
(Chile)

Antofagasta
8050
San Felix
(Chile)
San Ambrosio
(Chile)

PARAGUAY

Asunción

Rapa

San Miguel
de Tucumán

Porto
Alegre

Roggeveen
Basin

Arch. de
Juan Fernández
(Chile)

Córdoba

URUGUAY

Aconcagua
6962
Valparaíso
Santiago

Rosario
Buenos
Aires
Montevideo
Río de la Plata

Southwest

Challenger Fracture Zone

Concepción

ARGENTINA

Pacific

Menard Fracture Zone

ATLANTIC

Basin

Pacific-Antarctic Ridge

OCEAN

6212

Southeast
Pacific Basin

Punta Arenas
C. de Hornos
Est. de Magallanes
Tierra del Fuego
Drake Passage

Falkland Is.
(U.K.)

South Georgia
(U.K.)

1:35 000 000

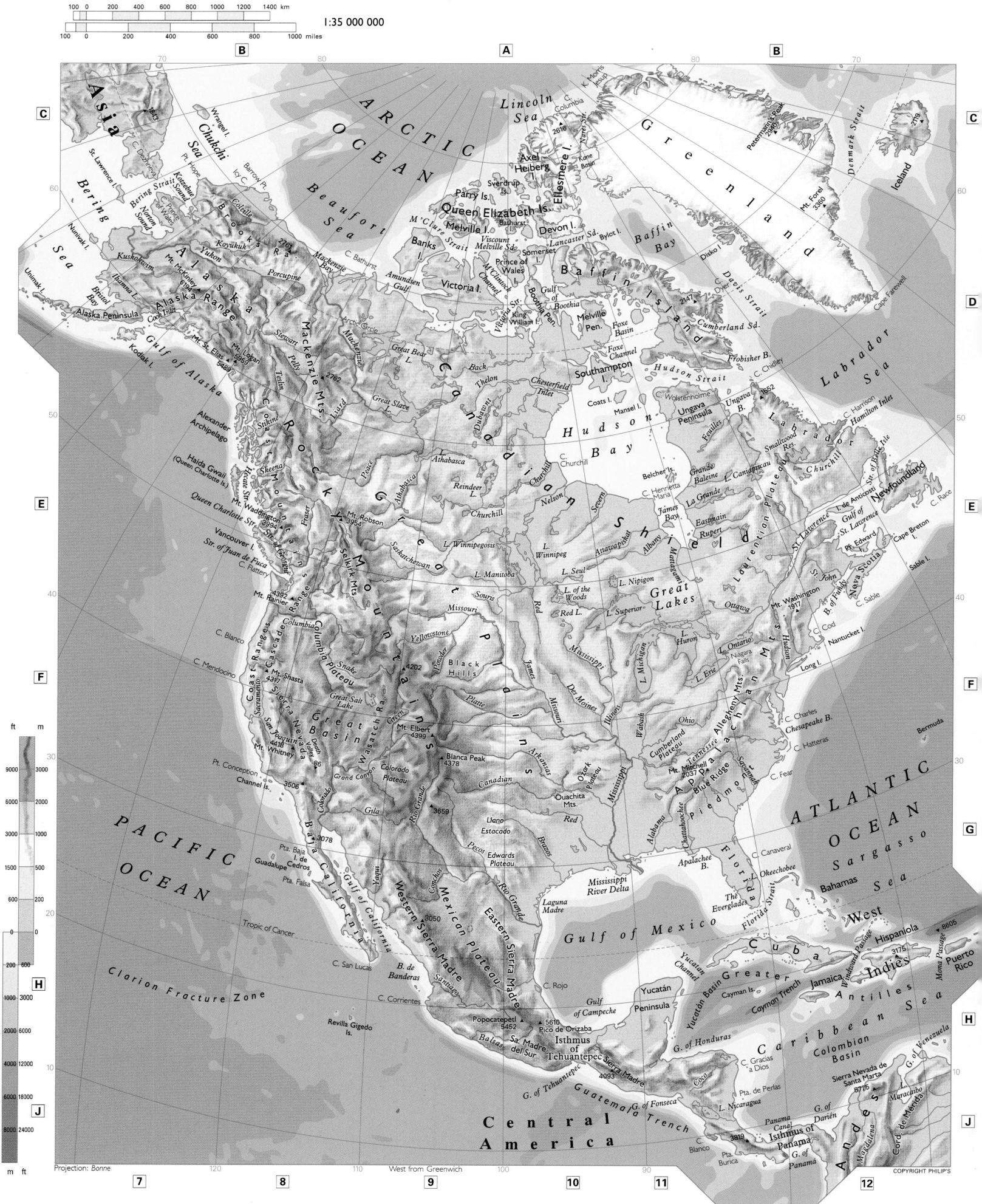

Projection: Bonne

West from Greenwich

COPYRIGHT PHILIP'S

1:35 000 000

100 0 200 400 600 800 1000 1200 1400 km
100 0 200 400 600 800 1000 miles

ARCTIC OCEAN

RUSSIA
Asia
St. Lawrence I.
Bering Strait
Bering Sea

GREENLAND
(Denmark)
ICELAND
Reykjavik
Denmark Strait

Queen Elizabeth Is.
Ellesmere I.
Baffin Bay

Beaufort Sea

Yukon
ALASKA
(U.S.A.)
Porcupine
Fairbanks
Anchorage
Kodiak I.
Gulf of Alaska

Victoria I.

NORTHWEST
Arctic Circle
YUKON TERRITORY
Whitehorse
Juneau

NUNAVUT
Baffin Island
Davis Strait
Nuuk

Great Bear L.
Mackenzie
Back
TERRITORIES
Yellowknife
Great Slave L.
Liard

Hudson Strait
Iqaluit

CANADA

BRITISH COLUMBIA
Skeena
Fraser
Peace
Athabasca
ALBERTA
Edmonton
Calgary
Saskatchewan
SASKATCHEWAN
Regina

Churchill
MANITOBA
Nelson
L. Winnipeg
Winnipeg

Hudson Bay

Eastmain
QUÉBEC
St. Lawrence
NEWFOUNDLAND & LABRADOR
St. John's
St-Pierre et Miquelon (Fr.)
PRINCE EDWARD I.
Charlottetown
NEW BRUNSWICK
Fredericton
NOVA SCOTIA
Halifax
Québec
Montréal
MAINE
Augusta
VER.
N.H. Concord
MASS. Boston
Providence

Victoria
Vancouver
Olympia
WASHINGTON
Seattle
Portland
Salem
OREGON
Columbia

ONTARIO
L. Superior
L. Huron
L. Michigan
L. Ontario
TORONTO
Ottawa
Buffalo
NEW YORK
Detroit
Cleveland
PHILADELPHIA
NEW YORK
Hartford
CONN.
R.I.

MONTANA
Helena
IDAHO
Boise
Snake
WYOMING

NORTH DAKOTA
Bismarck
SOUTH DAKOTA
MINNESOTA
Minneapolis
St. Paul
WISCONSIN
Madison
MICHIGAN
Lansing
Milwaukee
CHICAGO
Toledo
Erie
Pittsburgh
PA.
Columbus
OHIO
INDIANA
Indianapolis
Cincinnati
W.V.
WASHINGTON D.C.
Baltimore
MD.
DEL.
Richmond
VIRGINIA

Sacramento
SAN FRANCISCO
San Jose
Carson City
Salt Lake City
UTAH
NEVADA
Las Vegas
CALIFORNIA
LOS ANGELES
San Diego
Tijuana
Mexicali

Denver
COLORADO
NEBRASKA
Lincoln
Kansas City
Topeka
KANSAS
IOWA
ILLINOIS
Springfield
St. Louis
MISSOURI
KENTUCKY
Nashville
TENNESSEE
Memphis

Raleigh
NORTH CAROLINA
Columbia
SOUTH CAROLINA
Charlotte
Charleston
Bermuda (U.K.)

Santa Fe
Albuquerque
ARIZONA
NEW MEXICO
Phoenix
Tucson
El Paso
Ciudad Juárez

OKLAHOMA
Oklahoma City
ARKANSAS
Little Rock
Jackson
MISSISSIPPI
Birmingham
ALABAMA
Montgomery
ATLANTA
GEORGIA

UNITED STATES

PACIFIC OCEAN

Guadalupe (Mex.)

Hermosillo
Guaymas

DALLAS-FT. WORTH
TEXAS
Austin
HOUSTON
San Antonio
Rio Grande

Baton Rouge
LOUISIANA
New Orleans

Jacksonville
Tallahassee
FLORIDA
Orlando
Tampa
St. Petersburg
MIAMI

ATLANTIC OCEAN

BAHAMAS
Nassau
Turks & Caicos Is. (U.K.)

Tropic of Cancer
Culiacán
Monterrey
Torreón

Gulf of Mexico
Havana
CUBA
Florida Str.

DOMINICAN REP.
San Juan
PUERTO RICO (U.S.A.)

MEXICO

Revilla Gigedo Is. (Mex.)

San Luis Potosí
León
Querétaro
Guadalajara
MÉXICO
Toluca
Puebla
Acapulco

Mérida

Belmopan
BELIZE

Cayman Is. (U.K.)
JAMAICA
Kingston
HAITI
Port-au-Prince
Santo Domingo

Caribbean Sea

GUATEMALA
Guatemala
San Salvador
EL SALVADOR
HONDURAS
Tegucigalpa
NICARAGUA
Managua
L. Nicaragua
COSTA RICA
San José
PANAMÁ
Panamá

Maracaibo
Barranquilla
VENEZUELA

COLOMBIA
Medellín
South America

Projection: Bonne
West from Greenwich
COPYRIGHT PHILIP'S

■ MÉXICO Capital Cities

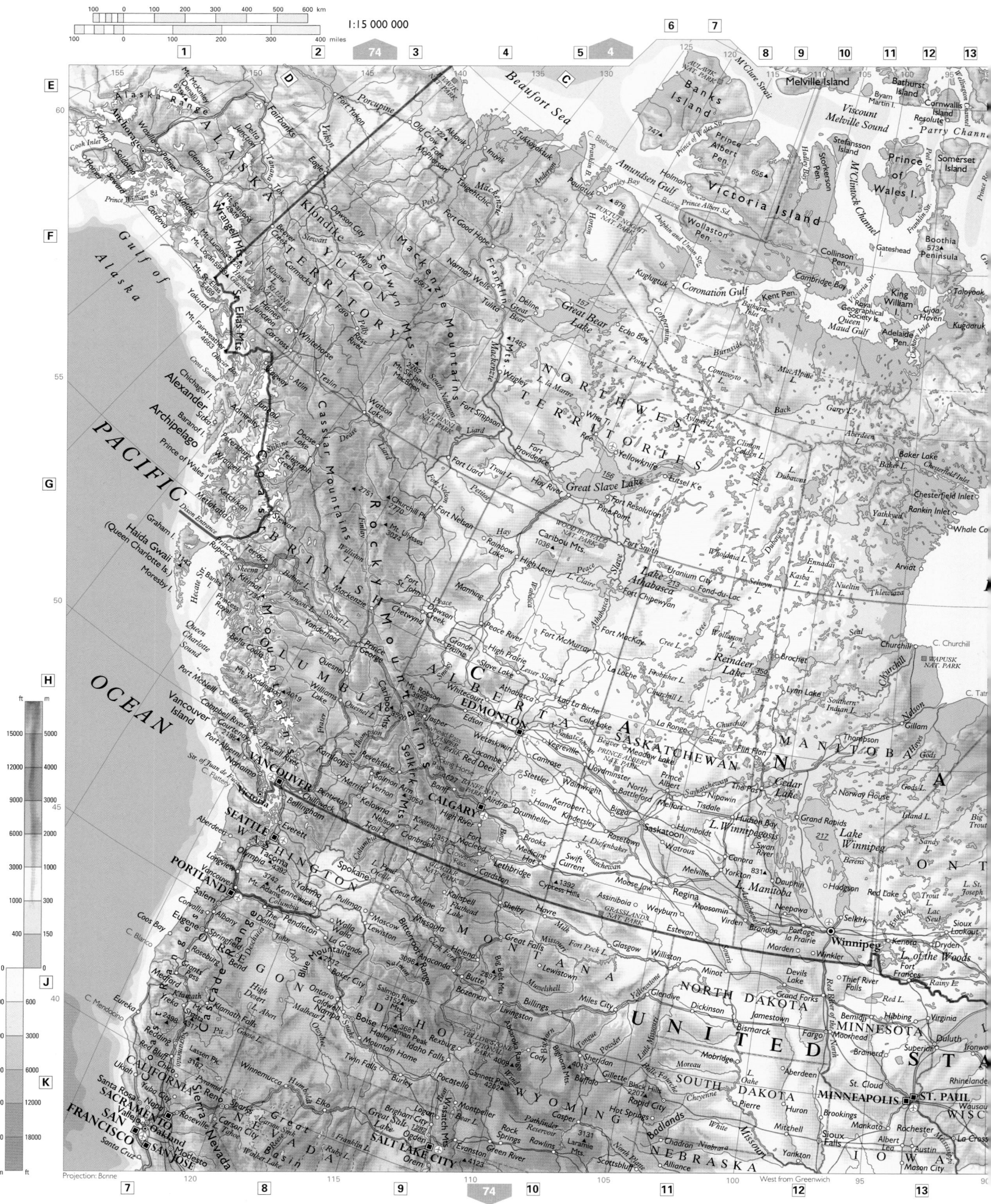

1:15 000 000

Projection: Bonne

NORTHERN CANADA
continuation northwards on same scale as main map

Main map labels (clockwise / by region):

15 16 17 18 19 20 21

ARCTIC OCEAN

GREENLAND (Denmark)

Baffin Bay

Lancaster Sound

Nunavik

Bylot I.

Pond Inlet

Arctic Bay

Borden Pen.

Nanisivik

Clyde River

C. Adair

C. Raper

Davis Strait

B a f f i n   I s l a n d

AUYUITTUQ NAT. PARK

Cumberland Peninsula

Pangnirtung

Qikiqtarjuaq

Home B.

C. Dyer

C. Mercy

Cumberland Sd.

Iqaluit

Pond Inlet

Iglulik

Hall Beach

Rowley

Fury and Hecla Str.

Spicer Is.

Prince Charles I.

Air Force I.

Melville Peninsula

Foxe Basin

Koukdjuak

Netilling L.

Amadjuak

Meta Incognita Peninsula

Frobisher Bay

Hall Peninsula

Resolution I.

Salisbury

Kimmirut

Kinngait

Mill I.

Vansittart I.

C. Dorchester

N U N A V U T

Foxe Channel

Foxe Pen.

Southampton I.

Coral Harbour

Bell Pen.

Nottingham I.

Charles I.

Digges Is.

Salluit

Ivujivik

Coats I.

Mansel I.

Repulse Bay

Ross Welcome Sd.

Isthmus

HUDSON STRAIT

Akpatok I.

Quaqtaq

Kangiqsujuaq

Cratère du Nouveau-Québec

642

657

Ungava Bay

Kangirsuk

Arnaud

Kangiqsualujjuaq

Hebron

Nain

Hopedale

Péninsule d'Ungava

Puvirnituq

Inukjuak

Smith I.

L. Payne

Feuilles

L. Minto

Kuujjuaq

Leaf

TORNGAT MTS. NAT. PARK

C. Chidley

Killiniq I.

Mt. Caubvick

1652

George

Baleine

Kangiqsualujjuaq

257

Ottawa Is.

King George Is.

Sleeper Is.

Bakers Dozen Is.

Sanikiluaq

Belcher Is.

C. Henrietta Maria

Kuujjuarapik

Grande Baleine

L. Bienville

L. à l'Eau Claire

Kanaaupscow

La Grande

LABRADOR

Labrador Sea

3809

C. Harrison

Rigolet

NEWFOUNDLAND & LABRADOR

Cartwright

Port Hope Simpson

1128

North West River

Happy Valley-Goose Bay

Smallwood Res.

Churchill Falls

Churchill

Schefferville

Kawawachikamach

Petitsikapau L.

Esker

Labrador City

Fermont

Wabush

Caniapiscau

1135

Mts. Otish

HUDSON BAY

Peawanuck

Winisk

Attawapiskat

Akimiski I.

Charlton

Eastmain

Wemindji

Chisasibi

Twin Is.

James Bay

Pte. Louis XIV

Fort Albany

Moosonee

Waskaganish

Rupert

Eastmain

Nemiscau

Albanel

L. Mistassini

Gagnon

1104

Manicouagan

Manicouagan Rés.

Fort George

ONTARIO

Attawapiskat

Lansdowne House

Fort Hope

Ogoki

Nakina

Geraldton

Nipigon

Thunder Bay

L. Superior

Houghton 183

Marquette

Escanaba

Green Bay

Menominee

MILWAUKEE

Grand Rapids

L. Michigan

Traverse City

Cadillac

Manistique

Petoskey

Sheboygan

Saginaw

Flint

Lansing

Sarnia

London

DETROIT

Toledo

Windsor

CLEVELAND

Erie

PENNSYLVANIA

Jamestown

Buffalo

Niagara Falls

TORONTO

Hamilton

Kitchener

L. Ontario

ROCHESTER

Syracuse

Elmira

Binghamton

NEW YORK

Albany

Springfield

HARTFORD

CONN.

New Haven

PROVIDENCE

MASS.

BOSTON

C. Cod

Lowell

Manchester

NEW HAMPSHIRE

VERMONT

MAINE

Augusta

Bangor

Portland

Lewiston

Montpelier

Burlington

Champlain

Ogdensburg

Cornwall

OTTAWA

Hull

Brockville

Kingston

Belleville

Oshawa

Peterborough

Barrie

Owen Sound

Orillia

Georgian Bay

L. Huron

Manitoulin I.

Parry Sound

Huntsville

North Bay

Nipissing

Pembroke

Mont-Laurier

Sudbury

Elliot Lake

Sault Ste. Marie

Wawa

Chapleau

New Liskeard

Kirkland Lake

Timmins

Cochrane

Kapuskasing

Hearst

Marathon

Rés. Cabonga

QUÉBEC

MONTRÉAL

Trois-Rivières

Shawinigan

Joliette

Granby

Sherbrooke

Drummondville

St-Hyacinthe

Victoriaville

Thetford Mines

Lévis

St-Georges

Woodstock

Fredericton

Saint John

Bay of Fundy

NEW BRUNSWICK

Miramichi

Moncton

Edmundston

Campbellton

Bathurst

Rivière-du-Loup

Rimouski

Matane

Pén. de la Gaspésie

Gaspé

Chaleur B.

1288

Baie-Comeau

Sept-Îles

Port-Cartier

Dét. de Jacques-Cartier

Î. d'Anticosti

Havre-St-Pierre

Natashquan

Romaine

St-Augustin

Blanc-Sablon

Strait of Belle Isle

St. Anthony

Belle Isle

L'Anse aux Meadows

Grey Is.

Baie Verte

Deer Lake

Corner Brook

Stephenville

Channel-Port aux Basques

Cabot Strait

Long Range Mts.

Gander

Grand Falls-Windsor

Lewisporte

Bonavista

Carbonear

St. John's

Placentia

Avalon Pen.

C. Race

NEWFOUNDLAND

Gulf of St. Lawrence

ST. PIERRE et MIQUELON (Fr.)

Îs. de la Madeleine

PRINCE EDWARD I.

Charlottetown

Summerside

Northumberland Str.

Cape Breton I.

Sydney

Glace Bay

Port Hawkesbury

NOVA SCOTIA

New Glasgow

Antigonish

Truro

Amherst

Dartmouth

Halifax

Bridgewater

Liverpool

Yarmouth

Digby

Kentville

C. Sable

Sable I. (Nova Scotia)

6309

ATLANTIC OCEAN

St. Lawrence (St-Laurent)

Chicoutimi

Jonquière

Alma

Roberval

L. St-Jean

Saguenay

Dolbeau-Mistassini

Chibougamau

1172

Rés. Gouin

Val-d'Or

Rouyn-Noranda

Amos

Matagami

L. Matagami

La Tuque

Grand Falls

COPYRIGHT PHILIP'S

Inset map (NORTHERN CANADA):

ARCTIC OCEAN

North Magnetic Pole 2011

1626

C. Thomas Hubbard

C. Columbia

Lincoln Sea

Alert

GREENLAND (KALAALLIT NUNAAT) (Denmark)

Kronprins Frederik Land

2170

Kap York

Peary Land

Petermann Gletscher

Nares Strait

Kane Basin

Humboldt Gletscher (Sermersuaq)

Knud Rasmussen Land

Qaanaaq (Thule)

Uummannaq (Dundas)

Lauge Koch Kyst

Melville Bugt

QUTTINIRPAAQ NAT. PARK

2616

Barbeau Pk.

Lake Hazen

Tanquary Fjord

Greely Fjord

Eureka

Axel Heiberg Island

2210

Ellesmere Island

Amund Ringnes I.

Ellef Ringnes I.

Meighen I.

C. Isachsen

Sverdrup Islands

King Christian I.

Mackenzie King I.

Borden Island

Brock I.

Prince Patrick Island

Eglinton I.

Emerald I.

Lougheed I.

776

Melville Island

Parry Islands

McClure Strait

N.W.T.

Queen Elizabeth Islands

N U N A V U T

Norwegian Bay

Graham I.

Cornwall I.

Grinnell Pen.

Grise Fiord

Jones Sound

Coburg I.

Devon Island

1951

Wellington Channel

Cornwallis Island

Resolute

Bathurst Island

Byam Martin I.

Lowther I.

Stefansson Island

Prince of Wales I.

Somerset Island

Parry Channel

Lancaster Sound

Viscount Melville Sound

Prince Regent Inlet

Boothia Pen.

Baffin Bay

2469

SIRMILIK NAT. PARK

Bylot I.

Pond Inlet

Nanisivik

Arctic Bay

Borden Pen.

Prince of Wales Icefield

Agassiz Icecap

Qeqertarsuaq

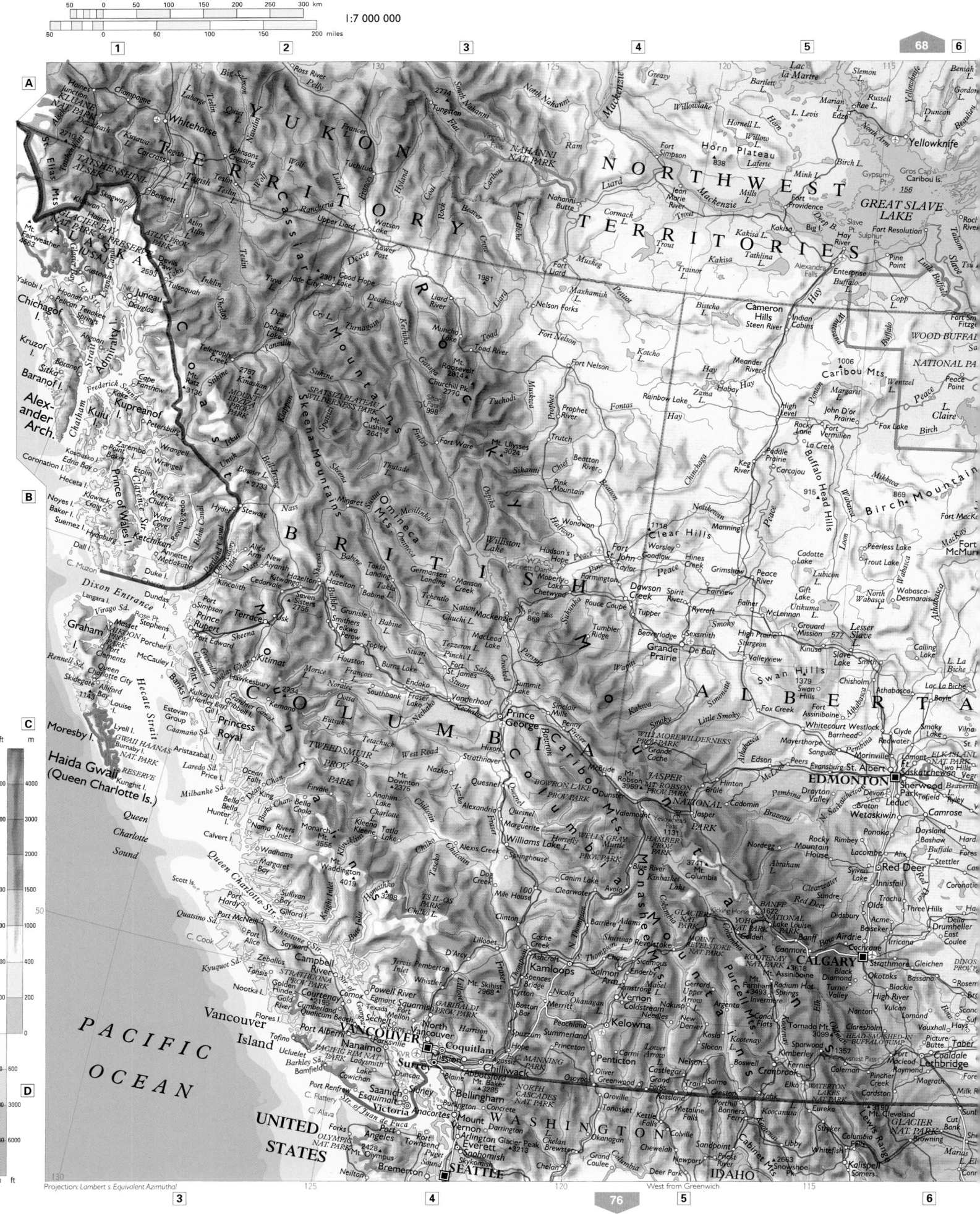

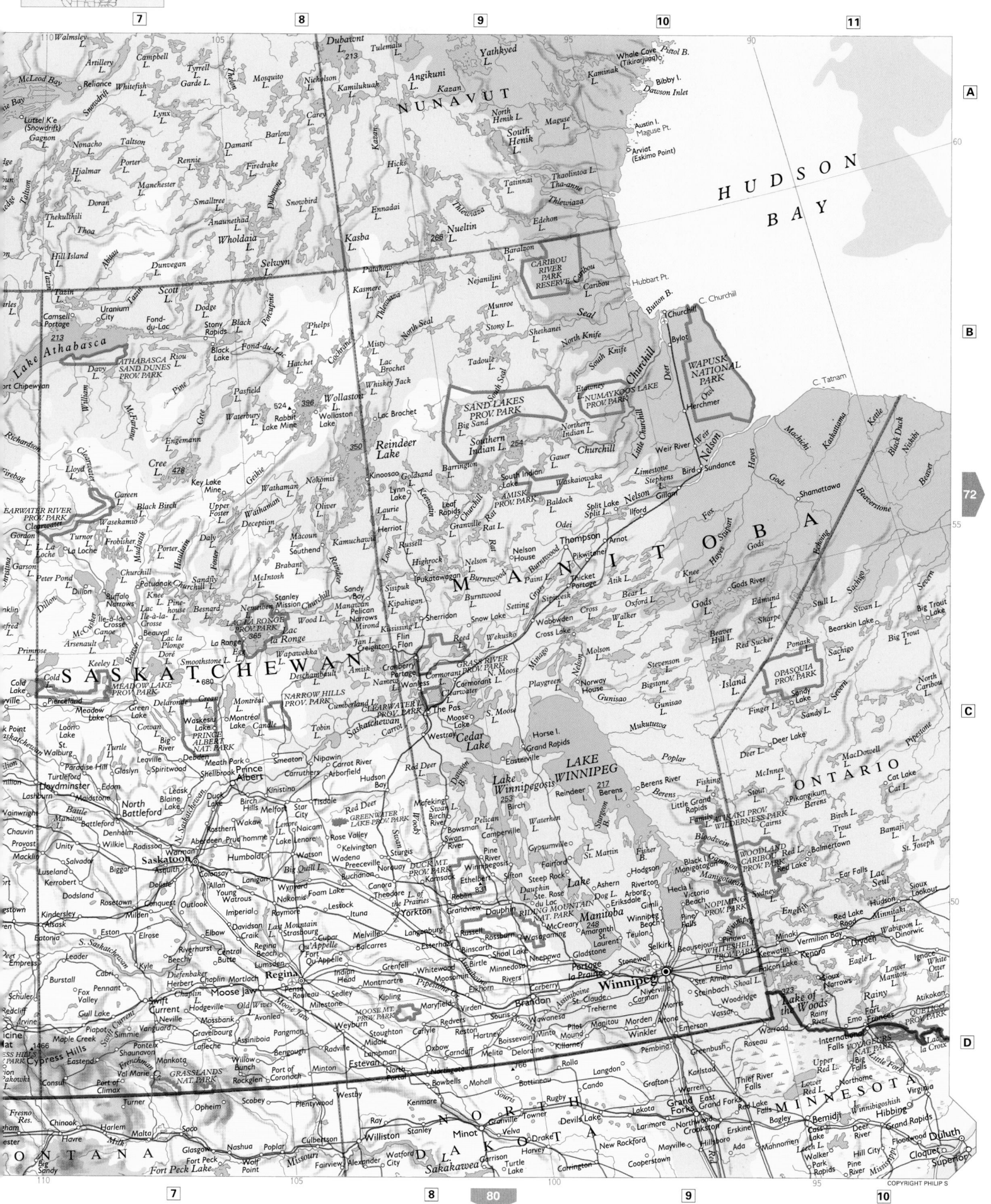

1:7 000 000

Projection: Lambert's Equivalent Azimuthal

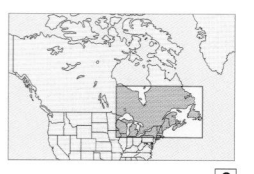

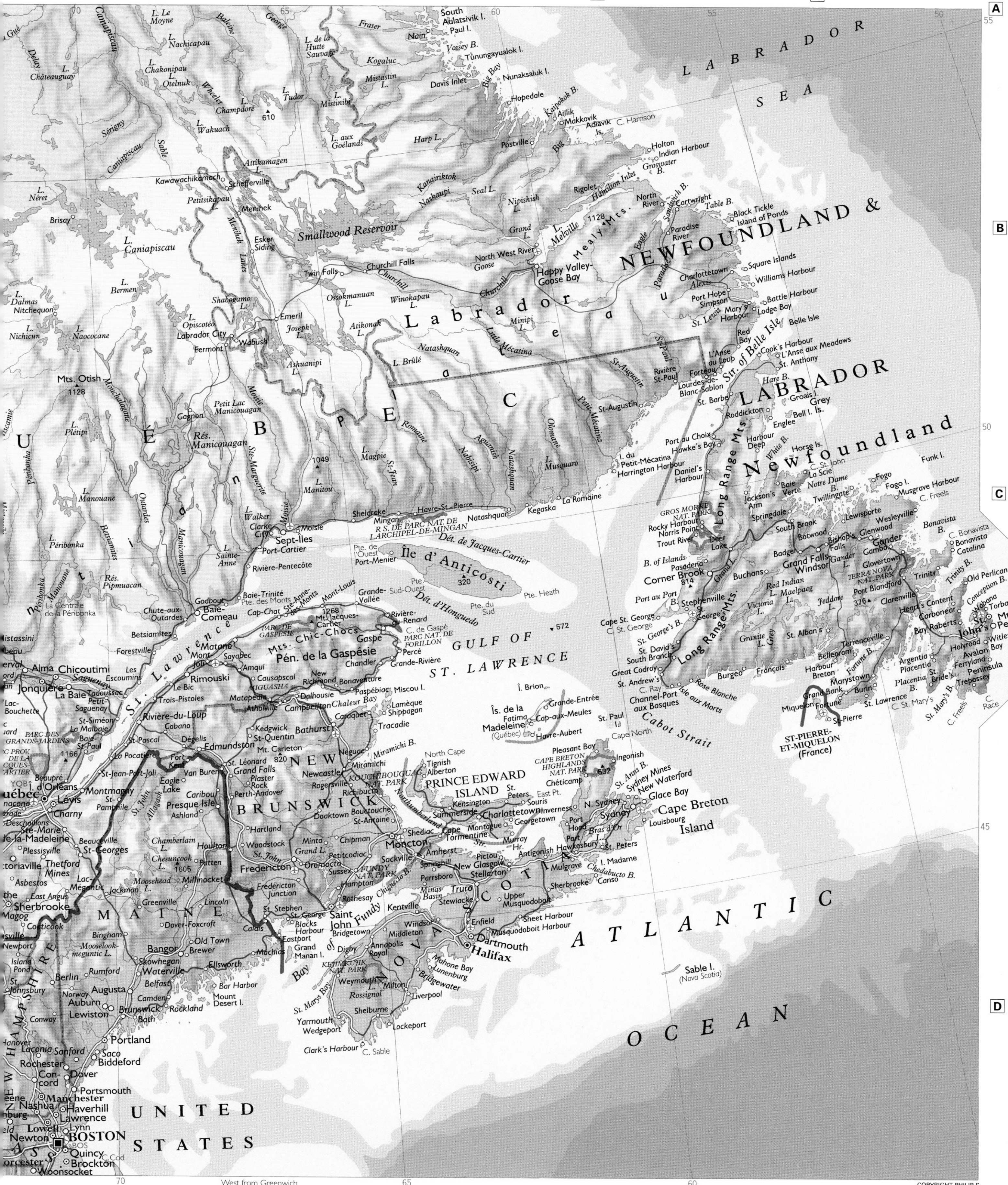
6
69
7
8
9
A
B
C
D
LABRADOR SEA
NEWFOUNDLAND & LABRADOR
Labrador
Newfoundland
Q U E B E C
Plateau du Labrador
GULF OF ST. LAWRENCE
ATLANTIC OCEAN
UNITED STATES
NEW BRUNSWICK
NOVA SCOTIA
PRINCE EDWARD ISLAND
MAINE
NEW HAMPSHIRE
Nain
Hopedale
Makkovik
Postville
Rigolet
Cartwright
Happy Valley-Goose Bay
North West River
Churchill Falls
Smallwood Reservoir
Schefferville
Labrador City
Wabush
Fermont
Mealy Mts.
Mts. Otish
Rés. Manicouagan
Sept-Îles
Port-Cartier
Baie-Comeau
Natashquan
Havre-St-Pierre
Blanc-Sablon
St. Anthony
Str. of Belle Isle
Long Range Mts.
Corner Brook
Stephenville
Grand Falls-Windsor
Gander
Channel-Port aux Basques
St. John's
Cabot Strait
Île d'Anticosti
Gaspé
Pén. de la Gaspésie
Chaleur Bay
Rimouski
St. Lawrence
Chicoutimi
Québec
Lévis
Sherbrooke
Edmundston
Fredericton
Saint John
Moncton
Bathurst
Charlottetown
Cape Breton Island
Sydney
Glace Bay
Halifax
Dartmouth
Truro
Yarmouth
Bay of Fundy
Îs. de la Madeleine
Sable I. (Nova Scotia)
ST-PIERRE-ET-MIQUELON (France)
Bangor
Augusta
Portland
Manchester
BOSTON
C. Cod
C. Race
C. Sable
70
65
60
55
50
45
West from Greenwich

100   0   100   200   300   400   500 km
1:15 000 000
100   0   50   100   150   200   250   300   350 miles

PACIFIC OCEAN

Anchorage
3363 miles
5412 km
Washington D.C.
2010 miles
3234 km
2438 miles
3923 km
San Francisco
2785 miles
4492 km
2395 miles
3854 km
Honolulu
Tropic of Cancer

BRITISH COLUMBIA
Kelowna
VANCOUVER
Penticton
Chilliwack
Vancouver
Bellingham
Everett
ALBERTA
Medicine Hat
Milk
Trail
Cranbrook
Shelby
C. Flattery
Victoria
SEATTLE
Tacoma
WASHINGTON
Spokane
Coeur d'Alene
Kalispell
Great Falls
MONTANA
Grays Harb.
Aberdeen
Olympia
Centralia
Wenatchee
Ellensburg
Yakima
Pullman
Flathead Lake
2108
Mt. Rainier
Moscow
Lewiston
Missoula
Longview
Vancouver
Columbia
Pendleton
Grangeville
Helena
Butte
Anaconda
Bozeman
Billings
Livingston
PORTLAND
McMinnville
Salem
The Dalles
La Grande
IDAHO
3086
Corvallis
Albany
Eugene
Springfield
Bend
Payette
Caldwell
Nampa
Boise
Idaho Falls
Pocatello
WYOMING
Coos Bay
OREGON
Roseburg
Ontario
Mountain Home
Twin Falls
Burley
Montpelier
Grants Pass
Medford
Klamath Falls
Rupert
Bear L.
Logan
Brigham City
Evanston
Eureka
Mt. Shasta
4317
Goose L.
Winnemucca
Humboldt R.
Elko
Great Salt Lake
SALT LAKE CITY
C. Mendocino
Redding
Red Bluff
Honey L.
Pyramid L.
Reno
Sparks
NEVADA
Ogden
Ely
Provo
Orem
UTAH
Chico
Yuba City
Carson City
Tahoe
Walker Lake
Nephi
Pt. Arena
Ukiah
Roseville
SACRAMENTO
Santa Rosa
Napa
Vallejo
Stockton
Hawthorne
Tonopah
Richfield
Grand Junction
SAN FRANCISCO
Oakland
Concord
Modesto
Merced
YOSEMITE NAT. PARK
Moab
Montrose
SAN JOSE
Santa Cruz
Salinas
Monterey
Fresno
Mt. Whitney
SEQUOIA NAT. PARK
CALIFORNIA
Visalia
Tulare
LAS VEGAS
Cedar City
ZION NAT. PARK
L. Powell
Cortez
Paso Robles
San Luis Obispo
Bakersfield
Ridgecrest
Henderson
Lake Mead
GRAND CANYON NAT. PARK
Grand Canyon
Colorado Plateau
Farming
Santa Maria
Santa Barbara
Mojave Desert
Bullhead City
Kingman
Flagstaff
Humphreys Peak
3851
Winslow
Gallup
Oxnard
Glendale
Pasadena
Barstow
Lake Havasu City
Prescott
Payson
LOS ANGELES
SAN BERNARDINO
Riverside
Palm Springs
Long Beach
Anaheim
Mission Viejo
Salton Sea
Glendale
PHOENIX
Mesa
Globe
ARIZONA
San Diego
Oceanside
El Centro
Yuma
Casa Grande
Safford
Silver City
TIJUANA
MEXICALI
Sonoran Desert
Tucson
SONORA
Nogales

ALASKA
on same scale

ARCTIC OCEAN
RUSSIA
Penzhino
Arctic Circle
CHUKCHI SEA
Point Hope
Cape Lisburne
Barrow
Pt. Barrow
Wainwright
North Slope
Koryakskoye Nagorye
2453
Anadyr
Chukotskiy Poluostrov
Uelen
Mys Dezhneva (East Cape)
Bering Strait
Kotzebue
Kobuk
De Long Mts.
1489
Baird Mts.
Prudhoe Bay
Colville
BROOKS RANGE
Endicott Mts.
2446
Philip Smith Mts.
Davidson Mts.
Tilichiki
Providenyia
Mys Chukotskiy
Little Diomede I. (U.S.A.)
Cape Prince of Wales
Shungnak
Schwatka Mts.
2682
Wiseman
Kovacha
St. Lawrence I. (U.S.A.)
533
658
Teller
Nome
Council
Selawik
Old Crow
Fort McPherson
Porcupine
Mys Oyutorski
Mys Navarin
Norton Sound
Nulato
Koyukuk
Ray Mts.
Yukon
Yukon Flats
Circle
BERING SEA
St. Matthew I.
Stuart I.
Emmonak
Kaltag
Kaiyah Mts.
College
Fairbanks
Eielson
Eagle
Dawson City
Klondike
Cape Romanzof
Hooper Bay
Yukon Delta
Kotlik
Unalakleet
Nenana
Anderson
Mt. Harper
1994
Tok
YUKON
Nunivak I.
611
Etolin Str.
Bethel
Kuskokwim
Holy Cross
Kuskokwim Mountains
Mt. McKinley (Denali)
6194
Mt. Hayes
4216
ALASKA RANGE
Beaver Creek
Cormacks
St. Paul I.
Pribilof Is.
St. George I.
Kulbuck Mts.
Tikchik Lakes
Iliamna Lake
Mt. Foraker
5304
Copper Center
Mt. Sanford
4949
Healy
Palmer
WASILLA
Kenai
Anchorage
Chugach Mts.
Mt. Blackburn
4996
Cordova
Valdez
Whittier
Prince William Sound
Mt. St. Elias
5489
Hubbard Glacier
Haines Junction
Whitehorse
Near Islands
Attu I.
345
Agattu I.
Rat Islands
Kiska I.
ALEUTIAN ISLANDS
Andreanof Islands
Amchitka I.
Kanaga I.
Adak I.
Atka I.
1533
Amlia I.
Seguam
Islands of Four Mountains
Umnak I.
2036
Dutch Harbor
Unalaska
Fox Islands
Unimak I.
Shishaldin Volcano
2587
Sanak I.
ALASKA PENINSULA
Shumagin Is.
Dillingham
Bristol Bay
Becharof Lake
2153
Afognak I.
Kodiak I.
Kodiak
Shelikof Strait
1362
Trinity Is.
Chirikof I.
Gulf of Alaska
Yakutat
Malaspina Glacier
Chichagof I.
SITKA
Alexander

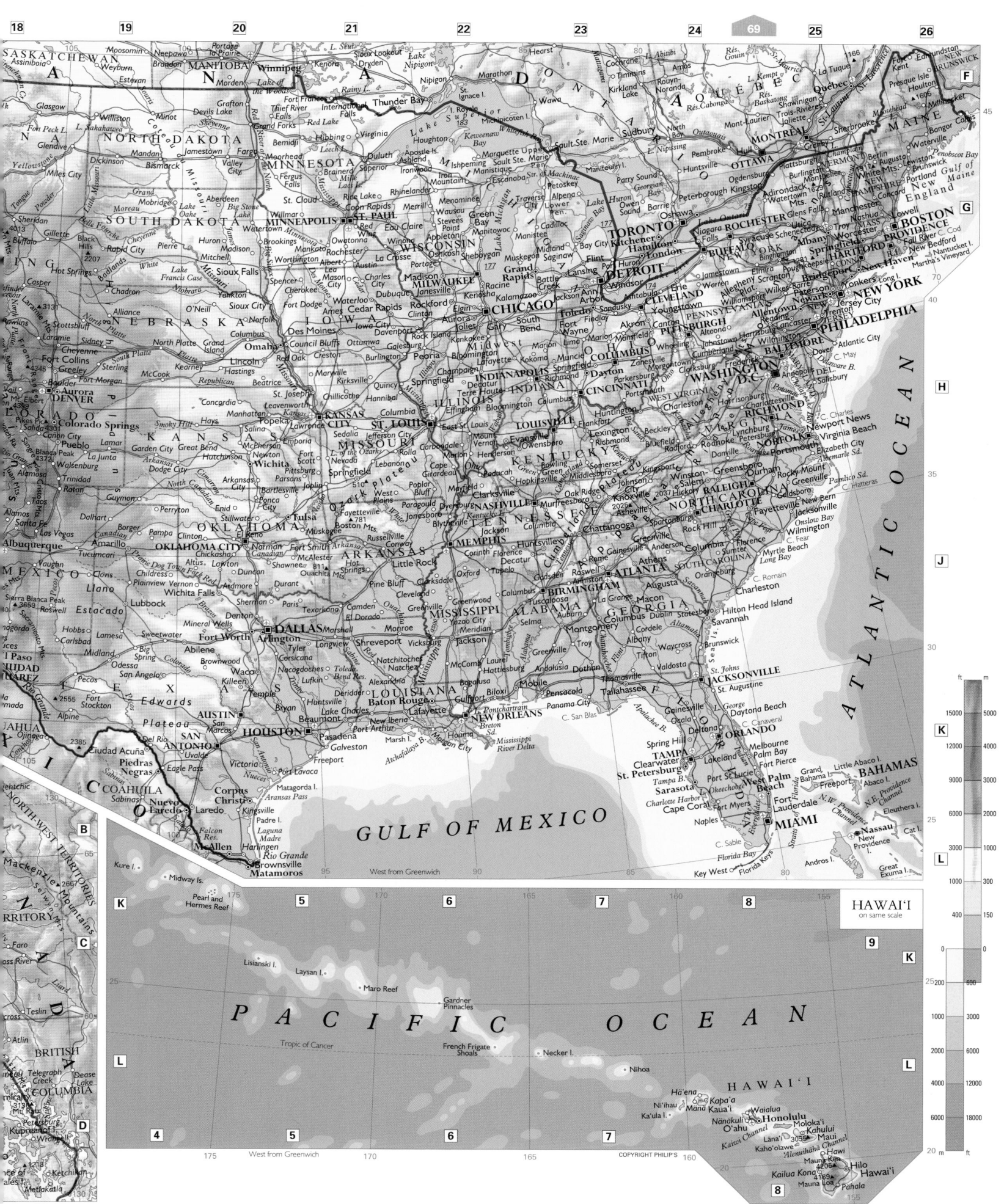

GULF OF MEXICO

ATLANTIC OCEAN

HAWAI'I
on same scale

PACIFIC OCEAN

COPYRIGHT PHILIP'S

1:6 700 000

1:2 500 000

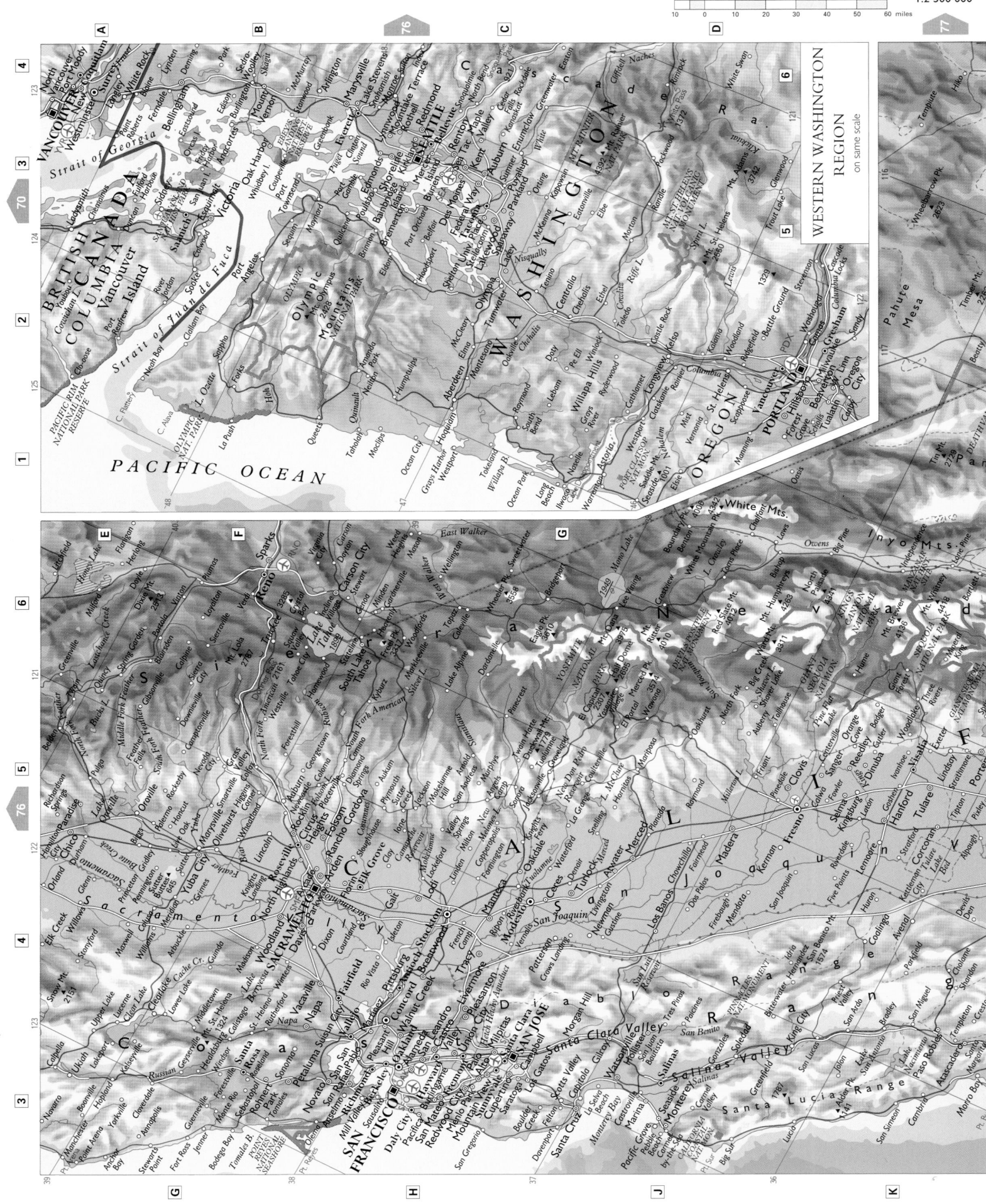

WESTERN WASHINGTON
REGION
on same scale

Lava fields

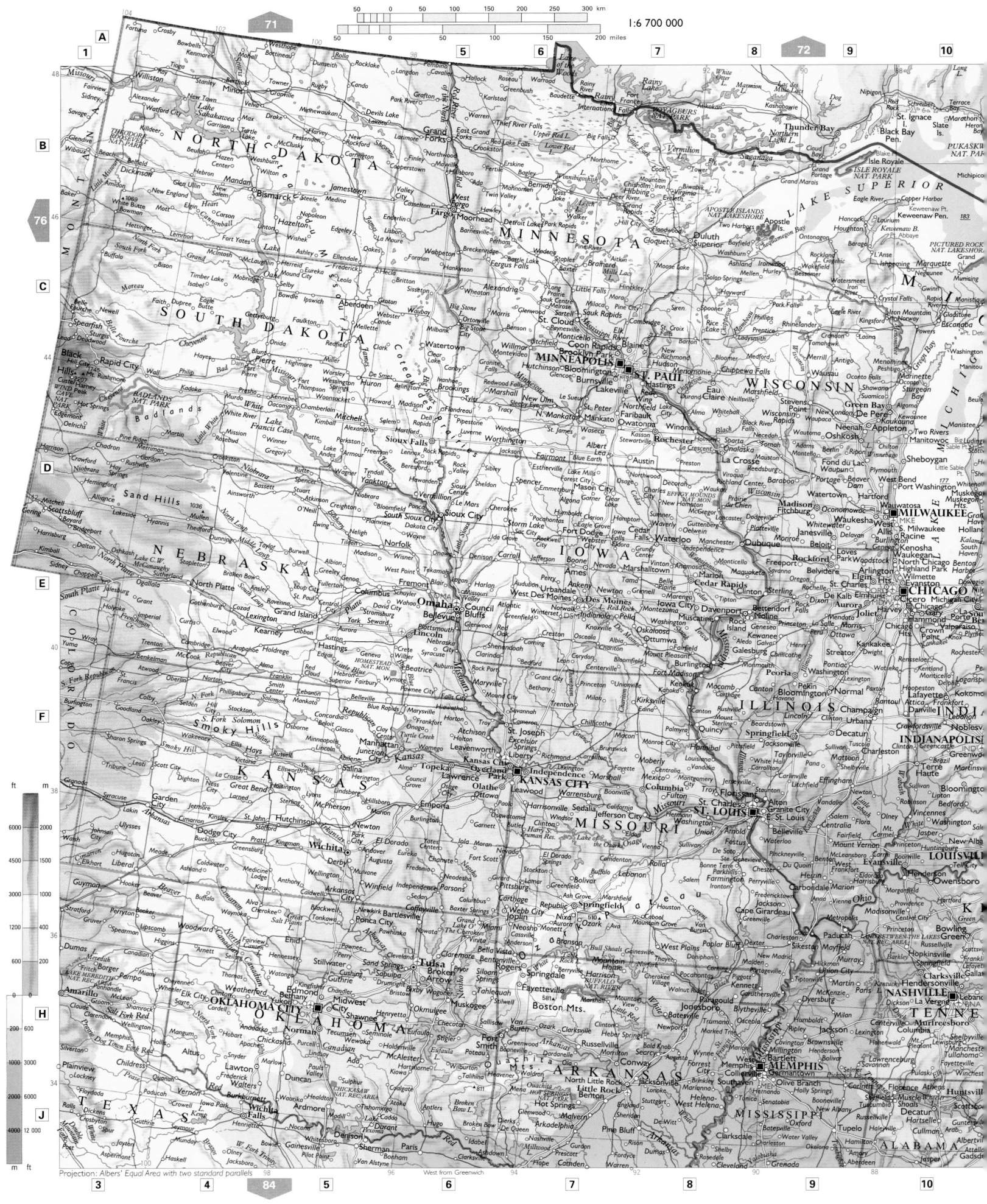

1:6 700 000

Projection: Albers' Equal Area with two standard parallels

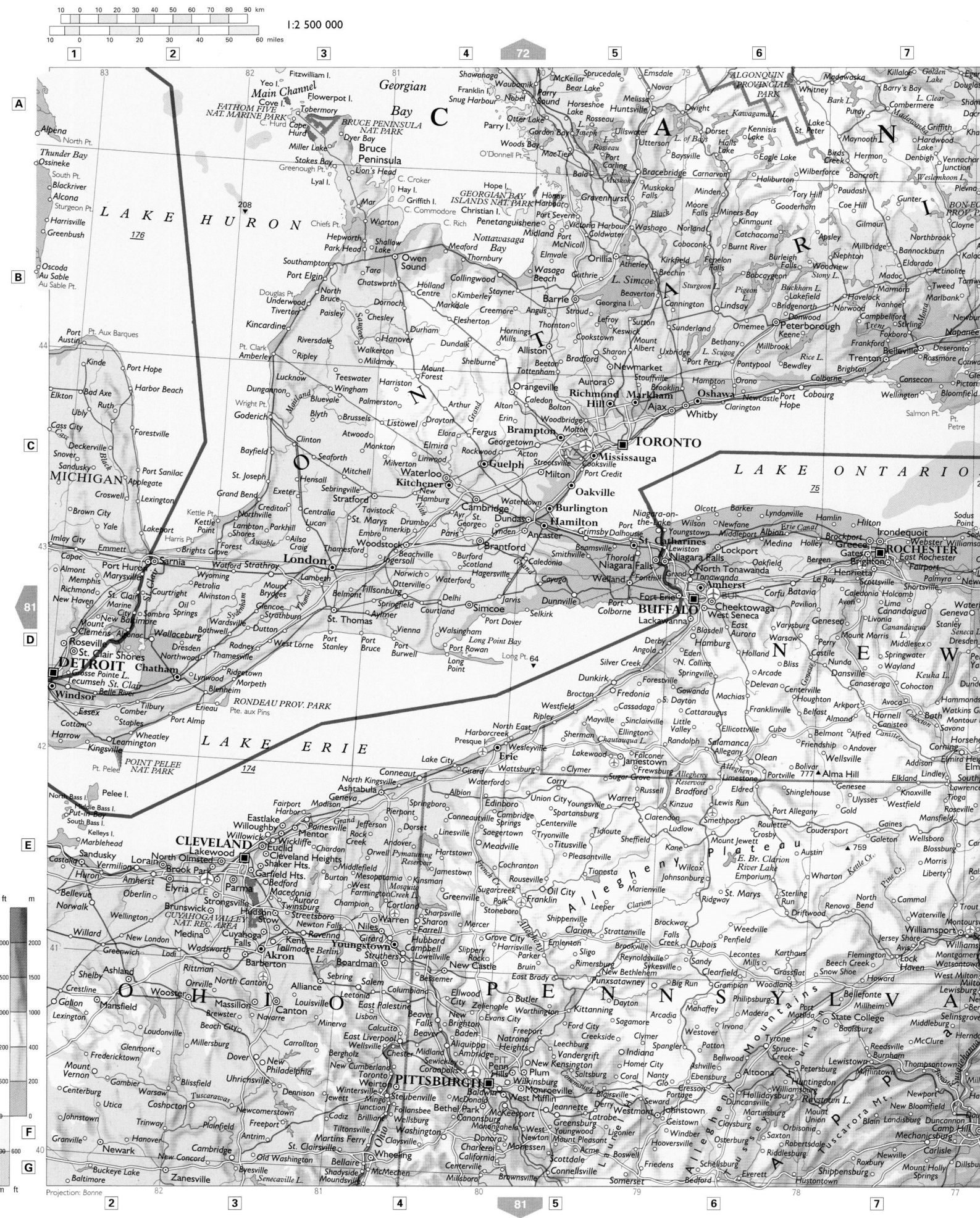

1:2 500 000

Projection: Bonne

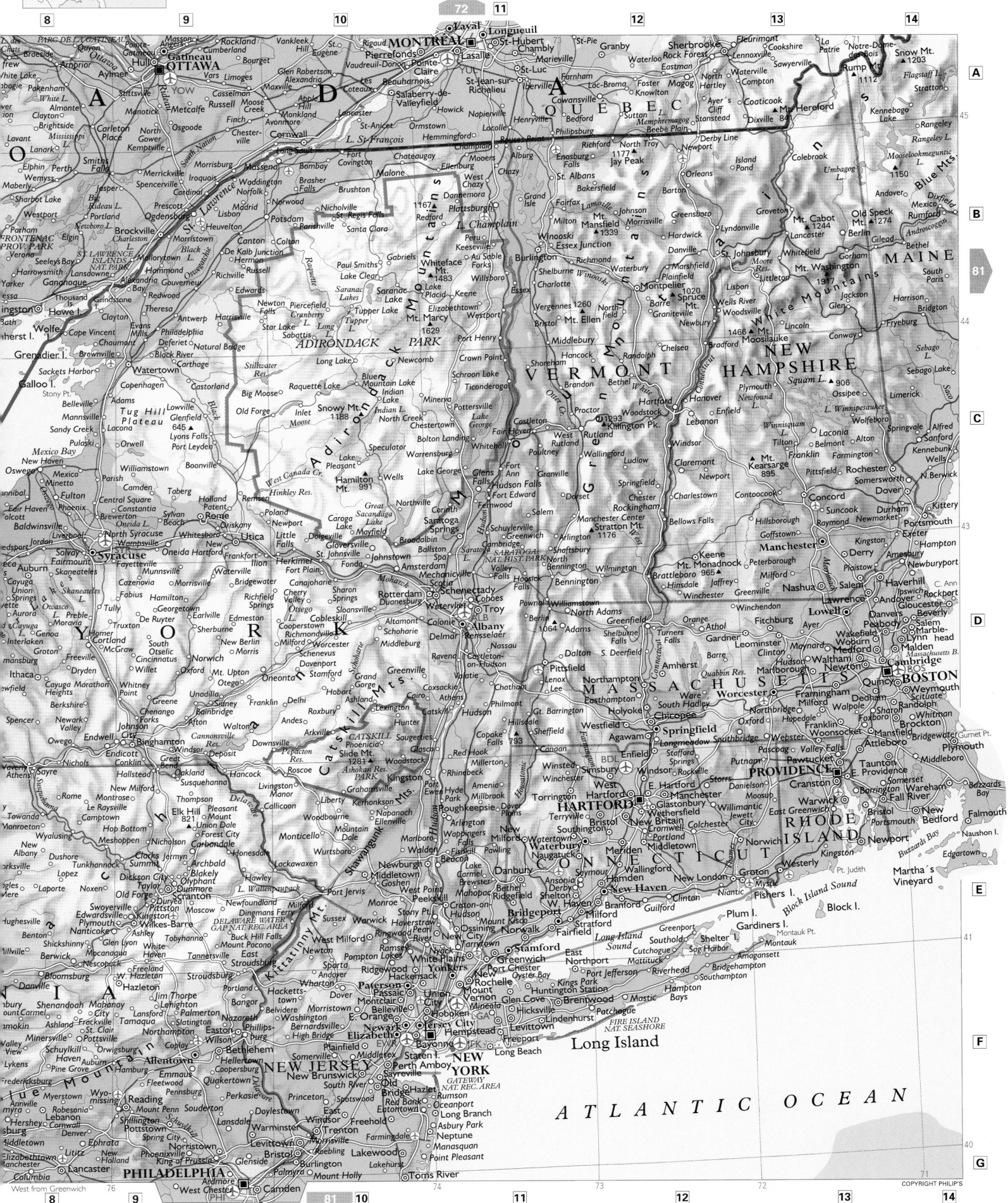

Projection: Albers' Equal Area with two standard parallels

West from Greenwich

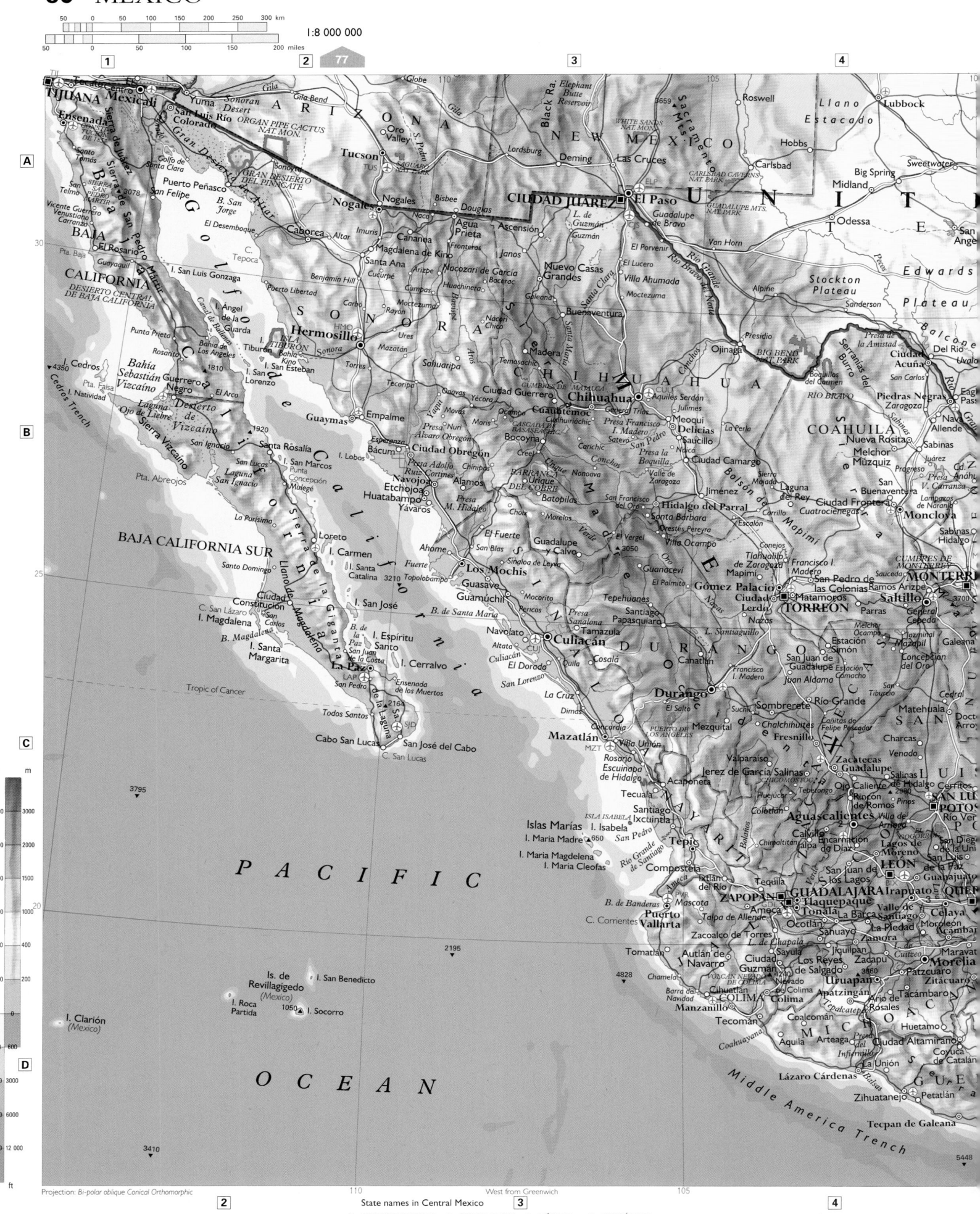

1:8 000 000

50   0   50   100   150   200   250   300 km

50   0   50   100   150   200 miles

Projection: Bi-polar oblique Conical Orthomorphic

State names in Central Mexico

1 DISTRITO FEDERAL   3 GUANAJUATO   5 MÉXICO   7 QUERÉTARO
2 AGUASCALIENTES   4 HIDALGO   6 MORELOS   8 TLAXCALA

West from Greenwich

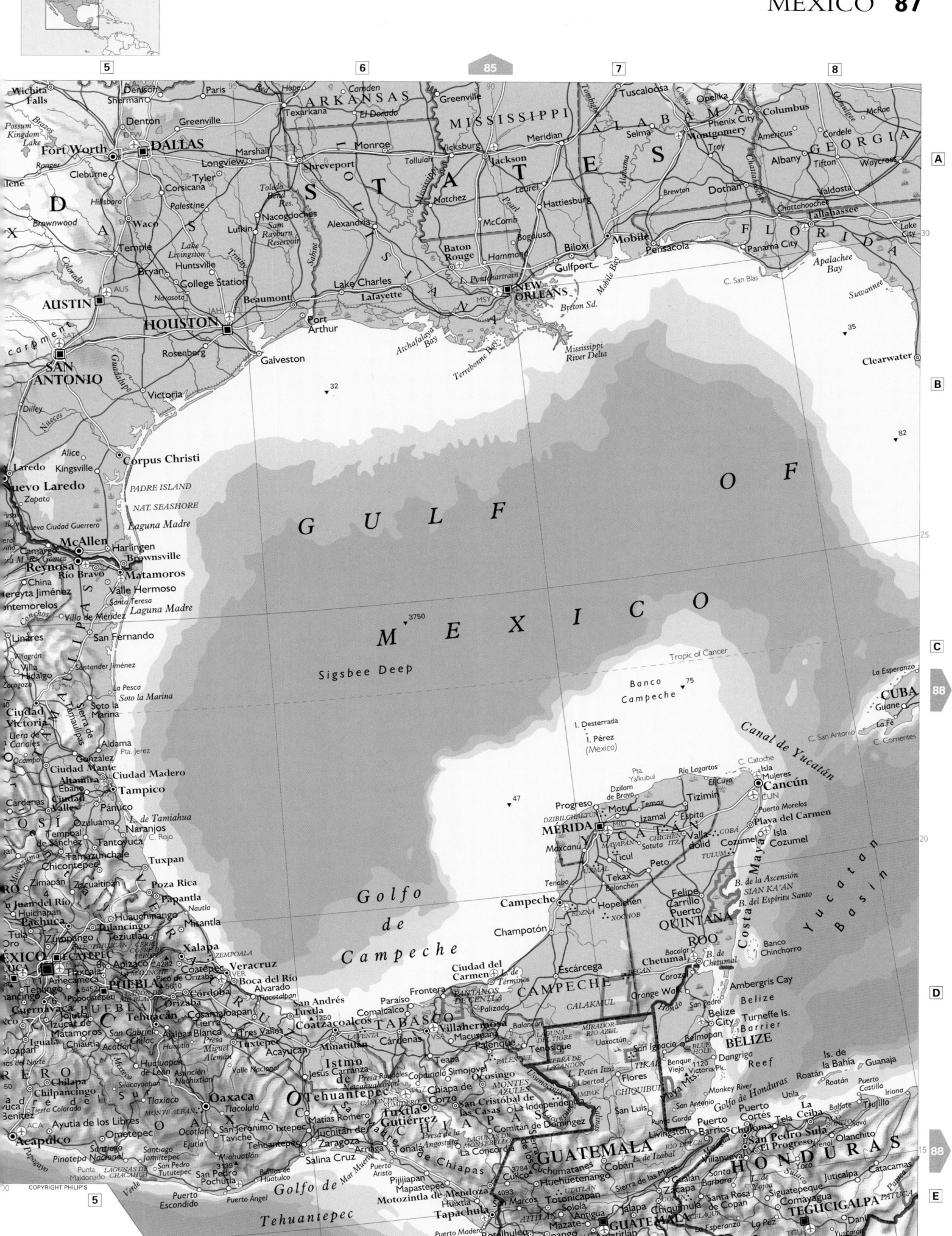

JAMAICA
1:3 000 000

GUADELOUPE AND MARTINIQUE
1:2 000 000

1:8 000 0

CARIBBEAN SEA

Gulf of Mexico

PACIFIC OCEAN

MEXICO

GUATEMALA

BELIZE

HONDURAS

EL SALVADOR

NICARAGUA

COSTA RICA

PANAMA

CUBA

JAMAICA

U.S.A.

FLORIDA

MARTINIQUE (Fr.)

GUADELOUPE (Fr.)

5

PUERTO RICO d
1:3 000 000
10 0 10 20 30 40 50 km
10 0 10 20 30 miles

VIRGIN ISLANDS e
1:2 000 000
10 0 10 20 30 km
10 0 10 20 miles

ATLANTIC OCEAN

PUERTO RICO
(U.S.A.)

Aguadilla • Isabela • Barceloneta
Arecibo • Manati • Vega • SAN JUAN
Baja • Bayamón • Carolina • Rio Grande • Dewey
Mayagüez • San Sebastián • Utuado • Caguas • Fajardo • Culebra
Adjuntas • Cordillera Central • Cayey • Humacao • Naguabo • Vieques
San German • Cerro • Coamo • Esperanza
Yauco • Ponce • Yabucoa
Pta. Aguila • Guanica • Guayama
I. Caja de Muertos

Virgin Islands
(U.K.)
The Settlement
Rufling Pt. • Anegada • East Pt.
Jost Van • Great Camanoe
Dyke I. • Guana I. • Virgin Gorda
Virgin Is. • Tortola • Spanish Town
(U.S.A.) • Road Town • Beef I. • Peter I.
Charlotte • Cruz • St. John I.
Amalie • Bay • Thomas I.

ST. LUCIA f
1:1 000 000
5 0 5 10 km
5 0 5 10 miles

Cap Point • Pte. Hardy
Gros Islet • Esperance Bay
Castries • Marquis
Girard
Anse la Raye • Millet • Dennery
Canaries • Trou Gras Pt.
Soufrière • Mt. Gimie • Micoud
Soufrière Bay • Petit Piton • Vierge Pt.
Gros Piton Pt. • Gros Piton • UVF
Choiseul • **ST. LUCIA**
Laborie • Vieux Fort
C. Moule à Chique

ATLANTIC OCEAN
Crab Hill • North Point
Spring Hall • Boscobelle
Fustic • Portland • Belleplaine
Speightstown • Bathsheba
Westmoreland • Bridgefield • Martin's Bay
Holetown • Jackson • Massiah
Black Rock • Ellerton • Street • Six Cross Roads
Bridgetown • Ivy • Edey • The Crane
Carlisle Bay • Worthing • Oistins • St. Martins
Bay • Chancery Lane • South Point
BARBADOS

BARBADOS g
1:1 000 000
5 0 5 10 km
5 0 5 10 miles

MAS

ATLANTIC OCEAN

New Bight • Cat I.
San Salvador I.
Conception I.
Rum Cay
Long I.
Clarence Town • Samana Cay
Crooked I.
Plana Cays
Albert Town • Snug Corner • Mayaguana I.
Acklins I.
Mira por vos Cay
Hogsty Reef
Little Inagua I.
Turks & Caicos Is.
Caicos Is. (U.K.)
Cockburn Town • Turks Is.
Great Inagua I.
Lake Rose • Matthew Town
INAGUA
Mouchoir Bank
Silver Bank
Navidad Bank

Tropic of Cancer
Crooked I. Passage
Caicos Passage

Moa
Baracoa
Maisí
GUANTÁNAMO
BAY (U.S.A.)
Cap-Haïtien
Port-de-Paix
Gonaïves
Fort Liberté • Puerto Plata • Santiago de los Caballeros
HAITI • **DOMINICAN REP.**
PORT-AU-PRINCE • La Vega • San Francisco de Macoris
Les Cayes • SANTO DOMINGO
Hispaniola
Beata Ridge
Muertas Trough
Antilles

Milwaukee Deep 8605
Puerto Rico Trench

Bayamón • SAN JUAN
Arecibo • Carolina • Virgin Is.
Ponce • **PUERTO RICO** (U.S.A.) • Fajardo • St. Thomas • Tortola • Virgin Gorda • Anegada
Mayagüez • Caguas • Guayama • Culebra • Charlotte Amalie • Road Town • Sombrero (U.K.)
Isla Mona • Vieques • Virgin Is. (U.S.A.) • Anguilla (U.K.)
St. Croix • St. Martin (Fr.)
Christiansted • St. Maarten (Neth.) • St-Barthélemy (Fr.)
Frederiksted • St. Eustatius • Barbuda
St. Kitts & Nevis • **ANTIGUA & BARBUDA**
Basseterre • Antigua • St. John's
Montserrat
Redonda • **GUADELOUPE** (Fr.)
Ste-Rose • Le Moule • La Désirade
Basse-Terre • Pointe-à-Pitre • Marie-Galante (Fr.)
Grand-Bourg
I. des Saintes
Portsmouth • **DOMINICA**
Roseau • Dominica Passage
Mt. Pelée • Martinique Passage
Fort-de-France • Ste-Marie
MARTINIQUE (Fr.) • Le Robert • Rivière-Pilote
St. Lucia Channel
Castries • **ST. LUCIA**
Soufrière • UVF
St. Vincent Passage
Soufrière • St. Vincent • Speightstown
Kingstown • **BARBADOS**
Bequia • Bridgetown
ST. VINCENT & THE GRENADINES
The Grenadines • Tobago
Carriacou • **GRENADA**
St. George's

Leeward Islands
Windward Islands
Lesser Antilles

CARIBBEAN SEA
Venezuelan Basin
Aves Ridge

Colombian Basin

ABC Islands / **Lesser Antilles**
Oranjestad • Aruba (Neth.) • Curaçao • Bonaire
Willemstad
Is. Las Aves • Is. Los Roques (Ven.)
I. Orchila (Ven.)
I. Blanquilla (Ven.)
Is. Los Hermanos
Is. Los Testigos
Tobago
Scarborough
NUEVA ESPARTA
I. de Margarita • Port of Spain
Pta. Gallinas
GUAJIRA
Pen. de la Guajira
COLOMBIA
Ríohacha • Uribia
Santa Marta • Maicao
Punta Cardón • Coro
Punta Fijo • La Vela
MÉDANOS DE CORO
Puerto Cumarebo
FALCÓN
Tucacas • Puerto Cabello
CARACAS • La Guaira
MARACAY • VALENCIA
Maracaibo • Cabimas
LARA • CARABOBO • MIRANDA
BARQUISIMETO • **VALENCIA** • Villa de Cura
ZULIA • TRUJILLO • PORTUGUESA
Lago de Maracaibo
MÉRIDA • **BARINAS**
San Cristóbal • Cúcuta • Táchira
VENEZUELA
SUCRE
Cumaná • Barcelona
TRINIDAD & TOBAGO
Trinidad • Arima • San Fernando
MONAGAS
DELTA AMACURO
Maturín • Tucupita
ANZOÁTEGUI
GUÁRICO
Ciudad Guayana
Ciudad Bolívar
Orinoco

COPYRIGHT PHILIP'S

92

West from Greenwich

ft: 6000 12 000 18 000 24 000
m: 2000 4000 6000 8000
4000 3000 2000 1500 1000 400 200 0
12 000 9000 6000 4500 3000 1200 600

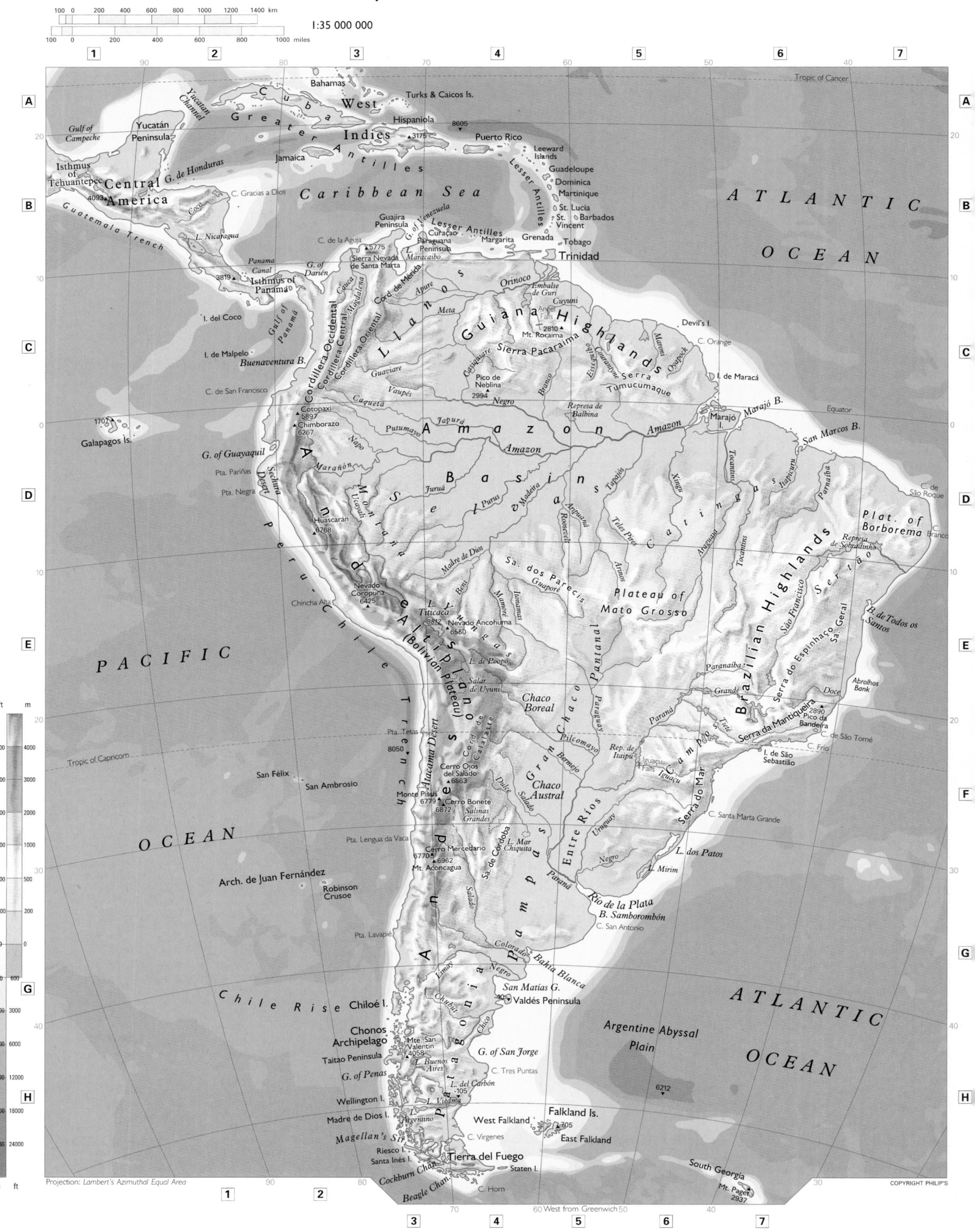

100 0 200 400 600 800 1000 1200 1400 km

1:35 000 000

100 0 200 400 600 800 1000 miles

Projection: Lambert's Azimuthal Equal Area

COPYRIGHT PHILIP'S

1:35 000 000

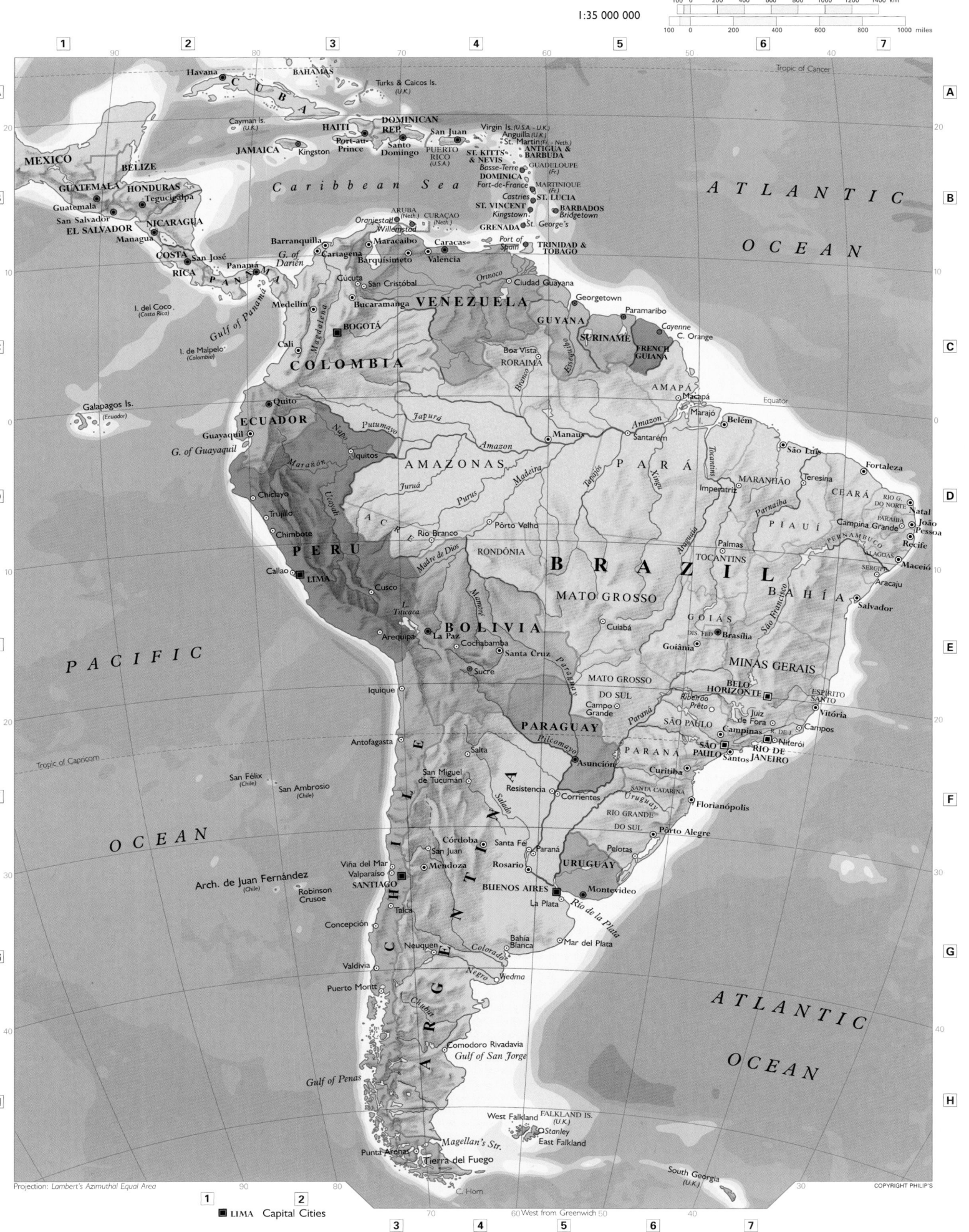

100 0 200 400 600 800 1000 1200 1400 km

100 0 200 400 600 800 1000 miles

| 1 | 2 | 3 | 4 | 5 | 6 | 7 |

A

Havana
BAHAMAS
Tropic of Cancer

C U B A

Cayman Is.
(U.K.)

HAITI
DOMINICAN
REP.
San Juan
Virgin Is. (U.S.A. - U.K.)
Anguilla (U.K.)
St. Martin (Fr. - Neth.)
ANTIGUA &
BARBUDA

B

MEXICO
BELIZE
GUATEMALA
HONDURAS
Tegucigalpa
Guatemala
San Salvador
EL SALVADOR
NICARAGUA
Managua

Port-au-
Prince
Santo
Domingo
Kingston
JAMAICA
PUERTO
RICO
(U.S.A)
ST. KITTS
& NEVIS
Basse-Terre
GUADELOUPE
(Fr.)
DOMINICA
Fort-de-France
MARTINIQUE
(Fr.)
Castries
ST. LUCIA
ST. VINCENT
Kingstown
BARBADOS
Bridgetown
GRENADA
St. George's

A T L A N T I C

O C E A N

Caribbean Sea

COSTA
RICA
San José
Panamá

P A N A M A

I. del Coco
(Costa Rica)

Barranquilla
G. of
Darién
Cartagena
Maracaibo
Caracas
Barquisimeto
Valencia
ARUBA
(Neth.)
Oranjestad
CURAÇAO
(Neth.)
Willemstad
Port of
Spain
TRINIDAD &
TOBAGO

C

I. de Malpelo
(Colombia)
Gulf of Panama

Medellín
Cúcuta
San Cristóbal
Bucaramanga
VENEZUELA
Orinoco
Ciudad Guayana
Georgetown
Paramaribo
Cayenne
C. Orange

Cali
BOGOTÁ
GUYANA
SURINAME
FRENCH
GUIANA

COLOMBIA
Boa Vista
RORAIMA
Essequibo
AMAPÁ

D

Galapagos Is.
(Ecuador)

Quito
ECUADOR
Guayaquil
G. of Guayaquil

Napo
Putumayo
Japurá
Equator
Macapá
Marajó
Belém

Marañón
Iquitos
AMAZONAS
Amazon
Manaus
Santarém

São Luís
Fortaleza

Juruá
Purus
Madeira
Tapajós
Xingu
Tocantins
P A R Á
MARANHÃO
Teresina
CEARÁ
RIO G.
DO NORTE
Natal

Chiclayo
Trujillo
A C R E
Rio Branco
Pôrto Velho
Imperatriz
Parnaíba
PIAUÍ
PARAÍBA
João
Pessoa
Recife

Chimbote
Ucayali
PERU
RONDÔNIA
Madre de Dios
Palmas
TOCANTINS
PERNAMBUCO
ALAGOAS
Maceió

10

Callao
LIMA
Cusco
Mamoré
B R A Z I L
SERGIPE
Aracaju

L. Titicaca
BOLIVIA
MATO GROSSO
GOIÁS
São Francisco
BAHÍA
Salvador

E

Arequipa
La Paz
Cochabamba
Santa Cruz
Cuiabá
DIS. FED.
Brasília
Goiânia

Sucre
MINAS GERAIS

Iquique
MATO GROSSO
DO SUL
Campo
Grande
Ribeirão
Prêto
BELO
HORIZONTE
Juiz
de Fora
ESPÍRITO
SANTO
Vitória

P A C I F I C

PARAGUAY
Paraná
SÃO PAULO
Campinas
Campos
R. DE J.
Niterói
RIO DE
JANEIRO

F

Tropic of Capricorn
San Félix
(Chile)
San Ambrosio
(Chile)

Antofagasta
Salta
Pilcomayo
Asunción
PARANÁ
SÃO
PAULO
Santos
Curitiba

San Miguel
de Tucumán
A R G E N T I N A
Resistencia
Corrientes
SANTA CATARINA
Uruguay
Florianópolis
RIO GRANDE
DO SUL

G

O C E A N

Arch. de Juan Fernández
(Chile)

Córdoba
Santa Fé
Paraná
Pôrto Alegre
Pelotas
URUGUAY

Viña del Mar
Valparaíso
SANTIAGO
San Juan
Mendoza
Rosario
Montevideo

Robinson
Crusoe
Talca
BUENOS AIRES
La Plata
Rio de la Plata

Concepción
Bahía
Blanca
Mar del Plata

Neuquén
Colorado

Valdivia
Negro
Viedma

Puerto Montt
C H I L E

40

Chubut
A T L A N T I C

Comodoro Rivadavia
Gulf of San Jorge

Gulf of Penas

O C E A N

H

West Falkland
FALKLAND IS.
(U.K.)
Stanley
East Falkland

Magellan's Str.
Punta Arenas
Tierra del Fuego
South Georgia
(U.K.)
C. Horn

Projection: Lambert's Azimuthal Equal Area

60 West from Greenwich 50

COPYRIGHT PHILIP'S

■ LIMA   Capital Cities

| 1 | 2 | 3 | 4 | 5 | 6 | 7 |

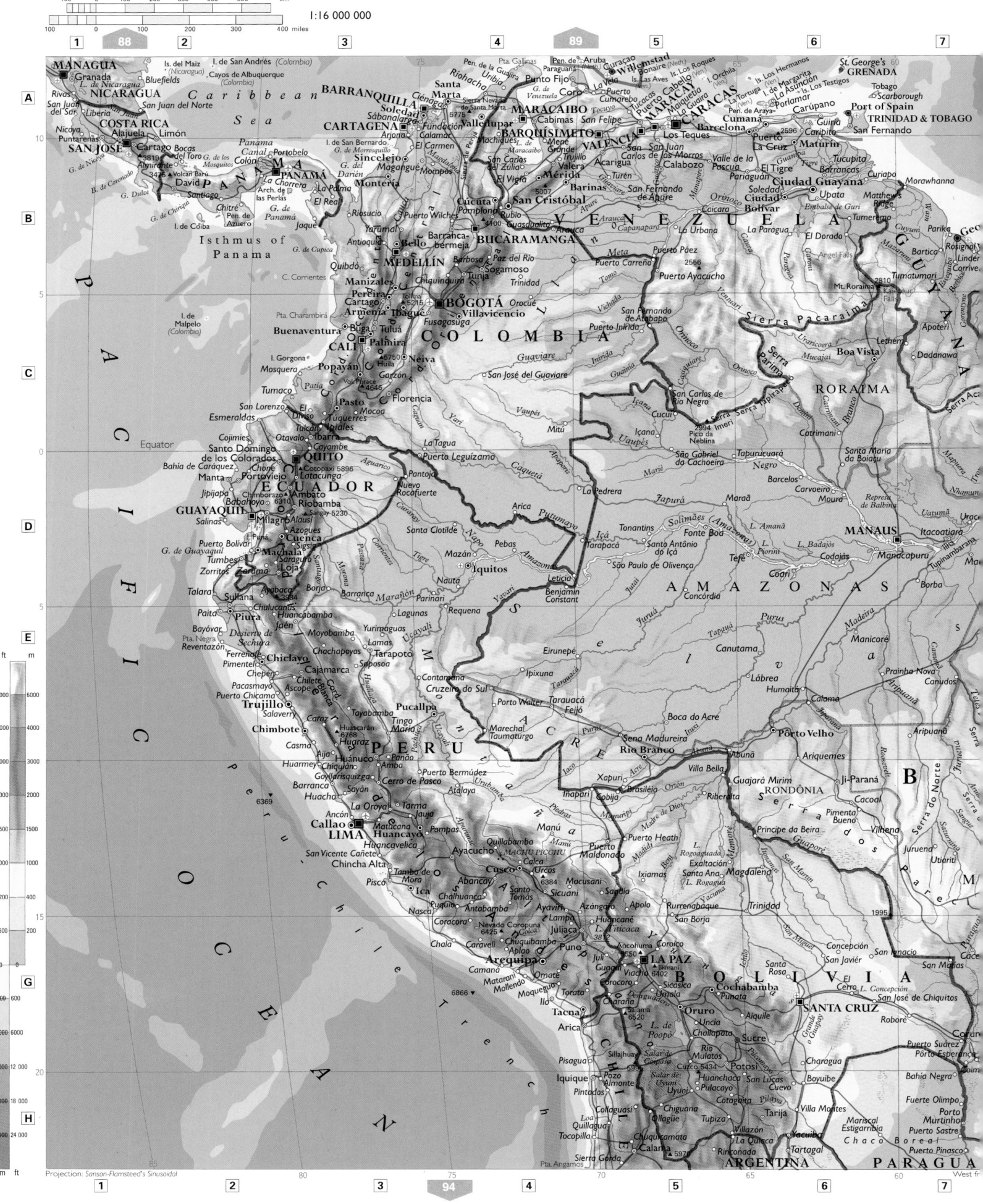

100 0 100 200 300 400 500 km
100 0 100 200 300 400 miles

1:16 000 000

Projection: Sanson-Flamsteed's Sinusoidal

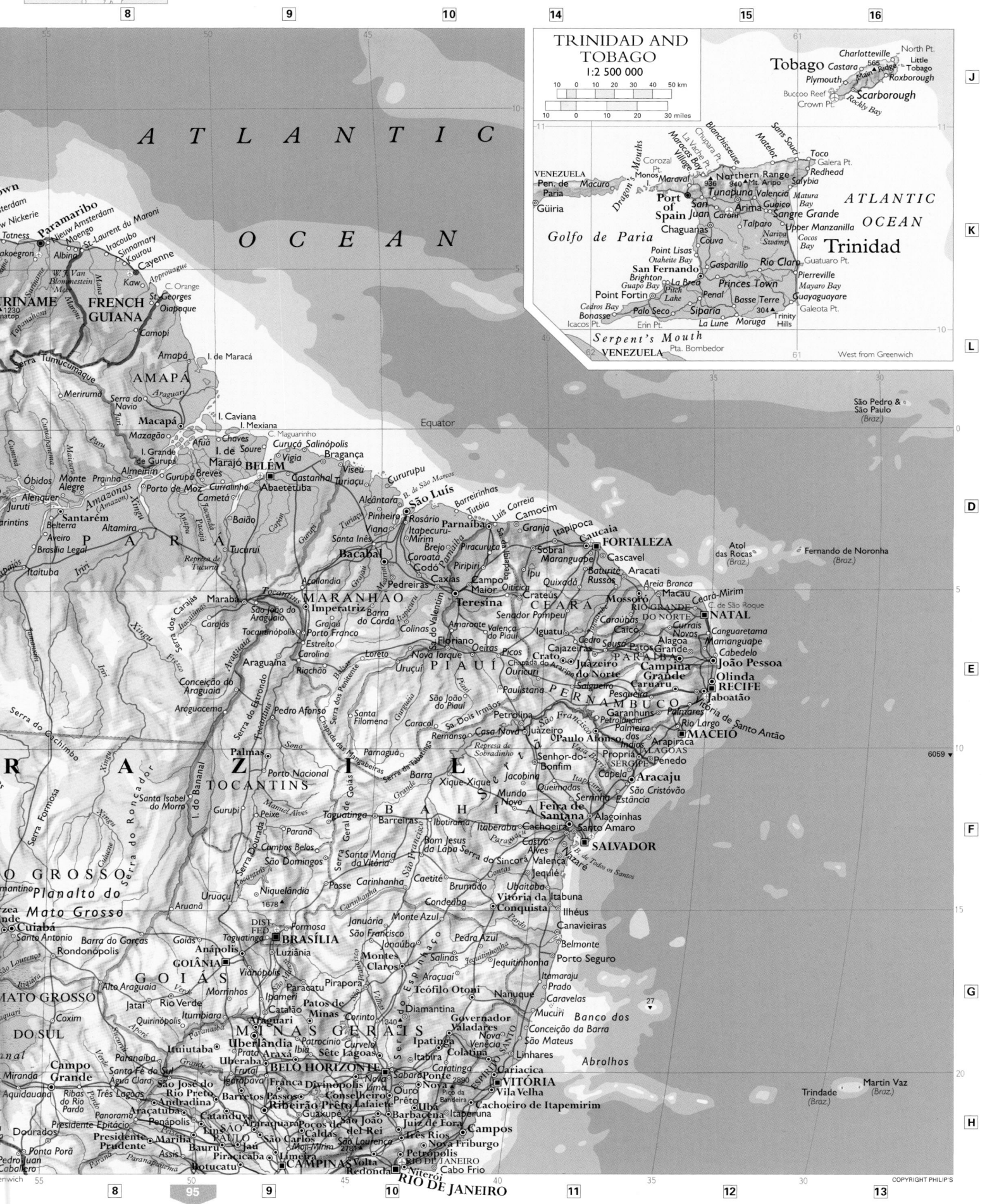

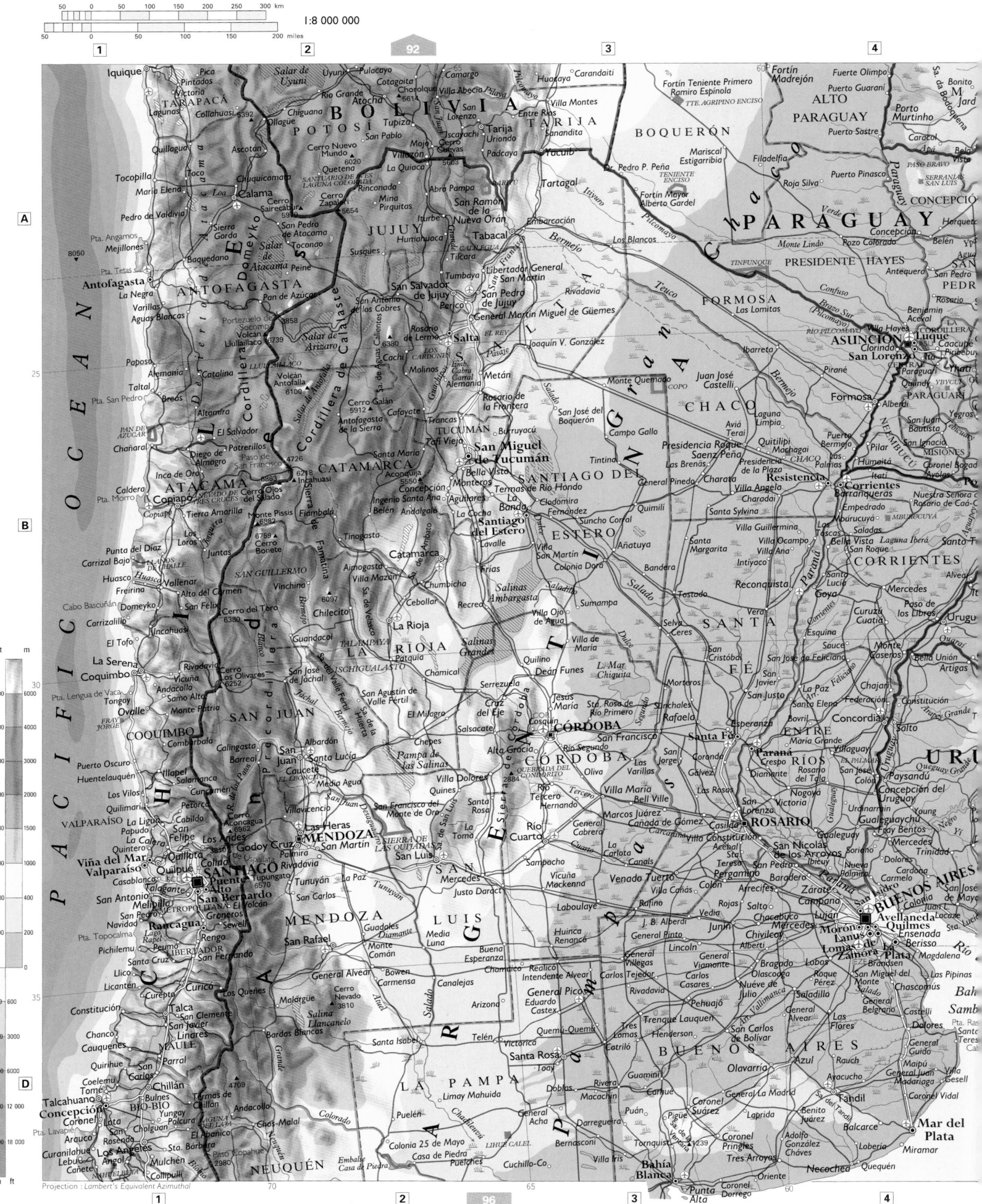

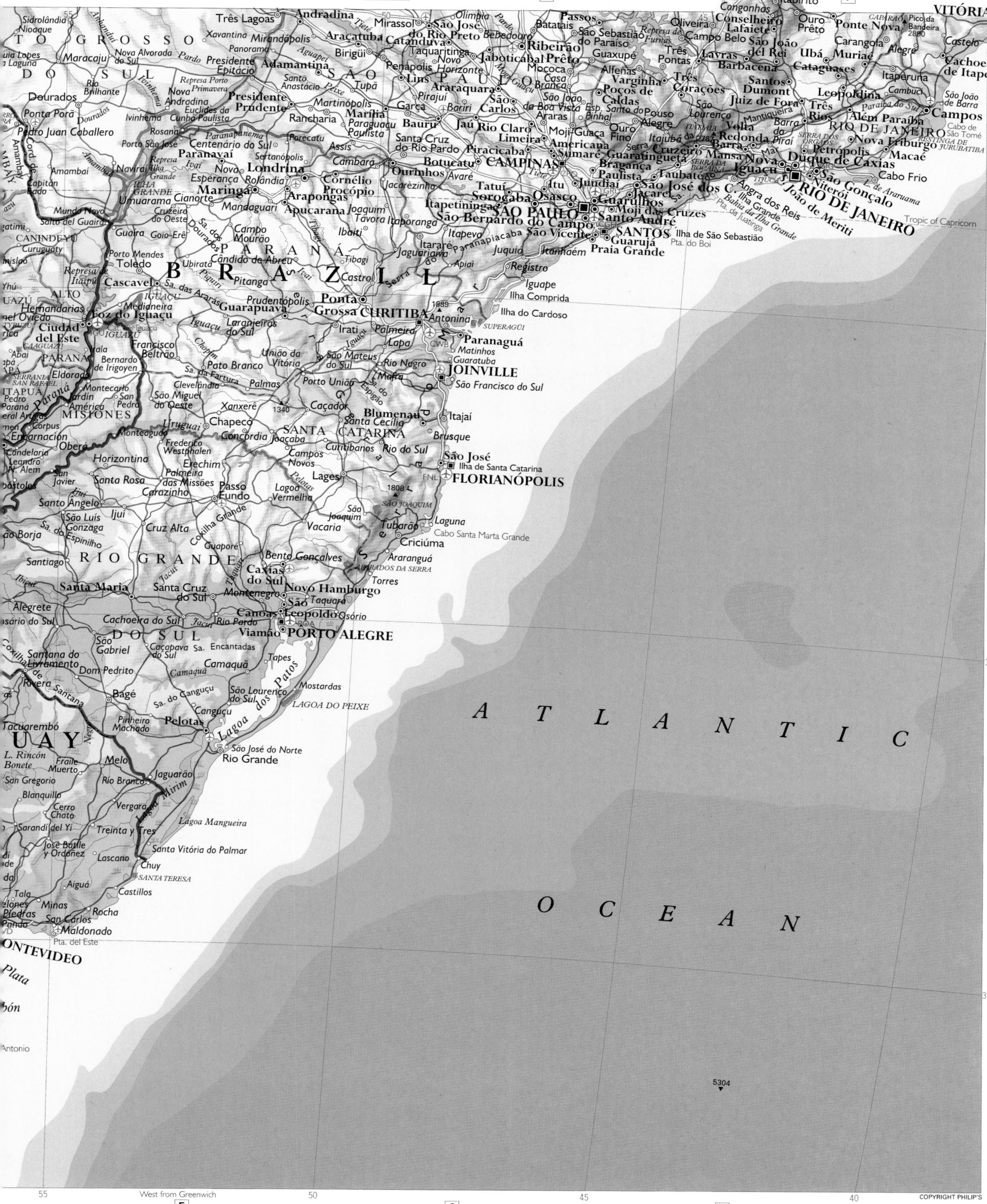

93

5   6   7

BELO
HORIZONTE
CNF
Betim Contagem   Itabirito
VITÓRIA
Vila
Velha
Sidrolândia
Nioaque   Congonhas
Três Lagoas   Andradina   Mirasol   Passos   Oliveira Conselheiro   Ouro   Ponte Nova   Pico da   Guarapari
São José   Batatais   São Sebastião   Campo Belo São João   Prêto   Bandeira   Castelo
Xavantina Mirandópolis   do Rio   Prêto   do Paraíso   Guaxupé   del Rei Ubá Muriaé   Cachoeiro
Aracatuba Catanduva   Ribeirão   Alfenas Varginha   Santos   Cataguases   de Itapemirim
O   G R O S S O   Birigüi   Taquaritinga   Casa   Três   Barbacena   Itaperuna
ua Lopes   Panorama   Penapolis   Horizonte   Branca   Corações   Juiz de Fora   Leopoldina   Campos
Maracaju   Nova Alvorada   Presidente   Jaboticabal Prêto   Poços de   Pouso   Cambu
Nova Sul   Pardo   Epitácio Adamantina   Lins   P A U L O   Caldas   Pinhal   São João
Dourados   Santo   Presidente   Garça   Santa   Moji-Guaçu Esp. Santo do   RIO DE JANEIRO
Ponta Porã   Anastácio   Prudente   Bauru   Piracicaba   Americana   Itajubá   Redonda
Pedro Juan Caballero   Marília Jaú Rio Claro   Limeira   Cruzeiro   Mansa   Petrópolis   Macaé
B R A Z I L   CAMPINAS   Guaratinguetá   Barra   Cabo Frio
Paranavaí   Londrina   Itu Jundiaí   Taubaté   Nova   Niterói
Maringá   Tatuí Osasco   São José dos C.   Iguaçu   São Gonçalo
Apucarana SÃO PAULO Guarulhos Tropic of Capricorn
P A R A N Á   São Bernardo do Campo Santo André
SANTOS
Ponta   Guarujá
Grossa CURITIBA
Cascavel   Paranaguá
Foz do Iguaçu   JOINVILLE
Ciudad   São Francisco do Sul
del Este
Blumenau
S A N T A   Itajaí
C A T A R I N A
São José
FLORIANÓPOLIS
Ilha de Santa Catarina
R I O   G R A N D E
Criciúma
Cabo Santa Marta Grande
Caxias
do Sul
Santa Maria   Novo Hamburgo
Torres
D O   S U L   Canoas
Viamão PORTO ALEGRE
A T L A N T I C
Bagé   LAGOA DO PEIXE
Pelotas
U A Y   Rio Grande
Jaguarão
Mirim
O C E A N
Chuy
Maldonado
ONTEVIDEO

COPYRIGHT PHILIP'S
West from Greenwich
5   6   7

1:16 000 000

ATLANTIC OCEAN

Argentine Abyssal Plain

PACIFIC OCEAN

BOLIVIA

PARAGUAY

BRAZIL

URUGUAY

A R G E N T I N A

C H I L E

P A T A G O N I A

Tropic of Capricorn

RIO DE JANEIRO
SÃO PAULO
CAMPINAS
CURITIBA
JOINVILLE
FLORIANÓPOLIS
PORTO ALEGRE
ASUNCIÓN
CÓRDOBA
MENDOZA
SANTIAGO
BUENOS AIRES
MONTEVIDEO
ROSARIO
Mar del Plata
Bahía Blanca
Neuquén
Valdivia
Puerto Montt
Comodoro Rivadavia
Río Gallegos
Punta Arenas
Ushuaia
Antofagasta
La Serena
Valparaíso
San Miguel de Tucumán
Santiago del Estero
La Rioja
San Juan
San Luis
Santa Fe
Paraná
La Plata
Pen. Valdés
Tierra del Fuego
Isla Grande de Tierra del Fuego

FALKLAND ISLANDS
(ISLAS MALVINAS) (U.K.)
West Falkland
East Falkland
Stanley
Port Darwin

South Georgia (U.K.)
Grytviken
Mt. Paget

C. Horn (Cabo de Hornos)

Projection: Sanson-Flamsteed's Sinusoidal

West from Greenwich

COPYRIGHT PHILIP'S

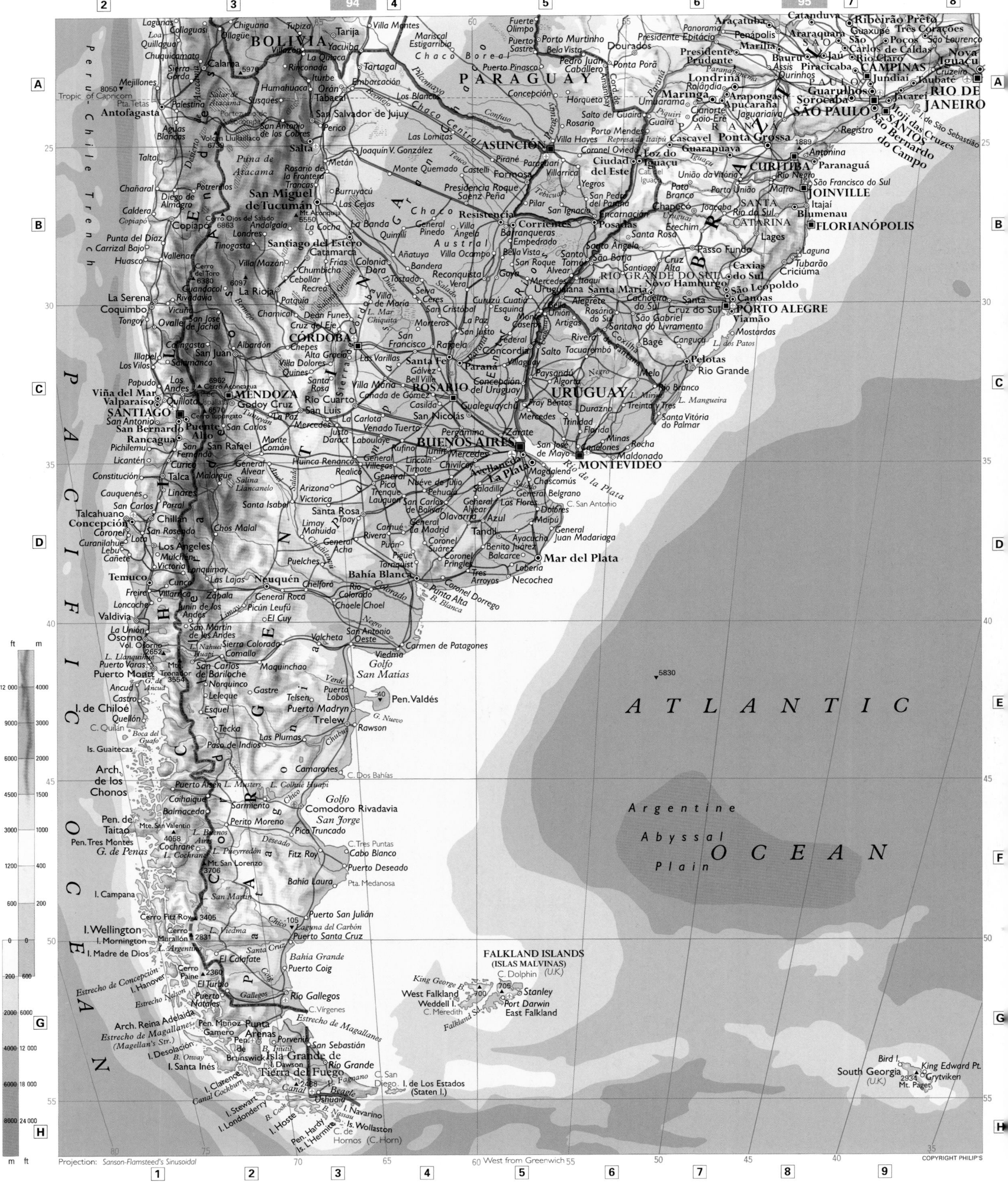

INDEX TO WORLD MAPS

The index contains the names of all the principal places and features shown on the World Maps. Each name is followed by an additional entry in italics giving the country or region within which it is located. The alphabetical order of names composed of two or more words is governed primarily by the first word, then by the second, and then by the country or region name that follows. This is an example of the rule:

Mīr Kūh *Iran*	26°22N 58°55E	**47** E8
Mīr Shahdād *Iran*	26°15N 58°29E	**47** E8
Mira *Italy*	45°26N 12°8E	**22** B5
Mira por vos Cay *Bahamas*	22°9N 74°30W	**89** B5

Physical features composed of a proper name (Erie) and a description (Lake) are positioned alphabetically by the proper name. The description is positioned after the proper name and is usually abbreviated:

Erie, L. *N. Amer.*	42°15N 81°0W	**82** D4

Where a description forms part of a settlement or administrative name, however, it is always written in full and put in its true alphabetical position:

Mount Morris *U.S.A.*	42°44N 77°52W	**82** D7

Names beginning with M' and Mc are indexed as if they were spelled Mac. Names beginning St. are alphabetized under Saint, but Sankt, Sint, Sant', Santa and San are all spelt in full and are alphabetized accordingly. If the same place name occurs two or more times in the index and all are in the same country, each is followed by the name of the administrative subdivision in which it is located.

The geographical co-ordinates which follow each name in the index give the latitude and longitude of each place. The first co-ordinate indicates latitude – the distance north or south of the Equator. The second co-ordinate indicates longitude – the distance east or west of the Greenwich Meridian. Both latitude and longitude are measured in degrees and minutes (there are 60 minutes in a degree).

The latitude is followed by N(orth) or S(outh) and the longitude by E(ast) or W(est).

The number in bold type which follows the geographical co-ordinates refers to the number of the map page where that feature or place will be found. This is usually the largest scale at which the place or feature appears.

The letter and figure that are immediately after the page number give the grid square on the map page, within which the feature is situated. The letter represents the latitude and the figure the longitude. A lower-case letter immediately after the page number refers to an inset map on that page.

In some cases the feature itself may fall within the specified square, while the name is outside. This is usually the case only with features that are larger than a grid square.

Rivers are indexed to their mouths or confluences, and carry the symbol ➔ after their names. The following symbols are also used in the index: ■ country, ☑ overseas territory or dependency, ☐ first-order administrative area, △ national park, ◠ other park (provincial park, nature reserve or game reserve), ✖ (LHR) principal airport (and location identifier), ⊙ Australian aboriginal land.

Abbreviations used in the index

A.C.T. – Australian Capital Territory
A.R. – Autonomous Region
Afghan. – Afghanistan
Afr. – Africa
Ala. – Alabama
Alta. – Alberta
Amer. – America(n)
Ant. – Antilles
Arch. – Archipelago
Ariz. – Arizona
Ark. – Arkansas
Atl. Oc. – Atlantic Ocean
B. – Baie, Bahía, Bay, Bucht, Bugt
B.C. – British Columbia
Bangla. – Bangladesh
Barr. – Barrage
Bos.-H. – Bosnia-Herzegovina
C. – Cabo, Cap, Cape, Coast
C.A.R. – Central African Republic
C. Prov. – Cape Province
Calif. – California
Cat. – Catarata
Cent. – Central
Chan. – Channel
Colo. – Colorado
Conn. – Connecticut
Cord. – Cordillera
Cr. – Creek
Czech. – Czech Republic
D.C. – District of Columbia
Del. – Delaware
Dem. – Democratic
Dep. – Dependency
Des. – Desert
Dét. – Détroit
Dist. – District
Dj. – Djebel
Dom. Rep. – Dominican Republic

E. – East
El Salv. – El Salvador
Eq. Guin. – Equatorial Guinea
Est. – Estrecho
Falk. Is. – Falkland Is.
Fd. – Fjord
Fla. – Florida
Fr. – French
G. – Golfe, Golfo, Gulf, Guba, Gebel
Ga. – Georgia
Gt. – Great, Greater
Guinea-Biss. – Guinea-Bissau
H.K. – Hong Kong
H.P. – Himachal Pradesh
Hants. – Hampshire
Harb. – Harbor, Harbour
Hd. – Head
Hts. – Heights
I.(s). – Île, Ilha, Insel, Isla, Island, Isle
Ill. – Illinois
Ind. – Indiana
Ind. Oc. – Indian Ocean
Ivory C. – Ivory Coast
J. – Jabal, Jebel
Jaz. – Jazīrah
Junc. – Junction
K. – Kap, Kapp
Kans. – Kansas
Kep. – Kepulauan
Ky. – Kentucky
L. – Lac, Lacul, Lago, Lagoa, Lake, Limni, Loch, Lough
La. – Louisiana
Ld. – Land
Liech. – Liechtenstein
Lux. – Luxembourg
Mad. P. – Madhya Pradesh
Madag. – Madagascar
Man. – Manitoba
Mass. – Massachusetts

Md. – Maryland
Me. – Maine
Medit. S. – Mediterranean Sea
Mich. – Michigan
Minn. – Minnesota
Miss. – Mississippi
Mo. – Missouri
Mont. – Montana
Mozam. – Mozambique
Mt.(s) – Mont, Montaña, Mountain
Mte. – Monte
Mti. – Monti
N. – Nord, Norte, North, Northern, Nouveau, Nahal, Nahr
N.B. – New Brunswick
N.C. – North Carolina
N. Cal. – New Caledonia
N. Dak. – North Dakota
N.H. – New Hampshire
N.I. – North Island
N.J. – New Jersey
N. Mex. – New Mexico
N.S. – Nova Scotia
N.S.W. – New South Wales
N.W.T. – North West Territory
N.Y. – New York
N.Z. – New Zealand
Nac. – Nacional
Nat. – National
Nebr. – Nebraska
Neths. – Netherlands
Nev. – Nevada
Nfld & L. – Newfoundland and Labrador
Nic. – Nicaragua
O. – Oued, Ouadi
Occ. – Occidentale
Okla. – Oklahoma
Ont. – Ontario
Or. – Orientale

Oreg. – Oregon
Os. – Ostrov
Oz. – Ozero
P. – Pass, Passo, Pasul, Pulau
P.E.I. – Prince Edward Island
Pa. – Pennsylvania
Pac. Oc. – Pacific Ocean
Papua N.G. – Papua New Guinea
Pass. – Passage
Peg. – Pegunungan
Pen. – Peninsula, Péninsule
Phil. – Philippines
Pk. – Peak
Plat. – Plateau
Prov. – Province, Provincial
Pt. – Point
Pta. – Ponta, Punta
Pte. – Pointe
Qué. – Québec
Queens. – Queensland
R. – Rio, River
R.I. – Rhode Island
Ra. – Range
Raj. – Rajasthan
Recr. – Recreational, Récréatif
Reg. – Region
Rep. – Republic
Res. – Reserve, Reservoir
Rhld-Pfz. – Rheinland-Pfalz
S. – South, Southern, Sur
Si. Arabia – Saudi Arabia
S.C. – South Carolina
S. Dak. – South Dakota
S.I. – South Island
S. Leone – Sierra Leone
Sa. – Serra, Sierra
Sask. – Saskatchewan
Scot. – Scotland
Sd. – Sound
Sev. – Severnaya
Sib. – Siberia

Sprs. – Springs
St. – Saint
Sta. – Santa
Ste. – Sainte
Sto. – Santo
Str. – Strait, Stretto
Switz. – Switzerland
Tas. – Tasmania
Tenn. – Tennessee
Terr. – Territory, Territoire
Tex. – Texas
Tg. – Tanjung
Trin. & Tob. – Trinidad & Tobago
U.A.E. – United Arab Emirates
U.K. – United Kingdom
U.S.A. – United States of America
Ut. P. – Uttar Pradesh
Va. – Virginia
Vdkhr. – Vodokhranilishche
Vdskh. – Vodoskhovyshche
Vf. – Vîrful
Vic. – Victoria
Vol. – Volcano
Vt. – Vermont
W. – Wadi, West
W. Va. – West Virginia
Wall. & F. Is. – Wallis and Futuna Is.
Wash. – Washington
Wis. – Wisconsin
Wlkp. – Wielkopolski
Wyo. – Wyoming
Yorks. – Yorkshire

A

A Coruña Spain 43°20N 8°25W 21 A1
A Estrada Spain 42°43N 8°27W 21 A1
A Fonsagrada Spain 43°8N 7°4W 21 A2
A Shau Vietnam 16°6N 107°22E 38 D6
Aabenraa Denmark 55°3N 9°25E 9 J13
Aachen Germany 50°45N 6°6E 16 C4
Aalborg Denmark 57°2N 9°54E 9 H13
Aalen Germany 48°51N 10°6E 16 D6
Aalst Belgium 50°56N 4°2E 15 D4
Aalten Neths. 51°56N 6°35E 15 C6
Aalter Belgium 51°5N 3°28E 15 C3
Äänekoski Finland 62°36N 25°44E 8 E21
Aarau Switz. 47°23N 8°4E 20 C8
Aare → Switz. 47°33N 8°14E 20 C8
Aarhus Denmark 56°8N 10°11E 9 H14
Aarschot Belgium 50°59N 4°49E 15 D4
Aba China 32°59N 101°42E 34 A3
Aba Nigeria 5°10N 7°19E 52 G7
Abaco I. Bahamas 26°25N 77°10W 88 A4
Ābādān Iran 30°22N 48°20E 47 D6
Ābādeh Iran 31°8N 52°40E 47 D7
Abadla Algeria 31°2N 2°45W 52 B5
Abaetetuba Brazil 1°40S 48°50W 93 D9
Abagnar Qi = Xilinhot China 43°52N 116°2E 32 C9
Abah, Tanjung Indonesia 8°46S 115°38E 37 K18
Abai Paraguay 25°58S 55°54W 95 B4
Abakan Russia 53°40N 91°10E 27 D10
Abancay Peru 13°35S 72°55W 92 F4
Abang, Gunung Indonesia 8°16S 115°25E 37 J18
Abariringa Kiribati 2°50S 171°40W 64 H10
Abarqū Iran 31°10N 53°20E 47 D7
Abashiri Japan 44°0N 144°15E 28 B12
Abashiri-Wan Japan 44°0N 144°30E 28 C12
Ābay = Nîl el Azraq → Sudan 15°38N 32°31E 53 E12
Abay Kazakhstan 49°38N 72°53E 26 E8
Abaya, L. Ethiopia 6°30N 37°50E 49 F2
Abaza Russia 52°39N 90°6E 26 D10
'Abbāsābād Iran 33°34N 58°23E 47 C8
Abbay = Nîl el Azraq → Sudan 15°38N 32°31E 53 E12
Abbaye, Pt. U.S.A. 46°58N 88°8W 80 B9
Abbé, L. Ethiopia 11°8N 41°47E 49 E3
Abbeville France 50°6N 1°49E 20 A4
Abbeville Ala., U.S.A. 31°34N 85°15W 85 F12
Abbeville La., U.S.A. 29°58N 92°8W 84 G8
Abbeville S.C., U.S.A. 34°11N 82°23W 85 D13
Abbeyfeale Ireland 52°23N 9°18W 10 D2
Abbeyleix Ireland 52°54N 7°22W 10 D4
Abbot Ice Shelf Antarctica 73°0S 92°0W 5 D16
Abbotsford Canada 49°5N 122°20W 70 D4
Abbottabad Pakistan 34°10N 73°15E 42 B5
ABC Islands W. Indies 12°15N 69°0W 89 D6
Abd al Kūrī Yemen 12°5N 52°20E 49 E5
Ābdar Iran 30°16N 55°19E 47 D7
'Abdolābād Iran 34°12N 56°30E 47 C8
Abdulpur Bangla. 24°15N 88°59E 43 G13
Abéché Chad 13°50N 20°35E 53 F10
Abel Tasman △ N.Z. 40°59S 173°3E 59 D4
Abengourou Ivory C. 6°42N 3°27W 52 G5
Åbenrå = Aabenraa Denmark 55°3N 9°25E 9 J13
Abeokuta Nigeria 7°3N 3°19E 52 G6
Aberaeron U.K. 52°15N 4°15W 13 E3
Aberayron = Aberaeron U.K. 52°15N 4°15W 13 E3
Aberchirder U.K. 57°34N 2°37W 11 D6
Abercorn Australia 25°12S 151°5E 63 D5
Aberdare U.K. 51°43N 3°27W 13 F4
Aberdaugleddau = Milford Haven U.K. 51°42N 5°7W 13 F2
Aberdeen Australia 32°9S 150°56E 63 E5
Aberdeen Canada 52°20N 106°8W 71 C7
Aberdeen S. Africa 32°28S 24°2E 56 D3
Aberdeen U.K. 57°9N 2°5W 11 D6
Aberdeen Idaho, U.S.A. 42°57N 112°50W 76 E7
Aberdeen Md., U.S.A. 39°31N 76°10W 81 F15
Aberdeen Miss., U.S.A. 33°49N 88°33W 85 E10
Aberdeen S. Dak., U.S.A. 45°28N 98°29W 80 C4
Aberdeen Wash., U.S.A. 46°59N 123°50W 78 D3
Aberdeen, City of □ U.K. 57°10N 2°10W 11 D6
Aberdeen L. Canada 64°30N 99°0W 68 E12
Aberdeenshire □ U.K. 57°17N 2°36W 11 D6
Aberdovey = Aberdyfi U.K. 52°33N 4°3W 13 E3
Aberdyfi U.K. 52°33N 4°3W 13 E3
Aberfeldy U.K. 56°37N 3°51W 11 E5
Aberfoyle U.K. 56°11N 4°23W 11 E4
Abergavenny U.K. 51°49N 3°1W 13 F4
Abergele U.K. 53°17N 3°35W 12 D4
Abergwaun = Fishguard U.K. 52°0N 4°58W 13 E3
Aberhonddu = Brecon U.K. 51°57N 3°23W 13 F4
Abermaw = Barmouth U.K. 52°44N 4°4W 12 E3
Abernathy U.S.A. 33°50N 101°51W 84 E4
Aberpennar = Mountain Ash U.K. 51°40N 3°23W 13 F4
Abert, L. U.S.A. 42°38N 120°14W 76 E3
Abertawe = Swansea U.K. 51°37N 3°57W 13 F4
Aberteifi = Cardigan U.K. 52°5N 4°40W 13 E3
Aberystwyth U.K. 52°25N 4°5W 13 E3
Abhā Si. Arabia 18°0N 42°34E 49 D3
Abhar Iran 36°9N 49°13E 47 B6
Abhayapuri India 26°24N 90°38E 43 F14
Abidjan Ivory C. 5°26N 3°58W 52 G5
Abilene Kans., U.S.A. 38°55N 97°13W 80 F5
Abilene Tex., U.S.A. 32°28N 99°43W 84 E5
Abingdon U.K. 51°40N 1°17W 13 F6
Abingdon U.S.A. 36°43N 81°59W 81 G13
Abington Reef Australia 18°0S 149°35E 62 B4
Abitau → Canada 59°53N 109°3W 71 B7
Abitibi → Canada 51°3N 80°55W 72 B3
Abitibi, L. Canada 48°40N 79°40W 72 C4
Abkhaz Republic = Abkhazia □ Georgia 43°12N 41°5E 19 F7
Abkhazia □ Georgia 43°12N 41°5E 19 F7
Abminga Australia 26°8S 134°51E 63 D1
Åbo = Turku Finland 60°30N 22°19E 9 F20
Abohar India 30°10N 74°10E 42 D6
Abomey Benin 7°10N 2°5E 52 G6
Abong-Mbang Cameroon 4°0N 13°8E 54 D2
Abou-Deïa Chad 11°20N 19°20E 53 F9
Aboyne U.K. 57°4N 2°47W 11 D6
Abra Pampa Argentina 22°43S 65°42W 94 A2
Abraham L. Canada 52°15N 116°35W 70 C5
Abreojos, Pta. Mexico 26°50N 113°40W 86 B2
Abrolhos, Banco dos Brazil 18°0S 38°0W 90 E7
Abrud Romania 46°19N 23°5E 17 E12
Absaroka Range U.S.A. 44°45N 109°50W 76 D9
Abu India 24°41N 72°50E 42 G5
Abū al Abyad U.A.E. 24°11N 53°50E 47 E7
Abū al Khaşīb Iraq 30°25N 48°0E 46 D5
Abū 'Alī Si. Arabia 27°20N 49°27E 47 E6
Abū 'Alī → Lebanon 34°25N 35°50E 48 A4
Abu Dhabi = Abū Ẓāby U.A.E. 24°28N 54°22E 47 E7
Abū Du'ān Syria 36°25N 38°15E 46 B3
Abu el Gaīn, W. → Egypt 29°35N 33°30E 48 F2
Abu Ga'da, W. → Egypt 29°15N 32°53E 48 F1
Abū Ḩadrīyah Si. Arabia 27°20N 48°58E 47 E6
Abu Hamed Sudan 19°32N 33°13E 53 E12
Abū Kamāl Syria 34°30N 41°0E 46 C4
Abū Madd, Ra's Si. Arabia 24°50N 37°7E 46 E3
Abū Mūsā U.A.E. 25°52N 55°3E 47 E7
Abū Qaşr Si. Arabia 30°21N 38°34E 46 D3
Abu Shagara, Ras Sudan 21°4N 37°19E 53 D13
Abu Simbel Egypt 22°18N 31°40E 53 D12
Abū Şukhayr Iraq 31°54N 44°30E 46 D5
Abū Zabad Sudan 12°25N 29°10E 53 F11
Abū Ẓāby U.A.E. 24°28N 54°22E 47 E7
Abū Zeydābād Iran 33°54N 51°45E 47 C6
Abuja Nigeria 9°5N 7°32E 52 G7
Abukuma-Gawa → Japan 38°6N 140°52E 28 E10
Abukuma-Sammyaku Japan 37°30N 140°45E 28 F10
Abunã Brazil 9°40S 65°20W 92 E5
Abunã → Brazil 9°41S 65°20W 92 E5
Abut Hd. N.Z. 43°7S 170°15E 59 E3
Abyei ⊠ Sudan 9°30N 28°30E 53 G11
Ābyek Iran 36°4N 50°33E 47 B6
Acadia △ U.S.A. 44°20N 68°13W 81 C19
Açailândia Brazil 4°57S 47°0W 93 D9
Acajutla El Salv. 13°36N 89°50W 88 D2
Acámbaro Mexico 20°2N 100°44W 86 D4
Acaponeta Mexico 22°30N 105°22W 86 C3
Acapulco Mexico 16°51N 99°55W 87 D5
Acaraí, Serra Brazil 1°50N 57°50W 92 C7
Acarigua Venezuela 9°33N 69°12W 92 B5
Acatlán Mexico 18°12N 98°3W 87 D5
Acayucán Mexico 17°57N 94°55W 87 D6
Accomac U.S.A. 37°43N 75°40W 81 G16
Accra Ghana 5°35N 0°6W 52 G5
Accrington U.K. 53°45N 2°22W 12 D5
Acebal Argentina 33°20S 60°50W 94 C3
Aceh □ Indonesia 4°15N 97°30E 36 D1
Achalpur India 21°22N 77°32E 44 D3
Acharnes Greece 38°5N 23°44E 23 E10
Acheloos → Greece 38°19N 21°7E 23 E9
Acheng China 45°30N 126°58E 33 B14
Acher India 23°10N 72°32E 42 H5
Achill Hd. Ireland 53°58N 10°15W 10 C1
Achill I. Ireland 53°58N 10°1W 10 C1
Achinsk Russia 56°20N 90°20E 27 D10
Acireale Italy 37°37N 15°10E 22 F6
Ackerman U.S.A. 33°19N 89°11W 85 E10
Acklins I. Bahamas 22°30N 74°0W 89 B5
Acme Canada 51°33N 113°30W 70 C6
Acme U.S.A. 40°8N 79°26W 82 F5
Aconcagua, Cerro Argentina 32°39S 70°0W 94 C2
Aconquija, Mt. Argentina 27°0S 66°0W 94 B2
Açores, Is. dos Atl. Oc. 38°0N 27°0W 52 a
Acornhoek S. Africa 24°37S 31°2E 57 B5
Acraman, L. Australia 32°2S 135°23E 63 E2
Acre = 'Akko Israel 32°55N 35°4E 48 C4
Acre □ Brazil 9°1S 71°0W 92 E4
Acre → Brazil 8°45S 67°22W 92 E5
Actinolite Canada 44°32N 77°19W 82 B7
Acton Canada 43°38N 80°3W 82 C4
Ad Dammām Si. Arabia 26°20N 50°5E 47 E6
Ad Dāmūr Lebanon 33°43N 35°27E 48 B4
Ad Dawādimī Si. Arabia 24°35N 44°15E 46 E5
Ad Dawḩah Qatar 25°15N 51°35E 47 E6
Ad Dawr Iraq 34°27N 43°47E 46 C4
Ad Dhakhīrah Qatar 25°44N 51°33E 47 E6
Ad Dir'īyah Si. Arabia 24°44N 46°35E 46 E5
Ad Dīwānīyah Iraq 32°0N 45°0E 46 D5
Ad Dujayl Iraq 33°51N 44°14E 46 C5
Ad Duwayd Si. Arabia 30°15N 42°17E 46 D4
Ada Minn., U.S.A. 47°18N 96°31W 80 B5
Ada Okla., U.S.A. 34°46N 96°41W 84 D6
Adabiya Egypt 29°53N 32°28E 48 F1
Adair, C. Canada 71°30N 71°34W 69 C17
Adaja → Spain 41°32N 4°52W 21 B3
Adak U.S.A. 51°45N 176°45W 74 E4
Adak I. U.S.A. 51°45N 176°45W 74 E4
Adamaoua, Massif de l' Cameroon 7°20N 12°20E 53 G8
Adamawa Highlands = Adamaoua, Massif de l' Cameroon 7°20N 12°20E 53 G8
Adamello, Mte. Italy 46°9N 10°30E 20 C9
Adaminaby Australia 36°0S 148°45E 63 F4
Adams Mass., U.S.A. 42°38N 73°7W 83 D11
Adams N.Y., U.S.A. 43°49N 76°1W 83 C8
Adams Wis., U.S.A. 43°57N 89°49W 80 D9
Adams, Mt. U.S.A. 46°12N 121°30W 78 D5
Adam's Bridge Sri Lanka 9°15N 79°40E 45 K4
Adams L. Canada 51°10N 119°40W 70 C5
Adam's Peak Sri Lanka 6°48N 80°30E 45 L5
'Adan Yemen 12°45N 45°0E 49 E4
Adana Turkey 37°0N 35°16E 46 B2
Adang, Ko Thailand 6°33N 99°18E 39 J2
Adapazarı = Sakarya Turkey 40°48N 30°25E 19 F5
Adarama Sudan 17°10N 34°52E 53 E12
Adare Ireland 52°34N 8°47W 10 D3
Adare, C. Antarctica 71°0S 171°0E 5 D11
Adaut Indonesia 8°8S 131°7E 37 F8
Adavale Australia 25°52S 144°32E 63 D3
Adda → Italy 45°8N 9°53E 20 D8
Addatigala India 17°31N 82°3E 44 F6
Addis Ababa = Addis Abeba Ethiopia 9°2N 38°42E 49 F2
Addis Abeba Ethiopia 9°2N 38°42E 49 F2
Addison U.S.A. 42°1N 77°14W 82 D7
Addo S. Africa 33°32S 25°45E 56 D4
Addo △ S. Africa 33°30S 25°50E 56 D4
Ādeh Iran 37°42N 45°11E 46 B5
Adel U.S.A. 31°8N 83°25W 85 F13
Adelaide Australia 34°52S 138°30E 63 E2
Adelaide S. Africa 32°42S 26°20E 56 D4
Adelaide I. Antarctica 67°15S 68°30W 5 C17
Adelaide Pen. Canada 68°15N 97°30W 68 D12
Adelaide River Australia 13°15S 131°7E 60 B5
Adelaide Village Bahamas 25°0N 77°31W 88 A4
Adelanto U.S.A. 34°35N 117°22W 79 L9
Adele I. Australia 15°32S 123°9E 60 C3
Adélie, Terre Antarctica 68°0S 140°0E 5 C10
Adelie Land = Adélie, Terre Antarctica 68°0S 140°0E 5 C10
Aden = 'Adan Yemen 12°45N 45°0E 49 E4
Aden, G. of Ind. Oc. 12°30N 47°30E 49 E4
Adendorp S. Africa 32°15S 24°30E 56 D3
Adh Dhayd U.A.E. 25°17N 55°53E 47 E7
Adhoi India 23°26N 70°32E 42 H4
Adi Indonesia 4°15S 133°30E 37 E8
Adieu, C. Australia 32°0S 132°10E 61 F5
Adieu Pt. Australia 15°14S 124°35E 60 C3
Adige → Italy 45°9N 12°20E 22 B5
Adigrat Ethiopia 14°20N 39°26E 49 E2
Adilabad India 19°33N 78°20E 44 E4
Adirondack ⌂ U.S.A. 44°0N 74°20W 83 C10
Adirondack Mts. U.S.A. 44°0N 74°0W 83 C10
Adis Abeba = Addis Abeba Ethiopia 9°2N 38°42E 49 F2
Adjuntas Puerto Rico 18°10N 66°43W 89 d
Adlavik Is. Canada 55°0N 58°40W 73 B8
Admiralty G. Australia 14°20S 125°55E 60 B4
Admiralty Gulf ☼ Australia 14°16S 125°52E 60 B4
Admiralty I. U.S.A. 57°30N 134°30W 70 B2
Admiralty Inlet Canada 72°30N 86°0W 69 C14
Admiralty Is. Papua N. G. 2°0S 147°0E 58 B7
Adolfo González Chaves Argentina 38°2S 60°5W 94 D3
Adolfo Ruiz Cortines, Presa Mexico 27°15N 109°6W 86 B3
Adonara Indonesia 8°15S 123°5E 37 F6
Adoni India 15°33N 77°18E 45 G3
Adour → France 43°32N 1°32W 20 E3
Adra India 23°30N 86°42E 43 H12
Adra Spain 36°43N 3°3W 21 D4
Adrano Italy 37°40N 14°50E 22 F6
Adrar Algeria 27°51N 0°11E 52 C5
Adrar Mauritania 20°30N 7°30W 52 D3
Adrar des Iforas Africa 19°40N 1°40E 52 E6
Adrian Mich., U.S.A. 41°54N 84°2W 81 E11
Adrian Tex., U.S.A. 35°16N 102°40W 84 D3
Adriatic Sea Medit. S. 43°0N 16°0E 22 C6
Adua Indonesia 1°45S 129°50E 37 E7
Adur India 9°8N 76°40E 45 K3
Adwa Ethiopia 14°15N 38°52E 49 E2
Adygea □ Russia 45°0N 40°0E 19 F7
Adzhar Republic = Ajaria □ Georgia 41°30N 42°0E 19 F7
Adzopé Ivory C. 6°7N 3°49W 52 G5
Ægean Sea Medit. S. 38°30N 25°0E 23 E11
Aerhtai Shan Mongolia 46°40N 92°45E 30 B7
Afaahiti Tahiti 17°45S 149°17W 59 d
'Afak Iraq 32°4N 45°15E 46 C5
Afareaitu Moorea 17°33S 149°47W 59 d
Afghanistan ■ Asia 33°0N 65°0E 40 C4
Aflou Algeria 34°7N 2°3E 52 B6
Afognak I. U.S.A. 58°15N 152°30W 74 D9
Africa 10°0N 20°0E 50 E6
'Afrīn Syria 36°32N 36°50E 46 B3
Afton N.Y., U.S.A. 42°14N 75°32W 83 D9
Afton Wyo., U.S.A. 42°44N 110°56W 76 E8
Afuá Brazil 0°15S 50°20W 93 D8
'Afula Israel 32°37N 35°17E 48 C4
Afyon Turkey 38°45N 30°33E 19 G5
Afyonkarahisar = Afyon Turkey 38°45N 30°33E 19 G5
Āgā Jarī Iran 30°42N 49°50E 47 D6
Agadés = Agadez Niger 16°58N 7°59E 52 E7
Agadez Niger 16°58N 7°59E 52 E7
Agadir Morocco 30°28N 9°55W 52 B4
Agalega Is. Mauritius 11°0S 57°0E 3 E12
Agar India 23°40N 76°2E 42 H7
Agar → India 21°0N 82°57E 44 D6
Agartala India 23°50N 91°23E 41 H17
Agassiz Canada 49°14N 121°46W 70 D4
Agassiz Icecap Canada 80°15N 76°0W 69 A16
Agats Indonesia 5°33S 138°0E 37 F9
Agatti I. India 10°50N 72°12E 45 J1
Agattu I. U.S.A. 52°25N 173°35E 74 E2
Agawam U.S.A. 42°5N 72°37W 83 D12
Agboville Ivory C. 5°55N 4°15W 52 G5
Ağdam Azerbaijan 40°0N 46°58E 46 B5
Agde France 43°19N 3°28E 20 E5
Agen France 44°12N 0°38E 20 D4
Āgh Kand Iran 37°15N 48°4E 47 B6
Aghios Efstratios Greece 39°34N 24°58E 23 E11
Aghiou Orous, Kolpos Greece 40°6N 24°0E 23 D11
Aginskoye Russia 51°6N 114°32E 27 D12
Agnew Australia 28°1S 120°31E 61 E3
Agori India 24°33N 82°57E 43 G10
Agra India 27°17N 77°58E 42 F7
Ağri Turkey 39°44N 43°3E 19 G7
Agri → Italy 40°13N 16°44E 22 D7
Ağri Daği Turkey 39°50N 44°15E 46 B5
Ağri Karakose = Ağri Turkey 39°44N 43°3E 19 G7
Agrigento Italy 37°19N 13°34E 22 F5
Agrinio Greece 38°37N 21°27E 23 E9
Agua Caliente Mexico 32°29N 116°59W 79 N10
Agua Caliente Springs U.S.A. 32°56N 116°19W 79 N10
Água Clara Brazil 20°25S 52°45W 93 H8
Agua Fria ⌂ U.S.A. 34°14N 112°0W 77 J8
Agua Hechicera Mexico 32°28N 116°15W 79 N10
Agua Prieta Mexico 31°18N 109°34W 86 A3
Aguadilla Puerto Rico 18°26N 67°10W 89 d
Aguadulce Panama 8°15N 80°32W 88 E3
Aguanga U.S.A. 33°27N 116°51W 79 M10
Aguanish Canada 50°14N 62°2W 73 B7
Aguanish → Canada 50°13N 62°5W 73 B7
Aguapey → Argentina 29°7S 56°36W 94 B4
Aguaray Guazú → Paraguay 24°47S 57°19W 94 A4
Aguarico → Ecuador 0°59S 75°11W 92 D3
Aguaro-Guariquito △ Venezuela 8°20N 66°35W 89 E6
Aguas Blancas Chile 24°15S 69°55W 94 A2
Aguas Calientes, Sierra de Argentina 25°26S 66°40W 94 B2
Aguascalientes Mexico 21°53N 102°18W 86 C4
Aguascalientes □ Mexico 22°0N 102°20W 86 C4
Aguila, Punta Puerto Rico 17°57N 67°13W 89 d
Aguilares Argentina 27°26S 65°35W 94 B2
Águilas Spain 37°23N 1°35W 21 D5
Aguja, C. de la Colombia 11°18N 74°12W 90 B3
Agujereada, Pta. Puerto Rico 18°30N 67°8W 89 d
Agulhas, C. S. Africa 34°52S 20°0E 56 D3
Agung, Gunung Indonesia 8°20S 115°28E 37 J18
Aguni-Jima Japan 26°30N 127°10E 29 L3
Agusan → Phil. 9°0N 125°30E 37 C7
Aha Mts. Botswana 19°45S 21°0E 56 A3
Ahaggar Algeria 23°0N 6°30E 52 D7
Ahai Dam China 27°21N 100°30E 34 D3
Ahar Iran 38°35N 47°0E 46 B5
Ahipara B. N.Z. 35°5S 173°5E 59 A4
Ahiri India 19°30N 80°0E 44 E5
Ahmad Wal Pakistan 29°18N 65°58E 42 E1
Ahmadabad India 23°0N 72°40E 42 H5
Aḩmadābād Khorāsān, Iran 35°3N 60°50E 47 C9
Aḩmadābād Khorāsān, Iran 35°49N 59°42E 47 C8
Aḩmadī Iran 27°56N 56°42E 47 E8
Ahmadnagar India 19°7N 74°46E 44 E2
Ahmadpur India 18°40N 76°57E 44 E3
Ahmadpur East Pakistan 29°12N 71°10E 42 E4
Ahmadpur Lamma Pakistan 28°19N 70°3E 42 E4
Ahmedabad = Ahmadabad India 23°0N 72°40E 42 H5
Ahmednagar = Ahmadnagar India 19°7N 74°46E 44 E2
Ahome Mexico 25°55N 109°11W 86 B3
Ahoskie U.S.A. 36°17N 76°59W 85 C16
Ahram Iran 28°52N 51°16E 47 D6
Ahuachapán El Salv. 13°54N 89°52W 88 D2
Ahvāz Iran 31°20N 48°40E 47 D6
Ahvenanmaa = Åland Finland 60°15N 20°0E 9 F19
Aḩwar Yemen 13°30N 46°40E 49 E4
Ai → India 26°26N 90°44E 43 F14
Ai-Ais Namibia 27°54S 17°59E 56 C2
Ai-Ais and Fish River Canyon △ Namibia 24°45S 17°15E 56 B2
Aichi □ Japan 35°0N 137°15E 29 G8
Aigrettes, Pte. des Réunion 21°3S 55°13E 55 c
Aiguá Uruguay 34°13S 54°46W 95 C5
Aigues-Mortes France 43°35N 4°12E 20 E6
Aihui = Heihe China 50°10N 127°30E 31 A14
Aija Peru 9°50S 77°45W 92 E3
Aikawa Japan 38°2N 138°15E 28 E9
Aiken U.S.A. 33°34N 81°43W 85 E14
Ailao Shan China 24°0N 101°20E 34 F3
Aileron Australia 22°39S 133°20E 62 C1
Aillik Canada 55°11N 59°18W 73 A8
Ailsa Craig Canada 43°8N 81°33W 82 C3
Ailsa Craig U.K. 55°15N 5°6W 11 F3
Aim Russia 59°0N 133°55E 27 D14
Aimogasta Argentina 28°33S 66°50W 94 B2
Aïn Ben Tili Mauritania 25°59N 9°27W 52 C4
Aïn Sefra Algeria 32°47N 0°37W 52 B5
Ain Sudr Egypt 29°50N 33°6E 48 F2
Aïn Témouchent Algeria 35°16N 1°8W 52 A5
Ainaži Latvia 57°50N 24°24E 9 H21
Ainsworth U.S.A. 42°33N 99°52W 80 D4
Aiquile Bolivia 18°10S 65°10W 92 G5
Aïr Niger 18°30N 8°0E 52 E7
Air Force I. Canada 67°58N 74°5W 69 D17
Air Hitam Malaysia 1°55N 103°11E 39 M4
Airdrie Canada 51°18N 114°2W 70 C6
Airdrie U.K. 55°52N 3°57W 11 F5
Aire → U.K. 53°43N 0°55W 12 D7
Airlie Beach Australia 20°16S 148°43E 62 b
Aisne → France 49°26N 2°50E 20 B5
Ait India 25°54N 79°14E 43 G8
Aitkin U.S.A. 46°32N 93°42W 80 B7
Aitutaki Cook Is. 18°52S 159°45W 65 J12
Aiud Romania 46°19N 23°44E 17 E12
Aix-en-Provence France 43°32N 5°27E 20 E6
Aix-la-Chapelle = Aachen Germany 50°45N 6°6E 16 C4
Aix-les-Bains France 45°41N 5°53E 20 D6
Aizawl India 23°40N 92°44E 41 H18
Aizkraukle Latvia 56°36N 25°11E 9 H21
Aizpute Latvia 56°43N 21°40E 9 H19
Aizuwakamatsu Japan 37°30N 139°56E 28 F9
Ajaccio France 41°55N 8°40E 20 F8
Ajaigarh India 24°52N 80°16E 43 G9
Ajalpan Mexico 18°22N 97°15W 87 D5
Ajanta India 20°30N 75°48E 44 D2
Ajanta Ra. India 20°28N 75°50E 44 D2
Ajari Rep. = Ajaria □ Georgia 41°30N 42°0E 19 F7
Ajaria □ Georgia 41°30N 42°0E 19 F7
Ajax Canada 43°50N 79°1W 82 C5
Ajdābiyā Libya 30°54N 20°4E 53 B10
Ajka Hungary 47°4N 17°31E 17 E9
'Ajlūn Jordan 32°18N 35°47E 48 C4
'Ajlūn □ Jordan 32°18N 35°47E 48 C4
'Ajmān U.A.E. 25°25N 55°30E 47 E7
Ajmer India 26°28N 74°37E 42 F6
Ajnala India 31°50N 74°48E 42 D6
Ajo U.S.A. 32°22N 112°52W 77 K7
Ajo, C. de Spain 43°31N 3°35W 21 A4
Akabira Japan 43°33N 142°5E 28 C11
Akalkot India 17°32N 76°13E 44 F3
Akan △ Japan 43°20N 144°20E 28 C12
Akaroa N.Z. 43°49S 172°59E 59 E4
Akashi Japan 34°45N 134°58E 29 G7
Akbarpur Bihar, India 24°39N 83°58E 43 G10
Akbarpur Ut. P., India 26°25N 82°32E 43 F10
Akçakale Turkey 36°41N 38°56E 46 B3
Akelamo Indonesia 1°35N 129°40E 37 D7
Akeru → India 17°25N 80°5E 44 F5
Aketi Dem. Rep. of the Congo 2°38N 23°47E 54 D4
Akhisar Turkey 38°56N 27°48E 23 E12
Akhnur India 32°52N 74°45E 43 C6
Akhtyrka = Okhtyrka Ukraine 50°25N 35°0E 19 D5
Aki Japan 33°30N 133°54E 29 H6
Akimiski I. Canada 52°50N 81°30W 72 B3
Akiōta Japan 34°36N 132°19E 29 G6
Akita Japan 39°45N 140°7E 28 E10
Akita □ Japan 39°40N 140°30E 28 E10
Akjoujt Mauritania 19°45N 14°15W 52 E3
Akkaraipattu Sri Lanka 7°13N 81°51E 45 L5
Akkeshi Japan 43°2N 144°51E 28 C12
'Akko Israel 32°55N 35°4E 48 C4
Aklavik Canada 68°12N 135°0W 68 D4
Aklera India 24°26N 76°32E 42 G7
Akō Japan 34°45N 134°24E 29 G7
Akola Maharashtra, India 20°42N 77°2E 44 D3
Akola Maharashtra, India 19°32N 74°3E 44 E2
Akordat Eritrea 15°30N 37°40E 49 D2
Akot India 21°10N 77°10E 44 D3
Akpatok I. Canada 60°25N 68°8W 69 E18
Åkrahamn Norway 59°15N 5°10E 9 G11
Akranes Iceland 64°19N 22°5W 8 D2
Akron Colo., U.S.A. 40°10N 103°13W 76 F12
Akron Ohio, U.S.A. 41°5N 81°31W 82 E3
Aksai Chin China 35°15N 79°55E 43 B8
Aksaray Turkey 38°25N 34°2E 46 B2
Aksay = Aqsay Kazakhstan 51°11N 53°0E 19 D9
Akşehir Turkey 38°18N 31°30E 46 B1
Akşehir Gölü Turkey 38°30N 31°25E 19 G5
Aksu China 41°5N 80°10E 30 C5
Aksum Ethiopia 14°5N 38°40E 49 E2
Aktsyabrski Belarus 52°38N 28°53E 17 B15
Aktyubinsk = Aqtöbe Kazakhstan 50°17N 57°10E 19 D10
Akure Nigeria 7°15N 5°5E 52 G7
Akuressa Sri Lanka 6°5N 80°29E 45 L5
Akureyri Iceland 65°40N 18°6W 8 D4
Akuseki-Shima Japan 29°27N 129°37E 29 K4
Akyab = Sittwe Burma 20°18N 92°45E 41 J18
Al 'Adan = 'Adan Yemen 12°45N 45°0E 49 E4
Al Aḩsā = Hasa Si. Arabia 25°50N 49°0E 47 E6
Al Ajfar Si. Arabia 27°26N 43°0E 46 E4
Al Amādīyah Iraq 37°5N 43°30E 46 B4
Al 'Amārah Iraq 31°55N 47°15E 46 D5
Al Anbār □ Iraq 33°25N 42°0E 46 C4
Al 'Aqabah Jordan 29°31N 35°0E 48 F4
Al 'Aqabah □ Jordan 29°30N 35°0E 48 F4
Al Arak Syria 34°38N 38°35E 46 C3
Al 'Aramah Si. Arabia 25°30N 46°0E 46 E5
Al 'Arţāwīyah Si. Arabia 26°31N 45°20E 46 E5
Al 'Āşimah = 'Ammān □ Jordan 31°40N 36°30E 48 D5
Al 'Assāfīyah Si. Arabia 28°17N 38°59E 46 D3
Al 'Awdah Si. Arabia 25°32N 45°41E 46 E5
Al 'Ayn Si. Arabia 25°4N 38°6E 46 E3
Al 'Ayn U.A.E. 24°15N 55°45E 47 E7
Al 'Azīzīyah Iraq 32°54N 45°4E 46 C5
Al Bāb Syria 36°23N 37°29E 46 B3
Al Bad' Si. Arabia 28°28N 35°1E 46 D2
Al Bada'i' Si. Arabia 26°2N 43°33E 46 E4
Al Bādī Iraq 35°56N 41°32E 46 C4
Al Baḩrah Kuwait 29°40N 47°52E 46 D5
Al Baḩral Mayyit = Dead Sea Asia 31°30N 35°30E 48 D4
Al Balqā' □ Jordan 32°5N 35°45E 48 C4
Al Bārūk, J. Lebanon 33°39N 35°40E 48 B4
Al Başrah Iraq 30°30N 47°50E 46 D5
Al Baţḩā Iraq 31°6N 45°53E 46 D5
Al Batrūn Lebanon 34°15N 35°40E 48 A4
Al Bayḑā Libya 32°50N 21°44E 53 B10
Al Biqā Lebanon 34°10N 36°10E 48 A5
Al Bi'r Si. Arabia 28°51N 36°16E 46 D3
Al Bukayrīyah Si. Arabia 26°9N 43°40E 46 E4
Al Burayj Syria 34°15N 36°46E 48 A5
Al Faḑilī Si. Arabia 26°58N 49°10E 47 E6
Al Fallūjah Iraq 33°20N 43°55E 46 C4
Al Fāw Iraq 30°0N 48°30E 47 D6
Al Fujayrah U.A.E. 25°7N 56°18E 47 E8
Al Ghammās Iraq 31°45N 44°37E 46 D5
Al Ghazālah Si. Arabia 26°48N 41°19E 46 E4
Al Ghadaf, W. → Jordan 31°26N 36°43E 48 D5
Al Ḩadīthah Iraq 34°0N 41°13E 46 C4
Al Ḩadīthah Si. Arabia 31°28N 37°8E 48 D6
Al Ḩaḑr Iraq 35°35N 42°44E 46 C4
Al Hājānah Syria 33°20N 36°33E 48 B5
Al Ḩajar al Gharbī Oman 24°10N 56°15E 47 E8
Al Hāmad Si. Arabia 31°30N 39°30E 46 D3
Al Ḩamdānīyah Syria 35°25N 36°50E 46 C3
Al Ḩamīdīyah Syria 34°42N 35°57E 48 A4

Al Ḥammār Iraq 30°57N 46°51E 46 D5
Al Ḥamrā' Si. Arabia 24°2N 38°55E 46 E3
Al Ḥamzah Iraq 31°43N 44°58E 46 D5
Al Ḥanākīyah Si. Arabia 24°51N 40°31E 46 E4
Al Harūj al Aswad Libya 27°0N 17°10E 53 C9
Al Ḥasakah Syria 36°35N 40°45E 46 B4
Al Ḥayy Iraq 32°5N 46°5E 46 C5
Al Ḥijarah Asia 30°0N 44°0E 46 D4
Al Ḥillah Iraq 32°30N 44°25E 46 C5
Al Hindīyah Iraq 32°30N 44°10E 46 C5
Al Hirmil Lebanon 34°26N 36°24E 48 A5
Al Hoceïma Morocco 35°8N 3°58W 52 A5
Al Ḥudaydah Yemen 14°50N 43°0E 49 E3
Al Ḥudūd ash Shamālīyah ☐ Si. Arabia 29°10N 42°30E 46 D4
Al Hufūf Si. Arabia 25°25N 49°45E 47 E6
Al Ḥumayḍah Si. Arabia 29°14N 34°56E 46 D2
Al Ḥunayy Si. Arabia 25°58N 48°45E 47 E6
Al Īsāwīyah Si. Arabia 30°43N 37°59E 46 D3
Al Jafr Jordan 30°18N 36°14E 48 E5
Al Jāfūrah Si. Arabia 25°0N 50°15E 47 E7
Al Jaghbūb Libya 29°42N 24°38E 53 C10
Al Jahrah Kuwait 29°25N 47°40E 46 D5
Al Jalāmīd Si. Arabia 31°20N 40°6E 46 D3
Al Jamalīyah Qatar 25°37N 51°5E 47 E6
Al Janūb ☐ Lebanon 33°20N 35°20E 48 B4
Al Jawf Libya 24°10N 23°24E 53 D10
Al Jawf Si. Arabia 29°55N 39°40E 46 D3
Al Jawf ☐ Si. Arabia 29°30N 39°30E 46 D3
Al Jazair = Algeria ■ Africa 28°30N 2°0E 52 C6
Al Jazirah Iraq 33°30N 44°0E 46 C5
Al Jithāmīyah Si. Arabia 27°41N 41°43E 46 E4
Al Jubayl Si. Arabia 27°0N 49°50E 47 E6
Al Jubaylah Si. Arabia 24°55N 46°25E 46 E5
Al Jubb Si. Arabia 27°11N 42°17E 46 E4
Al Junaynah Sudan 13°27N 22°45E 53 F10
Al Kabā'ish Iraq 30°58N 47°0E 46 D5
Al Karak Jordan 31°11N 35°42E 48 D4
Al Karak ☐ Jordan 31°0N 36°0E 48 E5
Al Kāẓimīyah Iraq 33°22N 44°18E 46 C5
Al Khābūrah Oman 23°57N 57°5E 47 F8
Al Khafji Si. Arabia 28°24N 48°29E 47 E6
Al Khalīl West Bank 31°32N 35°6E 48 D4
Al Khāliṣ Iraq 33°49N 44°32E 46 C5
Al Kharsānīyah Si. Arabia 27°13N 49°18E 47 E6
Al Khaṣab Oman 26°14N 56°15E 47 E8
Al Khawr Qatar 25°41N 51°30E 47 E6
Al Khiḍr Iraq 31°12N 45°33E 46 D5
Al Khiyām Lebanon 33°20N 35°36E 48 B4
Al Khubar Si. Arabia 26°17N 50°12E 47 E6
Al Khums Libya 32°40N 14°17E 53 B8
Al Kiswah Syria 33°23N 36°14E 48 B5
Al Kūfah Iraq 32°2N 44°24E 46 C5
Al Kufrah Libya 24°17N 23°15E 53 D10
Al Kuhayfiyah Si. Arabia 27°12N 43°3E 46 E4
Al Kūt Iraq 32°30N 46°0E 46 C5
Al Kuwayt Kuwait 29°30N 48°0E 46 D5
Al Labwah Lebanon 34°11N 36°20E 48 A5
Al Lādhiqīyah Syria 35°30N 35°45E 46 C2
Al Līth Si. Arabia 20°9N 40°15E 49 C3
Al Liwā' Oman 24°31N 56°36E 47 E8
Al Luḥayyah Yemen 15°45N 42°40E 49 D3
Al Madīnah Iraq 30°57N 47°16E 46 D5
Al Madīnah Si. Arabia 24°35N 39°52E 46 E3
Al Mafraq Jordan 32°17N 36°14E 48 C5
Al Mafraq ☐ Jordan 32°17N 36°15E 48 C5
Al Maghreb = Morocco ■ N. Afr. 32°0N 5°50W 52 B4
Al Maḥmūdīyah Iraq 33°3N 44°21E 46 C5
Al Majma'ah Si. Arabia 25°57N 45°22E 46 E5
Al Makhruq, W. → Jordan 31°28N 37°0E 48 D6
Al Makḥūl Si. Arabia 26°37N 42°39E 46 E4
Al Manāmah Bahrain 26°10N 50°30E 47 E6
Al Maqwa' Kuwait 29°10N 47°59E 46 D5
Al Marāḥ Si. Arabia 25°35N 49°35E 47 E6
Al Marj Libya 32°25N 20°30E 53 B10
Al Maṭlā Kuwait 29°24N 47°40E 46 D5
Al Mawṣil Iraq 36°15N 43°5E 46 B4
Al Mayādin Syria 35°1N 40°27E 46 C4
Al Mazār Jordan 31°4N 35°41E 48 D4
Al Midhnab Si. Arabia 25°50N 44°18E 46 E5
Al Minā' Lebanon 34°24N 35°49E 48 A4
Al Miqdādīyah Iraq 34°0N 45°0E 46 C5
Al Mubarraz Si. Arabia 25°30N 49°40E 47 E6
Al Mudawwarah Jordan 29°19N 36°0E 48 F5
Al Mughayrā' U.A.E. 24°5N 53°32E 47 E7
Al Muḥarraq Bahrain 26°15N 50°40E 47 E6
Al Mukallā Yemen 14°33N 49°2E 49 E4
Al Mukhā Yemen 13°18N 43°15E 49 E3
Al Musayjīd Si. Arabia 24°5N 39°5E 46 E3
Al Musayyib Iraq 32°49N 44°20E 46 C5
Al Muthanná ☐ Iraq 30°30N 45°15E 46 D5
Al Muwayliḥ Si. Arabia 27°40N 35°30E 46 E2
Al Qādisīyah ☐ Iraq 32°0N 45°0E 46 D5
Al Qā'im Iraq 34°21N 41°7E 46 C4
Al Qalībah Si. Arabia 28°24N 37°42E 46 D3
Al Qāmishlī Syria 37°2N 41°14E 46 B4
Al Qaryatayn Syria 34°12N 37°13E 48 A6
Al Qaṣīm ☐ Si. Arabia 26°0N 43°0E 46 E4
Al Qaṭ'ā Syria 34°40N 40°48E 46 C4
Al Qaṭīf Si. Arabia 26°35N 50°0E 47 E6
Al Qatrānah Jordan 31°12N 36°6E 48 D5
Al Qaṭrūn Libya 24°56N 15°3E 53 D9
Al Qayṣūmah Si. Arabia 28°20N 46°7E 46 D5
Al Qunayṭirah Syria 33°5N 35°45E 48 B4
Al Qunfudhah Si. Arabia 19°3N 41°4E 49 D3
Al Qurayyāt Si. Arabia 31°20N 37°20E 46 D3
Al Qurnah Iraq 31°1N 47°25E 46 D5
Al Quṣayr Iraq 30°39N 45°50E 46 D5
Al Quṣayr Syria 34°31N 36°34E 48 A5
Al Qutayfah Syria 33°44N 36°36E 48 B5
Al Quwaysimah Jordan 31°55N 35°57E 48 D4
Al 'Ubaylah Si. Arabia 21°59N 50°57E 49 C5
Al 'Udaylīyah Si. Arabia 25°8N 49°18E 47 E6
Al 'Ulā Si. Arabia 26°35N 38°0E 46 E3
Al 'Uqayr Si. Arabia 25°40N 50°15E 47 E6
Al 'Uwaynid Si. Arabia 24°50N 46°0E 46 E5
Al 'Uwayqīlah Si. Arabia 30°30N 42°10E 46 D4
Al 'Uyūn Ḥijāz, Si. Arabia 24°33N 39°35E 46 E3
Al 'Uyūn Najd, Si. Arabia 26°30N 43°50E 46 E4
Al 'Uzayr Iraq 31°19N 47°25E 46 D5
Al Wajh Si. Arabia 26°10N 36°30E 46 E3
Al Wakrah Qatar 25°10N 51°40E 47 E6
Al Waqbah Si. Arabia 28°48N 45°33E 46 D5
Al Wari'āh Si. Arabia 27°51N 47°25E 46 E5
Al Yaman = Yemen ■ Asia 15°0N 44°0E 49 E3
Ala Dağ Turkey 37°44N 35°9E 46 B2
Ala Tau Asia 45°30N 80°40E 30 B5
Ala Tau Shankou = Dzungarian Gate Asia 45°10N 82°0E 30 B5
Alabama ☐ U.S.A. 33°0N 87°0W 85 E11
Alabama → U.S.A. 31°8N 87°57W 85 F11
Alabaster U.S.A. 33°15N 86°49W 85 E11
Alaçam Dağları Turkey 39°18N 28°49E 23 E13
Alacant = Alicante Spain 38°23N 0°30W 21 C5
Alachua U.S.A. 29°47N 82°30W 85 G13
Alagoa Grande Brazil 7°3S 35°35W 93 E11
Alagoas ☐ Brazil 9°0S 36°0W 93 E11
Alagoinhas Brazil 12°7S 38°20W 93 F11
Alaheaieatnu = Altaelva → Norway 69°54N 23°17E 8 B20
Alajuela Costa Rica 10°2N 84°8W 88 D3
Alaknanda → India 30°8N 78°36E 43 D8
Alakurtti Russia 66°58N 30°25E 8 C24
Alamarvdasht Iran 27°37N 52°59E 47 E7
Alameda U.S.A. 35°11N 106°37W 77 J10
Alamo U.S.A. 37°22N 115°10W 79 H11
Alamogordo U.S.A. 32°54N 105°57W 77 K11
Alamos Mexico 27°1N 108°56W 86 B3
Alamosa U.S.A. 37°28N 105°52W 77 H11
Alampur India 15°55N 78°6E 45 G4
Åland Finland 60°15N 20°0E 9 F19
Aland India 17°36N 76°35E 44 F3
Ålands hav Europe 60°0N 19°30E 9 G18
Alandur India 13°0N 80°15E 45 H5
Alania = North Ossetia ☐ Russia 43°30N 44°30E 19 F7
Alanya Turkey 36°38N 32°0E 46 B1
Alapayevsk Russia 57°52N 61°42E 26 D7
Alappuzha India 9°30N 76°28E 45 K3
Alaşehir Turkey 38°23N 28°30E 23 E13
Alaska ☐ U.S.A. 64°0N 154°0W 74 C9
Alaska, G. of Pac. Oc. 58°0N 145°0W 68 F3
Alaska Peninsula U.S.A. 56°0N 159°0W 74 D8
Alaska Range U.S.A. 62°50N 151°0W 68 E1
Älät Azerbaijan 39°58N 49°25E 47 B6
Alatau Shan = Ala Tau Asia 45°30N 80°40E 30 B5
Alatyr Russia 54°55N 46°35E 18 D8
Alausi Ecuador 2°0S 78°50W 92 D3
Alava, C. U.S.A. 48°10N 124°44W 78 B2
Alavo = Alavus Finland 62°35N 23°36E 8 E20
Alavus Finland 62°35N 23°36E 8 E20
Alawa ✿ Australia 15°42S 134°39E 62 B1
Alawoona Australia 34°45S 140°30E 63 E3
Alayawarra ✿ Australia 22°0S 134°30E 62 C1
'Alayh Lebanon 33°46N 35°33E 48 B4
Alba Italy 44°42N 8°2E 20 D8
Alba-Iulia Romania 46°8N 23°39E 17 E12
Albacete Spain 39°0N 1°50W 21 C5
Albacutya, L. Australia 35°45S 141°58E 63 F3
Albanel, L. Canada 50°55N 73°12W 72 B5
Albania ■ Europe 41°0N 20°0E 23 D9
Albany Australia 35°1S 117°58E 61 G2
Albany Ga., U.S.A. 31°35N 84°10W 85 F12
Albany N.Y., U.S.A. 42°39N 73°45W 83 D11
Albany Oreg., U.S.A. 44°38N 123°6W 76 D2
Albany Tex., U.S.A. 32°44N 99°18W 84 E5
Albany → Canada 52°17N 81°31W 72 B3
Albardón Argentina 31°20S 68°30W 94 C2
Albatross B. Australia 12°45S 141°30E 62 A3
Albemarle U.S.A. 35°21N 80°12W 85 D14
Albemarle Sd. U.S.A. 36°5N 76°0W 85 C16
Alberche → Spain 39°58N 4°46W 21 C3
Alberdi Paraguay 26°14S 58°20W 94 B4
Alberga → Australia 27°6S 135°33E 63 D2
Albert, L. Africa 1°30N 31°0E 54 D6
Albert, L. Australia 35°30S 139°10E 63 F2
Albert Edward Ra. Australia 18°17S 127°57E 60 C4
Albert Lea U.S.A. 43°39N 93°22W 80 D7
Albert Nile → Uganda 3°36N 32°2E 54 D6
Albert Town Bahamas 22°37N 74°33W 89 B5
Alberta ☐ Canada 54°40N 115°0W 70 C6
Alberti Argentina 35°1S 60°16W 94 D3
Albertinia S. Africa 34°11S 21°34E 56 D3
Alberton Canada 46°50N 64°0W 73 C7
Albertville France 45°40N 6°22E 20 D7
Albertville U.S.A. 34°16N 86°13W 85 D11
Albi France 43°56N 2°9E 20 E5
Albia U.S.A. 41°2N 92°48W 80 E7
Albina Suriname 5°37N 54°15W 93 B8
Albina, Ponta Angola 15°52S 11°44E 56 A1
Albion Mich., U.S.A. 42°15N 84°45W 81 D11
Albion Nebr., U.S.A. 41°42N 98°0W 80 E4
Albion Pa., U.S.A. 41°53N 80°22W 82 E4
Alborán Medit. S. 35°57N 3°0W 21 E4
Ålborg = Aalborg Denmark 57°2N 9°54E 9 H13
Alborz, Reshteh-ye Kūhhā-ye Iran 36°0N 52°0E 47 C7
Albufeira Portugal 37°5N 8°15W 21 D1
Albuquerque U.S.A. 35°5N 106°39W 77 J10
Albuquerque, Cayos de Caribbean 12°10N 81°50W 88 D3
Alburg U.S.A. 44°59N 73°18W 83 B11
Albury Australia 36°3S 146°56E 63 F4
Alcalá de Henares Spain 40°28N 3°22W 21 B4
Alcalá la Real Spain 37°27N 3°57W 21 D4
Álcamo Italy 37°59N 12°55E 22 F5
Alcañiz Spain 41°2N 0°8W 21 B5
Alcântara Brazil 2°20S 44°30W 93 D10
Alcántara, Embalse de Spain 39°44N 6°50W 21 C2
Alcantarilla Spain 37°59N 1°12W 21 D5
Alcaraz, Sierra de Spain 38°40N 2°20W 21 C4
Alcaudete Spain 37°35N 4°5W 21 D3
Alcázar de San Juan Spain 39°24N 3°12W 21 C4
Alchevsk Ukraine 48°30N 38°45E 19 E6
Alcira = Alzira Spain 39°9N 0°30W 21 C5
Alcova U.S.A. 42°34N 106°43W 76 E10
Alcoy Spain 38°43N 0°30W 21 C5
Aldabra Is. Seychelles 9°22S 46°28E 51 G8
Aldama Mexico 22°55N 98°4W 87 C5
Aldan Russia 58°40N 125°30E 27 D13
Aldan → Russia 63°28N 129°35E 27 C13
Aldeburgh U.K. 52°10N 1°37E 13 E9
Alder Pk. U.S.A. 35°53N 121°22W 78 K5
Alderney U.K. 49°42N 2°11W 13 H5
Aldershot U.K. 51°15N 0°44W 13 F7
Aledo U.S.A. 41°12N 90°45W 80 E8
Aleg Mauritania 17°3N 13°55W 52 E3
Alegre Brazil 20°50S 41°30W 95 A7
Alegrete Brazil 29°40S 56°0W 95 B4
Aleksandriya = Oleksandriya Ukraine 50°37N 26°19E 17 C14
Aleksandrov Gay Russia 50°9N 48°34E 19 D8
Aleksandrovsk-Sakhalinskiy Russia 50°50N 142°20E 31 A17
Aleksandry, Zemlya Russia 80°25N 48°0E 26 A5
Além Paraíba Brazil 21°52S 42°41W 95 A7
Alemania Argentina 25°40S 65°30W 94 B2
Alemania Chile 25°10S 69°55W 94 B2
Alençon France 48°27N 0°4E 20 B4
Alenquer Brazil 1°56S 54°46W 93 D8
'Alenuihähä Channel U.S.A. 20°30N 156°0W 75 L8
Aleppo = Ḥalab Syria 36°10N 37°15E 46 B3
Aléria France 42°5N 9°26E 20 E9
Alert Canada 83°2N 60°0W 69 A20
Aleru India 17°39N 79°3E 44 F4
Alès France 44°9N 4°5E 20 D6
Alessándria Italy 44°54N 8°37E 20 D8
Ålesund Norway 62°28N 6°12E 8 E12
Aleutian Basin Pac. Oc. 57°0N 177°0E 64 B9
Aleutian Is. Pac. Oc. 52°0N 175°0W 64 B10
Aleutian Range U.S.A. 60°0N 154°0W 74 D9
Aleutian Trench Pac. Oc. 48°0N 180°0E 4 D17
Alexander U.S.A. 47°51N 103°39W 80 B2
Alexander, Mt. Australia 28°58S 120°16E 61 E3
Alexander Arch. U.S.A. 56°0N 136°0W 68 F4
Alexander Bay S. Africa 28°40S 16°30E 56 C2
Alexander City U.S.A. 32°56N 85°58W 85 E12
Alexander I. Antarctica 69°0S 70°0W 5 C17
Alexandra Australia 37°8S 145°40E 63 F4
Alexandra N.Z. 45°14S 169°25E 59 F2
Alexandra Channel Burma 14°7N 93°13E 45 G11
Alexandra Falls Canada 60°29N 116°18W 70 A5
Alexandria = El Iskandarîya Egypt 31°13N 29°58E 53 B11
Alexandria B.C., Canada 52°35N 122°27W 70 C4
Alexandria Ont., Canada 45°19N 74°38W 83 A10
Alexandria Romania 43°57N 25°24E 17 G13
Alexandria S. Africa 33°38S 26°28E 56 D4
Alexandria U.K. 55°59N 4°35W 11 F4
Alexandria La., U.S.A. 31°18N 92°27W 84 F8
Alexandria Minn., U.S.A. 45°53N 95°22W 80 C6
Alexandria S. Dak., U.S.A. 43°39N 97°47W 80 D5
Alexandria Bay U.S.A. 44°20N 75°55W 83 B9
Alexandrina, L. Australia 35°25S 139°10E 63 F2
Alexandroupoli Greece 40°50N 25°54E 23 D11
Alexis → Canada 52°33N 56°8W 73 B8
Alexis Creek Canada 52°10N 123°20W 70 C4
Aleysk Russia 52°40N 83°0E 26 D9
Alfenas Brazil 21°20S 46°10W 95 A6
Alford Aberds., U.K. 57°14N 2°41W 11 D6
Alford Lincs., U.K. 53°15N 0°10E 12 D8
Alfred Maine, U.S.A. 43°29N 70°43W 83 C14
Alfred N.Y., U.S.A. 42°16N 77°48W 82 D7
Alfreton U.K. 53°6N 1°24W 12 D6
Ålgård Norway 58°46N 5°53E 9 G11
Algarve Portugal 36°58N 8°20W 21 D1
Algeciras Spain 36°9N 5°28W 21 D3
Algemesí Spain 39°11N 0°27W 21 C5
Alger Algeria 36°42N 3°8E 52 A6
Algeria ■ Africa 28°30N 2°0E 52 C6
Algha Kazakhstan 49°53N 57°20E 19 E10
Alghero Italy 40°33N 8°19E 22 D3
Algiers = Alger Algeria 36°42N 3°8E 52 A6
Algoa B. S. Africa 33°50S 25°45E 56 D4
Algoma U.S.A. 44°36N 87°26W 80 C10
Algona U.S.A. 43°4N 94°14W 80 D6
Algonac U.S.A. 42°37N 82°32W 82 D2
Algonquin ⌂ Canada 45°50N 78°30W 72 C4
Algorta Uruguay 32°25S 57°23W 96 C5
Alhucemas = Al Hoceïma Morocco 35°8N 3°58W 52 A5
'Alī al Gharbī Iraq 32°30N 46°45E 46 C5
'Alī ash Sharqī Iraq 32°7N 46°44E 46 C5
Äli Bayramlı = Şirvan Azerbaijan 39°59N 48°52E 47 B6
'Alī Khēl Afghan. 33°57N 69°43E 42 C3
Alī Shāh Iran 38°9N 45°50E 46 B5
'Alīābād Golestān, Iran 36°40N 54°33E 47 B7
'Alīābād Khorāsān, Iran 32°30N 57°30E 47 C8
'Alīābād Kordestān, Iran 35°4N 46°58E 46 C5
'Alīābād Yazd, Iran 31°41N 53°49E 47 D7
Aliağa Turkey 38°47N 26°59E 23 E12
Aliakmonas → Greece 40°30N 22°36E 23 D10
Alibag India 18°38N 72°56E 44 E1
Alicante Spain 38°23N 0°30W 21 C5
Alice S. Africa 32°48S 26°55E 56 D4
Alice U.S.A. 27°45N 98°5W 84 H5
Alice → Queens., Australia 24°2S 144°50E 62 C3
Alice → Queens., Australia 15°35S 142°20E 62 B3
Alice Arm Canada 55°29N 129°31W 70 B3
Alice Springs Australia 23°40S 133°50E 62 C1
Alicedale S. Africa 33°15S 26°4E 56 D4
Aliceville U.S.A. 33°8N 88°9W 85 E10
Aliganj India 27°30N 79°10E 43 F8
Aligarh Raj., India 25°55N 76°15E 42 G7
Aligarh Ut. P., India 27°55N 78°10E 42 F8
Alīgūdarz Iran 33°25N 49°45E 47 C6
Alingsås Sweden 57°56N 12°31E 9 H15
Alipur Pakistan 29°25N 70°55E 42 E4
Alipur Duar India 26°30N 89°35E 41 F16
Aliquippa U.S.A. 40°37N 80°15W 82 F4
Alishan Taiwan 23°31N 120°48E 35 F13
Alitus = Alytus Lithuania 54°24N 24°3E 9 J21
Aliwal North S. Africa 30°45S 26°45E 56 D4
Alix Canada 52°24N 113°11W 70 C6
Aljustrel Portugal 37°55N 8°10W 21 D1
Alkmaar Neths. 52°37N 4°45E 15 B4
All American Canal U.S.A. 32°45N 115°15W 79 N11
Allagadda India 15°8N 78°30E 45 G4
Allagash → U.S.A. 47°5N 69°3W 81 B19
Allah Dad Pakistan 25°38N 67°34E 42 G2
Allahabad India 25°25N 81°58E 43 G9
Allan Canada 51°53N 106°4W 71 C7
Allanridge S. Africa 27°45S 26°40E 56 C4
Allegany U.S.A. 42°6N 78°30W 82 D6
Allegheny → U.S.A. 40°27N 80°1W 82 F5
Allegheny Mts. U.S.A. 38°15N 80°10W 81 F13
Allegheny Plateau U.S.A. 41°30N 78°30W 81 E14
Allegheny Res. U.S.A. 41°50N 79°0W 82 E6
Allègre, Pte. Guadeloupe 16°22N 61°46W 88 b
Allen, Bog of Ireland 53°15N 7°0W 10 C5
Allen, L. Ireland 54°8N 8°4W 10 B3
Allendale U.S.A. 33°1N 81°18W 85 E14
Allende Mexico 28°20N 100°51W 86 B4
Allentown U.S.A. 40°37N 75°29W 83 F9
Alleppey = Alappuzha India 9°30N 76°28E 45 K3
Aller → Germany 52°56N 9°12E 16 B5
Alleynes B. Barbados 13°13N 59°39W 89 g
Alliance Nebr., U.S.A. 42°6N 102°52W 80 D2
Alliance Ohio, U.S.A. 40°55N 81°6W 82 F3
Allier → France 46°57N 3°4E 20 C5
Alliford Bay Canada 53°12N 131°58W 70 C2
Alligator Pond Jamaica 17°52N 77°34W 88 a
Allinagaram India 10°2N 77°36E 45 J3
Alliston Canada 44°9N 79°52W 82 B5
Alloa U.K. 56°7N 3°47W 11 E5
Allora Australia 28°2S 152°0E 63 D5
Alluitsup Paa Greenland 60°30N 45°35W 4 C5
Allur India 14°40N 80°4E 45 G5
Alluru Kottapatnam India 15°24N 80°7E 45 G5
Alma Canada 48°35N 71°40W 73 C5
Alma Ga., U.S.A. 31°33N 82°28W 85 F13
Alma Kans., U.S.A. 39°1N 96°17W 80 F5
Alma Mich., U.S.A. 43°23N 84°39W 81 D11
Alma Nebr., U.S.A. 40°6N 99°22W 80 E4
Alma Wis., U.S.A. 44°20N 91°55W 80 C8
Alma Ata = Almaty Kazakhstan 43°15N 76°57E 30 C4
Alma Hill U.S.A. 42°2N 78°0W 82 D7
Almaden Australia 17°22S 144°40E 62 B3
Almadén Spain 38°49N 4°52W 21 C3
Almalyk = Olmaliq Uzbekistan 40°50N 69°35E 26 E7
Almanor, L. U.S.A. 40°14N 121°9W 76 F3
Almansa Spain 38°51N 1°5W 21 C5
Almanzor, Pico Spain 40°15N 5°18W 21 B3
Almanzora → Spain 37°14N 1°46W 21 D5
Almaty Kazakhstan 43°15N 76°57E 30 C4
Almazán Spain 41°30N 2°30W 21 B4
Almeirim Brazil 1°30S 52°34W 93 D8
Almelo Neths. 52°22N 6°42E 15 B6
Almendralejo Spain 38°41N 6°26W 21 C2
Almere Neths. 52°20N 5°15E 15 B5
Almería Spain 36°52N 2°27W 21 D4
Almirante Panama 9°10N 82°30W 88 E3
Almond U.S.A. 42°19N 77°44W 82 D7
Almont U.S.A. 42°55N 83°3W 82 D1
Almonte Canada 45°14N 76°12W 83 A8
Almora India 29°38N 79°40E 43 E8
Alness U.K. 57°41N 4°16W 11 D4
Alnmouth U.K. 55°24N 1°37W 12 B6
Alnwick U.K. 55°24N 1°42W 12 B6
Alon Burma 22°12N 95°5E 41 H19
Alor Indonesia 8°15S 124°30E 37 F6
Alor Setar Malaysia 6°7N 100°22E 39 J3
Alot India 23°56N 75°40E 42 H6
Aloysius, Mt. Australia 26°0S 128°38E 61 E4
Alpaugh U.S.A. 35°53N 119°29W 78 K7
Alpena U.S.A. 45°4N 83°27W 82 A1
Alpha Australia 23°39S 146°37E 62 C4
Alpha Ridge Arctic 84°0N 118°0W 4 A2
Alphen aan den Rijn Neths. 52°7N 4°40E 15 B4
Alpine Ariz., U.S.A. 33°51N 109°9W 77 K9
Alpine Calif., U.S.A. 32°50N 116°46W 79 N10
Alpine Tex., U.S.A. 30°22N 103°40W 84 F3
Alps Europe 46°30N 9°30E 16 E5
Alpurrurulam Australia 20°59S 137°50E 62 C2
Alsace ☐ France 48°15N 7°25E 20 B7
Alsask Canada 51°21N 109°59W 71 C7
Alsasua Spain 42°54N 2°10W 21 A4
Alsek → U.S.A. 59°10N 138°12W 70 B1
Alsta Norway 65°58N 12°40E 8 D15
Alston U.K. 54°49N 2°25W 12 C5
Alta Norway 69°57N 23°10E 8 B20
Alta Gracia Argentina 31°40S 64°30W 94 C3
Alta Sierra U.S.A. 35°42N 118°33W 79 K8
Altaelva → Norway 69°54N 23°17E 8 B20
Altafjorden Norway 70°5N 23°5E 8 A20
Altai = Aerhtai Shan Mongolia 46°40N 92°45E 30 B7
Altai = Gorno-Altay ☐ Russia 51°0N 86°0E 26 D9
Altamaha → U.S.A. 31°20N 81°20W 85 F14
Altamira Brazil 3°12S 52°10W 93 D8
Altamira Chile 25°47S 69°51W 94 B2
Altamira Mexico 22°24N 97°55W 87 C5
Altamont U.S.A. 42°42N 74°2W 83 D10
Altamura Italy 40°49N 16°33E 22 D7
Altanbulag Mongolia 50°16N 106°30E 30 A10
Altar Mexico 30°43N 111°44W 86 A2
Altar, Gran Desierto de Mexico 31°50N 114°10W 86 B2
Altata Mexico 24°40N 107°55W 86 C3
Altavista U.S.A. 37°6N 79°17W 81 G14
Altay China 47°48N 88°10E 30 B6
Altay Mongolia 46°22N 96°15E 30 B8
Altea Spain 38°38N 0°2W 21 C5
Altiplano Bolivia 17°0S 68°0W 92 G5
Alto Araguaia Brazil 17°15S 53°20W 93 G8
Alto Cuchumatanes = Cuchumatanes, Sierra de los Guatemala 15°35N 91°25W 88 C1
Alto del Carmen Chile 28°46S 70°30W 94 B1
Alto Molocue Mozam. 15°50S 37°35E 55 H7
Alto Paraguay ☐ Paraguay 21°0S 58°30W 94 A4
Alto Paraná ☐ Paraguay 25°30S 54°50W 95 B5
Alton Canada 43°54N 80°5W 82 C4
Alton U.K. 51°9N 0°59W 13 F7
Alton Ill., U.S.A. 38°53N 90°11W 80 F8
Alton N.H., U.S.A. 43°27N 71°13W 83 C13
Altona Canada 49°6N 97°33W 71 D9
Altoona U.S.A. 40°31N 78°24W 82 F6
Altun Kupri Iraq 35°45N 44°9E 46 C5
Altun Shan China 38°30N 88°0E 30 D6
Alturas U.S.A. 41°29N 120°32W 76 F3
Altus U.S.A. 34°38N 99°20W 84 D5
Alucra Turkey 40°22N 38°47E 19 F6
Alūksne Latvia 57°24N 27°3E 9 H22
Alunite U.S.A. 35°59N 114°55W 79 K12
Alur India 15°24N 77°15E 45 E3
Alusi Indonesia 7°35S 131°40E 37 F8
Alutgama Sri Lanka 6°26N 79°59E 45 L4
Alutnuwara Sri Lanka 7°19N 80°59E 45 L5
Aluva = Alwaye India 10°8N 76°24E 45 J3
Alva U.S.A. 36°48N 98°40W 84 C5
Alvarado Mexico 18°46N 95°46W 87 D5
Alvarado U.S.A. 32°24N 97°13W 84 E6
Alvaro Obregón, Presa Mexico 27°52N 109°52W 86 B3
Alvear Argentina 29°5S 56°30W 94 B4
Alvesta Sweden 56°54N 14°35E 9 H16
Alvinston Canada 42°49N 81°52W 82 D3
Älvkarleby Sweden 60°34N 17°26E 9 F17
Alvord Desert U.S.A. 42°30N 118°25W 76 E4
Älvsbyn Sweden 65°40N 21°0E 8 D19
Alwar India 27°38N 76°34E 42 F7
Alwaye India 10°8N 76°24E 45 J3
Alxa Zuoqi China 38°50N 105°40E 32 E3
Alyangula Australia 13°55S 136°30E 62 A2
Alyata = Älät Azerbaijan 39°58N 49°25E 47 B6
Alyth U.K. 56°38N 3°13W 11 E5
Alytus Lithuania 54°24N 24°3E 9 J21
Alzada U.S.A. 45°2N 104°25W 76 D11
Alzamay Russia 55°33N 98°39E 27 D10
Alzira Spain 39°9N 0°30W 21 C5
Am Timan Chad 11°0N 20°10E 53 F10
Amadeus, L. Australia 24°54S 131°0E 61 D5
Amâdi South Sudan 5°29N 30°25E 53 G12
Amadjuak L. Canada 65°0N 71°8W 69 E17
Amagansett U.S.A. 40°59N 72°9W 83 F12
Amagi Japan 33°25N 130°39E 29 H5
Amahai Indonesia 3°20S 128°55E 37 E7
Amaile Samoa 13°59S 171°22W 59 b
Amakusa = Hondo Japan 32°27N 130°12E 29 H5
Amakusa-Shotō Japan 32°15N 130°10E 29 H5
Åmål Sweden 59°3N 12°42E 9 G15
Amalapuram India 16°35N 81°55E 45 F5
Amaliada Greece 37°47N 21°22E 23 F9
Amalner India 21°5N 75°5E 44 D2
Amamapare Indonesia 4°53S 136°38E 37 E9
Amambaí Brazil 23°5S 55°13W 95 A4
Amambaí → Brazil 23°22S 53°56W 95 A5
Amambay ☐ Paraguay 23°0S 56°0W 95 A4
Amambay, Cordillera de S. Amer. 23°0S 55°45W 95 A4
Amami Japan 28°22N 129°27E 29 K4
Amami-Guntō Japan 27°16N 129°21E 29 L4
Amami-Ō-Shima Japan 28°16N 129°21E 29 K4
Aman, Pulau Malaysia 5°16N 100°24E 39 c
Amaná, L. Brazil 2°35S 64°40W 92 D6
Amanat → India 24°7N 84°4E 43 G11
Amanda Park U.S.A. 47°28N 123°55W 78 C3
Amankeldi Kazakhstan 50°10N 65°10E 26 D7
Amapá Brazil 2°5N 50°50W 93 C8
Amapá ☐ Brazil 1°40N 52°0W 93 C8
Amarante Brazil 6°14S 42°50W 93 E10
Amaranth Canada 50°36N 98°43W 71 C9
Amaravati → India 11°0N 78°15E 45 J4
Amargosa → U.S.A. 36°14N 116°51W 79 J10
Amargosa Desert U.S.A. 36°40N 116°30W 79 J10
Amargosa Range U.S.A. 36°20N 116°45W 79 J10
Amarillo U.S.A. 35°13N 101°50W 84 D4
Amarkantak India 22°40N 81°45E 43 H9
Amarnath India 19°12N 73°22E 44 E1
Amaro, Mte. Italy 42°5N 14°5E 22 C6
Amarpur India 25°5N 87°0E 43 G12
Amarwara India 22°18N 79°10E 43 H8
Amasya Turkey 40°40N 35°50E 19 F6
Amata Australia 26°9S 131°9E 61 E5
Amatikulu S. Africa 29°3S 31°33E 57 C5
Amatitlán Guatemala 14°29N 90°38W 88 D1
Amay Belgium 50°33N 5°19E 15 D5
Amazon = Amazonas → S. Amer. 0°5S 50°0W 93 D8
Amazonas ☐ Brazil 5°0S 65°0W 92 E6
Amazonas → S. Amer. 0°5S 50°0W 93 D8
Ambad India 19°38N 75°50E 44 E2
Ambagarh Chowki India 20°47N 80°43E 44 D5
Ambah India 26°43N 78°13E 42 F8
Ambajogal India 18°44N 76°23E 44 E3
Ambala India 30°23N 76°56E 42 D7
Ambalangoda Sri Lanka 6°15N 80°5E 45 L5
Ambalantota Sri Lanka 6°7N 81°1E 45 L5
Ambalapulai India 9°25N 76°25E 45 K3
Ambalavao Madag. 21°50S 46°56E 55 J9
Ambanja Madag. 13°40S 48°27E 55 G9
Ambarchik Russia 69°40N 162°20E 27 C17
Ambasamudram India 8°43N 77°25E 45 K3

Ambato Ecuador 1°5S 78°42W 92 D3
Ambato, Sierra de Argentina 28°25S 66°10W 94 B2
Ambatolampy Madag. 19°20S 47°35E 55 H9
Ambatondrazaka Madag. 17°55S 48°28E 55 H9
Amberg Germany 49°26N 11°52E 16 D6
Ambergris Cay Belize 18°0N 87°55W 87 D7
Amberley Canada 44°2N 81°42W 82 B3
Amberley N.Z. 43°9S 172°44E 59 E4
Ambikapur India 23°15N 83°15E 43 H10
Ambilobé Madag. 13°10S 49°3E 55 G9
Amble U.K. 55°20N 1°36W 12 B6
Ambleside U.K. 54°26N 2°58W 12 C5
Ambo Peru 10°5S 76°10W 92 F3
Ambohitra Madag. 12°30S 49°10E 55 G9
Amboise France 47°24N 1°2E 20 C4
Ambon Indonesia 3°43S 128°12E 37 E7
Ambositra Madag. 20°31S 47°25E 55 J9
Ambovombe Madag. 25°11S 46°5E 55 K9
Amboy U.S.A. 34°33N 115°45W 79 L11
Amboyna Cay S. China Sea 7°50N 112°50E 36 C4
Ambridge U.S.A. 40°36N 80°14W 82 F4
Ambriz Angola 7°48S 13°8E 54 F2
Ambur India 12°48N 78°43E 45 H4
Amchitka I. U.S.A. 51°32N 179°0E 74 E3
Amderma Russia 69°45N 61°30E 26 C7
Amdhi India 23°51N 81°27E 43 H9
Amdo China 32°20N 91°40E 30 E7
Ameca Mexico 20°33N 104°2W 86 C4
Ameca → Mexico 20°41N 105°18W 86 C3
Amecameca de Juárez Mexico 19°8N 98°46W 87 D5
Amed Indonesia 8°19S 115°39E 37 J18
Ameland Neths. 53°27N 5°45E 15 A5
Amenia U.S.A. 41°51N 73°33W 83 E11
America-Antarctica Ridge S. Ocean 59°0S 16°0W 5 B2
American Falls U.S.A. 42°47N 112°51W 76 E7
American Falls Res. U.S.A. 42°47N 112°52W 76 E7
American Fork U.S.A. 40°23N 111°48W 76 F8
American Highland Antarctica 73°0S 75°0E 5 D6
American Samoa ☒ Pac. Oc. 14°20S 170°0W 59 b
American Samoa △ Amer. Samoa 14°15S 170°28W 59 b
Americana Brazil 22°45S 47°20W 95 A6
Americus U.S.A. 32°4N 84°14W 85 E12
Amersfoort Neths. 52°9N 5°23E 15 B5
Amersfoort S. Africa 26°59S 29°53E 57 C4
Amery Basin S. Ocean 68°15S 74°30E 5 C6
Amery Ice Shelf Antarctica 69°30S 72°0E 5 C6
Ames U.S.A. 42°2N 93°37W 80 D7
Amesbury U.S.A. 42°51N 70°56W 83 D14
Amet India 25°18N 73°56E 42 G5
Amga Russia 60°50N 132°0E 27 C14
Amga → Russia 62°38N 134°32E 27 C14
Amgaon India 21°22N 80°22E 44 D5
Amgu Russia 45°45N 137°15E 28 B8
Amgun → Russia 52°56N 139°38E 27 D14
Amherst Canada 45°48N 64°8W 73 C7
Amherst Mass., U.S.A. 42°23N 72°31W 83 D12
Amherst N.Y., U.S.A. 42°59N 78°48W 82 D6
Amherst Ohio, U.S.A. 41°24N 82°14W 82 E2
Amherst I. Canada 44°8N 76°43W 83 B8
Amherstburg Canada 42°6N 83°6W 72 D3
Amiata, Mte. Italy 42°53N 11°37E 22 C4
Amidon U.S.A. 46°29N 103°19W 80 B2
Amiens France 49°54N 2°16E 20 B5
Amindivi Is. India 11°23N 72°23E 45 J1
Amini I. India 11°6N 72°45E 45 J1
Aminuis Namibia 23°43S 19°21E 56 B2
Amīrābād Iran 33°20N 46°16E 46 C5
Amirante Is. Seychelles 6°0S 53°0E 24 J7
Amisk ⌓ Canada 56°43N 98°0W 71 B9
Amisk L. Canada 54°35N 102°15W 71 C8
Amistad, Presa de la Mexico 29°26N 101°3W 86 B4
Amistad ⌓ U.S.A. 29°32N 101°12W 84 G4
Amite U.S.A. 30°44N 90°30W 85 F9
Amla India 21°56N 78°7E 42 J8
Amlapura Indonesia 8°27S 115°37E 37 J18
Amlia I. U.S.A. 52°4N 173°30W 74 E5
Amlwch U.K. 53°24N 4°20W 12 D3
'Ammān Jordan 31°57N 35°52E 48 D4
'Ammān □ Jordan 31°40N 36°30E 48 D5
'Ammān ✈ (AMM) Jordan 31°45N 36°2E 48 D5
Ammanford U.K. 51°48N 3°59W 13 F4
Ammassalik = Tasiilaq Greenland 65°40N 37°20W 4 C6
Ammochostos = Famagusta Cyprus 35°8N 33°55E 46 C2
Ammon U.S.A. 43°28N 111°58W 76 E8
Amnat Charoen Thailand 15°51N 104°38E 38 E5
Amnura Bangla. 24°37N 88°25E 43 G13
Amo Jiang → China 23°0N 101°50E 34 F3
Āmol Iran 36°23N 52°20E 47 B7
Amorgos Greece 36°50N 25°57E 23 F11
Amory U.S.A. 33°59N 88°29W 85 E10
Amos Canada 48°35N 78°5W 72 C4
Åmot Norway 59°57N 9°54E 9 G13
Amoy = Xiamen China 24°25N 118°4E 35 E12
Ampang Malaysia 3°8N 101°45E 39 L3
Ampani India 19°35N 82°38E 44 E6
Ampanihy Madag. 24°40S 44°45E 55 J8
Ampenan Indonesia 8°34S 116°4E 37 K18
Amper → Germany 48°29N 11°55E 16 D6
Amphoe Kathu Thailand 7°55N 98°21E 39 a
Amphoe Thalang Thailand 8°1N 98°20E 39 a
Amqui Canada 48°28N 67°27W 73 C6
Amrabad India 16°23N 78°50E 45 F4
Amravati India 20°55N 77°45E 44 D3
Amreli India 21°35N 71°17E 42 J4
Amritsar India 31°35N 74°57E 42 D6
Amroha India 28°53N 78°30E 43 E8
Amsterdam U.S.A. 42°56N 74°11W 83 D10
Amsterdam I. = Nouvelle Amsterdam, Î. Ind. Oc. 38°30S 77°30E 3 F13
Amstetten Austria 48°7N 14°51E 16 D8
Amudarya → Uzbekistan 43°58N 59°34E 26 E6
Amund Ringnes I. Canada 78°20N 96°25W 69 B12
Amundsen Abyssal Plain S. Ocean 65°0S 125°0W 5 C14
Amundsen Basin Arctic 87°30N 80°0E 4 A
Amundsen Gulf Canada 71°0N 124°0W 68 C7
Amundsen Ridges S. Ocean 69°15S 123°0W 5 C14
Amundsen-Scott Antarctica 90°0S 166°0E 5 E
Amundsen Sea Antarctica 72°0S 115°0W 5 D15
Amuntai Indonesia 2°28S 115°25E 36 E5
Amur → Russia 52°56N 141°10E 27 D15
Amurang Indonesia 1°5N 124°40E 37 D6
Amursk Russia 50°14N 136°54E 27 D14
Amyderya = Amudarya → Uzbekistan 43°58N 59°34E 26 E6
An Bien Vietnam 9°45N 105°0E 39 H5
An Hoa Vietnam 15°40N 108°5E 38 E7
An Khe Vietnam 13°57N 108°51E 38 F7
An Nabatīyah at Tahta Lebanon 33°23N 35°27E 48 B4
An Nabk Syria 34°2N 36°44E 48 A5
An Nafūd Si. Arabia 28°15N 41°0E 46 D4
An Najaf Iraq 32°3N 44°15E 46 C5
An Nāṣirīyah Iraq 31°0N 46°15E 46 D5
An Nhon = Binh Dinh Vietnam 13°55N 109°7E 38 F7
An Nu'ayrīyah Si. Arabia 27°30N 48°30E 47 E6
An Nu'mānīyah Iraq 32°32N 45°25E 46 C5
An Ros = Rush Ireland 53°31N 6°6W 10 C5
An Thoi, Quan Dao Vietnam 9°58N 104°0E 39 H5
Anabar → Russia 73°8N 113°36E 27 B12
Anaconda U.S.A. 46°8N 112°57W 76 C7
Anacortes U.S.A. 48°30N 122°37W 78 B4
Anadarko U.S.A. 35°4N 98°15W 84 D5
Anadolu Turkey 39°0N 30°0E 19 G5
Anadyr Russia 64°35N 177°20E 27 C18
Anadyr → Russia 64°55N 176°5E 27 C18
Anadyrskiy Zaliv Russia 64°0N 180°0E 27 C19
'Ānah Iraq 34°25N 42°0E 46 C4
Anaheim U.S.A. 33°50N 117°55W 79 M9
Anahim Lake Canada 52°28N 125°18W 70 C3
Anai Mudi India 10°12N 77°4E 45 J3
Anaimalai Hills India 10°20N 76°40E 45 J3
Anakapalle India 17°42N 83°6E 44 F6
Anakie Australia 23°32S 147°45E 62 C4
Analalava Madag. 14°35S 48°0E 55 G9
Anambar → Pakistan 30°15N 68°50E 42 D3
Anambas, Kepulauan Indonesia 3°20N 106°30E 36 D3
Anambas Is. = Anambas, Kepulauan Indonesia 3°20N 106°30E 36 D3
Anamosa U.S.A. 42°7N 91°17W 80 D8
Anamur Turkey 36°8N 32°58E 46 B2
Anan Japan 33°54N 134°40E 29 H7
Anand India 22°32N 72°59E 42 H5
Anandapuram India 14°5N 75°12E 45 G2
Anandpur India 21°16N 86°13E 44 D8
Anangu Pitjantjatjara ☼ Australia 27°0S 132°0E 61 E5
Anantapur India 14°39N 77°42E 45 G3
Anantnag India 33°45N 75°10E 43 C6
Ananyiv Ukraine 47°44N 29°58E 17 E15
Anápolis Brazil 16°15S 48°50W 93 G9
Anapu → Brazil 1°53S 50°53W 93 D8
Anār Iran 30°55N 55°13E 47 D7
Anārak Iran 33°25N 53°40E 47 C7
Anas → India 23°26N 74°0E 42 H5
Anatolia = Anadolu Turkey 39°0N 30°0E 19 G5
Añatuya Argentina 28°20S 62°50W 94 B3
Anatye ☼ Australia 22°29S 137°3E 62 C2
Anaunethad L. Canada 60°55N 104°25W 71 A8
Anbyŏn N. Korea 39°1N 127°35E 33 E14
Ancaster Canada 43°13N 79°59W 82 C5
Anchor Bay U.S.A. 38°48N 123°34W 78 G3
Anchorage U.S.A. 61°13N 149°54W 68 E2
Anchuthengu India 8°40N 76°46E 45 K3
Anci China 39°20N 116°40E 32 E9
Ancohuma, Nevado Bolivia 16°0S 68°50W 92 G5
Ancón Peru 11°50S 77°10W 92 F3
Ancona Italy 43°38N 13°30E 22 C5
Ancud Chile 42°0S 73°50W 96 E2
Ancud, G. de Chile 42°0S 73°0W 96 E2
Anda China 46°24N 125°19E 31 B14
Andacollo Argentina 37°10S 70°42W 94 D1
Andacollo Chile 30°14S 71°6W 94 C1
Andalgalá Argentina 27°40S 66°30W 94 B2
Åndalsnes Norway 62°35N 7°43E 8 E12
Andalucía □ Spain 37°35N 5°0W 21 D3
Andalusia = Andalucía □ Spain 37°35N 5°0W 21 D3
Andalusia U.S.A. 31°18N 86°29W 85 F11
Andaman & Nicobar Is. □ India 10°0N 93°0E 45 K11
Andaman Is. Ind. Oc. 12°30N 92°45E 45 H11
Andaman Sea Ind. Oc. 13°0N 96°0E 36 B1
Andamooka Australia 30°27S 137°9E 63 E2
Andapa Madag. 14°39S 49°39E 55 G9
Andara Namibia 18°2S 21°9E 56 A3
Andenes Norway 69°19N 16°18E 8 B17
Andenne Belgium 50°28N 5°5E 15 D5
Anderson Alaska, U.S.A. 64°25N 149°15W 74 C10
Anderson Calif., U.S.A. 40°27N 122°18W 76 F2
Anderson Ind., U.S.A. 40°10N 85°41W 81 E11
Anderson Mo., U.S.A. 36°39N 94°27W 80 G6
Anderson S.C., U.S.A. 34°31N 82°39W 85 D13
Anderson → Canada 69°42N 129°0W 68 D6
Anderson I. India 12°46N 92°43E 45 H11
Andes U.S.A. 42°12N 74°47W 83 D10
Andes, Cord. de los S. Amer. 20°0S 68°0W 92 H5
Andfjorden Norway 69°10N 16°20E 8 B17
Andhra, L. India 18°54N 73°32E 44 E1
Andhra Pradesh □ India 18°0N 79°0E 44 F4
Andijon Uzbekistan 41°10N 72°15E 30 C3
Andikíthira = Antikythira Greece 35°52N 23°15E 23 G10
Andīmeshk Iran 32°27N 48°21E 47 C6
Andizhan = Andijon Uzbekistan 41°10N 72°15E 30 C3
Andoany Madag. 13°25S 48°16E 55 G9
Andol India 17°51N 78°4E 44 F4
Andola India 16°57N 76°50E 44 F3
Andong S. Korea 36°40N 128°43E 33 F15
Andorra ■ Europe 42°30N 1°30E 20 E4
Andorra La Vella Andorra 42°31N 1°32E 20 E4
Andover U.K. 51°12N 1°29W 13 F6
Andover Kans., U.S.A. 37°43N 97°7W 80 G5
Andover Maine, U.S.A. 44°38N 70°45W 83 B14
Andover Mass., U.S.A. 42°40N 71°8W 83 D13
Andover N.J., U.S.A. 40°59N 74°45W 83 F10
Andover N.Y., U.S.A. 42°10N 77°48W 82 D7
Andover Ohio, U.S.A. 41°36N 80°34W 82 E4
Andøya Norway 69°10N 15°50E 8 B16
Andradina Brazil 20°54S 51°23W 93 H8
Andreanof Is. U.S.A. 51°30N 176°0W 74 E4
Andrews S.C., U.S.A. 33°27N 79°34W 85 E15
Andrews Tex., U.S.A. 32°19N 102°33W 84 E3
Ándria Italy 41°13N 16°17E 22 D7
Andros Greece 37°50N 24°57E 23 F11
Andros I. Bahamas 24°30N 78°0W 88 B4
Andros Town Bahamas 24°43N 77°47W 88 B4
Androscoggin → U.S.A. 43°58N 69°52W 83 C14
Androth I. India 10°50N 73°41E 45 J1
Andselv Norway 69°4N 18°34E 8 B18
Andújar Spain 38°3N 4°5W 21 C3
Andulo Angola 11°25S 16°45E 54 G3
Anegada Br. Virgin Is. 18°45N 64°20W 89 e
Anegada Passage W. Indies 18°15N 63°45W 89 C7
Aneto, Pico de Spain 42°37N 0°40E 21 A6
Anfu China 27°21N 114°40E 35 D10
Ang Thong Thailand 14°35N 100°31E 38 E3
Ang Thong, Ko Thailand 9°37N 99°41E 39 b
Ang Thong, Mu Ko △ Thailand 9°40N 99°43E 39 b
Angamos, Punta Chile 23°1S 70°32W 94 A1
Angara → Russia 58°5N 94°20E 27 D10
Angarsk Russia 52°30N 104°0E 30 A9
Angas Hills Australia 23°0S 127°50E 60 D4
Angaston Australia 34°30S 139°8E 63 E2
Ånge Sweden 62°31N 15°35E 8 E16
Ángel, Salto = Angel Falls Venezuela 5°57N 62°30W 92 B6
Ángel de la Guarda, I. Mexico 29°20N 113°25W 86 B2
Angel Falls Venezuela 5°57N 62°30W 92 B6
Angeles Phil. 15°9N 120°33E 37 A6
Ängelholm Sweden 56°15N 12°50E 9 H15
Angels Camp U.S.A. 38°4N 120°32W 78 G6
Ångermanälven → Sweden 64°0N 17°20E 8 E17
Ångermanland Sweden 63°36N 17°45E 8 E17
Angers Canada 45°31N 75°29W 83 A9
Angers France 47°30N 0°35W 20 C3
Ängesån → Sweden 66°16N 22°47E 8 C20
Angikuni L. Canada 62°12N 99°59W 71 A9
Angkor Cambodia 13°22N 103°50E 38 F4
Angledool Australia 29°5S 147°55E 63 D4
Anglesey U.K. 53°17N 4°20W 12 D3
Anglesey, Isle of □ U.K. 53°16N 4°18W 12 D3
Angleton U.S.A. 29°10N 95°26W 84 G7
Angmagssalik = Tasiilaq Greenland 65°40N 37°20W 4 C6
Ango Dem. Rep. of the Congo 4°10N 26°5E 54 D5
Angoche Mozam. 16°8S 39°55E 55 H7
Angol Chile 37°56S 72°45W 94 D1
Angola Ind., U.S.A. 41°38N 85°0W 81 E11
Angola N.Y., U.S.A. 42°38N 79°2W 82 D5
Angola ■ Africa 12°0S 18°0E 55 G3
Angoulême France 45°39N 0°10E 20 D4
Angoumois France 45°50N 0°25E 20 D3
Angra do Heroismo Azores 38°39N 27°13W 52 a
Angra dos Reis Brazil 23°0S 44°10W 95 A7
Angtassom Cambodia 11°1N 104°41E 39 G5
Anguang China 45°15N 123°45E 33 B12
Anguilla ☒ W. Indies 18°14N 63°5W 89 C7
Angul India 20°51N 85°6E 44 D7
Anguo China 38°28N 115°15E 32 E8
Angurugu Australia 14°0S 136°25E 62 A2
Angus Canada 44°19N 79°53W 82 B5
Angus □ U.K. 56°46N 2°56W 11 E6
Angwa → Zimbabwe 16°0S 30°23E 57 A5
Anhanduí → Brazil 21°46S 52°9W 95 A5
Anholt Denmark 56°42N 11°33E 9 H14
Anhua China 28°23N 111°12E 35 C8
Anhui □ China 32°0N 117°0E 35 B11
Anhwei = Anhui □ China 32°0N 117°0E 35 B11
Anichab Namibia 21°0S 14°46E 56 B1
Animas → U.S.A. 36°43N 108°13W 77 H9
Anin Burma 15°36N 97°50E 38 E1
Anjalankoski Finland 60°45N 26°51E 8 F22
Anjangaon India 21°10N 77°20E 44 D3
Anjar = Hawsh Mūssá Lebanon 33°45N 35°55E 48 B4
Anjar India 23°6N 70°10E 42 H4
Anjengo = Anchuthengu India 8°40N 76°46E 45 K3
Anji China 30°46N 119°40E 35 B12
Anjidiv I. India 14°40N 74°10E 45 G2
Anjou France 47°20N 0°15W 20 C3
Anjouan Comoros Is. 12°15S 44°20E 55 a
Anju N. Korea 39°36N 125°40E 33 E13
Ankaboa, Tanjona Madag. 21°58S 43°20E 55 J8
Ankang China 32°40N 109°1E 32 H5
Ankara Turkey 39°57N 32°54E 19 G5
Ankaratra Madag. 19°25S 47°12E 55 H9
Ankazoabo Madag. 22°18S 44°31E 55 J8
Ankeny U.S.A. 41°44N 93°36W 80 E7
Ankleshwar India 21°38N 73°3E 44 D1
Ankola India 14°40N 74°18E 45 G2
Anlong China 25°2N 105°27E 34 E5
Anlong Veng Cambodia 14°14N 104°5E 38 E5
Anlu China 31°15N 113°45E 35 B9
Anmyeondo S. Korea 36°25N 126°25E 33 F14
Ann, C. U.S.A. 42°38N 70°35W 83 D14
Ann Arbor U.S.A. 42°17N 83°45W 81 D12
Anna U.S.A. 37°28N 89°15W 80 G9
Annaba Algeria 36°50N 7°46E 52 A7
Annalee → Ireland 54°2N 7°24W 10 B4
Annam = Trung-Phan Vietnam 17°0N 109°0E 38 D6
Annamitique, Chaîne Asia 17°0N 106°40E 38 D6
Annan U.K. 54°59N 3°16W 11 G5
Annan → U.K. 54°58N 3°16W 11 G5
Annapolis U.S.A. 38°59N 76°30W 81 F15
Annapolis Royal Canada 44°44N 65°32W 73 D6
Annapurna Nepal 28°34N 83°50E 43 E10
Annean, L. Australia 26°54S 118°14E 61 E2
Annecy France 45°55N 6°8E 20 D7
Annette I. U.S.A. 55°9N 131°28W 70 B2
Annigeri India 15°26N 75°26E 45 G2
Anning China 24°55N 102°26E 34 E4
Anniston U.S.A. 33°39N 85°50W 85 E12
Annobón Atl. Oc. 1°25S 5°36E 51 G4
Annotto B. Jamaica 18°17N 76°45W 88 a
Annville U.S.A. 40°20N 76°31W 83 F8
Anping Hebei, China 38°15N 115°30E 32 E8
Anping Liaoning, China 41°5N 123°30E 33 D12
Anpu Gang China 21°25N 109°50E 34 G7
Anqing China 30°30N 117°3E 35 B11
Anqiu China 36°25N 119°10E 33 F10
Anren China 26°43N 113°18E 35 D9
Ansai China 36°50N 109°20E 32 F5
Ansan S. Korea 37°21N 126°52E 33 F14
Ansbach Germany 49°28N 10°34E 16 D6
Anse Boileau Seychelles 4°43S 55°29E 55 b
Anse la Raye St. Lucia 13°55N 61°3W 89 f
Anse Royale Seychelles 4°44S 55°31E 55 b
Anshan China 41°5N 122°58E 33 D12
Anshun China 26°18N 105°57E 34 D5
Ansley U.S.A. 41°18N 99°23W 80 E4
Anson U.S.A. 32°45N 99°54W 84 E5
Anson B. Australia 13°20S 130°6E 60 B5
Ansongo Mali 15°25N 0°35E 52 E6
Ansonia U.S.A. 41°21N 73°5W 83 E11
Anstruther U.K. 56°14N 2°41W 11 E6
Ansudu Indonesia 2°11S 139°22E 37 E9
Antabamba Peru 14°40S 73°0W 92 F4
Antagarh India 20°6N 81°9E 44 D5
Antakya = Hatay Turkey 36°14N 36°10E 46 B3
Antalaha Madag. 14°57S 50°20E 55 G10
Antalya Turkey 36°52N 30°45E 19 G5
Antalya Körfezi Turkey 36°15N 31°30E 19 G5
Antananarivo Madag. 18°55S 47°31E 55 H9
Antarctic Pen. Antarctica 67°0S 60°0W 5 C18
Antarctica 90°0S 0°0 5 E3
Antep = Gaziantep Turkey 37°6N 37°23E 46 B3
Antequera Paraguay 24°8S 57°7W 94 A4
Antequera Spain 37°5N 4°33W 21 D3
Antero, Mt. U.S.A. 38°41N 106°15W 76 G10
Anthony Kans., U.S.A. 37°9N 98°2W 80 G4
Anthony N. Mex., U.S.A. 32°0N 106°36W 77 K10
Anti Atlas Morocco 30°0N 8°30W 52 C4
Anti-Lebanon = Sharqi, Al Jabal ash Lebanon 33°40N 36°10E 48 B5
Antibes France 43°34N 7°6E 20 E7
Anticosti, Î. d' Canada 49°30N 63°0W 73 C7
Antigo U.S.A. 45°9N 89°9W 80 C9
Antigonish Canada 45°38N 61°58W 73 C7
Antigua Guatemala 14°34N 90°41W 88 D1
Antigua W. Indies 17°0N 61°50W 89 C7
Antigua & Barbuda ■ W. Indies 17°20N 61°48W 89 C7
Antikythira Greece 35°52N 23°15E 23 G10
Antilla Cuba 20°40N 75°50W 88 B4
Antilles = West Indies Cent. Amer. 15°0N 65°0W 89 D7
Antioch U.S.A. 38°1N 121°48W 78 G5
Antioquia Colombia 6°40N 75°55W 92 B3
Antipodes Is. Pac. Oc. 49°45S 178°40E 64 M9
Antlers U.S.A. 34°14N 95°37W 84 D7
Antofagasta Chile 23°50S 70°30W 94 A1
Antofagasta □ Chile 24°0S 69°0W 94 A2
Antofagasta de la Sierra Argentina 26°5S 67°20W 94 B2
Antofalla Argentina 25°30S 68°5W 94 B2
Antofalla, Salar de Argentina 25°40S 67°45W 94 B2
Anton U.S.A. 33°49N 102°10W 84 E3
Antonina Brazil 25°26S 48°42W 95 B6
Antrim U.K. 54°43N 6°14W 10 B5
Antrim U.S.A. 40°7N 81°21W 82 F3
Antrim □ U.K. 54°56N 6°25W 10 B5
Antrim, Mts. of U.K. 55°3N 6°14W 10 A5
Antrim Plateau Australia 18°8S 128°20E 60 C4
Antsalova Madag. 18°40S 44°37E 55 H8
Antsirabe Madag. 19°55S 47°2E 55 H9
Antsiranana Madag. 12°25S 49°20E 55 G9
Antsohihy Madag. 14°50S 47°59E 55 G9
Antu China 42°30N 128°20E 33 C15
Antwerp = Antwerpen Belgium 51°13N 4°25E 15 C4
Antwerp U.S.A. 44°12N 75°37W 83 B9
Antwerpen Belgium 51°13N 4°25E 15 C4
Antwerpen □ Belgium 51°15N 4°40E 15 C4
Anupgarh India 29°10N 73°10E 42 E5
Anuppur India 23°6N 81°41E 43 H9
Anuradhapura Sri Lanka 8°22N 80°28E 45 K5
Anurrete ☼ Australia 20°50S 135°38E 62 C2
Anveh Iran 27°23N 54°11E 47 E7
Anvers = Antwerpen Belgium 51°13N 4°25E 15 C4
Anvers I. Antarctica 64°30S 63°40W 5 C17
Anwen China 29°4N 120°26E 35 C13
Anxi Fujian, China 25°2N 118°12E 35 E12
Anxi Gansu, China 40°30N 95°43E 30 C8
Anxian China 31°40N 104°25E 34 B5
Anxiang China 29°27N 112°11E 35 C9
Anxious B. Australia 33°24S 134°45E 63 E1
Anyang China 36°5N 114°21E 32 F8
Anyang S. Korea 37°23N 126°55E 33 F14
Anyer Indonesia 6°4S 105°53E 37 G11
Anyi Jiangxi, China 28°49N 115°25E 35 C10
Anyi Shanxi, China 35°2N 111°2E 32 G6
Anyuan China 25°9N 115°21E 35 E10
Anyue China 30°9N 105°50E 34 B5
Anza U.S.A. 33°35N 116°39W 79 M10
Anze China 36°10N 112°12E 32 F7
Anzhero-Sudzhensk Russia 56°10N 86°0E 26 D9
Ánzio Italy 41°27N 12°37E 22 D5
Ao Makham Thailand 7°50N 98°24E 39 a
Ao Phangnga △ Thailand 8°10N 98°32E 39 a
Aoga-Shima Japan 32°28N 139°46E 29 H9
Aohan Qi China 43°18N 119°43E 33 C10
Aoji N. Korea 42°31N 130°23E 33 C16
Aomen = Macau China 22°12N 113°33E 35 F9
Aomori Japan 40°45N 140°45E 28 D10
Aomori □ Japan 40°45N 140°40E 28 D10
tAonach, An = Nenagh Ireland 52°52N 8°11W 10 D3
Aonla India 28°16N 79°11E 43 E8
Aorai, Mt. Tahiti 17°34S 149°30W 59 d
Aoraki Mount Cook N.Z. 43°36S 170°9E 59 E3
Aoral, Phnum Cambodia 12°0N 104°15E 39 G5
Aosta Italy 45°45N 7°20E 20 D7
Aotearoa = New Zealand ■ Oceania 40°0S 176°0E 59 D6
Aoukâr Mauritania 17°40N 10°0W 52 E4
Aozou, Couloir d' Chad 22°0N 19°0E 53 D9
Apá → S. Amer. 22°6S 58°2W 94 A4
Apache U.S.A. 34°54N 98°22W 84 D5
Apache Junction U.S.A. 33°25N 111°33W 77 K8
Apalachee B. U.S.A. 30°0N 84°0W 85 G13
Apalachicola U.S.A. 29°43N 84°59W 85 G12
Apalachicola → U.S.A. 29°43N 84°58W 85 G12
Apaporis → Colombia 1°23S 69°25W 92 D5
Aparados da Serra △ Brazil 29°10S 50°8W 95 B5
Aparri Phil. 18°22N 121°38E 37 A6
Apatity Russia 67°34N 33°22E 8 C25
Apatula = Finke Australia 25°34S 134°35E 62 D1
Apatzingán Mexico 19°5N 102°21W 86 D4
Apeldoorn Neths. 52°13N 5°57E 15 B5
Apennines = Appennini Italy 44°30N 10°0E 22 B4
Api Nepal 30°0N 80°57E 30 F5
Apia Samoa 13°50S 171°50W 59 b
Apiacás, Serra dos Brazil 9°50S 57°0W 92 E7
Apies → S. Africa 25°15S 28°8E 57 C4
Apizaco Mexico 19°25N 98°8W 87 D5
Aplao Peru 16°0S 72°40W 92 G4
Apo, Mt. Phil. 6°53N 125°14E 37 C7
Apollonia = Sūsah Libya 32°52N 21°59E 53 B10
Apolo Bolivia 14°30S 68°30W 92 F5
Apopa El Salv. 13°48N 89°10W 88 D2
Aporé → Brazil 19°27S 50°57W 93 G8
Apostle Is. U.S.A. 47°0N 90°40W 80 B8
Apostle Islands ⌓ U.S.A. 46°55N 91°0W 80 B8
Apóstoles Argentina 28°0S 56°0W 95 B4
Apostolos Andreas, C. Cyprus 35°42N 34°35E 46 C2
Apoteri Guyana 4°2N 58°32W 92 C7
Appalachian Mts. U.S.A. 38°0N 80°0W 81 G14
Appennini Italy 44°30N 10°0E 22 B4
Apple Hill Canada 45°13N 74°46W 83 A10
Apple Valley U.S.A. 34°32N 117°14W 79 L9
Appleby-in-Westmorland U.K. 54°35N 2°29W 12 C5
Appledore U.K. 51°3N 4°13W 13 F3
Appleton U.S.A. 44°16N 88°25W 80 C9
Approuague → Fr. Guiana 4°30N 51°57W 93 C8
Aprília Italy 41°36N 12°39E 22 D5
Apsley Canada 44°45N 78°6W 82 B6
Apucarana Brazil 23°55S 51°33W 95 A5
Apure → Venezuela 7°37N 66°25W 92 B5
Apurímac → Peru 12°17S 73°56W 92 F4
Āq Qālā Iran 37°10N 54°30E 47 B7
Aqaba = Al 'Aqabah Jordan 29°31N 35°0E 48 F4
Aqaba, G. of Red Sea 29°0N 34°40E 46 D2
'Aqabah, Khalīj al = Aqaba, G. of Red Sea 29°0N 34°40E 46 D2
'Aqdā Iran 32°26N 53°37E 47 C7
'Aqrah Iraq 36°46N 43°45E 46 B4
Aqsay Kazakhstan 51°11N 53°0E 19 D9
Aqtaū Kazakhstan 43°39N 51°12E 19 F9
Aqtöbe Kazakhstan 50°17N 57°10E 19 D10
Aqtoghay Kazakhstan 46°57N 79°40E 26 E8
Aqua = Sokhumi Georgia 43°0N 41°0E 19 F7
Aquidauana Brazil 20°30S 55°50W 93 H7
Aquila Mexico 18°36N 103°30W 86 D4
Aquiles Serdán Mexico 28°36N 105°53W 86 B3
Aquin Haiti 18°16N 73°24W 89 C5
Aquitain, Bassin France 44°0N 0°30W 20 D3
Ar Horqin Qi China 43°45N 120°0E 33 C11
Ar Rafīd Syria 32°57N 35°52E 48 C4
Ar Raḥḥālīyah Iraq 32°44N 43°23E 46 C4
Ar Ramādī Iraq 33°25N 43°20E 46 C4
Ar Ramthā Jordan 32°34N 36°0E 48 C5
Ar Raqqah Syria 35°59N 39°8E 46 C3
Ar Rashidiya = Er Rachidia Morocco 31°58N 4°20W 52 B5
Ar Rass Si. Arabia 25°50N 43°40E 46 E4
Ar Rayyān Qatar 25°17N 51°25E 47 E6
Ar Rifā'ī Iraq 31°50N 46°10E 46 D5
Ar Riyāḍ Si. Arabia 24°41N 46°42E 46 E5
Ar Ru'ays Qatar 26°8N 51°12E 47 E6
Ar Rukhaymīyah Iraq 29°22N 45°38E 46 D5
Ar Rumaythah Iraq 31°31N 45°12E 46 D5

Ar Ruṣāfah *Syria* 35°45N 38°49E **46** C3
Ar Ruṭbah *Iraq* 33°0N 40°15E **46** C4
Ara *India* 25°35N 84°32E **43** G11
Arab *U.S.A.* 34°19N 86°30W **85** D11
'Arab, Bahr el ➤
  South Sudan 9°0N 29°30E **53** G11
Arab, Shatt al = *Asia* 29°57N 48°34E **47** D6
'Arabābād *Iran* 33°2N 57°41E **47** C8
Arabia *Asia* 25°0N 45°0E **24** F6
Arabian Desert = Es Sahrâ' Esh
  Sharqîya *Egypt* 27°30N 32°30E **53** C12
Arabian Gulf = Persian Gulf
  Asia 27°0N 50°0E **47** E6
Arabian Sea *Ind. Oc.* 16°0N 65°0E **24** G8
Aracaju *Brazil* 10°55S 37°4W **93** F11
Aracati *Brazil* 4°30S 37°44W **93** D11
Araçatuba *Brazil* 21°10S 50°30W **95** A5
Aracena *Spain* 37°53N 6°38W **21** D2
Araçuaí *Brazil* 16°52S 42°4W **93** G10
'Arad *Israel* 31°15N 35°12E **48** D4
Arad *Romania* 46°10N 21°20E **17** E11
Arādān *Iran* 35°21N 52°30E **47** C7
Arafura Sea *E. Indies* 9°0S 135°0E **58** B6
Aragón □ *Spain* 41°25N 0°40W **21** B5
Aragón ➤ *Spain* 42°13N 1°44W **21** A5
Araguacema *Brazil* 8°50S 49°20W **93** E9
Araguaia ➤ *Brazil* 5°21S 48°41W **93** E9
Araguaína *Brazil* 7°12S 48°12W **93** E9
Araguari *Brazil* 18°38S 48°11W **93** G9
Araguari ➤ *Brazil* 1°15N 49°55W **93** C9
Arain *India* 26°27N 75°2E **42** F6
Arak *Algeria* 25°20N 3°45E **52** C6
Arāk *Iran* 34°0N 49°40E **47** C6
Arakan = Rakhine □
  Burma 19°0N 94°15E **41** K18
Arakan Coast *Burma* 19°0N 94°0E **41** K19
Arakan Yoma *Burma* 20°0N 94°40E **41** K19
Arakkonam *India* 13°7N 79°43E **45** H4
Araks = Aras, Rūd-e ➤
  Asia 40°5N 48°29E **46** B5
Aral *Kazakhstan* 46°41N 61°45E **26** E7
Aral Sea *Asia* 45°0N 58°20E **26** E7
Aral Tengizi = Aral Sea
  Asia 45°0N 58°20E **26** E7
Aralsk = Aral *Kazakhstan* 46°41N 61°45E **26** E7
Aralskoye More = Aral Sea
  Asia 45°0N 58°20E **26** E7
Aramac *Australia* 22°58S 145°14E **62** C4
Aran ➤ *India* 19°55N 78°12E **44** E4
Aran I. = Arranmore
  Ireland 55°0N 8°30W **10** A3
Aran Is. *Ireland* 53°6N 9°38W **10** C2
Aranda de Duero *Spain* 41°39N 3°42W **21** B4
Arandān *Iran* 35°23N 46°55E **46** C5
Arani *India* 12°43N 79°19E **45** H4
Aranjuez *Spain* 40°1N 3°40W **21** B4
Aranos *Namibia* 24°9S 19°7E **56** C2
Aransas Pass *U.S.A.* 27°55N 97°9W **84** H6
Aranyaprathet *Thailand* 13°41N 102°30E **38** F4
Arapahoe *U.S.A.* 40°18N 99°54W **80** E4
Arapey Grande ➤
  Uruguay 30°55S 57°49W **94** C4
Arapgir *Turkey* 39°5N 38°30E **46** B3
Arapiraca *Brazil* 9°45S 36°39W **93** E11
Arapongas *Brazil* 23°29S 51°28W **95** A5
Ar'ar *Si. Arabia* 30°59N 41°2E **46** D4
Araranguá *Brazil* 29°0S 49°30W **95** B6
Araraquara *Brazil* 21°50S 48°0W **93** H9
Araras, Serra das *Brazil* 25°0S 53°10W **95** B5
Ararat *Australia* 37°16S 142°58E **63** F3
Ararat, Mt. = Ağrı Dağı
  Turkey 39°50N 44°15E **46** B5
Araria *India* 26°9N 87°33E **43** F12
Araripe, Chapada do
  Brazil 7°20S 40°0W **93** E11
Araruama, L. de *Brazil* 22°53S 42°12W **95** A7
Aras, Rūd-e ➤ *Asia* 40°5N 48°29E **46** B5
Arauca *Colombia* 7°0N 70°40W **92** B4
Arauca ➤ *Venezuela* 7°24N 66°35W **92** B5
Arauco *Chile* 37°16S 73°25W **94** D1
Aravalli Range *India* 25°0N 73°30E **42** G5
Araxá *Brazil* 19°35S 46°55W **93** G9
Araya, Pen. de *Venezuela* 10°40N 64°0W **92** A6
Arba Minch *Ethiopia* 6°0N 37°30E **49** F2
Arbat *Iraq* 35°25N 45°35E **46** C5
Árbatax *Italy* 39°56N 9°42E **22** E3
Arbil *Iraq* 36°15N 44°5E **46** B5
Arborfield *Canada* 53°6N 103°39W **71** C8
Arborg *Canada* 50°54N 97°13W **71** C9
Arbroath *U.K.* 56°34N 2°35W **11** E6
Arbuckle *U.S.A.* 39°1N 122°3W **78** F4
Arcade *U.S.A.* 42°32N 78°25W **82** D6
Arcadia *Fla., U.S.A.* 27°13N 81°52W **85** H14
Arcadia *La., U.S.A.* 32°33N 92°55W **84** E8
Arcadia *Pa., U.S.A.* 40°47N 78°51W **82** F6
Arcata *U.S.A.* 40°52N 124°5W **76** F1
Archangel = Arkhangelsk
  Russia 64°38N 40°36E **18** B7
Archbald *U.S.A.* 41°30N 75°32W **83** E9
Archer ➤ *Australia* 13°28S 141°41E **62** A3
Archer B. *Australia* 13°20S 141°30E **62** A3
Archer Bend = Mungkan
  Kandju △ *Australia* 13°35S 142°52E **62** A3
Arches △ *U.S.A.* 38°45N 109°25W **76** G9
Archipel-de-Mingan △
  Canada 50°13N 63°10W **73** B7
Archipélago Los Roques △
  Venezuela 11°50N 66°44W **89** D6
Arckaringa Cr. ➤
  Australia 28°10S 135°22E **63** D2
Arco *U.S.A.* 43°38N 113°18W **76** E7
Arcos de la Frontera
  Spain 36°45N 5°49W **21** D3
Arcot *India* 12°53N 79°20E **45** H4
Arctic Bay *Canada* 73°1N 85°7W **69** C14
Arctic Mid-Ocean Ridge
  Arctic 87°0N 90°0E **4** A
Arctic Ocean *Arctic* 78°0N 160°0W **4** B18

Arctic Red River = Tsiigehtchic
  Canada 67°15N 134°0W **68** D5
Arctowski *Antarctica* 62°30S 58°0W **5** C18
Arda ➤ *Bulgaria* 41°40N 26°30E **23** D12
Ardabīl *Iran* 38°15N 48°18E **47** B6
Ardabīl □ *Iran* 38°15N 48°20E **47** B6
Ardakān = Sepīdān *Iran* 30°20N 52°5E **47** D7
Ardakān *Iran* 32°19N 53°59E **47** C7
Ardara *Ireland* 54°46N 8°25W **10** B3
Ardee *Ireland* 53°52N 6°33W **10** C5
Arden *Canada* 44°43N 76°56W **82** B8
Arden *Calif., U.S.A.* 38°36N 121°33W **78** G5
Arden *Nev., U.S.A.* 36°1N 115°14W **79** J11
Ardenne *Belgium* 49°50N 5°5E **15** E5
Ardennes = Ardenne
  Belgium 49°50N 5°5E **15** E5
Arderin *Ireland* 53°2N 7°39W **10** C4
Ardestān *Iran* 33°20N 52°25E **47** C7
Ardfert *Ireland* 52°20N 9°47W **10** D2
Ardglass *U.K.* 54°16N 5°36W **10** B6
Ardivachar Pt. *U.K.* 57°23N 7°26N **11** D1
Ardlethan *Australia* 34°22S 146°53E **63** E4
Ardmore *Okla., U.S.A.* 34°10N 97°8W **84** D6
Ardmore *Pa., U.S.A.* 40°2N 75°17W **83** F9
Ardnamurchan, Pt. of
  U.K. 56°43N 6°14W **11** E2
Ardnave Pt. *U.K.* 55°53N 6°20W **11** F2
Ardrossan *Australia* 34°26S 137°53E **63** E2
Ardrossan *U.K.* 55°39N 4°49N **11** F4
Ards Pen. *U.K.* 54°33N 5°34W **10** B6
Arecibo *Puerto Rico* 18°29N 66°43W **89** d
Areia Branca *Brazil* 5°0S 37°0W **93** E11
Arena, Pt. *U.S.A.* 38°57N 123°44W **78** G3
Arenal *Honduras* 15°21N 86°50W **88** C2
Arendal *Norway* 58°28N 8°46E **9** G13
Arequipa *Peru* 16°20S 71°30W **92** G4
Arévalo *Spain* 41°3N 4°43W **21** B3
Arezzo *Italy* 43°25N 11°53E **22** C4
Arga *Turkey* 38°21N 37°59E **46** B3
Arganda del Rey *Spain* 40°19N 3°26W **21** B4
Argarapa ✿ *Australia* 22°20S 134°58E **62** C1
Argenta *Canada* 50°11N 116°56W **70** C5
Argentan *France* 48°45N 0°1W **20** B3
Argentário, Mte. *Italy* 42°24N 11°9E **22** C4
Argentia *Canada* 47°18N 53°58W **73** C9
Argentina ■ *S. Amer.* 35°0S 66°0W **96** D3
Argentine Basin *Atl. Oc.* 45°0S 45°0W **96** H5
Argentino, L. *Argentina* 50°10S 73°0W **96** G2
Argeş ➤ *Romania* 44°5N 26°38E **17** F14
Arghandab ➤ *Afghan.* 31°30N 64°15E **42** D1
Argolikos Kolpos *Greece* 37°20N 22°52E **23** F10
Argos *Greece* 37°40N 22°43E **23** F10
Argostoli *Greece* 38°11N 20°29E **23** E9
Arguello, Pt. *U.S.A.* 34°35N 120°39W **79** L6
Argun ➤ *Russia* 53°20N 121°28E **31** A13
Argungu *Nigeria* 12°40N 4°31E **52** F6
Argyle, L. *Australia* 16°20S 128°40E **60** C4
Argyll & Bute □ *U.K.* 56°13N 5°28W **11** E3
Århus = Aarhus *Denmark* 56°8N 10°11E **9** H14
Ariadnoye *Russia* 45°8N 134°25E **28** B7
Ariamsvlei *Namibia* 28°9S 19°51E **56** C2
Ariana *Tunisia* 36°52N 10°12E **53** A8
Arica *Chile* 18°32S 70°20W **92** G4
Arica *Colombia* 2°0S 71°50W **92** D4
Arid, C. *Australia* 34°1S 123°10E **61** F3
Arida *Japan* 34°5N 135°8E **29** G7
Aride *Seychelles* 4°13S 55°40E **55** b
Ariège ➤ *France* 43°30N 1°25E **20** E4
Arima *Trin. & Tob.* 10°38N 61°17W **93** K15
Arinos ➤ *Brazil* 10°25S 58°20W **92** F7
Ario de Rosales *Mexico* 19°12N 101°43W **86** D4
Aripo, Mt. *Trin. & Tob.* 10°45N 61°15W **93** K15
Aripuanã *Brazil* 9°25S 60°30W **92** E6
Aripuanã ➤ *Brazil* 5°7S 60°25W **92** E6
Ariquemes *Brazil* 9°55S 63°6W **92** E6
Arisaig *U.K.* 56°55N 5°51W **11** E3
Aristazabal I. *Canada* 52°40N 129°10W **70** C3
Ariyalur *India* 11°8N 79°8E **45** J4
Arizaro, Salar de
  Argentina 24°40S 67°50W **94** A2
Arizona *Argentina* 35°45S 65°25W **94** D2
Arizona □ *U.S.A.* 34°0N 112°0W **77** J8
Arizpe *Mexico* 30°20N 110°10W **86** A2
'Arjah *Si. Arabia* 24°43N 44°17E **46** E5
Arjeplog *Sweden* 66°3N 17°54E **8** C17
Arjepluovve = Arjeplog
  Sweden 66°3N 17°54E **8** C17
Arjona *Colombia* 10°14N 75°22W **92** A3
Arjuna *Indonesia* 7°49S 112°34E **37** G15
Arka *Russia* 60°15N 142°0E **27** C15
Arkadelphia *U.S.A.* 34°7N 93°4W **84** D8
Arkaig, L. *U.K.* 56°59N 5°10W **11** E3
Arkalgud *India* 12°46N 76°3E **45** H3
Arkalyk = Arqalyk
  Kazakhstan 50°13N 66°50E **26** D7
Arkansas □ *U.S.A.* 35°0N 92°30W **84** D8
Arkansas ➤ *U.S.A.* 33°47N 91°4W **84** E9
Arkansas City *U.S.A.* 37°4N 97°2W **80** G5
Arkaroola *Australia* 30°20S 139°22E **63** E2
Arkhangelsk *Russia* 64°38N 40°36E **18** B7
Arki *India* 31°9N 76°58E **42** D7
Arklow *Ireland* 52°48N 6°10W **10** D5
Arkport *U.S.A.* 42°24N 77°42W **82** D7
Arkticheskiy, Mys *Russia* 81°10N 95°0E **27** A10
Arlanzón ➤ *Spain* 42°3N 4°17W **21** A3
Arlbergpass *Austria* 47°9N 10°12E **16** E6
Arlbergtunnel *Austria* 47°9N 10°12E **16** E6
Arles *France* 43°41N 4°40E **20** E6
Arlington *S. Africa* 28°1S 27°53E **57** D4
Arlington *N.Y., U.S.A.* 41°42N 73°54W **83** E11
Arlington *Oreg., U.S.A.* 45°43N 120°12W **76** D3
Arlington *S. Dak., U.S.A.* 44°22N 97°8W **80** C5
Arlington *Tex., U.S.A.* 32°44N 97°6W **84** E6
Arlington *Vt., U.S.A.* 43°5N 73°9W **83** C11
Arlington *Wash., U.S.A.* 48°12N 122°8W **78** B4
Arlington Heights
  U.S.A. 42°5N 87°59W **80** D10

Arlit *Niger* 19°0N 7°38E **52** E7
Arlon *Belgium* 49°42N 5°49E **15** E5
Arlparra *Australia* 22°11S 134°30E **62** C1
Arltunga *Australia* 23°26S 134°41E **62** C1
Armadale *Australia* 32°9S 116°0E **61** F2
Armagh *U.K.* 54°21N 6°39W **10** B5
Armagh □ *U.K.* 54°18N 6°37W **10** B5
Armando Bermudez △
  Dom. Rep. 19°3N 71°0W **89** C5
Armavir *Russia* 45°2N 41°7E **19** E7
Armenia *Colombia* 4°35N 75°45W **92** C3
Armenia ■ *Asia* 40°20N 45°0E **19** F7
Armidale *Australia* 30°30S 151°40E **63** E5
Armori *India* 20°28N 79°59E **44** D4
Armour *U.S.A.* 43°19N 98°21W **80** D4
Armstrong *B.C., Canada* 50°25N 119°10W **70** C5
Armstrong *Ont., Canada* 50°18N 89°4W **72** B2
Armur *India* 18°48N 78°16E **44** E4
Arnarfjörður *Iceland* 65°48N 23°40W **8** D2
Arnaud ➤ *Canada* 59°59N 69°46W **69** F18
Arnauti, C. *Cyprus* 35°6N 32°17E **46** C2
Arnett *U.S.A.* 36°8N 99°46W **84** C5
Arnhem *Neths.* 51°58N 5°55E **15** C5
Arnhem, C. *Australia* 12°20S 137°30E **62** A2
Arnhem B. *Australia* 12°20S 136°10E **62** A2
Arnhem Land ✿
  Australia 12°50S 134°50E **62** A1
Arno ➤ *Italy* 43°41N 10°17E **22** C4
Arno Bay *Australia* 33°54S 136°34E **63** E2
Arnold *U.K.* 53°1N 1°7W **12** D6
Arnold *Calif., U.S.A.* 38°15N 120°21W **78** G6
Arnold *Mo., U.S.A.* 38°26N 90°23W **80** F8
Arnot *Canada* 55°56N 96°41N **71** B9
Arnøya *Norway* 70°9N 20°40E **8** A19
Arnprior *Canada* 45°26N 76°21W **83** A8
Arnsberg *Germany* 51°24N 8°5E **16** C5
Aroa, Pte. *Moorea* 17°28S 149°46W **59** d
Aroab *Namibia* 26°41S 19°39E **56** C2
Aron *India* 25°57N 77°56E **42** G6
Aros ➤ *Mexico* 29°9N 107°57W **86** B3
Arqalyk *Kazakhstan* 50°13N 66°50E **26** D7
Arrah = Ara *India* 25°35N 84°32E **43** G11
Arrah *Ivory C.* 6°40N 3°58E **52** G5
Arran *U.K.* 55°34N 5°12W **11** F3
Arranmore *Ireland* 55°0N 8°30W **10** A3
Arras *France* 50°17N 2°46E **20** A5
Arrecife *Canary Is.* 28°57N 13°37W **52** C3
Arrecifes *Argentina* 34°6S 60°9W **94** C3
Arrée, Mts. d' *France* 48°26N 3°55W **20** B2
Arriaga *Mexico* 16°14N 93°54W **87** D6
Arrilalah *Australia* 23°43S 143°54E **62** C3
Arrino *Australia* 29°30S 115°40E **61** E2
Arrow, L. *Ireland* 54°3N 8°19W **10** B3
Arrowtown *N.Z.* 44°57S 168°50E **59** F2
Arroyo Grande *U.S.A.* 35°7N 120°35W **79** K6
Ars *Iran* 37°9N 47°46E **46** B5
Arsenault L. *Canada* 55°6N 108°32W **71** B7
Arsenev *Russia* 44°10N 133°15E **28** B6
Arsikere *India* 13°15N 76°15E **45** H3
Arta *Greece* 39°8N 21°2E **23** E9
Arteaga *Mexico* 18°28N 102°25W **86** D4
Artem *Russia* 43°22N 132°13E **28** C6
Artemovsk *Russia* 54°45N 93°35E **27** D10
Artemovsk *Ukraine* 48°35N 38°0E **19** E6
Artesia = Mosomane
  Botswana 24°2S 26°19E **56** B4
Artesia *U.S.A.* 32°51N 104°24W **77** K11
Arthur *Canada* 43°50N 80°32W **82** C4
Arthur ➤ *Australia* 41°2S 144°40E **63** G3
Arthur Cr. ➤ *Australia* 22°30S 136°25E **62** C2
Arthur Pt. *Australia* 22°7S 150°3E **62** C5
Arthur River *Australia* 33°20S 117°2E **61** F2
Arthur's Pass *N.Z.* 42°54S 171°35E **59** E3
Arthur's Pass △ *N.Z.* 42°53S 171°42E **59** E3
Arthur's Town *Bahamas* 24°38N 75°42W **89** B4
Artigas *Antarctica* 62°30S 58°0W **5** C18
Artigas *Uruguay* 30°20S 56°30W **94** C4
Artillery L. *Canada* 63°9N 107°52W **71** A7
Artois *France* 50°20N 2°30E **20** A5
Arts Bogd Uul *Mongolia* 44°40N 102°20E **32** B2
Artsyz *Ukraine* 46°4N 29°26E **17** E15
Artux *China* 39°40N 76°10E **30** D4
Artvin *Turkey* 41°14N 41°44E **19** F7
Artyk *Russia* 64°12N 145°6E **27** C15
Aru, Kepulauan *Indonesia* 6°0S 134°30E **37** F8
Aru Is. = Aru, Kepulauan
  Indonesia 6°0S 134°30E **37** F8
Arua *Uganda* 3°1N 30°58E **54** D6
Aruanã *Brazil* 14°54S 51°10W **93** F8
Aruba ☑ *W. Indies* 12°30N 70°0W **89** D6
Arué *Tahiti* 17°31S 149°30W **59** d
Arun ➤ *Nepal* 26°55N 87°10E **43** F12
Arun ➤ *U.K.* 50°49N 0°33W **13** G7
Arunachal Pradesh □
  India 28°0N 95°0E **41** F19
Aruppukkottai *India* 9°31N 78°8E **45** K4
Arusha *Tanzania* 3°20S 36°47E **54** E7
Aruvi ➤ *Sri Lanka* 8°48N 79°53E **45** K4
Aruwimi ➤
  Dem. Rep. of the Congo 1°13N 23°36E **54** D4
Arvada *Colo., U.S.A.* 39°48N 105°5W **76** G11
Arvada *Wyo., U.S.A.* 44°39N 106°8W **76** D10
Arvakalu *Sri Lanka* 8°20N 79°58E **45** K4
Arvayheer *Mongolia* 46°15N 102°48E **30** B9
Arvi *India* 20°59N 78°16E **44** D4
Arviat *Canada* 61°6N 93°59W **71** A10
Arvidsjaur *Sweden* 65°35N 19°7E **8** D18
Arvika *Sweden* 59°40N 12°36E **9** G15
Arvin *U.S.A.* 35°12N 118°50W **79** K8
Arwal *India* 25°15N 84°41E **43** G11
Arxan *China* 47°11N 119°57E **31** B12
Āštīyān *Iran* 34°31N 50°0E **47** C6
Arys *Kazakhstan* 42°26N 68°48E **26** E7
Arzamas *Russia* 55°27N 43°55E **18** C5
Aranzah *U.A.E.* 24°47N 52°34E **47** E7
Aş Şafā *Syria* 33°10N 37°0E **48** B6
Aş Saffānīyah *Si. Arabia* 27°55N 48°50E **47** E6
As Safīrah *Syria* 36°5N 37°21E **46** B3
Aş Şahm *Oman* 24°10N 56°53E **47** E8

As Sājir *Si. Arabia* 25°11N 44°36E **46** E5
As Salamīyah *Syria* 35°1N 37°2E **46** C3
As Salmān *Iraq* 30°30N 44°32E **46** D5
As Salṭ *Jordan* 32°2N 35°43E **48** C4
As Samāwah *Iraq* 31°15N 45°15E **46** D5
As Sanamayn *Syria* 33°3N 36°10E **48** B5
As Sukhnah *Syria* 34°52N 38°52E **46** C3
As Sulaymānīyah *Iraq* 35°35N 45°29E **46** C5
As Sulaymī *Si. Arabia* 26°17N 41°21E **46** E4
As Sulayyil *Si. Arabia* 20°27N 45°34E **49** C4
As Summān *Si. Arabia* 25°0N 47°0E **46** E5
As Suwaydā' *Syria* 32°40N 36°30E **48** C5
As Suwaydā' □ *Syria* 32°45N 36°45E **48** C5
As Suwayq *Oman* 23°51N 57°26E **47** F8
Aş Şuwayrah *Iraq* 32°55N 45°0E **46** C5
Asab *Namibia* 25°30S 18°0E **56** C2
Asad, Buḩayrat al *Syria* 36°0N 38°15E **46** C3
Asahi *Japan* 35°43N 140°39E **29** E10
Asahi-Gawa ➤ *Japan* 34°36N 133°58E **29** G6
Asahigawa = Asahikawa
  Japan 43°46N 142°22E **28** C11
Asahikawa *Japan* 43°46N 142°22E **28** C11
Asaluyeh *Iran* 27°29N 52°37E **47** E7
Asamankese *Ghana* 5°50N 0°40W **52** G5
Asan ➤ *India* 26°37N 78°24E **43** F8
Asansol *India* 23°40N 87°1E **43** H12
Asau *Samoa* 13°27S 172°33W **59** b
Asbesberg *S. Africa* 29°0S 23°0E **56** D3
Asbestos *Canada* 45°47N 71°58W **73** C5
Asbury Park *U.S.A.* 40°13N 74°1W **83** F10
Ascension, B. de la
  Mexico 19°40N 87°30W **87** D7
Ascension I. *Atl. Oc.* 7°57S 14°23W **51** G2
Aschaffenburg *Germany* 49°58N 9°6E **16** D5
Aschersleben *Germany* 51°45N 11°29E **16** C6
Ascó *Spain* 41°11N 0°41E **21** B6
Áscoli Piceno *Italy* 42°51N 13°34E **22** C5
Ascope *Peru* 7°46S 79°8W **92** E3
Ascotán *Chile* 21°45S 68°17W **94** A2
Aseb *Eritrea* 13°0N 42°40E **49** E3
Asela *Ethiopia* 8°0N 39°0E **47** F2
Asenovgrad *Bulgaria* 42°1N 24°51E **23** C11
Asgabat = Ashgabat
  Turkmenistan 37°58N 58°24E **47** B8
Asti *Italy* 44°54N 8°12E **20** D8
Astipalea *Greece* 36°32N 26°22E **23** F12
Astorga *Spain* 42°29N 6°8W **21** A2
Astoria *U.S.A.* 46°11N 123°50W **78** D3
Astrakhan *Russia* 46°25N 48°5E **19** E8
Astrebla Downs
  Australia 24°12S 140°34E **62** C3
Asturias □ *Spain* 43°15N 6°0W **21** A3
Asunción *Paraguay* 25°10S 57°30W **94** B4
Asunción Nochixtlán
  Mexico 17°28N 97°14W **87** D5
Aswân *Egypt* 24°4N 32°57E **53** D12
Aswan High Dam = Sadd el Aali
  Egypt 23°54N 32°54E **53** D12
Asyût *Egypt* 27°11N 31°4E **53** C12
At Ṭafīlah *Jordan* 30°45N 35°30E **48** E4
At Ṭafīlah □ *Jordan* 30°45N 35°30E **48** E4
Aṭ Ṭā'if *Si. Arabia* 21°5N 40°27E **49** C3
Aṭ Ta'mīm □ *Iraq* 35°30N 44°0E **46** C5
Aṭ Ṭīrāq *Si. Arabia* 27°19N 44°33E **46** E5
Aṭ Ṭubayq *Si. Arabia* 29°30N 37°0E **46** D3
Aṭ Ṭunayb *Jordan* 31°48N 35°57E **48** D4
Atacama *Chile* 27°30S 70°0W **94** B2
Atacama, Desierto de
  Chile 24°0S 69°20W **94** A2
Atacama, Salar de *Chile* 23°30S 68°20W **94** A2
Atakeye ✿ *Australia* 22°30S 133°45E **60** D5
Atakpamé *Togo* 7°31N 1°13E **52** G6
Atalaya *Peru* 10°45S 73°50W **92** F4
Atami *Japan* 35°5N 139°4E **29** G9
Atamyrat *Turkmenistan* 37°50N 65°12E **26** F7
Atapupu *Indonesia* 9°0S 124°51E **37** F6
Aṭār *Mauritania* 20°30N 13°5W **52** D3
Atari *Pakistan* 30°56N 74°2E **42** D6
Atascadero *U.S.A.* 35°29N 120°40W **78** K6
Atasū *Kazakhstan* 48°30N 71°0E **26** E8
Atatürk Barajı *Turkey* 37°28N 38°30E **19** G6
Atauro *E. Timor* 8°10S 125°30E **37** F7
Atbara *Sudan* 17°42N 33°59E **53** E12
'Atbara, Nahr ➤ *Sudan* 17°40N 33°56E **53** E12
Atbasar *Kazakhstan* 51°48N 68°20E **26** D7
Atchafalaya B. *U.S.A.* 29°25N 91°25W **84** G9
Atchison *U.S.A.* 39°34N 95°7W **80** F6
Ateshān *Iran* 35°35N 52°37E **47** C7
Ath *Belgium* 50°38N 3°47E **15** D3
Athabasca *Canada* 54°45N 113°20W **70** C6
Athabasca ➤ *Canada* 58°40N 110°50W **71** B6
Athabasca, L. *Canada* 59°15N 109°15W **71** B7
Athabasca Sand Dunes △
  Canada 59°4N 108°43W **71** B7
Athagarh *India* 20°32N 85°37E **44** D7
Athboy *Ireland* 53°36N 6°56W **10** C5
Athenry *Ireland* 53°18N 8°44W **10** C3
Athens *Ala., U.S.A.* 34°48N 86°58W **85** D11
Athens *Ga., U.S.A.* 33°57N 83°23W **85** D13
Athens *N.Y., U.S.A.* 42°16N 73°49W **83** D11
Athens *Ohio, U.S.A.* 39°20N 82°6W **81** F12
Athens *Pa., U.S.A.* 41°57N 76°31W **83** E8
Athens *Tenn., U.S.A.* 35°27N 84°36W **85** D12
Athens *Tex., U.S.A.* 32°12N 95°51W **84** E7
Atherley *Canada* 44°37N 79°20W **82** B5
Atherton *Australia* 17°17S 145°30E **62** B4
Athlone *Ireland* 53°25N 7°56W **10** C4
Athmallik *India* 20°43N 84°32E **44** D7
Athni *India* 16°44N 75°6E **44** F2
Athol *U.S.A.* 42°36N 72°14W **83** D12
Atholl, Forest of *U.K.* 56°51N 3°50E **11** E5
Atholville *Canada* 47°59N 66°43W **73** C6
Athos *Greece* 40°9N 24°22E **23** D11
Athy *Ireland* 53°0N 7°0W **10** C5
Ati *Chad* 13°13N 18°20E **53** F9
Atik L. *Canada* 55°15N 96°0W **71** B9
Atikaki △ *Canada* 51°30N 95°31W **71** C9
Atikameg ➤ *Canada* 52°30N 82°46W **72** B3
Atikokan *Canada* 48°45N 91°37W **72** C1

Atikonak L. Canada 52°40N 64°32W 73 B7
Atimaono Tahiti 17°46S 149°28W 59 d
Atirampattinam India 10°28N 79°20E 45 J4
Atiu Cook Is. 20°S 158°10W 65 J12
Atka Russia 60°50N 151°48E 27 C16
Atka I. U.S.A. 52°7N 174°30W 74 E5
Atkinson U.S.A. 42°32N 98°59W 80 D4
Atlanta U.S.A. 33°7N 94°10W 84 D7
Atlantic U.S.A. 41°24N 95°1W 80 E6
Atlantic City U.S.A. 39°21N 74°27W 81 F16
Atlantic-Indian Basin
 Antarctica 60°0S 30°0E 5 B4
Atlantic Ocean 0°0 20°0W 2 D8
Atlantis S. Africa 33°34S 18°29E 56 D2
Atlas Mts. = Haut Atlas
 Morocco 32°30N 5°0W 52 B4
Atlin Canada 59°31N 133°41W 70 B2
Atlin, L. Canada 59°26N 133°45W 70 B2
Atlin △ Canada 59°10N 134°30W 70 B2
Atmakur Andhra Pradesh,
 India 18°45N 78°39E 44 E4
Atmakur Andhra Pradesh,
 India 14°37N 79°40E 45 G4
Atmakur Andhra Pradesh,
 India 15°53N 78°35E 45 G4
Atmore U.S.A. 31°2N 87°29W 85 F11
Atoka U.S.A. 34°23N 96°8W 84 D6
Atolia U.S.A. 35°19N 117°37W 79 K9
Atqasuk U.S.A. 70°28N 157°24W 74 A8
Atrai → Bangla. 24°7N 89°22E 43 G13
Atrak = Atrek →
 Turkmenistan 37°35N 53°58E 47 B8
Atrauli India 28°2N 78°20E 42 E8
Atrek → Turkmenistan 37°35N 53°58E 47 B8
Atsuta Japan 43°24N 141°26E 28 C10
Attalla U.S.A. 34°1N 86°6W 85 D11
Attapeu Laos 14°48N 106°50E 38 E6
Attawapiskat Canada 52°56N 82°24W 72 B3
Attawapiskat → Canada 52°57N 82°18W 72 B3
Attawapiskat L. Canada 52°18N 87°54W 72 B2
Attica Ind., U.S.A. 40°18N 87°15W 80 E10
Attica Ohio, U.S.A. 41°4N 82°53W 82 E2
Attikamagen L. Canada 55°0N 66°30W 73 B6
Attleboro U.S.A. 41°57N 71°17W 83 E13
Attock Pakistan 33°52N 72°20E 42 C5
Attopu = Attapeu Laos 14°48N 106°50E 38 E6
Attu I. U.S.A. 52°55N 172°55E 74 E2
Attur India 11°35N 78°30E 45 J4
Atuel → Argentina 36°17S 66°50W 94 D2
Åtvidaberg Sweden 58°12N 16°0E 9 G17
Atwater U.S.A. 37°21N 120°37W 78 H6
Atwood Canada 43°40N 81°1W 82 C3
Atwood U.S.A. 39°48N 101°3W 80 F3
Atyraū Kazakhstan 47°5N 52°0E 19 E9
Au Sable U.S.A. 44°25N 83°20W 82 B1
Au Sable → U.S.A. 44°25N 83°20W 81 C12
Au Sable Forks U.S.A. 44°27N 73°41W 83 B11
Au Sable Pt. U.S.A. 44°20N 83°20W 82 B1
Auas Honduras 15°29N 84°20W 88 C3
Auasberg Namibia 22°37S 17°13E 56 B2
Aubagne France 43°17N 5°37E 20 E6
Aube → France 48°34N 3°43E 20 B5
Auberry U.S.A. 37°7N 119°29W 78 H7
Auburn Ala., U.S.A. 32°36N 85°29W 85 E12
Auburn Calif., U.S.A. 38°54N 121°4W 78 G5
Auburn Ind., U.S.A. 41°22N 85°4W 81 E11
Auburn Maine, U.S.A. 44°6N 70°14W 81 C18
Auburn N.Y., U.S.A. 42°56N 76°34W 83 D8
Auburn Nebr., U.S.A. 40°23N 95°51W 80 E6
Auburn Pa., U.S.A. 40°36N 76°6W 83 F8
Auburn Wash., U.S.A. 47°18N 122°14W 78 C4
Auburn Ra. Australia 25°15S 150°30E 63 D5
Auburndale U.S.A. 28°4N 81°48W 85 G14
Aubusson France 45°57N 2°11E 20 D5
Auch France 43°39N 0°36E 20 E4
Auchterarder U.K. 56°18N 3°41W 11 E5
Auchtermuchty U.K. 56°18N 3°13W 11 E5
Auckland N.Z. 36°52S 174°46E 59 B5
Auckland Is. Pac. Oc. 50°40S 166°5E 64 N8
Aude → France 43°13N 3°14E 20 E5
Auden Canada 50°14N 87°53W 72 B2
Audubon U.S.A. 41°43N 94°56W 80 E6
Augathella Australia 25°48S 146°35E 63 D4
Aughnacloy U.K. 54°25N 6°59W 10 B5
Aughrim Ireland 53°18N 8°19W 10 C3
Augrabies Falls S. Africa 28°35S 20°20E 56 C3
Augrabies Falls △
 S. Africa 28°35S 20°22E 56 C3
Augsburg Germany 48°25N 10°52E 16 D6
Augusta Australia 34°19S 115°9E 61 F2
Augusta Italy 37°13N 15°13E 22 F6
Augusta Ark., U.S.A. 35°17N 91°22W 84 D9
Augusta Ga., U.S.A. 33°28N 81°58W 85 E14
Augusta Kans., U.S.A. 37°41N 96°59W 80 G5
Augusta Maine, U.S.A. 44°19N 69°47W 81 C19
Augusta Mont., U.S.A. 47°30N 112°24W 76 C7
Augustów Poland 53°51N 23°0E 17 B12
Augustus, Mt. Australia 24°20S 116°50E 61 D2
Augustus I. Australia 15°20S 124°30E 60 C3
Aujuittuq = Grise Fiord
 Canada 76°25N 82°57W 69 B15
Aukštaitija △ Lithuania 55°15N 26°0E 9 J22
Aukum U.S.A. 38°34N 120°43W 78 G6
Aul India 20°41N 86°39E 44 D8
Aulavik △ Canada 73°42N 119°55W 68 C8
Auld, L. Australia 22°25S 123°50E 60 D3
Ault U.S.A. 40°35N 104°44W 76 F11
Aundah India 19°32N 77°3E 44 E3
Aundh India 17°33N 74°23E 44 F2
Aunis France 46°5N 0°50W 20 C3
Aunu'u Amer. Samoa 14°20S 170°31W 59 b
Auponhia Indonesia 1°58S 125°27E 37 E7
Aur, Pulau Malaysia 2°35N 104°10E 39 L5
Auraiya India 26°28N 79°33E 43 F8
Aurangabad Bihar, India 24°45N 84°18E 43 G11
Aurangabad Maharashtra,
 India 19°50N 75°23E 44 E2
Aurich Germany 53°28N 7°28E 16 B4
Aurillac France 44°55N 2°26E 20 D5

Aurora Canada 44°0N 79°28W 82 C5
Aurora S. Africa 32°40S 18°29E 56 D2
Aurora Colo., U.S.A. 39°43N 104°49W 76 G11
Aurora Ill., U.S.A. 41°45N 88°19W 80 E9
Aurora Mo., U.S.A. 36°58N 93°43W 80 G7
Aurora N.Y., U.S.A. 42°45N 76°42W 83 D8
Aurora Ohio, U.S.A. 41°21N 81°20W 82 E3
Aurukun Australia 13°20S 141°45E 62 A3
Aurukun ۞ Australia 13°36S 141°48E 62 A3
Aus Namibia 26°35S 16°12E 56 D2
Ausa India 18°15N 76°30E 44 E3
Ausable → Canada 43°19N 81°46W 82 C3
Auschwitz = Oświęcim
 Poland 50°2N 19°11E 17 C10
Auski Roadhouse
 Australia 22°22S 118°41E 60 D2
Austen Harbour India 12°55N 92°45E 45 H11
Austin Minn., U.S.A. 43°40N 92°58W 80 D7
Austin Nev., U.S.A. 39°30N 117°4W 76 G5
Austin Pa., U.S.A. 41°38N 78°6W 82 E6
Austin Tex., U.S.A. 30°17N 97°45W 84 F6
Austin, L. Australia 27°40S 118°0E 61 E2
Austin I. Canada 61°10N 94°0W 71 A10
Austra Norway 65°8N 11°55E 8 D14
Austral Is. = Tubuaï, Îs.
 French Polynesia 25°0S 150°0W 65 K13
Austral Seamount Chain
 Pac. Oc. 24°0S 150°0W 65 K13
Australia ■ Oceania 23°0S 135°0E 58 D6
Australian-Antarctic Basin
 S. Ocean 60°0S 120°0E 5 C9
Australian Capital Territory □
 Australia 35°30S 149°0E 63 F4
Australind Australia 33°17S 115°42E 61 F2
Austria ■ Europe 47°0N 14°0E 16 E8
Austvågøya Norway 68°20N 14°40E 8 B16
Autlán de Navarro
 Mexico 19°46N 104°22W 86 D4
Autun France 46°58N 4°17E 20 C6
Auvergne □ France 45°20N 3°15E 20 D5
Auvergne, Mts. d' France 45°20N 2°55E 20 D5
Auxerre France 47°48N 3°32E 20 C5
Auyuittuq △ Canada 67°30N 66°0W 69 D18
Av-Dovurak Russia 51°17N 91°35E 27 D10
Ava U.S.A. 36°57N 92°40W 80 G7
Avallon France 47°30N 3°53E 20 C5
Avalon U.S.A. 33°21N 118°20W 79 M8
Avalon Pen. Canada 47°30N 53°20W 73 C9
Avanigadda India 16°0N 80°56E 45 G5
Avanos Turkey 38°43N 34°51E 46 B2
Avaré Brazil 23°4S 48°58W 95 A6
Avawatz Mts. U.S.A. 35°40N 116°30W 79 K10
Aveiro Brazil 3°10S 55°5W 93 D7
Aveiro Portugal 40°37N 8°38E 21 B1
Āvej Iran 35°40N 49°15E 47 C6
Avellino Italy 40°54N 14°47E 22 D6
Avenal U.S.A. 36°0N 120°8W 78 K6
Avery U.S.A. 47°15N 115°49W 76 C6
Aves, I. de W. Indies 15°45N 63°55W 89 C7
Aves, Is. las Venezuela 12°0N 67°30W 89 D6
Avesta Sweden 60°9N 16°10E 9 F17
Aveyron → France 44°5N 1°16E 20 D4
Avezzano Italy 42°2N 13°25E 22 C5
Aviá Terai Argentina 26°45S 60°50W 94 B3
Aviemore U.K. 57°12N 3°50W 11 D5
Avignon France 43°57N 4°50E 20 E6
Ávila Spain 40°39N 4°43W 21 B3
Avila Beach U.S.A. 35°11N 120°44W 79 K6
Avilés Spain 43°35N 5°57W 21 A3
Avis U.S.A. 41°11N 77°19W 82 E7
Avissawella Sri Lanka 6°56N 80°11E 45 L5
Avoca U.S.A. 42°25N 77°25W 82 D7
Avoca → Australia 35°40S 143°43E 63 F3
Avoca → Ireland 52°48N 6°10W 10 D5
Avola Canada 51°45N 119°19W 70 C5
Avola Italy 36°56N 15°7E 22 F6
Avon U.S.A. 42°55N 77°45W 82 D7
Avon → Australia 31°40S 116°7E 61 F2
Avon → Bristol, U.K. 51°29N 2°41W 13 F5
Avon → Dorset, U.K. 50°44N 1°46W 13 G6
Avon → Warks., U.K. 52°0N 2°8W 13 E5
Avon Park U.S.A. 27°36N 81°31W 85 H14
Avonlea Canada 50°0N 105°0W 71 D8
Avonmore Canada 45°10N 74°58W 83 A10
Avonmouth U.K. 51°30N 2°42W 13 F5
Avranches France 48°40N 1°20W 20 B3
Awa-Shima Japan 38°27N 139°14E 28 E9
A'waj → Syria 33°23N 36°20E 48 B5
Awaji-Shima Japan 34°30N 134°50E 29 G7
'Awālī Bahrain 26°0N 50°30E 47 E6
Awantipur India 33°55N 75°3E 43 C6
Awarja → India 17°5N 76°15E 44 F3
Awasa Ethiopia 7°2N 38°28E 49 F2
Awash Ethiopia 9°1N 40°10E 49 F3
Awatere → N.Z. 41°37S 174°10E 59 D5
Awbārī Libya 26°46N 12°57E 53 C8
Awbārī, Idehan Libya 27°10N 11°30E 53 C8
Awe, L. U.K. 56°17N 5°16W 11 E3
Awjilah Libya 29°8N 21°7E 53 C10
Axe → U.K. 50°42N 3°4W 13 F5
Axel Heiberg I. Canada 80°0N 90°0W 69 B14
Axim Ghana 4°51N 2°15W 52 H5
Axios → Greece 40°57N 22°35E 23 D10
Axminster U.K. 50°46N 3°0W 13 G4
Ayabaca Peru 4°40S 79°53W 92 D3
Ayabe Japan 35°20N 135°20E 29 G7
Ayacucho Argentina 37°5S 58°20W 94 D4
Ayacucho Peru 13°0S 74°0W 92 F4
Ayaguz = Ayaköz
 Kazakhstan 48°10N 80°10E 30 B5
Ayakkum Hu China 37°30N 89°20E 30 D6
Ayaköz Kazakhstan 48°10N 80°10E 30 B5
Ayakudi India 10°28N 77°56E 45 J3
Ayamonte Spain 37°12N 7°24W 21 D2
Ayan Russia 56°30N 138°16E 27 D14
Ayaviri Peru 14°50S 70°35W 92 F4
Aydın Turkey 37°51N 27°51E 23 F12

Aydingkol Hu China 42°40N 89°15E 30 C6
Ayer U.S.A. 42°34N 71°35W 83 D13
Ayer Hitam Malaysia 5°24N 100°16E 39 c
Ayer's Cliff Canada 45°10N 72°3W 83 A12
Ayers Rock = Uluru
 Australia 25°23S 131°5E 61 E5
Ayeyarwady = Irrawaddy →
 Burma 15°50N 95°6E 41 M19
Aykhal Russia 66°0N 111°30E 27 C12
Aykino Russia 62°15N 49°56E 18 B8
Aylesbury U.K. 51°49N 0°49W 13 F7
Aylmer Canada 42°46N 80°59W 82 D4
Aylmer, L. Canada 64°5N 108°30W 68 E10
'Ayn, Wādī al Oman 22°15N 55°28E 47 F7
Ayn Dār Si. Arabia 25°55N 49°10E 47 E7
Ayn Zālah Iraq 36°45N 42°35E 46 B4
Ayolas Paraguay 27°10S 56°59W 94 B4
Ayon, Ostrov Russia 69°50N 169°0E 27 C17
'Ayoûn el 'Atroûs
 Mauritania 16°38N 9°37W 52 E4
Ayr Australia 19°35S 147°25E 62 B4
Ayr Canada 43°17N 80°27W 82 C4
Ayr U.K. 55°28N 4°38W 11 F4
Ayr → U.K. 55°28N 4°38W 11 F4
Ayre, Pt. of I. of Man 54°25N 4°21W 12 C3
Ayton Australia 15°56S 145°22E 62 B4
Aytos Bulgaria 42°42N 27°16E 23 C12
Ayu, Kepulauan Indonesia 0°35N 131°5E 37 D8
Ayutla Guatemala 14°40N 92°10W 88 D1
Ayutla de los Libres
 Mexico 16°54N 99°13W 87 D5
Ayutthaya = Phra Nakhon Si
 Ayutthaya Thailand 14°25N 100°30E 38 E3
Ayvacık Turkey 39°36N 26°24E 23 E12
Ayvalık Turkey 39°20N 26°46E 23 E12
Az Zabadānī Syria 33°43N 36°5E 48 B5
Az Zāhirīyah West Bank 31°25N 34°58E 48 D3
Az Zahrān Si. Arabia 26°10N 50°7E 47 E6
Az Zarqā Jordan 32°5N 36°4E 48 C5
Az Zarqā' U.A.E. 24°53N 53°4E 47 E7
Az Zarqā □ Jordan 32°5N 36°4E 48 C5
Az Zāwiyah Libya 32°52N 12°56E 53 B8
Az Zibār Iraq 36°52N 44°4E 46 B5
Az Zilfī Si. Arabia 26°12N 44°52E 46 E5
Az Zubayr Iraq 30°26N 47°40E 46 D5
Azad Kashmir □ Pakistan 33°50N 73°50E 43 C5
Azamgarh India 26°5N 83°13E 43 F10
Azángaro Peru 14°55S 70°13W 92 F4
Azaouad Mali 19°0N 3°0W 52 E5
Azangaro Peru 14°55S 70°13W 92 F4
Azar Shahr Iran 37°45N 45°59E 46 B5
Azarān Iran 37°25N 47°16E 46 B5
Azārbāyjān = Azerbaijan ■
 Asia 40°20N 48°0E 19 F8
Āzārbāyjān-e Gharbī □
 Iran 37°0N 44°30E 46 B5
Āzārbāyjān-e Sharqī □
 Iran 37°20N 47°0E 46 B5
Azare Nigeria 11°55N 10°10E 52 F8
A'zāz Syria 36°36N 37°4E 46 B3
Azbine = Aïr Niger 18°30N 8°0E 52 E7
Azerbaijan ■ Asia 40°20N 48°0E 19 F8
Azogues Ecuador 2°35S 78°0W 92 D3
Azores = Açores, Is. dos
 Atl. Oc. 38°0N 27°0W 52 a
Azov Russia 47°3N 39°25E 19 E6
Azov, Sea of Europe 46°0N 36°30E 19 E6
Azovskoye More = Azov, Sea of
 Europe 46°0N 36°30E 19 E6
Azraq ash Shīshān Jordan 31°50N 36°49E 48 D5
Aztec U.S.A. 36°49N 107°59W 77 H10
Azua de Compostela
 Dom. Rep. 18°25N 70°44W 89 C5
Azuaga Spain 38°16N 5°39W 21 C3
Azuero, Pen. de Panama 7°30N 80°30W 88 E3
Azul Argentina 36°42S 59°43W 94 D4
Azumino Japan 36°20N 137°50E 29 F8
Azusa U.S.A. 34°8N 117°52W 79 L9
Azzel Matti, Sebkra
 Algeria 26°10N 0°43E 52 C6

B

Ba Be △ Vietnam 22°25N 105°37E 38 A5
Ba Don Vietnam 17°45N 106°26E 38 D6
Ba Dong Vietnam 9°40N 106°33E 39 H6
Ba Ngoi Vietnam 11°54N 109°10E 39 G7
Ba Ria Vietnam 10°30N 107°10E 39 G6
Ba Tri Vietnam 10°2N 106°36E 39 G6
Ba Vi △ Vietnam 21°1N 105°22E 38 B5
Ba Xian = Bazhou China 39°8N 116°22E 32 E9
Baa Indonesia 10°50S 123°0E 60 B3
Baalbek = Ba'labakk
 Lebanon 34°0N 36°10E 48 B5
Baardheere Somalia 2°20N 42°27E 49 G3
Baarle-Nassau Belgium 51°27N 4°56E 15 C4
Bab el Mandeb Red Sea 12°35N 43°25E 49 E3
Bābā, Koh-i- Afghan. 34°30N 67°0E 40 B5
Baba Budan Hills India 13°30N 75°44E 45 H2
Baba Burnu Turkey 39°29N 26°2E 23 E12
Bābā Kalū Iran 30°7N 50°49E 47 D6
Babadag Romania 44°53N 28°44E 17 F15
Babaeski Turkey 41°26N 27°6E 23 D12
Babahoyo Ecuador 1°40S 79°30W 92 D3
Babai = Sarju → India 28°10N 82°21E 43 E10
Babar Indonesia 8°0S 129°30E 37 F7
Babar Pakistan 31°7N 69°32E 42 D3
Babarkach Pakistan 29°45N 68°0E 42 E3
Babb U.S.A. 48°51N 113°27W 76 B7
Baberu India 25°33N 80°43E 43 G9
Babi Besar, Pulau
 Malaysia 2°25N 103°59E 39 L4
Babian Jiang → China 22°55N 101°47E 34 F3
Bābīl □ Iraq 32°34N 44°22E 46 C5
Babinda Australia 17°20S 145°56E 62 B4
Babine Canada 55°22N 126°37W 70 B3
Babine → Canada 55°45N 127°44W 70 B3
Babine L. Canada 54°48N 126°0W 70 C3
Babo Indonesia 2°30S 133°30E 37 E8

Bābol Iran 36°40N 52°50E 47 B7
Bābol Sar Iran 36°45N 52°45E 47 B7
Baboua C.A.R. 5°49N 14°58E 54 C2
Babruysk Belarus 53°10N 29°15E 17 B15
Babuhri India 26°49N 69°43E 42 F3
Babusar Pass Pakistan 35°12N 73°59E 43 B5
Babuyan Chan. Phil. 18°40N 121°30E 37 A6
Babylon Iraq 32°34N 44°22E 46 C5
Bac Can Vietnam 22°8N 105°49E 34 F5
Bac Giang Vietnam 21°16N 106°11E 34 G6
Bac Lieu Vietnam 9°17N 105°43E 39 H5
Bac Ninh Vietnam 21°13N 106°4E 34 G6
Bac Phan Vietnam 22°0N 105°0E 34 G5
Bacabal Brazil 4°15S 44°45W 93 D10
Bacalar Mexico 18°43N 88°27W 87 D7
Bacan, Kepulauan
 Indonesia 0°35S 127°30E 37 E7
Bacarra Phil. 18°15N 120°37E 37 A6
Bacău Romania 46°35N 26°55E 17 E14
Bacerac Mexico 30°18N 108°50W 86 A3
Bach Long Vi, Dao
 Vietnam 20°10N 107°40E 38 B6
Bach Ma △ Vietnam 16°11N 107°49E 38 D6
Bachhwara India 25°35N 85°54E 43 G11
Back → Canada 65°10N 104°0W 68 D11
Bacolod Phil. 10°40N 122°57E 37 B6
Bacuk Malaysia 6°4N 102°25E 39 J4
Bácum Mexico 27°33N 110°5W 86 B2
Bād Iran 33°41N 52°1E 47 C7
Bad → U.S.A. 44°21N 100°22W 80 C3
Bad Axe U.S.A. 43°48N 83°0W 82 C2
Bad Ischl Austria 47°44N 13°38E 16 E7
Bad Kissingen Germany 50°11N 10°4E 16 C6
Bada Barabil India 22°7N 85°24E 43 H11
Badagara = Vadakara
 India 11°35N 75°40E 45 J2
Badain Jaran Shamo
 China 40°23N 102°0E 30 C9
Badajós, L. Brazil 3°15S 62°50W 92 D6
Badajoz Spain 38°50N 6°59W 21 C2
Badakhshān □ Afghan. 36°30N 71°0E 40 A7
Badaling China 40°20N 116°0E 32 D9
Badalzai Afghan. 29°50N 65°35E 42 E1
Badami India 15°55N 75°41E 45 G2
Badampahar India 22°10N 86°10E 44 C8
Badanah Si. Arabia 30°58N 41°30E 46 D4
Badarinath India 30°45N 79°30E 43 D8
Badas, Kepulauan
 Indonesia 0°45N 107°5E 36 D3
Baddo → Pakistan 28°0N 64°20E 40 F4
Bade Indonesia 7°10S 139°35E 37 F9
Baden Austria 48°1N 16°13E 16 D9
Baden Austria 40°38N 80°14W 82 F4
Baden-Baden Germany 48°44N 8°13E 16 D5
Baden-Württemberg □
 Germany 48°20N 8°40E 16 D5
Badgam India 34°1N 74°45E 43 B6
Badgastein Austria 47°7N 13°9E 16 E7
Badger Canada 49°0N 56°4W 73 C8
Badger U.S.A. 36°38N 119°1W 78 J7
Bādghīs □ Afghan. 35°0N 63°0E 40 B3
Badgingarra △ Australia 30°23S 115°22E 61 F2
Badin Pakistan 24°38N 68°54E 42 G3
Badlands U.S.A. 43°55N 102°30W 80 D2
Badlands △ U.S.A. 43°38N 102°56W 80 D2
Badnera India 20°48N 77°44E 44 D3
Badrah Iraq 33°6N 45°58E 46 C5
Badrain Jaran Shamo
 China 40°40N 103°20E 32 D2
Badrinath India 30°44N 79°29E 43 D8
Badu Australia 10°7S 142°11E 62 a
Badulla Sri Lanka 7°1N 81°7E 45 L5
Badung, Bukit Indonesia 8°49S 115°10E 37 K18
Badung, Selat Indonesia 8°40S 115°22E 37 K18
Badvel India 14°45N 79°3E 45 G4
Baena Spain 37°37N 4°20W 21 D3
Baengnyeongdo
 S. Korea 37°57N 124°40E 33 F13
Baeza Spain 37°57N 3°25W 21 D4
Bafatá Guinea-Biss. 12°8N 14°40E 52 F3
Baffin B. N. Amer. 72°0N 64°0W 66 B13
Baffin I. Canada 68°0N 75°0W 69 D17
Bafing → Mali 13°49N 10°50E 52 F3
Bafliyūn Syria 36°37N 36°59E 46 B3
Bafoulabé Mali 13°50N 10°55E 52 F3
Bafoussam Cameroon 5°28N 10°25E 54 C2
Bāfq Iran 31°40N 55°25E 47 D7
Bafra Turkey 41°34N 35°54E 19 F6
Bāft Iran 29°15N 56°38E 47 D8
Bafwasende
 Dem. Rep. of the Congo 1°3N 27°5E 54 D5
Bagaha India 27°6N 84°5E 44 A7
Bagalkot India 16°10N 75°40E 45 G2
Bagamoyo Tanzania 6°28S 38°55E 54 F7
Bagan Datoh Malaysia 3°59N 100°47E 39 L3
Bagan Serai Malaysia 5°1N 100°32E 39 K3
Baganga Phil. 7°34N 126°33E 37 C7
Bagani Namibia 18°7S 21°41E 56 A3
Bagansiapiapi Indonesia 2°12N 100°50E 36 D2
Bagasra India 21°30N 71°0E 42 J4
Bagaud India 22°19N 75°53E 42 H6
Bagdad U.S.A. 34°35N 115°53W 79 L11
Bagdarin Russia 54°26N 113°36E 27 D12
Bagé Brazil 31°20S 54°15W 95 C5
Bagenalstown Ireland 52°42N 6°58W 10 D5
Bagepalli India 13°47N 77°47E 45 H3
Bageshwar India 29°51N 79°46E 43 E8
Bagevadi India 16°35N 75°58E 44 F2
Baggs U.S.A. 41°2N 107°39W 76 F10
Bagh Pakistan 33°59N 73°45E 43 C5
Baghain → India 25°32N 81°1E 43 G9
Bagheria Italy 38°5N 13°30E 22 E5
Baghlān Afghan. 32°12N 68°46E 40 A6
Baghlān □ Afghan. 36°0N 68°30E 40 B6
Bagley U.S.A. 47°32N 95°24W 80 B6
Baglung Nepal 28°16N 83°36E 43 E10
Bago = Pegu Burma 17°20N 96°29E 41 L20
Bagodar India 24°5N 85°52E 43 G11
Bagrationovsk Russia 54°23N 20°39E 9 J19

Baguio Phil. 16°26N 120°34E 37 A6
Bahadurganj India 26°16N 87°49E 43 F12
Bahadurgarh India 28°40N 76°57E 42 E7
Bahama, Canal Viejo de
 W. Indies 22°10N 77°30W 88 B4
Bahamas ■ N. Amer. 24°0N 75°0W 89 B5
Bahār Iran 34°54N 48°26E 47 C6
Baharampur India 24°2N 88°27E 43 G13
Baharu Pandan = Pandan
 Malaysia 1°32N 103°46E 39 d
Bahawalnagar Pakistan 30°0N 73°15E 42 E5
Bahawalpur Pakistan 29°24N 71°40E 42 E4
Bäherden Turkmenistan 38°25N 57°26E 47 B8
Baheri India 28°45N 79°34E 43 E8
Bahgul → India 27°45N 79°36E 43 F8
Bahía = Salvador Brazil 13°0S 38°30W 93 F11
Bahía □ Brazil 12°0S 42°0W 93 F10
Bahía, Is. de la Honduras 16°45N 86°15W 88 C2
Bahía Blanca Argentina 38°35S 62°13W 94 D3
Bahía de Caráquez
 Ecuador 0°40S 80°27W 92 D2
Bahía de Los Angeles
 Mexico 28°56N 113°34W 86 B2
Bahía Kino Mexico 28°47N 111°58W 86 B2
Bahía Laura Argentina 48°10S 66°30W 96 F3
Bahía Negra Paraguay 20°5S 58°5W 92 H7
Bahir Dar Ethiopia 11°37N 37°10E 49 E2
Bahmanzād Iran 31°15N 51°47E 47 D6
Bahraich India 27°38N 81°37E 43 F9
Bahrain ■ Asia 26°0N 50°35E 47 E6
Bahror India 27°51N 76°20E 42 F7
Bāhū Kalāt Iran 25°43N 61°25E 47 E9
Bai Bung, Mui = Ca Mau, Mui
 Vietnam 8°38N 104°44E 39 H5
Bai Thuong Vietnam 19°54N 105°23E 38 C5
Baião Brazil 2°40S 49°40W 93 D9
Baïbokoum Chad 7°46N 15°43E 53 G9
Baicheng China 45°38N 122°42E 33 B12
Baidoa = Baydhabo
 Somalia 3°8N 43°30E 49 G3
Baie-Comeau Canada 49°12N 68°10W 73 C6
Baie-St-Paul Canada 47°28N 70°32W 73 C5
Baie Ste-Anne Seychelles 4°18S 55°45E 55 b
Baie-Trinité Canada 49°25N 67°20W 73 C6
Baie Verte Canada 49°55N 56°12W 73 C8
Baihar India 22°6N 80°33E 43 H9
Baihe Hubei, China 32°50N 110°5E 32 H6
Baihe Jilin, China 42°27N 128°9E 33 C15
Baihetan Dam China 27°11N 102°54E 34 D4
Ba'ījī Iraq 35°0N 43°30E 46 C4
Baijnath India 29°55N 79°37E 43 E8
Baikal, L. = Baykal, Oz.
 Russia 53°0N 108°0E 27 D11
Baikonur = Bayqonyr
 Kazakhstan 45°40N 63°20E 26 E7
Baikunthpur India 23°15N 82°33E 43 H10
Bailadila, Mt. India 18°43N 81°15E 44 E5
Baile Átha Fhirdhia = Ardee
 Ireland 53°52N 6°33W 10 C5
Baile Átha Í = Athy Ireland 53°0N 7°0W 10 C5
Baile Átha Luain = Athlone
 Ireland 53°25N 7°56W 10 C4
Baile Átha Troim = Trim
 Ireland 53°33N 6°48W 10 C5
Baile Brigín = Balbriggan
 Ireland 53°37N 6°11W 10 C5
Baile Sear = Baleshare
 U.K. 57°31N 7°22W 11 D1
Băileşti Romania 44°1N 23°20E 17 F12
Bailhongal India 15°55N 74°53E 45 G2
Bailieborough Ireland 53°56N 6°59W 10 C5
Baima China 33°0N 100°26E 34 A3
Bainbridge Ga., U.S.A. 30°55N 84°35W 85 F12
Bainbridge N.Y., U.S.A. 42°18N 75°29W 83 D9
Bainbridge Island
 U.S.A. 47°38N 122°32W 78 C4
Baine China 42°0N 128°0E 31 C14
Baing Indonesia 10°14S 120°34E 37 F6
Bainiu China 34°20N 112°32E 32 G7
Ba'ir Jordan 30°45N 36°55E 48 E5
Bairiki = Tarawa Kiribati 1°30N 173°0E 64 G9
Bairin Youqi China 43°30N 118°35E 33 C10
Bairin Zuoqi China 43°58N 119°15E 33 C10
Bairnsdale Australia 37°48S 147°36E 63 F4
Baisha China 34°20N 112°32E 32 G7
Baisha Li China 19°12N 109°20E 38 C7
Baishan = Hunjiang
 China 41°54N 126°26E 33 D14
Baishan China 42°43N 127°14E 33 C14
Baitadi Nepal 29°35N 80°25E 43 E9
Baitarani → India 20°45N 86°48E 44 D8
Baiyin China 36°45N 104°14E 32 F3
Baiyü China 31°16N 98°50E 34 B2
Baiyu Shan China 37°15N 107°30E 32 F4
Baj Baj India 22°30N 88°5E 43 H13
Baja Hungary 46°12N 18°59E 17 E10
Baja, Pta. Mexico 29°58N 115°49W 86 B1
Baja California Mexico 31°10N 115°12W 86 A1
Baja California □ Mexico 30°0N 115°0W 86 B2
Baja California Sur □
 Mexico 25°50N 111°50W 86 B2
Bajag India 22°40N 81°21E 43 H9
Bajana India 23°7N 71°49E 42 H4
Bajatrejo Indonesia 8°29S 114°19E 37 K18
Bajawa Indonesia 8°47S 120°59E 37 F6
Bajera Indonesia 8°31S 115°2E 37 J18
Bäjgīrān Iran 37°36N 58°24E 47 B8
Bajimba, Mt. Australia 29°17S 152°6E 63 D5
Bajo Boquete Panama 8°46N 82°27W 88 E3
Bajo Nuevo Caribbean 15°40N 78°50W 88 C4
Bajoga Nigeria 10°57N 11°20E 53 F8
Bajool Australia 23°40S 150°35E 62 C5
Bakel Senegal 14°56N 12°20W 52 F3
Baker Calif., U.S.A. 35°16N 116°4W 79 K10
Baker Mont., U.S.A. 46°22N 104°17W 76 C11
Baker, L. Canada 64°0N 96°0W 68 E12
Baker, Mt. U.S.A. 48°50N 121°49W 76 B3

Baker City *U.S.A.* 44°47N 117°50W **76** D5
Baker I. *Pac. Oc.* 0°01N 176°35W **64** G10
Baker I. *U.S.A.* 55°20N 133°40W **70** B2
Baker L. *Australia* 26°54S 126°5E **61** E4
Baker Lake *Canada* 64°20N 96°3W **68** E12
Bakers Creek *Australia* 21°13S 149°7E **62** C4
Bakers Dozen Is. *Canada* 56°45N 78°45W **72** A4
Bakersfield *Calif., U.S.A.* 35°23N 119°1W **79** K8
Bakersfield *Vt., U.S.A.* 44°45N 72°48W **83** B12
Bakharden = Bäherden
  Turkmenistan 38°25N 57°26E **47** B8
Bākhtarān = Kermānshāh
  Iran 34°23N 47°0E **46** C5
Bākhtarān = Kermānshāh □
  Iran 34°0N 46°30E **46** C5
Bakhtegän, Daryācheh-ye
  Iran 29°40N 53°50E **47** D7
Bakhtegän △ *Iran* 29°51N 53°40E **47** D7
Bakkafjörður *Iceland* 66°2N 14°48W **8** C6
Bakkageröi *Iceland* 65°31N 13°49W **8** D7
Bakony *Hungary* 47°10N 17°30E **17** E9
Bakony Forest = Bakony
  Hungary 47°10N 17°30E **17** E9
Bakouma *C.A.R.* 5°40N 22°56E **54** C4
Bakswaho *India* 24°15N 79°18E **43** G8
Bakutis Coast *Antarctica* 74°0S 120°0W **5** D15
Baky = Bakı *Azerbaijan* 40°29N 49°56E **47** A6
Bala *Canada* 45°1N 79°37W **82** A5
Bala *U.K.* 52°54N 3°36W **12** E4
Bala, L. *U.K.* 52°53N 3°37W **12** E4
Balabac I. *Phil.* 8°0N 117°0E **36** C5
Balabac Str. *E. Indies* 7°53N 117°5E **36** C5
Balabagh *Afghan.* 34°25N 70°12E **42** B4
Ba'labakk *Lebanon* 34°0N 36°10E **48** B5
Balabalangan, Kepulauan
  Indonesia 2°20S 117°30E **36** E5
Balad *Iraq* 34°0N 44°9E **46** C5
Balad Rūz *Iraq* 33°42N 45°5E **46** C5
Bālādeh *Färs, Iran* 29°17N 51°56E **47** D6
Bālādeh *Māzandaran, Iran* 36°12N 51°48E **47** B6
Balaghat *India* 21°49N 80°12E **44** D5
Balaghat Ra. *India* 18°50N 76°30E **44** E3
Balaguer *Spain* 41°50N 0°50E **21** B6
Balaklava *Ukraine* 44°30N 33°30E **19** F5
Balakovo *Russia* 52°4N 47°55E **18** D8
Balamau *India* 27°10N 80°21E **43** F9
Balancán *Mexico* 17°48N 91°32W **87** D6
Balangir *India* 20°43N 83°35E **44** D6
Balapur *India* 20°40N 76°45E **44** D3
Balashov *Russia* 51°30N 43°10E **19** D7
Balasinor *India* 22°57N 73°23E **42** H5
Balasore = Baleshwar
  India 21°35N 87°3E **44** D8
Balaton *Hungary* 46°50N 17°40E **17** E9
Balbina, Represa de *Brazil* 2°0S 59°30W **92** D7
Balboa *Panama* 8°57N 79°34W **88** E4
Balbriggan *Ireland* 53°37N 6°11W **10** C5
Balcarce *Argentina* 38°0S 58°10W **94** D4
Balcarres *Canada* 50°50N 103°35W **71** C8
Balchik *Bulgaria* 43°28N 28°11E **23** C13
Balclutha *N.Z.* 46°15S 169°45E **59** G2
Balcones Escarpment
  U.S.A. 29°30N 99°15W **84** G5
Bald I. *Australia* 34°57S 118°27E **61** F2
Bald Knob *U.S.A.* 35°19N 91°34W **84** D9
Baldock L. *Canada* 56°33N 97°57W **71** B9
Baldwin *Mich., U.S.A.* 43°54N 85°51W **81** D11
Baldwin *Pa., U.S.A.* 40°21N 79°58W **82** F5
Baldwinsville *U.S.A.* 43°10N 76°20W **83** C8
Baldy Peak *U.S.A.* 33°54N 109°34W **77** K9
Baleares, Is. *Spain* 39°30N 3°0E **21** C7
Baleares, Is. = Baleares, Is.
  Spain 39°30N 3°0E **21** C7
Baleine → *Canada* 58°15N 67°40W **73** A6
Baleine, Petite R. de la →
  Canada 56°0N 76°45W **72** A4
Baler *Phil.* 15°46N 121°34E **37** A6
Baleshare *U.K.* 57°31N 7°22W **11** D1
Baleshwar *India* 21°35N 87°3E **44** D8
Baley *Russia* 51°36N 116°37E **27** D12
Balfate *Honduras* 15°48N 86°25W **88** C2
Balgo *Australia* 20°9S 127°58E **60** D4
Balharshah *India* 19°50N 79°23E **44** E4
Bali *India* 25°11N 73°17E **42** G5
Bali *Indonesia* 8°20S 115°0E **37** J18
Bali □ *Indonesia* 8°20S 115°0E **37** J17
Bali, Selat *Indonesia* 8°18S 114°25E **37** J17
Bali Barat △ *Indonesia* 8°12S 114°35E **37** J17
Bali Sea *Indonesia* 8°0S 115°0E **37** J17
Baliapal *India* 21°40N 87°17E **43** J12
Baliguda *India* 20°12N 83°55E **44** D6
Balik Pulau *Malaysia* 5°21N 100°14E **39** c
Balıkesir *Turkey* 39°39N 27°53E **23** E12
Balikpapan *Indonesia* 1°10S 116°55E **36** E5
Balimbing *Phil.* 5°5N 119°58E **37** C5
Baling *Malaysia* 5°41N 100°55E **39** K3
Balkan Mts. = Stara Planina
  Bulgaria 43°15N 23°0E **23** C10
Balkanabat *Turkmenistan* 39°30N 54°22E **47** B7
Balkhash = Balqash
  Kazakhstan 46°50N 74°50E **26** E8
Balkhash, Ozero = Balqash Köli
  Kazakhstan 46°0N 74°50E **30** B3
Balkonda *India* 18°52N 78°12E **44** E4
Balladonia *Australia* 32°27S 123°51E **61** F3
Ballaghaderreen *Ireland* 53°55N 8°34W **10** C3
Ballarat *Australia* 37°33S 143°50E **63** F3
Ballard, L. *Australia* 29°20S 120°40E **61** E3
Ballater *U.K.* 57°3N 3°3W **11** D5
Ballenas, Canal de
  Mexico 29°10N 113°29W **86** B2
Balleny Is. *Antarctica* 66°30S 163°0E **5** C11
Ballia *India* 25°46N 84°12E **43** G11
Ballina *Australia* 28°50S 153°31E **63** D5
Ballina *Ireland* 54°7N 9°9W **10** B2
Ballinasloe *Ireland* 53°20N 8°13W **10** C3

Ballincollig *Ireland* 51°53N 8°33W **10** E3
Ballinger *U.S.A.* 31°45N 99°57W **84** F5
Ballinrobe *Ireland* 53°38N 9°13W **10** C2
Ballinskelligs B. *Ireland* 51°48N 10°13W **10** E1
Ballston Spa *U.S.A.* 43°0N 73°51W **83** D11
Ballyboghil *Ireland* 53°32N 6°16W **10** C5
Ballybunion *Ireland* 52°31N 9°40W **10** D2
Ballycanew *Ireland* 52°37N 6°19W **10** D5
Ballycastle *U.K.* 55°12N 6°15W **10** A5
Ballyclare *U.K.* 54°46N 6°0W **10** B5
Ballycroy △ *Ireland* 54°5N 9°50W **10** B2
Ballydehob *Ireland* 51°34N 9°28W **10** E2
Ballygawley *U.K.* 54°27N 7°2W **10** B4
Ballyhaunis *Ireland* 53°46N 8°46W **10** C3
Ballyheige *Ireland* 52°23N 9°49W **10** D2
Ballymena *U.K.* 54°52N 6°17W **10** B5
Ballymote *Ireland* 54°5N 8°31W **10** B3
Ballynahinch *U.K.* 54°24N 5°54W **10** B6
Ballyporeen *Ireland* 52°16N 8°6W **10** D3
Ballyquintin Pt. *U.K.* 54°20N 5°30W **10** B6
Ballyshannon *Ireland* 54°30N 8°11W **10** B3
Balmaceda *Chile* 46°0S 71°50W **96** F2
Balmertown *Canada* 51°4N 93°41W **71** C10
Balmoral *Australia* 37°15S 141°48E **63** F3
Balmorhea *U.S.A.* 30°59N 103°45W **84** F3
Balochistan = Baluchistan □
  Pakistan 27°30N 65°0E **40** F4
Balod *India* 20°44N 81°13E **44** D5
Balodar *Australia* 28°47S 147°56E **63** D4
Balotra *India* 25°50N 72°14E **42** G5
Balqash *Kazakhstan* 46°50N 74°50E **26** E8
Balrampur *India* 27°30N 82°20E **43** F10
Balranald *Australia* 34°38S 143°33E **63** E3
Balsas → *Brazil* 7°15S 44°35W **93** E9
Balsas → *Mexico* 17°55N 102°10W **86** D4
Balsas del Norte *Mexico* 18°0N 99°46W **87** D5
Balta *Ukraine* 47°56N 29°45E **17** D15
Bălți *Moldova* 47°48N 27°58E **17** E14
Baltic Sea *Europe* 57°0N 19°0E **9** H18
Baltimore *Ireland* 51°29N 9°22W **10** E2
Baltimore *Md., U.S.A.* 39°17N 76°36W **81** F15
Baltimore *Ohio, U.S.A.* 39°51N 82°36W **82** G2
Baltinglass *Ireland* 52°56N 6°43W **10** D5
Baltit *Pakistan* 36°15N 74°40E **43** A6
Baltiysk *Russia* 54°41N 19°58E **9** J18
Baluchistan □ *Pakistan* 27°30N 65°0E **40** F4
Balurghat *India* 25°15N 88°44E **43** G13
Balvi *Latvia* 57°8N 27°15E **9** H22
Balya *Turkey* 39°44N 27°35E **23** E12
Balykchy *Kyrgyzstan* 42°26N 76°12E **30** C4
Balyqshy *Kazakhstan* 47°4N 51°52E **19** E9
Bam *Iran* 29°7N 58°14E **47** D8
Bama *China* 24°8N 107°12E **34** E6
Bama *Nigeria* 11°33N 13°41E **53** F8
Bamaga *Australia* 10°50S 142°25E **62** A3
Bamaji L. *Canada* 51°9N 91°25W **72** B1
Bamako *Mali* 12°34N 7°55W **52** F4
Bambari *C.A.R.* 5°40N 20°35E **54** C4
Bambaroo *Australia* 18°50S 146°10E **62** B4
Bamberg *Germany* 49°54N 10°54E **16** D6
Bamberg *U.S.A.* 33°18N 81°2W **85** E14
Bamenda *Cameroon* 5°57N 10°11E **54** C1
Bamfield *Canada* 48°45N 125°10W **70** D3
Bāmīān □ *Afghan.* 35°0N 67°0E **40** B5
Bamiancheng *China* 43°15N 124°2E **33** C13
Bamou △ *Iran* 29°45N 52°35E **47** D7
Bampūr *Iran* 27°15N 60°21E **47** E9
Bampūr → *Iran* 27°24N 59°0E **47** E8
Ban Ao Tu Khun *Thailand* 8°9N 98°20E **39** a
Ban Ban *Laos* 19°31N 103°30E **38** C4
Ban Bang Hin *Thailand* 9°32N 98°35E **39** H2
Ban Bang Khu *Thailand* 7°57N 98°23E **39** a
Ban Bang Rong *Thailand* 8°3N 98°25E **39** a
Ban Bo Phut *Thailand* 9°33N 100°2E **39** b
Ban Chaweng *Thailand* 9°32N 100°3E **39** b
Ban Chiang *Thailand* 17°30N 103°10E **38** D4
Ban Chiang Klang
  Thailand 19°25N 100°55E **38** C3
Ban Choho *Thailand* 15°2N 102°9E **38** E4
Ban Dan Lan Hoi *Thailand* 17°0N 99°35E **38** D2
Ban Don = Surat Thani
  Thailand 9°6N 99°20E **39** H2
Ban Don *Vietnam* 12°53N 107°48E **38** F6
Ban Don, Ao → *Thailand* 9°20N 99°25E **39** H2
Ban Dong *Thailand* 19°30N 100°59E **38** C3
Ban Hong *Thailand* 18°18N 98°50E **38** C2
Ban Hua Thanon *Thailand* 9°26N 100°1E **39** b
Ban Kantang *Thailand* 7°25N 99°31E **39** J2
Ban Karon *Thailand* 7°51N 98°18E **39** a
Ban Kata *Thailand* 7°50N 98°18E **39** a
Ban Keun *Laos* 18°22N 102°35E **38** C4
Ban Khai *Thailand* 12°46N 101°18E **38** F3
Ban Kheun *Laos* 20°13N 101°7E **38** B3
Ban Khlong Khian *Thailand* 8°10N 98°26E **39** a
Ban Khlong Kua *Thailand* 6°57N 100°8E **39** J3
Ban Khuan *Thailand* 8°20N 98°25E **39** a
Ban Ko Yai Chim
  Thailand 11°17N 99°26E **39** G2
Ban Laem *Thailand* 13°13N 99°59E **38** F2
Ban Lamai *Thailand* 9°28N 100°3E **39** b
Ban Le Kathe *Thailand* 15°49N 98°53E **38** E2
Ban Lo Po Noi *Thailand* 8°1N 98°34E **39** a
Ban Mae Chedi *Thailand* 19°11N 99°31E **38** C2
Ban Mae Nam *Thailand* 9°34N 100°0E **39** b
Ban Mae Sariang
  Thailand 18°10N 97°56E **38** C1
Ban Mê Thuột = Buon Ma Thuot
  Vietnam 12°40N 108°3E **38** F7
Ban Mi *Thailand* 15°3N 100°32E **38** E3
Ban Muang Mo *Laos* 19°4N 103°58E **38** C4
Ban Na Bo *Thailand* 9°19N 99°41E **39** b
Ban Na San *Thailand* 8°53N 99°52E **39** H2
Ban Na Tong *Laos* 20°56N 101°47E **38** B3
Ban Nam Bac *Laos* 20°38N 102°20E **38** B4
Ban Nammi *Laos* 17°7N 105°40E **38** D5

Ban Nong Bok *Laos* 17°5N 104°48E **38** D5
Ban Nong Pling *Thailand* 15°40N 100°10E **38** E3
Ban Pak Chan *Thailand* 10°32N 98°51E **39** G2
Ban Patong *Thailand* 7°54N 98°18E **39** a
Ban Phai *Thailand* 16°4N 102°44E **38** D4
Ban Phak Chit *Thailand* 9°0N 98°24E **39** a
Ban Pong *Thailand* 13°50N 99°55E **38** F2
Ban Rawai *Thailand* 7°47N 98°20E **39** a
Ban Ron Phibun *Thailand* 8°9N 99°51E **39** H2
Ban Sakhu *Thailand* 8°4N 98°18E **39** a
Ban Sanam Chai *Thailand* 7°33N 100°25E **39** J3
Ban Tak *Thailand* 17°2N 99°4E **38** D2
Ban Tako *Thailand* 14°5N 102°40E **38** E4
Ban Tha Nun *Thailand* 8°12N 98°18E **39** a
Ban Tha Rua *Thailand* 7°59N 98°22E **39** a
Ban Tha Yu *Thailand* 8°17N 98°22E **39** a
Ban Thong Krut *Thailand* 9°25N 99°57E **39** b
Ban Xien Kok *Laos* 20°54N 100°39E **38** B3
Ban Yen Nhan *Vietnam* 20°57N 106°2E **38** B6
Banaba *Kiribati* 0°45S 169°50E **64** H8
Banagher *Ireland* 53°11N 7°59W **10** C3
Banalia
  Dem. Rep. of the Congo 1°32N 25°5E **54** D5
Banam *Cambodia* 11°20N 105°17E **39** G5
Bananal, I. do *Brazil* 11°30S 50°30W **93** F8
Bananga *India* 6°57N 93°54E **45** L11
Banaras = Varanasi *India* 25°22N 83°0E **43** G10
Banas → *Gujarat, India* 23°45N 71°25E **42** H4
Banas → *Mad. P., India* 24°15N 81°30E **43** G9
Bânâs, Ras *Egypt* 23°N 35°59E **53** D13
Banbridge *U.K.* 54°22N 6°16W **10** B5
Banbury *U.K.* 52°4N 1°20W **13** E6
Banchory *U.K.* 57°3N 2°29W **11** D6
Bancroft *Canada* 45°3N 77°51W **82** A7
Band Bonī *Iran* 25°30N 59°33E **47** E8
Band Qīr *Iran* 31°39N 48°53E **47** D6
Banda *Mad. P., India* 24°3N 78°57E **43** G8
Banda *Maharashtra, India* 15°49N 73°52E **45** G1
Banda *U. P., India* 25°30N 80°26E **43** G9
Banda, Kepulauan
  Indonesia 4°37S 129°50E **37** E7
Banda Aceh *Indonesia* 5°35N 95°20E **36** C1
Banda Banda, Mt.
  Australia 31°10S 152°28E **63** E5
Banda Elat *Indonesia* 5°40S 133°5E **37** F8
Banda Is. = Banda, Kepulauan
  Indonesia 4°37S 129°50E **37** E7
Banda Sea *Indonesia* 6°0S 130°0E **37** F8
Bandai-Asahi △ *Japan* 37°38N 140°0E **28** F10
Bandai-San *Japan* 37°36N 140°4E **28** F10
Bandān *Iran* 31°23N 60°44E **47** D9
Bandanaira *Indonesia* 4°32S 129°54E **37** E7
Bandanwara *India* 26°9N 74°38E **42** F6
Bandar = Machilipatnam
  India 16°12N 81°8E **45** F5
Bandar-e Abbās *Iran* 27°15N 56°15E **47** E8
Bandar-e Anzalī *Iran* 37°30N 49°30E **47** B6
Bandar-e Bushehr = Büshehr
  Iran 28°55N 50°55E **47** D6
Bandar-e Chārak *Iran* 26°45N 54°20E **47** E7
Bandar-e Deylam *Iran* 30°30N 50°45E **47** D6
Bandar-e Emām Khomeynī
  Iran 30°30N 49°5E **47** D6
Bandar-e Lengeh *Iran* 26°35N 54°58E **47** E7
Bandar-e Maqām *Iran* 26°56N 53°29E **47** E7
Bandar-e Ma'shur *Iran* 30°35N 49°10E **47** D6
Bandar-e Rīg *Iran* 29°29N 50°38E **47** D6
Bandar-e Torkeman *Iran* 37°0N 54°10E **47** B7
Bandar Labuan *Malaysia* 5°20N 115°14E **36** C5
Bandar Lampung
  Indonesia 5°20S 105°10E **36** F3
Bandar Maharani = Muar
  Malaysia 2°3N 102°34E **39** L4
Bandar Penggaram = Batu Pahat
  Malaysia 1°50N 102°56E **39** M4
Bandar Seri Begawan
  Brunei 4°52N 115°0E **36** D5
Bandar Sri Aman
  Malaysia 1°15N 111°32E **36** D4
Bandeira, Pico da *Brazil* 20°26S 41°47W **95** A7
Bandera *Argentina* 28°55S 62°20W **94** B3
Banderas, B. de *Mexico* 20°40N 105°25W **86** C3
Bandhavgarh *India* 23°40N 81°2E **44** C5
Bandhavgarh △ *India* 23°45N 81°10E **44** C5
Bandi → *India* 26°12N 75°47E **42** F6
Bandia → *India* 19°2N 80°28E **44** E5
Bandikui *India* 27°3N 76°34E **42** F7
Bandipur △ *India* 11°45N 76°30E **45** H3
Bandırma *Turkey* 40°20N 28°0E **23** D13
Bandjarmasin = Banjarmasin
  Indonesia 3°20S 114°35E **36** E4
Bandon *Ireland* 51°44N 8°44W **10** E3
Bandon → *Ireland* 51°43N 8°37W **10** E3
Bandundu
  Dem. Rep. of the Congo 3°15S 17°22E **54** E3
Bandung *Indonesia* 6°54S 107°36E **37** G12
Bāneh *Iran* 35°59N 45°53E **46** C5
Banes *Cuba* 21°0N 75°42W **89** B4
Banff *Canada* 51°10N 115°34W **70** C5
Banff *U.K.* 57°40N 2°33W **11** D6
Banff △ *Canada* 51°30N 116°15W **70** C5
Bang Fai → *Laos* 16°57N 104°45E **38** D5
Bang Hieng → *Laos* 16°10N 105°10E **38** D5
Bang Krathum *Thailand* 16°34N 100°18E **38** D3
Bang Lamung *Thailand* 13°3N 100°56E **38** F3
Bang Lang △ *Thailand* 5°57N 101°20E **39** K3
Bang Lang Res. *Thailand* 6°6N 101°17E **39** J3
Bang Mun Nak *Thailand* 16°2N 100°23E **38** D3
Bang Pa In *Thailand* 14°14N 100°38E **38** E3
Bang Rakam *Thailand* 16°45N 100°7E **38** D3
Bang Saphan *Thailand* 11°14N 99°28E **39** G2
Bang Thao *Thailand* 7°59N 98°18E **39** a
Banga → *India* 21°34N 88°52E **43** J13
Bangalore *India* 12°59N 77°40E **45** H3
Banganapalle *India* 15°19N 78°14E **45** G4
Banganga → *India* 27°6N 77°25E **42** F6
Bangaon *India* 23°0N 88°47E **43** H13
Bangassou *C.A.R.* 4°55N 23°7E **54** D4
Banggai *Indonesia* 1°34S 123°30E **37** E6

Banggai, Kepulauan
  Indonesia 1°40S 123°30E **37** E6
Banggai Arch. = Banggai,
  Kepulauan *Indonesia* 1°40S 123°30E **37** E6
Banggi, Pulau *Malaysia* 7°17N 117°12E **36** C5
Banghāzī *Libya* 32°11N 20°3E **53** B10
Bangka *Sulawesi, Indonesia* 1°50N 125°5E **37** D7
Bangka *Sumatera, Indonesia* 2°0S 105°50E **36** E3
Bangka, Selat *Indonesia* 2°30S 105°30E **36** E3
Bangka-Belitung □
  Indonesia 2°30S 107°0E **36** E3
Bangkalan *Indonesia* 7°2S 112°46E **37** G15
Bangkang *Burma* 22°4N 99°1E **34** F2
Bangkinang *Indonesia* 0°18N 101°5E **36** D2
Bangko *Indonesia* 2°5S 102°9E **36** E2
Bangkok, Bight of
  Thailand 12°55N 100°30E **38** F3
Bangla = Paschimbanga □
  India 23°0N 88°0E **43** H13
Bangladesh ■ *Asia* 24°0N 90°0E **41** H17
Bangli *Indonesia* 8°27S 115°21E **37** J18
Bangong Co *China* 33°45N 78°43E **43** C8
Bangor *Down, U.K.* 54°40N 5°40W **10** B6
Bangor *Gwynedd, U.K.* 53°14N 4°8W **12** D3
Bangor *Maine, U.S.A.* 44°48N 68°46W **81** C19
Bangor *Pa., U.S.A.* 40°52N 75°13W **83** F9
Bangued *Phil.* 17°40N 120°37E **37** A6
Bangui *C.A.R.* 4°23N 18°35E **54** D3
Bangweulu, L. *Zambia* 11°0S 30°0E **54** G6
Banhine △ *Mozam.* 22°49S 32°55E **57** B5
Bani *Dom. Rep.* 18°16N 70°22W **89** C5
Banī Sa'd *Iraq* 33°34N 44°32E **46** C5
Banihal Pass *India* 33°30N 75°12E **43** C6
Bāniyās *Syria* 35°10N 36°0E **46** C3
Banja Luka *Bos.-H.* 44°49N 17°11E **22** B7
Banjar *India* 31°38N 77°21E **42** D7
Banjar → *India* 22°36N 80°22E **43** H9
Banjarmasin *Indonesia* 3°20S 114°35E **36** E4
Banjul *Gambia* 13°28N 16°40W **52** F2
Banka *India* 24°53N 86°55E **43** G12
Bankipore *India* 25°35N 85°10E **41** G14
Bankot *India* 17°55N 73°12E **44** F1
Banks I. = Moa *Australia* 10°11S 142°16E **62** a
Banks I. *B.C., Canada* 53°20N 130°0W **70** C3
Banks I. *N.W.T., Canada* 73°15N 121°30W **68** C7
Banks Pen. *N.Z.* 43°45S 173°15E **59** E4
Banks Str. *Australia* 40°40S 148°10E **63** G4
Bankura *India* 23°11N 87°18E **43** H12
Banmankhi *India* 25°53N 87°11E **43** G12
Bann → *Armagh, U.K.* 54°30N 6°31W **10** B5
Bann → *L'derry., U.K.* 55°8N 6°41W **10** A5
Bannang Sata *Thailand* 6°16N 101°16E **39** J3
Banning *U.S.A.* 33°56N 116°53W **79** M10
Bannockburn *Canada* 44°39N 77°33W **82** B7
Bannockburn *U.K.* 56°5N 3°55W **11** E5
Bannu *Pakistan* 33°0N 70°18E **40** C7
Bano *India* 22°40N 84°55E **43** H11
Bansagar Dam *India* 24°11N 81°17E **44** B5
Bansgaon *India* 26°33N 83°21E **43** F10
Banská Bystrica
  Slovak Rep. 48°46N 19°14E **17** D10
Banswara *India* 23°32N 74°24E **42** H6
Bantaeng *Indonesia* 5°32S 119°56E **37** F5
Banteay Prei Nokor
  Cambodia 11°56N 105°40E **39** G5
Banten □ *Indonesia* 6°30S 106°0E **37** G11
Bantry *Ireland* 51°41N 9°27W **10** E2
Bantry B. *Ireland* 51°37N 9°44W **10** E2
Bantva *India* 21°29N 70°12E **42** J4
Bantval *India* 12°55N 75°0E **45** H2
Banyak, Kepulauan
  Indonesia 2°10N 97°10E **36** D1
Banyo *Cameroon* 6°52N 11°45E **54** C2
Banyuwangi *Indonesia* 8°13S 114°21E **37** J17
Banzare Coast *Antarctica* 68°0S 125°0E **5** C9
Bao Ha *Vietnam* 22°11N 104°21E **34** F5
Bao Lac *Vietnam* 22°57N 105°40E **34** A5
Bao Loc *Vietnam* 11°32N 107°48E **39** G6
Bao'an *China* 22°34N 113°52E **31** a
Baocheng *China* 33°12N 106°56E **34** H4
Baode *China* 39°1N 111°5E **32** E6
Baoding *China* 38°50N 115°28E **32** E8
Baoji *China* 34°20N 107°5E **32** G4
Baojing *China* 28°45N 109°41E **34** C7
Baokang *China* 31°54N 111°12E **35** B8
Baotou *China* 40°32N 110°2E **32** D6
Baoxing *China* 30°24N 102°56E **34** B4
Baoying *China* 33°17N 119°20E **33** H10
Baoyou = Ledong *China* 18°41N 109°5E **38** C7
Bap *India* 27°23N 72°18E **42** F5
Bapatla *India* 15°55N 80°30E **45** G5
Bāqerābād *Iran* 33°2N 51°58E **47** C6
Ba'qūbah *Iraq* 33°45N 44°50E **46** C5
Baquedano *Chile* 23°20S 69°52W **94** A2
Bar *Montenegro* 42°8N 19°6E **23** C8
Bar *Ukraine* 49°4N 27°40E **17** D14
Bar Bigha *India* 25°21N 85°47E **43** G11
Bar Harbor *U.S.A.* 44°23N 68°13W **81** C19
Bar-le-Duc *France* 48°47N 5°10E **20** B6
Bara Banki *India* 26°55N 81°43E **43** F9
Barabai *Indonesia* 2°32S 115°34E **36** E5
Baraboo *U.S.A.* 43°28N 89°45W **80** D9
Baracoa *Cuba* 20°20N 74°30W **89** B5
Baradā → *Syria* 33°33N 36°34E **48** B5
Baradero *Argentina* 33°52S 59°29W **94** C4
Barabona *Dom. Rep.* 18°13N 71°7W **89** C5
Barail Range *India* 25°15N 93°20E **41** G18
Barakaldo *Spain* 43°18N 2°59W **21** A4
Barakar → *India* 24°7N 83°44E **43** G11
Barakot *India* 21°33N 84°59E **43** J11
Baralaba *Australia* 24°13S 149°50E **62** C4
Baralzon L. *Canada* 60°0N 98°3W **71** B9
Baramati *India* 18°11N 74°33E **44** D2
Baramba *India* 20°25N 85°23E **44** D7

Baramula *India* 34°15N 74°20E **43** B6
Baran *India* 25°9N 76°40E **42** G7
Baran → *Pakistan* 25°13N 68°17E **42** G3
Baranavichy *Belarus* 53°10N 26°0E **17** B14
Baranof *U.S.A.* 57°5N 134°50W **70** B2
Baranof I. *U.S.A.* 57°0N 135°0W **68** F4
Barapasi *Indonesia* 2°15S 137°5E **37** E9
Barasat *India* 22°46N 88°31E **43** H13
Barat Daya, Kepulauan
  Indonesia 7°30S 128°0E **37** F7
Baratang I. *India* 12°13N 92°45E **45** H11
Barataria B. *U.S.A.* 29°20N 89°55W **85** G10
Barauda *India* 23°33N 75°15E **42** H6
Baraut *India* 29°13N 77°7E **42** E7
Barbacena *Brazil* 21°15S 43°56W **95** A7
Barbados ■ *W. Indies* 13°10N 59°30W **89** g
Barbas, C. *W. Sahara* 22°20N 16°42W **52** D2
Barbastro *Spain* 42°2N 0°5E **21** A6
Barbeau Pk. *Canada* 81°54N 75°1W **69** A4
Barberton *S. Africa* 25°42S 31°2E **57** C5
Barberton *U.S.A.* 41°1N 81°39W **82** E3
Barbosa *Colombia* 5°57N 73°37W **92** B4
Barbourville *U.S.A.* 36°52N 83°53W **81** G12
Barbuda *W. Indies* 17°30N 61°40W **89** C7
Barcaldine *Australia* 23°43S 145°6E **62** C4
Barcellona Pozzo di Gotto
  Italy 38°9N 15°13E **22** E6
Barcelona *Venezuela* 10°10N 64°40W **92** A6
Barceloneta *Puerto Rico* 18°27N 66°32W **89** d
Barcelos *Brazil* 1°0S 63°0W **92** D6
Barcoo → *Australia* 25°30S 142°50E **62** D3
Bardaï *Chad* 21°25N 17°0E **53** D9
Bardas Blancas *Argentina* 35°49S 69°45W **94** D2
Bardawīl, Sabkhet el
  Egypt 31°10N 33°15E **48** D2
Barddhaman *India* 23°14N 87°39E **43** H12
Bardejov *Slovak Rep.* 49°18N 21°15E **17** D11
Bardera = Baardheere
  Somalia 2°20N 42°27E **49** G3
Bardīyah *Libya* 31°45N 25°5E **53** B10
Bardoli *India* 21°12N 73°5E **44** D1
Bardsey I. *U.K.* 52°45N 4°47W **12** E3
Bardstown *U.S.A.* 37°49N 85°28W **81** G11
Bareilly *India* 28°22N 79°27E **43** E8
Barela *India* 23°6N 80°3E **43** H9
Barents Sea *Arctic* 73°0N 39°0E **4** B9
Barfleur, Pte. de *France* 49°42N 1°16W **20** B3
Bargara *Australia* 24°50S 152°25E **62** C5
Bargarh *India* 21°20N 83°37E **44** D6
Bargi Dam *India* 22°59N 80°0E **44** C5
Barh *India* 25°29N 85°46E **43** G11
Barharwa *India* 24°52N 87°47E **43** G12
Barhi *India* 24°15N 85°25E **43** G11
Bari *India* 26°39N 77°39E **42** F7
Bari *Italy* 41°8N 16°51E **22** D7
Bari Doab *Pakistan* 30°20N 73°0E **42** D5
Bari Sadri *India* 24°28N 74°30E **42** G6
Barīdī, Ra's *Si. Arabia* 24°17N 37°31E **46** E3
Barīm *Yemen* 12°39N 43°25E **50** E8
Barinas *Venezuela* 8°36N 70°15W **92** B4
Baring, C. *Canada* 70°0N 117°30W **68** D8
Baripada *India* 21°57N 86°45E **44** D8
Barisal *Bangla.* 22°45N 90°20E **41** H17
Barisal □ *Bangla.* 22°45N 90°20E **41** H17
Barisan, Pegunungan
  Indonesia 3°30S 102°15E **36** E2
Barito → *Indonesia* 4°0S 114°50E **36** E4
Baritú △ *Argentina* 23°43S 64°40W **94** A3
Barjūj, Wadi → *Libya* 25°26N 12°12E **53** C8
Bark L. *Canada* 45°27N 77°51W **82** A7
Barkakana *India* 23°37N 85°29E **43** H11
Barkam *China* 31°51N 102°28E **34** B4
Barker *U.S.A.* 43°20N 78°33W **82** C6
Barkley, L. *U.S.A.* 37°1N 88°14W **85** C10
Barkley Sound *Canada* 48°50N 125°10W **70** D3
Barkly East *S. Africa* 30°58S 27°33E **56** E4
Barkly Homestead
  Australia 19°52S 135°50E **62** B2
Barkly Tableland
  Australia 17°50S 136°40E **62** B2
Barkly West *S. Africa* 28°5S 24°31E **56** D3
Barkol Kazak Zizhixian
  China 43°37N 93°2E **30** C7
Bârlad *Romania* 46°15N 27°38E **17** E14
Bârlad → *Romania* 45°38N 27°32E **17** F14
Barlee, L. *Australia* 29°15S 119°30E **61** E2
Barlee, Mt. *Australia* 24°38S 128°13E **61** D4
Barletta *Italy* 41°19N 16°17E **22** D7
Barlovento *C. Verde Is.* 17°0N 25°0W **52** b
Barlow L. *Canada* 62°0N 103°0W **71** A8
Barmedman *Australia* 34°9S 147°21E **63** E4
Barmer *India* 25°45N 71°20E **42** G4
Barmera *Australia* 34°15S 140°28E **63** E3
Barmouth *U.K.* 52°44N 4°4W **12** E3
Barna → *India* 25°21N 83°3E **43** G10
Barnagar *India* 23°7N 75°19E **42** H6
Barnala *India* 30°23N 75°33E **42** D6
Barnard Castle *U.K.* 54°33N 1°55W **12** C6
Barnaul *Russia* 53°20N 83°40E **26** D9
Barnesville *Ga., U.S.A.* 33°3N 84°9W **85** E12
Barnesville *Minn., U.S.A.* 46°43N 96°28W **80** B5
Barnet □ *U.K.* 51°38N 0°9W **13** F7
Barneveld *Neths.* 52°7N 5°36E **15** B5
Barnhart *U.S.A.* 31°8N 101°10W **84** F4
Barnsley *U.K.* 53°34N 1°27W **12** D6
Barnstable *U.S.A.* 41°42N 70°18W **81** E18
Barnstaple *U.K.* 51°5N 4°4W **13** F3
Barnstaple Bay = Bideford Bay
  U.K. 51°5N 4°20W **13** F3
Barnwell *U.S.A.* 33°15N 81°23W **85** E14
Baro *Nigeria* 8°35N 6°18E **52** G7
Baroda = Vadodara *India* 22°20N 73°10E **42** H5
Baroda *India* 25°29N 76°35E **42** G7
Baroe *S. Africa* 33°13S 24°33E **56** D3
Baron Ra. *Australia* 23°30S 127°45E **60** D4
Barong *China* 31°3N 99°20E **34** B2
Barotseland *Zambia* 15°0S 24°0E **55** H4

Barpali India 21°11N 83°35E 44 D6
Barpeta India 26°20N 91°10E 41 F17
Barqa Libya 27°0N 23°0E 53 C10
Barques, Pt. Aux U.S.A. 44°4N 82°58W 82 B2
Barquísimeto Venezuela 10°4N 69°19W 92 A5
Barr Smith Range
  Australia 27°4S 120°20E 61 E3
Barra Brazil 11°5S 43°10W 93 F10
Barra U.K. 57°0N 7°29W 11 E1
Barra, Sd. of U.K. 57°4N 7°25W 11 D1
Barra de Navidad
  Mexico 19°12N 104°41W 86 D4
Barra do Corda Brazil 5°30S 45°10W 93 E9
Barra do Garças Brazil 15°54S 52°16W 93 G8
Barra do Piraí Brazil 22°30S 43°50W 95 A7
Barra Falsa, Pta. da
  Mozam. 22°58S 35°37E 57 B6
Barra Hd. U.K. 56°47N 7°40W 11 E1
Barra Mansa Brazil 22°35S 44°12W 95 A7
Barraba Australia 30°21S 150°35E 63 E5
Barranca Lima, Peru 10°45S 77°50W 92 F3
Barranca Loreto, Peru 4°50S 76°50W 92 D3
Barranca del Cobre △
  Mexico 27°18N 107°40W 86 B3
Barrancabermeja Colombia 7°0N 73°50W 92 B4
Barrancas Venezuela 8°55N 62°5W 92 B6
Barrancos Portugal 38°10N 6°58W 21 C2
Barranqueras Argentina 27°30S 59°0W 94 B4
Barranquilla Colombia 11°0N 74°50W 92 A4
Barraute Canada 48°26N 77°38W 72 C4
Barre Mass., U.S.A. 42°25N 72°6W 83 D12
Barre Vt., U.S.A. 44°12N 72°30W 83 B12
Barreal Argentina 31°33S 69°28W 94 C2
Barreiras Brazil 12°8S 45°0W 93 F10
Barreirinhas Brazil 2°30S 42°50W 93 D10
Barren, Nosy Madag. 18°25S 43°40E 55 H8
Barren I. India 12°16N 93°51E 45 H11
Barretos Brazil 20°30S 48°35W 93 H9
Barrhead Canada 54°10N 114°24W 70 C6
Barrie Canada 44°24N 79°40W 82 B5
Barrier Ra. Australia 31°0S 141°30E 63 E3
Barrière Canada 51°12N 120°7W 70 C4
Barrington U.S.A. 41°44N 71°18W 83 E13
Barrington L. Canada 56°55N 100°15W 71 B8
Barrington Tops Australia 32°6S 151°28E 63 E5
Barringun Australia 29°1S 145°41E 63 D4
Barron U.S.A. 45°24N 91°51W 80 C8
Barrow U.S.A. 71°18N 156°47W 74 A8
Barrow → Ireland 52°25N 6°58W 10 D5
Barrow, Pt. U.S.A. 71°23N 156°29W 74 A8
Barrow Creek Australia 21°30S 133°55E 62 C1
Barrow I. Australia 20°45S 115°20E 60 D2
Barrow-in-Furness U.K. 54°7N 3°14W 12 C4
Barrow Pt. Australia 14°20S 144°40E 62 A3
Barrow Ra. Australia 26°0S 127°40E 61 E4
Barrow Str. Canada 74°20N 95°0W 4 B3
Barry U.K. 51°24N 3°16W 13 F4
Barry's Bay Canada 45°29N 77°41W 82 A7
Barsat Pakistan 36°10N 72°45E 43 A5
Barsi India 18°10N 75°50E 44 E2
Barsoi India 25°48N 87°57E 41 G15
Barstow U.S.A. 34°54N 117°1W 79 L9
Bartica Guyana 6°25N 58°40W 92 B7
Bartle Frere Australia 17°27S 145°50E 62 B4
Bartlesville U.S.A. 36°45N 95°59W 84 C7
Bartlett Calif., U.S.A. 36°29N 118°2W 78 J8
Bartlett Tenn., U.S.A. 35°12N 89°52W 85 D10
Bartlett, L. Canada 63°5N 118°20W 70 A5
Barton U.S.A. 44°45N 72°11W 83 B12
Barton upon Humber
  U.K. 53°41N 0°25W 12 D7
Bartow U.S.A. 27°54N 81°50W 85 H14
Barú, Volcan Panama 8°55N 82°35W 88 E3
Barung, Nusa Indonesia 8°30S 113°30E 37 H15
Baruun Urt Mongolia 46°46N 113°15E 31 B11
Baruunsuu Mongolia 43°43N 105°35E 32 C3
Barwani India 22°2N 74°57E 42 H6
Barysaw Belarus 54°17N 28°28E 17 A15
Barzán Iraq 36°55N 44°3E 46 B5
Bāsa'idū Iran 26°35N 55°20E 47 E7
Basal Pakistan 33°33N 72°13E 42 C5
Basankusa
  Dem. Rep. of the Congo 1°5N 19°50E 54 D3
Basarabeasca Moldova 46°21N 28°58E 17 E15
Basarabia = Bessarabiya
  Moldova 47°0N 28°10E 17 E15
Basawa Afghan. 34°15N 70°50E 42 B4
Bascuñán, C. Chile 28°52S 71°35W 94 B1
Basel Switz. 47°35N 7°35E 20 C7
Bashākerd, Kūhhā-ye
  Iran 26°42N 58°35E 47 E8
Bashaw Canada 52°35N 112°58W 70 C6
Bāshī Iran 28°41N 51°4E 47 D6
Bashkir Republic =
  Bashkortostan □
  Russia 54°0N 57°0E 18 D10
Bashkortostan □ Russia 54°0N 57°0E 18 D10
Basilan I. Phil. 6°35N 122°0E 37 C6
Basilan Str. Phil. 6°50N 122°0E 37 C6
Basildon U.K. 51°34N 0°28E 13 F8
Basim = Washim India 20°3N 77°0E 44 D3
Basin U.S.A. 44°23N 108°2W 76 D9
Basingstoke U.K. 51°15N 1°5W 13 F6
Baskatong, Rés. Canada 46°46N 75°50W 72 C4
Basle = Basel Switz. 47°35N 7°35E 20 C7
Basmat India 19°15N 77°12E 44 E3
Basoda India 23°52N 77°54E 42 H7
Basque Provinces = País Vasco □
  Spain 42°50N 2°45W 21 A4
Basra = Al Baṣrah Iraq 30°30N 47°50E 46 D5
Bass Str. Australia 39°15S 146°30E 63 F4
Bassano Canada 50°48N 112°20W 70 C6
Bassano del Grappa Italy 45°46N 11°44E 22 B4
Bassas da India Ind. Oc. 22°0S 39°0E 57 B6
Basse-Pointe Martinique 14°52N 61°8W 88 c
Basse-Terre Guadeloupe 16°0N 61°44W 88 b
Basse Terre Trin. & Tob. 10°7N 61°19W 93 K15
Basses, Pte. des Guadeloupe 15°52N 61°17W 88 b

Basseterre
  St. Kitts & Nevis 17°17N 62°43W 89 C7
Bassett U.S.A. 42°35N 99°32W 80 D4
Bassi India 30°44N 76°21E 42 D7
Bastak Iran 27°15N 54°25E 47 E7
Basti India 26°52N 82°55E 43 F10
Bastia France 42°40N 9°30E 20 E8
Bastogne Belgium 50°1N 5°43E 15 D5
Bastrop La., U.S.A. 32°47N 91°55W 84 E9
Bastrop Tex., U.S.A. 30°7N 97°19W 84 F6
Basuo = Dongfang
  China 18°50N 108°33E 38 C7
Bat Yam Israel 32°2N 34°44E 48 C3
Bataan □ Phil. 14°40N 120°25E 37 B6
Batabanó Cuba 22°41N 82°18W 88 B3
Batabanó, G. de Cuba 22°30N 82°30W 88 B3
Batac Phil. 18°3N 120°34E 37 A6
Batagai Russia 67°38N 134°38E 27 C14
Batala India 31°48N 75°12E 42 D6
Batamay Russia 63°30N 129°15E 27 C13
Batang China 30°1N 99°0E 34 B2
Batang Indonesia 6°55S 109°45E 37 G13
Batangafo C.A.R. 7°25N 18°20E 54 C3
Batangas Phil. 13°35N 121°10E 37 B6
Batavia U.S.A. 43°0N 78°11W 82 D6
Batchelor Australia 13°4S 131°1E 60 B5
Batemans B. Australia 35°40S 150°12E 63 F5
Batemans Bay Australia 35°44S 150°11E 63 F5
Batesburg-Leesville
  U.S.A. 33°54N 81°33W 85 E14
Batesville Ark., U.S.A. 35°46N 91°39W 84 D9
Batesville Miss., U.S.A. 34°19N 89°57W 85 D10
Batesville Tex., U.S.A. 28°58N 99°37W 84 G5
Bath Canada 44°11N 76°47W 83 B8
Bath U.K. 51°23N 2°22W 13 F5
Bath Maine, U.S.A. 43°55N 69°49W 81 D19
Bath N.Y., U.S.A. 42°20N 77°19W 82 D7
Bath & North East Somerset □
  U.K. 51°21N 2°27W 13 F5
Batheay Cambodia 11°59N 104°57E 39 G5
Bathsheba Barbados 13°13N 59°32W 89 g
Bathurst Australia 33°25S 149°31E 63 E4
Bathurst Canada 47°37N 65°43W 73 C6
Bathurst S. Africa 33°30S 26°50E 56 D4
Bathurst, C. Canada 70°34N 128°0W 68 C6
Bathurst B. Australia 14°16S 144°25E 62 A3
Bathurst Harb. Australia 43°15S 146°10E 63 G4
Bathurst I. Australia 11°30S 130°10E 60 B5
Bathurst I. Canada 76°0N 100°30W 69 B11
Bathurst Inlet Canada 66°50N 108°1W 68 D10
Batiki Fiji 17°48S 179°10E 59 a
Batlow Australia 35°31S 148°9E 63 F4
Batman Turkey 37°55N 41°5E 46 B4
Baṭn al Ghūl Jordan 29°36N 35°56E 48 F4
Batna Algeria 35°34N 6°15E 52 A7
Baton Rouge U.S.A. 30°27N 91°11W 84 F9
Batong, Ko Thailand 6°32N 99°12E 39 J2
Batopilas Mexico 27°1N 107°44W 86 B3
Batouri Cameroon 4°30N 14°25E 54 D2
Båtsfjord Norway 70°38N 29°39E 8 A23
Battambang = Batdambang
  Cambodia 13°7N 103°12E 38 F4
Batti Malv India 8°50N 92°51E 45 K11
Batticaloa Sri Lanka 7°43N 81°45E 45 L5
Battipáglia Italy 40°37N 14°58E 22 D6
Battle U.K. 50°55N 0°30E 13 G8
Battle → Canada 52°43N 108°15W 71 C7
Battle Creek U.S.A. 42°19N 85°11W 81 D11
Battle Ground U.S.A. 45°47N 122°32W 78 E4
Battle Harbour Canada 52°16N 55°35W 73 B8
Battle Lake U.S.A. 46°17N 95°43W 80 B6
Battle Mountain U.S.A. 40°38N 116°56W 76 F5
Battleford Canada 52°45N 108°15W 71 C7
Batu Ethiopia 6°55N 39°45E 49 F2
Batu Malaysia 3°15N 101°40E 39 L3
Batu, Kepulauan Indonesia 0°30S 98°25E 36 E1
Batu Ferringhi Malaysia 5°28N 100°15E 39 c
Batu Gajah Malaysia 4°28N 101°3E 39 K3
Batu Is. = Batu, Kepulauan
  Indonesia 0°30S 98°25E 36 E1
Batu Pahat Malaysia 1°50N 102°56E 39 M4
Batu Puteh, Gunung
  Malaysia 4°15N 101°31E 39 K3
Batuata Indonesia 6°12S 122°42E 37 F6
Batugondang, Tanjung
  Indonesia 8°6S 114°29E 37 J17
Batumi Georgia 41°39N 41°44E 19 F7
Batur, Gunung Indonesia 8°14S 115°23E 37 J18
Batura Sar Pakistan 36°30N 74°31E 43 A6
Baturaja Indonesia 4°11S 104°15E 36 E2
Baturité Brazil 4°28S 38°45W 93 D11
Baturiti Indonesia 8°19S 115°11E 37 J18
Bau Malaysia 1°25N 110°9E 36 D4
Baubau Indonesia 5°25S 122°38E 37 F6
Baucau E. Timor 8°27S 126°27E 37 F7
Bauchi Nigeria 10°22N 9°48E 52 F7
Bauda India 20°32N 84°24E 44 D7
Baudette U.S.A. 48°43N 94°36W 80 A6
Bauhinia Australia 24°35S 149°18E 62 C4
Baukau = Baucau
  E. Timor 8°27S 126°27E 37 F7
Bauld, C. Canada 51°38N 55°26W 69 G20
Bauru Brazil 22°10S 49°0W 95 A6
Bausi India 24°48N 87°1E 43 G12
Bauska Latvia 56°24N 24°15E 9 H21
Bautzen Germany 51°10N 14°26E 16 C8
Bavānāt Iran 30°28N 53°27E 47 D7
Bavaria = Bayern □
  Germany 48°50N 12°0E 16 D6
Bavispe → Mexico 29°15N 109°11W 86 B3

Bawdwin Burma 23°5N 97°20E 41 H20
Bawean Indonesia 5°46S 112°35E 36 F4
Bawku Ghana 11°3N 0°19W 52 F5
Bawlake Burma 19°11N 97°21E 41 K20
Bawolung China 28°50N 101°16E 34 C3
Baxley U.S.A. 31°47N 82°21W 85 F13
Baxter U.S.A. 46°21N 94°17W 80 B6
Baxter Springs U.S.A. 37°2N 94°44W 80 G6
Baxter State △ U.S.A. 46°5N 68°57W 81 B19
Bay City Mich., U.S.A. 43°36N 83°54W 81 D12
Bay City Tex., U.S.A. 28°59N 95°58W 84 G7
Bay Minette U.S.A. 30°53N 87°46W 85 F11
Bay Roberts Canada 47°36N 53°16W 73 C9
Bay St. Louis U.S.A. 30°19N 89°20W 85 F10
Bay Springs U.S.A. 31°59N 89°17W 85 F10
Bay View N.Z. 39°25S 176°50E 59 C6
Bayamo Cuba 20°20N 76°40W 88 B4
Bayamón Puerto Rico 18°24N 66°9W 89 d
Bayan Har Shan China 34°0N 98°0E 30 E8
Bayan Hot = Alxa Zuoqi
  China 38°50N 105°40E 32 E3
Bayan Lepas Malaysia 5°17N 100°16E 39 c
Bayan Obo China 41°52N 109°59E 32 D5
Bayan-Ovoo = Erdenetsogt
  Mongolia 42°55N 106°5E 32 C4
Bayana India 26°55N 77°18E 42 F7
Bayanaūyl Kazakhstan 50°45N 75°45E 26 D8
Bayanhongor Mongolia 46°8N 102°43E 30 B9
Bayard N. Mex., U.S.A. 32°46N 108°8W 77 K9
Bayard Nebr., U.S.A. 41°45N 103°20W 80 E2
Baybay Phil. 10°40N 124°55E 37 B6
Baydaratskaya Guba
  Russia 69°0N 67°30E 26 C7
Baydhabo Somalia 3°8N 43°30E 49 G3
Bayern □ Germany 48°50N 12°0E 16 D6
Bayeux France 49°17N 0°42W 20 B3
Bayfield Canada 43°34N 81°42W 82 C3
Bayfield U.S.A. 46°49N 90°49W 80 B8
Bayındır Turkey 38°13N 27°39E 23 E12
Baykal, Oz. Russia 53°0N 108°0E 27 D11
Baykan Turkey 38°7N 41°44E 46 B4
Baymak Russia 52°36N 58°19E 18 D10
Baynes Mts. Namibia 17°15S 13°0E 56 A1
Baymbong Phil. 16°30N 121°10E 37 A6
Bayonne France 43°30N 1°28W 20 E3
Bayovar Peru 5°50S 81°0W 92 E2
Bayqongyr Kazakhstan 45°40N 63°20E 26 E7
Bayram-Ali = Baýramaly
  Turkmenistan 37°37N 62°10E 47 B9
Baýramaly Turkmenistan 37°37N 62°10E 47 B9
Bayramiç Turkey 39°48N 26°36E 23 E12
Bayreuth Germany 49°56N 11°35E 16 D6
Bayrūt Lebanon 33°53N 35°31E 48 B4
Bays, L. of Canada 45°15N 79°4W 82 A5
Baysville Canada 45°9N 79°7W 82 A5
Baytown U.S.A. 29°43N 94°59W 84 G7
Baza Spain 37°30N 2°47W 21 D4
Bazaruto, I. do Mozam. 21°40S 35°28E 57 B6
Bazaruto △ Mozam. 21°42S 35°26E 57 B6
Bazhong China 31°52N 106°46E 34 B6
Bazhou China 39°8N 116°22E 32 E9
Bazmān, Kūh-e Iran 28°4N 60°1E 47 D9
Bé, Nosy Madag. 13°25S 48°15E 55 G9
Beach U.S.A. 46°58N 104°0W 80 B2
Beach City U.S.A. 40°39N 81°35W 82 F3
Beachport Australia 37°29S 140°0E 63 F3
Beachville Canada 43°5N 80°49W 82 C4
Beachy Hd. U.K. 50°44N 0°15E 13 G8
Beacon Australia 30°26S 117°52E 61 F2
Beacon U.S.A. 41°30N 73°58W 83 E11
Beaconsfield Australia 41°11S 146°48E 63 G4
Beagle, Canal S. Amer. 55°0S 68°30W 96 H3
Beagle Bay Australia 16°58S 122°40E 60 C3
Beagle Bay ◇ Australia 16°53S 122°40E 60 C3
Beagle G. Australia 12°15S 130°25E 60 B5
Béal an Átha = Ballina
  Ireland 54°7N 9°9W 10 B2
Béal Átha na Sluaighe =
  Ballinasloe Ireland 53°20N 8°13W 10 C3
Beals Cr. → U.S.A. 32°10N 100°51W 84 E4
Beamsville Canada 43°12N 79°28W 82 C5
Bear → Calif., U.S.A. 38°56N 121°36W 78 G5
Bear → Utah, U.S.A. 41°30N 112°8W 74 G17
Bear I. Ireland 51°38N 9°50W 10 E2
Bear L. Canada 55°8N 96°0W 71 B9
Bear L. U.S.A. 41°59N 111°21W 76 F8
Bear Lake Canada 45°27N 79°35W 82 A5
Beardmore Canada 49°36N 87°57W 72 C2
Beardmore Glacier
  Antarctica 84°30S 170°0E 5 E11
Beardstown U.S.A. 40°1N 90°26W 80 E8
Bearma → India 24°20N 79°51E 43 G8
Béarn France 43°20N 0°30W 20 E3
Bearpaw Mts. U.S.A. 48°12N 109°30W 76 B9
Bearskin Lake Canada 53°58N 91°2W 72 B1
Beas → India 31°10N 74°59E 42 D6
Beata, C. Dom. Rep. 17°40N 71°30W 89 C5
Beata, I. Dom. Rep. 17°34N 71°31W 89 C5
Beatrice U.S.A. 40°16N 96°45W 80 E5
Beatrice, C. Australia 14°20S 136°55E 62 A2
Beatton → Canada 56°15N 120°45W 70 B4
Beatton River Canada 57°26N 121°20W 70 B4
Beatty U.S.A. 36°54N 116°46W 78 J10
Beau Bassin Mauritius 20°13S 57°27E 55 d
Beauce, Plaine de la
  France 48°10N 1°45E 20 B4
Beauceville Canada 46°13N 70°46W 73 C5
Beaudesert Australia 27°59S 153°0E 63 D5
Beaufort Malaysia 5°30N 115°40E 36 C5
Beaufort N.C., U.S.A. 34°43N 76°40W 85 D16
Beaufort S.C., U.S.A. 32°26N 80°40W 85 E14
Beaufort Sea Arctic 72°0N 140°0W 66 B5
Beaufort West S. Africa 32°18S 22°36E 56 D3
Beauharnois Canada 45°20N 73°52W 83 A11
Beaulieu → Canada 62°3N 113°11W 70 A6
Beauly U.K. 57°30N 4°28W 11 D4
Beauly → U.K. 57°29N 4°27W 11 D4
Beaumaris U.K. 53°16N 4°6W 12 D3
Beaumont Belgium 50°15N 4°14E 15 D4

Beaumont Calif., U.S.A. 33°57N 116°59W 79 M9
Beaumont Tex., U.S.A. 30°5N 94°6W 84 F7
Beaune France 47°2N 4°50E 20 C6
Beaupré Canada 47°3N 70°54W 73 C5
Beauraing Belgium 50°7N 4°57E 15 D4
Beausejour Canada 50°5N 96°35W 71 C9
Beauvais France 49°25N 2°8E 20 B5
Beauval Canada 55°9N 107°37W 71 B7
Beaver Okla., U.S.A. 36°49N 100°31W 84 C4
Beaver Pa., U.S.A. 40°42N 80°19W 82 F4
Beaver Utah, U.S.A. 38°17N 112°38W 76 G7
Beaver → B.C., Canada 59°52N 124°20W 70 B4
Beaver → Ont., Canada 55°55N 87°48W 72 A2
Beaver → Sask., Canada 55°26N 107°45W 71 B7
Beaver → U.S.A. 36°35N 99°30W 84 C5
Beaver City U.S.A. 40°8N 99°50W 80 E4
Beaver Creek Canada 63°0N 141°0W 68 E3
Beaver Dam U.S.A. 43°28N 88°50W 80 D9
Beaver Falls U.S.A. 40°46N 80°20W 82 F4
Beaver Hill L. Canada 54°5N 94°50W 71 C10
Beaver I. U.S.A. 45°40N 85°33W 81 C11
Beavercreek U.S.A. 39°43N 84°11W 81 F11
Beaverhill L. Canada 53°27N 112°32W 70 C6
Beaverlodge Canada 55°11N 119°29W 70 B5
Beaverstone → Canada 54°59N 89°25W 72 B2
Beaverton Canada 44°26N 79°9W 82 B5
Beaverton U.S.A. 45°29N 122°48W 78 E4
Beawar India 26°3N 74°18E 42 F6
Bebedouro Brazil 21°0S 48°25W 95 A6
Bebera, Tanjung
  Indonesia 8°44S 115°51E 37 K18
Becán Mexico 18°34N 89°31W 87 D7
Bécancour Canada 46°20N 72°26W 81 B17
Beccles U.K. 52°27N 1°35E 13 E9
Bečej Serbia 45°36N 20°3E 23 B9
Béchar Algeria 31°38N 2°18W 52 B5
Becharof L. U.S.A. 57°56N 156°23W 74 D8
Beckley U.S.A. 37°47N 81°11W 81 G13
Beddouza, C. Morocco 32°33N 9°9E 52 B4
Bedford Canada 45°7N 72°59W 83 A12
Bedford S. Africa 32°40S 26°10E 56 D4
Bedford U.K. 52°8N 0°28W 13 E7
Bedford Ind., U.S.A. 38°52N 86°29W 80 F10
Bedford Iowa, U.S.A. 40°40N 94°44W 80 E6
Bedford Ohio, U.S.A. 41°23N 81°32W 82 E3
Bedford Pa., U.S.A. 40°1N 78°30W 82 F6
Bedford Va., U.S.A. 37°20N 79°31W 81 G14
Bedford, C. Australia 15°14S 145°21E 62 B4
Bedourie Australia 24°30S 139°30E 62 C2
Bedti → India 14°50N 74°44E 45 G2
Bedugul Indonesia 8°17S 115°10E 37 J18
Bedum Neths. 53°18N 6°36E 15 A6
Beebe Plain Canada 45°1N 72°9W 83 A12
Beech Creek U.S.A. 41°5N 77°36W 82 E7
Beechy Canada 50°53N 107°24W 71 C7
Beed = Bir India 18°46N 74°4E 44 E2
Beef I. Br. Virgin Is. 18°26N 64°30W 89 e
Beenleigh Australia 27°43S 153°10E 63 D5
Be'er Menuḥa Israel 30°19N 35°8E 46 D2
Be'er Sheva Israel 31°15N 34°48E 48 D3
Beersheba = Be'er Sheva
  Israel 31°15N 34°48E 48 D3
Beestekraal S. Africa 25°23S 27°38E 57 C4
Beeston U.K. 52°56N 1°14W 12 E6
Beeton Canada 44°5N 79°47W 82 B5
Beeville U.S.A. 28°24N 97°45W 84 G6
Befale
  Dem. Rep. of the Congo 0°25N 20°45E 54 D4
Bega Australia 36°41S 149°51E 63 F4
Begusarai India 25°24N 86°9E 43 G12
Behähäd Iran 32°24N 59°47E 47 C8
Behbehän Iran 30°30N 50°15E 47 D6
Behm Canal U.S.A. 55°10N 131°0W 70 B2
Behshahr Iran 36°45N 53°35E 47 B7
Bei Jiang → China 23°2N 112°58E 35 F9
Bei Shan China 41°30N 96°0E 30 C8
Bei'an China 48°10N 126°20E 31 B14
Beibei China 29°47N 106°22E 34 C6
Beichuan China 31°55N 104°39E 34 B5
Beihai China 21°28N 109°6E 34 G7
Beijing □ China 39°55N 116°20E 32 E9
Beilen Neths. 52°52N 6°27E 15 B6
Beiliu China 22°41N 110°21E 35 F8
Beilpajah Australia 32°54S 143°52E 63 E3
Beinn na Faoghla = Benbecula
  U.K. 57°26N 7°21W 11 D1
Beipan Jiang → China 25°54N 106°36E 34 E6
Beipiao China 41°52N 120°32E 33 D11
Beira Mozam. 19°50S 34°52E 55 H6
Beirut = Bayrūt Lebanon 33°53N 35°31E 48 B4
Beiseker Canada 51°23N 113°32W 70 C6
Beit Lāḥīyā Gaza Strip 31°33N 34°30E 48 D3
Beitaolaizhao China 44°58N 125°58E 33 B13
Beitbridge Zimbabwe 22°12S 30°0E 55 J6
Beizhen = Binzhou
  China 37°20N 118°2E 33 F10
Beizhen China 41°38N 121°54E 33 D11
Beizhengzhen China 44°31N 123°30E 33 B12
Beja Portugal 38°2N 7°53W 21 C2
Béja Tunisia 36°43N 9°12E 52 A7
Bejaïa Algeria 36°42N 5°2E 52 A7
Béjar Spain 40°23N 5°46W 21 B3
Bejestān Iran 34°30N 58°5E 47 C8
Bekaa Valley = Al Biqā
  Lebanon 34°10N 36°10E 48 A5
Bekasi Indonesia 6°14S 106°59E 37 G12
Békéscsaba Hungary 46°40N 21°5E 17 E11
Bekok Malaysia 2°20N 103°7E 39 L4
Bela India 25°50N 82°0E 43 G10
Bela Pakistan 26°12N 66°20E 42 F2
Bela Bela S. Africa 24°51S 28°19E 57 B4
Bela Crkva Serbia 44°55N 21°27E 23 B9
Bela Vista Brazil 22°12S 56°20W 94 A4
Bela Vista Mozam. 26°10S 32°44E 57 D5
Belan → India 24°2N 81°45E 43 G9
Belarus ■ Europe 53°30N 27°0E 17 B14

Belau = Palau ■ Palau 7°30N 134°30E 58 A6
Belawan Indonesia 3°33N 98°32E 36 D1
Belaya → Russia 54°40N 56°0E 18 C9
Belaya Tserkov = Bila Tserkva
  Ukraine 49°45N 30°10E 17 D16
Belaya Zemlya, Ostrova
  Russia 81°36N 62°18E 26 A7
Belcher Is. Canada 56°15N 78°45W 72 A3
Belden U.S.A. 40°2N 121°17W 78 E5
Belebey Russia 54°7N 54°7E 18 D9
Beledweyne Somalia 4°30N 45°5E 49 G4
Belém Brazil 1°20S 48°30W 93 D9
Belén Argentina 27°40S 67°5W 94 B2
Belén Paraguay 23°30S 57°6W 94 A4
Belen U.S.A. 34°40N 106°46W 77 J10
Belet Uen = Beledweyne
  Somalia 4°30N 45°5E 49 G4
Belev Russia 53°50N 36°5E 18 D6
Belfair U.S.A. 47°27N 122°50W 78 C4
Belfast = eMakhazeni
  S. Africa 25°42S 30°2E 57 C5
Belfast U.K. 54°37N 5°56W 10 B6
Belfast Maine, U.S.A. 44°26N 69°1W 81 C17
Belfast N.Y., U.S.A. 42°21N 78°7W 82 D6
Belfast L. U.K. 54°40N 5°50W 10 B6
Belfield U.S.A. 46°53N 103°12W 80 B2
Belfort France 47°38N 6°52E 20 C7
Belfry U.S.A. 45°9N 109°1W 76 D9
Belgaum India 15°55N 74°35E 45 G2
Belgium ■ Europe 50°30N 5°0E 15 D4
Belgorod Russia 50°35N 36°35E 19 D6
Belgorod-Dnestrovskiy = Bilhorod-
  Dnistrovskyy Ukraine 46°11N 30°23E 19 E5
Belgrade = Beograd
  Serbia 44°50N 20°37E 23 B9
Belgrade U.S.A. 45°47N 111°11W 76 D8
Belgrano Antarctica 77°52S 34°37W 5 D1
Belhaven U.S.A. 35°33N 76°37W 85 D16
Beli Drim → Europe 42°6N 20°25E 23 C9
Belimbing Indonesia 8°24S 115°2E 37 J18
Belinyu Indonesia 1°35S 105°50E 36 E3
Beliton Is. = Belitung
  Indonesia 3°10S 107°50E 36 E3
Belitung Indonesia 3°10S 107°50E 36 E3
Belize ■ Cent. Amer. 17°0N 88°30W 87 D7
Belize Barrier Reef Belize 17°9N 88°3W 87 D7
Belize City Belize 17°25N 88°0W 87 D7
Belkovskiy, Ostrov
  Russia 75°32N 135°44E 27 B14
Bell → Canada 49°48N 77°38W 72 C4
Bell I. Canada 50°46N 55°35W 73 B8
Bell-Irving → Canada 56°12N 129°5W 70 B3
Bell Peninsula Canada 63°50N 82°0W 69 E15
Bell Ville Argentina 32°40S 62°40W 94 C3
Bella Bella Canada 52°10N 128°10W 70 C3
Bella Coola Canada 52°25N 126°40W 70 C3
Bella Unión Uruguay 30°15S 57°40W 94 C4
Bella Vista Corrientes,
  Argentina 28°33S 59°0W 94 B4
Bella Vista Tucuman,
  Argentina 27°10S 65°25W 94 B2
Bellaire U.S.A. 40°1N 80°45W 82 F4
Bellary India 15°10N 76°56E 45 G3
Bellata Australia 29°53S 149°46E 63 D4
Belle Fourche U.S.A. 44°40N 103°51W 80 C2
Belle Fourche → U.S.A. 44°26N 102°18W 80 C2
Belle Glade U.S.A. 26°41N 80°40W 85 H14
Belle-Île France 47°20N 3°10W 20 C2
Belle Isle Canada 51°57N 55°25W 73 B8
Belle Isle, Str. of Canada 51°30N 56°30W 73 B8
Belle Plaine Canada 54°9N 92°17W 80 E7
Belle River Canada 42°18N 82°43W 82 D2
Bellefontaine U.S.A. 40°22N 83°46W 81 E12
Bellefonte U.S.A. 40°55N 77°47W 82 F7
Belleoram Canada 47°31N 55°25W 73 C8
Belleplaine Barbados 13°15N 59°34W 89 g
Belleville Canada 44°10N 77°23W 82 B7
Belleville Ill., U.S.A. 38°31N 89°59W 80 F9
Belleville Kans., U.S.A. 39°50N 97°38W 80 F5
Belleville N.J., U.S.A. 40°47N 74°9W 83 F10
Belleville N.Y., U.S.A. 43°46N 76°10W 83 C8
Bellevue Canada 49°35N 114°22W 70 D6
Bellevue Idaho, U.S.A. 43°28N 114°16W 76 E6
Bellevue Nebr., U.S.A. 41°9N 95°54W 80 E6
Bellevue Ohio, U.S.A. 41°17N 82°51W 82 E2
Bellevue Wash., U.S.A. 47°37N 122°12W 78 C4
Bellin = Kangirsuk
  Canada 60°0N 70°0W 69 F18
Bellingen Australia 30°25S 152°50E 63 E5
Bellingham U.S.A. 48°46N 122°29W 78 B4
Bellingshausen Abyssal Plain
  S. Ocean 64°0S 90°0W 5 C16
Bellingshausen Sea
  Antarctica 66°0S 80°0W 5 C17
Bellinzona Switz. 46°11N 9°1E 20 C8
Bello Colombia 6°20N 75°33W 92 B3
Bellows Falls U.S.A. 43°8N 72°27W 83 C12
Bellpat Pakistan 29°0N 68°5E 42 E3
Belluno Italy 46°9N 12°13E 22 A5
Bellwood U.S.A. 40°36N 78°20W 82 F6
Belmont Canada 42°53N 81°5W 82 D3
Belmont S. Africa 29°28S 24°22E 56 D3
Belmont U.S.A. 42°14N 78°2W 82 D6
Belmonte Brazil 16°0S 39°0W 93 G11
Belmopan Belize 17°18N 88°30W 87 D7
Belmullet Ireland 54°14N 9°58W 10 B2
Belo Horizonte Brazil 19°55S 43°56W 93 G10
Belo-Tsiribihina Madag. 19°40S 44°30E 55 H8
Belogorsk Russia 51°0N 128°20E 27 D13
Beloit Kans., U.S.A. 39°28N 98°6W 80 F4
Beloit Wis., U.S.A. 42°31N 89°2W 80 D9
Belokorovichi Ukraine 51°7N 28°2E 17 C15
Belomorsk Russia 64°35N 34°54E 18 B5
Belonia India 23°15N 91°30E 41 H17
Belorussia = Belarus ■
  Europe 53°30N 27°0E 17 B14
Belovo Russia 54°30N 86°0E 26 D9

Beloyarskiy *Russia* 63°42N 66°40E **26 C7**
Beloye, Ozero *Russia* 60°10N 37°35E **18 B6**
Beloye More *Russia* 66°30N 38°0E **18 A6**
Belozersk *Russia* 60°1N 37°45E **18 B6**
Belpre *U.S.A.* 39°17N 81°34W **81 F13**
Belrain *India* 28°23N 80°55E **43 E9**
Belt *U.S.A.* 47°23N 110°55W **76 C8**
Beltana *Australia* 30°48S 138°25E **63 E2**
Belterra *Brazil* 2°45S 55°0W **93 D8**
Belton *U.S.A.* 31°3N 97°28W **84 F6**
Belton L. *U.S.A.* 31°6N 97°28W **84 F6**
Beltsy = Bălți *Moldova* 47°48N 27°58E **17 E14**
Belturbet *Ireland* 54°6N 7°26W **10 B4**
Belukha *Russia* 49°50N 86°50E **30 B6**
Beluran *Malaysia* 5°48N 117°35E **36 C5**
Belushya Guba *Russia* 71°32N 52°19E **26 B6**
Belvidere *Ill., U.S.A.* 42°15N 88°50W **80 D9**
Belvidere *N.J., U.S.A.* 40°50N 75°5W **83 F9**
Belyando → *Australia* 21°38S 146°50E **62 C4**
Belyando Crossing
    Australia 21°32S 146°51E **62 C4**
Belyuen *Australia* 12°34S 130°42E **60 B5**
Belyy, Ostrov *Russia* 73°30N 71°0E **26 B8**
Belyy Yar *Russia* 58°26N 84°39E **26 D9**
Belzoni *U.S.A.* 33°11N 90°29W **85 E9**
Bembéréke *Benin* 10°11N 2°43E **52 G6**
Bemetara *India* 21°42N 81°32E **43 J9**
Bemidji *U.S.A.* 47°28N 94°53W **80 B6**
Ben *Iran* 32°32N 50°45E **47 C6**
Ben Cruachan *U.K.* 56°26N 5°8W **11 E3**
Ben Dearg *U.K.* 57°47N 4°56W **11 D4**
Ben En △ *Vietnam* 19°37N 105°30E **38 C5**
Ben Gardane *Tunisia* 33°11N 11°11E **53 B8**
Ben Hope *U.K.* 58°25N 4°36W **11 C4**
Ben Lawers *U.K.* 56°32N 4°14W **11 E4**
Ben Lomond *N.S.W.,*
    Australia 30°1S 151°43E **63 E5**
Ben Lomond *Tas.,*
    Australia 41°38S 147°42E **63 G4**
Ben Lomond *U.K.* 56°11N 4°38W **11 E4**
Ben Lomond △ *Australia* 41°33S 147°39E **63 G4**
Ben Luc *Vietnam* 10°39N 106°29E **39 G6**
Ben Macdhui *U.K.* 57°4N 3°40W **11 D5**
Ben Mhor *U.K.* 57°15N 7°18W **11 D1**
Ben More *Argyll & Bute,*
    U.K. 56°26N 6°1W **11 E2**
Ben More *Stirling, U.K.* 56°23N 4°32W **11 E4**
Ben More Assynt *U.K.* 58°8N 4°52W **11 C4**
Ben Nevis *U.K.* 56°48N 5°1W **11 E3**
Ben Quang *Vietnam* 17°3N 106°55E **38 D6**
Ben Vorlich *U.K.* 56°21N 4°14W **11 E4**
Ben Wyvis *U.K.* 57°40N 4°35W **11 D4**
Bena *Nigeria* 11°20N 5°50E **52 F7**
Benalla *Australia* 36°30S 146°0E **63 F4**
Benares = Varanasi *India* 25°22N 83°0E **43 G10**
Benavente *Spain* 42°2N 5°43W **21 A3**
Benavides *U.S.A.* 27°36N 98°25W **84 H5**
Benbecula *U.K.* 57°26N 7°21W **11 D1**
Benbonyathe Hill
    Australia 30°25S 139°11E **63 E2**
Bend *U.S.A.* 44°4N 121°19W **76 D3**
Bender Beyla *Somalia* 9°30N 50°48E **49 F5**
Bendery = Tighina
    Moldova 46°50N 29°30E **17 E15**
Bendigo *Australia* 36°40S 144°15E **63 F3**
Benê Beraq *Israel* 32°6N 34°51E **48 C3**
Benevento *Italy* 41°8N 14°45E **22 D6**
Beng Mealea *Cambodia* 13°28N 104°14E **38 F5**
Bengal, Bay of *Ind. Oc.* 15°0N 90°0E **41 M17**
Bengaluru = Bangalore
    India 12°59N 77°40E **45 H3**
Bengbu *China* 32°58N 117°20E **33 H9**
Benghazi = Banghāzī
    Libya 32°11N 20°3E **53 B10**
Bengkalis *Indonesia* 1°30N 102°10E **39 M4**
Bengkulu *Indonesia* 3°50S 102°12E **36 E2**
Bengkulu □ *Indonesia* 3°48S 102°16E **36 E2**
Bengough *Canada* 49°25N 105°10W **71 D7**
Benguela *Angola* 12°37S 13°25E **55 G2**
Benguérua, I. *Mozam.* 21°58S 35°28E **57 B6**
Beni *Dem. Rep. of the Congo* 0°30N 29°27E **54 D5**
Beni → *Bolivia* 10°23S 65°24W **92 F5**
Beni Mellal *Morocco* 32°21N 6°21W **52 B4**
Beni Suef *Egypt* 29°5N 31°6E **53 C12**
Benidorm *Spain* 38°33N 0°9W **21 C5**
Benin ■ *Africa* 10°0N 2°0E **52 G6**
Benin, Bight of *W. Afr.* 5°0N 3°0E **52 H6**
Benin City *Nigeria* 6°20N 5°31E **52 G7**
Benito Juárez *Argentina* 37°40S 59°43W **94 D4**
Benjamin Aceval
    Paraguay 24°58S 57°34W **94 A4**
Benjamin Constant *Brazil* 4°40S 70°15W **92 D4**
Benjamin Hill *Mexico* 30°9N 111°7W **86 A2**
Benkelman *U.S.A.* 40°3N 101°32W **80 E3**
Bennett *Canada* 59°51N 135°0W **70 B2**
Bennett, L. *Australia* 22°50S 131°2E **60 D5**
Bennetta, Ostrov
    Russia 76°21N 148°56E **27 B15**
Bennettsville *U.S.A.* 34°37N 79°41W **85 D15**
Bennington *N.H., U.S.A.* 43°0N 71°55W **83 D11**
Bennington *Vt., U.S.A.* 42°53N 73°12W **83 D11**
Benom *Malaysia* 3°50N 102°6E **39 L4**
Benoni *S. Africa* 26°11S 28°18E **57 C4**
Benque Viejo del Carmen
    Belize 17°5N 89°8W **87 D7**
Benson *Ariz., U.S.A.* 31°58N 110°18W **77 L8**
Benson *Minn., U.S.A.* 45°19N 95°36W **80 C6**
Bent *Iran* 26°20N 59°31E **47 E8**
Benteng *Indonesia* 6°10S 120°30E **37 F6**
Bentinck I. *Australia* 17°3S 139°35E **62 B2**
Bentinck I. *Burma* 11°45N 98°3E **39 G2**
Bentley Subglacial Trench
    Antarctica 80°0S 115°0W **5 E15**
Bento Gonçalves *Brazil* 29°10S 51°31W **95 B5**
Benton *Ark., U.S.A.* 34°34N 92°35W **84 D8**
Benton *Calif., U.S.A.* 37°48N 118°32W **78 H8**
Benton *Ill., U.S.A.* 38°0N 88°55W **80 F9**

Benton *Pa., U.S.A.* 41°12N 76°23W **83 E8**
Benton Harbor *U.S.A.* 42°6N 86°27W **80 D10**
Bentong *Malaysia* 3°31N 101°55E **39 L3**
Bentonville *U.S.A.* 36°22N 94°13W **84 C7**
Benue → *Nigeria* 7°48N 6°46E **52 G7**
Benxi *China* 41°20N 123°48E **33 D12**
Beo *Indonesia* 4°25N 126°50E **37 D7**
Beograd *Serbia* 44°50N 20°37E **23 B9**
Beolgyo *S. Korea* 34°51N 127°21E **33 G14**
Beppu *Japan* 33°15N 131°30E **29 H5**
Beqa *Fiji* 18°23S 178°8E **59 a**
Beqaa Valley = Al Biqâ
    Lebanon 34°10N 36°10E **48 A5**
Ber Mota *India* 23°27N 68°34E **42 H3**
Bera, Tasik *Malaysia* 3°5N 102°38E **39 L4**
Berach → *India* 25°15N 75°2E **42 G6**
Berastagi *Indonesia* 3°11N 98°31E **39 L2**
Berat *Albania* 40°43N 19°59E **23 D8**
Berau = Tanjungredeb
    Indonesia 2°9N 117°29E **36 D5**
Berau, Teluk *Indonesia* 2°30S 132°30E **37 E8**
Berber *Sudan* 18°0N 34°0E **53 E12**
Berbera *Somalia* 10°30N 45°2E **49 E4**
Berbérati *C.A.R.* 4°15N 15°40E **54 D3**
Berbice → *Guyana* 6°20N 57°32W **92 B7**
Berdichev = Berdychiv
    Ukraine 49°57N 28°30E **17 D15**
Berdsk *Russia* 54°47N 83°2E **26 D9**
Berdyansk *Ukraine* 46°45N 36°50E **19 E6**
Berdychiv *Ukraine* 49°57N 28°30E **17 D15**
Berea *U.S.A.* 37°34N 84°17W **81 G11**
Berebere *Indonesia* 2°25N 128°45E **37 D7**
Berehove *Ukraine* 48°15N 22°35E **17 D12**
Bereket *Turkmenistan* 39°16N 55°32E **47 B7**
Berekum *Ghana* 7°29N 2°34W **52 G5**
Berens → *Canada* 52°25N 97°2W **71 C9**
Berens I. *Canada* 52°18N 97°18W **71 C9**
Berens River *Canada* 52°25N 97°0W **71 C9**
Beresford *U.S.A.* 43°5N 96°47W **80 D5**
Berestechko *Ukraine* 50°22N 25°5E **17 C13**
Bereza = Byaroza
    Belarus 52°31N 24°51E **17 B13**
Berezhany *Ukraine* 49°26N 24°58E **17 D13**
Berezina = Byarezina →
    Belarus 52°33N 30°14E **17 B16**
Bereznik *Russia* 62°51N 42°40E **18 B7**
Berezniki *Russia* 59°24N 56°46E **18 C10**
Berezovo *Russia* 64°0N 65°0E **26 C7**
Berga *Spain* 42°6N 1°48E **21 A6**
Bergama *Turkey* 39°8N 27°11E **23 E12**
Bérgamo *Italy* 45°41N 9°43E **20 D8**
Bergaon *India* 20°41N 80°27E **44 D5**
Bergen *Neths.* 52°40N 4°43E **15 B4**
Bergen *Norway* 60°20N 5°20E **8 F11**
Bergen *U.S.A.* 43°5N 77°57W **82 C7**
Bergen op Zoom *Neths.* 51°28N 4°18E **15 C4**
Bergerac *France* 44°51N 0°30E **20 D4**
Bergholz *U.S.A.* 40°31N 80°53W **82 F4**
Bergville *S. Africa* 28°52S 29°18E **57 C4**
Berhala, Selat *Indonesia* 1°0S 104°15E **36 E2**
Berhampore = Baharampur
    India 24°2N 88°27E **43 G13**
Berhampur = Brahmapur
    India 19°15N 84°54E **44 E7**
Bering Glacier *U.S.A.* 60°20N 143°30W **74 C11**
Bering Sea *Pac. Oc.* 58°0N 171°0W **66 D2**
Bering Strait *Pac. Oc.* 65°30N 169°0W **74 B6**
Beringovskiy *Russia* 63°3N 179°19E **27 C18**
Berisso *Argentina* 34°56S 57°50W **94 C4**
Berja *Spain* 36°50N 2°56W **21 D4**
Berkner I. *Antarctica* 79°30S 50°0W **5 D18**
Berkshire □ *U.K.* 42°19N 76°11W **83 D8**
Berkshire Downs *U.K.* 51°33N 1°29W **13 F6**
Berlin *Md., U.S.A.* 38°20N 75°13W **81 F16**
Berlin *N.H., U.S.A.* 44°28N 71°11W **83 B13**
Berlin *N.Y., U.S.A.* 42°42N 73°23W **83 D11**
Berlin *Wis., U.S.A.* 43°58N 88°57W **80 D9**
Berlin L. *U.S.A.* 41°3N 81°0W **82 E4**
Bermejo → *Formosa,*
    Argentina 26°51S 58°23W **94 B4**
Bermejo → *San Juan,*
    Argentina 32°30S 67°30W **94 C2**
Bermejo, Paso = Uspallata, P. de
    Argentina 32°37S 69°22W **94 C2**
Bermen, L. *Canada* 53°35N 68°55W **73 B6**
Bermuda ☑ *Atl. Oc.* 32°18N 64°45W **67 F13**
Bern *Switz.* 46°57N 7°28E **20 C7**
Bernalillo *U.S.A.* 35°18N 106°33W **77 J10**
Bernardo de Irigoyen
    Argentina 26°15S 53°40W **95 B5**
Bernardsville *U.S.A.* 40°43N 74°34W **83 F10**
Bernasconi *Argentina* 37°55S 63°44W **94 D3**
Bernburg *Germany* 51°47N 11°44E **16 C6**
Berne = Bern *Switz.* 46°57N 7°28E **20 C7**
Berneray *U.K.* 57°43N 7°11W **11 D1**
Bernier I. *Australia* 24°50S 113°12E **61 D1**
Bernina, Piz *Switz.* 46°20N 9°54E **20 D8**
Beroun *Czech Rep.* 49°57N 14°5E **16 D8**
Berri *Australia* 34°14S 140°35E **63 E3**
Berriane *Algeria* 32°50N 3°46E **52 B6**
Berry *Australia* 34°46S 150°43E **63 E5**
Berry *France* 46°50N 2°0E **20 C5**
Berry Is. *Bahamas* 25°40N 77°50W **88 A4**
Berryessa, L. *U.S.A.* 38°31N 122°6W **78 G4**
Berryville *U.S.A.* 36°22N 93°34W **84 C8**
Berseba *Namibia* 26°0S 17°46E **56 C2**
Bershad *Ukraine* 48°22N 29°31E **17 D15**
Berthold *U.S.A.* 48°19N 101°44W **80 A3**
Berthoud *U.S.A.* 40°19N 105°5W **76 F11**
Bertoua *Cameroon* 4°30N 13°45E **54 D2**
Bertraghboy B. *Ireland* 53°22N 9°54W **10 C2**
Beruwala *Sri Lanka* 6°30N 80°0E **45 L4**
Berwick *U.S.A.* 41°3N 76°14W **83 E8**
Berwick-upon-Tweed *U.K.* 55°46N 2°0W **12 B6**
Berwyn Mts. *U.K.* 52°54N 3°26W **12 E4**
Besal *Pakistan* 35°4N 73°56E **43 B5**
Besalampy *Madag.* 16°43S 44°29E **55 H8**
Besançon *France* 47°15N 6°2E **20 C7**

Besar *Indonesia* 2°40S 116°0E **36 E5**
Besnard L. *Canada* 55°25N 106°0W **71 B7**
Besni *Turkey* 37°41N 37°52E **46 B3**
Besor, N. → *Egypt* 31°28N 34°22E **48 D3**
Bessarabia *Moldova* 47°0N 28°10E **17 E15**
Bessarabka = Basarabeasca
    Moldova 46°21N 28°58E **17 E15**
Bessemer *Ala., U.S.A.* 33°24N 86°58W **85 E11**
Bessemer *Mich., U.S.A.* 46°29N 90°3W **80 B8**
Bessemer *Pa., U.S.A.* 40°59N 80°30W **82 F4**
Beswick *Australia* 14°34S 132°53E **60 B5**
Beswick *Australia* 14°31S 132°51E **60 B5**
Bet She'an *Israel* 32°30N 35°30E **48 C4**
Bet Shemesh *Israel* 31°44N 35°0E **48 D4**
Betanzos *Spain* 43°15N 8°12W **21 A1**
Bétaré Oya *Cameroon* 5°40N 14°5E **54 C2**
Bethal *S. Africa* 26°27S 29°28E **57 C4**
Bethanien *Namibia* 26°31S 17°8E **56 C2**
Bethany *Canada* 44°11N 78°34W **82 B6**
Bethany *Mo., U.S.A.* 40°16N 94°2W **80 E6**
Bethany *Okla., U.S.A.* 35°31N 97°38W **84 D6**
Bethel *Alaska, U.S.A.* 60°48N 161°45W **74 C7**
Bethel *Conn., U.S.A.* 41°22N 73°25W **83 E11**
Bethel *Maine, U.S.A.* 44°25N 70°47W **83 B14**
Bethel *Vt., U.S.A.* 43°50N 72°38W **83 C12**
Bethel Park *U.S.A.* 40°19N 80°2W **82 F4**
Bethlehem *S. Africa* 28°14S 28°18E **57 C4**
Bethlehem *U.S.A.* 40°37N 75°23W **83 F9**
Bethulie *S. Africa* 30°30S 25°59E **56 D4**
Béthune *France* 50°30N 2°38E **20 A5**
Betioky *Madag.* 23°48S 44°20E **55 J8**
Betong *Malaysia* 1°24N 111°31E **36 D4**
Betong *Thailand* 5°45N 101°5E **39 K3**
Betoota *Australia* 25°45S 140°42E **62 D3**
Betpaqdala *Kazakhstan* 45°45N 70°30E **30 B3**
Betroka *Madag.* 23°16S 46°0E **55 J9**
Betsiamites *Canada* 48°56N 68°40W **73 C6**
Betsiamites → *Canada* 48°56N 68°38W **73 C6**
Bettendorf *U.S.A.* 41°32N 90°30W **80 E8**
Bettiah *India* 26°48N 84°33E **43 F11**
Betul *India* 21°58N 77°59E **44 D3**
Betws-y-Coed *U.K.* 53°5N 3°48W **12 D4**
Beulah *Mich., U.S.A.* 44°38N 86°6W **80 C10**
Beulah *N. Dak., U.S.A.* 47°16N 101°47W **80 B3**
Beveren *Belgium* 51°12N 4°16E **15 C4**
Beverley *Australia* 32°9S 116°56E **61 F2**
Beverley *U.K.* 53°51N 0°26W **12 D7**
Beverly *U.S.A.* 42°33N 70°53W **83 D14**
Beverly Hills *U.S.A.* 28°55N 82°28W **85 G13**
Bewas → *India* 23°59N 79°21E **43 H8**
Bexhill *U.K.* 50°51N 0°29E **13 G8**
Beyänlü *Iran* 36°0N 47°51E **46 C5**
Beyneu *Kazakhstan* 45°18N 55°9E **19 E10**
Beypazari *Turkey* 40°10N 31°56E **19 F5**
Beypore → *India* 11°10N 75°47E **45 J2**
Beyşehir Gölü *Turkey* 37°41N 31°33E **46 B1**
Bezwada = Vijayawada
    India 16°31N 80°39E **44 F5**
Bhabua *India* 25°3N 83°37E **43 G10**
Bhachau *India* 23°20N 70°16E **42 H4**
Bhadar → *Gujarat, India* 22°17N 72°20E **42 H5**
Bhadar → *Gujarat, India* 21°27N 69°47E **42 J3**
Bhadarwah *India* 32°58N 75°46E **43 C6**
Bhadgaon = Bhaktapur
    Nepal 27°38N 85°24E **43 F11**
Bhadohi *India* 25°25N 82°34E **43 G10**
Bhadra *India* 29°8N 75°14E **42 E6**
Bhadra → *India* 14°0N 75°20E **45 H2**
Bhadrachalam *India* 17°40N 80°53E **44 F5**
Bhadrak *India* 21°10N 86°30E **44 D8**
Bhadran *India* 22°19N 72°6E **42 H5**
Bhadravati *India* 13°49N 75°40E **45 H2**
Bhag *Pakistan* 29°2N 67°42E **42 E2**
Bhagalpur *India* 25°10N 87°0E **43 G12**
Bhagirathi → *Paschimbanga,*
    India 23°25N 88°23E **43 H13**
Bhagirathi → *Uttarakhand,*
    India 30°8N 78°35E **43 D8**
Bhainsa *India* 19°10N 77°58E **44 E3**
Bhakkar *Pakistan* 31°40N 71°5E **42 D4**
Bhakra Dam *India* 31°30N 76°45E **42 D7**
Bhaktapur *Nepal* 27°38N 85°24E **43 F11**
Bhalki *India* 18°2N 77°13E **44 E3**
Bhamo *Burma* 24°15N 97°15E **41 G20**
Bhamragarh *India* 19°30N 80°40E **44 E5**
Bhandara *India* 21°5N 79°42E **44 D4**
Bhanpura *India* 24°31N 75°44E **42 G6**
Bhanrer Ra. *India* 23°40N 79°45E **43 H8**
Bhaptiahi *India* 26°19N 86°44E **43 F12**
Bharat = India ■ *Asia* 20°0N 78°0E **40 K11**
Bharatpur *Chhattisgarh,*
    India 23°44N 81°46E **43 H9**
Bharatpur *Raj., India* 27°15N 77°30E **42 F7**
Bharatpur *Nepal* 27°34N 84°10E **43 F11**
Bharno *India* 23°14N 84°53E **43 H11**
Bharraig = Barra *U.K.* 57°0N 7°29W **11 E1**
Bharraig, Caolas = Barra, Sd. of
    U.K. 57°4N 7°25W **11 D1**
Bharuch *India* 21°47N 73°0E **44 D1**
Bhatarsaigh = Vatersay
    U.K. 56°55N 7°32W **11 E1**
Bhatghar L. *India* 18°10N 73°48E **44 E1**
Bhatkal *India* 13°58N 74°35E **45 H2**
Bhatpara *India* 22°50N 88°25E **43 H13**
Bhattu *India* 29°36N 75°19E **42 E6**
Bhaun *Pakistan* 32°55N 72°40E **42 C5**
Bhaunagar = Bhavnagar
    India 21°45N 72°10E **44 D1**
Bhavani *India* 11°27N 77°43E **45 J3**
Bhavnagar *India* 21°45N 72°10E **44 D1**
Bhawanipatna *India* 19°55N 83°10E **44 E5**
Bhawari *India* 25°42N 73°4E **42 G5**
Bhayavadar *India* 21°51N 70°15E **42 J4**
Bhearnaraigh = Berneray
    U.K. 57°43N 7°11W **11 D1**
Bhera *Pakistan* 32°29N 72°57E **42 C5**

Bheri → *Nepal* 28°47N 81°18E **43 E9**
Bhikangaon *India* 21°52N 75°57E **42 J6**
Bhilai = Bhilainagar-Durg
    India 21°13N 81°26E **44 D5**
Bhilainagar-Durg *India* 21°13N 81°26E **44 D5**
Bhilsa = Vidisha *India* 23°28N 77°53E **42 H7**
Bhilwara *India* 25°25N 74°38E **42 G6**
Bhima → *India* 16°25N 77°17E **44 F3**
Bhimavaram *India* 16°30N 81°30E **45 F5**
Bhimbar *Pakistan* 32°59N 74°3E **43 C6**
Bhind *India* 26°30N 78°46E **43 F8**
Bhinga *India* 27°43N 81°56E **43 F9**
Bhinmal *India* 25°0N 72°15E **42 G5**
Bhisho *S. Africa* 32°50S 27°23E **56 D4**
Bhiwandi *India* 19°20N 73°0E **44 E1**
Bhiwani *India* 28°50N 76°9E **42 E7**
Bhogava → *India* 22°26N 72°20E **42 H5**
Bhojpur *Nepal* 27°10N 87°3E **43 F12**
Bhokardan *India* 20°16N 75°46E **44 D2**
Bhola *Bangla.* 22°45N 90°35E **41 H17**
Bholari *Pakistan* 25°19N 68°13E **42 G3**
Bhongir *India* 17°30N 78°56E **44 F4**
Bhopal *India* 23°20N 77°30E **42 H7**
Bhopalpatnam *India* 18°52N 80°23E **44 E5**
Bhor *India* 18°12N 73°53E **44 E1**
Bhuban *India* 20°53N 85°50E **44 D7**
Bhubaneshwar *India* 20°15N 85°50E **44 D7**
Bhuj *India* 23°15N 69°49E **42 H3**
Bhumiphol Res. *Thailand* 17°20N 98°40E **38 D2**
Bhusawal *India* 21°3N 75°46E **44 D2**
Bhutan ■ *Asia* 27°25N 90°30E **41 F17**
Biafra, B. of = Bonny, Bight of
    Africa 3°30N 9°20E **54 D1**
Biak *Indonesia* 1°10S 136°6E **37 E9**
Biała Podlaska *Poland* 52°4N 23°6E **17 B12**
Białogard *Poland* 54°2N 15°58E **16 A8**
Białystok *Poland* 53°10N 23°10E **17 B12**
Biaora *India* 23°56N 76°56E **42 H7**
Biārjmand *Iran* 36°6N 55°53E **47 B7**
Biaro *Indonesia* 2°5N 125°26E **37 D7**
Biarritz *France* 43°29N 1°33W **20 E3**
Bibai *Japan* 43°19N 141°52E **28 C10**
Bibby I. *Canada* 61°55N 93°0W **71 A10**
Biberach *Germany* 48°5N 9°47E **16 D5**
Bibile *Sri Lanka* 7°10N 81°25E **45 L5**
Bicester *U.K.* 51°54N 1°9W **13 F6**
Bicheno *Australia* 41°52S 148°18E **63 G4**
Bichia *India* 22°27N 80°42E **43 H9**
Bickerton I. *Australia* 13°45S 136°10E **62 A2**
Bid = Bir *India* 19°4N 75°46E **44 E2**
Bida *Nigeria* 9°3N 5°58E **52 G7**
Bidar *India* 17°55N 77°35E **44 F3**
Biddeford *U.S.A.* 43°30N 70°28W **81 D18**
Bideford *U.K.* 51°1N 4°13W **13 F3**
Bideford Bay *U.K.* 51°5N 4°20W **13 F3**
Bidhuna *India* 26°49N 79°31E **43 F8**
Bidokht *Iran* 34°20N 58°46E **47 C8**
Bidor *Malaysia* 4°6N 101°15E **39 K3**
Bidyadanga *Australia* 18°45S 121°43E **60 C3**
Bié, Planalto de *Angola* 12°0S 16°0E **55 G3**
Bieber *U.S.A.* 41°7N 121°8W **76 F3**
Biel *Switz.* 47°8N 7°14E **20 C7**
Bielefeld *Germany* 52°1N 8°33E **16 B5**
Biella *Italy* 45°34N 8°3E **20 D8**
Bielsk Podlaski *Poland* 52°47N 23°12E **17 B12**
Bielsko-Biała *Poland* 49°50N 19°2E **17 D10**
Bien Hoa *Vietnam* 10°57N 106°49E **39 G6**
Bienne = Biel *Switz.* 47°8N 7°14E **20 C7**
Bienville, L. *Canada* 55°5N 72°40W **72 A5**
Biesbosch △ *Neths.* 51°45N 4°48E **15 C4**
Biesiesfontein *S. Africa* 30°57S 17°58E **56 D2**
Big → *Canada* 54°50N 58°55W **73 B8**
Big B. *Canada* 55°43N 60°35W **73 A7**
Big Bear City *U.S.A.* 34°16N 116°51W **79 L10**
Big Bear Lake *U.S.A.* 34°15N 116°56W **79 L10**
Big Belt Mts. *U.S.A.* 46°30N 111°25W **76 C8**
Big Bend *Swaziland* 26°50S 31°58E **57 C5**
Big Bend △ *U.S.A.* 29°20N 103°5W **84 G3**
Big Black → *U.S.A.* 32°3N 91°4W **85 F9**
Big Blue → *U.S.A.* 39°35N 96°34W **80 F5**
Big Buddha
    Hong Kong, China 22°15N 113°54E **31 a**
Big Creek *U.S.A.* 37°11N 119°14W **78 H7**
Big Cypress △ *U.S.A.* 26°0N 81°10W **85 H14**
Big Desert *Australia* 35°45S 141°10E **63 F3**
Big Falls *U.S.A.* 48°12N 93°48W **80 A7**
Big Fork → *U.S.A.* 48°31N 93°43W **80 A7**
Big Horn Mts. = Bighorn Mts.
    U.S.A. 44°25N 107°0W **76 D10**
Big I. *Canada* 61°7N 116°45W **70 A5**
Big Lake *U.S.A.* 31°12N 101°28W **84 F4**
Big Moose *U.S.A.* 43°49N 74°58W **83 C10**
Big Muddy Cr. →
    U.S.A. 48°8N 104°36W **76 B11**
Big Pine *U.S.A.* 37°10N 118°17W **78 H8**
Big Piney *U.S.A.* 42°32N 110°7W **76 E8**
Big Quill L. *Canada* 51°55N 104°50W **71 C8**
Big Rapids *U.S.A.* 43°42N 85°29W **81 D11**
Big Rideau L. *Canada* 44°40N 76°15W **83 B8**
Big River *Canada* 53°50N 107°0W **71 C7**
Big Run *U.S.A.* 40°57N 78°55W **82 F6**
Big Sable Pt. *U.S.A.* 44°3N 86°1W **80 C10**
Big Salmon → *Canada* 61°52N 134°55W **70 A2**
Big Sand L. *Canada* 57°45N 99°45W **71 B9**
Big Sandy *U.S.A.* 48°11N 110°7W **76 B8**
Big Sandy → *U.S.A.* 38°25N 82°36W **81 F12**
Big Sandy Cr. = Sandy Cr. →
    U.S.A. 41°51N 109°47W **76 F9**
Big Sandy Cr. → *U.S.A.* 38°7N 102°29W **76 G12**
Big Sioux → *U.S.A.* 42°29N 96°27W **80 D5**
Big South Fork △
    U.S.A. 36°27N 84°47W **85 C12**
Big Spring *U.S.A.* 32°15N 101°28W **84 E4**
Big Stone City *U.S.A.* 45°18N 96°28W **80 C5**
Big Stone Gap *U.S.A.* 36°52N 82°47W **81 G12**
Big Stone L. *U.S.A.* 45°30N 96°35W **80 C6**
Big Sur *U.S.A.* 36°15N 121°48W **78 J5**
Big Timber *U.S.A.* 45°50N 109°57W **76 D9**
Big Trout L. *Canada* 53°40N 90°0W **72 B2**

Big Trout Lake *Canada* 53°45N 90°0W **72 B2**
Biğa *Turkey* 40°13N 27°14E **23 D12**
Bigadiç *Turkey* 39°22N 28°7E **23 E13**
Biggar *Canada* 52°4N 108°0W **71 C7**
Biggar *U.K.* 55°38N 3°32W **11 F5**
Bigge I. *Australia* 14°35S 125°10E **60 B4**
Biggenden *Australia* 25°31S 152°4E **63 D5**
Biggleswade *U.K.* 52°5N 0°14W **13 E7**
Biggs *U.S.A.* 39°25N 121°43W **78 F5**
Bighorn *U.S.A.* 46°10N 107°27W **76 C10**
Bighorn → *U.S.A.* 46°10N 107°28W **76 C10**
Bighorn Canyon △
    U.S.A. 45°10N 108°0W **76 D9**
Bighorn L. *U.S.A.* 44°55N 108°15W **76 D9**
Bighorn Mts. *U.S.A.* 44°25N 107°0W **76 D10**
Bigstone L. *Canada* 53°42N 95°44W **71 C9**
Bihać *Bos.-H.* 44°49N 15°57E **16 F8**
Bihar *India* 25°5N 85°40E **43 G11**
Bihar □ *India* 25°0N 86°0E **43 G12**
Bihariganj *India* 25°44N 86°59E **43 G12**
Bihor, Munții *Romania* 46°29N 22°47E **17 E12**
Bijagós, Arquipélago dos
    Guinea-Biss. 11°15N 16°10W **52 F2**
Bijaipur *India* 26°2N 77°20E **42 F7**
Bijapur *Chhattisgarh, India* 18°50N 80°50E **44 E5**
Bijapur *Karnataka, India* 16°50N 75°55E **44 F2**
Bījār *Iran* 35°52N 47°35E **46 C5**
Bijauri *Nepal* 28°6N 82°20E **43 E10**
Bijawar *India* 24°38N 79°30E **43 G8**
Bijeljina *Bos.-H.* 44°46N 19°14E **23 B8**
Bijie *China* 27°20N 105°16E **34 D5**
Bijnor *India* 29°27N 78°11E **42 E8**
Bikaner *India* 28°2N 73°18E **42 E5**
Bikapur *India* 26°30N 82°7E **43 F10**
Bikeqi *China* 40°43N 111°20E **32 D6**
Bikfayyā *Lebanon* 33°55N 35°41E **48 B4**
Bikin *Russia* 46°50N 134°20E **28 A7**
Bikin → *Russia* 46°51N 134°2E **28 A7**
Bikini Atoll *Marshall Is.* 12°0N 167°30E **64 F8**
Bikita *Zimbabwe* 20°6S 31°41E **57 B5**
Bīkkū Bīttī *Libya* 22°0N 19°12E **53 D9**
Bila Tserkva *Ukraine* 49°45N 30°10E **17 D16**
Bilara *India* 26°14N 73°53E **42 F5**
Bilaspur *Chhattisgarh,*
    India 22°2N 82°15E **43 H10**
Bilaspur *Punjab, India* 31°19N 76°50E **42 D7**
Bilauk Taungdan *Thailand* 13°0N 99°0E **38 F2**
Bilauri *Nepal* 28°41N 80°21E **43 E9**
Bilbao *Spain* 43°16N 2°56W **21 A4**
Bilbo = Bilbao *Spain* 43°16N 2°56W **21 A4**
Bíldudalur *Iceland* 65°41N 23°36W **8 D2**
Bílé Karpaty *Europe* 49°5N 18°0E **17 D9**
Bilecik *Turkey* 40°5N 30°5E **19 F5**
Bilgram *India* 27°11N 80°2E **43 F9**
Bilhaur *India* 26°51N 80°5E **43 F9**
Bilhorod-Dnistrovskyy
    Ukraine 46°11N 30°23E **19 E5**
Bilibino *Russia* 68°3N 166°20E **27 C17**
Bilimora *India* 20°45N 72°57E **44 D1**
Bililuna *Australia* 19°37S 127°41E **60 C4**
Billings *U.S.A.* 45°47N 108°30W **76 D9**
Billiton Is. = Belitung
    Indonesia 3°10S 107°50E **36 E3**
Bilma *Niger* 18°50N 13°30E **53 E8**
Bilma, Grand Erg de *Niger* 18°30N 14°0E **53 E8**
Biloela *Australia* 24°24S 150°31E **62 C5**
Biloli *India* 18°46N 77°44E **44 E3**
Biloxi *U.S.A.* 30°24N 88°53W **85 F10**
Bilpa Morea Claypan
    Australia 25°0S 140°0E **62 D3**
Biltine *Chad* 14°40N 20°50E **53 F10**
Bim Son *Vietnam* 20°4N 105°51E **38 B5**
Bima *Indonesia* 8°22S 118°49E **37 F5**
Bimbo *C.A.R.* 4°15N 18°33E **54 D3**
Bimini Is. *Bahamas* 25°42N 79°25W **88 A4**
Bin Xian *Heilongjiang,*
    China 45°42N 127°32E **33 B14**
Bin Xian *Shaanxi, China* 35°2N 108°4E **32 G5**
Bina-Etawah *India* 24°13N 78°14E **42 G8**
Binalong *Australia* 34°40S 148°39E **63 E4**
Bīnālūd, Kūh-e *Iran* 36°30N 58°30E **47 B8**
Binatang = Bintangau
    Malaysia 2°10N 111°40E **36 D4**
Binche *Belgium* 50°26N 4°10E **15 D4**
Binchuan *China* 25°42N 100°38E **34 E3**
Bindki *India* 26°2N 80°36E **43 F9**
Bindura *Zimbabwe* 17°18S 31°18E **55 H6**
Bingara *Australia* 29°52S 150°36E **63 D5**
Bingaram I. *India* 10°56N 72°17E **45 J1**
Bingham *U.S.A.* 45°3N 69°53W **81 C19**
Binghamton *U.S.A.* 42°6N 75°55W **83 D8**
Bingöl *Turkey* 38°53N 40°29E **46 B4**
Binh Dinh *Vietnam* 13°55N 109°7E **38 F7**
Binh Son *Vietnam* 15°20N 108°40E **38 E7**
Binhai *China* 34°2N 119°49E **33 G10**
Binjai *Indonesia* 3°20N 98°30E **36 D1**
Binka *India* 21°2N 83°48E **44 D6**
Binnaway *Australia* 31°28S 149°24E **63 E4**
Binongko *Indonesia* 5°57S 124°2E **37 F6**
Binscarth *Canada* 50°37N 101°17W **71 C8**
Bintan *Indonesia* 1°0N 104°0E **36 D2**
Bintangau *Malaysia* 2°10N 111°40E **36 D4**
Bintulu *Malaysia* 3°10N 113°0E **36 D4**
Bintuni *Indonesia* 2°7S 133°32E **37 E8**
Binyang *China* 23°12N 108°47E **34 F7**
Binzert = Bizerte *Tunisia* 37°15N 9°50E **53 A7**
Binzhou *China* 37°20N 118°2E **33 F10**
Bío Bío □ *Chile* 37°35S 72°0W **94 D1**
Biobío → *Chile* 36°49S 73°10W **94 D1**
Bioko *Eq. Guin.* 3°30N 8°40E **54 D1**
Bir *India* 19°4N 75°46E **44 E2**
Bîr Abu Muḥammad
    Egypt 29°44N 34°14E **48 F3**
Bi'r al Butayyiḥāt *Jordan* 29°47N 35°20E **48 F4**
Bi'r al Mārī *Jordan* 30°4N 35°33E **48 E4**
Bi'r al Qaṭṭār *Jordan* 30°4N 35°43E **48 E4**
Bîr Atrun *Sudan* 18°15N 26°40E **53 E11**
Bîr Beîḑa *Egypt* 30°25N 34°29E **48 E3**
Bîr el ʻAbd *Egypt* 31°2N 33°0E **48 D2**

Bîr el Biarât *Egypt* 29°30N 34°43E 48 F3
Bîr el Duweidar *Egypt* 30°56N 32°32E 48 E1
Bîr el Garârât *Egypt* 31°3N 33°34E 48 D2
Bîr el Heisi *Egypt* 29°22N 34°36E 48 F3
Bîr el Jafir *Egypt* 30°50N 32°41E 48 E1
Bîr el Mâlhi *Egypt* 30°38N 33°19E 48 E2
Bîr el Thamâda *Egypt* 30°12N 33°27E 48 E2
Bîr Gebeil Hisn *Egypt* 30°2N 33°18E 48 E2
Bi'r Ghadîr *Syria* 34°6N 37°3E 48 A6
Bîr Hasana *Egypt* 30°29N 33°46E 48 E2
Bîr Kaseiba *Egypt* 31°0N 33°17E 48 E2
Bîr Lahfân *Egypt* 31°0N 33°51E 48 E2
Bîr Madkûr *Egypt* 30°44N 32°33E 48 E1
Bîr Mogreïn *Mauritania* 25°10N 11°25W 52 C3
Bi'r Mutribah *Kuwait* 29°54N 47°17E 46 D5
Bîr Qatia *Egypt* 30°58N 32°45E 48 E1
Bîr Shalatein *Egypt* 23°5N 35°25E 53 D13
Bîrák *Libya* 27°31N 14°20E 53 C8
Biratnagar *Nepal* 26°27N 87°17E 43 F12
Birch → *Canada* 58°28N 112°17W 70 B6
Birch Hills *Canada* 52°59N 105°25W 71 C7
Birch I. *Canada* 52°26N 99°54W 71 C9
Birch L. *N.W.T., Canada* 62°4N 116°33W 70 A5
Birch L. *Ont., Canada* 51°23N 92°18W 72 B1
Birch Mts. *Canada* 57°30N 113°10W 70 B6
Birch River *Canada* 52°24N 101°6W 71 C8
Birchip *Australia* 35°56S 142°55E 63 F3
Bird *Canada* 56°30N 94°13W 71 B10
Bird I. = Aves, I. de
  W. Indies 15°45N 63°55W 89 C7
Bird I. *S. Georgia* 54°0S 38°3W 96 G9
Birds Creek *Canada* 45°6N 77°52W 82 A7
Birdsville *Australia* 25°51S 139°20E 62 D2
Birdum Cr. → *Australia* 15°14S 133°0E 60 C5
Birecik *Turkey* 37°2N 38°0E 46 B3
Birein *Israel* 30°50N 34°28E 48 E3
Bireuen *Indonesia* 5°14N 96°39E 36 C1
Birganj *Nepal* 27°1N 84°52E 43 F11
Birigüi *Brazil* 21°18S 50°16W 95 A5
Bîrjand *Iran* 32°53N 59°13E 47 C8
Birkenhead *U.K.* 53°23N 3°2W 12 D4
Bîrlad = Bârlad *Romania* 46°15N 27°38E 17 E14
Birmingham *U.K.* 52°29N 1°52W 13 E6
Birmingham *U.S.A.* 33°31N 86°48W 85 E11
Birmingham Int. ✈ (BHX)
  U.K. 52°26N 1°45W 13 E6
Birmitrapur *India* 22°24N 84°46E 44 C7
Birni Nkonni *Niger* 13°55N 5°15E 52 F7
Birnin Kebbi *Nigeria* 12°32N 4°12E 52 F6
Birobidzhan *Russia* 48°50N 132°50E 31 B15
Birr *Ireland* 53°6N 7°54W 10 C4
Birrie → *Australia* 29°43S 146°37E 63 D4
Birsilpur *India* 28°11N 72°15E 42 E5
Birsk *Russia* 55°25N 55°30E 18 C10
Birtle *Canada* 50°30N 101°5W 71 C8
Birur *India* 13°30N 75°55E 40 N9
Biržai *Lithuania* 56°11N 24°45E 9 H21
Bisa *Indonesia* 1°15S 127°28E 37 E7
Bisalpur *India* 28°14N 79°48E 43 E8
Bisbee *U.S.A.* 31°27N 109°55W 77 L9
Biscarrosse *France* 44°22N 1°20W 20 D3
Biscay, B. of *Atl. Oc.* 45°0N 2°0W 20 D1
Biscayne B. *U.S.A.* 25°40N 80°12W 85 J14
Biscoe Is. *Antarctica* 66°0S 67°0W 5 C17
Biscotasing *Canada* 47°18N 82°9W 72 C3
Bishan *China* 29°33N 106°12E 34 C6
Bishkek *Kyrgyzstan* 42°54N 74°46E 30 C3
Bishnupur *India* 23°8N 87°20E 43 H12
Bisho = Bhisho *S. Africa* 32°50S 27°23E 56 D4
Bishop *Calif., U.S.A.* 37°22N 118°24W 78 H8
Bishop *Tex., U.S.A.* 27°35N 97°48W 84 H6
Bishop Auckland *U.K.* 54°39N 1°40W 12 C6
Bishop's Falls *Canada* 49°2N 55°30W 73 C8
Bishop's Stortford *U.K.* 51°52N 0°10E 13 F8
Biskra *Algeria* 34°50N 5°44E 52 B7
Bismarck *U.S.A.* 46°48N 100°47W 80 B3
Bismarck Arch.
  Papua N. G. 2°30S 150°0E 58 B7
Bison *U.S.A.* 45°31N 102°28W 80 C2
Bisotûn *Iran* 34°23N 47°26E 46 C5
Bissagos = Bijagós, Arquipélago
  dos *Guinea-Biss.* 11°15N 16°10W 52 F2
Bissam Cuttack *India* 19°31N 83°31E 44 E6
Bissau *Guinea-Biss.* 11°45N 15°45W 52 F2
Bistcho L. *Canada* 59°45N 118°50W 70 B5
Bistriţa *Romania* 47°9N 24°35E 17 E13
Bistriţa → *Romania* 46°30N 26°57E 17 E14
Biswan *India* 27°29N 81°2E 43 F9
Bitam *Gabon* 2°5N 11°25E 54 D2
Bitkine *Chad* 11°59N 18°13E 53 F9
Bitlis *Turkey* 38°20N 42°3E 46 B4
Bitola *Macedonia* 41°1N 21°20E 23 D9
Bitolj = Bitola *Macedonia* 41°1N 21°20E 23 D9
Bitra I. *India* 11°33N 72°9E 45 J1
Bitter Creek *U.S.A.* 41°33N 108°33W 76 F9
Bitterfontein *S. Africa* 31°1S 18°32E 56 D2
Bitterroot → *U.S.A.* 46°52N 114°7W 76 C6
Bitterroot Range *U.S.A.* 46°0N 114°20W 76 C6
Bitterwater *U.S.A.* 36°23N 121°0W 78 J6
Biu *Nigeria* 10°40N 12°3E 53 F8
Biwa-Ko *Japan* 35°15N 136°10E 29 G8
Biwabik *U.S.A.* 47°32N 92°21W 80 B7
Bixby *U.S.A.* 35°57N 95°53W 84 D7
Biyang *China* 32°38N 113°21E 32 H7
Biysk *Russia* 52°40N 85°0E 26 D9
Bizana *S. Africa* 30°50S 29°52E 57 D4
Bizen *Japan* 34°43N 134°8E 29 G7
Bizerte *Tunisia* 37°15N 9°50E 53 A7
Bjargtangar *Iceland* 65°30N 24°30W 8 D1
Bjelovar *Croatia* 45°56N 16°49E 22 B7
Björneborg = Pori *Finland* 61°29N 21°48E 8 F19
Bjørnevatn *Norway* 69°40N 30°0E 8 B23
Bjørnøya *Arctic* 74°30N 19°0E 4 B8
Black = Da → *Vietnam* 21°15N 105°20E 34 G5
Black → *Canada* 44°42N 79°19W 82 B5
Black → *Ariz., U.S.A.* 33°44N 110°13W 77 K8
Black → *Ark., U.S.A.* 35°38N 91°20W 84 D9
Black → *La., U.S.A.* 31°16N 91°50W 84 F9
Black → *Mich., U.S.A.* 42°59N 82°27W 82 D2

Black → *N.Y., U.S.A.* 43°59N 76°4W 83 C8
Black → *Wis., U.S.A.* 43°57N 91°22W 80 D8
Black Bay Pen. *Canada* 48°38N 88°21W 72 C2
Black Birch L. *Canada* 56°53N 107°45W 71 B7
Black Canyon of the Gunnison △
  U.S.A. 38°40N 107°35W 76 G10
Black Diamond *Canada* 50°45N 114°14W 70 C6
Black Duck → *Canada* 56°51N 89°2W 72 A2
Black Forest = Schwarzwald
  Germany 48°30N 8°20E 16 D5
Black Forest *U.S.A.* 39°0N 104°43W 76 G11
Black Hd. *Ireland* 53°9N 9°16W 10 C2
Black Hills *U.S.A.* 44°0N 103°45W 80 D2
Black I. *Canada* 51°12N 96°30W 71 C9
Black L. *Canada* 59°12N 105°15W 71 B7
Black L. *Mich., U.S.A.* 45°28N 84°16W 81 C11
Black L. *N.Y., U.S.A.* 44°31N 75°36W 83 B9
Black Lake *Canada* 59°11N 105°20W 71 B7
Black Mesa *U.S.A.* 36°58N 102°58W 84 C3
Black Mt. = Mynydd Du
  U.K. 51°52N 3°50W 13 F4
Black Mts. *U.K.* 51°55N 3°7W 13 F4
Black Range *U.S.A.* 33°15N 107°50W 77 K10
Black River *Jamaica* 18°0N 77°50W 88 a
Black River *U.S.A.* 44°0N 75°47W 83 C9
Black River Falls *U.S.A.* 44°18N 90°51W 80 D8
Black Rock *Barbados* 13°7N 59°37W 89 g
Black Rock Desert
  U.S.A. 41°10N 118°50W 76 F4
Black Sea *Eurasia* 43°30N 35°0E 19 F6
Black Tickle *Canada* 53°28N 55°45W 73 B8
Black Volta → *Africa* 8°41N 1°33W 52 G5
Black Warrior →
  U.S.A. 32°32N 87°51W 85 E11
Blackall *Australia* 24°25S 145°45E 62 C4
Blackball *N.Z.* 42°22S 171°26E 59 E3
Blackbraes △ *Australia* 19°10S 144°10E 62 B3
Blackbull *Australia* 17°55S 141°45E 62 B3
Blackburn *U.K.* 53°45N 2°29W 12 D5
Blackburn, Mt. *U.S.A.* 61°44N 143°26W 74 C11
Blackburn with Darwen □
  U.K. 53°45N 2°29W 12 D5
Blackdown Tableland △
  Australia 23°52S 149°8E 62 C4
Blackfoot *U.S.A.* 43°11N 112°21W 76 E7
Blackfoot → *U.S.A.* 46°52N 113°53W 76 C7
Blackfoot Res. *U.S.A.* 42°55N 111°39W 76 E8
Blackpool *U.K.* 53°49N 3°3W 12 D4
Blackpool □ *U.K.* 53°49N 3°3W 12 D4
Blackriver *U.S.A.* 44°46N 83°17W 82 B1
Blacks Harbour *Canada* 45°3N 66°49W 73 C6
Blacksburg *U.S.A.* 37°14N 80°25W 81 G13
Blacksod B. *Ireland* 54°6N 10°0W 10 B1
Blackstairs Mt. *Ireland* 52°33N 6°48W 10 D5
Blackstone *U.S.A.* 37°5N 78°0W 81 G14
Blackstone Ra. *Australia* 26°0S 128°30E 61 E4
Blackwater = West Road →
  Canada 53°18N 122°53W 70 C4
Blackwater *Australia* 23°35S 148°53E 62 C4
Blackwater → *Meath,*
  Ireland 53°39N 6°41W 10 C4
Blackwater → *Waterford,*
  Ireland 52°4N 7°52W 10 D4
Blackwater → *U.K.* 54°31N 6°35W 10 B5
Blackwell *U.S.A.* 36°48N 97°17W 84 C6
Blackwells Corner
  U.S.A. 35°37N 119°47W 79 K7
Bladensburg △ *Australia* 22°30S 142°59E 62 C3
Blaenau Ffestiniog *U.K.* 53°0N 3°56W 12 E4
Blaenau Gwent □ *U.K.* 51°48N 3°12W 13 F4
Blagdarnoye = Blagodarnyy
  Russia 45°7N 43°37E 19 E7
Blagodarnyy *Russia* 45°7N 43°37E 19 E7
Blagoevgrad *Bulgaria* 42°2N 23°5E 23 C10
Blagoveshchensk
  Russia 50°20N 127°30E 31 A14
Blahkiuh *Indonesia* 8°31S 115°12E 37 J18
Blain *U.S.A.* 40°20N 77°31W 82 F7
Blaine *Minn., U.S.A.* 45°10N 93°13W 80 C7
Blaine *Wash., U.S.A.* 48°59N 122°45W 78 B4
Blaine Lake *Canada* 52°51N 106°52W 71 C7
Blair *U.S.A.* 41°33N 96°8W 80 E5
Blair Athol *Australia* 22°42S 147°31E 62 C4
Blair Atholl *U.K.* 56°46N 3°50W 11 E5
Blairgowrie *U.K.* 56°35N 3°21W 11 E5
Blairsden *U.S.A.* 39°47N 120°37W 78 F6
Blairsville *U.S.A.* 40°26N 79°16W 82 F5
Blakang Mati, Pulau
  Singapore 1°15N 103°50E 39 d
Blake Pt. *U.S.A.* 48°11N 88°25W 80 A9
Blakely *Ga., U.S.A.* 31°23N 84°56W 85 F12
Blakely *Pa., U.S.A.* 41°28N 75°37W 83 E9
Blambangan, Semenanjung
  Indonesia 8°42S 114°29E 37 K17
Blanc, Mont *Europe* 45°48N 6°50E 20 D7
Blanca, B. *Argentina* 39°10S 61°30W 96 D4
Blanca Peak *U.S.A.* 37°35N 105°29W 77 H11
Blanche, C. *Australia* 33°1S 134°9E 63 E1
Blanche, L. *S. Austral.,*
  Australia 29°15S 139°40E 63 D2
Blanche, L. *W. Austral.,*
  Australia 22°25S 123°17E 60 D3
Blanchisseuse
  Trin. & Tob. 10°48N 61°18W 93 K15
Blanco *S. Africa* 33°55S 22°23E 56 D3
Blanco *U.S.A.* 30°6N 98°25W 84 F5
Blanco → *Argentina* 30°20S 68°42W 94 C2
Blanco, C. *Costa Rica* 9°34N 85°8W 88 E2
Blanco, C. *U.S.A.* 42°51N 124°34W 76 E1
Blanda → *Iceland* 65°37N 20°9W 8 D3
Blandford Forum *U.K.* 50°51N 2°9W 13 G5
Blanding *U.S.A.* 37°37N 109°29W 77 H9
Blanes *Spain* 41°40N 2°48E 21 B7
Blankenberge *Belgium* 51°20N 3°9E 15 C3
Blanquilla, I. *Venezuela* 11°51N 64°37W 89 D7
Blanquillo *Uruguay* 32°53S 55°37W 95 C4
Blantyre *Malawi* 15°45S 35°0E 55 H7
Blarney *Ireland* 51°56N 8°33W 10 E3

Blasdell *U.S.A.* 42°48N 78°50W 82 D6
Blåvands Huk *Denmark* 55°33N 8°4E 9 J13
Blaydon *U.K.* 54°58N 1°42W 12 C6
Blayney *Australia* 33°32S 149°14E 63 E4
Blaze, Pt. *Australia* 12°56S 130°11E 60 B5
Blekinge *Sweden* 56°25N 15°20E 9 H16
Blenheim *Canada* 42°20N 82°0W 82 D3
Blenheim *N.Z.* 41°38S 173°57E 59 D5
Bletchley *U.K.* 51°59N 0°44W 13 F7
Blida *Algeria* 36°30N 2°49E 52 A6
Bligh Sound *N.Z.* 44°47S 167°32E 59 F1
Bligh Water *Fiji* 17°0S 178°0E 59 a
Blind River *Canada* 46°10N 82°58W 72 C3
Bliss *Idaho, U.S.A.* 42°56N 114°57W 76 E6
Bliss *N.Y., U.S.A.* 42°34N 78°15W 82 D6
Blissfield *U.S.A.* 41°50N 83°52W 81 E12
Blitar *Indonesia* 8°5S 112°11E 37 H15
Block I. *U.S.A.* 41°11N 71°35W 83 E13
Block Island Sd. *U.S.A.* 41°15N 71°40W 83 E13
Bloemfontein *S. Africa* 29°6S 26°7E 56 C4
Bloemhof *S. Africa* 27°38S 25°32E 56 D4
Blois *France* 47°35N 1°20E 20 C4
Blönduós *Iceland* 65°40N 20°12W 8 D3
Blongas *Indonesia* 8°53S 116°2E 37 K19
Bloodvein → *Canada* 51°47N 96°43W 71 C9
Bloody Foreland *Ireland* 55°10N 8°17W 10 A3
Bloomer *U.S.A.* 45°6N 91°29W 80 C8
Bloomfield *Canada* 43°59N 77°14W 82 C7
Bloomfield *Iowa, U.S.A.* 40°45N 92°25W 80 E7
Bloomfield *N. Mex.,*
  U.S.A. 36°43N 107°59W 77 H10
Bloomfield *Nebr., U.S.A.* 42°36N 97°39W 80 D5
Bloomington *Ill., U.S.A.* 40°28N 89°0W 80 E9
Bloomington *Ind.,*
  U.S.A. 39°10N 86°32W 80 F10
Bloomington *Minn.,*
  U.S.A. 44°50N 93°17W 80 C7
Bloomsburg *U.S.A.* 41°0N 76°27W 83 F8
Bloomsbury *Australia* 20°48S 148°38E 62 b
Blora *Indonesia* 6°57S 111°25E 37 G14
Blossburg *U.S.A.* 41°41N 77°4W 82 E7
Blouberg *S. Africa* 23°8S 28°59E 57 B4
Blountstown *U.S.A.* 30°27N 85°3W 85 F12
Blue Earth *U.S.A.* 43°38N 94°6W 80 D6
Blue Hole △ *Belize* 17°24N 87°30W 88 C2
Blue Mesa Res. *U.S.A.* 38°28N 107°20W 76 G10
Blue Mountain Lake
  U.S.A. 43°51N 74°27W 83 C10
Blue Mountain Pk. *Jamaica* 18°3N 76°36W 88 a
Blue Mt. *U.S.A.* 40°30N 76°30W 83 F8
Blue Mts. *Jamaica* 18°3N 76°36W 88 a
Blue Mts. *Maine, U.S.A.* 44°50N 70°35W 83 B14
Blue Mts. *Oreg., U.S.A.* 45°0N 118°20W 76 D4
Blue Mud Bay *Australia* 13°25S 136°2E 62 A2
Blue Nile = Nîl el Azraq →
  Sudan 15°38N 32°31E 53 E12
Blue Rapids *U.S.A.* 39°41N 96°39W 80 F5
Blue Ridge *U.S.A.* 36°40N 80°50W 81 G15
Blue River *Canada* 52°6N 119°18W 70 C5
Bluefield *U.S.A.* 37°15N 81°17W 81 G13
Bluefields *Nic.* 12°20N 83°50W 88 D3
Bluevale *Canada* 43°51N 81°15W 82 C3
Bluff *N.Z.* 46°37S 168°20E 59 G2
Bluff *U.S.A.* 37°17N 109°33W 77 H9
Bluff Knoll *Australia* 34°24S 118°15E 61 F2
Bluff Pt. *Australia* 27°50S 114°5E 61 E1
Bluffton *Ind., U.S.A.* 40°44N 85°11W 81 E11
Bluffton *S.C., U.S.A.* 32°14N 80°52W 85 E14
Blumenau *Brazil* 27°0S 49°0W 95 B6
Blunt *U.S.A.* 44°31N 99°59W 80 C4
Bly *U.S.A.* 42°24N 121°3W 76 E3
Blyde River Canyon △
  S. Afr. 24°37S 31°2E 57 B5
Blyth *Canada* 43°44N 81°26W 82 C3
Blyth *U.K.* 55°8N 1°31W 12 B6
Blythe *U.S.A.* 33°37N 114°36W 79 M12
Blytheville *U.S.A.* 35°56N 89°55W 85 D10
Bo *S. Leone* 7°55N 11°50W 52 G3
Bo Duc *Vietnam* 11°58N 106°50E 39 G6
Bo Hai *China* 39°0N 119°0E 33 E10
Bo Hai Haixia *Asia* 38°25N 121°10E 33 E11
Bo Xian = Bozhou *China* 33°55N 115°41E 32 H8
Boa Vista *Brazil* 2°48N 60°30W 92 C6
Boa Vista *C. Verde Is.* 16°0N 22°49W 52 b
Boaco *Nic.* 12°29N 85°35W 88 D2
Bo'ai *China* 35°10N 113°3E 32 G7
Boalsburg *U.S.A.* 40°47N 77°49W 82 F7
Boane *Mozam.* 26°6S 32°19E 57 D5
Boao *China* 19°8N 110°34E 38 C8
Boardman *U.S.A.* 41°2N 80°40W 82 E4
Boath *U.S.A.* 19°20N 78°20E 44 E4
Bobadah *Australia* 32°19S 146°41E 63 E4
Bobai *China* 22°17N 109°59E 34 F7
Bobbili *India* 18°35N 83°30E 44 E6
Bobcaygeon *Canada* 44°33N 78°33W 82 B6
Boblad *India* 17°13N 75°26E 44 F2
Bobo-Dioulasso
  Burkina Faso 11°8N 4°13W 52 F5
Bobonong *Botswana* 21°58S 28°20E 57 B4
Bóbr → *Poland* 52°4N 15°4E 16 B8
Bobraomby, Tanjon' i
  Madag. 12°40S 49°10E 55 G9
Bobruysk = Babruysk
  Belarus 53°10N 29°15E 17 B15
Boby, Pic *Madag.* 22°12S 46°55E 55 J9
Boca del Río *Mexico* 19°5N 96°4W 87 D5
Boca do Acre *Brazil* 8°50S 67°27W 92 E5
Boca Raton *U.S.A.* 26°21N 80°5W 85 H14
Bocas del Dragón = Dragon's
  Mouths *Trin. & Tob.* 11°0N 61°50W 93 K15
Bocas del Toro *Panama* 9°15N 82°20W 88 E3
Bochnia *Poland* 49°58N 20°27E 17 D11
Bochum = Senwabarana
  S. Africa 23°17S 29°7E 57 B4
Bochum *Germany* 51°28N 7°13E 16 C4
Bocoyna *Mexico* 27°52N 107°35W 86 B3
Bodaybo *Russia* 57°50N 114°0E 27 D12

Boddam *U.K.* 59°56N 1°17W 11 B7
Boddington *Australia* 32°50S 116°30E 61 F2
Bodega Bay *U.S.A.* 38°20N 123°3W 78 G3
Boden *Sweden* 65°50N 21°42E 8 D19
Bodensee *Europe* 47°35N 9°25E 20 C8
Bodh Gaya *India* 24°41N 84°59E 43 G11
Bodhan *India* 18°40N 77°44E 44 E3
Bodinayakkanur *India* 10°2N 77°10E 45 J3
Bodmin *U.K.* 50°28N 4°43W 13 G3
Bodmin Moor *U.K.* 50°33N 4°36W 13 G3
Bodø *Norway* 67°17N 14°24E 8 C16
Bodrog → *Hungary* 48°11N 21°22E 17 D11
Bodrum *Turkey* 37°3N 27°30E 23 F12
Boende
  Dem. Rep. of the Congo 0°24S 21°12E 54 E4
Boerne *U.S.A.* 29°47N 98°44W 84 G5
Boesmans → *S. Africa* 33°42S 26°39E 56 D4
Bogalusa *U.S.A.* 30°47N 89°52W 85 F10
Bogan → *Australia* 30°20S 146°55E 63 D4
Bogan Gate *Australia* 33°7S 147°49E 63 E4
Bogantungan *Australia* 23°41S 147°17E 62 C4
Bogata *U.S.A.* 33°28N 95°13W 84 E7
Bogda Shan *China* 43°35N 89°40E 30 C6
Boggabilla *Australia* 28°36S 150°24E 63 D5
Boggabri *Australia* 30°45S 150°5E 63 E5
Boggeragh Mts. *Ireland* 52°2N 8°55W 10 D3
Boglan = Solhan *Turkey* 38°57N 41°3E 46 B4
Bognor Regis *U.K.* 50°47N 0°40W 13 G7
Bogo *Phil.* 11°3N 124°0E 37 B6
Bogong, Mt. *Australia* 36°47S 147°17E 63 F4
Bogor *Indonesia* 6°36S 106°48E 37 G12
Bogotá *Colombia* 4°34N 74°0W 92 C4
Bogotol *Russia* 56°15N 89°50E 26 D9
Bogra *Bangla.* 24°51N 89°22E 41 G16
Boguchany *Russia* 58°40N 97°30E 27 D10
Bogué *Mauritania* 16°45N 14°10W 52 E3
Bohemian Forest = Böhmerwald
  Germany 49°8N 13°14E 16 D7
Böhmerwald *Germany* 49°8N 13°14E 16 D7
Bohol □ *Phil.* 9°50N 124°10E 37 C6
Bohol Sea *Phil.* 9°0N 124°0E 37 C6
Bohorok *Indonesia* 3°30N 98°12E 39 L2
Bohuslän *Sweden* 58°25N 12°0E 9 G15
Boi, Pta. do *Brazil* 23°55S 45°15W 95 A6
Boiaçu *Brazil* 0°27S 61°46W 92 D6
Boigu *Australia* 9°16S 142°12E 62 a
Boileau, C. *Australia* 17°40S 122°7E 60 C3
Boipariguda *India* 18°46N 82°26E 44 E6
Boise *U.S.A.* 43°37N 116°13W 76 E5
Boise City *U.S.A.* 36°44N 102°31W 84 C3
Boissevain *Canada* 49°15N 100°5W 71 D8
Bojador, C. *W. Sahara* 26°0N 14°30W 52 C3
Bojana → *Albania* 41°52N 19°22E 23 D8
Bojnūrd *Iran* 37°30N 57°20E 47 B8
Bojonegoro *Indonesia* 7°11S 111°54E 37 G14
Bokaro *India* 23°46N 85°55E 43 H11
Boké *Guinea* 10°56N 14°17W 52 F3
Bokhara → *Australia* 29°55S 146°42E 63 D4
Boknafjorden *Norway* 59°14N 5°40E 9 G11
Bokor △ *Cambodia* 10°50N 104°1E 39 G5
Bokoro *Chad* 12°25N 17°14E 53 F9
Bokpyin *Burma* 11°18N 98°42E 39 G2
Bokungu
  Dem. Rep. of the Congo 0°35S 22°50E 54 E4
Bolan → *Pakistan* 28°38N 67°42E 42 E2
Bolan Pass *Pakistan* 29°50N 67°20E 40 E5
Bolaños → *Mexico* 21°12N 104°5W 86 C4
Bolbec *France* 49°30N 0°30E 20 B4
Boldājī *Iran* 31°56N 51°3E 47 D6
Bole *China* 44°55N 81°37E 30 C5
Bolekhiv *Ukraine* 49°0N 23°57E 17 D12
Bolesławiec *Poland* 51°17N 15°37E 16 C8
Bolgatanga *Ghana* 10°44N 0°53W 52 F5
Bolgrad = Bolhrad
  Ukraine 45°40N 28°32E 17 F15
Bolhrad *Ukraine* 45°40N 28°32E 17 F15
Bolinao *Phil.* 16°23N 119°54E 37 A5
Bolivar *Mo., U.S.A.* 37°37N 93°25W 80 G7
Bolivar *N.Y., U.S.A.* 42°4N 78°10W 82 D6
Bolivar *Tenn., U.S.A.* 35°12N 89°0W 85 D10
Bolivar, Pico *Venezuela* 8°32N 71°2W 89 E5
Bolivia ■ *S. Amer.* 17°6S 64°0W 92 G6
Bolivian Plateau = Altiplano
  Bolivia 17°0S 68°0W 92 G5
Bollnäs *Sweden* 61°21N 16°24E 8 F17
Bollon *Australia* 28°2S 147°29E 63 D4
Bolmen *Sweden* 56°55N 13°40E 9 H15
Bolobo
  Dem. Rep. of the Congo 2°6S 16°20E 54 E3
Bologna *Italy* 44°29N 11°20E 22 B4
Bologoye *Russia* 57°55N 34°5E 18 C5
Bolomba
  Dem. Rep. of the Congo 0°35N 19°0E 54 D3
Bolonchén *Mexico* 20°1N 89°45W 87 D7
Boloven, Cao Nguyen
  Laos 15°10N 106°30E 38 E6
Bolpur *India* 23°40N 87°45E 43 H12
Bolsena, L. di *Italy* 42°36N 11°56E 22 C4
Bolshevik, Ostrov
  Russia 78°30N 102°0E 27 B11
Bolshoy Anyuy →
  Russia 68°30N 160°49E 27 C17
Bolshoy Begichev, Ostrov
  Russia 74°20N 112°30E 27 B12
Bolshoy Kamen *Russia* 43°7N 132°19E 28 C6
Bolshoy Kavkaz = Caucasus
  Mountains *Eurasia* 42°50N 44°0E 19 F7
Bolshoy Lyakhovskiy, Ostrov
  Russia 73°35N 142°0E 27 B15
Bolshoy Tyuters, Ostrov
  Russia 59°51N 27°13E 9 G22
Bolsward *Neths.* 53°3N 5°32E 15 A5
Bolt Head *U.K.* 50°12N 3°48E 13 G4
Bolton *Canada* 43°54N 79°45W 82 C5
Bolton *U.K.* 53°35N 2°26W 12 D5
Bolton Landing *U.S.A.* 43°32N 73°35W 83 C11
Bolu *Turkey* 40°45N 31°35E 19 F5
Bolungavík *Iceland* 66°9N 23°15W 8 C2
Boluo *China* 23°3N 114°21E 35 F10

Bolvadin *Turkey* 38°45N 31°4E 46 B1
Bolzano *Italy* 46°31N 11°22E 22 A4
Bom Jesus da Lapa
  Brazil 13°15S 43°25W 93 F10
Boma *Dem. Rep. of the Congo* 5°50S 13°4E 54 F2
Bombala *Australia* 36°56S 149°15E 63 F4
Bombay *U.S.A.* 44°56N 74°34W 83 B10
Bombedor, Pta. *Venezuela* 9°53N 61°37W 93 L15
Bomberai, Semenanjung
  Indonesia 3°0S 133°0E 37 E8
Bomboma
  Dem. Rep. of the Congo 2°25N 18°55E 54 D3
Bomi *China* 29°50N 95°45E 30 F8
Bømlo *Norway* 59°37N 5°13E 9 G11
Bompoka *India* 8°15N 93°13E 45 K11
Bomu → *C.A.R.* 4°40N 22°30E 54 D4
Bon, C. = Ra's at Tib *Tunisia* 37°1N 11°2E 22 F4
Bon Acceuil *Mauritius* 20°10S 57°39E 55 d
Bon Echo △ *Canada* 44°55N 77°16W 82 B7
Bon Sar Pa *Vietnam* 12°24N 107°35E 38 F6
Bonāb *Iran* 36°35N 48°41E 47 B6
Bonaigarh *India* 21°50N 84°57E 43 J11
Bonaire *W. Indies* 12°10N 68°15W 89 D6
Bonampak *Mexico* 16°44N 91°5W 87 D6
Bonang *Australia* 37°11S 148°41E 63 F4
Bonanza *Nic.* 13°54N 84°35W 88 D3
Bonaparte Arch.
  Australia 14°0S 124°30E 60 B3
Bonar Bridge *U.K.* 57°54N 4°20W 11 D4
Bonasse *Trin. & Tob.* 10°5N 61°54W 93 K15
Bonaventure *Canada* 48°5N 65°32W 73 C6
Bonavista *Canada* 48°40N 53°5W 73 C9
Bonavista, C. *Canada* 48°42N 53°5W 73 C9
Bonavista B. *Canada* 48°45N 53°25W 73 C9
Bondo
  Dem. Rep. of the Congo 3°55N 23°53E 54 D4
Bondokodi *Indonesia* 9°35S 119°0E 60 A2
Bondoukou *Ivory C.* 8°2N 2°47W 52 G5
Bondowoso *Indonesia* 7°55S 113°49E 37 G15
Bone, Teluk *Indonesia* 4°10S 120°50E 37 E6
Bonerate *Indonesia* 7°25S 121°5E 37 F6
Bonerate, Kepulauan
  Indonesia 6°30S 121°10E 37 F6
Bo'ness *U.K.* 56°1N 3°37W 11 E5
Bonete, Cerro *Argentina* 27°55S 68°40W 94 B2
Bong Son = Hoai Nhon
  Vietnam 14°28N 109°1E 38 E7
Bongaigaon *India* 26°28N 90°34E 30 F7
Bongandanga
  Dem. Rep. of the Congo 1°24N 21°3E 54 D4
Bongor *Chad* 10°35N 15°20E 53 F9
Bongos, Massif des *C.A.R.* 8°40N 22°25E 54 D4
Bonham *U.S.A.* 33°35N 96°11W 84 E6
Bonifacio *France* 41°24N 9°10E 20 F8
Bonifacio, Bouches de
  Medit. S. 41°12N 9°15E 22 D3
Bonin Is. = Ogasawara Gunto
  Pac. Oc. 27°0N 142°0E 64 E6
Bonn *Germany* 50°46N 7°6E 16 C4
Bonne Terre *U.S.A.* 37°55N 90°33W 80 G8
Bonners Ferry *U.S.A.* 48°42N 116°19W 76 B5
Bonney, L. *Australia* 37°50S 140°20E 63 F3
Bonnie Rock *Australia* 30°29S 118°22E 61 F2
Bonny, Bight of *Africa* 3°30N 9°20E 54 D1
Bonnyrigg *U.K.* 55°53N 3°6W 11 F5
Bonnyville *Canada* 54°20N 110°45W 71 C6
Bonoi *Indonesia* 1°45S 137°41E 37 E9
Bonsall *U.S.A.* 33°16N 117°14W 79 M9
Bontang *Indonesia* 0°10N 117°30E 36 D5
Bonthe *S. Africa* 34°5S 20°28E 56 E3
Bonthe *S. Leone* 7°30N 12°33W 52 G3
Bontoc *Phil.* 17°7N 120°58E 37 A6
Bonython Ra. *Australia* 23°40S 128°45E 60 D4
Boodjamulla △ *Australia* 18°15S 138°6E 62 B2
Bookabie *Australia* 31°50S 132°41E 61 F5
Booker *U.S.A.* 36°27N 100°32W 84 C4
Booligal *Australia* 33°58S 144°53E 63 E3
Böön Tsagaan Nuur
  Mongolia 45°35N 99°9E 30 B8
Boonah *Australia* 27°58S 152°41E 63 D5
Boone *Iowa, U.S.A.* 42°4N 93°53W 80 D7
Boone *N.C., U.S.A.* 36°13N 81°41W 85 C14
Booneville *Ark., U.S.A.* 35°8N 93°55W 84 D8
Booneville *Miss., U.S.A.* 34°39N 88°34W 85 D10
Boonville *Calif., U.S.A.* 39°1N 123°22W 78 F3
Boonville *Ind., U.S.A.* 38°3N 87°16W 80 F10
Boonville *Mo., U.S.A.* 38°58N 92°44W 80 F7
Boonville *N.Y., U.S.A.* 43°29N 75°20W 83 C9
Boorabbin △ *Australia* 31°3S 120°10E 61 F3
Boorindal *Australia* 30°22S 146°11E 63 E4
Boorowa *Australia* 34°28S 148°44E 63 E4
Boosaaso *Somalia* 11°12N 49°18E 49 E4
Boothia, Gulf of *Canada* 71°0N 90°0W 68 B2
Boothia Pen. *Canada* 71°0N 94°0W 68 C13
Bootle *U.K.* 53°28N 3°1W 12 D4
Booué *Gabon* 0°5S 11°55E 54 E2
Boquilla, Presa de la
  Mexico 27°31N 105°30W 86 B3
Boquillas del Carmen
  Mexico 29°11N 102°58W 86 B4
Bor *Serbia* 44°5N 22°7E 23 B10
Bôr *South Sudan* 6°10N 31°40E 53 G12
Bor Mashash *Israel* 31°7N 34°50E 48 D3
Bora Bora
  French Polynesia 16°30S 151°45W 65 J12
Borah Peak *U.S.A.* 44°8N 113°47W 76 D7
Boraha, Nosy *Madag.* 16°50S 49°55E 55 H9
Borås *Sweden* 57°43N 12°56E 9 H15
Borāzjān *Iran* 29°22N 51°10E 47 D6
Borba *Brazil* 4°12S 59°34W 92 D7
Borborema, Planalto da
  Brazil 7°0S 37°0W 90 D7
Bord Khūn-e Now *Iran* 28°3N 51°28E 47 D6
Borda, C. *Australia* 35°45S 136°34E 63 F2
Bordeaux *France* 44°50N 0°36W 20 D3
Borden *Australia* 34°3S 118°27E 61 F2
Borden-Carleton *Canada* 46°18N 63°47W 73 C7
Borden I. *Canada* 78°30N 111°30W 69 B9
Borden Pen. *Canada* 73°0N 83°0W 69 C15

Border Ranges △
  Australia 28°24S 152°56E 63 D5
Borders = Scottish Borders □
  U.K. 55°35N 2°50W 11 F6
Bordertown Australia 36°19S 140°45E 63 F3
Borðeyri Iceland 65°12N 21°6W 8 D3
Bordj Flye Ste-Marie
  Algeria 27°19N 2°32W 52 C5
Bordj in Eker Algeria 24°9N 5°3E 52 D7
Bordj Mokhtar Algeria 21°20N 0°56E 52 D6
Bordj Omar Driss Algeria 28°10N 6°40E 52 C7
Borehamwood U.K. 51°40N 0°15W 13 F7
Borgampad India 17°39N 80°52E 44 F5
Borgarnes Iceland 64°32N 21°55W 8 D3
Børgefjellet Norway 65°20N 13°45E 8 D15
Borger Neths. 52°54N 6°44E 15 B6
Borger U.S.A. 35°39N 101°24W 84 D4
Borgholm Sweden 56°52N 16°39E 9 H17
Borhoyn Tal Mongolia 43°50N 111°58E 32 C6
Borikhane Laos 18°33N 103°43E 38 C4
Borisoglebsk Russia 51°27N 42°5E 19 D7
Borisov = Barysaw
  Belarus 54°17N 28°28E 17 A15
Borja Peru 4°20S 77°40W 92 D3
Borkou Chad 18°15N 18°50E 53 E9
Borkum Germany 53°34N 6°40E 16 B4
Borlänge Sweden 60°29N 15°26E 9 F16
Borley, C. Antarctica 66°15S 52°30E 5 C5
Borneo E. Indies 1°0N 115°0E 36 D5
Bornholm Denmark 55°10N 15°0E 9 J16
Borobudur △ Indonesia 7°36S 110°12E 37 G14
Borogontsy Russia 62°42N 131°8E 27 C14
Borohoro Shan China 44°6N 83°10E 30 C5
Boron U.S.A. 35°0N 117°39W 79 L9
Borongan Phil. 11°37N 125°26E 37 B7
Borovichi Russia 58°25N 33°55E 18 C5
Borrego Springs
  U.S.A. 33°15N 116°23W 79 M10
Borrisokane Ireland 53°0N 8°7W 10 D3
Borroloola Australia 16°4S 136°17E 62 B2
Borşa Romania 47°41N 24°50E 17 E13
Borsad India 22°25N 72°54E 42 H5
Bortala = Bole China 44°55N 81°37E 30 C5
Borth U.K. 52°29N 4°2W 13 E3
Börüjerd Iran 33°55N 48°50E 47 C6
Boryeong S. Korea 36°21N 126°36E 33 F14
Boryslav Ukraine 49°18N 23°28E 17 D12
Borzya Russia 50°24N 116°31E 31 A12
Bosa Italy 40°18N 8°30E 22 D3
Bosanska Gradiška
  Bos.-H. 45°10N 17°15E 22 B7
Boscastle U.K. 50°41N 4°42W 13 G3
Boscobelle Barbados 13°17N 59°35W 89 g
Bose China 23°53N 106°35E 34 F6
Boseong S. Korea 34°46N 127°5E 33 G14
Boshan China 36°28N 117°49E 33 F9
Boshof S. Africa 28°31S 25°13E 56 C4
Boshrūyeh Iran 33°50N 57°30E 47 C8
Bosna → Bos.-H.
Bosna i Hercegovina = Bosnia-
  Herzegovina ■ Europe 44°0N 18°0E 22 B7
Bosnia-Herzegovina ■
  Europe 44°0N 18°0E 22 B7
Bosnik Indonesia 1°5S 136°10E 37 E9
Bosobolo
  Dem. Rep. of the Congo 4°15N 19°50E 54 D3
Bosque Farms U.S.A. 35°51N 106°42W 77 J10
Bosra = Buşra ash Shām
  Syria 32°30N 36°25E 48 C5
Bossangoa C.A.R. 6°35N 17°30E 54 C3
Bossier City U.S.A. 32°31N 93°44W 84 E8
Bossiesvlei Namibia 25°1S 16°44E 56 C2
Bosso Niger 13°43N 13°19E 53 F8
Bostan Pakistan 30°26N 67°2E 42 D2
Bostānābād Iran 37°50N 46°50E 46 B5
Bosten Hu China 41°55N 87°40E 30 C6
Boston U.K. 52°59N 0°2W 12 E7
Boston Bar Canada 49°52N 121°30W 70 D4
Boston Mts. U.S.A. 35°42N 93°15W 84 D8
Boswell Canada 49°28N 116°45W 70 D5
Boswell U.S.A. 40°10N 79°2W 82 F5
Botad India 22°15N 71°40E 42 H4
Botene Laos 17°35N 101°12E 38 D3
Bothaville S. Africa 27°23S 26°34E 56 C4
Bothnia, G. of Europe 62°0N 20°0E 8 F19
Bothwell Australia 42°20S 147°1E 63 G4
Bothwell Canada 42°38N 81°52W 82 D3
Botletle → Botswana 20°10S 23°15E 56 B3
Botoşani Romania 47°42N 26°41E 17 E14
Botou Burkina Faso 12°42N 1°59E 52 F6
Botou China 38°4N 116°34E 32 E9
Botshabelo S. Africa 29°14S 26°44E 56 C4
Botswana ■ Africa 22°0S 24°0E 56 B3
Bottineau U.S.A. 48°50N 100°27W 80 A3
Botucatu Brazil 22°55S 48°30W 95 A6
Botum Sakor △ Cambodia 11°5N 103°15E 39 G4
Botwood Canada 49°6N 55°23W 73 C8
Bou Saâda Algeria 35°11N 4°9E 52 A6
Bouaflé Ivory C. 7°1N 5°47W 52 G4
Bouaké Ivory C. 7°40N 5°2W 52 G4
Bouar C.A.R. 6°0N 15°40E 54 C3
Bouârfa Morocco 32°32N 1°58W 52 B5
Boucaut B. Australia 12°0S 134°25E 62 A1
Bouctouche Canada 46°30N 64°45W 73 C7
Bougainville, C. Australia 13°57S 126°4E 60 B4
Bougainville I. Papua N. G. 6°0S 155°0E 58 B8
Bougainville Reef
  Australia 15°30S 147°5E 62 B4
Bougie = Bejaïa Algeria 36°42N 5°2E 52 A7
Bougouni Mali 11°30N 7°20W 52 F4
Bouillon Belgium 49°44N 5°3E 15 E5
Boulder Colo., U.S.A. 40°1N 105°17W 76 F11
Boulder Mont., U.S.A. 46°14N 112°7W 76 C7
Boulder City U.S.A. 35°58N 114°49W 79 K12
Boulder Creek U.S.A. 37°7N 122°7W 78 H4
Boulder Dam = Hoover Dam
  U.S.A. 36°1N 114°44W 79 K12
Boulia Australia 22°52S 139°51E 62 C2

Boulogne-sur-Mer France 50°42N 1°36E 20 A4
Boulsa Burkina Faso 12°39N 0°34W 52 F5
Boultoum Niger 14°45N 10°25E 53 F8
Bouma △ Fiji 16°50S 179°52E 59 a
Boun Neua Laos 21°38N 101°54E 38 B3
Boun Tai Laos 21°23N 101°58E 38 B3
Bouna Ivory C. 9°10N 3°0W 52 G5
Boundary Peak U.S.A. 37°51N 118°21W 78 H8
Boundiali Ivory C. 9°30N 6°20W 52 G4
Bountiful U.S.A. 40°53N 111°52W 76 F8
Bounty Is. Pac. Oc. 48°0S 178°30E 64 M9
Bounty Trough Pac. Oc. 46°0S 178°0E 64 M9
Bourbonnais France 46°28N 3°0E 20 C5
Bourdel L. Canada 56°43N 74°10W 72 A5
Bourem Mali 17°0N 0°24W 52 E5
Bourg-en-Bresse France 46°13N 5°12E 20 C6
Bourg-St-Maurice France 45°35N 6°46E 20 D7
Bourgas = Burgas
  Bulgaria 42°33N 27°29E 23 C12
Bourges France 47°9N 2°25E 20 C5
Bourget Canada 45°26N 75°9W 83 A9
Bourgogne □ France 47°0N 4°50E 20 C6
Bourke Australia 30°8S 145°55E 63 E4
Bourne U.K. 52°47N 0°22W 12 E7
Bournemouth U.K. 50°43N 1°52W 13 G6
Bournemouth □ U.K. 50°43N 1°52W 13 G6
Bouse U.S.A. 33°56N 114°0W 79 M13
Bousso Chad 10°34N 16°52E 53 F9
Bouvet I. = Bouvetøya
  Antarctica 54°26S 3°24E 2 G10
Bouvetøya Antarctica 54°26S 3°24E 2 G10
Bovill U.S.A. 46°51N 116°24W 76 C5
Bovril Argentina 31°21S 59°26W 94 C4
Bow → Canada 49°57N 111°41W 70 C6
Bow Island Canada 49°50N 111°23W 76 B8
Bowbells U.S.A. 48°48N 102°15W 80 A2
Bowdle U.S.A. 45°27N 99°39W 80 C4
Bowelling Australia 33°25S 116°30E 61 F2
Bowen Argentina 35°0S 67°31W 94 D2
Bowen Australia 20°0S 148°16E 62 J6
Bowen Mts. Australia 37°0S 147°50E 63 F4
Bowers Basin Pac. Oc. 53°45N 176°0E 4 D16
Bowers Ridge Pac. Oc. 54°0N 180°0E 4 D17
Bowie Ariz., U.S.A. 32°19N 109°29W 77 K9
Bowie Tex., U.S.A. 33°34N 97°51W 84 E6
Bowkān Iran 36°31N 46°12E 46 B5
Bowland, Forest of U.K. 54°0N 2°30W 12 D5
Bowling Green Ky.,
  U.S.A. 36°59N 86°27W 80 G10
Bowling Green Ohio,
  U.S.A. 41°23N 83°39W 81 E12
Bowling Green, C.
  Australia 19°19S 147°25E 62 B4
Bowling Green Bay △
  Australia 19°26S 146°57E 62 B4
Bowman U.S.A. 46°11N 103°24W 80 B2
Bowman I. Antarctica 65°0S 104°0E 5 C8
Bowmanville = Clarington
  Canada 43°55N 78°41W 82 C6
Bowmore U.K. 55°45N 6°17W 11 F2
Bowral Australia 34°26S 150°27E 63 E5
Bowraville Australia 30°37S 152°52E 63 E5
Bowron → Canada 54°3N 121°50W 70 C4
Bowron Lake = Canada 53°10N 121°5W 70 C4
Bowser L. Canada 56°30N 129°30W 70 B3
Bowsman Canada 52°14N 101°12W 71 C8
Box Cr. → Australia 34°10S 143°50E 63 E3
Boxmeer Neths. 51°38N 5°56E 15 C5
Boxtel Neths. 51°36N 5°20E 15 C5
Boyang China 29°0N 116°38E 35 C11
Boyce U.S.A. 31°23N 92°40W 84 F8
Boyd L. Canada 52°46N 76°42W 72 B4
Boyle Canada 54°35N 112°49W 70 C6
Boyle Ireland 53°59N 8°18W 10 C3
Boyne → Ireland 53°43N 6°15W 10 C5
Boyne City U.S.A. 45°13N 85°1W 81 C11
Boynton Beach U.S.A. 26°32N 80°4W 85 H14
Boyoma, Chutes
  Dem. Rep. of the Congo 0°35N 25°23E 50 F6
Boysen Res. U.S.A. 43°25N 108°11W 76 E9
Boyuibe Bolivia 20°25S 63°17W 92 G6
Boyup Brook Australia 33°50S 116°23E 61 F2
Boz Dağları Turkey 38°20N 28°0E 23 E13
Bozburun Turkey 36°43N 28°4E 23 F13
Bozcaada Turkey 39°49N 26°3E 23 E12
Bozdoğan Turkey 37°40N 28°17E 23 F13
Bozeman U.S.A. 45°41N 111°2W 76 D8
Bozhou China 33°55N 115°41E 32 H8
Bozoum C.A.R. 6°25N 16°35E 54 C3
Bozyazı Turkey 36°6N 33°0E 46 B2
Bra Italy 44°42N 7°51E 20 D7
Brabant □ Belgium 50°46N 4°30E 15 D4
Brabant L. Canada 55°58N 103°43W 71 B8
Brač Croatia 43°20N 16°40E 22 C7
Bracadale, L. U.K. 57°20N 6°30W 11 D2
Bracciano, L. di Italy 42°7N 12°14E 22 C5
Bracebridge Canada 45°2N 79°19W 82 A5
Bräcke Sweden 62°45N 15°26E 8 E16
Brackettville U.S.A. 29°19N 100°25W 84 G4
Bracknell U.K. 51°25N 0°43W 13 F7
Bracknell Forest □ U.K. 51°25N 0°44W 13 F7
Brad Romania 46°10N 22°50E 17 E12
Bradenton U.S.A. 27°30N 82°34W 85 H13
Bradford Canada 44°7N 79°34W 82 B5
Bradford U.K. 53°47N 1°45W 12 D6
Bradford Pa., U.S.A. 41°58N 78°38W 82 E6
Bradford Vt., U.S.A. 43°59N 72°9W 83 C12
Bradley Ark., U.S.A. 33°6N 93°39W 84 E8
Bradley Calif., U.S.A. 35°52N 120°48W 78 K6
Brady U.S.A. 31°9N 99°20W 84 F5
Braeside Canada 45°28N 76°24W 83 A8
Braga Portugal 41°35N 8°25W 21 B1
Bragado Argentina 35°2S 60°27W 94 D3
Bragança Brazil 1°0S 47°2W 93 D9
Bragança Portugal 41°48N 6°50W 21 B2
Bragança Paulista Brazil 22°55S 46°32W 95 A6
Brahestad = Raahe
  Finland 64°40N 24°28E 8 D21

Brahmanbaria Bangla. 23°58N 91°15E 41 H17
Brahmani → India 20°39N 86°46E 44 D8
Brahmapur India 19°15N 84°54E 44 E7
Brahmaputra → Asia 23°40N 90°35E 43 H13
Braich-y-pwll U.K. 52°47N 4°46W 12 E3
Braidwood Australia 35°27S 149°49E 63 F4
Brainerd U.S.A. 46°22N 94°12W 80 B6
Braintree U.K. 51°53N 0°34E 13 F8
Braintree U.S.A. 42°13N 71°0W 83 D14
Brak → S. Africa 29°35S 22°55E 56 D3
Brakwater Namibia 22°28S 17°3E 56 B2
Bramhapuri India 20°36N 79°52E 44 D4
Brampton Canada 43°45N 79°45W 82 C5
Brampton U.K. 54°57N 2°44W 12 C5
Brampton I. Australia 20°49S 149°16E 62 b
Branco → Brazil 1°20S 61°50W 92 D6
Branco, C. Brazil 7°9S 34°47W 90 D7
Brandberg Namibia 21°10S 14°33E 56 B1
Brandberg △ Namibia 21°10S 14°30E 56 B1
Brandenburg = Neubrandenburg
  Germany 53°33N 13°15E 16 B7
Brandenburg Germany 52°25N 12°33E 16 B7
Brandenburg □ Germany 52°50N 13°0E 16 B7
Brandfort S. Africa 28°40S 26°30E 56 C4
Brandon Canada 49°50N 99°57W 71 D9
Brandon U.S.A. 43°48N 73°6W 83 C11
Brandon B. Ireland 52°17N 10°8W 10 D1
Brandon Mt. Ireland 52°15N 10°15W 10 D1
Brandsen Argentina 35°10S 58°15W 94 D4
Brandvlei S. Africa 30°25S 20°30E 56 D3
Branford U.S.A. 41°17N 72°49W 83 E12
Braniewo Poland 54°25N 19°50E 17 A10
Bransfield Str. Antarctica 63°0S 59°0W 5 C18
Branson U.S.A. 36°39N 93°13W 80 G7
Brantford Canada 43°10N 80°15W 82 C4
Bras d'Or L. Canada 45°50N 60°50W 73 C7
Brasher Falls U.S.A. 44°49N 74°47W 83 B10
Brasil = Brazil ■ S. Amer. 12°0S 50°0W 93 F9
Brasil, Planalto Brazil 18°0S 46°30W 90 E6
Brasiléia Brazil 11°0S 68°45W 92 F5
Brasília Brazil 15°47S 47°55W 93 G9
Brasília Legal Brazil 3°49S 55°36W 93 D7
Braslaw Belarus 55°38N 27°0E 9 J22
Braşov Romania 45°38N 25°35E 17 F13
Brasschaat Belgium 51°19N 4°27E 15 C4
Brassey, Banjaran
  Malaysia 5°0N 117°15E 36 D5
Brassey Ra. Australia 25°8S 122°15E 61 E3
Brasstown Bald U.S.A. 34°53N 83°49W 85 D13
Brastad Sweden 58°23N 11°30E 9 G14
Bratislava Slovak Rep. 48°10N 17°7E 17 D9
Bratsk Russia 56°10N 101°30E 27 D11
Bratskoye Vdkhr.
  Russia 56°0N 101°40E 27 D11
Brattleboro U.S.A. 42°51N 72°34W 83 D12
Braunau Austria 48°15N 13°3E 16 D7
Braunschweig Germany 52°15N 10°31E 16 B6
Braunton U.K. 51°7N 4°10W 13 F3
Brava C. Verde Is. 15°0N 24°40W 52 b
Bravo del Norte, Rio = Grande,
  Rio → N. Amer. 25°58N 97°9W 84 J6
Brawley U.S.A. 32°59N 115°31W 79 N11
Bray Ireland 53°13N 6°7W 10 C5
Bray, Mt. Australia 14°0S 134°30E 62 A1
Bray, Pays de France 49°46N 1°26E 20 B4
Brazeau → Canada 52°55N 115°14W 70 C5
Brazil U.S.A. 39°32N 87°8W 80 F10
Brazil ■ S. Amer. 12°0S 50°0W 93 F9
Brazilian Highlands = Brasil,
  Planalto Brazil 18°0S 46°30W 90 E6
Brazo Sur → S. Amer. 25°21S 57°42W 94 B4
Brazos → U.S.A. 28°53N 95°23W 84 G7
Brazzaville Congo 4°9S 15°12E 54 E3
Brčko Bos.-H. 44°54N 18°46E 23 B8
Bré = Bray Ireland 53°13N 6°7W 10 C5
Breaden, L. Australia 25°51S 125°28E 61 E4
Breaksea Sd. N.Z. 45°35S 166°35E 59 F1
Bream B. N.Z. 35°56S 174°28E 59 A5
Bream Hd. N.Z. 35°51S 174°36E 59 A5
Breas Chile 25°29S 70°24W 94 B1
Brebes Indonesia 6°52S 109°3E 37 G13
Brechin Canada 44°32N 79°10W 82 B5
Brechin U.K. 56°44N 2°39W 11 E6
Brecht Belgium 51°21N 4°38E 15 C4
Breckenridge Colo.,
  U.S.A. 39°29N 106°3W 76 G10
Breckenridge Minn.,
  U.S.A. 46°16N 96°35W 80 B5
Breckenridge Tex., U.S.A. 32°45N 98°54W 84 E5
Breckland U.K. 52°30N 0°40E 13 E8
Brecon U.K. 51°57N 3°23W 13 F4
Brecon Beacons U.K. 51°53N 3°26W 13 F4
Brecon Beacons △ U.K. 51°50N 3°30W 13 F4
Breda Neths. 51°35N 4°45E 15 C4
Bredasdorp S. Africa 34°33S 20°2E 56 D3
Bree Belgium 51°8N 5°35E 15 C5
Bregenz Austria 47°30N 9°45E 16 E5
Breiðafjörður Iceland 65°15N 23°15W 8 D2
Brejo Brazil 3°41S 42°47W 93 D10
Bremen Germany 53°4N 8°47E 16 B5
Bremer Bay Australia 34°21S 119°20E 61 F2
Bremer I. Australia 12°5S 136°45E 62 A2
Bremerhaven Germany 53°33N 8°36E 16 B5
Bremerton U.S.A. 47°34N 122°37W 78 C4
Brenham U.S.A. 30°10N 96°24W 84 F6
Brennerpass Austria 47°2N 11°30E 16 E6
Brent U.S.A. 32°56N 87°10W 85 E11
Brentwood U.K. 51°37N 0°19E 13 F8
Brentwood Calif., U.S.A. 37°56N 121°42W 78 H5
Brentwood N.Y., U.S.A. 40°47N 73°15W 83 F11
Bréscia Italy 45°33N 10°15E 20 D9
Breskens Neths. 51°23N 3°33E 15 C3
Breslau = Wrocław Poland 51°5N 17°5E 17 C9
Bresse France 46°43N 11°39E 22 A4
Bressanone Italy 46°43N 11°39E 22 A4
Bressay U.K. 60°9N 1°6W 11 A7
Brest Belarus 52°10N 23°40E 17 B12
Brest France 48°24N 4°31W 20 B1
Brest □ Belarus 52°30N 26°10E 17 B13

Brest-Litovsk = Brest
  Belarus 52°10N 23°40E 17 B12
Bretagne □ France 48°10N 3°0W 20 B2
Breton Canada 53°7N 114°28W 70 C6
Breton Sd. U.S.A. 29°35N 89°15W 85 G10
Brett, C. N.Z. 35°10S 174°20E 59 A5
Brevard U.S.A. 35°14N 82°44W 85 D13
Breves Brazil 1°40S 50°29W 93 D8
Brewarrina Australia 30°0S 146°51E 63 E4
Brewer U.S.A. 44°48N 68°46W 81 C19
Brewer, Mt. U.S.A. 36°44N 118°28W 78 J8
Brewster N.Y., U.S.A. 41°24N 73°36W 83 E11
Brewster Ohio, U.S.A. 40°43N 81°36W 82 F3
Brewster Wash., U.S.A. 48°6N 119°47W 76 B4
Brewster, Kap = Kangikajik
  Greenland 70°7N 22°0W 4 B6
Brewton U.S.A. 31°7N 87°4W 85 F11
Breyten S. Africa 26°16S 30°0E 57 C5
Bria C.A.R. 6°30N 21°58E 54 C4
Briançon France 44°54N 6°39E 20 D7
Bribie I. Australia 27°0S 153°10E 63 D5
Bribri Costa Rica 9°38N 82°50W 88 E3
Bridgefield Barbados 13°9N 59°36W 89 g
Bridgehampton U.S.A. 40°56N 72°19W 83 F12
Bridgend S. Africa 28°40S 26°30E 56 C4
Bridgend U.K. 51°30N 3°34W 13 F4
Bridgend □ U.K. 51°36N 3°36W 13 F4
Bridgenorth Canada 44°23N 78°23W 82 B6
Bridgeport Calif., U.S.A. 38°15N 119°14W 78 G7
Bridgeport Conn., U.S.A. 41°11N 73°12W 83 E11
Bridgeport N.Y., U.S.A. 43°9N 75°58W 83 C9
Bridgeport Nebr., U.S.A. 41°40N 103°6W 80 E2
Bridgeport Tex., U.S.A. 33°13N 97°45W 84 E6
Bridger U.S.A. 45°18N 108°55W 76 D9
Bridgeton U.S.A. 39°26N 75°14W 81 F16
Bridgetown Australia 33°58S 116°7E 61 F2
Bridgetown Barbados 13°6N 59°37W 89 g
Bridgetown Canada 44°55N 65°18W 73 D6
Bridgewater Australia 42°44S 147°14E 63 G4
Bridgewater Canada 44°25N 64°31W 73 D7
Bridgewater Mass.,
  U.S.A. 41°59N 70°58W 83 E14
Bridgewater N.Y., U.S.A. 42°53N 75°15W 83 D9
Bridgewater, C. Australia 38°23S 141°23E 63 F3
Bridgnorth U.K. 52°32N 2°25W 13 E5
Bridgton U.S.A. 44°3N 70°42W 83 B14
Bridgwater U.K. 51°8N 2°59W 13 F5
Bridgwater B. U.K. 51°15N 3°15W 13 F4
Bridlington U.K. 54°5N 0°12W 12 C7
Bridlington B. U.K. 54°4N 0°10W 12 C7
Bridport Australia 40°59S 147°23E 63 G4
Bridport U.K. 50°44N 2°45W 13 G5
Brig Switz. 46°18N 7°59E 20 C7
Brigg U.K. 53°34N 0°28W 12 D7
Brigham City U.S.A. 41°31N 112°1W 76 F7
Bright Australia 36°42S 146°56E 63 F4
Brighton Australia 35°5S 138°30E 63 F2
Brighton Canada 44°2N 77°44W 82 B7
Brighton Trin. & Tob. 10°15N 61°39W 93 K15
Brighton U.K. 50°49N 0°7W 13 G7
Brighton Colo., U.S.A. 39°59N 104°49W 76 G11
Brighton U.S.A. 43°8N 77°34W 82 C7
Brightside Canada 45°7N 76°29W 83 A8
Brilliant Canada 40°15N 80°39W 82 F4
Brindisi Italy 40°39N 17°55E 23 D7
Brinkley U.S.A. 34°53N 91°12W 84 D9
Brinnon U.S.A. 47°41N 122°54W 78 C4
Brion, Î. Canada 47°46N 61°26W 73 C7
Brisay Canada 54°26N 70°31W 73 B5
Brisbane Australia 27°25S 153°2E 63 D5
Brisbane → Australia 27°24S 153°9E 63 D5
Bristol U.K. 51°26N 2°35W 13 F5
Bristol Conn., U.S.A. 41°40N 72°57W 83 E12
Bristol Pa., U.S.A. 40°6N 74°51W 83 F10
Bristol R.I., U.S.A. 41°40N 71°16W 83 E13
Bristol Tenn., U.S.A. 36°36N 82°11W 85 C13
Bristol Vt., U.S.A. 44°8N 73°4W 83 B11
Bristol, City of □ U.K. 51°27N 2°36W 13 F5
Bristol B. U.S.A. 58°0N 160°0W 74 D8
Bristol Channel U.K. 51°18N 4°30W 13 F3
Bristol I. Antarctica 58°45S 28°0W 5 B1
Bristol L. U.S.A. 34°28N 115°41W 79 L11
Bristow U.S.A. 35°50N 96°23W 84 D6
Britain = Great Britain
  Europe 54°0N 2°15W 6 E5
British Columbia □
  Canada 55°0N 125°15W 70 C3
British Indian Ocean Terr. =
  Chagos Arch. ☑ Ind. Oc. 6°0S 72°0E 25 J9
British Isles Europe 54°0N 4°0W 6 E5
British Mts. N. Amer. 68°50N 140°0W 74 B12
British Virgin Is. ☑
  W. Indies 18°30N 64°30W 89 e
Brits S. Africa 25°37S 27°48E 57 C4
Britstown S. Africa 30°37S 23°30E 56 E3
Britt Canada 45°46N 80°34W 72 C3
Brittany = Bretagne □
  France 48°10N 3°0W 20 B2
Britton U.S.A. 45°48N 97°45W 80 C5
Brive-la-Gaillarde France 45°10N 1°32E 20 D4
Brixen = Bressanone
  Italy 46°43N 11°39E 22 A4
Brixham U.K. 50°23N 3°31W 13 G4
Brno Czech Rep. 49°10N 16°35E 17 D9
Broach = Bharuch India 21°47N 73°0E 44 D1
Broad → U.S.A. 34°1N 81°4W 85 D14
Broad Arrow Australia 30°23S 121°15E 61 F3
Broad B. U.K. 58°14N 6°18W 11 C2
Broad Haven Ireland 54°20N 9°55W 10 B2
Broad Law U.K. 55°30N 3°21W 11 F5
Broad Pk. = Faichan Kangri
  India 35°48N 76°34E 43 B7
Broad Sd. Australia 22°0S 149°45E 62 C4
Broadalbin U.S.A. 43°4N 74°12W 83 C10
Broadback → Canada 51°21N 78°52W 72 B4
Broadhurst Ra. Australia 22°30S 122°30E 60 D3
Broads, The U.K. 52°45N 1°30E 12 E9
Broadus U.S.A. 45°27N 105°25W 76 D11
Brochet Canada 57°53N 101°40W 71 B8
Brochet, L. Canada 58°36N 101°35W 71 B8
Brock I. Canada 77°52N 114°19W 69 B9

Brocken Germany 51°47N 10°37E 16 C6
Brockport U.S.A. 43°13N 77°56W 82 C7
Brockton U.S.A. 42°5N 71°1W 83 D13
Brockville Canada 44°35N 75°41W 83 B9
Brockway Mont.,
  U.S.A. 47°18N 105°45W 76 C11
Brockway Pa., U.S.A. 41°15N 78°47W 82 E6
Brocton U.S.A. 42°23N 79°26W 82 D5
Brodeur Pen. Canada 72°30N 88°10W 69 C14
Brodick U.K. 55°35N 5°9W 11 F3
Brodnica Poland 53°15N 19°25E 17 B10
Brody Ukraine 50°5N 25°10E 17 C13
Brogan U.S.A. 44°15N 117°31W 76 D5
Broken Arrow U.S.A. 36°3N 95°48W 84 C7
Broken Bow Nebr.,
  U.S.A. 41°24N 99°38W 80 E4
Broken Bow Okla., U.S.A. 34°2N 94°44W 84 D7
Broken Bow Lake U.S.A. 34°9N 94°40W 84 D7
Broken Hill Australia 31°58S 141°29E 63 E3
Broken Ridge Ind. Oc. 30°0S 94°0E 64 L1
Broken River Ra. Australia 21°0S 148°22E 62 b
Bromo Tengger Semeru △
  Indonesia 7°56S 112°57E 37 H15
Bromsgrove U.K. 52°21N 2°2W 13 E5
Brønderslev Denmark 57°16N 9°57E 9 H13
Bronkhorstspruit
  S. Africa 25°46S 28°45E 57 C4
Brønnøysund Norway 65°28N 12°14E 8 D15
Brook Park U.S.A. 41°23N 81°48W 82 E3
Brookhaven U.S.A. 31°35N 90°26W 85 F9
Brookings Oreg., U.S.A. 42°3N 124°17W 76 E1
Brookings S. Dak., U.S.A. 44°19N 96°48W 80 C5
Brooklin Canada 43°55N 78°55W 82 C6
Brooklyn Park U.S.A. 45°6N 93°23W 80 C7
Brooks Canada 50°35N 111°55W 70 C6
Brooks Range U.S.A. 68°0N 152°0W 74 B9
Brooksville U.S.A. 28°33N 82°23W 85 G13
Brookton Australia 32°22S 117°0E 61 F2
Brookville U.S.A. 41°10N 79°5W 82 E5
Broom, L. U.K. 57°55N 5°15W 11 D3
Broome Australia 18°0S 122°15E 60 C3
Brora U.K. 58°0N 3°52W 11 C5
Brora → U.K. 58°0N 3°51W 11 C5
Brosna → Ireland 53°14N 7°58W 10 C4
Brothers U.S.A. 43°49N 120°36W 76 E3
Brough U.K. 54°32N 2°18W 12 C5
Brough Hd. U.K. 59°8N 3°20W 11 B5
Broughton Island = Qikiqtarjuaq
  Canada 67°33N 63°0W 69 D19
Brown, L. Australia 31°5S 118°15E 61 F2
Brown, Pt. Australia 32°32S 133°50E 63 E1
Brown City U.S.A. 43°13N 82°59W 82 C2
Brown Willy U.K. 50°35N 4°37W 13 G3
Brownfield U.S.A. 33°11N 102°17W 84 E3
Browning U.S.A. 48°34N 113°1W 76 B7
Brownsville Oreg.,
  U.S.A. 44°24N 122°59W 76 D2
Brownsville Pa., U.S.A. 40°1N 79°53W 82 F5
Brownsville Tenn.,
  U.S.A. 35°36N 89°16W 85 D10
Brownsville Tex., U.S.A. 25°54N 97°30W 84 J6
Brownville U.S.A. 44°0N 75°59W 83 C9
Brownwood U.S.A. 31°43N 98°59W 84 F5
Browse I. Australia 14°7S 123°33E 60 B3
Bruas Malaysia 4°30N 100°47E 39 K3
Bruay-la-Buissière France 50°29N 2°33E 20 A5
Bruce, Mt. Australia 22°37S 118°8E 60 D2
Bruce Pen. Canada 45°0N 81°30W 82 B3
Bruce Peninsula △
  Canada 45°14N 81°36W 82 A3
Bruce Rock Australia 31°52S 118°8E 61 F2
Bruck an der Leitha
  Austria 48°1N 16°47E 17 D9
Bruck an der Mur Austria 47°24N 15°16E 16 E8
Brue → U.K. 51°13N 2°59W 13 F5
Bruges = Brugge Belgium 51°13N 3°13E 15 C3
Brugge Belgium 51°13N 3°13E 15 C3
Bruin U.S.A. 41°3N 79°43W 82 E5
Brûk, W. el → Egypt 30°15N 33°50E 48 E2
Brûlé Canada 53°15N 117°58W 70 C5
Brûlé, L. Canada 53°35N 64°4W 73 B7
Brumado Brazil 14°14S 41°40W 93 F10
Brumunddal Norway 60°53N 10°56E 8 F14
Bruneau U.S.A. 42°53N 115°48W 76 E6
Bruneau → U.S.A. 42°56N 115°57W 76 E6
Brunei = Bandar Seri Begawan
  Brunei 4°52N 115°0E 36 D5
Brunei ■ Asia 4°50N 115°0E 36 D5
Brunner, L. N.Z. 42°37S 171°27E 59 E3
Brunssum Neths. 50°57N 5°59E 15 D5
Brunswick = Braunschweig
  Germany 52°15N 10°31E 16 B6
Brunswick Ga., U.S.A. 31°10N 81°30W 85 F14
Brunswick Maine,
  U.S.A. 43°55N 69°58W 81 D19
Brunswick Md., U.S.A. 39°19N 77°38W 81 F15
Brunswick Mo., U.S.A. 39°26N 93°8W 80 F7
Brunswick Ohio, U.S.A. 41°14N 81°51W 82 E3
Brunswick, Pen. de Chile 53°30S 71°30W 96 G2
Brunswick B. Australia 15°15S 124°50E 60 C3
Brunswick Junction
  Australia 33°15S 115°50E 61 F2
Brunt Ice Shelf Antarctica 75°30S 25°0W 5 D2
Brus Laguna Honduras 15°47N 84°35W 88 C3
Brush U.S.A. 40°15N 103°37W 76 F12
Brushton U.S.A. 44°50N 74°31W 83 B10
Brusque Brazil 27°5S 49°0W 95 B6
Brussels Canada 43°44N 81°15W 82 C3
Bruthen Australia 37°42S 147°50E 63 F4
Bryan Ohio, U.S.A. 41°28N 84°33W 81 E11
Bryan Tex., U.S.A. 30°40N 96°22W 84 F6
Bryan, Mt. Australia 33°30S 139°5E 63 E2
Bryansk Russia 53°13N 34°25E 18 D4
Bryce Canyon △ U.S.A. 37°30N 112°10W 77 H7
Bryne Norway 58°44N 5°38E 9 G11
Bryson City U.S.A. 35°26N 83°27W 85 D13
Bsharri Lebanon 34°15N 36°0E 48 A5
Bū Baqarah U.A.E. 25°35N 56°25E 47 E8
Bu Craa W. Sahara 26°45N 12°50W 52 C3

Bū Ḩaşā *U.A.E.* 23°30N 53°20E **47** F7
Bua *Fiji* 16°48S 178°37E **59** a
Bua Yai *Thailand* 15°33N 102°26E **38** E4
Buan *S. Korea* 35°44N 126°44E **33** G14
Buapinang *Indonesia* 4°40S 121°30E **37** E6
Bubi → *Zimbabwe* 22°20S 31°7E **57** B5
Būbiyān *Kuwait* 29°45N 48°15E **47** D6
Buca *Fiji* 16°38S 179°52E **59** a
Bucaramanga *Colombia* 7°0N 73°0W **92** B4
Bucasia *Australia* 21°2S 149°10E **62** b
Buccaneer Arch.
  Australia 16°7S 123°20E **60** C3
Buccoo Reef *Trin. & Tob.* 11°10N 60°51W **93** J16
Buchach *Ukraine* 49°5N 25°25E **17** D13
Buchan *U.K.* 57°32N 2°21W **11** D6
Buchan Ness *U.K.* 57°29N 1°46W **11** D7
Buchanan *Canada* 51°40N 102°45W **71** C8
Buchanan *Liberia* 5°57N 10°2W **52** G3
Buchanan, L. *Queens.,*
  Australia 21°35S 145°52E **62** C4
Buchanan, L. *W. Austral.,*
  Australia 25°33S 123°2E **61** E3
Buchanan, L. *U.S.A.* 30°45N 98°25W **84** F5
Buchanan Cr. →
  Australia 19°13S 136°33E **62** B2
Buchans *Canada* 48°50N 56°52W **73** C8
Bucharest = Bucureşti
  Romania 44°27N 26°10E **17** F14
Bucheon *S. Korea* 37°28N 126°45E **33** F14
Buchon, Pt. *U.S.A.* 35°15N 120°54W **78** K6
Buck Hill Falls *U.S.A.* 41°11N 75°16W **83** E9
Buckeye Lake *U.S.A.* 39°55N 82°29W **82** G2
Buckhannon *U.S.A.* 39°0N 80°8W **81** F13
Buckhaven *U.K.* 56°11N 3°3W **11** E5
Buckhorn L. *Canada* 44°29N 78°23W **82** B6
Buckie *U.K.* 57°41N 2°58W **11** D6
Buckingham *Canada* 45°37N 75°24W **72** C4
Buckingham *U.K.* 51°59N 0°57W **13** F7
Buckingham B.
  Australia 12°10S 135°40E **62** A2
Buckingham Canal *India* 14°0N 80°5E **45** H5
Buckinghamshire □ *U.K.* 51°53N 0°55W **13** F7
Buckle Hd. *Australia* 14°26S 127°52E **60** B4
Buckleboo *Australia* 32°54S 136°12E **63** E2
Buckley *U.K.* 53°10N 3°5W **12** D4
Buckley → *Australia* 20°10S 138°49E **62** C2
Bucklin *U.S.A.* 37°33N 99°38W **80** G4
Bucks L. *U.S.A.* 39°54N 121°12W **78** F5
Bucureşti *Romania* 44°27N 26°10E **17** F14
Bucyrus *U.S.A.* 40°48N 82°59W **81** E12
Budalin *Burma* 22°20N 95°10E **41** H19
Budaun *India* 28°5N 79°10E **43** E8
Budd Coast *Antarctica* 68°0S 112°0E **5** C8
Bude *U.K.* 50°49N 4°34W **13** G3
Budennovsk *Russia* 44°50N 44°10E **19** F7
Budge Budge = Baj Baj
  India 22°30N 88°5E **43** H13
Budgewoi *Australia* 33°13S 151°34E **63** E5
Budjala
  Dem. Rep. of the Congo 2°50N 19°40E **54** D3
Budo-Sungai Padi △
  Thailand 6°19N 101°42E **39** J3
Buellton *U.S.A.* 34°37N 120°12W **79** L6
Buena Esperanza
  Argentina 34°45S 65°15W **94** C2
Buena Park *U.S.A.* 33°52N 117°59W **79** M9
Buena Vista *Colo.,*
  U.S.A. 38°51N 106°8W **76** G10
Buena Vista *Va., U.S.A.* 37°44N 79°21W **81** G14
Buena Vista Lake Bed
  U.S.A. 35°12N 119°18W **79** K7
Buenaventura *Colombia* 3°53N 77°4W **92** C3
Buenaventura *Mexico* 29°51N 107°29W **86** B3
Buenos Aires *Costa Rica* 9°10N 83°20W **88** E3
Buenos Aires □ *Argentina* 36°30S 60°0W **94** D4
Buenos Aires, L. = General
  Carrera, L. *S. Amer.* 46°35S 72°0W **96** F2
Buffalo *Mo., U.S.A.* 37°39N 93°6W **80** G7
Buffalo *N.Y., U.S.A.* 42°53N 78°53W **82** D6
Buffalo *Okla., U.S.A.* 36°50N 99°38W **84** C5
Buffalo *S. Dak., U.S.A.* 45°35N 103°33W **80** C2
Buffalo *Wyo., U.S.A.* 44°21N 106°42W **76** D10
Buffalo → *Canada* 60°5N 115°5W **70** A5
Buffalo → *S. Africa* 28°43S 30°37E **57** C5
Buffalo △ *U.S.A.* 36°14N 92°36W **84** C8
Buffalo Head Hills
  Canada 57°25N 115°55W **70** B5
Buffalo L. *Alta., Canada* 52°27N 112°54W **70** C6
Buffalo L. *N.W.T.,*
  Canada 60°12N 115°25W **70** A5
Buffalo Narrows *Canada* 55°51N 108°29W **71** B7
Buffels → *S. Africa* 29°36S 17°3E **56** C2
Buford *U.S.A.* 34°7N 83°59W **85** D12
Bug = Buh → *Ukraine* 46°59N 31°58E **19** E5
Bug → *Poland* 52°31N 21°5E **17** B11
Buga *Colombia* 4°0N 76°15W **92** C3
Bugel, Tanjung *Indonesia* 6°26S 111°3E **37** G14
Bugsuk I. *Phil.* 8°12N 117°18E **36** C5
Bugulma *Russia* 54°33N 52°48E **18** D9
Buguruslan *Russia* 53°39N 52°26E **18** D9
Buh → *Ukraine* 46°59N 31°58E **19** E5
Buhera *Zimbabwe* 19°18S 31°29E **57** A5
Buhl *U.S.A.* 42°36N 114°46W **76** E6
Builth Wells *U.K.* 52°9N 3°25W **13** E4
Buir Nur *Mongolia* 47°50N 117°42E **31** B12
Buji *China* 22°37N 114°5E **31** a
Bujumbura *Burundi* 3°16S 29°18E **54** E5
Bukachacha *Russia* 52°55N 116°50E **27** D12
Bukavu
  Dem. Rep. of the Congo 2°20S 28°52E **54** E5
Bukhara = Buxoro
  Uzbekistan 39°48N 64°25E **26** F7
Bukhoro = Buxoro
  Uzbekistan 39°48N 64°25E **26** F7
Bukhtarma Res. = Zaysan Köli
  Kazakhstan 48°0N 83°0E **26** E9
Bukit Bendera *Malaysia* 5°25N 100°15E **39** c
Bukit Mertajam *Malaysia* 5°22N 100°28E **39** c
Bukit Nil *Malaysia* 1°22N 104°12E **39** d

Bukit Tengah *Malaysia* 5°22N 100°25E **39** c
Bukittinggi *Indonesia* 0°20S 100°20E **36** E2
Bukkapatnam *India* 14°14N 77°46E **45** G3
Bukoba *Tanzania* 1°20S 31°49E **54** E6
Bula *Indonesia* 3°6S 130°30E **37** E8
Bula *Phil.* 12°40N 123°52E **37** B6
Bulan *Phil.* 12°40N 123°52E **37** B6
Buldan *Turkey* 38°2N 28°50E **23** E13
Buldana *India* 20°30N 76°18E **44** D3
Buldir I. *U.S.A.* 52°21N 175°56E **74** E3
Bulgan *Mongolia* 48°45N 103°34E **30** B9
Bulgar *Russia* 54°57N 49°4E **18** D8
Bulgaria ■ *Europe* 42°35N 25°30E **23** C11
Buli, Teluk *Indonesia* 0°48N 128°25E **37** D7
Buliluyan, C. *Phil.* 8°20N 117°15E **36** C5
Bulkley → *Canada* 55°15N 127°40W **70** B3
Bull Shoals L. *U.S.A.* 36°22N 92°35W **84** C8
Bulleringa △ *Australia* 17°39S 143°56E **62** B3
Bullhead City *U.S.A.* 35°8N 114°32W **79** K12
Büllingen *Belgium* 50°25N 6°16E **15** D6
Bullock Creek *Australia* 17°43S 144°31E **62** B3
Bulloo → *Australia* 28°43S 142°30E **63** D3
Bulloo L. *Australia* 28°43S 142°25E **63** D3
Bulls *N.Z.* 40°10S 175°24E **59** D5
Bulman *Australia* 13°39S 134°20E **62** A1
Bulnes *Chile* 36°42S 72°19W **94** D1
Bulsar = Valsad *India* 20°40N 72°58E **44** D1
Bultfontein *S. Africa* 28°18S 26°10E **56** D4
Bulukumba *Indonesia* 5°33S 120°11E **37** F6
Bulun *Russia* 70°37N 127°30E **27** B13
Bumba
  Dem. Rep. of the Congo 2°13N 22°30E **54** D4
Bumbah, Khalīj *Libya* 32°20N 23°15E **53** B10
Bumhpa Bum *Burma* 26°51N 97°14E **41** F20
Bunaken *Indonesia* 1°37N 124°46E **37** D6
Bunbury *Australia* 33°20S 115°35E **61** F2
Bunclody *Ireland* 52°39N 6°40W **10** D5
Buncrana *Ireland* 55°8N 7°27W **10** A4
Bundaberg *Australia* 24°54S 152°22E **63** C5
Bundey → *Australia* 21°46S 135°37E **62** C2
Bundi *India* 25°30N 75°35E **42** G6
Bundjalung △ *Australia* 29°16S 153°21E **63** D5
Bundoran *Ireland* 54°28N 8°18W **10** B3
Bung Kan *Thailand* 18°23N 103°37E **38** C4
Bungay *U.K.* 52°27N 1°28E **13** E9
Bungil Cr. → *Australia* 27°5S 149°5E **63** D4
Bungle Bungle = Purnululu △
  Australia 17°20S 128°20E **60** C4
Bungo-Suidō *Japan* 33°0N 132°15E **29** H6
Bungotakada *Japan* 33°35N 131°25E **29** H5
Bunia
  Dem. Rep. of the Congo 1°35N 30°20E **54** D6
Bunji *Pakistan* 35°45N 74°40E **43** B6
Bunkie *U.S.A.* 30°57N 92°11W **84** F8
Bunnell *U.S.A.* 29°28N 81°16W **85** G14
Buntok *Indonesia* 1°40S 114°58E **36** E4
Bunya Mts. △ *Australia* 26°51S 151°34E **63** D5
Bunyu *Indonesia* 3°35N 117°50E **36** D5
Buol *Indonesia* 1°15N 121°32E **37** D6
Buon Brieng *Vietnam* 13°9N 108°12E **38** F7
Buon Ho *Vietnam* 12°57N 108°18E **38** F7
Buon Ma Thuot *Vietnam* 12°40N 108°3E **38** F7
Buong Long *Cambodia* 13°44N 106°59E **38** F6
Buorkhaya, Mys
  Russia 71°50N 132°40E **27** B14
Buqayq *Si. Arabia* 26°0N 49°45E **47** E6
Bur Acaba = Buurhakaba
  Somalia 3°12N 44°20E **49** G3
Bûr Safâga *Egypt* 26°43N 33°57E **46** E2
Bûr Sa'îd *Egypt* 31°16N 32°18E **53** B12
Bûr Sûdân *Sudan* 19°32N 37°9E **53** E13
Burakin *Australia* 30°31S 117°10E **61** F2
Burang *China* 30°15N 81°10E **30** D5
Burao = Burco *Somalia* 9°32N 45°32E **49** F4
Burāq *Syria* 33°11N 36°29E **48** B5
Burathum *Nepal* 28°4N 84°50E **43** E11
Buraydah *Si. Arabia* 26°20N 43°59E **46** E4
Burco *Somalia* 9°32N 45°32E **49** F4
Burda *India* 25°50N 77°35E **42** G7
Burdekin → *Australia* 19°38S 147°25E **62** B4
Burdur *Turkey* 37°45N 30°17E **19** G5
Burdwan = Barddhaman
  India 23°14N 87°39E **43** H12
Bure *Ethiopia* 10°40N 37°4E **49** E2
Bure → *U.K.* 52°38N 1°43E **12** E9
Bureskoye Vdkhr.
  Russia 50°16N 130°20E **27** D14
Burg el Arab *Egypt* 30°54N 29°32E **53** B11
Burgas *Bulgaria* 42°33N 27°29E **23** C12
Burgeo *Canada* 47°37N 57°38W **73** C8
Burgersdorp *S. Africa* 31°0S 26°20E **56** D4
Burgess, Mt. *Canada* 30°50S 121°5E **61** F3
Burghead *U.K.* 57°43N 3°30W **11** D5
Burgos *Spain* 42°21N 3°41W **21** A4
Burgsvik *Sweden* 57°3N 18°19E **9** H18
Burgundy = Bourgogne □
  France 47°0N 4°50E **20** C6
Burhaniye *Turkey* 39°30N 26°58E **23** E12
Burhanpur *India* 21°18N 76°14E **44** D3
Burhi Gandak → *India* 25°20N 86°37E **43** G12
Burias I. *Phil.* 12°55N 123°5E **37** B6
Burica, Pta. *Costa Rica* 8°3N 82°51W **88** E3
Burien *U.S.A.* 47°28N 122°20W **78** C4
Buriram *Thailand* 15°0N 103°0E **38** E4
Burkburnett *U.S.A.* 34°6N 98°34W **84** D5
Burke → *Australia* 23°12S 139°33E **62** C2
Burke Chan. *Canada* 52°10N 127°30W **70** C3
Burketown *Australia* 17°45S 139°33E **62** B2
Burkina Faso ■ *Africa* 12°0N 1°0W **52** F5
Burk's Falls *Canada* 45°37N 79°24W **72** C4
Burleigh Falls *Canada* 44°33N 78°12W **82** B6
Burley *U.S.A.* 42°32N 113°48W **76** E7
Burlingame *U.S.A.* 37°35N 122°21W **78** H4
Burlington *Canada* 43°18N 79°45W **82** C5

Burlington *Colo.,*
  U.S.A. 39°18N 102°16W **76** G12
Burlington *Iowa, U.S.A.* 40°49N 91°14W **80** E8
Burlington *Kans., U.S.A.* 38°12N 95°45W **80** F7
Burlington *N.C., U.S.A.* 36°6N 79°26W **85** C15
Burlington *N.J., U.S.A.* 40°4N 74°51W **83** F10
Burlington *Vt., U.S.A.* 44°29N 73°12W **83** B11
Burlington *Wash.,*
  U.S.A. 48°28N 122°20W **78** B4
Burlington *Wis., U.S.A.* 42°41N 88°17W **80** D9
Burma ■ *Asia* 21°0N 96°30E **41** J20
Burnaby I. *Canada* 52°25N 131°19W **70** C2
Burnet *U.S.A.* 30°45N 98°14W **84** F5
Burney *U.S.A.* 40°53N 121°40W **76** F3
Burnham *U.S.A.* 40°38N 77°34W **82** F7
Burnham-on-Sea *U.K.* 51°14N 3°0W **13** F4
Burnie *Australia* 41°4S 145°56E **63** G4
Burnley *U.K.* 53°47N 2°14W **12** D5
Burns *U.S.A.* 43°35N 119°3W **76** E4
Burns Junction *U.S.A.* 42°47N 117°51W **76** E5
Burns Lake *Canada* 54°14N 125°45W **70** C3
Burnside → *Canada* 66°51N 108°4W **68** D10
Burnside, L. *Australia* 25°22S 123°0E **61** E3
Burnsville *U.S.A.* 44°47N 93°17W **80** C7
Burnt River *Canada* 44°41N 78°42W **82** B6
Burntwood → *Canada* 56°8N 96°34W **71** B9
Burntwood L. *Canada* 55°22N 100°26W **71** B8
Burqān *Kuwait* 29°0N 47°57E **46** D5
Burqin *China* 47°43N 87°0E **30** B6
Burra *Australia* 33°40S 138°55E **63** E2
Burray *U.K.* 58°51N 2°54W **11** C6
Burren △ *Ireland* 53°9N 9°5W **10** C2
Burren Junction *Australia* 30°7S 148°58E **63** E4
Burrinjuck, L. *Australia* 35°0S 148°36E **63** F4
Burro, Serranías del
  Mexico 28°56N 102°5W **86** B4
Burrow Hd. *U.K.* 54°41N 4°24W **11** G4
Burrum Coast △
  Australia 25°13S 152°36E **63** D5
Burruyacú *Argentina* 26°30S 64°40W **94** B3
Burry Port *U.K.* 51°41N 4°15W **13** F3
Bursa *Turkey* 40°15N 29°5E **23** D13
Burstall *Canada* 50°39N 109°54W **71** C7
Burton *Ohio, U.S.A.* 41°28N 81°8W **82** E3
Burton *S.C., U.S.A.* 32°26N 80°43W **85** E14
Burton, L. *Canada* 54°45N 78°20W **72** B4
Burton upon Trent *U.K.* 52°48N 1°38W **12** E6
Buru *Indonesia* 3°30S 126°30E **37** E7
Burūn, Râs *Egypt* 31°14N 33°7E **48** D2
Burundi ■ *Africa* 3°15S 30°0E **54** E5
Burutu *Nigeria* 5°20N 5°29E **52** G7
Burwell *U.S.A.* 41°47N 99°8W **80** E4
Burwick *U.K.* 58°45N 2°58E **11** C5
Bury *U.K.* 53°35N 2°17W **12** D5
Bury St. Edmunds *U.K.* 52°15N 0°43E **13** E8
Buryatia □ *Russia* 53°0N 110°0E **27** D12
Busan *S. Korea* 35°5N 129°0E **33** G15
Busaso = Boosaaso
  Somalia 11°12N 49°18E **49** E4
Buşayrah *Syria* 35°9N 40°26E **46** C4
Büshehr *Iran* 28°55N 50°55E **47** D6
Büshehr □ *Iran* 28°20N 51°45E **47** D6
Bushire = Büshehr *Iran* 28°55N 50°55E **47** D6
Businga
  Dem. Rep. of the Congo 3°16N 20°59E **54** D4
Buşra ash Shām *Syria* 32°30N 36°25E **48** C5
Busselton *Australia* 33°42S 115°15E **61** F2
Bussum *Neths.* 52°16N 5°10E **15** B5
Busto Arsízio *Italy* 45°37N 8°51E **20** D8
Busu Djanoa
  Dem. Rep. of the Congo 1°43N 21°23E **54** D4
Busuanga I. *Phil.* 12°10N 120°0E **37** B6
Busungbiu *Indonesia* 8°16S 114°58E **37** J17
Buta *Dem. Rep. of the Congo* 2°50N 24°53E **54** D4
Butare *Rwanda* 2°31S 29°52E **54** E5
Butaritari *Kiribati* 3°30N 174°0E **64** G9
Bute *U.K.* 55°48N 5°2W **11** F3
Bute Inlet *Canada* 50°40N 124°53W **70** C4
Butembo
  Dem. Rep. of the Congo 0°9N 29°18E **54** D5
Butha-Buthe *Lesotho* 28°47S 28°14E **57** C4
Butler *Mo., U.S.A.* 38°16N 94°20W **80** F6
Butler *Pa., U.S.A.* 40°52N 79°54W **82** F5
Buton *Indonesia* 5°0S 122°45E **37** E6
Butte *Mont., U.S.A.* 46°0N 112°32W **76** C7
Butte *Nebr., U.S.A.* 42°58N 98°51W **80** D4
Butte Creek → *U.S.A.* 39°12N 121°56W **78** F5
Butterworth = Gcuwa
  S. Africa 32°20S 28°11E **57** D4
Butterworth *Malaysia* 5°24N 100°23E **39** c
Buttevant *Ireland* 52°14N 8°40W **10** D3
Buttfield, Mt. *Australia* 24°45S 128°9E **61** D4
Button B. *Canada* 58°45N 94°23W **71** B10
Buttonwillow *U.S.A.* 35°24N 119°28W **79** K7
Butty Hd. *Australia* 33°54S 121°39E **61** F3
Butuan *Phil.* 8°57N 125°33E **37** C7
Butung = Buton *Indonesia* 5°0S 122°45E **37** E6
Buturlinovka *Russia* 50°50N 40°35E **19** D7
Butwal *Nepal* 27°33N 83°31E **43** F10
Buxar *India* 25°34N 83°58E **43** G10
Buxoro *Uzbekistan* 39°48N 64°25E **26** F7
Buxtehude *Germany* 53°28N 9°39E **16** B5
Buxton *U.K.* 53°16N 1°54W **12** D6
Buy *Russia* 58°28N 41°28E **18** C7
Buyant-Uhaa *Mongolia* 44°55N 110°11E **32** B6
Buyo, L. de *Ivory C.* 6°16N 7°10W **52** G4
Büyük Menderes →
  Turkey 37°28N 27°11E **23** F12
Büyükçekmece *Turkey* 41°2N 28°35E **23** D13
Buyun Shan *China* 40°4N 122°43E **33** D12
Buzău *Romania* 45°10N 26°50E **17** F14
Buzău → *Romania* 45°26N 27°44E **17** F14
Buzen *Japan* 33°35N 131°5E **29** H5
Buzi → *Mozam.* 19°50S 34°43E **55** H6
Büzmeyin *Turkmenistan* 38°3N 58°12E **47** B8
Buzuluk *Russia* 52°48N 52°12E **18** D9
Buzzards Bay *U.S.A.* 41°45N 70°37W **83** E14

Byam Martin I. *Canada* 75°15N 104°15W **69** B11
Byarezina → *Belarus* 52°33N 30°14E **17** B16
Byaroza *Belarus* 52°31N 24°51E **17** B13
Byblos = Jubayl *Lebanon* 34°5N 35°39E **48** A4
Bydgoszcz *Poland* 53°10N 18°0E **17** B9
Byelorussia = Belarus ■
  Europe 53°30N 27°0E **17** B14
Byers *U.S.A.* 39°43N 104°14W **76** G11
Byesville *U.S.A.* 39°58N 81°32W **82** G3
Byfield △ *Australia* 22°52S 150°45E **62** C5
Bykhaw *Belarus* 53°31N 30°14E **17** B16
Bykhov = Bykhaw
  Belarus 53°31N 30°14E **17** B16
Bylas *U.S.A.* 33°8N 110°7W **77** K8
Bylot *Canada* 58°25N 94°8W **71** B10
Bylot I. *Canada* 73°13N 78°34W **69** C16
Byram *U.S.A.* 32°11N 90°15W **85** E9
Byrd, C. *Antarctica* 69°38S 76°7W **5** C17
Byrock *Australia* 30°40S 146°27E **63** E4
Byron, C. *Australia* 28°43S 153°38E **63** D5
Byron Bay *Australia* 28°43S 153°37E **63** D5
Byrranga, Gory *Russia* 75°0N 100°0E **27** B11
Byrranga Mts. = Byrranga, Gory
  Russia 75°0N 100°0E **27** B11
Byske *Sweden* 64°57N 21°11E **8** D19
Byskeälven → *Sweden* 64°57N 21°13E **8** D19
Bytom *Poland* 50°25N 18°54E **17** C10
Bytów *Poland* 54°10N 17°30E **17** A9

C

C.W. McConaughy, L.
  U.S.A. 41°14N 101°40W **80** E3
Ca → *Vietnam* 18°45N 105°45E **38** C5
Ca Mau *Vietnam* 9°7N 105°8E **39** H5
Ca Mau, Mui *Vietnam* 8°38N 104°44E **39** H5
Ca Na *Vietnam* 11°20N 108°54E **39** G7
Caacupé *Paraguay* 25°23S 57°5W **94** B4
Caaguazú □ *Paraguay* 26°5S 55°31W **95** B4
Caála *Angola* 12°46S 15°30E **55** G3
Caamaño Sd. *Canada* 52°55N 129°25W **70** C3
Caazapá *Paraguay* 26°8S 56°19W **94** B4
Caazapá □ *Paraguay* 26°10S 56°0W **95** B4
Cabanatuan *Phil.* 15°30N 120°58E **37** A6
Cabano *Canada* 47°40N 68°56W **73** C6
Cabazon *U.S.A.* 33°55N 116°47W **79** M10
Cabedelo *Brazil* 7°0S 34°50W **93** E12
Cabhán, An = Cavan
  Ireland 54°0N 7°22W **10** B4
Cabildo *Chile* 32°30S 71°5W **94** C1
Cabimas *Venezuela* 10°23N 71°25W **92** A4
Cabinda *Angola* 5°33S 12°11E **54** F2
Cabinda □ *Angola* 5°0S 12°30E **54** F2
Cabinet Mts. *U.S.A.* 48°10N 115°50W **76** B6
Cabo Blanco *Argentina* 47°15S 65°47W **96** F3
Cabo Frio *Brazil* 22°51S 42°3W **95** A7
Cabo Pantoja *Peru* 1°0S 75°10W **92** D3
Cabo San Lucas *Mexico* 22°53N 109°54W **86** C3
Cabo Verde = Cape Verde Is. ■
  Atl. Oc. 16°0N 24°0W **52** b
Cabonga, Réservoir
  Canada 47°20N 76°40W **72** C4
Cabool *U.S.A.* 37°7N 92°6W **80** G8
Caboolture *Australia* 27°5S 152°58E **63** D5
Cabora Bassa Dam = Cahora
  Bassa, Lago de *Mozam.* 15°20S 32°50E **55** H6
Caborca *Mexico* 30°37N 112°6W **86** A2
Cabot, Mt. *U.S.A.* 44°30N 71°25W **83** B13
Cabot Hd. *Canada* 45°14N 81°17W **82** A3
Cabot Str. *Canada* 47°15N 59°40W **73** C8
Cabra *Spain* 37°30N 4°28W **21** D3
Cabra I. *India* 7°18N 93°50E **45** L11
Cabrera *Spain* 39°8N 2°57E **21** C7
Cabri *Canada* 50°35N 108°25W **71** C7
Cabriel → *Spain* 39°14N 1°3W **21** C5
Caçador *Brazil* 26°47S 51°0W **95** B5
Čačak *Serbia* 43°54N 20°20E **23** C9
Caçapava do Sul *Brazil* 30°30S 53°30W **95** C5
Cáceres *Brazil* 16°5S 57°40W **92** G7
Cáceres *Spain* 39°26N 6°23W **21** C2
Cache Bay *Canada* 46°22N 80°0W **72** C4
Cache Cr. → *U.S.A.* 38°42N 121°42W **78** G5
Cache Creek *Canada* 50°48N 121°19W **70** C4
Cachi *Argentina* 25°5S 66°10W **94** B2
Cachimbo, Serra do *Brazil* 9°30S 55°30W **93** E7
Cachinal de la Sierra
  Chile 24°58S 69°32W **94** A2
Cachoeira *Brazil* 12°30S 39°0W **93** F11
Cachoeira do Sul *Brazil* 30°3S 52°53W **95** C5
Cachoeiro de Itapemirim
  Brazil 20°51S 41°7W **95** A7
Cacoal *Brazil* 11°32S 61°18W **92** F6
Cacólo *Angola* 10°9S 19°21E **54** G3
Caconda *Angola* 13°48S 15°8E **55** G3
Caddo *U.S.A.* 34°7N 96°16W **84** D6
Cader Idris *U.K.* 52°42N 3°53W **13** E4
Cadereyta de Jiménez
  Mexico 25°36N 100°0W **86** B5
Cadibarrawirracanna, L.
  Australia 28°52S 135°27E **63** D2
Cadillac *U.S.A.* 44°15N 85°24W **81** C11
Cadiz *Phil.* 10°57N 123°15E **37** B6
Cádiz *Spain* 36°30N 6°20W **21** D2
Cadiz *Calif., U.S.A.* 34°30N 115°28W **79** L11
Cadiz *Ohio, U.S.A.* 40°22N 81°0W **82** F4
Cádiz, G. de *Spain* 36°40N 7°0W **21** D2
Cadiz L. *U.S.A.* 34°18N 115°24W **79** L11
Cadney Park *Australia* 27°55S 134°3E **63** D1
Cadomin *Canada* 53°2N 117°20W **70** C5
Cadoux *Australia* 30°46S 117°7E **61** F2
Caen *France* 49°10N 0°22W **20** B3
Caerdydd = Cardiff *U.K.* 51°29N 3°10W **13** F4
Caerfyrddin = Carmarthen
  U.K. 51°52N 4°19W **13** F3
Caergybi = Holyhead
  U.K. 53°18N 4°38W **12** D3
Caernarfon *U.K.* 53°8N 4°16W **12** D3
Caernarfon B. *U.K.* 53°4N 4°40W **12** D3

Caernarvon = Caernarfon
  U.K. 53°8N 4°16W **12** D3
Caerphilly *U.K.* 51°35N 3°13W **13** F4
Caerphilly □ *U.K.* 51°37N 3°12W **13** F4
Caesarea *Israel* 32°30N 34°53E **48** C3
Caetité *Brazil* 13°50S 42°32W **93** F10
Cafayate *Argentina* 26°2S 66°0W **94** B2
Cafu *Angola* 16°30S 15°8E **56** B2
Cagayan de Oro *Phil.* 8°30N 124°40E **37** C6
Cágliari *Italy* 39°13N 9°7E **22** E3
Cágliari, G. di *Italy* 39°8N 9°11E **22** E3
Cagúan → *Colombia* 0°8S 74°18W **92** D4
Caguas *Puerto Rico* 18°14N 66°2W **89** d
Caha Mts. *Ireland* 51°45N 9°40W **10** E2
Cahama *Angola* 16°17S 14°19E **56** A1
Cahir *Ireland* 52°22N 7°56W **10** D4
Cahirciveen *Ireland* 51°56N 10°14W **10** E1
Cahora Bassa, Lago de
  Mozam. 15°20S 32°50E **55** H6
Cahore Pt. *Ireland* 52°33N 6°12W **10** D5
Cahors *France* 44°27N 1°27E **20** D4
Cahul *Moldova* 45°50N 28°15E **17** F15
Cai Bau, Dao *Vietnam* 21°10N 107°27E **34** G6
Cai Be *Vietnam* 10°20N 106°2E **39** G6
Cai Nuoc *Vietnam* 8°56N 105°1E **39** H5
Caia *Mozam.* 17°51S 35°24E **55** H7
Caianda *Angola* 11°2S 23°31E **54** G4
Caibarién *Cuba* 22°30N 79°30W **88** B4
Caicara *Venezuela* 7°38N 66°10W **92** B5
Caicó *Brazil* 6°20S 37°0W **93** E11
Caicos Is. *Turks & Caicos* 21°40N 71°40W **89** B5
Caicos Passage *W. Indies* 22°45N 72°45W **89** B5
Caidian *China* 30°35N 114°2E **35** B10
Caiguna *Australia* 32°16S 125°29E **61** F4
Caird Coast *Antarctica* 75°0S 25°0W **5** D1
Cairn Gorm *U.K.* 57°7N 3°39W **11** D5
Cairngorm Mts. *U.K.* 57°6N 3°42W **11** D5
Cairngorms △ *U.K.* 57°10N 3°50W **11** D5
Cairnryan *U.K.* 54°59N 5°1W **11** G3
Cairns *Australia* 16°57S 145°45E **62** B4
Cairns L. *Canada* 51°42N 94°30W **71** C10
Cairo = El Qâhira *Egypt* 30°2N 31°13E **53** B12
Cairo *Ga., U.S.A.* 30°52N 84°13W **85** F12
Cairo *Ill., U.S.A.* 37°0N 89°11W **80** G9
Cairo *N.Y., U.S.A.* 42°18N 74°0W **83** D11
Caiseal = Cashel *Ireland* 52°30N 7°53W **10** D4
Caisleán an Bharraigh = Castlebar
  Ireland 53°52N 9°18W **10** C2
Caithness *U.K.* 58°25N 3°35W **11** C5
Caithness, Ord of *U.K.* 58°8N 3°36W **11** C5
Caja de Muertos, I.
  Puerto Rico 17°54N 66°32W **89** d
Cajamarca *Peru* 7°5S 78°28W **92** E3
Cajàzeiras *Brazil* 6°52S 38°30W **93** E11
Calabar *Nigeria* 4°57N 8°20E **52** H7
Calabogie *Canada* 45°18N 76°43W **83** A8
Calabozo *Venezuela* 9°0N 67°28W **92** B5
Calábria □ *Italy* 39°0N 16°30E **22** E7
Calahorra *Spain* 42°18N 1°59W **21** A5
Calais *France* 50°57N 1°56E **20** A4
Calais *U.S.A.* 45°11N 67°17W **81** C20
Calakmul △ *Mexico* 18°14N 89°48W **87** D7
Calalaste, Cord. de
  Argentina 25°0S 67°0W **94** B2
Calama *Brazil* 8°0S 62°50W **92** E6
Calama *Chile* 22°30S 68°55W **94** A2
Calamar *Colombia* 10°15N 74°55W **92** A4
Calamian Group *Phil.* 11°50N 119°55E **37** B5
Calamocha *Spain* 40°50N 1°17W **21** B5
Calang *Indonesia* 4°37N 95°37E **36** D1
Calanscio, Sarïr *Libya* 27°30N 22°30E **53** C10
Calapan *Phil.* 13°25N 121°7E **37** B6
Călăraşi *Romania* 44°12N 27°20E **17** F14
Calatayud *Spain* 41°20N 1°40W **21** B5
Calauag *Phil.* 13°55N 122°15E **37** B6
Calavite, C. *Phil.* 13°26N 120°20E **37** B6
Calbayog *Phil.* 12°4N 124°38E **37** B6
Calca *Peru* 13°22S 72°0W **92** F4
Calcasieu L. *U.S.A.* 29°55N 93°18W **84** G8
Calcium *U.S.A.* 44°1N 75°50W **83** B9
Calcutta *U.S.A.* 40°40N 80°34W **82** F4
Caldas da Rainha *Portugal* 39°24N 9°8W **21** C1
Calder → *U.K.* 53°44N 1°22W **12** D6
Caldera *Chile* 27°5S 70°55W **94** B1
Caldwell *Idaho, U.S.A.* 43°40N 116°41W **76** E5
Caldwell *Kans., U.S.A.* 37°2N 97°37W **80** G6
Caldwell *Tex., U.S.A.* 30°32N 96°42W **84** F6
Caledon *Canada* 43°51N 79°51W **82** C5
Caledon *S. Africa* 34°14S 19°26E **56** E2
Caledon → *S. Africa* 30°31S 26°5E **56** D4
Caledon B. *Australia* 12°45S 137°0E **62** A2
Caledonia *Canada* 43°7N 79°58W **82** C5
Caledonia *U.S.A.* 42°58N 77°51W **82** D7
Calemba *Angola* 16°0S 15°44E **56** B2
Calen *Australia* 20°56S 148°48E **62** b
Caletones *Chile* 34°6S 70°27W **94** C1
Calexico *U.S.A.* 32°40N 115°30W **79** N11
Calf of Man *I. of Man* 54°3N 4°48W **12** C3
Calgary *Canada* 51°0N 114°10W **70** C6
Calhoun *U.S.A.* 34°30N 84°57W **85** D12
Cali *Colombia* 3°25N 76°35W **92** C3
Calicut = Kozhikode
  India 11°15N 75°43E **45** J2
Caliente *U.S.A.* 37°37N 114°31W **77** H6
California *Mo., U.S.A.* 38°38N 92°34W **80** F7
California *Pa., U.S.A.* 40°4N 79°54W **82** F5
California, Baja, T.N. = Baja
  California □ *Mexico* 30°0N 115°0W **86** B2
California, Baja, T.S. = Baja
  California Sur □
  Mexico 25°50N 111°50W **86** B2
California, G. de *Mexico* 27°0N 111°0W **86** B2
California City *U.S.A.* 35°10N 117°55W **79** K9
California Hot Springs
  U.S.A. 35°51N 118°41W **79** K8
Calilegua △ *Argentina* 23°36S 64°50W **94** B3
Calingasta *Argentina* 31°15S 69°30W **94** C2
Calipatria *U.S.A.* 33°8N 115°31W **79** M11
Calistoga *U.S.A.* 38°35N 122°35W **78** G4

Calitzdorp *S. Africa* 33°33S 21°42E **56** D3
Callabonna, L. *Australia* 29°40S 140°5E **63** D3
Callan *Ireland* 52°32N 7°24W **10** D4
Callander *U.K.* 56°15N 4°13W **11** E4
Callicoon *U.S.A.* 41°46N 75°3W **83** E9
Calling Lake *Canada* 55°15N 113°12W **70** B6
Calliope *Australia* 24°0S 151°16E **62** C5
Calne *U.K.* 51°26N 2°0W **13** F6
Calola *Angola* 16°25S 17°48E **56** B2
Caloundra *Australia* 26°45S 153°10E **63** D5
Calpella *U.S.A.* 39°14N 123°12W **78** F3
Calpine *U.S.A.* 39°40N 120°27W **78** F6
Calstock *Canada* 49°47N 84°9W **72** C3
Caltagirone *Italy* 37°14N 14°31E **22** F6
Caltanissetta *Italy* 37°29N 14°4E **22** F6
Calulo *Angola* 10°1S 14°56E **54** G2
Calvert → *Australia* 16°17S 137°44E **62** B2
Calvert I. *Canada* 51°30N 128°0W **70** C3
Calvert Ra. *Australia* 24°0S 122°30E **60** D3
Calvi *France* 42°34N 8°45E **20** E8
Calvià *Spain* 39°34N 2°31E **21** C7
Calvillo *Mexico* 21°51N 102°43W **86** C4
Calvinia *S. Africa* 31°28S 19°45E **56** D2
Calwa *U.S.A.* 36°42N 119°46W **78** J7
Cam → *U.K.* 52°21N 0°16E **13** E8
Cam Lam = Ba Ngoi
   Vietnam 11°54N 109°10E **39** G7
Cam Pha *Vietnam* 21°7N 107°18E **34** G6
Cam Ranh *Vietnam* 11°54N 109°12E **39** G7
Cam Xuyen *Vietnam* 18°15N 106°0E **38** C6
Camabatela *Angola* 8°20S 15°26E **54** F3
Camacupa *Angola* 11°58S 17°22E **55** G3
Camagüey *Cuba* 21°20N 77°55W **88** B4
Camaná *Peru* 16°30S 72°50W **92** G4
Camanche Res. *U.S.A.* 38°14N 121°1W **78** G6
Camaquã *Brazil* 30°51S 51°49W **95** C5
Camaquã → *Brazil* 31°17S 51°47W **95** C5
Camargo *Mexico* 26°19N 98°50W **87** B5
Camarillo *U.S.A.* 34°13N 119°2W **79** L7
Camarón, C. *Honduras* 16°0N 85°5W **88** C2
Camarones *Argentina* 44°50S 65°40W **96** E3
Camas *U.S.A.* 45°35N 122°24W **78** E4
Camas Valley *U.S.A.* 43°2N 123°40W **76** E2
Camballin *Australia* 17°59S 124°12E **60** C3
Cambará *Brazil* 23°2S 50°5W **95** A5
Cambay = Khambhat
   India 22°23N 72°33E **42** H5
Cambay, G. of = Khambhat, G. of
   India 20°45N 72°30E **40** J8
Cambodia ■ *Asia* 12°15N 105°0E **38** F5
Camborne *U.K.* 50°12N 5°19W **13** G2
Cambrai *France* 50°11N 3°14E **20** A5
Cambria *U.S.A.* 35°34N 121°5W **78** K5
Cambrian Mts. *U.K.* 52°3N 3°57W **13** E4
Cambridge *Canada* 43°23N 80°15W **82** C4
Cambridge *Jamaica* 18°18N 77°54W **88** a
Cambridge *N.Z.* 37°54S 175°29E **59** B5
Cambridge *U.K.* 52°12N 0°8E **13** E8
Cambridge *Minn., U.S.A.* 45°34N 93°13W **80** C7
Cambridge *N.Y., U.S.A.* 43°2N 73°22W **83** C11
Cambridge *Nebr., U.S.A.* 40°17N 100°10W **80** E3
Cambridge *Ohio, U.S.A.* 40°2N 81°35W **82** F3
Cambridge Bay *Canada* 69°10N 105°0W **68** D11
Cambridge G. *Australia* 14°55S 128°15E **60** B4
Cambridge Springs *U.S.A.* 41°48N 80°4W **82** E4
Cambridgeshire □ *U.K.* 52°25N 0°7W **13** E7
Cambuci *Brazil* 21°35S 41°55W **95** A7
Cambundi-Catembo
   Angola 10°10S 17°35E **54** G3
Camden *Australia* 32°28S 24°25E **56** D3
Camden *Australia* 34°1S 150°43E **63** E5
Camden *Ala., U.S.A.* 31°59N 87°17W **85** F11
Camden *Ark., U.S.A.* 33°35N 92°50W **84** E8
Camden *Maine, U.S.A.* 44°13N 69°4W **81** C19
Camden *N.J., U.S.A.* 39°55N 75°7W **83** G9
Camden *N.Y., U.S.A.* 43°20N 75°45W **83** C9
Camden *S.C., U.S.A.* 34°16N 80°36W **85** D14
Camden Sd. *Australia* 15°27S 124°25E **60** C3
Camdenton *U.S.A.* 38°1N 92°45W **80** F7
Camelford *U.K.* 50°37N 4°42W **13** G3
Cameron *Ariz., U.S.A.* 35°53N 111°25W **77** J8
Cameron *La., U.S.A.* 29°48N 93°20W **84** G8
Cameron *Mo., U.S.A.* 39°44N 94°14W **80** F6
Cameron *Tex., U.S.A.* 30°51N 96°59W **84** F6
Cameron Highlands
   Malaysia 4°27N 101°22E **39** K3
Cameron Hills *Canada* 59°48N 118°0W **70** B5
Cameroon ■ *Africa* 6°0N 12°30E **53** G7
Cameroun, Mt. *Cameroon* 4°13N 9°10E **54** D1
Cametá *Brazil* 2°12S 49°30W **93** D9
Camilla *U.S.A.* 31°14N 84°12W **85** F12
Caminha *Portugal* 41°50N 8°50W **21** B1
Camino *U.S.A.* 38°44N 120°41W **78** G6
Cammal *U.S.A.* 41°24N 77°28W **82** E7
Camocim *Brazil* 2°55S 40°50W **93** D10
Camooweal *Australia* 19°56S 138°7E **62** B2
Camooweal Caves △
   Australia 20°1S 138°11E **62** C2
Camopi *Fr. Guiana* 3°12N 52°17W **93** C8
Camorta *India* 8°8N 93°30E **45** K11
Camp Hill *U.S.A.* 40°14N 76°55W **82** F8
Camp Nelson *U.S.A.* 36°8N 118°39W **79** J8
Camp Pendleton *U.S.A.* 33°13N 117°24W **79** M9
Camp Verde *U.S.A.* 34°34N 111°51W **77** J8
Camp Wood *U.S.A.* 29°40N 100°1W **84** G4
Campana *Argentina* 34°10S 58°55W **94** C4
Campana, I. *Chile* 48°20S 75°20W **96** F1
Campánia □ *Italy* 41°0N 14°30E **22** D6
Campbell *S. Africa* 28°48S 23°44E **56** D3
Campbell *Calif., U.S.A.* 37°17N 121°57W **78** H5
Campbell *Ohio, U.S.A.* 41°5N 80°37W **82** E4
Campbell I. *Pac. Oc.* 52°30S 169°0E **64** N8
Campbell L. *Canada* 63°14N 106°55W **71** A7
Campbell Plateau *S. Ocean* 50°0S 170°0E **5** A11
Campbell River *Canada* 50°5N 125°20W **70** C3
Campbellford *Canada* 44°18N 77°48W **82** B7
Campbellpur *Pakistan* 33°46N 72°26E **42** C5
Campbellsville *U.S.A.* 37°21N 85°20W **81** G11
Campbellton *Canada* 47°57N 66°43W **73** C6
Campbelltown *Australia* 34°4S 150°49E **63** E5
Campbeltown *U.K.* 55°26N 5°36W **11** F3
Campeche *Mexico* 19°51N 90°32W **87** D6
Campeche □ *Mexico* 19°0N 90°30W **87** D6
Campeche, Golfo de
   Mexico 19°30N 93°0W **87** D6
Camperdown *Australia* 38°14S 143°9E **63** F3
Camperville *Canada* 51°59N 100°9W **71** C8
Câmpina *Romania* 45°10N 25°45E **17** F13
Campina Grande *Brazil* 7°20S 35°47W **93** E11
Campinas *Brazil* 22°50S 47°0W **95** A6
Campo Grande *Brazil* 20°25S 54°40W **93** H8
Campo Maior *Brazil* 4°50S 42°12W **93** D10
Campo Mourão *Brazil* 24°3S 52°22W **95** A5
Campobasso *Italy* 41°34N 14°39E **22** D6
Campos *Brazil* 21°50S 41°20W **95** A7
Campos Belos *Brazil* 13°10S 47°3W **93** F9
Campos Novos *Brazil* 27°21S 51°50W **95** B5
Camptonville *U.S.A.* 39°27N 121°3W **78** F5
Camptown *U.S.A.* 41°44N 76°14W **83** E8
Câmpulung *Romania* 45°17N 25°3E **17** F13
Camrose *Canada* 53°0N 112°50W **70** C6
Camsell Portage *Canada* 59°37N 109°15W **71** B7
Çan *Turkey* 40°2N 27°3E **23** D12
Can Gio *Vietnam* 10°25N 106°58E **39** G6
Can Tho *Vietnam* 10°2N 105°46E **39** G5
Canaan *U.S.A.* 42°2N 73°20W **83** D11
Canacona *India* 15°1N 74°4E **45** G2
Canada ■ *N. Amer.* 60°0N 100°0W **68** G11
Canada Abyssal Plain
   Arctic 80°0N 140°0W **4** B18
Canada Basin *Arctic* 75°0N 145°0W **4** B18
Cañada de Gómez
   Argentina 32°40S 61°30W **94** C3
Canadian *U.S.A.* 35°55N 100°23W **84** D4
Canadian → *U.S.A.* 35°28N 95°3W **84** D7
Canadian Shield *Canada* 53°0N 75°0W **66** D12
Canajoharie *U.S.A.* 42°54N 74°35W **83** D10
Çanakkale *Turkey* 40°8N 26°24E **23** D12
Çanakkale Boğazı
   Turkey 40°17N 26°32E **23** D12
Canal Flats *Canada* 50°10N 115°48W **70** C5
Canalejas *Argentina* 35°15S 66°34W **94** D2
Canals *Argentina* 33°35S 62°53W **94** C3
Canandaigua *U.S.A.* 42°54N 77°17W **82** D7
Canandaigua L. *U.S.A.* 42°47N 77°19W **82** D7
Cananea *Mexico* 31°0N 110°18W **86** A2
Canarias, Is. *Atl. Oc.* 28°30N 16°0W **52** C2
Canaries *St. Lucia* 13°55N 61°4W **89** f
Canarreos, Arch. de los
   Cuba 21°35N 81°40W **88** B3
Canary Is. = Canarias, Is.
   Atl. Oc. 28°30N 16°0W **52** C2
Canaseraga *U.S.A.* 42°27N 77°45W **82** D7
Canatlán *Mexico* 24°31N 104°47W **86** C4
Canaveral, C. *U.S.A.* 28°27N 80°32W **85** G14
Canaveral △ *U.S.A.* 28°28N 80°34W **85** G14
Canavieiras *Brazil* 15°39S 39°0W **93** G11
Canberra *Australia* 35°15S 149°8E **63** F4
Canby *Calif., U.S.A.* 41°27N 120°52W **76** F3
Canby *Minn., U.S.A.* 44°43N 96°16W **80** C5
Canby *Oreg., U.S.A.* 45°16N 122°42W **78** E4
Cancún *Mexico* 21°8N 86°44W **87** C7
Candela *Argentina* 27°29S 55°44W **95** B4
Candelo *Australia* 36°47S 149°43E **63** F4
Candi Dasa *Indonesia* 8°30S 115°34E **37** J18
Candia = Iraklio *Greece* 35°20N 25°12E **23** G11
Candle L. *Canada* 53°50N 105°18W **71** C7
Candlemas I. *Antarctica* 57°3S 26°40W **5** B1
Cando *U.S.A.* 48°32N 99°12W **80** A4
Canea = Chania *Greece* 35°30N 24°4E **23** G11
Canelones *Uruguay* 34°32S 56°17W **95** C4
Cañete *Chile* 37°50S 73°30W **94** D1
Cangas del Narcea *Spain* 43°10N 6°32W **21** A2
Cangnan *China* 27°30N 120°23E **35** D13
Cangshan *China* 34°50N 118°2E **33** G10
Canguaretama *Brazil* 6°20S 35°5W **93** E11
Canguçu *Brazil* 31°22S 52°43W **95** C5
Canguçu, Serra do *Brazil* 31°20S 52°40W **95** C5
Cangxi *China* 31°47N 105°59E **34** B5
Cangzhou *China* 38°19N 116°52E **32** E9
Caniapiscau → *Canada* 56°40N 69°30W **73** A6
Caniapiscau, L. *Canada* 54°10N 69°55W **73** B6
Canicattì *Italy* 37°21N 13°51E **22** F5
Canim Lake *Canada* 51°47N 120°54W **70** C4
Canindeyu □ *Paraguay* 24°10S 55°0W **95** A5
Canisteo *U.S.A.* 42°16N 77°36W **82** D7
Canisteo → *U.S.A.* 42°7N 77°8W **82** D7
Cañitas de Felipe Pescador
   Mexico 23°36N 102°43W **86** C4
Çankırı *Turkey* 40°40N 33°37E **19** F5
Canmore *Canada* 51°7N 115°18W **70** C5
Cann River *Australia* 37°35S 149°7E **63** F4
Canna *U.K.* 57°3N 6°33W **11** D2
Cannanore = Kannur
   India 11°53N 75°27E **45** J2
Cannanore Is. *India* 10°30N 72°30E **45** J1
Cannes *France* 43°32N 7°1E **20** E7
Canning Town = Port Canning
   India 22°23N 88°40E **43** H13
Cannington *Canada* 44°20N 79°2W **82** B5
Cannock *U.K.* 52°41N 2°1W **13** E5
Cannonball → *U.S.A.* 46°26N 100°35W **80** B3
Cannondale Mt.
   Australia 25°13S 148°57E **62** D4
Cannonsville Res. *U.S.A.* 42°4N 75°22W **83** D9
Cannonvale *Australia* 20°17S 148°43E **62** b
Canoas *Brazil* 29°56S 51°11W **95** B5
Canoe L. *Canada* 55°10N 108°15W **71** B7
Cañon City *U.S.A.* 38°27N 105°14W **76** G11
Cañón de Río Blanco △
   Mexico 18°43N 97°15W **87** D5
Canonniers Pt. *Mauritius* 20°2S 57°32E **55** d
Canora *Canada* 51°40N 102°30W **71** C8
Canowindra *Australia* 33°35S 148°38E **63** E4
Canso *Canada* 45°20N 61°0W **73** C7
Cantabria □ *Spain* 43°10N 4°0W **21** A4
Cantabrian Mts. = Cantábrica,
   Cordillera *Spain* 43°0N 5°10W **21** A3
Cantábrica, Cordillera
   Spain 43°0N 5°10W **21** A3
Cantal, Plomb du *France* 45°3N 2°45E **20** D5
Canterbury *Australia* 25°23S 141°53E **62** D3
Canterbury *U.K.* 51°16N 1°6E **13** F9
Canterbury Bight *N.Z.* 44°16S 171°55E **59** F4
Canterbury Plains *N.Z.* 43°55S 171°22E **59** E3
Cantil *U.S.A.* 35°18N 117°58W **79** K9
Canton *Ga., U.S.A.* 34°14N 84°29W **85** D12
Canton *Ill., U.S.A.* 40°33N 90°2W **80** E8
Canton *Miss., U.S.A.* 32°37N 90°2W **85** E9
Canton *Mo., U.S.A.* 40°8N 91°32W **80** E8
Canton *N.Y., U.S.A.* 44°36N 75°10W **83** B9
Canton *Ohio, U.S.A.* 40°48N 81°23W **82** F3
Canton *S. Dak., U.S.A.* 43°18N 96°35W **80** D5
Canton L. *U.S.A.* 36°6N 98°35W **84** C5
Canudos *Brazil* 7°13S 58°5W **92** E7
Canumã → *Brazil* 3°55S 59°10W **92** D7
Canutama *Brazil* 6°30S 64°20W **92** E6
Canutillo *U.S.A.* 31°55N 106°36W **84** F1
Canvey *U.K.* 51°31N 0°37E **13** F8
Canyon *U.S.A.* 34°59N 101°55W **84** D4
Canyon De Chelly △
   U.S.A. 36°10N 109°20W **77** H9
Canyonlands △ *U.S.A.* 38°15N 110°0W **77** G9
Canyons of the Ancients △
   U.S.A. 37°30N 108°55W **77** H9
Canyonville *U.S.A.* 42°56N 123°17W **76** E2
Cao Bang *Vietnam* 22°40N 106°15E **34** F6
Cao He → *China* 40°10N 124°32E **33** D13
Cao Lanh *Vietnam* 10°27N 105°38E **39** G5
Cao Xian *China* 34°50N 115°35E **32** G8
Cap-aux-Meules *Canada* 47°23N 61°52W **73** C7
Cap-Chat *Canada* 49°6N 66°40W **73** C6
Cap-de-la-Madeleine
   Canada 46°22N 72°31W **72** C5
Cap-Haïtien *Haiti* 19°40N 72°20W **89** C5
Cap Pt. *St. Lucia* 14°7N 60°57W **89** f
Capac *U.S.A.* 43°1N 82°56W **82** D2
Capanaparo → *Venezuela* 7°1N 67°7W **92** B5
Cape → *Australia* 20°59S 146°51E **62** C4
Cape Arid △ *Australia* 33°58S 123°13E **61** F3
Cape Barren I. *Australia* 40°25S 148°15E **63** G4
Cape Breton Highlands △
   Canada 46°50N 60°40W **73** C7
Cape Breton I. *Canada* 46°0N 60°30W **73** C7
Cape Charles *U.S.A.* 37°16N 76°1W **81** G15
Cape Coast *Ghana* 5°5N 1°15W **52** G5
Cape Cod △ *U.S.A.* 41°56N 70°6W **81** E18
Cape Coral *U.S.A.* 26°33N 81°57W **85** H14
Cape Crawford *Australia* 16°41S 135°43E **62** B2
Cape Dorset = Kinngait
   Canada 64°14N 76°32W **69** E16
Cape Fear → *U.S.A.* 33°53N 78°1W **85** D15
Cape Girardeau *U.S.A.* 37°19N 89°32W **80** G9
Cape Hatteras △ *U.S.A.* 35°30N 75°28W **85** D17
Cape Hillsborough △
   Australia 20°54S 149°2E **62** b
Cape Le Grand △
   Australia 33°54S 122°26E **61** F3
Cape Lookout △ *U.S.A.* 35°45N 76°25W **85** D16
Cape May *U.S.A.* 38°56N 74°56W **81** F16
Cape May Point *U.S.A.* 38°56N 74°58W **81** F16
Cape Melville △
   Australia 14°26S 144°28E **62** A3
Cape Range △ *Australia* 22°3S 114°0E **60** D1
Cape St. George *Canada* 48°28N 59°14W **73** C7
Cape Tormentine *Canada* 46°8N 63°47W **73** C7
Cape Upstart △ *Australia* 19°45S 147°48E **62** B4
Cape Verde Is. ■ *Atl. Oc.* 16°0N 24°0W **52** b
Cape Vincent *U.S.A.* 44°8N 76°20W **83** B8
Cape York Peninsula
   Australia 12°0S 142°30E **62** A3
Capela *Brazil* 10°30S 37°0W **93** F11
Capella *Australia* 23°2S 148°1E **62** C4
Capesterre-Belle-Eau
   Guadeloupe 16°4N 61°36W **88** b
Capesterre-de-Marie-Galante
   Guadeloupe 15°53N 61°14W **88** b
Capim → *Brazil* 1°40S 47°47W **93** D9
Capitan *U.S.A.* 33°35N 105°35W **77** K11
Capitán Arturo Prat
   Antarctica 63°0S 61°0W **5** C17
Capitol Reef △ *U.S.A.* 38°15N 111°10W **77** G8
Capitola *U.S.A.* 36°59N 121°57W **78** J5
Capraia *Italy* 43°2N 9°50E **20** E8
Capri *Italy* 40°33N 14°14E **22** D6
Capricorn Coast
   Australia 23°16S 150°49E **62** C5
Capricorn Group
   Australia 23°30S 151°55E **62** C5
Capricorn Ra. *Australia* 23°20S 116°50E **60** D2
Caprivi □ *Namibia* 18°0S 23°30E **56** B4
Caprivi Strip *Namibia* 18°0S 23°0E **56** B3
Captains Flat *Australia* 35°35S 149°27E **63** F4
Capulin Volcano △
   U.S.A. 36°47N 103°58W **84** C3
Caquetá → *Colombia* 1°15S 69°15W **92** D5
Car Nicobar *India* 9°10N 92°47E **45** K11
Caracal *Romania* 44°8N 24°22E **17** F13
Caracas *Venezuela* 10°30N 66°55W **92** A5
Caracol *Belize* 16°45N 89°6W **88** C2
Caracol *Mato Grosso do Sul,
   Brazil* 22°18S 57°1W **94** A4
Caracol *Piauí, Brazil* 9°15S 43°22W **93** E10
Carajas *Brazil* 6°5S 50°23W **93** E8
Carajás, Serra dos *Brazil* 6°0S 51°30W **93** E8
Carangola *Brazil* 20°44S 42°5W **95** A7
Caransebes *Romania* 45°28N 22°18E **17** F12
Caraquet *Canada* 47°48N 64°57W **73** C6
Caratasca, L. de
   Honduras 15°20N 83°40W **88** C3
Caratinga *Brazil* 19°50S 42°10W **93** G10
Caraúbas *Brazil* 5°43S 37°33W **93** E11
Caravaca de la Cruz *Spain* 38°8N 1°52W **21** C5
Caravelas *Brazil* 17°45S 39°15W **93** G11
Caraveli *Peru* 15°45S 73°25W **92** G4
Caravelle, Presqu'île de la
   Martinique 14°46N 60°48W **88** c
Caraz *Peru* 9°3S 77°47W **92** E3
Carazinho *Brazil* 28°16S 52°46W **95** B5
Carballiño *Spain* 42°13N 8°41W **21** A1
Carberry *Canada* 49°50N 99°25W **71** D9
Carbó *Mexico* 29°42N 110°58W **86** B2
Carbón, L. del *Argentina* 49°35S 68°21W **90** G3
Carbonara, C. *Italy* 39°6N 9°31E **22** E3
Carbondale *Colo.,
   U.S.A.* 39°24N 107°13W **76** G10
Carbondale *Ill., U.S.A.* 37°44N 89°13W **80** G9
Carbondale *Pa., U.S.A.* 41°35N 75°30W **83** E9
Carbonear *Canada* 47°42N 53°13W **73** C9
Carbónia *Italy* 39°10N 8°30E **22** E3
Carcajou *Canada* 57°47N 117°6W **70** B5
Carcarana → *Argentina* 32°27N 60°48W **94** C3
Carcasse, C. *Haiti* 18°30N 74°28W **89** C5
Carcassonne *France* 43°13N 2°20E **20** E5
Carcross *Canada* 60°13N 134°45W **70** A2
Cardamon Hills *India* 9°30N 77°15E **45** K3
Cardamom Mts. = Kravanh, Chuor
   Phnum *Cambodia* 12°0N 103°32E **39** G4
Cárdenas *Cuba* 23°0N 81°30W **88** B3
Cárdenas *San Luis Potosí,
   Mexico* 22°0N 99°38W **87** C5
Cárdenas *Tabasco, Mexico* 17°59N 93°22W **87** D6
Cardiff *U.K.* 51°29N 3°10W **13** F4
Cardiff □ *U.K.* 51°31N 3°12W **13** F4
Cardiff-by-the-Sea
   U.S.A. 33°1N 117°17W **79** M9
Cardigan *U.K.* 52°5N 4°40W **13** E3
Cardigan B. *U.K.* 52°30N 4°30W **13** E3
Cardinal *Canada* 44°47N 75°23W **83** B9
Cardona *Uruguay* 33°53S 57°18W **94** C4
Cardoso, Ilha do *Brazil* 25°8S 47°58W **95** B5
Cardston *Canada* 49°15N 113°20W **70** D6
Cardwell *Australia* 18°14S 146°2E **62** B4
Careen L. *Canada* 57°0N 108°11W **71** B7
Carei *Romania* 47°40N 22°29E **17** E12
Carey *Australia* 29°0S 122°15E **61** E3
Carey, L. *Australia* 29°0S 122°15E **61** E3
Carey L. *Canada* 62°12N 102°55W **71** A8
Carhué *Argentina* 37°10S 62°50W **94** D3
Caria *Turkey* 37°20N 28°10E **23** F13
Cariacica *Brazil* 20°16S 40°25W **93** H10
Caribbean Sea *W. Indies* 15°0N 75°0W **89** D5
Cariboo Mts. *Canada* 53°0N 121°0W **70** C4
Caribou *U.S.A.* 46°52N 68°1W **81** B19
Caribou → *Man.,
   Canada* 59°20N 94°44W **71** B10
Caribou → *N.W.T.,
   Canada* 61°27N 125°45W **70** A3
Caribou I. *Canada* 47°22N 85°49W **72** C2
Caribou Is. *Canada* 61°55N 113°15W **70** A6
Caribou L. *Man., Canada* 59°21N 96°10W **71** B9
Caribou L. *Ont., Canada* 50°25N 89°5W **72** B2
Caribou Mts. *Canada* 59°12N 115°40W **70** B5
Caribou River △ *Canada* 59°35N 96°35W **71** B9
Carichic *Mexico* 27°56N 107°3W **86** B3
Carinda *Australia* 30°28S 147°41E **63** E4
Carinhanha *Brazil* 14°15S 44°46W **93** F10
Carinhanha → *Brazil* 14°20S 43°47W **93** F10
Carinthia = Kärnten □
   Austria 46°52N 13°30E **16** E8
Caripito *Venezuela* 10°8N 63°6W **92** A6
Carleton, Mt. *Canada* 47°23N 66°53W **73** C6
Carleton Place *Canada* 45°8N 76°9W **83** A8
Carletonville *S. Africa* 26°23S 27°22E **56** C4
Carlin *U.S.A.* 40°43N 116°7W **76** F5
Carlingford L. *U.K.* 54°3N 6°9W **10** B5
Carlinville *U.S.A.* 39°17N 89°53W **80** F9
Carlisle *U.K.* 54°54N 2°56W **12** C5
Carlisle *U.S.A.* 40°12N 77°12W **82** F7
Carlisle B. *Barbados* 13°5N 59°37W **89** g
Carlisle I. *Australia* 20°49S 149°18E **62** b
Carlos Casares *Argentina* 35°32S 61°20W **94** D3
Carlos Tejedor *Argentina* 35°25S 62°25W **94** D3
Carlow *Ireland* 52°50N 6°56W **10** D5
Carlow □ *Ireland* 52°43N 6°50W **10** D5
Carlsbad *Calif., U.S.A.* 33°10N 117°21W **79** M9
Carlsbad *N. Mex.,
   U.S.A.* 32°25N 104°14W **77** K11
Carlsbad Caverns △
   U.S.A. 32°10N 104°35W **77** K11
Carluke *U.K.* 55°45N 3°50W **11** F5
Carlyle *Canada* 49°40N 102°20W **71** D8
Carmacks *Canada* 62°5N 136°16W **68** E4
Carman *Canada* 49°30N 98°0W **71** D9
Carmarthen *U.K.* 51°52N 4°19W **13** F3
Carmarthen B. *U.K.* 51°40N 4°30W **13** F3
Carmarthenshire □ *U.K.* 51°55N 4°13W **13** F3
Carmaux *France* 44°3N 2°10E **20** D5
Carmel *U.S.A.* 41°26N 73°41W **83** E11
Carmel, Mt. = Hä Karmel, Har
   Israel 32°44N 35°3E **48** C4
Carmel-by-the-Sea
   U.S.A. 36°33N 121°55W **78** J5
Carmel Valley *U.S.A.* 36°29N 121°43W **78** J5
Carmelo *Uruguay* 34°0S 58°20W **94** C4
Carmen *Paraguay* 27°13S 56°12W **95** B4
Carmen, I. *Mexico* 25°57N 111°12W **86** B2
Carmen de Patagones
   Argentina 40°50S 63°0W **96** E4
Carmensa *Argentina* 35°15S 67°40W **94** D2
Carmi *Canada* 49°36N 119°8W **70** D5
Carmi *U.S.A.* 38°5N 88°10W **80** F9
Carmila *Australia* 21°55S 149°24E **62** C4
Carmona *Costa Rica* 10°0N 85°15W **88** E2
Carmona *Spain* 37°28N 5°42W **21** D3
Carn Ban *U.K.* 57°7N 4°15W **11** D4
Carn Eige *U.K.* 57°17N 5°8W **11** D3
Carnamah *Australia* 29°41S 115°53E **61** E2
Carnarvon *Australia* 24°51S 113°42E **61** D1
Carnarvon *S. Africa* 30°56S 22°8E **56** D3
Carnarvon △ *Australia* 24°54S 148°2E **62** C4
Carnarvon Ra. *Queens.,
   Australia* 25°15S 148°30E **62** D4
Carnarvon Ra. *W. Austral.,
   Australia* 25°20S 120°45E **61** E3
Carnatic *India* 9°40N 77°50E **45** K3
Carnation *U.S.A.* 47°39N 121°55W **78** C5
Carncastle *U.K.* 54°54N 5°53W **10** B6
Carndonagh *Ireland* 55°16N 7°15W **10** A4
Carnduff *Canada* 49°10N 101°50W **71** D8
Carnegie *U.S.A.* 40°24N 80°5W **82** F4
Carnegie, L. *Australia* 26°5S 122°30E **61** E3
Carnegie Ridge *Pac. Oc.* 1°0S 87°0W **65** H19
Carney I. *Antarctica* 74°0S 121°0W **5** D14
Carnic Alps = Karnische Alpen
   Europe 46°36N 13°0E **16** E7
Carniche Alpi = Karnische Alpen
   Europe 46°36N 13°0E **16** E7
Carnot *C.A.R.* 4°59N 15°56E **54** D3
Carnot, C. *Australia* 34°57S 135°38E **63** E2
Carnot B. *Australia* 17°20S 122°15E **60** C3
Carnoustie *U.K.* 56°30N 2°42W **11** E6
Carnsore Pt. *Ireland* 52°10N 6°22W **10** D5
Caro *U.S.A.* 43°29N 83°24W **81** D12
Caroga Lake *U.S.A.* 43°8N 74°28W **83** C10
Carolina *Brazil* 7°10S 47°30W **93** E9
Carolina *Puerto Rico* 18°23N 65°58W **89** d
Carolina *S. Africa* 26°5S 30°6E **57** C5
Caroline I. *Kiribati* 9°58S 150°13W **65** H12
Caroline Is. *Micronesia* 8°0N 150°0E **64** G6
Caroni → *Venezuela* 8°21N 62°43W **92** B6
Caroní *Trin. & Tob.* 10°34N 61°23W **93** K15
Caronie = Nébrodi, Monti
   Italy 37°54N 14°35E **22** F6
Caroona *Australia* 31°24S 150°26E **63** E5
Carpathians *Europe* 49°30N 21°0E **17** D11
Carpentaria, G. of *Australia* 14°0S 139°0E **62** A2
Carpentras *France* 44°3N 5°2E **20** D6
Carpi *Italy* 44°47N 10°53E **22** B4
Carpinteria *U.S.A.* 34°24N 119°31W **79** L7
Carr Boyd Ra. *Australia* 16°15S 128°35E **60** C4
Carra, L. *Ireland* 53°41N 9°14W **10** C2
Carrabelle *U.S.A.* 29°51N 84°40W **85** G12
Carraig Mhachaire Rois =
   Carrickmacross *Ireland* 53°59N 6°43W **10** C5
Carraig na Siúire =
   Carrick-on-Suir *Ireland* 52°21N 7°24W **10** D4
Carranya ○ *Australia* 19°13S 127°46E **60** C4
Carrara *Italy* 44°5N 10°6E **20** D9
Carrauntoohill *Ireland* 52°0N 9°45W **10** D2
Carrick-on-Shannon
   Ireland 53°57N 8°7W **10** C3
Carrick-on-Suir *Ireland* 52°21N 7°24W **10** D4
Carrickfergus *U.K.* 54°43N 5°49W **10** B6
Carrickmacross *Ireland* 53°59N 6°43W **10** C5
Carrieton *Australia* 32°25S 138°31E **63** E2
Carrigaline *Ireland* 51°48N 8°23W **10** E3
Carrillo *Mexico* 26°54N 103°55W **86** B4
Carrington *U.S.A.* 47°27N 99°8W **80** B4
Carrizal Bajo *Chile* 28°5S 71°20W **94** B1
Carrizalillo *Chile* 29°5S 71°30W **94** B1
Carrizo Cr. → *U.S.A.* 36°55N 103°55W **77** H12
Carrizo Plain △ *U.S.A.* 35°11N 119°47W **78** K7
Carrizo Springs *U.S.A.* 28°31N 99°52W **84** G5
Carrizozo *U.S.A.* 33°38N 105°53W **77** K11
Carroll *U.S.A.* 42°4N 94°52W **80** D6
Carrollton *Ga., U.S.A.* 33°35N 85°5W **85** E12
Carrollton *Ill., U.S.A.* 39°18N 90°24W **80** F8
Carrollton *Ky., U.S.A.* 38°41N 85°11W **81** F11
Carrollton *Mo., U.S.A.* 39°22N 93°30W **80** F7
Carrollton *Ohio, U.S.A.* 40°34N 81°5W **82** F3
Carron → *U.K.* 57°53N 4°22W **11** D4
Carron, L. *U.K.* 57°22N 5°35W **11** D3
Carrot → *Canada* 53°50N 101°17W **71** C8
Carrot River *Canada* 53°17N 103°35W **71** C8
Carruthers *Canada* 52°52N 109°16W **71** C7
Carson *Calif., U.S.A.* 33°49N 118°16W **79** M8
Carson *N. Dak., U.S.A.* 46°25N 101°34W **80** B3
Carson → *U.S.A.* 39°45N 118°40W **78** F8
Carson City *U.S.A.* 39°10N 119°46W **78** F7
Carson Sink *U.S.A.* 39°50N 118°25W **76** G4
Cartagena *Colombia* 10°25N 75°33W **92** A3
Cartagena *Spain* 37°38N 0°59W **21** D5
Cartago *Colombia* 4°45N 75°55W **92** C3
Cartago *Costa Rica* 9°50N 83°55W **88** E3
Cartersville *U.S.A.* 34°10N 84°48W **85** D12
Carterton *N.Z.* 41°2S 175°31E **59** D5
Carthage *Tunisia* 36°52N 10°20E **22** F4
Carthage *Ill., U.S.A.* 40°25N 91°8W **80** E8
Carthage *Mo., U.S.A.* 37°11N 94°19W **80** G6
Carthage *N.Y., U.S.A.* 43°59N 75°37W **83** C9
Carthage *Tex., U.S.A.* 32°9N 94°20W **84** E7
Cartier I. *Australia* 12°31S 123°29E **60** B3
Cartwright *Canada* 53°41N 56°58W **73** B8
Caruaru *Brazil* 8°15S 35°55W **93** E11
Carúpano *Venezuela* 10°39N 63°15W **92** A6
Caruthersville *U.S.A.* 36°11N 89°39W **85** C10
Carvoeiro *Brazil* 1°30S 61°59W **92** D6
Carvoeiro, C. *Portugal* 39°21N 9°24W **21** C1
Cary *U.S.A.* 35°47N 78°46W **85** D15
Cas-gwent = Chepstow
   U.K. 51°38N 2°41W **13** F5
Casa de Piedra *Argentina* 38°5S 67°28W **94** D2
Casa de Piedra, Embalse
   Argentina 38°5S 67°28W **94** D2
Casa Grande *U.S.A.* 32°53N 111°45W **77** K8
Casa Nova *Brazil* 9°25S 41°5W **93** E10
Casablanca *Chile* 33°20S 71°25W **94** C1
Casablanca *Morocco* 33°36N 7°36W **52** B4
Cascada de Basaseachic △
   Mexico 28°9N 108°15W **86** B3
Cascade *Seychelles* 4°39S 55°29E **55** b
Cascade *Idaho, U.S.A.* 44°31N 116°2W **76** D5
Cascade *Mont., U.S.A.* 47°16N 111°42W **76** C8
Cascade Locks *U.S.A.* 45°40N 121°54W **78** E5
Cascade Ra. *U.S.A.* 47°0N 121°30W **78** D5
Cascade Res. *U.S.A.* 44°32N 116°3W **76** D5
Cascais *Portugal* 38°41N 9°25W **21** C1
Cascavel *Brazil* 24°57S 53°28W **95** A5

Cáscina *Italy* 43°41N 10°33E **22 C4**
Casco B. *U.S.A.* 43°45N 70°0W **81 D19**
Caserta *Italy* 41°4N 14°20E **22 D6**
Casey *Antarctica* 66°0S 76°0E **5 C8**
Caseyr, Raas = Asir, Ras
  Somalia 11°55N 51°10E **49 E5**
Cashel *Ireland* 52°30N 7°53W **10 D4**
Casiguran *Phil.* 16°22N 122°7E **37 A6**
Casilda *Argentina* 33°10S 61°10W **94 C3**
Casino *Australia* 28°52S 153°3E **63 D5**
Casiquiare → *Venezuela* 2°1N 67°7W **92 C5**
Casma *Peru* 9°30S 78°20W **92 E3**
Casmalia *U.S.A.* 34°50N 120°32W **79 L6**
Casnewydd = Newport
  U.K. 51°35N 3°0W **13 F5**
Caspe *Spain* 41°14N 0°1W **21 B5**
Casper *U.S.A.* 42°51N 106°19W **76 E10**
Caspian Depression *Eurasia* 47°0N 48°0E **19 E8**
Caspian Sea *Eurasia* 43°0N 50°0E **19 F9**
Cass City *U.S.A.* 43°36N 83°10W **82 C1**
Cass Lake *U.S.A.* 47°23N 94°37W **80 B6**
Cassadaga *U.S.A.* 42°20N 79°19W **82 D5**
Casselman *Canada* 45°19N 75°5W **83 A9**
Casselton *U.S.A.* 46°54N 97°13W **80 B5**
Cassiar Mts. *Canada* 59°30N 130°30W **70 B2**
Cassino *Italy* 41°30N 13°49E **22 D5**
Cassville *U.S.A.* 36°41N 93°52W **80 G7**
Castaic *U.S.A.* 34°30N 118°38W **79 L8**
Castalia *U.S.A.* 41°24N 82°49W **82 E2**
Castanhal *Brazil* 1°18S 47°55W **93 D9**
Castara *Trin. & Tob.* 11°17N 60°42W **93 J16**
Castell-Nedd = Neath
  U.K. 51°39N 3°48W **13 F4**
Castellammare di Stábia
  Italy 40°42N 14°29E **22 D6**
Castelli *Argentina* 36°7S 57°47W **94 D4**
Castelló de la Plana *Spain* 39°58N 0°3W **21 C5**
Castelo *Brazil* 20°33S 41°14W **95 A7**
Castelo Branco *Portugal* 39°50N 7°31W **21 C2**
Castelsarrasin *France* 44°2N 1°7E **20 E4**
Casterton *Australia* 37°30S 141°30E **63 F3**
Castile *U.S.A.* 42°38N 78°3W **82 D6**
Castilla-La Mancha □
  Spain 39°30N 3°30W **21 C4**
Castilla y Leon □ *Spain* 42°0N 5°0W **21 B3**
Castillos *Uruguay* 34°12S 53°52W **95 C5**
Castle Dale *U.S.A.* 39°13N 111°1W **76 G8**
Castle Douglas *U.K.* 54°56N 3°56W **11 G5**
Castle Rock *Colo.*,
  U.S.A. 39°22N 104°51W **76 G11**
Castle Rock *Wash.*,
  U.S.A. 46°17N 122°54W **78 D4**
Castlebar *Ireland* 53°52N 9°18W **10 C2**
Castlebay *U.K.* 56°57N 7°31W **11 E1**
Castleblayney *Ireland* 54°7N 6°44W **10 B5**
Castlecomer *Ireland* 52°48N 7°14W **10 D4**
Castlederg *U.K.* 54°42N 7°36W **10 B4**
Castleford *U.K.* 53°43N 1°21W **12 D6**
Castlegar *Canada* 49°20N 117°40W **70 D5**
Castleisland *Ireland* 52°14N 9°28W **10 D2**
Castlemaine *Australia* 37°2S 144°12E **63 F3**
Castlemaine *Ireland* 52°10N 9°42W **10 D2**
Castlepollard *Ireland* 53°41N 7°19W **10 C4**
Castlerea *Ireland* 53°46N 8°29W **10 C3**
Castlereagh → *Australia* 30°12S 147°32E **63 E4**
Castlereagh B. *Australia* 12°10S 135°10E **62 A2**
Castleton *U.S.A.* 43°37N 73°11W **83 C11**
Castleton-on-Hudson
  U.S.A. 42°31N 73°45W **83 D11**
Castletown *I. of Man* 54°5N 4°38W **12 C3**
Castletown Bearhaven
  Ireland 51°39N 9°55W **10 E2**
Castor *Canada* 52°15N 111°50W **70 C6**
Castor → *Canada* 53°24N 78°58W **72 B4**
Castorland *U.S.A.* 43°53N 75°31W **83 C9**
Castres *France* 43°37N 2°13E **20 E5**
Castricum *Neths.* 52°33N 4°40E **15 B4**
Castries *St. Lucia* 14°2N 60°58W **89 f**
Castro *Brazil* 24°45S 50°0W **95 A6**
Castro *Chile* 42°30S 73°50W **96 E2**
Castro Alves *Brazil* 12°46S 39°33W **93 F11**
Castro Valley *U.S.A.* 37°41N 122°5W **78 H4**
Castroville *U.S.A.* 36°46N 121°45W **78 J5**
Castuera *Spain* 38°43N 5°37W **21 C3**
Cat Ba, Dao *Vietnam* 20°50N 107°0E **38 B6**
Cat Ba △ *Vietnam* 20°47N 107°3E **38 B6**
Cat I. *Bahamas* 24°30N 75°30W **89 B4**
Cat L. *Canada* 51°40N 91°50W **72 B1**
Cat Lake *Canada* 51°40N 91°50W **72 B1**
Cat Tien △ *Vietnam* 11°25N 107°17E **39 G6**
Catacamas *Honduras* 14°54N 85°56W **88 D2**
Cataguases *Brazil* 21°23S 42°39W **95 A7**
Catalão *Brazil* 18°10S 47°57W **93 G9**
Catánia *Italy* 37°30N 15°6E **22 F6**
Catanzaro *Italy* 38°54N 16°35E **22 E7**
Catarman *Phil.* 12°28N 124°35E **37 B6**
Catatumbo-Bari △
  Colombia 9°3N 73°12W **89 E5**
Catchacoma *Canada* 44°44N 78°19W **82 B6**
Cateel *Phil.* 7°47N 126°24E **37 C7**
Catembe *Mozam.* 26°0S 32°33E **57 C5**
Caterham *U.K.* 51°15N 0°4W **13 F7**
Cathair na Mart = Westport
  Ireland 53°48N 9°31W **10 C2**
Cathcart *S. Africa* 32°18S 27°10E **56 E4**
Cathedral City *U.S.A.* 33°47N 116°28W **79 M10**
Cathlamet *U.S.A.* 46°12N 123°23W **78 D3**

Catlettsburg *U.S.A.* 38°25N 82°36W **81 F12**
Catoche, C. *Mexico* 21°35N 87°5W **87 C7**
Catriló *Argentina* 36°26S 63°24W **94 D3**
Catrimani *Brazil* 0°27N 61°41W **92 C6**
Catrimani → *Brazil* 0°28N 61°44W **92 C6**
Catskill *U.S.A.* 42°14N 73°52W **83 D11**
Catskill △ *U.S.A.* 42°8N 74°39W **83 D10**
Catskill Mts. *U.S.A.* 42°10N 74°25W **83 D10**
Catt, Mt. *Australia* 13°49S 134°23E **62 A1**
Cattaraugus *U.S.A.* 42°20N 78°52W **82 D6**
Catterick *U.K.* 54°23N 1°37W **12 C6**
Catuala *Angola* 16°25S 19°2E **56 A2**
Catuane *Mozam.* 26°48S 32°18E **57 C5**
Caubvick, Mt. = Iberville, Mt. d'
  Canada 58°50N 63°50W **69 F19**
Cauca → *Colombia* 8°54N 74°28W **92 B4**
Caucaia *Brazil* 3°40S 38°35W **93 D11**
Caucasus Mountains
  Eurasia 42°50N 44°0E **19 F7**
Caucete *Argentina* 31°38S 68°20W **94 C2**
Caungula *Angola* 8°26S 18°38E **54 F3**
Cauquenes *Chile* 36°0S 72°22W **94 D1**
Caura → *Venezuela* 7°38N 64°53W **92 B6**
Causapscal *Canada* 48°19N 67°12W **73 C6**
Cauvery → *India* 11°9N 78°52E **45 J4**
Caux, Pays de *France* 49°38N 0°35E **20 B4**
Cavalier *U.S.A.* 48°48N 97°37W **80 A6**
Cavan *Ireland* 54°0N 7°22W **10 B4**
Cavan □ *Ireland* 54°1N 7°16W **10 C4**
Cave Creek *U.S.A.* 33°50N 111°57W **77 K8**
Cavendish *Australia* 37°31S 142°2E **63 F3**
Caviana, I. *Brazil* 0°10N 50°10W **93 C8**
Cawndilla L. *Australia* 32°30S 142°15E **63 E3**
Cawnpore = Kanpur
  India 26°28N 80°20E **43 F9**
Caxias *Brazil* 4°55S 43°20W **93 D10**
Caxias do Sul *Brazil* 29°10S 51°10W **95 B5**
Cay Sal Bank *Bahamas* 23°45N 80°0W **88 B4**
Cayambe *Ecuador* 0°3N 78°8W **92 C3**
Cayenne *Fr. Guiana* 5°5N 52°18W **93 B8**
Cayey *Puerto Rico* 18°7N 66°10W **89 d**
Cayman Brac *Cayman Is.* 19°43N 79°49W **88 C4**
Cayman Is. □ *W. Indies* 19°40N 80°30W **88 C3**
Cayman Trench *Caribbean* 17°0N 83°0W **66 H11**
Cayuga *Canada* 42°59N 79°50W **82 D5**
Cayuga *U.S.A.* 42°54N 76°44W **83 D8**
Cayuga Heights *U.S.A.* 42°27N 76°29W **83 D8**
Cayuga L. *U.S.A.* 42°41N 76°41W **83 D8**
Cazenovia *U.S.A.* 42°56N 75°51W **83 D9**
Cazombo *Angola* 11°54S 22°56E **55 G4**
Ceanannus Mor = Kells
  Ireland 53°44N 6°53W **10 C5**
Ceará = Fortaleza *Brazil* 3°45S 38°35W **93 D11**
Ceará □ *Brazil* 5°0S 40°0W **93 E11**
Ceará-Mirim *Brazil* 5°38S 35°25W **93 E11**
Ceatharlach = Carlow
  Ireland 52°50N 6°56W **10 D5**
Cébaco, I. de *Panama* 7°33N 81°9W **88 E3**
Cebollar *Argentina* 29°10S 66°35W **94 B2**
Cebu *Phil.* 10°18N 123°54E **37 B6**
Cecil Plains *Australia* 27°30S 151°11E **63 D5**
Cedar → *U.S.A.* 41°17N 91°21W **80 E8**
Cedar City *U.S.A.* 37°41N 113°4W **77 H7**
Cedar Creek Res. *U.S.A.* 32°11N 96°4W **84 E6**
Cedar Falls *Iowa, U.S.A.* 42°32N 92°27W **80 D7**
Cedar Falls *Wash.,*
  U.S.A. 47°25N 121°45W **78 C5**
Cedar Key *U.S.A.* 29°8N 83°2W **85 G13**
Cedar L. *Canada* 53°10N 100°0W **71 C9**
Cedar Park *U.S.A.* 30°30N 97°49W **84 F6**
Cedar Rapids *U.S.A.* 41°59N 91°40W **80 E8**
Cedartown *U.S.A.* 34°1N 85°15W **85 D12**
Cedarvale *Canada* 55°1N 128°22W **70 B3**
Cedarville *S. Africa* 30°23S 29°3E **57 D4**
Cedral *Mexico* 23°50N 100°45W **86 C4**
Cedro *Brazil* 6°34S 39°3W **93 E11**
Cedros, I. *Mexico* 28°12N 115°15W **86 B1**
Cedros B. *Trin. & Tob.* 10°16N 61°54W **93 K15**
Ceduna *Australia* 32°7S 133°46E **63 E1**
Ceel Gaal *Somalia* 10°58N 50°20E **49 E5**
Ceel Waaq *Kenya* 2°49N 40°56E **54 D8**
Ceeldheere *Somalia* 3°50N 47°8E **49 G4**
Ceerigaabo *Somalia* 10°35N 47°20E **49 E4**
Cefalù *Italy* 38°2N 14°1E **22 E6**
Cegléd *Hungary* 47°11N 19°47E **17 E10**
Ceheng *China* 24°58N 105°48E **34 E5**
Cekik *Indonesia* 8°12S 114°27E **37 J17**
Celaque △ *Honduras* 14°30N 88°43W **88 D2**
Celaya *Mexico* 20°31N 100°37W **86 C4**
Celebes = Sulawesi
  Indonesia 2°0S 120°0E **37 E6**
Celebes Sea *Indonesia* 3°0N 123°0E **37 D6**
Celina *U.S.A.* 40°33N 84°35W **81 E11**
Celje *Slovenia* 46°16N 15°18E **16 E8**
Celle *Germany* 52°37N 10°4E **16 B6**
Celtic Sea *Atl. Oc.* 50°9N 9°34W **14 F2**
Cenderawasih, Teluk
  Indonesia 3°0S 135°20E **37 E9**
Cengong *China* 27°13N 108°44E **34 D7**
Centennial *U.S.A.* 39°34N 104°52W **76 G11**
Center *N. Dak., U.S.A.* 47°7N 101°18W **80 B3**
Center *Tex., U.S.A.* 31°48N 94°11W **84 F7**
Centerburg *U.S.A.* 40°18N 82°42W **82 F2**
Centerville *Calif., U.S.A.* 36°44N 119°30W **78 J7**
Centerville *Iowa, U.S.A.* 40°44N 92°52W **80 E8**
Centerville *Pa., U.S.A.* 40°3N 79°59W **82 F5**
Centerville *Tenn., U.S.A.* 35°47N 87°28W **85 D11**
Centerville *Tex., U.S.A.* 31°16N 95°59W **84 F7**
Central = Tsentralnyy □
  Russia 52°0N 40°0E **26 D4**
Central □ *Botswana* 22°0S 26°30E **56 B4**
Central, Cordillera *Colombia* 5°0N 75°0W **92 C4**
Central, Cordillera
  Costa Rica 10°10N 84°5W **88 D3**
Central, Cordillera
  Dom. Rep. 19°15N 71°0W **89 C5**
Central, Cordillera
  Puerto Rico 18°8N 66°35W **89 d**

Central African Rep. ■
  Africa 7°0N 20°0E **53 G9**
Central America *America* 12°0N 85°0W **66 H11**
Central Australia ◇
  Australia 22°30S 128°30E **60 D4**
Central Bedfordshire □
  U.K. 52°5N 0°20W **13 E7**
Central Butte *Canada* 50°48N 106°31W **71 C7**
Central City *Colo.,*
  U.S.A. 39°48N 105°31W **76 G11**
Central City *Ky., U.S.A.* 37°18N 87°7W **80 G10**
Central City *Nebr., U.S.A.* 41°7N 98°0W **80 E4**
Central Desert ◇
  Australia 19°56S 130°46E **60 C5**
Central Japan Int. ✈ (NGO)
  Japan 34°53N 136°45E **29 G8**
Central Kalahari ◇
  Botswana 22°36S 23°58E **56 B3**
Central Makran Range
  Pakistan 26°30N 64°15E **40 F4**
Central Pacific Basin
  Pac. Oc. 8°0N 175°0W **64 G10**
Central Patricia *Canada* 51°30N 90°9W **72 B1**
Central Point *U.S.A.* 42°23N 122°55W **76 E2**
Central Russian Uplands
  Europe 54°0N 36°0E **6 E13**
Central Siberian Plateau
  Russia 65°0N 105°0E **24 B12**
Central Square *U.S.A.* 43°17N 76°9W **83 C8**
Centralia *Canada* 43°17N 81°28W **82 C3**
Centralia *Ill., U.S.A.* 38°32N 89°8W **80 F9**
Centralia *Mo., U.S.A.* 39°13N 92°8W **80 F8**
Centralia *Wash., U.S.A.* 46°43N 122°58W **78 D4**
Centre de Flacq *Mauritius* 20°12S 57°43E **55 d**
Centreville *N.S., U.S.A.* 42°28N 78°14W **82 D6**
Centreville *Pa., U.S.A.* 41°44N 79°45W **82 E5**
Cenxi *China* 22°57N 110°57E **35 F8**
Cephalonia = Kefalonia
  Greece 38°15N 20°30E **23 E9**
Cepu *Indonesia* 7°9S 111°35E **37 G14**
Ceram = Seram *Indonesia* 3°10S 129°0E **37 E7**
Ceram Sea = Seram Sea
  Indonesia 2°30S 128°30E **37 E7**
Ceredigion □ *U.K.* 52°16N 4°15W **13 E3**
Ceres *Argentina* 29°55S 61°55W **94 B3**
Ceres *S. Africa* 33°21S 19°18E **56 D2**
Ceres *U.S.A.* 37°35N 120°57W **78 H6**
Cerf *Seychelles* 4°38S 55°40E **55 b**
Cerignola *Italy* 41°17N 15°53E **22 D6**
Cerigo = Kythira *Greece* 36°8N 23°0E **23 F10**
Çerkezköy *Turkey* 41°17N 28°0E **23 D12**
Cerralvo, I. *Mexico* 24°15N 109°55W **86 C3**
Cerritos *Mexico* 22°25N 100°16W **86 C4**
Cerro Chato *Uruguay* 33°6S 55°8W **95 C4**
Cerro Cofre de Perote △
  Mexico 19°29N 97°8W **87 D5**
Cerro Corá △ *Paraguay* 22°35S 56°2W **95 A4**
Cerro de Pasco *Peru* 10°45S 76°10W **92 F3**
Cerro el Copey △
  Venezuela 10°59N 63°53W **89 D7**
Cerro Hoya △ *Panama* 7°17N 80°45W **88 E3**
Cerro Saroche △
  Venezuela 10°8N 69°38W **89 D6**
Cerventes *Australia* 30°31S 115°3E **61 F2**
Cervera *Spain* 41°40N 1°16E **21 B6**
Cesena *Italy* 44°8N 12°15E **22 B5**
Cēsis *Latvia* 57°18N 25°15E **9 H21**
Česká Rep. = Czech Rep. ■
  Europe 50°0N 15°0E **16 D8**
České Budějovice
  Czech Rep. 48°55N 14°25E **16 D8**
Českomoravská Vrchovina
  Czech Rep. 49°30N 15°40E **16 D8**
Çeşme *Turkey* 38°20N 26°23E **23 E12**
Cessnock *Australia* 32°50S 151°21E **63 E5**
Cetinje *Montenegro* 42°23N 18°59E **23 C8**
Cetraro *Italy* 39°31N 15°55E **22 E6**
Ceuta *N. Afr.* 35°52N 5°18W **21 E3**
Cévennes *France* 44°10N 3°50E **20 D5**
Ceyhan *Turkey* 37°4N 35°47E **46 B2**
Ceylanpınar *Turkey* 36°50N 40°2E **46 B4**
Ceylon = Sri Lanka ■ *Asia* 7°30N 80°50E **45 L5**
Cha-am *Thailand* 12°48N 99°58E **38 F2**
Chacabuco *Argentina* 34°40S 60°27W **94 C3**
Chachapoyas *Peru* 6°15S 77°50W **92 E3**
Chachoengsao *Thailand* 13°42N 101°5E **38 F3**
Chachran *Pakistan* 28°55N 70°30E **42 E4**
Chachro *Pakistan* 25°5N 70°15E **42 G4**
Chaco □ *Argentina* 26°30S 61°0W **94 B3**
Chaco □ *Paraguay* 26°0S 60°0W **94 B4**
Chaco → *U.S.A.* 36°46N 108°39W **77 H9**
Chaco △ *Argentina* 27°0S 59°30W **94 B4**
Chaco Austral *S. Amer.* 27°0S 61°30W **96 B4**
Chaco Boreal *S. Amer.* 22°0S 60°0W **92 H6**
Chaco Central *S. Amer.* 24°0S 61°0W **96 A4**
Chaco Culture △ *U.S.A.* 36°3N 107°58W **77 H10**
Chacon, C. *U.S.A.* 54°42N 132°0W **70 C2**
Chad ■ *Africa* 15°0N 17°15E **53 F8**
Chad, L. = Tchad, L. *Chad* 13°30N 14°30E **53 F8**
Chadileuvú → *Argentina* 37°46S 66°0W **94 D2**
Chadobets → *Russia* 58°45N 130°38E **27 D14**
Chadron *U.S.A.* 42°50N 103°0W **80 D2**
Chadyr-Lunga = Ciadâr-Lunga
  Moldova 46°3N 28°51E **17 E15**
Chae Hom *Thailand* 18°43N 99°35E **38 C2**
Chae Son △ *Thailand* 18°42N 99°10E **38 C2**
Chaem → *Thailand* 18°11N 98°38E **38 C2**
Chaeryŏng *N. Korea* 38°24N 125°36E **33 E13**
Chagai Hills = Chāh Gay Hills
  Afghan. 29°30N 64°0E **40 E3**
Chagda *Russia* 58°45N 130°38E **27 D14**
Chaghcharān *Afghan.* 34°31N 65°15E **40 B4**
Chagos Arch. ◇ *Ind. Oc.* 6°0S 72°0E **25 J9**
Chagres △ *Panama* 9°33N 79°37W **88 E4**
Chaguanas *Trin. & Tob.* 10°30N 61°26W **93 K15**
Chang, Ko *Thailand* 12°0N 102°23E **39 G4**
Chang, Ko *Thailand* 9°50N 98°27E **39 H2**
Ch'ang Chiang = Chang Jiang →
  China 31°48N 121°10E **35 B13**
Chang Jiang → *China* 31°48N 121°10E **35 B13**
Chang-won *S. Korea* 35°16N 128°37E **33 G15**

Chahār Mahāll va Bakhtīārī □
  Iran 32°0N 49°0E **47 C6**
Chai Badan *Thailand* 15°12N 101°8E **38 E3**
Chaibasa *India* 22°42N 85°49E **43 H11**
Chainat *Thailand* 15°11N 100°8E **38 E3**
Chainpur *Nepal* 27°17N 87°19E **43 F12**
Chaiya *Thailand* 9°23N 99°14E **39 H2**
Chaiyaphum *Thailand* 15°48N 102°2E **38 E4**
Chaj Doab *Pakistan* 32°15N 73°0E **42 C5**
Chajari *Argentina* 30°42S 58°0W **94 C4**
Chak Amru *Pakistan* 32°22N 75°11E **42 C6**
Chakar → *Pakistan* 29°29N 68°2E **42 E3**
Chakari *Zimbabwe* 18°5S 29°51E **57 A4**
Chakhānsūr *Afghan.* 31°10N 62°0E **40 D3**
Chakonipau, L. *Canada* 56°18N 68°30W **73 A6**
Chakradharpur *India* 22°45N 85°40E **43 H11**
Chakrata *India* 30°42N 77°51E **42 D7**
Chakwal *Pakistan* 32°56N 72°53E **42 C5**
Chala *Peru* 15°48S 74°20W **92 G4**
Chalakudi *India* 10°18N 76°20E **45 J3**
Chalchihuites *Mexico* 23°29N 103°53W **86 C4**
Chalcis = Chalkida
  Greece 38°27N 23°42E **23 E10**
Chaleur B. *Canada* 47°55N 65°30W **73 C6**
Chalfant *U.S.A.* 37°32N 118°21W **78 H8**
Chalhuanca *Peru* 14°15S 73°15W **92 F4**
Chaling *China* 26°58N 113°30E **35 D9**
Chalisgaon *India* 20°30N 75°10E **44 D2**
Chalk River *Canada* 46°1N 77°27W **72 C4**
Chalkida *Greece* 38°27N 23°42E **23 E10**
Chalky Inlet *N.Z.* 46°3S 166°31E **59 G1**
Challakere *India* 14°19N 76°39E **45 G3**
Challapata *Bolivia* 18°53S 66°50W **92 G5**
Challenger Deep *Pac. Oc.* 11°30N 142°0E **64 F6**
Challenger Fracture Zone
  Pac. Oc. 35°0S 105°0W **65 L17**
Challis *U.S.A.* 44°30N 114°14W **76 D6**
Chalmette *U.S.A.* 29°56N 89°57W **85 G10**
Chaloem Rattanakosin △
  Thailand 14°40N 99°17E **38 E2**
Chalon-sur-Saône *France* 46°48N 4°50E **20 C6**
Chalong *Thailand* 7°50N 98°22E **39 a**
Châlons-en-Champagne
  France 48°58N 4°20E **20 B6**
Chama *U.S.A.* 36°54N 106°35W **77 H10**
Chamaicó *Argentina* 35°3S 64°58W **94 D3**
Chaman *Pakistan* 30°58N 66°25E **40 D5**
Chamba *India* 32°35N 76°10E **42 C7**
Chambal → *India* 26°29N 79°15E **43 F8**
Chamberlain *U.S.A.* 43°49N 99°20W **80 D4**
Chamberlain → *Australia* 15°30S 127°54E **60 C4**
Chamberlain L. *U.S.A.* 46°14N 69°19W **81 B19**
Chambers *U.S.A.* 35°11N 109°26W **77 J9**
Chambersburg *U.S.A.* 39°56N 77°40W **81 F15**
Chambéry *France* 45°34N 5°55E **20 D6**
Chambeshi → *Zambia* 11°53S 29°48E **54 G6**
Chambly *Canada* 45°27N 73°17W **83 A11**
Chambord *Canada* 48°25N 72°6E **73 C5**
Chamchamal *Iraq* 35°32N 44°50E **46 C5**
Chamela *Mexico* 19°32N 105°5W **86 D3**
Chamical *Argentina* 30°22S 66°27W **94 C2**
Chamkar Luong
  Cambodia 11°0N 103°45E **39 G4**
Chamoli *India* 30°24N 79°21E **43 D8**
Chamonix-Mont Blanc
  France 45°55N 6°51E **20 D7**
Chamouchouane =
  Ashuapmushuan →
  Canada 48°37N 72°20W **72 C5**
Champa *India* 22°2N 82°43E **43 H10**
Champagne *Canada* 60°49N 136°30W **70 A1**
Champagne *France* 48°40N 4°20E **20 B6**
Champaign *U.S.A.* 40°7N 88°15W **80 E9**
Champaner *India* 22°29N 73°32E **42 H5**
Champassak *Laos* 14°53S 105°52E **38 E5**
Champawat *India* 29°20N 80°6E **43 E9**
Champdoré, L. *Canada* 55°55N 65°49W **73 A6**
Champion *U.S.A.* 41°19N 80°51W **82 E4**
Champlain *U.S.A.* 44°59N 73°27W **83 B11**
Champlain, L. *U.S.A.* 44°40N 73°20W **83 B11**
Champotón *Mexico* 19°21N 90°43W **87 D6**
Champua *India* 22°5N 85°40E **43 H11**
Chamrajnagar *India* 11°52N 76°52E **45 J3**
Chana *Thailand* 6°55N 100°44E **39 J3**
Chañaral *Chile* 26°23S 70°40W **94 B1**
Chanārān *Iran* 36°39N 59°6E **47 B8**
Chanasma *India* 23°44N 72°5E **42 H5**
Chancery Lane *Barbados* 13°3N 59°30W **89 g**
Chanco *Chile* 35°44S 72°32W **94 D1**
Chand *India* 21°57N 79°7E **43 J8**
Chandan Chauki *India* 28°33N 80°47E **43 E9**
Chandannagar *India* 22°52N 88°24E **43 H13**
Chandausi *India* 28°27N 78°49E **43 E8**
Chandeleur Is. *U.S.A.* 29°55N 88°57W **85 G10**
Chandeleur Sd. *U.S.A.* 29°55N 89°0W **85 G10**
Chandigarh *India* 30°43N 76°47E **42 D7**
Chandil *India* 22°58N 86°3E **43 H12**
Chandler *Australia* 27°0S 133°19E **63 D1**
Chandler *Canada* 48°18N 64°46W **73 C7**
Chandler *Ariz., U.S.A.* 33°18N 111°50W **77 K8**
Chandler *Okla., U.S.A.* 35°42N 96°53W **84 H6**
Chandod *India* 21°59N 73°28E **42 J5**
Chandpur *Bangla.* 23°8N 90°45E **41 H17**
Chandragiri *India* 13°35N 79°19E **45 H4**
Chandrapur *India* 19°57N 79°25E **44 H4**
Chandrupatla *India* 18°33N 80°42E **44 E5**
Chānf *Iran* 26°38N 60°29E **47 E9**
Chang *Pakistan* 26°59N 68°30E **42 F3**
Chang, Ko *Thailand* 12°0N 102°23E **39 G4**
Chang Jiang → *China* 31°48N 121°10E **35 B13**

Changan *China* 22°48N 113°48E **31 a**
Changanacheri *India* 9°25N 76°31E **45 K3**
Changanassery = Changanacheri
  India 9°25N 76°31E **45 K3**
Changane → *Mozam.* 24°30S 33°30E **57 B5**
Changbai *China* 41°25N 128°5E **33 D15**
Changbai Shan *China* 42°20N 129°0E **33 C15**
Changchik'ou = Zhangjiakou
  China 40°48N 114°55E **32 D8**
Ch'angchou = Changzhou
  China 31°47N 119°58E **35 B12**
Changchun *China* 43°57N 125°17E **33 C13**
Changchunling *China* 45°18N 125°27E **33 B13**
Changde *China* 29°4N 111°35E **35 C8**
Changdo-ri *N. Korea* 38°30N 127°40E **33 E14**
Changfeng *China* 32°28N 117°10E **35 A11**
Changge *China* 34°13N 113°46E **34 G7**
Changhua *China* 30°12N 119°12E **35 B12**
Changhua *Taiwan* 24°2N 120°30E **35 F13**
Changhŭngni *N. Korea* 40°24N 128°19E **33 D15**
Changji *China* 44°1N 87°19E **30 C6**
Changjiang *China* 19°20N 108°55E **38 C7**
Changjiang Shuiku
  China 22°29N 113°27E **31 a**
Changjin *N. Korea* 40°23N 127°15E **33 D14**
Changjin-ho *N. Korea* 40°30N 127°15E **33 D14**
Changle *China* 25°59N 119°27E **35 E12**
Changli *China* 39°40N 119°13E **35 E10**
Changling *China* 44°20N 123°58E **33 B12**
Changlun *Malaysia* 6°25N 100°26E **39 J3**
Changning *Hunan, China* 26°28N 112°22E **35 D9**
Changning *Sichuan,*
  China 28°40N 104°56E **34 C5**
Changning *Yunnan, China* 24°45N 99°30E **34 E2**
Changping *China* 40°14N 116°12E **32 D9**
Changsha *China* 28°12N 113°0E **35 C9**
Changshan *China* 28°55N 118°27E **35 C12**
Changshan Qundao
  China 39°11N 122°32E **33 E12**
Changshou *China* 29°50N 107°4E **34 C6**
Changshu *China* 31°38N 120°43E **35 B13**
Changshun *China* 26°3N 106°25E **34 D6**
Changtai *China* 24°35N 117°42E **35 E11**
Changting *China* 25°50N 116°22E **35 E11**
Changtu *China* 42°46N 124°6E **33 C13**
Changuinola *Panama* 9°26N 82°31W **88 E3**
Changwu *Guangxi Zhuangzu,*
  China 23°25N 111°17E **35 F8**
Changwu *Shaanxi, China* 35°10N 107°45E **32 G4**
Changxing *China* 31°0N 119°55E **35 B12**
Changyang *China* 30°30N 111°10E **35 B8**
Changyi *China* 36°40N 119°30E **33 F10**
Changyŏn *N. Korea* 38°15N 125°6E **33 E13**
Changyuan *China* 35°15N 114°42E **32 G8**
Changzhi *China* 36°10N 113°6E **32 F7**
Changzhou *China* 31°47N 119°58E **35 B12**
Chanhanga *Angola* 16°0S 14°8E **56 A1**
Chania *Greece* 35°30N 24°4E **23 G11**
Chanion, Kolpos *Greece* 35°33N 23°55E **23 G10**
Channagiri *India* 14°2N 75°58E **45 G2**
Channapatna *India* 12°40N 77°15E **45 H3**
Channel Is. *U.K.* 49°19N 2°24E **13 H5**
Channel Is. *U.S.A.* 33°40N 119°15W **79 M7**
Channel Islands △
  U.S.A. 34°0N 119°24W **79 L7**
Channel-Port aux Basques
  Canada 47°30N 59°9W **73 C8**
Channel Tunnel *Europe* 51°0N 1°30E **13 F9**
Channing *U.S.A.* 35°41N 102°20W **84 D3**
Chantada *Spain* 42°36N 7°46W **21 A2**
Chanthaburi *Thailand* 12°38N 102°12E **38 F4**
Chantrey Inlet *Canada* 67°48N 96°20W **68 B10**
Chanute *U.S.A.* 37°41N 95°27W **80 G6**
Chao Hu *China* 31°30N 117°30E **35 B11**
Chao Phraya →
  Thailand 13°40N 100°31E **38 F3**
Chao Phraya Lowlands
  Thailand 15°30N 100°0E **38 E3**
Chaocheng *China* 36°4N 115°37E **32 F8**
Chaohu *China* 31°38N 117°58E **35 B11**
Chaoyang *Guangdong,*
  China 23°17N 116°30E **35 F11**
Chaoyang *Liaoning,*
  China 41°35N 120°22E **33 D11**
Chaozhou *China* 23°42N 116°32E **35 F11**
Chapayev *Kazakhstan* 50°25N 51°10E **19 D9**
Chapais *Canada* 49°47N 74°51W **72 C5**
Chapala, L. de *Mexico* 20°15N 103°0W **86 C4**
Chapayev = Chapayev
  Kazakhstan 50°25N 51°10E **19 D9**
Chapayevsk *Russia* 53°0N 49°40E **18 D9**
Chapecó *Brazil* 27°14S 52°41W **95 B5**
Chapel Hill *U.S.A.* 35°55N 79°4W **85 D15**
Chapleau *Canada* 47°50N 83°24W **72 C3**
Chaplin *Canada* 50°28N 106°40W **71 C7**
Chaplin L. *Canada* 50°22N 106°36W **71 C7**
Chappell *U.S.A.* 41°6N 102°28W **80 E2**
Chapra = Chhapra *India* 25°48N 84°44E **43 G11**
Chara *Russia* 56°54N 118°20E **27 D12**
Charadai *Argentina* 27°35S 59°55W **94 B4**
Charagua *Bolivia* 19°45S 63°10W **92 G6**
Charambirá, Punta
  Colombia 4°16N 77°32W **92 C3**
Charaña *Bolivia* 17°30S 69°25W **92 G5**
Charanwala *India* 27°51N 72°10E **42 F5**
Charata *Argentina* 27°13S 61°14W **94 B3**
Charcas *Mexico* 23°8N 101°7W **86 C4**
Charcot I. *Antarctica* 70°0S 70°0W **5 C17**
Chard *U.K.* 50°52N 2°58E **13 G5**
Chardon *U.S.A.* 41°35N 81°12W **82 E3**
Chardzhou = Türkmenabat
  Turkmenistan 39°6N 63°34E **47 B9**
Charente → *France* 45°57N 1°5W **20 D3**
Chari → *Chad* 12°58N 14°31E **53 F8**
Chārīkār *Afghan.* 35°0N 69°10E **40 B6**
Chariton → *U.S.A.* 39°19N 92°58W **80 F8**
Chärjew = Türkmenabat
  Turkmenistan 39°6N 63°34E **47 B9**

Charkhari *India* 25°24N 79°45E **43** G8
Charkhi Dadri *India* 28°37N 76°17E **42** E7
Charleroi *Belgium* 50°24N 4°27E **15** D4
Charleroi *U.S.A.* 40°9N 79°57W **82** F5
Charles, C. *U.S.A.* 37°7N 75°58W **81** G16
Charles, Peak *Australia* 32°52S 121°11E **61** F3
Charles City *U.S.A.* 43°4N 92°41W **80** D7
Charles I. *Canada* 62°39N 74°15W **69** E17
Charles L. *Canada* 59°50N 110°33W **71** B6
Charles Town *U.S.A.* 39°17N 77°52W **81** F15
Charlesbourg *Canada* 46°51N 71°16W **81** B18
Charleston *Ill., U.S.A.* 39°30N 88°10W **80** F9
Charleston *Miss., U.S.A.* 34°1N 90°4W **85** D9
Charleston *Mo., U.S.A.* 36°55N 89°21W **80** G9
Charleston *S.C., U.S.A.* 32°46N 79°56W **85** E15
Charleston *W. Va.,*
  U.S.A. 38°21N 81°38W **81** F13
Charleston L. *Canada* 44°32N 76°0W **83** B9
Charleston Peak
  U.S.A. 36°16N 115°42W **79** J11
Charlestown *Ireland* 53°58N 8°48W **10** C3
Charlestown *S. Africa* 27°26S 29°53E **57** C4
Charlestown *Ind.,*
  U.S.A. 38°27N 85°40W **81** F11
Charlestown *N.H.,*
  U.S.A. 43°14N 72°25W **83** C12
Charlestown of Aberlour
  U.K. 57°28N 3°14W **11** D5
Charleville *Australia* 26°24S 146°15E **63** D4
Charleville *Ireland* 52°21N 8°40W **10** D3
Charleville-Mézières
  France 49°44N 4°40E **20** B6
Charlevoix *U.S.A.* 45°19N 85°16W **81** C11
Charlotte *Mich., U.S.A.* 42°34N 84°50W **81** D11
Charlotte *N.C., U.S.A.* 35°13N 80°50W **85** D14
Charlotte *Vt., U.S.A.* 44°19N 73°16W **83** B11
Charlotte Amalie
  U.S. Virgin Is. 18°21N 64°56W **89** e
Charlotte Harbor *U.S.A.* 26°57N 82°4W **85** H13
Charlotte L. *Canada* 52°12N 125°19W **70** C3
Charlottesville *U.S.A.* 38°2N 78°30W **81** F14
Charlottetown *Nfld. & L.,*
  Canada 52°46N 56°7W **73** B8
Charlottetown *P.E.I.,*
  Canada 46°14N 63°8W **73** C7
Charlotteville
  Trin. & Tob. 11°20N 60°33W **93** J16
Charlton *Australia* 36°16S 143°24E **63** F3
Charlton I. *Canada* 52°0N 79°20W **72** B4
Charny *Canada* 46°43N 71°15W **81** A18
Charolles *France* 46°27N 4°16E **20** C6
Charre *Mozam.* 17°13S 35°10E **55** H7
Charsadda *Pakistan* 34°17N 71°44E **42** B4
Charters Towers *Australia* 20°5S 146°13E **62** C4
Chartres *France* 48°29N 1°30E **20** B4
Chascomús *Argentina* 35°30S 58°0W **94** D4
Chase *Canada* 50°50N 119°41W **70** C5
Chashma Barrage
  Pakistan 32°27N 71°20E **42** C4
Chāt *Iran* 37°59N 55°16E **47** B7
Châteaubriant *France* 47°43N 1°23W **20** C3
Chateaugay *U.S.A.* 44°56N 74°5W **83** B10
Châteauguay, L. *Canada* 56°26N 70°3W **73** A5
Châteaulin *France* 48°11N 4°8W **20** B1
Châteauroux *France* 46°50N 1°40E **20** C4
Châteaux, Pte. des
  Guadeloupe 16°15N 61°10W **88** b
Châtellerault *France* 46°50N 0°30E **20** C4
Chatham = Miramichi
  Canada 47°2N 65°28W **73** C6
Chatham *Canada* 42°24N 82°11W **82** D2
Chatham *U.K.* 51°22N 0°32E **13** F8
Chatham *U.S.A.* 42°21N 73°36W **83** D11
Chatham Is. *Pac. Oc.* 44°0S 176°40W **64** M10
Chatham Rise *Pac. Oc.* 43°30S 180°0E **64** M10
Chatmohar *Bangla.* 24°15N 89°15E **43** G13
Chatra *India* 24°12N 84°56E **43** G11
Chatrapur *India* 19°22N 85°2E **44** E7
Chats, L. des *Canada* 45°30N 76°20W **83** A8
Chatsworth *Canada* 44°27N 80°54W **82** B4
Chāttāgām = Chittagong
  Bangla. 22°19N 91°48E **41** H17
Chattahoochee *U.S.A.* 30°42N 84°51W **85** F12
Chattahoochee →
  U.S.A. 30°54N 84°57W **85** F12
Chatteris *U.K.* 52°28N 0°2E **13** E8
Chatturat *Thailand* 15°40N 101°51E **38** E3
Chau Doc *Vietnam* 10°42N 105°7E **39** G5
Chaukan Pass *Burma* 27°8N 97°10E **41** F20
Chaumont *France* 48°7N 5°8E **20** B6
Chaumont *U.S.A.* 44°4N 76°8W **83** B8
Chaunskaya G. *Russia* 69°0N 169°0E **27** C17
Chaura *India* 8°27N 93°2E **45** K11
Chautara *Nepal* 27°46N 85°42E **43** F11
Chautauqua L. *U.S.A.* 42°10N 79°24W **82** D5
Chauvin *Canada* 52°45N 110°10W **71** C6
Chavakachcheri *Sri Lanka* 9°43N 80°12E **45** K5
Chaves *Brazil* 0°15S 49°55W **93** D9
Chaves *Portugal* 41°45N 7°32W **21** B2
Chawang *Thailand* 8°25N 99°30E **39** H2
Chaykovskiy *Russia* 56°47N 54°9E **18** C9
Chazy *U.S.A.* 44°53N 73°26E **83** B11
Cheb *Czech Rep.* 50°9N 12°28E **16** C7
Cheboksary *Russia* 56°8N 47°12E **18** C8
Cheboygan *U.S.A.* 45°39N 84°29W **81** C11
Chech, Erg *Africa* 25°0N 2°15W **52** D5
Chechenia □ *Russia* 43°30N 45°29E **19** F8
Checheno-Ingush Republic =
  Chechenia □ *Russia* 43°30N 45°29E **19** F8
Chechnya = Chechenia □
  Russia 43°30N 45°29E **19** F8
Checotah *U.S.A.* 35°28N 95°31W **84** D7
Chedabucto B. *Canada* 45°25N 61°8W **73** C7
Cheduba I. *Burma* 18°45N 93°40E **41** K18
Cheektowaga *U.S.A.* 42°54N 78°45W **82** D6
Cheepie *Australia* 26°33S 145°1E **63** D4
Chegdomyn *Russia* 51°7N 133°1E **27** D14

Chegga *Mauritania* 25°27N 5°40W **52** C4
Chegutu *Zimbabwe* 18°10S 30°14E **55** H6
Chehalis *U.S.A.* 46°40N 122°58W **78** D4
Chehalis → *U.S.A.* 46°57N 123°50W **78** D3
Cheju = Jeju *S. Korea* 33°31N 126°32E **33** H14
Cheju-do = Jeju-do
  S. Korea 33°29N 126°34E **33** H14
Chek Lap Kok *China* 22°18N 113°56E **31** a
Chek Lap Kok ✈ (HKG)
  China 22°19N 113°57E **31** a
Chekiang = Zhejiang □
  China 29°0N 120°0E **35** C13
Chela, Sa. da *Angola* 16°20S 13°20E **56** A1
Chelan *U.S.A.* 47°51N 120°1W **76** C3
Chelan, L. *U.S.A.* 48°11N 120°30W **76** B3
Cheleken = Hazar
  Turkmenistan 39°34N 53°16E **19** G9
Cheleken Yarymadasy
  Turkmenistan 39°30N 53°15E **47** B7
Chelforó *Argentina* 39°0S 66°33W **96** D3
Chelkar = Shalqar
  Kazakhstan 47°48N 59°39E **26** E6
Chelm *Poland* 51°8N 23°30E **17** C12
Chelmno *Poland* 53°20N 18°30E **17** B10
Chelmsford *U.K.* 51°44N 0°29E **13** F8
Chelsea *Australia* 38°5S 145°8E **63** F4
Chelsea *U.S.A.* 43°59N 72°27W **83** C12
Cheltenham *U.K.* 51°54N 2°4W **13** F5
Chelyabinsk *Russia* 55°10N 61°24E **26** D7
Chelyuskin, C. = Chelyuskin, Mys
  Russia 77°30N 103°0E **27** B11
Chelyuskin, Mys *Russia* 77°30N 103°0E **27** B11
Chemainus *Canada* 48°55N 123°42W **78** B3
Chemba *Mozam.* 17°9S 34°53E **55** H6
Chemin Grenier *Mauritius* 20°29S 57°28E **55** d
Chemnitz *Germany* 50°51N 12°54E **16** C7
Chemult *U.S.A.* 43°14N 121°47W **76** E3
Chen, Gora *Russia* 65°16N 141°50E **27** C15
Chenab → *Pakistan* 30°23N 71°2E **42** D4
Chenab Nagar *Pakistan* 31°45N 72°55E **42** D5
Chenango Forks *U.S.A.* 42°15N 75°51W **83** D9
Chenchiang = Zhenjiang
  China 32°11N 119°26E **35** A12
Cheney *U.S.A.* 47°30N 117°35W **76** C5
Cheng Xian *China* 33°43N 105°42E **34** H3
Chengalpattu *India* 12°42N 79°58E **45** H4
Chengbu *China* 26°18N 110°16E **35** D8
Chengcheng *China* 35°8N 109°56E **32** G5
Chengchou = Zhengzhou
  China 34°45N 113°34E **32** G7
Chengde *China* 40°59N 117°58E **33** D9
Chengdong Hu *China* 32°15N 116°20E **35** A11
Chengdu *China* 30°38N 104°2E **34** B5
Chenggong *China* 24°52N 102°56E **34** E4
Chenggu *China* 33°10N 107°21E **34** A6
Chenghai *China* 23°30N 116°42E **35** F11
Chengjiang *China* 24°39N 103°0E **34** E4
Chengkou *China* 31°54N 108°31E **34** B7
Chengmai *China* 19°50N 109°58E **38** C7
Chengshan Jiao *China* 37°25N 122°44E **33** F12
Ch'engtu = Chengdu
  China 30°38N 104°2E **34** B5
Chengwu *China* 34°58N 115°50E **32** G8
Chengxi Hu *China* 32°15N 116°10E **35** A11
Chengyang *China* 36°18N 120°21E **33** F11
Chenjiagang *China* 34°23N 119°47E **33** G10
Chenkaladi *Sri Lanka* 7°47N 81°35E **45** L5
Chennai *India* 13°8N 80°19E **45** H5
Chenxi *China* 28°2N 110°12E **35** C8
Chenzhou *China* 25°47N 113°1E **35** E9
Cheò, Eilean a' = Skye
  U.K. 57°15N 6°10W **11** D2
Cheo Reo *Vietnam* 13°20N 108°25E **38** F7
Cheom Ksan *Cambodia* 14°13N 104°56E **38** E5
Cheonan *S. Korea* 36°48N 127°9E **33** F14
Cheongdo *S. Korea* 35°38N 128°42E **33** G15
Cheongju *S. Korea* 36°39N 127°27E **33** F14
Cheorwon *S. Korea* 38°15N 127°10E **33** E14
Chepén *Peru* 7°15S 79°23W **92** E3
Chepes *Argentina* 31°20S 66°35W **94** C2
Chepo *Panama* 9°10N 79°6W **88** E4
Chepstow *U.K.* 51°38N 2°41W **13** F5
Chequamegon B. *U.S.A.* 46°39N 90°51W **80** B8
Cher → *France* 47°21N 0°29E **20** C4
Cheraw *U.S.A.* 34°42N 79°53W **85** D15
Cherbourg *France* 49°39N 1°40W **20** B3
Cherdyn *Russia* 60°24N 56°29E **18** B10
Cheremkhovo *Russia* 53°8N 103°1E **30** A9
Cherepovets *Russia* 59°5N 37°55E **18** C6
Chergui, Chott ech *Algeria* 34°21N 0°25E **52** B6
Cherial *India* 17°55N 78°59E **44** F4
Cherikov = Cherykaw
  Belarus 53°32N 31°20E **17** B16
Cheriyam I. *India* 10°9N 73°40E **45** J1
Cherkasy *Ukraine* 49°27N 32°4E **19** E5
Cherkessk *Russia* 44°15N 42°5E **19** F7
Cherla *India* 18°5N 80°49E **44** E5
Cherlak *Russia* 54°15N 74°55E **26** D8
Chernaya *Russia* 70°30N 89°10E **27** B9
Chernigov = Chernihiv
  Ukraine 51°28N 31°20E **18** D5
Chernigovka *Russia* 44°19N 132°34E **28** B6
Chernihiv *Ukraine* 51°28N 31°20E **18** D5
Chernivtsi *Ukraine* 48°15N 25°52E **17** D13
Chernobyl = Chornobyl
  Ukraine 51°20N 30°15E **17** C16
Chernogorsk *Russia* 53°49N 91°18E **27** D10
Chernovtsy = Chernivtsi
  Ukraine 48°15N 25°52E **17** D13
Chernyakhovsk *Russia* 54°36N 21°48E **9** J19
Chernyshevskiy *Russia* 63°0N 112°30E **27** C12
Cherokee *Iowa, U.S.A.* 42°45N 95°33W **80** D6
Cherokee *Okla., U.S.A.* 36°45N 98°21W **84** C5
Cherokee Village *U.S.A.* 36°17N 91°31W **84** C9
Cherokees, Grand Lake O' The
  U.S.A. 36°28N 94°55W **84** C7
Cherrapunji *India* 25°17N 91°47E **41** G17
Cherry Valley *U.S.A.* 42°48N 74°45W **83** D10
Cherskiy *Russia* 68°45N 161°18E **27** C17

Cherskogo Khrebet
  Russia 65°0N 143°0E **27** C15
Cherthala *India* 9°42N 76°20E **45** K3
Cherven *Belarus* 53°45N 28°28E **17** B15
Chervonohrad *Ukraine* 50°25N 24°10E **17** C13
Cherwell → *U.K.* 51°44N 1°14W **13** F6
Cherykaw *Belarus* 53°32N 31°20E **17** B16
Chesapeake *U.S.A.* 36°49N 76°16W **81** G15
Chesapeake B. *U.S.A.* 38°0N 76°10W **81** F14
Cheshire East □ *U.K.* 53°15N 2°15W **12** D5
Cheshire West and Chester □
  U.K. 53°15N 2°40W **12** D5
Cheshskaya Guba *Russia* 67°20N 47°0E **18** A8
Cheshunt *U.K.* 51°43N 0°1W **13** F7
Chesil Beach *U.K.* 50°37N 2°33W **13** G5
Chesley *Canada* 44°17N 81°5W **82** B3
Chester *U.K.* 53°12N 2°53W **12** D5
Chester *Calif., U.S.A.* 40°19N 121°14W **76** F3
Chester *Ill., U.S.A.* 37°55N 89°49W **80** G9
Chester *Mont., U.S.A.* 48°31N 110°58W **76** B8
Chester *Pa., U.S.A.* 39°51N 75°22W **81** F16
Chester *S.C., U.S.A.* 34°43N 81°12W **85** D14
Chester *Vt., U.S.A.* 43°16N 72°36W **83** C12
Chester *W. Va., U.S.A.* 40°37N 80°34W **82** F4
Chester-le-Street *U.K.* 54°51N 1°34W **12** C6
Chesterfield *U.K.* 53°15N 1°25W **12** D6
Chesterfield, Îs. *N. Cal.* 19°52S 158°15E **58** C8
Chesterfield Inlet
  Canada 63°30N 90°45W **68** E13
Chesterton Ra. *Australia* 25°30S 147°27E **63** D4
Chesterton Range △
  Australia 26°16S 147°22E **63** D4
Chestertown *U.S.A.* 43°40N 73°48W **83** C11
Chesterville *Canada* 45°6N 75°14W **83** A9
Chesuncook L. *U.S.A.* 46°0N 69°21W **81** C19
Chetamale *India* 10°43N 92°33E **45** J11
Chéticamp *Canada* 46°37N 60°59W **73** C7
Chetlat I. *India* 11°42N 72°42E **45** J1
Chetumal *Mexico* 18°30N 88°20E **87** D7
Chetumal, B. de
  Cent. Amer. 18°40N 88°10W **87** D7
Chetwynd *Canada* 55°45N 121°36W **70** B4
Cheung Chau *China* 22°13N 114°1E **31** a
Cheviot, The *U.K.* 55°29N 2°9W **12** B5
Cheviot Hills *U.K.* 55°20N 2°30W **12** B5
Cheviot Ra. *Australia* 25°20S 143°45E **62** D3
Chew Bahir *Ethiopia* 4°40N 36°50E **49** G2
Chewelah *U.S.A.* 48°17N 117°43W **76** B5
Cheyenne *Okla., U.S.A.* 35°37N 99°40W **84** D5
Cheyenne *Wyo., U.S.A.* 41°8N 104°49W **76** F11
Cheyenne → *U.S.A.* 44°41N 101°18W **80** C3
Cheyenne Wells
  U.S.A. 38°49N 102°21W **76** G12
Cheyne B. *Australia* 34°35S 118°50E **61** F2
Cheyur *India* 12°21N 80°0E **45** H5
Chhabra *India* 24°40N 76°54E **42** G7
Chhaktala *India* 22°6N 74°11E **42** H6
Chhapra *India* 25°48N 84°44E **43** G11
Chhata *India* 27°42N 77°30E **42** F7
Chhatarpur *Jharkhand,*
  India 24°23N 84°11E **43** G11
Chhatarpur *Mad. P., India* 24°55N 79°35E **43** G8
Chhati *India* 20°47N 81°40E **44** D5
Chhattisgarh □ *India* 22°0N 82°0E **43** J10
Chhep *Cambodia* 13°45N 105°24E **38** F5
Chhindwara *Mad. P., India* 23°3N 79°29E **43** H8
Chhindwara *Mad. P., India* 22°2N 78°59E **43** H8
Chhinhdipada *India* 21°6N 84°54E **44** D7
Chhlong *Cambodia* 12°15N 105°58E **39** F5
Chhota Tawa → *India* 22°14N 76°36E **42** H7
Chhoti Kali Sindh →
  India 24°2N 75°31E **42** G6
Chhuikhadan *India* 21°32N 80°59E **43** J9
Chhuk *Cambodia* 10°46N 104°28E **39** G5
Chi → *Thailand* 15°11N 104°43E **38** E5
Chi Thanh *Vietnam* 13°17N 109°16E **38** F7
Chiai *Taiwan* 23°29N 120°25E **35** F13
Chiali *Taiwan* 23°9N 120°10E **35** F13
Chiang Dao *Thailand* 19°22N 98°58E **38** C2
Chiang Dao, Doi *Thailand* 19°23N 98°54E **38** C2
Chiang Kham *Thailand* 19°32N 100°18E **38** C3
Chiang Khan *Thailand* 17°52N 101°36E **38** D3
Chiang Khong *Thailand* 20°17N 100°24E **34** H4
Chiang Mai *Thailand* 18°47N 98°59E **38** C2
Chiang Rai *Thailand* 19°52N 99°50E **34** H2
Chiang Saen *Thailand* 20°16N 100°5E **34** H3
Chiapa de Corzo *Mexico* 16°42N 93°0W **87** D6
Chiapas □ *Mexico* 16°30N 92°30W **87** D6
Chiapas, Sa. Madre de
  Mexico 15°40N 93°0W **87** D6
Chiautla de Tapia
  Mexico 18°18N 98°36W **87** D5
Chiávari *Italy* 44°19N 9°19E **20** D8
Chiavenna *Italy* 46°19N 9°24E **20** D8
Chiba *Japan* 35°30N 140°7E **29** G10
Chiba □ *Japan* 35°30N 140°20E **29** G10
Chibabava *Mozam.* 20°17S 33°35E **57** B5
Chibemba *Cunene, Angola* 15°48S 14°8E **55** H2
Chibemba *Huíla, Angola* 16°20S 15°20E **56** A2
Chibi *Zimbabwe* 20°18S 30°25E **57** B5
Chibia *Angola* 15°10S 13°42E **55** H2
Chibougamau *Canada* 49°56N 74°24W **72** C5
Chibougamau, L. *Canada* 49°50N 74°20W **72** C5
Chibuk *Nigeria* 10°52N 12°50E **53** F8
Chibuto *Mozam.* 24°40S 33°33E **57** B5
Chic-Chocs, Mts. *Canada* 48°55N 66°0W **73** C6
Chicacole = Srikakulam
  India 18°14N 83°58E **44** E6
Chicago Heights *U.S.A.* 41°30N 87°38W **80** E10
Chichagof I. *U.S.A.* 57°30N 135°30W **68** F4
Chichaoua *Morocco* 31°32N 8°44W **52** B4
Chichawatni *Pakistan* 30°32N 72°42E **42** D5
Chichén-Itzá *Mexico* 20°37N 88°35W **87** C7
Chicheng *China* 40°55N 115°55E **32** D8
Chichester *U.K.* 50°50N 0°47W **13** G7
Chichester Ra. *Australia* 22°12S 119°15E **60** D2
Chichibu *Japan* 35°59N 139°10E **29** F9
Chichibu-Tama-Kai △
  Japan 35°52N 138°42E **29** G9

Ch'ich'ihaerh = Qiqihar
  China 47°26N 124°0E **31** B13
Chicholi *India* 22°1N 77°40E **42** H8
Chickasaw △ *U.S.A.* 34°26N 97°0W **84** D6
Chickasha *U.S.A.* 35°3N 97°58W **84** D6
Chiclana de la Frontera
  Spain 36°26N 6°9W **21** D2
Chiclayo *Peru* 6°42S 79°50W **92** E3
Chico *U.S.A.* 39°44N 121°50W **78** F5
Chico → *Chubut, Argentina* 44°0S 67°0W **96** E3
Chico → *Santa Cruz,*
  Argentina 50°0S 68°30W **96** F3
Chicoa *Mozam.* 15°36S 32°20E **57** A5
Chicomo *Mozam.* 24°31S 34°6E **57** B5
Chicomostoc *Mexico* 22°28N 102°46W **86** C4
Chicontepec *Mexico* 20°58N 98°10W **87** C5
Chicopee *U.S.A.* 42°9N 72°37E **83** D12
Chicoutimi *Canada* 48°28N 71°5W **73** C5
Chicualacuala *Mozam.* 22°6S 31°42E **57** B5
Chidambaram *India* 11°20N 79°45E **45** J4
Chidenguele *Mozam.* 24°55S 34°11E **57** B5
Chidley, C. *Canada* 60°23N 64°26W **69** E19
Chiducuane *Mozam.* 24°35S 34°25E **57** B5
Chiede *Angola* 17°15S 16°22E **56** A2
Chiefs Pt. *Canada* 44°41N 81°18W **82** B3
Chiem Hoa *Vietnam* 22°12N 105°17E **38** A5
Chiemsee *Germany* 47°53N 12°28E **16** E7
Chiengmai = Chiang Mai
  Thailand 18°47N 98°59E **38** C2
Chiese → *Italy* 45°8N 10°25E **20** D9
Chieti *Italy* 42°21N 14°10E **22** C6
Chifeng *China* 42°18N 118°58E **33** C10
Chignecto B. *Canada* 45°30N 64°40W **73** C7
Chiguana *Bolivia* 21°0S 67°58W **94** A2
Chigwell *U.K.* 51°37N 0°6E **13** F8
Chihli, G. of = Bo Hai
  China 39°0N 119°0E **33** E10
Chihuahua *Mexico* 28°38N 106°5W **86** B3
Chihuahua □ *Mexico* 28°30N 106°0W **86** B3
Chiili = Shïeli *Kazakhstan* 44°20N 66°15E **26** E7
Chik Bollapur *India* 13°25N 77°45E **45** H3
Chikalda *India* 21°24N 77°19E **44** D3
Chikhli *Ahmadabad, India* 20°45N 73°4E **44** D1
Chikhli *Maharashtra, India* 20°20N 76°18E **44** D3
Chikmagalur *India* 13°15N 75°45E **45** H2
Chiknayakanhalli *India* 13°26N 76°37E **45** H3
Chikodi *India* 16°26N 74°38E **45** F2
Chilapa *Mexico* 17°36N 99°10W **87** D5
Chilas *Pakistan* 35°25N 74°5E **43** B6
Chilaw *Sri Lanka* 7°30N 79°50E **45** L4
Chilcotin → *Canada* 51°44N 122°23W **70** C4
Childers *Australia* 25°15S 152°17E **63** D5
Childress *U.S.A.* 34°25N 100°13W **84** D4
Chile ■ *S. Amer.* 35°0S 72°0W **96** D2
Chile Rise *Pac. Oc.* 38°0S 92°0W **65** L18
Chilecito *Argentina* 29°10S 67°30W **94** B2
Chilete *Peru* 7°10S 78°50W **92** E3
Chililabombwe *Zambia* 12°18S 27°43E **55** G5
Chilim *Pakistan* 35°5N 75°5E **43** B6
Chilin = Jilin *China* 43°44N 126°30E **33** C14
Chilka L. *India* 19°40N 85°25E **44** E7
Chilko → *Canada* 52°0N 123°40W **70** C4
Chilko L. *Canada* 51°20N 124°10W **70** C4
Chillagoe *Australia* 17°7S 144°33E **62** B3
Chillán *Chile* 36°40S 72°10W **94** D1
Chillicothe *Ill., U.S.A.* 40°55N 89°29W **80** E9
Chillicothe *Mo., U.S.A.* 39°48N 93°33W **80** F7
Chillicothe *Ohio, U.S.A.* 39°20N 82°59W **81** F12
Chilliwack *Canada* 49°10N 121°54W **70** D4
Chilo *India* 19°40N 85°25E **44** E7
Chiloane, I. *Mozam.* 20°40S 34°55E **57** B5
Chiloé, I. de *Chile* 42°30S 73°50W **96** E2
Chilpancingo *Mexico* 17°33N 99°30W **87** D5
Chiltern Hills *U.K.* 51°40N 0°53W **13** F7
Chilton *U.S.A.* 44°2N 88°10W **80** C9
Chilung *Taiwan* 25°3N 121°45E **35** E13
Chilwa, L. *Malawi* 15°15S 35°40E **55** H7
Chimaltitán *Mexico* 21°35N 103°50W **86** C4
Chimán *Panama* 8°45N 78°40W **88** E4
Chimanimani *Zimbabwe* 19°48S 32°52E **57** A5
Chimanimani △ *Zimbabwe* 19°48S 33°0E **57** A5
Chimay *Belgium* 50°3N 4°20E **15** D4
Chimayo *U.S.A.* 36°0N 105°56W **77** J11
Chimborazo *Ecuador* 1°29S 78°55W **92** D3
Chimbote *Peru* 9°0S 78°35W **92** E3
Chimboy *Uzbekistan* 42°57N 59°47E **26** E6
Chimkent = Shymkent
  Kazakhstan 42°18N 69°36E **26** E7
Chimoio *Mozam.* 19°4S 33°30E **55** H6
Chimur *India* 20°30N 79°23E **44** D4
Chin □ *Burma* 22°0N 93°0E **41** J18
Chin Hills *Burma* 22°30N 93°30E **41** H18
Chin Ling Shan = Qinling Shandi
  China 33°50N 108°10E **32** H5
China *Mexico* 25°42N 99°14W **87** B5
China ■ *Asia* 30°0N 110°0E **31** E11
China, Great Plain of
  Asia 35°0N 115°0E **24** E13
China Lake *U.S.A.* 35°44N 117°37W **79** K9
Chinan = Jinan *China* 36°38N 117°1E **32** F9
Chinandega *Nic.* 12°35N 87°12W **88** D2
Chinati Peak *U.S.A.* 29°57N 104°29W **84** G2
Chincha Alta *Peru* 13°25S 76°7W **92** F3
Chinchaga → *Canada* 58°53N 118°20W **70** B5
Chinchilla *Australia* 26°45S 150°38E **63** D5
Chincholi *India* 17°28N 77°26E **44** E3
Chinchorro, Banco
  Mexico 18°35N 87°22W **87** D7
Chinchou = Jinzhou
  China 41°5N 121°3E **33** D11
Chincoteague *U.S.A.* 37°56N 75°23W **81** G16
Chinde *Mozam.* 18°35S 36°30E **55** H7
Chindwin → *Burma* 21°26N 95°15E **41** J19
Chineni *India* 33°2N 75°15E **43** C6
Chingola *Zambia* 12°31S 27°53E **55** G5
Chingune *Mozam.* 20°33S 34°58E **57** B5

Chinhanguanine *Mozam.* 25°21S 32°30E **57** C5
Chinhoyi *Zimbabwe* 17°20S 30°8E **55** H6
Chiniot *Pakistan* 31°45N 73°0E **42** D5
Chinipas *Mexico* 27°23N 108°32W **86** B3
Chinji *Pakistan* 32°42N 72°22E **42** C5
Chinju = Jinju *S. Korea* 35°12N 128°2E **33** G15
Chinko → *C.A.R.* 4°50N 23°53E **54** D4
Chinle *U.S.A.* 36°9N 109°33W **77** H9
Chinmen *Taiwan* 24°26N 118°19E **35** E13
Chinmen Tao *Taiwan* 24°26N 118°22E **35** E12
Chinnamanur *India* 9°50N 77°24E **45** K3
Chinnampo = Namp'o
  N. Korea 38°52N 125°10E **33** E13
Chino *Japan* 35°59N 138°9E **29** G9
Chino *U.S.A.* 34°1N 117°41W **79** L9
Chino Valley *U.S.A.* 34°45N 112°27W **77** J7
Chinon *France* 47°10N 0°15E **20** C4
Chinook *U.S.A.* 48°35N 109°14W **76** B9
Chinook Trough *Pac. Oc.* 44°0N 175°0W **64** C10
Chinsura = Chunchura
  India 22°53N 88°27E **43** H13
Chintalapudi *India* 17°4N 80°59E **44** F5
Chintamani *India* 13°26N 78°3E **45** H4
Chióggia *Italy* 45°13N 12°17E **22** B5
Chios *Greece* 38°27N 26°9E **23** E12
Chipata *Zambia* 13°38S 32°28E **55** G6
Chipindo *Angola* 13°49S 15°48E **55** G3
Chipinge *Zimbabwe* 20°13S 32°28E **55** J6
Chipley *U.S.A.* 30°47N 85°32W **85** F12
Chiplun *India* 17°31N 73°34E **44** F1
Chipman *Canada* 46°6N 65°53W **73** C6
Chippenham *U.K.* 51°27N 2°6W **13** F5
Chippewa → *U.S.A.* 44°25N 92°5W **80** C7
Chippewa Falls *U.S.A.* 44°56N 91°24W **80** C8
Chipping Norton *U.K.* 51°56N 1°32W **13** F6
Chiputneticook Lakes
  N. Amer. 45°35N 67°35W **81** C20
Chiquián *Peru* 10°10S 77°0W **92** F3
Chiquibul △ *Belize* 16°49N 88°52W **88** C2
Chiquimula *Guatemala* 14°51N 89°37W **88** D2
Chiquinquira *Colombia* 5°37N 73°50W **92** B4
Chirala *India* 15°50N 80°26E **45** G5
Chirawa *India* 28°14N 75°42E **42** E6
Chirchiq *Uzbekistan* 41°29N 69°35E **26** E7
Chiredzi *Zimbabwe* 21°0S 31°38E **57** B5
Chiricahua △ *U.S.A.* 32°0N 109°20W **77** K9
Chiricahua Peak *U.S.A.* 31°51N 109°18W **77** L9
Chirikof I. *U.S.A.* 55°50N 155°40W **74** D8
Chirimiri *India* 23°15N 82°20E **43** H10
Chiripó Grande, Cerro
  Costa Rica 9°29N 83°29W **88** E3
Chirundu *Zimbabwe* 16°3S 28°50E **57** A4
Chisapani *Nepal* 28°37N 81°16E **43** E9
Chisasibi *Canada* 53°50N 79°0W **72** B4
Ch'ishan *Taiwan* 22°44N 120°31E **35** F13
Chisholm *Canada* 54°55N 114°10W **70** C6
Chisholm *U.S.A.* 47°29N 92°53W **80** B7
Chishtian Mandi *Pakistan* 29°50N 72°55E **42** E5
Chishui *China* 28°30N 105°48E **34** C5
Chishui He → *China* 28°49N 105°50E **34** C5
Chisimaio = Kismaayo
  Somalia 0°22S 42°32E **49** H3
Chișinău *Moldova* 47°2N 28°50E **17** E15
Chisos Mts. *U.S.A.* 29°5N 103°15W **84** G3
Chistopol *Russia* 55°25N 50°38E **18** C9
Chita *Russia* 52°0N 113°35E **31** A11
Chitapur *India* 17°10N 77°5E **44** F3
Chitose *Japan* 42°49N 141°39E **28** C10
Chitradurga *India* 14°14N 76°24E **45** G3
Chitrakot *India* 19°10N 81°40E **44** E5
Chitral *Pakistan* 35°50N 71°56E **40** B7
Chitravati → *India* 14°45N 78°15E **45** G4
Chitré *Panama* 7°59N 80°27W **88** E3
Chittagong *Bangla.* 22°19N 91°48E **41** H17
Chittagong □ *Bangla.* 24°5N 91°0E **41** G17
Chittaurgarh *India* 24°52N 74°38E **42** G6
Chittoor *India* 13°15N 79°5E **45** H4
Chittur *India* 10°40N 76°45E **45** J3
Chitungwiza *Zimbabwe* 18°0S 31°6E **55** H6
Chiusi *Italy* 43°1N 11°57E **22** C4
Chivasso *Italy* 45°11N 7°53E **20** D7
Chivilcoy *Argentina* 34°55S 60°0W **94** C4
Chixi *China* 22°0N 112°58E **35** G9
Chkalov = Orenburg
  Russia 51°45N 55°6E **18** D10
Chloride *U.S.A.* 35°25N 114°12W **79** K12
Cho-do *N. Korea* 38°30N 124°40E **33** E13
Cho Phuoc Hai *Vietnam* 10°26N 107°18E **39** G6
Chobe △ *Botswana* 18°37S 24°23E **56** A4
Chocolate Mts. *U.S.A.* 33°15N 115°15W **79** M11
Choctawhatchee →
  U.S.A. 30°25N 86°8W **85** F11
Chodavaram *Andhra Pradesh,*
  India 17°50N 82°57E **44** F6
Chodavaram *Andhra Pradesh,*
  India 17°27N 81°46E **44** F5
Choele Choel *Argentina* 39°11S 65°40W **96** D3
Choghā Zanbil *Iran* 32°4N 48°32E **47** C6
Choiseul *St. Lucia* 13°47N 61°3W **89** f
Choiseul *Solomon Is.* 7°0S 156°40E **58** B8
Choix *Mexico* 26°43N 108°17W **86** B3
Chojnice *Poland* 53°42N 17°32E **17** B9
Chok Chai *Thailand* 14°44N 102°10E **38** E4
Chōkai-San *Japan* 39°6N 140°3E **28** E10
Choke Canyon Res.
  U.S.A. 28°30N 98°20W **84** G5
Chokurdakh *Russia* 70°38N 147°55E **27** B15
Chokwé *Mozam.* 24°32S 32°59E **57** B5
Cholame *U.S.A.* 35°44N 120°18W **78** K6
Cholet *France* 47°4N 0°52E **20** C3
Cholguan *Chile* 37°10S 72°3W **94** D1
Choloma *Honduras* 15°37N 87°57W **88** C2
Choluteca *Honduras* 13°20N 87°14W **88** D2
Choluteca → *Honduras* 13°0N 87°20W **88** D2
Chom Bung *Thailand* 13°37N 99°36E **38** F2
Chom Thong *Thailand* 18°25N 98°41E **38** C2
Choma *Zambia* 16°48S 26°59E **55** H5

Chomolungma = Everest, Mt.
Nepal 28°5N 86°58E **43** E12
Chomun *India* 27°15N 75°40E **42** F6
Chomutov *Czech Rep.* 50°28N 13°23E **16** C7
Chon Buri *Thailand* 13°21N 101°1E **38** F3
Chon Thanh *Vietnam* 11°24N 106°36E **39** G6
Chone *Ecuador* 0°40S 80°0W **92** D3
Chong Kai *Cambodia* 13°57N 103°35E **38** F4
Chong Mek *Thailand* 15°10N 105°27E **38** E5
Chong Phangan *Thailand* 9°39N 100°0E **39** b
Chong Samui *Thailand* 9°21N 99°50E **39** b
Chongde *China* 30°32N 120°26E **35** B13
Ch'ŏngjin *N. Korea* 41°47N 129°50E **33** D15
Chŏngju *N. Korea* 39°40N 125°5E **33** E13
Chongli *China* 40°58N 115°15E **32** D8
Chongming *China* 31°38N 121°23E **35** B13
Chongming Dao *China* 31°40N 121°30E **35** B13
Chŏngp'yŏng *N. Korea* 39°47N 127°23E **33** E14
Chongqing *Chongqing,*
China 29°35N 106°25E **34** C6
Chongqing *Sichuan,*
China 30°38N 103°40E **34** B4
Chongqing Shi □ *China* 30°0N 108°0E **34** C6
Chongren *China* 27°46N 116°3E **35** D11
Chonguene *Mozam.* 25°3S 33°49E **57** C5
Chongyi *China* 25°45N 114°29E **35** E10
Chongzuo *China* 22°23N 107°20E **34** F6
Chonogol *Mongolia* 45°54N 115°22E **32** B8
Chonos, Arch. de los *Chile* 45°0S 75°0W **96** F2
Chop *Ukraine* 48°26N 22°12E **17** D12
Chopda *India* 21°20N 75°15E **44** D2
Chopim → *Brazil* 25°35S 53°5W **95** B5
Chor *Pakistan* 25°31N 69°46E **42** G3
Chora Sfakion *Greece* 35°15N 24°9E **23** G11
Chorbat La *India* 34°42N 76°37E **43** B7
Chorley *U.K.* 53°39N 2°38W **12** D5
Chornobyl *Ukraine* 51°20N 30°15E **17** C16
Chorolque, Cerro *Bolivia* 20°59S 66°5W **94** A2
Chorregon *Australia* 22°40S 143°32E **62** C3
Chorro el Indio △
Venezuela 7°43N 72°9W **89** E5
Chortkiv *Ukraine* 49°2N 25°46E **17** D13
Chorzów *Poland* 50°18N 18°57E **17** C10
Chos-Malal *Argentina* 37°20S 70°15W **94** D1
Ch'osan *N. Korea* 40°50N 125°47E **33** D13
Choszczno *Poland* 53°7N 15°25E **16** B8
Choteau *U.S.A.* 47°49N 112°11W **76** C7
Chotila *India* 22°23N 71°15E **42** H4
Chotta Udepur *India* 22°19N 74°1E **42** H6
Chowchilla *U.S.A.* 37°7N 120°16W **78** H6
Choybalsan *Mongolia* 48°4N 114°30E **31** B11
Choyr *Mongolia* 46°24N 108°30E **31** B10
Christchurch *N.Z.* 43°33S 172°47E **59** E4
Christchurch *U.K.* 50°44N 1°47W **13** G6
Christian I. *Canada* 44°50N 80°12W **82** B4
Christian Sd. *U.S.A.* 55°56N 134°40W **75** D13
Christiana *S. Africa* 27°52S 25°8E **56** C4
Christiansted
U.S. Virgin Is. 17°45N 64°42W **89** C7
Christie B. *Canada* 62°32N 111°10W **71** A6
Christina → *Canada* 56°40N 111°3W **71** B6
Christmas Cr. →
Australia 18°29S 125°23E **60** C4
Christmas I. = Kiritimati
Kiribati 1°58N 157°27W **65** G12
Christmas I. *Ind. Oc.* 10°30S 105°40E **64** J2
Christopher, L. *Australia* 24°49S 127°42E **61** D4
Chū = Shū *Kazakhstan* 43°36N 73°42E **26** E8
Chu → *Vietnam* 19°53N 105°45E **38** C5
Chu Lai *Vietnam* 15°28N 108°45E **38** E7
Chu Mom Ray △
Vietnam 14°29N 107°38E **38** E6
Chu Se *Vietnam* 13°40N 108°8E **38** F7
Chuadanga *Bangla.* 23°38N 88°51E **43** H13
Chuak, Ko *Thailand* 9°28N 99°41E **39** b
Ch'uanchou = Quanzhou
China 24°55N 118°34E **35** E12
Chuankou *China* 34°20N 110°59E **32** G6
Chubbuck *U.S.A.* 42°55N 112°28W **76** E7
Chūbu □ *Japan* 36°45N 137°30E **29** F8
Chūbu-Sangaku △
Japan 36°30N 137°40E **29** F8
Chubut → *Argentina* 43°20S 65°5W **96** E3
Chuchi L. *Canada* 55°12N 124°30W **70** B4
Chuda *India* 22°29N 71°41E **42** H4
Chudskoye, Ozero *Russia* 58°13N 27°30E **9** G22
Chugach Mts. *U.S.A.* 60°45N 147°0W **74** C10
Chūgoku □ *Japan* 35°0N 133°0E **29** G6
Chūgoku-Sanchi *Japan* 35°0N 133°0E **29** G6
Chugwater *U.S.A.* 41°46N 104°50W **76** F11
Chukchi Plateau *Arctic* 78°0N 165°0W **4** B17
Chukchi Sea *Russia* 68°0N 175°0W **27** C19
Chukotskiy Mys *Russia* 64°14N 173°8W **74** C5
Chukotskiy Poluostrov
Russia 66°0N 174°0W **74** B5
Chukotskoye Nagorye
Russia 68°0N 175°0E **27** C18
Chula Vista *U.S.A.* 32°38N 117°5W **79** N9
Chulband → *India* 20°40N 79°54E **44** D4
Chulucanas *Peru* 5°8S 80°10W **92** E2
Chulym → *Russia* 57°43N 83°51E **26** D9
Chum Phae *Thailand* 16°40N 102°6E **38** D4
Chum Saeng *Thailand* 15°55N 100°15E **38** E3
Chumar *India* 32°40N 78°35E **43** C8
Chumbicha *Argentina* 29°0S 66°10W **94** B2
Chumikan *Russia* 54°40N 135°10E **27** D14
Chumphon *Thailand* 10°35N 99°14E **39** G2
Chuna → *Russia* 57°47N 94°37E **27** D10
Chun'an *China* 29°35N 119°3E **35** C12
Chuncheon *S. Korea* 37°58N 127°44E **33** F14
Chunchura *India* 22°53N 88°27E **43** H13
Chunggang-ŭp
N. Korea 41°48N 126°48E **33** D14
Chunghwa *N. Korea* 38°52N 125°47E **33** E13
Chungju *S. Korea* 36°58N 127°58E **33** F14
Chungking = Chongqing
China 29°35N 106°25E **34** C6
Chungli *Taiwan* 24°57N 121°13E **35** E13
Chungt'iaoshan = Zhongtiao Shan
China 35°0N 111°10E **32** G6

Chungyang Shanmo
Taiwan 23°10N 121°0E **35** F13
Chunian *Pakistan* 30°57N 74°0E **42** D6
Chunya *Tanzania* 8°30S 33°27E **54** F6
Chunyang *China* 43°38N 129°23E **33** C15
Chupara Pt. *Trin. & Tob.* 10°49N 61°22W **93** K15
Chuquibamba *Peru* 15°47S 72°44W **92** G4
Chuquicamata *Chile* 22°15S 69°0W **94** A2
Chur *Switz.* 46°52N 9°32E **20** C8
Churachandpur *India* 24°20N 93°40E **41** G18
Church Stretton *U.K.* 52°32N 2°48W **13** E5
Churchill *Canada* 58°47N 94°11W **71** B10
Churchill → *Man.,*
Canada 58°47N 94°12W **71** B10
Churchill → *Nfld. & L.,*
Canada 53°19N 60°10W **73** B7
Churchill, C. *Canada* 58°46N 93°12W **71** B10
Churchill Falls *Canada* 53°36N 64°19W **73** B7
Churchill L. *Canada* 55°55N 108°20W **71** B7
Churchill Pk. *Canada* 58°10N 125°10W **70** B3
Churki *India* 23°50N 83°12E **43** H10
Churu *India* 28°20N 74°50E **42** E6
Churún Merú = Angel Falls
Venezuela 5°57N 62°30W **92** B6
Chushal *India* 33°40N 78°40E **43** C8
Chuska Mts. *U.S.A.* 36°15N 108°50W **77** H9
Chusovoy *Russia* 58°22N 57°50E **18** C10
Chute-aux-Outardes
Canada 49°7N 68°24W **73** C6
Chuuk = Truk *Micronesia* 7°25N 151°46E **64** G7
Chuvash Republic = Chuvashia □
Russia 55°30N 47°0E **18** C8
Chuvashia □ *Russia* 55°30N 47°0E **18** C8
Chuwārtah *Iraq* 35°43N 45°34E **46** C5
Chuxiong *China* 25°2N 101°28E **34** E3
Chuy *Uruguay* 33°41S 53°27W **95** C5
Chuzhou *China* 32°19N 118°20E **35** A12
Ci Xian *China* 36°20N 114°25E **32** F8
Ciadâr-Lunga *Moldova* 46°3N 28°51E **17** E15
Ciamis *Indonesia* 7°20S 108°21E **37** G13
Cianjur *Indonesia* 6°49S 107°8E **37** G12
Cianorte *Brazil* 23°37S 52°37W **95** A5
Cibola *U.S.A.* 33°17N 114°42W **79** M12
Cicia *Fiji* 17°45S 179°18W **59** a
Ciéagas del Cataumbo △
Venezuela 9°25N 71°54W **89** E5
Ciechanów *Poland* 52°52N 20°38E **17** B11
Ciego de Ávila *Cuba* 21°50N 78°50W **88** B4
Ciénaga *Colombia* 11°1N 74°15W **92** A4
Cienfuegos *Cuba* 22°10N 80°30W **88** B3
Cieszyn *Poland* 49°45N 18°35E **17** D10
Cieza *Spain* 38°17N 1°23W **21** C5
Cihuatlán *Mexico* 19°14N 104°35W **86** D4
Cijara, Embalse de *Spain* 39°18N 4°52W **21** C3
Cijulang *Indonesia* 7°42S 108°27E **37** G13
Cilacap *Indonesia* 7°43S 109°0E **37** G13
Cili *China* 29°30N 111°8E **35** C8
Cill Airne = Killarney
Ireland 52°4N 9°30W **10** D2
Cill Chainnigh = Kilkenny
Ireland 52°39N 7°15W **10** D4
Cill Dara = Kildare *Ireland* 53°9N 6°55W **10** C5
Cill Droichid = Celbridge
Ireland 53°20N 6°32W **10** C5
Cill Mhantáin = Wicklow
Ireland 52°59N 6°3W **10** D5
Cilo Daği *Turkey* 37°28N 43°55E **19** G7
Cima *U.S.A.* 35°14N 115°30W **79** K11
Cimarron *Kans., U.S.A.* 37°48N 100°21W **80** G3
Cimarron *N. Mex.,*
U.S.A. 36°31N 104°55W **77** H11
Cimarron → *U.S.A.* 36°10N 96°16W **84** C6
Cimişlia *Moldova* 46°34N 28°44E **17** E15
Cimone, Mte. *Italy* 44°12N 10°42E **22** B4
Cinca → *Spain* 41°26N 0°21E **21** B6
Cincar *Bos.-H.* 43°55N 17°5E **22** C7
Cincinnati *U.S.A.* 39°9N 84°27W **81** F11
Cincinnatus *U.S.A.* 42°33N 75°54W **83** D9
Çine *Turkey* 37°37N 28°2E **23** F13
Ciney *Belgium* 50°18N 5°5E **15** D5
Cinque I. *India* 11°16N 92°42E **45** J11
Cinto, Mte. *France* 42°24N 8°54E **20** E8
Circle *Alaska, U.S.A.* 65°50N 144°4W **74** B11
Circle *Mont., U.S.A.* 47°25N 105°35W **76** C11
Circleville *U.S.A.* 39°36N 82°57W **81** F12
Cirebon *Indonesia* 6°45S 108°32E **37** G13
Cirencester *U.K.* 51°43N 1°57W **13** F6
Citlaltépetl = Orizaba, Pico de
Mexico 18°58N 97°15W **87** D5
Citrus Heights *U.S.A.* 38°42N 121°17W **78** G5
Citrusdal *S. Africa* 32°35S 19°0E **56** D2
Città di Castello *Italy* 43°27N 12°14E **22** C5
Ciudad Acuña *Mexico* 29°18N 100°55W **86** B4
Ciudad Altamirano
Mexico 18°20N 100°40W **86** D4
Ciudad Anáhuac *Mexico* 27°14N 100°7W **86** B4
Ciudad Bolívar *Venezuela* 8°5N 63°36W **92** B6
Ciudad Camargo
Mexico 27°40N 105°10W **86** B3
Ciudad Cortés *Costa Rica* 8°55N 84°0W **88** E3
Ciudad del Carmen
Mexico 18°38N 91°50W **87** D6
Ciudad del Este *Paraguay* 25°30S 54°50W **95** B5
Ciudad Delicias = Delicias
Mexico 28°13N 105°28W **86** B3
Ciudad Frontera *Mexico* 26°56N 101°27W **86** B4
Ciudad Guayana *Venezuela* 8°0N 62°30W **92** B6
Ciudad Guerrero
Mexico 28°33N 107°30W **86** B3
Ciudad Guzmán *Mexico* 19°41N 103°29W **86** D4
Ciudad Juárez *Mexico* 31°44N 106°29W **86** A3
Ciudad Lerdo *Mexico* 25°32N 103°32W **86** B4
Ciudad Madero *Mexico* 22°19N 97°50W **87** C5
Ciudad Mante *Mexico* 22°44N 98°59W **87** C5
Ciudad Obregón *Mexico* 27°29N 109°56W **86** B3
Ciudad Real *Spain* 38°59N 3°55W **21** C4
Ciudad Rodrigo *Spain* 40°35N 6°32W **21** B2
Ciudad Valles *Mexico* 21°59N 99°1W **87** C5

Ciudad Victoria *Mexico* 23°44N 99°8W **87** C5
Civitanova Marche *Italy* 43°18N 13°44E **22** C5
Civitavécchia *Italy* 42°6N 11°48E **22** C4
Cizre *Turkey* 37°19N 42°10E **46** B4
Clackmannanshire □
U.K. 56°10N 3°43W **11** E5
Clacton-on-Sea *U.K.* 51°47N 1°11E **13** F9
Claire, L. *Canada* 58°35N 112°5W **70** B6
Clairton *U.S.A.* 40°18N 79°53W **82** F5
Clallam Bay *U.S.A.* 48°15N 124°16W **78** B2
Clanton *U.S.A.* 32°51N 86°38W **85** E11
Clanwilliam *S. Africa* 32°11S 18°52E **56** D2
Clara *Ireland* 53°21N 7°37W **10** C4
Claraville *U.S.A.* 35°24N 118°20W **79** K8
Clare *Australia* 33°50S 138°37E **63** E2
Clare *U.S.A.* 43°49N 84°46W **81** D11
Clare □ *Ireland* 52°45N 9°0W **10** D3
Clare → *Ireland* 53°20N 9°2W **10** C2
Clare I. *Ireland* 53°47N 10°0W **10** C1
Claremont *Calif., U.S.A.* 34°6N 117°43W **79** L9
Claremont *N.H., U.S.A.* 43°23N 72°20W **83** C12
Claremont Pt. *Australia* 14°1S 143°41E **62** A3
Claremore *U.S.A.* 36°19N 95°36W **84** C7
Claremorris *Ireland* 53°45N 9°0W **10** C3
Clarence → *Australia* 29°25S 153°22E **63** D5
Clarence → *N.Z.* 42°10S 173°56E **59** E4
Clarence, I. *Chile* 54°0S 72°0W **96** G2
Clarence I. *Antarctica* 61°10S 54°0W **5** C18
Clarence Str. *Australia* 12°0S 131°0E **60** B5
Clarence Town *Bahamas* 23°6N 74°59W **89** B5
Clarendon *Pa., U.S.A.* 41°47N 79°6W **82** E5
Clarendon *Tex., U.S.A.* 34°56N 100°53W **84** D4
Clarenville *Canada* 48°10N 54°1W **73** C9
Claresholm *Canada* 50°2N 113°33W **70** D6
Clarie Coast *Antarctica* 68°0S 135°0E **5** C9
Clarinda *U.S.A.* 40°44N 95°2W **80** E6
Clarington *Canada* 43°55N 78°41W **82** C6
Clarion *Iowa, U.S.A.* 42°44N 93°44W **80** D7
Clarion *Pa., U.S.A.* 41°13N 79°23W **82** E5
Clarion → *U.S.A.* 41°7N 79°41W **82** E5
Clarion Fracture Zone
Pac. Oc. 20°0N 120°0W **66** H7
Clark *U.S.A.* 44°53N 97°44W **80** C5
Clark, Pt. *Canada* 44°4N 81°45W **82** B3
Clark Fork *U.S.A.* 48°9N 116°11W **76** B5
Clark Fork → *U.S.A.* 48°9N 116°15W **76** B5
Clarkdale *U.S.A.* 34°46N 112°3W **77** J7
Clarke City *Canada* 50°12N 66°38W **73** B6
Clarke I. *Australia* 40°32S 148°10E **63** G4
Clarke Ra. *Australia* 20°40S 148°30E **62** b
Clarks Fork Yellowstone →
U.S.A. 45°32N 108°50W **76** D9
Clark's Harbour *Canada* 43°25N 65°38W **73** D6
Clarks Hill L. = J. Strom Thurmond
L. *U.S.A.* 33°40N 82°12W **85** E13
Clarks Summit *U.S.A.* 41°30N 75°42W **83** E9
Clarksburg *U.S.A.* 39°17N 80°30W **81** F13
Clarksdale *U.S.A.* 34°12N 90°35W **85** D9
Clarkston *U.S.A.* 46°25N 117°3W **76** C5
Clarksville *Ark., U.S.A.* 35°28N 93°28W **84** D8
Clarksville *Tenn., U.S.A.* 36°32N 87°21W **85** C11
Clarksville *Tex., U.S.A.* 33°37N 95°3W **84** E7
Clatskanie *U.S.A.* 46°6N 123°12W **78** D3
Claude *U.S.A.* 35°7N 101°22W **84** D4
Claveria *Phil.* 18°37N 121°4E **37** A6
Clay *U.S.A.* 38°17N 121°10W **78** G5
Clay Center *U.S.A.* 39°23N 97°8W **80** F5
Claypool *U.S.A.* 33°25N 110°51W **77** K8
Claysburg *U.S.A.* 40°17N 78°27W **82** F6
Claysville *U.S.A.* 40°7N 80°25W **82** F4
Clayton *N. Mex., U.S.A.* 36°27N 103°11W **77** H12
Clayton *N.Y., U.S.A.* 44°14N 76°5W **83** B8
Clear, C. *Ireland* 51°25N 9°32W **10** E2
Clear, L. *Canada* 45°26N 77°12W **82** A7
Clear Hills *Canada* 56°40N 119°30W **70** B5
Clear I. *Ireland* 51°26N 9°30W **10** E2
Clear L. *U.S.A.* 39°2N 122°47W **78** F4
Clear Lake *Iowa, U.S.A.* 43°8N 93°23W **80** D7
Clear Lake *S. Dak., U.S.A.* 44°45N 96°41W **80** C5
Clear Lake Res. *U.S.A.* 41°56N 121°5W **76** F3
Clearfield *Pa., U.S.A.* 41°2N 78°27W **82** E6
Clearfield *Utah, U.S.A.* 41°7N 112°2W **76** F7
Clearlake *U.S.A.* 38°57N 122°38W **78** G4
Clearwater *Canada* 51°38N 120°2W **70** C4
Clearwater *U.S.A.* 27°59N 82°48W **85** H13
Clearwater → *Alta.,*
Canada 52°22N 114°57W **70** C6
Clearwater → *Alta.,*
Canada 56°44N 111°23W **71** B6
Clearwater L. *Canada* 53°34N 99°49W **71** C9
Clearwater Lake △
Canada 54°0N 101°0W **71** C8
Clearwater Mts. *U.S.A.* 46°5N 115°20W **76** C6
Clearwater River △
Canada 56°55N 109°10W **71** B7
Cleburne *U.S.A.* 32°21N 97°23W **84** E6
Clee Hills *U.K.* 52°26N 2°35W **13** E5
Cleethorpes *U.K.* 53°33N 0°3W **12** D7
Cleeve Cloud *U.K.* 51°56N 2°0W **13** F6
Clemson *U.S.A.* 34°41N 82°50W **85** D13
Clerke Reef *Australia* 17°22S 119°20E **60** C2
Clermont *Australia* 22°49S 147°39E **62** C4
Clermont *U.S.A.* 28°33N 81°46W **85** G14
Clermont-Ferrand *France* 45°46N 3°4E **20** D5
Clervaux *Lux.* 50°4N 6°2E **15** D6
Clevedon *U.K.* 51°26N 2°52W **13** F5
Cleveland *Miss., U.S.A.* 33°45N 90°43W **85** E9
Cleveland *Ohio, U.S.A.* 41°29N 81°41W **82** E3
Cleveland *Okla., U.S.A.* 36°19N 96°28W **84** C6
Cleveland *Tenn., U.S.A.* 35°10N 84°53W **85** D12
Cleveland *Tex., U.S.A.* 30°21N 95°5W **84** F7
Cleveland, C. *Australia* 19°11S 147°1E **62** B4
Cleveland, Mt. *U.S.A.* 48°56N 113°51W **76** B7
Cleveland Heights *U.S.A.* 41°31N 81°33W **82** E3
Cleveland Ra. *Brazil* 26°24S 52°23W **95** B5
Clew B. *Ireland* 53°50N 9°49W **10** C2
Clewiston *U.S.A.* 26°45N 80°56W **85** H14

Clifden *Ireland* 53°29N 10°1W **10** C1
Clifden *N.Z.* 46°1S 167°42E **59** G1
Cliffdell *U.S.A.* 46°56N 121°5W **78** D5
Cliffy Hd. *Australia* 35°1S 116°29E **61** G2
Clifton *Australia* 27°59S 151°53E **63** D5
Clifton *Ariz., U.S.A.* 33°3N 109°18W **77** K9
Clifton *Colo., U.S.A.* 39°7N 108°25W **76** G9
Clifton *Tex., U.S.A.* 31°47N 97°35W **84** F6
Clifton Beach *Australia* 16°46S 145°39E **62** B4
Clinch → *U.S.A.* 35°53N 84°29W **85** D12
Clingmans Dome
U.S.A. 35°34N 83°30W **85** D13
Clint *U.S.A.* 31°35N 106°14W **84** F1
Clinton *B.C., Canada* 51°6N 121°35W **70** C4
Clinton *Ont., Canada* 43°37N 81°32W **82** C3
Clinton *N.Z.* 46°12S 169°23E **59** G2
Clinton *Ark., U.S.A.* 35°36N 92°28W **84** D8
Clinton *Conn., U.S.A.* 41°17N 72°32W **83** E12
Clinton *Ill., U.S.A.* 40°9N 88°57W **80** E9
Clinton *Ind., U.S.A.* 39°40N 87°24W **80** F10
Clinton *Iowa, U.S.A.* 41°51N 90°12W **80** E8
Clinton *Mass., U.S.A.* 42°25N 71°41W **83** D13
Clinton *Miss., U.S.A.* 32°20N 90°20W **85** E9
Clinton *Mo., U.S.A.* 38°22N 93°46W **80** F7
Clinton *N.C., U.S.A.* 35°0N 78°22W **85** D15
Clinton *Okla., U.S.A.* 35°31N 98°58W **84** D5
Clinton *S.C., U.S.A.* 34°29N 81°53W **85** D14
Clinton *Tenn., U.S.A.* 36°6N 84°8W **85** C12
Clinton *Wash., U.S.A.* 47°59N 122°21W **78** C4
Clinton, C. *Australia* 22°30S 150°45E **62** C5
Clinton Colden L.
Canada 63°58N 107°27W **68** E10
Clipperton, Î. *Pac. Oc.* 10°18N 109°13W **65** F17
Clipperton Fracture Zone
Pac. Oc. 19°0N 122°0W **65** G16
Clisham *U.K.* 57°58N 6°49W **11** D2
Clitheroe *U.K.* 53°53N 2°22W **12** D5
Clo-oose *Canada* 48°39N 124°49W **78** B2
Cloates, Pt. *Australia* 22°43S 113°40E **60** D1
Clocolan *S. Africa* 28°55S 27°34E **57** C4
Clodomira *Argentina* 27°35S 64°14W **94** B3
Cloghaneely *Ireland* 55°8N 8°5W **10** A3
Clogher Hd. *Ireland* 53°48N 6°14W **10** C5
Clonakilty *Ireland* 51°37N 8°53W **10** E3
Clonakilty B. *Ireland* 51°35N 8°51W **10** E3
Cloncurry *Australia* 20°40S 140°28E **62** C3
Cloncurry *Ireland* 53°25N 6°48W **10** C5
Cloncurry → *Australia* 18°37S 140°40E **62** B3
Clondalkin *Ireland* 53°19N 6°25W **10** C5
Clones *Ireland* 54°11N 7°15W **10** B4
Clonmel *Ireland* 52°21N 7°42W **10** D4
Cloppenburg *Germany* 52°50N 8°3E **16** B5
Cloquet *U.S.A.* 46°43N 92°28W **80** B7
Clorinda *Argentina* 25°16S 57°45W **94** B4
Cloud Peak *U.S.A.* 44°23N 107°11W **76** D10
Cloudcroft *U.S.A.* 32°58N 105°45W **77** K11
Cloverdale *U.S.A.* 38°48N 123°1W **78** G4
Clovis *Calif., U.S.A.* 36°49N 119°42W **78** J7
Clovis *N. Mex., U.S.A.* 34°24N 103°12W **77** J12
Cloyne *Canada* 44°49N 77°11W **82** B7
Cluain Meala = Clonmel
Ireland 52°21N 7°42W **10** D4
Cluj-Napoca *Romania* 46°47N 23°38E **17** E12
Clunes *Australia* 37°20S 143°45E **63** F3
Clutha → *N.Z.* 46°20S 169°49E **59** G2
Clwyd → *U.K.* 53°19N 3°31W **12** D4
Clyde *Canada* 54°9N 113°39W **70** C6
Clyde *N.Z.* 45°12S 169°20E **59** F2
Clyde *U.S.A.* 43°5N 76°52W **82** C8
Clyde → *U.K.* 55°55N 4°30W **11** F4
Clyde, Firth of *U.K.* 55°22N 5°1W **11** F3
Clyde River *Canada* 70°30N 68°30W **69** C18
Clydebank *U.K.* 55°54N 4°23W **11** F4
Clymer *N.Y., U.S.A.* 42°1N 79°37W **82** D5
Clymer *Pa., U.S.A.* 40°40N 79°1W **82** D5
Coachella *U.S.A.* 33°41N 116°10W **79** M10
Coachella Canal
U.S.A. 32°43N 114°57W **79** N12
Coahoma *U.S.A.* 32°18N 101°18W **84** E4
Coahuayana → *Mexico* 18°41N 103°45W **86** D4
Coahuila □ *Mexico* 27°20N 102°0W **86** B4
Coal → *Canada* 59°39N 126°57W **70** B3
Coalcomán *Mexico* 18°47N 103°9W **86** D4
Coaldale *Canada* 49°45N 112°35W **70** D6
Coalgate *U.S.A.* 34°32N 96°13W **84** D6
Coalinga *U.S.A.* 36°9N 120°21W **78** J6
Coalisland *U.K.* 54°33N 6°42W **10** B5
Coalville *U.K.* 52°44N 1°23W **12** E6
Coalville *U.S.A.* 40°55N 111°24W **76** F8
Coamo *Puerto Rico* 18°5N 66°22W **89** d
Coari *Brazil* 4°8S 63°7W **92** D6
Coast Mts. *Canada* 55°0N 129°20W **70** C3
Coast Ranges *U.S.A.* 39°0N 123°0W **78** G4
Coatbridge *U.K.* 55°52N 4°6W **11** F4
Coatepec *Mexico* 19°27N 96°58W **87** D5
Coatepeque *Guatemala* 14°46N 91°55W **88** D1
Coatesville *U.S.A.* 39°59N 75°50W **81** F16
Coaticook *Canada* 45°10N 71°46W **83** A13
Coats I. *Canada* 62°30N 83°0W **69** E15
Coats Land *Antarctica* 77°0S 25°0W **5** D1
Coatzacoalcos *Mexico* 18°7N 94°25W **87** D6
Cobá *Mexico* 20°31N 87°45W **87** C7
Cobalt *Canada* 47°25N 79°42W **72** C4
Cobán *Guatemala* 15°30N 90°21W **88** C1
Cobar *Australia* 31°27S 145°48E **63** E4
Cóbh, An = Cobh *Ireland* 51°51N 8°17W **10** E3
Cobija *Bolivia* 11°0S 68°50W **92** F5
Cobleskill *U.S.A.* 42°41N 74°29W **83** D10
Coboconk *Canada* 44°39N 78°48W **82** B6
Cobourg *Canada* 43°58N 78°10W **82** C6
Cobourg Pen. *Australia* 11°20S 132°15E **60** B5
Cobram *Australia* 35°54S 145°40E **63** F4
Coburg *Germany* 50°15N 10°58E **16** C6
Coburg I. *Canada* 75°57N 79°26W **69** B16
Cocanada = Kakinada
India 16°57N 82°11E **44** F6
Cochabamba *Bolivia* 17°26S 66°10W **92** G5
Cochin = Kochi *India* 9°58N 76°20E **45** Q10
Cochin China = Nam-Phan
Vietnam 10°30N 106°0E **39** G6

Cochran *U.S.A.* 32°23N 83°21W **85** E13
Cochrane *Alta., Canada* 51°11N 114°30W **70** C6
Cochrane *Ont., Canada* 49°0N 81°0W **72** C3
Cochrane *Chile* 47°15S 72°33W **96** F2
Cochrane, L. *Chile* 47°10S 72°0W **96** F2
Cochranton *U.S.A.* 41°31N 80°3W **82** E4
Cockburn *Australia* 32°5S 141°0E **63** E3
Cockburn, Canal *Chile* 54°30S 72°0W **96** G2
Cockburn I. *Canada* 45°55N 83°22W **72** C3
Cockburn Ra. *Australia* 15°46S 128°0E **60** C4
Cockermouth *U.K.* 54°40N 3°22W **12** C4
Cockpit Country, The
Jamaica 18°15N 77°45W **88** a
Coco → *Cent. Amer.* 15°0N 83°8W **88** D3
Coco, I. del *Pac. Oc.* 5°25N 87°55W **65** G19
Coco Channel *Asia* 13°45N 93°10E **45** H11
Cocoa *U.S.A.* 28°21N 80°44W **85** G14
Cocobeach *Gabon* 0°59N 9°34E **54** D1
Cocos B. *Trin. & Tob.* 10°24N 61°2W **93** K15
Cocos I. = Coco, I. del
Pac. Oc. 5°25N 87°55W **65** G19
Cocos Is. *Ind. Oc.* 12°10S 96°55E **64** J1
Cocos Ridge *Pac. Oc.* 4°0N 88°0W **65** G19
Cod, C. *U.S.A.* 42°5N 70°10W **81** D18
Codajás *Brazil* 3°55S 62°0W **92** D6
Codó *Brazil* 4°30S 43°55W **93** D10
Cody *U.S.A.* 44°32N 109°3W **76** D9
Coe Hill *Canada* 44°52N 77°50W **82** B7
Coelemu *Chile* 36°30S 72°48W **94** D1
Coen *Australia* 13°52S 143°12E **62** A3
Coeur d'Alene *U.S.A.* 47°41N 116°46W **76** C5
Coeur d'Alene L. *U.S.A.* 47°32N 116°49W **76** C5
Coevorden *Neths.* 52°40N 6°44E **15** B6
Coffeyville *U.S.A.* 37°2N 95°37W **80** G6
Coffin B. *Australia* 34°38S 135°28E **63** E2
Coffin Bay *Australia* 34°37S 135°29E **63** E2
Coffin Bay △ *Australia* 34°34S 135°19E **63** E2
Coffin Bay Peninsula
Australia 34°32S 135°15E **63** E2
Coffs Harbour *Australia* 30°16S 153°5E **63** E5
Cognac *France* 45°41N 0°20W **20** D3
Cohocton *U.S.A.* 42°30N 77°30W **82** D7
Cohocton → *U.S.A.* 42°9N 77°6W **82** D7
Cohoes *U.S.A.* 42°46N 73°42W **83** D11
Cohuna *Australia* 35°45S 144°15E **63** F3
Coiba, I. de *Panama* 7°30N 81°40W **88** E3
Coig → *Argentina* 51°0S 69°10W **96** G3
Coigeach, Rubha *U.K.* 58°6N 5°26W **11** C3
Coihaique *Chile* 45°30S 71°45W **96** F2
Coimbatore *India* 11°2N 76°59E **45** J3
Coimbra *Brazil* 19°55S 57°48W **92** G7
Coimbra *Portugal* 40°15N 8°27W **21** B1
Coín *Spain* 36°40N 4°48W **21** D3
Coipasa, Salar de *Bolivia* 19°26S 68°9W **92** G5
Cojimies *Ecuador* 0°20N 80°0W **92** C3
Cojutepequé *El Salv.* 13°41N 88°54W **88** D2
Cokeville *U.S.A.* 42°5N 110°57W **76** E8
Colac *Australia* 38°21S 143°35E **63** F3
Colachel = Kolachel *India* 8°10N 77°15E **45** K3
Colatina *Brazil* 19°32S 40°37W **93** G10
Colbeck, C. *Antarctica* 77°6S 157°48E **5** D13
Colborne *Canada* 44°0N 77°53W **82** C7
Colby *U.S.A.* 39°24N 101°3W **80** F3
Colca → *Peru* 15°55S 72°43W **92** G4
Colchester *U.K.* 51°54N 0°55E **13** F8
Colchester *U.S.A.* 41°35N 72°20W **83** E12
Cold L. *Canada* 54°33N 110°5W **71** C7
Cold Lake *Canada* 54°27N 110°10W **71** C6
Coldstream *Canada* 50°13N 119°11W **70** C5
Coldstream *U.K.* 55°39N 2°15W **11** F6
Coldwater *Canada* 44°42N 79°40W **82** B5
Coldwater *Kans., U.S.A.* 37°16N 99°20W **80** G4
Coldwater *Mich., U.S.A.* 41°57N 85°0W **81** E11
Colebrook *U.S.A.* 44°54N 71°30W **83** B13
Coleman *Canada* 49°40N 114°30W **70** D6
Coleman *U.S.A.* 31°50N 99°26W **84** F5
Coleman → *Australia* 15°6S 141°38E **62** B3
Colenso *S. Africa* 28°44S 29°50E **57** D4
Coleraine *Australia* 37°36S 141°40E **63** F3
Coleraine *U.K.* 55°8N 6°41W **10** A5
Coleridge, L. *N.Z.* 43°17S 171°30E **59** E3
Coleroon → *India* 11°25N 79°50E **45** J4
Colesberg *S. Africa* 30°45S 25°5E **56** E4
Coleville *U.S.A.* 38°34N 119°30W **78** G7
Colfax *Calif., U.S.A.* 39°6N 120°57W **78** F6
Colfax *La., U.S.A.* 31°31N 92°42W **84** F8
Colfax *Wash., U.S.A.* 46°53N 117°22W **76** C5
Colhué Huapi, L.
Argentina 45°30S 69°0W **96** F3
Coligny *S. Africa* 26°17S 26°15E **57** C4
Colima *Mexico* 19°14N 103°43W **86** D4
Colima □ *Mexico* 19°10N 104°0W **86** D4
Colima, Nevado de
Mexico 19°33N 103°38W **86** D4
Colina *Chile* 33°13S 70°45W **94** C1
Colinas *Brazil* 6°0S 44°10W **93** E10
Coll *U.K.* 56°39N 6°34W **11** E2
Collahuasi *Chile* 21°5S 68°45W **94** A2
Collarenebri *Australia* 29°33S 148°34E **63** D4
College *U.S.A.* 64°52N 147°49W **74** C10
College Station *U.S.A.* 30°37N 96°21W **84** F6
Collie *Australia* 33°22S 116°8E **61** F2
Collier B. *Australia* 16°10S 124°15E **60** C3
Collier Range △ *Australia* 24°39S 119°7E **61** D2
Collierville *U.S.A.* 35°3N 89°40W **85** D10
Collina, Passo di *Italy* 44°2N 10°56E **22** B4
Collingwood *Canada* 44°29N 80°13W **82** B4
Collingwood *N.Z.* 40°41S 172°40E **59** D4
Collins *Canada* 50°17N 89°27W **72** B2
Collins Bay *Canada* 44°14N 76°36W **83** B8
Collinson Pen. *Canada* 69°58N 101°24W **68** D11
Collinsville *Australia* 20°30S 147°56E **62** C4
Collipulli *Chile* 37°55S 72°30W **94** D1
Collooney *Ireland* 54°11N 8°29W **10** B3
Colmar *France* 48°5N 7°20E **20** B7
Colo → *Australia* 33°25S 150°52E **63** E5

Cologne = Köln *Germany* 50°56N 6°57E **16** C4
Coloma *U.S.A.* 38°48N 120°53W **78** G6
Colomb-Béchar = Béchar
  Algeria 31°38N 2°18W **52** B5
Colombia ■ *S. Amer.* 3°45N 73°0W **92** C4
Colombian Basin *Caribbean* 14°0N 76°0W **88** D4
Colombo *Sri Lanka* 6°56N 79°58E **45** L4
Colón *B. Aires, Argentina* 33°53S 61°7W **94** C3
Colón *Entre Ríos,*
  Argentina 32°12S 58°10W **94** C4
Colón *Cuba* 22°42N 80°54W **88** B3
Colón *Panama* 9°20N 79°54W **88** E4
Colón, Arch. de *Ecuador* 0°0 91°0W **90** D1
Colonia del Sacramento
  Uruguay 34°25S 57°50W **94** C4
Colonia Dora *Argentina* 28°34S 62°59W **94** B3
Colonial Beach *U.S.A.* 38°15N 76°58W **81** F15
Colonie *U.S.A.* 42°43N 73°50W **83** D11
Colonsay *Canada* 51°59N 105°52W **71** C7
Colonsay *U.K.* 56°5N 6°12W **11** E2
Colorado □ *U.S.A.* 39°30N 105°30W **76** G11
Colorado → *Argentina* 39°50S 62°8W **96** D4
Colorado → *N. Amer.* 31°45N 114°40W **77** L6
Colorado → *U.S.A.* 28°36N 95°59W **84** G7
Colorado City *U.S.A.* 32°24N 100°52W **84** E4
Colorado Plateau *U.S.A.* 37°0N 111°0W **77** H8
Colorado River Aqueduct
  U.S.A. 33°50N 117°23W **79** L12
Colorado Springs
  U.S.A. 38°50N 104°49W **76** G11
Colotlán *Mexico* 22°6N 103°16W **86** C4
Colstrip *U.S.A.* 45°53N 106°38W **76** D10
Colton *U.S.A.* 44°33N 74°56W **83** B10
Columbia *Ky., U.S.A.* 37°6N 85°18W **81** G11
Columbia *La., U.S.A.* 32°6N 92°5W **84** E8
Columbia *Miss., U.S.A.* 31°15N 89°50W **85** F10
Columbia *Mo., U.S.A.* 38°57N 92°20W **80** F7
Columbia *Pa., U.S.A.* 40°2N 76°30W **83** F8
Columbia *S.C., U.S.A.* 34°0N 81°2W **85** D11
Columbia *Tenn., U.S.A.* 35°37N 87°2W **85** D11
Columbia → *N. Amer.* 46°15N 124°5W **78** D2
Columbia, C. *Canada* 83°6N 69°57W **69** A18
Columbia, District of □
  U.S.A. 38°55N 77°0W **81** F15
Columbia, Mt. *Canada* 52°8N 117°20W **70** C5
Columbia Basin *U.S.A.* 46°45N 119°5W **76** C4
Columbia Falls *U.S.A.* 48°23N 114°11W **76** B6
Columbia Mts. *Canada* 52°0N 119°0W **70** C5
Columbia Plateau *U.S.A.* 44°0N 117°30W **76** E5
Columbiana *U.S.A.* 40°53N 80°42W **82** F4
Columbretes, Is. *Spain* 39°50N 0°50E **21** C6
Columbus *Ga., U.S.A.* 32°28N 84°59W **85** E12
Columbus *Ind., U.S.A.* 39°13N 85°55W **81** F11
Columbus *Kans., U.S.A.* 37°10N 94°50W **80** G6
Columbus *Miss., U.S.A.* 33°30N 88°25W **85** E10
Columbus *Mont., U.S.A.* 45°38N 109°15W **76** D9
Columbus *N. Mex.,*
  U.S.A. 31°50N 107°38W **77** L10
Columbus *Nebr., U.S.A.* 41°26N 97°22W **80** E5
Columbus *Ohio, U.S.A.* 39°58N 83°0W **81** F12
Columbus *Tex., U.S.A.* 29°42N 96°33W **84** G6
Colusa *U.S.A.* 39°13N 122°1W **78** F4
Colville *U.S.A.* 48°33N 117°54W **76** B5
Colville → *U.S.A.* 70°25N 150°30W **4** A9
Colville, C. *N.Z.* 36°29S 175°21E **59** B5
Colwood *Canada* 48°26N 123°29W **78** B3
Colwyn Bay *U.K.* 53°18N 3°44W **12** D4
Comácchio *Italy* 44°42N 12°11E **22** B5
Comalcalco *Mexico* 18°16N 93°13W **87** D6
Comallo *Argentina* 41°0S 70°5W **96** E2
Comanche *U.S.A.* 31°54N 98°36W **84** F5
Comandante Ferraz
  Antarctica 62°30S 58°0W **5** C18
Comayagua *Honduras* 14°25N 87°37W **88** D2
Combahee → *U.S.A.* 32°31N 80°31W **85** E14
Combarbalá *Chile* 31°11S 71°2W **94** C1
Combe Martin *U.K.* 51°12N 4°3W **13** F3
Comber *Canada* 42°14N 82°33W **82** D2
Comber *U.K.* 54°33N 5°45W **10** B6
Combermere *Canada* 45°22N 77°37W **82** A7
Comblain-au-Pont
  Belgium 50°29N 5°35E **15** D5
Comeragh Mts. *Ireland* 52°18N 7°34W **10** D4
Comet *Australia* 23°36S 148°38E **62** C4
Comilla *Bangla.* 23°28N 91°10E **41** H17
Comino, C. *Italy* 40°32N 9°49E **22** D3
Comitán de Domínguez
  Mexico 16°15N 92°8W **87** D6
Commerce *Ga., U.S.A.* 34°12N 83°28W **85** D13
Commerce *Tex., U.S.A.* 33°15N 95°54W **84** E7
Committee B. *Canada* 68°30N 86°30W **69** D14
Commodore, C. *Canada* 44°47N 80°54W **82** B4
Commonwealth B.
  Antarctica 67°0S 144°0E **5** C10
Commoron Cr. →
  Australia 28°22S 150°8E **63** D5
Communism Pk. = imeni Ismail
  Samani, Pik *Tajikistan* 39°0N 72°2E **26** F8
Como *Italy* 45°47N 9°5E **20** D8
Como, Lago di *Italy* 46°0N 9°11E **20** D8
Comodoro Rivadavia
  Argentina 45°50S 67°40W **96** F3
Comorin, C. = Kannyakumari
  India 8°3N 77°40E **45** K3
Comoros ■ *Ind. Oc.* 12°10S 44°15E **55** a
Comox *Canada* 49°42N 124°55W **70** D4
Compiègne *France* 49°24N 2°50E **20** B5
Compostela *Mexico* 21°14N 104°55W **86** C4
Comprida, I. *Brazil* 24°50S 47°42W **95** A6
Compton *Canada* 45°14N 71°49W **83** A13
Compton *U.S.A.* 33°53N 118°13W **79** M8
Comrat *Moldova* 46°18N 28°40E **17** E15
Con Cuong *Vietnam* 19°2N 104°54E **38** C5
Con Dao △ *Vietnam* 8°42N 106°35E **39** H6
Con Son, Dao *Vietnam* 8°41N 106°37E **39** H6
Conakry *Guinea* 9°29N 13°49W **52** G3
Conara *Australia* 41°50S 147°26E **63** G4
Concarneau *France* 47°52N 3°56W **20** C2
Conceição da Barra
  Brazil 18°35S 39°45W **93** G11

Conceição do Araguaia
  Brazil 8°0S 49°2W **93** E9
Concepción *Argentina* 27°20S 65°35W **94** B2
Concepción *Bolivia* 16°15S 62°8W **92** G6
Concepción *Chile* 36°50S 73°0W **94** D1
Concepción *Paraguay* 23°22S 57°26W **94** A4
Concepción □ *Chile* 37°0S 72°30W **94** D1
Concepción, Est. de *Chile* 50°30S 74°55W **96** G2
Concepción, L. *Bolivia* 17°20S 61°20W **92** G6
Concepción, Pta.
  Mexico 26°53N 111°50W **86** B2
Concepción del Oro
  Mexico 24°38N 101°25W **86** C4
Concepción del Uruguay
  Argentina 32°35S 58°20W **94** C4
Conception, Pt. *U.S.A.* 34°27N 120°28W **79** L6
Conception B. *Canada* 47°45N 53°0W **73** C9
Conception B. *Namibia* 23°55S 14°22E **56** B1
Conception I. *Bahamas* 23°52N 75°9W **89** B4
Conchas Dam *U.S.A.* 35°22N 104°11W **77** J11
Concho *U.S.A.* 34°28N 109°36W **77** J9
Concho → *U.S.A.* 31°34N 99°43W **84** F5
Conchos → *Chihuahua,*
  Mexico 29°35N 104°25W **86** B4
Conchos → *Tamaulipas,*
  Mexico 24°55N 97°38W **87** B5
Concord *Calif., U.S.A.* 37°59N 122°2W **78** H4
Concord *N.C., U.S.A.* 35°25N 80°35W **85** D14
Concord *N.H., U.S.A.* 43°12N 71°32W **83** C13
Concordia *Antarctica* 75°6S 123°23E **5** D9
Concórdia *Argentina* 31°20S 58°2W **94** C4
Concórdia *Amazonas,*
  Brazil 4°36S 66°36W **92** D5
Concórdia *Sta. Catarina,*
  Brazil 27°14S 52°1W **95** B5
Concordia *Mexico* 23°17N 106°4W **86** C3
Concordia *U.S.A.* 39°34N 97°40W **80** F5
Concrete *U.S.A.* 48°32N 121°45W **76** B3
Condamine *Australia* 26°56S 150°9E **63** D5
Condé *France* 45°9N 98°6W **80** C4
Condeúba *Brazil* 14°52S 42°0W **93** F10
Condobolin *Australia* 33°4S 147°6E **63** E4
Condon *U.S.A.* 45°14N 120°11W **76** D3
Conegliano *Italy* 45°53N 12°18E **22** B5
Conejos *Mexico* 26°14N 103°53W **86** B4
Confuso → *Paraguay* 25°9S 57°34W **94** B4
Conghua *China* 23°36N 113°31E **35** F9
Congjiang *China* 25°43N 108°52E **34** E7
Congleton *U.K.* 53°10N 2°13W **12** D5
Congo (Brazzaville) = Congo ■
  Africa 1°0S 16°0E **54** E3
Congo (Kinshasa) = Congo, Dem.
  Rep. of the ■ *Africa* 3°0S 23°0E **54** E4
Congo ■ *Africa* 1°0S 16°0E **54** E3
Congo → *Africa* 6°4S 12°24E **54** F2
Congo, Dem. Rep. of the ■
  Africa 3°0S 23°0E **54** E4
Congo Basin *Africa* 0°10S 24°30E **54** E4
Congonhas *Brazil* 20°30S 43°52W **95** A7
Congress *U.S.A.* 34°9N 112°51W **77** J7
Coniston *Canada* 46°29N 80°51W **72** C3
Conjeeveram = Kanchipuram
  India 12°52N 79°45E **45** H4
Conklin *Canada* 55°38N 111°5W **71** B6
Conklin *U.S.A.* 42°2N 75°49W **83** D9
Conn, L. *Ireland* 54°3N 9°15W **10** B2
Connacht □ *Ireland* 53°43N 9°12W **10** C2
Conneaut *U.S.A.* 41°57N 80°34W **82** E4
Conneautville *U.S.A.* 41°45N 80°22W **82** E4
Connecticut □ *U.S.A.* 41°30N 72°45W **83** E12
Connecticut → *U.S.A.* 41°16N 72°20W **83** E12
Connell *U.S.A.* 46°40N 118°52W **76** C4
Connellsville *U.S.A.* 40°1N 79°35W **82** F5
Connemara *Ireland* 53°29N 9°45W **10** C2
Connemara △ *Ireland* 53°32N 9°52W **10** C2
Connersville *U.S.A.* 39°39N 85°8W **81** F11
Connors Ra. *Australia* 21°40S 149°10E **62** C4
Conquest *Canada* 51°32N 107°14W **71** C7
Conrad *U.S.A.* 48°10N 111°57W **76** B8
Conran, C. *Australia* 37°49S 148°44E **63** F4
Conroe *U.S.A.* 30°19N 95°27W **84** F7
Consecon *Canada* 44°0N 77°31W **82** C7
Conselheiro Lafaiete
  Brazil 20°40S 43°48W **95** A7
Consett *U.K.* 54°51N 1°50W **12** C6
Consort *Canada* 52°1N 110°46W **71** C6
Constance = Konstanz
  Germany 47°40N 9°10E **16** E5
Constance, L. = Bodensee
  Europe 47°35N 9°25E **20** C8
Constanţa *Romania* 44°14N 28°38E **17** F15
Constantine *Algeria* 36°25N 6°42E **52** A7
Constitución *Chile* 35°20S 72°30W **94** D1
Constitución *Uruguay* 31°0S 57°50W **94** C4
Constitución de 1857 △
  Mexico 32°4N 115°55W **86** A1
Consul *Canada* 49°20N 109°30W **71** D7
Contact *U.S.A.* 41°46N 114°45W **76** F6
Contai *India* 21°54N 87°46E **43** J12
Contamana *Peru* 7°19S 74°55W **92** E4
Contas → *Brazil* 14°17S 39°1W **93** F11
Contoocook *U.S.A.* 43°13N 71°45W **83** C13
Contra Costa *Mozam.* 25°9S 33°30E **57** C5
Contwoyto L. *Canada* 65°42N 110°50W **68** D9
Conway = Conwy →
  U.K. 53°17N 3°50W **12** D4
Conway *Australia* 20°24S 148°41E **62** b
Conway *Canada* 44°6N 76°54W **82** B8
Conway *Ark., U.S.A.* 35°5N 92°26W **84** D8
Conway *N.H., U.S.A.* 43°59N 71°7W **83** C13
Conway *S.C., U.S.A.* 33°51N 79°3W **85** E15
Conway, C. *Australia* 20°34S 148°46E **62** b
Conway, L. *Australia* 28°17S 135°35E **63** D2
Conwy *U.K.* 53°17N 3°50W **12** D4
Conwy □ *U.K.* 53°10N 3°44W **12** D4
Conwy → *U.K.* 53°17N 3°50W **12** D4

Coober Pedy *Australia* 29°1S 134°43E **63** D1
Cooch Behar = Koch Bihar
  India 26°22N 89°29E **41** F16
Cooinda *Australia* 13°15S 130°5E **60** B5
Cook *Australia* 30°37S 130°25E **61** F5
Cook, B. *Chile* 55°10S 70°0W **96** H3
Cook, Mt. = Aoraki Mount Cook
  N.Z. 43°36S 170°9E **59** E3
Cook Inlet *U.S.A.* 60°0N 152°0W **68** F1
Cook Is. ☑ *Pac. Oc.* 17°0S 160°0W **65** J12
Cook Strait *N.Z.* 41°15S 174°29E **59** D5
Cookeville *U.S.A.* 36°10N 85°30W **85** C12
Cookhouse *S. Africa* 32°44S 25°47E **56** D4
Cooks Harbour *Canada* 51°36N 55°52W **73** B8
Cookshire *Canada* 45°25N 71°38W **83** A13
Cookstown *Canada* 44°11N 79°42W **82** B5
Cookstown *U.K.* 54°38N 6°45W **10** B5
Cooktown *Australia* 15°30S 145°16E **62** B4
Coolabah *Australia* 31°1S 146°43E **63** E4
Cooladdi *Australia* 26°37S 145°23E **63** D4
Coolah *Australia* 31°48S 149°41E **63** E4
Coolamon *Australia* 34°46S 147°8E **63** E4
Coolgardie *Australia* 30°55S 121°8E **61** F3
Coolidge *U.S.A.* 32°59N 111°31W **77** K8
Coolidge Dam *U.S.A.* 33°10N 110°32W **77** K8
Cooma *Australia* 36°12S 149°8E **63** F4
Coon Rapids *U.S.A.* 45°9N 93°19W **80** C7
Coonabarabran
  Australia 31°14S 149°18E **63** E4
Coonamble *Australia* 30°56S 148°27E **63** E4
Coonana *Australia* 31°0S 123°0E **61** F3
Coonana ⊙ *Australia* 30°51S 122°53E **61** F3
Coondapoor *India* 13°42N 74°40E **45** H2
Cooninnie, L. *Australia* 26°4S 139°59E **63** D2
Coonoor *India* 11°21N 76°45E **45** J3
Cooper *U.S.A.* 33°23N 95°42W **84** E7
Cooper Cr. → *Australia* 28°29S 137°46E **63** D2
Cooper Ridge *Pac. Oc.* 10°0N 150°30W **65** G12
Cooperstown *N. Dak.,*
  U.S.A. 47°27N 98°8W **80** B4
Cooperstown *N.Y.,*
  U.S.A. 42°42N 74°56W **83** D10
Coorabie *Australia* 31°54S 132°18E **61** F5
Coorong, The *Australia* 35°50S 139°20E **63** F2
Coorow *Australia* 29°53S 116°2E **61** E2
Cooroy *Australia* 26°22S 152°54E **63** D5
Coos Bay *U.S.A.* 43°22N 124°13W **76** E1
Cootamundra *Australia* 34°36S 148°1E **63** E4
Cootehill *Ireland* 54°4N 7°5W **10** B4
Copahue Paso *Argentina* 37°49S 71°8W **94** D1
Copainalá *Mexico* 17°4N 93°10W **87** D6
Copake *U.S.A.* 42°7N 73°31W **83** D11
Copán *Honduras* 14°50N 89°9W **88** D2
Cope *U.S.A.* 39°40N 102°51W **76** G12
Copenhagen *U.S.A.* 43°54N 75°41W **83** C9
Copiapó *Chile* 27°30S 70°20W **94** B1
Copiapó → *Chile* 27°19S 70°56W **94** B1
Coplay *U.S.A.* 40°44N 75°29W **83** F9
Copo △ *Argentina* 25°53S 61°44W **94** B3
Copp L. *Canada* 60°14N 114°40W **70** A6
Coppename → *Suriname* 5°48N 55°55W **93** B7
Copper Canyon = Barranca del
  Cobre △ *Mexico* 27°18N 107°40W **86** B3
Copper Center *U.S.A.* 61°58N 145°18W **74** C10
Copper Harbor *U.S.A.* 47°28N 87°53W **80** B10
Copperas Cove *U.S.A.* 31°8N 97°54W **84** F6
Coppermine = Kugluktuk
  Canada 67°50N 115°5W **68** D8
Coppermine → *Canada* 67°49N 116°4W **68** D8
Copperopolis *U.S.A.* 37°58N 120°38W **78** H6
Coquet → *U.K.* 55°20N 1°32W **12** B6
Coquille *U.S.A.* 43°11N 124°11W **76** E1
Coquimbo *Chile* 30°0S 71°20W **94** C1
Coquimbo □ *Chile* 31°0S 71°0W **94** C1
Coquitlam *Canada* 49°17N 122°45W **70** D4
Corabia *Romania* 43°48N 24°30E **17** G13
Coracora *Peru* 15°5S 73°45W **92** G4
Coraki *Australia* 28°59S 153°17E **63** D5
Coral *U.S.A.* 40°29N 79°10W **82** F5
Coral Bay *Australia* 23°8S 113°46E **60** D1
Coral Harbour *Canada* 64°8N 83°10W **69** E15
Coral Sea *Pac. Oc.* 15°0S 150°0E **64** J7
Coral Sea Basin *Pac. Oc.* 14°0S 152°0E **64** J7
Coral Sea Islands Terr. □
  Australia 20°0S 155°0E **58** C8
Coral Springs *U.S.A.* 26°16N 80°16W **85** H14
Coraopolis *U.S.A.* 40°31N 80°10W **82** F4
Corato *Italy* 41°9N 16°25E **22** D7
Corbett △ *India* 29°30N 79°0E **43** E8
Corbin *U.S.A.* 36°57N 84°6W **81** G11
Corby *U.K.* 52°30N 0°41W **13** E7
Corcaigh = Cork *Ireland* 51°54N 8°29W **10** E3
Corcoran *U.S.A.* 36°6N 119°33W **78** J7
Corcovado △ *Costa Rica* 8°33N 83°35W **88** E3
Corcubión *Spain* 42°56N 9°12W **21** A1
Cordele *U.S.A.* 31°58N 83°47W **85** F13
Cordell *U.S.A.* 35°17N 98°59W **84** D5
Córdoba *Argentina* 31°20S 64°10W **94** C3
Córdoba *Mexico* 18°53N 96°56W **87** D5
Córdoba *Spain* 37°50N 4°50W **21** D3
Córdoba □ *Argentina* 31°22S 64°15W **94** C3
Córdoba, Sierra de
  Argentina 31°10S 64°25W **94** C3
Cordova *U.S.A.* 60°33N 145°45W **68** E2
Corella *Australia* 19°34S 140°47E **62** B3
Corentyne → *S. Amer.* 5°50N 57°8W **92** B7
Corfield *Australia* 21°40S 143°21E **62** C3
Corfu = Kerkyra *Greece* 39°38N 19°50E **25** A3
Corfu □ *U.S.A.* 42°57N 78°24W **82** D6
Coria *Spain* 39°58N 6°33W **21** C2
Corigliano Cálabro *Italy* 39°36N 16°31E **22** E7
Coringa Is. *Australia* 16°58S 149°58E **62** B4
Corinth = Korinthos
  Greece 37°56N 22°55E **23** F10
Corinth *Miss., U.S.A.* 34°56N 88°31W **85** D10
Corinth *N.Y., U.S.A.* 43°15N 73°49W **83** C11

Corinth, G. of = Korinthiakos
  Kolpos *Greece* 38°16N 22°30E **23** E10
Corinto *Brazil* 18°20S 44°30W **93** G10
Corinto *Nic.* 12°30N 87°10W **88** D2
Cork *Ireland* 51°54N 8°29W **10** E3
Cork □ *Ireland* 51°57N 8°40W **10** E3
Cork Harbour *Ireland* 51°47N 8°16W **10** E3
Çorlu *Turkey* 41°11N 27°49E **23** D12
Cormack L. *Canada* 60°56N 121°37W **70** A4
Cormorant *Canada* 54°14N 100°35W **71** C8
Cormorant L. *Canada* 54°15N 100°50W **71** C8
Corn Is. = Maíz, Is. del
  Nic. 12°15N 83°4W **88** D3
Cornélio Procópio *Brazil* 23°7S 50°40W **95** A5
Corner Brook *Canada* 48°57N 57°58W **73** C8
Cornești *Moldova* 47°21N 28°1E **17** E15
Corning *Ark., U.S.A.* 36°25N 90°35W **85** C9
Corning *Calif., U.S.A.* 39°56N 122°11W **76** G2
Corning *Iowa, U.S.A.* 40°59N 94°44W **80** E6
Corning *N.Y., U.S.A.* 42°9N 77°3W **82** D7
Cornwall *Canada* 45°2N 74°44W **83** A10
Cornwall *U.S.A.* 40°17N 76°25W **83** F8
Cornwall □ *U.K.* 50°26N 4°40W **13** G3
Cornwall I. *Canada* 77°37N 94°38W **69** B13
Cornwallis I. *Canada* 75°8N 95°0W **69** B13
Corny Pt. *Australia* 34°55S 137°0E **63** E2
Coro *Venezuela* 11°25N 69°41W **92** A5
Coroatá *Brazil* 4°8S 44°0W **93** D10
Corocoro *Bolivia* 17°15S 68°28W **92** G5
Coroico *Bolivia* 16°0S 67°50W **92** G5
Coromandel *N.Z.* 36°45S 175°31E **59** B5
Coromandel Coast *India* 12°30N 81°0E **45** H5
Corona *Calif., U.S.A.* 33°53N 117°34W **79** M9
Corona *N. Mex., U.S.A.* 34°15N 105°36W **77** J11
Coronado *U.S.A.* 32°41N 117°10W **79** N9
Coronado, B. de *Costa Rica* 9°0N 83°40W **88** E3
Coronados, Is. Los
  Mexico 32°26N 117°19W **79** N9
Coronation *Canada* 52°5N 111°27W **70** C6
Coronation Gulf *Canada* 68°25N 110°0W **68** D10
Coronation I. *Antarctica* 60°45S 46°0W **5** C18
Coronation Is. *Australia* 14°57S 124°55E **60** B3
Coronda *Argentina* 31°58S 60°56W **94** C3
Coronel *Chile* 37°0S 73°10W **94** D1
Coronel Bogado
  Paraguay 27°11S 56°18W **94** B4
Coronel Dorrego
  Argentina 38°40S 61°10W **94** D3
Coronel Oviedo *Paraguay* 25°24S 56°30W **94** B4
Coronel Pringles
  Argentina 38°0S 61°30W **94** D3
Coronel Suárez *Argentina* 37°30S 61°52W **94** D3
Coronel Vidal *Argentina* 37°28S 57°45W **94** D4
Coropuna, Nevado *Peru* 15°30S 72°41W **92** G4
Corowa *Australia* 35°58S 146°21E **63** F4
Corozal □ *Belize* 18°23N 88°23W **87** D7
Corozal Pt. *Trin. & Tob.* 10°45N 61°37W **93** K15
Corpus *Argentina* 27°10S 55°30W **94** B4
Corpus Christi *U.S.A.* 27°47N 97°24W **84** H6
Corpus Christi, L. *U.S.A.* 28°2N 97°52W **84** G6
Corraun Pen. *Ireland* 53°54N 9°54W **10** C2
Corrib, L. *Ireland* 53°27N 9°16W **10** C2
Corrientes *Argentina* 27°30S 58°45W **94** B4
Corrientes □ *Argentina* 28°0S 57°0W **94** B4
Corrientes → *Argentina* 30°42S 59°38W **94** C4
Corrientes → *Peru* 3°43S 74°35W **92** D4
Corrientes, C. *Colombia* 5°30N 77°34W **92** B3
Corrientes, C. *Cuba* 21°43N 84°30W **88** B3
Corrientes, C. *Mexico* 20°25N 105°42W **86** C3
Corrigan *U.S.A.* 31°0N 94°52W **84** F7
Corrigin *Australia* 32°0S 117°53E **61** F2
Corriverton *Guyana* 5°55N 57°20W **92** B7
Corry *U.S.A.* 41°55N 79°39W **82** E5
Corse *France* 42°0N 9°0E **20** F8
Corse, C. *France* 43°1N 9°25E **20** E8
Corsica = Corse □ *France* 42°0N 9°0E **20** F8
Corsicana *U.S.A.* 32°6N 96°28W **84** E6
Corte *France* 42°19N 9°11E **20** E8
Cortés, Mar de = California, G. de
  Mexico 27°0N 111°0W **86** B2
Cortez *U.S.A.* 37°21N 108°35W **77** H9
Córthaidh, Inis = Enniscorthy
  Ireland 52°30N 6°34W **10** D5
Cortland *N.Y., U.S.A.* 42°36N 76°11W **83** D8
Cortland *Ohio, U.S.A.* 41°20N 80°44W **82** E4
Çorum *Turkey* 40°30N 34°57E **19** F5
Corumbá *Brazil* 19°0S 57°30W **92** G7
Corunna = A Coruña
  Spain 43°20N 8°25W **21** A1
Corvallis *U.S.A.* 44°34N 123°16W **76** D2
Corvette, L. de la *Canada* 53°25N 73°3W **72** B5
Corvo *Azores* 39°43N 31°8W **52** a
Corydon *U.S.A.* 40°46N 93°19W **80** E7
Cosalá *Mexico* 24°23N 106°41W **86** C3
Cosamaloapan de Carpio
  Mexico 18°22N 95°48W **87** D5
Cosenza *Italy* 39°18N 16°15E **22** E7
Coshocton *U.S.A.* 40°16N 81°51W **82** F3
Cosmo Newberry
  Australia 28°0S 122°54E **61** E3
Cosmo Newberry ⊙
  Australia 27°59S 122°53E **61** E3
Cosmonaut Sea *S. Ocean* 66°30S 40°0E **5** C5
Coso Junction *U.S.A.* 36°3N 117°57W **79** J9
Coso Pk. *U.S.A.* 36°13N 117°44W **79** J9
Cosquín *Argentina* 31°15S 64°30W **94** C3
Costa Blanca *Spain* 38°25N 0°10W **21** C5
Costa Brava *Spain* 41°30N 3°0E **21** B7
Costa Cálida *Spain* 37°30N 1°30W **21** D5
Costa Daurada *Spain* 41°12N 1°15E **21** B6
Costa de la Luz *Spain* 36°15N 5°58W **21** D2
Costa del Azahar *Spain* 39°39N 0°13W **21** B6
Costa del Sol *Spain* 36°30N 4°30W **21** D3
Costa Maya *Mexico* 18°44N 87°42W **87** D7
Costa Mesa *U.S.A.* 33°38N 117°55W **79** M9
Costa Rica ■ *Cent. Amer.* 10°0N 84°0W **88** E3
Costa Smeralda *Italy* 41°5N 9°35E **22** D3
Costa Verde *Spain* 43°22N 4°14W **21** A3

Cosumnes → *U.S.A.* 38°16N 121°26W **78** G5
Cotabato *Phil.* 7°14N 124°15E **37** C6
Cotagaita *Bolivia* 20°45S 65°40W **94** A2
Côte d'Azur *France* 43°25N 7°10E **20** E7
Côte-d'Ivoire = Ivory Coast ■
  Africa 7°30N 5°0W **52** G4
Coteau des Prairies
  U.S.A. 45°20N 97°50W **80** C5
Coteau du Missouri
  U.S.A. 47°0N 100°0W **80** B4
Cotentin *France* 49°15N 1°30W **20** B3
Cotonou *Benin* 6°20N 2°25E **52** G6
Cotopaxi *Ecuador* 0°40S 78°30W **92** D3
Cotswold Hills *U.K.* 51°42N 2°10W **13** F5
Cottage Grove *U.S.A.* 43°48N 123°3W **76** E2
Cottam *Canada* 42°8N 82°45W **82** D2
Cottbus *Germany* 51°45N 14°20E **16** C8
Cottonwood *U.S.A.* 34°45N 112°1W **77** J7
Cotulla *U.S.A.* 28°26N 99°14W **84** G5
Coudersport *U.S.A.* 41°46N 78°1W **82** E6
Couedic, C. du *Australia* 36°5S 136°40E **63** F2
Coulee City *U.S.A.* 47°37N 119°17W **76** C4
Coulee Dam Nat. Recr. Area =
  Lake Roosevelt △
  U.S.A. 48°5N 118°14W **76** B4
Coulman I. *Antarctica* 73°35S 170°0E **5** D11
Coulonge → *Canada* 45°52N 76°46W **72** C4
Coulterville *U.S.A.* 37°43N 120°12W **78** H6
Council *Alaska, U.S.A.* 64°53S 163°41W **74** C7
Council *Idaho, U.S.A.* 44°44N 116°26W **76** D5
Council Bluffs *U.S.A.* 41°16N 95°52W **80** E6
Council Grove *U.S.A.* 38°40N 96°29W **80** F5
Coupeville *U.S.A.* 48°13N 122°41W **78** B4
Courantyne = Corentyne →
  S. Amer. 5°50N 57°8W **92** B7
Courcelles *Belgium* 50°28N 4°22E **15** D4
Courtenay *Canada* 49°45N 125°0W **70** D4
Courtland *Canada* 42°51N 80°38W **82** D4
Courtland *U.S.A.* 38°20N 121°34W **78** G5
Courtrai = Kortrijk
  Belgium 50°50N 3°17E **15** D3
Courtright *Canada* 42°49N 82°28W **82** D2
Coushatta *U.S.A.* 32°1N 93°21W **84** E8
Coutts Crossing
  Australia 29°49S 152°55E **63** D5
Couva *Trin. & Tob.* 10°25N 61°27W **93** K15
Couvin *Belgium* 50°3N 4°29E **15** D4
Cove I. *Canada* 45°17N 81°44W **82** A3
Coventry *U.K.* 52°25N 1°28W **13** E6
Covilhã *Portugal* 40°17N 7°31W **21** B2
Covington *Ga., U.S.A.* 33°36N 83°51W **85** E13
Covington *Ky., U.S.A.* 39°5N 84°30W **81** F11
Covington *Tenn., U.S.A.* 35°34N 89°39W **85** D10
Covington *Va., U.S.A.* 37°47N 79°59W **81** G14
Cowal, L. *Australia* 33°40S 147°25E **63** E4
Cowan, L. *Australia* 31°45S 121°45E **61** F3
Cowan L. *Canada* 54°0N 107°15W **71** C7
Cowangie *Australia* 35°12S 141°26E **63** F3
Cowansville *Canada* 45°14N 72°46W **83** A12
Coward Springs
  Australia 29°24S 136°49E **63** D2
Cowcowing Lakes
  Australia 30°55S 117°20E **61** F2
Cowdenbeath *U.K.* 56°7N 3°21W **11** E5
Cowell *Australia* 33°39S 136°56E **63** E2
Cowes *U.K.* 50°45N 1°18W **13** G6
Cowichan L. *Canada* 48°53N 124°17W **78** B2
Cowlitz → *U.S.A.* 46°6N 122°55W **78** D4
Cowra *Australia* 33°49S 148°42E **63** E4
Coxilha Grande *Brazil* 28°18S 51°30W **95** B5
Coxim *Brazil* 18°30S 54°55W **93** G8
Cox's Bazar *Bangla.* 21°26N 91°59E **41** J17
Coyote Wells *U.S.A.* 32°44N 115°58W **79** N11
Coyuca de Benítez *Mexico* 17°2N 100°4W **87** D4
Coyuca de Catalán
  Mexico 18°20N 100°39W **86** D4
Cozad *U.S.A.* 40°52N 99°59W **80** E4
Cozumel *Mexico* 20°31N 86°55W **87** C7
Cozumel, Isla *Mexico* 20°30N 86°40W **87** C7
Crab Hill *Barbados* 13°19N 59°38W **89** g
Cracow = Kraków
  Poland 50°4N 19°57E **17** C10
Cracow *Australia* 25°17S 150°17E **63** D5
Cradle Mt.-Lake St. Clair △
  Australia 41°49S 147°56E **63** G4
Cradock *Australia* 32°6S 138°31E **63** E2
Cradock *S. Africa* 32°8S 25°36E **56** D4
Craig *U.S.A.* 40°31N 107°33W **76** F10
Craigavon *U.K.* 54°27N 6°23W **10** B5
Craik *Canada* 51°3N 105°49W **71** C7
Crailsheim *Germany* 49°8N 10°5E **16** D6
Craiova *Romania* 44°21N 23°48E **17** F12
Cramsie *Australia* 23°20S 144°15E **62** C3
Cranberry L. *U.S.A.* 44°11N 74°50W **83** B10
Cranberry Portage
  Canada 54°35N 101°23W **71** C8
Cranbrook *Australia* 34°18S 117°33E **61** F2
Cranbrook *Canada* 49°30N 115°46W **70** D5
Crandon *U.S.A.* 45°34N 88°54W **80** C9
Crane *Oreg., U.S.A.* 43°25N 118°35W **76** E4
Crane *Tex., U.S.A.* 31°24N 102°21W **84** F3
Crane, The *Barbados* 13°6N 59°27W **89** g
Cranganore *India* 10°13N 76°13E **45** J3
Cranston *U.S.A.* 41°47N 71°26W **83** E13
Crater L. *U.S.A.* 42°56N 122°6W **76** E2
Crater Lake △ *U.S.A.* 42°55N 122°10W **76** E2
Craters of the Moon △
  U.S.A. 43°25N 113°30W **76** E7
Crateús *Brazil* 5°10S 40°39W **93** E10
Crato *Brazil* 7°10S 39°25W **93** E11
Craven, L. *Canada* 54°20S 76°56W **80** D7
Crawford *U.S.A.* 42°41N 103°25W **80** D2
Crawfordsville *U.S.A.* 40°2N 86°54W **80** E10
Crawley *U.K.* 51°7N 0°11W **13** F7
Crazy Mts. *U.S.A.* 46°12N 110°20W **76** C8
Crean L. *Canada* 54°5N 106°9W **71** C7
Crediton *Canada* 43°17N 81°33W **82** C3
Crediton *U.K.* 50°47N 3°40W **13** G4
Cree → *Canada* 58°57N 105°47W **71** B7

Cree → U.K. 54°55N 4°25W 11 G4
Cree L. Canada 57°30N 106°30W 71 B7
Creede U.S.A. 37°51N 106°56W 77 H10
Creekside U.S.A. 40°40N 79°11W 82 F5
Creemore Canada 44°19N 80°6W 82 B4
Creighton Canada 54°45N 101°54W 71 C8
Creighton U.S.A. 42°28N 97°54W 80 D5
Crema Italy 45°22N 9°41E 20 D8
Cremona Italy 45°7N 10°2E 20 D9
Cres Croatia 44°58N 14°25E 16 F8
Crescent City U.S.A. 41°45N 124°12W 76 F1
Crespo Argentina 32°2S 60°19W 94 C3
Cresson U.S.A. 40°28N 78°36W 82 F6
Crestline Calif., U.S.A. 34°14N 117°18W 79 L9
Crestline Ohio, U.S.A. 40°47N 82°44W 82 F2
Creston Canada 49°10N 116°31W 70 D5
Creston Calif., U.S.A. 35°32N 120°33W 78 K6
Creston Iowa, U.S.A. 41°4N 94°22W 80 E7
Crestview Calif., U.S.A. 37°46N 118°58W 78 H8
Crestview Fla., U.S.A. 30°46N 86°34W 85 F11
Crete = Kriti Greece 35°15N 25°0E 23 G11
Crete U.S.A. 40°38N 96°58W 80 E5
Creus, C. de Spain 42°20N 3°19E 21 A7
Creuse → France 47°0N 0°34E 20 C4
Crewe U.K. 53°6N 2°26W 12 D5
Crewkerne U.K. 50°53N 2°48W 13 G5
Crianlarich U.K. 56°24N 4°37W 11 E4
Criciúma Brazil 28°40S 49°23W 95 B6
Crieff U.K. 56°22N 3°50W 11 E5
Crimea □ Ukraine 45°0N 33°10E 19 E5
Crimean Pen. = Krymskyy
  Pivostriv Ukraine 45°0N 34°0E 19 F5
Crişul Alb → Romania 46°42N 21°17E 17 E11
Crişul Negru →
  Romania 46°42N 21°16E 17 E11
Crna → Macedonia 41°33N 21°59E 23 D9
Crna Gora = Montenegro ■
  Europe 42°40N 19°20E 23 C8
Crna Gora Macedonia 42°10N 21°30E 23 C9
Crna Reka = Crna →
  Macedonia 41°33N 21°59E 23 D9
Croagh Patrick Ireland 53°46N 9°40W 10 C2
Croatia ■ Europe 45°20N 16°0E 16 F9
Crocker, Banjaran
  Malaysia 5°40N 116°30E 36 C5
Crockett U.S.A. 31°19N 95°27W 84 F7
Crocodile = Umgwenya →
  Mozam. 25°14S 32°18E 57 D5
Crocodile → S. Africa 24°12S 26°53E 56 B4
Crocodile Is. Australia 12°3S 134°58E 62 A1
Crohy Hd. Ireland 54°55N 8°26W 10 B3
Croix, L. la Canada 48°20N 92°15W 72 C1
Croker, C. Australia 10°58S 132°35E 60 B5
Croker, C. Canada 44°58N 80°59W 82 B4
Croker I. Australia 11°12S 132°32E 60 B5
Croker Islands Seas ◎
  Australia 11°20S 132°30E 60 B5
Cromarty U.K. 57°40N 4°2W 11 D4
Cromer U.K. 52°56N 1°17E 12 E9
Cromwell N.Z. 45°3S 169°14E 59 F2
Cromwell U.S.A. 41°36N 72°39W 83 E12
Crook U.K. 54°43N 1°45W 12 C6
Crooked → Canada 54°50N 122°54W 70 C4
Crooked → U.S.A. 44°32N 121°16W 76 D3
Crooked I. Bahamas 22°50N 74°10W 89 B5
Crooked Island Passage
  Bahamas 22°55N 74°35W 89 B5
Crookston Minn., U.S.A. 47°47N 96°37W 80 B5
Crookston Nebr., U.S.A. 42°56N 100°45W 80 D3
Crookwell Australia 34°28S 149°24E 63 E4
Crosby U.K. 53°30N 3°3W 12 D4
Crosby N. Dak., U.S.A. 48°55N 103°18W 80 A2
Crosby Pa., U.S.A. 41°45N 78°23W 82 E6
Crosbyton U.S.A. 33°40N 101°14W 84 E4
Cross City U.S.A. 29°38N 83°7W 85 G13
Cross Fell U.K. 54°43N 2°28W 12 C5
Cross L. Canada 54°45N 97°30W 71 C9
Cross Lake Canada 54°37N 97°47W 71 C9
Cross Sound U.S.A. 58°0N 135°0W 68 F4
Crossett U.S.A. 33°8N 91°58W 84 E9
Crosshaven Ireland 51°47N 8°17W 10 E3
Crossmaglen U.K. 54°5N 6°36W 10 B5
Crossmolina Ireland 54°6N 9°20W 10 B2
Crossville U.S.A. 35°57N 85°2W 85 D12
Croswell U.S.A. 43°16N 82°37W 82 C2
Croton-on-Hudson
  U.S.A. 41°12N 73°55W 83 E11
Crotone Italy 39°5N 17°8E 22 E7
Crow → Canada 59°41N 124°20W 70 B4
Crow Agency U.S.A. 45°36N 107°28W 76 D10
Crow Hd. Ireland 51°35N 10°9W 10 E1
Crowell U.S.A. 33°59N 99°43W 84 E5
Crowley U.S.A. 30°13N 92°22W 84 F8
Crowley, L. U.S.A. 37°53N 118°42W 78 H8
Crown Point Ind., U.S.A. 41°25N 87°22W 80 E10
Crown Point N.Y.,
  U.S.A. 43°57N 73°26W 83 C11
Crown Pt. Trin. & Tob. 11°18N 60°51W 93 J16
Crownpoint U.S.A. 35°41N 108°9W 77 J9
Crows Landing U.S.A. 37°23N 121°6W 78 H5
Crows Nest Australia 27°16S 152°4E 63 D5
Crowsnest Pass Canada 49°40N 114°40W 70 D6
Croydon Australia 18°13S 142°14E 62 B3
Croydon □ U.K. 51°22N 0°5W 13 F7
Crozet, Îs. Ind. Oc. 46°27S 52°0E 3 G12
Crusheen Ireland 52°57N 8°53W 10 D3
Cruz, C. Cuba 19°50N 77°50W 88 C4
Cruz Alta Brazil 28°45S 53°40W 95 B5
Cruz Bay U.S. Virgin Is. 18°20N 64°48W 89 e
Cruz del Eje Argentina 30°45S 64°50W 94 C3
Cruzeiro Brazil 22°33S 45°0W 95 A7
Cruzeiro do Oeste Brazil 23°46S 53°4W 95 A5
Cruzeiro do Sul Brazil 7°35S 72°35W 92 E4
Cry L. Canada 58°45N 129°0W 70 B3
Crystal Bay U.S.A. 39°15N 120°0W 78 F7
Crystal Brook Australia 33°21S 138°12E 63 E2
Crystal City U.S.A. 28°41N 99°50W 84 G5
Crystal Falls U.S.A. 46°5N 88°20W 80 B9

Crystal River U.S.A. 28°54N 82°35W 85 G13
Crystal Springs U.S.A. 31°59N 90°21W 85 F9
Csongrád Hungary 46°43N 20°12E 17 E11
Cu Lao Hon Vietnam 10°54N 108°18E 39 G7
Cua Rao Vietnam 19°16N 104°27E 38 C5
Cuamato Angola 17°2S 15°7E 56 A2
Cuamba Mozam. 14°45S 36°22E 55 G7
Cuando → Angola 17°30S 23°15E 55 H4
Cuando = Kwando →
  Angola 16°25S 20°0E 56 A3
Cuando Cubango □
  Angola 16°25S 20°0E 56 A3
Cuangar Angola 17°36S 18°39E 56 A2
Cuango = Kwango →
  Dem. Rep. of the Congo 3°14S 17°22E 54 E3
Cuanza → Angola 9°21S 13°9E 54 F2
Cuarto → Argentina 33°25S 63°2W 94 C3
Cuatrociénegas Mexico 26°59N 102°5W 86 B4
Cuauhtémoc Mexico 28°25N 106°52W 86 B3
Cuba N. Mex., U.S.A. 36°1N 107°4W 77 H10
Cuba N.Y., U.S.A. 42°13N 78°17W 82 D6
Cuba ■ W. Indies 22°0N 79°0W 88 B4
Cubango → Africa 18°50S 22°25E 56 A3
Cuc Phuong △ Vietnam 20°17N 105°38E 38 B5
Cuchumatanes, Sierra de los
  Guatemala 15°35N 91°25W 88 C1
Cuckfield U.K. 51°1N 0°8W 13 F7
Cucuí Brazil 1°12N 66°50W 92 C5
Cucurpé Mexico 30°20N 110°43W 86 A2
Cuddalore India 11°46N 79°45E 45 J4
Cuddapah India 14°30N 78°47E 45 G4
Cuddapan, L. Australia 25°45S 141°26E 62 D3
Cue Australia 27°25S 117°54E 61 E2
Cuenca Ecuador 2°50S 79°9W 92 D3
Cuenca Spain 40°5N 2°10W 21 B4
Cuenca, Serranía de Spain 39°55N 1°50W 21 C5
Cuernavaca Mexico 18°55N 99°15W 87 D5
Cuero U.S.A. 29°6N 97°17W 84 G6
Cueva de la Quebrada del Toro △
  Venezuela 10°46N 69°3W 89 D6
Cuevas del Almanzora
  Spain 37°18N 1°58W 21 D5
Cuevo Bolivia 20°15S 63°30W 92 H6
Cuiabá Brazil 15°30S 56°0W 93 G7
Cuiabá → Brazil 17°5S 56°36W 93 G7
Cuihangcun China 22°27N 113°32E 31 a
Cuijk Neths. 51°44N 5°50E 15 C5
Cuilco Guatemala 15°24N 91°58W 88 C1
Cuillin Hills U.K. 57°13N 6°15W 11 D2
Cuillin Sd. U.K. 57°4N 6°20W 11 D2
Cuilo = Kwilu →
  Dem. Rep. of the Congo 3°22S 17°22E 54 E3
Cuito → Angola 18°1S 20°48E 56 A3
Cuitzeo, L. de Mexico 19°55N 101°5W 86 D4
Cukai Malaysia 4°13N 103°25E 39 K4
Culbertson U.S.A. 48°9N 104°31W 76 B11
Culcairn Australia 35°41S 147°3E 63 F4
Culebra Puerto Rico 18°19N 65°18W 89 d
Culgoa → Australia 29°56S 146°20E 63 D4
Culgoa Flood Plain △
  Australia 28°58S 147°5E 63 D4
Culiacán Mexico 24°50N 107°23W 86 C3
Culiacán → Mexico 24°30N 107°42W 86 C3
Culik Indonesia 8°21S 115°37E 37 J18
Culion Phil. 11°54N 119°58E 37 B6
Cullarin Ra. Australia 34°30S 149°30E 63 E4
Cullen U.K. 57°42N 2°49W 11 D6
Cullen Pt. Australia 11°57S 141°54E 62 A3
Cullera Spain 39°9N 0°17W 21 C5
Cullman U.S.A. 34°11N 86°51W 85 D11
Cullompton U.K. 50°51N 3°24W 13 G4
Culpeper U.S.A. 38°30N 78°0W 81 F14
Culuene → Brazil 12°56S 52°51W 93 F8
Culver, Pt. Australia 32°54S 124°43E 61 F3
Culverden N.Z. 42°47S 172°49E 59 E4
Cumaná Venezuela 10°30N 64°5W 92 A6
Cumberland B.C., Canada 49°40N 125°0W 70 D4
Cumberland Ont., Canada 45°29N 75°24W 83 A9
Cumberland U.S.A. 39°39N 78°46W 81 F14
Cumberland → U.S.A. 37°9N 88°25W 80 G9
Cumberland, L. U.S.A. 36°52N 85°9W 81 G11
Cumberland Gap △
  U.S.A. 36°36N 83°40W 81 G12
Cumberland I. U.S.A. 30°50N 81°25W 85 F14
Cumberland Is. Australia 20°35S 149°10E 62 b
Cumberland Island △
  U.S.A. 30°12N 81°24W 85 F14
Cumberland L. Canada 54°3N 102°18W 71 C8
Cumberland Pen. Canada 67°0N 64°0W 69 D19
Cumberland Plateau
  U.S.A. 36°0N 85°0W 85 D12
Cumberland Sd. Canada 65°30N 66°0W 69 D18
Cumbernauld U.K. 55°57N 3°58W 11 F5
Cumborah Australia 29°40S 147°45E 63 D4
Cumbres de Majalca △
  Mexico 28°48N 106°30W 86 B3
Cumbres de Monterrey △
  Mexico 25°26N 100°25W 86 B4
Cumbria □ U.K. 54°42N 2°52W 12 C5
Cumbrian Mts. U.K. 54°30N 3°0W 12 C5
Cumbum India 15°40N 79°10E 45 G4
Cuminá → Brazil 1°30S 56°0W 93 D7
Cummings Mt. U.S.A. 35°2N 118°34W 79 K8
Cummins Australia 34°16S 135°43E 63 E2
Cumnock Australia 32°59S 148°46E 63 E4
Cumnock U.K. 55°28N 4°17W 11 F4
Cumpas Mexico 30°2N 109°48W 86 B3
Cumpra Chile 38°55S 72°2W 96 D2
Cuncumén Chile 31°53S 70°38W 94 C1
Cundeelee ◎ Australia 30°43S 123°25E 61 F3
Cunderdin Australia 31°37S 117°12E 61 F2
Cunene → Angola 17°20S 11°50E 56 A1
Cúneo Italy 44°23N 7°32E 20 D7
Cung Son Vietnam 13°2N 108°58E 38 F7
Çüngüş Turkey 38°13N 39°17E 46 B3
Cunnamulla Australia 28°2S 145°38E 63 D4
Cupar Canada 50°57N 104°10W 71 C8
Cupar U.K. 56°19N 3°1W 11 E5
Cupertino U.S.A. 37°19N 122°2W 78 H4
Cupica, G. de Colombia 6°25N 77°30W 92 B3

Curaçao W. Indies 12°10N 69°0W 89 D6
Curanilahue Chile 37°29S 73°28W 94 D1
Curaray → Peru 2°20S 74°5W 92 D4
Curepipe Mauritius 20°19S 57°31E 55 d
Curepto Chile 35°8S 72°1W 94 D1
Curiapo Venezuela 8°33N 61°5W 92 B6
Curicó Chile 34°55S 71°20W 94 C1
Curieuse Seychelles 4°15S 55°44E 55 b
Curitiba Brazil 25°20S 49°10W 95 B6
Curitibanos Brazil 27°18S 50°36W 95 B5
Currabubula Australia 31°16S 150°44E 63 E5
Currais Novos Brazil 6°13S 36°30W 93 E11
Curral Velho C. Verde Is. 16°8N 22°48W 52 b
Curralinho Brazil 1°45S 49°46W 93 D9
Currane, L. Ireland 51°49N 10°4W 10 E1
Currant U.S.A. 38°44N 115°28W 76 G6
Currawinya △ Australia 28°55S 144°27E 63 D3
Current → U.S.A. 36°15N 90°55W 84 C9
Currie Australia 39°56S 143°53E 63 F3
Currie U.S.A. 40°16N 114°45W 76 F6
Curtea de Argeş
  Romania 45°12N 24°42E 17 F13
Curtin Springs Australia 25°20S 131°45E 61 E5
Curtis U.S.A. 40°38N 100°31W 80 E3
Curtis Group Australia 39°30S 146°37E 63 F4
Curtis I. Australia 23°35S 151°10E 62 C5
Curuápanema → Brazil 2°25S 55°2W 93 D7
Curuçá Brazil 0°43S 47°50W 93 D9
Curuguaty Paraguay 24°31S 55°42W 95 A4
Çürüksu Çayi = Büyük
  Menderes → Turkey 37°28N 27°11E 23 F12
Curup Indonesia 3°26S 102°13E 36 E2
Cururupu Brazil 1°50S 44°50W 93 D10
Curuzú Cuatiá Argentina 29°50S 58°5W 94 B4
Curvelo Brazil 18°45S 44°27W 93 G10
Cusco Peru 13°32S 72°0W 92 F4
Cushendall U.K. 55°5N 6°4W 10 A5
Cushing U.S.A. 35°59N 96°46W 84 D6
Cushing, Mt. Canada 57°35N 126°57W 70 B3
Cusihuiriáchic Mexico 28°14N 106°50W 86 B3
Custer U.S.A. 43°46N 103°36W 80 D2
Cut Bank U.S.A. 48°38N 112°20W 76 B7
Cutchogue U.S.A. 41°1N 72°30W 83 E12
Cuthbert U.S.A. 31°46N 84°48W 85 F12
Cutler U.S.A. 36°31N 119°17W 78 J7
Cuttaburra → Australia 29°43S 144°22E 63 D3
Cuttack India 20°25N 85°57E 44 D7
Cuvier, C. Australia 23°14S 113°22E 61 D1
Cuvier I. N.Z. 36°27S 175°50E 59 B5
Cuxhaven Germany 53°51N 8°41E 16 B5
Cuyahoga Falls U.S.A. 41°8N 81°29W 82 E3
Cuyahoga Valley △
  U.S.A. 41°24N 81°33W 82 E3
Cuyo Phil. 10°51N 121°2E 37 B6
Cuyuni → Guyana 6°23N 58°41W 92 B7
Cuzco = Cusco Peru 13°32S 72°0W 92 F4
Cuzco Bolivia 20°0S 66°50W 92 H5
Cwmbran U.K. 51°39N 3°2W 13 F4
Cyclades Greece 37°0N 24°30E 23 F11
Cygnet Australia 43°8S 147°1E 63 G4
Cynthiana U.S.A. 38°23N 84°18W 81 F11
Cypress Hills Canada 49°40N 109°30W 71 D7
Cypress Hills △ Canada 49°40N 109°30W 71 D7
Cyprus ■ Asia 35°0N 33°0E 46 C2
Cyrenaica = Barqa Libya 27°0N 23°0E 53 C10
Cyrene Libya 32°53N 21°52E 53 B10
Czar Canada 52°27N 110°50W 71 C6
Czech Rep. ■ Europe 50°0N 15°0E 16 D8
Częstochowa Poland 50°49N 19°7E 17 C10

D

Da → Vietnam 21°15N 105°20E 34 G5
Da Hinggan Ling China 48°0N 121°0E 31 B13
Da Lat Vietnam 11°56N 108°25E 39 G7
Da Nang Vietnam 16°4N 108°13E 38 D7
Da Qaidam China 37°50N 95°15E 30 D8
Da Yunhe → Hopei,
  China 39°10N 117°10E 33 E9
Da Yunhe → Jiangsu,
  China 34°25N 120°5E 33 G11
Da'an China 45°30N 124°7E 33 B13
Daan Viljoen △ Namibia 22°2S 16°45E 56 B2
Daba Shan China 32°0N 109°0E 34 B7
Dabbagh, Jabal Si. Arabia 27°52N 35°45E 46 E2
Dabhoi India 22°10N 73°20E 42 H5
Dabie Shan China 31°20N 115°20E 35 B10
Dabola Guinea 10°50N 11°5W 52 F3
Dabu China 24°22N 116°41E 35 E11
Dabugam India 19°27N 82°26E 44 E6
Dabung Malaysia 5°23N 102°1E 39 K4
Dacca = Dhaka Bangla. 23°43N 90°26E 43 H14
Dachang China 32°13N 118°45E 35 A12
Dachaoshan Dam China 24°1N 100°22E 34 E3
Dachigam △ India 34°10N 75°0E 42 B6
Dacre Canada 45°22N 76°57W 82 A8
Dadanawa Guyana 2°50N 59°30W 92 C7
Dade City U.S.A. 28°22N 82°11W 85 G13
Dadhar Pakistan 29°28N 67°39E 42 E2
Dadnah U.A.E. 25°32N 56°22E 47 E8
Dadra & Nagar Haveli □
  India 20°5N 73°0E 44 D1
Dadri = Charkhi Dadri
  India 28°37N 76°17E 42 E7
Dadu Pakistan 26°45N 67°45E 42 F2
Dadu He → China 29°31N 103°44E 34 C5
Daegu S. Korea 35°50N 128°37E 33 G15
Daejeon S. Korea 36°20N 127°28E 33 F14
Daeseong S. Korea 33°8N 126°17E 33 H14
Daet Phil. 14°2N 122°55E 37 B6
Dafang China 27°0N 105°39E 34 D5
Dafeng China 33°30N 120°45E 33 H11
Dagana Senegal 16°30N 15°35W 52 E2
Dagestan □ Russia 42°30N 47°0E 19 F8
Daggett U.S.A. 34°52N 116°52W 79 L10
Daghestan Republic = Dagestan □
  Russia 42°30N 47°0E 19 F8
Dağlıq Qarabağ = Nagorno-
  Karabakh □ Azerbaijan 39°55N 46°45E 46 B5

Dagö = Hiiumaa Estonia 58°50N 22°45E 9 G20
Dagu China 38°59N 117°40E 33 E9
Daguan China 27°43N 103°56E 34 D4
Dagupan Phil. 16°3N 120°20E 37 A6
Dahab Egypt 28°31N 34°31E 46 D2
Dahanu India 19°58N 72°44E 44 D1
Dahivadi India 17°43N 74°33E 44 F2
Dahlak Kebir Eritrea 15°50N 40°10E 49 D3
Dahlonega U.S.A. 34°32N 83°59W 85 D13
Dahod India 22°50N 74°15E 42 H6
Dahong Shan China 31°25N 113°0E 35 B9
Dahongliutan China 35°45N 79°20E 43 B8
Dahra Libya 29°30N 17°50E 53 C9
Dahūk Iraq 36°50N 43°1E 46 B3
Dai Hao Vietnam 18°1N 106°25E 38 C6
Dai-Sen Japan 35°22N 133°32E 29 G6
Dai Shan China 30°25N 122°10E 35 B14
Dai Xian China 39°4N 112°58E 32 E7
Daicheng China 38°42N 116°38E 32 E9
Daikondi = Dāykondī □
  Afghan. 34°0N 66°0E 40 C5
Dailekh Nepal 28°50N 81°44E 43 E9
Daingean Ireland 53°18N 7°17W 10 C4
Daingean, An = Dingle
  Ireland 52°9N 10°17W 10 D1
Dainkog China 32°30N 97°58E 34 A1
Daintree Australia 16°20S 145°20E 62 B4
Daintree △ Australia 16°8S 145°2E 62 B4
Daiō-Misaki Japan 34°15N 136°45E 29 G8
Daisen Japan 39°27N 140°29E 28 E10
Daisen-Oki △ Japan 35°23N 133°34E 29 G6
Daisetsu-Zan Japan 43°30N 142°57E 28 C11
Daisetsu-Zan △ Japan 43°30N 142°55E 28 C11
Daitari India 21°10N 85°46E 44 D7
Daiyun Shan China 25°50N 118°15E 35 E12
Dajarra Australia 21°42S 139°30E 62 C2
Dajiawa China 37°9N 119°0E 33 F10
Dajin Chuan → China 31°16N 101°59E 34 B3
Dak Dam Cambodia 12°20N 107°21E 38 F6
Dak Nhe Vietnam 15°28N 107°48E 38 E6
Dak Pek Vietnam 15°4N 107°44E 38 E6
Dak Song Vietnam 12°19N 107°35E 39 F6
Dak Sui Vietnam 14°55N 107°43E 38 E6
Dakar Senegal 14°34N 17°29W 52 F2
Dakhla W. Sahara 23°50N 15°53W 52 D2
Dakhla, El Wâhât el
  Egypt 25°30N 28°50E 53 C11
Dakoank India 7°2N 93°43E 45 L11
Dakor India 22°45N 73°11E 42 H5
Dakota City U.S.A. 42°25N 96°25W 80 D5
Đakovica = Gjakovë
  Kosovo 42°22N 20°26E 23 C9
Dalachi China 36°48N 105°0E 32 F3
Dalai Nur China 43°20N 116°45E 32 C9
Dālakī Iran 29°26N 51°17E 47 D6
Dalälven → Sweden 60°12N 16°43E 9 F17
Dalaman → Turkey 36°41N 28°43E 23 F13
Dalandzadgad Mongolia 43°27N 104°30E 32 C3
Dalap-Uliga-Darrit = Majuro
  Marshall Is. 7°9N 171°12E 64 G9
Dalarna Sweden 61°0N 14°0E 8 F16
Dalay Mongolia 43°28N 103°30E 32 C2
Dālbandīn Pakistan 29°0N 64°23E 40 E4
Dalbeattie U.K. 54°56N 3°50W 11 G5
Dalbeg Australia 20°16S 147°18E 62 C4
Dalby Australia 27°10S 151°17E 63 D5
Dale City U.S.A. 38°38N 77°19W 81 F15
Dale Hollow L. U.S.A. 36°32N 85°27W 85 C12
Dalgān Iran 27°31N 59°19E 47 E8
Dalhart U.S.A. 36°4N 102°31W 84 C3
Dalhousie Canada 48°5N 66°26W 73 C6
Dalhousie India 32°38N 75°58E 42 C6
Dali Shaanxi, China 34°48N 109°58E 32 G5
Dali Yunnan, China 25°40N 100°10E 34 E3
Dalian China 38°50N 121°40E 33 E11
Daliang Shan China 28°0N 102°45E 34 D4
Daling He → China 40°55N 121°40E 33 D11
Dāliyat el Karmel Israel 32°43N 35°2E 48 C4
Dallas Oreg., U.S.A. 44°55N 123°19W 76 D2
Dallas Tex., U.S.A. 32°47N 96°48W 84 E6
Dalles, The U.S.A. 45°36N 121°10W 76 D3
Dalmā U.A.E. 24°30N 52°20E 47 E7
Dalmacia Croatia 43°20N 17°0E 22 C7
Dalmas, L. Canada 53°30N 71°50W 73 B5
Dalmatia = Dalmacija
  Croatia 43°20N 17°0E 22 C7
Dalmau India 26°4N 81°2E 43 F9
Dalmellington U.K. 55°19N 4°23W 11 F4
Dalnegorsk Russia 44°32N 135°33E 28 B8
Dalnerechensk Russia 45°50N 133°40E 28 B6
Dalnevostochnyy □
  Russia 67°0N 140°0E 27 C14
Daloa Ivory C. 7°0N 6°30W 52 G4
Dalou Shan China 28°15N 107°0E 34 C6
Dalry U.K. 55°42N 4°43W 11 F4
Dalrymple, L. Australia 20°40S 147°0E 62 C4
Dalrymple, Mt. Australia 21°1S 148°39E 62 b
Dalsland Sweden 58°50N 12°15E 9 G15
Daltenganj India 24°0N 84°4E 43 H11
Dalton Mass., U.S.A. 42°28N 73°11W 83 D11
Dalton-in-Furness U.K. 54°10N 3°11W 12 C4
Dalvík Iceland 65°58N 18°32W 8 D4
Dálvvadis = Jokkmokk
  Sweden 66°35N 19°50E 8 C18
Dalwallinu Australia 30°17S 116°40E 61 F2
Daly → Australia 13°35S 130°19E 60 B5
Daly L. Canada 56°32N 105°39W 71 B7
Daly River Australia 13°46S 130°42E 60 B5
Daly River-Port Keats ◎
  Australia 14°13S 129°36E 60 B4
Daly Waters Australia 16°15S 133°24E 62 B1

Dāmaneh Iran 33°1N 50°29E 47 C6
Damanganga → India 20°25N 72°56E 44 D1
Damanhûr Egypt 31°0N 30°30E 53 B12
Damant L. Canada 61°45N 105°5W 71 A7
Damar Indonesia 7°7S 128°40E 37 F7
Damara C.A.R. 4°58N 18°42E 54 D3
Damaraland Namibia 20°0S 15°0E 56 B2
Damascus = Dimashq
  Syria 33°30N 36°18E 48 B5
Damaturu Nigeria 11°45N 11°55E 54 B2
Damāvand Iran 35°47N 52°0E 47 C7
Damāvand, Qolleh-ye
  Iran 35°56N 52°10E 47 C7
Damba Angola 6°44S 15°20E 54 F3
Dâmbovita → Romania 44°12N 26°26E 17 F14
Dambulla Sri Lanka 7°51N 80°39E 45 L5
Dame Marie Haiti 18°34N 74°26W 89 C5
Dāmghān Iran 36°10N 54°17E 47 B7
Damiel Spain 39°4N 3°37W 21 C4
Damietta = Dumyât
  Egypt 31°24N 31°48E 53 B12
Daming China 36°15N 115°6E 32 F8
Damīr Qābū Syria 36°58N 41°51E 46 B4
Dammam = Ad Dammām
  Si. Arabia 26°20N 50°5E 47 E6
Damodar → India 23°17N 87°35E 43 H12
Damoh India 23°50N 79°28E 43 H8
Dampier Australia 20°41S 116°42E 60 D2
Dampier, Selat Indonesia 0°40S 131°0E 37 E8
Dampier Arch. Australia 20°38S 116°32E 60 D2
Damrei, Chuor Phnum
  Cambodia 11°30N 103°0E 39 G4
Damyang S. Korea 35°19N 126°59E 33 G14
Dana Indonesia 11°0S 121°15E 37 F6
Dana Jordan 30°41N 35°37E 48 E4
Dana Nepal 28°32N 83°37E 43 E10
Dana, L. Canada 50°53N 77°20W 72 B4
Dana, Mt. U.S.A. 37°54N 119°12W 78 H7
Danakil Desert Ethiopia 12°45N 41°0E 49 E3
Danané Ivory C. 7°16N 8°9W 52 G4
Danba China 30°54N 101°48E 34 B3
Danbury U.S.A. 41°24N 73°28W 83 E11
Danby L. U.S.A. 34°13N 115°5W 79 L11
Dand Afghan. 31°28N 65°32E 42 D1
Dandeldhura Nepal 29°20N 80°35E 43 E9
Dandeli India 15°5N 74°30E 45 G2
Dandenong Australia 38°0S 145°15E 63 F4
Dandong China 40°10N 124°20E 33 D13
Danfeng China 33°45N 110°25E 32 H6
Dangan Liedao China 22°0N 114°8E 35 F10
Danger Is. = Pukapuka
  Cook Is. 10°53S 165°49W 65 J11
Danger Pt. S. Africa 34°40S 19°17E 56 E2
Dangla Shan = Tanggula Shan
  China 32°40N 92°10E 30 E7
Dangrek, Mts. = Dangrek, Phnom
  Thailand 14°20N 104°0E 38 E5
Dangrek, Phnom
  Thailand 14°20N 104°0E 38 E5
Dangriga Belize 17°0N 88°13W 87 D7
Dangshan China 34°27N 116°22E 35 G10
Dangtu China 31°32N 118°25E 35 B12
Dangyang China 30°52N 111°44E 35 B8
Daniel U.S.A. 42°52N 110°4W 76 E8
Daniel's Harbour Canada 50°13N 57°35W 73 B8
Danielskuil S. Africa 28°11S 23°33E 56 C3
Danielson U.S.A. 41°48N 71°53W 83 E13
Danilov Russia 58°16N 40°13E 18 C7
Daning China 36°28N 110°45E 32 F6
Danjiangkou China 32°31N 111°30E 35 A8
Danjiangkou Shuiku
  China 32°32N 111°0E 35 A8
Dank Oman 23°33N 56°16E 47 F8
Dankhar Gompa India 32°10N 78°10E 42 C8
Danleng China 30°1N 103°31E 34 B4
Danlí Honduras 14°4N 86°35W 88 D2
Danmark = Denmark ■
  Europe 55°45N 10°0E 9 J14
Dannemora U.S.A. 44°43N 73°44W 83 B11
Dannevirke N.Z. 40°12S 176°8E 59 D6
Dannhauser S. Africa 28°0S 30°3E 57 C5
Dansville U.S.A. 42°34N 77°42W 82 D7
Danta India 24°11N 72°46E 42 G5
Dantan India 21°57N 87°20E 43 J12
Dante = Xaafuun Somalia 10°25N 51°16E 49 E5
Dantewara India 18°53N 81°27E 44 E5
Danube = Dunărea →
  Europe 45°20N 29°40E 17 F15
Danvers U.S.A. 42°34N 70°56W 83 D14
Danville Ill., U.S.A. 40°8N 87°37W 80 E10
Danville Ky., U.S.A. 37°39N 84°46W 81 G11
Danville Pa., U.S.A. 40°58N 76°37W 83 F8
Danville Va., U.S.A. 36°36N 79°23W 81 G14
Danville Vt., U.S.A. 44°25N 72°9W 83 B12
Danyang China 32°0N 119°31E 35 B12
Danzhai China 26°11N 107°48E 34 D6
Danzhou China 19°31N 109°33E 38 C7
Danzig = Gdańsk Poland 54°22N 18°40E 17 A10
Dao Xian China 25°36N 111°31E 35 E8
Daocheng China 29°0N 100°18E 34 C3
Dapaong Togo 10°55N 0°16E 52 F6
Dapoli India 17°46N 73°11E 44 F1
Daqing China 46°35N 125°0E 31 B13
Daqq-e Sorkh, Kavīr Iran 33°45N 52°50E 47 C7
Daqu Shan China 30°25N 122°20E 35 B14
Dar Banda Africa 8°0N 23°0E 50 F6
Dar el Beida = Casablanca
  Morocco 33°36N 7°36W 52 B4
Dar es Salaam Tanzania 6°50S 39°12E 54 F7
Dar Mazār Iran 29°14N 57°20E 47 D8
Dar'ā Syria 32°55N 36°10E 48 C5
Dar'ā □ Syria 32°55N 36°10E 48 C5
Dārāb Iran 28°50N 54°30E 47 D7
Daraban Pakistan 31°44N 70°20E 42 D4
Daraj Libya 30°10N 10°28E 53 B8
Dārān Iran 33°0N 50°17E 47 C6
Dārayyā Syria 33°28N 36°15E 48 B5
Darband Pakistan 34°20N 72°50E 42 B5

Darband, Küh-e *Iran* 31°34N 57°8E **47** D8
Darbhanga *India* 26°15N 85°55E **43** F11
D'Arcy *Canada* 50°33N 122°29W **70** C4
Dardanelle *Ark., U.S.A.* 35°13N 93°9W **84** D8
Dardanelle *Calif., U.S.A.* 38°20N 119°50W **78** G7
Dardanelles = Çanakkale Boğazı
  Turkey 40°17N 26°32E **23** D12
Dârestän *Iran* 29°9N 58°42E **47** D8
Dârfûr *Sudan* 13°40N 24°0E **53** F10
Dargai *Pakistan* 34°25N 71°55E **42** B4
Dargaville *N.Z.* 35°57S 173°52E **59** A4
Darhan *Mongolia* 49°37N 106°21E **30** B10
Darhan Muminggan
  China 41°40N 110°28E **32** D6
Darıca *Turkey* 40°45N 29°23E **23** D13
Darién, G. del *Colombia* 9°0N 77°0W **92** B3
Darién △ *Panama* 7°36N 77°57W **88** E4
Dariganga = Ovoot
  Mongolia 45°21N 113°45E **32** B7
Daringbadi *India* 19°54N 84°8E **44** E7
Darjeeling = Darjiling
  India 27°3N 88°18E **43** F13
Darjiling *India* 27°3N 88°18E **43** F13
Darkan *Australia* 33°20S 116°43E **61** F2
Darkhana *Pakistan* 30°39N 72°11E **42** D5
Darkhazīneh *Iran* 31°54N 48°39E **47** D6
Darkot Pass *Pakistan* 36°45N 73°26E **43** A5
Darling → *Australia* 34°4S 141°54E **63** E3
Darling Downs *Australia* 27°30S 150°30E **63** D5
Darling Ra. *Australia* 32°30S 116°20E **61** F2
Darlington *U.K.* 54°32N 1°33W **12** C6
Darlington *U.S.A.* 34°18N 79°52W **85** D15
Darlington □ *U.K.* 54°32N 1°33W **12** C6
Darlington, L. *S. Africa* 33°10S 25°9E **56** D4
Darlot, L. *Australia* 27°48S 121°35E **61** E3
Darłowo *Poland* 54°25N 16°25E **16** A9
Darmstadt *Germany* 49°51N 8°39E **16** D5
Darnah *Libya* 32°45N 22°45E **53** B10
Darnall *S. Africa* 29°23S 31°18E **57** D5
Darnley *Australia* 9°35S 143°46E **62** a
Darnley, C. *Antarctica* 68°0S 69°0E **5** C6
Darnley B. *Canada* 69°30N 123°30W **68** D7
Darr → *Australia* 23°39S 143°50E **62** C3
Darra Pezu *Pakistan* 32°19N 70°44E **42** C4
Darrequeira *Argentina* 37°42S 63°10W **94** D3
Darrington *U.S.A.* 48°15N 121°36W **76** B3
Darsi *India* 15°46N 79°44E **45** G4
Dart → *U.K.* 50°24N 3°39W **13** G4
Dartmoor *U.K.* 50°38N 3°57W **13** G4
Dartmoor △ *U.K.* 50°37N 3°59W **13** G4
Dartmouth *Canada* 44°40N 63°30W **73** D7
Dartmouth *U.K.* 50°21N 3°36W **13** G4
Dartmouth, L. *Australia* 26°4S 145°18E **63** D4
Darvel, Teluk = Lahad Datu, Telok
  Malaysia 4°50N 118°20E **37** D5
Darwen *U.K.* 53°42N 2°29W **12** D5
Darwendale *Zimbabwe* 17°41S 30°33E **57** B5
Darwha *India* 20°15N 77°45E **44** D3
Darwin *Australia* 12°25S 130°51E **60** B5
Darwin *U.S.A.* 36°15N 117°35W **79** J9
Darya Khan *Pakistan* 31°48N 71°6E **42** D4
Daryapur *India* 20°55N 77°20E **44** D3
Daryoi Amu = Amudarya →
  Uzbekistan 43°58N 59°34E **26** E6
Dās *U.A.E.* 25°20N 53°30E **47** E7
Dashen, Ras *Ethiopia* 13°8N 38°26E **49** E2
Dashetai *China* 41°0N 109°5E **32** D5
Dashiqiao *China* 40°38N 122°30E **33** D12
Dashköpri *Turkmenistan* 36°16N 62°8E **47** B9
Dasht → *Pakistan* 25°10N 61°40E **40** G2
Daska *Pakistan* 32°20N 74°20E **42** C6
Daşoguz *Turkmenistan* 41°49N 59°58E **26** E6
Dasuya *India* 31°49N 75°38E **42** D6
Datça *Turkey* 36°46N 27°40E **23** F12
Date *Japan* 42°28N 140°52E **28** C10
Datia *India* 25°39N 78°27E **43** G8
Datian *China* 25°40N 117°50E **35** E11
Datong *Anhui, China* 30°48N 117°44E **35** B11
Datong *Qinghai, China* 36°20N 102°50E **30** D9
Datong *Shanxi, China* 40°6N 113°18E **32** D7
Dattakhel *Pakistan* 32°54N 69°46E **42** C3
Dattapur = Dhamangaon
  India 20°48N 78°9E **44** D4
Datu, Tanjung *Indonesia* 2°5N 109°39E **36** D3
Datu Piang *Phil.* 7°2N 124°30E **37** C6
Datuk, Tanjung = Datu, Tanjung
  Indonesia 2°5N 109°39E **36** D3
Daud Khel *Pakistan* 32°53N 71°34E **42** C4
Daudnagar *India* 25°2N 84°24E **43** G11
Daugava → *Latvia* 57°4N 24°3E **9** H21
Daugavpils *Latvia* 55°53N 26°32E **9** J22
Daulatabad *India* 19°57N 75°15E **44** E2
Daulpur *India* 26°45N 77°59E **42** F7
Daund *India* 18°26N 74°40E **44** D2
Daung Kyun *Burma* 12°13N 98°4E **39** F1
Dauphin *Canada* 51°9N 100°5W **71** C8
Dauphin *U.S.A.* 40°22N 76°56W **82** F8
Dauphin, L. *Canada* 51°20N 99°45W **71** C9
Dauphiné *France* 45°15N 5°25E **20** D6
Dausa *India* 26°52N 76°20E **42** F7
Davangere *India* 14°25N 75°55E **45** G2
Davao *Phil.* 7°0N 125°40E **37** C7
Davao G. *Phil.* 6°30N 125°48E **37** C7
Dāvar Panāh = Sarāvān
  Iran 27°25N 62°15E **47** E9
Davenport *Calif., U.S.A.* 37°1N 122°12W **78** H4
Davenport *Iowa, U.S.A.* 41°32N 90°35W **80** E8
Davenport *Wash., U.S.A.* 47°39N 118°9W **76** C4
Davenport Ra. *Australia* 20°28S 134°0E **62** C1
Davenport Range △
  Australia 20°36S 134°22E **62** C1
Daventry *U.K.* 52°16N 1°10W **13** E6
David *Panama* 8°30N 82°30W **88** E3
David City *U.S.A.* 41°15N 97°8W **80** E5
David Glacier *Antarctica* 75°20S 162°0E **5** D11
David Gorodok = Davyd Haradok
  Belarus 52°4N 27°8E **17** B14
Davidson *Canada* 51°16N 105°59W **71** C7
Davidson Mts. *U.S.A.* 68°41N 142°22W **74** B11

Davis *Antarctica* 68°34S 77°55E **5** C6
Davis *U.S.A.* 38°33N 121°44W **78** G5
Davis Dam *U.S.A.* 35°12N 114°34W **79** K12
Davis Inlet *Canada* 55°50N 60°59W **73** A7
Davis Mts. *U.S.A.* 30°50N 103°55W **84** F3
Davis Sea *Antarctica* 66°0S 92°0E **5** C7
Davis Str. *N. Amer.* 65°0N 58°0W **69** D19
Davos *Switz.* 46°48N 9°49E **20** C8
Davy L. *Canada* 58°53N 108°18W **71** B7
Davyd Haradok *Belarus* 52°4N 27°8E **17** B14
Dawei = Tavoy *Burma* 14°2N 98°12E **38** E2
Dawes Ra. *Australia* 24°40S 150°40E **62** C5
Dawlish *U.K.* 50°35N 3°28W **13** G4
Dawna Ra. *Burma* 16°30N 98°30E **38** D2
Dawros Hd. *Ireland* 54°50N 8°33W **10** B3
Dawson *U.S.A.* 31°46N 84°27W **85** F12
Dawson, I. *Chile* 53°50S 70°50W **96** G2
Dawson B. *Canada* 52°53N 100°49W **71** C8
Dawson City *Canada* 64°10N 139°30W **68** E4
Dawson Creek *Canada* 55°45N 120°15W **70** B4
Dawson Inlet *Canada* 61°50N 93°25W **71** A10
Dawson Ra. *Australia* 24°30S 149°48E **62** C4
Dawu *Hubei, China* 31°34N 114°7E **35** B9
Dawu *Sichuan, China* 30°55N 101°10E **34** B3
Daxian *China* 31°15N 107°23E **34** B6
Daxin *China* 22°50N 107°11E **34** F6
Daxindian *China* 37°30N 120°50E **33** F11
Daxinggou *China* 43°25N 129°40E **33** C15
Daxue Shan *Sichuan,*
  China 30°30N 101°30E **34** B3
Daxue Shan *Yunnan,*
  China 23°42N 99°48E **34** F2
Dayao *China* 25°43N 101°20E **34** E3
Daye *China* 30°6N 114°58E **35** B10
Dayi *China* 30°41N 103°29E **34** B4
Dāykondī □ *Afghan.* 34°0N 66°0E **40** C5
Daylesford *Australia* 37°21S 144°9E **63** F3
Dayong *China* 29°11N 110°30E **35** C8
Dayr az Zawr *Syria* 35°20N 40°5E **46** C4
Daysland *Canada* 52°50N 112°20W **70** C6
Dayton *Nev., U.S.A.* 39°14N 119°36W **78** F7
Dayton *Ohio, U.S.A.* 39°45N 84°12W **81** F11
Dayton *Pa., U.S.A.* 40°53N 79°15W **82** F5
Dayton *Tenn., U.S.A.* 35°30N 85°1W **85** D12
Dayton *Wash., U.S.A.* 46°19N 117°59W **76** C5
Dayton *Wyo., U.S.A.* 44°53N 107°16W **76** D10
Daytona Beach *U.S.A.* 29°13N 81°1W **85** G14
Dayu *China* 25°24N 114°22E **35** E10
Dayville *U.S.A.* 44°28N 119°32W **76** D4
Dazhu *China* 30°41N 107°15E **34** B6
Dazu *China* 29°40N 105°42E **34** C5
De Aar *S. Africa* 30°39S 24°0E **56** D3
De Funiak Springs
  U.S.A. 30°43N 86°7W **85** F11
De Grey → *Australia* 20°12S 119°13E **60** D2
De Haan *Belgium* 51°16N 3°2E **15** C3
De Hoop △ *S. Africa* 34°30S 20°28E **56** D3
De Kalb Junction *U.S.A.* 44°30N 75°16W **83** B9
De Land *U.S.A.* 29°2N 81°18W **85** G14
De Leon *U.S.A.* 32°7N 98°32W **84** E5
De Long Mts. *U.S.A.* 68°10N 163°30W **74** B7
De Panne *Belgium* 51°6N 2°34E **15** C2
De Pere *U.S.A.* 44°27N 88°4W **80** C9
De Queen *U.S.A.* 34°2N 94°21W **84** D7
De Quincy *U.S.A.* 30°27N 93°26W **84** F8
De Ruyters *U.S.A.* 42°45N 75°53W **83** D9
De Smet *U.S.A.* 44°23N 97°33W **80** C5
De Soto *U.S.A.* 38°8N 90°34W **80** F8
De Tour Village *U.S.A.* 46°0N 83°56W **81** B12
De Witt *U.S.A.* 34°18N 91°20W **84** D9
Dead Sea *Asia* 31°30N 35°30E **48** D4
Deadwood *U.S.A.* 44°23N 103°44W **80** C2
Deadwood L. *Canada* 59°10N 128°30W **70** B3
Deal *U.K.* 51°13N 1°25E **13** F9
Deal I. *Australia* 39°30S 147°20E **63** F4
Dealesville *S. Africa* 28°41S 25°44E **56** D4
De'an *China* 29°21N 115°46E **35** C10
Dean → *Canada* 52°49N 126°58W **70** C3
Dean, Forest of *U.K.* 51°45N 2°33W **13** F5
Dean Chan. *Canada* 52°30N 127°15W **70** C3
Deán Funes *Argentina* 30°20S 64°20W **94** C3
Dease → *Canada* 59°56N 128°32W **70** B3
Dease L. *Canada* 58°40N 130°5W **70** B2
Dease Lake *Canada* 58°25N 130°6W **70** B2
Death Valley *U.S.A.* 36°15N 116°50W **79** J10
Death Valley △ *U.S.A.* 36°29N 117°6W **79** J9
Death Valley Junction
  U.S.A. 36°20N 116°25W **79** J10
Deatnu = Tana →
  Norway 70°30N 28°14E **8** A23
Debagram *India* 23°41N 88°18E **43** H13
Debao *China* 23°21N 106°46E **34** F6
Debar *Macedonia* 41°31N 20°30E **23** D9
Debden *Canada* 53°30N 106°50W **71** C7
Debica *Poland* 50°2N 21°25E **17** C11
DeBolt *Canada* 55°12N 118°1W **70** B5
Deborah East, L.
  Australia 30°45S 119°30E **61** F2
Deborah West, L.
  Australia 30°45S 119°5E **61** F2
Debre Markos *Ethiopia* 10°20N 37°40E **49** E2
Debre Tabor *Ethiopia* 11°50N 38°26E **49** E2
Debre Zeyit *Ethiopia* 8°50N 39°0E **49** F2
Debrecen *Hungary* 47°33N 21°42E **17** E11
Decatur *Ala., U.S.A.* 34°36N 86°59W **85** D11
Decatur *Ga., U.S.A.* 33°47N 84°18W **85** D12
Decatur *Ill., U.S.A.* 39°51N 88°57W **80** F10
Decatur *Ind., U.S.A.* 40°50N 84°56W **81** E11
Decatur *Tex., U.S.A.* 33°14N 97°35W **84** E6
Deccan *India* 18°0N 79°0E **44** F4
Deception Bay *Australia* 27°10S 153°5E **63** D5
Deception I. *Antarctica* 63°0S 60°15W **5** C17
Deception L. *Canada* 56°33N 104°13W **71** B8
Dechang *China* 27°25N 102°11E **34** D4
Dechhu *India* 26°46N 72°20E **42** F5
Děčín *Czech Rep.* 50°47N 14°12E **16** C8
Deckerville *U.S.A.* 43°32N 82°44W **82** C2
Decorah *U.S.A.* 43°18N 91°48W **80** D8
Dedéagach = Alexandroupoli
  Greece 40°50N 25°54E **23** D11

Dee → *Aberds., U.K.* 57°9N 2°5W **11** D6
Dee → *Dumf. & Gall., U.K.* 54°51N 4°3W **11** G4
Dee → *Wales, U.K.* 53°22N 3°17W **12** D4
Deep B. *Canada* 61°15N 116°35W **70** A5
Deep Bay = Shenzhen Wan
  China 22°27N 113°55E **31** a
Deepwater *Australia* 29°25S 151°51E **63** D5
Deer → *Canada* 58°23N 94°13W **71** B10
Deer L. *Canada* 52°40N 94°20W **71** C10
Deer Lake *Nfld. & L.,*
  Canada 49°11N 57°27W **73** C8
Deer Lake *Ont., Canada* 52°36N 94°20W **71** C10
Deer Lodge *U.S.A.* 46°24N 112°44W **76** C7
Deer Park *U.S.A.* 47°57N 117°28W **76** C5
Deer River *U.S.A.* 47°20N 93°48W **80** B7
Deeragun *Australia* 19°16S 146°33E **62** B4
Deerdepoort *S. Africa* 24°37N 26°27E □
Defiance *U.S.A.* 41°17N 84°22W **81** E11
Degana *India* 26°50N 74°20E **42** F6
Dêgê *China* 31°44N 98°39E **34** B2
Dégelis *Canada* 47°30N 68°35W **73** C6
Deggendorf *Germany* 48°50N 12°57E **16** D7
Degh → *Pakistan* 31°3N 73°21E **42** D5
Deh Bīd *Iran* 30°39N 53°11E **47** D7
Deh Dasht *Iran* 30°47N 50°33E **47** D6
Deh-e Shīr *Iran* 31°29N 53°45E **47** D7
Dehaj *Iran* 30°42N 54°53E **47** D7
Dehak *Iran* 27°11N 62°37E **47** E9
Dehdez *Iran* 31°43N 50°17E **47** D6
Dehej *India* 21°44N 72°40E **42** J5
Dehestān *Iran* 28°30N 55°35E **47** D7
Dehgāh *Iran* 35°17N 47°25E **46** C5
Dehibat *Tunisia* 32°0N 10°47E **53** B8
Dehiwala *Sri Lanka* 6°50N 79°51E **45** L4
Dehlorān *Iran* 32°41N 47°16E **46** C5
Dehnow-e Kūhestān *Iran* 27°58N 58°32E **47** E8
Dehra Dun *India* 30°20N 78°4E **42** D8
Dehri *India* 24°50N 84°15E **43** G11
Dehua *China* 25°26N 118°14E **35** E12
Dehui *China* 44°30N 125°40E **33** B13
Deinze *Belgium* 50°59N 3°32E **15** D3
Deir al Balah *Gaza Strip* 31°25N 34°21E **48** D3
Dej *Romania* 47°10N 23°52E **17** E12
Dejiang *China* 28°18N 108°7E **34** C7
Deka → *Zimbabwe* 18°4S 26°42E **56** A4
DeKalb *U.S.A.* 41°56N 88°46W **80** E9
Dekese
  Dem. Rep. of the Congo 3°24S 21°24E **54** E4
Del Mar *U.S.A.* 32°58N 117°16W **79** N9
Del Norte *U.S.A.* 37°41N 106°21W **77** H10
Del Rio *U.S.A.* 29°22N 100°54W **84** G4
Delambre I. *Australia* 20°26S 117°5E **60** D2
Delano *U.S.A.* 35°46N 119°15W **79** K7
Delano Peak *U.S.A.* 38°22N 112°22W **76** G7
Delareyville *S. Africa* 26°41S 25°26E **56** C4
Delaronde L. *Canada* 54°3N 107°3W **71** C7
Delavan *U.S.A.* 42°38N 88°39W **80** D9
Delaware *U.S.A.* 40°18N 83°4W **81** E12
Delaware □ *U.S.A.* 39°0N 75°20W **81** F16
Delaware → *U.S.A.* 39°15N 75°20W **83** G9
Delaware B. *U.S.A.* 39°0N 75°10W **81** F16
Delaware Water Gap △
  U.S.A. 41°10N 74°55W **83** E10
Delay → *Canada* 56°56N 71°28W **73** A5
Delegate *Australia* 37°4S 148°56E **63** F4
Delevan *U.S.A.* 42°29N 78°29W **82** D6
Delft *Neths.* 52°1N 4°22E **15** B4
Delft I. *Sri Lanka* 9°30N 79°40E **45** K4
Delfzijl *Neths.* 53°20N 6°55E **15** A6
Delgado, C. *Mozam.* 10°45S 40°40E **54** G8
Delgerhet *Mongolia* 45°50N 110°30E **32** B6
Delgo *Sudan* 20°6N 30°40E **53** D12
Delhi *Canada* 42°51N 80°30W **82** D4
Delhi *La., U.S.A.* 32°28N 91°30W **84** E9
Delhi *N.Y., U.S.A.* 42°17N 74°55W **83** D10
Delia *Canada* 51°38N 112°23W **70** C6
Delice *Turkey* 39°54N 34°2E **19** G5
Delicias *Mexico* 28°13N 105°28W **86** B3
Delījān *Iran* 33°59N 50°40E **47** C6
Déline *Canada* 65°11N 123°25W **68** D7
Delingha *China* 37°23N 97°23E **30** D8
Delisle *Canada* 51°55N 107°8W **71** C7
Delldonga, Ostrova
  Russia 76°40N 149°20E **27** B15
Deloraine *Australia* 41°30S 146°40E **63** G4
Deloraine *Canada* 49°15N 100°29W **71** D8
Delphi *U.S.A.* 40°36N 86°41W **80** E10
Delphos *U.S.A.* 40°51N 84°21W **81** E11
Delportshoop *S. Africa* 28°22S 24°20E **56** C3
Delray Beach *U.S.A.* 26°28N 80°4W **85** H14
Delta *Colo., U.S.A.* 38°44N 108°4W **76** G9
Delta *Utah, U.S.A.* 39°21N 112°35W **76** G7
Delta Dunărea △
  Romania 45°15N 29°25E **17** F15
Delta Junction *U.S.A.* 64°2N 145°44W **68** E2
Deltona *U.S.A.* 28°54N 81°16W **85** G14
Delungra *Australia* 29°39S 150°51E **63** D5
Delvada *India* 20°46N 71°2E **42** J4
Delvinë *Albania* 39°59N 20°6E **23** E9
Demak *Indonesia* 6°53S 110°38E **37** G14
Demanda, Sierra de la
  Spain 42°15N 3°0W **21** A4
Demavend = Damāvand,
  Qolleh-ye *Iran* 35°56N 52°10E **47** C7
Dembidolo *Ethiopia* 8°34N 34°50E **49** F1
Demchok *India* 32°42N 79°29E **43** C8
Demer → *Belgium* 50°57N 4°42E **15** D4
Deming *N. Mex.,*
  U.S.A. 32°16N 107°46W **77** K10
Deming *Wash., U.S.A.* 48°50N 122°13W **78** B4
Demini → *Brazil* 0°46S 62°56W **92** D6
Demirci *Turkey* 39°2N 28°38E **23** E13
Demirköy *Turkey* 41°49N 27°45E **23** D12
Demopolis *U.S.A.* 32°31N 87°50W **85** E11
Dempo *Indonesia* 4°2S 103°15E **36** E2

Den Bosch = 's-Hertogenbosch
  Neths. 51°42N 5°17E **15** C5
Den Burg *Neths.* 53°3N 4°47E **15** A4
Den Chai *Thailand* 17°59N 100°4E **38** D3
Den Haag = 's-Gravenhage
  Neths. 52°7N 4°17E **15** B4
Den Helder *Neths.* 52°57N 4°45E **15** B4
Den Oever *Neths.* 52°56N 5°2E **15** B5
Denair *U.S.A.* 37°32N 120°48W **78** H6
Denali = McKinley, Mt.
  U.S.A. 63°4N 151°0W **68** E1
Denau = Denov
  Uzbekistan 38°16N 67°54E **26** F7
Denbigh *Canada* 45°8N 77°15W **82** A7
Denbigh *U.K.* 53°12N 3°25W **12** D4
Denbighshire □ *U.K.* 53°8N 3°22W **12** D4
Dendang *Indonesia* 3°7S 107°56E **36** E3
Dendermonde *Belgium* 51°2N 4°5E **15** C4
Dengchuan *China* 25°59N 100°3E **34** E3
Dengfeng *China* 34°25N 113°2E **32** G7
Dengkou *China* 40°18N 106°55E **32** D4
Dengzhou *China* 32°34N 112°4E **35** A9
Denham *Australia* 25°56S 113°31E **61** E1
Denham, Mt. *Jamaica* 18°13N 77°32W **88** a
Denham Ra. *Australia* 21°55S 147°46E **62** C4
Denham Sd. *Australia* 25°45S 113°15E **61** E1
Denholm *Canada* 52°39N 108°1W **71** C7
Denia *Spain* 38°49N 0°8E **21** C6
Denial B. *Australia* 32°14S 133°32E **63** E1
Deniliquin *Australia* 35°30S 144°58E **63** F3
Denimoo = Fort Resolution
  Canada 61°10N 113°40W **70** A6
Denison *Iowa, U.S.A.* 42°1N 95°21W **80** D6
Denison *Tex., U.S.A.* 33°45N 96°33W **84** E6
Denison Plains *Australia* 18°35S 128°0E **60** C4
Deniyaya *Sri Lanka* 6°21N 80°33E **45** L5
Denizli *Turkey* 37°42N 29°2E **19** G4
Denman Glacier *Antarctica* 66°45S 100°0E **5** C8
Denmark *Australia* 34°59S 117°25E **61** F2
Denmark ■ *Europe* 55°45N 10°0E **9** J14
Denmark Str. *Atl. Oc.* 66°0N 30°0W **66** C17
Dennery *St. Lucia* 13°55N 60°54W **89** f
Dennison *U.S.A.* 40°24N 81°19W **82** F3
Denny *U.K.* 56°1N 3°55W **11** E5
Denov *Uzbekistan* 38°16N 67°54E **26** F7
Denpasar *Indonesia* 8°39S 115°13E **37** K18
Denpasar ✈ (DPS)
  Indonesia 8°44S 115°10E **37** K18
Denton *Mont., U.S.A.* 47°19N 109°57W **76** C9
Denton *Tex., U.S.A.* 33°13N 97°8W **84** E6
D'Entrecasteaux, Pt.
  Australia 34°50S 115°57E **61** F2
D'Entrecasteaux △
  Australia 34°20S 115°33E **61** F2
D'Entrecasteaux Is.
  Papua N. G. 9°0S 151°0E **58** B8
Denver *Colo., U.S.A.* 39°42N 104°59W **76** G11
Denver *Pa., U.S.A.* 40°14N 76°8W **83** F8
Denver City *U.S.A.* 32°58N 102°50W **84** E3
Deoband *India* 29°42N 77°43E **42** E7
Deobhog *India* 19°53N 82°44E **44** E6
Deodrug *India* 16°26N 76°55E **45** F3
Deogarh *Odisha, India* 21°32N 84°45E **44** D7
Deogarh *Raj., India* 25°32N 73°54E **42** G5
Deoghar *India* 24°30N 86°42E **43** G12
Deolali *India* 19°58N 73°50E **44** E1
Deoli = Devli *India* 25°50N 75°20E **42** G6
Deora *India* 26°22N 70°55E **42** F4
Deori *India* 23°24N 79°1E **43** H8
Deoria *India* 26°31N 83°48E **43** F10
Deosai Mts. *Pakistan* 35°40N 75°0E **43** B6
Deosri *India* 26°46N 90°29E **43** F14
Depalpur *India* 22°51N 75°33E **42** H6
Deposit *U.S.A.* 42°4N 75°25W **83** D9
Depuch I. *Australia* 20°37S 117°44E **60** D2
Deputatskiy *Russia* 69°18N 139°54E **27** C14
Dêqên *China* 28°34N 98°51E **34** C2
Deqing *China* 23°8N 111°42E **35** F8
Dera Ghazi Khan *Pakistan* 30°5N 70°43E **42** D4
Dera Ismail Khan
  Pakistan 31°50N 70°50E **42** D4
Derabugti *Pakistan* 29°2N 69°9E **42** E3
Derawar Fort *Pakistan* 28°46N 71°20E **42** E4
Derbent *Russia* 42°5N 48°15E **19** F8
Derby *Australia* 17°18S 123°38E **60** C3
Derby *U.K.* 52°56N 1°28W **12** E6
Derby *Conn., U.S.A.* 41°19N 73°5W **83** E11
Derby *Kans., U.S.A.* 37°33N 97°16W **80** G5
Derby *N.Y., U.S.A.* 42°41N 78°58W **82** D6
Derby City □ *U.K.* 52°56N 1°28W **12** E6
Derby Line *U.S.A.* 45°0N 72°6W **83** B12
Derbyshire □ *U.K.* 53°11N 1°38W **12** D6
Derdepoort *S. Africa* 24°38S 26°24E **56** B4
Dereham *U.K.* 52°41N 0°57E **13** E8
Derg → *U.K.* 54°44N 7°26W **10** B4
Derg, L. *Ireland* 53°0N 8°20W **10** D3
Deridder *U.S.A.* 30°51N 93°17W **84** F8
Dermott *U.S.A.* 33°32N 91°26W **84** E9
Dêrong *China* 28°44N 99°9E **34** C2
Derry = Londonderry *U.K.* 55°0N 7°20W **10** B4
Derry = Londonderry □
  U.K. 55°0N 7°20W **10** B4
Derry *N.H., U.S.A.* 42°53N 71°19W **83** D13
Derry *Pa., U.S.A.* 40°20N 79°18W **82** F5
Derryveagh Mts. *Ireland* 54°56N 8°11W **10** B3
Derwent → *Cumb., U.K.* 54°39N 3°33W **12** C4
Derwent → *Derby, U.K.* 52°57N 1°28W **12** E6
Derwent → *N. Yorks.,*
  U.K. 53°45N 0°58W **12** D7
Derwent Water *U.K.* 54°35N 3°9W **12** C4
Des Moines *Iowa, U.S.A.* 41°35N 93°37W **80** E7
Des Moines *N. Mex.,*
  U.S.A. 36°46N 103°50W **77** H12
Des Moines *Wash.,*
  U.S.A. 47°24N 122°19W **78** C4
Des Moines → *U.S.A.* 40°23N 91°25W **80** E8
Desaguadero →
  Argentina 34°30S 66°46W **94** C2
Desaguadero → *Bolivia* 16°35S 69°5W **92** G5

Desaru *Malaysia* 1°31N 104°17E **39** d
Descanso, Pta. *Mexico* 32°21N 117°3W **79** N9
Deschaillons-sur-St-Laurent
  Canada 46°32N 72°7W **73** C5
Deschambault L.
  Canada 54°50N 103°30W **71** C8
Deschutes → *U.S.A.* 45°38N 120°55W **76** D3
Dese *Ethiopia* 11°5N 39°40E **49** E2
Deseado → *Argentina* 47°45S 65°54W **96** F3
Deseronto *Canada* 44°12N 77°3W **82** B7
Desert Center *U.S.A.* 33°43N 115°24W **79** M11
Desert Hot Springs
  U.S.A. 33°58N 116°30W **79** M10
Deshnok *India* 27°48N 73°21E **42** F5
Desierto Central de Baja
  California *Mexico* 29°40N 114°50W **86** B2
Desna → *Ukraine* 50°33N 30°32E **17** C16
Desolación, I. *Chile* 53°0S 74°0W **96** G2
Despeñaperros, Paso
  Spain 38°24N 3°30W **21** C4
Dessau *Germany* 51°51N 12°14E **16** C7
Dessye = Dese *Ethiopia* 11°5N 39°40E **49** E2
D'Estrees B. *Australia* 35°55S 137°45E **63** F2
Desuri *India* 25°18N 73°35E **42** G5
Det Udom *Thailand* 14°54N 105°5E **38** E5
Dete *Zimbabwe* 18°38S 26°50E **56** A4
Detmold *Germany* 51°56N 8°52E **16** C5
Detour, Pt. *U.S.A.* 45°40N 86°40W **80** C10
Detroit *U.S.A.* 42°19N 83°12W **82** D1
Detroit Lakes *U.S.A.* 46°49N 95°51W **80** B6
Deua △ *Australia* 35°32S 149°46E **63** F4
Deurne *Neths.* 51°27N 5°49E **15** C5
Deutsche Bucht *Germany* 54°15N 8°0E **16** A5
Deutschland = Germany ■
  Europe 51°0N 10°0E **16** C6
Deva *Romania* 45°53N 22°55E **17** F12
Devakottai *India* 9°55N 78°45E **45** K4
Devaprayag *India* 30°13N 78°35E **43** D8
Devarkonda *India* 16°42N 78°56E **44** F4
Deventer *Neths.* 52°15N 6°10E **15** B6
Deveron → *U.K.* 57°41N 2°32W **11** D6
Devgad I. *India* 14°48N 74°5E **45** G2
Devgadh Bariya *India* 22°40N 73°55E **42** H5
Devgarh *India* 16°23N 73°23E **45** F1
Devi → *India* 19°59N 86°24E **44** E8
Devikot *India* 26°42N 71°12E **42** F4
Devils Den *U.S.A.* 35°46N 119°58W **78** K7
Devils Hole = Death Valley △
  U.S.A. 36°29N 117°6W **79** J9
Devils Lake *U.S.A.* 48°7N 98°52W **80** A4
Devils Paw *Canada* 58°47N 134°0W **70** B2
Devils Postpile △ *U.S.A.* 37°37N 119°5W **78** H7
Devil's Pt. *Sri Lanka* 9°26N 80°6E **45** K5
Devils Tower *U.S.A.* 44°35N 104°42W **76** D11
Devils Tower △ *U.S.A.* 44°48N 104°55W **76** D11
Devine *U.S.A.* 29°8N 98°54W **84** G5
Devipattinam *India* 9°23N 78°54E **45** K4
Devizes *U.K.* 51°22N 1°58W **13** F6
Devli *India* 25°50N 75°20E **42** G6
Devon *Canada* 53°24N 113°44W **70** C6
Devon □ *U.K.* 50°50N 3°40W **13** G4
Devon I. *Canada* 75°10N 85°0W **69** B15
Devonport *Australia* 41°10S 146°22E **63** G4
Devonport *N.Z.* 36°49S 174°49E **59** B5
Devrukh *India* 17°3N 73°37E **44** F1
Dewas *India* 22°59N 76°3E **42** H7
Dewetsdorp *S. Africa* 29°33S 26°39E **56** D4
Dewey *Puerto Rico* 18°18N 65°18W **89** d
Dexing *China* 28°46N 117°30E **35** C11
Dexter *Maine, U.S.A.* 45°1N 69°18W **81** C19
Dexter *Mo., U.S.A.* 36°48N 89°57W **80** G9
Dexter *N. Mex., U.S.A.* 33°12N 104°22W **77** K11
Dey-Dey, L. *Australia* 29°12S 131°4E **61** E5
Deyang *China* 31°3N 104°27E **34** B5
Deyhūk *Iran* 33°15N 57°30E **47** C8
Deyyer *Iran* 27°55N 51°55E **47** E6
Dez → *Iran* 31°39N 48°52E **47** D6
Dezadeash L. *Canada* 60°28N 136°58W **70** A1
Dezfūl *Iran* 32°20N 48°30E **47** C6
Dezhneva, Mys *Russia* 66°5N 169°40W **27** C19
Dezhou *China* 37°26N 116°18E **32** F9
Dhadhar → *India* 24°56N 85°24E **43** G11
Dhahiriya = Az Zāhirīyah
  West Bank 31°25N 34°58E **48** D3
Dhahran = Az Zahrān
  Si. Arabia 26°10N 50°7E **47** E6
Dhak *Pakistan* 32°25N 72°33E **42** C5
Dhaka *Bangla.* 23°43N 90°26E **43** H14
Dhaka □ *Bangla.* 24°25N 90°25E **43** G14
Dhamangaon *India* 20°48N 78°9E **44** D4
Dhamār *Yemen* 14°30N 44°20E **49** E3
Dhampur *India* 29°19N 78°33E **43** E8
Dhamra *India* 20°47N 86°58E **44** D8
Dhamtari *India* 20°42N 81°35E **44** D5
Dhanbad *India* 23°50N 86°30E **43** H12
Dhangarhi *Nepal* 28°55N 80°40E **43** E9
Dhankuta *Nepal* 26°55N 87°40E **43** F12
Dhanora *India* 20°20N 80°22E **44** D5
Dhanpuri *India* 23°13N 81°30E **44** G9
Dhanushkodi *India* 9°11N 79°24E **45** K4
Dhar *India* 22°35N 75°26E **42** H6
Dharampur *India* 22°13N 75°18E **42** H6
Dharamsala = Dharmsala
  India 32°16N 76°23E **42** C7
Dharan *Nepal* 26°49N 87°17E **43** F12
Dharangaon *India* 21°1N 75°16E **44** D2
Dharapuram *India* 10°45N 77°34E **45** J3
Dhariwal *India* 31°57N 75°19E **42** D6
Dharla → *Bangla.* 25°46N 89°42E **43** G13
Dharmapuri *India* 12°10N 78°10E **45** H4
Dharmavaram *India* 14°29N 77°44E **45** G3
Dharmjaygarh *India* 22°28N 83°13E **43** H10
Dharni *India* 21°33N 76°53E **42** J7
Dharur *India* 18°3N 76°8E **44** E3
Dharwad *India* 15°30N 75°4E **45** G2
Dhasan → *India* 25°48N 79°24E **43** G8
Dhaulagiri *Nepal* 28°39N 83°28E **43** E10
Dhebar, L. *India* 24°10N 74°0E **42** G6

Dhenkanal *India* 20°45N 85°35E **44** D7
Dhī Qār □ *Iraq* 31°00N 46°15E **46** D5
Dhībān *Jordan* 31°30N 35°46E **48** D4
Dhilwan *India* 31°31N 75°21E **42** D6
Dhodhekánisos = Dodecanese
　Greece 36°35N 27°0E **23** F12
Dholka *India* 22°44N 72°29E **42** H5
Dhond = Daund *India* 18°26N 74°40E **44** E2
Dhoraji *India* 21°45N 70°37E **42** J4
Dhorpatan *Nepal* 28°29N 83°4E **43** E10
Dhrangadhra *India* 22°59N 71°31E **42** H4
Dhrol *India* 22°33N 70°25E **42** H4
Dhuburi *India* 26°2N 89°59E **41** F16
Dhule *India* 20°58N 74°50E **44** D2
Di Linh *Vietnam* 11°35N 108°4E **39** G7
Di Linh, Cao Nguyen
　Vietnam 11°30N 108°0E **39** G7
Diablo Range *U.S.A.* 37°20N 121°25W **78** J5
Diafarabé *Mali* 14°9N 4°57W **52** F5
Diamante *Argentina* 32°5S 60°40W **94** C3
Diamante → *Argentina* 34°30S 66°46W **94** C2
Diamantina *Brazil* 18°17S 43°40W **93** G10
Diamantina →
　Australia 26°45S 139°10E **63** D2
Diamantina △ *Australia* 23°33S 141°23E **62** C3
Diamantino *Brazil* 14°30S 56°30W **93** F7
Diamond Bar *U.S.A.* 34°1N 117°48W **79** L9
Diamond Harbour *India* 22°11N 88°14E **43** H13
Diamond Is. *Australia* 17°25S 151°5E **62** B5
Diamond Mts. *U.S.A.* 39°40N 115°50W **76** G6
Diamond Springs
　U.S.A. 38°42N 120°49W **78** G6
Dian Chi *China* 24°50N 102°43E **34** E4
Dianbai *China* 21°33N 111°0E **35** G8
Diancheng *China* 21°30N 111°4E **35** G8
Dianjiang *China* 30°24N 107°20E **34** B6
Diaoyu Dao = Senkaku-Shotō
　E. China Sea 25°45N 123°30E **29** M1
Diaoyu Tai = Senkaku-Shotō
　E. China Sea 25°45N 123°30E **29** M1
Diavolo, Mt. *India* 12°40N 92°56E **45** H11
Diba = Dibbā al Ḩiṣn
　U.A.E. 25°45N 56°16E **47** E8
Dibai *India* 28°13N 78°15E **42** E8
Dibaya
　Dem. Rep. of the Congo 6°30S 22°57E **54** F4
Dibaya-Lubue
　Dem. Rep. of the Congo 4°12S 19°54E **54** E3
Dibbā al Ḩiṣn *U.A.E.* 25°45N 56°16E **47** E8
Dibbeen △ *Jordan* 32°20N 35°45E **48** C4
D'Iberville, Lac *Canada* 55°55N 73°15W **72** A5
Dibete *Botswana* 23°45S 26°32E **56** B4
Dibrugarh *India* 27°29N 94°55E **41** F19
Dickens *U.S.A.* 33°37N 100°50W **84** E4
Dickinson *U.S.A.* 46°53N 102°47W **80** B3
Dickson *U.S.A.* 36°5N 87°23W **85** C11
Dickson City *U.S.A.* 41°28N 75°36W **83** E9
Didiéni *Mali* 13°53N 8°6W **52** F4
Didsbury *Canada* 51°35N 114°10W **70** C6
Didwana *India* 27°23N 74°36E **42** F6
Diefenbaker, L. *Canada* 51°0N 106°55W **71** C7
Diego de Almagro *Chile* 26°22S 70°3W **94** B1
Diego Suarez = Antsiranana
　Madag. 12°25S 49°20E **55** G9
Diekirch *Lux.* 49°52N 6°10E **15** E6
Dien Ban *Vietnam* 15°53N 108°16E **38** E7
Dien Bien Phu *Vietnam* 21°20N 103°0E **34** G4
Dien Chau, Vinh *Vietnam* 19°0N 105°55E **38** C5
Dien Khanh *Vietnam* 12°15N 109°6E **39** F7
Dieppe *France* 49°54N 1°4E **20** B4
Dierks *U.S.A.* 34°7N 94°1W **84** D7
Diest *Belgium* 50°58N 5°4E **15** D5
Dif *Somalia* 0°59N 40°58E **49** G3
Differdange *Lux.* 49°31N 5°54E **15** E5
Dig *India* 27°28N 77°20E **42** F7
Digby *Canada* 44°38N 65°50W **73** D6
Digges Is. *Canada* 62°40N 77°50W **69** E16
Diggi *India* 26°22N 75°26E **42** F6
Dighinala *Bangla.* 23°15N 92°5E **41** H18
Dighton *U.S.A.* 38°29N 100°28W **80** F3
Diglur *India* 18°34N 77°33E **44** E3
Digne-les-Bains *France* 44°5N 6°12E **20** D7
Digos *Phil.* 6°45N 125°20E **37** C7
Digranes *Iceland* 66°4N 14°44W **8** C6
Digras *India* 20°6N 77°45E **44** D3
Digul → *Indonesia* 7°7S 138°42E **37** F9
Dihang = Brahmaputra →
　Asia 23°40N 90°35E **43** H13
Dijlah, Nahr → *Asia* 31°0N 47°25E **46** D5
Dijon *France* 47°20N 5°3E **20** C6
Dikhil *Djibouti* 11°8N 42°20E **49** E3
Dikkil = Dikhil *Djibouti* 11°8N 42°20E **49** E3
Diksmuide *Belgium* 51°2N 2°52E **15** C2
Dikson *Russia* 73°40N 80°5E **26** B9
Dikti Oros *Greece* 35°8N 25°30E **23** G11
Dila *Ethiopia* 6°21N 38°22E **49** F2
Dili *E. Timor* 8°39S 125°34E **37** F7
Diligent Strait *India* 12°11N 92°57E **45** H11
Dilley *U.S.A.* 28°40N 99°10W **84** G5
Dillingham *U.S.A.* 59°3N 158°28W **74** D8
Dillon *Canada* 55°56N 108°35W **71** B7
Dillon *Mont., U.S.A.* 45°13N 112°38W **76** D7
Dillon *S.C., U.S.A.* 34°25N 79°22W **85** D15
Dillon → *Canada* 55°56N 108°56W **71** B7
Dillsburg *U.S.A.* 40°7N 77°2W **82** F7
Dilolo
　Dem. Rep. of the Congo 10°28S 22°18E **54** G4
Dimapur *India* 25°54N 93°45E **30** F7
Dimas *Mexico* 23°43N 106°47W **86** C3
Dimashq *Syria* 33°30N 36°18E **48** B5
Dimashq □ *Syria* 33°30N 36°30E **48** B5
Dimbaza *S. Africa* 32°50S 27°14E **57** D4
Dimboola *Australia* 36°28S 142°7E **63** F3
Dîmbovita = Dâmbovita →
　Romania 44°12N 26°22E **17** F14
Dimbulah *Australia* 17°8S 145°4E **62** B4
Dimitrovgrad *Bulgaria* 42°5N 25°35E **23** C11

Dimitrovgrad *Russia* 54°14N 49°39E **18** D8
Dimitrovo = Pernik
　Bulgaria 42°35N 23°2E **23** C10
Dimmitt *U.S.A.* 34°33N 102°19W **84** D3
Dimona *Israel* 31°2N 35°1E **48** D4
Dinagat I. *Phil.* 10°10N 125°40E **37** B7
Dinajpur *Bangla.* 25°33N 88°43E **41** G16
Dinan *France* 48°28N 2°2W **20** B2
Dīnān Āb *Iran* 32°4N 56°49E **47** C8
Dinant *Belgium* 50°16N 4°55E **15** D4
Dinapur *India* 25°38N 85°5E **43** G11
Dīnār, Kūh-e *Iran* 30°42N 51°46E **47** D6
Dinara Planina *Croatia* 44°0N 16°30E **22** C7
Dinard *France* 48°38N 2°6W **20** B2
Dinaric Alps = Dinara Planina
　Croatia 44°0N 16°30E **22** C7
Dinbych-y-Pysgod = Tenby
　U.K. 51°40N 4°42W **13** F3
Dindi → *India* 16°24N 78°15E **45** F4
Dindigul *India* 10°25N 78°0E **45** J4
Dindori *India* 22°57N 81°5E **43** H9
Ding Xian = Dingzhou
　China 38°30N 114°59E **32** E8
Dinga *Pakistan* 25°26N 67°10E **42** G2
Ding'an *China* 19°42N 110°19E **38** C8
Dingbian *China* 37°35N 107°32E **32** F4
Dingle *Ireland* 52°9N 10°17W **10** D1
Dingle B. *Ireland* 52°3N 10°20W **10** D1
Dingle Pen. *Ireland* 52°12N 10°5W **10** D1
Dingmans Ferry *U.S.A.* 41°13N 74°55W **83** E10
Dingnan *China* 24°45N 115°0E **35** E10
Dingo *Australia* 23°38S 149°19E **62** C4
Dingtao *China* 35°5N 115°35E **32** G9
Dingwall *U.K.* 57°36N 4°26W **11** D4
Dingxiang *China* 38°30N 112°58E **32** E7
Dingyuan *China* 32°32N 117°41E **35** A11
Dingzhou *China* 38°30N 114°59E **32** E8
Dinh, Mui *Vietnam* 11°22N 109°1E **39** G7
Dinh Lap *Vietnam* 21°33N 107°6E **34** G6
Dinin → *Ireland* 52°43N 7°18W **10** D4
Dinira △ *Venezuela* 9°57N 70°6W **89** E6
Dinokwe *Botswana* 23°29S 26°37E **56** B4
Dinorwic *Canada* 49°41N 92°30W **71** D10
Dinosaur △ *Canada* 50°47N 111°30W **70** C6
Dinosaur △ *U.S.A.* 40°30N 108°45W **76** F9
Dinuba *U.S.A.* 36°32N 119°23W **78** J7
Diourbel *Senegal* 14°39N 16°12W **52** F2
Dipalpur *Pakistan* 30°40N 73°39E **42** D5
Diplo *Pakistan* 24°35N 69°35E **42** G3
Dipolog *Phil.* 8°36N 123°20E **37** C6
Dipperu △ *Australia* 21°56S 148°42E **62** C4
Dir *Pakistan* 35°8N 71°59E **40** B7
Dire Dawa *Ethiopia* 9°35N 41°45E **49** F3
Dirfís Oros *Greece* 38°40N 23°54E **23** E10
Diriamba *Nic.* 11°51N 86°19W **88** D2
Dirk Hartog I. *Australia* 25°50S 113°5E **61** E1
Dirranbandi *Australia* 28°33S 148°17E **63** D4
Disa *India* 24°18N 72°10E **42** G5
Disappointment, C.
　U.S.A. 46°18N 124°5W **78** D2
Disappointment, L.
　Australia 23°20S 122°40E **60** D3
Disaster B. *Australia* 37°15S 149°58E **63** F4
Discovery B. *Australia* 38°10S 140°40E **63** F3
Discovery B. *China* 22°18N 114°1E **31** a
Disko = Qeqertarsuaq
　Greenland 69°45N 53°30W **4** C5
Disney Reef *Tonga* 19°17S 174°7W **59** c
Disneyland Hong Kong
　China 22°18N 114°2E **31** a
Diss *U.K.* 52°23N 1°7E **13** E9
Disteghil Sar *Pakistan* 36°20N 75°12E **43** A6
District of Columbia □
　U.S.A. 38°55N 77°0W **81** F15
Distrito Federal □ *Brazil* 15°45S 47°45W **93** G9
Distrito Federal □
　Mexico 19°15N 99°10W **87** D5
Diu *India* 20°45N 70°58E **42** J4
Divándarreh *Iran* 35°55N 47°2E **46** C5
Divi Pt. *India* 15°59N 81°9E **45** G5
Divide *U.S.A.* 45°45N 112°45W **76** D7
Dividing Ra. *Australia* 27°45S 116°0E **61** E2
Divinópolis *Brazil* 20°10S 44°54W **93** H10
Divnoye *Russia* 45°55N 43°21E **19** E7
Divo *Ivory C.* 5°48N 5°15W **52** G4
Dīwāl Kol *Afghan.* 34°23N 67°52E **42** B2
Dixie Mt. *U.S.A.* 39°55N 120°16W **78** F6
Dixon *Calif., U.S.A.* 38°27N 121°49W **78** G5
Dixon *Ill., U.S.A.* 41°50N 89°29W **80** E9
Dixon Entrance *U.S.A.* 54°30N 132°0W **68** G5
Dixville *Canada* 45°4N 71°46W **83** A13
Diyālā □ *Iraq* 33°45N 44°50E **46** C5
Diyālā → *Iraq* 33°13N 44°30E **46** C5
Diyarbakır *Turkey* 37°55N 40°18E **46** B4
Diyodar *India* 24°8N 71°50E **42** G4
Djamba *Angola* 16°45S 13°58E **56** A1
Djambala *Congo* 2°32S 14°30E **54** E2
Djanet *Algeria* 24°35N 9°32E **52** D7
Djawa = Jawa *Indonesia* 7°0S 110°0E **36** F3
Djelfa *Algeria* 34°40N 3°15E **52** B6
Djerba, Î. de *Tunisia* 33°50N 10°48E **53** B8
Djerid, Chott *Tunisia* 33°42N 8°30E **52** B7
Djibouti *Djibouti* 11°30N 43°5E **49** E3
Djibouti ■ *Africa* 12°0N 43°0E **49** E3
Djolu *Dem. Rep. of the Congo* 0°35N 22°5E **54** D4
Djougou *Benin* 9°40N 1°45E **52** G6
Djoum *Cameroon* 2°41N 12°35E **54** D2
Djourab, Erg du *Chad* 16°40N 18°50E **53** E9
Djukbinj △ *Australia* 12°11S 131°2E **60** B5
Djúpivogur *Iceland* 64°39N 14°17W **8** D6
Dmitriya Lapteva, Proliv
　Russia 73°0N 140°0E **27** B15
Dnepr = Dnipro →
　Ukraine 46°30N 32°18E **19** E5
Dneprodzerzhinsk =
　Dniprodzerzhynsk
　Ukraine 48°32N 34°37E **19** E5
Dnepropetrovsk = Dnipropetrovsk
　Ukraine 48°30N 35°0E **19** E6

Dnestr = Dnister →
　Europe 46°18N 30°17E **17** E16
Dnieper = Dnipro →
　Ukraine 46°30N 32°18E **19** E5
Dniester = Dnister →
　Europe 46°18N 30°17E **17** E16
Dnipro → *Ukraine* 46°30N 32°18E **19** E5
Dniprodzerzhynsk
　Ukraine 48°32N 34°37E **19** E5
Dnipropetrovsk *Ukraine* 48°30N 35°0E **19** E6
Dnister → *Europe* 46°18N 30°17E **17** E16
Dno *Russia* 57°50N 29°58E **9** H23
Dnyapro = Dnipro →
　Ukraine 46°30N 32°18E **19** E5
Do Gonbadān = Gachsārān
　Iran 30°15N 50°45E **47** D6
Doaktown *Canada* 46°33N 66°8W **73** C6
Doan Hung *Vietnam* 21°30N 105°10E **34** G5
Doba *Chad* 8°40N 16°50E **53** G9
Dobandi *Pakistan* 31°13N 66°50E **42** D2
Dobbyn *Australia* 19°44S 140°2E **62** B3
Dobele *Latvia* 56°37N 23°16E **9** H20
Doberai, Jazirah *Indonesia* 1°25S 133°0E **37** E8
Doblas *Argentina* 37°5S 64°0W **94** D3
Dobo *Indonesia* 5°45S 134°15E **37** F8
Doboj *Bos.-H.* 44°46N 18°4E **23** B8
Dobrich *Bulgaria* 43°37N 27°49E **23** C12
Dobruja *Europe* 44°30N 28°15E **17** F15
Dobrush *Belarus* 52°25N 31°22E **17** B16
Doc, Mui *Vietnam* 17°58N 106°30E **38** D6
Docker River = Kaltukatjara
　Australia 24°52S 129°5E **61** D4
Doctor Arroyo *Mexico* 23°40N 100°11W **86** C4
Doctor Pedro P. Peña
　Paraguay 22°27S 62°21W **94** A3
Doda *India* 33°10N 75°34E **43** C6
Doda, L. *Canada* 49°25N 75°13W **72** C4
Doda Betta *India* 11°24N 76°44E **45** J3
Dodballapur *India* 13°18N 77°32E **45** H3
Dodecanese *Greece* 36°35N 27°0E **23** F12
Dodge City *U.S.A.* 37°45N 100°1W **80** G3
Dodge L. *Canada* 59°50N 105°36W **71** B7
Dodgeville *U.S.A.* 42°58N 90°8W **80** D8
Dodoma *Tanzania* 6°8S 35°45E **54** F7
Dodsland *Canada* 51°50N 108°45W **71** C7
Dodson *U.S.A.* 48°24N 108°15W **76** B9
Doesburg *Neths.* 52°1N 6°9E **15** B6
Doetinchem *Neths.* 51°59N 6°18E **15** C6
Dog Creek *Canada* 51°35N 122°14W **70** C4
Dog L. *Man., Canada* 51°2N 98°31W **71** C9
Dog L. *Ont., Canada* 48°48N 89°30W **72** C2
Dogran *Pakistan* 31°48N 73°35E **42** D5
Doğubayazıt *Turkey* 39°31N 44°5E **46** B5
Doha = Ad Dawḩah
　Qatar 25°15N 51°35E **47** E6
Dohazari *Bangla.* 22°10N 92°5E **41** H18
Dohrighat *India* 26°16N 83°31E **43** F10
Doi *Indonesia* 2°14N 127°49E **37** D7
Doi Inthanon *Thailand* 18°35N 98°29E **38** C2
Doi Inthanon △ *Thailand* 18°33N 98°34E **38** C2
Doi Luang *Thailand* 18°30N 101°0E **38** C3
Doi Luang △ *Thailand* 19°22N 99°35E **38** C2
Doi Phukha △ *Thailand* 19°8N 101°9E **38** C3
Doi Saket *Thailand* 18°52N 99°9E **38** C2
Doi Suthep Pui △
　Thailand 18°49N 98°53E **38** C2
Doi Toa *Thailand* 17°55N 98°30E **38** C2
Dois Irmãos, Sa. *Brazil* 9°0S 42°30W **93** E10
Dokdo = Liancourt Rocks
　Asia 37°15N 131°52E **29** F5
Dokkum *Neths.* 53°20N 5°59E **15** A5
Dokri *Pakistan* 27°25N 68°7E **42** F3
Dolak, Pulau *Indonesia* 8°0S 138°30E **37** F9
Dolbeau-Mistassini
　Canada 48°53N 72°14W **73** C5
Dole *France* 47°7N 5°31E **20** C6
Dolgellau *U.K.* 52°45N 3°53W **12** E4
Dolgelley = Dolgellau
　U.K. 52°45N 3°53W **12** E4
Dolinsk *Russia* 47°21N 142°48E **27** E15
Dollard *Neths.* 53°20N 7°10E **15** A7
Dolo *Ethiopia* 4°11N 42°3E **49** G3
Dolomites = Dolomiti
　Italy 46°23N 11°51E **22** A4
Dolomiti *Italy* 46°23N 11°51E **22** A4
Dolores *Argentina* 36°20S 57°40W **94** D4
Dolores *Uruguay* 33°34S 58°15W **94** C4
Dolores *U.S.A.* 37°28N 108°30W **77** H9
Dolores → *U.S.A.* 38°49N 109°17W **76** G9
Dolphin, C. *Falk. Is.* 51°10S 59°0W **96** G5
Dolphin and Union Str.
　Canada 69°5N 114°45W **68** D9
Dom Pedrito *Brazil* 31°0S 54°40W **95** C5
Domariaganj → *India* 26°17N 83°44E **43** F10
Dombarovskiy *Russia* 50°46N 59°32E **26** D6
Dombås *Norway* 62°4N 9°8E **8** E13
Dombes *France* 45°20N 5°1E **20** C6
Domel I. = Letsôk-aw Kyun
　Burma 11°30N 98°25E **39** G2
Domeyko *Chile* 29°0S 71°0W **94** B1
Domeyko, Cordillera
　Chile 24°30S 69°0W **94** A2
Dominador *Chile* 24°21S 69°20W **94** A2
Dominica ■ *W. Indies* 15°20N 61°20W **89** C7
Dominica Passage
　W. Indies 15°10N 61°20W **89** C7
Dominican Rep. ■
　W. Indies 19°0N 70°30W **89** C5
Domodóssola *Italy* 46°7N 8°17E **20** C8
Domville, Mt. *Australia* 28°1S 151°15E **63** D5
Don → *India* 16°20N 76°15E **45** F3
Don → *Russia* 47°4N 39°18E **19** E6
Don → *Aberds., U.K.* 57°11N 2°5W **11** D6
Don → *S. Yorks., U.K.* 53°41N 0°52W **12** D7

Don, C. *Australia* 11°18S 131°46E **60** B5
Don Benito *Spain* 38°53N 5°51W **21** C3
Don Figuereroa Mts.
　Jamaica 18°5N 77°36W **88** a
Don Sak *Thailand* 9°18N 99°41E **39** b
Donaghadee *U.K.* 54°39N 5°33W **10** B6
Donaghmore *Ireland* 52°52N 7°36W **10** D4
Donald *Australia* 36°23S 143°0E **63** F3
Donaldsonville *U.S.A.* 30°6N 90°59W **84** F9
Donalsonville *U.S.A.* 31°3N 84°53W **85** F12
Donau = Dunărea →
　Europe 45°20N 29°40E **17** F15
Donauwörth *Germany* 48°43N 10°47E **16** D6
Doncaster *U.K.* 53°32N 1°6W **12** D6
Dondo *Angola* 9°45S 14°25E **54** F2
Dondo, Teluk *Indonesia* 0°50N 120°30E **37** D6
Dondra Head *Sri Lanka* 5°55N 80°40E **45** M5
Donegal *Ireland* 54°39N 8°5W **10** B3
Donegal □ *Ireland* 54°53N 8°0W **10** B4
Donegal B. *Ireland* 54°31N 8°49W **10** B3
Donets → *Russia* 47°33N 40°55E **19** E7
Donets Basin *Ukraine* 49°0N 38°0E **6** F13
Donetsk *Ukraine* 48°0N 37°45E **19** E6
Dong Ba Thin *Vietnam* 12°8N 109°13E **39** F7
Dong Dang *Vietnam* 21°54N 106°42E **34** G6
Dong Giam *Vietnam* 19°25N 105°31E **38** C5
Dong Ha *Vietnam* 16°55N 107°8E **38** D6
Dong Hene *Laos* 16°40N 105°18E **38** D5
Dong Hoi *Vietnam* 17°29N 106°36E **38** D6
Dong Jiang → *China* 23°6N 114°0E **35** F10
Dong Khe *Vietnam* 22°26N 106°27E **38** A6
Dong Phayayen
　Thailand 14°20N 101°22E **38** E3
Dong Ujimqin Qi *China* 45°32N 116°55E **32** B9
Dong Van *Vietnam* 23°16N 105°22E **38** A5
Dong Xoai *Vietnam* 11°32N 106°55E **39** G6
Dong'an *China* 26°23N 111°12E **35** D8
Dongara *Australia* 29°14S 114°57E **61** E1
Dongargarh *India* 21°10N 80°40E **44** D5
Dongbei *China* 45°0N 125°0E **33** D13
Dongchuan *China* 26°8N 103°1E **34** D4
Dongfang *China* 18°50N 108°33E **38** C7
Dongfeng *China* 42°40N 125°34E **33** C13
Donggala *Indonesia* 0°30S 119°40E **37** E5
Donggan *China* 23°22N 105°9E **34** F5
Donggang *China* 39°52N 124°10E **33** E13
Dongguan *China* 22°58N 113°44E **35** F9
Dongguang *China* 37°50N 116°30E **32** F9
Donghae *S. Korea* 37°29N 129°7E **33** F15
Donghai Dao *China* 21°0N 110°15E **35** G8
Dongjingcheng *China* 44°5N 129°10E **33** B15
Dongkou *China* 27°6N 110°35E **35** D8
Donglan *China* 24°30N 107°21E **34** E6
Dongliao He → *China* 42°58N 123°32E **33** C12
Dongliu *China* 30°13N 116°55E **35** B11
Dongmen *China* 22°20N 107°48E **34** F6
Dongning *China* 44°2N 131°5E **33** B16
Dongnyi *China* 28°3N 100°1E **34** C3
Dongola *Sudan* 19°9N 30°22E **53** E12
Dongping *China* 35°55N 116°20E **32** G9
Dongsha Dao
　S. China Sea 20°45N 116°43E **35** G11
Dongshan *China* 23°43N 117°30E **35** F11
Dongsheng *China* 39°50N 110°0E **32** E6
Dongtai *China* 32°51N 120°21E **33** H11
Dongting Hu *China* 29°18N 112°45E **35** C9
Dongtou *China* 27°51N 121°10E **35** D13
Dongxiang *China* 28°11N 116°34E **35** C11
Dongxing *China* 21°34N 108°0E **34** G7
Dongyang *China* 29°13N 120°15E **35** C13
Dongying *China* 37°37N 118°37E **33** F10
Dongyinggang *China* 37°37N 118°37E **33** F10
Dongzhi *China* 30°9N 117°0E **35** B11
Donington, C. *Australia* 34°45S 136°0E **63** E2
Doniphan *U.S.A.* 36°37N 90°50W **80** G8
Donna *U.S.A.* 26°9N 98°4W **84** H5
Donnaconda *Canada* 46°41N 71°41W **73** C5
Donnelly's Crossing
　N.Z. 35°42S 173°38E **59** A4
Donner Pass *U.S.A.* 39°19N 120°20W **78** F6
Donnybrook *Australia* 33°34S 115°48E **61** F2
Donnybrook *S. Africa* 29°59S 29°48E **57** D4
Donora *U.S.A.* 40°11N 79°52W **82** F5
Donostia = Donostia-San
　Sebastián *Spain* 43°17N 1°58W **21** A5
Donostia-San Sebastián
　Spain 43°17N 1°58W **21** A5
Donwood *Canada* 44°19N 78°16W **82** B6
Doomadgee *Australia* 17°56S 138°49E **62** B2
Doomadgee ۞ *Australia* 17°56S 138°49E **62** B2
Doon → *U.K.* 55°27N 4°39W **11** F4
Doon Doon ۞ *Australia* 16°18S 128°14E **60** C4
Dora, L. *Australia* 22°0S 123°0E **60** D3
Dora Báltea → *Italy* 45°11N 8°3E **20** D8
Doran L. *Canada* 61°13N 108°6W **71** A7
Dorchester *U.K.* 50°42N 2°27W **13** G5
Dorchester, C. *Canada* 65°27N 77°27W **69** D16
Dordabis *Namibia* 22°52S 17°38E **56** B2
Dordogne □ *France* 45°2N 0°36W **20** D3
Dordogne → *France* 45°2N 0°36W **20** D3
Dordrecht *Neths.* 51°48N 4°39E **15** C4
Dordrecht *S. Africa* 31°20S 27°3E **56** D4
Doré L. *Canada* 54°46N 107°17W **71** C7
Dori *Burkina Faso* 14°3N 0°2W **52** F5
Doring → *S. Africa* 31°54S 18°39E **56** E2
Doringbos *S. Africa* 31°59S 19°16E **56** E2
Dorking *U.K.* 51°14N 0°19W **13** F7
Dornakal *India* 17°27N 80°10E **44** F5
Dornbirn *Austria* 47°25N 9°45E **16** E5
Dornie *U.K.* 57°17N 5°31W **11** D3
Dornoch *Canada* 44°18N 80°51W **82** B4
Dornoch *U.K.* 57°53N 4°2W **11** D4
Dornoch Firth *U.K.* 57°51N 4°4W **11** D4
Dornogovĭ □ *Mongolia* 44°0N 110°0E **32** B6
Doro, Kavo *Greece* 38°9N 24°38E **23** E11
Dorohoi *Romania* 47°56N 26°23E **17** E14
Döröö Nuur *Mongolia* 48°0N 93°0E **30** B7
Dorr *Iran* 33°17N 50°38E **47** C6
Dorre I. *Australia* 25°13S 113°12E **61** E1

Dorrigo *Australia* 30°20S 152°44E **63** E5
Dorris *U.S.A.* 41°58N 121°55W **76** F3
Dorset *Canada* 45°14N 78°54W **82** A6
Dorset *Ohio, U.S.A.* 41°40N 80°40W **82** E4
Dorset *Vt., U.S.A.* 43°15N 73°5W **83** C11
Dorset □ *U.K.* 50°45N 2°26W **13** G5
Dortmund *Germany* 51°30N 7°28E **16** C4
Dörtyol *Turkey* 36°50N 36°13E **46** B3
Dorūneh *Iran* 35°10N 57°18E **47** C8
Dos Bahías, C. *Argentina* 44°58S 65°32W **96** E3
Dos Hermanas *Spain* 37°16N 5°55W **21** D3
Dos Palos *U.S.A.* 36°59N 120°37W **78** J6
Dosso *Niger* 13°0N 3°13E **52** F6
Dothan *U.S.A.* 31°13N 85°24W **85** F12
Doty *U.S.A.* 46°38N 123°17W **78** D3
Douai *France* 50°21N 3°4E **15** D3
Douala *Cameroon* 4°0N 9°45E **54** D1
Douarnenez *France* 48°6N 4°21W **20** B1
Double Island Pt.
　Australia 25°56S 153°11E **63** D5
Double Mountain Fork →
　U.S.A. 33°16N 100°0W **84** E4
Doubs □ *France* 46°53N 5°1E **20** C6
Doubs → *France* 46°53N 5°1E **20** C6
Doubtful Sd. *N.Z.* 45°20S 166°49E **59** F1
Doubtless B. *N.Z.* 34°55S 173°26E **59** A4
Douglas *Canada* 45°31N 76°56W **82** A8
Douglas *I. of Man* 54°10N 4°28W **12** C3
Douglas *S. Africa* 29°4S 23°46E **56** C3
Douglas *Ariz., U.S.A.* 31°21N 109°33W **77** L9
Douglas *Ga., U.S.A.* 31°31N 82°51W **85** F13
Douglas *Wyo., U.S.A.* 42°45N 105°24W **76** E11
Douglas Apsley △
　Australia 41°45S 148°11E **63** G4
Douglas Chan. *Canada* 53°40N 129°20W **70** C3
Douglas Pt. *Canada* 44°19N 81°37W **82** B3
Douglasville *U.S.A.* 33°45N 84°45W **85** E12
Doumen *China* 22°10N 113°18E **35** F9
Dounreay *U.K.* 58°35N 3°44W **11** C5
Dourada, Serra *Brazil* 13°10S 48°45W **93** F9
Dourados *Brazil* 22°9S 54°50W **95** A5
Dourados → *Brazil* 21°58S 54°18W **95** A5
Dourados, Serra dos
　Brazil 23°30S 53°30W **95** A5
Douro → *Europe* 41°8N 8°40W **21** B1
Dove → *U.K.* 52°51N 1°36W **12** E6
Dove Creek *U.S.A.* 37°46N 108°54W **77** H9
Dover *Australia* 43°18S 147°2E **63** G4
Dover *U.K.* 51°7N 1°19E **13** F9
Dover *Del., U.S.A.* 39°10N 75°32W **81** F16
Dover *N.H., U.S.A.* 43°12N 70°56W **83** C14
Dover *N.J., U.S.A.* 40°53N 74°34W **83** F10
Dover *Ohio, U.S.A.* 40°32N 81°29W **82** F3
Dover, Pt. *Australia* 32°32S 125°32E **61** F4
Dover, Str. of *Europe* 51°0N 1°30E **13** G9
Dover-Foxcroft *U.S.A.* 45°11N 69°13W **81** C19
Dover Plains *U.S.A.* 41°43N 73°35W **83** E11
Dovey = Dyfi → *U.K.* 52°32N 4°3W **13** E3
Dovrefjell *Norway* 62°15N 9°33E **8** E13
Dow Rūd *Iran* 33°28N 49°4E **47** C6
Dowagiac *U.S.A.* 41°59N 86°6W **80** E10
Dowerin *Australia* 31°12S 117°2E **61** F2
Dowgha'i *Iran* 36°54N 58°32E **47** B8
Dowlatābād *Kermān, Iran* 28°20N 56°40E **47** D8
Dowlatābād *Khorāsān,
　Iran* 35°16N 59°29E **47** C8
Down □ *U.K.* 54°23N 6°2W **10** B5
Downey *U.S.A.* 42°26N 112°7W **76** E7
Downham Market *U.K.* 52°37N 0°23E **13** E8
Downieville *U.S.A.* 39°34N 120°50W **78** F6
Downpatrick *U.K.* 54°20N 5°43W **10** B6
Downpatrick Hd. *Ireland* 54°20N 9°21W **10** B2
Downsville *U.S.A.* 42°5N 75°0W **83** D9
Downton, Mt. *Canada* 52°42N 124°52W **70** C4
Dowsāri *Iran* 28°25N 57°59E **47** D8
Doyle *U.S.A.* 40°2N 120°6W **78** E6
Doylestown *U.S.A.* 40°21N 75°10W **83** F9
Dozois, Rés. *Canada* 47°30N 77°5W **72** C4
Dra Khel *Pakistan* 27°58N 66°45E **42** F2
Drâa, C. *Morocco* 28°47N 11°0W **52** C3
Drâa, Hamada du *Algeria* 28°0N 6°0W **52** C4
Drâa, Oued → *Morocco* 28°40N 11°10W **52** C3
Drachten *Neths.* 53°7N 6°5E **15** A6
Drăgăşani *Romania* 44°39N 24°17E **17** F13
Dragichyn *Belarus* 52°15N 25°8E **17** B13
Dragoman, Prokhod
　Bulgaria 42°58N 22°53E **23** C10
Dragon's Mouths
　Trin. & Tob. 11°0N 61°50W **93** K15
Draguignan *France* 43°32N 6°27E **20** E7
Drain *U.S.A.* 43°40N 123°19W **76** E2
Drake *U.S.A.* 47°55N 100°23W **80** B3
Drake Passage *S. Ocean* 58°0S 68°0W **5** B17
Drakensberg *S. Africa* 31°0S 28°0E **57** D4
Drama *Greece* 41°9N 24°10E **23** D11
Drammen *Norway* 59°42N 10°12E **9** G14
Drangajökull *Iceland* 66°9N 22°15W **8** C2
Dras *India* 34°25N 75°48E **43** B6
Drau = Drava → *Croatia* 45°33N 18°55E **23** B8
Drava → *Croatia* 45°33N 18°55E **23** B8
Drayton *Canada* 43°46N 80°40W **82** C4
Drayton Valley *Canada* 53°12N 114°58W **70** C6
Drenthe □ *Neths.* 52°52N 6°40E **15** B6
Dresden *Canada* 42°35N 82°11W **82** D2
Dresden *Germany* 51°3N 13°44E **16** C7
Dresden *U.S.A.* 42°41N 76°57W **82** D8
Dreux *France* 48°44N 1°23E **20** B4
Driffield *U.K.* 54°0N 0°26W **12** C7
Driftwood *U.S.A.* 41°20N 78°8W **82** E6
Driggs *U.S.A.* 43°44N 111°6W **76** E8
Drin → *Albania* 41°39N 19°38E **23** C8
Drina → *Bos.-H.* 44°53N 19°21E **23** B8
Drøbak *Norway* 59°39N 10°39E **9** G14
Drobeta-Turnu Severin
　Romania 44°39N 22°41E **17** F12
Drochia *Moldova* 48°2N 27°48E **17** D14
Drogheda *Ireland* 53°43N 6°22W **10** C5
Drogichin = Dragichyn
　Belarus 52°15N 25°8E **17** B13
Drogobych = Drohobych
　Ukraine 49°20N 23°30E **17** D12

Drohobych *Ukraine* 49°20N 23°30E **17 D12**
Droichead Átha = Drogheda
  Ireland 53°43N 6°22W **10 C5**
Droichead na Bandan = Bandon
  Ireland 51°44N 8°44W **10 E3**
Droichead Nua = Newbridge
  Ireland 53°11N 6°48W **10 C5**
Droitwich *U.K.* 52°16N 2°8W **13 E5**
Drôme → *France* 44°46N 4°46E **20 D6**
Dromedary, C. *Australia* 36°17S 150°10E **63 F5**
Dromore *Down, U.K.* 54°25N 6°9W **10 B5**
Dromore *Tyrone, U.K.* 54°31N 7°28W **10 B4**
Dromore West *Ireland* 54°15N 8°52W **10 B3**
Dronfield *U.K.* 53°19N 1°27W **12 D6**
Dronning Maud Land
  Antarctica 72°30S 12°0E **5 D3**
Dronten *Neths.* 52°32N 5°43E **15 B5**
Druk Yul = Bhutan ■
  Asia 27°25N 90°30E **41 F17**
Drumbo *Canada* 43°16N 80°35W **82 C4**
Drumcliff *Ireland* 54°20N 8°29W **10 B3**
Drumheller *Canada* 51°25N 112°40W **70 C6**
Drummond *U.S.A.* 46°40N 113°9W **76 C7**
Drummond I. *U.S.A.* 46°1N 83°39W **72 C4**
Drummond Pt. *Australia* 34°9S 135°16E **63 E2**
Drummond Ra.
  Australia 23°45S 147°10E **62 C4**
Drummondville *Canada* 45°55N 72°25W **72 C5**
Drumright *U.S.A.* 35°59N 96°36W **84 D6**
Druskininkai *Lithuania* 54°3N 23°58E **9 J20**
Drut → *Belarus* 53°8N 30°5E **17 B16**
Druzhina *Russia* 68°14N 145°18E **27 C15**
Dry Harbour Mts. *Jamaica* 18°19N 77°24W **88 a**
Dry Tortugas *U.S.A.* 24°38N 82°55W **85 J13**
Dryander △ *Australia* 20°13S 148°34E **62 b**
Dryden *Canada* 49°47N 92°50W **71 D10**
Dryden *U.S.A.* 42°30N 76°18W **83 D8**
Drygalski I. *Antarctica* 66°0S 92°0E **5 C7**
Drygalski Ice Tongue
  Antarctica 75°24S 163°30E **5 D11**
Drysdale → *Australia* 13°59S 126°51E **60 B4**
Drysdale I. *Australia* 11°41S 136°0E **62 A2**
Drysdale River △
  Australia 14°56S 127°2E **60 B4**
Du Gué → *Canada* 57°21N 70°45W **72 A5**
Du He → *China* 32°48N 110°40E **35 A8**
Du Quoin *U.S.A.* 38°1N 89°14W **80 G1**
Du'an *China* 23°59N 108°3E **34 F7**
Duanesburg *U.S.A.* 42°45N 74°11W **83 D10**
Duaringa *Australia* 23°42S 149°42E **62 C4**
Duarte, Pico *Dom. Rep.* 19°2N 70°59W **89 C5**
Dubãsari *Moldova* 47°15N 29°10E **17 E15**
Dubãsari Vdkhr. *Moldova* 47°30N 29°0E **17 E15**
Dubawnt → *Canada* 64°33N 100°6W **71 A8**
Dubawnt L. *Canada* 63°8N 101°28W **71 A8**
Dubbo *Australia* 32°11S 148°35E **63 E4**
Dublin, Ga., U.S.A. 32°32N 82°54W **85 E13**
Dublin *Tex., U.S.A.* 32°5N 98°21W **84 E5**
Dublin □ *Ireland* 53°24N 6°20W **10 C5**
Dubno *Ukraine* 50°25N 25°45E **17 C13**
DuBois *Idaho, U.S.A.* 44°10N 112°14W **76 D7**
DuBois *Pa., U.S.A.* 41°7N 78°46W **82 E6**
Dubossary = Dubãsari
  Moldova 47°15N 29°10E **17 E15**
Dubossary Vdkhr. = Dubãsari
  Vdkhr. *Moldova* 47°30N 29°0E **17 E15**
Dubovka *Russia* 49°5N 44°50E **19 E7**
Dubrajpur *India* 23°48N 87°25E **43 H12**
Dubréka *Guinea* 9°46N 13°31W **52 G3**
Dubrovitsa = Dubrovytsya
  Ukraine 51°31N 26°35E **17 C14**
Dubrovnik *Croatia* 42°39N 18°6E **23 C8**
Dubrovytsya *Ukraine* 51°31N 26°35E **17 C14**
Dubuque *U.S.A.* 42°30N 90°41W **80 D8**
Duc Tho *Vietnam* 18°32N 105°35E **38 C5**
Duchang *China* 29°18N 116°12E **35 C11**
Duchesne *U.S.A.* 40°10N 110°24W **76 F8**
Duchess *Australia* 21°20S 139°50E **62 C2**
Ducie I. *Pac. Oc.* 24°40S 124°48W **65 K15**
Duck → *Canada* 36°2N 87°52W **85 C11**
Duck Cr. → *Australia* 22°37S 116°53E **60 D2**
Duck Lake *Canada* 52°50N 106°16W **71 C7**
Duck Mountain △
  Canada 51°45N 101°0W **71 C8**
Duckwall, Mt. *U.S.A.* 37°58N 120°7W **78 H6**
Dudhi *India* 24°15N 83°10E **43 G10**
Dudley *U.K.* 52°31N 2°5W **13 E5**
Dudna → *India* 19°17N 76°54E **44 E3**
Dudwa *India* 28°30N 80°41E **43 E9**
Dudwa △ *India* 28°30N 80°40E **43 E9**
Duero = Douro → *Europe* 41°8N 8°40W **21 B1**
Dufftown *U.K.* 57°27N 3°8W **11 D5**
Dugi Otok *Croatia* 44°0N 15°3E **16 G8**
Duisburg *Germany* 51°26N 6°45E **16 C4**
Duiwelskloof = Modjadjiskloof
  S. Africa 23°42S 30°10E **57 B5**
Dujiangyan *China* 31°2N 103°38E **34 B4**
Dükdamin *Iran* 35°59N 57°43E **47 C8**
Dukelský Průsmyk
  Slovak Rep. 49°25N 21°42E **17 D11**
Dukhãn *Qatar* 25°25N 50°50E **47 E6**
Duki *Pakistan* 30°14N 68°25E **40 D6**
Duku *Nigeria* 10°43N 10°43E **53 F8**
Dulan *China* 36°0N 97°11E **30 D8**
Dulce *U.S.A.* 36°56N 107°0W **77 H10**
Dulce → *Argentina* 30°32S 62°33W **94 C3**
Dulce, G. *Costa Rica* 8°40N 83°20W **88 E3**
Dulf *Iraq* 35°7N 45°51E **46 C5**
Duliu *China* 39°2N 116°55E **32 E9**
Dullewala *Pakistan* 31°50N 71°25E **42 D4**
Dullstroom *S. Africa* 25°27S 30°7E **57 C5**
Dulq Maghār *Syria* 36°22N 38°39E **46 B3**
Duluth *U.S.A.* 46°47N 92°6W **80 B7**
Dum Duma *India* 27°40N 95°40E **41 F19**
Dūmā *Syria* 33°34N 36°24E **48 B5**
Dumaguete *Phil.* 9°17N 123°15E **37 C6**
Dumai *Indonesia* 1°35N 101°28E **36 D2**
Dumaran *Phil.* 10°33N 119°50E **37 B5**

Dumas *Ark., U.S.A.* 33°53N 91°29W **84 E9**
Dumas *Tex., U.S.A.* 35°52N 101°58W **84 D4**
Dumayr *Syria* 33°39N 36°42E **48 B5**
Dumbarton *U.K.* 55°57N 4°33W **11 F4**
Dumbleyung *Australia* 33°17S 117°42E **61 F2**
Dumfries *U.K.* 55°4N 3°37W **11 F5**
Dumfries & Galloway □
  U.K. 55°9N 3°58W **11 F5**
Dumka *India* 24°12N 87°15E **43 G12**
Dumoine → *Canada* 46°13N 77°51W **72 C4**
Dumoine, L. *Canada* 46°55N 77°55W **72 C4**
Dumont d'Urville
  Antarctica 66°40S 140°0E **5 C10**
Dumont d'Urville Sea
  S. Ocean 63°30S 138°0E **5 C9**
Dumyât *Egypt* 31°24N 31°48E **53 B12**
Dún Dealgan = Dundalk
  Ireland 54°1N 6°24W **10 B5**
Dún Garbhán = Dungarvan
  Ireland 52°5N 7°37W **10 D4**
Duna = Dunãrea →
  Europe 45°20N 29°40E **17 F15**
Dunagiri *India* 30°31N 79°52E **43 D8**
Dunaj = Dunãrea →
  Europe 45°20N 29°40E **17 F15**
Dunakeszi *Hungary* 47°37N 19°8E **17 E10**
Dunãrea → *Europe* 45°20N 29°40E **17 F15**
Dunaújváros *Hungary* 46°58N 18°57E **17 E10**
Dunav = Dunãrea →
  Europe 45°20N 29°40E **17 F15**
Dunay *Russia* 42°52N 132°22E **28 C6**
Dunback *N.Z.* 45°23S 170°36E **59 F3**
Dunbar *U.K.* 56°0N 2°31W **11 E6**
Dunblane *U.K.* 56°11N 3°58W **11 E5**
Duncan *Canada* 48°45N 123°40W **78 B3**
Duncan *Ariz., U.S.A.* 32°43N 109°6W **77 K9**
Duncan *Okla., U.S.A.* 34°30N 97°57W **84 D6**
Duncan, L. *Canada* 53°29N 77°58W **72 B4**
Duncan, L. *Canada* 62°51N 113°58W **70 A6**
Duncan Passage *India* 11°0N 92°0E **45 J11**
Duncan Town *Bahamas* 22°15N 75°45W **88 B4**
Duncannon *U.S.A.* 40°23N 77°2W **82 F7**
Duncansby Head *U.K.* 58°38N 3°1W **11 C5**
Duncansville *U.S.A.* 40°25N 78°26W **82 F6**
Dund-Us *Mongolia* 48°1N 91°38E **30 B7**
Dundalk *Canada* 44°10N 80°24W **82 B4**
Dundalk *Ireland* 54°1N 6°24W **10 B5**
Dundalk *U.S.A.* 39°15N 76°31W **81 F15**
Dundalk Bay *Ireland* 53°55N 6°15W **10 C5**
Dundas = Uummannaq
  Greenland 77°33N 68°52W **69 B18**
Dundas *Canada* 43°17N 79°59W **82 D5**
Dundas, L. *Australia* 32°35S 121°50E **61 F3**
Dundas I. *Canada* 54°30N 130°50W **70 C2**
Dundas Str. *Australia* 11°15S 131°35E **60 B5**
Dundee *S. Africa* 28°11S 30°15E **57 C5**
Dundee *U.K.* 56°28N 2°59W **11 E6**
Dundee *U.S.A.* 42°32N 76°59W **82 D8**
Dundee City □ *U.K.* 56°30N 2°58W **11 E6**
Dundgovi □ *Mongolia* 45°10N 106°0E **32 B4**
Dundrum *U.K.* 54°16N 5°52W **10 B6**
Dundrum B. *U.K.* 54°13N 5°47W **10 B6**
Dunedin *N.Z.* 45°50S 170°33E **59 F3**
Dunedin *U.S.A.* 28°1N 82°46W **85 G13**
Dunfanaghy *Ireland* 55°11N 7°58W **10 A4**
Dunfermline *U.K.* 56°5N 3°27W **11 E5**
Dungannon *Canada* 43°51N 81°36W **82 C3**
Dungannon *U.K.* 54°31N 6°46W **10 B5**
Dungarpur *India* 23°52N 73°45E **42 H5**
Dungarvan *Ireland* 52°5N 7°37W **10 D4**
Dungarvan Harbour
  Ireland 52°4N 7°35W **10 D4**
Dungeness *U.K.* 50°54N 0°59E **13 G8**
Dungiven *U.K.* 54°56N 6°56W **10 B5**
Dunglow *Ireland* 54°57N 8°21W **10 B3**
Dungo, L. do *Angola* 17°15S 19°0E **56 A2**
Dungog *Australia* 32°22S 151°46E **63 E5**
Dungu
  Dem. Rep. of the Congo 3°40N 28°32E **54 D5**
Dungun *Malaysia* 4°45N 103°25E **39 K4**
Dunhua *China* 43°20N 128°14E **33 C15**
Dunhuang *China* 40°8N 94°36E **30 C7**
Dunk I. *Australia* 17°59S 146°29E **62 B4**
Dunkeld *Australia* 33°25S 149°29E **63 E4**
Dunkeld *U.K.* 56°34N 3°35W **11 E5**
Dunkerque *France* 51°2N 2°20E **20 A5**
Dunkery Beacon *U.K.* 51°9N 3°36W **13 F4**
Dunkirk = Dunkerque
  France 51°2N 2°20E **20 A5**
Dunkirk *U.S.A.* 42°29N 79°20W **82 D5**
Dunleer *Ireland* 53°50N 6°24W **10 C5**
Dunmanus B. *Ireland* 51°31N 9°50W **10 E2**
Dunmanway *Ireland* 51°43N 9°6W **10 E2**
Dunmarra *Australia* 16°42S 133°25E **62 B1**
Dunmore *U.S.A.* 41°25N 75°38W **83 E9**
Dunmore East *Ireland* 52°9N 7°0W **10 D5**
Dunmore Town
  Bahamas 25°30N 76°39W **88 A4**
Dunn *U.S.A.* 35°19N 78°37W **85 D15**
Dunnellon *U.S.A.* 29°3N 82°28W **85 G13**
Dunnet Hd. *U.K.* 58°40N 3°21W **11 C5**
Dunning *U.S.A.* 41°50N 100°6W **80 E3**
Dunnville *Canada* 42°54N 79°36W **82 D5**
Dunolly *Australia* 36°51S 143°44E **63 F3**
Dunoon *U.K.* 55°57N 4°56W **11 F4**
Duns *U.K.* 55°47N 2°20W **11 F6**
Dunseith *U.S.A.* 48°50N 100°3W **80 A3**
Dunshaughlin *Ireland* 53°31N 6°33W **10 C5**
Dunsmuir *U.S.A.* 41°13N 122°16W **76 F2**
Dunstable *U.K.* 51°53N 0°32W **13 F7**
Dunstan Mts. *N.Z.* 44°53S 169°35E **59 F2**
Dunster *Canada* 53°8N 119°50W **70 C5**
Dunvegan *U.K.* 57°27N 6°35W **11 D2**
Dunvegan L. *Canada* 60°8N 107°10W **71 A7**
Duolun *China* 42°12N 116°28E **32 C9**
Duong Dong *Vietnam* 10°13N 103°58E **39 G4**
Dupree *U.S.A.* 45°4N 101°35W **80 C3**
Dupuyer *U.S.A.* 48°13N 112°30W **76 B7**
Durack → *Australia* 15°33S 127°52E **60 C4**

Durack Ra. *Australia* 16°50S 127°40E **60 C4**
Durack River *Australia* 15°33S 127°39E **60 C4**
Durance → *France* 43°55N 4°45E **20 E6**
Durand *U.S.A.* 44°38N 91°58W **80 C8**
Durango *Mexico* 24°3N 104°39W **86 C4**
Durango □ *Mexico* 37°16N 107°53W **77 H10**
Durango □ *Mexico* 24°50N 105°20W **86 C4**
Durant *Miss., U.S.A.* 33°4N 89°51W **85 E10**
Durant *Okla., U.S.A.* 33°59N 96°25W **84 E6**
Durazno *Uruguay* 33°25S 56°31W **94 C4**
Durazzo = Durrës
  Albania 41°19N 19°28E **23 D8**
Durban *S. Africa* 29°49S 31°1E **57 C5**
Durban ✈ (DIA) *S. Africa* 29°37S 31°7E **57 C5**
Durbuy *Belgium* 50°21N 5°28E **15 D5**
Düren *Germany* 50°48N 6°29E **16 C4**
Durg = Bhilainagar-Durg
  India 21°13N 81°26E **44 D5**
Durgapur *India* 23°30N 87°20E **43 H12**
Durham *Canada* 44°10N 80°49W **82 B4**
Durham *U.K.* 54°47N 1°34W **12 C6**
Durham *Calif., U.S.A.* 39°39N 121°48W **78 F5**
Durham *N.C., U.S.A.* 35°59N 78°54W **85 D15**
Durham *N.H., U.S.A.* 43°8N 70°56W **83 C14**
Durham □ *U.K.* 54°42N 1°45W **12 C6**
Durlas = Thurles *Ireland* 52°41N 7°49W **10 D4**
Durmã *Si. Arabia* 24°37N 46°8E **46 E5**
Durmitor *Montenegro* 43°10N 19°0E **23 C8**
Durness *U.K.* 58°34N 4°45W **11 C4**
Durrës *Albania* 41°19N 19°28E **23 D8**
Durrow *Ireland* 52°51N 7°24W **10 D4**
Dursey I. *Ireland* 51°36N 10°12W **10 E1**
Dursley *U.K.* 51°40N 2°21W **13 F5**
Dursunbey *Turkey* 39°35N 28°37E **23 E13**
Durūz, Jabal ad *Jordan* 32°35N 36°40E **48 C5**
D'Urville, Tanjung
  Indonesia 1°28S 137°54E **37 E9**
D'Urville I. *N.Z.* 40°50S 173°55E **59 D4**
Duryea *U.S.A.* 41°20N 75°45W **83 E9**
Dushak *Turkmenistan* 37°13N 60°1E **47 B9**
Dushan *China* 25°48N 107°30E **34 E6**
Dushanbe *Tajikistan* 38°33N 68°48E **26 F7**
Dushore *U.S.A.* 41°31N 76°24W **83 E8**
Dusky Sd. *N.Z.* 45°47S 166°30E **59 F1**
Dussejour, C. *Australia* 14°45S 128°13E **60 B4**
Düsseldorf *Germany* 51°14N 6°47E **16 C4**
Dutch Harbor *U.S.A.* 53°53N 166°32W **74 E6**
Dutlwe *Botswana* 23°58S 23°46E **56 B3**
Dutton *Canada* 42°39N 81°30W **82 D3**
Dutton → *Australia* 20°44S 143°10E **62 C3**
Dutywa *S. Africa* 32°8S 28°18E **57 D4**
Duwayhin, Khawr
  U.A.E. 24°20N 51°25E **47 E6**
Duyfken Pt. *Australia* 12°33S 141°38E **62 A3**
Duyun *China* 26°18N 107°29E **34 D6**
Dvina, Severnaya →
  Russia 64°32N 40°30E **18 B7**
Dvinsk = Daugavpils
  Latvia 55°53N 26°32E **9 J22**
Dvinskaya Guba *Russia* 65°0N 39°0E **18 B6**
Dwarka *India* 22°18N 69°8E **42 H3**
Dwellingup *Australia* 32°43S 116°4E **61 F2**
Dwight *Canada* 45°20N 79°1W **82 A5**
Dwight *U.S.A.* 41°5N 88°26W **80 E9**
Dyatlovo = Dzyatlava
  Belarus 53°28N 25°28E **17 B13**
Dyce *U.K.* 57°13N 2°12W **11 D6**
Dyer, C. *Canada* 66°37N 61°16W **69 D19**
Dyer Bay *Canada* 45°10N 81°20W **82 A3**
Dyer Plateau *Antarctica* 70°45S 65°30W **5 D17**
Dyersburg *U.S.A.* 36°3N 89°23W **85 C10**
Dyfi → *U.K.* 52°32N 4°3W **13 E3**
Dymer *Ukraine* 50°47N 30°18E **17 C16**
Dysart *Australia* 22°32S 148°23E **62 C4**
Dzaoudzi *Mayotte* 12°47S 45°16E **55 a**
Dzavhan Gol →
  Mongolia 48°54N 93°23E **30 B7**
Dzerzhinsk *Russia* 56°14N 43°30E **18 C7**
Dzhalinda *Russia* 53°26N 124°0E **27 D13**
Dzhambul = Taraz
  Kazakhstan 42°54N 71°22E **30 C3**
Dzhankoy *Ukraine* 45°40N 34°20E **19 E5**
Dzhezkazgan = Zhezqazghan
  Kazakhstan 47°44N 67°40E **26 E7**
Dzhizak = Jizzax
  Uzbekistan 40°6N 67°50E **26 E7**
Dzhugdzur, Khrebet
  Russia 57°30N 138°0E **27 D14**
Dzhungarskiye Vorota =
  Dzungarian Gate *Asia* 45°10N 82°0E **30 B5**
Działdowo *Poland* 53°15N 20°15E **17 B11**
Dzibilchaltún *Mexico* 21°10N 89°35W **87 C7**
Dzierżoniów *Poland* 50°45N 16°39E **17 C9**
Dzilam de Bravo *Mexico* 21°24N 88°53W **87 C7**
Dzükija △ *Lithuania* 54°10N 24°30E **9 J21**
Dzungarian Basin = Junggar Pendi
  China 44°30N 86°0E **30 C6**
Dzungarian Gate *Asia* 45°10N 82°0E **30 B5**
Dzüünbayan *Mongolia* 44°29N 110°2E **32 B6**
Dzüünharaa *Mongolia* 48°52N 106°28E **30 B10**
Dzüünmod *Mongolia* 47°45N 106°58E **30 B10**
Dzyarzhynsk *Belarus* 53°40N 27°1E **17 B14**
Dzyatlava *Belarus* 53°28N 25°28E **17 B13**

E

E.C. Manning △ *Canada* 49°5N 120°45W **70 D4**
Eabamet L. *Canada* 51°30N 87°46W **72 B2**
Eabametoong *Canada* 51°30N 88°0W **72 B2**
Éadan Doire = Edenderry
  Ireland 53°21N 7°4W **10 C4**
Eads *U.S.A.* 38°29N 102°47W **76 G12**
Eagar *U.S.A.* 34°6N 109°17W **77 J9**
Eagle *Alaska, U.S.A.* 64°47N 141°12W **68 C5**
Eagle *Colo., U.S.A.* 39°39N 106°50W **76 G10**
Eagle → *Canada* 53°36N 57°26W **73 B8**
Eagle Butte *U.S.A.* 45°0N 101°10W **80 C3**
Eagle Grove *U.S.A.* 42°40N 93°54W **80 D7**
Eagle L. *Canada* 49°42N 93°13W **71 D10**

Eagle L. *Calif., U.S.A.* 40°39N 120°45W **76 F3**
Eagle L. *Maine, U.S.A.* 46°20N 69°22W **81 B19**
Eagle Lake *Canada* 45°8N 78°29W **82 A6**
Eagle Lake *Maine, U.S.A.* 47°3N 68°36W **81 B19**
Eagle Lake *Tex., U.S.A.* 29°35N 96°20W **84 G6**
Eagle Mountain
  U.S.A. 33°49N 115°27W **79 M11**
Eagle Nest *U.S.A.* 36°33N 105°16W **77 H11**
Eagle Pass *U.S.A.* 28°43N 100°30W **84 G4**
Eagle Pk. *U.S.A.* 38°10N 119°25W **78 G7**
Eagle Pt. *Australia* 16°11S 124°23E **60 C3**
Eagle River *Mich., U.S.A.* 47°25N 88°18W **80 B9**
Eagle River *Wis., U.S.A.* 45°55N 89°15W **80 C9**
Eaglehawk *Australia* 36°44S 144°15E **63 F3**
Eagles Mere *U.S.A.* 41°25N 76°33W **83 E8**
Ear Falls *Canada* 50°38N 93°13W **71 C10**
Earlimart *U.S.A.* 35°53N 119°16W **79 K7**
Earn → *U.K.* 56°21N 3°18W **11 E5**
Earn, L. *U.K.* 56°23N 4°13W **11 E4**
Earnslaw, Mt. *N.Z.* 44°32S 168°27E **59 F2**
Earth *U.S.A.* 34°14N 102°24W **84 D3**
Easley *U.S.A.* 34°50N 82°36W **85 D13**
East Anglia *U.K.* 52°30N 1°0E **12 E9**
East Angus *Canada* 45°30N 71°40W **73 C5**
East Antarctica *Antarctica* 80°0S 90°0E **5 D7**
East Aurora *U.S.A.* 42°46N 78°37W **82 D6**
East Ayrshire □ *U.K.* 55°26N 4°11W **11 F4**
East Bengal *Bangla.* 24°0N 90°0E **41 G17**
East Beskids = Vychodné Beskydy
  Europe 49°20N 22°0E **17 D11**
East Brady *U.S.A.* 40°59N 79°37W **82 F5**
East Branch Clarion River L.
  U.S.A. 41°35N 78°35W **82 E6**
East C. = Dezhneva, Mys
  Russia 66°5N 169°40W **27 C19**
East C. *N.Z.* 37°42S 178°35E **59 B7**
East Caroline Basin
  Pac. Oc. 4°0N 146°45E **64 G6**
East Chicago *U.S.A.* 41°38N 87°27W **80 E10**
East China Sea *Asia* 30°0N 126°0E **31 F14**
East Coulee *Canada* 51°23N 112°27W **70 C6**
East Dereham = Dereham
  U.K. 52°41N 0°57E **13 E8**
East Dunbartonshire □
  U.K. 55°57N 4°13W **11 F4**
East Falkland *Falk. Is.* 51°30S 58°30W **96 G5**
East Grand Forks *U.S.A.* 47°56N 97°1W **80 B5**
East Greenwich *U.S.A.* 41°40N 71°27W **83 E13**
East Grinstead *U.K.* 51°7N 0°3E **13 F8**
East Hartford *U.S.A.* 41°46N 72°39W **83 E12**
East Haydon *Australia* 18°0S 141°30E **62 B3**
East Helena *U.S.A.* 46°35N 111°56W **76 C8**
East Indies *Asia* 0°0 120°0E **24 J14**
East Kilbride *U.K.* 55°47N 4°11W **11 F4**
East Lansing *U.S.A.* 42°44N 84°29W **81 D11**
East Liverpool *U.S.A.* 40°37N 80°35W **82 F4**
East London *S. Africa* 33°0S 27°55E **57 D4**
East Lothian □ *U.K.* 55°58N 2°44W **11 F6**
East Main = Eastmain
  Canada 52°10N 78°30W **72 B4**
East Mariana Basin
  Pac. Oc. 12°0N 153°0E **64 F7**
East Northport *U.S.A.* 40°53N 73°20W **83 F11**
East Orange *U.S.A.* 40°46N 74°12W **83 F10**
East Pacific Rise *Pac. Oc.* 15°0S 110°0W **65 J17**
East Palestine *U.S.A.* 40°50N 80°33W **82 F4**
East Pine *Canada* 55°48N 120°12W **70 B4**
East Providence *U.S.A.* 41°49N 71°23W **83 E13**
East Pt. *Br. Virgin Is.* 18°40N 64°18W **89 e**
East Pt. *Canada* 46°27N 61°58W **73 C7**
East Renfrewshire □ *U.K.* 55°46N 4°21W **11 F4**
East Retford = Retford
  U.K. 53°19N 0°56W **12 D7**
East Riding of Yorkshire □
  U.K. 53°55N 0°30W **12 D7**
East Rochester *U.S.A.* 43°7N 77°29W **82 C7**
East St. Louis *U.S.A.* 38°37N 90°9W **80 F8**
East Schelde = Oosterschelde →
  Neths. 51°33N 4°0E **15 C4**
East Sea = Japan, Sea of
  Asia 40°0N 135°0E **28 E7**
East Siberian Sea *Russia* 73°0N 160°0E **27 B17**
East Stroudsburg *U.S.A.* 41°1N 75°11W **83 E9**
East Sussex □ *U.K.* 50°56N 0°19E **13 G8**
East Tasman Plateau
  Pac. Oc. 43°30S 152°0E **64 M7**
East Tawas *U.S.A.* 44°17N 83°29W **81 C12**
East Timor ■ *Asia* 8°50S 126°0E **37 F7**
East Toorale *Australia* 30°27S 145°28E **63 E4**
East Walker → *U.S.A.* 38°52N 119°10W **78 G7**
East Windsor *U.S.A.* 40°17N 74°34W **83 F10**
Eastbourne *N.Z.* 41°19S 174°55E **59 D5**
Eastbourne *U.K.* 50°46N 0°18E **13 G8**
Eastend *Canada* 49°32N 108°50W **71 D7**
Easter Fracture Zone
  Pac. Oc. 25°0S 115°0W **65 K16**
Easter I. = Pascua, I. de
  Chile 27°7S 109°23W **65 K17**
Eastern Cape □ *S. Africa* 32°0S 26°0E **56 D4**
Eastern Cr. → *Australia* 20°40S 141°35E **62 C3**
Eastern Desert = Es Sahrâ' Esh
  Sharqîya *Egypt* 27°30N 32°30E **53 C12**
Eastern Ghats *India* 14°0N 78°50E **45 N11**
Eastern Group = Lau Group
  Fiji 17°0S 178°30W **59 a**
Eastern Group *Australia* 33°30S 124°30E **61 F3**
Eastern Guruma ☉
  Australia 22°0S 117°30E **60 D2**
Eastern Transvaal =
  Mpumalanga □ *S. Africa* 26°0S 30°0E **57 B5**
Easterville *Canada* 53°8N 99°49W **71 C9**
Easthampton *U.S.A.* 42°16N 72°40W **83 D12**
Eastlake *U.S.A.* 41°40N 81°26W **82 E3**
Eastland *U.S.A.* 32°24N 98°49W **84 E5**
Eastleigh *U.K.* 50°58N 1°21W **13 G6**
Eastmain *Canada* 52°10N 78°30W **72 B4**
Eastmain → *Canada* 52°27N 78°26W **72 B4**
Eastman *Canada* 45°18N 72°19W **83 A12**

Eastman *U.S.A.* 32°12N 83°11W **85 E13**
Easton *Md., U.S.A.* 38°47N 76°5W **81 F15**
Easton *Pa., U.S.A.* 40°41N 75°13W **83 F9**
Easton *Wash., U.S.A.* 47°14N 121°11W **78 C5**
Eastport *U.S.A.* 44°56N 67°0W **81 C20**
Eastsound *U.S.A.* 48°42N 122°55W **78 B4**
Eaton *U.S.A.* 40°32N 104°42W **76 F11**
Eatonia *Canada* 51°13N 109°25W **71 C7**
Eatonton *U.S.A.* 33°20N 83°23W **85 E13**
Eatontown *U.S.A.* 40°19N 74°4W **83 F10**
Eatonville *U.S.A.* 46°52N 122°16W **78 D4**
Eau Claire *U.S.A.* 44°49N 91°30W **80 C8**
Eau Claire, L. à l' *Canada* 56°10N 74°25W **72 A5**
Eauripik Rise *Pac. Oc.* 2°0N 142°0E **64 G6**
Ebano *Mexico* 22°13N 98°24W **87 C5**
Ebbw Vale *U.K.* 51°46N 3°12W **13 F4**
Ebeltoft *Denmark* 56°12N 10°41E **9 H14**
Ebensburg *U.S.A.* 40°29N 78°44W **82 F6**
Eberswalde-Finow
  Germany 52°50N 13°49E **16 B7**
Ebetsu *Japan* 43°7N 141°34E **28 C10**
Ebey's Landing △
  U.S.A. 48°12N 122°41W **78 B4**
Ebian *China* 29°11N 103°13E **34 C4**
Ebinur Hu *China* 44°55N 82°55E **30 C5**
Ebolowa *Cameroon* 2°55N 11°10E **54 D2**
Ebonda
  Dem. Rep. of the Congo 2°12N 22°21E **54 D4**
Ebre = Ebro → *Spain* 40°43N 0°54E **21 B6**
Ebro → *Spain* 40°43N 0°54E **21 B6**
Ecatepec de Morelos
  Mexico 19°36N 99°3W **87 D5**
Ecbatana = Hamadãn
  Iran 34°52N 48°32E **47 C6**
Eceabat *Turkey* 40°11N 26°21E **23 D12**
Ech Chéliff *Algeria* 36°10N 1°20E **52 A6**
Echigo-Sammyaku
  Japan 36°50N 139°50E **29 F9**
Echizen *Japan* 35°50N 136°10E **29 G8**
Echizen-Misaki *Japan* 35°59N 135°57E **29 G7**
Echo Bay *N.W.T., Canada* 66°5N 117°55W **68 D8**
Echo Bay *Ont., Canada* 46°29N 84°4W **72 C3**
Echoing → *Canada* 55°51N 92°5W **72 B1**
Echternach *Lux.* 49°49N 6°25E **15 E6**
Echuca *Australia* 36°10S 144°45E **63 F3**
Écija *Spain* 37°30N 5°10W **21 D3**
Eclipse I. *Australia* 35°5S 117°58E **61 G2**
Eclipse Is. *Australia* 13°54S 126°19E **60 B4**
Eclipse Sd. *Canada* 72°38N 79°0W **69 C11**
Ecuador ■ *S. Amer.* 2°0S 78°0W **92 D3**
Ed Da'ein *Sudan* 11°26N 26°9E **54 B5**
Ed Damazin *Sudan* 11°46N 34°21E **53 F12**
Ed Dâmer *Sudan* 17°27N 34°0E **53 E12**
Ed Dar el Beida = Casablanca
  Morocco 33°36N 7°36W **52 B4**
Ed Debba *Sudan* 18°0N 30°51E **53 E12**
Ed Déffa *Egypt* 30°40N 26°30E **53 B11**
Ed Dueim *Sudan* 14°0N 32°10E **53 F12**
Edam *Canada* 53°11N 108°46W **71 C7**
Edam *Neths.* 52°31N 5°3E **15 B5**
Edapally *India* 11°19N 78°3E **45 J4**
Eday *U.K.* 59°11N 2°47W **11 B6**
Eddrachillis B. *U.K.* 58°17N 5°14W **11 C3**
Eddystone *U.K.* 50°11N 4°16W **13 G3**
Eddystone Pt. *Australia* 40°59S 148°20E **63 G4**
Ede *Neths.* 52°4N 5°40E **15 B5**
Edehon L. *Canada* 60°25N 97°15W **71 A9**
Eden *Australia* 37°3S 149°55E **63 F4**
Eden *N.C., U.S.A.* 36°29N 79°53W **85 G6**
Eden *N.Y., U.S.A.* 42°39N 78°55W **82 D6**
Eden *Tex., U.S.A.* 31°13N 99°51W **84 F5**
Eden → *U.K.* 54°57N 3°1W **12 C4**
Edenburg *S. Africa* 29°43S 25°58E **56 C4**
Edendale *S. Africa* 29°39S 30°18E **57 C5**
Edenderry *Ireland* 53°21N 7°4W **10 C4**
Edenton *U.S.A.* 36°4N 76°39W **85 C16**
Edenville *S. Africa* 27°37S 27°34E **57 C4**
Eder → *Germany* 51°12N 9°28E **16 C5**
Edessa *Greece* 40°48N 22°5E **23 D10**
Edfu = Idfû *Egypt* 24°55N 32°49E **53 D12**
Edgar *U.S.A.* 40°22N 97°58W **80 E5**
Edgartown *U.S.A.* 41°23N 70°31W **83 E14**
Edge Hill *U.K.* 52°8N 1°26W **13 E6**
Edgefield *U.S.A.* 33°47N 81°56W **85 E14**
Edgeley *U.S.A.* 46°22N 98°43W **80 B4**
Edgemont *U.S.A.* 43°18N 103°50W **80 D2**
Edgeøya *Svalbard* 77°45N 22°30E **4 B9**
Édhessa = Edessa *Greece* 40°48N 22°5E **23 D10**
Edievale *N.Z.* 45°49S 169°22E **59 F2**
Edina *U.S.A.* 40°10N 92°11W **80 E7**
Edinboro *U.S.A.* 41°52N 80°8W **82 E4**
Edinburg *U.S.A.* 26°18N 98°10W **84 H5**
Edinburgh, City of □ *U.K.* 55°57N 3°17W **11 F5**
Edineţ *Moldova* 48°9N 27°18E **17 D14**
Edirne *Turkey* 41°40N 26°34E **23 D12**
Edison *U.S.A.* 48°33N 122°27W **78 B4**
Edithburgh *Australia* 35°5S 137°43E **63 F2**
Edmeston *U.S.A.* 42°42N 75°15W **83 D9**
Edmond *U.S.A.* 35°39N 97°29W **84 D6**
Edmonds *U.S.A.* 47°48N 122°22W **78 C4**
Edmonton *Australia* 17°2S 145°46E **62 B4**
Edmonton *Canada* 53°30N 113°30W **70 C6**
Edmund L. *Canada* 54°45N 93°17W **72 B1**
Edmundston *Canada* 47°23N 68°20W **73 C6**
Edna *U.S.A.* 28°59N 96°39W **84 G6**
Edremit *Turkey* 39°34N 27°0E **23 E12**
Edremit Körfezi *Turkey* 39°30N 26°45E **23 E12**
Edson *Canada* 53°35N 116°28W **70 C5**
Eduardo Castex
  Argentina 35°50S 64°18W **94 D3**
Eduardo Frei *Antarctica* 62°30S 58°0W **5 C18**
Edward → *Australia* 35°5S 143°30E **63 F3**
Edward, L. *Africa* 0°25S 29°40E **54 E5**
Edward VII Land
  Antarctica 80°0S 150°0W **5 E13**
Edwards *Calif., U.S.A.* 34°50N 117°40W **79 L9**
Edwards *N.Y., U.S.A.* 44°20N 75°15W **83 B9**
Edwards Plateau *U.S.A.* 30°45N 101°20W **84 F4**
Edwardsville *U.S.A.* 41°15N 75°56W **83 E9**

Edzná *Mexico* 19°39N 90°19W **87** D6
Edzo *Canada* 62°49N 116°4W **70** A5
Eeklo *Belgium* 51°11N 3°33E **15** C3
Eenhana *Namibia* 17°30S 16°23E **56** A2
Eesti = Estonia ■ *Europe* 58°30N 25°30E **9** G21
Effigy Mounds △ *U.S.A.* 43°5N 91°11W **80** D8
Effingham *U.S.A.* 39°7N 88°33W **80** F9
Égadi, Ísole *Italy* 37°55N 12°16E **22** F5
Egan Range *U.S.A.* 39°35N 114°55W **76** G6
Eganville *Canada* 45°32N 77°5W **82** A7
Eger = Cheb *Czech Rep.* 50°9N 12°28E **16** C7
Eger *Hungary* 47°53N 20°27E **17** E11
Egersund *Norway* 58°26N 6°1E **9** G12
Egg L. *Canada* 55°5N 105°30W **71** B7
Éghezée *Belgium* 50°35N 4°55E **15** C4
Egilsstaðir *Iceland* 65°16N 14°25E **8** D6
Egio *Greece* 38°15N 22°5E **23** E10
Eglinton I. *Canada* 75°48N 118°30W **69** B8
Egmont *Canada* 49°45N 123°56W **70** D4
Egmont, C. *N.Z.* 39°16S 173°45E **59** C4
Egmont, Mt. = Taranaki, Mt.
   N.Z. 39°17S 174°5E **59** C5
Egmont △ *N.Z.* 39°17S 174°4E **59** C5
Egra *India* 21°54N 87°32E **43** J12
Eğridir *Turkey* 37°52N 30°51E **19** G5
Eğridir Gölü *Turkey* 37°53N 30°50E **46** B1
Egvekinot *Russia* 66°19N 179°50W **27** C19
Egypt ■ *Africa* 28°0N 31°0E **53** C12
Ehime □ *Japan* 33°30N 132°40E **29** H6
Ehrenberg *U.S.A.* 33°36N 114°31W **79** M12
Eibar *Spain* 43°11N 2°28W **21** A4
Eidsvold *Australia* 25°25S 151°12E **63** D5
Eidsvoll *Norway* 60°19N 11°14E **9** F14
Eielson *U.S.A.* 64°40N 147°4W **74** C10
Eifel *Germany* 50°15N 6°50E **16** C4
Eigg *U.K.* 56°54N 6°10W **11** E2
Eighty Mile Beach
   Australia 19°30S 120°40E **60** C3
Eil, L. *U.K.* 56°51N 5°16W **11** E3
Eildon, L. *Australia* 37°10S 146°0E **63** F4
Eilean Siar □ *U.K.* 57°30N 7°10W **11** D1
Einasleigh *Australia* 18°32S 144°5E **62** B3
Einasleigh → *Australia* 17°30S 142°17E **62** B3
Eindhoven *Neths.* 51°26N 5°28E **15** C5
Eire = Ireland ■ *Europe* 53°50N 7°52W **10** C4
Eiríksjökull *Iceland* 64°46N 20°24W **8** D3
Eiriosgaigh = Eriskay *U.K.* 57°4N 7°18W **11** D1
Eirunepé *Brazil* 6°35S 69°53W **92** E5
Eiseb → *Namibia* 20°33S 20°59E **56** B2
Eisenach *Germany* 50°58N 10°19E **16** C6
Eisenerz *Austria* 47°32N 14°54E **16** E8
Eivissa *Spain* 38°54N 1°26E **21** C6
Ejutla *Mexico* 16°34N 96°44W **87** D5
Ekalaka *U.S.A.* 45°53N 104°33W **76** D11
Ekaterinburg = Yekaterinburg
   Russia 56°50N 60°30E **26** D7
Ekenäs = Raasepori
   Finland 60°0N 23°26E **9** G20
Eketahuna *N.Z.* 40°38S 175°43E **59** D5
Ekibastuz *Kazakhstan* 51°50N 75°10E **26** D8
Eksjö *Sweden* 57°40N 14°58E **9** H16
Ekuma → *Namibia* 18°40S 16°2E **56** A2
Ekwan → *Canada* 53°12N 82°15W **72** B3
Ekwan Pt. *Canada* 53°16N 82°7W **72** B3
El Aaiún *W. Sahara* 27°9N 13°12W **52** C3
El Abanico *Chile* 37°20S 71°31W **94** D1
El Alamein *Egypt* 30°48N 28°58E **53** B11
El 'Aqaba, W. → *Egypt* 30°7N 33°54E **48** E2
El Arīḥā *West Bank* 31°52N 35°27E **48** D4
El 'Arīsh *Egypt* 31°8N 33°50E **48** D2
El 'Arīsh, W. → *Egypt* 31°8N 33°47E **48** D2
El Asnam = Ech Chéliff
   Algeria 36°10N 1°20E **52** A6
El Bayadh *Algeria* 33°40N 1°1E **52** B6
El Bluff *Nic.* 11°59N 83°40W **88** D3
El Cajon *U.S.A.* 32°48N 116°58W **79** N10
El Calafate *Argentina* 50°19S 72°15W **96** G2
El Campo *U.S.A.* 29°12N 96°16W **84** G6
El Capitan *U.S.A.* 37°44N 119°38E **78** H7
El Carbón *Honduras* 15°25N 85°32W **88** C2
El Carmen *Colombia* 9°43N 75°8W **92** B3
El Centro *U.S.A.* 32°48N 115°34W **79** N11
El Cerro *Bolivia* 17°30S 61°40W **92** G6
El Compadre *Mexico* 32°20N 116°14W **79** N10
El Cuy *Argentina* 39°55S 68°25W **96** D3
El Cuyo *Mexico* 21°31N 87°41W **87** C7
El Daheir *Egypt* 31°13N 34°10E **48** D3
El Descanso *Mexico* 32°12N 116°58W **79** N10
El Desemboque *Mexico* 30°33N 113°1W **86** A2
El Diviso *Colombia* 1°22N 78°14W **92** C3
El Djouf *Mauritania* 21°25N 6°40W **52** D4
El Dorado *Mexico* 24°17N 107°21W **86** C3
El Dorado *Ark., U.S.A.* 33°12N 92°40W **84** E8
El Dorado *Kans., U.S.A.* 37°49N 96°52W **80** G5
El Dorado *Venezuela* 6°55N 61°37W **92** B6
El Dorado Springs *U.S.A.* 37°52N 94°1W **80** G6
El Escorial *Spain* 40°35N 4°7W **21** B3
El Faiyûm *Egypt* 29°19N 30°50E **53** C12
El Fâsher *Sudan* 13°33N 25°26E **53** F11
El Ferrol = Ferrol *Spain* 43°29N 8°15W **21** A1
El Fuerte *Mexico* 26°25N 108°39W **86** B3
El Geneina = Al Junaynah
   Sudan 13°27N 22°45E **53** F10
El Gezira □ *Sudan* 15°0N 33°0E **53** F12
El Gogorrón △ *Mexico* 21°49N 100°57W **86** C4
El Goléa *Algeria* 30°30N 2°50E **52** B6
El Guácharo △ *Venezuela* 10°8N 63°21W **89** D7
El Guache △ *Venezuela* 9°45N 69°30W **89** E6
El Iskandarîya *Egypt* 31°13N 29°58E **53** B11
El Istiwa'iya *Sudan* 5°0N 28°0E **53** G11
El Jadida *Morocco* 33°11N 8°17W **52** B4
El Jardal *Honduras* 14°54N 88°50W **88** D2
El Kef □ *Tunisia* 36°0N 9°0E **53** A7
El Khârga *Egypt* 25°30N 30°33E **53** C12
El Khartûm *Sudan* 15°31N 32°35E **53** E12
El Khartûm Baḥrî *Sudan* 15°40N 32°31E **53** E12
El Kuntilla *Egypt* 30°1N 34°45E **48** E3
El Leoncito △ *Argentina* 31°58S 69°10W **94** C2

El Lucero *Mexico* 30°37N 106°31W **86** A3
El Maestrazgo *Spain* 40°30N 0°25W **21** B5
El Mahalla el Kubra *Egypt* 31°0N 31°0E **53** B12
El Malpais △ *U.S.A.* 34°53N 108°0W **77** J10
El Mansûra *Egypt* 31°0N 31°19E **53** B12
El Ménia = El Goléa
   Algeria 30°30N 2°50E **52** B6
El Milagro *Argentina* 30°59S 65°59W **94** C2
El Minyâ *Egypt* 28°7N 30°33E **53** C12
El Obeid *Sudan* 13°8N 30°10E **53** F12
El Odaiya *Sudan* 12°8N 28°12E **53** F11
El Oro *Mexico* 19°51N 100°7W **87** D4
El Oued *Algeria* 33°20N 6°58E **52** B7
El Palmar △ *Argentina* 32°10S 58°31W **94** C4
El Paso *U.S.A.* 31°45N 106°29W **84** F1
El Paso de Robles = Paso Robles
   U.S.A. 35°38N 120°41W **78** K6
El Pinacate y Gran Desierto de
   Altar = Gran Desierto del
   Pinacate △ *Mexico* 31°51N 113°32W **86** A2
El Portal *U.S.A.* 37°41N 119°47W **78** H7
El Porvenir *Mexico* 31°15N 105°51W **86** A3
El Progreso *Honduras* 15°26N 87°51W **88** C2
El Puerto de Santa María
   Spain 36°36N 6°13W **21** D2
El Qantara *Egypt* 30°51N 32°20E **48** E1
El Quseima *Egypt* 30°40N 34°15E **48** E3
El Real de Santa María
   Panama 8°0N 77°40W **92** B3
El Reno *U.S.A.* 35°32N 97°57W **75** H20
El Rey △ *Argentina* 24°40S 64°34W **94** A3
El Río *U.S.A.* 34°14N 119°10W **79** L7
El Rosario *Mexico* 30°1N 115°45W **86** A1
El Salto *Mexico* 23°47N 105°22W **86** C3
El Salvador ■ *Cent. Amer.* 13°50N 89°0W **88** D2
El Sauce *Nic.* 13°0N 86°40W **88** D2
El Suweis *Egypt* 29°58N 32°31E **53** C12
El Tamarâni, W. → *Egypt* 29°40N 34°28E **48** E3
El Thamad *Egypt* 29°40N 34°28E **48** F3
El Tigre *Venezuela* 8°44N 64°15W **92** B6
El Tîh, Gebel *Egypt* 29°40N 33°50E **48** F2
El Tofo *Chile* 29°22S 71°18W **94** B1
El Tránsito *Chile* 28°52S 70°17W **94** B1
El Tûr *Egypt* 28°14N 33°36E **46** D2
El Turbio *Argentina* 51°45S 72°5W **96** G2
El Uqsur *Egypt* 25°41N 32°38E **53** C12
El Vergel *Mexico* 26°28N 106°22W **86** B3
El Vigía *Venezuela* 8°38N 71°39W **92** B4
El Wabeira *Egypt* 29°34N 33°6E **48** F2
El Wuz *Sudan* 15°5N 30°7E **53** F12
Elamanchili *India* 17°33N 82°50E **44** F6
Elat *Israel* 29°30N 34°56E **48** F3
Elâzığ *Turkey* 38°37N 39°14E **46** B3
Elba *Italy* 42°46N 10°17E **22** C4
Elba *U.S.A.* 31°25N 86°4W **85** F11
Elbasan *Albania* 41°9N 20°9E **23** D9
Elbe → *Europe* 53°50N 9°0E **16** B5
Elbert, Mt. *U.S.A.* 39°7N 106°27W **76** G10
Elberton *U.S.A.* 34°7N 82°52W **85** D13
Elbeuf *France* 49°17N 1°2E **20** B4
Elbing = Elblag *Poland* 54°10N 19°25E **17** A10
Elbistan *Turkey* 38°13N 37°15E **46** B3
Elblag *Poland* 54°10N 19°25E **17** A10
Elbow *Canada* 51°7N 106°35W **71** C7
Elbrus *Russia* 43°21N 42°30E **19** F7
Elburz Mts. = Alborz, Reshteh-ye
   Kūhhā-ye *Iran* 36°0N 52°0E **47** C7
Elche *Spain* 38°15N 0°42W **21** C5
Elcho I. *Australia* 11°55S 135°45E **62** A2
Elda *Spain* 38°29N 0°47W **21** C5
Elde → *Germany* 53°7N 11°15E **16** B6
Eldon *Mo., U.S.A.* 38°21N 92°35W **80** F7
Eldon *Wash., U.S.A.* 47°33N 123°3W **78** C3
Eldora *U.S.A.* 42°22N 93°5W **80** D7
Eldorado *Argentina* 26°28S 54°43W **95** B5
Eldorado *Canada* 44°35N 77°31W **82** B7
Eldorado *Ill., U.S.A.* 37°49N 88°26W **80** G9
Eldorado *Tex., U.S.A.* 30°52N 100°36W **84** F4
Eldoret *Kenya* 0°30N 35°17E **54** D7
Eldred *U.S.A.* 41°58N 78°23W **82** E6
Eleanora, Pk. *Australia* 32°57S 121°9E **61** F3
Elefantes → *Africa* 24°10S 32°40E **57** C5
Elektrostal *Russia* 55°41N 38°32E **18** C6
Elemi Triangle *Africa* 5°0N 35°20E **54** D7
Elephant Butte Res.
   U.S.A. 33°9N 107°11W **77** K10
Elephant I. *Antarctica* 61°0S 55°0W **5** C18
Elephant Pass *Sri Lanka* 9°35N 80°25E **45** K5
Eleuthera I. *Bahamas* 25°0N 76°20W **88** B4
Elgin *Canada* 44°36N 76°13W **83** B8
Elgin *U.K.* 57°39N 3°19W **11** D5
Elgin *Ill., U.S.A.* 42°2N 88°17W **80** D9
Elgin *N. Dak., U.S.A.* 46°24N 101°51W **80** B3
Elgin *Oreg., U.S.A.* 45°34N 117°55W **76** D5
Elgin *Tex., U.S.A.* 30°21N 97°22W **84** F6
Elgon, Mt. *Africa* 1°10N 34°30E **54** D6
Eliase *Indonesia* 8°21S 130°48E **37** F8
Elim *Namibia* 17°48S 15°31E **56** A2
Elim *S. Africa* 34°35S 19°45E **56** E2
Elista *Russia* 46°16N 44°14E **19** E7
Elizabeth *Australia* 34°42S 138°41E **63** E2
Elizabeth *U.S.A.* 40°39N 74°12W **83** F10
Elizabeth City *U.S.A.* 36°18N 76°14W **85** C16
Elizabethton *U.S.A.* 36°21N 82°13W **85** C13
Elizabethtown *Ky.,
   U.S.A.* 37°42N 85°52W **81** G11
Elizabethtown *N.Y.,
   U.S.A.* 44°13N 73°36W **83** B11
Elizabethtown *Pa., U.S.A.* 40°9N 76°36W **83** F8
Elk *Poland* 53°50N 22°21E **17** B12
Elk → *Canada* 49°11N 115°14W **70** D5
Elk → *U.S.A.* 34°46N 87°16W **85** D11
Elk City *U.S.A.* 35°25N 99°25W **84** D5
Elk Creek *U.S.A.* 39°36N 122°32W **78** F4
Elk Grove *U.S.A.* 38°25N 121°22W **78** G5
Elk Island △ *Canada* 53°35N 112°59W **70** C6
Elk Lake *Canada* 47°40N 80°25W **72** C3
Elk Point *Canada* 53°54N 110°55W **71** C6

Elk River *Idaho, U.S.A.* 46°47N 116°11W **76** C5
Elk River *Minn., U.S.A.* 45°18N 93°35W **80** C7
Elkedra → *Australia* 21°8S 136°22E **62** C2
Elkhart *Ind., U.S.A.* 41°41N 85°58W **81** E11
Elkhart *Kans., U.S.A.* 37°0N 101°54W **80** G3
Elkhorn *Canada* 49°59N 101°14W **71** D8
Elkhorn → *U.S.A.* 41°8N 96°19W **80** E5
Elkhovo *Bulgaria* 42°10N 26°35E **23** C12
Elkin *U.S.A.* 36°15N 80°51W **85** C14
Elkins *U.S.A.* 38°55N 79°51W **81** F14
Elkland *U.S.A.* 41°59N 77°19W **82** E7
Elko *Canada* 49°20N 115°10W **70** D5
Elko *U.S.A.* 40°50N 115°46W **76** F6
Elkton *U.S.A.* 43°49N 83°11W **82** C2
Ellas = Greece ■ *Europe* 40°0N 23°0E **23** E9
Ellef Ringnes I. *Canada* 78°30N 102°2W **69** B11
Ellen, Mt. *U.S.A.* 38°6N 110°48W **76** G8
Ellenburg *U.S.A.* 44°54N 73°48W **83** B11
Ellendale *U.S.A.* 46°0N 98°32W **80** B4
Ellensburg *U.S.A.* 46°59N 120°34W **76** C3
Ellenville *U.S.A.* 41°43N 74°24W **83** E10
Ellerton *Barbados* 13°7N 59°33W **89** g
Ellery, Mt. *Australia* 37°28S 148°47E **63** F4
Ellesmere, L. *N.Z.* 43°47S 172°28E **59** G4
Ellesmere I. *Canada* 79°30N 80°0W **69** B16
Ellesmere Island = Quttinirpaaq △
   Canada 82°13N 72°13W **69** A17
Ellesmere Port *U.K.* 53°17N 2°54W **12** D5
Ellice Is. = Tuvalu ■
   Pac. Oc. 8°0S 178°0E **58** B10
Ellicottville *U.S.A.* 42°17N 78°40W **82** D6
ElliTot *U.S.A.* 42°13N 79°6W **82** D5
Elliot *Australia* 17°33S 133°32E **62** B1
Elliot *S. Africa* 31°22S 27°48E **57** D4
Elliot Lake *Canada* 46°25N 82°35W **72** C3
Elliotdale = Xhora
   S. Africa 31°55S 28°38E **57** E4
Ellis *U.S.A.* 38°56N 99°34W **80** F4
Elliston *Australia* 33°39S 134°53E **63** E1
Ellisville *U.S.A.* 31°36N 89°12W **85** F10
Ellon *U.K.* 57°22N 2°4W **11** D6
Ellora *India* 20°1N 75°10E **44** D2
Ellore = Eluru *India* 16°48N 81°8E **44** F5
Ellsworth *Kans., U.S.A.* 38°44N 98°14W **80** F4
Ellsworth *Maine, U.S.A.* 44°33N 68°25W **81** C19
Ellsworth Land *Antarctica* 66°0S 53°0E **5** D5
Ellsworth Mts. *Antarctica* 78°30S 85°0W **5** D16
Ellwood City *U.S.A.* 40°52N 80°17W **82** F4
Elma *Canada* 49°52N 95°55W **71** D9
Elma *U.S.A.* 47°0N 123°25W **78** D3
Elmalı *Turkey* 36°44N 29°56E **19** G4
Elmhurst *U.S.A.* 41°53N 87°56W **80** E10
Elmira *Canada* 43°36N 80°33W **82** C4
Elmira *U.S.A.* 42°6N 76°48W **82** D8
Elmira Heights *U.S.A.* 42°8N 76°50W **82** D8
Elmore *Australia* 36°30S 144°37E **63** F3
Elmshorn *Germany* 53°43N 9°40E **16** B5
Elmvale *Canada* 44°35N 79°52W **82** B5
Elora *Canada* 43°41N 80°26W **82** C4
Eloy *U.S.A.* 32°45N 111°33W **77** K8
Elphin *Canada* 44°55N 76°37W **83** B8
Elpitiya *Sri Lanka* 6°17N 80°10E **45** L5
Elrose *Canada* 51°12N 108°0W **71** C7
Elsby △ *Australia* 14°55S 133°10E **60** B5
Elsie *U.S.A.* 45°52N 123°36W **78** E3
Elsinore = Helsingør
   Denmark 56°2N 12°35E **9** H15
Eltanin Fracture Zone System
   S. Ocean 54°0S 130°0W **5** B14
Eltham *N.Z.* 39°26S 174°19E **59** C5
Eluru *India* 16°48N 81°8E **44** F5
Elvas *Portugal* 38°50N 7°10W **21** C2
Elverum *Norway* 60°53N 11°34E **8** F14
Elvire → *Australia* 17°51S 128°11E **60** C4
Elvire, Mt. *Australia* 29°22S 119°36E **61** E2
Elwell, L. = Tiber Res.
   U.S.A. 48°19N 111°6W **76** B8
Elwood *Ind., U.S.A.* 40°17N 85°50W **81** E11
Elwood *Nebr., U.S.A.* 40°36N 99°52W **80** E4
Elx = Elche *Spain* 38°15N 0°42W **21** C5
Ely *U.K.* 52°24N 0°16E **13** E8
Ely *Minn., U.S.A.* 47°55N 91°51W **80** B8
Ely *Nev., U.S.A.* 39°15N 114°54W **76** G6
Elyria *U.S.A.* 41°22N 82°7W **82** E2
Emāmrūd *Iran* 36°30N 55°0E **47** B7
eMbalenhle *S. Africa* 26°32S 29°4E **57** D4
Embarcación *Argentina* 23°10S 64°0W **94** A3
Embetsu *Japan* 44°44N 141°47E **28** B10
Embi *Kazakhstan* 48°50N 58°8E **26** E6
Embi → *Kazakhstan* 46°55N 53°28E **19** E9
Embro *Canada* 43°9N 80°54W **82** C4
Embrun *France* 44°34N 6°30E **20** D7
Emden *Germany* 53°21N 7°12E **16** B4
Emei Shan *China* 29°32N 103°46E **34** C4
Emeishan *China* 29°31N 103°23E **34** C4
Emerald *Australia* 23°32S 148°10E **62** C4
Emerald I. *Canada* 76°48N 114°10W **69** B9
Emerson *Canada* 49°0N 97°10W **71** D9
Emet *Turkey* 39°20N 29°15E **23** E13
Emgwenya *S. Africa* 25°40S 30°18E **57** D5
Emi Koussi *Chad* 19°45N 18°55E **53** E9
Emine, Nos *Bulgaria* 42°40N 27°56E **23** C12
Emissi, Tarso *Chad* 21°27N 18°36E **53** D9
Emlenton *U.S.A.* 41°11N 79°43W **82** E5
Emmaus *S. Africa* 29°2S 25°15E **56** C4
Emmaus *U.S.A.* 40°32N 75°30W **83** F9
Emmeloord *Neths.* 52°44N 5°46E **15** B5
Emmen *Neths.* 52°48N 6°57E **15** B6
Emmet *Australia* 24°45S 144°30E **62** C3
Emmetsburg *U.S.A.* 43°7N 94°41W **80** D6
Emmett *Idaho, U.S.A.* 43°52N 116°30W **76** E5
Emmett *Mich., U.S.A.* 42°59N 82°46W **82** D2
Emmiganuru = Yemmiganur
   India 15°44N 77°29E **45** G3
Emmonak *U.S.A.* 62°47N 164°31W **74** C7
Emo *Canada* 48°38N 93°50W **71** D10

Empalme *Mexico* 27°58N 110°51W **86** B2
Empangeni *S. Africa* 28°50S 31°52E **57** C5
Empedrado *Argentina* 28°0S 58°46W **94** B4
Emperor Seamount Chain
   Pac. Oc. 40°0N 170°0E **64** D9
Emperor Trough *Pac. Oc.* 43°0N 175°30E **64** C9
Emporia *Kans., U.S.A.* 38°25N 96°11W **80** F5
Emporia *Va., U.S.A.* 36°42N 77°32W **81** G15
Emporium *U.S.A.* 41°31N 78°14W **82** E6
Empress *Canada* 50°57N 110°0W **71** C7
Empty Quarter = Rub' al Khālī
   Si. Arabia 19°0N 48°0E **49** D4
Ems → *Germany* 53°20N 7°12E **16** B4
Emsdale *Canada* 45°32N 79°19E **82** A5
Emu *China* 43°40N 128°6E **33** C15
Emu Park *Australia* 23°13S 150°50E **62** C5
eMuziwezinto *S. Africa* 30°15S 30°45E **57** D5
'En 'Avrona *Israel* 29°43N 35°0E **48** F4
'En Boqeq *Israel* 31°12N 35°21E **47** D4
'En Gedi *Israel* 31°28N 35°25E **47** D4
En Nahud *Sudan* 12°45N 28°25E **53** F11
Ena *Japan* 35°25N 137°25E **29** G8
Enard B. *U.K.* 58°5N 5°20W **11** C3
Enare träsk = Inarijärvi
   Finland 69°0N 28°0E **8** B23
Enarotali *Indonesia* 3°55S 136°21E **37** E9
Encampment *U.S.A.* 41°12N 106°47W **76** F10
Encantadas, Serra *Brazil* 30°40S 53°0W **95** C5
Encarnación *Paraguay* 27°15S 55°50W **95** B4
Encarnación de Díaz
   Mexico 21°31N 102°14W **86** C4
Encinitas *U.S.A.* 33°3N 117°17W **79** M9
Encino *U.S.A.* 34°39N 105°28W **77** J11
Encounter B. *Australia* 35°45S 138°45E **63** F2
Endako *Canada* 54°6N 125°2W **70** C3
Endau Rompin △
   Malaysia 2°27N 103°45E **39** L4
Ende *Indonesia* 8°45S 121°40E **37** F6
Endeavour Str. *Australia* 10°45S 142°0E **62** A3
Enderbury *Kiribati* 3°8S 171°5W **64** H10
Enderby *Canada* 50°35N 119°10W **70** C5
Enderby Abyssal Plain
   S. Ocean 60°0S 40°0E **5** C5
Enderby I. *Australia* 20°35S 116°30E **60** D2
Enderby Land *Antarctica* 66°0S 53°0E **5** C5
Enderlin *U.S.A.* 46°38N 97°36W **80** B5
Endicott *U.S.A.* 42°6N 76°4W **83** D8
Endicott Mts. *U.S.A.* 68°0N 152°0W **74** B9
Endwell *U.S.A.* 42°6N 76°2W **83** D8
Endyalgout I. *Australia* 11°40S 132°35E **60** B5
Eneabba *Australia* 29°45S 115°16E **61** E2
Enewetak Atoll
   Marshall Is. 11°30N 162°15E **64** F8
Enez *Turkey* 40°45N 26°5E **23** D12
Enfer, Pte. d' *Martinique* 14°22N 60°54W **88** c
Enfield *Canada* 44°56N 63°32W **73** D7
Enfield *Conn., U.S.A.* 41°58N 72°36E **83** E12
Enfield *N.C., U.S.A.* 36°11N 77°41W **85** C16
Enfield *N.H., U.S.A.* 43°39N 72°9W **83** C12
Engadin *Switz.* 46°45N 10°10E **20** C9
Engaño, C. *Dom. Rep.* 18°30N 68°20W **89** C6
Engaño, C. *Phil.* 18°35N 122°23E **37** A6
Engaru *Japan* 44°3N 143°31E **28** B11
Engcobo = Ngcobo
   S. Africa 31°37S 28°0E **57** D4
Engels *Russia* 51°28N 46°6E **19** D8
Enggano *Indonesia* 5°20S 102°40E **36** F2
England *U.S.A.* 34°33N 91°58W **84** D9
England □ *U.K.* 53°0N 2°0W **13** E5
Englee *Canada* 50°45N 56°5W **73** B8
Englehart *Canada* 47°49N 79°52W **72** C4
English → *Canada* 49°12N 91°5W **71** C10
English Bazar = Ingraj Bazar
   India 24°58N 88°10E **43** G13
English Channel *Europe* 50°0N 2°0W **13** G6
English Company's Is., The
   Australia 11°50S 136°32E **62** A2
English River *Canada* 49°14N 91°0W **72** C1
Enid *U.S.A.* 36°24N 97°53W **84** C6
Eniwa *Japan* 43°0N 141°30E **28** C10
Enkhuizen *Neths.* 52°42N 5°17E **15** B5
Enle *China* 24°0N 101°9E **34** F3
Enna *Italy* 37°34N 14°16E **22** F6
Ennadai L. *Canada* 60°58N 101°20W **71** A8
Ennedi *Chad* 17°15N 22°0E **53** E10
Enngonia *Australia* 29°21S 145°50E **63** D4
Ennis *Ireland* 52°51N 8°59W **10** D3
Ennis *Mont., U.S.A.* 45°21N 111°44W **76** D8
Ennis *Tex., U.S.A.* 32°20N 96°38W **84** E6
Enniscorthy *Ireland* 52°30N 6°34W **10** D5
Enniskillen *U.K.* 54°21N 7°39W **10** B4
Ennistimon *Ireland* 52°57N 9°17W **10** D2
Enns → *Austria* 48°14N 14°32E **16** D8
Eno *Finland* 62°47N 30°10E **8** E24
Enontekiö *Finland* 68°23N 23°37E **8** B20
Enosburg Falls *U.S.A.* 44°55N 72°48W **83** B12
Enping *China* 22°16N 112°21E **35** F9
Enriquillo, L. *Dom. Rep.* 18°20N 71°40W **89** C5
Enschede *Neths.* 52°13N 6°53E **15** B6
Ensenada *Argentina* 34°55S 57°55W **94** C4
Ensenada *Mexico* 31°52N 116°37W **86** A1
Ensenada de los Muertos
   Mexico 23°59N 109°51W **86** C2
Enshi *China* 30°18N 109°29E **34** B7
Entebbe *Uganda* 0°4N 32°28E **54** D6
Enterprise *Canada* 60°47N 115°45W **70** A5
Enterprise *Ala., U.S.A.* 31°19N 85°51W **85** F12
Enterprise *Oreg., U.S.A.* 45°25N 117°17W **76** D5
Entre Ríos *Bolivia* 21°30S 64°25W **94** A3
Entre Ríos □ *Argentina* 30°30S 58°30W **94** C4
Entroncamento *Portugal* 39°28N 8°28W **21** C1
Enugu *Nigeria* 6°20N 7°30E **52** G7
Enumclaw *U.S.A.* 47°12N 121°59W **78** C5
Eochaill = Youghal
   Ireland 51°56N 7°52W **10** E4
Eólie, Ís. *Italy* 38°30N 14°57E **22** E6
Epe *Neths.* 52°21N 5°59E **15** B5
Épernay *France* 49°3N 3°56E **20** B5
Ephesus *Turkey* 37°55N 27°22E **23** F12

Ephraim *U.S.A.* 39°22N 111°35W **76** G8
Ephrata *Pa., U.S.A.* 40°11N 76°11W **83** F8
Ephrata *Wash., U.S.A.* 47°19N 119°33W **76** C4
Épinal *France* 48°10N 6°27E **20** B7
Epsom *U.K.* 51°19N 0°16W **13** F7
Epukiro *Namibia* 21°40S 19°9E **56** B2
Equatoria = El Istiwa'iya
   Sudan 5°0N 28°0E **53** G11
Equatorial Guinea ■ *Africa* 2°0N 8°0E **54** D1
Er Hai *China* 25°48N 100°11E **34** E3
Er Rachidia *Morocco* 31°58N 4°20W **52** B5
Er Rahad *Sudan* 12°45N 30°32E **53** F12
Er Rif *Morocco* 35°1N 4°1W **52** A5
Erandol *India* 20°56N 75°20E **44** D2
Erāwadī Myit = Irrawaddy →
   Burma 15°50N 95°6E **41** M19
Erāwadī Myitwanya = Irrawaddy,
   Mouths of the *Burma* 15°30N 95°0E **41** M19
Erawan △ *Thailand* 14°25N 98°58E **38** E2
Erbil = Arbīl *Iraq* 36°15N 44°5E **46** B5
Erçek *Turkey* 38°39N 43°36E **46** B4
Erciyaş Dağı *Turkey* 38°30N 35°30E **46** B2
Érd *Hungary* 47°22N 18°56E **17** E10
Erdao Jiang → *China* 42°37N 128°0E **33** C14
Erdek *Turkey* 40°23N 27°47E **23** D12
Erdene = Ulaan-Uul
   Mongolia 46°4N 100°49E **32** B6
Erdenet *Mongolia* 49°2N 104°5E **30** B9
Erdenetsogt *Mongolia* 42°55N 106°5E **32** C4
Erebus, Mt. *Antarctica* 77°35S 167°0E **5** D11
Erechim *Brazil* 27°35S 52°15W **95** B5
Ereğli *Konya, Turkey* 37°31N 34°4E **46** B2
Ereğli *Zonguldak, Turkey* 41°15N 31°24E **19** F5
Erenhot *China* 43°48N 112°2E **32** C7
Eresma → *Spain* 41°26N 4°45W **21** B3
Erfenisdam *S. Africa* 28°30S 26°50E **56** C4
Erfurt *Germany* 50°58N 11°2E **16** C6
Ergani *Turkey* 38°17N 39°49E **46** B3
Ergel *Mongolia* 43°8N 109°5E **32** C5
Ergeni Vozvyshennost
   Russia 47°0N 44°0E **19** E7
Ērgļi *Latvia* 56°54N 25°38E **9** H21
Ergun He = Argun →
   Russia 53°20N 121°28E **31** A13
Ergun Youqi *China* 50°15N 120°11E **31** A13
Erhlin *Taiwan* 23°54N 120°22E **35** F13
Eriboll, L. *U.K.* 58°30N 4°42W **11** C4
Érice *Italy* 38°2N 12°35E **22** E5
Erie *U.S.A.* 42°8N 80°5W **82** D4
Erie, L. *N. Amer.* 42°15N 81°0W **82** D4
Erie Canal *U.S.A.* 43°5N 78°43W **82** C7
Erieau *Canada* 42°16N 81°57W **82** D3
Erigavo = Ceerigaabo
   Somalia 10°35N 47°20E **49** E4
Eriksdale *Canada* 50°52N 98°7W **71** C9
Erimanthos *Greece* 37°57N 21°50E **23** F9
Erimo-Misaki *Japan* 41°50N 143°15E **28** D11
Erin *Canada* 43°45N 80°7W **82** C4
Erin Pt. *Trin. & Tob.* 10°3N 61°39W **93** K15
Erinpura *India* 25°9N 73°3E **42** G5
Eriskay *U.K.* 57°4N 7°18W **11** D1
Eritrea ■ *Africa* 14°0N 38°30E **49** D2
Erlangen *Germany* 49°36N 11°0E **16** D6
Erldunda *Australia* 25°14S 133°12E **62** D1
Ermelo *Neths.* 52°18N 5°35E **15** B5
Ermelo *S. Africa* 26°31S 29°59E **57** D4
Ermenek *Turkey* 36°38N 33°0E **46** B2
Ermoupoli *Greece* 37°28N 24°57E **23** F11
Ernakulam *India* 9°59N 76°22E **45** K3
Erne → *Ireland* 54°30N 8°16W **10** B3
Erne, Lower L. *U.K.* 54°28N 7°47W **10** B4
Erne, Upper L. *U.K.* 54°14N 7°32W **10** B4
Ernest Giles Ra. *Australia* 27°0S 123°45E **61** E3
Erode *India* 11°24N 77°45E **45** J3
Eromanga *Australia* 26°40S 143°11E **63** D3
Erongo *Namibia* 21°39S 15°58E **56** B2
Erongo *Namibia* 22°0S 15°0E **56** B2
Erongo □ *Namibia* 22°0S 15°0E **56** B2
Erramala Hills *India* 15°30N 78°15E **45** G4
Errenteria *Spain* 43°19N 1°54W **21** A5
Errigal *Ireland* 55°2N 8°6W **10** A3
Errinundra △ *Australia* 37°20S 148°47E **63** F4
Erris Hd. *Ireland* 54°17N 10°0W **10** B1
Erskine *U.S.A.* 47°40N 96°0W **80** B6
Ertan Shuiku *China* 27°5N 101°52E **34** D3
Ertis = Irtysh → *Russia* 61°4N 68°52E **26** C7
Erwin *U.S.A.* 36°9N 82°25W **85** C13
Erzgebirge *Germany* 50°27N 12°55E **16** C7
Erzin *Russia* 50°15N 95°10E **27** D10
Erzincan *Turkey* 39°46N 39°30E **46** B3
Erzurum *Turkey* 39°57N 41°15E **46** B4
Es Sahrâ' Esh Sharqîya
   Egypt 27°30N 32°30E **53** C12
Es Sînâ' *Egypt* 29°0N 34°0E **48** F2
Esan-Misaki *Japan* 41°40N 141°10E **28** D10
Esashi *Hokkaidō, Japan* 44°56N 142°35E **28** B11
Esashi *Hokkaidō, Japan* 41°52N 140°7E **28** D10
Esbjerg *Denmark* 55°29N 8°29E **9** J13
Esbo = Espoo *Finland* 60°12N 24°40E **9** F21
Escalante *U.S.A.* 37°47N 111°36W **77** H8
Escalante → *U.S.A.* 37°24N 110°57W **77** H8
Escalón *Mexico* 26°45N 104°20W **86** B4
Escambia → *U.S.A.* 30°32N 87°11W **85** F11
Escanaba *U.S.A.* 45°45N 87°4W **80** C10
Escárcega *Mexico* 18°37N 90°43W **87** D6
Esch-sur-Alzette *Lux.* 49°32N 6°0E **15** E6
Escondido *U.S.A.* 33°7N 117°5W **79** M9
Escuinapa de Hidalgo
   Mexico 22°50N 105°50W **86** C3
Escuintla *Guatemala* 14°20N 90°48W **88** D1
Esenguly *Turkmenistan* 37°37N 53°59E **26** F6
Eşfahān *Iran* 32°39N 51°43E **47** C6
Eşfahān □ *Iran* 32°50N 51°50E **47** C6
Esfarāyen *Iran* 37°4N 57°30E **47** B8
Esfideh *Iran* 33°39N 59°46E **47** C8
Esh Sham = Dimashq
   Syria 33°30N 36°18E **48** B5
Esha Ness *U.K.* 60°29N 1°38W **11** A7
Eshan *China* 24°11N 102°24E **34** E4

Eshkol △ Israel 31°20N 34°30E 48 D3
Eshowe S. Africa 28°50S 31°30E 57 C5
Esigodini Zimbabwe 20°18S 28°56E 57 B4
Esil = Ishim → Russia 57°45N 71°10E 26 D8
Esk → Dumf. & Gall., U.K. 54°58N 3°2W 11 G5
Esk → N. Yorks., U.K. 54°30N 0°37W 12 C7
Eskān Iran 26°48N 63°9E 47 E9
Esker Siding Canada 53°53N 66°25W 73 B6
Eskifjörður Iceland 65°3N 13°55W 8 D7
Eskilstuna Sweden 59°22N 16°32E 9 G17
Eskimo Point = Arviat
   Canada 61°6N 93°59W 71 A10
Eskişehir Turkey 39°50N 30°30E 19 G5
Esla → Spain 41°29N 6°3W 21 B2
Eslāmābād-e Gharb Iran 34°10N 46°30E 46 C5
Eslāmshahr Iran 35°40N 51°10E 47 C6
Eşme Turkey 38°23N 28°58E 23 E13
Esmeraldas Ecuador 1°0N 79°40W 92 C3
Esna = Isna Egypt 25°17N 32°30E 51 C12
Esnagi L. Canada 48°36N 84°33W 72 C3
España = Spain ■ Europe 39°0N 4°0W 21 B4
Espanola Canada 46°15N 81°46W 72 C3
Espanola U.S.A. 35°59N 106°5W 77 J10
Esparza Costa Rica 9°59N 84°40W 88 E3
Esperance Australia 33°45S 121°55E 61 F3
Esperance B. Australia 33°48S 121°55E 61 F3
Esperance Harbour
   St. Lucia 14°4N 60°55W 89 f
Esperanza Antarctica 65°0S 55°0W 5 C18
Esperanza Argentina 31°29S 61°3W 94 C3
Esperanza Puerto Rico 18°6N 65°28W 89 d
Espichel, C. Portugal 38°22N 9°16E 21 C1
Espigão, Serra do Brazil 26°35S 50°30W 95 B5
Espinazo, Sierra del = Espinhaço,
   Serra do Brazil 17°30S 43°30W 93 G10
Espinhaço, Serra do
   Brazil 17°30S 43°30W 93 G10
Espinilho, Serra do Brazil 28°30S 55°0W 95 B5
Espírito Santo □ Brazil 20°0S 40°45W 93 H10
Espírito Santo do Pinhal
   Brazil 22°10S 46°46W 95 A6
Espiritu Santo Vanuatu 15°15S 166°50E 58 C9
Espíritu Santo, B. del
   Mexico 19°20N 87°35W 87 D7
Espíritu Santo, I.
   Mexico 24°30N 110°22W 86 C2
Espita Mexico 21°1N 88°19W 87 C7
Espoo Finland 60°12N 24°40E 9 F21
Espungabera Mozam. 20°29S 32°45E 57 B5
Esquel Argentina 42°55S 71°20W 96 E2
Esquimalt Canada 48°26N 123°25W 78 B3
Esquina Argentina 30°0S 59°30W 94 C4
Essaouira Morocco 31°32N 9°42W 52 B4
Essen Belgium 51°28N 4°28E 15 C4
Essen Germany 51°28N 7°2E 16 C4
Essendon, Mt. Australia 25°0S 120°29E 61 E3
Essequibo → Guyana 6°50N 58°30W 92 B7
Essex Canada 42°10N 82°49W 82 D2
Essex Calif., U.S.A. 34°44N 115°15W 79 L11
Essex N.Y., U.S.A. 44°19N 73°21W 83 B11
Essex □ U.K. 51°54N 0°27E 13 F8
Essex Junction U.S.A. 44°29N 73°7W 83 B11
Esslingen Germany 48°44N 9°18E 16 D5
Estación Camacho
   Mexico 24°25N 102°18W 86 C4
Estación Simón Mexico 24°42N 102°35W 86 C4
Estados, I. de Los
   Argentina 54°40S 64°30W 96 G4
Eştahbānāt Iran 29°8N 54°4E 47 D7
Estância Brazil 11°16S 37°26W 93 F11
Estancia U.S.A. 34°46N 106°4W 77 J10
Estārm Iran 28°21N 58°21E 47 D8
Estcourt S. Africa 29°0S 29°53E 57 C4
Este △ Dom. Rep. 18°14N 68°42W 89 C6
Estelí Nic. 13°9N 86°22W 88 D2
Esterhazy Canada 50°37N 102°5W 71 C8
Estevan Canada 49°10N 102°59W 71 D8
Estevan Group Canada 53°3N 129°38W 70 C3
Estherville U.S.A. 43°24N 94°50W 80 D7
Eston Canada 51°8N 108°40W 71 C7
Estonia ■ Europe 58°30N 25°30E 9 G21
Estreito Brazil 6°32S 47°25W 93 E9
Estrela, Serra da Portugal 40°10N 7°45W 21 B2
Estremoz Portugal 38°51N 7°39W 21 C2
Estrondo, Serra do Brazil 7°20S 48°0W 93 E9
Esztergom Hungary 47°47N 18°44E 17 E10
Et Tidra Mauritania 19°45N 16°20W 52 E2
Etah India 27°35N 78°40E 43 F8
Étampes France 48°26N 2°10E 20 B5
Etanga Namibia 17°55S 13°0E 56 A1
Etawah India 26°48N 79°6E 43 F8
Etawney L. Canada 57°50N 96°50W 71 B9
Etchojoa Mexico 26°55N 109°38W 86 B3
eThekwini = Durban
   S. Africa 29°49S 31°1E 57 C5
Ethel U.S.A. 46°32N 122°46W 78 D4
Ethelbert Canada 51°32N 100°25W 71 C8
Ethiopia ■ Africa 8°0N 40°0E 49 F3
Ethiopian Highlands
   Ethiopia 10°0N 37°0E 49 F2
Etive, L. U.K. 56°29N 5°10W 11 E3
Etna Italy 37°50N 14°55E 22 F6
Etolin Strait U.S.A. 60°20N 165°15W 74 C6
Etosha ☼ Namibia 19°0S 16°0E 56 A2
Etosha Pan Namibia 18°40S 16°30E 56 A2
Etowah U.S.A. 35°20N 84°32W 85 D12
Etrek Turkmenistan 37°36N 54°46E 47 B7
Ettelbruck Lux. 49°51N 6°5E 15 E6
Ettrick Water → U.K. 55°31N 2°55W 11 F6
Etzná-Tixmucuy = Edzná
   Mexico 19°39N 90°19W 87 D6
Eua Tonga 21°22S 174°56W 59 c
Euboea = Evia Greece 38°30N 24°0E 23 E11
Eucla Australia 31°41S 128°52E 61 F4
Euclid U.S.A. 41°34N 81°32W 82 E3
Eucumbene, L. Australia 36°2S 148°40E 63 F4
Eudora U.S.A. 33°7N 91°16W 84 E9
Eufaula Ala., U.S.A. 31°54N 85°9W 85 F12
Eufaula Okla., U.S.A. 35°17N 95°35W 84 D7

Eufaula L. U.S.A. 35°18N 95°21W 84 D7
Eugene U.S.A. 44°5N 123°4W 76 D2
Eugowra Australia 33°22S 148°24E 63 E4
Eulo Australia 28°10S 145°3E 63 D4
Eungella △ Australia 20°57S 148°40E 62 b
Eunice La., U.S.A. 30°30N 92°25W 84 F8
Eunice N. Mex., U.S.A. 32°26N 103°10W 77 K12
Eupen Belgium 50°37N 6°3E 15 D6
Euphrates = Furāt, Nahr al →
   Asia 31°0N 47°25E 46 D5
Eureka Canada 80°0N 85°56W 69 B14
Eureka Calif., U.S.A. 40°47N 124°9W 76 F1
Eureka Kans., U.S.A. 37°49N 96°17W 80 G5
Eureka Mont., U.S.A. 48°53N 115°3W 76 B6
Eureka Nev., U.S.A. 39°31N 115°58W 76 G6
Eureka S. Dak., U.S.A. 45°46N 99°38W 80 C4
Eureka, Mt. Australia 26°35S 121°35E 61 E3
Eureka Sd. Canada 79°0N 85°0W 69 B15
Euroa Australia 36°44S 145°35E 63 F4
Europa, Île Ind. Oc. 22°20S 40°22E 57 B7
Europa, Picos de Spain 43°10N 4°49W 21 A3
Europa, Pt. Gib. 36°3N 5°21W 21 D3
Europe 50°0N 20°0E 6 E10
Europoort Neths. 51°57N 4°10E 15 C4
Eustis U.S.A. 28°51N 81°41W 85 G14
Eutsuk L. Canada 53°20N 126°45W 70 C3
Evale Angola 16°33S 15°44E 56 A2
Evans U.S.A. 40°23N 104°41W 76 F11
Evans, L. Canada 50°50N 77°0W 72 B4
Evans City U.S.A. 40°46N 80°4W 82 F4
Evans Head Australia 29°7S 153°27E 63 D5
Evansburg Canada 53°36N 114°59W 70 C5
Evanston U.S.A. 41°16N 110°58W 76 F8
Evansville U.S.A. 37°58N 87°35W 80 G10
Evaz Iran 27°46N 53°59E 47 E7
Eveleth U.S.A. 47°28N 92°32W 80 B7
Evensk Russia 62°12N 159°30E 27 C16
Everard, L. Australia 31°30S 135°0E 63 E2
Everard Ranges Australia 27°5S 132°28E 61 E5
Everest, Mt. Nepal 28°5N 86°58E 43 E12
Everett Pa., U.S.A. 40°1N 78°23W 82 F6
Everett Wash., U.S.A. 47°59N 122°12W 78 C4
Everglades, The U.S.A. 25°50N 81°0W 85 J14
Everglades △ U.S.A. 25°30N 81°0W 85 J14
Everglades City U.S.A. 25°52N 81°23W 85 J14
Evergreen Ala., U.S.A. 31°26N 86°57W 85 F11
Evergreen Mont., U.S.A. 48°14N 114°17W 76 B6
Evesham U.K. 52°6N 1°56W 13 E6
Evia Greece 38°30N 24°0E 23 E11
Evje Norway 58°36N 7°51E 9 G12
Évora Portugal 38°33N 7°57W 21 C2
Evowghlī Iran 38°43N 45°13E 46 B5
Évreux France 49°3N 1°8E 20 B4
Evros → Greece 41°40N 26°34E 23 D12
Évry France 48°38N 2°27E 20 B5
Évvoia = Evia Greece 38°30N 24°0E 23 E11
Ewe, L. U.K. 57°49N 5°38W 11 D3
Ewing U.S.A. 42°16N 98°21W 80 D4
Ewo Congo 0°48S 14°45E 54 E2
Exaltación Bolivia 13°10S 65°20W 92 F5
Excelsior Springs U.S.A. 39°20N 94°13W 80 F6
Exe → U.K. 50°41N 3°29W 13 G4
Exeter Canada 43°21N 81°29W 82 C3
Exeter U.K. 50°43N 3°31W 13 G4
Exeter Calif., U.S.A. 36°18N 119°9W 78 J7
Exeter N.H., U.S.A. 42°59N 70°57W 83 D14
Exmoor Canada 51°12N 3°45W 13 F4
Exmoor △ U.K. 51°8N 3°42W 13 F4
Exmouth Australia 21°54S 114°10E 60 D1
Exmouth U.K. 50°37N 3°25W 13 G4
Exmouth G. Australia 22°15S 114°15E 60 D1
Exmouth Plateau Ind. Oc. 19°0S 114°0E 64 J3
Expedition △ Australia 25°4S 149°7E 63 D4
Expedition Ra. Australia 24°30S 149°12E 62 C4
Extremadura □ Spain 39°30N 6°5W 21 C2
Exuma Sound Bahamas 24°30N 76°20W 88 B4
Eyasi, L. Tanzania 3°30S 35°0E 54 E7
Eye Pen. U.K. 58°13N 6°10W 11 C2
Eyemouth U.K. 55°52N 2°5W 11 F6
Eyjafjallajökull Iceland 63°38N 19°36W 8 E4
Eyjafjörður Iceland 66°15N 18°30W 8 C4
Eyl Somalia 8°0N 49°50E 49 F4
Eyre (North), L.
   Australia 28°30S 137°20E 63 D2
Eyre (South), L.
   Australia 29°18S 137°25E 63 D2
Eyre, L. Australia 29°30S 137°26E 58 D6
Eyre Mts. N.Z. 45°25S 168°25E 59 F2
Eyre Pen. Australia 33°30S 136°17E 63 E2
Eysturoy Færoe Is. 62°13N 6°54W 8 E9
Eyvān = Jūy Zar Iran 33°50N 46°18E 46 C5
Eyvānkī Iran 35°24N 51°56E 47 C6
Ezhou China 30°23N 114°50E 35 B10
Ezine Turkey 39°48N 26°20E 23 E12

F

F.Y.R.O.M. = Macedonia ■
   Europe 41°53N 21°40E 23 D9
Faaa Tahiti 17°34S 149°35W 59 d
Faaone Tahiti 17°40S 149°21W 59 d
Fabala Guinea 9°44N 9°5W 52 G4
Fabens U.S.A. 31°30N 106°10W 84 F1
Fabius U.S.A. 42°50N 75°59W 83 D9
Fabriano Italy 43°20N 12°54E 22 C5
Fachi Niger 18°6N 11°34E 53 E8
Fada Chad 17°13N 21°34E 53 E10
Fada-n-Gourma
   Burkina Faso 12°10N 0°30E 52 F6
Faddeyevskiy, Ostrov
   Russia 76°0N 144°0E 27 B15
Fadghāmī Syria 35°53N 40°52E 46 C4
Faenza Italy 44°17N 11°53E 22 B4
Færoe Is. = Føroyar ☑
   Atl. Oc. 62°0N 7°0W 8 F9
Fāgāras Romania 45°48N 24°58E 17 F13
Fagersta Sweden 60°1N 15°46E 9 F16
Fagnano, L. Argentina 54°30S 68°0W 96 G3
Fahlīān Iran 30°11N 51°28E 47 D6

Fahraj Kermān, Iran 29°0N 59°0E 47 D8
Fahraj Yazd, Iran 31°46N 54°36E 47 D7
Fai Tsi Long Vietnam 21°0N 107°30E 34 B6
Faial Azores 38°34N 28°42W 52 a
Faichan Kangri India 35°48N 76°34E 43 B7
Fair Haven N.Y., U.S.A. 43°18N 76°42W 83 C8
Fair Haven Vt., U.S.A. 43°36N 73°16W 83 C11
Fair Hd. U.K. 55°14N 6°9W 10 A5
Fair Isle U.K. 59°32N 1°38W 11 B7
Fair Oaks U.S.A. 38°39N 121°16W 78 G5
Fairbanks U.S.A. 64°51N 147°43W 68 E2
Fairbury U.S.A. 40°8N 97°11W 80 E5
Fairfax U.S.A. 40°40N 73°1W 83 B11
Fairfield Calif., U.S.A. 38°15N 122°3W 78 G4
Fairfield Conn., U.S.A. 41°9N 73°16W 83 E11
Fairfield Idaho, U.S.A. 43°21N 114°44W 76 E6
Fairfield Ill., U.S.A. 38°23N 88°22W 80 F9
Fairfield Iowa, U.S.A. 40°56N 91°57W 80 E8
Fairfield Tex., U.S.A. 31°44N 96°10W 84 F6
Fairford Canada 51°37N 98°38W 71 C9
Fairhope U.S.A. 30°31N 87°54W 85 F11
Fairlie N.Z. 44°5S 170°49E 59 F3
Fairmead U.S.A. 37°5N 120°10W 78 H6
Fairmont Minn., U.S.A. 43°39N 94°28W 80 D7
Fairmont W. Va., U.S.A. 39°29N 80°9W 81 F13
Fairmount Calif., U.S.A. 34°45N 118°26W 79 L8
Fairmount N.Y., U.S.A. 43°3N 76°12W 83 C8
Fairplay U.S.A. 39°15N 106°2W 76 G10
Fairport U.S.A. 43°6N 77°27W 82 C7
Fairport Harbor U.S.A. 41°45N 81°17W 82 E3
Fairview Canada 56°5N 118°25W 70 B5
Fairview Mont., U.S.A. 47°51N 104°3W 76 C11
Fairview Okla., U.S.A. 36°16N 98°29W 84 C5
Fairweather, Mt. U.S.A. 58°55N 137°32W 70 B1
Faisalabad Pakistan 31°30N 73°5E 42 D5
Faith U.S.A. 45°2N 102°2W 80 C2
Faizabad India 26°45N 82°10E 43 F10
Faizpur India 21°14N 75°49E 44 D2
Fajardo Puerto Rico 18°20N 65°39W 89 d
Fajr, W. → Si. Arabia 29°10N 38°10E 46 D3
Fakenham U.K. 52°51N 0°51E 12 E8
Fakfak Indonesia 2°55S 132°18E 37 E8
Faku China 42°32N 123°21E 33 C12
Falaise France 48°54N 0°12W 20 B3
Falam Burma 23°0N 93°45E 41 H18
Falcón, Presa Mexico 26°35N 99°10W 87 B5
Falcon Lake Canada 49°42N 95°15W 71 D9
Falcon Res. U.S.A. 26°34N 99°10W 84 H5
Falconara Maríttima
   Italy 43°37N 13°24E 22 C5
Falcone, C. del Italy 40°58N 8°12E 22 D3
Falconer U.S.A. 42°7N 79°13W 82 D5
Falefa Samoa 13°54S 171°31W 59 b
Falelatai Samoa 13°55S 171°59W 59 b
Falelima Samoa 13°32S 172°41W 59 b
Faleshty = Fălești
   Moldova 47°32N 27°44E 17 E14
Fălești Moldova 47°32N 27°44E 17 E14
Falfurrias U.S.A. 27°14N 98°9W 84 H5
Falher Canada 55°44N 117°15W 70 B5
Falkenberg Sweden 56°54N 12°30E 9 H15
Falkirk U.K. 56°0N 3°47W 11 F5
Falkirk □ U.K. 55°58N 3°49W 11 F5
Falkland U.K. 56°16N 3°12W 11 E5
Falkland Is. ☑ Atl. Oc. 51°30S 59°0W 96 G5
Falkland Is. △ Falk. Is. 52°0S 60°0W 96 G5
Fall River U.S.A. 41°43N 71°10W 83 E13
Fallbrook U.S.A. 33°23N 117°15W 79 M9
Fallon U.S.A. 39°28N 118°47W 76 G4
Falls City U.S.A. 40°3N 95°36W 80 E6
Falls Creek U.S.A. 41°9N 78°48W 82 E6
Falmouth Jamaica 18°30N 77°40W 88 a
Falmouth U.K. 50°9N 5°5W 13 G2
Falmouth U.S.A. 41°33N 70°37W 83 E14
Falsa, Pta. Mexico 27°51N 115°3W 86 B1
False B. S. Africa 34°15S 18°40E 56 E2
False Divi Pt. India 15°43N 80°50E 45 G5
False Pt. India 20°18N 86°48E 44 D8
Falso, C. Honduras 15°12N 83°21W 88 C3
Falster Denmark 54°45N 11°55E 9 J14
Fălticeni Romania 47°21N 26°20E 17 E14
Falun Sweden 60°37N 15°37E 8 F16
Famagusta Cyprus 35°8N 33°55E 46 C2
Famatina, Sierra de
   Argentina 27°30S 68°0W 94 B2
Family L. Canada 51°54N 95°27W 71 C9
Famoso U.S.A. 35°37N 119°12W 79 K7
Fan Xian China 35°55N 115°38E 32 G8
Fanad Hd. Ireland 55°17N 7°38W 10 A4
Fang Thailand 19°55N 99°13E 38 C2
Fang Xian China 32°3N 110°40E 35 A8
Fangchang China 31°5N 118°4E 35 B12
Fangcheng China 33°18N 112°59E 34 H7
Fangchenggang China 21°42N 108°21E 34 G7
Fangliao Taiwan 22°22N 120°38E 35 F13
Fangshan Beijing, China 39°41N 116°0E 32 E9
Fangshan Shanxi, China 38°3N 111°25E 32 E6
Fangzi China 36°33N 119°10E 33 F10
Fanjiatun China 43°40N 125°15E 33 C13
Fanling China 22°30N 114°8E 31 a
Fannich, L. U.K. 57°38N 4°59W 11 D4
Fannūj Iran 26°35N 59°38E 47 E8
Fanø Denmark 55°25N 8°25E 9 J13
Fano Italy 43°50N 13°1E 22 C5
Fanshi China 39°12N 113°20E 32 E7
Fao = Al Fāw Iraq 30°0N 48°30E 47 D6
Faqirwali Pakistan 29°27N 73°0E 42 E5
Far East = Dalnevostochnyy □
   Russia 67°0N 140°0E 27 C14
Far East Asia 40°0N 130°0E 24 E14
Faradje
   Dem. Rep. of the Congo 3°50N 29°45E 54 D5
Farafangana Madag. 22°49S 47°50E 55 J9
Farāh Afghan. 32°20N 62°7E 40 C3
Farāh □ Afghan. 32°25N 62°10E 40 C3
Faranah Guinea 10°3N 10°45W 52 F3
Farasān, Jazā'ir Si. Arabia 16°45N 41°55E 49 D3
Farasan Is. = Farasān, Jazā'ir
   Si. Arabia 16°45N 41°55E 49 D3

Fareham U.K. 50°51N 1°11W 13 G6
Farewell, C. N.Z. 40°29S 172°43E 59 D4
Farewell C. = Nunap Isua
   Greenland 59°48N 43°55W 66 D15
Farghona Uzbekistan 40°23N 71°19E 26 E8
Fargo U.S.A. 46°53N 96°48W 80 B5
Fār'iah, W. al →
   West Bank 32°12N 35°27E 48 C4
Faribault U.S.A. 44°18N 93°16W 80 C7
Faridabad India 28°26N 77°19E 42 E6
Faridkot India 30°44N 74°45E 42 D6
Faridpur Bangla. 23°15N 89°55E 43 H13
Faridpur India 28°13N 79°33E 43 E8
Farīmān Iran 35°40N 59°49E 47 C8
Farleigh Australia 21°4S 149°8E 62 b
Farmerville U.S.A. 32°47N 92°24W 84 E8
Farmingdale U.S.A. 40°12N 74°10W 83 F10
Farmington Canada 55°54N 120°30W 70 B4
Farmington Calif.,
   U.S.A. 37°55N 120°59W 78 H6
Farmington Maine,
   U.S.A. 44°40N 70°9W 81 C18
Farmington Mo., U.S.A. 37°47N 90°25W 80 G8
Farmington N.H., U.S.A. 43°24N 71°4W 83 C13
Farmington N. Mex.,
   U.S.A. 36°44N 108°12W 77 H9
Farmington Utah,
   U.S.A. 40°59N 111°53W 76 F8
Farmington → U.S.A. 41°51N 72°38W 83 E12
Farmville U.S.A. 37°18N 78°24W 81 G14
Farne Is. U.K. 55°38N 1°37W 12 B6
Farnham Canada 45°17N 72°59W 83 A12
Farnham, Mt. Canada 50°29N 116°30W 70 C5
Faro Brazil 2°10S 56°39W 92 D7
Faro Canada 62°11N 133°22W 68 E5
Faro Portugal 37°2N 7°55W 21 D2
Färö Sweden 57°55N 19°5E 9 H18
Farquhar, C. Australia 23°50S 113°36E 61 D1
Farrars Cr. → Australia 25°35S 140°43E 62 D3
Farrāshband Iran 28°57N 52°5E 47 D7
Farrell U.S.A. 41°13N 80°30W 82 E4
Farrokhī Iran 33°50N 59°31E 47 C8
Farrukhabad India 27°24N 79°34E 44 A4
Fārs □ Iran 29°30N 55°0E 47 D7
Farsala Greece 39°17N 22°23E 23 E10
Fārsī Iran 27°58N 50°11E 47 E6
Farson U.S.A. 42°7N 109°26W 76 E9
Farsund Norway 58°5N 6°55E 9 G12
Fartak, Râs Si. Arabia 28°5N 34°34E 46 D2
Fartak, Ra's Yemen 15°38N 52°15E 49 D5
Fartura, Serra da Brazil 26°21S 52°52W 95 B5
Fārūj Iran 37°14N 58°14E 47 B8
Farvel, Kap = Nunap Isua
   Greenland 59°48N 43°55W 66 D15
Farwell U.S.A. 34°23N 103°2W 84 D3
Fasā Iran 29°0N 53°39E 47 D7
Fasano Italy 40°50N 17°22E 22 D7
Fastiv Ukraine 50°7N 29°57E 17 C15
Fastnet Rock Ireland 51°22N 9°37W 10 E2
Fastov = Fastiv Ukraine 50°7N 29°57E 17 C15
Fatagartuting, Tanjung
   Indonesia 2°46S 131°57E 37 E8
Fatehabad Haryana, India 29°31N 75°27E 42 E6
Fatehabad Ut. P., India 27°1N 78°19E 42 F8
Fatehgarh India 27°25N 79°35E 43 F8
Fatehpur Bihar, India 24°38N 85°14E 43 G11
Fatehpur Raj., India 28°0N 74°40E 42 F6
Fatehpur Ut. P., India 25°56N 81°13E 43 G9
Fatehpur Ut. P., India 27°10N 81°13E 43 F9
Fatehpur Sikri India 27°6N 77°40E 42 F6
Fathom Five △ Canada 45°17N 81°40W 82 A3
Fatima Canada 47°24N 61°53W 73 C7
Faulkton U.S.A. 45°2N 99°8W 80 C4
Faure I. Australia 25°52S 113°50E 61 E1
Fauresmith S. Africa 29°44S 25°17E 56 C4
Fauske Norway 67°17N 15°25E 8 C16
Favara Italy 37°19N 13°39E 22 F5
Favignana Italy 37°56N 12°20E 22 F5
Fawcett, Pt. Australia 11°46S 130°2E 60 B5
Fawn → Canada 55°20N 87°35W 72 A2
Fawnskin U.S.A. 34°16N 116°56W 79 L10
Faxaflói Iceland 64°29N 23°0W 8 D2
Faya-Largeau Chad 17°58N 19°6E 53 E9
Fayd Si. Arabia 27°1N 42°52E 46 E4
Fayette Ala., U.S.A. 33°41N 87°50W 85 E11
Fayette Mo., U.S.A. 39°9N 92°41W 80 F7
Fayette N.Y., U.S.A. 42°48N 76°48W 83 D8
Fayetteville Ark., U.S.A. 36°4N 94°10W 84 C7
Fayetteville N.C., U.S.A. 35°3N 78°53W 85 D15
Fayetteville Tenn., U.S.A. 35°9N 86°34W 85 D11
Faylakah Kuwait 29°27N 48°20E 47 D6
Fazilka India 30°27N 74°2E 42 D6
Fazilpur Pakistan 29°18N 70°29E 42 E4
Fderik Mauritania 22°40N 12°45W 52 D3
Feakle Ireland 52°56N 8°40W 10 D3
Feale → Ireland 52°27N 9°37W 10 D2
Fear, C. U.S.A. 33°50N 77°58W 85 E16
Feather → U.S.A. 38°47N 121°36W 78 G5
Feather Falls U.S.A. 39°36N 121°16W 78 F5
Featherston N.Z. 41°6S 175°20E 59 D5
Fécamp France 49°45N 0°22E 20 B4
Fedala = Mohammedia
   Morocco 33°44N 7°21W 52 B4
Federación Argentina 31°0S 57°55W 94 C4
Féderal Argentina 30°57S 58°48W 94 C4
Federal Way U.S.A. 47°18N 122°19W 78 C4
Fedeshkūh Iran 28°49N 53°50E 47 D7
Fehmarn Germany 54°27N 11°7E 16 A6
Fehmarn Belt Europe 54°35N 11°20E 9 J14
Fehmarn Belt = Fehmarn Bælt
   Europe 54°35N 11°20E 9 J14
Fei Xian China 35°18N 117°59E 35 G9
Feicheng China 36°14N 116°45E 32 F9
Feidong China 31°55N 117°35E 35 B11
Feijó Brazil 8°9S 70°21W 92 E4
Feilding N.Z. 40°13S 175°35E 59 D5
Feira de Santana Brazil 12°15S 38°57W 93 F11

Feixi China 31°43N 117°59E 35 B11
Feixiang China 36°30N 114°45E 32 F8
Feldkirch Austria 47°15N 9°37E 16 E5
Félicité Seychelles 4°19S 55°52E 55 b
Felipe Carrillo Puerto
   Mexico 19°38N 88°3W 87 D7
Felixburg Zimbabwe 19°29S 30°51E 57 A5
Felixstowe U.K. 51°58N 1°23E 13 F9
Felton U.S.A. 37°3N 122°4W 78 H4
Femer Bælt = Fehmarn Bælt
   Europe 54°35N 11°20E 9 J14
Femunden Norway 62°10N 11°53E 8 E14
Fen He → China 35°36N 110°42E 32 G6
Fenelon Falls Canada 44°32N 78°45W 82 B6
Feng Xian Jiangsu, China 34°43N 116°35E 32 G9
Feng Xian Shaanxi, China 33°54N 106°40E 32 H4
Fengcheng Jiangxi,
   China 28°12N 115°48E 35 C10
Fengcheng Liaoning,
   China 40°28N 124°5E 33 D13
Fengdu China 29°55N 107°48E 34 C6
Fengfeng China 36°28N 114°8E 32 F8
Fenggang China 27°57N 107°47E 34 D6
Fenghua China 29°40N 121°25E 35 C13
Fenghuang China 27°57N 109°29E 34 D7
Fengjie China 31°3N 109°31E 34 B7
Fengkai China 23°24N 111°30E 35 F8
Fengkang Taiwan 22°12N 120°41E 35 F13
Fengle China 31°29N 112°29E 35 B9
Fenglin Taiwan 23°45N 121°26E 35 F13
Fengning China 41°10N 116°33E 32 D9
Fengqing China 24°38N 99°55E 34 E2
Fengqiu China 35°2N 114°25E 32 G8
Fengrun China 39°48N 118°8E 33 E10
Fengshan Guangxi Zhuangzu,
   China 24°39N 109°15E 34 E7
Fengshan Guangxi Zhuangzu,
   China 24°31N 107°3E 34 E6
Fengshan Taiwan 22°38N 120°21E 35 F13
Fengshun China 23°46N 116°10E 35 F11
Fengtai China 32°50N 116°40E 35 A11
Fengtongzhai △ China 30°32N 102°54E 34 B4
Fengxian China 34°29N 107°23E 32 G4
Fengxin China 28°41N 115°18E 35 C10
Fengyang China 32°51N 117°29E 33 H9
Fengyi Taiwan 25°37N 100°20E 34 E3
Fengyüan Taiwan 24°10N 120°35E 35 E13
Fengzhen China 40°25N 113°2E 32 D7
Fenoarivo Atsinanana
   Madag. 17°22S 49°25E 55 H9
Fens, The U.K. 52°38N 0°2W 12 E7
Fenton U.S.A. 42°48N 83°42W 81 D12
Fenxi China 36°40N 111°31E 32 F6
Fenyang China 37°18N 111°48E 32 F6
Fenyi China 27°45N 114°47E 35 D10
Feodosiya Ukraine 45°2N 35°16E 19 E6
Ferbane Ireland 53°16N 7°50W 10 C4
Ferdows Iran 33°58N 58°2E 47 C8
Ferfer Somalia 5°4N 45°9E 49 F4
Fergana = Farghona
   Uzbekistan 40°23N 71°19E 26 E8
Fergus Canada 43°43N 80°24W 82 C4
Fergus Falls U.S.A. 46°17N 96°4W 80 B5
Ferizaj Kosovo 42°23N 21°10E 23 C9
Ferkéssédougou Ivory C. 5°35N 5°6W 52 G4
Ferland Canada 50°19N 88°27W 72 B2
Ferlo, Vallée du Senegal 15°15N 14°15W 52 E3
Fermanagh □ U.K. 54°21N 7°40W 10 B4
Fermo Italy 43°9N 13°43E 22 C5
Fermont Canada 52°47N 67°5W 73 B6
Fermoy Ireland 52°9N 8°16W 10 D3
Fernández Argentina 27°55S 63°50W 94 B3
Fernandina Beach
   U.S.A. 30°40N 81°27W 85 F14
Fernando de Noronha
   Brazil 4°0S 33°10W 93 D12
Fernando Póo = Bioko
   Eq. Guin. 3°30N 8°40E 54 D1
Ferndale Canada 44°58N 81°17W 82 B3
Ferndale U.S.A. 48°51N 122°36W 78 B4
Fernie Canada 49°30N 115°5W 70 D5
Fernlees Australia 23°51S 148°7E 62 C4
Fernley U.S.A. 39°36N 119°15W 76 G4
Fernwood U.S.A. 43°16N 73°38W 83 C11
Feroke India 11°9N 75°46E 45 J2
Ferozepore = Firozpur
   India 30°55N 74°40E 42 D6
Ferrara Italy 44°50N 11°35E 22 B4
Ferreñafe Peru 6°42S 79°50W 92 E3
Ferret, C. France 44°38N 1°15W 20 D3
Ferriday U.S.A. 31°38N 91°33W 84 F9
Ferrol Spain 43°29N 8°15W 21 A1
Ferron U.S.A. 39°5N 111°8W 76 G8
Ferryland Canada 47°2N 52°53W 73 C9
Fertile U.S.A. 47°32N 96°17W 80 B5
Fès Morocco 34°0N 5°0W 52 B5
Fessenden U.S.A. 47°39N 99°38W 80 B4
Festus U.S.A. 38°13N 90°24W 80 F8
Feteşti Romania 44°22N 27°51E 17 F14
Fethiye Turkey 36°36N 29°6E 19 G4
Fetlar U.K. 60°36N 0°52W 11 A8
Feuilles → Canada 58°47N 70°4W 69 F17
Fez = Fès Morocco 34°0N 5°0W 52 B5
Fezzan Libya 27°0N 13°0E 53 C8
Fiambalá Argentina 27°45S 67°37W 94 B2
Fianarantsoa Madag. 21°26S 47°5E 55 J9
Ficksburg S. Africa 28°51S 27°53E 57 C4
Field → Australia 23°48S 138°0E 62 C2
Field I. Australia 12°5S 132°23E 60 B5
Fier Albania 40°43N 19°33E 23 D8
Fife □ U.K. 56°16N 3°1W 11 E5
Fife Ness U.K. 56°17N 2°35W 11 E6
Fifth Cataract Sudan 18°22N 33°50E 53 E12
Figeac France 44°37N 2°2E 20 D5
Figueira da Foz Portugal 40°7N 8°54W 21 B1
Figueres Spain 42°18N 2°58E 21 A7
Figuig Morocco 32°5N 1°11W 52 B5
Fiji ■ Pac. Oc. 17°20S 179°0E 59 a
Filabus Zimbabwe 20°34S 29°20E 57 B4

Filadelfia *Paraguay* 22°21S 60°2W **94** A3
Filchner Ice Shelf *Antarctica* 79°0S 40°0W **5** D1
Filey *U.K.* 54°12N 0°18W **12** C7
Filey B. *U.K.* 54°12N 0°15W **12** C7
Filiatra *Greece* 37°9N 21°35E **23** F9
Filingué *Niger* 14°21N 3°22E **52** F6
Filipstad *Sweden* 59°43N 14°9E **9** G16
Fillmore *Calif., U.S.A.* 34°24N 118°55W **79** L8
Fillmore *Utah, U.S.A.* 38°58N 112°20W **76** G7
Fimbul Ice Shelf *S. Ocean* 69°30S 1°0W **5** C2
Finch *Canada* 45°11N 75°7W **83** A9
Finch Hatton *Australia* 20°25S 148°39E **62** b
Findhorn → *U.K.* 57°38N 3°38W **11** D5
Findlay *U.S.A.* 41°2N 83°39W **81** E12
Fine *U.S.A.* 44°14N 75°8W **83** B9
Finger L. *Canada* 53°33N 93°30W **72** B1
Finger Lakes *U.S.A.* 42°40N 76°30W **83** D8
Fíngoè *Mozam.* 15°55S 31°50E **55** G6
Finisterre, C. = Fisterra, C.
  Spain 42°50N 9°19W **21** A1
Finke *Australia* 25°34S 134°35E **62** D1
Finke Gorge △ *Australia* 24°8S 132°49E **60** D5
Finland ■ *Europe* 63°0N 27°0E **8** E22
Finland, G. of *Europe* 60°0N 26°0E **9** G22
Finlay → *Canada* 57°0N 125°10W **70** B3
Finley *Australia* 35°38S 145°35E **63** F4
Finley *U.S.A.* 47°31N 97°50W **80** B5
Finn → *Ireland* 54°51N 7°28W **10** B4
Finnigan, Mt. *Australia* 15°49S 145°17E **62** B4
Finniss, C. *Australia* 33°8S 134°51E **63** E1
Finnmark *Norway* 69°37N 23°57E **8** B20
Finnsnes *Norway* 69°14N 18°0E **8** B18
Finspång *Sweden* 58°43N 15°47E **9** G16
Fiora → *Italy* 42°20N 11°34E **22** C4
Fiordland △ *N.Z.* 45°46S 167°0E **59** F1
Fiq *Syria* 32°46N 35°41E **48** C4
Firat = Furāt, Nahr al →
  Asia 31°0N 47°25E **46** D5
Fire Island △ *U.S.A.* 40°38N 73°8W **83** F11
Firebag → *Canada* 57°45N 111°21W **71** B6
Firebaugh *U.S.A.* 36°52N 120°27W **78** J6
Firedrake L. *Canada* 61°25N 104°30W **71** A8
Firenze *Italy* 43°46N 11°15E **22** C4
Firk, Sha'ib → *Iraq* 30°59N 44°34E **46** D5
Firozabad *India* 27°10N 78°25E **43** F8
Firozpur *India* 30°55N 74°40E **42** D6
Firozpur-Jhirka *India* 27°48N 76°57E **42** F7
Fīrūzābād *Iran* 28°52N 52°35E **47** D7
Fīrūzkūh *Iran* 35°50N 52°50E **47** C7
Firvale *Canada* 52°27N 126°13W **70** C3
Fish → *Namibia* 28°7S 17°10E **56** C2
Fish → *S. Africa* 31°30S 20°16E **56** D3
Fish River Canyon
  Namibia 27°40S 17°35E **56** C2
Fisher B. *Canada* 51°35N 97°13W **71** C9
Fishers I. *U.S.A.* 41°15N 72°0W **83** E13
Fishguard *U.K.* 52°0N 4°58W **13** E3
Fishing L. *Canada* 52°10N 95°24W **71** C9
Fishkill *U.S.A.* 41°32N 73°54W **83** E11
Fisterra, C. *Spain* 42°50N 9°19W **21** A1
Fitchburg *Mass., U.S.A.* 42°35N 71°48W **83** D13
Fitchburg *Wis., U.S.A.* 42°58N 89°28W **80** D9
Fitz Roy *Argentina* 47°0S 67°0W **96** F3
Fitz Roy, Cerro *Argentina* 49°17S 73°5W **96** F2
Fitzgerald *Canada* 59°51N 111°36W **70** B6
Fitzgerald *U.S.A.* 31°43N 83°15W **85** F13
Fitzgerald River △
  Australia 33°53S 119°55E **61** F3
Fitzmaurice → *Australia* 14°45S 130°5E **60** B5
Fitzroy → *Queens.,*
  Australia 23°32S 150°52E **62** C5
Fitzroy → *W. Austral.,*
  Australia 17°31S 123°35E **60** C3
Fitzroy Crossing *Australia* 18°9S 125°38E **60** C4
Fitzwilliam I. *Canada* 45°30N 81°45W **82** A3
Fiume = Rijeka *Croatia* 45°20N 14°21E **16** F8
Five Points *U.S.A.* 36°26N 120°6W **78** J6
Fizi *Dem. Rep. of the Congo* 4°17S 28°55E **54** E5
Flagstaff *U.S.A.* 35°12N 111°39W **77** J8
Flagstaff L. *U.S.A.* 45°12N 70°18W **83** A14
Flaherty I. *Canada* 56°15N 79°15W **72** A4
Flåm *Norway* 60°50N 7°7E **8** F12
Flambeau → *U.S.A.* 45°18N 91°14W **80** C8
Flamborough Hd. *U.K.* 54°7N 0°5W **12** C7
Flaming Gorge △
  U.S.A. 41°10N 109°25W **76** F9
Flaming Gorge Res.
  U.S.A. 41°10N 109°25W **76** F9
Flamingo, Teluk *Indonesia* 5°30S 138°0E **37** F9
Flanders = Flandre *Europe* 50°50N 2°30E **15** B9
Flandre *Europe* 50°50N 2°30E **15** B9
Flandre-Occidentale = West-
  Vlaanderen □ *Belgium* 51°0N 3°0E **15** D2
Flandre-Orientale = Oost-
  Vlaanderen □ *Belgium* 51°5N 3°50E **15** C3
Flandreau *U.S.A.* 44°3N 96°36W **80** C5
Flanigan *U.S.A.* 40°10N 119°53W **78** E7
Flannan Is. *U.K.* 58°9N 7°52W **11** C1
Flåsjön *Sweden* 64°5N 15°40E **8** D16
Flat → *Canada* 61°33N 125°18W **70** A3
Flat I. *Mauritius* 19°53S 57°35E **55** d
Flathead L. *U.S.A.* 47°51N 114°8W **76** C6
Flattery, C. *Australia* 14°58S 145°21E **62** A4
Flattery, C. *U.S.A.* 48°23N 124°29W **78** B2
Flatwoods *U.S.A.* 38°31N 82°43W **81** F12
Fleetwood *U.S.A.* 40°27N 75°49W **83** F9
Fleetwood *U.K.* 53°55N 3°1W **12** D4
Flekkefjord *Norway* 58°18N 6°39E **9** G12
Flemington *U.S.A.* 41°7N 77°28W **82** E7
Flensburg *Germany* 54°47N 9°27E **16** A5
Flers *France* 48°47N 0°33W **20** B3
Flesherton *Canada* 44°16N 80°33W **82** B4
Flesko, Tanjung *Indonesia* 0°29N 124°30E **37** D6
Fleurieu Pen. *Australia* 35°40S 138°5E **63** F2
Flevoland □ *Neths.* 52°30N 5°30E **15** B5
Flin Flon *Canada* 54°46N 101°53W **71** C8
Flinders → *Australia* 17°36S 140°36E **62** B3
Flinders B. *Australia* 34°19S 115°19E **61** F2
Flinders Group *Australia* 14°11S 144°15E **62** A3

Flinders I. *S. Austral.,*
  Australia 33°44S 134°41E **63** E1
Flinders I. *Tas., Australia* 40°0S 148°0E **63** G4
Flinders Ranges
  Australia 31°30S 138°30E **63** E2
Flinders Reefs *Australia* 17°37S 148°31E **62** B4
Flint *U.K.* 53°15N 3°8W **12** D4
Flint *U.S.A.* 43°1N 83°41W **81** D12
Flint → *U.S.A.* 30°57N 84°34W **85** F12
Flint I. *Kiribati* 11°26S 151°48W **65** J12
Flintshire □ *U.K.* 53°17N 3°17W **12** D4
Flodden *U.K.* 55°37N 2°8W **12** B5
Floodplains △ *Sri Lanka* 8°10N 81°10E **45** K5
Floodwood *U.S.A.* 46°56N 92°55W **80** B7
Flora *Australia* 38°40N 88°29W **80** F9
Florala *U.S.A.* 31°0N 86°20W **85** F11
Florence = Firenze *Italy* 43°46N 11°15E **22** C4
Florence *Ala., U.S.A.* 34°48N 87°41W **85** D11
Florence *Ariz., U.S.A.* 33°2N 111°23W **77** K8
Florence *Colo., U.S.A.* 38°23N 105°8W **76** G11
Florence *Oreg., U.S.A.* 43°58N 124°7W **76** D1
Florence *S.C., U.S.A.* 34°12N 79°46W **85** D15
Florence, L. *Australia* 28°53S 138°9E **63** D2
Florencia *Colombia* 1°36N 75°36W **92** C3
Florennes *Belgium* 50°15N 4°35E **15** D4
Florenville *Belgium* 49°40N 5°19E **15** E5
Flores *Azores* 39°26N 31°13W **52** a
Flores *Guatemala* 16°59N 89°50W **88** C2
Flores *Indonesia* 8°35S 121°0E **37** F6
Flores I. *Canada* 49°20N 126°10W **70** D3
Flores Sea *Indonesia* 6°30S 120°0E **37** F6
Floreşti *Moldova* 47°53N 28°17E **17** E15
Floresville *U.S.A.* 29°8N 98°10W **84** G5
Floriano *Brazil* 6°50S 43°0W **93** E10
Florianópolis *Brazil* 27°30S 48°30W **95** B6
Florida *Cuba* 21°32N 78°14W **88** B4
Florida *Uruguay* 34°7S 56°10W **95** C4
Florida □ *U.S.A.* 28°0N 82°0W **85** G14
Florida, Straits of *U.S.A.* 25°0N 80°0W **88** B4
Florida B. *U.S.A.* 25°0N 80°45W **88** B3
Florida Keys *U.S.A.* 24°40N 81°0W **85** J14
Florin *U.S.A.* 38°30N 121°24W **78** G5
Florina *Greece* 40°48N 21°26E **23** D9
Florissant *U.S.A.* 38°47N 90°19W **80** F8
Florø *Norway* 61°35N 5°1E **8** F11
Flower Station *Canada* 45°10N 76°41W **83** A8
Flowerpot I. *Canada* 45°18N 81°38W **82** A3
Floydada *U.S.A.* 33°59N 101°20W **84** E4
Fluk *Indonesia* 1°42S 127°44E **37** E7
Flushing =
  Vlissingen
  Neths. 51°26N 3°34E **15** C3
Fly → *Papua N. G.* 8°25S 143°0E **58** B7
Flying Fish, C. *Antarctica* 72°6S 102°29W **5** D15
Foa *Tonga* 19°45S 174°18W **59** c
Foam Lake *Canada* 51°40N 103°32W **71** C8
Foça *Turkey* 38°39N 26°46E **23** E12
Fochabers *U.K.* 57°37N 3°6W **11** D5
Focşani *Romania* 45°41N 27°15E **17** F14
Fogang *China* 23°52N 113°30E **35** F9
Fóggia *Italy* 41°27N 15°34E **22** D6
Fogo *Canada* 49°43N 54°17W **73** C9
Fogo *C. Verde Is.* 15°5N 24°20W **52** b
Fogo I. *Canada* 49°40N 54°5W **73** C9
Föhr *Germany* 54°43N 8°30E **16** A5
Foix *France* 42°58N 1°38E **20** E4
Folda *Nord-Trøndelag,*
  Norway 64°32N 10°30E **8** D14
Folda *Nordland, Norway* 67°38N 14°50E **8** C16
Foley *Botswana* 21°34S 27°21E **56** B4
Foley *U.S.A.* 30°24N 87°41W **85** F11
Foleyet *Canada* 48°15N 82°25W **72** C3
Folgefonna *Norway* 60°3N 6°23E **9** F12
Foligno *Italy* 42°57N 12°42E **22** C5
Folkestone *U.K.* 51°5N 1°12E **13** F9
Folkston *U.S.A.* 30°50N 82°0W **85** F13
Follansbee *U.S.A.* 40°19N 80°35W **82** F4
Folsom *U.S.A.* 38°40N 121°9W **78** G5
Folsom L. *U.S.A.* 38°42N 121°9W **78** G5
Fomboni *Comoros Is.* 12°18S 43°46E **55** a
Fond-du-Lac *Canada* 59°19N 107°12W **71** B7
Fond du Lac *U.S.A.* 43°47N 88°27W **80** D9
Fond-du-Lac → *Canada* 59°17N 106°0W **71** B7
Fonda *U.S.A.* 42°57N 74°22W **83** D10
Fondi *Italy* 41°21N 13°25E **22** D5
Fongafale *Tuvalu* 8°31S 179°13E **58** B10
Fonsagrada = A Fonsagrada
  Spain 43°8N 7°4W **21** A2
Fonseca, G. de
  Cent. Amer. 13°10N 87°40W **88** D2
Fontainebleau *France* 48°24N 2°40E **20** B5
Fontana *U.S.A.* 34°6N 117°26W **79** L9
Fontas → *Canada* 58°14N 121°48W **70** B4
Fonte Boa *Brazil* 2°33S 66°0W **92** D5
Fontenay-le-Comte
  France 46°28N 0°48W **20** C3
Fontenelle Res. *U.S.A.* 42°1N 110°3W **76** E8
Fontur *Iceland* 66°23N 14°32W **8** C6
Fonuafo'ou *Tonga* 20°19S 175°25W **59** c
Fonualei *Tonga* 18°1S 174°19W **59** c
Foochow = Fuzhou
  China 26°5N 119°16E **35** D12
Foping *China* 33°41N 108°0E **32** H5
Foraker, Mt. *U.S.A.* 62°58N 151°24W **74** C9
Forbes *Australia* 33°22S 148°0E **63** E4
Forbesganj *India* 26°17N 87°18E **43** F12
Ford City *Calif., U.S.A.* 35°9N 119°27W **79** K7
Ford City *Pa., U.S.A.* 40°46N 79°32W **82** F5
Førde *Norway* 61°27N 5°53E **8** F11
Fords Bridge *Australia* 29°41S 145°29E **63** D4
Fordyce *U.S.A.* 33°49N 92°25W **84** E8
Forel, Mt. *Greenland* 66°52N 36°55W **4** C6
Foremost *Canada* 49°26N 111°34W **70** D6
Forest *Canada* 43°6N 82°0W **82** C3
Forest City *Iowa, U.S.A.* 43°16N 93°39W **80** D7
Forest City *N.C., U.S.A.* 35°20N 81°52W **85** D14
Forest City *Pa., U.S.A.* 41°39N 75°28W **83** E9
Forest Grove *U.S.A.* 45°31N 123°7W **78** E3
Forestburg *Canada* 52°35N 112°1W **70** C6

Foresthill *U.S.A.* 39°1N 120°49W **78** F6
Forestier Pen. *Australia* 43°0S 148°0E **63** G4
Forestville *Canada* 48°48N 69°2W **73** C6
Forestville *Calif., U.S.A.* 38°28N 122°54W **78** G4
Forestville *N.Y., U.S.A.* 42°28N 79°10W **82** D5
Forfar *U.K.* 56°39N 2°53W **11** E6
Forillon △ *Canada* 48°46N 64°12W **73** C7
Forks *U.S.A.* 47°57N 124°23W **78** C2
Forksville *U.S.A.* 41°29N 76°35W **83** E8
Forlì *Italy* 44°13N 12°3E **22** B5
Forman *U.S.A.* 46°7N 97°38W **80** B5
Formby Pt. *U.K.* 53°33N 3°6W **12** D4
Formentera *Spain* 38°43N 1°27E **21** C6
Formentor, C. de *Spain* 39°58N 3°13E **21** C7
Former Yugoslav Republic of
  Macedonia = Macedonia ■
  Europe 41°53N 21°40E **23** D9
Fórmia *Italy* 41°15N 13°37E **22** D5
Formosa = Taiwan ■
  Asia 23°30N 121°0E **35** F13
Formosa *Argentina* 26°15S 58°10W **94** B4
Formosa *Brazil* 15°32S 47°20W **93** G9
Formosa □ *Argentina* 25°0S 60°0W **94** B4
Formosa, Serra *Brazil* 12°0S 55°0W **93** F8
Formosa B. = Ungwana B.
  Kenya 2°45S 40°20E **54** C5
Føroyar ☑ *Atl. Oc.* 62°0N 7°0W **8** F9
Forres *U.K.* 57°37N 3°37W **11** D5
Forrest *Australia* 30°51S 128°6E **61** F4
Forrest, Mt. *Australia* 24°48S 127°45E **61** D4
Forrest City *U.S.A.* 35°1N 90°47W **85** D9
Forsayth *Australia* 18°33S 143°34E **62** B3
Forssa *Finland* 60°49N 23°38E **8** F20
Forst *Germany* 51°45N 14°37E **16** C8
Forster *Australia* 32°12S 152°31E **63** E5
Forsyth *U.S.A.* 46°16N 106°41W **76** C10
Fort Abbas *Pakistan* 29°12N 72°52E **42** E5
Fort Albany *Canada* 52°15N 81°35W **72** B3
Fort Assiniboine *Canada* 54°20N 114°45W **70** C6
Fort Augustus *U.K.* 57°9N 4°42W **11** D4
Fort Beaufort *S. Africa* 32°46S 26°40E **56** D4
Fort Benton *U.S.A.* 47°49N 110°40W **76** C8
Fort Bragg *U.S.A.* 39°26N 123°48W **76** G2
Fort Bridger *U.S.A.* 41°19N 110°23W **76** F8
Fort Chipewyan *Canada* 58°42N 111°8W **71** B6
Fort Clatsop = Lewis and Clark △
  U.S.A. 46°8N 123°53W **78** D3
Fort Collins *U.S.A.* 40°35N 105°5W **76** F11
Fort-Coulonge *Canada* 45°50N 76°45W **72** C4
Fort Covington *U.S.A.* 44°59N 74°29W **83** B10
Fort Dauphin = Taolanaro
  Madag. 25°2S 47°0E **55** K9
Fort Davis *U.S.A.* 30°35N 103°54W **84** F3
Fort-de-France *Martinique* 14°36N 61°5W **88** c
Fort Defiance *U.S.A.* 35°45N 109°5W **77** J9
Fort Dodge *U.S.A.* 42°30N 94°11W **80** D6
Fort Edward *U.S.A.* 43°16N 73°35W **83** C11
Fort Erie *Canada* 42°54N 78°56W **82** D6
Fort Fairfield *U.S.A.* 46°46N 67°50W **81** B20
Fort Frances *Canada* 48°36N 93°24W **71** D10
Fort Franklin = Déline
  Canada 65°11N 123°25W **68** B7
Fort Garland *U.S.A.* 37°26N 105°26W **77** H11
Fort George = Chisasibi
  Canada 53°50N 79°0W **72** B4
Fort Good Hope *Canada* 66°14N 128°40W **68** B6
Fort Hancock *U.S.A.* 31°18N 105°51W **84** F2
Fort Hope = Eabametoong
  Canada 51°30N 88°0W **72** B2
Fort Irwin *U.S.A.* 35°16N 116°41W **79** K10
Fort Kent *U.S.A.* 47°15N 68°36W **81** B19
Fort Klamath *U.S.A.* 42°42N 122°0W **76** D3
Fort Laramie *U.S.A.* 42°13N 104°31W **76** E11
Fort Liard *Canada* 60°14N 123°30W **70** A4
Fort Liberté *Haiti* 19°42N 71°51W **89** C5
Fort Lupton *U.S.A.* 40°5N 104°49W **76** F11
Fort MacKay *Canada* 57°12N 111°41W **70** B6
Fort Macleod *Canada* 49°45N 113°30W **70** D6
Fort McMurray *Canada* 56°44N 111°7W **70** B6
Fort McPherson *Canada* 67°30N 134°55W **68** B5
Fort Madison *U.S.A.* 40°38N 91°27W **80** E8
Fort Meade *U.S.A.* 27°45N 81°48W **85** H14
Fort Morgan *U.S.A.* 40°15N 103°48W **76** F12
Fort Myers *U.S.A.* 26°39N 81°52W **85** H14
Fort Nelson *Canada* 58°50N 122°44W **70** B4
Fort Nelson → *Canada* 59°32N 124°0W **70** B4
Fort Norman = Tulita
  Canada 64°57N 125°30W **68** B6
Fort Payne *U.S.A.* 34°26N 85°43W **85** D12
Fort Peck *U.S.A.* 48°1N 106°27W **76** B10
Fort Peck Dam *U.S.A.* 48°0N 106°26W **76** C10
Fort Peck L. *U.S.A.* 48°0N 106°26W **76** C10
Fort Pierce *U.S.A.* 27°27N 80°20W **85** H14
Fort Pierre *U.S.A.* 44°21N 100°22W **80** C3
Fort Plain *U.S.A.* 42°56N 74°37W **83** D10
Fort Portal *Uganda* 0°40N 30°20E **54** D6
Fort Providence *Canada* 61°3N 117°40W **70** A5
Fort Qu'Appelle *Canada* 50°45N 103°50W **71** C8
Fort Resolution *Canada* 61°10N 113°40W **70** A6
Fort Ross *U.S.A.* 38°32N 123°13W **78** G3
Fort Rupert = Waskaganish
  Canada 51°30N 78°40W **72** B4
Fort St. James *Canada* 54°30N 124°10W **70** C4
Fort St. John *Canada* 56°15N 120°50W **70** B4
Fort Saskatchewan
  Canada 53°40N 113°15W **70** C6
Fort Scott *U.S.A.* 37°50N 94°42W **80** G7
Fort Severn *Canada* 56°0N 87°40W **72** A2
Fort Shevchenko
  Kazakhstan 44°35N 50°23E **19** F9
Fort Simpson *Canada* 61°45N 121°15W **70** A4
Fort Smith *Canada* 60°0N 111°51W **70** B6
Fort Smith *U.S.A.* 35°23N 94°25W **84** D7
Fort Stockton *U.S.A.* 30°53N 102°53W **84** F3
Fort Sumner *U.S.A.* 34°28N 104°15W **77** J11
Fort Thompson *U.S.A.* 44°3N 99°26W **80** C4
Fort Union △ *U.S.A.* 35°54N 105°0W **77** J11
Fort Valley *U.S.A.* 32°33N 83°53W **85** E13
Fort Vermilion *Canada* 58°24N 116°0W **70** B5
Fort Walton Beach
  U.S.A. 30°25N 86°36W **85** F11

Fort Ware *Canada* 57°26N 125°41W **70** B3
Fort Wayne *U.S.A.* 41°4N 85°9W **81** E11
Fort William *U.K.* 56°49N 5°7W **11** E3
Fort Worth *U.S.A.* 32°43N 97°19W **84** E6
Fort Yates *U.S.A.* 46°5N 100°38W **80** B3
Fort Yukon *U.S.A.* 66°34N 145°16W **68** B5
Fortaleza *Brazil* 3°45S 38°35W **93** D11
Forteau *Canada* 51°28N 56°58W **73** B8
Fortescue → *Australia* 21°0S 116°4E **60** D2
Fortescue River Roadhouse
  Australia 21°17S 116°8E **60** D2
Forth → *U.K.* 56°9N 3°50W **11** E5
Forth, Firth of *U.K.* 56°5N 2°55W **11** E6
Fortine *U.S.A.* 48°46N 114°54W **76** B6
Fortrose *U.K.* 57°35N 4°9W **11** D4
Fortuna *Calif., U.S.A.* 40°36N 124°9W **76** F1
Fortuna *N. Dak., U.S.A.* 48°55N 103°47W **80** A2
Fortune *Canada* 47°4N 55°50W **73** C8
Fortune B. *Canada* 47°30N 55°22W **73** C8
Forūr *Iran* 26°17N 54°32E **47** E7
Fosen *Norway* 63°50N 10°20E **8** E14
Fosnavåg *Norway* 62°22N 5°38E **8** E11
Fossano *Italy* 44°33N 7°43E **20** D7
Fossil *U.S.A.* 45°0N 120°9W **76** D3
Fossil Butte △ *U.S.A.* 41°50N 110°27W **76** F8
Foster → *Canada* 45°17N 72°30W **83** A12
Foster → *Canada* 55°47N 105°49W **71** B7
Fosters Ra. *Australia* 21°35S 133°48E **62** C1
Fostoria *U.S.A.* 41°10N 83°25W **81** E12
Fougères *France* 48°21N 1°14W **20** B3
Foul Pt. *Sri Lanka* 8°35N 81°18E **45** K5
Foula *U.K.* 60°10N 2°5W **11** A6
Foulness I. *U.K.* 51°36N 0°55E **13** F8
Fouman *Cameroon* 5°45N 10°50E **53** G7
Foumbouni *Comoros Is.* 11°51S 43°29E **55** a
Fountain *U.S.A.* 38°41N 104°42W **76** G11
Fountain Hills *U.S.A.* 33°37N 111°43W **77** K8
Fountain Springs
  U.S.A. 35°54N 118°51W **79** K8
Four Mountains, Is. of
  U.S.A. 53°0N 170°0W **74** E5
Fouriesburg *S. Africa* 28°38S 28°14E **56** C4
Fourni *Greece* 37°36N 26°32E **23** F12
Fouta Djallon *Guinea* 11°20N 12°10W **52** F3
Foux, Cap-à- *Haiti* 19°43N 73°27W **89** C5
Foveaux Str. *N.Z.* 46°42S 168°10E **59** G2
Fowey *U.K.* 50°20N 4°39W **13** G3
Fowler *Calif., U.S.A.* 36°38N 119°41W **78** J7
Fowler *Colo., U.S.A.* 38°8N 104°2W **76** G11
Fowler, Pt. *Australia* 32°2S 132°3E **61** F5
Fowlers B. *Australia* 31°59S 132°34E **61** F5
Fowman *Iran* 37°13N 49°19E **47** B6
Fox → *Canada* 56°3N 93°18W **71** B10
Fox Creek *Canada* 54°24N 116°48W **70** C5
Fox Is. *U.S.A.* 53°0N 168°0W **74** E6
Fox Lake *Canada* 58°28N 114°31W **70** B6
Fox Valley *Canada* 50°30N 109°25W **71** C7
Foxboro *Canada* 44°14N 77°26W **82** B7
Foxboro *U.S.A.* 42°4N 71°16W **83** D13
Foxdale *Australia* 20°22S 148°35E **62** b
Foxe Basin *Canada* 66°0N 77°0W **69** D16
Foxe Chan. *Canada* 65°0N 80°0W **69** E16
Foxe Pen. *Canada* 65°0N 76°0W **69** E16
Foxford *Ireland* 53°59N 9°7W **10** C2
Foxton *N.Z.* 40°29S 175°18E **59** D5
Foyle, Lough *U.K.* 55°7N 7°4W **10** A4
Foynes *Ireland* 52°37N 9°7W **10** D2
Foz do Cunene *Angola* 17°15S 11°48E **56** A1
Foz do Iguaçu *Brazil* 25°30S 54°30W **95** B5
Frackville *U.S.A.* 40°47N 76°14W **83** F8
Framingham *U.S.A.* 42°18N 71°24W **83** D13
Franca *Brazil* 20°33S 47°30W **93** H9
Francavilla Fontana
  Italy 40°32N 17°35E **22** D7
France ■ *Europe* 47°0N 3°0E **20** C5
Frances *Australia* 36°41S 140°55E **63** F3
Frances → *Canada* 60°16N 129°10W **70** A3
Frances L. *Canada* 61°23N 129°30W **70** A3
Franceville *Gabon* 1°40S 13°32E **54** E2
Franche-Comté □ *France* 46°50N 5°55E **20** C6
Francis Case, L. *U.S.A.* 43°4N 98°34W **80** D4
Francisco Beltrão *Brazil* 26°5S 53°4W **95** B5
Francisco Ignacio Madero *Coahuila,*
  Mexico 25°48N 103°18W **86** B4
Francisco Ignacio Madero *Durango,*
  Mexico 24°26N 104°18W **86** C4
Francisco Ignacio Madero, Presa
  Mexico 28°10N 105°37W **86** B3
Francistown *Botswana* 21°7S 27°33E **57** B4
François *Canada* 47°35N 56°45W **73** C8
François L. *Canada* 54°0N 125°30W **70** C3
Francois Peron △
  Australia 25°42S 113°33E **61** E1
Francs Pk. *U.S.A.* 43°58N 109°20W **76** E9
Franeker *Neths.* 53°12N 5°33E **15** A5
Frank Hann △ *Australia* 32°52S 120°19E **61** F3
Frankford *Canada* 44°12N 77°36W **82** B7
Frankfort *S. Africa* 27°17S 28°30E **57** C4
Frankfort *Ind., U.S.A.* 40°17N 86°31W **80** E10
Frankfort *Kans., U.S.A.* 39°42N 96°25W **80** F5
Frankfort *Ky., U.S.A.* 38°12N 84°52W **81** F11
Frankfort *N.Y., U.S.A.* 43°2N 75°4W **83** D9
Frankfurt *Brandenburg,*
  Germany 52°20N 14°32E **16** B8
Frankfurt *Hessen, Germany* 50°7N 8°41E **16** C5
Fränkische Alb *Germany* 49°10N 11°23E **16** D6
Frankland → *Australia* 35°0S 116°48E **61** G2
Franklin *Ky., U.S.A.* 36°43N 86°35W **80** G10
Franklin *La., U.S.A.* 29°48N 91°30W **84** G9
Franklin *Mass., U.S.A.* 42°5N 71°24W **83** D13
Franklin *N.H., U.S.A.* 43°27N 71°39W **83** C13
Franklin *N.Y., U.S.A.* 42°20N 75°9W **83** D9
Franklin *Nebr., U.S.A.* 40°6N 98°57W **80** E4
Franklin *Pa., U.S.A.* 41°24N 79°50W **82** E5
Franklin *Va., U.S.A.* 36°41N 76°56W **81** G15
Franklin *W. Va., U.S.A.* 38°39N 79°20W **81** F14
Franklin B. *Canada* 69°45N 126°0W **68** B6
Franklin D. Roosevelt L.
  U.S.A. 48°18N 118°9W **76** B4
Franklin-Gordon Wild Rivers △
  Australia 42°19S 145°51E **63** G4

Franklin I. *Antarctica* 76°10S 168°30E **5** D11
Franklin I. *Canada* 45°24N 80°20W **82** A4
Franklin L. *U.S.A.* 40°25N 115°22W **76** F6
Franklin Mts. *Canada* 65°0N 125°0W **68** B6
Franklin Str. *Canada* 72°0N 96°0W **68** A10
Franklinton *U.S.A.* 30°51N 90°9W **85** F9
Franklinville *U.S.A.* 42°20N 78°27W **82** D6
Frankston *Australia* 38°8S 145°8E **63** F4
Fransfontein *Namibia* 20°12S 15°1E **56** B2
Frantsa Iosifa, Zemlya
  Arctic 82°0N 55°0E **26** A6
Franz *Canada* 48°25N 84°30W **72** C3
Franz Josef Land = Frantsa Iosifa,
  Zemlya *Arctic* 82°0N 55°0E **26** A6
Fraser → *B.C., Canada* 49°7N 123°11W **78** A3
Fraser → *Nfld. & L.,*
  Canada 56°39N 62°10W **73** A7
Fraser, Mt. *Australia* 25°35S 118°20E **61** E2
Fraser I. *Australia* 25°15S 153°10E **63** D5
Fraser Lake *Canada* 54°0N 124°50W **70** C4
Fraserburg *S. Africa* 31°55S 21°30E **56** E3
Fraserburgh *U.K.* 57°42N 2°1W **11** D6
Fraserdale *Canada* 49°55N 81°37W **72** C3
Fray Bentos *Uruguay* 33°10S 58°15W **94** C4
Fray Jorge △ *Chile* 30°42S 71°40W **94** C1
Frazier Downs ♦
  Australia 18°48S 121°42E **60** C3
Fredericia *Denmark* 55°34N 9°45E **9** J13
Frederick *Md., U.S.A.* 39°25N 77°25W **81** F15
Frederick *Okla., U.S.A.* 34°23N 99°1W **84** D5
Frederick *S. Dak., U.S.A.* 45°50N 98°31W **80** C4
Fredericksburg *Pa.,*
  U.S.A. 40°27N 76°26W **83** F8
Fredericksburg *Tex.,*
  U.S.A. 30°16N 98°52W **84** F5
Fredericksburg *Va.,*
  U.S.A. 38°18N 77°28W **81** F15
Fredericktown *Mo.,*
  U.S.A. 37°34N 90°18W **80** G8
Fredericktown *Ohio,*
  U.S.A. 40°29N 82°33W **82** F2
Frederico Westphalen
  Brazil 27°22S 53°24W **95** B5
Fredericton *Canada* 45°57N 66°40W **73** C6
Fredericton Junction
  Canada 45°41N 66°40W **73** C6
Frederikshåb = Paamiut
  Greenland 62°0N 49°43W **4** C5
Frederikshamn = Hamina
  Finland 60°34N 27°12E **8** F22
Frederikshavn *Denmark* 57°28N 10°31E **9** H14
Frederiksted
  U.S. Virgin Is. 17°43N 64°53W **89** C7
Fredonia *Ariz., U.S.A.* 36°57N 112°32W **77** H7
Fredonia *Kans., U.S.A.* 37°32N 95°49W **80** G6
Fredonia *N.Y., U.S.A.* 42°26N 79°20W **82** D5
Fredrikstad *Norway* 59°13N 10°57E **9** G14
Free State □ *S. Africa* 28°30S 27°0E **56** C4
Freehold *U.S.A.* 40°16N 74°17W **83** F10
Freeland *U.S.A.* 41°1N 75°54W **83** E9
Freels, C. *Nfld. & L.,*
  Canada 49°15N 53°30W **73** C9
Freels, C. *Nfld. & L.,*
  Canada 46°37N 53°32W **73** C9
Freeman *Calif., U.S.A.* 35°35N 117°53W **79** K9
Freeman *S. Dak., U.S.A.* 43°21N 97°26W **80** D5
Freeport *Bahamas* 26°30N 78°47W **88** A4
Freeport *Ill., U.S.A.* 42°17N 89°36W **80** D9
Freeport *N.Y., U.S.A.* 40°39N 73°35W **83** F11
Freeport *Ohio, U.S.A.* 40°12N 81°15W **82** F3
Freeport *Pa., U.S.A.* 40°41N 79°41W **82** F5
Freeport *Tex., U.S.A.* 28°57N 95°21W **84** G7
Freetown *S. Leone* 8°30N 13°17W **52** G3
Freeville *U.S.A.* 42°30N 76°20W **83** D8
Frégate, I. de la *Canada* 53°15N 74°45W **72** B5
Fregenal de la Sierra
  Spain 38°10N 6°39W **21** C2
Fregon *Australia* 26°45S 132°1E **61** E5
Freibourg = Fribourg
  Switz. 46°49N 7°9E **20** C7
Freiburg *Germany* 47°59N 7°51E **16** E4
Freire *Chile* 38°54S 72°38W **96** D2
Freirina *Chile* 28°30S 71°10W **94** B1
Freising *Germany* 48°24N 11°45E **16** D6
Freistadt *Austria* 48°30N 14°30E **16** D8
Fréjus *France* 43°25N 6°44E **20** E7
Fremantle *Australia* 32°7S 115°47E **61** F2
Fremont *Calif., U.S.A.* 37°32N 121°57W **78** H4
Fremont *Mich., U.S.A.* 43°28N 85°57W **81** D11
Fremont *Nebr., U.S.A.* 41°26N 96°30W **80** E5
Fremont *Ohio, U.S.A.* 41°21N 83°7W **81** E12
Fremont → *U.S.A.* 38°24N 110°42W **76** G8
French Camp *U.S.A.* 37°53N 121°16W **78** H5
French Cays = Plana Cays
  Bahamas 22°38N 73°30W **89** B5
French Creek → *U.S.A.* 41°24N 79°50W **82** E5
French Frigate Shoals
  U.S.A. 23°45N 166°10W **75** L6
French Guiana ☑ *S. Amer.* 4°0N 53°0W **93** C8
French Polynesia ☑
  Pac. Oc. 20°0S 145°0W **65** J13
French Riviera = Côte d'Azur
  France 43°25N 7°10E **20** E7
Frenchman Cr. →
  N. Amer. 48°31N 107°10W **76** B10
Frenchman Cr. →
  U.S.A. 40°14N 100°50W **80** E3
Fresco → *Brazil* 7°15S 51°30W **93** E8
Freshfield, C. *Antarctica* 68°25S 151°10E **5** C10
Fresnillo *Mexico* 23°10N 102°53W **86** C4
Fresno *U.S.A.* 36°44N 119°47W **78** J7
Fresno Res. *U.S.A.* 48°36N 109°57W **76** B9
Frew → *Australia* 20°0S 135°38E **62** C2
Frewsburg *U.S.A.* 42°3N 79°10W **82** D5
Freycinet △ *Australia* 42°11S 148°19E **63** G4
Freycinet Pen. *Australia* 42°13S 148°25E **63** G4
Fria *Guinea* 10°27N 13°38W **52** F3
Fria, C. *Namibia* 18°0S 12°0E **56** A1

Friant *U.S.A.* 36°59N 119°43W **78** J7
Frías *Argentina* 28°40S 65°5W **94** B2
Fribourg *Switz.* 46°49N 7°9E **20** C7
Fribourg □ *Switz.* 46°40N 7°0E **20** C7
Friday Harbor *U.S.A.* 48°32N 123°1W **78** B3
Friedens *U.S.A.* 40°3N 78°59W **82** F6
Friedrichshafen *Germany* 47°39N 9°30E **16** E5
Friendship *U.S.A.* 42°12N 78°8W **82** D6
Friesland □ *Neths.* 53°5N 5°50E **15** A5
Frigate *Seychelles* 4°35S 55°56E **55** b
Frio → *U.S.A.* 28°26N 98°11W **84** G5
Frio, C. *Brazil* 22°50S 41°50W **90** F6
Friona *U.S.A.* 34°38N 102°43W **84** D3
Frisco *U.S.A.* 33°8N 96°49W **84** E6
Fritch *U.S.A.* 35°38N 101°36W **84** D4
Frobisher B. *Canada* 62°30N 66°0W **69** E18
Frobisher Bay = Iqaluit
  Canada 63°44N 68°31W **69** E18
Frobisher L. *Canada* 56°20N 108°15W **71** B7
Frohavet *Norway* 64°0N 9°30E **8** E13
Frome *U.K.* 51°14N 2°19W **13** F5
Frome → *U.K.* 50°41N 2°6W **13** G5
Frome, L. *Australia* 30°45S 139°45E **63** E2
Front Range *U.S.A.* 40°25N 105°45W **76** F11
Front Royal *U.S.A.* 38°55N 78°12W **81** F14
Frontenac △ *Canada* 44°32N 76°30W **83** B8
Frontera *Mexico* 18°32N 92°38W **87** D6
Fronteras *Mexico* 30°56N 109°31W **86** A3
Frosinone *Italy* 41°38N 13°19E **22** D5
Frostburg *U.S.A.* 39°39N 78°56W **81** F14
Frostisen *Norway* 68°14N 17°10E **8** B17
Frøya *Norway* 63°43N 8°40E **8** E13
Fruita *U.S.A.* 39°9N 108°44W **76** G9
Frunze = Bishkek
  Kyrgyzstan 42°54N 74°46E **30** C3
Frutal *Brazil* 20°0S 49°0W **93** H9
Frýdek-Místek
  Czech Rep. 49°40N 18°20E **17** D10
Fryeburg *U.S.A.* 44°1N 70°59W **83** B14
Fu Jiang → *China* 30°0N 106°16E **34** C6
Fu Xian = Wafangdian
  China 39°38N 121°58E **33** E11
Fu Xian *China* 36°0N 109°20E **32** G5
Fu'an *China* 27°11N 119°36E **35** D12
Fubian *China* 31°17N 102°22E **34** B4
Fucheng *China* 37°50N 116°10E **32** F9
Fuchou = Fuzhou *China* 26°5N 119°16E **35** D12
Fuchū *Japan* 34°34N 133°14E **29** G6
Fuchuan *China* 24°50N 111°5E **35** E8
Fuding *China* 27°20N 120°12E **35** D13
Fuengirola *Spain* 36°32N 4°41W **21** D3
Fuentes de Oñoro *Spain* 40°33N 6°52W **21** B2
Fuerte → *Mexico* 25°54N 109°22W **86** B3
Fuerte Olimpo *Paraguay* 21°0S 57°51W **94** A4
Fuerteventura *Canary Is.* 28°30N 14°0W **52** C3
Fufeng *China* 34°22N 108°0E **32** G5
Fugou *China* 27°5N 98°47E **34** D2
Fugou *China* 34°3N 114°25E **32** G8
Fugu *China* 39°2N 111°3E **32** E6
Fuhai *China* 47°2N 87°25E **30** B6
Fuḥaymī *Iraq* 34°16N 42°10E **46** C4
Fuidhaigh = Wiay *U.K.* 57°24N 7°13W **11** D1
Fuji *Japan* 35°9N 138°39E **29** G9
Fuji-Hakone-Izu △
  Japan 35°15N 138°45E **29** G9
Fuji-San *Japan* 35°22N 138°44E **29** G9
Fuji-Yoshida *Japan* 35°30N 138°46E **29** G9
Fujian □ *China* 26°0N 118°0E **35** E12
Fujin *China* 47°16N 132°1E **31** B15
Fujinomiya *Japan* 35°10N 138°40E **29** G9
Fujisawa *Japan* 35°22N 139°29E **29** G9
Fujiyama, Mt. = Fuji-San
  Japan 35°22N 138°44E **29** G9
Fukagawa *Japan* 43°43N 142°2E **28** C11
Fukien = Fujian □ *China* 26°0N 118°0E **35** E12
Fukuchiyama *Japan* 35°19N 135°9E **29** G7
Fukue *Japan* 32°41N 128°51E **29** H4
Fukue-Shima *Japan* 32°40N 128°45E **29** H4
Fukui *Japan* 36°5N 136°10E **29** F8
Fukui □ *Japan* 36°0N 136°12E **29** G8
Fukuoka *Japan* 33°39N 130°21E **29** H5
Fukuoka □ *Japan* 33°30N 131°0E **29** H5
Fukushima *Japan* 37°44N 140°28E **28** F10
Fukushima □ *Japan* 37°30N 140°15E **28** F10
Fukuyama *Japan* 34°35N 133°20E **29** G6
Fulaga *Fiji* 19°8S 178°33W **59** a
Fulda *Germany* 50°32N 9°40E **16** C5
Fulda → *Germany* 51°25N 9°39E **16** C5
Fulford Harbour *Canada* 48°47N 123°27W **78** B3
Fuliang *China* 29°23N 117°14E **35** C11
Fuling *China* 29°43N 107°17E **34** C6
Fullerton *Calif., U.S.A.* 33°53N 117°56W **79** M9
Fullerton *Nebr., U.S.A.* 41°22N 97°58W **80** E5
Fulongquan *China* 44°20N 124°42E **33** B13
Fulton *Mo., U.S.A.* 38°52N 91°57W **80** F8
Fulton *N.Y., U.S.A.* 43°19N 76°25W **83** C8
Fumin *China* 25°10N 102°20E **34** E4
Funabashi *Japan* 35°45N 140°0E **29** G10
Funafuti = Fongafale
  Tuvalu 8°31S 179°13E **58** B10
Funan *China* 32°39N 115°42E **35** A10
Funchal *Madeira* 32°38N 16°54W **52** B2
Fundación *Colombia* 10°31N 74°11W **92** A4
Fundão *Portugal* 40°8N 7°30W **21** B2
Fundy, B. of *Canada* 45°0N 66°0W **73** D6
Fundy △ *Canada* 45°35N 65°10W **73** D6
Funhalouro *Mozam.* 23°3S 34°25E **57** B5
Funing *Hebei, China* 39°53N 119°12E **33** E10
Funing *Jiangsu, China* 33°45N 119°50E **33** H10
Funing *Yunnan, China* 23°35N 105°45E **34** F5
Funtua *Nigeria* 11°30N 7°18E **52** F7
Fuping *Hebei, China* 38°48N 114°12E **32** E8
Fuping *Shaanxi, China* 34°42N 109°10E **32** G5
Fuqing *China* 25°41N 119°21E **35** E12
Fuquan *China* 26°40N 107°27E **34** D6
Furano *Japan* 43°21N 142°23E **28** C11
Furāt, Nahr al → *Asia* 31°0N 47°25E **46** D5
Fürg *Iran* 28°18N 55°13E **47** D7

Furnas, Represa de
  Brazil 20°50S 45°30W **95** A6
Furneaux Group
  Australia 40°10S 147°50E **63** G4
Furqlus *Syria* 34°36N 37°8E **48** A6
Fürstenwalde *Germany* 52°22N 14°3E **16** B8
Fürth *Germany* 49°28N 10°59E **16** D6
Furukawa = Ōsaki
  Japan 38°34N 140°58E **28** E10
Fury and Hecla Str.
  Canada 69°56N 84°0W **69** D15
Fusagasugá *Colombia* 4°21N 74°22W **92** C4
Fushan *Shandong, China* 37°30N 121°15E **33** F11
Fushan *Shanxi, China* 35°58N 111°51E **32** G6
Fusong *China* 42°20N 127°15E **33** C14
Fushun *Liaoning, China* 41°50N 123°56E **33** D12
Fushun *Sichuan, China* 29°13N 104°52E **34** C5
Fusui *China* 22°40N 107°56E **34** F6
Futian *China* 22°32N 114°4E **31** a
Fuxian Hu *China* 24°30N 102°53E **34** E4
Fuxin *China* 42°5N 121°48E **33** C11
Fuyang *Anhui, China* 33°0N 115°48E **32** H8
Fuyang *Zhejiang, China* 30°5N 119°57E **35** B12
Fuyang He → *China* 38°12N 117°0E **32** E9
Fuying Dao *China* 26°34N 120°9E **35** D13
Fuyong *China* 22°40N 113°49E **31** a
Fuyu *Heilongjiang, China* 47°49N 124°27E **31** B13
Fuyu *Jilin, China* 45°12N 124°43E **33** B13
Fuyuan *China* 25°40N 104°16E **34** E5
Fuyun *China* 47°0N 89°28E **30** B6
Fuzhou = Linchuan
  China 27°57N 116°15E **35** D11
Fuzhou *China* 26°5N 119°16E **35** D12
Fyn *Denmark* 55°20N 10°30E **9** J14
Fyne, L. *U.K.* 55°59N 5°23W **11** F3

G

Gaalkacyo *Somalia* 6°30N 47°30E **49** F4
Gabba *Australia* 9°45S 142°38E **62** a
Gabela *Angola* 11°0S 14°24E **54** G2
Gabès *Tunisia* 33°53N 10°2E **53** B8
Gabès, G. de *Tunisia* 34°0N 10°30E **53** B8
Gabon ■ *Africa* 0°10S 10°0E **54** E2
Gaborone *Botswana* 24°45S 25°57E **56** B4
Gabriels *U.S.A.* 44°26N 74°12W **83** B10
Gābrīk *Iran* 25°44N 58°28E **47** E8
Gabrovo *Bulgaria* 42°52N 25°19E **23** C11
Gāch Sār *Iran* 36°7N 51°19E **47** B6
Gachsārān *Iran* 30°15N 50°45E **47** D6
Gad Hinglaj *India* 16°14N 74°21E **45** F2
Gadag *India* 15°30N 75°45E **45** G2
Gadap *Pakistan* 25°5N 67°28E **42** G2
Gadarwara *India* 22°50N 78°50E **43** H8
Gadhada *India* 22°0N 71°35E **42** J4
Gadra *Pakistan* 25°40N 70°38E **42** G4
Gadsden *U.S.A.* 34°1N 86°1W **85** D11
Gadwal *India* 16°10N 77°50E **45** F3
Gaffney *U.S.A.* 35°5N 81°39W **85** D14
Gafsa *Tunisia* 34°24N 8°43E **53** B7
Gagaria *India* 25°43N 70°46E **42** G4
Găgăuzia □ *Moldova* 46°10N 28°40E **17** E15
Gagnoa *Ivory C.* 6°56N 5°16W **52** G4
Gagnon *Canada* 51°50N 68°5W **73** B6
Gagnon, L. *Canada* 62°3N 110°27W **71** A6
Gahmar *India* 25°27N 83°49E **43** G10
Gai Xian = Gaizhou
  China 40°22N 122°20E **33** D12
Gail *U.S.A.* 32°46N 101°27W **84** E4
Gaillimh = Galway *Ireland* 53°17N 9°3W **10** C2
Gaines *U.S.A.* 41°46N 77°35W **82** E7
Gainesville *Fla., U.S.A.* 29°40N 82°20W **85** G13
Gainesville *Ga., U.S.A.* 34°18N 83°50W **85** D13
Gainesville *Mo., U.S.A.* 36°36N 92°26W **80** G7
Gainesville *Tex., U.S.A.* 33°38N 97°8W **84** E6
Gainsborough *U.K.* 53°24N 0°46W **12** D7
Gairdner, L. *Australia* 31°30S 136°0E **63** E2
Gairloch *U.K.* 57°43N 5°41W **11** D3
Gairloch, L. *U.K.* 57°43N 5°45W **11** D3
Gaizhou *China* 40°22N 122°20E **33** D12
Gaj → *Pakistan* 26°26N 67°21E **42** F2
Gajendragarh *India* 15°44N 75°59E **45** G2
Gakuch *Pakistan* 36°7N 73°45E **43** A5
Gal Oya △ *Sri Lanka* 7°0N 81°20E **45** L5
Gal Oya Res. *Sri Lanka* 7°5N 81°30E **45** L5
Galán, Cerro *Argentina* 25°55S 66°52W **94** B2
Galápagos = Colón, Arch. de
  Ecuador 0°0 91°0W **90** D1
Galapagos Fracture Zone
  Pac. Oc. 3°0N 110°0W **65** G17
Galapagos Rise *Pac. Oc.* 15°0S 95°0W **65** J18
Galashiels *U.K.* 55°37N 2°49W **11** F6
Galați *Romania* 45°27N 28°2E **17** F15
Galatina *Italy* 40°10N 18°10E **23** D8
Galax *U.S.A.* 36°40N 80°56W **81** G13
Galbín Goví *Mongolia* 43°0N 107°0E **32** C4
Galcaio = Gaalkacyo
  Somalia 6°30N 47°30E **49** F4
Galdhøpiggen *Norway* 61°38N 8°18E **8** F13
Galeana *Chihuahua,
  Mexico* 30°7N 107°38W **86** A3
Galeana *Nuevo León,
  Mexico* 24°50N 100°4W **86** A3
Galela *Indonesia* 1°50N 127°49E **37** D7
Galeota Pt. *Trin. & Tob.* 10°8N 60°59W **93** K16
Galera Pt. *Trin. & Tob.* 10°49N 60°54W **93** K16
Galesburg *U.S.A.* 40°57N 90°22W **80** E8
Galestan □ *Iran* 37°30N 56°0E **47** B8
Galeton *U.S.A.* 41°44N 77°39W **82** E7
Galich *Russia* 58°22N 42°24E **18** C7
Galicia □ *Spain* 42°43N 7°45W **21** A2
Galilee = Hagalil *Israel* 32°53N 35°18E **48** C4
Galilee, L. *Australia* 22°20S 145°50E **62** C4
Galilee, Sea of = Yam Kinneret
  Israel 32°45N 35°35E **48** C4
Galion *U.S.A.* 40°44N 82°47W **82** F2
Galiuro Mts. *U.S.A.* 32°30N 110°20W **77** K8

Galiwinku *Australia* 12°2S 135°34E **62** A2
Gallan Hd. *U.K.* 58°15N 7°2W **11** C1
Gallatin *U.S.A.* 36°24N 86°27W **85** C11
Galle *Sri Lanka* 6°5N 80°10E **45** L5
Gállego → *Spain* 41°39N 0°51W **21** B5
Gallegos → *Argentina* 51°35S 69°0W **96** G3
Galley Hd. *Ireland* 51°32N 8°55W **10** E3
Gallinas, Pta. *Colombia* 12°28N 71°40W **92** A4
Gallipoli = Gelibolu
  Turkey 40°28N 26°43E **23** D12
Gallipoli *Italy* 40°3N 17°58E **23** D8
Gallipolis *U.S.A.* 38°49N 82°12W **81** F12
Galloo I. *U.S.A.* 43°55N 76°25W **83** C8
Galloway *U.K.* 55°1N 4°29W **11** F4
Galloway, Mull of *U.K.* 54°39N 4°52W **11** G4
Gallup *U.S.A.* 35°32N 108°45W **77** J9
Galmudug *Somalia* 6°30N 48°0E **49** F4
Galoya *Sri Lanka* 8°10N 80°55E **45** K5
Galt *U.S.A.* 38°15N 121°18W **78** G5
Galty Mts. *Ireland* 52°22N 8°10W **10** D3
Galtymore *Ireland* 52°21N 8°11W **10** D3
Galugāh *Iran* 36°43N 53°48E **47** B7
Galva *U.S.A.* 41°10N 90°3W **80** E8
Galveston *U.S.A.* 29°18N 94°48W **84** G7
Galveston B. *U.S.A.* 29°36N 94°50W **84** G7
Gálvez *Argentina* 32°0S 61°14W **94** C3
Galway *Ireland* 53°17N 9°3W **10** C2
Galway □ *Ireland* 53°22N 9°1W **10** C2
Galway B. *Ireland* 53°13N 9°10W **10** C2
Gam → *Vietnam* 21°55N 105°12E **38** B5
Gamagōri *Japan* 34°50N 137°14E **29** G8
Gambat *Pakistan* 27°17N 68°26E **42** F3
Gambhir → *India* 26°58N 77°27E **42** F6
Gambia ■ *W. Afr.* 13°25N 16°0W **52** F2
Gambia → *W. Afr.* 13°28N 16°34W **52** F2
Gambier *U.S.A.* 40°22N 82°23W **82** F2
Gambier, C. *Australia* 11°56S 130°57E **60** B5
Gambier, Is.
  French Polynesia 23°8S 134°58W **65** K14
Gambier Is. *Australia* 35°3S 136°30E **63** F2
Gambo *Canada* 48°47N 54°13W **73** C9
Gamboli *Pakistan* 29°53N 68°24E **42** E3
Gamboma *Congo* 1°55S 15°52E **54** E3
Gamka → *S. Africa* 33°18S 21°39E **56** D3
Gamkab → *Namibia* 28°4S 17°54E **56** D2
Gamlakarleby = Kokkola
  Finland 63°50N 23°8E **8** E20
Gammon → *Canada* 51°24N 95°44W **71** C9
Gammon Ranges △
  Australia 30°38S 139°8E **63** E2
Gampaha *Sri Lanka* 7°5N 79°59E **45** L4
Gampola *Sri Lanka* 7°10N 80°34E **45** L5
Gamtoos → *S. Africa* 33°58S 25°1E **56** D4
Gamzigrad-Romuliana
  Serbia 43°53N 22°11E **23** C10
Gan Jiang → *China* 29°15N 116°0E **35** C11
Ganado *U.S.A.* 35°43N 109°33W **77** J9
Gananoque *Canada* 44°20N 76°10W **83** B8
Ganāveh *Iran* 29°35N 50°35E **47** D6
Gäncä *Azerbaijan* 40°45N 46°20E **19** F8
Gancheng *China* 18°51N 108°37E **38** C7
Gand = Gent *Belgium* 51°2N 3°42E **15** C3
Ganda *Angola* 13°3S 14°35E **55** G2
Gandajika
  Dem. Rep. of the Congo 6°46S 23°58E **54** F4
Gandak → *India* 25°39N 85°13E **43** G11
Gandava *Pakistan* 28°32N 67°32E **42** E2
Gander *Canada* 48°58N 54°35W **73** C9
Gander L. *Canada* 48°58N 54°35W **73** C9
Gandhi Sagar *India* 24°40N 75°40E **42** G6
Gandhinagar *India* 23°15N 72°45E **42** H5
Gandia *Spain* 38°58N 0°9W **21** C5
Ganedidalem = Gani
  Indonesia 0°48S 128°14E **37** E7
Ganga → *India* 23°20N 90°30E **43** H14
Ganga Sagar *India* 21°38N 88°5E **43** J13
Gangakher *India* 18°57N 76°45E **44** E3
Gangan → *India* 28°38N 78°58E **43** E8
Ganganagar *India* 29°56N 73°56E **42** E5
Gangapur *Maharashtra,
  India* 19°41N 75°1E **44** E2
Gangapur *Raj., India* 26°32N 76°49E **42** F7
Gangaw *Burma* 22°5N 94°5E **41** H19
Gangawati *India* 15°30N 76°36E **45** G3
Gangdisê Shan *China* 31°20N 81°0E **43** D9
Ganges = Ganga →
  India 23°20N 90°30E **43** H14
Ganges *Canada* 48°51N 123°31W **70** D4
Ganges, Mouths of the
  India 21°30N 90°0E **43** J14
Ganggyeong *S. Korea* 36°10N 127°0E **33** F14
Gangneung *S. Korea* 37°45N 128°54E **33** F15
Gangoh *India* 29°46N 77°18E **42** E7
Gangotri *India* 30°50N 79°10E **43** D8
Gangotri *India* 30°50N 79°10E **43** D8
Gangseong *S. Korea* 38°24N 128°30E **33** E15
Gangtok *India* 27°20N 88°37E **41** F16
Gangu *China* 34°40N 105°15E **32** G3
Gangyao *China* 44°12N 126°37E **33** B14
Gani *Indonesia* 0°48S 128°14E **37** E7
Ganj *India* 27°45N 78°57E **43** F8
Ganluo *China* 28°58N 102°58E **34** C4
Gannett Peak *U.S.A.* 43°11N 109°39W **76** E9
Ganquan *China* 36°20N 109°20E **32** F5
Ganshui *China* 28°40N 106°40E **34** C6
Gansu □ *China* 36°0N 104°0E **32** G3
Ganta *Liberia* 7°15N 8°59W **52** G4
Gantheaume, C. *Australia* 36°4S 137°32E **63** F2
Gantheaume B. *Australia* 27°40S 114°10E **61** E1
Gantsevichi = Hantsavichy
  Belarus 52°49N 26°30E **17** B14
Ganyem = Genyem
  Indonesia 2°46S 140°12E **37** E10
Ganyu *China* 34°50N 119°8E **33** G10
Ganzhou *China* 25°51N 114°56E **35** E10
Gao *Mali* 16°15N 0°5W **52** E5
Gao Xian *China* 28°21N 104°32E **34** C5

Gao'an *China* 28°26N 115°17E **35** C10
Gaobeidian *China* 39°19N 115°51E **32** E8
Gaocheng *China* 38°2N 114°49E **32** E8
Gaochun *China* 31°20N 118°49E **35** B12
Gaohebu *China* 30°43N 116°49E **35** B11
Gaokeng *China* 27°40N 113°58E **35** D9
Gaolan Dao *China* 21°55N 113°10E **35** G9
Gaoligong Shan *China* 24°45N 98°45E **34** E2
Gaomi *China* 36°20N 119°42E **33** F10
Gaoping *China* 35°45N 112°55E **32** G7
Gaotang *China* 36°50N 116°15E **32** F9
Gaoua *Burkina Faso* 10°20N 3°8W **52** F5
Gaoual *Guinea* 11°45N 13°25W **52** F3
Gaoxiong = Kaohsiung
  Taiwan 22°35N 120°16E **35** F13
Gaoyang *China* 38°40N 115°45E **32** E8
Gaoyao *China* 23°3N 112°27E **35** F9
Gaoyou *China* 32°47N 119°26E **35** A12
Gaoyou Hu *China* 32°45N 119°20E **33** H10
Gaoyuan *China* 37°8N 117°58E **33** F9
Gaozhou *China* 21°58N 110°50E **35** G8
Gap *France* 44°33N 6°5E **20** D7
Gapat → *India* 24°30N 82°28E **43** G10
Gapuwiyak *Australia* 12°25S 135°43E **62** A2
Gar *China* 32°10N 79°58E **30** E4
Gara, L. *Ireland* 53°57N 8°26W **10** C3
Garabogazköl Aylagy
  Turkmenistan 41°0N 53°30E **19** F9
Garachiné *Panama* 8°0N 78°12W **88** E4
Garagum *Turkmenistan* 39°30N 60°0E **47** B8
Garah *Australia* 29°5S 149°38E **63** D4
Garanhuns *Brazil* 8°50S 36°30W **93** E11
Garautha *India* 25°34N 79°18E **43** G8
Garawa ◇ *Australia* 16°43S 136°51E **62** B2
Garberville *U.S.A.* 40°6N 123°48W **76** F2
Garbiyang *India* 30°8N 80°54E **43** D9
Garda, L. di *Italy* 45°40N 10°41E **22** B4
Garde L. *Canada* 62°50N 106°13W **71** A7
Garden City *Ga., U.S.A.* 32°6N 81°9W **85** E14
Garden City *Kans.,
  U.S.A.* 37°58N 100°53W **80** G3
Garden City *Tex., U.S.A.* 31°52N 101°29W **84** F4
Garden Grove *U.S.A.* 33°47N 117°55W **79** M9
Gardēz *Afghan.* 33°37N 69°9E **42** C3
Gardiner *Maine, U.S.A.* 44°14N 69°47W **81** C19
Gardiner *Mont., U.S.A.* 45°2N 110°22W **76** D8
Gardiners I. *U.S.A.* 41°6N 72°6W **83** E12
Gardner *U.S.A.* 42°34N 71°59W **83** D13
Gardner Canal *Canada* 53°27N 128°8W **70** C3
Gardner Pinnacles
  U.S.A. 25°0N 167°55W **75** L6
Gardnerville *U.S.A.* 38°56N 119°45W **78** G7
Gardo = Qardho *Somalia* 9°30N 49°6E **49** F4
Garey *U.S.A.* 34°53N 120°19W **79** L6
Garfield *U.S.A.* 47°1N 117°9W **76** C5
Garforth *U.K.* 53°47N 1°24W **12** D6
Gargantua, C. *Canada* 47°36N 85°2W **81** B11
Gargett *Australia* 21°9S 148°46E **62** b
Garhchiroli *India* 20°10N 80°0E **44** D5
Garhshankar *India* 31°13N 76°11E **42** D7
Garhwa *India* 24°11N 83°47E **43** G10
Gari *Russia* 59°27N 62°20E **26** D7
Garibaldi △ *Canada* 49°50N 122°40W **70** D4
Gariep, L. *S. Africa* 30°40S 25°40E **56** D4
Garies *S. Africa* 30°32S 17°59E **56** D2
Garig Gunak Barlu △
  Australia 11°26S 131°58E **60** B5
Garigliano → *Italy* 41°13N 13°45E **22** D5
Garissa *Kenya* 0°25S 39°40E **54** E7
Garland *Tex., U.S.A.* 32°54N 96°38W **84** E6
Garland *Utah, U.S.A.* 41°45N 112°10W **76** F7
Garmāb *Iran* 35°25N 56°45E **47** C8
Garmisch-Partenkirchen
  Germany 47°30N 11°6E **16** E6
Garmsār *Iran* 35°20N 52°25E **47** C7
Garner *U.S.A.* 43°6N 93°36W **80** D7
Garnett *U.S.A.* 38°17N 95°14W **80** F6
Garo Hills *India* 25°30N 90°30E **43** G14
Garoe = Garoowe *Somalia* 8°25N 48°33E **49** F4
Garonne → *France* 45°2N 0°36W **20** D3
Garoowe *Somalia* 8°25N 48°33E **49** F4
Garot *India* 24°19N 75°41E **42** G6
Garoua *Cameroon* 9°19N 13°21E **53** G8
Garrauli *India* 25°5N 79°22E **43** G8
Garrison *Mont., U.S.A.* 46°31N 112°49W **76** C7
Garrison *N. Dak., U.S.A.* 47°40N 101°25W **80** B3
Garrison Res. = Sakakawea, L.
  U.S.A. 47°30N 101°25W **80** B3
Garron Pt. *U.K.* 55°3N 5°59W **10** A6
Garry → *U.K.* 56°44N 3°47W **11** E5
Garry, L. *Canada* 65°58N 100°18W **68** D11
Garson L. *Canada* 56°19N 110°2W **71** B6
Garstang *U.K.* 53°55N 2°46W **12** D5
Garu *India* 23°40N 84°14E **43** H11
Garub *Namibia* 26°37S 16°0E **56** C2
Garut *Indonesia* 7°14S 107°53E **37** G12
Garvie Mts. *N.Z.* 45°30S 168°50E **59** F2
Garwa = Garoua
  Cameroon 9°19N 13°21E **53** G8
Garwa *India* 24°11N 83°47E **43** G10
Gary *U.S.A.* 41°36N 87°20W **80** E10
Garzê *China* 31°38N 100°1E **34** B3
Garzón *Colombia* 2°10N 75°40W **92** C3
Gas-San *Japan* 38°32N 140°1E **28** E10
Gasan Kuli = Esenguly
  Turkmenistan 37°37N 53°59E **26** F6
Gascogne *France* 43°45N 0°20E **20** E4
Gascogne, G. de *Europe* 44°0N 2°0W **20** D2
Gascony = Gascogne
  France 43°45N 0°20E **20** E4
Gascoyne → *Australia* 24°52S 113°37E **61** D1
Gascoyne Junction
  Australia 25°2S 115°17E **61** E2
Gashaka *Nigeria* 7°20N 11°29E **53** G8
Gashua *Nigeria* 12°54N 11°0E **53** F8
Gasparillo *Trin. & Tob.* 10°18N 61°26W **93** K15
Gaspé *Canada* 48°52N 64°30W **73** C7
Gaspé, C. de *Canada* 48°48N 64°7W **73** C7
Gaspé Pen. = Gaspésie, Pén. de la
  Canada 48°45N 65°40W **73** C6

Gaspésie, Pén. de la
  Canada 48°45N 65°40W **73** C6
Gaspésie △ *Canada* 48°55N 66°10W **73** C6
Gasteiz = Vitoria-Gasteiz
  Spain 42°50N 2°41W **21** A4
Gastonia *U.S.A.* 35°16N 81°11W **85** D14
Gastre *Argentina* 42°20S 69°15W **96** E3
Gata, C. de *Spain* 36°41N 2°13W **21** D4
Gata, Sierra de *Spain* 40°20N 6°45W **21** B2
Gataga → *Canada* 58°35N 126°59W **70** B3
Gatchina *Russia* 59°35N 30°9E **9** G24
Gatehouse of Fleet *U.K.* 54°53N 4°12W **11** G4
Gates *U.S.A.* 43°9N 77°42W **82** C7
Gateshead I. *Canada* 70°36N 100°26W **68** C11
Gatesville *U.S.A.* 31°26N 97°45W **84** F6
Gateshead *U.K.* 54°57N 1°35W **12** C6
Gatineau *Canada* 45°29N 75°39W **83** A9
Gatineau → *Canada* 45°27N 75°42W **72** C4
Gatineau △ *Canada* 45°40N 76°0W **72** C4
Gatton *Australia* 27°32S 152°17E **63** D5
Gatún, L. *Panama* 9°7N 79°56W **88** E4
Gatwick, London ✈ (LGW)
  U.K. 51°10N 0°11W **13** F7
Gatyana *S. Africa* 32°16S 28°31E **57** E4
Gau *Fiji* 18°2S 179°18E **59** a
Gauer L. *Canada* 57°0N 97°50W **71** B9
Gauhati = Guwahati
  India 26°10N 91°45E **41** F17
Gauja → *Latvia* 57°10N 24°16E **9** H21
Gaujas △ *Latvia* 57°10N 24°35E **9** H21
Gaula → *Norway* 63°21N 10°14E **8** E14
Gauri Phanta *India* 28°41N 80°36E **43** E9
Gauribidanur *India* 13°37N 77°32E **45** H3
Gaustatoppen *Norway* 59°48N 8°40E **9** G13
Gauteng □ *S. Africa* 26°0S 28°0E **57** C4
Gāv Koshī *Iran* 28°38N 57°12E **47** D8
Gāvakān *Iran* 29°37N 53°10E **47** D7
Gāvāter *Iran* 25°10N 61°31E **47** E9
Gāvbandī *Iran* 27°12N 53°4E **47** E7
Gavdos *Greece* 34°50N 24°5E **23** G11
Gaviota *U.S.A.* 34°29N 120°13W **79** L6
Gāvkhūnī, Bāṭlāq-e *Iran* 32°6N 52°52E **47** C7
Gävle *Sweden* 60°40N 17°9E **8** F17
Gawachab *Namibia* 27°4S 17°55E **56** C2
Gawilgarh Hills *India* 21°15N 76°45E **44** D3
Gawler *Australia* 34°30S 138°42E **63** E2
Gawler Ranges *Australia* 32°30S 135°45E **63** E2
Gaxun Nur *China* 42°22N 100°30E **30** B9
Gay *Russia* 51°27N 58°27E **18** D10
Gaya *India* 24°47N 85°4E **43** G11
Gaya *Niger* 11°52N 3°28E **52** F6
Gaylord *U.S.A.* 45°2N 84°41W **81** C11
Gayndah *Australia* 25°35S 151°32E **63** D5
Gaysin = Haysyn
  Ukraine 48°57N 29°25E **17** D15
Gayvoron = Hayvoron
  Ukraine 48°22N 29°52E **17** D15
Gaza *Gaza Strip* 31°30N 34°28E **48** D3
Gaza □ *Mozam.* 23°10S 32°45E **57** B5
Gaza Strip □ *Asia* 31°29N 34°25E **48** D3
Gazanjyk = Bereket
  Turkmenistan 39°16N 55°32E **47** B7
Gāzbor *Iran* 28°5N 58°51E **47** D8
Gaziantep *Turkey* 37°6N 37°23E **46** B3
Gazimağusa = Famagusta
  Cyprus 35°8N 33°55E **46** C2
Gbadolite
  Dem. Rep. of the Congo 4°17N 21°1E **54** D4
Gbarnga *Liberia* 7°19N 9°13W **52** G4
Gcoverega *Botswana* 19°8S 24°18E **56** A3
Gcuwa *S. Africa* 32°20S 28°11E **57** D4
Gdańsk *Poland* 54°22N 18°40E **17** A10
Gdańska, Zatoka *Poland* 54°30N 19°20E **17** A10
Gdov *Russia* 58°48N 27°55E **9** G22
Gdynia *Poland* 54°35N 18°33E **17** A10
Gebe *Indonesia* 0°5N 129°25E **37** D7
Gebze *Turkey* 40°47N 29°25E **23** D13
Gedaref *Sudan* 14°2N 35°28E **53** F13
Gede, Tanjung *Indonesia* 6°46S 105°12E **37** G11
Gediz → *Turkey* 38°35N 26°48E **23** E12
Gedser *Denmark* 54°35N 11°55E **9** J14
Gedung, Pulau *Malaysia* 5°17N 100°23E **39** c
Geegully Cr. →
  Australia 18°32S 123°41E **60** C3
Geel *Belgium* 51°10N 4°59E **15** C4
Geelong *Australia* 38°10S 144°22E **63** F3
Geelvink B. = Cenderawasih,
  Teluk *Indonesia* 3°0S 135°20E **37** E9
Geelvink Chan. *Australia* 28°30S 114°0E **61** E1
Geesthacht *Germany* 53°26N 10°22E **16** B6
Geidam *Nigeria* 12°57N 11°57E **53** F8
Geikie → *Canada* 57°45N 103°52W **71** B8
Geikie Gorge △ *Australia* 18°3S 125°41E **60** C4
Geistown *U.S.A.* 40°18N 78°52W **82** F6
Gejiu *China* 23°20N 103°10E **34** F4
Gel, Meydān-e *Iran* 29°4N 54°50E **47** D7
Gela *Italy* 37°4N 14°15E **22** F6
Gelang Patah *Malaysia* 1°27N 103°35E **39** d
Gelderland □ *Neths.* 52°5N 6°10E **15** B6
Geldrop *Neths.* 51°25N 5°32E **15** C5
Geleen *Neths.* 50°57N 5°49E **15** D5
Gelib = Jilib *Somalia* 0°29N 42°46E **49** G3
Gelibolu *Turkey* 40°28N 26°43E **23** D12
Gelsenkirchen *Germany* 51°32N 7°6E **16** C4
Gelugur *Malaysia* 5°22N 100°18E **39** c
Gemas *Malaysia* 2°37N 102°36E **39** L4
Gembloux *Belgium* 50°34N 4°43E **15** D4
Gemena
  Dem. Rep. of the Congo 3°13N 19°48E **54** D3
Gemerek *Turkey* 39°15N 36°10E **46** B3
Gemlik *Turkey* 40°26N 29°9E **23** D13
Gemsbok △ *Botswana* 25°5S 21°1E **56** C3
Genale → *Ethiopia* 6°2N 39°1E **49** F2
General Acha *Argentina* 37°20S 64°38W **94** D3
General Alvear *B. Aires,
  Argentina* 36°0S 60°0W **94** D4
General Alvear *Mendoza,
  Argentina* 35°0S 67°40W **94** D2
General Artigas
  Paraguay 26°52S 56°16W **94** B4

General Belgrano *Argentina* 36°35S 58°47W **94** D4
General Bernardo O'Higgins *Antarctica* 63°0S 58°3W **5** C18
General Cabrera *Argentina* 32°53S 63°52W **94** C3
General Carrera, L. *S. Amer.* 46°35S 72°0W **96** F2
General Cepeda *Mexico* 25°21N 101°22W **86** B4
General Guido *Argentina* 36°40S 57°50W **94** D4
General Juan Madariaga *Argentina* 37°0S 57°0W **94** D4
General La Madrid *Argentina* 37°17S 61°20W **94** D3
General MacArthur *Phil.* 11°18N 125°28E **37** B7
General Martin Miguel de Güemes *Argentina* 24°50S 65°0W **94** A3
General Pico *Argentina* 35°45S 63°50W **94** D3
General Pinedo *Argentina* 27°15S 61°20W **94** B3
General Pinto *Argentina* 34°45S 61°50W **94** C3
General Roca *Argentina* 39°2S 67°35W **96** D3
General Santos *Phil.* 6°5N 125°14E **37** C7
General Treviño *Mexico* 26°14N 99°29W **87** B5
General Trias *Mexico* 28°21N 106°22W **86** B3
General Viamonte *Argentina* 35°1S 61°3W **94** D3
General Villegas *Argentina* 35°5S 63°0W **94** D3
Genesee *Idaho, U.S.A.* 46°33N 116°56W **76** C5
Genesee *Pa., U.S.A.* 41°59N 77°54W **82** E7
Geneseo *Ill., U.S.A.* 41°27N 90°9W **80** E8
Geneseo *N.Y., U.S.A.* 42°48N 77°49W **82** D7
Geneva = Genève *Switz.* 46°12N 6°9E **20** C7
Geneva *Ala., U.S.A.* 31°2N 85°52W **85** F12
Geneva *N.Y., U.S.A.* 42°52N 76°59W **82** D8
Geneva *Nebr., U.S.A.* 40°32N 97°36W **80** E6
Geneva *Ohio, U.S.A.* 41°48N 80°57W **82** E4
Geneva, L. = Léman, L. *Europe* 46°26N 6°30E **20** C7
Genève *Switz.* 46°12N 6°9E **20** C7
Gengma *China* 23°32N 99°20E **34** F2
Genhe *China* 50°47N 121°31E **31** A13
Genil → *Spain* 37°42N 5°19W **21** D3
Genk *Belgium* 50°58N 5°32E **15** D5
Gennargentu, Mti. del *Italy* 40°1N 9°19E **22** D3
Genoa = Génova *Italy* 44°25N 8°57E **20** D8
Genoa *Australia* 37°29S 149°35E **63** F4
Genoa *N.Y., U.S.A.* 42°40N 76°32W **83** D8
Genoa *Nebr., U.S.A.* 41°27N 97°44W **80** E5
Genoa *Nev., U.S.A.* 39°2N 119°50W **78** F7
Génova *Italy* 44°25N 8°57E **20** D8
Génova, G. di *Italy* 44°0N 9°0E **22** C3
Genriyetty, Ostrov *Russia* 77°6N 156°30E **27** B16
Gent *Belgium* 51°2N 3°42E **15** C3
Genteng *Jawa Barat, Indonesia* 7°22S 106°24E **37** G12
Genteng *Jawa Timur, Indonesia* 8°22S 114°9E **37** J17
Genyem *Indonesia* 2°46S 140°12E **37** E10
Geochang *S. Korea* 35°41N 127°55E **33** G14
Geographe B. *Australia* 33°30S 115°15E **61** F2
Geographe Chan. *Australia* 24°30S 113°0E **61** D1
Georga, Zemlya *Russia* 80°30N 49°0E **26** A5
George *S. Africa* 33°58S 22°29E **56** D3
George → *Canada* 58°49N 66°10W **73** A6
George, L. *N.S.W., Australia* 35°10S 149°25E **63** F4
George, L. *S. Austral., Australia* 37°25S 140°0E **63** F3
George, L. *W. Austral., Australia* 22°45S 123°40E **60** D3
George, L. *Fla., U.S.A.* 29°17N 81°36W **85** G14
George, L. *N.Y., U.S.A.* 43°37N 73°33W **83** C11
George Gill Ra. *Australia* 24°22S 131°45E **60** D5
George Pt. *Australia* 20°6S 148°36E **62** b
George River = Kangiqsualujjuaq *Canada* 58°30N 65°59W **69** F18
George Sound *N.Z.* 44°52S 167°25E **59** F1
George Town *Australia* 41°6S 146°49E **63** G4
George Town *Bahamas* 23°33N 75°47W **88** B4
George Town *Cayman Is.* 19°20N 81°24W **88** C3
George Town *Malaysia* 5°25N 100°20E **39** c
George V Land *Antarctica* 69°0S 148°0E **5** C10
George VI Sound *Antarctica* 71°0S 68°0W **5** D17
George West *U.S.A.* 28°20N 98°7W **84** G5
Georgetown = Janjanbureh *Gambia* 13°30N 14°47W **52** F3
Georgetown *Australia* 18°17S 143°33E **62** B3
Georgetown *Ont., Canada* 43°40N 79°56W **82** C5
Georgetown *P.E.I., Canada* 46°13N 62°24W **73** C7
Georgetown *Guyana* 6°50N 58°12W **92** B7
Georgetown *Calif., U.S.A.* 38°54N 120°50W **78** G6
Georgetown *Colo., U.S.A.* 39°42N 105°42W **76** G11
Georgetown *Ky., U.S.A.* 38°13N 84°33W **81** F11
Georgetown *N.Y., U.S.A.* 42°46N 75°44W **83** D9
Georgetown *Ohio, U.S.A.* 38°52N 83°54W **81** F12
Georgetown *S.C., U.S.A.* 33°23N 79°17W **85** E15
Georgetown *Tex., U.S.A.* 30°38N 97°41W **84** F6
Georgia □ *U.S.A.* 32°50N 83°15W **85** E13
Georgia ■ *Asia* 42°0N 43°0E **19** F7
Georgia, Str. of *N. Amer.* 49°25N 124°0W **78** A3
Georgia Basin *S. Ocean* 55°45S 35°30W **5** B1
Georgian B. *Canada* 45°15N 81°0W **82** A4
Georgian Bay Islands △ *Canada* 44°53N 79°52W **82** B5
Georgievka *Kazakhstan* 49°19N 84°34E **26** E9
Georgina → *Australia* 23°30S 139°47E **62** C2
Georgina I. *Canada* 44°22N 79°17W **82** B5
Georgiyevka *Russia* 44°12N 43°28E **19** F7
Gera *Germany* 50°53N 12°4E **16** C7
Geraardsbergen *Belgium* 50°45N 3°53E **15** D3
Geral, Serra *Brazil* 26°25N 50°0W **95** B6

Geral de Goiás, Serra *Brazil* 12°0S 46°0W **93** F9
Geraldine *U.S.A.* 47°36N 110°16W **76** C8
Geraldton *Australia* 28°48S 114°32E **61** E1
Geraldton *Canada* 49°44N 87°10W **72** C2
Gerdine, Mt. *U.S.A.* 61°35N 152°27W **74** C9
Gereshk *Afghan.* 31°47N 64°35E **40** D4
Gerik *Malaysia* 5°50N 101°15E **39** K3
Gering *U.S.A.* 41°50N 103°40W **80** E2
Gerlach *U.S.A.* 40°39N 119°21W **76** F4
German Bight = Deutsche Bucht *Germany* 54°15N 8°0E **16** A5
Germansen Landing *Canada* 55°43N 124°40W **70** B4
Germantown *U.S.A.* 35°5N 89°49W **85** D10
Germany ■ *Europe* 51°0N 10°0E **16** C6
Germi *Iran* 39°1N 48°3E **47** B6
Gerokgak *Indonesia* 8°11S 114°27E **37** J17
Gerona = Girona *Spain* 41°58N 2°46E **21** B7
Gerrard *Canada* 50°30N 117°17W **70** C5
Gersoppa Falls *India* 14°12N 74°46E **45** G2
Gertak Sanggul *Malaysia* 5°17N 100°12E **39** c
Gertak Sanggul, Tanjung *Malaysia* 5°16N 100°11E **39** c
Gerung *Indonesia* 8°43S 116°7E **37** K19
Geser *Indonesia* 3°50S 130°54E **37** E8
Gettysburg *Pa., U.S.A.* 39°50N 77°14W **81** F15
Gettysburg *S. Dak., U.S.A.* 45°1N 99°57W **80** C4
Getxo *Spain* 43°21N 2°59W **21** A4
Getz Ice Shelf *Antarctica* 75°0S 130°0W **5** D14
Gevrai *India* 19°16N 75°45E **44** E2
Geyser *U.S.A.* 47°16N 110°30W **76** C8
Geyserville *U.S.A.* 38°42N 122°54W **78** G4
Gezhouba Dam *China* 30°40N 111°27E **35** B8
Ghadaf, W. al → *Iraq* 32°56N 43°30E **46** C4
Ghadāmis *Libya* 30°11N 9°29E **53** B8
Ghaggar → *India* 29°30N 74°53E **42** E6
Ghaghara → *India* 25°45N 84°40E **43** G11
Ghaghat → *Bangla.* 25°19N 89°38E **43** G13
Ghagra *India* 23°17N 84°33E **43** H11
Ghagra → *India* 27°29N 81°9E **43** F9
Ghallamane *Mauritania* 23°15N 10°0W **52** D4
Ghana ■ *W. Afr.* 8°0N 1°0W **52** G5
Ghanpokhara *Nepal* 28°17N 84°14E **43** E11
Ghansor *India* 22°39N 80°1E **43** H9
Ghanzi *Botswana* 21°50S 21°34E **56** B3
Ghanzi □ *Botswana* 22°30S 22°0E **56** B3
Gharb Bahr el Ghazāl = Western Bahr el Ghazâl □ *South Sudan* 7°30N 25°30E **50** F6
Ghardaïa *Algeria* 32°20N 3°37E **52** B6
Gharm *Tajikistan* 39°0N 70°20E **26** F8
Gharyān *Libya* 32°10N 13°0E **53** B8
Ghāt *Libya* 24°59N 10°11E **53** D8
Ghatal *India* 22°40N 87°46E **43** H12
Ghatampur *India* 26°8N 80°13E **43** F9
Ghatgaon *India* 21°24N 85°53E **44** D7
Ghatprabha → *India* 16°15N 75°20E **45** F2
Ghats, Eastern *India* 14°0N 78°50E **45** H4
Ghats, Western *India* 14°0N 75°0E **45** H2
Ghatsila *India* 22°36N 86°29E **43** H12
Ghaţţī *Si. Arabia* 31°16N 37°31E **46** D3
Ghawdex = Gozo *Malta* 36°3N 14°15E **22** F6
Ghazal, Bahr el → *Chad* 13°0N 15°47E **53** F9
Ghazal, Bahr el → *South Sudan* 9°31N 30°25E **53** G12
Ghaziabad *India* 28°42N 77°26E **42** E7
Ghazipur *India* 25°38N 83°35E **43** G10
Ghaznī *Afghan.* 33°30N 68°28E **42** C3
Ghaznī □ *Afghan.* 32°10N 68°20E **40** C6
Ghent = Gent *Belgium* 51°2N 3°42E **15** C3
Gherghe Gheorghiu-Dej = Onești *Romania* 46°17N 26°47E **17** E14
Ghīnah, Wādī al → *Si. Arabia* 30°27N 38°14E **46** D3
Ghizar → *Pakistan* 36°15N 73°43E **43** A5
Ghod → *India* 18°30N 74°35E **44** E2
Ghogha *India* 21°40N 72°20E **44** D1
Ghotaru *India* 27°20N 70°1E **42** F4
Ghotki *Pakistan* 28°5N 69°21E **42** E3
Ghowr □ *Afghan.* 34°0N 64°20E **40** C4
Ghughri *India* 22°39N 80°41E **43** H9
Ghugus *India* 19°58N 79°12E **44** E4
Ghulam Mohammad Barrage *Pakistan* 25°30N 68°20E **42** G3
Ghūrīān *Afghan.* 34°17N 61°25E **40** B2
Gia Dinh *Vietnam* 10°49N 106°42E **39** G6
Gia Lai = Plei Ku *Vietnam* 13°57N 108°0E **38** F7
Gia Nghia *Vietnam* 11°58N 107°42E **39** G6
Gia Ngoc *Vietnam* 14°50N 108°58E **38** E7
Gia Vuc *Vietnam* 14°42N 108°34E **38** E7
Giamama = Jamaame *Somalia* 0°4N 42°44E **49** G3
Gianitsa *Greece* 40°46N 22°24E **23** D10
Giant Forest *U.S.A.* 36°36N 118°43W **78** J8
Giant Sequoia △ *U.S.A.* 36°10N 118°35W **78** K8
Giants Causeway *U.K.* 55°16N 6°29W **10** A5
Giant's Tank *Sri Lanka* 8°51N 80°2E **45** K5
Gianyar *Indonesia* 8°32S 115°20E **37** K18
Giarabub = Al Jaghbūb *Libya* 29°42N 24°38E **53** C10
Giarre *Italy* 37°43N 15°11E **22** F6
Gibara *Cuba* 21°9N 76°11W **88** B4
Gibbon *U.S.A.* 40°45N 98°51W **80** E4
Gibe II *Ethiopia* 8°0N 37°30E **49** F2
Gibe III *Ethiopia* 7°0N 37°30E **49** F2
Gibeon *Namibia* 25°9S 17°43E **56** C2
Gibraltar ☑ *Europe* 36°7N 5°22W **21** D3
Gibraltar, Str. of *Medit. S.* 35°55N 5°40W **21** E3
Gibraltar Range △ *Australia* 29°31S 152°19E **63** D5
Gibson Desert *Australia* 24°0S 126°0E **60** D4
Gibsons *Canada* 49°24N 123°32W **70** D4
Gibsonville *U.S.A.* 39°46N 120°54W **78** F6
Giddalur *India* 15°20N 78°57E **45** G4
Giddings *U.S.A.* 30°11N 96°56W **84** F6
Giebnegáisi = Kebnekaise *Sweden* 67°53N 18°33E **8** C18

Giessen *Germany* 50°34N 8°41E **16** C5
Gīfān *Iran* 37°54N 57°28E **47** B8
Gift Lake *Canada* 55°53N 115°49W **70** B5
Gifu *Japan* 35°30N 136°45E **29** G8
Gifu □ *Japan* 35°40N 137°0E **29** G8
Giganta, Sa. de la *Mexico* 26°0N 111°39W **86** B2
Gigha *U.K.* 55°42N 5°44W **11** F3
Gíglio *Italy* 42°20N 10°52E **22** C4
Gijón *Spain* 43°32N 5°42W **21** A3
Gil I. *Canada* 53°12N 129°15W **70** C3
Gila → *U.S.A.* 32°43N 114°33W **77** K6
Gila Bend *U.S.A.* 32°57N 112°43W **77** K7
Gila Bend Mts. *U.S.A.* 33°10N 113°0W **77** K7
Gila Cliff Dwellings △ *U.S.A.* 33°12N 108°16W **77** K9
Gīlān □ *Iran* 37°0N 50°0E **47** B6
Gilbert → *Australia* 16°35S 141°15E **62** B3
Gilbert Is. *Kiribati* 1°0N 172°0E **58** A10
Gilbert River *Australia* 18°9S 142°52E **62** B3
Gilbert Seamounts *Pac. Oc.* 52°50N 150°10W **4** D18
Gilead *U.S.A.* 44°24N 70°59W **83** B14
Gilford I. *Canada* 50°40N 126°30W **70** C3
Gilgandra *Australia* 31°43S 148°39E **63** E4
Gilgit *India* 35°50N 74°15E **43** B6
Gilgit → *Pakistan* 35°44N 74°37E **43** B6
Gilgit-Baltistan □ *Pakistan* 36°30N 73°0E **43** A5
Gilimanuk *Indonesia* 8°10S 114°26E **37** J17
Gillam *Canada* 56°20N 94°40W **71** B10
Gillen, L. *Australia* 26°11S 124°38E **61** E3
Gilles, L. *Australia* 32°50S 136°45E **63** E2
Gillette *U.S.A.* 44°18N 105°30W **76** D11
Gilliat *Australia* 20°40S 141°28E **62** C3
Gillingham *U.K.* 51°23N 0°33E **13** F8
Gilmer *U.S.A.* 32°44N 94°57W **84** E7
Gilmore, L. *Australia* 32°29S 121°37E **61** F3
Gilmour *Canada* 44°48N 77°37W **82** B7
Gilroy *U.S.A.* 37°1N 121°34W **78** H5
Gimcheon *S. Korea* 36°11N 128°4E **33** F15
Gimhae *S. Korea* 35°14N 128°53E **33** G15
Gimhwa *S. Korea* 38°17N 127°28E **33** E14
Gimie, Mt. *St. Lucia* 13°54N 61°0W **89** f
Gimje *S. Korea* 35°48N 126°45E **33** G14
Gimli *Canada* 50°40N 97°0W **71** C9
Gin → *Sri Lanka* 6°5N 80°7E **45** L5
Gin Gin *Australia* 25°0S 151°58E **63** D5
Gingee *India* 12°15N 79°25E **45** H4
Gingin *Australia* 31°22S 115°54E **61** F2
Gingindlovu *S. Africa* 29°2S 31°30E **57** C5
Ginir *Ethiopia* 7°6N 40°40E **49** F3
Giohar = Jawhar *Somalia* 2°48N 45°30E **49** G4
Giona, Oros *Greece* 38°38N 22°14E **23** E10
Gir □ *India* 21°0N 71°0E **42** J4
Gir Hills *India* 21°0N 71°0E **42** J4
Girab *India* 26°2N 70°38E **42** F4
Girâfi, W. → *Egypt* 29°58N 34°39E **48** F3
Girard *St. Lucia* 13°59N 60°57W **89** D7
Girard *Kans., U.S.A.* 37°31N 94°51W **80** G6
Girard *Ohio, U.S.A.* 41°9N 80°42W **82** E4
Girard *Pa., U.S.A.* 42°0N 80°19W **82** E4
Girdle Ness *U.K.* 57°9N 2°3W **11** D6
Giresun *Turkey* 40°55N 38°30E **19** F6
Girga *Egypt* 26°17N 31°55E **53** C12
Giri → *India* 30°28N 77°41E **42** D7
Giridih *India* 24°10N 86°21E **43** G12
Girne = Kyrenia *Cyprus* 35°20N 33°20E **46** C2
Giron = Kiruna *Sweden* 67°52N 20°15E **8** C19
Girona *Spain* 41°58N 2°46E **21** B7
Gironde → *France* 45°32N 1°7W **20** D3
Girraween △ *Australia* 28°46S 151°54E **63** D5
Girringun △ *Australia* 18°15S 145°32E **62** B4
Giru *Australia* 19°30S 147°5E **62** B4
Girvan *U.K.* 55°14N 4°51W **11** F4
Gisborne *N.Z.* 38°39S 178°5E **59** C7
Gisenyi *Rwanda* 1°41S 29°15E **54** E5
Gislaved *Sweden* 57°19N 13°32E **9** H15
Gitega *Burundi* 3°26S 29°56E **54** E5
Githio *Greece* 36°46N 22°34E **23** F10
Giuba = Juba → *Somalia* 1°30N 42°35E **49** G3
Giurgiu *Romania* 43°52N 25°57E **17** G13
Giyani *S. Africa* 23°19S 30°43E **57** B5
Gizab *Afghan.* 33°22N 66°17E **42** C1
Gizhiga *Russia* 62°3N 160°30E **27** C17
Gizhiginskaya Guba *Russia* 61°0N 158°0E **27** C16
Gizycko *Poland* 54°2N 21°48E **17** A11
Gjakovë *Kosovo* 42°22N 20°26E **23** C9
Gjirokastër *Albania* 40°7N 20°10E **23** D9
Gjoa Haven *Canada* 68°38N 95°53W **68** D12
Gjøvik *Norway* 60°47N 10°43E **8** F14
Glace Bay *Canada* 46°11N 59°58W **73** C8
Glacier △ *Canada* 51°15N 117°30W **70** C5
Glacier △ *U.S.A.* 48°42N 113°48W **76** B7
Glacier Bay *U.S.A.* 58°40N 136°0W **68** F4
Glacier Bay △ *U.S.A.* 58°45N 136°30W **70** B1
Glacier Peak *U.S.A.* 48°7N 121°7W **78** B5
Gladewater *U.S.A.* 32°33N 94°56W **84** E7
Gladstone *Queens., Australia* 23°52S 151°16E **62** C5
Gladstone *S. Austral., Australia* 33°15S 138°22E **63** E2
Gladstone *Canada* 50°13N 98°57W **71** C9
Gladwin *U.S.A.* 43°59N 84°29W **81** D11
Glagah *Indonesia* 8°13S 114°18E **37** J17
Glåma = Glomma → *Norway* 59°12N 10°57E **9** G14
Gláma *Iceland* 65°48N 23°0W **8** D2
Glamis *U.S.A.* 32°55N 115°5W **79** N11
Glamorgan, Vale of □ *U.K.* 51°28N 3°25W **13** F4
Glasco *Kans., U.S.A.* 39°22N 97°50W **80** F5
Glasco *N.Y., U.S.A.* 42°3N 73°57W **83** D11
Glasgow *U.K.* 55°51N 4°15W **11** F4
Glasgow *Ky., U.S.A.* 37°0N 85°55W **81** G11
Glasgow *Mont., U.S.A.* 48°12N 106°38W **76** B10
Glasgow, City of □ *U.K.* 55°51N 4°12W **11** F4

Glasgow Int. ✈ (GLA) *U.K.* 55°51N 4°21W **11** F4
Glaslyn *Canada* 53°22N 108°21W **71** C7
Glastonbury *U.K.* 51°9N 2°43W **13** F5
Glastonbury *U.S.A.* 41°43N 72°37W **83** E12
Glazov *Russia* 58°9N 52°40E **18** C9
Gleichen *Canada* 50°52N 113°3W **70** C6
Gleiwitz = Gliwice *Poland* 50°22N 18°41E **17** C10
Glen *U.S.A.* 44°7N 71°11W **83** B13
Glen Affric *U.K.* 57°17N 5°1W **11** D3
Glen Canyon *U.S.A.* 37°30N 110°40W **77** H8
Glen Canyon △ *U.S.A.* 37°15N 111°0W **77** H8
Glen Canyon Dam *U.S.A.* 36°57N 111°29W **77** H8
Glen Coe *U.K.* 56°40N 5°0W **11** E3
Glen Cove *U.S.A.* 40°51N 73°38W **83** F11
Glen Garry *U.K.* 57°3N 5°7W **11** D3
Glen Innes *Australia* 29°44S 151°44E **63** D5
Glen Lyon *U.S.A.* 41°10N 76°5W **83** E8
Glen Mor *U.K.* 57°9N 4°37W **11** D4
Glen Moriston *U.K.* 57°11N 4°52W **11** D4
Glen Robertson *Canada* 45°22N 74°30W **83** A10
Glen Spean *U.K.* 56°53N 4°40W **11** E4
Glen Ullin *U.S.A.* 46°49N 101°50W **80** B3
Glenbeigh *Ireland* 52°3N 9°58W **10** D2
Glencoe *Canada* 42°45N 81°43W **82** D3
Glencoe *S. Africa* 28°11S 30°11E **57** C5
Glencoe *U.S.A.* 44°46N 94°9W **80** C6
Glencolumbkille *Ireland* 54°43N 8°42W **10** B3
Glendale *U.S.A.* 33°32N 112°11W **77** K7
Glendive *U.S.A.* 47°7N 104°43W **76** C11
Glendo *U.S.A.* 42°30N 105°2W **76** E11
Glenelg → *Australia* 38°4S 140°59E **63** F3
Glenfield *U.S.A.* 43°43N 75°24W **83** C9
Glengad Hd. *Ireland* 55°20N 7°10W **10** A4
Glengarriff *Ireland* 51°45N 9°34W **10** E2
Glenmont *U.S.A.* 40°31N 82°6W **82** F2
Glenmorgan *Australia* 27°14S 149°42E **63** D4
Glenn *U.S.A.* 39°31N 122°1W **78** F4
Glennallen *U.S.A.* 62°7N 145°33W **68** E2
Glennamaddy *Ireland* 53°37N 8°33W **10** C3
Glenns Ferry *U.S.A.* 42°57N 115°18W **76** E6
Glenora *Canada* 44°2N 77°3W **82** B7
Glenorchy *Australia* 42°49S 147°18E **63** G4
Glenore *Australia* 17°50S 141°12E **62** B3
Glenreagh *Australia* 30°2S 153°1E **63** E5
Glenrock *U.S.A.* 42°52N 105°52W **76** E11
Glenrothes *U.K.* 56°12N 3°10W **11** E5
Glens Falls *U.S.A.* 43°19N 73°39W **83** C11
Glenside *U.S.A.* 40°6N 75°9W **83** F9
Glenties *Ireland* 54°48N 8°17W **10** B3
Glenveagh △ *Ireland* 55°3N 8°1W **10** A3
Glenville *U.S.A.* 38°56N 80°50W **81** F13
Glenwood *Canada* 49°0N 54°58W **73** C9
Glenwood *Ark., U.S.A.* 34°20N 93°33W **84** D8
Glenwood *Iowa, U.S.A.* 41°3N 95°45W **80** E6
Glenwood *Minn., U.S.A.* 45°39N 95°23W **80** C6
Glenwood *Wash., U.S.A.* 46°1N 121°17W **78** D5
Glenwood Springs *U.S.A.* 39°33N 107°19W **76** G10
Glettinganes *Iceland* 65°30N 13°37W **8** D7
Glin *Ireland* 52°34N 9°17W **10** D2
Gliwice *Poland* 50°22N 18°41E **17** C10
Globe *U.S.A.* 33°24N 110°47W **77** K8
Głogów *Poland* 51°37N 16°5E **16** C9
Glomma → *Norway* 59°12N 10°57E **9** G14
Glorieuses, Îs. *Ind. Oc.* 11°30S 47°20E **55** G9
Glossop *U.K.* 53°27N 1°56W **12** D6
Gloucester *Australia* 32°0S 151°59E **63** E5
Gloucester *U.K.* 51°53N 2°15W **13** F5
Gloucester *U.S.A.* 42°37N 70°40W **83** D14
Gloucester I. *Australia* 20°0S 148°30E **62** b
Gloucester Island △ *Australia* 20°2S 148°30E **62** b
Gloucester Point *U.S.A.* 37°15N 76°30W **81** G15
Gloucestershire □ *U.K.* 51°46N 2°15W **13** F5
Gloversville *U.S.A.* 43°3N 74°21W **83** C10
Glovertown *Canada* 48°40N 54°3W **73** C9
Glusk *Belarus* 52°53N 28°41E **17** B15
Glyn Ebwy = Ebbw Vale *U.K.* 51°46N 3°12W **13** F4
Gmünd *Austria* 48°45N 15°0E **16** D8
Gmunden *Austria* 47°55N 13°48E **16** E7
Gniezno *Poland* 52°30N 17°35E **17** B9
Gnowangerup *Australia* 33°58S 117°59E **61** F2
Go Cong *Vietnam* 10°22N 106°40E **39** G6
Goa *India* 15°33N 73°59E **45** G1
Goa □ *India* 15°33N 73°59E **45** G1
Goalen Hd. *Australia* 36°33S 150°4E **63** F5
Goalpara *India* 26°10N 90°40E **41** F17
Goaltor *India* 22°43N 87°10E **43** H12
Goalundo Ghat *Bangla.* 23°50N 89°47E **43** H13
Goat Fell *U.K.* 55°38N 5°11W **11** F3
Goba *Ethiopia* 7°1N 39°59E **49** F2
Goba *Mozam.* 26°15S 32°13E **57** D5
Gobabis *Namibia* 22°30S 19°0E **56** C2
Gobi *Asia* 44°0N 110°0E **32** C6
Gobichettipalayam *India* 11°31N 77°21E **45** J3
Gobō *Japan* 33°53N 135°10E **29** H7
Gochas *Namibia* 24°59S 18°55E **56** C2
Godalming *U.K.* 51°11N 0°36W **13** F7
Godavari → *India* 16°25N 82°18E **44** F6
Godavari Pt. *India* 17°0N 82°20E **44** F6
Godbout *Canada* 49°20N 67°38W **73** C6
Godda *India* 24°50N 87°13E **43** G12
Goderich *Canada* 43°45N 81°41W **82** C3
Godfrey Ra. *Australia* 24°0S 117°0E **61** D2
Godhavn = Qeqertarsuaq *Greenland* 69°15N 53°38W **4** C5
Godhra *India* 22°49N 73°40E **42** H5
Godoy Cruz *Argentina* 32°56S 68°52W **94** C2
Gods → *Canada* 56°22N 92°51W **72** A1
Gods L. *Canada* 54°40N 94°15W **72** B1
Gods River *Canada* 54°50N 94°5W **71** C10
Godthåb = Nuuk *Greenland* 64°10N 51°35W **67** C14
Goeie Hoop, Kaap die = Good Hope, C. of *S. Africa* 34°24S 18°30E **56** D2

Goéland, L. au *Canada* 49°50N 76°48W **72** C4
Goélands, L. aux *Canada* 55°27N 64°17W **73** A7
Goeree *Neths.* 51°50N 4°0E **15** C3
Goes *Neths.* 51°30N 3°55E **15** C3
Goffstown *U.S.A.* 43°1N 71°36W **83** C13
Gogama *Canada* 47°35N 81°43W **72** C3
Gogebic, L. *U.S.A.* 46°30N 89°35W **80** B9
Gogra = Ghaghara → *India* 25°45N 84°40E **43** G11
Gogriâl *South Sudan* 8°30N 28°8E **53** G11
Gohana *India* 29°8N 76°42E **42** E7
Goharganj *India* 23°1N 77°41E **42** H7
Goi → *India* 22°4N 74°46E **42** H6
Goiânia *Brazil* 16°43S 49°20W **93** G9
Goiás *Brazil* 15°55S 50°10W **93** G8
Goiás □ *Brazil* 12°10S 48°0W **93** F9
Goio-Erê *Brazil* 24°12S 53°1W **95** A5
Gojō *Japan* 34°21N 135°42E **29** G7
Gojra *Pakistan* 31°10N 72°40E **42** D5
Gokak *India* 16°11N 74°52E **45** F2
Gokarn *India* 14°33N 74°17E **45** G2
Gökçeada *Turkey* 40°10N 25°50E **23** D11
Gökova Körfezi *Turkey* 36°55N 27°50E **23** F12
Göksu → *Turkey* 36°19N 34°5E **46** B2
Gokteik *Burma* 22°26N 97°0E **41** H20
Gokurt *Pakistan* 29°40N 67°26E **42** E2
Gokwe *Zimbabwe* 18°7S 28°58E **57** A4
Gola *India* 28°3N 80°32E **43** E9
Golakganj *India* 26°8N 89°52E **43** F13
Golan Heights = Hagolan *Syria* 33°0N 35°45E **48** C4
Goläshkerd *Iran* 27°59N 57°16E **47** E8
Golconda *India* 17°24N 78°23E **44** F4
Golconda *U.S.A.* 40°58N 117°30W **76** F5
Gold *U.S.A.* 41°52N 77°50W **82** E7
Gold Beach *U.S.A.* 42°25N 124°25W **76** E1
Gold Coast *W. Afr.* 4°0N 1°40W **52** H5
Gold Hill *U.S.A.* 42°26N 123°3W **76** E2
Gold River *Canada* 49°46N 126°3W **70** D3
Golden *Canada* 51°20N 116°59W **70** C5
Golden B. *N.Z.* 40°40S 172°50E **59** D4
Golden Gate Highlands △ *S. Africa* 28°40S 28°40E **57** C4
Golden Hinde *Canada* 49°40N 125°44W **70** D3
Golden Lake *Canada* 45°34N 77°21W **82** A7
Golden Rock *India* 10°45N 78°48E **45** J4
Golden Spike △ *U.S.A.* 41°37N 112°33W **76** F7
Golden Vale *Ireland* 52°33N 8°17W **10** D3
Goldendale *U.S.A.* 45°49N 120°50W **76** D3
Goldfield *U.S.A.* 37°42N 117°14W **77** H5
Goldsand L. *Canada* 57°2N 101°8W **71** B8
Goldsboro *U.S.A.* 35°23N 77°59W **85** D16
Goldsmith *U.S.A.* 31°59N 102°37W **84** F3
Goldthwaite *U.S.A.* 31°27N 98°34W **84** F5
Goleniów *Poland* 53°35N 14°50E **16** B8
Golestān □ *Iran* 37°20N 55°25E **47** B7
Golestānak *Iran* 30°36N 54°14E **47** D7
Goleta *U.S.A.* 34°27N 119°50W **79** L7
Golfito *Costa Rica* 8°41N 83°5W **88** E3
Golfo Aranci *Italy* 40°59N 9°38E **22** D3
Golfo de Santa Clara *Mexico* 31°42N 114°30W **86** A2
Goliad *U.S.A.* 28°40N 97°23W **84** G6
Golmud *China* 36°25N 94°53E **30** D7
Golpäyegän *Iran* 33°27N 50°18E **47** C6
Golra *Pakistan* 33°37N 72°56E **42** C5
Golspie *U.K.* 57°58N 3°59W **11** D5
Goma *Dem. Rep. of the Congo* 1°37S 29°10E **54** E5
Gomal Pass *Pakistan* 31°56N 69°20E **42** D3
Gomati → *India* 25°32N 83°11E **43** G10
Gombe *Nigeria* 10°19N 11°2E **53** F8
Gomel = Homyel *Belarus* 52°28N 31°0E **17** B16
Gomera *Canary Is.* 28°7N 17°14W **52** F2
Gómez Palacio *Mexico* 25°34N 103°30W **86** B4
Gomīshān *Iran* 37°4N 54°6E **47** B7
Gomogomo *Indonesia* 6°39S 134°43E **37** F8
Gomoh *India* 23°52N 86°10E **43** H12
Gompa = Ganta *Liberia* 7°15N 8°59W **52** G4
Gonābād *Iran* 34°15N 58°45E **47** C8
Gonaïves *Haiti* 19°20N 72°42W **89** C5
Gonâve, G. de la *Haiti* 19°29N 72°42W **89** C5
Gonâve, Île de la *Haiti* 18°51N 73°3W **89** C5
Gonbad-e Kāvūs *Iran* 37°20N 55°25E **47** B7
Gonda *India* 27°9N 81°58E **43** F9
Gondal *India* 21°58N 70°52E **42** J4
Gonder *Ethiopia* 12°39N 37°30E **49** E2
Gondia *India* 21°23N 80°10E **44** D5
Gönen *Turkey* 40°6N 27°39E **23** D12
Gong Xian *China* 28°23N 104°47E **34** C5
Gong'an *China* 30°7N 112°12E **35** B9
Gongbei *China* 22°12N 113°32E **31** a
Gongchangling *China* 41°7N 123°27E **33** D12
Gongcheng *China* 24°50N 110°49E **35** E8
Gongga Shan *China* 29°40N 101°55E **34** C3
Gonggar *China* 29°23N 91°7E **30** F7
Gongguan *China* 21°48N 109°36E **34** G7
Gonghe *China* 36°18N 100°32E **30** D9
Gongju *S. Korea* 36°15N 127°17E **33** F14
Gongming *China* 22°47N 113°53E **31** a
Gongolgon *Australia* 30°21S 146°54E **63** E4
Gongshan *China* 27°43N 98°29E **34** D2
Gongtan *China* 28°55N 108°28E **34** C7
Gongyi *China* 34°45N 112°58E **32** G7
Goni *Nigeria* 11°30N 12°15E **53** F8
Gonjo *China* 30°50N 98°15E **34** B2
Gonzales *Calif., U.S.A.* 36°30N 121°26W **78** J5
Gonzales *Tex., U.S.A.* 29°30N 97°27W **84** G6
González *Mexico* 22°48N 98°25W **87** C5
Good Hope, C. of *S. Africa* 34°24S 18°30E **56** D2
Good Hope Lake *Canada* 59°16N 129°18W **70** B3
Gooderham *Canada* 44°54N 78°21W **82** B6
Goodhouse *S. Africa* 28°57S 18°13E **56** C2
Gooding *U.S.A.* 42°56N 114°43W **76** E6
Goodland *U.S.A.* 39°21N 101°43W **80** F3
Goodlands *Mauritius* 20°2S 57°39E **55** d
Goodlow *Canada* 56°20N 120°8W **70** B4
Goodooga *Australia* 29°3S 147°28E **63** D4
Goodsprings *U.S.A.* 35°49N 115°27W **79** K11

Goole U.K. 53°42N 0°53W 12 D7
Goolgowi Australia 33°58S 145°41E 63 E4
Goomalling Australia 31°15S 116°49E 61 F2
Goomeri Australia 26°12S 152°6E 63 D5
Goondiwindi Australia 28°30S 150°21E 63 D5
Goongarrie, L. Australia 30°3S 121°9E 61 F3
Goongarrie △ Australia 30°7S 121°30E 61 F3
Goonyella Australia 21°47S 147°58E 62 C4
Goose → Canada 53°20N 60°35W 73 B7
Goose Creek U.S.A. 32°59N 80°2W 85 E14
Goose L. U.S.A. 41°56N 120°26W 76 F3
Gooty India 15°7N 77°41E 45 G3
Gop India 22°5N 69°50E 42 H3
Gopalganj India 26°28N 84°55E 43 F11
Göppingen Germany 48°42N 9°39E 16 D5
Gorakhpur India 26°47N 83°23E 43 F10
Goražde Bos.-H. 43°38N 18°58E 23 C8
Gorda, Pta. Nic. 14°20N 83°10W 88 D3
Gordan B. Australia 11°35S 130°10E 60 B5
Gordon U.S.A. 42°48N 102°12W 80 D2
Gordon → Australia 42°27S 145°30E 63 G4
Gordon Bay Canada 45°2N 79°47W 82 A5
Gordon L. Alta., Canada 56°30N 110°25W 71 B6
Gordon L. N.W.T., Canada 63°5N 113°11W 70 A6
Gordonvale Australia 17°5S 145°50E 62 B4
Goré Chad 7°59N 16°31E 53 G9
Gore Ethiopia 8°12N 35°32E 49 F2
Gore N.Z. 46°5S 168°58E 59 G2
Gore Bay Canada 45°57N 82°28W 72 C3
Gorey Ireland 52°41N 6°18W 10 D5
Gorg Iran 29°29N 59°43E 47 D8
Gorgān Iran 36°55N 54°30E 47 B7
Gorgona, I. Colombia 3°0N 78°10W 92 C3
Gorham U.S.A. 44°23N 71°10W 83 B13
Goribidnur = Gauribidanur India 13°37N 77°32E 45 H3
Goriganga → India 29°45N 80°23E 43 E9
Gorinchem Neths. 51°50N 4°59E 15 C4
Goris Armenia 39°31N 46°22E 19 G8
Gorizia Italy 45°56N 13°37E 22 B5
Gorkiy = Nizhniy Novgorod Russia 56°20N 44°0E 18 C7
Gorkovskoye Vdkhr. Russia 57°2N 43°4E 18 C7
Gorleston U.K. 52°35N 1°44E 13 E9
Görlitz Germany 51°9N 14°58E 16 C8
Gorlovka = Horlivka Ukraine 48°19N 38°5E 19 E6
Gorman U.S.A. 34°47N 118°51W 79 L8
Gorna Dzhumayo = Blagoevgrad Bulgaria 42°2N 23°5E 23 C10
Gorna Oryakhovitsa Bulgaria 43°7N 25°40E 23 C11
Gorno-Altay □ Russia 51°0N 86°0E 26 D9
Gorno-Altaysk Russia 51°50N 86°5E 26 D9
Gornozavodsk Russia 46°33N 141°50E 27 E15
Gornyatski Russia 67°32N 64°3E 18 A11
Gornyy Russia 44°57N 133°59E 28 B6
Gorodenka = Horodenka Ukraine 48°41N 25°29E 17 D13
Gorodok = Horodok Ukraine 49°46N 23°32E 17 D12
Gorodok = Horokhiv Ukraine 50°30N 24°45E 17 C13
Gorong, Kepulauan Indonesia 3°59S 131°25E 37 E8
Gorongose → Mozam. 20°30S 34°40E 57 B5
Gorongoza △ Mozam. 18°50S 34°29E 57 A5
Gorontalo Indonesia 0°35N 123°5E 37 D6
Gorontalo □ Indonesia 0°50N 122°20E 37 D6
Gort Ireland 53°3N 8°49W 10 C3
Gorumahisani India 22°20N 86°24E 44 C8
Goryeong S. Korea 35°44N 128°15E 33 G15
Gorzów Wielkopolski Poland 52°43N 15°15E 16 B8
Gosford Australia 33°23S 151°18E 63 E5
Goshen Calif., U.S.A. 36°21N 119°25W 78 J7
Goshen Ind., U.S.A. 41°35N 85°50W 81 E11
Goshen N.Y., U.S.A. 41°24N 74°20W 83 E10
Goshogawara Japan 40°48N 140°27E 28 D10
Goslar Germany 51°54N 10°25E 16 C6
Gospič Croatia 44°35N 15°23E 16 F8
Gosport U.K. 50°48N 1°9W 13 G6
Gosse → Australia 19°32S 134°37E 62 B1
Göta älv → Sweden 57°42N 11°54E 9 H14
Göta kanal Sweden 58°30N 15°58E 9 G16
Götaland Sweden 57°30N 14°30E 9 H16
Göteborg Sweden 57°43N 11°59E 9 H14
Gotha Germany 50°56N 10°42E 16 C6
Gothenburg = Göteborg Sweden 57°43N 11°59E 9 H14
Gothenburg U.S.A. 40°56N 100°10W 80 E3
Gotland Sweden 57°30N 18°33E 9 H18
Gotō = Fukue Japan 32°41N 128°51E 29 H4
Gotō-Rettō Japan 32°55N 129°5E 29 H4
Gotska Sandön Sweden 58°24N 19°15E 9 G18
Gōtsu Japan 35°0N 132°14E 29 G6
Göttingen Germany 51°31N 9°55E 16 C5
Gottwaldov = Zlín Czech Rep. 49°14N 17°40E 17 D9
Goubangzi China 41°20N 121°52E 33 D11
Gouda Neths. 52°1N 4°42E 15 B4
Gouin, Rés. Canada 48°35N 74°40W 72 C5
Goulburn Australia 34°44S 149°44E 63 E4
Goulburn Is. Australia 11°40S 133°20E 62 A1
Goulimine Morocco 28°56N 10°0W 52 C3
Goundam Mali 16°27N 3°40W 52 E5
Gourits → S. Africa 34°21S 21°52E 56 D3
Gourock U.K. 55°57N 4°49W 11 F4
Gouverneur U.S.A. 44°20N 75°28W 83 B9
Gove Peninsula Australia 12°17S 136°49E 62 A2
Governador Valadares Brazil 18°15S 41°57W 93 G10
Governor's Harbour Bahamas 25°10N 76°14W 88 A4
Govindgarh India 24°23N 81°18E 43 G9
Gowan Ra. Australia 25°0S 145°0E 62 D4
Gowanda U.S.A. 42°28N 78°56W 82 D6

Gower U.K. 51°35N 4°10W 13 F3
Gowna, L. Ireland 53°51N 7°34W 10 C4
Goya Argentina 29°10S 59°10W 94 B4
Goyang S. Korea 37°39N 126°50E 33 F14
Goyder Lagoon Australia 27°3S 138°58E 63 D2
Goyllarisquizga Peru 10°31S 76°24W 92 F3
Goz Beïda Chad 12°10N 21°20E 53 F10
Gozo Malta 36°3N 14°15E 22 F6
Graaff-Reinet S. Africa 32°13S 24°32E 56 D3
Gračac Croatia 44°18N 15°57E 16 F8
Gracias a Dios, C. Honduras 15°0N 83°10W 88 D3
Graciosa Azores 39°4N 28°0W 52 a
Grado Spain 43°23N 6°4W 21 A2
Grady U.S.A. 34°49N 103°19W 77 J12
Grafham Water U.K. 52°19N 0°18W 13 E7
Grafton Australia 29°38S 152°58E 63 D5
Grafton N. Dak., U.S.A. 48°25N 97°25W 80 A5
Grafton W. Va., U.S.A. 39°21N 80°2W 81 F13
Graham Canada 49°20N 90°30W 72 C1
Graham U.S.A. 33°6N 98°35W 84 E5
Graham, Mt. U.S.A. 32°42N 109°52W 77 K9
Graham Bell, Ostrov = Greem-Bell, Ostrov Russia 81°0N 62°0E 26 A7
Graham I., B.C., Canada 53°40N 132°30W 70 C2
Graham I. Nunavut, Canada 77°25N 90°30W 69 B13
Graham Land Antarctica 65°0S 64°0W 5 C17
Grahamstown S. Africa 33°19S 26°31E 56 D4
Grahamsville U.S.A. 41°51N 74°33W 83 E10
Grain Coast W. Afr. 4°20N 10°0W 52 H3
Grajagan Indonesia 8°35S 114°13E 37 K17
Grajaú Brazil 5°50S 46°4W 93 E9
Grajaú → Brazil 3°41S 44°48W 93 D10
Grampian U.S.A. 40°58N 78°37W 82 F6
Grampian Highlands = Grampian Mts. U.K. 56°50N 4°0W 11 E5
Grampian Mts. U.K. 56°50N 4°0W 11 E5
Grampians, The Australia 37°15S 142°20E 63 F3
Gran Canaria Canary Is. 27°55N 15°35W 52 C2
Gran Chaco S. Amer. 25°0S 61°0W 94 B3
Gran Desierto del Pinacate △ Mexico 31°51N 113°32W 86 A2
Gran Paradiso Italy 45°33N 7°17E 20 D7
Gran Sasso d'Itália Italy 42°27N 13°42E 22 C5
Granada Nic. 11°58N 86°0W 88 D2
Granada Spain 37°10N 3°35W 21 D4
Granada U.S.A. 38°4N 102°19W 76 G12
Granard Ireland 53°47N 7°30W 10 C4
Granbury U.S.A. 32°27N 97°47W 84 E6
Granby Canada 45°25N 72°45W 83 A12
Granby U.S.A. 40°5N 105°56W 76 F11
Grand → Canada 42°51N 79°34W 82 D5
Grand → Mo., U.S.A. 39°23N 93°7W 80 F7
Grand → S. Dak., U.S.A. 45°40N 100°45W 80 C3
Grand-Anse = Portsmouth Dominica 15°34N 61°27W 89 C7
Grand Bahama I. Bahamas 26°40N 78°30W 88 A4
Grand Baie Mauritius 20°0S 57°35E 55 d
Grand Bank Canada 47°6N 55°48W 73 C8
Grand Bassam Ivory C. 5°10N 3°49W 52 G5
Grand Bend Canada 43°18N 81°45W 82 C3
Grand-Bourg Guadeloupe 15°53N 61°19W 88 b
Grand Canal = Da Yunhe China 39°10N 117°10E 33 E9
Grand Canyon U.S.A. 36°3N 112°9W 77 H7
Grand Canyon △ U.S.A. 36°15N 112°30W 77 H7
Grand Canyon-Parashant △ U.S.A. 36°30N 113°45W 77 H7
Grand Cayman Cayman Is. 19°20N 81°20W 88 C3
Grand Coulee U.S.A. 47°57N 119°0W 76 C4
Grand Coulee Dam U.S.A. 47°57N 118°59W 76 C4
Grand Falls Canada 48°56N 55°40W 73 C8
Grand Falls-Windsor Canada 48°56N 55°40W 73 C8
Grand Forks Canada 49°0N 118°30W 70 D5
Grand Forks U.S.A. 47°55N 97°3W 80 B5
Grand Gorge U.S.A. 42°21N 74°29W 83 D10
Grand Haven U.S.A. 43°4N 86°13W 80 D10
Grand I. Mich., U.S.A. 46°31N 86°40W 80 B10
Grand I. N.Y., U.S.A. 43°0N 78°58W 82 D6
Grand Island U.S.A. 40°55N 98°21W 80 E4
Grand Isle La., U.S.A. 29°14N 90°0W 85 G9
Grand Isle Vt., U.S.A. 44°43N 73°18W 83 B11
Grand Junction U.S.A. 39°4N 108°33W 76 G9
Grand L. N.B., Canada 45°57N 66°7W 73 C6
Grand L. Nfld. & L., Canada 49°0N 57°30W 73 C8
Grand L. Nfld. & L., Canada 53°40N 60°30W 73 B7
Grand L. U.S.A. 29°55N 92°47W 84 G8
Grand Lake U.S.A. 40°15N 105°49W 76 F11
Grand Manan I. Canada 44°45N 66°52W 73 D6
Grand Marais Mich., U.S.A. 46°40N 85°59W 81 B11
Grand Marais Minn., U.S.A. 47°45N 90°25W 72 C1
Grand-Mère Canada 46°36N 72°40W 72 C5
Grand Portage U.S.A. 47°58N 89°41W 80 B9
Grand Prairie U.S.A. 32°45N 96°59W 84 E6
Grand Rapids Canada 53°12N 99°19W 71 C9
Grand Rapids Mich., U.S.A. 42°58N 85°40W 81 D11
Grand Rapids Minn., U.S.A. 47°14N 93°31W 80 B7
Grand St-Bernard, Col du Europe 45°50N 7°10E 20 D7
Grand Staircase-Escalante △ U.S.A. 37°25N 111°33W 77 H8
Grand Teton U.S.A. 43°54N 110°50W 76 E8
Grand Teton △ U.S.A. 43°50N 110°70W 76 E8
Grand Union Canal U.K. 52°7N 0°53W 13 E7
Grande → Jujuy, Argentina 24°20S 65°2W 94 A2
Grande → Mendoza, Argentina 36°52S 69°45W 94 D2

Grande → Bolivia 15°51S 64°39W 92 G6
Grande → Bahia, Brazil 11°30S 44°30W 93 F10
Grande → Minas Gerais, Brazil 20°6S 51°4W 93 H8
Grande, B. Argentina 50°30S 68°20W 96 G3
Grande, Rio → N. Amer. 25°58N 97°9W 84 J6
Grande Anse Seychelles 4°18S 55°45E 55 b
Grande Baleine → Canada 55°16N 77°47W 72 A4
Grande Cache Canada 53°53N 119°8W 70 C5
Grande Comore Comoros Is. 11°35S 43°20E 55 a
Grande-Entrée Canada 47°30N 61°40W 73 C7
Grande Prairie Canada 55°10N 118°50W 70 B5
Grande-Rivière Canada 48°26N 64°30W 73 C7
Grande-Terre Guadeloupe 16°20N 61°25W 88 b
Grande-Vallée Canada 49°14N 65°8W 73 C6
Grande Vigie, Pte. de la Guadeloupe 16°32N 61°27W 88 b
Grandfalls U.S.A. 31°20N 102°51W 84 F3
Grands-Jardins △ Canada 47°41N 70°51W 73 C5
Grandview Canada 51°10N 100°42W 71 C8
Grandview U.S.A. 46°15N 119°54W 76 D4
Graneros Chile 34°5S 70°45W 94 C1
Grangemouth U.K. 56°1N 3°42W 11 E5
Granger U.S.A. 41°35N 109°58W 76 F9
Grangeville U.S.A. 45°56N 116°7W 76 D5
Granisle Canada 54°53N 126°13W 70 C3
Granite City U.S.A. 38°42N 90°8W 80 F8
Granite Falls U.S.A. 44°49N 95°33W 80 C6
Granite L. Canada 48°8N 57°5W 73 C8
Granite Mt. U.S.A. 33°5N 116°28W 79 M10
Granite Pk. U.S.A. 45°10N 109°48W 76 D9
Graniteville U.S.A. 44°8N 72°29W 83 B12
Granity N.Z. 41°39S 171°51E 59 D3
Granja Brazil 3°7S 40°50W 93 D10
Granollers Spain 41°39N 2°18E 21 B7
Grant U.S.A. 40°50N 101°43W 80 E3
Grant, Mt. U.S.A. 38°34N 118°48W 76 G4
Grant City U.S.A. 40°29N 94°25W 80 E6
Grant I. Australia 11°10S 132°52E 60 B5
Grant Range U.S.A. 38°30N 115°25E 76 G6
Grantham U.K. 52°55N 0°38W 12 E7
Grantown-on-Spey U.K. 57°20N 3°36W 11 J10
Grants U.S.A. 35°9N 107°52W 77 J10
Grants Pass U.S.A. 42°26N 123°19W 76 E2
Grantsville U.S.A. 40°36N 112°28W 76 F7
Granville France 48°50N 1°35W 20 B3
Granville N. Dak., U.S.A. 48°16N 100°47W 80 A3
Granville N.Y., U.S.A. 43°24N 73°16W 83 C11
Granville Ohio, U.S.A. 40°4N 82°31W 82 F2
Granville L. Canada 56°18N 100°30W 71 B8
Graskop S. Africa 24°56S 30°49E 57 B5
Grass → Canada 56°3N 96°33W 71 B9
Grass Range U.S.A. 47°2N 108°48W 76 C9
Grass River △ Canada 54°40N 100°50W 71 C8
Grass Valley Calif., U.S.A. 39°13N 121°4W 78 F6
Grass Valley Oreg., U.S.A. 45°22N 120°47W 76 D3
Grasse France 43°38N 6°56E 20 E7
Grassflat U.S.A. 41°0N 78°6W 82 E6
Grasslands △ Canada 49°11N 107°38W 71 D7
Grassy Australia 40°3S 144°5E 63 G3
Graulhet France 43°45N 1°59E 20 E4
Gravelbourg Canada 49°50N 106°35W 71 D7
's-Gravenhage Neths. 52°7N 4°17E 15 B4
Gravenhurst Canada 44°52N 79°20W 82 B5
Gravesend Australia 29°35S 150°20E 63 D5
Gravesend U.K. 51°26N 0°22E 13 F8
Gravois, Pointe-à- Haiti 16°15N 73°56W 89 C5
Grayling U.S.A. 44°40N 84°43W 81 C11
Grays U.K. 51°28N 0°21E 13 F8
Grays Harbor U.S.A. 46°59N 124°1W 76 D1
Grays L. U.S.A. 43°4N 111°26W 76 E8
Grays River U.S.A. 46°21N 123°37W 78 D3
Greasy L. Canada 62°55N 122°12W 70 A4
Great Abaco I. = Abaco I. Bahamas 26°25N 77°10W 88 A4
Great Artesian Basin Australia 23°0S 144°0E 62 C3
Great Australian Bight Australia 33°30S 130°0E 61 F5
Great Bahama Bank Bahamas 23°15N 78°0W 88 B4
Great Barrier I. N.Z. 36°11S 175°25E 59 B5
Great Barrier Reef Australia 18°0S 146°50E 62 B4
Great Barrier Reef △ Australia 20°0S 150°0E 62 B4
Great Barrington U.S.A. 42°12N 73°22W 83 D11
Great Basalt Wall △ Australia 19°52S 145°43E 62 B4
Great Basin U.S.A. 40°0N 117°0W 76 G5
Great Basin △ U.S.A. 38°56N 114°15W 76 G6
Great Basses Sri Lanka 6°11N 81°29E 45 L5
Great Bear → Canada 65°0N 126°0W 68 B7
Great Bear L. Canada 65°30N 120°0W 68 B8
Great Belt = Store Bælt Denmark 55°20N 11°0E 9 J14
Great Bend Kans., U.S.A. 38°22N 98°46W 80 F4
Great Bend Pa., U.S.A. 41°58N 75°45W 83 E9
Great Blasket I. Ireland 52°6N 10°32W 10 D1
Great Britain Europe 54°0N 2°15W 6 E5
Great Camanoe Br. Virgin Is. 18°30N 64°35W 89 e
Great Channel Asia 6°0N 94°0E 45 L11
Great Coco I. = Koko Kyunzu Burma 14°7N 93°22E 45 G11
Great Codroy Canada 47°51N 59°16W 73 C8
Great Divide, The = Great Dividing Ra. Australia 23°0S 146°0E 62 C4
Great Divide Basin U.S.A. 42°0N 108°0W 76 E9
Great Dividing Ra. Australia 23°0S 146°0E 62 C4
Great Driffield = Driffield U.K. 54°0N 0°26W 12 C7

Great Exuma I. Bahamas 23°30N 75°50W 88 B4
Great Falls U.S.A. 47°30N 111°17W 76 C8
Great Fish = Groot-Vis → S. Africa 33°28S 27°5E 56 D4
Great Guana Cay Bahamas 24°0N 76°20W 88 B4
Great Himalayan △ India 31°30N 77°30E 42 D7
Great Inagua I. Bahamas 21°0N 73°20W 89 B5
Great Indian Desert = Thar Desert India 28°0N 72°0E 42 F5
Great Karoo S. Africa 31°55S 21°0E 56 D3
Great Khingan Mts. = Da Hinggan Ling China 48°0N 121°0E 31 B13
Great Lake Australia 41°50S 146°40E 63 G4
Great Lakes N. Amer. 46°0N 84°0W 66 E11
Great Limpopo Transfrontier △ Africa 23°0S 31°45E 57 B5
Great Malvern U.K. 52°7N 2°18W 13 E5
Great Miami → U.S.A. 39°7N 84°49W 81 F11
Great Nicobar India 7°0N 93°50E 45 L11
Great Ormes Head U.K. 53°20N 3°52W 12 D4
Great Ouse → U.K. 52°48N 0°21E 12 E8
Great Palm I. Australia 18°45S 146°40E 62 B4
Great Pedro Bluff Jamaica 17°51N 77°44W 88 a
Great Pee Dee → U.S.A. 33°21N 79°10W 85 E15
Great Plains N. Amer. 47°0N 105°0W 66 D9
Great Ruaha → Tanzania 7°56S 37°52E 54 F7
Great Sacandaga L. U.S.A. 43°6N 74°16W 83 C10
Great Saint Bernard Pass = Grand St-Bernard, Col du Europe 45°50N 7°10E 20 D7
Great Salt Desert = Kavīr, Dasht-e Iran 34°30N 55°0E 47 C7
Great Salt L. U.S.A. 41°15N 112°40W 76 F7
Great Salt Lake Desert U.S.A. 40°50N 113°30W 76 F7
Great Salt Plains L. U.S.A. 36°45N 98°8W 84 C5
Great Sand Dunes △ U.S.A. 37°48N 105°45W 77 H11
Great Sandy → Australia 26°13S 153°2E 63 D5
Great Sandy Desert Australia 21°0S 124°0E 60 D3
Great Sangi = Sangihe, Pulau Indonesia 3°35N 125°30E 37 D7
Great Sea Reef Fiji 16°15S 179°0E 59 a
Great Sitkin I. U.S.A. 52°3N 176°6W 74 E4
Great Skellig Ireland 51°47N 10°33W 10 E1
Great Slave L. Canada 61°23N 115°38W 70 A5
Great Smoky Mts. △ U.S.A. 35°40N 83°40W 85 D13
Great Stour = Stour → U.K. 51°18N 1°22E 13 F9
Great Victoria Desert Australia 29°30S 126°30E 61 E4
Great Wall Antarctica 62°30S 58°0W 5 C18
Great Wall China 38°30N 109°30E 32 E5
Great Whernside U.K. 54°10N 1°58W 12 C6
Great Yarmouth U.K. 52°37N 1°44E 13 E9
Great Zab = Zāb al Kabīr → Iraq 36°1N 43°24E 46 B4
Greater Antilles W. Indies 17°40N 74°0W 89 C5
Greater London □ U.K. 51°31N 0°6W 13 F7
Greater Manchester □ U.K. 53°30N 2°15W 12 D5
Greater Sunda Is. Indonesia 7°0S 112°0E 36 F4
Gredos, Sierra de Spain 40°20N 5°0W 21 B3
Greece U.S.A. 43°13N 77°41W 82 C7
Greece ■ Europe 40°0N 23°0E 23 E9
Greeley Colo., U.S.A. 40°25N 104°42W 76 F11
Greeley Nebr., U.S.A. 41°33N 98°32W 80 E4
Greely Fd. Canada 80°30N 85°0W 69 A15
Greem-Bell, Ostrov Russia 81°0N 62°0E 26 A7
Green → Ky., U.S.A. 37°54N 87°30W 80 G10
Green → Utah, U.S.A. 38°11N 109°53W 76 G9
Green B. U.S.A. 45°0N 87°30W 80 C10
Green Bay U.S.A. 44°31N 88°0W 80 C9
Green C. Australia 37°13S 150°1E 63 F5
Green Cove Springs U.S.A. 29°59N 81°42W 85 G14
Green I. = Lütao Taiwan 22°40N 121°30E 35 F13
Green Lake Canada 54°17N 107°47W 71 C7
Green Mts. U.S.A. 43°45N 72°45W 83 C12
Green River Utah, U.S.A. 38°59N 110°10W 76 G8
Green River Wyo., U.S.A. 41°32N 109°28W 76 F9
Green Valley U.S.A. 31°52N 110°56W 77 L8
Greenbank U.S.A. 48°6N 122°34W 78 B4
Greenbush Mich., U.S.A. 44°35N 83°19W 82 B1
Greenbush Minn., U.S.A. 48°42N 96°11W 80 A5
Greencastle U.S.A. 39°38N 86°52W 80 F10
Greene U.S.A. 42°20N 75°46W 83 D9
Greeneville U.S.A. 36°10N 82°50W 85 D13
Greenfield Calif., U.S.A. 36°19N 121°15W 78 J5
Greenfield Calif., U.S.A. 35°15N 119°0W 79 K8
Greenfield Ind., U.S.A. 39°47N 85°46W 81 F11
Greenfield Iowa, U.S.A. 41°18N 94°28W 80 E6
Greenfield Mass., U.S.A. 42°35N 72°36W 83 D12
Greenfield Mo., U.S.A. 37°25N 93°51W 80 G7
Greenland ☑ N. Amer. 66°0N 45°0W 67 C15
Greenland Sea Arctic 73°0N 10°0W 4 B7
Greenock U.K. 55°57N 4°46W 11 F4
Greenore Ireland 54°1N 6°9W 10 B5
Greenore Pt. Ireland 52°14N 6°19W 10 D5
Greenough Australia 28°58S 114°43E 61 E1
Greenough → Australia 28°51S 114°38E 61 E1
Greenough Pt. Canada 44°58N 81°26W 82 B3
Greenport U.S.A. 41°6N 72°22W 83 E12
Greensboro Ga., U.S.A. 33°35N 83°11W 85 E13
Greensboro N.C., U.S.A. 36°4N 79°48W 85 C15
Greensboro Vt., U.S.A. 44°36N 72°18W 83 B12
Greensburg Ind., U.S.A. 39°20N 85°29W 81 F11
Greensburg Kans., U.S.A. 37°36N 99°18W 80 G4
Greensburg Pa., U.S.A. 40°18N 79°33W 82 F5

Greenstone Pt. U.K. 57°55N 5°37W 11 D3
Greenvale Australia 18°59S 145°7E 62 B4
Greenville Liberia 5°1N 9°6W 52 G4
Greenville Ala., U.S.A. 31°50N 86°38W 85 F11
Greenville Calif., U.S.A. 40°8N 120°57W 78 E6
Greenville Maine, U.S.A. 45°28N 69°35W 81 C19
Greenville Mich., U.S.A. 43°11N 85°15W 81 D11
Greenville Miss., U.S.A. 33°24N 91°4W 85 E9
Greenville Mo., U.S.A. 37°8N 90°27W 80 G8
Greenville N.C., U.S.A. 35°37N 77°23W 85 D16
Greenville N.H., U.S.A. 42°46N 71°49W 83 D13
Greenville N.Y., U.S.A. 42°25N 74°1W 83 D10
Greenville Ohio, U.S.A. 40°6N 84°38W 81 E11
Greenville Pa., U.S.A. 41°24N 80°23W 82 E4
Greenville S.C., U.S.A. 34°51N 82°24W 85 D13
Greenville Tex., U.S.A. 33°8N 96°7W 84 E6
Greenwater Lake △ Canada 52°32N 103°30W 71 C8
Greenwich Conn., U.S.A. 41°2N 73°38W 83 E11
Greenwich N.Y., U.S.A. 43°5N 73°30W 83 C11
Greenwich Ohio, U.S.A. 41°2N 82°31W 82 E2
Greenwood Canada 49°10N 118°40W 70 D5
Greenwood Ark., U.S.A. 35°13N 94°16W 84 D7
Greenwood Ind., U.S.A. 39°37N 86°7W 80 F10
Greenwood Miss., U.S.A. 33°31N 90°11W 85 E9
Greenwood S.C., U.S.A. 34°12N 82°10W 85 D13
Greenwood, Mt. Australia 13°48S 130°4E 60 B5
Gregory U.S.A. 43°14N 99°26W 80 D4
Gregory → Australia 17°53S 139°17E 62 B2
Gregory, L. S. Austral., Australia 28°55S 139°0E 63 D2
Gregory, L. W. Austral., Australia 20°0S 127°40E 60 D4
Gregory, L. W. Austral., Australia 25°38S 119°58E 61 E2
Gregory △ Australia 15°38S 131°15E 60 C5
Gregory Downs Australia 18°35S 138°45E 62 B2
Gregory Ra. Queens., Australia 19°30S 143°40E 62 B3
Gregory Ra. W. Austral., Australia 21°20S 121°12E 60 D3
Greifswald Germany 54°5N 13°23E 16 A7
Greiz Germany 50°39N 12°10E 16 C7
Gremikha Russia 67°59N 39°47E 18 A6
Grenaa Denmark 56°25N 10°53E 9 H14
Grenada U.S.A. 33°47N 89°49W 85 E10
Grenada ■ W. Indies 12°10N 61°40W 89 D7
Grenadier I. U.S.A. 44°3N 76°22W 83 B8
Grenadines, The St. Vincent 12°40N 61°20W 89 D7
Grenen Denmark 57°44N 10°40E 9 H14
Grenfell Australia 33°52S 148°8E 63 E4
Grenfell Canada 50°30N 102°56W 71 C8
Grenoble France 45°12N 5°42E 20 D6
Grenville, C. Australia 12°0S 143°13E 62 A3
Grenville Chan. Canada 53°40N 129°46W 70 C3
Gresham U.S.A. 45°30N 122°25W 78 E4
Gresik Indonesia 7°13S 112°38E 37 G15
Gretna U.K. 55°0N 3°3W 11 F5
Grevenmacher Lux. 49°41N 6°26E 15 E6
Grey → Canada 47°34N 57°6W 73 C8
Grey → N.Z. 42°27S 171°12E 59 E3
Grey, C. Australia 13°0S 136°35E 62 A2
Grey Is. Canada 50°50N 55°35W 69 G20
Grey Ra. Australia 27°0S 143°30E 63 D3
Greybull U.S.A. 44°30N 108°3W 76 D9
Greymouth N.Z. 42°29S 171°13E 59 E3
Greystones Ireland 53°9N 6°5W 10 C5
Greytown N.Z. 41°5S 175°29E 59 D5
Greytown S. Africa 29°1S 30°36E 57 C5
Gribbell I. Canada 53°23N 129°0W 70 C3
Gridley U.S.A. 39°22N 121°42W 78 F5
Griekwastad S. Africa 28°49S 23°15E 56 C3
Griffin U.S.A. 33°15N 84°16W 85 E12
Griffith Australia 34°18S 146°2E 63 E4
Griffith Canada 45°15N 77°10W 82 A7
Griffith I. Canada 44°50N 80°55W 82 B4
Grimaylov = Hrymayliv Ukraine 49°20N 26°5E 17 D14
Grimes U.S.A. 39°4N 121°54W 78 F5
Grimsay U.K. 57°29N 7°14W 11 D1
Grimsby Canada 43°12N 79°34W 82 C5
Grimsby U.K. 53°34N 0°5W 12 D7
Grimsey Iceland 66°33N 17°58W 8 C5
Grimshaw Canada 56°10N 117°40W 70 B5
Grimstad Norway 58°20N 8°35E 9 G13
Grindstone I. U.S.A. 44°17N 76°27W 83 B8
Grinnell U.S.A. 41°45N 92°43W 80 E7
Grinnell Pen. Canada 76°40N 95°0W 69 B13
Griomasaigh = Grimsay U.K. 57°29N 7°14W 11 D1
Gris-Nez, C. France 50°52N 1°35E 20 A4
Grise Fiord Canada 76°25N 82°57W 69 B15
Groais I. Canada 50°55N 55°35W 73 B8
Groblersdal S. Africa 25°15S 29°25E 57 C4
Grodno = Hrodna Belarus 53°42N 23°52E 17 B12
Grodzyanka = Hrodzyanka Belarus 53°31N 28°42E 17 B15
Groesbeck U.S.A. 31°31N 96°32W 84 F6
Grójec Poland 51°50N 20°58E 17 C11
Grong Norway 64°25N 12°8E 8 D15
Groningen Neths. 53°15N 6°35E 15 A6
Groningen □ Neths. 53°16N 6°40E 15 A6
Groom U.S.A. 35°12N 101°6W 84 D4
Groot → S. Africa 33°45S 24°36E 56 D3
Groot-Berg → S. Africa 32°47S 18°8E 56 D2
Groot-Brakrivier S. Africa 34°2S 22°18E 56 D3
Groot Karasberge Namibia 27°20S 18°40E 56 D2
Groot Kei → S. Africa 32°41S 28°22E 57 D4
Groot-Vis → S. Africa 33°28S 27°5E 56 D4
Grootdrink S. Africa 28°33S 21°42E 56 C3
Groote Eylandt Australia 14°0S 136°40E 62 A2
Groote Peel △ Neths. 51°22N 5°49E 15 C5
Grootfontein Namibia 19°31S 18°6E 56 B2
Grootlaagte → Africa 20°55S 21°27E 56 B3
Grootvloer → S. Africa 30°0S 20°40E 56 D3

Gros C. Canada 61°59N 113°32W 70 A6
Gros Islet St. Lucia 14°5N 60°58W 89 f
Gros Morne △ Canada 49°40N 57°50W 73 C8
Gros Piton St. Lucia 13°49N 61°5W 89 f
Gros Piton Pt. St. Lucia 13°49N 61°5W 89 f
Grosse Point U.S.A. 42°23N 82°54W 82 D2
Grosser Arber Germany 49°6N 13°8E 16 D7
Grosseto Italy 42°46N 11°8E 22 C4
Grossglockner Austria 47°5N 12°40E 16 E7
Groswater B. Canada 54°20N 57°40W 73 B8
Groton Conn., U.S.A. 41°21N 72°5W 83 E12
Groton N.Y., U.S.A. 42°36N 76°22W 83 D8
Groton S. Dak., U.S.A. 45°27N 98°6W 80 C4
Grouard Mission Canada 55°33N 116°9W 70 B5
Groundhog → Canada 48°45N 82°58W 72 C3
Grouw Neths. 53°5N 5°51E 15 A5
Grove City U.S.A. 41°10N 80°5W 82 E4
Grove Hill U.S.A. 31°42N 87°47W 85 F11
Groveland U.S.A. 37°50N 120°14W 78 H6
Grover Beach U.S.A. 35°7N 120°37W 79 K6
Groves U.S.A. 29°57N 93°54W 84 G8
Groveton U.S.A. 44°36N 71°31W 83 B13
Grovetown U.S.A. 33°27N 82°12W 85 E13
Groznyy Russia 43°20N 45°45E 19 F8
Grudziądz Poland 53°30N 18°47E 17 B10
Gruinard B. U.K. 57°56N 5°35W 11 D3
Grundy Center U.S.A. 42°22N 92°47W 80 D7
Gruver U.S.A. 36°16N 101°24W 84 C4
Gryazi Russia 52°30N 39°58E 18 D6
Gryazovets Russia 58°50N 40°10E 18 C7
Grytviken S. Georgia 54°19S 36°33W 96 G9
Gua India 22°18N 85°20E 43 H11
Gua Musang Malaysia 4°53N 101°58E 39 K3
Guacanayabo, G. de Cuba 20°40N 77°20W 88 B4
Guachípas → Argentina 25°40S 65°30W 94 B2
Guadalajara Mexico 20°40N 103°20W 86 C4
Guadalajara Spain 40°37N 3°12W 21 B4
Guadalcanal Solomon Is. 9°32S 160°12E 58 B9
Guadales Argentina 34°30S 67°55W 94 C2
Guadalete → Spain 36°35N 6°13W 21 D2
Guadalquivir → Spain 36°47N 6°22W 21 D2
Guadalupe = Guadeloupe ☑
  W. Indies 16°15N 61°40W 88 b
Guadalupe Mexico 22°45N 102°31W 86 C4
Guadalupe U.S.A. 34°58N 120°34W 79 L6
Guadalupe U.S.A. 28°27N 96°47W 84 G6
Guadalupe, Sierra de
  Spain 39°28N 5°30W 21 C3
Guadalupe de Bravo
  Mexico 31°23N 106°7W 86 A3
Guadalupe I. Pac. Oc. 29°0N 118°50W 66 G8
Guadalupe Mts. △
  U.S.A. 31°40N 104°30W 84 F2
Guadalupe Peak U.S.A. 31°50N 104°52W 84 F2
Guadalupe y Calvo
  Mexico 26°6N 106°58W 86 B3
Guadarrama, Sierra de
  Spain 41°0N 4°0W 21 B4
Guadeloupe ☑ W. Indies 16°20N 61°40W 88 b
Guadeloupe △ Guadeloupe 16°10N 61°40W 88 b
Guadeloupe Passage
  W. Indies 16°50N 62°15W 89 C7
Guadiana → Portugal 37°14N 7°22W 21 D2
Guadix Spain 37°18N 3°11W 21 D4
Guafo, Boca del Chile 43°35S 74°0W 96 E2
Guaico Trin. & Tob. 10°35N 61°9W 93 K15
Guainía → Colombia 2°1N 67°7W 92 C5
Guaíra Brazil 24°5S 54°10W 95 A5
Guaíra □ Paraguay 25°45S 56°30W 94 B4
Guaire = Gorey Ireland 52°41N 6°18W 10 D5
Guaitecas, Is. Chile 44°0S 74°30W 96 E2
Guajará-Mirim Brazil 10°50S 65°20W 92 F5
Guajira, Pen. de la
  Colombia 12°0N 72°0W 92 A4
Gualán Guatemala 15°8N 89°22W 88 C2
Gualeguay Argentina 33°10S 59°14W 94 C4
Gualeguaychú Argentina 33°3S 59°31W 94 C4
Gualequay → Argentina 33°19S 59°39W 94 C4
Guam ☑ Pac. Oc. 13°27N 144°45E 64 F6
Guamini Argentina 37°1S 62°28W 94 D3
Guamúchil Mexico 25°28N 108°6W 86 B3
Guana I. Br. Virgin Is. 18°30N 64°30W 89 e
Guanabacoa Cuba 23°8N 82°18W 88 B3
Guanacaste, Cordillera de
  Costa Rica 10°40N 85°4W 88 D2
Guanacaste △ Costa Rica 10°57N 85°30W 88 D2
Guanacevi Mexico 25°56N 105°57W 86 B3
Guanahani = San Salvador I.
  Bahamas 24°0N 74°30W 89 B5
Guanaja Honduras 16°30N 85°55W 88 C2
Guanajay Cuba 22°56N 82°42W 88 B3
Guanajuato Mexico 21°1N 101°15W 86 C4
Guanajuato □ Mexico 21°0N 101°0W 86 C4
Guandacol Argentina 29°30S 68°40W 94 B2
Guandi Shan China 37°53N 111°29E 32 F6
Guane Cuba 22°10N 84°7W 88 B3
Guang'an China 30°28N 106°35E 34 B6
Guangchang China 26°50N 116°21E 35 D11
Guangde China 30°54N 119°25E 35 B12
Guangdong □ China 23°0N 113°0E 35 F9
Guangfeng China 28°20N 118°15E 35 C12
Guanghan China 30°58N 104°17E 34 B5
Guangling China 39°47N 114°22E 32 E8
Guangnan China 24°5N 105°4E 34 E5
Guangning China 23°45N 112°40E 35 F9
Guangrao China 37°5N 118°25E 33 F10
Guangshui China 31°37N 114°0E 35 B9
Guangshun China 26°8N 106°21E 34 D6
Guangwu China 37°48N 105°57E 32 F3
Guangxi Zhuangzu Zizhiqu □
  China 24°0N 109°0E 34 F7
Guangyuan China 32°26N 105°51E 32 H3
Guangze China 27°30N 117°12E 35 D11
Guanica Puerto Rico 17°58N 66°55W 89 d
Guanipa → Venezuela 9°56N 62°26W 92 B6
Guanling China 25°56N 105°35E 34 E5
Guannan China 34°8N 119°21E 33 G10
Guantánamo Cuba 20°10N 75°14W 89 B4

Guantánamo B. Cuba 19°59N 75°10W 89 C4
Guantao China 36°42N 115°25E 32 F8
Guanting Shuiku China 40°14N 115°35E 32 D8
Guanyang China 25°30N 111°8E 35 E8
Guanyun China 34°20N 119°18E 33 G10
Guapay = Grande →
  Bolivia 15°51S 64°39W 92 G6
Guápiles Costa Rica 10°10N 83°46W 88 D3
Guapo B. Trin. & Tob. 10°12N 61°41W 93 K15
Guaporé Brazil 28°51S 51°54W 95 B5
Guaporé → Brazil 11°55S 65°4W 92 F5
Guaqui Bolivia 16°41S 68°54W 92 G5
Guaramacal △ Venezuela 9°13N 70°12W 89 E5
Guarapari Brazil 20°40S 40°30W 95 A7
Guarapuava Brazil 25°20S 51°30W 95 B5
Guaratinguetá Brazil 22°49S 45°9W 95 A6
Guaratuba Brazil 25°53S 48°38W 95 B6
Guarda Portugal 40°32N 7°20W 21 B2
Guardafui, C. = Asir, Ras
  Somalia 11°55N 51°10E 49 E5
Guárico □ Venezuela 8°40N 66°35W 92 B5
Guarujá Brazil 24°2S 46°25W 95 A6
Guarulhos Brazil 23°29S 46°33W 95 A6
Guasave Mexico 25°34N 108°27W 86 B3
Guasdualito Venezuela 7°15N 70°44W 92 B4
Guatemala Guatemala 14°40N 90°22W 88 D1
Guatemala ■ Cent. Amer. 15°40N 90°30W 88 C1
Guatemala Basin Pac. Oc. 11°0N 95°0W 65 F18
Guatemala Trench
  Pac. Oc. 14°0N 95°0W 66 H10
Guatopo △ Venezuela 10°5N 66°30W 89 D6
Guatuaro Pt.
  Trin. & Tob. 10°19N 60°59W 93 K16
Guaviare → Colombia 4°3N 67°44W 92 C5
Guaxupé Brazil 21°10S 47°5W 95 A6
Guayaguayare
  Trin. & Tob. 10°8N 61°2W 93 K15
Guayama Puerto Rico 17°59N 66°7W 89 d
Guayaquil Ecuador 2°15S 79°52W 92 D3
Guayaquil Mexico 29°59N 115°4W 86 B1
Guayaquil, G. de Ecuador 3°10S 81°0W 92 D2
Guaymas Mexico 27°56N 110°54W 86 B2
Gubbi India 13°19N 76°56E 45 H3
Gubkin Russia 51°17N 37°32E 19 D6
Gubkinskiy Russia 64°27N 76°36E 26 C8
Gucheng China 32°20N 111°30E 35 A8
Gudalur India 11°30N 76°29E 45 J3
Gudbrandsdalen Norway 61°33N 10°10E 8 F14
Guddu Barrage Pakistan 28°30N 69°50E 42 E3
Gudivada India 16°30N 81°3E 45 F5
Gudiyattam India 12°57N 78°55E 45 H4
Gudur India 14°12N 79°55E 45 H4
Guecho = Getxo Spain 43°21N 2°59W 21 A4
Guékédou Guinea 8°40N 10°5W 52 G3
Guelmine = Goulimine
  Morocco 28°56N 10°0W 52 C3
Guelph Canada 43°35N 80°20W 82 C4
Guerara Algeria 32°51N 4°22E 52 B6
Guéret France 46°11N 1°51E 20 C4
Guerneville U.S.A. 38°30N 123°0W 78 G4
Guernica = Gernika-Lumo
  Spain 43°19N 2°40W 21 A4
Guernsey U.K. 49°26N 2°35W 13 H5
Guernsey U.S.A. 42°16N 104°45W 76 E11
Guerrero □ Mexico 17°40N 100°0W 87 D5
Gügher Iran 29°28N 56°27E 47 D8
Gui Jiang → China 23°30N 111°15E 35 F8
Guia Lopes da Laguna
  Brazil 21°26S 56°7W 95 A4
Guiana Highlands
  S. Amer. 5°10N 60°40W 90 C4
Guichi China 30°39N 117°27E 35 B11
Guiding China 26°34N 107°11E 34 D6
Guidong China 26°7N 113°57E 35 D9
Guidónia-Montecélio Italy 42°1N 12°45E 22 C5
Guigang China 23°8N 109°35E 34 F7
Guijá Mozam. 24°27S 33°0E 57 B5
Guildford U.K. 51°14N 0°34W 13 F7
Guilford U.S.A. 41°17N 72°41W 83 E12
Guilin China 25°18N 110°15E 35 E8
Guillaume-Delisle, L.
  Canada 56°15N 76°17W 72 A4
Guimarães Portugal 41°28N 8°24W 21 B1
Guimaras □ Phil. 10°35N 122°37E 37 B6
Guinda U.S.A. 38°50N 122°12W 78 G4
Guinea Africa 8°0N 8°0E 50 F4
Guinea ■ W. Afr. 10°20N 11°30W 52 F3
Guinea, Gulf of Atl. Oc. 3°0N 2°30E 51 F4
Guinea-Bissau ■ Africa 12°0N 15°0W 52 F3
Güines Cuba 22°50N 82°0W 88 B3
Guingamp France 48°34N 3°10W 20 B2
Guiping China 23°21N 110°2E 35 F8
Güiria Venezuela 10°32N 62°18W 93 K14
Guiuan Phil. 11°5N 125°55E 37 B7
Guixi China 28°16N 117°15E 35 C11
Guiyang Guizhou, China 26°32N 106°40E 34 D6
Guiyang Hunan, China 25°46N 112°42E 35 D9
Guizhou □ China 27°0N 107°0E 34 D6
Gujar Khan Pakistan 33°16N 73°19E 42 C5
Gujarat □ India 23°20N 71°0E 42 H4
Gujiao China 37°54N 112°8E 32 F7
Gujranwala Pakistan 32°10N 74°12E 42 C6
Gujrat Pakistan 32°40N 74°2E 42 C6
Gulbarga India 17°20N 76°50E 45 L3
Gulbene Latvia 57°8N 26°52E 9 H22
Guledagudda India 16°3N 75°48E 45 F2
Gulf, The = Persian Gulf
  Asia 27°0N 50°0E 47 E6
Gulf Islands △ U.S.A. 30°10N 87°10W 85 F11
Gulfport U.S.A. 30°22N 89°6W 85 F10
Gulgong Australia 32°20S 149°49E 63 E4
Gulian China 52°56N 122°21E 31 A13
Gulin China 28°1N 105°50E 34 C5
Gulistan Pakistan 30°30N 66°35E 42 D2
Gulja = Yining China 43°58N 81°10E 30 C5
Gull Lake Canada 50°10N 108°29W 71 C7
Güllük Turkey 37°14N 27°35E 23 F12

Gulmarg India 34°3N 74°25E 43 B6
Gülshat Kazakhstan 46°38N 74°21E 26 C8
Gulu Uganda 2°48N 32°17E 54 D6
Gumal → Pakistan 31°40N 71°50E 42 D4
Gumel Nigeria 12°39N 9°22E 52 F7
Gumi S. Korea 36°10N 128°12E 33 F15
Gumla India 23°3N 84°33E 43 H11
Gumlu Australia 19°53S 147°41E 62 B4
Gumma □ Japan 36°30N 138°20E 29 F9
Gumzai Indonesia 5°28S 134°42E 37 F8
Guna India 24°40N 77°19E 42 G7
Gunbalanya Australia 12°20S 133°4E 60 B5
Gundabooka △ Australia 30°30S 145°20E 63 E4
Gundarehi India 20°57N 81°17E 44 D5
Gundlakamma → India 15°30N 80°15E 45 G5
Gundlupet India 11°48N 76°41E 45 J3
Gunisao → Canada 53°56N 97°53W 71 C9
Gunisao L. Canada 53°33N 96°15W 71 C9
Gunjyal Pakistan 32°20N 71°55E 42 C4
Gunnbjørn Fjeld
  Greenland 68°55N 29°47W 4 C6
Gunnedah Australia 30°59S 150°15E 63 E5
Gunnewin Australia 25°59S 148°33E 63 D4
Gunningbar Cr. →
  Australia 31°14S 147°6E 63 E4
Gunnison Colo., U.S.A. 38°33N 106°56W 76 G10
Gunnison Utah, U.S.A. 39°9N 111°49W 76 G8
Gunnison → U.S.A. 39°4N 108°35W 76 G9
Gunsan S. Korea 35°59N 126°45E 33 G14
Gunter Canada 44°52N 77°32W 82 B7
Guntersville U.S.A. 34°21N 86°18W 85 D11
Guntong Malaysia 4°36N 101°3E 39 K3
Guntur India 16°23N 80°30E 45 F5
Gunung Ciremay △
  Indonesia 6°53S 108°24E 37 G13
Gunungapi Indonesia 6°45S 126°30E 37 F7
Gunungsitoli Indonesia 1°15N 97°30E 36 D1
Gunupur India 19°5N 83°50E 44 E6
Gunza Angola 10°50S 13°50E 54 G2
Guo He → China 32°59N 117°10E 33 H9
Guoyang China 33°32N 116°12E 32 H9
Gupis Pakistan 36°15N 73°20E 43 A5
Gurbantünggüt Shamo
  China 45°8N 87°20E 30 B6
Gurdaspur India 32°5N 75°31E 42 C6
Gurdon U.S.A. 33°55N 93°9W 84 E8
Gurgaon India 28°27N 77°1E 42 E7
Gurgueia → Brazil 6°50S 43°24W 93 E10
Gurha India 25°12N 71°39E 42 G4
Guri, Embalse de
  Venezuela 7°50N 62°52W 92 B6
Gurkha Nepal 28°5N 84°40E 43 E11
Gurla Mandhata = Naimona'nyi
  Feng China 30°26N 81°18E 43 D9
Gurley Australia 29°45S 149°48E 63 D4
Gurnet Point U.S.A. 42°1N 70°34W 83 D14
Gurun Malaysia 5°49N 100°27E 39 K3
Gürün Turkey 38°43N 37°15E 19 G6
Gurupá Brazil 1°25S 51°35W 93 D8
Gurupá, I. Grande de
  Brazil 1°25S 51°45W 93 D8
Gurupi Brazil 11°43S 49°4W 93 F9
Gurupi → Brazil 1°13S 46°6W 93 D9
Guruwe Zimbabwe 16°40S 30°42E 57 A5
Gurvan Sayhan Uul
  Mongolia 43°50N 104°0E 32 C3
Guryev = Atyraū
  Kazakhstan 47°5N 52°0E 19 E9
Gusau Nigeria 12°12N 6°40E 52 F7
Gushan China 39°50N 123°35E 33 E12
Gushgy = Serhetabat
  Turkmenistan 35°20N 62°18E 47 C9
Gushi China 32°11N 115°41E 35 A10
Gusinoozersk Russia 51°16N 106°27E 27 D11
Gustavus U.S.A. 58°25N 135°44W 70 B1
Gustine U.S.A. 37°16N 121°0W 78 H6
Güstrow Germany 53°47N 12°10E 16 B7
Gütersloh Germany 51°54N 8°24E 16 C5
Gutha Australia 28°58S 115°55E 61 E2
Guthalungra Australia 19°52S 147°50E 62 B4
Guthrie Canada 44°28N 79°32W 82 B5
Guthrie Okla., U.S.A. 35°53N 97°25W 84 D6
Guthrie Tex., U.S.A. 33°37N 100°19W 84 E4
Gutian China 26°32N 118°43E 35 D12
Guttenberg U.S.A. 42°47N 91°6W 80 D8
Gutu Zimbabwe 19°41S 31°9E 57 A5
Guwahati India 26°10N 91°45E 41 F17
Guy Fawkes River △
  Australia 30°0S 152°20E 63 D5
Guyana ■ S. Amer. 5°0N 59°0W 92 C7
Guyane française = French
  Guiana ☑ S. Amer. 4°0N 53°0W 93 C8
Guyang China 41°0N 110°5E 32 D6
Guyenne France 44°30N 0°40E 20 D4
Guymon U.S.A. 36°41N 101°29W 84 C4
Guyra Australia 30°15S 151°40E 63 E5
Guyuan Hebei, China 41°37N 115°40E 32 D8
Guyuan Ningxia Huizu,
  China 36°0N 106°20E 32 F4
Güzelyurt = Morphou
  Cyprus 35°12N 32°59E 46 C2
Guzhang China 28°42N 109°58E 34 C7
Guzhen China 33°22N 117°18E 33 H9
Guzmán, L. de Mexico 31°20N 107°30W 86 A3
Gwa Burma 17°36N 94°34E 41 L19
Gwabegar Australia 30°37S 148°59E 63 E4
Gwädar Pakistan 25°10N 62°18E 40 G3
Gwaii Haanas △
  Canada 52°21N 131°26W 70 C2
Gwalior India 26°12N 78°10E 42 F8
Gwanda Zimbabwe 20°55S 29°0E 55 J5
Gwangju S. Korea 35°9N 126°54E 33 G14
Gwanju = Gwangju
  S. Korea 35°9N 126°54E 33 G14
Gweebarra B. Ireland 54°51N 8°23W 10 B3
Gweedore Ireland 55°3N 8°14W 10 A3
Gweru Zimbabwe 19°28S 29°45E 55 H5

Gwinn U.S.A. 46°19N 87°27W 80 B10
Gwydir → Australia 29°27S 149°48E 63 D4
Gwynedd □ U.K. 52°52N 4°10W 12 E3
Gyandzha = Gäncä
  Azerbaijan 40°45N 46°20E 19 F8
Gyangzê China 29°5N 89°47E 30 F6
Gyaring Hu China 34°50N 97°40E 30 E8
Gydanskiy Poluostrov
  Russia 70°0N 78°0E 26 C8
Gyeongju S. Korea 35°51N 129°14E 33 G15
Gympie Australia 26°11S 152°38E 63 D5
Gyöngyös Hungary 47°48N 19°56E 17 E10
Győr Hungary 47°41N 17°40E 17 E9
Gypsum Pt. Canada 61°53N 114°35W 70 A5
Gypsumville Canada 51°45N 98°40W 71 C9
Gyula Hungary 46°38N 21°17E 17 E11
Gyumri Armenia 40°47N 43°50E 19 F7
Gyzylarbat = Serdar
  Turkmenistan 39°4N 56°23E 47 B8
Gyzyletrek = Etrek
  Turkmenistan 37°36N 54°46E 47 B7

H

Ha 'Arava → Israel 30°50N 35°20E 48 E4
Ha Coi Vietnam 21°26N 107°46E 34 G6
Ha Dong Vietnam 20°58N 105°46E 34 G5
Ha Giang Vietnam 22°50N 104°59E 34 F5
Hä Karmel, Har Israel 32°44N 35°3E 48 C4
Ha Karmel △ Israel 32°45N 35°5E 48 C4
Ha Long = Hong Gai
  Vietnam 20°57N 107°5E 34 G6
Ha Long, Vinh Vietnam 20°56N 107°3E 38 B6
Ha Tien Vietnam 10°23N 104°29E 39 G5
Ha Tinh Vietnam 18°20N 105°54E 38 C5
Ha Trung Vietnam 19°58N 105°50E 38 C5
Haaksbergen Neths. 52°9N 6°45E 15 B6
Ha'ano Tonga 19°41S 174°18W 59 c
Ha'apai Group Tonga 19°47S 174°27W 59 c
Haapiti Moorea 17°34S 149°52W 59 d
Haapsalu Estonia 58°56N 23°30E 9 G20
Haarlem Neths. 52°23N 4°39E 15 B4
Haast → N.Z. 43°50S 169°2E 59 E2
Haast Bluff Australia 23°22S 132°0E 60 D5
Haasts Bluff △ Australia 23°25S 131°55E 60 D5
Hab → Pakistan 24°53N 66°41E 42 G3
Hab Nadi Chauki Pakistan 25°0N 66°50E 42 G2
Habahe China 48°3N 86°23E 30 B6
Habay Canada 58°50N 118°44W 70 B5
Ḥabbāniyah Iraq 33°17N 43°29E 46 C4
Habirag China 42°17N 115°42E 32 C8
Ḥabshān U.A.E. 23°50N 53°37E 47 F7
Haboro Japan 44°22N 141°42E 28 B10
Hachijō-Jima Japan 33°5N 139°45E 29 H9
Hachiman = Gujō Japan 35°45N 136°57E 29 G8
Hachinohe Japan 40°30N 141°29E 28 D10
Hachiōji Japan 35°40N 139°20E 29 G9
Hackettstown U.S.A. 40°51N 74°50W 83 F10
Hadali Pakistan 32°16N 72°11E 42 C5
Hadarba, Ras Sudan 22°4N 36°51E 53 D13
Hadarom □ Israel 31°0N 35°0E 48 E4
Hadd, Ra's al Oman 22°35N 59°50E 49 C6
Haddington U.K. 55°57N 2°47W 11 F6
Hadejia Nigeria 12°30N 10°5E 52 F7
Hadera Israel 32°27N 34°55E 48 C3
Hadera, N. → Israel 32°28N 34°52E 48 C3
Haderslev Denmark 55°15N 9°30E 9 J13
Hadgaon India 19°30N 77°40E 44 E3
Hadhramaut = Ḥaḍramawt □
  Yemen 15°30N 49°30E 49 D4
Ḥadīboh Yemen 12°39N 54°2E 49 E5
Hadley B. Canada 72°31N 108°12W 68 C10
Hadong S. Korea 35°5N 127°44E 33 G14
Ḥaḍramawt □ Yemen 15°30N 49°30E 49 D4
Ḥadrāniyah Iraq 35°38N 43°14E 46 C4
Hadrian's Wall U.K. 55°0N 2°30W 12 B5
Hae, Ko Thailand 7°44N 98°22E 39 a
Haean S. Korea 38°3N 125°45E 33 E13
Hä'ena U.S.A. 22°14N 159°34W 75 L8
Haenam S. Korea 34°34N 126°35E 33 G14
Haenertsburg S. Africa 24°0S 29°50E 57 B4
Haerhpin = Harbin
  China 45°48N 126°40E 33 B14
Hafar al Bāṭin Si. Arabia 28°32N 45°52E 46 D5
Ḥafirat al 'Aydā Si. Arabia 26°26N 39°12E 46 E3
Ḥafit Oman 23°59N 55°49E 47 F7
Hafizabad Pakistan 32°5N 73°40E 42 C5
Haflong India 25°10N 93°5E 41 G18
Haft Gel Iran 31°30N 49°32E 47 D6
Hagalil Israel 32°53N 35°18E 48 C4
Hagari → India 15°40N 77°0E 45 G3
Hagemeister I. U.S.A. 58°39N 160°54W 74 D7
Hagen Germany 51°21N 7°27E 16 C4
Hagerman U.S.A. 33°7N 104°20W 77 K11
Hagerman Fossil Beds △
  U.S.A. 42°48N 114°57W 76 E6
Hagerstown U.S.A. 39°39N 77°43W 81 F15
Hagersville Canada 42°58N 80°3W 82 D4
Hagfors Sweden 60°3N 13°45E 9 F15
Hagi Japan 34°30N 131°22E 29 G5
Hagolan Syria 33°0N 35°45E 48 C4
Hagondange France 49°16N 6°11E 20 B7
Hags Hd. Ireland 52°57N 9°28W 10 D2
Hague, C. de la France 49°44N 1°56W 20 B3
Hague, The = 's-Gravenhage
  Neths. 52°7N 4°17E 15 B4
Haguenau France 48°49N 7°47E 20 B7

Ḥā'il Si. Arabia 27°28N 41°45E 46 E4
Ḥā'il □ Si. Arabia 26°40N 41°40E 46 E4
Hailar China 49°10N 119°38E 31 B12
Hailey U.S.A. 43°31N 114°19W 76 E6
Haileybury Canada 47°30N 79°38W 72 C4
Hailin China 44°37N 129°30E 33 B15
Hailing Dao China 21°35N 111°47E 35 G8
Hailun China 47°28N 126°50E 31 B14
Hailuoto Finland 65°3N 24°45E 8 D21
Haimen Guangdong,
  China 23°15N 116°38E 35 F11
Haimen Jiangsu, China 31°52N 121°10E 35 B13
Hainan □ China 19°0N 109°30E 38 C7
Hainan Dao China 19°0N 109°30E 38 C7
Hainan Str. = Qiongzhou Haixia
  China 20°10N 110°15E 38 B8
Hainaut □ Belgium 50°30N 4°0E 15 D4
Haines Alaska, U.S.A. 59°14N 135°26W 70 B1
Haines Oreg., U.S.A. 44°55N 117°56W 76 D5
Haines City U.S.A. 28°7N 81°38W 85 G14
Haines Junction Canada 60°45N 137°30W 70 A1
Haining China 30°28N 120°40E 35 B13
Haiphong Vietnam 20°47N 106°41E 34 G6
Haitan Dao China 25°30N 119°45E 35 D12
Haiti ■ W. Indies 19°0N 72°30W 89 C5
Haiya Sudan 18°20N 36°21E 53 E13
Haiyan Qinghai, China 36°53N 100°59E 30 D9
Haiyan Zhejiang, China 30°28N 120°58E 35 B13
Haiyang China 36°47N 121°9E 33 F11
Haiyuan Guangxi Zhuangzu,
  China 22°8N 107°35E 34 F6
Haiyuan Ningxia Huizu,
  China 36°35N 105°52E 32 F3
Haizhou China 34°37N 119°7E 33 G10
Haizhou Wan China 34°50N 119°20E 33 G10
Haj Ali Qoli, Kavīr Iran 35°55N 54°50E 47 C7
Hajdúböszörmény
  Hungary 47°40N 21°30E 17 E11
Haji Ibrahim Iraq 36°40N 44°30E 46 B5
Ḥājjīābād Iran 33°37N 60°0E 47 C9
Hajipur India 25°45N 85°13E 43 G11
Ḥajjah Yemen 15°42N 43°36E 49 D3
Ḥājjīābād Iran 28°19N 55°55E 47 D7
Ḥājjīābād-e Zarrīn Iran 33°9N 54°51E 47 C7
Hajnówka Poland 52°47N 23°35E 17 B12
Hakkâri Turkey 37°34N 43°44E 46 B5
Hakken-Zan Japan 34°10N 135°54E 29 G7
Hakkōda San Japan 40°50N 141°0E 28 D10
Hakodate Japan 41°45N 140°44E 28 D10
Hakos Namibia 23°15S 16°21E 56 B2
Hakskeenpan S. Africa 26°48S 20°13E 56 D3
Haku-San Japan 36°9N 136°46E 29 F8
Haku-San △ Japan 36°15N 136°45E 29 F8
Hakui Japan 36°53N 136°47E 29 F8
Hakusan Japan 36°31N 136°34E 29 F8
Hala Pakistan 25°43N 68°20E 40 G6
Ḥalab Syria 36°10N 37°15E 46 B3
Ḥalabjah Iraq 35°10N 45°58E 46 C5
Halaib Sudan 22°12N 36°30E 53 D13
Halaib Triangle Africa 22°30N 35°20E 53 D13
Ḥalāt 'Ammār Si. Arabia 29°10N 36°4E 46 D3
Halba Lebanon 34°34N 36°6E 48 A5
Halberstadt Germany 51°54N 11°3E 16 C6
Halcombe N.Z. 40°8S 175°30E 59 D5
Halcon, Mt. Phil. 13°16N 121°0E 37 B6
Halden Norway 59°9N 11°23E 9 G14
Haldia Bangla. 22°1N 88°3E 43 H13
Haldwani India 29°31N 79°30E 43 E8
Hale → Australia 24°56S 135°53E 62 C2
Halesowen U.K. 52°27N 2°3W 13 E5
Halesworth U.K. 52°20N 1°31E 13 E9
Haleyville U.S.A. 34°14N 87°37W 85 D11
Half Dome U.S.A. 37°44N 119°32E 78 H7
Halfmoon Bay N.Z. 46°50S 168°5E 59 G2
Halfway → Canada 56°12N 121°32W 70 B4
Halia India 24°50N 82°19E 43 G10
Haliburton Canada 45°3N 78°30W 82 A6
Halifax Australia 18°32S 146°22E 62 B4
Halifax Canada 44°38N 63°35W 73 D7
Halifax U.K. 53°43N 1°52W 12 D6
Halifax U.S.A. 40°25N 76°55W 82 F8
Halifax B. Australia 18°50S 147°0E 62 B4
Halifax I. Namibia 26°38S 15°4E 56 C2
Halik Shan China 42°20N 81°22E 30 C5
Halīl → Iran 27°40N 58°30E 47 E8
Halimun = Indonesia 6°42S 106°26E 37 G11
Halkida = Chalkida
  Greece 38°27N 23°42E 23 E10
Halkirk U.K. 58°30N 3°29W 11 C5
Hall Beach Canada 68°46N 81°12W 69 D15
Hall Pen. Canada 63°30N 66°0W 69 E18
Hall Pt. Australia 15°40S 124°23E 60 C3
Halland Sweden 57°8N 12°47E 9 H15
Ḥallāniyat, Jazā'ir al
  Oman 17°30N 55°58E 49 D6
Hallasan S. Korea 33°22N 126°32E 33 H14
Halle Germany 51°30N 11°56E 16 C6
Hällefors Sweden 59°47N 14°31E 9 G16
Hallett Australia 33°25S 138°55E 63 E2
Hallettsville U.S.A. 29°27N 96°57W 84 G6
Halley Antarctica 75°35S 26°39W 5 D1
Hallia → India 16°55N 79°20E 44 F4
Hallim S. Korea 33°24N 126°15E 33 H14
Hallingdalselva →
  Norway 60°23N 9°35E 8 F13
Hallock U.S.A. 48°47N 96°57W 80 A5
Halls Creek Australia 18°16S 127°38E 60 C4
Halls Gap Australia 37°8S 142°34E 63 F3
Halls Lake Canada 45°7N 78°45W 82 A6
Hallsberg Sweden 59°5N 15°7E 9 G16
Hallstead U.S.A. 41°58N 75°45W 83 E9
Halmahera Indonesia 0°40N 128°0E 37 D7
Halmstad Sweden 56°41N 12°52E 9 H15
Halong Bay = Ha Long, Vinh
  Vietnam 20°56N 107°3E 38 B6
Hälsingborg = Helsingborg
  Sweden 56°3N 12°42E 9 H15

Hälsingland Sweden 61°40N 16°5E 8 F17
Halstead U.K. 51°57N 0°40E 13 F8
Haltiatunturi Finland 69°17N 21°18E 8 B19
Halton □ U.K. 53°22N 2°45W 12 D5
Haltwhistle U.K. 54°58N 2°26W 12 C5
Ḥālūl Qatar 25°40N 52°40E 47 E7
Halvad India 23°1N 71°11E 42 H4
Ḥalvān Iran 33°57N 56°15E 47 C8
Hamab Namibia 28°7S 19°16E 56 C2
Hamada Japan 34°56N 132°4E 29 G6
Hamadān Iran 34°52N 48°32E 47 C6
Hamadān □ Iran 35°0N 49°0E 47 C6
Ḥamāh Syria 35°5N 36°40E 46 C3
Hamamatsu Japan 34°45N 137°45E 29 G8
Hamar Norway 60°48N 11°7E 8 F14
Hamâta, Gebel Egypt 24°17N 35°0E 46 E2
Hamatonbetsu Japan 45°10N 142°20E 28 B11
Hambantota Sri Lanka 6°10N 81°10E 45 L5
Hamber ⌂ Canada 52°20N 118°0W 70 C5
Hamburg Germany 53°33N 9°59E 16 B5
Hamburg Ark., U.S.A. 33°14N 91°48W 84 E9
Hamburg N.Y., U.S.A. 42°43N 78°50W 82 D6
Hamburg Pa., U.S.A. 40°33N 75°59W 83 F9
Ḥamḍ, W. al → Si. Arabia 24°55N 36°20E 46 E3
Hamden U.S.A. 41°23N 72°54W 83 E12
Häme Finland 61°38N 25°10E 8 F21
Hämeenlinna Finland 61°0N 24°28E 8 F21
Hamelin Pool Australia 26°22S 114°20E 61 E1
Hameln Germany 52°6N 9°21E 16 B5
Hamerkaz □ Israel 32°15N 34°55E 48 C3
Hamersley Ra. Australia 22°0S 117°45E 60 D2
Hamhŭng N. Korea 39°54N 127°30E 33 E14
Hami China 42°55N 93°25E 30 C7
Hamilton Australia 37°45S 142°2E 63 F3
Hamilton Canada 43°15N 79°50W 82 C5
Hamilton N.Z. 37°47S 175°19E 59 B5
Hamilton U.K. 55°46N 4°2W 11 F4
Hamilton Ala., U.S.A. 34°9N 87°59W 85 D11
Hamilton Mont., U.S.A. 46°15N 114°10W 76 C6
Hamilton N.Y., U.S.A. 42°50N 75°33W 83 D9
Hamilton Ohio, U.S.A. 39°24N 84°34W 81 F11
Hamilton Tex., U.S.A. 31°42N 98°7W 84 F5
Hamilton → Queens., Australia 23°30S 139°47E 62 C2
Hamilton → S. Austral., Australia 26°40S 135°19E 63 D2
Hamilton City U.S.A. 39°45N 122°1W 78 F4
Hamilton I. Australia 20°21S 148°56E 62 b
Hamilton Inlet Canada 54°0N 57°30W 73 B8
Hamilton Mt. U.S.A. 43°25N 74°22W 83 C10
Hamina Finland 60°34N 27°12E 8 F22
Hamirpur H.P., India 31°41N 76°31E 42 D7
Hamirpur Ut. P., India 25°57N 80°9E 43 G9
Hamlet U.S.A. 34°53N 79°42W 85 D15
Hamley Bridge Australia 34°17S 138°35E 63 E2
Hamlin = Hameln Germany 52°6N 9°21E 16 B5
Hamlin N.Y., U.S.A. 43°17N 77°55W 82 C7
Hamlin Tex., U.S.A. 32°53N 100°8W 84 E4
Hamm Germany 51°40N 7°50E 16 C4
Ḥammār, Hawr al Iraq 30°50N 47°10E 46 D5
Hammerfest Norway 70°39N 23°41E 8 A20
Hammond Ind., U.S.A. 41°38N 87°30W 80 E10
Hammond La., U.S.A. 30°30N 90°28W 85 F9
Hammond N.Y., U.S.A. 44°27N 75°42W 83 B9
Hammondsport U.S.A. 42°25N 77°13W 82 D7
Hammonton U.S.A. 39°39N 74°48W 81 F16
Hampden N.Z. 45°18S 170°50E 59 F3
Hampi India 15°18N 76°28E 45 G3
Hampshire □ U.K. 51°7N 1°23W 13 F6
Hampshire Downs U.K. 51°15N 1°10W 13 F6
Hampton N.B., Canada 45°32N 65°51W 73 C6
Hampton Ont., Canada 43°58N 78°45W 82 C6
Hampton Ark., U.S.A. 33°32N 92°28W 84 E8
Hampton Iowa, U.S.A. 42°45N 93°13W 80 D7
Hampton N.H., U.S.A. 42°57N 70°50W 83 D14
Hampton S.C., U.S.A. 32°52N 81°7W 85 E14
Hampton Va., U.S.A. 37°2N 76°21W 81 G15
Hampton Bays U.S.A. 40°53N 72°30W 83 F12
Hampton Tableland Australia 32°0S 127°0E 61 F4
Hamyang S. Korea 35°32N 127°42E 33 G14
Han Jiang → China 23°25N 116°40E 35 F11
Han Pijesak Bos.-H. 44°5N 18°57E 23 B8
Han Shui → China 30°34N 114°17E 35 B10
Hanak Si. Arabia 25°32N 37°0E 46 E3
Hanamaki Japan 39°23N 141°7E 28 E10
Hanau Germany 50°7N 8°56E 16 C5
Hanbogd = Ihbulag Mongolia 43°11N 107°10E 32 C4
Hancheng China 35°31N 110°25E 32 G6
Hanchuan China 30°40N 113°50E 35 B9
Hancock Mich., U.S.A. 47°8N 88°35W 80 B9
Hancock N.Y., U.S.A. 41°57N 75°17W 83 E9
Hancock Vt., U.S.A. 43°55N 72°50W 83 C12
Handa Japan 34°53N 136°55E 29 G8
Handa I. U.K. 58°23N 5°11W 11 C3
Handan China 36°35N 114°28E 32 F8
Handwara India 34°21N 74°20E 43 B6
Hanegev Israel 30°50N 35°0E 48 E4
Hanford U.S.A. 36°20N 119°39W 78 J7
Hanford Reach ⌂ U.S.A. 46°40N 119°30W 76 C4
Hang Chat Thailand 18°20N 99°21E 38 C2
Hangang → S. Korea 37°50N 126°30E 33 F14
Hangayn Nuruu Mongolia 47°30N 99°0E 30 B8
Hangchou = Hangzhou China 30°18N 120°11E 35 B13
Hanggin Houqi China 40°58N 107°4E 32 D4
Hanggin Qi China 39°52N 108°50E 32 E5
Hangu China 39°18N 117°53E 33 E9
Hangzhou China 30°18N 120°11E 35 B13
Hangzhou Wan China 30°15N 120°45E 35 B13
Hanh Mongolia 51°32N 100°35E 30 A9
Hanhongor Mongolia 43°55N 104°28E 32 C3
Hania = Chania Greece 35°30N 24°4E 23 G11
Ḥanīdh Si. Arabia 26°35N 48°38E 47 E6
Ḥanīsh Yemen 13°45N 42°46E 49 E3
Hanjiang China 25°26N 119°6E 35 E12
Hankinson U.S.A. 46°4N 96°54W 80 B5
Hankö Finland 59°50N 22°57E 9 G20
Hankou China 30°35N 114°30E 35 B10
Hanksville U.S.A. 38°22N 110°43W 76 G8
Hanle India 32°42N 79°4E 43 C8
Hanmer Springs N.Z. 42°32S 172°50E 59 E4
Hann → Australia 17°26S 126°17E 60 C4
Hann, Mt. Australia 15°45S 126°0E 60 C4
Hanna Canada 51°40N 111°54W 70 C6
Hanna U.S.A. 41°52N 106°34W 76 F10
Hannah B. Canada 51°40N 80°0W 72 B4
Hannibal Mo., U.S.A. 39°42N 91°22W 80 F8
Hannibal N.Y., U.S.A. 43°19N 76°35W 83 C8
Hannover Germany 52°22N 9°46E 16 B5
Hanoi Vietnam 21°5N 105°55E 34 G5
Hanover = Hannover Germany 52°22N 9°46E 16 B5
Hanover Canada 44°9N 81°2W 82 B3
Hanover S. Africa 31°4S 24°29E 56 D3
Hanover N.H., U.S.A. 43°42N 72°17W 83 C12
Hanover Ohio, U.S.A. 40°4N 82°16W 82 F2
Hanover Pa., U.S.A. 39°48N 76°59W 81 F15
Hanover, I. Chile 51°0S 74°50W 96 G2
Hans Lollik I. U.S. Virgin Is. 18°24N 64°53W 89 e
Hansdiha India 24°36N 87°5E 43 G12
Hanshou China 28°56N 111°50E 35 C8
Hansi H.P., India 32°27N 77°50E 42 C7
Hansi Haryana, India 29°10N 75°57E 42 E6
Hanson, L. Australia 31°0S 136°15E 63 E2
Hanting China 36°46N 119°12E 33 F10
Hantsavichy Belarus 52°49N 26°30E 17 B14
Hanumangarh India 29°35N 74°19E 42 E6
Hanyin China 32°54N 108°28E 32 H5
Hanyuan China 29°21N 102°40E 34 C4
Hanzhong China 33°10N 107°1E 34 A6
Hanzhuang China 34°33N 117°23E 33 G9
Haoxue China 30°3N 112°24E 35 B9
Haparanda Sweden 65°52N 24°8E 8 D21
Happy U.S.A. 34°45N 101°52W 84 D4
Happy Camp U.S.A. 41°48N 123°23W 76 F2
Happy Valley-Goose Bay Canada 53°15N 60°20W 73 B7
Hapsu N. Korea 41°13N 128°51E 33 D15
Hapur India 28°45N 77°45E 42 E7
Ḥaql Si. Arabia 29°10N 34°58E 48 F3
Har Indonesia 5°16S 133°14E 37 F8
Har-Ayrag Mongolia 45°47N 109°16E 32 B5
Har Hu China 38°20N 97°38E 30 D8
Har Us Nuur Mongolia 48°0N 92°0E 30 B7
Har Yehuda Israel 31°35N 34°57E 48 D3
Ḥaraḍ Si. Arabia 24°22N 49°0E 49 C4
Haramosh Pakistan 35°50N 74°54E 43 B6
Haranomachi = Minamisōma Japan 37°38N 140°58E 28 F10
Harar = Harer Ethiopia 9°20N 42°8E 49 F3
Harare Zimbabwe 17°43S 31°2E 55 H6
Harazé Chad 9°57N 20°48E 53 G10
Harbhanga India 20°38N 84°36E 44 D7
Harbin China 45°48N 126°40E 33 B14
Harbor Beach U.S.A. 43°51N 82°39W 82 C2
Harborcreek U.S.A. 42°9N 79°57W 82 D5
Harbour Breton Canada 47°29N 55°50W 73 C8
Harbour Deep Canada 50°25N 56°32W 73 B8
Harda India 22°27N 77°5E 42 H7
Hardangerfjorden Norway 60°5N 6°0E 9 F12
Hardangervidda Norway 60°7N 7°20E 8 F12
Hardap □ Namibia 24°0S 17°0E 56 B2
Hardap ⌂ Namibia 24°29S 17°45E 56 B2
Hardap Dam Namibia 24°32S 17°50E 56 B2
Hardenberg Neths. 52°34N 6°37E 15 B6
Harderwijk Neths. 52°21N 5°38E 15 B5
Hardey → Australia 22°45S 116°8E 60 D2
Hardin U.S.A. 45°44N 107°37W 76 D10
Harding S. Africa 30°35S 29°55E 57 D4
Harding Ra. Australia 16°17S 124°55E 60 C3
Hardisty Canada 52°40N 111°18W 70 C6
Hardoi India 27°26N 80°6E 43 F9
Hardwar = Haridwar India 29°58N 78°9E 42 E8
Hardwick U.S.A. 44°30N 72°22W 83 B12
Hardwood Lake Canada 45°12N 77°26W 82 A7
Hardy, Pen. Chile 55°30S 68°20W 96 H3
Hardy, Pte. St. Lucia 14°6N 60°56W 89 f
Hare B. Canada 51°15N 55°45W 73 B8
Hareid Norway 62°22N 6°1E 8 E12
Harer Ethiopia 9°20N 42°8E 49 F3
Hargeisa Somalia 9°30N 44°2E 49 F3
Hari → Indonesia 1°16S 104°5E 36 E2
Haridwar India 29°58N 78°9E 42 E8
Harihar India 14°32N 75°44E 45 G2
Hariharpur Garhi Nepal 27°19N 85°29E 43 F11
Harim, Jabal al Oman 25°58N 56°14E 47 E8
Haringhata → Bangla. 22°0N 89°58E 41 J16
Haripad India 9°14N 76°28E 45 K3
Harīr, W. al → Syria 32°44N 35°59E 48 C4
Harīrūd → Asia 37°24N 60°38E 47 B9
Härjedalen Sweden 62°22N 13°5E 8 E15
Harlan Iowa, U.S.A. 41°39N 95°19W 80 E6
Harlan Ky., U.S.A. 36°51N 83°19W 81 G12
Harlech U.K. 52°52N 4°6W 12 E3
Harlem U.S.A. 48°32N 108°47W 76 B9
Harlingen Neths. 53°11N 5°25E 15 A5
Harlingen U.S.A. 26°12N 97°42W 84 H6
Harlow U.K. 51°46N 0°8E 13 F8
Harlowton U.S.A. 46°26N 109°50W 76 C9
Harnai India 17°48N 73°6E 44 F1
Harnai Pakistan 30°6N 67°56E 42 D2
Harney Basin U.S.A. 43°0N 119°30W 76 E4
Harney L. U.S.A. 43°14N 119°8W 76 E4
Harney Peak U.S.A. 43°52N 103°32W 80 D2
Härnösand Sweden 62°38N 17°55E 8 E17
Haroldswick U.K. 60°48N 0°50W 11 A8
Harp L. Canada 55°5N 61°50W 73 A7
Harpanahalli India 14°47N 76°2E 45 G3
Harper Liberia 4°25N 7°43W 52 H4
Harper, Mt. U.S.A. 64°14N 143°51W 74 C11
Harrai India 22°37N 79°13E 43 H8
Harrand Pakistan 29°28N 70°3E 42 E4
Harricana → Canada 50°56N 79°32W 72 B4
Harriman U.S.A. 35°56N 84°33W 85 D12
Harrington Harbour Canada 50°31N 59°30W 73 B8
Harris U.K. 57°50N 6°55W 11 D2
Harris, L. Australia 31°10S 135°10E 63 E2
Harris, Sd. of U.K. 57°44N 7°6W 11 D1
Harris Pt. Canada 43°6N 82°9W 82 C2
Harrisburg Ill., U.S.A. 37°44N 88°32W 80 G9
Harrisburg Nebr., U.S.A. 41°33N 103°44W 80 E2
Harrisburg Pa., U.S.A. 40°16N 76°53W 82 F8
Harrismith S. Africa 28°15S 29°8E 57 C4
Harrison Ark., U.S.A. 36°14N 93°7W 84 C8
Harrison Maine, U.S.A. 44°7N 70°39W 83 B14
Harrison Nebr., U.S.A. 42°41N 103°53W 80 D2
Harrison, C. Canada 54°55N 57°55W 73 B8
Harrison Bay U.S.A. 70°40N 151°0W 74 A9
Harrison L. Canada 49°33N 121°50W 70 D4
Harrisonburg U.S.A. 38°27N 78°52W 81 F14
Harrisonville U.S.A. 38°39N 94°21W 80 F6
Harriston Canada 43°57N 80°53W 82 C4
Harrisville Mich., U.S.A. 44°39N 83°17W 82 B1
Harrisville N.Y., U.S.A. 44°9N 75°19W 83 B9
Harrisville Pa., U.S.A. 41°8N 80°0W 82 E5
Harrodsburg U.S.A. 37°46N 84°51W 81 G11
Harrogate U.K. 54°0N 1°33W 12 C6
Harrow Canada 42°2N 82°55W 82 D2
Harrowsmith Canada 44°24N 76°40W 83 B8
Harry S. Truman Res. U.S.A. 38°16N 93°24W 80 F7
Harsīn Iran 34°18N 47°33E 46 C5
Harstad Norway 68°48N 16°30E 8 B17
Harsud India 22°6N 76°44E 42 H7
Hart U.S.A. 43°42N 86°22W 80 D10
Hart, L. Australia 31°10S 136°25E 63 E2
Hartbees → S. Africa 28°45S 20°32E 56 C3
Hartford Conn., U.S.A. 41°46N 72°41W 83 E12
Hartford Ky., U.S.A. 37°27N 86°55W 80 G10
Hartford S. Dak., U.S.A. 43°38N 96°57W 80 D5
Hartford Vt., U.S.A. 43°40N 72°20W 83 C12
Hartford Wis., U.S.A. 43°19N 88°22W 80 D9
Hartford City U.S.A. 40°27N 85°22W 81 E11
Hartland Canada 46°20N 67°32W 73 C6
Hartland Pt. U.K. 51°1N 4°32W 13 F3
Hartlepool U.K. 54°42N 1°13W 12 C6
Hartlepool □ U.K. 54°42N 1°17W 12 C6
Hartley Bay Canada 53°25N 129°15W 70 C3
Hartmannberge Namibia 17°0S 13°0E 56 A1
Hartney Canada 49°30N 100°35W 71 D8
Harts → S. Africa 28°24S 24°17E 56 C3
Harts Range Australia 23°6S 134°55E 62 C1
Hartselle U.S.A. 34°27N 86°56W 85 D11
Hartshorne U.S.A. 34°51N 95°34W 84 D7
Hartstown U.S.A. 41°33N 80°23W 82 E4
Hartsville U.S.A. 34°23N 80°4W 85 D14
Hartswater S. Africa 27°34S 24°43E 56 C3
Hartwell U.S.A. 34°21N 82°56W 85 D13
Harunabad Pakistan 29°35N 73°8E 42 E5
Harur India 12°3N 78°29E 45 H4
Harvand Iran 28°25N 55°43E 47 D7
Harvey Australia 33°5S 115°54E 61 F2
Harvey U.S.A. 47°47N 99°56W 80 B4
Harwich U.K. 51°56N 1°17E 13 F9
Haryana □ India 29°0N 76°10E 42 E7
Haryn → Belarus 52°7N 27°17E 17 B14
Harz Germany 51°38N 10°44E 16 C6
Hasa Si. Arabia 25°50N 49°0E 47 E6
Ḥasā, W. al → Jordan 31°4N 35°29E 48 D4
Ḥasanābād Iran 32°8N 52°44E 47 C7
Hasanparti India 18°4N 79°32E 44 E4
Ḥasb, W. → Iraq 31°45N 44°17E 46 D5
Hasdo → India 21°44N 82°44E 43 J10
Hashimoto Japan 34°19N 135°37E 29 G7
Hashtjerd Iran 35°52N 50°40E 47 C6
Hashtpur = Tālesh Iran 37°58N 48°58E 47 B6
Haskell U.S.A. 33°10N 99°44W 84 E5
Haskovo = Khaskovo Bulgaria 41°56N 25°30E 23 D11
Haslemere U.K. 51°5N 0°43W 13 F7
Hassan India 13°0N 76°5E 45 H3
Hasselt Belgium 50°56N 5°21E 15 D5
Hassi Messaoud Algeria 31°51N 6°1E 52 B7
Hässleholm Sweden 56°10N 13°46E 9 H15
Hastings N.Z. 39°39S 176°52E 59 C6
Hastings U.K. 50°51N 0°35E 13 G8
Hastings Mich., U.S.A. 42°39N 85°17W 81 D11
Hastings Minn., U.S.A. 44°44N 92°51W 80 C7
Hastings Nebr., U.S.A. 40°35N 98°23W 80 E4
Hastings Ra. Australia 31°15S 152°14E 63 E5
Hat Lot Vietnam 21°15N 104°7E 38 B5
Hat Yai Thailand 7°1N 100°27E 39 J3
Hatanbulag = Ergel Mongolia 43°8N 109°5E 32 C5
Hatay Turkey 36°14N 36°10E 46 B3
Hatch U.S.A. 32°40N 107°9W 77 K10
Hatchet L. Canada 58°36N 103°40W 71 B8
Hateruma-Shima Japan 24°3N 123°47E 29 M1
Hatfield Australia 33°54S 143°49E 63 E3
Hatgal Mongolia 50°26N 100°9E 30 A9
Hathras India 27°36N 78°6E 42 F8
Hatia Bangla. 22°30N 91°5E 41 H17
Hatia Nepal 27°43N 87°21E 43 F12
Hatid India 17°17N 75°3E 44 F2
Hato Mayor Dom. Rep. 18°46N 69°15W 89 C6
Hatra = Al Ḥaḍr Iraq 35°35N 42°44E 46 C4
Hatta India 24°7N 79°36E 43 G8
Hatta U.A.E. 24°45N 56°4E 47 E8
Hattah Australia 34°48S 142°17E 63 E3
Hattah Kulkyne △ Australia 34°16S 142°33E 63 E3
Hatteras, C. U.S.A. 35°14N 75°32W 85 D17
Hattiesburg U.S.A. 31°20N 89°17W 85 F10
Hatvan Hungary 47°40N 19°45E 17 E10
Hau → Vietnam 9°30N 106°13E 39 H6
Haugesund Norway 59°23N 5°13E 9 G11
Haukipudas Finland 65°12N 25°20E 8 D21
Haultain → Canada 55°51N 106°46W 71 B7
Hauraki G. N.Z. 36°35S 175°5E 59 B5
Haut Atlas Morocco 32°30N 5°0W 52 B4
Hautes Fagnes = Hohes Venn Belgium 50°30N 6°5E 15 D6
Hauts Plateaux Algeria 35°0N 1°0E 52 B6
Havana = La Habana Cuba 23°8N 82°22W 88 B3
Havana U.S.A. 40°18N 90°4W 80 E8
Havant U.K. 50°51N 0°58W 13 G7
Havasor = Kığzı Turkey 38°18N 43°25E 46 B4
Havasu, L. U.S.A. 34°18N 114°28W 79 L12
Havelian Pakistan 34°2N 73°10E 42 B5
Havelock Canada 44°26N 77°53W 82 B7
Havelock N.Z. 41°17S 173°48E 59 D4
Havelock U.S.A. 34°53N 76°54W 85 D16
Havelock I. India 11°58N 93°0E 45 J11
Haverfordwest U.K. 51°48N 4°58W 13 F3
Haverhill U.K. 52°5N 0°28E 13 E8
Haverhill U.S.A. 42°47N 71°5W 83 D13
Haveri India 14°53N 75°24E 45 G2
Haverstraw U.S.A. 41°12N 73°58W 83 E11
Havirga Mongolia 45°41N 113°5E 32 B7
Havířov Czech Rep. 49°46N 18°20E 17 D10
Havlíčkův Brod Czech Rep. 49°36N 15°33E 16 D8
Havre U.S.A. 48°33N 109°41W 76 B9
Havre-Aubert Canada 47°12N 61°56W 73 C7
Havre-St.-Pierre Canada 50°18N 63°33W 73 B7
Haw → U.S.A. 35°36N 79°3W 85 D15
Hawai'i U.S.A. 19°30N 155°30W 75 M8
Hawai'i □ U.S.A. 19°30N 156°30W 75 M8
Hawaiian Is. Pac. Oc. 20°30N 156°0W 65 E12
Hawaiian Ridge Pac. Oc. 24°0N 165°0W 65 E11
Hawarden U.S.A. 43°0N 96°29W 80 D5
Hawea, L. N.Z. 44°28S 169°19E 59 F2
Hawera N.Z. 39°35S 174°19E 59 C5
Hawi U.S.A. 20°14N 155°50W 75 L8
Hawick U.K. 55°26N 2°47W 11 F6
Hawk Junction Canada 48°5N 84°38W 72 C3
Hawke B. N.Z. 39°25S 177°20E 59 C6
Hawker Australia 31°59S 138°22E 63 E2
Hawke's Bay Canada 50°36N 57°10W 73 B8
Hawkesbury Canada 45°37N 74°37W 72 C5
Hawkesbury I. Canada 53°37N 129°3W 70 C3
Hawkesbury Pt. Australia 11°55S 134°5E 62 A1
Hawkinsville U.S.A. 32°17N 83°28W 85 E13
Hawley Minn., U.S.A. 46°53N 96°19W 80 B5
Hawley Pa., U.S.A. 41°28N 75°11W 83 E9
Ḥawrān, W. → Iraq 33°58N 42°34E 46 C4
Hawsh Mūssá Lebanon 33°45N 35°55E 48 B4
Hawthorne U.S.A. 38°32N 118°38W 76 G4
Hay Australia 34°30S 144°51E 63 E3
Hay → Australia 24°50S 138°0E 62 C2
Hay → Canada 60°50N 116°26W 70 A5
Hay, C. Australia 14°5S 129°29E 60 B4
Hay I. Canada 44°53N 80°58W 82 B4
Hay L. Canada 58°50N 118°50W 70 B5
Hay-on-Wye U.K. 52°5N 3°8W 13 E4
Hay Point Australia 21°18S 149°17E 62 C4
Hay River Canada 60°51N 115°44W 70 A5
Hay Springs U.S.A. 42°41N 102°41W 80 D2
Hayachine-San Japan 39°34N 141°29E 28 E10
Hayastan = Armenia ■ Asia 40°20N 45°0E 19 F7
Haydān, W. al → Jordan 31°29N 35°34E 48 D4
Hayden U.S.A. 40°30N 107°16W 76 F10
Hayes U.S.A. 44°23N 101°1W 80 C3
Hayes → Canada 57°3N 92°12W 72 A1
Hayes, Mt. U.S.A. 63°37N 146°43W 74 C10
Hayes Creek Australia 13°43S 131°22E 60 B5
Hayle U.K. 50°11N 5°26W 13 G2
Hayling I. U.K. 50°48N 0°59W 13 G7
Hayman I. Australia 20°4S 148°53E 62 b
Hayrabolu Turkey 41°12N 27°5E 23 D12
Hays Canada 50°6N 111°48W 70 C6
Hays U.S.A. 38°53N 99°20W 80 F4
Haysyn Ukraine 48°57N 29°25E 17 D15
Hayvoron Ukraine 48°22N 29°52E 17 D15
Hayward Calif., U.S.A. 37°40N 122°4W 78 H4
Hayward Wis., U.S.A. 46°1N 91°29W 80 B8
Haywards Heath U.K. 51°0N 0°5W 13 G7
Hazafon □ Israel 32°40N 35°20E 48 C4
Hazar Turkmenistan 39°34N 53°16E 19 G9
Hazārān, Kūh-e Iran 29°35N 57°20E 47 D8
Hazard U.S.A. 37°15N 83°12W 81 G12
Hazaribag India 23°58N 85°26E 43 H11
Hazaribag Road India 24°12N 85°57E 43 G11
Hazelton Canada 55°20N 127°42W 70 B3
Hazelton U.S.A. 46°29N 100°17W 80 B3
Hazen U.S.A. 47°18N 101°38W 80 B3
Hazen, L. Canada 81°47N 71°1W 69 A17
Hazlehurst Ga., U.S.A. 31°52N 82°36W 85 F13
Hazlehurst Miss., U.S.A. 31°52N 90°24W 85 F9
Hazlet U.S.A. 40°25N 74°12W 83 F10
Hazleton U.S.A. 40°57N 75°59W 83 F9
Hazlett, L. Australia 21°30S 128°48E 60 D4
Hazro Turkey 38°15N 40°47E 46 B4
He Xian = Hezhou China 24°27N 111°30E 35 E8
He Xian China 31°45N 118°20E 35 B12
Head of Bight Australia 31°30S 131°25E 61 F5
Head-Smashed-In Buffalo Jump Canada 49°44N 113°37W 70 D6
Healdsburg U.S.A. 38°37N 122°52W 78 G4
Healdton U.S.A. 34°14N 97°29W 84 D6
Healesville Australia 37°35S 145°30E 63 F4
Healy U.S.A. 63°52N 148°58W 74 C10
Heany Junction Zimbabwe 20°6S 28°54E 57 B4
Heard I. Ind. Oc. 53°6S 72°36E 3 G13
Hearne U.S.A. 30°53N 96°36W 84 F6
Hearst Canada 49°40N 83°41W 72 C3
Heart → U.S.A. 46°46N 100°50W 80 B3
Heart's Content Canada 47°54N 53°27W 73 C9
Heath, Pte. Canada 49°8N 61°40W 73 C7
Heavener U.S.A. 34°53N 94°36W 84 D7
Hebbronville U.S.A. 27°18N 98°41W 84 H5
Hebei □ China 39°0N 116°0E 32 E9
Hebel Australia 28°58S 147°47E 63 D4
Heber U.S.A. 32°44N 115°32W 79 N11
Heber Springs U.S.A. 35°30N 92°2W 84 D8
Hebgen L. U.S.A. 44°52N 111°20W 76 D8
Hebi China 35°57N 114°7E 32 G8
Hebrides U.K. 57°30N 7°0W 6 D4
Hebrides, Sea of the U.K. 57°5N 7°0W 11 D2
Hebron = Al Khalīl West Bank 31°32N 35°6E 48 D4
Hebron Canada 58°5N 62°30W 69 F19
Hebron N. Dak., U.S.A. 46°54N 102°3W 80 B2
Hebron Nebr., U.S.A. 40°10N 97°35W 80 E5
Hecate Str. Canada 53°10N 130°30W 70 C2
Heceta I. U.S.A. 55°46N 133°40W 70 B2
Hechi China 24°40N 108°2E 34 E7
Hechuan China 30°2N 106°12E 34 B6
Hecla U.S.A. 45°53N 98°9W 80 C4
Hecla I. Canada 51°10N 96°43W 71 C9
Hede Sweden 62°23N 13°30E 8 E15
Hedemora Sweden 60°18N 15°58E 9 F16
Heerde Neths. 52°24N 6°2E 15 B6
Heerenveen Neths. 52°57N 5°55E 15 B5
Heerhugowaard Neths. 52°40N 4°51E 15 B4
Heerlen Neths. 50°55N 5°58E 15 D5
Ḥefa Israel 32°46N 35°0E 48 C4
Ḥefa □ Israel 32°40N 35°0E 48 C4
Hefei China 31°52N 117°18E 35 B11
Hefeng China 29°55N 109°52E 34 C7
Hegang China 47°20N 130°19E 31 B15
Hei Ling Chau China 22°15N 114°2E 31 a
Heichengzhen China 36°24N 106°3E 32 F4
Heidelberg Germany 49°24N 8°42E 16 D5
Heidelberg S. Africa 34°6S 20°59E 56 D3
Heidelberg S. Africa 26°30S 28°21E 57 C4
Heihe China 50°10N 127°30E 31 A14
Heijing China 25°22N 101°44E 34 E3
Heilbron S. Africa 27°16S 27°59E 57 C4
Heilbronn Germany 49°9N 9°13E 16 D5
Heilongjiang □ China 48°0N 126°0E 31 B14
Heilunkiang = Heilongjiang □ China 48°0N 126°0E 31 B14
Heimaey Iceland 63°26N 20°17W 8 E3
Heinola Finland 61°13N 26°2E 8 F22
Heinze Chaung Burma 14°42N 97°52E 38 E1
Heinze Kyun Burma 14°25N 97°45E 38 E1
Heishan China 41°40N 122°5E 33 D12
Heishui Liaoning, China 42°8N 119°30E 33 C10
Heishui Sichuan, China 32°4N 103°2E 34 A4
Hejaz = Ḥijāz Si. Arabia 24°0N 40°0E 46 E3
Hejian China 38°25N 116°5E 32 E9
Hejiang China 28°43N 105°46E 34 C5
Hejin China 35°35N 110°42E 32 G6
Hekimhan Turkey 38°50N 37°55E 46 B3
Hekla Iceland 63°56N 19°35W 8 E4
Hekou Gansu, China 36°10N 103°26E 32 F2
Hekou Guangdong, China 23°13N 112°45E 35 F9
Hekou Yunnan, China 22°30N 103°59E 34 F4
Helan Shan China 38°30N 105°55E 32 E3
Helen Atoll Palau 2°40N 132°0E 37 D8
Helena U.S.A. 46°36N 112°2W 76 C7
Helena -West Helena U.S.A. 34°32N 90°36W 85 D9
Helendale U.S.A. 34°44N 117°19W 79 L9
Helensburgh U.K. 56°1N 4°43W 11 E4
Helensville N.Z. 36°41S 174°29E 59 B5
Helenvale Australia 15°43S 145°14E 62 B4
Helgeland Norway 66°7N 13°29E 8 C15
Helgoland Germany 54°10N 7°53E 16 A4
Heligoland = Helgoland Germany 54°10N 7°53E 16 A4
Heligoland B. = Deutsche Bucht Germany 54°15N 8°0E 16 A5
Hell Hole Gorge △ Australia 25°31S 144°12E 62 D3
Hella Iceland 63°50N 20°24W 8 E3
Hellas = Greece ■ Europe 40°0N 23°0E 23 E9
Hellertown U.S.A. 40°35N 75°21W 83 F9
Hellespont = Çanakkale Boğazı Turkey 40°17N 26°32E 23 D12
Hellevoetsluis Neths. 51°50N 4°8E 15 C4
Hellín Spain 38°31N 1°40W 21 C5
Hells Canyon ⌂ U.S.A. 45°30N 117°45W 76 D5
Helmand □ Afghan. 31°20N 64°0E 40 D4
Helmand → Afghan. 31°12N 61°34E 40 D2
Helmeringhausen Namibia 25°54S 16°57E 56 C2
Helmond Neths. 51°29N 5°41E 15 C5
Helmsdale U.K. 58°7N 3°39W 11 C5
Helmsdale → U.K. 58°8N 3°43W 11 C5
Helong China 42°40N 129°0E 33 C15
Helper U.S.A. 39°41N 110°51W 76 G8
Helsingborg Sweden 56°3N 12°42E 9 H15
Helsingør Denmark 56°2N 12°35E 9 H15
Helston U.K. 50°6N 5°17W 13 G2
Helvellyn U.K. 54°32N 3°1W 12 C4
Helwân Egypt 29°50N 31°20E 53 C12
Hemavati → India 12°30N 76°20E 45 H3
Hemel Hempstead U.K. 51°44N 0°28W 13 F7
Hemet U.S.A. 33°45N 116°58W 79 M10
Hemingford U.S.A. 42°19N 103°4W 80 D2
Hemis △ India 34°10N 77°15E 42 B7
Hemmingford Canada 45°3N 73°35W 83 A11
Hempstead N.Y., U.S.A. 40°42N 73°37W 83 F11
Hempstead Tex., U.S.A. 30°6N 96°5W 84 F6
Hemse Sweden 57°15N 18°22E 9 H18
Henan □ China 34°0N 114°0E 32 H8
Henares → Spain 40°24N 3°30W 21 B4
Henashi-Misaki Japan 40°37N 139°51E 28 D9
Henderson Argentina 36°18S 61°43W 94 D3
Henderson Ky., U.S.A. 37°50N 87°35W 80 G10
Henderson N.C., U.S.A. 36°20N 78°25W 85 C15
Henderson N.Y., U.S.A. 43°50N 76°10W 83 C8
Henderson Tenn., U.S.A. 35°26N 88°38W 85 D10
Henderson Tex., U.S.A. 32°9N 94°48W 84 E7
Henderson I. Pac. Oc. 24°22S 128°19W 65 K15
Hendersonville N.C., U.S.A. 35°19N 82°28W 85 D13
Hendersonville Tenn., U.S.A. 36°18N 86°37W 85 C11
Hendījān Iran 30°14N 49°43E 47 D6
Hendorābī Iran 26°40N 53°37E 47 E7
Heng Jiang → China 28°40N 104°25E 34 C5
Heng Xian China 22°40N 109°17E 34 F7
Hengcheng China 38°18N 106°28E 32 E4
Hëngch'un Taiwan 22°0N 120°44E 35 F13
Hengdaohezi China 44°52N 129°0E 33 B15

Hengduan Shan *China* 28°30N 98°50E **34** C2
Hengelo *Neths.* 52°16N 6°48E **15** B6
Henggang *China* 22°39N 114°12E **31** a
Hengmen *China* 22°33N 113°35E **31** a
Hengshan *Hunan, China* 27°16N 112°45E **35** D9
Hengshan *Shaanxi, China* 37°58N 109°5E **32** F5
Hengshui *China* 37°41N 115°40E **32** F8
Hengyang *China* 26°59N 112°22E **35** D9
Henley-on-Thames *U.K.* 51°32N 0°54W **13** F7
Henlopen, C. *U.S.A.* 38°48N 75°6W **81** F16
Hennenman *S. Africa* 27°59S 27°1E **56** C4
Hennessey *U.S.A.* 36°6N 97°54W **84** C6
Henri Pittier △ *Venezuela* 10°26N 67°37W **89** D6
Henrietta *N.Y., U.S.A.* 43°4N 77°37W **82** C7
Henrietta *Tex., U.S.A.* 33°49N 98°12W **84** E5
Henrietta, Ostrov = Genriyetty,
　Ostrov *Russia* 77°6N 156°30E **27** B16
Henrietta Maria, C.
　Canada 55°9N 82°20W **72** A3
Henry *U.S.A.* 41°7N 89°22W **80** E9
Henry Ice Rise *Antarctica* 80°35S 62°0W **5** D17
Henry Lawrence I. *India* 12°9N 93°5E **45** H11
Henryetta *U.S.A.* 35°27N 95°59W **84** D7
Henryville *Canada* 45°8N 73°11W **83** A11
Hensall *Canada* 43°26N 81°30W **82** C3
Hentiesbaai *Namibia* 22°8S 14°18E **56** B1
Hentiyn Nuruu
　Mongolia 48°30N 108°30E **31** B10
Henty *Australia* 35°30S 147°3E **63** F4
Henzada *Burma* 17°38N 95°26E **41** L19
Heping *China* 24°29N 115°0E **35** E10
Heppner *U.S.A.* 45°21N 119°33W **76** D4
Hepu *China* 21°40N 109°12E **34** G7
Hepworth *Canada* 44°37N 81°9W **82** B3
Heqing *China* 26°37N 100°11E **34** D3
Hequ *China* 39°20N 111°15E **32** E6
Heradsflói *Iceland* 65°42N 14°12W **8** D6
Heradsvötn → *Iceland* 65°45N 19°25W **8** D4
Heraklion = Iraklio
　Greece 35°20N 25°12E **23** G11
Herald Cays *Australia* 16°58S 149°9E **62** B4
Herāt *Afghan.* 34°20N 62°7E **40** B3
Herāt □ *Afghan.* 35°0N 62°0E **40** B3
Herbert *Canada* 50°30N 107°10W **71** C7
Herbert → *Australia* 18°31S 146°17E **62** B4
Herberton *Australia* 17°20S 145°25E **62** B4
Herbertsdale *S. Africa* 34°1S 21°46E **56** D3
Herceg-Novi *Montenegro* 42°30N 18°33E **23** C8
Herchmer *Canada* 57°22N 94°10W **71** B10
Herdubreid *Iceland* 65°11N 16°21W **8** D5
Hereford *U.K.* 52°4N 2°43W **13** E5
Hereford *U.S.A.* 34°49N 102°24W **84** D3
Herefordshire □ *U.K.* 52°8N 2°40W **13** E5
Herentals *Belgium* 51°12N 4°51E **15** C4
Herford *Germany* 52°7N 8°39E **16** B5
Herington *U.S.A.* 38°40N 96°57W **80** F5
Herkimer *U.S.A.* 43°2N 74°59W **83** D10
Herlen → *Asia* 48°48N 117°0E **31** B12
Herlong *U.S.A.* 40°8N 120°8W **78** F6
Herm *U.K.* 49°30N 2°28W **13** H5
Hermann *U.S.A.* 38°42N 91°27W **80** F8
Hermannsburg *Australia* 23°57S 132°45E **60** D5
Hermanus *S. Africa* 34°27S 19°12E **56** D2
Hermidale *Australia* 31°30S 146°42E **63** E4
Hermiston *U.S.A.* 45°51N 119°17W **76** D4
Hermon *Canada* 45°6N 77°37W **82** A7
Hermon *U.S.A.* 44°28N 75°14W **83** B9
Hermon, Mt. = Shaykh, J. ash
　Lebanon 33°25N 35°50E **48** B4
Hermosillo *Mexico* 29°10N 111°0W **86** B2
Hernád → *Hungary* 47°56N 21°8E **17** D11
Hernandarias *Paraguay* 25°20S 54°40W **95** B5
Hernandez *U.S.A.* 36°24N 120°46W **78** J6
Hernando *Argentina* 32°28S 63°40W **94** C3
Hernando *U.S.A.* 34°50N 90°0W **85** D10
Herndon *U.S.A.* 40°43N 76°51W **82** F8
Herne Bay *U.K.* 51°21N 1°8E **13** F9
Herning *Denmark* 56°8N 8°58E **9** H13
Heroica Caborca = Caborca
　Mexico 30°37N 112°6W **86** A2
Heroica Nogales = Nogales
　Mexico 31°19N 110°56W **86** A2
Heron Bay *Canada* 48°40N 86°25W **72** C2
Heron I. *Australia* 23°27S 151°55E **62** C5
Herreid *U.S.A.* 45°50N 100°4W **80** C3
Herrin *U.S.A.* 37°48N 89°2W **80** G9
Herriot *Canada* 56°22N 101°16W **71** B8
Herschel I. *Canada* 69°35N 139°5W **4** C1
Hershey *U.S.A.* 40°17N 76°39W **83** F8
Herstal *Belgium* 50°40N 5°38E **15** D5
Hertford *U.K.* 51°48N 0°4W **13** F7
Hertfordshire □ *U.K.* 51°51N 0°5W **13** F7
's-Hertogenbosch *Neths.* 51°42N 5°17E **15** C5
Hertzogville *S. Africa* 28°9S 25°30E **56** C4
Hervey B. *Australia* 25°0S 152°52E **62** C5
Herzliyya *Israel* 32°10N 34°50E **48** C3
Heşar *Fārs, Iran* 29°52N 50°16E **47** D6
Heşar *Markazi, Iran* 35°50N 49°12E **47** C6
Heshan *Guangdong, China* 22°34N 113°4E **35** F9
Heshan *Guangxi Zhuangzu,*
　China 23°50N 108°53E **34** F7
Heshui *China* 35°48N 108°0E **32** G5
Heshun *China* 37°22N 113°32E **32** F7
Hesperia *U.S.A.* 34°25N 117°18W **79** L9
Hesse = Hessen □ *Germany* 50°30N 9°0E **16** C5
Hessen □ *Germany* 50°30N 9°0E **16** C5
Hetauda *Nepal* 27°25N 85°2E **43** F11
Hetch Hetchy Aqueduct
　U.S.A. 37°29N 122°19W **78** H5
Hetta Enontekiö *Finland* 68°23N 23°37E **8** B20
Hettinger *U.S.A.* 46°0N 102°42W **80** B2
Heuksando *S. Korea* 34°40N 125°30E **33** G13
Heunghae *S. Korea* 36°12N 129°21E **33** F15
Heuvelton *U.S.A.* 44°37N 75°25W **83** B9
Hewitt *U.S.A.* 31°28N 97°12W **84** F6
Hexham *U.K.* 54°58N 2°4W **12** C5
Hexi *Yunnan, China* 24°9N 102°38E **34** E4
Hexi *Zhejiang, China* 27°5N 119°38E **35** D12

Hexigten Qi *China* 43°18N 117°30E **33** C9
Heydarābād *Iran* 30°33N 55°38E **47** D7
Heysham *U.K.* 54°3N 2°53W **12** C5
Heyuan *China* 23°39N 114°40E **35** F10
Heywood *Australia* 38°8S 141°37E **63** F3
Heze *China* 35°14N 115°20E **32** G8
Hezhang *China* 27°8N 104°41E **34** D5
Hezhou *China* 24°27N 111°30E **35** E8
Hi Vista *U.S.A.* 34°45N 117°46W **79** L9
Hiawatha *U.S.A.* 39°51N 95°32W **80** F6
Hibbing *U.S.A.* 47°25N 92°56W **80** B7
Hibernia Reef *Australia* 12°0S 123°23E **60** B3
Hickman *U.S.A.* 36°34N 89°11W **80** G9
Hickory *U.S.A.* 35°44N 81°21W **85** D14
Hicks, Pt. *Australia* 37°49S 149°17E **63** F4
Hicks L. *Canada* 61°25N 100°0W **71** A9
Hicksville *U.S.A.* 40°46N 73°32W **83** F11
Hida-Gawa → *Japan* 35°26N 137°3E **29** G8
Hida-Sammyaku *Japan* 36°30N 137°40E **29** F8
Hidaka *Japan* 42°30N 142°10E **28** C11
Hidaka-Sammyaku
　Japan 42°35N 142°45E **28** C11
Hidalgo □ *Mexico* 20°30N 99°0W **87** C5
Hidalgo del Parral
　Mexico 26°56N 105°40W **86** B3
Hierro *Canary Is.* 27°44N 18°0W **52** C2
Higashiajima-San
　Japan 37°40N 140°10E **28** F10
Higashiōsaka *Japan* 34°39N 135°37E **29** G7
Higgins *U.S.A.* 36°7N 100°2W **84** C4
Higgins Corner *U.S.A.* 39°2N 121°5W **78** F5
High Bridge *U.S.A.* 40°40N 74°54W **83** F10
High Desert *U.S.A.* 43°40N 120°20W **76** E3
High Island Res. *China* 22°22N 114°21E **31** a
High Level *Canada* 58°31N 117°8W **70** B5
High Point *U.S.A.* 35°57N 80°0W **85** D15
High Prairie *Canada* 55°30N 116°30W **70** B5
High River *Canada* 50°30N 113°50W **70** C6
High Tatra = Tatry
　Slovak Rep. 49°20N 20°0E **17** D11
High Veld *Africa* 27°0S 27°0E **50** J6
High Wycombe *U.K.* 51°37N 0°45W **13** F7
Highland □ *U.K.* 57°17N 4°21W **11** D4
Highland Park *U.S.A.* 42°11N 87°48W **80** D10
Highmore *U.S.A.* 44°31N 99°27W **80** C4
Highrock L. *Canada* 55°45N 100°30W **71** B8
Higüey *Dom. Rep.* 18°37N 68°42W **89** C6
Hiiumaa *Estonia* 58°50N 22°45E **9** G20
Hijārah, Şahrā' al *Iraq* 30°25N 44°30E **46** D5
Hijāz *Si. Arabia* 24°0N 40°0E **46** E3
Hijo = Tagum *Phil.* 7°33N 125°53E **37** C7
Hikari *Japan* 33°58N 131°58E **29** H5
Hiko *U.S.A.* 37°32N 115°14W **78** H11
Hikone *Japan* 35°15N 136°10E **29** G8
Hikurangi *Gisborne, N.Z.* 37°55S 178°4E **59** C6
Hikurangi *Northland,*
　N.Z. 35°36S 174°17E **59** A5
Hildesheim *Germany* 52°9N 9°56E **16** B5
Hill → *Australia* 30°23S 115°3E **61** F2
Hill City *Idaho, U.S.A.* 43°18N 115°3W **76** E6
Hill City *Kans., U.S.A.* 39°22N 99°51W **80** F4
Hill City *Minn., U.S.A.* 46°59N 93°36W **80** B7
Hill City *S. Dak., U.S.A.* 43°56N 103°35W **80** D2
Hill Island L. *Canada* 60°30N 109°50W **71** A7
Hillaby, Mt. *Barbados* 13°12N 59°35W **89** g
Hillcrest *Barbados* 13°13N 59°31W **89** g
Hillegom *Neths.* 52°18N 4°35E **15** B4
Hillsboro *Kans., U.S.A.* 38°21N 97°12W **80** F5
Hillsboro *N. Dak., U.S.A.* 47°26N 97°3W **80** B5
Hillsboro *Ohio, U.S.A.* 39°12N 83°37W **81** F12
Hillsboro *Oreg., U.S.A.* 45°31N 122°59W **78** E4
Hillsboro *Tex., U.S.A.* 32°1N 97°8W **84** E6
Hillsborough *Grenada* 12°28N 61°28W **89** D7
Hillsborough *U.S.A.* 43°7N 71°54W **83** C13
Hillsborough Channel
　Australia 20°56S 149°15E **62** b
Hillsdale *Mich., U.S.A.* 41°56N 84°38W **81** E11
Hillsdale *N.Y., U.S.A.* 42°11N 73°32W **83** D11
Hillsport *Canada* 49°27N 85°34W **72** C2
Hillston *Australia* 33°30S 145°31E **63** E4
Hilo *U.S.A.* 19°44N 155°5W **75** M8
Hilton *U.S.A.* 43°17N 77°48W **82** C7
Hilton Head Island
　U.S.A. 32°13N 80°45W **85** E14
Hilversum *Neths.* 52°14N 5°10E **15** B5
Himachal Pradesh □ *India* 31°30N 77°0E **42** D7
Himalaya *Asia* 29°0N 84°0E **43** E11
Himalchuli *Nepal* 28°27N 84°38E **43** E11
Himatnagar *India* 23°37N 72°57E **42** H5
Himeji *Japan* 34°50N 134°40E **29** G7
Himi *Japan* 36°50N 136°55E **29** F8
Ḩimş *Syria* 34°40N 36°45E **48** A5
Ḩimş □ *Syria* 34°30N 37°0E **48** A5
Hin Khom, Laem *Thailand* 9°25N 99°56E **39** b
Hinche *Haiti* 19°9N 72°1W **89** C5
Hinchinbrook I.
　Australia 18°20S 146°15E **62** B4
Hinchinbrook Island △
　Australia 18°14S 146°6E **62** B4
Hinckley *U.K.* 52°33N 1°22W **13** E6
Hinckley *U.S.A.* 46°1N 92°56W **80** B7
Hindaun *India* 26°44N 77°5E **42** F7
Hindmarsh, L. *Australia* 36°5S 141°55E **63** F3
Hindol *India* 20°40N 85°10E **44** D7
Hindu Bagh *Pakistan* 30°56N 67°50E **42** D2
Hindu Kush *Asia* 36°0N 71°0E **40** B7
Hindupur *India* 13°49N 77°32E **45** H3
Hines Creek *Canada* 56°20N 118°40W **70** B5
Hinesville *U.S.A.* 31°51N 81°36W **85** F14
Hinganghat *India* 20°30N 78°52E **44** D4
Hingham *U.S.A.* 48°33N 110°25W **76** B8
Hingir *India* 21°57N 83°41E **43** J10
Hingoli *India* 19°41N 77°15E **44** E3
Hinna = Imi *Ethiopia* 6°28N 42°10E **47** F3
Hinnøya *Norway* 68°35N 15°50E **8** B16
Hinojosa del Duque *Spain* 38°30N 5°9W **21** C3
Hinthada = Henzada
　Burma 17°38N 95°26E **41** L19

Hinton *Canada* 53°26N 117°34W **70** C5
Hinton *U.S.A.* 37°40N 80°54W **81** G13
Hios = Chios *Greece* 38°27N 26°9E **23** E12
Hirado *Japan* 33°22N 129°33E **29** H4
Hirakud Dam *India* 21°32N 83°45E **44** D6
Hiran → *India* 23°6N 79°21E **43** H8
Hirapur *India* 24°22N 79°13E **43** G8
Hirara = Miyakojima
　Japan 24°48N 125°17E **29** M2
Hiratsuka *Japan* 35°19N 139°21E **29** G9
Hirekerur *India* 14°28N 75°23E **45** G2
Hiroo *Japan* 42°17N 143°19E **28** C11
Hirosaki *Japan* 40°34N 140°28E **28** D10
Hiroshima *Japan* 34°24N 132°30E **29** G6
Hiroshima □ *Japan* 34°50N 133°0E **29** G6
Hisar *India* 29°12N 75°45E **42** E6
Hisb, Sha'ib → = Ḩasb, W. →
　Iraq 31°45N 44°17E **46** D5
Hiṣmá *Si. Arabia* 28°30N 36°0E **46** D3
Hispaniola *W. Indies* 19°0N 71°0W **89** C5
Hīt *Iraq* 33°38N 42°49E **46** C4
Hita *Japan* 33°20N 130°58E **29** H5
Hitachi *Japan* 36°36N 140°39E **29** F10
Hitchin *U.K.* 51°58N 0°16W **13** F7
Hitiaa *Tahiti* 17°36S 149°18W **59** d
Hitoyoshi *Japan* 32°13N 130°45E **29** H5
Hitra *Norway* 63°30N 8°45E **8** E13
Hiva Oa *French Polynesia* 9°45S 139°0W **65** H14
Hixon *Canada* 53°25N 122°35W **70** C4
Ḩiyyon, N. → *Israel* 30°25N 35°10E **48** E4
Hjalmar L. *Canada* 61°33N 109°25W **71** A7
Hjälmaren *Sweden* 59°18N 15°40E **9** G16
Hjørring *Denmark* 57°29N 9°59E **9** H13
Hjort Trench *S. Ocean* 58°0S 157°30E **5** B10
Hkakabo Razi *Burma* 28°25N 97°23E **34** C1
Hlobane *S. Africa* 27°42S 31°0E **57** C5
Hluhluwe *S. Africa* 28°1S 32°15E **57** C5
Hluhluwe △ *S. Africa* 22°10S 32°5E **57** C5
Hlyboka *Ukraine* 48°5N 25°56E **17** D13
Ho *Ghana* 6°37N 0°27E **52** G6
Ho Chi Minh City = Thanh Pho Ho
　Chi Minh *Vietnam* 10°58N 106°40E **39** G6
Ho Hoa Binh *Vietnam* 20°50N 105°0E **34** G5
Ho Thac Ba *Vietnam* 21°42N 105°1E **38** A5
Ho Thuong *Vietnam* 19°32N 105°48E **38** C5
Hoa Binh *Vietnam* 20°50N 105°20E **38** B5
Hoa Hiep *Vietnam* 11°34N 105°51E **39** G5
Hoai Nhon *Vietnam* 14°28N 109°1E **38** E7
Hoang Lien → *Vietnam* 21°30N 105°32E **38** B5
Hoang Lien Son *Vietnam* 22°0N 104°0E **34** F4
Hoanib → *Namibia* 19°27S 12°46E **56** A2
Hoare B. *Canada* 65°17N 62°30W **69** D19
Hoarusib → *Namibia* 19°3S 12°36E **56** A2
Hobart *Australia* 42°50S 147°21E **63** G4
Hobart *U.S.A.* 35°1N 99°6W **84** D5
Hobbs *U.S.A.* 32°42N 103°8W **77** K12
Hobbs Coast *Antarctica* 74°50S 131°0W **5** D14
Hobe Sound *U.S.A.* 27°4N 80°8W **85** H14
Hobro *Denmark* 56°39N 9°46E **9** H13
Hoburgen *Sweden* 56°55N 18°7E **9** H18
Hobyo *Somalia* 5°25N 48°30E **49** F4
Hochfeld *Namibia* 21°28S 17°58E **56** B2
Hodaka-Dake *Japan* 36°17N 137°39E **29** F8
Hodeida = Al Ḩudaydah
　Yemen 14°50N 43°0E **49** E3
Hodgeville *Canada* 50°7N 106°58W **71** C7
Hodgson *Canada* 51°13N 97°36W **71** C9
Hódmezövásárhely
　Hungary 46°28N 20°22E **17** E11
Hodna, Chott el *Algeria* 35°26N 4°43E **52** A6
Hodonín *Czech Rep.* 48°50N 17°10E **17** D9
Hoek van Holland *Neths.* 52°0N 4°7E **15** C4
Hoengseong *S. Korea* 37°29N 127°59E **33** F14
Hoeryong *N. Korea* 42°30N 129°45E **33** C15
Hoeyang *N. Korea* 38°43N 127°36E **33** E14
Hof *Germany* 50°19N 11°55E **16** C6
Hofmeyr *S. Africa* 31°39S 25°50E **56** E4
Höfn *Iceland* 64°15N 15°13W **8** D6
Hofors *Sweden* 60°31N 16°15E **9** F17
Hofsjökull *Iceland* 64°49N 18°48W **8** D4
Höfu *Japan* 34°3N 131°34E **29** G5
Hogan Group *Australia* 39°13S 147°1E **63** F4
Hogarth, Mt. *Australia* 21°48S 136°58E **62** C2
Hoge Kempen △ *Belgium* 51°6N 5°35E **15** C5
Hoge Veluwe △ *Neths.* 52°5N 5°46E **15** B5
Hogenakai Falls *India* 12°6N 77°50E **45** H3
Hoggar = Ahaggar *Algeria* 23°0N 6°30E **52** D7
Hogsty Reef *Bahamas* 21°41N 73°48W **89** B5
Hoh → *U.S.A.* 47°45N 124°29W **78** C2
Hoh Xil Shan *China* 36°30N 89°0E **30** D6
Hohenwald *U.S.A.* 35°33N 87°33W **85** D11
Hoher Rhön = Rhön
　Germany 50°24N 9°58E **16** C5
Hohes Venn *Belgium* 50°30N 6°5E **15** D6
Hoi An *Vietnam* 15°30N 108°19E **38** E7
Hoi Xuan *Vietnam* 20°25N 105°9E **38** B5
Hoisington *U.S.A.* 38°31N 98°47W **80** F4
Hōjō *Japan* 33°58N 132°46E **29** H6
Hokianga Harbour *N.Z.* 35°31S 173°22E **59** A4
Hokitika *N.Z.* 42°42S 171°0E **59** E3
Hokkaidō □ *Japan* 43°30N 143°0E **28** C11
Hokuto *Japan* 41°49N 140°39E **28** D10
Holalkere *India* 14°2N 76°11E **45** G3
Holbrook *Australia* 35°42S 147°18E **63** F4
Holbrook *U.S.A.* 34°54N 110°10W **77** J8
Holcomb *U.S.A.* 42°54N 77°25W **82** D7
Holden *U.S.A.* 39°6N 112°16W **76** G7
Holdenville *U.S.A.* 35°5N 96°24W **84** D6
Holdrege *U.S.A.* 40°26N 99°23W **80** E4
Hole-Narsipur *India* 12°48N 76°16E **45** H3
Holetown *Barbados* 13°11N 59°38W **89** g
Holguín *Cuba* 20°50N 76°20W **88** B4
Hollams Bird I. *Namibia* 24°40S 14°30E **56** B1
Holland = Netherlands ■
　Europe 52°0N 5°30E **15** C5
Holland *Mich., U.S.A.* 42°47N 86°7W **80** D10
Holland *N.Y., U.S.A.* 42°38N 78°32W **82** D6

Holland Centre *Canada* 44°23N 80°47W **82** B4
Holland Patent *U.S.A.* 43°14N 75°15W **83** C9
Hollandale *U.S.A.* 33°10N 90°51W **85** E9
Holley *U.S.A.* 43°14N 78°2W **82** C6
Hollidaysburg *U.S.A.* 40°26N 78°24W **82** F6
Hollis *U.S.A.* 34°41N 99°55W **84** D5
Hollister *Calif., U.S.A.* 36°51N 121°24W **78** J5
Hollister *Idaho, U.S.A.* 42°21N 114°35W **76** E6
Holly Hill *U.S.A.* 29°16N 81°3W **85** G14
Holly Springs *U.S.A.* 34°46N 89°27W **85** D10
Hollywood *Ireland* 53°6N 6°35W **10** B6
Holman *Canada* 70°44N 117°44W **68** C8
Hólmavík *Iceland* 65°42N 21°40W **8** D3
Holmen *U.S.A.* 43°58N 91°15W **80** D8
Holmes Reefs *Australia* 16°27S 148°0E **62** B4
Holmsund *Sweden* 63°41N 20°20E **8** E19
Holon *Israel* 32°2N 34°46E **48** C3
Holroyd → *Australia* 14°10S 141°36E **62** A3
Holstebro *Denmark* 56°22N 8°37E **9** H13
Holsworthy *U.K.* 50°48N 4°22W **13** G3
Holton *Canada* 54°31N 57°12W **73** B8
Holton *U.S.A.* 39°28N 95°44W **80** F6
Holtville *U.S.A.* 32°49N 115°23W **79** N11
Holwerd *Neths.* 53°22N 5°54E **15** A5
Holy Cross *U.S.A.* 62°12N 159°46W **74** C8
Holy I. *Anglesey, U.K.* 53°17N 4°37W **12** D3
Holy I. *Northumberland,*
　U.K. 55°40N 1°47W **12** B6
Holyhead *U.K.* 53°18N 4°38W **12** D3
Holyoke *Colo., U.S.A.* 40°35N 102°18W **76** F12
Holyoke *Mass., U.S.A.* 42°12N 72°37W **83** D12
Holyrood *Canada* 47°27N 53°8W **73** C9
Homalin *Burma* 24°55N 95°0E **41** G19
Homand *Iran* 32°28N 59°37E **47** C8
Homathko → *Canada* 51°0N 124°56W **70** C4
Hombori *Mali* 15°20N 1°38W **52** E5
Home B. *Canada* 68°40N 67°10W **69** D18
Home Hill *Australia* 19°43S 147°25E **62** B4
Home Reef *Tonga* 18°59S 174°47W **59** c
Homedale *U.S.A.* 43°37N 116°56W **76** E5
Homer *Alaska, U.S.A.* 59°39N 151°33W **68** F1
Homer *La., U.S.A.* 32°48N 93°4W **84** E8
Homer *N.Y., U.S.A.* 42°38N 76°10W **83** D8
Homer City *U.S.A.* 40°32N 79°10W **82** F5
Homestead *Australia* 20°20S 145°40E **62** C4
Homestead *U.S.A.* 25°28N 80°29W **85** J14
Homestead △ *U.S.A.* 40°17N 96°50W **80** E6
Homnabad *India* 17°45N 77°11E **44** F3
Homoine *Mozam.* 23°55S 35°8E **57** B6
Homs = Ḩimş *Syria* 34°40N 36°45E **48** A5
Homyel *Belarus* 52°28N 31°0E **17** B16
Hon Chong *Vietnam* 10°25N 104°30E **39** G5
Hon Hai *Vietnam* 10°0N 109°0E **39** H7
Hon Me *Vietnam* 19°23N 105°56E **38** C5
Honan = Henan □ *China* 34°0N 114°0E **32** H8
Honavar *India* 14°17N 74°27E **45** G2
Honbetsu *Japan* 43°7N 143°37E **28** C11
Honcut *U.S.A.* 39°20N 121°32W **78** F5
Honda, Bahía *Cuba* 22°58N 83°10W **88** B3
Hondeklipbaai *S. Africa* 30°19S 17°17E **56** D2
Hondo *Japan* 32°27N 130°12E **29** H5
Hondo *U.S.A.* 29°21N 99°9W **84** G5
Hondo, Río → *Belize* 18°25N 88°21W **87** D7
Honduras ■ *Cent. Amer.* 14°40N 86°30W **88** D2
Honduras, G. de *Caribbean* 16°50N 87°0W **88** C2
Hønefoss *Norway* 60°10N 10°18E **9** F14
Honesdale *U.S.A.* 41°34N 75°16W **83** E9
Honey Harbour *Canada* 44°52N 79°49W **82** B5
Honey L. *U.S.A.* 40°15N 120°19W **78** E6
Honfleur *France* 49°25N 0°13E **20** B4
Hong → *Vietnam* 20°16N 106°34E **38** B5
Hong Gai *Vietnam* 20°57N 107°5E **34** G6
Hong He → *China* 32°25N 115°35E **32** H8
Hong Hu *China* 29°54N 113°24E **35** C9
Hong Kong □ *China* 22°11N 114°14E **31** a
Hong Kong Int. ✈ (HKG)
　China 22°19N 113°57E **31** a
Hong'an *China* 31°20N 114°40E **35** B10
Hongcheon *S. Korea* 37°44N 127°53E **33** F14
Honghai Wan *China* 22°40N 115°0E **35** F10
Honghe *China* 23°25N 102°25E **34** F4
Honghu *China* 29°50N 113°30E **35** C9
Hongjiang *China* 27°7N 109°59E **34** D7
Honglïu He → *China* 38°0N 109°50E **32** F5
Hongor *Mongolia* 45°45N 112°50E **32** B7
Hongseong *S. Korea* 36°37N 126°38E **33** F14
Hongshan *China* 30°18N 117°58E **35** B11
Hongshui He → *China* 23°48N 109°30E **34** F7
Hongtong *China* 36°16N 111°40E **32** F6
Honguedo, Détroit d'
　Canada 49°15N 64°0W **73** C7
Hongwon *N. Korea* 40°0N 127°56E **33** E14
Hongya *China* 29°57N 103°22E **34** C4
Hongyuan *China* 32°51N 102°40E **34** A4
Hongze Hu *China* 33°15N 118°35E **33** H10
Honiara *Solomon Is.* 9°27S 159°57E **58** B8
Honiton *U.K.* 50°47N 3°11W **13** G4
Honjō = Yurihonjō
　Japan 39°23N 140°3E **28** E10
Honnali *India* 14°15N 75°40E **45** G2
Honningsvåg *Norway* 70°59N 25°59E **8** A21
Honolulu *U.S.A.* 21°19N 157°52W **75** L8
Honshū *Japan* 36°0N 138°0E **28** F9
Hood, Mt. *U.S.A.* 45°23N 121°42W **76** D3
Hood, Pt. *Australia* 34°23S 119°34E **61** F2
Hood River *U.S.A.* 45°43N 121°31W **76** D3
Hoodsport *U.S.A.* 47°24N 123°9W **78** C3
Hoogeveen *Neths.* 52°44N 6°28E **15** B6
Hoogezand-Sappemeer
　Neths. 53°9N 6°45E **15** A6
Hooghly = Hugli → *India* 21°56N 88°4E **43** J13
Hooghly-Chinsura = Chunchura
　India 22°53N 88°27E **43** H13
Hook Hd. *Ireland* 52°7N 6°56W **10** D5
Hook I. *Australia* 20°4S 148°57E **62** b
Hook of Holland = Hoek van
　Holland *Neths.* 52°0N 4°7E **15** C4
Hooker *U.S.A.* 36°52N 101°13W **84** C4
Hooker Creek = Lajamanu
　Australia 18°23S 130°38E **60** C5

Hooker Creek ○ *Australia* 18°6S 130°23E **60** C5
Hoonah *U.S.A.* 58°7N 135°27W **70** B1
Hooper Bay *U.S.A.* 61°32N 166°6W **74** C6
Hoopeston *U.S.A.* 40°28N 87°40W **80** E10
Hoopstad *S. Africa* 27°50S 25°55E **56** C4
Hoorn *Neths.* 52°38N 5°4E **15** B5
Hoover *U.S.A.* 33°24N 86°49W **85** E11
Hoover Dam *U.S.A.* 36°1N 114°44W **79** K12
Hooversville *U.S.A.* 40°9N 78°55W **82** F6
Hop Bottom *U.S.A.* 41°42N 75°46W **83** E9
Hope *Canada* 49°25N 121°25W **70** D4
Hope *Ariz., U.S.A.* 33°43N 113°42W **79** M13
Hope *Ark., U.S.A.* 33°40N 93°36W **84** E8
Hope, L. *S. Austral.,*
　Australia 28°24S 139°18E **63** D2
Hope, L. *W. Austral.,*
　Australia 32°35S 120°15E **61** F3
Hope, Pt. *U.S.A.* 68°21N 166°47W **66** C3
Hope I. *Canada* 44°55N 80°11W **82** B4
Hope Town *Bahamas* 26°35N 76°57W **88** A4
Hope Vale *Australia* 15°16S 145°20E **62** B4
Hope Vale ○ *Australia* 15°8S 145°15E **62** B4
Hopedale *Canada* 55°28N 60°13W **73** A7
Hopedale *U.S.A.* 42°8N 71°33W **83** D13
Hopefield *S. Africa* 33°3S 18°22E **56** D2
Hopei = Hebei □ *China* 39°0N 116°0E **32** E9
Hopelchén *Mexico* 19°46N 89°51W **87** D7
Hopetoun *Vic., Australia* 35°42S 142°22E **63** F3
Hopetoun *W. Austral.,*
　Australia 33°57S 120°7E **61** F3
Hopetown *S. Africa* 29°34S 24°3E **56** C3
Hopewell *U.S.A.* 37°18N 77°17W **81** G15
Hopkins, L. *Australia* 24°15S 128°35E **60** D4
Hopkinsville *U.S.A.* 36°52N 87°29W **80** G10
Hopland *U.S.A.* 38°58N 123°7W **78** G3
Hoquiam *U.S.A.* 46°59N 123°53W **78** D3
Horana *Sri Lanka* 6°43N 80°4E **45** L5
Hordern Hills *Australia* 20°15S 130°0E **60** D5
Horinger *China* 40°28N 111°48E **32** D6
Horizontina *Brazil* 27°37S 54°19W **95** B5
Horlick Mts. *Antarctica* 84°0S 102°0W **5** E15
Horlivka *Ukraine* 48°19N 38°5E **19** E6
Hormak *Iran* 29°58N 60°51E **47** D9
Hormoz *Iran* 27°35N 55°0E **47** E7
Hormoz, Jaz.-ye *Iran* 27°8N 56°28E **47** E8
Hormozgān □ *Iran* 27°30N 56°0E **47** E8
Hormuz, Kūh-e *Iran* 27°27N 55°10E **47** E7
Hormuz, Str. of *The Gulf* 26°30N 56°30E **47** E8
Horn *Austria* 48°39N 15°40E **16** D8
Horn → *Canada* 61°30N 118°1W **70** A5
Horn, Cape = Hornos, C. de
　Chile 55°50S 67°30W **96** H3
Horn Head *Ireland* 55°14N 8°0W **10** A3
Horn I. *Australia* 10°37S 142°17E **62** A3
Horn Plateau *Canada* 62°15N 119°15W **70** A5
Hornavan *Sweden* 66°15N 17°30E **8** C17
Hornbeck *U.S.A.* 31°20N 93°24W **84** F8
Hornbrook *U.S.A.* 41°55N 122°33W **76** F2
Horncastle *U.K.* 53°13N 0°7W **12** D7
Hornell *U.S.A.* 42°20N 77°40W **82** D7
Hornell L. *Canada* 62°20N 119°25W **70** A5
Hornepayne *Canada* 49°14N 84°48W **72** C3
Hornings Mills *Canada* 44°9N 80°12W **82** B4
Hornitos *U.S.A.* 37°30N 120°14W **78** H6
Hornos, C. de *Chile* 55°50S 67°30W **96** H3
Hornsby *Australia* 33°42S 151°2E **63** B5
Hornsea *U.K.* 53°55N 0°11W **12** D7
Horobetsu = Noboribetsu
　Japan 42°24N 141°6E **28** C10
Horodenka *Ukraine* 48°41N 25°29E **17** D13
Horodok *Khmelnytskyy,*
　Ukraine 49°10N 26°34E **17** D14
Horodok *Lviv, Ukraine* 49°46N 23°32E **17** D12
Horokhiv *Ukraine* 50°30N 24°45E **17** C13
Horqin Youyi Qianqi
　China 46°5N 122°3E **33** A12
Horqin Zuoyi Zhongqi
　China 44°8N 123°18E **33** B12
Horqueta *Paraguay* 23°15S 56°55W **94** A4
Horse C. → *U.S.A.* 41°57N 103°58W **76** F12
Horse I. *Canada* 53°20N 99°6W **71** C9
Horse Is. *Canada* 50°15N 55°50W **73** B8
Horsefly L. *Canada* 52°25N 121°0W **70** C4
Horseheads *U.S.A.* 42°10N 76°49W **82** D8
Horsens *Denmark* 55°52N 9°51E **9** J13
Horseshoe Lake *Canada* 45°17N 79°51W **82** A5
Horsham *Australia* 36°44S 142°13E **63** F3
Horsham *U.K.* 51°4N 0°20W **13** F7
Horta *Azores* 38°32N 28°38W **52** a
Horten *Norway* 59°25N 10°32E **9** G14
Horti *India* 17°7N 75°47E **44** F2
Horton *U.S.A.* 39°40N 95°32W **80** F6
Horton → *Canada* 69°56N 126°52W **68** C6
Horwood L. *Canada* 48°5N 82°20W **72** C3
Hosapete = Hospet *India* 15°15N 76°20E **45** G3
Hosdrug = Kanhangad
　India 12°21N 74°58E **45** H2
Hosdurga *India* 13°49N 76°17E **45** H3
Ḩoseynābād *Khuzestān,*
　Iran 32°45N 48°20E **47** C6
Ḩoseynābād *Kordestān,*
　Iran 35°33N 47°8E **46** C5
Hoshangabad *India* 22°45N 77°45E **42** H7
Hoshiarpur *India* 31°30N 75°58E **42** D6
Hoskote *India* 13°4N 77°48E **45** H3
Hosmer *U.S.A.* 45°34N 99°28W **80** C4
Hospet *India* 15°15N 76°20E **45** G3
Hoste, I. *Chile* 55°0S 69°0W **96** H3
Hosur *India* 12°43N 77°49E **45** H3
Hot *Thailand* 18°8N 98°29E **38** C2
Hot Creek Range
　U.S.A. 38°40N 116°0W **76** G5
Hot Springs *Ark., U.S.A.* 34°31N 93°3W **84** D8
Hot Springs *S. Dak.,*
　U.S.A. 43°26N 103°29W **80** D2
Hot Springs △ *U.S.A.* 34°31N 93°3W **84** D8
Hotagen *Sweden* 63°59N 14°12E **8** E16
Hotan *China* 37°25N 79°55E **30** D4
Hotan He → *China* 40°22N 80°56E **30** C5
Hotazel *S. Africa* 27°17S 22°58E **56** C3

Hotchkiss U.S.A. 38°48N 107°43W 76 G10
Hotham, C. Australia 12°2S 131°18E 60 B5
Hoting Sweden 64°8N 16°15E 8 D17
Hotte, Massif de la Haiti 18°30N 73°45W 89 C5
Hottentotsbaai Namibia 26°8S 14°59E 56 C1
Hou Hai China 22°32N 113°56E 31 a
Houei Sai Laos 20°18N 100°26E 34 G3
Houffalize Belgium 50°8N 5°48E 15 D5
Houghton Mich., U.S.A. 47°7N 88°34W 80 B9
Houghton N.Y., U.S.A. 42°25N 78°10W 82 D6
Houghton L. U.S.A. 44°21N 84°44W 81 C11
Houghton-le-Spring U.K. 54°51N 1°28W 12 C6
Houhora Heads N.Z. 34°49S 173°9E 59 A4
Houlton U.S.A. 46°8N 67°51W 81 B20
Houma China 35°36N 111°20E 32 G6
Houma U.S.A. 29°36N 90°43W 85 G9
Housatonic → U.S.A. 41°10N 73°7W 83 E11
Houston Canada 54°25N 126°39W 70 C3
Houston Mo., U.S.A. 37°22N 91°58W 80 G8
Houston Tex., U.S.A. 29°45N 95°21W 84 G7
Hout = Mogwadi →
  S. Africa 23°4S 29°36E 57 B4
Houtkraal S. Africa 30°23S 24°5E 56 D3
Houtman Abrolhos
  Australia 28°43S 113°48E 61 E1
Hovd = Dund-Us Mongolia 48°1N 91°38E 30 B7
Hove U.K. 50°50N 0°10W 13 G7
Hovenweep △ U.S.A. 37°20N 109°0W 77 H9
Hoveyzeh Iran 31°27N 48°4E 47 D6
Hövsgöl Mongolia 43°37N 109°39E 32 C5
Hövsgöl Nuur Mongolia 51°0N 100°30E 30 A9
Howar, Wadi → Sudan 17°30N 27°8E 53 E11
Howard Australia 25°16S 152°32E 63 D5
Howard Pa., U.S.A. 41°1N 77°40W 82 F7
Howard S. Dak., U.S.A. 44°1N 97°32W 80 C5
Howe U.S.A. 43°48N 113°0W 76 E7
Howe, C. Australia 37°30S 150°0E 63 F5
Howe, West Cape
  Australia 35°8S 117°36E 61 G2
Howe I. Canada 44°16N 76°17W 83 B8
Howell U.S.A. 42°36N 83°56W 81 D12
Howick Canada 45°11N 73°51W 83 A11
Howick S. Africa 29°28S 30°14E 57 C5
Howick Group Australia 14°20S 145°30E 62 A4
Howitt, L. Australia 27°40S 138°40E 63 D2
Howland I. Pac. Oc. 0°48N 176°38W 64 G10
Höxter Germany 51°46N 9°22E 16 C5
Hoy U.K. 58°50N 3°15W 11 C5
Høyanger Norway 61°13N 6°4E 8 F12
Hoyerswerda Germany 51°26N 14°14E 16 C8
Hoylake U.K. 53°24N 3°10W 12 D4
Hpa-an = Pa-an Burma 16°51N 97°40E 41 L20
Hpunan Pass Asia 27°30N 96°55E 41 F20
Hpyu = Pyu Burma 18°30N 96°28E 41 K20
Hradec Králové
  Czech Rep. 50°15N 15°50E 16 C8
Hrodna Belarus 53°42N 23°52E 17 B12
Hrodzyanka Belarus 53°31N 28°42E 17 B15
Hron → Slovak Rep. 47°49N 18°45E 17 E10
Hrvatska = Croatia ■
  Europe 45°20N 16°0E 16 F9
Hrymayliv Ukraine 49°20N 26°5E 17 D14
Hsenwi Burma 23°22N 97°55E 41 H20
Hsiamen = Xiamen
  China 24°25N 118°4E 35 E12
Hsian = Xi'an China 34°15N 109°0E 32 G5
Hsinchu Taiwan 24°48N 120°58E 35 E13
Hsinhailien = Lianyungang
  China 34°40N 119°11E 33 G10
Hsinkai = Bhamo
  Burma 24°15N 97°15E 41 G20
Hsinying Taiwan 23°21N 120°17E 35 F13
Hsopket Burma 23°11N 98°26E 34 F2
Hsüchou = Xuzhou
  China 34°18N 117°10E 33 G9
Htawei = Tavoy Burma 14°2N 98°12E 38 E2
Hu Xian China 34°8N 108°42E 32 G5
Hua Hin Thailand 12°34N 99°58E 38 F2
Hua Muang Laos 20°13N 103°52E 38 B4
Hua Shan China 34°28N 110°4E 32 G6
Hua Xian Henan, China 35°30N 114°30E 32 G6
Hua Xian Shaanxi, China 34°30N 109°48E 32 G5
Hua'an China 25°1N 117°32E 35 E11
Huab → Namibia 20°52S 13°25E 56 A2
Huacheng China 24°4N 115°37E 35 E10
Huachinera Mexico 30°9N 108°55W 86 A3
Huacho Peru 11°10S 77°35W 92 F3
Huade China 41°55N 113°59E 32 D7
Huadian China 43°0N 126°40E 33 C14
Huadu China 23°22N 113°12E 35 F9
Huahine, Î.
  French Polynesia 16°46S 150°58W 65 J12
Huai Hat △ Thailand 16°52N 104°17E 38 D5
Huai He → China 33°0N 118°30E 35 A12
Huai Kha Khaeng △
  Thailand 15°20N 98°55E 38 E2
Huai Nam Dang △
  Thailand 19°30N 98°30E 38 C2
Huai Yot Thailand 7°45N 99°37E 39 J2
Huai'an Hebei, China 40°30N 114°20E 32 D8
Huai'an Jiangsu, China 33°30N 119°10E 33 H10
Huaibei China 34°0N 116°48E 32 G9
Huaibin China 32°32N 115°27E 35 A10
Huaide = Gongzhuling
  China 43°30N 124°40E 33 C13
Huaidezhen China 43°48N 124°50E 33 C13
Huaihua China 27°32N 109°57E 34 D7
Huaiji China 23°55N 112°12E 35 F9
Huainan China 32°38N 116°58E 35 A11
Huaining China 30°24N 116°40E 35 B11
Huairen China 39°48N 113°20E 32 E7
Huairou China 40°20N 116°35E 32 D9
Huaiyang China 33°40N 114°52E 32 H8
Huaiyin China 33°30N 119°2E 33 H10
Huaiyuan Anhui, China 32°55N 117°10E 33 H9
Huaiyuan Guangxi Zhuangzu,
  China 24°31N 108°22E 34 E7
Huajuapán de León
  Mexico 17°48N 97°46W 87 D5

Hualapai Peak U.S.A. 35°5N 113°54W 79 K13
Hualien Taiwan 23°59N 121°36E 35 E13
Huallaga → Peru 5°15S 75°30W 92 E3
Huambo Angola 12°42S 15°54E 55 G3
Huan Jiang → China 34°28N 109°0E 32 G5
Huan Xian China 36°33N 107°7E 32 F4
Huancabamba Peru 5°10S 79°15W 92 E3
Huancane Peru 15°10S 69°44W 92 G5
Huancavelica Peru 12°50S 75°5W 92 F3
Huancayo Peru 12°5S 75°12W 92 F3
Huanchaca Bolivia 20°15S 66°40W 92 H5
Huang Hai = Yellow Sea
  China 35°0N 123°0E 33 G12
Huang He → China 37°55N 118°50E 33 F11
Huang Xian China 37°38N 120°30E 33 F11
Huangdao China 36°0N 120°7E 33 G11
Huanggang China 30°29N 114°52E 35 B10
Huangguoshu China 26°0N 105°40E 34 E5
Huanghua China 38°22N 117°20E 33 E9
Huanghuagang China 38°20N 117°54E 33 E9
Huangling China 35°34N 109°15E 32 G5
Huanglong China 35°30N 109°59E 32 G5
Huanglong △ China 32°44N 103°50E 34 A4
Huanglongtan China 32°40N 110°33E 35 A8
Huangmei China 30°5N 115°56E 35 B10
Huangping China 26°50N 114°22E 35 B10
Huangping China 26°52N 107°54E 34 D6
Huangshan Anhui, China 30°8N 118°9E 35 B12
Huangshan Anhui,
  China 29°42N 118°25E 35 C12
Huangshi China 30°10N 115°3E 35 B10
Huangsongdian China 43°45N 127°25E 33 C14
Huangyan China 28°38N 121°19E 35 C13
Huangyangsi China 26°33N 111°39E 35 D8
Huaning China 24°17N 102°56E 34 E4
Huanjiang China 24°50N 108°18E 34 E7
Huanren China 41°23N 125°20E 33 D13
Huantai China 36°58N 117°56E 33 F9
Huanuco Peru 9°55S 76°15W 92 E3
Huaping China 26°46N 101°25E 34 D3
Huaraz Peru 9°30S 77°32W 92 E3
Huarmey Peru 10°5S 78°5W 92 F3
Huarong China 29°29N 112°30E 35 C9
Huascarán, Nevado Peru 9°7S 77°37W 92 E3
Huasco Chile 28°30S 71°15W 94 B1
Huasco → Chile 28°27S 71°13W 94 B1
Huasna U.S.A. 35°6N 120°24W 79 K6
Huatabampo Mexico 26°50N 109°38W 86 B3
Huauchinango Mexico 20°12N 98°3W 87 C5
Huautla de Jiménez
  Mexico 18°8N 96°51W 87 D5
Huaxi China 26°25N 106°40E 34 D6
Huayin China 34°35N 110°5E 32 G6
Huayuan China 28°37N 109°29E 34 C7
Huazhou China 21°33N 110°33E 35 G8
Hubballi = Hubli India 15°22N 75°15E 45 G2
Hubbard Ohio, U.S.A. 41°9N 80°34W 82 E4
Hubbard Tex., U.S.A. 31°51N 96°48W 84 F6
Hubbard Glacier Canada 60°18N 139°22W 68 E4
Hubbart Pt. Canada 59°21N 94°41W 71 B10
Hubei □ China 31°0N 112°0E 35 B9
Hubli India 15°22N 75°15E 45 G2
Huch'ang N. Korea 41°25N 127°2E 33 D14
Hucknall U.K. 53°3N 1°13W 12 D6
Huddersfield U.K. 53°39N 1°47W 12 D6
Hudiksvall Sweden 61°43N 17°10E 8 F17
Hudson Canada 50°6N 92°9W 72 B1
Hudson Mass., U.S.A. 42°23N 71°34W 83 D13
Hudson N.Y., U.S.A. 42°15N 73°46W 83 D11
Hudson Wis., U.S.A. 44°58N 92°45W 80 C7
Hudson Wyo., U.S.A. 42°54N 108°35W 76 E9
Hudson → U.S.A. 40°42N 74°2W 83 F10
Hudson, C. Antarctica 68°21S 153°45E 5 C10
Hudson Bay Nunavut,
  Canada 60°0N 86°0W 69 F14
Hudson Bay Sask.,
  Canada 52°51N 102°23W 71 C8
Hudson Falls U.S.A. 43°18N 73°35W 83 C11
Hudson Mts. Antarctica 74°32S 99°20W 5 D16
Hudson Str. Canada 62°0N 70°0W 69 E18
Hudson's Hope Canada 56°0N 121°54W 70 B4
Hue Vietnam 16°30N 107°35E 38 D6
Huehuetenango
  Guatemala 15°20N 91°28W 88 C1
Huejúcar Mexico 22°21N 103°13W 86 C4
Huelva Spain 37°18N 6°57W 21 D2
Huentelauquén Chile 31°38S 71°33W 94 C1
Huerta, Sa. de la
  Argentina 31°10S 67°30W 94 C2
Huesca Spain 42°8N 0°25W 21 A5
Huetamo Mexico 18°35N 100°53W 86 D4
Hugh → Australia 25°1S 134°1E 62 D1
Hughenden Australia 20°52S 144°10E 62 C3
Hughesville U.S.A. 41°14N 76°44W 83 E8
Hugli → India 21°56N 88°4E 43 J13
Hugo Colo., U.S.A. 39°8N 103°28W 76 G12
Hugo Okla., U.S.A. 34°1N 95°31W 84 D7
Hugoton U.S.A. 37°11N 101°21W 80 G3
Hui Xian = Huixian
  China 35°27N 113°12E 32 G7
Hui Xian China 33°50N 106°4E 32 H4
Hui'an China 25°1N 118°43E 35 E12
Hui'anbu China 37°28N 106°38E 32 F4
Huichang China 25°32N 115°45E 35 E10
Huichapan Mexico 20°23N 99°39W 87 C5
Huichon N. Korea 40°10N 126°16E 33 D14
Huidong Guangdong,
  China 22°58N 114°43E 35 F10
Huidong Sichuan, China 26°34N 102°35E 34 D4
Huifa He → China 43°0N 127°50E 33 C14
Huila, Nevado del Colombia 3°0N 76°0W 92 C3
Huilai China 23°0N 116°18E 35 F11
Huili China 26°35N 102°17E 34 D4
Huimin China 37°27N 117°28E 33 F9
Huinan China 42°40N 126°2E 33 C14
Huinca Renancó
  Argentina 34°51S 64°22W 94 C3

Huining China 35°38N 105°0E 32 G3
Huinong China 39°5N 106°35E 32 E4
Huishui China 26°7N 106°38E 34 D6
Huiting China 34°5N 116°5E 32 G9
Huitong China 26°51N 109°45E 34 D7
Huixian China 35°27N 113°12E 32 G7
Huixtla Mexico 15°9N 92°28W 87 D6
Huize China 26°24N 103°15E 34 D5
Huizhou China 23°0N 114°23E 35 F10
Hukawng Valley Burma 26°30N 96°30E 41 F20
Hukeri India 16°14N 74°36E 45 F2
Hukou China 29°45N 116°21E 35 C11
Hukuntsi Botswana 23°58S 21°45E 56 B3
Ḥulayfā' Si. Arabia 25°58N 40°45E 46 E4
Hulin China 45°48N 132°59E 31 B15
Hulin He → China 45°0N 122°10E 33 B12
Hull = Kingston upon Hull
  U.K. 53°45N 0°21W 12 D7
Hull Canada 45°26N 75°43W 83 A9
Hull → U.K. 53°44N 0°20W 12 D7
Hulst Neths. 51°17N 4°2E 15 C4
Huludao China 40°45N 120°50E 33 D11
Hulun Nur China 49°0N 117°30E 31 B12
Hulunbuir = Hailar
  China 49°10N 119°38E 31 B12
Huma, Tanjung Malaysia 5°29N 100°16E 39 c
Humacao Puerto Rico 18°9N 65°50W 89 d
Humahuaca Argentina 23°10S 65°25W 94 A2
Humaitá Brazil 7°35S 63°1W 92 E6
Humaitá Paraguay 27°2S 58°31W 94 B4
Humansdorp S. Africa 34°2S 24°46E 56 D3
Humbe Angola 16°40S 14°55E 56 A1
Humber → U.K. 53°42N 0°27W 12 D7
Humboldt Canada 52°15N 105°9W 71 C7
Humboldt Iowa, U.S.A. 42°44N 94°13W 80 D6
Humboldt Tenn., U.S.A. 35°50N 88°55W 85 D10
Humboldt → U.S.A. 39°59N 118°36W 76 F4
Humboldt Gletscher = Sermersuaq
  Greenland 79°30N 62°0W 69 B4
Hume U.S.A. 36°48N 118°54W 78 J8
Hume, L. Australia 36°0S 147°5E 63 F4
Humen China 22°50N 113°40E 31 a
Humenné Slovak Rep. 48°55N 21°50E 17 D11
Hyndman U.S.A. 39°49N 78°43W 82 F6
Humphreys, Mt. U.S.A. 37°17N 118°40W 78 H8
Humphreys Peak
  U.S.A. 35°21N 111°41W 77 J8
Humptulips U.S.A. 47°14N 123°57W 78 C3
Hūn Libya 29°2N 16°0E 53 C9
Hun Jiang → China 40°50N 125°38E 33 D13
Húnaflói Iceland 65°50N 20°50W 8 D3
Hunan □ China 27°30N 112°0E 35 D9
Hunchun China 42°52N 130°28E 33 C16
Hundewali Pakistan 31°55N 72°38E 42 D5
Hundred Mile House
  Canada 51°38N 121°18W 70 C4
Hunedoara Romania 45°40N 22°50E 17 F12
Hung Yen Vietnam 20°39N 106°4E 34 G9
Hunga Ha'apai Tonga 20°41S 175°7W 59 c
Hungary ■ Europe 47°20N 19°20E 17 E10
Hungary, Plain of Europe 47°0N 20°0E 6 F10
Hungerford Australia 28°58S 144°24E 63 D3
Hŭngnam N. Korea 39°49N 127°45E 33 E14
Hungt'ou Hsü = Lan Yü
  Taiwan 22°4N 121°25E 35 F13
Hunjiang China 41°54N 126°28E 33 D14
Hunsberge Namibia 27°45S 17°12E 56 C2
Hunsrück Germany 49°56N 7°27E 16 D4
Hunstanton U.K. 52°56N 0°29E 12 E8
Hunsur India 12°16N 76°16E 45 H3
Hunter → Australia 42°13N 74°13W 83 D10
Hunter I. Australia 40°30S 144°45E 63 G3
Hunter I. Canada 51°55N 128°0W 70 C3
Hunter Ra. Australia 32°45S 150°15E 63 E5
Hunterville N.Z. 39°56S 175°35E 59 C5
Huntingburg U.S.A. 38°18N 86°57W 80 F10
Huntingdon U.K. 52°20N 0°11W 13 E7
Huntingdon U.S.A. 40°30N 78°1W 82 F6
Huntington Ind., U.S.A. 40°53N 85°30W 81 E11
Huntington N.Y., U.S.A. 40°52N 73°26W 83 F11
Huntington Oreg.,
  U.S.A. 44°21N 117°16W 76 D5
Huntington Utah,
  U.S.A. 39°20N 110°58W 76 G8
Huntington W. Va.,
  U.S.A. 38°25N 82°27W 81 F12
Huntington Beach
  U.S.A. 33°40N 118°5W 79 M9
Huntly N.Z. 37°34S 175°11E 59 B5
Huntly U.K. 57°27N 2°47W 11 D6
Huntsville Canada 45°20N 79°14W 82 A5
Huntsville Ala., U.S.A. 34°44N 86°35W 85 H11
Huntsville Tex., U.S.A. 30°43N 95°33W 84 F7
Hunyuan China 39°42N 113°42E 32 E7
Hunza → India 35°54N 74°20E 43 B6
Huo Shan China 36°26N 111°52E 32 F6
Huo Xian = Huozhou
  China 36°36N 111°42E 32 F6
Huolin Gol China 45°32N 119°38E 33 B10
Huong Khe Vietnam 18°13N 105°41E 38 C5
Huonville Australia 43°0S 147°5E 63 G4
Huoqiu China 32°20N 116°12E 35 A11
Huoshan China 31°25N 116°20E 35 B11
Huozhou China 36°36N 111°42E 32 F6
Hupeh = Hubei □ China 31°0N 112°0E 35 B9
Ḥūr Iran 30°50N 57°7E 47 D8
Ḥuraymīla Si. Arabia 25°8N 46°8E 46 E5
Hurd, C. Canada 45°13N 81°44W 82 A3
Hure Qi China 42°45N 121°45E 33 C11
Hurghada Egypt 27°15N 33°50E 53 C12
Hurley N. Mex., U.S.A. 32°42N 108°8W 77 K9
Hurley Wis., U.S.A. 46°27N 90°11W 80 B8
Huron Calif., U.S.A. 36°12N 120°6W 78 J6
Huron Ohio, U.S.A. 41°24N 82°33W 82 E2
Huron S. Dak., U.S.A. 44°22N 98°13W 80 C4
Huron, L. U.S.A. 44°30N 82°40W 82 B2
Huron East Canada 43°37N 81°18W 82 C3

Hurricane U.S.A. 37°11N 113°17W 77 H7
Hurunui → N.Z. 42°54S 173°18E 59 E4
Húsavík Iceland 66°3N 17°21W 8 C5
Huşi Romania 46°41N 28°7E 17 E15
Hustadvika Norway 63°0N 7°0E 8 E12
Hustontown U.S.A. 40°3N 78°2W 82 F6
Hutchinson Kans., U.S.A. 38°5N 97°56W 80 F5
Hutchinson Minn.,
  U.S.A. 44°54N 94°22W 80 C6
Hutiao Xia China 27°43N 100°9E 34 D3
Hutte Sauvage, L. de la
  Canada 56°15N 64°45W 73 A7
Hutton, Mt. Australia 25°51S 148°20E 63 D4
Huwaki Indonesia 7°55S 126°30E 37 F7
Huy Belgium 50°31N 5°15E 15 D5
Huzhou China 30°51N 120°8E 35 B13
Huzurabad India 18°12N 79°25E 44 E4
Huzurnagar India 16°54N 79°53E 44 E4
Hvammstangi Iceland 65°24N 20°57W 8 D3
Hvar Croatia 43°11N 16°28E 22 C7
Hvítá → Iceland 64°30N 21°58W 8 D3
Hwacheon-Cheosuji
  S. Korea 38°5N 127°50E 33 E14
Hwang Ho = Huang He →
  China 37°55N 118°50E 33 F10
Hwange Zimbabwe 18°18S 26°30E 55 H5
Hwange △ Zimbabwe 19°0S 26°30E 56 A4
Hwlffordd = Haverfordwest
  U.K. 51°48N 4°58W 13 F3
Hyannis Mass., U.S.A. 41°39N 70°17W 81 E18
Hyannis Nebr., U.S.A. 42°0N 101°46W 80 E3
Hyargas Nuur Mongolia 49°0N 93°0E 30 B7
Hydaburg U.S.A. 55°15N 132°50W 70 B2
Hyde Park U.S.A. 41°47N 73°56W 83 E11
Hyden Australia 32°24S 118°53E 61 F2
Hyder U.S.A. 55°55N 130°5W 70 B2
Hyderabad India 17°22N 78°29E 44 F4
Hyderabad Pakistan 25°23N 68°24E 42 G3
Hydra Greece 37°20N 23°28E 23 F10
Hyères France 43°8N 6°9E 20 E7
Hyères, Îs. d' France 43°0N 6°20E 20 E7
Hyesan N. Korea 41°20N 128°10E 33 D15
Hyland → Canada 59°52N 128°12W 70 B3
Hyndman U.S.A. 43°45N 114°8W 76 E6
Hyōgo □ Japan 35°15N 134°50E 29 G7
Hyrum U.S.A. 41°38N 111°51W 76 F8
Hysham U.S.A. 46°18N 107°14W 76 C10
Hythe U.K. 51°4N 1°5E 13 F9
Hyūga Japan 32°25N 131°35E 29 H5
Hyvinge = Hyvinkää
  Finland 60°38N 24°50E 8 F21
Hyvinkää Finland 60°38N 24°50E 8 F21

I

I-n-Gall Niger 16°51N 7°1E 52 E7
Iaco → Brazil 9°3S 68°34W 92 E5
Ialomiţa → Romania 44°42N 27°51E 17 F14
Iaşi Romania 47°10N 27°40E 17 E14
Ib → India 21°34N 83°48E 43 J10
Iba Phil. 15°22N 120°0E 37 A6
Ibadan Nigeria 7°22N 3°58E 52 G6
Ibagué Colombia 4°20N 75°20W 92 C3
Ibar → Serbia 43°43N 20°45E 23 C9
Ibaraki □ Japan 36°10N 140°10E 29 F10
Ibarra Ecuador 0°21N 78°7W 92 C3
Ibb Yemen 14°2N 44°10E 49 E3
Ibenga → Congo 2°19N 18°9E 54 D3
Iberian Peninsula Europe 40°0N 5°0W 6 H5
Iberville Canada 45°19N 73°17W 83 A11
Iberville, Mt. d' Canada 58°50N 63°50W 69 F19
Ibiá Brazil 19°30S 46°30W 93 G9
Ibiapaba, Sa. da Brazil 4°0S 41°30W 93 D10
Ibicuí → Brazil 29°25S 56°47W 95 B4
Ibicuy Argentina 33°55S 59°10W 94 C4
Ibiza = Eivissa Spain 38°54N 1°26E 21 C6
Ibonma Indonesia 3°29S 133°31E 37 E8
Ibotirama Brazil 12°13S 43°12W 93 F10
Ibrāhīm → Lebanon 34°4N 35°38E 48 A4
'Ibrī Oman 23°14N 56°30E 47 F8
Ibu Indonesia 1°35N 127°33E 37 D7
Ibusuki Japan 31°12N 130°40E 29 J5
Ica Peru 14°0S 75°48W 92 F3
Içá → Brazil 2°55S 67°58W 92 D5
Icacos Pt. Trin. & Tob. 10°3N 61°57W 93 K15
Içana Brazil 0°21N 67°19W 92 C5
Içana → Brazil 0°26N 67°19W 92 C5
İçel Turkey 36°51N 34°36E 46 B2
Iceland ■ Europe 64°45N 19°0W 8 D4
Iceland Basin Atl. Oc. 61°0N 19°0W 4 C7
Icelandic Plateau Arctic 64°0N 10°0W 4 C7
Ichalkaranji India 16°40N 74°33E 44 F2
Ichchapuram India 19°10N 84°40E 44 E7
Ichhawar India 23°1N 77°1E 42 H7
Ichihara Japan 35°28N 140°5E 29 G10
Ichilo → Bolivia 15°57S 64°50W 92 G6
Ichinohe Japan 40°13N 141°17E 28 D10
Ichinomiya Japan 35°18N 136°48E 29 G8
Ichinoseki Japan 38°55N 141°8E 28 E10
Içoguz Turkmenistan 40°11N 58°24E 26 E6
Icy C. U.S.A. 70°20N 161°52W 66 B3
Ida Grove U.S.A. 42°21N 95°28W 80 D6
Idabel U.S.A. 33°54N 94°50W 84 E7
Idaho □ U.S.A. 45°0N 115°0W 76 D6
Idaho City U.S.A. 43°50N 115°50W 76 E6
Idaho Falls U.S.A. 43°30N 112°2W 76 E7
Idalia △ Australia 24°49S 144°36E 62 C3
Idar-Oberstein Germany 49°43N 7°16E 16 D4
Idensalmi = Iisalmi
  Finland 63°32N 27°10E 8 E22
Idfû Egypt 24°55N 32°49E 53 D12
Idhra = Hydra Greece 37°20N 23°28E 23 F10
Idi Indonesia 5°2N 97°37E 36 C1
Idi, Oros = Psiloritis, Oros
  Greece 35°15N 24°45E 23 G11
Idiofa Dem. Rep. of the Congo 4°55S 19°42E 54 E3

Idlib Syria 35°55N 36°36E 46 C3
Idria U.S.A. 36°25N 120°41W 78 J6
Idutywa = Dutywa
  S. Africa 32°8S 28°18E 57 D4
Ieper Belgium 50°51N 2°53E 15 D2
Ierapetra Greece 35°1N 25°44E 23 G11
Iesi Italy 43°31N 13°14E 22 C5
Ifakara Tanzania 8°8S 36°41E 54 F7
'Ifāl, W. al → Si. Arabia 28°7N 35°3E 46 D2
Ife Nigeria 7°30N 4°31E 52 G6
Iffley Australia 18°53S 141°12E 62 B3
Iforas, Adrar des Africa 19°40N 1°40E 52 E6
Ifould, L. Australia 30°52S 132°6E 61 F5
Igarapava Brazil 20°3S 47°47W 93 H9
Igarka Russia 67°30N 86°33E 26 C9
Igatpuri India 19°40N 73°35E 44 E1
Iglésias Italy 39°19N 8°32E 22 E3
Igloolik = Iglulik
  Canada 69°20N 81°49W 69 D15
Igluligaarjuk = Chesterfield Inlet
  Canada 63°30N 90°45W 68 E13
Iglulik Canada 69°20N 81°49W 69 D15
Ignace Canada 49°30N 91°40W 72 C1
İğneada Burnu Turkey 41°53N 28°2E 23 D13
Igoumenitsa Greece 39°32N 20°18E 23 E9
Igrim Russia 63°12N 64°30E 26 C7
Iguaçu → Brazil 25°36S 54°36W 95 B5
Iguaçu, Cat. del Brazil 25°41S 54°26W 95 B5
Iguaçu △ Brazil 25°30S 54°0W 95 B5
Iguaçu Falls = Iguaçu, Cat. del
  Brazil 25°41S 54°26W 95 B5
Iguala Mexico 18°21N 99°32W 87 D5
Igualada Spain 41°37N 1°37E 21 B6
Iguassu = Iguaçu →
  Brazil 25°36S 54°36W 95 B5
Iguatu Brazil 6°20S 39°18W 93 E11
Iguazú △ Argentina 25°42S 54°22W 95 B5
Iguidi, Erg Africa 27°0N 7°0W 52 C4
Iharana Madag. 13°25S 50°0E 55 G10
Ihbulag Mongolia 43°11N 107°10E 32 C4
Iheya-Shima Japan 27°4N 127°58E 29 L3
Ihosy Madag. 22°24S 46°8E 55 J9
Ii Finland 65°19N 25°22E 8 D21
Ii-Shima Japan 26°43N 127°47E 29 L3
Iida Japan 35°35N 137°50E 29 G8
Iijoki → Finland 65°20N 25°20E 8 D21
Iisalmi Finland 63°32N 27°10E 8 E22
Iiyama Japan 36°51N 138°22E 29 F9
Iizuka Japan 33°38N 130°42E 29 H5
Ijâfene Mauritania 20°40N 8°0W 52 D4
Ijebu-Ode Nigeria 6°47N 3°58E 52 G6
IJmuiden Neths. 52°28N 4°35E 15 B4
Ijo älv = Iijoki → Finland 65°20N 25°20E 8 D21
IJssel → Neths. 52°35N 5°50E 15 B5
IJsselmeer Neths. 52°45N 5°20E 15 B5
Ijuí Brazil 28°23S 53°55W 95 B5
Ijui → Brazil 27°58S 55°20W 95 B4
Ikare Nigeria 7°32N 5°40E 52 G7
Ikaria Greece 37°35N 26°10E 23 F12
Ikeda Japan 34°1N 133°48E 29 G6
Ikela Dem. Rep. of the Congo 1°6S 23°6E 54 E4
Iki Japan 33°45N 129°42E 29 H4
Ikopa → Madag. 16°45S 46°40E 55 H9
Ikparjuk = Arctic Bay
  Canada 73°1N 85°7W 69 C14
Iksan S. Korea 35°59N 127°0E 33 G14
Ikuntji = Haasts Bluff
  Australia 23°22S 132°0E 60 D5
Ilagan Phil. 17°7N 121°53E 37 A6
Īlām Iran 33°36N 46°36E 46 C5
Ilam Nepal 26°58N 87°58E 43 F12
Īlām □ Iran 33°0N 47°0E 46 C5
Ilan Taiwan 24°45N 121°44E 35 E13
Ilanskiy Russia 56°14N 96°3E 27 D10
Ilawa Poland 53°36N 19°34E 17 B10
Ilayangudi India 9°34N 78°37E 45 K4
Ile → Kazakhstan 45°53N 77°10E 28 B4
Île-à-la-Crosse Canada 55°27N 107°53W 71 B7
Île-à-la-Crosse, Lac
  Canada 55°40N 107°45W 71 B7
Île-de-France □ France 49°0N 2°20E 20 B5
Ilebo Dem. Rep. of the Congo 4°17S 20°55E 54 E4
Ilek Russia 51°32N 53°21E 26 D6
Ilek → Russia 51°30N 53°22E 26 D6
Ilesha Nigeria 7°37N 4°40E 52 G6
Ilford Canada 56°4N 95°35W 71 B9
Ilfracombe Australia 23°30S 144°30E 62 C3
Ilfracombe U.K. 51°12N 4°8W 13 F3
Ilha Grande, Represa
  Brazil 23°10S 53°5W 95 A5
Ilha Grande △ Brazil 23°10S 53°20W 95 A5
Ilhéus Brazil 14°49S 39°2W 93 F11
Ili = Ile → Kazakhstan 45°53N 77°10E 28 B4
Iliamna L. U.S.A. 59°30N 155°0W 74 D8
Iligan Phil. 8°12N 124°13E 37 C6
Ilion U.S.A. 43°1N 75°2W 83 D9
Ilkal India 15°57N 76°8E 45 G3
Ilkeston U.K. 52°58N 1°19W 12 E6
Ilkley U.K. 53°56N 1°48W 12 D6
Illampu = Ancohuma, Nevado
  Bolivia 16°0S 68°50W 92 G5
Illana B. Phil. 7°35N 123°45E 37 C6
Illapel Chile 32°0S 71°10W 94 C1
Iller → Germany 48°23N 9°58E 16 D6
Illimani, Nevada Bolivia 16°30S 67°50W 92 G5
Illinois □ U.S.A. 40°15N 89°30W 80 E9
Illinois → U.S.A. 38°58N 90°28W 80 F8
Illizi Algeria 26°31N 8°32E 52 C7
Ilma, L. Australia 29°13S 127°46E 61 E4
Ilmajoki Finland 62°44N 22°34E 8 E20
Ilmen, Ozero Russia 58°15N 31°10E 18 C5
Ilo Peru 17°40S 71°20W 92 G4
Iloilo Phil. 10°45N 122°33E 37 B6
Ilomantsi Finland 62°38N 30°57E 8 E24
Ilorin Nigeria 8°30N 4°35E 52 G6
Ilwaco U.S.A. 46°19N 124°3W 78 D2
Imabari Japan 34°4N 133°0E 29 G6
Imandra, Ozero Russia 67°30N 33°0E 8 C25

Imari *Japan* 33°15N 129°52E **29 H4**
Imatra *Finland* 61°12N 28°48E **8 F23**
imeni 26 Bakinskikh Komissarov
= Neftçala *Azerbaijan* 39°19N 49°12E **47 B6**
imeni 26 Bakinskikh Komissarov
Turkmenistan 39°22N 54°10E **47 B7**
imeni Ismail Samani, Pik
Tajikistan 39°0N 72°2E **26 F8**
Imeri, Serra *Brazil* 0°50N 65°25W **92 C5**
Imfolozi △ *S. Africa* 28°18S 31°50E **57 C5**
Imi *Ethiopia* 6°28N 42°10E **49 F3**
Imlay *U.S.A.* 40°40N 118°9W **76 F4**
Imlay City *U.S.A.* 43°2N 83°5W **82 D1**
Immingham *U.K.* 53°37N 0°13W **12 D7**
Immokalee *U.S.A.* 26°25N 81°25W **85 H14**
Imola *Italy* 44°20N 11°42E **22 B4**
Imperatriz *Brazil* 5°30S 47°29W **93 E9**
Impéria *Italy* 43°53N 8°3E **20 E8**
Imperial *Canada* 51°21N 105°28W **71 C7**
Imperial *Calif., U.S.A.* 32°51N 115°34W **79 N11**
Imperial *Nebr., U.S.A.* 40°31N 101°39W **80 E3**
Imperial Beach *U.S.A.* 32°35N 117°6W **79 N9**
Imperial Dam *U.S.A.* 32°55N 114°25W **79 N12**
Imperial Res. *U.S.A.* 32°53N 114°28W **79 N12**
Imperial Valley *U.S.A.* 33°0N 115°30W **79 N11**
Imperieuse Reef
Australia 17°36S 118°50E **60 C2**
Impfondo *Congo* 1°40N 18°0E **54 D3**
Imphal *India* 24°48N 93°56E **41 G18**
Imroz = Gökçeada
Turkey 40°10N 25°50E **23 D11**
Imuris *Mexico* 30°47N 110°52W **86 A2**
Imuruan B. *Phil.* 10°40N 119°10E **37 B5**
In Guezzam *Algeria* 19°37N 5°52E **52 E7**
In Salah *Algeria* 27°10N 2°32E **52 C6**
Ina *Japan* 35°50N 137°55E **29 G8**
Inagua △ *Bahamas* 21°5N 73°24W **89 B5**
Inangahua *N.Z.* 41°52S 171°59E **59 D3**
Inanwatan *Indonesia* 2°8S 132°10E **37 E8**
Iñapari *Peru* 11°0S 69°40W **92 F5**
Inari *Finland* 68°54N 27°1E **8 B22**
Inarijärvi *Finland* 69°0N 28°0E **8 B23**
Inawashiro-Ko *Japan* 37°29N 140°6E **28 F10**
tInbhear Mór, An = Arklow
Ireland 52°48N 6°10W **10 D5**
Inca *Spain* 39°43N 2°54E **21 C7**
Inca de Oro *Chile* 26°45S 69°54W **94 B2**
Incahuasi *Argentina* 27°2S 68°18W **94 B2**
Incahuasi *Chile* 29°12S 71°5W **94 B1**
İnce Burun *Turkey* 42°7N 34°56E **19 F5**
Incesu *Turkey* 38°38N 35°11E **46 B2**
Incheon *S. Korea* 37°27N 126°40E **33 F14**
İncirliova *Turkey* 37°50N 27°41E **23 F12**
Incline Village *U.S.A.* 39°10N 119°58W **78 F7**
Incomáti → *Mozam.* 25°46S 32°43E **57 C5**
Indalsälven → *Sweden* 62°36N 17°30E **8 E17**
Indaw *Burma* 24°15N 96°5E **41 G20**
Independence *Calif.,*
U.S.A. 36°48N 118°12W **78 J8**
Independence *Iowa,*
U.S.A. 42°28N 91°54W **80 D9**
Independence *Kans.,*
U.S.A. 37°14N 95°42W **80 G6**
Independence *Ky.,*
U.S.A. 38°57N 84°33W **81 F11**
Independence *Mo., U.S.A.* 39°6N 94°25W **80 F6**
Independence Fjord
Greenland 82°10N 29°0W **4 A6**
Independence Mts.
U.S.A. 41°20N 116°0W **76 F5**
Index *U.S.A.* 47°50N 121°33W **78 C5**
Indi *India* 17°10N 75°58E **44 F2**
India ■ *Asia* 20°0N 78°0E **40 K11**
Indian → *U.S.A.* 27°59N 80°34W **85 H14**
Indian Cabins *Canada* 59°52N 117°40W **70 B5**
Indian Harbour *Canada* 54°27N 57°13W **73 B8**
Indian Head *Canada* 50°30N 103°41W **71 C8**
Indian L. *U.S.A.* 43°46N 74°16W **83 C10**
Indian Lake *U.S.A.* 43°47N 74°16W **83 C10**
Indian Springs *U.S.A.* 36°35N 115°40W **79 J11**
Indiana *U.S.A.* 40°37N 79°9W **82 F5**
Indiana □ *U.S.A.* 40°0N 86°0W **81 F11**
Indianapolis *U.S.A.* 39°46N 86°9W **80 F2**
Indianola *Iowa, U.S.A.* 41°22N 93°34W **80 E7**
Indianola *Miss., U.S.A.* 33°27N 90°39W **85 E9**
Indiga *Russia* 67°38N 49°9E **18 A8**
Indigirka → *Russia* 70°48N 148°54E **27 B15**
Indio *U.S.A.* 33°43N 116°13W **79 M10**
Indira Gandhi Canal *India* 28°0N 72°0E **42 F5**
Indira Pt. *India* 6°44N 93°49E **45 L11**
Indira Sagar *India* 22°15N 76°40E **42 H7**
Indo-China *Asia* 15°0N 102°0E **24 G12**
Indonesia ■ *Asia* 5°0S 115°0E **36 F5**
Indore *India* 22°42N 75°53E **42 H6**
Indramayu *Indonesia* 6°20S 108°19E **37 G13**
Indravati → *India* 19°20N 80°20E **44 E5**
Indre → *France* 47°16N 0°11E **20 C4**
Indulkana *Australia* 26°58S 133°5E **63 D1**
Indus → *Pakistan* 24°20N 67°47E **42 G2**
Indus, Mouths of the
Pakistan 24°0N 68°0E **42 H3**
Inebolu *Turkey* 41°55N 33°40E **19 F5**
Infiernillo, Presa del
Mexico 18°35N 101°50W **86 D4**
Inga, Barrage d'
Dem. Rep. of the Congo 5°39S 13°39E **54 F2**
Ingenio Santa Ana
Argentina 27°25S 65°40W **94 B2**
Ingersoll *Canada* 43°4N 80°55W **82 C4**
Ingham *Australia* 18°43S 146°10E **62 B4**
Ingleborough *U.K.* 54°10N 2°22W **12 C5**
Inglewood *Queens.,*
Australia 28°25S 151°2E **63 D5**
Inglewood *Vic., Australia* 36°29S 143°53E **63 F3**
Inglewood *N.Z.* 39°9S 174°14E **59 C5**
Ingólfshöfði *Iceland* 63°48N 16°39W **8 E5**
Ingolstadt *Germany* 48°46N 11°26E **16 D6**
Ingomar *U.S.A.* 46°35N 107°23W **76 C10**
Ingonish *Canada* 46°42N 60°18W **73 C7**

Ingraj Bazar *India* 24°58N 88°10E **43 G13**
Ingrid Christensen Coast
Antarctica 69°30S 76°0E **5 C6**
Ingulec = Inhulec
Ukraine 47°42N 33°14E **19 E5**
Ingushetia □ *Russia* 43°20N 44°50E **19 F8**
Ingwavuma *S. Africa* 27°9S 31°59E **57 C5**
Inhaca *Mozam.* 26°1S 32°57E **57 C5**
Inhaca Pen. *Mozam.* 26°13S 32°55E **57 C5**
Inhafenga *Mozam.* 20°36S 33°53E **57 B5**
Inhambane *Mozam.* 23°54S 35°30E **57 B6**
Inhambane □ *Mozam.* 22°30S 34°20E **57 B5**
Inharrime *Mozam.* 24°30S 35°0E **57 B6**
Inharrime → *Mozam.* 24°30S 35°0E **57 B6**
Inhulec *Ukraine* 47°42N 33°14E **19 E5**
Ining = Yining *China* 43°58N 81°10E **30 C5**
Inírida → *Colombia* 3°55N 67°52W **92 C5**
Inis = Ennis *Ireland* 52°51N 8°59W **10 D3**
Inishbofin *Ireland* 53°37N 10°13W **10 C1**
Inisheer *Ireland* 53°3N 9°32W **10 C2**
Inishfree B. *Ireland* 55°4N 8°23W **10 A3**
Inishkea North *Ireland* 54°9N 10°11W **10 B1**
Inishkea South *Ireland* 54°7N 10°12W **10 B1**
Inishmaan *Ireland* 53°5N 9°35W **10 C2**
Inishmore *Ireland* 53°8N 9°45W **10 C2**
Inishmurray *Ireland* 54°26N 8°39W **10 B3**
Inishowen Pen. *Ireland* 55°14N 7°15W **10 A4**
Inishshark *Ireland* 53°37N 10°16W **10 C1**
Inishturk *Ireland* 53°42N 10°7W **10 C1**
Inishvickillane *Ireland* 52°3N 10°37W **10 D1**
Injinoo ◎ *Australia* 10°56S 142°15E **62 A3**
Injune *Australia* 25°53S 148°32E **63 D4**
Inklin → *N. Amer.* 58°50N 133°10W **70 B2**
Inland Kaikoura Ra.
N.Z. 41°59S 173°41E **59 D4**
Inland Sea = Setonaikai
Japan 34°20N 133°30E **29 G6**
Inle L. *Burma* 20°30N 96°58E **41 J20**
Inlet *U.S.A.* 43°45N 74°48W **83 C10**
Inn → *Austria* 48°35N 13°28E **16 D7**
Innamincka *Australia* 27°44S 140°46E **63 D3**
Inner Hebrides *U.K.* 57°0N 6°30W **11 E2**
Inner Mongolia = Nei Mongol
Zizhiqu □ *China* 42°0N 112°0E **32 D7**
Inner Sound *U.K.* 57°30N 5°55W **11 D3**
Innerkip *Canada* 43°13N 80°42W **82 C4**
Innetalling I. *Canada* 56°0N 79°0W **72 A4**
Innisfail *Australia* 17°33S 146°5E **62 B4**
Innisfail *Canada* 52°2N 113°57W **70 C6**
In'noshima *Japan* 34°19N 133°10E **29 G6**
Innsbruck *Austria* 47°16N 11°23E **16 E6**
Inny → *Ireland* 53°32N 7°51W **10 C4**
Inongo
Dem. Rep. of the Congo 1°55S 18°30E **54 E3**
Inoucdjouac = Inukjuak
Canada 58°25N 78°15W **69 F16**
Inowrocław *Poland* 52°50N 18°12E **17 B10**
Inscription, C. *Australia* 25°29S 112°59E **61 E1**
Insein *Burma* 16°50N 96°5E **41 L20**
Inta *Russia* 66°5N 60°8E **18 A11**
Intendente Alvear
Argentina 35°12S 63°32W **94 D3**
Interlaken *Switz.* 46°41N 7°50E **20 C7**
Interlaken *U.S.A.* 42°37N 76°44W **83 D8**
International Falls
U.S.A. 48°36N 93°25W **80 A7**
Interview I. *India* 12°55N 92°43E **45 H11**
Intiyaco *Argentina* 28°43S 60°5W **94 B3**
Inukjuak *Canada* 58°25N 78°15W **69 F16**
Inútil, B. *Chile* 53°30S 70°15W **96 G2**
Inuvik *Canada* 68°16N 133°40W **68 D5**
Inveraray *U.K.* 56°14N 5°5W **11 E3**
Inverbervie *U.K.* 56°51N 2°17W **11 E6**
Invercargill *N.Z.* 46°24S 168°24E **59 G2**
Inverclyde □ *U.K.* 55°55N 4°49W **11 F4**
Inverell *Australia* 29°45S 151°8E **63 D5**
Invergordon *U.K.* 57°41N 4°10W **11 D4**
Inverloch *Australia* 38°38S 145°45E **63 F4**
Invermere *Canada* 50°30N 116°2W **70 C5**
Inverness *Canada* 46°15N 61°19W **73 C7**
Inverness *U.K.* 57°29N 4°13W **11 D4**
Inverness *U.S.A.* 28°50N 82°20W **85 G13**
Inverurie *U.K.* 57°17N 2°23W **11 D6**
Investigator Group
Australia 34°45S 134°20E **63 E1**
Investigator Str. *Australia* 35°30S 137°0E **63 F2**
Inya *Russia* 50°28N 86°37E **26 D9**
Inyangani *Zimbabwe* 18°5S 32°50E **55 H6**
Inyantue *Zimbabwe* 18°33S 26°39E **56 A4**
Inyo Mts. *U.S.A.* 36°40N 118°0W **78 J9**
Inyokern *U.S.A.* 35°39N 117°49W **79 K9**
Inza *Russia* 53°55N 46°25E **18 D8**
Iō-Jima *Japan* 30°48N 130°18E **29 J5**
Ioannina *Greece* 39°42N 20°47E **23 E9**
Iola *U.S.A.* 37°55N 95°24W **80 G6**
Iona *U.K.* 56°20N 6°25W **11 E2**
Ione *U.S.A.* 38°21N 120°56W **78 G6**
Ionia *U.S.A.* 42°59N 85°4W **81 D11**
Ionian Is. = Ionioi Nisoi
Greece 38°40N 20°0E **23 E9**
Ionian Sea *Medit. S.* 37°30N 17°30E **23 E7**
Ionioi Nisoi *Greece* 38°40N 20°0E **23 E9**
Ios *Greece* 36°41N 25°20E **23 F11**
Iowa □ *U.S.A.* 42°18N 93°30W **80 D7**
Iowa → *U.S.A.* 41°10N 91°1W **80 E8**
Iowa City *U.S.A.* 41°40N 91°32W **80 E8**
Iowa Falls *U.S.A.* 42°31N 93°16W **80 D7**
Iowa Park *U.S.A.* 33°57N 98°40W **84 E5**
Ipameri *Brazil* 17°44S 48°9W **93 G9**
Ipatinga *Brazil* 19°32S 42°30W **93 G10**
Ipiales *Colombia* 0°50N 77°37W **92 C3**
Ipin = Yibin *China* 28°45N 104°32E **34 C5**
Ipixuna *Brazil* 7°0S 71°40W **92 E4**
Ipoh *Malaysia* 4°35N 101°5E **39 K3**
Ippy *C.A.R.* 6°5N 21°7E **54 C4**
Ipsala *Turkey* 40°55N 26°23E **23 D12**
Ipswich *Australia* 27°35S 152°40E **63 D5**
Ipswich *U.K.* 52°4N 1°10E **13 E9**
Ipswich *Mass., U.S.A.* 42°41N 70°50W **83 D14**

Ipswich *S. Dak., U.S.A.* 45°27N 99°2W **80 C4**
Ipu *Brazil* 4°23S 40°44W **93 D10**
Iqaluit *Canada* 63°44N 68°31W **69 E18**
Iqaluktuutiaq = Cambridge Bay
Canada 69°10N 105°0W **68 D11**
Iquique *Chile* 20°19S 70°5W **92 H4**
Iquitos *Peru* 3°45S 73°10W **92 D4**
Irabu-Jima *Japan* 24°50N 125°10E **29 M2**
Iracoubo *Fr. Guiana* 5°30N 53°10W **93 B8**
Irafshān *Iran* 26°42N 61°56E **47 E9**
Iráklio *Greece* 35°20N 25°12E **23 G11**
Iráklio = Iraklio *Greece* 35°20N 25°12E **23 G11**
Iráklion = Iraklio *Greece* 35°20N 25°12E **23 G11**
Irala *Paraguay* 25°55S 54°35W **95 B5**
Iran ■ *Asia* 33°0N 53°0E **47 C7**
Iran, Pegunungan
Malaysia 2°20N 114°50E **36 D4**
Iran Ra. = Iran, Pegunungan
Malaysia 2°20N 114°50E **36 D4**
Iranamadu Tank *Sri Lanka* 9°23N 80°29E **45 K5**
Īrānshahr *Iran* 27°15N 60°40E **47 E9**
Irapuato *Mexico* 20°41N 101°28W **86 C4**
Iraq ■ *Asia* 33°0N 44°0E **46 C5**
Irati *Brazil* 25°25S 50°38W **95 B5**
Irazú, Volcan *Costa Rica* 10°28N 84°42E **88 D3**
Irbid *Jordan* 32°35N 35°48E **48 C4**
Irbid □ *Jordan* 32°30N 35°50E **48 C5**
Irebu *Dem. Rep. of the Congo* 0°40S 17°46E **54 E3**
Ireland ■ *Europe* 53°50N 7°52W **10 C4**
Iri = Iksan *S. Korea* 35°59N 127°0E **33 G14**
Irian Jaya = Papua □
Indonesia 4°0S 137°0E **37 E9**
Irian Jaya Barat □
Indonesia 2°5S 132°50E **37 E8**
Iringa *Tanzania* 7°48S 35°43E **54 F7**
Irinjalakuda *India* 10°21N 76°14E **45 J3**
Iriomote △ *Japan* 24°29N 123°53E **29 M1**
Iriomote-Jima *Japan* 24°19N 123°48E **29 M1**
Iriona *Honduras* 15°57N 85°11W **88 C2**
Iriri → *Brazil* 3°52S 52°37W **93 D8**
Irish Sea *Europe* 53°38N 4°48W **12 D3**
Irkutsk *Russia* 52°18N 104°20E **30 A9**
Irma *Canada* 52°55N 111°14W **71 C6**
Irō-Zaki *Japan* 34°36N 138°51E **29 G9**
Iron Baron *Australia* 32°58S 137°11E **63 E2**
Iron Gate = Portile de Fier
Europe 44°44N 22°30E **17 F12**
Iron Knob *Australia* 32°46S 137°8E **63 E2**
Iron Mountain *U.S.A.* 45°49N 88°4W **80 C9**
Iron Range △ *Australia* 12°34S 143°18E **62 A3**
Iron River *U.S.A.* 46°6N 88°39W **80 B9**
Irondequoit *U.S.A.* 43°13N 77°35W **82 C7**
Ironton *Mo., U.S.A.* 37°36N 90°38W **80 G9**
Ironton *Ohio, U.S.A.* 38°32N 82°41W **81 F12**
Ironwood *U.S.A.* 46°27N 90°9W **80 B8**
Ironwood Forest △
U.S.A. 32°32N 111°28W **77 K8**
Iroquois *Canada* 44°51N 75°19W **83 B9**
Iroquois Falls *Canada* 48°46N 80°41W **72 C3**
Irpin *Ukraine* 50°30N 30°15E **17 C16**
Irrara Cr. → *Australia* 29°35S 145°31E **63 D4**
Irrawaddy □ *Burma* 17°0N 95°0E **41 L19**
Irrawaddy → *Burma* 15°50N 95°6E **41 M19**
Irrawaddy, Mouths of the
Burma 15°30N 95°0E **41 M19**
Irricana *Canada* 51°19N 113°37W **70 C6**
Irrunytju *Australia* 26°3S 128°56E **61 E4**
Irtysh → *Russia* 61°4N 68°52E **26 C7**
Irún *Spain* 43°20N 1°52W **21 A5**
Irunea = Pamplona-Iruña
Spain 42°48N 1°38W **21 A5**
Irvine *Canada* 49°57N 110°16W **71 D6**
Irvine *U.K.* 55°37N 4°41W **11 F4**
Irvine *Calif., U.S.A.* 33°41N 117°46W **79 M9**
Irvine *Ky., U.S.A.* 37°42N 83°58W **81 G12**
Irvinestown *U.K.* 54°28N 7°39W **10 B4**
Irving *U.S.A.* 32°48N 96°56W **84 E6**
Irvona *U.S.A.* 40°46N 78°33W **82 F6**
Irwin → *Australia* 29°15S 114°54E **61 E1**
Irymple *Australia* 34°14S 142°8E **63 E3**
Isa Khel *Pakistan* 32°41N 71°17E **42 C4**
Isaac → *Australia* 22°55S 149°20E **62 C4**
Isabel *U.S.A.* 45°24N 101°26W **80 C3**
Isabel, I. *Mexico* 21°51N 105°55W **86 C3**
Isabela *Phil.* 6°40N 121°59E **37 C6**
Isabela *Puerto Rico* 18°30N 67°2W **89 d**
Isabela, Cord. *Nic.* 13°30N 85°25W **88 D2**
Isabella Ra. *Australia* 21°0S 121°4E **60 D3**
Isachsen, C. *Canada* 79°20N 105°28W **69 B10**
Isachsen Mt. *Antarctica* 72°8S 26°6E **5 D4**
Ísafjarðardjúp *Iceland* 66°10N 23°0W **8 C2**
Ísafjörður *Iceland* 66°5N 23°9W **8 C2**
Isagarh *India* 24°48N 77°51E **42 G7**
Isahaya *Japan* 32°52N 130°2E **29 H5**
Isan → *India* 26°51N 80°7E **43 F9**
Isana = Içana → *Brazil* 0°26N 67°19W **92 C5**
Isar → *Germany* 48°48N 12°57E **16 D7**
Íschia *Italy* 40°44N 13°57E **22 D5**
Ischigualasto △ *Argentina* 30°0S 68°0W **94 B2**
Isdell → *Australia* 16°27S 124°51E **60 C3**
Ise *Japan* 34°25N 136°45E **29 G8**
Ise-Shima △ *Japan* 34°25N 136°48E **29 G8**
Ise-Wan *Japan* 34°43N 136°43E **29 G8**
Isère → *France* 44°59N 4°51E **20 D6**
Isérnia *Italy* 41°36N 14°14E **22 D6**
Isfahan = Eşfahān *Iran* 32°39N 51°43E **47 C6**
Ishigaki *Japan* 24°20N 124°10E **29 M2**
Ishigaki-Shima *Japan* 24°20N 124°10E **29 M2**
Ishikari-Gawa →
Japan 43°15N 141°23E **28 C10**
Ishikari-Sammyaku
Japan 43°30N 143°0E **28 C11**
Ishikari-Wan *Japan* 43°25N 141°1E **28 C10**
Ishikawa *Japan* 26°25N 127°49E **29 L3**
Ishikawa □ *Japan* 36°30N 136°30E **29 F8**
Ishim *Russia* 56°10N 69°30E **26 D7**
Ishim → *Russia* 57°45N 71°10E **26 D8**
Ishinomaki *Japan* 38°32N 141°20E **28 E10**
Ishioka *Japan* 36°11N 140°16E **29 F10**

Ishkoman *Pakistan* 36°30N 73°50E **43 A5**
Ishpeming *U.S.A.* 46°29N 87°40W **80 B10**
Isil Kul *Russia* 54°55N 71°16E **26 D8**
iSimangaliso → *S. Africa* 27°50S 32°32E **57 C5**
Isiro *Dem. Rep. of the Congo* 2°53N 27°40E **54 D5**
Isisford *Australia* 24°15S 144°21E **62 C3**
İskenderun *Turkey* 36°32N 36°10E **46 B3**
İskenderun Körfezi
Turkey 36°40N 35°50E **19 G6**
İskür → *Bulgaria* 43°45N 24°25E **23 C11**
Iskut → *Canada* 56°45N 131°49W **70 B2**
Isla → *U.K.* 56°32N 3°20W **11 E5**
Isla Coiba △ *Panama* 7°33N 81°36W **88 E3**
Isla de Salamanca △
Colombia 10°59N 74°40W **89 D5**
Isla Gorge △ *Australia* 25°10S 149°57E **62 D4**
Isla Isabel △ *Mexico* 21°54N 105°58W **86 C3**
Isla Tiburón y San Esteban △
Mexico 29°0N 112°27W **86 B2**
Isla Vista *U.S.A.* 34°25N 119°53W **79 L7**
Islam Headworks
Pakistan 29°49N 72°33E **42 E5**
Islamabad *Pakistan* 33°40N 73°10E **42 C5**
Islamgarh *Pakistan* 27°51N 70°48E **42 F4**
Islamkot *Pakistan* 24°42N 70°13E **42 G4**
Islampur *Bihar, India* 25°9N 85°12E **43 G11**
Islampur *Maharashtra,*
India 17°2N 74°20E **44 F2**
Islampur *Paschimbanga,*
India 26°16N 88°12E **43 F13**
Island = Iceland ■ *Europe* 64°45N 19°0W **8 D4**
Island L. *Canada* 53°47N 94°25W **71 C10**
Island Lagoon *Australia* 31°30S 136°40E **63 E2**
Island Pond *U.S.A.* 44°49N 71°53W **83 B13**
Islands, B. of *Canada* 49°11N 58°15W **73 C8**
Islands, B. of *N.Z.* 35°15S 174°6E **59 A5**
Islay *U.K.* 55°46N 6°10W **11 F2**
Isle → *France* 44°55N 0°15W **20 D3**
Isle aux Morts *Canada* 47°35N 59°0W **73 C8**
Isle of Wight □ *U.K.* 50°41N 1°17W **13 G6**
Isle Royale △ *U.S.A.* 48°0N 88°55W **80 B9**
Isleton *U.S.A.* 38°10N 121°37W **78 G5**
Ismail = Izmayil *Ukraine* 45°22N 28°46E **17 F15**
Ismâ'iliya *Egypt* 30°37N 32°18E **53 B12**
Isna *Egypt* 25°17N 32°30E **53 C12**
Isparta *Turkey* 37°47N 30°30E **19 G5**
İspica *Italy* 36°47N 14°55E **22 F6**
Israel ■ *Asia* 32°0N 34°50E **48 D3**
Issoire *France* 45°32N 3°15E **20 D5**
Issyk-Kul = Balykchy
Kyrgyzstan 42°26N 76°12E **30 C4**
Issyk-Kul, Ozero = Ysyk-Köl
Kyrgyzstan 42°25N 77°15E **26 E8**
Istiea *Greece* 38°57N 23°9E **23 E10**
Isto, Mt. *U.S.A.* 69°12N 143°48W **74 B11**
Istokpoga, L. *U.S.A.* 27°23N 81°17W **85 H14**
Istra *Croatia* 45°10N 14°0E **16 F7**
Istres *France* 43°31N 4°59E **20 E6**
Istria = Istra *Croatia* 45°10N 14°0E **16 F7**
Itá *Paraguay* 25°29S 57°21W **94 B4**
Itaberaba *Brazil* 12°32S 40°18W **93 F10**
Itabira *Brazil* 19°37S 43°13W **93 G10**
Itabirito *Brazil* 20°15S 43°48W **95 A7**
Itabuna *Brazil* 14°48S 39°16W **93 F11**
Itacaunas → *Brazil* 5°21S 49°8W **93 E9**
Itacoatiara *Brazil* 3°8S 58°25W **92 D7**
Itaipú, Represa de *Brazil* 25°30S 54°30W **95 B5**
Itaituba *Brazil* 4°10S 55°50W **93 D7**
Itajaí *Brazil* 27°50S 48°39W **95 B6**
Itajubá *Brazil* 22°24S 45°30W **95 A6**
Itala △ *S. Africa* 27°30S 31°7E **57 C5**
Italy ■ *Europe* 42°0N 13°0E **22 C5**
Itamaraju *Brazil* 17°4S 39°32W **93 G11**
Itapecuru Mirim *Brazil* 3°24S 44°20W **93 D10**
Itaperuna *Brazil* 21°10S 41°54W **95 A7**
Itapetininga *Brazil* 23°36S 48°7W **95 A6**
Itapeva *Brazil* 23°59S 48°59W **95 A6**
Itapicuru → *Bahia,*
Brazil 11°47S 37°32W **93 F11**
Itapicuru → *Maranhão,*
Brazil 2°52S 44°12W **93 D10**
Itapipoca *Brazil* 3°30S 39°35W **93 D11**
Itapuá □ *Paraguay* 26°40S 55°40W **95 B4**
Itaquí *Brazil* 29°8S 56°30W **94 B4**
Itararé *Brazil* 24°6S 49°23W **95 A6**
Itarsi *India* 22°36N 77°51E **42 H7**
Itatí *Argentina* 27°16S 58°15W **94 B4**
Itatiaia △ *Brazil* 22°22S 44°38W **95 A7**
Itchen → *U.K.* 50°55N 1°22W **13 G6**
Itezhi Tezhi, L. *Zambia* 15°30S 25°30E **55 H5**
Ithaca = Ithaki *Greece* 38°25N 20°40E **23 E9**
Ithaca *U.S.A.* 42°27N 76°30W **83 D8**
Ithaki *Greece* 38°25N 20°40E **23 E9**
Itiquira → *Brazil* 17°18S 56°44W **93 G7**
Itiyuro → *Argentina* 22°40S 63°50W **94 A3**
Itō *Japan* 34°58N 139°5E **29 G9**
Itoigawa *Japan* 37°2N 137°51E **29 F8**
Itonamas → *Bolivia* 12°28S 64°24W **92 F6**
Ittoqqortoormiit *Greenland* 70°20N 23°0W **4 B6**
Itu *Brazil* 23°17S 47°15W **95 A6**
Itu Aba I. *S. China Sea* 10°23N 114°21E **36 B4**
Ituiutaba *Brazil* 19°0S 49°25W **93 G9**
Itumbiara *Brazil* 18°20S 49°10W **93 G9**
Ituna *Canada* 51°10N 103°24W **71 C8**
Iturbe *Argentina* 23°0S 65°25W **94 A2**
Iturup, Ostrov *Russia* 45°0N 148°0E **27 E15**
Ituxi → *Brazil* 7°18S 64°51W **92 E6**
Itzehoe *Germany* 53°55N 9°31E **16 B5**
Ivaí → *Brazil* 23°18S 53°42W **95 A5**
Ivalo *Finland* 68°38N 27°35E **8 B22**
Ivalojoki → *Finland* 68°40N 27°40E **8 B22**
Ivanava *Belarus* 52°7N 25°29E **17 B13**
Ivanhoe *Australia* 32°56S 144°20E **63 E3**
Ivanhoe *Canada* 44°77N 77°20W **82 B7**
Ivanhoe *Calif., U.S.A.* 36°23N 119°13W **78 J7**
Ivanhoe *Minn., U.S.A.* 44°28N 96°15W **80 C6**
Ivano-Frankivsk
Ukraine 48°40N 24°40E **17 D13**
Ivanovo = Ivanava
Belarus 52°7N 25°29E **17 B13**

Ivanovo *Russia* 57°5N 41°0E **18 C7**
Ivatsevichy *Belarus* 52°43N 25°21E **17 B13**
Ivdel *Russia* 60°42N 60°24E **18 B11**
Iveragh Pen. *Ireland* 51°52N 10°15W **10 E1**
Ivinheima → *Brazil* 23°14S 53°42W **95 A5**
Ivinhema *Brazil* 22°10S 53°37W **95 A5**
Ivory Coast *W. Afr.* 4°20N 5°0W **52 H4**
Ivory Coast ■ *Africa* 7°30N 5°0W **52 G4**
Ivrea *Italy* 45°28N 7°52E **20 D7**
Ivujivik *Canada* 62°24N 77°55W **69 E16**
Ivvavik △ *Canada* 69°6N 139°30W **68 D4**
Ivybridge *U.K.* 50°23N 3°56W **13 G4**
Iwaizumi *Japan* 39°50N 141°45E **28 E10**
Iwaki *Japan* 37°3N 140°55E **29 F10**
Iwakuni *Japan* 34°15N 132°8E **29 G6**
Iwamizawa *Japan* 43°12N 141°46E **28 C10**
Iwanai *Japan* 42°58N 140°30E **28 C10**
Iwata *Japan* 34°42N 137°51E **29 G8**
Iwate □ *Japan* 39°30N 141°30E **28 E10**
Iwate-San *Japan* 39°51N 141°0E **28 E10**
Iwo *Nigeria* 7°39N 4°9E **52 G6**
Iwŏn *N. Korea* 40°19N 128°39E **33 D15**
Ixiamas *Bolivia* 13°50S 68°5W **92 F5**
Ixopo *S. Africa* 30°11S 30°5E **57 D5**
Ixtepec *Mexico* 16°34N 95°6W **87 D5**
Ixtlán del Rio *Mexico* 21°2N 104°22W **86 C4**
Iyo *Japan* 33°45N 132°45E **29 H6**
Izabal, L. de *Guatemala* 15°30N 89°10W **88 C2**
Izamal *Mexico* 20°56N 89°1W **87 C7**
Izena-Shima *Japan* 26°56N 127°56E **29 L3**
Izhevsk *Russia* 56°51N 53°14E **18 C9**
Izhma → *Russia* 65°19N 52°54E **18 A9**
Izmayil *Ukraine* 45°22N 28°46E **17 F15**
İzmir *Turkey* 38°25N 27°8E **23 E12**
İzmit = Kocaeli *Turkey* 40°45N 29°50E **19 F4**
İznik Gölü *Turkey* 40°27N 29°30E **23 D13**
Izra *Syria* 32°51N 36°15E **48 C5**
Izu-Hantō *Japan* 34°45N 139°0E **29 G9**
Izu-Shotō *Japan* 34°30N 140°0E **29 G10**
Izúcar de Matamoros
Mexico 18°36N 98°28W **87 D5**
Izumi *Japan* 32°5N 130°22E **29 H5**
Izumi-Sano *Japan* 34°23N 135°18E **29 G7**
Izumo *Japan* 35°20N 132°46E **29 G6**
Izyaslav *Ukraine* 50°5N 26°50E **17 C14**

J

J.F.K. Int. ✈ (JFK)
U.S.A. 40°38N 73°47W **83 F11**
J. Strom Thurmond L.
U.S.A. 33°40N 82°12W **85 E13**
Ja-ela *Sri Lanka* 7°5N 79°53E **45 L4**
Jabalpur *India* 23°9N 79°58E **43 H8**
Jabālya *Gaza Strip* 31°32N 34°29E **48 D3**
Jabbūl *Syria* 36°4N 37°30E **46 B3**
Jabiru *Australia* 12°40S 132°53E **60 B5**
Jablah *Syria* 35°20N 36°0E **46 C3**
Jablonec nad Nisou
Czech Rep. 50°43N 15°10E **16 C8**
Jaboatão *Brazil* 8°7S 35°1W **93 E11**
Jaboticabal *Brazil* 21°15S 48°17W **95 A6**
Jaca *Spain* 42°35N 0°33W **21 A5**
Jacareí *Brazil* 23°20S 46°0W **95 A6**
Jacarèzinho *Brazil* 23°5S 49°58W **95 A6**
Jack River △ *Australia* 14°58S 144°19E **62 A3**
Jackman *U.S.A.* 45°37N 70°15W **81 C18**
Jacksboro *U.S.A.* 33°13N 98°10W **84 E5**
Jackson *Barbados* 13°7N 59°36W **89 g**
Jackson *Ala., U.S.A.* 31°31N 87°53W **85 F11**
Jackson *Calif., U.S.A.* 38°21N 120°46W **78 G6**
Jackson *Ky., U.S.A.* 37°33N 83°23W **81 G12**
Jackson *Mich., U.S.A.* 42°15N 84°24W **81 D11**
Jackson *Minn., U.S.A.* 43°37N 95°1W **80 D6**
Jackson *Miss., U.S.A.* 32°18N 90°12W **85 E9**
Jackson *Mo., U.S.A.* 37°23N 89°40W **80 G9**
Jackson *N.H., U.S.A.* 44°10N 71°11W **83 B13**
Jackson *Ohio, U.S.A.* 39°3N 82°39W **81 F12**
Jackson *Tenn., U.S.A.* 35°37N 88°49W **85 D10**
Jackson *Wyo., U.S.A.* 43°29N 110°46W **76 E8**
Jackson B. *N.Z.* 43°58S 168°42E **59 E2**
Jackson L. *U.S.A.* 43°52N 110°36W **76 E8**
Jacksons *N.Z.* 42°46S 171°32E **59 E3**
Jackson's Arm *Canada* 49°52N 56°47W **73 C8**
Jacksonville *Ala., U.S.A.* 33°49N 85°46W **85 E12**
Jacksonville *Ark., U.S.A.* 34°52N 92°7W **84 D8**
Jacksonville *Calif.,*
U.S.A. 37°52N 120°24W **78 H6**
Jacksonville *Fla., U.S.A.* 30°20N 81°39W **85 F14**
Jacksonville *Ill., U.S.A.* 39°44N 90°14W **80 F9**
Jacksonville *N.C.,*
U.S.A. 34°45N 77°26W **85 D16**
Jacksonville *Tex., U.S.A.* 31°58N 95°17W **84 F7**
Jacksonville Beach
U.S.A. 30°17N 81°24W **85 F14**
Jacmel *Haiti* 18°14N 72°32W **89 C5**
Jacob Lake *U.S.A.* 36°43N 112°13W **77 H7**
Jacobabad *Pakistan* 28°20N 68°29E **42 E3**
Jacobina *Brazil* 11°11S 40°30W **93 F10**
Jacques-Cartier, Dét. de
Canada 50°0N 63°30W **73 C7**
Jacques-Cartier, Mt.
Canada 48°57N 66°0W **73 C6**
Jacques-Cartier △
Canada 47°15N 71°33W **73 C5**
Jacuí → *Brazil* 30°2S 51°15W **95 C5**
Jacumba *U.S.A.* 32°37N 116°11W **79 N10**
Jacundá → *Brazil* 1°57S 50°26W **93 D8**
Jadcherla *India* 16°46N 78°9E **44 F4**
Jade City *Canada* 59°15N 129°37W **70 B3**
Jade Dragon Snow Mt. = Yulong
Xueshan *China* 26°10N 100°10E **34 D3**
Jade Mt. = Yü Shan
Taiwan 23°25N 120°52E **35 F13**
Jaén *Peru* 5°25S 78°40W **92 E3**
Jaén *Spain* 37°44N 3°43W **21 D4**
Jafarabad *India* 20°52N 71°22E **42 J4**
Jaffa = Tel Aviv-Yafo
Israel 32°4N 34°48E **48 C3**

Jaffa, C. Australia 36°58S 139°40E 63 F2
Jaffna Sri Lanka 9°45N 80°2E 45 K5
Jaffrey U.S.A. 42°49N 72°2W 83 D12
Jagadhri India 30°10N 77°20E 42 D7
Jagadishpur India 25°30N 84°21E 43 G11
Jagat Nepal 28°19N 84°53E 43 E11
Jagdalpur India 19°3N 82°0E 44 E6
Jagdaqi China 50°25N 124°7E 31 A13
Jagersfontein S. Africa 29°44S 25°27E 56 D4
Jaghīn → Iran 27°17N 57°13E 47 E8
Jagodina Serbia 44°5N 21°15E 23 C9
Jagraon India 30°50N 75°25E 42 D6
Jagtial India 18°50N 79°0E 44 E4
Jaguariaíva Brazil 24°10S 49°50W 95 A6
Jaguaribe → Brazil 4°25S 37°45W 93 D11
Jagüey Grande Cuba 22°35N 81°7W 88 B3
Jahanabad India 25°13N 84°59E 43 G11
Jahazpur India 25°37N 75°17E 42 G6
Jahrom Iran 28°30N 53°31E 47 D7
Jaigarh India 17°17N 73°13E 44 F1
Jaijon India 31°21N 76°9E 42 D7
Jailolo Indonesia 1°5N 127°30E 37 D7
Jailolo, Selat Indonesia 0°5N 129°5E 37 D7
Jaipur India 27°0N 75°50E 42 F6
Jais India 26°15N 81°32E 43 F9
Jaisalmer India 26°55N 70°54E 42 F4
Jaisinghnagar India 23°38N 78°34E 43 H8
Jaitaran India 26°12N 73°56E 42 F5
Jaithari India 23°14N 78°37E 43 H8
Jajarkot Nepal 28°42N 82°14E 43 E10
Jājarm Iran 36°58N 56°27E 47 B8
Jajpur India 20°53N 86°22E 44 D8
Jakam → India 23°54N 74°13E 42 H6
Jakhal India 29°48N 75°50E 42 E6
Jakhau India 23°13N 68°43E 42 H3
Jakobstad = Pietarsaari
  Finland 63°40N 22°43E 8 E20
Jal U.S.A. 32°7N 103°12W 77 K12
Jalājil Si. Arabia 25°40N 45°27E 46 E5
Jalālābād Afghan. 34°30N 70°29E 42 B4
Jalalabad India 27°41N 79°42E 43 F8
Jalalpur Jattan Pakistan 32°38N 74°11E 42 C6
Jalama U.S.A. 34°29N 120°29W 79 L6
Jalandhar = Jullundur
  India 31°20N 75°40E 42 D6
Jalapa Guatemala 14°39N 89°59W 88 D2
Jalapa Enríquez = Xalapa
  Mexico 19°32N 96°55W 87 D5
Jalasjärvi Finland 62°29N 22°47E 8 E20
Jalaun India 26°8N 79°25E 43 F8
Jaldhaka → Bangla. 26°16N 89°16E 43 F13
Jalesar India 27°29N 78°19E 42 F8
Jaleswar Nepal 26°38N 85°48E 43 F11
Jalgaon India 21°0N 75°42E 44 D2
Jalibah Iraq 30°35N 46°32E 46 D5
Jalingo Nigeria 8°55N 11°25E 53 G8
Jalisco □ Mexico 20°20N 103°40W 86 D4
Jalkot Pakistan 35°14N 73°24E 43 B5
Jalna India 19°48N 75°38E 44 E2
Jalón → Spain 41°47N 1°4W 21 B5
Jalor India 25°21N 72°37E 42 G5
Jalpa Mexico 21°32N 102°58W 86 C4
Jalpaiguri India 26°32N 88°46E 41 F16
Jalpan Mexico 21°14N 99°29W 87 C5
Jaluit I. Marshall Is. 6°0N 169°30E 64 G8
Jalūlā Iraq 34°16N 45°10E 46 C5
Jamaame Somalia 0°4N 42°44E 49 G3
Jamaica ■ W. Indies 18°10N 77°30W 88 a
Jamalpur Bangla. 24°52N 89°56E 41 G16
Jamalpur India 25°18N 86°28E 43 G12
Jamalpurganj India 23°2N 87°59E 43 H13
Jamanxim → Brazil 4°43S 56°18W 93 D7
Jambewangi Indonesia 8°17S 114°7E 37 J17
Jambi Indonesia 1°38S 103°30E 36 E2
Jambi □ Indonesia 1°30S 102°30E 36 E2
Jambongan, Pulau
  Malaysia 6°45N 117°20E 36 C5
Jambusar India 22°3N 72°51E 42 H5
James → S. Dak., U.S.A. 42°52N 97°18W 80 D5
James → Va., U.S.A. 36°56N 76°27W 81 G15
James B. Canada 54°0N 80°0W 72 B3
James Ranges Australia 24°10S 132°30E 60 D5
James Ross I. Antarctica 63°58S 57°50W 5 C18
Jamesabad Pakistan 25°17N 69°15E 42 G3
Jamestown Australia 33°10S 138°32E 63 E2
Jamestown S. Africa 31°6S 26°45E 56 D4
Jamestown N. Dak.,
  U.S.A. 46°54N 98°42W 80 B4
Jamestown N.Y., U.S.A. 42°6N 79°14W 82 D5
Jamestown Pa., U.S.A. 41°29N 80°27W 82 E4
Jamīlābād Iran 34°24N 48°28E 47 C6
Jamira → India 21°35N 88°28E 43 J13
Jamkhandi India 16°30N 75°15E 44 F2
Jamkhed India 18°43N 75°19E 44 E2
Jammalamadugu India 14°51N 78°25E 45 G4
Jammu India 32°43N 74°54E 42 C6
Jammu & Kashmir □
  India 34°25N 77°0E 43 B7
Jamnagar India 22°30N 70°6E 42 H4
Jamner India 20°45N 75°52E 44 D2
Jamni → India 25°13N 78°35E 43 G8
Jampur Pakistan 29°39N 70°40E 42 E4
Jamrud Pakistan 33°59N 71°24E 42 C4
Jämsä Finland 61°53N 25°10E 8 F21
Jamshedpur India 22°44N 86°12E 43 H12
Jamtara India 23°59N 86°49E 43 H12
Jämtland Sweden 63°31N 14°0E 8 E16
Jan L. Canada 54°56N 102°55W 71 C8
Jan Mayen Arctic 71°0N 9°0W 4 B7
Janakpur Nepal 26°42N 85°55E 44 A7
Janaúba Brazil 15°48S 43°19W 93 G10
Jand Pakistan 33°30N 72°6E 42 C5
Jandanku ○ Australia 16°20S 135°45E 62 B2
Jandaq Iran 34°3N 54°22E 47 C7
Jandola Pakistan 32°20N 70°9E 42 C4
Jandowae Australia 26°45S 151°7E 63 D5
Janesville U.S.A. 42°41N 89°1W 80 D9
Jangamo Mozam. 24°6S 35°21E 57 B6
Janghai India 25°33N 82°19E 43 G10

Jangheung S. Korea 34°41N 126°52E 33 G14
Jangipur India 24°28N 88°4E 43 G12
Jangoon India 17°44N 79°5E 44 F4
Janjanbureh Gambia 13°30N 14°47W 52 F3
Janjgir India 22°1N 82°34E 43 J10
Janos Mexico 30°54N 108°10W 86 A3
Januária Brazil 15°25S 44°25W 93 G10
Janûb Sînî □ Egypt 29°30N 33°50E 48 F2
Janwada India 18°0N 77°29E 44 E3
Jaora India 23°40N 75°10E 42 H6
Japan ■ Asia 36°0N 136°0E 29 G8
Japan, Sea of Asia 40°0N 135°0E 28 E7
Japan Trench Pac. Oc. 32°0N 142°0E 64 D6
Japen = Yapen Indonesia 1°50S 136°0E 37 E9
Japla India 24°33N 84°1E 43 G11
Japurá → Brazil 3°8S 65°46W 92 D5
Jaquarão Brazil 32°34S 53°23W 95 C5
Jaqué Panama 7°27N 78°8W 88 E4
Jarábulus Syria 36°49N 38°1E 46 B3
Jarama → Spain 40°24N 3°32W 21 B4
Jaranwala Pakistan 31°15N 73°26E 42 D5
Jarash Jordan 32°17N 35°54E 48 C4
Jarash □ Jordan 32°17N 35°54E 48 C4
Jardim Brazil 21°28S 56°2W 94 A4
Jardín América Argentina 27°3S 55°14W 95 B4
Jardine River △ Australia 11°9S 142°21E 62 A3
Jardines de la Reina, Arch. de los
  Cuba 20°50N 78°50W 88 B4
Jargalang China 43°5N 122°55E 33 C12
Jari → Brazil 1°9S 51°54W 93 D8
Jarīr, W. al → Si. Arabia 25°38N 42°30E 46 E4
Jarosław Poland 50°2N 22°42E 17 C12
Jarrahdale Australia 32°24S 116°5E 61 F2
Jarrahi → Iran 30°49N 48°48E 47 D6
Jartai China 39°45N 105°48E 32 E3
Järvenpää Finland 60°29N 25°5E 8 F21
Jarvis Canada 42°53N 80°6W 82 D4
Jarvis I. Pac. Oc. 0°15S 160°5W 65 H11
Jarwa India 27°38N 82°30E 43 F10
Jasdan India 22°2N 71°12E 42 H4
Jashpurnagar India 22°54N 84°9E 43 H11
Jasidih India 24°31N 86°39E 43 G12
Jāsimīyah Iraq 33°45N 44°41E 46 C5
Jasin Malaysia 2°20N 102°26E 39 L4
Jāsk Iran 25°38N 57°45E 47 E8
Jasło Poland 49°45N 21°30E 17 D11
Jaso India 24°30N 80°29E 43 G9
Jasper Alta., Canada 52°55N 118°5W 70 C5
Jasper Ont., Canada 44°52N 75°57W 83 B9
Jasper Ala., U.S.A. 33°50N 87°17W 85 E11
Jasper Fla., U.S.A. 30°31N 82°57W 85 F13
Jasper Ind., U.S.A. 38°24N 86°56W 80 F10
Jasper Tex., U.S.A. 30°56N 94°1W 84 F7
Jasper △ Canada 52°50N 118°8W 70 C5
Jasrasar India 27°43N 73°49E 42 F5
Jászberény Hungary 47°30N 19°55E 17 E10
Jataí Brazil 17°58S 51°48W 93 G8
Jath India 17°3N 75°13E 44 F2
Jati Pakistan 24°20N 68°19E 42 G3
Jatibarang Indonesia 6°28S 108°18E 37 G13
Jatiluwih Indonesia 8°23S 115°8E 37 J18
Játiva = Xàtiva Spain 38°59N 0°32W 21 C5
Jaú Brazil 22°10S 48°30W 95 A6
Jauja Peru 11°45S 75°15W 92 F3
Jaunpur India 25°46N 82°44E 43 G10
Jauja Somalia 2°48N 45°30E 49 G4
Jawoyn ○ Australia 14°16S 132°28E 60 B5
Java = Jawa Indonesia 7°0S 110°0E 36 F3
Java Sea Indonesia 4°35S 107°15E 36 E3
Java Trench Ind. Oc. 9°0S 105°0E 36 F3
Javadi Hills India 12°40N 78°40E 45 H4
Javla India 17°18N 75°9E 44 F2
Jawa Indonesia 7°0S 110°0E 36 F3
Jawa Barat □ Indonesia 7°0S 107°0E 37 G12
Jawa Tengah □ Indonesia 7°0S 110°0E 37 G14
Jawa Timur □ Indonesia 8°0S 113°0E 37 G15
Jawad India 24°36N 74°51E 42 G6
Jawhar India 19°55N 73°14E 44 E1
Jawhar Somalia 2°48N 45°30E 49 G4
Jawoyn ○ Australia 14°16S 132°28E 60 B5
Jay Peak U.S.A. 44°55N 72°32W 83 B12
Jaya, Puncak Indonesia 3°57S 137°17E 37 E9
Jayanti India 26°45N 89°40E 41 F16
Jayapura Indonesia 2°28S 140°38E 37 E10
Jayawijaya, Pegunungan
  Indonesia 5°0S 139°0E 37 F9
Jaynagar India 26°43N 86°9E 43 F12
Jaypur = Jeypore India 18°50N 82°38E 44 E6
Jayrūd Syria 33°49N 36°44E 46 C3
Jayton U.S.A. 33°15N 100°34W 84 E4
Jāz Mūrīān, Hāmūn-e
  Iran 27°20N 58°55E 47 E8
Jazireh-ye Shīf Iran 29°4N 50°54E 47 D6
Jazminal Mexico 24°52N 101°24W 86 C4
Jazzīn Lebanon 33°31N 35°35E 48 B4
Jean U.S.A. 35°47N 115°20W 79 K11
Jean Marie River
  Canada 61°32N 120°38W 70 A4
Jean-Rabel Haiti 19°50N 73°5W 89 C5
Jeanerette U.S.A. 29°55N 91°40W 84 G9
Jeanette, Ostrov = Zhannetty,
  Ostrov Russia 76°43N 158°0E 27 B16
Jeannette U.S.A. 40°20N 79°36W 82 F5
Jebāl Bārez, Kūh-e Iran 28°30N 58°20E 47 D8
Jebel, Bahr el →
  South Sudan 9°30N 30°25E 53 G12
Jebel Ali = Minā' Jabal 'Alī
  U.A.E. 25°2N 55°8E 47 E7
Jecheon S. Korea 37°8N 128°12E 33 F15
Jedburgh U.K. 55°29N 2°33W 11 F6
Jedda = Jiddah Si. Arabia 21°29N 39°10E 49 C2
Jeddore L. Canada 48°3N 55°55W 73 C8
Jędrzejów Poland 50°35N 20°15E 17 C11
Jefferson Iowa, U.S.A. 42°1N 94°23W 80 D6
Jefferson Ohio, U.S.A. 41°44N 80°46W 82 E4
Jefferson Tex., U.S.A. 32°46N 94°21W 84 E7
Jefferson, Mt. Nev.,
  U.S.A. 38°47N 116°56W 76 G5
Jefferson, Mt. Oreg.,
  U.S.A. 44°41N 121°48W 76 D3

Jefferson City Mo., U.S.A. 38°34N 92°10W 80 F7
Jefferson City Tenn.,
  U.S.A. 36°7N 83°30W 85 C13
Jeffersontown U.S.A. 38°12N 85°35W 81 F11
Jeffersonville U.S.A. 38°17N 85°44W 81 F11
Jeffrey City U.S.A. 42°30N 107°49W 76 E10
Jega Nigeria 12°15N 4°23E 52 F6
Jeju S. Korea 33°31N 126°32E 33 H14
Jeju-do S. Korea 33°29N 126°34E 33 H14
Jēkabpils Latvia 56°29N 25°57E 9 H21
Jekyll I. U.S.A. 31°4N 81°25W 85 F14
Jelenia Góra Poland 50°50N 15°45E 16 C8
Jelgava Latvia 56°41N 23°49E 9 H20
Jember Indonesia 8°11S 113°41E 37 H15
Jena Germany 50°54N 11°35E 16 C6
Jena U.S.A. 31°41N 92°8W 84 F8
Jengish Chokoso = Pobedy, Pik
  Kyrgyzstan 42°0N 79°58E 30 C4
Jenin West Bank 32°28N 35°18E 48 C4
Jenkins U.S.A. 37°10N 82°38W 81 G12
Jenner U.S.A. 38°27N 123°7W 78 G3
Jennings U.S.A. 30°13N 92°40W 84 F8
Jeong-eup S. Korea 35°35N 126°50E 33 G14
Jeongseon S. Korea 37°20N 128°45E 33 F15
Jeonju S. Korea 35°50N 127°4E 33 G14
Jepara Indonesia 7°40S 109°14E 37 G14
Jeparit Australia 36°8S 142°1E 63 F3
Jequié Brazil 13°51S 40°5W 93 F10
Jequitinhonha Brazil 16°30S 41°0W 93 G10
Jequitinhonha →
  Brazil 15°51S 38°53W 93 G11
Jerada Morocco 34°17N 2°10W 52 B5
Jerantut Malaysia 3°56N 102°22E 39 L4
Jerejak, Pulau Malaysia 5°19N 100°19E 39 c
Jérémie Haiti 18°40N 74°10W 89 C5
Jerez, Pta. Mexico 22°58N 97°40W 87 C5
Jerez de García Salinas
  Mexico 22°39N 103°0W 86 C4
Jerez de la Frontera Spain 36°41N 6°7W 21 D2
Jerez de los Caballeros
  Spain 38°20N 6°45W 21 C2
Jericho = El Arīḥā
  West Bank 31°52N 35°27E 48 D4
Jericho Australia 23°38S 146°6E 62 C4
Jerid, Chott el = Djerid, Chott
  Tunisia 33°42N 8°30E 52 B7
Jerilderie Australia 35°20S 145°41E 63 F4
Jermyn U.S.A. 41°32N 75°33W 83 E9
Jerome U.S.A. 42°44N 114°31W 76 E6
Jerramungup Australia 33°55S 118°55E 61 F2
Jersey U.K. 49°11N 2°7W 13 H5
Jersey Shore U.S.A. 41°12N 77°15W 82 E7
Jerseyville U.S.A. 39°7N 90°20W 80 F8
Jervis B. Australia 35°8S 150°46E 63 F5
Jervis Inlet Canada 50°0N 123°57W 70 C4
Jesi = Iesi Italy 43°31N 13°14E 22 C5
Jessore Bangla. 23°10N 89°10E 41 H16
Jesup U.S.A. 31°36N 81°53W 85 F14
Jesús Carranza Mexico 17°26N 95°2W 87 D5
Jesús María Argentina 30°59S 64°5W 94 C3
Jetmore U.S.A. 38°4N 99°54W 80 F4
Jetpur India 21°45N 70°10E 42 J4
Jevnaker Norway 60°15N 10°26E 9 F14
Jewett U.S.A. 40°22N 81°2W 82 F3
Jewett City U.S.A. 41°36N 71°59W 83 E13
Jeyḥūnābād Iran 34°58N 48°59E 47 C6
Jeypore India 18°50N 82°38E 44 E6
Jha Jha India 24°46N 86°22E 43 G12
Jhaarkand = Jharkhand □
  India 24°0N 85°50E 43 H11
Jhabua India 22°46N 74°36E 42 H6
Jhajjar India 28°37N 76°42E 42 E7
Jhal Pakistan 28°17N 67°27E 42 E2
Jhal Jhao Pakistan 26°20N 65°35E 40 F4
Jhalawar India 24°40N 76°10E 42 G7
Jhalida India 23°22N 85°58E 43 H11
Jhalrapatan India 24°33N 76°10E 42 G7
Jhang Maghiana
  Pakistan 31°15N 72°22E 42 D5
Jhansi India 25°30N 78°36E 43 G8
Jhargram India 22°27N 86°59E 43 H12
Jharia India 23°45N 86°26E 43 H12
Jharkhand □ India 24°0N 85°50E 43 H11
Jharsuguda India 21°56N 84°5W 44 D7
Jhelum Pakistan 33°0N 73°45E 42 C5
Jhelum → Pakistan 31°20N 72°10E 42 D5
Jhilmilli India 23°24N 82°51E 43 H10
Jhudo Pakistan 24°58N 69°18E 42 G3
Jhunjhunun India 28°10N 75°30E 42 E6
Ji-Paraná Brazil 10°52S 62°57W 92 F6
Ji Xian China 36°7N 110°40E 32 F6
Jia Xian Henan, China 33°59N 113°12E 32 H7
Jia Xian Shaanxi, China 38°12N 110°28E 32 E6
Jiahe China 25°38N 112°19E 35 E9
Jiaji = Qionghai China 19°15N 110°26E 38 C8
Jialing Jiang → China 29°30N 106°20E 34 C6
Jiamusi China 46°40N 130°26E 31 B15
Ji'an Jiangxi, China 27°6N 114°59E 35 D10
Ji'an Jilin, China 41°5N 126°10E 33 D14
Jianchang China 40°55N 120°35E 33 D11
Jianchuan China 26°38N 99°55E 34 D2
Jiande China 29°23N 119°15E 35 C12
Jian'an China 28°0N 117°0E 35 C11
Jiangbei China 29°40N 106°34E 34 C6
Jiangcheng China 22°36N 101°52E 34 F3
Jiangchuan China 24°8N 102°39E 34 E4
Jiangdi China 26°57N 103°37E 34 D4
Jiangdu China 32°30N 119°36E 35 A12
Jiange China 32°4N 105°32E 34 A5
Jianghua China 25°0N 111°47E 35 E8
Jiangjin China 29°14N 106°14E 34 C6
Jiangkou China 27°40N 108°49E 34 D7
Jiangle China 26°42N 117°23E 35 D11
Jiangmen China 22°32N 113°0E 35 F9
Jiangning China 31°55N 118°50E 35 B12
Jiangshan China 28°40N 118°37E 35 C12
Jiangsu □ China 33°0N 120°0E 35 H11
Jiangxi □ China 27°30N 116°0E 35 D11

Jiangyan China 32°30N 120°7E 35 A13
Jiangyin China 31°54N 120°17E 35 B13
Jiangyong China 25°20N 111°22E 35 E8
Jiangyou China 31°44N 104°43E 34 B5
Jianhe China 26°37N 108°31E 34 D7
Jianli China 29°46N 112°56E 35 C9
Jianning China 26°50N 116°50E 35 D11
Jian'ou China 27°3N 118°17E 35 D12
Jianping China 41°53N 119°42E 33 D10
Jianshi China 30°37N 109°38E 34 B7
Jianshui China 23°36N 102°43E 34 F4
Jianyang Fujian, China 27°20N 118°5E 35 D12
Jianyang Sichuan, China 30°24N 104°33E 34 B5
Jiao Xian = Jiaozhou
  China 36°18N 120°1E 33 F11
Jiaohe Hebei, China 38°2N 116°20E 32 E9
Jiaohe Jilin, China 43°40N 127°22E 33 C14
Jiaoling China 24°41N 116°12E 35 E11
Jiaonan China 35°52N 119°58E 33 G10
Jiaozhou China 36°18N 120°1E 33 F11
Jiaozhou Wan China 36°5N 120°10E 33 F11
Jiaozuo China 35°16N 113°12E 32 G7
Jiawang China 34°28N 117°26E 33 G9
Jiaxiang China 35°25N 116°20E 32 G9
Jiaxing China 30°49N 120°45E 35 B13
Jiayi = Chiai Taiwan 23°29N 120°25E 35 F13
Jiayu China 29°55N 113°55E 35 C9
Jiayuguan China 39°49N 98°18E 30 D8
Jibuti = Djibouti ■ Africa 12°0N 43°0E 49 E3
Jicarón, I. Panama 7°10N 81°50W 88 E3
Jiddah Si. Arabia 21°29N 39°10E 49 C2
Jido India 29°2N 94°58E 41 E19
Jieshou China 33°18N 115°22E 32 H8
Jiexiu China 37°2N 111°55E 32 F6
Jieyang China 23°35N 116°21E 35 F11
Jigalong Australia 23°21S 120°47E 60 D3
Jigalong ○ Australia 23°21S 120°46E 60 D3
Jigni India 25°45N 79°25E 43 G8
Jihlava Czech Rep. 49°28N 15°35E 16 D8
Jihlava → Czech Rep. 48°55N 16°36E 17 D9
Jijiga Ethiopia 9°20N 42°50E 49 F3
Jilib Somalia 0°29N 42°46E 49 G3
Jilin China 43°44N 126°30E 33 C14
Jilin □ China 44°0N 127°0E 33 C14
Jilong = Chilung Taiwan 25°3N 121°45E 35 E13
Jim Thorpe U.S.A. 40°52N 75°44W 83 F9
Jima Ethiopia 7°40N 36°47E 49 F2
Jimbaran, Teluk Indonesia 8°46S 115°9E 37 K18
Jiménez Mexico 27°8N 104°54W 86 B4
Jimeta Nigeria 9°17N 12°28E 54 C2
Jimo China 36°23N 120°30E 33 F11
Jin Jiang → China 28°24N 115°48E 35 C10
Jin Xian = Jinzhou
  China 38°55N 121°42E 33 E11
Jinan China 36°38N 117°1E 32 F9
Jinchang China 38°30N 102°10E 30 D9
Jincheng China 35°29N 112°50E 32 G7
Jinchuan China 31°30N 102°3E 34 B4
Jind India 29°19N 76°22E 42 E7
Jindabyne Australia 36°25S 148°35E 63 F4
Jinding China 22°22N 113°33E 31 a
Jindo S. Korea 34°28N 126°15E 33 G14
Jindřichův Hradec
  Czech Rep. 49°10N 15°2E 16 D8
Jing He → China 34°27N 109°4E 32 G5
Jing Shan China 31°0N 111°35E 34 B7
Jing Xian China 30°38N 118°25E 35 B12
Jing'an China 28°50N 115°17E 35 C10
Jingbian China 37°20N 108°30E 32 F5
Jingchuan China 35°20N 107°20E 32 G4
Jingde China 30°15N 118°27E 35 B12
Jingdezhen China 29°20N 117°11E 35 C11
Jingdong China 24°23N 100°47E 34 E3
Jinggangshan China 26°58N 114°15E 35 D10
Jinggu China 23°35N 100°41E 34 F3
Jinghai Guangdong,
  China 22°59N 116°31E 35 F11
Jinghai Tianjin, China 38°55N 116°55E 32 E9
Jinghong China 22°0N 100°45E 34 F3
Jinghong Dam China 22°10N 100°46E 34 F3
Jingjiang China 32°2N 120°16E 35 A13
Jingle China 38°20N 111°55E 32 E6
Jingmen China 31°0N 112°10E 35 B9
Jingning China 35°30N 105°43E 32 G3
Jingpo Hu China 43°55N 128°55E 33 C15
Jingshan China 31°1N 113°7E 35 B9
Jingtai China 37°10N 104°6E 32 F3
Jingtanggang China 39°10N 119°13E 33 E10
Jingxi China 23°8N 106°27E 34 F6
Jingyang China 34°30N 108°50E 32 G5
Jingyu China 42°25N 126°45E 33 C14
Jingyuan China 36°30N 104°40E 32 F3
Jingzhou Hubei, China 30°21N 112°11E 35 B9
Jingzhou Hunan, China 26°33N 109°40E 34 D7
Jingziguan China 33°15N 111°0E 34 A7
Jinhua China 29°8N 119°38E 35 C12

Jintur India 19°37N 76°42E 44 E3
Jinxi Jiangxi, China 27°56N 116°45E 35 D11
Jinxi Liaoning, China 40°52N 120°50E 33 D11
Jinxian China 28°26N 116°17E 35 C11
Jinxiang China 35°5N 116°22E 32 G9
Jinyang China 27°28N 103°5E 34 D4
Jinyun China 28°35N 120°5E 35 C13
Jinzhai China 31°40N 115°53E 35 B10
Jinzhong China 37°42N 112°46E 32 F7
Jinzhou Liaoning, China 38°55N 121°42E 33 E11
Jinzhou Liaoning, China 41°5N 121°3E 33 D11
Jiparaná → Brazil 8°3S 62°52W 92 E6
Jipijapa Ecuador 1°0S 80°40W 92 D2
Jiquilpan Mexico 19°59N 102°43W 86 D4
Jirisan S. Korea 35°20N 127°44E 33 G14
Jiroft Iran 28°45N 57°50E 47 D8
Jishan China 35°34N 110°58E 32 G6
Jishou China 28°21N 109°43E 34 C7
Jisr ash Shughūr Syria 35°49N 36°18E 46 C3
Jitarning Australia 32°48S 117°57E 61 F2
Jitra Malaysia 6°16N 100°25E 39 J3
Jiu → Romania 43°47N 23°48E 17 F12
Jiudengkou China 39°56N 106°40E 32 E4
Jiujiang Guangdong, China 22°50N 113°0E 35 F9
Jiujiang Jiangxi, China 29°42N 115°58E 35 C10
Jiuling Shan China 28°40N 114°40E 35 C10
Jiulong China 28°57N 101°31E 34 C3
Jiuquan China 39°50N 98°20E 30 D8
Jiutai China 44°10N 125°50E 33 B13
Jiuxincheng China 39°17N 115°59E 32 E8
Jiuzhaigou △ China 33°8N 103°52E 34 A4
Jiwani Pakistan 25°1N 61°44E 40 G2
Jixi Anhui, China 30°5N 118°34E 35 B12
Jixi Heilongjiang, China 45°20N 130°50E 33 B16
Jiyang China 37°0N 117°12E 33 F9
Jiyuan China 35°7N 112°57E 32 G7
Jīzān Si. Arabia 17°0N 42°20E 49 D3
Jize China 36°54N 114°56E 32 F8
Jizhou China 37°35N 115°30E 32 F8
Jizl, Wādī al → Si. Arabia 25°39N 38°25E 46 E3
Jizô-Zaki Japan 35°34N 133°20E 29 G6
Jizzax Uzbekistan 40°6N 67°50E 26 E7
Joaçaba Brazil 27°5S 51°31W 95 B5
João Pessoa Brazil 7°10S 34°52W 93 E12
Joaquín V. González
  Argentina 25°10S 64°0W 94 B3
Jobat India 22°25N 74°34E 42 H6
Jodhpur India 26°23N 73°8E 42 F5
Jodiya India 22°42N 70°18E 42 H4
Joensuu Finland 62°37N 29°49E 8 E23
Jöetsu Japan 37°12N 138°10E 29 F9
Jofane Mozam. 21°15S 34°18E 57 B5
Jog Falls = Gersoppa Falls
  India 14°12N 74°46E 45 G2
Jogbani India 26°25N 87°15E 43 F12
Jõgeva Estonia 58°45N 26°24E 9 G22
Jogjakarta = Yogyakarta
  Indonesia 7°49S 110°22E 37 G14
Johannesburg S. Africa 26°11S 28°2E 57 D4
Johannesburg U.S.A. 35°22N 117°38W 79 K9
Johilla → India 23°37N 81°14E 43 H9
John Crow Mts. Jamaica 18°5N 76°25W 88 a
John Day U.S.A. 44°25N 118°57W 76 D4
John Day → U.S.A. 45°44N 120°39W 76 D3
John Day Fossil Beds △
  U.S.A. 44°33N 119°38W 76 D4
John D'or Prairie Canada 58°30N 115°8W 70 B5
John H. Kerr Res.
  U.S.A. 36°36N 78°18W 85 C15
John o' Groats U.K. 58°38N 3°4W 11 C5
Johnnie U.S.A. 36°25N 116°5W 79 J10
John's Ra. Australia 21°55S 133°23E 62 C1
Johnson U.S.A. 44°38N 72°41W 83 B12
Johnson City Kans.,
  U.S.A. 37°34N 101°45W 80 G3
Johnson City N.Y., U.S.A. 42°7N 75°58W 83 D9
Johnson City Tenn.,
  U.S.A. 36°19N 82°21W 85 C13
Johnson City Tex., U.S.A. 30°17N 98°25W 84 F5
Johnsonburg U.S.A. 41°29N 78°41W 82 E6
Johnsondale U.S.A. 35°58N 118°32W 79 K8
Johnsons Crossing
  Canada 60°29N 133°18W 70 A2
Johnston, L. Australia 32°25S 120°30E 61 F3
Johnston Falls = Mambilima Falls
  Zambia 10°31S 28°45E 54 G5
Johnston I. Pac. Oc. 17°10N 169°8W 65 F11
Johnstone Str. Canada 50°28N 126°0W 70 C3
Johnstown Ireland 52°45N 7°33W 10 D4
Johnstown N.Y., U.S.A. 43°0N 74°22W 83 C10
Johnstown Ohio, U.S.A. 40°9N 82°41W 82 F2
Johnstown Pa., U.S.A. 40°20N 78°55W 82 F6
Johor □ Malaysia 2°5N 103°20E 39 M4
Johor, Selat Asia 1°28N 103°47E 39 d
Johor Bahru Malaysia 1°28N 103°46E 39 d
Jõhvi Estonia 59°22N 27°27E 9 G22
Joinville Brazil 26°15S 48°55W 95 B6
Joinville I. Antarctica 65°0S 55°30W 5 C18
Jojutla Mexico 18°37N 99°11W 87 D5
Jokkmokk Sweden 66°35N 19°50E 8 C18
Jökulsá á Bru → Iceland 65°40N 14°16W 8 D6
Jökulsá á Fjöllum →
  Iceland 66°10N 16°30W 8 C5
Jökulsárgljúfur △ Iceland 65°56N 16°31W 8 D5
Jolfa Āzarbājān-e Sharqī,
  Iran 38°58N 45°38E 46 B5
Jolfa Eşfahan, Iran 32°58N 51°37E 47 C6
Joliet U.S.A. 41°32N 88°5W 80 E9
Joliette Canada 46°3N 73°24W 72 C5
Jolo Phil. 6°0N 121°0E 37 C6
Jolon U.S.A. 35°58N 121°9W 78 K5
Jombang Indonesia 7°33S 112°14E 37 G15
Jomda China 31°28N 98°12E 34 B2
Jonava Lithuania 55°8N 24°12E 9 J21
Jones Sound Canada 76°0N 85°0W 69 B15
Jonesboro Ark., U.S.A. 35°50N 90°42W 85 D9
Jonesboro La., U.S.A. 32°15N 92°43W 84 E8
Joniškis Lithuania 56°13N 23°35E 9 H20
Jönköping Sweden 57°45N 14°8E 9 H16

Jonquière *Canada* 48°27N 71°14W **73** C5
Joplin *U.S.A.* 37°6N 94°31W **80** G6
Jora *India* 26°20N 77°49E **42** F6
Jordan *Mont., U.S.A.* 47°19N 106°55W **76** C10
Jordan *N.Y., U.S.A.* 43°4N 76°29W **83** C8
Jordan ■ *Asia* 31°0N 36°0E **48** D4
Jordan → *Asia* 31°48N 35°32E **48** D4
Jordan Valley *U.S.A.* 42°59N 117°3W **76** E5
Jorhat *India* 26°45N 94°12E **41** F19
Jörn *Sweden* 65°4N 20°1E **8** D19
Jorong *Indonesia* 3°58S 114°56E **36** E4
Jørpeland *Norway* 59°3N 6°1E **9** G12
Jorquera → *Chile* 28°3S 69°58W **94** B2
Jos *Nigeria* 9°53N 8°51E **52** G7
José Batlle y Ordóñez
   Uruguay 33°20S 55°10W **95** C4
Joseph, L. *Canada* 45°10N 79°44W **82** A5
Joseph Bonaparte G.
   Australia 14°35S 128°50E **60** B4
Joseph L. *Canada* 52°45N 65°18W **73** B6
Joshinath *India* 30°34N 79°34E **43** D8
Joshinetsu-Kōgen △
   Japan 36°42N 138°32E **29** F9
Joshua Tree *U.S.A.* 34°8N 116°19W **79** L10
Joshua Tree △ *U.S.A.* 33°55N 116°0W **79** M10
Jost Van Dyke I.
   Br. Virgin Is. 18°29N 64°47W **89** e
Jostedalsbreen *Norway* 61°40N 6°59E **8** F12
Jotunheimen *Norway* 61°35N 8°25E **8** F13
Joubertberge *Namibia* 18°30S 14°0E **56** A1
Jourdanton *U.S.A.* 28°55N 98°33W **84** G5
Jovellanos *Cuba* 22°40N 81°10W **88** B3
Ju Xian *China* 36°35N 118°20E **33** F10
Juan Aldama *Mexico* 24°19N 103°21W **86** C4
Juan Bautista Alberdi
   Argentina 34°26S 61°48W **94** C3
Juan de Fuca, Str of.
   N. Amer. 48°15N 124°0W **78** B3
Juán de Nova *Ind. Oc.* 17°3S 43°45E **57** A7
Juan Fernández, Arch. de
   Pac. Oc. 33°50S 80°0W **90** G2
Juan José Castelli
   Argentina 25°27S 60°57W **94** B3
Juan L. Lacaze *Uruguay* 34°26S 57°25W **94** C4
Juankoski *Finland* 63°3N 28°19E **8** E23
Juárez *Mexico* 27°37N 100°44W **86** B4
Juárez, Sa. de *Mexico* 32°0N 115°50W **86** A1
Juàzeiro *Brazil* 9°30S 40°30W **93** E10
Juàzeiro do Norte *Brazil* 7°10S 39°18W **93** E11
Juba *South Sudan* 4°50N 31°35E **53** H12
Juba → *Somalia* 1°30N 42°35E **49** G3
Jubail = Al Jubayl
   Si. Arabia 27°0N 49°50E **47** E6
Jubany *Antarctica* 62°30S 58°0W **5** C18
Jubany *Lebanon* 34°5N 35°39E **48** A4
Jubbah *Si. Arabia* 28°2N 40°56E **46** D4
Jubbal *India* 31°5N 77°40E **42** D7
Jubbulpore = Jabalpur
   India 23°9N 79°58E **43** H8
Jubilee L. *Australia* 29°0S 126°50E **61** E4
Juby, C. *Morocco* 28°0N 12°59W **52** C3
Júcar = Xúquer → *Spain* 39°5N 0°10W **21** C5
Júcaro *Cuba* 21°37N 78°51W **88** B4
Juchitán de Zaragoza
   Mexico 16°26N 95°1W **87** D5
Judea = Har Yehuda
   Israel 31°35N 34°57E **48** D3
Judith → *U.S.A.* 47°44N 109°39W **76** C9
Judith, Pt. *U.S.A.* 41°22N 71°29W **83** E13
Judith Gap *U.S.A.* 46°41N 109°45W **76** C9
Juigalpa *Nic.* 12°6N 85°26W **88** D2
Juiz de Fora *Brazil* 21°43S 43°19W **95** A7
Jujuy □ *Argentina* 23°20S 65°40W **94** A2
Julesburg *U.S.A.* 40°59N 102°16W **76** F12
Juli *Peru* 16°10S 69°25W **92** G5
Julia Cr. → *Australia* 20°0S 141°11E **62** C3
Julia Creek *Australia* 20°39S 141°44E **62** C3
Juliaca *Peru* 15°25S 70°10W **92** G4
Julian *U.S.A.* 33°4N 116°38W **79** M10
Julian, L. *Canada* 54°25N 77°57W **72** B4
Julianatop *Suriname* 3°40N 56°30W **93** C7
Julianehåb = Qaqortoq
   Greenland 60°43N 46°0W **4** C5
Julimes *Mexico* 28°25N 105°27W **86** B3
Jullundur *India* 31°20N 75°40E **42** D6
Julu *China* 37°15N 115°2E **32** F8
Jumbo Pk. *U.S.A.* 36°12N 114°11W **79** J12
Jumentos Cays *Bahamas* 23°0N 75°40W **88** B4
Jumilla *Spain* 38°28N 1°19W **21** C5
Jumla *Nepal* 29°15N 82°13E **43** E10
Jumna = Yamuna →
   India 25°30N 81°53E **43** G9
Jumunjin *S. Korea* 37°55N 128°54E **33** F15
Junagadh *India* 21°30N 70°30E **42** J4
Junan *China* 35°12N 118°53E **33** G10
Junction *Tex., U.S.A.* 30°29N 99°46W **84** F5
Junction *Utah, U.S.A.* 38°14N 112°13W **77** G7
Junction B. *Australia* 11°52S 133°55E **62** A1
Junction City *Kans., U.S.A.* 39°2N 96°50W **80** F5
Junction City *Oreg.,*
   U.S.A. 44°13N 123°12W **76** D2
Junction Pt. *Australia* 11°45S 133°50E **62** A1
Jundah *Australia* 24°46S 143°2E **62** C3
Jundiaí *Brazil* 24°30S 47°0W **95** A6
Juneau *U.S.A.* 58°18N 134°25W **70** B2
Junee *Australia* 34°53S 147°35E **63** E4
Jungar Qi *China* 39°49N 110°57E **32** E6
Jungfrau *Switz.* 46°32N 7°58E **20** C4
Junggar Pendi *China* 44°30N 86°0E **30** C6
Jungshahi *Pakistan* 24°52N 67°44E **42** G2
Juniata → *U.S.A.* 40°24N 77°1W **82** F7
Junín *Argentina* 34°33S 60°57W **94** C3
Junín de los Andes
   Argentina 39°45S 71°0W **96** D2
Jūniyah *Lebanon* 33°59N 35°38E **48** B4
Junlian *China* 28°8N 104°29E **34** C5
Junnar *India* 19°12N 73°58E **44** E1
Juntas *Chile* 28°24S 69°58W **94** B2
Juntura *U.S.A.* 43°45N 118°5W **76** E4

Jur, Nahr el →
   South Sudan 8°45N 29°15E **53** G11
Jura = Jura, Mts. du *Europe* 46°40N 6°5E **20** C7
Jura = Schwäbische Alb
   Germany 48°20N 9°30E **16** D5
Jura *U.K.* 56°0N 5°50W **11** F3
Jura, Mts. du *Europe* 46°40N 6°5E **20** C7
Jura, Sd. of *U.K.* 55°57N 5°45W **11** F3
Jurbarkas *Lithuania* 55°4N 22°46E **9** J20
Jurien Bay *Australia* 30°18S 115°2E **61** F2
Jūrmala *Latvia* 56°58N 23°34E **9** H20
Jurong *China* 31°57N 119°9E **35** B12
Juruá → *Brazil* 2°37S 65°44W **92** D5
Juruena *Brazil* 13°0S 58°10W **92** F7
Juruena → *Brazil* 7°20S 58°3W **92** E7
Juruti *Brazil* 2°9S 56°4W **93** D7
Justo Daract *Argentina* 33°52S 65°12W **94** C2
Jutaí → *Brazil* 2°43S 66°57W **92** D5
Juticalpa *Honduras* 14°40N 86°12W **88** D2
Jutland = Jylland *Denmark* 56°25N 9°30E **9** H13
Juuka *Finland* 63°13N 29°17E **8** E23
Juventud, I. de la *Cuba* 21°40N 82°40W **88** B3
Jūy Zar *Iran* 33°50N 46°18E **46** C5
Juye *China* 35°22N 116°5E **32** G9
Jwaneng *Botswana* 24°45S 24°50E **55** J4
Jylland *Denmark* 56°25N 9°30E **9** H13
Jyväskylä *Finland* 62°14N 25°50E **8** E21

K

K2 *Pakistan* 35°58N 76°32E **43** B7
Kaakha = Kaka
   Turkmenistan 37°21N 59°36E **47** B8
Kaap Plateau *S. Africa* 28°30S 24°0E **56** C3
Kaapkruis *Namibia* 21°55S 13°57E **56** C1
Kabaena *Indonesia* 5°15S 122°0E **37** F6
Kabala *S. Leone* 9°38N 11°37W **52** G3
Kabale *Uganda* 1°15S 30°0E **54** E6
Kabalo *Dem. Rep. of the Congo* 6°0S 27°0E **54** F5
Kabambare
   Dem. Rep. of the Congo 4°41S 27°39E **54** E5
Kabanjahe *Indonesia* 3°6N 98°30E **36** D1
Kabankalan *Phil.* 9°59N 122°49E **37** C6
Kabara *Fiji* 18°59S 178°56W **59** a
Kabardino-Balkaria □
   Russia 43°30N 43°30E **19** F7
Kabarega Falls = Murchison Falls
   Uganda 2°15N 31°30E **54** D6
Kabasalan *Phil.* 7°47N 122°44E **37** C6
Kabat *Indonesia* 8°16S 114°19E **37** J17
Kabbani → *India* 12°3N 76°54E **45** H3
Kabin Buri *Thailand* 13°57N 101°43E **38** F3
Kabinakagami L. *Canada* 48°54N 84°25W **72** C3
Kabinda
   Dem. Rep. of the Congo 6°19S 24°20E **54** F4
Kabompo → *Zambia* 14°11S 23°11E **55** G4
Kabongo
   Dem. Rep. of the Congo 7°22S 25°33E **54** F5
Kabrît, G. el *Egypt* 29°42N 33°16E **48** F2
Kabūd Gonbad *Iran* 37°5N 59°45E **47** B8
Kābul *Afghan.* 34°28N 69°11E **42** B3
Kābul □ *Afghan.* 34°30N 69°0E **40** B6
Kābul → *Pakistan* 33°55N 72°14E **42** C5
Kaburuang *Indonesia* 3°50N 126°30E **37** D7
Kabwe *Zambia* 14°30S 28°29E **55** G5
Kachchh, Gulf of *India* 22°50N 69°15E **42** H3
Kachchh, Rann of *India* 24°0N 70°0E **42** H4
Kachchhidhana *India* 21°44N 78°46E **43** J8
Kachikau *Botswana* 18°8S 24°26E **56** A3
Kachin □ *Burma* 26°0N 97°30E **34** D1
Kachīry *Kazakhstan* 53°10N 75°50E **26** D8
Kachnara *India* 23°50N 75°6E **42** H6
Kachot *Cambodia* 11°30N 103°3E **39** G4
Kaçkar *Turkey* 40°45N 41°10E **19** F7
Kadaiyanallur *India* 9°3N 77°22E **45** K3
Kadan Kyun *Burma* 12°30N 98°20E **38** F2
Kadanai → *Afghan.* 31°22N 65°45E **42** D1
Kadavu *Fiji* 19°0S 178°15E **59** a
Kadavu Passage *Fiji* 18°45S 178°0E **59** a
Kade *Ghana* 6°7N 0°56W **52** G5
Kadhimain = Al Kāẓimīyah
   Iraq 33°22N 44°18E **46** C5
Kadi *India* 23°18N 72°23E **42** H5
Kadina *Australia* 33°55S 137°43E **63** E2
Kadipur *India* 26°10N 82°23E **43** F10
Kadirabad *India* 19°51N 75°54E **44** E2
Kadiri *India* 14°12N 78°13E **45** G4
Kadirli *Turkey* 37°23N 36°5E **46** B3
Kadiyevka = Stakhanov
   Ukraine 48°35N 38°40E **19** E6
Kadmat I. *India* 11°14N 72°47E **45** J1
Kadoka *U.S.A.* 43°50N 101°31W **80** D3
Kadoma *Zimbabwe* 18°20S 29°52E **55** H5
Kaduna *Nigeria* 10°30N 7°21E **52** F7
Kadur *India* 13°34N 76°1E **45** H3
Kaédi *Mauritania* 16°9N 13°28W **52** E3
Kaeng Khoi *Thailand* 14°35N 101°0E **38** E3
Kaeng Krachan △
   Thailand 12°57N 99°23E **38** F2
Kaeng Krung △ *Thailand* 9°30N 98°50E **39** H2
Kaeng Tana △ *Thailand* 15°25N 105°32E **38** E5
Kaesŏng *N. Korea* 37°58N 126°35E **33** F14
Kāf *Si. Arabia* 31°25N 37°29E **46** D3
Kafan = Kapan *Armenia* 39°18N 46°27E **46** B5
Kafanchan *Nigeria* 9°40N 8°20E **52** G7
Kafin *Nigeria* 13°34N 76°1E **45** H3
Kafue *Zambia* 15°46S 28°9E **55** H5
Kafue → *Zambia* 15°30S 29°0E **55** H5
Kaga *Afghan.* 34°14N 70°10E **42** B4
Kaga Bandoro *C.A.R.* 7°0N 19°10E **54** C3
Kagawa □ *Japan* 34°15N 134°0E **29** G7
Kagera □ *Uganda* 0°57S 31°47E **54** E6
Kağızman *Turkey* 40°5N 43°10E **46** B4
Kagoshima *Japan* 31°35N 130°33E **29** J5
Kagoshima □ *Japan* 31°30N 130°30E **29** J5
Kahak *Iran* 36°6N 49°46E **47** B6
Kahan *Pakistan* 29°18N 68°54E **42** E3
Kahang *Malaysia* 2°12N 103°32E **39** L4

Kahayan → *Indonesia* 3°40S 114°0E **36** E4
Kahemba
   Dem. Rep. of the Congo 7°18S 18°55E **54** F3
Kahnūj *Iran* 27°55N 57°40E **47** E8
Kahoka *U.S.A.* 40°25N 91°44W **80** E8
Kaho'olawe *U.S.A.* 20°33N 156°37W **75** L8
Kahramanmaraş *Turkey* 37°37N 36°53E **46** B3
Kâhta *Turkey* 37°48N 38°38E **46** B3
Kahului *U.S.A.* 20°54N 156°28W **75** L8
Kahurangi △ *N.Z.* 41°10S 172°32E **59** D4
Kahuta *Pakistan* 33°35N 73°24E **42** C5
Kai, Kepulauan *Indonesia* 5°55S 132°45E **37** F8
Kai Besar *Indonesia* 5°35S 133°0E **37** F8
Kai Is. = Kai, Kepulauan
   Indonesia 5°55S 132°45E **37** F8
Kai Kecil *Indonesia* 5°45S 132°40E **37** F8
Kai Xian *China* 31°11N 108°21E **34** B7
Kaiapoi *N.Z.* 43°24S 172°40E **59** E4
Kaidu He → *China* 41°46N 86°31E **30** C6
Kaieteur Falls *Guyana* 5°1N 59°10W **92** B7
Kaifeng *China* 34°48N 114°21E **32** G8
Kaihua *China* 29°12N 118°20E **35** C12
Kaijiang *China* 31°7N 107°55E **34** B6
Kaikohe *N.Z.* 35°25N 173°49E **59** A4
Kaikoura *N.Z.* 42°25S 173°43E **59** E4
Kailash = Kangrinboqe Feng
   China 31°0N 81°25E **43** D9
Kaili *China* 26°33N 107°59E **34** D6
Kailu *China* 43°38N 121°18E **33** C11
Kailua Kona *U.S.A.* 19°39N 155°59W **75** M8
Kaimana *Indonesia* 3°39S 133°45E **37** E8
Kaimanawa Mts. *N.Z.* 39°15S 175°56E **59** C5
Kaimganj *India* 27°33N 79°24E **43** F8
Kaimur Hills *India* 24°30N 82°0E **43** G10
Kainab → *Namibia* 28°32S 19°34E **56** C2
Kainji Res. *Nigeria* 10°1N 4°40E **52** F6
Kainuu □ *Finland* 64°30N 29°7E **8** D23
Kaipara Harbour *N.Z.* 36°25S 174°14E **59** B5
Kaiping *China* 22°23N 112°42E **35** F9
Kaipokok B. *Canada* 54°54N 59°47W **73** B8
Kaira *India* 22°45N 72°50E **42** H5
Kairana *India* 29°24N 77°15E **42** E7
Kaironi *Indonesia* 0°47S 133°40E **37** E8
Kairouan *Tunisia* 35°45N 10°5E **53** A8
Kaiserslautern *Germany* 49°26N 7°45E **16** D4
Kaitaia *N.Z.* 35°8S 173°17E **59** A4
Kaitangata *N.Z.* 46°17S 169°51E **59** G2
Kaithal *India* 29°48N 76°26E **42** E7
Kaitu → *Pakistan* 33°10N 70°30E **42** C4
Kaiwi Channel *U.S.A.* 21°15N 157°30W **75** L8
Kaiyang *China* 27°4N 106°59E **34** D6
Kaiyuan *Liaoning, China* 42°28N 124°1E **33** C13
Kaiyuan *Yunnan, China* 23°40N 103°12E **34** F4
Kaiyuh Mts. *U.S.A.* 64°30N 158°0W **74** C8
Kajaani *Finland* 64°17N 27°46E **8** D22
Kajabbi *Australia* 20°0S 140°1E **62** C3
Kajana = Kajaani
   Finland 64°17N 27°46E **8** D22
Kajang *Malaysia* 2°59N 101°48E **39** L3
Kajo Kaji *South Sudan* 3°58N 31°40E **53** H12
Kaka *Turkmenistan* 37°21N 59°36E **47** B8
Kakabeka Falls *Canada* 48°24N 89°37W **72** C2
Kakadu △ *Australia* 12°0S 132°3E **60** B5
Kakamas *S. Africa* 28°45S 20°33E **56** C3
Kakamega *Kenya* 0°20N 34°46E **54** D6
Kakana *India* 9°7N 92°48E **45** K11
Kakanui Mts. *N.Z.* 45°10S 170°30E **59** F3
Kakdwip *India* 21°53N 88°11E **43** J13
Kake = Akiōta *Japan* 34°36N 132°19E **29** G6
Kake *U.S.A.* 56°59N 133°57W **70** B2
Kakegawa *Japan* 34°45N 138°1E **29** G9
Kakeroma-Jima *Japan* 28°8N 129°14E **29** K4
Kakhak *Iran* 34°9N 58°38E **47** C8
Kakhovka *Ukraine* 46°45N 33°30E **19** E5
Kakhovske Vdskh. *Ukraine* 47°5N 34°0E **19** E5
Kakinada *India* 16°57N 82°11E **44** F6
Kakisa *Canada* 60°56N 117°25W **70** A5
Kakisa → *Canada* 61°3N 118°10W **70** A5
Kakisa L. *Canada* 60°56N 117°43W **70** A5
Kakogawa *Japan* 34°46N 134°51E **29** G7
Kakwa → *Canada* 54°37N 118°28W **70** C5
Kāl Gūsheh *Iran* 30°59N 58°12E **47** D8
Kal Sefīd *Iran* 34°52N 47°23E **46** C5
Kala Oya → *Sri Lanka* 8°20N 79°45E **45** K4
Kalaallit Nunaat = Greenland ☑
   N. Amer. 66°0N 45°0W **67** C15
Kalabagh *Pakistan* 33°0N 71°28E **42** C4
Kalabahi *Indonesia* 8°13S 124°31E **37** F6
Kalach *Russia* 50°22N 41°0E **19** D7
Kaladan → *Burma* 20°20N 93°5E **41** J18
Kaladar *Canada* 44°37N 77°5W **82** B7
Kalahari *Africa* 24°0S 21°30E **56** B3
Kalahari Gemsbok △
   S. Africa 25°30S 20°30E **56** C3
Kalajoki *Finland* 64°12N 24°10E **8** D21
Kalakamati *Botswana* 20°40S 27°25E **57** B4
Kalakan *Russia* 55°15N 116°45E **27** D12
K'alak'unlun Shank'ou =
   Karakoram Pass *Asia* 35°33N 77°50E **43** B7
Kalam *Pakistan* 35°34N 72°30E **43** B5
Kalama *U.S.A.* 46°1N 122°51W **78** E4
Kalámai = Kalamata
   Greece 37°3N 22°10E **23** F10
Kalamata *Greece* 37°3N 22°10E **23** F10
Kalamazoo *U.S.A.* 42°17N 85°35W **81** D11
Kalamazoo → *U.S.A.* 42°40N 86°10W **80** D10
Kalamb *India* 18°3N 74°48E **44** E2
Kalamnuri *India* 19°35N 77°0E **44** E3
Kalan *Turkey* 39°7N 39°32E **46** B3
Kalāntarī *Iran* 32°10N 54°8E **47** C7
Kalao *Indonesia* 7°21S 121°0E **37** F6
Kalaotoa *Indonesia* 7°20S 121°50E **37** F6
Kalasin *Thailand* 16°26N 103°30E **38** D4
Kālat *Iran* 25°29N 59°22E **47** E9
Kalat *Pakistan* 29°8N 66°31E **40** E5
Kalāteh *Iran* 36°33N 55°41E **47** B7
Kalāteh-ye Ganj *Iran* 27°31N 57°55E **47** E8
Kalbā *U.A.E.* 25°5N 56°22E **47** E8
Kalbarri *Australia* 27°40S 114°10E **61** E1
Kalbarri △ *Australia* 27°51S 114°30E **61** E1

Kalburgi = Gulbarga
   India 17°20N 76°50E **44** F3
Kalce *Slovenia* 45°54N 14°13E **16** E8
Kale *Turkey* 37°27N 28°49E **23** F13
Kalegauk Kyun *Burma* 15°33N 97°35E **38** E1
Kalemie
   Dem. Rep. of the Congo 5°55S 29°9E **54** F5
Kalewa *Burma* 23°10N 94°15E **41** H19
Kalgan → *India* 20°54N 156°28W **75** L8
Kalghatgi *India* 15°11N 74°58E **45** G2
Kalgoorlie-Boulder
   Australia 30°40S 121°22E **61** F3
Kali → *India* 29°8N 79°5E **43** E8
Kali Sindh → *India* 25°32N 76°17E **42** G6
Kaliakra, Nos *Bulgaria* 43°21N 28°30E **23** C13
Kalianda *Indonesia* 5°50S 105°45E **36** F3
Kalibo *Phil.* 11°43N 122°22E **37** B6
Kalimantan *Indonesia* 0°0 114°0E **36** E4
Kalimantan Barat □
   Indonesia 0°0 110°30E **36** E4
Kalimantan Selatan □
   Indonesia 2°30S 115°30E **36** E5
Kalimantan Tengah □
   Indonesia 2°0S 113°30E **36** E4
Kalimantan Timur □
   Indonesia 1°30N 116°30E **36** D5
Kálimnos *Greece* 37°0N 27°0E **23** F12
Kalimpong *India* 27°4N 88°35E **43** F13
Kalinadi → *India* 14°50N 74°7E **45** G2
Kaliningrad *Russia* 54°42N 20°32E **9** J19
Kalinkavichy *Belarus* 52°12N 29°20E **17** B15
Kalinkovichi = Kalinkavichy
   Belarus 52°12N 29°20E **17** B15
Kalispell *U.S.A.* 48°12N 114°19W **76** B6
Kalisz *Poland* 51°45N 18°8E **17** C10
Kaliveli Tank *India* 12°5N 79°50E **45** H5
Kalix *Sweden* 65°53N 23°12E **8** D20
Kalix → *Sweden* 65°50N 23°11E **8** D20
Kalka *India* 30°46N 76°57E **42** D7
Kalkarindji *Australia* 17°30S 130°47E **60** C5
Kalkaska *U.S.A.* 44°44N 85°11W **81** C11
Kalkfeld *Namibia* 20°57S 16°14E **56** B2
Kalkfontein *Botswana* 22°4S 20°57E **56** B3
Kalkrand *Namibia* 24°1S 17°35E **56** B2
Kallakurichchi *India* 11°44N 79°1E **45** J4
Kallam *India* 18°36N 76°2E **44** E3
Kallavesi *Finland* 62°58N 27°30E **8** E22
Kallidaikurichi *India* 8°38N 77°31E **45** K3
Kallsjön *Sweden* 63°38N 13°0E **8** E15
Kalmar *Sweden* 56°40N 16°20E **9** H17
Kalmunai *Sri Lanka* 7°25N 81°49E **45** L5
Kalmykia □ *Russia* 46°5N 46°1E **19** E8
Kalna *India* 23°13N 88°25E **43** H13
Kalnai *India* 22°46N 83°30E **43** H10
Kalocsa *Hungary* 46°32N 19°0E **17** E10
Kalol *Gujarat, India* 22°37N 73°31E **42** H5
Kalol *Gujarat, India* 23°15N 72°33E **42** H5
Kalpeni I. *India* 10°5N 73°38E **45** J1
Kalpi *India* 26°8N 79°47E **43** F8
Kalpitiya *Sri Lanka* 8°14N 79°46E **45** K4
Kalputhi I. *India* 10°49N 72°10E **45** J1
Kalrayan Hills *India* 11°45N 78°40E **45** J4
Kalsubai *India* 19°35N 73°45E **44** E1
Kaltag *U.S.A.* 64°20N 158°43W **74** C8
Kaltukatjara *Australia* 24°52S 129°5E **61** D4
Kalu *Pakistan* 25°5N 67°39E **42** G2
Kaluga *Russia* 54°35N 36°10E **18** D6
Kalulushi *Zambia* 12°50S 28°3E **55** G5
Kalumburu *Australia* 13°55S 126°35E **60** B4
Kalumburu ◎ *Australia* 14°17S 126°38E **60** B4
Kalush *Ukraine* 49°3N 24°23E **17** D13
Kalutara *Sri Lanka* 6°35N 80°0E **45** L5
Kalwakurti *India* 16°41N 78°30E **44** F4
Kalya *Russia* 60°15N 59°59E **18** B10
Kalyan *Maharashtra, India* 20°30N 74°3E **44** D2
Kalyan *Maharashtra, India* 19°15N 73°9E **44** E1
Kalyandurg *India* 14°33N 77°6E **45** G3
Kalyani *India* 17°52N 76°57E **44** F3
Kalyansingapuram *India* 19°30N 83°19E **44** E6
Kama *Japan* 33°33N 130°49E **29** H5
Kama → *Russia* 55°45N 52°0E **18** C9
Kamaishi *Japan* 39°16N 141°53E **28** E10
Kamalapuram *India* 14°35N 78°49E **45** G4
Kamalia *Pakistan* 30°44N 72°42E **42** D5
Kamananjab *Namibia* 19°35S 14°51E **56** B2
Kamaran *Yemen* 15°21N 42°35E **49** D3
Kamareddi *India* 18°19N 78°21E **44** E4
Kamativi *Zimbabwe* 18°20S 27°6E **56** A4
Kambalda West
   Australia 31°10S 121°37E **61** F3
Kambam *India* 9°45N 77°16E **45** K3
Kambangan, Nusa
   Indonesia 7°40S 108°10E **37** G13
Kambar *Pakistan* 27°37N 68°1E **42** F3
Kambarka *Russia* 56°15N 54°11E **18** C9
Kambove
   Dem. Rep. of the Congo 10°51S 26°33E **54** G5
Kamchatka, Poluostrov
   Russia 57°0N 160°0E **27** D17
Kamchatka Pen. = Kamchatka,
   Poluostrov *Russia* 57°0N 160°0E **27** D17
Kamchiya → *Bulgaria* 43°4N 27°44E **23** C12
Kameda-Hantō *Japan* 41°50N 140°0E **28** D10
Kamen *Russia* 53°50N 81°30E **26** D9
Kamen-Rybolov *Russia* 44°46N 132°2E **28** B5
Kamenjak, Rt *Croatia* 44°47N 13°55E **16** F7
Kamenka *Russia* 65°58N 44°0E **18** A7
Kamenka Bugskaya =
   Kamyanka-Buzka
   Ukraine 50°8N 24°16E **17** C13
Kamensk Uralskiy *Russia* 56°25N 62°2E **26** D7
Kamenskoye *Russia* 62°45N 165°30E **27** C17
Kameoka *Japan* 35°0N 135°35E **29** G7
Kamiah *U.S.A.* 46°14N 116°2W **76** C5
Kamieskroon *S. Africa* 30°9S 17°56E **56** E2
Kamilukuak L. *Canada* 62°22N 101°40W **71** A8
Kamin-Kashyrskyy
   Ukraine 51°39N 24°56E **17** C13

Kamina
   Dem. Rep. of the Congo 8°45S 25°0E **54** F5
Kaminak L. *Canada* 62°10N 95°0W **71** A10
Kaminoyama *Japan* 38°9N 140°17E **28** E10
Kamla → *India* 25°35N 86°36E **43** G12
Kamloops *Canada* 50°40N 120°20W **70** C4
Kamo *Japan* 37°39N 139°3E **28** F9
Kamoke *Pakistan* 32°4N 74°4E **42** C6
Kampala *Uganda* 0°20N 32°32E **54** D6
Kampar *Malaysia* 4°18N 101°9E **39** K3
Kampar → *Indonesia* 0°30N 103°8E **36** D2
Kampen *Neths.* 52°33N 5°53E **15** B5
Kampene
   Dem. Rep. of the Congo 3°36S 26°40E **54** E5
Kamphaeng Phet
   Thailand 16°28N 99°30E **38** D2
Kampong Cham
   Cambodia 12°0N 105°30E **39** G5
Kampong Chhnang
   Cambodia 12°20N 104°35E **39** F5
Kampong Pengerang
   Malaysia 1°22N 104°7E **39** d
Kampong Punggai
   Malaysia 1°27N 104°18E **39** d
Kampong Saom
   Cambodia 10°38N 103°30E **39** G4
Kampong Saom, Chaak
   Cambodia 10°50N 103°32E **39** G4
Kampong Tanjong Langsat
   Malaysia 1°28N 104°1E **39** d
Kampong Telok Ramunia
   Malaysia 1°22N 104°15E **39** d
Kampot *Cambodia* 10°36N 104°10E **39** G5
Kampuchea = Cambodia ■
   Asia 12°15N 105°0E **38** F5
Kampung Air Putih
   Malaysia 4°15N 103°10E **39** K4
Kampung Jerangau
   Malaysia 4°50N 103°10E **39** K4
Kampung Raja *Malaysia* 5°45N 102°35E **39** K4
Kampungbaru = Tolitoli
   Indonesia 1°5N 120°50E **37** D6
Kamrau, Teluk *Indonesia* 3°30S 133°36E **37** E8
Kamsack *Canada* 51°34N 101°54W **71** C8
Kamsar *Guinea* 10°40N 14°36W **52** F3
Kamskoye Vdkhr. *Russia* 58°41N 56°7E **18** C10
Kamthi *India* 21°9N 79°19E **44** D4
Kamuchawie L. *Canada* 56°18N 101°59W **71** B8
Kamui-Misaki *Japan* 43°20N 140°21E **28** C10
Kamyanets-Podilskyy
   Ukraine 48°45N 26°40E **17** D14
Kamyanka-Buzka
   Ukraine 50°8N 24°16E **17** C13
Kāmyārān *Iran* 34°47N 46°56E **46** C5
Kamyshin *Russia* 50°10N 45°24E **19** D8
Kanaaupscow → *Canada* 54°2N 76°30W **72** B4
Kanab *U.S.A.* 37°3N 112°32W **77** H7
Kanab Cr. → *U.S.A.* 36°24N 112°38W **77** H7
Kanacea *Lau Group, Fiji* 17°15S 179°6W **59** a
Kanacea *Taveuni, Fiji* 16°59S 179°56E **59** a
Kanaga I. *U.S.A.* 51°45N 177°22W **74** E4
Kanagi *Japan* 40°54N 140°27E **28** D10
Kanairiktok → *Canada* 55°2N 60°18W **73** A7
Kanakapura *India* 12°33N 77°28E **45** H3
Kananga
   Dem. Rep. of the Congo 5°55S 22°18E **54** F4
Kanash *Russia* 55°30N 47°32E **18** C8
Kanaskat *U.S.A.* 47°19N 121°54W **78** C5
Kanastraíon, Ákra = Paliouri,
   Akra *Greece* 39°57N 23°45E **23** E10
Kanawha → *U.S.A.* 38°50N 82°9W **81** F12
Kanazawa *Japan* 36°30N 136°38E **29** F8
Kanchanaburi *Thailand* 14°2N 99°31E **38** E2
Kanchenjunga *Nepal* 27°50N 88°10E **43** F13
Kanchenjunga △ *India* 27°42N 88°8E **43** F13
Kanchipuram *India* 12°52N 79°45E **45** H4
Kandaghat *India* 30°59N 77°7E **42** D7
Kandahar *India* 18°52N 77°12E **44** E3
Kandahār *Afghan.* 31°32N 65°43E **40** D4
Kandahār □ *Afghan.* 31°0N 65°0E **40** D4
Kandalaksha *Russia* 67°9N 32°30E **8** C25
Kandalakshskiy Zaliv
   Russia 66°0N 35°0E **18** A6
Kandangan *Indonesia* 2°50S 115°20E **36** E5
Kandavu = Kadavu *Fiji* 19°0S 178°15E **59** a
Kandavu Passage = Kadavu
   Passage *Fiji* 18°45S 178°0E **59** a
Kandhkot *Pakistan* 28°16N 69°8E **42** E3
Kandhla *India* 29°18N 77°19E **42** E7
Kandi *Benin* 11°7N 2°55E **52** F6
Kandi *India* 23°58N 88°5E **43** H13
Kandiaro *Pakistan* 27°4N 68°13E **42** F3
Kandla *India* 23°0N 70°10E **42** H4
Kandos *Australia* 32°45S 149°58E **63** E4
Kandreho *Madag.* 17°29S 46°6E **57** B8
Kandy *Sri Lanka* 7°18N 80°43E **45** L5
Kane *U.S.A.* 41°40N 78°49W **82** E6
Kane Basin *Greenland* 79°1N 70°0W **69** B18
Kangān *Fārs, Iran* 27°50N 52°3E **47** E7
Kangān *Hormozgān, Iran* 25°48N 57°28E **47** E8
Kangar *Malaysia* 6°27N 100°12E **39** J3
Kangaroo I. *Australia* 35°45S 137°0E **63** F2
Kangaroo Mts. *Australia* 23°29S 141°51E **62** C3
Kangasala *Finland* 61°28N 24°4E **8** F21
Kangāvar *Iran* 34°40N 48°0E **46** C5
Kangding *China* 30°2N 101°57E **34** B3
Kangean, Kepulauan
   Indonesia 6°55S 115°23E **36** F5
Kangean Is. = Kangean,
   Kepulauan *Indonesia* 6°55S 115°23E **36** F5
Kanggye *N. Korea* 41°0N 126°35E **33** D14
Kangiqcik *Greenland* 70°7N 22°0W **4** B6
Kangiqliniq = Rankin Inlet
   Canada 62°30N 93°0W **68** E13
Kangiqsualujjuaq
   Canada 58°30N 65°59W **69** F18
Kangiqsujuaq *Canada* 61°30N 72°0W **69** E17
Kangiqtugaapik = Clyde River
   Canada 70°30N 68°30W **69** C18

Kangirsuk Canada 60°0N 70°0W 69 F18
Kangkar Chemaran
  Malaysia 1°34N 104°12E 39 d
Kangkar Sungai Tiram
  Malaysia 1°35N 103°55E 39 d
Kangkar Teberau
  Malaysia 1°32N 103°51E 39 d
Kangping China 42°43N 123°18E 33 C12
Kangra India 32°6N 76°16E 42 C7
Kangrinboqe Feng China 31°0N 81°25E 43 D9
Kangto China 27°50N 92°35E 41 F18
Kanha △ India 22°15N 80°40E 43 H9
Kanhan → India 21°4N 79°34E 44 D4
Kanhangad India 12°21N 74°58E 45 H2
Kanhar → India 24°28N 83°8E 43 G10
Kaniapiskau = Caniapiscau →
  Canada 56°40N 69°30W 73 A6
Kaniapiskau, L. = Caniapiscau, L.
  Canada 54°10N 69°55W 73 B6
Kanigiri India 15°24N 79°31E 45 G4
Kanin, Poluostrov Russia 68°0N 45°0E 18 A8
Kanin Nos, Mys Russia 68°39N 43°32E 18 A7
Kanin Pen. = Kanin, Poluostrov
  Russia 68°0N 45°0E 18 A8
Kaniva Australia 36°22S 141°18E 63 F3
Kanjut Sar Pakistan 36°7N 75°25E 43 A6
Kankaanpää Finland 61°44N 22°50E 8 F20
Kankakee U.S.A. 41°7N 87°52W 80 E10
Kankakee → U.S.A. 41°23N 88°15W 80 E9
Kankan Guinea 10°23N 9°15W 52 F4
Kankendy = Xankändi
  Azerbaijan 39°52N 46°49E 46 B5
Kanker India 20°10N 81°40E 44 D5
Kankesanturai Sri Lanka 9°49N 80°2E 45 K5
Kankroli India 25°4N 73°53E 42 G5
Kanmaw Kyun Burma 11°40N 98°28E 39 G2
Kannapolis U.S.A. 35°30N 80°37W 85 D14
Kannauj India 27°3N 79°56E 43 F8
Kanniyakumari India 8°5N 77°34E 45 K3
Kannod India 22°45N 76°40E 40 H10
Kannur India 11°53N 75°27E 45 J2
Kannyakumari India 8°3N 77°40E 45 K3
Kano Nigeria 12°2N 8°30E 52 F7
Kan'onji Japan 34°7N 133°39E 29 G6
Kanowit Malaysia 2°14N 112°20E 36 D4
Kanoya Japan 31°25N 130°50E 29 J5
Kanpetlet Burma 21°10N 93°59E 41 J18
Kanpur India 26°28N 80°20E 43 F9
Kansas □ U.S.A. 38°30N 99°0W 80 F4
Kansas → U.S.A. 39°7N 94°37W 80 F6
Kansas City Kans., U.S.A. 39°7N 94°38W 80 F6
Kansas City Mo., U.S.A. 39°6N 94°35W 80 F6
Kansk Russia 56°20N 95°37E 27 D10
Kansu = Gansu □ China 36°0N 104°0E 32 G3
Kantaphor India 22°35N 76°34E 42 H7
Kantharalak Thailand 14°39N 104°39E 38 E5
Kantli → India 21°54N 87°46E 43 J12
Kantli → Japan 36°15N 139°30E 29 F9
Kantō □ Japan 36°15N 139°30E 29 F9
Kantō-Sanchi Japan 35°59N 138°50E 29 G9
Kanturk Ireland 52°11N 8°54W 10 D3
Kanuma Japan 36°34N 139°42E 29 F9
Kanus Namibia 27°50S 18°39E 56 D2
Kanye Botswana 24°55S 25°28E 56 B4
Kao Tonga 19°40S 175°1W 59 c
Kao Phara Thailand 8°3N 98°22E 39 a
Kaohsiung Taiwan 22°35N 120°16E 35 F13
Kaokoveld Namibia 19°15S 14°30E 56 A1
Kaolack Senegal 14°5N 16°8W 52 F2
Kaoshan China 44°38N 124°50E 33 B13
Kapa'a U.S.A. 22°5N 159°19W 75 L8
Kapadvanj India 23°5N 73°0E 42 H5
Kapan Armenia 39°18N 46°27E 46 B5
Kapanga
  Dem. Rep. of the Congo 8°30S 22°40E 54 F4
Kapchagai = Qapshaghay
  Kazakhstan 43°51N 77°14E 26 E8
Kapela = Velika Kapela
  Croatia 45°10N 15°5E 16 F8
Kapfenberg Austria 47°26N 15°18E 16 E8
Kapiri Mposhi Zambia 13°59S 28°43E 55 G5
Kāpīsā □ Afghan. 35°0N 69°20E 40 B6
Kapiskau → Canada 52°47N 81°55W 72 B3
Kapit Malaysia 2°0N 112°55E 36 D4
Kapiti I. N.Z. 40°50S 174°56E 59 D5
Kaplan U.S.A. 30°0N 92°17W 84 F8
Kapoe Thailand 9°34N 98°32E 39 H2
Kapoeta South Sudan 4°50N 33°35E 53 H12
Kaposvár Hungary 46°25N 17°47E 17 E9
Kapowsin U.S.A. 46°59N 122°13W 78 D4
Kapps Namibia 22°32S 17°18E 56 C2
Kapsan N. Korea 41°4N 128°19E 33 D15
Kapsukas = Marijampolė
  Lithuania 54°33N 23°19E 9 J20
Kaptai L. Bangla. 22°40N 92°20E 41 H18
Kapuas → Indonesia 0°25S 109°20E 36 E3
Kapuas Hulu, Pegunungan
  Malaysia 1°30N 113°30E 36 D4
Kapuas Hulu Ra. = Kapuas Hulu,
  Pegunungan Malaysia 1°30N 113°30E 36 D4
Kapunda Australia 34°20S 138°56E 63 E2
Kapuni N.Z. 39°29S 174°8E 59 C5
Kapurthala India 31°23N 75°25E 42 D6
Kapuskasing Canada 49°25N 82°30W 72 C3
Kapuskasing → Canada 49°49N 82°0W 72 C3
Kaputar, Mt. Australia 30°15S 150°10E 63 E5
Kara Russia 69°10N 65°0E 26 C7
Kara Bogaz Gol, Zaliv =
  Garabogazköl Aylagy
  Turkmenistan 41°0N 53°30E 19 F9
Kara-Kala = Garrygala
  Turkmenistan 38°31N 56°29E 47 B8
Kara Kalpak Republic =
  Qoraqalpoghiston □
  Uzbekistan 43°0N 58°0E 26 E6
Kara Kum = Garagum
  Turkmenistan 39°30N 60°0E 47 B8
Kara Sea Russia 75°0N 70°0E 26 B8
Karabiğa Turkey 40°23N 27°17E 23 D12

Karabük Turkey 41°12N 32°37E 19 F5
Karaburun Turkey 38°41N 26°28E 23 E12
Karabutak = Qarabutaq
  Kazakhstan 50°0N 60°14E 26 E7
Karacabey Turkey 40°12N 28°21E 23 D13
Karacasu Turkey 37°43N 28°35E 23 F13
Karachey-Cherkessia □
  Russia 43°40N 41°30E 19 F7
Karad India 17°15N 74°10E 44 F2
Karaganda = Qaraghandy
  Kazakhstan 49°50N 73°10E 30 B3
Karagayly = Qaraghayly
  Kazakhstan 49°26N 76°0E 26 E8
Karaginskiy, Ostrov
  Russia 58°45N 164°0E 27 D17
Karagiye, Vpadina
  Kazakhstan 43°27N 51°45E 19 F9
Karagiye Depression = Karagiye,
  Vpadina Kazakhstan 43°27N 51°45E 19 F9
Karagola Road India 25°29N 87°23E 43 G12
Karaikal India 10°59N 79°50E 45 J4
Karaikkudi India 10°5N 78°45E 45 J4
Karaitivu I. Sri Lanka 9°45N 79°52E 45 K4
Karaj Iran 35°48N 51°0E 47 C6
Karajarri ☉ Australia 19°0S 122°30E 60 C3
Karak Malaysia 3°25N 102°2E 39 L4
Karakalpakstan =
  Qoraqalpoghiston □
  Uzbekistan 43°0N 58°0E 26 E6
Karakelong Indonesia 4°35N 126°50E 37 D7
Karakitang Indonesia 3°14N 125°28E 37 D7
Karakol Kyrgyzstan 42°30N 78°20E 30 C4
Karakoram Pass Asia 35°33N 77°50E 43 B7
Karakoram Ra. Pakistan 35°30N 77°0E 43 B7
Karakuwisa Namibia 18°56S 19°40E 56 A2
Karalon Russia 57°5N 115°50E 27 D12
Karama Jordan 31°57N 35°35E 48 D4
Karaman Turkey 37°14N 33°13E 46 B2
Karamay China 45°30N 84°58E 30 B5
Karambu Indonesia 3°53S 116°6E 36 E5
Karamea Bight N.Z. 41°22S 171°40E 59 D3
Karamnasa → India 25°31N 83°52E 43 G10
Karān Si. Arabia 27°43N 49°49E 47 E6
Karand Iran 34°16N 46°15E 46 C5
Karanganyar Indonesia 7°38S 109°37E 37 G13
Karangasem = Amlapura
  Indonesia 8°27S 115°37E 37 J18
Karanja Maharashtra,
  India 21°11N 78°24E 44 D4
Karanja Maharashtra,
  India 20°29N 77°31E 44 D3
Karanjia India 21°47N 85°58E 43 J11
Karas □ Namibia 27°0S 17°30E 56 C2
Karasburg Namibia 28°0S 18°44E 56 C2
Karasino Russia 66°50N 86°50E 26 C9
Karasjok Norway 69°27N 25°30E 8 B21
Karasuk Russia 53°44N 78°2E 26 D8
Karasuyama Japan 36°39N 140°9E 29 F10
Karatau, Khrebet = Qarataū
  Kazakhstan 43°30N 69°30E 26 E7
Karatax Shan China 35°57N 81°0E 30 D5
Karativu Sri Lanka 8°22N 79°47E 45 K4
Karatsu Japan 33°26N 129°58E 29 H5
Karaul Russia 70°6N 82°15E 26 B9
Karauli India 26°30N 77°4E 42 F7
Karawang Indonesia 6°30S 107°15E 37 G12
Karawanken Europe 46°30N 14°40E 16 E8
Karayazı Turkey 39°41N 42°9E 19 G7
Karazhal = Qarazhal
  Kazakhstan 48°2N 70°49E 26 E8
Karbalā' Iraq 32°36N 44°3E 46 C5
Karcag Hungary 47°19N 20°57E 17 E11
Karcha → Pakistan 34°45N 76°10E 43 B7
Karchana India 25°17N 81°56E 43 G9
Karditsa Greece 39°23N 21°54E 23 E9
Kärdla Estonia 59°0N 22°45E 9 G20
Kardzhali = Kŭrdzhali
  Bulgaria 41°38N 25°21E 23 D11
Kareeberge S. Africa 30°59S 21°50E 56 D3
Kareha → India 25°44N 86°21E 43 G12
Kareima Sudan 18°30N 31°49E 53 E12
Karelia □ Russia 65°30N 32°30E 18 A5
Karelian Republic = Karelia □
  Russia 65°30N 32°30E 18 A5
Karera India 25°32N 78°9E 42 G8
Kārevāndar Iran 27°53N 60°44E 47 E9
Kargasok Russia 59°3N 80°53E 26 D9
Kargat Russia 55°10N 80°15E 26 D9
Kargil India 34°32N 76°12E 43 B7
Kargopol Russia 61°30N 38°58E 18 B6
Kariba, L. Zimbabwe 16°40S 28°25E 55 H5
Kariba Dam Zimbabwe 16°30S 28°35E 55 H5
Kariba Gorge Zambia 16°30S 28°50E 55 H5
Karibib Namibia 22°0S 15°56E 56 B2
Karijini △ Australia 23°8S 118°15E 60 D2
Karimata, Kepulauan
  Indonesia 1°25S 109°0E 36 E3
Karimata, Selat Indonesia 2°0S 108°40E 36 E3
Karimata Is. = Karimata,
  Kepulauan Indonesia 1°25S 109°0E 36 E3
Karimnagar India 18°26N 79°10E 44 E4
Karimun, Pulau Indonesia 1°3N 103°22E 39 d
Karimun Kecil, Pulau
  Indonesia 1°8N 103°22E 39 d
Karimunjawa, Kepulauan
  Indonesia 5°50S 110°30E 36 F4
Karin Somalia 10°50N 45°52E 49 E4
Karīt Iran 33°29N 56°55E 47 C8
Kariya Japan 34°58N 137°1E 29 G8
Karjala Finland 62°0N 30°25E 8 F24
Karjat India 18°33N 75°0E 44 E2
Karkaralinsk = Qarqaraly
  Kazakhstan 49°26N 75°30E 30 B4
Karkheh → Iran 31°2N 47°29E 46 D5
Karkinitska Zatoka
  Ukraine 45°56N 33°0E 19 E5

Karkinitskiy Zaliv = Karkinitska
  Zatoka Ukraine 45°56N 33°0E 19 E5
Karkuk = Kirkūk Iraq 35°30N 44°21E 46 C5
Karlantijpa North ☉
  Australia 19°27S 133°33E 60 C5
Karlantijpa South ☉
  Australia 20°31S 133°9E 60 D5
Karleby = Kokkola
  Finland 63°50N 23°8E 8 E20
Karlovac Croatia 45°31N 15°36E 16 F8
Karlovo Bulgaria 42°38N 24°47E 23 C11
Karlovy Vary Czech Rep. 50°13N 12°51E 16 C7
Karlsbad = Karlovy Vary
  Czech Rep. 50°13N 12°51E 16 C7
Karlsena, Mys Russia 77°0N 67°42E 26 B7
Karlshamn Sweden 56°10N 14°51E 9 H16
Karlskoga Sweden 59°28N 14°33E 9 G16
Karlskrona Sweden 56°10N 15°35E 9 H16
Karlsruhe Germany 49°0N 8°23E 16 D5
Karlstad Sweden 59°23N 13°30E 9 G15
Karlstad U.S.A. 48°35N 96°31W 80 A5
Karmala India 18°25N 75°12E 44 E2
Karmi'el Israel 32°55N 35°18E 48 C4
Karnak Egypt 25°43N 32°39E 53 C12
Karnal India 29°42N 77°2E 42 E7
Karnali → Nepal 28°45N 81°16E 43 E9
Karnaphuli Res. = Kaptai L.
  Bangla. 22°40N 92°20E 41 H18
Karnaprayag India 30°16N 79°15E 43 D8
Karnataka □ India 13°15N 77°0E 45 H3
Karnes City U.S.A. 28°53N 97°54W 84 G6
Karnische Alpen Europe 46°36N 13°0E 16 E7
Kärnten □ Austria 46°52N 13°30E 16 E8
Karon, Ao Thailand 7°51N 98°17E 39 a
Karonga Malawi 9°57S 33°55E 54 F6
Karoo △ S. Africa 32°18S 22°27E 56 D3
Karoonda Australia 35°1S 139°59E 63 F2
Karor Pakistan 31°15N 70°59E 42 D4
Karora Sudan 17°44N 38°15E 53 E13
Karpathos Greece 35°37N 27°10E 23 G12
Karpinsk Russia 59°45N 60°1E 18 C11
Karpogory Russia 64°0N 44°27E 18 B7
Karpuz Burnu = Apostolos
  Andreas, C. Cyprus 35°42N 34°35E 46 C2
Karratha Australia 20°44S 116°52E 60 D2
Kars Turkey 40°40N 43°5E 19 F7
Karsakpay Kazakhstan 47°55N 66°40E 26 E7
Karshi = Qarshi
  Uzbekistan 38°53N 65°48E 26 F7
Karsiyang India 26°56N 88°18E 43 F13
Karsog India 31°23N 77°12E 42 D7
Kartala Comoros Is. 11°45S 43°21E 55 a
Kartaly Russia 53°3N 60°40E 26 D7
Kartapur India 31°27N 75°32E 42 D6
Karthaus U.S.A. 41°8N 78°9W 82 E6
Karufa Indonesia 3°50S 133°20E 37 E8
Karumba Australia 17°31S 140°50E 62 B3
Kärün → Iran 30°26N 48°10E 47 D6
Karungu Kenya 0°50S 34°10E 54 E6
Karur India 10°59N 78°2E 45 J4
Karviná Czech Rep. 49°53N 18°31E 17 D10
Karwan → India 27°26N 78°4E 42 F8
Karwar India 14°55N 74°13E 45 G2
Karwi India 25°12N 80°57E 43 G9
Karymskoye Russia 51°36N 114°21E 27 D12
Kasai →
  Dem. Rep. of the Congo 3°30S 16°10E 54 E3
Kasaji
  Dem. Rep. of the Congo 10°25S 23°27E 55 G4
Kasama Zambia 10°16S 31°9E 54 G6
Kasan-dong N. Korea 41°18N 126°55E 33 D14
Kasandra Kolpos Greece 40°5N 23°30E 23 D10
Kasane Namibia 17°34S 24°50E 56 A3
Kasaragod India 12°30N 74°58E 45 H2
Kasba L. Canada 60°20N 102°10W 71 A8
Käseh Garān Iran 34°5N 46°2E 46 C5
Kasempa Zambia 13°30S 25°44E 55 G5
Kasenga
  Dem. Rep. of the Congo 10°20S 28°45E 55 G5
Kasese Uganda 0°13N 30°3E 54 D6
Kasganj India 27°48N 78°42E 43 F8
Kashabowie Canada 48°40N 90°26W 72 C1
Kashaf Iran 35°58N 61°7E 47 C9
Kāshān Iran 34°5N 51°30E 47 C6
Kashechewan Canada 52°18N 81°37W 72 B3
Kashgar = Kashi China 39°30N 76°2E 30 D4
Kashi China 39°30N 76°2E 30 D4
Kashipur Odisha, India 19°16N 83°3E 44 E6
Kashipur Uttarakhand,
  India 29°15N 79°0E 43 E8
Kashiwazaki Japan 37°22N 138°33E 29 F9
Kashk-e Kohneh Afghan. 34°55N 62°30E 40 B3
Kashkū'īyeh Iran 30°31N 55°40E 47 D7
Kāshmar Iran 35°16N 58°0E 47 C8
Kashmir Asia 34°0N 76°0E 43 C7
Kashmor Pakistan 28°28N 69°32E 42 E3
Kashun Noerh = Gaxun Nur
  China 42°22N 100°30E 30 C9
Kasiari India 22°8N 87°14E 43 H12
Kasimov Russia 54°55N 41°20E 18 D7
Kasiruta Indonesia 0°25S 127°12E 37 E7
Kaskaskia → U.S.A. 37°58N 89°57W 80 G9
Kaskattama → Canada 57°3N 90°4W 71 B10
Kaskinen Finland 62°22N 21°15E 8 E19
Kaskö = Kaskinen
  Finland 62°22N 21°15E 8 E19
Kaslo Canada 49°55N 116°55W 70 D5
Kasmere L. Canada 59°34N 101°10W 71 B8
Kasongo
  Dem. Rep. of the Congo 4°30S 26°33E 54 E5
Kasongo Lunda
  Dem. Rep. of the Congo 6°35S 16°49E 54 F3
Kasos Greece 35°20N 26°55E 23 G12
Kassalâ Sudan 15°30N 36°0E 53 E13
Kassel Germany 51°18N 9°26E 16 C5
Kasson U.S.A. 44°2N 92°45W 80 C7
Kastamonu Turkey 41°25N 33°43E 19 F5
Kasterlee Belgium 51°15N 4°59E 15 C4
Kastoria Greece 40°30N 21°19E 23 D9
Kastrom Mefa'a = Umm al Rasas
  Jordan 31°30N 35°55E 48 D4

Kasumi Japan 35°38N 134°38E 29 G7
Kasur Pakistan 31°5N 74°25E 42 D6
Kata, Ao Thailand 7°48N 98°18E 39 a
Kata Tjuta Australia 25°20S 130°50E 61 E5
Katahdin, Mt. U.S.A. 45°54N 68°56W 81 C19
Kataka = Cuttack India 20°25N 85°57E 44 D7
Katanga
  Dem. Rep. of the Congo 8°0S 25°0E 54 F5
Katangi India 21°56N 79°50E 44 D4
Katanning Australia 33°40S 117°33E 61 F2
Katchall India 7°57N 93°22E 45 L11
Katerini Greece 40°18N 22°37E 23 D10
Katghora India 22°30N 82°33E 43 H9
Katha Burma 24°10N 96°30E 41 G20
Katherîna, Gebel Egypt 28°30N 33°57E 46 D2
Katherine Australia 14°27S 132°20E 60 B5
Katherine Gorge = Nitmiluk △
  Australia 14°6S 132°15E 60 B5
Kathi India 21°47N 74°3E 42 J6
Kathiawar India 22°20N 71°0E 42 H4
Kathmandu Nepal 27°45N 85°20E 43 F11
Kathua India 32°23N 75°34E 42 C6
Katihar India 25°34N 87°36E 43 G12
Katima Mulilo Namibia 17°28S 24°13E 56 A3
Katingan = Mendawai →
  Indonesia 3°30S 113°0E 36 E4
Katiola Ivory C. 8°10N 5°10W 52 G4
Katiti ☉ Australia 25°1S 131°11E 61 E5
Katmandu = Kathmandu
  Nepal 27°45N 85°20E 43 F11
Katni India 23°51N 80°24E 43 H9
Katol India 21°17N 78°38E 44 D4
Katoomba Australia 33°41S 150°19E 63 E5
Katowice Poland 50°17N 19°5E 17 C10
Katrine, L. U.K. 56°15N 4°30W 11 E4
Katrineholm Sweden 59°0N 16°12E 9 G17
Katsina Nigeria 13°0N 7°32E 52 F7
Katsumoto Japan 33°51N 129°42E 29 H4
Katsuura Japan 35°10N 140°20E 29 G10
Katsuyama Japan 36°3N 136°30E 29 F8
Kattegat Denmark 56°40N 11°20E 9 H14
Katwa India 23°30N 88°5E 43 H13
Katwijk Neths. 52°12N 4°24E 15 B4
Kau-Ye Kyun Burma 11°1N 98°32E 39 G2
Kaua'i U.S.A. 22°3N 159°30W 75 L8
Kaudom △ Namibia 18°45S 20°51E 56 A3
Kaufman U.S.A. 32°35N 96°19W 84 E6
Kauhajoki Finland 62°25N 22°10E 8 E20
Kaukauna U.S.A. 44°17N 88°17W 80 C9
Kaukauveld Namibia 20°0S 20°15E 56 B3
Ka'ula I. U.S.A. 21°40N 160°33W 75 L7
Kaunas Lithuania 54°54N 23°54E 9 J20
Kaunia Bangla. 25°46N 89°26E 43 G13
Kautokeino Norway 69°0N 23°4E 8 B20
Kauwapur India 27°31N 82°18E 43 F10
Kavacha Russia 60°16N 169°51E 27 C17
Kavala Greece 40°57N 24°28E 23 D11
Kavalerovo Russia 44°15N 135°4E 28 B7
Kavali India 14°55N 80°1E 45 G5
Kavār Iran 29°11N 52°44E 47 D7
Kavaratti I. India 10°34N 72°37E 45 J1
Kavaratti India 10°33N 72°38E 45 J1
Kavi India 22°12N 72°38E 42 H5
Kavimba Botswana 18°2S 24°38E 56 A3
Kavīr, Dasht-e Iran 34°30N 55°0E 47 C7
Kavīr ∩ Iran 34°40N 52°0E 47 C7
Kaw Fr. Guiana 4°30N 52°15W 93 C8
Kawagama L. Canada 45°18N 78°45W 82 A6
Kawagoe Japan 35°55N 139°29E 29 G9
Kawaguchi Japan 35°52N 139°45E 29 G9
Kawah Ijen △ Indonesia 8°3S 114°14E 37 H15
Kawanoe = Shikokuchūō
  Japan 34°1N 133°34E 29 G6
Kawardha India 22°0N 81°17E 43 J9
Kawasi Indonesia 1°38S 127°28E 37 E7
Kawawachikamach
  Canada 54°48N 66°50W 73 B6
Kawerau N.Z. 38°7S 176°42E 59 C6
Kawhia N.Z. 38°4S 174°49E 59 C5
Kawhia Harbour N.Z. 38°5S 174°51E 59 C5
Kawio, Kepulauan
  Indonesia 4°30N 125°30E 37 D7
Kawthaung Burma 10°5N 98°36E 39 H2
Kawthoolei = Kayin □
  Burma 18°0N 97°30E 41 L20
Kawthule = Kayin □
  Burma 18°0N 97°30E 41 L20
Kaya Burkina Faso 13°4N 1°10W 52 F5
Kayah □ Burma 19°15N 97°15E 41 K20
Kayak I. U.S.A. 59°56N 144°23W 74 D11
Kayamkulam India 9°10N 76°33E 45 K3
Kayan → Indonesia 2°55N 117°35E 36 D5
Kaycee U.S.A. 43°43N 106°38W 76 E10
Kayeli Indonesia 3°20S 127°10E 37 E7
Kayenta U.S.A. 36°44N 110°15W 77 H8
Kayes Mali 14°25N 11°30W 52 F3
Kayin □ Burma 18°0N 97°30E 41 L20
Kayoa Indonesia 0°1N 127°28E 37 D7
Kayseri Turkey 38°45N 35°30E 46 B2
Kaysville U.S.A. 41°2N 111°56W 76 F8
Kayts Sri Lanka 9°42N 79°51E 45 K4
Kazachye Russia 70°52N 135°58E 27 B14
Kazakhstan ■ Asia 50°0N 70°0E 26 E8
Kazan Russia 55°50N 49°10E 18 C8
Kazan → Canada 64°2N 95°29W 71 A9
Kazan-Rettō Pac. Oc. 25°0N 141°0E 64 E6
Kazanlŭk Bulgaria 42°38N 25°20E 23 C11
Kazatin = Kozyatyn
  Ukraine 49°45N 28°50E 17 D15
Kāzerūn Iran 29°38N 51°40E 47 D6
Kazi Magomed = Qazimämmäd
  Azerbaijan 40°3N 49°0E 47 A6
Kazipet India 17°58N 79°30E 44 E4
Kazuno Japan 40°10N 140°45E 28 D10
Kazym → Russia 63°54N 65°50E 26 C7
Kea Greece 37°35N 24°22E 23 F11
Keady U.K. 54°15N 6°42W 10 B5
Kearney U.S.A. 40°42N 99°5W 80 E4
Kearney Australia 20°10S 128°4E 60 D4

Kearny U.S.A. 33°3N 110°55W 77 K8
Kearsarge, Mt. U.S.A. 43°22N 71°50W 83 C13
Keban Turkey 38°50N 38°50E 19 G6
Keban Baraji Turkey 38°41N 38°33E 46 B3
Kebnekaise Sweden 67°53N 18°33E 8 C18
Kebri Dehar Ethiopia 6°45N 44°17E 49 F3
Kebumen Indonesia 7°42S 109°40E 37 G13
Kechika → Canada 59°41N 127°12W 70 B3
Kecskemét Hungary 46°57N 19°42E 17 E10
Kedah □ Malaysia 5°50N 100°40E 39 K3
Kedainiai Lithuania 55°15N 24°2E 9 J21
Kedarnath India 30°44N 79°4E 43 D8
Kedgwick Canada 47°40N 67°20W 73 C6
Kediri Indonesia 7°51S 112°1E 37 G15
Keeler U.S.A. 36°29N 117°52W 78 J9
Keeley L. Canada 54°54N 108°8W 71 C7
Keeling Is. = Cocos Is.
  Ind. Oc. 12°10S 96°55E 64 J1
Keelung = Chilung
  Taiwan 25°3N 121°45E 35 E13
Keene Canada 44°15N 78°10W 82 B6
Keene Calif., U.S.A. 35°13N 118°33W 79 K8
Keene N.H., U.S.A. 42°56N 72°17W 83 D12
Keene N.Y., U.S.A. 44°16N 73°46W 83 B11
Keep River △ Australia 15°49S 129°8E 60 C4
Keeper Hill Ireland 52°45N 8°16E 10 D3
Keerweer, C. Australia 14°0S 141°32E 62 A3
Keeseville U.S.A. 44°29N 73°30W 83 B11
Keetmanshoop Namibia 26°35S 18°8E 56 C2
Keewatin Canada 49°46N 94°34W 71 D10
Keewatin → Canada 56°29N 100°46W 71 B8
Kefalonia Greece 38°15N 20°30E 23 E9
Kefamenanu Indonesia 9°28S 124°29E 37 F6
Kefar Sava Israel 32°11N 34°54E 48 C3
Keffi Nigeria 8°55N 7°43E 52 G7
Keflavík Iceland 64°2N 22°35W 8 D2
Keg River Canada 57°54N 117°55W 70 B5
Kegalla Sri Lanka 7°15N 80°21E 45 L5
Kegaska Canada 50°9N 61°18W 73 B7
Keighley U.K. 53°52N 1°54W 12 D6
Keila Estonia 59°18N 24°25E 9 G21
Keimoes S. Africa 28°41S 20°59E 56 C3
Keitele Finland 63°10N 26°20E 8 E22
Keith Australia 36°6S 140°20E 63 F3
Keith U.K. 57°32N 2°57W 11 D6
Keiyasi Fiji 17°53S 177°46E 59 a
Keizer U.S.A. 44°57N 123°1W 76 D2
Kejimkujik △ Canada 44°25N 65°25W 73 D6
Kejserr Franz Joseph Fd.
  Greenland 73°30N 24°30W 4 B6
Kekri India 26°0N 75°10E 42 G6
Kelan China 38°43N 111°31E 32 E6
Kelang = Klang Malaysia 3°2N 101°26E 39 L3
Kelani Ganga → Sri Lanka 6°58N 79°50E 45 L4
Kelantan □ Malaysia 5°10N 102°0E 39 K4
Kelantan → Malaysia 6°13N 102°14E 39 J4
Kelkit Turkey 40°45N 36°32E 19 F6
Kellerberrin Australia 31°36S 117°38E 61 F2
Kellett, C. Canada 72°0N 126°0W 4 B1
Kelleys I. U.S.A. 41°36N 82°42W 82 E2
Kellogg U.S.A. 47°32N 116°7W 76 C5
Kells Ireland 53°44N 6°53W 10 C5
Kélo Chad 9°10N 15°45E 53 G9
Kelowna Canada 49°50N 119°25W 70 D5
Kelsey Creek Australia 20°26S 148°31E 62 b
Kelseyville U.S.A. 38°59N 122°50W 78 G4
Kelso N.Z. 45°54S 169°15E 59 F2
Kelso U.K. 55°36N 2°26W 11 F6
Kelso U.S.A. 46°9N 122°54W 78 D4
Keluang = Kluang
  Malaysia 2°3N 103°18E 39 L4
Kelvington Canada 52°10N 103°30W 71 C8
Kem → Russia 64°57N 34°41E 18 B5
Kema Indonesia 1°22N 125°8E 37 D7
Kemah Turkey 39°32N 39°5E 46 B3
Kemaman Malaysia 4°12N 103°18E 39 K4
Kemano Canada 53°35N 128°0W 70 C3
Kemasik Malaysia 4°25N 103°27E 39 K4
Kemerovo Russia 55°20N 86°5E 26 D9
Kemi Finland 65°44N 24°34E 8 D21
Kemi älv = Kemijoki →
  Finland 65°47N 24°32E 8 D21
Kemi träsk = Kemijärvi
  Finland 66°43N 27°22E 8 C22
Kemijärvi Finland 66°43N 27°22E 8 C22
Kemijoki → Finland 65°47N 24°32E 8 D21
Kemmerer U.S.A. 41°48N 110°32W 76 F8
Kemp, L. U.S.A. 33°46N 99°9W 84 E5
Kemp Land Antarctica 69°0S 55°0E 5 C5
Kempas Malaysia 1°33N 103°42E 39 d
Kempsey Australia 31°1S 152°50E 63 E5
Kempt, L. Canada 47°25N 74°22W 72 C5
Kempten Germany 47°45N 10°17E 16 E6
Kempton Australia 42°31S 147°12E 63 G4
Kemptville Canada 45°0N 75°38W 83 B9
Ken → India 25°13N 80°27E 43 G9
Kenai U.S.A. 60°33N 151°16W 68 E1
Kenai Mts. U.S.A. 60°0N 150°0W 74 D9
Kendai India 22°45N 82°37E 43 H10
Kendal Indonesia 6°56S 110°14E 37 G14
Kendal U.K. 54°20N 2°44W 12 C5
Kendall Australia 31°35S 152°44E 63 E5
Kendall → Australia 14°4S 141°35E 62 A3
Kendallville U.S.A. 41°27N 85°16W 81 E11
Kendari Indonesia 3°50S 122°30E 37 E6
Kendawangan Indonesia 2°32S 110°17E 36 E4
Kendi, Pulau Malaysia 5°13N 100°11E 39 c
Kendrapara India 20°35N 86°30E 44 D8
Kendrew S. Africa 32°32S 24°30E 56 D3
Kene Thao Laos 17°44N 101°10E 38 D3
Kenedy U.S.A. 28°49N 97°51W 84 G6
Kenema S. Leone 7°50N 11°14E 52 G3
Keng Kok Laos 16°26N 105°12E 38 D5
Keng Tawng Burma 20°45N 98°18E 41 J21
Keng Tung Burma 21°18N 99°39E 38 B2
Kenhardt S. Africa 29°19S 21°12E 56 D3
Kenitra Morocco 34°15N 6°40W 52 B4
Kenli China 37°30N 118°20E 33 F10

Kenmare Ireland 51°53N 9°36W 10 E2
Kenmare U.S.A. 48°41N 102°5W 80 A2
Kenmare River → Ireland 51°48N 9°51W 10 E2
Kennebago Lake U.S.A. 45°4N 70°40W 83 A14
Kennebec U.S.A. 43°54N 99°52W 80 D4
Kennebec → U.S.A. 43°45N 69°46W 81 D19
Kennebunk U.S.A. 43°23N 70°33W 83 C14
Kennedy Zimbabwe 18°52S 27°10E 56 A4
Kennedy Channel Arctic 80°50N 66°0W 69 A18
Kennedy Ra. Australia 24°45S 115°10E 61 D2
Kennedy Range △ Australia 24°34S 115°2E 61 D2
Kennemerduinen △ Neths. 52°27N 4°33E 15 B4
Kennet → U.K. 51°27N 0°57W 13 F7
Kenneth Ra. Australia 23°50S 117°8E 61 D2
Kennett U.S.A. 36°14N 90°3W 80 G8
Kennewick U.S.A. 46°12N 119°7W 76 C4
Kennisis Lake Canada 45°13N 78°36W 82 A6
Kenogami → Canada 51°6N 84°28W 72 B3
Kenora Canada 49°47N 94°29W 71 D10
Kenosha U.S.A. 42°35N 87°49W 80 D10
Kensington Canada 46°28N 63°34W 73 C7
Kent Ohio, U.S.A. 41°9N 81°22W 82 E3
Kent Tex., U.S.A. 31°4N 104°13W 84 F2
Kent Wash., U.S.A. 47°22N 122°14W 78 C4
Kent □ U.K. 51°12N 0°40E 13 F8
Kent Group Australia 39°30S 147°20E 63 F4
Kent Pen. Canada 68°30N 107°0W 68 D10
Kentaū Kazakhstan 43°32N 68°36E 26 E7
Kentland U.S.A. 40°46N 87°27W 80 E10
Kenton U.S.A. 40°39N 83°37W 81 E12
Kentucky □ U.S.A. 37°0N 84°0W 81 G11
Kentucky → U.S.A. 38°41N 85°11W 81 F11
Kentucky L. U.S.A. 37°1N 88°16W 80 G9
Kentville Canada 45°6N 64°29W 73 C7
Kentwood U.S.A. 30°56N 90°31W 85 F9
Kenya ■ Africa 1°0N 38°0E 54 D7
Kenya, Mt. Kenya 0°10S 37°18E 54 E7
Kenyir, Tasik Malaysia 5°1N 102°54E 39 K4
Keo Neua, Deo Vietnam 18°23N 105°10E 38 C5
Keokuk U.S.A. 40°24N 91°24W 80 E8
Keoladeo △ India 27°0N 77°20E 42 F7
Keonjhargarh India 21°28N 85°35E 43 J11
Kep Cambodia 10°29N 104°19E 39 G5
Kep Vietnam 21°24N 106°16E 38 B6
Kep △ Cambodia 10°30N 104°18E 39 G5
Kepala Batas Malaysia 5°31N 100°26E 39 c
Kepi Indonesia 6°32S 139°19E 37 F9
Kerala □ India 11°0N 76°15E 45 J3
Kerama-Rettō Japan 26°5N 127°15E 29 L3
Keran Pakistan 34°35N 73°59E 43 B5
Kerang Australia 35°40S 143°55E 63 F3
Keraudren, C. Australia 19°58S 119°45E 60 C2
Kerch Ukraine 45°20N 36°20E 19 E6
Kerepakupai-Meru = Angel Falls Venezuela 5°57N 62°30W 92 B6
Kerguelen Ind. Oc. 49°15S 69°10E 3 G13
Kerian, Kuala Malaysia 5°10N 100°25E 39 c
Kericho Kenya 0°22S 35°15E 54 E7
Kerinci Indonesia 1°40S 101°15E 36 E2
Kerki = Atamyrat Turkmenistan 37°50N 65°12E 26 F7
Kerkrade Neths. 50°53N 6°4E 15 D6
Kerkyra Greece 39°38N 19°50E 23 E8
Kermadec Is. Pac. Oc. 30°0S 178°15W 58 E11
Kermadec Trench Pac. Oc. 30°30S 176°0W 64 L10
Kermān Iran 30°15N 57°1E 47 D8
Kerman U.S.A. 36°43N 120°4W 78 J6
Kermān □ Iran 30°0N 57°0E 47 D8
Kermān, Bīābān-e Iran 28°45N 59°45E 47 D8
Kermānshāh Iran 34°23N 47°0E 46 C5
Kermānshāh □ Iran 34°0N 46°30E 46 C5
Kermit U.S.A. 31°52N 103°6W 84 F3
Kern → U.S.A. 35°16N 119°18W 79 K7
Kernow = Cornwall □ U.K. 50°26N 4°40W 13 G3
Kernville U.S.A. 35°45N 118°26W 79 K8
Keroh Malaysia 5°43N 101°1E 39 K3
Kerrera U.K. 56°24N 5°33W 11 E3
Kerrobert Canada 51°56N 109°8W 71 C7
Kerrville U.S.A. 30°3N 99°8W 84 F5
Kerry □ Ireland 52°7N 9°35W 10 D2
Kerry Hd. Ireland 52°25N 9°56W 10 D2
Kerulen = Herlen → Asia 48°48N 117°0E 31 B12
Kerzaz Algeria 29°29N 1°37W 52 C5
Kesagami → Canada 51°40N 79°45W 72 B4
Kesagami L. Canada 50°23N 80°15W 72 B3
Keşan Turkey 40°49N 26°38E 23 D12
Kesennuma Japan 38°54N 141°35E 28 E10
Keshit Iran 29°43N 58°17E 47 D8
Kesigi = Kosgi India 15°51N 77°16E 45 G3
Keskal India 20°5N 81°35E 44 D5
Kestenga Russia 65°50N 31°45E 8 D24
Keswick U.K. 54°36N 3°8W 12 C4
Ket → Russia 58°55N 81°32E 26 D9
Ketapang Jawa Timur, Indonesia 8°9S 114°23E 37 J17
Ketapang Kalimantan Barat, Indonesia 1°55S 110°0E 36 E4
Ketchikan U.S.A. 55°21N 131°39W 70 B2
Ketchum U.S.A. 43°41N 114°22W 76 E6
Ketef, Khalîg Umm el Egypt 23°40N 35°35E 46 F2
Keti Bandar Pakistan 24°8N 67°27E 42 G2
Ketri India 28°1N 75°50E 42 E6
Kętrzyn Poland 54°7N 21°22E 17 A11
Kettering U.K. 52°24N 0°43W 13 E7
Kettering U.S.A. 39°41N 84°10W 81 F11
Kettle → Canada 56°40N 89°34W 71 B11
Kettle Falls U.S.A. 48°37N 118°3W 76 B4
Kettle Point Canada 43°10N 82°1W 82 C2
Kettle Pt. Canada 43°13N 82°1W 82 C2
Kettleman City U.S.A. 36°1N 119°58W 78 J7
Keuka L. U.S.A. 42°30N 77°9W 82 D7
Keuruu Finland 62°16N 24°41E 8 E21
Kewanee U.S.A. 41°14N 89°56W 80 E9
Keware Nepal 27°57N 83°47E 43 F10
Kewaunee U.S.A. 44°27N 87°31W 80 C10
Keweenaw B. U.S.A. 47°0N 88°15W 80 B9
Keweenaw Pen. U.S.A. 47°15N 88°15W 80 B9
Keweenaw Pt. U.S.A. 47°25N 87°43W 80 B10
Key, L. Ireland 54°0N 8°15W 10 C3
Key Lake Mine Canada 57°5N 105°32W 71 B7
Key Largo U.S.A. 25°5N 80°27W 85 J14
Key West U.S.A. 24°33N 81°48W 88 B3
Keynsham U.K. 51°24N 2°29W 13 F5
Keyser U.S.A. 39°26N 78°59W 81 F14
Kezhma Russia 58°59N 101°9E 27 D11
Kezi Zimbabwe 20°58S 28°32E 57 B4
Kgalagadi □ Botswana 24°30S 22°0E 56 B3
Kgalagadi Transfrontier ⌂ Africa 25°10S 21°0E 56 C3
Khabarovsk Russia 48°30N 135°5E 31 B16
Khabr △ Iran 28°51N 56°22E 47 D8
Khābūr → Syria 35°17N 40°35E 46 C4
Khachmas = Xaçmaz Azerbaijan 41°31N 48°42E 19 F8
Khachrod India 23°25N 75°20E 42 H6
Khadro Pakistan 26°11N 68°50E 42 F3
Khadzhilyangar = Dahongliutan China 35°45N 79°20E 43 B8
Khaga India 25°47N 81°7E 43 G9
Khagaria India 25°30N 86°32E 43 G12
Khaipur Pakistan 29°34N 72°17E 42 E5
Khair India 27°57N 77°46E 42 F7
Khairabad India 27°33N 80°47E 43 F9
Khairagarh India 21°27N 81°2E 43 J9
Khairpur Pakistan 27°32N 68°49E 42 F3
Khairpur Nathan Shah Pakistan 27°6N 67°44E 42 F2
Khairwara India 23°58N 73°38E 42 H5
Khaisor → Pakistan 31°17N 68°59E 42 D3
Khajuraho India 24°51N 79°55E 43 G8
Khajuri Kach Pakistan 32°4N 69°51E 42 C3
Khakassia □ Russia 53°0N 90°0E 26 D9
Khakhea Botswana 24°48S 23°22E 56 B3
Khalafābād Iran 30°54N 49°24E 47 D6
Khalilabad India 26°48N 83°5E 43 F10
Khalīlī Iran 27°38N 53°17E 47 E7
Khalkhāl Iran 37°37N 48°32E 47 B6
Khalkís = Chalkida Greece 38°27N 23°42E 23 E10
Khalmer Yu Russia 67°58N 65°1E 26 C7
Khalturin Russia 58°40N 48°50E 18 C8
Khalūf Oman 20°30N 58°13E 49 C6
Kham Keut Laos 18°15N 104°43E 38 C5
Khamaria India 23°5N 80°48E 43 H9
Khambhaliya India 22°14N 69°41E 42 H3
Khambhat India 22°23N 72°33E 42 H5
Khambhat, G. of India 20°45N 72°30E 40 J8
Khamgaon India 20°42N 76°37E 44 D3
Khamīr Iran 26°57N 55°36E 47 E7
Khamir Yemen 16°2N 44°0E 49 D3
Khamīs Mushayţ Si. Arabia 18°18N 42°44E 49 D3
Khammam India 17°11N 80°6E 44 F5
Khamsa Egypt 30°27N 32°23E 48 E1
Khan → Namibia 22°37S 14°56E 56 B2
Khān Abū Shāmat Syria 33°39N 36°53E 48 B5
Khān Azād Iraq 33°7N 44°22E 46 C5
Khān Mujiddah Iraq 32°21N 43°48E 46 C4
Khān Shaykhūn Syria 35°26N 36°38E 46 C3
Khan Tengri, Pik Asia 42°12N 80°10E 30 C5
Khān Yūnis Gaza Strip 31°21N 34°18E 48 D3
Khanai Pakistan 30°30N 67°8E 42 D2
Khānaqīn Iraq 34°23N 45°25E 46 C5
Khānbāghī Iran 36°10N 55°25E 47 B7
Khandwa India 21°49N 76°22E 44 D3
Khandyga Russia 62°42N 135°35E 27 C14
Khanewal Pakistan 30°20N 71°55E 42 D4
Khangah Dogran Pakistan 31°50N 73°37E 42 D5
Khangchendzonga = Kanchenjunga △ India 27°42N 88°8E 43 F13
Khanh Duong Vietnam 12°44N 108°44E 38 F7
Khaniá = Chania Greece 35°30N 24°4E 23 G11
Khaniadhana India 25°1N 78°8E 42 G8
Khanka, L. Asia 45°0N 132°24E 28 B6
Khankendy = Xankändi Azerbaijan 39°52N 46°49E 46 B5
Khanna India 30°42N 76°16E 42 D7
Khanozai Pakistan 30°37N 67°19E 42 D2
Khanpur Pakistan 28°42N 70°35E 42 E4
Khanty-Mansiysk Russia 61°0N 69°0E 26 C7
Khao Khitchakut △ Thailand 12°50N 102°10E 38 F4
Khao Laem △ Thailand 14°56N 98°31E 38 E2
Khao Laem Res. Thailand 14°50N 98°30E 38 E2
Khao Lak △ Malaysia 8°38N 98°18E 39 H2
Khao Luang △ Thailand 8°34N 99°42E 39 H2
Khao Nam Khang △ Thailand 6°32N 100°35E 39 J3
Khao Phlu Thailand 9°29N 99°59E 39 b
Khao Pu -Khao Ya △ Thailand 7°26N 99°57E 39 J2
Khao Sam Roi Yot △ Thailand 12°13N 99°57E 39 F2
Khao Sok △ Thailand 8°55N 98°38E 39 H2
Khao Yai △ Thailand 14°21N 101°29E 38 E3
Khaoen Si Nakarin △ Thailand 14°47N 99°0E 38 E2
Khapalu Pakistan 35°10N 76°20E 43 B7
Khapcheranga Russia 49°42N 112°24E 27 E12
Khaptao △ Nepal 29°20N 81°10E 43 E9
Kharaghoda India 23°11N 71°46E 42 H4
Kharagpur India 22°20N 87°25E 43 H12
Kharan Kalat Pakistan 28°34N 65°21E 40 E4
Kharānaq Iran 32°20N 54°45E 47 C7
Kharda India 18°40N 75°34E 44 E2
Khardung La India 34°20N 77°43E 43 B7
Kharg = Khārk, Jazīreh-ye Iran 29°15N 50°28E 47 D6
Khârga, El Wâhât el Egypt 25°10N 30°35E 53 C12
Khargon India 21°45N 75°40E 44 D2
Khari → India 25°54N 74°31E 42 G6
Kharian Pakistan 32°49N 73°52E 42 C5
Khariar India 20°17N 82°46E 44 D6
Khārk, Jazīreh-ye Iran 29°15N 50°28E 47 D6
Kharkiv Ukraine 49°58N 36°20E 19 E6
Kharkov = Kharkiv Ukraine 49°58N 36°20E 19 E6
Kharovsk Russia 59°56N 40°13E 18 C7
Kharsawangarh India 22°48N 85°50E 43 H11
Kharta Turkey 40°55N 29°7E 23 D13
Khartoum = El Khartûm Sudan 15°31N 32°35E 53 E12
Khartum Canada 45°15N 77°5W 82 A7
Khasan Russia 42°25N 130°40E 28 C5
Khāsh Iran 28°15N 61°15E 47 D9
Khashm el Girba Sudan 14°59N 35°58E 53 F13
Khaskovo Bulgaria 41°56N 25°30E 23 D11
Khat, Laem Thailand 8°6N 98°26E 39 a
Khatanga Russia 72°0N 102°20E 27 B11
Khatanga → Russia 72°55N 106°0E 27 B11
Khatauli India 29°17N 77°43E 42 E7
Khatra India 22°59N 86°51E 43 H12
Khātūnābād Iran 30°1N 55°25E 47 D7
Khatyrka Russia 62°3N 175°15E 27 C18
Khavda India 23°51N 69°43E 42 H3
Khawr Fakkān U.A.E. 25°21N 56°22E 47 E8
Khaybar, Ḩarrat Si. Arabia 25°30N 39°45E 46 E4
Khāzimiyah Iraq 34°46N 43°37E 46 C4
Khe Bo Vietnam 19°8N 104°41E 38 C5
Khe Long Vietnam 21°29N 104°46E 38 B5
Khe Sanh Vietnam 16°37N 106°45E 38 D6
Khed Maharashtra, India 17°43N 73°27E 44 F1
Khed Maharashtra, India 18°51N 73°56E 44 E1
Khed Brahma India 24°7N 73°5E 42 G5
Khekra India 28°52N 77°20E 42 E7
Khemarak Phouminville = Krong Kaoh Kong Cambodia 11°37N 102°59E 39 G4
Khemisset Morocco 33°50N 6°1W 52 B4
Khemmarat Thailand 16°10N 105°15E 38 D5
Khenāmān Iran 30°27N 56°29E 47 D8
Khenchela Algeria 35°28N 7°11E 52 A7
Khersān → Iran 31°33N 50°22E 47 D6
Kherson Ukraine 46°35N 32°35E 19 E5
Kheta → Russia 71°54N 102°6E 27 B11
Khewari Pakistan 26°36N 68°52E 42 F3
Khilchipur India 24°2N 76°34E 42 G7
Khilok Russia 51°30N 110°45E 27 D12
Khíos = Chios Greece 38°27N 26°9E 23 E12
Khirsadoh India 22°11N 78°47E 43 H8
Khiuma = Hiiumaa Estonia 58°50N 22°45E 9 G20
Khiva = Xiva Uzbekistan 41°30N 60°18E 26 E7
Khlong Khlung Thailand 16°12N 99°43E 38 D2
Khlong Lan △ Thailand 16°12N 99°13E 38 D2
Khlong Phanom △ Thailand 8°45N 98°38E 39 H2
Khmelnik Ukraine 49°33N 27°58E 17 D14
Khmelnytskyy Ukraine 49°23N 27°0E 17 D14
Khmelnytskyy □ Ukraine 49°50N 26°40E 17 D14
Khmer Rep. = Cambodia ■ Asia 12°15N 105°0E 38 F5
Khoai, Hon Vietnam 8°26N 104°50E 39 H5
Khobar = Al Khubar Si. Arabia 26°17N 50°12E 47 E6
Khodoriv Ukraine 49°24N 24°19E 17 D13
Khodzent = Khŭjand Tajikistan 40°17N 69°37E 26 E7
Khojak Pass Afghan. 30°51N 66°34E 42 D2
Khok Kloi Thailand 8°17N 98°19E 39 a
Khok Pho Thailand 6°43N 101°6E 39 J3
Khok Samrong Thailand 15°3N 100°43E 38 E3
Kholm Russia 57°10N 31°15E 18 C5
Kholmsk Russia 47°40N 142°5E 27 E15
Khomas □ Namibia 23°30S 17°0E 56 B2
Khomas Hochland Namibia 22°40S 16°0E 56 B2
Khomeyn Iran 33°40N 50°7E 47 C6
Khomeynī Shahr Iran 32°41N 51°31E 47 C6
Khomodino Botswana 22°46S 23°52E 56 B3
Khon Kaen Thailand 16°30N 102°47E 38 D4
Khong → Cambodia 13°32N 105°58E 38 F5
Khong Sedone Laos 15°34N 105°49E 38 E5
Khonuu Russia 66°30N 143°12E 27 C15
Khoper → Russia 49°30N 42°20E 19 D6
Khorāsān-e Janūb □ Iran 32°0N 59°0E 47 C8
Khorāsān-e Razavī □ Iran 35°0N 59°0E 47 C8
Khorāsān-e Shemālī □ Iran 37°0N 57°0E 47 B8
Khorat = Nakhon Ratchasima Thailand 14°59N 102°12E 38 E4
Khorat, Cao Nguyen Thailand 15°30N 102°50E 38 E4
Khorixas Namibia 20°16S 14°59E 56 B1
Khorramābād Khorāsān, Iran 35°6N 57°57E 47 C8
Khorramābād Lorestān, Iran 33°30N 48°25E 47 C6
Khorramshahr Iran 30°29N 48°15E 47 D6
Khorugh Tajikistan 37°30N 71°36E 26 F8
Khosravī Iran 30°48N 51°28E 47 D6
Khosrowābād Khuzestān, Iran 30°10N 48°25E 47 D6
Khosrowābād Kordestān, Iran 35°31N 47°38E 46 C5
Khost Pakistan 30°13N 67°35E 42 D2
Khosūyeh Iran 28°32N 54°26E 47 D7
Khotang Nepal 27°1N 86°51E 43 F12
Khotyn Ukraine 48°31N 26°27E 17 D14
Khouribga Morocco 32°58N 6°57W 52 B4
Khowst Afghan. 33°22N 69°58E 42 C3
Khowst □ Afghan. 33°20N 70°0E 40 C6
Khoyniki Belarus 51°54N 29°55E 17 C15
Khram, Ko Thailand 12°42N 100°47E 38 F3
Khuan Wa Thailand 7°53N 98°17E 39 a
Khudzhand = Khŭjand Tajikistan 40°17N 69°37E 26 E7
Khuff Si. Arabia 24°55N 44°53E 46 E5
Khūgīānī Afghan. 31°34N 66°32E 42 D2
Khuis Botswana 26°40S 21°49E 56 C3
Khuiyala India 27°9N 70°25E 42 F4
Khŭjand Tajikistan 40°17N 69°37E 26 E7
Khujner India 23°47N 76°36E 42 H7
Khukhan Thailand 14°42N 104°12E 38 E5
Khulna Bangla. 22°45N 89°34E 41 H16
Khulna □ Bangla. 22°25N 89°35E 41 H16
Khumago Botswana 20°26S 24°32E 56 B3
Khunjerab △ Pakistan 36°40N 75°30E 43 A6
Khunjerab Pass = Kinjirap Daban Asia 36°40N 75°25E 40 A9
Khūnsorkh Iran 27°9N 56°7E 47 E8
Khunti India 23°5N 85°17E 43 H11
Khūr Iran 32°55N 58°18E 47 C8
Khurai India 24°3N 78°23E 42 G8
Khurayş Si. Arabia 25°6N 48°2E 47 E6
Khurda India 20°11N 85°37E 44 D7
Khurja India 28°15N 77°58E 42 E7
Khūrmāl Iraq 35°18N 46°2E 46 C5
Khurr, Wādī al Iraq 32°3N 43°52E 46 C4
Khūsf Iran 32°46N 58°53E 47 C8
Khushab Pakistan 32°20N 72°20E 42 C5
Khust Ukraine 48°10N 23°18E 17 D12
Khutse ⌂ Botswana 23°31S 24°12E 56 B3
Khuzdar Pakistan 27°52N 66°30E 42 F2
Khūzestān □ Iran 31°0N 49°0E 47 D6
Khvāf Iran 34°33N 60°8E 47 C9
Khvājeh Iran 38°9N 46°35E 46 B5
Khvānsār Iran 29°56N 54°8E 47 D7
Khvor Iran 33°45N 55°0E 47 C7
Khvorgū Iran 27°34N 56°27E 47 E8
Khvormūj Iran 28°40N 51°30E 47 D6
Khvoy Iran 38°35N 45°0E 46 B5
Khwae Noi → Thailand 14°1N 99°32E 38 E2
Khyber Pakhtunkhwa □ Pakistan 34°0N 72°0E 42 C4
Khyber Pass Afghan. 34°10N 71°8E 42 B4
Kia Fiji 16°16S 179°8E 59 a
Kiadho → India 19°37N 77°40E 44 E3
Kiama Australia 34°40S 150°50E 63 E5
Kiamba Phil. 6°2N 124°46E 37 C6
Kiangsi = Jiangxi □ China 27°30N 116°0E 35 D11
Kiangsu = Jiangsu □ China 33°0N 120°0E 33 H11
Kibombo Dem. Rep. of the Congo 3°57S 25°53E 54 E5
Kibre Mengist Ethiopia 5°54N 38°59E 49 F2
Kıbrıs = Cyprus ■ Asia 35°0N 33°0E 46 C2
Kibwezi Kenya 2°27S 37°57E 54 E7
Kichha → India 28°41N 79°18E 43 E8
Kichmengskiy Gorodok Russia 59°59N 45°48E 18 B8
Kicking Horse Pass Canada 51°28N 116°16W 70 C5
Kidal Mali 18°26N 1°22E 52 E6
Kidderminster U.K. 52°24N 2°15W 13 E5
Kidnappers, C. N.Z. 39°38S 177°5E 59 C6
Kidsgrove U.K. 53°5N 2°14W 12 D5
Kidston Australia 18°52S 144°8E 62 B3
Kiel Germany 54°19N 10°8E 16 A6
Kiel Canal = Nord-Ostsee-Kanal Germany 54°12N 9°32E 16 A5
Kielce Poland 50°52N 20°42E 17 C11
Kielder Water U.K. 55°11N 2°31W 12 B5
Kieler Bucht Germany 54°35N 10°25E 16 A6
Kiev = Kyyiv Ukraine 50°30N 30°28E 17 C16
Kiffa Mauritania 16°37N 11°24W 52 E3
Kifrī Iraq 34°45N 45°0E 46 C5
Kigali Rwanda 1°59S 30°4E 54 E6
Kigoma-Ujiji Tanzania 4°55S 29°36E 54 E5
Kığzı Turkey 38°18N 43°25E 46 B4
Kihnu Estonia 58°9N 24°1E 9 G21
Kii-Sanchi Japan 34°20N 136°0E 29 G8
Kii-Suidō Japan 33°40N 134°45E 29 H7
Kikaiga-Shima Japan 28°19N 129°59E 29 K4
Kikiak = Rigolet Canada 54°10N 58°23W 73 B8
Kikinda Serbia 45°50N 20°30E 23 B9
Kikládhes = Cyclades Greece 37°0N 24°30E 23 F11
Kikuchi Japan 32°59N 130°47E 29 H5
Kikwit Dem. Rep. of the Congo 5°0S 18°45E 54 F3
Kilakkarai India 9°12N 78°47E 45 K4
Kilar India 33°6N 76°25E 42 C7
Kilbeggan Ireland 53°22N 7°30W 10 C4
Kilbrannan Sd. U.K. 55°37N 5°26W 11 F3
Kilbuck Mts. U.S.A. 60°36N 159°53W 74 C8
Kilchu N. Korea 40°57N 129°25E 33 D15
Kilcoy Australia 26°59S 152°30E 63 D5
Kildare Ireland 53°9N 6°55W 10 C5
Kildare □ Ireland 53°10N 6°50W 10 C5
Kildinstroy Russia 68°48N 33°6E 8 B25
Kilfinnane Ireland 52°21N 8°28W 10 D3
Kilgarvan Ireland 51°54N 9°27W 10 E2
Kilgore U.S.A. 32°23N 94°53W 84 E7
Kilifi Kenya 3°40S 39°48E 54 E7
Kilimanjaro Tanzania 3°7S 37°20E 54 E7
Kilindini Kenya 4°4S 39°40E 54 E7
Kilinochchi Sri Lanka 9°24N 80°25E 45 K5
Kilis Turkey 36°42N 37°6E 46 B3
Kiliya Ukraine 45°28N 29°16E 17 F15
Kilkee Ireland 52°41N 9°39W 10 D2
Kilkeel U.K. 54°7N 5°55W 10 B5
Kilkenny Ireland 52°39N 7°15W 10 D4
Kilkenny □ Ireland 52°35N 7°15W 10 D4
Kilkieran B. Ireland 53°20N 9°41W 10 C2
Kilkis Greece 40°58N 22°57E 23 D10
Killala Ireland 54°13N 9°13W 10 B2
Killala B. Ireland 54°16N 9°8W 10 B2
Killaloe Canada 45°33N 77°25W 82 A7
Killaloe Ireland 52°48N 8°28W 10 D3
Killarney Australia 28°20S 152°18E 63 D5
Killarney Canada 49°10N 99°40W 71 D9
Killarney Ireland 52°4N 9°30W 10 D2
Killarney △ Ireland 52°0N 9°33W 10 D2
Killary Harbour Ireland 53°38N 9°52W 10 C2
Killdeer U.S.A. 47°22N 102°45W 80 B2
Killeen U.S.A. 31°7N 97°44W 84 F6
Killin U.K. 56°28N 4°19W 11 E4
Killington Pk. U.S.A. 43°36N 72°49W 83 C12
Killini Greece 37°54N 22°25E 23 F10
Killiniq I. Canada 60°24N 64°37W 69 E19
Killorglin Ireland 52°6N 9°47W 10 D2
Killybegs Ireland 54°38N 8°26W 10 B3
Kilmarnock U.K. 55°37N 4°29W 11 F4
Kilmore Australia 37°25S 144°53E 63 F3
Kilmore Quay Ireland 52°10N 6°36W 10 D5
Kilosa Tanzania 6°48S 37°0E 54 F7
Kilrush Ireland 52°38N 9°29W 10 D2
Kiltan I. India 11°29N 73°0E 45 J1
Kilwa Kivinje Tanzania 8°45S 39°25E 54 F7
Kilwinning U.K. 55°39N 4°43W 11 F4
Kim U.S.A. 37°15N 103°21W 77 H12
Kimaam Indonesia 7°58S 138°53E 37 F9
Kimba Australia 33°8S 136°23E 63 E2
Kimball Nebr., U.S.A. 41°14N 103°40W 80 E2
Kimball S. Dak., U.S.A. 43°45N 98°57W 80 D4
Kimberley Australia 16°20S 127°0E 60 C4
Kimberley B.C., Canada 49°40N 115°59W 70 D5
Kimberley Ont., Canada 44°23N 80°32W 82 B4
Kimberley S. Africa 28°43S 24°46E 56 C3
Kimberly U.S.A. 42°32N 114°22W 76 E6
Kimch'aek N. Korea 40°40N 129°10E 33 D15
Kimhae = Gimhae S. Korea 35°14N 128°53E 33 G15
Kimmirut Canada 62°50N 69°50W 69 E18
Kimpese Dem. Rep. of the Congo 5°35S 14°26E 54 F2
Kimry Russia 56°55N 37°15E 18 C6
Kinabalu, Gunung Malaysia 6°3N 116°14E 36 C5
Kinaskan L. Canada 57°38N 130°8W 70 B2
Kinbasket L. Canada 52°0N 118°10W 70 C5
Kincardine Canada 44°10N 81°40W 82 B3
Kincolith Canada 55°0N 129°57W 70 C3
Kinde U.S.A. 43°56N 83°0W 82 C2
Kinder Scout U.K. 53°24N 1°52W 12 D6
Kindersley Canada 51°30N 109°10W 71 C7
Kindia Guinea 10°0N 12°52W 52 F3
Kindu Dem. Rep. of the Congo 2°55S 25°50E 54 E5
Kineshma Russia 57°30N 42°5E 18 C7
King, L. Australia 33°10S 119°35E 61 F2
King, Mt. Australia 25°10S 147°30E 62 D4
King Christian I. Canada 77°48N 101°40W 69 B11
King City U.S.A. 36°13N 121°8W 78 J5
King Cr. → Australia 24°35S 139°30E 62 C2
King Edward → Australia 14°14S 126°35E 60 B4
King Edward Point S. Georgia 54°17S 36°30W 96 G9
King Frederick VI Land = Kong Frederik VI.s Kyst Greenland 63°0N 43°0W 4 C5
King George B. Falk. Is. 51°30S 60°30W 96 G4
King George I. Antarctica 60°0S 60°0W 5 C18
King George Is. Canada 57°20N 80°30W 69 F15
King George Sd. Australia 35°5S 118°0E 61 G2
King I. = Kadan Kyun Burma 12°30N 98°20E 38 F2
King I. Australia 39°50S 144°0E 63 F3
King I. Canada 52°10N 127°40W 70 C3
King Khalid Military City = Madinat al Malik Khālid al Askarīyah Si. Arabia 27°54N 45°31E 46 E5
King Leopold Ranges Australia 17°30S 125°45E 60 C4
King of Prussia U.S.A. 40°5N 75°23W 83 F9
King Sd. Australia 16°50S 123°20E 60 C3
King Sejong Antarctica 62°30S 58°0W 5 C18
King Shaka = Durban ✈ (DIA) S. Africa 29°37S 31°27E 57 C5
King William I. Canada 69°10N 97°25W 68 D12
King William's Town S. Africa 32°51S 27°22E 56 D4
Kingaok = Bathurst Inlet Canada 66°50N 108°1W 68 D10
Kingaroy Australia 26°32S 151°51E 63 D5
Kingfisher U.S.A. 35°52N 97°56W 84 D6
Kingirbān Iraq 34°40N 44°54E 46 C5
Kingisepp = Kuressaare Estonia 58°15N 22°30E 9 G20
Kingisepp Russia 59°25N 28°40E 9 G23
Kingman Ariz., U.S.A. 35°12N 114°4W 79 K12
Kingman Kans., U.S.A. 37°39N 98°7W 80 G4
Kingoonya Australia 30°55S 135°19E 63 E2
Kingri Pakistan 30°27N 69°49E 42 D3
Kings → U.S.A. 36°3N 119°50W 78 J7
Kings Canyon Australia 24°15S 131°34E 60 D5
Kings Canyon △ U.S.A. 36°50N 118°40W 78 J8
King's Lynn U.K. 52°45N 0°24E 12 E8
Kings Park U.S.A. 40°53N 73°16W 83 F11
Kings Peak U.S.A. 40°46N 110°23W 76 F8
Kingsbridge U.K. 50°17N 3°47W 13 G4
Kingsburg U.S.A. 36°31N 119°33W 78 J7
Kingscote Australia 35°40S 137°38E 63 F2
Kingscourt Ireland 53°54N 6°48W 10 C5
Kingsford U.S.A. 45°48N 88°4W 80 C9
Kingsland U.S.A. 30°48N 81°41W 85 F14
Kingsport U.S.A. 36°33N 82°33W 85 C13
Kingston Canada 44°14N 76°30W 83 B8
Kingston Jamaica 17°55N 76°50W 88 a
Kingston N.Z. 45°20S 168°43E 59 F2
Kingston N.H., U.S.A. 42°56N 71°3W 83 D13
Kingston N.Y., U.S.A. 41°56N 73°59W 83 E11
Kingston Pa., U.S.A. 41°16N 75°54W 83 E9
Kingston R.I., U.S.A. 41°29N 71°30W 83 E13
Kingston Pk. U.S.A. 35°44N 115°55W 79 K11
Kingston South East Australia 36°51S 139°55E 63 F2
Kingston upon Hull U.K. 53°45N 0°21W 12 D7
Kingston upon Hull □ U.K. 53°45N 0°21W 12 D7
Kingstown St. Vincent 13°10N 61°10W 89 D7
Kingstree U.S.A. 33°40N 79°50W 85 E15
Kingsville Canada 42°2N 82°45W 82 D2

Kingsville *U.S.A.* 27°31N 97°52W **84** H6
Kingussie *U.K.* 57°6N 4°2W **11** D4
Kingwood *U.S.A.* 30°2N 95°16W **84** F7
Kınık *Turkey* 39°6N 27°24E **23** E12
Kinistino *Canada* 52°57N 105°2W **71** C7
Kinjirap Daban *Asia* 36°40N 75°25E **40** A9
Kinkala *Congo* 4°18S 14°49E **54** E2
Kinki □ *Japan* 33°45N 136°0E **29** H8
Kinleith *N.Z.* 38°20S 175°56E **59** C5
Kinlochleven *U.K.* 56°43N 5°0W **11** E4
Kinmount *Canada* 44°48N 78°45W **82** B6
Kinna *Sweden* 57°32N 12°42E **9** H15
Kinnairds Hd. *U.K.* 57°43N 2°1W **11** D6
Kinngait *Canada* 64°14N 76°32W **69** E16
Kinniyai *Sri Lanka* 8°29N 81°11E **45** K5
Kino Nuevo *Mexico* 28°52N 112°33W **86** B2
Kinoje → *Canada* 52°8N 81°25W **72** B3
Kinomoto *Japan* 35°30N 136°13E **29** G8
Kinoosao *Canada* 57°5N 102°1W **71** B8
Kinross *U.K.* 56°13N 3°25W **11** E5
Kinsale *Ireland* 51°42N 8°31W **10** E3
Kinsale, Old Hd. of *Ireland* 51°37N 8°33W **10** E3
Kinsha = Chang Jiang → *China* 31°48N 121°10E **35** B13
Kinshasa *Dem. Rep. of the Congo* 4°20S 15°15E **54** E3
Kinsley *U.S.A.* 37°55N 99°25W **80** G4
Kinsman *U.S.A.* 41°26N 80°35W **82** E4
Kinston *U.S.A.* 35°16N 77°35W **85** D16
Kintamani *Indonesia* 8°14S 115°19E **37** J18
Kintore *U.K.* 57°14N 2°20W **11** D6
Kintore Ra. *Australia* 23°15S 128°47E **60** D4
Kintyre *U.K.* 55°30N 5°35W **11** F3
Kintyre, Mull of *U.K.* 55°17N 5°47W **11** F3
Kinushseo → *Canada* 55°15N 83°45W **72** A3
Kinuso *Canada* 55°20N 115°25W **70** B5
Kinvarra *Ireland* 53°8N 8°56W **10** C3
Kinwat *India* 19°38N 78°12E **44** E4
Kinzua *U.S.A.* 41°52N 78°58W **82** E6
Kiosk *Canada* 46°6N 78°53W **72** C4
Kiowa *Kans., U.S.A.* 37°1N 98°29W **80** G4
Kiowa *Okla., U.S.A.* 34°43N 95°54W **84** D7
Kipahigan L. *Canada* 55°20N 101°55W **71** B8
Kiparissia *Greece* 37°15N 21°40E **23** F9
Kiparissiakos Kolpos *Greece* 37°25N 21°25E **23** F9
Kipawa, L. *Canada* 46°50N 79°0W **72** C4
Kipling *Canada* 50°6N 102°38W **71** C8
Kippure *Ireland* 53°11N 6°21W **10** C5
Kipushi *Dem. Rep. of the Congo* 11°48S 27°12E **55** G5
Kirandul *India* 18°33N 81°10E **44** E5
Kirensk *Russia* 57°50N 107°55E **27** D11
Kirghiz Range *Asia* 42°40N 73°40E **30** C3
Kirghizia = Kyrgyzstan ■ *Asia* 42°0N 75°0E **26** E8
Kirgiziya Steppe *Eurasia* 50°0N 55°0E **19** E10
Kiri Buru *India* 22°0N 85°0E **44** D7
Kiribati ■ *Pac. Oc.* 3°0S 180°0E **58** E10
Kırıkkale *Turkey* 39°51N 33°32E **19** G5
Kirillov *Russia* 59°49N 38°24E **18** C6
Kirin = Jilin *China* 43°44N 126°30E **33** C14
Kirindi Oya → *Sri Lanka* 6°15N 81°20E **45** L5
Kirinyaga = Kenya, Mt. *Kenya* 0°10S 37°18E **54** E7
Kirirom △ *Cambodia* 11°18N 104°5E **39** G5
Kirishima *Japan* 31°44N 130°46E **29** J5
Kirishima Yaku △ *Japan* 31°24N 130°50E **29** J5
Kiritimati *Kiribati* 1°58N 157°27W **65** G12
Kirkby *U.K.* 53°30N 2°54W **12** D5
Kirkby-in-Ashfield *U.K.* 53°6N 1°14W **12** D6
Kirkby Lonsdale *U.K.* 54°12N 2°36W **12** C5
Kirkby Stephen *U.K.* 54°29N 2°21W **12** C5
Kirkcaldy *U.K.* 56°7N 3°9W **11** E5
Kirkcudbright *U.K.* 54°50N 4°2W **11** G4
Kirkenes *Norway* 69°40N 30°5E **8** B24
Kirkfield *Canada* 44°34N 78°59W **82** B6
Kirkintilloch *U.K.* 55°56N 4°8W **11** F4
Kirkjubæjarklaustur *Iceland* 63°47N 18°4W **8** E4
Kirkkonummi *Finland* 60°8N 24°26E **9** F21
Kirkland *U.S.A.* 47°40N 122°12W **78** C4
Kirkland Lake *Canada* 48°9N 80°2W **72** C3
Kırklareli *Turkey* 41°44N 27°15E **23** D12
Kirksville *U.S.A.* 40°12N 92°35W **80** E7
Kirkūk *Iraq* 35°30N 44°21E **46** C5
Kirkwall *U.K.* 58°59N 2°58W **11** C6
Kirkwood *S. Africa* 33°22S 25°15E **56** D4
Kirlampudi *India* 17°12N 82°12E **44** F6
Kirov *Russia* 58°35N 49°40E **18** C8
Kirovabad = Gäncä *Azerbaijan* 40°45N 46°20E **19** F8
Kirovograd = Kirovohrad *Ukraine* 48°35N 32°20E **19** E5
Kirovohrad *Ukraine* 48°35N 32°20E **19** E5
Kirovsk *Russia* 67°32N 33°41E **18** A5
Kirovskiy *Kamchatka, Russia* 54°27N 155°42E **27** D16
Kirovskiy *Primorsk, Russia* 45°7N 133°30E **28** B6
Kirriemuir *U.K.* 56°41N 3°1W **11** E5
Kirsanov *Russia* 52°35N 42°40E **18** D7
Kırşehir *Turkey* 39°14N 34°5E **46** B2
Kirthar △ *Pakistan* 25°45N 67°30E **42** F2
Kirthar Range *Pakistan* 27°0N 67°0E **42** F2
Kirtland *U.S.A.* 36°44N 108°21W **77** H9
Kiruna *Sweden* 67°52N 20°15E **8** C19
Kiryū *Japan* 36°24N 139°20E **29** F9
Kisangani *Dem. Rep. of the Congo* 0°35N 25°15E **54** D5
Kisar *Indonesia* 8°5S 127°10E **37** F7
Kisarazu *Japan* 35°23N 139°55E **29** G9
Kiselevsk *Russia* 54°5N 86°39E **26** D9
Kish = Qeys *Iran* 26°32N 53°58E **47** E7
Kishanganga → *Pakistan* 34°18N 73°28E **43** B5
Kishanganj *India* 26°3N 88°14E **43** F13
Kishangarh *Raj., India* 26°34N 74°52E **42** F6
Kishangarh *Raj., India* 27°50N 70°30E **42** F4
Kishinev = Chişinău *Moldova* 47°2N 28°50E **17** E15

Kishiwada *Japan* 34°28N 135°22E **29** G7
Kishtwar *India* 33°20N 75°48E **42** C6
Kisii *Kenya* 0°40S 34°45E **54** E6
Kiska I. *U.S.A.* 51°59N 177°30E **74** E3
Kiskőrös *Hungary* 46°37N 19°20E **17** E10
Kiskunfélegyháza *Hungary* 46°42N 19°53E **17** E10
Kiskunhalas *Hungary* 46°28N 19°37E **17** E10
Kislovodsk *Russia* 43°50N 42°45E **19** F7
Kismaayo *Somalia* 0°22S 42°32E **49** H3
Kiso-Gawa → *Japan* 35°20N 136°45E **29** G8
Kiso-Sammyaku *Japan* 35°45N 137°45E **29** G8
Kisofukushima *Japan* 35°52N 137°43E **29** G8
Kisofukushima *Japan* 35°52N 137°43E **29** G8
Kissamos *Guinea* 9°5N 10°5W **52** G3
Kissimmee *U.S.A.* 28°18N 81°24W **85** G14
Kissimmee → *U.S.A.* 27°9N 80°52W **85** H14
Kississing L. *Canada* 55°10N 101°20W **71** B8
Kisumu *Kenya* 0°3S 34°45E **54** E6
Kit Carson *U.S.A.* 38°46N 102°48W **76** G12
Kita *Mali* 13°5N 9°25W **52** F4
Kitaibaraki *Japan* 36°50N 140°45E **29** F10
Kitakami *Japan* 39°20N 141°10E **28** E10
Kitakami-Gawa → *Japan* 38°25N 141°19E **28** E10
Kitakami-Sammyaku *Japan* 39°30N 141°30E **28** E10
Kitakata *Japan* 37°39N 139°52E **28** F9
Kitakyūshū *Japan* 33°50N 130°50E **29** H5
Kitale *Kenya* 1°0N 35°0E **54** D7
Kitami *Japan* 43°48N 143°54E **28** C11
Kitami-Sammyaku *Japan* 44°22N 142°43E **28** B11
Kitchener *Canada* 43°27N 80°29W **82** C4
Kitee *Finland* 62°5N 30°8E **8** E24
Kitega = Gitega *Burundi* 3°26S 29°56E **54** E5
Kíthira = Kythira *Greece* 36°8N 23°0E **23** F10
Kithnos *Greece* 37°26N 24°27E **23** F11
Kitimat *Canada* 54°3N 128°38W **70** C3
Kitinen → *Finland* 67°14N 27°27E **8** C22
Kitsuki *Japan* 33°25N 131°37E **29** H5
Kittakittaooloo, L. *Australia* 28°3S 138°14E **63** D2
Kittanning *U.S.A.* 40°49N 79°31W **82** F5
Kittatinny Mt. *U.S.A.* 41°19N 74°39W **83** F10
Kittery *U.S.A.* 43°5N 70°45W **83** C14
Kittilä *Finland* 67°40N 24°51E **8** C21
Kitui *Kenya* 1°17S 38°0E **54** E7
Kitwanga *Canada* 55°6N 128°4W **70** B3
Kitwe *Zambia* 12°54S 28°13E **55** G5
Kivarli *India* 24°33N 72°46E **42** G5
Kivertsi *Ukraine* 50°50N 25°28E **17** C13
Kivu, L. *Dem. Rep. of the Congo* 1°48S 29°0E **54** E5
Kiwirrkurra *Australia* 22°49S 127°45E **60** D4
Kiwirrkurra ◉ *Australia* 22°49S 127°45E **60** D4
Kiyev = Kyyiv *Ukraine* 50°30N 30°28E **17** C16
Kiyevskoye Vdkhr. = Kyyivske Vdskh. *Ukraine* 51°0N 30°25E **17** C16
Kizel *Russia* 59°3N 57°40E **18** C10
Kizil Irmak → *Turkey* 41°44N 35°58E **19** F6
Kizil Jilga *China* 35°26N 78°50E **43** B8
Kızıldağ △ *Turkey* 38°5N 31°20E **46** B1
Kızıltepe *Turkey* 37°12N 40°35E **46** B4
Kizlyar *Russia* 43°51N 46°40E **19** F8
Kizyl-Arvat = Serdar *Turkmenistan* 39°4N 56°23E **47** B8
Kjölur *Iceland* 64°50N 19°25W **8** D4
Kladno *Czech Rep.* 50°10N 14°7E **16** C8
Klaeng *Thailand* 12°47N 101°39E **38** F3
Klagenfurt *Austria* 46°38N 14°20E **16** E8
Klaipėda *Lithuania* 55°43N 21°10E **9** J19
Klaksvík *Færoe Is.* 62°14N 6°35W **8** E9
Klamath → *U.S.A.* 41°33N 124°5W **76** F1
Klamath Falls *U.S.A.* 42°13N 121°46W **76** E3
Klamath Mts. *U.S.A.* 41°50N 123°20W **76** F2
Klamono *Indonesia* 1°8S 131°30E **37** E8
Klang *Malaysia* 3°2N 101°26E **39** L3
Klappan → *Canada* 58°0N 129°43W **70** B3
Klarälven → *Sweden* 59°23N 13°32E **9** G15
Klatovy *Czech Rep.* 49°23N 13°18E **16** D7
Klawer *S. Africa* 31°44S 18°36E **56** D2
Klazienaveen *Neths.* 52°44N 7°0E **15** B6
Kleena Kleene *Canada* 52°0N 124°59W **70** C4
Klein-Karas *Namibia* 27°33S 18°7E **56** C2
Kleinbegin *S. Africa* 28°54S 21°40E **56** C3
Klerksdorp *S. Africa* 26°53S 26°38E **56** C4
Kletsk = Klyetsk *Belarus* 53°5N 26°45E **17** B14
Kletskiy *Russia* 49°16N 43°11E **19** E7
Klickitat *U.S.A.* 45°49N 121°9W **76** D3
Klickitat → *U.S.A.* 45°42N 121°17W **78** E5
Klinaklini → *Canada* 51°21N 125°40W **70** C3
Klip → *S. Africa* 27°3S 29°3E **57** D4
Klipdale *S. Africa* 34°19S 19°57E **56** D2
Klipplaat *S. Africa* 33°1S 24°22E **56** D3
Kłodzko *Poland* 50°28N 16°38E **17** C9
Klondike *Canada* 64°0N 139°26W **68** E4
Klong Wang Chao △ *Thailand* 16°20N 99°9E **38** D2
Kluane △ *Canada* 60°45N 139°30W **70** A1
Kluane L. *Canada* 61°15N 138°40W **68** E4
Kluang *Malaysia* 2°3N 103°18E **39** L4
Kluczbork *Poland* 50°58N 18°12E **17** C10
Klukwan *U.S.A.* 59°24N 135°54W **70** B1
Klungkung *Indonesia* 8°32S 115°24E **37** K18
Klyetsk *Belarus* 53°5N 26°45E **17** B14
Klyuchevskaya, Gora *Russia* 55°50N 160°30E **27** D17
Klyuchi *Russia* 56°18N 160°51E **27** D17
Knaresborough *U.K.* 54°1N 1°28W **12** C6
Knee L. *Man., Canada* 55°3N 94°45W **72** A1
Knee L. *Sask., Canada* 55°51N 107°0W **71** B7
Knight Inlet *Canada* 50°45N 125°40W **70** C3
Knighton *U.K.* 52°21N 3°3W **13** E4
Knights Ferry *U.S.A.* 37°50N 120°40W **78** H6
Knights Landing *U.S.A.* 38°48N 121°43W **78** G5
Knob, C. *Australia* 34°32S 119°16E **61** F2
Knockmealdown Mts. *Ireland* 52°14N 7°56W **10** D4

Knokke-Heist *Belgium* 51°21N 3°17E **15** C3
Knossos *Greece* 35°16N 25°10E **23** G11
Knowlton *Canada* 45°13N 72°31W **83** A12
Knox *U.S.A.* 41°18N 86°37W **80** E10
Knox Coast *Antarctica* 66°30S 108°0E **5** C8
Knoxville *Iowa, U.S.A.* 41°19N 93°6W **80** E7
Knoxville *Pa., U.S.A.* 41°57N 77°27W **82** E7
Knoxville *Tenn., U.S.A.* 35°58N 83°55W **85** D13
Knud Rasmussen Land *Greenland* 78°0N 60°0W **69** B20
Knysna *S. Africa* 34°2S 23°2E **56** D3
Ko Kha *Thailand* 18°11N 99°24E **38** C2
Ko Tarutao △ *Thailand* 6°31N 99°26E **39** J2
Ko Yao *Thailand* 8°7N 98°35E **39** a
Koartac = Quaqtaq *Canada* 60°55N 69°40W **69** E18
Koba *Indonesia* 6°37S 134°37E **37** F8
Kobarid *Slovenia* 46°15N 13°30E **16** E7
Kobayashi *Japan* 31°56N 130°59E **29** J5
Kōbe *Japan* 34°41N 135°13E **29** G7
Kōbi-Sho *E. China Sea* 25°56N 123°41E **29** M1
Koblenz *Germany* 50°21N 7°36E **16** C4
Kobryn *Belarus* 52°15N 24°22E **17** B13
Kobuk → *U.S.A.* 66°54N 160°38W **74** B7
Kocaeli *Turkey* 40°45N 29°50E **19** F4
Kočani *Macedonia* 41°55N 22°25E **23** D10
Koch Bihar *India* 26°22N 89°29E **41** F16
Kochas *India* 25°15N 83°56E **43** G10
Kochi *India* 9°58N 76°20E **45** K3
Kōchi *Japan* 33°30N 133°35E **29** H6
Kōchi □ *Japan* 33°40N 133°30E **29** H6
Kochiu = Gejiu *China* 23°20N 103°10E **34** D5
Kodala *India* 19°38N 84°57E **44** E7
Kodarma *India* 24°28N 85°36E **43** G11
Koddiyar B. *Sri Lanka* 8°33N 81°15E **45** K5
Kodiak *U.S.A.* 57°47N 152°24W **74** D9
Kodiak I. *U.S.A.* 57°30N 152°45W **74** D9
Kodikkarai = Point Calimere *India* 10°17N 79°49E **45** J4
Kodinar *India* 20°46N 70°46E **42** J4
Kodinsk *Russia* 58°40N 99°10E **27** D10
Kodlipet *India* 12°48N 75°53E **45** H2
Kodungallur = Cranganore *India* 10°13N 76°13E **45** J3
Koedoesberge *S. Africa* 32°40S 20°11E **56** D3
Koes *Namibia* 26°0S 19°15E **56** C2
Koffiefontein *S. Africa* 29°30S 25°0E **56** C4
Kofiau *Indonesia* 1°11S 129°50E **37** E7
Kōfu *Japan* 35°40N 138°30E **29** G9
Koga *Japan* 36°11N 139°43E **29** F9
Kogaluc → *Canada* 56°12N 61°44W **73** A7
Køge *Denmark* 55°27N 12°11E **9** J15
Kogon *Uzbekistan* 39°43N 64°33E **26** F7
Koh-i-Khurd △ *Afghan.* 33°30N 65°59E **42** C1
Koh-i-Maran *Pakistan* 29°18N 66°50E **42** E2
Koh Ker *Cambodia* 13°47N 104°32E **38** F5
Koh Wai *Thailand* 11°54N 102°25E **39** H4
Kohat *Pakistan* 33°40N 71°29E **42** C4
Kohima *India* 25°35N 94°10E **41** G19
Kohkīlūyeh va Būyer Aḥmadī □ *Iran* 31°30N 50°30E **47** D6
Kohler Ra. *Antarctica* 77°0S 110°0W **5** D15
Kohlu *Pakistan* 29°54N 69°15E **42** E3
Kohtla-Järve *Estonia* 59°20N 27°20E **9** G22
Koi Sanjaq *Iraq* 36°5N 44°38E **46** B5
Koihoa *India* 8°12N 93°29E **45** K11
Koilkuntla *India* 15°14N 78°19E **45** G4
Koillismaa *Finland* 65°44N 28°36E **8** D23
Koin *N. Korea* 40°28N 126°18E **33** D14
Kojō *N. Korea* 38°58N 127°58E **33** E14
Kojonup *Australia* 33°48S 117°10E **61** F2
Kojūr *Iran* 36°23N 51°43E **47** B6
Kon Ka Kinh △ *Vietnam* 14°19N 107°23E **38** E6
Kon Tum *Vietnam* 14°24N 108°0E **38** E7
Kon Tum, Plateau du *Vietnam* 14°30N 108°30E **38** E7
Konar □ *Afghan.* 34°30N 71°3E **40** B7
Konarak *India* 19°54N 86°7E **44** E8
Konāri *Iran* 28°13N 51°36E **47** D6
Konch *India* 26°0N 79°10E **43** G8
Kondagaon *India* 19°35N 81°35E **44** E5
Kondinin *Australia* 32°34S 118°8E **61** F2
Kondoa *Tanzania* 4°55S 35°50E **54** E7
Kondopoga *Russia* 62°12N 34°17E **18** B5
Kondratyevo *Russia* 57°22N 98°15E **27** D10
Kondukur *India* 15°12N 79°57E **45** G4
Köneürgench *Turkmenistan* 42°19N 59°10E **26** E6
Konevo *Russia* 62°8N 39°20E **18** B6
Kong = Khong → *Cambodia* 13°32N 105°58E **38** F5
Kong *Ivory C.* 8°54N 4°36W **52** G5
Kong, Koh *Cambodia* 11°20N 103°0E **39** G4
Kong Christian IX.s Land *Greenland* 68°0N 36°0W **4** C6
Kong Christian X.s Land *Greenland* 74°0N 29°0W **4** B6
Kong Frederik IX.s Land *Greenland* 67°0N 52°0W **4** C5
Kong Frederik VI.s Kyst *Greenland* 63°0N 43°0W **4** C5
Kong Frederik VIII.s Land *Greenland* 78°30N 26°0W **4** B6
Kong Oscar Fjord *Greenland* 72°20N 24°0W **4** B6
Konglu *Burma* 27°13N 97°57E **41** F20
Kongola *Namibia* 17°45S 23°20E **56** A3
Kongolo *Dem. Rep. of the Congo* 5°22S 27°0E **54** F5
Kongsberg *Norway* 59°39N 9°39E **9** G13
Kongsvinger *Norway* 60°12N 12°2E **9** F18
Kongur Shan *China* 38°34N 75°18E **30** D4
Konin *Poland* 52°12N 18°15E **17** B10
Konjic *Bos.-H.* 43°42N 17°58E **23** C7
Konkiep *Namibia* 26°49S 17°15E **56** D2
Konnur *India* 16°14N 74°49E **45** F2
Konosha *Russia* 61°0N 40°5E **18** B7
Kōnosu *Japan* 36°3N 139°31E **29** F9
Kononop *Ukraine* 51°12N 33°7E **19** D5

Konqi He → *China* 41°0N 86°0E **30** C6
Końskie *Poland* 51°15N 20°23E **17** C11
Konstanz *Germany* 47°40N 9°10E **16** E5
Kont *Iran* 26°55N 61°50E **47** E9
Konta *India* 17°48N 81°23E **44** F5
Kontagora *Nigeria* 10°23N 5°27E **52** F7
Kontiolahti *Finland* 62°46N 29°50E **8** E23
Konya *Turkey* 37°52N 32°35E **46** B2
Koocanusa, L. *Canada* 49°20N 115°15W **76** B6
Kookynie *Australia* 29°17S 121°22E **61** E3
Koolyanobbing *Australia* 30°48S 119°36E **61** F2
Koonibba *Australia* 31°54S 133°25E **63** E1
Koorawatha *Australia* 34°2S 148°33E **63** E4
Koorda *Australia* 30°48S 117°35E **61** F2
Kooskia *U.S.A.* 46°9N 115°59W **76** C6
Kootenay → *U.S.A.* 49°19N 117°39W **70** D5
Kootenay △ *Canada* 51°0N 116°0W **70** C5
Kootenay L. *Canada* 49°45N 116°50W **70** D5
Kootjieskolk *S. Africa* 31°15S 20°21E **56** D3
Kopaonik *Serbia* 43°10N 20°50E **23** C9
Kópavogur *Iceland* 64°6N 21°55W **8** D3
Koper *Slovenia* 45°31N 13°44E **16** F7
Kopervik *Norway* 59°17N 5°17E **9** G11
Kopet Dagh *Asia* 38°0N 58°0E **47** B8
Kopeysk *Russia* 55°7N 61°37E **26** D7
Kopi *Australia* 33°24S 135°40E **63** E2
Köping *Sweden* 59°31N 16°3E **9** G17
Koppa *India* 13°33N 75°21E **45** H2
Koppal *India* 15°23N 76°5E **45** G3
Koppeh Dāgh = Kopet Dagh *Asia* 38°0N 58°0E **47** B8
Koppies *S. Africa* 27°20S 27°30E **57** C4
Koprivnica *Croatia* 46°12N 16°45E **22** A7
Köprülü △ *Turkey* 37°20N 31°5E **46** B1
Kopychyntsi *Ukraine* 49°7N 25°58E **17** D13
Korab *Macedonia* 41°44N 20°40E **23** D9
Koral *India* 21°50N 73°12E **42** J5
Korangal *India* 17°6N 77°38E **44** E3
Koraput *India* 18°50N 82°40E **44** E6
Korba *India* 22°20N 82°45E **43** H10
Korbu, Gunung *Malaysia* 4°41N 101°18E **39** K3
Korçë *Albania* 40°37N 20°50E **23** D9
Korčula *Croatia* 42°56N 16°57E **22** C7
Kord Kūy *Iran* 36°48N 54°7E **47** B7
Kord Sheykh *Iran* 28°31N 52°53E **47** D7
Kordestān □ *Iran* 36°0N 47°0E **46** C5
Kordofân *Sudan* 13°0N 29°0E **53** F11
Korea, North ■ *Asia* 40°0N 127°0E **33** E14
Korea, South ■ *Asia* 36°0N 128°0E **33** G15
Korea Bay *Korea* 39°0N 124°0E **33** E13
Korea Strait *Asia* 34°0N 129°30E **33** H15
Koregaon *India* 17°40N 74°10E **44** F2
Korets *Ukraine* 50°40N 27°5E **17** C14
Korff Ice Rise *Antarctica* 79°0S 69°30W **5** D17
Korhogo *Ivory C.* 9°29N 5°28W **52** G4
Korinthiakos Kolpos *Greece* 38°16N 22°30E **23** E10
Korinthos *Greece* 37°56N 22°55E **23** F10
Kōriyama *Japan* 37°24N 140°23E **28** F10
Korla *China* 41°45N 86°4E **30** C6
Korneshty = Corneşti *Moldova* 47°21N 28°1E **17** E15
Koro *Fiji* 17°19S 179°23E **59** a
Koro *Ivory C.* 8°32N 7°30W **52** G4
Koro Sea *Fiji* 17°30S 179°45W **59** a
Korogwe *Tanzania* 5°5S 38°25E **54** F7
Korolevu *Fiji* 18°12S 177°46E **59** a
Koronadal *Phil.* 6°12N 124°51E **37** C6
Körös → *Hungary* 46°43N 20°12E **17** E11
Korosten *Ukraine* 50°54N 28°36E **17** C15
Korostyshev *Ukraine* 50°19N 29°4E **17** C15
Korovou *Fiji* 17°47S 178°32E **59** a
Koroyanitu △ *Fiji* 17°40S 177°35E **59** a
Korsakov *Russia* 46°36N 142°42E **27** E15
Korshunovo *Russia* 58°37N 110°10E **27** D12
Korsør *Denmark* 55°20N 11°9E **9** J14
Kortrijk *Belgium* 50°50N 3°17E **15** D3
Korwai *India* 24°7N 78°5E **42** G8
Koryakskoye Nagorye *Russia* 61°0N 171°0E **27** C18
Kos *Greece* 36°50N 27°15E **23** F12
Kosan *N. Korea* 38°52N 127°25E **33** E14
Kościan *Poland* 52°5N 16°40E **17** B9
Kosciusko *U.S.A.* 33°4N 89°35W **85** E10
Kosciuszko, Mt. *Australia* 36°27S 148°16E **63** F4
Kosgi *Andhra Pradesh, India* 16°58N 77°43E **44** F3
Kosgi *Andhra Pradesh, India* 15°51N 77°16E **45** G3
Kosha *Sudan* 20°50N 30°30E **53** D12
K'oshih = Kashi *China* 39°30N 76°2E **30** D4
Koshiki-Rettō *Japan* 31°45N 129°49E **29** J4
Kosi *India* 27°48N 77°29E **42** F7
Kosi → *India* 28°41N 78°57E **43** E8
Košice *Slovak Rep.* 48°42N 21°15E **17** D11
Koslan *Russia* 63°34N 49°14E **18** B8
Kosŏng *N. Korea* 38°40N 128°22E **33** E15
Kosovo ■ *Europe* 42°30N 21°0E **23** C9
Kosovska Mitrovica = Mitrovicë *Kosovo* 42°54N 20°52E **23** C9
Kossou, L. de *Ivory C.* 6°59N 5°31W **52** G4
Koster *S. Africa* 25°52S 26°54E **57** D4
Kôstî *Sudan* 13°8N 32°43E **53** F12
Kostopil *Ukraine* 50°51N 26°22E **17** C14
Kostroma *Russia* 57°50N 40°58E **18** C7
Kostrzyn *Poland* 52°35N 14°39E **16** B8
Koszalin *Poland* 54°11N 16°8E **16** A9
Kot Addu *Pakistan* 30°30N 71°0E **42** D4
Kot Kapura *India* 30°35N 74°50E **42** D6
Kot Moman *Pakistan* 32°13N 73°0E **42** C5
Kot Sultan *Pakistan* 30°46N 70°56E **42** D4
Kota *India* 25°14N 75°49E **42** G6
Kota Barrage *India* 25°6N 75°51E **42** G6
Kota Belud *Malaysia* 6°21N 116°26E **36** C5
Kota Bharu *Malaysia* 6°7N 102°14E **39** J4
Kota Kinabalu *Malaysia* 6°0N 116°4E **36** C5
Kota Tinggi *Malaysia* 1°44N 103°53E **39** M4

Kotaagung *Indonesia* 5°38S 104°29E **36** F2
Kotabaru *Indonesia* 3°20S 116°20E **36** E5
Kotabumi *Indonesia* 4°49S 104°54E **36** E2
Kotamobagu *Indonesia* 0°57N 124°31E **37** D6
Kotapad *India* 19°9N 82°21E **44** E6
Kotapinang *Indonesia* 1°53N 100°5E **36** D1
Kotcho L. *Canada* 59°7N 121°12W **70** B4
Kotdwara *India* 29°45N 78°32E **43** E8
Kotelnich *Russia* 58°22N 48°24E **18** C8
Kotelnikovo *Russia* 47°38N 43°8E **19** E7
Kotelnyy, Ostrov *Russia* 75°10N 139°0E **27** B14
Kothapet *India* 19°21N 79°28E **44** E4
Kothari → *India* 25°20N 75°4E **42** G6
Kothi *Chhattisgarh, India* 23°21N 82°3E **43** H10
Kothi *Mad. P., India* 24°45N 80°40E **43** G9
Kotiro *Pakistan* 26°17N 67°13E **42** F2
Kotka *Finland* 60°28N 26°58E **8** F22
Kotlas *Russia* 61°17N 46°43E **18** B8
Kotli *Pakistan* 33°30N 73°55E **42** C5
Kotlik *U.S.A.* 63°2N 163°33W **74** C7
Kotma *India* 23°12N 81°58E **43** H9
Kotor *Montenegro* 42°25N 18°47E **23** C8
Kotovsk *Ukraine* 47°45N 29°35E **17** E15
Kotputli *India* 27°43N 76°12E **42** F7
Kotri *Pakistan* 25°22N 68°22E **42** G3
Kotri → *India* 19°15N 80°35E **44** E5
Kottagudem *India* 17°30N 80°40E **44** F5
Kottayam *India* 9°35N 76°33E **45** K3
Kotto → *C.A.R.* 4°14N 22°2E **54** D4
Kottur *India* 10°34N 76°56E **45** J3
Kotturu *India* 14°45N 76°10E **45** G3
Kotu Group *Tonga* 20°0S 174°45W **59** c
Kotuy → *Russia* 71°54N 102°6E **27** B11
Kotzebue *U.S.A.* 66°53N 162°39W **74** B7
Kotzebue Sound *U.S.A.* 66°20N 163°0W **74** B7
Kouchibouguac △
    Canada 46°50N 65°0W **73** C6
Koudougou *Burkina Faso* 12°10N 2°20W **52** F5
Kougaberge *S. Africa* 33°48S 23°50E **56** D3
Kouilou → *Congo* 4°10S 12°5E **54** E2
Koukdjuak → *Canada* 66°43N 73°0W **69** D17
Koula Moutou *Gabon* 1°15S 12°25E **54** E2
Koulen = Kulen
    Cambodia 13°50N 104°40E **38** F5
Koumala *Australia* 21°38S 149°15E **62** C4
Koumra *Chad* 8°50N 17°35E **53** G9
Kountze *U.S.A.* 30°22N 94°19W **84** F7
Kourou *Fr. Guiana* 5°9N 52°39W **93** B8
Kouroussa *Guinea* 10°45N 9°45W **52** F4
Kousseri *Cameroon* 12°0N 14°55E **53** F8
Koutiala *Mali* 12°25N 5°23W **52** F4
Kouvola *Finland* 60°52N 26°43E **8** F22
Kovdor *Russia* 67°34N 30°24E **8** C24
Kovel *Ukraine* 51°11N 24°38E **17** C13
Kovilpatti *India* 9°10N 77°50E **45** K3
Kovrov *Russia* 56°25N 41°25E **18** C7
Kovur *Andhra Pradesh, India* 17°3N 81°39E **44** F5
Kovur *Andhra Pradesh,
    India* 14°30N 80°1E **45** G5
Kowanyama *Australia* 15°29S 141°44E **62** B3
Kowanyama ✿ *Australia* 15°20S 141°47E **62** B3
Kowŏn *N. Korea* 39°26N 127°14E **33** E14
Koyampattur = Coimbatore
    India 11°2N 76°59E **45** J3
Köyceğiz *Turkey* 36°57N 28°40E **23** F13
Koyukuk → *U.S.A.* 64°55N 157°32W **74** C8
Koza = Okinawa *Japan* 26°19N 127°46E **29** L3
Kozan *Turkey* 37°26N 35°50E **46** B2
Kozani *Greece* 40°19N 21°47E **23** D9
Kozhikode *India* 11°15N 75°43E **45** J2
Kozhva *Russia* 65°10N 57°0E **18** A10
Kōzu-Shima *Japan* 34°13N 139°10E **29** G9
Kozyatyn *Ukraine* 49°45N 28°50E **17** D15
Kozyrevsk *Russia* 56°3N 159°51E **27** D16
Kpalimé *Togo* 6°57N 0°44E **52** G6
Kra, Isthmus of = Kra, Kho Khot
    Thailand 10°15N 99°30E **39** G2
Kra, Kho Khot *Thailand* 10°15N 99°30E **39** G2
Kra Buri *Thailand* 10°22N 98°46E **39** G2
Kraai → *S. Africa* 30°40S 26°45E **56** D4
Krabi *Thailand* 8°4N 98°55E **39** H2
Kracheh = Kratie
    Cambodia 12°32N 106°10E **38** F6
Kragan *Indonesia* 6°43S 111°38E **37** G14
Kragerø *Norway* 58°52N 9°25E **9** G13
Kragujevac *Serbia* 44°2N 20°56E **23** B9
Krakatau = Rakata, Pulau
    Indonesia 6°10S 105°20E **37** G11
Krakatoa = Rakata, Pulau
    Indonesia 6°10S 105°20E **37** G11
Krakor *Cambodia* 12°32N 104°12E **38** F5
Kraków *Poland* 50°4N 19°57E **17** C10
Kraksaan *Indonesia* 7°43S 113°23E **37** G16
Kralanh *Cambodia* 13°35N 103°25E **38** F4
Kraljevo *Serbia* 43°44N 20°41E **23** C9
Kramatorsk *Ukraine* 48°50N 37°30E **19** E6
Kramfors *Sweden* 62°55N 17°48E **8** E17
Kranj *Slovenia* 46°16N 14°22E **16** E8
Krankskop *S. Africa* 28°0S 30°47E **57** C5
Krasavino *Russia* 60°58N 46°29E **18** B8
Krasieo Res. *Thailand* 14°49N 99°30E **38** E2
Kraskino *Russia* 42°44N 130°48E **28** C5
Kraśnik *Poland* 50°55N 22°15E **17** C12
Krasnoarmeysk *Russia* 51°0N 45°42E **26** D5
Krasnodar *Russia* 45°5N 39°0E **19** E6
Krasnokamsk *Russia* 58°4N 55°48E **18** C10
Krasnoperekopsk *Ukraine* 46°0N 33°54E **19** E5
Krasnorechenskiy
    Russia 44°41N 135°14E **28** B7
Krasnoselkup *Russia* 65°20N 82°10E **26** C9
Krasnoturinsk *Russia* 59°46N 60°12E **18** C11
Krasnoufimsk *Russia* 56°36N 57°38E **18** C10
Krasnouralsk *Russia* 58°21N 60°3E **18** C11
Krasnovishersk *Russia* 60°23N 57°3E **18** B10
Krasnoyarsk *Russia* 56°8N 93°0E **27** D10
Krasnoyarskoye Vdkhr.
    Russia 56°0N 92°30E **27** D10
Krasnyy Kut *Russia* 50°50N 47°0E **19** D8

Krasnyy Luch *Ukraine* 48°13N 39°0E **19** E6
Krasnyy Yar *Russia* 46°43N 48°23E **19** E8
Kratie *Cambodia* 12°32N 106°10E **38** F6
Krau *Indonesia* 3°19S 140°5E **37** E10
Kravanh, Chuor Phnum
    Cambodia 12°0N 103°32E **39** G4
Krefeld *Germany* 51°20N 6°33E **16** C4
Kremenchuk *Ukraine* 49°5N 33°25E **19** E5
Kremenchuksk Vdskh.
    Ukraine 49°20N 32°30E **19** E5
Kremenets *Ukraine* 50°8N 25°43E **17** C13
Kremmling *U.S.A.* 40°4N 106°24W **76** F10
Krems *Austria* 48°25N 15°36E **16** D8
Kretinga *Lithuania* 55°53N 21°15E **9** J19
Krichev = Krychaw
    Belarus 53°40N 31°41E **17** B16
Kril'on, Mys *Russia* 45°53N 142°5E **28** B11
Krishna → *India* 15°57N 80°59E **45** G5
Krishnagiri *India* 12°32N 78°16E **45** H4
Krishnanagar *India* 23°24N 88°33E **43** H13
Krishnaraja Sagar *India* 12°20N 76°30E **45** H3
Kristiansand *Norway* 58°8N 8°1E **9** G13
Kristianstad *Sweden* 56°2N 14°9E **9** H16
Kristiansund *Norway* 63°7N 7°45E **8** E12
Kristiinankaupunki
    Finland 62°16N 21°21E **8** E19
Kristinehamn *Sweden* 59°18N 14°7E **9** G16
Kristinestad = Kristiinankaupunki
    Finland 62°16N 21°21E **8** E19
Kriti *Greece* 35°15N 25°0E **23** G11
Krivoy Rog = Kryvyy Rih
    Ukraine 47°51N 33°20E **19** E5
Krk *Croatia* 45°8N 14°40E **16** F8
Krokodil = Umgwenya →
    Mozam. 25°14S 32°18E **57** C5
Krong Kaoh Kong
    Cambodia 11°37N 102°59E **39** G4
Kronprins Frederik Land
    Greenland 81°0N 45°0W **4** B5
Kronprins Olav Kyst
    Antarctica 69°0S 42°0E **5** C5
Kronprinsesse Märtha Kyst
    Antarctica 73°30S 10°0W **5** D2
Kronshtadt *Russia* 59°57N 29°51E **18** B4
Kroonstad *S. Africa* 27°43S 27°19E **56** C4
Kropotkin *Russia* 45°28N 40°28E **19** E7
Krosno *Poland* 49°42N 21°46E **17** D11
Krotoszyn *Poland* 51°42N 17°23E **17** C9
Kruger △ *S. Africa* 24°50S 26°10E **57** B4
Kruisfontein *S. Africa* 33°59S 24°43E **56** D3
Krupki *Belarus* 54°19N 29°8E **17** A15
Kruševac *Serbia* 43°35N 21°28E **23** C9
Krychaw *Belarus* 53°40N 31°41E **17** B16
Krymskiy Poluostrov = Krymskyy
    Pivostriv *Ukraine* 45°0N 34°0E **19** F5
Krymskyy Pivostriv
    Ukraine 45°0N 34°0E **19** F5
Kryvyy Rih *Ukraine* 47°51N 33°20E **19** E5
Ksar el Kebir *Morocco* 35°0N 6°0W **52** B4
Ksar es Souk = Er Rachidia
    Morocco 31°58N 4°20W **52** B5
Kuah *Malaysia* 6°19N 99°51E **39** J2
Kuala Belait *Malaysia* 4°35N 114°11E **36** D4
Kuala Berang *Malaysia* 5°5N 103°1E **39** K4
Kuala Dungun = Dungun
    Malaysia 4°45N 103°25E **39** K4
Kuala Kangsar *Malaysia* 4°46N 100°56E **39** K3
Kuala Kelawang *Malaysia* 2°56N 102°5E **39** L4
Kuala Kerai *Malaysia* 5°30N 102°12E **39** K4
Kuala Kubu Bharu
    Malaysia 3°34N 101°39E **39** L3
Kuala Lipis *Malaysia* 4°10N 102°3E **39** K4
Kuala Lumpur *Malaysia* 3°9N 101°41E **39** L3
Kuala Nerang *Malaysia* 6°16N 100°37E **39** J3
Kuala Pilah *Malaysia* 2°45N 102°15E **39** L4
Kuala Rompin *Malaysia* 2°49N 103°29E **39** L4
Kuala Selangor *Malaysia* 3°20N 101°15E **39** L3
Kuala Sepetang *Malaysia* 4°49N 100°28E **39** K3
Kuala Terengganu
    Malaysia 5°20N 103°8E **39** K4
Kualajelai *Indonesia* 2°58S 110°46E **36** E4
Kualakapuas *Indonesia* 2°55S 114°20E **36** E4
Kualakurun *Indonesia* 1°10S 113°50E **36** E4
Kualapembuang
    Indonesia 3°14S 112°38E **36** E4
Kualasimpang *Indonesia* 4°17N 98°3E **36** D1
Kuancheng *China* 40°37N 118°30E **33** D10
Kuandang *Indonesia* 0°56N 123°1E **37** D6
Kuandian *China* 40°45N 124°45E **33** D13
Kuanshan *Taiwan* 23°3N 121°9E **35** F13
Kuantan *Malaysia* 3°49N 103°20E **39** L4
Kuba = Quba *Azerbaijan* 41°21N 48°32E **19** F8
Kuban → *Russia* 45°20N 37°30E **19** E6
Kubokawa = Shimanto
    Japan 33°12N 133°8E **29** H6
Kubu *Indonesia* 8°16S 115°35E **37** J18
Kubutambahan *Indonesia* 8°5S 115°10E **37** J18
Kucar, Tanjung
    Indonesia 8°39S 114°34E **37** K18
Kuchaman *India* 27°13N 74°47E **42** F6
Kuchchaveli *Sri Lanka* 8°49N 81°6E **45** K5
Kuchinda *India* 21°44N 84°21E **43** J11
Kuching *Malaysia* 1°33N 110°25E **36** D4
Kuchino-eruba-Jima
    Japan 30°28N 130°12E **29** J5
Kuchino-Shima *Japan* 29°57N 129°55E **29** K4
Kuchinotsu *Japan* 32°36N 130°11E **29** H5
Kucing = Kuching
    Malaysia 1°33N 110°25E **36** D4
Kud → *Pakistan* 26°5N 66°20E **42** F2
Kuda *India* 23°10N 71°15E **42** H4
Kudal *India* 16°2N 73°41E **45** F1
Kudalier → *India* 18°35N 79°48E **44** E4
Kudat *Malaysia* 6°55N 116°55E **36** C5
Kudremukh *India* 13°15N 75°20E **45** H2
Kudus *Indonesia* 6°48S 110°51E **37** G14

Kudymkar *Russia* 59°1N 54°39E **18** C9
Kueiyang = Guiyang
    China 26°32N 106°40E **34** D6
Kufra Oasis = Al Kufrah
    Libya 24°17N 23°15E **53** D10
Kufstein *Austria* 47°35N 12°11E **16** E7
Kugaaruk = Pelly Bay
    Canada 68°38N 89°50W **69** D14
Kugluktuk *Canada* 67°50N 115°5W **68** D8
Kugong I. *Canada* 56°18N 79°50W **72** A4
Küh Dasht *Iran* 33°32N 47°36E **46** C5
Kühak *Iran* 27°12N 63°10E **47** E9
Kuhan *Pakistan* 28°19N 67°14E **42** E2
Kūhbonān *Iran* 31°23N 56°19E **47** D8
Kühestak *Iran* 26°47N 57°2E **47** E8
Kuhin *Iran* 36°22N 49°40E **47** B6
Kūhīrī *Iran* 26°55N 61°2E **47** E9
Kuhmo *Finland* 64°7N 29°31E **8** D23
Kuhn Chae △ *Thailand* 19°8N 99°24E **38** C2
Kühpāyeh *Esfahan, Iran* 32°44N 52°20E **47** C7
Kühpāyeh *Kermān, Iran* 30°35N 57°15E **47** D8
Kui Buri *Thailand* 12°3N 99°52E **39** F2
Kuibyshev → *Thailand* 12°10N 99°37E **39** F2
Kuichong *China* 22°38N 114°25E **31** a
Kuiseb → *Namibia* 22°59S 14°31E **56** B1
Kuito *Angola* 12°22S 16°55E **55** G3
Kuiu I. *U.S.A.* 57°45N 134°10W **70** B2
Kujang *N. Korea* 39°57N 126°1E **33** E14
Kuji *Japan* 40°11N 141°46E **28** D10
Kujū-San *Japan* 33°5N 131°15E **29** H5
Kukës *Albania* 42°5N 20°27E **23** C9
Kukup *Malaysia* 1°20N 103°27E **39** d
Kukup, Pulau *Malaysia* 1°18N 103°27E **39** d
Kula *Turkey* 38°32N 28°40E **23** E13
K'ula Shan *Bhutan* 28°14N 90°36E **30** F7
Kulachi *Pakistan* 31°56N 70°27E **42** D4
Kulai *Malaysia* 1°44N 103°35E **39** M4
Kulasekarappattinam *India* 8°20N 78°5E **45** K4
Kuldīga *Latvia* 56°58N 21°59E **9** H19
Kulen *Cambodia* 13°50N 104°40E **38** F5
Kulgam *India* 33°36N 75°2E **43** C6
Kulgera *Australia* 25°50S 133°18E **62** D1
Kulim *Malaysia* 5°22N 100°34E **39** K3
Kulin *Australia* 32°40S 118°2E **61** F2
Kulittalai *India* 10°55N 78°25E **45** J4
Kulkayu = Hartley Bay
    Canada 53°25N 129°15W **70** C3
Kullu *India* 31°58N 77°6E **42** D7
Kŭlob *Tajikistan* 37°55N 69°50E **26** F7
Kulsary = Qulsary
    Kazakhstan 46°59N 54°1E **19** E9
Kulti *India* 23°43N 86°50E **43** H12
Kulunda *Russia* 52°35N 78°57E **26** D8
Kulungar *Afghan.* 34°0N 69°2E **42** C3
Kulvand *Iran* 31°21N 54°35E **47** D7
Kulwin *Australia* 35°2S 142°42E **63** F3
Kulyab = Kŭlob *Tajikistan* 37°55N 69°50E **26** F7
Kuma → *Russia* 44°55N 47°0E **19** F8
Kumagaya *Nigeria* 13°8N 10°38E **53** F8
Kumagaya *Japan* 36°9N 139°22E **29** F9
Kumai *Indonesia* 2°44S 111°43E **36** E4
Kumamba, Kepulauan
    Indonesia 1°36S 138°45E **37** E9
Kumamoto *Japan* 32°45N 130°45E **29** H5
Kumamoto □ *Japan* 32°55N 130°55E **29** H5
Kumanovo *Macedonia* 42°9N 21°42E **23** C9
Kumara *N.Z.* 42°37S 171°12E **59** E3
Kumara Roadhouse
    Australia 24°41S 119°32E **61** D2
Kumasi *Ghana* 6°41N 1°38W **52** G5
Kumba *Cameroon* 4°36N 9°24E **54** D1
Kumbakonam *India* 10°58N 79°25E **45** J4
Kumbarilla *Australia* 27°15S 150°55E **63** D5
Kumbhraj *India* 24°22N 77°3E **42** G7
Kumbia *Australia* 26°41S 151°39E **63** D5
Kumbukkan Oya →
    Sri Lanka 6°35N 81°40E **45** L5
Kŭmch'on *N. Korea* 38°10N 126°29E **33** E14
Kume-Shima *Japan* 26°20N 126°47E **29** L3
Kumertau *Russia* 52°45N 55°57E **18** D10
Kumharsain *India* 31°19N 77°27E **42** D7
Kumo *Nigeria* 10°1N 11°12E **53** F8
Kumo älv = Kokemäenjoki →
    Finland 61°32N 21°44E **8** F19
Kumon Bum *Burma* 26°30N 97°15E **41** F20
Kumta *India* 14°29N 74°32E **45** G3
Kumtag Shamo *China* 39°40N 92°0E **30** D7
Kuna *U.S.A.* 43°30N 116°25W **76** E5
Kunashir, Ostrov *Russia* 44°0N 146°0E **27** E15
Kunchha *Nepal* 28°8N 84°20E **43** E11
Kunda *Estonia* 59°30N 26°34E **9** G22
Kunda *India* 25°43N 81°31E **43** G9
Kundar → *Pakistan* 31°56N 69°19E **42** D3
Kundian *Pakistan* 32°27N 71°28E **42** C4
Kundla *India* 21°21N 71°25E **42** J4
Kunene □ *Namibia* 20°0S 14°0E **56** A1
Kung, Ao *Thailand* 8°5N 98°24E **39** a
Kunga → *Bangla.* 21°46N 89°30E **43** J13
Kunghit I. *Canada* 52°6N 131°3W **70** C2
Kungrad = Qŭnghirot
    Uzbekistan 43°2N 58°50E **26** E6
Kungsbacka *Sweden* 57°30N 12°5E **9** H15
Kungur *Russia* 57°25N 56°57E **18** C10
Kungurri *Australia* 21°4S 148°45E **62** b
Kunhar → *Pakistan* 34°20N 73°30E **43** B5
Kuningan *Indonesia* 6°59S 108°29E **37** G13
Kunlong *Burma* 23°20N 98°50E **34** F2
Kunlun Shan *Asia* 36°0N 86°30E **30** D6
Kunlun Shankou *China* 35°38N 94°4E **30** D7
Kunming *China* 25°1N 102°41E **34** E4
Kunmunya ✿ *Australia* 15°26S 124°42E **60** D3
Kunshan *China* 31°22N 120°58E **35** B13
Kununurra *Australia* 15°40S 128°50E **60** C4
Kunwari → *India* 26°26N 79°11E **43** F8
Kunya-Urgench = Köneürgench
    Turkmenistan 42°19N 59°10E **26** E6
Kuopio *Finland* 62°53N 27°35E **8** E22

Kupa → *Croatia* 45°28N 16°24E **16** F9
Kupang *Indonesia* 10°19S 123°39E **37** F6
Kupreanof I. *U.S.A.* 56°50N 133°30W **70** B2
Kupyansk-Uzlovoi
    Ukraine 49°40N 37°43E **19** E6
Kuqa *China* 41°35N 82°30E **30** C5
Kür → *Azerbaijan* 39°29N 49°15E **19** G8
Kür Dili *Azerbaijan* 39°3N 49°13E **47** B6
Kura = Kür → *Azerbaijan* 39°29N 49°15E **19** G8
Kuranda *Australia* 16°48S 145°35E **62** B4
Kuranga *India* 22°4N 69°10E **42** H3
Kurashiki *Japan* 34°40N 133°50E **29** G6
Kurayn *Si. Arabia* 27°39N 49°50E **47** E6
Kurayoshi *Japan* 35°26N 133°50E **29** G6
Kŭrchatov *Kazakhstan* 50°45N 78°32E **26** D8
Kurduvadi *India* 18°8N 75°29E **44** E2
Kürdzhali *Bulgaria* 41°38N 25°21E **23** D11
Kure *Japan* 34°14N 132°32E **29** G6
Kure I. *U.S.A.* 28°25N 178°25W **75** K4
Kuressaare *Estonia* 58°15N 22°30E **9** G20
Kurgan *Russia* 55°26N 65°18E **26** D7
Kuri *India* 26°37N 70°43E **42** F4
Kuria Maria Is. = Ḩallāniyat,
    Jazā'ir al *Oman* 17°30N 55°58E **49** D6
Kurichchi *India* 11°36N 77°35E **45** J3
Kuridala *Australia* 21°16S 140°29E **62** C3
Kurigram *Bangla.* 25°49N 89°39E **41** G16
Kurikka *Finland* 62°36N 22°24E **8** E20
Kuril Basin *Pac. Oc.* 47°0N 150°0E **4** E15
Kuril Is. = Kurilskiye Ostrova
    Russia 45°0N 150°0E **27** E16
Kuril-Kamchatka Trench
    Pac. Oc. 44°0N 153°0E **64** C7
Kurilsk *Russia* 45°14N 147°53E **27** E15
Kurilskiye Ostrova
    Russia 45°0N 150°0E **27** E16
Kurino *Japan* 31°57N 130°43E **29** J5
Kurinskaya Kosa = Kür Dili
    Azerbaijan 39°3N 49°13E **47** B6
Kurkheda *India* 20°37N 80°12E **44** D5
Kurkuta ✿ *Australia* 24°0S 127°56E **60** D4
Kurnool *India* 15°45N 78°0E **45** G4
Kuro-Shima *Kagoshima,
    Japan* 30°50N 129°57E **29** J4
Kuro-Shima *Okinawa,
    Japan* 24°14N 124°1E **29** M2
Kurow *N.Z.* 44°44S 170°29E **59** F3
Kurram → *Pakistan* 32°36N 71°20E **42** C4
Kurri Kurri *Australia* 32°50S 151°28E **63** E5
Kurrimine *Australia* 17°47S 146°6E **62** B4
Kurse Korhi *India* 20°14N 80°46E **44** D5
Kurseong = Karsiyang
    India 26°56N 88°18E **43** F13
Kurshskiy Zaliv *Russia* 55°9N 21°6E **9** J19
Kursk *Russia* 51°42N 36°11E **18** D6
Kuruçay *Turkey* 39°39N 38°29E **46** B3
Kurukshetra = Thanesar
    India 30°1N 76°52E **42** D7
Kuruktag *China* 41°0N 89°0E **30** C6
Kuruman *S. Africa* 27°28S 23°28E **56** C3
Kuruman → *S. Africa* 26°56S 20°39E **56** C3
Kurume *Japan* 33°15N 130°30E **29** H5
Kurunegala *Sri Lanka* 7°30N 80°23E **45** L5
Kurya *Russia* 61°42N 57°9E **18** B10
Kus Gölü *Turkey* 40°10N 27°55E **23** D12
Kuşadası *Turkey* 37°52N 27°15E **23** F12
Kusamba *Indonesia* 8°34S 115°27E **37** K18
Kusatsu *Japan* 36°37N 138°36E **29** F9
Kusawa L. *Canada* 60°20N 136°13W **70** A1
Kushalgarh *India* 23°10N 74°27E **42** H6
Kushalnagar *India* 12°14N 75°57E **45** H2
Kushikino *Japan* 31°44N 130°16E **29** J5
Kushima *Japan* 31°29N 131°14E **29** J5
Kushimoto *Japan* 33°28N 135°47E **29** H7
Kushiro *Japan* 43°0N 144°25E **28** C12
Kushiro-Gawa →
    Japan 42°59N 144°23E **28** C12
Kushiro Shitsugen △
    Japan 43°9N 144°26E **28** C12
Kūshk *Iran* 28°46N 56°51E **47** D8
Kushka = Serhetabat
    Turkmenistan 35°20N 62°18E **47** C9
Kushol *India* 33°40N 76°36E **43** C7
Kushtia *Bangla.* 23°55N 89°5E **41** H16
Kushva *Russia* 58°18N 59°45E **18** C10
Kuskokwim → *U.S.A.* 60°5N 162°25W **74** C7
Kuskokwim B. *U.S.A.* 59°45N 162°25W **74** C7
Kuskokwim Mts. *U.S.A.* 62°30N 156°0W **74** C8
Kusmi *India* 23°17N 83°55E **43** H10
Kusŏng *N. Korea* 39°59N 125°15E **33** E13
Kussharo-Ko *Japan* 43°38N 144°21E **28** C12
Kustanay = Qostanay
    Kazakhstan 53°10N 63°35E **26** D7
Kut, Ko *Thailand* 11°40N 102°35E **39** G4
Kuta *Indonesia* 8°43S 115°11E **37** K18
Kütahya *Turkey* 39°30N 30°2E **19** G5
Kutaisi *Georgia* 42°19N 42°40E **19** F7
Kutaraja = Banda Aceh
    Indonesia 5°35N 95°20E **36** C1
Kutch, Gulf of = Kachchh, Gulf of
    India 22°50N 69°15E **42** H3
Kutch, Rann of = Kachchh, Rann
    of *India* 24°0N 70°0E **42** H4
Kutiyana *India* 21°36N 70°2E **42** J4
Kutno *Poland* 52°15N 19°23E **17** B10
Kutru *India* 19°5N 80°46E **44** E5
Kutse *Botswana* 21°7S 22°16E **56** B3
Kuttabul *Australia* 21°1S 148°54E **62** b
Kutu *Dem. Rep. of the Congo* 2°40S 18°11E **54** E3
Kutum *Sudan* 14°10N 24°40E **53** F10
Kuujjuaq *Canada* 58°6N 68°15W **69** F18
Kuujjuarapik *Canada* 55°20N 77°35W **72** A4
Kuusamo *Finland* 65°57N 29°8E **8** D23
Kuusankoski *Finland* 60°55N 26°38E **8** F22
Kuwait = Al Kuwayt
    Kuwait 29°30N 48°0E **46** D5
Kuwait ■ *Asia* 29°30N 47°30E **46** D5
Kuwana *Japan* 35°5N 136°43E **29** G8
Kuwana → *India* 26°25N 83°15E **43** F10

Kuybyshev = Samara
    Russia 53°8N 50°6E **18** D9
Kuybyshev *Russia* 55°27N 78°19E **26** D8
Kuybyshevskoye Vdkhr.
    Russia 55°2N 49°30E **18** C8
Kuye He → *China* 38°23N 110°46E **32** E6
Kūyeh *Iran* 38°45N 47°57E **46** B5
Kuyto, Ozero *Russia* 65°6N 31°20E **8** D24
Kuytun *China* 44°25N 85°0E **30** C5
Kuyumba *Russia* 60°58N 96°59E **27** C10
Kuzey Anadolu Dağları
    Turkey 41°0N 36°45E **19** F6
Kuzhithurai *India* 8°18N 77°11E **45** K3
Kuznetsk *Russia* 53°12N 46°40E **18** D8
Kuzomen *Russia* 66°22N 36°50E **18** A6
Kvænangen *Norway* 70°5N 21°15E **8** A19
Kvaløya *Norway* 69°40N 18°30E **8** B18
Kvarner *Croatia* 44°50N 14°10E **16** F8
Kvarnerič *Croatia* 44°43N 14°37E **16** F8
Kwabhaca *S. Africa* 30°51S 29°0E **57** E4
Kwai = Khwae Noi →
    Thailand 14°1N 99°32E **38** E2
Kwajalein *Marshall Is.* 9°5N 167°20E **64** G8
Kwakhanai *Botswana* 21°39S 21°16E **56** B3
Kwakoegron *Suriname* 5°12N 55°25W **93** B7
KwaMashu *S. Africa* 29°45S 30°58E **57** C5
Kwando → *Africa* 18°27S 23°32E **56** B3
Kwangdaeri *N. Korea* 40°34N 127°33E **33** D14
Kwango →
    Dem. Rep. of the Congo 3°14S 17°22E **54** E3
Kwangsi-Chuang = Guangxi
    Zhuangzu Zizhiqu □
    China 24°0N 109°0E **34** F7
Kwangtung = Guangdong □
    China 23°0N 113°0E **35** F9
Kwataboahegan →
    Canada 51°9N 80°50W **72** B3
Kwatisore *Indonesia* 3°18S 134°50E **37** E8
KwaZulu Natal □ *S. Africa* 29°0S 30°0E **57** C5
Kweichow = Guizhou □
    China 27°0N 107°0E **34** D6
Kwekwe *Zimbabwe* 18°58S 29°48E **55** H5
Kweneng □ *Botswana* 24°0S 25°0E **56** B3
Kwidzyn *Poland* 53°44N 18°55E **17** B10
Kwilu →
    Dem. Rep. of the Congo 3°22S 17°22E **54** E3
Kwinana *Australia* 32°15S 115°47E **61** F2
Kwoka *Indonesia* 0°31S 132°27E **37** E8
Kyabra Cr. → *Australia* 25°36S 142°55E **63** D3
Kyabram *Australia* 36°19S 145°4E **63** F4
Kyaikto *Burma* 17°20N 97°3E **38** D1
Kyaing Tong = Keng Tung
    Burma 21°18N 99°39E **38** B2
Kyakhta *Russia* 50°30N 106°25E **27** D11
Kyancutta *Australia* 33°8S 135°33E **63** E2
Kyaukpadaung *Burma* 20°52N 95°8E **41** J19
Kyaukpyu *Burma* 19°28N 93°30E **41** K18
Kyaukse *Burma* 21°36N 96°10E **41** J20
Kyburz *U.S.A.* 38°47N 120°18W **78** G6
Kyelang *India* 32°35N 77°2E **42** C7
Kyle *Canada* 50°50N 108°2W **71** C7
Kyle *U.S.A.* 29°59N 97°53W **84** F6
Kyle of Lochalsh *U.K.* 57°17N 5°44W **11** D3
Kymijoki → *Finland* 60°30N 26°55E **8** F22
Kymmene älv = Kymijoki →
    Finland 60°30N 26°55E **8** F22
Kyneton *Australia* 37°10S 144°29E **63** F3
Kynuna *Australia* 21°37S 141°55E **62** C3
Kyō-ga-Saki *Japan* 35°45N 135°15E **29** G7
Kyoga, L. *Uganda* 1°35N 33°0E **54** D6
Kyogle *Australia* 28°40S 153°0E **63** D5
Kyŏngju = Gyeongju
    S. Korea 35°51N 129°14E **33** G15
Kyŏngsŏng *N. Korea* 41°35N 129°36E **33** D15
Kyonpyaw *Burma* 17°12N 95°10E **41** L19
Kyōto *Japan* 35°0N 135°45E **29** G7
Kyōto □ *Japan* 35°15N 135°45E **29** G7
Kypros = Cyprus ■ *Asia* 35°0N 33°0E **46** C2
Kyrenia *Cyprus* 35°20N 33°19E **46** C2
Kyrgyzstan ■ *Asia* 42°0N 75°0E **26** E8
Kyro älv = Kyrönjoki →
    Finland 63°14N 21°45E **8** E19
Kyrönjoki → *Finland* 63°14N 21°45E **8** E19
Kythira *Greece* 36°8N 23°0E **23** F10
Kyunhla *Burma* 23°25N 95°15E **41** H19
Kyuquot Sound *Canada* 50°2N 127°22W **70** D3
Kyūshū *Japan* 33°0N 131°0E **29** H5
Kyūshū □ *Japan* 33°0N 131°0E **29** H5
Kyushu-Palau Ridge
    Pac. Oc. 20°0N 136°0E **64** E5
Kyūshū-Sanchi *Japan* 32°35N 131°17E **29** H5
Kyustendil *Bulgaria* 42°16N 22°41E **23** C10
Kyusyur *Russia* 70°19N 127°30E **27** B13
Kyyiv *Ukraine* 50°30N 30°28E **17** C16
Kyyivske Vdskh. *Ukraine* 51°0N 30°25E **17** C16
Kyzyl *Russia* 51°50N 94°30E **30** A7
Kyzyl Kum *Uzbekistan* 42°30N 65°0E **26** E7
Kyzyl Kyya *Kyrgyzstan* 40°16N 72°8E **26** E8
Kyzyl Orda = Qyzylorda
    Kazakhstan 44°48N 65°28E **26** E7

L

La Alcarria *Spain* 40°31N 2°45W **21** B4
La Amistad △ *Cent. Amer.* 9°28N 83°18W **88** E3
La Asunción *Venezuela* 11°2N 63°53W **92** A6
La Baie *Canada* 48°19N 70°53W **73** C5
La Banda *Argentina* 27°45S 64°10W **94** B3
La Barca *Mexico* 20°17N 102°34W **86** C4
La Barge *U.S.A.* 42°16N 110°12W **76** E8
La Barra *Nic.* 12°54N 83°33W **88** D3
La Belle *U.S.A.* 26°46N 81°26W **85** H14
La Biche → *Canada* 59°57N 123°50W **70** B4
La Biche, L. *Canada* 54°50N 112°3W **70** C6
La Brea *Trin. & Tob.* 10°15N 61°37W **93** K15
La Calera *Chile* 32°50S 71°10W **94** C1
La Campana △ *Chile* 32°58S 71°14W **94** C1
La Carlota *Argentina* 33°30S 63°20W **94** C3

La Ceiba Honduras 15°40N 86°50W 88 C2
La Chaux-de-Fonds Switz. 47°7N 6°50E 20 C7
La Chorrera Panama 8°53N 79°47W 88 E4
La Cocha Argentina 27°50S 65°40W 94 B2
La Concepción Panama 8°31N 82°37W 88 E3
La Concordia Mexico 16°5N 92°38W 87 D6
La Coruña = A Coruña
  Spain 43°20N 8°25W 21 A1
La Crescent U.S.A. 43°50N 91°18W 80 D8
La Crete Canada 58°11N 116°24W 70 B5
La Crosse Kans., U.S.A. 38°32N 99°18W 80 F4
La Crosse Wis., U.S.A. 43°48N 91°15W 80 D8
La Cruz Costa Rica 11°4N 85°39W 88 D2
La Cruz Mexico 23°55N 106°54W 86 C3
La Désirade Guadeloupe 16°18N 61°3W 88 b
La Digue Seychelles 4°20S 55°51E 55 b
La Esperanza Cuba 22°46N 83°44W 88 B3
La Esperanza Honduras 14°15N 88°10W 88 D2
La Estrada = A Estrada
  Spain 42°43N 8°27W 21 A1
La Fayette U.S.A. 34°42N 85°17W 85 D12
La Fé Cuba 22°2N 84°15W 88 B3
La Follette U.S.A. 36°23N 84°7W 85 C12
La Gi Vietnam 10°40N 107°45E 39 G6
La Grande U.S.A. 45°20N 118°5W 76 D4
La Grande → Canada 53°50N 79°0W 72 B5
La Grande 3, Rés. Canada 53°40N 75°10W 72 B4
La Grande 4, Rés. Canada 54°0N 73°15W 72 B5
La Grange Calif., U.S.A. 37°42N 120°27W 78 H6
La Grange Ga., U.S.A. 33°2N 85°2W 85 E12
La Grange Ky., U.S.A. 38°24N 85°22W 81 F11
La Grange Tex., U.S.A. 29°54N 96°52W 84 G6
La Guaira Venezuela 10°36N 66°56W 92 A5
La Habana Cuba 23°8N 82°22W 88 B3
La Independencia Mexico 16°15N 92°1W 87 D6
La Isabela Dom. Rep. 19°58N 71°2W 89 C5
La Junta U.S.A. 37°59N 103°33W 76 H12
La Libertad = Puerto Libertad
  Mexico 29°55N 112°43W 86 B2
La Libertad Guatemala 16°47N 90°7W 88 C1
La Ligua Chile 32°30S 71°16W 94 C1
La Línea de la Concepción
  Spain 36°15N 5°23W 21 D3
La Loche Canada 56°29N 109°26W 71 B7
La Louvière Belgium 50°27N 4°10E 15 D4
La Lune Trin. & Tob. 10°3N 61°22W 93 K15
La Malbaie Canada 47°40N 70°10W 73 C5
La Malinche △ Mexico 19°15N 98°3W 87 D5
La Mancha Spain 39°10N 2°54W 21 C4
La Martre, L. Canada 63°15N 117°55W 70 A5
La Mercy = Durban ✈ (DIA)
  S. Africa 29°37S 31°7E 57 C5
La Mesa Mexico 32°30N 116°57W 79 N10
La Mesa U.S.A. 32°46N 117°1W 79 N9
La Mesilla U.S.A. 32°16N 106°48W 77 K10
La Moure U.S.A. 46°21N 98°18W 80 B4
La Negra Chile 23°46S 70°18W 94 A1
La Oroya Peru 11°32S 75°54W 92 F3
La Palma Canary Is. 28°40N 17°50W 52 C2
La Palma Panama 8°15N 78°0W 88 E4
La Palma del Condado
  Spain 37°21N 6°38W 21 D2
La Paloma Chile 30°35S 71°0W 94 C1
La Pampa □ Argentina 36°50S 66°0W 94 D2
La Paragua Venezuela 6°50N 63°20W 92 B6
La Paz Entre Ríos,
  Argentina 30°50S 59°45W 94 C4
La Paz San Luis, Argentina 33°30S 67°20W 94 C2
La Paz Bolivia 16°20S 68°10W 92 G5
La Paz Honduras 14°20N 87°47W 88 D2
La Paz Mexico 24°10N 110°18W 86 C2
La Paz Centro Nic. 12°20N 86°41W 88 D2
La Pedrera Colombia 1°18S 69°43W 92 D5
La Pérade Canada 46°35N 72°12W 73 C5
La Perla Mexico 28°18N 104°32W 86 B4
La Perouse Str. Asia 45°40N 142°0E 28 B11
La Pesca Mexico 23°46N 97°47W 87 C5
La Piedad Mexico 20°21N 102°0W 86 C4
La Pine U.S.A. 43°40N 121°30W 76 E3
La Plata Argentina 35°0S 57°55W 94 C4
La Pocatière Canada 47°22N 70°2W 73 C5
La Porte U.S.A. 29°40N 95°1W 84 G7
La Purísima Mexico 26°10N 112°4W 86 B2
La Push U.S.A. 47°55N 124°38W 78 C2
La Quiaca Argentina 22°5S 65°35W 94 A2
La Rioja Argentina 29°20S 67°0W 94 B2
La Rioja □ Argentina 29°30S 67°0W 94 B2
La Rioja □ Spain 42°20N 2°20W 21 A4
La Robla Spain 42°50N 5°41W 21 A3
La Roche-en-Ardenne
  Belgium 50°11N 5°35E 15 D5
La Roche-sur-Yon France 46°40N 1°25W 20 C3
La Rochelle France 46°10N 1°9W 20 C3
La Roda Spain 39°13N 2°15W 21 C4
La Romaine Canada 50°13N 60°40W 73 B7
La Romana Dom. Rep. 18°27N 68°57W 89 C6
La Ronge Canada 55°5N 105°20W 71 B7
La Rumorosa Mexico 32°34N 116°6W 79 N10
La Salle U.S.A. 41°20N 89°6W 80 E9
La Sarre Canada 48°45N 79°15W 72 C4
La Scie Canada 49°57N 55°36W 73 C8
La Selva Beach U.S.A. 36°56N 121°51W 78 J5
La Serena Chile 29°55S 71°10W 94 B1
La Seu d'Urgell Spain 42°22N 1°23E 21 A6
La Seyne-sur-Mer France 43°7N 5°52E 20 E6
La Soufrière St. Vincent 13°20N 61°11W 89 D7
La Spézia Italy 44°7N 9°50E 20 D8
La Tagua Colombia 0°3N 74°40W 92 C4
La Tortuga, I. Venezuela 11°0N 65°22W 89 D6
La Tuque Canada 47°30N 72°50W 72 C5
La Unión Chile 40°10S 73°0W 96 E2
La Unión El Salv. 13°20N 87°50W 88 D2
La Unión Mexico 17°58N 101°49W 86 D4
La Urbana Venezuela 7°8N 66°56W 92 B5
La Vache Pt.
  Trin. & Tob. 10°47N 61°28W 93 K15
La Vall d'Uixó Spain 39°49N 0°15W 21 C5
La Vega Dom. Rep. 19°20N 70°30W 89 C5

La Vela de Coro
  Venezuela 11°27N 69°34W 92 A5
La Venta Mexico 18°5N 94°3W 87 D6
La Vergne U.S.A. 36°1N 86°35W 85 C11
La Villa Joiosa = Villajoyosa
  Spain 38°30N 0°12W 21 C5
Laascaanood = Las Anod
  Somalia 8°26N 47°19E 49 F4
Labasa Fiji 16°30S 179°27E 59 a
Labdah = Leptis Magna
  Libya 32°40N 14°12E 53 B8
Labe = Elbe → Europe 53°50N 9°0E 16 B5
Labé Guinea 11°24N 12°16W 52 F3
Laberge, L. Canada 61°11N 135°12W 70 A1
Labinsk Russia 44°40N 40°48E 19 F7
Labis Malaysia 2°22N 103°2E 39 L4
Laborie St. Lucia 13°45N 61°2W 89 f
Laboulaye Argentina 34°10S 63°30W 94 C3
Labrador Canada 53°20N 61°0W 73 B7
Labrador City Canada 52°57N 66°55W 73 B6
Labrador Sea Atl. Oc. 57°0N 54°0W 69 F21
Lábrea Brazil 7°15S 64°51W 92 E6
Labuan □ Malaysia 5°20N 115°12E 36 C4
Labuha Indonesia 0°30S 127°30E 37 E7
Labuhan Indonesia 6°22S 105°50E 37 G11
Labuhanbajo Indonesia 8°28S 119°54E 37 F6
Labuhanbilik Indonesia 2°31N 100°10E 39 L3
Labuk, Telok Malaysia 6°10N 117°50E 36 C5
Labyrinth, L. Australia 30°40S 135°11E 63 E2
Labytnangi Russia 66°39N 66°21E 18 A12
Lac-Bouchette Canada 48°16N 72°11W 73 C5
Lac-Édouard Canada 47°40N 72°16W 73 C5
Lac La Biche Canada 54°45N 111°58W 70 C6
Lac la Martre = Wha Ti
  Canada 63°8N 117°16W 68 E8
Lac La Ronge Canada 55°9N 104°41W 71 B7
Lac-Mégantic Canada 45°35N 70°53W 73 C5
Lac Thien Vietnam 12°25N 108°11E 38 F7
Lacanau France 44°58N 1°5W 20 D3
Lacantún → Mexico 16°36N 90°39W 87 D6
Laccadive Is. = Lakshadweep Is.
  India 10°0N 72°30E 45 J1
Lacepede B. Australia 36°40S 139°40E 63 F2
Lacepede Is. Australia 16°55S 122°0E 60 C3
Lacey U.S.A. 47°7N 122°49W 78 C4
Lachhmangarh India 27°50N 75°4E 42 F6
Lachi Pakistan 33°25N 71°20E 42 C4
Lachlan → Australia 34°22S 143°55E 63 E3
Lachute Canada 45°39N 74°21W 72 C5
Lackagh Hills Ireland 54°16N 8°10W 10 B3
Lackawanna U.S.A. 42°50N 78°50W 82 D6
Lackawaxen U.S.A. 41°29N 74°59W 83 E10
Lacolle Canada 45°5N 73°22W 83 A11
Lacombe Canada 52°30N 113°44W 70 C6
Lacona U.S.A. 43°39N 76°10W 83 C8
Laconia U.S.A. 43°32N 71°28W 83 C13
Ladakh Ra. India 34°0N 78°0E 43 C8
Ladismith S. Africa 33°28S 21°15E 56 D3
Lādīz Iran 28°55N 61°15E 47 D9
Ladnun India 27°38N 74°25E 42 F6
Ladoga, L. = Ladozhskoye Ozero
  Russia 61°15N 30°30E 8 F24
Ladozhskoye Ozero
  Russia 61°15N 30°30E 8 F24
Lady Elliott I. Australia 24°7S 152°42E 62 C5
Lady Frere S. Africa 31°42S 27°14E 56 D4
Lady Grey S. Africa 30°43S 27°13E 56 D4
Ladybrand S. Africa 29°9S 27°29E 56 C4
Ladysmith Canada 49°0N 123°49W 78 B3
Ladysmith S. Africa 28°32S 29°46E 57 C4
Ladysmith U.S.A. 45°28N 91°12W 80 C8
Lae Papua N. G. 6°40S 147°2E 58 B7
Laem Ngop Thailand 12°10N 102°26E 39 F4
Laem Son △ Thailand 9°29N 98°24E 39 H2
Læsø Denmark 57°15N 11°5E 9 H14
Lafayette Ind., U.S.A. 40°25N 86°54W 80 E10
Lafayette La., U.S.A. 30°14N 92°1W 84 F8
Lafayette Tenn., U.S.A. 36°31N 86°2W 85 C11
Laferte → Canada 61°53N 117°44W 70 A5
Lafia Nigeria 8°30N 8°34E 52 G7
Laflèche Canada 49°45N 106°40W 71 D7
Laful India 7°10N 93°52E 45 L11
Lagan → U.K. 54°36N 5°55W 10 B6
Lagarfljót → Iceland 65°40N 14°18W 8 D6
Lagdo, L. de Cameroon 8°40N 14°0E 53 G8
Lågen → Oppland, Norway 61°8N 10°25E 8 F14
Lågen → Vestfold, Norway 59°3N 10°3E 9 G14
Lages Brazil 27°48S 50°20W 95 B5
Laghouat Algeria 33°50N 2°59E 52 B6
Lagoa do Peixe △ Brazil 31°12S 50°50W 95 C5
Lagoa Vermelha Brazil 28°13S 51°32W 95 B5
Lagonoy G. Phil. 13°35S 123°50E 37 B6
Lagos Portugal 37°5N 8°41W 21 D1
Lagos de Moreno
  Mexico 21°21N 101°55W 86 C4
Lagrange = Bidyadanga
  Australia 18°45S 121°43E 60 C3
Lagrange B. Australia 18°38S 121°42E 60 C3
Laguna Brazil 28°30S 48°50W 95 B6
Laguna U.S.A. 35°2N 107°25W 77 J10
Laguna, Sa. de la
  Mexico 23°35N 109°55W 86 C3
Laguna Beach U.S.A. 33°33N 117°47W 79 M9
Laguna de la Restinga △
  Venezuela 10°58N 64°0W 89 D6
Laguna de Lachuá △
  Guatemala 15°55N 90°40W 88 C1
Laguna del Laja △ Chile 37°27S 71°20W 94 D1
Laguna del Tigre △
  Guatemala 17°32N 90°56W 88 C1
Laguna Limpia Argentina 26°32S 59°45W 94 B4
Lagunas Chile 21°0S 69°45W 94 A2
Lagunas Peru 5°10S 75°35W 92 E3
Lagunas de Chacahua △
  Mexico 16°0N 97°43W 87 D5
Lagunas de Montebello △
  Mexico 16°4N 91°42W 87 D6
Lahad Datu Malaysia 5°0N 118°20E 37 D5
Lahad Datu, Telok
  Malaysia 4°50N 118°20E 37 D5

Lahan Sai Thailand 14°25N 102°52E 38 E4
Lahanam Laos 16°16N 105°16E 38 D5
Lahar India 26°12N 78°57E 43 F8
Laharpur India 27°43N 80°56E 43 F9
Lahat Indonesia 3°45S 103°30E 36 E2
Lahewa Indonesia 1°22N 97°12E 36 D1
Lāhījān Iran 37°10N 50°6E 47 B6
Lahn → Germany 50°19N 7°37E 16 C4
Laholm Sweden 56°30N 13°2E 9 H15
Lahore Pakistan 31°32N 74°22E 42 D6
Lahri Pakistan 29°11N 68°13E 42 E3
Lāhrūd Iran 38°30N 47°52E 46 B5
Lahti Finland 60°58N 25°40E 8 F21
Lahtis = Lahti Finland 60°58N 25°40E 8 F21
Lahugala Kitulana △
  Sri Lanka 6°50N 81°40E 45 L5
Laï Chad 9°25N 16°18E 53 G9
Lai Chau Vietnam 22°5N 103°3E 34 F4
Lai'an China 32°28N 118°30E 35 A12
Laibin China 23°42N 109°14E 34 F7
Laifeng China 29°27N 109°20E 34 C7
Laila = Layla Si. Arabia 22°10N 46°40E 49 C4
Laingsburg S. Africa 33°9S 20°52E 56 E3
Lainioälven → Sweden 67°35N 22°40E 8 C20
Lairg U.K. 58°2N 4°24W 11 C4
Laiwu China 36°15N 117°40E 33 F9
Laixi China 36°50N 120°31E 33 F11
Laiyang China 36°59N 120°45E 33 F11
Laiyuan China 39°20N 114°40E 32 E8
Laizhou China 37°8N 119°57E 33 F10
Laizhou Wan China 37°30N 119°30E 33 F10
Lajamanu Australia 18°23S 130°38E 60 C5
Lak Sao Laos 18°11N 104°59E 38 C5
Lakaband Pakistan 31°2N 69°15E 42 D3
Lake U.S.A. 44°33N 110°24W 76 D8
Lake Alpine U.S.A. 38°29N 120°0W 78 G7
Lake Andes U.S.A. 43°9N 98°32W 80 D4
Lake Arthur U.S.A. 30°5N 92°41W 84 F8
Lake Bindegolly △
  Australia 28°0S 144°12E 63 D3
Lake Cargelligo Australia 33°15S 146°22E 63 E4
Lake Charles U.S.A. 30°14N 93°13W 84 F8
Lake City Colo., U.S.A. 38°2N 107°19W 76 G10
Lake City Fla., U.S.A. 30°11N 82°38W 85 F13
Lake City Mich., U.S.A. 44°20N 85°13W 81 C11
Lake City Minn., U.S.A. 44°27N 92°16W 80 C7
Lake City Pa., U.S.A. 42°1N 80°21W 82 D4
Lake City S.C., U.S.A. 33°52N 79°45W 85 E15
Lake Cowichan Canada 48°49N 124°3W 78 B3
Lake District △ U.K. 54°30N 3°21W 12 C4
Lake Elsinore U.S.A. 33°38N 117°20W 79 M9
Lake Eyre △ Australia 28°40S 137°31E 63 D2
Lake Gairdner △
  Australia 31°41S 135°51E 63 E2
Lake George U.S.A. 43°26N 73°43W 83 C11
Lake Grace Australia 33°7S 118°28E 61 F2
Lake Gregory ♡
  Australia 20°12S 127°27E 60 D4
Lake Harbour = Kimmirut
  Canada 62°50N 69°50W 69 E18
Lake Havasu City
  U.S.A. 34°27N 114°22W 79 L12
Lake Hughes U.S.A. 34°41N 118°26W 79 L8
Lake Isabella U.S.A. 35°38N 118°28W 79 K8
Lake Jackson U.S.A. 29°3N 95°27W 84 G7
Lake King Australia 33°5S 119°45E 61 F2
Lake Lenore Canada 52°24N 104°59W 71 C8
Lake Louise Canada 51°30N 116°10W 70 C5
Lake Mackay ♡
  Australia 21°48S 129°46E 60 D4
Lake Mead △ U.S.A. 36°30N 114°22W 79 K12
Lake Meredith △
  U.S.A. 35°50N 101°50W 84 D4
Lake Mills U.S.A. 43°25N 93°32W 80 D7
Lake Placid U.S.A. 44°17N 73°59W 83 B11
Lake Pleasant U.S.A. 43°28N 74°25W 83 C10
Lake Providence U.S.A. 32°48N 91°10W 84 E9
Lake Roosevelt △ U.S.A. 48°5N 118°14W 76 B4
Lake St. Peter Canada 45°18N 78°2W 82 A6
Lake Stevens U.S.A. 48°1N 122°4W 78 B4
Lake Superior △ Canada 47°45N 84°45W 72 C3
Lake Torrens △
  Australia 30°55S 137°40E 63 E2
Lake Village U.S.A. 33°20N 91°17W 84 E9
Lake Wales U.S.A. 27°54N 81°35W 85 H14
Lake Worth U.S.A. 26°37N 80°3W 85 H14
Lakeba Fiji 18°13S 178°47W 59 a
Lakeba Passage Fiji 18°0S 178°45W 59 a
Lakefield Canada 44°25N 78°16W 82 B6
Lakefield △ Australia 15°24S 144°06E 62 B3
Lakehurst U.S.A. 40°1N 74°19W 83 F10
Lakeland Australia 15°49S 144°57E 62 B3
Lakeland U.S.A. 28°3N 81°57W 85 G14
Lakemba = Lakeba Fiji 18°13S 178°47W 59 a
Lakeport Calif., U.S.A. 39°3N 122°55W 78 F4
Lakeport Mich., U.S.A. 43°7N 82°30W 82 C2
Lakes Entrance Australia 37°50S 148°0E 63 F4
Lakeside Calif., U.S.A. 32°52N 116°55W 79 N10
Lakeside Nebr., U.S.A. 42°3N 102°26W 80 D2
Lakeview U.S.A. 42°11N 120°21W 76 E3
Lakeville U.S.A. 44°39N 93°14W 80 C7
Lakewood Colo., U.S.A. 39°42N 105°4W 76 G11
Lakewood N.J., U.S.A. 40°6N 74°13W 83 F10
Lakewood N.Y., U.S.A. 42°6N 79°19W 82 D5
Lakewood Ohio, U.S.A. 41°28N 81°47W 82 E7
Lakewood Wash.,
  U.S.A. 47°11N 122°32W 78 C4
Lakha India 26°9N 70°54E 42 F4
Lakhimpur India 27°57N 80°46E 43 F9
Lakhisarai India 25°11N 86°5E 43 G12
Lakhnadon India 22°36N 79°36E 43 H8
Lakhnau = Lucknow
  India 26°50N 81°0E 43 F9
Lakhonpheng Laos 15°54N 105°34E 38 E5
Lakhpat India 23°48N 68°47E 42 H3
Lakin U.S.A. 37°57N 101°15W 80 G3
Lakitusaki → Canada 54°21N 82°25W 72 B3
Lakki Pakistan 32°36N 70°55E 42 C4
Lakonikos Kolpos
  Greece 36°40N 22°40E 23 F10

Lakor Indonesia 8°15S 128°17E 37 F7
Lakota Ivory C. 5°50N 5°30W 52 G4
Lakota U.S.A. 48°2N 98°21W 80 A4
Laksar India 29°46N 78°3E 42 E8
Lakselv Norway 70°2N 25°0E 8 A21
Laksettipet India 18°52N 79°13E 44 E4
Lakshadweep □ India 10°0N 72°30E 45 J1
Lakshadweep Is. India 10°0N 72°30E 45 J1
Lakshmanpur India 22°58N 83°3E 43 H10
Lakshmeshwar India 15°9N 75°28E 45 G2
Lakshmikantapur India 22°5N 88°20E 43 H13
Lala Musa Pakistan 32°40N 73°57E 42 C5
Lalaghat India 24°30N 92°40E 41 G18
Lalganj India 25°52N 85°13E 43 G11
Lalgola India 24°25N 88°15E 43 G13
L'Albufera Spain 39°20N 0°27W 21 C5
Lalī Iran 32°21N 49°6E 47 C6
Lalibela Ethiopia 12°3N 39°0E 49 E2
Lalin China 45°12N 127°0E 33 B14
Lalín Spain 42°40N 8°5W 21 A1
Lalin He → China 45°32N 125°40E 33 B13
Lalitpur India 24°42N 78°28E 43 G8
Lalitpur Nepal 27°40N 85°20E 43 F11
Lalkua India 29°5N 79°31E 43 E8
Lalsot India 26°34N 76°20E 42 F7
Lam Nam Nan △
  Thailand 17°55N 100°28E 38 D3
Lam Pao Res. Thailand 16°50N 103°15E 38 D4
Lama Kara Togo 9°30N 1°15E 52 G6
Lamae Thailand 9°32N 99°2E 39 H2
Lamaing Burma 15°25N 97°53E 38 K11
Lamar Colo., U.S.A. 38°5N 102°37W 76 G12
Lamar Mo., U.S.A. 37°30N 94°16W 80 G6
Lamas Peru 6°28S 76°31W 92 E3
Lamayuru India 34°25N 76°56E 43 B7
Lambaréné Gabon 0°41S 10°12E 54 E2
Lambasa = Labasa Fiji 16°30S 179°27E 59 a
Lambay I. Ireland 53°29N 6°1W 10 C5
Lambert's Bay S. Africa 32°5S 18°17E 56 E2
Lame Deer U.S.A. 45°37N 106°40W 76 D10
Lamego Portugal 41°5N 7°52W 21 B2
Lamèque Canada 47°45N 64°38W 73 C7
Lameroo Australia 35°19S 140°33E 63 F3
Lamesa U.S.A. 32°44N 101°58W 84 E4
Lamia Greece 38°55N 22°26E 23 E10
Lamington △ Australia 28°13S 153°12E 63 D5
Lammermuir Hills U.K. 55°50N 2°40W 11 F6
Lamoille → U.S.A. 44°38N 73°13W 83 B11
Lamon B. Phil. 14°30N 122°20E 37 B6
Lamont Canada 53°46N 112°50W 70 C6
Lamont Calif., U.S.A. 35°15N 118°55W 79 K8
Lamont Wyo., U.S.A. 42°13N 107°29W 76 E10
Lampa Peru 15°22S 70°22W 92 G4
Lampang Thailand 18°16N 99°32E 38 C2
Lampasas U.S.A. 31°4N 98°11W 84 F5
Lampazos de Naranjo
  Mexico 27°1N 100°31W 86 B4
Lampedusa Medit. S. 35°36N 12°40E 22 G5
Lampeter U.K. 52°7N 4°4W 13 E3
Lamphun Thailand 18°40N 99°2E 38 C2
Lampione Medit. S. 35°33N 12°20E 22 G5
Lampman Canada 49°25N 102°50W 71 D8
Lampung □ Indonesia 5°30S 104°30E 36 F2
Lamta India 22°8N 80°7E 43 H9
Lamu Kenya 2°16S 40°55E 54 E8
Lamy U.S.A. 35°29N 105°53W 77 J11
Lan Xian China 38°15N 111°35E 32 E6
Lan Yü Taiwan 22°4N 121°25E 35 F13
Lāna'i U.S.A. 20°50N 156°55W 75 L8
Lanak La China 34°27N 79°32E 43 B8
Lanak'o Shank'ou = Lanak La
  China 34°27N 79°32E 43 B8
Lanark Canada 45°1N 76°22W 83 A8
Lanark U.K. 55°40N 3°47W 11 F5
Lanbi Kyun Burma 10°50N 98°20E 39 G2
Lancang China 22°36N 99°58E 34 F2
Lancang Jiang → China 21°40N 101°10E 34 G3
Lancashire □ U.K. 53°50N 2°48W 12 D5
Lancaster Canada 45°10N 74°30W 83 A10
Lancaster U.K. 54°3N 2°48W 12 C5
Lancaster Calif., U.S.A. 34°42N 118°8W 79 L8
Lancaster Ky., U.S.A. 37°37N 84°35W 81 G11
Lancaster N.H., U.S.A. 44°29N 71°34W 83 B13
Lancaster Ohio, U.S.A. 39°43N 82°36W 81 F12
Lancaster Pa., U.S.A. 40°2N 76°19W 83 F8
Lancaster S.C., U.S.A. 34°43N 80°46W 85 D14
Lancaster Wis., U.S.A. 42°51N 90°43W 80 D8
Lancaster Sd. Canada 74°13N 84°0W 69 C15
Lancelin Australia 31°0S 115°18E 61 F2
Lanchow = Lanzhou
  China 36°1N 103°52E 32 F2
Lanciano Italy 42°14N 14°23E 22 C6
Lancun China 36°25N 120°10E 33 F11
Land Between the Lakes △
  U.S.A. 36°25N 88°0W 85 C11
Landeck Austria 47°9N 10°34E 16 E6
Lander U.S.A. 42°50N 108°44W 76 E9
Lander → Australia 22°0S 132°0E 60 D5
Landes France 44°0N 1°0W 20 D3
Landfall I. India 13°40N 93°2E 45 H11
Landi Kotal Pakistan 34°7N 71°6E 42 B4
Landisburg U.S.A. 40°21N 77°19W 82 F7
Landmannalaugar Iceland 63°59N 19°4W 8 E4
Land's End U.K. 50°4N 5°44W 13 G2
Landsborough Cr. →
  Australia 22°28S 144°35E 62 C3
Landshut Germany 48°34N 12°8E 16 D7
Lanesboro U.S.A. 41°57N 75°34W 83 E9
Lanett U.S.A. 32°52N 85°12W 85 E12
Lang Shan China 41°0N 106°30E 32 D4
Lang Son Vietnam 21°52N 106°42E 34 G4
Lang Suan Thailand 9°57N 99°4E 39 H2
La'nga Co China 30°45N 81°15E 43 D9
Langar Iran 35°23N 60°2E 47 C9
Langara I. Canada 54°14N 133°1W 70 C2
Langarūd Iran 37°11N 50°8E 47 B6
Langdai China 26°6N 105°21E 34 D5

Langdon U.S.A. 48°45N 98°22W 80 A4
Langeberg S. Africa 33°55S 21°0E 56 D3
Langeberge S. Africa 28°15S 22°33E 56 D3
Langeland Denmark 54°56N 10°48E 9 J14
Langfang China 39°30N 116°41E 32 E9
Langholm U.K. 55°9N 3°0W 11 F5
Langjökull Iceland 64°39N 20°12W 8 D3
Langkawi, Pulau Malaysia 6°25N 99°45E 39 J2
Langklip S. Africa 28°12S 20°20E 56 D3
Langkon Malaysia 6°30N 116°40E 36 C5
Langley Canada 49°7N 122°39W 78 A4
Langøya Norway 68°45N 14°50E 8 B16
Langreo Spain 43°18N 5°40W 21 A3
Langres France 47°52N 5°20E 20 C6
Langres, Plateau de France 47°45N 5°3E 20 C6
Langsa Indonesia 4°30N 97°57E 36 D1
Langtang △ Nepal 28°10N 85°30E 43 E11
Langtou China 40°1N 124°19E 33 D13
Langtry U.S.A. 29°49N 101°34W 84 G4
Langu Thailand 6°53N 99°47E 39 J2
Languedoc France 43°58N 3°55E 20 E5
Langwang China 22°38N 113°27E 31 a
Langxi China 31°10N 119°12E 35 B12
Langzhong China 31°38N 105°58E 34 B5
Lanigan Canada 51°51N 105°2W 71 C7
Lanjigarh India 19°43N 83°23E 44 E6
Lankao China 34°48N 114°50E 32 G8
Länkäran Azerbaijan 38°48N 48°52E 47 B6
Lannion France 48°46N 3°29W 20 B2
L'Annonciation Canada 46°25N 74°55W 72 C5
Lanping China 26°28N 99°15E 34 D2
Lansang △ Thailand 16°45N 99°0E 38 D2
Lansdale U.S.A. 40°14N 75°17W 83 F9
Lansdowne Australia 31°48S 152°30E 63 E5
Lansdowne Canada 44°24N 76°1W 83 B8
Lansdowne India 29°50N 78°41E 43 E8
Lansdowne House = Neskantaga
  Canada 52°14N 87°53W 72 B2
L'Anse U.S.A. 46°45N 88°27W 80 B9
L'Anse au Loup Canada 51°32N 56°50W 73 B8
L'Anse aux Meadows
  Canada 51°36N 55°32W 73 B8
Lansford U.S.A. 40°50N 75°53W 83 F9
Lanshan China 25°24N 112°10E 35 E9
Lanshantou China 35°5N 119°20E 33 G10
Länsi-Turunmaa Finland 60°18N 22°18E 9 F20
Lansing U.S.A. 42°44N 84°33W 81 D11
Lanta, Ko Thailand 7°35N 99°3E 39 J2
Lantau I. China 22°15N 113°56E 31 a
Lantian China 34°11N 109°20E 32 G5
Lanusei Italy 39°52N 9°34E 22 E3
Lanxi China 29°13N 119°28E 35 C12
Lanzarote Canary Is. 29°0N 13°40W 52 C3
Lanzhou China 36°1N 103°52E 32 F2
Lao Cai Vietnam 22°30N 103°57E 34 F4
Laoag Phil. 18°7N 120°34E 37 A6
Laoang Phil. 12°32N 125°8E 37 B7
Laoha He → China 43°25N 120°35E 33 C11
Laohekou China 32°22N 111°38E 34 A8
Laois □ Ireland 52°57N 7°27W 10 D4
Laon France 49°33N 3°35E 20 B5
Laona U.S.A. 45°34N 88°40W 80 C9
Laos ■ Asia 17°45N 105°0E 38 D5
Lapa Brazil 25°46S 49°44W 95 B6
Lapeer U.S.A. 43°3N 83°19W 81 D12
Lapland = Lappland Europe 68°7N 24°0E 8 B21
LaPorte Ind., U.S.A. 41°36N 86°43W 80 E10
Laporte Pa., U.S.A. 41°25N 76°30W 83 E8
Lappeenranta Finland 61°3N 28°12E 8 F23
Lappland Europe 68°7N 24°0E 8 B21
Lappo = Lapua Finland 62°58N 23°0E 8 E20
Laprida Argentina 37°34S 60°45W 94 D3
Lâpseki Turkey 40°20N 26°41E 23 D12
Laptev Sea Russia 76°0N 125°0E 27 B13
Lapua Finland 62°58N 23°0E 8 E20
L'Aquila Italy 42°22N 13°22E 22 C5
Lār Iran 27°40N 54°14E 47 E7
Laramie U.S.A. 41°19N 105°35W 76 F11
Laramie Mts. U.S.A. 42°0N 105°30W 76 F11
Laranda = Karaman
  Turkey 37°14N 33°13E 46 B2
Laranjeiras do Sul Brazil 25°23S 52°23W 95 B5
Larantuka Indonesia 8°21S 122°55E 37 F6
Larat Indonesia 7°0S 132°0E 37 F8
Larder Lake Canada 48°5N 79°40W 72 C4
Laredo U.S.A. 27°30N 99°30W 84 H5
Laredo Sd. Canada 52°30N 128°53W 70 C3
Largo U.S.A. 27°54N 82°47W 85 H13
Largs U.K. 55°47N 4°52W 11 F4
Lariang Indonesia 1°26S 119°17E 37 E5
Larimore U.S.A. 47°54N 97°38W 80 B5
Larisa Greece 39°36N 22°27E 23 E10
Larkana Pakistan 27°32N 68°18E 42 F3
Larnaca Cyprus 34°55N 33°38E 46 C2
Larne U.K. 54°51N 5°51W 10 B6
Larned U.S.A. 38°11N 99°6W 80 F4
Larose U.S.A. 29°34N 90°23W 85 G9
Larrimah Australia 15°35S 133°12E 60 C5
Larsen Ice Shelf Antarctica 67°0S 62°0W 5 C17
Larvik Norway 59°4N 10°2E 8 G14
Las Animas U.S.A. 38°4N 103°13W 76 G12
Las Anod Somalia 8°26N 47°19E 49 F4
Las Brenãs Argentina 27°5S 61°7W 94 B3
Las Cejas Argentina 26°53S 64°44W 96 B4
Las Chimeneas Mexico 32°8N 116°5W 79 N10
Las Cruces U.S.A. 32°19N 106°47W 77 K10
Las Flores Argentina 36°10S 59°7W 94 D4
Las Heras Argentina 32°51S 68°49W 94 C2
Las Lajas Argentina 38°30S 70°25W 96 D2
Las Lomitas Argentina 24°43S 60°35W 94 A3
Las Palmas Argentina 27°8S 58°45W 94 B4
Las Palmas Canary Is. 28°7N 15°26W 52 C2
Las Palmas → Mexico 32°26N 116°54W 79 N10
Las Piedras Uruguay 34°44S 56°14W 95 C4
Las Pipinas Argentina 35°30S 57°19W 94 D4
Las Plumas Argentina 43°40S 67°15W 96 E3
Las Rosas Argentina 32°30S 61°35W 94 C3
Las Tablas Panama 7°49N 80°14W 88 E3

136 Las Toscas

Las Toscas Argentina 28°21S 59°18W 94 B4
Las Tunas Cuba 20°58N 76°59W 88 B4
Las Varillas Argentina 31°50S 62°50W 94 C3
Las Vegas U.S.A. 35°36N 105°13W 77 J11
Lascano Uruguay 33°35S 54°12W 95 C5
Lash-e Joveyn Afghan. 31°45N 61°30E 40 D2
Lashio Burma 22°56N 97°45E 41 H20
Lashburn Canada 53°10N 109°40W 71 C7
Lashkar India 26°10N 78°10E 42 F8
Läsjerd Iran 35°24N 53°4E 47 C7
Lassen Pk. U.S.A. 40°29N 121°30W 76 F3
Lassen Volcanic △
U.S.A. 40°30N 121°20W 76 F3
Lastchance Cr. →
U.S.A. 40°2N 121°15W 78 E5
Lastoursville Gabon 0°55S 12°38E 54 E2
Lastovo Croatia 42°46N 16°55E 22 C7
Lat Yao Thailand 15°45N 99°48E 38 E2
Latacunga Ecuador 0°50S 78°35W 92 D3
Latady I. Antarctica 70°45S 74°35W 5 D17
Latakia = Al Lādhiqīyah
Syria 35°30N 35°45E 46 C2
Latchford Canada 47°20N 79°50W 72 C4
Late Tonga 18°48S 174°39W 59 c
Latehar India 23°45N 84°30E 43 H11
Latham Australia 29°44S 116°20E 61 E2
Lathi India 27°43N 71°23E 42 F4
Lathrop Wells U.S.A. 36°39N 116°24W 79 J10
Latina Italy 41°28N 12°52E 22 D5
Latium = Lazio □ Italy 42°10N 12°30E 22 D5
Laton U.S.A. 36°26N 119°41W 78 J7
Latouche Treville, C.
Australia 18°27S 121°49E 60 C3
Latrobe Australia 41°14S 146°30E 63 G4
Latrobe Australia 40°19N 79°23W 82 F5
Latur India 18°25N 76°40E 44 E3
Latvia ■ Europe 56°50N 24°0E 9 H21
Lau Group Fiji 17°0S 178°30W 59 a
Lauchhammer Germany 51°29N 13°47E 16 C7
Lauge Koch Kyst
Greenland 75°45N 57°45W 69 B20
Laughlin U.S.A. 35°10N 114°34W 79 K12
Laukaa Finland 62°24N 25°56E 8 E21
Launceston Australia 41°24S 147°8E 63 G4
Launceston U.K. 50°38N 4°22W 13 G3
Laune → Ireland 52°7N 9°47W 10 D2
Launglon Bok Burma 13°50N 97°54E 38 F1
Laura Australia 15°32S 144°32E 62 B3
Laurel Miss., U.S.A. 31°41N 89°8W 85 F10
Laurel Mont., U.S.A. 45°40N 108°46W 76 D9
Laurel Hill U.S.A. 40°14N 79°6W 82 F5
Laurencekirk U.K. 56°50N 2°28W 11 E6
Laurens U.S.A. 34°30N 82°1W 85 D13
Laurentian Plateau Canada 52°0N 70°0W 73 B6
Lauria Italy 40°2N 15°50E 22 E6
Laurie L. Canada 56°35S 101°57W 71 B8
Laurinburg U.S.A. 34°47N 79°28W 85 D15
Laurium U.S.A. 47°14N 88°27W 80 B9
Lausanne Switz. 46°32N 6°38E 20 C7
Laut Indonesia 4°45N 108°0E 36 D3
Laut, Pulau Indonesia 3°40S 116°10E 36 E5
Laut Kecil, Kepulauan
Indonesia 4°45S 115°40E 36 E5
Lautoka Fiji 17°37S 177°27E 59 a
Lauwersmeer △ Neths. 53°22N 6°11E 15 A6
Lava Beds △ U.S.A. 41°40N 121°30W 76 F3
Lavagh More Ireland 54°46N 8°6W 10 B3
Laval France 48°4N 0°48W 20 B3
Lavalle Argentina 28°15S 65°15W 94 B2
Lāvān Iran 26°48N 53°22E 47 E7
Lavant Canada 45°3N 76°42W 83 A8
Lāvar Meydān Iran 30°20N 54°30E 47 D7
Laverton Australia 28°44S 122°29E 61 E3
Lavras Brazil 21°20S 45°0W 95 A7
Lavrio Greece 37°40N 24°4E 23 F11
Lavumisa Swaziland 27°20S 31°55E 57 D5
Lawaki Fiji 17°40S 178°35E 59 a
Lawas Malaysia 4°55N 115°25E 36 D5
Lawele Indonesia 5°13S 122°57E 37 F6
Lawn Hill = Boodjamulla △
Australia 18°15S 138°6E 62 B2
Lawqah Si. Arabia 29°49N 42°45E 46 D4
Lawrence N.Z. 45°55S 169°41E 59 F2
Lawrence Ind., U.S.A. 39°50N 86°2W 80 F10
Lawrence Kans., U.S.A. 38°58N 95°14W 80 F6
Lawrence Mass., U.S.A. 42°43N 71°10W 83 D13
Lawrenceburg Ind.,
U.S.A. 39°6N 84°52W 81 F11
Lawrenceburg Tenn.,
U.S.A. 35°14N 87°20W 85 D11
Lawrenceville Ga.,
U.S.A. 33°57N 83°59W 85 E13
Lawrenceville Pa., U.S.A. 41°59N 77°8W 82 E7
Laws U.S.A. 37°24N 118°20W 78 H8
Lawton U.S.A. 34°37N 98°25W 84 D5
Lawu Indonesia 7°40S 111°13E 37 G14
Laxford, L. U.K. 58°24N 5°6W 11 C3
Laxiwa Dam China 36°4N 101°11E 30 D9
Layla Si. Arabia 22°10N 46°40E 47 C5
Laylān Iraq 35°18N 44°31E 46 C5
Laysan I. U.S.A. 25°50N 171°50W 75 K5
Layton U.S.A. 41°4N 111°58W 76 F8
Laytonville U.S.A. 39°41N 123°29W 76 G2
Lazarev Russia 52°13N 141°30E 27 D15
Lazarev Sea S. Ocean 67°30S 3°0W 5 C2
Lázaro Cárdenas
Mexico 17°55N 102°11W 86 D4
Lazio □ Italy 42°10N 12°30E 22 D5
Lazo Russia 43°25N 133°55E 28 C6
Le Bic Canada 48°20N 68°41W 73 C6
Le Creusot France 46°48N 4°24E 20 C6
Le François Martinique 14°38N 60°57W 88 c
Le Gosier Guadeloupe 16°14N 61°29W 88 b
Le Gris Gris Mauritius 20°31S 57°32E 55 d
Le Havre France 49°30N 0°5E 20 B4
Le Lamentin Martinique 14°35N 61°2W 88 c
Le Mans France 48°0N 0°10E 20 C4
Le Marin Martinique 14°27N 60°55W 88 c

Le Mars U.S.A. 42°47N 96°10W 80 D5
Le Mont-St-Michel France 48°40N 1°30W 20 B3
Le Moule Guadeloupe 16°20N 61°22W 88 b
Le Moyne, L. Canada 56°45N 68°47W 73 A6
Le Port Réunion 20°56S 55°18E 55 c
Le Prêcheur Martinique 14°50N 61°12W 88 c
Le Puy-en-Velay France 45°3N 3°52E 20 D5
Le Raysville U.S.A. 41°50N 76°10W 83 E8
Le Robert Martinique 14°40N 60°56W 88 c
Le Roy U.S.A. 42°58N 77°59W 82 D7
Le St-Esprit Martinique 14°34N 60°56W 88 c
Le Sueur U.S.A. 44°28N 93°55W 80 C7
Le Tampon Réunion 21°16S 55°32E 55 c
Le Thuy Vietnam 17°14N 106°49E 38 D6
Le Touquet-Paris-Plage
France 50°30N 1°36E 20 A4
Le Tréport France 50°3N 1°20E 20 A4
Le Verdon-sur-Mer France 45°33N 1°4W 20 D3
Lea → U.K. 51°31N 0°1E 13 F8
Leach Cambodia 12°21N 103°46E 39 F4
Leader Canada 50°50N 109°30W 71 C7
Leadville U.S.A. 39°15N 106°18W 76 G10
Leaf → U.S.A. 30°59N 88°44W 85 F10
Leaf Rapids Canada 56°30N 99°59W 71 B9
League City U.S.A. 29°31N 95°6W 84 C7
Leamington Canada 42°3N 82°36W 82 D2
Leamington U.S.A. 39°32N 112°17W 76 G7
Leamington Spa = Royal
Leamington Spa U.K. 52°18N 1°31W 13 E6
Le'an China 27°22N 115°48E 35 D10
Leandro Norte Alem
Argentina 27°34S 55°15W 95 B4
Leane, L. Ireland 52°2N 9°32W 10 D2
Learmonth Australia 22°13S 114°10E 60 D1
Leask Canada 53°5N 106°45W 71 C7
Leatherhead U.K. 51°18N 0°20W 13 F7
Leavdnja = Lakselv Norway 70°2N 25°0E 8 A21
Leavenworth Kans.,
U.S.A. 39°19N 94°55W 80 F6
Leavenworth Wash.,
U.S.A. 47°36N 120°40W 76 C3
Lebak Phil. 6°32N 124°5E 37 C6
Lebam U.S.A. 46°34N 123°33W 78 D3
Lebanon Ind., U.S.A. 40°3N 86°28W 80 E10
Lebanon Kans., U.S.A. 39°49N 98°33W 80 F4
Lebanon Ky., U.S.A. 37°34N 85°15W 81 G11
Lebanon Mo., U.S.A. 37°41N 92°40W 80 G7
Lebanon N.H., U.S.A. 43°39N 72°15W 83 C12
Lebanon Oreg., U.S.A. 44°32N 122°55W 76 D2
Lebanon Pa., U.S.A. 40°20N 76°26W 83 F8
Lebanon Tenn., U.S.A. 36°12N 86°18W 85 C11
Lebanon ■ Asia 34°0N 36°0E 48 B5
Lebec U.S.A. 34°51N 118°52W 79 L8
Lebel-sur-Quévillon
Canada 49°3N 76°59W 72 C4
Lębork Poland 54°33N 17°46E 17 A9
Lebrija Spain 36°53N 6°5W 21 D2
Lebu Chile 37°40S 73°47W 94 D1
Lecce Italy 40°23N 18°11E 23 D8
Lecco Italy 45°51N 9°23E 20 D8
Lech → Germany 48°43N 10°56E 16 D6
Lechang China 25°10N 113°20E 35 E9
Lecontes Mills U.S.A. 41°5N 78°17W 82 E6
Ledang, Gunung
Malaysia 2°22N 102°37E 39 L4
Ledong China 18°41N 109°5E 38 C7
Leduc Canada 53°15N 113°30W 70 C6
Lee U.S.A. 42°19N 73°15W 83 D11
Lee → Ireland 51°53N 8°56W 10 E3
Lee Vining U.S.A. 37°58N 119°7W 78 H7
Leech L. U.S.A. 47°10N 94°24W 80 B6
Leechburg U.S.A. 40°37N 79°36W 82 F5
Leeds U.K. 53°48N 1°33W 12 D6
Leeds U.S.A. 33°33N 86°33W 85 E11
Leek Neths. 53°10N 6°24E 15 A6
Leek U.K. 53°7N 2°1W 12 D5
Leeman Australia 29°57S 114°58E 61 E1
Leeper U.S.A. 41°22N 79°18W 82 E5
Leer Germany 53°13N 7°26E 16 B4
Leesburg U.S.A. 28°49N 81°53W 85 G14
Leesville U.S.A. 31°8N 93°16W 84 F8
Leeton Australia 34°33S 146°23E 63 E4
Leetonia U.S.A. 40°53N 80°45W 82 F4
Leeu Gamka S. Africa 32°47S 21°59E 56 E3
Leeuwarden Neths. 53°15N 5°48E 15 A5
Leeuwin, C. Australia 34°20S 115°9E 61 F2
Leeuwin Naturaliste △
Australia 34°6S 115°3E 61 F2
Leeward Is. Atl. Oc. 16°30N 63°30W 89 C7
Lefkada Greece 38°40N 20°43E 23 E9
Lefkosia = Nicosia
Cyprus 35°10N 33°25E 46 C2
Lefroy Canada 44°16N 79°34W 82 B5
Lefroy, L. Australia 31°21S 121°40E 61 F3
Legazpi Phil. 13°10N 123°45E 37 B6
Legendre I. Australia 20°22S 116°55E 60 D2
Leghorn = Livorno Italy 43°33N 10°19E 22 C4
Legian Indonesia 8°42S 115°10E 37 K18
Legionowo Poland 52°25N 20°50E 17 B11
Legnago Italy 45°11N 11°18E 22 B4
Legnica Poland 51°12N 16°10E 16 C9
Leh India 34°9N 77°35E 43 B7
Lehigh Acres U.S.A. 26°36N 81°39W 85 H14
Lehighton U.S.A. 40°50N 75°43W 83 F9
Lehututu Botswana 23°54S 21°55E 56 C3
Lei Shui → China 26°55N 112°35E 35 D9
Leiah Pakistan 30°58N 70°58E 42 D4
Leibo China 28°11N 103°34E 34 C4
Leicester U.K. 52°38N 1°8W 13 E6
Leicester City □ U.K. 52°38N 1°9W 13 E6
Leicestershire □ U.K. 52°41N 1°17W 13 E6
Leichhardt → Australia 17°35S 139°48E 62 B2
Leichhardt Ra. Australia 20°46S 147°40E 62 C4

Leiden Neths. 52°9N 4°30E 15 B4
Leie → Belgium 51°2N 3°45E 15 C3
Leimus Nic. 14°40N 84°3W 88 D3
Leine → Germany 52°43N 9°36E 16 B5
Leinster Australia 27°51S 120°36E 61 E3
Leinster □ Ireland 53°3N 7°8W 10 C4
Leinster, Mt. Ireland 52°37N 6°46W 10 D5
Leipzig Germany 51°18N 12°22E 16 C7
Leiria Portugal 39°46N 8°53W 21 C1
Leirvik Norway 59°47N 5°28E 9 G11
Leishan China 26°15N 108°20E 34 D7
Leisler, Mt. Australia 23°23S 129°20E 60 D4
Leith Hill U.K. 51°11N 0°22W 13 F7
Leitir Ceanainn = Letterkenny
Ireland 54°57N 7°45W 10 B4
Leitrim Ireland 54°0N 8°5W 10 B3
Leitrim □ Ireland 54°8N 8°0W 10 B4
Leixlip Ireland 53°22N 6°30W 10 C5
Leiyang China 26°27N 112°45E 35 D9
Leizhou China 20°52N 110°8E 35 G8
Leizhou Bandao China 21°0N 110°0E 34 G7
Leizhou Wan China 20°50N 110°20E 35 G8
Lek → Neths. 51°54N 4°35E 15 C4
Leka Norway 65°5N 11°35E 8 D14
Leland Mich., U.S.A. 45°1N 85°45W 81 C11
Leland Miss., U.S.A. 33°24N 90°54W 85 E9
Leleque Argentina 42°28S 71°0W 96 E2
Leling China 37°44N 117°13E 33 F9
Lelystad Neths. 52°30N 5°25E 15 B5
Léman, L. Europe 46°26N 6°30E 20 C7
Lembar Indonesia 8°45S 116°4E 37 K19
Lembongan, Nusa
Indonesia 8°40S 115°27E 37 K18
Lembuak Indonesia 8°36S 116°11E 37 K19
Lemesós = Limassol
Cyprus 34°42N 33°1E 46 C2
Lemhi Ra. U.S.A. 44°0N 113°0W 76 D7
Lemmer Neths. 52°51N 5°43E 15 B5
Lemmon U.S.A. 45°57N 102°10W 80 C2
Lemon Grove U.S.A. 32°44N 117°1W 79 N9
Lemoore U.S.A. 36°18N 119°46W 78 J7
Lemvig Denmark 56°33N 8°20E 9 H13
Lena → Russia 72°52N 126°40E 27 B13
Lenadoon Pt. Ireland 54°18N 9°3W 10 B2
Lenggong Malaysia 5°6N 100°58E 39 K3
Lengshuijiang China 27°40N 111°26E 35 D8
Lengshuitan China 26°27N 111°35E 35 D8
Lengua de Vaca, Pta.
Chile 30°14S 71°38W 94 C1
Leninogorsk = Ridder
Kazakhstan 50°20N 83°30E 26 D9
Leninsk Russia 48°40N 45°15E 19 E8
Leninsk-Kuznetskiy
Russia 54°44N 86°10E 26 D9
Lenkoran = Länkäran
Azerbaijan 38°48N 48°52E 47 B6
Lenmalu Indonesia 1°45S 130°15E 37 E8
Lennox U.S.A. 43°21N 96°53W 80 D5
Lennoxville Canada 45°22N 71°51W 83 A13
Lenoir U.S.A. 35°55N 81°32W 85 D14
Lenoir City U.S.A. 35°48N 84°16W 85 D12
Lenore L. Canada 52°30N 104°59W 71 C8
Lenox U.S.A. 42°22N 73°17W 83 D11
Lens France 50°26N 2°50E 20 A5
Lensk Russia 60°48N 114°55E 27 C12
Lentini Italy 37°17N 15°0E 22 F6
Lenwood U.S.A. 34°53N 117°7W 79 L9
Lenya Burma 11°33N 98°57E 39 G2
Leoben Austria 47°22N 15°5E 16 E8
Leodhais = Lewis U.K. 58°9N 6°40W 11 C2
Leola U.S.A. 45°43N 98°56W 80 C4
Leominster U.K. 52°14N 2°43W 13 E5
Leominster U.S.A. 42°32N 71°46W 83 D13
León Mexico 21°6N 101°41W 86 C4
León Nic. 12°27N 86°51W 88 D2
León Spain 42°38N 5°34W 21 A3
León □ Spain 42°40N 5°55W 21 B3
León, Montes de Spain 42°30N 6°18W 21 A2
Leonardville Namibia 23°29S 18°49E 56 B2
Leone Amer. Samoa 14°23S 170°48W 59 b
Leongatha Australia 38°30S 145°58E 63 F4
Leonora Australia 28°49S 121°19E 61 E3
Leopoldina Brazil 21°28S 42°40W 95 A7
Leopoldsburg Belgium 51°7N 5°13E 15 C5
Leoti U.S.A. 38°29N 101°21W 80 F3
Leova Moldova 46°28N 28°15E 17 E15
Leoville Canada 53°39N 107°33W 71 C7
Lepel = Lyepyel Belarus 54°50N 28°40E 9 J23
Leping China 28°47N 117°7E 35 C11
Lépo, L. do Angola 17°0S 19°0E 56 A2
Leppävirta Finland 62°29N 27°46E 8 E22
Leptis Magna Libya 32°40N 14°12E 53 B8
Leribe Lesotho 28°51S 28°3E 57 C4
Lérida = Lleida Spain 41°37N 0°39E 21 B6
Les Sables-d'Olonne
France 46°30N 1°45W 20 C3
Lesbos Greece 39°10N 26°20E 23 E12
Leshan China 29°33N 103°41E 34 C4
Leshukonskoye Russia 64°54N 45°46E 18 B8
Leskov I. Antarctica 56°0S 28°0W 5 B1
Leskovac Serbia 43°0N 21°58E 23 C9
Lesopilnoye Russia 46°44N 134°20E 28 A7
Lesotho ■ Africa 29°40S 28°0E 57 C4
Lesozavodsk Russia 45°30N 133°29E 28 B6
Lesse → Belgium 50°15N 4°54E 15 D4
Lesse et Lomme △ Belgium 50°8N 5°9E 15 D5
Lesser Antilles W. Indies 15°0N 61°0W 89 D7
Lesser Slave L. Canada 55°30N 115°25W 70 B5
Lesser Sunda Is. Indonesia 8°0S 120°0E 37 F6
Lessines Belgium 50°42N 3°50E 15 D3
Lestock Canada 51°19N 103°59W 71 C8
Lesuer △ Australia 30°11S 115°10E 61 F2
Lesueur I. Australia 13°50S 127°17E 60 B4

Lésvos = Lesbos Greece 39°10N 26°20E 23 E12
Leszno Poland 51°50N 16°30E 17 C9
Letaba → S. Africa 23°59S 31°50E 57 B5
Letchworth U.K. 51°59N 0°13W 13 F7
Lethbridge Canada 49°45N 112°45W 70 D6
Lethem Guyana 3°20N 59°50W 92 C7
Leti, Kepulauan Indonesia 8°10S 128°0E 37 F7
Leti Is. = Leti, Kepulauan
Indonesia 8°10S 128°0E 37 F7
Letiahau → Botswana 21°16S 24°0E 56 B3
Leticia Colombia 4°9S 70°0W 92 D5
Leting China 39°23N 118°55E 33 E10
Letjiesbos S. Africa 32°34S 22°16E 56 D3
Letlhakane Botswana 21°27S 25°30E 56 B4
Letlhakeng Botswana 24°0S 24°59E 56 B3
Letpadan Burma 17°45N 95°45E 41 L19
Letpan Burma 19°28N 94°10E 41 K19
Letsôk-aw Kyun Burma 11°30N 98°25E 39 G2
Letterkenny Ireland 54°57N 7°45W 10 B4
Leucadia U.S.A. 33°4N 117°18W 79 M9
Leuchars U.K. 56°24N 2°53W 11 E6
Leuser, Gunung Indonesia 3°46N 97°12E 36 D1
Leuven Belgium 50°52N 4°42E 15 D4
Leuze-en-Hainaut Belgium 50°36N 3°37E 15 D3
Levanger Norway 63°45N 11°19E 8 E14
Levelland U.S.A. 33°35N 102°23W 84 E3
Leven U.K. 56°12N 3°0W 11 E6
Leven, L. U.K. 56°12N 3°22W 11 E5
Leveque C. Australia 16°20S 123°0E 60 C3
Levice Slovak Rep. 48°13N 18°35E 17 D10
Levin N.Z. 40°37S 175°18E 59 D5
Lévis Canada 46°48N 71°9W 73 C5
Levis, L. Canada 62°37N 117°58W 70 A5
Levittown N.Y., U.S.A. 40°44N 73°31W 83 F11
Levittown Pa., U.S.A. 40°9N 74°51W 83 F10
Levka Oros Greece 35°18N 24°3E 23 G11
Levkás = Lefkada Greece 38°40N 20°43E 23 E9
Levskigrad = Karlovo
Bulgaria 42°38N 24°47E 23 C11
Levuka Fiji 17°34S 179°0E 59 a
Lewes U.K. 50°52N 0°1E 13 G8
Lewes U.S.A. 38°46N 75°9W 81 F16
Lewis U.K. 58°9N 6°40W 11 C2
Lewis → U.S.A. 45°51N 122°48W 78 E4
Lewis, Butt of U.K. 58°31N 6°16W 11 C2
Lewis and Clark △
U.S.A. 46°8N 123°53W 78 D3
Lewis Ra. Australia 20°3S 128°50E 60 D4
Lewis Range U.S.A. 48°5N 113°5W 76 B7
Lewis Run U.S.A. 41°52N 78°40W 82 E6
Lewisburg Pa., U.S.A. 40°58N 76°54W 82 F8
Lewisburg Tenn., U.S.A. 35°27N 86°48W 85 D11
Lewisburg W. Va.,
U.S.A. 37°48N 80°27W 81 G13
Lewisporte Canada 49°15N 55°3W 73 C8
Lewiston Idaho, U.S.A. 46°25N 117°1W 76 C5
Lewiston Maine, U.S.A. 44°6N 70°13W 81 C18
Lewiston N.Y., U.S.A. 43°11N 79°3W 82 C5
Lewistown Mont., U.S.A. 47°4N 109°26W 76 C9
Lewistown Pa., U.S.A. 40°36N 77°34W 82 F7
Lexington Ill., U.S.A. 40°39N 88°47W 80 E9
Lexington Ky., U.S.A. 38°3N 84°30W 81 F11
Lexington Mich., U.S.A. 43°16N 82°32W 82 C2
Lexington Mo., U.S.A. 39°11N 93°52W 80 F7
Lexington N.C., U.S.A. 35°49N 80°15W 85 D14
Lexington Nebr., U.S.A. 40°47N 99°45W 80 E4
Lexington Ohio, U.S.A. 40°41N 82°35W 82 F2
Lexington S.C., U.S.A. 33°59N 81°11W 85 E14
Lexington Tenn., U.S.A. 35°39N 88°24W 85 D10
Lexington Va., U.S.A. 37°47N 79°27W 81 G14
Lexington Park U.S.A. 38°16N 76°27W 81 F15
Leyburn U.K. 54°19N 1°48W 12 C6
Leye China 24°48N 106°29E 34 E6
Leyland U.K. 53°42N 2°43W 12 D5
Leyte Phil. 11°0N 125°0E 37 B7
Lezhë Albania 41°47N 19°39E 23 D8
Lezhi China 30°19N 104°58E 34 B5
Lhasa China 29°25N 90°58E 30 F7
Lhazê China 29°5N 87°38E 30 F6
Lhokkruet Indonesia 4°55N 95°24E 36 D1
Lhokseumawe Indonesia 5°10N 97°10E 36 C1
Li Thailand 17°48N 98°57E 38 D2
Li Jiang → China 24°40N 110°40E 35 E8
Li Jiang △ China 24°38N 110°38E 35 E8
Li Shan China 35°30N 111°56E 32 G6
Li Shui → China 29°24N 112°1E 35 C9
Li Xian Gansu, China 34°10N 105°5E 32 G3
Li Xian Hebei, China 38°30N 115°35E 32 E8
Li Xian Hunan, China 29°36N 111°42E 35 C8
Liao He → China 41°0N 121°50E 33 D11
Liacheng China 36°28N 115°58E 32 F8
Liangcheng Nei Monggol Zizhiqu,
China 40°28N 112°25E 32 D7
Liangcheng Shandong,
China 35°32N 119°37E 33 G10
Liangdang China 33°56N 106°18E 32 H4
Lianghe China 24°40N 98°20E 34 E2
Lianghekou China 29°11N 108°44E 34 C7
Liangping China 30°38N 107°47E 34 B6
Liangpran Indonesia 1°4N 114°23E 36 D4
Lianhua China 27°3N 113°54E 35 D9
Lianhua Shan China 23°40N 115°48E 35 F10
Lianjiang Fujian, China 26°12N 119°27E 35 D12
Lianjiang Guangdong,
China 21°40N 110°20E 35 G8
Lianping China 24°26N 114°30E 35 E10
Lianshan China 24°38N 112°8E 35 E9
Lianshanguan China 40°53N 123°43E 33 D12
Lianshui China 33°42N 119°20E 33 H10
Lianyuan China 27°40N 111°38E 35 D8
Lianyungang China 34°40N 119°11E 33 G10
Lianzhou China 24°51N 112°22E 35 E9
Liao He → China 41°0N 121°50E 33 D11
Liaocheng China 36°28N 115°58E 32 F8
Liaodong Bandao China 40°0N 122°30E 33 E12
Liaodong Wan China 40°20N 121°10E 33 D11

Liaoning □ China 41°40N 122°30E 33 D12
Liaotung, G. of = Liaodong Wan
China 40°20N 121°10E 33 D11
Liaoyang China 41°15N 122°58E 33 D12
Liaoyuan China 42°58N 125°2E 33 C13
Liaozhong China 41°23N 122°50E 33 D12
Liard → Canada 61°51N 121°18W 70 A4
Liard River Canada 59°25N 126°5W 70 B3
Liari Pakistan 25°37N 66°30E 42 G2
Libanggaon Nepal 28°18N 82°38E 43 E10
Libau = Liepāja Latvia 56°30N 21°0E 9 H19
Libby U.S.A. 48°23N 115°33W 76 B6
Libenge
Dem. Rep. of the Congo 3°40N 18°55E 54 D3
Liberal U.S.A. 37°3N 100°55W 80 G3
Liberec Czech Rep. 50°47N 15°7E 16 C8
Liberia Costa Rica 10°40N 85°30W 88 D2
Liberia ■ W. Afr. 6°30N 9°30W 52 G4
Libertador □ Chile 34°15S 70°45W 94 C1
Liberty Mo., U.S.A. 39°15N 94°25W 80 F6
Liberty N.Y., U.S.A. 41°48N 74°45W 83 E10
Liberty Pa., U.S.A. 41°34N 77°6W 82 E7
Liberty Tex., U.S.A. 30°3N 94°48W 84 F7
Liberty-Newark Int. ✈ (EWR)
U.S.A. 40°42N 74°10W 83 F10
Líbiya, Sahrâ' Africa 25°0N 25°0E 53 C10
Libo China 25°22N 107°53E 34 E6
Libobo, Tanjung Indonesia 0°54S 128°28E 37 E7
Libode S. Africa 31°33S 29°2E 57 D4
Libong, Ko Thailand 7°15N 99°23E 39 J2
Libourne France 44°55N 0°14W 20 D3
Libramont Belgium 49°55N 5°23E 15 E5
Libreville Gabon 0°25N 9°26E 54 D1
Libya ■ N. Afr. 27°0N 17°0E 53 C9
Libyan Desert = Líbîya, Sahrâ'
Africa 25°0N 25°0E 53 C10
Libyan Plateau = Ed Déffa
Egypt 30°40N 26°30E 53 B11
Licantén Chile 35°55S 72°0W 94 D1
Licata Italy 37°6N 13°56E 22 F5
Licheng China 36°28N 113°20E 32 F7
Lichfield U.K. 52°41N 1°49E 13 E6
Lichinga Mozam. 13°13S 35°11E 55 G7
Lichtenburg S. Africa 26°8S 26°8E 56 D4
Lichuan Hubei, China 30°18N 108°57E 34 B7
Lichuan Jiangxi, China 27°18N 116°55E 35 D11
Licking → U.S.A. 39°6N 84°30W 81 F11
Lida Belarus 53°53N 25°15E 17 B13
Lidköping Sweden 58°31N 13°7E 9 G15
Liebig, Mt. Australia 23°18S 131°22E 60 D5
Liechtenstein ■ Europe 47°8N 9°35E 20 C8
Liège Belgium 50°38N 5°35E 15 D5
Liège □ Belgium 50°32N 5°35E 15 D5
Liegnitz = Legnica Poland 51°12N 16°10E 16 C9
Lieksa Finland 63°18N 30°2E 8 E24
Lienyünchiangshih =
Lianyungang China 34°40N 119°11E 33 G10
Lienz Austria 46°50N 12°46E 16 E7
Liepāja Latvia 56°30N 21°0E 9 H19
Lier Belgium 51°7N 4°34E 15 C4
Lietuva = Lithuania ■
Europe 55°30N 24°0E 9 J21
Lièvre → Canada 45°31N 75°26W 72 C4
Liffey → Ireland 53°21N 6°13W 10 C5
Lifford Ireland 54°51N 7°29W 10 B4
Lifudzin Russia 44°21N 134°58E 28 B7
Lightning Ridge Australia 29°22S 148°0E 63 D4
Ligonier U.S.A. 40°15N 79°14W 82 F5
Liguria □ Italy 44°30N 8°50E 20 D8
Ligurian Sea Medit. S. 43°20N 9°0E 22 C3
Lihou Reefs and Cays
Australia 17°25S 151°40E 62 B5
Lihué Calel △ Argentina 38°0S 65°10W 94 D2
Lijiang China 26°55N 100°20E 34 D3
Lik → Laos 18°31N 102°30E 38 C4
Likasi
Dem. Rep. of the Congo 10°55S 26°48E 54 G5
L'Île-Rousse France 42°38N 8°57E 20 E8
Liling China 27°42N 113°29E 35 D9
Lille France 50°38N 3°3E 20 A5
Lille Bælt Denmark 55°20N 9°45E 9 J13
Lillehammer Norway 61°8N 10°30E 8 F14
Lillesand Norway 58°15N 8°23E 9 G13
Lillian Pt. Australia 27°40S 126°6E 61 E4
Lillooet Canada 50°44N 121°57W 70 C4
Lillooet → Canada 49°15N 121°57W 70 D4
Lilongwe Malawi 14°0S 33°48E 55 G6
Liloy Phil. 8°4N 122°39E 37 C6
Lim → Europe 43°45N 19°15E 23 C8
Lima Mont., U.S.A. 44°38N 112°36W 76 D7
Lima N.Y., U.S.A. 42°54N 77°36W 82 D7
Lima Ohio, U.S.A. 40°44N 84°6W 81 E11
Lima → Portugal 41°41N 8°50W 21 B1
Limassol Cyprus 34°42N 33°1E 46 C2
Limavady U.K. 55°3N 6°56W 10 A5
Limay → Argentina 39°0S 68°0W 96 D3
Limay Mahuida
Argentina 37°10S 66°45W 94 D2
Limbang Malaysia 4°42N 115°6E 36 D5
Limbaži Latvia 57°31N 24°42E 9 H21
Limbdi India 22°34N 71°51E 42 H4
Limbe Cameroon 4°1N 9°10E 54 D1
Limburg Germany 50°22N 8°4E 16 C5
Limburg □ Belgium 51°2N 5°25E 15 C5
Limburg □ Neths. 51°20N 5°55E 15 C5
Limeira Brazil 22°35S 47°28W 95 A6
Limerick Ireland 52°40N 8°37W 10 D3
Limerick U.S.A. 43°41N 70°48W 83 C14
Limerick □ Ireland 52°30N 8°50W 10 D3
Limestone U.S.A. 42°2N 78°38W 82 D6
Limestone → Canada 56°31N 94°7W 71 B10
Limfjorden Denmark 56°55N 9°0E 9 H13
Limia = Lima → Portugal 41°41N 8°50W 21 B1
Limingen Norway 64°48N 13°35E 8 D15
Limmen Bight Australia 14°40S 135°35E 62 A2
Limmen Bight →
Australia 15°7S 135°44E 62 B2

Limnos Greece 39°50N 25°5E 23 E11
Limoges Canada 45°20N 75°16W 83 A9
Limoges France 45°50N 1°15E 20 D4
Limón Costa Rica 10°0N 83°2W 88 E3
Limon U.S.A. 39°16N 103°41W 76 G12
Limousin □ France 45°30N 1°30E 20 D5
Limoux France 43°4N 2°12E 20 E5
Limpopo □ S. Africa 24°5S 29°0E 57 B4
Limpopo → Africa 25°5S 33°30E 57 C5
Limuru Kenya 1°2S 36°35E 54 E7
Lin Xian China 37°57N 110°58E 32 F6
Lin'an China 30°15N 119°42E 35 B12
Linares Chile 35°50S 71°40W 94 D1
Linares Mexico 24°52N 99°34W 87 C5
Linares Spain 38°10N 3°40W 21 C4
Lincang China 23°58N 100°1E 34 F3
Lincheng China 37°25N 114°30E 32 F8
Linchuan China 27°57N 116°15E 35 D11
Lincoln = Beamsville
 Canada 43°12N 79°28W 82 C5
Lincoln Argentina 34°55S 61°30W 94 C3
Lincoln N.Z. 43°38S 172°30E 59 E4
Lincoln U.K. 53°14N 0°32W 12 D7
Lincoln Calif., U.S.A. 38°54N 121°17W 78 G5
Lincoln Ill., U.S.A. 40°9N 89°22W 80 E9
Lincoln Kans., U.S.A. 39°3N 98°9W 80 F5
Lincoln Maine, U.S.A. 45°22N 68°30W 81 C19
Lincoln N.H., U.S.A. 44°3N 71°40W 83 B13
Lincoln N. Mex., U.S.A. 33°30N 105°23W 77 K11
Lincoln Nebr., U.S.A. 40°49N 96°41W 80 E5
Lincoln City U.S.A. 44°57N 124°1W 76 D1
Lincoln Hav = Lincoln Sea
 Arctic 84°0N 55°0W 69 A21
Lincoln Sea Arctic 84°0N 55°0W 69 A21
Lincolnshire □ U.K. 53°14N 0°32W 12 D7
Lincolnshire Wolds U.K. 53°26N 0°13W 12 D7
Lincolnton U.S.A. 35°29N 81°16W 85 D14
Linda U.S.A. 39°8N 121°34W 78 F5
Lindeman I. Australia 20°27S 149°3E 62 b
Lindeman Islands △
 Australia 20°28S 149°5E 62 b
Linden Guyana 6°0N 58°10W 92 B7
Linden Ala., U.S.A. 32°18N 87°48W 85 E11
Linden Calif., U.S.A. 38°1N 121°5W 78 G5
Linden Tex., U.S.A. 33°1N 94°22W 84 E7
Lindenhurst U.S.A. 40°41N 73°23W 83 F11
Lindesnes Norway 57°58N 7°3E 9 H12
Lindi Tanzania 9°58S 39°38E 54 F7
Lindi →
 Dem. Rep. of the Congo 0°33N 25°5E 54 D5
Lindley S. Africa 42°1N 77°8W 82 D7
Lindos Greece 36°6N 28°4E 23 F13
Lindsay Canada 44°22N 78°43W 82 B6
Lindsay Calif., U.S.A. 36°12N 119°5W 78 J7
Lindsay Okla., U.S.A. 34°50N 97°38W 84 D6
Lindsborg U.S.A. 38°35N 97°40W 80 F5
Line Islands Pac. Oc. 7°0N 160°0W 65 H12
Linesville U.S.A. 41°39N 80°26W 82 E4
Linfen China 36°3N 111°30E 32 F6
Ling Xian Hunan, China 26°29N 113°48E 35 D9
Ling Xian Shandong,
 China 37°22N 116°30E 32 F9
Lingal India 16°17N 78°31E 45 F4
Linganamakki Res. India 14°6N 74°52E 45 G2
Lingao China 19°56N 109°42E 38 C7
Lingayen Phil. 16°1N 120°14E 37 A6
Lingayen G. Phil. 16°10N 120°15E 37 A6
Lingbao China 34°31N 110°51E 32 G6
Lingbi China 33°33N 117°33E 33 H9
Lingchuan Guangxi Zhuangzu,
 China 25°26N 110°21E 35 E8
Lingchuan Shanxi, China 35°45N 113°12E 32 G7
Lingding Yang China 22°25N 113°44E 31 a
Lingen Germany 52°31N 7°19E 16 B4
Lingga Indonesia 0°12S 104°37E 36 E2
Lingga, Kepulauan
 Indonesia 0°10S 104°30E 36 E2
Lingga Arch. = Lingga, Kepulauan
 Indonesia 0°10S 104°30E 36 E2
Linghai China 41°11N 121°22E 33 D11
Lingle U.S.A. 42°8N 104°21W 76 E11
Lingqiu China 39°28N 114°22E 32 E8
Lingshan China 22°25N 109°18E 34 F7
Lingshi China 36°48N 111°48E 32 F6
Lingshou China 38°20N 114°20E 32 E8
Lingshui China 18°27N 110°0E 38 C8
Lingsugur India 16°10N 76°31E 45 F3
Lingtai China 35°0N 107°40E 32 G4
Linguère Senegal 15°25N 15°5W 52 E2
Lingui China 25°12N 110°2E 35 E8
Lingwu China 38°6N 106°20E 32 E4
Lingyuan China 41°10N 119°15E 33 D10
Lingyun China 25°2N 106°35E 34 E6
Linhai China 28°50N 121°8E 35 C13
Linhares Brazil 19°25S 40°4W 93 G10
Linhe China 40°48N 107°20E 32 D4
Linjiang China 41°50N 127°0E 33 D14
Linköping Sweden 58°28N 15°36E 9 G16
Linkou China 45°15N 130°18E 33 B16
Linli China 29°27N 111°30E 35 C8
Linnhe, L. U.K. 56°36N 5°25W 11 E3
Linosa Medit. S. 35°51N 12°50E 22 G5
Linqing China 36°50N 115°42E 32 F8
Linqu China 36°25N 118°30E 33 F10
Linquan China 33°5N 115°17E 35 A10
Lins Brazil 21°40S 49°44W 95 A6
Linshu China 34°53N 118°38E 33 G10
Linshui China 30°21N 106°57E 34 B6
Linstead Jamaica 18°8N 77°2W 88 a
Lintao China 35°26N 103°58E 32 G2
Linton Ind., U.S.A. 39°2N 87°10W 80 F10
Linton N. Dak., U.S.A. 46°16N 100°14W 80 B3
Lintong China 34°20N 109°10E 32 G5
Linwood Canada 43°35N 80°43W 82 C4
Linwu China 25°19N 112°31E 35 E9
Linxi Hebei, China 39°42N 118°26E 33 E10
Linxi Liaoning, China 43°36N 118°2E 33 C10

Linxia China 35°36N 103°10E 30 D9
Linxiang China 29°28N 113°23E 35 C9
Linyanti → Africa 17°50S 25°5E 56 A4
Linyi Shandong, China 37°13N 116°54E 32 F9
Linyi Shandong, China 35°5N 118°21E 33 G10
Linying China 33°48N 113°56E 32 H7
Linz Austria 48°18N 14°18E 16 D8
Linzhenzhen China 36°30N 109°59E 32 F5
Linzhou China 36°4N 113°49E 32 F7
Linzi China 36°50N 118°20E 33 F10
Lion, G. du France 43°10N 4°0E 20 E6
Lions, G. of = Lion, G. du
 France 43°10N 4°0E 20 E6
Lion's Head Canada 44°58N 81°15W 82 B3
Lipa Phil. 13°57N 121°10E 37 B6
Lipari Italy 38°26N 14°58E 22 E6
Lipari, Is. = Eólie, Ís. Italy 38°30N 14°57E 22 E6
Lipcani Moldova 48°14N 26°48E 17 D14
Liperi Finland 62°31N 29°24E 8 E23
Lipetsk Russia 52°37N 39°35E 18 D6
Liping China 26°15N 109°7E 34 D7
Lipkany = Lipcani
 Moldova 48°14N 26°48E 17 D14
Lipovets Ukraine 49°12N 29°1E 17 D15
Lippe → Germany 51°39N 6°36E 16 C4
Lipscomb U.S.A. 36°14N 100°16W 84 C4
Liptrap, C. Australia 38°50S 145°55E 63 F4
Lipu China 24°30N 110°22E 35 E8
Lira Uganda 2°17N 32°57E 54 D6
Liria = Lliria Spain 39°37N 0°35W 21 C5
Lisala Dem. Rep. of the Congo 2°12N 21°38E 54 D4
Lisbon N. Dak., U.S.A. 46°27N 97°41W 80 B5
Lisbon N.H., U.S.A. 44°13N 71°55W 83 B13
Lisbon N.Y., U.S.A. 44°43N 75°19W 83 B9
Lisbon Ohio, U.S.A. 40°46N 80°46W 82 F4
Lisbon Falls U.S.A. 44°0N 70°4W 81 D10
Lisburn U.K. 54°31N 6°3W 10 B5
Lisburne, C. U.S.A. 68°53N 166°13W 74 B6
Liscannor B. Ireland 52°55N 9°24W 10 D2
Lisdoonvarna Ireland 53°2N 9°18W 10 C2
Lishe Jiang → China 24°15N 101°35E 34 E3
Lishi China 37°31N 111°8E 32 F6
Lishu China 43°20N 124°18E 33 C13
Lishui Jiangsu, China 31°38N 119°2E 35 B12
Lishui Zhejiang, China 28°28N 119°54E 35 C12
Lisianski I. U.S.A. 26°2N 174°0W 75 K5
Lisichansk = Lysychansk
 Ukraine 48°55N 38°30E 19 E6
Lisieux France 49°10N 0°12E 20 B4
Liski Russia 51°3N 39°30E 19 D6
Lismore Australia 28°44S 153°21E 63 D5
Lismore Ireland 52°8N 7°55W 10 D4
Lista Norway 58°7N 6°39E 9 G12
Lister, Mt. Antarctica 78°0S 162°0E 5 D11
Liston Australia 28°39S 152°6E 63 D5
Listowel Canada 43°44N 80°58W 82 C4
Listowel Ireland 52°27N 9°29W 10 D2
Litang Guangxi Zhuangzu,
 China 23°12N 109°8E 34 F7
Litang Sichuan, China 30°1N 100°17E 34 B3
Litang Qu → China 28°4N 101°32E 34 C3
Litani → Lebanon 33°20N 35°15E 48 B4
Litchfield Calif., U.S.A. 40°24N 120°23W 78 E6
Litchfield Conn., U.S.A. 41°45N 73°11W 83 E11
Litchfield Ill., U.S.A. 39°11N 89°39W 80 F9
Litchfield Minn., U.S.A. 45°8N 94°32W 80 C6
Litchfield △ Australia 13°14S 131°1E 60 B5
Lithgow Australia 33°25S 150°8E 63 E5
Lithino, Akra Greece 34°55N 24°44E 23 G11
Lithuania ■ Europe 55°30N 24°0E 9 J21
Lititz U.S.A. 40°9N 76°18W 83 F8
Litoměřice Czech Rep. 50°33N 14°10E 16 C8
Little Abaco Bahamas 26°50N 77°30W 88 A4
Little Andaman I. India 10°45N 92°30E 45 J11
Little Barrier I. N.Z. 36°12S 175°8E 59 B5
Little Basses Sri Lanka 6°24N 81°43E 45 L5
Little Belt Mts. U.S.A. 46°40N 110°45W 76 C8
Little Bighorn Battlefield △
 U.S.A. 45°34N 107°25W 76 D10
Little Blue → U.S.A. 39°42N 96°41W 80 F5
Little Buffalo → Canada 61°0N 113°46W 70 A6
Little Cayman Cayman Is. 19°41N 80°3W 88 C3
Little Churchill →
 Canada 57°30N 95°22W 71 B9
Little Coco I. Burma 14°0N 93°13E 45 H11
Little Colorado →
 U.S.A. 36°12N 111°48W 77 H8
Little Current Canada 45°55N 82°0W 72 C3
Little Current → Canada 50°57N 84°36W 72 B3
Little Diomede I. U.S.A. 65°45N 168°56W 74 B6
Little Falls Minn., U.S.A. 45°59N 94°22W 80 C6
Little Falls N.Y., U.S.A. 43°3N 74°51W 83 C10
Little Fork → U.S.A. 48°31N 93°35W 80 A7
Little Grand Rapids
 Canada 52°0N 95°29W 71 C9
Little Humboldt →
 U.S.A. 41°1N 117°43W 76 F5
Little Inagua I. Bahamas 21°40N 73°50W 89 B5
Little Karoo S. Africa 33°45S 21°0E 56 E3
Little Khingan Mts. = Xiao
 Hinggan Ling China 49°0N 127°0E 33 B14
Little Lake U.S.A. 35°56N 117°55W 79 K9
Little Laut Is. = Laut Kecil,
 Kepulauan Indonesia 4°45S 115°40E 36 E5
Little Mecatina = Petit-
 Mécatina → Canada 50°40N 59°30W 73 B8
Little Minch U.K. 57°35N 6°45W 11 D2
Little Missouri →
 U.S.A. 47°36N 102°25W 80 B2
Little Nicobar India 7°20N 93°40E 45 L11
Little Ouse → U.K. 52°22N 1°12E 13 E9
Little Rann India 23°25N 71°25E 42 H4
Little Red → U.S.A. 35°11N 91°27W 84 D9
Little River N.Z. 43°45S 172°49E 59 E4
Little Rock U.S.A. 34°45N 92°17W 84 D8
Little Sable Pt. U.S.A. 43°38N 86°33W 80 D10
Little Sioux → U.S.A. 41°48N 96°4W 80 E5
Little Smoky → Canada 54°44N 117°11W 70 C5
Little Snake → U.S.A. 40°27N 108°26W 76 F9

Little Tobago
 Trin. & Tob. 11°18N 60°30W 93 J16
Little Valley U.S.A. 42°15N 78°48W 82 D6
Little Wabash → U.S.A. 37°55N 88°5W 80 G9
Little White → U.S.A. 43°40N 100°40W 80 D3
Little Zab = Zāb aş Şaghīr →
 Iraq 35°17N 43°29E 46 C4
Littlefield U.S.A. 33°55N 102°20W 84 E3
Littlehampton U.K. 50°49N 0°32W 13 G7
Littleton U.S.A. 44°18N 71°46W 83 B13
Liu He → China 40°55N 121°35E 33 D11
Liu Jiang → China 23°55N 109°30E 34 F7
Liuba China 33°38N 106°55E 34 A6
Liucheng China 24°38N 109°14E 34 E7
Liugou China 40°57N 118°15E 33 D10
Liuhe China 42°17N 125°43E 33 C13
Liuheng Dao China 29°40N 122°5E 35 C14
Liujiang China 24°26N 109°11E 34 E7
Liukang Tenggaja = Sabalana,
 Kepulauan Indonesia 6°45S 118°50E 37 F5
Liupan Shan China 35°39N 106°12E 32 G4
Liupanshui China 26°38N 104°48E 34 D5
Liuwa Plain Zambia 14°20S 22°30E 55 G4
Liuyang China 28°10N 113°37E 35 C9
Liuzhou China 24°22N 109°22E 34 E7
Liuzhuang China 33°12N 120°18E 33 H11
Livadia Greece 38°27N 22°54E 23 E10
Live Oak Calif., U.S.A. 39°17N 121°40W 78 F5
Live Oak Fla., U.S.A. 30°18N 82°59W 85 F13
Lively Canada 46°26N 81°9W 81 B13
Livermore U.S.A. 37°41N 121°47W 78 H5
Livermore, Mt. U.S.A. 30°38N 104°11W 84 F2
Livermore Falls U.S.A. 44°29N 70°11W 81 C18
Liverpool Australia 33°54S 150°58E 63 B5
Liverpool Canada 44°5N 64°41W 73 D7
Liverpool U.K. 53°25N 3°0W 12 D4
Liverpool U.S.A. 43°6N 76°13W 83 C8
Liverpool Bay U.K. 53°30N 3°20W 12 D4
Liverpool Ra. Australia 31°50S 150°30E 63 E5
Livingston Guatemala 15°50N 88°50W 88 C2
Livingston U.K. 55°54N 3°30W 11 F5
Livingston Ala., U.S.A. 32°35N 88°11W 85 E10
Livingston Calif., U.S.A. 37°23N 120°43W 78 H6
Livingston Mont.,
 U.S.A. 45°40N 110°34W 76 D8
Livingston S.C., U.S.A. 33°38N 81°7W 85 E14
Livingston Tenn., U.S.A. 36°23N 85°19W 85 C12
Livingston Tex., U.S.A. 30°43N 94°56W 84 F7
Livingston, L. U.S.A. 30°50N 95°10W 84 F7
Livingston Manor
 U.S.A. 41°54N 74°50W 83 E10
Livingstone Zambia 17°46S 25°52E 55 H5
Livny Russia 52°30N 37°30E 18 D6
Livonia Mich., U.S.A. 42°23N 83°23W 81 D12
Livonia N.Y., U.S.A. 42°49N 77°40W 82 D7
Livorno Italy 43°33N 10°19E 22 C4
Livramento Brazil 30°55S 55°30W 95 C4
Lixi China 26°23N 101°59E 34 D3
Lixian China 31°28N 103°13E 34 B4
Lixin China 33°8N 116°13E 35 A11
Liyang China 31°26N 119°28E 35 B12
Lizard I. Australia 14°42S 145°30E 62 A4
Lizard Pt. U.K. 49°57N 5°13W 13 H2
Ljubljana Slovenia 46°4N 14°33E 16 E8
Ljungan → Sweden 62°18N 17°23E 8 E17
Ljungby Sweden 56°49N 13°55E 9 H15
Ljusdal Sweden 61°46N 16°3E 8 F17
Ljusnan → Sweden 61°12N 17°8E 8 F17
Ljusne Sweden 61°13N 17°7E 8 F17
Llancanelo, Salina
 Argentina 35°40S 69°8W 94 D2
Llandeilo U.K. 51°53N 3°59W 13 F4
Llandovery U.K. 51°59N 3°48W 13 F4
Llandrindod Wells U.K. 52°14N 3°22W 13 E4
Llandudno U.K. 53°19N 3°50W 12 D4
Llanelli U.K. 51°41N 4°10W 13 F3
Llanes Spain 43°25N 4°50W 21 A3
Llanfair-ym-Muallt = Builth Wells
 U.K. 52°9N 3°25W 13 E4
Llangollen U.K. 52°58N 3°11W 12 E4
Llanidloes U.K. 52°27N 3°31W 13 E4
Llano U.S.A. 30°45N 98°41W 84 F5
Llano → U.S.A. 30°39N 98°26W 84 F5
Llano Estacado U.S.A. 33°30N 103°0W 84 E3
Llanos S. Amer. 5°0N 71°35W 92 C4
Llanos de Challe △ Chile 28°8S 71°1W 94 B1
Llanquihue, L. Chile 41°10S 72°50W 96 E1
Llanwrtyd Wells U.K. 52°7N 3°38W 13 E4
Lleida Spain 41°37N 0°39E 21 B6
Llera de Canales Mexico 23°19N 99°1W 87 C5
Lleyn Peninsula U.K. 52°51N 4°36W 12 E3
Llico Chile 34°46S 72°5W 94 C1
Lliria Spain 39°37N 0°35W 21 C5
Llobregat → Spain 41°19N 2°5E 21 B7
Lloret de Mar Spain 41°41N 2°53E 21 B7
Lloyd B. Australia 12°45S 143°27E 62 A3
Lloyd L. Canada 57°22N 108°57W 71 B7
Lloydminster Canada 53°17N 110°0W 71 C7
Llucmajor Spain 39°29N 2°53E 21 C7
Llullaillaco, Volcán
 S. Amer. 24°43S 68°30W 94 A2
Llullaillaco △ Chile 24°50S 68°51W 94 A2
Lo → Vietnam 21°18N 105°25E 38 B5
Loa U.S.A. 38°24N 111°39W 76 G8
Loa → Chile 21°26S 70°41W 94 A1
Loaita I. S. China Sea 10°41N 114°25E 36 B4
Loange →
 Dem. Rep. of the Congo 4°17S 20°2E 54 E4
Lobamba Swaziland 26°28S 31°12E 57 C5
Lobatse Botswana 25°12S 25°40E 56 C4
Lobería Argentina 38°10S 58°40W 94 D4
Lobito Angola 12°18S 13°35E 55 G2
Lobos Argentina 35°10S 59°0W 94 D4
Lobos, I. Mexico 27°20N 110°36W 86 B2
Loc Binh Vietnam 21°46N 106°54E 38 B6
Loc Ninh Vietnam 11°50N 106°34E 39 G6
Locarno Switz. 46°10N 8°47E 20 C8
Loch Garman = Wexford
 Ireland 52°20N 6°28W 10 D5

Loch Lomond and the Trossachs △
 U.K. 56°10N 4°40W 11 E4
Lochaber U.K. 56°59N 5°1W 11 E3
Locharbriggs U.K. 55°7N 3°35W 11 F5
Lochboisdale U.K. 57°9N 7°20W 11 D1
Loche, L. La Canada 56°30N 109°30W 71 B7
Lochem Neths. 52°9N 6°26E 15 B6
Loches France 47°7N 1°0E 20 C4
Lochgilphead U.K. 56°2N 5°26W 11 E3
Lochinver U.K. 58°9N 5°14W 11 C3
Lochmaddy U.K. 57°36N 7°10W 11 D1
Lochnagar Australia 23°33S 145°38E 62 C4
Lochnagar U.K. 56°57N 3°15W 11 E5
Lochy, L. U.K. 57°0N 4°53W 11 E4
Lock Australia 33°34S 135°46E 63 E2
Lock Haven U.S.A. 41°8N 77°28W 82 E7
Lockeford U.S.A. 38°10N 121°9W 78 G5
Lockeport Canada 43°47N 65°4W 73 D6
Lockerbie U.K. 55°7N 3°21W 11 F5
Lockhart U.S.A. 29°53N 97°40W 84 G6
Lockhart, L. Australia 33°15S 119°3E 61 F2
Lockhart River Australia 12°58S 143°30E 62 A3
Lockhart River ♦
 Australia 12°47S 143°20E 62 A3
Lockney U.S.A. 34°7N 101°27W 84 D4
Lockport U.S.A. 43°10N 78°42W 82 C6
Lod Israel 31°57N 34°54E 48 D3
Lodeinoye Pole Russia 60°44N 33°33E 18 B5
Lodge Bay Canada 52°14N 55°51W 73 B8
Lodge Grass U.S.A. 45°19N 107°22W 76 D10
Lodhran Pakistan 29°32N 71°30E 42 E4
Lodi Italy 45°19N 9°30E 20 B8
Lodi Calif., U.S.A. 38°8N 121°16W 78 G5
Lodi Ohio, U.S.A. 41°2N 82°1W 82 E3
Lodja Dem. Rep. of the Congo 3°30S 23°23E 54 E4
Lodwar Kenya 3°7N 35°36E 54 D7
Łódź Poland 51°45N 19°27E 17 C10
Loei Thailand 17°29N 101°35E 38 D3
Loeriesfontein S. Africa 31°0S 19°26E 56 E2
Lofoten Norway 68°30N 13°59E 8 B16
Logan Iowa, U.S.A. 41°39N 95°47W 80 E6
Logan Ohio, U.S.A. 39°32N 82°25W 81 F12
Logan Utah, U.S.A. 41°44N 111°50W 76 F8
Logan W. Va., U.S.A. 37°51N 81°59W 81 G13
Logan, Mt. Canada 60°34N 140°23W 68 E3
Logandale U.S.A. 36°36N 114°29W 79 J12
Logansport Ind., U.S.A. 40°45N 86°22W 80 E10
Logansport La., U.S.A. 31°58N 94°0W 84 F8
Logone → Chad 12°6N 15°2E 53 F9
Logroño Spain 42°28N 2°27W 21 A4
Lohardaga India 23°27N 84°45E 43 H11
Loharia India 23°45N 74°14E 42 H6
Loharu India 28°27N 75°49E 42 E6
Lohri Wah → Pakistan 27°27N 67°37E 42 F2
Loikaw Burma 19°40N 97°17E 41 K20
Loimaa Finland 60°50N 23°5E 8 F20
Loir → France 47°33N 0°32W 20 C3
Loire → France 47°16N 2°10W 20 C2
Loja Ecuador 3°59S 79°16W 92 D3
Loja Spain 37°10N 4°10W 21 D3
Loji = Kawasi Indonesia 1°38S 127°28E 37 E7
Lojung China 24°27N 109°36E 34 E7
Lokan tekojärvi Finland 67°55N 27°35E 8 C22
Lokeren Belgium 51°6N 3°59E 15 C3
Lokgwabe Botswana 24°10S 21°50E 56 B3
Lokitaung Kenya 4°12N 35°48E 54 D7
Lokoja Nigeria 7°47N 6°45E 52 G7
Lokolo →
 Dem. Rep. of the Congo 1°43S 18°23E 54 E3
Lola, Mt. U.S.A. 39°26N 120°22W 78 F6
Lolland Denmark 54°45N 11°30E 9 J14
Lolo U.S.A. 46°45N 114°5W 76 C6
Lom Bulgaria 43°48N 23°12E 23 C10
Lom Kao Thailand 16°53N 101°14E 38 D3
Lom Sak Thailand 16°47N 101°15E 38 D3
Loma U.S.A. 47°56N 110°30W 76 C8
Loma Linda U.S.A. 34°3N 117°16W 79 L9
Lomaloma Fiji 17°17S 178°59W 59 a
Lomami →
 Dem. Rep. of the Congo 0°46N 24°16E 54 D4
Lomas de Zamora
 Argentina 34°45S 58°24W 94 C4
Lombadina Australia 16°31S 122°54E 60 C3
Lombárdia □ Italy 45°40N 9°30E 20 B8
Lombardy = Lombárdia □
 Italy 45°40N 9°30E 20 B8
Lomblen Indonesia 8°30S 123°32E 37 F6
Lombok Indonesia 8°45S 116°30E 36 F5
Lombok, Selat Indonesia 8°30S 115°50E 37 K18
Lomé Togo 6°9N 1°20E 52 G6
Lomela
 Dem. Rep. of the Congo 2°19S 23°15E 54 E4
Lomela →
 Dem. Rep. of the Congo 0°15S 20°40E 54 E4
Lommel Belgium 51°14N 5°19E 15 C5
Lomond Canada 50°24N 112°36W 70 C6
Lomond, L. U.K. 56°8N 4°38W 11 E4
Lomonosov Ridge Arctic 88°0N 140°0E 4 A
Lomphat Cambodia 13°30N 106°59E 38 F6
Lompobatang Indonesia 5°24S 119°56E 37 F5
Lompoc U.S.A. 34°38N 120°28W 79 L6
Łomża Poland 53°10N 22°2E 17 B12
Lon, Ko Thailand 7°47N 99°15E 39 J2
Lonavale India 18°46N 73°29E 44 E1
Loncoche Chile 39°20S 72°50W 96 D2
Londa India 15°30N 74°30E 45 G2
London Canada 42°59N 81°15W 82 D3
London Ky., U.S.A. 37°8N 84°5W 81 G11
London Ohio, U.S.A. 39°53N 83°27W 81 F12
London, Greater □ U.K. 51°36N 0°5W 13 F7
London Gatwick ✈ (LGW)
 U.K. 51°10N 0°11W 13 F7
London Stansted ✈ (STN)
 U.K. 51°54N 0°14E 13 F8
Londonderry U.K. 55°0N 7°20W 10 B4
Londonderry □ U.K. 55°0N 7°20W 10 B4
Londonderry, C.
 Australia 13°45S 126°55E 60 B4
Londonderry, I. Chile 55°0S 71°0W 96 H2

Londres Argentina 27°43S 67°7W 96 B3
Londrina Brazil 23°18S 51°10W 95 A5
Lone Pine U.S.A. 36°36N 118°4W 78 J8
Lonely Mine Zimbabwe 19°30S 28°49E 57 A4
Long B. U.S.A. 33°35N 78°45W 85 E15
Long Beach Calif.,
 U.S.A. 33°46N 118°11W 79 M8
Long Beach N.Y., U.S.A. 40°35N 73°39W 83 F11
Long Beach Wash.,
 U.S.A. 46°21N 124°3W 78 D2
Long Branch U.S.A. 40°18N 74°0W 83 F11
Long Creek U.S.A. 44°43N 119°6W 76 D4
Long Eaton U.K. 52°53N 1°15W 12 E6
Long I. Australia 20°22S 148°51E 62 b
Long I. Bahamas 23°20N 75°10W 89 B4
Long I. Canada 54°50N 79°20W 72 B4
Long I. Ireland 51°30N 9°34W 10 E2
Long I. U.S.A. 40°45N 73°30W 83 F11
Long Island Sd. U.S.A. 41°10N 73°0W 83 E11
Long L. Canada 49°30N 86°50W 72 C2
Long L. U.S.A. 44°0N 74°23W 83 C10
Long Lake U.S.A. 43°58N 74°25W 83 C10
Long Point Canada 42°34N 80°25W 82 D4
Long Point B. Canada 42°40N 80°10W 82 D4
Long Prairie U.S.A. 45°59N 94°52W 80 C6
Long Prairie → U.S.A. 46°20N 94°36W 80 B6
Long Pt. Ont., Canada 42°35N 80°2W 82 D4
Long Pt. Ont., Canada 43°56N 76°53W 83 C8
Long Range Mts. Canada 49°30N 57°30W 73 C8
Long Reef Australia 14°1S 125°48E 60 B4
Long Sault Canada 45°2N 74°53W 83 A10
Long Str. = Longa, Proliv
 Russia 70°0N 175°0E 27 C18
Long Thanh Vietnam 10°47N 106°57E 39 G6
Long Xian China 34°55N 106°55E 32 G4
Long Xuyen Vietnam 10°19N 105°28E 39 G5
Longa, Proliv Russia 70°0N 175°0E 27 C18
Long'an China 23°10N 107°40E 34 F6
Longbenton U.K. 55°1N 1°31W 12 B6
Longboat Key U.S.A. 27°23N 82°39W 85 H13
Longchang China 29°18N 105°15E 34 C5
Longchuan Guangdong,
 China 24°5N 115°17E 35 E10
Longchuan Yunnan, China 24°23N 97°58E 34 E1
Longde China 35°30N 106°20E 32 G4
Longford Australia 41°32S 147°3E 63 G4
Longford Ireland 53°43N 7°49W 10 C4
Longford □ Ireland 53°42N 7°45W 10 C4
Longford, An = Longford
 Ireland 53°43N 7°49W 10 C4
Longhai China 24°25N 117°46E 35 E11
Longhua Guangdong, China 22°39N 114°0E 31 a
Longhua Hebei, China 41°18N 117°45E 33 D9
Longhui China 27°7N 111°2E 35 D8
Longiram Indonesia 0°5S 115°45E 36 E5
Longjing China 42°46N 129°25E 33 C15
Longkou Jiangxi, China 26°8N 115°10E 35 D10
Longkou Shandong,
 China 37°40N 120°18E 33 F11
Longlac Canada 49°45N 86°25W 72 C2
Longli China 26°25N 106°58E 34 D6
Longlin China 24°47N 105°20E 34 E5
Longling China 24°37N 98°39E 34 E2
Longmeadow U.S.A. 42°3N 72°34W 83 D12
Longmen China 23°43N 114°18E 35 F10
Longmen Shiku China 34°28N 112°28E 32 G7
Longming China 22°59N 107°7E 34 F6
Longmont U.S.A. 40°10N 105°6W 76 F11
Longnan China 24°55N 114°47E 35 E10
Longnawan Indonesia 1°51N 114°55E 36 D4
Longquan China 28°7N 119°10E 35 C12
Longreach Australia 23°28S 144°14E 62 C3
Longshan China 29°29N 109°23E 34 C7
Longsheng China 25°48N 110°0E 35 E8
Longtan Dam China 25°5N 107°0E 34 E6
Longview Tex., U.S.A. 32°30N 94°44W 84 E7
Longview Wash., U.S.A. 46°8N 122°57W 78 D4
Longxi China 34°53N 104°40E 32 G3
Longxue Dao China 22°41N 113°38E 31 a
Longyan China 25°10N 117°0E 35 E11
Longyearbyen Svalbard 78°13N 15°40E 4 B8
Longyou China 29°1N 119°8E 35 C12
Longzhou China 22°22N 106°50E 34 F6
Lonoke U.S.A. 34°47N 91°54W 84 D9
Lonquimay Chile 38°26S 71°14W 96 D2
Lons-le-Saunier France 46°40N 5°31E 20 C6
Looe U.K. 50°22N 4°28W 13 G3
Lookout, C. Canada 55°18N 83°56W 72 A3
Lookout, C. U.S.A. 34°35N 76°32W 85 D16
Loon → Alta., Canada 57°8N 115°3W 70 B5
Loon → Man., Canada 52°30N 101°59W 71 B8
Loon Lake Canada 54°2N 109°10W 71 C7
Loongana Australia 30°52S 127°5E 61 F4
Loop Hd. Ireland 52°34N 9°56W 10 D2
Lop China 37°3N 80°11E 30 D5
Lop Nor = Lop Nur China 40°20N 90°10E 30 C7
Lop Nur China 40°20N 90°10E 30 C7
Lopatina, Gora Russia 50°47N 143°10E 27 D15
Lopatka, Mys Russia 50°52N 156°40E 27 D16
Lopburi Thailand 14°48N 100°37E 38 E3
Lopez, C. Gabon 0°47S 8°40E 54 E1
Lopphavet Norway 70°27N 21°15E 8 A19
Lora → Afghan. 31°35N 66°32E 40 D4
Lora, Hāmūn-i- Pakistan 29°38N 64°58E 40 E4
Lora Cr. → Australia 28°10S 135°22E 63 D2
Lora del Río Spain 37°39N 5°33W 21 D3
Lorain U.S.A. 41°28N 82°11W 82 E2
Loralai Pakistan 30°20N 68°41E 42 D3
Lorca Spain 37°41N 1°42W 21 D5
Lord Howe I. Pac. Oc. 31°33S 159°6E 58 E8
Lord Howe Rise Pac. Oc. 30°0S 162°30E 64 L8
Lord Loughborough I.
 Burma 10°25N 97°54E 39 G1
Lordsburg U.S.A. 32°21N 108°43W 77 K9
Lorestān □ Iran 33°30N 48°40E 47 C6
Loreto Brazil 7°5S 45°10W 93 E9
Loreto Mexico 26°0N 111°21W 86 B2
Lorient France 47°45N 3°23W 20 C2

Lormi *India* 22°17N 81°41E **43** H9
Lorn *U.K.* 56°26N 5°10W **11** E3
Lorn, Firth of *U.K.* 56°20N 5°40W **11** E3
Lorne *Australia* 38°33S 143°59E **63** F3
Lorraine □ *France* 48°53N 6°0E **20** B7
Los Alamos *Calif., U.S.A.* 34°44N 120°17W **79** L6
Los Alamos *N. Mex., U.S.A.* 35°53N 106°19W **77** J10
Los Altos *U.S.A.* 37°23N 122°7W **78** H4
Los Andes *Chile* 32°50S 70°40W **94** C1
Los Angeles *Chile* 37°28S 72°23W **94** D1
Los Angeles *U.S.A.* 35°22N 118°5W **79** K9
Los Angeles Aqueduct *U.S.A.* 35°22N 118°5W **79** K9
Los Banos *U.S.A.* 37°4N 120°51W **78** H6
Los Blancos *Argentina* 23°40S 62°30W **94** A3
Los Cabos Int. ✈ (SJD) *Mexico* 23°9N 109°43W **86** C3
Los Cardones △ *Argentina* 25°8S 65°55W **94** B2
Los Chiles *Costa Rica* 11°2N 84°43W **88** D3
Los Gatos *U.S.A.* 37°14N 121°59W **78** H5
Los Haïtises △ *Dom. Rep.* 19°4N 69°36W **89** C6
Los Hermanos, Is. *Venezuela* 11°45N 64°25W **89** D7
Los Loros *Chile* 27°50S 70°6W **94** B1
Los Lunas *U.S.A.* 34°48N 106°44W **77** J10
Los Mochis *Mexico* 25°45S 108°57W **86** B3
Los Olivos *U.S.A.* 34°40N 120°7W **79** L6
Los Palacios *Cuba* 22°35N 83°15W **88** B3
Los Queñes *Chile* 35°1S 70°48W **94** D1
Los Reyes de Salgado *Mexico* 19°35N 102°29W **86** D4
Los Roques, Is. *Venezuela* 11°50N 66°45W **89** D6
Los Teques *Venezuela* 10°21N 67°2W **92** A5
Los Testigos, Is. *Venezuela* 11°23S 63°6W **92** A6
Los Vilos *Chile* 32°10S 71°30W **94** C1
Lošinj *Croatia* 44°30N 14°30E **16** F8
Loskop Dam *S. Africa* 25°23S 29°20E **57** C4
Lossiemouth *U.K.* 57°42N 3°17W **11** D5
Lostwithiel *U.K.* 50°24N 4°41W **13** G3
Lot → *France* 44°18N 0°20E **20** D4
Lota *Chile* 37°5S 73°10W **94** D1
Loţfābād *Iran* 37°32N 59°20E **47** B8
Lothair *S. Africa* 26°22S 30°27E **57** C5
Lotta → *Europe* 68°42N 31°6E **8** B24
Lotung *Taiwan* 24°41N 121°46E **35** E13
Loubomo *Congo* 4°9S 12°47E **54** E2
Loudi *China* 27°42N 111°59E **35** D8
Loudonville *U.S.A.* 40°38N 82°14W **82** F2
Louga *Senegal* 15°45N 16°5W **52** E2
Loughborough *U.K.* 52°47N 1°11W **12** E6
Lougheed I. *Canada* 77°26N 105°6W **69** B10
Loughrea *Ireland* 53°12N 8°33W **10** C3
Loughros More B. *Ireland* 54°48N 8°32W **10** B3
Louis Trichardt *S. Africa* 23°1S 29°43E **57** B4
Louis XIV, Pte. *Canada* 54°37N 79°45W **72** B4
Louisa *U.S.A.* 38°7N 82°36W **81** F12
Louisbourg *Canada* 45°55N 60°0W **73** C8
Louisburgh *Ireland* 53°46N 9°49W **10** C2
Louise I. *Canada* 52°55N 131°50W **70** C2
Louiseville *Canada* 46°20N 72°56W **72** C5
Louisiade Arch. *Papua N. G.* 11°10S 153°0E **58** C8
Louisiana *U.S.A.* 39°27N 91°3W **80** F8
Louisiana □ *U.S.A.* 30°50N 92°0W **84** F9
Louisville *Ky., U.S.A.* 38°15N 85°46W **81** F11
Louisville *Miss., U.S.A.* 33°7N 89°3W **85** E10
Louisville *Ohio, U.S.A.* 40°50N 81°16W **82** F3
Louisville Ridge *Pac. Oc.* 31°0S 172°30W **64** L10
Loulé *Portugal* 37°9N 8°0W **21** D1
Loup City *U.S.A.* 41°17N 98°58W **80** E4
Loups Marins, Lacs des *Canada* 56°30N 73°45W **72** A5
Lourdes *France* 43°6N 0°3W **20** E3
Lourdes-de-Blanc-Sablon *Canada* 51°24N 57°12W **73** B8
Louth *Australia* 30°30S 145°8E **63** E4
Louth *Ireland* 53°58N 6°32W **10** C5
Louth *U.K.* 53°22N 0°1W **12** D7
Louth □ *Ireland* 53°56N 6°34W **10** C5
Louvain = Leuven *Belgium* 50°52N 4°42E **15** D4
Louwsburg *S. Africa* 27°37S 31°7E **57** C5
Lovech *Bulgaria* 43°8N 24°42E **23** C11
Loveland *U.S.A.* 40°24N 105°5W **76** F11
Lovell *U.S.A.* 44°50N 108°24W **76** D9
Lovelock *U.S.A.* 40°11N 118°28W **76** F4
Loviisa *Finland* 60°28N 26°12E **8** F22
Lovina *Indonesia* 8°9S 115°1E **37** J18
Loving *U.S.A.* 32°17N 104°6W **77** K11
Lovington *U.S.A.* 32°57N 103°21W **77** K12
Lovisa = Loviisa *Finland* 60°28N 26°12E **8** F22
Low, L. *Canada* 52°29N 76°17W **72** B4
Low Pt. *Australia* 32°25S 127°25E **61** F4
Low Tatra = Nízké Tatry *Slovak Rep.* 48°55N 19°30E **17** D10
Lowell *U.S.A.* 42°38N 71°19W **83** D13
Lowellville *U.S.A.* 41°2N 80°32W **82** E4
Löwen → *Namibia* 26°51S 18°17E **56** D2
Lower Alkali L. *U.S.A.* 41°16N 120°2W **76** F3
Lower Arrow L. *Canada* 49°40N 118°5W **70** D5
Lower California = Baja California *Mexico* 31°10N 115°12W **86** A1
Lower Hutt *N.Z.* 41°10S 174°55E **59** D5
Lower Lake *U.S.A.* 38°55N 122°37W **78** G4
Lower Manitou L. *Canada* 49°15N 93°0W **71** D10
Lower Post *Canada* 59°58N 128°30W **70** B3
Lower Red L. *U.S.A.* 47°58N 95°0W **80** B6
Lower Saxony = Niedersachsen □ *Germany* 52°50N 9°0E **16** B5
Lower Tunguska = Tunguska, Nizhnyaya → *Russia* 65°48N 88°4E **27** C9
Lowestoft *U.K.* 52°29N 1°45E **13** E9
Lowgar □ *Afghan.* 34°0N 69°0E **40** B6
Lowther I. *Canada* 74°33N 97°30W **69** C12
Lowville *U.S.A.* 43°47N 75°29W **83** C9
Loxton *Australia* 34°28S 140°31E **63** E3
Loxton *S. Africa* 31°30S 22°22E **56** D3

Loyalton *U.S.A.* 39°41N 120°14W **78** F6
Loyalty Is. = Loyauté, Îs. *N. Cal.* 20°50S 166°30E **58** D9
Loyang = Luoyang *China* 34°40N 112°26E **32** G7
Loyauté, Îs. *N. Cal.* 20°50S 166°30E **58** D9
Loyev = Loyew *Belarus* 51°56N 30°46E **17** C16
Loyew *Belarus* 51°56N 30°46E **17** C16
Ltalaltuma ◎ *Australia* 23°57S 132°25E **60** D5
Lü Shan *China* 29°30N 115°55E **35** C10
Lü Shan △ *China* 29°26N 115°52E **35** C10
Lu Wo *China* 22°33N 114°6E **31** a
Luachimo *Angola* 7°23S 20°48E **54** F4
Luajan → *India* 24°44N 85°1E **43** G11
Lualaba → *Dem. Rep. of the Congo* 0°26N 25°20E **54** D5
Lu'an *China* 31°45N 116°29E **35** B11
Luan Chau *Vietnam* 21°38N 103°24E **34** G4
Luan He → *China* 39°20N 119°5E **33** E10
Luan Xian *China* 39°40N 118°40E **33** E10
Luancheng *Guangxi Zhuangzu, China* 22°48N 108°55E **34** F7
Luancheng *Hebei, China* 37°53N 114°40E **32** F8
Luanda *Angola* 8°50S 13°15E **54** F2
Luang, Doi *Thailand* 18°30N 101°15E **38** C3
Luang, Thale *Thailand* 7°30N 100°15E **39** J3
Luang Nam Tha *Laos* 20°58N 101°30E **34** A3
Luang Prabang *Laos* 19°52N 102°10E **34** H4
Luangwa → *Zambia* 14°25S 30°25E **55** G6
Luangwa Valley *Zambia* 13°30S 31°30E **55** G6
Luangwe = Loange → *Dem. Rep. of the Congo* 4°17S 20°2E **54** E4
Luanne *China* 40°55N 117°40E **33** D9
Luanping *China* 40°53N 117°23E **33** D9
Luanshya *Zambia* 13°3S 28°28E **55** G5
Luapula → *Africa* 9°26S 28°33E **54** F5
Luarca *Spain* 43°32N 6°32W **21** A2
Luashi *Dem. Rep. of the Congo* 10°50S 23°36E **55** G4
Luau *Angola* 10°40S 22°10E **54** G4
Lubana, Ozero = Lubānas Ezers *Latvia* 56°45N 27°0E **9** H22
Lubānas Ezers *Latvia* 56°45N 27°0E **9** H22
Lubang Is. *Phil.* 13°50N 120°12E **37** B6
Lubango *Angola* 14°55S 13°30E **55** G2
Lubbock *U.S.A.* 33°35N 101°51W **84** E4
Lübeck *Germany* 53°52N 10°40E **16** B6
Lubero = Luofu *Dem. Rep. of the Congo* 0°10S 29°15E **54** E5
Lubilash → *Dem. Rep. of the Congo* 6°2S 23°45E **54** F4
Lubin *Poland* 51°24N 16°11E **16** C9
Lublin *Poland* 51°12N 22°38E **17** C12
Lubnān = Lebanon ■ *Asia* 34°0N 36°0E **48** B5
Lubnān, Jabal *Lebanon* 33°45N 35°40E **48** B4
Lubny *Ukraine* 50°3N 32°58E **26** D4
Lubudi *Dem. Rep. of the Congo* 9°57S 25°58E **54** F5
Lubuklinggau *Indonesia* 3°15S 102°55E **36** E2
Lubuksikaping *Indonesia* 0°10N 100°15E **36** D2
Lubumbashi *Dem. Rep. of the Congo* 11°40S 27°28E **55** G5
Lubutu *Dem. Rep. of the Congo* 0°45S 26°30E **54** E5
Lucan *Canada* 43°11N 81°24W **82** C3
Lucan *Ireland* 53°22N 6°28W **10** C5
Lucania, Mt. *Canada* 61°1N 140°27W **68** E3
Lucas Channel = Main Channel *Canada* 45°21N 81°45W **82** A3
Lucca *Italy* 43°50N 10°29E **22** C4
Luce Bay *U.K.* 54°45N 4°48W **11** G4
Lucea *Jamaica* 18°27N 78°10W **88** a
Lucedale *U.S.A.* 30°56N 88°35W **85** F10
Lucena *Phil.* 13°56N 121°37E **37** B6
Lucena *Spain* 37°27N 4°31W **21** D3
Lučenec *Slovak Rep.* 48°18N 19°42E **17** D10
Lucerne = Luzern *Switz.* 47°3N 8°18E **20** C8
Lucerne *U.S.A.* 39°6N 122°48W **78** F4
Lucerne Valley *U.S.A.* 34°27N 116°57W **79** L10
Lucheng *China* 36°20N 113°11E **32** F7
Luchuan *China* 22°21N 110°12E **35** F8
Lucia *U.S.A.* 36°2N 121°33W **78** J5
Lucinda *Australia* 18°32S 146°20E **62** B4
Luckenwalde *Germany* 52°5N 13°10E **16** B7
Luckhoff *S. Africa* 29°44S 24°43E **56** C3
Lucknow *Canada* 43°57N 81°31W **82** C3
Lucknow *India* 26°50N 81°0E **43** F9
Lüda = Dalian *China* 38°50N 121°40E **33** E11
Lüderitz *Namibia* 26°41S 15°8E **56** D2
Lüderitzbaai *Namibia* 26°36S 15°8E **56** C2
Ludhiana *India* 30°57N 75°56E **42** D6
Ludian *China* 27°10N 103°33E **34** D4
Luding Qiao *China* 29°53N 102°12E **34** C4
Ludington *U.S.A.* 43°57N 86°27W **80** D10
Ludlow *U.K.* 52°22N 2°42W **13** E5
Ludlow *Calif., U.S.A.* 34°43N 116°10W **79** L10
Ludlow *Pa., U.S.A.* 41°43N 78°56W **82** E6
Ludlow *Vt., U.S.A.* 43°24N 72°42W **83** C12
Ludvika *Sweden* 60°8N 15°14E **9** F16
Ludwigsburg *Germany* 48°53N 9°11E **16** D5
Ludwigshafen *Germany* 49°29N 8°26E **16** D5
Luena Flats *Zambia* 14°47S 23°17E **55** G4
Lüeyang *China* 33°22N 106°10E **34** A6
Lufeng *Guangdong, China* 22°57N 115°38E **35** F10
Lufeng *Yunnan, China* 25°0N 102°5E **34** E4
Lufira → *Dem. Rep. of the Congo* 9°30S 27°0E **54** F5
Lufkin *U.S.A.* 31°21N 94°44W **84** F7
Luga *Russia* 58°40N 29°55E **9** G23
Lugano *Switz.* 46°1N 8°57E **20** C8
Lugansk = Luhansk *Ukraine* 48°38N 39°15E **19** E6
Lugenda → *Mozam.* 11°25S 38°33E **55** G4
Lugh = Luuq *Somalia* 3°48N 42°34E **49** G3
Lugnaquilla *Ireland* 52°58N 6°28W **10** D5
Lugo *Italy* 44°25N 11°54E **22** B4
Lugo *Spain* 43°2N 7°35W **21** A2

Lugoj *Romania* 45°42N 21°57E **17** F11
Lugovoy = Qulan *Kazakhstan* 42°55N 72°43E **26** E8
Luhansk *Ukraine* 48°38N 39°15E **19** E6
Luhe *China* 32°19N 118°50E **35** A12
Luhuo *China* 31°21N 100°48E **34** B3
Lui → *Angola* 8°21S 17°33E **54** F3
Luiana *Angola* 17°25S 22°59E **56** A3
Luiana → *Angola* 17°24S 23°3E **55** H4
Luichow Pen. = Leizhou Bandao *China* 21°0N 110°0E **34** G7
Luimneach = Limerick *Ireland* 52°40N 8°37W **10** D3
Luing *U.K.* 56°14N 5°39W **11** E3
Luis Correia *Brazil* 3°0S 41°35W **93** D10
Luitpold Coast *Antarctica* 78°30S 32°0W **5** D1
Luiza *Dem. Rep. of the Congo* 7°40S 22°30E **54** F4
Luján *Argentina* 34°45S 59°5W **94** C4
Lujiang *China* 31°20N 117°15E **35** B11
Lukang *Taiwan* 24°1N 120°22E **35** E13
Lukanga Swamp *Zambia* 14°30S 27°40E **55** G5
Lukenie → *Dem. Rep. of the Congo* 3°0S 18°50E **54** E3
Lukla *Nepal* 27°42N 86°43E **43** F12
Lukolela *Dem. Rep. of the Congo* 26°21N 105°16E **34** D5
Lukosi *Zimbabwe* 18°30S 26°30E **55** H5
Luków *Poland* 51°55N 22°23E **17** C12
Lülang Shan *China* 38°0N 111°15E **32** F6
Luleå *Sweden* 65°35N 22°10E **8** D20
Luleälven → *Sweden* 65°35N 22°10E **8** D20
Lüleburgaz *Turkey* 41°23N 27°22E **23** D12
Luliang *China* 25°0N 103°40E **34** E4
Luling *U.S.A.* 29°41N 97°39W **84** G6
Lulong *China* 39°53N 118°51E **33** E10
Lulonga → *Dem. Rep. of the Congo* 1°0N 18°10E **54** D3
Lulua → *Dem. Rep. of the Congo* 4°30S 20°30E **54** E4
Luma *Amer. Samoa* 14°16S 169°33W **59** b
Lumajang *Indonesia* 8°8S 113°13E **37** H15
Lumbala N'guimbo *Angola* 14°18S 21°18E **55** G4
Lumberton *N.C., U.S.A.* 34°37N 79°0W **85** D15
Lumberton *Tex., U.S.A.* 30°16N 94°12W **84** F7
Lumsden *Canada* 50°39N 104°52W **71** C8
Lumsden *N.Z.* 45°44S 168°27E **59** F2
Lumut *Malaysia* 4°13N 100°37E **39** K3
Lumut, Tanjung *Indonesia* 3°50S 105°58E **36** E3
Luna *India* 23°43N 69°16E **42** H3
Lunan *China* 24°40N 103°18E **34** E4
Lunavada *India* 23°8N 73°37E **42** H5
Lund *Sweden* 55°44N 13°12E **9** J15
Lundazi *Zambia* 12°20S 33°7E **55** G6
Lundu *Malaysia* 1°40N 109°50E **36** D3
Lundy *U.K.* 51°10N 4°41W **13** F3
Lune → *U.K.* 54°0N 2°51W **12** C5
Lüneburg *Germany* 53°15N 10°24E **16** B6
Lüneburg Heath = Lüneburger Heide *Germany* 53°10N 10°12E **16** B6
Lüneburger Heide *Germany* 53°10N 10°12E **16** B6
Lunenburg *Canada* 44°22N 64°18W **73** D7
Lunéville *France* 48°36N 6°30E **20** B7
Lunglei *India* 22°55N 92°45E **41** H18
Luni *India* 26°0N 73°6E **42** G5
Luni → *India* 24°41N 71°14E **42** G4
Luninets = Luninyets *Belarus* 52°15N 26°50E **17** B14
Luning *U.S.A.* 38°30N 118°11W **76** G4
Luninyets *Belarus* 52°15N 26°50E **17** B14
Lunkaransar *India* 28°29N 73°44E **42** E5
Luo He → *China* 34°35N 110°20E **32** G6
Luocheng *China* 24°48N 108°53E **34** E7
Luochuan *China* 35°45N 109°26E **32** G5
Luoci *China* 25°19N 102°18E **34** E4
Luodian *China* 25°24N 106°43E **34** E6
Luoding *China* 22°45N 111°40E **35** F8
Luofu *Dem. Rep. of the Congo* 0°10S 29°15E **54** E5
Luohe *China* 33°32N 114°2E **32** H8
Luojiang *China* 31°18N 104°33E **34** B5
Luonan *China* 34°5N 110°10E **32** G6
Luoning *China* 34°35N 111°40E **32** G6
Luoshan *China* 32°13N 114°30E **35** A10
Luotian *China* 30°46N 115°22E **35** B10
Luoxiao Shan *China* 26°30N 114°1E **35** D10
Luoyang *China* 34°40N 112°26E **32** G7
Luoyuan *China* 26°28N 119°30E **35** D12
Luozigou *China* 43°42N 130°18E **33** C16
Lupoing *China* 24°53N 104°21E **34** E5
Luquan *Hebei, China* 38°4N 114°17E **32** E8
Luquan *Yunnan, China* 25°35N 102°28E **34** E4
Luque *Paraguay* 25°19S 57°25W **94** B4
Luquillo, Sierra de *Puerto Rico* 18°20N 65°47W **89** d
Luray *U.S.A.* 38°40N 78°28W **81** F14
Lurgan *U.K.* 54°27N 6°20W **10** B5
Lusaka *Zambia* 15°28S 28°16E **55** H5
Lusambo *Dem. Rep. of the Congo* 4°58S 23°28E **54** E4
Luseland *Canada* 52°5N 109°24W **71** C7
Lushan *Henan, China* 33°45N 112°55E **32** H7
Lushan *Sichuan, China* 30°12N 102°52E **34** B4
Lushi *China* 34°3N 111°3E **32** G6
Lushnjë *Albania* 40°55N 19°41E **23** D8
Lushui *China* 25°58N 98°44E **34** E2
Lüshun *China* 38°45N 121°15E **33** E11
Lusk *U.S.A.* 42°46N 104°27W **76** E11
Lūt, Dasht-e *Iran* 31°30N 58°0E **47** D8
Luta = Dalian *China* 38°50N 121°40E **33** E11
Lütao *Taiwan* 22°40N 121°30E **35** F13
Lutherstadt Wittenberg *Germany* 51°53N 12°39E **16** C7
Luton *U.K.* 51°53N 0°24W **13** F7
Luton □ *U.K.* 51°53N 0°24W **13** F7
Lutsel K'e *Canada* 62°24N 110°44W **71** A6
Lutsk *Ukraine* 50°50N 25°15E **17** C13
Lutto = Lotta → *Europe* 68°42N 31°6E **8** B24
Lützow Holmbukta *Antarctica* 69°10S 37°30E **5** C4
Lutzputs *S. Africa* 28°3S 20°40E **56** D3
Luuq *Somalia* 3°48N 42°34E **49** G3

Luverne *Ala., U.S.A.* 31°43N 86°16W **85** F11
Luverne *Minn., U.S.A.* 43°39N 96°13W **80** D5
Luvua → *Dem. Rep. of the Congo* 6°50S 27°30E **54** F5
Luvuhu → *S. Africa* 22°25S 31°18E **57** B5
Luwuk *Indonesia* 0°56S 122°47E **37** E6
Luxembourg *Lux.* 49°37N 6°9E **15** E6
Luxembourg □ *Belgium* 49°58N 5°30E **15** E5
Luxembourg ■ *Europe* 49°45N 6°0E **15** E5
Luxembourg ✈ (LUX) *Lux.* 49°37N 6°10E **15** E6
Luxi *Hunan, China* 28°20N 110°7E **35** C8
Luxi *Yunnan, China* 24°27N 98°36E **34** E2
Luxian *China* 29°29N 105°24E **34** C5
Luxor = El Uqsur *Egypt* 25°41N 32°38E **53** C12
Luyi *China* 33°50N 115°35E **32** H8
Luykau = Loikaw *Burma* 19°40N 97°17E **41** K20
Luza *Russia* 60°39N 47°10E **18** B8
Luzern *Switz.* 47°3N 8°18E **20** C8
Luzhai *China* 24°29N 109°42E **34** E7
Luzhi *China* 26°21N 105°16E **34** D5
Luzhou *China* 28°52N 105°20E **34** C5
Luziânia *Brazil* 16°20S 48°0W **93** G9
Luzon *Phil.* 16°0N 121°0E **37** A6
Luzon Strait *Asia* 21°0N 120°40E **35** G13
Lviv *Ukraine* 49°50N 24°0E **17** D13
Lvov = Lviv *Ukraine* 49°50N 24°0E **17** D13
Lyakhavichy *Belarus* 53°2N 26°32E **17** B14
Lyakhovskiye, Ostrova *Russia* 73°40N 141°0E **27** B15
Lyal I. *Canada* 44°57N 81°24W **82** B3
Lybster *U.K.* 58°18N 3°15W **11** C5
Lyckele *Sweden* 64°38N 18°40E **8** D18
Lydda = Lod *Israel* 31°57N 34°54E **48** D3
Lydenburg *S. Africa* 25°10S 30°29E **57** C5
Lydia *Turkey* 38°48N 28°19E **23** E13
Lyell *N.Z.* 41°48S 172°4E **59** D4
Lyell I. *Canada* 52°40N 131°35W **70** C2
Lyepyel *Belarus* 54°50N 28°40E **9** J23
Lykens *U.S.A.* 40°34N 76°42W **83** F8
Lyman *U.S.A.* 41°20N 110°18W **76** F8
Lyme B. *U.K.* 50°42N 2°53W **13** G4
Lyme Regis *U.K.* 50°43N 2°57W **13** G5
Lymington *U.K.* 50°45N 1°32W **13** G6
Łyna → *Poland* 54°37N 21°14E **17** A11
Lynchburg *U.S.A.* 37°25N 79°9W **81** G14
Lynd → *Australia* 16°28S 143°18E **62** B3
Lynd Ra. *Australia* 25°30S 149°20E **63** D4
Lynden *Canada* 43°14N 80°9W **82** C4
Lynden *U.S.A.* 48°57N 122°27W **78** B4
Lyndhurst *Australia* 30°15S 138°18E **63** E2
Lyndon → *Australia* 23°29S 114°6E **61** D1
Lyndonville *N.Y., U.S.A.* 43°20N 78°23W **82** C6
Lyndonville *Vt., U.S.A.* 44°31N 72°1W **83** B12
Lyngen *Norway* 69°45N 20°30E **8** B19
Lynher Reef *Australia* 15°27S 121°55E **60** C3
Lynn *U.S.A.* 42°28N 70°57W **83** D14
Lynn Canal *U.S.A.* 58°50N 135°15W **74** D12
Lynn Haven *U.S.A.* 30°15N 85°39W **85** F12
Lynn Lake *Canada* 56°51N 101°3W **71** B8
Lynnwood *U.S.A.* 47°49N 122°18W **78** C4
Lynton *U.K.* 51°13N 3°50W **13** F4
Lyntupy *Belarus* 55°4N 26°23E **9** J22
Lynx L. *Canada* 62°25N 106°15W **71** A7
Lyon *France* 45°46N 4°50E **20** D6
Lyonnais *France* 45°45N 4°15E **20** D6
Lyons = Lyon *France* 45°46N 4°50E **20** D6
Lyons *Ga., U.S.A.* 32°12N 82°19W **85** E13
Lyons *Kans., U.S.A.* 38°21N 98°12W **80** F4
Lyons *N.Y., U.S.A.* 43°5N 77°0W **82** C8
Lyons → *Australia* 25°2S 115°9E **61** E2
Lyons Falls *U.S.A.* 43°37N 75°22W **83** C9
Lys = Leie → *Belgium* 51°2N 3°45E **15** C3
Lysva *Russia* 58°7N 57°49E **18** C10
Lysychansk *Ukraine* 48°55N 38°30E **19** E6
Lytham St. Anne's *U.K.* 53°45N 3°0W **12** D4
Lyttelton *N.Z.* 43°35S 172°44E **59** E4
Lytton *Canada* 50°13N 121°31W **70** C4
Lyubertsy *Russia* 55°40N 37°51E **18** C6
Lyuboml *Ukraine* 51°11N 24°4E **17** C13

M

Ma → *Vietnam* 19°47N 105°56E **34** H5
Ma On Shan *China* 22°24N 114°10E **31** a
Ma'adaba *Jordan* 31°43N 35°47E **48** D4
Ma'alot-Tarshiha *Israel* 33°1N 35°17E **48** B4
Maamba *Zambia* 17°17S 26°28E **56** A4
Ma'ān *Jordan* 30°12N 35°44E **48** E4
Ma'ān □ *Jordan* 30°0N 36°0E **48** F5
Maanselkä *Finland* 63°52N 28°32E **8** C23
Ma'anshan *China* 31°44N 118°29E **35** B12
Maarianhamina = Mariehamn *Finland* 60°5N 19°55E **9** F18
Ma'arrat an Nu'mān *Syria* 35°43N 36°43E **46** C3
Maas → *Neths.* 51°45N 4°32E **15** C4
Maaseik *Belgium* 51°6N 5°45E **15** C5
Maasin *Phil.* 10°8N 124°50E **37** B6
Maastricht *Neths.* 50°50N 5°40E **15** D5
Maave *Mozam.* 21°4S 34°47E **57** B5
Mababe Depression *Botswana* 18°50S 24°15E **56** A3
Mabel L. *Canada* 50°35N 118°43W **70** C5
Maberly *Canada* 44°50N 76°32W **83** B8
Mabian *China* 28°47N 103°37E **34** C4
Mablethorpe *U.K.* 53°20N 0°15E **12** D8
Mabuasehube △ *Botswana* 25°5S 21°10E **56** C3
Mabuiag *Australia* 9°55S 142°11E **62** a
Mac Bac *Vietnam* 9°46N 106°7E **39** H6
Macachín *Argentina* 37°10S 63°43W **94** D3
Macaé *Brazil* 22°20S 41°43W **95** A7
McAlester *U.S.A.* 34°56N 95°46W **84** D7
McAllen *U.S.A.* 26°12N 98°14W **84** H5

MacAlpine L. *Canada* 66°32N 102°45W **68** C12
Macamic *Canada* 48°45N 79°0W **72** C4
Macao = Macau *China* 22°12N 113°33E **35** F9
Macapá *Brazil* 0°5N 51°4W **93** C8
Macarao △ *Venezuela* 10°22N 67°7W **89** D6
McArthur → *Australia* 15°54S 136°40E **62** B2
McArthur, Port *Australia* 16°4S 136°23E **62** B2
Macau *Brazil* 5°15S 36°40W **93** E11
Macau *China* 22°12N 113°33E **35** F9
McBride *Canada* 53°20N 120°19W **70** C4
McCall *U.S.A.* 44°55N 116°6W **76** D5
McCamey *U.S.A.* 31°8N 102°14W **84** F3
McCammon *U.S.A.* 42°39N 112°12W **76** E7
McCauley I. *Canada* 53°40N 130°15W **70** C2
McCleary *U.S.A.* 47°3N 123°16W **78** C3
Macclenny *U.S.A.* 30°17N 82°7W **85** F13
Macclesfield *U.K.* 53°15N 2°8W **12** D5
M'Clintock Chan. *Canada* 72°0N 102°0W **68** C11
McClintock Ra. *Australia* 18°44S 127°38E **60** C4
McCloud *U.S.A.* 41°15N 122°8W **76** F2
McCluer I. *Australia* 11°5S 133°0E **60** B5
McClure *U.S.A.* 40°42N 77°19W **82** F7
McClure, L. *U.S.A.* 37°35N 120°16W **78** H6
M'Clure Str. *Canada* 75°0N 119°0W **69** C8
McClusky *U.S.A.* 47°29N 100°27W **80** B3
McComb *U.S.A.* 31°15N 90°27W **85** F9
McCook *U.S.A.* 40°12N 100°38W **80** E3
McCreary *Canada* 50°47N 99°29W **71** C9
McCullough Mt. *U.S.A.* 35°35N 115°13W **79** K11
McCusker → *Canada* 55°32N 108°39W **71** B7
McDermitt *U.S.A.* 41°59N 117°43W **76** F5
McDonald *U.S.A.* 40°22N 80°14W **82** F4
Macdonald, L. *Australia* 23°30S 129°0E **60** D4
McDonald Is. *Ind. Oc.* 53°0S 73°0E **3** G13
MacDonnell Ranges *Australia* 23°40S 133°0E **60** D5
MacDowell L. *Canada* 52°15N 92°45W **72** B1
Macduff *U.K.* 57°40N 2°31W **11** D6
Macedonia *U.S.A.* 41°19N 81°31W **82** E3
Macedonia □ *Greece* 40°39N 22°0E **23** D10
Macedonia ■ *Europe* 41°53N 21°40E **23** D9
Maceió *Brazil* 9°40S 35°41W **93** E11
Macerata *Italy* 43°18N 13°27E **22** C5
McFarland *U.S.A.* 35°41N 119°14W **79** K7
McFarlane → *Canada* 59°12N 107°58W **71** B7
Macfarlane, L. *Australia* 32°0S 136°40E **63** E2
McGehee *U.S.A.* 33°38N 91°24W **84** E9
McGill *U.S.A.* 39°23N 114°47W **76** G6
Macgillycuddy's Reeks *Ireland* 51°58N 9°45W **10** E2
McGraw *U.S.A.* 42°36N 76°8W **83** D8
McGregor *U.S.A.* 43°1N 91°11W **80** D8
McGregor Ra. *Australia* 27°0S 142°45E **63** D3
McGuire, Mt. *Australia* 20°18S 148°23E **62** b
Mach *Pakistan* 29°50N 67°20E **42** E2
Māch Kowr *Iran* 25°48N 61°28E **47** E9
Machado = Jiparaná → *Brazil* 8°3S 62°52W **92** E6
Machagai *Argentina* 26°56S 60°2W **94** B3
Machakos *Kenya* 1°30S 37°15E **54** E7
Machala *Ecuador* 3°20S 79°57W **92** D3
Machanga *Mozam.* 20°59S 35°0E **57** B6
Machattie, L. *Australia* 24°50S 139°48E **62** C2
Machava *Mozam.* 25°54S 32°28E **57** C5
Macheke *Zimbabwe* 18°5S 31°51E **57** A5
Macheng *China* 31°12N 115°2E **35** B10
Macherla *India* 16°29N 79°26E **44** F4
Machgaon *India* 20°5N 86°17E **44** D8
Machhu → *India* 23°6N 70°46E **42** H4
Machiara △ *Pakistan* 34°40N 73°30E **42** B5
Machias *Maine, U.S.A.* 44°43N 67°28W **81** C20
Machias *N.Y., U.S.A.* 42°25N 78°29W **82** D6
Machichi → *Canada* 57°3N 92°6W **71** B10
Machilipatnam *India* 16°12N 81°8E **45** F5
Machiques *Venezuela* 10°4N 72°34W **92** A4
Machu Picchu *Peru* 13°8S 72°30W **92** F4
Machynlleth *U.K.* 52°35N 3°50E **13** E4
Macia *Mozam.* 25°2S 33°8E **57** C5
McIlwraith Ra. *Australia* 13°50S 143°20E **62** A3
McInnes L. *Canada* 52°13N 93°45W **71** C10
McIntosh *U.S.A.* 45°55N 101°21W **80** C3
McIntosh L. *Canada* 55°45N 105°0W **71** B8
Macintosh Ra. *Australia* 27°39S 125°32E **61** E4
Macintyre → *Australia* 28°37S 150°47E **63** D5
Mackay *Australia* 21°8S 149°11E **62** K7
Mackay *U.S.A.* 43°55N 113°37W **76** E7
MacKay → *Canada* 57°10N 111°38W **70** B6
Mackay, L. *Australia* 22°30S 129°0E **60** D4
McKay Ra. *Australia* 23°0S 122°30E **60** D3
McKeesport *U.S.A.* 40°20N 79°51W **82** F5
McKellar *Canada* 45°30N 79°55W **82** A5
McKenna *U.S.A.* 46°56N 122°33W **78** D4
Mackenzie = Linden *Guyana* 6°0N 58°10W **92** B7
Mackenzie *Canada* 55°20N 123°5W **70** B4
McKenzie *U.S.A.* 36°8N 88°31W **85** C10
Mackenzie → *Australia* 23°38S 149°46E **62** C4
McKenzie → *U.S.A.* 44°7N 123°6W **76** D2
Mackenzie Bay *Canada* 69°0N 137°30W **66** C6
Mackenzie King I. *Canada* 77°45N 111°0W **69** B9
Mackenzie Mts. *Canada* 64°0N 130°0W **68** C6
Mackinac, Straits of *U.S.A.* 45°50N 84°40W **81** C11
Mackinaw City *U.S.A.* 45°47N 84°44W **81** C11
McKinlay *Australia* 21°16S 141°18E **62** C3
McKinlay → *Australia* 20°50S 141°28E **62** C3
McKinley, Mt. *U.S.A.* 63°4N 151°0W **68** E1
McKinley Sea *Arctic* 82°0N 0°0 **4** A7
McKinney *U.S.A.* 33°12N 96°37W **84** E6
McKittrick *U.S.A.* 35°18N 119°37W **79** K7
Macklin *Canada* 52°20N 109°56W **71** C7
Macksville *Australia* 30°40S 152°56E **63** E5
McLaughlin *U.S.A.* 45°49N 100°49W **80** C3
Maclean *Australia* 29°26S 153°16E **63** D5

McLean U.S.A. 35°14N 100°36W 84 D4
McLeansboro U.S.A. 38°6N 88°32W 80 F9
Maclear S. Africa 31°2S 28°23E 57 D4
Macleay → Australia 30°56S 153°0E 63 E5
McLennan Canada 55°42N 116°50W 70 B5
McLeod → Canada 54°9N 115°44W 70 C5
MacLeod, L. Australia 24°9S 113°47E 61 D1
MacLeod B. Canada 62°53N 110°0W 71 A7
MacLeod Lake Canada 54°58N 123°0W 70 C4
McLoughlin, Mt. U.S.A. 42°27N 122°19W 76 E2
McMechen U.S.A. 39°57N 80°44W 82 G4
McMinnville Oreg., U.S.A. 45°13N 123°12W 76 D2
McMinnville Tenn., U.S.A. 35°41N 85°46W 85 D12
McMurdo Antarctica 77°51S 166°37E 5 D11
McMurdo Sd. Antarctica 77°0S 170°0E 5 D11
McMurray = Fort McMurray Canada 56°44N 111°7W 70 B6
McMurray U.S.A. 48°19N 122°14W 78 B4
Maçobere Mozam. 21°13S 32°47E 57 B5
Macodoene Mozam. 23°32S 35°5E 57 B6
Macomb U.S.A. 40°27N 90°40W 80 E8
Mâcon France 46°19N 4°50E 20 C6
Macon Ga., U.S.A. 32°51N 83°38W 85 E13
Macon Miss., U.S.A. 33°7N 88°34W 85 E10
Macon Mo., U.S.A. 39°44N 92°28W 80 F7
Macoun L. Canada 56°32N 103°40W 71 B8
Macovane Mozam. 21°30S 35°2E 57 B6
McPherson U.S.A. 38°22N 97°40W 80 F5
McPherson Pk. U.S.A. 34°53N 119°53W 79 L7
McPherson Ra. Australia 28°15S 153°15E 63 D5
Macquarie → Australia 30°7S 147°24E 63 E4
Macquarie Harbour Australia 42°15S 145°23E 63 G4
Macquarie I. Pac. Oc. 54°36S 158°55E 64 N7
Macquarie Ridge S. Ocean 57°0S 159°0E 5 B10
MacRobertson Land Antarctica 71°0S 64°0E 5 D6
Macroom Ireland 51°54N 8°57W 10 E3
MacTier Canada 45°8N 79°47W 82 A5
Macuira △ Colombia 12°9N 71°21W 89 D5
Macumba → Australia 27°52S 137°12E 63 D2
Macuro Venezuela 10°42N 61°55W 93 K15
Macusani Peru 14°4S 70°29W 92 F4
Macuspana Mexico 17°46N 92°36W 87 D6
Macusse Angola 17°48S 20°23E 56 A3
Ma'dabā □ Jordan 31°43N 35°47E 48 D4
Madadeni S. Africa 27°43S 30°3E 57 C5
Madagascar ■ Africa 20°0S 47°0E 55 J9
Madā'in Sālih Si. Arabia 26°46N 37°57E 46 E3
Madakasira India 13°56N 77°16E 45 H3
Madama Niger 22°0N 13°40E 53 D8
Madame, I. Canada 45°30N 60°58W 73 C7
Madanapalle India 13°33N 78°28E 45 H4
Madang Papua N. G. 5°12S 145°49E 58 B7
Madaripur Bangla. 23°19N 90°15E 41 H17
Madauk Burma 17°56N 96°52E 41 L20
Madawaska Canada 45°30N 78°0W 82 A7
Madawaska → Canada 45°27N 76°21W 82 A7
Madaya Burma 22°12N 96°10E 41 H20
Maddalena Italy 41°16N 9°23E 22 D3
Maddur India 12°36N 77°4E 45 H3
Madeira Atl. Oc. 32°50N 17°0W 52 B2
Madeira → Brazil 3°22S 58°45W 92 D7
Madeleine, Îs. de la Canada 47°30N 61°40W 73 C7
Madera Mexico 29°12N 108°7W 86 B3
Madera Calif., U.S.A. 36°57N 120°3W 78 J6
Madera Pa., U.S.A. 40°49N 78°26W 82 F6
Madgaon India 15°12N 73°58E 45 G1
Madha India 18°0N 75°30E 44 F2
Madhavpur India 21°15N 69°58E 42 J3
Madhepura India 26°11N 86°23E 43 F12
Madhira India 16°55N 80°22E 44 F5
Madhubani India 26°21N 86°7E 43 F12
Madhugiri India 13°40N 77°12E 45 H3
Madhupur India 24°16N 86°39E 43 G12
Madhya Pradesh □ India 22°50N 78°0E 42 J8
Madidi → Bolivia 12°32S 66°52W 92 F5
Madikeri India 12°30N 75°45E 45 H2
Madikwe ⌂ S. Africa 27°38S 32°15E 57 C5
Madill U.S.A. 34°6N 96°46W 84 D6
Madimba Dem. Rep. of the Congo 4°58S 15°5E 54 E3
Ma'din Syria 35°45N 39°36E 46 C3
Madinat al Malik Khālid al Askarīyah Si. Arabia 27°54N 45°31E 46 E5
Madingou Congo 4°10S 13°33E 54 E2
Madison Calif., U.S.A. 38°41N 121°59W 78 G5
Madison Fla., U.S.A. 30°28N 83°25W 85 F13
Madison Ind., U.S.A. 38°44N 85°23W 81 F11
Madison Nebr., U.S.A. 41°50N 97°27W 80 E5
Madison Ohio, U.S.A. 41°46N 81°3W 82 E3
Madison S. Dak., U.S.A. 44°0N 97°7W 80 C5
Madison Wis., U.S.A. 43°4N 89°24W 80 D9
Madison → U.S.A. 45°56N 111°31W 76 D8
Madison Heights U.S.A. 37°25N 79°8W 81 G14
Madisonville Ky., U.S.A. 37°20N 87°30W 80 G10
Madisonville Tex., U.S.A. 30°57N 95°55W 84 F7
Madista Botswana 21°15S 25°6E 56 B4
Madiun Indonesia 7°38S 111°32E 37 G14
Madoc Canada 44°30N 77°28W 82 B7
Madoi China 34°46N 98°18E 30 E8
Madona Latvia 56°53N 26°5E 9 H22
Madrakah, Ra's al Oman 19°0N 57°50E 49 D6
Madras = Chennai India 13°8N 80°19E 45 H5
Madras = Tamil Nadu □ India 11°0N 77°0E 45 J3
Madras U.S.A. 44°38N 121°8W 76 D3
Madre, L. U.S.A. 25°15N 97°30W 84 J6
Madre, Sierra Phil. 17°0N 122°0E 37 A6
Madre de Dios → Bolivia 10°59S 66°8W 92 F5
Madre de Dios, I. Chile 50°20S 75°10W 96 G1
Madre del Sur, Sierra Mexico 17°30N 100°0W 87 D5
Madre Occidental, Sierra Mexico 27°0N 107°0W 86 B3
Madre Oriental, Sierra Mexico 25°0N 100°0W 86 C5
Madri India 24°16N 73°32E 42 G5
Madrid U.S.A. 44°45N 75°8W 83 B9
Madura Australia 31°55S 127°0E 61 F4
Madura Indonesia 7°30S 114°0E 37 G15
Madura, Selat Indonesia 7°30S 113°20E 37 G15
Madura Oya △ Sri Lanka 7°20N 81°10E 45 L5
Madurai India 9°55N 78°10E 45 K4
Madurantakam India 12°30N 79°50E 45 H4
Mae Chan Thailand 20°9N 99°52E 38 B2
Mae Charim △ Thailand 18°17N 100°59E 38 C3
Mae Hong Son Thailand 19°16N 97°56E 38 C2
Mae Khlong → Thailand 13°24N 100°0E 38 F3
Mae Moei △ Thailand 17°26N 98°7E 38 D2
Mae Phang △ Thailand 19°7N 99°13E 38 C2
Mae Phrik Thailand 17°27N 99°7E 38 D2
Mae Ping △ Thailand 17°37N 98°51E 38 D2
Mae Ramat Thailand 16°58N 98°31E 38 D2
Mae Rim Thailand 18°54N 98°57E 38 C2
Mae Sai Thailand 20°20N 99°55E 34 G2
Mae Sot Thailand 16°43N 98°34E 38 D2
Mae Suai Thailand 19°39N 99°33E 34 H2
Mae Tha Thailand 18°28N 99°8E 38 C2
Mae Tup Res. Thailand 17°52N 98°45E 38 D2
Mae Wa △ Thailand 17°23N 99°16E 38 D2
Mae Wong △ Thailand 15°54N 99°12E 38 E2
Mae Yom △ Thailand 18°43N 100°15E 38 C3
Maebaru Japan 33°33N 130°12E 29 H5
Maebashi Japan 36°24N 139°4E 29 F9
Maelpaeg L. Canada 48°20N 56°30W 73 C8
Maesteg U.K. 51°36N 3°40W 13 F4
Maestra, Sierra Cuba 20°15N 77°0W 88 B4
Maevatanana Madag. 16°56S 46°49E 55 H9
Mafadi S. Africa 29°12S 29°21E 57 C4
Mafeking = Mafikeng S. Africa 25°50S 25°38E 56 C4
Mafeking Canada 52°40N 101°10W 71 C8
Mafeteng Lesotho 29°51S 27°15E 56 C4
Maffra Australia 37°53S 146°58E 63 F4
Mafia I. Tanzania 7°45S 39°50E 54 F7
Mafikeng S. Africa 25°50S 25°38E 56 C4
Mafra Brazil 26°10S 49°55W 95 B6
Mafra Portugal 38°55N 9°20W 21 C1
Magadan Russia 59°38N 150°50E 27 D16
Magadi India 12°58N 77°14E 45 H3
Magaliesburg S. Africa 26°0S 27°32E 57 C4
Magallanes, Estrecho de Chile 52°30S 75°0W 96 G2
Magangué Colombia 9°14N 74°45W 92 B4
Magdagachi Russia 53°27N 125°48E 27 D13
Magdalen Is. = Madeleine, Îs. de la Canada 47°30N 61°40W 73 C7
Magdalena Argentina 35°5S 57°30W 94 D4
Magdalena Bolivia 13°13S 63°57W 92 F6
Magdalena U.S.A. 34°7N 107°15W 77 J10
Magdalena → Colombia 11°6N 74°51W 92 A4
Magdalena, B. Mexico 24°35N 112°0W 86 C2
Magdalena, I. Mexico 24°40N 112°15W 86 C2
Magdalena, Llano de Mexico 25°0N 111°25W 86 C2
Magdalena de Kino Mexico 30°38N 110°57W 86 A2
Magdeburg Germany 52°7N 11°38E 16 B6
Magdelaine Cays Australia 16°33S 150°18E 62 B5
Magee U.S.A. 31°52N 89°44W 85 F10
Magelang Indonesia 7°29S 110°13E 37 G14
Magellan's Str. = Magallanes, Estrecho de Chile 52°30S 75°0W 96 G2
Magenta, L. Australia 33°30S 119°2E 61 F2
Magerøya Norway 71°3N 25°40E 8 A21
Maggiore, Lago Italy 45°57N 8°39E 20 D8
Maggotty Jamaica 18°9N 77°46W 88 a
Maghâgha Egypt 28°38N 30°50E 53 C12
Maghera U.K. 54°51N 6°41W 10 B5
Magherafelt U.K. 54°45N 6°37W 10 B5
Maghreb N. Afr. 32°0N 4°0W 50 C3
Magistralnyy Russia 56°16N 107°36E 27 D11
Magnetic Pole (North) Arctic 82°18N 113°24W 4 A2
Magnetic Pole (South) Antarctica 64°8S 138°8E 5 C9
Magnitogorsk Russia 53°27N 59°4E 18 D10
Magnolia Ark., U.S.A. 33°16N 93°14W 84 E8
Magnolia Miss., U.S.A. 31°9N 90°28W 85 F9
Mago Fiji 17°26S 179°8W 59 a
Magog Canada 45°18N 72°9W 83 A12
Magpie, L. Canada 51°0N 64°41W 73 B7
Magrath Canada 49°25N 112°50W 70 D6
Maguan China 23°0N 104°21E 34 F5
Maguarinho, C. Brazil 0°15S 48°30W 93 D9
Magude Mozam. 25°2S 32°40E 57 C5
Mağusa = Famagusta Cyprus 35°8N 33°55E 46 C2
Maguse L. Canada 61°37N 95°10W 71 A9
Maguse Pt. Canada 61°20N 93°50W 71 A10
Magvana India 23°13N 69°22E 42 H3
Magwe Burma 20°10N 95°0E 41 J19
Magyarorszag = Hungary ■ Europe 47°20N 19°20E 17 E10
Maha Oya Sri Lanka 7°31N 81°22E 45 L5
Maha Sarakham Thailand 16°12N 103°16E 38 D4
Mahābād Iran 36°50N 45°45E 46 B5
Mahabaleshwar India 17°58N 73°43E 44 F1
Mahabalipuram India 12°37N 80°11E 45 H5
Mahabharat Lekh Nepal 28°30N 82°0E 43 E10
Mahabo Madag. 20°23S 44°40E 55 J8
Mahad India 18°6N 73°29E 44 E1
Mahadeo Hills India 22°20N 78°30E 43 H8
Mahadeopur India 18°48N 80°0E 44 E5
Mahaffey U.S.A. 40°53N 78°44W 82 F6
Mahajan India 28°48N 73°56E 42 E5
Mahajanga Madag. 15°40S 46°25E 55 H9
Mahakam → Indonesia 0°35S 117°17E 36 E5
Mahalapye Botswana 23°1S 26°51E 56 B4
Mahale Mts. Tanzania 6°20S 30°0E 54 F6
Maḥallāt Iran 33°55N 50°30E 47 C6
Māhān Iran 30°5N 57°18E 47 D8
Mahan → India 23°30N 82°50E 43 H10
Mahanadi → India 20°20N 86°25E 44 D8
Mahananda → India 25°12N 87°52E 43 G12
Mahanoro Madag. 19°54S 48°48E 55 H9
Mahanoy City U.S.A. 40°49N 76°9W 83 F8
Maharashtra □ India 20°30N 75°30E 44 D2
Mahasamund India 21°6N 82°6E 44 D6
Mahasham, W. → Egypt 30°15N 34°10E 48 E3
Mahattat ash Shīdīyah Jordan 29°55N 35°55E 48 F4
Mahattat 'Unayzah Jordan 30°30N 35°47E 48 E4
Mahaweli Ganga → Sri Lanka 8°27N 81°13E 45 K5
Mahaxay Laos 17°22N 105°12E 38 D5
Mahbubabad India 17°42N 80°2E 44 F5
Mahbubnagar India 16°45N 77°59E 44 F3
Mahda U.A.E. 25°20N 56°15E 47 E8
Maḥḍah Oman 24°24N 55°59E 47 E7
Mahdia Tunisia 35°28N 11°0E 53 A8
Mahe Jammu & Kashmir, India 33°10N 78°32E 43 C8
Mahé Pondicherry, India 11°42N 75°34E 45 J2
Mahé Seychelles 5°0S 55°30E 55 b
Mahé ✕ (SEZ) Seychelles 4°40S 55°31E 55 b
Mahébourg Mauritius 20°24S 57°42E 55 d
Mahendra Giri India 8°20N 77°30E 45 K3
Mahendragarh India 28°17N 76°14E 42 E7
Mahendranagar Nepal 28°55N 80°20E 43 E9
Mahenge Tanzania 8°45S 36°41E 54 F7
Maheno N.Z. 45°10S 170°50E 59 F3
Mahesana India 23°39N 72°26E 42 H5
Maheshwar India 22°11N 75°35E 42 H6
Mahgawan India 26°29N 78°37E 43 F8
Mahi → India 22°15N 72°55E 42 H5
Mahia Pen. N.Z. 39°9S 177°55E 59 C6
Mahikeng = Mafikeng S. Africa 25°50S 25°38E 56 C4
Mahilyow Belarus 53°55N 30°18E 17 B16
Mahim India 19°39N 72°44E 44 E1
Mahina Tahiti 17°30S 149°27W 59 d
Mahinerangi, L. N.Z. 45°50S 169°56E 59 F2
Mahmud Kot Pakistan 30°16N 71°0E 42 D4
Mahnomen U.S.A. 47°19N 95°58W 80 B6
Maho Sri Lanka 7°49N 80°16E 45 L5
Mahoba India 25°15N 79°55E 43 G8
Mahón = Maó Spain 39°53N 4°16E 21 C8
Mahone Bay Canada 44°27N 64°23W 73 D7
Mahongo ⌂ Namibia 18°0S 23°15E 56 A3
Mahopac U.S.A. 41°22N 73°45W 83 E11
Mahuva India 21°5N 71°48E 42 J4
Mai-Ndombe, L. Dem. Rep. of the Congo 2°0S 18°20E 54 E3
Mai Thon, Ko Thailand 7°40N 98°28E 39 a
Maicuru → Brazil 2°14S 54°17W 93 D8
Maidan Khula Afghan. 33°36N 69°50E 42 C3
Maidenhead U.K. 51°31N 0°42W 13 F7
Maidstone Canada 53°5N 109°20W 71 C7
Maidstone U.K. 51°16N 0°32E 13 F8
Maiduguri Nigeria 12°0N 13°20E 53 F8
Maigh Nuad = Maynooth Ireland 53°23N 6°34W 10 C5
Maihar India 24°16N 80°45E 43 G9
Maikala Ra. India 22°0N 81°0E 44 D5
Mailani India 28°17N 80°21E 43 E9
Mailsi Pakistan 29°48N 72°15E 42 E5
Main → Germany 50°0N 8°18E 16 C5
Main → U.K. 54°48N 6°18W 10 B5
Main Channel Canada 45°21N 81°45W 82 A3
Main Range △ Australia 28°11S 152°27E 63 D5
Main Ridge Trin. & Tob. 11°16N 60°40W 93 J16
Maindargi India 17°28N 76°18E 44 F3
Maine France 48°20N 0°15W 20 C3
Maine □ U.S.A. 45°20N 69°0W 81 C19
Maine → Ireland 52°9N 9°45W 10 D2
Maine, G. of U.S.A. 43°0N 68°30W 75 G26
Maingkwan Burma 26°15N 96°37E 41 F20
Mainistir na Corann = Midleton Ireland 51°55N 8°10W 10 E3
Mainit, L. Phil. 9°31N 125°30E 37 C7
Mainland Orkney, U.K. 58°59N 3°8W 11 C5
Mainland Shet., U.K. 60°15N 1°22W 11 A7
Mainpuri India 27°18N 79°4E 43 F8
Maintirano Madag. 18°3S 44°1E 55 H8
Mainz Germany 50°1N 8°14E 16 C5
Maio C. Verde Is. 15°10N 23°10W 52 b
Maipú Argentina 36°52S 57°50W 94 D4
Maiquetía Venezuela 10°36N 66°57W 92 A5
Mairabari India 26°30N 92°22E 41 F18
Maisi Cuba 20°17N 74°9W 89 B5
Maisi, Pta. de Cuba 20°10N 74°10W 89 B5
Maitland N.S.W., Australia 32°33S 151°36E 63 E5
Maitland S. Austral., Australia 34°23S 137°40E 63 E2
Maitland → Canada 43°45N 81°43W 82 C3
Maitri Antarctica 70°0S 3°0W 5 D3
Maiyuan China 25°34N 117°28E 35 E11
Maíz, Is. del Nic. 12°15N 83°4W 88 D3
Maizuru Japan 35°25N 135°22E 29 G7
Majalengka Indonesia 6°50S 108°13E 37 G13
Majene Indonesia 3°38S 118°57E 37 E5
Majiang China 26°28N 107°32E 34 D6
Majorca = Mallorca Spain 39°30N 3°0E 21 C7
Majuro Marshall Is. 7°9N 171°12E 64 G9
Mak, Ko Thailand 11°49N 102°29E 39 G4
Maka Senegal 13°40N 14°10W 52 F3
Makaha Zimbabwe 17°20S 32°39E 57 A5
Makalamabedi Botswana 20°19S 23°51E 56 B3
Makale Indonesia 3°6S 119°51E 37 E5
Makalu Asia 27°55N 87°8E 43 F12
Makalu-Barun △ Nepal 27°45N 87°10E 43 F12
Makarikari = Makgadikgadi Salt Pans Botswana 20°40S 25°45E 56 B4
Makarov Basin Arctic 87°0N 150°0W 4 A
Makarovo Russia 57°40N 107°45E 27 D11
Makassar Indonesia 5°10S 119°20E 37 F5
Makassar, Selat Indonesia 1°0S 118°20E 37 E5
Makassar, Str. of = Makassar, Selat Indonesia 1°0S 118°20E 37 E5
Makat = Maqat Kazakhstan 47°39N 53°19E 19 E9
Makedonija = Macedonia ■ Europe 41°53N 21°40E 23 D9
Makeni S. Leone 8°55N 12°5W 52 G3
Makeyevka = Makiyivka Ukraine 48°0N 38°0E 19 E6
Makgadikgadi △ Botswana 20°27S 24°47E 56 B3
Makgadikgadi Salt Pans Botswana 20°40S 25°45E 56 B4
Makhachkala Russia 43°0N 47°30E 19 F8
Makhado = Louis Trichardt S. Africa 23°1S 29°43E 57 B4
Makham, Ao Thailand 7°51N 98°25E 39 a
Makhfar al Buşayyah Iraq 30°0N 46°10E 46 D5
Makhmūr Iraq 35°46N 43°35E 46 C4
Makhtal India 16°30N 77°31E 45 E3
Makian Indonesia 0°20N 127°20E 37 D7
Makīnsk Kazakhstan 52°37N 70°26E 26 D8
Makira = San Cristóbal Solomon Is. 10°30S 161°0E 58 C9
Makiyivka Ukraine 48°0N 38°0E 19 E6
Makkah Si. Arabia 21°30N 39°54E 49 C2
Makkovik Canada 55°10N 59°10W 73 A8
Makó Hungary 46°14N 20°33E 17 E11
Makogai Fiji 17°28S 179°0E 59 a
Makokou Gabon 0°40N 12°50E 54 D2
Makrai India 22°2N 77°0E 42 H7
Makran Coast Range Pakistan 25°40N 64°0E 40 G4
Makrana India 27°2N 74°46E 42 F6
Makri India 19°46N 81°55E 44 E5
Mākū Iran 39°15N 44°31E 46 B5
Makunda Botswana 22°30S 20°7E 56 B3
Makung Taiwan 23°34N 119°34E 35 F12
Makurazaki Japan 31°15N 130°20E 29 J5
Makurdi Nigeria 7°43N 8°35E 52 G7
Makushin Volcano U.S.A. 53°53N 166°55W 74 E6
Makūyeh Iran 28°7N 53°9E 47 D7
Makwassie S. Africa 27°17S 26°0E 56 C4
Makwiro Zimbabwe 17°58S 30°25E 57 A5
Mal B. Ireland 52°50N 9°30W 10 D2
Mala = Mallow Ireland 52°8N 8°39W 10 D3
Mala ✪ Australia 21°39S 130°45E 60 D5
Mala, Pta. Panama 7°28N 80°2W 88 E3
Malabar Coast India 11°0N 75°0E 45 J2
Malacca, Straits of Indonesia 3°0N 101°0E 39 L3
Malad City U.S.A. 42°12N 112°15W 76 E7
Maladzyechna Belarus 54°20N 26°50E 17 A14
Málaga Spain 36°43N 4°23W 21 D3
Malagasy Rep. = Madagascar ■ Africa 20°0S 47°0E 55 J9
Malaimbandy Madag. 20°20S 45°36E 55 J9
Malaita Solomon Is. 9°0S 161°0E 58 B9
Malakal South Sudan 9°33N 31°40E 53 G12
Malakanagiri India 18°21N 81°54E 44 E5
Malakand Pakistan 34°40N 71°55E 42 B4
Malakula Vanuatu 16°15S 167°30E 58 C9
Malakwal Pakistan 32°34N 73°13E 42 C5
Malamala Indonesia 3°21S 120°55E 37 E6
Malanda Australia 17°22S 145°35E 62 B4
Malang Indonesia 7°59S 112°45E 37 G15
Malangen Norway 69°24N 18°37E 8 B18
Malangwa Nepal 26°52N 85°34E 43 F11
Malanje Angola 9°36S 16°17E 54 F3
Malappuram India 11°7N 76°11E 45 J3
Mälaren Sweden 59°30N 17°10E 9 G17
Malargüe Argentina 35°32S 69°30W 94 D2
Malartic Canada 48°9N 78°9W 72 C4
Malaryta Belarus 51°50N 24°3E 17 C13
Malaspina Glacier U.S.A. 59°50N 140°30W 74 D11
Malatya Turkey 38°25N 38°20E 46 B3
Malawi ■ Africa 11°55S 34°0E 55 G6
Malawi, L. Africa 12°30S 34°30E 55 G6
Malay Pen. Asia 7°25N 100°0E 39 J3
Malaya Vishera Russia 58°55N 32°25E 18 C5
Malaybalay Phil. 8°5N 125°7E 37 C7
Malāyer Iran 34°19N 48°51E 47 C6
Malaysia ■ Asia 5°0N 110°0E 39 K4
Malazgirt Turkey 39°10N 42°33E 46 B4
Malbon Australia 21°5S 140°17E 62 C3
Malbooma Australia 30°41S 134°11E 63 E1
Malbork Poland 54°3N 19°1E 17 B10
Malcolm Australia 28°51S 121°25E 61 E3
Malcolm, Pt. Australia 33°48S 123°45E 61 F3
Maldah India 25°2N 88°9E 43 G13
Maldegem Belgium 51°14N 3°26E 15 C3
Malden U.S.A. 36°34N 89°57W 80 G9
Malden I. Kiribati 4°3S 155°1W 65 H12
Maldives ■ Ind. Oc. 5°0N 73°0E 25 H9
Maldon U.K. 51°44N 0°42E 13 F8
Maldonado Uruguay 34°59S 55°0W 95 C5
Maldonado, Pta. Mexico 16°20N 98°33W 87 D5
Malé Karpaty Slovak Rep. 48°30N 17°20E 17 D9
Maleas, Akra Greece 36°28N 23°7E 23 F10
Malebo, Pool Africa 4°17S 15°20E 54 E3
Malegaon India 20°30N 74°38E 44 D2
Malek Kandī Iran 37°9N 46°6E 46 B5
Malema Mozam. 14°57S 37°20E 55 G7
Maler Kotla India 30°32N 75°58E 42 D6
Malgomaj Sweden 64°40N 16°30E 8 D17
Malha Sudan 15°8N 25°10E 53 E11
Malhargarh India 24°17N 74°59E 42 G6
Malheur → U.S.A. 44°4N 116°59W 76 D5
Malheur L. U.S.A. 43°20N 118°48W 76 E4
Mali ■ Africa 17°0N 3°0W 52 E5
Mali → Burma 25°42N 97°30E 41 G20
Mali Kyun Burma 13°0N 98°20E 38 F2
Malibu U.S.A. 34°2N 118°41W 79 L8
Maliku = Minicoy I. India 8°17N 73°2E 45 K1
Maliku Indonesia 0°39S 123°16E 37 E6
Malili Indonesia 2°42S 121°6E 37 E6
Malimba, Mts. Dem. Rep. of the Congo 7°30S 29°30E 54 F5
Malin Hd. Ireland 55°23N 7°23W 10 A4
Malin Pen. Ireland 55°20N 7°17W 10 A4
Malindi Kenya 3°12S 40°5E 54 E8
Malines = Mechelen Belgium 51°2N 4°29E 15 C4
Malino Indonesia 1°0N 121°0E 37 D6
Malipo China 23°7N 104°42E 34 F5
Malita Phil. 6°19N 125°39E 37 C7
Maliwun Burma 10°17N 98°40E 39 G2
Maliya India 23°5N 70°46E 42 H4
Malkapur India 20°53N 76°12E 44 D3
Malkara Turkey 40°53N 26°53E 23 D12
Malkhangiri = Malakanagiri India 18°21N 81°54E 44 E5
Mallacoota Inlet Australia 37°34S 149°40E 63 F4
Mallaig U.K. 57°0N 5°50W 11 D3
Mallawan India 27°4N 80°12E 43 F9
Mallawi Egypt 27°44N 30°44E 53 C12
Mallicolo = Malakula Vanuatu 16°15S 167°30E 58 C9
Mallorca Spain 39°30N 3°0E 21 C7
Mallorytown Canada 44°29N 75°53W 83 B9
Mallow Ireland 52°8N 8°39W 10 D3
Malmberget Sweden 67°11N 20°40E 8 C19
Malmédy Belgium 50°25N 6°2E 15 D6
Malmesbury S. Africa 33°28S 18°41E 56 D2
Malmivaara = Malmberget Sweden 67°11N 20°40E 8 C19
Malmö Sweden 55°36N 12°59E 9 J15
Malolo Fiji 17°45S 177°11E 59 a
Malolos Phil. 14°50N 120°49E 37 B6
Malolotja ⌂ Swaziland 26°4S 31°6E 57 C5
Malone U.S.A. 44°51N 74°18W 83 B10
Malong China 25°24N 103°34E 34 E4
Måløy Norway 61°57N 5°6E 8 F11
Malpaso, Presa = Netzahualcóyotl, Presa Mexico 17°8N 93°35W 87 D6
Malpelo, I. de Colombia 4°3N 81°35W 92 C2
Malprabha → India 16°20N 76°5E 45 F3
Malpur India 23°21N 73°27E 42 H5
Malpura India 26°17N 75°23E 42 F6
Malsiras India 17°52N 74°55E 44 F2
Malta Idaho, U.S.A. 42°18N 113°22W 76 E7
Malta Mont., U.S.A. 48°21N 107°52W 76 B10
Malta ■ Europe 35°55N 14°26E 22 G6
Maltahöhe Namibia 24°55S 17°0E 56 B2
Malton U.K. 54°8N 0°49W 12 C7
Maluku Indonesia 1°0S 127°0E 37 E7
Maluku □ Indonesia 3°0S 128°0E 37 E7
Maluku Sea = Molucca Sea Indonesia 0°0 125°0E 37 E6
Malur India 13°0N 77°55E 45 H3
Malvalli India 12°28N 77°8E 45 H3
Malvan India 16°2N 73°30E 45 F1
Malvern U.S.A. 34°22N 92°49W 84 D8
Malvern Hills U.K. 52°0N 2°19W 13 E5
Malvinas, Is. = Falkland Is. ☑ Atl. Oc. 51°30S 59°0W 96 G5
Malyn Ukraine 50°46N 29°3E 17 C15
Malyy Lyakhovskiy, Ostrov Russia 74°7N 140°36E 27 B15
Malyy Taymyr, Ostrov Russia 78°6N 107°15E 27 B11
Mama Russia 58°18N 112°54E 27 D12
Mamanguape Brazil 6°50S 35°4W 93 E11
Mamanuca Group Fiji 17°35S 177°5E 59 a
Mamarr Mitlā Egypt 30°2N 32°54E 48 E1
Mamasa Indonesia 2°55S 119°20E 37 E5
Mamberamo → Indonesia 2°0S 137°50E 37 E9
Mambilima Falls Zambia 10°31S 28°45E 54 G5
Mamburao Phil. 13°13N 120°39E 37 B6
Mameigwess L. Canada 52°35N 87°50W 72 B2
Mamili △ Namibia 18°2S 24°1E 56 A3
Mammoth U.S.A. 32°43N 110°39W 77 K8
Mammoth Cave △ U.S.A. 37°8N 86°13W 80 G10
Mamoré → Bolivia 10°23S 65°53W 92 F5
Mamou Guinea 10°15N 12°0W 52 F3
Mamoudzou Mayotte 12°48S 45°14E 55 a
Mamuju Indonesia 2°41S 118°50E 37 E5
Mamuno Botswana 22°16S 20°1E 56 B3
Man Ivory C. 7°30N 7°40W 52 G4
Man → India 17°31N 75°32E 44 F2
Man, I. of India 8°28N 93°36E 45 K11
Man, I. of U.K. 54°15N 4°30W 12 C3
Man-Bazar India 23°4N 86°39E 43 H12
Man Na Burma 23°27N 97°19E 41 H20
Mänä U.S.A. 22°2N 159°47W 75 L8
Mana → Fr. Guiana 5°45N 53°55W 93 B8
Manaar, G. of = Mannar, G. of Asia 8°30N 79°0E 45 K4
Manacapuru Brazil 3°16S 60°37W 92 D6
Manacor Spain 39°34N 3°13E 21 C7
Manado Indonesia 1°29N 124°51E 37 D6
Managua Nic. 12°6N 86°20W 88 D2
Managua, L. de Nic. 12°20N 86°30W 88 D2
Manakara Madag. 22°8S 48°1E 55 J9
Manali India 32°16N 77°10E 42 C7
Manama = Al Manāmah Bahrain 26°10N 50°30E 47 E6
Mananjary Madag. 21°13S 48°20E 55 J9
Manantavadi India 11°49N 76°1E 45 J3
Manantenina Madag. 24°17S 47°19E 55 J9
Manaos = Manaus Brazil 3°0S 60°0W 92 D7
Manapire → Venezuela 7°42N 66°7W 92 B5
Manapouri N.Z. 45°34S 167°39E 59 F1
Manapouri, L. N.Z. 45°32S 167°32E 59 F1
Manapparai India 10°36N 78°25E 45 J4
Manar → India 18°50N 77°20E 44 E3
Manār, Jabal Yemen 14°2N 44°17E 49 E3
Manas China 44°17N 86°10E 30 C6
Manas → India 26°12N 90°40E 41 F17
Manas He → China 45°38N 85°12E 30 B6
Manaslu Nepal 28°33N 84°33E 43 E11
Manasquan U.S.A. 40°8N 74°3W 83 F10
Manassa U.S.A. 37°11N 105°56W 77 H11
Manatí Puerto Rico 18°26N 66°29W 89 d
Manaus Brazil 3°0S 60°0W 92 D7

Manawan L. Canada 55°24N 103°14W 71 B8
Manbij Syria 36°31N 37°57E 46 B3
Manchegorsk Russia 67°54N 32°58E 26 C4
Manchester U.K. 53°29N 2°12W 12 D5
Manchester Calif., U.S.A. 38°58N 123°41W 78 G3
Manchester Conn., U.S.A. 41°47N 72°31W 83 E12
Manchester Ga., U.S.A. 32°51N 84°37W 85 E12
Manchester Iowa, U.S.A. 42°29N 91°27W 80 D8
Manchester Ky., U.S.A. 37°9N 83°46W 81 G12
Manchester N.H., U.S.A. 42°59N 71°28W 83 D13
Manchester N.Y., U.S.A. 42°56N 77°16W 82 D7
Manchester Pa., U.S.A. 40°4N 76°43W 83 F8
Manchester Tenn., U.S.A. 35°29N 86°5W 85 D11
Manchester Vt., U.S.A. 43°10N 73°5W 83 C11
Manchester Int. ✈ (MAN) U.K. 53°21N 2°17W 12 D5
Manchester L. Canada 61°28N 107°29W 71 A7
Manchhar L. Pakistan 26°25N 67°39E 42 F2
Manchuria = Dongbei China 45°0N 125°0E 33 D13
Manchurian Plain China 47°0N 124°0E 24 D14
Mand → India 21°42N 83°15E 43 J10
Mand → Iran 28°20N 52°30E 47 D7
Mandaguari Brazil 23°32S 51°42W 95 A5
Mandah = Töhöm Mongolia 44°27N 108°2E 32 B5
Mandal Norway 58°2N 7°25E 9 G12
Mandala, Puncak Indonesia 4°44S 140°20E 37 E10
Mandalay Burma 22°0N 96°4E 41 J20
Mandale = Mandalay Burma 22°0N 96°4E 41 J20
Mandalgarh India 25°12N 75°6E 42 G6
Mandalgovĭ Mongolia 45°45N 106°10E 32 B4
Mandan U.S.A. 46°50N 100°54W 80 B3
Mandar, Teluk Indonesia 3°32S 119°21E 37 E5
Mandaue Phil. 10°20N 123°56E 37 B6
Mandeville Jamaica 18°2N 77°31W 88 a
Mandi India 31°39N 76°58E 42 D7
Mandi Burewala Pakistan 30°9N 72°41E 42 D5
Mandi Dabwali India 29°58N 74°42E 42 E6
Mandimba Mozam. 14°20S 35°40E 55 G7
Mandioli Indonesia 0°40S 127°20E 37 E7
Mandla India 22°39N 80°30E 43 H9
Mandorah Australia 12°32S 130°42E 60 B5
Mandra Pakistan 33°23N 73°12E 42 C5
Mandritsara Madag. 15°50S 48°49E 55 H9
Mandsaur India 24°3N 75°8E 42 G6
Mandurah Australia 32°36S 115°48E 61 F2
Mandvi India 22°51N 69°22E 42 H3
Mandya India 12°30N 77°0E 45 H3
Mandzai Pakistan 30°55N 67°6E 42 D2
Maneh Iran 37°39N 57°7E 47 B8
Maner → India 18°30N 79°40E 44 E4
Maneroo Cr. → Australia 23°21S 143°53E 62 C3
Manfalût Egypt 27°20N 30°52E 53 C12
Manfredónia Italy 41°38N 15°55E 22 D6
Mangabeiras, Chapada das Brazil 10°0S 46°30W 93 F9
Mangaia Cook Is. 21°55S 157°55W 65 K12
Mangalagiri India 16°26N 80°36E 45 F5
Mangalia Romania 43°50N 28°35E 17 G15
Mangalore India 12°55N 74°47E 45 H2
Mangaluru = Mangalore India 12°55N 74°47E 45 H2
Mangalvedha India 17°31N 75°28E 44 F2
Mangan India 27°31N 88°32E 43 F13
Mangaon India 18°15N 73°20E 44 E1
Mangarrayi ○ Australia 15°5S 133°10E 62 B1
Mangawan India 24°41N 81°33E 43 G9
Mangaweka N.Z. 39°48S 175°47E 59 C5
Manggar Indonesia 2°50S 108°10E 36 E3
Manggawitu Indonesia 4°8S 133°32E 37 E8
Mangghystaŭ Tübegi Kazakhstan 44°30N 52°30E 26 E6
Manggis Indonesia 8°29S 115°31E 37 J18
Mangkalihat, Tanjung Indonesia 1°2N 118°59E 37 D5
Mangkururrpa ○ Australia 20°35S 129°43E 60 D4
Mangla Pakistan 33°7N 73°39E 42 C5
Mangla Dam Pakistan 33°9N 73°44E 43 C5
Manglaur India 29°44N 77°49E 42 E7
Mangnai China 37°52N 91°43E 30 D7
Mangnai Zhen China 38°24N 90°14E 30 D7
Mango Togo 10°20N 0°30E 52 F6
Mango Tonga 20°17S 174°29W 59 c
Mangoche Malawi 14°25S 35°16E 55 G7
Mangoky → Madag. 21°29S 43°41E 55 J8
Mangole Indonesia 1°50S 125°55E 37 E6
Mangonui N.Z. 35°1S 173°32E 59 A4
Mangrol Mad. P., India 21°7N 70°7E 42 J4
Mangrol Raj., India 25°20N 76°31E 42 G6
Mangrul Pir India 20°19N 77°21E 44 D3
Mangueira, L. da Brazil 33°0S 52°50W 95 C5
Mangum U.S.A. 34°53N 99°30W 84 D5
Manguri Australia 28°58S 134°22E 63 A1
Mangyshlak, Poluostrov = Mangghystaŭ Tübegi Kazakhstan 44°30N 52°30E 26 E6
Manhattan U.S.A. 39°11N 96°35W 80 F5
Manhiça Mozam. 25°23S 32°49E 57 C5
Manica Mozam. 18°58S 32°59E 57 A5
Manica □ Mozam. 19°10S 33°45E 57 A5
Manicoré Brazil 5°48S 61°16W 92 E6
Manicouagan → Canada 49°30N 68°30W 73 C6
Manicouagan, Rés. Canada 51°5N 68°40W 73 B6
Maniĩfah Si. Arabia 27°44N 49°0E 47 E6
Manifold, C. Australia 22°41S 150°50E 62 C5
Maniganggo China 31°56N 99°10E 34 B3
Manigotagan Canada 51°6N 96°18W 71 C9
Manigotagan → Canada 51°7N 96°20W 71 C9
Manihari India 25°21N 87°38E 43 G12

Manihiki Cook Is. 10°24S 161°1W 65 J11
Manihiki Plateau Pac. Oc. 11°0S 164°0W 65 J11
Manikpur India 25°4N 81°7E 43 G9
Manila U.S.A. 40°59N 109°43W 76 F9
Manila B. Phil. 14°40N 120°35E 37 B6
Manilla Australia 30°45S 150°43E 63 E5
Maningrida Australia 12°3S 134°13E 62 A1
Manipur □ India 25°0N 94°0E 41 G19
Manipur → Burma 23°45N 94°20E 41 H19
Manisa Turkey 38°38N 27°30E 23 E12
Manistee U.S.A. 44°15N 86°19W 80 C10
Manistee → U.S.A. 44°15N 86°21W 80 C10
Manistique U.S.A. 45°57N 86°15W 80 C10
Manitoba □ Canada 53°30N 97°0W 71 B9
Manitoba, L. Canada 51°0N 98°45W 71 C9
Manitou Canada 49°15N 98°32W 71 D9
Manitou, L. Canada 50°55N 65°17W 73 B6
Manitou Is. U.S.A. 45°8N 86°0W 80 C10
Manitou L. Canada 52°43N 109°43W 71 C7
Manitou Springs U.S.A. 38°52N 104°55W 76 G11
Manitoulin I. Canada 45°40N 82°30W 72 C3
Manitouwadge Canada 49°8N 85°48W 72 C2
Manitowoc U.S.A. 44°5N 87°40W 80 C10
Maniyachi India 8°51N 77°55E 45 K3
Manizales Colombia 5°5N 75°32W 92 B3
Manjacaze Mozam. 24°45S 34°0E 57 B5
Manjakandriana Madag. 18°55S 47°47E 55 H9
Manjhand Pakistan 25°50N 68°10E 42 G3
Manjimup Australia 34°15S 116°6E 61 F2
Manjlegaon India 19°9N 76°14E 44 E3
Manjra → India 18°49N 77°52E 44 E3
Mankato Kans., U.S.A. 39°47N 98°13W 80 F4
Mankato Minn., U.S.A. 44°10N 94°0W 80 C6
Mankayane Swaziland 26°40S 31°4E 57 C5
Mankera Pakistan 31°23N 71°26E 42 D4
Mankota Canada 49°25N 107°5W 71 D7
Mankulam Sri Lanka 9°8N 80°26E 45 K5
Manlay = Üydzin Mongolia 44°9N 107°0E 32 B4
Manmad India 20°18N 74°28E 44 D2
Mann Ranges Australia 26°6S 130°5E 61 E5
Manna Indonesia 4°25S 102°55E 36 E2
Mannahill Australia 32°25S 140°0E 63 E3
Mannar Sri Lanka 9°1N 79°54E 45 K4
Mannar, G. of Asia 8°30N 79°0E 45 K4
Mannar I. Sri Lanka 9°5N 79°45E 45 K4
Mannargudi India 10°45N 79°51E 45 J4
Mannheim Germany 49°29N 8°29E 16 D5
Manning Canada 56°53N 117°39W 70 B5
Manning Oreg., U.S.A. 45°45N 123°13W 78 E3
Manning S.C., U.S.A. 33°42N 80°13W 85 E14
Mannum Australia 34°50S 139°20E 63 E2
Manohar India 22°23N 85°12E 43 H11
Manokwari Indonesia 0°54S 134°0E 37 E8
Manombo Madag. 22°57S 43°28E 55 J8
Manono Dem. Rep. of the Congo 7°15S 27°25E 54 F5
Manono Samoa 13°50S 172°5W 59 b
Manorhamilton Ireland 54°18N 8°11W 10 B3
Manosque France 43°49N 5°47E 20 E6
Manotick Canada 45°13N 75°41W 83 A9
Manouane → Canada 49°30N 71°10W 73 C5
Manouane, L. Canada 50°45N 70°45W 73 B5
Manp'o N. Korea 41°6N 126°24E 33 D14
Manpojin = Manp'o N. Korea 41°6N 126°24E 33 D14
Manpur Chhattisgarh, India 23°17N 83°35E 43 H10
Manpur Mad. P., India 22°26N 75°37E 42 H6
Manresa Spain 41°48N 1°50E 21 B6
Mansa Gujarat, India 23°27N 72°45E 42 H5
Mansa Punjab, India 30°0N 75°27E 42 E6
Mansa Zambia 11°13S 28°55E 54 G5
Mansehra Pakistan 34°20N 73°15E 42 B5
Mansel I. Canada 62°0N 80°0W 69 E15
Mansfield Australia 37°4S 146°6E 63 F4
Mansfield U.K. 53°9N 1°11W 12 D6
Mansfield La., U.S.A. 32°2N 93°43W 84 E8
Mansfield Mass., U.S.A. 42°2N 71°13W 83 D13
Mansfield Ohio, U.S.A. 40°45N 82°31W 82 F2
Mansfield Pa., U.S.A. 41°48N 77°5W 82 E7
Mansfield Tex., U.S.A. 32°33N 97°8W 84 E6
Mansfield, Mt. U.S.A. 44°33N 72°49W 83 B12
Manson Creek Canada 55°37N 124°32W 70 B4
Manta Ecuador 1°0S 80°40W 92 D2
Mantalingajan, Mt. Phil. 8°55N 117°45E 36 C5
Manteca U.S.A. 37°48N 121°13W 78 H5
Manteo U.S.A. 35°55N 75°40W 85 D17
Mantes-la-Jolie France 48°58N 1°41E 20 B4
Mantha India 19°40N 76°23E 44 E3
Manthani India 18°40N 79°35E 44 E4
Manti U.S.A. 39°16N 111°38W 76 G8
Mantiqueira, Serra da Brazil 22°0S 44°0W 95 A7
Mantova Italy 45°9N 10°48E 22 B4
Mänttä Vilppula Finland 62°3N 24°40E 8 E21
Mantua = Mántova Italy 45°9N 10°48E 22 B4
Manú Peru 12°10S 70°51W 92 F4
Manú → Peru 12°16S 70°55W 92 F4
Manu'a Is. Amer. Samoa 14°13S 169°35W 59 b
Manuel Alves → Brazil 11°19S 48°28W 93 F9
Manui Indonesia 3°35S 123°5E 37 E6
Manukau N.Z. 37°0S 174°52E 59 B5
Manvi India 15°57N 76°59E 45 G3
Manwath India 19°19N 76°32E 44 E3
Many U.S.A. 31°34N 93°29W 84 F8
Manyallaluk ○ Australia 14°16S 132°49E 60 B5
Manych-Gudilo, Ozero Russia 46°24N 42°38E 19 E7
Manyoni Tanzania 5°45S 34°55E 54 F6
Manzai Pakistan 32°12N 70°15E 42 C4
Manzanar ○ U.S.A. 36°44N 118°9W 78 J7

Manzanares Spain 39°2N 3°22W 21 C4
Manzanillo Cuba 20°20N 77°31W 88 B4
Manzanillo Mexico 19°3N 104°20W 86 D4
Manzanillo, Pta. Panama 9°30N 79°40W 88 E4
Manzano Mts. U.S.A. 34°40N 106°20W 77 J10
Manzariyeh Iran 34°53N 50°50E 47 C6
Manzhouli China 49°35N 117°25E 31 B12
Manzini Swaziland 26°30S 31°25E 57 C5
Manzouli = Manzhouli China 49°35N 117°25E 31 B12
Maó Spain 39°53N 4°16E 21 C8
Maoke, Pegunungan Indonesia 3°40S 137°30E 37 E9
Maolin China 43°58N 123°30E 33 C12
Maoming China 21°50N 110°54E 35 G8
Maopi T'ou China 21°56N 120°43E 35 G13
Maoxian China 31°41N 103°49E 34 B4
Maoxing China 45°28N 124°40E 33 B13
Mapam Yumco China 30°45N 81°28E 43 D9
Mapastepec Mexico 15°26N 92°54W 87 D6
Mapia, Kepulauan Indonesia 0°50N 134°20E 37 D8
Mapimí Mexico 25°49N 103°51W 86 B4
Mapimí, Bolsón de Mexico 27°0N 104°15W 86 B4
Maping China 31°34N 113°32E 35 B9
Mapinhane Mozam. 22°20S 35°0E 57 B6
Maple Creek Canada 49°55N 109°29W 71 D7
Maple Valley U.S.A. 47°25N 122°3W 78 C4
Mapleton U.S.A. 44°2N 123°52W 76 D2
Mapoon ○ Australia 11°44S 142°8E 62 A3
Mapuca India 15°36N 73°46E 45 G1
Mapuera → Brazil 1°5S 57°2W 92 D7
Mapulanguene Mozam. 24°29S 32°6E 57 B5
Mapungubwe △ S. Africa 22°15S 29°22E 57 B4
Maputo Mozam. 25°58S 32°32E 57 C5
Maputo □ Mozam. 26°0S 32°25E 57 C5
Maputo, B. de Mozam. 25°50S 32°45E 57 C5
Maputo → Mozam. 26°23S 32°48E 57 C5
Maqat Kazakhstan 47°39N 53°19E 19 E9
Maqên China 34°24N 100°6E 30 E9
Maqên Gangri China 34°55N 99°18E 30 E8
Maqiaohe China 44°40N 130°30E 33 B16
Maqnā Si. Arabia 28°25N 34°50E 46 D2
Maqteïr Mauritania 21°50N 11°40W 52 D3
Maqu China 33°52N 101°42E 30 E9
Maquan He = Brahmaputra → Asia 23°40N 90°35E 43 H13
Maquela do Zombo Angola 6°0S 15°15E 54 F3
Maquinchao Argentina 41°15S 68°50W 96 E3
Maquoketa U.S.A. 42°4N 90°40W 80 D8
Mar Canada 44°49N 81°12W 82 B3
Mar, Serra do Brazil 25°30S 49°0W 95 B6
Mar Chiquita, L. Argentina 30°40S 62°50W 94 C3
Mar del Plata Argentina 38°0S 57°30W 94 D4
Mar Menor Spain 37°40N 0°45W 21 D5
Maraã Brazil 1°52S 65°25W 92 D5
Maraa Tahiti 17°46S 149°34W 59 d
Marabá Brazil 5°20S 49°5W 93 E9
Maraboon, L. Australia 23°41S 148°0E 62 C4
Maracá, I. de Brazil 2°10N 50°30W 93 C8
Maracaibo Venezuela 10°40N 71°37W 92 A4
Maracaibo, L. de Venezuela 9°40N 71°30W 92 B4
Maracaju Brazil 21°38S 55°9W 95 A4
Maracas Bay Village Trin. & Tob. 10°46N 61°28W 93 K15
Maracay Venezuela 10°15N 67°28W 92 A5
Marādah Libya 29°15N 19°15E 53 C9
Maradi Niger 13°29N 7°20E 52 F7
Marāgheh Iran 37°30N 46°12E 46 B5
Marāh Si. Arabia 25°0N 45°35E 46 E5
Marajó, I. de Brazil 1°0S 49°30W 93 D9
Marākand Iran 38°51N 45°16E 46 B5
Marakele △ S. Africa 24°30S 25°30E 57 D4
Maralinga Australia 30°13S 131°32E 61 F5
Maralinga Tjarutja ○ Australia 29°30S 131°0E 61 E5
Marambio Antarctica 64°0S 56°0W 5 C18
Maran Malaysia 3°35N 102°45E 39 L4
Marana U.S.A. 32°27N 111°13W 77 K8
Maranboy Australia 14°40S 132°39E 60 B5
Marand Iran 38°30N 45°45E 46 B5
Marang Malaysia 5°12N 103°13E 39 K4
Maranguape Brazil 3°55S 38°50W 93 D11
Maranhão = São Luís Brazil 2°39S 44°15W 93 D10
Maranhão □ Brazil 5°0S 46°0W 93 E9
Maranoa → Australia 27°50S 148°37E 63 D4
Marañón → Peru 4°30S 73°35W 92 D4
Marão Mozam. 24°18S 34°2E 57 B5
Maraş = Kahramanmaraş Turkey 37°37N 36°53E 46 B3
Marathon Australia 20°51S 143°32E 62 C3
Marathon Canada 48°44N 86°23W 72 C2
Marathon N.Y., U.S.A. 42°27N 76°2W 83 D8
Marathon Tex., U.S.A. 30°12N 103°15W 84 F3
Maratua Indonesia 2°10N 118°35E 37 D5
Maraval Trin. & Tob. 10°42N 61°31W 93 K15
Maravatío Mexico 19°54N 100°27W 86 D4
Marāwih U.A.E. 24°18N 53°18E 47 E7
Marbella Spain 36°30N 4°57W 21 D3
Marble Bar Australia 21°9S 119°44E 60 D2
Marblehead Mass., U.S.A. 42°29N 70°51W 83 D14
Marblehead Ohio, U.S.A. 41°32N 82°44W 82 E2
Marburg Germany 50°47N 8°46E 16 C5
Marca, Pta. do Angola 16°31S 11°43E 55 H2
March U.K. 52°33N 0°5E 13 E8
Marche France 46°5N 1°20E 20 C4
Marche-en-Famenne Belgium 50°14N 5°19E 15 D5
Marchena Spain 37°18N 5°23W 21 D3
Marco Island U.S.A. 25°58N 81°44W 85 J14
Marcos Juárez Argentina 32°42S 62°5W 94 C3

Marcus Baker, Mt. U.S.A. 61°26N 147°45W 74 C10
Marcus I. = Minami-Tori-Shima Pac. Oc. 24°20N 153°58E 64 E7
Marcy, Mt. U.S.A. 44°7N 73°56W 83 B11
Mardan Pakistan 34°20N 72°0E 42 B5
Mardie Australia 21°12S 115°59E 60 D2
Mardin Turkey 37°20N 40°43E 46 B4
Maree, L. U.K. 57°40N 5°26W 11 D3
Mareeba Australia 16°59S 145°28E 62 B4
Mareetsane S. Africa 26°9S 25°25E 56 C4
Marek = Stanke Dimitrov Bulgaria 42°17N 23°9E 23 C10
Marengo U.S.A. 41°48N 92°4W 80 E7
Marfa U.S.A. 30°19N 104°1W 84 F2
Margao = Madgaon India 15°12N 73°58E 45 G1
Margaret → Australia 18°9S 125°41E 60 C4
Margaret Bay Canada 51°20N 127°35W 70 C3
Margaret L. Canada 58°56N 115°25W 70 B5
Margaret River Australia 33°57S 115°4E 61 F2
Margarita, I. de Venezuela 11°0N 64°0W 92 A6
Margaritovo Russia 43°25S 134°45E 28 C7
Margate S. Africa 30°50S 30°20E 57 D5
Margate U.K. 51°23N 1°23E 13 F9
Marghilon Uzbekistan 40°27N 71°42E 26 E8
Märgow, Dasht-e Afghan. 30°40N 62°30E 40 D3
Marguerite Canada 52°30N 122°25W 70 C4
Mari El □ Russia 56°30N 48°0E 18 C8
Mari Indus Pakistan 32°57N 71°34E 42 C4
Mari Republic = Mari El □ Russia 56°30N 48°0E 18 C8
María Elena Chile 22°18S 69°40W 94 A2
María Grande Argentina 31°45S 59°55W 94 C4
Maria I. N. Terr., Australia 14°52S 135°45E 62 A2
Maria I. Tas., Australia 42°35S 148°0E 63 G4
Maria Island △ Australia 42°38S 148°5E 63 G4
Maria van Diemen, C. N.Z. 34°29S 172°40E 59 A4
Mariala △ Australia 25°57S 145°2E 63 D4
Marian Australia 21°9S 148°57E 62 b
Marian L. Canada 63°0N 116°15W 70 A5
Mariana Trench Pac. Oc. 13°0N 145°0E 64 F6
Marianna Ark., U.S.A. 34°46N 90°46W 85 D9
Marianna Fla., U.S.A. 30°46N 85°14W 85 F12
Marias → U.S.A. 47°56N 110°30W 76 C8
Marias, Is. Mexico 21°25N 106°28W 86 C3
Mariato, Punta Panama 7°12N 80°52W 88 E3
Maribor Slovenia 46°36N 15°40E 16 E8
Marico → Africa 23°35S 26°57E 56 B4
Maricopa Ariz., U.S.A. 33°4N 112°3W 77 K7
Maricopa Calif., U.S.A. 35°4N 119°24W 79 K7
Marié → Brazil 0°27S 66°26W 92 D5
Marie Byrd Land Antarctica 79°30S 125°0W 5 D14
Marie-Galante Guadeloupe 15°56N 61°16W 88 b
Mariecourt = Kangiqsujuaq Canada 61°30N 72°0W 69 E17
Mariehamn Finland 60°5N 19°55E 9 F18
Mariembourg Belgium 50°6N 4°31E 15 D4
Mariental Namibia 24°36S 18°0E 56 B2
Marienville U.S.A. 41°28N 79°8W 82 E5
Mariestad Sweden 58°43N 13°50E 9 G15
Marietta Ga., U.S.A. 33°57N 84°33W 85 E12
Marietta Ohio, U.S.A. 39°25N 81°27W 81 F13
Marieville Canada 45°26N 73°10W 83 A11
Mariinsk Russia 56°10N 87°20E 26 D9
Marijampolė Lithuania 54°33N 23°19E 9 J20
Marília Brazil 22°13S 50°0W 95 A6
Marín Spain 42°23N 8°42W 21 A1
Marina U.S.A. 36°41N 121°48W 78 J5
Marinduque Phil. 13°25N 122°0E 37 B6
Marine City U.S.A. 42°43N 82°30W 82 D2
Marinette U.S.A. 45°6N 87°38W 80 C10
Maringá Brazil 23°26S 52°2W 95 A5
Marion Ala., U.S.A. 32°38N 87°19W 85 E11
Marion Ark., U.S.A. 35°13N 90°12W 80 H9
Marion Ill., U.S.A. 37°44N 88°56W 80 G9
Marion Ind., U.S.A. 40°32N 85°40W 81 E11
Marion Iowa, U.S.A. 42°2N 91°36W 80 D8
Marion Kans., U.S.A. 38°21N 97°1W 80 F5
Marion N.C., U.S.A. 35°41N 82°1W 85 D13
Marion Ohio, U.S.A. 40°35N 83°8W 81 E12
Marion S.C., U.S.A. 34°11N 79°24W 85 D15
Marion Va., U.S.A. 36°50N 81°31W 81 G13
Marion, L. U.S.A. 33°28N 80°10W 85 E14
Mariposa U.S.A. 37°29N 119°58W 78 H7
Mariscal Estigarribia Paraguay 22°3S 60°40W 94 A3
Maritime Alps = Maritimes, Alpes Europe 44°10N 7°10E 20 D7
Maritimes, Alpes Europe 44°10N 7°10E 20 D7
Maritsa = Evros → Greece 41°40N 26°34E 23 D12
Mariupol Ukraine 47°5N 37°31E 19 E6
Mariusa △ Venezuela 9°24N 61°27W 89 E7
Marīvān Iran 35°30N 46°25E 46 C5
Marj 'Uyūn Lebanon 33°21N 35°34E 48 B4
Marka Somalia 1°48N 44°15E 49 G3
Markam China 29°42N 98°38E 34 C2
Markapur India 15°44N 79°19E 45 G4
Markazī □ Iran 34°0N 49°30E 47 C6
Markdale Canada 44°19N 80°39W 82 B4
Marked Tree U.S.A. 35°32N 90°25W 85 D9
Market Drayton U.K. 52°54N 2°29W 12 E5
Market Harborough U.K. 52°29N 0°55W 13 E7
Market Rasen U.K. 53°24N 0°20W 12 D7
Markham, Mt. Antarctica 83°0S 164°0E 5 E11
Markleeville U.S.A. 38°42N 119°47W 78 G7
Markovo Russia 64°40N 170°24E 27 C17
Marks Russia 51°45N 46°50E 18 D8
Marksville U.S.A. 31°8N 92°4W 84 F8
Marla Australia 27°19S 133°33E 63 D1
Marlbank Canada 44°26N 77°6W 82 B7
Marlboro U.S.A. 41°36N 73°59W 83 E11
Marlborough Australia 22°46S 149°52E 62 C4
Marlborough U.K. 51°25N 1°43W 13 F6
Marlborough U.S.A. 42°21N 71°33W 83 D13

Marlborough Downs U.K. 51°27N 1°53W 13 F6
Marlin U.S.A. 31°18N 96°54W 84 F6
Marlow U.K. 51°34N 0°46W 13 F7
Marlow U.S.A. 34°39N 97°58W 84 D5
Marmagao India 15°25N 73°56E 45 G1
Marmara Turkey 40°35N 27°34E 23 D12
Marmara, Sea of = Marmara Denizi Turkey 40°45N 28°15E 23 D13
Marmara Denizi Turkey 40°45N 28°15E 23 D13
Marmaris Turkey 36°50N 28°14E 23 F13
Marmion, Mt. Australia 29°16S 119°50E 61 E2
Marmion L. Canada 48°55N 91°20W 72 C1
Marmolada, Mte. Italy 46°26N 11°51E 22 A4
Marmora Canada 44°28N 77°41W 82 B7
Marne → France 48°47N 2°29E 20 B5
Maro Reef U.S.A. 25°25N 170°35W 75 K5
Maroantsetra Madag. 15°26S 49°44E 55 H9
Maroelaboom Namibia 19°15S 18°53E 56 A2
Marondera Zimbabwe 18°5S 31°42E 55 H6
Maroni → Fr. Guiana 5°30N 54°0W 93 B8
Maroochydore Australia 26°29S 153°5E 63 D5
Maroona Australia 37°27S 142°54E 63 F3
Maroua Cameroon 10°40N 14°20E 53 F8
Marovoay Madag. 16°6S 46°39E 55 H9
Marquard S. Africa 28°40S 27°28E 56 C4
Marquesas Fracture Zone Pac. Oc. 9°0S 125°0W 65 H10
Marquesas Is. = Marquises, Îs. French Polynesia 9°30S 140°0W 65 H14
Marquette U.S.A. 46°33N 87°24W 80 B10
Marquis St. Lucia 14°2N 60°54W 89 f
Marquises, Îs. French Polynesia 9°30S 140°0W 65 H14
Marra, Djebel Sudan 13°10N 24°22E 53 F10
Marracuene Mozam. 25°45S 32°35E 57 C5
Marrakech Morocco 31°9N 8°0W 52 B4
Marrawah Australia 40°55S 144°42E 63 G3
Marree Australia 29°39S 138°1E 63 D2
Marrimane Mozam. 22°58S 33°34E 57 B5
Marromeu Mozam. 18°15S 36°25E 57 A6
Marromeu → Mozam. 19°0S 36°0E 57 A6
Marrowie Cr. → Australia 33°23S 145°40E 63 E4
Marrupa Mozam. 13°8S 37°30E 55 G7
Mars Hill U.S.A. 46°31N 67°52W 81 B20
Marsá 'Alam Egypt 25°5N 34°54E 49 B1
Marsá Matrûh Egypt 31°19N 27°9E 53 B11
Marsabit Kenya 2°18N 38°0E 54 D7
Marsala Italy 37°48N 12°26E 22 F5
Marsden Australia 33°47S 147°32E 63 E4
Marseille France 43°18N 5°23E 20 E6
Marseilles = Marseille France 43°18N 5°23E 20 E6
Marsh I. U.S.A. 29°34N 91°53W 84 G9
Marshall Ark., U.S.A. 35°55N 92°38W 84 D8
Marshall Mich., U.S.A. 42°16N 84°58W 81 D11
Marshall Minn., U.S.A. 44°27N 95°47W 80 C6
Marshall Mo., U.S.A. 39°7N 93°12W 80 F7
Marshall Tex., U.S.A. 32°33N 94°23W 84 E7
Marshall → Australia 22°59S 136°59E 62 C2
Marshall Is. ■ Pac. Oc. 9°0N 171°0E 58 A10
Marshalltown U.S.A. 42°3N 92°55W 80 D7
Marshbrook Zimbabwe 18°33S 31°9E 57 A5
Marshfield Mo., U.S.A. 37°15N 92°54W 80 G7
Marshfield Vt., U.S.A. 44°20N 72°20W 83 B12
Marshfield Wis., U.S.A. 44°40N 90°10W 80 C8
Marshūn Iran 36°19N 49°23E 47 B6
Märsta Sweden 59°37N 17°52E 9 G17
Mart U.S.A. 31°33N 96°50W 84 F6
Martaban Burma 16°30N 97°35E 41 L20
Martaban, G. of Burma 16°5N 96°30E 41 L20
Martapura Kalimantan Selatan, Indonesia 3°22S 114°47E 36 E4
Martapura Sumatera Selatan, Indonesia 4°19S 104°22E 36 E2
Marte R. Gómez, Presa Mexico 26°10N 99°0W 87 B5
Martelange Belgium 49°49N 5°43E 15 E5
Marthapal India 19°24N 81°74E 44 E5
Martha's Vineyard U.S.A. 41°25N 70°38W 83 E14
Martigny Switz. 46°6N 7°3E 20 C7
Martigues France 43°24N 5°4E 20 E6
Martin Slovak Rep. 49°6N 18°58E 17 D10
Martin S. Dak., U.S.A. 43°11N 101°44W 80 D3
Martin Tenn., U.S.A. 36°21N 88°51W 85 G10
Martin L. U.S.A. 32°41N 85°55W 85 E12
Martina Franca Italy 40°42N 17°20E 22 D7
Martinborough N.Z. 41°14S 175°29E 59 D5
Martinez Calif., U.S.A. 38°1N 122°8W 78 G4
Martinez Ga., U.S.A. 33°31N 82°5W 85 E13
Martinique ☑ W. Indies 14°40N 61°0W 88 c
Martinique Passage W. Indies 15°15N 61°0W 89 C7
Martinópolis Brazil 22°11S 51°12W 95 A5
Martins Bay Barbados 13°12N 59°29W 89 g
Martins Ferry U.S.A. 40°6N 80°44W 82 F4
Martinsburg Pa., U.S.A. 40°19N 78°20W 82 F6
Martinsburg W. Va., U.S.A. 39°27N 77°58W 81 F15
Martinsville Ind., U.S.A. 39°26N 86°25W 80 F10
Martinsville Va., U.S.A. 36°41N 79°52W 81 G14
Marton N.Z. 40°4S 175°23E 59 D5
Martos Spain 37°44N 3°58W 21 D4
Martu ○ Australia 22°30S 122°30E 60 D3
Marudi Malaysia 4°11N 114°19E 36 D4
Maruf Afghan. 31°30N 67°6E 40 D5
Marugame Japan 34°15N 133°40E 29 G6
Marunga Angola 17°28S 20°2E 56 B3
Maruwa ○ Australia 22°30S 127°30E 60 D4
Marv Dasht Iran 29°50N 52°40E 47 D7
Marvast Iran 30°30N 54°15E 47 D7
Marvel Loch Australia 31°28S 119°29E 61 F2
Marwar India 25°43N 73°45E 42 G5
Mary Turkmenistan 37°40N 61°50E 28 F7
Maryborough = Portlaoise Ireland 53°2N 7°18W 10 C4
Maryborough Queens., Australia 25°31S 152°37E 63 D5

Maryborough *Vic.,* Australia 37°3S 143°44E **63** F3
Maryfield Canada 49°50N 101°35W **71** D8
Maryland □ *U.S.A.* 39°0N 76°30W **81** F15
Maryland Junction Zimbabwe 17°45S 30°31E **55** H6
Maryport *U.K.* 54°44N 3°28W **12** C4
Mary's Harbour Canada 52°18N 55°51W **73** B8
Marystown Canada 47°10N 55°10W **73** C8
Marysville *Calif., U.S.A.* 39°9N 121°35W **78** F5
Marysville *Kans., U.S.A.* 39°51N 96°39W **80** F5
Marysville *Mich., U.S.A.* 42°54N 82°29W **82** D2
Marysville *Ohio, U.S.A.* 40°14N 83°22W **81** E12
Marysville *Wash., U.S.A.* 48°3N 122°11W **78** B4
Maryville *Mo., U.S.A.* 40°21N 94°52W **80** E6
Maryville *Tenn., U.S.A.* 35°46N 83°58W **85** D13
Masada Israel 31°18N 35°21E **48** D4
Masai Malaysia 1°29N 103°55E **39** d
Masai Steppe Tanzania 4°30S 36°30E **54** C4
Masaka Uganda 0°21S 31°45E **54** E6
Masalembo, Kepulauan Indonesia 5°35S 114°30E **36** F4
Masalima, Kepulauan Indonesia 5°4S 117°5E **36** F5
Masamba Indonesia 2°30S 120°15E **37** E6
Masan S. Korea 35°11N 128°32E **33** G15
Masandam, Ra's Oman 26°30N 56°30E **47** E8
Masasi Tanzania 10°45S 38°52E **54** G7
Masaya Nic. 12°0N 86°7W **88** D2
Masbate Phil. 12°21N 123°36E **37** B6
Mascara Algeria 35°26N 0°6E **52** A6
Mascarene Is. *Ind. Oc.* 22°0S 55°0E **50** J9
Mascota Mexico 20°32N 104°49W **86** C4
Masela Indonesia 8°9S 129°51E **37** F7
Maseru Lesotho 29°18S 27°30E **56** C4
Mashābih Si. Arabia 25°35N 36°30E **46** E3
Mashan China 23°40N 108°11E **34** F7
Mashang China 36°48N 117°57E **33** F9
Mashatu △ Botswana 22°45S 29°55E **57** B4
Masherbrum Pakistan 35°38N 76°18E **43** B7
Mashhad Iran 36°20N 59°35E **47** B8
Mashīz Iran 29°56N 56°37E **47** D8
Māshkel, Hāmūn-i- *Pakistan* 28°20N 62°56E **47** D9
Mashki Chāh Pakistan 29°5N 62°30E **40** E3
Mashonaland Zimbabwe 16°30S 31°0E **55** H6
Mashonaland Central □ *Zimbabwe* 17°30S 31°0E **57** A5
Mashonaland East □ *Zimbabwe* 18°0S 32°0E **57** A5
Mashonaland West □ *Zimbabwe* 17°30S 29°30E **57** A4
Mashrakh India 26°7N 84°48E **43** F11
Masi Manimba *Dem. Rep. of the Congo* 4°40S 17°54E **54** E3
Masig Australia 9°45S 143°24E **62** a
Masindi Uganda 1°40N 31°43E **54** D6
Maşīrah, Jazīrat Oman 21°0N 58°50E **47** C6
Maşīrah, Khalīj Oman 20°10N 58°10E **49** C6
Masisi *Dem. Rep. of the Congo* 1°23S 28°49E **54** E5
Masjed Soleyman Iran 31°55N 49°18E **47** D6
Mask, L. Ireland 53°36N 9°22W **10** C2
Maski India 15°56N 76°46E **45** G3
Maskin Oman 23°44N 56°52E **47** F8
Masoala, Tanjon' i *Madag.* 15°59S 50°13E **55** H10
Masohi = Amahai *Indonesia* 3°20S 128°55E **37** E7
Mason *Nev., U.S.A.* 38°56N 119°8W **78** G7
Mason *Tex., U.S.A.* 30°45N 99°14W **84** F5
Mason City U.S.A. 43°9N 93°12W **80** D7
Masqat Oman 23°37N 58°36E **49** C6
Massa Italy 44°1N 10°9E **20** D9
Massachusetts □ *U.S.A.* 42°30N 72°0W **83** D13
Massachusetts B. *U.S.A.* 42°25N 70°50W **83** D14
Massakory Chad 13°0N 15°49E **53** F9
Massangena Mozam. 21°34S 33°0E **57** B5
Massango Angola 8°2S 16°21E **54** F3
Massawa = Mitsiwa *Eritrea* 15°35N 39°25E **49** D2
Massena U.S.A. 44°56N 74°54W **83** B10
Massenya Chad 11°21N 16°9E **53** F9
Masset Canada 54°2N 132°10W **70** C2
Massiah Street Barbados 13°9N 59°29W **89** g
Massif Central France 44°55N 3°0E **20** D5
Massillon U.S.A. 40°48N 81°32W **82** F3
Massinga Mozam. 23°15S 35°22E **57** B6
Massingir Mozam. 23°51S 32°4E **57** B5
Masson-Angers Canada 45°32N 75°25W **83** A9
Masson I. Antarctica 66°10S 93°20E **5** C7
Mastanli = Momchilgrad *Bulgaria* 41°33N 25°23E **23** D11
Masterton N.Z. 40°56S 175°39E **59** D5
Mastic U.S.A. 40°47N 72°54W **83** F12
Mastuj Pakistan 36°20N 72°36E **43** A5
Mastung Pakistan 29°50N 66°56E **40** E5
Masty Belarus 53°27N 24°38E **17** B13
Masuda Japan 34°40N 131°51E **29** G5
Masuku = Franceville *Gabon* 1°40S 13°32E **54** E2
Masurian Lakes = Mazurski, Pojezierze *Poland* 53°50N 21°0E **17** B11
Masvingo Zimbabwe 20°8S 30°49E **55** J6
Maşyāf Syria 35°4N 36°20E **46** C3
Mata-au = Clutha → *N.Z.* 46°20S 169°49E **59** G2
Matabeleland Zimbabwe 18°0S 27°0E **55** H5
Matachewan Canada 47°56N 80°39W **72** C3
Matadi *Dem. Rep. of the Congo* 5°52S 13°31E **54** F2
Matagalpa Nic. 13°0N 85°58W **88** D2
Matagami Canada 49°45N 77°34W **72** C4
Matagami, L. Canada 49°50N 77°40W **72** C4
Matagorda B. U.S.A. 28°40N 96°12W **84** G6
Matagorda I. U.S.A. 28°15N 96°30W **84** G6
Mataiea Tahiti 17°46S 149°25W **59** d
Matak Indonesia 3°18N 106°16E **36** D3

Matale Sri Lanka 7°30N 80°37E **45** L5
Matam Senegal 15°34N 13°17W **52** E3
Matamoros *Coahuila, Mexico* 25°32N 103°15W **86** B4
Matamoros *Tamaulipas, Mexico* 25°53N 97°30W **87** B5
Ma'ţan as Sarra Libya 21°45N 22°0E **53** D10
Matane Canada 48°50N 67°33W **73** C6
Matang China 23°30N 104°7E **34** F5
Matanomadh India 23°33N 68°57E **42** H3
Matanzas Cuba 23°0N 81°40W **88** B3
Matapa Botswana 23°11S 24°39E **56** B3
Matapan, C. = Tenaro, Akra *Greece* 36°22N 22°27E **23** F10
Matapédia Canada 48°0N 66°59W **73** C6
Matara Sri Lanka 5°58N 80°30E **45** M5
Mataram Indonesia 8°35S 116°7E **37** K19
Matarani Peru 17°0S 72°10W **92** G4
Mataranka Australia 14°55S 133°4E **60** B5
Matarma, Râs Egypt 30°27N 32°44E **48** E1
Mataró Spain 41°32N 2°29E **21** B7
Matatiele S. Africa 30°20S 28°49E **57** D4
Mataura N.Z. 46°11S 168°51E **59** G2
Matavai, B. de Tahiti 17°30S 149°23W **59** d
Matehuala Mexico 23°39N 100°39W **86** C4
Mateke Hills Zimbabwe 21°48S 31°0E **55** J6
Matelot Trin. & Tob. 10°50N 61°7W **93** K15
Matera Italy 40°40N 16°36E **22** D7
Mathis U.S.A. 28°6N 97°50W **84** G6
Mathraki Greece 39°48N 19°31E **23** E8
Mathura India 27°30N 77°40E **42** F7
Mati Phil. 6°55N 126°15E **37** C7
Matiali India 26°56N 88°49E **43** F13
Matías Romero Mexico 16°53N 95°2W **87** D5
Matiri Ra. N.Z. 41°38S 172°20E **59** D4
Matjiesfontein S. Africa 33°14S 20°35E **56** D3
Matla → India 21°40N 88°40E **43** J13
Matlamanyane Botswana 19°33S 25°57E **56** A4
Matli Pakistan 25°2N 68°39E **42** G3
Matlock U.K. 53°9N 1°33W **12** D6
Mato Grosso □ *Brazil* 14°0S 55°0W **93** F8
Mato Grosso, Planalto do *Brazil* 15°0S 55°0W **93** G8
Mato Grosso do Sul □ *Brazil* 18°0S 55°0W **93** G8
Matochkin Shar, Proliv *Russia* 73°23N 55°12E **26** B6
Matola Mozam. 25°57S 32°27E **57** C5
Matopo Hills Zimbabwe 20°36S 28°20E **55** J5
Matosinhos Portugal 41°11N 8°42W **21** B1
Matroosberg S. Africa 33°23S 19°40E **56** D2
Maţruḥ Oman 23°37N 58°30E **49** C6
Matsu Tao Taiwan 26°8N 119°56E **35** E13
Matsue Japan 35°25N 133°10E **29** G6
Matsum, Ko Thailand 9°22N 99°59E **39** b
Matsumae Japan 41°26N 140°7E **28** D10
Matsumae-Hantō *Japan* 41°30N 140°15E **28** D10
Matsumoto Japan 36°15N 138°0E **29** F9
Matsusaka Japan 34°34N 136°32E **29** G8
Matsushima Japan 38°20N 141°10E **28** E10
Matsuura Japan 33°20N 129°49E **29** H4
Matsuyama Japan 33°45N 132°45E **29** H6
Mattagami → Canada 50°43N 81°29W **72** B3
Mattancheri India 9°50N 76°15E **45** K3
Mattawa Canada 46°20N 78°45W **72** C4
Matterhorn Switz. 45°58N 7°39E **20** D7
Matthew Town Bahamas 20°57N 73°40W **89** B5
Matthews Ridge Guyana 7°37N 60°10W **92** B6
Mattice Canada 49°40N 83°20W **72** C3
Mattili India 18°33N 82°12E **44** E6
Mattituck U.S.A. 40°59N 72°32W **83** F12
Mattō = Hakusan *Japan* 36°31N 136°34E **29** F8
Mattoon U.S.A. 39°29N 88°23W **80** F9
Matuba Mozam. 24°28S 32°49E **57** B5
Matucana Peru 11°55S 76°25W **92** F3
Matugama Sri Lanka 6°31N 80°7E **45** L5
Matuku Fiji 19°10S 179°44E **59** a
Matún = Khowst *Afghan.* 33°22N 69°58E **42** C3
Matura B. Trin. & Tob. 10°39N 61°1W **93** K15
Maturín Venezuela 9°45N 63°11W **92** B6
Mau *Mad. P., India* 26°17N 78°41E **43** F8
Mau *Ut. P., India* 25°56N 83°33E **43** G10
Mau *Ut. P., India* 25°17N 81°23E **43** G9
Mau Ranipur India 25°16N 79°8E **43** G8
Maubeuge France 50°17N 3°57E **20** A6
Maubin Burma 16°44N 95°39E **41** L19
Maud, Pt. Australia 23°6S 113°45E **60** D1
Maud Rise S. Ocean 66°0S 3°0E **5** C3
Maués Brazil 3°20S 57°45W **92** D7
Mauganj India 24°50N 81°55E **43** G9
Maughold Hd. I. of Man 54°18N 4°18W **12** C3
Maui U.S.A. 20°48N 156°20W **75** L8
Maulamyaing = Moulmein *Burma* 16°30N 97°40E **41** L20
Maule □ *Chile* 36°5S 72°30W **94** D1
Maumee U.S.A. 41°34N 83°39W **81** E12
Maumee → U.S.A. 41°42N 83°28W **81** E12
Maumere Indonesia 8°38S 122°13E **37** F6
Maun Botswana 20°0S 23°26E **56** B3
Mauna Kea U.S.A. 19°50N 155°28W **75** M8
Mauna Loa U.S.A. 19°30N 155°35W **75** M8
Maunath Bhanjan = Mau *India* 25°56N 83°33E **43** G10
Maungmagan Kyunzu *Burma* 14°0N 97°48E **38** E1
Maupin U.S.A. 45°11N 121°5W **76** D3
Maurepas, L. U.S.A. 30°15N 90°30W **85** F9
Maurice, L. Australia 29°30S 131°0E **61** E5
Mauricie △ Canada 46°45N 73°0W **72** C5
Mauritania ■ Africa 20°50N 10°0W **52** E3
Mauritius ■ *Ind. Oc.* 20°0S 57°0E **55** d
Mauston U.S.A. 43°48N 90°5W **80** D8
Mavli India 24°45N 73°55E **42** G5
Mawai India 22°30N 81°4E **43** H9
Mawana India 29°6N 77°58E **42** E7

Mawand Pakistan 29°33N 68°38E **42** E3
Mawjib, W. al → *Jordan* 31°28N 35°36E **48** D4
Mawkmai Burma 20°14N 97°37E **41** J20
Mawlaik Burma 23°40N 94°26E **41** H19
Mawlamyine = Moulmein *Burma* 16°30N 97°40E **41** L20
Mawqaq Si. Arabia 27°25N 41°8E **46** E4
Mawson Antarctica 67°30S 62°53E **5** C6
Mawson Coast Antarctica 68°30S 63°0E **5** C6
Max U.S.A. 47°49N 101°18W **80** B3
Maxcanú Mexico 20°35N 90°0W **87** C6
Maxesibeni S. Africa 30°49S 29°23E **57** D4
Maxhamish L. Canada 59°50N 123°17W **70** B4
Maxixe Mozam. 23°54S 35°17E **57** B6
Maxville Canada 45°17N 74°51W **83** A10
Maxwell U.S.A. 39°17N 122°11W **78** F4
Maxwelton Australia 20°43S 142°41E **62** C3
May, C. U.S.A. 38°56N 74°58W **81** F16
May Pen Jamaica 17°58N 77°15W **88** a
Maya → Russia 60°28N 134°28E **27** D14
Maya Mts. Belize 16°30N 89°0W **87** D7
Mayabandar India 12°56N 92°56E **45** H11
Mayaguana I. Bahamas 22°30N 72°44W **89** B5
Mayagüez Puerto Rico 18°12N 67°9W **89** d
Mayāmey Iran 36°24N 55°42E **47** B7
Mayang China 27°53N 109°49E **34** D7
Mayanup Australia 33°57S 116°27E **61** F2
Mayapán Mexico 20°29N 89°11W **87** C7
Mayari Cuba 20°40N 75°41W **89** B4
Mayaro B. Trin. & Tob. 10°14N 60°59W **93** K16
Mayavaram = Mayiladuthurai *India* 11°3N 79°42E **45** J4
Maybell U.S.A. 40°31N 108°5W **76** F9
Maybole U.K. 55°21N 4°42W **11** F4
Maydān Iraq 34°55N 45°37E **46** C5
Mayenne → France 47°30N 0°32W **20** C3
Mayer U.S.A. 34°24N 112°14W **77** J7
Mayerthorpe Canada 53°57N 115°8W **70** C5
Mayfield *Ky., U.S.A.* 36°44N 88°38W **80** G9
Mayfield *N.Y., U.S.A.* 43°6N 74°16W **83** C10
Mayhill U.S.A. 32°53N 105°29W **77** K11
Maykop Russia 44°35N 40°10E **19** F7
Maymyo Burma 22°2N 96°28E **38** A1
Maynard *Mass., U.S.A.* 42°26N 71°27W **83** D13
Maynard *Wash., U.S.A.* 47°59N 122°55W **78** C4
Maynard Hills Australia 28°28S 119°49E **61** E2
Mayne → Australia 23°40S 141°55E **62** C3
Maynooth Canada 45°13N 77°56W **82** A7
Maynooth Ireland 53°23N 6°34W **10** C5
Mayo Canada 63°38N 135°57W **68** E4
Mayo □ Ireland 53°53N 9°3W **10** C2
Mayon Volcano Phil. 13°15N 123°41E **37** B6
Mayor I. N.Z. 37°16S 176°17E **59** B6
Mayotte ☑ *Ind. Oc.* 12°50S 45°10E **55** a
Maysān □ Iraq 31°55N 47°15E **46** D5
Maysville U.S.A. 38°39N 83°46W **81** F12
Mayu Indonesia 1°30N 126°30E **37** D7
Mayuram = Mayiladuthurai *India* 11°3N 79°42E **45** J4
Mayville *N. Dak., U.S.A.* 47°30N 97°20W **80** B5
Mayville *N.Y., U.S.A.* 42°15N 79°30W **82** D5
Mazabuka Zambia 15°52S 27°44E **55** H5
Mazagán = El Jadida *Morocco* 33°11N 8°17W **52** B4
Mazagão Brazil 0°7S 51°16W **93** D8
Mazán Peru 3°30S 73°0W **92** D4
Māzandarān □ *Iran* 36°30N 52°0E **47** B7
Mazapil Mexico 24°39N 101°34W **86** C4
Mazar China 36°32N 77°1E **30** D4
Mazara del Vallo Italy 37°39N 12°35E **22** F5
Mazarrón Spain 37°38N 1°19W **21** D5
Mazaruni → Guyana 6°25N 58°35W **92** B7
Mazatán Mexico 29°0N 110°8W **86** B2
Mazatenango Guatemala 14°35N 91°30W **88** D1
Mazatlán Mexico 23°13N 106°25W **86** C3
Mažeikiai Lithuania 56°20N 22°20E **9** H20
Māzhān Iran 32°30N 59°0E **47** C8
Mazīnān Iran 36°19N 56°56E **47** B8
Mazoe → Mozam. 16°20S 33°30E **55** H6
Mazurski, Pojezierze *Poland* 53°50N 21°0E **17** B11
Mazyr Belarus 51°59N 29°15E **17** B15
Mba Fiji 17°33S 177°41E **59** a
Mbabane Swaziland 26°18S 31°6E **57** C5
Mbaïki C.A.R. 3°53N 18°1E **54** D3
Mbala Zambia 8°46S 31°24E **54** F6
Mbalabala Zimbabwe 20°27S 29°3E **57** B4
Mbale Uganda 1°8N 34°12E **54** D6
Mbalmayo Cameroon 3°33N 11°33E **54** D2
Mbandaka *Dem. Rep. of the Congo* 0°1N 18°18E **54** D3
Mbanza Congo Angola 6°18S 14°16E **54** F2
Mbanza Ngungu *Dem. Rep. of the Congo* 5°12S 14°53E **54** F2
Mbarara Uganda 0°35S 30°40E **54** E6
Mbengga = Beqa *Fiji* 18°23S 178°8E **59** a
Mbeya Tanzania 8°54S 33°29E **54** F6
Mbhashe → S. Africa 32°15S 28°54E **57** D4
Mbini = Río Muni □ *Eq. Guin.* 1°30N 10°0E **54** D2
Mbizi Zimbabwe 21°23S 31°1E **57** B5
Mbombela S. Africa 25°29S 30°59E **57** D5
Mbouda Cameroon 5°38N 10°15E **52** G8
M'boukou, L. de Cameroon 6°23N 12°50E **54** C2
Mbour Senegal 14°22N 16°54W **52** F2
Mbuji-Mayi *Dem. Rep. of the Congo* 6°9S 23°40E **54** F4
Mburucuyá Argentina 28°1S 58°14W **94** B4
Mburucuyá △ Argentina 28°1S 58°12W **94** B4
Mchinji Malawi 13°47S 32°58E **55** G6
Mdantsane S. Africa 32°56S 27°46E **57** D4
Mead, L. U.S.A. 36°0N 114°44W **79** J12
Meade U.S.A. 37°17N 100°20W **80** G3
Meade River = Atqasuk *U.S.A.* 70°28N 157°24W **74** A8
Meadow Lake Canada 54°10N 108°26W **71** C7
Meadow Lake △ Canada 54°27N 109°0W **71** C7
Meadow Valley Wash → *U.S.A.* 36°40N 114°34W **79** J12

Meadville U.S.A. 41°39N 80°9W **82** E4
Meaford Canada 44°36N 80°35W **82** B4
Meakan Dake Japan 43°15N 144°0E **28** C11
Mealy Mts. Canada 53°10N 58°0W **73** B8
Meander River Canada 59°2N 117°42W **70** B5
Meares, C. U.S.A. 45°37N 124°0W **76** D1
Mearim → Brazil 3°4S 44°35W **93** D10
Meath □ Ireland 53°40N 6°57W **10** C5
Meath Park Canada 53°27N 105°22W **71** C7
Meaux France 48°58N 2°50E **20** B5
Mebechi-Gawa → *Japan* 40°31N 141°31E **28** D10
Mebulu, Tanjung *Indonesia* 8°50S 115°5E **37** K18
Mecca = Makkah *Si. Arabia* 21°30N 39°54E **49** C2
Mecca U.S.A. 33°34N 116°5W **79** M10
Mechanicsburg U.S.A. 40°13N 77°1W **82** F8
Mechanicville U.S.A. 42°54N 73°41W **83** D11
Mechelen Belgium 51°2N 4°29E **15** C4
Mecheria Algeria 33°35N 0°18W **52** B5
Mecklenburg Germany 53°33N 11°40E **16** B7
Mecklenburger Bucht *Germany* 54°20N 11°40E **16** A6
Meconta Mozam. 14°59S 39°50E **55** G7
Medak India 18°1N 78°15E **44** E4
Medan Indonesia 3°40N 98°38E **36** D1
Médanos de Coro △ *Venezuela* 11°35N 69°44W **89** D6
Medanosa, Pta. Argentina 48°8S 66°0W **96** F3
Medawachchiya Sri Lanka 8°30N 80°30E **45** K5
Medchal India 17°37N 78°29E **44** F4
Médéa Algeria 36°12N 2°50E **52** A6
Medellín Colombia 6°15N 75°35W **92** B3
Medelpad Sweden 62°33N 16°30E **8** E17
Medemblik Neths. 52°46N 5°8E **15** B5
Medford *Oreg., U.S.A.* 42°19N 122°52W **76** E2
Medford *Wis., U.S.A.* 45°9N 90°20W **80** C8
Medgidia Romania 44°15N 28°19E **17** F15
Media Agua Argentina 31°58S 68°25W **94** C2
Media Luna Argentina 34°45S 66°44W **94** C2
Medianeira Brazil 25°17S 54°5W **95** B5
Mediaş Romania 46°9N 24°22E **17** E13
Medicine Bow U.S.A. 41°54N 106°12W **76** F10
Medicine Bow Mts. *U.S.A.* 40°40N 106°0W **76** F10
Medicine Hat Canada 50°0N 110°45W **71** D6
Medicine Lake U.S.A. 48°30N 104°30W **76** B11
Medicine Lodge U.S.A. 37°17N 98°35W **80** G4
Medina = Al Madīnah *Si. Arabia* 24°35N 39°52E **46** E3
Medina *N. Dak., U.S.A.* 46°54N 99°18W **80** B4
Medina *N.Y., U.S.A.* 43°13N 78°23W **82** C6
Medina *Ohio, U.S.A.* 41°8N 81°52W **82** E3
Medina → U.S.A. 29°16N 98°29W **84** G5
Medina del Campo Spain 41°18N 4°55W **21** B3
Medina L. U.S.A. 29°32N 98°56W **84** G5
Medina Sidonia Spain 36°28N 5°57W **21** D3
Medinipur India 22°25N 87°21E **43** H12
Mediterranean Sea Europe 35°0N 15°0E **6** H7
Médoc France 45°10N 0°50W **20** D3
Medveditsa → Russia 49°35N 42°41E **19** E7
Medvezhi, Ostrava *Russia* 71°0N 161°0E **27** B17
Medvezhyegorsk Russia 63°0N 34°25E **18** B5
Medway □ U.K. 51°25N 0°32E **13** F8
Medway → U.K. 51°27N 0°46E **13** F8
Meekatharra Australia 26°32S 118°29E **61** E2
Meeker U.S.A. 40°2N 107°55W **76** F10
Meerut India 29°1N 77°42E **42** E7
Meeteetse U.S.A. 44°9N 108°52W **76** D9
Mega Ethiopia 3°57N 38°19E **49** G2
Megara Greece 37°58N 23°22E **23** F10
Megasini India 21°38N 86°21E **43** J12
Meghalaya □ *India* 25°50N 91°0E **41** G17
Meghna → Bangla. 22°50N 90°50E **41** H17
Megion Russia 61°3N 76°6E **26** C8
Mégiscane, L. Canada 48°35N 75°55W **72** C4
Meharry, Mt. Australia 22°59S 118°35E **60** D2
Mehekar India 20°9N 76°34E **44** D3
Mehlville U.S.A. 38°31N 90°19W **80** F9
Mehndawal India 26°58N 83°5E **43** F10
Mehr Jān Iran 33°50N 55°6E **47** C7
Mehrābād Iran 36°53N 47°55E **46** B5
Mehrān Iran 33°7N 46°10E **46** C5
Mehrān → Iran 26°45N 55°26E **47** E7
Mehrgarh Pakistan 29°30N 67°30E **42** E2
Mehrīz Iran 31°35N 54°28E **47** D7
Mei Jiang → China 24°25N 116°35E **35** E11
Mei Xian China 34°18N 107°55E **32** G4
Meicheng China 29°29N 119°16E **35** C12
Meichengzhen China 29°9N 111°40E **35** C8
Meichuan China 30°8N 115°31E **35** B10
Meighen I. Canada 80°0N 99°30W **69** B12
Meigu China 28°16N 103°20E **34** C4
Meihekou China 42°32N 125°40E **33** C13
Meiktila Burma 20°53N 95°54E **41** J19
Meili Xue Shan China 28°30N 98°39E **34** C2
Meimyu = Maymyo *Burma* 22°2N 96°28E **38** A1
Meishan China 30°3N 103°23E **34** B4
Meissen Germany 51°9N 13°29E **16** C7
Meitan China 27°45N 107°29E **34** D6
Meizhou China 24°16N 116°6E **35** E11
Meja India 25°9N 82°7E **43** G10
Mejillones Chile 23°10S 70°30W **94** A1
Mekele Ethiopia 13°33N 39°30E **49** E2
Mekerghene, Sebkra *Algeria* 26°21N 1°30E **52** C6
Mekhtar Pakistan 30°30N 69°15E **40** D6
Meknès Morocco 33°57N 5°33W **52** B4
Mekong → Asia 9°30N 106°15E **39** H6
Mekongga Indonesia 3°39S 121°15E **37** E6
Mekvari = Kür → *Azerbaijan* 39°29N 49°15E **19** G8
Melagiri Hills India 12°20N 77°30E **45** H3
Melaka Malaysia 2°15N 102°15E **39** L4
Melaka □ *Malaysia* 2°15N 102°15E **39** L4
Melanesia Pac. Oc. 4°0S 155°0E **64** H7

Melanesian Basin *Pac. Oc.* 0°5N 160°35E **64** G8
Melapalaiyam India 8°39N 77°44E **45** K3
Melaya Indonesia 8°17S 114°30E **37** J17
Melbourne U.S.A. 28°5N 80°37W **85** G14
Melchor Múzquiz *Mexico* 27°53N 101°31W **86** B4
Melchor Ocampo *Mexico* 24°51N 101°39W **86** C4
Melekeok Palau 7°27N 134°38E **64** G5
Mélèzes → Canada 57°40N 69°29W **72** A5
Melfort Canada 52°50N 104°37W **71** C8
Melhus Norway 63°17N 10°18E **8** E14
Melilla N. Afr. 35°21N 2°57W **21** E4
Melipilla Chile 33°42S 71°15W **94** C1
Melissa Canada 45°24N 79°14W **82** A5
Melita Canada 49°15N 101°0W **71** D8
Melitopol Ukraine 46°50N 35°22E **19** E6
Melk Austria 48°13N 15°20E **16** D8
Mellansel Sweden 63°26N 18°19E **8** E18
Mellen U.S.A. 46°20N 90°40W **80** B8
Mellerud Sweden 58°41N 12°28E **9** G15
Mellette U.S.A. 45°9N 98°30W **80** C4
Melo Uruguay 32°20S 54°10W **95** C5
Melolo Indonesia 9°53S 120°40E **37** F6
Melouprey Cambodia 13°48N 105°16E **38** F5
Melrhir, Chott Algeria 34°13N 6°30E **52** B7
Melrose Australia 32°42S 146°57E **63** E4
Melrose U.K. 55°36N 2°43W **11** F6
Melrose *Minn., U.S.A.* 45°40N 94°49W **80** C6
Melrose *N. Mex., U.S.A.* 34°26N 103°38W **77** J12
Melstone U.S.A. 46°36N 107°52W **76** C10
Melton Mowbray U.K. 52°47N 0°54W **12** E7
Melun France 48°32N 2°39E **20** B5
Melung Nepal 27°31N 86°3E **43** F12
Melur India 10°2N 78°23E **45** J4
Melville Canada 50°55N 102°50W **71** C8
Melville, C. Australia 14°11S 144°30E **62** A3
Melville, L. Canada 53°30N 60°0W **73** B8
Melville B. Australia 12°0S 136°45E **62** A2
Melville B. Greenland 75°30N 63°0W **69** B19
Melville I. Australia 11°30S 131°0E **60** B5
Melville I. Canada 75°30N 112°0W **69** B8
Melville Pen. Canada 68°0N 84°0W **69** D15
Melvin, Lough Ireland 54°26N 8°10W **10** B3
Memba Mozam. 14°11S 40°30E **55** G8
Memboro Indonesia 9°30S 119°30E **60** A2
Memel = Klaipėda *Lithuania* 55°43N 21°10E **9** J19
Memel S. Africa 27°38S 29°36E **57** C4
Memmingen Germany 47°58N 10°10E **16** E6
Mempawah Indonesia 0°30N 109°5E **36** D3
Memphis *Mich., U.S.A.* 42°54N 82°46W **82** D2
Memphis *Tenn., U.S.A.* 35°8N 90°2W **85** D9
Memphis *Tex., U.S.A.* 34°44N 100°33W **84** D4
Memphrémagog, L. *N. Amer.* 45°8N 72°17W **83** B12
Mena U.S.A. 34°35N 94°15W **84** D7
Menado = Manado *Indonesia* 1°29N 124°51E **37** D6
Menai Strait U.K. 53°11N 4°13W **12** D3
Ménaka Mali 15°59N 2°18E **52** E6
Menan = Chao Phraya → *Thailand* 13°40N 100°31E **38** F3
Menard U.S.A. 30°55N 99°47W **84** F5
Menard Fracture Zone *Pac. Oc.* 43°0S 97°0W **65** M18
Mendaña Fracture Zone *Pac. Oc.* 16°0S 91°0W **65** J18
Mendawai → Indonesia 3°30S 113°0E **36** E4
Mende France 44°31N 3°30E **20** D5
Mendeleyev Ridge Arctic 80°0N 178°0W **4** B17
Mendhar India 33°35N 74°10E **43** C6
Mendip Hills U.K. 51°17N 2°40W **13** F5
Mendocino, C. U.S.A. 40°26N 124°25W **76** F1
Mendocino Fracture Zone *Pac. Oc.* 40°0N 142°0W **65** D13
Mendota *Calif., U.S.A.* 36°45N 120°23W **78** J6
Mendota *Ill., U.S.A.* 41°33N 89°7W **80** E9
Mendoyo Indonesia 8°23S 114°42E **37** J17
Mendoza Argentina 32°50S 68°52W **94** C2
Mendoza □ Argentina 33°0S 69°0W **94** C2
Mene Grande Venezuela 9°49N 70°56W **92** B4
Menemen Turkey 38°34N 27°3E **23** E12
Menen Belgium 50°47N 3°7E **15** D3
Mengcheng China 33°12N 116°36E **34** H9
Mengdingjie China 23°31N 98°58E **34** F2
Menggala Indonesia 4°30S 105°15E **36** E3
Menghai China 21°49N 100°55E **34** G3
Mengjin China 34°55N 112°45E **32** G7
Mengla China 21°20N 101°25E **34** G3
Menglian China 22°21N 99°27E **34** F2
Mengshan China 24°14N 110°55E **35** E8
Mengyin China 35°40N 117°58E **33** G9
Mengzhe China 22°2N 100°15E **34** F3
Mengzi China 23°20N 103°22E **34** F4
Menifee U.S.A. 33°41N 117°10W **79** M9
Menihek Canada 54°28N 56°36W **73** B6
Menihek L. Canada 54°0N 67°0W **73** B6
Menin = Menen *Belgium* 50°47N 3°7E **15** D3
Menindee Australia 32°20S 142°25E **63** E3
Menindee L. Australia 32°20S 142°25E **63** E3
Meningie Australia 35°50S 139°18E **63** F2
Menjangan, Pulau *Indonesia* 8°7S 114°31E **37** J17
Menlo Park U.S.A. 37°27N 122°12W **78** H4
Menongue Angola 14°48S 17°52E **55** G3
Menorca Spain 40°0N 4°0E **21** C8
Mentakab Malaysia 3°29N 102°21E **39** L4
Mentawai, Kepulauan *Indonesia* 2°0S 99°0E **36** E1
Menton France 43°50N 7°29E **20** E7
Mentor U.S.A. 41°40N 81°21W **82** E3
Menzelinsk Russia 55°47N 53°11E **18** C9
Menzies Australia 29°40S 121°2E **61** E3

Meob B. *Namibia* 24°25S 14°34E **56** B1
Meoqui *Mexico* 28°17N 105°29W **86** B3
Meppel *Neths.* 52°42N 6°12E **15** B6
Merak *Indonesia* 6°10N 106°26E **37** F12
Meramangye, L.
  Australia 28°25S 132°13E **61** E5
Meran = Merano *Italy* 46°40N 11°9E **22** A4
Merano *Italy* 46°40N 11°9E **22** A4
Merauke *Indonesia* 8°29S 140°24E **37** F10
Merbein *Australia* 34°10S 142°2E **63** E3
Merca = Marka *Somalia* 1°48N 44°50E **49** G3
Merced *U.S.A.* 37°18N 120°29W **78** H6
Merced → *U.S.A.* 37°21N 120°59W **78** H6
Merced Pk. *U.S.A.* 37°36N 119°24W **78** H7
Mercedes B. Aires,
  Argentina 34°40S 59°30W **94** C4
Mercedes Corrientes,
  Argentina 29°10S 58°5W **94** B4
Mercedes San Luis,
  Argentina 33°40S 65°21W **94** C2
Mercedes *Uruguay* 33°12S 58°0W **94** C4
Merceditas *Chile* 28°20S 70°35W **94** B1
Mercer *N.Z.* 37°16S 175°5E **59** B5
Mercer *U.S.A.* 41°14N 80°15W **82** E4
Mercer Island *U.S.A.* 47°34N 122°13W **78** C4
Mercury *U.S.A.* 36°40N 115°59W **79** J11
Mercy, C. *Canada* 65°0N 63°30W **69** E19
Mere *U.K.* 51°6N 2°16W **13** F5
Merebuk, Gunung
  Indonesia 8°13S 114°39E **37** J17
Meredith, C. *Falk. Is.* 52°15S 60°40W **96** G4
Meredith, L. *U.S.A.* 35°43N 101°33W **84** D4
Mergui *Burma* 12°26N 98°34E **38** F2
Mergui Arch. = Myeik Kyunzu
  Burma 11°30N 97°30E **39** G1
Mérida *Mexico* 20°58N 89°37W **87** C7
Mérida *Spain* 38°55N 6°25W **21** C2
Mérida *Venezuela* 8°24N 71°8W **92** B4
Mérida, Cord. de *Venezuela* 9°0N 71°0W **92** B4
Meriden *U.K.* 52°26N 1°38W **13** E6
Meriden *U.S.A.* 41°32N 72°48W **83** E12
Meridian Calif., U.S.A. 39°9N 121°55W **78** F5
Meridian Idaho, U.S.A. 43°37N 116°24W **76** E5
Meridian Miss., U.S.A. 32°22N 88°42W **85** E10
Merinda *Australia* 20°2S 148°11E **62** C4
Merir *Palau* 4°10N 132°30E **37** D8
Merirumã *Brazil* 1°15N 54°50W **93** C8
Merkel *U.S.A.* 32°28N 100°1W **84** E4
Mermaid Reef *Australia* 17°6S 119°36E **60** C2
Meroe *India* 7°33N 93°33E **45** L11
Merowe Dam *Sudan* 18°35N 31°56E **53** E12
Merredin *Australia* 31°28S 118°18E **61** F2
Merrick *U.K.* 55°8N 4°28W **11** F4
Merrickville *Canada* 44°55N 75°50W **83** B9
Merrill Oreg., U.S.A. 42°1N 121°36W **76** E3
Merrill Wis., U.S.A. 45°11N 89°41W **80** C9
Merrimack → *U.S.A.* 42°49N 70°49W **83** D14
Merriman *U.S.A.* 42°55N 101°42W **80** D3
Merritt *Canada* 50°10N 120°45W **70** C4
Merritt Island *U.S.A.* 28°21N 80°42W **85** G5
Merriwa *Australia* 32°6S 150°22E **63** E5
Merry I. *Canada* 55°29N 77°31W **72** A4
Merryville *U.S.A.* 30°45N 93°33W **84** F8
Mersea I. *U.K.* 51°47N 0°58E **13** F8
Merseburg *Germany* 51°22N 11°59E **16** C6
Mersey → *U.K.* 53°25N 3°1W **12** D4
Merseyside □ *U.K.* 53°31N 3°2W **12** D4
Mersin = İçel *Turkey* 36°51N 34°36E **46** B2
Mersing *Malaysia* 2°25N 103°50E **39** L4
Merta *India* 26°39N 74°4E **42** F5
Merta Road *India* 26°43N 73°55E **42** F5
Merthyr Tydfil *U.K.* 51°45N 3°22W **13** F4
Merthyr Tydfil □ *U.K.* 51°46N 3°21W **13** F4
Mértola *Portugal* 37°40N 7°40W **21** D2
Mertz Glacier *Antarctica* 67°30S 144°45E **5** C10
Mertzon *U.S.A.* 31°16N 100°49W **84** F4
Meru *Kenya* 0°3N 37°40E **54** D7
Meru *Tanzania* 3°15S 36°46E **54** E7
Meru Betiri △ *Indonesia* 8°27S 113°51E **37** H15
Mesa *U.S.A.* 33°25N 111°50W **77** K8
Mesa Verde △ *U.S.A.* 37°11N 108°29W **77** H9
Mesada = Masada *Israel* 31°18N 35°21E **48** D4
Mesgouez, L. *Canada* 51°20N 75°0W **72** B5
Meshed = Mashhad *Iran* 36°20N 59°35E **47** B8
Meshgīn Shahr *Iran* 38°30N 47°45E **46** B5
Meshoppen *U.S.A.* 41°36N 76°3W **83** E8
Mesilinka → *Canada* 56°6N 124°30W **70** B4
Mesologi *Greece* 38°21N 21°28E **23** E9
Mesopotamia = Al Jazirah
  Iraq 33°30N 44°0E **46** C5
Mesopotamia *U.S.A.* 41°27N 80°57W **82** E4
Mesquite *U.S.A.* 36°48N 114°4W **77** H6
Messaad *Algeria* 34°8N 3°30E **52** B6
Messalo → *Mozam.* 12°25S 39°15E **55** G7
Messina
  S. Africa 22°20S 30°5E **57** B5
Messina *Italy* 38°11N 15°34E **22** E6
Messina, Str. di *Italy* 38°15N 15°35E **22** F6
Messini *Greece* 37°4N 22°1E **23** F10
Messiniakos Kolpos
  Greece 36°45N 22°5E **23** F10
Mesta = Nestos →
  Europe 40°54N 24°49E **23** D11
Meta → *S. Amer.* 6°12N 67°28W **92** B5
Meta Incognita Pen.
  Canada 62°45N 68°30W **69** E18
Metabetchouan *Canada* 48°26N 71°52W **73** C5
Metaline Falls *U.S.A.* 48°52N 117°22W **76** B5
Metán *Argentina* 25°30S 65°0W **94** B3
Metcalfe *Canada* 45°14N 75°28W **83** A9
Metema *Ethiopia* 12°58N 36°12E **49** E2
Methven *N.Z.* 43°38S 171°40E **59** E3
Metlakatla *U.S.A.* 55°8N 131°35W **68** F5
Metropolis *U.S.A.* 37°9N 88°44W **80** G9
Metropolitana □ *Chile* 33°30S 70°50W **94** C1
Mettuppalaiyam *India* 11°18N 76°59E **45** J3
Mettur *India* 11°48N 77°47E **45** J3
Metu *Ethiopia* 8°18N 35°35E **49** F2

Metz *France* 49°8N 6°10E **20** B7
Meulaboh *Indonesia* 4°11N 96°3E **36** D1
Meureudu *Indonesia* 5°19N 96°10E **36** C1
Meuse → *Europe* 50°45N 5°41E **15** D5
Mexia *U.S.A.* 31°41N 96°29W **84** F6
Mexiana, I. *Brazil* 0°0 49°30W **93** D9
Mexicali *Mexico* 32°40N 115°30W **79** N11
Mexican Plateau *Mexico* 25°0N 104°0W **66** G9
Mexican Water *U.S.A.* 36°57N 109°32W **77** H9
Mexico *Maine, U.S.A.* 44°34N 70°33W **83** B14
Mexico *Mo., U.S.A.* 39°10N 91°53W **80** F8
Mexico *N.Y., U.S.A.* 43°28N 76°14W **83** C8
México □ *Mexico* 19°20N 99°30W **87** D5
Mexico ■ *Cent. Amer.* 25°0N 105°0W **86** C4
Mexico, G. of *Cent. Amer.* 25°0N 90°0W **87** C7
Mexico B. *U.S.A.* 43°35N 76°20W **83** C8
Meydān-e Naftūn *Iran* 31°56N 49°18E **47** D6
Meydani, Ra's-e *Iran* 25°24N 59°6E **47** E8
Meyers Chuck *U.S.A.* 55°45N 132°15W **70** B2
Meymaneh *Afghan.* 35°53N 64°38E **40** B4
Mezen *Russia* 65°50N 44°20E **18** A7
Mezen → *Russia* 65°44N 44°22E **18** A7
Mézenc, Mt. *France* 44°54N 4°11E **20** D6
Mezhdurechensk *Russia* 53°41N 88°3E **26** D9
Mezhdurechenskiy
  Russia 59°36N 65°56E **26** D7
Mezőkövesd *Hungary* 47°49N 20°35E **17** E11
Mezőtúr *Hungary* 47°1N 20°41E **17** E11
Mezquital *Mexico* 23°29N 104°23W **86** C4
Mezquital → *Mexico* 28°25S 32°26E **57** C5
Mfolozi → *S. Africa* 28°25S 32°26E **57** C5
Mhow *India* 22°33N 75°50E **42** H6
Miahuatlán *Mexico* 16°20N 96°36W **87** D5
Miami Okla., U.S.A. 36°53N 94°53W **84** C7
Miami Tex., U.S.A. 35°42N 100°38W **84** D4
Mian Xian *China* 33°10N 106°32E **34** A6
Mianchi *China* 34°48N 111°48E **32** G6
Miandarreh *Iran* 35°37N 53°39E **47** C7
Miandowāb *Iran* 37°0N 46°5E **46** B5
Miandrivazo *Madag.* 19°31S 45°29E **55** H9
Mīāneh *Iran* 37°30N 47°40E **46** B5
Mianning *China* 28°32N 102°9E **34** C4
Mianwali *Pakistan* 32°38N 71°28E **42** C4
Mianyang *China* 31°22N 104°47E **34** B5
Mianzhu *China* 31°22N 104°7E **34** B5
Miao Ling *China* 26°55N 107°30E **34** D6
Miaodao Qundao
  China 38°10N 120°45E **33** E11
Miaoli *Taiwan* 24°37N 120°49E **35** E13
Miass *Russia* 54°59N 60°6E **18** D11
Mica *S. Africa* 24°10S 30°48E **57** C5
Michalovce *Slovak Rep.* 48°47N 21°58E **17** D11
Michigan □ *U.S.A.* 44°0N 85°0W **81** C11
Michigan, L. *U.S.A.* 44°0N 87°0W **80** D10
Michigan City *U.S.A.* 41°43N 86°54W **80** E10
Michipicoten I. *Canada* 47°40N 85°40W **72** C2
Michoacán □ *Mexico* 19°10N 101°50W **86** D4
Michurin *Bulgaria* 42°9N 27°51E **23** C12
Michurinsk *Russia* 52°58N 40°27E **18** D7
Micoud *St. Lucia* 13°49N 60°54W **89** f
Micronesia *Pac. Oc.* 11°0N 160°0E **64** G7
Micronesia, Federated States of ■
  Pac. Oc. 9°0N 150°0E **58** A8
Mid-Indian Ridge *Ind. Oc.* 30°0S 75°0E **64** M1
Mid-Oceanic Ridge *Ind. Oc.* 42°0S 90°0E **64** M1
Mid-Pacific Seamounts
  Pac. Oc. 18°0N 177°0W **64** F10
Midai *Indonesia* 3°0N 107°47E **36** D3
Midale *Canada* 49°25N 103°20W **71** D8
Middelburg *Neths.* 51°30N 3°36E **15** C3
Middelburg Eastern Cape,
  S. Africa 31°30S 25°0E **56** E4
Middelburg Mpumalanga,
  S. Africa 25°49S 29°28E **57** C4
Middelpos *S. Africa* 31°55S 20°13E **56** E3
Middelwit *S. Africa* 24°51S 27°3E **56** B4
Middle Alkali L. *U.S.A.* 41°27N 120°5W **76** F3
Middle America Trench =
  Guatemala Trench
  Pac. Oc. 14°0N 95°0W **66** D10
Middle Andaman I.
  India 12°30N 92°30E **45** H11
Middle Bass I. *U.S.A.* 41°41N 82°48W **82** E2
Middle East Asia 35°0N 40°0E **24** E5
Middle Fork Feather →
  U.S.A. 38°33N 121°30W **78** F5
Middle I. *Australia* 34°6S 123°11E **61** F3
Middle Loup → *U.S.A.* 41°17N 98°24W **80** E4
Middleboro *U.S.A.* 41°54N 70°55W **83** E14
Middleburg Fla., U.S.A. 30°4N 81°52W **85** F14
Middleburg Pa., U.S.A. 40°47N 77°3W **82** F7
Middleburgh *U.S.A.* 42°36N 74°20W **83** D10
Middlebury *U.S.A.* 44°1N 73°10W **83** B11
Middlefield *U.S.A.* 41°27N 81°4W **82** E3
Middlemount *Australia* 22°50S 148°40E **62** C4
Middleport N.Y., U.S.A. 43°13N 78°29W **82** C6
Middleport Ohio, U.S.A. 39°0N 82°3W **81** F12
Middlesboro *U.S.A.* 36°36N 83°43W **81** G12
Middlesbrough *U.K.* 54°35N 1°13W **12** C6
Middlesbrough □ *U.K.* 54°28N 1°13W **12** C6
Middlesex *Belize* 17°2N 88°31W **88** C2
Middlesex N.J., U.S.A. 40°36N 74°30W **83** F10
Middlesex N.Y., U.S.A. 42°42N 77°16W **82** D7
Middleton *Australia* 22°22S 141°32E **62** C3
Middleton *Canada* 44°57N 65°4W **73** D6
Middleton Cr. →
  Australia 22°35S 141°51E **62** C3
Middleton I. *U.S.A.* 59°26N 146°20W **74** D10
Middleton *U.K.* 54°17N 6°51W **10** B5
Middletown Calif.,
  U.S.A. 38°45N 122°37W **78** G4
Middletown Conn.,
  U.S.A. 41°34N 72°39W **83** E12
Middletown N.Y.,
  U.S.A. 41°27N 74°25W **83** E10
Middletown Ohio,
  U.S.A. 39°31N 84°24W **81** F11
Middletown Pa., U.S.A. 40°12N 76°44W **83** F8
Midge Point *Australia* 20°39S 148°43E **62** b
Midhurst *Canada* 44°26N 79°43W **82** B5

Midhurst *U.K.* 50°59N 0°44W **13** G7
Midi, Canal du → *France* 43°45N 1°21E **20** E4
Midland *Australia* 31°54S 115°1E **61** F2
Midland *Canada* 44°45N 79°50W **82** B5
Midland Calif., U.S.A. 33°52N 114°48W **79** M12
Midland Mich., U.S.A. 43°37N 84°14W **81** D11
Midland Pa., U.S.A. 40°39N 80°27W **82** F4
Midland Tex., U.S.A. 32°0N 102°3W **84** F3
Midleton *Ireland* 51°55N 8°10W **10** E3
Midlothian *U.S.A.* 32°30N 97°0W **84** E6
Midlothian □ *U.K.* 55°51N 3°5W **11** F5
Midnapore = Medinipur
  India 22°25N 87°21E **43** H12
Midu *China* 25°18N 100°30E **34** E3
Midway Is. *Pac. Oc.* 28°13N 177°22W **75** K4
Midway Wells *U.S.A.* 32°41N 115°7W **79** N11
Midwest *U.S.A.* 42°0N 90°0W **75** B9
Midwest Wyo., U.S.A. 43°25N 106°16W **76** E10
Midwest City *U.S.A.* 35°27N 97°24W **84** D6
Midyat *Turkey* 37°25N 41°23E **46** B4
Midzör *Bulgaria* 43°24N 22°40E **23** C10
Mie □ *Japan* 34°30N 136°10E **29** G8
Międzychód *Poland* 52°35N 15°53E **16** B8
Międzyrzec Podlaski
  Poland 51°58N 22°45E **17** C12
Mielec *Poland* 50°15N 21°25E **17** C11
Mienga *Angola* 17°12S 19°48E **56** B2
Miercurea-Ciuc *Romania* 46°21N 25°48E **17** E13
Mieres *Spain* 43°18N 5°48W **21** A3
Mifflintown *U.S.A.* 40°34N 77°24W **82** F7
Mifraz Ḥefa *Israel* 32°52N 35°0E **48** C4
Migang Shan *China* 35°32N 106°13E **32** G4
Miguasha △ *Canada* 48°5N 66°26W **73** C6
Miguel Alemán, Presa
  Mexico 18°15N 96°32W **87** D5
Miguel Hidalgo, Presa
  Mexico 26°30N 108°34W **86** B3
Mihara *Japan* 34°24N 133°5E **29** G6
Mikhaylovgrad = Montana
  Bulgaria 43°27N 23°16E **23** C10
Mikhaylovka *Russia* 50°3N 43°5E **19** D7
Mikines *Greece* 37°43N 22°46E **23** F10
Mikkeli *Finland* 61°43N 27°15E **8** F22
Mikkwa → *Canada* 58°25N 114°46W **70** B6
Mikonos = Mykonos
  Greece 37°30N 25°25E **23** F11
Mikun *Russia* 62°20N 50°0E **18** B9
Milaca *U.S.A.* 45°45N 93°39W **80** C7
Milagro *Ecuador* 2°11S 79°36W **92** D3
Milan Mo., U.S.A. 40°12N 93°7W **80** E7
Milan Tenn., U.S.A. 35°55N 88°46W **85** D10
Milazzo *Italy* 38°13N 15°15E **22** E6
Milbank *U.S.A.* 45°13N 96°38W **80** C5
Milbanke Sd. *Canada* 52°19N 128°33W **70** C3
Milden *Canada* 51°29N 107°32W **71** C7
Mildenhall *U.K.* 52°21N 0°32E **13** E8
Mildmay *Canada* 44°3N 81°7W **82** B3
Mildura *Australia* 34°13S 142°9E **63** E3
Mile *China* 24°28N 103°20E **34** E4
Miles *Australia* 26°40S 150°9E **63** D5
Miles City *U.S.A.* 46°25N 105°51W **76** C11
Milestone *Canada* 49°59N 104°31W **71** D8
Miletus *Turkey* 37°30N 27°18E **23** F12
Milford Calif., U.S.A. 40°10N 120°22W **78** E6
Milford Conn., U.S.A. 41°14N 73°3W **83** E11
Milford Del., U.S.A. 38°55N 75°26W **81** F16
Milford Mass., U.S.A. 42°8N 71°31W **83** D13
Milford N.H., U.S.A. 42°50N 71°39W **83** D13
Milford Pa., U.S.A. 41°19N 74°48W **83** E10
Milford Utah, U.S.A. 38°24N 113°1W **76** G7
Milford Haven *U.K.* 51°42N 5°7W **13** F2
Milford Sound *N.Z.* 44°41S 167°47E **59** F1
Milh, Baḥr al = Razāzah, Buḥayrat
  ar Iraq 32°40N 43°35E **46** C4
Milikapiti *Australia* 11°26S 130°40E **60** B5
Miling *Australia* 30°30S 116°17E **61** F2
Milk River *Canada* 49°10N 112°5W **70** D6
Mill I. *Antarctica* 66°0S 101°30E **5** C8
Mill I. *Canada* 63°58N 77°47W **69** E16
Millau *France* 44°8N 3°4E **20** D5
Millbridge *Canada* 44°41N 77°36W **82** B7
Millbrook *Canada* 44°10N 78°29W **82** B6
Millbrook Ala., U.S.A. 32°29N 86°22W **85** E11
Millbrook N.Y., U.S.A. 41°47N 73°42W **83** E11
Mille Lacs, L. des *Canada* 48°45N 90°35W **72** C1
Mille Lacs L. *U.S.A.* 46°15N 93°39W **80** B7
Milledgeville *U.S.A.* 33°5N 83°14W **85** E13
Millen *U.S.A.* 32°48N 81°57W **85** E14
Millennium I. = Caroline I.
  Kiribati 9°58S 150°13W **65** H12
Miller *U.S.A.* 44°31N 98°59W **80** C4
Miller Lake *Canada* 45°6N 81°26W **82** A3
Millersburg Ohio, U.S.A. 40°33N 81°55W **82** F3
Millersburg Pa., U.S.A. 40°32N 76°58W **82** F8
Millerton *U.S.A.* 41°57N 73°31W **83** E11
Millerton L. *U.S.A.* 37°1N 119°41W **78** J7
Millet *St. Lucia* 13°55N 60°59W **89** f
Millheim *U.S.A.* 40°54N 77°29W **82** F7
Millicent *Australia* 37°34S 140°21E **63** F3
Millington *U.S.A.* 35°20N 89°53W **85** D10
Millinocket *U.S.A.* 45°39N 68°43W **81** C19
Millmerran *Australia* 27°53S 151°16E **63** D5
Millom *U.K.* 54°13N 3°16W **12** C4
Mills L. *Canada* 61°30N 118°20W **70** A5
Millsboro *U.S.A.* 40°0N 80°0W **82** G5
Millstream Chichester △
  Australia 21°35S 117°6E **60** D2
Millstreet *Ireland* 52°4N 9°4W **10** D2
Milltown Malbay *Ireland* 52°52N 9°24W **10** D2
Millville N.J., U.S.A. 39°24N 75°2W **81** F16
Millville Pa., U.S.A. 41°7N 76°32W **83** E8
Millwood L. *U.S.A.* 33°42N 93°58W **84** E8
Milne → *Australia* 21°10S 137°33E **62** C2
Milo *U.S.A.* 45°15N 68°59W **81** C19
Milos *Greece* 36°44N 24°25E **23** F11

Milparinka *Australia* 29°46S 141°57E **63** D3
Milpitas *U.S.A.* 37°26N 121°55W **78** H5
Milton N.S., Canada 44°4N 64°45W **73** D7
Milton Ont., Canada 43°31N 79°53W **82** C5
Milton *N.Z.* 46°7S 169°59E **59** G2
Milton Calif., U.S.A. 38°3N 120°51W **78** G6
Milton Fla., U.S.A. 30°38N 87°3W **85** F11
Milton Pa., U.S.A. 41°1N 76°51W **82** F8
Milton Vt., U.S.A. 44°38N 73°7W **83** B11
Milton-Freewater
  U.S.A. 45°56N 118°23W **76** D4
Milton Keynes *U.K.* 52°1N 0°44W **13** E7
Milton Keynes □ *U.K.* 52°1N 0°44W **13** E7
Miluo *China* 29°0N 112°59E **35** C9
Milverton *Canada* 43°34N 80°55W **82** C4
Milwaukee *U.S.A.* 43°2N 87°54W **80** D10
Milwaukee Deep *Atl. Oc.* 19°50N 68°0W **89** C6
Milwaukie *U.S.A.* 45°26N 122°38W **78** E4
Mimili *Australia* 27°0S 132°42E **61** E5
Min Jiang → *Fujian,*
  China 26°0N 119°35E **35** E12
Min Jiang → *Sichuan,*
  China 28°45N 104°40E **34** C5
Min Xian *China* 34°25N 104°5E **32** G3
Mina *U.S.A.* 38°24N 118°7W **78** G4
Mīnā Jabal 'Alī *U.A.E.* 25°2N 55°8E **47** E7
Mina Pirquitas *Argentina* 22°40S 66°30W **94** A2
Mīnā Su'ud *Si. Arabia* 28°45N 48°28E **47** D6
Mīnā'al Aḥmadī *Kuwait* 29°5N 48°10E **47** D6
Minago → *Canada* 54°33N 98°59W **71** C9
Minaki *Canada* 49°59N 94°40W **71** D10
Minamata *Japan* 32°10N 130°30E **29** H5
Minami-Arapusa △
  Japan 35°30N 138°9E **29** G9
Minami-Tori-Shima
  Pac. Oc. 24°20N 153°58E **64** E7
Minamiaizu *Japan* 37°12N 139°46E **29** F9
Minamiawaji *Japan* 34°10N 134°42E **29** H7
Minamisōma *Japan* 37°38N 140°58E **28** F10
Minas *Uruguay* 34°20S 55°10W **95** C4
Minas, Sierra de las
  Guatemala 15°9N 89°31W **88** C2
Minas Basin *Canada* 45°20N 64°12W **73** C7
Minas Gerais □ *Brazil* 18°50S 46°0W **93** G9
Minatitlán *Mexico* 17°59N 94°31W **87** D6
Minbu *Burma* 20°10N 94°52E **41** J19
Minchinabad *Pakistan* 30°10N 73°34E **42** D5
Mindanao *Phil.* 8°0N 125°0E **37** C7
Mindanao Sea = Bohol Sea
  Phil. 9°0N 124°0E **37** C6
Mindanao Trench *Pac. Oc.* 12°0N 126°6E **37** B7
Mindelo *C. Verde Is.* 16°24N 25°0W **52** b
Minden *Canada* 44°55N 78°43W **82** B6
Minden *Germany* 52°17N 8°55E **16** B5
Minden La., U.S.A. 32°37N 93°17W **84** E8
Minden Nev., U.S.A. 38°57N 119°46W **78** G7
Mindibungu = Billiluna
  Australia 19°37S 127°41E **60** C4
Mindiptana *Indonesia* 5°55S 140°22E **37** F10
Mindoro *Phil.* 13°0N 121°0E **37** B6
Mindoro Str. *Phil.* 12°30N 120°30E **37** B6
Mine *Japan* 34°12N 131°7E **29** G5
Minehead *U.K.* 51°12N 3°29W **13** F4
Mineola N.Y., U.S.A. 40°44N 73°38W **83** F11
Mineola Tex., U.S.A. 32°40N 95°29W **84** E7
Mineral King *U.S.A.* 36°27N 118°36W **78** J8
Mineral Wells *U.S.A.* 32°48N 98°7W **84** E5
Miners Bay *Canada* 44°49N 78°46W **82** B6
Minersville *U.S.A.* 40°41N 76°16W **83** F8
Minerva N.Y., U.S.A. 43°47N 73°59W **83** C11
Minerva Ohio, U.S.A. 40°44N 81°6W **82** F3
Minetto *U.S.A.* 43°24N 76°28W **83** C8
Minfeng *China* 37°4N 82°46E **30** D5
Mingäçevir Su Anbarı
  Azerbaijan 40°57N 46°50E **19** F8
Mingan *Canada* 50°20N 64°0W **73** B7
Mingechaurskoye Vdkhr. =
  Mingäçevir Su Anbarı
  Azerbaijan 40°57N 46°50E **19** F8
Mingela *Australia* 19°52S 146°38E **62** B4
Mingenew *Australia* 29°12S 115°21E **61** E2
Mingera Cr. → *Australia* 20°38S 137°45E **62** C2
Minggang *China* 32°24N 114°3E **35** A10
Mingguang *China* 32°46N 117°59E **35** A11
Mingin *Burma* 22°50N 94°30E **41** H19
Minglun *China* 25°10N 108°21E **34** E7
Mingo Junction *U.S.A.* 40°19N 80°37W **82** F4
Mingora *Pakistan* 34°48N 72°22E **43** B5
Mingshan *China* 30°3N 103°10E **34** B4
Mingteke Daban = Mintaka Pass
  Pakistan 37°0N 74°58E **43** A6
Mingxi *China* 26°18N 117°12E **35** D11
Mingyuegue *China* 43°2N 128°50E **33** C15
Minhe *China* 36°9N 102°45E **30** D9
Minho = Miño → *Spain* 41°52N 8°40W **21** A2
Minho *Portugal* 41°25N 8°20W **21** B1
Minhou *China* 26°0N 119°15E **35** E12
Minicoy I. *India* 8°17N 73°2E **45** K1
Minidoka *U.S.A.* 42°45N 113°29W **76** E7
Minigwal, L. *Australia* 29°31S 123°14E **61** E3
Minilya → *Australia* 23°45S 114°0E **61** D1
Minilya Roadhouse
  Australia 23°55S 114°0E **61** D1
Minipi L. *Canada* 52°25N 60°45W **73** B7
Minjilang *Australia* 11°8S 132°3E **60** B5
Mink L. *Canada* 61°54N 117°40W **70** A5
Minna *Nigeria* 9°37N 6°30E **52** G7
Minneapolis Kans., U.S.A. 39°8N 97°42W **80** F5
Minneapolis Minn.,
  U.S.A. 44°57N 93°16W **80** C7
Minnedosa *Canada* 50°14N 99°50W **71** C9
Minnesota □ *U.S.A.* 46°0N 94°15W **80** B6
Minnesota → *U.S.A.* 44°54N 93°9W **80** C7
Minnewaukan *U.S.A.* 48°4N 99°15W **80** A4
Minnipa *Australia* 32°51S 135°9E **63** E2
Minnitaki L. *Canada* 49°57N 92°10W **72** C1
Mino *Japan* 35°32N 136°55E **29** G8
Miño → *Spain* 41°52N 8°40W **21** A2
Minorca = Menorca *Spain* 40°0N 4°0E **21** C8
Minot *U.S.A.* 48°14N 101°18W **80** A3

Minqin *China* 38°38N 103°20E **32** E2
Minqing *China* 26°15N 118°50E **35** D12
Minsk *Belarus* 53°52N 27°30E **17** B14
Mińsk Mazowiecki
  Poland 52°10N 21°33E **17** B11
Mintabie *Australia* 27°15S 133°7E **63** D1
Mintaka Pass *Pakistan* 37°0N 74°58E **43** A6
Minto *Canada* 46°5N 66°5W **73** C6
Minto, L. *Canada* 57°13N 75°0W **72** A5
Minton *Canada* 49°10N 104°35W **71** D8
Minturn *U.S.A.* 39°35N 106°26W **76** G10
Minudasht *Iran* 37°17N 56°7E **47** B8
Minusinsk *Russia* 53°43N 91°20E **27** D10
Minutang *India* 28°15N 96°30E **41** E20
Minvoul *Gabon* 2°9N 12°8E **54** D2
Minya Konka = Gongga Shan
  China 29°40N 101°55E **34** C3
Miraj *India* 16°50N 74°45E **44** L9
Miram Shah *Pakistan* 33°0N 70°2E **42** C4
Miramar *Argentina* 38°15S 57°50W **94** D4
Miramar *Mozam.* 23°50S 35°35E **57** C6
Miramichi *Canada* 47°2N 65°28W **73** C6
Miramichi B. *Canada* 47°15N 65°0W **73** C7
Miranda *Brazil* 20°10S 56°15W **93** H7
Miranda → *Brazil* 19°25S 57°20W **93** G7
Miranda de Ebro *Spain* 42°41N 2°57W **21** A4
Miranda do Douro
  Portugal 41°30N 6°16W **21** B2
Mirandópolis *Brazil* 21°9S 51°6W **95** A5
Mirani *Australia* 21°8S 148°53E **62** b
Mirassol *Brazil* 20°46S 49°28W **95** A6
Mirbāṭ *Oman* 17°0N 54°45E **49** D5
Miri *Malaysia* 4°23N 113°59E **36** D4
Mirialguda *India* 16°52N 79°35E **44** F4
Miriam Vale *Australia* 24°20S 151°33E **62** C5
Mirigama *Sri Lanka* 7°15N 80°8E **45** L5
Mirim, L. *S. Amer.* 32°45S 52°50W **95** C5
Miriuwung Gajerrong ☼
  Australia 15°0S 128°45E **60** C4
Mīrjāveh *Iran* 29°1N 61°30E **47** D9
Mirnyy *Antarctica* 66°50S 92°30E **5** C14
Mirnyy *Russia* 62°33N 113°53E **27** C12
Mirokhan *Pakistan* 27°46N 68°6E **42** F3
Mirond L. *Canada* 55°6N 102°47W **71** B8
Mirpur *Pakistan* 33°32N 73°56E **43** C5
Mirpur Batoro *Pakistan* 24°44N 68°16E **42** G3
Mirpur Bibiwari *Pakistan* 28°33N 67°44E **42** E2
Mirpur Khas *Pakistan* 25°30N 69°0E **42** G3
Mirpur Sakro *Pakistan* 24°33N 67°41E **42** G2
Mirs Bay = Tai Pang Wan
  China 22°33N 114°24E **31** a
Mirtağ *Turkey* 38°23N 41°56E **46** B4
Mirtoo Sea *Greece* 37°0N 23°20E **23** F10
Miryang *S. Korea* 35°31N 128°44E **33** G15
Mirzapur *India* 25°10N 82°34E **43** G10
Mirzapur-cum-Vindhyachal
  = Mirzapur *India* 25°10N 82°34E **43** G10
Misantla *Mexico* 19°56N 96°50W **87** D5
Misawa *Japan* 40°41N 141°24E **28** D10
Miscou I. *Canada* 47°57N 64°31W **73** C7
Misha *India* 7°59N 93°20E **45** L10
Mish'āb, Ra's al
  Si. Arabia 28°15N 48°43E **47** D6
Mishan *China* 45°37N 131°48E **28** B5
Mishawaka *U.S.A.* 41°40N 86°11W **80** E10
Mishima *Japan* 35°10N 138°52E **29** G9
Misión *Mexico* 32°6N 116°53W **79** N10
Misiones □ *Argentina* 27°0S 55°0W **95** B5
Misiones □ *Paraguay* 27°0S 56°0W **94** B4
Miskah *Si. Arabia* 24°49N 42°56E **46** E4
Miskitos, Cayos *Nic.* 14°26N 82°50W **88** D3
Miskolc *Hungary* 48°7N 20°50E **17** D11
Misool *Indonesia* 1°52S 130°10E **37** E8
Miṣr = Egypt ■ *Africa* 28°0N 31°0E **53** C12
Miṣrātah *Libya* 32°24N 15°3E **53** B9
Missanabie *Canada* 48°20N 84°6W **72** C3
Missinaibi → *Canada* 50°43N 81°29W **72** B3
Missinaibi L. *Canada* 48°23N 83°40W **72** C3
Mission *Canada* 49°10N 122°15W **70** D4
Mission S. Dak., U.S.A. 43°18N 100°39W **80** D3
Mission Tex., U.S.A. 26°13N 98°20W **84** H5
Mission Beach *Australia* 17°53S 146°6E **62** B4
Mission Viejo *U.S.A.* 33°36N 117°40W **79** M9
Missisa L. *Canada* 52°20N 85°7W **72** B2
Missisicabi → *Canada* 51°14N 79°31W **72** B4
Mississagi → *Canada* 46°15N 83°9W **72** C3
Mississippi □ *U.S.A.* 33°0N 90°0W **85** E10
Mississippi → *U.S.A.* 29°9N 89°15W **85** G10
Mississippi L. *Canada* 45°5N 76°10W **83** A8
Mississippi River Delta
  U.S.A. 29°10N 89°15W **85** G10
Mississippi Sd. *U.S.A.* 30°20N 89°0W **85** G10
Missoula *U.S.A.* 46°52N 114°1W **76** C6
Missouri □ *U.S.A.* 38°25N 92°30W **80** F7
Missouri → *U.S.A.* 38°49N 90°7W **80** F8
Missouri City *U.S.A.* 29°37N 95°32W **84** G7
Missouri Valley *U.S.A.* 41°34N 95°53W **80** E6
Mist *U.S.A.* 45°59N 123°15W **78** E3
Mistassibi → *Canada* 48°53N 72°13W **73** B5
Mistassini *Canada* 48°53N 72°12W **73** C5
Mistassini → *Canada* 48°42N 72°20W **73** C5
Mistassini, L. *Canada* 51°0N 73°30W **72** B5
Mistastin L. *Canada* 55°57N 63°20W **73** A7
Mistinibi, L. *Canada* 55°56N 64°17W **73** A7
Mistissini *Canada* 48°53N 72°12W **73** C5
Misty L. *Canada* 58°53N 101°40W **71** B8
Misurata = Miṣrātah
  Libya 32°24N 15°3E **53** B9

Mitchell *Australia* 26°29S 147°58E **63** D4
Mitchell *Canada* 43°28N 81°12W **82** C3
Mitchell *Nebr., U.S.A.* 41°57N 103°49W **80** E2
Mitchell *Oreg., U.S.A.* 44°34N 120°9W **76** D3
Mitchell *S. Dak., U.S.A.* 43°43N 98°2W **80** D4
Mitchell → *Australia* 15°12S 141°35E **62** B3
Mitchell, Mt. *U.S.A.* 35°46N 82°16W **85** D13
Mitchell-Alice Rivers △
  Australia 15°28S 142°5E **62** B3
Mitchell Ra. *Australia* 12°49S 135°36E **62** A2
Mitchelstown *Ireland* 52°15N 8°16W **10** D3
Mitha Tiwana *Pakistan* 32°13N 72°6E **42** C5
Mithi *Pakistan* 24°44N 69°48E **42** G3
Mithrao *Pakistan* 27°28N 69°40E **42** F3
Mitilíni *Greece* 39°6N 26°35E **23** E12
Mitla Pass = Mamarr Mitlā
  Egypt 30°2N 32°54E **48** E1
Mito *Japan* 36°20N 140°30E **29** F10
Mitrovicë *Kosovo* 42°54N 20°52E **23** C9
Mitsamiouli *Comoros Is.* 11°20S 43°16E **55** a
Mitsiwa *Eritrea* 15°35N 39°25E **49** D2
Mitsukaidō *Japan* 36°1N 139°59E **29** F9
Mittagong *Australia* 34°28S 150°29E **63** E5
Mittimatalik = Pond Inlet
  Canada 72°40N 77°0W **69** C16
Mitú *Colombia* 1°15N 70°13W **92** C4
Mitumba, Mts.
  Dem. Rep. of the Congo 7°0S 27°30E **54** F5
Mitwaba
  Dem. Rep. of the Congo 8°2S 27°17E **54** F5
Mixteco → *Mexico* 18°11N 98°30W **87** D5
Miyagi □ *Japan* 38°15N 140°45E **28** E10
Miyah, W. el → *Syria* 34°44N 39°57E **46** C3
Miyake-Jima *Japan* 34°5N 139°30E **29** G9
Miyako *Japan* 39°40N 141°59E **28** E10
Miyako-Jima *Japan* 24°45N 125°20E **29** M2
Miyako-Rettō *Japan* 24°24N 125°0E **29** M2
Miyakojima *Japan* 24°48N 125°17E **29** M2
Miyakonojō *Japan* 31°40N 131°5E **29** J5
Miyani *India* 21°50N 69°26E **42** J3
Miyanoura-Dake *Japan* 30°20N 130°31E **29** J5
Miyazaki *Japan* 31°56N 131°30E **29** J5
Miyazaki □ *Japan* 32°30N 131°30E **29** H5
Miyazu *Japan* 35°35N 135°10E **29** G7
Miyet, Bahr el = Dead Sea
  Asia 31°30N 35°30E **48** D4
Miyi *China* 26°47N 102°9E **34** D4
Miyoshi *Japan* 34°48N 132°51E **29** G6
Miyun *China* 40°28N 116°50E **32** D9
Miyun Shuiku *China* 40°30N 117°0E **33** D9
Mizdah *Libya* 31°30N 13°0E **53** B8
Mizen Hd. *Cork, Ireland* 51°27N 9°50W **10** E2
Mizen Hd. *Wicklow, Ireland* 52°51N 6°4W **10** D5
Mizhi *China* 37°47N 110°12E **32** F6
Mizoram □ *India* 23°30N 92°40E **41** H18
Mizpe Ramon *Israel* 30°34N 34°49E **48** E3
Mizuho *Antarctica* 70°30S 41°0E **5** D5
Mizusawa = Ōshū *Japan* 39°8N 141°8E **28** E10
Mjölby *Sweden* 58°20N 15°10E **9** G16
Mjøsa *Norway* 60°40N 11°0E **8** F14
Mkhaya △ *Swaziland* 26°34S 31°45E **57** C5
Mkhuze △ *S. Africa* 29°27S 29°30E **57** C4
Mkomazi → *S. Africa* 30°12S 30°50E **57** D5
Mkuze *S. Africa* 27°10S 32°0E **57** C5
Mladá Boleslav *Czech Rep.* 50°27N 14°53E **16** C8
Mlange = Mulanje, Mt.
  Malawi 16°2S 35°33E **55** H7
Mława *Poland* 53°9N 20°25E **17** B11
Mlawula △ *Swaziland* 26°12S 32°2E **57** C5
Mljet *Croatia* 42°43N 17°30E **22** C7
Mmabatho *S. Africa* 25°49S 25°30E **56** C4
Mo i Rana *Norway* 66°20N 14°7E **8** C16
Moa *Australia* 10°11S 142°16E **62** a
Moa *Cuba* 20°40N 74°56W **89** B4
Moa *Indonesia* 8°0S 128°0E **37** F7
Moa → *S. Leone* 6°59N 11°36W **52** G3
Moab *U.S.A.* 38°35N 109°33W **76** G9
Moala *Fiji* 18°36S 179°53E **59** a
Moama *Australia* 36°7S 144°46E **63** F3
Moamba *Mozam.* 25°36S 32°15E **57** D5
Moapa *U.S.A.* 36°40N 114°37W **79** J12
Moate *Ireland* 53°24N 7°44W **10** C4
Mobārakābād *Iran* 28°24N 53°20E **47** D7
Mobaye *C.A.R.* 4°25N 21°5E **54** D4
Moberly *U.S.A.* 39°25N 92°26W **80** F7
Moberly Lake *Canada* 55°50N 121°44W **70** B4
Mobile *U.S.A.* 30°41N 88°3W **85** F10
Mobile B. *U.S.A.* 30°30N 88°0W **85** F11
Mobridge *U.S.A.* 45°32N 100°26W **80** C3
Moc Chau *Vietnam* 20°50N 104°38E **38** B5
Moc Hoa *Vietnam* 10°46N 105°56E **39** G5
Moçambique = Mozambique ■
  Africa 19°0S 35°0E **55** H7
Moçambique *Mozam.* 15°3S 40°42E **55** H8
Moce *Fiji* 18°40S 178°29W **59** a
Mocanaqua *U.S.A.* 41°9N 76°8W **83** E8
Moce *Fiji* 18°40S 178°29W **59** a
Mochima △ *Venezuela* 10°30N 64°5W **89** D7
Mochudi *Botswana* 24°27S 26°7E **56** B4
Mocimboa da Praia
  Mozam. 11°25S 40°20E **54** G8
Moclips *U.S.A.* 47°14N 124°13W **78** C2
Mocoa *Colombia* 1°7N 76°35W **92** C3
Mococa *Brazil* 21°28S 47°0W **95** A6
Mocorito *Mexico* 25°29N 107°55W **86** B3
Moctezuma *Mexico* 29°48N 109°42W **86** B3
Moctezuma → *Mexico* 21°59N 98°34W **87** C5
Mocuba *Mozam.* 16°54S 36°57E **55** H7
Modane *France* 45°12N 6°40E **20** D7
Modasa *India* 23°30N 73°21E **42** H5
Modder → *S. Africa* 29°2S 24°37E **56** D3
Modderrivier *S. Africa* 29°2S 24°38E **56** D3
Módena *Italy* 44°40N 10°55E **22** B4
Modena *U.S.A.* 37°48N 113°56W **77** H7
Modesto *U.S.A.* 37°39N 121°0W **78** H6
Módica *Italy* 36°52N 14°46E **22** F6
Modimolle *S. Africa* 24°42S 28°22E **57** B4
Modjadjiskloof *S. Africa* 23°42S 30°10E **57** B5
Moe *Australia* 38°12S 146°19E **63** F4
Moengo *Suriname* 5°45N 54°20W **93** B8

Moenjodaro = Mohenjodaro
  Pakistan 27°19N 68°7E **42** F3
Moffat *U.K.* 55°21N 3°27W **11** F5
Moga *India* 30°48N 75°8E **42** D6
Mogadishu = Muqdisho
  Somalia 2°2N 45°25E **49** G4
Mogador = Essaouira
  Morocco 31°32N 9°42W **52** B4
Mogalakwena →
  S. Africa 22°38S 28°40E **57** B4
Mogami-Gawa → *Japan* 38°45N 140°0E **28** E10
Mogaung *Burma* 25°20N 97°0E **41** G20
Mogi-Mirim *Brazil* 22°29S 47°0W **93** H9
Mogilev = Mahilyow
  Belarus 53°55N 30°18E **17** B16
Mogilev-Podolskiy = Mohyliv-
  Podilskyy *Ukraine* 48°26N 27°48E **17** D14
Mogocha *Russia* 53°40N 119°50E **27** D12
Mogoditshane *Botswana* 24°37S 25°51E **56** B4
Mogok *Burma* 23°0N 96°40E **41** H20
Mogollon Rim *U.S.A.* 34°10N 110°50W **77** J8
Mogumber *Australia* 31°2S 116°3E **61** F2
Mogwadi → *S. Africa* 23°4S 29°36E **57** B4
Mohács *Hungary* 45°58N 18°41E **17** F10
Mohala *India* 20°35N 80°44E **44** D5
Mohales Hoek *Lesotho* 30°7S 27°26E **56** D4
Mohali *India* 30°47N 76°41E **42** D7
Mohall *U.S.A.* 48°46N 101°31W **80** A3
Mohammadābād *Iran* 37°52N 59°5E **47** B8
Mohammedia *Morocco* 33°44N 7°21W **52** B4
Mohana *India* 19°27N 84°14E **44** G8
Mohana → *India* 24°43N 85°0E **43** G11
Mohave, L. *U.S.A.* 35°12N 114°34W **79** K12
Mohawk → *U.S.A.* 42°47N 73°41W **83** D11
Mohéli *Comoros Is.* 12°20S 43°40E **55** a
Mohenjodaro *Pakistan* 27°19N 68°7E **42** F3
Moher, Cliffs of *Ireland* 52°58N 9°27W **10** D2
Mohicanville Res. *U.S.A.* 40°45N 82°9W **82** F2
Mohns Ridge *Arctic* 72°30N 5°0W **4** B7
Mohsenābād *Iran* 36°40N 59°35E **47** B8
Mohyliv-Podilskyy
  Ukraine 48°26N 27°48E **17** D14
Moidart, L. *U.K.* 56°47N 5°52W **11** E3
Moinabad *India* 17°44N 77°16E **44** F3
Moisaküla *Estonia* 58°3N 25°12E **9** G21
Moisie *Canada* 50°12N 66°1W **73** B6
Moisie → *Canada* 50°14N 66°5W **73** B6
Mojave *U.S.A.* 35°3N 118°10W **79** K8
Mojave Desert *U.S.A.* 35°0N 116°30W **79** L10
Moji das Cruzes *Brazil* 23°31S 46°11W **95** A6
Moji-Guaçu → *Brazil* 20°53S 48°10W **95** A6
Mojiang *China* 23°37N 101°35E **34** F3
Mojo *Bolivia* 21°48S 65°33W **94** A2
Mojokerto *Indonesia* 7°28S 112°26E **37** G15
Mokala △ *S. Africa* 29°10S 24°10E **56** C3
Mokameh *India* 25°24N 85°55E **43** G11
Mokau *N.Z.* 38°42S 174°39E **59** C5
Mokelumne → *U.S.A.* 38°13N 121°28W **78** G5
Mokelumne Hill *U.S.A.* 38°18N 120°43W **78** G6
Mokhotlong *Lesotho* 29°22S 29°2E **57** C4
Mokoan, L. *Australia* 36°25S 146°5E **63** C4
Mokokchung *India* 26°15N 94°30E **41** F19
Mokolo → *S. Africa* 23°14S 27°43E **57** B4
Mokopane *S. Africa* 24°10S 28°55E **57** B4
Mokra Gora *Europe* 42°50N 20°30E **23** C9
Mol *Belgium* 51°11N 5°5E **15** C5
Molakalmuru *India* 14°55N 76°50E **45** G3
Molchanovo *Russia* 57°40N 83°50E **26** D9
Mold *U.K.* 53°9N 3°8W **12** D4
Moldavia = Moldova ■
  Europe 47°0N 28°0E **17** E15
Moldavia *Romania* 46°30N 27°0E **17** E14
Molde *Norway* 62°45N 7°9E **8** E12
Moldova ■ *Europe* 47°0N 28°0E **17** E15
Moldoveanu, Vf.
  Romania 45°36N 24°45E **17** F13
Mole → *U.K.* 51°24N 0°21W **13** F7
Molepolole *Botswana* 24°28S 25°28E **56** B4
Molfetta *Italy* 41°12N 16°36E **22** D7
Moline *U.S.A.* 41°30N 90°31W **80** E8
Molinos *Argentina* 25°28S 66°15W **94** B2
Mollendo *Peru* 17°0S 72°0W **92** G4
Mollerin, L. *Australia* 30°30S 117°35E **61** F2
Molodechno = Maladzyechna
  Belarus 54°20N 26°50E **17** A14
Molodezhnaya *Antarctica* 67°40S 45°51E **5** C9
Moloka'i *U.S.A.* 21°8N 157°0W **75** L8
Molokai Fracture Zone
  Pac. Oc. 28°0N 125°0W **65** E15
Molong *Australia* 33°5S 148°54E **63** E4
Molopo → *Africa* 28°30S 20°12E **56** D3
Molson L. *Canada* 54°22N 96°40W **71** C9
Molteno *S. Africa* 31°22S 26°22E **56** D4
Molu *Indonesia* 6°45S 131°40E **37** F8
Molucca Sea *Indonesia* 0°0 125°0E **37** E6
Moluccas = Maluku
  Indonesia 1°0S 127°0E **37** E7
Moma *Mozam.* 16°47S 39°4E **55** H7
Mombasa *Kenya* 4°3S 39°40E **54** E7
Mombetsu *Japan* 44°21N 143°22E **28** B11
Momchilgrad *Bulgaria* 41°33N 25°23E **23** D11
Mompós *Colombia* 9°14N 74°26W **92** B4
Møn *Denmark* 54°57N 12°20E **9** J15
Mon □ *Burma* 16°0N 97°30E **41** L20
Mona, Canal de la = Mona
  Passage *W. Indies* 18°30N 67°45W **89** C6
Mona, Isla *Puerto Rico* 18°5N 67°54W **89** C6
Mona, Pta. *Costa Rica* 9°37N 82°36W **88** E3
Mona Passage *W. Indies* 18°30N 67°45W **89** C6
Monaca *U.S.A.* 40°41N 80°17W **82** F4
Monaco ■ *Europe* 43°46N 7°23E **20** E7
Monadhliath Mts. *U.K.* 57°10N 4°4W **11** D4
Monadnock, Mt. *U.S.A.* 42°52N 72°7W **83** D12
Monaghan *Ireland* 54°15N 6°57W **10** B5

Monaghan □ *Ireland* 54°11N 6°56W **10** B5
Monahans *U.S.A.* 31°36N 102°54W **84** F3
Monar, L. *U.K.* 57°26N 5°8W **11** D3
Monaragala *Sri Lanka* 6°52N 81°22E **45** L5
Monarch Mt. *Canada* 51°55N 125°57W **70** C3
Monashee Mts. *Canada* 51°0N 118°43W **70** C5
Monasterevin *Ireland* 53°8N 7°4W **10** C4
Monastir = Bitola
  Macedonia 41°1N 21°20E **23** D9
Monastir *Tunisia* 35°50N 10°49E **53** A8
Monbetsu = Hidaka
  Japan 42°30N 142°10E **28** C11
Moncayo, Sierra del *Spain* 41°48N 1°50W **21** B5
Monchegorsk *Russia* 67°54N 32°58E **8** C25
Mönchengladbach
  Germany 51°11N 6°27E **16** C4
Monchique *Portugal* 37°19N 8°38W **21** D1
Moncks Corner *U.S.A.* 33°12N 80°1W **85** E14
Monclova *Mexico* 26°54N 101°25W **86** B4
Moncton *Canada* 46°7N 64°51W **73** C7
Mondego → *Portugal* 40°9N 8°52W **21** B1
Mondeodo *Indonesia* 3°34S 122°9E **37** E6
Mondlo *S. Africa* 27°59S 30°43E **57** C5
Mondoví *Italy* 44°23N 7°49E **20** D7
Mondrain I. *Australia* 34°9S 122°14E **61** F3
Moneague *Jamaica* 18°16N 77°7W **88** a
Moneron, Ostrov
  Russia 46°15N 141°16E **28** A10
Monessen *U.S.A.* 40°9N 79°54W **82** F5
Monett *U.S.A.* 36°55N 93°55W **80** G7
Moneymore *U.K.* 54°41N 6°40W **10** B5
Monforte de Lemos *Spain* 42°31N 7°33W **21** A2
Mong Hpayak *Burma* 20°52N 99°55E **38** B2
Mong Hsat *Shan, Burma* 21°54N 98°30E **34** G2
Mong Hsat *Shan, Burma* 21°53N 99°15E **38** B2
Mong Kung *Burma* 21°35N 97°35E **41** J20
Mong Nai *Burma* 20°32N 97°46E **41** J20
Mong Ping *Burma* 21°22N 99°2E **34** G2
Mong Tai = Shan □
  Burma 21°30N 98°30E **41** J21
Mong Ton *Burma* 20°17N 98°45E **41** J21
Mong Yai *Burma* 22°21N 98°3E **41** H21
Mong Yang *Burma* 21°50N 99°41E **38** B2
Mongalla *South Sudan* 5°8N 31°42E **53** G12
Mongers, L. *Australia* 29°25S 117°5E **61** E2
Monghyr = Munger
  India 25°23N 86°30E **43** G12
Mongibello = Etna *Italy* 37°50N 14°55E **22** F6
Mongo *Chad* 12°14N 18°43E **53** F9
Mongolia ■ *Asia* 47°0N 103°0E **30** B9
Mongolia, Plateau of
  Asia 45°0N 105°0E **24** D12
Mongu *Zambia* 15°16S 23°12E **55** H4
Mõngua *Angola* 16°43S 15°20E **56** A2
Monifieth *U.K.* 56°30N 2°48W **11** E6
Monkey Mia *Australia* 25°48S 113°43E **61** E1
Monkey River *Belize* 16°22N 88°29W **87** D7
Monkland *Canada* 45°11N 74°52W **83** A10
Monkoto
  Dem. Rep. of the Congo 1°38S 20°35E **54** E4
Monkton *Canada* 43°35N 81°5W **82** C3
Monmouth *U.K.* 51°48N 2°42W **13** F5
Monmouth *Ill., U.S.A.* 40°55N 90°39W **80** E8
Monmouth *Oreg.,
  U.S.A.* 44°51N 123°14W **76** D2
Monmouthshire □ *U.K.* 51°48N 2°54W **13** F5
Mono, Pta. *Nic.* 12°0N 83°30W **88** D3
Mono L. *U.S.A.* 38°1N 119°1W **78** H7
Monolith *U.S.A.* 35°7N 118°22W **79** K8
Monongahela *U.S.A.* 40°12N 79°56W **82** F5
Monópoli *Italy* 40°57N 17°18E **22** D7
Monos I. *Trin. & Tob.* 10°42N 61°44W **93** K15
Monroe *Ga., U.S.A.* 33°47N 83°43W **85** E13
Monroe *La., U.S.A.* 32°30N 92°7W **84** E8
Monroe *Mich., U.S.A.* 41°55N 83°24W **81** E12
Monroe *N.C., U.S.A.* 34°59N 80°33W **85** D14
Monroe *N.Y., U.S.A.* 41°20N 74°11W **83** E10
Monroe *Utah, U.S.A.* 38°38N 112°7W **76** G7
Monroe *Wash., U.S.A.* 47°51N 121°58W **78** C5
Monroe *Wis., U.S.A.* 42°36N 89°38W **80** D9
Monroe City *U.S.A.* 39°39N 91°44W **80** F8
Monroeton *U.S.A.* 41°43N 76°29W **83** E8
Monroeville *Ala., U.S.A.* 31°31N 87°20W **85** F11
Monroeville *Pa., U.S.A.* 40°26N 79°45W **82** F5
Monrovia *Liberia* 6°18N 10°47W **52** G3
Mons *Belgium* 50°27N 3°58E **15** D3
Monse *Indonesia* 4°7S 123°15E **37** E6
Mont-de-Marsan *France* 43°54N 0°31W **20** E3
Mont-Joli *Canada* 48°37N 68°10W **73** C6
Mont-Laurier *Canada* 46°35N 75°30W **72** C4
Mont-Louis *Canada* 49°15N 65°44W **73** C6
Mont-St-Michel, Le
  France 48°40N 1°30W **20** B3
Mont-Tremblant △
  Canada 46°30N 74°30W **72** C5
Montagu *S. Africa* 33°45S 20°8E **56** E3
Montagu I. *Antarctica* 58°25S 26°20W **5** B1
Montague *Canada* 46°10N 62°39W **73** C7
Montague, I. *Mexico* 31°45N 114°48W **86** A2
Montague I. *U.S.A.* 60°0N 147°30W **74** D7
Montague Ra. *Australia* 27°15S 119°30E **61** E2
Montague Sd. *Australia* 14°28S 125°20E **60** B4
Montálbán *Spain* 40°50N 0°45W **21** B5
Montalvo *U.S.A.* 34°15N 119°12W **79** L7
Montana *Bulgaria* 43°27N 23°16E **23** C10
Montaña *Peru* 6°0S 73°0W **92** E4
Montana □ *U.S.A.* 47°0N 110°0W **76** C9
Montargis *France* 47°59N 2°43E **20** C5
Montauban *France* 44°2N 1°21E **20** D4
Montauk *U.S.A.* 41°3N 71°57W **83** E13
Montauk Pt. *U.S.A.* 41°4N 71°52W **83** E13
Montbéliard *France* 47°31N 6°48E **20** C7
Montceau-les-Mines
  France 46°40N 4°23E **20** C6
Montclair *U.S.A.* 40°49N 74°12W **83** F10
Monte Albán *Mexico* 17°2N 96°46W **87** D5
Monte Alegre *Brazil* 2°0S 54°0W **93** D8
Monte Azul *Brazil* 15°9S 42°53W **93** G10
Monte-Carlo *Monaco* 43°44N 7°25E **20** E7

Monte Caseros *Argentina* 30°10S 57°50W **94** C4
Monte Comán *Argentina* 34°40S 67°53W **94** C2
Monte Cristi *Dom. Rep.* 19°52N 71°39W **89** C5
Monte Lindo →
  Paraguay 23°56S 57°12W **94** A4
Monte Patria *Chile* 30°42S 70°58W **94** C1
Monte Quemado
  Argentina 25°53S 62°41W **94** B3
Monte Rio *U.S.A.* 38°28N 123°0W **78** G4
Monte Santu, C. di *Italy* 40°5N 9°44E **22** D3
Monte Vista *U.S.A.* 37°35N 106°9W **77** H10
Monteagudo *Argentina* 27°14S 54°8W **95** B5
Montebello *Canada* 45°40N 74°55W **72** C5
Montebello Is. *Australia* 20°30S 115°45E **60** D2
Montecarlo *Argentina* 26°34S 54°47W **95** B5
Montecito *U.S.A.* 34°26N 119°40W **79** L7
Montecristi *Ecuador* 1°0S 80°40W **92** D2
Montecristo *Italy* 42°20N 10°19E **22** C4
Montego Bay *Jamaica* 18°28N 77°55W **88** a
Montélimar *France* 44°33N 4°45E **20** D6
Montello *U.S.A.* 43°48N 89°20W **80** D9
Montemorelos *Mexico* 25°12N 99°49W **87** B5
Montenegro *Brazil* 29°39S 51°29W **95** B5
Montenegro ■ *Europe* 42°40N 19°20E **23** C8
Montepuez *Mozam.* 13°8S 38°59E **55** G7
Monterey *U.S.A.* 36°37N 121°55W **78** J5
Monterey B. *U.S.A.* 36°45N 122°0W **78** J5
Montería *Colombia* 8°46N 75°53W **92** B3
Monteros *Argentina* 27°11S 65°30W **94** B2
Monterrey *Mexico* 25°40N 100°19W **86** B4
Montes Azules △ *Mexico* 16°21N 91°3W **87** D6
Montes Claros *Brazil* 16°30S 43°50W **93** G10
Montesano *U.S.A.* 46°59N 123°36W **78** D3
Montesilvano *Italy* 42°29N 14°8E **22** C6
Montevideo *Uruguay* 34°50S 56°11W **95** C4
Montevideo *U.S.A.* 44°57N 95°43W **80** C6
Montezuma *U.S.A.* 41°35N 92°32W **80** E7
Montezuma Castle △
  U.S.A. 34°39N 111°45W **77** J8
Montgomery *U.K.* 52°34N 3°8W **13** E4
Montgomery *Ala.,
  U.S.A.* 32°23N 86°19W **85** E11
Montgomery *Pa., U.S.A.* 41°10N 76°53W **82** E8
Montgomery *W. Va.,
  U.S.A.* 38°11N 81°19W **81** F13
Montgomery City *U.S.A.* 38°59N 91°30W **80** F8
Monticello *Ark., U.S.A.* 33°38N 91°47W **84** E9
Monticello *Fla., U.S.A.* 30°33N 83°52W **85** F13
Monticello *Ind., U.S.A.* 40°45N 86°46W **81** E9
Monticello *Iowa, U.S.A.* 42°15N 91°12W **80** D8
Monticello *Ky., U.S.A.* 36°50N 84°51W **81** G11
Monticello *Minn., U.S.A.* 45°18N 93°48W **80** C7
Monticello *Miss., U.S.A.* 31°33N 90°7W **85** F9
Monticello *N.Y., U.S.A.* 41°39N 74°42W **83** E10
Monticello *Utah, U.S.A.* 37°52N 109°21W **77** H9
Montijo *Portugal* 38°41N 8°54E **21** C1
Montilla *Spain* 37°36N 4°40W **21** D3
Montluçon *France* 46°22N 2°36E **20** C5
Montmagny *Canada* 46°58N 70°34W **73** C5
Montmartre *Canada* 50°14N 103°27W **71** C8
Montmorillon *France* 46°26N 0°50E **20** C4
Monto *Australia* 24°52S 151°6E **62** C5
Montongbuwoh *Indonesia* 8°33S 116°4E **37** K19
Montoro *Spain* 38°1N 4°27E **21** C3
Montour Falls *U.S.A.* 42°21N 76°51W **82** D8
Montoursville *U.S.A.* 41°15N 76°55W **82** E8
Montpelier *Idaho, U.S.A.* 42°19N 111°18W **76** E8
Montpelier *Vt., U.S.A.* 44°16N 72°35W **83** B12
Montpellier *France* 43°37N 3°52E **20** E5
Montréal → *Canada* 47°14N 84°39W **72** C3
Montréal L. *Canada* 54°20N 105°45W **71** C7
Montreal Lake *Canada* 54°3N 105°46W **71** C7
Montreux *Switz.* 46°26N 6°55E **20** C7
Montrose *U.K.* 56°44N 2°27W **11** E6
Montrose *Colo., U.S.A.* 38°29N 107°53W **76** G10
Montrose *Pa., U.S.A.* 41°50N 75°53W **83** E9
Monts, Pte. des *Canada* 49°20N 67°12W **73** C6
Montserrat ☑ *W. Indies* 16°40N 62°10W **89** C7
Monywa *Burma* 22°7N 95°11E **41** H19
Monze *Zambia* 16°17S 27°29E **55** H5
Monze, C. *Pakistan* 24°47N 66°37E **42** G2
Monzón *Spain* 41°52N 0°10E **21** B6
Mooers *U.S.A.* 44°58N 73°35W **83** B11
Mooi → *S. Africa* 28°45S 30°34E **57** C5
Mooi River *S. Africa* 29°13S 29°50E **57** C4
Mookgopong *S. Africa* 24°38S 28°44E **57** B4
Moomba *Australia* 28°6S 140°12E **63** A3
Moonah → *Australia* 22°3S 138°33E **62** C2
Moonda, L. *Australia* 25°52S 140°25E **62** D3
Moonie *Australia* 27°46S 150°20E **63** D5
Moonie → *Australia* 29°19S 148°43E **63** D4
Moonta *Australia* 34°6S 137°32E **63** E2
Moora *Australia* 30°37S 115°58E **61** F2
Moorcroft *U.S.A.* 44°16N 104°57W **76** D11
Moore → *Australia* 31°22S 115°30E **61** F2
Moore, L. *Australia* 29°50S 117°35E **61** E2
Moore Falls *Canada* 44°48N 78°48E **82** B6
Moore Park *Australia* 24°43S 152°17E **62** C5
Moore Res. *U.S.A.* 44°20N 71°53W **83** B13
Moore River △ *Australia* 31°7S 115°39E **61** F2
Moorefield *U.S.A.* 39°4N 78°58W **81** F14
Moorfoot Hills *U.K.* 55°44N 3°8W **11** F5
Moorhead *U.S.A.* 46°53N 96°45W **80** B5
Moorpark *U.S.A.* 34°17N 118°53W **79** L8
Moorreesburg *S. Africa* 33°6S 18°38E **56** D2
Moorrinya △ *Australia* 21°42S 144°58E **62** C3
Moosa → *Canada* 51°20N 80°25E **72** B3
Moose → *U.S.A.* 43°38N 75°24W **83** C9
Moose Creek *Canada* 45°15N 74°58W **83** A10
Moose Factory *Canada* 51°16N 80°32W **72** B3
Moose Jaw *Canada* 50°24N 105°30W **71** C7
Moose Jaw → *Canada* 50°34N 105°18W **71** C7
Moose Lake *Canada* 53°46N 100°8W **71** C8
Moose Lake *U.S.A.* 46°27N 92°46W **80** B7
Moose Mountain
  Canada 49°48N 102°25W **71** D8
Moosehead L. *U.S.A.* 45°38N 69°40W **81** C19
Mooselookmeguntic L.
  U.S.A. 44°55N 70°49W **83** B14

Moosilauke, Mt. *U.S.A.* 44°3N 71°40W **83** B13
Moosomin *Canada* 50°9N 101°40W **71** C8
Moosonee *Canada* 51°17N 80°39W **72** B3
Moosup *U.S.A.* 41°43N 71°53W **83** E13
Mopane *S. Africa* 22°37S 29°52E **57** B4
Mopipi *Botswana* 21°6S 24°55E **56** B3
Mopti *Mali* 14°30N 4°0W **52** F5
Moqor *Afghan.* 32°50N 67°42E **42** C2
Moquegua *Peru* 17°15S 70°46W **92** G4
Mora *Sweden* 61°2N 14°38E **8** F16
Mora *Minn., U.S.A.* 45°53N 93°18W **80** C7
Mora *N. Mex., U.S.A.* 35°58N 105°20W **77** J11
Moradabad *India* 28°50N 78°50E **43** E8
Morafenobe *Madag.* 17°50S 44°53E **55** H8
Moramanga *Madag.* 18°56S 48°12E **55** H9
Moran *Kans., U.S.A.* 37°55N 95°10W **80** G6
Moran *Wyo., U.S.A.* 43°50N 110°31W **76** E8
Moranbah *Australia* 22°1S 148°6E **62** C4
Morang = Biratnagar
  Nepal 26°27N 87°17E **43** F12
Morant Bay *Jamaica* 17°53N 76°25W **88** a
Morant Cays *Jamaica* 17°22N 76°0W **88** C4
Morant Pt. *Jamaica* 17°55N 76°12W **88** a
Morar *India* 26°14N 78°14E **42** F8
Morar, L. *U.K.* 56°57N 5°40W **11** E3
Moratuwa *Sri Lanka* 6°45N 79°55E **45** L4
Morava → *Serbia* 44°36N 21°4E **23** B9
Morava → *Slovak Rep.* 48°10N 16°59E **17** D9
Moravia *U.S.A.* 42°43N 76°25W **83** D8
Moravian Hts. = Českomoravská
  Vrchovina *Czech Rep.* 49°30N 15°40E **16** D8
Morawa *Australia* 29°13S 116°0E **61** E2
Morawhanna *Guyana* 8°30N 59°40W **92** B7
Moray □ *U.K.* 57°31N 3°18W **11** D5
Moray Firth *U.K.* 57°40N 3°52W **11** D5
Morbi *India* 22°50N 70°42E **42** H4
Morden *Canada* 49°15N 98°10W **71** D9
Mordovian Republic =
  Mordvinia □ *Russia* 54°20N 44°30E **18** D7
Mordvinia □ *Russia* 54°20N 44°30E **18** D7
Moreau → *U.S.A.* 45°18N 100°43W **80** C3
Morebeng *S. Africa* 23°30S 29°55E **57** B4
Morecambe *U.K.* 54°5N 2°52W **12** C5
Morecambe B. *U.K.* 54°7N 3°0W **12** C5
Moree *Australia* 29°28S 149°54E **63** D4
Morehead *U.S.A.* 38°11N 83°26W **81** F12
Morehead City *U.S.A.* 34°43N 76°43W **85** D16
Morel → *India* 26°13N 76°36E **42** F7
Morelia *Mexico* 19°42N 101°7W **86** D4
Morella *Australia* 23°0S 143°52E **62** C3
Morella *Spain* 40°35N 0°5W **21** B5
Morelos *Mexico* 26°42N 107°40W **86** B3
Morelos □ *Mexico* 18°45N 99°0W **87** D5
Moremi △ *Botswana* 19°18S 23°10E **56** A3
Morena *India* 26°30N 78°4E **42** F8
Morena, Sierra *Spain* 38°20N 4°0W **21** C3
Moreno Valley *U.S.A.* 33°56N 117°14W **79** M10
Moresby I. *Canada* 52°30N 131°40W **70** C2
Moreton I. *Australia* 27°10S 153°25E **63** D5
Moreton Island △
  Australia 27°2S 153°24E **63** D5
Morgan *U.S.A.* 41°2N 111°41W **76** F8
Morgan City *U.S.A.* 29°42N 91°12W **84** G9
Morgan Hill *U.S.A.* 37°8N 121°39W **78** H5
Morganfield *U.S.A.* 37°41N 87°55W **80** G10
Morganton *U.S.A.* 35°45N 81°41W **85** D14
Morgantown *U.S.A.* 39°38N 79°57W **81** F14
Morgenzon *S. Africa* 26°45S 29°36E **57** C4
Morghak *Iran* 29°7N 57°54E **47** D8
Morhar → *India* 25°29N 85°11E **43** G11
Mori *Japan* 42°6N 140°35E **28** C10
Moriarty *U.S.A.* 34°59N 106°3W **77** J10
Morice L. *Canada* 53°50N 127°40W **70** C3
Morinville *Canada* 53°49N 113°41W **70** C6
Morioka *Japan* 39°45N 141°8E **28** E10
Morioka *Mexico* 28°10N 108°32W **86** B3
Morlaix *France* 48°36N 3°52W **20** B2
Mormugao = Marmagao
  India 15°25N 73°56E **45** G1
Mornington *Australia* 38°15S 145°5E **63** F4
Mornington, I. *Chile* 49°50S 75°30W **96** F1
Mornington I. *Australia* 16°30S 139°30E **62** B2
Moro *Pakistan* 26°40N 68°0E **42** F3
Moro → *Pakistan* 29°42N 67°22E **42** E2
Moro G. *Phil.* 6°30N 123°0E **37** C6
Morocco ■ *N. Afr.* 32°0N 5°50W **52** B4
Morogoro *Tanzania* 6°50S 37°40E **54** F7
Moroleón *Mexico* 20°8N 101°12W **86** C4
Morombe *Madag.* 21°45S 43°22E **55** J8
Morón *Argentina* 34°39S 58°37W **94** C4
Morón *Cuba* 22°8N 78°39W **88** B4
Mörön *Mongolia* 49°38N 100°9E **30** B9
Morón de la Frontera
  Spain 37°6N 5°28W **21** D3
Morona → *Peru* 4°40S 77°10W **92** D3
Morondava *Madag.* 20°17S 44°17E **55** J8
Morongo Valley *U.S.A.* 34°3N 116°37W **79** L10
Moroni *Comoros Is.* 11°40S 43°16E **55** a
Moroni *U.S.A.* 39°32N 111°35W **76** G8
Morotai *Indonesia* 2°10N 128°30E **37** D7
Moroto *Uganda* 2°28N 34°42E **54** D6
Morpeth *Canada* 42°23N 81°50W **82** D3
Morpeth *U.K.* 55°10N 1°41W **12** B6
Morphou *Cyprus* 35°12N 32°59E **46** C4
Morrilton *U.S.A.* 35°9N 92°44W **84** D8
Morrinhos *Brazil* 17°45S 49°10W **93** G9
Morrinsville *N.Z.* 37°40S 175°32E **59** B5
Morris *Canada* 49°25N 97°22W **71** D9
Morris *Ill., U.S.A.* 41°22N 88°26W **80** E9
Morris *Minn., U.S.A.* 45°35N 95°55W **80** C6
Morris *N.Y., U.S.A.* 42°33N 75°15W **83** D9
Morris *Pa., U.S.A.* 41°35N 77°17W **82** E7
Morris, Mt. *Australia* 26°9S 131°4E **61** E5
Morris Jesup, Kap
  Greenland 83°40N 34°0W **66** A16
Morrisburg *Canada* 44°55N 75°7W **83** B9
Morristown *Ariz.,
  U.S.A.* 33°51N 112°37W **77** K7
Morristown *N.J., U.S.A.* 40°48N 74°29W **83** F10

Morristown *N.Y., U.S.A.* 44°35N 75°39W **83** B9
Morristown *Tenn.,*
 U.S.A. 36°13N 83°18W **85** C13
Morrisville *N.Y., U.S.A.* 42°53N 75°35W **83** D9
Morrisville *Pa., U.S.A.* 40°13N 74°47W **83** F10
Morrisville *Vt., U.S.A.* 44°34N 72°36W **83** B12
Morro, Pta. *Chile* 27°6S 71°0W **94** B1
Morro Bay *U.S.A.* 35°22N 120°51W **78** K6
Morrocoy △ *Venezuela* 10°48N 68°13W **89** D6
Morrosquillo, G. de
 Colombia 9°35N 75°40W **88** E4
Morrumbene *Mozam.* 23°31S 35°16E **57** B6
Morshansk *Russia* 53°28N 41°50E **18** D7
Morsi *India* 21°21N 78°0E **44** J10
Morteros *Argentina* 30°50S 62°0W **94** C3
Mortlach *Canada* 50°27N 106°4W **71** C7
Mortlake *Australia* 38°5S 142°50E **63** F3
Morton *Tex., U.S.A.* 33°44N 102°46W **84** E3
Morton *Wash., U.S.A.* 46°34N 122°17W **78** D4
Moruga *Trin. & Tob.* 10°4N 61°16W **93** K15
Morundah *Australia* 34°57S 146°19E **63** E4
Moruya *Australia* 35°58S 150°3E **63** F5
Morvan *France* 47°5N 4°3E **20** C6
Morven *Australia* 26°22S 147°5E **63** D4
Morvern *U.K.* 56°38N 5°44W **11** E3
Morwell *Australia* 38°10S 146°22E **63** F4
Morzhovets, Ostrov
 Russia 66°44N 42°35E **18** A7
Mosakahiken = Moose Lake
 Canada 53°46N 100°8W **71** C8
Moscos Is. *Burma* 14°0N 97°30E **38** F1
Moscow *Idaho, U.S.A.* 46°44N 117°0W **76** C5
Moscow *Pa., U.S.A.* 41°20N 75°31W **83** E9
Mosel → *Europe* 50°22N 7°36E **20** A7
Moselle = Mosel →
 Europe 50°22N 7°36E **20** A7
Moses Lake *U.S.A.* 47°8N 119°17W **76** C4
Mosgiel *N.Z.* 45°53S 170°21E **59** F3
Moshaweng → *S. Africa* 26°35S 22°50E **56** C3
Moshchnyy, Ostrov *Russia* 60°1N 27°50E **9** F22
Moshi *Tanzania* 3°22S 37°18E **54** E7
Moshupa *Botswana* 24°46S 25°29E **56** B4
Mosi-oa-Tunya = Victoria Falls
 Zimbabwe 17°58S 25°52E **55** H5
Mosjøen *Norway* 65°51N 13°12E **8** D15
Moskenesøya *Norway* 67°58N 13°0E **8** C15
Moskenstraumen
 Norway 67°47N 12°45E **8** C15
Mosomane *Botswana* 24°2S 26°19E **56** B4
Mosonmagyaróvár
 Hungary 47°52N 17°18E **17** E9
Mosquera *Colombia* 2°35N 78°24W **92** C3
Mosquero *U.S.A.* 35°47N 103°58W **77** J12
Mosquitia *Honduras* 15°20N 84°10W **88** C3
Mosquito Creek L.
 U.S.A. 41°18N 80°46W **82** E4
Mosquito L. *Canada* 62°35N 103°20W **71** A8
Mosquitos, G. de los
 Panama 9°15N 81°10W **88** E3
Moss *Norway* 59°27N 10°40E **9** G14
Moss Vale *Australia* 34°32S 150°25E **63** E5
Mossaka *Congo* 1°15S 16°45E **54** E3
Mossbank *Canada* 49°56N 105°56W **71** D7
Mossburn *N.Z.* 45°41S 168°15E **59** F2
Mosselbaai *S. Africa* 34°11S 22°8E **56** D3
Mossendjo *Congo* 2°55S 12°42E **54** E2
Mossgiel *Australia* 33°15S 144°5E **63** E3
Mossman *Australia* 16°21S 145°15E **62** B4
Mossoró *Brazil* 5°10S 37°15W **93** E11
Most *Czech Rep.* 50°31N 13°38E **16** C7
Mostaganem *Algeria* 35°54N 0°5E **52** A6
Mostar *Bos.-H.* 43°22N 17°50E **23** C7
Mostardas *Brazil* 31°2S 50°51W **95** C5
Mostiska = Mostyska
 Ukraine 49°48N 23°4E **17** D12
Mosty = Masty *Belarus* 53°27N 24°38E **17** B13
Mostyska *Ukraine* 49°48N 23°4E **17** D12
Mosul = Al Mawşil *Iraq* 36°15N 43°5E **46** B4
Motagua → *Guatemala* 15°44N 88°14W **88** C2
Motala *Sweden* 58°32N 15°1E **9** G16
Motaze *Mozam.* 24°48S 32°52E **57** B5
Moth *India* 25°43N 78°57E **43** G8
Motherwell *U.K.* 55°47N 3°58W **11** F5
Motihari *India* 26°30N 84°55E **43** F11
Motozintla de Mendoza
 Mexico 15°22N 92°14W **87** D6
Motril *Spain* 36°31N 3°37W **21** D4
Mott *U.S.A.* 46°23N 102°20W **80** B2
Motueka *N.Z.* 41°7S 173°1E **59** D4
Motueka → *N.Z.* 41°5S 173°1E **59** D4
Motul *Mexico* 21°6N 89°17W **87** C7
Mouchalagane →
 Canada 50°56N 68°41W **73** B6
Mouding *China* 25°20N 101°28E **34** E3
Moudros *Greece* 39°50N 25°18E **23** E11
Mouhoun = Black Volta →
 Africa 8°41N 1°33W **52** G5
Mouila *Gabon* 1°50S 11°0E **54** E2
Moulamein *Australia* 35°3S 144°1E **63** F3
Moule à Chique, C.
 St. Lucia 13°43N 60°57W **89** f
Moulins *France* 46°35N 3°19E **20** C5
Moulmein *Burma* 16°30N 97°40E **41** L20
Moulouya, O. → *Morocco* 35°5N 2°25W **52** B5
Moultrie *U.S.A.* 31°11N 83°47W **85** F13
Moultrie, L. *U.S.A.* 33°20N 80°5W **85** E14
Mound City *Mo., U.S.A.* 40°7N 95°14W **80** E6
Mound City *S. Dak.,*
 U.S.A. 45°44N 100°4W **80** C3
Moundou *Chad* 8°40N 16°10E **53** G9
Moundsville *U.S.A.* 39°55N 80°44W **82** G4
Moung *Cambodia* 12°46N 103°27E **38** F4
Mount Airy *U.S.A.* 36°31N 80°37W **85** C14
Mount Albert *Canada* 44°9N 79°19W **82** B5
Mount Aspiring △ *N.Z.* 44°19S 168°47E **59** F2
Mount Barker *S. Austral.,*
 Australia 35°5S 138°52E **63** F2
Mount Barker *W. Austral.,*
 Australia 34°38S 117°40E **61** F2

Mount Barnett Roadhouse
 Australia 16°39S 125°57E **60** C4
Mount Brydges *Canada* 42°54N 81°29W **82** D3
Mount Burr *Australia* 37°34S 140°26E **63** F3
Mount Carmel = Ha Karmel △
 Israel 32°45N 35°5E **48** C4
Mount Carmel *Ill.,*
 U.S.A. 38°25N 87°46W **80** F10
Mount Carmel *Pa.,*
 U.S.A. 40°47N 76°26W **83** F8
Mount Clemens *U.S.A.* 42°35N 82°53W **82** D2
Mount Coolon *Australia* 21°25S 147°25E **62** C4
Mount Desert I. *U.S.A.* 44°21N 68°20W **81** C19
Mount Dora *U.S.A.* 28°48N 81°38W **85** G14
Mount Ebenezer *Australia* 25°6S 132°34E **61** E5
Mount Edziza △ *Canada* 57°30N 130°45W **70** B2
Mount Field △ *Australia* 42°39S 146°35E **63** G4
Mount Fletcher *S. Africa* 30°40S 28°30E **57** D4
Mount Forest *Canada* 43°59N 80°43W **82** C4
Mount Frankland △
 Australia 31°47S 116°37E **61** F2
Mount Frederick ۞
 Australia 19°39S 129°18E **60** C4
Mount Gambier
 Australia 37°50S 140°46E **63** F3
Mount Garnet *Australia* 17°37S 145°6E **62** B4
Mount Holly *U.S.A.* 39°59N 74°47W **83** G10
Mount Holly Springs
 U.S.A. 40°7N 77°12W **82** F7
Mount Hope *N.S.W.,*
 Australia 32°51S 145°51E **63** E4
Mount Hope *S. Austral.,*
 Australia 34°7S 135°23E **63** E2
Mount Isa *Australia* 20°42S 139°26E **62** C2
Mount James ۞
 Australia 24°51S 116°54E **61** D2
Mount Jewett *U.S.A.* 41°44N 78°39W **82** E6
Mount Kaputar △
 Australia 30°16S 150°10E **63** E5
Mount Kisco *U.S.A.* 41°12N 73°44W **83** E11
Mount Laguna *U.S.A.* 32°52N 116°25W **79** N10
Mount Larcom *Australia* 23°48S 150°59E **62** C5
Mount Lofty Ranges
 Australia 34°35S 139°5E **63** E2
Mount Magnet *Australia* 28°2S 117°47E **61** E2
Mount Maunganui *N.Z.* 37°40S 176°14E **59** B6
Mount Molloy *Australia* 16°42S 145°20E **62** B4
Mount Morgan
 Australia 23°40S 150°25E **62** C5
Mount Morris *U.S.A.* 42°44N 77°52W **82** D7
Mount Pearl *Canada* 47°31N 52°47W **73** C9
Mount Penn *U.S.A.* 40°20N 75°54W **83** F9
Mount Perry *Australia* 25°13S 151°42E **63** D5
Mount Pleasant *Iowa,*
 U.S.A. 40°58N 91°33W **80** E8
Mount Pleasant *Mich.,*
 U.S.A. 43°36N 84°46W **81** D11
Mount Pleasant *Pa.,*
 U.S.A. 40°9N 79°33W **82** F5
Mount Pleasant *S.C.,*
 U.S.A. 32°47N 79°52W **85** E15
Mount Pleasant *Tenn.,*
 U.S.A. 35°32N 87°12W **85** D11
Mount Pleasant *Tex.,*
 U.S.A. 33°9N 94°58W **84** E7
Mount Pleasant *Utah,*
 U.S.A. 39°33N 111°27W **76** G8
Mount Pocono *U.S.A.* 41°7N 75°22W **83** E9
Mount Rainier △
 U.S.A. 46°55N 121°50W **78** D5
Mount Revelstoke △
 Canada 51°5N 118°30W **70** C5
Mount Robson △ *Canada* 53°0N 119°0W **70** C5
Mount St. Helens △
 U.S.A. 46°14N 122°11W **78** D4
Mount Selinda *Zimbabwe* 20°24S 32°43E **57** B5
Mount Shasta *U.S.A.* 41°19N 122°19W **76** F2
Mount Signal *U.S.A.* 32°39N 115°37W **79** N11
Mount Sterling *Ill.,*
 U.S.A. 39°59N 90°45W **80** F8
Mount Sterling *Ky.,*
 U.S.A. 38°4N 83°56W **81** F12
Mount Surprise
 Australia 18°10S 144°17E **62** B3
Mount Union *U.S.A.* 40°23N 77°53W **82** F7
Mount Upton *U.S.A.* 42°26N 75°23W **83** D9
Mount Vernon *Ill.,*
 U.S.A. 38°19N 88°55W **80** F9
Mount Vernon *Ind.,*
 U.S.A. 37°56N 87°54W **75** H22
Mount Vernon *Ohio,*
 U.S.A. 40°23N 82°29W **82** F2
Mount Vernon *Wash.,*
 U.S.A. 48°25N 122°20W **78** B4
Mount William △
 Australia 40°56S 148°14E **63** G4
Mountain Ash *U.K.* 51°40N 3°23W **13** F4
Mountain Center
 U.S.A. 33°42N 116°44W **79** M10
Mountain City *Nev.,*
 U.S.A. 41°50N 115°58W **76** F6
Mountain City *Tenn.,*
 U.S.A. 36°29N 81°48W **85** C14
Mountain Dale *U.S.A.* 41°41N 74°32W **83** E10
Mountain Grove *U.S.A.* 37°8N 92°16W **80** G7
Mountain Home *Ark.,*
 U.S.A. 36°20N 92°23W **84** C8
Mountain Home *Idaho,*
 U.S.A. 43°8N 115°41W **76** E6
Mountain Iron *U.S.A.* 47°32N 92°37W **80** B7
Mountain Pass *U.S.A.* 35°29N 115°35W **79** K11
Mountain View *Ark.,*
 U.S.A. 35°52N 92°7W **84** D8
Mountain View *Calif.,*
 U.S.A. 37°23N 122°5W **78** H4
Mountain Zebra △
 S. Africa 32°14S 25°27E **56** D4
Mountainair *U.S.A.* 34°31N 106°15W **77** J10
Mountbellew *Ireland* 53°28N 8°31W **10** C3

Mountlake Terrace
 U.S.A. 47°47N 122°18W **78** C4
Mountmellick *Ireland* 53°7N 7°20W **10** C4
Mountrath *Ireland* 53°0N 7°28W **10** D4
Moura *Australia* 24°35S 149°58E **62** C4
Moura *Brazil* 1°32S 61°38W **92** D6
Moura *Portugal* 38°7N 7°30W **21** C2
Mourdi, Dépression du
 Chad 18°10N 23°0E **53** E10
Mourilyan *Australia* 17°35S 146°3E **62** B4
Mourne → *U.K.* 54°52N 7°26W **10** B4
Mourne Mts. *U.K.* 54°10N 6°0W **10** B5
Mouscron *Belgium* 50°45N 3°12E **15** D3
Moussoro *Chad* 13°41N 16°35E **53** F9
Moutong *Indonesia* 0°28N 121°13E **37** D6
Movas *Mexico* 28°10N 109°25W **86** B3
Moville *Ireland* 55°11N 7°3W **10** A4
Mowandjum *Australia* 17°22S 123°40E **60** C3
Moy → *Ireland* 54°8N 9°8W **10** B2
Moya *Comoros Is.* 12°18S 44°18E **55** a
Moyale *Kenya* 3°30N 39°4E **54** D7
Moyen Atlas *Morocco* 33°0N 5°0W **52** B4
Moyo *Indonesia* 8°10S 117°40E **36** F5
Moyobamba *Peru* 6°0S 77°0W **92** E3
Moyyero → *Russia* 68°44N 103°42E **27** C11
Moyynqum *Kazakhstan* 44°12N 71°0E **28** E8
Moyynty *Kazakhstan* 47°10N 73°18E **26** E8
Mozambique = Moçambique
 Mozam. 15°3S 40°42E **55** H8
Mozambique ■ *Africa* 19°0S 35°0E **55** H7
Mozambique Chan.
 Africa 17°30S 42°30E **57** A7
Mozdok *Russia* 43°45N 44°48E **19** F7
Mozdūrān *Iran* 36°9N 60°35E **47** B9
Mozhnābād *Iran* 34°7N 60°6E **47** C9
Mozyr = Mazyr *Belarus* 51°59N 29°15E **17** B15
Mpanda *Tanzania* 6°23S 31°1E **54** F6
Mphoeng *Zimbabwe* 21°10S 27°51E **57** B4
Mpika *Zambia* 11°51S 31°25E **55** G6
Mpumalanga *S. Africa* 29°50S 30°33E **57** D5
Mpumalanga □ *S. Africa* 26°0S 30°0E **57** C5
Mpwapwa *Tanzania* 6°23S 36°30E **54** F7
Mqanduli *S. Africa* 31°49S 28°45E **57** D4
Msaken *Tunisia* 35°49N 10°33E **53** A8
M'sila *Algeria* 35°46N 4°30E **52** A6
Mstislavl = Mstsislaw
 Belarus 54°0N 31°50E **17** A16
Mstsislaw *Belarus* 54°0N 31°50E **17** A16
Mtamvuna = Mthamvuna →
 S. Africa 31°6S 30°12E **57** D5
Mthamvuna → *S. Africa* 31°6S 30°12E **57** D5
Mthatha *S. Africa* 31°36S 28°49E **57** D4
Mtubatuba *S. Africa* 28°30S 32°8E **57** C5
Mtwalume *S. Africa* 30°30S 30°38E **57** D5
Mtwara-Mikindani
 Tanzania 10°20S 40°20E **54** G8
Mu Gia, Deo *Vietnam* 17°40N 105°47E **38** D5
Mu Ko Chang △
 Thailand 11°59N 102°22E **39** G4
Mu Ko Surin *Thailand* 9°30N 97°55E **39** H1
Mu Us Shamo *China* 39°0N 109°0E **32** E5
Muang Beng *Laos* 20°23N 101°46E **34** G3
Muang Chiang Rai = Chiang Rai
 Thailand 19°52N 99°50E **34** H2
Muang Et *Laos* 20°49N 104°1E **38** B5
Muang Hiam *Laos* 20°5S 103°22E **38** B4
Muang Hongsa *Laos* 19°43N 101°20E **38** C3
Muang Houn *Laos* 20°8N 101°23E **34** G3
Muang Kau *Laos* 15°6N 105°47E **38** E5
Muang Khao *Laos* 19°38N 103°32E **38** C4
Muang Khong *Laos* 14°7N 105°51E **38** E5
Muang Khoua *Laos* 21°5N 102°31E **34** G4
Muang Liap *Laos* 18°29N 101°40E **38** C3
Muang Mai *Thailand* 8°5N 98°21E **39** a
Muang May *Laos* 14°49N 106°56E **38** E6
Muang Na Mo *Laos* 21°3N 101°49E **34** G3
Muang Ngeun *Laos* 20°36N 101°3E **34** G3
Muang Ngoi *Laos* 20°43N 102°41E **34** G4
Muang Nong *Laos* 16°22N 106°30E **38** D6
Muang Ou Neua *Laos* 22°18N 101°48E **34** F3
Muang Ou Tay *Laos* 22°7N 101°48E **34** F3
Muang Pak Beng *Laos* 19°54N 101°8E **34** H3
Muang Phalane *Laos* 16°39N 105°34E **38** D5
Muang Phiang *Laos* 19°6N 101°32E **38** C3
Muang Phine *Laos* 16°32N 106°2E **38** D6
Muang Saiapoun *Laos* 18°24N 101°31E **38** C3
Muang Sing *Laos* 21°11N 101°9E **34** G3
Muang Son *Laos* 20°27N 103°19E **38** B4
Muang Soui *Laos* 19°33N 102°52E **38** C4
Muang Va *Laos* 21°53N 102°19E **34** G4
Muang Va *Laos* 18°18N 101°20E **34** G3
Muang Xai *Laos* 20°42N 101°59E **34** G3
Muang Xamteu *Laos* 19°59N 104°38E **38** C5
Muar *Malaysia* 2°3N 102°34E **39** L4
Muarabungo *Indonesia* 1°28S 102°52E **36** E2
Muaraenim *Indonesia* 3°40S 103°50E **36** E2
Muarajuloi *Indonesia* 0°12S 114°3E **36** E4
Muarakaman *Indonesia* 0°2S 116°45E **36** E5
Muaratebo *Indonesia* 1°30S 102°26E **36** E2
Muaratembesi *Indonesia* 1°42S 103°8E **36** E2
Muarateweh *Indonesia* 0°58S 114°52E **36** E4
Mubarakpur *India* 26°6N 83°18E **43** F10
Mubarraz = Al Mubarraz
 Si. Arabia 25°30N 49°40E **47** E6
Mubi *Nigeria* 10°18N 13°16E **53** F8
Mucajaí → *Brazil* 2°25N 60°52W **92** C6
Muchinga Mts. *Zambia* 11°30S 31°30E **55** G6
Muchuan *China* 28°57N 103°53E **34** C4
Muck *U.K.* 56°50N 6°15W **11** E2
Muckadilla *Australia* 26°35S 148°23E **63** D4
Muckaty ۞ *Australia* 18°37S 133°52E **62** B1
Muckle Flugga *U.K.* 60°51N 0°54W **11** A8
Mucuri *Brazil* 18°0S 39°36W **93** G11
Mucusso *Angola* 18°1S 21°25E **56** B3
Mudanjiang *China* 44°38N 129°30E **33** B15
Mudanya *Turkey* 40°25N 28°50E **23** D13
Muddebihal *India* 16°20N 76°8E **45** F3
Muddy Cr. → *U.S.A.* 38°24N 110°42W **76** G8
Mudgee *Australia* 32°32S 149°31E **63** E4

Mudhol *Andhra Pradesh,*
 India 18°58N 77°55E **44** E3
Mudhol *Karnataka, India* 16°21N 75°17E **45** F2
Mudigere *India* 13°8N 75°38E **45** H2
Mudjatik → *Canada* 56°1N 107°36W **71** B7
Mudukulattur *India* 9°21N 78°31E **45** K4
Mudumu △ *Namibia* 18°5S 23°29E **56** A3
Mueller Ranges
 Australia 18°18S 126°46E **60** C4
Muerto, Mar *Mexico* 16°10N 94°10W **87** D6
Mufu Shan *China* 29°20N 114°30E **35** C10
Mufulira *Zambia* 12°32S 28°15E **55** G5
Mughal Sarai *India* 25°18N 83°7E **43** G10
Mughayrā' *Si. Arabia* 29°17N 37°41E **46** D3
Mugi *Japan* 33°40N 134°25E **29** H7
Muğla *Turkey* 37°15N 28°22E **23** F13
Mugu *Nepal* 29°45N 82°30E **43** E10
Mugu Karnali → *Nepal* 29°38N 81°51E **43** E9
Muhammad, Râs *Egypt* 27°44N 34°16E **46** E2
Muhammad Qol *Sudan* 20°53N 37°9E **53** D13
Muhammadabad *India* 26°4N 83°25E **43** F10
Mühlhausen *Germany* 51°12N 10°27E **16** C6
Mühlig Hofmann fjell
 Antarctica 72°30S 5°0E **5** D3
Muhos *Finland* 64°47N 25°59E **8** D21
Muhu *Estonia* 58°36N 23°11E **9** G20
Mui Wo *China* 22°16N 113°59E **31** a
Muileann gCearr, An = Mullingar
 Ireland 53°31N 7°21W **10** C4
Muine Bheag = Bagenalstown
 Ireland 52°42N 6°58W **10** D5
Muineachán = Monaghan
 Ireland 54°15N 6°57W **10** B5
Muir, L. *Australia* 34°30S 116°40E **61** F2
Muir of Ord *U.K.* 57°32N 4°28W **11** D4
Mujeres, I. *Mexico* 21°13N 86°43W **88** B2
Muka, Tanjung *Malaysia* 5°28N 100°11E **39** c
Mukacheve *Ukraine* 48°27N 22°45E **17** D12
Mukachevo = Mukacheve
 Ukraine 48°27N 22°45E **17** D12
Mukah *Malaysia* 2°55N 112°5E **36** D4
Mukandwara *India* 24°49N 75°59E **42** G6
Mukawwa, Geziret *Egypt* 23°55N 35°53E **46** E2
Mukdahan *Thailand* 16°32N 104°43E **38** D5
Mukdahan △ *Thailand* 16°26N 104°45E **38** D5
Mukden = Shenyang
 China 41°48N 123°27E **33** D12
Mukerian *India* 31°57N 75°37E **42** D6
Mukher *India* 18°42N 77°22E **44** E3
Mukinbudin *Australia* 30°55S 118°5E **61** F2
Muko Phetra △ *Thailand* 6°57N 99°33E **39** J2
Mukomuko *Indonesia* 2°30S 101°10E **36** E2
Muktinath *Nepal* 28°49N 83°53E **43** E10
Muktsar *India* 30°30N 74°30E **42** D6
Mukur = Moqor *Afghan.* 32°50N 67°42E **42** C2
Mukutawa → *Canada* 53°10N 97°24W **71** C9
Mul *India* 20°4N 79°40E **44** D4
Mula *Spain* 38°3N 1°33W **21** C5
Mula → *India* 18°34N 74°21E **44** E2
Mula → *Pakistan* 27°57N 67°36E **42** F2
Mulanje, Mt. *Malawi* 16°2S 35°33E **55** H7
Mulbagal *India* 13°10N 78°24E **45** H4
Mulchatna → *U.S.A.* 59°40N 157°7W **74** D8
Mulchén *Chile* 37°45S 72°20W **94** D1
Mulde → *Germany* 51°53N 12°15E **16** C7
Mule Creek Junction
 U.S.A. 43°23N 104°13W **76** E11
Mulegé *Mexico* 26°53N 111°59W **86** B2
Muleshoe *U.S.A.* 34°13N 102°43W **84** D3
Mulgrave *Canada* 45°38N 61°31W **73** C7
Mulgrave I. = Badu
 Australia 10°7S 142°11E **62** a
Mulhacén *Spain* 37°4N 3°20W **21** D4
Mulhouse *France* 47°40N 7°20E **20** C7
Muli *China* 27°52N 101°8E **34** D3
Mulifanua *Samoa* 13°50S 171°59W **59** b
Muling *China* 44°35N 130°10E **33** B16
Mulki *India* 13°6N 74°48E **45** H2
Mull *U.K.* 56°25N 5°56W **11** E3
Mull, Sound of *U.K.* 56°30N 5°50W **11** E3
Mullaittivu *Sri Lanka* 9°15N 80°49E **45** K5
Mullen *U.S.A.* 42°3N 101°1W **80** D3
Mullengudgery *Australia* 31°43S 147°23E **63** E4
Mullens *U.S.A.* 37°35N 81°23W **81** G13
Muller, Pegunungan
 Indonesia 0°30N 113°30E **36** D4
Mullet Pen. *Ireland* 54°13N 10°2W **10** B1
Mullewa *Australia* 28°29S 115°30E **61** E2
Mulligan → *Australia* 25°0S 139°0E **62** D2
Mullingar *Ireland* 53°31N 7°21W **10** C4
Mullins *U.S.A.* 34°12N 79°15W **85** D15
Mullumbimby *Australia* 28°30S 153°30E **63** D5
Mulonga Plain *Zambia* 16°45S 24°0E **55** H4
Mulroy B. *Ireland* 55°15N 7°46W **10** A4
Mulshi L. *India* 18°30N 73°48E **44** E1
Multai *India* 21°50N 78°21E **44** D4
Multan *Pakistan* 30°15N 71°36E **42** D4
Mulug *India* 18°11N 79°57E **44** E4
Mulvane *U.S.A.* 37°29N 97°15W **80** G5
Mulwala, L. *Australia* 35°59S 146°1E **63** C4
Mun → *Thailand* 15°19N 105°30E **38** E5
Muna *Indonesia* 5°0S 122°30E **37** F6
Munabao *India* 25°45N 70°17E **42** G4
Munamagi *Estonia* 57°43N 27°4E **9** H22
Munaung *Burma* 18°45N 93°40E **41** K18
Munaung I. = Cheduba I.
 Burma 18°45N 93°40E **41** K18
Muncan *Indonesia* 8°34S 115°11E **37** K18
Muncar *Indonesia* 8°26S 114°20E **37** J17
Munchen-Gladbach =
 Mönchengladbach
 Germany 51°11N 6°27E **16** C4
Muncho Lake *Canada* 59°0N 125°50W **70** B3
Munch'ŏn *N. Korea* 39°14N 127°19E **33** E14
Muncie *U.S.A.* 40°12N 85°23W **81** E11
Muncoonie L. West
 Australia 25°12S 138°40E **62** D2
Mundabbera *Australia* 25°36S 151°18E **63** D5
Mundakayam *India* 9°30N 76°50E **45** K3

Mundal *Sri Lanka* 7°48N 79°48E **45** L4
Munday *U.S.A.* 33°27N 99°38W **84** E5
Münden *Germany* 51°25N 9°38E **16** C5
Mundiwindi *Australia* 23°47S 120°9E **60** D3
Mundo Novo *Brazil* 11°50S 40°29W **93** F10
Mundra *India* 22°54N 69°48E **42** H3
Mundrabilla *Australia* 31°52S 127°51E **61** F4
Muneru → *India* 16°45N 80°3E **44** F5
Mungallala *Australia* 26°28S 147°34E **63** D4
Mungallala Cr. →
 Australia 28°53S 147°5E **63** D4
Mungana *Australia* 17°8S 144°27E **62** B3
Mungaoli *India* 24°24N 78°7E **42** G8
Mungbere
 Dem. Rep. of the Congo 2°36N 28°28E **54** D5
Mungeli *India* 22°4N 81°41E **43** H9
Munger *India* 25°23N 86°30E **43** G12
Mungerannie *Australia* 28°1S 138°39E **63** A2
Mungilli ۞ *Australia* 25°14S 124°17E **61** E3
Mungkan Kandju △
 Australia 13°35S 142°52E **62** A3
Mungkarta ۞ *Australia* 20°22S 134°2E **62** C1
Munising *U.S.A.* 46°25N 86°40W **80** B10
Munku-Sardyk *Russia* 51°45N 100°20E **27** D11
Munnsville *U.S.A.* 42°58N 75°35W **83** D9
Muñoz Gamero, Pen.
 Chile 52°30S 73°5W **96** G2
Munroe L. *Canada* 59°13N 98°35W **71** B9
Munsan *S. Korea* 37°51N 126°48E **33** F14
Münster *Germany* 51°58N 7°37E **16** C4
Munster □ *Ireland* 52°18N 8°44W **10** D3
Muntadgin *Australia* 31°45S 118°33E **61** F2
Muntok *Indonesia* 2°5S 105°10E **36** E3
Muong Nhie *Vietnam* 22°12N 102°28E **34** F4
Muong Sen *Vietnam* 19°24N 104°8E **38** C5
Muong Te *Vietnam* 22°24N 102°49E **34** F4
Muong Xia *Vietnam* 20°19N 104°50E **38** B5
Muonio *Finland* 67°57N 23°40E **8** C20
Muonio älv = Muonionjoki →
 Finland 67°11N 23°34E **8** C20
Muonioälven = Muonionjoki →
 Finland 67°11N 23°34E **8** C20
Muonionjoki → *Finland* 67°11N 23°34E **8** C20
Mupa → *Mozam.* 18°58S 35°54E **57** A6
Muping *China* 37°22N 121°36E **33** F11
Muqdisho *Somalia* 2°2N 45°25E **49** G4
Mur → *Austria* 46°18N 16°52E **17** E9
Murakami *Japan* 38°14N 139°29E **28** E9
Muralag = Prince of Wales I.
 Australia 10°40S 142°10E **62** a
Murallón, Cerro *Chile* 49°48S 73°30W **96** F2
Murang'a *Kenya* 0°45S 37°9E **54** E7
Murashi *Russia* 59°30N 49°0E **18** C8
Murat → *Turkey* 38°46N 40°0E **19** G7
Muratlı *Turkey* 41°10N 27°29E **23** D12
Murayama *Japan* 38°30N 140°25E **28** E10
Murchison → *Australia* 27°45S 114°0E **61** E1
Murchison, Mt.
 Antarctica 73°25S 166°20E **5** D11
Murchison Falls *Uganda* 2°15N 31°30E **54** D6
Murchison Ra. *Australia* 20°0S 134°10E **62** C1
Murchison Roadhouse
 Australia 27°39S 116°14E **61** E2
Murcia *Spain* 38°5N 1°10W **21** D5
Murcia □ *Spain* 37°50N 1°30W **21** D5
Murdo *U.S.A.* 43°53N 100°43W **80** D3
Murdoch Pt. *Australia* 14°37S 144°55E **62** A3
Mureş → *Romania* 46°15N 20°13E **17** E11
Mureşul = Mureş →
 Romania 46°15N 20°13E **17** E11
Murewa *Zimbabwe* 17°39S 31°47E **57** A5
Murfreesboro *N.C.,*
 U.S.A. 36°27N 77°6W **85** C16
Murfreesboro *Tenn.,*
 U.S.A. 35°51N 86°24W **85** D11
Murgap *Tajikistan* 38°10N 74°2E **26** F8
Murgap → *Turkmenistan* 38°18N 61°12E **47** B9
Murgenella *Australia* 11°34S 132°56E **60** B5
Murgha Kibzai *Pakistan* 30°44N 69°25E **42** D3
Murghob = Murgap
 Tajikistan 38°10N 74°2E **26** F8
Murgon *Australia* 26°15S 151°54E **63** D5
Muri *India* 23°22N 85°52E **43** H11
Muria *Indonesia* 6°36S 110°53E **37** G14
Muriaé *Brazil* 21°8S 42°23W **95** A7
Müritz *Germany* 53°25N 12°42E **16** B7
Murliganj *India* 25°54N 86°59E **43** G12
Murmansk *Russia* 68°57N 33°10E **8** B25
Murmashi *Russia* 68°47N 32°42E **8** B25
Murom *Russia* 55°35N 42°3E **18** C7
Muroran *Japan* 42°25N 141°0E **28** C10
Muroto *Japan* 33°18N 134°9E **29** H7
Muroto-Misaki *Japan* 33°15N 134°10E **29** H7
Murphy *U.S.A.* 43°13N 116°33W **76** E5
Murphys *U.S.A.* 38°8N 120°28W **78** G6
Murray *Australia* 9°56S 144°2E **62** a
Murray *Ky., U.S.A.* 36°37N 88°19W **80** G9
Murray *Utah, U.S.A.* 40°40N 111°53W **76** F8
Murray → *Australia* 35°20S 139°22E **63** F2
Murray, L. *U.S.A.* 34°3N 81°13W **85** D14
Murray Bridge *Australia* 35°6S 139°14E **63** F2
Murray Fracture Zone
 Pac. Oc. 35°0N 130°0W **65** D14
Murray Harbour *Canada* 46°0N 62°28W **73** C7
Murray River △
 Australia 34°23S 140°32E **63** E3
Murraysburg *S. Africa* 31°58S 23°47E **56** C3
Murree *Pakistan* 33°56N 73°28E **42** C5
Murrieta *U.S.A.* 33°33N 117°13W **79** M9
Murrumbidgee →
 Australia 34°43S 143°12E **63** E3
Murrumburrah
 Australia 34°32S 148°22E **63** E4
Murrurundi *Australia* 31°42S 150°51E **63** E5
Murshidabad *India* 24°11N 88°19E **43** G13
Murtazapur *India* 20°40N 77°25E **44** D3
Murtle L. *Canada* 52°8N 119°38W **70** C5
Murtoa *Australia* 36°35S 142°28E **63** F3
Murud *India* 18°19N 72°58E **44** E1

Mururoa
  French Polynesia 21°52S 138°55W **65** K14
Murwara *India* 23°46N 80°28E **43** H9
Murwillumbah *Australia* 28°18S 153°27E **63** D5
Murzûq *Libya* 25°53N 13°57E **53** C8
Murzûq, Idehân *Libya* 24°50N 13°51E **53** D8
Mürzzuschlag *Austria* 47°36N 15°41E **16** E8
Mus *India* 9°14N 92°47E **45** K11
Muş *Turkey* 38°45N 41°30E **46** B4
Mûsa, Gebel *Egypt* 28°33N 33°59E **46** D2
Musa Khel *Pakistan* 30°59N 69°52E **42** D3
Mûsa Qal'eh *Afghan.* 32°20N 64°50E **40** C4
Musafirkhana *India* 26°22N 81°48E **43** F9
Musala *Bulgaria* 42°13N 23°37E **23** C10
Musala *Indonesia* 1°41N 98°28E **36** D1
Musan *N. Korea* 42°12N 129°12E **33** C15
Musay'id *Qatar* 25°0N 51°33E **47** E6
Muscat = Masqat *Oman* 23°37N 58°36E **49** C6
Muscatine *U.S.A.* 41°25N 91°3W **80** E8
Muscle Shoals *U.S.A.* 34°45N 87°40W **85** D11
Musgrave Harbour
  Canada 49°27N 53°58W **73** C9
Musgrave Ranges
  Australia 26°0S 132°0E **61** E5
Mushie
  Dem. Rep. of the Congo 2°56S 16°55E **54** E3
Musi → *India* 16°41N 79°40E **44** F4
Musi → *Indonesia* 2°20S 104°56E **36** E2
Musina *S. Africa* 22°20S 30°5E **57** B5
Musiri *India* 10°56N 78°27E **45** J4
Muskeg → *Canada* 60°20N 123°20W **70** A4
Muskegon *U.S.A.* 43°14N 86°16W **80** D10
Muskegon → *U.S.A.* 43°14N 86°21W **80** D10
Muskegon Heights
  U.S.A. 43°12N 86°16W **80** D10
Muskogee *U.S.A.* 35°45N 95°22W **84** D7
Muskoka, L. *Canada* 45°0N 79°25W **82** B5
Muskoka Falls *Canada* 44°59N 79°17W **82** B5
Muskwa → *Canada* 58°47N 122°48W **70** B4
Muslimiyah *Syria* 36°19N 37°12E **46** B3
Musoma *Tanzania* 1°30S 33°48E **54** E6
Musquaro, L. *Canada* 50°38N 61°5W **73** B7
Musquodoboit Harbour
  Canada 44°50N 63°9W **73** D7
Musselburgh *U.K.* 55°57N 3°2W **11** F5
Musselshell → *U.S.A.* 47°21N 107°57W **76** C10
Mussende *Angola* 10°32S 16°5E **54** G3
Mussoorie *India* 30°27N 78°6E **42** D8
Mussuco *Angola* 17°2S 19°3E **56** A2
Mustafakemalpaşa
  Turkey 40°2N 28°24E **23** D13
Mustang *India* 29°10N 83°55E **43** E10
Musters, L. *Argentina* 45°20S 69°25W **96** F3
Musudan *N. Korea* 40°50N 129°43E **33** D15
Muswellbrook *Australia* 32°16S 150°56E **63** E5
Mût *Egypt* 25°28N 28°58E **53** C11
Mut *Turkey* 36°40N 33°28E **46** B2
Mutanda *Mozam.* 21°0S 33°34E **57** B5
Mutare *Zimbabwe* 18°58S 32°38E **55** H6
Mutawintji △ *Australia* 31°10S 142°30E **63** E3
Muting *Indonesia* 7°23S 140°20E **37** F10
Mutki = Mirtağ *Turkey* 38°23N 41°56E **46** B4
Mutoko *Zimbabwe* 17°24S 32°13E **57** A5
Mutoray *Russia* 60°56N 101°0E **27** C11
Mutsamudu *Comoros Is.* 12°10S 44°25E **55** a
Mutsu *Japan* 41°5N 140°55E **28** D10
Mutsu-Wan *Japan* 41°5N 140°55E **28** D10
Muttaburra *Australia* 22°38S 144°29E **62** C3
Mutton I. *Ireland* 52°49N 9°32W **10** D2
Muttukuru *India* 14°16N 80°6E **45** G5
Mutur *Sri Lanka* 8°27N 81°16E **45** K5
Muweilih *Egypt* 30°42N 34°19E **48** E3
Muy Muy *Nic.* 12°39N 85°36W **88** D2
Muynak *Uzbekistan* 43°44N 59°10E **26** E6
Muyunkum, Peski = Moyynqum
  Kazakhstan 44°12N 71°0E **30** C3
Muz Tag *China* 36°25N 87°25E **30** D6
Muzaffarabad *Pakistan* 34°25N 73°30E **43** B5
Muzaffargarh *Pakistan* 30°5N 71°14E **42** D4
Muzaffarnagar *India* 29°26N 77°40E **42** E7
Muzaffarpur *India* 26°7N 85°23E **43** F11
Muzafirpur *Pakistan* 30°58N 69°9E **42** D3
Muzhi *Russia* 65°25N 64°40E **18** A11
Muztagh-Ata *China* 38°17N 75°7E **30** D4
Mvuma *Zimbabwe* 19°16S 30°30E **55** H6
Mwali = Mohéli
  Comoros Is. 12°20S 43°40E **55** a
Mwanza
  Dem. Rep. of the Congo 7°55S 26°43E **54** F5
Mwanza *Tanzania* 2°30S 32°58E **54** E6
Mweelrea *Ireland* 53°39N 9°49W **10** C2
Mweka
  Dem. Rep. of the Congo 4°50S 21°34E **54** E4
Mwene-Ditu
  Dem. Rep. of the Congo 6°35S 22°27E **54** F4
Mwenga
  Dem. Rep. of the Congo 3°1S 28°28E **54** E5
Mweru, L. *Zambia* 9°0S 28°40E **54** F5
Mwinilunga *Zambia* 11°43S 24°25E **55** G4
My Son *Vietnam* 15°48N 108°7E **38** E7
My Tho *Vietnam* 10°29N 106°23E **39** G6
Myajlar *India* 26°15N 70°20E **42** F4
Myanaung *Burma* 18°18N 95°22E **41** K19
Myanmar = Burma ■
  Asia 21°0N 96°30E **41** J20
Myaungmya *Burma* 16°30N 94°40E **41** L19
Mycenæ = Mikines
  Greece 37°43N 22°46E **23** F10
Myeik = Mergui *Burma* 12°26N 98°34E **38** F2
Myeik Kyunzu *Burma* 11°30N 97°30E **39** G1
Myerstown *U.S.A.* 40°22N 76°19W **83** F8
Myingyan *Burma* 21°30N 95°20E **41** J19
Myitkyina *Burma* 25°24N 97°26E **41** G20
Mykines *Færoe Is.* 62°7N 7°35W **8** E9
Mykolayiv *Ukraine* 46°58N 32°0E **19** E5
Mykonos *Greece* 37°30N 25°25E **23** F11
Mymensingh *Bangla.* 24°45N 90°24E **41** G17
Mynydd Du *U.K.* 51°52N 3°50W **13** F4
Mýrdalsjökull *Iceland* 63°40N 19°6W **8** E4

Myrtle Beach *U.S.A.* 33°42N 78°53W **85** E15
Myrtle Creek *U.S.A.* 43°1N 123°17W **76** E2
Myrtle Point *U.S.A.* 43°4N 124°8W **76** E1
Mysia *Turkey* 39°50N 27°0E **23** E12
Mysore = Karnataka □
  India 13°15N 77°0E **45** H3
Mysore *India* 12°17N 76°41E **45** H3
Mystic *U.S.A.* 41°21N 71°58W **83** E13
Mysuru = Mysore *India* 12°17N 76°41E **45** H3
Myszków *Poland* 50°45N 19°22E **17** C10
Mytishchi *Russia* 55°50N 37°50E **18** C6
Mývatn *Iceland* 65°36N 17°0W **8** D5
Mzimkulu → *S. Africa* 30°44S 30°28E **57** D5
Mzimvubu → *S. Africa* 31°38S 29°33E **57** D4
Mzuzu *Malawi* 11°30S 33°55E **54** G6

N

Na Clocha Liatha = Greystones
  Ireland 53°9N 6°5W **10** C5
Na Haeo △ *Thailand* 17°31N 100°58E **38** D3
Na Hearadh = Harris
  U.K. 57°50N 6°55W **11** D2
Na Hearadh, Caolas = Harris, Sd.
  of *U.K.* 57°44N 7°6W **11** D1
Na Noi *Thailand* 18°19N 100°43E **38** C3
Na Phao *Laos* 17°35N 105°44E **38** D5
Na Sam *Vietnam* 22°3N 106°37E **34** F6
Na Thon *Thailand* 9°32N 99°56E **39** b
Naab → *Germany* 49°1N 12°2E **16** D6
Naantali *Finland* 60°29N 22°2E **9** F20
Naas *Ireland* 53°12N 6°40W **10** C5
Nababeep *S. Africa* 29°36S 17°46E **56** C2
Nabadwip = Navadwip
  India 23°34N 88°20E **43** H13
Nabawa *Australia* 28°30S 114°48E **61** E1
Nabberu, L. *Australia* 25°50S 120°30E **61** E3
Naberezhnyye Chelny
  Russia 55°42N 52°19E **18** C9
Nabeul *Tunisia* 36°30N 10°44E **53** A8
Nabha *India* 30°26N 76°14E **42** D7
Nabîd *Iran* 29°40N 57°38E **47** D8
Nabire *Indonesia* 3°15S 135°26E **37** E9
Nabisar *Pakistan* 25°8N 69°40E **42** G3
Nabisipi → *Canada* 50°14N 62°13W **73** B7
Nāblus = Nābulus
  West Bank 32°14N 35°15E **48** C4
Naboomspruit *S. Africa* 24°32S 28°40E **57** B4
Nabouwalu *Fiji* 17°0S 178°45E **59** a
Nābulus *West Bank* 32°14N 35°15E **48** C4
Nacala *Mozam.* 14°32S 40°34E **55** G8
Nacaome *Honduras* 13°31N 87°30W **88** D2
Naches *U.S.A.* 46°44N 120°42W **78** D6
Naches → *U.S.A.* 46°38N 120°31W **78** D6
Nachicapau, L. *Canada* 56°40N 68°5W **73** A6
Nachingwea *Tanzania* 10°23S 38°49E **54** G7
Nachna *India* 27°34N 71°41E **42** F4
Nachuge *India* 10°47N 92°21E **45** J11
Nacimiento, L. *U.S.A.* 35°46N 120°53W **78** K6
Naco *Mexico* 31°19N 109°56W **86** A3
Nacogdoches *U.S.A.* 31°36N 94°39W **84** F7
Nácori Chico *Mexico* 29°40N 108°57W **86** B3
Nacozari de García
  Mexico 30°25N 109°38W **86** A3
Nacula *Fiji* 16°54S 177°27E **59** a
Nada = Danzhou *China* 19°31N 109°33E **38** C7
Nådendal = Naantali
  Finland 60°29N 22°2E **9** F20
Nadi *Fiji* 17°42S 177°20E **59** a
Nadiad *India* 22°41N 72°56E **42** H5
Nadûshan *Iran* 32°2N 53°35E **47** C7
Nadvirna *Ukraine* 48°37N 24°30E **17** D13
Nadvoitsy *Russia* 63°52N 34°14E **18** B5
Nadvornaya = Nadvirna
  Ukraine 48°37N 24°30E **17** D13
Nadym *Russia* 65°35N 72°42E **26** C8
Nadym → *Russia* 66°12N 72°0E **26** C8
Nærbø *Norway* 58°40N 5°39E **9** G11
Næstved *Denmark* 55°13N 11°44E **9** J14
Nafpaktos *Greece* 38°24N 21°50E **23** E9
Nafplio *Greece* 37°33N 22°50E **23** F10
Naft-e Safid *Iran* 31°40N 49°17E **47** D6
Naftshahr *Iran* 34°0N 45°30E **46** C5
Nafud Desert = An Nafûd
  Si. Arabia 28°15N 41°0E **46** E4
Naga *Phil.* 13°38N 123°15E **37** B6
Nagagami *Canada* 50°23N 84°20W **72** B3
Nagahama *Japan* 35°23N 136°16E **29** G8
Nagai *Japan* 38°6N 140°2E **28** E10
Nagaland □ *India* 26°0N 94°30E **41** G19
Nagano *Japan* 36°40N 138°10E **29** F9
Nagano □ *Japan* 36°15N 138°0E **29** F9
Nagaoka *Japan* 37°27N 138°51E **29** F9
Nagaon *India* 26°20N 92°50E **41** F18
Nagappattinam *India* 10°46N 79°51E **45** J4
Nagar → *Bangla.* 24°27N 89°12E **43** G13
Nagar Karnul *India* 16°29N 78°26E **45** F4
Nagar Parkar *Pakistan* 24°28N 70°46E **42** G4
Nagaram *India* 18°21N 80°26E **44** E5
Nagarhole △ *India* 12°0N 76°10E **45** J3
Nagarjuna Sagar *India* 16°35N 79°17E **45** H4
Nagari Hills *India* 13°3N 79°45E **45** H4
Nagasaki *Japan* 32°47N 129°50E **29** H4
Nagasaki □ *Japan* 32°50N 129°40E **29** H4
Nagaur *India* 27°15N 73°45E **42** F5
Nagbhir *India* 20°34N 79°55E **44** D4
Nagda *India* 23°27N 75°25E **42** H6
Nagercoil *India* 8°12N 77°26E **45** K3
Nagîneh *Iran* 34°20N 57°15E **47** C8
Nagir *Pakistan* 36°12N 74°42E **43** A6
Nagod *India* 24°34N 80°36E **43** G9
Nagod *India* 24°17S 151°15E **62** C5
Nagorno-Karabakh □
  Azerbaijan 39°55N 46°45E **46** B5

Nagornyy *Russia* 55°58N 124°57E **27** D13
Nagoya *Japan* 35°10N 136°50E **29** G8
Nagoya ✈ (NGO) *Japan* 34°53N 136°45E **29** G8
Nagpur *India* 21°8N 79°10E **44** D4
Nagqu *China* 31°29N 92°3E **30** E7
Nagua *Dom. Rep.* 19°23N 69°50W **89** C6
Naguabo *Puerto Rico* 18°13N 65°44W **89** d
Nagurunguru ⊜
  Australia 16°45S 129°45E **60** C4
Nagykanizsa *Hungary* 46°28N 17°0E **17** E9
Nagykőrös *Hungary* 47°5N 19°48E **17** E10
Naha *Japan* 26°13N 127°42E **29** L3
Nahan *India* 30°33N 77°18E **42** D7
Nahanni △ *Canada* 61°36N 125°41W **70** A4
Nahanni Butte *Canada* 61°2N 123°31W **70** A4
Nahargarh *Mad. P., India* 24°10N 75°14E **42** G6
Nahargarh *Raj., India* 24°55N 76°50E **42** G7
Nahariyya *Israel* 33°1N 35°5E **46** C2
Nahâvand *Iran* 34°10N 48°22E **47** C6
Nahuel Huapi, L.
  Argentina 41°0S 71°32W **96** E2
Nahuelbuta △ *Chile* 37°44S 72°57W **94** D1
Nai Yong *Thailand* 8°14N 98°22E **39** a
Naicá *Mexico* 27°53N 105°31E **86** B3
Naicam *Canada* 52°30N 104°30W **71** C8
Naikoon △ *Canada* 53°55N 131°55W **70** C2
Naikul *India* 21°20N 84°58E **44** D7
Naimisharanya *India* 27°21N 80°30E **43** F9
Naimona'nyi Feng *China* 30°26N 81°18E **43** D9
Nain *Canada* 56°34N 61°40W **73** A7
Nā'în *Iran* 32°54N 53°0E **47** C7
Naini Tal *India* 29°30N 79°30E **43** E8
Nainpur *India* 22°30N 80°10E **43** H9
Nainwa *India* 25°46N 75°51E **42** G6
Nairai *Fiji* 17°49S 179°15E **59** a
Nairn *U.K.* 57°35N 3°53W **11** D5
Nairobi *Kenya* 1°17S 36°48E **54** E7
Naissaar *Estonia* 59°34N 24°29E **9** G21
Naitaba *Fiji* 17°0S 179°16W **59** a
Naivasha *Kenya* 0°40S 36°30E **54** E7
Najaf = An Najaf *Iraq* 32°3N 44°15E **46** C5
Najafābād *Iran* 32°40N 51°15E **47** C6
Najd *Si. Arabia* 26°30N 42°0E **49** B3
Najibabad *India* 29°40N 78°20E **42** E8
Najin *N. Korea* 42°12N 130°15E **33** C16
Najmah *Si. Arabia* 26°42N 50°6E **47** E6
Najrān *Si. Arabia* 17°34N 44°18E **49** D3
Naju *S. Korea* 35°3N 126°43E **33** G14
Nakadōri-Shima *Japan* 32°57N 129°4E **29** H4
Nakaminato *Japan* 36°21N 140°36E **29** F10
Nakamura = Shimanto
  Japan 32°59N 132°56E **29** H6
Nakano *Japan* 36°45N 138°22E **29** F9
Nakano-Shima *Japan* 29°51N 129°52E **29** K4
Nakashibetsu *Japan* 43°33N 144°59E **28** C12
Nakfa *Eritrea* 16°40N 38°32E **49** D2
Nakha Yai, Ko *Thailand* 8°3N 98°28E **39** a
Nakhichevan = Naxçivan
  Azerbaijan 39°12N 45°15E **46** B5
Nakhichevan Rep. = Naxçivan □
  Azerbaijan 39°25N 45°26E **46** B5
Nakhl *Egypt* 29°55N 33°43E **48** F2
Nakhl-e Taqī *Iran* 27°28N 52°36E **47** E7
Nakhodka *Russia* 42°53N 132°54E **28** C6
Nakhon Nayok *Thailand* 14°12N 101°13E **38** E3
Nakhon Pathom *Thailand* 13°49N 100°3E **38** F3
Nakhon Phanom
  Thailand 17°23N 104°43E **38** D5
Nakhon Ratchasima
  Thailand 14°59N 102°12E **38** E4
Nakhon Sawan *Thailand* 15°35N 100°10E **38** E3
Nakhon Si Thammarat
  Thailand 8°29N 100°0E **39** H3
Nakhon Thai *Thailand* 17°5N 100°44E **38** D3
Nakhtarana *India* 23°20N 69°15E **42** H3
Nakina *Canada* 50°10N 86°40W **72** B2
Nakodar *India* 31°8N 75°31E **42** D6
Naktong → *S. Korea* 35°7N 128°57E **33** G15
Nakuru *Kenya* 0°15S 36°4E **54** E7
Nakusp *Canada* 50°20N 117°45W **70** C5
Nal *Pakistan* 27°40N 66°12E **42** F2
Nal → *Pakistan* 25°20N 65°30E **42** G1
Nalázi *Mozam.* 24°3S 33°20E **57** B5
Nalchik *Russia* 43°30N 43°33E **19** F7
Nalgonda *India* 17°6N 79°15E **44** F4
Nalhati *India* 24°17N 87°52E **43** G12
Naliya *India* 23°16N 68°50E **42** H3
Nallamalai Hills *India* 15°30N 78°50E **45** G4
Nam Can *Vietnam* 8°46N 104°59E **39** H5
Nam-ch'on *N. Korea* 38°15N 126°26E **33** E14
Nam Co *China* 30°30N 90°45E **30** E7
Nam Dinh *Vietnam* 20°25N 106°5E **34** G6
Nam Du, Quan Dao
  Vietnam 9°41N 104°21E **39** H5
Nam Hke → *Burma* 25°34N 95°41E **34** G2
Nam Loi → *Burma* 21°3N 99°39E **34** G3
Nam Nao △ *Thailand* 16°44N 101°32E **38** D3
Nam Ngum Res. *Laos* 18°35N 102°34E **38** C4
Nam Phong *Thailand* 16°42N 102°52E **38** D4
Nam Theun Res. *Laos* 17°51N 105°3E **38** D5
Nam Tok *Thailand* 14°21N 99°4E **38** E2
Nam Un Res. *Thailand* 17°13N 103°44E **38** D4
Namacunde *Angola* 17°18S 15°50E **56** A2
Namacurra *Mozam.* 17°30S 36°50E **57** B6
Namak, Daryācheh-ye
  Iran 34°30N 52°0E **47** C7
Namak, Kavir-e *Iran* 34°30N 57°30E **47** C8
Namakkal *India* 11°13N 78°13E **45** J4
Namakzār, Daryācheh-ye
  Iran 34°0N 60°30E **47** C9
Namaland *Namibia* 26°0S 17°0E **56** B2
Namangan *Uzbekistan* 41°0N 71°40E **30** C3
Namapa *Mozam.* 13°43S 39°50E **55** G7
Namaqua △ *S. Africa* 30°0S 17°25E **56** D2
Namaqualand *S. Africa* 30°0S 17°25E **56** D2
Namber *Indonesia* 1°2S 134°49E **37** E8
Nambour *Australia* 26°32S 152°58E **63** D5
Nambouwalu = Nabouwalu
  Fiji 17°0S 178°45E **59** a

Nambucca Heads
  Australia 30°37S 153°0E **63** E5
Nambung △ *Australia* 30°30S 115°5E **61** F2
Namcha Barwa *China* 29°40N 95°10E **30** F8
Namche Bazar *Nepal* 27°51N 86°47E **43** F12
Namchonjŏm = Nam-ch'on
  N. Korea 38°15N 126°26E **33** E14
Namenalala *Fiji* 17°8S 179°9E **59** a
Namew L. *Canada* 54°14N 101°56W **71** C8
Namgia *India* 31°48N 78°40E **43** D8
Namhkam *Burma* 23°50N 97°41E **34** E1
Namib Desert *Namibia* 22°30S 15°0E **56** B2
Namib-Naukluft ⌂
  Namibia 24°40S 15°16E **56** B2
Namibe *Angola* 15°7S 12°11E **55** H2
Namibe □ *Angola* 16°35S 12°30E **56** A1
Namibia ■ *Africa* 22°0S 18°9E **56** B2
Namibwoestyn = Namib Desert
  Namibia 22°30S 15°0E **56** B2
Namjeju *S. Korea* 33°14N 126°33E **33** H14
Namlea *Indonesia* 3°18S 127°5E **37** E7
Namoi → *Australia* 30°12S 149°30E **63** E4
Nampa *U.S.A.* 43°34N 116°34W **76** E5
Nampo *N. Korea* 38°52N 125°10E **33** E13
Nampō-Shotō *Japan* 32°0N 140°0E **29** J10
Nampula *Mozam.* 15°6S 39°15E **55** H7
Namrole *Indonesia* 3°46S 126°46E **37** E7
Namse Shankou *China* 30°0N 82°25E **43** E10
Namsen → *Norway* 64°28N 11°37E **8** D14
Namsos *Norway* 64°29N 11°30E **8** D14
Namtok Chat Trakan △
  Thailand 17°17N 100°40E **38** D3
Namtok Huay Yang △
  Thailand 11°35N 99°30E **39** G2
Namtok Mae Surin △
  Thailand 18°55N 98°2E **38** C2
Namtok Ngao △ *Thailand* 9°58N 98°46E **39** H2
Namtok Phlew △
  Thailand 12°33N 102°13E **38** F4
Namtok Yong △ *Thailand* 8°15N 98°45E **39** H2
Namtsy *Russia* 62°43N 129°37E **27** C13
Namtu *Burma* 23°5N 97°28E **41** H20
Namu *Canada* 51°52N 127°50W **70** C3
Namuka-i-Lau *Fiji* 18°53S 178°37W **59** a
Namur *Belgium* 50°27N 4°52E **15** D4
Namur □ *Belgium* 50°17N 5°0E **15** D4
Namutoni *Namibia* 18°49S 16°55E **56** A2
Namwon *S. Korea* 35°23N 127°23E **33** G14
Namyang *N. Korea* 42°57N 129°52E **33** C15
Nan → *Thailand* 18°48N 100°46E **38** C3
Nan → *Thailand* 15°42N 100°9E **38** E3
Nan-ch'ang = Nanchang
  China 28°42N 115°55E **35** C10
Nan Ling *China* 25°0N 112°30E **35** E8
Nan Xian *China* 29°20N 112°22E **35** C9
Nanaimo *Canada* 49°10N 124°0W **70** D4
Nänäkuli *U.S.A.* 21°24N 158°9W **75** L8
Nanam *N. Korea* 41°44N 129°40E **33** D15
Nan'an *China* 24°59N 118°21E **35** E12
Nanango *Australia* 26°40S 152°0E **63** D5
Nan'ao *China* 23°28N 117°5E **35** F11
Nanao *Japan* 37°0N 137°0E **29** F8
Nanbu *China* 31°18N 106°3E **34** B6
Nanchang *China* 28°42N 115°55E **35** C10
Nancheng *China* 27°33N 116°35E **35** D11
Nanching = Nanjing
  China 32°2N 118°47E **35** A12
Nanchong *China* 30°43N 106°2E **34** B6
Nanchuan *China* 29°9N 107°6E **34** C6
Nancowry *India* 7°59N 93°32E **45** L11
Nanda Devi *India* 30°23N 79°59E **43** D8
Nanda Devi △ *India* 30°30N 79°50E **43** D8
Nanda Kot *India* 30°17N 80°5E **43** D9
Nandan
  Japan 34°10N 134°42E **29** G7
Nandan *China* 24°58N 107°29E **34** E6
Nanded *India* 19°10N 77°20E **44** E3
Nandewar Ra. *Australia* 30°15S 150°35E **63** E5
Nandgaon *India* 20°19N 74°39E **44** D2
Nandi = Nadi *Fiji* 17°42S 177°20E **59** a
Nandi *Zimbabwe* 20°58S 31°44E **57** B5
Nandigama *India* 16°47N 80°18E **44** F5
Nandigram *India* 22°1N 87°58E **43** H12
Nandikotkur *India* 15°52N 78°18E **45** G4
Nandura *India* 20°52N 76°25E **44** D3
Nandurbar *India* 21°20N 74°15E **44** D2
Nandyal *India* 15°30N 78°30E **45** G4
Nanfeng *Guangdong,*
  China 23°45N 111°47E **35** F8
Nanfeng *Jiangxi, China* 27°12N 116°28E **35** D11
Nang Rong *Thailand* 14°38N 102°48E **38** E4
Nanga-Eboko *Cameroon* 4°41N 12°22E **54** D2
Nanga Parbat *Pakistan* 35°10N 74°35E **43** B6
Nangapinoh *Indonesia* 0°20S 111°44E **36** E4
Nangarhar □ *Afghan.* 34°20N 70°0E **40** B7
Nangatayap *Indonesia* 1°32S 110°34E **36** E4
Nangong *China* 37°23N 115°22E **32** F8
Nanguneri *India* 8°29N 77°40E **45** K3
Nanhua *China* 25°13N 101°21E **34** E3
Nanhuang *China* 36°58N 121°48E **33** F11
Nanhui *China* 31°5N 121°44E **35** B13
Nanisivik *Canada* 73°2N 84°33W **69** C15
Nanjangud *India* 12°6N 76°43E **45** H3
Nanji Shan *China* 27°57N 121°4E **35** D13
Nanjian *China* 25°2N 100°25E **34** E3
Nanjiang *China* 32°28N 106°51E **34** A6
Nanjing *Fujian, China* 24°25N 117°20E **35** E11
Nanjing *Jiangsu, China* 32°2N 118°47E **35** A12
Nankang *China* 25°40N 114°45E **35** E10
Nanking = Nanjing
  China 32°2N 118°47E **35** A12
Nankoku *Japan* 33°39N 133°44E **29** H6
Nanlang *China* 22°30N 113°32E **31** a
Nanling *China* 30°55N 118°20E **35** B12
Nannial *India* 19°4N 79°38E **44** E4
Nanning *China* 22°48N 108°20E **34** F7
Nannup *Australia* 33°59S 115°48E **61** F2

Nanpan Jiang → *China* 25°10N 106°5E **34** E6
Nanpara *India* 27°52N 81°33E **43** F9
Nanping *Fujian, China* 26°38N 118°10E **35** D12
Nanping *Henan, China* 29°55N 112°3E **35** C9
Nanri Dao *China* 25°15N 119°25E **35** E12
Nansei-Shotō = Ryūkyū-Rettō
  Japan 26°0N 126°0E **29** M3
Nansen Basin *Arctic* 84°0N 50°0E **4** A10
Nansen Sd. *Canada* 81°0N 91°0W **69** A13
Nansha *China* 22°45N 113°34E **31** a
Nansha Port *China* 22°40N 113°40E **31** a
Nanshan *China* 18°19N 109°10E **38** C7
Nanshan I. *S. China Sea* 10°45N 115°49E **36** B5
Nantawarrinna ⊜
  Australia 30°49S 138°58E **63** B2
Nantes *France* 47°12N 1°33W **20** C3
Nanticoke *U.S.A.* 41°12N 76°0W **83** E8
Nanton *Canada* 50°21N 113°46W **70** C6
Nantong *China* 32°1N 120°52E **35** A13
Nantou *China* 22°32N 113°55E **31** a
Nant'ou *Taiwan* 23°55N 120°41E **35** F13
Nantucket *U.S.A.* 41°17N 70°6W **81** E18
Nantucket I. *U.S.A.* 41°16N 70°5W **81** E18
Nantwich *U.K.* 53°4N 2°31W **12** D5
Nanty Glo *U.S.A.* 40°28N 78°50W **82** F6
Nanuku Passage *Fiji* 17°0S 179°15W **59** a
Nanuque *Brazil* 17°50S 40°21W **93** G10
Nanusa, Kepulauan
  Indonesia 4°45N 127°1E **37** D7
Nanutarra Roadhouse
  Australia 22°32S 115°30E **60** D2
Nanxi *China* 28°54N 104°59E **34** C5
Nanxiong *China* 25°6N 114°15E **35** E10
Nanyang *China* 33°11N 112°30E **32** H7
Nanyi Hu *China* 31°5N 119°0E **35** B12
Nanyuki *Kenya* 0°2N 37°4E **54** D7
Nanzhang *China* 31°45N 111°50E **35** B8
Nanzhao *China* 33°30N 112°20E **32** H7
Nao, C. de la *Spain* 38°44N 0°14E **21** C6
Naococane, L. *Canada* 52°50N 70°45W **73** B5
Naozhou Dao *China* 20°55N 110°20E **35** G8
Napa *U.S.A.* 38°18N 122°17W **78** G4
Napa → *U.S.A.* 38°10N 122°19W **78** G4
Napanee *Canada* 44°15N 77°0W **82** B8
Napanoch *U.S.A.* 41°44N 74°22W **83** E10
Nape *Laos* 18°18N 105°6E **38** C5
Nape Pass = Keo Neua, Deo
  Vietnam 18°23N 105°10E **38** C5
Napier *N.Z.* 39°30S 176°56E **59** C6
Napier Broome B.
  Australia 14°2S 126°37E **60** B4
Napier Pen. *Australia* 12°4S 135°43E **62** A2
Napierville *Canada* 45°11N 73°25W **83** A11
Naples = Nápoli *Italy* 40°50N 14°15E **22** D6
Naples *U.S.A.* 26°8N 81°48W **85** H14
Napo *China* 23°22N 105°50E **34** F5
Napo → *Peru* 3°20S 72°40W **92** D4
Napoleon *N. Dak., U.S.A.* 46°30N 99°46W **80** B4
Napoleon *Ohio, U.S.A.* 41°23N 84°8W **81** E11
Nápoli *Italy* 40°50N 14°15E **22** D6
Naqadeh *Iran* 36°57N 45°23E **46** B5
Naqb, Ra's an *Jordan* 29°48N 35°44E **48** F4
Naqqâsh *Iran* 35°40N 49°6E **47** C6
Nara *Japan* 34°40N 135°49E **29** G7
Nara *Mali* 15°10N 7°20W **52** E4
Nara □ *Japan* 34°30N 136°0E **29** G8
Nara Canal *Pakistan* 24°30N 69°20E **42** G3
Nara Visa *U.S.A.* 35°37N 103°6W **77** J12
Naracoorte *Australia* 36°58S 140°45E **63** F3
Naradhan *Australia* 33°34S 146°17E **63** E4
Naraini *India* 25°11N 80°29E **43** G9
Naranjos *Mexico* 21°21N 97°41W **87** C5
Narasannapeta *India* 18°25N 84°3E **44** E7
Narasapur *India* 16°26N 81°40E **45** F5
Narasaraopet *India* 16°14N 80°4E **45** F5
Narathiwat *Thailand* 6°30N 101°48E **39** J3
Narayanpatnam *India* 18°53N 83°10E **44** E7
Narayangadh = Bharatpur
  Nepal 27°34N 84°10E **43** F11
Narayanganj *Bangla.* 23°40N 90°33E **41** H17
Narayanpet *India* 16°45N 77°30E **44** F3
Narberth *U.K.* 51°47N 4°44W **13** F3
Narbonne *France* 43°11N 3°0E **20** E5
Narcondam I. *India* 13°20N 94°16E **45** G11
Nardîn *Iran* 37°3N 55°59E **47** B7
Nardò *Italy* 40°11N 18°2E **23** D8
Narembeen *Australia* 32°7S 118°24E **61** F2
Nares Str. *Arctic* 80°0N 70°0W **69** B18
Naretha *Australia* 31°0S 124°45E **61** F3
Narew → *Poland* 52°26N 20°41E **17** B11
Nari → *Pakistan* 28°0N 67°40E **42** F2
Narin *Afghan.* 36°5N 69°0E **40** A6
Narita *Japan* 35°47N 140°19E **29** G10
Nariva Swamp
  Trin. & Tob. 10°26N 61°4W **93** K15
Narmada → *India* 21°38N 72°36E **42** J5
Narmada Canal *India* 22°20N 73°44E **42** J5
Narnaul *India* 28°5N 76°11E **42** E7
Narodnaya *Russia* 65°5N 59°58E **18** A10
Narooma *Australia* 36°14S 150°4E **63** F5
Narowal *Pakistan* 32°6N 74°52E **42** C6
Narrabri *Australia* 30°19S 149°46E **63** E4
Narran → *Australia* 28°37S 148°12E **63** D4
Narrandera *Australia* 34°42S 146°31E **63** E4
Narrogin *Australia* 32°58S 117°14E **61** F2
Narromine *Australia* 32°12S 148°12E **63** E4
Narrow Hills △ *Canada* 54°0N 104°37W **71** C8
Narsampet *India* 17°57N 79°58E **44** F4
Narsimhapur *India* 22°54N 79°14E **43** H8
Narsinghgarh *India* 23°45N 76°40E **42** H7
Narsinghpur *India* 20°28N 85°5E **44** D7
Narsipatnam *India* 17°40N 82°37E **44** F6
Naruto = Sanmu *Japan* 34°11N 134°37E **29** G7
Narva *Estonia* 59°23N 28°12E **18** C4
Narva → *Russia* 59°27N 28°2E **9** G23
Narva Bay = Narva Laht
  Estonia 59°35N 27°35E **9** G22
Narva Laht *Estonia* 59°35N 27°35E **9** G22

Narvik *Norway* 68°28N 17°26E **8** B17
Narwana *India* 29°39N 76°6E **42** E7
Narwinbi ✪ *Australia* 16°7S 136°17E **62** B2
Naryan-Mar *Russia* 67°42N 53°12E **18** A9
Narym *Russia* 59°0N 81°30E **26** D9
Naryn *Kyrgyzstan* 41°26N 75°58E **30** C4
Naryn Qum *Kazakhstan* 47°30N 49°0E **26** E5
Nás, An = Naas *Ireland* 53°12N 6°40W **10** C5
Nasa *Norway* 66°29N 15°23E **8** C16
Nasau *Fiji* 17°19S 179°27E **59** a
Nasca *Peru* 14°50S 74°57W **92** F4
Nasca Ridge *Pac. Oc.* 20°0S 80°0W **65** K19
Naseby *N.Z.* 45°1S 170°10E **59** F3
Naselle *U.S.A.* 46°22N 123°49W **78** D3
Naser, Buheirat en *Egypt* 23°0N 32°30E **53** D12
Nashik = Nasik *India* 19°58N 73°50E **44** E1
Nashua *Mont., U.S.A.* 48°8N 106°22W **76** B10
Nashua *N.H., U.S.A.* 42°45N 71°28W **83** D13
Nashville *Ark., U.S.A.* 33°57N 93°51W **84** E8
Nashville *Ga., U.S.A.* 31°12N 83°15W **85** F13
Nashville *Tenn., U.S.A.* 36°10N 86°47W **85** C11
Nasik *India* 19°58N 73°50E **44** E1
Nasirabad *India* 26°15N 74°45E **42** F6
Nasirabad *Pakistan* 28°23N 68°24E **42** E3
Nasiri = Ahvāz *Iran* 31°20N 48°40E **47** D6
Nasiriyah = An Nāşirīyah *Iraq* 31°0N 46°15E **46** D5
Naskaupi ➛ *Canada* 53°47N 60°51W **73** B7
Naşrābād *Iran* 34°8N 51°26E **47** C6
Naşriān-e Pā'īn *Iran* 32°52N 46°52E **46** C5
Nass ➛ *Canada* 55°0N 129°40W **70** C3
Nassau *Bahamas* 25°5N 77°20W **88** A4
Nassau *U.S.A.* 42°31N 73°37W **83** D11
Nassau, B. *Chile* 55°20S 68°0W **96** H3
Nasser, L. = Naser, Buheirat en *Egypt* 23°0N 32°30E **53** D12
Nässjö *Sweden* 57°39N 14°42E **9** H16
Nastapoka ➛ *Canada* 56°55N 76°33W **72** A4
Nastapoka, Is. *Canada* 56°55N 76°50W **72** A4
Nasushiobara *Japan* 36°58N 140°3E **29** F10
Nata *Botswana* 20°12S 26°12E **56** B4
Nata ➛ *Botswana* 20°14S 26°10E **56** B4
Natal *Brazil* 5°47S 35°13W **93** E11
Natal *Indonesia* 0°35N 99°7E **36** D1
Natal Drakensberg = uKhahlamba Drakensberg ⌓ *S. Africa* 29°27S 29°30E **57** C4
Naţanz *Iran* 33°30N 51°55E **47** C6
Natashquan *Canada* 50°14N 61°46W **73** B7
Natashquan ➛ *Canada* 50°7N 61°50W **73** B7
Natchez *U.S.A.* 31°34N 91°24W **84** F9
Natchitoches *U.S.A.* 31°46N 93°5W **84** F8
Natewa B. *Fiji* 16°35S 179°40E **59** a
Nathalia *Australia* 36°1S 145°13E **63** F4
Nathdwara *India* 24°55N 73°50E **42** G5
Natimuk *Australia* 36°42S 142°0E **63** F3
Nation ➛ *Canada* 55°30N 123°32W **70** B4
National City *U.S.A.* 32°40N 117°5W **79** N9
Natitingou *Benin* 10°20N 1°26E **52** F6
Natividad, I. *Mexico* 27°52N 115°11W **86** B1
Natkyizin *Burma* 14°57N 97°59E **38** E1
Natron, L. *Tanzania* 2°20S 36°0E **54** E7
Natrona Heights *U.S.A.* 40°37N 79°44W **82** F5
Natukanaoka Pan *Namibia* 18°40S 15°45E **56** A2
Natuna Besar, Kepulauan *Indonesia* 4°0N 108°15E **36** D3
Natuna Is. = Natuna Besar, Kepulauan *Indonesia* 4°0N 108°15E **36** D3
Natuna Selatan, Kepulauan *Indonesia* 2°45N 109°0E **36** D3
Natural Bridge *U.S.A.* 44°5N 75°30W **83** B9
Natural Bridges ⌓ *U.S.A.* 37°36N 110°0W **77** H9
Naturaliste, C. *Tas., Australia* 40°50S 148°15E **63** G4
Naturaliste, C. *W. Austral., Australia* 33°32S 115°0E **61** F2
Naturaliste Plateau *Ind. Oc.* 34°0S 112°0E **64** L3
Nau Qala *Afghan.* 34°5N 68°5E **42** B3
Naugatuck *U.S.A.* 41°30N 73°3W **83** E11
Naujaat = Repulse Bay *Canada* 66°30N 86°30W **69** D14
Naumburg *Germany* 51°9N 11°47E **16** C6
Naupada *India* 18°34N 84°18E **44** E7
Nauru ■ *Pac. Oc.* 1°0S 166°0E **58** B9
Naushahra = Nowshera *Pakistan* 34°0N 72°0E **40** C8
Naushahro *Pakistan* 26°50N 68°7E **42** F3
Naushon I. *U.S.A.* 41°29N 70°45W **83** E14
Nausori *Fiji* 18°2S 178°32E **59** a
Nauta *Peru* 4°31S 73°35W **92** D4
Nautanwa *India* 27°20N 83°25E **43** F10
Naute ⌓ *Namibia* 26°55S 17°57E **56** C2
Nautla *Mexico* 20°13N 96°47W **87** C5
Nava *Mexico* 28°25N 100°45W **86** B4
Navadwip *India* 23°34N 88°20E **43** H13
Navahrudak *Belarus* 53°40N 25°50E **17** B13
Navajo Res. *U.S.A.* 36°48N 107°36W **77** H10
Navalgund *India* 15°34N 75°22E **45** G2
Navalmoral de la Mata *Spain* 39°52N 5°33W **21** C3
Navan *Ireland* 53°39N 6°41W **10** C5
Navarin, Mys *Russia* 62°15N 179°5E **27** C18
Navarino, I. *Chile* 55°0S 67°40W **96** H3
Navarra ☐ *Spain* 42°40N 1°40W **21** A5
Navarre *U.S.A.* 40°43N 81°31W **82** F3
Navarro ➛ *U.S.A.* 39°11N 123°45W **78** F3
Navasota *U.S.A.* 30°23N 96°5W **84** F6
Navassa I. *W. Indies* 18°30N 75°0W **89** C5
Naver ➛ *U.K.* 58°32N 4°14W **11** C4
Navibandar *India* 21°26N 69°48E **42** J3
Navidad *Chile* 33°57S 71°50W **94** C1
Naviraí *Brazil* 23°8S 54°13W **95** A5
Naviti *Fiji* 17°7S 177°15E **59** a
Navlakhi *India* 22°58N 70°28E **42** H4
Năvodari *Romania* 44°19N 28°36E **17** F15
Navoi *Uzbekistan* 40°9N 65°22E **26** E7
Navojoa *Mexico* 27°6N 109°26W **86** B3
Navolato *Mexico* 24°47N 107°42W **86** C3
Navsari *India* 20°57N 72°59E **44** D1
Navua *Fiji* 18°12S 178°11E **59** a
Nawa Kot *Pakistan* 28°21N 71°24E **42** E4
Nawab Khan *Pakistan* 30°17N 69°12E **42** D3
Nawabganj *Ut. P., India* 26°56N 81°14E **43** F9
Nawabganj *Ut. P., India* 28°32N 79°40E **43** E8
Nawabshah *Pakistan* 26°15N 68°25E **42** F3
Nawada *India* 24°50N 85°33E **43** G11
Nawakot *Nepal* 27°55N 85°10E **43** F11
Nawalgarh *India* 27°50N 75°15E **42** F6
Nawanshahr *India* 32°33N 74°48E **43** C6
Nawapara *India* 20°46N 82°33E **44** D6
Nawar, Dasht-i- *Afghan.* 33°52N 68°0E **42** C3
Nawoiy = Navoi *Uzbekistan* 40°9N 65°22E **26** E7
Naxçıvan *Azerbaijan* 39°12N 45°15E **46** B5
Naxçıvan ☐ *Azerbaijan* 39°25N 45°26E **46** B5
Naxos *Greece* 37°8N 25°25E **23** F11
Nay, Mui *Vietnam* 12°54N 109°26E **38** F7
Nāy Band *Būshehr, Iran* 27°20N 52°40E **47** E7
Nāy Band *Khorāsān, Iran* 32°20N 57°34E **47** C8
Nay Pyi Taw = Naypyidaw *Burma* 19°44N 96°12E **30** H8
Nayagarh *India* 20°8N 85°6E **44** D7
Nayakhan *Russia* 61°56N 159°0E **27** C16
Nayarit ☐ *Mexico* 22°0N 105°0W **86** C4
Nayau *Fiji* 18°6S 178°10E **59** a
Nayong *China* 26°50N 105°20E **34** D5
Nayoro *Japan* 44°21N 142°28E **28** B11
Naypyidaw *Burma* 19°44N 96°12E **30** H8
Nayudupeta *India* 13°54N 79°54E **45** H4
Nayyāl, W. ➛ *Si. Arabia* 28°35N 39°4E **46** D3
Nazaré *Brazil* 13°2S 39°0W **93** F11
Nazareth = Nazerat *Israel* 32°42N 35°17E **48** C4
Nazareth *U.S.A.* 40°44N 75°19W **83** F9
Nazarovo *Russia* 57°2N 90°40E **27** D10
Nazas *Mexico* 25°14N 104°8W **86** B4
Nazas ➛ *Mexico* 25°12N 104°12W **86** B4
Nazca = Nasca *Peru* 14°50S 74°57W **92** F4
Naze, The *U.K.* 51°53N 1°18E **13** F9
Nazerat *Israel* 32°42N 35°17E **48** C4
Nāzīk *Iran* 39°1N 45°4E **46** B5
Nazilli *Turkey* 37°55N 28°15E **23** F13
Nazko *Canada* 53°1N 123°37W **70** C4
Nazko ➛ *Canada* 53°7N 123°34W **70** C4
Nazret *Ethiopia* 8°32N 39°22E **49** F2
Ndalatando *Angola* 9°12S 14°48E **54** F2
Ndélé *C.A.R.* 8°25N 20°36E **54** C4
Ndjamena *Chad* 12°10N 15°0E **53** F8
Ndola *Zambia* 13°0S 28°34E **55** G5
Ndomo ⌓ *S. Africa* 26°52S 32°15E **57** C5
Ndoto Mts. *Kenya* 2°0N 37°0E **54** D7
Neagh, Lough *U.K.* 54°37N 6°25W **10** B5
Neah Bay *U.S.A.* 48°22N 124°37W **78** B2
Neale, L. *Australia* 24°15S 130°0E **60** D5
Neales ➛ *Australia* 28°8S 136°47E **63** D2
Near Is. *U.S.A.* 52°30N 174°0E **74** E2
Neath *U.K.* 51°39N 3°48W **13** F4
Neath Port Talbot ☐ *U.K.* 51°42N 3°45W **13** F4
Nebine Cr. ➛ *Australia* 29°27S 146°56E **63** D4
Nebitdag = Balkanabat *Turkmenistan* 39°30N 54°22E **47** B7
Nebo *Australia* 21°42S 148°42E **62** C4
Nebraska ☐ *U.S.A.* 41°30N 99°30W **80** E4
Nebraska City *U.S.A.* 40°41N 95°52W **80** E6
Nébrodi, Monti *Italy* 37°54N 14°35E **22** F6
Necedah *U.S.A.* 44°2N 90°4W **80** C8
Nechako ➛ *Canada* 53°55N 122°42W **70** C4
Neches ➛ *U.S.A.* 29°58N 93°51W **84** G8
Neckar ➛ *Germany* 49°27N 8°29E **16** D5
Necker I. *U.S.A.* 23°35N 164°42W **75** L7
Necochea *Argentina* 38°30S 58°50W **94** D4
Nederland = Netherlands ■ *Europe* 52°0N 5°30E **15** C5
Needles *Canada* 49°53N 118°7W **70** D5
Needles *U.S.A.* 34°51N 114°37W **79** L12
Needles, The *U.K.* 50°39N 1°35W **13** G6
Neembucú ☐ *Paraguay* 27°0S 58°0W **94** B4
Neemuch = Nimach *India* 24°30N 74°56E **42** G6
Neenah *U.S.A.* 44°11N 88°28W **80** C9
Neepawa *Canada* 50°15N 99°30W **71** C9
Neftçala *Azerbaijan* 39°19N 49°12E **47** B6
Neftegorsk *Russia* 53°1N 142°58E **27** D15
Neftekumsk *Russia* 44°46N 44°50E **19** F7
Nefteyugansk *Russia* 61°5N 72°42E **26** C8
Nefyn *U.K.* 52°56N 4°31W **12** E3
Negapatam = Nagappattinam *India* 10°46N 79°51E **45** J4
Negara *Indonesia* 8°22S 114°37E **37** J17
Negaunee *U.S.A.* 46°30N 87°36W **80** B10
Negele *Ethiopia* 5°20N 39°36E **49** F2
Negeri Sembilan ☐ *Malaysia* 2°45N 102°10E **39** L4
Negev Desert = Hanegev *Israel* 30°50N 35°0E **48** E4
Negombo *Sri Lanka* 7°12N 79°50E **45** L4
Negotin *Serbia* 44°16N 22°37E **23** B10
Negra, Pta. *Mauritania* 22°54N 16°18W **52** D2
Negra, Pta. *Peru* 6°6S 81°10W **92** E2
Negrais, C. = Maudin Sun *Burma* 16°0N 94°30E **41** M19
Negril *Jamaica* 18°22N 78°20W **88** a
Negro ➛ *Argentina* 41°2S 62°47W **96** E4
Negro ➛ *Brazil* 3°0S 60°0W **92** D7
Negro ➛ *Uruguay* 33°24S 58°22W **94** C4
Negros *Phil.* 9°30N 122°40E **37** C6
Neguac *Canada* 47°15N 65°5W **73** C6
Nehalem ➛ *U.S.A.* 45°40N 123°56W **78** E3
Nehāvand *Iran* 35°56N 49°31E **47** C6
Nehbandān *Iran* 31°35N 60°5E **47** D9
Nehe *China* 48°29N 124°50E **31** B13
Nei Mongol Zizhiqu ☐ *China* 42°0N 112°0E **32** D7
Neiafu *Tonga* 18°39S 173°59W **59** c
Neiges, Piton des *Réunion* 21°5S 55°29E **55** c
Neijiang *China* 29°35N 104°55E **34** C5
Neilingding Dao *China* 22°25N 113°48E **31** a
Neill I. *India* 11°50N 93°3E **45** J11
Neillsville *U.S.A.* 44°34N 90°36W **80** C8
Neilton *U.S.A.* 47°25N 123°53W **78** C3
Neiqiu *China* 37°15N 114°30E **32** F8
Neiva *Colombia* 2°56N 75°18W **92** C3
Neixiang *China* 33°10N 111°52E **32** H6
Nejanilini L. *Canada* 59°33N 97°48W **71** B9
Nejd = Najd *Si. Arabia* 26°30N 42°0E **49** B3
Nekā *Iran* 36°39N 53°19E **47** B7
Nekemte *Ethiopia* 9°4N 36°30E **49** F2
Neksø *Denmark* 55°4N 15°8E **9** J16
Nelamangala *India* 13°6N 77°24E **45** H3
Nelia *Australia* 20°39S 142°12E **62** C3
Neligh *U.S.A.* 42°8N 98°2W **80** D4
Nelkan *Russia* 57°40N 136°4E **27** D14
Nellikuppam *India* 11°46N 79°43E **45** J4
Nellore *India* 14°27N 79°59E **45** G4
Nelson *Canada* 49°30N 117°20W **70** D5
Nelson *N.Z.* 41°18S 173°16E **59** D4
Nelson *U.K.* 53°50N 2°13W **12** D5
Nelson *Ariz., U.S.A.* 35°31N 113°19W **77** J7
Nelson *Nev., U.S.A.* 35°42N 114°49W **79** K12
Nelson ➛ *Canada* 54°33N 98°2W **71** C9
Nelson, C. *Australia* 38°26S 141°32E **63** F3
Nelson, Estrecho *Chile* 51°30S 75°0W **96** G2
Nelson Forks *Canada* 59°30N 124°0W **70** B4
Nelson House *Canada* 55°47N 98°51W **71** B9
Nelson L. *Canada* 55°48N 100°7W **71** B8
Nelson Lakes △ *N.Z.* 41°55S 172°44E **59** D4
Nelspoort *S. Africa* 32°7S 23°0E **56** D3
Nelspruit = Mbombela *S. Africa* 25°29S 30°59E **57** C5
Néma *Mauritania* 16°40N 7°15W **52** E4
Neman = Nemunas ➛ *Lithuania* 55°25N 21°10E **9** J19
Nembrala *Indonesia* 10°53S 122°50E **60** B3
Nemeiben L. *Canada* 55°20N 105°20W **71** B7
Nemiscau *Canada* 51°18N 76°54W **72** B4
Nemiscau, L. *Canada* 51°25N 76°40W **72** B4
Nemunas ➛ *Lithuania* 55°25N 21°10E **9** J19
Nemuro *Japan* 43°20N 145°35E **28** C12
Nemuro-Kaikyō *Japan* 43°30N 145°30E **28** C12
Nen Jiang ➛ *China* 45°28N 124°30E **33** B13
Nenagh *Ireland* 52°52N 8°11W **10** D3
Nenana *U.S.A.* 64°34N 149°5W **74** C10
Nenasi *Malaysia* 3°9N 103°23E **39** L4
Nene ➛ *U.K.* 52°49N 0°11E **13** E8
Nenjiang *China* 49°10N 125°10E **31** B14
Neodesha *U.S.A.* 37°25N 95°41W **80** G6
Neora Valley △ *India* 27°0N 88°45E **43** F13
Neosho *U.S.A.* 36°52N 94°22W **80** G6
Neosho ➛ *U.S.A.* 36°48N 95°18W **84** C7
Nepal ■ *Asia* 28°0N 84°30E **43** F11
Nepalganj *Nepal* 28°5N 81°40E **43** E9
Nepalganj Road *India* 28°1N 81°41E **43** E9
Nephi *U.S.A.* 39°43N 111°50W **76** G8
Nephin *Ireland* 54°1N 9°22W **10** B2
Nephin Beg Range *Ireland* 54°0N 9°40W **10** C2
Neptune *U.S.A.* 40°13N 74°2W **83** F10
Neqāb *Iran* 36°42N 57°25E **47** B8
Nerang *Australia* 27°58S 153°20E **63** D5
Nerchinsk *Russia* 52°0N 116°39E **27** D12
Néret, L. *Canada* 54°45N 70°44W **73** B5
Neretva ➛ *Croatia* 43°1N 17°27E **23** C7
Neringa *Lithuania* 55°20N 21°5E **9** J19
Neris ➛ *Lithuania* 55°8N 24°16E **9** J21
Neryungri *Russia* 57°38N 124°28E **27** D13
Nescopeck *U.S.A.* 41°3N 76°12W **83** E8
Neskantaga *Canada* 52°14N 87°53W **72** B2
Neskaupstaður *Iceland* 65°9N 13°42W **8** D7
Ness, L. *U.K.* 57°15N 4°32W **11** D4
Ness City *U.S.A.* 38°27N 99°54W **80** F4
Nesterov = Zhovkva *Ukraine* 50°4N 23°58E **17** C12
Nestos ➛ *Europe* 40°54N 24°49E **23** D11
Nesvizh = Nyasvizh *Belarus* 53°14N 26°38E **17** B14
Netanya *Israel* 32°20N 34°51E **48** C3
Netarhat *India* 23°29N 84°16E **43** H11
Nete ➛ *Belgium* 51°7N 4°14E **15** C4
Netherdale *Australia* 21°10S 148°33E **62** b
Netherlands ■ *Europe* 52°0N 5°30E **15** C5
Netherlands Antilles = ABC Islands *W. Indies* 12°15N 69°0W **89** D6
Netrang *India* 21°39N 73°21E **42** J5
Nettilling L. *Canada* 66°30N 71°0W **69** D17
Netzahualcóyotl, Presa *Mexico* 17°8N 93°35W **87** D6
Neubrandenburg *Germany* 53°33N 13°15E **16** B7
Neuchâtel *Switz.* 47°0N 6°55E **20** C7
Neuchâtel, Lac de *Switz.* 46°53N 6°50E **20** C7
Neufchâteau *Belgium* 49°50N 5°25E **15** E5
Neumayer *Antarctica* 71°0S 68°30W **5** D17
Neumünster *Germany* 54°4N 9°58E **16** A5
Neunkirchen *Germany* 49°20N 7°9E **16** D4
Neuquén *Argentina* 38°55S 68°0W **96** D3
Neuquén ☐ *Argentina* 38°0S 69°50W **94** D2
Neuruppin *Germany* 52°55N 12°48E **16** B7
Neuse ➛ *U.S.A.* 35°6N 76°29W **85** D16
Neusiedler See *Austria* 47°50N 16°47E **17** E9
Neustrelitz *Germany* 53°21N 13°4E **16** B7
Neva ➛ *Russia* 59°56N 30°20E **18** C5
Nevada *Iowa, U.S.A.* 42°1N 93°27W **80** D7
Nevada *Mo., U.S.A.* 37°51N 94°22W **80** G6
Nevada ☐ *U.S.A.* 39°0N 117°0W **76** G5
Nevada City *U.S.A.* 39°16N 121°1W **78** F6
Nevado, Cerro *Argentina* 35°30S 68°32W **94** D2
Nevado de Colima = Volcán de Colima △ *Mexico* 19°30N 103°40W **86** D4
Nevado de Tres Cruces △ *Chile* 27°13S 69°5W **94** B2
Nevasa *India* 19°34N 75°0E **44** E2
Nevel *Russia* 56°0N 29°55E **18** C4
Nevelsk *Russia* 46°40N 141°51E **27** E15
Nevers *France* 47°0N 3°9E **20** C5
Nevertire *Australia* 31°50S 147°44E **63** E4
Neville *Canada* 49°58N 107°39W **71** D7
Nevinnomyssk *Russia* 44°40N 42°0E **19** F7
Nevis *St. Kitts & Nevis* 17°0N 62°30W **89** C7
Nevşehir *Turkey* 38°33N 34°40E **46** B2
Nevyansk *Russia* 57°30N 60°13E **18** C11
New ➛ *U.S.A.* 38°10N 81°12W **81** F13
New Aiyansh *Canada* 55°12N 129°4W **70** B3
New Albany *Ind., U.S.A.* 38°18N 85°49W **81** F11
New Albany *Miss., U.S.A.* 34°29N 89°0W **85** D10
New Albany *Pa., U.S.A.* 41°36N 76°27W **83** E8
New Amsterdam *Guyana* 6°15N 57°36W **92** B7
New Baltimore *U.S.A.* 42°41N 82°44W **82** D2
New Bedford *U.S.A.* 41°38N 70°56W **83** E14
New Berlin *N.Y., U.S.A.* 42°37N 75°20W **83** D9
New Berlin *Pa., U.S.A.* 40°50N 76°57W **82** F8
New Bern *U.S.A.* 35°7N 77°3W **85** D16
New Bethlehem *U.S.A.* 41°0N 79°20W **82** F5
New Bight *Bahamas* 24°19N 75°24W **89** B4
New Bloomfield *U.S.A.* 40°25N 77°11W **82** F7
New Boston *U.S.A.* 33°28N 94°25W **84** E7
New Braunfels *U.S.A.* 29°42N 98°8W **84** G5
New Brighton *N.Z.* 43°29S 172°43E **59** E4
New Brighton *U.S.A.* 40°42N 80°19W **82** F4
New Britain *Papua N. G.* 5°50S 150°20E **58** B8
New Britain *U.S.A.* 41°40N 72°47W **83** E12
New Brunswick *U.S.A.* 40°30N 74°27W **83** F10
New Brunswick ☐ *Canada* 46°50N 66°30W **73** C6
New Caledonia ☒ *Pac. Oc.* 21°0S 165°0E **58** D9
New Caledonia Trough *Pac. Oc.* 30°0S 165°0E **64** L8
New Castile = Castilla-La Mancha ☐ *Spain* 39°30N 3°30W **21** C4
New Castle *Ind., U.S.A.* 39°55N 85°22W **81** F11
New Castle *Pa., U.S.A.* 41°0N 80°21W **82** F4
New City *U.S.A.* 41°9N 73°59W **83** E11
New Concord *U.S.A.* 39°59N 81°54W **82** G3
New Cumberland *U.S.A.* 40°30N 80°36W **82** F4
New Cuyama *U.S.A.* 34°57N 119°38W **79** L7
New Denver *Canada* 50°0N 117°25W **70** D5
New Don Pedro Res. *U.S.A.* 37°43N 120°24W **78** H6
New England *U.S.A.* 43°0N 71°0W **75** G25
New England *N. Dak., U.S.A.* 46°32N 102°52W **80** B2
New England Ra. *Australia* 30°20S 151°45E **63** E5
New Forest △ *U.K.* 50°53N 1°34W **13** G6
New Galloway *U.K.* 55°5N 4°9W **11** F4
New Glasgow *Canada* 45°35N 62°36W **73** C7
New Guinea *Oceania* 4°0S 136°0E **58** B6
New Hamburg *Canada* 43°23N 80°42W **82** C4
New Hampshire ☐ *U.S.A.* 44°0N 71°30W **83** C13
New Hampton *U.S.A.* 43°3N 92°19W **80** D7
New Hanover *S. Africa* 29°22S 30°31E **57** C5
New Hartford *U.S.A.* 43°4N 75°18W **83** C9
New Haven *Conn., U.S.A.* 41°18N 72°55W **83** E12
New Haven *Mich., U.S.A.* 42°44N 82°48W **82** D2
New Haven *N.Y., U.S.A.* 43°28N 76°18W **83** C8
New Hazelton *Canada* 55°20N 127°30W **70** B3
New Hebrides = Vanuatu ■ *Pac. Oc.* 15°0S 168°0E **58** C9
New Holland *U.S.A.* 40°6N 76°5W **83** F8
New Iberia *U.S.A.* 30°1N 91°49W **84** F9
New Ireland *Papua N. G.* 3°20S 151°50E **58** B8
New Jersey ☐ *U.S.A.* 40°0N 74°30W **81** F16
New Kensington *U.S.A.* 40°34N 79°46W **82** F5
New Lexington *U.S.A.* 39°43N 82°13W **81** F12
New Liskeard *Canada* 47°31N 79°41W **72** C4
New London *Conn., U.S.A.* 41°22N 72°6W **83** E12
New London *Ohio, U.S.A.* 41°5N 82°24W **82** E2
New London *Wis., U.S.A.* 44°23N 88°45W **80** C9
New Madrid *U.S.A.* 36°36N 89°32W **80** G9
New Martinsville *U.S.A.* 39°39N 80°52W **81** F13
New Meadows *U.S.A.* 44°58N 116°18W **76** D5
New Melones L. *U.S.A.* 37°57N 120°31W **78** H6
New Mexico ☐ *U.S.A.* 34°30N 106°0W **77** J11
New Milford *Conn., U.S.A.* 41°35N 73°25W **83** E11
New Milford *Pa., U.S.A.* 41°52N 75°44W **83** E9
New Norcia *Australia* 30°57S 116°13E **61** F2
New Norfolk *Australia* 42°46S 147°2E **63** G4
New Philadelphia *U.S.A.* 40°30N 81°27W **82** F3
New Plymouth *N.Z.* 39°4S 174°5E **59** C5
New Plymouth *U.S.A.* 43°58N 116°49W **76** E5
New Port Richey *U.S.A.* 28°16N 82°43W **85** G13
New Providence *Bahamas* 25°25N 77°35W **88** A4
New Quay *U.K.* 52°13N 4°21W **13** E3
New Radnor *U.K.* 52°15N 3°9W **13** E4
New Richmond *Canada* 48°15N 65°45W **73** C6
New Richmond *U.S.A.* 45°7N 92°32W **80** C7
New River Gorge ⌓ *U.S.A.* 37°53N 81°5W **81** G13
New Roads *U.S.A.* 30°42N 91°26W **84** F9
New Rochelle *U.S.A.* 40°55N 73°46W **83** F11
New Rockford *U.S.A.* 47°41N 99°8W **80** B4
New Romney *U.K.* 50°59N 0°57E **13** G8
New Ross *Ireland* 52°23N 6°57W **10** D5
New Salem *U.S.A.* 46°51N 101°25W **80** B3
New Scone = Scone *U.K.* 56°25N 3°24W **11** E5
New Siberian I. = Novaya Sibir, Ostrov *Russia* 75°10N 150°0E **27** B16
New Siberian Is. = Novosibirskiye Ostrova *Russia* 75°0N 142°0E **27** B15
New Smyrna Beach *U.S.A.* 29°1N 80°56W **85** G14
New South Wales ☐ *Australia* 33°0S 146°0E **63** E4
New Tecumseth = Alliston *Canada* 44°9N 79°52W **82** B5
New Town *U.S.A.* 47°59N 102°30W **80** B2
New Tredegar *U.K.* 51°44N 3°16W **13** F4
New Ulm *U.S.A.* 44°19N 94°28W **80** C6
New Waterford *Canada* 46°13N 60°4W **73** C7
New Westminster *Canada* 49°13N 122°55W **78** A4
New York ☐ *U.S.A.* 43°0N 75°0W **83** D9
New York J.F. Kennedy Int. ✈ (JFK) *U.S.A.* 40°38N 73°47W **83** F11
New Zealand ■ *Oceania* 40°0S 176°0E **59** D6
Newaj ➛ *India* 24°24N 76°49E **42** G7
Newark *Del., U.S.A.* 39°41N 75°46W **81** F16
Newark *N.J., U.S.A.* 40°44N 74°10W **83** F10
Newark *N.Y., U.S.A.* 43°3N 77°6W **82** C7
Newark *Ohio, U.S.A.* 40°3N 82°24W **82** F2
Newark Liberty Int. ✈ (EWR) *U.S.A.* 40°42N 74°10W **83** F10
Newark-on-Trent *U.K.* 53°5N 0°48W **12** D7
Newark Valley *U.S.A.* 42°14N 76°11W **83** D8
Newberg *U.S.A.* 45°18N 122°58W **76** D2
Newberry *Mich., U.S.A.* 46°21N 85°30W **81** B11
Newberry *S.C., U.S.A.* 34°17N 81°37W **85** D14
Newberry Springs *U.S.A.* 34°50N 116°41W **79** L10
Newboro L. *Canada* 44°38N 76°20W **83** B8
Newbridge *Ireland* 53°11N 6°48W **10** C5
Newburgh *Canada* 44°19N 76°52W **82** B8
Newburgh *U.S.A.* 41°30N 74°1W **83** E10
Newbury *U.K.* 51°24N 1°20W **13** F6
Newbury *N.H., U.S.A.* 43°19N 72°3W **83** B12
Newbury *Vt., U.S.A.* 44°5N 72°4W **83** B12
Newburyport *U.S.A.* 42°49N 70°53W **83** D14
Newcastle *Australia* 33°0S 151°46E **63** E5
Newcastle *N.B., Canada* 47°1N 65°38W **73** C6
Newcastle *Ont., Canada* 43°55N 78°35W **72** D4
Newcastle *Ireland* 52°27N 9°3W **10** D2
Newcastle *S. Africa* 27°45S 29°58E **57** C4
Newcastle *U.K.* 54°13N 5°54W **10** B6
Newcastle *Calif., U.S.A.* 38°53N 121°8W **78** G5
Newcastle *Wyo., U.S.A.* 43°50N 104°11W **76** E11
Newcastle Emlyn *U.K.* 52°2N 4°28W **13** E3
Newcastle Ra. *Australia* 15°45S 130°15E **60** C5
Newcastle-under-Lyme *U.K.* 53°1N 2°14W **12** D5
Newcastle-upon-Tyne *U.K.* 54°58N 1°36W **12** C6
Newcastle Waters *Australia* 17°30S 133°28E **62** B1
Newcomb *U.S.A.* 43°58N 74°10W **83** C10
Newcomerstown *U.S.A.* 40°16N 81°36W **82** F3
Newdegate *Australia* 33°6S 119°0E **61** F2
Newell *Australia* 16°20S 145°16E **62** B4
Newell *U.S.A.* 44°43N 103°25W **80** C2
Newenham, C. *U.S.A.* 58°39N 162°11W **74** D7
Newfane *U.S.A.* 43°17N 78°43W **82** C6
Newfield *U.S.A.* 42°18N 76°33W **83** D8
Newfound L. *U.S.A.* 43°40N 71°47W **83** C13
Newfoundland *Canada* 49°0N 55°0W **73** C8
Newfoundland *U.S.A.* 41°18N 75°19W **83** E9
Newfoundland & Labrador ☐ *Canada* 52°0N 58°0W **73** B8
Newhaven *U.K.* 50°47N 0°3E **13** G8
Newkirk *U.S.A.* 36°53N 97°3W **84** C6
Newlyn *U.K.* 50°6N 5°34W **13** G2
Newman *Australia* 23°18S 119°45E **60** D2
Newman *U.S.A.* 37°19N 121°1W **78** H5
Newmarket *Canada* 44°3N 79°28W **82** B5
Newmarket *Ireland* 52°13N 9°0W **10** D2
Newmarket *U.K.* 52°15N 0°25E **13** E8
Newmarket *U.S.A.* 43°5N 70°56W **83** C14
Newnan *U.S.A.* 33°23N 84°48W **85** E12
Newport *Ireland* 53°53N 9°33W **10** C2
Newport *I. of W., U.K.* 50°42N 1°17W **13** G6
Newport *Newport, U.K.* 51°35N 3°0W **13** F5
Newport *Ark., U.S.A.* 35°37N 91°16W **84** D9
Newport *Ky., U.S.A.* 39°5N 84°29W **81** F11
Newport *N.H., U.S.A.* 43°22N 72°10W **83** C12
Newport *N.Y., U.S.A.* 43°11N 75°1W **83** C9
Newport *Oreg., U.S.A.* 44°39N 124°3W **76** D1
Newport *Pa., U.S.A.* 40°29N 77°8W **82** F7
Newport *R.I., U.S.A.* 41°29N 71°19W **83** E13
Newport *Tenn., U.S.A.* 35°58N 83°11W **85** D13
Newport *Vt., U.S.A.* 44°56N 72°13W **83** B12
Newport *Wash., U.S.A.* 48°11N 117°3W **76** B5
Newport ☐ *U.K.* 51°33N 3°1W **13** F4
Newport Beach *U.S.A.* 33°37N 117°56W **79** M9
Newport News *U.S.A.* 36°58N 76°25W **81** G15
Newport Pagnell *U.K.* 52°5N 0°43W **13** E7
Newquay *U.K.* 50°25N 5°6W **13** G2
Newry *U.K.* 54°11N 6°21W **10** B5
Newry Islands △ *Australia* 20°51S 148°56E **62** b
Newton *Ill., U.S.A.* 38°59N 88°10W **80** F9
Newton *Iowa, U.S.A.* 41°42N 93°3W **80** E7
Newton *Kans., U.S.A.* 38°3N 97°21W **80** F5
Newton *Miss., U.S.A.* 32°19N 89°10W **85** E10
Newton *N.C., U.S.A.* 35°40N 81°13W **85** D14
Newton *N.J., U.S.A.* 41°3N 74°45W **83** E10
Newton *Tex., U.S.A.* 30°51N 93°46W **84** F8
Newton Abbot *U.K.* 50°32N 3°37W **13** G4
Newton Aycliffe *U.K.* 54°37N 1°34W **12** C6
Newton Falls *N.Y., U.S.A.* 44°12N 74°59W **83** B10
Newton Falls *Ohio, U.S.A.* 41°11N 80°59W **82** E4
Newton Stewart *U.K.* 54°57N 4°30W **11** G4
Newtonmore *U.K.* 57°4N 4°8W **11** D4
Newtown *U.K.* 52°31N 3°19W **13** E4
Newtownabbey *U.K.* 54°40N 5°56W **10** B6
Newtownards *U.K.* 54°36N 5°42W **10** B6
Newtownbarry = Bunclody *Ireland* 52°39N 6°40W **10** D5
Newtownstewart *U.K.* 54°43N 7°23W **10** B4
Newville *U.S.A.* 40°10N 77°24W **82** F7
Neya *Russia* 58°21N 43°49E **18** C7
Neyrīz *Iran* 29°15N 54°19E **47** D7
Neyshābūr *Iran* 36°10N 58°50E **47** B8
Neyveli *India* 11°32N 79°29E **45** J4
Neyyattinkara *India* 8°26N 77°5E **45** K3
Nezhin = Nizhyn *Ukraine* 51°5N 31°55E **19** D5
Nezperce *U.S.A.* 46°14N 116°14W **76** C5

Nga, Laem *Thailand* 7°55N 98°27E **39 a**
Ngaanyatjarra ☉
Australia 22°40S 127°0E **60 D4**
Ngabang *Indonesia* 0°23N 109°55E **36 D3**
Ngaborodamlu, Tanjung
Indonesia 6°56S 134°11E **37 F8**
N'Gage *Angola* 7°46S 15°15E **54 F3**
Ngaliwurru Nungali ☉
Australia 15°42S 130°4E **60 C5**
Ngalurrtju ☉ *Australia* 22°44S 132°5E **60 D5**
Ngami Depression
Botswana 20°30S 22°46E **56 B3**
Ngamring *China* 29°14N 87°10E **30 F6**
Nganglong Kangri *China* 33°0N 81°0E **43 C9**
Ngao *Thailand* 18°46N 99°59E **38 C2**
Ngaoundéré *Cameroon* 7°15N 13°35E **54 C2**
Ngapara *N.Z.* 44°57S 170°46E **59 F3**
Ngarluma ☉ *Australia* 21°30S 118°30E **60 D2**
Ngawi *Indonesia* 7°24S 111°26E **37 G14**
Ngcobo *S. Africa* 31°37S 28°0E **57 D4**
Nghia Lo *Vietnam* 21°33N 104°28E **34 G5**
Ngoring Hu *China* 34°55N 97°5E **30 E8**
Ngorongoro *Tanzania* 3°11S 35°32E **54 E7**
Nguigmi *Niger* 14°20N 13°20E **53 F8**
Nguiu *Australia* 11°46S 130°38E **60 B5**
Ngukurr *Australia* 14°44S 134°44E **62 A1**
Ngum → *Laos* 18°31N 102°32E **38 C4**
Ngundu *Zimbabwe* 18°11S 31°15E **57 A5**
Nguru *Nigeria* 12°56N 10°29E **53 F8**
Nguyen Binh *Vietnam* 22°39N 105°56E **34 F5**
Ngwaketse ☉ *Botswana* 25°0S 25°0E **56 C3**
Nha Bang *Vietnam* 10°37N 105°0E **39 G5**
Nha Trang *Vietnam* 12°16N 109°10E **39 F7**
Nhacoongo *Mozam.* 24°18S 35°14E **57 B6**
Nhamundá → *Brazil* 2°12S 56°41W **93 D7**
Nhangulaze, L. *Mozam.* 24°0S 34°30E **57 B5**
Nharnuwangga, Wajarri and
Ngarlawangga ☉
Australia 24°50S 118°0E **61 D2**
Nhill *Australia* 36°18S 141°40E **63 F3**
Nho Quan *Vietnam* 20°18N 105°45E **34 G5**
Nhulunbuy *Australia* 12°10S 137°20E **62 A2**
Niafounké *Mali* 16°0N 4°5W **52 E5**
Niagara Falls *Canada* 43°7N 79°5W **82 C5**
Niagara Falls *U.S.A.* 43°5N 79°4W **82 C6**
Niagara-on-the-Lake
Canada 43°15N 79°4W **82 C5**
Niah *Malaysia* 3°58N 113°46E **36 D4**
Niamey *Niger* 13°27N 2°6E **52 F6**
Niangara
Dem. Rep. of the Congo 3°42N 27°50E **54 D5**
Niantic *U.S.A.* 41°20N 72°11W **83 E12**
Nias *Indonesia* 1°0N 97°30E **36 D1**
Nibāk *Si. Arabia* 24°25N 50°50E **47 E7**
Nicaragua ■ *Cent. Amer.* 11°40N 85°30W **88 D2**
Nicaragua, L. de *Nic.* 12°0N 85°30W **88 D2**
Nicastro *Italy* 38°59N 16°19E **22 E7**
Nice *France* 43°42N 7°14E **20 E7**
Niceville *U.S.A.* 30°31N 86°30W **85 F11**
Nichicun, L. *Canada* 53°5N 71°0W **73 B5**
Nichinan *Japan* 31°38N 131°23E **29 J5**
Nicholás, Canal *Caribbean* 23°30N 80°5W **88 B3**
Nicholas Channel = Nicholás,
Canal *Caribbean* 23°30N 80°5W **88 B3**
Nicholasville *U.S.A.* 37°53N 84°34W **81 G11**
Nichols *U.S.A.* 42°1N 76°22W **83 D8**
Nicholson *Australia* 18°2S 128°54E **60 C4**
Nicholson *U.S.A.* 41°37N 75°47W **83 E9**
Nicholson → *Australia* 17°31S 139°36E **62 B2**
Nicholson L. *Canada* 62°40N 102°40W **71 A8**
Nicholson Ra. *Australia* 27°15S 116°45E **61 E2**
Nicholville *U.S.A.* 44°41N 74°39W **83 B10**
Nicobar Is. *Ind. Oc.* 8°0N 93°30E **45 L11**
Nicola *Canada* 50°12N 120°40W **70 C4**
Nicolls Town *Bahamas* 25°8N 78°0W **88 A4**
Nicosia *Cyprus* 35°10N 33°25E **46 C2**
Nicoya *Costa Rica* 10°9N 85°27W **88 D2**
Nicoya, G. de *Costa Rica* 10°0N 85°0W **88 E3**
Nicoya, Pen. de *Costa Rica* 9°45S 85°40W **88 E2**
Nidd → *U.K.* 53°59N 1°23W **12 D6**
Niedersachsen □ *Germany* 52°50N 9°0E **16 B5**
Niekerkshoop *S. Africa* 29°19S 22°51E **56 D3**
Niemen = Nemunas →
Lithuania 55°25N 21°10E **9 J19**
Nienburg *Germany* 52°39N 9°13E **16 B5**
Nieu Bethesda *S. Africa* 31°51S 24°34E **56 D3**
Nieuw Amsterdam
Suriname 5°53N 55°5W **93 B7**
Nieuw Nickerie *Suriname* 6°0N 56°59W **93 B7**
Nieuwoudtville *S. Africa* 31°23S 19°7E **56 E2**
Nieuwpoort *Belgium* 51°8N 2°45E **15 C2**
Niğde *Turkey* 37°58N 34°40E **46 B2**
Nigel *S. Africa* 26°27S 28°25E **57 D4**
Niger ■ *W. Afr.* 17°30N 10°0E **52 E7**
Niger → *W. Afr.* 5°33N 6°33E **52 G7**
Nigeria ■ *W. Afr.* 8°30N 8°0E **52 G7**
Nighasin *India* 28°14N 80°52E **43 E9**
Nightcaps *N.Z.* 45°57S 168°2E **59 F2**
Nihoa *U.S.A.* 23°6N 161°58W **75 L7**
Nihon = Japan ■ *Asia* 36°0N 136°0E **29 G8**
Nii-Jima *Japan* 34°20N 139°15E **29 G9**
Niigata *Japan* 37°58N 139°0E **28 F9**
Niigata □ *Japan* 37°15N 138°45E **29 F9**
Niihama *Japan* 33°55N 133°16E **29 H6**
Ni'ihau *U.S.A.* 21°54N 160°9W **75 L7**
Niimi *Japan* 34°59N 133°28E **29 G6**
Niitsu *Japan* 37°48N 139°7E **28 F9**
Nijil *Jordan* 30°32N 35°33E **48 E4**
Nijkerk *Neths.* 52°13N 5°30E **15 B5**
Nijverdal *Neths.* 52°22N 6°28E **15 B6**
Nīk Pey *Iran* 36°50N 48°10E **47 B6**
Nikaweratiya *Sri Lanka* 7°45N 80°7E **45 L5**
Nikel *Russia* 69°24N 30°13E **8 B24**
Nikiniki *Indonesia* 9°49S 124°30E **60 A3**
Nikkō *Japan* 36°45N 139°35E **29 F9**
Nikkō △ *Japan* 36°56N 139°37E **29 F9**
Nikolayev = Mykolayiv
Ukraine 46°58N 32°0E **19 E5**

Nikolayevsk *Russia* 50°0N 45°35E **19 E8**
Nikolayevsk-na-Amur
Russia 53°8N 140°44E **27 D15**
Nikolskoye *Russia* 55°12N 166°0E **27 D17**
Nikopol *Ukraine* 47°35N 34°25E **19 E5**
Nīkshahr *Iran* 26°15N 60°10E **47 E9**
Nikšić *Montenegro* 42°50N 18°57E **23 C8**
Nîl, Nahr en → *Africa* 30°10N 31°6E **53 B12**
Nîl el Abyad → *Sudan* 15°38N 32°31E **53 E12**
Nîl el Azraq → *Sudan* 15°38N 32°31E **53 E12**
Nila *Indonesia* 6°44S 129°31E **37 F7**
Nilakkottai *India* 10°10N 77°52E **45 J3**
Niland *U.S.A.* 33°14N 115°31W **79 M11**
Nilanga *India* 18°6N 76°46E **44 E3**
Nile = Nîl, Nahr en →
Africa 30°10N 31°6E **53 B12**
Niles *Mich., U.S.A.* 41°50N 86°15W **80 E10**
Niles *Ohio, U.S.A.* 41°11N 80°46W **82 E4**
Nileshwar *India* 12°15N 75°6E **45 H2**
Nilgiri Hills *India* 11°30N 76°30E **45 J3**
Nim Ka Thana *India* 27°44N 75°48E **42 F6**
Nimach *India* 24°30N 74°56E **42 G6**
Nimbahera *India* 24°37N 74°45E **42 G6**
Nîmes *France* 43°50N 4°23E **20 E6**
Nimfaíon, Ákra = Pines, Akra
Greece 40°5N 24°20E **23 D11**
Nimmitabel *Australia* 36°29S 149°15E **63 F4**
Nīnawā *Iraq* 36°25N 43°10E **46 B4**
Nīnawā □ *Iraq* 36°15N 43°0E **46 B4**
Nindigully *Australia* 28°21S 148°50E **63 D4**
Nine Degree Channel *India* 9°0N 73°0E **45 K1**
Ninepin Group *China* 22°16N 114°21E **31 a**
Nineveh = Nīnawā *Iraq* 36°25N 43°10E **46 B4**
Ning Xian *China* 35°30N 107°58E **32 G4**
Ningaloo Marine ☉
Australia 22°23S 113°32E **60 D1**
Ning'an *China* 44°22N 129°20E **33 B15**
Ningbo *China* 29°51N 121°28E **35 C13**
Ningcheng *China* 41°32N 119°53E **33 D10**
Ningde *China* 26°38N 119°23E **35 D12**
Ningdu *China* 26°25N 115°59E **35 D10**
Ningguang *China* 26°42N 113°55E **35 D9**
Ningguo *China* 30°35N 119°0E **35 B12**
Ninghai *China* 29°15N 121°27E **35 C13**
Ninghua *China* 26°14N 116°45E **35 D11**
Ningjin *China* 37°35N 114°57E **32 F8**
Ningjing Shan *China* 31°0N 98°20E **34 C2**
Ninglang *China* 27°20N 100°55E **34 D3**
Ningling *China* 34°25N 115°22E **32 G8**
Ningming *China* 22°8N 107°4E **34 F6**
Ningnan *China* 27°5N 102°36E **34 D4**
Ningpo = Ningbo
China 29°51N 121°28E **35 C13**
Ningqiang *China* 32°47N 106°15E **32 H4**
Ningshan *China* 33°21N 108°21E **34 A7**
Ningsia Hui A.R. = Ningxia Huizu
Zizhiqu □ *China* 38°0N 106°0E **32 F4**
Ningwu *China* 39°0N 112°18E **32 E7**
Ningxia Huizu Zizhiqu □
China 38°0N 106°0E **32 F4**
Ningxiang *China* 28°15N 112°30E **35 C9**
Ningyang *China* 35°47N 116°45E **32 G9**
Ningyuan *China* 25°37N 111°57E **35 E8**
Ninh Binh *Vietnam* 20°15N 105°55E **34 G5**
Ninh Giang *Vietnam* 20°44N 106°24E **38 B6**
Ninh Hoa *Vietnam* 12°30N 109°7E **38 F7**
Ninh Ma *Vietnam* 12°48N 109°21E **38 F7**
Ninove *Belgium* 50°51N 4°2E **15 D4**
Nioaque *Brazil* 21°5S 55°50W **95 A4**
Niobrara *U.S.A.* 42°45N 98°2W **80 D4**
Niobrara → *U.S.A.* 42°46N 98°3W **80 D4**
Nioro du Sahel *Mali* 15°15N 9°30W **52 E4**
Niort *France* 46°19N 0°29W **20 C3**
Nipani *India* 16°20N 74°25E **45 F2**
Nipawin *Canada* 53°20N 104°0W **71 C8**
Nipigon *Canada* 49°0N 88°17W **72 C2**
Nipigon, L. *Canada* 49°50N 88°30W **72 C2**
Nipishish L. *Canada* 54°12N 60°45W **73 B7**
Nipissing, L. *Canada* 46°20N 80°0W **72 C4**
Nipomo *U.S.A.* 35°3N 120°29W **79 K6**
Nipton *U.S.A.* 35°28N 115°16W **79 K11**
Niquelândia *Brazil* 14°33S 48°23W **93 F9**
Nīr *Iran* 38°2N 47°59E **46 B5**
Nira → *India* 17°58N 75°8E **44 F2**
Nirasaki *Japan* 35°42N 138°27E **29 G9**
Nirmal *India* 19°3N 78°20E **44 E4**
Nirmali *India* 26°20N 86°35E **43 F12**
Niš *Serbia* 43°19N 21°58E **23 C9**
Nisa *Turkmenistan* 37°59N 58°11E **47 B8**
Nisāb *Si. Arabia* 29°11N 44°43E **46 D5**
Nisāb *Yemen* 14°25N 46°29E **49 E4**
Nishino'omote *Japan* 30°43N 130°59E **29 J5**
Nishiwaki *Japan* 34°59N 134°58E **29 G7**
Niskibi → *Canada* 56°29N 88°9W **72 A2**
Nisqually → *U.S.A.* 47°7N 122°42W **78 C4**
Nissum Bredning *Denmark* 56°40N 8°20E **9 H13**
Nistru = Dnister →
Europe 46°18N 30°17E **17 E16**
Nisutlin → *Canada* 60°14N 132°34W **70 A2**
Nitchequon *Canada* 53°10N 70°58W **73 B5**
Nith → *Canada* 43°12N 80°23W **82 C4**
Nith → *U.K.* 55°14N 3°33W **11 F5**
Nitmiluk △ *Australia* 14°6S 132°15E **60 B5**
Nitra *Slovak Rep.* 48°19N 18°4E **17 D10**
Nitra → *Slovak Rep.* 47°46N 18°10E **17 E10**
Niue ☑ *Pac. Oc.* 19°2S 169°54W **65 J11**
Niulan Jiang → *China* 27°30N 103°5E **34 D4**
Niut *Indonesia* 0°55N 109°54E **36 D4**
Niutou Shan *China* 29°5N 121°59E **35 C13**
Niuzhuang *China* 40°58N 122°28E **33 D12**
Nivala *Finland* 63°56N 24°57E **8 E21**
Nivelles *Belgium* 50°35N 4°20E **15 D4**
Nivernais *France* 47°15N 3°30E **20 C5**
Niverville *Canada* 49°36N 97°3W **71 D9**
Niwas *India* 23°3N 80°26E **43 H9**
Nixa *U.S.A.* 37°3N 93°18W **80 G7**
Nixon *U.S.A.* 29°16N 97°46W **84 G6**
Nizam Sagar *India* 18°10N 77°58E **44 E3**

Nizamabad *India* 18°45N 78°7E **44 E4**
Nizamghat *India* 28°20N 95°45E **41 E19**
Nizhne Kolymsk
Russia 68°34N 160°55E **27 C17**
Nizhnekamsk *Russia* 55°38N 51°49E **18 C9**
Nizhneudinsk *Russia* 54°54N 99°3E **27 D10**
Nizhnevartovsk *Russia* 60°56N 76°38E **26 C8**
Nizhniy Bestyakh
Russia 61°57N 129°54E **27 C13**
Nizhniy Novgorod *Russia* 56°20N 44°0E **18 C7**
Nizhniy Tagil *Russia* 57°55N 59°57E **18 C10**
Nizhyn *Ukraine* 51°5N 31°55E **19 D5**
Nizip *Turkey* 37°5N 37°50E **46 B3**
Nízké Tatry *Slovak Rep.* 48°55N 19°30E **17 D10**
Nizwá *Oman* 22°56N 57°32E **49 C6**
Njazidja = Grande Comore
Comoros Is. 11°35S 43°20E **55 a**
Njombe *Tanzania* 9°20S 34°50E **54 F6**
Nkandla *S. Africa* 28°37S 31°5E **57 C5**
Nkawkaw *Ghana* 6°36N 0°49W **52 G5**
Nkhotakota *Malawi* 12°56S 34°15E **55 G6**
Nkongsamba *Cameroon* 4°55N 9°55E **54 D1**
Nkurenkuru *Namibia* 17°42S 18°32E **56 A2**
Nmai → *Burma* 25°30N 97°25E **34 F2**
Noakhali *Bangla.* 22°48N 91°10E **41 H17**
Nobel *Canada* 45°25N 80°6W **82 A4**
Nobeoka *Japan* 32°36N 131°41E **29 H5**
Noblesville *U.S.A.* 40°3N 86°1W **80 E10**
Noboribetsu *Japan* 42°24N 141°6E **28 C10**
Noccundra *Australia* 27°50S 142°36E **63 D3**
Nocera Inferiore *Italy* 40°44N 14°38E **22 D6**
Nocona *U.S.A.* 33°47N 97°44W **84 E6**
Noda *Japan* 35°56N 139°52E **29 G9**
Nogales *Mexico* 31°19N 110°56W **86 A2**
Nogales *U.S.A.* 31°21N 110°56W **77 L8**
Nōgata *Japan* 33°48N 130°44E **29 H5**
Noggerup *Australia* 33°32S 116°5E **61 F2**
Noginsk *Russia* 64°30N 90°50E **27 C10**
Nogliki *Russia* 51°50N 143°10E **27 D15**
Nogoa → *Australia* 23°40S 147°55E **62 C4**
Nogoyá *Argentina* 32°24S 59°48W **94 C4**
Nohar *India* 29°11N 74°49E **42 E6**
Nohta *India* 23°40N 79°34E **43 H8**
Noires, Mts. *France* 48°11N 3°40W **20 B2**
Noirmoutier, Î. de *France* 46°58N 2°10W **20 C2**
Nojane *Botswana* 23°15S 20°14E **56 B3**
Nojima-Zaki *Japan* 34°54N 139°53E **29 G9**
Nok Kundi *Pakistan* 28°50N 62°45E **40 E3**
Nok Ta Phao, Ko *Thailand* 9°23N 99°40E **39 b**
Nokaneng *Botswana* 19°40S 22°17E **56 B3**
Nokia *Finland* 61°30N 23°30E **8 F20**
Nokomis *Canada* 51°35N 105°0W **71 C8**
Nokomis L. *Canada* 57°0N 103°0W **71 B8**
Nola *C.A.R.* 3°35N 16°4E **54 D3**
Noma Omuramba →
Namibia 18°52S 20°53E **56 A3**
Nombre de Dios *Panama* 9°34N 79°28W **88 E4**
Nome *U.S.A.* 64°30N 165°25W **74 C6**
Nomgon *Mongolia* 42°50N 105°8E **32 C3**
Nomo-Zaki *Japan* 32°35N 129°44E **29 H4**
Nomuka *Tonga* 20°17S 174°48W **59 c**
Nomuka Group *Tonga* 20°20S 174°48W **59 c**
Nonacho L. *Canada* 61°42N 109°40W **71 A7**
Nonda *Australia* 20°40S 142°28E **62 C3**
Nong Chang *Thailand* 15°23N 99°51E **38 E2**
Nong Han Res. *Thailand* 17°11N 104°9E **38 D5**
Nong Het *Laos* 19°29N 103°59E **38 C4**
Nong Khai *Thailand* 17°50N 102°46E **38 D4**
Nong'an *China* 44°25N 125°5E **33 B13**
Nongoma *S. Africa* 27°58S 31°35E **57 C5**
Nongsa *Indonesia* 1°11N 104°8E **39 d**
Nonoava *Mexico* 27°28N 106°44W **86 B3**
Nonsan *S. Korea* 36°12N 127°5E **33 F14**
Noonamah *Australia* 12°40S 131°4E **60 B5**
Noondie, L. *Australia* 28°30S 120°30E **61 E2**
Noonkanbah ☉
Australia 18°30S 124°50E **60 C3**
Noord Brabant □ *Neths.* 51°40N 5°0E **15 C5**
Noord Holland □ *Neths.* 52°30N 4°45E **15 B4**
Noordbeveland *Neths.* 51°35N 3°50E **15 C3**
Noordoostpolder *Neths.* 52°45N 5°45E **15 B5**
Noordwijk *Neths.* 52°14N 4°26E **15 B4**
Noosa Heads *Australia* 26°25S 153°6E **63 D5**
Nootka I. *Canada* 49°32N 126°42W **70 D3**
Nopiming △ *Canada* 50°30N 95°37W **71 C9**
Noralee *Canada* 53°59N 126°26W **70 C3**
Noranda = Rouyn-Noranda
Canada 48°20N 79°0W **72 C4**
Norco *U.S.A.* 33°56N 117°33W **79 M9**
Nord-Ostsee-Kanal
Germany 54°12N 9°32E **16 A5**
Nordaustlandet *Svalbard* 79°14N 23°0E **4 B9**
Nordegg *Canada* 52°29N 116°5W **70 C5**
Norderney *Germany* 53°42N 7°9E **16 B4**
Norderstedt *Germany* 53°42N 10°1E **16 B5**
Nordfjord *Norway* 61°55N 5°30E **8 F11**
Nordfriesische Inseln
Germany 54°40N 8°20E **16 A5**
Nordhausen *Germany* 51°30N 10°47E **16 C6**
Norðoyar *Færoe Is.* 62°17N 6°35W **8 E9**
Nordkapp *Norway* 71°10N 25°50E **8 A21**
Nordkapp *Svalbard* 80°31N 20°0E **4 A9**
Nordkinnhalvøya
Norway 70°55N 27°40E **8 A22**
Nordrhein-Westfalen □
Germany 51°45N 7°30E **16 C4**
Nordvik *Russia* 74°2N 111°32E **27 B12**
Nore → *Ireland* 52°25N 6°58W **10 D4**
Noreland *Canada* 44°43N 78°48W **82 B6**
Norfolk = Simcoe
Canada 42°50N 80°23W **82 D4**
Norfolk *N.Y., U.S.A.* 44°48N 74°59W **83 B10**
Norfolk *Nebr., U.S.A.* 42°2N 97°25W **80 D5**
Norfolk *Va., U.S.A.* 36°50N 76°17W **81 G15**
Norfolk □ *U.K.* 52°39N 0°54E **13 E8**
Norfolk Broads △ *U.K.* 52°30N 1°15E **13 E9**
Norfolk I. *Pac. Oc.* 28°58S 168°3E **58 D9**
Norfolk Ridge *Pac. Oc.* 29°0S 168°0E **64 K8**
Norfork L. *U.S.A.* 36°15N 92°14W **84 C8**

Norge = Norway ■ *Europe* 63°0N 11°0E **8 E14**
Norilsk *Russia* 69°20N 88°6E **27 C9**
Norma, Mt. *Australia* 20°55S 140°42E **62 C3**
Normal *U.S.A.* 40°31N 88°59W **80 E9**
Norman *U.S.A.* 35°13N 97°26W **84 D6**
Norman → *Australia* 19°18S 141°51E **62 B3**
Norman Wells *Canada* 65°17N 126°51W **68 D6**
Normanby → *Australia* 14°23S 144°10E **62 A3**
Normandie *France* 48°45N 0°10E **20 B4**
Normandin *Canada* 48°49N 72°31W **72 C5**
Normandy = Normandie
France 48°45N 0°10E **20 B4**
Normanhurst, Mt.
Australia 25°4S 122°30E **61 E3**
Normanton *Australia* 17°40S 141°10E **62 B3**
Norman Wells *Canada* 49°0N 79°22W **72 C4**
Norquay *Canada* 51°53N 102°5W **71 C8**
Norquinco *Argentina* 41°51S 70°55W **96 E2**
Norrbottens län □ *Sweden* 66°50N 20°0E **8 C19**
Norris Point *Canada* 49°31N 57°53W **73 C8**
Norristown *U.S.A.* 40°7N 75°21W **83 F9**
Norrköping *Sweden* 58°37N 16°11E **9 G17**
Norrland *Sweden* 62°15N 15°45E **8 E16**
Norrtälje *Sweden* 59°46N 18°42E **9 G18**
Norseman *Australia* 32°8S 121°43E **61 F3**
Norsk *Russia* 52°30N 130°5E **27 D14**
Norte, Serra do *Brazil* 11°20S 59°0W **92 F7**
Norte, C. *Brazil* 1°40N 49°55W **93 C9**
North, C. *Canada* 47°2N 60°20W **73 C7**
North Adams *U.S.A.* 42°42N 73°7W **83 D11**
North America 40°0N 100°0W **66 F10**
North Andaman I. *India* 13°15N 92°55E **45 H11**
North Arm *Canada* 62°0N 114°30W **70 A5**
North Augusta *U.S.A.* 33°30N 81°59W **85 E14**
North Australian Basin
Ind. Oc. 14°30S 116°30E **64 J3**
North Ayrshire □ *U.K.* 55°45N 4°44W **11 F4**
North Bass I. *U.S.A.* 41°40N 82°56W **82 E2**
North Battleford *Canada* 52°50N 108°17W **71 C7**
North Bay *Canada* 46°20N 79°30W **72 C4**
North Belcher Is. *Canada* 56°50N 79°50W **72 A4**
North Bend *Oreg.,
U.S.A.* 43°24N 124°14W **76 E1**
North Bend *Pa., U.S.A.* 41°20N 77°42W **82 E7**
North Bend *Wash.,
U.S.A.* 47°30N 121°47W **78 C5**
North Bennington
U.S.A. 42°56N 73°15W **83 D11**
North Berwick *U.K.* 56°4N 2°42W **11 E6**
North Berwick *U.S.A.* 43°18N 70°44W **83 C14**
North Brother I. *India* 10°59N 92°40E **45 J11**
North Bruce *Canada* 44°22N 81°26W **82 B3**
North C. *Canada* 47°5N 64°0W **73 C7**
North C. *N.Z.* 34°23S 173°4E **59 A4**
North Canadian →
U.S.A. 35°22N 95°37W **84 D7**
North Canton *U.S.A.* 40°53N 81°24W **82 F3**
North Cape = Nordkapp
Norway 71°10N 25°50E **8 A21**
North Caribou L. *Canada* 52°50N 90°40W **72 B1**
North Carolina □ *U.S.A.* 35°30N 80°0W **85 D15**
North Cascades △
U.S.A. 48°45N 121°10W **76 B3**
North Channel *Canada* 46°0N 83°0W **72 C3**
North Channel *U.K.* 55°13N 5°52W **11 F3**
North Charleston
U.S.A. 32°53N 79°58W **85 E15**
North Chicago *U.S.A.* 42°19N 87°51W **80 D10**
North Collins *U.S.A.* 42°35N 78°56W **82 D6**
North Creek *U.S.A.* 43°42N 73°59W **83 C11**
North Dakota □ *U.S.A.* 47°30N 100°15W **80 B3**
North Downs *U.K.* 51°19N 0°21E **13 F8**
North East *U.S.A.* 42°13N 79°50W **82 D5**
North East □ *Botswana* 20°45S 27°30E **57 B4**
North East Frontier Agency =
Arunachal Pradesh □
India 28°0N 95°0E **41 F19**
North East Lincolnshire □
U.K. 53°34N 0°2W **12 D7**
North Esk → *U.K.* 56°46N 2°24W **11 E6**
North European Plain
Europe 55°0N 25°0E **6 E10**
North Foreland *U.K.* 51°22N 1°28E **13 F9**
North Fork *U.S.A.* 37°14N 119°21W **78 H7**
North Fork American →
U.S.A. 38°57N 120°59W **78 G5**
North Fork Feather →
U.S.A. 38°33N 121°30W **78 F5**
North Fork Grand →
U.S.A. 45°47N 102°16W **80 C2**
North Fork Red →
U.S.A. 34°24N 99°14W **84 D5**
North Frisian Is. = Nordfriesische
Inseln *Germany* 54°40N 8°20E **16 A5**
North Gower *Canada* 45°8N 75°43W **83 A9**
North Hd. *Australia* 30°14S 114°59E **61 F1**
North Henik L. *Canada* 61°45N 97°40W **71 A9**
North Highlands *U.S.A.* 38°40N 121°23W **78 G5**
North I. *India* 10°8N 72°20E **45 J1**
North I. *N.Z.* 38°0S 175°0E **59 C5**
North I. *Seychelles* 4°25S 55°13E **55 b**
North Kingsville *U.S.A.* 41°54N 80°42W **82 E4**
North Knife → *Canada* 58°53N 94°45W **71 B10**
North Koel → *India* 24°45N 83°50E **43 G10**
North Korea ■ *Asia* 40°0N 127°0E **33 E14**
North Lakhimpur *India* 27°14N 94°7E **41 F19**
North Lanarkshire □
U.K. 55°52N 3°56W **11 F5**
North Lincolnshire □
U.K. 53°36N 0°30W **12 D7**
North Little Rock *U.S.A.* 34°45N 92°15W **84 D8**
North Loup → *U.S.A.* 41°17N 98°24W **80 E4**
North Magnetic Pole
Arctic 82°18N 113°24W **4 A2**
North Mankato *U.S.A.* 44°10N 94°2W **80 C6**
North Minch *U.K.* 58°5N 5°55W **11 C3**
North Moose L. *Canada* 54°3N 100°12W **71 C8**
North Myrtle Beach
U.S.A. 33°48N 78°42W **85 E15**
North Nahanni →
Canada 62°15N 123°20W **70 A4**

North Olmsted *U.S.A.* 41°25N 81°56W **82 E3**
North Ossetia □ *Russia* 43°30N 44°30E **19 F7**
North Pagai, I. = Pagai Utara,
Pulau *Indonesia* 2°35S 100°0E **36 E2**
North Palisade *U.S.A.* 37°6N 118°31W **78 H8**
North Platte *U.S.A.* 41°8N 100°46W **80 E3**
North Platte → *U.S.A.* 41°7N 100°42W **80 E3**
North Pole *Arctic* 90°0N 0°0 **4 A**
North Portal *Canada* 49°0N 102°33W **71 D8**
North Powder *U.S.A.* 45°2N 117°55W **76 D5**
North Pt. *Barbados* 13°20N 59°37W **89 g**
North Pt. *Trin. & Tob.* 11°21N 60°31W **93 J16**
North Pt. *U.S.A.* 45°2N 83°16W **82 A1**
North Reef I. *India* 13°5N 92°43E **45 H11**
North Rhine Westphalia =
Nordrhein-Westfalen □
Germany 51°45N 7°30E **16 C4**
North River *Canada* 53°49N 57°6W **73 B8**
North Ronaldsay *U.K.* 59°22N 2°26W **11 B6**
North Saskatchewan →
Canada 53°15N 105°5W **71 C7**
North Sea *Europe* 56°0N 4°0E **6 D6**
North Seal → *Canada* 58°50N 98°7W **71 B9**
North Sentinel I. *India* 11°33N 92°15E **45 J11**
North Slope ☆ *U.S.A.* 69°15N 152°0W **74 B9**
North Somerset □ *U.K.* 51°24N 2°45W **13 F5**
North Sydney *Canada* 46°12N 60°15W **73 C7**
North Syracuse *U.S.A.* 43°8N 76°7W **83 C8**
North Taranaki Bight
N.Z. 38°50S 174°15E **59 C5**
North Thompson →
Canada 50°40N 120°20W **70 C4**
North Tonawanda *U.S.A.* 43°2N 78°53W **82 C6**
North Troy *U.S.A.* 45°0N 72°24W **83 B12**
North Twin I. *Canada* 53°20N 80°0W **72 B4**
North Tyne → *U.K.* 55°0N 2°8W **12 B5**
North Uist *U.K.* 57°40N 7°15W **11 D1**
North Vancouver *Canada* 49°19N 123°4W **78 A3**
North Vernon *U.S.A.* 39°0N 85°38W **81 F11**
North Wabasca L.
Canada 56°0N 113°55W **70 B6**
North Walsham *U.K.* 52°50N 1°22E **12 E9**
North West = Severo-Zapadnyy □
Russia 65°0N 40°0E **26 C4**
North West □ *Botswana* 19°0S 22°30E **56 A3**
North-West □ *S. Africa* 27°0S 25°0E **56 C4**
North West C. *Australia* 21°45S 114°9E **60 D1**
North West Christmas I. Ridge
Pac. Oc. 6°30N 165°0W **65 F11**
North West Frontier = Khyber
Pakhtunkhwa □
Pakistan 34°0N 72°0E **42 C4**
North West Highlands
U.K. 57°33N 4°58W **11 D4**
North West River *Canada* 53°30N 60°10W **73 B7**
North Wildwood *U.S.A.* 39°0N 74°48W **81 F16**
North York Moors *U.K.* 54°23N 0°53W **12 C7**
North York Moors △
U.K. 54°27N 0°51W **12 C7**
North Yorkshire □ *U.K.* 54°15N 1°25W **12 C6**
Northallerton *U.K.* 54°20N 1°26W **12 C6**
Northam *Australia* 31°35S 116°42E **61 F2**
Northam *S. Africa* 24°56S 27°18E **56 B4**
Northampton *Australia* 28°27S 114°33E **61 E1**
Northampton *U.K.* 52°15N 0°53W **13 E7**
Northampton *Mass.,
U.S.A.* 42°19N 72°38W **83 D12**
Northampton *Pa., U.S.A.* 40°41N 75°30W **83 F9**
Northamptonshire □
U.K. 52°16N 0°55W **13 E7**
Northbridge *U.S.A.* 42°9N 71°39W **83 D13**
Northbrook *Canada* 44°44N 77°9W **82 B7**
Northcliffe *Australia* 34°39S 116°7E **61 F2**
Northeast Pacific Basin
Pac. Oc. 32°0N 145°0W **65 D13**
Northeast Providence Channel
W. Indies 26°0N 76°0W **88 A4**
Northern = Limpopo □
S. Africa 24°5S 29°0E **57 B4**
Northern Areas = Gilgit-
Baltistan □ *Pakistan* 36°30N 73°0E **43 A5**
Northern Cape □ *S. Africa* 30°0S 20°0E **56 C3**
Northern Circars *India* 17°30N 82°30E **44 F6**
Northern Indian L.
Canada 57°20N 97°20W **71 B9**
Northern Ireland □ *U.K.* 54°45N 7°0W **10 B5**
Northern Lau Group *Fiji* 17°30S 178°59W **59 a**
Northern Light L. *Canada* 48°15N 90°39W **72 C1**
Northern Marianas ☑
Pac. Oc. 17°0N 145°0E **64 F6**
Northern Province □
S. Africa 24°0S 29°0E **57 B4**
Northern Range
Trin. & Tob. 10°46N 61°15W **93 K15**
Northern Sporades
Greece 39°15N 23°30E **23 E10**
Northern Territory □
Australia 20°0S 133°0E **60 D5**
Northfield *Minn., U.S.A.* 44°27N 93°9W **80 C7**
Northfield *Vt., U.S.A.* 44°9N 72°40W **83 B12**
Northgate *Canada* 49°0N 102°16W **71 D8**
Northland □ *N.Z.* 35°30S 173°30W **59 A4**
Northome *U.S.A.* 47°52N 94°17W **80 B6**
Northport *Ala., U.S.A.* 33°14N 87°35W **85 E11**
Northport *Wash., U.S.A.* 48°55N 117°48W **76 B5**
Northumberland □ *U.K.* 55°12N 2°0W **12 B6**
Northumberland, C.
Australia 38°5S 140°40E **63 F3**
Northumberland Is.
Australia 21°30S 149°50E **62 C4**
Northumberland Str.
Canada 46°20N 64°0W **73 C7**
Northville *Canada* 43°10N 81°56W **82 C3**
Northville *U.S.A.* 43°13N 74°11W **83 C10**
Northwest Pacific Basin
Pac. Oc. 32°0N 165°0W **64 D8**
Northwest Providence Channel
W. Indies 26°0N 78°0W **88 A4**
Northwest Territories □
Canada 63°0N 118°0W **68 D8**

Northwich U.K. 53°15N 2°31W 12 D5
Northwood Iowa, U.S.A. 43°27N 93°13W 80 D7
Northwood N. Dak., U.S.A. 47°44N 97°34W 80 B5
Norton U.S.A. 39°50N 99°53W 80 F4
Norton Sd. U.S.A. 63°50N 164°0W 74 C7
Norwalk Calif., U.S.A. 33°54N 118°4W 79 M8
Norwalk Conn., U.S.A. 41°7N 73°22W 83 E11
Norwalk Iowa, U.S.A. 41°29N 93°41W 80 E7
Norwalk Ohio, U.S.A. 41°15N 82°37W 82 E2
Norway Maine, U.S.A. 44°13N 70°32W 81 C18
Norway Mich., U.S.A. 45°47N 87°55W 80 C10
Norway ■ Europe 63°0N 11°0E 8 E14
Norway House Canada 53°59N 97°50W 71 C9
Norwegian B. Canada 77°30N 90°0W 69 B14
Norwegian Basin Atl. Oc. 68°0N 2°0W 4 C7
Norwegian Sea Atl. Oc. 66°0N 1°0E 8 B6
Norwich Canada 42°59N 80°36W 82 D4
Norwich U.K. 52°38N 1°18E 13 E9
Norwich Conn., U.S.A. 41°31N 72°5W 83 E12
Norwich N.Y., U.S.A. 42°32N 75°32W 83 D9
Norwood Canada 44°23N 77°59W 82 B7
Norwood U.S.A. 44°45N 75°0W 83 B10
Nosappu-Misaki Japan 45°26N 141°39E 28 C12
Noshiro Japan 40°12N 140°0E 28 D10
Noṣratābād Iran 29°55N 60°0E 47 D8
Noss Hd. U.K. 58°28N 3°3W 11 C5
Nossob → S. Africa 26°55S 20°45E 56 C3
Nosy Varika Madag. 20°35S 48°32E 55 J9
Noteć → Poland 52°44N 15°26E 16 B8
Notikewin → Canada 57°2N 117°38W 70 B5
Noto-Hantō Japan 37°15N 136°40E 29 F8
Notodden Norway 59°35N 9°17E 9 G13
Notre Dame B. Canada 49°45N 55°30W 73 C8
Notre-Dame-de-Koartac = Quaqtaq Canada 60°55N 69°40W 69 E18
Notre-Dame-des-Bois Canada 45°24N 71°4W 83 A13
Notre-Dame-d'Ivugivic = Ivujivik Canada 62°24N 77°55W 69 E16
Notre-Dame-du-Nord Canada 47°36N 79°30W 72 C4
Nottawasaga B. Canada 44°35N 80°15W 82 B4
Nottaway → Canada 51°22N 78°55W 72 B4
Nottingham U.K. 52°58N 1°10W 12 E6
Nottingham, City of □ U.K. 52°58N 1°10W 12 E6
Nottingham I. Canada 63°20N 77°55W 69 E16
Nottinghamshire □ U.K. 53°10N 1°3W 12 D6
Nottoway → U.S.A. 36°33N 76°55W 81 G15
Notwane → Botswana 23°35S 26°58E 56 B4
Nouâdhibou Mauritania 20°54N 17°0W 52 D2
Nouâdhibou, Râs Mauritania 20°50N 17°0W 52 D2
Nouakchott Mauritania 18°9N 15°58W 52 E2
Nouméa N. Cal. 22°17S 166°30E 58 D9
Noupoort S. Africa 31°10S 24°57E 56 D3
Nouveau Comptoir = Wemindji Canada 53°0N 78°49W 72 B4
Nouvelle Amsterdam, Î. Ind. Oc. 38°30S 77°30E 3 F13
Nouvelle-Calédonie = New Caledonia ☒ Pac. Oc. 21°0S 165°0E 58 D9
Nova Esperança Brazil 23°8S 52°24W 95 A5
Nova Friburgo Brazil 22°16S 42°30W 95 A7
Nova Iguaçu Brazil 22°45S 43°28W 95 A7
Nova Iorque Brazil 7°0S 44°5W 93 E10
Nova Lamego Guinea-Biss. 12°19N 14°11W 52 F3
Nova Mambone Mozam. 21°0S 35°3E 57 B6
Nova Scotia □ Canada 45°10N 63°0W 73 C7
Nova Sofala Mozam. 20°7S 34°42E 57 B5
Nova Venécia Brazil 18°45S 40°24W 93 G10
Nova Zagora Bulgaria 42°32N 26°1E 23 C11
Novar Canada 45°27N 79°15W 82 A5
Novara Italy 45°28N 8°38E 20 D8
Novato U.S.A. 38°6N 122°35W 78 G4
Novaya Ladoga Russia 60°7N 32°16E 18 B5
Novaya Lyalya Russia 59°4N 60°45E 18 C11
Novaya Sibir, Ostrov Russia 75°10N 150°0E 27 B16
Novaya Zemlya Russia 75°0N 56°0E 26 B6
Nové Zámky Slovak Rep. 48°2N 18°8E 17 D10
Novgorod = Velikiy Novgorod Russia 58°30N 31°25E 18 C5
Novgorod-Severskiy = Novhorod-Siverskyy Ukraine 52°2N 33°10E 18 D5
Novhorod-Siverskyy Ukraine 52°2N 33°10E 18 D5
Novi Lígure Italy 44°46N 8°47E 20 D8
Novi Pazar Serbia 43°12N 20°28E 23 C9
Novi Sad Serbia 45°18N 19°52E 23 B8
Novo Hamburgo Brazil 29°37S 51°7W 95 B5
Novo Mesto Slovenia 45°47N 15°12E 22 B6
Novoaltaysk Russia 53°30N 84°0E 26 D9
Novocherkassk Russia 47°27N 40°15E 19 E7
Novodvinsk Russia 64°25N 40°42E 18 B7
Novogrudok = Navahrudak Belarus 53°40N 25°50E 17 B13
Novohrad-Volynskyy Ukraine 50°34N 27°35E 17 C14
Novokachalinsk Russia 45°5N 132°0E 28 B5
Novokuybyshevsk Russia 53°7N 49°58E 18 D8
Novokuznetsk Russia 53°45N 87°10E 26 D9
Novolazarevskaya Antarctica 71°0S 12°0E 5 D3
Novomoskovsk Russia 54°5N 38°15E 18 D6
Novorossiysk Russia 44°43N 37°46E 19 F6
Novorybnoye Russia 72°50N 105°50E 27 B11
Novoselytsya Ukraine 48°14N 26°15E 17 D14
Novoshakhtinsk Russia 47°46N 39°58E 19 E6
Novosibirsk Russia 55°0N 83°5E 26 D9
Novosibirskiye Ostrova Russia 75°0N 142°0E 27 B15
Novotroitsk Russia 51°10N 58°15E 18 D10
Novouzensk Russia 50°32N 48°17E 19 D8
Novovolynsk Ukraine 50°45N 24°4E 17 C13
Novska Croatia 45°19N 17°0E 22 B7
Novvy Bor Russia 66°43N 52°19E 18 A9
Novyy Port Russia 67°40N 72°30E 26 C8

Novyy Urengoy Russia 65°48N 76°52E 26 C8
Nowa Sól Poland 51°48N 15°44E 16 C8
Nowata U.S.A. 36°42N 95°38W 84 C7
Nowbarān Iran 35°8N 49°42E 47 C6
Nowghāb Iran 33°53N 59°4E 47 C8
Nowgong = Nagaon India 26°20N 92°50E 41 F18
Nowgong India 25°4N 79°27E 43 G8
Nowra Australia 34°53S 150°35E 63 E5
Nowrangapur India 19°14N 82°33E 44 E6
Nowshera Pakistan 34°0N 72°0E 40 C8
Nowy Sącz Poland 49°40N 20°41E 17 D11
Nowy Targ Poland 49°29N 20°2E 17 D11
Nowy Tomyśl Poland 52°19N 16°10E 16 B9
Noxen U.S.A. 41°25N 76°4W 83 E8
Noyabr'sk Russia 64°34N 76°21E 26 C8
Noyon France 49°34N 2°59E 20 B5
Noyon Mongolia 43°2N 102°4E 32 C2
Nqutu S. Africa 28°13S 30°32E 57 C5
Nsanje Malawi 16°55S 35°12E 55 H7
Nsawam Ghana 5°50N 0°24W 52 G5
Ntaria ⊙ Australia 24°0S 132°41E 60 D5
Nu Jiang → China 29°58N 97°25E 34 E2
Nu Shan China 26°0N 99°20E 34 E2
Nuba Mts. = Nubah, Jibalan Sudan 12°0N 31°0E 53 F12
Nubah, Jibalan Sudan 12°0N 31°0E 53 F12
Nubia Africa 21°0N 32°0E 50 D7
Nubian Desert = Nûbîya, Es Sahrâ en Sudan 21°30N 33°30E 53 D12
Nûbîya, Es Sahrâ en Sudan 21°30N 33°30E 53 D12
Nuboai Indonesia 2°10S 136°30E 37 E9
Nubra → India 34°35N 77°35E 43 B7
Nueces → U.S.A. 27°51N 97°30W 84 H6
Nueltin L. Canada 60°30N 99°30W 71 A9
Nuestra Señora del Rosario de Caá-Catí Argentina 27°45S 57°36W 94 B4
Nueva Ciudad Guerrero Mexico 26°34N 99°12W 87 B5
Nueva Gerona Cuba 21°53N 82°49W 88 B3
Nueva Palmira Uruguay 33°52S 58°20W 94 C4
Nueva Rosita Mexico 27°57N 101°13W 86 B4
Nueva San Salvador El Salv. 13°40N 89°18W 88 D2
Nuéve de Julio Argentina 35°30S 61°0W 94 D3
Nuevitas Cuba 21°30N 77°20W 88 B4
Nuevo, G. Argentina 43°0S 64°30W 96 E4
Nuevo Casas Grandes Mexico 30°25N 107°55W 86 A3
Nuevo Laredo Mexico 27°30N 99°31W 87 B5
Nuevo León □ Mexico 25°20N 100°0W 86 C5
Nuevo Rocafuerte Ecuador 0°55S 75°27W 92 D3
Nugget Pt. N.Z. 46°27S 169°50E 59 G2
Nuhaka N.Z. 39°3S 177°45E 59 C6
Nukey Bluff Australia 32°26S 135°29E 63 E2
Nukhayb Iraq 32°4N 42°3E 46 C4
Nuku Hiva French Polynesia 8°54S 140°6W 65 H13
Nuku'alofa Tonga 21°10S 175°12W 59 c
Nukus Uzbekistan 42°27N 59°41E 26 E6
Nulato U.S.A. 64°43N 158°6W 74 C8
Nullagine Australia 21°53S 120°7E 60 D3
Nullagine → Australia 21°20S 120°20E 60 D3
Nullarbor Australia 31°28S 130°55E 61 F5
Nullarbor △ Australia 32°39S 130°0E 61 F5
Nullarbor Plain Australia 31°10S 129°0E 61 F4
Numalla, L. Australia 28°43S 144°20E 63 D3
Numan Nigeria 9°29N 12°3E 53 G8
Numata Japan 36°45N 139°4E 29 F9
Numaykoos Lake ☐ Canada 57°52N 95°58W 71 B9
Numazu Japan 35°7N 138°51E 29 G9
Numbulwar Australia 14°15S 135°45E 62 A2
Numfoor Indonesia 1°0S 134°50E 37 E8
Numurkah Australia 36°5S 145°26E 63 F4
Nunaksaluk I. Canada 55°49N 60°20W 73 A7
Nunap Isua Greenland 59°48N 43°55W 66 D15
Nunavik Greenland 71°50N 54°25W 69 C21
Nunavut □ Canada 66°0N 85°0W 69 C15
Nunda U.S.A. 42°35N 77°56W 82 D7
Nuneaton U.K. 52°32N 1°27N 13 E6
Nungarin Australia 31°12S 118°6E 61 F2
Nunivak I. U.S.A. 60°10N 166°30W 74 C6
Nunkun India 33°57N 76°2E 43 C7
Núoro Italy 40°20N 9°20E 22 D3
Nuozhadu Dam China 22°39N 100°25E 34 F3
Nûr Iran 36°33N 52°1E 47 B7
Nūrābād Hormozgān, Iran 27°47N 57°12E 47 E8
Nūrābād Lorestān, Iran 34°4N 47°58E 46 C5
Nuremberg = Nürnberg Germany 49°27N 11°3E 16 D6
Nuri Mexico 28°5N 109°22W 86 B3
Nuriootpa Australia 34°27S 139°0E 63 E2
Nūristān □ Afghan. 35°20N 71°0E 40 B7
Nurmes Finland 63°33N 29°10E 8 E23
Nürnberg Germany 49°27N 11°3E 16 D6
Nurpur Pakistan 31°53N 71°54E 42 D4
Nurran, L. = Terewah, L. Australia 29°52S 147°35E 63 D4
Nurrari Lakes Australia 29°1S 130°5E 61 E5
Nusa Dua Indonesia 8°48S 115°14E 37 K18
Nusa Tenggara Barat □ Indonesia 8°50S 117°30E 36 F5
Nusa Tenggara Timur □ Indonesia 9°30S 122°0E 37 F6
Nusaybin Turkey 37°3N 41°10E 19 G7
Nuṣeirat Gaza Strip 31°27N 34°24E 48 D3
Nushki Pakistan 29°35N 66°0E 42 E2
Nuuk Greenland 64°10N 51°35W 69 C14
Nuupere, Pte. Moorea 17°36S 149°47W 59 d
Nuwara Eliya Sri Lanka 6°58N 80°48E 45 L5
Nuwaybʿ, W. an → Si. Arabia 29°18N 34°57E 48 F3
Nuweiba' Egypt 28°59N 34°39E 46 D2
Nuwerus S. Africa 31°8S 18°24E 56 D2
Nuweveldberge S. Africa 32°10S 21°45E 56 E3

Nuyts, Pt. Australia 35°4S 116°38E 61 G2
Nuyts Arch. Australia 32°35S 133°20E 63 E1
Nxai Pan △ Botswana 19°50S 24°46E 56 A3
Nxaunxau Botswana 18°57S 21°4E 56 A3
Nyabing Australia 33°33S 118°9E 61 F2
Nyack U.S.A. 41°5N 73°55W 83 E11
Nyahururu Kenya 0°2N 36°27E 54 D7
Nyaingêntanglha Shan China 30°0N 90°0E 30 F7
Nyâlâ Sudan 12°2N 24°58E 53 F10
Nyalam China 28°32N 86°4E 30 F6
Nyandoma Russia 61°40N 40°12E 18 B7
Nyangana Namibia 18°0S 20°40E 56 A3
Nyasa, L. = Malawi, L. Africa 12°30S 34°30E 55 G6
Nyasvizh Belarus 53°14N 26°38E 17 B14
Nyaungdon = Yandoon Burma 17°0N 95°40E 41 L19
Nyazepetrovsk Russia 56°3N 59°36E 18 C10
Nybro Sweden 56°44N 15°55E 9 H16
Nyda Russia 66°40N 72°58E 26 C8
Nyeboe Land Greenland 82°0N 57°0W 69 A20
Nyingchi China 29°32N 94°25E 30 F7
Nyíregyháza Hungary 47°58N 21°47E 17 E11
Nykarleby = Uusikaarlepyy Finland 63°32N 22°31E 8 E20
Nykøbing Nordjylland, Denmark 56°48N 8°51E 9 H13
Nykøbing Sjælland, Denmark 54°56N 11°52E 9 J14
Nykøbing Sjælland, Denmark 55°55N 11°40E 9 J14
Nyköping Sweden 58°45N 17°1E 9 G17
Nylstroom = Modimolle S. Africa 24°42S 28°22E 57 B4
Nymagee Australia 32°7S 146°20E 63 E4
Nymboida △ Australia 29°38S 152°26E 63 D5
Nynäshamn Sweden 58°54N 17°57E 9 G17
Nyngan Australia 31°30S 147°8E 63 E4
Nyoma Rap India 33°10N 78°40E 43 C8
Nyoman = Nemunas → Lithuania 55°25N 21°10E 9 J19
Nysa Poland 50°30N 17°22E 17 C9
Nysa → Europe 52°4N 14°46E 16 B8
Nyslott = Savonlinna Finland 61°52N 28°53E 8 F23
Nyssa U.S.A. 43°53N 117°0W 76 E5
Nystad = Uusikaupunki Finland 60°47N 21°25E 8 F19
Nyunzu Dem. Rep. of the Congo 5°57S 27°58E 54 F5
Nyurba Russia 63°17N 118°28E 27 C12
Nzega Tanzania 4°10S 33°12E 54 C6
Nzérékoré Guinea 7°49N 8°48W 52 G4
Nzeto Angola 7°10S 12°52E 54 F2
Nzwani = Anjouan Comoros Is. 12°15S 44°20E 55 a

O

O Le Pupū Pu'e △ Samoa 13°59S 171°43W 59 b
Ō-Shima Hokkaidō, Japan 41°30N 139°22E 28 D9
Ō-Shima Shizuoka, Japan 34°44N 139°24E 29 G9
Oa, Mull of U.K. 55°35N 6°20W 11 F2
Oacoma U.S.A. 43°48N 99°24W 80 D4
Oahe, L. U.S.A. 44°27N 100°24W 80 C3
Oahe Dam U.S.A. 44°27N 100°24W 80 C3
O'ahu U.S.A. 21°28N 157°58W 75 L8
Oak Harbor U.S.A. 48°18N 122°39W 78 B4
Oak Hill U.S.A. 37°59N 81°9W 81 G13
Oak Island U.S.A. 33°55N 78°10W 85 E15
Oak Ridge U.S.A. 36°1N 84°16W 85 C12
Oak View U.S.A. 34°24N 119°18W 79 L7
Oakan-Dake Japan 43°27N 144°10E 28 C12
Oakdale Calif., U.S.A. 37°46N 120°51W 78 H6
Oakdale La., U.S.A. 30°49N 92°40W 84 F8
Oakes U.S.A. 46°8N 98°6W 80 B4
Oakesdale U.S.A. 47°8N 117°15W 76 C5
Oakey Australia 27°25S 151°43E 63 D5
Oakfield U.S.A. 43°4N 78°16W 82 C6
Oakham U.K. 52°40N 0°43W 13 E7
Oakhurst U.S.A. 37°19N 119°40W 78 H7
Oakland U.S.A. 37°48N 122°16W 78 H4
Oakley Idaho, U.S.A. 42°15N 113°53W 76 E7
Oakley Kans., U.S.A. 39°8N 100°51W 80 F3
Oakover → Australia 21°0S 120°40E 60 D3
Oakridge U.S.A. 43°45N 122°28W 76 E2
Oakville Canada 43°27N 79°41W 82 C5
Oakville U.S.A. 46°51N 123°14W 78 D3
Oamaru N.Z. 45°5S 170°59E 59 F3
Oasis Calif., U.S.A. 37°29N 117°55W 78 H9
Oasis Calif., U.S.A. 33°28N 116°6W 79 M10
Oates Land Antarctica 69°0S 160°0E 5 C11
Oatman U.S.A. 35°1N 114°19W 79 K12
Oaxaca Mexico 17°3N 96°43W 87 D5
Oaxaca □ Mexico 17°0N 96°30W 87 D5
Ob → Russia 66°45N 69°30E 26 C7
Oba Canada 49°4N 84°7W 72 C3
Obama Japan 35°30N 135°45E 29 G7
Oban U.K. 56°25N 5°29W 11 E3
Obbia = Hobyo Somalia 5°25N 48°30E 49 F4
Oberá Argentina 27°21S 55°2W 95 B4
Oberhausen Germany 51°28N 6°51E 16 C4
Oberlin Kans., U.S.A. 39°49N 100°32W 80 F3
Oberlin La., U.S.A. 30°37N 92°46W 84 F8
Oberlin Ohio, U.S.A. 41°18N 82°13W 82 E2
Oberon Australia 33°45S 149°52E 63 E4
Obi, Kepulauan Indonesia 1°23S 127°45E 37 E7
Óbidos Brazil 1°50S 55°30W 93 D7
Obihiro Japan 42°56N 143°12E 28 C11
Obilatu Indonesia 1°25S 127°20E 37 E7
Obluchye Russia 49°1N 131°4E 27 E14
Obo C.A.R. 5°20N 26°32E 54 D5
Obo Canada 51°38N 85°58W 72 B2
Oboa, L. Canada 50°50N 87°10W 72 B2
Obozerskaya = Obozerskiy Russia 63°34N 40°21E 18 B7
Obozerskiy Russia 63°34N 40°21E 18 B7
Observatory Inlet Canada 55°10N 129°54W 70 B3

Obshchi Syrt Russia 52°0N 53°0E 6 E16
Obskaya Guba Russia 69°0N 73°0E 26 C8
Obuasi Ghana 6°17N 1°40W 52 G5
Ocala U.S.A. 29°11N 82°8W 85 G13
Ocampo Chihuahua, Mexico 28°11N 108°23W 86 B3
Ocampo Tamaulipas, Mexico 22°50N 99°20W 87 C5
Ocaña Spain 39°55N 3°30W 21 C4
Occidental, Cordillera Colombia 5°0N 76°0W 92 C3
Occidental, Grand Erg Algeria 30°20N 1°0E 52 B6
Ocean City Md., U.S.A. 38°20N 75°5W 81 F16
Ocean City N.J., U.S.A. 39°17N 74°35W 81 F16
Ocean City Wash., U.S.A. 47°4N 124°10W 78 C2
Ocean Falls Canada 52°18N 127°48W 70 C3
Ocean I. = Banaba Kiribati 0°45S 169°50E 64 H8
Ocean Park U.S.A. 46°30N 124°3W 78 D2
Oceano U.S.A. 35°6N 120°37W 79 K6
Oceanport U.S.A. 40°19N 74°3W 83 F10
Oceanside U.S.A. 33°12N 117°23W 79 M9
Ochil Hills U.K. 56°14N 3°40W 11 E5
Ocho Rios Jamaica 18°24N 77°6W 88 a
Ocilla U.S.A. 31°36N 83°15W 85 F13
Ocmulgee → U.S.A. 31°58N 82°33W 85 F13
Ocniţa Moldova 48°25N 27°30E 17 D14
Oconee → U.S.A. 31°58N 82°33W 85 F13
Oconomowoc U.S.A. 43°7N 88°30W 80 D9
Oconto U.S.A. 44°53N 87°52W 80 C2
Oconto Falls U.S.A. 44°52N 88°9W 80 C1
Ocosingo Mexico 16°53N 92°6W 87 D6
Ocotal Nic. 13°41N 86°31W 88 D2
Ocotlán Jalisco, Mexico 20°21N 102°46W 86 C4
Ocotlán Oaxaca, Mexico 16°48N 96°40W 87 D5
Ōda Japan 35°11N 132°30E 29 G6
Ódáðahraun Iceland 65°5N 17°0W 8 D5
Ōdaejin N. Korea 41°34N 129°40E 28 D8
Odate Japan 40°16N 140°34E 28 D10
Odawara Japan 35°20N 139°6E 29 G9
Odda Norway 60°3N 6°35E 9 F12
Odei → Canada 56°6N 96°54W 71 B9
Ödemiş Turkey 38°15N 28°0E 23 E13
Odendaalsrus S. Africa 27°48S 26°45E 56 C4
Odense Denmark 55°22N 10°23E 9 J14
Oder → Europe 53°33N 14°38E 16 B8
Odesa Ukraine 46°30N 30°45E 19 E5
Odessa = Odesa Ukraine 46°30N 30°45E 19 E5
Odessa Canada 44°17N 76°43W 83 B8
Odessa Tex., U.S.A. 31°52N 102°23W 84 F3
Odessa Wash., U.S.A. 47°20N 118°41W 76 C4
Odiakwe Botswana 20°12S 25°17E 56 B4
Odienné Ivory C. 9°30N 7°34W 52 G4
Odintsovo Russia 55°40N 37°16E 18 C6
Odisha □ India 20°0N 84°0E 44 E7
O'Donnell Pt. Canada 45°5N 80°5W 82 A4
Odorheiu Secuiesc Romania 46°21N 25°21E 17 E13
Odra = Oder → Europe 53°33N 14°38E 16 B8
Odzi Zimbabwe 19°0S 32°20E 57 A5
Odzi → Zimbabwe 19°45S 32°23E 57 A5
Oecussi = Pante Macassar E. Timor 9°30S 123°58E 37 F6
Oeiras Brazil 7°0S 42°8W 93 E10
Oelrichs U.S.A. 43°11N 103°14W 80 D2
Oelwein U.S.A. 42°41N 91°55W 80 D8
Oeno I. Pac. Oc. 24°0S 131°0W 65 K14
Oenpelli = Gunbalanya Australia 12°20S 133°4E 60 B5
Ofanto → Italy 41°22N 16°13E 22 D7
Offa Nigeria 8°13N 4°42E 52 G6
Offaly □ Ireland 53°15N 7°30W 10 C4
Offenbach Germany 50°6N 8°44E 16 C5
Offenburg Germany 48°28N 7°56E 16 D4
Officer Cr. → Australia 27°46S 132°30E 61 E5
Ofolanga Tonga 19°38S 174°27W 59 c
Ofotfjorden Norway 68°27N 17°0E 8 B17
Ofu Amer. Samoa 14°11S 169°41W 59 b
Ōfunato Japan 39°4N 141°43E 28 E10
Oga Japan 39°55N 139°50E 28 E9
Oga-Hantō Japan 39°58N 139°47E 28 E9
Ogaden Ethiopia 7°30N 45°30E 49 F3
Ōgaki Japan 35°21N 136°37E 29 G8
Ogallala U.S.A. 41°8N 101°43W 80 E3
Ogasawara Gunto Pac. Oc. 27°0N 142°0E 64 E6
Ogbomosho Nigeria 8°1N 4°11E 52 G6
Ogden U.S.A. 41°13N 111°58W 76 F8
Ogdensburg U.S.A. 44°42N 75°30W 83 B9
Ogea Driki Fiji 19°12S 178°27W 59 a
Ogea Levu Fiji 19°8S 178°24W 59 a
Ogeechee → U.S.A. 31°50N 81°3W 85 F14
Ogilby U.S.A. 32°49N 114°50W 79 N12
Óglio → Italy 45°2N 10°39E 22 B4
Ogmore Australia 22°37S 149°35E 62 C4
Ogoki Canada 51°38N 85°58W 72 B2
Ogoki → Canada 51°38N 85°57W 72 B2
Ogoki L. Canada 50°50N 87°10W 72 B2
Ogoki Res. Canada 50°45N 88°15W 72 B2
Ogooué → Gabon 1°0S 9°0E 54 E1
Ogowe = Ogooué → Gabon 1°0S 9°0E 54 E1
Ogre Latvia 56°49N 24°36E 9 H21
Ogurja Ada Turkmenistan 38°55N 53°2E 47 B7
Ohai N.Z. 45°55S 168°0E 59 F2
Ohakune N.Z. 39°24S 175°24E 59 C5
Ohangwena □ Namibia 17°30S 17°0E 56 B2
Ohata Japan 41°24N 141°10E 28 D10
Ohau, L. N.Z. 44°15S 169°53E 59 F2
Ohio □ U.S.A. 40°15N 82°45W 82 F2
Ohio → U.S.A. 36°59N 89°8W 80 G9
Ohře → Czech Rep. 50°30N 14°10E 16 C8
Ohrid Macedonia 41°8N 20°52E 23 D9
Ohridsko Jezero Macedonia 41°8N 20°52E 23 D9
Ohrigstad S. Africa 24°39S 30°36E 57 B5
Oi Qu → China 28°37N 98°16E 34 C2
Oiapoque Brazil 3°50N 51°50W 93 C8
Oikou China 38°35N 117°42E 33 E9
Oil City U.S.A. 41°26N 79°42W 82 E5

Oil Springs Canada 42°47N 82°7W 82 D2
Oildale U.S.A. 35°25N 119°1W 79 K7
Oise → France 49°0N 2°4E 20 B5
Oistins Barbados 13°4N 59°33W 89 g
Oistins B. Barbados 13°4N 59°33W 89 g
Ōita Japan 33°14N 131°36E 29 H5
Ōita □ Japan 33°15N 131°30E 29 H5
Oiticica Brazil 5°3S 41°5W 93 E10
Ojai U.S.A. 34°27N 119°15W 79 L7
Ojhar India 20°6N 73°56E 44 D1
Ojinaga Mexico 29°34N 104°25W 86 B4
Ojiya Japan 37°18N 138°48E 29 F9
Ojo Caliente Mexico 22°34N 102°15W 86 C4
Ojo de Liebre, L. Mexico 27°45N 114°15W 86 B2
Ojos del Salado, Cerro Argentina 27°0S 68°40W 94 B2
Oka → Russia 56°20N 43°59E 18 C7
Okaba Indonesia 8°6S 139°42E 37 F9
Okahandja Namibia 22°0S 16°59E 56 B2
Okakarara Namibia 20°35S 17°27E 56 B2
Okanagan L. Canada 50°0N 119°30W 70 D5
Okandja Gabon 0°35S 13°45E 54 E2
Okanogan U.S.A. 48°22N 119°35W 76 B4
Okanogan → U.S.A. 48°6N 119°44W 76 B4
Okanogan Range N. Amer. 49°0N 119°55W 70 D5
Okaputa Namibia 20°5S 17°0E 56 B2
Okara Pakistan 30°50N 73°31E 42 D5
Okaukuejo Namibia 19°10S 16°0E 56 B2
Okavango □ Namibia 18°0S 19°30E 56 A2
Okavango Delta Botswana 18°45S 22°45E 56 A3
Okavango Swamp = Okavango Delta Botswana 18°45S 22°45E 56 A3
Okaya Japan 36°5N 138°10E 29 F9
Okayama Japan 34°40N 133°54E 29 G6
Okayama □ Japan 35°0N 133°50E 29 G6
Okazaki Japan 34°57N 137°10E 29 G8
Okeechobee U.S.A. 27°15N 80°50W 85 H14
Okeechobee, L. U.S.A. 27°0N 80°50W 85 H14
Okefenokee △ U.S.A. 30°45N 82°18W 85 F13
Okefenokee Swamp U.S.A. 30°40N 82°20W 85 F13
Okehampton U.K. 50°44N 4°0W 13 G4
Okha India 22°27N 69°4E 42 H3
Okha Russia 53°40N 143°0E 27 D15
Okhotsk Russia 59°20N 143°10E 27 D15
Okhotsk, Sea of Asia 55°0N 145°0E 27 D15
Okhotskiy Perevoz Russia 61°52N 135°35E 27 C14
Okhtyrka Ukraine 50°25N 35°0E 19 D5
Oki-Shotō Japan 36°5N 133°15E 29 F6
Okiep S. Africa 29°39S 17°53E 56 C2
Okinawa Japan 26°19N 127°46E 29 L3
Okinawa □ Japan 26°40N 128°0E 29 L4
Okinawa-Guntō Japan 26°40N 128°0E 29 L4
Okinawa-Jima Japan 26°32N 128°0E 29 L4
Okino-erabu-Shima Japan 27°21N 128°33E 29 L4
Oklahoma □ U.S.A. 35°20N 97°30W 84 D6
Oklahoma City U.S.A. 35°30N 97°30W 84 D6
Okmulgee U.S.A. 35°37N 95°58W 84 D7
Oknitsa = Ocniţa Moldova 48°25N 27°30E 17 D14
Okolona U.S.A. 34°0N 88°45W 85 E10
Okombahe Namibia 21°23S 15°22E 56 B2
Okotoks Canada 50°43N 113°58W 70 C6
Oksovskiy Russia 62°33N 39°57E 18 B6
Oktyabrsk = Qandyaghash Kazakhstan 49°28N 57°25E 19 E10
Oktyabrskiy = Aktsyabrski Belarus 52°38N 28°53E 17 B15
Oktyabrskiy Bashkortostan, Russia 54°28N 53°28E 18 D9
Oktyabrskiy Kamchatka, Russia 52°39N 156°14E 27 D16
Oktyabrskoy Revolyutsii, Ostrov Russia 79°30N 97°0E 27 B10
Okuru N.Z. 43°55S 168°55E 59 E2
Okushiri-Tō Japan 42°15N 139°30E 28 C9
Okwa → Botswana 22°30S 23°0E 56 B3
Ola Russia 59°35N 151°17E 27 D16
Ólafsfjörður Iceland 66°4N 18°39W 8 C4
Ólafsvík Iceland 64°53N 23°43W 8 D2
Olancha U.S.A. 36°17N 118°1W 79 J8
Olancha Pk. U.S.A. 36°16N 118°7W 79 J8
Olanchito Honduras 15°30N 86°30W 88 C2
Öland Sweden 56°45N 16°38E 9 H17
Olary Australia 32°18S 140°19E 63 E3
Olascoaga Argentina 35°15S 60°39W 94 D3
Olathe U.S.A. 38°53N 94°49W 80 F7
Olavarría Argentina 36°55S 60°20W 94 D3
Oława Poland 50°57N 17°20E 17 C9
Ólbia Italy 40°55N 9°31E 22 D3
Olcott U.S.A. 43°20N 78°42W 82 C6
Old Bahama Chan. = Bahama, Canal Viejo de W. Indies 22°10N 77°30W 88 B4
Old Baldy Pk. = San Antonio, Mt. U.S.A. 34°17N 117°38W 79 L9
Old Bridge U.S.A. 40°25N 74°22W 83 F10
Old Castile = Castilla y Leon □ Spain 42°0N 5°0W 21 B3
Old Crow Canada 67°30N 139°55W 68 D4
Old Dale U.S.A. 34°8N 115°47W 79 L11
Old Forge N.Y., U.S.A. 43°43N 74°58W 83 C10
Old Forge Pa., U.S.A. 41°22N 75°45W 83 E9
Old Mapoon ⊙ Australia 11°5S 142°22E 62 A3
Old Perlican Canada 48°5N 53°1W 73 C9
Old Speck Mt. U.S.A. 44°34N 70°57W 83 B14
Old Town U.S.A. 44°56N 68°39W 81 C19
Old Washington U.S.A. 40°2N 81°27W 82 F3
Old Wives L. Canada 50°5N 106°0W 71 C7
Oldbury U.K. 51°38N 2°33W 13 F5
Oldcastle Ireland 53°46N 7°10W 10 C4
Oldenburg Germany 53°9N 8°13E 16 B5
Oldenzaal Neths. 52°19N 6°53E 15 B6
Oldham U.K. 53°33N 2°7W 12 D5

Oldman → Canada 49°57N 111°42W 70 D6
Oldmeldrum U.K. 57°20N 2°19W 11 D6
Olds Canada 51°50N 114°10W 70 C6
Öldziyt Mongolia 44°40N 109°1E 32 B5
Olean U.S.A. 42°5N 78°26W 82 D6
Olekma → Russia 60°22N 120°42E 27 C13
Olekminsk Russia 60°25N 120°30E 27 C13
Oleksandriya Ukraine 50°37N 26°19E 17 C14
Olema U.S.A. 38°3N 122°47W 78 G4
Olenegorsk Russia 68°9N 33°18E 8 B25
Olenek Russia 68°28N 112°18E 27 C12
Olenek → Russia 73°0N 120°10E 27 B13
Oléron, Î. d' France 45°55N 1°15W 20 D3
Oleśnica Poland 51°13N 17°22E 17 C9
Olevsk Ukraine 51°12N 27°39E 17 C14
Olga, L. Canada 49°47N 77°15W 72 C4
Olgas, The = Kata Tjuta
  Australia 25°20S 130°50E 61 E5
Ölgiy Mongolia 48°56N 89°57E 30 B6
Olhão Portugal 37°3N 7°48W 21 D2
Olifants = Elefantes →
  Africa 24°10S 32°40E 57 B5
Olifants → Namibia 25°30S 19°30E 56 B2
Olifantshoek S. Africa 27°57S 22°42E 56 C3
Ólimbos, Óros = Olympos Oros
  Greece 40°6N 22°23E 23 D10
Olímpia Brazil 20°44S 48°54W 95 A6
Olinda Brazil 8°1S 34°51W 93 E12
Oliva Argentina 32°0S 63°38W 94 C3
Olivares, Cerro los
  Argentina 30°18S 69°55W 94 C2
Olive Branch U.S.A. 34°57N 89°49W 85 D10
Olivehurst U.S.A. 39°6N 121°34W 78 F5
Olivenza Spain 38°41N 7°9W 21 C2
Oliver Canada 49°13N 119°37W 70 D5
Oliver L. Canada 56°56N 103°22W 71 B8
Ollagüe Chile 21°15S 68°10W 94 A2
Olmaliq Uzbekistan 40°50N 69°35E 26 E7
Olney Ill., U.S.A. 38°44N 88°5W 80 F9
Olney Tex., U.S.A. 33°22N 98°45W 84 E5
Olomane → Canada 50°14N 60°37W 73 B7
Olomouc Czech Rep. 49°38N 17°12E 17 D9
Olonets Russia 61°0N 32°54E 18 B5
Olongapo Phil. 14°50N 120°18E 37 B6
Olosega Amer. Samoa 14°10S 169°37W 59 b
Olosenga = Swains I.
  Amer. Samoa 11°11S 171°4W 65 J11
Olot Spain 42°11N 2°30E 21 A7
Olovyannaya Russia 50°58N 115°35E 27 D12
Oloy → Russia 66°29N 159°29E 27 C16
Olsztyn Poland 53°48N 20°29E 17 B11
Olt → Romania 43°43N 24°51E 17 G13
Olteniţa Romania 44°7N 26°42E 17 F14
Olton U.S.A. 34°11N 102°8W 84 D3
Oluan Pi Taiwan 21°53N 120°51E 35 G13
Olympia Greece 37°39N 21°39E 23 F9
Olympia U.S.A. 47°3N 122°53W 78 D4
Olympic △ U.S.A. 47°45N 123°43W 78 C3
Olympic Dam Australia 30°30S 136°55E 63 E2
Olympic Mts. U.S.A. 47°55N 123°45W 78 C3
Olympus Cyprus 34°56N 32°52E 46 C2
Olympus, Mt. = Olymbos Oros
  Greece 40°6N 22°23E 23 D10
Olympus, Mt. = Uludağ
  Turkey 40°4N 29°13E 23 D13
Olympus, Mt. U.S.A. 47°48N 123°43W 78 C3
Olyphant U.S.A. 41°27N 75°36W 83 E9
Olyutorskiy, Mys
  Russia 59°55N 170°27E 27 D18
Om → Russia 54°59N 73°22E 26 D8
Om Koi Thailand 17°48N 98°22E 38 D2
Ōma Japan 41°45N 141°5E 28 D10
Ōmachi Japan 36°30N 137°50E 29 F8
Ōmae-Zaki Japan 34°36N 138°14E 29 G9
Ōmagari = Daisen
  Japan 39°27N 140°29E 28 E10
Omagh U.K. 54°36N 7°19W 10 B4
Omagh □ U.K. 54°35N 7°15W 10 B4
Omaha U.S.A. 41°17N 95°58W 80 E6
Omak U.S.A. 48°25N 119°31W 76 B4
Omalur India 11°44N 78°4E 45 J4
Oman ■ Asia 23°0N 58°0E 49 C6
Oman, G. of Asia 24°30N 58°30E 47 E8
Omaruru Namibia 21°26S 16°0E 56 B2
Omaruru → Namibia 22°7S 14°15E 56 B1
Omate Peru 16°45S 71°0W 92 G4
Ombai, Selat Indonesia 8°30S 124°50E 37 F6
Omboué Gabon 1°35S 9°15E 54 E1
Ombrone → Italy 42°42N 11°5E 22 C4
Omdurmân Sudan 15°40N 32°28E 53 E12
Omemee Canada 44°18N 78°33W 82 B6
Ometepe, I. de Nic. 11°32N 85°35W 88 D2
Ometepec Mexico 16°41N 98°25W 87 D5
Ominato Japan 41°17N 141°10E 28 D10
Omineca → Canada 56°3N 124°16W 70 B4
Omineca Mts. Canada 56°30N 125°30W 70 B3
Omitara Namibia 22°16S 18°2E 56 B2
Ōmiya = Saitama Japan 35°54N 139°38E 29 G9
Ommen Neths. 52°31N 6°26E 15 B6
Ömnögovĭ □ Mongolia 43°15N 104°0E 32 C3
Omo → Ethiopia 6°25N 36°10E 49 F2
Omolon → Russia 68°42N 158°36E 27 C16
Omono-Gawa → Japan 39°46N 140°3E 28 E10
Ompha Canada 45°0N 76°50W 83 B8
Omsk Russia 55°0N 73°12E 26 D8
Omsukchan Russia 62°32N 155°48E 27 C16
Ōmu Japan 44°34N 142°58E 28 B11
Omul, Vf. Romania 45°27N 25°29E 17 F13
Ōmura Japan 32°56N 129°57E 29 H4
Omuramba Omatako →
  Namibia 17°45S 20°25E 56 A2
Omuramba Ovambo →
  Namibia 18°45S 16°59E 56 A2
Omusati □ Namibia 18°30S 15°0E 56 A1
Omuta Japan 33°5N 130°26E 29 H5
Omuthiya Namibia 17°45S 16°13E 56 A2
Onaga U.S.A. 39°29N 96°10W 80 F5

Onalaska U.S.A. 43°53N 91°14W 80 D8
Onancock U.S.A. 37°43N 75°45W 81 G16
Onangue, L. Gabon 0°57S 10°4E 54 E2
Onaping L. Canada 47°3N 81°30W 72 C3
Onavas Mexico 28°31N 109°35W 86 B3
Onawa U.S.A. 42°2N 96°6W 80 D5
Oncócua Angola 16°30S 13°25E 56 A1
Onda Spain 39°55N 0°17W 21 C5
Ondangwa Namibia 17°57S 16°4E 56 A2
Ondjiva Angola 16°48S 15°50E 56 A2
Öndörhaan Mongolia 47°19N 110°39E 31 B11
Öndverðarnes Iceland 64°52N 24°0W 8 D2
One Arm Point Australia 16°26S 123°3E 60 C3
One Arm Point ○
  Australia 16°31S 122°53E 60 C3
One Tree Australia 34°11S 144°43E 63 E3
Oneata Fiji 18°26S 178°25W 59 a
Onega Russia 64°0N 38°10E 18 B6
Onega → Russia 63°58N 38°2E 18 B6
Onega, G. of = Onezhskaya Guba
  Russia 64°24N 36°38E 18 B6
Onega, L. = Onezhskoye Ozero
  Russia 61°44N 35°22E 18 B6
Oneida U.S.A. 43°6N 75°39W 83 C9
Oneida L. U.S.A. 43°12N 75°54W 83 C9
O'Neill U.S.A. 42°27N 98°39W 80 D4
Onekotan, Ostrov
  Russia 49°25N 154°45E 27 E16
Oneonta U.S.A. 42°27N 75°4W 83 D9
Oneşti Romania 46°11N 26°47E 17 E14
Onezhskaya Guba Russia 64°24N 36°38E 18 B6
Onezhskoye Ozero Russia 61°44N 35°22E 18 B6
Ongarue N.Z. 38°42S 175°19E 59 C5
Ongea Levu = Ogea Levu
  Fiji 19°8S 178°24W 59 a
Ongers → S. Africa 31°4S 23°13E 56 D3
Ongerup Australia 33°58S 118°28E 61 F2
Ongi Mongolia 45°27N 103°54E 32 B2
Ongjin N. Korea 37°56N 125°21E 33 F13
Ongkharak Thailand 14°8N 101°1E 38 E3
Ongniud Qi China 43°0N 118°38E 33 C10
Ongole India 15°33N 80°2E 45 G5
Ongon = Havirga
  Mongolia 45°41N 113°5E 32 B7
Ongwediva Namibia 17°47S 15°46E 56 A2
Onida U.S.A. 44°42N 100°4W 80 C3
Onilahy → Madag. 23°34S 43°45E 55 J8
Onitsha Nigeria 6°6N 6°42E 52 G7
Ono Fiji 18°55S 178°29E 59 a
Onoda Japan 33°59N 131°11E 29 G5
Onslow Australia 21°40S 115°12E 60 D2
Onslow B. U.S.A. 34°20N 77°15W 85 D16
Ontake-San Japan 35°53N 137°29E 29 G8
Ontario Calif., U.S.A. 34°4N 117°39W 79 L9
Ontario Oreg., U.S.A. 44°2N 116°58W 76 D5
Ontario □ Canada 48°0N 83°0W 72 B2
Ontario, L. N. Amer. 43°20N 78°0W 82 C7
Ontonagon U.S.A. 46°52N 89°19W 80 B9
Onyx U.S.A. 35°41N 118°14W 79 K8
Oodnadatta Australia 27°33S 135°30E 63 D2
Ooldea Australia 30°27S 131°50E 61 F5
Oombulgurri Australia 15°15S 127°45E 60 C4
Oombulgurri ○
  Australia 15°10S 127°50E 60 C4
Oorindi Australia 20°40S 141°1E 62 C3
Oost-Vlaanderen □
  Belgium 51°5N 3°50E 15 C3
Oostende Belgium 51°15N 2°54E 15 C2
Oosterhout Neths. 51°39N 4°47E 15 C4
Oosterschelde → Neths. 51°33N 4°0E 15 C4
Oosterwolde Neths. 53°0N 6°17E 15 B6
Oosterschelde △ Neths. 51°40N 3°40E 15 C3
Ootacamund = Udagamandalam
  India 11°30N 76°44E 45 J3
Ootsa L. Canada 53°50N 126°2W 70 C3
Ooty = Udagamandalam
  India 11°30N 76°44E 45 J3
Op Luang △ Thailand 18°12N 98°32E 38 C2
Opala Dem. Rep. of the Congo 0°40S 24°20E 54 E4
Opanake Sri Lanka 6°35N 80°40E 45 L5
Opasatika Canada 49°30N 82°50W 72 C3
Opasquia △ Canada 53°33N 93°5W 72 B1
Opava Czech Rep. 49°57N 17°58E 17 D9
Opelika U.S.A. 32°39N 85°23W 85 E12
Opelousas U.S.A. 30°32N 92°5W 84 F8
Opémisca, L. Canada 49°56N 74°52W 72 C5
Opheim U.S.A. 48°51N 106°24W 76 B10
Ophthalmia Ra.
  Australia 23°15S 119°30E 60 D2
Opinaca → Canada 52°15N 78°2W 72 B4
Opinaca, Rés. Canada 52°39N 76°20W 72 B4
Opinnagau → Canada 54°12N 82°25W 72 B3
Opiscotéo, L. Canada 53°10N 68°10W 73 B6
Opobo Nigeria 4°35N 7°34E 52 H7
Opole Poland 50°42N 17°58E 17 C9
Oponono L. Namibia 18°8S 15°45E 56 A2
Oporto = Porto Portugal 41°8N 8°40W 21 B1
Opotiki N.Z. 38°1S 177°19E 59 C6
Opp U.S.A. 31°17N 86°16W 85 F11
Oppdal Norway 62°35N 9°41E 8 E13
Opportunity U.S.A. 47°39N 117°15W 76 C5
Opua N.Z. 35°19S 174°9E 59 A5
Opunake N.Z. 39°26S 173°52E 59 C4
Opuwo Namibia 18°3S 13°45E 56 A1
Oracle U.S.A. 32°37N 110°46W 77 K8
Oradea Romania 47°2N 21°58E 17 E11
Öræfajökull Iceland 64°2N 16°39W 8 D5
Orai India 25°58N 79°30E 43 G8
Oral = Zhayyq →
  Kazakhstan 47°0N 51°48E 19 E9
Oral Kazakhstan 51°20N 51°20E 19 D9
Oran Algeria 35°45N 0°39W 52 A5
Orange Australia 33°15S 149°7E 63 E4
Orange France 44°8N 4°47E 20 D6
Orange Calif., U.S.A. 33°47N 117°51W 79 M9
Orange Mass., U.S.A. 42°35N 72°19W 83 D12
Orange Tex., U.S.A. 30°6N 93°44W 84 F8
Orange Va., U.S.A. 38°15N 78°7W 81 F14
Orange → S. Africa 28°41S 16°28E 56 D2

Orange, C. Brazil 4°20N 51°30W 93 C8
Orange Cove U.S.A. 36°38N 119°19W 78 J7
Orange Free State = Free State □
  S. Africa 28°30S 27°0E 56 C4
Orange Grove U.S.A. 27°58N 97°56W 84 H6
Orange Walk Belize 18°6N 88°33W 87 D7
Orangeburg U.S.A. 33°30N 80°52W 85 E14
Orangeville Canada 43°55N 80°5W 82 C4
Orango Guinea-Biss. 11°5N 16°0W 52 F2
Oranienburg Germany 52°45N 13°14E 16 B7
Oranje = Orange →
  S. Africa 28°41S 16°28E 56 C2
Oranjemund Namibia 28°38S 16°29E 56 C2
Oranjerivier S. Africa 29°40S 24°12E 56 D3
Oranjestad Aruba 12°32N 70°2W 89 D5
Orapa Botswana 21°15S 25°30E 55 J5
Oras Phil. 12°9N 125°28E 37 B7
Orbetello Italy 42°27N 11°13E 22 C4
Orbisonia U.S.A. 40°15N 77°54W 82 F7
Orbost Australia 37°40S 148°29E 63 F4
Orcadas Antarctica 60°44S 44°37W 5 C18
Orcas I. U.S.A. 48°42N 122°56W 78 B4
Orchard City U.S.A. 38°50N 107°58W 76 G10
Orchard Homes U.S.A. 46°55N 114°4W 76 C6
Orchid I. = Lan Yü
  Taiwan 22°4N 121°25E 35 F13
Orchila, I. Venezuela 11°48N 66°10W 89 D6
Orcutt U.S.A. 34°52N 120°27W 79 L6
Ord U.S.A. 41°36N 98°56W 80 E4
Ord → Australia 15°33S 128°15E 60 C4
Ord, Mt. Australia 17°20S 125°34E 60 C4
Ord Mts. U.S.A. 34°39N 116°45W 79 L10
Orderville U.S.A. 37°17N 112°38W 77 H7
Ordos = Mu Us Shamo
  China 39°0N 109°0E 32 E5
Ordu Turkey 40°55N 37°53E 19 F6
Ordway U.S.A. 38°13N 103°46W 76 G12
Ore Mts. = Erzgebirge
  Germany 50°27N 12°55E 16 C7
Örebro Sweden 59°20N 15°18E 9 G16
Oregon U.S.A. 42°1N 89°20W 80 D9
Oregon □ U.S.A. 44°0N 121°0W 76 E3
Oregon City U.S.A. 45°21N 122°36W 78 E4
Oregon Dunes △ U.S.A. 43°40N 124°10W 76 E1
Orekhovo-Zuyevo Russia 55°50N 38°55E 18 C6
Orel Russia 52°57N 36°3E 18 D6
Orem U.S.A. 40°19N 111°42W 76 F8
Ören Turkey 37°3N 27°57E 23 F12
Orenburg Russia 51°45N 55°6E 18 D10
Orense = Ourense Spain 42°19N 7°55W 21 A2
Orepuki N.Z. 46°19S 167°46E 59 G1
Orestes Pereyra Mexico 26°30N 105°39W 86 B3
Orestiada Greece 41°30N 26°33E 23 D12
Orford Ness U.K. 52°5N 1°35E 13 E9
Organ Pipe Cactus △
  U.S.A. 32°0N 112°52W 77 K7
Orgaz Spain 39°39N 3°53E 21 C4
Orgeyev = Orhei
  Moldova 47°24N 28°50E 17 E15
Orhaneli Turkey 39°54N 28°59E 23 E13
Orhangazi Turkey 40°29N 29°18E 23 D13
Orhei Moldova 47°24N 28°50E 17 E15
Orhon Gol → Mongolia 50°21N 106°0E 30 A10
Oriental, Cordillera
  Colombia 6°0N 73°0W 92 B4
Oriental, Grand Erg Algeria 30°0N 6°30E 52 B7
Oriente Argentina 38°44S 60°37W 94 D3
Orihuela Spain 38°7N 0°55W 21 C5
Orillia Canada 44°40N 79°24W 82 B5
Orinoco → Venezuela 9°15N 61°30W 92 B6
Orion Canada 49°27N 110°49W 71 D6
Oriskany U.S.A. 43°10N 75°20W 83 C9
Orissa = Odisha □ India 20°0N 84°0E 44 E7
Orissaare Estonia 58°34N 23°5E 9 G20
Oristano Italy 39°54N 8°36E 22 E3
Oristano, G. di Italy 39°50N 8°29E 22 E3
Orizaba Mexico 18°51N 97°6W 87 D5
Orizaba, Pico de Mexico 18°58N 97°15W 87 D5
Orkanger Norway 63°18N 9°52E 8 E13
Orkhon = Orhon Gol →
  Mongolia 50°21N 106°0E 30 A10
Orkla → Norway 63°18N 9°51E 8 E13
Orkney S. Africa 26°58S 26°40E 56 D4
Orkney □ U.K. 59°2N 3°13W 11 B5
Orkney Is. U.K. 59°0N 3°0W 11 B6
Orland U.S.A. 39°45N 122°12W 78 F4
Orléanais France 48°0N 2°0E 20 C5
Orléans France 47°54N 1°52E 20 C4
Orleans U.S.A. 44°49N 72°12W 83 B12
Orléans, Î. d' Canada 46°54N 70°58W 73 C5
Ormara Pakistan 25°16N 64°33E 40 G4
Ormoc Phil. 11°0N 124°37E 37 B6
Ormond N.Z. 38°33S 177°56E 59 C6
Ormond Beach U.S.A. 29°17N 81°3W 85 G14
Ormskirk U.K. 53°35N 2°54W 12 D5
Ormstown Canada 45°8N 74°0W 83 A11
Oro N. Korea 40°1N 127°27E 33 D14
Oro → Mexico 25°35N 105°2W 86 B3
Oro Grande U.S.A. 34°36N 117°20W 79 L9
Oro Valley U.S.A. 32°26N 110°58W 77 K8
Orocué Colombia 4°48N 71°20W 92 C4
Orofino U.S.A. 46°29N 116°15W 76 C5
Orohena, Mt. Tahiti 17°37S 149°28W 59 d
Orol Dengizi = Aral Sea
  Asia 45°0N 58°20E 26 E7
Oromocto Canada 45°54N 66°29W 73 C6
Orono Canada 43°59N 78°37W 82 C6
Oronsay U.K. 56°1N 6°15W 11 E2
Oroquieta Phil. 8°32N 123°44E 37 C6
Orosei Italy 40°23N 9°42E 22 D3
Orosháza Hungary 46°32N 20°42E 17 E11
Orotukan Russia 62°16N 151°42E 27 C16
Oroville Calif., U.S.A. 39°31N 121°33W 78 F5
Oroville Wash., U.S.A. 48°56N 119°26W 76 B4
Oroville, L. U.S.A. 39°33N 121°29W 78 F5
Orroroo Australia 32°43S 138°38E 63 E2

Orrville U.S.A. 40°50N 81°46W 82 F3
Orsha Belarus 54°30N 30°25E 18 D5
Orsk Russia 51°12N 58°34E 18 D10
Orşova Romania 44°41N 22°25E 17 F12
Ortaca Turkey 36°49N 28°45E 23 F13
Ortegal, C. Spain 43°43N 7°52W 21 A2
Orthez France 43°29N 0°48W 20 E3
Ortigueira Spain 43°40N 7°50W 21 A2
Orting U.S.A. 47°6N 122°12W 78 C4
Ortles Italy 46°31N 10°33E 20 C9
Ortón → Bolivia 10°50S 67°0W 92 F5
Ortonville U.S.A. 45°19N 96°27W 80 C5
Orūmīyeh Iran 37°40N 45°0E 46 B5
Orūmīyeh, Daryācheh-ye
  Iran 37°50N 45°30E 46 B5
Oruro Bolivia 18°0S 67°9W 92 G5
Orust Sweden 58°10N 11°40E 9 G14
Oruzgān □ Afghan. 33°0N 66°0E 40 C5
Orvieto Italy 42°43N 12°7E 22 C5
Orwell N.Y., U.S.A. 43°35N 75°50W 83 C9
Orwell Ohio, U.S.A. 41°32N 80°52W 82 E4
Orwell → U.K. 51°59N 1°18E 13 F9
Orwigsburg U.S.A. 40°38N 76°6W 83 F8
Oryakhovo Bulgaria 43°40N 23°57E 23 C10
Oryol = Orel Russia 52°57N 36°3E 18 D6
Osa Russia 57°17N 55°26E 18 C10
Osa, Pen. de Costa Rica 8°0N 84°0W 88 E3
Osage U.S.A. 43°17N 92°49W 80 D7
Osage → U.S.A. 38°36N 91°57W 80 F8
Osage City U.S.A. 38°38N 95°50W 80 F6
Ōsaki Japan 38°34N 140°58E 28 E10
Osawatomie U.S.A. 38°31N 94°57W 80 F6
Osborne U.S.A. 39°26N 98°42W 80 F4
Osceola Ark., U.S.A. 35°42N 89°58W 85 D10
Osceola Iowa, U.S.A. 41°2N 93°46W 80 E7
Oscoda U.S.A. 44°26N 83°20W 82 B1
Ösel = Saaremaa Estonia 58°30N 22°30E 9 G20
Osgoode Canada 45°8N 75°36W 83 A9
Osh Kyrgyzstan 40°37N 72°49E 30 C3
Oshakati Namibia 17°45S 15°40E 56 A2
Oshana □ Namibia 17°50S 15°40E 56 A2
Oshawa Canada 43°50N 78°50W 82 C6
Oshigambo Namibia 17°45S 16°5E 56 A2
Oshika-Hantō Japan 38°20N 141°30E 28 E10
Oshikoto □ Namibia 18°30S 17°0E 56 A2
Oshivelo Namibia 18°37S 17°10E 56 A2
Oshkosh Nebr., U.S.A. 41°24N 102°21W 80 E2
Oshkosh Wis., U.S.A. 44°1N 88°33W 80 D9
Oshmyany = Ashmyany
  Belarus 54°26N 25°52E 17 A13
Oshnovīyeh Iran 37°2N 45°6E 46 B5
Oshogbo Nigeria 7°48N 4°37E 52 G6
Oshtorīnān Iran 34°1N 48°38E 47 C6
Ōshū Japan 39°8N 141°8E 28 E10
Oshwe
  Dem. Rep. of the Congo 3°25S 19°28E 54 E3
Osijek Croatia 45°34N 18°41E 23 B8
Osipovichi = Asipovichy
  Belarus 53°19N 28°33E 17 B15
Osiyan India 26°43N 72°55E 42 F5
Osizweni S. Africa 27°49S 30°7E 57 C5
Oskaloosa U.S.A. 41°18N 92°39W 80 E7
Oskarshamn Sweden 57°15N 16°27E 9 H17
Oskélanéo Canada 48°5N 75°15W 72 C4
Öskemen Kazakhstan 50°0N 82°36E 26 D9
Oslofjorden Norway 59°20N 10°35E 9 G14
Osmanabad India 18°5N 76°10E 44 E3
Osmaniye Turkey 37°5N 36°10E 46 B3
Osmannagar India 18°32N 79°20E 44 E4
Osnabrück Germany 52°17N 8°3E 16 B5
Osogbo = Oshogbo Nigeria 7°48N 4°37E 52 G6
Osório Brazil 29°53S 50°17W 95 B5
Osorno Chile 40°25S 73°0W 96 E2
Osorno, Vol. Chile 41°0S 72°30W 96 D2
Osoyoos Canada 49°0N 119°30W 70 D5
Osøyro Norway 60°9N 5°30E 8 F11
Ospika → Canada 56°20N 124°0W 70 B4
Osprey Reef Australia 13°52S 146°36E 62 A4
Oss Neths. 51°46N 5°32E 15 C5
Ossa, Mt. Australia 41°52S 146°3E 63 G4
Ossa, Oros Greece 39°47N 22°42E 23 E10
Ossabaw I. U.S.A. 31°50N 81°5W 85 F14
Ossining U.S.A. 41°10N 73°55W 83 E11
Ossipee U.S.A. 43°41N 71°7W 83 C13
Ossokmanuan L. Canada 53°25N 65°0W 73 B7
Ossora Russia 59°20N 163°13E 27 D17
Ostend = Oostende
  Belgium 51°15N 2°54E 15 C2
Oster Ukraine 50°57N 30°53E 17 C16
Österbotten = Pohjanmaa □
  Finland 62°58N 22°50E 8 E20
Osterburg U.S.A. 40°16N 78°31W 82 F6
Österdalälven → Sweden 60°30N 15°7E 8 F15
Østerdalen Norway 61°40N 10°50E 8 F14
Østermyra = Seinäjoki
  Finland 62°40N 22°51E 8 E20
Österreich = Austria ■
  Europe 47°0N 14°0E 16 E8
Östersund Sweden 63°10N 14°38E 8 E16
Ostfriesische Inseln
  Germany 53°42N 7°0E 16 B4
Ostrava Czech Rep. 49°51N 18°18E 17 D10
Ostróda Poland 53°42N 19°58E 17 B10
Ostroh Ukraine 50°20N 26°30E 17 C14
Ostrołęka Poland 53°4N 21°32E 17 B11
Ostrów Mazowiecka
  Poland 52°50N 21°51E 17 B11
Ostrów Wielkopolski
  Poland 51°36N 17°44E 17 C9
Ostrowiec-Świętokrzyski
  Poland 50°55N 21°22E 17 C11
Ostuni Italy 40°44N 17°35E 23 D7
Ōsumi-Kaikyō Japan 30°55N 131°0E 29 J5
Ōsumi-Shotō Japan 30°30N 130°0E 29 J5
Osuna Spain 37°14N 5°8W 21 D3
Oswegatchie → U.S.A. 44°42N 75°30W 83 B9
Oswego U.S.A. 43°27N 76°31W 83 C8
Oswego → U.S.A. 43°27N 76°30W 83 C8
Oswestry U.K. 52°52N 3°3W 12 E4

Oświęcim Poland 50°2N 19°11E 17 C10
Otago □ N.Z. 45°15S 170°0E 59 F2
Otago Harbour N.Z. 45°47S 170°42E 59 F3
Otaheite B. Trin. & Tob. 10°15N 61°30W 93 K15
Ōtake Japan 34°12N 132°13E 29 G6
Otaki N.Z. 40°45S 175°10E 59 D5
Otaru Japan 43°10N 141°0E 28 C10
Otaru-Wan = Ishikari-Wan
  Japan 43°25N 141°1E 28 C10
Otavalo Ecuador 0°13N 78°20W 92 C3
Otavi Namibia 19°40S 17°24E 56 A2
Ōtawara Japan 36°50N 140°5E 29 F10
Otchinjau Angola 16°30S 13°56E 56 A1
Otego U.S.A. 42°23N 75°10W 83 D9
Otelnuk, L. Canada 56°9N 68°12W 73 A6
Othello U.S.A. 46°50N 119°10W 76 C4
Otish, Mts. Canada 52°22N 70°30E 73 B5
Otjinene Namibia 21°8S 18°46E 56 B2
Otjiwarongo Namibia 20°30S 16°33E 56 B2
Otjozondjupa □ Namibia 21°0S 17°0E 56 B2
Oto Tolu Group Tonga 20°21S 174°32W 59 c
Otoineppu Japan 44°44N 142°16E 28 B11
Otorohanga N.Z. 38°12S 175°14E 59 C5
Otoskwin → Canada 52°13N 88°6W 72 B2
Otra → Norway 58°9N 8°1E 9 G13
Otranto Italy 40°9N 18°28E 23 D8
Otranto, C. d' Italy 40°7N 18°30E 23 D8
Otranto, Str. of Italy 40°15N 18°40E 23 D8
Otse S. Africa 25°2S 25°45E 56 D4
Otsego L. U.S.A. 42°45N 74°53W 83 D10
Ōtsu Japan 35°0N 135°50E 29 G7
Ōtsuki Japan 35°36N 138°57E 29 G9
Ottappalam India 10°46N 76°23E 45 J3
Ottawa = Outaouais →
  Canada 45°27N 74°8W 72 C5
Ottawa Canada 45°26N 75°42W 83 A9
Ottawa Ill., U.S.A. 41°21N 88°51W 80 E9
Ottawa Kans., U.S.A. 38°37N 95°16W 80 F6
Ottawa Is. Canada 59°35N 80°10W 69 F15
Otter Cr. → U.S.A. 44°13N 73°17W 83 B11
Otter Lake Canada 45°17N 79°56W 82 A5
Otterville Canada 42°55N 80°36W 82 D4
Ottery St. Mary U.K. 50°44N 3°17W 13 G4
Ottosdal S. Africa 26°46S 25°59E 56 D4
Ottumwa U.S.A. 41°1N 92°25W 80 E7
Oturkpo Nigeria 7°16N 8°8E 52 G7
Otway, B. Chile 53°30S 74°0W 96 G2
Otway, C. Australia 38°52S 143°30E 63 F3
Otwock Poland 52°5N 21°20E 17 B11
Ou → Laos 20°4N 102°13E 38 B4
Ou-Sammyaku Japan 39°20N 140°35E 28 E10
Ouachita → U.S.A. 31°38N 91°49W 84 F9
Ouachita, L. U.S.A. 34°34N 93°12W 84 D8
Ouachita Mts. U.S.A. 34°30N 94°30W 84 D7
Ouagadougou
  Burkina Faso 12°25N 1°30W 52 F5
Ouahigouya Burkina Faso 13°31N 2°25W 52 F5
Ouahran = Oran Algeria 35°45N 0°39W 52 A5
Ouallene Algeria 24°41N 1°11E 52 D6
Ouarâne Mauritania 21°0N 10°30W 52 D3
Ouargla Algeria 31°59N 5°16E 52 B7
Ouarra → C.A.R. 5°5N 24°26E 54 C4
Ouarzazate Morocco 30°55N 6°50W 52 B4
Oubangi →
  Dem. Rep. of the Congo 0°30S 17°50E 54 E3
Ouddorp Neths. 51°50N 3°57E 15 C3
Oude Rijn → Neths. 52°12N 4°24E 15 B4
Oudenaarde Belgium 50°50N 3°37E 15 D3
Oudtshoorn S. Africa 33°35S 22°14E 56 E3
Ouessant, Î. d' France 48°28N 5°6W 20 B1
Ouesso Congo 1°37N 16°5E 54 D3
Ouest, Pte. de l' Canada 49°52N 64°40W 73 C7
Ouezzane Morocco 34°51N 5°35W 52 B4
Oughter, L. Ireland 54°1N 7°28W 10 B4
Oughterard Ireland 53°26N 9°18W 10 C2
Ouidah Benin 6°25N 2°0E 52 G6
Oujda Morocco 34°41N 1°55W 52 B5
Oulainen Finland 64°17N 24°47E 8 D21
Oulu Finland 65°1N 25°29E 8 D21
Oulujärvi Finland 64°25N 27°15E 8 D22
Oulujoki → Finland 65°1N 25°30E 8 D21
Oum Chalouba Chad 15°48N 20°46E 53 E10
Oum Hadjer Chad 13°18N 19°41E 53 F9
Ounasjoki → Finland 66°31N 25°40E 8 C21
Ounguati Namibia 22°0S 15°46E 56 B2
Ounianga Kébir Chad 19°4N 20°29E 53 E10
Our → Lux. 49°55N 6°5E 15 E6
Ouray U.S.A. 38°1N 107°40W 77 G10
Ourense Spain 42°19N 7°55W 21 A2
Ouricuri Brazil 7°53S 40°5W 93 E10
Ourinhos Brazil 23°0S 49°54W 95 A6
Ouro Fino Brazil 22°16S 46°25W 95 A6
Ouro Prêto Brazil 20°20S 43°30W 95 A7
Ourthe → Belgium 50°29N 5°35E 15 D5
Ouse → E. Sussex, U.K. 50°47N 0°4E 13 G8
Ouse → N. Yorks., U.K. 53°44N 0°55W 12 D7
Outaouais → Canada 45°27N 74°8W 72 C5
Outapi Namibia 17°30S 15°0E 56 A2
Outardes → Canada 49°24N 69°30W 73 C6
Outer Hebrides U.K. 57°30N 7°15W 11 D1
Outjo Namibia 20°5S 16°7E 56 B2
Outlook Canada 51°30N 107°0W 71 C7
Outokumpu Finland 62°43N 29°1E 8 E23
Ouyen Australia 35°1S 142°22E 63 F3
Ovalau Fiji 17°40S 178°48E 59 a
Ovalle Chile 30°33S 71°18W 94 C1
Ovamboland Namibia 18°30S 16°0E 56 A2
Overflakkee Neths. 51°44N 4°10E 15 C4
Overijssel □ Neths. 52°25N 6°35E 15 B6
Overland Park U.S.A. 38°58N 94°40W 80 F6
Overlander Roadhouse
  Australia 26°19S 114°28E 61 E1
Overton U.S.A. 36°33N 114°27W 79 J12
Övertorneå Sweden 66°23N 23°38E 8 C20
Ovid U.S.A. 42°41N 76°49W 83 D8
Oviedo Spain 43°25N 5°50W 21 A3
Ovišrags Latvia 57°33N 21°44E 9 H19
Övöot Mongolia 45°21N 113°45E 32 B7
Övör Hangay □ Mongolia 45°0N 102°30E 32 B2

Øvre Årdal Norway 61°19N 7°48E 8 F12
Ovruch Ukraine 51°25N 28°45E 17 C15
Owaka N.Z. 46°27S 169°40E 59 G2
Owambo = Ovamboland
  Namibia 18°30S 16°0E 56 A2
Owasco L. U.S.A. 42°50N 76°31W 83 D8
Owase Japan 34°7N 136°12E 29 G8
Owatonna U.S.A. 44°5N 93°14W 80 C7
Owbeh Afghan. 34°28N 63°10E 40 B3
Owego U.S.A. 42°6N 76°16W 83 D8
Owen Sound Canada 44°35N 80°55W 82 B4
Owen Stanley Ra.
  Papua N. G. 8°30S 147°0E 58 B7
Oweniny → Ireland 54°8N 9°34W 10 B2
Owens → U.S.A. 36°32N 117°59W 78 J9
Owens L. U.S.A. 36°26N 117°57W 79 J9
Owensboro U.S.A. 37°46N 87°7W 80 G10
Owl → Canada 57°51N 92°44W 71 B10
Owo Nigeria 7°10N 5°39E 52 G7
Owosso U.S.A. 43°0N 84°10W 81 D11
Owyhee U.S.A. 41°57N 116°6W 76 F5
Owyhee → U.S.A. 43°49N 117°2W 76 E5
Owyhee, L. U.S.A. 43°38N 117°14W 76 E5
Ox Mts. = Slieve Gamph
  Ireland 54°6N 9°0W 10 B3
Öxarfjörður Iceland 66°15N 16°45W 8 C5
Oxbow Canada 49°14N 102°10W 71 D8
Oxelösund Sweden 58°43N 17°5E 9 G17
Oxford N.Z. 43°18S 172°11E 59 E4
Oxford U.K. 51°46N 1°15W 13 F6
Oxford Mass., U.S.A. 42°7N 71°52W 83 D13
Oxford Miss., U.S.A. 34°22N 89°31W 85 D10
Oxford N.C., U.S.A. 36°19N 78°35W 85 C15
Oxford N.Y., U.S.A. 42°27N 75°36W 83 D9
Oxford Ohio, U.S.A. 39°31N 84°45W 81 F11
Oxford L. Canada 54°51N 95°37W 71 C9
Oxfordshire □ U.K. 51°48N 1°16W 13 F6
Oxnard U.S.A. 34°12N 119°11W 79 L7
Oxus = Amudarya →
  Uzbekistan 43°58N 59°34E 26 E6
Oya Malaysia 2°55N 111°55E 36 D4
Oyama Japan 36°18N 139°48E 29 F9
Oyem Gabon 1°34N 11°31E 54 D2
Oyen Canada 51°22N 110°28W 71 C6
Oykel → U.K. 57°56N 4°26W 11 D4
Oymyakon Russia 63°25N 142°44E 27 C15
Oyo Nigeria 7°46N 3°56E 52 G6
Oyster Bay U.S.A. 40°52N 73°32W 83 F11
Ōyūbari Japan 43°1N 142°5E 28 C11
Ozamiz Phil. 8°15N 123°50E 37 C6
Ozar = Ojhar India 20°6N 73°56E 44 D1
Ozark Ala., U.S.A. 31°28N 85°39W 85 F12
Ozark Ark., U.S.A. 35°29N 93°50W 84 D8
Ozark Mo., U.S.A. 37°1N 93°12W 80 G7
Ozark Plateau U.S.A. 37°20N 91°40W 80 G8
Ozarks, L. of the U.S.A. 38°12N 92°38W 80 F7
Ózd Hungary 48°14N 20°15E 17 D11
Ozernovskiy Russia 51°30N 156°31E 27 D16
Ozette, L. U.S.A. 48°6N 124°38W 78 B2
Ozieri Italy 40°35N 9°0E 22 D3
Ozona U.S.A. 30°43N 101°12W 84 F4
Ozuluama Mexico 21°40N 97°51W 87 C5

P

Pa-an Burma 16°51N 97°40E 41 L20
Pa Mong Dam Thailand 18°0N 102°22E 38 D4
Pa Sak → Thailand 15°30N 101°0E 38 E3
Paamiut Greenland 62°0N 49°43W 4 C5
Paarl S. Africa 33°45S 18°56E 56 D2
Pab Hills Pakistan 26°30N 66°45E 42 F2
Pabaidh = Pabbay U.K. 57°46N 7°14W 11 D1
Pabbay U.K. 57°46N 7°14W 11 D1
Pabianice Poland 51°40N 19°20E 17 C10
Pabna Bangla. 24°1N 89°18E 41 G16
Pacaja → Brazil 1°56S 50°50W 93 D8
Pacaraima, Sa. S. Amer. 4°0N 62°30W 92 C6
Pacasmayo Peru 7°20S 79°35W 92 E3
Pachitea → Peru 8°46S 74°33W 92 E4
Pachmarhi India 22°28N 78°26E 43 H8
Pachora India 20°38N 75°29E 44 D2
Pachpadra India 25°58N 72°10E 42 G5
Pachuca Mexico 20°7N 98°44W 87 C5
Pacific Antarctic Ridge
  Pac. Oc. 43°0S 115°0W 5 B13
Pacific Grove U.S.A. 36°38N 121°56W 78 J5
Pacific Ocean 10°0N 140°0W 65 G14
Pacific Rim △ Canada 48°40N 124°45W 78 B2
Pacitan Indonesia 8°12S 111°7E 37 H14
Packwood U.S.A. 46°36N 121°40W 78 D5
Padaido, Kepulauan
  Indonesia 1°15S 136°30E 37 E9
Padampur India 20°59N 83°4E 44 D6
Padang Riau, Indonesia 1°0N 102°30E 39 M4
Padang Sumatera Barat,
  Indonesia 1°0S 100°20E 36 E2
Padang Endau Malaysia 2°40N 103°38E 39 L4
Padangpanjang Indonesia 0°40S 100°20E 36 E2
Padangsidempuan
  Indonesia 1°30N 99°15E 36 D1
Paddle Prairie Canada 57°57N 117°29W 70 B5
Paderborn Germany 51°42N 8°45E 16 C5
Paderoo India 18°5N 82°40E 44 E6
Padma India 24°12N 85°22E 43 G11
Pádova Italy 45°25N 11°53E 22 B4
Padra India 22°15N 73°7E 42 H5
Padrauna India 26°54N 83°59E 43 F10
Padre I. U.S.A. 27°10N 97°25W 84 H6
Padre Island ○ U.S.A. 27°0N 97°25W 84 H6
Padstow U.K. 50°33N 4°58W 13 G3
Padua = Pádova Italy 45°25N 11°53E 22 B4
Paducah Ky., U.S.A. 37°5N 88°37W 80 G9
Paducah Tex., U.S.A. 34°1N 100°18W 84 D4
Padwa India 18°27N 82°47E 44 E6
Paea Tahiti 17°41S 149°35W 59 d
Paektu-san N. Korea 41°59N 128°4E 33 D15
Paeroa N.Z. 37°23S 175°41E 59 B5
Pafúri Mozam. 22°28S 31°17E 57 B5

Pag Croatia 44°25N 15°3E 16 F8
Pagadian Phil. 7°55N 123°30E 37 C6
Pagai Selatan, Pulau
  Indonesia 3°0S 100°15E 36 E2
Pagai Utara, Pulau
  Indonesia 2°35S 100°0E 36 E2
Pagalu = Annobón Atl. Oc. 1°25S 5°36E 51 G4
Pagara India 24°22N 80°1E 43 G9
Pagastikos Kolpos Greece 39°15S 23°0E 23 E10
Pagatan Indonesia 3°33S 115°59E 36 E5
Page U.S.A. 36°57N 111°27W 77 H8
Paget, Mt. S. Georgia 54°26S 36°31W 96 G9
Pagosa Springs U.S.A. 37°16N 107°1W 77 H10
Pagri China 27°45N 89°10E 30 F6
Pagwa River Canada 50°2N 85°14W 72 B2
Pāhala U.S.A. 19°12N 155°29W 75 M8
Pahang □ Malaysia 3°30N 102°45E 39 L4
Pahang → Malaysia 3°30N 103°9E 39 L4
Pahiatua N.Z. 40°27S 175°50E 59 D5
Pahokee U.S.A. 26°50N 80°40W 85 H14
Pahrump U.S.A. 36°12N 115°59W 79 J11
Pahute Mesa U.S.A. 37°20N 116°45W 78 H10
Pai Thailand 19°19N 98°27E 38 C2
Paicines U.S.A. 36°44N 121°17W 78 J5
Paide Estonia 58°53N 25°33E 9 G21
Paignton U.K. 50°26N 3°35W 13 G4
Päijänne Finland 61°30N 25°30E 8 F21
Pailani India 25°45N 80°26E 43 G9
Pailin Cambodia 12°46N 102°36E 38 F4
Painan Indonesia 1°21S 100°34E 36 E2
Painesville U.S.A. 41°43N 81°15W 82 E3
Paint Hills = Wemindji
  Canada 53°0N 78°49W 72 B4
Paint L. Canada 55°28N 97°57W 71 B9
Painted Desert U.S.A. 36°0N 111°0W 77 H8
Paintsville U.S.A. 37°49N 82°48W 81 G12
País Vasco □ Spain 42°50N 2°45W 21 A4
Paisley Canada 44°18N 81°16W 82 B3
Paisley U.K. 55°50N 4°25W 11 F4
Paisley U.S.A. 42°42N 120°32W 76 E3
Paita Peru 5°11S 81°9W 92 E2
Paithan India 19°29N 75°23E 44 E2
Paizhou China 30°12N 113°55E 35 B9
Pajares, Puerto de Spain 42°58N 5°46W 21 A3
Pak Lay Laos 18°15N 101°27E 38 C3
Pak Ou Laos 20°3N 102°12E 38 B4
Pak Phanang Thailand 8°21N 100°12E 39 H3
Pak Sane Laos 18°22N 103°39E 38 C4
Pak Song Laos 15°11N 106°14E 38 E6
Pak Suang Laos 19°58N 102°15E 38 C4
Pak Tam Chung China 22°24N 114°19E 31 a
Pak Thong Chai Thailand 14°43N 102°1E 38 E4
Pakala India 13°29N 79°8E 45 H4
Pakaur India 24°38N 87°51E 43 G12
Pakch'ŏn N. Korea 39°44N 125°35E 33 E13
Pakenham Canada 45°18N 76°18W 83 A8
Pakhuis S. Africa 32°9S 19°5E 56 D2
Pakistan ■ Asia 30°0N 70°0E 42 E4
Pakkading Laos 18°19N 103°59E 38 C4
Pakokku Burma 21°20N 95°0E 41 J19
Pakowki L. Canada 49°20N 111°0W 71 D6
Pakpattan Pakistan 30°25N 73°27E 42 D5
Paktīā □ Afghan. 33°30N 69°15E 40 C6
Paktīkā □ Afghan. 32°30N 69°0E 40 C6
Pakwach Uganda 2°28N 31°27E 54 D6
Pakxe Laos 15°5N 105°52E 38 E5
Pal Lahara India 21°27N 85°11E 43 J11
Pala Chad 9°25N 15°5E 53 G9
Pala U.S.A. 33°22N 117°5W 79 M9
Palacios U.S.A. 28°42N 96°13W 84 G6
Palagruža Croatia 42°24N 16°15E 22 C7
Palakkad India 10°46N 76°42E 45 J3
Palakol India 16°31N 81°46E 45 F5
Palalankwe India 10°52N 92°29E 45 J11
Palam India 19°0N 77°0E 44 E3
Palampur India 32°10N 76°30E 42 C7
Palana Australia 39°45S 147°55E 63 F4
Palana Russia 59°10N 159°59E 27 D16
Palanan Phil. 17°8N 122°29E 37 A6
Palanan Pt. Phil. 17°17N 122°30E 37 A6
Palandri Pakistan 33°42N 73°40E 43 C5
Palanga Lithuania 55°58N 21°3E 9 J19
Palangkaraya Indonesia 2°16S 113°56E 36 E4
Palani India 10°30N 77°33E 45 J3
Palani Hills India 10°14N 77°33E 45 J3
Palanpur India 24°10N 72°25E 42 G5
Palapye Botswana 22°30S 27°7E 56 B4
Palas → India 12°27N 80°13E 45 H5
Palasponga India 21°47N 85°34E 43 J11
Palatka Russia 60°6N 150°54E 27 C16
Palatka U.S.A. 29°39N 81°38W 85 G14
Palau ■ Palau 7°30N 134°30E 58 A6
Palauk Burma 13°10N 98°40E 38 F2
Palaw Burma 12°58N 98°39E 38 F2
Palawan Phil. 9°30N 118°30E 36 C5
Palayankottai India 8°45N 77°45E 45 K3
Paldiski Estonia 59°23N 24°9E 9 G21
Paleleh Indonesia 1°10N 121°50E 37 D6
Palembang Indonesia 3°0S 104°50E 36 E2
Palencia Spain 42°1N 4°34W 21 A3
Palenque Mexico 17°29N 92°1W 87 D6
Palermo Italy 38°7N 13°22E 22 E5
Palermo U.S.A. 39°26N 121°33W 78 F5
Palestina Chile 23°50S 69°47W 96 A3
Palestine Asia 32°0N 35°0E 48 D4
Palestine U.S.A. 31°46N 95°38W 84 F7
Paletwa Burma 21°10N 92°50E 41 J18
Palghat = Palakkad India 10°46N 76°42E 45 J3
Palgrave, Mt. Australia 23°22S 115°58E 60 D2
Pali India 25°50N 73°20E 42 G5
Palikir Micronesia 6°55N 158°9E 64 G7
Paliouri, Akra Greece 39°57N 23°45E 23 E10
Palisades Res. U.S.A. 43°20N 111°12W 76 E8
Paliseul Belgium 49°54N 5°8E 15 E5
Palitana India 21°32N 71°49E 42 J4

Palizada Mexico 18°15N 92°5W 87 D6
Palk Bay Asia 9°30N 79°15E 45 K4
Palk Strait Asia 10°0N 79°45E 45 K4
Palkānah Iraq 35°49N 44°26E 46 C5
Palkonda India 18°36N 83°48E 44 E6
Palkonda Ra. India 13°50N 79°20E 45 H4
Palkot India 22°53N 84°39E 43 H11
Pallanza = Verbánia Italy 45°56N 8°33E 20 D8
Pallarenda Australia 19°12S 146°46E 62 B4
Palleru → India 16°45N 80°2E 44 F5
Pallinup → Australia 34°27S 118°50E 61 F2
Pallu India 28°59N 74°14E 42 E6
Palm Bay U.S.A. 28°2N 80°35W 85 G14
Palm Beach U.S.A. 26°43N 80°2W 85 H14
Palm Coast U.S.A. 29°35N 81°12W 85 G14
Palm Desert U.S.A. 33°43N 116°22W 79 M10
Palm-Grove ○ Australia 24°57S 149°21E 62 C4
Palm Is. Australia 18°40S 146°35E 62 B4
Palm Springs U.S.A. 33°50N 116°33W 79 M10
Palma, B. de Spain 39°30N 2°39E 21 C7
Palma de Mallorca Spain 39°35N 2°39E 21 C7
Palma Soriano Cuba 20°15N 76°0W 88 B4
Palmaner India 13°12N 78°45E 45 H4
Palmares Brazil 8°41S 35°28W 93 E11
Palmas Brazil 26°29S 52°0W 95 B5
Palmas, C. Liberia 4°27N 7°46W 52 H4
Pálmas, G. di Italy 39°0N 8°30E 22 E3
Palmdale U.S.A. 34°35N 118°7W 79 L8
Palmeira das Missões
  Brazil 27°55S 53°17W 95 B5
Palmeira dos Índios
  Brazil 9°25S 36°37W 93 E11
Palmer Antarctica 64°35S 65°0W 5 C17
Palmer U.S.A. 61°36N 149°7W 68 E2
Palmer → Australia 16°0S 142°26E 62 B3
Palmer Arch. Antarctica 64°15S 65°0W 5 C17
Palmer Lake U.S.A. 39°7N 104°55W 76 G11
Palmer Land Antarctica 73°0S 63°0W 5 D18
Palmerston Australia 12°31S 130°59E 60 B5
Palmerston Canada 43°50N 80°51W 82 C4
Palmerston N.Z. 45°29S 170°43E 59 F3
Palmerston North N.Z. 40°21S 175°39E 59 D5
Palmerton U.S.A. 40°48N 75°37W 83 F9
Palmetto U.S.A. 27°31N 82°34W 85 H13
Palmi Italy 38°21N 15°51E 22 E6
Palmira Argentina 32°59S 68°34W 94 C2
Palmira Colombia 3°32N 76°16W 92 C3
Palmyra = Tudmur Syria 34°36N 38°15E 46 C3
Palmyra Mo., U.S.A. 39°48N 91°32W 80 F8
Palmyra N.J., U.S.A. 40°0N 75°1W 83 F9
Palmyra N.Y., U.S.A. 43°5N 77°18W 82 C7
Palmyra Pa., U.S.A. 40°18N 76°36W 83 F8
Palmyra Is. Pac. Oc. 5°52N 162°5W 65 G11
Palmyra Pt. India 20°46N 87°1E 44 D8
Palo Alto U.S.A. 37°27N 122°10W 78 H4
Palo Seco Trin. & Tob. 10°4N 61°36W 93 K15
Palo Verde U.S.A. 33°26N 114°44W 79 M12
Palo Verde △ Costa Rica 10°21N 85°21W 88 D2
Palomar Mt. U.S.A. 33°22N 116°50W 79 M10
Palopo Indonesia 3°0S 120°16E 37 E6
Palos, C. de Spain 37°38N 0°40W 21 D5
Palos Verdes, Pt. U.S.A. 33°46N 118°25W 79 M8
Palos Verdes Estates
  U.S.A. 33°48N 118°23W 79 M8
Palu Indonesia 1°0S 119°52E 37 E5
Palu Turkey 38°45N 40°0E 46 B3
Paluma Ra. Australia 19°9S 146°22E 62 B4
Palwal India 28°8N 77°19E 42 E7
Pamanukan Indonesia 6°16S 107°49E 37 G12
Pamban I. India 9°15N 79°20E 45 K4
Pamekasan Indonesia 7°10S 113°28E 37 G15
Pamenang Indonesia 8°24S 116°6E 37 J19
Pamiers France 43°7N 1°39E 20 E4
Pamir Tajikistan 37°40N 73°0E 26 F8
Pamlico → U.S.A. 35°20N 76°28W 85 D16
Pamlico Sd. U.S.A. 35°20N 76°0W 85 D17
Pampa U.S.A. 35°32N 100°58W 84 D4
Pampa de las Salinas
  Argentina 32°1S 66°58W 94 C2
Pampanua Indonesia 4°16S 120°8E 37 E6
Pampas Argentina 35°0S 63°0W 94 D3
Pampas Peru 12°20S 74°50W 92 F4
Pamplona Colombia 7°23N 72°39W 92 B4
Pamplona-Iruña Spain 42°48N 1°38W 21 A5
Pampoenpoort S. Africa 31°3S 22°40E 56 D3
Pan de Azúcar Chile 24°5S 68°10W 94 A2
Pan de Azúcar △ Chile 26°0S 70°40W 94 B1
Pan Xian China 25°46N 104°38E 34 E5
Pana U.S.A. 39°23N 89°5W 80 F9
Panaca U.S.A. 37°47N 114°23W 77 H6
Panadura Sri Lanka 6°47N 79°53E 45 L4
Panaitan Indonesia 6°36S 105°12E 37 G11
Panaji India 15°25N 73°50E 45 G1
Panamá Panama 9°0N 79°25W 88 E4
Panama Sri Lanka 6°45N 81°48E 45 L5
Panama ■ Cent. Amer. 8°48N 79°55W 88 E4
Panamá, G. de Panama 8°4N 79°20W 88 E4
Panama, Isthmus of
  Cent. Amer. 9°0N 79°0W 88 E4
Panama Basin Pac. Oc. 5°0N 83°30W 65 G19
Panama Canal Panama 9°10N 79°37W 88 E4
Panama City U.S.A. 30°10N 85°40W 85 F12
Panamint Range U.S.A. 36°20N 117°20W 79 J9
Panamint Springs
  U.S.A. 36°20N 117°28W 79 J9
Panão Peru 9°55S 75°55W 92 E3
Panay Phil. 11°10N 122°30E 37 B6
Panay G. Phil. 11°0N 122°30E 37 B6
Pančevo Serbia 44°52N 20°41E 23 B9
Panch'iao Taiwan 25°1N 121°27E 35 E13
Panda Mozam. 24°2S 34°45E 57 C5
Pandan Malaysia 1°32N 103°46E 39 d
Pandan Phil. 11°45N 122°10E 37 B6
Pandan Tampoi = Tampoi
  Malaysia 1°30N 103°39E 39 d
Pandegelang Indonesia 6°25S 106°5E 37 G12
Pandhana India 21°42N 76°13E 42 J7
Pandharkawada India 20°1N 78°32E 44 D4

Pandharpur India 17°41N 75°20E 44 F2
Pandhurna India 21°36N 78°35E 44 D4
Pando Uruguay 34°44S 56°0W 95 C4
Pando, L. = Hope, L.
  Australia 28°24S 139°18E 63 D2
Pandora Costa Rica 9°43N 83°3W 88 E3
Panevėžys Lithuania 55°42N 24°25E 9 J21
Pang Sida △ Thailand 14°5N 102°17E 38 E4
Pangandaran Indonesia 7°40S 108°39E 37 G13
Pangandaran △
  Indonesia 7°43S 108°42E 37 G13
Pangani Tanzania 5°25S 38°58E 54 F7
Pangfou = Bengbu
  China 32°58N 117°20E 33 H9
Pangga, Tanjung
  Indonesia 8°54S 116°2E 37 K19
Panghsang = Bangkang
  Burma 22°4N 99°1E 34 F2
Pangjiabu China 40°38N 115°26E 32 D8
Pangkah, Tanjung
  Indonesia 6°51S 112°33E 37 G15
Pangkai Burma 22°49N 98°39E 34 F2
Pangkajene Indonesia 4°46S 119°34E 37 E5
Pangkalanbrandan
  Indonesia 4°1N 98°20E 36 D1
Pangkalanbuun Indonesia 2°41S 111°37E 36 E4
Pangkalpinang Indonesia 2°0S 106°0E 36 E3
Pangkor, Pulau Malaysia 4°13N 100°34E 39 K3
Pangniqtuuq = Pangnirtung
  Canada 66°8N 65°43W 69 D18
Pangnirtung Canada 66°8N 65°43W 69 D18
Pangody Russia 65°52N 74°27E 26 C8
Pangong Tso = Bangong Co
  China 33°45N 78°43E 43 C8
Panguitch U.S.A. 37°50N 112°26W 77 H7
Pangutaran Group Phil. 6°18N 120°34E 37 C6
Panhala India 16°49N 74°7E 44 F2
Panhandle U.S.A. 35°21N 101°23W 84 D4
Pani Mines India 22°29N 73°50E 42 H5
Panikota I. India 20°46N 71°21E 42 J4
Panipat India 29°25N 77°2E 42 E7
Panjal Range = Pir Panjal Range
  India 32°30N 76°50E 42 C7
Panjgur Pakistan 27°0N 64°5E 40 F4
Panjhra → India 21°13N 74°57E 44 D2
Panjim = Panaji India 15°25N 73°50E 45 G1
Panjin China 41°3N 122°2E 33 D12
Panjnad → Pakistan 28°57N 70°30E 42 E4
Panjnad Barrage Pakistan 29°22N 71°15E 42 E4
Panjwai Afghan. 31°26N 65°27E 42 D1
Panmunjŏm N. Korea 37°59N 126°38E 33 F14
Panna India 24°40N 80°15E 43 G9
Panna △ India 24°40N 80°0E 43 G8
Panna Hills India 24°40N 81°15E 43 G9
Pannawonica Australia 21°39S 116°19E 60 D2
Pano Akil Pakistan 27°51N 69°7E 42 F3
Panorama Brazil 21°21S 51°51W 95 A5
Panruti India 11°46N 79°35E 45 J4
Pansemal India 21°39N 74°42E 42 J6
Panshan = Panjin China 41°3N 122°2E 33 D12
Panshi China 42°58N 126°5E 33 C14
Pantanal Brazil 17°30S 57°40W 92 H7
Pantanos de Centla ○
  Mexico 18°25N 92°25W 87 D6
Pantar Indonesia 8°28S 124°10E 37 F6
Pante Macassar E. Timor 9°30S 123°58E 37 F6
Pantelleria Italy 36°50N 11°57E 22 F4
Pánuco Mexico 22°3N 98°10W 87 C5
Panvel India 18°59N 73°4E 44 E1
Panzhihua China 26°33N 101°44E 34 D3
Paola U.S.A. 38°35N 94°53W 80 F6
Paonia U.S.A. 38°52N 107°36W 76 G10
Paopao Moorea 17°30S 149°49W 59 d
Paoting = Baoding
  China 38°50N 115°28E 32 E8
Paot'ou = Baotou China 40°32N 110°2E 32 D6
Paoua C.A.R. 7°9N 16°20E 54 C3
Pápa Hungary 47°22N 17°30E 17 E9
Papa Stour U.K. 60°20N 1°42W 11 A7
Papa Westray U.K. 59°20N 2°55W 11 B6
Papagayo → Mexico 16°46N 99°43W 87 D5
Papagayo, G. de
  Costa Rica 10°30N 85°50W 88 D2
Papagni → India 15°35N 77°45E 45 G3
Papakura N.Z. 37°4S 174°59E 59 B5
Papantla Mexico 20°27N 97°19W 87 C5
Papar Malaysia 5°45N 116°0E 36 C5
Papara Tahiti 17°43S 149°31W 59 d
Paparoa △ N.Z. 42°7S 171°26E 59 E3
Papeete Tahiti 17°32S 149°34W 59 d
Papenoo Tahiti 17°30S 149°25W 59 d
Papenoo → Tahiti 17°30S 149°25W 59 d
Papetoai Moorea 17°29S 149°52W 59 d
Paposo Chile 25°0S 70°30W 94 B1
Papua □ Indonesia 4°0S 137°0E 37 E9
Papua, G. of Papua N. G. 9°0S 144°50E 58 B7
Papua New Guinea ■
  Oceania 8°0S 145°0E 58 B7
Papudo Chile 32°29S 71°27W 94 C1
Papun Burma 18°2N 97°30E 41 K20
Papunya Australia 23°15S 131°54E 60 D5
Pará = Belém Brazil 1°20S 48°30W 93 D9
Pará □ Brazil 3°20S 52°0W 93 D8
Paraburdoo Australia 23°14S 117°32E 60 D2
Paracatu Brazil 17°10S 46°50W 93 G9
Paracel Is. S. China Sea 15°50N 112°0E 36 A4
Parachilna Australia 31°10S 138°21E 63 E2
Parachinar Pakistan 33°55N 70°5E 42 C4
Paradip India 20°15N 86°35E 44 D8
Paradise Calif., U.S.A. 39°46N 121°37W 78 F5
Paradise Nev., U.S.A. 36°9N 115°10W 79 J11
Paradise → Canada 53°27N 57°19W 73 B8
Paradise Hill Canada 53°32N 109°28W 71 C7
Paradise River Canada 53°27N 57°17W 73 B8
Paradise Valley U.S.A. 41°30N 117°32W 76 F5
Paragould U.S.A. 36°3N 90°29W 85 C9
Paragua → Venezuela 6°55N 62°55W 92 B6
Paraguaçu → Brazil 12°45S 38°54W 93 F11
Paraguaçu Paulista
  Brazil 22°22S 50°35W 95 A5

Paraguaná, Pen. de
  Venezuela 12°0N 70°0W 92 A5
Paraguarí Paraguay 25°36S 57°0W 94 B4
Paraguarí □ Paraguay 26°0S 57°10W 94 B4
Paraguay ■ S. Amer. 23°0S 57°0W 94 A4
Paraguay → Paraguay 27°18S 58°38W 94 B4
Paraíba = João Pessoa
  Brazil 7°10S 34°52W 93 E12
Paraíba □ Brazil 7°0S 36°0W 93 E11
Paraíba do Sul → Brazil 21°37S 41°3W 95 A7
Paraíso Mexico 18°24N 93°14W 87 D6
Parak Iran 27°38N 52°25E 47 E7
Parakou Benin 9°25N 2°40E 52 G6
Paralkote India 19°0N 80°41E 44 E5
Páramos del Batallón y La Negra △
  Venezuela 8°1N 71°55W 89 E5
Paramushir, Ostrov
  Russia 50°24N 156°0E 27 D16
Paran → Israel 30°20N 35°10E 48 E4
Paraná Argentina 31°45S 60°30W 94 C3
Paraná Brazil 12°30S 47°48W 93 F9
Paraná □ Brazil 24°30S 51°0W 95 A4
Paraná → Argentina 33°43S 59°15W 94 C4
Paranaguá Brazil 25°30S 48°30W 95 B6
Paranaíba Brazil 19°40S 51°11W 93 G8
Paranaíba → Brazil 20°6S 51°4W 93 H8
Paranapanema → Brazil 22°40S 53°9W 95 A5
Paranapiacaba, Serra do
  Brazil 24°31S 48°35W 95 A6
Paranavaí Brazil 23°4S 52°56W 95 A5
Parang Maguindanao, Phil. 7°23N 124°16E 37 C6
Parang Sulu, Phil. 5°55N 120°54E 37 C6
Parangippettai India 11°30N 79°38E 45 J4
Parângul Mare, Vf.
  Romania 45°20N 23°37E 17 F12
Paranthan Sri Lanka 9°26N 80°24E 45 K5
Paraparaumu N.Z. 40°57S 175°3E 59 D5
Parbati → Mad. P., India 25°50N 76°30E 42 G7
Parbati → Raj., India 26°54N 77°53E 42 F7
Parbhani India 19°8N 76°52E 44 E3
Parchim Germany 53°26N 11°52E 16 B6
Pardes Hanna-Karkur
  Israel 32°28N 34°57E 48 C3
Pardo → Bahia, Brazil 15°40S 39°0W 93 G11
Pardo → Mato Grosso,
  Brazil 21°46S 52°9W 95 A5
Pardoo Roadhouse
  Australia 20°6S 119°3E 60 D2
Pardubice Czech Rep. 50°3N 15°45E 16 C8
Pare Indonesia 7°43S 112°12E 37 G15
Parecis, Serra dos Brazil 13°0S 60°0W 92 F7
Paren Russia 62°30N 163°15E 27 C17
Parenda India 18°16N 75°28E 44 E2
Parent Canada 47°55N 74°35W 72 C5
Parent, L. Canada 48°31N 77°1W 72 C4
Parepare Indonesia 4°0S 119°40E 37 E5
Parga Greece 39°15N 20°29E 23 E9
Pargas = Länsi-Turunmaa
  Finland 60°18N 22°18E 9 F20
Pargi India 17°11N 77°53E 44 E3
Parham Canada 44°39N 76°43W 83 B8
Paria → 36°52N 111°36W 77 H8
Paria, G. de Venezuela 10°20N 62°0W 89 D7
Pariaguán Venezuela 8°51N 64°34W 92 B6
Paricutín, Cerro Mexico 19°28N 102°15W 86 D4
Parigi Indonesia 0°50S 120°5E 37 E6
Parika Guyana 6°50N 58°20W 92 B7
Parikkala Finland 61°33N 29°31E 8 F23
Parima, Serra Brazil 2°30N 64°0W 92 C6
Parinari Peru 4°35S 74°25W 92 D4
Pariñas, Pta. Peru 4°30S 82°0W 90 D2
Parintins Brazil 2°40S 56°50W 93 D7
Pariparit Kyun Burma 14°52N 93°41E 45 G11
Paris Canada 43°12N 80°25W 82 C4
Paris Idaho, U.S.A. 42°14N 111°24W 76 E8
Paris Ky., U.S.A. 38°13N 84°15W 81 F11
Paris Tenn., U.S.A. 36°18N 88°19W 85 C10
Paris Tex., U.S.A. 33°40N 95°33W 84 E7
Parish U.S.A. 43°25N 76°8W 83 C8
Parishville U.S.A. 44°38N 74°49W 83 B10
Pariti Indonesia 10°1S 123°45E 60 B3
Park → U.S.A. 48°45N 122°18W 78 B4
Park City U.S.A. 37°48N 97°20W 80 G5
Park Falls U.S.A. 45°56N 90°27W 80 C8
Park Head Canada 44°36N 81°9W 82 B3
Park Hills U.S.A. 37°51N 90°51W 80 G8
Park Range U.S.A. 40°41N 106°41W 76 F10
Park Rapids U.S.A. 46°55N 95°4W 80 B6
Park River U.S.A. 48°24N 97°45W 80 A5
Park Rynie S. Africa 30°25S 30°45E 57 E5
Parkā Bandar Iran 25°55N 59°35E 47 E8
Parkal India 18°12N 79°43E 44 E4
Parkano Finland 62°1N 23°0E 8 E20
Parker Ariz., U.S.A. 34°9N 114°17W 79 L12
Parker Pa., U.S.A. 41°5N 79°41W 82 E5
Parker Dam U.S.A. 34°18N 114°8W 79 L12
Parkersburg U.S.A. 39°16N 81°34W 81 F13
Parkes Australia 33°9S 148°11E 63 E4
Parkfield U.S.A. 35°54N 120°26W 78 K6
Parkhill Canada 43°15N 81°38W 82 C3
Parkland U.S.A. 47°9N 122°26W 78 C4
Parkston U.S.A. 43°24N 97°59W 80 D5
Parksville Canada 49°20N 124°21W 70 D4
Parkway U.S.A. 38°32N 121°26W 78 G5
Parla Spain 40°14N 3°46W 21 B4
Parlakimidi India 18°45N 84°5E 44 E7
Parli India 18°50N 76°35E 44 E3
Parma Italy 44°48N 10°20E 20 D9
Parma Idaho, U.S.A. 43°47N 116°57W 76 E5
Parma Ohio, U.S.A. 41°24N 81°43W 82 E3
Parnaíba Brazil 2°54S 41°47W 93 D10
Parnaíba → Brazil 3°0S 41°50W 93 D10
Parnassos Greece 38°35N 22°30E 23 E10
Parner India 19°0N 74°26E 44 E2
Pärnu Estonia 58°28N 24°33E 9 G21
Paro Dzong Bhutan 27°23N 89°53E 43 F13
Parola India 20°47N 75°7E 44 D2

Paroo → *Australia* 31°28S 143°32E **63** E3
Paros *Greece* 37°5N 25°12E **23** F11
Parowan *U.S.A.* 37°51N 112°50W **77** H7
Parral *Chile* 36°10S 71°52W **94** D1
Parramatta *Australia* 33°48S 151°1E **63** B5
Parras *Mexico* 25°25N 102°11W **86** B4
Parrett → *U.K.* 51°12N 3°1W **13** F4
Parris I. *U.S.A.* 32°20N 80°41W **85** E14
Parrsboro *Canada* 45°30N 64°25W **73** C7
Parry Channel *Canada* 74°15N 94°0W **69** C13
Parry I. *Canada* 45°18N 80°10W **82** A4
Parry Is. *Canada* 77°0N 110°0W **69** B10
Parry Sound *Canada* 45°20N 80°0W **82** A5
Parsnip → *Canada* 55°10N 123°2W **70** B4
Parsons *U.S.A.* 37°20N 95°16W **80** G6
Parsons Ra. *Australia* 13°30S 135°15E **62** A2
Partabpur *India* 20°0N 80°42E **44** E5
Partinico *Italy* 38°3N 13°7E **22** E5
Partizansk *Russia* 43°8N 133°9E **27** E14
Partridge I. *Canada* 55°59N 87°37W **72** A2
Partry Mts. *Ireland* 53°40N 9°28W **10** C2
Partur *India* 19°40N 76°14E **44** E3
Paru → *Brazil* 1°33S 52°38W **93** D8
Parur *India* 10°13N 76°14E **45** J3
Parvān □ *Afghan.* 35°0N 69°0E **40** B6
Parvatipuram *India* 18°50N 83°25E **44** E6
Parvatsar *India* 26°52N 74°49E **42** F6
Parys *S. Africa* 26°52S 27°29E **56** C4
Pas, The *Canada* 53°45N 101°15W **71** C8
Pasadena *Canada* 49°1N 57°36W **73** C8
Pasadena *U.S.A.* 29°43N 95°13W **84** G7
Pasaje → *Argentina* 25°39S 63°56W **94** B3
Pasar *Indonesia* 8°27S 114°54E **37** J17
Pasargadae *Iran* 30°11N 53°10E **47** D7
Pascagoula *U.S.A.* 30°21N 88°33W **85** F10
Pascagoula → *U.S.A.* 30°23N 88°37W **85** F10
Pașcani *Romania* 47°14N 26°45E **17** E14
Paschimbanga □ *India* 23°0N 88°0E **43** H13
Pasco *U.S.A.* 46°14N 119°6W **76** C4
Pasco I. *Australia* 20°57S 115°20E **60** D2
Pascoag *U.S.A.* 41°57N 71°42W **83** E13
Pascua, I. de *Chile* 27°7S 109°23W **65** K17
Pasfield L. *Canada* 58°24N 105°20W **71** B7
Pasir Mas *Malaysia* 6°2N 102°8E **39** J4
Pasir Putih *Malaysia* 5°50N 102°24E **39** K4
Pasirian *Indonesia* 8°13S 113°8E **37** H15
Paskūh *Iran* 27°34N 61°39E **47** E9
Pasley, C. *Australia* 33°52S 123°35E **61** F3
Pašman *Croatia* 43°58N 15°20E **16** G8
Pasni *Pakistan* 25°15N 63°27E **40** G3
Paso Bravo △ *Paraguay* 22°32S 57°55W **94** A4
Paso Cantinela *Mexico* 32°33N 115°47W **79** N11
Paso de Indios *Argentina* 43°55S 69°0W **96** E3
Paso de los Libres
  Argentina 29°44S 57°10W **94** B4
Paso de los Toros
  Uruguay 32°45S 56°30W **94** C4
Paso Robles *U.S.A.* 35°38N 120°41W **78** K6
Paspébiac *Canada* 48°3N 65°17W **73** C6
Pasrur *Pakistan* 32°16N 74°43E **42** C6
Passage East *Ireland* 52°14N 7°0W **10** D5
Passage West *Ireland* 51°52N 8°21W **10** E3
Passau *Germany* 48°34N 13°28E **16** D7
Passero, C. *Italy* 36°41N 15°10E **22** F6
Passo Fundo *Brazil* 28°10S 52°20W **95** B5
Passos *Brazil* 20°45S 46°37W **93** H9
Pastavy *Belarus* 55°4N 26°50E **9** J22
Pastaza → *Peru* 4°50S 76°52W **92** D3
Pasto *Colombia* 1°13N 77°17W **92** C3
Pasuruan *Indonesia* 7°40S 112°44E **37** G15
Patagonia *Argentina* 45°0S 69°0W **96** F3
Patagonia *U.S.A.* 31°33N 110°45W **77** L8
Patambar *Iran* 29°45N 60°17E **47** D9
Patan = Lalitpur *Nepal* 27°40N 85°20E **43** F11
Patan = Somnath *India* 20°53N 70°22E **42** J4
Patan *Gujarat, India* 23°54N 72°14E **42** H5
Patan *Maharashtra, India* 17°22N 73°57E **44** F1
Patani *Indonesia* 0°20N 128°50E **37** D7
Pataudi *India* 28°18N 76°48E **42** E7
Patchewollock *Australia* 35°22S 142°12E **63** F3
Patchogue *U.S.A.* 40°46N 73°1W **83** F11
Patea *N.Z.* 39°45S 174°30E **59** C5
Patensie *S. Africa* 33°46S 24°49E **56** D3
Paternò *Italy* 37°34N 14°54E **22** F6
Pateros *U.S.A.* 48°3N 119°54W **76** B4
Paterson *U.S.A.* 40°54N 74°9W **83** F10
Paterson Ra. *Australia* 21°45S 122°10E **60** D3
Pathankot *India* 32°18N 75°45E **42** C6
Pathardi *India* 19°10N 75°11E **44** E2
Pathein = Bassein
  Burma 16°45N 94°30E **41** L19
Pathfinder Res. *U.S.A.* 42°28N 106°51W **76** E10
Pathiu *Thailand* 10°42N 99°19E **39** G2
Pathri *India* 19°15N 76°27E **44** E3
Pathum Thani *Thailand* 14°1N 100°32E **38** E3
Pati *Indonesia* 6°45S 111°1E **37** G14
Patia → *Colombia* 2°13N 78°40W **92** C3
Patiala *Punjab, India* 30°23N 76°26E **42** D7
Patiala *Ut. P., India* 27°43N 79°1E **43** F8
Patkai Bum *India* 27°0N 95°30E **41** F19
Patmos *Greece* 37°21N 26°36E **23** F12
Patna *India* 25°35N 85°12E **43** G11
Patnagarh *India* 20°43N 83°9E **44** D6
Pato Branco *Brazil* 26°13S 52°40W **95** B5
Patong, Ao *Thailand* 7°54N 98°17E **39** a
Patos *Brazil* 6°55S 37°16W **93** E11
Patos, L. dos *Brazil* 31°20S 51°0W **95** C5
Patos, Río de los →
  Argentina 31°18S 69°25W **94** C2
Patos de Minas *Brazil* 18°35S 46°32W **93** G9
Patquía *Argentina* 30°2S 66°55W **94** C2
Patra *Greece* 38°14N 21°47E **23** E9
Patraikos Kolpos *Greece* 38°17N 21°30E **23** E9
Patras = Patra *Greece* 38°14N 21°47E **23** E9
Patriot Hills *Antarctica* 82°20S 81°25W **5** E16
Patrocínio *Brazil* 18°57S 47°0W **93** G9
Pattadakal *India* 16°1N 75°42E **45** G2
Pattani *Thailand* 6°48N 101°15E **39** J3
Pattaya *Thailand* 12°52N 100°55E **38** F3

Patten *U.S.A.* 46°0N 68°38W **81** B19
Patterson *Calif., U.S.A.* 37°28N 121°8W **78** H5
Patterson *La., U.S.A.* 29°42N 91°18W **84** G9
Patterson, Mt. *U.S.A.* 38°29N 119°20W **78** G7
Patti *Punjab, India* 31°17N 74°54E **42** D6
Patti *Ut. P., India* 25°55N 82°12E **43** G10
Pattoki *Pakistan* 31°5N 73°52E **42** D5
Patton *U.S.A.* 40°38N 78°39W **82** F6
Pattukkottai *India* 10°25N 79°20E **45** J4
Patuakhali *Bangla.* 22°20N 90°25E **41** H17
Patuanak *Canada* 55°55N 107°43W **71** B7
Patuca → *Honduras* 15°50N 84°18W **88** C3
Patuca, Punta *Honduras* 15°49N 84°14W **88** C3
Patuca △ *Honduras* 14°30N 85°30W **88** D2
Patur *India* 20°27N 76°56E **44** D3
Patvinsuo △ *Finland* 63°7N 30°45E **8** E24
Pátzcuaro *Mexico* 19°31N 101°38W **86** D4
Pau *France* 43°19N 0°25W **20** E3
Paudash *Canada* 44°59N 77°58W **82** B7
Pauk *Burma* 21°27N 94°30E **41** J19
Paul I. *Canada* 56°30N 61°20W **73** A7
Paul Smiths *U.S.A.* 44°26N 74°15W **83** B10
Paulatuk *Canada* 69°25N 124°0W **68** D7
Paulding Bay *S. Ocean* 66°0S 118°0E **5** C8
Paulistana *Brazil* 8°9S 41°9W **93** E10
Paulo Afonso *Brazil* 9°21S 38°15W **93** E11
Paulpietersburg *S. Africa* 27°23S 30°50E **57** C5
Pauls Valley *U.S.A.* 34°44N 97°13W **84** D6
Pauma Valley *U.S.A.* 33°16N 116°58W **79** M10
Pauni *India* 20°48N 79°40E **44** D4
Pauri *India* 30°9N 78°47E **43** D8
Pavagada *India* 14°6N 77°16E **45** G3
Pāveh *Iran* 35°3N 46°22E **46** C5
Pavia *Italy* 45°7N 9°8E **20** D8
Pavilion *U.S.A.* 42°52N 78°1W **82** D6
Pāvilosta *Latvia* 56°53N 21°14E **9** H19
Pavlodar *Kazakhstan* 52°33N 77°0E **26** D8
Pavlograd = Pavlohrad
  Ukraine 48°30N 35°52E **19** E6
Pavlohrad *Ukraine* 48°30N 35°52E **19** E6
Pavlovo *Russia* 55°58N 43°5E **18** C7
Pavlovsk *Russia* 50°26N 40°5E **19** D7
Pavlovskaya *Russia* 46°17N 39°47E **19** E6
Pawai, Pulau *Singapore* 1°11N 103°44E **39** d
Pawayan *India* 28°4N 80°6E **43** E9
Pawhuska *U.S.A.* 36°40N 96°20W **84** C6
Pawling *U.S.A.* 41°34N 73°36W **83** E11
Pawnee *U.S.A.* 36°20N 96°48W **84** C6
Pawnee City *U.S.A.* 40°7N 96°9W **80** E5
Pawtucket *U.S.A.* 41°53N 71°23W **83** E13
Paxi *Greece* 39°14N 20°12E **23** E9
Paxton *U.S.A.* 40°27N 88°6W **80** E9
Payakumbuh *Indonesia* 0°20S 100°35E **36** E2
Payette *U.S.A.* 44°5N 116°56W **76** D5
Payne Bay = Kangirsuk
  Canada 60°0N 70°0W **69** F18
Payne L. *Canada* 59°30N 74°30W **69** F17
Paynes Find *Australia* 29°15S 117°42E **61** E2
Paynesville *Australia* 45°23N 94°43W **80** C6
Paysandú *Uruguay* 32°19S 58°8W **94** C4
Payson *Ariz., U.S.A.* 34°14N 111°20W **77** J8
Payson *Utah, U.S.A.* 40°3N 111°44W **76** F8
Paz → *Guatemala* 13°44N 90°10W **88** D1
Paz, B. de la *Mexico* 24°9N 110°25W **86** C2
Pāzanān *Iran* 30°35N 49°59E **47** D6
Pazardzhik *Bulgaria* 42°12N 24°20E **23** C11
Pe Ell *U.S.A.* 46°34N 123°18W **78** D3
Peabody *U.S.A.* 42°31N 70°56W **83** D14
Peace → *Canada* 59°0N 111°25W **70** B6
Peace Point *Canada* 59°7N 112°27W **70** B6
Peace River *Canada* 56°15N 117°18W **70** B5
Peach Springs *U.S.A.* 35°32N 113°25W **77** J7
Peachland *Canada* 49°47N 119°45W **70** D5
Peachtree City *U.S.A.* 33°25N 84°35W **85** E12
Peak, The = Kinder Scout
  U.K. 53°24N 1°52W **12** D6
Peak Charles △ *Australia* 32°42S 121°10E **61** F3
Peak District *U.K.* 53°24N 1°46W **12** D6
Peak Hill *Australia* 32°47S 148°11E **63** E4
Peak Ra. *Australia* 22°50S 148°20E **62** C4
Peake Cr. → *Australia* 28°2S 136°7E **63** D2
Peale, Mt. *U.S.A.* 38°26N 109°14W **76** G9
Pearblossom *U.S.A.* 34°30N 117°55W **79** L9
Pearl → *U.S.A.* 30°11N 89°32W **85** F10
Pearl and Hermes Reef
  U.S.A. 27°55N 175°45W **75** K4
Pearl Banks *Sri Lanka* 8°45N 79°45E **45** K4
Pearl River = Zhu Jiang →
  China 22°45N 113°37E **35** F9
Pearl River *U.S.A.* 41°4N 74°2W **83** E10
Pearl River Bridge *China* 22°15N 113°48E **31** a
Pearsall *U.S.A.* 28°54N 99°6W **84** G5
Peary Land *Greenland* 82°40N 33°0W **4** A6
Pease → *U.S.A.* 34°12N 99°2W **84** D5
Peawanuck *Canada* 55°15N 85°12W **72** A2
Pebane *Mozam.* 17°10S 38°8E **55** H7
Pebas *Peru* 3°10S 71°46W **92** D4
Pebble Beach *U.S.A.* 36°34N 121°57W **78** J5
Peć = Pejë *Kosovo* 42°40N 20°17E **23** C9
Pechenga *Russia* 69°29N 31°4E **8** B24
Pechenizhyn *Ukraine* 48°30N 24°48E **17** D13
Pechora *Russia* 65°10N 57°11E **18** A10
Pechora → *Russia* 68°13N 54°15E **18** A9
Pechorskaya Guba *Russia* 68°40N 54°0E **18** A9
Pechory *Russia* 57°48N 27°40E **9** H22
Pecos *U.S.A.* 35°35N 105°41W **77** J11
Pecos *Tex., U.S.A.* 31°26N 103°30W **84** F3
Pecos → *U.S.A.* 29°42N 101°22W **84** G4
Pécs *Hungary* 46°5N 18°15E **17** E10
Pedasi *Panama* 7°32N 80°3W **88** E3
Pedda Bellara *India* 19°4N 78°49E **44** E4
Peddapalli *India* 18°40N 79°24E **44** E4
Peddapuram *India* 17°6N 82°8E **44** F6
Pedder, L. *Australia* 42°55S 146°10E **63** G4
Peddie *S. Africa* 33°14S 27°7E **57** D4
Pedernales *Dom. Rep.* 18°2N 71°44W **89** C5
Pedirka Desert *Australia* 26°40S 135°14E **63** D2
Pedra Azul *Brazil* 16°2S 41°17W **93** G10
Pedra Lume *C. Verde Is.* 16°40N 22°52W **52** b

Pedreiras *Brazil* 4°32S 44°40W **93** D10
Pedro Afonso *Brazil* 9°0S 48°10W **93** E9
Pedro Cays *Jamaica* 17°5N 77°48W **88** C4
Pedro de Valdivia *Chile* 22°55S 69°38W **94** A2
Pedro Juan Caballero
  Paraguay 22°30S 55°40W **95** A4
Pee Dee = Great Pee Dee →
  U.S.A. 33°21N 79°10W **85** E15
Peebinga *Australia* 34°52S 140°57E **63** E3
Peebles *U.K.* 55°40N 3°11W **11** F5
Peekskill *U.S.A.* 41°17N 73°55W **83** E11
Peel I. of Man *54°13N 4°40W **12** C3
Peel → *Australia* 30°50S 150°29E **63** E5
Peel → *Canada* 67°0N 135°0W **68** D5
Peel Sd. *Canada* 73°0N 96°0W **68** C12
Peera Peera Poolanna L.
  Australia 26°30S 138°0E **63** D2
Peerless Lake *Canada* 56°37N 114°40W **70** B6
Peers *Canada* 53°40N 116°0W **70** C5
Pegasus Bay *N.Z.* 43°20S 173°10E **59** E4
Pegu *Burma* 17°20N 96°29E **41** L20
Pegu Yoma *Burma* 19°0N 96°0E **41** K20
Pehuajó *Argentina* 35°45S 62°0W **94** D3
Pei Xian *China* 34°44N 116°55E **32** G9
Peikang *Taiwan* 23°34N 120°18E **35** F13
Peine *Chile* 23°45S 68°8W **94** A2
Peine *Germany* 52°19N 10°14E **16** B6
Peipus, L. = Chudskoye, Ozero
  Russia 58°13N 27°30E **9** G22
Peixe *Brazil* 12°0S 48°40W **93** F9
Peixe → *Brazil* 21°31S 51°58W **95** A5
Pejë *Kosovo* 42°40N 20°17E **23** C9
Pekalongan *Indonesia* 6°53S 109°40E **37** G13
Pekan *Malaysia* 3°30N 103°25E **39** L4
Pekan Nenas *Malaysia* 1°31N 103°31E **39** d
Pekanbaru *Indonesia* 0°30N 101°15E **36** D2
Pekin *China* 40°35N 89°40W **80** E9
Pekin *U.S.A.* 8°25S 114°49E **37** J17
Pekutatan *Indonesia* 8°25S 114°49E **37** J17
Pelabuhan Ratu, Teluk
  Indonesia 7°5S 106°30E **37** G12
Pelagie, Is. *Italy* 35°39N 12°33E **22** G5
Pelaihari *Indonesia* 3°55S 114°45E **36** E4
Peleaga, Vf. *Romania* 45°22N 22°55E **17** F12
Pelée, Mt. *Martinique* 14°48N 61°10W **88** c
Pelee, Pt. *Canada* 41°54N 82°31W **72** D3
Pelee I. *Canada* 41°47N 82°40W **82** E2
Peleng *Indonesia* 1°20S 123°30E **37** E6
Pelentong *Malaysia* 1°32N 103°49E **39** d
Pelican *U.S.A.* 57°58N 136°14W **70** B1
Pelican L. *Canada* 52°28N 100°20W **71** C8
Pelican Narrows
  Canada 55°10N 102°56W **71** B8
Peliješac *Croatia* 42°55N 17°25E **22** C7
Pelkosenniemi *Finland* 67°6N 27°28E **8** C22
Pella *S. Africa* 29°1S 19°6E **56** C2
Pella *U.S.A.* 41°25N 92°55W **80** E7
Pello *Finland* 66°47N 23°59E **8** C20
Pelly → *Canada* 62°47N 137°19W **70** A1
Pelly Bay *Canada* 68°38N 89°50W **69** D14
Peloponnesos □ *Greece* 37°10N 22°0E **23** F10
Pelorus Sd. *N.Z.* 40°59S 173°59E **59** D4
Pelotas *Brazil* 31°42S 52°23W **95** C5
Pelotas → *Brazil* 27°28S 51°55W **95** B5
Pelvoux, Massif du *France* 44°52N 6°20E **20** D7
Pemalang *Indonesia* 6°53S 109°23E **37** G13
Pemanggil, Pulau
  Malaysia 2°37N 104°21E **39** L5
Pematangsiantar *Indonesia* 2°57N 99°5E **36** D1
Pemba *Mozam.* 12°58S 40°30E **55** G8
Pemba I. *Tanzania* 5°0S 39°45E **54** F7
Pemberton *Australia* 34°30S 116°0E **61** F2
Pemberton *Canada* 50°25N 122°50W **70** C4
Pembina → *Canada* 54°45N 114°17W **70** C6
Pembroke *Canada* 45°50N 77°7W **72** C4
Pembroke *U.K.* 51°41N 4°55W **13** F3
Pembrokeshire □ *U.K.* 51°52N 4°56W **13** F3
Pembrokeshire Coast △
  U.K. 51°50N 5°2W **13** F2
Pen *India* 18°45N 73°5E **44** E1
Pen-y-bont ar Ogwr = Bridgend
  U.K. 51°30N 3°34W **13** F4
Pen-y-Ghent *U.K.* 54°10N 2°14W **12** C5
Penal *Trin. & Tob.* 10°9N 61°29W **93** K15
Penang = Pinang *Malaysia* 5°25N 100°15E **39** c
Penápolis *Brazil* 21°30S 50°0W **95** A6
Peñarroya-Pueblonuevo
  Spain 38°19N 5°16W **21** C3
Penarth *U.K.* 51°26N 3°11W **13** F4
Peñas, C. de *Spain* 43°42N 5°52W **21** A3
Peñas, G. de *Chile* 47°0S 75°0W **96** F2
Pench → *India* 21°17N 79°10E **44** D4
Pench △ *India* 21°45N 79°20E **43** J8
Pench'i = Benxi *China* 41°20N 123°48E **33** D12
Pend Oreille → *U.S.A.* 49°4N 117°37W **76** B5
Pend Oreille, L. *U.S.A.* 48°10N 116°21W **76** B5
Pendembu *S. Leone* 9°7N 11°14W **52** G3
Pender B. *Australia* 16°45S 122°42E **60** C3
Pendleton *U.S.A.* 45°40N 118°47W **76** D4
Pendra *India* 22°46N 81°57E **43** H9
Penedo *Brazil* 10°15S 36°36W **93** F11
Penelokan *Indonesia* 8°17S 115°22E **37** J18
Penetanguishene *Canada* 44°50N 79°55W **82** B5
Penfield *U.S.A.* 41°13N 78°35W **82** E6
Penfro = Pembroke *U.K.* 51°41N 4°55W **13** F3
Peng Chau *China* 22°17N 114°2E **31** a
Peng'an *China* 31°2N 106°22E **34** B6
Penganga → *India* 19°53N 79°9E **44** E4
P'enghu Ch'üntou
  Taiwan 23°34N 119°30E **35** F12
Penglai *China* 37°48N 120°42E **33** F11
Pengshan *China* 30°14N 103°56E **34** B4
Pengshui *China* 29°17N 108°12E **34** C7
Penguin *Australia* 41°8S 146°6E **63** G4
Pengxi *China* 30°44N 105°45E **34** B5
Pengze *China* 29°52N 116°32E **35** C11
Pengzhou *China* 31°4N 103°32E **34** B4
Peniche *Portugal* 39°19N 9°22W **21** C1
Penida, Nusa *Indonesia* 8°45S 115°30E **37** K18
Peninsular Malaysia □
  Malaysia 4°0N 102°0E **39** L4

Penitente, Serra do *Brazil* 8°45S 46°20W **93** E9
Penkridge *U.K.* 52°44N 2°6W **12** E5
Penmarch, Pte. de *France* 47°48N 4°22W **20** C1
Penn Hills *U.S.A.* 40°28N 79°52W **82** F5
Penn Yan *U.S.A.* 42°40N 77°3W **82** D7
Pennant *Canada* 50°32N 108°14W **71** C7
Penner → *India* 14°35N 80°10E **45** G5
Pennines *U.K.* 54°45N 2°27W **12** C5
Pennington *U.S.A.* 39°15N 121°47W **78** F5
Pennsburg *U.S.A.* 40°23N 75°29W **83** F9
Pennsylvania □ *U.S.A.* 40°45N 77°30W **81** E15
Penny *Canada* 53°51N 121°20W **70** C4
Penobscot → *U.S.A.* 44°30N 68°48W **81** C19
Penobscot B. *U.S.A.* 44°35N 68°50W **81** C19
Penola *Australia* 37°25S 140°48E **63** F3
Penong *Australia* 31°56S 133°1E **61** F5
Penonomé *Panama* 8°31N 80°21W **88** E3
Penrhyn *Cook Is.* 9°0S 158°0W **65** H12
Penrith *Australia* 33°43S 150°38E **63** E5
Penrith *U.K.* 54°40N 2°45W **12** C5
Penryn *U.K.* 50°9N 5°7W **13** G2
Pensacola *U.S.A.* 30°25N 87°13W **85** F11
Pensacola Mts. *Antarctica* 84°0S 40°0W **5** E1
Pense *Canada* 50°25N 104°59W **71** C8
Penshurst *Australia* 37°49S 142°20E **63** F3
Penticton *Canada* 49°30N 119°38W **70** D5
Pentland *Australia* 20°32S 145°25E **62** C4
Pentland Firth *U.K.* 58°43N 3°10W **11** C5
Pentland Hills *U.K.* 55°48N 3°25W **11** F5
Penukonda *India* 14°5N 77°38E **45** G3
Penza *Russia* 53°15N 45°5E **18** D8
Penzance *U.K.* 50°7N 5°33W **13** G2
Penzhino *Russia* 63°30N 167°55E **27** C17
Penzhinskaya Guba
  Russia 61°30N 163°0E **27** C17
Peoria *Ariz., U.S.A.* 33°43N 112°14W **77** K7
Peoria *Ill., U.S.A.* 40°42N 89°36W **80** E9
Pepacton Res. *U.S.A.* 42°5N 74°58W **83** D10
Pepani → *S. Africa* 25°49S 22°47E **56** C3
Pera Hd. *Australia* 12°55S 141°37E **62** A3
Perabumulih *Indonesia* 3°27S 104°15E **36** E2
Perak □ *Malaysia* 5°0N 101°0E **39** K3
Perak → *Malaysia* 4°0N 100°50E **39** K3
Perancak *Indonesia* 8°24S 114°37E **37** J17
Peräpohjola *Finland* 66°16N 26°10E **8** C22
Percé *Canada* 48°31N 64°13W **73** C7
Perche, Collines du *France* 48°30N 0°40E **20** B4
Percival Lakes *Australia* 21°25S 125°0E **60** D4
Percy Is. *Australia* 21°39S 150°16E **62** C5
Perdido, Mte. *Spain* 42°40N 0°5E **21** A6
Perdu, Mt. = Perdido, Mte.
  Spain 42°40N 0°5E **21** A6
Pereira *Colombia* 4°49N 75°43W **92** C3
Peremul Par *India* 11°10N 72°4E **45** J1
Perenjori *Australia* 29°26S 116°16E **61** E2
Pereyaslav-Khmelnytskyy
  Ukraine 50°3N 31°28E **19** D5
Pérez, I. *Mexico* 22°24N 89°42W **87** C7
Pergamino *Argentina* 33°52S 60°30W **94** C3
Pergau → *Malaysia* 5°23N 102°2E **39** K3
Perham *U.S.A.* 46°36N 95°34W **80** B6
Perhentian, Kepulauan
  Malaysia 5°54N 102°42E **39** K4
Péribonka → *Canada* 48°45N 72°5W **73** C5
Péribonka, La Centrale de
  Canada 49°30N 71°10W **73** C5
Perico *Argentina* 24°20S 65°5W **94** A2
Pericos *Mexico* 25°3N 107°42W **86** B3
Périgueux *France* 45°10N 0°42E **20** D4
Perijá, Sierra de *Colombia* 9°30N 73°3W **92** B4
Perijá △ *Venezuela* 9°30N 72°55W **89** E5
Peringat *Malaysia* 6°2N 102°17E **39** K4
Periyakulam *India* 10°5N 77°30E **45** K3
Periyar → *India* 10°15N 76°10E **45** J3
Periyar, L. *India* 9°25N 77°10E **45** K3
Periyar △ *India* 9°25N 77°10E **45** K3
Perkasie *U.S.A.* 40°22N 75°18W **83** F9
Perlas, Arch. de las
  Panama 8°41N 79°7W **88** E4
Perlas, Punta de *Nic.* 12°30N 83°30W **88** D3
Perlis □ *Malaysia* 6°30N 100°15E **39** J2
Perm *Russia* 58°0N 56°10E **18** C10
Pernambuco = Recife
  Brazil 8°0S 35°0W **93** E12
Pernambuco □ *Brazil* 8°0S 37°0W **93** E11
Pernatty Lagoon
  Australia 31°30S 137°12E **63** E2
Pernik *Bulgaria* 42°35N 23°2E **23** C10
Peron Is. *Australia* 13°9S 130°4E **60** B5
Peron Pen. *Australia* 26°0S 113°10E **61** E1
Perow *Canada* 54°35N 126°10W **70** C3
Perpignan *France* 42°42N 2°53E **20** E5
Perris *U.S.A.* 33°47N 117°14W **79** M9
Perry *Fla., U.S.A.* 30°7N 83°35W **85** F13
Perry *Ga., U.S.A.* 32°28N 83°44W **85** E13
Perry *Iowa, U.S.A.* 41°51N 94°6W **80** E6
Perry *N.Y., U.S.A.* 42°42N 78°0W **82** D7
Perry *Okla., U.S.A.* 36°17N 97°14W **84** C6
Perryton *U.S.A.* 36°24N 100°48W **84** C4
Perryville *U.S.A.* 37°43N 89°52W **80** G9
Persepolis *Iran* 29°55N 52°50E **47** D7
Pershotravensk *Ukraine* 50°13N 27°40E **17** C14
Persia = Iran ■ *Asia* 33°0N 53°0E **47** C7
Persian Gulf *Asia* 27°0N 50°0E **47** E6
Perth *Australia* 31°57S 115°52E **61** F2
Perth *Canada* 44°55N 76°15W **83** B8
Perth *U.K.* 56°24N 3°26W **11** E5
Perth & Kinross □ *U.K.* 56°45N 3°55W **11** E5
Perth Amboy *U.S.A.* 40°30N 74°15W **83** F10
Perth-Andover *Canada* 46°44N 67°42W **73** C6
Peru *Ind., U.S.A.* 40°45N 86°4W **81** E11
Peru *N.Y., U.S.A.* 44°35N 73°32W **83** B11
Peru ■ *S. Amer.* 4°0S 75°0W **92** D4
Peru Basin *Pac. Oc.* 20°0S 95°0W **65** J18
Peru-Chile Trench *Pac. Oc.* 20°0S 72°0W **92** G3
Perúgia *Italy* 43°7N 12°23E **22** C5

Pervomaysk *Ukraine* 48°10N 30°46E **19** E5
Pervouralsk *Russia* 56°59N 59°59E **18** C10
Pésaro *Italy* 43°54N 12°55E **22** C5
Pescadores = P'enghu Ch'üntou
  Taiwan 23°34N 119°30E **35** F12
Pescara *Italy* 42°28N 14°13E **22** C6
Peshawar *Pakistan* 34°2N 71°37E **42** B4
Peshkopi *Albania* 41°41N 20°25E **23** D9
Peshtigo *U.S.A.* 45°3N 87°45W **80** C10
Pesqueira *Brazil* 8°20S 36°42W **93** E11
Petah Tiqwa *Israel* 32°6N 34°53E **48** C3
Petaling Jaya *Malaysia* 3°4N 101°42E **39** L3
Petaluma *U.S.A.* 38°14N 122°39W **78** G4
Pétange *Lux.* 49°33N 5°55E **15** E5
Petaro *Pakistan* 25°31N 68°18E **42** G3
Petatlán *Mexico* 17°31N 101°16W **86** D4
Petauke *Zambia* 14°14S 31°20E **55** G6
Petawawa *Canada* 45°54N 77°17W **72** C4
Petén Itzá, L. *Guatemala* 16°58N 89°50W **88** C2
Peter I. *Br. Virgin Is.* 18°22N 64°35W **89** e
Peter I. Øy *Antarctica* 69°0S 91°0W **5** C16
Peter Pond L. *Canada* 55°55N 108°44W **71** B7
Peterbell *Canada* 48°36N 83°21W **72** C3
Peterborough *Australia* 32°58S 138°51E **63** E2
Peterborough *Canada* 44°20N 78°20W **82** B6
Peterborough *U.K.* 52°35N 0°15W **13** E7
Peterborough *U.S.A.* 42°53N 71°57W **83** D13
Peterborough □ *U.K.* 52°35N 0°15W **13** E7
Peterculter *U.K.* 57°6N 2°16W **11** D6
Peterhead *U.K.* 57°31N 1°48W **11** D7
Peterlee *U.K.* 54°47N 1°20W **12** C6
Petermann ۞ *Australia* 24°58S 130°0E **61** E4
Petermann Gletscher
  Greenland 80°30N 60°0W **69** A20
Petermann Ranges
  Australia 26°0S 130°30E **61** E5
Petersburg *Alaska,*
  U.S.A. 56°48N 132°58W **68** F5
Petersburg *Pa., U.S.A.* 40°34N 78°3W **82** F6
Petersburg *Va., U.S.A.* 37°14N 77°24W **81** G15
Petersburg *W. Va., U.S.A.* 39°1N 79°5W **81** F14
Petersfield *U.K.* 51°1N 0°56W **13** F7
Petit-Canal *Guadeloupe* 16°25N 61°31W **88** b
Petit-Goâve *Haiti* 18°27N 72°51W **89** C5
Petit Lac Manicouagan
  Canada 51°25N 67°40W **73** B6
Petit-Mécatina →
  Canada 50°40N 59°30W **73** B8
Petit-Mécatina, Î. du
  Canada 50°30N 59°25W **73** B8
Petit Piton *St. Lucia* 13°51N 61°5W **89** f
Petit-Saguenay *Canada* 48°15N 70°4W **73** C5
Petitcodiac *Canada* 45°57N 65°11W **73** C6
Petite Terre, Îles de la
  Guadeloupe 16°13N 61°9W **88** b
Petitot → *Canada* 60°14N 123°29W **70** A4
Petitsikapau L. *Canada* 54°37N 66°25W **73** B6
Petlad *India* 22°30N 72°45E **42** H5
Peto *Mexico* 20°8N 88°55W **87** C7
Petone *N.Z.* 41°13S 174°53E **59** D5
Petoskey *U.S.A.* 45°22N 84°57W **81** C11
Petra *Jordan* 30°20N 35°22E **48** E4
Petra, Ostrov *Russia* 76°15N 118°30E **27** B12
Petra Velikogo, Zaliv
  Russia 42°40N 132°0E **28** C6
Petre, Pt. *Canada* 43°50N 77°9W **82** C7
Petrich *Bulgaria* 41°24N 23°13E **23** D10
Petrified Forest △ *U.S.A.* 35°0N 109°30W **77** J9
Petrikov = Pyetrikaw
  Belarus 52°11N 28°29E **17** B15
Petrolândia *Brazil* 9°5S 38°20W **93** E11
Petrolia *Canada* 42°54N 82°9W **82** D2
Petrolina *Brazil* 9°24S 40°30W **93** E10
Petropavl *Kazakhstan* 54°53N 69°13E **26** D7
Petropavlovsk = Petropavl
  Kazakhstan 54°53N 69°13E **26** D7
Petropavlovsk-Kamchatskiy
  Russia 53°3N 158°43E **27** D16
Petrópolis *Brazil* 22°33S 43°9W **95** A7
Petroșani *Romania* 45°28N 23°20E **17** F12
Petrovaradin *Serbia* 45°16N 19°55E **23** B8
Petrovsk *Russia* 52°22N 45°19E **18** D8
Petrovsk-Zabaykalskiy
  Russia 51°20N 108°55E **27** D11
Petrozavodsk *Russia* 61°41N 34°20E **18** B5
Petrus Steyn *S. Africa* 27°38S 28°8E **57** C4
Petrusburg *S. Africa* 29°4S 25°26E **56** C4
Peumo *Chile* 34°21S 71°12W **94** C1
Peureulak *Indonesia* 4°48N 97°45E **36** D1
Pevek *Russia* 69°41N 171°19E **27** C18
Pforzheim *Germany* 48°52N 8°41E **16** D5
Pha Taem △ *Thailand* 15°32N 105°30E **38** E5
Phagwara *India* 31°10N 75°40E **42** D6
Phala *Botswana* 23°45S 26°50E **56** C4
Phalaborwa *S. Africa* 23°57S 31°7E **57** B5
Phalera = Phulera *India* 26°52N 75°16E **42** F6
Phalodi *India* 27°12N 72°24E **42** F5
Phaltan *India* 17°59N 74°26E **44** F2
Phaluai, Ko *Thailand* 9°32N 99°41E **39** b
Phan *Thailand* 19°28N 99°43E **38** C2
Phan Rang-Thap Cham
  Vietnam 11°34N 109°0E **39** G7
Phan Ri Cua *Vietnam* 11°16N 108°40E **39** G7
Phan Si Pan *Vietnam* 22°18N 103°46E **38** A4
Phan Thiet *Vietnam* 11°1N 108°9E **39** G7
Phan Thiet, Vinh
  Vietnam 10°53N 108°5E **39** G7
Phan Wa, Laem *Thailand* 7°47N 98°25E **39** a
Phanat Nikhom
  Thailand 13°27N 101°11E **38** F3
Phangan, Ko *Thailand* 9°45N 100°0E **39** H3
Phangnga *Thailand* 8°28N 98°30E **39** H2
Phangnga, Ao *Thailand* 8°9N 98°33E **39** a
Phanom Sarakham
  Thailand 13°45N 101°21E **38** F3
Phaphund *India* 26°36N 79°28E **43** F8
Pharenda *India* 27°5N 83°17E **43** F10
Pharr *U.S.A.* 26°12N 98°11W **84** H5

Phatthalung	*Thailand*	7°39N 100°6E	**39 J3**
Phayam, Ko	*Thailand*	9°44N 98°25E	**39 H2**
Phayao	*Thailand*	19°11N 99°55E	**38 C2**
Phelps	*U.S.A.*	42°58N 77°3W	**82 D7**
Phelps L.	*Canada*	59°15N 103°15W	**71 B8**
Phenix City	*U.S.A.*	32°28N 85°1W	**85 E12**
Phet Buri = Phetchaburi			
	Thailand	13°1N 99°55E	**38 F2**
Phetchabun	*Thailand*	16°25N 101°8E	**38 D3**
Phetchabun, Thiu Khao			
	Thailand	16°0N 101°20E	**38 E3**
Phetchaburi	*Thailand*	13°1N 99°55E	**38 F2**
Phi Phi, Ko	*Thailand*	7°45N 98°46E	**39 J2**
Phiafay	*Laos*	14°48N 106°0E	**38 E6**
Phibun Mangsahan			
	Thailand	15°14N 105°14E	**38 E5**
Phichai	*Thailand*	17°22N 100°10E	**38 D3**
Phichit	*Thailand*	16°26N 100°22E	**38 D3**
Philadelphia *Miss.,*			
	U.S.A.	32°46N 89°7W	**85 E10**
Philadelphia *N.Y., U.S.A.*		44°9N 75°43W	**83 D9**
Philadelphia *Pa., U.S.A.*		39°57N 75°9W	**83 G9**
Philip	*U.S.A.*	44°2N 101°40W	**80 C3**
Philip Smith Mts. *U.S.A.*		68°0N 148°0W	**74 B10**
Philippeville	*Belgium*	50°12N 4°33E	**15 D4**
Philippi	*U.S.A.*	39°9N 80°3W	**81 F13**
Philippi L.	*Australia*	24°20S 138°55E	**62 C2**
Philippine Basin *Pac. Oc.*		17°0N 132°0E	**64 F5**
Philippine Sea *Pac. Oc.*		12°0N 123°0E	**37 B6**
Philippine Trench = Mindanao			
Trench	*Pac. Oc.*	12°0N 126°6E	**37 B7**
Philippines ■	*Asia*	12°0N 123°0E	**37 B6**
Philippolis	*S. Africa*	30°15S 25°16E	**56 D4**
Philippopolis = Plovdiv			
	Bulgaria	42°8N 24°44E	**23 C11**
Philipsburg	*Canada*	45°2N 73°5W	**83 A11**
Philipsburg *Mont.,*			
	U.S.A.	46°20N 113°18W	**76 C7**
Philipsburg *Pa., U.S.A.*		40°54N 78°13W	**82 F6**
Philipstown = Daingean			
	Ireland	53°18N 7°17W	**10 C4**
Philipstown	*S. Africa*	30°28S 24°30E	**56 E3**
Phillip I.	*Australia*	38°30S 145°12E	**63 F4**
Phillips	*U.S.A.*	45°42N 90°24W	**80 C8**
Phillipsburg *Kans., U.S.A.*		39°45N 99°19W	**80 F5**
Phillipsburg *N.J., U.S.A.*		40°42N 75°12W	**83 F9**
Philmont	*U.S.A.*	42°15N 73°39W	**83 D11**
Philomath	*U.S.A.*	44°32N 123°22W	**76 D2**
Phimai	*Thailand*	15°13N 102°30E	**38 E4**
Phitsanulok	*Thailand*	16°50N 100°12E	**38 D3**
Phnom Kulen △			
	Cambodia	13°38N 104°15E	**38 F5**
Phnom Penh	*Cambodia*	11°33N 104°55E	**39 G5**
Phnum Penh = Phnom Penh			
	Cambodia	11°33N 104°55E	**39 G5**
Pho, Laem	*Thailand*	6°55N 101°19E	**39 J3**
Phoenicia	*U.S.A.*	42°5N 74°14W	**83 D10**
Phoenix	*Mauritius*	20°17S 57°30E	**55 d**
Phoenix *Ariz., U.S.A.*		33°26N 112°4W	**77 K7**
Phoenix *N.Y., U.S.A.*		43°14N 76°18W	**83 C8**
Phoenix Is.	*Kiribati*	3°30S 172°0W	**64 H10**
Phoenixville	*U.S.A.*	40°8N 75°31W	**83 F9**
Phon	*Thailand*	15°49N 102°30E	**38 E4**
Phong →	*Thailand*	16°23N 102°56E	**38 D4**
Phong Nha -Ke Bang △			
	Vietnam	17°30N 106°10E	**38 D6**
Phong Saly	*Laos*	21°42N 102°9E	**34 G4**
Phong Tho	*Vietnam*	22°32N 103°21E	**38 A4**
Phonhong	*Laos*	18°30N 102°25E	**38 C4**
Phonsavan	*Laos*	19°27N 103°10E	**38 C4**
Phonum	*Thailand*	8°49N 98°48E	**39 H2**
Phosphate Hill	*Australia*	21°53S 139°58E	**62 C2**
Photharam	*Thailand*	13°41N 99°51E	**38 F2**
Phra Nakhon Si Ayutthaya			
	Thailand	14°25N 100°30E	**38 E3**
Phra Thong, Ko	*Thailand*	9°5N 98°17E	**39 H2**
Phrae	*Thailand*	18°7N 100°9E	**38 C3**
Phrom Phiram	*Thailand*	17°2N 100°12E	**38 D3**
Phrom Thep, Laem	*Thailand*	7°45N 98°19E	**39 a**
Phu Bia	*Laos*	19°10N 103°0E	**38 C4**
Phu Chong -Na Yoi △			
	Thailand	14°25N 105°30E	**38 E5**
Phu Hin Rong Kla △			
	Thailand	17°0N 100°59E	**38 D3**
Phu Kao -Phu Phan Kham △			
	Thailand	16°53N 102°31E	**38 D4**
Phu Kradung △	*Thailand*	17°2N 101°44E	**38 D3**
Phu Loi	*Laos*	20°14N 103°14E	**38 B4**
Phu Luang △	*Thailand*	17°15N 101°29E	**38 D3**
Phu Ly	*Vietnam*	20°35N 105°50E	**34 G5**
Phu My	*Vietnam*	14°15N 109°5E	**38 E7**
Phu Pha Man △			
	Thailand	16°44N 101°50E	**38 D3**
Phu Phan △	*Thailand*	17°0N 103°56E	**38 D4**
Phu Quoc, Dao	*Vietnam*	10°20N 104°0E	**39 G4**
Phu Sa Dok Bua △			
	Thailand	16°11N 104°45E	**38 D5**
Phu Sang △	*Thailand*	19°35N 100°19E	**38 C3**
Phu Tho	*Vietnam*	21°24N 105°13E	**34 G5**
Phu Wiang △	*Thailand*	16°39N 102°24E	**38 D4**
Phuc Yen	*Vietnam*	21°16N 105°45E	**34 G5**
Phuket	*Thailand*	7°53N 98°24E	**39 a**
Phuket, Ko	*Thailand*	8°0N 98°22E	**39 a**
Phul	*India*	30°19N 75°14E	**42 D6**
Phulad	*India*	25°38N 73°49E	**42 G5**
Phulbani	*India*	20°28N 84°14E	**44 D7**
Phulchari	*Bangla.*	25°11N 89°37E	**43 G13**
Phulera	*India*	26°52N 75°16E	**42 F6**
Phulpur	*India*	25°31N 82°49E	**43 G10**
Phunphin	*Thailand*	9°7N 99°12E	**39 H2**
Phuntsholing	*Bhutan*	26°51N 89°28E	**41 F16**
Phuphrabat	*Thailand*	17°40N 102°45E	**38 D4**
Phuthaditjhaba	*S. Africa*	28°25S 28°48E	**57 D4**
Phyu = Pyu	*Burma*	18°30N 96°28E	**41 K20**
Pia ○	*Australia*	27°7S 116°23E	**61 E2**
Piacenza	*Italy*	45°1N 9°40E	**20 D8**
Piai, Tanjung	*Malaysia*	1°17N 103°30E	**39 d**
Pian Cr. →	*Australia*	30°2S 148°12E	**63 E4**
Pianosa	*Italy*	42°35N 10°5E	**22 C4**
Piao'ertun	*China*	41°50N 123°47E	**33 D12**
Piapot	*Canada*	49°59N 109°8W	**71 D7**
Piatra Neamţ	*Romania*	46°56N 26°21E	**17 E14**
Piauí □	*Brazil*	7°0S 43°0W	**93 E10**
Piauí →	*Brazil*	6°38S 42°42W	**93 E10**
Piave →	*Italy*	45°32N 12°44E	**22 B5**
Pibor Post	*South Sudan*	6°47N 33°3E	**53 G12**
Picardie □	*France*	49°50N 3°0E	**20 B5**
Picardy = Picardie □			
	France	49°50N 3°0E	**20 B5**
Picayune	*U.S.A.*	30°32N 89°41W	**85 F10**
Pichhor	*India*	25°58N 78°20E	**43 G8**
Pichilemu	*Chile*	34°22S 72°0W	**94 C1**
Pichor	*India*	25°11N 78°11E	**42 G8**
Pickerel L.	*Canada*	48°40N 91°25W	**72 C1**
Pickering	*U.K.*	54°15N 0°46W	**12 C7**
Pickering, Vale of *U.K.*		54°14N 0°45W	**12 C7**
Pickle Lake	*Canada*	51°30N 90°12W	**72 B1**
Pickwick L.	*U.S.A.*	35°4N 88°15W	**85 D10**
Pico	*Azores*	38°28N 28°20W	**52 a**
Pico Bonito △	*Honduras*	15°34N 86°48W	**88 C2**
Pico Truncado	*Argentina*	46°40S 68°0W	**96 F3**
Picos	*Brazil*	7°5S 41°28W	**93 E10**
Picton	*Canada*	44°1N 77°9W	**82 B7**
Picton	*N.Z.*	41°18S 174°3E	**59 D5**
Pictou	*Canada*	45°41N 62°42W	**73 C7**
Picture Butte	*Canada*	49°55N 112°45W	**70 D6**
Pictured Rocks ○			
	U.S.A.	46°30N 86°30W	**80 B10**
Picún Leufú	*Argentina*	39°30S 69°5W	**96 D3**
Pidurutalagala	*Sri Lanka*	7°10N 80°50E	**45 L5**
Piedmont = Piemonte □			
	Italy	45°0N 8°0E	**20 D7**
Piedmont *Ala., U.S.A.*		33°55N 85°37W	**85 E12**
Piedmont *S.C., U.S.A.*		34°42N 82°28W	**85 F11**
Piedras Negras	*Mexico*	28°42N 100°31W	**86 B4**
Pieksämäki	*Finland*	62°18N 27°10E	**8 E22**
Pielinen	*Finland*	63°15N 29°40E	**8 E23**
Piemonte □	*Italy*	45°0N 8°0E	**20 D7**
Pienaarsrivier	*S. Africa*	25°15S 28°18E	**57 C4**
Piercefield	*U.S.A.*	44°13N 74°35W	**83 B10**
Pierceland	*Canada*	54°20N 109°46W	**71 C7**
Pierpont	*U.S.A.*	41°45N 80°34W	**82 E4**
Pierre	*U.S.A.*	44°22N 100°21W	**80 C3**
Pierrefonds	*Canada*	45°29N 73°51W	**83 A11**
Pierreville	*Trin. & Tob.*	10°16N 61°0W	**93 K16**
Piet Retief	*S. Africa*	27°1S 30°50E	**57 C5**
Pietarsaari	*Finland*	63°40N 22°43E	**8 E20**
Pietermaritzburg *S. Africa*		29°35S 30°25E	**57 C5**
Pietersburg = Polokwane			
	S. Africa	23°54S 29°25E	**57 B4**
Pietrosul, Vf. *Maramureş,*			
	Romania	47°35N 24°43E	**17 E13**
Pietrosul, Vf. *Suceava,*			
	Romania	47°12N 25°18E	**17 E13**
Pigeon I.	*India*	14°2N 74°20E	**45 G2**
Pigeon L.	*Canada*	53°0N 78°30W	**82 B6**
Piggott	*U.S.A.*	36°23N 90°11W	**85 C9**
Pigüe	*Argentina*	37°36S 62°25W	**94 D3**
Pihani	*India*	27°36N 80°15E	**43 F9**
Pihlajavesi	*Finland*	61°45N 28°45E	**8 F23**
Pijijiapan	*Mexico*	15°42N 93°14W	**87 D6**
Pikangikum	*Canada*	51°49N 94°0W	**71 C10**
Pikes Peak	*U.S.A.*	38°50N 105°3W	**76 G11**
Piketberg	*S. Africa*	32°55S 18°40E	**56 E2**
Pikeville	*U.S.A.*	37°29N 82°31W	**81 G12**
Pikou	*China*	39°18N 122°22E	**33 E12**
Pikwitonei	*Canada*	55°35N 97°9W	**71 B9**
Piła	*Poland*	53°10N 16°48E	**17 B9**
Pilanesberg △ *S. Africa*		25°15S 27°4E	**56 D4**
Pilani	*India*	28°22N 75°33E	**42 E6**
Pilar	*Paraguay*	26°50S 58°20W	**94 B4**
Pilaya →	*Bolivia*	20°55S 64°4W	**92 H6**
Pilbara	*Australia*	21°15S 118°16E	**60 D2**
Pilcomayo →	*Paraguay*	25°21S 57°42W	**94 B4**
Pilgrim's Rest	*S. Africa*	24°55S 30°44E	**57 B5**
Pilibhit	*India*	28°40N 79°50E	**43 E8**
Pilica →	*Poland*	51°52N 21°17E	**17 C11**
Pilipinas = Philippines ■			
	Asia	12°0N 123°0E	**37 B6**
Pilkhawa	*India*	28°43N 77°42E	**42 E7**
Pilliga	*Australia*	30°21S 148°54E	**63 E4**
Pilos	*Greece*	36°55N 21°42E	**23 F9**
Pilot Mound	*Canada*	49°15N 98°54W	**71 D9**
Pilot Point	*U.S.A.*	33°24N 96°58W	**84 E6**
Pilot Rock	*U.S.A.*	45°29N 118°50W	**76 D4**
Pima	*U.S.A.*	32°54N 109°50W	**77 K9**
Pimba	*Australia*	31°18S 136°46E	**63 E2**
Pimenta Bueno	*Brazil*	11°35S 61°10W	**92 F6**
Pimentel	*Peru*	6°45S 79°55W	**92 E3**
Pimpri Chinchwad *India*		18°37N 73°47E	**44 E1**
Pin Valley △	*India*	31°50N 77°50E	**42 D7**
Pinang	*Malaysia*	5°25N 100°15E	**39 c**
Pinang □	*Malaysia*	5°20N 100°20E	**39 K3**
Pinar del Rio	*Cuba*	22°26N 83°40W	**88 B3**
Pinarhisar	*Turkey*	41°37N 27°30E	**23 D12**
Pinatubo, Mt.	*Phil.*	15°8N 120°21E	**37 A6**
Pinawa	*Canada*	50°9N 95°50W	**71 C9**
Pinchang	*China*	31°36N 107°3E	**34 B6**
Pincher Creek	*Canada*	49°30N 113°57W	**70 D6**
Pinchi L.	*Canada*	54°38N 124°30W	**70 C4**
Pinckneyville	*U.S.A.*	38°5N 89°23W	**80 F9**
Pińczów	*Poland*	50°32N 20°32E	**17 C11**
Pindar	*Australia*	28°30S 115°47E	**61 E2**
Pindera Downs ○			
	Australia	29°24S 142°37E	**63 A3**
Pindi Gheb	*Pakistan*	33°14N 72°21E	**42 C5**
Pindos Oros	*Greece*	40°0N 21°0E	**23 E9**
Pindus Mts. = Pindos Oros			
	Greece	40°0N 21°0E	**23 E9**
Pine → *B.C., Canada*		56°8N 120°43W	**70 B4**
Pine → *Sask., Canada*		58°50N 105°38W	**71 B7**
Pine Bluff	*U.S.A.*	34°13N 92°1W	**84 D8**
Pine Bluffs	*U.S.A.*	41°11N 104°4W	**76 F11**
Pine City	*U.S.A.*	45°50N 92°59W	**80 C7**
Pine Cr. →	*U.S.A.*	41°10N 77°16W	**82 E7**
Pine Creek	*Australia*	13°50S 131°50E	**60 B5**
Pine Falls	*Canada*	50°34N 96°11W	**71 C9**
Pine Flat L.	*U.S.A.*	36°50N 119°20W	**78 J7**
Pine Grove	*U.S.A.*	40°33N 76°23W	**83 F8**
Pine Hill	*Australia*	23°38S 146°57E	**62 C4**
Pine Island Glacier			
	Antarctica	76°0S 100°0W	**5 D15**
Pine Pass	*Canada*	55°25N 122°42W	**70 B4**
Pine Point	*Canada*	60°50N 114°28W	**70 A6**
Pine Ridge	*U.S.A.*	43°2N 102°33W	**80 D2**
Pine River	*Canada*	51°45N 100°30W	**71 C8**
Pine River	*U.S.A.*	46°43N 94°24W	**80 B6**
Pine Valley	*U.S.A.*	32°50N 116°32W	**79 N10**
Pinecrest	*U.S.A.*	38°12N 120°1W	**78 G6**
Pinedale *Calif., U.S.A.*		36°50N 119°48W	**78 J7**
Pinedale *Wyo., U.S.A.*		42°52N 109°52W	**76 E9**
Pinega →	*Russia*	64°30N 44°19E	**18 B8**
Pinehouse L.	*Canada*	55°32N 106°35W	**71 B7**
Pineimuta →	*Canada*	52°8N 88°33W	**72 B2**
Pinerolo	*Italy*	44°53N 7°21E	**20 D7**
Pines, Akra	*Greece*	40°5N 24°20E	**23 D11**
Pinetop-Lakeside *U.S.A.*		34°9N 109°58W	**77 J9**
Pineville	*S. Africa*	31°19N 92°26W	**84 F8**
Ping →	*Thailand*	15°42N 100°9E	**38 E3**
Pingaring	*Australia*	32°40S 118°32E	**61 F2**
Pingba	*China*	26°23N 106°12E	**34 D6**
Pingbian	*China*	23°0N 103°45E	**34 F4**
Pingchuan	*China*	27°35N 101°55E	**34 D3**
Pingding	*China*	37°47N 113°38E	**32 F7**
Pingdingshan	*China*	33°43N 113°27E	**32 H7**
Pingdu	*China*	36°42N 119°59E	**33 F10**
Pingelly	*Australia*	32°32S 117°5E	**61 F2**
Pingguo	*China*	23°19N 107°36E	**34 F6**
Pinghe	*China*	24°17N 117°21E	**35 E11**
Pinghu	*China*	30°40N 121°2E	**35 B13**
Pingjiang	*China*	28°45N 113°36E	**35 C9**
Pingle	*China*	24°40N 110°40E	**35 E8**
Pingli	*China*	32°27N 109°22E	**34 A7**
Pingliang	*China*	35°35N 106°31E	**32 G4**
Pinglu	*China*	39°31N 112°30E	**32 E7**
Pingluo	*China*	38°52N 106°30E	**32 E4**
Pingnan *Fujian, China*		26°55N 119°0E	**35 D12**
Pingnan *Guangxi Zhuangzu,*			
	China	23°33N 110°22E	**35 F8**
Pingquan	*China*	41°1N 118°37E	**33 D10**
Pingrup	*Australia*	33°32S 118°29E	**61 F2**
Pingshan	*China*	28°39N 104°3E	**34 C5**
Pingtang	*China*	25°31N 119°47E	**35 E12**
Pingtang	*China*	25°49N 107°17E	**34 E6**
P'ingtung	*Taiwan*	22°38N 120°30E	**35 F13**
Pingwu	*China*	32°25N 104°30E	**32 H3**
Pingxiang *Guangxi Zhuangzu,*			
	China	22°6N 106°46E	**34 F6**
Pingxiang *Jiangxi, China*		27°43N 113°48E	**35 D9**
Pingyao	*China*	37°12N 112°10E	**32 F7**
Pingyi	*China*	35°30N 117°35E	**33 G9**
Pingyin	*China*	36°20N 116°25E	**32 F9**
Pingyuan *Guangdong,*			
	China	24°37N 115°57E	**35 E10**
Pingyuan *Shandong,*			
	China	37°10N 116°22E	**32 F9**
Pingyuanjie	*China*	23°45N 103°48E	**34 F4**
Pinheiro	*Brazil*	2°31S 45°5W	**93 D9**
Pinheiro Machado *Brazil*		31°34S 53°23W	**95 C5**
Pinhel	*Portugal*	40°50N 7°1W	**21 B2**
Pini	*Indonesia*	0°10N 98°40E	**36 D1**
Pinios →	*Greece*	39°55S 22°41E	**23 E10**
Pinjarra	*Australia*	32°37S 115°52E	**61 F2**
Pink Mountain *Canada*		57°3N 122°52W	**70 B4**
Pinnacle Is. = Senkaku-Shotō			
	E. China Sea	25°45N 123°30E	**29 M1**
Pinnacles ○	*U.S.A.*	36°25N 121°12W	**78 J5**
Pinnaroo	*Australia*	35°17S 140°53E	**63 F3**
Pinon Hills	*U.S.A.*	34°26N 117°39W	**79 L9**
Pinos	*Mexico*	22°18N 101°34W	**86 C4**
Pinos, Mt.	*U.S.A.*	34°49N 119°8W	**79 L7**
Pinos Pt.	*U.S.A.*	36°38N 121°57W	**77 H3**
Pinrang	*Indonesia*	3°46S 119°41E	**37 E5**
Pins, Pte. aux	*Canada*	42°15N 81°51W	**82 D3**
Pinsk	*Belarus*	52°10N 26°1E	**17 B14**
Pintados	*Chile*	20°35S 69°40W	**92 H5**
Pinyang	*China*	27°42N 120°31E	**35 D13**
Pinyug	*Russia*	60°5N 48°0E	**18 B8**
Pioche	*U.S.A.*	37°56N 114°27W	**77 H6**
Piombino	*Italy*	42°55N 10°32E	**22 C4**
Pioner, Ostrov	*Russia*	79°50N 92°0E	**27 B10**
Piopiotaki = Milford Sd.			
	N.Z.	44°41S 167°47E	**59 F1**
Piorini, L.	*Brazil*	3°15S 62°35W	**92 D6**
Piotrków Trybunalski			
	Poland	51°23N 19°43E	**17 C10**
Pip	*Iran*	26°45N 60°10E	**47 E9**
Pipar	*India*	26°25N 73°31E	**42 F5**
Pipar Road	*India*	26°27N 73°27E	**42 F5**
Piparia *Mad. P., India*		22°45N 78°23E	**42 H8**
Piparia *Mad. P., India*		21°49N 77°37E	**42 J7**
Pipestone	*U.S.A.*	44°0N 96°19W	**80 D5**
Pipestone →	*Canada*	52°53N 89°23W	**72 B2**
Pipestone Cr. →			
	Canada	49°38N 100°15W	**71 D8**
Piplan	*Pakistan*	32°17N 71°21E	**42 C4**
Piploda	*India*	23°37N 74°56E	**42 H6**
Pipmuacan, Rés. *Canada*		49°45N 70°30W	**73 C5**
Pippingarra	*Australia*	20°27S 118°42E	**60 D2**
Piquiri →	*Brazil*	24°3S 54°14W	**95 A5**
Pir Panjal Range *India*		32°30N 76°50E	**42 C7**
Pir Sohrāb	*Iran*	25°44N 60°54E	**47 E9**
Piracicaba	*Brazil*	22°45S 47°40W	**95 A6**
Piracuruca	*Brazil*	3°50S 41°50W	**93 D10**
Pirae	*Tahiti*	17°31S 149°32W	**59 d**
Pirajui	*Brazil*	21°59S 49°29W	**95 A6**
Pirané	*Argentina*	25°42S 59°6W	**94 B4**
Piranhas	*Brazil*	17°20S 44°56W	**93 F9**
Pirawa	*India*	24°10N 76°2E	**42 G7**
Pirgos	*Greece*	37°40N 21°27E	**23 F9**
Piribebuy	*Paraguay*	25°26S 57°2W	**94 B4**
Pirimapun	*Indonesia*	6°20S 138°24E	**37 F9**
Pirin Planina	*Bulgaria*	41°40N 23°30E	**23 D10**
Pirineos = Pyrénées			
	Europe	42°45N 0°18E	**20 E4**
Piripiri	*Brazil*	4°15S 41°46W	**93 D10**
Pirlangimpi	*Australia*	11°24S 130°26E	**60 B5**
Pirmasens	*Germany*	49°12N 7°36E	**16 D4**
Pirot	*Serbia*	43°9N 22°33E	**23 C10**
Piru	*Indonesia*	3°4S 128°12E	**37 E7**
Piru	*U.S.A.*	34°25N 118°48W	**79 L8**
Pisa	*Italy*	43°43N 10°23E	**22 C4**
Pisagua	*Chile*	19°40S 70°15W	**92 G4**
Pisco	*Peru*	13°50S 76°12W	**92 F3**
Písek	*Czech Rep.*	49°19N 14°10E	**16 D8**
Pishan	*China*	37°30N 78°33E	**30 D4**
Pīshīn	*Iran*	26°6N 61°47E	**47 E9**
Pishin	*Pakistan*	30°35N 67°0E	**42 D2**
Pishin Lora →	*Pakistan*	29°9N 64°5E	**42 E1**
Pising	*Indonesia*	5°8S 121°53E	**37 F6**
Pismo Beach	*U.S.A.*	35°9N 120°38W	**79 K6**
Pissis, Cerro	*Argentina*	27°45S 68°48W	**94 B2**
Pistóia	*Italy*	43°55N 10°54E	**22 C4**
Pistol B.	*Canada*	62°25N 92°37W	**71 A10**
Pisuerga →	*Spain*	41°33N 4°52W	**21 B3**
Pit →	*U.S.A.*	40°47N 122°6W	**76 F2**
Pitarpunga L.	*Australia*	34°24S 143°30E	**63 E3**
Pitcairn I.	*Pac. Oc.*	25°5S 130°5W	**65 K14**
Pitch L.	*Trin. & Tob.*	10°14N 61°39W	**93 K15**
Piteå	*Sweden*	65°20N 21°25E	**8 D19**
Piteälven →	*Sweden*	65°20N 21°25E	**8 D19**
Piteşti	*Romania*	44°52N 24°54E	**17 F13**
Pithapuram	*India*	17°10N 82°15E	**44 F6**
Pithara	*Australia*	30°20S 116°35E	**61 F2**
Pithora	*India*	21°16N 82°31E	**44 D6**
Pithoragarh	*India*	29°35N 80°13E	**43 E9**
Pithoro	*Pakistan*	25°31N 69°23E	**42 G3**
Pitlochry	*U.K.*	56°42N 3°44W	**11 E5**
Pitt I.	*Canada*	53°30N 129°50W	**70 C3**
Pitti I.	*India*	10°50N 72°38E	**45 J1**
Pittsburg *Calif., U.S.A.*		38°2N 121°53W	**78 G5**
Pittsburg *Kans., U.S.A.*		37°25N 94°42W	**80 G6**
Pittsburg *Tex., U.S.A.*		33°0N 94°59W	**84 E7**
Pittsburgh	*U.S.A.*	40°26N 79°58W	**82 F5**
Pittsfield *Ill., U.S.A.*		39°36N 90°49W	**80 F8**
Pittsfield *Maine, U.S.A.*		44°47N 69°23W	**81 C19**
Pittsfield *Mass., U.S.A.*		42°27N 73°15W	**83 D11**
Pittsfield *N.H., U.S.A.*		43°18N 71°20E	**83 C13**
Pittston	*U.S.A.*	41°19N 75°47W	**83 E9**
Pittsworth	*Australia*	27°41S 151°37E	**63 D5**
Pituri →	*Australia*	22°35S 138°30E	**62 C2**
Piura	*Peru*	5°15S 80°38W	**92 E2**
Piuthan	*Nepal*	28°7N 82°56E	**43 E10**
Pixian	*China*	30°48N 103°52E	**34 B4**
Pixley	*U.S.A.*	35°58N 119°18W	**78 K7**
Pizhou = Pei Xian *China*		34°44N 116°55E	**32 G9**
Pizhou	*China*	34°18N 117°57E	**33 G9**
Placentia	*Canada*	47°20N 54°0W	**73 C9**
Placentia B.	*Canada*	47°0N 54°40W	**73 C9**
Placerville	*U.S.A.*	38°44N 120°48W	**78 G6**
Placetas	*Cuba*	22°15N 79°44W	**88 B4**
Plaine des Jarres *Laos*		19°27N 103°10E	**38 C4**
Plainfield *N.J., U.S.A.*		40°37N 74°25W	**83 F10**
Plainfield *Ohio, U.S.A.*		40°13N 81°43W	**82 F3**
Plainfield *Vt., U.S.A.*		44°17N 72°26W	**83 B12**
Plains *Mont., U.S.A.*		47°28N 114°53W	**76 C6**
Plains *Tex., U.S.A.*		33°11N 102°50W	**84 E3**
Plainview *Nebr., U.S.A.*		42°21N 97°47W	**80 D5**
Plainview *Tex., U.S.A.*		34°11N 101°43W	**84 D4**
Plainwell	*U.S.A.*	42°27N 85°38W	**81 D11**
Plaistow	*U.S.A.*	42°50N 71°6W	**83 D13**
Plaka, Akra	*Greece*	35°11N 26°19E	**23 G12**
Plana Cays	*Bahamas*	22°38N 73°30W	**89 B5**
Planada	*U.S.A.*	37°16N 120°19W	**78 H6**
Plano	*U.S.A.*	33°1N 96°42W	**84 E6**
Plant City	*U.S.A.*	28°1N 82°7W	**85 G13**
Plaquemine	*U.S.A.*	30°17N 91°14W	**84 F9**
Plasencia	*Spain*	40°3N 6°8W	**21 B2**
Plaster City	*U.S.A.*	32°47N 115°51W	**79 N11**
Plaster Rock	*Canada*	46°53N 67°22W	**73 C6**
Plastun	*Russia*	44°45N 136°19E	**28 B8**
Plata, Río de la →			
	S. Amer.	34°45S 57°30W	**94 C4**
Plátani →	*Italy*	37°23N 13°16E	**22 F5**
Platte	*U.S.A.*	43°23N 98°51W	**80 D4**
Platte → *Mo., U.S.A.*		39°16N 94°50W	**80 F6**
Platte → *Nebr., U.S.A.*		41°4N 95°53W	**80 E6**
Platteville	*U.S.A.*	42°44N 90°29W	**80 D8**
Plattsburgh	*U.S.A.*	44°42N 73°28W	**83 B11**
Plattsmouth	*U.S.A.*	41°1N 95°53W	**80 E6**
Plauen	*Germany*	50°30N 12°8E	**16 C7**
Plavinas	*Latvia*	56°35N 25°46E	**9 H21**
Playa del Carmen *Mexico*		20°37N 87°4W	**87 C7**
Playgreen L.	*Canada*	54°0N 98°15W	**71 C9**
Pleasant Bay	*Canada*	46°51N 60°48W	**73 C7**
Pleasant Hill	*U.S.A.*	37°57N 122°4W	**78 H4**
Pleasant Mount *U.S.A.*		41°44N 75°26W	**83 E9**
Pleasanton *Calif., U.S.A.*		37°39N 121°52W	**78 H5**
Pleasanton *Tex., U.S.A.*		28°58N 98°29W	**84 G5**
Pleasantville *N.J.,*			
	U.S.A.	39°24N 74°32W	**81 F16**
Pleasantville *Pa., U.S.A.*		41°35N 79°34W	**82 E5**
Plei Ku	*Vietnam*	13°57N 108°0E	**38 F7**
Plenty →	*Australia*	23°25S 136°31E	**62 C2**
Plenty, B. of	*N.Z.*	37°45S 177°0E	**59 B6**
Plentywood	*U.S.A.*	48°47N 104°34W	**76 B11**
Plesetsk	*Russia*	62°43N 40°20E	**18 B7**
Plessisville	*Canada*	46°14N 71°47W	**73 C5**
Plétipi, L.	*Canada*	51°44N 70°6W	**73 B5**
Pleven	*Bulgaria*	43°26N 24°37E	**23 C11**
Plevlja = Pljevlja *Montenegro*			
Plevna	*Canada*	44°58N 76°59W	**82 B8**
Pljevlja	*Montenegro*	43°21N 19°21E	**23 C8**
Plock	*Poland*	52°32N 19°40E	**17 B10**
Plöckenstein	*Germany*	48°46N 13°51E	**16 D7**
Ploiești	*Romania*	44°57N 26°5E	**17 F14**
Plonge, Lac la	*Canada*	55°8N 107°20W	**71 B7**
Plovdiv	*Bulgaria*	42°8N 24°44E	**23 C11**
Plover Cove Res. *China*		22°28N 114°15E	**31 a**
Plum	*U.S.A.*	40°29N 79°47W	**82 F5**
Plum I.	*U.S.A.*	41°11N 72°12W	**83 E12**
Plumas	*U.S.A.*	39°45N 120°4W	**78 F6**
Plummer	*U.S.A.*	47°20N 116°53W	**76 C5**
Plumridge Lakes			
	Australia	29°26S 125°16E	**61 E4**
Plumtree	*Zimbabwe*	20°27S 27°55E	**55 J5**
Plungė	*Lithuania*	55°53N 21°59E	**9 J19**
Plymouth	*Trin. & Tob.*	11°14N 60°48W	**93 J16**
Plymouth	*U.K.*	50°22N 4°10W	**13 G3**
Plymouth *Calif., U.S.A.*		38°29N 120°51W	**78 G6**
Plymouth *Ind., U.S.A.*		41°21N 86°19W	**80 E10**
Plymouth *Mass., U.S.A.*		41°57N 70°40W	**83 E14**
Plymouth *N.C., U.S.A.*		35°52N 76°43W	**85 D16**
Plymouth *N.H., U.S.A.*		43°46N 71°41W	**83 C13**
Plymouth *Pa., U.S.A.*		41°14N 75°57W	**83 E9**
Plymouth *Wis., U.S.A.*		43°45N 87°59W	**80 D10**
Plympton-Wyoming = Wyoming			
	Canada	42°57N 82°7W	**82 D2**
Plynlimon = Pumlumon Fawr			
	U.K.	52°28N 3°46W	**13 E4**
Plyusa	*Russia*	58°28N 29°27E	**9 G23**
Plzeň	*Czech Rep.*	49°45N 13°22E	**16 D7**
Pmere Nyente ○			
	Australia	24°15S 136°10E	**62 C2**
Po →	*Italy*	44°57N 12°4E	**22 B5**
Po Hai = Bo Hai *China*		39°0N 119°0E	**33 E10**
Pobeda	*Russia*	65°12N 146°12E	**27 C15**
Pobedy, Pik	*Kyrgyzstan*	42°0N 79°58E	**30 C4**
Pocahontas *Ark., U.S.A.*		36°16N 90°58W	**85 C9**
Pocahontas *Iowa, U.S.A.*		42°44N 94°40W	**80 D6**
Pocatello	*U.S.A.*	42°52N 112°27W	**76 E7**
Pocomoke City	*U.S.A.*	38°5N 75°34W	**81 F16**
Poços de Caldas *Brazil*		21°50S 46°33W	**95 A6**
Podgorica	*Montenegro*	42°30N 19°19E	**23 C8**
Podile	*India*	15°37N 79°37E	**45 G4**
Podilska Vysochyna			
	Ukraine	49°0N 28°0E	**17 D14**
Podolsk	*Russia*	55°25N 37°30E	**18 C6**
Podporozhye	*Russia*	60°55N 34°2E	**18 B5**
Pofadder	*S. Africa*	29°10S 19°22E	**56 D2**
Pogranichnyy	*Russia*	44°25N 131°24E	**28 B5**
Poh	*Indonesia*	0°46S 122°51E	**37 E6**
Pohang	*S. Korea*	36°1N 129°23E	**33 F15**
Pohjanmaa □	*Finland*	62°58N 22°50E	**8 E20**
Pohnpei	*Micronesia*	6°55N 158°10E	**64 G7**
Pohri	*India*	25°32N 77°22E	**42 G6**
Poinsett, C.	*Antarctica*	65°42S 113°18E	**5 C8**
Point Arena	*U.S.A.*	38°55N 123°41W	**78 G3**
Point Baker	*U.S.A.*	56°21N 133°37W	**70 B2**
Point Calimere	*India*	10°17N 79°49E	**45 J4**
Point Fortin	*Trin. & Tob.*	10°10N 61°42W	**93 K15**
Point Hope	*U.S.A.*	68°21N 166°47W	**74 B6**
Point L.	*Canada*	65°15N 113°4W	**68 B9**
Point Lisas	*Trin. & Tob.*	10°24N 61°29W	**93 K15**
Point Pedro	*Sri Lanka*	9°50N 80°15E	**45 K5**
Point Pelee △	*Canada*	41°57N 82°31W	**82 E2**
Point Pleasant *N.J., U.S.A.*		40°5N 74°4W	**83 F10**
Point Pleasant *W. Va.,*			
	U.S.A.	38°51N 82°8W	**81 F12**
Point Reyes ○	*U.S.A.*	38°10N 122°55W	**78 G2**
Pointe-à-Pitre	*Guadeloupe*	16°15N 61°32W	**88 b**
Pointe-au-Pic = La Malbaie			
	Canada	47°40N 70°10W	**73 C5**
Pointe-Claire	*Canada*	45°26N 73°50W	**83 A11**
Pointe-Gatineau	*Canada*	45°27N 75°41W	**83 A9**
Pointe-Noire	*Congo*	4°48S 11°53E	**54 E2**
Pointe-Noire	*Guadeloupe*	16°14N 61°47W	**88 b**
Poipet	*Cambodia*	13°39N 102°33E	**38 F4**
Poisonbush Ra.			
	Australia	22°30S 121°30E	**60 D3**
Poissonnier Pt. *Australia*		19°57S 119°10E	**60 C2**
Poitiers	*France*	46°35N 0°20E	**20 C4**
Poitou	*France*	46°40N 0°10W	**20 C3**
Pojoaque	*U.S.A.*	35°54N 106°1W	**77 J10**
Pokaran	*India*	27°0N 71°50E	**42 F4**
Pokataroo	*Australia*	29°30S 148°36E	**63 D4**
Pokhara	*Nepal*	28°14N 83°58E	**43 E10**
Poko *Dem. Rep. of the Congo*		3°7N 26°52E	**54 D5**
Pokrovsk	*Russia*	61°29N 129°0E	**27 C13**
Pola = Pula	*Croatia*	44°54N 13°57E	**16 F7**
Polacca	*U.S.A.*	35°50N 110°23W	**77 J8**
Polan	*Iran*	25°30N 61°10E	**47 E9**
Poland	*U.S.A.*	43°13N 75°3W	**83 C9**
Poland ■	*Europe*	52°0N 20°0E	**17 C10**
Polar Bear △	*Canada*	55°0N 83°45W	**72 A2**
Polatsk	*Belarus*	55°30N 28°50E	**9 J23**
Polavaram	*India*	17°15N 81°38E	**44 F5**
Polcura	*Chile*	37°17S 71°43W	**94 D1**
Polesye = Pripet Marshes			
	Europe	52°10N 27°10E	**17 B15**
Polevskoy	*Russia*	56°26N 60°11E	**18 C11**
Police	*Poland*	53°33N 14°33E	**16 B8**
Police, Pte.	*Seychelles*	4°51S 55°32E	**55 b**
Poligiros	*Greece*	40°23N 23°25E	**23 D10**
Polillo Is.	*Phil.*	14°56N 122°0E	**37 B6**
Polk	*U.S.A.*	41°22N 79°56W	**82 E5**
Pollachi	*India*	10°35N 77°0E	**45 J3**
Pollnovat	*Russia*	63°50N 65°54E	**26 C7**
Polokwane	*S. Africa*	23°54S 29°25E	**57 B4**
Polokwane →	*S. Africa*	22°25S 30°5E	**57 B5**
Polonnaruwa	*Sri Lanka*	7°56N 81°0E	**45 L5**
Polonne	*Ukraine*	50°6N 27°30E	**17 C14**
Polonnoye = Polonne			
	Ukraine	50°6N 27°30E	**17 C14**
Polson	*U.S.A.*	47°41N 114°9W	**76 C6**
Poltava	*Ukraine*	49°35N 34°35E	**19 E5**
Pôltsamaa	*Estonia*	58°39N 25°58E	**9 G21**
Polunochnoye	*Russia*	60°52N 60°25E	**26 C7**
Polur	*India*	12°32N 79°11E	**45 H4**
Pôlva	*Estonia*	58°3N 27°3E	**9 G22**
Polyarny	*Russia*	69°8N 33°20E	**8 B25**
Polyarnyye Zori *Russia*		67°22N 32°30E	**8 C25**
Polynesia	*Pac. Oc.*	10°0S 162°0W	**65 F11**
Polynésie française = French			
	Polynesia ■ *Pac. Oc.*	20°0S 145°0W	**65 J13**
Pombal	*Portugal*	39°55N 8°40W	**21 C1**
Pomene	*Mozam.*	22°53S 35°33E	**57 B6**
Pomeroy *Ohio, U.S.A.*		39°2N 82°2W	**81 F12**
Pomeroy *Wash., U.S.A.*		46°28N 117°36W	**76 C5**
Pomézia	*Italy*	41°40N 12°30E	**22 D5**
Pomona	*Australia*	26°22S 152°52E	**63 D5**
Pomona	*U.S.A.*	34°4N 117°45W	**79 L9**

Pomorskie, Pojezierze
Poland 53°40N 16°37E **17** B9
Pompeys Pillar *U.S.A.* 45°59N 107°57W **76** D10
Pompeys Pillar △ *U.S.A.* 46°0N 108°0W **76** D10
Pompton Lakes *U.S.A.* 41°0N 74°17W **83** F10
Ponape = Pohnpei
Micronesia 6°55N 158°10E **64** G7
Ponask L. *Canada* 54°0N 92°41W **72** B1
Ponca *U.S.A.* 42°34N 96°43W **80** D5
Ponca City *U.S.A.* 36°42N 97°5W **84** C6
Ponce *Puerto Rico* 18°1N 66°37W **89** d
Ponchatoula *U.S.A.* 30°26N 90°26W **85** F9
Poncheville, L. *Canada* 50°10N 76°55W **72** B4
Pond *U.S.A.* 35°43N 119°20W **79** K7
Pond Inlet *Canada* 72°40N 77°0W **69** C16
Pondicherry = Puducherry
India 11°59N 79°50E **45** J4
Ponds, I. of *Canada* 53°27N 55°52W **73** B8
Ponferrada *Spain* 42°32N 6°35W **21** A2
Ponnaiyar → *India* 11°50N 79°45E **45** J4
Ponneri *India* 13°20N 80°15E **45** J2
Ponnani *India* 10°45N 75°59E **45** J2
Ponnuru *India* 16°5N 80°34E **45** F5
Ponoka *Canada* 52°42N 113°40W **70** C6
Ponorogo *Indonesia* 7°52S 111°27E **37** G14
Ponoy *Russia* 67°0N 41°13E **18** A7
Ponoy → *Russia* 66°59N 41°17E **18** A7
Ponta Delgada *Azores* 37°44N 25°40W **52** a
Ponta Grossa *Brazil* 25°7S 50°10W **95** B5
Ponta Porã *Brazil* 22°20S 55°35W **95** A4
Pontarlier *France* 46°54N 6°20E **20** C7
Pontchartrain, L. *U.S.A.* 30°5N 90°5W **85** F9
Ponte Nova *Brazil* 20°25S 42°54W **95** A7
Ponteix *Canada* 49°46N 107°29W **71** D7
Pontevedra *Spain* 42°26N 8°40W **21** A1
Pontiac *Ill., U.S.A.* 40°53N 88°38W **80** E9
Pontiac *Mich., U.S.A.* 42°38N 83°18W **81** D12
Pontian Kechil *Malaysia* 1°29N 103°23E **39** d
Pontianak *Indonesia* 0°3S 109°15E **36** E3
Pontine Is. = Ponziane, Ísole
Italy 40°55N 12°57E **22** D5
Pontine Mts. = Kuzey Anadolu
Dağları *Turkey* 41°0N 36°45E **19** F6
Pontivy *France* 48°5N 2°58W **20** B2
Pontoise *France* 49°3N 2°5E **20** B5
Ponton → *Canada* 58°27N 116°11W **70** B5
Pontypool *Canada* 44°6N 78°38W **82** B6
Pontypool *U.K.* 51°42N 3°2W **13** F4
Pontypridd *U.K.* 51°36N 3°20W **13** F4
Ponziane, Ísole *Italy* 40°55N 12°57E **22** D5
Poochera *Australia* 32°43S 134°51E **63** E1
Poole *U.K.* 50°43N 1°59W **13** G6
Poole □ *U.K.* 50°43N 1°59W **13** G6
Poona = Pune *India* 18°29N 73°57E **44** E1
Poonamallee *India* 13°3N 80°10E **45** H5
Pooncarie *Australia* 33°22S 142°31E **63** E3
Poopelloe L. *Australia* 31°40S 144°0E **63** E3
Poopó, L. de *Bolivia* 18°30S 67°35W **92** G5
Popayán *Colombia* 2°27N 76°36W **92** C3
Poperinge *Belgium* 50°51N 2°42E **15** D2
Popiltah L. *Australia* 33°10S 141°42E **63** E3
Popio L. *Australia* 33°10S 141°52E **63** E3
Poplar *U.S.A.* 48°7N 105°12W **76** B11
Poplar → *Canada* 53°0N 97°19W **71** C9
Poplar Bluff *U.S.A.* 36°46N 90°24W **80** G8
Poplarville *U.S.A.* 30°51N 89°32W **85** F10
Popocatépetl, Volcán
Mexico 19°2N 98°38W **87** D5
Popokabaka
Dem. Rep. of the Congo 5°41S 16°40E **54** F3
Poprad *Slovak Rep.* 49°3N 20°18E **17** D11
Porali → *Pakistan* 25°58N 66°26E **42** G2
Porcher I. *Canada* 53°50N 130°30W **70** C2
Porcupine → *Canada* 59°11N 104°46W **71** B8
Porcupine → *U.S.A.* 66°34N 145°19W **68** D2
Porcupine Gorge △
Australia 20°22S 144°26E **62** C3
Pordenone *Italy* 45°57N 12°39E **22** B5
Pori *Finland* 61°29N 21°48E **8** F19
Porkhov *Russia* 57°45N 29°38E **9** H23
Porlamar *Venezuela* 10°57N 63°51W **92** A6
Pormpuraaw *Australia* 14°59S 141°26E **62** A3
Pormpuraaw ◎
Australia 14°55S 141°47E **62** A3
Poronaysk *Russia* 49°13N 143°0E **31** B17
Poroshiri-Dake *Japan* 42°41N 142°52E **28** C11
Porpoise B. *Antarctica* 66°0S 127°0E **5** C9
Porsangerfjorden *Norway* 70°40N 25°40E **8** A21
Porsgrunn *Norway* 59°10N 9°40E **9** G13
Port Alberni *Canada* 49°14N 124°50W **70** D4
Port Alfred *S. Africa* 33°36S 26°55E **56** D4
Port Alice *Canada* 50°20N 127°25W **70** C3
Port Allegany *U.S.A.* 41°48N 78°17W **82** E6
Port Allen *U.S.A.* 30°27N 91°12W **85** F9
Port Alma *Australia* 23°38S 150°53E **62** C5
Port Alma *Canada* 42°10N 82°14W **82** D2
Port Angeles *U.S.A.* 48°7N 123°27W **78** B3
Port Antonio *Jamaica* 18°10N 76°26W **88** a
Port Aransas *U.S.A.* 27°50N 97°4W **84** H6
Port Arthur *Australia* 43°7S 147°50E **63** G4
Port Arthur *U.S.A.* 29°54N 93°56W **84** G8
Port au Choix *Canada* 50°43N 57°22W **73** B8
Port au Port B. *Canada* 48°40N 58°50W **73** C8
Port-au-Prince *Haiti* 18°40N 72°20W **89** C5
Port Augusta *Australia* 32°30S 137°50E **63** E2
Port Austin *U.S.A.* 44°3N 83°1W **82** B2
Port Blair *India* 11°40N 92°45E **45** J11
Port Blandford *Canada* 48°20N 54°10W **73** C9
Port Bradshaw *Australia* 12°30S 137°20E **62** A2
Port Broughton
Australia 33°37S 137°56E **63** E2
Port Bruce *Canada* 42°39N 81°0W **82** D3
Port Burwell *Canada* 42°40N 80°48W **82** D4
Port Campbell *India* 11°56N 92°37E **45** J11
Port Canning *India* 22°23N 88°40E **43** H13
Port Carling *Canada* 45°7N 79°35W **82** A5
Port-Cartier *Canada* 50°2N 66°50W **73** B6
Port Chalmers *N.Z.* 45°49S 170°30E **59** F3
Port Charlotte *U.S.A.* 26°59N 82°6W **85** H13

Port Chester *U.S.A.* 41°0N 73°40W **83** F11
Port Clements *Canada* 53°40N 132°10W **70** C2
Port Clinton *U.S.A.* 41°31N 82°56W **81** E12
Port Colborne *Canada* 42°50N 79°10W **82** D5
Port Coquitlam *Canada* 49°15N 122°45W **78** A4
Port Cornwallis *India* 13°17N 93°5E **45** H11
Port Credit *Canada* 43°33N 79°35W **82** C5
Port Curtis *Australia* 23°57S 151°20E **62** C5
Port Dalhousie *Canada* 43°13N 79°16W **82** C5
Port Darwin *Australia* 12°24S 130°45E **60** B5
Port Darwin *Falk. Is.* 51°50S 59°0W **96** G5
Port Davey *Australia* 43°16S 145°55E **63** G4
Port-de-Paix *Haiti* 19°50N 72°50W **89** C5
Port Dickson *Malaysia* 2°30N 101°49E **39** L3
Port Douglas *Australia* 16°30S 145°30E **62** B4
Port Dover *Canada* 42°47N 80°12W **82** D4
Port Edward *Canada* 54°12N 130°10W **70** C2
Port Elgin *Canada* 44°25N 81°25W **82** B3
Port Elizabeth *S. Africa* 33°58S 25°40E **56** D4
Port Ellen *U.K.* 55°38N 6°11W **11** F2
Port Erin *I. of Man* 54°5N 4°45W **12** C3
Port Essington *Australia* 11°15S 132°10E **60** B5
Port Ewen *U.S.A.* 41°54N 73°59W **83** E11
Port Fairy *Australia* 38°22S 142°12E **63** F3
Port Gamble *U.S.A.* 47°51N 122°34W **78** C4
Port-Gentil *Gabon* 0°40S 8°50E **54** E1
Port Germein *Australia* 33°1S 138°1E **63** E2
Port Ghalib *Egypt* 25°20N 34°50E **46** E2
Port Gibson *U.S.A.* 31°58N 90°59W **84** F9
Port Glasgow *U.K.* 55°56N 4°41W **11** F4
Port Harcourt *Nigeria* 4°40N 7°10E **52** H7
Port Hardy *Canada* 50°41N 127°30W **70** C3
Port Harrison = Inukjuak
Canada 58°25N 78°15W **69** F16
Port Hawkesbury
Canada 45°36N 61°22W **73** C7
Port Hedland *Australia* 20°25S 118°35E **60** D2
Port Henry *U.S.A.* 44°3N 73°28W **83** B11
Port Hood *Canada* 46°0N 61°32W **73** C7
Port Hope *Canada* 43°56N 78°20W **82** C6
Port Hope *U.S.A.* 43°57N 82°43W **82** C2
Port Hope Simpson
Canada 52°33N 56°18W **73** B8
Port Hueneme *U.S.A.* 34°7N 119°12W **79** L7
Port Huron *U.S.A.* 42°58N 82°26W **82** D2
Port Jefferson *U.S.A.* 40°57N 73°3W **83** F11
Port Jervis *U.S.A.* 41°22N 74°41W **83** E10
Port Kenny *Australia* 33°10S 134°41E **63** E1
Port Láirge = Waterford
Ireland 52°15N 7°8W **10** D4
Port Lavaca *U.S.A.* 28°37N 96°38W **84** G6
Port Leyden *U.S.A.* 43°35N 75°21W **83** C9
Port Lincoln *Australia* 34°42S 135°52E **63** E2
Port Loko *S. Leone* 8°48N 12°46W **52** G3
Port-Louis *Guadeloupe* 16°28N 61°32W **88** b
Port Louis *Mauritius* 20°10S 57°30E **55** d
Port MacDonnell
Australia 38°5S 140°48E **63** F3
Port McNeill *Canada* 50°35N 127°6W **70** C3
Port Macquarie
Australia 31°25S 152°25E **63** E5
Port Maria *Jamaica* 18°22N 76°54W **88** a
Port Matilda *U.S.A.* 40°48N 78°3W **82** F6
Port McNicoll *Canada* 44°44N 79°48W **82** B5
Port Mellon *Canada* 49°32N 123°31W **70** D4
Port-Menier *Canada* 49°51N 64°15W **73** C7
Port Moody *Canada* 49°17N 122°51W **78** A4
Port Morant *Jamaica* 17°54N 76°19W **88** a
Port Moresby *Papua N. G.* 9°24S 147°8E **58** B7
Port Musgrave *Australia* 11°55S 141°50E **62** A3
Port Neches *U.S.A.* 30°0N 93°59W **84** G8
Port Nolloth *S. Africa* 29°17S 16°52E **56** C2
Port Nouveau-Québec =
Kangiqsualujjuaq
Canada 58°30N 65°59W **69** F18
Port of Climax *Canada* 49°10N 108°20W **71** D7
Port of Coronach *Canada* 49°7N 105°31W **71** D7
Port of Spain
Trin. & Tob. 10°40N 61°31W **93** K15
Port Orange *U.S.A.* 29°9N 80°59W **85** G14
Port Orchard *U.S.A.* 47°32N 122°38W **78** C4
Port Orford *U.S.A.* 42°45N 124°30W **76** E1
Port Pegasus *N.Z.* 47°12S 167°41E **59** G1
Port Perry *Canada* 44°6N 78°56W **82** B6
Port Phillip B. *Australia* 38°10S 144°50E **63** F3
Port Pirie *Australia* 33°10S 138°1E **63** E2
Port Renfrew *Canada* 48°30N 124°20W **78** B2
Port Roper *Australia* 14°45S 135°25E **62** A2
Port Rowan *Canada* 42°40N 80°30W **82** D4
Port Safaga = Bûr Safâga
Egypt 26°43N 33°57E **46** E2
Port Said = Bûr Sa'îd
Egypt 31°16N 32°18E **53** B12
Port St. Joe *U.S.A.* 29°49N 85°18W **85** G12
Port St. Johns = Umzimvubu
S. Africa 31°38S 29°33E **57** D4
Port St. Lucie *U.S.A.* 27°18N 80°21W **85** H14
Port Sanilac *U.S.A.* 43°26N 82°33W **82** C2
Port Severn *Canada* 44°48N 79°43W **82** B5
Port Shepstone *S. Africa* 30°44S 30°28E **57** D5
Port Simpson *Canada* 54°30N 130°20W **70** C2
Port Stanley = Stanley
Falk. Is. 51°40S 59°51W **96** G5
Port Stanley *Canada* 42°40N 81°10W **82** D3
Port Sudan = Bûr Sûdân
Sudan 19°32N 37°9E **53** E13
Port Sulphur *U.S.A.* 29°29N 89°42W **85** G10
Port Talbot *U.K.* 51°35N 3°47W **13** F4
Port Townsend *U.S.A.* 48°7N 122°45W **78** B4
Port-Vendres *France* 42°32N 3°8E **20** E5
Port Vila *Vanuatu* 17°45S 168°18E **58** C9
Port Vladimir *Russia* 69°25N 33°6E **8** B25
Port Wakefield *Australia* 34°12S 138°10E **63** E2
Port Washington
U.S.A. 43°23N 87°53W **80** D10
Porta Orientalis *Romania* 45°6N 22°18E **17** F12
Portacloy *Ireland* 54°20N 9°48W **10** B2
Portadown *U.K.* 54°25N 6°27W **10** B5
Portaferry *U.K.* 54°23N 5°33W **10** B6

Portage *Pa., U.S.A.* 40°23N 78°41W **82** F6
Portage *Wis., U.S.A.* 43°33N 89°28W **80** D9
Portage la Prairie
Canada 49°58N 98°18W **71** D9
Portageville *U.S.A.* 36°26N 89°42W **80** G9
Portalegre *Portugal* 39°19N 7°25E **21** C2
Portales *U.S.A.* 34°11N 103°20W **77** J12
Portarlington *Ireland* 53°9N 7°14W **10** C4
Portbou *Spain* 42°25N 3°9E **21** A7
Porter L. *N.W.T., Canada* 61°41N 108°5W **71** A7
Porter L. *Sask., Canada* 56°20N 107°20W **71** B7
Porterville *S. Africa* 33°0S 19°0E **56** D2
Porterville *U.S.A.* 36°4N 119°1W **78** J8
Porth Tywyn = Burry Port
U.K. 51°41N 4°15W **13** F3
Porthcawl *U.K.* 51°29N 3°42W **13** F4
Porthill *U.S.A.* 48°59N 116°30W **76** B5
Porthmadog *U.K.* 52°55N 4°8W **12** E3
Portile de Fier *Europe* 44°44N 22°30E **17** F12
Portimão *Portugal* 37°8N 8°32W **21** D1
Portishead *U.K.* 51°29N 2°46W **13** F5
Portknockie *U.K.* 57°42N 2°51W **11** D6
Portland *N.S.W., Australia* 33°20S 150°0E **63** E5
Portland *Vic., Australia* 38°20S 141°35E **63** F3
Portland *Canada* 44°42N 76°12W **83** B8
Portland *Conn., U.S.A.* 41°34N 72°38W **83** E12
Portland *Maine, U.S.A.* 43°39N 70°16W **81** D18
Portland *Mich., U.S.A.* 42°52N 84°54W **81** D11
Portland *Oreg., U.S.A.* 45°32N 122°37W **78** E4
Portland *Pa., U.S.A.* 40°55N 75°6W **83** F9
Portland *Tex., U.S.A.* 27°53N 97°20W **84** H6
Portland, I. of *U.K.* 50°33N 2°26W **13** G5
Portland B. *Australia* 38°15S 141°45E **63** F3
Portland Bight *Jamaica* 17°52N 77°5W **88** a
Portland Bill *U.K.* 50°31N 2°28W **13** G5
Portland Canal *U.S.A.* 55°56N 130°0W **70** B2
Portland Int. ✈ **(PDX)**
U.S.A. 45°35N 122°36W **78** E4
Portland Pt. *Jamaica* 17°42N 77°11W **88** a
Portlaoise *Ireland* 53°2N 7°18W **10** C4
Portmadoc = Porthmadog
U.K. 52°55N 4°8W **12** E3
Portmore *Jamaica* 17°53N 76°53W **88** a
Porto *France* 42°16N 8°42E **20** E8
Porto *Portugal* 41°8N 8°40W **21** B1
Porto Alegre *Brazil* 30°5S 51°10W **95** C5
Porto de Moz *Brazil* 1°41S 52°13W **93** D8
Porto Empédocle *Italy* 37°17N 13°32E **22** F5
Porto Esperança *Brazil* 19°37S 57°29W **92** G7
Porto Franco *Brazil* 6°20S 47°24W **93** E9
Porto Inglês *C. Verde Is.* 15°21N 23°10W **52** b
Porto Mendes *Brazil* 24°30S 54°15W **95** A5
Porto Murtinho *Brazil* 21°45S 57°55W **92** H7
Porto Nacional *Brazil* 10°40S 48°30W **93** F9
Porto-Novo *Benin* 6°23N 2°42E **52** G6
Porto Primavera, Represa
Brazil 22°10S 52°45W **95** A5
Porto Santo, I. de
Madeira 33°45N 16°25W **52** B2
Porto São José *Brazil* 22°43S 53°10W **95** A5
Porto Seguro *Brazil* 16°26S 39°5W **93** G11
Porto Tórres *Italy* 40°50N 8°24E **22** D3
Porto União *Brazil* 26°10S 51°10W **95** B5
Porto-Vecchio *France* 41°35N 9°16E **20** F8
Porto Velho *Brazil* 8°46S 63°54W **92** E6
Porto Walter *Brazil* 8°15S 72°40W **92** E4
Portobelo *Panama* 9°35N 79°42W **88** E4
Portoferráio *Italy* 42°48N 10°20E **22** C4
Portola *U.S.A.* 39°49N 120°28W **78** F6
Portoscuso *Italy* 39°12N 8°24E **22** E3
Portoviejo *Ecuador* 1°7S 80°28W **92** D2
Portpatrick *U.K.* 54°51N 5°7W **11** G3
Portree *U.K.* 57°25N 6°12W **11** D2
Portrush *U.K.* 55°12N 6°40W **10** A5
Portsmouth *Dominica* 15°34N 61°27W **89** C7
Portsmouth *U.K.* 50°48N 1°6W **13** G6
Portsmouth *N.H., U.S.A.* 43°5N 70°45W **83** C14
Portsmouth *Ohio, U.S.A.* 38°44N 82°57W **81** F12
Portsmouth *R.I., U.S.A.* 41°36N 71°15W **83** E13
Portsmouth *Va., U.S.A.* 36°58N 76°23W **81** G15
Portsmouth □ *U.K.* 50°48N 1°6W **13** G6
Portsoy *U.K.* 57°41N 2°41W **11** D6
Portstewart *U.K.* 55°11N 6°43W **10** A5
Porttipahdan tekojärvi
Finland 68°5N 26°40E **8** B22
Portugal ■ *Europe* 40°0N 8°0W **21** C1
Portumna *Ireland* 53°6N 8°14W **10** C3
Portville *U.S.A.* 42°3N 78°20W **82** D6
Poruma *Australia* 10°2S 143°4E **62** a
Porvenir *Chile* 53°10S 70°16W **96** G2
Posadas *Argentina* 27°30S 55°50W **95** B4
Posht-e Badam *Iran* 33°2N 55°23E **47** C7
Poso *Indonesia* 1°20S 120°55E **37** E6
Poso, Danau *Indonesia* 1°52S 120°35E **37** E6
Posse *Brazil* 14°4S 46°18W **93** F9
Possession I. *Antarctica* 72°4S 172°0E **5** D11
Possum Kingdom L.
U.S.A. 32°52N 98°26W **84** E5
Post *U.S.A.* 33°12N 101°23W **84** E4
Post Falls *U.S.A.* 47°43N 116°57W **76** C5
Postavy = Pastavy *Belarus* 55°4N 26°50E **9** J22
Poste-de-la-Baleine =
Kuujjuarapik *Canada* 55°20N 77°35W **72** A4
Postmasburg *S. Africa* 28°18S 23°5E **56** D3
Postojna *Slovenia* 45°46N 14°12E **16** F8
Poston *U.S.A.* 34°0N 114°24W **79** M12
Postville *Canada* 54°54N 59°47W **73** B8
Posyet *Russia* 42°39N 130°48E **28** C5
Potchefstroom *S. Africa* 26°41S 27°7E **56** D4
Poteau *U.S.A.* 35°3N 94°37W **84** D7
Poteet *U.S.A.* 29°2N 98°35W **84** G5
Potenza *Italy* 40°38N 15°48E **22** D6
Poteriteri, L. *N.Z.* 46°5S 167°10E **59** G1
Potgietersrus = Mokopane
S. Africa 24°10S 28°55E **57** B4
Poti *Georgia* 42°10N 41°38E **19** F7
Potiskum *Nigeria* 11°39N 11°2E **53** F8
Potomac → *U.S.A.* 38°0N 76°23W **81** F14
Potosí *Bolivia* 19°38S 65°50W **92** G5

Potosi Mt. *U.S.A.* 35°57N 115°29W **79** K11
Pototan *Phil.* 10°54N 122°38E **37** B6
Potrerillos *Chile* 26°30S 69°30W **94** B2
Potsdam *Germany* 52°25N 13°4E **16** B7
Potsdam *U.S.A.* 44°40N 74°59W **83** B10
Pottangi *India* 18°34N 82°58E **44** E6
Potterville *U.S.A.* 42°37N 84°44W **81** D11
Pottersville *U.S.A.* 43°43N 73°50W **83** C11
Pottstown *U.S.A.* 40°15N 75°39W **83** F9
Pottsville *U.S.A.* 40°41N 76°12W **83** F8
Pottuvil *Sri Lanka* 6°55N 81°50E **45** L5
Poughkeepsie *U.S.A.* 41°42N 73°56W **83** E11
Poulaphouca Res. *Ireland* 53°8N 6°30W **10** C5
Poulsbo *U.S.A.* 47°44N 122°38W **78** C4
Poultney *U.S.A.* 43°31N 73°14W **83** C11
Poulton-le-Fylde *U.K.* 53°51N 2°58W **12** D5
Pouso Alegre *Brazil* 22°14S 45°57W **95** A6
Pouthisat *Cambodia* 12°34N 103°50E **38** F4
Považská Bystrica
Slovak Rep. 49°8N 18°27E **17** D10
Povenets *Russia* 62°50N 34°50E **18** B5
Poverty B. *N.Z.* 38°43S 178°2E **59** C7
Póvoa de Varzim *Portugal* 41°25N 8°46W **21** B1
Povorotnyy, Mys *Russia* 42°40N 133°2E **28** C6
Povungnituk = Puvirnituq
Canada 60°2N 77°10W **69** E16
Powassan *Canada* 46°5N 79°25W **72** C4
Poway *U.S.A.* 32°58N 117°2W **79** N9
Powder → *U.S.A.* 46°45N 105°26W **76** C11
Powder River *U.S.A.* 43°2N 106°59W **76** E10
Powell *U.S.A.* 44°45N 108°46W **76** D9
Powell, L. *U.S.A.* 36°57N 111°29W **77** H8
Powell River *Canada* 49°50N 124°35W **70** D4
Powers *U.S.A.* 45°41N 87°32W **80** C10
Pownal *U.S.A.* 42°45N 73°14W **83** D11
Powys □ *U.K.* 52°20N 3°20W **13** E4
Poyang Hu *China* 29°5N 116°20E **35** C11
Poyarkovo *Russia* 49°36N 128°41E **27** E13
Poza Rica *Mexico* 20°33N 97°27E **87** C5
Požarevac *Serbia* 44°35N 21°18E **23** B9
Poznań *Poland* 52°25N 16°55E **17** B9
Pozo *U.S.A.* 35°20N 120°24W **79** K6
Pozo Almonte *Chile* 20°10S 69°50W **92** H5
Pozo Colorado *Paraguay* 23°30S 58°45W **94** A4
Pozoblanco *Spain* 38°23N 4°51W **21** C3
Pozzuoli *Italy* 40°49N 14°7E **22** D6
Prachin Buri *Thailand* 14°0N 101°25E **38** F3
Prado *Brazil* 17°20S 39°13W **93** G11
Prahita → *India* 19°0N 79°55E **44** E4
Praia *C. Verde Is.* 15°2N 23°34W **52** b
Prainha *Brazil* 1°45S 53°30W **93** D8
Prainha Nova *Brazil* 7°10S 60°30W **92** E6
Prairie *Australia* 20°50S 144°35E **62** C3
Prairie City *U.S.A.* 44°28N 118°43W **76** D4
Prairie Dog Town Fork Red →
U.S.A. 34°34N 99°58W **84** D5
Prairie du Chien *U.S.A.* 43°3N 91°9W **80** D8
Prairies, L. of the
Canada 51°16N 101°32W **71** C8
Prambanan △ *Indonesia* 7°45S 110°28E **37** G14
Pran Buri *Thailand* 12°23N 99°55E **38** F2
Prapat *Indonesia* 2°41N 98°58E **36** D1
Praslin *Seychelles* 4°18S 55°45E **55** b
Prata *Brazil* 19°25S 48°54W **93** G9
Pratabpur *India* 23°28N 83°15E **43** H10
Pratapgarh *Raj., India* 24°2N 74°40E **42** G6
Pratapgarh *Ut. P., India* 25°56N 81°59E **43** G9
Pratas = Dongsha Dao
S. China Sea 20°45N 116°43E **35** G11
Prato *Italy* 43°53N 11°6E **22** C4
Pratt *U.S.A.* 37°39N 98°44W **80** G4
Prattville *U.S.A.* 32°28N 86°29W **85** E11
Pravara → *India* 19°35N 74°45E **44** E2
Pravia *Spain* 43°30N 6°12W **21** A2
Praya *Indonesia* 8°39S 116°17E **36** F5
Prayag = Allahabad
India 25°25N 81°58E **43** G9
Preah Vihear *Cambodia* 14°23N 104°41E **38** E5
Preble *U.S.A.* 42°44N 76°8W **83** D8
Precipice △ *Australia* 25°18S 150°5E **63** D5
Precordillera *Argentina* 30°0S 69°1W **94** C3
Preeceville *Canada* 51°57N 102°40W **71** C8
Preiļi *Latvia* 56°18N 26°43E **9** H22
Premont *U.S.A.* 27°22N 98°7W **84** H5
Prentice *U.S.A.* 45°33N 90°17W **80** C8
Preobrazheniye *Russia* 42°54N 133°54E **28** C6
Preparis I. = Pariparit Kyun
Burma 14°52N 93°41E **45** G11
Preparis North Channel
Ind. Oc. 15°27N 94°5E **45** G11
Preparis South Channel
Ind. Oc. 14°33N 93°30E **45** G11
Přerov *Czech Rep.* 49°28N 17°27E **17** D9
Prescott *Canada* 44°45N 75°30W **83** B9
Prescott *Ariz., U.S.A.* 34°33N 112°28W **77** J7
Prescott *Ark., U.S.A.* 33°48N 93°23W **84** E8
Prescott Valley *U.S.A.* 34°40N 112°18W **77** J7
Preservation Inlet *N.Z.* 46°8S 166°35E **59** G1
Presho *U.S.A.* 43°54N 100°3W **80** D3
Presidencia de la Plaza
Argentina 27°0S 59°50W **94** B4
Presidencia Roque Saenz Peña
Argentina 26°45S 60°30W **94** B3
Presidente Epitácio *Brazil* 21°56S 52°6W **93** H8
Presidente Hayes □
Paraguay 24°0S 59°0W **94** A4
Presidente Prudente
Brazil 22°5S 51°25W **95** A5
Presidio *Mexico* 29°34N 104°22W **86** B4
Presidio *U.S.A.* 29°34N 104°22W **84** G2
Prešov *Slovak Rep.* 49°0N 21°15E **17** D11
Prespa, L. = Prespansko Jezero
Macedonia 40°55N 21°0E **23** D9
Prespansko Jezero
Macedonia 40°55N 21°0E **23** D9
Presque I. *U.S.A.* 42°9N 80°6W **82** D4
Presque Isle *U.S.A.* 46°41N 68°1W **81** B19
Prestatyn *U.K.* 53°20N 3°24W **12** D4

Presteigne *U.K.* 52°17N 3°0W **13** E5
Preston *Canada* 43°23N 80°21W **82** C4
Preston *U.K.* 53°46N 2°42W **12** D5
Preston *Idaho, U.S.A.* 42°6N 111°53W **76** E8
Preston *Minn., U.S.A.* 43°40N 92°5W **80** D7
Preston *C., Australia* 20°51S 116°12E **60** D2
Prestonburg *U.S.A.* 37°40N 82°47W **81** G12
Prestwick *U.K.* 55°29N 4°37W **11** F4
Pretoria *S. Africa* 25°44S 28°12E **57** C4
Preveza *Greece* 38°57N 20°45E **23** E9
Prey Veng *Cambodia* 11°35N 105°29E **39** G5
Pribilof Is. *U.S.A.* 57°0N 170°0W **74** D6
Příbram *Czech Rep.* 49°41N 14°2E **16** D8
Price *U.S.A.* 39°36N 110°49W **76** G8
Price, C. *India* 13°34N 93°3E **45** H11
Price I. *Canada* 52°23N 128°41W **70** C3
Prichard *U.S.A.* 30°44N 88°5W **85** F10
Priekule *Latvia* 56°26N 21°35E **9** H19
Prienai *Lithuania* 54°38N 23°57E **9** J20
Prieska *S. Africa* 29°40S 22°42E **56** C3
Priest L. *U.S.A.* 48°35N 116°52W **76** B5
Priest River *U.S.A.* 48°11N 116°55W **76** B5
Priest Valley *U.S.A.* 36°10N 120°39W **78** J6
Prievidza *Slovak Rep.* 48°46N 18°36E **17** D10
Prikaspiyskaya Nizmennost =
Caspian Depression
Eurasia 47°0N 48°0E **19** E8
Prilep *Macedonia* 41°21N 21°32E **23** D9
Priluki = Pryluky
Ukraine 50°30N 32°24E **19** D5
Prime Seal I. *Australia* 40°3S 147°43E **63** G4
Primo Tapia *Mexico* 32°16N 116°54W **79** N10
Primorskiy Kray □ *Russia* 45°0N 135°0E **28** B7
Primrose L. *Canada* 54°55N 109°45W **71** C7
Prince Albert *Canada* 53°15N 105°50W **71** C7
Prince Albert *S. Africa* 33°12S 22°2E **56** D3
Prince Albert △ *Canada* 54°0N 106°25W **71** C7
Prince Albert Mts.
Antarctica 76°0S 161°30E **5** D11
Prince Albert Pen.
Canada 72°30N 116°0W **68** C8
Prince Albert Sd. *Canada* 70°25N 115°0W **68** D8
Prince Alfred, C. *Canada* 74°20N 124°40W **4** B1
Prince Charles I.
Canada 67°47N 76°12W **69** D16
Prince Charles Mts.
Antarctica 72°0S 67°0E **5** D6
Prince Edward Fracture Zone
Ind. Oc. 46°0S 35°0E **5** A4
Prince Edward I. □
Canada 46°20N 63°20W **73** C7
Prince Edward Is. *Ind. Oc.* 46°35S 38°0E **3** G11
Prince George *Canada* 53°55N 122°50W **70** C4
Prince of Wales, C.
U.S.A. 65°36N 168°5W **74** B6
Prince of Wales I.
Australia 10°40S 142°10E **62** A3
Prince of Wales I. *Canada* 73°0N 99°0W **68** C12
Prince of Wales I.
U.S.A. 55°47N 132°50W **68** F5
Prince of Wales Icefield
Canada 78°15N 79°0W **69** B16
Prince of Wales Str.
Canada 73°0N 117°0W **68** C8
Prince Patrick I. *Canada* 77°0N 120°0W **69** B8
Prince Regent Inlet
Canada 73°0N 90°0W **69** C14
Prince Rupert *Canada* 54°20N 130°20W **70** C2
Prince William Sd.
U.S.A. 60°40N 147°0W **68** E2
Princes Town
Trin. & Tob. 10°16N 61°23W **93** K15
Princess Charlotte B.
Australia 14°25S 144°0E **62** A3
Princess Elizabeth Trough
S. Ocean 64°10S 83°0E **5** C7
Princess May Ranges
Australia 15°30S 125°30E **60** C4
Princess Royal I. *Canada* 53°0N 128°40W **70** C3
Princeton *Canada* 49°27N 120°30W **70** D4
Princeton *Calif., U.S.A.* 39°24N 122°1W **78** F4
Princeton *Ill., U.S.A.* 41°23N 89°28W **80** E9
Princeton *Ind., U.S.A.* 38°21N 87°34W **80** F10
Princeton *Ky., U.S.A.* 37°7N 87°53W **80** G10
Princeton *Mo., U.S.A.* 40°24N 93°35W **80** E7
Princeton *N.J., U.S.A.* 40°21N 74°39W **83** F10
Princeton *W. Va., U.S.A.* 37°22N 81°6W **81** G13
Principe São Tomé & Príncipe* 1°37N 7°25E **50 F4
Principe da Beira *Brazil* 12°20S 64°30W **92** F6
Prineville *U.S.A.* 44°18N 120°51W **76** D3
Prins Harald Kyst *Antarctica* 70°0S 35°1E **5** D4
Prinsesse Astrid Kyst
Antarctica 70°45S 12°30E **5** D3
Prinsesse Ragnhild Kyst
Antarctica 70°15S 27°30E **5** D4
Prinzapolca *Nic.* 13°20N 83°35W **88** D3
Priozersk *Russia* 61°2N 30°7E **8** F24
Pripet = Prypyat →
Europe 51°20N 30°15E **17** C16
Pripet Marshes *Europe* 52°10N 27°10E **17** B15
Pripyat Marshes = Pripet Marshes
Europe 52°10N 27°10E **17** B15
Pripyats = Prypyat →
Europe 51°20N 30°15E **17** C16
Prishtinë *Kosovo* 42°40N 21°13E **23** C9
Priština = Prishtinë
Kosovo 42°40N 21°13E **23** C9
Privas *France* 44°45N 4°37E **20** D6
Privolzhskaya Vozvyshennost
Russia 51°0N 46°0E **19** D8
Privolzhskiy □ *Russia* 56°0N 50°0E **18** D6
Prizren *Kosovo* 42°13N 20°45E **23** C9
Probolinggo *Indonesia* 7°46S 113°13E **37** G15
Proctor *U.S.A.* 43°40N 73°2W **83** C11
Proddatur *India* 14°45N 78°30E **45** G4
Profondeville *Belgium* 50°23N 4°52E **15** D4
Progreso *Coahuila,*
Mexico 27°28N 100°59W **86** B4
Progreso *Yucatán, Mexico* 21°20N 89°40W **87** C7

Progress *Antarctica* 66°22S 76°22E **5 C12**
Progress *Russia* 49°45N 129°37E **27 E13**
Prokopyevsk *Russia* 54°0N 86°45E **26 D9**
Prokuplje *Serbia* 43°16N 21°36E **23 C9**
Prome *Burma* 18°49N 95°13E **41 K19**
Prophet → *Canada* 58°48N 122°40W **70 B4**
Prophet River *Canada* 58°6N 122°43W **70 B4**
Propriá *Brazil* 10°13S 36°51W **93 F11**
Propriano *France* 41°41N 8°52E **20 F8**
Proserpine *Australia* 20°21S 148°36E **62 b**
Prosna → *Poland* 52°6N 17°44E **17 C9**
Prospect *U.S.A.* 43°18N 75°9W **83 C9**
Prosser *U.S.A.* 46°12N 119°46W **76 C4**
Prostějov *Czech Rep.* 49°30N 17°9E **17 D9**
Proston *Australia* 26°8S 151°32E **63 D5**
Provence *France* 43°40N 5°46E **20 E6**
Providence *Ky., U.S.A.* 37°24N 87°46W **80 G10**
Providence *R.I., U.S.A.* 41°49N 71°24W **83 E13**
Providence *Canada* 45°41N 82°15W **72 C3**
Providence Mts.
U.S.A. 35°10N 115°15W **79 K11**
Providencia, I. de
Colombia 13°25N 81°26W **88 D3**
Provideniya *Russia* 64°23N 173°18W **27 C19**
Provins *France* 48°33N 3°15E **20 B5**
Provo *U.S.A.* 40°14N 111°39W **76 F8**
Provost *Canada* 52°25N 110°20W **71 C6**
Prudhoe Bay *U.S.A.* 70°18N 148°22W **74 A10**
Prudhoe I. *Australia* 21°19S 149°41E **62 C4**
Prud'homme *Canada* 52°20N 105°54W **71 C7**
Pruszków *Poland* 52°9N 20°49E **17 B11**
Prut → *Romania* 45°28N 28°10E **17 F15**
Pruzhany *Belarus* 52°33N 24°28E **17 B13**
Prydz B. *Antarctica* 69°0S 74°0E **5 C6**
Pryluky *Ukraine* 50°30N 32°24E **19 D5**
Pryor *U.S.A.* 36°19N 95°19W **84 C7**
Prypyat → *Europe* 51°20N 30°15E **17 C16**
Przemyśl *Poland* 49°50N 22°45E **17 D12**
Przhevalsk = Karakol
Kyrgyzstan 42°30N 78°20E **30 C4**
Psara *Greece* 38°37N 25°38E **23 E11**
Psiloritis, Oros *Greece* 35°15N 24°45E **23 G11**
Pskov *Russia* 57°50N 28°25E **9 H23**
Ptich = Ptsich → *Belarus* 52°9N 28°52E **17 B15**
Ptolemaida *Greece* 40°30N 21°43E **23 D9**
Ptsich → *Belarus* 52°9N 28°52E **17 B15**
Pu Xian *China* 36°24N 111°6E **32 F6**
Pua *Thailand* 19°11N 100°55E **38 C3**
Puán *Argentina* 37°30S 62°45W **94 D3**
Pu'an *China* 25°46N 104°57E **34 E5**
Pu'apu'a *Samoa* 13°34S 172°9W **59 b**
Pubei *China* 22°16N 109°31E **34 F7**
Pucallpa *Peru* 8°25S 74°30W **92 E4**
Pucheng *China* 27°59N 118°31E **35 D12**
Puch'on = Bucheon
S. Korea 37°28N 126°45E **33 F14**
Pudasjärvi *Finland* 65°23N 26°53E **8 D22**
Puding *China* 26°18N 105°44E **34 D5**
Pudozh *Russia* 61°48N 36°32E **18 B6**
Pudu = Suizhou *China* 31°42N 113°24E **35 B9**
Puducherry *India* 11°59N 79°50E **45 J4**
Pudukkottai *India* 10°28N 78°47E **45 J4**
Puebla *Mexico* 19°3N 98°12W **87 D5**
Puebla □ *Mexico* 18°50N 98°0W **87 D5**
Pueblo *U.S.A.* 38°16N 104°37W **76 G11**
Puelches *Argentina* 38°5S 65°51W **94 D2**
Puelén *Argentina* 37°32S 67°38W **94 D2**
Puente Alto *Chile* 33°32S 70°35W **94 C1**
Puente-Genil *Spain* 37°22N 4°47W **21 D3**
Pu'er *China* 23°0N 101°15E **34 D3**
Puerca, Pta. *Puerto Rico* 18°13N 65°36W **89 d**
Puerco → *U.S.A.* 34°22N 107°50W **77 J10**
Puerto Aisén *Chile* 45°27S 73°0W **96 F2**
Puerto Ángel *Mexico* 15°40N 96°29W **87 D5**
Puerto Arista *Mexico* 15°56N 93°48W **87 D6**
Puerto Armuelles *Panama* 8°20N 82°51W **88 E3**
Puerto Ayacucho
Venezuela 5°40N 67°35W **92 B5**
Puerto Barrios *Guatemala* 15°40N 88°32W **88 C2**
Puerto Bermejo
Argentina 26°55S 58°34W **94 B4**
Puerto Bermúdez *Peru* 10°20S 74°58W **92 F4**
Puerto Bolívar *Ecuador* 3°19S 79°55W **92 D3**
Puerto Cabello *Venezuela* 10°28N 68°1W **92 A5**
Puerto Cabezas *Nic.* 14°0N 83°30W **88 D3**
Puerto Cabo Gracias á Dios
Nic. 15°0N 83°10W **88 D3**
Puerto Carreño *Colombia* 6°12N 67°22W **92 B5**
Puerto Castilla *Honduras* 16°0N 86°0W **88 C2**
Puerto Chicama *Peru* 7°45S 79°20W **92 E3**
Puerto Coig *Argentina* 50°54S 69°15W **96 G3**
Puerto Cortés *Honduras* 15°51N 88°0W **88 C2**
Puerto Cumarebo
Venezuela 11°29N 69°30W **92 A5**
Puerto de los Ángeles △
Mexico 23°39N 105°45W **86 C3**
Puerto del Rosario
Canary Is. 28°30N 13°52W **52 C3**
Puerto Deseado *Argentina* 47°55S 66°0W **96 F3**
Puerto Escondido *Mexico* 15°50N 97°3W **87 D5**
Puerto Heath *Bolivia* 12°34S 68°39W **92 F5**
Puerto Inírida *Colombia* 3°53N 67°52W **92 C5**
Puerto Juárez *Mexico* 21°11N 86°49W **87 C7**
Puerto La Cruz *Venezuela* 10°13N 64°38W **92 A6**
Puerto Leguízamo
Colombia 0°12S 74°46W **92 D4**
Puerto Lempira
Honduras 15°16N 83°46W **88 C3**
Puerto Libertad *Mexico* 29°55N 112°43W **86 B2**
Puerto Limón *Colombia* 3°23N 73°30W **92 C4**
Puerto Lobos *Argentina* 42°0S 65°3W **96 E3**
Puerto Madryn *Argentina* 42°48S 65°4W **96 E3**
Puerto Maldonado *Peru* 12°30S 69°10W **92 F5**
Puerto Manatí *Cuba* 21°22N 76°50W **88 B4**
Puerto Montt *Chile* 41°28S 73°0W **96 E2**
Puerto Morazán *Nic.* 12°51N 87°11W **88 D2**
Puerto Morelos *Mexico* 20°50N 86°52W **87 C7**
Puerto Natales *Chile* 51°45S 72°15W **96 G2**

Puerto Oscuro *Chile* 31°24S 71°35W **94 C1**
Puerto Padre *Cuba* 21°13N 76°35W **88 B4**
Puerto Páez *Venezuela* 6°13N 67°28W **92 B5**
Puerto Peñasco *Mexico* 31°20N 113°33W **86 A2**
Puerto Pinasco *Paraguay* 22°36S 57°50W **94 A4**
Puerto Plata *Dom. Rep.* 19°48N 70°45W **89 C5**
Puerto Princesa *Phil.* 9°46N 118°45E **37 C5**
Puerto Quepos *Costa Rica* 9°29N 84°6W **88 E3**
Puerto Rico ☑ *W. Indies* 18°15N 66°45W **89 d**
Puerto Rico Trench
Atl. Oc. 19°50N 66°0W **89 C6**
Puerto San Julián
Argentina 49°18S 67°43W **96 F3**
Puerto Santa Cruz
Argentina 50°0S 68°32W **96 G3**
Puerto Sastre *Paraguay* 22°2S 57°55W **94 A4**
Puerto Suárez *Bolivia* 18°58S 57°52W **92 G7**
Puerto Vallarta *Mexico* 20°37N 105°15W **86 C3**
Puerto Varas *Chile* 41°19S 72°59W **96 E2**
Puerto Wilches *Colombia* 7°21N 73°54W **92 B4**
Puertollano *Spain* 38°43N 4°7W **21 C3**
Pueu *Tahiti* 17°44S 149°13W **59 d**
Pueyrredón, L. *Argentina* 47°20S 72°0W **96 F2**
Puffin I. *Ireland* 51°50N 10°24W **10 E1**
Pugachev *Russia* 52°0N 48°49E **18 D8**
Pugal *India* 28°30N 72°48E **42 E5**
Puge *China* 27°20N 102°31E **34 D4**
Puget Sound *U.S.A.* 47°50N 122°30W **78 C4**
Pugŏdong *N. Korea* 42°5N 130°0E **33 C16**
Pūgūnzī *Iran* 25°49N 59°10E **47 E8**
Puigcerdà *Spain* 42°24N 1°50E **21 A6**
Puijiang *China* 30°14N 103°30E **34 B4**
Pujiang *China* 29°29N 119°54E **35 C12**
Pujon-ho *N. Korea* 40°35N 127°35E **33 D14**
Pukaki, L. *N.Z.* 44°4S 170°1E **59 F3**
Pukapuka *Cook Is.* 10°53S 165°49W **65 J11**
Pukaskwa △ *Canada* 48°20N 86°0W **72 C2**
Pukatawagan *Canada* 55°45N 101°20W **71 B8**
Pukchin *N. Korea* 40°12N 125°45E **33 D13**
Pukch'ŏng *N. Korea* 40°14N 128°10E **33 D15**
Pukekohe *N.Z.* 37°12S 174°55E **59 B5**
Pukhrayan *India* 26°14N 79°51E **43 F8**
Puksubaek-san
N. Korea 40°42N 127°45E **33 D14**
Pula *Croatia* 44°54N 13°57E **16 F7**
Pulacayo *Bolivia* 20°25S 66°41W **92 H5**
Pulandian *China* 39°25N 121°58E **33 E11**
Pulaski *N.Y., U.S.A.* 43°34N 76°8W **83 C8**
Pulaski *Tenn., U.S.A.* 35°12N 87°2W **85 D11**
Pulaski *Va., U.S.A.* 37°3N 80°47W **81 G13**
Pulau → *Indonesia* 5°50S 138°15E **37 F9**
Pulau Gili *Indonesia* 8°21S 116°1E **37 J19**
Pulawy *Poland* 51°23N 21°59E **17 C11**
Pule *U.S.A.* 39°48N 121°29W **78 F5**
Pulgaon *India* 20°44N 78°21E **44 D4**
Pulicat *India* 13°25N 80°19E **45 H5**
Pulicat L. *India* 13°40N 80°15E **45 H5**
Pulivendla *India* 14°25N 78°14E **45 G4**
Puliyangudi *India* 9°11N 77°24E **45 K3**
Pullman *U.S.A.* 46°44N 117°10W **76 C5**
Pulog, Mt. *Phil.* 16°40N 120°50E **37 A6**
Pultusk *Poland* 52°43N 21°6E **17 B11**
Pumlumon Fawr *U.K.* 52°28N 3°46W **13 E4**
Puná, I. *Ecuador* 2°55S 80°5W **92 D2**
Punaauia *Tahiti* 17°37S 149°34W **59 d**
Punakaiki *N.Z.* 42°7S 171°20E **59 E3**
Punakha Dzong *Bhutan* 27°42N 89°52E **41 F16**
Punalur *India* 9°0N 76°56E **45 K3**
Punasar *India* 27°6N 73°6E **42 F5**
Punata *Bolivia* 17°32S 65°50W **92 G5**
Punch *India* 33°48N 74°4E **43 C6**
Punch → *Pakistan* 33°12N 73°40E **42 C5**
Punda Maria *S. Africa* 22°40S 31°5E **57 B5**
Pune *India* 18°29N 73°57E **44 E1**
P'ungsan *N. Korea* 40°50N 128°9E **33 D15**
Puning *China* 23°20N 116°12E **35 F11**
Punjab □ *India* 31°0N 76°0E **42 D7**
Punjab □ *Pakistan* 32°0N 72°30E **42 E6**
Puno *Peru* 15°55S 70°3W **92 G4**
Punpun → *India* 25°31N 85°18E **43 G11**
Punta, Cerro de
Puerto Rico 18°10N 66°37W **89 d**
Punta Alta *Argentina* 38°53S 62°4W **96 D4**
Punta Arenas *Chile* 53°10S 71°0W **96 G2**
Punta del Díaz *Chile* 28°0S 70°45W **94 B1**
Punta Gorda *Belize* 16°10N 88°45W **87 D7**
Punta Gorda *U.S.A.* 26°56N 82°3W **85 H13**
Punta Prieta *Mexico* 28°58N 114°17W **86 B2**
Puntarenas *Costa Rica* 10°0N 84°50W **88 E3**
Puntland *Somalia* 9°0N 50°0E **49 F4**
Punto Fijo *Venezuela* 11°50N 70°13W **92 A4**
Punxsutawney *U.S.A.* 40°57N 78°59W **82 F6**
Pupuan *Indonesia* 8°19S 115°0E **37 J18**
Puqi *China* 29°40N 113°50E **35 C9**
Puquio *Peru* 14°45S 74°10W **92 F4**
Pur → *Russia* 67°31N 77°55E **26 C8**
Puracé, Vol. *Colombia* 2°21N 76°23W **92 C3**
Puralia = Puruliya *India* 23°17N 86°24E **43 H12**
Puranpur *India* 28°31N 80°9E **43 E9**
Purbalingga *Indonesia* 7°23S 109°21E **37 G13**
Purbeck, Isle of *U.K.* 50°39N 1°59W **13 G5**
Purcell *U.S.A.* 35°1N 97°22W **84 D6**
Purcell Mts. *Canada* 49°55N 116°15W **70 D5**
Purdy *Canada* 45°19N 77°44W **82 A7**
Puri *India* 19°50N 85°58E **44 E7**
Purmerend *Neths.* 52°32N 4°58E **15 B4**
Purna → *India* 19°6N 77°2E **44 E3**
Purnia *India* 25°45N 87°31E **43 G12**
Purnululu △ *Australia* 17°20S 128°20E **60 C4**
Pursat = Pouthisat
Cambodia 12°34N 103°50E **38 F4**
Purukcahu *Indonesia* 0°35S 114°35E **36 E4**
Puruliya *India* 23°17N 86°24E **43 H12**
Purus → *Brazil* 3°42S 61°28W **92 D6**
Puruvesi *Finland* 61°50N 29°30E **8 F23**
Purvis *U.S.A.* 31°9N 89°25W **85 F10**
Purwa *India* 26°28N 80°47E **43 F9**
Purwakarta *Indonesia* 6°35S 107°29E **37 G12**
Purwo, Tanjung
Indonesia 8°44S 114°21E **37 K18**

Purwodadi *Indonesia* 7°7S 110°55E **37 G14**
Purwokerto *Indonesia* 7°25S 109°14E **37 G13**
Puryŏng *N. Korea* 42°5N 129°43E **33 C15**
Pus → *India* 19°55N 77°55E **44 E3**
Pusa *India* 25°59N 85°41E **43 G11**
Pusad *India* 19°56N 77°36E **44 E3**
Pusan = Busan *S. Korea* 35°5N 129°0E **33 G15**
Pushkin *Russia* 59°45N 30°25E **9 C6**
Pushkino *Russia* 51°16N 47°0E **19 D8**
Put-in-Bay *U.S.A.* 41°39N 82°49W **82 E2**
Putahow L. *Canada* 59°54N 100°40W **71 B8**
Putao *Burma* 27°28N 97°30E **41 F20**
Putaruru *N.Z.* 38°2S 175°50E **59 C5**
Puteran *Indonesia* 7°5S 114°0E **37 G15**
Putian *China* 25°23N 119°0E **35 E12**
Putignano *Italy* 40°51N 17°7E **22 D7**
Puting, Tanjung *Indonesia* 3°31S 111°46E **36 E4**
Putnam *U.S.A.* 41°55N 71°55W **83 E13**
Putorana, Gory *Russia* 69°0N 95°0E **27 C10**
Putrajaya *Malaysia* 2°55N 101°40E **39 L3**
Puttalam *Sri Lanka* 8°1N 79°55E **45 K5**
Puttalam Lagoon
Sri Lanka 8°15N 79°45E **45 K4**
Puttgarden *Germany* 54°30N 11°10E **16 A6**
Puttur *Andhra Pradesh,
India* 13°27N 79°33E **45 H4**
Puttur *Karnataka, India* 12°46N 75°12E **45 H2**
Putumayo → *S. Amer.* 3°7S 67°58W **92 D5**
Putuo *China* 29°56N 122°20E **35 C8**
Putussibau *Indonesia* 0°50N 112°56E **36 D4**
Puvirnituq *Canada* 60°2N 77°10W **69 E16**
Puy-de-Dôme *France* 45°46N 2°57E **20 D5**
Puyallup *U.S.A.* 47°12N 122°18W **78 C4**
Puyang *China* 35°40N 115°1E **32 G8**
Pūzeh Rig *Iran* 27°20N 58°40E **47 E8**
Pweto
Dem. Rep. of the Congo 8°25S 28°51E **54 F5**
Pwllheli *U.K.* 52°53N 4°25W **12 E3**
Pyaozero, Ozero *Russia* 66°5N 30°58E **8 C24**
Pyapon *Burma* 16°20N 95°40E **41 L19**
Pyasina → *Russia* 73°30N 87°0E **27 B9**
Pyatigorsk *Russia* 44°2N 43°6E **19 F7**
Pyay = Prome *Burma* 18°49N 95°13E **41 K19**
Pye = Prome *Burma* 18°49N 95°13E **41 K19**
Pyeongtaek *S. Korea* 37°1N 127°4E **33 F14**
Pyetrikaw *Belarus* 52°11N 28°29E **17 B15**
Pyhäjoki *Finland* 64°28N 24°14E **8 D21**
Pyin-Oo-Lwin = Maymyo
Burma 22°2N 96°28E **38 A1**
Pyinmana *Burma* 19°45N 96°12E **41 K20**
Pymatuning Res. *U.S.A.* 41°30N 80°28W **82 E4**
Pyŏktong *N. Korea* 40°50N 125°50E **33 D13**
Pyŏngang *N. Korea* 38°24N 127°17E **33 E14**
P'yŏngsong *N. Korea* 39°14N 125°52E **33 E13**
P'yŏngyang *N. Korea* 39°0N 125°30E **33 E13**
Pyote *U.S.A.* 31°32N 103°8W **84 F3**
Pyramid L. *U.S.A.* 40°1N 119°35W **76 F4**
Pyramid Pk. *U.S.A.* 36°25N 116°37W **79 J10**
Pyrénées *Europe* 42°45N 0°18E **20 E4**
Pyu *Burma* 18°30N 96°28E **41 K20**

Q

Qaanaaq *Greenland* 77°30N 69°10W **69 B18**
Qachasnek *S. Africa* 30°6S 28°42E **57 D4**
Qa'el Jafr *Jordan* 30°20N 36°25E **48 E5**
Qa'emābād *Iran* 31°44N 60°2E **47 D9**
Qā'emshahr *Iran* 36°30N 52°53E **47 B7**
Qagan Nur *Jilin, China* 45°15N 124°18E **33 B13**
Qagan Nur *Nei Monggol Zizhiqu,
China* 43°30N 114°55E **32 C8**
Qahar Youyi Zhongqi
China 41°12N 112°40E **32 D7**
Qahremānshahr = Kermānshāh
Iran 34°23N 47°0E **46 C5**
Qaidam Pendi *China* 37°0N 95°0E **30 D8**
Qajarīyeh *Iran* 31°1N 48°22E **47 D6**
Qala-i-Jadid = Spīn Būldak
Afghan. 31°1N 66°25E **42 D2**
Qala Viala *Pakistan* 30°49N 67°17E **42 D2**
Qala Yangi *Afghan.* 34°20N 66°30E **42 B2**
Qal'at al Akhḍar *Si. Arabia* 28°4N 37°9E **46 E3**
Qal'at Dīzah *Iraq* 36°11N 45°7E **46 B5**
Qal'at Şālih *Iraq* 31°31N 47°16E **46 D5**
Qal'at Sukkar *Iraq* 31°51N 46°5E **46 D5**
Qamani'tuaq = Baker Lake
Canada 64°20N 96°3W **68 E12**
Qamdo *China* 31°15N 97°6E **34 B1**
Qamea *Fiji* 16°45S 179°45W **59 a**
Qamruddin Karez
Pakistan 31°45N 68°20E **42 D3**
Qandahār = Kandahār
Afghan. 31°32N 65°43E **40 D4**
Qandahār = Kandahār □
Afghan. 31°0N 65°0E **40 D4**
Qandyaghash
Kazakhstan 49°28N 57°25E **19 E10**
Qapān *Iran* 37°40N 55°47E **47 B7**
Qapshaghay *Kazakhstan* 43°51N 77°14E **26 E8**
Qara Qash → *China* 35°0N 78°30E **43 B8**
Qaraghandy *Kazakhstan* 49°50N 73°10E **30 B3**
Qaraghayly *Kazakhstan* 49°26N 76°0E **26 E8**
Qārah *Si. Arabia* 29°55N 40°3E **46 D4**
Qaratau *Ongtüstik Qazaqstan,
Kazakhstan* 43°30N 69°30E **26 E7**
Qarataū *Zhambyl,
Kazakhstan* 43°10N 70°28E **26 E8**
Qarazhal *Kazakhstan* 48°12N 70°49E **26 E8**
Qarchak *Iran* 35°25N 51°34E **47 C6**
Qardho *Somalia* 9°30N 49°6E **49 F4**
Qareh → *Iran* 39°25N 47°22E **46 B5**
Qareh Tekān *Iran* 36°38N 49°29E **47 B6**
Qarnein *U.A.E.* 24°56N 52°52E **47 E7**
Qarqan He → *China* 39°30N 88°30E **30 D6**
Qarqaraly *Kazakhstan* 49°26N 75°30E **30 B4**
Qarshi *Uzbekistan* 38°53N 65°48E **26 F7**
Qartabā *Lebanon* 34°4N 35°50E **48 A4**

Qārūh *Kuwait* 28°49N 48°46E **47 D6**
Qaryat al Gharab *Iraq* 31°27N 44°48E **46 D5**
Qaryat al 'Ulyā *Si. Arabia* 27°33N 47°42E **46 E5**
Qasr 'Amra *Jordan* 31°48N 36°35E **46 D3**
Qaşr-e Qand *Iran* 26°15N 60°45E **47 E9**
Qaşr-e Shīrīn *Iran* 34°31N 45°35E **46 C5**
Qasr Farâfra *Egypt* 27°0N 28°1E **53 C11**
Qasurittuq = Resolute
Canada 74°42N 94°54W **69 C13**
Qatanā *Syria* 33°26N 36°4E **48 B5**
Qatar ■ *Asia* 25°30N 51°15E **47 E6**
Qatlish *Iran* 37°50N 57°19E **47 B8**
Qattâra, Munkhafed el
Egypt 29°30N 27°30E **53 C11**
Qattâra Depression = Qattâra,
Munkhafed el *Egypt* 29°30N 27°30E **53 C11**
Qawām al Ḥamzah = Al Ḥamzah
Iraq 31°43N 44°58E **46 D5**
Qāyen *Iran* 33°40N 59°10E **47 C8**
Qazaqstan = Kazakhstan ■
Asia 50°0N 70°0E **26 E8**
Qazimämmäd *Azerbaijan* 40°3N 49°0E **47 A6**
Qazvīn *Iran* 36°15N 50°0E **47 B6**
Qazvīn □ *Iran* 36°20N 50°0E **47 B6**
Qena *Egypt* 26°10N 32°43E **53 C12**
Qeqertarsuaq *Greenland* 69°45N 53°30W **4 C5**
Qeqertarsuaq *Greenland* 69°15N 53°38W **4 C5**
Qeshlāq *Iran* 34°55N 46°28E **46 C5**
Qeshm *Iran* 26°55N 56°10E **47 E8**
Qeys *Iran* 26°32N 53°58E **47 E7**
Qezel Owzen → *Iran* 36°45N 49°22E **47 B6**
Qezi'ot *Israel* 30°52N 34°26E **48 E3**
Qi Xian *China* 34°40N 114°48E **32 G8**
Qian Gorlos *China* 45°5N 124°42E **33 B13**
Qian Hai *China* 22°32N 113°54E **31 a**
Qian Xian *China* 34°31N 108°15E **32 G5**
Qian'an *China* 40°0N 118°41E **33 E10**
Qiancheng *China* 27°12N 109°50E **34 D7**
Qianjiang *Guangxi Zhuangzu,
China* 23°38N 108°58E **34 F7**
Qianjiang *Hubei, China* 30°24N 112°55E **35 B9**
Qianjiang *Sichuan, China* 29°33N 108°41E **34 C7**
Qianjin *China* 47°34N 133°4E **31 B15**
Qianshan *Anhui, China* 30°37N 116°35E **35 B11**
Qianshan *Guangdong,
China* 22°15N 113°31E **31 a**
Qianwei *China* 29°13N 103°56E **34 C4**
Qianxi *China* 27°3N 106°3E **34 D6**
Qianyang *Hunan, China* 27°18N 110°10E **35 D8**
Qianyang *Shaanxi, China* 34°40N 107°8E **32 G4**
Qianyang *Zhejiang,
China* 30°11N 119°25E **35 B12**
Qi'ao *China* 22°25N 113°39E **31 a**
Qi'ao Dao *China* 22°25N 113°38E **31 a**
Qiaocun *China* 39°56N 112°58E **32 E7**
Qiaojia *China* 26°56N 102°58E **34 D4**
Qichun *China* 30°18N 115°25E **35 B10**
Qidong *Hunan, China* 26°49N 112°7E **35 D9**
Qidong *Jiangsu, China* 31°48N 121°38E **35 B13**
Qiemo *China* 38°8N 85°32E **30 D6**
Qijiang *China* 28°57N 106°35E **34 C6**
Qijiaojing *China* 43°28N 91°36E **30 C6**
Qikiqtarjuaq *Canada* 67°33N 63°0W **69 D19**
Qila Saifullāh *Pakistan* 30°45N 68°17E **42 D3**
Qilian Shan *China* 38°30N 96°0E **30 D8**
Qimen *China* 29°50N 117°42E **35 C11**
Qin He → *China* 35°1N 113°22E **32 G7**
Qin Jiang → *Guangxi Zhuangzu,
China* 21°53N 108°35E **34 F7**
Qin Jiang → *Jiangxi,
China* 26°15N 115°55E **35 D10**
Qin Ling = Qinling Shandi
China 33°50N 108°10E **32 H5**
Qin'an *China* 34°48N 105°40E **32 G3**
Qing Xian *China* 38°35N 116°45E **32 E9**
Qingcheng *China* 37°15N 117°40E **33 F9**
Qingcheng Shan *China* 30°58N 103°31E **34 B4**
Qingchuan *China* 32°36N 105°9E **32 H3**
Qingdao *China* 36°5N 120°20E **33 F11**
Qingfeng *China* 35°52N 115°8E **32 G8**
Qinghai □ *China* 36°0N 98°0E **30 D8**
Qinghai Hu *China* 36°40N 100°10E **30 D9**
Qinghecheng *China* 41°28N 124°15E **33 D13**
Qinghemen *China* 41°48N 121°25E **33 D11**
Qingjian *China* 37°8N 110°8E **32 F6**
Qingjiang = Huaiyin
China 33°30N 119°2E **33 H10**
Qingliu *China* 26°11N 116°48E **35 D11**
Qinglong *China* 25°49N 105°12E **34 E5**
Qingping *China* 26°39N 107°47E **34 D6**
Qingshui *China* 34°48N 106°8E **32 G4**
Qingshuihe *China* 39°55N 111°35E **32 E6**
Qingtian *China* 28°1N 120°15E **35 C13**
Qingtongxia *China* 38°2N 106°3E **32 E4**
Qingtongxia Shuiku
China 37°50N 105°58E **32 F3**
Qingxi *China* 27°8N 108°43E **34 D7**
Qingxu *China* 37°34N 112°22E **32 F7**
Qingyang *Anhui, China* 30°38N 117°50E **35 B11**
Qingyang *Gansu, China* 36°2N 107°55E **32 F4**
Qingyi Jiang → *China* 29°32N 103°44E **34 C4**
Qingyuan *Guangdong,
China* 23°40N 112°59E **35 F9**
Qingyuan *Liaoning,
China* 42°10N 124°55E **33 C13**
Qingyun *China* 37°45N 117°20E **33 F9**
Qingzhen *China* 26°31N 106°25E **34 D6**
Qinhuangdao *China* 39°56N 119°30E **33 E10**
Qinling Shandi *China* 33°50N 108°10E **32 H5**
Qinshui *China* 35°40N 112°8E **32 G7**
Qinyang = Jiyuan *China* 35°7N 112°57E **32 G7**
Qinyuan *China* 36°29N 112°20E **32 F7**
Qinzhou *China* 21°58N 108°38E **34 F7**
Qionghai *China* 19°15N 110°26E **38 C8**
Qiongshan *China* 19°51N 110°26E **38 C8**
Qiongzhou Haixia *China* 20°10N 110°15E **38 B8**
Qiqihar *China* 47°26N 124°0E **31 B13**
Qira *China* 37°0N 80°48E **30 D5**
Qiraïya, W. → *Egypt* 30°27N 34°0E **48 E3**
Qiryat Ata *Israel* 32°47N 35°6E **48 C4**
Qiryat Gat *Israel* 31°32N 34°46E **48 D3**
Qiryat Mal'akhi *Israel* 31°44N 34°44E **48 D3**
Qiryat Shemona *Israel* 33°13N 35°35E **48 B4**
Qiryat Yam *Israel* 32°51N 35°4E **48 C4**
Qishan *China* 34°25N 107°38E **32 G4**
Qitai *China* 44°2N 89°35E **30 C6**
Qitaihe *China* 45°48N 130°51E **28 B5**
Qiubei *China* 24°2N 104°12E **34 E5**
Qixia *China* 37°17N 120°52E **33 F11**
Qiyang *China* 26°35N 111°50E **35 D8**
Qızılağac Körfäzi *Azerbaijan* 39°9N 49°0E **47 B6**
Qods *Iran* 35°45N 51°15E **47 C6**
Qojūr *Iran* 36°12N 47°55E **46 B5**
Qom *Iran* 34°40N 51°0E **47 C6**
Qom □ *Iran* 34°40N 51°0E **47 C6**
Qomolangma Feng = Everest, Mt.
Nepal 28°5N 86°58E **43 E12**
Qomsheh *Iran* 32°0N 51°55E **47 C6**
Qoqek = Tacheng *China* 46°40N 82°58E **30 B5**
Qoqon = Qŭqon
Uzbekistan 40°31N 70°56E **26 E8**
Qoraqalpoghistan □
Uzbekistan 43°0N 58°0E **26 E6**
Qorveh *Iran* 35°10N 47°48E **46 C5**
Qosshaghyl *Kazakhstan* 46°40N 54°0E **19 E9**
Qostanay *Kazakhstan* 53°10N 63°35E **26 D7**
Qu Jiang → *China* 30°1N 106°24E **34 B6**
Qu Xian *China* 30°48N 106°58E **34 B6**
Quabbin Res. *U.S.A.* 42°20N 72°20W **83 D12**
Quairading *Australia* 32°0S 117°21E **61 F2**
Quakertown *U.S.A.* 40°26N 75°21W **83 F9**
Qualicum Beach
Canada 49°22N 124°26W **70 D4**
Quambatook *Australia* 35°49S 143°34E **63 F3**
Quambone *Australia* 30°57S 147°53E **63 E4**
Quamby *Australia* 20°22S 140°17E **62 C3**
Quan Long = Ca Mau
Vietnam 9°7N 105°8E **39 H5**
Quanah *U.S.A.* 34°18N 99°44W **84 D5**
Quang Ngai *Vietnam* 15°13N 108°58E **38 E7**
Quang Tri *Vietnam* 16°45N 107°13E **38 D6**
Quang Yen *Vietnam* 20°56N 106°52E **34 G6**
Quannan *China* 24°45N 114°33E **35 E10**
Quantico *U.S.A.* 38°31N 77°17W **81 F15**
Quantock Hills *U.K.* 51°8N 3°10W **13 F4**
Quanyang *China* 42°21N 127°32E **33 C14**
Quanzhou *Fujian, China* 24°55N 118°34E **35 E12**
Quanzhou *Guangxi Zhuangzu,
China* 25°57N 111°5E **35 E8**
Qu'Appelle → *Canada* 50°33N 103°53W **71 C8**
Quaqtaq *Canada* 60°55N 69°40W **69 E18**
Quarai *Brazil* 30°15S 56°20W **94 C4**
Quartu Sant'Élena *Italy* 39°15N 9°10E **22 E3**
Quartzsite *U.S.A.* 33°40N 114°13W **79 M12**
Quatre Bornes *Mauritius* 20°15S 57°28E **55 d**
Quatsino Sd. *Canada* 50°25N 127°58W **70 C3**
Quba *Azerbaijan* 41°21N 48°32E **19 F8**
Qūchān *Iran* 37°10N 58°27E **47 B8**
Queanbeyan *Australia* 35°17S 149°14E **63 F4**
Québec *Canada* 46°52N 71°13W **73 C5**
Québec □ *Canada* 48°0N 74°0W **73 B6**
Quebrada del Condorito △
Argentina 31°49S 64°40W **94 C3**
Queen Alexandra Ra.
Antarctica 85°0S 170°0E **5 E11**
Queen Charlotte City
Canada 53°15N 132°2W **70 C2**
Queen Charlotte Is. = Haida Gwaii
Canada 53°20N 132°10W **70 C2**
Queen Charlotte Sd.
Canada 51°0N 128°0W **70 C3**
Queen Charlotte Strait
Canada 50°45N 127°10W **70 C3**
Queen Elizabeth Is.
Canada 76°0N 95°0W **69 B13**
Queen Mary Land *Antarctica* 70°0S 95°0E **5 D7**
Queen Maud G.
Canada 68°15N 102°30W **68 D11**
Queen Maud Land = Dronning
Maud Land *Antarctica* 72°30S 12°0E **5 D3**
Queen Maud Mts.
Antarctica 86°0S 160°0W **5 E12**
Queens Channel *Australia* 15°0S 129°30E **60 C4**
Queenscliff *Australia* 38°16S 144°39E **63 F3**
Queensland □ *Australia* 22°0S 142°0E **62 C3**
Queenstown *Australia* 42°4S 145°35E **63 G4**
Queenstown *N.Z.* 45°1S 168°40E **59 F2**
Queenstown *S. Africa* 31°52S 26°52E **56 D4**
Queets *U.S.A.* 47°32N 124°19W **78 C2**
Queguay Grande →
Uruguay 32°9S 58°9W **94 C4**
Queimadas *Brazil* 11°0S 39°38W **93 F11**
Quelimane *Mozam.* 17°53S 36°58E **55 H7**
Quellón *Chile* 43°7S 73°37W **96 E2**
Quelpart = Jeju-do
S. Korea 33°29N 126°34E **33 H14**
Quemado *N. Mex.,
U.S.A.* 34°20N 108°30W **77 J9**
Quemado *Tex., U.S.A.* 28°56N 100°37W **84 G4**
Quemoy = Chinmen
Taiwan 24°26N 118°19E **35 E13**
Quemú-Quemú *Argentina* 36°3S 63°36W **94 D3**
Quepem *India* 15°13N 74°3E **45 G2**
Quequén *Argentina* 38°30S 58°30W **94 D4**
Querétaro *Mexico* 20°36N 100°23W **86 C4**
Querétaro □ *Mexico* 21°0N 99°55W **86 C5**
Queshan *China* 32°55N 114°2E **35 A10**
Quesnel *Canada* 53°0N 122°30W **70 C4**
Quesnel → *Canada* 52°58N 122°29W **70 C4**
Quesnel L. *Canada* 52°30N 121°20W **70 C4**
Questa *U.S.A.* 36°42N 105°36W **77 H11**
Quetico △ *Canada* 48°30N 91°45W **72 C1**
Quetta *Pakistan* 30°15N 66°55E **42 D2**
Quetzaltenango
Guatemala 14°50N 91°30W **88 D1**

Qufar *Si. Arabia* 27°26N 41°37E **46** E4
Qufu *China* 35°36N 116°58E **32** G9
Qui Nhon *Vietnam* 13°40N 109°13E **38** F7
Quibala *Angola* 10°46S 14°59E **54** G2
Quibaxe *Angola* 8°24S 14°27E **54** F2
Quibdó *Colombia* 5°42N 76°40W **92** B3
Quiberon *France* 47°29N 3°9W **20** C2
Quiet L. *Canada* 61°5N 133°5W **70** A2
Quiindy *Paraguay* 25°58S 57°14W **94** B4
Quilá *Mexico* 24°23N 107°13W **86** C3
Quilcene *U.S.A.* 43°15S 74°30W **94** F2
Quilcene *U.S.A.* 47°49N 122°53W **78** C4
Quilimarí *Chile* 32°5S 71°30W **94** C1
Quilino *Argentina* 30°14S 64°29W **94** C3
Quillabamba *Peru* 12°50S 72°50W **92** F4
Quillagua *Chile* 21°40S 69°40W **94** A2
Quillota *Chile* 32°54S 71°16W **94** C1
Quilmes *Argentina* 34°43S 58°15W **94** C4
Quilon = Kollam *India* 8°50N 76°38E **45** K3
Quilpie *Australia* 26°35S 144°11E **63** D3
Quilpué *Chile* 33°5S 71°33W **94** C1
Quimilí *Argentina* 27°40S 62°30W **94** B3
Quimper *France* 48°0N 4°9W **20** B1
Quimperlé *France* 47°53N 3°33W **20** C2
Quinault → *U.S.A.* 47°21N 124°18W **78** C2
Quincy *Calif., U.S.A.* 39°56N 120°57W **78** F6
Quincy *Fla., U.S.A.* 30°35N 84°34W **85** F3
Quincy *Ill., U.S.A.* 39°56N 91°23W **80** F8
Quincy *Wash., U.S.A.* 47°14N 119°51W **76** C4
Quines *Argentina* 32°13S 65°48W **94** C2
Quintana Roo □ *Mexico* 19°40N 88°30W **87** D7
Quintanar de la Orden
    Spain 39°36N 3°5W **21** C4
Quintero *Chile* 32°45S 71°30W **94** C1
Quirihue *Chile* 36°15S 72°35W **94** D1
Quirindi *Australia* 31°28S 150°40E **63** E5
Quirinópolis *Brazil* 18°32S 50°30W **93** G8
Quissanga *Mozam.* 12°24S 40°28E **55** G8
Quissico *Mozam.* 24°42S 34°44E **57** B5
Quitilipi *Argentina* 26°50S 60°13W **94** B3
Quitman *U.S.A.* 30°47N 83°34W **85** F13
Quito *Ecuador* 0°15S 78°35W **92** D3
Quixadá *Brazil* 4°55S 39°0W **93** D11
Qujing *China* 25°32N 103°41E **34** E4
Qulan *Kazakhstan* 42°55N 72°43E **26** E8
Qul'ān, Jazā'ir *Egypt* 24°22N 35°31E **46** E2
Qulsary *Kazakhstan* 46°59N 54°1E **19** E9
Qumbu *S. Africa* 31°10S 28°48E **57** D4
Quneitra = Al Qunayţirah
    Syria 33°5N 35°45E **48** B4
Qŭnghirot *Uzbekistan* 43°2N 58°50E **26** E6
Qu'nyido *China* 31°15N 98°6E **34** B2
Quoin I. *Australia* 14°54S 129°32E **60** B4
Quoin Pt. *S. Africa* 34°46S 19°37E **56** E2
Quorn *Australia* 32°25S 138°5E **63** E2
Qŭqon *Uzbekistan* 40°31N 70°56E **26** E8
Qurnat as Sawdā' *Lebanon* 34°18N 36°6E **48** A5
Quşaybā' *Si. Arabia* 26°53N 43°35E **46** E4
Quşaybah *Iraq* 34°24N 40°59E **46** C4
Quseir *Egypt* 26°7N 34°16E **46** E2
Quseir Amra = Qasr 'Amra
    Jordan 31°48N 36°35E **46** D3
Qūshchī *Iran* 37°59N 45°3E **46** B5
Qutang Gorge = Qutang Xia
    China 31°0N 109°40E **34** B7
Qutang Xia *China* 31°0N 109°40E **34** B7
Quthing *Lesotho* 30°25S 27°36E **57** E4
Qūţīābād *Iran* 35°47N 48°30E **47** C6
Quttinirpaaq △ *Canada* 82°13N 72°13W **69** A17
Quwo *China* 35°38N 111°25E **32** G6
Quyang *China* 38°35N 114°40E **32** E8
Quynh Nhai *Vietnam* 21°49N 103°33E **38** B4
Quyon *Canada* 45°31N 76°14W **83** A8
Quzhou *China* 28°57N 118°54E **35** C12
Quzi *China* 36°20N 107°20E **32** F4
Qyzylorda *Kazakhstan* 44°48N 65°28E **26** E7

R

Ra, Ko *Thailand* 9°13N 98°16E **39** H2
Raahe *Finland* 64°40N 24°28E **8** D21
Raalte *Neths.* 52°23N 6°16E **15** B6
Raasay *U.K.* 57°25N 6°4W **11** D2
Raasay, Sd. of *U.K.* 57°30N 6°8W **11** D2
Raasepori *Finland* 60°0N 23°26E **9** G20
Rába → *Hungary* 47°38N 17°38E **17** E9
Rabat *Malta* 35°53N 14°24E **22** G6
Rabat *Morocco* 34°2N 6°48W **52** B4
Rabaul *Papua N. G.* 4°24S 152°18E **58** B8
Rabbit Flat *Australia* 20°11S 130°1E **60** D5
Rabbit Lake Mine *Canada* 58°4N 104°1W **71** B8
Rabi *Fiji* 16°30S 179°59W **59** a
Rābigh *Si. Arabia* 22°50N 39°5E **49** C2
Râbniţa *Moldova* 47°45N 29°0E **17** E15
Rābor *Iran* 29°17N 56°55E **47** D8
Rabwah = Chenab Nagar
    Pakistan 31°45N 72°55E **42** D5
Race, C. *Canada* 46°40N 53°5W **73** C9
Rach Gia *Vietnam* 10°5N 105°5E **39** G5
Rach Soi *Vietnam* 9°57N 105°7E **39** H5
Racha Noi, Ko *Thailand* 7°30N 98°19E **39** J2
Racha Yai, Ko *Thailand* 7°36N 98°21E **39** J2
Rachid *Mauritania* 18°45N 11°35W **52** E3
Racibórz *Poland* 50°7N 18°18E **17** C10
Racine *U.S.A.* 42°44N 87°47W **80** D10
Rackerby *U.S.A.* 39°26N 121°22W **78** F5
Rădăuţi *Romania* 47°50N 25°59E **17** E13
Radcliff *U.S.A.* 37°51N 85°57W **81** G11
Radcliff *U.S.A.* 50°25N 24°32E **17** C13
Radekhiv *Ukraine* 50°25N 24°32E **17** C13
Radekhov = Radekhiv
    Ukraine 50°25N 24°32E **17** C13
Radford *U.S.A.* 37°8N 80°34W **81** G13
Radhanpur *India* 23°50N 71°38E **42** H4
Radhwa, Jabal *Si. Arabia* 24°34N 38°18E **46** E3
Radisson *Qué., Canada* 53°47N 77°37W **72** B4
Radisson *Sask., Canada* 52°30N 107°20W **71** C7
Radium Hot Springs
    Canada 50°35N 116°2W **70** C5

Radnor Forest *U.K.* 52°17N 3°10W **13** E4
Radom *Poland* 51°23N 21°12E **17** C11
Radomsko *Poland* 51°5N 19°28E **17** C10
Radomyshl *Ukraine* 50°30N 29°12E **17** C15
Radstock, C. *Australia* 33°12S 134°20E **63** E1
Raduzhnyy *Russia* 62°5N 77°28E **26** C8
Radviliškis *Lithuania* 55°49N 23°33E **9** J20
Radville *Canada* 49°30N 104°15W **71** D8
Rae *Canada* 62°50N 116°3W **70** A5
Rae Bareli *India* 26°18N 81°20E **43** F9
Rae Isthmus *Canada* 66°40N 87°30W **69** D14
Raeren *Belgium* 50°41N 6°7E **15** D6
Raeside, L. *Australia* 29°20S 122°0E **61** E3
Raetihi *N.Z.* 39°25S 175°17E **59** C5
Rafaela *Argentina* 31°10S 61°30W **94** C3
Rafah *Gaza Strip* 31°18N 34°14E **48** D3
Rafhā *Si. Arabia* 29°35N 43°35E **46** D4
Rafsanjān *Iran* 30°30N 56°5E **47** D8
Raft Pt. *Australia* 16°4S 124°26E **60** C3
Râga *South Sudan* 8°28N 25°41E **53** G11
Ragachow *Belarus* 53°8N 30°5E **17** B16
Ragama *Sri Lanka* 7°0N 79°50E **40** R11
Ragged, Mt. *Australia* 33°27S 123°25E **61** F3
Ragged Pt. *Barbados* 13°10N 59°26W **89** g
Raghunathpalli *India* 22°14N 84°48E **43** H11
Raghunathpur *India* 23°33N 86°40E **43** H12
Raglan *N.Z.* 37°55S 174°55E **59** B5
Ragusa *Italy* 36°55N 14°44E **22** F6
Raha *Indonesia* 4°55S 123°0E **37** E6
Rahaeng = Tak *Thailand* 16°52N 99°8E **38** D2
Rahat *Israel* 31°24N 34°45E **48** D3
Rahatgarh *India* 23°47N 78°22E **43** H8
Rahimyar Khan *Pakistan* 28°30N 70°25E **42** E4
Rāhjerd *Iran* 34°22N 50°22E **47** C6
Rahon *India* 31°3N 76°7E **42** D7
Rahuri *India* 19°23N 74°39E **44** E2
Rai, Hon *Vietnam* 9°48N 104°38E **39** H5
Raiatéa, Î.
    French Polynesia 16°50S 151°25W **65** J12
Raichur *India* 16°10N 77°20E **45** L10
Raiganj *India* 25°37N 88°10E **43** G13
Raigarh *India* 21°56N 83°25E **44** D6
Raighar *India* 19°51N 82°6E **44** E6
Raijua *Indonesia* 10°37S 121°36E **37** F6
Raikot *India* 30°41N 75°42E **42** D6
Railton *Australia* 41°25S 146°28E **63** G4
Rainbow Bridge △
    U.S.A. 37°5N 110°58W **77** H8
Rainbow Lake *Canada* 58°30N 119°23W **70** B5
Rainier *U.S.A.* 46°53N 122°41W **78** D4
Rainier, Mt. *U.S.A.* 46°52N 121°46W **78** D5
Rainy L. *Canada* 48°42N 93°10W **71** D10
Rainy River *Canada* 48°43N 94°29W **71** D10
Raippaluoto *Finland* 63°13N 21°14E **8** E19
Raipur *India* 21°17N 81°45E **44** D5
Rairakhol *India* 21°4N 84°21E **44** D7
Raisen *India* 23°20N 77°48E **42** H8
Raisio *Finland* 60°28N 22°11E **9** F20
Raj Nandgaon *India* 21°5N 81°5E **44** D5
Raj Nilgiri *India* 21°28N 86°46E **43** J12
Raja, Ujung *Indonesia* 3°40N 96°25E **36** D1
Raja Ampat, Kepulauan
    Indonesia 0°30S 130°0E **37** E8
Rajahmundry *India* 17°1N 81°48E **44** F5
Rajaji △ *India* 30°10N 78°20E **42** D8
Rajampet *India* 14°11N 79°10E **45** G4
Rajang → *Malaysia* 2°30N 112°0E **36** D4
Rajanpur *Pakistan* 29°6N 70°19E **42** E4
Rajapalaiyam *India* 9°25N 77°35E **45** K3
Rajapur *India* 16°40N 73°31E **44** F1
Rajasthan □ *India* 26°45N 73°30E **42** F5
Rajasthan Canal = Indira Gandhi
    Canal *India* 28°0N 72°0E **42** F5
Rajauri *India* 33°25N 74°21E **43** C6
Rajendranagar *India* 17°18N 78°27E **44** F4
Rajgarh *Mad. P., India* 24°2N 76°45E **42** G7
Rajgarh *Raj., India* 27°14N 76°38E **42** F7
Rajgarh *Raj., India* 28°40N 75°25E **42** E6
Rajghat Dam *India* 24°45N 78°20E **44** B4
Rajgir *India* 25°2N 85°25E **43** G11
Rajim *India* 20°58N 81°53E **44** D5
Rajkot *India* 22°15N 70°56E **42** H4
Rajmahal Hills *India* 24°30N 87°30E **43** G12
Rajpipla *India* 21°50N 73°30E **44** D1
Rajpur *India* 22°18N 74°21E **42** H6
Rajpura *India* 30°25N 76°32E **42** D7
Rajsamand = Kankroli
    India 25°4N 73°53E **42** G5
Rajshahi *Bangla.* 24°22N 88°39E **41** G16
Rajshahi □ *Bangla.* 25°0N 89°0E **43** G13
Rajula *India* 21°3N 71°26E **42** J4
Rajur *India* 20°7N 78°58E **44** D4
Rajura *India* 19°47N 79°22E **44** E4
Rakaia *N.Z.* 43°45S 172°1E **59** E4
Rakaia → *N.Z.* 43°36S 172°15E **59** E4
Rakan, Ra's *Qatar* 26°10N 51°20E **47** E6
Rakaposhi *Pakistan* 36°10N 74°25E **43** A6
Rakata, Pulau *Indonesia* 6°10S 105°20E **37** G11
Rakhine □ *Burma* 19°0N 94°15E **41** K18
Rakhiv *Ukraine* 48°3N 24°12E **17** D13
Rakhni *Pakistan* 30°4N 69°56E **42** D3
Rakhni → *Pakistan* 29°31N 69°36E **42** E3
Rakiraki *Fiji* 17°22S 178°11E **59** a
Rakitnoye *Russia* 45°36N 134°17E **28** B7
Rakiura = Stewart I.
    N.Z. 46°58S 167°54E **59** G1
Rakops *Botswana* 21°1S 24°28E **56** B3
Rakvere *Estonia* 59°20N 26°25E **9** G22
Raleigh *U.S.A.* 35°47N 78°39W **85** D15
Ralik Chain *Pac. Oc.* 8°0N 168°0E **64** G8
Ralls *U.S.A.* 33°41N 101°24W **84** E4
Ralston *U.S.A.* 41°30N 76°57W **82** E8
Ram → *Canada* 62°1N 123°41W **70** A4
Rama *Nic.* 12°9N 84°15W **88** D3
Ramachandrapuram *India* 16°50N 82°4E **44** F6
Ramagiri Udayagiri *India* 19°8N 84°18E **44** E7
Ramagundam *India* 18°55N 79°15E **44** E4
Ramakona *India* 21°43N 78°50E **43** J8

Raman *Thailand* 6°29N 101°18E **39** J3
Ramanathapuram *India* 9°25N 78°55E **45** K4
Ramanujganj *India* 23°48N 83°42E **43** H10
Ramas C. *India* 15°5N 73°55E **45** G1
Ramat Gan *Israel* 32°4N 34°48E **48** C3
Ramatlhabama *S. Africa* 25°37S 25°33E **56** C4
Ramban *India* 33°14N 75°12E **43** C6
Rambi = Rabi *Fiji* 16°30S 179°59W **59** a
Rambipuji *Indonesia* 8°12S 113°37E **37** H15
Ramdurg *India* 15°58N 75°22E **45** G2
Rame Hd. *Australia* 37°47S 149°30E **63** F4
Ramechhap *Nepal* 27°25N 86°10E **43** F12
Rameswaram *India* 9°17N 79°18E **45** K4
Ramganga → *India* 27°5N 79°58E **43** F8
Ramgarh *Jharkhand,
    India* 23°40N 85°35E **43** H11
Ramgarh *Raj., India* 27°16N 75°14E **42** F6
Ramgarh *Raj., India* 27°30N 70°36E **42** F4
Rāmhormoz *Iran* 31°15N 49°35E **47** D6
Ramīān *Iran* 37°3N 55°16E **47** B7
Ramla *Israel* 31°55N 34°52E **48** D3
Ramnad = Ramanathapuram
    India 9°25N 78°55E **45** K4
Ramnagar *Jammu & Kashmir,
    India* 32°47N 75°18E **43** C6
Ramnagar *Uttarakhand,
    India* 29°24N 79°7E **43** E8
Râmnicu Sărat *Romania* 45°26N 27°3E **17** F14
Râmnicu Vâlcea *Romania* 45°9N 24°21E **17** F13
Ramona *U.S.A.* 33°2N 116°52W **79** M10
Ramore *Canada* 48°30N 80°25W **72** C3
Ramotswa *Botswana* 24°50S 25°52E **56** C4
Rampur *H.P., India* 31°26N 77°43E **42** D7
Rampur *Mad. P., India* 23°25N 73°53E **42** H5
Rampur *Odisha, India* 21°48N 83°58E **44** D6
Rampur *Ut. P., India* 28°50N 79°5E **43** E8
Rampur Hat *India* 24°10N 87°50E **43** G12
Rampura *India* 24°30N 75°27E **42** G6
Ramrama Tola *India* 21°52N 79°55E **43** J8
Ramree I. *Burma* 19°0N 93°40E **41** K19
Ramsar *Iran* 36°53N 50°41E **47** B6
Ramsey *I. of Man* 54°20N 4°22W **12** C3
Ramsey *U.S.A.* 41°4N 74°9W **83** E10
Ramsey L. *Canada* 47°13N 82°15W **72** C3
Ramsgate *U.K.* 51°20N 1°25E **13** F9
Ramtek *India* 21°20N 79°15E **44** D4
Rana Pratap Sagar Dam
    India 24°58N 75°38E **42** G6
Ranaghat *India* 23°15N 88°35E **43** H13
Ranahu *Pakistan* 25°55N 69°45E **42** G3
Ranau *Malaysia* 6°2N 116°40E **36** C5
Rancagua *Chile* 34°10S 70°50W **94** C1
Rancheria → *Canada* 60°13N 129°7W **70** A3
Ranchester *U.S.A.* 44°54N 107°10W **76** D10
Ranchi *India* 23°19N 85°27E **43** H11
Rancho Cordova *U.S.A.* 38°36N 121°18W **78** G5
Rancho Cucamonga
    U.S.A. 34°10N 117°30W **79** L9
Randalstown *U.K.* 54°45N 6°19W **10** B5
Rander *India* 21°14N 72°47E **44** D1
Randers *Denmark* 56°29N 10°1E **9** H14
Randfontein *S. Africa* 26°8S 27°45E **57** D4
Randle *U.S.A.* 46°32N 121°57W **78** D5
Randolph *Mass., U.S.A.* 42°10N 71°2W **83** D13
Randolph *N.Y., U.S.A.* 42°10N 78°59W **82** D6
Randolph *Utah, U.S.A.* 41°40N 111°11W **76** F8
Randolph *Vt., U.S.A.* 43°55N 72°40W **83** C12
Randsburg *U.S.A.* 35°22N 117°39W **79** K9
Råneälven → *Sweden* 65°50N 22°20E **8** D20
Rangae *Thailand* 6°19N 101°44E **39** J3
Rangaunu B. *N.Z.* 34°51S 173°15E **59** A4
Rangeley *U.S.A.* 44°58N 70°39W **83** B14
Rangeley L. *U.S.A.* 44°55N 70°43W **83** B14
Rangely *U.S.A.* 40°5N 108°48W **76** F9
Ranger *U.S.A.* 32°28N 98°41W **84** E5
Rangia *India* 26°28N 91°38E **41** F17
Rangiora *N.Z.* 43°19S 172°36E **59** E4
Rangitaiki → *N.Z.* 37°54S 176°49E **59** B6
Rangitata → *N.Z.* 43°45S 171°15E **59** E3
Rangitoto ke te tonga = D'Urville I.
    N.Z. 40°50S 173°55E **59** D4
Rangkasbitung
    Indonesia 6°21S 106°15E **37** G12
Rangoon *Burma* 16°45N 96°20E **41** L20
Rangpur *Bangla.* 25°42N 89°22E **41** G16
Rangsang *Indonesia* 1°20N 103°5E **39** M4
Ranibennur *India* 14°35N 75°30E **45** G2
Raniganj *Paschimbanga,
    India* 23°40N 87°5E **41** H15
Raniganj *Ut. P., India* 27°3N 82°13E **43** F9
Ranikhet *India* 29°39N 79°25E **43** E8
Ranippettai *India* 12°56N 79°23E **45** H4
Raniwara *India* 24°50N 72°10E **42** G5
Rāniyah *Iraq* 36°15N 44°53E **46** B5
Ranka *India* 23°59N 83°47E **43** H10
Ranken → *Australia* 20°31S 137°36E **62** C2
Rankin *U.S.A.* 31°13N 101°56W **84** F4
Rankin Inlet *Canada* 62°30N 93°0W **68** E13
Rankins Springs
    Australia 33°49S 146°14E **63** E4
Rannoch, L. *U.K.* 56°38N 4°48W **11** E4
Rannoch Moor *U.K.* 56°38N 4°48W **11** E4
Ranohira *Madag.* 22°29S 45°24E **55** J9
Ranong *Thailand* 9°56N 98°40E **39** H2
Ranpur *India* 20°5N 85°20E **44** D7
Rānsa *Iran* 33°39N 48°18E **47** C6
Ransiki *Indonesia* 1°30S 134°10E **37** E8
Rantau Abang *Malaysia* 4°52N 103°24E **39** K4
Rantauprapat *Indonesia* 2°15N 99°50E **36** D1
Rantemario *Indonesia* 3°15S 119°57E **37** E5
Ranthambore △ *India* 26°0N 76°30E **42** F7
Rantoul *U.S.A.* 40°19N 88°9W **80** E9
Raohe *China* 46°47N 134°0E **28** A7
Raoping *China* 23°42N 117°1E **35** F11
Raoyang *China* 38°15N 115°45E **32** E8
Rap, Ko *Thailand* 9°19N 99°58E **39** b

Rapa *French Polynesia* 27°35S 144°20W **65** K13
Rapa Nui = Pascua, I. de
    Chile 27°7S 109°23W **65** K17
Rapallo *Italy* 44°21N 9°14E **20** D8
Rapar *India* 23°34N 70°38E **42** H4
Rāpch *Iran* 25°40N 59°15E **47** E8
Rapel, Lago *Chile* 34°20S 71°14W **94** C1
Rapid City *U.S.A.* 44°5N 103°14W **80** C2
Rapid River *U.S.A.* 45°55N 86°58W **80** C10
Rapla *Estonia* 59°1N 24°52E **9** G21
Rapti → *India* 26°18N 83°41E **43** F10
Raquette → *U.S.A.* 45°0N 74°42W **83** B10
Raquette Lake *U.S.A.* 43°49N 74°40E **83** C10
Rara △ *Nepal* 29°30N 82°10E **43** E10
Rarotonga *Cook Is.* 21°30S 160°0W **65** K12
Ra's al 'Ayn *Syria* 36°45N 40°12E **46** B4
Ra's al Khaymah *U.A.E.* 25°50N 55°59E **47** E7
Ra's at Tib *Tunisia* 37°1N 11°2E **22** F4
Rasa, Pta. *Argentina* 36°20S 56°41W **94** D4
Raseiniai *Lithuania* 55°25N 23°5E **9** J20
Rashmi *India* 25°4N 74°22E **42** G6
Rasht *Iran* 37°20N 49°40E **47** B6
Rasi Salai *Thailand* 15°20N 104°9E **38** E5
Rasipuram *India* 11°30N 78°15E **45** J4
Raskot *Nepal* 29°14N 81°39E **43** E9
Rason L. *Australia* 28°45S 124°25E **61** E3
Rasra *India* 25°50N 83°50E **43** G10
Rasua Garhi *Nepal* 28°17N 85°23E **43** E11
Rasul *Pakistan* 32°42N 73°34E **42** C5
Rat → *Canada* 49°35N 97°10W **71** D9
Rat Buri = Ratchaburi
    Thailand 13°30N 99°54E **38** F2
Rat Islands *U.S.A.* 52°0N 178°0E **74** E3
Rat L. *Canada* 56°10N 99°40W **71** B9
Ratangarh *India* 28°5N 74°35E **42** E6
Raţāwī *Iraq* 30°38N 47°13E **46** D5
Ratchaburi *Thailand* 13°30N 99°54E **38** F2
Rath *India* 25°36N 79°37E **43** G8
Rath Luirc = Charleville
    Ireland 52°21N 8°40W **10** D3
Rathangan *Ireland* 53°14N 7°0W **10** C4
Rathdrum *Ireland* 52°56N 6°14W **10** D5
Rathenow *Germany* 52°37N 12°19E **16** B7
Rathkeale *Ireland* 52°32N 8°56W **10** D3
Rathlin I. *U.K.* 55°18N 6°14W **10** A5
Rathmelton *Ireland* 55°2N 7°39W **10** A4
Ratibor = Racibórz
    Poland 50°7N 18°18E **17** C10
Ratlam *India* 23°20N 75°0E **42** H6
Ratmanova Ostrov
    Russia 65°46N 169°6W **74** B6
Ratnagiri *India* 16°57N 73°18E **44** F1
Ratnapura *Sri Lanka* 6°40N 80°20E **45** L5
Ratodero *Pakistan* 27°48N 68°18E **42** F3
Raton *U.S.A.* 36°54N 104°24W **77** H11
Rattaphum *Thailand* 7°8N 100°16E **39** J3
Rattray Hd. *U.K.* 57°38N 1°50W **11** D7
Ratz, Mt. *Canada* 57°23N 132°12W **70** B2
Raub *Malaysia* 3°47N 101°52E **39** L3
Rauch *Argentina* 36°45S 59°5W **94** D4
Raudales *Mexico* 17°27N 93°39W **87** D6
Raufarhöfn *Iceland* 66°27N 15°57W **8** C6
Raufoss *Norway* 60°44N 10°37E **8** F14
Rauma *Finland* 61°10N 21°30E **8** F19
Raumo = Rauma *Finland* 61°10N 21°30E **8** F19
Raung, Gunung *Indonesia* 8°8S 114°3E **37** J17
Raurkela *India* 22°14N 84°50E **43** H11
Rausu-Dake *Japan* 44°4N 145°7E **28** B12
Rava-Ruska *Ukraine* 50°15N 23°42E **17** C12
Rava Russkaya = Rava-Ruska
    Ukraine 50°15N 23°42E **17** C12
Ravalli *U.S.A.* 47°17N 114°11W **76** C6
Ravānsar *Iran* 34°43N 46°40E **46** C5
Rāvar *Iran* 31°20N 56°51E **47** D8
Ravena *U.S.A.* 42°28N 73°49W **83** D11
Ravenna *Italy* 44°25N 12°12E **22** B5
Ravenna *Nebr., U.S.A.* 41°1N 98°55W **80** E4
Ravenna *Ohio, U.S.A.* 41°9N 81°15W **82** E3
Ravensburg *Germany* 47°46N 9°36E **16** E5
Ravenshoe *Australia* 17°37S 145°29E **62** B4
Ravensthorpe *Australia* 33°35S 120°2E **61** F3
Ravenswood *Australia* 20°6S 146°54E **62** C4
Ravenswood *U.S.A.* 38°57N 81°46W **81** F13
Raver *India* 21°15N 76°2E **44** D3
Ravi → *Pakistan* 30°35N 71°49E **42** D4
Rawalpindi *Pakistan* 33°38N 73°8E **42** C5
Rawang *Malaysia* 3°20N 101°35E **39** L3
Rawene *N.Z.* 35°25S 173°32E **59** A4
Rawi, Ko *Thailand* 6°33N 99°14E **39** J2
Rawlinna *Australia* 30°58S 125°28E **61** F4
Rawlins *U.S.A.* 41°47N 107°14W **76** F10
Rawlinson Ra. *Australia* 24°40S 128°30E **61** D4
Rawson *Argentina* 43°15S 65°5W **96** E3
Raxaul *India* 26°59N 84°51E **43** F11
Ray *U.S.A.* 48°21N 103°10W **80** A2
Ray, C. *Canada* 47°33N 59°15W **73** C8
Ray Mts. *U.S.A.* 66°0N 152°0W **74** B9
Raya Ring, Ko *Thailand* 7°30N 98°29E **39** a
Rayachoti *India* 14°4N 78°50E **45** G4
Rayadurg *India* 14°40N 76°50E **45** G3
Rayagada *India* 19°15N 83°20E **44** E6
Raychikhinsk *Russia* 49°46N 129°25E **27** E13
Rāyen *Iran* 29°34N 57°26E **47** D8
Rayleigh *U.K.* 51°36N 0°37E **13** F8
Raymond *Canada* 49°30N 112°35W **70** D6
Raymond *Calif., U.S.A.* 37°13N 119°54W **78** H7
Raymond *N.H., U.S.A.* 43°2N 71°11W **83** C13
Raymond *Wash., U.S.A.* 46°41N 123°44W **78** D3
Raymondville *U.S.A.* 26°29N 97°47W **84** H6
Raymore *Canada* 51°25N 104°31W **71** C8
Rayón *Mexico* 29°43N 110°35W **86** B2
Rayong *Thailand* 12°40N 101°20E **38** F3
Raystown L. *U.S.A.* 40°25N 78°5W **82** F6
Rayville *U.S.A.* 32°29N 91°46W **84** E9
Raz, Pte. du *France* 48°2N 4°47W **20** C1
Razan *Iran* 35°23N 49°2E **47** C6

Razāzah, Buḩayrat ar
    Iraq 32°40N 43°35E **46** C4
Razāzah, L. = Razāzah, Buḩayrat
    ar *Iraq* 32°40N 43°35E **46** C4
Razdel'naya = Rozdilna
    Ukraine 46°50N 30°2E **17** E16
Razdolnoye *Russia* 43°30N 131°52E **28** C5
Razeh *Iran* 32°47N 48°9E **47** C6
Razgrad *Bulgaria* 43°33N 26°34E **23** C12
Razim, Lacul *Romania* 44°50N 29°0E **17** F15
Razmak *Pakistan* 32°45N 69°50E **42** C3
Re, Cu Lao *Vietnam* 15°22N 109°8E **38** E7
Ré, Î. de *France* 46°12N 1°30W **20** C3
Reading *U.K.* 51°27N 0°58W **13** F7
Reading *U.S.A.* 40°20N 75°56W **83** F9
Reading □ *U.K.* 51°27N 0°58W **13** F7
Realicó *Argentina* 35°0S 64°15W **94** D3
Ream *Cambodia* 10°34N 103°39E **39** G4
Ream △ *Cambodia* 10°30N 103°45E **39** G4
Reay Forest *U.K.* 58°22N 4°55W **11** C4
Rebecca, L. *Australia* 30°0S 122°15E **61** F3
Rebi *Indonesia* 6°23S 134°7E **37** F8
Rebiana, Sahrâ' *Libya* 24°30N 21°0E **53** D10
Reboly *Russia* 63°49N 30°47E **8** E24
Rebun-Tō *Japan* 45°23N 141°2E **28** B10
Recherche, Arch. of the
    Australia 34°15S 122°50E **61** F3
Rechna Doab *Pakistan* 31°35N 73°30E **42** D5
Rechytsa *Belarus* 52°21N 30°24E **17** B16
Recife *Brazil* 8°0S 35°0W **93** E12
Recife *Seychelles* 4°36S 55°42E **55** b
Reckong Peo *India* 31°32N 78°16E **42** D8
Reconquista *Argentina* 29°10S 59°45W **94** B4
Recreo *Argentina* 29°25S 65°10W **94** B2
Red → *U.S.A.* 31°1N 91°45W **84** F9
Red Bank *U.S.A.* 40°21N 74°5W **83** F10
Red Bay *Canada* 51°44N 56°25W **73** B8
Red Bluff *U.S.A.* 40°11N 122°15W **76** F2
Red Bluff Res. *U.S.A.* 31°54N 103°55W **77** L12
Red Cliffs *Australia* 34°19S 142°11E **63** E3
Red Cloud *U.S.A.* 40°5N 98°32W **80** E4
Red Creek *U.S.A.* 43°14N 76°45W **83** C8
Red Deer *Canada* 52°20N 113°50W **70** C6
Red Deer → *Alta.,
    Canada* 50°58N 110°0W **71** C7
Red Deer → *Man.,
    Canada* 52°53N 101°1W **71** C8
Red Deer L. *Canada* 52°55N 101°20W **71** C8
Red Hook *U.S.A.* 41°55N 73°53W **83** E11
Red Indian L. *Canada* 48°35N 57°0W **73** C8
Red L. *Canada* 51°3N 93°49W **71** C10
Red Lake *Canada* 51°3N 93°49W **71** C10
Red Lake Falls *U.S.A.* 47°53N 96°16W **80** B5
Red Lake Road *U.S.A.* 49°59N 93°25W **71** C10
Red Lodge *U.S.A.* 45°11N 109°15W **76** D9
Red Mountain *U.S.A.* 35°37N 117°38W **79** K9
Red Oak *U.S.A.* 41°1N 95°14W **80** E6
Red River of the North →
    N. Amer. 49°0N 97°15W **80** A5
Red Rock *Canada* 48°55N 88°15W **72** C2
Red Rock, L. *U.S.A.* 41°22N 92°59W **80** E7
Red Rocks Pt. *Australia* 32°13S 127°32E **61** F4
Red Sea *Asia* 25°0N 36°0E **49** C2
Red Slate Mt. *U.S.A.* 37°31N 118°52W **78** H8
Red Sucker L. *Canada* 54°9N 93°40W **72** B1
Red Tower Pass = Turnu Roşu, P.
    Romania 45°33N 24°17E **17** F13
Red Wing *U.S.A.* 44°34N 92°31W **80** C7
Redang, Pulau *Malaysia* 5°49N 103°2E **39** K4
Redange *Lux.* 49°46N 5°52E **15** E5
Redcar *U.K.* 54°37N 1°4W **12** C6
Redcar & Cleveland □
    U.K. 54°29N 1°0W **12** C7
Redcliff *Canada* 50°10N 110°50W **76** A8
Redcliffe *Australia* 27°12S 153°6E **63** D5
Redcliffe, Mt. *Australia* 28°30S 121°30E **61** E3
Reddersburg *S. Africa* 29°41S 26°10E **56** D4
Redding *U.S.A.* 40°35N 122°24W **76** F2
Redditch *U.K.* 52°18N 1°55E **13** E6
Redfield *U.S.A.* 44°53N 98°31W **80** C4
Redford *U.S.A.* 44°38N 73°48W **83** B11
Redhead *Trin. & Tob.* 10°44N 60°58W **93** K16
Redlands *U.S.A.* 34°4N 117°11W **79** M9
Redmond *Oreg., U.S.A.* 44°17N 121°11W **76** D3
Redmond *Wash., U.S.A.* 47°40N 122°7W **78** C4
Redon *France* 47°40N 2°6W **20** C2
Redonda *Antigua & B.* 16°58N 62°19W **89** C7
Redondela *Spain* 42°15N 8°38W **21** A1
Redondo Beach *U.S.A.* 33°50N 118°23W **79** M8
Redoubt Volcano
    U.S.A. 60°29N 152°45W **74** C9
Redruth *U.K.* 50°14N 5°14W **13** G2
Redvers *Canada* 49°35N 101°40W **71** D8
Redwater *Canada* 53°55N 113°6W **70** C6
Redwood *U.S.A.* 44°18N 75°48W **83** B9
Redwood △ *U.S.A.* 41°40N 124°5W **76** F1
Redwood City *U.S.A.* 37°30N 122°15W **78** H4
Redwood Falls *U.S.A.* 44°32N 95°7W **80** C6
Ree, L. *Ireland* 53°35N 8°0W **10** C3
Reed City *U.S.A.* 43°53N 85°31W **81** D11
Reed L. *Canada* 54°38N 100°30W **71** C8
Reedley *U.S.A.* 36°36N 119°27W **78** J7
Reedsburg *U.S.A.* 43°32N 90°0W **80** D8
Reedsport *U.S.A.* 43°42N 124°6W **76** E1
Reedsville *U.S.A.* 40°39N 77°35W **82** F7
Reefton *N.Z.* 42°6S 171°51E **59** E3
Reese → *U.S.A.* 40°48N 117°4W **76** F5
Refugio *U.S.A.* 28°18N 97°17W **84** G6
Regensburg *Germany* 49°1N 12°6E **16** D7
Reggâne = Zaouiet Reggâne
    Algeria 26°32N 0°3E **52** C6
Réggio di Calábria *Italy* 38°6N 15°39E **22** E6
Réggio nell'Emília *Italy* 44°43N 10°36E **22** B4
Reghin *Romania* 46°46N 24°42E **17** E13
Regina *Canada* 50°27N 104°35W **71** C8
Regina Beach *Canada* 50°47N 105°0W **71** C8
Registro *Brazil* 24°29S 47°49W **95** A6
Rehar → *India* 23°55N 82°40E **43** H10

Rehli India 23°38N 79°5E 43 H8
Rehoboth Namibia 23°15S 17°4E 56 B2
Rehovot Israel 31°54N 34°48E 48 D3
Reichenbach Germany 50°37N 12°17E 16 C7
Reidsville U.S.A. 36°21N 79°40W 85 C15
Reigate U.K. 51°14N 0°12W 13 F7
Reims France 49°15N 4°1E 20 B6
Reina Adelaida, Arch.
  Chile 52°20S 74°0W 96 G2
Reindeer → Canada 55°36N 103°11W 71 B8
Reindeer I. Canada 52°30N 98°0W 71 C9
Reindeer L. Canada 57°15N 102°15W 71 B8
Reinga, C. N.Z. 34°25S 172°43E 59 A4
Reinosa Spain 43°2N 4°15W 21 A3
Reitz S. Africa 27°48S 28°29E 57 C4
Reivilo S. Africa 27°36S 24°8E 56 C3
Reliance Canada 63°0N 109°20W 71 A7
Remanso Brazil 9°41S 42°4W 93 E10
Remarkable, Mt.
  Australia 32°48S 138°10E 63 E2
Rembang Indonesia 6°42S 111°21E 37 G14
Remedios Panama 8°15N 81°50W 88 E3
Remeshk Iran 26°55N 58°50E 47 E8
Remich Lux. 49°32N 6°22E 15 E6
Ren Xian China 37°8N 114°40E 32 F8
Rendang Indonesia 8°26S 115°25E 37 J18
Rendsburg Germany 54°17N 9°39E 16 A5
Renfrew Canada 45°30N 76°40W 83 A8
Renfrewshire □ U.K. 55°49N 4°38W 11 F4
Rengat Indonesia 0°30S 102°45E 36 E2
Rengo Chile 34°24S 70°50W 94 C1
Renhua China 25°5N 113°40E 35 E9
Renhuai China 27°48N 106°24E 34 D6
Reni = Taranagar India 28°43N 74°50E 42 E6
Reni Ukraine 45°28N 28°15E 17 F15
Renigunta India 13°38N 79°30E 45 H4
Renmark Australia 34°11S 140°43E 63 E3
Rennell Sd. Canada 53°23N 132°35W 70 C2
Renner Springs Australia 18°20S 133°47E 62 B1
Rennes France 48°7N 1°41W 20 B3
Rennick Glacier
  Antarctica 70°30S 161°45E 5 D11
Rennie L. Canada 61°32N 105°35W 71 A7
Reno U.S.A. 39°31N 119°48W 78 F7
Reno → Italy 44°38N 12°16E 22 B5
Renovo U.S.A. 41°20N 77°45W 82 E7
Renqiu China 38°43N 116°5E 32 E9
Renshou China 29°59N 104°9E 34 C5
Rensselaer Ind., U.S.A. 40°57N 87°9W 80 E10
Rensselaer N.Y., U.S.A. 42°38N 73°45W 83 D11
Renton U.S.A. 47°28N 122°12W 78 C4
Renukoot India 24°12N 83°2E 43 G10
Reotipur India 25°33N 83°45E 43 G10
Repalle India 16°2N 80°45E 45 F5
Republic Mo., U.S.A. 37°7N 93°29W 80 G7
Republic Wash., U.S.A. 48°39N 118°44W 76 B4
Republican → U.S.A. 39°4N 96°48W 80 F5
Repulse B. Australia 20°35S 148°46E 62 b
Repulse Bay Canada 66°30N 86°30W 69 D14
Requena Peru 5°5S 73°52W 92 E4
Requena Spain 39°30N 1°4W 21 C5
Reserve U.S.A. 33°43N 108°45W 77 K9
Resht = Rasht Iran 37°20N 49°40E 47 B6
Resistencia Argentina 27°30S 59°0W 94 B4
Reşiţa Romania 45°18N 21°53E 17 F11
Reso = Raisio Finland 60°28N 22°11E 9 F20
Resolute Canada 74°42N 94°54W 69 C13
Resolution I. Canada 61°30N 65°0W 69 E19
Resolution I. N.Z. 45°40S 166°40E 59 F1
Ressano Garcia Mozam. 25°25S 32°0E 57 C5
Reston Canada 49°33N 101°6W 71 D8
Retalhuleu Guatemala 14°33N 91°46W 88 D1
Retford U.K. 53°19N 0°56W 12 D7
Rethimno Greece 35°18N 24°30E 23 G11
Reti Pakistan 28°5N 69°48E 42 E3
Réunion ☑ Ind. Oc. 21°0S 56°0E 55 c
Reus Spain 41°10N 1°5E 21 B6
Reutlingen Germany 48°29N 9°12E 16 D5
Reval = Tallinn Estonia 59°22N 24°48E 9 G21
Revda Russia 56°48N 59°57E 18 C10
Revelganj India 25°50N 84°40E 43 G11
Revelstoke Canada 51°0N 118°10W 70 C5
Reventazón Peru 6°10S 80°58W 92 E2
Revillagigedo, Is. de
  Pac. Oc. 18°40N 112°0W 86 D2
Rewa India 24°33N 81°25E 43 G9
Rewari India 28°15N 76°40E 42 E7
Rexburg U.S.A. 43°49N 111°47W 76 E8
Rey, I. del Panama 8°20N 78°30W 88 E4
Rey, L. del Mexico 27°1N 103°26W 86 B4
Rey Malabo Eq. Guin. 3°45N 8°50E 54 D1
Reyes, Pt. U.S.A. 38°0N 123°0W 78 H3
Reyðarfjörður Iceland 65°2N 14°13W 8 D6
Reykjahlíð Iceland 65°40N 16°55W 8 D5
Reykjanes Iceland 63°48N 22°40W 8 E2
Reykjavík Iceland 64°10N 21°57W 8 D3
Reynolds Ra. Australia 22°30S 133°0E 60 D5
Reynoldsville U.S.A. 41°6N 78°53W 82 E6
Reynosa Mexico 26°7N 98°18W 87 B5
Rēzekne Latvia 56°30N 27°17E 9 H22
Rezvan Iran 27°34N 56°6E 47 E8
Rhayader U.K. 52°18N 3°29W 13 E4
Rhein → Europe 51°52N 6°2E 15 C6
Rhein-Main-Donau-Kanal
  Germany 49°1N 11°27E 16 D6
Rheine Germany 52°17N 7°26E 16 B4
Rheinland-Pfalz □ Germany 50°0N 7°0E 16 C4
Rhin = Rhein → Europe 51°52N 6°2E 15 C6
Rhine = Rhein → Europe 51°52N 6°2E 15 C6
Rhinebeck U.S.A. 41°56N 73°55W 83 E11
Rhineland-Palatinate =
  Rheinland-Pfalz □
  Germany 50°0N 7°0E 16 C4
Rhinelander U.S.A. 45°38N 89°25W 80 C9
Rhinns Pt. U.K. 55°40N 6°29W 11 F2
Rhir, Cap Morocco 30°38N 9°54W 52 B4
Rhode Island □ U.S.A. 41°40N 71°30W 83 E13
Rhodes Greece 36°15N 28°10E 23 F13

Rhodope Mts. = Rhodopi Planina
  Bulgaria 41°40N 24°20E 23 D11
Rhodopi Planina
  Bulgaria 41°40N 24°20E 23 D11
Rhön Germany 50°24N 9°58E 16 C5
Rhondda U.K. 51°39N 3°31W 13 F4
Rhondda Cynon Taff □
  U.K. 51°42N 3°27W 13 F4
Rhône □ France 45°54N 4°35E 20 C6
Rhône → France 43°28N 4°42E 20 E6
Rhum = Rùm U.K. 57°0N 6°20W 11 E2
Rhydaman = Ammanford
  U.K. 51°48N 3°59W 13 F4
Rhyl U.K. 53°20N 3°29W 12 D4
Riachão Brazil 7°20S 46°37W 93 E9
Riang, Laem Thailand 8°7N 98°27E 39 a
Riasi India 33°10N 74°50E 43 C6
Riau □ Indonesia 0°0 102°35E 36 E2
Riau, Kepulauan □
  Indonesia 0°30N 104°20E 36 D2
Riau Arch. = Riau, Kepulauan □
  Indonesia 0°30N 104°20E 36 D2
Ribadeo Spain 43°35N 7°5W 21 A2
Ribas do Rio Pardo
  Brazil 20°27S 53°46W 93 H8
Ribble → U.K. 53°52N 2°25W 12 D5
Ribe Denmark 55°19N 8°44E 9 J13
Ribeira Grande C. Verde Is. 17°0N 25°4W 52 b
Ribeirão Prêto Brazil 21°10S 47°50W 95 A6
Riberalta Bolivia 11°0S 66°0W 92 F5
Riccarton N.Z. 43°32S 172°37E 59 E4
Rice U.S.A. 34°5N 114°51W 79 L12
Rice L. Canada 44°12N 78°10W 82 B6
Rice Lake U.S.A. 45°30N 91°44W 80 C8
Rich, C. Canada 44°43N 80°38W 82 B4
Richards Bay S. Africa 28°48S 32°6E 57 C5
Richardson → Canada 58°25N 111°14W 71 B6
Richardson Lakes
  U.S.A. 44°46N 70°58W 81 C18
Richardson Springs
  U.S.A. 39°51N 121°46W 78 F5
Riche, C. Australia 34°36S 118°47E 61 F2
Richey U.S.A. 47°39N 105°4W 76 C11
Richfield U.S.A. 38°46N 112°5W 76 G7
Richfield Springs U.S.A. 42°51N 74°59W 83 D10
Richford U.S.A. 45°0N 72°40W 83 B12
Richibucto Canada 46°42N 64°54W 73 C7
Richland Ga., U.S.A. 32°5N 84°40W 85 E12
Richland Wash., U.S.A. 46°17N 119°18W 76 C4
Richland Center U.S.A. 43°21N 90°23W 80 D8
Richlands U.S.A. 37°6N 81°48W 81 G13
Richmond Australia 20°43S 143°8E 62 C3
Richmond N.Z. 41°20S 173°12E 59 D4
Richmond U.K. 54°25N 1°43W 12 C6
Richmond Calif., U.S.A. 37°56N 122°21W 78 H4
Richmond Ind., U.S.A. 39°50N 84°53W 81 F11
Richmond Ky., U.S.A. 37°45N 84°18W 81 G11
Richmond Mich., U.S.A. 42°49N 82°45W 82 D2
Richmond Mo., U.S.A. 39°17N 93°58W 80 F7
Richmond Tex., U.S.A. 29°35N 95°46W 84 G7
Richmond Utah, U.S.A. 41°56N 111°48W 76 F8
Richmond Va., U.S.A. 37°33N 77°27W 81 G15
Richmond Vt., U.S.A. 44°24N 72°59W 83 B12
Richmond Hill Canada 43°52N 79°27W 82 C5
Richmond Ra. Australia 29°0S 152°45E 63 D5
Richmondville U.S.A. 42°38N 74°33W 83 D10
Richtersveld △ S. Africa 28°15S 17°10E 56 C2
Richville U.S.A. 44°25N 75°23W 83 B9
Richwood U.S.A. 38°14N 80°32W 81 F13
Ridder Kazakhstan 50°20N 83°30E 26 D9
Riddlesburg U.S.A. 40°9N 78°15W 82 F6
Rideau → Canada 45°27N 75°42W 83 A9
Ridgecrest U.S.A. 35°38N 117°40W 79 K9
Ridgefield Conn., U.S.A. 41°17N 73°30W 83 E11
Ridgefield Wash., U.S.A. 45°49N 122°45W 78 E4
Ridgeland Miss., U.S.A. 32°26N 90°8W 85 E9
Ridgeland S.C., U.S.A. 32°29N 80°59W 85 E14
Ridgetown Canada 42°26N 81°52W 82 D3
Ridgewood U.S.A. 40°59N 74°7W 83 F10
Ridgway U.S.A. 41°25N 78°44W 82 E6
Riding Mountain △
  Canada 50°50N 100°0W 71 C9
Ridley, Mt. Australia 33°12S 122°7E 61 F3
Riebeek-Oos S. Africa 33°10S 26°10E 56 E4
Ried Austria 48°14N 13°30E 16 D7
Riesa Germany 51°17N 13°17E 16 C7
Rietbron S. Africa 32°54S 23°10E 56 E3
Rietfontein Namibia 21°58S 20°58E 56 B3
Rieti Italy 42°24N 12°51E 22 C5
Rif = Er Rif Morocco 35°1N 4°1W 52 A5
Riffe L. U.S.A. 46°32N 122°26W 78 D4
Rifle U.S.A. 39°32N 107°47W 76 G10
Rift Valley Africa 7°0N 30°0E 50 G7
Rīga Latvia 56°53N 24°8E 9 H21
Riga, G. of Latvia 57°40N 23°45E 9 H20
Rīgān Iran 28°37N 58°58E 47 D8
Rīgas Jūras Līcis = Riga, G. of
  Latvia 57°40N 23°45E 9 H20
Rigaud Canada 45°29N 74°18W 83 A10
Rigby U.S.A. 43°40N 111°55W 76 E8
Rīgestān Afghan. 30°15N 65°0E 40 D4
Riggins U.S.A. 45°25N 116°19W 76 D5
Rigolet Canada 54°10N 58°23W 73 B8
Rihand Dam India 24°9N 83°2E 43 G10
Riihimäki Finland 60°45N 24°48E 8 F21
Riiser-Larsen-halvøya
  Antarctica 68°0S 35°0E 5 C4
Riiser-Larsen Ice Shelf
  S. Ocean 74°0S 19°0W 5 D2
Riiser-Larsen Sea S. Ocean 67°30S 22°0E 5 C4
Rijeka Croatia 45°20N 14°21E 16 F8
Rijssen Neths. 52°19N 6°31E 15 B6
Rikuchū-Kaigan △
  Japan 39°20N 142°0E 28 E11
Rikuzentakada Japan 39°0N 141°40E 28 E11
Riley U.S.A. 43°32N 119°28W 76 E4
Rima → Nigeria 13°4N 5°10E 52 F7
Rimah, Wadi ar →
  Si. Arabia 26°5N 41°30E 46 E4

Rimau, Pulau Malaysia 5°15N 100°16E 39 c
Rimbey Canada 52°35N 114°15W 70 C6
Rimersburg U.S.A. 41°3N 79°30W 82 E5
Rímini Italy 44°3N 12°33E 22 B5
Rimouski Canada 48°27N 68°30W 73 C6
Rimrock U.S.A. 46°40N 121°7W 78 D5
Rinca Indonesia 8°45S 119°35E 37 F5
Rincón de Romos
  Mexico 22°14N 102°18W 86 C4
Rinconada Argentina 22°26S 66°10W 94 A2
Rind → India 25°53N 80°33E 43 G9
Ringas India 27°21N 75°34E 42 F6
Ringgold Is. Fiji 16°15S 179°25W 59 a
Ringkøbing Denmark 56°5N 8°15E 9 H13
Ringvassøya Norway 69°56N 19°15E 8 B18
Ringwood U.S.A. 41°7N 74°15W 83 E10
Rinjani, Gunung
  Indonesia 8°24S 116°28E 36 F5
Río Branco Brazil 9°58S 67°49W 92 E5
Río Branco Uruguay 32°40S 53°40W 95 C5
Río Bravo Mexico 25°59N 98°6W 87 B5
Río Bravo △ N. Amer. 29°2N 102°45W 86 B4
Río Bravo del Norte →
  Mexico 25°57N 97°9W 87 B5
Río Brilhante Brazil 21°48S 54°33W 95 A5
Río Claro Brazil 22°19S 47°35W 95 A6
Río Claro Trin. & Tob. 10°20N 61°10W 93 K15
Río Colorado Argentina 39°0S 64°0W 96 D4
Río Cuarto Argentina 33°10S 64°25W 94 C3
Río das Pedras Mozam. 23°8S 35°28E 57 B6
Rio de Janeiro □ Brazil 22°50S 43°0W 95 A7
Río do Sul Brazil 27°13S 49°37W 95 B6
Río Dulce △ Guatemala 15°43N 88°50W 88 C2
Río Gallegos Argentina 51°35S 69°15W 96 G3
Río Grande Argentina 53°50S 67°45W 96 G3
Río Grande Mexico 32°0S 52°20W 95 C5
Río Grande Mexico 23°50N 103°2W 86 C4
Río Grande Puerto Rico 18°23N 65°50W 89 d
Río Grande → N. Amer. 25°58N 97°9W 84 J6
Río Grande City U.S.A. 26°23N 98°49W 84 H5
Rio Grande de Santiago →
  Mexico 21°36N 105°26W 86 C3
Rio Grande do Norte □
  Brazil 5°40S 36°0W 93 E11
Río Grande do Sul □ Brazil 30°0S 53°0W 95 C5
Río Hato Panama 8°22N 80°10W 88 E3
Río Lagartos Mexico 21°36N 88°10W 87 C7
Río Largo Brazil 9°28S 35°50W 93 E11
Río Mulatos Bolivia 19°40S 66°50W 92 G5
Río Negro Brazil 26°0S 49°55W 95 B6
Río Muni □ Eq. Guin. 1°30N 10°0E 54 D2
Río Pardo Brazil 30°0S 52°30W 95 C5
Río Pilcomayo △ Argentina 25°5S 58°5W 94 B4
Río Plátano △ Honduras 15°45N 85°0W 88 C3
Río Rancho U.S.A. 35°14N 106°41W 77 J10
Río Segundo Argentina 31°40S 63°59W 94 C3
Río Tercero Argentina 32°15S 64°8W 94 C3
Río Verde Brazil 17°50S 51°0W 93 G8
Río Verde Mexico 21°56N 99°59W 87 C5
Río Vista U.S.A. 38°10N 121°42W 78 G5
Riobamba Ecuador 1°50S 78°45W 92 D3
Riohacha Colombia 11°33N 72°55W 92 A4
Riosucio Colombia 7°27N 77°7W 92 B3
Riou L. Canada 59°7N 106°25W 71 B7
Ripley Canada 44°4N 81°35W 82 B3
Ripley Calif., U.S.A. 33°32N 114°39W 79 M12
Ripley N.Y., U.S.A. 42°16N 79°43W 82 D5
Ripley Tenn., U.S.A. 35°45N 89°32W 85 D10
Ripley W. Va., U.S.A. 38°49N 81°43W 81 F13
Ripon U.K. 54°9N 1°31W 12 C6
Ripon Calif., U.S.A. 37°44N 121°7W 78 H5
Ripon Wis., U.S.A. 43°51N 88°50W 80 D9
Rishā', W. ar → Si. Arabia 25°33N 44°5E 46 E5
Rishikesh India 30°7N 78°19E 42 D8
Rishiri-Rebun-Sarobetsu △
  Japan 45°26N 141°30E 28 B10
Rishiri-Tō Japan 45°11N 141°15E 28 B10
Rishon le Ziyyon Israel 31°58N 34°48E 48 D3
Rison U.S.A. 33°58N 92°11W 84 E8
Risør Norway 58°43N 9°13E 9 G13
Rita Blanca Cr. →
  U.S.A. 35°40N 102°29W 84 D3
Ritchie's Arch. India 12°14N 93°10E 45 H11
Ritter, Mt. U.S.A. 37°41N 119°12W 78 H7
Rittman U.S.A. 40°58N 81°47W 82 F3
Ritzville U.S.A. 47°8N 118°23W 76 C4
Riva del Garda Italy 45°53N 10°50E 22 B4
Rivadavia B. Aires,
  Argentina 35°29S 62°59W 94 D3
Rivadavia Mendoza,
  Argentina 33°13S 68°30W 94 C2
Rivadavia Salta, Argentina 24°5S 62°54W 94 A3
Rivadavia Chile 29°57S 70°35W 94 B1
Rivas Nic. 11°30N 85°50W 88 D2
Rivash Iran 35°28N 58°26E 47 C8
Rivera Argentina 37°12S 63°14W 94 D3
Rivera Uruguay 31°0S 55°50W 95 C4
Riverbank U.S.A. 37°44N 120°56W 78 H6
Riverdale U.S.A. 36°26N 119°52W 78 J7
Riverhead U.S.A. 40°55N 72°40W 83 F12
Riverhurst Canada 50°55N 106°50W 71 C7
Rivers Canada 50°2N 100°14W 71 C8
Rivers Inlet Canada 51°42N 127°15W 70 C3
Riversdale Canada 44°5N 81°20W 82 B3
Riversdale S. Africa 34°7S 21°15E 56 E3
Riverside U.S.A. 33°59N 117°22W 79 M9
Riversleigh Australia 19°5S 138°40E 62 B2
Riverton Australia 34°10S 138°46E 63 E2
Riverton Canada 51°1N 97°0W 71 C9
Riverton N.Z. 46°21S 168°0E 59 G2
Riverton U.S.A. 43°2N 108°23W 76 E9
Riviera di Levante
  Italy 44°15N 9°30E 20 D8
Riviera di Ponente Italy 44°10N 8°20E 20 D8
Rivière-au-Renard
  Canada 48°59N 64°23W 73 C7

Rivière-du-Loup Canada 47°50N 69°30W 73 C6
Rivière-Pentecôte Canada 49°57N 67°1W 73 C6
Rivière-Pilote Martinique 14°26N 60°53W 88 c
Rivière St-Paul Canada 51°28N 57°45W 73 B8
Rivière-Salée Martinique 14°31N 61°0W 88 c
Rivne Ukraine 50°40N 26°10E 17 C14
Rivne □ Ukraine 51°15N 26°30E 17 C14
Rívoli Italy 45°3N 7°31E 20 D7
Rívoli B. Australia 37°32S 140°3E 63 F3
Riyadh = Ar Riyāḍ
  Si. Arabia 24°41N 46°42E 46 E5
Rize Turkey 41°0N 40°30E 19 F7
Rizhao China 35°25N 119°30E 33 G10
Rizzuto, C. Italy 38°53N 17°5E 22 E7
Rjukan Norway 59°54N 8°33E 9 G13
Road Town Br. Virgin Is. 18°27N 64°37W 89 e
Roan Plateau U.S.A. 39°20N 109°20W 76 G9
Roanne France 46°3N 4°4E 20 C6
Roanoke Ala., U.S.A. 33°9N 85°22W 85 E12
Roanoke Va., U.S.A. 37°16N 79°56W 81 G14
Roanoke → U.S.A. 35°57N 76°42W 85 D17
Roanoke I. U.S.A. 35°53N 75°39W 85 D17
Roanoke Rapids U.S.A. 36°28N 77°40W 85 C16
Roatán Honduras 16°18N 86°35W 88 C2
Robāt Sang Iran 35°35N 59°10E 47 C8
Robāţkarīm Iran 35°25N 50°59E 47 C6
Robben I. S. Africa 33°46S 18°22E 56 D2
Robbins I. Australia 40°42S 145°0E 63 G4
Robe → Australia 21°42S 116°15E 60 D2
Robe Australia 37°11S 139°45E 63 F2
Robert Bourassa, Rés.
  Canada 53°40N 76°55W 72 B4
Robert Lee U.S.A. 31°54N 100°29W 84 F4
Robertsdale U.S.A. 40°11N 78°6W 82 F6
Robertsganj India 24°44N 83°4E 43 G10
Robertson S. Africa 33°46S 19°50E 56 D2
Robertson I. Antarctica 65°15S 59°30W 5 C18
Robertson Ra. Australia 23°15S 121°0E 60 D3
Robertstown Australia 33°58S 139°5E 63 E2
Roberval Canada 48°32N 72°15W 72 C5
Robeson Chan. N. Amer. 82°0N 61°30W 69 A19
Robesonia U.S.A. 40°21N 76°8W 83 F8
Robinson U.S.A. 39°0N 87°44W 80 F10
Robinson → Australia 16°3S 137°16E 62 B2
Robinson Crusoe I.
  Pac. Oc. 33°38S 78°52W 90 F2
Robinson Ra. Australia 25°40S 119°0E 61 E2
Robinvale Australia 34°40S 142°45E 63 E3
Roblin Canada 51°14N 101°21W 71 C8
Roboré Bolivia 18°10S 59°45W 92 G7
Robson, Mt. Canada 53°10N 119°10W 70 C5
Robstown U.S.A. 27°47N 97°40W 84 H6
Roca, C. da Portugal 38°40N 9°31W 21 C1
Roca Partida, I. Mexico 19°1N 112°2W 86 D2
Rocas, Atol das Brazil 4°0S 34°1W 93 D12
Rocha Uruguay 34°30S 54°25W 95 C5
Rochdale U.K. 53°38N 2°9W 12 D5
Rochefort Belgium 50°9N 5°12E 15 D5
Rochefort France 45°56N 0°57W 20 D3
Rochelle U.S.A. 41°56N 89°4W 80 E9
Rocher River Canada 61°23N 112°44W 70 A6
Rochester U.K. 51°23N 0°31E 13 F8
Rochester Ind., U.S.A. 41°4N 86°13W 80 E10
Rochester Minn., U.S.A. 44°1N 92°28W 80 C7
Rochester N.H., U.S.A. 43°18N 70°59W 83 C14
Rochester N.Y., U.S.A. 43°10N 77°37W 82 C7
Rock → Canada 60°7N 127°7W 70 A3
Rock, The Australia 35°15S 147°2E 63 F4
Rock Creek U.S.A. 41°40N 80°52W 82 E4
Rock Falls U.S.A. 41°47N 89°41W 80 E9
Rock Hill U.S.A. 34°56N 81°1W 85 D14
Rock Island U.S.A. 41°30N 90°34W 80 E8
Rock Port U.S.A. 40°25N 95°31W 80 E6
Rock Rapids U.S.A. 43°26N 96°10W 80 D5
Rock Sound Bahamas 24°54N 76°12W 88 B4
Rock Springs Mont.,
  U.S.A. 46°49N 106°15W 76 C10
Rock Springs Wyo.,
  U.S.A. 41°35N 109°14W 76 F9
Rock Valley U.S.A. 43°12N 96°18W 80 D5
Rockall Atl. Oc. 57°37N 13°42W 6 D3
Rockdale Tex., U.S.A. 30°39N 97°0W 84 F6
Rockdale Wash., U.S.A. 47°22N 121°28W 78 C5
Rockeby = Mungkan Kandju △
  Australia 13°35S 142°52E 62 A3
Rockefeller Plateau
  Antarctica 76°0S 130°0W 5 E14
Rockford U.S.A. 42°16N 89°6W 80 D9
Rockglen Canada 49°11N 105°57W 71 D7
Rockhampton Australia 23°22S 150°32E 62 C5
Rockingham N.C.,
  U.S.A. 34°57N 79°46W 85 D15
Rockingham Vt., U.S.A. 43°11N 72°29W 83 C12
Rockingham B. Australia 18°5S 146°10E 62 B4
Rocklake U.S.A. 48°47N 99°15W 80 A4
Rockland Canada 45°33N 75°17W 83 A9
Rockland Idaho, U.S.A. 42°34N 112°53W 76 E7
Rockland Maine, U.S.A. 44°6N 69°7W 81 C19
Rockland Mich., U.S.A. 46°44N 89°11W 80 B9
Rocklin U.S.A. 38°48N 121°14W 78 G5
Rockly B. Trin. & Tob. 11°9N 60°46W 93 J16
Rockmart U.S.A. 34°1N 85°3W 85 D12
Rockport Mass., U.S.A. 42°39N 70°37W 83 D14
Rockport Tex., U.S.A. 28°2N 97°3W 84 G6
Rocksprings U.S.A. 30°1N 100°13W 84 G4
Rockville Conn., U.S.A. 41°52N 72°28W 83 E12
Rockville Md., U.S.A. 39°5N 77°9W 81 F15
Rockwall U.S.A. 32°56N 96°28W 84 E6
Rockwell City U.S.A. 42°24N 94°38W 80 D6
Rockwood Canada 43°37N 80°8W 82 C4
Rockwood Maine,
  U.S.A. 45°41N 69°45W 81 C19
Rockwood Tenn., U.S.A. 35°52N 84°41W 85 D12
Rocky Ford U.S.A. 38°3N 103°43W 76 G12
Rocky Gully Australia 34°30S 116°57E 61 F2
Rocky Harbour Canada 49°36N 57°55W 73 C8
Rocky Island L. Canada 46°55N 83°0W 72 C3
Rocky Lane Canada 58°31N 116°22W 70 B5
Rocky Mount U.S.A. 35°57N 77°48W 85 D16

Rocky Mountain △
  U.S.A. 40°25N 105°45W 76 F11
Rocky Mountain House
  Canada 52°22N 114°55W 70 C6
Rocky Mts. N. Amer. 49°0N 115°0W 76 B6
Rocky Point Namibia 19°3S 12°30E 56 B1
Rod Pakistan 28°10N 63°5E 40 E3
Rødbyhavn Denmark 54°39N 11°22E 9 J14
Roddickton Canada 50°51N 56°8W 73 B8
Rodez France 44°21N 2°33E 20 D5
Ródhos = Rhodes Greece 36°15N 28°10E 23 F13
Rodna ☉ Australia 23°45S 132°4E 60 D5
Rodney Canada 42°34N 81°41W 82 D3
Rodney, C. N.Z. 36°17S 174°50E 59 B5
Rodrigues Ind. Oc. 19°45S 63°20E 3 E13
Roe → U.K. 55°6N 6°59W 10 A5
Roebling U.S.A. 40°7N 74°47W 83 F10
Roebourne Australia 20°44S 117°9E 60 D2
Roebuck B. Australia 18°5S 122°20E 60 C3
Roebuck Roadhouse
  Australia 17°59S 122°36E 60 C3
Roermond Neths. 51°12N 6°0E 15 C6
Roes Welcome Sd. Canada 65°0N 87°0W 69 E14
Roeselare Belgium 50°57N 3°7E 15 D3
Rogachev = Ragachow
  Belarus 53°8N 30°5E 17 B16
Rogagua, L. Bolivia 13°43S 66°50W 92 F5
Rogatyn Ukraine 49°24N 24°36E 17 D13
Rogers U.S.A. 36°20N 94°7W 84 C7
Rogers City U.S.A. 45°25N 83°49W 81 C12
Rogersville Canada 46°44N 65°26W 73 C6
Roggan → Canada 54°24N 79°25W 72 B4
Roggan L. Canada 54°8N 77°50W 72 B4
Roggeveen Basin
  Pac. Oc. 31°30S 95°30W 65 L18
Roggeveldberge S. Africa 32°10S 20°10E 56 E3
Rogoaguado, L. Bolivia 13°0S 65°30W 92 F5
Rogojampi Indonesia 8°19S 114°17E 37 J17
Rogue → U.S.A. 42°26N 124°26W 76 E1
Roha India 18°26N 73°7E 44 E1
Rohnert Park U.S.A. 38°16N 122°40W 78 G4
Rohri Pakistan 27°45N 68°51E 42 F3
Rohri Canal Pakistan 26°15N 68°27E 42 F3
Rohtak India 28°55N 76°43E 42 E7
Roi Et Thailand 16°4N 103°40E 38 D4
Roja Latvia 57°29N 22°43E 9 H20
Rojas Argentina 34°10S 60°45W 94 C3
Rojo, C. Mexico 21°33N 97°20W 87 C5
Rokan → Indonesia 2°0N 100°50E 36 D2
Rokiškis Lithuania 55°55N 25°35E 9 J21
Rolândia Brazil 23°18S 51°23W 95 A5
Rolla Mo., U.S.A. 37°57N 91°46W 80 G8
Rolla N. Dak., U.S.A. 48°52N 99°37W 80 A4
Rolleston Australia 24°28S 148°35E 62 C4
Rollingstone Australia 19°2S 146°24E 62 B4
Roma Australia 26°32S 148°49E 63 D4
Roma Sweden 57°32N 18°26E 9 H18
Roma-Los Saenz U.S.A. 26°24N 99°1W 84 H5
Romain, C. U.S.A. 33°0N 79°22W 85 E15
Romaine → Canada 50°18N 63°47W 73 B7
Roman Romania 46°57N 26°55E 17 E14
Romang Indonesia 7°30S 127°20E 37 F7
Români Egypt 30°59N 32°38E 48 E1
Romania ■ Europe 46°0N 25°0E 17 F12
Romano, Cayo Cuba 22°0N 77°30W 88 B4
Romans-sur-Isère France 45°3N 5°3E 20 D6
Romanzof C. U.S.A. 61°49N 166°6W 74 C6
Romblon Phil. 12°33N 122°17E 37 B6
Rome Ga., U.S.A. 34°15N 85°10W 85 D12
Rome N.Y., U.S.A. 43°13N 75°27W 83 C9
Rome Pa., U.S.A. 41°51N 76°21W 83 E8
Romney U.S.A. 39°21N 78°45W 81 F14
Romney Marsh U.K. 51°2N 0°54E 13 F8
Rømø Denmark 55°10N 8°30E 9 J13
Romorantin-Lanthenay
  France 47°21N 1°45E 20 C4
Rompin → Malaysia 2°49N 103°29E 39 L4
Romsdalen Norway 62°25N 7°52E 8 E12
Romsey U.K. 51°0N 1°29E 13 F6
Ron India 15°40N 75°44E 45 G2
Ron Vietnam 17°53N 106°27E 38 D6
Rona U.K. 57°34N 5°59W 11 D3
Ronan U.S.A. 47°32N 114°6W 76 C6
Roncador, Cayos
  Colombia 13°32N 80°4W 88 D3
Roncador, Serra do
  Brazil 12°30S 52°30W 93 F8
Ronda Spain 36°46N 5°12W 21 D3
Rondane Norway 61°57N 9°50E 8 F13
Rondônia □ Brazil 11°0S 63°0W 92 F6
Rondonópolis Brazil 16°28S 54°38W 93 G8
Rondu Pakistan 35°32N 75°10E 43 B6
Rong, Koh Cambodia 10°45N 103°15E 39 G4
Rong Jiang → China 24°35N 109°20E 34 E7
Rong Xian China 22°50N 110°31E 35 F8
Rong'an China 25°14N 109°22E 34 E7
Rongcheng China 29°20N 105°32E 34 C5
Rongcheng China 37°9N 122°23E 33 F12
Ronge, L. la Canada 55°6N 105°17W 71 B7
Rongjiang China 25°57N 108°28E 34 E7
Rongshui China 25°5N 109°12E 34 E7
Rongxian China 29°23N 104°22E 34 C5
Rønne Denmark 55°6N 14°43E 9 J16
Ronne Ice Shelf Antarctica 77°30S 60°0W 5 D18
Ronsard, C. Australia 24°46S 113°10E 61 D1
Ronse Belgium 50°45N 3°35E 15 D3
Roodepoort S. Africa 26°11S 27°54E 57 D4
Roof Butte U.S.A. 36°28N 109°5W 77 H9
Rooiboklaagte → Namibia 20°50S 21°0E 56 B3
Rooniu, Mt. Tahiti 17°49S 149°12W 59 d
Roorkee India 29°52N 77°59E 42 E7
Roosendaal Neths. 51°32N 4°29E 15 C4
Roosevelt U.S.A. 40°18N 109°59W 76 F9
Roosevelt → Brazil 7°35S 60°20W 92 E6
Roosevelt, Mt. Canada 58°26N 125°20W 70 B3
Roosevelt I. Antarctica 79°30S 162°0W 5 D12
Roper → Australia 14°43S 135°27E 62 A2
Roper Bar Australia 14°44S 134°44E 62 A1
Roper River = St. Vidgeon's ☉
  Australia 14°47S 134°53E 62 A1

Roque Pérez *Argentina* 35°25S 59°24W **94** D4
Roquetas de Mar *Spain* 36°46N 2°36W **21** D4
Roraima □ *Brazil* 2°0N 61°30W **92** C6
Roraima, Mt. *Venezuela* 5°10N 60°40W **92** B6
Ros Comáin = Roscommon
  Ireland 53°38N 8°11W **10** C3
Ros Mhic Thriúin = New Ross
  Ireland 52°23N 6°57W **10** D5
Rosa, Monte *Europe* 45°57N 7°53E **20** D7
Rosalia *U.S.A.* 47°14N 117°22W **76** C5
Rosamond *U.S.A.* 34°52N 118°10W **79** L8
Rosario *Argentina* 33°0S 60°40W **94** C3
Rosário *Brazil* 3°0S 44°15W **93** D10
Rosario *Mexico* 22°58N 105°53W **86** C3
Rosario *Paraguay* 24°30S 57°35W **94** A4
Rosario de la Frontera
  Argentina 25°50S 65°0W **94** B3
Rosario de Lerma
  Argentina 24°59S 65°35W **94** A2
Rosario del Tala
  Argentina 32°20S 59°10W **94** C4
Rosário do Sul *Brazil* 30°15S 54°55W **95** C5
Rosarito *Baja Calif.,*
  Mexico 32°20N 117°2W **79** N9
Rosarito *Baja Calif.,*
  Mexico 28°38N 114°1W **86** B2
Roscoe *U.S.A.* 41°56N 74°55W **83** E10
Roscommon *Ireland* 53°38N 8°11W **10** C3
Roscommon □ *Ireland* 53°49N 8°23W **10** C3
Roscrea *Ireland* 52°57N 7°49W **10** D4
Rose → *Australia* 14°16S 135°45E **62** A2
Rose, L. *Bahamas* 21°0N 73°30W **89** B5
Rose Belle *Mauritius* 20°24S 57°36E **55** d
Rose Blanche *Canada* 47°38N 58°45W **73** C8
Rose Hill *Mauritius* 20°14S 57°27E **55** d
Rose Pt. *Canada* 54°11N 131°39W **70** C2
Rose Valley *Canada* 52°19N 103°49W **71** C8
Roseau *Dominica* 15°17N 61°24W **89** C7
Roseau *U.S.A.* 48°51N 95°46W **80** A6
Rosebery *Australia* 41°46S 145°33E **63** G4
Rosebud *S. Dak., U.S.A.* 43°14N 100°51W **80** D3
Rosebud *Tex., U.S.A.* 31°4N 96°59W **84** F6
Roseburg *U.S.A.* 43°13N 123°20W **76** E2
Rosedale *U.S.A.* 33°51N 91°2W **85** E9
Rosehearty *U.K.* 57°42N 2°7W **11** D6
Roseires Res. *Sudan* 11°51N 34°23E **53** F12
Roseland *U.S.A.* 38°25N 122°43W **78** G4
Rosemary *Canada* 50°46N 112°5W **70** C6
Rosenberg *U.S.A.* 29°34N 95°49W **84** G7
Rosenheim *Germany* 47°51N 12°7E **16** E7
Roses, G. de *Spain* 42°10N 3°15E **21** A7
Rosetown *Canada* 51°35N 107°59W **71** C7
Roseville *Calif., U.S.A.* 38°45N 121°17W **78** G5
Roseville *Mich., U.S.A.* 42°30N 82°56W **82** D2
Roseville *U.S.A.* 41°51N 76°57W **83** E8
Rosewood *Australia* 27°38S 152°36E **63** D5
Roshkhvār *Iran* 34°58N 59°37E **47** C8
Rosignano Maríttimo
  Italy 43°24N 10°28E **22** C4
Rosignol *Guyana* 6°15N 57°30W **92** B7
Roșiori de Vede *Romania* 44°9N 25°0E **17** F13
Roskilde *Denmark* 55°38N 12°3E **9** J15
Roslavl *Russia* 53°57N 32°55E **18** D5
Rosmead *S. Africa* 31°29S 25°8E **56** D4
Ross *Australia* 42°2S 147°30E **63** G4
Ross *N.Z.* 42°53S 170°49E **59** E3
Ross Dependency
  Antarctica 76°0S 170°0W **5** D12
Ross I. *Antarctica* 77°30S 168°0E **5** D11
Ross Ice Shelf *Antarctica* 80°0S 180°0E **5** E12
Ross L. *U.S.A.* 48°44N 121°4W **76** B3
Ross-on-Wye *U.K.* 51°54N 2°34W **13** F5
Ross River *Australia* 23°44S 134°30E **62** C1
Ross River *Canada* 62°30N 131°30W **70** A2
Ross Sea *Antarctica* 74°0S 178°0E **5** D11
Rossall Pt. *U.K.* 53°55N 3°3W **12** D4
Rossan Pt. *Ireland* 54°42N 8°47W **10** B3
Rossano *Italy* 39°36N 16°39E **22** E7
Rossburn *Canada* 50°40N 100°49W **71** C8
Rosseau *Canada* 45°16N 79°39W **82** A5
Rosseau, L. *Canada* 45°10N 79°35W **82** A5
Rosses, The *Ireland* 55°2N 8°20W **10** A3
Rossignol, L. *Canada* 52°43N 73°40W **72** B5
Rossignol L. *Canada* 44°12N 65°10W **73** D6
Rossiya = Russia ■
  Eurasia 62°0N 105°0E **27** C11
Rossland *Canada* 49°6N 117°50W **70** D5
Rosslare *Ireland* 52°17N 6°24W **10** D5
Rosslare Europort = Rosslare
  Harbour *Ireland* 52°15N 6°20W **10** D5
Rosslare Harbour *Ireland* 52°15N 6°20W **10** D5
Rossmore *Canada* 44°8N 77°23W **82** B7
Rosso *Mauritania* 16°40N 15°45W **52** E2
Rossosh *Russia* 50°15N 39°28E **19** D6
Rossvatnet *Norway* 65°45N 14°5E **8** D16
Røst *Norway* 67°32N 12°10E **8** C15
Rosthern *Canada* 52°40N 106°20W **71** C7
Rostock *Germany* 54°5N 12°8E **16** A7
Rostov *Don, Russia* 47°15N 39°45E **19** E6
Rostov *Yaroslavl, Russia* 57°14N 39°25E **18** C6
Roswell *Ga., U.S.A.* 34°2N 84°22W **85** D12
Roswell *N. Mex., U.S.A.* 33°24N 104°32W **77** K11
Rotan *U.S.A.* 32°51N 100°28W **84** E4
Rote *Indonesia* 10°50S 123°0E **37** F6
Rother → *U.K.* 50°59N 0°45E **13** G8
Rothera *Antarctica* 67°34S 68°8W **5** C17
Rotherham *U.K.* 53°26N 1°20W **12** D6
Rothes *U.K.* 57°32N 3°13W **11** D5
Rothesay *Canada* 45°23N 66°0W **73** C6
Rothesay *U.K.* 55°50N 5°3W **11** F3
Roti = Rote *Indonesia* 10°50S 123°0E **37** F6
Roto *Australia* 33°0S 145°30E **63** E4
Rotondo, Mte. *France* 42°14N 9°8E **20** E8
Rotoroa, L. *N.Z.* 41°55S 172°39E **59** D4
Rotorua *N.Z.* 38°9S 176°16E **59** C6
Rotorua, L. *N.Z.* 38°5S 176°18E **59** C6
Rotterdam *Neths.* 51°55N 4°30E **15** C4
Rotterdam *U.S.A.* 42°48N 74°1W **83** D10

Rottnest I. *Australia* 32°0S 115°27E **61** F2
Rottumeroog *Neths.* 53°33N 6°34E **15** A6
Rottweil *Germany* 48°9N 8°37E **16** D5
Rotuma *Fiji* 12°25S 177°5E **58** C10
Roubaix *France* 50°40N 3°10E **20** A5
Rouen *France* 49°27N 1°4E **20** B4
Rouleau *Canada* 50°10N 104°56W **71** C8
Roulpmaulpma ◌
  Australia 23°52S 133°0E **60** D5
Round I. *Mauritius* 19°51S 57°45E **55** d
Round Mountain *U.S.A.* 38°43N 117°4W **76** G5
Round Mt. *Australia* 30°26S 152°16E **63** E5
Round Rock *U.S.A.* 30°31N 97°41W **84** F6
Roundup *U.S.A.* 46°27N 108°33W **76** C9
Rousay *U.K.* 59°10N 3°2W **11** B5
Rouses Point *U.S.A.* 44°59N 73°22W **83** B11
Rouseville *U.S.A.* 41°28N 79°42W **82** E5
Rousse = Ruse *Bulgaria* 43°48N 25°59E **23** C12
Roussillon *France* 42°30N 2°35E **20** E5
Rouxville *S. Africa* 30°25S 26°50E **56** D4
Rouyn-Noranda *Canada* 48°20N 79°0W **72** C4
Rovaniemi *Finland* 66°29N 25°41E **8** C21
Rovereto *Italy* 45°53N 11°3E **22** B4
Rovigo *Italy* 45°4N 11°47E **22** B4
Rovinj *Croatia* 45°5N 13°40E **16** F7
Rovno = Rivne *Ukraine* 50°40N 26°10E **17** C14
Rovuma = Ruvuma →
  Tanzania 10°29S 40°28E **54** G8
Row'ān *Iran* 35°8N 48°51E **47** C6
Rowena *Australia* 29°48S 148°55E **63** D4
Rowley L. *Canada* 69°6N 77°52W **69** D16
Rowley Shoals *Australia* 17°30S 119°0E **60** C2
Roxas *Phil.* 11°36N 122°49E **37** B6
Roxboro *U.S.A.* 36°24N 78°59W **85** C15
Roxborough *Trin. & Tob.* 11°15N 60°35W **93** J16
Roxburgh *N.Z.* 45°33S 169°19E **59** F2
Roxbury *N.Y., U.S.A.* 42°17N 74°33W **83** D10
Roxbury *Pa., U.S.A.* 40°6N 77°39W **82** F7
Roxby Downs *Australia* 30°43S 136°46E **63** E2
Roy *Mont., U.S.A.* 47°20N 108°58W **76** C9
Roy *N. Mex., U.S.A.* 35°57N 104°12W **77** J11
Roy *Utah, U.S.A.* 41°10N 112°2W **76** F7
Royal Bardia △ *Nepal* 28°20N 81°20E **43** E9
Royal Canal *Ireland* 53°30N 7°13W **10** C4
Royal Chitawan △
  Nepal 26°30N 84°30E **43** F11
Royal Geographical Society Is.
  Canada 68°40N 100°15W **68** D11
Royal Leamington Spa
  U.K. 52°18N 1°31W **13** E6
Royal Natal △ *S. Africa* 28°43S 28°51E **57** C4
Royal Tunbridge Wells
  U.K. 51°7N 0°16E **13** F8
Royale, Isle *U.S.A.* 48°0N 88°54W **80** B9
Royan *France* 45°37N 1°2W **20** D3
Royston *U.K.* 52°3N 0°0 **13** E7
Rozdilna *Ukraine* 46°50N 30°2E **17** E16
Rozhyshche *Ukraine* 50°54N 25°15E **17** C13
Rtishchevo *Russia* 52°18N 43°46E **18** D7
Ruacana *Namibia* 17°27S 14°21E **56** A1
Ruahine Ra. *N.Z.* 39°55S 176°2E **59** C6
Ruapehu *N.Z.* 39°17S 175°35E **59** C5
Ruapuke I. *N.Z.* 46°46S 168°31E **59** G2
Ruâq, W. → *Egypt* 30°0N 33°49E **48** F2
Rub' al Khālī *Si. Arabia* 19°0N 48°0E **49** D4
Rubh a' Mhail *U.K.* 55°56N 6°8W **11** F2
Rubha Hunish *U.K.* 57°42N 6°20W **11** D2
Rubha Robhanais = Lewis, Butt of
  U.K. 58°31N 6°16W **11** C2
Rubicon → *U.S.A.* 38°53N 121°4W **78** G5
Rubio *Venezuela* 7°43N 72°22W **92** B4
Rubtsovsk *Russia* 51°30N 81°10E **30** A5
Ruby L. *U.S.A.* 40°10N 115°28W **76** F6
Ruby Mts. *U.S.A.* 40°30N 115°20W **76** F6
Rubyvale *Australia* 23°25S 147°42E **62** C4
Rucheng *China* 25°33N 113°38E **35** E9
Rūd Sar *Iran* 37°8N 50°18E **47** B6
Rudall *Australia* 33°43S 136°17E **63** E2
Rudall → *Australia* 22°34S 122°13E **60** D3
Rudall River △ *Australia* 22°38S 122°30E **60** D3
Rudbar *Iran* 36°48N 49°23E **47** B6
Rudewa *Namibia* 29°16S 19°3W **82**
Rudnyy *Kazakhstan* 52°57N 63°7E **26** D7
Rudolfa, Ostrov *Russia* 81°45N 58°30E **26** A6
Rudong *China* 32°20N 121°12E **35** A13
Rudraprayag *India* 28°59N 79°24E **43** E8
Rudyard *U.S.A.* 46°14N 84°36W **81** B11
Ruffling Pt. *Br. Virgin Is.* 18°44N 64°27W **89** e
Rufiji → *Tanzania* 7°50S 39°15E **54** F7
Rufino *Argentina* 34°20S 62°50W **94** C3
Rugao *China* 32°23N 120°31E **35** A13
Rugby *U.K.* 52°23N 1°16W **13** E6
Rugby *U.S.A.* 48°22N 100°0W **80** A4
Rügen *Germany* 54°22N 13°24E **16** A7
Ruhnu *Estonia* 57°48N 23°15E **9** H20
Ruhr → *Germany* 51°27N 6°43E **16** C4
Rui'an *China* 27°47N 120°40E **35** D13
Ruichang *China* 29°40N 115°39E **35** C10
Ruidoso *U.S.A.* 33°20N 105°41W **77** K11
Ruijin *China* 25°48N 116°0E **35** E10
Ruili *China* 24°6N 97°46E **34** E1
Rujm Tal'at al Jamā'ah
  Jordan 30°24N 35°30E **48** E4
Ruk *Pakistan* 27°50N 68°42E **42** F3
Rukhla *Pakistan* 32°27N 71°57E **42** C4
Ruki →
  Dem. Rep. of the Congo 0°5N 18°17E **54** E3
Rukumkot *Nepal* 28°37N 82°37E **43** E10
Rukwa □ *Tanzania* 8°0S 32°20E **54** F6
Rulhieres, C. *Australia* 13°56S 127°22E **60** B4
Rum *Jordan* 29°39N 35°26E **48** F4
Rùm *U.K.* 57°0N 6°20W **11** E2
Rum Cay *Bahamas* 23°40N 74°58W **89** B5
Rum Jungle *Australia* 13°0S 130°59E **60** B5
Rumāḥ *Si. Arabia* 25°29N 47°10E **46** E5
Rumania = Romania ■
  Europe 46°0N 25°0E **17** F12
Rumaylah *Iraq* 30°47N 47°37E **46** D5
Rumbêk *South Sudan* 6°54N 29°37E **53** G11
Rumford *U.S.A.* 44°33N 70°33W **83** B14

Rumia *Poland* 54°37N 18°25E **17** A10
Rumoi *Japan* 43°56N 141°39E **28** C10
Rumson *U.S.A.* 40°23N 74°0W **83** F11
Runan *China* 33°0N 114°30E **32** H8
Runanga *N.Z.* 42°25S 171°15E **59** E3
Runaway, C. *N.Z.* 37°32S 177°59E **59** B6
Runaway Bay *Jamaica* 18°27N 77°20W **88** a
Runcorn *U.K.* 53°21N 2°44W **12** D5
Rundu *Namibia* 17°52S 19°43E **56** A2
Rungwe *Tanzania* 9°11S 33°32E **50** G7
Rungwe, Mt. *Tanzania* 9°8S 33°40E **54** F6
Runton Ra. *Australia* 23°31S 123°6E **60** D3
Ruo Shui → *China* 41°0N 100°16E **32** B9
Ruokolahti *Finland* 61°17N 28°50E **8** F23
Ruoqiang *China* 38°55N 88°10E **30** D6
Rupa *India* 27°15N 92°21E **41** F18
Rupar *India* 31°2N 76°38E **42** D7
Rupat *Indonesia* 1°45N 101°40E **36** D2
Rupen → *India* 23°28N 71°31E **42** H4
Rupert *U.S.A.* 42°37N 113°41W **76** E7
Rupert → *Canada* 51°29N 78°45W **72** B4
Rupert B. *Canada* 51°35N 79°0W **72** B4
Rupert House = Waskaganish
  Canada 51°30N 78°40W **72** B4
Rupsa *India* 21°37N 87°1E **43** J12
Rurrenabaque *Bolivia* 14°30S 67°32W **92** F5
Ruschuk = Ruse
  Bulgaria 43°48N 25°59E **23** C12
Ruse *Bulgaria* 43°48N 25°59E **23** C12
Rush *Ireland* 53°31N 6°6W **10** C5
Rushan *China* 36°56N 121°30E **33** F11
Rushden *U.K.* 52°18N 0°35W **13** E7
Rushikulya → *India* 19°23N 85°5E **44** E7
Rushmore, Mt. *U.S.A.* 43°53N 103°28W **80** D3
Rushville *Ill., U.S.A.* 40°7N 90°34W **80** E8
Rushville *Ind., U.S.A.* 39°37N 85°27W **81** F11
Rushville *Nebr., U.S.A.* 42°43N 102°28W **80** D2
Russas *Brazil* 4°55S 37°50W **93** D11
Russell *Canada* 50°50N 101°20W **71** C8
Russell *Kans., U.S.A.* 38°54N 98°52W **80** F4
Russell *N.Y., U.S.A.* 44°27N 75°9W **83** B9
Russell *Pa., U.S.A.* 41°56N 79°8W **82** E5
Russell Cave △ *U.S.A.* 34°59N 85°49W **85** D12
Russell L. *Man., Canada* 56°15N 101°30W **71** B8
Russell L. *N.W.T., Canada* 63°5N 115°44W **70** A5
Russellkonda *India* 19°57N 84°42E **44** E7
Russellville *Ala., U.S.A.* 34°30N 87°44W **85** D11
Russellville *Ark., U.S.A.* 35°17N 93°8W **84** D8
Russellville *Ky., U.S.A.* 36°51N 86°53W **80** G10
Russia ■ *Eurasia* 62°0N 105°0E **27** C11
Russian → *U.S.A.* 38°27N 123°8W **78** G3
Rustam Shahr *Pakistan* 26°58N 66°6E **42** F2
Rustavi *Georgia* 41°30N 45°0E **19** F8
Rustenburg *S. Africa* 25°41S 27°14E **56** C4
Ruston *U.S.A.* 32°32N 92°38W **84** E8
Ruteng *Indonesia* 8°35S 120°30E **37** F6
Rutenga *Zimbabwe* 21°15S 30°44E **57** B5
Ruth *U.S.A.* 43°42N 82°45W **82** C2
Rutherford *U.S.A.* 38°26N 122°24W **78** G4
Rutland *U.S.A.* 43°37N 72°58W **83** C12
Rutland □ *U.K.* 52°38N 0°40W **13** E7
Rutland I. *India* 11°25N 92°10E **45** J11
Rutland Water *U.K.* 52°39N 0°38W **13** E7
Rutledge → *Canada* 61°4N 112°0W **71** A6
Rutledge L. *Canada* 61°33N 110°47W **71** A6
Rutog *China* 33°27N 79°42E **30** E4
Rutshuru
  Dem. Rep. of the Congo 1°13S 29°25E **54** E5
Ruvuma □ *Tanzania* 10°29S 40°28E **54** G8
Ruvuma → *Tanzania* 10°29S 40°28E **54** G8
Ruwais *U.A.E.* 24°5N 52°50E **47** E7
Ruwenzori *Africa* 0°30N 29°55E **54** D5
Ruya → *Zimbabwe* 16°27S 32°5E **57** A5
Ruyang *China* 34°9N 112°27E **32** G7
Ruyuan *China* 24°46N 113°16E **35** E9
Ruzhou *China* 34°11N 112°52E **32** G7
Ružomberok *Slovak Rep.* 49°3N 19°17E **17** D10
Rwanda ■ *Africa* 2°0S 30°0E **54** E5
Ryan, L. *U.K.* 55°0N 5°2W **11** G3
Ryazan *Russia* 54°40N 39°40E **18** D6
Ryazhsk *Russia* 53°45N 40°3E **18** D7
Rybachiy Poluostrov
  Russia 69°43N 32°0E **8** B25
Rybachye = Balykchy
  Kyrgyzstan 42°26N 76°12E **30** C4
Rybinsk *Russia* 58°5N 38°50E **18** C6
Rybinskoye Vdkhr.
  Russia 58°30N 38°25E **18** C6
Rybnitsa = Râbnița
  Moldova 47°45N 29°0E **17** E15
Rycroft *Canada* 55°45N 118°40W **70** B5
Ryde *U.K.* 50°43N 1°9W **13** G6
Ryderwood *U.S.A.* 46°23N 123°3W **78** D3
Rye → *U.K.* 54°11N 0°44W **12** C7
Rye Bay *U.K.* 50°52N 0°49E **13** G8
Rye Patch Res. *U.S.A.* 40°28N 118°19W **76** F4
Ryegate *U.S.A.* 46°18N 109°15W **76** C9
Ryley *Canada* 53°17N 112°26W **70** C6
Rylstone *Australia* 32°46S 149°58E **63** E4
Ryn Peski = Naryn Qum
  Kazakhstan 47°30N 49°0E **26** E5
Ryōtsu *Japan* 38°5N 138°28E **28** E9
Rypin *Poland* 53°3N 19°25E **17** B10
Ryūgasaki *Japan* 35°54N 140°11E **29** G10
Ryukyu Is. = Ryūkyū-Rettō
  Japan 26°0N 126°0E **29** M3
Ryūkyū-Rettō *Japan* 26°0N 126°0E **29** M3
Rzeszów *Poland* 50°5N 21°58E **17** C11
Rzhev *Russia* 56°20N 34°20E **18** C5

S

Sa Dec *Vietnam* 10°20N 105°46E **39** G5
Sa Kaeo *Thailand* 13°49N 102°4E **38** F4
Sa Pa *Vietnam* 22°20N 103°47E **38** A4
Sa'ad Shahr *Iran* 30°10N 53°5E **47** D7
Sa'ādatābād *Hormozgān,*
  Iran 28°3N 55°53E **47** D7
Sahara *Africa* 23°0N 5°0E **52** D6
Sa'ādatābād *Kermān, Iran* 29°40N 55°51E **47** D7

Saale → *Germany* 51°56N 11°54E **16** C6
Saalfeld *Germany* 50°38N 11°21E **16** C6
Saanich *Canada* 48°29N 123°26W **78** B3
Saar → *Europe* 49°41N 6°32E **15** E6
Saarbrücken *Germany* 49°14N 6°59E **16** D4
Saaremaa *Estonia* 58°30N 22°30E **9** G20
Saarijärvi *Finland* 62°43N 25°16E **8** E21
Sab 'Ābār *Syria* 33°46N 37°41E **46** C3
Saba *W. Indies* 17°38N 63°14W **89** C7
Šabac *Serbia* 44°48N 19°42E **23** B8
Sabadell *Spain* 41°28N 2°7E **21** B7
Sabah □ *Malaysia* 6°0N 117°0E **36** C5
Sabak Bernam *Malaysia* 3°46N 100°58E **39** L3
Sabalān, Kūhhā-ye *Iran* 38°15N 47°45E **46** B5
Sabalana, Kepulauan
  Indonesia 6°45S 118°50E **37** F5
Sabana de la Mar
  Dom. Rep. 19°7N 69°24W **89** C6
Sábanalarga *Colombia* 10°38N 74°55W **92** A4
Sabang *Indonesia* 5°50N 95°15E **36** C1
Sabari → *India* 17°35N 81°16E **44** F5
Sabarmati → *India* 22°18N 72°22E **42** H5
Sabattis *U.S.A.* 44°6N 74°40W **83** B10
Saberania *Indonesia* 2°5S 138°18E **37** E9
Sabhā *Libya* 27°9N 14°29E **53** C8
Sabi → *India* 28°29N 76°44E **42** E7
Sabie *S. Africa* 25°10S 30°48E **57** C5
Sabinal *U.S.A.* 29°19N 99°28W **84** G5
Sabinas *Mexico* 27°51N 101°7W **86** B4
Sabinas → *Mexico* 27°37N 100°42W **86** B4
Sabinas Hidalgo *Mexico* 26°30N 100°10W **86** B4
Sabine → *U.S.A.* 29°59N 93°47W **84** G8
Sabine L. *U.S.A.* 29°53N 93°51W **84** G8
Sabine Pass *U.S.A.* 29°44N 93°54W **84** G8
Sablayan *Phil.* 12°50N 120°50E **37** B6
Sable *Canada* 55°30N 68°21N **73** A6
Sable, C. *Canada* 43°29N 65°38W **73** D6
Sable, C. *U.S.A.* 25°9N 81°8W **88** A3
Sable I. *Canada* 44°0N 60°0W **73** D8
Sabrina Coast *Antarctica* 68°0S 120°0E **5** C9
Sabulubek *Indonesia* 1°36S 98°40E **36** E1
Sabzevār *Iran* 36°15N 57°40E **47** B8
Sabzvārān = Jiroft *Iran* 28°45N 57°50E **47** D8
Sac City *U.S.A.* 42°25N 95°0W **80** D6
Săcele *Romania* 45°37N 25°41E **17** F13
Sachigo → *Canada* 55°6N 88°58W **72** A2
Sachigo, L. *Canada* 53°50N 92°12W **72** B1
Sachimbo *Angola* 9°14S 20°16E **54** F4
Sachin *India* 21°5N 72°53E **44** D1
Sachsen □ *Germany* 50°55N 13°10E **16** C7
Sachsen-Anhalt □
  Germany 52°0N 12°0E **16** C7
Sackets Harbor *U.S.A.* 43°57N 76°7W **83** C8
Sackville *Canada* 45°54N 64°22W **73** C7
Saco *Maine, U.S.A.* 43°30N 70°27W **83** C14
Saco *Mont., U.S.A.* 48°28N 107°21W **76** B10
Sacramento *U.S.A.* 38°35N 121°29W **78** G5
Sacramento → *U.S.A.* 38°3N 121°56W **78** G5
Sacramento Mts.
  U.S.A. 32°30N 105°30W **77** K11
Sacramento Valley
  U.S.A. 39°30N 122°0W **78** G5
Sada-Misaki *Japan* 33°20N 132°5E **29** H6
Sadabad *India* 27°27N 78°3E **42** F8
Sadao *Thailand* 6°38N 100°26E **39** J3
Sadaseopet *India* 17°38N 77°59E **44** F3
Saddal el Aali *Egypt* 23°54N 32°54E **53** D12
Saddle Mt. *U.S.A.* 45°58N 123°41W **78** E3
Saddle Pk. *India* 13°9N 93°1E **45** H11
Sado *Japan* 38°0N 138°25E **28** E9
Sadra *India* 23°21N 72°43E **42** H5
Sadri *India* 25°11N 73°26E **42** G5
Sæby *Denmark* 57°21N 10°30E **9** H14
Saegertown *U.S.A.* 41°43N 80°9W **82** E4
Şafājah *Si. Arabia* 26°25N 39°0E **46** E3
Safata B. *Samoa* 14°0S 171°50W **59** b
Safed = Zefat *Israel* 32°58N 35°29E **48** C4
Safford *U.S.A.* 32°50N 109°43W **77** K9
Saffron Walden *U.K.* 52°1N 0°16E **13** E8
Safi *Morocco* 32°18N 9°20W **52** B4
Şafiābād *Iran* 36°45N 57°58E **47** B8
Safid Dasht *Iran* 33°27N 48°11E **47** C6
Safid Kūh *Afghan.* 34°45N 63°0E **40** B3
Safid Rūd → *Iran* 37°23N 50°11E **47** B6
Safipur *India* 26°44N 80°21E **43** F9
Safune *Samoa* 13°25S 172°21W **59** b
Şafwān *Iraq* 30°7N 47°43E **46** D5
Sag Harbor *U.S.A.* 41°0N 72°18W **83** F12
Saga *Japan* 33°15N 130°16E **29** H5
Saga □ *Japan* 33°15N 130°20E **29** H5
Sagae *Japan* 38°22N 140°17E **28** E10
Sagamore *U.S.A.* 40°46N 79°14W **82** F5
Saganaga L. *Canada* 48°14N 90°52W **80** A8
Saganthit Kyun *Burma* 11°56N 98°29E **39** G2
Sagar *Karnataka, India* 16°38N 76°48E **44** F3
Sagar *Karnataka, India* 14°14N 75°6E **45** G2
Sagar *Mad. P., India* 23°50N 78°44E **43** H8
Sagarmatha = Everest, Mt.
  Nepal 28°5N 86°58E **43** E12
Sagarmatha △ *Nepal* 27°55N 86°45E **43** E12
Saginaw *U.S.A.* 43°26N 83°56W **81** D12
Saginaw B. *U.S.A.* 43°50N 83°40W **81** D12
Saglouc = Salluit
  Canada 62°14N 75°38W **69** E16
Sagone *France* 42°14N 8°44E **20** E8
Sagua la Grande *Cuba* 22°50N 80°10W **88** B3
Saguache *U.S.A.* 38°5N 106°8W **76** G10
Saguaro △ *U.S.A.* 32°12N 110°38W **77** K8
Saguenay → *Canada* 48°22N 71°0W **73** C5
Sagunt = Sagunto *Spain* 39°42N 0°18W **21** C5
Sagunto *Spain* 39°42N 0°18W **21** C5
Sagwara *India* 23°41N 74°1E **42** H6
Sahagún *Spain* 42°18N 5°2W **21** A3
Sahand, Kūh-e *Iran* 37°44N 46°27E **46** B5
Sahara *Africa* 23°0N 5°0E **52** D6

Saharan Atlas = Saharien, Atlas
  Algeria 33°30N 1°0E **52** B6
Saharanpur *India* 29°58N 77°33E **42** E7
Saharien, Atlas *Algeria* 33°30N 1°0E **52** B6
Saharsa *India* 25°53N 86°36E **43** G12
Sahaswan *India* 28°5N 78°45E **43** E8
Saheira, W. el → *Egypt* 30°5N 33°25E **48** E2
Sahel *Africa* 16°0N 5°0E **52** E5
Sahibganj *India* 25°12N 87°40E **43** G12
Sāhilīyah *Iraq* 33°43N 42°42E **46** C4
Sahiwal *Pakistan* 30°45N 73°8E **42** D5
Şahneh *Iran* 34°29N 47°41E **46** C5
Sahrawi = Western Sahara ■
  Africa 25°0N 13°0W **52** D3
Sahuaripa *Mexico* 29°3N 109°14W **86** B3
Sahuarita *U.S.A.* 31°57N 110°58W **77** L8
Sahuayo de Díaz *Mexico* 20°4N 102°43W **86** C4
Sai → *India* 25°39N 82°47E **43** G10
Sai Buri *Thailand* 6°43N 101°45E **39** J3
Sai Thong △ *Thailand* 15°56N 101°10E **38** E3
Sai Yok △ *Thailand* 14°25N 98°40E **38** E2
Saibai I. *Australia* 9°25S 142°40E **62** a
Sa'id Bundās *South Sudan* 8°24N 24°48E **53** G10
Sa'īdābād = Sīrjān *Iran* 29°30N 55°45E **47** D7
Sa'īdābād *Iran* 36°8N 54°11E **47** B7
Saidpur *Bangla.* 25°48N 89°0E **41** G16
Saidpur *India* 25°33N 83°11E **43** G10
Saidu Sharif *Pakistan* 34°43N 72°24E **43** B5
Saigō *Japan* 36°12N 133°20E **29** F6
Saigon = Thanh Pho Ho Chi Minh
  Vietnam 10°58N 106°40E **39** G6
Saijō *Japan* 33°55N 133°11E **29** H6
Saikai △ *Japan* 33°12N 129°36E **29** H4
Saikhoa Ghat *India* 27°50N 95°40E **41** F19
Saiki *Japan* 32°58N 131°51E **29** H5
Sailana *India* 23°28N 74°55E **42** H6
Sailolof *Indonesia* 1°15S 130°46E **37** E8
Sailu *India* 19°28N 76°28E **44** E3
Saimaa *Finland* 61°15N 28°15E **8** F23
Saimen = Saimaa *Finland* 61°15N 28°15E **8** F23
Şa'in Dezh *Iran* 36°40N 46°25E **46** B5
St. Abb's Head *U.K.* 55°55N 2°8W **11** F6
St. Alban's *Canada* 47°51N 55°50W **73** C8
St. Albans *U.K.* 51°45N 0°19W **13** F7
St. Albans *Vt., U.S.A.* 44°49N 73°5W **83** B11
St. Albans *W. Va.,*
  U.S.A. 38°23N 81°50W **81** F13
St. Alban's Head *U.K.* 50°34N 2°4W **13** G5
St. Albert *Canada* 53°37N 113°32W **70** C6
St. Andrew's *Canada* 47°45N 59°15W **73** C8
St. Andrews *U.K.* 56°20N 2°47W **11** E6
St-Anicet *Canada* 45°8N 74°22W **83** A10
St. Annes *Canada* 49°40N 96°39W **71** D9
St. Anns B. *Canada* 46°22N 60°25W **73** C7
St. Ann's Bay *Jamaica* 18°26N 77°12W **88** a
St. Anthony *Canada* 51°22N 55°35W **73** B8
St. Anthony *U.S.A.* 43°58N 111°41W **76** E8
St-Antoine *Canada* 46°22N 64°45W **73** C7
St. Arnaud *Australia* 36°40S 143°16E **63** F3
St-Augustin *Canada* 51°13N 58°38W **73** B8
St-Augustin → *Canada* 51°16N 58°40W **73** B8
St. Augustine *U.S.A.* 29°54N 81°19W **85** G14
St. Austell *U.K.* 50°20N 4°47W **13** G3
St. Barbe *Canada* 51°12N 56°46W **73** B8
St-Barthélemy ☑
  W. Indies 17°50N 62°50W **89** C7
St. Barts = St-Barthélemy ☑
  W. Indies 17°50N 62°50W **89** C7
St. Bees Hd. *U.K.* 54°31N 3°38W **12** C4
St. Bees I. *Australia* 20°56S 149°26E **62** b
St-Benoît *Réunion* 21°2S 55°43E **55** c
St. Bride's *Canada* 46°56N 54°10W **73** C9
St. Brides B. *U.K.* 51°49N 5°9W **13** F2
St-Brieuc *France* 48°30N 2°46W **20** B2
St. Catharines *Canada* 43°10N 79°15W **82** C5
St. Catherines I. *U.S.A.* 31°40N 81°10W **85** F14
St. Catherine's Pt. *U.K.* 50°34N 1°18W **13** G6
St-Chamond *France* 45°28N 4°31E **20** D6
St. Charles *Ill., U.S.A.* 41°54N 88°19W **80** E9
St. Charles *Md., U.S.A.* 38°36N 76°56W **81** F15
St. Charles *Mo., U.S.A.* 38°47N 90°29W **80** F8
St. Charles *Va., U.S.A.* 36°48N 83°4W **81** G12
St. Christopher-Nevis = St. Kitts &
  Nevis ■ *W. Indies* 17°20N 62°40W **89** C7
St. Clair *Mich., U.S.A.* 42°50N 82°30W **82** D2
St. Clair *Pa., U.S.A.* 40°43N 76°12W **83** F8
St. Clair → *U.S.A.* 42°38N 82°31W **82** D2
St. Clair, L. *N. Amer.* 42°27N 82°39W **82** D2
St. Clairsville *U.S.A.* 40°5N 80°54W **82** F4
St. Claude *Canada* 49°40N 98°20W **71** D9
St. Clears *U.K.* 51°49N 4°31W **13** F3
St-Clet *Canada* 45°21N 74°13W **83** A10
St. Cloud *Fla., U.S.A.* 28°15N 81°17W **85** G14
St. Cloud *Minn., U.S.A.* 45°34N 94°10W **80** C7
St. Cricq, C. *Australia* 25°17S 113°6E **61** E1
St. Croix *U.S. Virgin Is.* 17°45N 64°45W **89** C7
St. Croix → *U.S.A.* 44°45N 92°48W **80** C7
St. Croix Falls *U.S.A.* 45°24N 92°38W **80** C7
St. David's *Canada* 48°12N 58°52W **73** C8
St. David's *U.K.* 51°53N 5°16W **13** F2
St. David's Head *U.K.* 51°54N 5°19W **13** F2
St-Denis *Réunion* 20°52S 55°27E **55** c
St-Denis (RUN) *Réunion* 20°52S 55°27E **55** c
St-Dizier *France* 48°38N 4°56E **20** B6
St. Elias, Mt. *U.S.A.* 60°18N 140°56W **68** E3
St. Elias Mts. *N. Amer.* 60°33N 139°28W **70** A1
St-Étienne *France* 45°27N 4°22E **20** D6
St. Eugène *Canada* 45°30N 74°28W **83** A10
St. Eustatius *W. Indies* 17°20N 63°0W **89** C7
St-Félicien *Canada* 48°40N 72°25W **72** C5
St-Flour *France* 45°2N 3°6E **20** D5
St. Francis *U.S.A.* 39°47N 101°48W **80** F3
St. Francis → *U.S.A.* 34°38N 90°36W **85** D9
St. Francis, C. *S. Africa* 34°14S 24°49E **56** E3
St. Francisville *U.S.A.* 30°47N 91°23W **84** F9
St-François, L. *Canada* 45°10N 74°22W **83** A10
St-Gabriel *Canada* 46°17N 73°24W **72** C5
St. Gallen = Sankt Gallen
  Switz. 47°26N 9°22E **20** C8

St-Gaudens *France*   43°6N 0°44E **20** E4
St. George *Australia*   28°1S 148°30E **63** D4
St. George *N.B., Canada*   45°11N 66°50W **73** C6
St. George *Ont., Canada*   43°15N 80°15W **82** C4
St. George *S.C., U.S.A.*   33°11N 80°35W **85** E14
St. George *Utah, U.S.A.*   37°6N 113°35W **77** H7
St. George, C. *Canada*   48°30N 59°16W **73** C8
St. George, C. *U.S.A.*   29°40N 85°5W **85** G12
St. George I. *U.S.A.*   56°35N 169°35W **74** D6
St. George's *Canada*   48°26N 58°31W **73** C8
St. George's *Grenada*   12°5N 61°43W **89** D7
St. George's B. *Canada*   48°24N 58°53W **73** C8
St. Georges Basin *N.S.W.,*
  Australia   35°7S 150°36E **63** F5
St. Georges Basin *W. Austral.,*
  Australia   15°23S 125°2E **60** C4
St. George's Channel *Europe* 52°0N 6°0W **10** E6
St. George's Channel
  India   7°15N 93°43E **45** L11
St. Georges Hd. *Australia* 35°12S 150°42E **63** F5
St. Gotthard P. = San Gottardo, P.
  del *Switz.*   46°33N 8°33E **20** C8
St. Helena *Atl. Oc.*   15°58S 5°42W **50** H3
St. Helena *U.S.A.*   38°30N 122°28W **78** G4
St. Helena, Mt. *U.S.A.*   38°40N 122°36W **78** G4
St. Helena B. *S. Africa*   32°40S 18°10E **56** D2
St. Helens *Australia*   41°20S 148°15E **63** G4
St. Helens *U.K.*   53°27N 2°44W **12** D5
St. Helens *U.S.A.*   45°52N 122°48W **78** E4
St. Helens, Mt. *U.S.A.*   46°12N 122°12W **78** D4
St. Helier *U.K.*   49°10N 2°7W **13** H5
St-Hyacinthe *Canada*   45°40N 72°58W **72** C5
St. Ignace *U.S.A.*   45°52N 84°44W **81** C11
St. Ignace I. *Canada*   48°45N 88°0W **72** C2
St. Ignatius *U.S.A.*   47°19N 114°6W **76** C6
St. Ives *Cambs., U.K.*   52°20N 0°4W **13** E7
St. Ives *Corn., U.K.*   50°12N 5°30W **13** G2
St. James *U.S.A.*   43°59N 94°38W **80** D6
St-Jean → *Canada*   50°17N 64°20W **73** B7
St-Jean, L. *Canada*   48°40N 72°0W **73** C5
St-Jean-Port-Joli *Canada* 47°15N 70°13W **73** C5
St-Jean-sur-Richelieu
  Canada   45°20N 73°20W **83** A11
St-Jérôme *Canada*   45°47N 74°0W **72** C5
St. John *Canada*   45°20N 66°8W **73** C6
St. John *U.S.A.*   38°0N 98°46W **80** F4
St. John → *N. Amer.*   45°12N 66°5W **81** C20
St. John, C. *Canada*   50°0N 55°32W **73** C9
St. John I. *U.S. Virgin Is.* 18°20N 64°42W **89** e
St. John's *Antigua & B.*   17°6N 61°51W **89** C7
St. John's *Canada*   47°35N 52°40W **73** C9
St. Johns *Ariz., U.S.A.*   34°30N 109°22W **77** J9
St. Johns *Mich., U.S.A.*   43°0N 84°33W **81** D11
St. Johns → *U.S.A.*   30°24N 81°24W **85** F14
St. John's Pt. *Ireland*   54°34N 8°27W **10** B3
St. Johnsbury *U.S.A.*   44°25N 72°1W **83** B12
St. Johnsville *U.S.A.*   43°0N 74°43W **83** C10
St. Joseph *Canada*   43°24N 81°42W **82** C3
St-Joseph *Martinique*   14°39N 61°4W **88** c
St-Joseph *Réunion*   21°22S 55°37E **55** c
St. Joseph *La., U.S.A.*   31°55N 91°14W **84** F9
St. Joseph *Mo., U.S.A.*   39°46N 94°50W **80** F7
St. Joseph → *U.S.A.*   42°7N 86°29W **80** D10
St. Joseph, I. *Canada*   46°12N 83°58W **72** C3
St. Joseph, L. *Canada*   51°10N 90°35W **72** B1
St. Kilda *U.K.*   57°49N 8°34W **14** C2
St. Kitts & Nevis ■
  W. Indies   17°20N 62°40W **89** C7
St. Laurent *Canada*   50°25N 97°58W **71** C9
St. Lawrence *Australia*   22°16S 149°31E **62** C4
St. Lawrence → *Canada*   46°54N 55°23W **73** C8
St. Lawrence → *Canada*   49°30N 66°0W **73** C6
St. Lawrence, Gulf of
  Canada   48°25N 62°0W **73** C7
St. Lawrence I. *U.S.A.*   63°30N 170°30W **74** C5
St. Lawrence Islands △
  Canada   44°27N 75°52W **83** B9
St. Léonard *Canada*   47°12N 67°58W **73** C6
St-Leu *Réunion*   21°9S 55°18E **55** c
St. Lewis → *Canada*   52°26N 56°11W **73** B8
St-Lô *France*   49°7N 1°5W **20** B3
St-Louis *Guadeloupe*   15°56N 61°19W **88** b
St-Louis *Réunion*   21°16S 55°25E **55** c
St. Louis *Senegal*   16°8N 16°27W **52** E2
St. Louis *U.S.A.*   38°37N 90°11W **80** F8
St. Louis → *U.S.A.*   46°44N 92°9W **80** B7
St-Luc *Canada*   45°22N 73°18W **83** A11
St. Lucia ■ *W. Indies*   14°0N 60°57W **89** f
St. Lucia, L. *S. Africa*   28°5S 32°30E **57** C5
St. Lucia △ *S. Africa*   28°6S 32°27E **57** C5
St. Lucia Channel
  W. Indies   14°15N 61°0W **89** D7
St. Maarten ☑ *W. Indies* 18°2N 63°5W **89** C7
St. Magnus B. *U.K.*   60°25N 1°35W **11** A7
St-Malo *France*   48°39N 2°1W **20** B2
St-Marc *Haiti*   19°10N 72°41W **89** C5
St. Maries *U.S.A.*   47°19N 116°35W **76** C5
St-Martin ☑ *W. Indies*   18°5N 63°5W **89** C7
St. Martin, C. *Martinique* 14°52N 61°14W **88** c
St. Martin, L. *Canada*   51°40N 98°30W **71** C9
St. Martins *Barbados*   13°5N 59°28W **89** g
St. Mary Is. *India*   13°20N 74°35E **45** H2
St. Mary Pk. *Australia*   31°32S 138°34E **63** E2
St. Marys *Australia*   41°35S 148°11E **63** G4
St. Marys *Canada*   43°20N 81°10W **82** C3
St. Mary's *Corn., U.K.*   49°55N 6°18W **13** H1
St. Mary's *Orkney, U.K.* 58°54N 2°54W **11** C6
St. Marys *Ga., U.S.A.*   30°44N 81°33W **85** F14
St. Marys *Pa., U.S.A.*   41°26N 78°34W **82** E6
St. Mary's, C. *Canada*   46°50N 54°12W **73** C9
St. Mary's B. *Canada*   46°50N 53°50W **73** C9
St. Mary's Bay *Canada*   44°25N 66°10W **73** D6
St-Mathieu, Pte. *France*   48°20N 4°45W **20** B1
St. Matthew I. *U.S.A.*   60°24N 172°42W **74** C5
St-Maurice → *Canada*   46°21N 72°31W **72** C5
St. Mawes *U.K.*   50°10N 5°2W **13** G2
St-Nazaire *France*   47°17N 2°12W **20** C2

St. Neots *U.K.*   52°14N 0°15W **13** E7
St-Omer *France*   50°45N 2°15E **20** A5
St-Pamphile *Canada*   46°58N 69°48W **73** C6
St-Pascal *Canada*   47°32N 69°48W **73** C6
St. Paul *Canada*   54°0N 111°17W **70** C6
St-Paul *Réunion*   20°59S 55°17E **55** c
St. Paul *Minn., U.S.A.*   44°56N 93°5W **80** C7
St. Paul *Nebr., U.S.A.*   41°13N 98°27W **80** E4
St-Paul → *Canada*   51°27N 57°42W **73** B8
St. Paul, Î. *Ind. Oc.*   38°55S 77°34E **3** F13
St. Paul I. *Canada*   47°12N 60°9W **73** C7
St. Paul I. *U.S.A.*   57°10N 170°15W **74** D5
St. Peter *U.S.A.*   44°20N 93°57W **80** C7
St. Peter Port *U.K.*   49°26N 2°33W **13** H5
St. Peters *N.S., Canada* 45°40N 60°53W **73** C7
St. Peters *P.E.I., Canada* 46°25N 62°35W **73** C7
St. Petersburg *U.S.A.*   27°46N 82°40W **85** H13
St-Phillippe *Réunion*   21°21S 55°44E **55** c
St-Pie *Canada*   45°30N 72°54W **83** A12
St-Pierre *Martinique*   14°45N 61°10W **88** c
St-Pierre *Réunion*   21°19S 55°28E **55** c
St-Pierre *St-P. & M.*   46°46N 56°12W **73** C8
St-Pierre, L. *Canada*   46°12N 72°52W **72** C5
St-Pierre-et-Miquelon ☑
  N. Amer.   46°55N 56°10W **73** C8
St-Quentin *Canada*   47°30N 67°23W **73** C6
St-Quentin *France*   49°50N 3°16E **20** B5
St. Regis *U.S.A.*   47°18N 115°6W **76** C6
St. Regis Falls *U.S.A.*   44°40N 74°32W **83** B10
St-Siméon *Canada*   47°51N 69°54W **73** C6
St. Simons I. *U.S.A.*   31°12N 81°15W **85** F14
St. Simons Island *U.S.A.* 31°9N 81°22W **85** F14
St. Stephen *Canada*   45°16N 67°17W **73** C6
St. Thomas *Canada*   42°45N 81°10W **82** D3
St. Thomas I.
  U.S. Virgin Is.   18°20N 64°55W **89** e
St-Tite *Canada*   46°45N 72°34W **72** C5
St-Trond = Sint-Truiden
  Belgium   50°48N 5°10E **15** D5
St-Tropez *France*   43°17N 6°38E **20** E7
St. Vidgeon's ☉ *Australia* 14°47S 134°53E **62** A1
St. Vincent = São Vicente
  C. Verde Is.   17°0N 25°0W **52** b
St. Vincent, G. *Australia* 35°0S 138°0E **63** F2
St. Vincent & the Grenadines ■
  W. Indies   13°0N 61°10W **89** D7
St. Vincent Passage
  W. Indies   13°30N 61°0W **89** D7
St-Vith *Belgium*   50°17N 6°9E **15** D6
St. Walburg *Canada*   53°39N 109°12W **71** C7
Saintala *India*   20°26N 83°20E **44** D8
Ste-Agathe-des-Monts
  Canada   46°3N 74°17W **72** C5
Ste-Anne *Guadeloupe*   16°13N 61°24W **88** b
Ste-Anne *Seychelles*   4°36S 55°31E **55** b
Ste-Anne, L. *Canada*   50°0N 67°42W **73** B6
Ste-Anne-des-Monts
  Canada   49°8N 66°30W **73** C6
Ste. Genevieve *U.S.A.*   37°59N 90°2W **80** G8
Ste-Marguerite →
  Canada   50°9N 66°36W **73** B6
Ste-Marie *Canada*   46°26N 71°0W **73** C5
Ste-Marie *Martinique*   14°48N 61°1W **88** c
Ste-Marie, Ile = Boraha, Nosy
  Madag.   16°50S 49°55E **55** H9
Ste-Rose *Guadeloupe*   16°20N 61°45W **88** b
Ste-Rose *Réunion*   21°8S 55°45E **55** c
Ste. Rose du Lac *Canada* 51°4N 99°30W **71** C9
Saintes *France*   45°45N 0°37W **20** D3
Saintes, Îs. des *Guadeloupe* 15°50N 61°35W **88** b
Saintfield *U.K.*   54°28N 5°49W **10** B6
Saintonge *France*   45°40N 0°50W **20** D3
Saipal *Nepal*   29°50N 81°40E **43** E9
Saipan *N. Marianas*   15°12N 145°45E **64** F6
Sairang *India*   23°50N 92°45E **41** H18
Sairecábur, Cerro *Bolivia* 22°43S 67°54W **94** A2
Saitama □ *Japan*   35°54N 139°38E **29** G9
Saitama □ *Japan*   36°25N 139°30E **29** F9
Saiyid *Pakistan*   33°7N 73°2E **42** C5
Sajama *Bolivia*   18°7S 69°0W **92** G5
Sajószentpéter *Hungary* 48°12N 20°44E **17** D11
Sajum *India*   33°20N 79°0E **43** C8
Sak → *S. Africa*   30°52S 20°25E **56** D3
Sakaide *Japan*   34°19N 133°50E **29** G6
Sakaiminato *Japan*   35°38N 133°11E **29** G6
Sakākah *Si. Arabia*   30°0N 40°8E **46** D4
Sakakawea, L. *U.S.A.*   47°30N 101°25W **80** B3
Sakami → *Canada*   53°40N 76°40W **72** B4
Sakami, L. *Canada*   53°15N 77°0W **72** B4
Sakartvelo = Georgia ■
  Asia   42°0N 43°0E **19** F7
Sakarya *Turkey*   40°48N 30°25E **19** F5
Sakashima-Guntō *Japan* 24°46N 124°0E **29** M2
Sakata *Japan*   38°55N 139°50E **28** E9
Sakchu *N. Korea*   40°23N 125°2E **33** D13
Sakha □ *Russia*   66°0N 130°0E **27** C14
Sakhalin *Russia*   51°0N 143°0E **27** D15
Sakhalinskiy Zaliv
  Russia   54°0N 141°0E **27** D15
Sakhi Gopal *India*   19°58N 85°50E **44** E7
Šakiai *Lithuania*   54°59N 23°2E **9** J20
Sakoli *India*   21°5N 79°59E **44** D4
Sakon Nakhon *Thailand* 17°10N 104°9E **38** D5
Sakrand *Pakistan*   26°10N 68°15E **42** F3
Sakri *Maharashtra, India* 21°2N 74°20E **44** D2
Sakri *Maharashtra, India* 26°13N 86°5E **43** F12
Sakrivier *S. Africa*   30°54S 20°28E **56** D3
Saksi *India*   22°2N 82°58E **43** H10
Sakuma *Japan*   35°3N 137°49E **29** G8
Sakurai *Japan*   34°30N 135°51E **29** G7
Sal → *Russia*   47°33N 43°0E **19** E7
Sal *C. Verde Is.*   16°45N 22°55E **52** b
Sal Rei *C. Verde Is.*   16°11N 22°53W **52** b
Sala *Sweden*   59°58N 16°35E **9** G17
Sala Consilina *Italy*   40°23N 15°36E **22** D6
Sala-y-Gómez *Pac. Oc.* 26°28S 105°28W **65** K17
Sala y Gómez Ridge
  Pac. Oc.   25°0S 98°0W **65** K18
Salaberry-de-Valleyfield
  Canada   45°15N 74°8W **83** A10

Salada, L. *Mexico*   32°20N 115°40W **77** K6
Saladas *Argentina*   28°15S 58°40W **94** B4
Saladillo *Argentina*   35°40S 59°55W **94** D4
Salado → *B. Aires,*
  Argentina   35°44S 57°22W **94** D4
Salado → *La Pampa,*
  Argentina   37°30S 67°0W **96** D3
Salado → *Santa Fe,*
  Argentina   31°40S 60°41W **94** C3
Salado → *Mexico*   26°52N 99°19W **84** H5
Salaga *Ghana*   8°31N 0°31W **52** G5
Sālah *Syria*   32°40N 36°45E **48** C5
Şalāḩ ad Dīn □ *Iraq*   34°35N 43°35E **46** C4
Salālah *Oman*   16°56N 53°59E **49** D5
Salamanca *Chile*   31°46S 70°59W **94** C1
Salamanca *Spain*   40°58N 5°39W **21** B3
Salamanca *U.S.A.*   42°10N 78°43W **82** D6
Salāmatābād *Iran*   35°39N 47°50E **46** C5
Salamina *Greece*   37°56N 23°30E **23** F10
Salar de Atacama *Chile* 23°30S 68°25W **94** A2
Salar de Uyuni *Bolivia* 20°30S 67°45W **92** H5
Salatiga *Indonesia*   7°19S 110°30E **37** G14
Salavat *Russia*   53°21N 55°55E **18** D10
Salaverry *Peru*   8°15S 79°0W **92** E3
Salawati *Indonesia*   1°7S 130°52E **37** E8
Salawin → *Thailand*   18°18N 97°40E **38** C1
Salaya *India*   22°19N 69°35E **42** H3
Salayar *Indonesia*   6°7S 120°30E **37** F6
Salcombe *U.K.*   50°14N 3°47W **13** G4
Saldanha *S. Africa*   33°0S 17°58E **56** D2
Saldanha B. *S. Africa*   33°6S 18°0E **56** D2
Saldus *Latvia*   56°38N 22°30E **9** H20
Sale *Australia*   38°6S 147°6E **63** F4
Salé *Morocco*   34°3N 6°48E **52** B4
Sale *U.K.*   53°26N 2°19W **12** D5
Salekhard *Russia*   66°30N 66°35E **26** C7
Salelologa *Samoa*   13°41S 172°11W **59** b
Salem *India*   11°40N 78°11E **45** J4
Salem *Ill., U.S.A.*   38°38N 88°57W **80** F9
Salem *Ind., U.S.A.*   38°36N 86°6W **80** F10
Salem *Mass., U.S.A.*   42°31N 70°53W **83** D14
Salem *Mo., U.S.A.*   37°39N 91°32W **80** G8
Salem *N.H., U.S.A.*   42°45N 71°12W **83** D13
Salem *N.J., U.S.A.*   39°34N 75°28W **81** F16
Salem *N.Y., U.S.A.*   43°10N 73°20W **83** C11
Salem *Ohio, U.S.A.*   40°54N 80°52W **82** F4
Salem *Oreg., U.S.A.*   44°56N 123°2W **76** D2
Salem *S. Dak., U.S.A.*   43°44N 97°23W **80** D5
Salem *Va., U.S.A.*   37°18N 80°3W **81** G13
Salerno *Italy*   40°41N 14°47E **22** D6
Salford *U.K.*   53°30N 2°18W **12** D5
Salgótarján *Hungary*   48°5N 19°47E **17** D10
Salgueiro *Brazil*   8°4S 39°6W **93** E11
Salher *India*   20°40N 73°55E **44** D1
Salibabu *Indonesia*   3°51N 126°40E **37** D7
Salibea = Salybia
  Trin. & Tob.   10°43N 61°2W **93** K15
Salida *U.S.A.*   38°32N 106°0W **76** G11
Salihli *Turkey*   38°28N 28°8E **23** E13
Salihorsk *Belarus*   52°51N 27°27E **17** B14
Salima *Malawi*   13°47S 34°28E **55** G6
Salina *Italy*   38°34N 14°50E **22** E6
Salina *Kans., U.S.A.*   38°50N 97°37W **80** F5
Salina *Utah, U.S.A.*   38°58N 111°51W **76** G8
Salina Cruz *Mexico*   16°10N 95°12W **87** D5
Salinas *Brazil*   16°10S 42°10W **93** G10
Salinas *Ecuador*   2°10S 80°58W **92** D2
Salinas *U.S.A.*   36°40N 121°39W **78** J5
Salinas → *Guatemala* 16°28N 90°31W **87** D6
Salinas → *U.S.A.*   36°45N 121°48W **78** J5
Salinas, B. de *Nic.*   11°4N 85°45W **88** D2
Salinas, Pampa de las
  Argentina   31°58S 66°42W **94** C2
Salinas Ambargasta
  Argentina   29°0S 65°0W **94** B3
Salinas de Hidalgo
  Mexico   22°38N 101°43W **86** C4
Salinas Grandes *Argentina* 30°0S 65°0W **94** C3
Salinas Pueblo Missions △
  U.S.A.   34°6N 106°4W **77** J10
Salinas Valley *U.S.A.*   36°15N 121°15W **78** J5
Saline → *Ark., U.S.A.*   33°10N 92°8W **84** E8
Saline → *Kans., U.S.A.* 38°52N 97°30W **80** F5
Salinópolis *Brazil*   0°40S 47°20W **93** D9
Salisbury *Australia*   34°46S 138°38E **63** E2
Salisbury *U.K.*   51°4N 1°47W **13** F6
Salisbury *Md., U.S.A.*   38°22N 75°36W **81** F16
Salisbury *N.C., U.S.A.*   35°40N 80°29W **85** D14
Salisbury I. *Canada*   63°30N 77°0W **69** E16
Salisbury Plain *U.K.*   51°14N 1°55W **13** F6
Şalkhad *Syria*   32°29N 36°43E **48** C5
Salla *Finland*   66°50N 28°49E **8** C23
Salliq = Coral Harbour
  Canada   64°8N 83°10W **69** E15
Sallisaw *U.S.A.*   35°28N 94°47W **84** D7
Salluit *Canada*   62°14N 75°38W **69** E16
Sallyana *Nepal*   28°22N 82°10E **43** E10
Salmās *Iran*   38°11N 44°47E **46** B5
Salmo *Canada*   49°10N 117°20W **70** D5
Salmon *U.S.A.*   45°11N 113°54W **76** D7
Salmon → *Canada*   54°3N 122°40W **70** C4
Salmon → *U.S.A.*   45°51N 116°47W **76** D5
Salmon Arm *Canada*   50°40N 119°15W **70** C5
Salmon Gums *Australia* 32°59S 121°38E **61** F3
Salmon Pt. *Canada*   43°52N 77°15W **82** C7
Salmon River Mts.
  U.S.A.   44°50N 115°30W **76** D6
Salmon River Res.
  U.S.A.   43°32N 75°55W **83** C9
Salo *Finland*   60°22N 23°10E **9** F20
Salome *U.S.A.*   33°47N 113°37W **79** M13
Salon *India*   26°2N 81°27E **43** F9
Salon-de-Provence *France* 43°39N 5°6E **20** E6
Salonica = Thessaloníki
  Greece   40°38N 22°58E **23** D10
Salonta *Romania*   46°49N 21°42E **17** E11
Salpausselkä *Finland*   61°3N 26°15E **8** F22
Salsacate *Argentina*   31°20S 65°5W **94** C2
Salsk *Russia*   46°28N 41°30E **19** E7

Salso → *Italy*   37°6N 13°57E **22** F5
Salt → *Canada*   60°0N 112°25W **70** B6
Salt → *U.S.A.*   33°23N 112°19W **77** K7
Salt Fork Red → *U.S.A.* 34°27N 99°21W **84** D5
Salt L. *Australia*   30°6S 142°8E **63** E3
Salt Lake City *U.S.A.*   40°45N 111°53W **76** F8
Salt Range *Pakistan*   32°30N 72°25E **42** C5
Salta *Argentina*   24°57S 65°25W **94** A2
Salta □ *Argentina*   24°48S 65°30W **94** A2
Saltash *U.K.*   50°24N 4°14W **13** G3
Saltburn by the Sea *U.K.* 54°35N 0°58W **12** C7
Saltcoats *U.K.*   55°38N 4°47W **11** F4
Saltee Is. *Ireland*   52°7N 6°37W **10** D5
Saltfjellet *Norway*   66°40N 15°15E **8** C16
Saltfjorden *Norway*   67°15N 14°10E **8** C16
Saltillo *Mexico*   25°25N 101°0W **86** B4
Salto *Argentina*   34°20S 60°15W **94** C3
Salto *Uruguay*   31°27S 57°50W **94** C4
Salto → *Italy*   42°26N 12°25E **22** C5
Salto del Guaira *Paraguay* 24°3S 54°17W **95** A5
Salton City *U.S.A.*   33°18N 115°57W **79** M11
Salton Sea *U.S.A.*   33°15N 115°45W **79** M11
Saltsburg *U.S.A.*   40°29N 79°27W **82** F5
Saluda → *U.S.A.*   34°1N 81°4W **85** D14
Salûm *Egypt*   31°31N 25°7E **53** B11
Salur *India*   18°27N 83°18E **44** E6
Salvador *Brazil*   13°0S 38°30W **93** F11
Salvador *Canada*   52°10N 109°32W **71** C7
Salvador, El ■ *Cent. Amer.* 13°50N 89°0W **88** D2
Salvador, L. *U.S.A.*   29°43N 90°15W **85** G9
Salween → *Burma*   16°31N 97°37E **41** L20
Salyan *Azerbaijan*   39°33N 48°59E **47** B6
Salybia *Trin. & Tob.*   10°43N 61°2W **93** K15
Salzach → *Austria*   48°12N 12°56E **16** D7
Salzburg *Austria*   47°48N 13°2E **16** E7
Salzgitter *Germany*   52°9N 10°19E **16** B6
Salzwedel *Germany*   52°52N 11°10E **16** B6
Sam *India*   26°50N 70°31E **42** F4
Sam Neua *Laos*   20°29N 104°5E **38** B5
Sam Ngao *Thailand*   17°18N 99°0E **38** D2
Sam Rayburn Res. *U.S.A.* 31°4N 94°5W **84** F7
Sam Rong, Laem *Thailand* 9°35N 100°4E **39** b
Sam Son *Vietnam*   19°44N 105°54E **38** C5
Sama de Langreo = Langreo
  Spain   43°18N 5°40W **21** A3
Samagaltay *Russia*   50°36N 95°3E **27** D10
Samales Group *Phil.*   6°0N 122°0E **37** C6
Samalkot *India*   17°3N 82°13E **44** F6
Samana *India*   30°10N 76°13E **42** D7
Samana Cays *Bahamas* 23°3N 73°45W **89** B5
Samangān □ *Afghan.*   36°15N 68°3E **40** B5
Samani *Japan*   42°7N 142°56E **28** C11
Samar *Phil.*   12°0N 125°0E **37** B7
Samara *Russia*   53°8N 50°6E **18** D9
Samaria = Shōmron
  West Bank   32°15N 35°13E **48** C4
Samarinda *Indonesia*   0°30S 117°9E **36** E5
Samarkand = Samarqand
  Uzbekistan   39°40N 66°55E **26** F7
Samarqand *Uzbekistan* 39°40N 66°55E **26** F7
Sāmarrā' *Iraq*   34°12N 43°52E **46** C4
Samastipur *India*   25°50N 85°50E **43** G11
Samba *India*   32°32N 75°10E **43** C6
Sambalpur *India*   21°28N 84°4E **44** D7
Sambar, Tanjung
  Indonesia   2°59S 110°19E **36** E4
Sambas *Indonesia*   1°20N 109°20E **36** D3
Sambava *Madag.*   14°16S 50°10E **55** G10
Sambhajinagar = Aurangabad
  India   19°50N 75°23E **44** E2
Sambhal *India*   28°35N 78°37E **43** E8
Sambhar *India*   26°52N 75°6E **42** F6
Sambhar L. *India*   26°55N 75°12E **42** F6
Sambiase *Italy*   38°58N 16°17E **22** E7
Sambir *Ukraine*   49°30N 23°10E **17** D12
Sambor *Cambodia*   12°46N 106°0E **38** F6
Samborombón, B.
  Argentina   36°5S 57°20W **94** D4
Samcheok *S. Korea*   37°30N 129°10E **33** F15
Samet, Ko *Thailand*   12°34N 101°27E **38** F3
Sammanturai *Sri Lanka* 7°36N 81°39E **45** L5
Samnah *Si. Arabia*   25°10N 37°15E **46** E3
Samo Alto *Chile*   30°22S 71°0W **94** C1
Samoa ■ *Pac. Oc.*   14°0S 172°0W **59** b
Samoan Is. *Pac. Oc.*   14°0S 171°0W **59** b
Samokov *Bulgaria*   42°18N 23°35E **23** C10
Samos *Greece*   37°45N 26°50E **23** F12
Samothráki = Mathraki
  Greece   39°48N 19°31E **23** E8
Samothraki *Greece*   40°28N 25°28E **23** D11
Sampacho *Argentina*   33°20S 64°50W **94** C3
Sampalan *Indonesia*   8°41S 115°34E **37** K18
Sampang *Indonesia*   7°11S 113°13E **37** G15
Sampit *Indonesia*   2°34S 113°0E **36** E4
Sampit, Teluk *Indonesia* 3°5S 113°3E **36** E4
Samrong *Cambodia*   14°15N 103°30E **38** E4
Samsø *Denmark*   55°50N 10°35E **9** J14
Samsun *Turkey*   41°15N 36°22E **19** F6
Samui, Ko *Thailand*   9°30N 100°0E **39** b
Samut Sakhon *Thailand* 13°31N 100°13E **38** F3
Samut Songkhram
  Thailand   13°24N 100°1E **38** F3
Samwari *Pakistan*   28°30N 66°46E **42** E2
San *Mali*   13°15N 4°57W **52** F5
San → *Cambodia*   13°32N 105°57E **38** F5
San → *Poland*   50°45N 21°51E **17** C11
San Agustín, C. *Phil.*   6°20N 126°13E **37** C7
San Agustín de Valle Fértil
  Argentina   30°35S 67°30W **94** C2
San Ambrosio *Pac. Oc.*   26°28S 79°53W **90** F3
San Andreas *U.S.A.*   38°12N 120°41W **78** G6
San Andrés, I. de
  Caribbean   12°42N 81°46W **88** D3
San Andres Mts. *U.S.A.* 33°0N 106°30W **77** K10
San Andrés Tuxtla
  Mexico   18°27N 95°13W **87** D5

San Antonio *Belize*   16°15N 89°2W **87** D7
San Antonio *Chile*   33°40S 71°40W **94** C1
San Antonio *N. Mex.,*
  U.S.A.   33°55N 106°52W **77** K10
San Antonio *Tex., U.S.A.* 29°25N 98°29W **84** G5
San Antonio → *U.S.A.* 28°30N 96°54W **84** G6
San Antonio, C.
  Argentina   36°15S 56°40W **94** D4
San Antonio, C. de *Cuba* 21°50N 84°57W **88** B3
San Antonio, Mt.
  U.S.A.   34°17N 117°38W **79** L9
San Antonio de los Baños
  Cuba   22°54N 82°31W **88** B3
San Antonio de los Cobres
  Argentina   24°10S 66°17W **94** A2
San Antonio Oeste
  Argentina   40°40S 65°0W **96** E4
San Ardo *U.S.A.*   36°1N 120°54W **78** J6
San Augustine *U.S.A.*   31°32N 94°7W **84** F7
San Benedetto del Tronto
  Italy   42°57N 13°53E **22** C5
San Benedicto, I.
  Mexico   19°18N 110°49W **86** D2
San Benito *U.S.A.*   26°8N 97°38W **84** H6
San Benito → *U.S.A.*   36°53N 121°34W **78** J5
San Benito Mt. *U.S.A.*   36°22N 120°37W **78** J6
San Bernardino *U.S.A.*   34°7N 117°19W **79** L9
San Bernardino Mts.
  U.S.A.   34°10N 116°45W **79** L10
San Bernardino Str.
  Phil.   12°30N 124°10E **37** B7
San Bernardo *Chile*   33°40S 70°50W **94** C1
San Bernardo, I. de
  Colombia   9°45N 75°50W **92** B3
San Blas *Mexico*   26°5N 108°46W **86** B3
San Blas, Arch. de
  Panama   9°50N 78°31W **88** E4
San Blas, C. *U.S.A.*   29°40N 85°21W **85** G12
San Borja *Bolivia*   14°50S 66°52W **92** F5
San Buenaventura = Ventura
  U.S.A.   34°17N 119°18W **79** L7
San Buenaventura
  Mexico   27°5N 101°32W **86** B4
San Carlos *Argentina*   33°50S 69°0W **94** C2
San Carlos *Chile*   36°10S 72°0W **94** D1
San Carlos *Baja Calif. S.,*
  Mexico   24°47N 112°7W **86** C2
San Carlos *Coahuila,*
  Mexico   29°1N 100°51W **86** B4
San Carlos *Nic.*   11°12N 84°50W **88** D3
San Carlos *Phil.*   10°29N 123°25E **37** B6
San Carlos *Uruguay*   34°46S 54°58W **95** C5
San Carlos *Venezuela*   9°40N 68°36W **92** B5
San Carlos de Bariloche
  Argentina   41°10S 71°25W **96** E2
San Carlos de Bolívar
  Argentina   36°15S 61°6W **94** D3
San Carlos del Zulia
  Venezuela   9°1N 71°55W **92** B4
San Carlos L. *U.S.A.*   33°11N 110°32W **77** K8
San Clemente *Chile*   35°30S 71°29W **94** D1
San Clemente *U.S.A.*   33°26N 117°37W **79** M9
San Clemente I. *U.S.A.* 32°53N 118°29W **79** N8
San Cristóbal *Argentina* 30°20S 61°10W **94** C3
San Cristóbal *Dom. Rep.* 18°25N 70°6W **89** C5
San Cristóbal *Solomon Is.* 10°30S 161°0E **58** C9
San Cristóbal *Venezuela* 7°46N 72°14W **92** B4
San Cristóbal de las Casas
  Mexico   16°45N 92°38W **87** D6
San Diego *Calif., U.S.A.* 32°42N 117°9W **79** N9
San Diego *Tex., U.S.A.*   27°46N 98°14W **84** H5
San Diego, C. *Argentina* 54°40S 65°10W **96** G3
San Diego de la Unión
  Mexico   21°28N 100°52W **86** C4
San Diego Int. ✈ (SAN)
  U.S.A.   32°44N 117°11W **79** N9
San Estanislao *Paraguay* 24°39S 56°26W **94** A4
San Felipe *Chile*   32°43S 70°42W **94** C1
San Felipe *Mexico*   31°1N 114°52W **86** A2
San Felipe *Venezuela*   10°20N 68°44W **92** A5
San Felipe → *U.S.A.*   33°12N 115°49W **79** M11
San Félix *Chile*   28°56S 70°28W **94** B1
San Félix *Pac. Oc.*   26°23S 80°0W **90** F2
San Fernando *Chile*   34°30S 71°0W **94** C1
San Fernando *Mexico*   24°51N 98°10W **87** C5
San Fernando *La Unión,*
  Phil.   16°40N 120°23E **37** A6
San Fernando *Pampanga,*
  Phil.   15°5N 120°37E **37** A6
San Fernando *Spain*   36°28N 6°17W **21** D2
San Fernando
  Trin. & Tob.   10°16N 61°28W **93** K15
San Fernando *U.S.A.*   34°17N 118°26W **79** L8
San Fernando de Apure
  Venezuela   7°54N 67°15W **92** B5
San Fernando de Atabapo
  Venezuela   4°3N 67°42W **92** C5
San Francisco *Argentina* 31°30S 62°5W **94** C3
San Francisco →
  U.S.A.   32°59N 109°22W **77** K9
San Francisco, C. de
  Colombia   6°18N 77°29W **90** C2
San Francisco, Paso de
  S. Amer.   27°0S 68°0W **94** B2
San Francisco de Macorís
  Dom. Rep.   19°19N 70°15W **89** C5
San Francisco del Monte de Oro
  Argentina   32°36S 66°8W **94** C2
San Francisco del Oro
  Mexico   26°52N 105°51W **86** B3
San Francisco Int. ✈ (SFO)
  U.S.A.   37°37N 122°22W **78** H4
San Gabriel *Chile*   33°47S 70°15W **94** C1
San Gabriel Chilac
  Mexico   18°19N 97°21W **87** D5
San Gabriel Mts. *U.S.A.* 34°17N 117°38W **79** L9
San Gavino Monreale
  Italy   39°33N 8°47E **22** E3

San German *Puerto Rico* 18°4N 67°4W **89 d**
San Gorgonio Mt.
U.S.A. 34°6N 116°50W **79 L10**
San Gottardo, P. del *Switz.* 46°33N 8°33E **20 C8**
San Gregorio *Uruguay* 32°37S 55°40W **95 C4**
San Gregorio *U.S.A.* 37°20N 122°23W **78 H4**
San Guillermo △
Argentina 27°50S 69°45W **94 B2**
San Ignacio *Belize* 17°10N 89°5W **87 D7**
San Ignacio *Bolivia* 16°20S 60°55W **92 G6**
San Ignacio *Mexico* 27°27N 112°51W **86 B2**
San Ignacio *Paraguay* 26°52S 57°3W **94 B4**
San Ignacio, L. *Mexico* 26°54N 113°13W **86 B2**
San Ildefonso, C. *Phil.* 16°0N 122°1E **37 A6**
San Isidro *Argentina* 34°29S 58°31W **94 C4**
San Jacinto *U.S.A.* 33°47N 116°57W **79 M10**
San Javier *Misiones,*
Argentina 27°55S 55°5W **95 B4**
San Javier *Santa Fe,*
Argentina 30°40S 59°55W **94 C4**
San Javier *Bolivia* 16°18S 62°30W **92 G6**
San Javier *Chile* 35°40S 71°45W **94 D1**
San Jerónimo Taviche
Mexico 16°44N 96°35W **87 D5**
San Joaquin *U.S.A.* 36°36N 120°11W **78 J6**
San Joaquin → *U.S.A.* 38°4N 121°51W **78 G5**
San Joaquin Valley
U.S.A. 37°20N 121°0W **78 J6**
San Jon *U.S.A.* 35°6N 103°20W **77 J12**
San Jorge *Argentina* 31°54S 61°50W **94 C3**
San Jorge, B. *Mexico* 31°20N 113°20W **86 A2**
San Jorge, G. *Argentina* 46°0S 66°0W **96 F3**
San José *Argentina* 32°12S 58°15W **94 C4**
San José *Costa Rica* 9°55N 84°2W **88 E3**
San José *Guatemala* 14°0N 90°50W **88 D1**
San Jose *Mind. Occ., Phil.* 12°27N 121°4E **37 B6**
San Jose *Nueva Ecija,*
Phil. 15°45N 120°55E **37 A6**
San Jose *U.S.A.* 37°20N 121°53W **78 H5**
San Jose → *U.S.A.* 34°25N 106°45W **77 J10**
San José, I. *Mexico* 25°0N 110°38W **86 C2**
San Jose de Buenavista
Phil. 10°45N 121°56E **37 B6**
San José de Chiquitos
Bolivia 17°53S 60°50W **92 G6**
San José de Feliciano
Argentina 30°26S 58°46W **94 C4**
San José de Jáchal
Argentina 30°15S 68°46W **94 C2**
San José de Mayo
Uruguay 34°27S 56°40W **94 C4**
San José del Cabo *Mexico* 23°3N 109°41W **86 C3**
San José del Guaviare
Colombia 2°35N 72°38W **92 C4**
San Juan *Argentina* 31°30S 68°30W **94 C2**
San Juan *Puerto Rico* 18°28N 66°7W **89 d**
San Juan *Trin. & Tob.* 10°39N 61°29W **93 K15**
San Juan □ *Argentina* 31°9S 69°0W **94 C2**
San Juan → *Argentina* 32°20S 67°25W **94 C2**
San Juan → *Nic.* 10°56N 83°42W **88 D3**
San Juan → *U.S.A.* 37°16N 110°26W **77 H8**
San Juan Bautista
Paraguay 26°37S 57°6W **94 B4**
San Juan Bautista
U.S.A. 36°51N 121°32W **78 J5**
San Juan Capistrano
U.S.A. 33°30N 117°40W **79 M9**
San Juan Cr. → *U.S.A.* 35°40N 120°22W **78 J5**
San Juan de Guadelupe
Mexico 24°38N 102°44W **86 C4**
San Juan de la Costa
Mexico 24°20N 110°41W **86 C2**
San Juan de los Lagos
Mexico 21°15N 102°18W **86 C4**
San Juan de los Morros
Venezuela 9°55N 67°21W **92 B5**
San Juan del Norte *Nic.* 10°58N 83°40W **88 D3**
San Juan del Norte, B. de
Nic. 11°0N 83°40W **88 D3**
San Juan del Río *Mexico* 20°23N 100°0W **87 C5**
San Juan del Sur *Nic.* 11°20N 85°51W **88 D2**
San Juan I. *U.S.A.* 48°32N 123°5W **78 B3**
San Juan Island △
U.S.A. 48°35N 123°8W **78 B4**
San Justo *Argentina* 30°47S 60°30W **94 C3**
San Kamphaeng *Thailand* 18°45N 99°8E **38 C2**
San Lázaro, C. *Mexico* 24°50N 112°18W **86 C2**
San Leandro *U.S.A.* 37°42N 122°9W **78 H4**
San Lorenzo *Argentina* 32°45S 60°45W **94 C3**
San Lorenzo *Ecuador* 1°15N 78°50W **92 C3**
San Lorenzo *Paraguay* 25°20S 57°32W **94 B4**
San Lorenzo → *Mexico* 24°15N 107°24W **86 C3**
San Lorenzo, I. *Mexico* 28°38N 112°51W **86 B2**
San Lorenzo, Mte.
Argentina 47°40S 72°20W **96 F2**
San Lucas = Cabo San Lucas
Mexico 22°53N 109°54W **86 C3**
San Lucas *Bolivia* 20°5S 65°7W **92 H5**
San Lucas *Mexico* 27°10N 112°14W **86 B2**
San Lucas *U.S.A.* 36°8N 121°1W **78 J5**
San Lucas, C. *Mexico* 22°52N 109°53W **86 C3**
San Luis *Argentina* 33°20S 66°20W **94 C2**
San Luis *Cuba* 22°17N 83°46W **88 B3**
San Luis *Guatemala* 16°14N 89°27W **88 C2**
San Luis *Ariz., U.S.A.* 32°29N 114°47W **77 K6**
San Luis *Colo., U.S.A.* 37°12N 105°25W **77 H11**
San Luis □ *Argentina* 34°0S 66°0W **94 C2**
San Luis, I. *Mexico* 29°58N 114°26W **86 B2**
San Luis, Sierra de
Argentina 32°30S 66°10W **94 C2**
San Luis de la Paz
Mexico 21°18N 100°31W **86 C4**
San Luis Obispo *U.S.A.* 35°17N 120°40W **79 K6**
San Luis Potosí *Mexico* 22°9N 100°59W **86 C4**
San Luis Potosí □ *Mexico* 22°10N 101°0W **86 C4**
San Luis Res. *U.S.A.* 37°4N 121°5W **78 H5**
San Luis Río Colorado
Mexico 32°29N 114°58W **86 A2**

San Manuel *U.S.A.* 32°36N 110°38W **77 K8**
San Marcos *Guatemala* 14°59N 91°52W **88 D1**
San Marcos *Calif., U.S.A.* 33°9N 117°10W **79 M9**
San Marcos *Tex., U.S.A.* 29°53N 97°56W **84 G6**
San Marino *San Marino* 43°55N 12°30E **16 G7**
San Marino ■ *Europe* 43°56N 12°25E **22 C5**
San Martín *Antarctica* 68°11S 67°0W **5 C17**
San Martín *Argentina* 33°5S 68°28W **94 C2**
San Martín → *Bolivia* 13°8S 63°43W **92 F6**
San Martín, L. *Argentina* 48°50S 72°50W **96 F2**
San Martín de los Andes
Argentina 40°10S 71°20W **96 E2**
San Mateo *U.S.A.* 37°34N 122°19W **78 H4**
San Matías *Bolivia* 16°25S 58°20W **92 G7**
San Matías, G. *Argentina* 41°30S 64°0W **96 E4**
San Miguel *El Salv.* 13°30N 88°12W **88 D2**
San Miguel *Panama* 8°27N 78°55W **88 E4**
San Miguel *U.S.A.* 35°45N 120°42W **78 J5**
San Miguel → *Bolivia* 13°52S 63°56W **92 F6**
San Miguel de Tucumán
Argentina 26°50S 65°20W **94 B2**
San Miguel del Monte
Argentina 35°23S 58°50W **94 D4**
San Miguel I. *U.S.A.* 34°2N 120°23W **79 L6**
San Nicolás de los Arroyos
Argentina 33°25S 60°10W **94 C3**
San Nicolas I. *U.S.A.* 33°15N 119°30W **79 M7**
San Onofre *U.S.A.* 33°22N 117°34W **79 M9**
San Pablo *Bolivia* 21°43S 66°38W **94 A2**
San Pablo *U.S.A.* 37°58N 122°21W **78 H4**
San Pedro *B. Aires,*
Argentina 33°40S 59°40W **94 C4**
San Pedro *Misiones,*
Argentina 26°30S 54°10W **95 B5**
San Pedro *Chile* 33°54S 71°28W **94 C1**
San Pedro *Ivory C.* 4°50N 6°33W **52 H4**
San Pedro *Mexico* 23°55N 110°17W **86 C2**
San Pedro □ *Paraguay* 24°0S 57°0W **94 A4**
San Pedro → *Chihuahua,*
Mexico 28°21N 105°25W **86 B3**
San Pedro → *Nayarit,*
Mexico 21°45N 105°30W **86 C3**
San Pedro → *U.S.A.* 32°59N 110°47W **77 K8**
San Pedro, Pta. *Chile* 25°30S 70°38W **94 B1**
San Pedro Channel
U.S.A. 33°30N 118°25W **79 M8**
San Pedro de Atacama
Chile 22°55S 68°15W **94 A2**
San Pedro de Jujuy
Argentina 24°12S 64°55W **94 A3**
San Pedro de las Colonias
Mexico 25°45N 102°59W **86 B4**
San Pedro de Macorís
Dom. Rep. 18°30N 69°18W **89 C6**
San Pedro del Norte *Nic.* 13°4N 84°33W **88 D3**
San Pedro del Paraná
Paraguay 26°43S 56°13W **94 B4**
San Pedro Mártir, Sa. de
Mexico 30°45N 115°13W **86 A1**
San Pedro Ocampo = Melchor
Ocampo *Mexico* 24°51N 101°39W **86 C4**
San Pedro Pochutla
Mexico 15°44N 96°28W **87 D5**
San Pedro Sula *Honduras* 15°30N 88°0W **88 C2**
San Pedro Tututepec
Mexico 16°9N 97°38W **87 D5**
San Pietro *Italy* 39°8N 8°17E **22 E3**
San Rafael *Argentina* 34°40S 68°21W **94 C2**
San Rafael *Calif., U.S.A.* 37°58N 122°32W **78 H4**
San Rafael *N. Mex.,*
U.S.A. 35°7N 107°53W **77 J10**
San Rafael Mt. *U.S.A.* 34°41N 119°52W **79 L7**
San Rafael Mts. *U.S.A.* 34°40N 119°50W **79 L7**
San Ramón de la Nueva Orán
Argentina 23°10S 64°20W **94 A3**
San Remo *Italy* 43°49N 7°46E **20 E7**
San Roque *Argentina* 28°25S 58°45W **94 B4**
San Roque *Spain* 36°17N 5°21W **21 D3**
San Rosendo *Chile* 37°16S 72°43W **94 D1**
San Saba *U.S.A.* 31°12N 98°43W **84 F5**
San Salvador *El Salv.* 13°40N 89°10W **88 D2**
San Salvador de Jujuy
Argentina 24°10S 64°48W **94 A3**
San Salvador I. *Bahamas* 24°0N 74°30W **89 B5**
San Sebastián = Donostia-San
Sebastián *Spain* 43°17N 1°58W **21 A5**
San Sebastián *Argentina* 53°10S 68°30W **96 G3**
San Sebastián *Puerto Rico* 18°20N 66°59W **89 d**
San Severo *Italy* 41°41N 15°23E **22 D6**
San Simeon *U.S.A.* 35°39N 121°11W **78 K5**
San Simon *U.S.A.* 32°16N 109°14W **77 K9**
San Telmo *Mexico* 30°58N 116°6W **86 A1**
San Tiburcio *Mexico* 24°8N 101°32W **86 C4**
San Valentin, Mte. *Chile* 46°30S 73°30W **96 F2**
San Vicente de Cañete
Peru 13°8S 76°30W **92 F3**
San Vicente de la Barquera
Spain 43°23N 4°29W **21 A3**
San Vito *Costa Rica* 8°50N 82°58W **88 E3**
Sana' = San'a' *Yemen* 15°27N 44°12E **49 D3**
San'a' *Yemen* 15°27N 44°12E **49 D3**
Sana → *Bos.-H.* 45°3N 16°23E **16 F9**
Sanaa → *Yemen* 15°27N 44°12E **49 D3**
Sanaga → *Cameroon* 3°35N 9°38E **54 D1**
Sanak I. *U.S.A.* 54°25N 162°40W **74 E7**
Sanalona, Presa *Mexico* 24°49N 107°7W **86 C3**
Sanana *Indonesia* 2°4S 125°58E **37 E7**
Sanand *India* 22°59N 72°25E **42 H5**
Sanandaj *Iran* 35°18N 47°1E **46 C5**
Sanandita *Bolivia* 21°40S 63°45W **94 A3**
Sanawad *India* 22°11N 76°5E **42 H7**
Sancha He → *China* 26°48N 106°7E **34 D6**
Sanchahe *China* 44°50N 126°2E **33 B14**
Sánchez *Dom. Rep.* 19°15N 69°36W **89 C6**
Sanchi *India* 23°28N 77°44E **42 H7**
Sanchor *India* 24°45N 71°55E **42 G4**
Sancti Spíritus *Cuba* 21°52N 79°33W **88 B4**

Sancy, Puy de *France* 45°32N 2°50E **20 D5**
Sand = Polokwane →
S. Africa 22°25S 30°5E **57 B5**
Sand Hills *U.S.A.* 42°10N 101°30W **80 D3**
Sand Lakes △ *Canada* 57°51N 98°32W **71 B9**
Sand Springs *U.S.A.* 36°9N 96°7W **84 C6**
Sanda *Japan* 34°53N 135°14E **29 G7**
Sandakan *Malaysia* 5°53N 118°4E **36 C5**
Sandan = Sambor
Cambodia 12°46N 106°0E **38 F6**
Sandanski *Bulgaria* 41°35N 23°16E **23 D10**
Sanday *U.K.* 59°16N 2°31W **11 B6**
Sanders *U.S.A.* 35°13N 109°20W **77 J9**
Sanderson *U.S.A.* 30°9N 102°24W **84 F3**
Sandersville *U.S.A.* 32°59N 82°48W **85 E13**
Sandfire Roadhouse
Australia 19°45S 121°15E **60 C3**
Sandfly L. *Canada* 55°43N 106°6W **71 B7**
Sandfontein *Namibia* 23°48S 19°1E **56 B2**
Sandheads, The *India* 21°10N 88°20E **43 J13**
Sandía *Peru* 14°10S 69°30W **92 F5**
Sandila *India* 27°5N 80°31E **43 F9**
Sandnes *Norway* 58°50N 5°45E **9 G11**
Sandnessjøen *Norway* 66°2N 12°38E **8 C15**
Sandoa
Dem. Rep. of the Congo 9°41S 23°0E **54 F4**
Sandomierz *Poland* 50°40N 21°43E **17 C11**
Sandover → *Australia* 21°43S 136°32E **62 C2**
Sandoway = Thandwe
Burma 18°20N 94°30E **41 K19**
Sandoy *Færoe Is.* 61°52N 6°46W **8 F9**
Sandpoint *U.S.A.* 48°17N 116°33W **76 B5**
Sandray *U.K.* 56°53N 7°31W **11 E1**
Sandringham *U.K.* 52°51N 0°31E **12 E8**
Sandstone *Australia* 27°59S 119°16E **61 E2**
Sandu *China* 26°0N 107°52E **34 E6**
Sandur *India* 15°6N 76°33E **45 F3**
Sandusky *Mich., U.S.A.* 43°25N 82°50W **82 C2**
Sandusky *Ohio, U.S.A.* 41°27N 82°42W **82 E2**
Sandveld *Namibia* 21°25S 20°0E **56 B3**
Sandviken *Sweden* 60°38N 16°46E **8 F17**
Sandwich, C. *Australia* 18°14S 146°18E **62 B4**
Sandwich B. *Canada* 53°40N 57°15W **73 B8**
Sandwich B. *Namibia* 23°25S 14°20E **56 B1**
Sandy *Oreg., U.S.A.* 45°24N 122°16W **78 E4**
Sandy *Pa., U.S.A.* 41°6N 78°46W **82 E6**
Sandy *Utah, U.S.A.* 40°32N 111°50W **76 F8**
Sandy Bay *Canada* 55°31N 102°19W **71 B8**
Sandy Bight *Australia* 33°50S 123°20E **61 F3**
Sandy C. *Queens.,*
Australia 24°42S 153°15E **62 C5**
Sandy C. *Tas., Australia* 41°25S 144°45E **63 G3**
Sandy Cay *Bahamas* 23°13N 75°18W **89 B4**
Sandy Cr. → *Australia* 31°54S 145°18E **63 B4**
Sandy Cr. → *U.S.A.* 41°51N 109°47W **76 F9**
Sandy Creek *U.S.A.* 43°38N 76°5W **83 C8**
Sandy L. *Canada* 53°2N 93°0W **72 B1**
Sandy Lake *Canada* 53°0N 93°15W **72 B1**
Sandy Point *India* 10°32N 92°22E **45 J11**
Sandy Valley *U.S.A.* 35°49N 115°38W **79 K11**
Sanford *Fla., U.S.A.* 28°48N 81°16W **85 G14**
Sanford *Maine, U.S.A.* 43°27N 70°47W **83 C14**
Sanford *N.C., U.S.A.* 35°29N 79°10W **85 D15**
Sanford → *Australia* 27°22S 115°53E **61 E2**
Sanford, Mt. *U.S.A.* 62°13N 144°8W **68 E3**
Sang-i-Masha *Afghan.* 33°8N 67°27E **42 C2**
Sanga → *Congo* 1°5S 17°0E **54 E3**
Sangamner *India* 19°37N 74°15E **44 E2**
Sangān *Iran* 34°23N 60°15E **47 C9**
Sangar *Afghan.* 32°56N 65°30E **42 C1**
Sangar *Russia* 64°2N 127°31E **27 C13**
Sangar Sarai *Afghan.* 34°27N 70°35E **42 B4**
Sangareddi *India* 17°38N 78°7E **44 F4**
Sangarh → *Pakistan* 30°43N 70°44E **42 D4**
Sangay *Ecuador* 2°0S 78°20W **92 D3**
Sangeang *Indonesia* 8°12S 119°6E **37 F5**
Sanger *U.S.A.* 36°42N 119°33W **78 J7**
Sangerhausen *Germany* 51°28N 11°18E **16 C6**
Sanggan He → *China* 38°12N 117°15E **32 E9**
Sanggau *Indonesia* 0°5N 110°30E **36 D4**
Sanghar *Pakistan* 26°2N 68°57E **42 F3**
Sangihe, Kepulauan
Indonesia 3°0N 125°30E **37 D7**
Sangihe, Pulau *Indonesia* 3°35N 125°30E **37 D7**
Sangiran □ *Indonesia* 7°27S 110°50E **37 G14**
Sangju *S. Korea* 36°25N 128°10E **33 F15**
Sangkapura *Indonesia* 5°52S 112°40E **36 F4**
Sangkha *Thailand* 14°37N 103°52E **38 E4**
Sangkhla Buri *Thailand* 14°57N 98°28E **38 E2**
Sangkulirang *Indonesia* 0°59N 117°58E **36 D5**
Sangla *Pakistan* 31°43N 73°23E **42 D5**
Sangli *India* 16°55N 74°33E **44 F2**
Sangmélima *Cameroon* 2°57N 12°1E **54 D2**
Sango *Zimbabwe* 18°44S 31°44E **57 A5**
Sangod *India* 24°55N 76°17E **42 G7**
Sangole *India* 17°26N 75°11E **44 F2**
Sangre de Cristo Mts.
U.S.A. 37°30N 105°20W **77 H11**
Sangre Grande
Trin. & Tob. 10°35N 61°8W **93 K15**
Sangrur *India* 30°14N 75°50E **42 D6**
Sangudo *Canada* 53°50N 114°54W **70 C6**
Sangue → *Brazil* 11°1S 58°39W **92 F7**
Sangzhi *China* 29°25N 110°12E **35 C8**
Sanibel *U.S.A.* 26°27N 82°1W **85 H13**
Sanin-Kaigan △ *Japan* 35°39N 134°37E **29 G7**
Sanirajak = Hall Beach
Canada 68°46N 81°12W **69 D15**
Sanjawi *Pakistan* 30°17N 68°21E **42 D3**
Sanjiang *China* 25°48N 109°37E **34 E7**
Sanjo *Japan* 37°37N 138°57E **28 F9**
Sankarankovil *India* 9°10N 77°35E **45 K3**
Sankeshwar *India* 16°23N 74°32E **45 F2**
Sankh → *India* 22°15N 84°48E **43 H11**
Sankt Gallen *Switz.* 47°26N 9°22E **20 C8**
Sankt Michel = Mikkeli
Finland 61°43N 27°15E **8 F22**

Sankt Moritz *Switz.* 46°30N 9°51E **20 C8**
Sankt Pölten *Austria* 48°12N 15°38E **16 D8**
Sankuru →
Dem. Rep. of the Congo 4°17S 20°25E **54 E4**
Sanliurfa *Turkey* 37°12N 38°50E **46 B3**
Sanlúcar de Barrameda
Spain 36°46N 6°21W **21 D2**
Sanmen *China* 29°5N 121°35E **35 C13**
Sanmenxia *China* 34°47N 111°12E **32 G6**
Sanming *China* 26°15N 117°40E **35 D11**
Sanmu *Japan* 34°11N 134°37E **29 G7**
Sanndraigh = Sandray
U.K. 56°53N 7°31W **11 E1**
Sannicandro Gargánico
Italy 41°50N 15°34E **22 D6**
Sânnicolau Mare
Romania 46°5N 20°39E **17 E11**
Sannieshof *S. Africa* 26°30S 25°47E **56 C4**
Sannin, J. *Lebanon* 33°57N 35°52E **48 B4**
Sanniquellie *Liberia* 7°19N 8°38W **52 G4**
Sano *Japan* 36°19N 139°35E **29 F9**
Sanok *Poland* 49°35N 22°10E **17 D12**
Sanqingshan △ *China* 28°54N 118°3E **35 C12**
Sanquhar *U.K.* 55°22N 3°54W **11 F5**
Sans Souci *Trin. & Tob.* 10°50N 61°0W **93 K16**
Sansha *China* 26°58N 120°12E **35 D13**
Sanshui *China* 23°10N 112°56E **35 F9**
Sansui *China* 26°58N 108°39E **34 D7**
Sant Antoni de Portmany
Spain 38°59N 1°19E **21 C6**
Sant Feliu de Guíxols *Spain* 41°45N 3°1E **21 B7**
Sant Jordi, G. de *Spain* 40°53N 1°2E **21 B6**
Santa Ana *Bolivia* 13°50S 65°40W **92 F5**
Santa Ana *El Salv.* 14°0N 89°31W **88 D2**
Santa Ana *Mexico* 30°33N 111°7W **86 A2**
Santa Ana *U.S.A.* 33°46N 117°52W **79 M9**
Santa Ana de los Ríos de Cuenca =
Cuenca *Ecuador* 2°50S 79°9W **92 D3**
Sant' Antíoco *Italy* 39°4N 8°27E **22 E3**
Santa Bárbara *Chile* 37°40S 72°1W **94 D1**
Santa Bárbara *Honduras* 14°53N 88°14W **88 D2**
Santa Bárbara *Mexico* 26°48N 105°49W **86 B3**
Santa Barbara *U.S.A.* 34°25N 119°42W **79 L7**
Santa Barbara Channel
U.S.A. 34°15N 120°0W **79 L7**
Santa Barbara I. *U.S.A.* 33°29N 119°2W **79 M7**
Santa Catalina, Gulf of
U.S.A. 33°10N 117°50W **79 N9**
Santa Catalina, I.
Mexico 25°40N 110°47W **86 B2**
Santa Catalina I.
U.S.A. 33°23N 118°25W **79 M8**
Santa Catarina □ *Brazil* 27°25S 48°30W **95 B6**
Santa Catarina, I. de
Brazil 27°30S 48°40W **95 B6**
Santa Cecília *Brazil* 26°56S 50°18W **95 B5**
Santa Clara *Cuba* 22°20N 80°0W **88 B4**
Santa Clara *Calif.,*
U.S.A. 37°21N 121°57W **78 H5**
Santa Clara *N.Y., U.S.A.* 44°38N 74°27W **83 B10**
Santa Clara *Utah, U.S.A.* 37°8N 113°39W **77 H7**
Santa Clara → *Mexico* 29°51N 107°6W **86 A3**
Santa Clara de Olimar
Uruguay 32°50S 54°54W **95 C5**
Santa Clara Valley
U.S.A. 36°50N 121°30W **78 J5**
Santa Clarita *U.S.A.* 34°24N 118°33W **79 L8**
Santa Clotilde *Peru* 2°33S 73°45W **92 D4**
Santa Cruz *Bolivia* 17°43S 63°10W **92 G6**
Santa Cruz *Chile* 34°38S 71°27W **94 C1**
Santa Cruz *Costa Rica* 10°15N 85°35W **88 D2**
Santa Cruz *Phil.* 14°20N 121°24E **37 B6**
Santa Cruz *U.S.A.* 36°58N 122°1W **78 J4**
Santa Cruz → *Argentina* 50°10S 68°20W **96 G3**
Santa Cruz de Mompox = Mompós
Colombia 9°14N 74°26W **92 B4**
Santa Cruz de Tenerife
Canary Is. 28°28N 16°15W **52 C2**
Santa Cruz del Norte
Cuba 23°9N 81°55W **88 B3**
Santa Cruz del Sur *Cuba* 20°44N 78°0W **88 B4**
Santa Cruz do Rio Pardo
Brazil 22°54S 49°37W **95 A6**
Santa Cruz do Sul *Brazil* 29°42S 52°25W **95 B5**
Santa Cruz I. *U.S.A.* 34°1N 119°43W **79 M7**
Santa Cruz Is. *Solomon Is.* 10°30S 166°0E **58 C9**
Santa Cruz Mts. *Jamaica* 17°58N 77°43W **88 a**
Santa Elena *Argentina* 30°58S 59°47W **94 C4**
Santa Elena, C.
Costa Rica 10°54N 85°56W **88 D2**
Santa Fé *Argentina* 31°35S 60°41W **94 C3**
Santa Fe *U.S.A.* 35°41N 105°57W **77 J11**
Santa Fé □ *Argentina* 31°50S 60°55W **94 C3**
Santa Fé do Sul *Brazil* 20°13S 50°56W **93 H8**
Santa Filomena *Brazil* 9°6S 45°50W **93 E9**
Santa Inês *Brazil* 13°17S 39°48W **93 F11**
Santa Inés, I. *Chile* 54°0S 73°0W **96 G2**
Santa Isabel *Argentina* 36°10S 66°54W **94 D2**
Santa Isabel do Morro
Brazil 11°34S 50°40W **93 F8**
Santa Lucía *Corrientes,*
Argentina 28°58S 59°5W **94 B4**
Santa Lucía *San Juan,*
Argentina 31°30S 68°30W **94 C2**
Santa Lucía *Uruguay* 34°27S 56°24W **94 C4**
Santa Lucia Range
U.S.A. 36°0N 121°20W **78 K5**
Santa Luzia *C. Verde Is.* 16°50N 24°35W **52 b**
Santa Margarita
Argentina 38°28S 61°35W **94 D3**
Santa Margarita *U.S.A.* 35°23N 120°37W **78 K6**
Santa Margarita →
U.S.A. 33°13N 117°23W **79 M9**
Santa Margarita, I.
Mexico 24°27N 111°50W **86 C2**
Santa Maria *U.S.A.* 34°57N 120°26W **79 L6**
Santa María → *Mexico* 31°0N 107°14W **86 A3**
Santa María, B. de *Mexico* 25°4N 108°6W **86 B3**
Santa Maria da Vitória
Brazil 13°24S 44°12W **93 F10**
Santa Maria di Léuca, C.
Italy 39°47N 18°22E **23 E8**
Santa Marta *Colombia* 11°15N 74°13W **92 A4**
Santa Marta, Sierra Nevada de
Colombia 10°55N 73°50W **92 A4**
Santa Marta Grande, C.
Brazil 28°43S 48°50W **95 B6**
Santa Maura = Lefkada
Greece 38°40N 20°43E **23 E9**
Santa Monica Mts. △
U.S.A. 34°4N 118°44W **79 L8**
Santa Paula *U.S.A.* 34°21N 119°4W **79 L7**
Santa Rosa *La Pampa,*
Argentina 36°40S 64°17W **94 D3**
Santa Rosa *San Luis,*
Argentina 32°21S 65°10W **94 C2**
Santa Rosa *Brazil* 27°52S 54°29W **95 B5**
Santa Rosa *Calif., U.S.A.* 38°26N 122°43W **78 G4**
Santa Rosa *N. Mex.,*
U.S.A. 34°57N 104°41W **77 J11**
Santa Rosa and San Jacinto Mts. △
U.S.A. 33°28N 116°20W **79 M10**
Santa Rosa de Copán
Honduras 14°47N 88°46W **88 D2**
Santa Rosa de Río Primero
Argentina 31°8S 63°20W **94 C3**
Santa Rosa del Sara
Bolivia 17°7S 63°35W **92 G6**
Santa Rosa I. *Calif.,*
U.S.A. 33°58N 120°6W **79 M6**
Santa Rosa I. *Fla.,*
U.S.A. 30°20N 86°50W **85 F11**
Santa Rosa Range
U.S.A. 41°45N 117°40W **76 F5**
Santa Rosalía *Mexico* 27°19N 112°17W **86 B2**
Santa Sylvina *Argentina* 27°50S 61°10W **94 B3**
Santa Tecla = Nueva San Salvador
El Salv. 13°40N 89°18W **88 D2**
Santa Teresa *Argentina* 33°25S 60°47W **94 C3**
Santa Teresa *Australia* 24°8S 134°22E **62 C1**
Santa Teresa *Mexico* 25°17N 97°51W **87 B5**
Santa Teresa △ *Uruguay* 33°57S 53°31W **95 C5**
Santa Teresita *Argentina* 36°32S 56°41W **94 D4**
Santa Vitória do Palmar
Brazil 33°32S 53°25W **95 C5**
Santa Ynez → *U.S.A.* 34°41N 120°36W **79 L6**
Santa Ynez Mts. *U.S.A.* 34°30N 120°0W **79 L6**
Santa Ysabel *U.S.A.* 33°7N 116°40W **79 M10**
Santai *China* 31°5N 104°58E **34 B5**
Santana, Coxilha de
Brazil 30°50S 55°35W **95 C4**
Santana do Livramento
Brazil 30°55S 55°30W **95 C4**
Santander *Spain* 43°27N 3°51W **21 A4**
Santander Jiménez
Mexico 24°13N 98°28W **87 C5**
Santanilla, Is. *Honduras* 17°22N 83°57W **88 C3**
Santaquin *U.S.A.* 39°59N 111°47W **76 G8**
Santarém *Brazil* 2°25S 54°42W **93 D8**
Santarém *Portugal* 39°12N 8°42W **21 C1**
Santaren Channel
W. Indies 24°0N 79°30W **88 B4**
Santee *U.S.A.* 32°50N 116°58W **79 N10**
Santee → *U.S.A.* 33°7N 79°17W **85 E15**
Santiago = Río Grande de
Santiago → *Mexico* 21°36N 105°26W **86 C3**
Santiago = São Tiago
C. Verde Is. 15°0N 23°40W **52 b**
Santiago *Brazil* 29°11S 54°52W **95 B5**
Santiago *Panama* 8°0N 81°0W **88 E3**
Santiago *Phil.* 16°41N 121°33E **37 A6**
Santiago → *Peru* 4°27S 77°38W **92 D3**
Santiago de Compostela
Spain 42°52N 8°37W **21 A1**
Santiago de Cuba *Cuba* 20°0N 75°49W **88 C4**
Santiago de los Caballeros
Dom. Rep. 19°30N 70°40W **89 C5**
Santiago del Estero
Argentina 27°50S 64°15W **94 B3**
Santiago del Estero □
Argentina 27°40S 63°15W **94 B3**
Santiago Ixcuintla
Mexico 21°49N 105°13W **86 C3**
Santiago Jamiltepec
Mexico 16°17N 97°49W **87 D5**
Santiago Papasquiaro
Mexico 25°3N 105°25W **86 C3**
Santiago Pinotepa Nacional
Mexico 16°19N 98°1W **87 D5**
Santiaguillo, L. de
Mexico 24°48N 104°48W **86 C4**
Santo Amaro *Brazil* 12°30S 38°43W **93 F11**
Santo Anastácio *Brazil* 21°58S 51°39W **95 A5**
Santo André *Brazil* 23°39S 46°29W **95 A6**
Santo Ângelo *Brazil* 28°15S 54°15W **95 B5**
Santo Antão *C. Verde Is.* 16°52N 25°10W **52 b**
Santo Antônio do Içá
Brazil 3°5S 67°57W **92 D5**
Santo Antônio do Leverger
Brazil 15°52S 56°5W **93 G7**
Santo Domingo
Dom. Rep. 18°30N 69°59W **89 C6**
Santo Domingo *Mexico* 25°29N 111°55W **86 B2**
Santo Domingo *Nic.* 12°14N 84°59W **88 D3**
Santo Domingo, Cay
Bahamas 21°25N 75°45W **88 B4**
Santo Domingo de los Colorados
Ecuador 0°15S 79°9W **92 D3**
Santo Domingo Pueblo
U.S.A. 35°31N 106°22W **77 J10**
Santo Domingo Tehuantepec =
Tehuantepec *Mexico* 16°21N 95°13W **87 D5**
Santo Tomás *Mexico* 31°33N 116°24W **86 A1**
Santo Tomás *Peru* 14°26S 72°8W **92 F4**

Santo Tomé *Argentina* 28°40S 56°5W **95 B4**
Santo Tomé de Guayana = Ciudad
 Guayana *Venezuela* 8°0N 62°30W **92 B6**
Santoña *Spain* 43°29N 3°27W **21 A4**
Santorini *Greece* 36°23N 25°27E **23 F11**
Santos *Brazil* 24°0S 46°20W **95 A6**
Santos Dumont *Brazil* 22°55S 43°10W **95 A7**
Santuario de Aves Laguna
 Colorada △ *Bolivia* 22°10S 67°45W **94 A2**
Sanuki *Japan* 34°19N 134°10E **29 G7**
Sanur *Indonesia* 8°41S 115°15E **37 K18**
Sanwer *India* 22°59N 75°50E **42 H6**
Sanxia Shuiku *China* 30°3N 107°58E **34 B6**
Sanxiang *China* 22°21N 113°25E **31 a**
Sanya *China* 18°14N 109°29E **38 C7**
Sanyuan *China* 34°35N 108°58E **32 G5**
São Bernardo do Campo
 Brazil 23°45S 46°34W **95 A6**
São Borja *Brazil* 28°39S 56°0W **95 B4**
São Carlos *Brazil* 22°0S 47°50W **95 A6**
São Cristóvão *Brazil* 11°1S 37°15W **93 F11**
São Domingos *Brazil* 13°25S 46°19W **93 F9**
São Filipe *C. Verde Is.* 15°2N 24°30W **52 b**
São Francisco *Brazil* 16°0S 44°50W **93 G10**
São Francisco → *Brazil* 10°30S 36°24W **93 F11**
São Francisco do Sul
 Brazil 26°15S 48°36W **95 B6**
São Gabriel *Brazil* 30°20S 54°20W **95 C5**
São Gonçalo *Brazil* 22°48S 43°5W **95 A7**
São João da Boa Vista
 Brazil 22°0S 46°52W **95 A6**
São João da Madeira
 Portugal 40°54N 8°30W **21 B1**
São João del Rei *Brazil* 21°8S 44°15W **95 A7**
São João do Araguaia
 Brazil 5°23S 48°46W **93 E9**
São João do Piauí *Brazil* 8°21S 42°15W **93 E10**
São Joaquim *Brazil* 28°18S 49°56W **95 B6**
São Joaquim → *Brazil* 28°12S 49°37W **95 B6**
São Jorge *Azores* 38°38N 28°3W **52 a**
São José *Brazil* 27°38S 48°39W **95 B5**
São José do Norte *Brazil* 32°1S 52°3W **95 C5**
São José do Rio Preto
 Brazil 20°50S 49°20W **95 A6**
São José dos Campos
 Brazil 23°7S 45°52W **95 A6**
São Leopoldo *Brazil* 29°50S 51°10W **95 B5**
São Lourenço *Brazil* 22°7S 45°3W **95 A6**
São Lourenço → *Brazil* 17°53S 57°27W **93 G7**
São Lourenço do Sul
 Brazil 31°22S 51°58W **95 C5**
São Luís *Brazil* 2°39S 44°15W **93 D10**
São Luís Gonzaga *Brazil* 28°25S 55°0W **95 B5**
São Marcos → *Brazil* 18°15S 47°37W **93 G9**
São Marcos, B. de *Brazil* 2°0S 44°0W **93 D10**
São Mateus *Brazil* 18°44S 39°50W **93 G11**
São Mateus do Sul *Brazil* 25°52S 50°23W **95 B5**
São Miguel *Azores* 37°47N 25°30W **52 a**
São Miguel do Oeste
 Brazil 26°45S 53°34W **95 B5**
São Nicolau *C. Verde Is.* 16°20N 24°20W **52 b**
São Paulo *Brazil* 22°0S 49°0W **95 A6**
São Paulo de Olivença
 Brazil 3°27S 68°48W **92 D5**
São Roque, C. de *Brazil* 5°30S 35°16W **93 E11**
São Sebastião, I. de
 Brazil 23°50S 45°18W **95 A6**
São Sebastião do Paraíso
 Brazil 20°54S 46°59W **95 A6**
São Tiago *C. Verde Is.* 15°0N 23°40W **52 b**
São Tomé
 São Tomé & Príncipe 0°10N 6°39E **50 F4**
São Tomé, C. de *Brazil* 22°0S 40°59W **95 A7**
São Tomé & Príncipe ■
 Africa 0°12N 6°39E **51 F4**
São Vicente *Brazil* 23°57S 46°23W **95 A6**
São Vicente *C. Verde Is.* 17°0N 25°0W **52 b**
São Vicente, C. de *Portugal* 37°0N 9°0W **21 D1**
Saona, I. *Dom. Rep.* 18°10N 68°40W **89 C6**
Saône → *France* 45°44N 4°50E **20 D6**
Saonek *Indonesia* 0°22S 130°55E **37 E8**
Sapam, Ao *Thailand* 8°0N 98°26E **39 a**
Saparua *Indonesia* 3°33S 128°40E **37 E7**
Sape *Indonesia* 8°34S 118°59E **37 F5**
Sapele *Nigeria* 5°50N 5°40E **52 G7**
Sapelo I. *U.S.A.* 31°25N 81°12W **85 F14**
Saposoa *Peru* 6°55S 76°45W **92 E3**
Sapphire *Australia* 23°28S 147°43E **62 C4**
Sappho *U.S.A.* 48°4N 124°16W **78 B2**
Sapporo *Japan* 43°0N 141°21E **28 C10**
Sapt Kosi → *Nepal* 26°32N 86°56E **43 F12**
Sapudi *Indonesia* 7°6S 114°20E **37 G16**
Sapulpa *U.S.A.* 35°59N 96°5W **84 D6**
Saqqez *Iran* 36°15N 46°20E **46 B5**
Sar Dasht *Āzarbāyjān-e Gharbī,*
 Iran 36°9N 45°28E **46 B5**
Sar Dasht *Khuzestān, Iran* 32°32N 48°52E **47 C6**
Sar-e Pol □ *Afghan.* 36°20N 65°50E **40 B4**
Sar Gachīneh = Yāsūj
 Iran 30°31N 51°31E **47 D6**
Sar Planina *Macedonia* 42°0N 21°0E **23 C9**
Sara Buri = Saraburi
 Thailand 14°30N 100°55E **38 E3**
Sarāb *Iran* 37°55N 47°40E **46 B5**
Sarābādī *Iraq* 33°1N 44°48E **44 C5**
Saraburi *Thailand* 14°30N 100°55E **38 E3**
Saradiya *India* 21°34N 70°2E **42 J4**
Saragossa = Zaragoza
 Spain 41°39N 0°53W **21 B5**
Saraguro *Ecuador* 3°35S 79°16W **92 D3**
Sarahs *Turkmenistan* 36°32N 61°13E **47 B9**
Sarai Naurang *Pakistan* 32°50N 70°47E **42 C4**
Saraikela *India* 22°42N 85°56E **43 H11**
Saraipali *India* 21°20N 82°59E **44 D6**
Sarajevo *Bos.-H.* 43°52N 18°26E **23 C8**
Sarakhs = Sarahs
 Turkmenistan 36°32N 61°13E **47 B9**
Saran, Gunung *Indonesia* 0°30S 111°25E **36 E4**
Saranac Lake *U.S.A.* 44°20N 74°10W **83 B10**
Saranac Lakes *U.S.A.* 44°20N 74°28W **83 B10**
Sarandí del Yí *Uruguay* 33°18S 55°38W **95 C4**
Sarandí Grande *Uruguay* 33°44S 56°20W **94 C4**
Sarangani B. *Phil.* 6°0N 125°13E **37 C7**
Sarangani Is. *Phil.* 5°25N 125°25E **37 C7**
Sarangarh *India* 21°30N 83°5E **44 D6**
Saransk *Russia* 54°10N 45°10E **18 D8**
Sarapul *Russia* 56°28N 53°48E **18 C9**
Sarasota *U.S.A.* 27°20N 82°32W **85 H13**
Saratoga *Calif., U.S.A.* 37°16N 122°2W **78 H4**
Saratoga *Wyo., U.S.A.* 41°27N 106°49W **76 F10**
Saratoga △ *U.S.A.* 43°0N 73°30W **83 D11**
Saratoga L. *U.S.A.* 43°1N 73°44W **83 C11**
Saratoga Springs *U.S.A.* 43°5N 73°47W **83 C11**
Saratok *Malaysia* 1°55N 111°17E **36 D4**
Saratov *Russia* 51°30N 46°2E **19 D8**
Sarāvān *Iran* 27°25N 62°15E **47 E9**
Saravane *Laos* 15°43N 106°25E **38 E6**
Sarawak □ *Malaysia* 2°0N 113°0E **36 D4**
Saray *Turkey* 41°26N 27°55E **23 D12**
Sarayköy *Turkey* 37°55N 28°54E **23 F13**
Sarbāz *Iran* 26°38N 61°19E **47 E9**
Sarbīsheh *Iran* 32°30N 59°40E **47 C8**
Sarda → *India* 27°21N 81°23E **43 F9**
Sardar Sarovar Dam
 India 21°50N 73°50E **44 D1**
Sardarshahr *India* 28°30N 74°29E **42 E6**
Sardegna □ *Italy* 40°0N 9°0E **22 D3**
Sardhana *India* 29°9N 77°39E **42 E7**
Sardinia = Sardegna □ *Italy* 40°0N 9°0E **22 D3**
Sardis *Turkey* 38°28N 27°58E **23 E12**
Sārdūīyeh = Dar Mazār
 Iran 29°14N 57°20E **47 D8**
Saren *Indonesia* 8°26S 115°34E **37 J18**
Sarera, G. of *Indonesia* 2°0S 135°0E **58 B6**
Sargasso Sea *Atl. Oc.* 27°0N 72°0W **66 G13**
Sargodha *Pakistan* 32°10N 72°40E **42 C5**
Sarh *Chad* 9°5N 18°23E **53 G9**
Sārī *Iran* 36°30N 53°4E **47 B7**
Saria *India* 21°38N 83°22E **43 J10**
Sariab *Pakistan* 30°6N 66°59E **42 D2**
Sarıgöl *Turkey* 38°14N 28°41E **23 E13**
Sarikei *Malaysia* 2°8N 111°30E **36 D4**
Sarila *India* 25°46N 79°41E **43 G8**
Sarina *Australia* 21°22S 149°13E **62 C4**
Sarita *U.S.A.* 27°13N 97°47W **84 M6**
Sariwŏn *N. Korea* 38°31N 125°46E **33 E13**
Sarju → *India* 27°21N 81°23E **43 F9**
Sark *U.K.* 49°25N 2°22W **13 H5**
Sarkari Tala *India* 27°39N 70°52E **42 F4**
Şarköy *Turkey* 40°36N 27°6E **23 D12**
Sarlat-la-Canéda *France* 44°54N 1°13E **20 D4**
Sarmi *Indonesia* 1°49S 138°44E **37 E9**
Sarmiento *Argentina* 45°35S 69°5W **96 F3**
Särna *Sweden* 61°41N 13°8E **8 F15**
Sarnia *Canada* 42°58N 82°23W **82 D2**
Sarolangun *Indonesia* 2°19S 102°42E **36 E2**
Saronikos Kolpos *Greece* 37°45N 23°45E **23 F10**
Saros Körfezi *Turkey* 40°30N 26°15E **23 D12**
Sarpsborg *Norway* 59°16N 11°7E **9 G14**
Sarqan *Kazakhstan* 45°24N 79°55E **30 B4**
Sarre = Saar → *Europe* 49°41N 6°32E **15 E6**
Sarreguemines *France* 49°5N 7°4E **20 B7**
Sartell *U.S.A.* 45°37N 94°12W **80 C6**
Sarthe → *France* 47°33N 0°31W **20 C3**
Saruna → *Pakistan* 26°31N 67°7E **42 F2**
Sarvar *India* 26°4N 75°0E **42 F6**
Sarvestān *Iran* 29°20N 53°10E **47 D7**
Sary-Tash *Kyrgyzstan* 39°44N 73°15E **26 F8**
Saryshaghan *Kazakhstan* 46°12N 73°38E **26 E8**
Sasan Gir *India* 21°10N 70°36E **42 J4**
Sasaram *India* 24°57N 84°5E **43 G11**
Sasebo *Japan* 33°10N 129°43E **29 H4**
Saser Kangri *India* 34°50N 77°50E **43 B7**
Saskatchewan □ *Canada* 54°40N 106°0W **71 C7**
Saskatchewan →
 Canada 53°37N 100°40W **71 C8**
Saskatoon *Canada* 52°10N 106°38W **71 C7**
Saskylakh *Russia* 71°55N 114°1E **27 B12**
Saslaya △ *Nic.* 13°45N 85°4W **88 D2**
Sasolburg *S. Africa* 26°46S 27°49E **57 C4**
Sasovo *Russia* 54°25N 41°55E **18 D7**
Sassandra *Ivory C.* 4°55N 6°8W **52 H4**
Sassandra → *Ivory C.* 4°58N 6°5W **52 H4**
Sássari *Italy* 40°43N 8°34E **22 D3**
Sassie *Australia* 10°2S 142°51E **62 a**
Sassnitz *Germany* 54°29N 13°39E **16 A7**
Sassuolo *Italy* 44°33N 10°47E **22 B4**
Sastamala *Finland* 61°20N 22°54E **8 F20**
Sasvad *India* 18°20N 74°2E **44 E2**
Sasyk, Ozero *Ukraine* 45°45N 29°40E **17 F15**
Sata-Misaki *Japan* 31°0N 130°40E **29 J5**
Satadougou *Mali* 12°25N 11°25W **52 F3**
Satakunta □ *Finland* 61°45N 23°0E **8 F20**
Satara *India* 17°44N 73°58E **44 F1**
Satara *S. Africa* 24°29S 31°47E **57 B5**
Satarwa *India* 23°55N 84°16E **43 H11**
Satevó *Mexico* 27°57N 106°7W **86 B3**
Satilla → *U.S.A.* 30°59N 81°29W **85 F14**
Satka *Russia* 55°3N 59°1E **18 C10**
Satmala Hills *Andhra Pradesh,*
 India 19°45N 78°45E **44 E4**
Satmala Hills *Maharashtra,*
 India 20°15N 74°40E **44 D2**
Satna *India* 24°35N 80°50E **43 G9**
Sátoraljaújhely *Hungary* 48°25N 21°41E **17 D11**
Satpura △ *India* 21°25N 76°10E **44 D3**
Satpura △ *India* 22°0N 78°15E **42 H8**
Satsuma-Sendai *Japan* 31°50N 130°20E **29 J5**
Satsuna-Shotō *Japan* 30°0N 130°0E **29 K5**
Sattahip *Thailand* 12°41N 100°54E **38 F3**
Sattenapalle *India* 16°25N 80°6E **45 F5**
Satui *Indonesia* 3°50S 115°27E **36 E5**
Satun *Thailand* 6°43N 100°2E **39 J3**
Satupa'itea *Samoa* 13°45S 172°18W **59 b**
Saturnina → *Brazil* 12°15S 58°10W **92 F7**
Sauce *Argentina* 30°5S 58°46W **94 C4**
Sauceda *Mexico* 25°46N 101°19W **86 B4**
Saucillo *Mexico* 28°1N 105°17W **86 B3**
Sauda *Norway* 59°40N 6°20E **9 G12**
Sauðarkrókur *Iceland* 65°45N 19°40W **8 D4**
Saudi Arabia ■ *Asia* 26°0N 44°0E **46 B3**
Sauerland *Germany* 51°12N 7°59E **16 C4**
Saugeen → *Canada* 44°30N 81°22W **82 B3**
Saugerties *U.S.A.* 42°5N 73°57W **83 D11**
Saugus *U.S.A.* 34°25N 118°32W **79 L8**
Sauk Centre *U.S.A.* 45°44N 94°57W **80 C6**
Sauk Rapids *U.S.A.* 45°35N 94°10W **80 C6**
Sault Ste. Marie *Canada* 46°30N 84°20W **72 C3**
Sault Ste. Marie *U.S.A.* 46°30N 84°21W **81 B11**
Saumlaki *Indonesia* 7°55S 131°20E **37 F8**
Saumur *France* 47°15N 0°5W **20 C3**
Saundatti *India* 15°47N 75°7E **45 G2**
Saunders, C. *N.Z.* 45°53S 170°45E **59 F3**
Saunders I. *Antarctica* 57°48S 26°28W **5 B1**
Saunders Pt. *Australia* 27°52S 125°38E **61 E4**
Saurimo *Angola* 9°40S 20°12E **54 F4**
Savá *Honduras* 15°32N 86°15W **88 C2**
Sava → *Serbia* 44°50N 20°26E **23 B9**
Savage *U.S.A.* 47°27N 104°21W **76 C11**
Savage I. = Niue ☑
 Pac. Oc. 19°2S 169°54W **65 J11**
Savage River *Australia* 41°31S 145°14E **63 G4**
Savai'i *Samoa* 13°28S 172°24W **59 b**
Savalou *Benin* 7°57N 1°58E **52 G6**
Savanna *U.S.A.* 42°5N 90°8W **80 D8**
Savanna-la-Mar *Jamaica* 18°10N 78°10W **88 a**
Savannah *Ga., U.S.A.* 32°5N 81°6W **85 E14**
Savannah *Mo., U.S.A.* 39°56N 94°50W **80 E6**
Savannah *Tenn., U.S.A.* 35°14N 88°15W **85 D10**
Savannah → *U.S.A.* 32°2N 80°53W **85 E14**
Savannakhet *Laos* 16°30N 104°49E **38 D5**
Savant L. *Canada* 50°16N 90°44W **72 B1**
Savant Lake *Canada* 50°14N 90°40W **72 B1**
Savantvadi *India* 15°55N 73°54E **45 G1**
Savanur *India* 14°59N 75°21E **45 G2**
Savarkundla = Kundla
 India 21°21N 71°25E **42 J4**
Savda *India* 21°9N 75°56E **44 D2**
Save → *Mozam.* 21°16S 34°0E **57 B5**
Sāveh *Iran* 35°2N 50°20E **47 C6**
Savelugu *Ghana* 9°38N 0°54W **52 G5**
Savo *Finland* 62°45N 27°30E **8 E22**
Savoie □ *France* 45°26N 6°25E **20 D7**
Savolax = Savo *Finland* 62°45N 27°30E **8 E22**
Savona *Italy* 44°17N 8°30E **20 D8**
Savonlinna *Finland* 61°52N 28°53E **8 F23**
Savoy = Savoie □ *France* 45°26N 6°25E **20 D7**
Savsjö *Sweden* 57°20N 14°40E **9 H16**
Savusavu *Fiji* 16°34S 179°15E **59 a**
Savusavu B. *Fiji* 16°45S 179°15E **59 a**
Sawahlunto *Indonesia* 0°40S 100°52E **36 E2**
Sawai *Indonesia* 3°0S 129°5E **37 E7**
Sawai Madhopur *India* 26°0N 76°25E **42 G7**
Sawaleke *Fiji* 17°59S 179°18E **59 a**
Sawang Daen Din
 Thailand 17°28N 103°28E **38 D4**
Sawankhalok *Thailand* 17°19N 99°50E **38 D2**
Sawara *Japan* 35°55N 140°30E **29 G10**
Sawatch Range *U.S.A.* 39°0N 106°30W **76 G10**
Sawel Mt. *U.K.* 54°50N 7°2W **10 B4**
Sawi *Thailand* 10°14N 99°5E **39 G2**
Sawtooth △ *U.S.A.* 44°0N 114°50W **76 D6**
Sawtooth Range *U.S.A.* 44°3N 114°58W **76 D6**
Sawu *Indonesia* 10°35S 121°50E **37 F6**
Sawu Sea *Indonesia* 9°30S 121°50E **37 F6**
Saxby → *Australia* 18°25S 140°53E **62 B3**
Saxmundham *U.K.* 52°13N 1°30E **13 E9**
Saxony = Sachsen □
 Germany 50°55N 13°10E **16 C7**
Saxony, Lower = Niedersachsen □
 Germany 52°50N 9°0E **16 B5**
Saxton *U.S.A.* 40°13N 78°15W **82 F6**
Sayabec *Canada* 48°35N 67°41W **73 C6**
Sayaboury *Laos* 19°15N 101°45E **38 C3**
Sayán *Peru* 11°8S 77°12W **92 F3**
Sayan, Vostochnyy *Russia* 54°0N 96°0E **27 D10**
Sayan, Zapadnyy *Russia* 52°30N 94°0E **30 A7**
Sayanogorsk *Russia* 53°5N 91°23E **27 D10**
Saydā *Lebanon* 33°35N 35°25E **48 B4**
Sayhandulaan = Öldziyt
 Mongolia 44°40N 109°1E **32 B5**
Sayhūt *Yemen* 15°12N 51°10E **49 D5**
Saylac *Somalia* 11°21N 43°30E **49 E3**
Saynshand = Buyant-Uhaa
 Mongolia 44°55N 110°11E **32 B6**
Sayre *Okla., U.S.A.* 35°18N 99°38W **84 D5**
Sayre *Pa., U.S.A.* 41°59N 76°32W **83 E8**
Sayreville *U.S.A.* 40°28N 74°22W **83 F10**
Sayula *Mexico* 19°52N 103°36W **86 D4**
Sayward *Canada* 50°21N 125°55W **70 C3**
Sazanit *Albania* 40°30N 19°20E **23 D8**
Sazin *Pakistan* 35°35N 73°30E **43 B5**
Sázava → *Czech Rep.* 49°53N 14°24E **16 D8**
Sazin *Pakistan* 35°35N 73°30E **43 B5**
Scafell Pike *U.K.* 54°27N 3°14W **12 C4**
Scalloway *U.K.* 60°9N 1°17W **11 A7**
Scalpay *U.K.* 57°18N 6°0W **11 D2**
Scandia *Canada* 50°20N 112°2W **70 C6**
Scandicci *Italy* 43°45N 11°11E **22 C4**
Scandinavia *Europe* 64°0N 12°0E **8 E15**
Scapa Flow *U.K.* 58°53N 3°3W **11 C5**
Scappoose *U.S.A.* 45°45N 122°53W **78 E4**
Scarba *U.K.* 56°11N 5°43W **11 E3**
Scarborough
 Trin. & Tob. 11°11N 60°42W **93 J16**
Scarborough *U.K.* 54°17N 0°24W **12 C7**
Scariff I. *Ireland* 51°44N 10°15W **10 E1**
Scarp *U.K.* 58°1N 7°8W **11 C1**
Sceebeli = Shabeelle →
 Somalia 2°0N 44°0E **49 G3**
Schaffhausen *Switz.* 47°42N 8°39E **20 C8**
Schagen *Neths.* 52°49N 4°48E **15 B4**
Schaghticoke *U.S.A.* 42°54N 73°35W **83 D11**
Schefferville *Canada* 54°48N 66°50W **73 B6**
Schelde → *Belgium* 51°15N 4°16E **15 C4**
Schell Creek Ra. *U.S.A.* 39°25N 114°40W **76 G6**
Schellsburg *U.S.A.* 40°3N 78°39W **82 F6**
Schenectady *U.S.A.* 42°49N 73°57W **83 D11**
Schenevus *U.S.A.* 42°33N 74°50W **83 D10**
Schiedam *Neths.* 51°55N 4°25E **15 C4**
Schiermonnikoog *Neths.* 53°30N 6°15E **15 A6**
Schiermonnikoog △
 Neths. 53°30N 6°15E **15 A6**
Schio *Italy* 45°43N 11°21E **22 B4**
Schleswig *Germany* 54°31N 9°34E **16 A5**
Schleswig-Holstein □
 Germany 54°30N 9°30E **16 A5**
Schœlcher *Martinique* 14°36N 61°7W **88 c**
Schoharie *U.S.A.* 42°40N 74°19W **83 D10**
Schoharie Cr. →
 U.S.A. 42°57N 74°18W **83 D10**
Schokland *Neths.* 52°38N 5°46E **15 B5**
Scholls *U.S.A.* 45°24N 122°56W **78 E4**
Schouten I. *Australia* 42°20S 148°20E **63 G4**
Schouten Is. = Supiori
 Indonesia 1°0S 136°0E **37 E9**
Schouwen *Neths.* 51°43N 3°45E **15 C3**
Schreiber *Canada* 48°45N 87°20W **72 C2**
Schroffenstein *Namibia* 27°11S 18°42E **56 C2**
Schroon Lake *U.S.A.* 43°50N 73°46W **83 C11**
Schuler *Canada* 50°20N 110°6W **71 C6**
Schumacher *Canada* 48°30N 81°16W **72 C3**
Schurz *U.S.A.* 38°57N 118°49W **76 G4**
Schuyler *U.S.A.* 41°27N 97°4W **80 E5**
Schuylerville *U.S.A.* 43°6N 73°35W **83 C11**
Schuylkill → *U.S.A.* 39°53N 75°12W **83 G9**
Schuylkill Haven *U.S.A.* 40°37N 76°11W **83 F8**
Schwäbische Alb *Germany* 48°20N 9°30E **16 D5**
Schwaner, Pegunungan
 Indonesia 1°0S 112°30E **36 E4**
Schwarzrand *Namibia* 25°37S 16°50E **56 C2**
Schwarzwald *Germany* 48°30N 8°20E **16 D5**
Schwatka Mts. *U.S.A.* 67°20N 156°30W **74 B8**
Schwedt *Germany* 53°3N 14°16E **16 B8**
Schweinfurt *Germany* 50°3N 10°14E **16 C6**
Schweizer-Reneke
 S. Africa 27°11S 25°18E **56 C4**
Schwenningen = Villingen-
 Schwenningen *Germany* 48°3N 8°26E **16 D5**
Schwerin *Germany* 53°36N 11°22E **16 B6**
Schwyz *Switz.* 47°2N 8°39E **20 C8**
Sciacca *Italy* 37°31N 13°3E **22 F5**
Scilla *Italy* 38°15N 15°43E **22 E6**
Scilly, Isles of *U.K.* 49°56N 6°22W **13 H1**
Scioto → *U.S.A.* 38°44N 83°1W **81 F12**
Scituate *U.S.A.* 42°12N 70°44W **83 D14**
Scobey *U.S.A.* 48°47N 105°25W **76 B11**
Scone *Australia* 32°5S 150°52E **63 E5**
Scone *U.K.* 56°25N 3°24W **11 E5**
Scoresbysund = Ittoqqortoormiit
 Greenland 70°20N 23°0W **4 B6**
Scotia *Calif., U.S.A.* 40°29N 124°6W **76 F1**
Scotia *N.Y., U.S.A.* 42°50N 73°58W **83 D11**
Scotia Sea *Antarctica* 56°5S 56°0W **5 B18**
Scotland *Canada* 43°1N 80°22W **82 C4**
Scotland □ *U.K.* 57°0N 4°0W **11 E5**
Scott *Antarctica* 77°0S 166°45E **5 D11**
Scott, C. *Australia* 13°30S 129°49E **60 B4**
Scott City *U.S.A.* 38°29N 100°54W **80 F3**
Scott Glacier *Antarctica* 66°15S 100°5E **5 C8**
Scott I. *Antarctica* 67°0S 179°0E **5 C11**
Scott Is. *Canada* 50°48N 128°40W **70 C3**
Scott L. *Canada* 59°55N 106°18W **71 B7**
Scott Reef *Australia* 14°0S 121°50E **60 B3**
Scottburgh *S. Africa* 30°15S 30°47E **57 D5**
Scottdale *U.S.A.* 40°6N 79°35W **82 F5**
Scottish Borders □ *U.K.* 55°35N 2°50W **11 F6**
Scotts Valley *U.S.A.* 37°3N 122°1W **78 H4**
Scottsbluff *U.S.A.* 41°52N 103°40W **80 E2**
Scottsboro *U.S.A.* 34°40N 86°2W **85 D11**
Scottsburg *U.S.A.* 38°41N 85°47W **81 F11**
Scottsdale *Australia* 41°9S 147°31E **63 G4**
Scottsdale *U.S.A.* 33°40N 111°53W **77 K8**
Scottsville *Ky., U.S.A.* 36°45N 86°11W **80 G10**
Scottsville *N.Y., U.S.A.* 43°2N 77°47W **82 C7**
Scottville *U.S.A.* 43°58N 86°17W **80 D10**
Scranton *U.S.A.* 41°25N 75°40W **83 E9**
Scugog, L. *Canada* 44°10N 78°55W **82 B6**
Scunthorpe *U.K.* 53°36N 0°39W **12 D7**
Scutari = Shkodër *Albania* 42°4N 19°32E **23 C8**
Sea Is. *U.S.A.* 31°30N 81°7W **85 F14**
Seabrook, L. *Australia* 30°55S 119°40E **61 F2**
Seaford *U.K.* 50°47N 0°7E **13 G8**
Seaford *U.S.A.* 38°39N 75°37W **81 F16**
Seaforth *Australia* 20°55S 148°57E **62 b**
Seaforth *Canada* 43°35N 81°25W **82 C3**
Seaforth, L. *U.K.* 57°52N 6°36W **11 D2**
Seagraves *U.S.A.* 32°57N 102°34W **84 E3**
Seaham *U.K.* 54°50N 1°20E **12 C6**
Seal → *Canada* 59°4N 94°48W **71 B10**
Seal L. *Canada* 54°20N 61°30W **73 B7**
Sealy *U.S.A.* 29°47N 96°9W **84 G6**
Searchlight *U.S.A.* 35°28N 114°55W **79 K12**
Searcy *U.S.A.* 35°15N 91°44W **84 D9**
Searles L. *U.S.A.* 35°44N 117°21W **79 K9**
Seascale *U.K.* 54°24N 3°29W **12 C4**
Seaside *Calif., U.S.A.* 36°37N 121°50W **78 J5**
Seaside *Oreg., U.S.A.* 46°0N 123°56W **78 E3**
Seaspray *Australia* 38°25S 147°15E **63 F4**
Seattle *U.S.A.* 47°36N 122°19W **78 C4**
Seattle-Tacoma Int. ✈ (SEA)
 U.S.A. 47°27N 122°18W **78 C4**
Seba *Indonesia* 10°29S 121°50E **60 B3**
Sebago L. *U.S.A.* 43°52N 70°34W **83 C14**
Sebago L. *U.S.A.* 43°51N 70°34W **83 C14**
Sebastián Vizcaíno, B.
 Mexico 28°0N 114°30W **86 B2**
Sebastopol = Sevastopol
 Ukraine 44°35N 33°30E **19 F5**
Sebastopol *U.S.A.* 38°24N 122°49W **78 G4**
Sebewaing *U.S.A.* 43°44N 83°27W **81 D12**
Sebha = Sabhā *Libya* 27°9N 14°29E **53 C8**
Sebinkarahisar *Turkey* 40°22N 38°28E **19 F6**
Sebring *Fla., U.S.A.* 27°30N 81°27W **85 H14**
Sebring *Ohio, U.S.A.* 40°55N 81°2W **82 F3**
Sebringville *Canada* 43°24N 81°4W **82 C3**
Sebta = Ceuta *N. Afr.* 35°52N 5°18W **21 E3**
Sebuku *Indonesia* 3°30S 116°25E **36 E5**
Sechelt *Canada* 49°25N 123°42W **70 D4**
Sechura, Desierto de *Peru* 6°0S 80°30W **92 E2**
Secretary I. *N.Z.* 45°15S 166°56E **59 F1**
Secunderabad *India* 17°28N 78°30E **44 F4**
Security *U.S.A.* 38°45N 104°45W **76 G11**
Sedalia *U.S.A.* 38°42N 93°14W **80 F7**
Sedan *France* 49°43N 4°57E **20 B6**
Sedan *U.S.A.* 37°8N 96°11W **80 G5**
Sedbergh *U.K.* 54°20N 2°31W **12 C5**
Seddon *N.Z.* 41°40S 174°7E **59 D5**
Seddonville *N.Z.* 41°33S 172°1E **59 D4**
Sedé Boqér *Israel* 30°52N 34°47E **48 E3**
Sedeh *Fārs, Iran* 30°45N 52°11E **47 D7**
Sedeh *Khorāsān, Iran* 33°20N 59°14E **47 C8**
Séderot *Israel* 31°32N 34°37E **48 D3**
Sédhiou *Senegal* 12°44N 15°30W **52 F2**
Sedley *Canada* 50°10N 104°0W **71 C8**
Sedona *U.S.A.* 34°52N 111°46W **77 J8**
Sedova, Pik *Russia* 73°29N 54°58E **26 B6**
Sedro-Woolley *U.S.A.* 48°30N 122°14W **78 B4**
Seeheim *Namibia* 26°50S 17°45E **56 C2**
Seeis *Namibia* 22°29S 17°39E **56 B2**
Seekoei → *S. Africa* 30°18S 25°1E **56 D4**
Seferihisar *Turkey* 38°10N 26°50E **23 E12**
Sefophe *Botswana* 22°11S 27°58E **57 B4**
Seg-ozero *Russia* 63°20N 33°46E **18 B5**
Segamat *Malaysia* 2°30N 102°50E **39 L4**
Segesta *Italy* 37°56N 12°50E **22 F5**
Seget *Indonesia* 1°24S 130°58E **37 E8**
Segezha *Russia* 63°44N 34°19E **18 B5**
Ségou *Mali* 13°30N 6°16W **52 F4**
Segovia = Coco →
 Cent. Amer. 15°0N 83°8W **88 D3**
Segovia *Spain* 40°57N 4°10W **21 B3**
Segre → *Spain* 41°40N 0°43E **21 B6**
Seguam I. *U.S.A.* 52°19N 172°30W **74 E5**
Séguéla *Ivory C.* 7°55N 6°40W **52 G4**
Seguin *U.S.A.* 29°34N 97°58W **84 G6**
Segundo → *Argentina* 30°53S 62°44W **94 C3**
Segura → *Spain* 38°3N 0°44W **21 C5**
Seh Konj, Kūh-e *Iran* 30°6N 57°30E **47 D8**
Seh Qal'eh *Iran* 33°40N 58°24E **47 C8**
Sehitwa *Botswana* 20°30S 22°30E **56 B3**
Sehlabathebe △ *Lesotho* 29°53S 29°7E **57 C4**
Sehore *India* 23°10N 77°5E **42 H7**
Sehwan *Pakistan* 26°28N 67°53E **42 F2**
Seikan Tunnel *Japan* 41°28N 140°10E **28 D10**
Seil *U.K.* 56°18N 5°38W **11 E3**
Seiland *Norway* 70°25N 23°15E **8 A20**
Seiling *U.S.A.* 36°9N 98°56W **84 C5**
Seinäjoki *Finland* 62°40N 22°51E **8 E20**
Seine → *France* 49°26N 0°26E **20 B4**
Seistan = Sīstān *Asia* 30°50N 61°0E **47 D9**
Seistan, Daryācheh-ye = Sīstān,
 Daryācheh-ye *Iran* 31°0N 61°0E **47 D9**
Sekayu *Indonesia* 2°51S 103°51E **36 E2**
Sekondi-Takoradi *Ghana* 4°58N 1°45W **52 H5**
Sekudai *Malaysia* 1°32N 103°39E **39 d**
Sekuma *Botswana* 24°36S 23°50E **56 B3**
Selah *U.S.A.* 46°39N 120°32W **76 C3**
Selangor □ *Malaysia* 3°10N 101°30E **39 L3**
Selaru *Indonesia* 8°9S 131°0E **37 F8**
Selatan, Selat *Malaysia* 5°15N 100°20E **39 c**
Selawik L. *U.S.A.* 66°30N 160°45W **74 B7**
Selby *U.K.* 53°47N 1°5W **12 D6**
Selby *U.S.A.* 45°31N 100°2W **80 C3**
Selçuk *Turkey* 37°56N 27°22E **23 F12**
Selden *U.S.A.* 39°33N 100°34W **80 F3**
Sele → *Italy* 40°29N 14°56E **22 D6**
Selebi-Phikwe *Botswana* 21°58S 27°48E **57 B4**
Selemdzha → *Russia* 51°42N 128°53E **27 D13**
Selenga = Selenge Mörön →
 Asia 52°16N 106°16E **30 A10**
Selenge Mörön → *Asia* 52°16N 106°16E **30 A10**
Seletan, Tanjung
 Indonesia 4°9S 114°40E **36 E4**
Sélibabi *Mauritania* 15°10N 12°15W **52 E3**
Seligman *U.S.A.* 35°20N 112°53W **77 J7**
Selîma *Sudan* 21°22N 29°19E **53 D11**
Selinda Spillway →
 Botswana 18°35S 23°10E **56 A3**
Selinsgrove *U.S.A.* 40°48N 76°52W **82 F8**
Selkirk *Man., Canada* 50°10N 96°55W **71 C9**
Selkirk *Ont., Canada* 42°49N 79°56W **82 D5**
Selkirk *U.K.* 55°33N 2°50W **11 F6**
Selkirk I. = Horse I.
 Canada 53°20N 99°6W **71 C9**
Selkirk Mts. *Canada* 51°15N 117°40W **68 C8**
Sellafield *U.K.* 54°25N 3°29W **12 C4**
Sells *U.S.A.* 31°55N 111°53W **77 L8**
Selma *Ala., U.S.A.* 32°25N 87°1W **85 E11**
Selma *Calif., U.S.A.* 36°34N 119°37W **78 J7**
Selma *N.C., U.S.A.* 35°32N 78°17W **85 D15**
Selmer *U.S.A.* 35°10N 88°36W **85 D10**
Selpele *Indonesia* 0°1S 130°5E **37 E8**
Selsey Bill *U.K.* 50°43N 0°47W **13 G7**
Seltso *Russia* 53°22N 34°4E **18 D5**
Selu *Indonesia* 7°32S 130°55E **37 F8**
Selva *Argentina* 29°50S 62°0W **94 B3**
Selva Lancandona = Montes
 Azules △ *Mexico* 16°21N 91°3W **87 D6**
Selvas *Brazil* 6°30S 67°0W **92 E5**
Selvagens, Ilhas *Madeira* 30°5N 15°55W **52 B2**
Selwyn L. *Canada* 60°0N 104°30W **71 B8**
Selwyn Mts. *Canada* 63°0N 130°0W **68 B6**
Selwyn Ra. *Australia* 21°10S 140°0E **62 C3**
Seman → *Albania* 40°47N 19°30E **23 D8**
Semarang *Indonesia* 7°0S 110°26E **37 G14**
Semarapura = Klungkung
 Indonesia 8°32S 115°24E **37 K18**
Sembung *Indonesia* 8°28S 115°11E **37 J18**

Semey *Kazakhstan* 50°30N 80°10E **30** A5
Seminoe Res. *U.S.A.* 42°9N 106°55W **76** E10
Seminole Okla., *U.S.A.* 35°14N 96°41W **84** D6
Seminole *Tex., U.S.A.* 32°43N 102°39W **84** E3
Seminole Draw →
   U.S.A. 32°27N 102°20W **84** E3
Semipalatinsk = Semey
   Kazakhstan 50°30N 80°10E **30** A5
Semirara Is. *Phil.* 12°0N 121°20E **37** B6
Semisopochnoi I. *U.S.A.* 51°55N 179°36E **74** E3
Semitau *Indonesia* 0°29N 111°57E **36** D4
Semmering P. *Austria* 47°41N 15°45E **16** E8
Semnān *Iran* 35°40N 53°23E **47** C7
Semnān □ *Iran* 36°0N 54°0E **47** C7
Semporna *Malaysia* 4°30N 118°33E **37** D5
Semuda *Indonesia* 2°51S 112°58E **36** E4
Sen → *Cambodia* 12°32N 104°28E **38** F5
Senā *Iran* 28°27N 51°36E **47** D6
Sena Madureira *Brazil* 9°5S 68°45W **92** E5
Senador Pompeu *Brazil* 5°40S 39°20W **93** E11
Senang, Pulau *Singapore* 1°11N 103°52E **39** d
Senanga *Zambia* 16°7S 23°16E **55** H4
Senatobia *U.S.A.* 34°37N 89°58W **85** D10
Sendai = Satsuma-Sendai
   Japan 31°50N 130°20E **29** J5
Sendai *Japan* 38°15N 140°53E **28** E10
Sendai-Wan *Japan* 38°15N 141°0E **28** E10
Sendhwa *India* 21°41N 75°6E **42** J6
Sendurjana *India* 21°32N 78°17E **44** D4
Seneca *U.S.A.* 34°41N 82°57W **85** D13
Seneca Falls *U.S.A.* 42°55N 76°48W **83** D8
Seneca L. *U.S.A.* 42°40N 76°54W **82** D7
Senecaville L. *U.S.A.* 39°55N 81°25W **82** G3
Senegal ■ *W. Afr.* 14°30N 14°30W **52** F3
Sénégal → *W. Afr.* 15°48N 16°32W **52** E2
Senegambia *Africa* 12°45N 12°0W **50** E2
Senekal *S. Africa* 28°20S 27°36E **57** C4
Senge Khambab = Indus →
   Pakistan 24°20N 67°47E **42** G2
Senggigi *Indonesia* 8°29S 116°2E **37** J19
Senhor-do-Bonfim
   Brazil 10°30S 40°10W **93** F10
Senigállia *Italy* 43°43N 13°13E **22** C5
Senj *Croatia* 45°0N 14°58E **16** F8
Senja *Norway* 69°25N 17°30E **8** B17
Senkaku-Shotō
   E. China Sea 25°45N 123°30E **29** M1
Senlis *France* 49°13N 2°35E **20** B5
Senmonorom *Cambodia* 12°27N 107°12E **38** F6
Senneterre *Canada* 48°25N 77°15W **72** C4
Seno *Laos* 16°35N 104°50E **38** D5
Senqu = Orange →
   S. Africa 28°41S 16°28E **56** C2
Sens *France* 48°11N 3°15E **20** B5
Senta *Serbia* 45°55N 20°3E **23** B9
Sentinel *U.S.A.* 32°52N 113°13W **77** K7
Senwabarana *S. Africa* 23°17S 29°7E **57** B4
Seo de Urgel = La Seu d'Urgell
   Spain 42°22N 1°23E **21** A6
Seogwipo *S. Korea* 33°13N 126°34E **33** H14
Seohara *India* 29°15N 78°33E **43** E8
Seonath → *India* 21°44N 82°28E **43** J10
Seondha *India* 26°9N 78°48E **43** F8
Seongnam *S. Korea* 37°26N 127°8E **33** F14
Seoni *India* 22°5N 79°30E **43** H8
Seoni Malwa *India* 22°27N 77°28E **42** H8
Seonsan *S. Korea* 36°14N 128°17E **33** F15
Seoriuarayan *India* 21°45N 82°34E **44** D6
Seosan *S. Korea* 36°47N 126°27E **33** F14
Sepīdān *Iran* 30°20N 52°5E **47** D7
Sepone *Laos* 16°45N 106°13E **38** D6
Sept-Îles *Canada* 50°13N 66°22W **73** B6
Sequim *U.S.A.* 48°5N 123°6W **78** B3
Sequoia ∆ *U.S.A.* 36°30N 118°30W **78** J8
Seraing *Belgium* 50°35N 5°32E **15** D5
Seram *Indonesia* 3°10S 129°0E **37** E7
Seram Sea *Indonesia* 2°30S 128°30E **37** E7
Serampore = Shrirampur
   India 22°44N 88°21E **43** H13
Serang *Indonesia* 6°8S 106°10E **37** G12
Serasan *Indonesia* 2°29N 109°4E **36** D3
Serbia ■ *Europe* 43°20N 20°0E **23** B9
Serdar *Turkmenistan* 39°4N 56°23E **47** B8
Serdobsk *Russia* 52°28N 44°10E **18** D7
Seremban *Malaysia* 2°43N 101°53E **39** L3
Sereth = Siret →
   Romania 45°24N 28°1E **17** F14
Sergeya Kirova, Ostrova
   Russia 77°30N 89°0E **27** B10
Sergino *Russia* 62°25N 65°12E **26** C7
Sergipe □ *Brazil* 10°30S 37°30W **93** F11
Sergiyev Posad *Russia* 56°20N 38°10E **18** C6
Serhetabat *Turkmenistan* 35°20N 62°18E **47** C9
Seria *Brunei* 4°37N 114°23E **36** D4
Serian *Malaysia* 1°10N 110°31E **36** D4
Serifos *Greece* 37°9N 24°30E **23** F11
Sérigny → *Canada* 56°47N 66°0W **73** A6
Seringapatam Reef
   Australia 13°38S 122°5E **60** B3
Seririt *Indonesia* 8°12S 114°56E **37** J17
Serkout *Algeria* 23°56N 6°47E **52** D7
Sermata *Indonesia* 8°15S 128°50E **37** F7
Sermersuaq *Greenland* 79°30N 62°0W **69** B19
Serov *Russia* 59°29N 60°35E **18** C11
Serowe *Botswana* 22°25S 26°43E **56** B4
Serpentine Lakes
   Australia 28°30S 129°10E **61** E4
Serpent's Mouth = Sierpe, Bocas de
   la *Venezuela* 10°0N 61°30W **93** L15
Serpukhov *Russia* 54°55N 37°28E **18** D6
Serra do Navio *Brazil* 0°59N 52°3W **93** C8
Serranía San Luís ∆
   Paraguay 22°35S 57°22W **94** A4
Serranía San Rafael ∆
   Paraguay 26°30S 56°0W **95** B4
Serres *Greece* 41°5N 23°31E **23** D10
Serrezuela *Argentina* 30°40S 65°20W **94** C2

Serrinha *Brazil* 11°39S 39°0W **93** F11
Sertanópolis *Brazil* 23°4S 51°2W **95** A5
Sêrtar *China* 32°20N 100°41E **34** A3
Serua *Indonesia* 6°18S 130°1E **37** F8
Serui *Indonesia* 1°53S 136°10E **37** E9
Serule *Botswana* 21°57S 27°20E **56** B4
Sesepe *Indonesia* 1°30S 127°59E **37** E7
Sesfontein *Namibia* 19°7S 13°39E **56** A1
Sesheke *Zambia* 17°29S 24°13E **56** A3
Setana *Japan* 42°26N 139°51E **28** C9
Sète *France* 43°25N 3°42E **20** E5
Sete Lagoas *Brazil* 19°27S 44°16W **93** G10
Seti → *Nepal* 28°59N 81°8E **43** E9
Sétif *Algeria* 36°9N 5°26E **52** A7
Seto *Japan* 35°14N 137°6E **29** G8
Setonaikai *Japan* 34°20N 133°30E **29** G6
Setonaikai ∆ *Japan* 34°15N 133°15E **29** G6
Settat *Morocco* 33°0N 7°40W **52** B4
Setting L. *Canada* 55°0N 98°38W **71** C9
Settle *U.K.* 54°5N 2°16W **12** C5
Settlement, The
   Br. Virgin Is. 18°43N 64°22W **89** e
Settlers *S. Africa* 25°2S 28°30E **57** C4
Setúbal *Portugal* 38°30N 8°58W **21** C1
Setúbal, B. de *Portugal* 38°40N 8°56W **21** C1
Seul, Lac *Canada* 50°20N 92°30W **72** B1
Sevan, Ozero = Sevana Lich
   Armenia 40°30N 45°20E **46** A5
Sevana Lich *Armenia* 40°30N 45°20E **46** A5
Sevastopol *Ukraine* 44°35N 33°30E **19** F5
Seven Sisters *Canada* 54°56N 128°10W **70** C3
Severn → *Canada* 56°2N 87°36W **72** A2
Severn → *U.K.* 51°35N 2°40W **13** F5
Severnaya Zemlya *Russia* 79°0N 100°0E **27** B11
Severnyye Uvaly *Russia* 60°0N 50°0E **18** C8
Severo-Kurilsk *Russia* 50°40N 156°8E **27** D16
Severo-Yeniseyskiy
   Russia 60°22N 93°1E **27** C10
Severo-Zapadnyy □ *Russia* 65°0N 40°0E **26** C4
Severobaykalsk *Russia* 55°39N 109°19E **27** D11
Severodvinsk *Russia* 64°27N 39°58E **18** B6
Severomorsk *Russia* 69°5N 33°27E **8** B25
Severouralsk *Russia* 60°9N 59°57E **18** B10
Seversk *Russia* 56°36N 84°49E **26** D9
Sevier → *U.S.A.* 39°4N 113°6W **76** G7
Sevier Desert *U.S.A.* 39°40N 112°45W **76** G7
Sevier L. *U.S.A.* 38°54N 113°9W **76** G7
Sevilla *Spain* 37°23N 5°58W **21** D2
Seville = Sevilla *Spain* 37°23N 5°58W **21** D2
Sevlievo *Bulgaria* 43°2N 25°6E **23** C11
Sewani *India* 28°58N 75°39E **42** E6
Seward *Alaska, U.S.A.* 60°7N 149°27W **68** F2
Seward *Nebr., U.S.A.* 40°55N 97°6W **80** E5
Seward *Pa., U.S.A.* 40°25N 79°1W **82** F5
Seward Peninsula *U.S.A.* 65°30N 166°0W **74** B6
Sewell *Chile* 34°10S 70°23W **94** C1
Sewer *Indonesia* 5°53S 134°40E **37** F8
Sewickley *U.S.A.* 40°32N 80°12W **82** F4
Sexsmith *Canada* 55°21N 118°47W **70** B5
Seychelles ■ *Ind. Oc.* 5°0S 56°0E **55** b
Seyðisfjörður *Iceland* 65°16N 13°57W **8** D7
Seydişehir *Turkey* 37°25N 31°51E **19** G5
Seydvān *Iran* 38°34N 45°2E **46** B5
Seyhan → *Turkey* 36°43N 34°53E **46** B2
Seym → *Ukraine* 51°27N 32°34E **19** D5
Seymour *Australia* 37°2S 145°10E **63** F4
Seymour *S. Africa* 32°33S 26°46E **57** D4
Seymour *Conn., U.S.A.* 41°24N 73°4W **83** E11
Seymour *Ind., U.S.A.* 38°58N 85°53W **81** F11
Seymour *Tex., U.S.A.* 33°35N 99°16W **84** E5
Sfântu Gheorghe
   Romania 45°52N 25°48E **17** F13
Sfax *Tunisia* 34°49N 10°48E **53** B8
Sha Tau Kok *China* 22°33N 114°13E **31** a
Sha Xi → *China* 26°35N 118°0E **35** D12
Sha Xian *China* 26°23N 117°45E **35** D11
Shaanxi □ *China* 35°0N 109°0E **32** G5
Shaba = Katanga □
   Dem. Rep. of the Congo 8°0S 25°0E **54** F5
Shabeelle → *Somalia* 2°0N 44°0E **49** G3
Shabogamo L. *Canada* 53°15N 66°30W **73** B6
Shabunda
   Dem. Rep. of the Congo 2°40S 27°16E **54** E5
Shache *China* 38°20N 77°10E **30** D4
Shackleton Fracture Zone
   S. Ocean 60°0S 60°0W **5** B18
Shackleton Ice Shelf
   Antarctica 66°0S 100°0E **5** C8
Shackleton Inlet *Antarctica* 83°0S 160°0E **5** E11
Shādegān *Iran* 30°40N 48°38E **47** D6
Shadi *China* 26°7N 114°47E **35** D10
Shadi *India* 33°24N 77°14E **43** C7
Shadrinsk *Russia* 56°5N 63°32E **26** D7
Shadyside *U.S.A.* 39°58N 80°45W **82** G4
Shafter *U.S.A.* 35°30N 119°16W **79** K7
Shaftesbury *U.K.* 51°0N 2°11W **13** F5
Shaftsbury *U.S.A.* 43°0N 73°11W **83** D11
Shagram *Pakistan* 36°24N 72°20E **43** A5
Shah Alam *Malaysia* 3°5N 101°32E **39** L3
Shah Alizai *Pakistan* 29°25N 66°33E **42** E2
Shah Bunder *Pakistan* 24°13N 67°56E **42** G2
Shahabad *Karnataka, India* 17°10N 76°54E **44** F3
Shahabad *Punjab, India* 30°10N 76°55E **42** D7
Shahabad *Raj., India* 27°36N 79°56E **43** F8
Shahabad *Ut. P., India* 27°36N 79°56E **43** F8
Shahada *India* 21°33N 74°30E **42** J6
Shahadpur *Pakistan* 25°55N 68°35E **42** G3
Shahapur *India* 15°50N 74°34E **45** G2
Shahbā' *Syria* 32°52N 36°38E **48** C5
Shahdād *Iran* 30°30N 57°40E **47** D8
Shahdād, Namakzār-e
   Iran 30°20N 58°20E **47** D8
Shahdadkot *Pakistan* 27°50N 67°55E **42** F2
Shahdol *India* 23°19N 81°26E **43** H9
Shahe *China* 37°0N 114°32E **32** F8
Shahganj *India* 26°3N 82°44E **43** F10
Shahgarh *India* 27°15N 69°50E **42** F3
Shāhīn Shahr *Iran* 32°49N 51°32E **47** C6
Shahjahanpur *India* 27°54N 79°57E **43** F8

Shahpur = Salmās *Iran* 38°11N 44°47E **46** B5
Shahpur *Karnataka, India* 16°40N 76°48E **44** F3
Shahpur *Mad. P., India* 22°12N 77°58E **42** H7
Shahpur *Baluchistan,*
   Pakistan 28°46N 68°27E **42** E3
Shahpur *Punjab, Pakistan* 32°17N 72°26E **42** C5
Shahpur Chakar *Pakistan* 26°9N 68°39E **42** F3
Shahpura *Mad. P., India* 23°10N 80°45E **43** H9
Shahpura *Raj., India* 25°38N 74°56E **42** G6
Shahr-e Bābak *Iran* 30°7N 55°9E **47** D7
Shahr-e Kord *Iran* 32°15N 50°55E **47** C6
Shāhrakht *Iran* 33°38N 60°16E **47** C9
Shāhrezā = Qomsheh *Iran* 32°0N 51°55E **47** D6
Shāhrig *Pakistan* 30°15N 67°40E **42** D2
Shāhrud = Emāmrūd *Iran* 36°30N 55°0E **47** B7
Shajapur *India* 23°27N 76°21E **42** H7
Shajing *China* 22°44N 113°48E **31** a
Shakargarh *Pakistan* 32°17N 75°10E **42** C6
Shakawe *Botswana* 18°28S 21°49E **56** A3
Shaker Heights *U.S.A.* 41°28N 81°32W **82** E3
Shakhtersk *Russia* 49°10N 142°8E **27** E15
Shakhty *Russia* 47°40N 40°16E **19** E7
Shakhunya *Russia* 57°40N 46°46E **18** C8
Shaki *Nigeria* 8°41N 3°21E **52** G6
Shakotan-Hantō *Japan* 43°10N 140°30E **28** C10
Shaksam Valley *Asia* 36°0N 76°20E **43** A7
Shallow Lake *Canada* 44°36N 81°5W **82** B3
Shalqar *Kazakhstan* 47°48N 59°39E **26** E6
Shaluli Shan *China* 30°40N 99°55E **34** B2
Shām *Iran* 26°39N 57°21E **47** E8
Shām, Bādiyat ash *Asia* 32°0N 40°0E **46** C3
Shamal Sīnī □ *Egypt* 30°30N 33°50E **48** E2
Shamattawa *Canada* 55°51N 92°5W **72** A1
Shamattawa → *Canada* 55°1N 85°23W **72** A2
Shamīl *Iran* 27°30N 56°55E **47** E8
Shāmkūh *Iran* 35°47N 57°50E **47** C8
Shamli *India* 29°32N 77°18E **42** E7
Shammar, Jabal *Si. Arabia* 27°40N 41°0E **46** E4
Shamo = Gobi *Asia* 44°0N 110°0E **32** C6
Shamo, L. *Ethiopia* 5°45N 37°30E **49** F2
Shamokin *U.S.A.* 40°47N 76°34W **83** F8
Shamrock *Canada* 45°23N 76°50W **83** A8
Shamrock *U.S.A.* 35°13N 100°15W **84** D4
Shan □ *Burma* 21°30N 98°30E **41** J21
Shan Xian *China* 34°50N 116°5E **32** G9
Shanchengzhen *China* 42°20N 125°20E **33** C13
Shāndak *Iran* 28°28N 60°27E **47** D9
Shandan *China* 38°45N 101°15E **30** D9
Shandon *U.S.A.* 35°39N 120°23W **78** K6
Shandong □ *China* 36°0N 118°0E **33** G10
Shandong Bandao *China* 37°0N 121°0E **33** F11
Shandur Pass *Pakistan* 36°4N 72°31E **43** A5
Shang Xian = Shangzhou
   China 33°50N 109°58E **32** H5
Shangani *Zimbabwe* 19°41S 29°20E **57** A4
Shangani → *Zimbabwe* 18°41S 27°10E **55** H5
Shangbancheng *China* 40°50N 118°1E **33** D10
Shangcheng *China* 31°47N 115°26E **35** B10
Shangdu *China* 41°30N 113°30E **32** D7
Shanggao *China* 28°17N 114°55E **35** C10
Shanghai Shi □ *China* 31°0N 121°30E **35** B13
Shanghang *China* 25°2N 116°23E **35** E11
Shanghe *China* 37°20N 117°10E **33** F9
Shanglin *China* 23°27N 108°33E **34** F7
Shangnan *China* 33°32N 110°50E **32** H6
Shangqiu *China* 34°26N 115°36E **32** G8
Shangrao *China* 28°25N 117°59E **35** C11
Shangri-La = Zhongdian
   China 27°48N 99°42E **34** D2
Shangshui *China* 33°32N 114°35E **32** H8
Shangsi *China* 22°8N 107°58E **34** F6
Shangyi *China* 41°4N 113°57E **32** D7
Shangyou *China* 25°48N 114°32E **35** E10
Shangyu *China* 30°3N 120°52E **35** B13
Shangzhi *China* 45°22N 127°56E **33** B14
Shangzhou *China* 33°50N 109°58E **32** H5
Shanhetun *China* 44°33N 127°15E **33** B14
Shanklin *U.K.* 50°38N 1°11W **13** G6
Shannon *N.Z.* 40°33S 175°25E **59** D5
Shannon → *Ireland* 52°35N 9°30W **10** D2
Shannon, Mouth of the
   Ireland 52°30N 9°55W **10** D2
Shannon ∆ *Australia* 34°35S 116°25E **61** F2
Shannonbridge *Ireland* 53°17N 8°3W **10** C3
Shansi = Shanxi □ *China* 37°0N 112°0E **32** F7
Shantar, Ostrov Bolshoy
   Russia 55°9N 137°40E **27** D14
Shantipur *India* 23°17N 88°25E **43** H13
Shantou *China* 23°18N 116°40E **35** F11
Shantung = Shandong □
   China 36°0N 118°0E **33** G10
Shanwei *China* 22°48N 115°22E **35** F10
Shanxi □ *China* 37°0N 112°0E **32** F7
Shanyang *China* 33°31N 109°55E **32** H5
Shanyin *China* 39°25N 112°56E **32** E7
Shaodong *China* 27°15N 111°43E **35** D8
Shaoguan *China* 24°48N 113°35E **35** E9
Shaoshan *China* 27°55N 112°33E **35** D9
Shaowu *China* 27°22N 117°28E **35** D11
Shaoxing *China* 30°0N 120°35E **35** C13
Shaoyang *Hunan, China* 26°59N 111°20E **35** D8
Shaoyang *Hunan, China* 27°14N 111°25E **35** D8
Shap *U.K.* 54°32N 2°40W **12** C5
Shaqra' *Si. Arabia* 25°15N 45°16E **46** E5
Sharafkhāneh *Iran* 38°11N 45°29E **46** B5
Sharavati → *India* 14°20N 74°25E **45** G2
Sharbot Lake *Canada* 44°46N 76°41W **83** B8
Shari *Japan* 43°55N 144°40E **28** C12
Sharjah = Ash Shāriqah
   U.A.E. 25°23N 55°26E **47** E7
Shark B. *Australia* 25°30S 113°32E **61** E1
Shark Bay ∆ *Australia* 25°30S 113°30E **61** E1
Sharm el Sheikh *Egypt* 27°53N 34°18E **53** C12
Sharon *Canada* 44°6N 79°26W **82** B5

Sharon *Mass., U.S.A.* 42°7N 71°11W **83** D13
Sharon *Pa., U.S.A.* 41°14N 80°31W **82** E4
Sharon Springs *Kans.,*
   U.S.A. 38°54N 101°45W **80** F3
Sharon Springs *N.Y.,*
   U.S.A. 42°48N 74°37W **83** D10
Sharp Pt. *Australia* 10°58S 142°43E **62** A3
Sharpe L. *Canada* 54°24N 93°40W **72** B1
Sharpsville *U.S.A.* 41°15N 80°29W **82** E4
Sharqi, Al Jabal ash
   Lebanon 33°40N 36°10E **48** B5
Sharya *Russia* 58°22N 45°20E **18** C8
Shashemene *Ethiopia* 7°13N 38°33E **49** F2
Shashi *Botswana* 21°15S 27°27E **57** B4
Shasta, Mt. *U.S.A.* 41°25N 122°12W **76** F2
Shasta L. *U.S.A.* 40°43N 122°25W **76** F2
Shatsky Rise *Pac. Oc.* 34°0N 157°0E **64** D7
Shatt al Arab *Asia* 29°57N 48°34E **47** D6
Shaunavon *Canada* 49°35N 108°25W **71** D7
Shaver L. *U.S.A.* 37°9N 119°18W **78** H7
Shaw → *Australia* 20°21S 119°17E **60** D2
Shaw I. *Australia* 20°30S 149°2E **62** b
Shawanaga *Canada* 45°31N 80°17W **82** A4
Shawangunk Mts.
   U.S.A. 41°35N 74°30W **83** E10
Shawano *U.S.A.* 44°47N 88°36W **80** C9
Shawmari, J. ash *Jordan* 30°35N 36°35E **48** E5
Shawnee *U.S.A.* 35°20N 96°55W **84** D6
Shay Gap *Australia* 20°30S 120°10E **60** D3
Shayang *China* 30°42N 112°29E **35** B9
Shaybārā *Si. Arabia* 25°26N 36°47E **46** E3
Shaykh, J. ash *Lebanon* 33°25N 35°50E **48** B4
Shaykh Miskīn *Syria* 32°49N 36°9E **48** C5
Shaykh Sa'd *Iraq* 32°34N 46°17E **46** C5
Shāzand *Iran* 33°56N 49°24E **47** C6
Shchūchīnsk *Kazakhstan* 52°56N 70°12E **26** D8
She Xian *Anhui, China* 29°50N 118°25E **35** C12
She Xian *Hebei, China* 36°30N 113°40E **32** F7
Shebele = Shabeelle →
   Somalia 2°0N 44°0E **49** G3
Sheboygan *U.S.A.* 43°46N 87°45W **80** D10
Shediac *Canada* 46°14N 64°32W **73** C7
Sheelin, L. *Ireland* 53°48N 7°20W **10** C4
Sheenjek → *U.S.A.* 66°45N 144°33W **74** B11
Sheep Haven *Ireland* 55°11N 7°52W **10** A4
Sheep Range *U.S.A.* 36°35N 115°15W **79** J11
Sheerness *U.K.* 51°26N 0°47E **13** F8
Sheet Harbour *Canada* 44°56N 62°31W **73** D7
Sheffield *U.K.* 53°23N 1°28W **12** D6
Sheffield *Ala., U.S.A.* 34°46N 87°41W **85** D11
Sheffield *Mass., U.S.A.* 42°5N 73°21W **83** D11
Sheffield *Pa., U.S.A.* 41°42N 79°3W **82** E5
Shegaon *India* 20°48N 76°47E **44** D3
Shehong *China* 30°54N 105°18E **34** B5
Sheikhpura *India* 25°9N 85°53E **43** G11
Shekhupura *Pakistan* 31°42N 73°58E **42** D5
Shekou *China* 22°30N 113°55E **31** a
Shelburne *N.S., Canada* 43°47N 65°20W **73** E6
Shelburne *Ont., Canada* 44°4N 80°15W **82** B4
Shelburne B. *Australia* 11°50S 142°50E **62** A3
Shelburne Falls *U.S.A.* 42°36N 72°45W **83** D12
Shelby *Mich., U.S.A.* 43°37N 86°22W **80** D10
Shelby *Miss., U.S.A.* 33°57N 90°46W **85** E9
Shelby *Mont., U.S.A.* 48°30N 111°51W **76** B8
Shelby *N.C., U.S.A.* 35°17N 81°32W **85** D14
Shelby *Ohio, U.S.A.* 40°53N 82°40W **82** F2
Shelbyville *Ill., U.S.A.* 39°24N 88°48W **80** F9
Shelbyville *Ind., U.S.A.* 39°31N 85°47W **81** F11
Shelbyville *Ky., U.S.A.* 38°13N 85°14W **81** F11
Shelbyville *Tenn., U.S.A.* 35°29N 86°28W **85** D11
Sheldon *U.S.A.* 43°11N 95°51W **80** D6
Sheldrake *Canada* 50°20N 64°51W **73** B7
Shelikhova, Zaliv *Russia* 59°30N 157°0E **27** D16
Shelikof Strait *U.S.A.* 57°30N 155°0W **74** D9
Shell Lakes *Australia* 29°20S 127°30E **61** E4
Shellbrook *Canada* 53°13N 106°24W **71** C7
Shellharbour *Australia* 34°31S 150°51E **63** E5
Shelter I. *U.S.A.* 41°4N 72°20W **83** E12
Shelton *Conn., U.S.A.* 41°19N 73°5W **83** E11
Shelton *Wash., U.S.A.* 47°13N 123°6W **78** C3
Shen Xian *China* 36°15N 115°40E **32** F8
Shenandoah *Iowa, U.S.A.* 40°46N 95°22W **80** E6
Shenandoah *Pa., U.S.A.* 40°49N 76°12W **83** F8
Shenandoah *Va., U.S.A.* 38°29N 78°37W **81** F14
Shenandoah → *U.S.A.* 39°19N 77°44W **81** F15
Shenandoah ∆ *U.S.A.* 38°35N 78°22W **81** F14
Shenchi *China* 39°8N 112°10E **32** E7
Shencottah *India* 8°59N 77°18E **45** K3
Shendam *Nigeria* 8°49N 9°30E **52** G7
Shendī *Sudan* 16°46N 33°22E **53** E12
Shendurni *India* 20°39N 75°36E **44** D2
Shengfang *China* 39°3N 116°42E **32** E9
Shengzhou *China* 29°35N 120°50E **35** C13
Shenjingzi *China* 44°40N 124°30E **33** B13
Shenmu *China* 38°50N 110°29E **32** E6
Shennongjia *China* 31°43N 110°44E **35** B8
Shenqiu *China* 33°25N 115°5E **32** H8
Shensi = Shaanxi □ *China* 35°0N 109°0E **32** G5
Shenyang *China* 41°48N 123°27E **33** D12
Shenzhen *China* 22°32N 114°5E **35** F10
Shenzhen Bao'an Int. ✈ (SZX)
   China 22°41N 113°49E **31** a
Shenzhen Shuiku *China* 22°34N 114°8E **31** a
Shenzhen Wan *China* 22°27N 113°55E **31** a
Sheo *India* 26°11N 71°15E **42** F4
Sheopur Kalan *India* 25°40N 76°40E **42** G7
Shepetivka *Ukraine* 50°10N 27°10E **17** C14
Shepparton *Australia* 36°23S 145°26E **63** F4
Sheppey, I. of *U.K.* 51°25N 0°48E **13** F8
Shepton Mallet *U.K.* 51°11N 2°33W **13** F5
Sheqi *China* 33°12N 112°57E **32** H7
Sher Qila *Pakistan* 36°7N 74°2E **43** A6
Sherborne *U.K.* 50°57N 2°31W **13** G5
Sherbro I. *S. Leone* 7°30N 12°40W **52** G3
Sherbrooke *N.S., Canada* 45°8N 61°59W **73** C7
Sherbrooke *Qué.,*
   Canada 45°28N 71°57W **83** A13

Sherburne *U.S.A.* 42°41N 75°30W **83** D9
Shergarh *India* 26°20N 72°18E **42** F5
Sherghati *India* 24°34N 84°47E **43** G11
Sheridan *Ark., U.S.A.* 34°19N 92°24W **84** D8
Sheridan *Wyo., U.S.A.* 44°48N 106°58W **76** D10
Sheringham *U.K.* 52°56N 1°13E **12** E9
Sherkin I. *Ireland* 51°28N 9°26W **10** E2
Sherkot *India* 29°22N 78°35E **43** E8
Sherlovaya Gora
   Russia 50°34N 116°15E **27** D12
Sherman *N.Y., U.S.A.* 42°9N 79°35W **82** D5
Sherman *Tex., U.S.A.* 33°38N 96°36W **84** E6
Sherpur *India* 25°34N 83°47E **43** G10
Sherridon *Canada* 55°8N 101°5W **71** B8
Shertallai = Cherthala
   India 9°42N 76°20E **45** K3
Sherwood Forest *U.K.* 53°6N 1°7W **12** D6
Sherwood Park *Canada* 53°31N 113°19W **70** C6
Sheslay → *Canada* 58°48N 132°5W **70** B2
Shethanei L. *Canada* 58°48N 97°50W **71** B9
Shetland □ *U.K.* 60°30N 1°30W **11** A7
Shetland Is. *U.K.* 60°30N 1°30W **11** A7
Shetrunji → *India* 21°19N 72°7E **42** J5
Sheung Shui *China* 22°31N 114°7E **31** a
Shevaroy Hills *India* 11°58N 78°12E **45** J4
Shevgaon *India* 19°9N 75°14E **44** E2
Shey-Phoksundo ∆
   Nepal 29°30N 82°45E **43** E10
Sheyang *China* 33°48N 120°29E **33** H11
Sheyenne → *U.S.A.* 47°2N 96°50W **80** B5
Shiashkotan, Ostrov
   Russia 48°49N 154°6E **27** E16
Shibām *Yemen* 15°59N 48°36E **49** D4
Shibata *Japan* 37°57N 139°20E **28** F9
Shibecha *Japan* 43°17N 144°36E **28** C12
Shibetsu *Hokkaidō,*
   Japan 43°30N 145°10E **28** C12
Shibetsu *Hokkaidō,*
   Japan 44°10N 142°23E **28** B11
Shibing *China* 27°2N 108°7E **34** D7
Shibogama L. *Canada* 53°35N 88°15W **72** B2
Shibushi *Japan* 31°25N 131°8E **29** J5
Shicheng *China* 26°22N 116°20E **35** D11
Shickshinny *U.S.A.* 41°9N 76°9W **83** E8
Shickshock Mts. = Chic-Chocs,
   Mts. *Canada* 48°55N 66°0W **73** C6
Shidao *China* 36°50N 122°25E **33** F12
Shidian *China* 24°40N 99°5E **34** E2
Shido = Sanuki *Japan* 34°19N 134°10E **29** G7
Shiel, L. *U.K.* 56°48N 5°34W **11** E3
Shield, C. *Australia* 13°20S 136°20E **62** A2
Shīeli *Kazakhstan* 44°20N 66°15E **26** E7
Shifang *China* 31°8N 104°10E **34** B5
Shiga □ *Japan* 35°20N 136°0E **29** G8
Shigu *China* 26°51N 99°56E **34** D2
Shiguaigou *China* 40°52N 110°15E **32** D6
Shihchiachuangi = Shijiazhuang
   China 38°2N 114°28E **32** E8
Shihezi *China* 44°15N 86°2E **30** C6
Shijiazhuang *China* 38°2N 114°28E **32** E8
Shijiu Hu *China* 31°25N 118°50E **35** B12
Shikarpur *India* 28°17N 78°7E **42** E8
Shikarpur *Pakistan* 27°57N 68°39E **42** F3
Shikohabad *India* 27°6N 78°36E **43** F8
Shikokochūō *Japan* 34°1N 133°34E **29** G7
Shikoku □ *Japan* 33°30N 133°30E **29** H6
Shikoku-Sanchi *Japan* 33°30N 133°30E **29** H6
Shikotan, Ostrov *Asia* 43°47N 146°44E **27** E15
Shikotsu-Ko *Japan* 42°45N 141°25E **28** C10
Shikotsu-Tōya ∆ *Japan* 44°4N 145°8E **28** C10
Shiliguri *India* 26°45N 88°25E **41** F16
Shiliu = Changjiang
   China 19°20N 108°55E **38** C7
Shilka *Russia* 52°0N 115°55E **27** D12
Shilka → *Russia* 53°20N 121°26E **27** D13
Shillelagh *Ireland* 52°45N 6°32W **10** D5
Shillington *U.S.A.* 40°18N 75°58W **83** F9
Shillong *India* 25°35N 91°53E **41** G17
Shilo *West Bank* 32°4N 35°18E **48** C4
Shilong *China* 23°5N 113°52E **35** F9
Shilou *China* 37°0N 110°48E **32** F6
Shimabara *Japan* 32°48N 130°20E **29** H5
Shimada *Japan* 34°49N 138°10E **29** G9
Shimane □ *Japan* 35°0N 132°30E **29** G6
Shimanovsk *Russia* 52°15N 127°30E **27** D13
Shimanto *Kōchi, Japan* 33°12N 133°8E **29** H6
Shimanto *Kōchi, Japan* 32°59N 132°56E **29** H6
Shimbiris *Somalia* 10°44N 47°14E **49** E4
Shimen *China* 29°35N 111°20E **35** C8
Shimenjie *China* 29°29N 116°48E **35** C11
Shimian *China* 29°17N 102°23E **34** C4
Shimizu *Japan* 35°0N 138°30E **29** G9
Shimla *India* 31°2N 77°9E **42** D7
Shimodate *Japan* 36°20N 139°55E **29** F9
Shimoga *India* 13°57N 75°32E **45** H2
Shimokita-Hantō *Japan* 41°20N 141°0E **28** D10
Shimonoseki *Japan* 33°58N 130°55E **29** H5
Shimpuru Rapids
   Namibia 17°45S 19°55E **56** A2
Shimsha → *India* 13°15N 77°10E **45** H3
Shin, L. *U.K.* 58°5N 4°30W **11** C4
Shinan *China* 22°49N 109°53E **34** F7
Shināṣ *Oman* 24°46N 56°28E **47** E8
Shīndand *Afghan.* 33°12N 62°8E **40** C3
Shinglehouse *U.S.A.* 41°58N 78°12W **82** E6
Shingū *Japan* 33°40N 135°55E **29** H7
Shingwidzi *S. Africa* 23°5S 31°25E **57** B5
Shinjō *Japan* 38°46N 140°18E **28** E10
Shinkolobwe
   Dem. Rep. of the Congo 11°10S 26°40E **54** G5
Shinshār *Syria* 34°36N 36°43E **48** A5
Shinyanga *Tanzania* 3°45S 33°27E **54** E6
Shio-no-Misaki *Japan* 33°25N 135°45E **29** H7
Shiogama *Japan* 38°19N 141°1E **28** E10
Shiojiri *Japan* 36°6N 137°58E **29** F8
Shipchenski Prokhod
   Bulgaria 42°45N 25°15E **23** C11
Shiphoirt, L. = Seaforth, L.
   U.K. 57°52N 6°36W **11** D2

Shiping *China* 23°45N 102°23E **34** F4
Shippagan *Canada* 47°45N 64°45W **73** C7
Shippensburg *U.S.A.* 40°3N 77°31W **82** F7
Shippenville *U.S.A.* 41°15N 79°28W **82** E5
Shiprock *U.S.A.* 36°47N 108°41W **77** H9
Shiqian *China* 27°32N 108°13E **34** D7
Shiqma, N. → *Israel* 31°37N 34°30E **48** D3
Shiquan *China* 33°5N 108°15E **34** A7
Shiquan He = Indus →
  Pakistan 24°20N 67°47E **42** G2
Shīr Kūh *Iran* 31°39N 54°3E **47** D7
Shiragami-Misaki
  Japan 41°24N 140°12E **28** D10
Shirakawa *Fukushima,*
  Japan 37°7N 140°13E **29** F10
Shirakawa *Gifu, Japan* 36°17N 136°56E **29** F8
Shirane-San *Gumma,*
  Japan 36°48N 139°22E **29** F9
Shirane-San *Yamanashi,*
  Japan 35°42N 138°9E **29** G9
Shiraoi *Japan* 42°33N 141°21E **28** C10
Shīrāz *Iran* 29°42N 52°30E **47** D7
Shire → *Africa* 17°42S 35°19E **55** F4
Shiren *China* 41°57N 126°34E **33** D14
Shiretoko △ *Japan* 44°15N 145°15E **28** B12
Shiretoko-Misaki *Japan* 44°21N 145°20E **28** B12
Shirinab → *Pakistan* 30°15N 66°28E **42** D2
Shiriya-Zaki *Japan* 41°25N 141°30E **28** D10
Shiroishi *Japan* 38°0N 140°37E **28** F10
Shirol *India* 16°47N 74°41E **44** F2
Shirpur *India* 21°21N 74°57E **44** D2
Shirshov Ridge *Pac. Oc.* 58°0N 170°0E **64** B8
Shīrvān *Iran* 37°30N 57°50E **47** B8
Shirwa, L. = Chilwa, L.
  Malawi 15°15S 35°40E **55** H7
Shishaldin Volcano
  U.S.A. 54°45N 163°58W **74** E7
Shishi *China* 24°44N 118°37E **35** E12
Shishou *China* 29°38N 112°22E **35** C9
Shitai *China* 30°12N 117°25E **35** B11
Shivamogga = Shimoga
  India 13°57N 75°32E **45** H2
Shivpuri *India* 25°26N 77°42E **42** G7
Shixian *China* 43°5N 129°50E **33** C15
Shixing *China* 24°46N 114°5E **35** E10
Shiyan *Guangdong, China* 22°42N 113°56E **31** a
Shiyan *Hubei, China* 32°35N 110°45E **35** A8
Shizhu *China* 29°58N 108°7E **34** C7
Shizong *China* 24°50N 104°0E **34** E5
Shizuoka *Japan* 34°57N 138°24E **29** G9
Shizuoka □ *Japan* 35°15N 138°40E **29** G9
Shklov = Shklow
  Belarus 54°16N 30°15E **17** A16
Shklow *Belarus* 54°16N 30°15E **17** A16
Shkodër *Albania* 42°4N 19°32E **23** D8
Shkumbini → *Albania* 41°2N 19°31E **23** D8
Shmidta, Ostrov *Russia* 81°0N 91°0E **27** A10
Shō-Gawa → *Japan* 36°47N 137°4E **29** F8
Shoal L. *Canada* 49°33N 95°1W **71** D9
Shoal Lake *Canada* 50°30N 100°35W **71** C8
Shōdo-Shima *Japan* 34°30N 134°15E **29** G7
Sholapur = Solapur *India* 17°43N 75°56E **44** F2
Shōmrōn *West Bank* 32°15N 35°13E **48** C4
Shoranur *India* 10°46N 76°19E **45** J3
Shorapur *India* 16°31N 76°48E **45** F3
Shoreham *U.S.A.* 43°53N 73°18W **83** C11
Shoreham by Sea *U.K.* 50°50N 0°16W **13** G7
Shori → *Pakistan* 28°29N 69°44E **42** E3
Shorkot *Pakistan* 30°50N 72°0E **42** D4
Shorkot Road *Pakistan* 30°47N 72°15E **42** D4
Shortt's I. *India* 20°47N 87°4E **44** D8
Shoshone *Calif., U.S.A.* 35°58N 116°16W **79** K10
Shoshone *Idaho, U.S.A.* 42°56N 114°25W **76** E6
Shoshone L. *U.S.A.* 44°22N 110°43W **76** D8
Shoshone Mts. *U.S.A.* 39°20N 117°25W **76** G5
Shoshong *Botswana* 22°56S 26°31E **56** B4
Shoshoni *U.S.A.* 43°14N 108°7W **76** E9
Shou Xian *China* 32°37N 116°42E **35** A11
Shouchang *China* 29°18N 119°12E **35** C12
Shouguang *China* 37°52N 118°45E **33** F10
Shouning *China* 27°27N 119°31E **35** D12
Shouyang *China* 37°54N 113°8E **32** F7
Show Low *U.S.A.* 34°15N 110°2W **77** J8
Shqipëria = Albania ■
  Europe 41°0N 20°0E **23** D9
Shreveport *U.S.A.* 32°31N 93°45W **84** E8
Shrewsbury *U.K.* 52°43N 2°45W **13** E5
Shri Mohangarh *India* 27°17N 71°18E **42** F4
Shrirampur *India* 22°44N 88°21E **43** H13
Shropshire □ *U.K.* 52°36N 2°45W **13** E5
Shū *Kazakhstan* 43°36N 73°42E **26** E8
Shuangbai *China* 24°42N 101°38E **34** E3
Shuangcheng *China* 45°20N 126°15E **33** B14
Shuangfeng *China* 27°29N 112°11E **35** D9
Shuanggou *China* 34°2N 117°30E **33** G9
Shuangjiang *China* 23°26N 99°58E **34** F2
Shuangliao *China* 43°29N 123°30E **33** C12
Shuangshanzi *China* 40°20N 119°8E **33** D10
Shuangyang *China* 43°28N 125°40E **33** C13
Shuangyashan *China* 46°28N 131°5E **31** B5
Shucheng *China* 31°28N 116°57E **35** B11
Shuiji *China* 27°15N 118°6E **35** D12
Shujalpur *India* 23°18N 76°46E **42** H7
Shukpa Kunzang *India* 34°22N 78°22E **43** B8
Shulan *China* 44°28N 127°0E **33** B14
Shule *China* 39°25N 76°3E **30** D4
Shule He → *China* 40°20N 92°50E **30** C7
Shumagin Is. *U.S.A.* 55°7N 160°30W **74** D7
Shumen *Bulgaria* 43°18N 26°55E **23** C12
Shumikha *Russia* 55°10N 63°15E **26** D7
Shunān *Japan* 34°3N 131°50E **29** G5
Shunchang *China* 26°54N 117°48E **35** D11
Shunde *China* 22°42N 113°14E **35** F9
Shungnak *U.S.A.* 66°52N 157°9W **74** B8
Shuo Xian = Shuozhou
  China 39°20N 112°33E **32** E7

Shuozhou *China* 39°20N 112°33E **32** E7
Shuqrā' *Yemen* 13°22N 45°44E **49** E4
Shūr → *Fārs, Iran* 28°30N 55°0E **47** D7
Shūr → *Kermān, Iran* 30°52N 57°37E **47** D8
Shūr → *Yazd, Iran* 31°45N 55°15E **47** D7
Shūr Āb *Iran* 34°23N 51°11E **47** C6
Shūr Gaz *Iran* 29°10N 59°20E **47** D8
Shūrāb *Iran* 33°43N 56°29E **47** C8
Shūrjestān *Iran* 31°24N 52°25E **47** D7
Shūrūgwi *Zimbabwe* 19°40S 30°0E **55** H6
Shūsf *Iran* 31°50N 60°5E **47** D9
Shūshtar *Iran* 32°0N 48°50E **47** D6
Shuswap L. *Canada* 50°55N 119°3W **70** C5
Shute Harbour △
  Australia 20°17S 148°47E **62** b
Shuyang *China* 34°10N 118°42E **33** G10
Shūzū *Iran* 29°52N 54°30E **47** D7
Shwebo *Burma* 22°30N 95°45E **41** H19
Shwegu *Burma* 24°15N 96°26E **41** G20
Shweli → *Burma* 23°45N 96°45E **41** H20
Shyamnagar *India* 13°21N 92°57E **45** H11
Shymkent *Kazakhstan* 42°18N 69°36E **26** E7
Shyok *India* 34°13N 78°12E **43** B8
Shyok → *Pakistan* 35°13N 75°53E **43** B6
Si Kiang = Xi Jiang →
  China 22°5N 113°20E **35** F9
Si Lanna △ *Thailand* 19°17N 99°12E **38** C2
Si Nakarin Res. *Thailand* 14°35N 99°0E **38** E2
Si-ngan = Xi'an *China* 34°15N 109°0E **32** G5
Si Phangnga *Thailand* 9°8N 98°29E **39** H2
Si Prachan *Thailand* 14°37N 100°9E **38** E3
Si Racha *Thailand* 13°10N 100°48E **38** F3
Si Sa Ket *Thailand* 15°8N 104°23E **38** E5
Siahan Glacier *Asia* 35°20N 77°30E **43** B7
Siahaf → *Pakistan* 29°3N 68°57E **42** E3
Siahan Range *Pakistan* 27°30N 64°40E **40** F4
Siak Sri Indrapura
  Indonesia 0°51N 102°0E **36** D2
Sialkot *Pakistan* 32°32N 74°30E **42** C6
Siam = Thailand ■ *Asia* 16°0N 102°0E **38** E4
Sian = Xi'an *China* 34°15N 109°0E **32** G5
Sian Ka'an △ *Mexico* 19°35N 87°40W **87** D7
Siantan *Indonesia* 3°10N 106°15E **36** D3
Siāreh *Iran* 28°5N 60°14E **47** D9
Siargao I. *Phil.* 9°52N 126°3E **37** C7
Siasi *Phil.* 5°34N 120°50E **37** C6
Siau *Indonesia* 2°50N 125°25E **37** D7
Šiauliai *Lithuania* 55°56N 23°15E **9** J20
Siavonga *Zambia* 16°33S 28°42E **57** A4
Sibâi, Gebel el *Egypt* 25°45N 34°10E **46** E2
Sibang *Indonesia* 8°34S 115°13E **37** K18
Sibay *Russia* 52°42N 58°39E **18** D10
Sibayi, L. *S. Africa* 27°20S 32°45E **57** C5
Šibenik *Croatia* 43°48N 15°54E **22** C6
Siberia = Sibirskiy □
  Russia 58°0N 90°0E **27** D10
Siberia *Russia* 60°0N 100°0E **24** B12
Siberut *Indonesia* 1°30S 99°0E **36** E1
Sibi *Pakistan* 29°30N 67°54E **42** E2
Sibirskiy □ *Russia* 58°0N 90°0E **27** D10
Sibirtsevo *Russia* 44°12N 132°26E **28** B5
Sibiti *Congo* 3°38S 13°19E **54** E2
Sibiu *Romania* 45°45N 24°9E **17** F13
Sibley *U.S.A.* 43°24N 95°45W **80** D6
Sibolga *Indonesia* 1°42N 98°45E **36** D1
Siborongborong *Indonesia* 2°13N 98°58E **39** L2
Sibsagar *India* 27°0N 94°36E **41** F19
Sibu *Malaysia* 2°18N 111°49E **36** D4
Sibuco *Phil.* 7°20N 122°10E **37** C6
Sibuguey B. *Phil.* 7°50N 122°45E **37** C6
Sibut *C.A.R.* 5°46N 19°10E **54** C3
Sibutu *Phil.* 4°45N 119°30E **37** D5
Sibutu Passage *E. Indies* 4°50N 120°0E **37** D6
Sibuyan I. *Phil.* 12°25N 122°40E **37** B6
Sibuyan Sea *Phil.* 12°30N 122°20E **37** B6
Sicamous *Canada* 50°49N 119°0W **70** C5
Siccus → *Australia* 31°55S 139°17E **63** E2
Sichon *Thailand* 9°0N 99°54E **39** H2
Sichuan □ *China* 30°30N 103°0E **34** B5
Sichuan Pendi *China* 31°0N 105°0E **34** B5
Sicilia *Italy* 37°30N 14°30E **22** F6
Sicily = Sicilia *Italy* 37°30N 14°30E **22** F6
Sicily, Str. of *Medit. S.* 37°35N 11°56E **22** F4
Sico → *Honduras* 15°58N 84°58W **88** C3
Sicuani *Peru* 14°21S 71°10W **92** F4
Siddapur *India* 14°20N 74°53E **45** G2
Siddhapur *India* 23°56N 72°25E **42** H5
Siddipet *India* 18°5N 78°51E **44** E4
Sidhauli *India* 27°17N 80°50E **43** F9
Sidhi *India* 24°25N 81°53E **43** G9
Sidi-bel-Abbès *Algeria* 35°13N 0°39W **52** A5
Sidi Ifni *Morocco* 29°29N 10°12W **52** C3
Sidikalang *Indonesia* 2°45N 98°19E **39** L2
Sidlaw Hills *U.K.* 56°32N 3°2W **11** E5
Sidley, Mt. *Antarctica* 77°2S 126°2W **5** D14
Sidmouth *U.K.* 50°40N 3°15W **13** G4
Sidmouth, C. *Australia* 13°25S 143°36E **62** A3
Sidney *Canada* 48°39N 123°24W **78** B3
Sidney *Mont., U.S.A.* 47°43N 104°9W **76** C11
Sidney *N.Y., U.S.A.* 42°19N 75°24W **83** D9
Sidney *Nebr., U.S.A.* 41°8N 102°59W **80** E2
Sidney *Ohio, U.S.A.* 40°17N 84°9W **81** E11
Sidney Lanier, L. *U.S.A.* 34°10N 84°4W **85** D12
Sidoarjo *Indonesia* 7°27S 112°43E **37** G15
Sidon = Saydā *Lebanon* 33°35N 35°25E **48** B4
Sidra = Surt *Libya* 31°11N 16°39E **53** B9
Sidra, G. of = Surt, Khalīj
  Libya 31°40N 18°30E **53** B9
Siedlce *Poland* 52°10N 22°20E **17** B12
Sieg → *Germany* 50°46N 7°6E **16** C4
Siegen *Germany* 50°51N 8°0E **16** C5
Siem Pang *Cambodia* 14°7N 106°23E **38** E6
Siem Reap = Siemreab
  Cambodia 13°20N 103°52E **38** F4
Siemreab *Cambodia* 13°20N 103°52E **38** F4
Siena *Italy* 43°19N 11°21E **22** C4
Sieradz *Poland* 51°37N 18°41E **17** C10
Sierpe, Bocas de la
  Venezuela 10°0N 61°30W **93** L15

Sierra Blanca *U.S.A.* 31°11N 105°22W **84** F2
Sierra Blanca Peak
  U.S.A. 33°23N 105°49W **77** K11
Sierra City *U.S.A.* 39°34N 120°38W **78** F6
Sierra Colorada *Argentina* 40°35S 67°50W **96** E3
Sierra de Agalta △
  Honduras 15°1N 85°48W **88** C2
Sierra de Bahoruco △
  Dom. Rep. 18°10N 71°25W **89** C5
Sierra de La Culata △
  Venezuela 8°45N 71°10W **89** E5
Sierra de Lancandón △
  Guatemala 16°59N 90°23W **88** C1
Sierra de las Quijadas △
  Argentina 32°29S 67°5W **94** C2
Sierra de San Luis △
  Venezuela 11°20N 69°43W **89** D6
Sierra de San Pedro Mártir △
  Mexico 31°10N 115°30W **86** A1
Sierra Gorda *Chile* 22°50S 69°15W **94** A2
Sierra Leone ■ *W. Afr.* 9°0N 12°0W **52** G3
Sierra Madre *Mexico* 16°0N 93°0W **87** D6
Sierra Madre Occidental
  Mexico 27°0N 107°0W **86** B3
Sierra Madre Oriental
  Mexico 25°0N 100°0W **86** C5
Sierra Mojada *Mexico* 27°18N 103°41W **86** B4
Sierra Nevada *Spain* 37°3N 3°15W **21** D4
Sierra Nevada *U.S.A.* 39°0N 120°30W **78** H8
Sierra Nevada △
  Venezuela 8°35N 70°45W **89** E5
Sierra Nevada de Santa Marta △
  Colombia 10°56N 73°36W **89** D5
Sierra Vista *U.S.A.* 31°33N 110°18W **77** L8
Sierraville *U.S.A.* 39°36N 120°22W **78** F6
Sifnos *Greece* 37°0N 24°45E **23** F11
Sifton *Canada* 51°21N 100°8W **71** C8
Sifton Pass *Canada* 57°52N 126°15W **70** B3
Sig *Algeria* 35°32N 0°12E **52** A5
Sigatoka *Fiji* 18°8S 177°32E **59** a
Sighetu-Marmației
  Romania 47°57N 23°52E **17** E12
Sighișoara *Romania* 46°12N 24°50E **17** E13
Sigiriya *Sri Lanka* 7°57N 80°45E **45** L5
Sigli *Indonesia* 5°25N 96°0E **36** C1
Siglufjörður *Iceland* 66°12N 18°55W **8** C4
Signal de Botrang *Belgium* 50°29N 6°1E **15** D6
Signy I. *Antarctica* 60°43S 45°36W **5** C18
Sigsig *Ecuador* 3°0S 78°50W **92** D3
Sigüenza *Spain* 41°3N 2°40W **21** B4
Siguiri *Guinea* 11°31N 9°10W **52** F4
Sigulda *Latvia* 57°10N 24°55E **9** H21
Siguniangshan *China* 31°15N 103°10E **34** B4
Sihawa *India* 20°19N 81°55E **44** D5
Sihong *China* 33°27N 118°16E **33** H10
Sihora *India* 23°29N 80°6E **43** H9
Sihui *China* 23°20N 112°40E **35** F9
Siikajoki → *Finland* 64°50N 24°43E **8** D21
Siikinjärvi *Finland* 63°4N 27°39E **8** E22
Sika *India* 22°26N 69°47E **42** H3
Sikanni Chief →
  Canada 57°47N 122°15W **70** B4
Sikao *Thailand* 7°34N 99°21E **39** J2
Sikar *India* 27°33N 75°10E **42** F6
Sikasso *Mali* 11°18N 5°35W **52** F4
Sikeston *U.S.A.* 36°53N 89°35W **80** G9
Sikhote Alin, Khrebet
  Russia 45°0N 136°0E **28** B8
Sikhote Alin Ra. = Sikhote Alin,
  Khrebet *Russia* 45°0N 136°0E **28** B8
Sikinos *Greece* 36°40N 25°8E **23** F11
Sikkim □ *India* 27°50N 88°30E **41** F16
Sil → *Spain* 42°27N 7°43W **21** A2
Silacayoapan *Mexico* 17°30N 98°9W **87** D5
Silawad *India* 21°54N 74°54E **42** J6
Silchar *India* 24°49N 92°48E **41** G18
Silent Valley △ *India* 11°10N 76°20E **45** J3
Siler City *U.S.A.* 35°44N 79°28W **85** D15
Sileru → *India* 17°49N 81°24E **44** F5
Silesia = Śląsk *Poland* 51°0N 16°30E **16** C9
Silgarhi Doti *Nepal* 29°15N 81°0E **43** E9
Silghat *India* 26°35N 93°0E **41** F18
Silhouette *Seychelles* 4°29S 55°12E **55** b
Silifke *Turkey* 36°22N 33°58E **46** B2
Siliguri = Shiliguri *India* 26°45N 88°25E **41** F16
Siling Co *China* 31°50N 89°20E **30** E6
Silistra *Bulgaria* 44°6N 27°19E **23** B12
Silivri *Turkey* 41°4N 28°14E **23** D13
Siljan *Sweden* 60°55N 14°45E **8** F16
Silkeborg *Denmark* 56°10N 9°32E **9** H13
Silkwood *Australia* 17°45S 146°2E **62** B4
Sillajhuay, Cordillera
  Chile 19°46S 68°40W **92** G5
Sillamäe *Estonia* 59°24N 27°45E **9** G22
Sillod *India* 20°18N 75°39E **44** D2
Silloth *U.K.* 54°52N 3°23W **12** C4
Siloam Springs *U.S.A.* 36°11N 94°32W **84** C7
Silopi *Turkey* 37°15N 42°27E **46** B4
Šilutė *Lithuania* 55°21N 21°33E **9** J19
Silvan *Turkey* 38°7N 41°2E **46** B4
Silvani *India* 23°18N 78°25E **43** H8
Silvassa *India* 20°16N 73°1E **44** D1
Silver City *U.S.A.* 32°46N 108°17W **77** K9
Silver Cr. → *U.S.A.* 43°16N 119°13W **76** E4
Silver Creek *U.S.A.* 42°33N 79°10W **82** D5
Silver L. *U.S.A.* 38°39N 120°6W **78** G6
Silver Lake *Calif., U.S.A.* 35°21N 116°7W **79** K10
Silver Lake *Oreg., U.S.A.* 43°8N 121°3W **76** E3
Silvermine Mts. *Ireland* 52°47N 8°15W **10** D3
Silverton *Colo., U.S.A.* 37°49N 107°40W **77** H10
Silverton *Tex., U.S.A.* 34°28N 101°19W **84** D4
Silvies → *U.S.A.* 43°34N 119°2W **76** E4
Simaltala *India* 24°43N 86°33E **43** G12
Simanggang = Bandar Sri Aman
  Malaysia 1°15N 111°32E **36** D4
Simao *China* 22°47N 101°5E **34** F3
Simard, L. *Canada* 47°40N 78°40W **72** C4
Simav *Turkey* 39°4N 28°58E **23** E13

Simbirsk = Ulyanovsk
  Russia 54°20N 48°25E **18** D8
Simcoe *Canada* 42°50N 80°23W **82** D4
Simcoe, L. *Canada* 44°25N 79°20W **82** B5
Simdega *India* 22°37N 84°31E **43** H11
Simeria *Romania* 45°51N 23°1E **17** F12
Simeulue *Indonesia* 2°45N 95°45E **36** D1
Simferopol *Ukraine* 44°55N 34°3E **19** F5
Simi *Greece* 36°35N 27°50E **23** F12
Simi Valley *U.S.A.* 34°16N 118°47W **79** L8
Simikot *Nepal* 30°0N 81°50E **43** E9
Simla = Shimla *India* 31°2N 77°9E **42** D7
Simlipal △ *India* 21°45N 86°30E **43** J12
Simmie *Canada* 49°56N 108°6W **71** D7
Simmler *U.S.A.* 35°21N 119°59W **79** K7
Simo älv = Simojoki →
  Finland 65°35N 25°1E **8** D21
Simojoki → *Finland* 65°35N 25°1E **8** D21
Simojovel *Mexico* 17°12N 92°38W **87** D6
Simpang Empat *Malaysia* 5°27N 100°29E **39** c
Simplonpass *Switz.* 46°15N 8°3E **20** C8
Simpson Desert *Australia* 25°0S 137°0E **62** D2
Simpson Desert △
  Australia 24°59S 138°21E **62** C2
Simpson Pen. *Canada* 68°34N 88°45W **69** D14
Simrishamn *Sweden* 55°33N 14°22E **9** J16
Simsbury *U.S.A.* 41°53N 72°48W **83** E12
Simushir, Ostrov *Russia* 46°50N 152°30E **27** E16
Sin Cowe I. *S. China Sea* 9°53N 114°19E **36** C4
Sina → *India* 17°30N 75°55E **44** F2
Sina Dhago *Somalia* 5°50N 47°0E **49** F4
Sinabang *Indonesia* 2°30N 96°24E **36** D1
Sinai = Es Sînâ' *Egypt* 29°0N 34°0E **48** F2
Sinai, Mt. = Mûsa, Gebel
  Egypt 28°33N 33°59E **46** D2
Sinaloa □ *Mexico* 25°0N 107°30W **86** C3
Sinaloa de Leyva
  Mexico 25°50N 108°14W **86** B3
Sinan *China* 27°56N 108°13E **34** D7
Sincelejo *Colombia* 9°18N 75°24W **92** B3
Sinch'ang *N. Korea* 40°7N 128°28E **33** D15
Sinch'ŏn *N. Korea* 38°17N 125°21E **33** E13
Sinclair *U.S.A.* 41°47N 107°7W **76** F10
Sinclair Mills *Canada* 54°5N 121°40W **70** C4
Sinclair's B. *U.K.* 58°31N 3°5W **11** C5
Sinclairville *U.S.A.* 42°16N 79°16W **82** D5
Sincorá, Serra do *Brazil* 13°30S 41°0W **93** F10
Sind = Sindh □ *Pakistan* 26°0N 69°0E **42** G3
Sind → *Jammu & Kashmir,*
  India 34°18N 74°45E **43** B6
Sind → *Mad. P., India* 26°26N 79°13E **43** F8
Sind Sagar Doab *Pakistan* 32°0N 71°30E **42** D4
Sindangan *Phil.* 8°10N 123°5E **37** C6
Sindangbarang *Indonesia* 7°27S 107°1E **37** G12
Sindewahi *India* 20°17N 79°39E **44** D4
Sindgi *India* 16°55N 76°14E **44** F3
Sindh = Indus →
  Pakistan 24°20N 67°47E **42** G2
Sindh □ *Pakistan* 26°0N 69°0E **42** G3
Sindhnur *India* 15°47N 76°46E **45** F3
Sindhuli Garhi *Nepal* 27°16N 85°58E **43** F11
Sindi *India* 20°48N 78°52E **44** D4
Sindri *India* 23°45N 86°42E **43** H12
Sines *Portugal* 37°56N 8°51W **21** D1
Sines, C. de *Portugal* 37°58N 8°53W **21** D1
Sing Buri *Thailand* 14°53N 100°25E **38** E3
Singa *Sudan* 13°10N 33°57E **53** F12
Singalila △ *India* 27°10N 88°5E **43** F13
Singanallur *India* 11°2N 77°1E **45** J3
Singapore, Straits of *Asia* 1°15N 104°0E **39** d
Singaraja *Indonesia* 8°7S 115°6E **37** J18
Singatoka = Sigatoka *Fiji* 18°8S 177°32E **59** a
Singida *Tanzania* 4°49S 34°48E **54** E6
Singkang *Indonesia* 4°8S 120°1E **37** E6
Singkawang *Indonesia* 1°0N 108°57E **36** D3
Singkep *Indonesia* 0°30S 104°25E **36** E2
Singkil *Indonesia* 2°17N 97°49E **39** L1
Singkuang *Indonesia* 1°3N 98°55E **39** L2
Singleton *Australia* 32°33S 151°0E **63** E5
Singleton, Mt. *N. Terr.,*
  Australia 22°0S 130°46E **60** D5
Singleton, Mt. *W. Austral.,*
  Australia 29°27S 117°15E **61** E2
Singoli *India* 25°0N 75°22E **42** G6
Singora = Songkhla
  Thailand 7°13N 100°37E **39** J3
Singrauli *India* 24°7N 82°23E **43** G10
Sinharaja *Sri Lanka* 6°25N 80°30E **45** L5
Sinhgarh *India* 18°22N 73°45E **44** E1
Sinhung *N. Korea* 40°11N 127°34E **33** D14
Sinjai *Indonesia* 5°7S 120°20E **37** F6
Sinjār *Iraq* 36°19N 41°52E **46** B4
Sinkat *Sudan* 18°55N 36°49E **53** E13
Sinkiang = Xinjiang Uygur
  Zizhiqu □ *China* 42°0N 86°0E **30** C6
Sinmak *N. Korea* 38°25N 126°14E **33** E14
Sinmi-do *N. Korea* 39°33N 124°53E **33** E13
Sinnamary *Fr. Guiana* 5°25N 53°0W **93** B8
Sinni → *Italy* 40°8N 16°41E **22** D7
Sinni → *Italy* 19°48N 74°0E **42** G2
Sinop *Turkey* 42°1N 35°11E **19** F6
Sinp'o *N. Korea* 40°0N 128°13E **33** E15
Sinsk *Russia* 61°8N 126°48E **27** C13
Sint-Hubert *Belgium* 50°2N 5°23E **15** D5
Sint-Niklaas *Belgium* 51°10N 4°8E **15** C4
Sint-Truiden *Belgium* 50°48N 5°10E **15** D5
Sintang *Indonesia* 0°5N 111°35E **36** D4
Sinton *U.S.A.* 28°2N 97°31W **84** G6
Sintra *Portugal* 38°47N 9°25W **21** C1
Sinŭiju *N. Korea* 40°5N 124°24E **33** D13
Siocon *Phil.* 7°40N 122°10E **37** C6
Sion *Switz.* 46°14N 7°20E **20** C7
Sion Mills *U.K.* 54°48N 7°29W **10** B4

tSionainn, An = Shannon →
  Ireland 52°35N 9°30W **10** D2
Sioux Center *U.S.A.* 43°5N 96°11W **80** D5
Sioux City *U.S.A.* 42°30N 96°24W **80** D5
Sioux Falls *U.S.A.* 43°33N 96°44W **80** D5
Sioux Lookout *Canada* 50°10N 91°50W **72** B1
Sioux Narrows *Canada* 49°25N 94°10W **71** D10
Sipadan *Malaysia* 4°6N 118°38E **37** D5
Siparia *Trin. & Tob.* 10°8N 61°31W **93** K15
Siping *China* 43°8N 124°21E **33** C13
Sipiwesk L. *Canada* 55°5N 97°35W **71** B9
Siple I. *Antarctica* 73°40S 125°10W **5** D14
Sipra → *India* 23°55N 75°28E **42** H6
Sipsongpanna = Xishuangbanna
  China 22°5N 101°1E **34** G3
Sipur *India* 21°11N 95°8E **41** K19
Sipura *Indonesia* 2°18S 99°40E **36** E1
Siquia → *Nic.* 12°10N 84°20W **88** D3
Siquijor *Phil.* 9°12N 123°35E **37** C6
Siquirres *Costa Rica* 10°6N 83°30W **88** D3
Şīr Abu Nu'ayr *U.A.E.* 25°20N 54°20E **47** E7
Şīr Banī Yās *U.A.E.* 24°19N 52°37E **47** E7
Sir Edward Pellew Group
  Australia 15°40S 137°10E **62** B2
Sir Graham Moore Is.
  Australia 13°53S 126°34E **60** B4
Sir James MacBrien, Mt.
  Canada 62°7N 127°41W **68** E6
Sira *India* 13°41N 76°49E **45** H3
Sira → *Norway* 58°23N 6°34E **9** G12
Siracusa *Italy* 37°4N 15°17E **22** F6
Sirajganj *Bangla.* 24°25N 89°47E **43** G13
Sirathu *India* 25°39N 81°19E **43** G9
Sīrdān *Iran* 36°39N 49°12E **47** B6
Siren *U.S.A.* 45°47N 92°24W **80** C7
Siret → *Romania* 45°24N 28°1E **17** F14
Sirghāyā *Syria* 33°51N 36°8E **48** B5
Sirikit Res. *Thailand* 17°45N 100°34E **38** C3
Sirinat △ *Thailand* 8°6N 98°17E **39** a
Sīrjān *Iran* 29°30N 55°45E **47** D7
Sirkali = Sirkazhi *India* 11°15N 79°41E **45** J4
Sirkazhi *India* 11°15N 79°41E **45** J4
Sirmaur *India* 24°51N 81°23E **43** G9
Sirmilik △ *Canada* 72°50N 80°35W **69** C15
Sirohi *India* 24°52N 72°53E **42** G5
Sironj *India* 24°5N 77°39E **42** G7
Siros = Ermoupoli
  Greece 37°28N 24°57E **23** F11
Sirpur *India* 19°29N 79°36E **44** E4
Sirr, Nafud as *Si. Arabia* 25°33N 44°35E **46** E5
Sirretta Pk. *U.S.A.* 35°56N 118°19W **79** K8
Sirri *Iran* 25°55N 54°32E **47** E7
Sirsa *India* 29°33N 75°4E **42** E6
Sirsa → *India* 26°51N 79°4E **43** F8
Sirsi *India* 14°40N 74°49E **45** G2
Sirsilla *India* 18°23N 78°50E **44** E4
Sirte = Surt *Libya* 31°11N 16°39E **53** B9
Siruguppa *India* 15°38N 76°54E **45** F3
Sirur *India* 18°50N 74°23E **44** E1
Şirvan *Azerbaijan* 39°59N 48°52E **47** B6
Sisak *Croatia* 45°30N 16°21E **16** F9
Sishen *S. Africa* 27°47S 22°59E **56** C3
Sishui *China* 35°42N 117°18E **33** G9
Sisipuk L. *Canada* 55°45N 101°50W **71** B8
Sisophon *Cambodia* 13°38N 102°59E **38** F4
Sisseton *U.S.A.* 45°40N 97°3W **80** C5
Sīstān *Asia* 30°50N 61°0E **47** D9
Sīstān, Daryācheh-ye *Iran* 31°0N 61°0E **47** D9
Sīstān va Balūchestān □
  Iran 27°0N 62°0E **47** D9
Sisters *U.S.A.* 44°18N 121°33W **76** D3
Sisters, The *Seychelles* 4°16S 55°52E **55** b
Siswa Bazar *India* 27°9N 83°46E **43** F10
Sitamarhi *India* 26°37N 85°30E **43** F11
Sitapur *India* 27°38N 80°45E **43** F9
Siteki *Swaziland* 26°32S 31°58E **57** D5
Sitges *Spain* 41°17N 1°47E **21** B6
Sitia *Greece* 35°13N 26°6E **23** G12
Sitito-Ozima Ridge *Pac. Oc.* 23°0N 143°0E **64** E6
Sitka *U.S.A.* 57°3N 135°20W **70** B1
Sitkaing = Sagaing
  Burma 21°52N 95°59E **41** J19
Sitoti *Botswana* 23°15S 23°40E **56** B3
Sittang Myit → *Burma* 17°20N 96°45E **41** L20
Sittard *Neths.* 51°0N 5°52E **15** C5
Sittingbourne *U.K.* 51°21N 0°45E **13** F8
Sittoung = Sittang Myit →
  Burma 17°20N 96°45E **41** L20
Sittwe *Burma* 20°18N 92°45E **41** J18
Si'umu *Samoa* 14°1S 171°48W **59** b
Siuna *Nic.* 13°37N 84°45E **88** D3
Siuri *India* 23°50N 87°34E **43** H12
Sivaganga *India* 9°50N 78°28E **45** K4
Sivagiri *India* 9°16N 77°26E **45** K3
Sivakasi *India* 9°24N 77°47E **45** K3
Sīvand *Iran* 30°5N 52°55E **47** D7
Sivas *Turkey* 39°43N 36°58E **46** B3
Sivasamudram *India* 12°16N 77°10E **45** H3
Siverek *Turkey* 37°50N 39°19E **46** B3
Sivomaskinskiy *Russia* 66°40N 62°35E **18** A11
Sivrihisar *Turkey* 39°30N 31°35E **19** G5
Sīwa *Egypt* 29°11N 25°31E **53** C11
Sīwa, El Wâhât es = Sīwa, El Wâhât es
  Egypt 29°10N 25°30E **50** D6
Siwa Oasis = Sīwa, El Wâhât es
  Egypt 29°10N 25°30E **50** D6
Siwalik Range *Nepal* 28°0N 83°0E **43** F10
Siwan *India* 26°13N 84°21E **43** F11
Siwana *India* 25°38N 72°25E **42** G5
Six Cross Roads *Barbados* 13°7N 59°28W **89** g
Sixian *China* 33°30N 117°50E **33** H9
Sixmilebridge *Ireland* 52°44N 8°46W **10** D3
Sixth Cataract *Sudan* 16°20N 32°42E **53** E12
Siyabuswa *S. Africa* 25°5S 29°3E **57** C4
Siyah Kuh, Kavīr-e *Iran* 32°55N 53°55E **47** C7
Siyang *China* 33°42N 118°40E **33** H10
Siziwang Qi *China* 41°25N 111°40E **32** D6
Sjælland *Denmark* 55°30N 11°30E **9** J14
Sjumen = Shumen
  Bulgaria 43°18N 26°55E **23** C12

Skadarsko Jezero Europe	42°10N 19°20E	23 C8	
Skaftafell Iceland	64°1N 17°0W	8 D5	
Skaftafell △ Iceland	64°9N 16°50W	8 D5	
Skagafjörður Iceland	65°54N 19°35W	8 D4	
Skagaströnd Iceland	65°50N 20°19W	8 D3	
Skagen Denmark	57°43N 10°35E	9 H14	
Skagerrak Denmark	57°30N 9°0E	9 H13	
Skagit → U.S.A.	48°23N 122°22W	78 B4	
Skagway U.S.A.	59°28N 135°19W	68 F4	
Skala-Podilska Ukraine	48°50N 26°15E	17 D14	
Skalat Ukraine	49°23N 25°55E	17 D13	
Skåne Sweden	55°59N 13°30E	9 J15	
Skaneateles U.S.A.	42°57N 76°26W	83 D8	
Skaneateles L. U.S.A.	42°51N 76°22W	83 D8	
Skardu Pakistan	35°20N 75°44E	43 B6	
Skarżysko-Kamienna Poland	51°7N 20°52E	17 C11	
Skeena → Canada	54°9N 130°5W	70 C2	
Skeena Mts. Canada	56°40N 128°30W	70 B3	
Skegness U.K.	53°9N 0°20E	12 D8	
Skeleton Coast Namibia	20°0S 13°0E	55 J2	
Skeleton Coast △ Namibia	20°0S 13°0E	56 B1	
Skellefteå Sweden	64°45N 20°50E	8 D19	
Skellefteälven → Sweden	64°45N 21°10E	8 D19	
Skelleftehamn Sweden	64°40N 21°9E	8 D19	
Skellig Michael = Great Skellig Ireland	51°47N 10°33W	10 E1	
Skerries Ireland	53°35N 6°8W	10 C5	
Skerries, The U.K.	53°25N 4°36W	12 D3	
Ski Norway	59°43N 10°52E	9 G14	
Skiathos Greece	39°12N 23°30E	23 E10	
Skibbereen Ireland	51°33N 9°16W	10 E2	
Skiddaw U.K.	54°39N 3°9W	12 C4	
Skidegate Canada	53°15N 132°1W	70 C2	
Skien Norway	59°12N 9°35E	9 G13	
Skierniewice Poland	51°58N 20°10E	17 C11	
Skihist, Mt. Canada	50°12N 121°54W	70 C4	
Skikda Algeria	36°50N 6°58E	52 A7	
Skipton U.K.	53°58N 2°3W	12 D5	
Skirmish Pt. Australia	11°59S 134°17E	62 A1	
Skiros Greece	38°55N 24°34E	23 E11	
Skive Denmark	56°33N 9°2E	9 H13	
Skjálfandafljót → Iceland	65°59N 17°25W	8 D5	
Skjálfandi Iceland	66°5N 17°30W	8 C5	
Skole Ukraine	49°3N 23°30E	17 D12	
Skopelos Greece	39°9N 23°47E	23 E10	
Skopje Macedonia	42°1N 21°26E	23 C9	
Skövde Sweden	58°24N 13°50E	9 G15	
Skovorodino Russia	54°0N 124°0E	27 D13	
Skowhegan U.S.A.	44°46N 69°43W	81 C19	
Skull Ireland	51°32N 9°34W	10 E2	
Skunk → U.S.A.	40°42N 91°7W	80 E8	
Skuodas Lithuania	56°16N 21°33E	9 H19	
Skvyra Ukraine	49°44N 29°40E	17 D15	
Skye U.K.	57°15N 6°10W	11 D2	
Skykomish U.S.A.	47°42N 121°22W	78 C5	
Skyros = Skiros Greece	38°55N 24°34E	23 E11	
Slade Point Australia	21°4S 149°13E	62 b	
Slade Pt. Australia	21°5S 149°13E	62 b	
Slættaratindur Faroe Is.	62°18N 7°1W	8 E9	
Slagelse Denmark	55°23N 11°19E	9 J14	
Slamet Indonesia	7°16S 109°8E	37 G13	
Slane Ireland	53°42N 6°33W	10 C5	
Slaney → Ireland	52°26N 6°33W	10 D5	
Slangberge S. Africa	31°32S 20°48E	56 D3	
Slate Is. Canada	48°40N 87°0W	72 C2	
Slatina Romania	44°28N 24°22E	17 F13	
Slatington U.S.A.	40°45N 75°37W	83 F9	
Slaton U.S.A.	33°26N 101°39W	84 E4	
Slave → Canada	61°18N 113°39W	70 A6	
Slave Coast W. Afr.	6°0N 2°30E	52 G6	
Slave Lake Canada	55°17N 114°43W	70 B6	
Slave Pt. Canada	61°11N 115°56W	70 A5	
Slavgorod Russia	53°1N 78°37E	26 D8	
Slavonski Brod Croatia	45°11N 18°1E	23 B8	
Slavuta Ukraine	50°15N 27°2E	17 C14	
Slavyanka Russia	42°53N 131°21E	28 C5	
Slavyanka = Slovyansk Ukraine	48°55N 37°36E	19 E6	
Slawharad Belarus	53°27N 31°0E	17 B16	
Slea Hd. Ireland	52°6N 10°27W	10 D1	
Sleaford U.K.	53°0N 0°24W	12 D7	
Sleaford B. Australia	34°55S 135°45E	63 E2	
Sleat, Sd. of U.K.	57°5N 5°47W	11 D3	
Sleeper Is. Canada	58°30N 81°0W	69 F15	
Sleeping Bear Dunes △ U.S.A.	44°50N 86°5W	80 C10	
Sleepy Eye U.S.A.	44°18N 94°43W	80 C6	
Slemon L. Canada	63°13N 116°4W	70 A5	
Slide Mt. U.S.A.	42°0N 74°25W	83 E10	
Slidell U.S.A.	30°17N 89°47W	85 F10	
Slieve Aughty Ireland	53°4N 8°30W	10 C3	
Slieve Bloom Ireland	53°4N 7°40W	10 C4	
Slieve Donard U.K.	54°11N 5°55W	10 B6	
Slieve Gamph Ireland	54°6N 9°0W	10 B3	
Slieve Gullion U.K.	54°7N 6°26W	10 B5	
Slieve League Ireland	54°40N 8°42W	10 B3	
Slieve Mish Ireland	52°12N 9°50W	10 D2	
Slievenamon Ireland	52°25N 7°34W	10 D4	
Sligeach = Sligo Ireland	54°16N 8°28W	10 B3	
Sligo Ireland	54°16N 8°28W	10 B3	
Sligo □ Ireland	54°8N 8°42W	10 B3	
Sligo B. Ireland	54°18N 8°40W	10 B3	
Slippery Rock U.S.A.	41°4N 80°3W	82 E4	
Slite Sweden	57°42N 18°48E	9 H18	
Sliven Bulgaria	42°42N 26°19E	23 C12	
Sloan U.S.A.	35°57N 115°13W	79 K11	
Sloansville U.S.A.	42°45N 74°22W	83 D10	
Slobodskoy Russia	58°40N 50°6E	18 C9	
Slobozia Romania	44°34N 27°23E	17 F14	
Slocan Canada	49°48N 117°28W	70 D5	
Slonim Belarus	53°4N 25°19E	17 B13	
Slough U.K.	51°30N 0°36W	13 F7	
Slough □ U.K.	51°30N 0°36W	13 F7	
Sloughhouse U.S.A.	38°26N 121°12W	78 G5	
Slovak Rep. ■ Europe	48°30N 20°0E	17 D10	
Slovakia = Slovak Rep. ■ Europe	48°30N 20°0E	17 D10	
Slovakian Ore Mts. = Slovenské Rudohorie Slovak Rep.	48°45N 20°0E	17 D10	
Slovenia ■ Europe	45°58N 14°30E	16 F8	
Slovenija = Slovenia Europe	45°58N 14°30E	16 F8	
Slovensko = Slovak Rep. ■ Europe	48°30N 20°0E	17 D10	
Slovenské Rudohorie Slovak Rep.	48°45N 20°0E	17 D10	
Slovyansk Ukraine	48°55N 37°36E	19 E6	
Sluch → Ukraine	51°37N 26°38E	17 C14	
Sluis Neths.	51°18N 3°23E	15 C3	
Słupsk Poland	54°30N 17°3E	17 A9	
Slurry S. Africa	25°49S 25°42E	56 C4	
Slutsk Belarus	53°2N 27°31E	17 B14	
Slyne Hd. Ireland	53°25N 10°10W	10 C1	
Slyudyanka Russia	51°40N 103°40E	27 D11	
Småland Sweden	57°15N 15°25E	9 H16	
Smalltree L. Canada	61°0N 105°0W	71 A8	
Smallwood Res. Canada	54°5N 64°30W	73 B7	
Smarhon Belarus	54°20N 26°24E	17 A14	
Smartt Syndicate Dam S. Africa	30°45S 23°10E	56 D3	
Smartville U.S.A.	39°13N 121°18W	78 F5	
Smeaton Canada	53°30N 104°49W	71 C8	
Smederevo Serbia	44°40N 20°57E	23 B9	
Smerwick Harbour Ireland	52°12N 10°23W	10 D1	
Smethport U.S.A.	41°49N 78°27W	82 E6	
Smidovich Russia	48°36N 133°49E	27 E14	
Smith Canada	55°10N 114°0W	70 B6	
Smith Center U.S.A.	39°47N 98°47W	80 F4	
Smith I. Canada	60°45N 78°25W	69 E16	
Smith I. India	13°20N 93°4E	45 H11	
Smith Islands △ Australia	20°40S 149°9E	62 b	
Smith River △ U.S.A.	41°55N 124°0W	76 F2	
Smithburne → Australia	17°3S 140°57E	62 B3	
Smithers Canada	54°45N 127°10W	70 C3	
Smithfield S. Africa	30°9S 26°30E	57 D4	
Smithfield N.C., U.S.A.	35°31N 78°21W	85 D15	
Smithfield Utah, U.S.A.	41°50N 111°50W	76 F8	
Smiths Falls Canada	44°55N 76°0W	83 B9	
Smithton Australia	40°53S 145°6E	63 G4	
Smithville Canada	43°6N 79°33W	82 C5	
Smithville U.S.A.	30°1N 97°10W	84 F6	
Smoke Creek Desert U.S.A.	40°30N 119°40W	76 F4	
Smoky → Canada	56°10N 117°21W	70 B5	
Smoky Bay Australia	32°22S 134°13E	63 E1	
Smoky Hill → U.S.A.	39°4N 96°48W	80 F5	
Smoky Hills U.S.A.	39°15N 99°30W	80 F4	
Smoky Lake Canada	54°10N 112°30W	70 C6	
Smøla Norway	63°23N 8°3E	8 E12	
Smolensk Russia	54°45N 32°5E	18 D5	
Smolikas, Oros Greece	40°9N 20°58E	23 D9	
Smolyan Bulgaria	41°36N 24°38E	23 D11	
Smooth Rock Falls Canada	49°17N 81°37W	72 C3	
Smoothstone L. Canada	54°40N 106°50W	71 C7	
Smorgon = Smarhon Belarus	54°20N 26°24E	17 A14	
Smyley I. Antarctica	72°55S 78°0W	5 D17	
Smyrna = İzmir Turkey	38°25N 27°8E	23 E12	
Smyrna U.S.A.	39°18N 75°36W	81 F16	
Snæfell Iceland	64°48N 15°34W	8 D6	
Snaefell I. of Man	54°16N 4°27W	12 C3	
Snæfellsjökull Iceland	64°49N 23°46W	8 D2	
Snake → U.S.A.	46°12N 119°2W	76 C4	
Snake I. Australia	38°47S 146°33E	63 F4	
Snake Range U.S.A.	39°0N 114°20W	76 G6	
Snake River Plain U.S.A.	42°50N 114°0W	76 E7	
Snåsavatnet Norway	64°12N 12°0E	8 D15	
Sneek Neths.	53°2N 5°40E	15 A5	
Sneem Ireland	51°50N 9°54W	10 E2	
Sneeuberge S. Africa	31°46S 24°20E	56 D3	
Snelling U.S.A.	37°31N 120°26W	78 H6	
Snežka Europe	50°41N 15°50E	16 C8	
Snizort, L. U.K.	57°33N 6°28W	11 D2	
Snøhetta Norway	62°19N 9°16E	8 E13	
Snohomish U.S.A.	47°55N 122°6W	78 C4	
Snoqualmie U.S.A.	47°31N 121°49W	78 C5	
Snoqualmie Pass U.S.A.	47°25N 121°25W	78 C5	
Snoul Cambodia	12°4N 106°26E	39 F6	
Snover U.S.A.	43°27N 82°58W	82 C2	
Snow Hill U.S.A.	38°11N 75°24W	81 F16	
Snow Lake Canada	54°52N 100°3W	71 C8	
Snow Mt. Calif., U.S.A.	39°23N 122°45W	78 F4	
Snow Mt. Maine, U.S.A.	45°18N 70°48W	83 A14	
Snow Shoe U.S.A.	41°2N 77°57W	82 E7	
Snowbird L. Canada	60°45N 103°0W	71 A8	
Snowdon U.K.	53°4N 4°5W	12 D3	
Snowdonia △ U.K.	53°7N 3°59W	12 D4	
Snowdrift = Łutsel K'e Canada	62°24N 110°44W	71 A6	
Snowdrift → Canada	62°24N 110°44W	71 A6	
Snowflake U.S.A.	34°30N 110°5W	77 J8	
Snowshoe Pk. U.S.A.	48°13N 115°41W	76 B6	
Snowtown Australia	33°46S 138°14E	63 E2	
Snowville U.S.A.	41°58N 112°43W	76 F7	
Snowy → Australia	37°46S 148°30E	63 F4	
Snowy Mt. U.S.A.	43°42N 74°23W	83 C10	
Snowy Mts. Australia	36°30S 148°20E	63 F4	
Snug Corner Bahamas	22°33N 73°52W	89 B5	
Snug Harbour Canada	45°22N 80°17W	82 A4	
Snyatyn Ukraine	48°27N 25°38E	17 D13	
Snyder Okla., U.S.A.	34°40N 98°57W	84 D5	
Snyder Tex., U.S.A.	32°44N 100°55W	84 E4	
Soalala Madag.	16°6S 45°20E	55 H9	
Soan → Pakistan	33°1N 71°44E	42 C4	
Sobat, Nahr → South Sudan	9°22N 31°33E	53 G12	
Sobhapur India	22°47N 78°17E	42 H8	
Sobradinho, Represa de Brazil	9°30S 42°0W	93 E10	
Sobral Brazil	3°50S 40°20W	93 D10	
Soc Giang Vietnam	22°54N 106°1E	34 F6	
Soc Trang Vietnam	9°37N 105°50E	39 H5	
Socastee U.S.A.	33°41N 78°59W	85 E15	
Soch'e = Shache China	38°20N 77°10E	30 D4	
Sochi Russia	43°35N 39°40E	19 F6	
Société, Îs. de la French Polynesia	17°0S 151°0W	65 J12	
Society Is. = Société, Îs. de la French Polynesia	17°0S 151°0W	65 J12	
Socompa, Portezuelo de Chile	24°27S 68°18W	94 A2	
Socorro N. Mex., U.S.A.	34°4N 106°54W	77 J10	
Socorro Tex., U.S.A.	31°39N 106°18W	84 F1	
Socorro, I. Mexico	18°45N 110°58W	86 D2	
Socotra Yemen	12°30N 54°0E	49 E5	
Soda L. U.S.A.	35°10N 116°4W	79 K10	
Soda Plains India	35°30N 79°0E	43 B8	
Soda Springs U.S.A.	42°39N 111°36W	76 E8	
Sodankylä Finland	67°29N 26°40E	8 C22	
Soddy-Daisy U.S.A.	35°17N 85°10W	85 D12	
Söderhamn Sweden	61°18N 17°10E	8 F17	
Söderköping Sweden	58°31N 16°20E	9 G17	
Södermanland Sweden	58°56N 16°55E	9 G17	
Södertälje Sweden	59°12N 17°39E	9 G17	
Sodiri Sudan	14°27N 29°0E	53 F11	
Sodwana Bay △ S. Africa	27°35S 32°43E	57 C5	
Soekmekaar = Morebeng S. Africa	23°30S 29°55E	57 B4	
Soest Neths.	52°9N 5°19E	15 B5	
Sofala □ Mozam.	19°30S 34°30E	57 A5	
Sofia = Sofiya Bulgaria	42°45N 23°20E	23 C10	
Sofia → Madag.	15°27S 47°23E	55 H9	
Sofiya Bulgaria	42°45N 23°20E	23 C10	
Sofu-Gan Japan	29°49N 140°21E	29 K10	
Sogamoso Colombia	5°43N 72°56W	92 B4	
Sogār Iran	25°53N 58°6E	47 E8	
Sogndalsfjøra Norway	61°14N 7°5E	8 F12	
Søgne Norway	58°5N 7°48E	9 G12	
Sognefjorden Norway	61°10N 5°50E	8 F11	
Soh Iran	33°26N 51°27E	47 C6	
Sohâg Egypt	26°33N 31°43E	53 C12	
Sohagpur India	22°42N 78°12E	42 H8	
Sohar = Şuḩār Oman	24°20N 56°40E	47 E8	
Sohela India	21°18N 83°24E	44 D6	
Soheuksando S. Korea	34°4N 125°7E	33 G13	
Soignies Belgium	50°35N 4°5E	15 D4	
Soissons France	49°25N 3°19E	20 B5	
Sôja Japan	34°40N 133°45E	29 G6	
Sojat India	25°55N 73°45E	42 G5	
Sokal Ukraine	50°31N 24°15E	17 C13	
Sokcho S. Korea	38°12N 128°36E	33 E15	
Söke Turkey	37°48N 27°28E	23 F12	
Sokhumi Georgia	43°0N 41°0E	19 F7	
Soko Is. China	22°10N 113°54E	31 a	
Sokodé Togo	9°0N 1°11E	52 G6	
Sokol Russia	59°30N 40°5E	18 C7	
Sokółka Poland	53°25N 23°30E	17 B12	
Sokołów Podlaski Poland	52°25N 22°15E	17 B12	
Sokoto Nigeria	13°2N 5°16E	52 F7	
Sol Iletsk Russia	51°10N 55°0E	18 D10	
Solan India	30°55N 77°7E	42 D7	
Solana Beach U.S.A.	32°58N 117°16W	79 N9	
Solander I. N.Z.	46°34S 166°54E	59 G1	
Solapur India	17°43N 75°56E	44 E2	
Soldotna U.S.A.	60°29N 151°3W	68 E1	
Soledad Colombia	10°55N 74°46W	92 A4	
Soledad U.S.A.	36°26N 121°20W	78 J5	
Soledad Venezuela	8°10N 63°34W	92 B6	
Solent, The U.K.	50°45N 1°25W	13 G6	
Solfonntaggen Norway	60°2N 6°57E	9 F12	
Solhan Turkey	38°57N 41°3E	46 B4	
Soligalich Russia	59°5N 42°10E	18 C7	
Soligorsk = Salihorsk Belarus	52°51N 27°27E	17 B14	
Solihull U.K.	52°26N 1°47W	13 E6	
Solikamsk Russia	59°38N 56°50E	18 C10	
Solimões = Amazonas → S. Amer.	0°5S 50°0W	93 D8	
Solingen Germany	51°10N 7°5E	16 C4	
Sollefteå Sweden	63°12N 17°20E	8 E17	
Sóller Spain	39°46N 2°43E	21 C7	
Solo → Indonesia	6°47S 112°22E	37 G15	
Sologne France	47°40N 1°45E	20 C4	
Solok Indonesia	0°45S 100°40E	36 E2	
Sololá Guatemala	14°49N 91°10W	88 D1	
Solomon, N. Fork → U.S.A.	39°29N 98°26W	80 F4	
Solomon, S. Fork → U.S.A.	39°25N 99°12W	80 F4	
Solomon Is. ■ Pac. Oc.	6°0S 155°0E	58 B8	
Solomon Rise Pac. Oc.	1°0N 157°0E	64 G7	
Solon China	46°32N 121°10E	31 B13	
Solon Springs U.S.A.	46°22N 91°49W	80 B8	
Solor Indonesia	8°27S 123°0E	37 F6	
Solothurn Switz.	47°13N 7°32E	20 C7	
Solovetskiye Ostrova Russia	65°5N 35°40E	18 B6	
Šolta Croatia	43°24N 16°15E	22 C7	
Solṭānābād Khorāsān, Iran	34°13N 59°58E	47 C8	
Solṭānābād Khorāsān, Iran	36°29N 58°5E	47 B8	
Solṭāniyeh Iran	36°20N 48°47E	47 B6	
Solunska Glava Macedonia	41°44N 21°31E	23 D9	
Solvang U.S.A.	34°36N 120°8W	79 L6	
Solvay U.S.A.	43°3N 76°13W	83 C8	
Sölvesborg Sweden	56°5N 14°35E	9 H16	
Solvychegodsk Russia	61°21N 46°56E	18 B8	
Solway Firth U.K.	54°49N 3°35W	12 C4	
Solwezi Zambia	12°11S 26°21E	55 G5	
Sōma Japan	37°40N 140°50E	28 F10	
Soma Turkey	39°10N 27°35E	23 E12	
Somabhula Zimbabwe	19°42S 29°40E	57 A4	
Somali Pen. Africa	7°0N 46°0E	50 F8	
Somalia ■ Africa	7°0N 47°0E	49 F4	
Somaliland □ Somalia	10°0N 46°0E	49 F4	
Sombor Serbia	45°46N 19°9E	23 B8	
Sombra Canada	42°43N 82°29W	82 D2	
Sombrerete Mexico	23°38N 103°39W	86 C4	
Sombrero Anguilla	18°37N 63°30W	89 C7	
Sombrero Channel India	7°41N 93°35E	45 L11	
Somdari India	25°47N 72°38E	42 G5	
Somers U.S.A.	48°5N 114°13W	76 B6	
Somerset Ky., U.S.A.	37°5N 84°36W	81 G11	
Somerset Mass., U.S.A.	41°47N 71°8W	83 E13	
Somerset Pa., U.S.A.	40°1N 79°5W	82 F5	
Somerset □ U.K.	51°9N 3°0W	13 F5	
Somerset East S. Africa	32°42S 25°35E	56 D4	
Somerset I. Canada	73°30N 93°0W	68 C13	
Somerset West S. Africa	34°8S 18°50E	56 D2	
Somersworth U.S.A.	43°16N 70°52W	83 C14	
Somerton U.S.A.	32°36N 114°43W	77 K6	
Somerville U.S.A.	40°35N 74°38W	83 F10	
Someş → Romania	47°49N 22°43E	17 D12	
Somme → France	50°11N 1°38E	20 A4	
Somnath India	20°53N 70°22E	42 J4	
Somosierra, Puerto de Spain	41°4N 3°35W	21 B4	
Somosomo Fiji	16°47S 179°58W	59 a	
Somosomo Str. Fiji	16°0S 180°0E	59 a	
Somoto Nic.	13°28N 86°37W	88 D2	
Somport, Túnel de Spain	42°48N 0°31W	20 E3	
Somvarpet India	12°36N 75°52E	45 H2	
Son → India	25°42N 84°52E	43 G11	
Son, Laem Thailand	7°59N 98°16E	39 a	
Son Ha Vietnam	15°3N 108°34E	38 E7	
Son La Vietnam	21°20N 103°50E	34 G4	
Son Tay Vietnam	21°8N 105°30E	34 G5	
Son Tinh Vietnam	15°10N 108°40E	38 E7	
Soná Panama	8°0N 81°20W	88 E3	
Sonamarg India	34°18N 75°21E	43 B6	
Sonamukhi India	23°18N 87°27E	43 H12	
Sonar → India	24°24N 79°56E	43 G8	
Sönch'ŏn N. Korea	39°48N 124°55E	33 E13	
Sondags → S. Africa	33°44S 25°51E	56 D4	
Sønderborg Denmark	54°55N 9°49E	9 J13	
Sóndrio Italy	46°10N 9°52E	20 C8	
Sondur → India	20°40N 82°1E	44 D6	
Sonepur India	20°55N 83°50E	44 D6	
Song Thailand	18°28N 100°11E	38 C3	
Song Cau Vietnam	13°27N 109°18E	38 F7	
Song Ma Vietnam	20°56N 103°53E	34 G4	
Song Xian China	34°12N 112°8E	32 G7	
Songadh India	21°9N 73°33E	44 D1	
Songan Indonesia	8°13S 115°24E	37 J18	
Songea Tanzania	10°40S 35°40E	54 G7	
Songgang China	22°46N 113°50E	31 a	
Songhua Hu China	43°35N 126°50E	33 C14	
Songhua Jiang → China	47°45N 132°30E	31 B15	
Songjiang China	31°1N 121°12E	35 B13	
Songjianghe China	42°10N 127°29E	33 C14	
Söngjin = Kimch'aek N. Korea	40°40N 129°10E	33 D15	
Songkan China	28°35N 106°52E	34 C6	
Songkhla Thailand	7°13N 100°37E	39 J3	
Songming China	25°12N 103°2E	34 E4	
Songnim N. Korea	38°45N 125°39E	33 E13	
Songo Mozam.	15°34S 32°38E	57 A5	
Songpan China	32°40N 103°30E	34 A4	
Songtao China	28°11N 109°10E	34 C7	
Songxi China	27°31N 118°44E	35 D12	
Songzi China	30°12N 111°45E	35 B8	
Sonhat India	23°29N 82°31E	43 H10	
Sonid Youqi China	42°45N 112°48E	32 C7	
Sonid Zuoqi China	43°50N 113°42E	32 C7	
Sonipat India	29°0N 77°5E	42 E7	
Sonkach India	22°59N 76°21E	42 H7	
Sonmiani Pakistan	25°25N 66°40E	42 G2	
Sonmiani B. Pakistan	25°15N 66°30E	42 G2	
Sono → Brazil	9°58S 48°11W	93 E9	
Sonora Calif., U.S.A.	38°18N 120°23W	78 G4	
Sonora Tex., U.S.A.	30°34N 100°39W	84 F4	
Sonora □ Mexico	29°20N 110°40W	86 B2	
Sonora → Mexico	29°5N 110°55W	86 B2	
Sonoran Desert U.S.A.	33°40N 113°30W	79 L12	
Sonoyta Mexico	31°51N 112°50W	86 A2	
Sonsonate El Salv.	13°43N 89°44W	88 D2	
Soochow = Suzhou China	31°19N 120°38E	35 B13	
Sooke Canada	48°13N 123°43W	78 B3	
Soomaaliya = Somalia ■ Africa	7°0N 47°0E	49 F4	
Sop Hao Laos	20°33N 104°27E	34 G5	
Sop Prap Thailand	17°53N 99°20E	38 D2	
Sopi Indonesia	2°34N 128°28E	37 D7	
Sopot Poland	54°27N 18°31E	17 A10	
Sopron Hungary	47°45N 16°32E	17 E9	
Sopur India	34°18N 74°27E	43 B6	
Sør-Rondane Antarctica	72°0S 25°0E	5 D4	
Sorab India	14°23N 75°6E	45 G2	
Sorada India	19°45N 84°26E	44 E7	
Sorah Pakistan	27°13N 68°56E	42 F3	
Soraon India	25°37N 81°51E	43 G9	
Sorel-Tracy Canada	46°0N 73°10W	72 C5	
Sórgono Italy	40°1N 9°6E	22 D3	
Soria Spain	41°43N 2°32W	21 B4	
Soriano Uruguay	33°24S 58°19W	94 C4	
Sorkh, Kuh-e Iran	35°40N 58°30E	47 C8	
Soroca Moldova	48°8N 28°12E	17 D15	
Sorocaba Brazil	23°31S 47°27W	95 A6	
Sorochinsk Russia	52°26N 53°10E	18 D9	
Soroki = Soroca Moldova	48°8N 28°12E	17 D15	
Sorong Indonesia	0°55S 131°15E	37 E8	
Soroti Uganda	1°43N 33°35E	54 D6	
Sørøya Norway	70°40N 22°30E	8 A20	
Sørøysundet Norway	70°25N 23°0E	8 A20	
Sorrell Australia	42°47S 147°34E	63 G4	
Sorrento Italy	40°37N 14°22E	22 D6	
Sorsele Sweden	65°31N 17°30E	8 D17	
Sorsogon Phil.	13°0N 124°0E	37 B6	
Sortavala Russia	61°42N 30°41E	8 F24	
Sortland Norway	68°42N 15°25E	8 B16	
Soscumica, L. Canada	50°15N 77°27W	72 B4	
Sosnogorsk Russia	63°37N 53°51E	18 B9	
Sosnowiec Poland	50°20N 19°10E	17 C10	
Sossus Vlei Namibia	24°40S 15°23E	56 B2	
Sôsura N. Korea	42°16N 130°36E	33 C16	
Sot → India	27°27N 79°37E	43 F8	
Sotavento C. Verde Is.	15°0N 24°0W	52 b	
Sotkamo Finland	64°8N 28°23E	8 D23	
Soto la Marina Mexico	23°46N 98°13W	87 C5	
Soto la Marina → Mexico	23°45N 97°45W	87 C5	
Sotuta Mexico	20°36N 89°1W	87 C7	
Souanké Congo	2°10N 14°3E	54 D2	
Soudas, Ormos Greece	35°25N 24°10E	23 G11	
Souderton U.S.A.	40°19N 75°19W	83 F9	
Soufrière Guadeloupe	16°5N 61°40W	88 b	
Soufrière St. Lucia	13°51N 61°3W	89 f	
Soufrière Bay Dominica	15°13N 61°22W	89 f	
Soukhouma Laos	14°38N 105°48E	38 E5	
Sound, The U.K.	50°20N 4°10W	13 G3	
Sound I. India	12°58N 92°78E	45 H11	
Sources, Mt. aux Lesotho	28°45S 28°50E	57 C4	
Soure Brazil	0°35S 48°30W	93 D9	
Souris Man., Canada	49°40N 100°20W	71 D8	
Souris P.E.I., Canada	46°21N 62°15W	73 C7	
Souris → N. Amer.	49°40N 99°34W	80 A4	
Sousa Brazil	6°45S 38°10W	93 E11	
Sousse Tunisia	35°50N 10°38E	53 A8	
Sout → S. Africa	31°35S 18°24E	56 D2	
South Africa ■ Africa	32°0S 23°0E	56 D3	
South America	10°0S 60°0W	90 E5	
South Andaman India	11°45N 92°10E	45 J11	
South Aulatsivik I. Canada	56°45N 61°30W	73 A7	
South Australia □ Australia	32°0S 139°0E	63 E2	
South Australian Basin Ind. Oc.	38°0S 126°0E	64 L4	
South Ayrshire □ U.K.	55°18N 4°41W	11 F4	
South Baldy Pk. U.S.A.	34°6N 107°11W	77 J10	
South Bass I. U.S.A.	41°39N 82°49W	82 E2	
South Bend Ind., U.S.A.	41°41N 86°15W	80 E10	
South Bend Wash., U.S.A.	46°40N 123°48W	78 D3	
South Boston U.S.A.	36°42N 78°54W	81 G14	
South Branch Canada	47°55N 59°2W	73 C8	
South Brook Canada	49°26N 56°5W	73 C8	
South Brother I. India	12°0N 93°37E	45 J11	
South Bruny I. Australia	43°20S 147°15E	63 G4	
South Carolina □ U.S.A.	34°0N 81°0W	85 D14	
South Charleston U.S.A.	38°22N 81°44W	81 F13	
South China Sea Asia	10°0N 113°0E	36 C4	
South Cumberland Is. △ Australia	20°42S 149°11E	62 b	
South Dakota □ U.S.A.	44°15N 100°0W	80 C4	
South Dayton U.S.A.	42°21N 79°3W	82 D5	
South Deerfield U.S.A.	42°29N 72°37W	83 D12	
South Downs U.K.	50°52N 0°25W	13 G7	
South Downs △ U.K.	50°50N 0°50W	13 G7	
South East □ Botswana	25°0S 25°40E	56 C4	
South East C. Australia	43°40S 146°50E	63 G4	
South East Is. Australia	34°17S 123°30E	61 F3	
South Esk → U.K.	56°43N 2°31W	11 E6	
South Fiji Basin Pac. Oc.	26°0S 175°0E	64 K9	
South Foreland U.K.	51°8N 1°24E	13 F9	
South Fork American → U.S.A.	38°57N 120°59W	78 G5	
South Fork Feather → U.S.A.	39°17N 121°36W	78 F5	
South Fork Grand → U.S.A.	45°43N 102°17W	80 C2	
South Fork Milk → U.S.A.	48°4N 106°19W	76 B10	
South Fork Republican → U.S.A.	40°3N 101°31W	80 E3	
South Georgia Antarctica	54°30S 37°0W	96 G9	
South Gloucestershire □ U.K.	51°32N 2°28W	13 F5	
South Hadley U.S.A.	42°16N 72°35W	83 D12	
South Haven U.S.A.	42°24N 86°16W	80 D10	
South Henik L. Canada	61°30N 97°20W	71 A9	
South Horr Kenya	2°12N 36°56E	54 D7	
South I. India	10°3N 72°17E	45 J1	
South I. N.Z.	44°0S 170°0E	59 F3	
South Indian Lake Canada	56°47N 98°56W	71 B9	
South Invercargill N.Z.	46°26S 168°23E	59 G2	
South Knife → Canada	58°55N 94°37W	71 B10	
South Koel → India	22°32N 85°14E	43 H11	
South Korea ■ Asia	36°0N 128°0E	33 G15	
South Lake Tahoe U.S.A.	38°57N 119°59W	78 G6	
South Lanarkshire □ U.K.	55°37N 3°53W	11 F5	
South Loup → U.S.A.	41°4N 98°39W	80 E4	
South Magnetic Pole Antarctica	64°8S 138°8E	5 C9	
South Milwaukee U.S.A.	42°55N 87°52W	80 D10	
South Molton U.K.	51°1N 3°51W	13 F4	
South Moose L. Canada	53°49N 100°1W	71 C8	
South Nahanni → Canada	61°3N 123°21W	70 A4	
South Nation → Canada	45°34N 75°6W	83 A9	
South Natuna Is. = Natuna Selatan, Kepulauan Indonesia	2°45N 109°0E	36 D3	
South Negril Pt. Jamaica	18°16N 78°22W	88 a	
South Orkney Is. Antarctica	63°0S 45°0W	5 C18	
South Ossetia □ Georgia	42°21N 44°2E	19 F7	
South Otselic U.S.A.	42°38N 75°46W	83 D9	
South Pagai, I. = Pagai Selatan, Pulau Indonesia	3°0S 100°15E	36 E2	
South Paris U.S.A.	44°14N 70°31W	83 B14	
South Pittsburg U.S.A.	35°1N 85°42W	85 D12	
South Platte → U.S.A.	41°7N 100°42W	80 E3	
South Pole Antarctica	90°0S 0°0	5 E	
South Porcupine Canada	48°30N 81°12W	72 C3	
South Portland U.S.A.	43°38N 70°15W	81 D18	
South Pt. Barbados	13°2N 59°32W	89 g	
South Pt. U.S.A.	44°52N 83°19W	82 B1	

South River Canada 45°52N 79°23W 72 C4
South River U.S.A. 40°27N 74°23W 83 F10
South Ronaldsay U.K. 58°48N 2°58W 11 C6
South Sandwich Is.
  Antarctica 57°0S 27°0W 5 B1
South Sandwich Trench
  Atl. Oc. 56°0S 24°0W 5 B1
South Saskatchewan →
  Canada 53°15N 105°5W 71 C7
South Seal → Canada 58°48N 98°8W 71 B9
South Sentinel I. India 10°59N 92°14E 45 J11
South Shetland Is.
  Antarctica 62°0S 59°0W 5 C18
South Shields U.K. 55°0N 1°25W 12 C6
South Sioux City U.S.A. 42°28N 96°24W 80 D5
South Sister U.S.A. 44°4N 121°51W 76 D3
South Sudan ■ Africa 8°0N 30°0E 53 G11
South Taranaki Bight
  N.Z. 39°40S 174°5E 59 C5
South Tasman Rise
  S. Ocean 48°0S 146°0E 5 A10
South Thompson →
  Canada 50°40N 120°20W 70 C4
South Twin I. Canada 53°7N 79°52W 72 B4
South Tyne → U.K. 54°59N 2°8W 12 C5
South Uist U.K. 57°20N 7°15W 11 D1
South Valley U.S.A. 35°1N 106°41W 77 J10
South Wellesley Is.
  Australia 16°58S 139°17E 62 B2
South West C. Australia 43°34S 146°3E 63 G4
South West C. N.Z. 47°17S 167°28E 59 G1
South Williamsport
  U.S.A. 41°13N 77°0W 82 E8
South Yorkshire □ U.K. 53°27N 1°36W 12 D6
Southampton Canada 44°30N 81°25W 82 B3
Southampton U.K. 50°54N 1°23W 13 G6
Southampton U.S.A. 40°53N 72°23W 83 F12
Southampton □ U.K. 50°54N 1°23W 13 G6
Southampton I. Canada 64°30N 84°0W 69 E15
Southaven U.S.A. 34°59N 90°0W 85 D9
Southbank U.S.A. 54°2N 125°46W 70 C3
Southbridge N.Z. 43°48S 172°16E 59 E4
Southbridge U.S.A. 42°5N 72°2W 83 D12
Southend Canada 56°19N 103°22W 71 B8
Southend-on-Sea U.K. 51°32N 0°44E 13 F8
Southend-on-Sea □ U.K. 51°32N 0°44E 13 F8
Southern = Yuzhnyy □
  Russia 44°0N 40°0E 26 E5
Southern Alps N.Z. 43°41S 170°11E 59 E3
Southern Cross Australia 31°12S 119°15E 61 F2
Southern Indian L.
  Canada 57°10N 98°30W 71 B9
Southern Lau Group Fiji 18°40S 178°40W 59 a
Southern Ocean 62°0S 60°0E 5 C6
Southern Pines U.S.A. 35°11N 79°24W 85 D15
Southern Uplands U.K. 55°28N 3°52W 11 F5
Southington U.S.A. 41°36N 72°53W 83 E12
Southland □ N.Z. 45°30S 168°0E 59 F1
Southold U.S.A. 41°4N 72°26W 83 E12
Southport Australia 27°58S 153°25E 63 D5
Southport U.K. 53°39N 3°0W 12 D4
Southport U.S.A. 42°3N 76°49W 82 D8
Southwest △ Australia 43°8S 146°49E 63 G4
Southwest Pacific Basin
  Pac. Oc. 40°0S 140°0W 5 A12
Southwold U.K. 52°20N 1°41E 13 E9
Southwood △ Australia 27°48S 150°8E 63 D5
Soutpansberg S. Africa 23°0S 29°30E 57 B4
Sovetsk Kaliningrad, Russia 55°6N 21°50E 9 J19
Sovetsk Kirov, Russia 57°38N 48°53E 18 C8
Sovetskaya Gavan
  Russia 48°58N 140°18E 27 E15
Sowma'eh Sarā Iran 37°17N 49°18E 47 B6
Sõya-Kaikyõ = La Perouse Str.
  Asia 45°40N 142°0E 28 B11
Sõya-Misaki Japan 45°30N 141°55E 28 B10
Soyo Angola 6°13S 12°20E 54 F2
Sozh → Belarus 51°57N 30°48E 17 B16
Spa Belgium 50°29N 5°53E 15 D5
Spaatz I. Antarctica 73°10S 75°0W 5 D17
Spain ■ Europe 39°0N 4°0W 21 B4
Spalding Australia 33°30S 138°37E 63 E2
Spalding U.K. 52°48N 0°9W 12 E7
Spanaway U.S.A. 47°6N 122°26W 78 C4
Spangler U.S.A. 40°39N 78°48W 82 F6
Spanish Canada 46°12N 82°20W 72 C3
Spanish Fork U.S.A. 40°7N 111°39W 76 F8
Spanish Town
  Br. Virgin Is. 18°26N 64°26W 89 e
Spanish Town Jamaica 18°0N 76°57W 88 a
Sparks U.S.A. 39°32N 119°45W 78 F7
Sparta = Spárti Greece 37°5N 22°25E 23 F10
Sparta Mich., U.S.A. 43°10N 85°42W 81 D11
Sparta N.J., U.S.A. 41°2N 74°38W 83 E10
Sparta Wis., U.S.A. 43°56N 90°49W 80 D8
Spartanburg U.S.A. 34°56N 81°57W 85 D14
Spárti Greece 37°5N 22°25E 23 F10
Spartivento, C. Calabria,
  Italy 37°55N 16°4E 22 F7
Spartivento, C. Sard., Italy 38°53N 8°50E 22 E3
Sparwood Canada 49°44N 114°53W 70 D6
Spassk Dalniy Russia 44°40N 132°48E 28 B6
Spatha, Ákra Greece 35°42N 23°43E 23 G10
Spatsizi → Canada 57°42N 128°7W 70 B3
Spatsizi Plateau Wilderness △
  Canada 57°40N 128°0W 70 B3
Spean → U.K. 56°55N 4°59W 11 E4
Spearfish U.S.A. 44°30N 103°52W 80 C2
Spearman U.S.A. 36°12N 101°12W 84 C4
Speculator U.S.A. 43°30N 74°22W 83 C10
Speightstown Barbados 13°15N 59°39W 89 g
Spence Bay = Taloyoak
  Canada 69°32N 93°32W 68 D13
Spencer Idaho, U.S.A. 44°22N 112°11W 76 D7
Spencer Iowa, U.S.A. 43°9N 95°9W 80 D6
Spencer N.Y., U.S.A. 42°13N 76°30W 83 D8
Spencer Nebr., U.S.A. 42°53N 98°42W 80 D4
Spencer, C. Australia 35°20S 136°53E 63 F2
Spencer B. Namibia 25°30S 14°47E 56 C1

Spencer G. Australia 34°0S 137°20E 63 E2
Spencerville Canada 44°51N 75°33W 83 B9
Spences Bridge Canada 50°25N 121°20W 70 C4
Spennymoor U.K. 54°42N 1°36W 12 C6
Spenser Mts. N.Z. 42°15S 172°45E 59 E4
Sperrin Mts. U.K. 54°50N 7°0W 10 B5
Spey → U.K. 57°40N 3°6W 11 D5
Speyer Germany 49°29N 8°25E 16 D5
Spezand Pakistan 29°59N 67°0E 42 E2
Spiddle Ireland 53°15N 9°18W 10 C2
Spinifex ◎ Australia 28°30S 128°30E 61 E4
Spirit Lake U.S.A. 46°15N 122°9W 78 D4
Spirit River Canada 55°45N 118°50W 70 B5
Spiritwood Canada 53°24N 107°33W 71 C7
Spithead U.K. 50°45N 1°10W 13 G6
Spitzbergen = Svalbard
  Arctic 78°0N 17°0E 4 B8
Spjelkavik Norway 62°28N 6°22E 8 E12
Split Croatia 43°31N 16°26E 22 C7
Split L. Canada 56°8N 96°15W 71 B9
Split Lake Canada 56°8N 96°15W 71 B9
Spofford U.S.A. 29°10N 100°25W 84 G4
Spokane U.S.A. 47°40N 117°24W 76 C5
Spoleto Italy 42°44N 12°44E 22 C5
Spooner U.S.A. 45°50N 91°53W 80 C8
Sporyy Navolok, Mys
  Russia 75°50N 68°40E 26 B7
Sprague U.S.A. 47°18N 117°59W 76 C5
Spratly I. S. China Sea 8°38N 111°55E 36 C4
Spratly Is. S. China Sea 8°20N 112°0E 36 C4
Spray U.S.A. 44°50N 119°48W 76 D4
Spree → Germany 52°32N 13°12E 16 B7
Sprengisandur Iceland 64°52N 18°7W 8 D4
Spring City U.S.A. 40°11N 75°33W 83 F9
Spring Creek U.S.A. 40°44N 115°35W 76 F6
Spring Garden U.S.A. 39°52N 120°47W 78 F6
Spring Hall Barbados 13°18N 59°36W 89 g
Spring Hill U.S.A. 28°27N 82°41W 85 G13
Spring Mts. U.S.A. 36°0N 115°45W 79 J11
Spring Valley U.S.A. 32°44N 116°59W 79 N10
Springbok S. Africa 29°42S 17°54E 56 C2
Springboro U.S.A. 41°48N 80°22W 82 E4
Springdale Canada 49°30N 56°6W 73 C8
Springdale U.S.A. 36°11N 94°8W 84 C7
Springer U.S.A. 36°22N 104°36W 77 H11
Springerville U.S.A. 34°8N 109°17W 77 J9
Springfield Canada 42°50N 80°56W 82 D4
Springfield N.Z. 43°19S 171°56E 59 E3
Springfield Colo.,
  U.S.A. 37°24N 102°37W 77 H12
Springfield Ill., U.S.A. 39°48N 89°39W 80 F9
Springfield Mass., U.S.A. 42°6N 72°35W 83 D12
Springfield Mo., U.S.A. 37°13N 93°17W 80 G7
Springfield Ohio, U.S.A. 39°55N 83°49W 81 F12
Springfield Oreg., U.S.A. 44°3N 123°1W 76 D2
Springfield Tenn., U.S.A. 36°31N 86°53W 85 C11
Springfield Vt., U.S.A. 43°18N 72°29W 83 C12
Springfontein S. Africa 30°15S 25°40E 56 D4
Springhill Canada 45°40N 64°4W 73 C7
Springhill U.S.A. 33°0N 93°28W 84 E8
Springhouse Canada 51°56N 122°7W 70 C4
Springlands = Corriverton
  Guyana 5°55N 57°20W 92 B7
Springs S. Africa 26°13S 28°25E 57 C4
Springsure Australia 24°8S 148°6E 62 C4
Springvale Australia 43°28N 70°48W 83 C14
Springville Calif., U.S.A. 36°8N 118°49W 78 J8
Springville N.Y., U.S.A. 42°31N 78°40W 82 D6
Springville Utah, U.S.A. 40°10N 111°37W 76 F8
Springwater U.S.A. 42°38N 77°35W 82 D7
Spruce-Creek U.S.A. 40°36N 78°9W 82 F6
Spruce Knob-Seneca Rocks △
  U.S.A. 38°50N 79°30W 81 F14
Spruce Mt. U.S.A. 44°12N 72°19W 83 B12
Sprucedale Canada 45°29N 79°28W 82 A5
Spur U.S.A. 33°28N 100°52W 84 E4
Spurn Hd. U.K. 53°35N 0°8E 12 D8
Spuzzum Canada 49°37N 121°23W 70 D4
Squam L. U.S.A. 43°45N 71°32W 83 C13
Squamish Canada 49°45N 123°10W 70 D4
Square Islands Canada 52°47N 55°47W 73 B8
Squires, Mt. Australia 26°14S 127°28E 61 E4
Srbija = Serbia ■ Europe 43°20N 20°0E 23 B9
Sre Ambel Cambodia 11°8N 103°46E 39 G4
Sre Khtum Cambodia 12°10N 106°52E 39 F6
Sre Umbell = Sre Ambel
  Cambodia 11°8N 103°46E 39 G4
Srebrenica Bos.-H. 44°6N 19°18E 23 B8
Sredinnyy Khrebet
  Russia 57°0N 160°0E 27 D17
Sredinnyy Ra. = Sredinnyy
  Khrebet Russia 57°0N 160°0E 27 D17
Srednekolymsk Russia 67°27N 153°40E 27 C16
Šrem Poland 52°6N 17°2E 17 B9
Sremska Mitrovica Serbia 44°59N 19°38E 23 B8
Srepok → Cambodia 13°33N 106°16E 38 F6
Sretensk Russia 52°10N 117°40E 27 D12
Sri Aman = Bandar Sri Aman
  Malaysia 1°15N 111°32E 36 D4
Sri Kalahasti India 13°45N 79°44E 45 H4
Sri Lanka ■ Asia 7°30N 80°50E 45 L5
Sri Pada = Adam's Peak
  Sri Lanka 6°48N 80°30E 45 L5
Sriharikota I. India 13°40N 80°20E 45 H5
Srikakulam India 18°14N 83°58E 44 E6
Srinagar India 34°5N 74°50E 43 B6
Srivardhan India 18°4N 73°3E 44 E1
Srivilliputtur India 9°31N 77°40E 45 K3
Srono Indonesia 8°24S 114°16E 37 J17
Srungavarapukota India 18°7N 83°32E 44 E5
Staaten → Australia 16°24S 141°17E 62 B3
Staaten River △
  Australia 16°15S 142°40E 62 B3
Stade Germany 53°35N 9°29E 16 B5
Stadskanaal Neths. 53°4N 6°55E 15 A6
Staffa U.K. 56°27N 6°21W 11 E2
Stafford U.K. 52°49N 2°7W 12 E5
Stafford U.S.A. 37°58N 98°36W 80 G4

Stafford Springs U.S.A. 41°57N 72°18W 83 E12
Staffordshire □ U.K. 52°53N 2°10W 12 E5
Staines U.K. 51°26N 0°29W 13 F7
Stakhanov Ukraine 48°35N 38°40E 19 E6
Stalowa Wola Poland 50°34N 22°3E 17 C12
Stalybridge U.K. 53°28N 2°3W 12 D5
Stamford Australia 21°15S 143°46E 62 C3
Stamford U.K. 52°39N 0°29W 13 E7
Stamford Conn., U.S.A. 41°3N 73°32W 83 E11
Stamford N.Y., U.S.A. 42°25N 74°38W 83 D10
Stamford Tex., U.S.A. 32°57N 99°48W 84 E5
Stampriet Namibia 24°20S 18°28E 56 B2
Stamps U.S.A. 33°22N 93°30W 84 E8
Standerton S. Africa 26°55S 29°7E 57 C4
Standish U.S.A. 43°59N 83°57W 81 D12
Stanford S. Africa 34°26S 19°29E 56 E2
Stanford U.S.A. 47°9N 110°13W 76 C8
Stanger S. Africa 29°27S 31°14E 57 C5
Stängelsån = Salpausselkä
  Finland 61°3N 26°15E 8 F22
Stanislaus → U.S.A. 37°40N 121°14W 78 H5
Stanke Dimitrov Bulgaria 42°17N 23°9E 23 C10
Stanley Australia 40°46S 145°19E 63 G4
Stanley Falk. Is. 51°40S 59°51W 96 G5
Stanley U.K. 54°53N 1°41W 12 C6
Stanley Idaho, U.S.A. 44°13N 114°56W 76 D6
Stanley N. Dak., U.S.A. 48°19N 102°23W 80 A2
Stanley N.Y., U.S.A. 42°48N 77°6W 82 D7
Stanley Mission U.S.A. 55°25N 104°33W 71 B8
Stanley Res. India 11°50N 77°40E 45 J3
Stanovoy Khrebet Russia 55°0N 130°0E 27 D14
Stanovoy Ra. = Stanovoy Khrebet
  Russia 55°0N 130°0E 27 D14
Stansmore Ra. Australia 21°23S 128°33E 60 D4
Stanstead, London ✈ (STN)
  U.K. 51°54N 0°14E 13 F8
Stanthorpe Australia 28°36S 151°59E 63 D5
Stanton U.S.A. 32°8N 101°48W 84 E4
Stanwood U.S.A. 48°15N 122°23W 78 B4
Staples Canada 42°10N 82°35W 82 D2
Staples U.S.A. 46°21N 94°48W 80 B7
Stapleton U.S.A. 41°29N 100°31W 80 E3
Star City Canada 52°50N 104°20W 71 C8
Star Lake U.S.A. 44°10N 75°2W 83 B9
Stara Planina Bulgaria 43°15N 23°0E 23 C10
Stara Zagora Bulgaria 42°26N 25°39E 23 C11
Starachowice Poland 51°3N 21°2E 17 C11
Staraya Russa Russia 57°58N 31°23E 18 C5
Starbuck I. Kiribati 5°37S 155°55W 65 H12
Starcke △ Australia 14°56S 145°2E 62 A4
Stargard Szczeciński
  Poland 53°20N 15°0E 16 B8
Staritsa Russia 56°33N 34°55E 18 C5
Starke U.S.A. 29°57N 82°7W 85 G13
Starkville U.S.A. 33°28N 88°49W 85 E10
Starogard Gdański
  Poland 53°59N 18°30E 17 B10
Starokonstantinov =
  Starokonstyantyniv
  Ukraine 49°48N 27°10E 17 D14
Starokonstyantyniv
  Ukraine 49°48N 27°10E 17 D14
Start Pt. U.K. 50°13N 3°39W 13 G4
Staryy Chartoriysk
  Ukraine 51°15N 25°54E 17 C13
Staryy Oskol Russia 51°19N 37°55E 19 D6
State College U.S.A. 40°48N 77°52W 82 F7
Stateline U.S.A. 38°57N 119°56W 78 G7
Staten, I. = Estados, I. de Los
  Argentina 54°40S 64°30W 96 G4
Staten I. U.S.A. 40°35N 74°9W 83 F10
Statesboro U.S.A. 32°27N 81°47W 85 E14
Statesville U.S.A. 35°47N 80°53W 85 D14
Statia = St. Eustatius
  W. Indies 17°20N 63°0W 89 C7
Stauffer U.S.A. 34°45N 119°3W 79 L7
Staunton Ill., U.S.A. 39°1N 89°47W 80 F9
Staunton Va., U.S.A. 38°9N 79°4W 81 F14
Stavanger Norway 58°57N 5°40E 9 G11
Staveley N.Z. 43°40S 171°32E 59 E3
Stavelot Belgium 50°23N 5°55E 15 D5
Stavern Norway 59°0N 10°1E 9 G14
Stavoren Neths. 52°53N 5°22E 15 B5
Stavropol Russia 45°5N 42°0E 19 E7
Stawell Australia 37°5S 142°47E 63 F3
Stawell → Australia 20°20S 142°55E 62 C3
Stayner Canada 44°25N 80°5W 82 B4
Stayton U.S.A. 44°48N 122°48W 76 D2
Steamboat Springs
  U.S.A. 40°29N 106°50W 76 F10
Steele U.S.A. 46°51N 99°55W 80 B4
Steelton U.S.A. 40°14N 76°50W 82 F8
Steen River Canada 59°40N 117°12W 70 B5
Steens Mt. U.S.A. 42°35N 118°40W 76 E4
Steenwijk Neths. 52°47N 6°7E 15 B6
Steep Pt. Australia 26°8S 113°8E 61 E1
Steep Rock Canada 51°30N 98°48W 71 C9
Stefanie L. = Chew Bahir
  Ethiopia 4°40N 36°50E 49 G2
Stefansson Bay Antarctica 67°20S 59°8E 5 C5
Stefansson I. Canada 73°20N 105°45W 69 C10
Steiermark □ Austria 47°26N 15°0E 16 E8
Steilacoom U.S.A. 47°10N 122°36W 78 C4
Steilrandberge Namibia 17°45S 13°20E 56 A1
Steinbach Canada 49°32N 96°40W 71 D9
Steinhausen Namibia 21°49S 18°20E 56 C2
Steinkjer Norway 64°1N 11°31E 8 D14
Steinkopf S. Africa 29°18S 17°43E 56 C2
Stellarton Canada 45°32N 62°30W 73 C7
Stellenbosch S. Africa 33°58S 18°50E 56 E2
Stendal Germany 52°36N 11°53E 16 B6
Steornabhaigh = Stornoway
  U.K. 58°13N 6°23W 11 C2
Stepanakert = Xankändi
  Azerbaijan 39°52N 46°49E 46 B5
Stephens Creek Australia 31°50S 141°30E 63 E3
Stephens I. Canada 54°10N 130°45W 70 C2
Stephens L. Canada 56°32N 95°0W 71 B9

Stephenville Canada 48°31N 58°35W 73 C8
Stephenville U.S.A. 32°13N 98°12W 84 E5
Steppe Asia 50°0N 50°0E 24 C7
Sterkstroom S. Africa 31°32S 26°32E 56 D4
Sterling Colo., U.S.A. 40°37N 103°13W 76 F12
Sterling Ill., U.S.A. 41°48N 89°42W 80 E9
Sterling Kans., U.S.A. 38°13N 98°12W 80 F4
Sterling City U.S.A. 31°51N 101°0W 84 F4
Sterling Heights U.S.A. 42°35N 83°2W 81 D12
Sterling Run U.S.A. 41°25N 78°12W 82 E6
Sterlitamak Russia 53°40N 56°0E 18 D10
Stettin = Szczecin Poland 53°27N 14°27E 16 B8
Stettiner Haff Germany 53°47N 14°15E 16 B8
Stettler Canada 52°19N 112°40W 70 C6
Steubenville U.S.A. 40°22N 80°37W 82 F4
Stevenage U.K. 51°55N 0°13W 13 F7
Stevens Point U.S.A. 44°31N 89°34W 80 C9
Stevenson U.S.A. 45°42N 121°53W 78 E5
Stevenson → Australia 27°6S 135°33E 63 D2
Stevenson L. Canada 53°55N 96°0W 71 C9
Stevensville U.S.A. 46°30N 114°5W 76 C6
Stewart Canada 55°56N 129°57W 70 B3
Stewart U.S.A. 39°5N 119°46W 78 F7
Stewart → Canada 63°19N 139°26W 68 E4
Stewart, C. Australia 11°57S 134°56E 62 A1
Stewart, I. Chile 54°50S 71°15W 96 G2
Stewart I. N.Z. 46°58S 167°54E 59 G1
Stewarts Point U.S.A. 38°39N 123°24W 78 G3
Stewartville U.S.A. 43°51N 92°29W 80 D7
Stewiacke Canada 45°9N 63°22W 73 C7
Steynsburg S. Africa 31°15S 25°49E 56 D4
Steyr Austria 48°3N 14°25E 16 D8
Steytlerville S. Africa 33°17S 24°19E 56 D3
Stigler U.S.A. 35°15N 95°8W 84 D7
Stikine → Canada 56°40N 132°30W 70 B2
Stilfontein S. Africa 26°51S 26°50E 56 C4
Stillwater N.Z. 42°27S 171°20E 59 E3
Stillwater N.Y., U.S.A. 42°55N 73°41W 83 D11
Stillwater Okla., U.S.A. 36°7N 97°4W 84 C6
Stillwater Range U.S.A. 39°50N 118°5W 76 G4
Stillwater Res. U.S.A. 43°54N 75°3W 83 C9
Stilwell U.S.A. 35°49N 94°38W 84 D7
Stînga Nistrului □
  Moldova 47°20N 29°15E 17 E15
Štip Macedonia 41°42N 22°10E 23 D10
Stirling Canada 44°18N 77°33W 82 B7
Stirling U.K. 56°8N 3°57W 11 E5
Stirling □ U.K. 56°12N 4°18W 11 E4
Stirling Ra. Australia 34°23S 118°0E 61 F2
Stirling Range △
  Australia 34°26S 118°20E 61 F2
Stittsville Canada 45°15N 75°55W 83 A9
Stjernøya Norway 70°20N 22°40E 8 A20
Stjørdalshalsen Norway 63°29N 10°51E 8 E14
Stockerau Austria 48°24N 16°12E 16 D9
Stockport U.K. 53°25N 2°9W 12 D5
Stocksbridge U.K. 53°29N 1°35W 12 D6
Stockton Calif., U.S.A. 37°58N 121°17W 78 H5
Stockton Kans., U.S.A. 39°26N 99°16W 80 F4
Stockton Mo., U.S.A. 37°42N 93°48W 80 G7
Stockton-on-Tees U.K. 54°35N 1°19W 12 C6
Stockton-on-Tees □ U.K. 54°35N 1°19W 12 C6
Stockton Plateau
  U.S.A. 30°30N 102°30W 84 F3
Stoeng Treng Cambodia 13°31N 105°58E 38 F5
Stoer, Pt. of U.K. 58°16N 5°23W 11 C3
Stoke-on-Trent U.K. 53°1N 2°11W 12 D5
Stoke-on-Trent □ U.K. 53°1N 2°11W 12 D5
Stokes △ Australia 33°45S 121°11E 61 F3
Stokes Bay Canada 45°0N 81°28W 82 B3
Stokes Pt. Australia 40°10S 143°56E 63 G3
Stokes Ra. Australia 15°50S 130°50E 60 C5
Stokksnes Iceland 64°14N 14°58W 8 D6
Stokmarknes Norway 68°34N 14°54E 8 B16
Stolac Bos.-H. 43°5N 17°59E 23 C7
Stolbovoy, Ostrov
  Russia 74°44N 135°14E 27 B14
Stolbtsy = Stowbtsy
  Belarus 53°30N 26°43E 17 B14
Stolin Belarus 51°53N 26°50E 17 C14
Stone U.K. 52°55N 2°9W 12 E5
Stoneboro U.S.A. 41°20N 80°7W 82 E4
Stonehaven U.K. 56°59N 2°12W 11 E6
Stonehenge Australia 24°22S 143°17E 62 C3
Stonehenge U.K. 51°9N 1°45W 13 F6
Stonewall Canada 50°10N 97°19W 71 C9
Stony I. U.S.A. 43°53N 76°19W 83 C8
Stony L. Man., Canada 58°51N 98°40W 71 B9
Stony L. Ont., Canada 44°30N 78°5W 82 B6
Stony Point U.S.A. 41°14N 73°59W 83 E11
Stony Pt. U.S.A. 43°50N 76°18W 83 C8
Stony Rapids Canada 59°16N 105°50W 71 B7
Stony Tunguska = Tunguska,
  Podkamennaya →
  Russia 61°50N 90°13E 27 C10
Stonyford U.S.A. 39°23N 122°33W 78 F4
Stora Lulevatten Sweden 67°10N 19°30E 8 C18
Storavan Sweden 65°45N 18°10E 8 D18
Stord Norway 59°52N 5°23E 9 G11
Store Bælt Denmark 55°20N 11°0E 9 J14
Storkerson Pen.
  Canada 72°30N 106°30W 68 C10
Storm B. Australia 43°10S 147°30E 63 G4
Storm Lake U.S.A. 42°39N 95°13W 80 D6
Stormberge S. Africa 31°16S 26°17E 56 D4
Stormsrivier S. Africa 33°59S 23°52E 56 E3
Stornoway U.K. 58°13N 6°23W 11 C2
Storozhinets = Storozhynets
  Ukraine 48°14N 25°45E 17 D13
Storozhynets Ukraine 48°14N 25°45E 17 D13
Storrs U.S.A. 41°49N 72°15W 83 E12
Storsjön Sweden 63°9N 14°30E 8 E16
Storuman Sweden 65°5N 17°10E 8 D17
Storuman, L. Sweden 65°13N 16°50E 8 D17
Stouffville Canada 43°58N 79°15W 82 C5
Stoughton Canada 49°40N 103°0W 71 D8
Stour → Dorset, U.K. 50°43N 1°47W 13 G6
Stour → Kent, U.K. 51°18N 1°22E 13 F9
Stour → Suffolk, U.K. 51°57N 1°4E 13 F9

Stourbridge U.K. 52°28N 2°8W 13 E5
Stout L. Canada 52°0N 94°40W 71 C10
Stove Pipe Wells Village
  U.S.A. 36°35N 117°11W 79 J9
Stow U.S.A. 41°10N 81°27W 82 E3
Stowbtsy Belarus 53°30N 26°43E 17 B14
Stowmarket U.K. 52°12N 1°0E 13 E9
Strabane U.K. 54°50N 7°27W 10 B4
Strahan Australia 42°9S 145°20E 63 G4
Stralsund Germany 54°18N 13°4E 16 A7
Strand S. Africa 34°9S 18°48E 56 D2
Stranda Møre og Romsdal,
  Norway 62°19N 6°58E 8 E12
Stranda Nord-Trøndelag,
  Norway 63°33N 10°14E 8 E14
Strangford L. U.K. 54°30N 5°37W 10 B6
Stranorlar Ireland 54°48N 7°46W 10 B4
Stranraer U.K. 54°54N 5°1W 11 G3
Strasbourg Canada 51°4N 104°55W 71 C8
Strasbourg France 48°35N 7°42E 20 B7
Stratford Canada 43°23N 81°0W 82 C4
Stratford N.Z. 39°20S 174°19E 59 C5
Stratford Calif., U.S.A. 36°11N 119°49W 78 J7
Stratford Conn., U.S.A. 41°12N 73°8W 83 E11
Stratford Tex., U.S.A. 36°20N 102°4W 84 C3
Stratford-upon-Avon
  U.K. 52°12N 1°42W 13 E6
Strath Spey U.K. 57°9N 3°49W 11 D5
Strathalbyn Australia 35°13S 138°53E 63 F2
Strathaven U.K. 55°40N 4°5W 11 F4
Strathcona △ Canada 49°38N 125°40W 70 D3
Strathmore Canada 51°5N 113°18W 70 C6
Strathmore U.K. 56°37N 3°7W 11 E5
Strathmore U.S.A. 36°9N 119°4W 78 J7
Strathnaver Canada 53°20N 122°33W 70 C4
Strathpeffer U.K. 57°35N 4°32W 11 D4
Strathroy Canada 42°58N 81°38W 82 D3
Strathy Pt. U.K. 58°36N 4°1W 11 C4
Strattanville U.S.A. 41°12N 79°19W 82 E5
Stratton U.S.A. 45°8N 70°26W 83 A14
Stratton Mt. U.S.A. 43°4N 72°55W 83 C12
Straubing Germany 48°52N 12°34E 16 D7
Straumnes Iceland 66°26N 23°8W 8 C2
Strawberry → U.S.A. 40°10N 110°24W 76 F8
Streaky B. Australia 32°48S 134°13E 63 E1
Streaky Bay Australia 32°51S 134°18E 63 E1
Streator U.S.A. 41°8N 88°50W 80 E9
Streetsboro U.S.A. 41°14N 81°21W 82 E3
Streetsville Canada 43°35N 79°42W 82 C5
Streng → Cambodia 13°12N 103°37E 38 F4
Streymoy Faroe Is. 62°8N 7°5W 8 E9
Strezhevoy Russia 60°42N 77°34E 26 C8
Strimonas → Greece 40°46N 23°51E 23 D10
Strokestown Ireland 53°47N 8°5W 10 C3
Stroma U.K. 58°41N 3°7W 11 C5
Strómboli Italy 38°47N 15°13E 22 E6
Stromeferry U.K. 57°21N 5°33W 11 D3
Stromness U.K. 58°58N 3°17W 11 C5
Stromsburg U.S.A. 41°7N 97°36W 80 E5
Strömstad Sweden 58°56N 11°10E 9 G14
Strömsund Sweden 63°51N 15°33E 8 E16
Strongsville U.S.A. 41°19N 81°50W 82 E3
Stronsay U.K. 59°7N 2°35W 11 B6
Stroud U.K. 51°45N 2°13W 13 F5
Stroud Road Australia 32°18S 151°57E 63 E5
Stroudsburg U.S.A. 40°59N 75°12W 83 F9
Struer Denmark 56°30N 8°35E 9 H13
Strugi Krasnyye Russia 58°21N 29°1E 9 G23
Strumica Macedonia 41°28N 22°41E 23 D10
Struthers Canada 48°41N 85°51W 72 C2
Struthers U.S.A. 41°4N 80°39W 82 E4
Stryker U.S.A. 48°41N 114°46W 76 B6
Stryy Ukraine 49°16N 23°48E 17 D12
Strzelecki Cr. →
  Australia 29°37S 139°59E 63 D2
Strzelecki Desert
  Australia 29°30S 140°0E 63 D3
Stuart Fla., U.S.A. 27°12N 80°15W 85 H14
Stuart Nebr., U.S.A. 42°36N 99°8W 80 D4
Stuart → Canada 54°0N 123°35W 70 C4
Stuart Bluff Ra. Australia 22°50S 131°52E 60 D5
Stuart I. U.S.A. 63°35N 162°30W 74 C7
Stuart L. Canada 54°30N 124°30W 70 C4
Stuart Ra. Australia 29°10S 134°56E 63 D1
Stull L. Canada 54°24N 92°34W 72 B1
Stung Treng = Stoeng Treng
  Cambodia 13°31N 105°58E 38 F5
Stupart → Canada 56°0N 93°25W 72 A1
Sturge I. Antarctica 67°26S 164°47E 5 C11
Sturgeon B. Canada 52°0N 97°50W 71 C9
Sturgeon Bay U.S.A. 44°50N 87°23W 80 C10
Sturgeon Falls Canada 46°25N 79°57W 72 C4
Sturgeon L. Alta., Canada 55°6N 117°32W 70 B5
Sturgeon L. Ont., Canada 50°0N 90°45W 72 C1
Sturgeon L. Ont., Canada 44°28N 78°43W 82 B6
Sturgis Canada 51°56N 102°36W 71 C8
Sturgis Mich., U.S.A. 41°48N 85°25W 81 E11
Sturgis S. Dak., U.S.A. 44°25N 103°31W 80 C2
Sturt △ Australia 27°1S 141°37E 63 D3
Sturt Cr. → Australia 19°8S 127°50E 60 C4
Sturt Stony Desert
  Australia 28°30S 141°0E 63 D3
Stutterheim S. Africa 32°33S 27°28E 56 D4
Stuttgart Germany 48°48N 9°11E 16 D5
Stuttgart U.S.A. 34°30N 91°33W 84 D9
Stuyvesant U.S.A. 42°23N 73°45W 83 D11
Stykkishólmur Iceland 65°2N 22°40W 8 D2
Styria = Steiermark □
  Austria 47°26N 15°0E 16 E8
Su Xian = Suzhou China 33°41N 116°59E 32 H9
Suakin Sudan 19°8N 37°20E 53 E13
Suamico U.S.A. 44°38N 88°2W 80 C9
Suan N. Korea 38°42N 126°22E 33 E14
Suana Indonesia 8°44S 115°36E 37 K18
Suar India 29°2N 79°3E 43 E8
Subā Si. Arabia 27°10N 35°40E 46 E2
Subang Indonesia 6°34S 107°45E 37 G12
Subansiri → India 26°48N 93°50E 41 F18
Subarnagiri India 19°50N 83°51E 44 E6
Subarnarekha → India 22°34N 87°24E 43 H12

Subayhah *Si. Arabia* 30°2N 38°50E **46** D3
Subi *Indonesia* 2°58N 108°50E **36** D3
Subotica *Serbia* 46°6N 19°39E **23** A8
Suceava *Romania* 47°38N 26°16E **17** E14
Suchan = Partizansk
  Russia 43°8N 133°9E **27** E14
Suchil *Mexico* 23°39N 103°54W **86** C4
Suchou = Suzhou
  China 31°19N 120°38E **35** B13
Süchow = Xuzhou
  China 34°18N 117°10E **33** G9
Suck → *Ireland* 53°17N 8°3W **10** C3
Sucre *Bolivia* 19°0S 65°15W **92** G5
Sucuriú → *Brazil* 20°47S 51°38W **93** H8
Sud, Pte. du *Canada* 49°3N 62°14W **73** C7
Sud-Ouest, Pte. *Canada* 49°23N 63°36W **73** C7
Sud Ouest, Pte. *Mauritius* 20°28S 57°18E **55** d
Sudan *U.S.A.* 34°4N 102°31W **84** D3
Sudan ■ *Africa* 15°0N 30°0E **53** E11
Sudbury *Canada* 46°30N 81°0W **72** C3
Sudbury *U.K.* 52°2N 0°45E **13** E8
Sudd *South Sudan* 8°20N 30°0E **53** G12
Sudeten Mts. = Sudety
  Europe 50°20N 16°45E **17** C9
Sudety *Europe* 50°20N 16°45E **17** C9
Suðuroy *Færoe Is.* 61°32N 6°50W **8** F9
Sudirman, Pegunungan
  Indonesia 4°30S 137°0E **37** E9
Sudong, Pulau *Singapore* 1°13N 103°44E **39** d
Sueca *Spain* 39°12N 0°21W **21** C5
Suemez I. *U.S.A.* 55°15N 133°20W **70** B2
Suez = El Suweis *Egypt* 29°58N 32°31E **53** C12
Suez, G. of = Suweis, Khalîg el
  Egypt 28°40N 33°0E **53** C12
Suez Canal = Suweis, Qanâ es
  Egypt 31°0N 32°20E **53** B12
Suffield *Canada* 50°12N 111°10W **70** C6
Suffolk *U.S.A.* 36°44N 76°35W **81** G15
Suffolk □ *U.K.* 52°16N 1°0E **13** E9
Sugag = Sagaing
  Burma 21°52N 95°59E **41** J19
Sugar Grove *U.S.A.* 41°59N 79°20W **82** E5
Sugarcreek *U.S.A.* 41°25N 79°52W **82** E5
Sugarive → *India* 26°16N 86°24E **43** F12
Sugluk = Salluit *Canada* 62°14N 75°38W **69** E16
Şuḩār *Oman* 24°20N 56°40E **47** E8
Sühbaatar *Mongolia* 50°17N 106°10E **30** A10
Sühbaatar □ *Mongolia* 45°30N 114°0E **32** B6
Suheli Par *India* 10°5N 72°17E **45** J1
Suhl *Germany* 50°36N 10°42E **16** C6
Sui *Pakistan* 28°37N 69°19E **42** E3
Sui Xian *China* 34°25N 115°2E **32** G8
Suichang *China* 28°29N 119°15E **35** C12
Suichuan *China* 26°20N 114°32E **35** D10
Suide *China* 37°30N 110°12E **32** F6
Suifenhe *China* 44°25N 131°10E **33** B16
Suihua *China* 46°32N 126°55E **31** B14
Suijiang *China* 28°40N 103°59E **34** C4
Suining *Hunan, China* 26°35N 110°10E **35** D8
Suining *Jiangsu, China* 33°56N 117°58E **33** H9
Suining *Sichuan, China* 30°26N 105°35E **34** B5
Suiping *China* 33°10N 113°59E **32** H7
Suir → *Ireland* 52°16N 7°9W **10** D4
Suisse = Switzerland ■
  Europe 46°30N 8°0E **20** C8
Suisun City *U.S.A.* 38°15N 122°2W **78** G4
Suixi *China* 21°19N 110°18E **35** G8
Suiyang *Guizhou, China* 27°58N 107°18E **34** D6
Suiyang *Heilongjiang,*
  China 44°30N 130°56E **33** B16
Suizhong *China* 40°21N 120°20E **33** D11
Suizhou *China* 31°42N 113°24E **35** B9
Sujangarh *India* 27°42N 74°31E **42** F6
Sujiatun *China* 41°39N 123°20E **33** D12
Sukabumi *Indonesia* 6°56S 106°50E **37** G12
Sukadana *Indonesia* 1°10S 110°0E **36** E4
Sukagawa *Japan* 37°17N 140°23E **29** F10
Sukamade *Indonesia* 8°30S 113°52E **37** H15
Sukaraja *Indonesia* 2°28S 110°25E **36** E4
Sukawati *Indonesia* 8°35S 115°17E **37** K18
Sukch'ŏn *N. Korea* 39°22N 125°35E **33** E13
Sukhona → *Russia* 61°15N 46°39E **18** C6
Sukhothai *Thailand* 17°1N 99°49E **38** D2
Sukhumi = Sokhumi
  Georgia 43°0N 41°0E **19** F7
Sukkur *Pakistan* 27°42N 68°54E **42** F3
Sukkur Barrage *Pakistan* 27°40N 68°50E **42** F3
Sukma *India* 18°24N 81°45E **44** E5
Sukri → *India* 25°4N 71°43E **42** G4
Sukumo *Japan* 32°56N 132°44E **29** H6
Sukunka → *Canada* 55°45N 121°15W **70** B4
Sula, Kepulauan *Indonesia* 1°45S 125°0E **37** E7
Sulaco → *Honduras* 15°2N 87°44W **88** C2
Sulaiman Range *Pakistan* 30°30N 69°50E **42** D3
Sülär *Iran* 31°53N 51°54E **47** D6
Sulawesi *Indonesia* 2°0S 120°0E **37** E6
Sulawesi Barat □ *Indonesia* 3°0S 119°0E **37** E5
Sulawesi Sea = Celebes Sea
  Indonesia 3°0N 123°0E **37** D6
Sulawesi Selatan □
  Indonesia 2°30S 120°0E **37** E6
Sulawesi Tengah □
  Indonesia 1°30S 121°0E **37** E6
Sulawesi Tenggara □
  Indonesia 3°50S 122°0E **37** E6
Sulawesi Utara □ *Indonesia* 1°0N 124°0E **37** D6
Sulima *S. Leone* 6°58N 11°32W **52** G3
Sulina *Romania* 45°10N 29°40E **17** F15
Sulitjelma *Norway* 67°9N 16°3E **8** C17
Sullana *Peru* 4°52S 80°39W **92** D2
Sullivan *Ill., U.S.A.* 39°36N 88°37W **80** F9
Sullivan *Ind., U.S.A.* 39°6N 87°24W **80** F10
Sullivan *Mo., U.S.A.* 38°13N 91°10W **80** F8
Sullivan Bay *Canada* 50°55N 126°50W **70** C3
Sullivan I. = Lanbi Kyun
  Burma 10°50N 98°20E **39** G2
Sullom Voe *U.K.* 60°27N 1°20W **11** A7
Sulphur *La., U.S.A.* 30°14N 93°23W **84** F8
Sulphur *Okla., U.S.A.* 34°31N 96°58W **84** D6

Sulphur Pt. *Canada* 60°56N 114°48W **70** A6
Sulphur Springs *U.S.A.* 33°8N 95°36W **84** E7
Sultan *Canada* 47°36N 82°47W **72** C3
Sultan *U.S.A.* 47°52N 121°49W **78** C5
Sultanábád = Arāk *Iran* 34°0N 49°40E **47** C6
Sultanpur *Mad. P., India* 23°9N 77°56E **42** H8
Sultanpur *Punjab, India* 31°13N 75°11E **42** D6
Sultanpur *Ut. P., India* 26°18N 82°4E **43** F10
Sulu Arch. *Phil.* 6°0N 121°0E **37** C6
Sulu Sea *E. Indies* 8°0N 120°0E **37** C6
Sulūq *Libya* 31°44N 20°14E **53** B10
Suluru *India* 13°42N 80°1E **45** H5
Sulzberger Ice Shelf
  Antarctica 78°0S 150°0W **5** E13
Sumalata *Indonesia* 1°0N 122°31E **37** D6
Sumampa *Argentina* 29°25S 63°29W **94** B3
Sumatera □ *Indonesia* 0°40N 100°20E **36** D2
Sumatera Barat □ *Indonesia* 1°0S 101°0E **36** E2
Sumatera Selatan □
  Indonesia 3°0S 104°0E **36** E2
Sumatera Utara □
  Indonesia 2°30N 98°0E **36** D1
Sumatra = Sumatera
  Indonesia 0°40N 100°20E **36** D2
Sumba *Indonesia* 9°45S 119°35E **37** F5
Sumba, Selat *Indonesia* 9°0S 118°40E **37** F5
Sumbawa *Indonesia* 8°26S 117°30E **36** F5
Sumbawa Besar *Indonesia* 8°30S 117°26E **36** F5
Sumbawanga □ *Tanzania* 8°0S 31°30E **54** F6
Sumbe *Angola* 11°10S 13°48E **54** G2
Sumburgh Hd. *U.K.* 59°52N 1°17W **11** B7
Sumdeo *India* 31°26N 78°44E **43** D8
Sumdo *China* 35°6N 78°41E **43** B8
Sumedang *Indonesia* 6°52S 107°55E **37** G12
Şumen = Shumen
  Bulgaria 43°18N 26°55E **23** C12
Sumenep *Indonesia* 7°1S 113°52E **37** G15
Sumgait = Sumqayit
  Azerbaijan 40°34N 49°38E **19** F8
Summer L. *U.S.A.* 42°50N 120°45W **76** E3
Summerland *Canada* 49°32N 119°41W **70** D5
Summerside *Canada* 46°24N 63°47W **73** C7
Summersville *U.S.A.* 38°17N 80°51W **81** F13
Summerville *Ga., U.S.A.* 34°29N 85°21W **85** D12
Summerville *S.C., U.S.A.* 33°1N 80°11W **85** E14
Summit Lake *Canada* 54°20N 122°40W **70** C4
Summit Peak *U.S.A.* 37°21N 106°42W **77** H10
Sumner *Iowa, U.S.A.* 42°51N 92°6W **80** D7
Sumner *Wash., U.S.A.* 47°12N 122°14W **78** C4
Sumoto *Japan* 34°21N 134°54E **29** G7
Šumperk *Czech Rep.* 49°59N 16°59E **17** D9
Sumqayit *Azerbaijan* 40°34N 49°38E **19** F8
Sumter *U.S.A.* 33°55N 80°21W **85** E14
Sumy *Ukraine* 50°57N 34°50E **19** D5
Sun City *S. Africa* 25°17S 27°3E **56** C4
Sun City Center *U.S.A.* 27°43N 82°21W **85** H13
Sun Kosi → *Nepal* 26°59N 87°8E **43** F12
Sun Lakes *U.S.A.* 33°10N 111°52W **77** K8
Sun Valley *U.S.A.* 43°42N 114°21W **76** E6
Sunagawa *Japan* 43°29N 141°55E **28** C10
Sunan *N. Korea* 39°15N 125°40E **33** E13
Sunart, L. *U.K.* 56°42N 5°43W **11** E3
Sunburst *U.S.A.* 48°53N 111°55W **76** B8
Sunbury *Australia* 37°35S 144°44E **63** F3
Sunbury *U.S.A.* 40°52N 76°48W **83** F8
Sunchales *Argentina* 30°58S 61°35W **94** C3
Suncheon *S. Korea* 34°52N 127°31E **33** G14
Suncho Corral *Argentina* 27°55S 63°27W **94** B3
Sunch'on *N. Korea* 39°25N 125°56E **33** E13
Suncook *U.S.A.* 43°8N 71°27W **83** C13
Sunda, Selat *Indonesia* 6°20S 105°30E **36** F3
Sunda Is. *Indonesia* 5°0S 105°0E **64** H2
Sunda Str. = Sunda, Selat
  Indonesia 6°20S 105°30E **36** F3
Sunda Trench = Java Trench
  Ind. Oc. 9°0S 105°0E **36** F3
Sundance *Canada* 56°32N 94°4W **71** B10
Sundance *U.S.A.* 44°24N 104°23W **76** D11
Sundar Nagar *India* 31°32N 76°53E **42** D7
Sundarbans *Asia* 22°0N 89°0E **41** J16
Sundarbans △ *India* 22°0N 89°0E **43** J13
Sundargarh *India* 22°4N 84°5E **44** C7
Sundays = Sondags →
  S. Africa 33°44S 25°51E **56** D4
Sunderland *Canada* 44°16N 79°4W **82** B5
Sunderland *U.K.* 54°55N 1°23W **12** C6
Sundown △ *Australia* 28°49S 151°38E **63** D5
Sundre *Canada* 51°49N 114°38W **70** C6
Sundsvall *Sweden* 62°23N 17°17E **8** E17
Sungai Acheh *Malaysia* 5°8N 100°30E **39** c
Sungai Kolok *Thailand* 6°2N 101°58E **39** J3
Sungai Lembing *Malaysia* 3°55N 103°3E **39** L4
Sungai Petani *Malaysia* 5°37N 100°30E **39** K3
Sungaigerong *Indonesia* 2°59S 104°52E **36** E2
Sungailiat *Indonesia* 1°51S 106°8E **36** E3
Sungaipenuh *Indonesia* 2°1S 101°20E **36** E2
Sungari = Songhua Jiang →
  China 47°45N 132°30E **31** B15
Sunghua Chiang = Songhua
  Jiang → *China* 47°45N 132°30E **31** B15
Sunland Park *U.S.A.* 31°50N 106°40W **77** L10
Sunndalsøra *Norway* 62°40N 8°33E **8** E13
Sunnyside *U.S.A.* 46°20N 120°0W **76** C4
Sunnyvale *U.S.A.* 37°23N 122°2W **78** H4
Suntar *Russia* 62°15N 117°30E **27** C12
Suomenselkä *Finland* 62°52N 24°0E **8** E21
Suomi = Finland ■ *Europe* 63°0N 27°0E **8** E22
Suomussalmi *Finland* 64°54N 29°10E **8** D23
Suoyarvi *Russia* 62°3N 32°20E **18** B5
Supai *U.S.A.* 36°15N 112°41W **77** H7
Supaul *India* 26°10N 86°40E **43** F12
Superior *Ariz., U.S.A.* 33°18N 111°6W **77** K8
Superior *Mont., U.S.A.* 47°12N 114°53W **76** C6
Superior *Nebr., U.S.A.* 40°1N 98°4W **80** E4
Superior *Wis., U.S.A.* 46°44N 92°6W **80** B7
Superior, L. *N. Amer.* 47°0N 87°0W **72** C2
Suphan Buri *Thailand* 14°14N 100°10E **38** E3
Suphan Dağı *Turkey* 38°54N 42°48E **46** B4
Supiori *Indonesia* 1°0S 136°0E **37** E9

Supung Shuiku *China* 40°35N 124°50E **33** D13
Süq ash Shuyūkh *Iraq* 30°53N 46°28E **46** D5
Süq Suwayq *Si. Arabia* 24°23N 38°27E **46** E3
Suqian *China* 33°54N 118°8E **33** H10
Suquṭra = Socotra *Yemen* 12°30N 54°0E **49** E5
Şūr *Lebanon* 33°19N 35°16E **48** B4
Şūr *Oman* 22°34N 59°32E **49** C6
Sur, Pt. *U.S.A.* 36°18N 121°54W **78** J5
Sura → *Russia* 56°6N 46°0E **18** C8
Surab *Pakistan* 28°25N 66°15E **42** E2
Surabaja = Surabaya
  Indonesia 7°17S 112°45E **37** G15
Surabaya *Indonesia* 7°17S 112°45E **37** G15
Surakarta *Indonesia* 7°35S 110°48E **37** G14
Surat *Australia* 27°10S 149°6E **63** D4
Surat *India* 21°12N 72°55E **44** D1
Surat Thani *Thailand* 9°6N 99°20E **39** H2
Suratgarh *India* 29°18N 73°55E **42** E5
Surathkal *India* 12°58N 74°46E **45** H2
Şuraymilā *Si. Arabia* 25°7N 46°7E **46** E5
Surendranagar *India* 22°45N 71°40E **42** H4
Surf *U.S.A.* 34°41N 120°36W **79** L6
Surfers Paradise *Australia* 28°0S 153°25E **63** D5
Surgana *India* 20°34N 73°37E **44** D1
Surgut *Russia* 61°14N 73°20E **26** C8
Suriapet *India* 17°10N 79°40E **44** F4
Surigao *Phil.* 9°47N 125°29E **37** C7
Surin *Thailand* 14°50N 103°34E **38** E4
Surinam = Suriname ■
  S. Amer. 4°0N 56°0W **93** C7
Suriname ■ *S. Amer.* 4°0N 56°0W **93** C7
Suriname → *Suriname* 5°50N 55°15W **93** B7
Surjagarh *India* 19°36N 80°25E **44** E5
Sürmaq *Iran* 31°3N 52°48E **47** D7
Surprise *U.S.A.* 33°38N 112°19W **77** K7
Surrey *Canada* 49°7N 122°45W **78** A4
Surrey □ *U.K.* 51°15N 0°31W **13** F7
Sursand *India* 26°39N 85°43E **43** F11
Sursar → *India* 26°14N 87°3E **43** F12
Surt *Libya* 31°11N 16°39E **53** B9
Surt, Khalīj *Libya* 31°40N 18°30E **53** B9
Surtanahu *Pakistan* 26°22N 70°0E **42** F4
Surtsey *Iceland* 63°20N 20°30W **8** E3
Suruga-Wan *Japan* 34°45N 138°30E **29** G9
Süsah *Libya* 32°52N 21°59E **53** B10
Susaki *Japan* 33°22N 133°17E **29** H6
Süsangerd *Iran* 31°35N 48°6E **47** D6
Susanville *U.S.A.* 40°25N 120°39W **76** F3
Susner *India* 23°57N 76°5E **42** H7
Susong *China* 30°10N 116°5E **35** B11
Susquehanna *U.S.A.* 41°57N 75°36W **83** E9
Susquehanna → *U.S.A.* 39°33N 76°5W **83** G8
Susques *Argentina* 23°35S 66°25W **94** A2
Sussex *Canada* 45°45N 65°37W **73** C6
Sussex *U.S.A.* 41°13N 74°37W **83** E10
Sussex, E. □ *U.K.* 51°0N 0°20E **13** G8
Sussex, W. □ *U.K.* 51°0N 0°30W **13** G7
Sustut → *Canada* 56°20N 127°30W **70** B3
Susuman *Russia* 62°47N 148°10E **27** C15
Susunu *Indonesia* 3°7S 133°39E **37** E8
Susurluk *Turkey* 39°54N 28°8E **23** E13
Sutay Uul *Asia* 46°35N 93°38E **30** B7
Sutherland *S. Africa* 32°24S 20°40E **56** D3
Sutherland *U.K.* 58°12N 4°50W **11** C4
Sutherland *U.S.A.* 41°10N 101°8W **80** E3
Sutherland Falls *N.Z.* 44°48S 167°46E **59** F1
Sutherlin *U.S.A.* 43°23N 123°19W **76** E2
Suthri *India* 23°3N 68°55E **42** H3
Sutlej → *Pakistan* 29°23N 71°3E **42** E4
Sutter *U.S.A.* 39°10N 121°45W **78** F5
Sutter Buttes *U.S.A.* 39°12N 121°49W **78** F5
Sutter Creek *U.S.A.* 38°24N 120°48W **78** G6
Sutton *Canada* 45°6N 72°37W **83** A12
Sutton *Nebr., U.S.A.* 40°36N 97°52W **80** E5
Sutton *W. Va., U.S.A.* 38°40N 80°43W **81** F13
Sutton → *Canada* 55°15N 83°45W **72** A3
Sutton Coldfield *U.K.* 52°35N 1°49W **13** E6
Sutton in Ashfield *U.K.* 53°8N 1°16W **12** D6
Sutton L. *Canada* 54°15N 84°42W **72** B3
Suttor → *Australia* 21°36S 147°2E **62** C4
Suttsu *Japan* 42°48N 140°14E **28** C10
Sutwik I. *U.S.A.* 56°34N 157°12W **74** D8
Suva *Fiji* 18°6S 178°30E **59** a
Suva Planina *Serbia* 43°10N 22°5E **23** C10
Suvorov Is. = Suwarrow Is.
  Cook Is. 13°15S 163°5W **65** J11
Suwałki *Poland* 54°8N 22°59E **17** A12
Suwannaphum *Thailand* 15°33N 103°47E **38** E4
Suwannee → *U.S.A.* 29°17N 83°10W **85** G13
Suwanose-Jima *Japan* 29°38N 129°43E **29** K4
Suwarrow Is. *Cook Is.* 13°15S 163°5W **65** J11
Suweis, Khalîg el *Egypt* 28°40N 33°0E **53** C12
Suweis, Qanâ es *Egypt* 31°0N 32°20E **53** B12
Suwon *S. Korea* 37°17N 127°1E **33** F14
Suzdal *Russia* 56°29N 40°26E **18** C7
Suzhou *Anhui, China* 33°41N 116°59E **32** H9
Suzhou *Jiangsu, China* 31°19N 120°38E **35** B13
Suzu *Japan* 37°25N 137°17E **29** F8
Suzu-Misaki *Japan* 37°31N 137°21E **29** F8
Suzuka *Japan* 34°55N 136°36E **29** G8
Svalbard *Arctic* 78°0N 17°0E **4** B8
Svalbard Radio = Longyearbyen
  Svalbard 78°13N 15°40E **4** B8
Svappavaara *Sweden* 67°40N 21°3E **8** C19
Svartisen *Norway* 66°40N 13°59E **8** C15
Svay Chek *Cambodia* 13°48N 102°58E **38** F4
Svay Rieng *Cambodia* 11°9N 105°45E **39** G5
Svealand *Sweden* 60°20N 15°0E **9** F16
Sveg *Sweden* 62°2N 14°21E **8** E16
Svendborg *Denmark* 55°4N 10°35E **9** J14
Sverdrup Chan. *Canada* 79°56N 96°25W **69** B12
Sverdrup Is. *Canada* 79°0N 97°0W **66** B10
Sverige = Sweden ■ *Europe* 57°0N 15°0E **9** H16
Svetlaya *Russia* 46°33N 138°18E **28** A9
Svetlogorsk = Svyetlahorsk
  Belarus 52°38N 29°46E **17** B15
Svir → *Russia* 60°30N 32°48E **18** B5
Svishtov *Bulgaria* 43°36N 25°23E **23** C11
Svislach *Belarus* 53°3N 24°2E **17** B13

Svizzera = Switzerland ■
  Europe 46°30N 8°0E **20** C8
Svobodnyy *Russia* 51°20N 128°0E **27** D13
Svolvær *Norway* 68°15N 14°34E **8** B16
Svyetlahorsk *Belarus* 52°38N 29°46E **17** B15
Swabian Alps = Schwäbische Alb
  Germany 48°20N 9°30E **16** D5
Swaffham *U.K.* 52°39N 0°42E **13** E8
Swains I. *Amer. Samoa* 11°11S 171°4W **65** J11
Swainsboro *U.S.A.* 32°36N 82°20W **85** E13
Swakop → *Namibia* 22°38S 14°36E **56** B2
Swakopmund *Namibia* 22°37S 14°30E **56** B1
Swale → *U.K.* 54°5N 1°20W **12** C6
Swamihalli *India* 14°52N 76°38E **45** G3
Swan → *Australia* 32°3S 115°45E **61** F2
Swan → *Canada* 52°30N 100°45W **71** C8
Swan Hill *Australia* 35°20S 143°33E **63** F3
Swan Hills *Canada* 54°43N 115°24W **70** C5
Swan Is. = Santanilla, Is.
  Honduras 17°22N 83°57W **88** C3
Swan L. *Man., Canada* 52°30N 100°40W **71** C8
Swan L. *Ont., Canada* 54°16N 91°11W **72** B1
Swan Ra. *U.S.A.* 48°0N 113°45W **76** C7
Swan River *Canada* 52°10N 101°16W **71** C8
Swanage *U.K.* 50°36N 1°58W **13** G6
Swansea *Australia* 42°8S 148°4E **63** G4
Swansea *Canada* 43°38N 79°28W **82** C5
Swansea *U.K.* 51°37N 3°57W **13** F4
Swansea □ *U.K.* 51°38N 4°3W **13** F3
Swartberge *S. Africa* 33°20S 22°0E **56** D3
Swartmodder *S. Africa* 28°1S 20°32E **56** C3
Swartnossob → *Namibia* 23°8S 18°42E **56** B2
Swartruggens *S. Africa* 25°39S 26°42E **56** D4
Swastika *Canada* 48°7N 80°6W **72** C3
Swat → *Pakistan* 34°40N 72°5E **43** B5
Swatow = Shantou
  China 23°18N 116°40E **35** F11
Swaziland ■ *Africa* 26°30S 31°30E **57** C5
Sweden ■ *Europe* 57°0N 15°0E **9** H16
Sweet Grass *U.S.A.* 48°59N 111°58W **76** B8
Sweet Home *U.S.A.* 44°24N 122°44W **76** D2
Sweetwater *Nev., U.S.A.* 38°27N 119°9W **78** G7
Sweetwater *Tenn.,*
  U.S.A. 35°36N 84°28W **85** D12
Sweetwater *Tex., U.S.A.* 32°28N 100°25W **84** E4
Sweetwater → *U.S.A.* 42°31N 107°2W **76** E10
Swellendam *S. Africa* 34°1S 20°26E **56** D3
Świdnica *Poland* 50°50N 16°30E **17** C9
Świdnik *Poland* 51°13N 22°39E **17** C12
Świebodzin *Poland* 52°15N 15°31E **16** B8
Świecie *Poland* 53°25N 18°30E **17** B10
Swift Current *Canada* 50°20N 107°45W **71** C7
Swift Current →
  Canada 50°38N 107°44W **71** C7
Swilly, L. *Ireland* 55°12N 7°33W **10** A4
Swindon *U.K.* 51°34N 1°46W **13** F6
Swindon □ *U.K.* 51°34N 1°46W **13** F6
Swinemünde = Świnoujście
  Poland 53°54N 14°16E **16** B8
Swinford *Ireland* 53°57N 8°58W **10** C3
Świnoujście *Poland* 53°54N 14°16E **16** B8
Switzerland ■ *Europe* 46°30N 8°0E **20** C8
Swoyerville *U.S.A.* 41°18N 75°53W **83** E9
Sydenham → *Canada* 42°33N 82°25W **82** D2
Sydney *Canada* 46°7N 60°7W **73** C7
Sydney *Australia* 33°52S 151°12E ...
Sydney L. *Canada* 50°41N 94°25W **71** C10
Sydney Mines *Canada* 46°18N 60°15W **73** C7
Sydprøven = Alluitsup Paa
  Greenland 60°30N 45°35W **4** C5
Sydra, G. of = Surt, Khalīj
  Libya 31°40N 18°30E **53** B9
Sykesville *U.S.A.* 41°3N 78°50W **82** E6
Syktyvkar *Russia* 61°45N 50°40E **18** B9
Sylacauga *U.S.A.* 33°10N 86°15W **85** E11
Sylarna *Sweden* 63°2N 12°13E **8** E15
Sylhet *Bangla.* 24°54N 91°52E **41** G17
Sylhet □ *Bangla.* 24°50N 91°50E **41** G17
Sylt *Germany* 54°54N 8°22E **16** A5
Sylvan Beach *U.S.A.* 43°12N 75°44W **83** C9
Sylvan Lake *Canada* 52°20N 114°3W **70** C6
Sylvania *Ga., U.S.A.* 32°45N 81°38W **85** E14
Sylvania *Ohio, U.S.A.* 41°43N 83°42W **81** E12
Sylvester *U.S.A.* 31°32N 83°50W **85** F13
Sym *Russia* 60°20N 88°18E **26** C9
Synnot Ra. *Australia* 16°30S 125°20E **60** C4
Syowa *Antarctica* 68°50S 37°0E **5** C5
Syracuse *Kans., U.S.A.* 37°59N 101°45W **80** G3
Syracuse *N.Y., U.S.A.* 43°3N 76°9W **83** C8
Syracuse *Nebr., U.S.A.* 40°39N 96°11W **80** E5
Syrdarya → *Kazakhstan* 46°3N 61°0E **26** E7
Syria ■ *Asia* 35°0N 38°0E **46** C3
Syrian Desert = Shām, Bādiyat ash
  Asia 32°0N 40°0E **46** C3
Syros = Ermoupoli
  Greece 37°28N 24°57E **23** F11
Syzran *Russia* 53°12N 48°30E **18** D8
Szczecin *Poland* 53°27N 14°27E **16** B8
Szczecinek *Poland* 53°43N 16°41E **17** B9
Szczeciński, Zalew = Stettiner Haff
  Germany 53°47N 14°15E **16** B8
Szczytno *Poland* 53°33N 21°0E **17** B11
Szechuan = Sichuan □
  China 30°30N 103°0E **34** B5
Szechuan Basin = Sichuan Pendi
  China 30°0N 105°0E **34** B5
Szeged *Hungary* 46°16N 20°10E **17** E11
Székesfehérvár *Hungary* 47°15N 18°25E **17** E10
Szekszárd *Hungary* 46°22N 18°42E **17** E10
Szentes *Hungary* 46°39N 20°21E **17** E11
Szolnok *Hungary* 47°10N 20°15E **17** E11
Szombathely *Hungary* 47°14N 16°38E **17** E9

T

Ta Khli *Thailand* 15°15N 100°21E **38** E3
Ta Lai *Vietnam* 11°24N 107°23E **39** G6
Ta Phraya △ *Thailand* 14°11N 102°49E **38** E4
Taamisaari = Raasepori
  Finland 60°0N 23°26E **9** G20
Tabacal *Argentina* 23°15S 64°15W **94** A3

Tabaco *Phil.* 13°22N 123°44E **37** B6
Ṭabah *Si. Arabia* 26°55N 42°38E **46** E4
Tabanan *Indonesia* 8°32S 115°8E **37** K18
Tabas *Khorāsān, Iran* 32°48N 60°12E **47** C9
Ṭabas *Yazd, Iran* 33°35N 56°55E **47** C8
Tabasará, Serranía de
  Panama 8°35N 81°40W **88** E3
Tabasco □ *Mexico* 18°0N 92°40W **87** D6
Tabāsīn *Iran* 31°12N 57°54E **47** D8
Tabatinga, Serra da
  Brazil 10°30S 44°0W **93** F10
Taber *Canada* 49°47N 112°8W **70** D6
Tablas I. *Phil.* 12°25N 122°2E **37** B6
Table, Pte. de la *Réunion* 21°14S 55°48E **55** c
Table B. *Canada* 53°40N 56°25W **73** B8
Table I. *Burma* 14°12N 93°22E **45** G11
Table Rock L. *U.S.A.* 36°36N 93°19W **80** G7
Tabletop, Mt. *Australia* 23°24S 147°11E **62** C4
Tábor *Czech Rep.* 49°25N 14°39E **16** D8
Tabora *Tanzania* 5°2S 32°50E **54** F6
Tabou *Ivory C.* 4°30N 7°20W **52** H4
Tabrīz *Iran* 38°7N 46°20E **46** B5
Tabuaeran *Kiribati* 3°51N 159°22W **65** G12
Tabūk *S. Arabia* 28°23N 36°36E **46** D3
Tabūk □ *Si. Arabia* 27°40N 36°50E **46** E3
Tacámbaro de Codallos
  Mexico 19°14N 101°28W **86** D4
Tacheng *China* 46°40N 82°58E **30** B5
Tach'i *Taiwan* 24°53N 121°17E **35** E13
Tachia *Taiwan* 24°25N 120°28E **35** E13
Tachilek *Burma* 20°26N 99°52E **38** B2
Tach'ing Shan = Daqing Shan
  China 40°40N 111°0E **32** D6
Tacloban *Phil.* 11°15N 124°58E **37** B6
Tacna *Peru* 18°0S 70°20W **92** G4
Tacoma *U.S.A.* 47°14N 122°26W **78** C4
Tacuarembó *Uruguay* 31°45S 56°0W **95** C4
Tademaït, Plateau du
  Algeria 28°30N 2°30E **52** C6
Tādepallegudem *India* 16°50N 81°30E **44** F5
Tadjoura *Djibouti* 11°50N 42°55E **49** E3
Tadmor *N.Z.* 41°27S 172°45E **59** D4
Tadoba △ *India* 20°30N 79°28E **44** D4
Tadoule L. *Canada* 58°36N 98°20W **71** B9
Tadoussac *Canada* 48°11N 69°42W **73** C6
Tadpatri *India* 14°55N 78°1E **45** G4
Tadzhikistan = Tajikistan ■
  Asia 38°30N 70°0E **26** F8
Taegu = Daegu
  S. Korea 35°50N 128°37E **33** G15
Taegwan *N. Korea* 40°13N 125°12E **33** D13
Taejŏn = Daejeon
  S. Korea 36°20N 127°28E **33** F14
Taen, Ko *Thailand* 9°22N 99°57E **39** b
Tafalla *Spain* 42°30N 1°41W **21** A5
Tafermaar *Indonesia* 6°47S 134°10E **37** F8
Tafi Viejo *Argentina* 26°43S 65°17W **94** B2
Tafīhān *Iran* 29°25N 52°39E **47** D7
Tafresh *Iran* 34°45N 49°57E **47** C6
Taft *Iran* 31°45N 54°14E **47** D7
Taft *Phil.* 11°57N 125°30E **37** B7
Taft *U.S.A.* 35°8N 119°28W **79** K7
Taftan *Pakistan* 29°0N 61°30E **42** E2
Taftān, Kūh-e *Iran* 28°40N 61°0E **47** D9
Tafwap *India* 7°23N 93°43E **45** L11
Taga *Samoa* 13°46S 172°28W **59** b
Taga Dzong *Bhutan* 27°5N 89°55E **41** F16
Taganrog *Russia* 47°12N 38°50E **19** E6
Tagbilaran *Phil.* 9°39N 123°51E **37** C6
Tagish *Canada* 60°19N 134°16W **70** A2
Tagish L. *Canada* 60°10N 134°20W **70** A2
Tagliamento → *Italy* 45°38N 13°6E **22** B5
Taguatinga *Brazil* 12°27S 46°22W **93** F10
Tagum *Phil.* 7°33N 125°53E **37** C7
Tagus = Tejo → *Europe* 38°40N 9°24W **21** C1
Tahakopa *N.Z.* 46°30S 169°23E **59** G2
Tahan, Gunung *Malaysia* 4°34N 102°17E **39** K4
Tahat *Algeria* 23°18N 5°33E **52** D7
Tāherī *Iran* 27°43N 52°20E **47** E7
Tahiti *French Polynesia* 17°37S 149°27W **59** d
Tahiti, I. *Tahiti* 17°37S 149°27W **59** d
Tahlequah *U.S.A.* 35°55N 94°58W **84** D7
Tahoe, L. *U.S.A.* 39°6N 120°2W **78** G6
Tahoe City *U.S.A.* 39°10N 120°9W **78** F6
Tahoka *U.S.A.* 33°10N 101°48W **84** E4
Taholah *U.S.A.* 47°21N 124°17W **78** C2
Tahoua *Niger* 14°57N 5°16E **52** F7
Tahrūd *Iran* 29°26N 57°49E **47** D8
Tahsis *Canada* 49°55N 126°40W **70** D3
Tahta *Egypt* 26°44N 31°32E **53** C12
Tahulandang *Indonesia* 2°27N 125°23E **37** D7
Tahuna *Indonesia* 3°38N 125°30E **37** D7
Tai Hu *China* 31°5N 120°10E **35** B12
Tai Mo Shan *China* 22°25N 114°7E **31** a
Tai O *China* 22°15N 113°52E **31** a
Tai Pang Wan *China* 22°33N 114°24E **31** a
Tai Po *China* 22°27N 114°10E **31** a
Tai Rom Yen △ *Thailand* 8°45N 99°30E **39** H2
Tai Yue Shan = Lantau I.
  China 22°15N 113°56E **31** a
Tai'an *China* 36°12N 117°8E **33** F9
Taiarapu, Presqu'île de
  Tahiti 17°47S 149°14W **59** d
Taibai Shan *China* 33°57N 107°45E **34** H4
Taibei = T'aipei *Taiwan* 25°4N 121°29E **35** E13
Taibus Qi *China* 41°54N 115°22E **32** D8
Taicang *China* 31°30N 121°5E **35** B13
T'aichung *Taiwan* 24°9N 120°37E **35** E13
Taieri → *N.Z.* 46°3S 170°12E **59** G3
Taigu *China* 37°28N 112°30E **32** F7
Taihang Shan *China* 36°0N 113°30E **32** G7
Taihape *N.Z.* 39°41S 175°48E **59** C5
Taihe *Anhui, China* 33°20N 115°42E **32** H8
Taihe *Jiangxi, China* 26°47N 114°52E **35** D10
Taihu *China* 30°22N 116°20E **35** B11
Taijiang *China* 26°39N 108°21E **34** D7
Taikang *China* 34°5N 114°50E **32** G8
Tailem Bend *Australia* 35°12S 139°29E **63** F2
T'ailuko *Taiwan* 24°9N 121°37E **35** E13

Taimyr Peninsula = Taimyr,
  Poluostrov *Russia* 75°0N 100°0E **27** B11
Tain *U.K.* 57°49N 4°4W **11** D4
T'ainan *Taiwan* 23°0N 120°10E **35** F13
Taining *China* 26°54N 117°9E **35** D11
Taipa *China* 22°10N 113°35E **31** a
T'aipei *Taiwan* 25°4N 121°29E **35** E13
Taiping *China* 30°15N 118°6E **35** B12
Taiping *Malaysia* 4°51N 100°44E **39** K3
Taipingchuan *China* 44°23N 123°11E **33** B12
Taipingzhen *China* 33°35N 111°42E **32** H6
Taishan *Guangdong*,
  China 22°14N 112°41E **35** F9
Taishan *Shandong, China* 36°25N 117°20E **33** F9
Taishun *China* 27°30N 119°42E **35** D12
Taitao, Pen. de *Chile* 46°30S 75°0W **96** F2
T'aitung *Taiwan* 22°43N 121°4E **35** F13
Taivalkoski *Finland* 65°33N 28°12E **8** D23
Taiwan ■ *Asia* 23°30N 121°0E **35** F13
Taiwan Strait *Asia* 24°40N 120°0E **35** E12
Taixing *China* 32°11N 120°0E **35** A13
Taiyiba *Israel* 32°36N 35°27E **48** C4
Taiyuan *China* 37°52N 112°33E **32** F7
Taizhong = T'aichung
  Taiwan 24°9N 120°37E **35** E13
Taizhou *Jiangsu, China* 32°28N 119°55E **35** A12
Taizhou *Zhejiang, China* 28°40N 121°24E **35** C13
Taizhou Liedao *China* 28°30N 121°55E **35** C13
Ta'izz *Yemen* 13°35N 44°2E **49** E3
Taj Mahal *India* 27°10N 78°2E **42** F8
Tājābād *Iran* 30°2N 54°24E **47** D7
Tajikistan ■ *Asia* 38°30N 70°0E **26** F8
Tajima = Minamiaizu
  Japan 37°12N 139°46E **29** F9
Tajo = Tejo → *Europe* 38°40N 9°24W **21** C1
Tak *Thailand* 16°52N 99°8E **38** D2
Takāb *Iran* 36°24N 47°7E **46** B5
Takachiho *Japan* 32°42N 131°18E **29** H5
Takachu *Botswana* 22°37S 21°58E **56** B3
Takada *Japan* 37°7N 138°15E **29** F9
Takahagi *Japan* 36°43N 140°45E **29** F10
Takaka *N.Z.* 40°51S 172°50E **59** D4
Takamaka *Seychelles* 4°50S 55°30E **55** b
Takamatsu *Japan* 34°20N 134°5E **29** G7
Takaoka *Japan* 36°47N 137°0E **29** F8
Takapuna *N.Z.* 36°47S 174°47E **59** B5
Takasaki *Japan* 36°20N 139°0E **29** F9
Takatsuki *Japan* 34°51N 135°37E **29** G7
Takayama *Japan* 36°18N 137°11E **29** F8
Take-Shima *Japan* 30°49N 130°26E **29** J5
Takefu = Echizen *Japan* 35°50N 136°10E **29** G8
Takengon *Indonesia* 4°45N 96°50E **36** D1
Takeo *Cambodia* 10°59N 104°47E **39** G5
Takeo *Japan* 33°12N 130°1E **29** H5
Takeshima = Liancourt Rocks
  Asia 37°15N 131°52E **29** F5
Tākestān *Iran* 36°0N 49°40E **47** C6
Taketa *Japan* 32°58N 131°24E **29** H5
Takh *India* 33°6N 77°32E **43** C7
Takhmau *Cambodia* 11°29N 104°57E **39** G5
Takht-e Soleyman *Iran* 36°36N 47°14E **46** B5
Takht-i-Sulaiman *Pakistan* 31°40N 69°58E **42** D3
Takikawa *Japan* 43°33N 141°54E **28** C10
Takla L. *Canada* 55°15N 125°45W **70** B3
Takla Landing *Canada* 55°30N 125°50W **70** B3
Taklamakan *China* 38°0N 83°0E **30** D5
Taklamakan Shamo =
  Taklamakan *China* 38°0N 83°0E **30** D5
Taksimo *Russia* 56°20N 114°52E **27** D12
Taku → *Canada* 58°30N 133°50W **70** B2
Takua Thung *Thailand* 8°24N 98°27E **39** a
Tal Halāl *Iran* 28°54N 55°1E **47** D7
Tala *Uruguay* 34°21S 55°46W **95** C4
Talagang *Pakistan* 32°55N 72°25E **42** C5
Talagante *Chile* 33°40S 70°50W **94** C1
Talaimannar *Sri Lanka* 9°6N 79°43E **45** K4
Talamanca, Cordillera de
  Cent. Amer. 9°20N 83°20W **88** E3
Talampaya △ *Argentina* 29°43S 67°42W **94** B2
Talara *Peru* 4°38S 81°18W **92** D2
Talas *Kyrgyzstan* 42°30N 72°13E **26** E8
Talâta *Egypt* 30°36N 32°20E **48** E1
Talaud, Kepulauan
  Indonesia 4°30N 126°50E **37** D7
Talaud Is. = Talaud, Kepulauan
  Indonesia 4°30N 126°50E **37** D7
Talavera de la Reina
  Spain 39°55N 4°46W **21** C3
Talayan *Phil.* 6°52N 124°24E **37** C6
Talbandh *India* 22°3N 86°20E **43** H12
Talbot, C. *Australia* 13°48S 126°43E **60** B4
Talbragar → *Australia* 32°12S 148°37E **63** E4
Talca *Chile* 35°28S 71°40W **94** D1
Talcahuano *Chile* 36°40S 73°10W **94** D1
Talcher *India* 21°0N 85°18E **44** D7
Taldy Kurgan = Taldyqorghan
  Kazakhstan 45°10N 78°45E **30** B4
Taldyqorghan *Kazakhstan* 45°10N 78°45E **30** B4
Tālesh *Iran* 37°58N 48°58E **47** B6
Tālesh, Kūhhā-ye *Iran* 37°42N 48°55E **47** B6
Talguppa *India* 14°13N 74°56E **45** G9
Tali Post *South Sudan* 5°55N 30°44E **53** G12
Taliabu *Indonesia* 1°50S 125°0E **37** E6
Talibon *Phil.* 10°9N 124°20E **37** B6
Talihina *U.S.A.* 34°45N 95°3W **84** D7
Talikota *India* 16°29N 76°17E **45** F3
Talipparamba *India* 12°3N 75°12E **45** H2
Taliwang *Indonesia* 8°50S 116°55E **36** F5
Talkot *Nepal* 29°37N 81°19E **43** E9
Tall 'Afar *Iraq* 36°22N 42°27E **46** B4
Tall Kalakh *Syria* 34°41N 36°15E **48** A5
Talladega *U.S.A.* 33°26N 86°6W **85** E11
Tallahassee *U.S.A.* 30°27N 84°17W **85** F12
Tallangatta *Australia* 36°15S 147°19E **63** F4
Tallering Pk. *Australia* 28°6S 115°37E **61** E2
Talli *Pakistan* 29°32N 68°8E **42** E3
Tallinn *Estonia* 59°22N 24°48E **9** G21
Tallmadge *U.S.A.* 41°6N 81°27W **82** E3
Tallulah *U.S.A.* 32°25N 91°11W **84** E9

Talnakh *Russia* 69°29N 88°22E **27** C9
Taloda *India* 21°34N 74°11E **44** D2
Taloyoak *Canada* 69°32N 93°32W **68** D13
Talpa de Allende
  Mexico 20°23N 104°51W **86** C4
Talparo *Trin. & Tob.* 10°30N 61°17W **93** K15
Talsi *Latvia* 57°10N 22°30E **9** H20
Taltal *Chile* 25°23S 70°33W **94** B1
Taltson → *Canada* 61°24N 112°46W **70** A6
Talwood *Australia* 28°29S 149°29E **63** D4
Talyawalka Cr. →
  Australia 32°28S 142°22E **63** E3
Tam Dao △ *Vietnam* 21°45N 105°45E **38** B5
Tam Ky *Vietnam* 15°34N 108°29E **38** E7
Tam Quan *Vietnam* 14°35N 109°3E **38** E7
Tama *U.S.A.* 41°58N 92°35W **80** E7
Tama Abu, Banjaran
  Malaysia 3°50N 115°5E **36** D5
Tamale *Ghana* 9°22N 0°50W **52** G5
Taman Negara △
  Malaysia 4°38N 102°26E **39** K4
Tamano *Japan* 34°29N 133°59E **29** G6
Tamanrasset *Algeria* 22°50N 5°30E **52** D7
Tamaqua *U.S.A.* 40°48N 75°58W **83** F9
Tamar → *U.K.* 50°27N 4°15W **13** G3
Tamarin *Mauritius* 20°19S 57°20E **55** d
Tamatave = Toamasina
  Madag. 18°10S 49°25E **55** H9
Tamaulipas □ *Mexico* 24°0N 98°45W **87** C5
Tamaulipas, Sierra de
  Mexico 23°30N 98°20W **87** C5
Tamazula *Mexico* 24°57N 106°57W **86** C3
Tamazunchale *Mexico* 21°16N 98°47W **87** C5
Tambacounda *Senegal* 13°45N 13°40W **52** F3
Tambelan, Kepulauan
  Indonesia 1°0N 107°30E **36** D3
Tambellup *Australia* 34°4S 117°37E **61** F2
Tambo *Australia* 24°54S 146°14E **62** C4
Tambo de Mora *Peru* 13°30S 76°8W **92** F3
Tambora *Indonesia* 8°12S 118°5E **36** F5
Tambov *Russia* 52°45N 41°28E **18** D7
Tambuku *Indonesia* 7°8S 113°40E **37** G15
Tâmega → *Portugal* 41°5N 8°21W **21** B1
Tamenglong *India* 25°0N 93°35E **41** G18
Tamiahua, L. de *Mexico* 21°35N 97°35W **87** C5
Tamil Nadu □ *India* 11°0N 77°0E **45** J3
Tamluk *India* 22°18N 87°58E **43** H12
Tammerfors = Tampere
  Finland 61°30N 23°50E **8** F20
Tampa *U.S.A.* 27°56N 82°27W **85** H13
Tampa, Tanjung
  Indonesia 8°55S 116°12E **37** K19
Tampa B. *U.S.A.* 27°50N 82°30W **85** H13
Tampere *Finland* 61°30N 23°50E **8** F20
Tampico *Mexico* 22°13N 97°51W **87** C5
Tampin *Malaysia* 2°28N 102°13E **39** L4
Tampoi *Malaysia* 1°30N 103°39E **39** d
Tamsagbulag *Mongolia* 47°14N 117°21E **31** B12
Tamu *Burma* 24°13N 94°12E **41** G19
Tamworth *Australia* 31°7S 150°58E **63** E5
Tamworth *Canada* 44°29N 77°0W **82** B8
Tamworth *U.K.* 52°39N 1°41W **13** E6
Tan An *Vietnam* 10°32N 106°25E **39** G6
Tan Chau *Vietnam* 10°48N 105°12E **39** G5
Tan Hiep *Vietnam* 10°27N 106°21E **39** G6
Tan-Tan *Morocco* 28°29N 11°1W **52** C3
Tan Yen *Vietnam* 22°4N 105°3E **38** A5
Tana → *Kenya* 2°32S 40°31E **54** E8
Tana → *Norway* 70°30N 28°14E **8** A23
Tana *Norway* 70°26N 28°24E **8** A23
Tana, L. *Ethiopia* 13°5N 37°30E **49** E2
Tanabe *Japan* 33°44N 135°22E **29** H7
Tanacross *U.S.A.* 63°40N 143°21W **74** a
Tanafjorden *Norway* 70°45N 28°25E **8** A23
Tanaga I. *U.S.A.* 51°48N 177°53W **74** E4
Tanah Merah *Malaysia* 5°48N 102°9E **39** K4
Tanahbala *Indonesia* 0°30S 98°30E **36** E1
Tanahgrogot *Indonesia* 1°55S 116°15E **36** E5
Tanahjampea *Indonesia* 7°10S 120°35E **37** F6
Tanahmasa *Indonesia* 0°12S 98°39E **36** E1
Tanahmerah *Indonesia* 6°5S 140°16E **37** F10
Tanakpur *India* 29°5N 80°7E **43** E9
Tanalwalla *Sri Lanka* 6°26N 81°8E **45** L5
Tanami Desert *Australia* 18°50S 132°0E **60** C5
Tanana *U.S.A.* 65°10N 152°4W **74** B9
Tanana → *U.S.A.* 65°10N 151°58W **68** D5
Tananarive = Antananarivo
  Madag. 18°55S 47°31E **55** H9
Tánaro → *Italy* 44°55N 8°40E **20** D8
Tancheng *China* 34°25N 118°20E **33** G10
Tanch'ŏn *N. Korea* 40°27N 128°54E **33** D15
Tanda *Ut. P., India* 26°33N 82°35E **43** F10
Tanda *Ut. P., India* 28°57N 78°56E **43** E8
Tandag *Phil.* 9°4N 126°9E **37** C7
Tandaué *Angola* 16°58S 18°5E **56** A2
Tandil *Argentina* 37°15S 59°6W **94** D4
Tandil, Sa. del *Argentina* 37°30S 59°0W **94** D4
Tandlianwala *Pakistan* 31°3N 73°9E **42** D5
Tando Adam *Pakistan* 25°45N 68°40E **42** G3
Tando Allahyar *Pakistan* 25°28N 68°43E **42** G3
Tando Bago *Pakistan* 24°47N 68°58E **42** G3
Tando Mohommed Khan
  Pakistan 25°8N 68°32E **42** G3
Tandou L. *Australia* 32°40S 142°5E **63** E3
Tandoureh △ *Iran* 37°50N 59°0E **47** B8
Tandragee *U.K.* 54°21N 6°24W **10** B5
Tandula → *India* 21°6N 81°14E **44** D5
Tandula Tank *India* 20°40N 81°12E **44** D5
Tandur *Andhra Pradesh,
  India* 19°11N 79°30E **44** E4
Tandur *Andhra Pradesh,
  India* 17°14N 77°35E **44** F3
Tane-ga-Shima *Japan* 30°30N 131°0E **29** J5
Taneatua *N.Z.* 38°4S 177°1E **59** C6
Tanen Tong Dan = Dawna Ra.
  Burma 16°30N 98°30E **38** D2
Tanezrouft *Algeria* 23°9N 0°11E **52** D6
Tang, Koh *Cambodia* 10°16N 103°7E **39** G4
Tang, Ra's-e *Iran* 25°21N 59°52E **47** E8

Tang Krasang *Cambodia* 12°34N 105°3E **38** F5
Tanga *Tanzania* 5°5S 39°2E **54** F7
Tangalla *Sri Lanka* 6°1N 80°48E **45** L5
Tanganyika, L. *Africa* 6°40S 30°0E **54** F6
Tangasseri *India* 8°53N 76°35E **45** K3
Tanger *Morocco* 35°50N 5°49W **52** A4
Tangerang *Indonesia* 6°11S 106°37E **37** G12
Tanggu *China* 39°2N 117°40E **33** E9
Tanggula Shan *China* 32°40N 92°10E **30** C7
Tanggula Shankou *China* 32°42N 92°27E **30** C7
Tanghe *China* 32°47N 112°50E **32** H7
Tanghla Range = Tanggula Shan
  China 32°40N 92°10E **30** C7
Tangi *India* 19°56N 85°24E **44** E7
Tangier = Tanger
  Morocco 35°50N 5°49W **52** A4
Tangjia *China* 22°22N 113°35E **31** a
Tangjia Wan *China* 22°21N 113°36E **31** a
Tangorin *Australia* 21°47S 144°12E **62** C3
Tangra Yumco *China* 31°0N 86°38E **30** D6
Tangshan *China* 39°38N 118°10E **33** E10
Tangtou *China* 35°28N 118°30E **33** G10
Tangxi *China* 29°3N 119°25E **35** C12
Tangyan He → *China* 28°54N 108°19E **34** C7
Tangyin *China* 35°54N 114°21E **32** G8
Taniantaweng Shan
  China 31°20N 98°0E **34** B2
Tanimbar, Kepulauan
  Indonesia 7°30S 131°30E **37** F8
Tanimbar Is. = Tanimbar,
  Kepulauan *Indonesia* 7°30S 131°30E **37** F8
Tanintharyi = Tenasserim
  Burma 12°6N 99°3E **39** F2
Tanjay *Phil.* 9°30N 123°5E **37** C6
Tanjong Pelepas *Malaysia* 1°21N 103°33E **39** d
Tanjore = Thanjavur
  India 10°48N 79°12E **45** J4
Tanjung *Kalimantan Selatan,
  Indonesia* 2°10S 115°25E **36** E5
Tanjung *Nusa Tenggara Barat,
  Indonesia* 8°21S 116°9E **37** J19
Tanjung Malim *Malaysia* 3°42N 101°31E **39** L3
Tanjung Tokong *Malaysia* 5°28N 100°18E **39** c
Tanjungbalai *Indonesia* 2°55N 99°44E **36** D1
Tanjungbatu *Indonesia* 2°23N 118°3E **36** D5
Tanjungkarang Telukbetung =
  Bandar Lampung
  Indonesia 5°20S 105°10E **36** F3
Tanjungpandan *Indonesia* 2°43S 107°38E **36** E3
Tanjungpinang *Indonesia* 1°5N 104°30E **36** D2
Tanjungredeb *Indonesia* 2°9N 117°29E **36** D5
Tanjungselor *Indonesia* 2°55N 117°25E **36** D5
Tank *Pakistan* 32°14N 70°25E **42** C4
Tankhala *India* 21°58N 73°47E **42** J5
Tankwa-Karoo △
  S. Africa 32°14S 19°50E **56** D2
Tannersville *U.S.A.* 41°3N 75°18W **83** E9
Tannu Ola *Asia* 51°0N 94°0E **27** D10
Tannum Sands *Australia* 23°57S 151°22E **62** C5
Tanout *Niger* 14°50N 8°55E **52** F7
Tanshui *Taiwan* 25°10N 121°28E **35** E13
Tansing *Nepal* 27°52N 83°33E **43** F10
Tanta *Egypt* 30°45N 30°57E **53** B12
Tantoyuca *Mexico* 21°21N 98°14W **87** C5
Tantung = Dandong
  China 40°10N 124°20E **33** D13
Tanuku *India* 16°45N 81°44E **44** F5
Tanunda *Australia* 34°30S 139°0E **63** E2
Tanur *India* 11°1N 75°52E **45** J2
Tanzania ■ *Africa* 6°0S 34°0E **54** F6
Tanzhou *China* 22°16N 113°28E **31** a
Tanzilla → *Canada* 58°8N 130°43W **70** B2
Tao 'an = Taonan
  China 45°22N 122°40E **33** B12
Tao'er He → *China* 45°45N 124°5E **33** B13
Taohua Dao *China* 29°50N 122°20E **35** C14
Taolanaro *Madag.* 25°2S 47°0E **55** K9
Taole *China* 38°48N 106°40E **32** E4
Taonan *China* 45°22N 122°40E **33** B12
Taos *U.S.A.* 36°24N 105°35W **77** H11
Taoudenni *Mali* 22°40N 3°55W **52** D5
Taoyuan *China* 28°55N 111°16E **35** C8
T'aoyüan *Taiwan* 25°0N 121°4E **35** E13
Tapa *Estonia* 59°15N 25°50E **9** G21
Tapa Shan = Daba Shan
  China 32°0N 109°0E **34** B7
Tapachula *Mexico* 14°54N 92°17W **87** E6
Tapah *Malaysia* 4°12N 101°15E **39** K3
Tapajós → *Brazil* 2°24S 54°41W **93** D8
Tapaktuan *Indonesia* 3°15N 97°10E **36** D1
Tapanahoni → *Suriname* 4°20N 54°25W **93** C8
Tapanui *N.Z.* 45°56S 169°18E **59** F2
Tapauá → *Brazil* 5°40S 64°21W **92** E6
Tapes *Brazil* 30°40S 51°23W **95** C5
Tapeta *Liberia* 6°29N 8°52W **52** G4
Taphan Hin *Thailand* 16°13N 100°26E **38** D3
Tapirapecó, Serra
  Venezuela 1°10N 65°0W **92** C6
Tapi Group *Phil.* 5°35N 120°50E **37** C6
Tapuae-o-Uenuku *N.Z.* 42°0S 173°39E **59** E4
Tapul Group *Phil.* 5°35N 120°50E **37** C6
Tapurucuará *Brazil* 0°24S 65°2W **92** D5
Taqtaq *Iraq* 35°53N 44°35E **46** C5
Taquara *Brazil* 29°36S 50°46W **95** B5
Tara *Australia* 27°17S 150°31E **63** D5
Tara *Canada* 44°28N 81°9W **82** B3
Tara *Russia* 56°55N 74°24E **26** D8
Tara → *Montenegro* 43°21N 18°51E **23** C8
Tarābulus *Lebanon* 34°31N 35°50E **48** A4
Tarābulus *Libya* 32°49N 13°7E **53** B8
Tarābulus *Libya* 31°0N 13°0E **53** B8
Taradehi *India* 23°18N 79°21E **43** H8
Tarakan *Indonesia* 3°20N 117°35E **36** D5
Tarama-Jima *Japan* 24°39N 124°42E **29** M2
Taran, Mys *Russia* 54°56N 19°59E **9** J18

Taranagar *India* 28°43N 74°50E **42** E6
Taranaki □ *N.Z.* 39°25S 174°30E **59** C5
Taranaki, Mt. *N.Z.* 39°17S 174°5E **59** C5
Tarancón *Spain* 40°1N 3°1W **21** B4
Táranto *Italy* 40°28N 17°14E **22** D7
Táranto, G. di *Italy* 40°8N 17°20E **22** D7
Tarapacá *Colombia* 2°56S 69°46W **92** D5
Tarapacá □ *Chile* 20°45S 69°30W **94** A2
Tarapoto *Peru* 6°30S 76°20W **92** E3
Tararua Ra. *N.Z.* 40°45S 175°25E **59** D5
Tarasaigh = Taransay
  U.K. 57°54N 7°0W **11** D1
Tarashcha *Ukraine* 49°30N 30°31E **17** D10
Tarauacá *Brazil* 8°6S 70°48W **92** E4
Tarauacá → *Brazil* 6°42S 69°48W **92** E5
Taravao *Tahiti* 17°43S 149°19W **59** d
Taravao, Isthme de
  Tahiti 17°43S 149°19W **59** d
Tarawa *Kiribati* 1°30N 173°0E **64** G9
Tarawera *N.Z.* 39°2S 176°36E **59** C6
Tarawera, L. *N.Z.* 38°13S 176°27E **59** C6
Taraz *Kazakhstan* 42°54N 71°22E **30** C3
Tarazona *Spain* 41°55N 1°43W **21** B5
Tarbagatay, Khrebet
  Kazakhstan 48°0N 83°0E **30** B5
Tarbat Ness *U.K.* 57°52N 3°47W **11** D5
Tarbela Dam *Pakistan* 34°8N 72°52E **42** B5
Tarbert *Ireland* 52°34N 9°22W **10** D2
Tarbert *Argyll & Bute., U.K.* 55°52N 5°25W **11** F3
Tarbert *W. Isles., U.K.* 57°54N 6°49W **11** D2
Tarbes *France* 43°15N 0°3E **20** E4
Tarboro *U.S.A.* 35°54N 77°32W **85** D16
Tarcoola *Australia* 30°44S 134°36E **63** E1
Tarcoon *Australia* 30°15S 146°43E **63** E4
Taree *Australia* 31°50S 152°30E **63** E5
Tarfaya *Morocco* 27°55N 12°55W **52** C3
Târgovişte *Romania* 44°55N 25°27E **17** F13
Târgu Jiu *Romania* 45°5N 23°19E **17** F12
Târgu Mureş *Romania* 46°31N 24°38E **17** E13
Tarif *U.A.E.* 24°3N 53°46E **47** E7
Tarifa *Spain* 36°1N 5°36W **21** D3
Tarija *Bolivia* 21°30S 64°40W **94** A3
Tarija □ *Bolivia* 21°30S 63°30W **94** A3
Tarim → *Indonesia* 2°55S 138°26E **37** E9
Tarim Basin = Tarim Pendi
  China 40°0N 84°0E **30** C5
Tarim He → *China* 39°30N 88°30E **30** D6
Tarim Pendi *China* 40°0N 84°0E **30** C5
Taritatu → *Indonesia* 2°54S 138°27E **37** E9
Tarka → *S. Africa* 32°10S 26°0E **56** D4
Tarka La *Bhutan* 27°12N 89°44E **43** F13
Tarkastad *S. Africa* 32°0S 26°16E **56** D4
Tarkhankut, Mys
  Ukraine 45°25N 32°30E **19** E5
Tarko Sale *Russia* 64°55N 77°50E **26** C8
Tarkwa *Ghana* 5°20N 2°0W **52** G5
Tarlac *Phil.* 15°29N 120°35E **37** A6
Tarma *Peru* 11°25S 75°45W **92** F3
Tarn □ *France* 44°5N 1°6E **20** E4
Târnăveni *Romania* 46°19N 24°13E **17** E13
Tarnobrzeg *Poland* 50°35N 21°41E **17** C11
Tarnów *Poland* 50°3N 21°0E **17** C11
Tarnowskie Góry *Poland* 50°27N 18°54E **17** C10
Tārom *Iran* 28°11N 55°46E **47** D7
Taroom *Australia* 25°36S 149°48E **63** D4
Taroudannt *Morocco* 30°30N 8°52W **52** B4
Tarpon Springs *U.S.A.* 28°9N 82°45W **85** G13
Tarrafal *C. Verde Is.* 15°18N 23°39W **52** b
Tarragona *Spain* 41°5N 1°17E **21** B6
Tarraleah *Australia* 42°17S 146°26E **63** G4
Tarrasa = Terrassa *Spain* 41°34N 2°1E **21** B7
Tarrytown *U.S.A.* 41°4N 73°52W **83** E11
Tarsus *Turkey* 36°58N 34°55E **46** B2
Tartagal *Argentina* 22°30S 63°50W **94** A3
Tartu *Estonia* 58°20N 26°44E **9** G22
Tarțūs *Syria* 34°55N 35°55E **46** C2
Tarumizu *Japan* 31°29N 130°42E **29** J5
Tarutao = Ko Tarutao △
  Thailand 6°33N 99°40E **39** J2
Tarutao, Ko *Thailand* 6°33N 99°40E **39** J2
Tarutung *Indonesia* 2°0N 98°54E **36** D1
Taseko → *Canada* 52°8N 123°45W **70** C4
Tasgaon *India* 17°2N 74°39E **44** F2
Tash-Kömür *Kyrgyzstan* 41°40N 72°10E **26** E8
Tashauz = Daşoguz
  Turkmenistan 41°49N 59°58E **26** E6
Tashi Chho Dzong = Thimphu
  Bhutan 27°31N 89°45E **41** F16
Tashkent = Toshkent
  Uzbekistan 41°20N 69°10E **26** E7
Tashtagol *Russia* 52°47N 87°53E **26** D9
Tasiilaq *Greenland* 65°40N 37°20W **4** C6
Tasikmalaya *Indonesia* 7°18S 108°12E **37** G13
Tåsjön *Sweden* 64°15N 15°40E **8** D16
Taskan *Russia* 62°59N 150°20E **27** C16
Tasman B. *N.Z.* 40°59S 173°25E **59** D4
Tasman Basin *Pac. Oc.* 46°0S 158°0E **64** M7
Tasman Mts. *N.Z.* 41°3S 172°25E **59** D4
Tasman Pen. *Australia* 43°10S 148°0E **63** G4
Tasman Sea *Pac. Oc.* 36°0S 160°0E **58** E9
Tasmania □ *Australia* 42°0S 146°30E **63** G4
Tasmanian Wilderness World
  Heritage Area △
  Australia 43°0S 146°0E **63** G4
Tassili n' Ajjer *Algeria* 25°47N 8°1E **52** C7
Tassili-Oua-n-Ahaggar
  Algeria 20°41N 5°30E **52** D7
Tat Ton △ *Thailand* 15°57N 102°2E **38** E4
Tata *Morocco* 29°46N 7°56W **52** C4
Tatabánya *Hungary* 47°32N 18°25E **17** E10
Tatahouine *Tunisia* 32°57N 10°29E **53** B8
Tatar Republic = Tatarstan □
  Russia 55°30N 51°30E **18** C9
Tatarbunary *Ukraine* 45°50N 29°39E **17** F15
Tatarsk *Russia* 55°14N 76°0E **26** D8
Tatarskiy Proliv *Russia* 50°0N 141°0E **27** E15

Tatarstan □ *Russia* 55°30N 51°30E **18** C9
Tatatua, Pte. *Tahiti* 17°44S 149°8W **59** d
Tateyama *Japan* 35°0N 139°50E **29** G9
Tathlina L. *Canada* 60°33N 117°39E **70** A5
Tathra *Australia* 36°44S 149°59E **63** F4
Tatinnai L. *Canada* 60°55N 97°40W **71** A9
Tatla Lake *Canada* 52°0N 124°20W **70** C4
Tatnam, C. *Canada* 57°16N 91°0W **71** B10
Tatra = Tatry *Slovak Rep.* 49°20N 20°0E **17** D11
Tatry *Slovak Rep.* 49°20N 20°0E **17** D11
Tatshenshini →
  Canada 59°28N 137°45W **70** B1
Tatshenshini-Alsek △
  Canada 59°55N 137°45W **70** B1
Tatsuno *Japan* 34°52N 134°33E **29** G7
Tatta = Thatta *Pakistan* 24°42N 67°55E **42** G2
Tatuí *Brazil* 23°25S 47°53W **95** A6
Tatum *U.S.A.* 33°16N 103°19W **77** K12
Tat'ung = Datong *China* 40°6N 113°18E **32** D7
Tatvan *Turkey* 38°31N 42°15E **46** B4
Ta'ū *Amer. Samoa* 14°15S 169°30W **59** b
Taubaté *Brazil* 23°0S 45°36W **95** A6
Tauern *Austria* 47°15N 12°40E **16** E7
Taumarunui *N.Z.* 38°53S 175°15E **59** C5
Taumaturgo *Brazil* 8°54S 72°51W **92** E4
Taung *S. Africa* 27°33S 24°47E **56** D3
Taungdwingyi *Burma* 20°1N 95°40E **41** J19
Taunggyi *Burma* 20°50N 97°0E **41** J20
Taungoo = Toungoo
  Burma 19°0N 96°30E **41** K20
Taungup *Burma* 18°51N 94°14E **41** K19
Taunsa *Pakistan* 30°42N 70°39E **42** D4
Taunsa Barrage *Pakistan* 30°42N 70°50E **42** D4
Taunton *U.K.* 51°1N 3°5W **13** F4
Taunton *U.S.A.* 41°54N 71°6W **83** E13
Taunus *Germany* 50°13N 8°34E **16** C5
Taupo *N.Z.* 38°41S 176°7E **59** C6
Taupo, L. *N.Z.* 38°46S 175°55E **59** C5
Tauragė *Lithuania* 55°14N 22°16E **9** J20
Tauranga *N.Z.* 37°42S 176°11E **59** B6
Tauranga Harb. *N.Z.* 37°30S 176°5E **59** B6
Taureau, Rés. *Canada* 46°46N 73°50W **72** C5
Taurianova *Italy* 38°21N 16°1E **22** E7
Taurus Mts. = Toros Dağları
  Turkey 37°0N 32°30E **46** B2
Tautira *Tahiti* 17°44S 149°9W **59** d
Tauyskaya Guba
  Russia 59°20N 150°20E **27** D16
Tavastehus = Hämeenlinna
  Finland 61°0N 24°28E **8** F21
Tavda *Russia* 58°7N 65°8E **26** D7
Tavda → *Russia* 57°47N 67°18E **26** D7
Taverner B. *Canada* 67°12N 72°25W **69** D17
Taveuni *Fiji* 16°51S 179°58W **59** a
Tavira *Portugal* 37°8N 7°40W **21** D2
Tavistock *Canada* 43°19N 80°50W **82** C4
Tavistock *U.K.* 50°33N 4°9W **13** G3
Tavoy *Burma* 14°2N 98°12E **38** E2
Tavoy Pt. *Burma* 13°32N 98°10E **38** E2
Tavrichanka *Russia* 43°18N 131°59E **28** C5
Tavua *Fiji* 17°37S 177°5E **59** a
Tavuki *Fiji* 19°7S 178°8E **59** a
Taw → *U.K.* 51°4N 4°4W **13** F3
Tawa → *India* 22°48N 77°48E **42** H8
Tawa Res. *India* 22°35N 78°5E **44** C4
Tawas City *U.S.A.* 44°16N 83°31W **81** C12
Tawau *Malaysia* 4°20N 117°55E **36** D5
Tawi-tawi I. *Phil.* 5°10N 120°0E **37** C6
Tawu *Taiwan* 22°22N 120°54E **35** F13
Taxco *Mexico* 18°33N 99°36W **87** D5
Taxila *Pakistan* 33°42N 72°52E **42** C5
Taxkorgan Tajik Zizhixian
  China 37°49N 75°14E **30** D4
Tay → *U.K.* 56°37N 3°38W **11** E5
Tay, Firth of *U.K.* 56°25N 3°8W **11** E5
Tay, L. *Australia* 32°55S 120°48E **61** F3
Tay, L. *U.K.* 56°32N 4°8W **11** E4
Tay △ *U.K.* 56°43N 3°59W **11** E5
Tay Ninh *Vietnam* 11°20N 106°5E **39** G6
Tayabamba *Peru* 8°15S 77°16W **92** E3
Taygetos Oros *Greece* 37°0N 22°23E **23** F10
Taylakova *Russia* 59°13N 74°0E **26** D8
Taylor *Canada* 56°13N 120°40W **70** B4
Taylor *Nebr., U.S.A.* 41°46N 99°23W **80** E4
Taylor *Pa., U.S.A.* 41°23N 75°43W **83** E9
Taylor *Tex., U.S.A.* 30°34N 97°25W **84** F6
Taylor, Mt. *U.S.A.* 35°14N 107°37W **77** J10
Taylorville *U.S.A.* 39°33N 89°18W **80** F9
Taymā *Si. Arabia* 27°35N 38°45E **46** E3
Taymyr, Oz. *Russia* 74°20N 102°0E **27** B11
Taymyr, Poluostrov
  Russia 75°0N 100°0E **27** B11
Taypaq *Kazakhstan* 49°0N 51°47E **19** E9
Tayport *U.K.* 56°27N 2°52W **11** E6
Tayrona △ *Colombia* 11°20N 74°2W **89** D5
Tayshet *Russia* 55°58N 98°1E **27** D10
Taytay *Phil.* 10°45N 119°30E **37** B5
Tāyyebād *Iran* 34°45N 60°45E **47** C9
Tāyyebād □ *Iran* 34°44N 60°44E **47** C9
Taz → *Russia* 67°32N 78°40E **26** C8
Taza *Morocco* 34°16N 4°6W **52** B5
Tāza Khurmātū *Iraq* 35°18N 44°20E **46** C5
Tazawa-Ko *Japan* 39°43N 140°40E **28** E10
Tazerbo *Libya* 25°45N 21°0E **53** C10
Tazin → *Canada* 59°48N 109°55W **71** B7
Tazin L. *Canada* 59°44N 108°42W **71** B7
Tazovskiy *Russia* 67°30N 78°44E **26** C8
Tbilisi *Georgia* 41°43N 44°50E **19** F7
Tchad = Chad ■ *Africa* 15°0N 17°15E **53** F8
Tchad, L. *Chad* 13°30N 14°30E **53** F8
Tch'eng-tou = Chengdu
  China 30°38N 104°2E **34** B5
Tchentlo L. *Canada* 55°15N 125°0W **70** B4
Tchibanga *Gabon* 2°45S 11°0E **54** E2
Tchogha Zanbil = Choghā Zanbil
  Iran 32°1N 48°32E **47** C6
Tch'ong-k'ing = Chongqing
  China 29°35N 106°25E **34** C6

Tczew *Poland* 54°8N 18°50E **17** A10
Te Anau, L. *N.Z.* 45°15S 167°45E **59** F1
Te Aroha *N.Z.* 37°32S 175°44E **59** B5
Te Awamutu *N.Z.* 38°1S 175°20E **59** C5
Te Ika a Maui = North I.
  N.Z. 38°0S 175°0E **59** C5
Te Kuiti *N.Z.* 38°20S 175°11E **59** C5
Te Puke *N.Z.* 37°46S 176°22E **59** B6
Te Waewae B. *N.Z.* 46°13S 167°33E **59** G1
Te Wai Pounamu = South I.
  N.Z. 44°0S 170°0E **59** F3
Teague *U.S.A.* 31°38N 96°17W **84** F6
Teahupoo *Tahiti* 17°50S 149°16W **59** d
Teapa *Mexico* 17°33N 92°57W **87** D6
Tebakang *Malaysia* 1°6N 110°30E **36** D4
Teberau → *Malaysia* 1°30N 103°42E **39** d
Tébessa *Algeria* 35°22N 8°8E **52** A7
Tebicuary → *Paraguay* 26°36S 58°16W **94** B4
Tebingtinggi *Riau,*
  Indonesia 1°0N 102°45E **36** E2
Tebingtinggi *Sumatera Utara,*
  Indonesia 3°20N 99°9E **36** D1
Tecate *Mexico* 32°34N 116°38W **79** N10
Tecka *Argentina* 43°29S 70°48W **96** E2
Tecomán *Mexico* 18°55N 103°53W **86** D4
Tecopa *U.S.A.* 35°51N 116°13W **79** K10
Tecoripa *Mexico* 28°37N 109°57W **86** B3
Tecuala *Mexico* 22°23N 105°27W **86** C3
Tecuci *Romania* 45°51N 27°27E **17** F14
Tecumseh *Canada* 42°19N 82°54W **82** D2
Tecumseh *Mich., U.S.A.* 42°0N 83°57W **81** D12
Tecumseh *Okla., U.S.A.* 35°15N 96°56W **84** D6
Tedzhen = Tejen
  Turkmenistan 37°23N 60°31E **26** F7
Tees → *U.K.* 54°37N 1°10W **12** C6
Tees B. *U.K.* 54°40N 1°9W **12** C6
Teeswater *Canada* 43°59N 81°17W **82** C3
Tefé *Brazil* 3°25S 64°50W **92** D6
Tegal *Indonesia* 6°52S 109°8E **37** G13
Tegallalang *Indonesia* 8°27S 115°17E **37** J18
Tegalsari *Indonesia* 8°25S 114°8E **37** J17
Tegid, L. = Bala, L. *U.K.* 52°53N 3°37W **12** E4
Tegucigalpa *Honduras* 14°5N 87°14W **88** D2
Tehachapi *U.S.A.* 35°8N 118°27W **79** K8
Tehachapi Mts. *U.S.A.* 35°0N 118°30W **79** L8
Tehoru *Indonesia* 3°23S 129°30E **37** E7
Tehrān □ *Iran* 35°30N 51°30E **47** C6
Tehri *India* 30°23N 78°29E **43** D8
Tehuacán *Mexico* 18°27N 97°23W **87** D5
Tehuantepec *Mexico* 16°21N 95°13W **87** D5
Tehuantepec, G. de
  Mexico 15°50N 95°12W **87** D5
Tehuantepec, Istmo de
  Mexico 17°15N 94°30W **87** D6
Teifi → *U.K.* 52°5N 4°41W **13** E3
Teign → *U.K.* 50°32N 3°32W **13** G4
Teignmouth *U.K.* 50°33N 3°31W **13** G4
Tejakula *Indonesia* 8°8S 115°20E **37** J18
Tejen *Turkmenistan* 37°23N 60°31E **26** F7
Tejen → *Turkmenistan* 37°24N 60°38W **26** F7
Tejo → *Europe* 38°40N 9°24W **21** C1
Tejon Pass *U.S.A.* 34°49N 118°53W **79** L8
Tekamah *U.S.A.* 41°47N 96°13W **80** E5
Tekapo, L. *N.Z.* 43°53S 170°33E **59** E3
Tekax *Mexico* 20°12N 89°17W **87** C7
Tekeli *Kazakhstan* 44°50N 79°0E **26** E8
Tekeze Dam *Ethiopia* 13°10N 38°45E **49** E2
Tekirdağ *Turkey* 40°58N 27°30E **23** D12
Tekkali *India* 18°37N 84°15E **44** E7
Tekoa *U.S.A.* 47°14N 117°4W **76** C5
Tekong Besar, Pulau
  Singapore 1°25N 104°3E **39** d
Tel → *India* 20°50N 83°54E **44** D6
Tel Aviv ✈ (TLV) *Israel* 32°5N 34°49E **48** C3
Tel Aviv-Yafo *Israel* 32°4N 34°48E **48** C3
Tel Lakhish *Israel* 31°34N 34°51E **48** D3
Tel Megiddo *Israel* 32°35N 35°11E **48** C4
Tela *Honduras* 15°40N 87°28W **88** C2
Telanaipura = Jambi
  Indonesia 1°38S 103°30E **36** E2
Telangana *India* 17°30N 78°30E **44** F4
Telavi *Georgia* 42°0N 45°30E **19** F8
Telegraph Creek *Canada* 58°0N 131°10W **70** B2
Telekhany = Tsyelyakhany
  Belarus 52°30N 25°46E **17** B13
Telemark *Norway* 59°15N 7°40E **9** G12
Telén *Argentina* 36°15S 65°31W **94** D2
Teleng *Iran* 25°47N 61°3E **47** E9
Teles Pires → *Brazil* 7°21S 58°3W **92** E7
Telescope Pk. *U.S.A.* 36°10N 117°5W **79** J9
Telford *U.K.* 52°40N 2°27W **13** E5
Telford and Wrekin □
  U.K. 52°45N 2°27W **12** E5
Telkwa *Canada* 54°41N 127°5W **70** C3
Tell City *U.S.A.* 37°57N 86°46W **80** G10
Teller *U.S.A.* 65°16N 166°22W **74** B6
Tellicherry = Thalassery
  India 11°45N 75°30E **45** J2
Telluride *U.S.A.* 37°56N 107°49W **77** H10
Teloloapán *Mexico* 18°21N 99°51W **87** D5
Telpos Iz *Russia* 63°16N 59°13E **18** B10
Telsen *Argentina* 42°30S 66°50W **96** E3
Telšiai *Lithuania* 55°59N 22°14E **9** J20
Teluk Anson = Teluk Intan
  Malaysia 4°3N 101°0E **39** K3
Teluk Bahang *Malaysia* 5°28N 100°13E **39** c
Teluk Betung = Bandar Lampung
  Indonesia 5°20S 105°10E **36** F3
Teluk Intan *Malaysia* 4°3N 101°0E **39** K3
Teluk Kumbar *Malaysia* 5°18N 100°14E **39** c
Telukbutun *Indonesia* 4°13N 108°12E **36** D3
Telukdalam *Indonesia* 0°33N 97°50E **36** D1
Tema *Ghana* 5°41N 0°0 **52** G5
Temagami, L. *Canada* 47°0N 80°10W **72** C3
Temax *Mexico* 21°9N 88°56W **87** C7
Temba *S. Africa* 25°20S 28°17E **57** D4
Tembagapura *Indonesia* 4°20S 137°0E **37** E9
Tembe △ *S. Africa* 26°51S 32°24E **57** C5
Temblor Range *U.S.A.* 35°20N 119°50W **79** K7

Teme → *U.K.* 52°11N 2°13W **13** E5
Temecula *U.S.A.* 33°30N 117°9W **79** M9
Temengor, Tasik
  Malaysia 5°24N 101°18E **39** K3
Temerloh *Malaysia* 3°27N 102°25E **39** L4
Teminabuan *Indonesia* 1°26S 132°1E **37** E8
Temir *Kazakhstan* 49°1N 57°14E **19** E10
Temirtau *Kazakhstan* 50°5N 72°56E **30** A3
Témiscamie → *Canada* 50°59N 73°5W **73** B5
Témiscaming *Canada* 46°44N 79°5W **72** C4
Témiscamingue, L.
  Canada 47°10N 79°25W **72** C4
Temosachic *Mexico* 28°57N 107°51W **86** B3
Tempe *U.S.A.* 33°24N 111°54W **77** K8
Tempiute *U.S.A.* 37°39N 115°38W **78** H11
Temple *U.S.A.* 31°6N 97°21W **84** F6
Temple B. *Australia* 12°15S 143°3E **62** A3
Templemore *Ireland* 52°47N 7°51W **10** D4
Templeton *U.S.A.* 35°33N 120°42W **78** K6
Templeton → *Australia* 21°0S 138°40E **62** C2
Tempoal de Sánchez
  Mexico 21°31N 98°23W **87** C5
Temuco *Chile* 38°45S 72°40W **96** D2
Temuka *N.Z.* 44°14S 171°17E **59** F3
Ten Degree Channel
  India 10°0N 92°30E **45** K11
Tenabo *Mexico* 20°3N 90°14W **87** C6
Tenaha *U.S.A.* 31°57N 94°15W **84** F7
Tenakee Springs *U.S.A.* 57°47N 135°13W **70** B1
Tenali *India* 16°15N 80°35E **45** F5
Tenancingo *Mexico* 18°58N 99°38W **87** D5
Tenango del Valle *Mexico* 19°7N 99°33W **87** D5
Tenaro, Akra *Greece* 36°22N 22°27E **23** F10
Tenasserim *Burma* 12°6N 99°3E **39** F2
Tenasserim □ *Burma* 14°0N 98°30E **38** F2
Tenasserim → *Burma* 12°24N 98°37E **38** F2
Tenby *U.K.* 51°40N 4°42W **13** F3
Tenda, Colle di *France* 44°7N 7°36E **20** D7
Tendaho *Ethiopia* 11°48N 40°54E **49** E3
Tendō *Japan* 38°20N 140°30E **28** E10
Tendukhera *India* 23°24N 79°33E **43** H8
Ténéré, Erg du *Niger* 17°35N 10°55E **53** E8
Tenerife *Canary Is.* 28°15N 16°35W **52** C2
Teng Xian *Guangxi Zhuangzu,*
  China 23°21N 110°56E **35** F8
Teng Xian *Shandong,*
  China 35°5N 117°10E **33** G9
Tengah, Kepulauan
  Indonesia 7°5S 118°15E **36** F5
Tengchong *China* 25°0N 98°28E **34** E2
Tengchowfu = Penglai
  China 37°48N 120°42E **33** F11
Tenggarong *Indonesia* 0°24S 116°58E **36** E5
Tengger Shamo *China* 38°0N 104°10E **32** F3
Tenggol, Pulau *Malaysia* 4°48N 103°41E **39** K4
Tengiz Köli *Kazakhstan* 50°30N 69°0E **30** A2
Tengzhou *China* 35°4N 117°9E **33** G9
Teniente Enciso △
  Paraguay 21°5S 61°8W **94** A3
Tenino *U.S.A.* 46°51N 122°51W **78** D4
Tenkasi *India* 8°55N 77°20E **45** K3
Tennant Creek *Australia* 19°30S 134°15E **62** B1
Tennessee □ *U.S.A.* 36°0N 86°30W **85** D11
Tennessee → *U.S.A.* 37°4N 88°34W **85** C10
Tenojoki = Tana →
  Norway 70°30N 28°14E **8** A23
Tenom *Malaysia* 5°4N 115°57E **36** C5
Tenosique *Mexico* 17°29N 91°26W **87** D6
Tenterden *U.K.* 51°4N 0°42E **13** F8
Tenterfield *Australia* 29°0S 152°0E **63** D5
Teófilo Otoni *Brazil* 17°50S 41°30W **93** G10
Tepa *Indonesia* 7°52S 129°31E **37** F7
Tepalcatepec → *Mexico* 18°35N 101°59W **86** D4
Tepehuanes *Mexico* 25°21N 105°44W **86** B3
Tepetongo *Mexico* 22°28N 103°9W **86** C4
Tepic *Mexico* 21°30N 104°54W **86** C4
Teplice *Czech Rep.* 50°40N 13°48E **16** C7
Tequila *Mexico* 20°54N 103°47W **86** C4
Ter → *Spain* 42°2N 3°12E **21** A7
Ter Apel *Neths.* 52°53N 7°5E **15** B7
Téra *Niger* 14°0N 0°45E **52** F6
Teraina *Kiribati* 4°43N 160°25W **65** G12
Terang *Australia* 38°15S 142°55E **63** F3
Terang, Teluk *Indonesia* 8°44S 116°0E **37** K19
Terceira *Azores* 38°43N 27°13W **52** a
Tercero → *Argentina* 32°58S 61°47W **94** C3
Terdal *India* 16°33N 75°3E **44** F2
Terebovlya *Ukraine* 49°18N 25°44E **17** D13
Terek → *Russia* 44°0N 47°30E **19** F8
Terengganu □ *Malaysia* 4°55N 103°0E **39** K4
Terepaima △ *Venezuela* 9°58N 69°17W **89** E6
Teresina *Brazil* 5°9S 42°45W **93** E10
Teressa *India* 8°15N 93°10E **45** K11
Terewah, L. *Australia* 29°52S 147°35E **63** D4
Teridgerie Cr. →
  Australia 30°25S 148°50E **63** E4
Termas de Río Hondo
  Argentina 27°29S 64°52W **94** B3
Términi Imerese *Italy* 37°59N 13°42E **22** F5
Términos, L. de *Mexico* 18°37N 91°33W **87** D6
Termiz *Uzbekistan* 37°15N 67°15E **26** F7
Térmoli *Italy* 42°0N 15°0E **22** C6
Ternate *Indonesia* 0°45N 127°25E **37** D7
Terneuzen *Neths.* 51°20N 3°50E **15** C3
Terney *Russia* 45°3N 136°37E **28** B8
Terni *Italy* 42°34N 12°37E **22** C5
Ternopil *Ukraine* 49°30N 25°40E **17** D13
Ternopil □ *Ukraine* 48°10N 25°10E **17** D13
Ternopol = Ternopil
  Ukraine 49°30N 25°40E **17** D13
Terowie *Australia* 33°8S 138°55E **63** E2
Terra Bella *U.S.A.* 35°58N 119°3W **79** K7
Terra Nova △ *Canada* 48°33N 53°55W **73** C9
Terrace *Canada* 54°30N 128°35W **70** C3
Terrace Bay *Canada* 48°47N 87°5W **72** C2
Terracina *Italy* 41°17N 13°15E **22** D5
Terralba *Italy* 39°43N 8°39E **22** E3

Terrassa *Spain* 41°34N 2°1E **21** B7
Terre Haute *U.S.A.* 39°28N 87°25W **80** F10
Terrebonne B. *U.S.A.* 29°5N 90°35W **85** G9
Terrell *U.S.A.* 32°44N 96°17W **84** E6
Terry *U.S.A.* 46°47N 105°19W **76** C11
Terschelling *Neths.* 53°25N 5°20E **15** A5
Teruel *Spain* 40°22N 1°8W **21** B5
Tervola *Finland* 66°6N 24°49E **8** C21
Teryaweynya L.
  Australia 32°18S 143°22E **63** E3
Teshio *Japan* 44°53N 141°44E **28** B10
Teshio-Gawa → *Japan* 44°53N 141°45E **28** B10
Tesiyn Gol → *Mongolia* 50°40N 93°20E **30** A7
Teslin *Canada* 60°10N 132°43W **70** A2
Teslin → *Canada* 61°34N 134°35W **70** A2
Teslin L. *Canada* 60°15N 132°57W **70** A2
Tessalit *Mali* 20°12N 1°0E **52** D6
Tessaoua *Niger* 13°47N 7°56E **52** F7
Test → *U.K.* 50°56N 1°29W **13** G6
Testigos, Is. Los *Venezuela* 11°23N 63°7W **89** D7
Tetachuck L. *Canada* 53°18N 125°55W **70** C3
Tetas, Pta. *Chile* 23°31S 70°38W **94** A1
Tete *Mozam.* 16°13S 33°33E **55** H6
Teterev → *Ukraine* 51°1N 30°5E **17** C16
Teteven *Bulgaria* 42°58N 24°17E **23** C11
Tethul → *Canada* 60°35N 112°12W **70** A6
Tetiyev *Ukraine* 49°22N 29°38E **17** D15
Tetlit Zheh = Fort McPherson
  Canada 67°30N 134°55W **68** D5
Teton → *U.S.A.* 47°56N 110°31W **76** C8
Tétouan *Morocco* 35°35N 5°21W **52** A4
Tetovo *Macedonia* 42°1N 20°59E **23** C9
Tetufera, Mt. *Tahiti* 17°40S 149°26W **59** d
Teuco → *Argentina* 25°35S 60°11W **94** B3
Teulon *Canada* 50°23N 97°16W **71** C9
Teun *Indonesia* 6°59S 129°8E **37** F7
Teuri-Tō *Japan* 44°26N 141°19E **28** B10
Teutoburger Wald *Germany* 52°5N 8°22E **16** B5
Tevere → *Italy* 41°44N 12°14E **22** D5
Teverya *Israel* 32°47N 35°32E **48** C4
Teviot → *U.K.* 55°29N 2°38W **11** F6
Tewantin *Australia* 26°27S 153°3E **63** D5
Tewkesbury *U.K.* 51°59N 2°9W **13** F5
Texada I. *Canada* 49°40N 124°25W **70** D4
Texarkana *Ark., U.S.A.* 33°26N 94°2W **84** E7
Texarkana *Tex., U.S.A.* 33°26N 94°3W **84** E7
Texas *Australia* 28°49S 151°9E **63** D5
Texas □ *U.S.A.* 31°40N 98°30W **84** F5
Texas City *U.S.A.* 29°24N 94°54W **84** G7
Texel *Neths.* 53°5N 4°50E **15** A4
Texline *U.S.A.* 36°23N 103°2W **84** C3
Texoma, L. *U.S.A.* 33°50N 96°34W **84** E6
Teyateyaneng *Lesotho* 29°7S 27°34E **55** K5
Tezin *Afghan.* 34°24N 69°30E **42** B3
Teziutlán *Mexico* 19°49N 97°21E **87** D5
Tezpur *India* 26°40N 92°45E **41** F18
Tezzeron L. *Canada* 54°43N 124°30W **70** C4
Tha-anne → *Canada* 60°31N 94°37W **71** A10
Tha Deua *Laos* 17°57N 102°53E **38** D4
Tha Deua *Laos* 19°26N 101°50E **38** C3
Tha Li *Thailand* 17°37N 101°25E **38** D3
Tha Pla *Thailand* 17°48N 100°32E **38** D3
Tha Rua *Thailand* 14°34N 100°44E **38** E3
Tha Sala *Thailand* 8°40N 99°56E **39** H2
Tha Song Yang *Thailand* 17°34N 97°55E **38** D1
Thaba Putsoa *Lesotho* 29°45S 28°0E **57** D4
Thaba-Tseka *Lesotho* 29°32S 28°36E **57** C4
Thabana Ntlenyana
  Lesotho 29°30S 29°16E **57** C4
Thabazimbi *S. Africa* 24°40S 27°21E **57** B4
Thādiq *Si. Arabia* 25°18N 45°52E **46** E5
Thai Binh *Vietnam* 20°35N 106°1E **34** G6
Thai Muang *Thailand* 8°24N 98°16E **39** H2
Thai Nguyen *Vietnam* 21°35N 105°55E **34** G5
Thailand ■ *Asia* 16°0N 102°0E **38** E4
Thailand, G. of *Asia* 11°30N 101°0E **39** G3
Thakhek *Laos* 17°25N 104°45E **38** D5
Thal *Pakistan* 33°28N 70°33E **42** C4
Thal Desert *Pakistan* 31°10N 71°30E **42** D4
Thala La = Hkakabo Razi
  Burma 28°25N 97°23E **34** C1
Thalabarivat *Cambodia* 13°33N 105°57E **38** F5
Thalang = Amphoe Thalang
  Thailand 8°1N 98°20E **39** a
Thalang *Thailand* 8°2N 98°20E **39** H2
Thalara *Nepal* 29°29N 80°59E **43** E9
Thalassery *India* 11°45N 75°30E **45** J2
Thale Sap Songkhla
  Thailand 7°12N 100°28E **39** J3
Thallon *Australia* 28°39S 148°49E **63** D4
Thalu, Ko *Thailand* 9°26N 99°54E **39** b
Tham Lot *Thailand* 19°34N 98°16E **38** C2
Thames → *N.Z.* 37°7S 175°34E **59** B5
Thames → *Canada* 42°20N 82°25W **82** D2
Thames → *U.K.* 51°29N 0°34E **13** F8
Thames Estuary *U.K.* 51°29N 0°52E **13** F8
Thamesford *Canada* 43°4N 81°0W **82** C4
Thamesville *Canada* 42°33N 81°59W **82** D3
Than *India* 22°34N 71°11E **42** H4
Than Kyun *Burma* 9°49N 98°4E **39** H1
Than Uyen *Vietnam* 22°0N 103°54E **38** B4
Thana Gazi *India* 27°25N 76°19E **42** F7
Thandla *India* 23°0N 74°34E **42** H6
Thandwe *Burma* 18°20N 94°30E **41** K19
Thane *India* 19°12N 72°59E **44** E1
Thanesar *India* 30°1N 76°52E **42** D7
Thanet, I. of *U.K.* 51°21N 1°20E **13** F9
Thangool *Australia* 24°38S 150°42E **62** C5
Thanh Hoa *Vietnam* 19°48N 105°46E **38** C5
Thanh Hung *Vietnam* 9°55N 105°43E **39** H5
Thanh Pho Ho Chi Minh
  Vietnam 10°58N 106°40E **39** G6
Thanh Thuy *Vietnam* 22°55N 104°51E **38** A5
Thanjavur *India* 10°48N 79°12E **45** J4
Thanlwin = Salween →
  Burma 16°31N 97°37E **41** L20

Thano Bula Khan
  Pakistan 25°22N 67°50E **42** G2
Thanya Buri *Thailand* 14°1N 100°45E **38** E3
Thaoge → *Botswana* 20°27S 22°36E **56** B3
Thaolintoa L. *Canada* 61°30N 96°25W **71** A9
Thap Lan △ *Thailand* 14°15N 102°16E **38** E4
Thap Sakae *Thailand* 11°30N 99°37E **39** G2
Thap Than *Thailand* 15°27N 99°54E **38** E2
Thar Desert *India* 28°0N 72°0E **42** F5
Tharad *India* 24°30N 71°44E **42** G4
Thargomindah *Australia* 27°58S 143°46E **63** D3
Tharp Fracture Zone
  S. Ocean 54°0S 135°0W **5** B14
Tharrawaddy *Burma* 17°38N 95°48E **41** L19
Tharthār, Buḥayrat ath
  Iraq 34°0N 43°15E **46** C4
Tharthar, L. = Tharthār, Buḥayrat
  ath *Iraq* 34°0N 43°15E **46** C4
Tharthār, W. ath → *Iraq* 34°32N 43°4E **46** C4
Thasos *Greece* 40°40N 24°40E **23** D11
That Khe *Vietnam* 22°16N 106°28E **34** F6
Thatcher *Ariz., U.S.A.* 32°51N 109°46W **77** K9
Thatcher *Colo., U.S.A.* 37°33N 104°7W **77** H11
Thaton *Burma* 16°55N 97°22E **41** L20
Thatta *Pakistan* 24°42N 67°55E **42** G2
Thaungdut *Burma* 24°30N 94°40E **41** G19
Thayawthadangy Kyun
  Burma 12°19N 98°0E **38** F1
Thayer *U.S.A.* 36°31N 91°33W **80** G8
Thayetmyo *Burma* 19°20N 95°10E **41** K19
Thazi *Burma* 21°0N 96°5E **41** J20
Thbeng Meanchey
  Cambodia 13°49N 104°58E **38** F5
The Bahamas ■ *N. Amer.* 24°0N 75°0W **89** B5
The Broads *U.K.* 52°45N 1°30E **12** E9
The Everglades *U.S.A.* 25°50N 81°0W **85** J14
The Gambia ■ *W. Afr.* 13°25N 16°0W **52** F2
The Gulf = Persian Gulf
  Asia 27°0N 50°0E **47** E6
The Hague = 's-Gravenhage
  Neths. 52°7N 4°17E **15** B4
The Pas *Canada* 53°45N 101°15W **71** C8
The Wash *U.K.* 52°58N 0°20E **12** E8
The Weald *U.K.* 51°4N 0°20E **13** F8
Thebes = Thiva *Greece* 38°19N 23°19E **23** E10
Thebes *Egypt* 25°40N 32°35E **53** C12
Thedford *U.S.A.* 41°59N 100°35W **80** E3
Theebine *Australia* 25°57S 152°34E **63** D5
Thekulthili L. *Canada* 61°3N 110°0W **71** A7
Thelon → *Canada* 64°16N 96°4W **71** A8
Theodore *Australia* 24°55S 150°3E **62** C5
Theodore *Canada* 51°26N 102°55W **71** C8
Theodore *U.S.A.* 30°33N 88°10W **85** F10
Theodore Roosevelt △
  U.S.A. 47°0N 103°25W **80** B2
Theodore Roosevelt L.
  U.S.A. 33°40N 111°10W **77** K8
Thepha *Thailand* 6°52N 100°58E **39** J3
Theresa *U.S.A.* 44°13N 75°48W **83** B9
Thermopolis *U.S.A.* 43°39N 108°13W **76** E9
Thermopylæ *Greece* 38°48N 22°35E **23** E10
Thessalon *Canada* 46°20N 83°30W **72** C3
Thessalonica, Gulf of =
  Thessaloniki Kolpos
  Greece 40°15N 22°45E **23** D10
Thessaloniki *Greece* 40°38N 22°58E **23** D10
Thessaloniki Kolpos
  Greece 40°15N 22°45E **23** D10
Thetford *U.K.* 52°25N 0°45E **13** E8
Thetford Mines *Canada* 46°8N 71°18W **73** C5
Theun → *Laos* 18°19N 104°0E **38** C5
Theunissen *S. Africa* 28°26S 26°43E **56** D4
Thevenard *Australia* 32°9S 133°38E **63** E1
Thibodaux *U.S.A.* 29°48N 90°49W **85** G9
Thicket Portage *Canada* 55°19N 97°42W **71** B9
Thief River Falls *U.S.A.* 48°7N 96°10W **80** A5
Thiel Mts. *Antarctica* 85°15S 91°0W **5** E16
Thiers *France* 45°52N 3°33E **20** D5
Thiès *Senegal* 14°50N 16°51W **52** F2
Thika *Kenya* 1°1S 37°5E **54** E7
Thimphu *Bhutan* 27°31N 89°45E **41** F16
Thina → *S. Africa* 31°18S 29°13E **57** D4
Þingvallavatn *Iceland* 64°11N 21°9W **8** D3
Thionville *France* 49°20N 6°10E **20** B7
Thira = Santorini *Greece* 36°23N 25°27E **23** F11
Third Cataract *Sudan* 19°42N 30°20E **53** E12
Thirsk *U.K.* 54°14N 1°19W **12** C6
Thiruvananthapuram
  India 8°41N 77°0E **45** K3
Thiruvarur *India* 10°46N 79°38E **45** J4
Thisted *Denmark* 56°58N 8°40E **9** H13
Thistle I. *Australia* 35°0S 136°8E **63** F2
Thithia = Cicia *Fiji* 17°45S 179°18W **59** a
Thiva *Greece* 38°19N 23°19E **23** E10
Þjórsá → *Iceland* 63°47N 20°48E **8** E3
Thlewiaza → *Canada* 60°29N 94°40W **71** A10
Thmar Puok *Cambodia* 13°57N 103°4E **38** F4
Tho Chu, Dao *Vietnam* 9°20N 103°28E **39** H4
Tho Vinh *Vietnam* 19°16N 105°42E **38** C5
Thoa → *Canada* 60°31N 109°47W **71** A7
Thoen *Thailand* 17°43N 99°12E **38** D2
Thoeng *Thailand* 19°41N 100°12E **38** C3
Thohoyandou *S. Africa* 22°58S 30°29E **55** J6
Thomas *U.S.A.* 35°45N 98°45W **84** D5
Thomas, L. *Australia* 26°4S 137°58E **63** D2
Thomas Hubbard, C.
  Canada 82°0N 94°25W **69** A13
Thomaston *U.S.A.* 32°53N 84°20W **85** E12
Thomasville *Ala., U.S.A.* 31°55N 87°44W **85** F11
Thomasville *Ga., U.S.A.* 30°50N 83°59W **85** F13
Thomasville *N.C., U.S.A.* 35°53N 80°5W **85** D14
Thompson *Canada* 55°45N 97°52W **71** B9
Thompson *U.S.A.* 41°52N 75°31W **83** E9
Thompson → *Canada* 50°15N 121°24W **70** C4
Thompson → *U.S.A.* 39°46N 93°37W **80** F7
Thompson Falls *U.S.A.* 47°36N 115°21W **76** C6
Thompson Pk. *U.S.A.* 41°0N 123°2W **76** F2
Thompson Springs
  U.S.A. 38°58N 109°43W **76** G9

Thompsontown *U.S.A.* 40°33N 77°14W **82** F7
Thomson *U.S.A.* 33°28N 82°30W **85** E13
Thomson → *Australia* 25°11S 142°53E **62** C3
Thong Yang *Thailand* 9°28N 99°56E **39** b
Thoothukudi = Tuticorin
  India 8°50N 78°12E **45** K4
Þórisvatn *Iceland* 64°20N 18°55W **8** D4
Thornaby on Tees *U.K.* 54°33N 1°18W **12** C6
Thornbury *Canada* 44°34N 80°26W **82** B4
Thorne *U.K.* 53°37N 0°57W **12** D7
Thornton *Canada* 44°16N 79°43W **82** B5
Thornton *U.S.A.* 39°52N 104°58W **76** G11
Thorold *Canada* 43°7N 79°12W **82** C5
Þórshöfn *Iceland* 66°12N 15°20W **8** C6
Thouin, C. *Australia* 20°20S 118°10E **60** D2
Thousand Islands *U.S.A.* 44°20N 76°0W **83** B9
Thousand Oaks *U.S.A.* 34°10N 118°50W **79** L8
Thrace *Turkey* 41°0N 27°0E **23** D12
Three Forks *U.S.A.* 45°54N 111°33W **76** D8
Three Gorges Dam
  China 30°45N 111°15E **35** B8
Three Gorges Res. = Sanxia
  Shuiku *China* 30°3N 107°58E **34** B6
Three Hills *Canada* 51°43N 113°15W **70** C6
Three Hummock I.
  Australia 40°25S 144°55E **63** G3
Three Pagodas Pass *Asia* 15°20N 98°30E **38** E2
Three Points, C. *Ghana* 4°42N 2°6W **52** H5
Three Rivers *Calif.,*
  U.S.A. 36°26N 118°54W **78** J8
Three Rivers *Tex., U.S.A.* 28°28N 98°11W **84** G5
Three Springs *Australia* 29°32S 115°45E **61** E2
Thrissur *India* 10°30N 76°18E **45** J3
Throssell, L. *Australia* 27°33S 124°10E **61** E3
Throssell Ra. *Australia* 22°3S 121°43E **60** D3
Thrushton △ *Australia* 27°47S 147°40E **63** D4
Thu Dau Mot *Vietnam* 10°58N 106°39E **39** G6
Thua → *Kenya* 1°31S 39°30E **54** E7
Thuamal Rampur *India* 19°23N 82°56E **44** E6
Thuan Hoa *Vietnam* 8°58N 105°30E **39** H5
Thubun Lakes *Canada* 61°30N 112°0W **71** A6
Thuin *Belgium* 50°20N 4°17E **15** D4
Thule = Qaanaaq
  Greenland 77°30N 69°10W **69** B18
Thule Air Base = Uummannaq
  Greenland 77°33N 68°52W **69** B18
Thun *Switz.* 46°45N 7°38E **20** C7
Thunder B. *U.S.A.* 45°0N 83°20W **82** B1
Thunder Bay *Canada* 48°20N 89°15W **72** C2
Thung Salaeng Luang △
  Thailand 16°43N 100°50E **38** D3
Thung Song *Thailand* 8°10N 99°40E **39** H2
Thungyai △ *Thailand* 15°20N 98°55E **38** E2
Thunkar *Bhutan* 27°55N 91°0E **41** F17
Thüringer Wald *Germany* 50°35N 11°0E **16** C6
Thuringowa △ *Australia* 19°18S 146°43E **62** B4
Thurles *Ireland* 52°41N 7°49W **10** D4
Thurrock □ *U.K.* 51°31N 0°23E **13** F8
Thursday I. *Australia* 10°30S 142°3E **62** A3
Thurso *Canada* 45°36N 75°15W **72** C4
Thurso *U.K.* 58°36N 3°32W **11** C5
Thurso → *U.K.* 58°36N 3°32W **11** C5
Thurston I. *Antarctica* 72°0S 100°0W **5** D16
Thutade L. *Canada* 57°0N 126°55W **70** B3
Ti-Tree *Australia* 22°5S 133°22E **62** C1
Tian Shan *Asia* 40°30N 76°0E **30** C4
Tianchang *China* 32°40N 119°0E **35** A12
Tiandeng *China* 23°6N 107°7E **34** F6
Tiandong *China* 23°36N 107°8E **34** F6
Tian'e *China* 25°1N 107°9E **34** E6
Tianhe *China* 24°48N 108°40E **34** E7
Tianjin *China* 39°7N 117°12E **33** E9
Tianjin Shi □ *China* 39°8N 117°12E **33** E9
Tianjun *China* 38°0N 98°30E **30** D8
Tianlin *China* 24°21N 106°12E **34** E6
Tianmen *China* 30°39N 113°9E **35** B9
Tianquan *China* 30°7N 102°43E **34** B4
Tianshifu *China* 41°17N 124°22E **33** D13
Tianshui *China* 34°32N 105°40E **32** G3
Tiantai *China* 29°10N 121°2E **35** C13
Tianyang *China* 18°18N 109°20E **38** C7
Tianyang *China* 23°42N 106°53E **34** F6
Tianzhen *China* 40°24N 114°5E **32** D8
Tianzhu *China* 26°54N 109°11E **34** D7
Tianzhuangtai *China* 40°43N 122°5E **33** D12
Tiarei *Tahiti* 17°32S 149°20W **59** d
Tiaret *Algeria* 35°20N 1°21E **52** A6
Tibagi *Brazil* 24°30S 50°24W **95** A5
Tibagi → *Brazil* 22°47S 51°1W **95** A5
Tībastī, Sarīr *Libya* 22°50N 18°30E **53** D9
Tibati *Cameroon* 6°22N 12°30E **54** C2
Tiber = Tevere → *Italy* 41°44N 12°14E **22** D5
Tiber Res. *U.S.A.* 48°19N 111°6W **76** B8
Tiberias = Teverya *Israel* 32°47N 35°32E **48** C4
Tiberias, L. = Yam Kinneret
  Israel 32°45N 35°35E **48** C4
Tibesti *Chad* 21°0N 17°30E **53** D9
Tibet = Xizang Zizhiqu □
  China 32°0N 88°0E **30** E6
Tibet, Plateau of *Asia* 32°0N 86°0E **24** E10
Tibnī *Syria* 35°36N 39°50E **46** C3
Tibooburra *Australia* 29°26S 142°1E **63** D3
Tibrikot *Nepal* 29°3N 82°48E **43** E10
Tiburón, I. *Mexico* 29°0N 112°25W **86** B2
Ticino → *Italy* 45°9N 9°14E **20** D8
Ticonderoga *U.S.A.* 43°51N 73°26W **83** C11
Ticul *Mexico* 20°24N 89°32W **87** C7
Tidaholm *Sweden* 58°12N 13°58E **9** G15
Tiddim *Burma* 23°28N 93°45E **41** H18
Tiden *India* 7°15N 93°33E **45** L11
Tidioute *U.S.A.* 41°41N 79°24W **82** E5
Tidjikja *Mauritania* 18°29N 11°35W **52** E3
Tidore *Indonesia* 0°40N 127°25E **37** D7
Tiefa *China* 42°28N 123°26E **33** C12
Tiegang Shuiku *China* 22°37N 113°53E **31** a
Tiel *Neths.* 51°53N 5°26E **15** C5
Tieli *China* 46°57N 128°3E **31** B14

Tieling *China* 42°20N 123°55E **33** C12
Tielt *Belgium* 51°0N 3°20E **15** C3
Tien Shan = Tian Shan
Asia 40°30N 76°0E **30** C4
Tien-tsin = Tianjin *China* 39°7N 117°12E **33** E9
Tien Yen *Vietnam* 21°20N 107°24E **38** B6
T'ienching = Tianjin
China 39°7N 117°12E **33** E9
Tienen *Belgium* 50°48N 4°57E **15** D4
Tientsin = Tianjin *China* 39°7N 117°12E **33** E9
Tieri *Australia* 23°2S 148°21E **62** C4
Tierra Amarilla *Chile* 27°28S 70°18W **94** B1
Tierra Amarilla *U.S.A.* 36°42N 106°33W **77** H10
Tierra Colorada *Mexico* 17°11N 99°32W **87** D5
Tierra de Campos *Spain* 42°10N 4°50W **21** A3
Tierra del Fuego, I. Grande de
Argentina 54°0S 69°0W **96** G3
Tiétar → *Spain* 39°50N 6°1W **21** C2
Tietê → *Brazil* 20°40S 51°35W **95** A5
Tiffin *U.S.A.* 41°7N 83°11W **81** E12
Tifton *U.S.A.* 31°27N 83°31W **85** F13
Tifu *Indonesia* 3°39S 126°24E **37** E7
Tiger Leaping Gorge = Hutiao Xia
China 27°13N 100°9E **34** D3
Tighina *Moldova* 46°50N 29°30E **17** E15
Tigil *Russia* 57°49N 158°40E **27** D16
Tigiria *India* 20°29N 85°31E **44** D7
Tignish *Canada* 46°58N 64°2W **73** C7
Tigre → *Peru* 4°30S 74°10W **92** D4
Tigre → *Venezuela* 9°20N 62°30W **92** B6
Tigris = Dijlah, Nahr →
Asia 31°0N 47°25E **46** D5
Tigyaing *Burma* 23°45N 96°10E **41** H20
Tihāmah *Asia* 15°3N 41°55E **49** D3
Tijara *India* 27°56N 76°31E **42** F7
Tijuana *Mexico* 32°32N 117°1W **79** N9
Tikal *Guatemala* 17°13N 89°24W **88** C2
Tikal △ *Guatemala* 17°23N 89°34W **88** C2
Tikamgarh *India* 24°44N 78°50E **43** G8
Tikchik Lakes *U.S.A.* 60°0N 159°0W **74** D8
Tikhoretsk *Russia* 45°56N 40°5E **19** E7
Tikhvin *Russia* 59°35N 33°30E **18** C5
Tikirarjuaq = Whale Cove
Canada 62°10N 92°34W **71** A10
Tikrīt *Iraq* 34°35N 43°37E **46** C4
Tiksi *Russia* 71°40N 128°45E **27** B13
Tilā' al 'Alī *Jordan* 32°0N 35°52E **48** D4
Tilamuta *Indonesia* 0°32N 122°23E **37** D6
Tilburg *Neths.* 51°31N 5°6E **15** C5
Tilbury *Canada* 42°17N 82°23W **82** D2
Tilbury *U.K.* 51°27N 0°22E **13** F8
Tilcara *Argentina* 23°36S 65°23W **94** A2
Tilden *U.S.A.* 42°3N 97°50W **80** D5
Tilhar *India* 28°0N 79°45E **43** F8
Tilichiki *Russia* 60°27N 166°5E **27** C17
Till → *U.K.* 55°41N 2°13W **12** B5
Tillamook *U.S.A.* 45°27N 123°51W **76** D2
Tillanchong I. *India* 8°30N 93°37E **45** K11
Tillsonburg *Canada* 42°53N 80°44W **82** D4
Tilos *Greece* 36°27N 27°27E **23** F12
Tilt → *U.K.* 56°46N 3°51W **11** E5
Tilton *U.S.A.* 43°27N 71°36W **83** C13
Tiltonsville *U.S.A.* 40°10N 80°41W **82** F4
Timanskiy Kryazh *Russia* 65°58N 50°5E **18** A9
Timaru *N.Z.* 44°23S 171°14E **59** F3
Timber Creek *Australia* 15°40S 130°29E **60** C5
Timber Lake *U.S.A.* 45°26N 101°5W **80** C3
Timber Mt. *U.S.A.* 37°6N 116°28W **78** H10
Timbué, Ponta *Mozam.* 18°47S 36°22E **57** A6
Timbuktu = Tombouctou
Mali 16°50N 3°0W **52** E5
Timika *Indonesia* 4°47S 136°32E **37** E9
Timimoun *Algeria* 29°14N 0°16E **52** C6
Timiris, Râs *Mauritania* 19°21N 16°30W **52** E2
Timiskaming, L. =
Témiscamingue, L.
Canada 47°10N 79°25W **72** C4
Timişoara *Romania* 45°43N 21°15E **17** F11
Timmins *Canada* 48°28N 81°25W **72** C3
Timok → *Serbia* 44°10N 22°40E **23** B10
Timoleague *Ireland* 51°39N 8°46W **10** E3
Timor *Asia* 9°0S 125°0E **37** F7
Timor Leste = East Timor ■
Asia 8°50S 126°0E **37** F7
Timor Sea *Ind. Oc.* 12°0S 127°0E **60** B4
Tin Can Bay *Australia* 25°56S 153°0E **63** D5
Tin Mt. *U.S.A.* 36°50N 117°10W **78** J9
Tin Shui Wai *China* 22°28N 114°0E **31** a
Tina → *S. Africa* 31°18S 29°13E **57** D4
Tina, Khalig el *Egypt* 31°10N 32°40E **48** D1
Tinaca Pt. *Phil.* 5°30N 125°25E **37** C7
Tindal *Australia* 14°31S 132°22E **60** B5
Tindivanam *India* 12°15N 79°41E **45** H4
Tindouf *Algeria* 27°42N 8°10W **52** C4
Tinfunque △ *Paraguay* 23°55S 60°17W **94** A3
Ting Jiang → *China* 24°45N 116°35E **35** E11
Tinggi, Pulau *Malaysia* 2°18N 104°7E **39** L5
Tingo María *Peru* 9°10S 75°54W **92** E3
Tingrela *Ivory C.* 10°27N 6°25W **52** F4
Tingri *China* 28°34N 86°38E **30** F6
Tinh Bien *Vietnam* 10°36N 104°57E **39** G5
Tinian *N. Marianas* 15°0N 145°38E **64** F6
Tinnevelly = Tirunelveli
India 8°45N 77°45E **45** K3
Tinogasta *Argentina* 28°5S 67°32W **94** B2
Tinos *Greece* 37°33N 25°8E **23** F11
Tinpahar *India* 24°59N 87°44E **43** G12
Tintina *Argentina* 27°2S 62°45W **94** B3
Tintinara *Australia* 35°48S 140°2E **63** F3
Tiobraid Árann = Tipperary
Ireland 52°28N 8°10W **10** D3
Tioga *N. Dak., U.S.A.* 48°24N 102°56W **80** A2
Tioga *Pa., U.S.A.* 41°55N 77°8W **82** E7
Tioman, Pulau *Malaysia* 2°50N 104°10E **39** L5
Tionesta *U.S.A.* 41°30N 79°28W **82** E5
Tipperary *Ireland* 52°28N 8°10W **10** D3
Tipperary □ *Ireland* 52°37N 7°55W **10** D4
Tipton *Calif., U.S.A.* 36°4N 119°19W **78** J7

Tipton *Iowa, U.S.A.* 41°46N 91°8W **80** E8
Tipton Mt. *U.S.A.* 35°32N 114°12W **79** K12
Tiptonville *U.S.A.* 36°23N 89°29W **85** C10
Tiptur *India* 13°15N 76°26E **45** H3
Tīrān *Iran* 32°45N 51°8E **47** C6
Tiranë *Albania* 41°18N 19°49E **23** D8
Tirari Desert *Australia* 28°22S 138°7E **63** D2
Tiraspol *Moldova* 46°55N 29°35E **17** E15
Tire *Turkey* 38°5N 27°45E **23** E12
Tirebolu *Turkey* 40°58N 38°45E **19** F6
Tiree *U.K.* 56°31N 6°55W **11** E2
Tiree, Passage of *U.K.* 56°30N 6°30W **11** E2
Tîrgovişte = Târgovişte
Romania 44°55N 25°27E **17** F13
Tîrgu Jiu = Târgu Jiu
Romania 45°5N 23°19E **17** F12
Tîrgu Mureş = Târgu Mureş
Romania 46°31N 24°38E **17** E13
Tirich Mir *Pakistan* 36°15N 71°55E **40** A7
Tiritiri o te Moana = Southern
Alps *N.Z.* 43°41S 170°11E **59** E3
Tirna → *India* 18°4N 76°57E **44** E3
Tirnavos *Greece* 39°45N 22°18E **23** E10
Tirodi *India* 21°40N 79°44E **44** D7
Tirol □ *Austria* 47°3N 10°43E **16** E6
Tirrukkovil *Sri Lanka* 7°7N 81°51E **45** L5
Tirso → *Italy* 39°53N 8°32E **22** E3
Tirttagangga *Indonesia* 8°24S 115°35E **37** J18
Tirthahalli *India* 13°42N 75°14E **45** H2
Tiruchchendur *India* 8°30N 78°11E **45** K4
Tiruchchirappalli *India* 10°45N 78°45E **45** J4
Tirukkoyilur *India* 11°57N 79°12E **45** J4
Tirumangalam *India* 9°49N 77°58E **45** K3
Tirumayam *India* 10°14N 78°45E **45** J4
Tirunelveli *India* 8°45N 77°45E **45** K3
Tirupati *India* 13°39N 79°25E **45** H4
Tiruppattur *Tamil Nadu,
India* 10°8N 78°37E **45** J4
Tiruppattur *Tamil Nadu,
India* 12°30N 78°30E **45** H4
Tiruppur *India* 11°5N 77°22E **45** J3
Tirur *India* 10°54N 75°55E **45** J2
Tiruttani *India* 13°11N 79°56E **45** H4
Tiruturaippundi *India* 10°32N 79°41E **45** J4
Tiruvadaimarudur *India* 11°2N 79°27E **45** J4
Tiruvalla *India* 9°23N 76°34E **45** K3
Tiruvallar *India* 13°9N 79°57E **45** H4
Tiruvannamalai *India* 12°15N 79°5E **45** H4
Tiruvettipuram *India* 12°39N 79°33E **45** H4
Tiruvottiyur *India* 13°10N 80°22E **45** H5
Tisa *India* 32°50N 76°9E **42** C7
Tisa → *Serbia* 45°15N 20°17E **23** B9
Tisdale *Canada* 52°50N 104°0W **71** C8
Tishomingo *U.S.A.* 34°14N 96°41W **84** D6
Tissamaharama *Sri Lanka* 6°17N 81°17E **45** L5
Tisza = Tisa → *Serbia* 45°15N 20°17E **23** B9
Tit-Ary *Russia* 71°55N 127°2E **27** B13
Tithwal *Pakistan* 34°21N 73°50E **43** B5
Titicaca, L. *S. Amer.* 15°30S 69°30W **92** G5
Titiwa *Nigeria* 12°14N 12°53E **53** F8
Titlagarh *India* 20°15N 83°11E **44** D6
Titule
Dem. Rep. of the Congo 3°15N 25°31E **54** D5
Titusville *Fla., U.S.A.* 28°37N 80°49W **85** G14
Titusville *Pa., U.S.A.* 41°38N 79°41W **82** E5
Tivaouane *Senegal* 14°56N 16°45W **52** F2
Tiverton *Canada* 44°16N 81°32W **82** B3
Tiverton *U.K.* 50°54N 3°29W **13** G4
Tivoli *Italy* 41°58N 12°45E **22** D5
Tiwi *Australia* 11°33S 130°42E **60** B5
Tizi-Ouzou *Algeria* 36°42N 4°3E **52** A6
Tizimín *Mexico* 21°9N 88°9W **87** C7
Tiznit *Morocco* 29°48N 9°45W **52** C4
Tjeggelvas *Sweden* 66°37N 17°45E **8** C17
Tjieggelvas = Tjeggelvas
Sweden 66°37N 17°45E **8** C17
Tjirebon = Cirebon
Indonesia 6°45S 108°32E **37** G13
Tjirrkarli ○ *Australia* 26°0S 125°28E **61** E4
Tjiuring *Indonesia* 8°25S 114°13E **37** J17
Tjörn *Sweden* 58°0N 11°35E **9** H14
Tjukayirla Roadhouse
Australia 27°9S 124°34E **61** E3
Tjurabalan ○ *Australia* 19°50S 128°0E **60** C4
Tlacotalpan *Mexico* 18°37N 95°40W **87** D5
Tlahualilo de Zaragoza
Mexico 26°7N 103°27W **86** B4
Tlaquepaque *Mexico* 20°39N 103°19W **86** C4
Tlaxcala *Mexico* 19°19N 98°14W **87** D5
Tlaxcala □ *Mexico* 19°25N 98°10W **87** D5
Tlaxiaco *Mexico* 17°25N 97°35W **87** D5
Tlemcen *Algeria* 34°52N 1°21W **52** B5
Tlokweng *Botswana* 24°40S 25°58E **56** B4
To Bong *Vietnam* 12°45N 109°16E **38** F7
Toad → *Canada* 59°25N 124°57W **70** B4
Toad River *Canada* 58°51N 125°14W **70** B3
Toamasina *Madag.* 18°10S 49°25E **55** H9
Toay *Argentina* 36°43S 64°38W **94** D3
Toba *China* 31°19N 97°42E **34** B1
Toba *Japan* 34°30N 136°51E **29** G8
Toba, Danau *Indonesia* 2°30N 98°30E **36** D1
Toba Kakar *Pakistan* 31°30N 69°0E **42** D3
Toba Tek Singh *Pakistan* 30°55N 72°25E **42** D5
Tobago *Trin. & Tob.* 11°10N 60°30W **93** J16
Tobelo *Indonesia* 1°45N 127°56E **37** D7
Tobercurry *Ireland* 54°3N 8°44W **10** B3
Tobermory *Canada* 45°12N 81°40W **82** A3
Tobermory *U.K.* 56°38N 6°5W **11** E2
Tobi *Palau* 2°40N 131°10E **37** D8
Tobi-Shima *Japan* 41°12N 139°34E **28** D9
Tobin, L. *Australia* 21°45S 125°49E **60** D4
Tobin L. *Canada* 53°35N 103°30W **71** C8
Toboali *Indonesia* 3°0S 106°25E **36** E3
Toboli *Indonesia* 0°38S 120°5E **37** E6
Tobolsk *Russia* 58°15N 68°10E **26** D7
Tobruk = Tubruq *Libya* 32°7N 23°55E **53** B10
Tobyhanna *U.S.A.* 41°11N 75°25W **83** E9
Tobyl = Tobol → *Russia* 58°10N 68°12E **26** D7

Tocantinópolis *Brazil* 6°20S 47°25W **93** E9
Tocantins □ *Brazil* 10°0S 48°0W **93** F9
Tocantins → *Brazil* 1°45S 49°10W **93** D9
Toccoa *U.S.A.* 34°35N 83°19W **85** D13
Tochi → *Pakistan* 32°49N 70°41E **42** C4
Tochigi *Japan* 36°25N 139°45E **29** F9
Tochigi □ *Japan* 36°45N 139°45E **29** F9
Toco *Trin. & Tob.* 10°49N 60°57W **93** K16
Toconao *Chile* 23°11S 68°1W **94** A2
Tocopilla *Chile* 22°5S 70°10W **94** A1
Tocumwal *Australia* 35°51S 145°31E **63** F4
Tocuyo → *Venezuela* 11°3N 68°23W **92** A5
Todd → *Australia* 24°52S 135°48E **62** C2
Todeli *Indonesia* 1°40S 124°27E **37** E6
Todgarh *India* 25°42N 73°58E **42** G5
Todos os Santos, B. de
Brazil 12°48S 38°38W **93** F11
Todos Santos *Mexico* 23°26N 110°13W **86** C2
Toe Hd. *U.K.* 57°50N 7°8W **11** D1
Tofield *Canada* 53°25N 112°40W **70** C6
Tofino *Canada* 49°11N 125°55W **70** D3
Tofua *Tonga* 19°45S 175°5W **59** c
Tōgane *Japan* 35°33N 140°22E **29** G10
Togian, Kepulauan
Indonesia 0°20S 121°50E **37** E6
Togliatti *Russia* 53°32N 49°24E **18** D8
Togo ■ *W. Afr.* 8°30N 1°35E **52** G6
Togtoh *China* 40°15N 111°10E **32** D6
Tohiea, Mt. *Moorea* 17°33S 149°49W **59** d
Tōhōku □ *Japan* 39°50N 141°45E **28** E10
Tōhōm *Mongolia* 44°27N 108°2E **32** B5
Toibalewe *India* 10°32N 92°30E **45** J11
Toinya *South Sudan* 6°17N 29°46E **53** G11
Toiyabe Range *U.S.A.* 39°30N 117°0W **76** G5
Tojikiston = Tajikistan ■
Asia 38°30N 70°0E **26** F8
Tōjō *Japan* 34°53N 133°16E **29** G6
Tok *U.S.A.* 63°20N 142°59W **68** E3
Tokachi-Dake *Japan* 43°17N 142°5E **28** C11
Tokachi-Gawa →
Japan 42°44N 143°42E **28** C11
Tokala *Indonesia* 1°30S 121°40E **37** E6
Tōkamachi *Japan* 37°8N 138°43E **29** F9
Tokanui *N.Z.* 46°34S 168°56E **59** G2
Tokara-Rettō *Japan* 29°37N 129°43E **29** K4
Tokarahi *N.Z.* 44°56S 170°39E **59** F3
Tokashiki-Shima *Japan* 26°11N 127°21E **29** L3
Tokat *Turkey* 40°22N 36°35E **19** F6
Tokch'ŏn *N. Korea* 39°45N 126°18E **33** E14
Tokdo = Liancourt Rocks
Asia 37°15N 131°52E **29** F5
Tokeland *U.S.A.* 46°42N 123°59W **78** D3
Tokelau Is. ☑ *Pac. Oc.* 9°0S 171°45W **64** H10
Tokmak *Kyrgyzstan* 42°49N 75°15E **26** E8
Toko Ra. *Australia* 23°5S 138°20E **62** C2
Tokoro-Gawa → *Japan* 44°7N 144°5E **28** B12
Toku *Tonga* 18°10S 174°11W **59** c
Tokuno-Shima *Japan* 27°56N 128°55E **29** L4
Tokushima *Japan* 34°4N 134°34E **29** G7
Tokushima □ *Japan* 33°55N 134°0E **29** H7
Tokuyama = Shunan
Japan 34°3N 131°50E **29** G5
Tōkyō *Japan* 35°43N 139°45E **29** G9
Tolaga Bay *N.Z.* 38°21S 178°20E **59** C7
Tolbukhin = Dobrich
Bulgaria 43°37N 27°49E **23** C12
Toledo *Brazil* 24°44S 53°45W **95** A5
Toledo *Spain* 39°50N 4°2E **21** C3
Toledo *Ohio, U.S.A.* 41°39N 83°33W **81** E12
Toledo *Oreg., U.S.A.* 44°37N 123°56W **76** D2
Toledo *Wash., U.S.A.* 46°26N 122°51W **78** D4
Toledo, Montes de *Spain* 39°33N 4°20W **21** C3
Toledo Bend Res. *U.S.A.* 31°11N 93°34W **84** F8
Tolga *Australia* 17°15S 145°29E **62** B4
Toliara *Madag.* 23°21S 43°40E **55** J8
Tolima *Colombia* 4°40N 75°19W **92** C3
Tolitoli *Indonesia* 1°5N 120°50E **37** D6
Tollhouse *U.S.A.* 37°1N 119°24W **78** H7
Tolmachevo *Russia* 58°56N 29°51E **9** G23
Tolo, Teluk *Indonesia* 2°20S 122°10E **37** E6
Tolo Harbour *China* 22°27N 114°12E **31** a
Tolyatti = Togliatti
Russia 53°32N 49°24E **18** D8
Tom Burke *S. Africa* 23°5S 28°0E **57** B4
Tom Price *Australia* 22°40S 117°48E **60** D2
Tomah *U.S.A.* 43°59N 90°30W **80** D8
Tomahawk *U.S.A.* 45°28N 89°44W **80** C9
Tomakomai *Japan* 42°38N 141°36E **28** C10
Tomales *U.S.A.* 38°15N 122°53W **78** G4
Tomales B. *U.S.A.* 38°15N 123°58W **78** G3
Tomanivi *Fiji* 17°37S 178°1E **59** a
Tomar *Portugal* 39°36N 8°25W **21** C1
Tomaszów Mazowiecki
Poland 51°30N 20°2E **17** C10
Tomatlán *Mexico* 19°56N 105°15W **86** D3
Tombador, Serra do *Brazil* 12°0S 58°0W **92** F7
Tombigbee → *U.S.A.* 31°8N 87°57W **85** F11
Tombouctou *Mali* 16°50N 3°0W **52** E5
Tombstone *U.S.A.* 31°43N 110°4W **77** L8
Tombua *Angola* 15°55S 11°55E **56** A1
Tomé *Chile* 36°36S 72°57W **94** D1
Tome *Japan* 38°40N 141°20E **28** E10
Tomelloso *Spain* 39°10N 3°2W **21** C4
Tomini *Indonesia* 0°30N 120°30E **37** D6
Tomini, Teluk *Indonesia* 0°10S 121°0E **37** E6
Tomintoul *U.K.* 57°15N 3°23W **11** D5
Tomkinson Ranges
Australia 26°11S 129°5E **61** E4
Tommot *Russia* 59°4N 126°20E **27** D13
Tomnop Ta Suos
Cambodia 11°20N 104°15E **39** G5
Tomo → *Colombia* 5°20N 67°48W **92** B5
Toms Place *U.S.A.* 37°34N 118°41W **78** H8
Toms River *U.S.A.* 39°58N 74°12W **83** G10
Tomsk *Russia* 56°30N 85°5E **26** D9
Tonalá *Chiapas, Mexico* 16°4N 93°45W **87** D6
Tonalá *Jalisco, Mexico* 20°37N 103°14W **86** C4
Tonantins *Brazil* 2°45S 67°45W **92** D5
Tonasket *U.S.A.* 48°42N 119°26W **76** B4

Tonawanda *U.S.A.* 43°1N 78°53W **82** D6
Toropets *Russia* 56°30N 31°40E **18** C5
Tororo *Uganda* 0°45N 34°12E **54** D6
Toros Dağları *Turkey* 37°0N 32°30E **46** B2
Torpa *India* 22°57N 85°6E **43** H11
Torquay *U.K.* 50°27N 3°32W **13** G4
Torrance *U.S.A.* 33°50N 118°20W **79** M8
Torre de Moncorvo
Portugal 41°12N 7°8W **21** B2
Torre del Greco *Italy* 40°47N 14°22E **22** D6
Torrejón de Ardoz *Spain* 40°27N 3°29W **21** B4
Torrelavega *Spain* 43°20N 4°5W **21** A3
Torremolinos *Spain* 36°38N 4°30W **21** D3
Torrens, L. *Australia* 31°0S 137°50E **63** E2
Torrens Cr. → *Australia* 22°23S 145°9E **62** C4
Torrens Creek *Australia* 20°48S 145°3E **62** C4
Torrent *Spain* 39°27N 0°28W **21** C5
Torreón *Mexico* 25°33N 103°26W **86** B4
Torres *Brazil* 29°21S 49°44W **95** B5
Torres *Mexico* 28°46N 110°47W **86** B2
Torres Strait *Australia* 9°50S 142°20E **62** a
Torres Vedras *Portugal* 39°5N 9°15W **21** C1
Torrevieja *Spain* 37°59N 0°42W **21** D5
Torrey *U.S.A.* 38°18N 111°25W **76** G8
Torridge → *U.K.* 51°0N 4°13W **13** G3
Torridon, L. *U.K.* 57°35N 5°50W **11** D3
Torrington *Conn., U.S.A.* 41°48N 73°7W **83** E11
Torrington *Wyo., U.S.A.* 42°4N 104°11W **76** E11
Tórshavn *Færoe Is.* 62°5N 6°56W **8** F9
Tortola *Br. Virgin Is.* 18°19N 64°45W **89** e
Tortosa *Spain* 40°49N 0°31E **21** B6
Tortue, Î. de la *Haiti* 20°5N 72°57W **89** B5
Tortuguero △ *Costa Rica* 10°25N 83°30W **88** D3
Torūd *Iran* 35°25N 55°5E **47** C7
Toruń *Poland* 53°2N 18°39E **17** B10
Tory Hill *Canada* 44°58N 78°16E **82** B6
Tory I. *Ireland* 55°16N 8°14W **10** A3
Tosa *Japan* 33°24N 133°23E **29** H6
Tosa-Shimizu *Japan* 32°52N 132°58E **29** H6
Tosa-Wan *Japan* 33°15N 133°30E **29** H6
Toscana □ *Italy* 43°25N 11°0E **22** C4
Toshka Lakes *Egypt* 22°50N 31°0E **53** D12
Toshkent *Uzbekistan* 41°20N 69°10E **26** E7
Tostado *Argentina* 29°15S 61°50W **94** B3
Tosu *Japan* 33°22N 130°31E **29** H5
Toteng *Botswana* 20°22S 22°58E **56** C3
Totma *Russia* 60°0N 42°40E **18** C7
Totnes *U.K.* 50°26N 3°42W **13** G4
Totness *Suriname* 5°53N 56°19W **93** B7
Totonicapán *Guatemala* 14°58N 91°12W **88** D1
Totoya, I. *Fiji* 18°57S 179°50W **59** a
Totten Glacier *Antarctica* 66°45S 116°10E **5** C8
Tottenham *Australia* 32°14S 147°21E **63** E4
Tottenham *Canada* 44°1N 79°49W **82** B5
Tottori *Japan* 35°30N 134°15E **29** G7
Tottori □ *Japan* 35°30N 134°12E **29** G7
Toubkal, Djebel *Morocco* 31°0N 8°0W **52** B4
Tougan *Burkina Faso* 13°11N 2°58W **52** F5
Touggourt *Algeria* 33°6N 6°4E **52** B7
Toul *France* 48°40N 5°53E **20** B6
Touliu *Taiwan* 23°42N 120°31E **35** F13
Toulon *France* 43°10N 5°55E **20** E6
Toulouse *France* 43°37N 1°27E **20** E4
Toummo *Niger* 22°45N 14°8E **53** D8
Tounan *Taiwan* 23°41N 120°28E **35** F13
Tounggoo *Burma* 19°0N 96°30E **41** K20
Touraine *France* 47°20N 0°30E **20** C4
Touran = Tūrān △ *Iran* 35°45N 56°30E **47** C8
Tourcoing *France* 50°42N 3°10E **20** A5
Touriñán, C. *Spain* 43°3N 9°18W **21** A1
Tournai *Belgium* 50°35N 3°25E **15** D3
Tournon-sur-Rhône *France* 45°4N 4°50E **20** D6
Tours *France* 47°22N 0°40E **20** C4
Toussoro, Mt. *C.A.R.* 9°7N 23°14E **54** C4
Touwsrivier *S. Africa* 33°20S 20°2E **56** D3
Towada *Japan* 40°37N 141°13E **28** D10
Towada-Hachimantai △
Japan 40°20N 140°53E **28** D10
Towada-Ko *Japan* 40°28N 140°55E **28** D10
Towanda *U.S.A.* 41°46N 76°27W **83** E8
Tower *U.S.A.* 47°48N 92°17W **80** B7
Towerhill Cr. →
Australia 22°28S 144°35E **62** C3
Towner *U.S.A.* 48°21N 100°25W **80** A3
Townsend *U.S.A.* 46°19N 111°31W **76** C8
Townshend I. *Australia* 22°10S 150°31E **62** C5
Townsville *Australia* 19°15S 146°45E **62** B4
Towraghondī *Afghan.* 35°13N 62°16E **40** B3
Towson *U.S.A.* 39°24N 76°36W **81** F15
Towuti, Danau *Indonesia* 2°45S 121°32E **37** E6
Tōya-Ko *Japan* 42°35N 140°51E **28** C10
Toyama *Japan* 36°40N 137°15E **29** F8
Toyama □ *Japan* 36°45N 137°30E **29** F8
Toyama-Wan *Japan* 37°0N 137°30E **29** F8
Toyapakeh *Indonesia* 8°41S 115°29E **37** K18
Toyohashi *Japan* 34°45N 137°25E **29** G8
Toyokawa *Japan* 34°48N 137°27E **29** G8
Toyooka *Japan* 35°35N 134°48E **29** G7
Toyota *Japan* 35°3N 137°7E **29** G8
Tozeur *Tunisia* 33°56N 8°8E **52** B7
Trá Lí = Tralee *Ireland* 52°16N 9°42W **10** D2
Trá Mhór = Tramore
Ireland 52°10N 7°10W **10** D4
Tra On *Vietnam* 9°58N 105°55E **39** H5
Tra Vinh *Vietnam* 9°50N 106°15E **39** H6
Trabzon *Turkey* 41°0N 39°45E **19** F6
Tracadie *Canada* 47°30N 64°55W **73** C7
Tracy *Canada* 46°1N 73°9W **72** C5
Tracy *Calif., U.S.A.* 37°44N 121°26W **78** H5
Tracy *Minn., U.S.A.* 44°14N 95°37W **80** C6
Trafalgar, C. *Spain* 36°10N 6°2W **21** D2
Trail *Canada* 49°5N 117°40W **70** D5
Trainor L. *Canada* 60°24N 120°17W **70** A4
Trakai *Lithuania* 54°30S 25°10E **9** J21
Tralee *Ireland* 52°16N 9°42W **10** D2
Tralee B. *Ireland* 52°17N 9°55W **10** D2
Tram Chim △ *Vietnam* 10°43N 105°31E **39** G5

Tramore *Ireland* 52°10N 7°10W **10** D4
Tramore B. *Ireland* 52°9N 7°10W **10** D4
Tran Ninh, Cao Nguyen *Laos* 19°30N 103°10E **38** C4
Tranås *Sweden* 58°3N 14°59E **9** G16
Trancas *Argentina* 26°11S 65°20W **94** B2
Trang *Thailand* 7°33N 99°38E **39** J2
Trangan *Indonesia* 6°40S 134°20E **37** F8
Trangie *Australia* 32°4S 148°0E **63** E4
Trani *Italy* 41°17N 16°25E **22** D7
Tranoroa *Madag.* 24°42S 45°4E **55** J9
Tranqueras *Uruguay* 31°13S 55°45W **95** C4
Transantarctic Mts. *Antarctica* 85°0S 170°0W **5** E12
Transilvania *Romania* 46°30N 24°0E **17** E12
Transilvanian Alps = Carpaţii Meridionali *Romania* 45°30N 25°0E **17** F13
Transnistria = Stînga Nistrului □ *Moldova* 47°20N 29°15E **17** E15
Transylvania = Transilvania *Romania* 46°30N 24°0E **17** E12
Trápani *Italy* 38°1N 12°29E **22** E5
Trapper Pk. *U.S.A.* 45°54N 114°18W **76** D6
Traralgon *Australia* 38°12S 146°34E **63** F4
Trasimeno, L. *Italy* 43°8N 12°6E **22** C5
Trat *Thailand* 12°14N 102°33E **39** F4
Tratani → *Pakistan* 29°19N 68°20E **42** E3
Traun *Austria* 48°14N 14°15E **16** D8
Travellers L. *Australia* 33°20S 142°0E **63** E3
Travemünde *Germany* 53°57N 10°52E **16** B6
Travers, Mt. *N.Z.* 42°1S 172°45E **59** E4
Traverse City *U.S.A.* 44°46N 85°38W **81** C11
Travis, L. *U.S.A.* 30°24N 97°55W **84** F6
Travnik *Bos.-H.* 44°17N 17°39E **23** B7
Trawbreaga B. *Ireland* 55°20N 7°25W **10** A4
Trébbia → *Italy* 45°4N 9°41E **20** D8
Třebíč *Czech Rep.* 49°14N 15°55E **16** D8
Trebinje *Bos.-H.* 42°44N 18°22E **23** C8
Trebonne *Australia* 18°37S 146°5E **62** B4
Trefaldwyn = Montgomery *U.K.* 52°34N 3°8W **13** E4
Trefynwy = Monmouth *U.K.* 51°48N 2°42W **13** F5
Tregaron *U.K.* 52°14N 3°56W **13** E4
Tregrosse Is. *Australia* 17°41S 150°43E **62** B5
Treherne *Canada* 49°38N 98°42W **71** D9
Treinta y Tres *Uruguay* 33°16S 54°17W **95** C5
Trelawney *Zimbabwe* 17°30S 30°30E **57** A5
Trelew *Argentina* 43°10S 65°20W **96** E3
Trelleborg *Sweden* 55°20N 13°10E **9** J15
Tremadog Bay *U.K.* 52°51N 4°18W **12** E3
Tremonton *U.S.A.* 41°43N 112°10W **76** F7
Tremp *Spain* 42°10N 0°52E **21** A6
Trenche → *Canada* 47°46N 72°53W **72** C5
Trenčín *Slovak Rep.* 48°52N 18°4E **17** D10
Trenggalek *Indonesia* 8°3S 111°43E **37** H14
Trenque Lauquen *Argentina* 36°5S 62°45W **94** D3
Trent → *Canada* 44°6N 77°34W **82** B7
Trent → *U.K.* 53°41N 0°42W **12** D7
Trento *Italy* 46°4N 11°8E **22** A4
Trenton *Canada* 44°10N 77°34W **82** B7
Trenton *Mo., U.S.A.* 40°5N 93°37W **80** E7
Trenton *N.J., U.S.A.* 40°14N 74°46W **83** F10
Trenton *Nebr., U.S.A.* 40°11N 101°1W **80** E3
Trepassey *Canada* 46°43N 53°25W **73** C9
Tres Arroyos *Argentina* 38°26S 60°20W **94** D3
Três Corações *Brazil* 21°44S 45°15W **95** A6
Três Lagoas *Brazil* 20°50S 51°43W **93** H8
Tres Lomas *Argentina* 36°27S 62°51W **94** D3
Tres Montes, C. *Chile* 46°50S 75°30W **96** F1
Tres Pinos *U.S.A.* 36°48N 121°19W **78** J5
Três Pontas *Brazil* 21°23S 45°29W **95** A6
Tres Puentes *Chile* 27°50S 70°15W **94** B1
Tres Puntas, C. *Argentina* 47°0S 66°0W **96** F3
Três Rios *Brazil* 22°6S 43°15W **95** A7
Tres Valles *Mexico* 18°15N 96°8W **87** D5
Tresco *U.K.* 49°57N 6°20W **13** H1
Treviso *Italy* 45°40N 12°15E **22** B5
Triabunna *Australia* 42°30S 147°55E **63** G4
Triangle *Zimbabwe* 21°2S 31°28E **57** B5
Tribal Areas □ *Pakistan* 33°0N 70°0E **42** C4
Tribulation, C. *Australia* 16°5S 145°29E **62** B4
Tribune *U.S.A.* 38°28N 101°45W **80** F3
Trichinopoly = Tiruchchirappalli *India* 10°45N 78°45E **45** J4
Trichur = Thrissur *India* 10°30N 76°18E **45** J3
Trichy = Tiruchchirappalli *India* 10°45N 78°45E **45** J4
Trida *Australia* 33°1S 145°1E **63** E4
Trier *Germany* 49°45N 6°38E **16** D4
Trieste *Italy* 45°40N 13°46E **22** B5
Triglav *Slovenia* 46°21N 13°50E **16** E7
Trikala *Greece* 39°34N 21°47E **23** E9
Trikora, Puncak *Indonesia* 4°15S 138°45E **37** E9
Trim *Ireland* 53°33N 6°48W **10** C5
Trimbak *India* 19°56N 73°33E **44** E1
Trimmu Dam *Pakistan* 31°10N 72°8E **42** D5
Trincomalee *Sri Lanka* 8°38N 81°15E **45** K5
Trindade *Atl. Oc.* 20°20S 29°50W **2** F8
Trindade *Brazil* 16°40S 49°30W **93** G9
Trinidad *Bolivia* 14°46S 64°50W **92** F6
Trinidad *Cuba* 21°48N 80°0W **88** B4
Trinidad *Trin. & Tob.* 10°30N 61°15W **93** K15
Trinidad *Uruguay* 33°30S 56°50W **94** C4
Trinidad *U.S.A.* 37°10N 104°31W **77** H11
Trinidad & Tobago ■ *W. Indies* 10°30N 61°20W **93** K15
Trinity *Canada* 48°59N 53°55W **73** C9
Trinity *U.S.A.* 30°57N 95°22W **84** F7
Trinity → *Calif., U.S.A.* 41°11N 123°42W **76** F2
Trinity → *Tex., U.S.A.* 29°45N 94°43W **84** G7
Trinity B. *Canada* 48°20N 53°10W **73** C9
Trinity Hills *Trin. & Tob.* 10°7N 61°7W **93** K15
Trinity Is. *U.S.A.* 56°33N 154°25W **74** D9
Trinity Range *U.S.A.* 40°10N 118°40W **76** F4
Trinkat *India* 8°5N 93°30E **45** K11
Trinkitat *Sudan* 18°45N 37°51E **53** E13
Trinway *U.S.A.* 40°9N 82°1W **82** F2
Triolet *Mauritius* 20°4S 57°32E **55** d
Tripoli = Tarābulus *Lebanon* 34°31N 35°50E **48** A4
Tripoli = Tarābulus *Libya* 32°49N 13°7E **53** B8
Tripoli *Greece* 37°31N 22°25E **23** F10
Tripolitania = Tarābulus *Libya* 31°0N 13°0E **53** B8
Tripura □ *India* 24°0N 92°0E **41** H18
Tristan da Cunha *Atl. Oc.* 37°6S 12°20W **51** K2
Trisul *India* 30°19N 79°47E **43** D8
Trivandrum = Thiruvananthapuram *India* 8°41N 77°0E **45** K3
Trnava *Slovak Rep.* 48°23N 17°35E **17** D9
Trochu *Canada* 51°50N 113°13W **70** C6
Trodely I. *Canada* 52°15N 79°26W **72** B4
Troglav *Croatia* 43°56N 16°36E **22** C7
Troilus, L. *Canada* 50°50N 74°35W **72** B5
Trois-Pistoles *Canada* 48°5N 69°10W **73** C6
Trois-Rivières *Canada* 46°25N 72°34W **72** C5
Trois-Rivières *Guadeloupe* 15°57N 61°40W **88** b
Troitsk *Russia* 54°10N 61°35E **26** D7
Troitsko Pechorsk *Russia* 62°40N 56°10E **18** B10
Troll *Antarctica* 72°0S 2°30E **5** D3
Trölladyngja *Iceland* 64°54N 17°16W **8** D5
Trollhättan *Sweden* 58°17N 12°20E **9** G15
Trollheimen *Norway* 62°46N 9°1E **8** E13
Trombetas → *Brazil* 1°55S 55°35W **93** D7
Tromsø *Norway* 69°40N 18°56E **8** B18
Tron *Thailand* 17°28N 100°7E **38** D3
Trona *U.S.A.* 35°46N 117°23W **79** K9
Tronador, Mte. *Argentina* 41°10S 71°50W **96** E2
Trøndelag *Norway* 64°17N 11°50E **8** D14
Trondheim *Norway* 63°36N 10°25E **8** E14
Trondheimsfjorden *Norway* 63°35N 10°30E **8** E14
Troon *U.K.* 55°33N 4°39W **11** F4
Tropic *U.S.A.* 37°37N 112°5W **77** H7
Trostan *U.K.* 55°3N 6°10W **10** A5
Trou Gras Pt. *St. Lucia* 13°51N 60°53W **89** f
Trout → *Canada* 61°19N 119°51W **70** A5
Trout L. *N.W.T., Canada* 60°40N 121°14W **70** A4
Trout L. *Ont., Canada* 51°20N 93°15W **71** C10
Trout Lake *Canada* 56°30N 114°32W **70** B6
Trout Lake *U.S.A.* 46°0N 121°32W **78** E5
Trout River *Canada* 49°29N 58°8W **73** C8
Trout Run *U.S.A.* 41°23N 77°3W **82** E7
Trouville-sur-Mer *France* 49°21N 0°5E **20** B4
Trowbridge *U.K.* 51°18N 2°12W **13** F5
Troy *Turkey* 39°57N 26°12E **23** E12
Troy *Ala., U.S.A.* 31°48N 85°58W **85** F12
Troy *Kans., U.S.A.* 39°47N 95°5W **80** F6
Troy *Mo., U.S.A.* 38°59N 90°59W **80** F8
Troy *Mont., U.S.A.* 48°28N 115°53W **76** B6
Troy *N.Y., U.S.A.* 42°44N 73°41W **83** D11
Troy *Ohio, U.S.A.* 40°2N 84°12W **81** E11
Troy *Pa., U.S.A.* 41°47N 76°47W **83** E8
Troyes *France* 48°19N 4°3E **20** B6
Truchas Pk. *U.S.A.* 35°58N 105°39W **77** J11
Trucial States = United Arab Emirates ■ *Asia* 23°50N 54°0E **47** F7
Truckee *U.S.A.* 39°20N 120°11W **78** F6
Trudovoye *Russia* 43°17N 132°5E **28** C6
Trujillo *Honduras* 16°0N 86°0W **88** C2
Trujillo *Peru* 8°6S 79°0W **92** E3
Trujillo *Spain* 39°28N 5°55W **21** C3
Trujillo *U.S.A.* 35°32N 104°42W **77** J11
Trujillo *Venezuela* 9°22N 70°38W **92** B4
Truk *Micronesia* 7°25N 151°46E **64** G7
Trumann *U.S.A.* 35°41N 90°31W **85** D9
Trumansburg *U.S.A.* 42°33N 76°40W **83** D8
Trumbull, Mt. *U.S.A.* 36°25N 113°19W **77** H7
Trundle *Australia* 32°53S 147°35E **63** E4
Trung Lon, Hon *Vietnam* 8°36N 106°8E **39** H6
Trung-Phan *Vietnam* 17°0N 109°0E **38** D6
Truro *Canada* 45°21N 63°14W **73** C7
Truro *U.K.* 50°16N 5°4W **13** G2
Truskavets *Ukraine* 49°17N 23°30E **17** D12
Trutch *Canada* 57°44N 122°57W **70** B4
Truth or Consequences *U.S.A.* 33°8N 107°15W **77** K10
Trutnov *Czech Rep.* 50°37N 15°54E **16** C8
Tryonville *U.S.A.* 41°42N 79°48W **82** E5
Tsandi *Namibia* 17°42S 14°50E **56** A1
Tsaratanana *Madag.* 16°47S 47°39E **55** G9
Tsau *Botswana* 20°8S 22°22E **56** B3
Tsavo *Kenya* 2°59S 38°28E **54** E7
Tsentralnyy □ *Russia* 52°0N 40°0E **26** D4
Tses *Namibia* 25°58S 18°8E **56** C2
Tsetserleg *Mongolia* 47°36N 101°32E **30** B9
Tsévié *Togo* 6°25N 1°20E **52** G6
Tshabong *Botswana* 26°2S 22°29E **56** C3
Tshane *Botswana* 24°5S 21°54E **56** B3
Tshela *Dem. Rep. of the Congo* 4°57S 13°4E **54** E2
Tshesebe *Botswana* 21°51S 27°32E **57** B4
Tshikapa *Dem. Rep. of the Congo* 6°28S 20°48E **54** F4
Tshwane = Pretoria *S. Africa* 25°44S 28°12E **57** C4
Tshwane *Botswana* 22°24S 22°1E **56** B3
Tsigara *Botswana* 20°22S 25°54E **56** B4
Tsihombe *Madag.* 25°10S 45°41E **55** K9
Tsiigehtchic *Canada* 67°15N 134°0W **68** D5
Ts'il-os ⌓ *Canada* 51°9N 123°59W **70** C4
Tsimlyansk Res. = Tsimlyanskoye Vdkhr. *Russia* 48°0N 43°0E **19** E7
Tsimlyanskoye Vdkhr. *Russia* 48°0N 43°0E **19** E7
Tsinan = Jinan *China* 36°38N 117°1E **32** F9
Tsineng *S. Africa* 27°5S 23°5E **56** C3
Tsinghai = Qinghai □ *China* 36°0N 98°0E **30** D8
Tsingtao = Qingdao *China* 36°5N 120°20E **33** F11
Tsirigo = Kythira *Greece* 36°8N 23°0E **23** F10
Tsitsikamma △ *S. Africa* 34°3S 23°40E **56** D3
Tskhinvali *Georgia* 42°14N 44°1E **19** F7
Tsna → *Russia* 54°55N 41°58E **18** D7
Tso Moriri, L. *India* 32°50N 78°20E **43** C8
Tsobis *Namibia* 19°27S 17°30E **56** A2
Tsodilo Hills *Botswana* 18°49S 21°43E **56** A3
Tsogttsetsiy = Baruunsuu *Mongolia* 43°43N 105°35E **32** C3
Tsolo *S. Africa* 31°18S 28°37E **57** D4
Tsomo *S. Africa* 32°0S 27°42E **57** D4
Tsu *Japan* 34°45N 136°25E **29** G8
Tsu L. *Canada* 60°40N 111°52W **70** A6
Tsuchiura *Japan* 36°5N 140°15E **29** F10
Tsugaru-Hantō *Japan* 41°0N 140°30E **28** D10
Tsugaru-Kaikyō *Japan* 41°35N 141°0E **28** D10
Tsumeb *Namibia* 19°9S 17°44E **56** A2
Tsumis *Namibia* 23°39S 17°29E **56** B2
Tsuruga *Japan* 35°45N 136°2E **29** G8
Tsurugi-San *Japan* 33°51N 134°6E **29** H7
Tsuruoka *Japan* 38°44N 139°50E **28** E9
Tsushima *Gifu, Japan* 35°10N 136°43E **29** G8
Tsushima *Nagasaki, Japan* 34°20N 129°20E **29** G4
Tsuyama *Japan* 35°3N 134°0E **29** G7
Tsyelyakhany *Belarus* 52°30N 25°46E **17** B13
Tuaim = Tuam *Ireland* 53°31N 8°51W **10** C3
Tual *Indonesia* 5°38S 132°44E **37** F8
Tualatin *U.S.A.* 45°23N 122°45W **78** E4
Tuam *Ireland* 53°31N 8°51W **10** C3
Tuamotu, Îs. *French Polynesia* 17°0S 144°0W **65** J13
Tuamotu Arch. = Tuamotu, Îs. *French Polynesia* 17°0S 144°0W **65** J13
Tuamotu Ridge *Pac. Oc.* 20°0S 138°0W **65** K14
Tuan Giao *Vietnam* 21°35N 103°25E **38** B4
Tuanfeng *China* 30°38N 114°52E **35** B10
Tuanxi *China* 27°28N 107°8E **34** D6
Tuao *Phil.* 17°45N 121°22E **37** A6
Tuapse *Russia* 44°5N 39°10E **19** F6
Tuatapere *N.Z.* 46°8S 167°41E **59** G1
Tuba City *U.S.A.* 36°8N 111°14W **77** H8
Tuban *Indonesia* 6°54S 112°3E **37** G15
Tubani *Botswana* 24°46S 24°18E **56** B3
Tubarão *Brazil* 28°30S 49°0W **95** B6
Tūbās *West Bank* 32°20N 35°22E **48** C4
Tubas → *Namibia* 22°54S 14°35E **56** B2
Tübingen *Germany* 48°31N 9°4E **16** D5
Tubou *Fiji* 18°13S 178°48W **59** a
Tubruq *Libya* 32°7N 23°55E **53** B10
Tubuaï, Îs. *French Polynesia* 25°0S 150°0W **65** K13
Tuc Trung *Vietnam* 11°1N 107°12E **39** G6
Tucacas *Venezuela* 10°48N 68°19W **92** A5
T'uch'ang *Taiwan* 24°35N 121°29E **35** E13
Tuchitua *Canada* 60°55N 129°13W **70** A3
Tuchodi → *Canada* 58°17N 123°42W **70** B4
Tuckanarra *Australia* 27°7S 118°5E **61** E2
Tucson *U.S.A.* 32°13N 110°58W **77** K8
Tucumán □ *Argentina* 26°48S 66°2W **94** B2
Tucumcari *U.S.A.* 35°10N 103°44W **77** J12
Tucupita *Venezuela* 9°2N 62°3W **92** B6
Tucuruí *Brazil* 3°42S 49°44W **93** D9
Tucuruí, Represa de *Brazil* 4°0S 49°30W **93** D9
Tudela *Spain* 42°4N 1°39W **21** A5
Tudmur *Syria* 34°36N 38°15E **46** C3
Tudor, L. *Canada* 55°50N 65°25W **73** A6
Tuen Mun *China* 22°24N 113°59E **31** a
Tug Hill Plateau *U.S.A.* 43°45N 75°50W **83** C9
Tugela → *S. Africa* 29°14S 31°30E **57** C5
Tugela Falls *S. Africa* 28°42S 29°51E **57** C4
Tuguegarao *Phil.* 17°35N 121°42E **37** A6
Tugur *Russia* 53°44N 136°45E **27** D14
Tui *Spain* 42°3N 8°39W **21** A1
Tukangbesi, Kepulauan *Indonesia* 6°0S 124°0E **37** F6
Tukarak I. *Canada* 56°15N 78°45W **72** A4
Tukayyid *Iraq* 29°47N 45°36E **46** D5
Tuktoyaktuk *Canada* 69°27N 133°2W **68** D5
Tuktut Nogait △ *Canada* 69°15N 122°0W **68** D7
Tukums *Latvia* 56°58N 23°10E **9** H20
Tukuyu *Tanzania* 9°17S 33°35E **54** F6
Tula *Hidalgo, Mexico* 20°3N 99°21W **87** C5
Tula *Tamaulipas, Mexico* 23°0N 99°43W **87** C5
Tula *Russia* 54°13N 37°38E **18** D6
Tulach Mhór = Tullamore *Ireland* 53°16N 7°31W **10** C4
Tulancingo *Mexico* 20°5N 98°22W **87** C5
Tulare *U.S.A.* 36°13N 119°21W **78** J7
Tulare Lake Bed *U.S.A.* 36°0N 119°48W **78** K7
Tularosa *U.S.A.* 33°5N 106°1W **77** K10
Tulbagh *S. Africa* 33°16S 19°6E **56** D2
Tulcán *Ecuador* 0°48N 77°43W **92** C3
Tulcea *Romania* 45°13N 28°46E **17** F15
Tulchyn *Ukraine* 48°41N 28°49E **17** D15
Tūleh *Iran* 34°35N 52°33E **47** C7
Tulemalu L. *Canada* 62°58N 99°25W **71** A9
Tulia *U.S.A.* 34°32N 101°46W **84** D4
Tulita *Canada* 64°57N 125°30W **68** E6
Ţūlkarm *West Bank* 32°19N 35°2E **48** C4
Tulla *Ireland* 52°53N 8°46W **10** D3
Tullahoma *U.S.A.* 35°22N 86°13W **85** D11
Tullamore *Australia* 32°39S 147°36E **63** E4
Tullamore *Ireland* 53°16N 7°31W **10** C4
Tulle *France* 45°16N 1°46E **20** D4
Tullow *Ireland* 52°49N 6°45W **10** D5
Tully *Australia* 17°56S 145°55E **62** B4
Tully *U.S.A.* 42°48N 76°7W **83** D8
Tulsa *U.S.A.* 36°10N 95°55W **84** C7
Tulsequah *Canada* 58°39N 133°35W **70** B2
Tuluá *Colombia* 4°6N 76°11W **92** C3
Tulum *Mexico* 20°13N 87°28W **87** C7
Tulun *Russia* 54°32N 100°35E **27** D11
Tulungagung *Indonesia* 8°5S 111°54E **37** H14
Tuma → *Nic.* 13°6N 84°35W **88** D3
Tumacacori ⌓ *U.S.A.* 31°35N 111°6W **77** L8
Tumaco *Colombia* 1°50N 78°45W **92** C3
Tumakuru = Tumkur *India* 13°18N 77°6E **45** H3
Tumatumari *Guyana* 5°20N 58°55W **92** B7
Tumba *Sweden* 59°12N 17°48E **9** G17
Tumba, L. *Dem. Rep. of the Congo* 0°50S 18°0E **54** E3
Tumbarumba *Australia* 35°44S 148°0E **63** F4
Tumbaya *Argentina* 23°50S 65°26W **94** A2
Tumbes *Peru* 3°37S 80°27W **92** D2
Tumbler Ridge *Canada* 55°8N 121°0W **70** B4
Tumby Bay *Australia* 34°21S 136°8E **63** E2
Tumd Youqi *China* 40°30N 110°30E **32** D6
Tumen *China* 43°0N 129°50E **28** C4
Tumen Jiang → *China* 42°20N 130°35E **33** C16
Tumeremo *Venezuela* 7°18N 61°30W **92** B6
Tumkur *India* 13°18N 77°6E **45** H3
Tump *Pakistan* 26°7N 62°16E **40** F3
Tumpat *Malaysia* 6°11N 102°10E **39** J4
Tumsar *India* 21°26N 79°45E **44** D4
Tumu *Ghana* 10°56N 1°56W **52** F5
Tumucumaque, Serra *Brazil* 2°0N 55°0W **93** C8
Tumut *Australia* 35°16S 148°13E **63** F4
Tumwater *U.S.A.* 47°1N 122°54W **78** C4
Tuna *India* 22°59N 70°5E **42** H4
Tunapuna *Trin. & Tob.* 10°38N 61°24W **93** K15
Tunas de Zaza *Cuba* 21°39N 79°34W **88** B4
Tunbridge Wells = Royal Tunbridge Wells *U.K.* 51°7N 0°16E **13** F8
Tunchang *China* 19°21N 110°5E **38** C8
Tuncurry *Australia* 32°17S 152°29E **63** E5
Tundla *India* 27°12N 78°17E **42** F8
Tundzha → *Bulgaria* 41°40N 26°35E **23** C11
Tung Chung *China* 22°17N 113°57E **31** a
Tunga → *India* 15°0N 75°50E **45** G2
Tungabhadra → *India* 15°57N 78°15E **45** G4
Tungabhadra Dam *India* 15°0N 75°50E **45** G2
Tungla *Nic.* 13°24N 84°21W **88** D3
Tungsha Tao = Dongsha Dao *S. China Sea* 20°45N 116°43E **35** G11
Tungshih *Taiwan* 24°12N 120°43E **35** E13
Tungsten *Canada* 61°57N 128°16W **70** A3
Tunguska, Nizhnyaya → *Russia* 65°48N 88°4E **27** C9
Tunguska, Podkamennaya → *Russia* 61°50N 90°13E **27** C10
Tuni *India* 17°22N 82°36E **44** F6
Tunica *U.S.A.* 34°41N 90°23W **85** D9
Tunis *Tunisia* 36°50N 10°11E **53** A8
Tunisia ■ *Africa* 33°30N 9°10E **53** A7
Tunja *Colombia* 5°33N 73°25W **92** B4
Tunkhannock *U.S.A.* 41°32N 75°57W **83** E9
Tunliu *China* 36°13N 112°52E **32** F7
Tunnel Creek △ *Australia* 17°41S 125°18E **60** C4
Tunnsjøen *Norway* 64°45N 13°25E **8** D15
Tunungayualok I. *Canada* 56°0N 61°0W **73** A7
Tunuyán *Argentina* 33°35S 69°0W **94** C2
Tunuyán → *Argentina* 33°33S 67°30W **94** C2
Tunxi = Huangshan *China* 30°8N 118°9E **35** B12
Tuo Jiang → *China* 28°50N 105°35E **34** C5
Tuolumne *U.S.A.* 37°58N 120°15W **78** H6
Tuolumne → *U.S.A.* 37°36N 121°13W **78** H5
Tūp Āghāj *Iran* 36°3N 47°50E **46** B5
Tupã *Brazil* 21°57S 50°28W **95** A5
Tupelo *U.S.A.* 34°16N 88°43W **85** D10
Tupinambarana, I. *Brazil* 3°0S 58°0W **92** D7
Tupiza *Bolivia* 21°30S 65°40W **94** A2
Tupman *U.S.A.* 35°18N 119°21W **79** K7
Tupper *Canada* 55°32N 120°1W **70** B4
Tupper L. *U.S.A.* 44°10N 74°32W **83** B10
Tupper Lake *U.S.A.* 44°14N 74°28W **83** B10
Tupungato, Cerro *S. Amer.* 33°15S 69°50W **94** C2
Tuquan *China* 45°18N 121°38E **33** B11
Túquerres *Colombia* 1°5N 77°37W **92** C3
Tura *Russia* 64°20N 100°17E **27** C11
Turabah *Si. Arabia* 28°20N 43°15E **46** D4
Tūrān *Iran* 35°39N 56°42E **47** C8
Turan *Russia* 51°55N 94°0E **27** D10
Tūrān △ *Iran* 35°45N 56°30E **47** C8
Ţurayf *Si. Arabia* 31°41N 38°39E **46** D3
Turda *Romania* 46°34N 23°47E **17** E12
Turek *Poland* 52°3N 18°30E **17** B10
Turén *Venezuela* 9°17N 69°6W **92** B5
Turfan = Turpan *China* 43°58N 89°10E **30** C6
Turfan Basin = Turpan Pendi *China* 42°40N 89°25E **30** C6
Turfan Depression = Turpan Pendi *China* 42°40N 89°25E **30** C6
Turgeon → *Canada* 50°0N 78°56W **72** C4
Tŭrgovishte *Bulgaria* 43°17N 26°38E **23** C12
Turgutlu *Turkey* 38°30N 27°43E **23** E12
Turgwe → *Zimbabwe* 21°31S 32°15E **57** B5
Turia → *Spain* 39°27N 0°19W **21** C5
Turiaçu *Brazil* 1°40S 45°19W **93** D9
Turiaçu → *Brazil* 1°36S 45°19W **93** D9
Turin = Torino *Italy* 45°3N 7°40E **20** D7
Turkana, L. *Africa* 3°30N 36°5E **54** D7
Turkestan = Türkistan *Kazakhstan* 43°17N 68°16E **26** E7
Turkey ■ *Eurasia* 39°0N 36°0E **19** G6
Turkey Creek = Warmun *Australia* 17°2S 128°12E **60** C4
Türkistan *Kazakhstan* 43°17N 68°16E **26** E7
Türkmenabat *Turkmenistan* 39°6N 63°34E **47** B9
Türkmenbashi *Turkmenistan* 40°5N 53°5E **47** A7
Turkmenistan ■ *Asia* 39°0N 59°0E **26** F6
Turks & Caicos Is. ☒ *W. Indies* 21°20N 71°20W **89** B5
Turks Island Passage *Turks & Caicos* 21°25N 71°19W **89** B5
Turku *Finland* 60°30N 22°19E **9** F20
Turkwel → *Kenya* 3°6N 36°6E **54** D7
Turlock *U.S.A.* 37°30N 120°51W **78** H6
Turnagain *Australia* 9°34S 142°17E **62** a
Turnagain → *Canada* 59°12N 127°35W **70** B3
Turnagain, C. *N.Z.* 40°28S 176°38E **59** D6
Turneffe Is. *Belize* 17°20N 87°50W **87** D7
Turner *U.S.A.* 48°51N 108°24W **76** B9
Turner Pt. *Australia* 11°47S 133°32E **62** A1
Turner Valley *Canada* 50°40N 114°17W **70** C6
Turners Falls *U.S.A.* 42°36N 72°33W **83** D12
Turnhout *Belgium* 51°19N 4°57E **15** C4
Turnor L. *Canada* 56°35N 108°35W **71** B7
Tŭrnovo = Veliko Tŭrnovo *Bulgaria* 43°5N 25°41E **23** C11
Turnu Măgurele *Romania* 43°46N 24°56E **17** G13
Turnu Roşu, P. *Romania* 45°33N 24°17E **17** F13
Turpan *China* 43°58N 89°10E **30** C6
Turpan Pendi *China* 42°40N 89°25E **30** C6
Turriff *U.K.* 57°32N 2°27W **11** D6
Tursāq *Iraq* 33°27N 45°47E **46** C5
Turtle Head I. *Australia* 10°56S 142°37E **62** A3
Turtle L. *Canada* 53°36N 108°38W **71** C7
Turtle Lake *U.S.A.* 47°31N 100°53W **80** B3
Turtleford *Canada* 53°23N 108°57W **71** C7
Turuépano △ *Venezuela* 10°34N 62°43W **89** D7
Turukhansk *Russia* 65°21N 88°5E **27** C9
Tuscaloosa *U.S.A.* 33°12N 87°34W **85** E11
Tuscany = Toscana □ *Italy* 43°25N 11°0E **22** C4
Tuscarawas → *U.S.A.* 40°24N 81°25W **82** F3
Tuscarora Mt. *U.S.A.* 40°55N 77°55W **82** F7
Tuscola *Ill., U.S.A.* 39°48N 88°17W **80** F9
Tuscola *Tex., U.S.A.* 32°12N 99°48W **84** E5
Tuscumbia *U.S.A.* 34°44N 87°42W **85** D11
Tuskegee *U.S.A.* 32°25N 85°42W **85** E12
Tuticorin *India* 8°50N 78°12E **45** K4
Tutóia *Brazil* 2°45S 42°20W **93** D10
Tutong *Brunei* 4°47N 114°40E **36** D4
Tutrakan *Bulgaria* 44°2N 26°40E **23** B12
Tuttle Creek L. *U.S.A.* 39°15N 96°36W **80** F5
Tuttlingen *Germany* 47°58N 8°48E **16** E5
Tutuala *E. Timor* 8°25S 127°15E **37** F7
Tutuila *Amer. Samoa* 14°19S 170°50W **59** b
Tutume *Botswana* 20°30S 27°5E **55** J5
Tuul Gol → *Mongolia* 48°30N 104°25E **30** B9
Tuva □ *Russia* 51°30N 95°0E **27** D10
Tuvalu ■ *Pac. Oc.* 8°0S 178°0E **58** B10
Tuvuca *Fiji* 17°40S 178°48W **59** a
Tuxpan *Mexico* 20°57N 97°24W **87** C5
Tuxtla Gutiérrez *Mexico* 16°45N 93°7W **87** D6
Tuy = Tui *Spain* 42°3N 8°39W **21** A1
Tuy Duc *Vietnam* 12°15N 107°27E **39** F6
Tuy Phong *Vietnam* 11°14N 108°43E **39** G7
Tuya L. *Canada* 59°7N 130°35W **70** B2
Tuyen Hoa *Vietnam* 17°50N 106°10E **38** D6
Tuyen Quang *Vietnam* 21°50N 105°10E **34** G5
Tūysarkān *Iran* 34°33N 48°27E **47** C6
Tuz Gölü *Turkey* 38°42N 33°18E **19** G5
Ţūz Khurmātū *Iraq* 34°56N 44°38E **46** C5
Tuzigoot △ *U.S.A.* 34°46N 112°2W **77** J7
Tuzla *Bos.-H.* 44°34N 18°41E **23** B8
Tver *Russia* 56°55N 35°59E **18** C6
Twain *U.S.A.* 40°1N 121°3W **78** E5
Twain Harte *U.S.A.* 38°2N 120°14W **78** G6
Twee River *Namibia* 25°27S 19°27E **56** C2
Tweed *Canada* 44°29N 77°19W **82** B7
Tweed → *U.K.* 55°45N 2°0W **11** F6
Tweed Heads *Australia* 28°10S 153°31E **63** D5
Tweedsmuir ⌓ *Canada* 53°0N 126°20W **70** C3
Twentynine Palms *U.S.A.* 34°8N 116°3W **79** L10
Twillingate *Canada* 49°42N 54°45W **73** C9
Twin Bridges *U.S.A.* 45°33N 112°20W **76** D7
Twin Falls *Canada* 53°30N 64°32W **73** B7
Twin Falls *U.S.A.* 42°34N 114°28W **76** E6
Twin Valley *U.S.A.* 47°16N 96°16W **80** B5
Twinsburg *U.S.A.* 41°19N 81°26W **82** E3
Twitchell Res. *U.S.A.* 34°59N 120°19W **79** L6
Two Harbors *U.S.A.* 47°2N 91°40W **80** B8
Two Hills *Canada* 53°43N 111°52W **70** C6
Two Rivers *U.S.A.* 44°9N 87°34W **80** C10
Two Rocks *Australia* 31°30S 115°35E **61** F2
Twofold B. *Australia* 37°8S 149°59E **63** F4
Twyfelfontein *Namibia* 20°34S 14°22E **56** B1
Tyachiv *Ukraine* 48°1N 23°35E **17** D12
Tychy *Poland* 50°9N 18°59E **17** C10
Tyler *Minn., U.S.A.* 44°17N 96°8W **80** C5
Tyler *Tex., U.S.A.* 32°21N 95°18W **84** E7
Tynda *Russia* 55°10N 124°43E **27** D13
Tyndall *U.S.A.* 43°0N 97°50W **80** D5
Tyne → *U.K.* 54°59N 1°32W **12** C6
Tyne & Wear □ *U.K.* 55°6N 1°17W **12** B6
Tynemouth *U.K.* 55°1N 1°26W **12** B6
Tyre = Sūr *Lebanon* 33°19N 35°16E **48** B4
Tyrifjorden *Norway* 60°2N 10°8E **9** F14
Tyrol = Tirol □ *Austria* 47°3N 10°43E **16** E6
Tyrone *U.S.A.* 40°40N 78°14W **82** F6
Tyrone □ *U.K.* 54°38N 7°11W **10** B4
Tyrrell → *Australia* 35°26S 142°51E **63** F3
Tyrrell, L. *Australia* 35°20S 142°50E **63** F3
Tyrrell L. *Canada* 63°7N 105°27W **71** A7
Tyrrhenian Sea *Medit. S.* 40°0N 12°30E **22** E5
Tysfjorden *Norway* 68°7N 16°25E **8** B17
Tyulgan *Russia* 52°22N 56°12E **18** D10
Tyumen *Russia* 57°11N 65°29E **26** D7
Tywi → *U.K.* 51°48N 4°21W **13** F3
Tywyn *U.K.* 52°35N 4°5W **13** E3
Tzaneen *S. Africa* 23°47S 30°9E **57** B5
Tzukong = Zigong *China* 29°15N 104°48E **34** C5

U

U.S.A. = United States of America ■ *N. Amer.* 37°0N 96°0W **75** H20
U.S. Virgin Is. ☒ *W. Indies* 18°20N 65°0W **89** e
Uaimh, An = Navan *Ireland* 53°39N 6°41W **10** C5
Uanle Uen = Wanleweyne *Somalia* 2°37N 44°54E **49** G3
Uatumã → *Brazil* 2°26S 57°37W **92** D7
Uaupés *Brazil* 0°8S 67°5W **92** D5
Uaupés → *Brazil* 0°2N 67°16W **92** C5
Uaxactún *Guatemala* 17°25N 89°29W **88** C2
Ubá *Brazil* 21°8S 43°0W **95** A7
Ubaitaba *Brazil* 14°18S 39°20W **93** F11
Ubangi = Oubangi → *Dem. Rep. of the Congo* 0°30S 17°50E **54** E3

Ubauro Pakistan 28°15N 69°45E **42 E3**
Ubayyiḍ, W. al → Iraq 32°34N 43°48E **46 C4**
Ube Japan 33°56N 131°15E **29 H5**
Úbeda Spain 38°3N 3°23W **21 C4**
Uberaba Brazil 19°50S 47°55W **93 G9**
Uberlândia Brazil 19°0S 48°20W **93 G9**
Ubly U.S.A. 43°42N 82°55W **82 C2**
Ubolratna Res. Thailand 16°45N 102°30E **38 D4**
Ubombo S. Africa 27°31S 32°4E **57 C5**
Ubon Ratchathani Thailand 15°15N 104°50E **38 E5**
Ubort → Belarus 52°6N 28°30E **17 B15**
Ubud Indonesia 8°30S 115°16E **37 J18**
Ubundu Dem. Rep. of the Congo 0°22S 25°30E **54 E5**
Ucayali → Peru 4°30S 73°30W **92 D4**
Uchab Namibia 19°47S 17°42E **56 A2**
Uchiura-Wan Japan 42°25N 140°40E **28 C10**
Uchquduq Uzbekistan 41°50N 62°50E **26 E7**
Uchur → Russia 58°48N 130°35E **27 D14**
Ucluelet Canada 48°57N 125°32W **70 D3**
Uda → Russia 54°42N 135°14E **27 D14**
Uda Walawe △ Sri Lanka 6°20N 81°0E **45 L5**
Udachnyy Russia 66°25N 112°24E **27 C12**
Udagamandalam India 11°30N 76°44E **45 J3**
Udainagar India 22°33N 76°13E **42 H7**
Udaipur India 24°36N 73°44E **42 G5**
Udaipur Garhi Nepal 27°0N 86°35E **43 F12**
Udala India 21°35N 86°34E **43 J12**
Udayagiri Andhra Pradesh, India 14°52N 79°19E **45 G4**
Udayagiri Odisha, India 20°8N 84°23E **44 D7**
Uddevalla Sweden 58°21N 11°55E **9 G14**
Uddjaure Sweden 65°56N 17°49E **8 D17**
Uden Neths. 51°40N 5°37E **15 C5**
Udgir India 18°25N 77°5E **44 E3**
Udhampur India 33°0N 75°5E **43 C6**
Údine Italy 46°3N 13°14E **22 A5**
Udintsev Fracture Zone S. Ocean 71°0S 145°0W **5 B13**
Udmurtia □ Russia 57°30N 52°30E **18 C9**
Udon Thani Thailand 17°29N 102°46E **38 D4**
Udong Cambodia 11°48N 104°45E **39 G5**
Udskaya Guba Russia 54°50N 135°45E **27 D14**
Udu Pt. Fiji 16°9S 179°57W **59 a**
Udumalaippettai India 10°35N 77°15E **45 J3**
Udupi India 13°25N 74°42E **45 H2**
Udva India 20°5N 73°0E **44 D1**
Udzungwa Range Tanzania 9°30S 35°10E **54 F7**
Ueda Japan 36°24N 138°16E **29 F9**
Uedineniya, Os. Russia 78°0N 85°0E **4 B12**
Uele → Dem. Rep. of the Congo 3°45N 24°45E **54 D4**
Uelen Russia 66°10N 170°0W **27 C19**
Uelzen Germany 52°57N 10°32E **16 B6**
Ufa Russia 54°45N 55°55E **18 D10**
Ufa → Russia 54°40N 56°0E **18 D10**
Ugab → Namibia 20°55S 13°30E **56 B1**
Ugalla → Tanzania 5°8S 30°42E **54 F6**
Uganda ■ Africa 2°0N 32°0E **54 D6**
Ugie S. Africa 31°10S 28°13E **57 D4**
Uglegorsk Russia 49°5N 142°2E **27 E15**
Ugljan Croatia 44°12N 15°10E **16 F8**
Ugolnye Kopi Russia 64°44N 177°42E **27 C18**
Uhlenhorst Namibia 23°45S 17°55E **56 B2**
Uhrichsville U.S.A. 40°24N 81°21W **82 F3**
Uibhist a Deas = South Uist U.K. 57°20N 7°15W **11 D1**
Uibhist a Tuath = North Uist U.K. 57°40N 7°15W **11 D1**
Uig U.K. 57°35N 6°21W **11 D2**
Uíge Angola 7°30S 14°40E **52 F2**
Uiha Tonga 19°54S 174°25W **59 c**
Uijeongbu S. Korea 37°44N 127°2E **33 F14**
Ŭiju N. Korea 40°15N 124°35E **33 D13**
Uinta Mts. U.S.A. 40°45N 110°30W **76 F8**
Uis Namibia 21°8S 14°49E **56 B1**
Uiseong S. Korea 36°21N 128°45E **33 F15**
Uitenhage S. Africa 33°40S 25°28E **56 D4**
Uithuizen Neths. 53°24N 6°41E **15 A6**
Ujh → India 32°10N 75°18E **43 C6**
Ujhani India 28°0N 79°6E **43 F8**
Uji-guntō Japan 31°15N 129°25E **29 J4**
Ujjain India 23°9N 75°43E **42 H6**
Ujung Kulon △ Indonesia 6°46S 105°19E **37 G11**
Ujung Pandang = Makassar Indonesia 5°10S 119°20E **37 F5**
Uka Russia 57°50N 162°0E **27 D17**
Ukai Sagar India 21°20N 73°43E **44 D1**
Uke-Shima Japan 28°2N 129°14E **29 K4**
uKhahlamba Drakensberg △ S. Africa 29°27S 29°30E **57 C4**
Ukhrul India 25°10N 94°25E **41 G19**
Ukhta Russia 63°34N 53°41E **18 B9**
Ukiah U.S.A. 39°9N 123°13W **78 F3**
Ukmergė Lithuania 55°15N 24°45E **9 J21**
Ukraine ■ Europe 49°0N 32°0E **19 E5**
Ukwi Botswana 23°29S 20°30E **56 C3**
Ulaan Nuur Mongolia 44°30N 103°40E **32 B2**
Ulaan-Uul Mongolia 46°4N 100°49E **32 B5**
Ulaanbaatar Mongolia 47°55N 106°53E **30 B10**
Ulaangom Mongolia 50°5N 92°10E **30 A7**
Ulaanjirem Mongolia 45°5N 105°30E **32 B3**
Ulak I. U.S.A. 51°22N 178°57W **74 E4**
Ulan Bator = Ulaanbaatar Mongolia 47°55N 106°53E **30 B10**
Ulan Ude Russia 51°45N 107°40E **31 A10**
Ulanhad = Chifeng China 42°18N 118°58E **33 C10**
Ulanhot = Horqin Youyi Qianqi China 46°5N 122°3E **33 A12**
Ulansuhai Nur China 40°53N 108°51E **32 D5**
Ulcinj Montenegro 41°58N 19°10E **23 D8**
Ulco S. Africa 28°21S 24°15E **56 C3**
Ule älv = Oulujoki → Finland 65°1N 25°30E **8 D21**
Ule träsk = Oulujärvi Finland 64°25N 27°15E **8 D22**

Uleåborg = Oulu Finland 65°1N 25°29E **8 D21**
Ulefoss Norway 59°17N 9°16E **9 G13**
Ulhasnagar India 19°15N 73°10E **44 E1**
Uliastay Mongolia 47°56N 97°28E **30 B8**
Uljin S. Korea 36°59N 129°24E **33 F15**
Ulladulla Australia 35°21S 150°29E **63 F5**
Ullapool U.K. 57°54N 5°9W **11 D3**
Ulleungdo S. Korea 37°30N 130°30E **29 F5**
Ullswater Canada 45°12N 79°29W **82 A5**
Ullswater U.K. 54°34N 2°52W **12 C5**
Ulmarra Australia 29°37S 153°4E **63 D5**
Ulricehamn Sweden 57°46N 13°26E **9 H15**
Ulsan S. Korea 35°20N 129°15E **33 G15**
Ulsta U.K. 60°30N 1°9W **11 A7**
Ulster □ U.K. 54°35N 6°30W **10 B5**
Ulubat Gölü Turkey 40°9N 28°35E **23 D13**
Uludağ Turkey 40°4N 29°13E **23 D13**
Ulundi S. Africa 28°20S 31°25E **57 C5**
Ulungur He → China 47°1N 87°24E **30 B6**
Ulungur Hu China 47°20N 87°10E **30 B6**
Uluru Australia 25°23S 131°5E **61 E5**
Uluru-Kata Tjuta △ Australia 25°19S 131°1E **61 E5**
Ulutau Kazakhstan 48°39N 67°1E **26 E7**
Uluwatu Indonesia 8°50S 115°5E **37 K18**
Ulva U.K. 56°29N 6°13W **11 E2**
Ulverston U.K. 54°13N 3°5W **12 C4**
Ulverstone Australia 41°11S 146°11E **63 G4**
Ulya Russia 59°10N 142°0E **27 D15**
Ulyanovsk Russia 54°20N 48°25E **18 D8**
Ulyasutay = Uliastay Mongolia 47°56N 97°28E **30 B8**
Ulysses Kans., U.S.A. 37°35N 101°22W **80 G3**
Ulysses Pa., U.S.A. 41°54N 77°46W **82 E7**
Ulysses, Mt. Canada 57°20N 124°5W **70 B4**
Umala Bolivia 17°25S 68°5W **92 G5**
'Umān = Oman ■ Asia 23°0N 58°0E **49 C6**
Uman Ukraine 48°40N 30°12E **17 D16**
Umaria India 23°35N 80°50E **43 H9**
Umarkhed India 19°37N 77°46E **44 E3**
Umarkot Pakistan 25°15N 69°40E **42 G3**
Umarpada India 21°27N 73°30E **42 J5**
Umatilla U.S.A. 45°55N 119°21W **76 D4**
Umba Russia 66°42N 34°11E **18 A5**
Umbagog L. U.S.A. 44°46N 71°3W **83 B13**
Umbakumba Australia 13°47S 136°50E **62 A2**
Umbrella Mts. N.Z. 45°35S 169°5E **59 F2**
Umeå Sweden 63°45N 20°20E **8 E19**
Umeälven → Sweden 63°45N 20°20E **8 E19**
Umera Indonesia 0°12S 129°37E **37 E7**
Umgwenya → Mozam. 25°14S 32°18E **57 C5**
Umiujaq Canada 56°33N 76°33W **72 A4**
Umkomaas S. Africa 30°13S 30°48E **57 D5**
Umlazi S. Africa 29°59S 30°54E **55 L6**
Umm ad Daraj, J. Jordan 32°18N 35°48E **48 C4**
Umm al Fahm Israel 32°31N 35°9E **48 C4**
Umm al Qaywayn U.A.E. 25°30N 55°35E **47 E7**
Umm al Qittan Jordan 32°18N 36°40E **48 C5**
Umm al Rasas Jordan 31°30N 35°55E **48 D4**
Umm Bāb Qatar 25°12N 50°48E **47 E6**
Umm Durman = Omdurmân Sudan 15°40N 32°28E **53 E12**
Umm el Fahm Israel 32°31N 35°9E **48 C4**
Umm Keddada Sudan 13°33N 26°35E **53 F11**
Umm Lajj Si. Arabia 25°0N 37°23E **46 E3**
Umm Qasr Iraq 30°1N 47°58E **46 D5**
Umm Ruwaba Sudan 12°50N 31°20E **53 F12**
Umm Tais △ Qatar 26°7N 51°15E **47 E6**
Umnak I. U.S.A. 53°15N 168°20W **74 E6**
Umniati → Zimbabwe 16°49S 28°45E **55 H5**
Umpqua → U.S.A. 43°40N 124°12W **76 E1**
Umred India 20°51N 79°18E **44 D4**
Umreth India 22°41N 73°4E **42 H5**
Umri India 19°2N 77°39E **44 E3**
Umtata = Mthatha S. Africa 31°36S 28°49E **57 D4**
Umuarama Brazil 23°45S 53°20W **95 A5**
Umvukwe Ra. Zimbabwe 16°45S 30°45E **55 H6**
Umzimvubu S. Africa 31°38S 29°33E **57 D4**
Umzinto = eMuziwezinto S. Africa 30°15S 30°45E **57 D5**
Una India 20°46N 71°8E **42 J4**
Una → Bos.-H. 45°0N 16°20E **16 F9**
Unadilla U.S.A. 42°20N 75°19W **83 D9**
Unalakleet U.S.A. 63°52N 160°47W **74 C7**
Unalaska U.S.A. 53°53N 166°32W **74 E6**
Unalaska I. U.S.A. 53°35N 166°50W **74 E6**
'Unayzah Si. Arabia 26°6N 43°58E **46 E4**
'Unayzah, J. Asia 32°12N 39°18E **46 C3**
Uncía Bolivia 18°25S 66°40W **92 G5**
Uncompahgre Peak U.S.A. 38°4N 107°28W **76 G10**
Uncompahgre Plateau U.S.A. 38°20N 108°15W **76 G9**
Undara Volcanic △ Australia 18°14S 144°41E **62 B3**
Underbool Australia 35°10S 141°51E **63 F3**
Underwood Canada 44°18N 81°29W **82 B3**
Ungarie Australia 33°38S 146°56E **63 E4**
Ungarra Australia 34°12S 136°2E **63 E2**
Ungava, Pén. d' Canada 60°0N 74°0W **69 F17**
Ungava B. Canada 59°30N 67°30W **69 F18**
Ungeny = Ungheni Moldova 47°11N 27°51E **17 E14**
Unggi N. Korea 42°16N 130°28E **33 C16**
Ungheni Moldova 47°11N 27°51E **17 E14**
União da Vitória Brazil 26°13S 51°5W **95 B5**
Unimak I. U.S.A. 54°45N 164°0W **74 E7**
Unimak Pass. U.S.A. 54°15N 164°30W **74 E7**
Union Miss., U.S.A. 32°34N 89°7W **85 E10**
Union Mo., U.S.A. 38°27N 91°0W **80 F8**
Union S.C., U.S.A. 34°43N 81°37W **85 D14**
Union City Calif., U.S.A. 37°36N 122°1W **78 H4**
Union City Pa., U.S.A. 41°54N 79°51W **82 E5**
Union City Tenn., U.S.A. 36°26N 89°3W **85 C10**
Union Dale U.S.A. 41°43N 75°29W **83 E9**
Union Gap U.S.A. 46°33N 120°28W **76 C3**
Union Springs Ala., U.S.A. 32°9N 85°43W **85 E12**

Union Springs N.Y., U.S.A. 42°50N 76°41W **83 D8**
Uniondale S. Africa 33°39S 23°7E **56 D3**
Uniontown U.S.A. 39°54N 79°44W **81 F14**
Unionville U.S.A. 40°29N 93°1W **80 E7**
United Arab Emirates ■ Asia 23°50N 54°0E **47 F7**
United Kingdom ■ Europe 53°0N 2°0W **14 E6**
United States of America ■ N. Amer. 37°0N 96°0W **75 H20**
Unity Canada 52°30N 109°5W **71 C7**
University Park U.S.A. 32°17N 106°45W **77 K10**
University Place U.S.A. 47°14N 122°33W **78 C4**
Unjha India 23°46N 72°24E **42 H5**
Unnao India 26°35N 80°30E **43 F9**
Unst U.K. 60°44N 0°53W **11 A8**
Unuk → Canada 56°5N 131°3W **70 B2**
Unzen-Amakusa △ Japan 32°15N 130°10E **29 H5**
Uong Bi Vietnam 21°2N 106°47E **38 B6**
Uotsuri-Shima E. China Sea 25°45N 123°29E **29 M1**
Uozu Japan 36°48N 137°24E **29 F8**
Upata Venezuela 8°1N 62°24W **92 B6**
Upemba, L. Dem. Rep. of the Congo 8°30S 26°20E **54 F5**
Upernavik Greenland 72°49N 56°20W **4 B5**
Upington S. Africa 28°25S 21°15E **56 C3**
Upleta India 21°46N 70°16E **42 J4**
'Upolu Samoa 13°58S 172°0W **59 b**
Upper Alkali L. U.S.A. 41°47N 120°8W **76 F3**
Upper Arrow L. Canada 50°30N 117°50W **70 C5**
Upper Daly ◌ Australia 14°26S 131°3E **60 B5**
Upper Darby U.S.A. 39°55N 75°16W **81 F16**
Upper Foster L. Canada 56°47N 105°20W **71 B7**
Upper Hutt N.Z. 41°8S 175°5E **59 D5**
Upper Klamath L. U.S.A. 42°25N 121°55W **76 E3**
Upper Lake U.S.A. 39°10N 122°54W **78 F4**
Upper Liard Canada 60°3N 128°54W **70 A3**
Upper Manzanilla Trin. & Tob. 10°31N 61°4W **93 K15**
Upper Missouri Breaks ◌ U.S.A. 47°50N 109°55W **76 C9**
Upper Musquodoboit Canada 45°10N 62°58W **73 C7**
Upper Red L. U.S.A. 48°8N 94°45W **80 A6**
Upper Sandusky U.S.A. 40°50N 83°17W **81 E12**
Upper Volta = Burkina Faso ■ Africa 12°0N 1°0W **52 F5**
Uppland Sweden 59°59N 17°48E **9 G17**
Uppsala Sweden 59°53N 17°38E **9 G17**
Upshi India 33°48N 77°52E **43 C7**
Upton U.S.A. 44°6N 104°38W **76 D11**
Uqsuqtuuq = Gjoa Haven Canada 68°38N 95°53W **68 D12**
Ur Iraq 30°55N 46°25E **46 D5**
Urad Qianqi China 40°40N 108°30E **32 D5**
Urahoro Japan 42°50N 143°40E **28 C11**
Urakawa Japan 42°9N 142°47E **28 C11**
Ural = Uralskiy □ Russia 64°0N 70°0E **26 C7**
Ural = Zhayyq → Kazakhstan 47°0N 51°48E **19 E9**
Ural Australia 33°21S 146°12E **63 E4**
Ural Mts. = Uralskie Gory Eurasia 60°0N 59°0E **18 C10**
Uralla Australia 30°37S 151°29E **63 E5**
Uralsk = Oral Kazakhstan 51°20N 51°20E **19 D9**
Uralskie Gory Eurasia 60°0N 59°0E **18 C10**
Uralskiy □ Russia 64°0N 70°0E **26 C7**
Urambo Tanzania 5°4S 32°0E **54 F6**
Urandangi Australia 21°32S 138°14E **62 C2**
Uranium City Canada 59°34N 108°37W **71 B7**
Urapuntja = Utopia Australia 22°14S 134°33E **62 C1**
Uraricoera → Brazil 3°2N 60°30W **92 C6**
Urasoe Japan 26°15N 127°43E **29 L3**
Uravakonda India 14°57N 77°12E **45 G3**
Urawa = Saitama Japan 35°54N 139°38E **29 G9**
Uray Russia 60°5N 65°15E **26 C7**
Utopia Australia 22°14S 134°33E **62 C1**
'Uray'irah Si. Arabia 25°57N 48°53E **47 E6**
Urbana Ill., U.S.A. 40°7N 88°12W **80 E9**
Urbana Ohio, U.S.A. 40°7N 83°45W **81 E12**
Urbandale U.S.A. 41°38N 93°43W **80 E7**
Urbino Italy 43°43N 12°38E **22 C5**
Urbión, Picos de Spain 42°1N 2°52W **21 A4**
Urcos Peru 13°40S 71°38W **92 F4**
Urdinarrain Argentina 32°37S 58°52W **94 C4**
Ure → U.K. 54°5N 1°20W **12 C6**
Urengoy Russia 65°58N 78°22E **26 C8**
Ures Mexico 29°26N 110°24W **86 B2**
Urewera △ N.Z. 38°29S 177°7E **59 C6**
Urfa = Sanliurfa Turkey 37°12N 38°50E **46 B3**
Urganch Uzbekistan 41°40N 60°41E **26 E7**
Urgench = Urganch Uzbekistan 41°40N 60°41E **26 E7**
Ürgüp Turkey 38°38N 34°56E **46 B2**
Uri India 34°8N 74°2E **43 B6**
Uribia Colombia 11°43N 72°16W **92 A4**
Uriondo Bolivia 21°41S 64°41W **94 A3**
Urique Mexico 27°13N 107°55W **86 B3**
Urique → Mexico 26°29N 107°58W **86 B3**
Urk Neths. 52°39N 5°36E **15 B5**
Urla Turkey 38°20N 26°47E **23 E12**
Urmia = Orūmīyeh Iran 37°40N 45°0E **46 B5**
Uroševac = Ferizaj Kosovo 42°23N 21°10E **23 C9**
Uroyan, Montanas de Puerto Rico 18°12N 66°50W **89 d**
Urrampinyi Iltjiltarri ◌ Australia 24°20S 132°10E **60 D5**
Uruaçu Brazil 14°30S 49°10W **93 F9**
Uruapan Mexico 19°24N 102°3W **86 D4**
Urubamba → Peru 10°43S 73°48W **92 F4**
Urucará Brazil 2°32S 57°45W **92 D7**
Uruçuí Brazil 7°20S 44°28W **93 E10**
Uruguai → Brazil 26°0S 53°30W **95 B5**
Uruguaiana Brazil 29°50S 57°0W **94 B4**
Uruguay ■ S. Amer. 32°30S 56°30W **94 C4**

Uruguay → S. Amer. 34°12S 58°18W **94 C4**
Urumchi = Ürümqi China 43°45N 87°45E **30 C6**
Ürümqi China 43°45N 87°45E **30 C6**
Uruna ◌ Australia 24°3S 133°1E **60 D5**
Urup, Ostrov Russia 46°0N 151°0E **27 E16**
Urzhar Kazakhstan 47°5N 81°38E **26 E9**
Usa → Russia 66°16N 59°49E **18 A10**
Uşak Turkey 38°43N 29°28E **19 G4**
Usakos Namibia 21°54S 15°31E **56 B2**
Usedom Germany 53°55N 14°2E **16 B8**
Useless Loop Australia 26°8S 113°23E **61 E1**
Ushakova, Ostrov Russia 82°0N 80°0E **27 A8**
Ushant = Ouessant, Î. d' France 48°28N 5°6W **20 B1**
'Ushayrah Si. Arabia 25°35N 45°47E **46 E5**
Ushibuka Japan 32°11N 130°1E **29 H5**
Ūshtöbe Kazakhstan 45°16N 78°0E **26 E8**
Ushuaia Argentina 54°50S 68°23W **96 G3**
Ushumun Russia 52°47N 126°32E **27 D13**
Usinsk Russia 65°57N 57°27E **18 A10**
Usk Canada 54°38N 128°26W **70 C3**
Usk → U.K. 51°33N 2°58W **13 F5**
Uska India 27°12N 83°7E **43 F10**
Usman Russia 52°5N 39°48E **18 D6**
Usolye-Sibirskoye Russia 52°48N 103°40E **27 D11**
Uspallata, P. de Argentina 32°37S 69°22W **94 C2**
Ussuriysk Russia 43°48N 131°59E **28 C5**
Ussurka Russia 45°12N 133°31E **28 B6**
Ust-Chaun Russia 68°47N 170°30E **27 C18**
Ust-Ilimsk Russia 58°3N 102°39E **27 D11**
Ust-Ishim Russia 57°45N 71°10E **26 D8**
Ust-Kamchatsk Russia 56°10N 162°28E **27 D17**
Ust-Kamenogorsk = Öskemen Kazakhstan 50°0N 82°36E **26 D9**
Ust-Khayryuzovo Russia 57°15N 156°45E **27 D16**
Ust-Kut Russia 56°50N 105°42E **27 D11**
Ust-Kuyga Russia 70°1N 135°43E **27 C14**
Ust-Maya Russia 60°30N 134°28E **27 C14**
Ust-Mil Russia 59°40N 133°11E **27 D14**
Ust-Nera Russia 64°35N 143°15E **27 C15**
Ust-Nyukzha Russia 56°34N 121°37E **27 D13**
Ust-Olenek Russia 73°0N 120°5E **27 B12**
Ust-Omchug Russia 61°9N 149°38E **27 C15**
Ust-Port Russia 69°40N 84°26E **26 C9**
Ust-Tsilma Russia 65°28N 52°11E **18 A9**
Ust-Urt = Ustyurt Plateau Asia 44°0N 55°0E **26 E6**
Ust-Usa Russia 66°2N 56°57E **18 A10**
Ust-Vorkuta Russia 67°24N 64°0E **18 A11**
Ústí nad Labem Czech Rep. 50°41N 14°3E **16 C8**
Ustica Italy 38°42N 13°11E **22 E5**
Ustinov = Izhevsk Russia 56°51N 53°14E **18 C9**
Ustyurt Plateau Asia 44°0N 55°0E **26 E6**
Usu China 44°27N 84°40E **30 C5**
Usuki Japan 33°8N 131°49E **29 H5**
Usulután El Salv. 13°25N 88°28W **88 D2**
Usumacinta → Mexico 18°24N 92°38W **87 D6**
Usumbura = Bujumbura Burundi 3°16S 29°18E **54 E5**
Usutu → Mozam. 26°48S 32°7E **57 C5**
Uta Indonesia 4°33S 136°0E **37 E9**
Utah □ U.S.A. 39°20N 111°30W **76 G8**
Utah L. U.S.A. 40°12N 111°48W **76 F8**
Utara, Selat Malaysia 5°28N 100°20E **39 c**
Utarni India 26°5N 71°58E **42 F4**
Utatlan Guatemala 15°2N 91°11W **88 C1**
Ute Creek → U.S.A. 35°21N 103°50W **77 J12**
Utena Lithuania 55°27N 25°40E **9 J21**
Uthai Thani Thailand 15°22N 100°3E **38 E3**
Uthal Pakistan 25°44N 66°40E **42 G2**
Utiariti Brazil 13°0S 58°10W **92 F7**
Utica N.Y., U.S.A. 43°6N 75°14W **83 C9**
Utica Ohio, U.S.A. 40°14N 82°27W **82 F2**
Utikuma L. Canada 55°50N 115°30W **70 B5**
Utila Honduras 16°6N 86°56W **88 C2**
Utkela India 20°6N 83°10E **44 D6**
Utnur India 19°22N 78°46E **44 E4**
Utopia Australia 22°14S 134°33E **62 C1**
Utraula India 27°19N 82°25E **43 F10**
Utrecht Neths. 52°5N 5°8E **15 B5**
Utrecht S. Africa 27°38S 30°20E **57 C5**
Utrecht □ Neths. 52°6N 5°7E **15 B5**
Utrera Spain 37°12N 5°48W **21 D3**
Utsjoki → Finland 69°51N 26°59E **8 B22**
Utsunomiya Japan 36°30N 139°50E **29 F9**
Uttar Pradesh □ India 27°0N 80°0E **43 F9**
Uttaradit Thailand 17°36N 100°5E **38 D3**
Uttarakhand □ India 30°0N 79°30E **43 D8**
Utterson Canada 45°12N 79°19W **82 A5**
Uttoxeter U.K. 52°54N 1°52W **12 E6**
Utuado Puerto Rico 18°16N 66°42W **89 d**
Uummannaq Avannaarsua, Greenland 77°33N 68°52W **69 B18**
Uummannaq Kitaa, Greenland 70°58N 52°17W **4 B5**
Uummannarsuaq = Nunap Isua Greenland 59°48N 43°55W **66 D15**
Uusikaarlepyy Finland 63°32N 22°31E **8 E20**
Uusikaupunki Finland 60°47N 21°25E **8 F19**
Uva Russia 56°59N 52°13E **18 C9**
Uvalde U.S.A. 29°13N 99°47W **84 G5**
Uvat Russia 59°5N 68°50E **26 D7**
Uvinza Tanzania 5°5S 30°24E **54 F6**
Uvira Dem. Rep. of the Congo 3°22S 29°3E **54 E5**
Uvs Nuur Mongolia 50°20N 92°30E **30 A7**
'Uwairidh, Ḥarrat al Si. Arabia 26°50N 38°0E **46 E3**
Uwajima Japan 33°10N 132°35E **29 H6**
Uweinat, Jebel Sudan 21°54N 24°58E **53 D10**
Uxbridge Canada 44°6N 79°7W **82 B5**
Uxin Qi China 38°50N 109°5E **32 E5**
Uxmal Mexico 20°22N 89°46W **87 C7**
Üydzin Mongolia 44°9N 107°0E **32 B4**
Uyo Nigeria 5°1N 7°53E **52 G7**
Uyûn Mûsa Egypt 29°53N 32°40E **48 F1**
Uyuni Bolivia 20°28S 66°47W **92 H5**
Uzbekistan ■ Asia 41°30N 65°0E **26 E7**

Uzboy → Turkmenistan 39°30N 55°0E **47 B7**
Uzen, Mal → Kazakhstan 49°4N 49°44E **19 E8**
Uzerche France 45°25N 1°34E **20 D4**
Uzh → Ukraine 51°15N 30°12E **17 C16**
Uzhgorod = Uzhhorod Ukraine 48°36N 22°18E **17 D12**
Uzhhorod Ukraine 48°36N 22°18E **17 D12**
Užice Serbia 43°55N 19°50E **23 C8**
Uzunköprü Turkey 41°16N 26°43E **23 D12**

V

Vaal → S. Africa 29°4S 23°38E **56 D3**
Vaal Dam S. Africa 27°0S 28°14E **57 C4**
Vaalwater S. Africa 24°15S 28°8E **57 B4**
Vaasa Finland 63°6N 21°38E **8 E19**
Vác Hungary 47°49N 19°10E **17 E10**
Vacaria Brazil 28°31S 50°52W **95 B5**
Vacaville U.S.A. 38°21N 121°59W **78 G5**
Vach = Vakh → Russia 60°45N 76°45E **26 C8**
Vache, Î. à Haiti 18°2N 73°35W **89 C5**
Vacoas Mauritius 20°18S 57°29E **55 d**
Vada India 19°39N 73°8E **44 E1**
Vadakara India 11°35N 75°40E **45 J2**
Vadnagar India 23°47N 72°40E **42 H5**
Vadodara India 22°20N 73°10E **42 H5**
Vadsø Norway 70°3N 29°50E **8 A23**
Vaduj India 17°36N 74°27E **44 F2**
Vaduz Liech. 47°8N 9°31E **20 C8**
Værøy Norway 67°40N 12°40E **8 C15**
Vágar Færoe Is. 62°5N 7°15W **8 E9**
Vágsfjorden Norway 68°50N 16°50E **8 B17**
Váh → Slovak Rep. 47°43N 18°7E **17 D9**
Vahsel B. Antarctica 75°0S 35°0W **5 D1**
Vähtjer = Gällivare Sweden 67°9N 20°40E **8 C19**
Vaigai → India 9°15N 79°10E **45 K4**
Vaihiria, L. Tahiti 17°40S 149°25W **59 d**
Vaijapur India 19°58N 74°45E **44 E2**
Vaikam India 9°45N 76°25E **45 K3**
Vail U.S.A. 39°40N 106°20W **76 G10**
Vaippar → India 9°0N 78°25E **45 K4**
Vairao Tahiti 17°47S 149°17W **59 d**
Vaisali → India 26°28N 78°53E **43 F8**
Vaitogi Amer. Samoa 14°24S 170°44W **59 b**
Vajpur India 21°24N 73°17E **44 D1**
Vakarai Sri Lanka 8°8N 81°26E **45 K5**
Vakh → Russia 60°45N 76°45E **26 C8**
Val-d'Or Canada 48°7N 77°47W **72 C4**
Val Marie Canada 49°15N 107°45W **71 D7**
Valaam Russia 61°22N 30°57E **8 F24**
Valahia Romania 44°35N 25°0E **17 F13**
Valaichenai Sri Lanka 7°54N 81°32E **45 L5**
Valandovo Macedonia 41°19N 22°34E **23 D10**
Valatie U.S.A. 42°24N 73°40W **83 D11**
Valcheta Argentina 40°40S 66°8W **96 E3**
Valdai Hills = Valdayskaya Vozvyshennost Russia 57°0N 33°30E **18 C5**
Valdayskaya Vozvyshennost Russia 57°0N 33°30E **18 C5**
Valdepeñas Spain 38°43N 3°25W **21 C4**
Valdés, Pen. Argentina 42°30S 63°45W **96 E4**
Valdez U.S.A. 61°7N 146°16W **68 E2**
Valdivia Chile 39°50S 73°14W **96 D2**
Valdivia Abyssal Plain S. Ocean 62°30S 70°0E **5 C6**
Valdosta U.S.A. 30°50N 83°17W **85 F13**
Valdres Norway 61°5N 9°5E **8 F13**
Vale U.S.A. 43°59N 117°15W **76 E5**
Vale of Glamorgan □ U.K. 51°28N 3°25W **13 F4**
Valemount Canada 52°50N 119°15W **70 C5**
Valença Brazil 13°20S 39°5W **93 F11**
Valença do Piauí Brazil 6°20S 41°45W **93 E10**
Valence France 44°57N 4°54E **20 D6**
Valencia Spain 39°27N 0°23W **21 C5**
Valencia Trin. & Tob. 10°39N 61°11W **93 K15**
Valencia U.S.A. 34°48N 106°43W **77 J10**
Valencia Venezuela 10°11N 68°0W **92 A5**
Valencia □ Spain 39°20N 0°40W **21 C5**
Valencia, G. de Spain 39°30N 0°20E **21 C6**
Valencia de Alcántara Spain 39°25N 7°14W **21 C2**
Valencia I. Ireland 51°54N 10°22W **10 E1**
Valenciennes France 50°20N 3°34E **20 A5**
Valentim, Sa. do Brazil 6°0S 43°30W **93 E10**
Valentin Russia 43°8N 134°17E **28 C7**
Valentine Nebr., U.S.A. 42°52N 100°33W **80 D3**
Valentine Tex., U.S.A. 30°35N 104°30W **84 F2**
Valera Venezuela 9°19N 70°37W **92 B4**
Valga Estonia 57°47N 26°2E **9 H22**
Valier U.S.A. 48°18N 112°16W **76 B7**
Valjevo Serbia 44°18N 19°53E **23 B8**
Valka Latvia 57°46N 26°3E **9 H22**
Valkeakoski Finland 61°16N 24°2E **8 F21**
Valkenswaard Neths. 51°21N 5°29E **15 C5**
Vall de Uxó = La Vall d'Uixó Spain 39°49N 0°15W **21 C5**
Valladolid Mexico 20°41N 88°12W **87 C7**
Valladolid Spain 41°38N 4°43W **21 B3**
Valle de la Pascua Venezuela 9°13N 66°0W **92 B5**
Valle de las Palmas Mexico 32°20N 116°43W **79 N10**
Valle de Santiago Mexico 20°23N 101°12W **86 C4**
Valle de Zaragoza Mexico 27°25N 105°50W **86 B3**
Valle Fértil, Sierra del Argentina 30°20S 68°0W **94 C2**
Valle Hermoso Mexico 25°35N 97°40W **87 B5**
Valle Nacional Mexico 17°47N 96°18W **87 D5**
Valledupar Colombia 10°29N 73°15W **92 A4**
Vallejo U.S.A. 38°7N 122°14W **78 G4**
Vallenar Chile 28°30S 70°50W **94 B1**
Valletta Malta 35°54N 14°31E **22 G6**
Valley Center U.S.A. 33°13N 117°2W **79 M9**
Valley City U.S.A. 46°55N 98°0W **80 B5**

Valley Falls *Oreg., U.S.A.* 42°29N 120°17W **76** E3
Valley Falls *R.I., U.S.A.* 41°54N 71°24W **83** E13
Valley of Flowers △ *India* 30°50N 79°40E **43** D8
Valley Springs *U.S.A.* 38°12N 120°50W **78** G6
Valley View *U.S.A.* 40°39N 76°33W **83** F8
Valley Wells *U.S.A.* 35°27N 115°46W **79** K11
Valleyview *Canada* 55°5N 117°17W **70** B5
Vallimanca, Arroyo
  Argentina 35°40S 59°10W **94** D4
Valls *Spain* 41°18N 1°15E **21** B6
Valmiera *Latvia* 57°37N 25°29E **9** H21
Valognes *France* 49°30N 1°28W **20** B3
Valona = Vlorë *Albania* 40°32N 19°28E **23** D8
Valozhyn *Belarus* 54°3N 26°30E **17** A14
Valparai *India* 10°22N 76°58E **45** J3
Valparaíso *Chile* 33°2S 71°40W **94** C1
Valparaíso *Mexico* 22°46N 103°34W **86** C4
Valparaiso *U.S.A.* 41°28N 87°4W **80** E10
Valparaíso □ *Chile* 33°2S 71°40W **94** C1
Valpoy *India* 15°32N 74°8E **45** G2
Vals → *S. Africa* 27°23S 26°30E **56** C4
Vals, Tanjung *Indonesia* 8°26S 137°25E **37** F9
Valsad *India* 20°40N 72°58E **44** D1
Valverde del Camino
  Spain 37°35N 6°47W **21** D2
Vambori *India* 19°17N 74°44E **44** E2
Vammala = Sastamala
  Finland 61°20N 22°54E **8** F20
Vamsadhara → *India* 18°21N 84°8E **44** E7
Van *Turkey* 38°30N 43°20E **46** B4
Van, L. = Van Gölü *Turkey* 38°30N 43°0E **46** B4
Van Alstyne *U.S.A.* 33°25N 96°35W **84** E6
Van Blommestein Meer
  Suriname 4°45N 55°5W **93** C7
Van Buren *Canada* 47°10N 67°55W **73** C6
Van Buren *Ark., U.S.A.* 35°26N 94°21W **84** D7
Van Buren *Maine,*
  U.S.A. 47°10N 67°58W **81** B20
Van Buren *Mo., U.S.A.* 37°0N 91°1W **80** G8
Van Canh *Vietnam* 13°37N 109°0E **38** F7
Van Diemen, C. *N. Terr.,*
  Australia 11°9S 130°24E **60** B5
Van Diemen, C. *Queens.,*
  Australia 16°30S 139°46E **62** B2
Van Diemen G. *Australia* 11°45S 132°0E **60** B5
Van Gölü *Turkey* 38°30N 43°0E **46** B4
Van Horn *U.S.A.* 31°3N 104°50W **84** F2
Van Ninh *Vietnam* 12°42N 109°14E **38** F7
Van Rees, Pegunungan
  Indonesia 2°35S 138°15E **37** E9
Van Tivu *India* 8°51N 78°15E **45** K4
Van Wert *U.S.A.* 40°52N 84°35W **81** E11
Van Yen *Vietnam* 21°4N 104°42E **34** G5
Van Zylsrus *S. Africa* 26°52S 22°4E **56** C3
Vanadzor *Armenia* 40°48N 44°30E **19** F7
Vanavara *Russia* 60°22N 102°16E **27** C11
Vancouver *Canada* 49°15N 123°7W **78** A3
Vancouver *U.S.A.* 45°38N 122°40W **78** E4
Vancouver, C. *Australia* 35°2S 118°11E **61** G2
Vancouver I. *Canada* 49°50N 126°0W **78** B2
Vancouver Int. ✈ (YVR)
  Canada 49°10N 123°10W **78** A3
Vandalia *Ill., U.S.A.* 38°58N 89°6W **80** F9
Vandalia *Mo., U.S.A.* 39°19N 91°29W **80** F8
Vandavasi *India* 12°30N 79°30E **45** H4
Vandeloos B. *Sri Lanka* 8°0N 81°45E **45** L5
Vandenberg Village
  U.S.A. 34°43N 120°28W **79** L6
Vandergrift *U.S.A.* 40°36N 79°34W **82** F5
Vanderhoof *Canada* 54°0N 124°0W **70** C4
Vanderkloof Dam *S. Africa* 30°4S 24°40E **56** D3
Vanderlin I. *Australia* 15°44S 137°2E **62** B2
Vänern *Sweden* 58°47N 13°30E **9** G15
Vänersborg *Sweden* 58°26N 12°19E **9** G15
Vang Vieng *Laos* 18°58N 102°32E **38** C4
Vangaindrano *Madag.* 23°21S 47°36E **55** J9
Vanguard *Canada* 49°55N 107°20W **71** D7
Vanino *Russia* 48°50N 140°5E **27** E15
Vanivilasa Sagara *India* 13°45N 76°30E **45** H3
Vaniyambadi *India* 12°46N 78°44E **45** H4
Vankleek Hill *Canada* 45°32N 74°40W **83** A10
Vännäs *Sweden* 63°58N 19°48E **8** E18
Vannes *France* 47°40N 2°47W **20** C2
Vannøya *Norway* 70°6N 19°50E **8** A18
Vanrhynsdorp *S. Africa* 31°36S 18°44E **56** D2
Vansada *India* 20°47N 73°25E **44** D1
Vansbro *Sweden* 60°32N 14°15E **9** F16
Vansittart B. *Australia* 14°3S 126°17E **60** B4
Vansittart I. *Canada* 65°50N 84°0W **69** D15
Vanua Balavu *Fiji* 17°12S 178°55W **59** a
Vanua Levu *Fiji* 16°33S 179°15E **59** a
Vanua Vara *Fiji* 18°22S 179°15W **59** a
Vanuatu ■ *Pac. Oc.* 15°0S 168°0E **58** C9
Vanwyksvlei *S. Africa* 30°18S 21°49E **56** D3
Vapi *India* 20°22N 72°54E **44** D1
Vapnyarka *Ukraine* 48°32N 28°45E **17** D15
Var → *France* 43°39N 7°12E **20** E7
Varada → *India* 15°0N 75°40E **45** G2
Varāmīn *Iran* 35°20N 51°39E **47** C6
Varāmīn □ *Iran* 35°18N 51°35E **47** B6
Varanasi *India* 25°22N 83°0E **43** G10
Varangerfjorden *Norway* 70°3N 29°25E **8** A23
Varangerhalvøya
  Norway 70°25N 29°30E **8** A23
Varaždin *Croatia* 46°20N 16°20E **16** E9
Varberg *Sweden* 57°6N 12°20E **9** H15
Vardak □ *Afghan.* 34°0N 68°0E **40** B6
Vardar = Axios →
  Greece 40°57N 22°35E **23** D10
Varde *Denmark* 55°38N 8°29E **9** J13
Vardø *Norway* 70°23N 31°5E **8** A24
Varella, Mui = Nay, Mui
  Vietnam 12°54N 109°26E **38** F7
Varèna *Lithuania* 54°12N 24°30E **9** J21
Varese *Italy* 45°48N 8°50E **20** D8
Varginha *Brazil* 21°33S 45°25W **95** A6
Varillas *Chile* 24°0S 70°10W **94** A1
Varkaus *Finland* 62°19N 27°50E **8** E22
Varna *Bulgaria* 43°13N 27°56E **23** C12

Varna → *India* 16°48N 74°32E **44** F2
Värnamo *Sweden* 57°10N 14°3E **9** H16
Várnjárga = Varangerhalvøya
  Norway 70°25N 29°30E **8** A23
Vars *Canada* 45°21N 75°21W **83** A9
Varysburg *U.S.A.* 42°46N 78°19W **82** D6
Varzaneh *Iran* 32°25N 52°40E **47** C7
Vasa = Vaasa *Finland* 63°6N 21°38E **8** E19
Vasa Barris → *Brazil* 11°10S 37°10W **93** F11
Vasai-Virar *India* 19°28N 72°48E **44** E1
Vascongadas = País Vasco □
  Spain 42°50N 2°45W **21** A4
Vasht = Khāsh *Iran* 28°15N 61°15E **47** D9
Vasilevichi *Belarus* 52°15N 29°50E **17** B16
Vasilkov = Vasylkiv
  Ukraine 50°7N 30°15E **17** C16
Vaslui *Romania* 46°38N 27°42E **17** E14
Vassar *Canada* 49°10N 95°55W **71** D9
Vassar *U.S.A.* 43°22N 83°35W **81** D12
Västerås *Sweden* 59°37N 16°38E **9** G17
Västerbotten *Sweden* 64°36N 20°4E **8** D19
Västerdalälven → *Sweden* 60°30N 15°7E **8** F16
Västervik *Sweden* 57°43N 16°33E **9** H17
Västmanland *Sweden* 59°45N 16°20E **9** G17
Vat Phou *Laos* 14°51N 105°49E **38** E5
Vatersay *U.K.* 56°55N 7°32W **11** E1
Vatiu = Atiu *Cook Is.* 20°0S 158°10W **65** J12
Vatnajökull *Iceland* 64°30N 16°48W **8** D5
Vatra-Dornei *Romania* 47°22N 25°22E **17** E13
Vatrak → *India* 23°9N 73°2E **42** H5
Vatu Vara *Fiji* 17°26S 179°31W **59** a
Vatulele *Fiji* 18°33S 177°37E **59** a
Vaudreuil-Dorion
  Canada 45°23N 74°3W **83** A10
Vaughn *Mont., U.S.A.* 47°33N 111°33W **76** C8
Vaughn *N. Mex.,*
  U.S.A. 34°36N 105°13W **77** J11
Vaujours L. *Canada* 55°27N 74°15W **72** A5
Vaupés = Uaupés →
  Brazil 0°2N 67°16W **92** C5
Vaupés □ *Colombia* 1°0N 71°0W **92** C4
Vauxhall *Canada* 50°5N 112°9W **70** C6
Vav *India* 24°22N 71°31E **42** G4
Vava'u *Tonga* 18°36S 174°0W **59** c
Vava'u Group *Tonga* 18°40S 174°0W **59** c
Vavuniya *Sri Lanka* 8°45N 80°30E **45** K5
Vawkavysk *Belarus* 53°9N 24°30E **17** B13
Vaxjö *Sweden* 56°52N 14°50E **9** H16
Vaygach, Ostrov *Russia* 70°0N 60°0E **26** C7
Veaikevárri = Svappavaara
  Sweden 67°40N 21°3E **8** C19
Vechte → *Neths.* 52°34N 6°6E **15** B6
Vedaranniyam *India* 10°25N 79°50E **45** J4
Vedea → *Romania* 43°42N 25°41E **17** G13
Vedia *Argentina* 34°30S 61°31W **94** C3
Veendam *Neths.* 53°5N 6°52E **15** A6
Veenendaal *Neths.* 52°2N 5°34E **15** B5
Vefsna → *Norway* 65°48N 13°10E **8** D15
Vega *Norway* 65°40N 11°55E **8** D14
Vega *U.S.A.* 35°15N 102°26W **84** D3
Vega Baja *Puerto Rico* 18°27N 66°23W **89** d
Vegreville *Canada* 53°30N 112°5W **70** C6
Vejer de la Frontera *Spain* 36°15N 5°59W **21** D3
Vejle *Denmark* 55°43N 9°30E **9** J13
Velachha *India* 21°26N 73°1E **44** D1
Velas, C. *Costa Rica* 10°21N 85°52W **88** D2
Velasco, Sierra de
  Argentina 29°20S 67°10W **94** B2
Velddrif *S. Africa* 32°42S 18°11E **56** D2
Velebit Planina *Croatia* 44°50N 15°20E **16** F8
Veles *Macedonia* 41°46N 21°47E **23** D9
Vélez-Málaga *Spain* 36°48N 4°5W **21** D3
Vélez Rubio *Spain* 37°41N 2°5W **21** D4
Velhas → *Brazil* 17°13S 44°49W **93** G10
Velika Kapela *Croatia* 45°10N 15°5E **16** F8
Velikaya → *Russia* 57°48N 28°10E **18** C4
Velikaya Kema *Russia* 45°30N 137°12E **28** B8
Veliki Ustyug *Russia* 60°47N 46°20E **18** B8
Velikiy Novgorod *Russia* 58°30N 31°25E **18** C5
Velikiye Luki *Russia* 56°25N 30°32E **18** C5
Veliko Tŭrnovo *Bulgaria* 43°5N 25°41E **23** C11
Velikonda Range *India* 14°45N 79°10E **45** G4
Vellar → *India* 11°30N 79°36E **45** J4
Velletri *Italy* 41°41N 12°47E **22** D5
Vellore *India* 12°57N 79°10E **45** H4
Velsk *Russia* 61°10N 42°5E **18** B7
Veluwezoom △ *Neths.* 52°5N 6°0E **15** B6
Velva *U.S.A.* 48°4N 100°56W **80** A3
Vembanad L. *India* 9°36N 76°15E **45** K3
Venado *Mexico* 22°56N 101°6W **86** C4
Venado Tuerto *Argentina* 33°50S 62°0W **94** C3
Vendée □ *France* 46°50N 1°35W **20** C3
Vendôme *France* 47°47N 1°3E **20** C4
Venézia *Italy* 45°27N 12°21E **22** B5
Venézia, G. di *Italy* 45°15N 13°0E **22** B5
Venezuela ■ *S. Amer.* 8°0N 66°0W **92** B5
Venezuela, G. de
  Venezuela 11°30N 71°0W **92** A4
Vengurla *India* 15°53N 73°45E **45** G1
Vengurla Rocks *India* 15°55N 73°22E **45** G1
Venice = Venézia *Italy* 45°27N 12°21E **22** B5
Venice *U.S.A.* 27°6N 82°27W **85** H13
Venkatagiri *India* 14°0N 79°35E **45** G4
Venkatapuram *India* 18°20N 80°30E **44** E5
Venlo *Neths.* 51°22N 6°11E **15** C6
Vennachar Junction
  Canada 45°5N 77°14W **82** A7
Vennesla *Norway* 58°15N 7°59E **9** G12
Venray *Neths.* 51°31N 6°0E **15** C6
Ventana, Sa. de la
  Argentina 38°0S 62°30W **94** D3
Ventersburg *S. Africa* 28°7S 27°9E **56** C4
Venterstad *S. Africa* 30°47S 25°48E **56** D4
Ventnor *U.K.* 50°36N 1°12W **13** G6

Ventotène *Italy* 40°47N 13°25E **22** D5
Ventoux, Mt. *France* 44°10N 5°17E **20** D6
Ventspils *Latvia* 57°25N 21°32E **9** H19
Ventuarí → *Venezuela* 3°58N 67°2W **92** C5
Ventucopa *U.S.A.* 34°50N 119°29W **79** L7
Ventura *U.S.A.* 34°17N 119°18W **79** L7
Vénus, Pte. *Tahiti* 17°29S 149°29W **59** d
Venus B. *Australia* 38°40S 145°42E **63** F4
Venustiano Carranza
  Mexico 30°25N 115°53W **86** A1
Venustiano Carranza, Presa
  Mexico 27°30N 100°37W **86** B4
Vera *Argentina* 29°30S 60°20W **94** B3
Vera *Spain* 37°15N 1°51W **21** D5
Veracruz *Mexico* 19°11N 96°8W **87** D5
Veracruz □ *Mexico* 19°0N 96°15W **87** D5
Veraval *India* 20°53N 70°27E **42** J4
Verbánia *Italy* 45°56N 8°33E **20** D8
Vercelli *Italy* 45°19N 8°25E **20** D8
Verdalsøra *Norway* 63°48N 11°30E **8** E14
Verde → *Argentina* 41°56S 65°5W **96** E3
Verde → *Goiás, Brazil* 18°1S 50°14W **93** G8
Verde → *Mato Grosso do Sul,*
  Brazil 21°25S 52°20W **93** H8
Verde → *Chihuahua,*
  Mexico 26°29N 107°11W **86** B3
Verde → *Jalisco, Mexico* 20°42N 103°14W **86** C4
Verde → *Oaxaca, Mexico* 15°59N 97°50W **87** D5
Verde → *Paraguay* 23°9S 57°37W **94** A4
Verde → *U.S.A.* 33°33N 111°40W **77** K8
Verde, Cay *Bahamas* 23°0N 75°5W **88** B4
Verden *Germany* 52°55N 9°14E **16** B5
Verdi *U.S.A.* 39°31N 119°59W **78** F7
Verdun *France* 49°9N 5°24E **20** B6
Vereeniging *S. Africa* 26°38S 27°57E **57** C4
Verga, C. *Guinea* 10°30N 14°10W **52** F3
Vergara *Uruguay* 32°56S 53°57W **95** C5
Vergemont Cr. →
  Australia 24°16S 143°16E **62** C3
Vergennes *U.S.A.* 44°10N 73°15W **83** B11
Veria *Greece* 40°34N 22°12E **23** D10
Verín *Spain* 41°57N 7°27W **21** B2
Verkhnetulomskoye Vdkhr.
  Russia 68°36N 31°12E **8** B24
Verkhnevilyuysk
  Russia 63°27N 120°18E **27** C13
Verkhniy Baskunchak
  Russia 48°14N 46°44E **19** E8
Verkhoyansk *Russia* 67°35N 133°25E **27** C14
Verkhoyansk Ra. =
  Verkhoyanskiy Khrebet
  Russia 66°0N 129°0E **27** C13
Verkhoyanskiy Khrebet
  Russia 66°0N 129°0E **27** C13
Vermilion *Canada* 53°20N 110°50W **70** C6
Vermilion *U.S.A.* 41°25N 82°22W **82** E2
Vermilion → *Canada* 53°22N 110°51W **71** C6
Vermilion B. *U.S.A.* 29°42N 92°0W **84** G9
Vermilion Bay *Canada* 49°51N 93°34W **71** D10
Vermilion L. *U.S.A.* 47°53N 92°26W **80** B7
Vermillion *U.S.A.* 42°47N 96°56W **80** D5
Vermillion → *Canada* 47°38N 72°56W **72** C5
Vermont □ *U.S.A.* 44°0N 73°0W **83** C12
Vernadsky *Antarctica* 65°0S 64°0W **5** C17
Vernal *U.S.A.* 40°27N 109°32W **76** F9
Vernalis *U.S.A.* 37°36N 121°17W **78** H5
Verner *Canada* 46°25N 80°8W **72** C3
Verneukpan *S. Africa* 30°0S 21°0E **56** E3
Vernon *Canada* 50°20N 119°15W **70** C5
Vernon *U.S.A.* 34°9N 99°17W **84** D5
Vernonia *U.S.A.* 45°52N 123°11W **78** E3
Vero Beach *U.S.A.* 27°38N 80°24W **85** H14
Véroia = Veria *Greece* 40°34N 22°12E **23** D10
Verona *Canada* 44°29N 76°42W **83** B8
Verona *Italy* 45°27N 10°59E **22** B4
Vert, C. *Senegal* 14°45N 17°30W **52** F2
Verulam *S. Africa* 29°38S 31°2E **57** C5
Verviers *Belgium* 50°37N 5°52E **15** D5
Veselovskoye Vdkhr.
  Russia 46°58N 41°25E **19** E7
Vesoul *France* 47°40N 6°11E **20** C7
Vesterålen *Norway* 68°45N 15°0E **8** B16
Vestfjorden *Norway* 67°55N 14°0E **8** C16
Vestmannaeyjar *Iceland* 63°27N 20°15W **8** E3
Vestvågøya *Norway* 68°18N 13°50E **8** B15
Vesuvio *Italy* 40°49N 14°26E **22** D6
Vesuvius, Mt. = Vesuvio
  Italy 40°49N 14°26E **22** D6
Veszprém *Hungary* 47°8N 17°57E **17** E9
Vetapalem *India* 15°47N 80°18E **45** G5
Vetlanda *Sweden* 57°24N 15°3E **9** H16
Vetlugu → *Russia* 56°36N 46°4E **18** C8
Vettore, Mte. *Italy* 42°49N 13°16E **22** C5
Veurne *Belgium* 51°5N 2°40E **15** C2
Veys *Iran* 31°30N 49°0E **47** D6
Vezhen *Bulgaria* 42°50N 24°20E **23** C11
Vi Thanh *Vietnam* 9°42N 105°26E **39** H5
Viacha *Bolivia* 16°39S 68°18W **92** G5
Viamão *Brazil* 30°5S 51°0W **95** C5
Viana *Brazil* 3°13S 45°0W **93** D10
Viana do Alentejo
  Portugal 38°17N 7°59W **21** C2
Viana do Castelo *Portugal* 41°42N 8°50W **21** B1
Vianden *Lux.* 49°56N 6°12E **15** E6
Viangchan = Vientiane
  Laos 17°58N 102°36E **38** D4
Vianópolis *Brazil* 16°40S 48°35W **93** G9
Viaréggio *Italy* 43°52N 10°14E **22** C4
Vibo Valéntia *Italy* 38°40N 16°6E **22** E7
Viborg *Denmark* 56°27N 9°23E **9** H13
Vic *Spain* 41°58N 2°19E **21** B7
Vicenza *Italy* 45°33N 11°33E **22** B4
Vich = Vic *Spain* 41°58N 2°19E **21** B7
Vichada → *Colombia* 4°55N 67°50W **92** C5
Vichy *France* 46°9N 3°26E **20** C5
Vicksburg *Ariz.,*
  U.S.A. 33°45N 113°45W **79** M13
Vicksburg *Miss., U.S.A.* 32°21N 90°53W **85** E9
Victor *India* 21°0N 71°30E **42** J4

Victor Harbor *Australia* 35°30S 138°37E **63** F2
Victoria *Argentina* 32°40S 60°10W **94** C3
Victoria *Canada* 48°30N 123°25W **78** B3
Victoria *Chile* 38°13S 72°20W **96** D2
Victoria *Kans., U.S.A.* 38°52N 99°9W **80** F4
Victoria *Tex., U.S.A.* 28°48N 97°0W **84** G6
Victoria *Seychelles* 4°38S 55°28E **55** b
Victoria □ *Australia* 37°0S 144°0E **63** F3
Victoria → *Australia* 15°10S 129°40E **60** C4
Victoria, Grand L.
  Canada 47°31N 77°30W **72** C4
Victoria, L. *Africa* 1°0S 33°0E **54** E6
Victoria, L. *Australia* 33°57S 141°15E **63** E3
Victoria, Mt. *Burma* 21°14N 93°55E **41** J18
Victoria Beach *Canada* 50°40N 96°35W **71** C9
Victoria de Durango = Durango
  Mexico 24°3N 104°39W **86** C4
Victoria de las Tunas = Las Tunas
  Cuba 20°58N 76°59W **88** B4
Victoria Falls *Zimbabwe* 17°58S 25°52E **55** H5
Victoria Harbour *Canada* 44°45N 79°45W **82** B5
Victoria I. *Canada* 71°0N 111°0W **68** D8
Victoria L. *Canada* 48°20N 57°27W **73** C8
Victoria Ld. *Antarctica* 75°0S 160°0E **5** D11
Victoria Pk. *Belize* 16°48N 88°37W **87** D7
Victoria River *Australia* 16°25S 131°0E **60** C5
Victoria Str. *Canada* 69°31N 100°30W **68** D11
Victoria West *S. Africa* 31°25S 23°4E **56** D3
Victoriaville *Canada* 46°4N 71°56W **73** C5
Victorica *Argentina* 36°20S 65°30W **94** D2
Victorville *U.S.A.* 34°32N 117°18W **79** L9
Vicuña *Chile* 30°0S 70°50W **94** C1
Vicuña Mackenna
  Argentina 33°53S 64°25W **94** C3
Vidal *U.S.A.* 34°7N 114°31W **79** L12
Vidalia *U.S.A.* 32°13N 82°25W **85** E13
Viddolatno = Vindelälven →
  Sweden 63°55N 19°50E **8** E18
Vidin *Bulgaria* 43°59N 22°50E **23** C10
Vidisha *India* 23°28N 77°53E **42** H7
Vidzy *Belarus* 55°23N 26°37E **9** J22
Viedma *Argentina* 40°50S 63°0W **96** E4
Viedma, L. *Argentina* 49°30S 72°30W **96** F2
Vielsalm *Belgium* 50°17N 5°54E **15** D5
Vieng Pou Kha *Laos* 20°41N 101°4E **34** G3
Vienna = Wien *Austria* 48°12N 16°22E **16** D9
Vienna *Canada* 42°41N 80°48W **82** D4
Vienna *Ill., U.S.A.* 37°25N 88°54W **80** G9
Vienna *Mo., U.S.A.* 38°11N 91°57W **80** F8
Vienne *France* 45°31N 4°53E **20** D6
Vienne → *France* 47°13N 0°5E **20** C4
Vientiane *Laos* 17°58N 102°36E **38** D4
Vientos, Paso de los
  Caribbean 20°0N 74°0W **89** C5
Vieques *Puerto Rico* 18°8N 65°25W **89** d
Vierge Pt. *St. Lucia* 13°49N 60°53W **89** f
Vierzon *France* 47°13N 2°5E **20** C5
Viet Quang *Vietnam* 22°30N 104°48E **34** F5
Viet Tri *Vietnam* 21°18N 105°25E **38** B5
Vietnam ■ *Asia* 19°0N 106°0E **38** C6
Vieux Fort *St. Lucia* 13°46N 60°58W **89** f
Vigan *Phil.* 17°35N 120°28E **37** A6
Vigévano *Italy* 45°19N 8°51E **20** D8
Vigia *Brazil* 0°50S 48°5W **93** D9
Vigo *Spain* 42°12N 8°41W **21** A1
Vihowa *Pakistan* 31°8N 70°30E **42** D4
Vihowa → *Pakistan* 31°8N 70°41E **42** D4
Vijayadurg *India* 16°30N 73°25E **44** F1
Vijayawada *India* 16°31N 80°39E **45** F5
Vijosë → *Albania* 40°37N 19°24E **23** D8
Vik *Iceland* 63°25N 19°1W **8** E4
Vikarabad *India* 17°20N 77°54E **44** E3
Vikeke = Viqueque
  E. Timor 8°52S 126°23E **37** F7
Viking *Canada* 53°7N 111°50W **70** C6
Vikna *Norway* 64°55N 10°58E **8** D14
Vila da Ribeira Brava
  C. Verde Is. 16°32N 24°25W **52** b
Vila do Bispo *Portugal* 37°5N 8°53W **21** D1
Vila Franca de Xira
  Portugal 38°57N 8°59W **21** C1
Vila Gomes da Costa
  Mozam. 24°20S 33°37E **57** B5
Vila Nova de Gaia *Portugal* 41°8N 8°37W **21** B1
Vila Real *Portugal* 41°17N 7°48W **21** B2
Vila-Real *Spain* 39°55N 0°3W **21** C5
Vila Real de Santo António
  Portugal 37°10N 7°28W **21** D2
Vila Velha *Brazil* 20°20S 40°17W **95** A7
Vilagarcía de Arousa
  Spain 42°34N 8°46W **21** A1
Vilaine → *France* 47°30N 2°27W **20** C2
Vilanandro, Tanjona
  Madag. 16°11S 44°27E **55** H8
Vilanculos *Mozam.* 22°1S 35°17E **57** B6
Vilanova i la Geltrú *Spain* 41°13N 1°40E **21** B6
Vilcheka, Ostrov *Russia* 80°0N 58°31E **26** B6
Vilcheka, Zemlya *Russia* 80°30N 60°30E **4** A11
Vileyka *Belarus* 54°30N 26°53E **17** A14
Vilhelmina *Sweden* 64°35N 16°39E **8** D17
Vilhena *Brazil* 12°40S 60°5W **92** F6
Viliya = Neris → *Lithuania* 55°8N 24°16E **9** J21
Viljandi *Estonia* 58°28N 25°30E **9** G21
Vilkitskogo, Proliv
  Russia 78°0N 103°0E **27** B11
Vilkovo = Vylkove
  Ukraine 45°28N 29°32E **17** F15
Villa Abecia *Bolivia* 21°0S 68°18W **94** A2
Villa Ana *Argentina* 28°28S 59°40W **94** B4
Villa Ángela *Argentina* 27°34S 60°45W **94** B3
Villa Bella *Bolivia* 10°25S 65°22W **92** F5
Villa Cañás *Argentina* 34°0S 61°35W **94** C3
Villa Constitución
  Argentina 33°15S 60°20W **94** C3
Villa de Arriaga *Mexico* 21°56N 101°20W **86** C4
Villa de María *Argentina* 29°55S 63°43W **94** B3
Villa de Méndez *Mexico* 25°7N 98°34W **87** C5
Villa Dolores *Argentina* 31°58S 65°15W **94** C2
Villa Gesell *Argentina* 37°15S 56°55W **94** D4

Villa Guillermina
  Argentina 28°15S 59°29W **94** B4
Villa Hayes *Paraguay* 25°5S 57°20W **94** B4
Villa Hidalgo *Mexico* 24°15N 99°26W **87** C5
Villa Iris *Argentina* 38°12S 63°12W **94** D3
Villa María *Argentina* 32°20S 63°10W **94** C3
Villa Mazán *Argentina* 28°40S 66°30W **94** B2
Villa Montes *Bolivia* 21°10S 63°30W **94** A3
Villa Ocampo *Argentina* 28°30S 59°20W **94** B4
Villa Ocampo *Mexico* 26°27N 105°31W **86** B3
Villa Ojo de Agua
  Argentina 29°30S 63°44W **94** B3
Villa San Martín
  Argentina 28°15S 64°9W **94** B3
Villa Unión *Mexico* 23°12N 106°14W **86** C3
Villacarrillo *Spain* 38°7N 3°3W **21** C4
Villach *Austria* 46°37N 13°51E **16** E7
Villagrán *Mexico* 24°29N 99°29W **87** C5
Villaguay *Argentina* 32°0S 59°0W **94** C4
Villahermosa *Mexico* 17°59N 92°55W **87** D6
Villajoyosa *Spain* 38°30N 0°12W **21** C5
Villalba *Spain* 43°26N 7°40W **21** A2
Villanueva *U.S.A.* 35°16N 105°22W **77** J11
Villanueva de la Serena
  Spain 38°59N 5°50W **21** C3
Villanueva y Geltrú = Vilanova i la
  Geltrú *Spain* 41°13N 1°40E **21** B6
Villarreal = Vila-Real
  Spain 39°55N 0°3W **21** C5
Villarrica *Chile* 39°15S 72°15W **96** D2
Villarrica *Paraguay* 25°40S 56°30W **94** B4
Villarrobledo *Spain* 39°18N 2°36W **21** C4
Villavicencio *Argentina* 32°28S 69°0W **94** C2
Villavicencio *Colombia* 4°9N 73°37W **92** C4
Villaviciosa *Spain* 43°32N 5°27W **21** A3
Villazón *Bolivia* 22°0S 65°35W **94** A2
Ville-Marie *Canada* 47°20N 79°30W **72** C4
Ville Platte *U.S.A.* 30°41N 92°17W **84** F8
Villena *Spain* 38°39N 0°52W **21** C5
Villeneuve-d'Ascq *France* 50°38N 3°9E **20** A5
Villeneuve-sur-Lot *France* 44°24N 0°42E **20** D4
Villiers *S. Africa* 27°2S 28°36E **57** C4
Villingen-Schwenningen
  Germany 48°3N 8°26E **16** D5
Villmanstrand = Lappeenranta
  Finland 61°3N 28°12E **8** F23
Villupuram *India* 11°59N 79°31E **45** J4
Vilna *Canada* 54°7N 111°55W **70** C6
Vilnius *Lithuania* 54°38N 25°19E **9** J21
Vilyuchinsk *Russia* 52°55N 158°24E **27** D16
Vilyuy → *Russia* 64°24N 126°26E **27** C13
Vilyuysk *Russia* 63°40N 121°35E **27** C13
Vilyuyskoye Vdkhr.
  Russia 63°0N 112°0E **27** C12
Viña del Mar *Chile* 33°0S 71°30W **94** C1
Vinarós *Spain* 40°30N 0°27E **21** B6
Vincennes *U.S.A.* 38°41N 87°32W **80** F10
Vincennes Bay *S. Ocean* 66°0S 109°0E **5** C8
Vincent *U.S.A.* 34°33N 118°11W **79** L8
Vinchina *Argentina* 28°45S 68°15W **94** B2
Vindelälven → *Sweden* 63°55N 19°50E **8** E18
Vindeln *Sweden* 64°12N 19°43E **8** D18
Vindhya Ra. *India* 22°50N 77°0E **42** H7
Vineland *U.S.A.* 39°29N 75°2W **81** F16
Vinh *Vietnam* 18°45N 105°38E **38** C5
Vinh Long *Vietnam* 10°16N 105°57E **39** G5
Vinh Moc *Vietnam* 21°18N 105°1E **38** B5
Vinh Yen *Vietnam* 21°21N 105°35E **34** G5
Vinita *U.S.A.* 36°39N 95°9W **84** C7
Vinkovci *Croatia* 45°19N 18°48E **23** B8
Vinnitsa = Vinnytsya
  Ukraine 49°15N 28°30E **17** D15
Vinnytsya *Ukraine* 49°15N 28°30E **17** D15
Vinson Massif *Antarctica* 78°35S 85°25W **5** D16
Vinton *Calif., U.S.A.* 39°48N 120°10W **78** F6
Vinton *Iowa, U.S.A.* 42°10N 92°1W **80** D7
Vinton *La., U.S.A.* 30°11N 93°35W **84** F8
Vinukonda *India* 16°4N 79°45E **45** F4
Violet Valley ☉ *Australia* 17°10S 127°55E **60** C4
Vioolsdrif *S. Africa* 28°46S 17°39E **56** C2
Viqueque *E. Timor* 8°52S 126°23E **37** F7
Virac *Phil.* 13°30N 124°20E **37** B6
Virachey *Cambodia* 13°59N 106°49E **38** F6
Virachey △ *Cambodia* 14°14N 106°55E **38** E6
Virago Sd. *Canada* 54°0N 132°30W **70** C2
Virajpet = Virarajendrapet
  India 12°10N 75°50E **45** H2
Viramgam *India* 23°5N 72°0E **42** H5
Virananşehir *Turkey* 37°13N 39°45E **46** B3
Virarajendrapet *India* 12°10N 75°50E **45** H2
Virawah *Pakistan* 24°31N 70°46E **42** G4
Virden *Canada* 49°50N 100°56W **71** D8
Vire *France* 48°50N 0°53W **20** B3
Virgenes, C. *Argentina* 52°19S 68°21W **96** G3
Virgin → *U.S.A.* 36°28N 114°21W **77** H6
Virgin Gorda *Br. Virgin Is.* 18°30N 64°26W **89** e
Virgin Is. (British) ☑
  W. Indies 18°30N 64°30W **89** e
Virgin Is. (U.S.) ☑ *W. Indies* 18°20N 65°0W **89** e
Virgin Islands ☉
  U.S. Virgin Is. 18°21N 64°43W **89** C7
Virginia *S. Africa* 28°8S 26°55E **56** D4
Virginia *U.S.A.* 47°31N 92°32W **80** B7
Virginia □ *U.S.A.* 37°30N 78°45W **81** G14
Virginia Beach *U.S.A.* 36°49N 76°9W **81** G16
Virginia City *Mont.,*
  U.S.A. 45°18N 111°56W **76** D7
Virginia City *Nev.,*
  U.S.A. 39°19N 119°39W **78** F7
Virginia Falls *Canada* 61°38N 125°42W **70** A3
Virginiatown *Canada* 48°9N 79°36W **72** C4
Viroqua *U.S.A.* 43°34N 90°53W **80** D8
Virovitica *Croatia* 45°51N 17°21E **22** B7
Virpur *India* 21°51N 70°42E **42** J4
Virton *Belgium* 49°35N 5°32E **15** E5
Virudunagar *India* 9°30N 77°58E **45** K3
Vis *Croatia* 43°4N 16°10E **22** C7

Visalia U.S.A. 36°20N 119°18W **78** J7
Visayan Sea Phil. 11°30N 123°30E **37** B6
Visby Sweden 57°37N 18°18E **9** H18
Viscount Melville Sd.
  Canada 74°10N 108°0W **69** C10
Visé Belgium 50°44N 5°41E **15** D5
Vise, Ostrov Russia 79°33N 76°50E **26** B8
Višegrad Bos.-H. 43°47N 19°17E **23** C8
Viseu Brazil 1°10S 46°5W **93** D9
Viseu Portugal 40°40N 7°55W **21** B2
Vishakhapatnam India 17°45N 83°20E **44** F6
Visnagar India 23°45N 72°32E **42** H5
Viso, Mte. Italy 44°38N 7°5E **20** D7
Visokoi I. Antarctica 56°43S 27°15W **5** B1
Vista U.S.A. 33°12N 117°14W **79** M9
Vistula = Wisła →
  Poland 54°22N 18°55E **17** A10
Vita India 17°17N 74°33E **44** F2
Vitebsk = Vitsyebsk
  Belarus 55°10N 30°15E **18** C5
Viterbo Italy 42°25N 12°6E **22** C5
Viti Levu Fiji 17°30S 177°30E **59** a
Vitigudino Spain 41°1N 6°26W **21** B2
Vitim Russia 59°28N 112°35E **27** D12
Vitim → Russia 59°26N 112°34E **27** D12
Vitória Brazil 20°20S 40°22W **93** H10
Vitória da Conquista
  Brazil 14°51S 40°51W **93** F10
Vitória de Santo Antão
  Brazil 8°10S 35°20W **93** E11
Vitoria-Gasteiz Spain 42°50N 2°41W **21** A4
Vitsyebsk Belarus 55°10N 30°15E **18** C5
Vittória Italy 36°57N 14°32E **22** F6
Vittório Véneto Italy 45°59N 12°18E **22** B5
Viveiro Spain 43°39N 7°38W **21** A2
Vivian U.S.A. 32°53N 93°59W **84** E8
Viwa Fiji 17°10S 177°58E **59** a
Vizcaíno, Desierto de
  Mexico 27°30N 113°45W **86** B2
Vizcaíno, Sierra Mexico 27°30N 114°0W **86** B2
Vize Turkey 41°34N 27°45E **23** D12
Vizianagaram India 18°6N 83°30E **44** E6
Vlaardingen Neths. 51°55N 4°21E **15** C4
Vladikavkaz Russia 43°0N 44°35E **19** F7
Vladimir Russia 56°15N 40°30E **18** C7
Vladimir Volynskiy = Volodymyr-
  Volynskyy Ukraine 50°50N 24°18E **17** C13
Vladivostok Russia 43°10N 131°53E **28** C5
Vlieland Neths. 53°16N 4°55E **15** A4
Vlissingen Neths. 51°26N 3°34E **15** C3
Vlorë Albania 40°32N 19°28E **23** D8
Vltava → Czech Rep. 50°21N 14°30E **16** D8
Vo Dat Vietnam 11°9N 107°31E **39** G6
Voe U.K. 60°21N 1°16W **11** A7
Vogelkop = Doberai, Jazirah
  Indonesia 1°25S 133°0E **37** E8
Vogelsberg Germany 50°31N 9°12E **16** C5
Voghera Italy 44°59N 9°1E **20** D8
Vohibinany Madag. 18°49S 49°4E **55** H9
Vohimarina = Iharana
  Madag. 13°25S 50°0E **55** G10
Vohimena, Tanjon' i
  Madag. 25°36S 45°8E **55** K9
Vohipeno Madag. 22°22S 47°51E **55** J9
Voi Kenya 3°25S 38°32E **54** E7
Voiron France 45°22N 5°35E **20** D6
Voisey B. Canada 56°15N 61°50W **73** A7
Vojmsjön Sweden 65°0N 16°24E **8** D17
Vojvodina □ Serbia 45°20N 20°0E **23** B9
Volborg U.S.A. 45°51N 105°41W **76** D11
Volcán de Colima △
  Mexico 19°30N 103°40W **86** D4
Volcano Is. = Kazan-Rettō
  Pac. Oc. 25°0N 141°0E **64** E6
Volda Norway 62°9N 6°5E **8** E12
Volga = Privolzhskiy □
  Russia 56°0N 50°0E **26** D6
Volga → Russia 46°0N 48°30E **19** E8
Volga Hts. = Privolzhskaya
  Vozvyshennost Russia 51°0N 46°0E **19** D8
Volgodonsk Russia 47°33N 42°5E **19** E7
Volgograd Russia 48°40N 44°25E **19** E7
Volgogradskoye Vdkhr.
  Russia 50°0N 45°20E **19** D8
Volkhov → Russia 60°8N 32°20E **18** B5
Volkovysk = Vawkavysk
  Belarus 53°9N 24°30E **17** B13
Volksrust S. Africa 27°24S 29°53E **57** C4
Volochanka Russia 71°0N 94°28E **27** B10
Volodymyr-Volynskyy
  Ukraine 50°50N 24°18E **17** C13
Vologda Russia 59°10N 39°45E **18** C6
Volos Greece 39°24N 22°59E **23** E10
Volosovo Russia 59°27N 29°32E **9** G23
Volovets Ukraine 48°43N 23°11E **17** D12
Volozhin = Valozhyn
  Belarus 54°3N 26°30E **17** A14
Volsk Russia 52°5N 47°22E **18** D8
Volta → Ghana 5°46N 0°41E **50** F4
Volta, L. Ghana 7°30N 0°0 E **52** G6
Volta Redonda Brazil 22°31S 44°5W **95** A7
Voltaire, C. Australia 14°16S 125°35E **60** B4
Volterra Italy 43°24N 10°51E **22** C4
Volturno → Italy 41°1N 13°55E **22** D5
Volyn □ Ukraine 51°15N 24°30E **17** C13
Volzhskiy Russia 48°56N 44°46E **19** E7
Vomo Fiji 17°30S 177°15E **59** a
Vopnafjörður Iceland 65°45N 14°50W **8** D6
Vorkuta Russia 67°48N 64°20E **18** A11
Vormsi Estonia 59°1N 23°13E **9** G20
Voronezh Russia 51°40N 39°10E **19** D6
Võrts järv Estonia 58°16N 26°3E **9** G22
Võru Estonia 57°48N 26°54E **9** H22
Vosges France 48°20N 7°10E **20** B7
Voss Norway 60°38N 6°26E **8** F12
Vostok Antarctica 78°30S 106°50E **5** D8
Vostok I. Kiribati 10°5S 152°23W **65** J12
Votkinsk Russia 57°0N 53°55E **18** C9

Votkinskoye Vdkhr.
  Russia 57°22N 55°12E **18** C10
Vouga → Portugal 40°41N 8°40W **21** B1
Voyageurs △ U.S.A. 48°32N 93°0W **80** A7
Voynitsa Russia 65°10N 30°20E **8** D24
Voyvozh Russia 62°56N 54°56E **26** C6
Vozhe, Ozero Russia 60°45N 39°0E **18** B6
Voznesensk Ukraine 47°35N 31°21E **19** E5
Voznesenye Russia 61°0N 35°28E **18** B6
Vrangel Russia 42°43N 133°5E **28** C6
Vrangelya, Ostrov Russia 71°0N 180°0E **27** B18
Vranje Serbia 42°34N 21°54E **23** C9
Vratsa Bulgaria 43°15N 23°30E **23** C10
Vrbas → Bos.-H. 45°8N 17°29E **22** B7
Vrbas Serbia 45°24N 19°41E **23** B8
Vrede S. Africa 27°24S 29°6E **57** C4
Vredefort S. Africa 27°0S 27°22E **56** D4
Vredenburg S. Africa 32°56S 18°0E **56** D2
Vredendal S. Africa 31°41S 18°35E **56** D2
Vriddhachalam India 11°30N 79°20E **45** J4
Vrindavan India 27°37N 77°40E **42** F7
Vršac Serbia 45°8N 21°30E **23** B9
Vryburg S. Africa 26°55S 24°45E **56** C3
Vryheid S. Africa 27°45S 30°47E **57** C5
Vu Liet Vietnam 18°43N 105°23E **38** C5
Vukovar Croatia 45°21N 18°59E **23** B8
Vuktyl Russia 63°52N 57°20E **26** C6
Vulcan Canada 50°25N 113°15W **70** C6
Vulcan Romania 45°23N 23°17E **17** F12
Vulcănești Moldova 45°41N 28°18E **17** F15
Vulcano Italy 38°24N 14°58E **22** E6
Vulkaneshty = Vulcănești
  Moldova 45°41N 28°18E **17** F15
Vung Tau Vietnam 10°21N 107°4E **39** G6
Vunidawa Fiji 17°50S 178°21E **59** a
Vunisea Fiji 19°3S 178°10E **59** a
Vyara India 21°8N 73°28E **44** D1
Vyartsilya Russia 62°8N 30°45E **8** E24
Vyatka = Kirov Russia 58°35N 49°40E **18** C8
Vyatka → Russia 55°37N 51°28E **18** C9
Vyatskiye Polyany Russia 56°14N 51°5E **18** C9
Vyazemskiy Russia 47°32N 134°45E **27** E14
Vyazma Russia 55°10N 34°15E **18** C5
Vyborg Russia 60°43N 28°47E **8** F23
Vychegda → Russia 61°18N 46°36E **18** B8
Vychodné Beskydy
  Europe 49°20N 22°0E **17** D11
Vyg-ozero Russia 63°47N 34°29E **18** B5
Vylkove Ukraine 45°28N 29°32E **17** F15
Vynohradiv Ukraine 48°9N 23°2E **17** D12
Vypin India 10°10N 76°15E **45** J3
Vyrnwy, L. U.K. 52°48N 3°31W **12** E4
Vyshniy Volochek Russia 57°30N 34°30E **18** C5
Vyshzha = imeni 26 Bakinskikh
  Komissarov
  Turkmenistan 39°22N 54°10E **47** B7
Vyškov Czech Rep. 49°17N 17°0E **17** D9
Vytegra Russia 61°0N 36°27E **18** B6

W

W.A.C. Bennett Dam
  Canada 56°2N 122°6W **70** B4
Wa Ghana 10°7N 2°25W **52** F5
Waal → Neths. 51°37N 5°0E **15** C5
Waalwijk Neths. 51°42N 5°4E **15** C5
Waanyi-Garawa ⦿
  Australia 18°2S 137°33E **62** B2
Wabakimi △ Canada 50°43N 89°29W **72** B2
Wabana Canada 47°40N 53°0W **73** C9
Wabasca → Canada 58°22N 115°20W **70** B5
Wabasca-Desmarais
  Canada 55°57N 113°56W **70** B6
Wabash U.S.A. 40°48N 85°49W **81** E11
Wabash → U.S.A. 37°48N 88°2W **80** G1
Wabigoon L. Canada 49°44N 92°44W **71** D10
Wabowden Canada 54°55N 98°38W **71** C9
Wabu Hu China 32°20N 116°50E **35** A11
Wabuk Pt. Canada 55°20N 85°5W **72** A2
Wabush Canada 52°55N 66°52W **73** B6
Waco U.S.A. 31°33N 97°9W **84** F6
Waconichi, L. Canada 50°8N 74°0W **72** B5
Wad Hamid Sudan 16°30N 32°45E **53** E12
Wad Medanî Sudan 14°28N 33°30E **53** F12
Wad Thana Pakistan 27°22N 66°23E **42** F2
Wadayama Japan 35°19N 134°52E **29** G7
Waddeneilanden Neths. 53°25N 5°10E **15** A5
Waddenzee Neths. 53°6N 5°10E **15** A5
Waddington, Mt.
  Canada 51°23N 125°15W **70** C3
Waddy Pt. Australia 24°58S 153°21E **63** C5
Wadebridge U.K. 50°31N 4°51E **13** G3
Wadena Canada 51°57N 103°47W **71** C8
Wadena U.S.A. 46°26N 95°8W **80** B6
Wadeye Australia 14°28S 129°52E **60** B4
Wadgaon India 18°44N 73°39E **44** E1
Wadhams Canada 51°30N 127°30W **70** C3
Wadhwan India 22°42N 71°41E **42** H4
Wadi India 17°4N 76°59E **44** F3
Wādī as Sīr Jordan 31°56N 35°49E **48** D4
Wadi Halfa Sudan 21°53N 31°19E **53** D12
Wādī Rum △ Jordan 29°30N 35°20E **48** F4
Wadian China 32°42N 112°29E **35** A9
Wadsworth Nev., U.S.A. 39°38N 119°17W **76** G4
Wadsworth Ohio, U.S.A. 41°2N 81°44W **82** E3
Waegwan S. Korea 35°59N 128°23E **33** G15
Wafangdian China 39°38N 121°58E **33** E11
Wafrah Kuwait 28°33N 47°56E **46** D5
Wagait ⦿ Australia 13°1S 130°5E **60** B5
Wageningen Neths. 51°58N 5°40E **15** C5
Wager B. Canada 65°26N 88°40W **69** D14
Wagga Wagga Australia 35°7S 147°24E **63** F4
Waghai India 20°46N 73°29E **44** D1
Waghete Indonesia 4°10S 135°50E **37** E9
Wagin Australia 33°17S 117°25E **61** F2
Wagner U.S.A. 43°5N 98°18W **80** D4
Wagon Mound U.S.A. 36°1N 104°42W **77** H11
Wagoner U.S.A. 35°58N 95°22W **84** D7

Wah Pakistan 33°45N 72°40E **42** C5
Wahai Indonesia 2°48S 129°35E **37** E7
Wâḥid Egypt 30°48N 32°21E **48** E1
Wahnai Afghan. 32°40N 65°50E **42** C1
Wahoo U.S.A. 41°13N 96°37W **80** E5
Wahpeton U.S.A. 46°16N 96°36W **80** B5
Wai India 17°56N 73°57E **44** F1
Waialua U.S.A. 21°34N 158°8W **75** L8
Waiau → N.Z. 42°47S 173°22E **59** E4
Waiawe Ganga →
  Sri Lanka 6°15N 81°0E **45** L5
Waibeem Indonesia 0°30S 132°59E **37** E8
Waigeo Indonesia 0°20S 130°40E **37** E8
Waihi N.Z. 37°23S 175°52E **59** B5
Waihou → N.Z. 37°15S 175°40E **59** B5
Waikabubak Indonesia 9°45S 119°25E **37** F5
Waikaremoana, L. N.Z. 38°49S 177°9E **59** C6
Waikari N.Z. 42°58S 172°41E **59** E4
Waikato → N.Z. 37°23S 174°43E **59** B5
Waikelo Indonesia 9°24S 119°19E **60** A2
Waikerie Australia 34°9S 140°0E **63** E3
Waikokopu N.Z. 39°3S 177°52E **59** C6
Waikouaiti N.Z. 45°36S 170°41E **59** F3
Waimakariri → N.Z. 43°24S 172°42E **59** E4
Waimate N.Z. 44°45S 171°3E **59** F3
Wainganga → India 18°50N 79°55E **44** E4
Waingapu Indonesia 9°35S 120°11E **37** F6
Waini → Guyana 8°20N 59°50W **92** B7
Wainwright Canada 52°50N 110°50W **71** C6
Wainwright U.S.A. 70°38N 160°2W **74** A7
Waiouru N.Z. 39°28S 175°41E **59** C5
Waipara N.Z. 43°3S 172°46E **59** E4
Waipawa N.Z. 39°56S 176°38E **59** C6
Waipiro N.Z. 38°2S 178°22E **59** C7
Waipoua Forest N.Z. 35°39S 173°33E **59** A4
Waipu N.Z. 35°59S 174°29E **59** A5
Waipukurau N.Z. 40°1S 176°33E **59** D6
Wairakei N.Z. 38°37S 176°6E **59** C6
Wairarapa, L. N.Z. 41°14S 175°15E **59** D5
Wairoa N.Z. 39°3S 177°25E **59** C6
Waitaki → N.Z. 44°56S 171°7E **59** F3
Waitangi N.Z. 35°16S 174°5E **59** A5
Waitara N.Z. 38°59S 174°15E **59** C5
Waitomo Caves N.Z. 38°16S 175°7E **59** C5
Waitsburg U.S.A. 46°16N 118°9W **76** C4
Waiuku N.Z. 37°15S 174°45E **59** B5
Wajima Japan 37°30N 137°0E **29** F8
Wajir Kenya 1°42N 40°5E **54** D8
Wakasa Japan 35°20N 134°24E **29** G7
Wakasa-Wan Japan 35°40N 135°30E **29** G7
Wakatipu, L. N.Z. 45°5S 168°33E **59** F2
Wakaw Canada 52°39N 105°44W **71** C7
Wakayama Japan 34°15N 135°15E **29** G7
Wakayama □ Japan 33°50N 135°30E **29** H7
Wake Forest U.S.A. 35°59N 78°30E **85** D15
WaKeeney U.S.A. 39°1N 99°53W **80** F4
Wakefield Jamaica 18°26N 77°42W **88** a
Wakefield N.Z. 41°24S 173°5E **59** D4
Wakefield U.K. 53°41N 1°29W **12** D6
Wakefield U.S.A. 46°29N 89°56W **80** B9
Wakkanai Japan 45°28N 141°35E **28** B10
Wakkerstroom S. Africa 27°24S 30°10E **57** C5
Wakool Australia 35°28S 144°23E **63** F3
Wakool → Australia 35°5S 143°33E **63** F3
Wakre Indonesia 0°19S 131°5E **37** E8
Wakuach, L. Canada 55°34N 67°32W **73** A6
Walagunya ⦿ Australia 23°10S 120°50E **60** D3
Walbrzych Poland 50°45N 16°18E **16** C9
Walbury Hill U.K. 51°21N 1°28W **13** F6
Walcha Australia 30°55S 151°31E **63** E5
Walcheren Neths. 51°30N 3°35E **15** C3
Walcott U.S.A. 41°46N 106°51W **76** F10
Waldburg Ra. Australia 24°40S 117°35E **61** D2
Walden Colo., U.S.A. 40°44N 106°17W **76** F10
Walden N.Y., U.S.A. 41°34N 74°11W **83** E10
Waldport U.S.A. 44°26N 124°4W **76** D1
Waldron U.S.A. 34°54N 94°5W **84** D7
Walebing Australia 30°41S 116°12E **61** F2
Wales □ U.K. 52°19N 4°43W **13** E3
Wales I. Canada 68°1N 86°40W **69** D14
Walgett Australia 30°0S 148°5E **63** E4
Walgreen Coast
  Antarctica 75°15S 105°0W **5** D15
Walker U.S.A. 47°6N 94°35W **80** B6
Walker, L. Canada 50°20N 67°11W **73** B6
Walker L. Canada 54°42N 95°57W **71** C9
Walker L. U.S.A. 38°42N 118°43W **76** G4
Walkerston Australia 21°11S 149°8E **62** b
Walkerton Canada 44°10N 81°10W **82** B3
Wall U.S.A. 44°0N 102°8W **80** C2
Walla Walla U.S.A. 46°4N 118°20W **76** C4
Wallace Idaho, U.S.A. 47°28N 115°56W **76** C6
Wallace N.C., U.S.A. 34°44N 77°59W **85** D16
Wallaceburg Canada 42°34N 82°23W **82** D2
Wallachia = Valahia
  Romania 44°35N 25°0E **17** F13
Wallal Australia 26°32S 146°7E **63** D4
Wallal Downs Australia 19°47S 120°40E **60** C3
Wallam Cr. → Australia 28°40S 147°20E **63** D4
Wallambin, L. Australia 30°57S 117°35E **61** F2
Wallangarra Australia 28°56S 151°58E **63** D5
Wallaroo Australia 33°56S 137°39E **63** E2
Wallenpaupack, L.
  U.S.A. 41°25N 75°15W **83** E9
Wallingford Conn.,
  U.S.A. 41°27N 72°50W **83** E12
Wallingford Vt., U.S.A. 43°28N 72°58W **83** C12
Wallis & Futuna, Îs. ⦿
  Pac. Oc. 13°18S 176°10W **58** C11
Wallula U.S.A. 46°5N 118°54W **76** C4
Wallumbilla Australia 26°33S 149°9E **63** D4

Walmsley L. Canada 63°25N 108°36W **71** A7
Walney, I. of U.K. 54°6N 3°15W **12** C4
Walnut Canyon △
  U.S.A. 35°15N 111°20W **77** J8
Walnut Creek U.S.A. 37°54N 122°4W **78** H4
Walnut Ridge U.S.A. 36°4N 90°57W **85** C9
Walpole Australia 34°58S 116°44E **61** F2
Walpole U.S.A. 42°9N 71°15W **83** D13
Walpole-Nornalup △
  Australia 35°0S 116°45E **61** G2
Walsall U.K. 52°35N 1°58W **13** E6
Walsenburg U.S.A. 37°38N 104°47W **77** H11
Walsh U.S.A. 37°23N 102°17W **77** H12
Walsh → Australia 16°31S 143°42E **62** B3
Walsingham Canada 42°40N 80°31W **82** D4
Waltair India 17°44N 83°23E **44** F6
Walter F. George Res.
  U.S.A. 31°38N 85°4W **85** F12
Walterboro U.S.A. 32°55N 80°40W **85** E14
Walters U.S.A. 34°22N 98°19W **84** D5
Waltman U.S.A. 43°4N 107°12W **76** E10
Walton U.S.A. 42°10N 75°8W **83** D9
Walton-on-the-Naze U.K. 51°51N 1°17E **13** F9
Walvis Bay Namibia 23°0S 14°28E **56** B1
Walvisbaai = Walvis Bay
  Namibia 23°0S 14°28E **56** B1
Wamba
  Dem. Rep. of the Congo 2°10N 27°57E **54** D5
Wamba Kenya 0°58N 37°19E **54** D7
Wambardi ⦿ Australia 16°2S 130°55E **60** C5
Wamego U.S.A. 39°12N 96°18W **80** F5
Wamena Indonesia 4°4S 138°57E **37** E9
Wampana Karlantijpa ⦿
  Australia 17°45S 132°10E **60** C5
Wampaya ⦿ Australia 17°20S 135°0E **62** B2
Wampsville U.S.A. 43°4N 75°42W **83** C9
Wamsutter U.S.A. 41°40N 107°58W **76** F10
Wamulan Indonesia 3°27S 126°7E **37** E7
Wan Tup Burma 21°13N 98°42E **34** G2
Wan Xian China 38°47N 115°7E **32** E8
Wana Pakistan 32°20N 69°32E **42** C3
Wanaaring Australia 29°38S 144°9E **63** D3
Wanaka N.Z. 44°42S 169°9E **59** F2
Wanaka, L. N.Z. 44°33S 169°7E **59** F2
Wan'an China 26°26N 114°49E **35** D10
Wanapitei L. Canada 46°45N 80°40W **72** C3
Wandel Sea = McKinley Sea
  Arctic 82°0N 0°0 E **4** A7
Wandhari Pakistan 27°42N 66°48E **42** F2
Wanding China 24°5N 98°4E **34** E2
Wandoan Australia 26°5S 149°55E **63** D4
Wandur Marine △ India 11°30N 92°30E **45** J11
Wanfu China 40°8N 122°38E **33** D12
Wang → Thailand 17°8S 179°0E **59** a
Wang Noi Thailand 14°13N 100°44E **38** E3
Wang Saphung Thailand 17°18N 101°46E **38** D3
Wang Thong Thailand 16°50N 100°26E **38** D3
Wanganella Australia 35°6S 144°49E **63** F3
Wanganui N.Z. 39°56S 175°3E **59** C5
Wangaratta Australia 36°21S 146°19E **63** F4
Wangary Australia 34°35S 135°29E **63** E2
Wangcang China 32°18N 106°20E **34** A6
Wangcheng China 28°22N 112°49E **35** C9
Wangcun China 36°41N 117°41E **33** F9
Wangdu China 38°40N 115°7E **32** E8
Wangerooge Germany 53°47N 7°54E **16** B4
Wangiwangi Indonesia 5°22S 123°37E **37** F6
Wangjiang China 30°10N 116°42E **35** B11
Wangmo China 25°11N 106°5E **34** E6
Wangqing China 43°12N 129°42E **33** C15
Wani India 20°5N 78°55E **44** E4
Wanimiyn ⦿ Australia 15°30S 130°49E **60** C5
Wanjina Wunggurr Wilinggin ⦿
  Australia 16°0S 127°0E **60** C4
Wankaner India 22°35N 70°57E **42** H4
Wanless Canada 54°11N 101°21W **71** C8
Wanleweyne Somalia 2°37N 44°54E **49** G3
Wanneroo Australia 31°42S 115°46E **61** F2
Wannian China 28°42N 117°4E **35** C11
Wanning China 18°48N 110°22E **38** C8
Wannoo Billabong Roadhouse
  Australia 27°25S 115°49E **61** E2
Wanon Niwat Thailand 17°38N 103°46E **38** D4
Wanqinsha China 22°43N 113°33E **31** a
Wanquan China 40°50N 114°40E **32** D8
Wanrong China 35°25N 110°50E **32** G6
Wanshan China 27°30N 109°12E **34** D7
Wanshan Qundao China 21°57N 113°45E **31** a
Wansheng China 28°57N 106°53E **34** C6
Wantage U.K. 51°35N 1°25W **13** F6
Wanxian China 30°42N 108°20E **34** B7
Wanyuan China 32°4N 108°3E **34** A7
Wanzai Guangdong, China 22°12N 113°31E **31** a
Wanzai Jiangxi, China 28°7N 114°30E **35** C10
Wapakoneta U.S.A. 40°34N 84°12W **81** E11
Wapato U.S.A. 46°27N 120°25W **76** C3
Wapawekka L. Canada 54°55N 104°40W **71** C8
Wapikopa L. Canada 52°56N 87°53W **72** B2
Wapiti → Canada 55°5N 118°18W **70** B5
Wappingers Falls
  U.S.A. 41°36N 73°55W **83** E11
Wapsipinicon → U.S.A. 41°44N 90°19W **80** E8
Wapusk △ Canada 57°46N 93°22W **71** B10
Warakurna ⦿ Australia 24°59S 128°17E **61** D4
Warangal India 17°58N 79°35E **44** F4
Waraseoni India 21°45N 80°2E **43** J9
Waratah Australia 41°30S 145°29E **63** G4
Waratah B. Australia 38°54S 146°5E **63** F4
Warburton Vic.,
  Australia 37°47S 145°42E **63** F4
Warburton W. Austral.,
  Australia 26°8S 126°35E **61** E4
Warburton ⦿ Australia 26°7S 126°34E **61** E4
Warburton → Australia 28°4S 137°28E **63** D2
Warburton Groove
  Australia 28°18S 137°8E **63** A2
Warburton Ra. Australia 25°55S 126°28E **61** E4
Ward N.Z. 41°49S 174°11E **59** D5
Ward → Australia 26°28S 146°6E **63** D4

Ward Mt. U.S.A. 37°12N 118°54W **78** H8
Warden S. Africa 27°50S 29°0E **57** C4
Wardha India 20°45N 78°39E **44** D4
Wardha → India 19°57N 79°11E **44** E4
Wardsville Canada 42°39N 81°45W **82** D3
Ware U.K. 51°49N 0°1E **13** F8
Ware U.S.A. 42°16N 72°14W **83** D12
Waregem Belgium 50°53N 3°27E **15** D3
Wareham U.S.A. 41°46N 70°43W **83** E14
Waremme Belgium 50°43N 5°15E **15** D5
Warialda Australia 29°29S 150°33E **63** D5
Warin Chamrap
  Thailand 15°12N 104°53E **38** E5
Warkopi Indonesia 1°12S 134°9E **37** E8
Warm Springs U.S.A. 38°10N 116°20W **77** G5
Warman Canada 52°19N 106°30W **71** C7
Warmbad = Bela Bela
  S. Africa 24°51S 28°19E **57** B4
Warmbad Namibia 28°25S 18°42E **56** D2
Warminster U.K. 51°12N 2°10W **13** F5
Warminster U.S.A. 40°12N 75°6W **83** F9
Warmun Australia 17°2S 128°12E **60** C4
Warner Mts. U.S.A. 41°40N 120°15W **76** F3
Warner Robins U.S.A. 32°37N 83°36W **85** E13
Waroona Australia 32°50S 115°58E **61** F2
Warora India 20°14N 79°1E **44** D4
Warrabri ⦿ Australia 21°1S 134°19E **62** C1
Warracknabeal Australia 36°9S 142°26E **63** F3
Warragul Australia 38°10S 145°58E **63** F4
Warrego → Australia 30°24S 145°21E **63** E4
Warrego Ra. Australia 24°58S 146°0E **62** C4
Warren Australia 31°42S 147°51E **63** E4
Warren Ark., U.S.A. 33°37N 92°4W **84** E8
Warren Mich., U.S.A. 42°28N 83°1W **81** D12
Warren Minn., U.S.A. 48°12N 96°46W **80** A5
Warren Ohio, U.S.A. 41°14N 80°49W **82** E4
Warren Pa., U.S.A. 41°51N 79°9W **82** E5
Warrenpoint U.K. 54°6N 6°15W **10** B5
Warrensburg Mo., U.S.A. 38°46N 93°44W **80** F7
Warrensburg N.Y.,
  U.S.A. 43°29N 73°46W **83** C11
Warrenton S. Africa 28°9S 24°47E **56** C3
Warrenton U.S.A. 46°10N 123°56W **78** D3
Warri Nigeria 5°30N 5°41E **52** G7
Warrington U.K. 53°24N 2°35W **12** D5
Warrington U.S.A. 30°23N 87°17W **85** F11
Warrington □ U.K. 53°24N 2°35W **12** D5
Warrnambool Australia 38°25S 142°30E **63** F3
Warroad U.S.A. 48°54N 95°19W **80** A6
Warruwi Australia 11°36S 133°20E **62** A1
Warsak Dam Pakistan 34°11N 71°19E **42** B4
Warsaw Ind., U.S.A. 41°14N 85°51W **81** E11
Warsaw N.Y., U.S.A. 42°45N 78°8W **82** D6
Warsaw Ohio, U.S.A. 40°20N 82°0W **82** F3
Warta → Poland 52°35N 14°39E **16** B8
Warthe = Warta →
  Poland 52°35N 14°39E **16** B8
Waru Indonesia 3°30S 130°36E **37** E8
Warud India 21°30N 78°16E **44** D4
Warumungu ⦿
  Australia 19°15S 134°44E **62** B1
Warwick Australia 28°10S 152°1E **63** D5
Warwick U.K. 52°18N 1°35W **13** E6
Warwick N.Y., U.S.A. 41°16N 74°22W **83** E10
Warwick R.I., U.S.A. 41°42N 71°28W **83** E13
Warwickshire □ U.K. 52°14N 1°38W **13** E6
Wasaga Beach Canada 44°31N 80°1W **82** B4
Wasagaming Canada 50°39N 99°58W **71** C9
Wasatch Ra. U.S.A. 40°0N 111°30W **76** F8
Wasbank S. Africa 28°15S 30°9E **57** C5
Wasco Calif., U.S.A. 35°36N 119°20W **79** K7
Wasco Oreg., U.S.A. 45°36N 120°42W **76** D3
Waseca U.S.A. 44°5N 93°30W **80** C7
Wasekamio L. Canada 56°45N 108°45W **71** B7
Wasgomura △ Sri Lanka 7°45N 81°0E **45** L5
Wash, The U.K. 52°58N 0°20E **12** E8
Washago Canada 44°45N 79°20W **82** B5
Washburn N. Dak.,
  U.S.A. 47°17N 101°2W **80** B3
Washburn Wis., U.S.A. 46°40N 90°54W **80** B8
Washim India 20°3N 77°0E **44** D3
Washington U.K. 54°55N 1°30W **12** C6
Washington Ga., U.S.A. 33°44N 82°44W **85** E13
Washington Ind., U.S.A. 38°40N 87°10W **80** F10
Washington Iowa, U.S.A. 41°18N 91°42W **80** E8
Washington Mo., U.S.A. 38°33N 91°1W **80** F8
Washington N.C., U.S.A. 35°33N 77°3W **85** D16
Washington N.J., U.S.A. 40°46N 74°59W **83** F10
Washington Pa., U.S.A. 40°10N 80°15W **82** F4
Washington Utah, U.S.A. 37°8N 113°31W **77** H7
Washington □ U.S.A. 47°30N 120°30W **76** C3
Washington, Mt.
  U.S.A. 44°16N 71°18W **83** B13
Washington Court House
  U.S.A. 39°32N 83°26W **81** F12
Washington I. U.S.A. 45°23N 86°54W **80** C10
Washougal U.S.A. 45°35N 122°21W **78** E4
Washpool △ Australia 29°22S 152°20E **63** D5
Wasian Indonesia 1°47S 133°19E **37** E8
Wasilla U.S.A. 61°35N 149°26W **68** C2
Wasior Indonesia 2°43S 134°30E **37** E8
Wasiri Indonesia 7°30S 126°30E **37** F7
Wāsiṭ □ Iraq 32°50N 45°35E **46** C5
Waskaganish Canada 51°30N 78°40W **72** B4
Waskaiowaka L. Canada 56°33N 96°23W **71** B9
Waskesiu Lake Canada 53°55N 106°5W **71** C7
Wasserkuppe Germany 50°29N 9°55E **16** C5
Waswanipi Canada 49°40N 76°29W **72** C4
Waswanipi, L. Canada 49°35N 76°40W **72** C4
Watampone Indonesia 4°29S 120°25E **37** E6
Watarrka △ Australia 24°20S 131°30E **60** D5
Water Park Pt. Australia 22°56S 150°47E **62** C5
Water Valley U.S.A. 34°10N 89°38W **85** D10
Waterberg Plateau
  Namibia 20°25S 17°18E **56** B2
Waterberge S. Africa 24°10S 28°0E **57** B4
Waterbury Conn., U.S.A. 41°33N 73°3W **83** E11
Waterbury Vt., U.S.A. 44°20N 72°46W **83** B12

Waterbury L. *Canada* 58°10N 104°22W **71 B8**
Waterdown *Canada* 43°20N 79°53W **82 C5**
Waterford *Canada* 42°56N 80°17W **82 D4**
Waterford *Ireland* 52°15N 7°8W **10 D4**
Waterford *Calif., U.S.A.* 37°38N 120°46W **78 H6**
Waterford *Pa., U.S.A.* 41°57N 79°59W **82 E5**
Waterford □ *Ireland* 52°10N 7°40W **10 D4**
Waterford Harbour *Ireland* 52°8N 6°58W **10 D5**
Waterhen L. *Canada* 52°10N 99°40W **71 C9**
Waterloo *Ont., Canada* 43°30N 80°32W **82 C4**
Waterloo *Qué., Canada* 45°22N 72°32W **83 A12**
Waterloo *Ill., U.S.A.* 38°20N 90°9W **80 F8**
Waterloo *Iowa, U.S.A.* 42°30N 92°21W **80 D7**
Waterloo *N.Y., U.S.A.* 43°59N 75°55W **83 D8**
Watersmeet *U.S.A.* 46°16N 89°11W **80 B9**
Waterton Lakes △
   Canada 48°45N 115°0W **70 D6**
Watertown *Conn., U.S.A.* 41°36N 73°7W **83 E11**
Watertown *N.Y., U.S.A.* 43°59N 75°55W **83 C9**
Watertown *S. Dak., U.S.A.* 44°54N 97°7W **80 C5**
Watertown *Wis., U.S.A.* 43°12N 88°43W **80 D9**
Waterval-Boven = Emgwenya
   S. Africa 25°40S 30°18E **57 C5**
Waterville *Canada* 45°16N 71°54W **83 A13**
Waterville *Maine, U.S.A.* 44°33N 69°38W **81 C19**
Waterville *N.Y., U.S.A.* 42°56N 75°23W **83 D9**
Waterville *Pa., U.S.A.* 41°19N 77°21W **82 E7**
Waterville *Wash., U.S.A.* 47°39N 120°4W **76 C3**
Watervliet *U.S.A.* 42°44N 73°42W **83 D11**
Wates *Indonesia* 7°51S 110°10E **37 G14**
Watford *Canada* 42°57N 81°53W **82 D3**
Watford *U.K.* 51°40N 0°24W **13 F7**
Watford City *U.S.A.* 47°48N 103°17W **80 B2**
Wathaman → *Canada* 57°16N 102°59W **71 B8**
Wathaman L. *Canada* 56°58N 103°44W **71 B8**
Watheroo *Australia* 30°15S 116°5E **61 F2**
Watheroo △ *Australia* 30°19S 115°64E **61 F2**
Wating *China* 35°40N 106°38E **32 G4**
Watkins Glen *U.S.A.* 42°23N 76°52W **82 D8**
Watling I. = San Salvador I.
   Bahamas 24°0N 74°30W **89 B5**
Watonga *U.S.A.* 35°51N 98°25W **84 D5**
Watrous *Canada* 51°40N 105°25W **71 C7**
Watrous *U.S.A.* 35°48N 104°59W **77 J11**
Watsa *Dem. Rep. of the Congo* 3°4N 29°30E **54 D5**
Watseka *U.S.A.* 40°47N 87°44W **80 E10**
Watson *Canada* 52°10N 104°30W **71 C8**
Watson Lake *Canada* 60°6N 128°49W **70 A3**
Watsontown *U.S.A.* 41°5N 76°52W **82 E8**
Watsonville *U.S.A.* 36°55N 121°45W **78 J5**
Wattiwarriganna Cr. →
   Australia 28°57S 136°10E **63 D2**
Watuata = Batuata
   Indonesia 6°12S 122°42E **37 F6**
Watubela, Kepulauan
   Indonesia 4°28S 131°35E **37 E8**
Watubela Is. = Watubela,
   Kepulauan *Indonesia* 4°28S 131°35E **37 E8**
Wau *South Sudan* 7°45N 28°1E **53 G11**
Waubamik *Canada* 45°27N 80°1W **82 A4**
Waubay *U.S.A.* 45°20N 97°18W **80 C5**
Wauchope *N.S.W.,*
   Australia 31°28S 152°45E **63 E5**
Wauchope *N. Terr.,*
   Australia 20°36S 134°15E **62 C1**
Wauchula *U.S.A.* 27°33N 81°49W **85 H14**
Waukarlycarly, L.
   Australia 21°18S 121°56E **60 D3**
Waukegan *U.S.A.* 42°22N 87°50W **80 D10**
Waukesha *U.S.A.* 43°1N 88°14W **80 D9**
Waukon *U.S.A.* 43°16N 91°29W **80 D8**
Waupaca *U.S.A.* 44°21N 89°5W **80 C9**
Waupun *U.S.A.* 43°38N 88°44W **80 D9**
Waurika *U.S.A.* 34°10N 98°0W **84 D6**
Wausau *U.S.A.* 44°58N 89°38W **80 C9**
Wautoma *U.S.A.* 44°4N 89°18W **80 C9**
Wauwatosa *U.S.A.* 43°2N 88°0W **80 D9**
Wave Hill = Kalkarindji
   Australia 17°30S 130°47E **60 C5**
Wave Rock △ *Australia* 32°26S 118°53E **61 F2**
Waveney → *U.K.* 52°35N 1°39E **13 E9**
Waverley *N.Z.* 39°46S 174°37E **59 C5**
Waverly *Iowa, U.S.A.* 42°44N 92°29W **80 D7**
Waverly *N.Y., U.S.A.* 42°1N 76°32W **83 E8**
Wavre *Belgium* 50°43N 4°38E **15 D4**
Wâw = Wau *South Sudan* 7°45N 28°1E **53 G11**
Wāw al Kabīr *Libya* 25°20N 16°43E **53 C9**
Wawa *Canada* 47°59N 84°47W **72 C3**
Wawanesa *Canada* 49°36N 99°40W **71 D9**
Wawona *U.S.A.* 37°32N 119°39W **78 H7**
Waxahachie *U.S.A.* 32°24N 96°51W **84 E6**
Way, L. *Australia* 26°45S 120°16E **61 E3**
Waya *Fiji* 17°19S 177°10E **59 a**
Waycross *U.S.A.* 31°13N 82°21W **85 F13**
Wayland *U.S.A.* 42°34N 77°35W **82 D7**
Wayne *Nebr., U.S.A.* 42°14N 97°1W **80 D5**
Wayne *W. Va., U.S.A.* 38°13N 82°27W **81 F4**
Waynesboro *Ga., U.S.A.* 33°6N 82°1W **85 E13**
Waynesboro *Miss.,*
   U.S.A. 31°40N 88°39W **85 F10**
Waynesboro *Pa., U.S.A.* 39°45N 77°35W **81 F15**
Waynesboro *Va., U.S.A.* 38°4N 78°53W **81 F14**
Waynesburg *U.S.A.* 39°54N 80°11W **81 F13**
Waynesville *U.S.A.* 35°28N 82°58W **85 D13**
Waynoka *U.S.A.* 36°35N 98°53W **84 C5**
Wazirabad *Pakistan* 32°30N 74°8E **42 C6**
Waziristan *Pakistan* 33°0N 70°0E **42 C4**
We *Indonesia* 5°51N 95°18E **36 C1**
Weald, The *U.K.* 51°4N 0°20E **13 F8**
Wear → *U.K.* 54°55N 1°23W **12 C6**
Weatherford *Okla.,*
   U.S.A. 35°32N 98°43W **84 D5**
Weatherford *Tex., U.S.A.* 32°46N 97°48W **84 E6**
Weaverville *U.S.A.* 40°44N 122°56W **76 F2**
Webb City *U.S.A.* 37°9N 94°28W **80 G6**
Webequie *Canada* 52°59N 87°21W **72 B2**
Webster *Mass., U.S.A.* 42°3N 71°53W **83 D13**
Webster *N.Y., U.S.A.* 43°13N 77°26W **82 C7**

Webster *S. Dak., U.S.A.* 45°20N 97°31W **80 C5**
Webster City *U.S.A.* 42°28N 93°49W **80 D7**
Webster Springs *U.S.A.* 38°29N 80°25W **81 F13**
Weda *Indonesia* 0°21N 127°50E **37 D7**
Weda, Teluk *Indonesia* 0°20N 128°0E **37 D7**
Weddell Abyssal Plain
   S. Ocean 65°0S 20°0W **5 C2**
Weddell I. *Falk. Is.* 51°50S 61°0W **96 G4**
Weddell Sea *Antarctica* 72°30S 40°0W **5 D1**
Wedderburn *Australia* 36°26S 143°33E **63 F3**
Wedgeport *Canada* 43°44N 65°59W **73 D6**
Wee Waa *Australia* 30°11S 149°26E **63 E4**
Weed *U.S.A.* 41°25N 122°23W **76 F2**
Weed Heights *U.S.A.* 38°59N 119°13W **78 G7**
Weedsport *U.S.A.* 43°2N 76°33W **83 C8**
Weedville *U.S.A.* 41°17N 78°30W **82 E6**
Weenen *S. Africa* 28°48S 30°7E **57 C5**
Weerribben △ *Neths.* 52°47N 5°58E **15 B5**
Weert *Neths.* 51°15N 5°43E **15 C5**
Wei He → *Hebei, China* 36°10N 115°45E **32 F8**
Wei He → *Shaanxi,*
   China 34°38N 110°15E **32 G6**
Weichang *China* 41°58N 117°49E **33 D9**
Weichuan *China* 34°20N 113°59E **32 G7**
Weiden *Germany* 49°41N 12°10E **16 D7**
Weifang *China* 36°44N 119°7E **33 F10**
Weihai *China* 37°30N 122°6E **33 F12**
Weihui *China* 35°25N 114°3E **32 G8**
Weimar *Germany* 50°58N 11°19E **16 C6**
Weinan *China* 34°31N 109°29E **32 G5**
Weining *China* 26°50N 104°17E **34 D5**
Weipa *Australia* 12°40S 141°50E **62 A3**
Weir → *Australia* 28°20S 149°50E **63 D4**
Weir → *Canada* 56°54N 93°21W **71 B10**
Weir River *Canada* 56°49N 94°6W **71 B10**
Weirton *U.S.A.* 40°24N 80°35W **82 F4**
Weiser *U.S.A.* 44°15N 116°58W **76 D5**
Weishan *Shandong, China* 34°47N 117°5E **33 G9**
Weishan *Yunnan, China* 25°12N 100°20E **34 E3**
Weishan Hu *China* 34°35N 117°14E **33 G9**
Weixi *China* 27°10N 99°10E **34 D2**
Weixin *China* 27°48N 105°3E **34 D5**
Weiyuan *Gansu, China* 35°7N 104°10E **32 G3**
Weiyuan *Sichuan, China* 29°35N 104°36E **34 C5**
Weizhou Dao *China* 21°0N 109°5E **34 G7**
Wejherowo *Poland* 54°35N 18°12E **17 A10**
Wekusko L. *Canada* 54°40N 99°50W **71 C9**
Welch *U.S.A.* 37°26N 81°35W **81 G13**
Welford △ *Australia* 25°5S 143°16E **62 D3**
Weligama *Sri Lanka* 5°58N 80°25E **45 M5**
Welkom *S. Africa* 28°0S 26°46E **56 C4**
Welland *Canada* 43°0N 79°15W **82 D5**
Welland → *U.K.* 52°51N 0°5W **13 E7**
Wellawaya *Sri Lanka* 6°44N 81°6E **45 L5**
Wellesley Is. *Australia* 16°42S 139°30E **62 B2**
Wellesley Islands ◎
   Australia 16°32S 139°23E **62 B2**
Wellingborough *U.K.* 52°19N 0°41W **13 E7**
Wellington *Australia* 32°35S 148°59E **63 E4**
Wellington *Canada* 43°57N 77°20W **82 C7**
Wellington *N.Z.* 41°19S 174°46E **59 D5**
Wellington *S. Africa* 33°38S 19°1E **56 D2**
Wellington *Somst., U.K.* 50°58N 3°13W **13 G4**
Wellington *Telford & Wrekin,*
   U.K. 52°42N 2°30W **13 E5**
Wellington *Colo., U.S.A.* 40°42N 105°0W **76 F11**
Wellington *Kans., U.S.A.* 37°16N 97°24W **80 G5**
Wellington *Nev., U.S.A.* 38°45N 119°23W **78 G7**
Wellington *Ohio, U.S.A.* 41°10N 82°13W **82 E2**
Wellington *Tex., U.S.A.* 34°51N 100°13W **84 D4**
Wellington, I. *Chile* 49°30S 75°0W **96 F2**
Wellington, L. *Australia* 38°6S 147°20E **63 F4**
Wellington Chan. *Canada* 75°0N 93°0W **69 C13**
Wells *U.K.* 51°13N 2°39W **13 F5**
Wells *Maine, U.S.A.* 43°20N 70°35W **83 C14**
Wells *N.Y., U.S.A.* 43°24N 74°17W **83 C10**
Wells *Nev., U.S.A.* 41°7N 114°58W **76 F6**
Wells, L. *Australia* 26°44S 123°15E **61 E3**
Wells, Mt. *Australia* 17°25S 127°8E **60 C4**
Wells Gray △ *Canada* 52°30N 120°15W **70 C4**
Wells-next-the-Sea *U.K.* 52°57N 0°51E **12 E8**
Wells River *U.S.A.* 44°9N 72°4W **83 B12**
Wellsboro *U.S.A.* 41°45N 77°18W **82 E7**
Wellsburg *U.S.A.* 40°16N 80°37W **82 F4**
Wellsville *N.Y., U.S.A.* 42°7N 77°57W **82 D7**
Wellsville *Ohio, U.S.A.* 40°36N 80°39W **82 F4**
Wellsville *Utah, U.S.A.* 41°38N 111°56W **76 F8**
Wellton *U.S.A.* 32°40N 114°8W **77 K6**
Wels *Austria* 48°9N 14°1E **16 D8**
Welshpool *U.K.* 52°39N 3°8W **13 E4**
Welwyn Garden City *U.K.* 51°48N 0°12W **13 F7**
Wem *U.K.* 52°52N 2°44W **12 E5**
Wemindji *Canada* 53°0N 78°49W **72 B4**
Wemyss *Canada* 44°52N 76°23W **83 B8**
Wen Xian *Gansu, China* 32°43N 104°36E **32 H3**
Wen Xian *Henan, China* 34°55N 113°5E **32 G7**
Wenatchee *U.S.A.* 47°25N 120°19W **76 C3**
Wenchang *China* 19°38N 110°42E **38 C8**
Wencheng *China* 27°46N 120°4E **35 D13**
Wenchi *Ghana* 7°46N 2°8W **52 G5**
Wenchow = Wenzhou
   China 28°0N 120°38E **35 D13**
Wenchuan *China* 31°22N 103°35E **34 B4**
Wenden *U.S.A.* 33°49N 113°33W **79 M13**
Wendeng *China* 37°15N 122°5E **33 F12**
Wendesi *Indonesia* 2°30S 134°17E **37 E8**
Wendover *U.S.A.* 40°44N 114°2W **76 F6**
Weng'an *China* 27°5N 107°25E **34 D6**
Wengcheng *China* 24°22N 113°50E **35 E9**
Wengyuan *China* 24°20N 114°9E **35 E10**
Wenling *China* 28°21N 121°20E **35 C13**
Wenlock → *Australia* 12°2S 141°55E **62 A3**
Wenshan *China* 23°20N 104°18E **34 F5**
Wenshang *China* 35°45N 116°30E **32 G9**
Wenshui *China* 37°26N 112°1E **32 F7**
Wensleydale *U.K.* 54°17N 2°0W **12 C6**
Wensu *China* 41°15N 80°10E **30 C5**
Wensum → *U.K.* 52°40N 1°15E **12 E8**

Wentworth *Australia* 34°2S 141°54E **63 E3**
Wentzel L. *Canada* 59°2N 114°28W **70 B6**
Wenut *Indonesia* 3°11S 133°19E **37 E8**
Wenxi *China* 35°20N 111°10E **32 G6**
Wenzhou *China* 28°0N 120°38E **35 D13**
Weott *U.S.A.* 40°20N 123°55W **76 F2**
Wepener *S. Africa* 29°42S 27°3E **56 C4**
Werda *Botswana* 25°24S 23°15E **56 C3**
Weri *Indonesia* 3°10S 132°38E **37 E8**
Werra → *Germany* 51°24N 9°39E **16 C5**
Werrimull *Australia* 34°25S 141°38E **63 E3**
Werris Creek *Australia* 31°18S 150°38E **63 E5**
Weser → *Germany* 53°36N 8°28E **16 B5**
Weslaco *U.S.A.* 26°10N 97°58W **84 H6**
Weslemkoon L. *Canada* 45°2N 77°25W **82 A7**
Wesleyville *Canada* 49°9N 53°33W **73 C9**
Wesleyville *U.S.A.* 42°9N 80°1W **82 D4**
Wessel, C. *Australia* 10°59S 136°46E **62 A2**
Wessel Is. *Australia* 11°10S 136°45E **62 A2**
Wessex *U.K.* 51°0N 2°0W **13 F5**
Wessington Springs
   U.S.A. 44°5N 98°34W **80 C4**
West *U.S.A.* 31°48N 97°6W **84 F6**
West → *U.S.A.* 42°52N 72°33W **83 D12**
West Allis *U.S.A.* 43°1N 88°0W **80 D9**
West Antarctica *Antarctica* 80°0S 90°0W **5 D15**
West Baines →
   Australia 15°38S 129°59E **60 C4**
West Bank ■ *Asia* 32°6N 35°13E **48 C4**
West Bend *U.S.A.* 43°25N 88°11W **80 D9**
West Bengal = Paschimbanga □
   India 23°0N 88°0E **43 H13**
West Berkshire □ *U.K.* 51°25N 1°17W **13 F6**
West Beskids = Západné Beskydy
   Europe 49°30N 19°0E **17 D10**
West Branch *U.S.A.* 44°17N 84°14W **81 C11**
West Branch Susquehanna →
   U.S.A. 40°53N 76°48W **83 F8**
West Bromwich *U.K.* 52°32N 1°59W **13 E6**
West Burra *U.K.* 60°5N 1°21W **11 A7**
West Canada Cr. →
   U.S.A. 43°1N 74°58W **83 C10**
West Caroline Basin
   Pac. Oc. 4°0N 138°0E **64 G5**
West Chazy *U.S.A.* 44°49N 73°28W **83 B11**
West Chester *U.S.A.* 39°58N 75°36W **83 G9**
West Coast = Namibia 21°53S 14°14E **56 B1**
West Coast △ *S. Africa* 33°13S 18°0E **56 D2**
West Columbia *U.S.A.* 29°9N 95°39W **84 G7**
West Covina *U.S.A.* 34°4N 117°54W **79 L9**
West Des Moines *U.S.A.* 41°35N 93°43W **80 E7**
West Dunbartonshire □
   U.K. 55°59N 4°30W **11 F4**
West End *Bahamas* 26°41N 78°58W **88 A4**
West Falkland *Falk. Is.* 51°40S 60°0W **96 G4**
West Fargo *U.S.A.* 46°52N 96°54W **80 B5**
West Fiji Basin *Pac. Oc.* 17°0S 173°0E **64 J9**
West Fjord = Vestfjorden
   Norway 67°55N 14°0E **8 C16**
West Fork Trinity →
   U.S.A. 32°48N 96°54W **84 E6**
West Frankfort *U.S.A.* 37°54N 88°55W **80 G9**
West Grand L. *U.S.A.* 45°14N 67°51W **81 C20**
West Hartford *U.S.A.* 41°45N 72°44W **83 E12**
West Haven *U.S.A.* 41°17N 72°57W **83 E12**
West Hazleton *U.S.A.* 40°58N 76°0W **83 F9**
West Hurley *U.S.A.* 41°59N 74°7W **83 E10**
West I. *India* 13°5N 92°54E **45 H11**
West Ice Shelf *Antarctica* 67°0S 85°0E **5 C7**
West Indies *Cent. Amer.* 15°0N 65°0W **89 D7**
West Jordan *U.S.A.* 40°36N 111°56W **76 F8**
West Linn *U.S.A.* 45°21N 122°36W **78 E4**
West Lorne *Canada* 42°36N 81°36W **82 D3**
West Lothian □ *U.K.* 55°54N 3°36W **11 F5**
West MacDonnell △
   Australia 23°38S 132°59E **60 D5**
West Mariana Basin
   Pac. Oc. 15°0N 137°0E **64 F5**
West Memphis *U.S.A.* 35°8N 90°10W **85 D9**
West Midlands □ *U.K.* 52°26N 2°0W **13 E6**
West Mifflin *U.S.A.* 40°21N 79°52W **82 F5**
West Milford *U.S.A.* 41°8N 74°22W **83 E10**
West Milton *U.S.A.* 41°1N 76°50W **82 E8**
West Monroe *U.S.A.* 32°31N 92°9W **84 E8**
West Newton *U.S.A.* 40°14N 79°46W **82 F5**
West Odessa *U.S.A.* 31°50N 102°30W **84 F3**
West Palm Beach *U.S.A.* 26°43N 80°3W **85 H14**
West Plains *U.S.A.* 36°44N 91°51W **80 G8**
West Point *Miss., U.S.A.* 33°36N 88°39W **85 E10**
West Point *N.Y., U.S.A.* 41°24N 73°58W **83 E11**
West Point *Nebr., U.S.A.* 41°51N 96°43W **80 E5**
West Point *Va., U.S.A.* 37°32N 76°48W **81 G15**
West Point L. *U.S.A.* 33°8N 85°0W **85 E12**
West Pt. = Ouest, Pte. de l'
   Canada 49°52N 64°40W **73 C7**
West Pt. *Australia* 35°1S 135°56E **63 F2**
West Road → *Canada* 53°18N 122°53W **70 C4**
West Rutland *U.S.A.* 43°36N 73°3W **83 C11**
West Schelde = Westerschelde →
   Neths. 51°25N 3°25E **15 C3**
West Seneca *U.S.A.* 42°51N 78°48W **82 D6**
West Siberian Plain *Russia* 62°0N 75°0E **24 B9**
West Sussex □ *U.K.* 50°55N 0°30W **13 G7**
West-Terschelling *Neths.* 53°22N 5°13E **15 A5**
West Valley City *U.S.A.* 38°45N 80°30W **81 F13**
West Virginia □ *U.S.A.* 38°45N 80°30W **81 F13**
West-Vlaanderen □ *Belgium* 51°0N 3°0E **15 D2**
West Walker → *U.S.A.* 38°54N 119°9W **78 G7**
West Wyalong *Australia* 33°56S 147°10E **63 E4**
West Yellowstone *U.S.A.* 44°40N 111°6W **76 D8**
West Yorkshire □ *U.K.* 53°45N 1°40W **12 D6**
Westall, Pt. *Australia* 32°55S 134°4E **63 E1**
Westbrook *U.S.A.* 43°41N 70°22W **81 D18**
Westby *Australia* 35°40N 117°24W **79 K9**
Westby *U.S.A.* 48°52N 104°3W **76 B3**
Westend *U.S.A.* 35°40N 117°24W **79 K9**
Westerland *Germany* 54°54N 8°17E **16 A5**
Westerly *U.S.A.* 41°22N 71°50W **83 E13**

Western Australia □
   Australia 25°0S 118°0E **61 E2**
Western Bahr el Ghazâl □
   South Sudan 7°30N 25°30E **50 F6**
Western Cape □ *S. Africa* 34°0S 20°0E **56 D3**
Western Dvina = Daugava →
   Latvia 57°4N 24°3E **9 H21**
Western Ghats *India* 14°0N 75°0E **45 H2**
Western Isles = Eilean Siar □
   U.K. 57°30N 7°10W **11 D1**
Western Sahara ■ *Africa* 25°0N 13°0W **52 D3**
Western Samoa = Samoa ■
   Pac. Oc. 14°0S 172°0W **59 b**
Western Sierra Madre = Madre
   Occidental, Sierra
   Mexico 27°0N 107°0W **86 B3**
Westernport *U.S.A.* 39°29N 79°3W **81 F14**
Westerschelde → *Neths.* 51°25N 3°25E **15 C3**
Westerwald *Germany* 50°38N 7°56E **16 C4**
Westfield *Mass., U.S.A.* 42°7N 72°45W **83 D12**
Westfield *N.Y., U.S.A.* 42°20N 79°35W **82 D5**
Westfield *Pa., U.S.A.* 41°55N 77°32W **82 E7**
Westhill *U.K.* 57°9N 2°19W **11 D6**
Westhope *U.S.A.* 48°55N 101°1W **80 A3**
Westland △ *N.Z.* 43°16S 170°16E **59 E2**
Westland Bight *N.Z.* 42°55S 170°5E **59 E3**
Westlock *Canada* 54°9N 113°55W **70 C6**
Westmar *Australia* 27°55S 149°44E **63 D4**
Westmeath □ *Ireland* 53°33N 7°34W **10 C4**
Westminster *Calif.,*
   U.S.A. 33°45N 118°0W **79 M8**
Westminster *Colo.,*
   U.S.A. 39°50N 105°2W **76 G11**
Westminster *Md.,*
   U.S.A. 39°34N 76°59W **81 F15**
Westmont *U.S.A.* 40°19N 78°58W **82 F6**
Westmoreland *Barbados* 13°13N 59°37W **89 g**
Westmorland *U.S.A.* 33°2N 115°37W **79 M11**
Weston *Oreg., U.S.A.* 45°49N 118°26W **76 D4**
Weston *W. Va., U.S.A.* 39°2N 80°28W **81 F13**
Weston I. *Canada* 52°33N 79°36W **72 B4**
Weston-super-Mare *U.K.* 51°21N 2°58W **13 F5**
Westover *U.S.A.* 40°45N 78°40W **82 F6**
Westport *Canada* 44°40N 76°25W **83 B8**
Westport *Ireland* 53°48N 9°31W **10 C2**
Westport *N.Z.* 41°46S 171°37E **59 D3**
Westport *N.Y., U.S.A.* 44°11N 73°26W **83 B11**
Westport *Oreg., U.S.A.* 46°8N 123°23W **78 D3**
Westport *Wash., U.S.A.* 46°53N 124°6W **78 D2**
Westray *Canada* 53°36N 101°24W **71 C8**
Westray *U.K.* 59°18N 3°0W **11 B5**
Westree *Canada* 47°26N 81°34W **72 C3**
Westville *U.S.A.* 39°38N 120°42W **78 F6**
Westwood *U.S.A.* 40°18N 121°0W **76 F3**
Wetar *Indonesia* 7°48S 126°30E **37 F7**
Wetaskiwin *Canada* 52°55N 113°24W **70 C6**
Wete *Tanzania* 5°4S 39°43E **54 F7**
Wetherby *U.K.* 53°56N 1°23W **12 D6**
Wethersfield *U.S.A.* 41°42N 72°40W **83 E12**
Wetteren *Belgium* 51°0N 3°53E **15 D3**
Wetzlar *Germany* 50°32N 8°31E **16 C5**
Wewoka *U.S.A.* 35°9N 96°30W **84 D6**
Wexford *Ireland* 52°20N 6°28W **10 D5**
Wexford □ *Ireland* 52°20N 6°25W **10 D5**
Wexford Harbour *Ireland* 52°20N 6°25W **10 D5**
Weyburn *Canada* 49°40N 103°50W **71 D8**
Weymouth *Canada* 44°30N 66°1W **73 D6**
Weymouth *U.K.* 50°37N 2°28W **13 G5**
Weymouth *U.S.A.* 42°13N 70°58W **83 D14**
Weymouth, C. *Australia* 12°37S 143°27E **62 A3**
Wha Ti *Canada* 63°8N 117°16W **68 E8**
Whakaari *N.Z.* 37°30S 177°13E **59 B6**
Whakatane *N.Z.* 37°57S 177°1E **59 B6**
Whale = Baleine →
   Canada 58°15N 67°40W **73 A6**
Whale B. *Burma* 11°37N 98°38E **39 G2**
Whale Cove *Canada* 62°10N 92°34W **71 A10**
Whales, B. of *Antarctica* 78°0S 160°0W **5 D12**
Whalsay *U.K.* 60°22N 0°59W **11 A8**
Whangamata *N.Z.* 37°12S 175°53E **59 B5**
Whangamomona *N.Z.* 39°8S 174°44E **59 C5**
Whanganui △ *N.Z.* 39°17S 174°53E **59 C5**
Whangarei *N.Z.* 35°43S 174°21E **59 A5**
Whangarei Harb. *N.Z.* 35°45S 174°28E **59 A5**
Wharekauri = Chatham Is.
   Pac. Oc. 44°0S 176°40W **64 M10**
Wharfe → *U.K.* 53°51N 1°9W **12 D6**
Wharfedale *U.K.* 54°6N 2°1W **12 C5**
Wharton *Canada* 40°54N 74°35W **83 F10**
Wharton *Pa., U.S.A.* 41°31N 78°1W **82 E6**
Wharton *Tex., U.S.A.* 29°19N 96°6W **84 G6**
Wharton Basin *Ind. Oc.* 22°0S 92°0E **64 K1**
Wheatland *Calif., U.S.A.* 39°1N 121°25W **78 F5**
Wheatland *Wyo., U.S.A.* 42°3N 104°58W **76 E11**
Wheatley *Canada* 42°6N 82°27W **82 D2**
Wheaton *Md., U.S.A.* 39°3N 77°3W **81 F15**
Wheaton *Minn., U.S.A.* 45°48N 96°30W **80 C5**
Wheelbarrow Pk.
   U.S.A. 37°26N 116°5W **78 H10**
Wheeler *Oreg., U.S.A.* 45°41N 123°53W **76 D1**
Wheeler *Tex., U.S.A.* 35°27N 100°16W **84 D4**
Wheeler → *Canada* 57°2N 67°13W **73 A6**
Wheeler L. *U.S.A.* 34°48N 87°23W **85 D11**
Wheeler Pk. *N. Mex.,*
   U.S.A. 36°34N 105°25W **77 H11**
Wheeler Pk. *Nev.,*
   U.S.A. 38°57N 114°15W **76 G6**
Wheeler Ridge *U.S.A.* 35°0N 118°57W **79 L8**
Wheelersburg *U.S.A.* 38°44N 82°51W **81 F12**
Wheeling *U.S.A.* 40°4N 80°43W **82 F4**
Whernside *U.K.* 54°14N 2°24W **12 C5**
Whiddy I. *Ireland* 51°41N 9°31W **10 E2**
Whim Creek *Australia* 20°50S 117°49E **60 D2**
Whiskey Jack L. *Canada* 58°23N 101°55W **71 B8**
Whiskeytown-Shasta-Trinity △
   U.S.A. 40°45N 122°15W **76 F2**
Whistleduck Cr. →
   Australia 20°15S 135°18E **62 C2**

Whistler *Canada* 50°7N 122°58W **70 C4**
Whitby *Canada* 43°52N 78°56W **82 C6**
Whitby *U.K.* 54°29N 0°37W **12 C7**
White → *Ark., U.S.A.* 33°57N 91°5W **84 E9**
White → *Ind., U.S.A.* 38°25N 87°45W **80 F10**
White → *S. Dak., U.S.A.* 43°42N 99°27W **80 D4**
White → *Tex., U.S.A.* 33°14N 100°56W **84 E4**
White → *Utah, U.S.A.* 40°4N 109°41W **76 F9**
White → *Vt., U.S.A.* 43°37N 72°20W **83 C12**
White → *Wash., U.S.A.* 47°12N 122°15W **78 C4**
White, L. *Australia* 21°9S 128°56E **60 D4**
White B. *Canada* 50°0N 56°35W **73 C8**
White Bird *U.S.A.* 45°46N 116°18W **76 D5**
White Butte *U.S.A.* 46°23N 103°18W **80 B2**
White City *U.S.A.* 39°26N 90°24W **80 F8**
White Cliffs *Australia* 30°50S 143°10E **63 E3**
White Hall *U.S.A.* 41°4N 75°47W **83 F9**
White Horse, Vale of *U.K.* 51°37N 1°30W **13 F6**
White I. = Whakaari
   N.Z. 37°30S 177°13E **59 B6**
White L. *Canada* 45°18N 76°31W **83 A8**
White L. *U.S.A.* 29°44N 92°30W **84 G8**
White Lake *Canada* 45°21N 76°29W **83 A8**
White Mountain Peak
   U.S.A. 37°38N 118°15W **79 H8**
White Mts. *Calif., U.S.A.* 37°30N 118°15W **78 H8**
White Mts. *N.H., U.S.A.* 44°15N 71°15W **83 B13**
White Mts. △ *Australia* 20°43S 145°12E **62 C4**
White Nile = Nîl el Abyad →
   Sudan 15°38N 32°31E **53 E12**
White Otter L. *Canada* 49°5N 91°55W **72 C1**
White Pass *U.S.A.* 46°38N 121°24W **78 D5**
White Plains *U.S.A.* 41°2N 73°46W **83 E11**
White River *Canada* 48°35N 85°20W **72 C2**
White River *U.S.A.* 43°34N 100°45W **80 D3**
White Rock *Canada* 49°2N 122°48W **78 A4**
White Rock *U.S.A.* 35°50N 106°12W **77 J10**
White Russia = Belarus ■
   Europe 53°30N 27°0E **17 B14**
White Sands △ *U.S.A.* 32°46N 106°20W **77 K10**
White Sea = Beloye More
   Russia 66°30N 38°0E **18 A6**
White Sulphur Springs *Mont.,*
   U.S.A. 46°33N 110°54W **76 C8**
White Sulphur Springs *W. Va.,*
   U.S.A. 37°48N 80°18W **81 G13**
White Swan *U.S.A.* 46°23N 120°44W **78 D6**
Whitecliffs *N.Z.* 43°26S 171°55E **59 E3**
Whitecourt *Canada* 54°10N 115°45W **70 C5**
Whiteface Mt. *U.S.A.* 44°22N 73°54W **83 B11**
Whitefield *U.S.A.* 44°23N 71°37W **83 B13**
Whitefish *U.S.A.* 48°25N 114°20W **76 B6**
Whitefish B. *U.S.A.* 46°40N 84°55W **72 C3**
Whitefish L. *Canada* 62°41N 106°48W **71 A7**
Whitefish Pt. *U.S.A.* 46°45N 84°59W **81 B11**
Whitegull, L. = Goélands, L. aux
   Canada 55°27N 64°17W **73 A7**
Whitehall *Mich., U.S.A.* 43°24N 86°21W **80 D10**
Whitehall *Mont., U.S.A.* 45°52N 112°6W **76 D7**
Whitehall *N.Y., U.S.A.* 43°33N 73°24W **83 C11**
Whitehall *Wis., U.S.A.* 44°22N 91°19W **80 C8**
Whitehaven *U.K.* 54°33N 3°35W **12 C4**
Whitehorse *Canada* 60°43N 135°3W **70 A1**
Whitemark *Australia* 40°7S 148°3E **63 G4**
Whiteriver *U.S.A.* 33°50N 109°58W **77 K9**
Whitesand → *Canada* 60°9N 115°45W **70 A5**
Whitesands *S. Africa* 34°23S 20°50E **56 D3**
Whitesboro *N.Y., U.S.A.* 43°7N 75°18W **83 C9**
Whitesboro *Tex., U.S.A.* 33°39N 96°54W **84 E6**
Whiteshell △ *Canada* 50°0N 95°40W **71 D9**
Whiteville *U.S.A.* 34°20N 78°42W **85 D15**
Whitewater *U.S.A.* 42°50N 88°44W **80 D9**
Whitewater Baldy
   U.S.A. 33°20N 108°39W **77 K9**
Whitewater L. *Canada* 50°50N 89°10W **72 B2**
Whitewood *Australia* 21°28S 143°30E **62 C3**
Whitewood *Canada* 50°20N 102°20W **71 C8**
Whithorn *U.K.* 54°44N 4°26W **11 G4**
Whitianga *N.Z.* 36°47S 175°41E **59 B5**
Whitman *U.S.A.* 42°5N 70°56W **83 D14**
Whitmore Mts.
   Antarctica 82°35S 104°30W **5 E15**
Whitney *Canada* 45°31N 78°14W **82 A6**
Whitney, Mt. *U.S.A.* 36°35N 118°18W **78 J8**
Whitney Point *U.S.A.* 42°20N 75°58W **83 D9**
Whitstable *U.K.* 51°21N 1°3E **13 F9**
Whitsunday I. *Australia* 20°15S 149°4E **62 b**
Whitsunday Islands △
   Australia 20°15S 149°0E **62 b**
Whittier *U.S.A.* 60°47N 148°41W **74 C10**
Whittlesea *Australia* 37°27S 145°9E **63 F4**
Wholdaia L. *Canada* 60°43N 104°20W **71 A8**
Whyalla *Australia* 33°2S 137°30E **63 E2**
Wiang Kosai △ *Thailand* 17°54N 99°29E **38 D2**
Wiang Sa *Thailand* 18°34N 100°45E **38 C3**
Wiarton *Canada* 44°40N 81°10W **82 B3**
Wiay *U.K.* 57°24N 7°13W **11 D1**
Wibaux *U.S.A.* 46°59N 104°11W **76 C11**
Wichian Buri *Thailand* 15°39N 101°7E **38 E3**
Wichita *U.S.A.* 37°42N 97°20W **80 G5**
Wichita Falls *U.S.A.* 33°54N 98°30W **84 E5**
Wick *U.K.* 58°26N 3°5W **11 C5**
Wickenburg *U.S.A.* 33°58N 112°44W **77 K7**
Wickepin *Australia* 32°50S 117°30E **61 F2**
Wickham *Australia* 20°42S 117°11E **60 D2**
Wickham, C. *Australia* 39°35S 143°57E **63 F3**
Wickliffe *U.S.A.* 41°36N 81°28W **82 E3**
Wicklow *Ireland* 52°59N 6°3W **10 D5**
Wicklow □ *Ireland* 52°57N 6°25W **10 D5**
Wicklow Hd. *Ireland* 52°58N 6°0W **10 D6**
Wicklow Mts. △ *Ireland* 53°6N 6°21W **10 C5**
Widgeegoara Cr. →
   Australia 28°51S 146°34E **63 D4**
Widgiemooltha *Australia* 31°30S 121°34E **61 F3**
Widnes *U.K.* 53°23N 2°45W **12 D5**
Wieluń *Poland* 51°15N 18°34E **17 C10**

174 Wiener Neustadt
INDEX TO WORLD MAPS

Wiener Neustadt Austria 47°49N 16°16E 16 E9
Wiesbaden Germany 50°4N 8°14E 16 C5
Wigan U.K. 53°33N 2°38W 12 D5
Wiggins Colo., U.S.A. 40°14N 104°4W 76 F11
Wiggins Miss., U.S.A. 30°51N 89°8W 85 F10
Wight, I. of U.K. 50°41N 1°17W 13 G6
Wigston U.K. 52°35N 1°6W 13 E6
Wigton U.K. 54°50N 3°10W 12 C4
Wigtown U.K. 54°53N 4°27W 11 G4
Wigtown B. U.K. 54°46N 4°15W 11 G4
Wik and Wikway People ✪ Australia 13°55S 142°28E 62 A3
Wilber U.S.A. 40°29N 96°58W 80 E5
Wilberforce Canada 45°2N 78°13W 82 A6
Wilberforce, C. Australia 11°54S 136°35E 62 A2
Wilburton U.S.A. 34°55N 95°19W 84 D7
Wilcannia Australia 31°30S 143°26E 63 E3
Wilcox U.S.A. 41°35N 78°41W 82 E6
Wildomar U.S.A. 33°36N 117°16W 79 M9
Wildrose U.S.A. 36°14N 117°11W 79 J9
Wildspitze Austria 46°53N 10°53E 16 E6
Wilge → S. Africa 27°3S 28°20E 57 C4
Wilhelm II Coast Antarctica 68°0S 90°0E 5 C7
Wilhelmshaven Germany 53°31N 8°7E 16 B5
Wilhelmstal Namibia 21°58S 16°21E 56 B2
Wilis Indonesia 7°51S 111°48E 37 G15
Wilkes-Barre U.S.A. 41°15N 75°53W 83 E9
Wilkes Land Antarctica 69°0S 120°0E 5 D9
Wilkie Canada 52°27N 108°42W 71 C7
Wilkins Ice Shelf Antarctica 70°30S 72°0W 5 C17
Wilkinsburg U.S.A. 40°26N 79°52W 82 F5
Wilkinson Lakes Australia 29°40S 132°39E 61 E5
Willandra Creek → Australia 33°22S 145°52E 63 E4
Willapa B. U.S.A. 46°40N 124°0W 78 D3
Willapa Hills U.S.A. 46°35N 123°25W 78 D3
Willard U.S.A. 41°3N 82°44W 82 E2
Willare Bridge Roadhouse Australia 17°43S 123°38E 60 C3
Willcox U.S.A. 32°15N 109°50W 77 K9
Willemstad Curaçao 12°5N 68°55W 89 D6
William → Canada 59°8N 109°19W 71 B7
William 'Bill' Dannelly Res. U.S.A. 32°6N 87°24W 85 E11
William Creek Australia 28°58S 136°22E 63 D2
Williams Australia 33°2S 116°52E 61 F2
Williams Ariz., U.S.A. 35°15N 112°11W 77 J7
Williams Calif., U.S.A. 39°9N 122°9W 78 F4
Williams Harbour Canada 52°33N 55°47W 73 B8
Williams Lake Canada 52°10N 122°10W 70 C4
Williamsburg Ky., U.S.A. 36°44N 84°10W 81 G11
Williamsburg Pa., U.S.A. 40°28N 78°12W 82 F6
Williamsburg Va., U.S.A. 37°16N 76°43W 81 G15
Williamson N.Y., U.S.A. 43°14N 77°11W 82 C7
Williamson W. Va., U.S.A. 37°41N 82°17W 81 G12
Williamsport U.S.A. 41°15N 77°1W 82 E7
Williamston U.S.A. 35°51N 77°4W 85 D16
Williamstown Ky., U.S.A. 38°38N 84°34W 81 F11
Williamstown Mass., U.S.A. 42°43N 73°12W 83 D11
Williamstown N.Y., U.S.A. 43°26N 75°53W 83 C9
Willimantic U.S.A. 41°43N 72°13W 83 E12
Willingboro U.S.A. 40°3N 74°54W 81 E16
Williston S. Africa 31°20S 20°53E 56 D3
Williston Fla., U.S.A. 29°23N 82°27W 85 G13
Williston N. Dak., U.S.A. 48°9N 103°37W 80 A2
Williston L. Canada 56°0N 124°0W 70 B4
Willits U.S.A. 39°25N 123°21W 76 G2
Willmar U.S.A. 45°7N 95°3W 80 C6
Willmore Wilderness ⌓ Canada 53°45N 119°30W 70 C5
Willoughby U.S.A. 41°39N 81°24W 82 E3
Willow Bunch Canada 49°20N 105°35W 71 D7
Willow L. Canada 62°10N 119°8W 70 A5
Willow Wall, The China 42°10N 122°0E 33 C12
Willowick U.S.A. 41°38N 81°28W 82 E3
Willowlake → Canada 62°42N 123°8W 70 A4
Willowmore S. Africa 33°15S 23°30E 56 D3
Willows U.S.A. 39°31N 122°12W 78 F4
Willowvale = Gatyana S. Africa 32°16S 28°31E 57 D4
Wills, L. Australia 21°25S 128°51E 60 D4
Wills Cr. → Australia 22°43S 140°2E 62 C3
Willsboro U.S.A. 44°21N 73°24W 83 B11
Willunga Australia 35°15S 138°30E 63 F2
Wilmington Australia 32°39S 138°7E 63 E2
Wilmington Del., U.S.A. 39°45N 75°33W 81 F16
Wilmington N.C., U.S.A. 34°14N 77°55W 85 D16
Wilmington Ohio, U.S.A. 39°27N 83°50W 81 F12
Wilmington Vt., U.S.A. 42°52N 72°52W 83 D12
Wilmslow U.K. 53°19N 2°13W 12 D5
Wilpattu △ Sri Lanka 8°20N 79°50E 45 K4
Wilpena Cr. → Australia 31°25S 139°29E 63 E2
Wilsall U.S.A. 45°59N 110°38W 76 D8
Wilson N.C., U.S.A. 35°44N 77°55W 85 D16
Wilson N.Y., U.S.A. 43°19N 78°50W 82 C6
Wilson Pa., U.S.A. 40°41N 75°15W 83 F9
Wilson → Australia 16°48S 128°16E 60 C4
Wilson Bluff Australia 31°41S 129°0E 61 F4
Wilson Inlet Australia 35°0S 117°22E 61 G2
Wilsons Promontory Australia 38°59S 146°23E 63 F4
Wilton U.S.A. 47°10N 100°47W 80 B3
Wilton → Australia 14°45S 134°33E 62 A1
Wiltshire □ U.K. 51°18N 1°53W 13 F6
Wiltz Lux. 49°57N 5°55E 15 E5
Wiluna Australia 26°36S 120°14E 61 E3
Wimborne Minster U.K. 50°48N 1°59W 13 G6
Wimmera → Australia 36°8S 141°56E 63 F3
Winburg S. Africa 28°30S 27°2E 56 C4
Winchendon U.S.A. 42°41N 72°3W 83 D12
Winchester U.K. 51°4N 1°18W 13 F6
Winchester Conn., U.S.A. 41°53N 73°9W 83 E11
Winchester Idaho, U.S.A. 46°14N 116°38W 76 C5
Winchester Ind., U.S.A. 40°10N 84°59W 81 E11
Winchester Ky., U.S.A. 37°59N 84°11W 81 G11
Winchester N.H., U.S.A. 42°46N 72°23W 83 D12
Winchester Tenn., U.S.A. 35°11N 86°7W 85 D11
Winchester Va., U.S.A. 39°11N 78°10W 81 F14
Wind → U.S.A. 43°12N 108°12W 76 E9
Wind Cave △ U.S.A. 43°32N 103°17W 80 D2
Wind River Range U.S.A. 43°0N 109°30W 76 E9
Windamere, L. Australia 32°48S 149°51E 63 B4
Windau = Ventspils Latvia 57°25N 21°32E 9 H19
Windber U.S.A. 40°14N 78°50W 82 F6
Winder U.S.A. 34°0N 83°45W 85 D13
Windermere U.K. 54°23N 2°55W 12 C5
Windhoek Namibia 22°35S 17°4E 56 B2
Windidda ✪ Australia 26°23S 122°12E 61 E3
Windjana Gorge △ Australia 17°51S 125°0E 60 C3
Windom U.S.A. 43°52N 95°7W 80 D6
Windorah Australia 25°24S 142°36E 62 D3
Window Rock U.S.A. 35°41N 109°3W 77 J9
Windrush → U.K. 51°43N 1°24W 13 F6
Windsor Australia 33°37S 150°50E 63 E5
Windsor N.S., Canada 44°59N 64°5W 73 D7
Windsor Ont., Canada 42°18N 83°0W 82 D2
Windsor U.K. 51°29N 0°36W 13 F7
Windsor Calif., U.S.A. 38°33N 122°49W 78 G4
Windsor Colo., U.S.A. 40°29N 104°54W 76 F11
Windsor Conn., U.S.A. 41°50N 72°39W 83 E12
Windsor Mo., U.S.A. 38°32N 93°31W 80 F7
Windsor N.Y., U.S.A. 42°5N 75°37W 83 D9
Windsor Vt., U.S.A. 43°29N 72°24W 83 C12
Windsor & Maidenhead □ U.K. 51°29N 0°40W 13 F7
Windsorton S. Africa 28°16S 24°44E 56 C3
Windward Is. W. Indies 13°0N 61°0W 89 D7
Windward Passage = Vientos, Paso de los Caribbean 20°0N 74°0W 89 C5
Winefred L. Canada 55°30N 110°30W 71 B6
Winfield U.S.A. 37°15N 96°59W 80 G5
Wingate Mts. Australia 14°25S 130°40E 60 B5
Wingellina = Irrunytju Australia 26°3S 128°56E 61 E4
Wingham Australia 31°48S 152°22E 63 E5
Wingham Canada 43°55N 81°20W 82 C3
Winisk → Canada 55°17N 85°5W 72 A2
Winisk L. Canada 52°55N 87°22W 72 B2
Wink U.S.A. 31°45N 103°9W 84 F3
Winkler Canada 49°10N 97°56W 71 D9
Winlock U.S.A. 46°30N 122°56W 78 D4
Winneba Ghana 5°25N 0°36W 52 G5
Winnebago, L. U.S.A. 44°0N 88°26W 80 D9
Winnecke Cr. → Australia 18°35S 131°34E 60 C5
Winnemucca U.S.A. 40°58N 117°44W 76 F5
Winnemucca L. U.S.A. 40°7N 119°21W 76 F4
Winner U.S.A. 43°22N 99°52W 80 D4
Winnett U.S.A. 47°0N 108°21W 76 C9
Winnfield U.S.A. 31°56N 92°38W 84 F8
Winnibigoshish, L. U.S.A. 47°27N 94°13W 80 B6
Winnipeg Canada 49°54N 97°9W 71 D9
Winnipeg → Canada 50°38N 96°19W 71 C9
Winnipeg, L. Canada 52°0N 97°0W 71 C9
Winnipeg Beach Canada 50°30N 96°58W 71 C9
Winnipegosis Canada 51°39N 99°55W 71 C9
Winnipegosis L. Canada 52°30N 100°0W 71 C9
Winnipesaukee, L. U.S.A. 43°38N 71°21W 83 C13
Winnisquam L. U.S.A. 43°33N 71°31W 83 C13
Winnsboro La., U.S.A. 32°10N 91°43W 84 E9
Winnsboro S.C., U.S.A. 34°23N 81°5W 85 D14
Winnsboro Tex., U.S.A. 32°58N 95°17W 84 E7
Winokapau, L. Canada 53°15N 62°50W 73 B7
Winona Minn., U.S.A. 44°3N 91°39W 80 C8
Winona Miss., U.S.A. 33°29N 89°44W 85 E10
Winooski U.S.A. 44°29N 73°11W 83 B11
Winooski → U.S.A. 44°32N 73°17W 83 B11
Winschoten Neths. 53°9N 7°3E 15 A7
Winsford U.K. 53°12N 2°31W 12 D5
Winslow = Bainbridge Island U.S.A. 47°38N 122°32W 78 C4
Winslow U.S.A. 35°2N 110°42W 77 J8
Winsted U.S.A. 41°55N 73°4W 83 E11
Winston-Salem U.S.A. 36°6N 80°15W 85 C14
Winter Garden U.S.A. 28°34N 81°35W 85 G14
Winter Haven U.S.A. 28°1N 81°44W 85 G14
Winter Park U.S.A. 28°36N 81°20W 85 G14
Winterhaven U.S.A. 32°44N 114°38W 79 N12
Winters U.S.A. 38°32N 121°58W 78 G5
Winterset U.S.A. 41°20N 94°1W 80 E6
Wintersville U.S.A. 40°23N 80°42W 82 F4
Winterswijk Neths. 51°58N 6°43E 15 C6
Winterthur Switz. 47°30N 8°44E 20 C8
Winthrop U.S.A. 48°28N 120°10W 76 B3
Winton Australia 22°24S 143°3E 62 C3
Winton N.Z. 46°8S 168°20E 59 G2
Wirlyajarrayi ✪ Australia 21°45S 132°35E 60 D5
Wirrulla Australia 32°24S 134°31E 63 E1
Wisbech U.K. 52°41N 0°9E 13 E8
Wisconsin □ U.S.A. 44°45N 89°30W 80 C9
Wisconsin → U.S.A. 43°0N 91°15W 80 D8
Wisconsin Rapids U.S.A. 44°23N 89°49W 80 C9
Wisdom U.S.A. 45°37N 113°27W 76 D7
Wiseman U.S.A. 67°25N 150°6W 74 B9
Wishaw U.K. 55°46N 3°54W 11 F5
Wishek U.S.A. 46°16N 99°33W 80 B4
Wisła → Poland 54°22N 18°55E 17 A10
Wismar Germany 53°54N 11°29E 16 B6
Wisner U.S.A. 41°59N 96°55W 80 E5
Witbank = eMalahleni S. Africa 25°51S 29°14E 57 C4
Witches Gorge = Wu Xia China 31°2N 110°10E 35 B8
Witdraai S. Africa 26°58S 20°48E 56 C3
Witham U.K. 51°48N 0°40E 13 F8
Witham → U.K. 52°59N 0°2W 12 E7
Withernsea U.K. 53°44N 0°1E 12 D8
Witjira △ Australia 26°22S 135°37E 63 D2
Witless Bay Canada 47°17N 52°50W 73 C9
Witney U.K. 51°48N 1°28W 13 F6
Witnossob → Namibia 23°55S 18°45E 56 C3
Witriver S. Africa 25°20S 31°0E 57 C5
Wittenberge Germany 53°0N 11°45E 16 B6
Wittenoom Australia 22°15S 118°20E 60 D2
Witvlei Namibia 22°23S 18°32E 56 B2
Wiwon N. Korea 40°54N 126°3E 33 D14
Wkra → Poland 52°27N 20°44E 17 B11
Wlingi Indonesia 8°5S 112°25E 37 H15
Włocławek Poland 52°40N 19°3E 17 B10
Włodawa Poland 51°33N 23°31E 17 C12
Wodian China 32°50N 112°35E 32 H7
Wodonga Australia 36°5S 146°50E 63 F4
Woinbogoin China 32°51N 98°39E 34 A2
Wokam Indonesia 5°45S 134°28E 37 F8
Woking U.K. 51°19N 0°34W 13 F7
Wokingham U.K. 51°24N 0°49W 13 F7
Wokingham □ U.K. 51°25N 0°51W 13 F7
Wolf → Canada 60°17N 132°33W 70 A2
Wolf Creek U.S.A. 47°0N 112°4W 76 C7
Wolf L. Canada 60°24N 131°40W 70 A2
Wolf Point U.S.A. 48°5N 105°39W 76 B11
Wolfe Creek Crater △ Australia 19°10S 127°47E 60 C4
Wolfe I. Canada 44°7N 76°20W 83 B8
Wolfeboro U.S.A. 43°35N 71°13W 83 C13
Wolfsberg Austria 46°50N 14°52E 16 E8
Wolfsburg Germany 52°25N 10°48E 16 B6
Wolin Poland 53°50N 14°37E 16 B8
Wollaston, Is. Chile 55°40S 67°30W 96 H3
Wollaston L. Canada 58°7N 103°10W 71 B8
Wollaston Lake Canada 58°3N 103°33W 71 B8
Wollaston Pen. Canada 69°30N 115°0W 68 D9
Wollongong Australia 34°25S 150°54E 63 E5
Wolmaransstad S. Africa 27°12S 25°59E 56 C4
Wolseley S. Africa 33°26S 19°7E 56 D2
Wolsey U.S.A. 44°25N 98°28W 80 C4
Wolstenholme, C. Canada 62°35N 77°30W 66 C12
Wolvega Neths. 52°52N 6°0E 15 B6
Wolverhampton U.K. 52°35N 2°7W 13 E5
Wondai Australia 26°20S 151°49E 63 D5
Wongalarroo L. Australia 31°32S 144°0E 63 E3
Wongan Hills Australia 30°51S 116°37E 61 F2
Wonju S. Korea 37°22N 127°58E 33 F14
Wonosari Indonesia 7°58S 110°36E 37 G14
Wonosobo Indonesia 7°22S 109°54E 37 G13
Wonowon Canada 56°44N 121°48W 70 B4
Wŏnsan N. Korea 39°11N 127°27E 33 E14
Wonthaggi Australia 38°37S 145°37E 63 F4
Wood Buffalo △ Canada 59°0N 113°41W 70 B6
Wood Is. Australia 16°24S 123°19E 60 C3
Wood L. Canada 55°17N 103°17W 71 B8
Woodah, I. Australia 13°27S 136°10E 62 A2
Woodbourne U.S.A. 41°46N 74°36W 83 E10
Woodbridge U.K. 52°6N 1°20E 13 E9
Woodburn Australia 29°6S 153°23E 63 A5
Woodburn U.S.A. 45°9N 122°51W 76 D2
Woodenbong Australia 28°24S 152°39E 63 D5
Woodend Australia 37°20S 144°33E 63 F3
Woodford Australia 26°58S 152°47E 63 D5
Woodfords U.S.A. 38°47N 119°50W 78 G7
Woodlake U.S.A. 36°25N 119°6W 78 J7
Woodland Calif., U.S.A. 38°41N 121°46W 78 G5
Woodland Maine, U.S.A. 45°9N 67°25W 81 C20
Woodland Pa., U.S.A. 41°0N 78°21W 82 F6
Woodland Wash., U.S.A. 45°54N 122°45W 78 E4
Woodland Caribou ⌓ Canada 51°0N 94°45W 71 C10
Woodlands, The U.S.A. 30°9N 95°29W 84 F7
Woodonga Australia 36°10S 146°50E 63 F4
Woodridge Canada 49°20N 96°9W 71 D9
Woodroffe, Mt. Australia 26°20S 131°45E 61 E5
Woods, L. Australia 17°50S 133°30E 62 B1
Woods, L. of the N. Amer. 49°15N 94°45W 71 D10
Woods Bay Canada 45°8N 79°59W 82 A5
Woodstock Australia 19°35S 146°50E 62 B4
Woodstock N.B., Canada 46°11N 67°37W 73 C6
Woodstock Ont., Canada 43°10N 80°45W 82 C4
Woodstock U.K. 51°51N 1°20W 13 F6
Woodstock Ill., U.S.A. 42°19N 88°27W 80 D9
Woodstock N.Y., U.S.A. 42°2N 74°7W 83 D10
Woodstock Vt., U.S.A. 43°37N 72°31W 83 C12
Woodsville U.S.A. 44°9N 72°2W 83 B13
Woodview Canada 44°35N 78°8W 82 B6
Woodville N.Z. 40°20S 175°53E 59 D5
Woodville Miss., U.S.A. 31°6N 91°18W 84 F9
Woodville Tex., U.S.A. 30°47N 94°25W 84 F7
Woodward U.S.A. 36°26N 99°24W 84 C5
Woody U.S.A. 35°42N 118°50W 79 K8
Woody → Canada 52°31N 100°51W 71 C8
Woolacombe U.K. 51°10N 4°13W 13 F3
Woolamai, C. Australia 38°30S 145°23E 63 F4
Wooler U.K. 55°33N 2°1W 12 B5
Woolgoolga Australia 30°6S 153°11E 63 E5
Woomera Australia 31°5S 136°50E 63 E2
Woonsocket R.I., U.S.A. 42°0N 71°31W 83 E13
Woonsocket S. Dak., U.S.A. 44°3N 98°17W 80 C4
Wooramel → Australia 25°47S 114°10E 61 E1
Wooramel Roadhouse Australia 25°45S 114°17E 61 E1
Wooroonooran △ Australia 16°25S 146°1E 62 B4
Wooster U.S.A. 40°48N 81°56W 82 F3
Worcester S. Africa 33°39S 19°27E 56 D2
Worcester U.K. 52°11N 2°12W 13 E5
Worcester Mass., U.S.A. 42°16N 71°48W 83 D13
Worcester N.Y., U.S.A. 42°36N 74°45W 83 D10
Worcestershire □ U.K. 52°13N 2°10W 13 E5
Workington U.K. 54°39N 3°33W 12 C4
Worksop U.K. 53°18N 1°7W 12 D6
Workum Neths. 52°59N 5°26E 15 B5
Worland U.S.A. 44°1N 107°57W 76 D10
Worms Germany 49°37N 8°21E 16 D5
Worsley Canada 56°31N 119°8W 70 B5
Wortham U.S.A. 31°47N 96°28W 84 F6
Worthing Barbados 13°5N 59°35W 89 g
Worthing U.K. 50°49N 0°21W 13 G7
Worthington Minn., U.S.A. 43°37N 95°36W 80 D6
Worthington Pa., U.S.A. 40°50N 79°38W 82 F5
Wosi Indonesia 0°15S 128°0E 37 E7
Wotjalum ✪ Australia 16°30S 123°45E 60 C3
Wotjobaluk ✪ Australia 37°0S 142°0E 63 C3
Wou-han = Wuhan China 30°31N 114°18E 35 B10
Wousi = Wuxi China 31°33N 120°18E 35 B13
Wowoni Indonesia 4°5S 123°5E 37 E6
Wrangel I. = Vrangelya, Ostrov Russia 71°0N 180°0E 27 B18
Wrangell U.S.A. 56°28N 132°23W 70 B2
Wrangell Mts. U.S.A. 61°30N 142°0W 68 E3
Wrath, C. U.K. 58°38N 5°1W 11 C3
Wray U.S.A. 40°5N 102°13W 76 F12
Wrekin, The U.K. 52°41N 2°32W 13 E5
Wrens U.S.A. 33°12N 82°23W 85 E13
Wrexham U.K. 53°3N 3°0W 12 D4
Wrexham □ U.K. 53°1N 2°58W 12 D5
Wright Fla., U.S.A. 30°27N 86°38W 85 F11
Wright Wyo., U.S.A. 43°45N 105°28W 76 E11
Wright Pt. Canada 43°48N 81°44W 82 C3
Wrightmyo India 11°47N 92°43E 45 J11
Wrightson, Mt. U.S.A. 31°42N 110°51W 77 L8
Wrightwood U.S.A. 34°22N 117°38W 79 L9
Wrigley Canada 63°16N 123°37W 68 E7
Wrocław Poland 51°5N 17°5E 17 C9
Września Poland 52°21N 17°36E 17 B9
Wu Jiang → China 29°40N 107°20E 34 C6
Wu Kau Tang China 22°30N 114°14E 31 a
Wu Xia China 31°2N 110°10E 35 B8
Wu'an China 36°40N 114°15E 32 F8
Wubalawun ✪ Australia 15°28S 133°1E 60 C5
Wubin Australia 30°6S 116°37E 61 F2
Wubu China 37°28N 110°42E 32 F6
Wuchang China 44°55N 127°5E 33 B14
Wucheng China 37°12N 116°20E 32 F9
Wuchuan Guangdong, China 21°33N 110°43E 35 G8
Wuchuan Guizhou, China 28°25N 108°3E 34 C7
Wuchuan Nei Monggol Zizhiqu, China 41°5N 111°28E 32 D6
Wuda China 39°29N 106°42E 32 E4
Wudang Shan China 32°23N 111°2E 35 A8
Wudi China 37°40N 117°35E 33 F9
Wuding China 25°24N 102°21E 34 E4
Wuding He → China 37°2N 110°23E 32 F6
Wudinna Australia 33°0S 135°22E 63 E2
Wudongde Dam China 26°20N 102°15E 34 D4
Wudu China 33°22N 104°54E 32 H3
Wufeng China 30°12N 110°42E 35 B8
Wugang China 26°44N 110°35E 35 D8
Wugong Shan China 27°30N 114°0E 35 D9
Wuguishan China 22°25N 113°25E 31 a
Wuguллar = Beswick Australia 14°34S 132°53E 60 B5
Wuhai China 39°39N 106°48E 32 E4
Wuhan China 30°31N 114°18E 35 B10
Wuhe China 33°10N 117°50E 33 H9
Wuhsi = Wuxi China 31°33N 120°18E 35 B13
Wuhu China 31°22N 118°21E 35 B12
Wujiang China 31°10N 120°38E 35 B13
Wukari Nigeria 7°51N 9°42E 52 G7
Wulajie China 44°6N 126°33E 33 B14
Wulanbulang China 41°5N 110°55E 32 D6
Wular L. India 34°20N 74°30E 43 B6
Wulian China 35°40N 119°12E 33 G10
Wulian Feng China 27°48N 103°36E 34 D4
Wuliang Shan China 24°30N 100°40E 34 E3
Wuliaru Indonesia 7°27S 131°0E 37 F8
Wuling Shan China 30°0N 110°0E 34 C7
Wulingyuan ⌓ China 29°20N 110°30E 35 C8
Wulong China 29°22N 107°43E 34 C6
Wulong △ China 31°8N 103°5E 34 B4
Wulumuchi = Ürümqi China 43°45N 87°45E 30 C6
Wumeng Shan China 26°48N 104°0E 34 D5
Wuming China 23°12N 108°18E 34 F7
Wuning China 29°17N 115°5E 35 C10
Wunna → India 20°18N 78°48E 44 D4
Wunnummin L. Canada 52°55N 89°10W 72 B2
Wuntho Burma 23°55N 95°45E 41 H19
Wupatki △ U.S.A. 35°35N 111°20W 77 J8
Wuping China 25°5N 116°5E 35 E11
Wuppertal Germany 51°16N 7°12E 16 C4
Wuppertal S. Africa 32°13S 19°12E 56 D2
Wuqing China 39°23N 117°4E 33 E9
Wurralibi ✪ Australia 15°43S 137°1E 62 B2
Wurtsboro U.S.A. 41°35N 74°29W 83 E10
Würzburg Germany 49°46N 9°55E 16 D5
Wushan China 34°43N 104°53E 32 G3
Wushi China 41°9N 79°13E 30 C4
Wutai China 38°40N 113°12E 32 E7
Wutai Shan China 39°3N 113°32E 32 E7
Wuting = Huimin China 37°27N 117°28E 33 F9
Wutong China 25°24N 110°4E 35 E8
Wutonghaolai China 42°50N 120°5E 33 C11
Wutongqiao China 29°22N 103°50E 34 C4
Wuwei Anhui, China 31°18N 117°54E 35 B11
Wuwei Gansu, China 37°57N 102°34E 30 D9
Wuxi Jiangsu, China 31°33N 120°18E 35 B13
Wuxi Sichuan, China 31°23N 109°35E 34 B7
Wuxiang China 36°49N 112°50E 32 F7
Wuxuan China 23°34N 109°38E 34 F7
Wuxue China 29°52N 115°30E 35 C10
Wuyang China 33°25N 113°35E 32 H7
Wuyi Hebei, China 37°46N 115°56E 32 F8
Wuyi Zhejiang, China 28°52N 119°50E 35 C12
Wuyi Shan China 27°0N 117°0E 35 D11
Wuyishan China 27°45N 118°0E 35 D12
Wuyishan △ China 27°55N 117°54E 35 D11
Wuyuan Jiangxi, China 29°15N 117°50E 35 C11
Wuyuan Nei Monggol Zizhiqu, China 41°2N 108°20E 32 D5
Wuzhai China 38°54N 111°48E 32 E6
Wuzhi Shan China 18°45N 109°45E 38 C7
Wuzhong China 38°2N 106°12E 32 E4
Wuzhou China 23°30N 111°18E 35 F8
Wuzishan = Tongshi China 18°30N 109°20E 38 C7
Wyaaba Cr. → Australia 16°27S 141°35E 62 B3
Wyalkatchem Australia 31°8S 117°22E 61 F2
Wyalusing U.S.A. 41°40N 76°16W 83 E8
Wyandotte U.S.A. 42°12N 83°9W 81 D12
Wyandra Australia 27°12S 145°56E 63 D4
Wyangala, L. Australia 33°54S 149°0E 63 E4
Wyara, L. Australia 28°42S 144°14E 63 D3
Wycheproof Australia 36°5S 143°17E 63 F3
Wycliffe Well Australia 20°48S 134°14E 62 C1
Wye → U.K. 51°38N 2°40W 13 F5
Wyemandoo Australia 28°28S 118°29E 61 E2
Wymondham U.K. 52°35N 1°7E 13 E9
Wymore U.S.A. 40°7N 96°40W 80 E5
Wyndham Australia 15°33S 128°3E 60 C4
Wyndham N.Z. 46°20S 168°51E 59 G2
Wynne U.S.A. 35°14N 90°47W 85 D9
Wynyard Australia 41°5S 145°44E 63 G4
Wynyard Canada 51°45N 104°10W 71 C8
Wyola L. Australia 29°8S 130°17E 61 E5
Wyoming Canada 42°57N 82°7W 82 D2
Wyoming □ U.S.A. 43°0N 107°30W 76 E10
Wyomissing U.S.A. 40°20N 75°59W 83 F9
Wyong Australia 33°14S 151°24E 63 E5
Wytheville U.S.A. 36°57N 81°5W 81 G13

X

Xaafuun Somalia 10°25N 51°16E 49 E5
Xaafuun, Ras Somalia 10°27N 51°24E 49 E5
Xaçmaz Azerbaijan 41°31N 48°42E 19 F8
Xai-Xai Mozam. 25°6S 33°31E 57 C5
Xaignabouri = Sayaboury Laos 19°15N 101°45E 38 C3
Xainza China 30°58N 88°35E 30 E6
Xalapa Mexico 19°32N 96°55W 87 D5
Xangongo Angola 16°45S 15°5E 56 A2
Xankändi Azerbaijan 39°52N 46°49E 46 B5
Xanthi Greece 41°10N 24°58E 23 D11
Xanxerê Brazil 26°53S 52°23W 95 B5
Xapuri Brazil 10°35S 68°35W 92 F5
Xar Moron He → China 43°25N 120°35E 33 C11
Xátiva Spain 38°59N 0°32W 21 C5
Xau, L. Botswana 21°15S 24°44E 56 B3
Xavantina Brazil 21°15S 52°48W 95 A5
Xebert China 44°2N 122°0E 33 B12
Xenia U.S.A. 39°41N 83°56W 81 F12
Xhora S. Africa 31°55S 28°38E 57 D4
Xhumo Botswana 21°7S 24°35E 56 B3
Xi Jiang → China 22°5N 113°20E 35 F9
Xi Ujimqin Qi China 44°32N 117°40E 33 B9
Xi Xian Henan, China 32°20N 114°43E 35 A10
Xi Xian Shanxi, China 36°41N 110°58E 32 F6
Xia Xian China 35°8N 111°12E 32 G6
Xiachengzi China 44°40N 130°18E 33 B16
Xiachuan Dao China 21°40N 112°40E 35 G9
Xiaguan China 25°32N 100°16E 30 F9
Xiajiang China 27°30N 115°10E 35 D10
Xiajin China 36°56N 116°0E 32 F9
Xiamen China 24°25N 118°4E 35 E12
Xi'an China 34°15N 109°0E 32 G5
Xian Xian China 38°12N 116°6E 32 E9
Xianfeng China 29°40N 109°8E 34 C7
Xiang Jiang → China 28°55N 112°50E 35 C9
Xiang Khouang Laos 19°17N 103°25E 38 C4
Xiangcheng Henan, China 33°50N 113°27E 32 H7
Xiangcheng Sichuan, China 28°53N 99°47E 34 C2
Xiangdu China 23°13N 106°58E 34 F6
Xiangfan China 32°2N 112°8E 35 A9
Xianggang = Hong Kong □ China 22°11N 114°14E 31 a
Xianghuang Qi China 42°2N 113°50E 32 C7
Xiangjiaba Dam China 28°37N 104°17E 34 C5
Xiangning China 35°58N 110°50E 32 G6
Xiangquan China 36°30N 113°1E 32 F7
Xiangquan He = Sutlej → Pakistan 29°23N 71°3E 42 E4
Xiangshan China 29°29N 121°51E 35 C13
Xiangshui China 34°12N 119°33E 33 G10
Xiangtan China 27°51N 112°54E 35 D9
Xiangxiang China 27°43N 112°28E 35 D9
Xiangyin China 28°38N 112°54E 35 C9
Xiangyun China 25°34N 100°35E 34 E3
Xiangzhou China 23°58N 109°40E 34 F7
Xianju China 28°51N 120°44E 35 C13
Xianning China 29°51N 114°16E 35 C10
Xianshui He → China 30°10N 100°59E 34 B3
Xiantao China 30°25N 113°25E 35 B9
Xianyang China 34°20N 108°40E 32 G5
Xianyou China 25°22N 118°38E 35 E12
Xiao Hinggan Ling China 49°0N 127°0E 31 B14
Xiao Xian China 34°15N 116°55E 32 G9
Xiaofeng China 30°35N 119°32E 35 B12
Xiaogan China 30°52N 113°55E 35 B9
Xiaojin China 30°59N 102°21E 34 B4
Xiaolan China 22°38N 113°13E 35 F9
Xiaoshan China 30°12N 120°18E 35 B13
Xiaowan Dam China 24°42N 100°5E 34 E3
Xiaowutai Shan China 39°51N 114°59E 32 E8
Xiaoyi China 37°8N 111°48E 32 F6

Xiapu *China* 26°54N 119°59E **35** D12
Xiashan = Zhanjiang *China* 21°15N 110°20E **35** G8
Xiawa *China* 42°35N 120°38E **33** C11
Xiayi *China* 34°15N 116°10E **32** G9
Xichang *China* 27°51N 102°19E **34** D4
Xichong *China* 30°57N 105°54E **34** B5
Xichou *China* 23°25N 104°42E **34** E5
Xichuan *China* 33°0N 111°30E **32** H6
Xide *China* 28°8N 102°19E **34** C4
Xiemahe *China* 31°38N 111°12E **35** B8
Xifei He → *China* 32°45N 116°40E **32** H9
Xifeng *Gansu, China* 35°40N 107°40E **32** G4
Xifeng *Guizhou, China* 27°7N 106°42E **34** D6
Xifeng *Liaoning, China* 42°42N 124°45E **33** C13
Xifengzhen = Xifeng *China* 35°40N 107°40E **32** G4
Xigazê *China* 29°5N 88°45E **30** F6
Xihe *China* 34°2N 105°20E **32** G3
Xihua *China* 33°45N 114°30E **32** H8
Xili Shuiku *China* 22°36N 113°57E **31** a
Xiliao He → *China* 43°32N 123°35E **33** C12
Xilin *China* 24°30N 105°6E **34** E5
Xiling Gorge = Xiling Xia *China* 30°54N 110°48E **35** B8
Xiling Xia *China* 30°54N 110°48E **35** B8
Xilinhot *China* 43°52N 116°2E **32** C9
Xiluodu Dam *China* 28°12N 103°34E **34** C4
Ximeng *China* 22°50N 99°27E **34** F2
Ximiao *China* 40°59N 100°12E **30** C9
Xin Jiang → *China* 28°45N 116°35E **35** C11
Xin Xian = Xinzhou *China* 38°22N 112°46E **32** E7
Xin'anjiang Shuiku *China* 29°33N 118°56E **35** C12
Xinavane *Mozam.* 25°2S 32°47E **57** C5
Xinbin *China* 41°40N 125°2E **33** D13
Xincai *China* 32°43N 114°58E **35** A10
Xinchang *China* 29°28N 120°52E **35** C13
Xincheng *Guangxi Zhuangzu, China* 24°5N 108°39E **34** E7
Xincheng *Jiangxi, China* 26°48N 114°6E **35** D10
Xinfeng *Guangdong, China* 24°5N 114°16E **35** E10
Xinfeng *Jiangxi, China* 27°7N 116°11E **35** D11
Xinfeng *Jiangxi, China* 25°27N 114°50E **35** E10
Xinfengjiang Shuiku *China* 23°52N 114°30E **35** F10
Xing Xian *China* 38°27N 111°7E **32** E6
Xing'an *Guangxi Zhuangzu, China* 25°38N 110°40E **35** E8
Xingan *Jiangxi, China* 27°46N 115°20E **35** D10
Xingcheng *China* 40°40N 120°45E **33** D11
Xingguo *China* 26°21N 115°21E **35** D10
Xinghe *China* 40°55N 113°55E **32** D7
Xinghua *China* 32°58N 119°48E **33** H10
Xinghua Wan *China* 25°15N 119°20E **35** E12
Xinglong *China* 40°25N 117°30E **33** D9
Xingning *China* 24°3N 115°42E **35** E10
Xingping *China* 34°20N 108°28E **32** G5
Xingren *China* 25°24N 105°11E **34** E5
Xingshan *China* 31°15N 110°45E **35** B8
Xingtai *China* 37°3N 114°32E **32** F8
Xingu → *Brazil* 1°30S 51°53W **93** D8
Xingwen *China* 28°22N 104°50E **34** C5
Xingxingxia *China* 41°47N 95°0E **30** C7
Xingyang *China* 34°45N 112°52E **32** G7
Xingyi *China* 25°3N 104°59E **34** E5
Xinhe *China* 37°30N 115°15E **32** F8
Xinhua *China* 27°42N 111°13E **35** D8
Xinhuang *China* 27°21N 109°12E **34** D7
Xinhui *China* 22°25N 113°0E **35** F9
Xining *China* 36°34N 101°40E **30** D9
Xinji *China* 37°55N 115°13E **32** F8
Xinjian *China* 28°37N 115°46E **35** C10
Xinjiang *China* 35°34N 111°11E **32** G6
Xinjiang Uygur Zizhiqu □ *China* 42°0N 86°0E **30** C6
Xinjin = Pulandian *China* 39°25N 121°58E **33** E11
Xinjin *China* 30°24N 103°47E **34** B4
Xinkai He → *China* 43°32N 123°35E **33** C12
Xinken *China* 22°39N 113°36E **31** a
Xinle *China* 38°25N 114°40E **32** E8
Xinlitun *China* 42°0N 122°8E **33** D12
Xinlong *China* 30°57N 100°12E **34** B3
Xinmi *China* 34°30N 113°25E **32** G7
Xinmin *China* 41°59N 122°50E **33** D12
Xinning *China* 26°28N 110°50E **35** D8
Xinping *China* 24°5N 101°59E **34** E3
Xinshao *China* 27°21N 111°26E **35** D8
Xintai *China* 35°55N 117°45E **33** G9
Xintian *China* 25°55N 112°13E **35** E9
Xinwan *China* 22°47N 113°40E **31** a
Xinxiang *China* 35°18N 113°50E **32** G7
Xinxing *China* 22°35N 112°15E **35** F9
Xinyang *China* 32°6N 114°3E **35** A10
Xinye *China* 32°30N 112°21E **35** A9
Xinyi *Guangdong, China* 22°25N 111°0E **35** F8
Xinyi *Nei Monggol Zizhiqu, China* 34°23N 118°21E **33** G10
Xinyu *China* 27°49N 114°58E **35** D10
Xinzheng *China* 34°20N 113°45E **32** G7
Xinzhou *Hainan, China* 19°43N 109°17E **38** C7
Xinzhou *Hubei, China* 30°50N 114°48E **35** B10
Xinzhou *Shanxi, China* 38°22N 112°46E **32** E7
Xiongyuecheng *China* 40°12N 122°5E **33** D11
Xiping *Henan, China* 33°22N 114°5E **32** H8
Xiping *Henan, China* 33°25N 111°8E **32** H6
Xiping *Zhejiang, China* 28°16N 119°29E **35** C12
Xique-Xique *Brazil* 10°50S 42°40W **93** F10
Xisha Qundao = Paracel Is. *S. China Sea* 15°50N 112°0E **36** A4
Xishuangbanna *China* 22°5N 101°1E **34** F3
Xishui *Guizhou, China* 28°19N 106°9E **34** C6
Xishui *Hubei, China* 30°30N 115°15E **35** B10
Xiu Shui → *China* 29°13N 116°0E **35** C10

Xiuning *China* 29°45N 118°10E **35** C12
Xiuren *China* 24°27N 110°12E **35** E8
Xiushan *China* 28°25N 108°57E **34** C7
Xiushui *China* 29°2N 114°33E **35** C10
Xiuwen *China* 26°49N 106°32E **34** D6
Xiuyan *China* 40°18N 123°11E **33** D12
Xixabangma Feng *China* 28°20N 85°40E **43** E11
Xixia *China* 33°25N 111°29E **32** H6
Xixiang *Guangdong, China* 22°34N 113°52E **31** a
Xixiang *Shaanxi, China* 33°0N 107°44E **32** H4
Xixón = Gijón *Spain* 43°32N 5°42W **21** A3
Xiyang *China* 37°38N 113°38E **32** F7
Xizang Zizhiqu □ *China* 32°0N 88°0E **30** E6
Xochob *Mexico* 19°21N 89°48W **87** D7
Xu Jiang → *China* 28°0N 116°25E **35** D11
Xuan Loc *Vietnam* 10°56N 107°14E **39** G6
Xuan'en *China* 30°0N 109°30E **34** C7
Xuanhan *China* 31°18N 107°38E **34** B6
Xuanhua *China* 40°40N 115°2E **32** D8
Xuanwei *China* 26°15N 103°59E **34** C5
Xuanzhou *China* 30°56N 118°43E **35** B12
Xuchang *China* 34°2N 113°48E **32** G7
Xuefeng Shan *China* 27°5N 110°35E **35** D8
Xuejiaping *China* 31°39N 110°16E **35** B8
Xun Jiang → *China* 23°35N 111°30E **35** F8
Xun Xian *China* 35°42N 114°33E **32** G8
Xundian *China* 25°36N 103°15E **34** E4
Xunwu *China* 24°54N 115°37E **35** E10
Xunyang *China* 32°48N 109°22E **32** H5
Xunyi *China* 35°8N 108°20E **32** G5
Xupu *China* 27°53N 110°32E **35** D8
Xushui *China* 39°2N 115°40E **32** E8
Xuwen *China* 20°20N 110°10E **35** G8
Xuyi *China* 32°55N 118°32E **35** A12
Xuyong *China* 28°10N 105°22E **34** C5
Xuzhou *China* 34°18N 117°10E **33** G9

Y

Y Drenewydd = Newtown *U.K.* 52°31N 3°19W **13** E4
Y Fenni = Abergavenny *U.K.* 51°49N 3°1W **13** F4
Y Gelli Gandryll = Hay-on-Wye *U.K.* 52°5N 3°8W **13** E4
Y Trallwng = Welshpool *U.K.* 52°39N 3°8W **13** E4
Ya Xian = Sanya *China* 18°14N 109°29E **38** C7
Yaamba *Australia* 23°8S 150°22E **62** C5
Ya'an *China* 29°58N 103°5E **34** C4
Yaapeet *Australia* 35°45S 142°3E **63** F3
Yablonovyy Khrebet *Russia* 53°0N 114°0E **27** D12
Yablonovyy Ra. = Yablonovyy Khrebet *Russia* 53°0N 114°0E **27** D12
Yabrai Shan *China* 39°40N 103°0E **32** E2
Yabrūd *Syria* 33°58N 36°39E **48** B5
Yabucoa *Puerto Rico* 18°3N 65°53W **89** d
Yacambú △ *Venezuela* 9°42N 69°27W **89** E6
Yacheng *China* 18°22N 109°6E **38** C7
Yacuiba *Bolivia* 22°0S 63°43W **94** A3
Yacuma → *Bolivia* 13°38S 65°23W **92** F5
Yadgir *India* 16°45N 77°5E **44** F3
Yadkin → *U.S.A.* 35°23N 80°4W **85** D14
Yadua *Fiji* 16°49S 178°18E **59** a
Yaeyama-Rettō *Japan* 24°30N 123°40E **29** M1
Yagasa Cluster *Fiji* 18°57S 178°28W **59** a
Yagodnoye *Russia* 62°33N 149°40E **27** C15
Yahk *Canada* 49°6N 116°10W **70** D5
Yahuma *Dem. Rep. of the Congo* 1°0N 23°10E **54** D4
Yaita *Japan* 36°48N 139°56E **29** F9
Yajiang *China* 30°2N 100°57E **34** B3
Yakeshi *China* 49°17N 120°44E **31** B13
Yakima *U.S.A.* 46°36N 120°31W **76** C3
Yakima → *U.S.A.* 46°15N 119°14W **76** C4
Yakishiri-Jima *Japan* 44°26N 141°25E **28** B10
Yakobi I. *U.S.A.* 58°0N 136°30W **70** B1
Yakovlevka *Russia* 44°26N 133°28E **28** B6
Yaku-Shima *Japan* 30°20N 130°30E **29** J5
Yakumo *Japan* 42°15N 140°16E **28** C10
Yakutat *U.S.A.* 59°33N 139°44W **68** F4
Yakutat B. *U.S.A.* 59°45N 140°45W **74** D11
Yakutia = Sakha □ *Russia* 66°0N 130°0E **27** C14
Yakutsk *Russia* 62°5N 129°50E **27** C13
Yala *Thailand* 6°33N 101°18E **39** J3
Yala △ *Sri Lanka* 6°20N 81°30E **45** L5
Yalata *Australia* 31°59S 132°26E **61** F5
Yalata △ *Australia* 31°35S 132°7E **61** F5
Yalboroo *Australia* 20°50S 148°40E **62** b
Yale *U.S.A.* 43°8N 82°48W **82** C2
Yalgorup △ *Australia* 32°39S 115°38E **61** F2
Yalinga *C.A.R.* 6°33N 23°10E **54** C4
Yalkabul, Pta. *Mexico* 21°32N 88°37W **87** C7
Yalleroi *Australia* 24°3S 145°42E **62** C4
Yalobusha → *U.S.A.* 33°33N 90°10W **85** E9
Yalong Jiang → *China* 26°40N 101°55E **34** D3
Yalova *Turkey* 40°41N 29°15E **23** D13
Yalpirakinu ⊙ *Australia* 22°24S 132°15E **60** D5
Yalta *Ukraine* 44°30N 34°10E **19** F5
Yalu Jiang → *China* 39°55N 124°19E **33** E13
Yam *Australia* 9°54S 142°46E **62** a
Yam Ha Melah = Dead Sea *Asia* 31°30N 35°30E **48** D4
Yam Kinneret *Israel* 32°45N 35°35E **48** C4
Yamada = Kama *Japan* 33°33N 130°49E **29** H5
Yamagata *Japan* 38°15N 140°15E **28** E10
Yamagata □ *Japan* 38°30N 140°0E **28** E10
Yamaguchi *Japan* 34°10N 131°32E **29** G5
Yamaguchi □ *Japan* 34°20N 131°40E **29** G5
Yamal, Poluostrov *Russia* 71°0N 70°0E **26** B8
Yamal Pen. = Yamal, Poluostrov *Russia* 71°0N 70°0E **26** B8
Yamanashi □ *Japan* 35°40N 138°40E **29** G9

Yamantau, Gora *Russia* 54°15N 58°6E **18** D10
Yamato Ridge *Sea of Japan* 39°20N 135°0E **28** E7
Yamba *Australia* 29°26S 153°23E **63** D5
Yambarran Ra. *Australia* 15°10S 130°25E **60** C5
Yâmbiô *South Sudan* 4°35N 28°16E **53** H11
Yambol *Bulgaria* 42°30N 26°30E **23** C12
Yamburg *Russia* 68°21N 77°8E **26** C8
Yamdena *Indonesia* 7°45S 131°20E **37** F8
Yame *Japan* 33°13N 130°35E **29** H5
Yamethin *Burma* 20°29N 96°18E **41** J20
Yamma Yamma, L. *Australia* 26°16S 141°20E **63** D3
Yampa → *U.S.A.* 40°32N 108°59W **76** F9
Yampi Sd. *Australia* 16°8S 123°38E **60** C3
Yampil *Moldova* 48°15N 28°15E **17** D15
Yampol = Yampil *Moldova* 48°15N 28°15E **17** D15
Yamu, Laem *Thailand* 7°59N 98°26E **39** a
Yamuna → *India* 25°30N 81°53E **43** G9
Yamunanagar *India* 30°7N 77°17E **42** D7
Yamzho Yumco *China* 28°48N 90°35E **30** F7
Yan Oya → *Sri Lanka* 9°0N 81°10E **45** K5
Yana → *Russia* 71°30N 136°0E **27** B14
Yanagawa *Japan* 33°10N 130°24E **29** H5
Yanai *Japan* 33°58N 132°7E **29** H6
Yan'an *China* 36°35N 109°26E **32** F5
Yanaul *Russia* 56°25N 55°0E **18** C10
Yanbian *China* 26°47N 101°31E **34** D3
Yanbu 'al Baḩr *Si. Arabia* 24°0N 38°5E **46** F3
Yanchang *China* 36°43N 110°1E **32** F6
Yancheng *Henan, China* 33°35N 114°0E **32** H8
Yancheng *Jiangsu, China* 33°23N 120°8E **33** H11
Yanchep *Australia* 31°33S 115°37E **61** F2
Yanchi *China* 37°48N 107°20E **32** F4
Yanchuan *China* 36°51N 110°10E **32** F6
Yandang Shan *China* 28°0N 120°35E **35** C13
Yandeyarra ⊙ *Australia* 21°17S 118°24E **60** D2
Yandicoogina *Australia* 22°49S 119°12E **60** D2
Yandoon *Burma* 17°0N 95°40E **41** L19
Yanfeng *China* 25°52N 101°8E **34** E3
Yang Xian *China* 33°15N 107°30E **34** A6
Yang-yang *S. Korea* 38°4N 128°38E **33** E15
Yangambi *Dem. Rep. of the Congo* 0°47N 24°24E **54** D4
Yangbi *China* 25°41N 99°58E **34** E2
Yangcheng *China* 35°28N 112°22E **32** G7
Yangch'ü = Taiyuan *China* 37°52N 112°33E **32** F7
Yangchun *China* 22°11N 111°48E **35** F8
Yanggao *China* 40°21N 113°55E **32** D7
Yanggu *China* 36°8N 115°43E **32** F8
Yangjiang *China* 21°50N 111°59E **35** G8
Yangliuqing *China* 39°2N 117°5E **33** E9
Yangon = Rangoon *Burma* 16°45N 96°20E **41** L20
Yangping *China* 31°12N 111°25E **35** B8
Yangpingguan *China* 32°58N 106°5E **34** A5
Yangquan *China* 37°58N 113°31E **32** F7
Yangshan *China* 24°30N 112°40E **35** E9
Yangshuo *China* 24°48N 110°29E **35** E8
Yangtse = Chang Jiang → *China* 31°48N 121°10E **35** B13
Yangtze Kiang = Chang Jiang → *China* 31°48N 121°10E **35** B13
Yangxin *China* 29°50N 115°12E **35** C10
Yangyuan *China* 40°1N 114°10E **32** D8
Yangzhong *China* 32°22N 119°22E **35** A12
Yangzhou *China* 32°21N 119°26E **35** A12
Yanhe *China* 28°31N 108°29E **34** C7
Yanji *China* 42°59N 129°30E **33** C15
Yanjin *China* 28°5N 104°18E **34** C5
Yanjing *China* 29°7N 98°33E **34** C2
Yankton *U.S.A.* 42°53N 97°23W **80** D5
Yankunytjatjara-Antakirinja ⊙ *Australia* 27°0S 134°30E **63** A1
Yanqi *China* 42°5N 86°35E **30** C6
Yanqing *China* 40°30N 115°58E **32** D8
Yanshan *Hebei, China* 38°4N 117°22E **33** E9
Yanshan *Jiangxi, China* 28°15N 117°41E **35** C11
Yanshan *Yunnan, China* 23°35N 104°20E **34** F5
Yanshou *China* 45°28N 128°22E **33** B15
Yantabulla *Australia* 29°21S 145°0E **63** D4
Yantai *China* 37°34N 121°22E **33** F11
Yantian *China* 22°35N 114°16E **31** a
Yanting *China* 31°11N 105°24E **34** B5
Yantongshan *China* 43°17N 126°0E **33** C14
Yanuca *Fiji* 18°24S 178°0E **59** a
Yanwa *China* 27°35N 98°55E **34** D2
Yanyuan *China* 27°25N 101°30E **34** D3
Yanzhou *China* 35°35N 116°49E **32** G9
Yao Xian *China* 34°55N 108°59E **32** G5
Yao Yai, Ko *Thailand* 8°7N 98°37E **39** a
Yao'an *China* 25°31N 101°18E **34** E3
Yaoundé *Cameroon* 3°50N 11°35E **54** D2
Yaowan *China* 34°15N 118°3E **33** G10
Yap *Pac. Oc.* 9°30N 138°10E **64** G5
Yapen *Indonesia* 1°50S 136°0E **37** E9
Yapen, Selat *Indonesia* 1°20S 136°10E **37** E9
Yapero *Indonesia* 4°59S 137°11E **37** E9
Yappar → *Australia* 18°22S 141°16E **62** B3
Yapuparra ⊙ *Australia* 27°15S 126°20E **61** E4
Yaqaga *Fiji* 16°35S 178°36E **59** a
Yaqui → *Mexico* 27°37N 110°39W **86** B2
Yar-Sale *Russia* 66°50N 70°50E **26** C8
Yaraka *Australia* 24°53S 144°3E **62** C3
Yaransk *Russia* 57°22N 47°49E **18** C8
Yare → *U.K.* 52°35N 1°38E **13** E9
Yaremcha *Ukraine* 48°27N 24°33E **17** D13
Yaren *Nauru* 0°33S 166°55E **57** B9
Yarensk *Russia* 62°11N 49°15E **18** B8
Yari → *Colombia* 0°20S 72°20W **92** D4
Yarkand = Shache *China* 38°20N 77°10E **30** D4
Yarkant He → *China* 40°26N 80°59E **30** C5
Yarker *Canada* 44°23N 76°46W **83** B8
Yarkhun → *Pakistan* 36°17N 72°30E **43** A5

Yarlung Ziangbo Jiang = Brahmaputra → *Asia* 23°40N 90°35E **43** H13
Yarmouth *Canada* 43°50N 66°7W **73** D6
Yarmūk → *Syria* 32°42N 35°40E **48** C4
Yaroslavl *Russia* 57°35N 39°55E **18** C6
Yarqa, W. → *Egypt* 30°0N 33°49E **48** F2
Yarra Yarra Lakes *Australia* 29°40S 115°45E **61** E2
Yarram *Australia* 38°29S 146°39E **63** F4
Yarraman *Australia* 26°50S 152°0E **63** D5
Yarras *Australia* 31°25S 152°20E **63** E5
Yarrie *Australia* 20°40S 120°12E **60** D3
Yartsevo *Russia* 60°20N 90°0E **27** C10
Yarumal *Colombia* 6°58N 75°24W **92** B3
Yasawa *Fiji* 16°47S 177°31E **59** a
Yasawa Group *Fiji* 17°0S 177°23E **59** a
Yaselda *Belarus* 52°7N 26°28E **17** B14
Yasin *Pakistan* 36°24N 73°23E **43** A5
Yasinski, L. *Canada* 53°16N 77°35W **72** B4
Yasinya *Ukraine* 48°16N 24°21E **17** D13
Yasothon *Thailand* 15°50N 104°10E **38** E5
Yass *Australia* 34°49S 148°54E **63** E4
Yāsūj *Iran* 30°31N 51°31E **47** D6
Yatağan *Turkey* 37°20N 28°10E **23** F13
Yates Center *U.S.A.* 37°53N 95°44W **80** G6
Yathkyed L. *Canada* 62°40N 98°0W **71** A9
Yatsushiro *Japan* 32°30N 130°40E **29** H5
Yauco *Puerto Rico* 18°2N 66°51W **89** d
Yaval *India* 21°10N 75°42E **44** D2
Yavari → *Peru* 4°21S 70°2W **92** D4
Yávaros *Mexico* 26°42N 109°31W **86** B3
Yavatmal *India* 20°20N 78°15E **44** D4
Yavne *Israel* 31°52N 34°45E **48** D3
Yavoriv *Ukraine* 49°55N 23°20E **17** D12
Yavorov = Yavoriv *Ukraine* 49°55N 23°20E **17** D12
Yawatahama *Japan* 33°27N 132°24E **29** H6
Yawri B. *S. Leone* 8°22N 13°0W **52** G3
Yaxi *China* 27°33N 106°41E **34** D6
Yaxian = Sanya *China* 18°14N 109°29E **38** C7
Yazd *Iran* 31°55N 54°27E **47** D7
Yazd □ *Iran* 32°0N 55°0E **47** D7
Yazd-e Khvāst *Iran* 31°31N 52°7E **47** D7
Yazman *Pakistan* 29°8N 71°45E **42** E4
Yazoo → *U.S.A.* 32°22N 90°54W **85** E9
Yazoo City *U.S.A.* 32°51N 90°25W **85** E9
Ybycuí △ *Paraguay* 26°5S 56°46W **94** B4
Ybytruzú △ *Paraguay* 25°51S 56°11W **95** B4
Ye *Burma* 15°15N 97°15E **38** E1
Ye Xian *China* 33°35N 113°25E **32** H7
Yebyu *Burma* 14°15N 98°13E **38** E1
Yecheng *China* 37°54N 77°26E **30** D4
Yecheon *S. Korea* 36°39N 128°27E **33** F15
Yecla *Spain* 38°35N 1°5W **21** C5
Yécora *Mexico* 28°20N 108°58W **86** B3
Yedintsy = Edineţ *Moldova* 48°9N 27°18E **17** D14
Yegros *Paraguay* 26°20S 56°25W **94** B4
Yehbuah *Indonesia* 8°23S 114°45E **37** J17
Yehuda, Midbar *Israel* 31°35N 35°15E **48** D4
Yei *South Sudan* 4°9N 30°40E **53** H12
Yekaterinburg *Russia* 56°50N 60°30E **26** D7
Yelandur *India* 12°6N 77°0E **45** H3
Yelarbon *Australia* 28°33S 150°38E **63** D5
Yelets *Russia* 52°40N 38°30E **18** D6
Yelin = Lingshui *China* 18°27N 110°0E **38** C8
Yelizavetgrad = Kirovohrad *Ukraine* 48°35N 32°20E **19** E5
Yelizovo *Russia* 53°11N 158°23E **27** D16
Yell *U.K.* 60°35N 1°5W **11** A7
Yell Sd. *U.K.* 60°33N 1°15W **11** A7
Yellamanchili = Elamanchili *India* 17°33N 82°50E **44** F6
Yellandu *India* 17°39N 80°23E **44** F5
Yellapur *India* 14°58N 74°43E **45** G2
Yellareddi *India* 18°12N 78°2E **44** E4
Yellow = Huang He → *China* 37°55N 118°50E **33** F10
Yellow Sea *China* 35°0N 123°0E **33** G12
Yellowhead Pass *Canada* 52°53N 118°25W **70** C5
Yellowknife *Canada* 62°27N 114°29W **70** A6
Yellowknife → *Canada* 62°31N 114°19W **70** A6
Yellowstone → *U.S.A.* 47°59N 103°59W **76** C12
Yellowstone △ *U.S.A.* 44°40N 110°30W **76** D8
Yellowstone L. *U.S.A.* 44°27N 110°22W **76** D8
Yelsk *Belarus* 51°50N 29°10E **17** C15
Yemen ■ *Asia* 15°0N 44°0E **49** E3
Yemmiganur *India* 15°44N 77°29E **45** G3
Yen Bai *Vietnam* 21°42N 104°52E **34** G5
Yenangyaung *Burma* 20°30N 95°0E **41** J19
Yenbo = Yanbu 'al Baḩr *Si. Arabia* 24°0N 38°5E **46** F3
Yenda *Australia* 34°13S 146°14E **63** E4
Yenice *Turkey* 39°55N 27°17E **23** E12
Yenisey → *Russia* 71°50N 82°40E **26** B9
Yeniseysk *Russia* 58°27N 92°13E **27** D10
Yeniseyskiy Zaliv *Russia* 72°20N 81°0E **26** B9
Yenyuka *Russia* 57°57N 121°15E **27** D13
Yeo → *U.K.* 51°2N 2°49W **13** G5
Yeo, L. *Australia* 28°0S 124°30E **61** E3
Yeo I. *Canada* 45°24N 81°48W **82** A3
Yeola *India* 20°2N 74°30E **44** D2
Yeong-wol *S. Korea* 37°11N 128°28E **33** F15
Yeongcheon *S. Korea* 35°58N 128°56E **33** G15
Yeongdeok *S. Korea* 36°24N 129°22E **33** F15
Yeongdong *S. Korea* 36°10N 127°46E **33** F14
Yeongju *S. Korea* 36°50N 128°40E **33** F15
Yeosu *S. Korea* 34°47N 127°45E **33** G14
Yeotmal = Yavatmal *India* 20°20N 78°15E **44** D4
Yeovil *U.K.* 50°57N 2°38W **13** G5
Yeppoon *Australia* 23°5S 150°47E **62** C5
Yerbent *Turkmenistan* 39°19N 58°36E **47** B8
Yerbogachen *Russia* 61°16N 108°0E **27** C11
Yerevan *Armenia* 40°10N 44°31E **46** A5
Yerington *U.S.A.* 38°59N 119°10W **76** G4

Yermo *U.S.A.* 34°54N 116°50W **79** L10
Yeropol *Russia* 65°15N 168°40E **27** C17
Yershov *Russia* 51°23N 48°27E **19** D8
Yes Tor *U.K.* 50°41N 4°0W **13** G4
Yesan *S. Korea* 36°41N 126°51E **33** F14
Yeso *U.S.A.* 34°26N 104°37W **77** J11
Yessey *Russia* 68°29N 102°10E **27** C11
Yetman *Australia* 28°56S 150°48E **63** D5
Yeu, Î. d' *France* 46°42N 2°20W **20** C2
Yevpatoriya *Ukraine* 45°15N 33°20E **19** E5
Yeysk *Russia* 46°40N 38°12E **19** E6
Yezd = Yazd *Iran* 31°55N 54°27E **47** D7
Ygatimi *Paraguay* 24°5S 55°40W **95** A4
Yhati *Paraguay* 25°45S 56°35W **94** B4
Yhú *Paraguay* 25°0S 56°0W **95** B4
Yi 'Allaq, G. *Egypt* 30°21N 33°31E **48** E2
Yi He → *China* 34°10N 118°8E **33** G10
Yi Xian *Anhui, China* 29°55N 117°57E **35** C11
Yi Xian *Hebei, China* 39°20N 115°30E **32** E8
Yi Xian *Liaoning, China* 41°30N 121°22E **33** D11
Yibin *China* 28°45N 104°32E **34** C5
Yichang *China* 30°40N 111°20E **35** B8
Yicheng *Henan, China* 31°41N 112°12E **35** B8
Yicheng *Shanxi, China* 35°42N 111°40E **32** G6
Yichuan *China* 36°2N 110°10E **32** F6
Yichun *Heilongjiang, China* 47°44N 128°52E **31** B14
Yichun *Jiangxi, China* 27°48N 114°22E **35** D10
Yidu *China* 36°43N 118°28E **33** F10
Yidun *China* 30°22N 99°21E **34** B2
Yifeng *China* 28°22N 114°45E **35** C10
Yihuang *China* 27°30N 116°12E **35** D11
Yijun *China* 35°28N 109°8E **32** G5
Yıldız Dağları *Turkey* 41°48N 27°36E **23** D12
Yilehuli Shan *China* 51°20N 124°20E **31** A13
Yiliang *Yunnan, China* 24°56N 103°11E **34** E4
Yiliang *Yunnan, China* 27°38N 104°2E **34** D5
Yilong *China* 31°34N 106°23E **34** B6
Yima *China* 34°44N 111°53E **32** G6
Yimen *China* 24°40N 102°10E **34** E4
Yimianpo *China* 45°7N 128°2E **33** B15
Yin Xu *China* 36°7N 114°18E **32** F8
Yi'nan *China* 35°31N 118°24E **33** G10
Yinchuan *China* 38°30N 106°15E **32** E4
Yindarlgooda, L. *Australia* 30°40S 121°52E **61** F3
Ying He → *China* 32°30N 116°30E **32** H9
Ying Xian *China* 39°32N 113°10E **32** E7
Yingcheng *China* 30°56N 113°35E **35** B9
Yingde *China* 24°10N 113°25E **35** E9
Yingjiang *China* 24°41N 97°55E **34** E1
Yingjing *China* 29°41N 102°52E **34** C4
Yingkou *China* 40°37N 122°18E **33** D12
Yingpanshui *China* 37°26N 104°18E **32** F3
Yingshan *Hubei, China* 30°41N 115°32E **35** B10
Yingshan *Sichuan, China* 31°4N 106°35E **34** B6
Yingshang *China* 32°38N 116°12E **35** A11
Yingtan *China* 28°12N 117°0E **35** C11
Yingualyalya ⊙ *Australia* 18°49S 129°12E **60** C4
Yining *China* 43°58N 81°10E **30** C5
Yininarra ⊙ *Australia* 20°53S 129°27E **60** D4
Yinjiang *China* 28°1N 108°21E **34** C7
Yinmabin *Burma* 22°10N 94°55E **41** H19
Yipinglang *China* 25°10N 101°52E **34** E3
Yirga Alem *Ethiopia* 6°48N 38°22E **49** F2
Yirrkala *Australia* 12°14S 136°56E **62** A2
Yishan *China* 24°28N 108°38E **34** E7
Yishui *China* 35°47N 118°30E **33** G10
Yitong *China* 43°13N 125°20E **33** C13
Yiwu *China* 29°20N 120°3E **35** C13
Yixing *China* 31°21N 119°48E **35** B12
Yiyang *Henan, China* 34°27N 112°10E **32** G7
Yiyang *Hunan, China* 28°35N 112°18E **35** C9
Yiyang *Jiangxi, China* 28°22N 117°20E **35** C11
Yizhang *China* 25°27N 112°57E **35** E9
Yizheng *China* 32°18N 119°10E **35** A12
Yli-Kitka *Finland* 66°8N 28°30E **8** C23
Ylitornio *Finland* 66°19N 23°39E **8** C20
Ylivieska *Finland* 64°4N 24°28E **8** D21
Yoakum *U.S.A.* 29°17N 97°9W **84** G6
Yog Pt. *Phil.* 14°6N 124°12E **37** B6
Yogyakarta *Indonesia* 7°49S 110°22E **37** G14
Yogyakarta □ *Indonesia* 7°48S 110°22E **37** G14
Yoho △ *Canada* 51°25N 116°30W **70** C5
Yojoa, L. de *Honduras* 14°53N 88°0W **88** D2
Yok Don △ *Vietnam* 12°50N 107°40E **38** F6
Yokadouma *Cameroon* 3°26N 14°55E **54** D2
Yokkaichi *Japan* 34°55N 136°38E **29** G8
Yoko *Cameroon* 5°32N 12°20E **54** C2
Yokohama *Japan* 35°27N 139°28E **29** G9
Yokosuka *Japan* 35°20N 139°40E **29** G9
Yokote *Japan* 39°20N 140°30E **28** E10
Yola *Nigeria* 9°10N 12°29E **53** G8
Yolaina, Cordillera de *Nic.* 11°30N 84°0W **88** D2
Yöloten *Turkmenistan* 37°18N 62°21E **47** B9
Yom → *Thailand* 15°35N 100°1E **38** E3
Yonago *Japan* 35°25N 133°19E **29** G6
Yonaguni-Jima *Japan* 24°27N 123°0E **29** M1
Yŏnan *N. Korea* 37°55N 126°11E **33** F14
Yonezawa *Japan* 37°57N 140°4E **28** F10
Yong Peng *Malaysia* 2°0N 103°3E **39** M4
Yong Sata *Thailand* 7°8N 99°41E **39** J2
Yong'an *China* 25°59N 117°25E **35** E11
Yongchang *China* 38°15N 101°40E **32** F2
Yongcheng *China* 33°55N 116°23E **32** H9
Yongchuan *China* 29°20N 105°55E **34** C5
Yongchun *China* 25°16N 118°3E **35** E12
Yongde *China* 24°5N 99°25E **34** E2
Yongden *China* 36°38N 103°25E **32** F2
Yongding *China* 24°43N 116°45E **35** E11
Yongfeng *China* 27°20N 115°22E **35** D10
Yongfu *China* 24°59N 109°59E **34** E7

Yonghe China 36°46N 110°38E **32 F6**
Yŏnghŭng N. Korea 39°31N 127°18E **33 E14**
Yongji Jilin, China 42°33N 126°13E **33 C14**
Yongji Shanxi, China 34°52N 110°28E **32 G6**
Yongjia China 28°10N 120°45E **35 C13**
Yongkang Yunnan, China 24°9N 99°20E **34 E2**
Yongkang Zhejiang, China 28°55N 120°2E **35 C13**
Yongnian China 36°47N 114°29E **32 F8**
Yongning Guangxi Zhuangzu, China 22°42N 108°28E **34 F7**
Yongning Ningxia Huizu, China 38°15N 106°14E **32 E4**
Yongping China 25°27N 99°38E **34 E2**
Yongren China 26°4N 101°40E **34 D3**
Yongshan China 28°11N 103°35E **34 C4**
Yongsheng China 26°38N 100°46E **34 D3**
Yongshun China 29°2N 109°51E **34 C7**
Yongtai China 25°49N 118°58E **35 E12**
Yongxin = Jinggangshan China 26°58N 114°15E **35 D10**
Yongxing China 26°9N 113°8E **35 D9**
Yongxiu China 29°2N 115°42E **35 C10**
Yongzhou China 26°17N 111°37E **35 D8**
Yonibana S. Leone 8°30N 12°19W **52 G3**
Yonne → France 48°23N 2°58E **20 B5**
York Australia 31°52S 116°47E **61 F2**
York U.K. 53°58N 1°6W **12 D6**
York Ala., U.S.A. 32°29N 88°18W **85 E10**
York Nebr., U.S.A. 40°52N 97°36W **80 E5**
York Pa., U.S.A. 39°58N 76°44W **81 F15**
York, C. Australia 10°42S 142°31E **62 A3**
York, City of □ U.K. 53°58N 1°6W **12 D6**
York, Kap Greenland 75°55N 66°25W **69 B18**
York, Vale of U.K. 54°15N 1°25W **12 C5**
York Sd. Australia 15°0S 125°5E **60 C4**
Yorke Pen. Australia 34°50S 137°40E **63 E2**
Yorkshire Dales △ U.K. 54°12N 2°10W **12 C5**
Yorkshire Wolds U.K. 54°8N 0°31W **12 C7**
Yorkton Canada 51°11N 102°28W **71 C8**
Yorkville U.S.A. 38°52N 123°13W **78 G3**
Yoro Honduras 15°9N 87°7W **88 C2**
Yoron-Jima Japan 27°2N 128°26E **29 L4**
Yos Sudarso, Pulau = Dolak, Pulau Indonesia 8°0S 138°30E **37 F9**
Yosemite △ U.S.A. 37°45N 119°40W **78 H7**
Yosemite Village U.S.A. 37°45N 119°35W **78 H7**
Yoshino-Kumano △ Japan 34°12N 135°55E **29 H8**
Yoshkar Ola Russia 56°38N 47°55E **18 C8**
Yotvata Israel 29°55N 35°2E **48 F4**
You Jiang → China 22°50N 108°6E **34 F6**
You Xian China 27°1N 113°17E **35 D9**
Youbou Canada 48°53N 124°13W **78 B2**
Youghal Ireland 51°56N 7°52W **10 E4**
Youghal B. Ireland 51°55N 7°49W **10 E4**
Young Australia 34°19S 148°18E **63 E4**
Young Canada 51°47N 105°45W **71 C7**
Young Uruguay 32°44S 57°36W **94 C4**
Young I. Antarctica 66°25S 162°24E **5 C11**
Younghusband, L. Australia 30°50S 136°5E **63 E2**
Younghusband Pen. Australia 36°0S 139°25E **63 F2**
Youngstown Canada 51°35N 111°10W **71 C6**
Youngstown N.Y., U.S.A. 43°15N 79°3W **82 C5**
Youngstown Ohio, U.S.A. 41°6N 80°39W **82 E4**
Youngsville U.S.A. 41°51N 79°19W **82 E5**
Youngwood U.S.A. 40°14N 79°34W **82 F5**
Youxi China 26°10N 118°13E **35 D12**
Youyang China 28°47N 108°42E **34 C7**
Youyu China 40°10N 112°20E **32 D7**
Yozgat Turkey 39°51N 34°47E **19 G5**
Ypacaraí △ Paraguay 25°18S 57°19W **94 B4**
Ypané → Paraguay 23°29S 57°19W **94 A4**
Ypres = Ieper Belgium 50°51N 2°53E **15 D2**
Yr Wyddgrug = Mold U.K. 53°9N 3°8W **12 D4**
Yreka U.S.A. 41°44N 122°38W **76 F2**
Ystad Sweden 55°26N 13°50E **9 J15**
Ysyk-Köl = Balykchy Kyrgyzstan 42°26N 76°12E **30 C4**
Ysyk-Köl Kyrgyzstan 42°25N 77°15E **26 E8**
Ythan → U.K. 57°19N 1°59W **11 D7**
Ytyk-Kyuyel Russia 62°30N 133°45E **27 C14**
Yu Jiang → China 22°50N 108°6E **34 F6**
Yü Shan Taiwan 23°25N 120°52E **35 F13**
Yu Xian = Yuzhou China 34°10N 113°28E **32 G7**
Yu Xian Hebei, China 39°50N 114°35E **32 E8**
Yu Xian Shanxi, China 38°5N 113°20E **32 E7**
Yuan Jiang → Hunan, China 28°55N 111°50E **35 C8**
Yuan Jiang → Yunnan, China 22°20N 103°59E **34 F4**
Yuan'an China 31°3N 111°34E **35 B8**
Yuanjiang Hunan, China 28°47N 112°21E **35 C9**
Yuanjiang Yunnan, China 23°32N 102°0E **34 F4**
Yüanli Taiwan 24°27N 120°39E **35 E13**
Yüanlin Taiwan 23°58N 120°30E **35 F13**
Yuanling China 28°29N 110°22E **35 C8**
Yuanmou China 25°42N 101°53E **34 E3**
Yuanping China 38°42N 112°46E **32 E7**
Yuanqu China 35°18N 111°40E **32 G6**
Yuanyang Henan, China 35°3N 113°58E **32 G7**
Yuanyang Yunnan, China 23°10N 102°43E **34 F4**
Yuba → U.S.A. 39°8N 121°36W **78 F5**
Yuba City U.S.A. 39°8N 121°37W **78 F5**
Yūbari Japan 43°4N 141°59E **28 C10**
Yūbetsu Japan 44°13N 143°50E **28 B11**
Yucatán □ Mexico 20°50N 89°0W **87 C7**
Yucatán, Canal de Caribbean 22°0N 86°30W **88 B2**
Yucatán, Península de Mexico 19°30N 89°0W **66 H11**
Yucatan Basin Cent. Amer. 19°0N 86°0W **87 D7**
Yucatan Channel = Yucatán, Canal de Caribbean 22°0N 86°30W **88 B2**
Yucca U.S.A. 34°52N 114°9W **79 L12**

Yucca Valley U.S.A. 34°8N 116°27W **79 L10**
Yucheng China 36°55N 116°32E **32 F9**
Yuci = Jinzhong China 37°42N 112°46E **32 F7**
Yudu China 25°59N 115°30E **35 E10**
Yuechi China 30°34N 106°25E **34 B6**
Yuen Long China 22°26N 114°2E **31 a**
Yuendumu Australia 22°16S 131°49E **60 D5**
Yuendumu ◎ Australia 22°21S 131°40E **60 D5**
Yueqing China 28°9N 120°59E **35 C13**
Yueqing Wan China 28°5N 121°20E **35 D13**
Yuexi Anhui, China 30°50N 116°20E **35 B11**
Yuexi Sichuan, China 28°37N 102°26E **34 C4**
Yueyang China 29°21N 113°5E **35 C9**
Yugan China 28°43N 116°37E **35 C11**
Yugorenok Russia 59°47N 137°40E **27 D14**
Yuhuan China 28°9N 121°12E **35 C13**
Yühuan Dao China 28°5N 121°15E **35 C13**
Yukon U.S.A. 35°31N 97°45W **84 D6**
Yukon → U.S.A. 62°32N 163°54W **74 C7**
Yukon Flats U.S.A. 66°40N 145°45W **74 B10**
Yukon Territory □ Canada 63°0N 135°0W **68 E5**
Yukta Russia 63°26N 105°42E **27 C11**
Yukuhashi Japan 33°44N 130°59E **29 H5**
Yulara Australia 25°10S 130°55E **61 E5**
Yule → Australia 20°41S 118°17E **60 D2**
Yuleba Australia 26°37S 149°24E **63 D4**
Yüli Taiwan 23°20N 121°18E **35 F13**
Yulin Guangxi Zhuangzu, China 22°40N 110°8E **35 F8**
Yulin Hainan, China 18°10N 109°31E **38 C7**
Yulin Shaanxi, China 38°20N 109°30E **32 E5**
Yulong Xueshan China 27°6N 100°10E **34 D3**
Yuma Ariz., U.S.A. 32°43N 114°37W **79 N12**
Yuma Colo., U.S.A. 40°8N 102°43W **76 F12**
Yuma, B. de Dom. Rep. 18°20N 68°35W **89 C6**
Yumen China 39°50N 97°30E **30 D8**
Yun Gui Gaoyuan China 26°0N 104°0E **34 E3**
Yun Ling Shan China 27°0N 99°20E **34 D2**
Yun Xian Hubei, China 32°50N 110°46E **32 H6**
Yun Xian Yunnan, China 24°27N 100°8E **34 E3**
Yuna Australia 28°20S 115°0E **61 E2**
Yunan China 23°12N 111°30E **35 F8**
Yuncheng Henan, China 35°36N 115°57E **32 G8**
Yuncheng Shanxi, China 35°2N 111°0E **32 G6**
Yunfu China 22°50N 112°5E **35 F9**
Yungang Shiku China 40°6N 113°7E **32 D7**
Yungas Bolivia 17°0S 66°0W **92 G5**
Yungay Chile 37°10S 72°5W **94 D1**
Yunhe China 28°8N 119°33E **35 C12**
Yunkai Dashan China 22°30N 111°0E **35 F8**
Yunkanjini ◎ Australia 22°33S 131°56E **60 D5**
Yunling Shan China 28°30N 98°50E **34 D2**
Yunlong China 25°57N 99°13E **34 E2**
Yunmeng China 31°2N 113°43E **35 B9**
Yunnan □ China 25°0N 102°0E **34 E4**
Yunta Australia 32°34S 139°36E **63 E2**
Yunxi China 33°0N 110°22E **34 H6**
Yunxiao China 23°59N 117°18E **35 F11**
Yunyang Chongqing, China 31°2N 108°51E **34 B7**
Yunyang Henan, China 33°26N 112°42E **35 A9**
Yupanqui Basin Pac. Oc. 19°0S 101°0W **65 J17**
Yuping China 27°13N 108°56E **34 D7**
Yuqing China 27°13N 107°53E **34 D6**
Yuraygir △ Australia 29°45S 153°15E **63 D5**
Yurga Russia 55°42N 84°51E **26 D9**
Yurihonjō Japan 39°23N 140°3E **28 E10**
Yurimaguas Peru 5°55S 76°7W **92 E3**
Yurubí △ Venezuela 10°26N 68°42W **89 D6**
Yuscarán Honduras 13°58N 86°45W **88 D2**
Yushan China 28°42N 118°10E **35 C12**
Yushanzhen China 29°28N 108°22E **34 C7**
Yushe China 37°4N 112°58E **32 F7**
Yushu Jilin, China 44°43N 126°38E **33 B14**
Yushu Qinghai, China 33°5N 96°55E **30 E8**
Yutai China 35°0N 116°45E **32 G9**
Yutian Hebei, China 39°53N 117°45E **33 E9**
Yutian Sinkiang-Uigur, China 36°52N 81°42E **30 D5**
Yuxarı Qarabağ = Nagorno-Karabakh □ Azerbaijan 39°55N 46°45E **46 B5**
Yuxi China 24°30N 102°35E **34 E4**
Yuyao China 30°3N 121°10E **35 B13**
Yuzawa Japan 39°10N 140°30E **28 E10**
Yuzhno-Kurilsk Russia 44°1N 145°51E **27 E15**
Yuzhno-Sakhalinsk Russia 46°58N 142°45E **31 B17**
Yuzhnyy □ Russia 44°0N 40°0E **26 E5**
Yuzhou China 34°10N 113°28E **32 G7**
Yvetot France 49°37N 0°44E **20 B4**

Z

Zāb al Kabīr → Iraq 36°1N 43°24E **46 B4**
Zāb aş Şaghīr → Iraq 35°17N 43°29E **46 C4**
Zabaykalsk Russia 49°40N 117°25E **27 E12**
Zābol Iran 31°0N 61°32E **47 D9**
Zābol □ Afghan. 32°0N 67°0E **40 D5**
Zābolī Iran 27°10N 61°35E **47 E9**
Zabrze Poland 50°18N 18°50E **17 C10**
Zacapa Guatemala 14°59N 89°31W **88 D2**
Zacapu Mexico 19°50N 101°43W **86 D4**
Zacatecas Mexico 22°47N 102°35W **86 C4**
Zacatecas □ Mexico 23°0N 103°0W **86 C4**
Zacatecoluca El Salv. 13°29N 88°51W **88 D2**
Zachary U.S.A. 30°39N 91°9W **84 F9**
Zacoalco de Torres Mexico 20°14N 103°35W **86 C4**
Zacualtipán Mexico 20°39N 98°36W **87 C5**
Zadar Croatia 44°8N 15°14E **16 F8**
Zadetkyi Kyun Burma 10°0N 98°25E **39 G2**
Zafarqand Iran 33°11N 52°29E **47 C7**
Zafra Spain 38°26N 6°30W **21 C2**
Żagań Poland 51°39N 15°22E **16 C8**
Zagaoua Chad 15°30N 22°24E **53 E10**
Zagazig Egypt 30°40N 31°30E **53 B12**

Zāgheh Iran 33°30N 48°42E **47 C6**
Zagreb Croatia 45°50N 15°58E **16 F9**
Zagros, Kūhhā-ye Iran 33°45N 48°5E **47 C6**
Zagros Mts. = Zagros, Kūhhā-ye Iran
Zāhedān Fārs, Iran 28°46N 53°52E **47 D7**
Zāhedān Sīstān va Balūchestān, Iran 29°30N 60°50E **47 D9**
Zahirabad India 17°43N 77°37E **44 F3**
Zahlah Lebanon 33°52N 35°50E **48 B4**
Zaïre = Congo → Africa 6°4S 12°24E **54 F2**
Zaječar Serbia 43°53N 22°18E **23 C10**
Zakamensk Russia 50°23N 103°17E **27 D11**
Zakhodnaya Dzvina = Daugava → Latvia 57°4N 24°3E **9 H21**
Zākhū Iraq 37°10N 42°50E **46 B4**
Zakinthos = Zakynthos Greece 37°47N 20°54E **23 F9**
Zakopane Poland 49°18N 19°57E **17 D10**
Zakynthos Greece 37°47N 20°54E **23 F9**
Zalaegerszeg Hungary 46°53N 16°47E **17 E9**
Zalantun China 48°0N 122°43E **31 B13**
Zalari Russia 53°33N 102°30E **27 D11**
Zalău Romania 47°12N 23°3E **17 E12**
Zaleshchiki = Zalishchyky Ukraine 48°45N 25°45E **17 D13**
Zalew Wiślany Poland 54°20N 19°50E **17 A10**
Zalingei Sudan 12°51N 23°29E **53 F10**
Zalishchyky Ukraine 48°45N 25°45E **17 D13**
Zama L. Canada 58°45N 119°5W **70 B5**
Zambeze → Africa 18°35S 36°20E **55 H7**
Zambezi = Zambeze → Africa 18°35S 36°20E **55 H7**
Zambezi Zambia 13°30S 23°15E **55 G4**
Zambia ■ Africa 15°0S 28°0E **55 G2**
Zamboanga Phil. 6°59N 122°3E **37 C6**
Zamora Mexico 19°59N 102°16W **86 D4**
Zamora Spain 41°30N 5°45E **21 B3**
Zamość Poland 50°43N 23°15E **17 C12**
Zamtang China 32°26N 101°6E **34 A3**
Zanda China 31°32N 79°50E **30 E4**
Zandvoort Neths. 52°22N 4°32E **15 B4**
Zanesville U.S.A. 39°56N 82°1W **82 G2**
Zangābād Iran 38°26N 46°44E **46 B5**
Zanjān Iran 36°40N 48°35E **47 B6**
Zanjān □ Iran 37°20N 49°30E **47 B6**
Zanjān → Iran 37°8N 47°47E **47 B6**
Zante = Zakynthos Greece 37°47N 20°54E **23 F9**
Zanthus Australia 31°2S 123°34E **61 F3**
Zanzibar Tanzania 6°12S 39°12E **54 F7**
Zaouiet El-Kala = Bordj Omar Driss Algeria 28°10N 6°40E **52 C7**
Zaouiet Reggâne Algeria 26°32N 0°3E **52 C6**
Zaoyang China 32°10N 112°45E **35 A9**
Zaozhuang China 34°50N 117°35E **33 G9**
Zap Suyu = Zāb al Kabīr → Iraq 36°1N 43°24E **46 B4**
Zapadnaya Dvina = Daugava → Latvia 57°4N 24°3E **9 H21**
Západné Beskydy Europe 49°30N 19°0E **17 D10**
Zapala Argentina 39°0S 70°5W **96 D2**
Zapaleri, Cerro Bolivia 22°49S 67°11W **94 A2**
Zapata U.S.A. 26°55N 99°16W **84 H5**
Zapolyarnyy Russia 69°26N 30°51E **8 B24**
Zapopán Mexico 20°43N 103°24W **86 C4**
Zaporizhzhya Ukraine 47°50N 35°10E **19 E6**
Zaporozhye = Zaporizhzhya Ukraine 47°50N 35°10E **19 E6**
Zara Turkey 39°58N 37°43E **46 B3**
Zaragoza Coahuila, Mexico 28°29N 100°55W **86 B4**
Zaragoza Nuevo León, Mexico 23°58N 99°46W **87 C5**
Zaragoza Spain 41°39N 0°53W **21 B5**
Zarand Kermān, Iran 30°46N 56°34E **47 D8**
Zarand Markazī, Iran 35°18N 50°25E **47 C6**
Zaranj Afghan. 30°55N 61°55E **40 D2**
Zarasai Lithuania 55°40N 26°20E **9 J22**
Zárate Argentina 34°7S 59°0W **94 C4**
Zard, Kūh-e Iran 32°22N 50°4E **47 C6**
Zāreh Iran 35°7N 49°9E **47 C6**
Zaria Nigeria 11°0N 7°40E **52 F7**
Zarind Iran 33°55N 46°10E **46 C5**
Zarqā', Nahr az → Jordan 32°10N 35°37E **48 C4**
Zarrīn Iran 32°46N 54°37E **47 C7**
Zaruma Ecuador 3°40S 79°38W **92 D3**
Żary Poland 51°37N 15°10E **16 C8**
Zarzis Tunisia 33°31N 11°2E **53 B8**
Zaskar → India 34°13N 77°20E **43 B7**
Zaskar Mts. India 33°15N 77°30E **43 C7**
Zastron S. Africa 30°18S 27°7E **56 D4**
Zavāreh Iran 33°29N 52°28E **47 C7**
Zave Zimbabwe 17°6S 30°1E **57 A5**
Zavitinsk Russia 50°10N 129°20E **27 D13**
Zavodovski I. Antarctica 56°0S 27°45W **5 B1**
Zawiercie Poland 50°30N 19°24E **17 C10**
Zāwiyat al Baydā = Al Bayda Libya 32°50N 21°44E **53 B10**
Zāyā Iraq 33°33N 44°13E **46 C5**
Zāyandeh → Iran 32°35N 52°0E **47 C7**
Zaysan Kazakhstan 47°28N 84°52E **30 B5**
Zaysan Köli Kazakhstan 48°0N 83°0E **26 E9**
Zayü China 28°48N 97°27E **41 E20**
Zbarazh Ukraine 49°43N 25°44E **17 D13**
Zdolbuniv Ukraine 50°30N 26°15E **17 C14**
Zduńska Wola Poland 51°37N 18°59E **17 C10**
Zeballos Canada 49°59N 126°50W **70 D3**
Zebediela S. Africa 24°20S 29°17E **57 B4**
Zeebrugge Belgium 51°19N 3°12E **15 C3**
Zeehan Australia 41°52S 145°25E **63 G4**
Zeeland □ Neths. 51°30N 3°50E **15 C3**
Zeerust S. Africa 25°31S 26°4E **56 C4**
Zefat Israel 32°58N 35°29E **48 C4**
Zeil, Mt. Australia 23°30S 132°23E **60 D5**
Zeila = Saylac Somalia 11°21N 43°30E **49 E3**
Zeist Neths. 52°5N 5°15E **15 B5**

Zeitz Germany 51°2N 12°7E **16 C7**
Zelenogorsk Russia 60°12N 29°43E **8 F23**
Zelenograd Russia 56°1N 37°12E **18 C6**
Zelienople U.S.A. 40°48N 80°8W **82 F4**
Zempoala Mexico 19°27N 96°23W **87 D5**
Zemun Serbia 44°51N 20°25E **23 B9**
Zengcheng China 23°13N 113°52E **35 F9**
Zenica Bos.-H. 44°10N 17°57E **23 B7**
Žepče Bos.-H. 44°28N 18°2E **23 B8**
Zevenaar Neths. 51°56N 6°5E **15 C6**
Zeya Russia 53°48N 127°14E **27 D13**
Zeya → Russia 51°42N 128°53E **27 D13**
Zeyskoye Vdkhr. Russia 54°30N 127°30E **27 D13**
Zêzere → Portugal 39°28N 8°20W **21 C1**
Zghartā Lebanon 34°21N 35°53E **48 A4**
Zgorzelec Poland 51°10N 15°0E **16 C8**
Zhabinka Belarus 52°13N 24°2E **17 B13**
Zhambyl = Taraz Kazakhstan 42°54N 71°22E **30 C3**
Zhangaözen Kazakhstan 43°18N 52°48E **19 F9**
Zhangaqazaly Kazakhstan 45°48N 62°6E **26 E7**
Zhangbei China 41°10N 114°45E **32 D8**
Zhangguangcai Ling China 45°0N 129°0E **33 B15**
Zhangjiabian China 22°33N 113°28E **31 a**
Zhangjiagang China 31°55N 120°30E **35 B13**
Zhangjiakou China 40°48N 114°55E **32 D8**
Zhangping China 25°17N 117°23E **35 E11**
Zhangpu China 24°8N 117°35E **35 E11**
Zhangshu China 28°4N 115°29E **35 C10**
Zhangye China 38°50N 100°23E **30 D9**
Zhangzhou China 24°30N 117°35E **35 E11**
Zhanhua China 37°40N 118°8E **33 F10**
Zhanjiang China 21°15N 110°20E **35 G8**
Zhannetty, Ostrov Russia 76°43N 158°0E **27 B16**
Zhanyi China 25°38N 103°48E **34 E4**
Zhanyu China 44°30N 122°30E **33 B12**
Zhao Xian China 37°43N 114°45E **32 F8**
Zhao'an China 23°41N 117°10E **35 F11**
Zhaocheng China 36°22N 111°38E **32 F6**
Zhaodong China 46°4N 125°59E **31 B13**
Zhaojue China 28°1N 102°49E **34 C4**
Zhaoping China 24°11N 110°48E **35 E8**
Zhaoqing China 23°0N 112°20E **35 F9**
Zhaotong China 27°20N 103°44E **34 D5**
Zhaoyang Hu China 35°0N 116°47E **32 G9**
Zhaoyuan Heilongjiang, China 45°27N 125°0E **33 B13**
Zhaoyuan Shandong, China 37°20N 120°23E **33 F11**
Zhari Namco China 31°6N 85°36E **30 E6**
Zhashkiv Ukraine 49°15N 30°5E **17 D16**
Zhashui China 33°40N 109°8E **32 H5**
Zhayylma Kazakhstan 51°37N 61°33E **26 D7**
Zhayyq → Kazakhstan 47°0N 51°48E **19 E9**
Zhdanov = Mariupol Ukraine 47°5N 37°31E **19 E6**
Zhecheng China 34°7N 115°20E **32 G8**
Zhegao China 31°46N 117°45E **35 B11**
Zhejiang □ China 29°0N 120°0E **35 C13**
Zheleznodorozhnyy Russia 62°35N 50°55E **18 B9**
Zheleznogorsk-Ilimskiy Russia 56°34N 104°8E **27 D11**
Zhen'an China 33°27N 109°9E **34 A7**
Zhenba China 32°34N 107°58E **34 A6**
Zhenfeng China 25°22N 105°40E **34 E5**
Zheng'an China 28°32N 107°27E **34 C6**
Zhengding China 38°8N 114°32E **32 E8**
Zhenghe China 27°20N 118°50E **35 D12**
Zhengyang China 32°37N 114°22E **35 A10**
Zhengyangguan China 32°30N 116°29E **35 A11**
Zhengzhou China 34°45N 113°34E **32 G7**
Zhenhai China 29°59N 121°42E **35 C13**
Zhenjiang China 32°11N 119°26E **35 A12**
Zhenkang China 23°58N 99°0E **34 F2**
Zhenlai China 45°50N 123°5E **33 B12**
Zhenning China 26°4N 105°45E **34 D5**
Zhenping Henan, China 33°10N 112°16E **35 A9**
Zhenping Shaanxi, China 31°59N 109°31E **34 B7**
Zhenxiong China 27°27N 104°50E **34 D5**
Zhenyuan Gansu, China 35°35N 107°30E **32 G4**
Zhenyuan Guizhou, China 27°7N 108°21E **34 D7**
Zhenyuan Yunnan, China 23°51N 100°59E **34 F3**
Zherong China 27°15N 119°52E **35 D12**
Zhetiqara Kazakhstan 52°11N 61°12E **26 D7**
Zhezqazghan Kazakhstan 47°44N 67°40E **26 E7**
Zhicheng China 30°25N 111°27E **35 B8**
Zhidan China 36°48N 108°48E **32 F5**
Zhigansk Russia 66°48N 123°27E **27 C13**
Zhijiang Hubei, China 30°31N 111°45E **35 B8**
Zhijiang Hunan, China 27°27N 109°42E **34 D7**
Zhijin China 26°37N 105°45E **34 D5**
Zhilinda Russia 70°0N 114°20E **27 C12**
Zhitomir = Zhytomyr Ukraine 50°20N 28°40E **17 C15**
Zhlobin Belarus 52°55N 30°0E **17 B16**
Zhmerynka Ukraine 49°2N 28°2E **17 D15**
Zhob Pakistan 31°20N 69°31E **42 D3**
Zhob → Pakistan 32°4N 69°50E **42 C3**
Zhodzina Belarus 54°5N 28°17E **17 A15**
Zhokhova, Ostrov Russia 76°4N 152°40E **27 B16**
Zhongba China 29°39N 84°10E **30 F5**
Zhongdian China 27°48N 99°42E **34 D2**
Zhongdong China 24°40N 107°47E **34 F6**
Zhongdu China 24°40N 109°40E **34 F7**
Zhongjiang China 30°53N 104°46E **34 B5**
Zhongning China 37°29N 105°40E **32 F3**
Zhongshan Antarctica 69°0S 39°50E **5 C6**
Zhongshan Guangdong, China 22°26N 113°20E **35 F9**
Zhongshan Guangxi Zhuangzu, China 24°29N 111°18E **35 E8**
Zhongshankong China 22°35N 113°29E **31 a**
Zhongtiao Shan China 35°0N 111°10E **32 G6**
Zhongwei China 37°30N 105°12E **32 F3**

Zhongxian China 30°18N 107°58E **34 B6**
Zhongxiang China 31°12N 112°34E **35 B9**
Zhongyang China 37°20N 111°11E **32 F6**
Zhosaly Kazakhstan 45°29N 64°4E **26 E7**
Zhoucun China 36°47N 117°48E **33 F9**
Zhoukou China 33°38N 114°38E **32 H8**
Zhoukoudian China 39°41N 115°56E **32 E8**
Zhouning China 27°12N 119°20E **35 D12**
Zhoushan China 30°1N 122°6E **35 C14**
Zhoushan Dao China 30°5N 122°10E **35 C14**
Zhouzhi China 34°10N 108°12E **32 G5**
Zhovkva Ukraine 50°4N 23°58E **17 C13**
Zhu Jiang → China 22°45N 113°37E **35 F9**
Zhuanghe China 39°40N 123°0E **33 E13**
Zhucheng China 36°0N 119°27E **33 G10**
Zhugqu China 33°40N 104°30E **32 H3**
Zhuhai China 22°17N 113°34E **35 F9**
Zhuji China 29°40N 120°10E **35 C13**
Zhujiang Kou China 22°20N 113°45E **31 a**
Zhumadian China 32°59N 114°2E **35 A10**
Zhuo Xian = Zhuozhou China 39°28N 115°58E **32 E8**
Zhuolu China 40°20N 115°12E **32 D8**
Zhuozhou China 39°28N 115°58E **32 E8**
Zhuozi China 41°0N 112°25E **32 D7**
Zhushan China 32°15N 110°13E **34 A8**
Zhuxi China 32°25N 109°40E **34 A7**
Zhuzhou China 27°49N 113°12E **35 D9**
Zhytomyr Ukraine 50°20N 28°40E **17 C15**
Zhytomyr □ Ukraine 50°50N 28°10E **17 C14**
Zi Shui → China 28°40N 112°40E **35 C9**
Ziarat Pakistan 30°25N 67°49E **42 D2**
Zibo China 36°47N 118°3E **33 F10**
Zichang China 37°18N 109°40E **32 F5**
Zidi = Wandhari Pakistan 27°42N 66°48E **42 F2**
Zielona Góra Poland 51°57N 15°31E **16 C8**
Zierikzee Neths. 51°40N 3°55E **15 C3**
Zigong China 29°15N 104°48E **34 C5**
Ziguéy Chad 14°43N 15°50E **53 F9**
Ziguinchor Senegal 12°35N 16°20W **52 F2**
Zihuatanejo Mexico 17°39N 101°33W **86 D4**
Zijin China 23°33N 115°8E **35 F10**
Žilina Slovak Rep. 49°12N 18°42E **17 D10**
Zillah Libya 28°17N 17°33E **53 C9**
Zima Russia 54°0N 102°5E **27 D11**
Zimapán Mexico 20°45N 99°21W **87 C5**
Zimbabwe ■ Africa 19°0S 30°0E **55 H6**
Zimbabwe Africa 20°16S 30°54E **55 H6**
Zimnicea Romania 43°40N 25°22E **17 G13**
Zinave △ Mozam. 21°35S 33°40E **57 B5**
Zinder Niger 13°48N 9°0E **52 F7**
Zion △ U.S.A. 37°15N 113°5W **77 H7**
Zirreh, Gowd-e Afghan. 29°45N 62°0E **40 E3**
Zitácuaro Mexico 19°24N 100°22W **86 D4**
Zitong China 31°37N 105°10E **34 B5**
Zitundo Mozam. 26°48S 32°47E **57 C5**
Ziway, L. Ethiopia 8°0N 38°50E **49 F2**
Zixi China 27°45N 117°4E **35 D11**
Zixing China 25°59N 113°21E **35 D9**
Ziyang Shaanxi, China 32°32N 108°31E **34 H5**
Ziyang Sichuan, China 30°6N 104°40E **34 B5**
Ziyuan China 26°2N 110°40E **35 D8**
Ziyun China 25°45N 106°5E **34 E6**
Zizhong China 29°48N 104°47E **34 C5**
Zlatograd Bulgaria 41°22N 25°7E **23 D11**
Zlatoust Russia 55°10N 59°40E **18 C10**
Zlín Czech Rep. 49°14N 17°40E **17 D9**
Zmeinogorsk Kazakhstan 51°10N 82°13E **26 D9**
Znojmo Czech Rep. 48°50N 16°2E **16 D9**
Zobeyrī Iran 34°10N 46°40E **46 C5**
Zoetermeer Neths. 52°3N 4°30E **15 B4**
Zogang China 29°55N 97°42E **34 C1**
Zohreh → Iran 30°16N 51°17E **47 D6**
Zolochiv Ukraine 49°45N 24°51E **17 D13**
Zomba Malawi 15°22S 35°19E **55 H7**
Zongo Dem. Rep. of the Congo 4°20N 18°35E **54 D3**
Zonguldak Turkey 41°28N 31°50E **19 F5**
Zongyang China 30°42N 117°12E **35 B11**
Zorritos Peru 3°43S 80°40W **92 D2**
Zou Xiang China 35°30N 116°58E **32 G9**
Zouar Chad 20°30N 16°32E **53 D9**
Zouérate = Zouîrât Mauritania 22°44N 12°21W **52 D3**
Zouîrât Mauritania 22°44N 12°21W **52 D3**
Zoutkamp Neths. 53°20N 6°18E **15 A6**
Zrenjanin Serbia 45°22N 20°23E **23 B9**
Zufār Oman 17°40N 54°0E **49 D5**
Zug Switz. 47°10N 8°31E **20 C8**
Zugspitze Germany 47°25N 10°59E **16 E6**
Zuid-Holland □ Neths. 52°0N 4°35E **15 C4**
Zuidbeveland Neths. 51°30N 3°50E **15 C3**
Zuidhorn Neths. 53°15N 6°23E **15 A6**
Zula Eritrea 15°17N 39°40E **49 D2**
Zumbo Mozam. 15°35S 30°26E **55 H6**
Zumpango Mexico 19°48N 99°6W **87 D5**
Zunhua China 40°18N 117°58E **33 D9**
Zuni Pueblo U.S.A. 35°4N 108°51W **77 J9**
Zunyi China 27°42N 106°53E **34 D6**
Zuo Jiang → China 22°50N 108°6E **34 F6**
Zuoquan China 37°1N 113°27E **32 F7**
Zuozhou China 22°56N 107°48E **34 F6**
Zurbāţīyah Iraq 33°9N 46°3E **46 C5**
Zürich Switz. 47°22N 8°32E **20 C8**
Zutphen Neths. 52°9N 6°12E **15 B6**
Zuurberg △ S. Africa 33°12S 25°33E **56 D4**
Zuwārah Libya 32°58N 12°1E **53 B8**
Zūzan Iran 34°22N 59°53E **47 C8**
Zvishavane Zimbabwe 20°17S 30°2E **55 H6**
Zvolen Slovak Rep. 48°33N 19°10E **17 D10**
Zwettl Austria 48°35N 15°9E **16 D8**
Zwickau Germany 50°44N 12°30E **16 C7**
Zwolle Neths. 52°31N 6°6E **15 B6**
Zwolle U.S.A. 31°38N 93°39W **84 F8**
Żyrardów Poland 52°3N 20°28E **17 B11**
Zyryan Kazakhstan 49°43N 84°20E **26 E9**
Zyryanka Russia 65°45N 150°51E **27 C16**
Zyryanovsk = Zyryan Kazakhstan 49°43N 84°20E **26 E9**
Żywiec Poland 49°42N 19°10E **17 D10**